AN AFRICAN SURVEY
REVISED 1956

AN AFRICAN SURVEY

REVISED 1956

A STUDY OF PROBLEMS ARISING IN
AFRICA SOUTH OF THE SAHARA

BY

LORD HAILEY

P.C., O.M., G.C.S.I., G.C.M.G., G.C.I.E.

Issued under the auspices of the
Royal Institute of International Affairs

OXFORD UNIVERSITY PRESS

LONDON   NEW YORK   TORONTO

1957

Oxford University Press, Amen House, London E.C.4

GLASGOW NEW YORK TORONTO MELBOURNE WELLINGTON
BOMBAY CALCUTTA MADRAS KARACHI
CAPE TOWN IBADAN NAIROBI ACCRA SINGAPORE

PRINTED IN GREAT BRITAIN
AT THE UNIVERSITY PRESS, OXFORD
BY CHARLES BATEY, PRINTER TO THE UNIVERSITY

PREFACE

IN a Foreword to *An African Survey* (1938) the late Lord Lothian explained that the work had owed its inception to a suggestion made by General Smuts in the course of the Rhodes Memorial Lecture delivered by him at Oxford in 1929. Africa, he then said, was developing under the control of a number of European Powers, and different and often conflicting principles were being applied by them in the administrative, social, educational, and legal fields. He pleaded accordingly for the compilation of a survey of conditions in Africa as a whole, so designed as to include also a review of the extent to which modern knowledge was being applied to African problems.

A Committee was subsequently formed, under the chairmanship of Lord Lothian, which arranged for the preparation of the Survey. It was from the first decided that this work, while giving all the information necessary for the appreciation of the problems under discussion, should treat the problems themselves in as objective a spirit as possible: '. . . the weight should lie in the full statement of fact rather than in the expression of opinion.' The execution of the work was made possible by a generous donation from the Carnegie Corporation of New York, supplemented at a later stage by the Rhodes Trustees. The Council of the Royal Institute of International Affairs acted as trustees for the funds of the Survey and placed the facilities of Chatham House at its disposal.

The Survey, published in November 1938, was reprinted in May 1939. In the course of 1940 the Government of the United Kingdom issued a White Paper explaining the grounds on which they had put forward the legislation embodied in the Colonial Development and Welfare Act of that year, itself an innovation of considerable importance in the field of British Colonial policy. In the course of this statement they announced that they had decided on the allocation of a separate sum for Colonial research, up to a maximum of £500,000 a year. They added: 'In reaching this decision we had in mind the proposal for special provision for research made by Lord Hailey in his *African Survey*, and we take this opportunity of acknowledging our debt to him for the suggestion.'

At the end of the Second World War suggestions were made from various quarters for the revision of the Survey of 1938, but conditions in Africa were changing very rapidly, and for some time it did not appear feasible to carry out a revision which would have any lasting value. A beginning in the task of revision was finally made in September 1952, but it soon became apparent that the result would be unsatisfactory unless the original work were largely rewritten. As the result, the present volume, though similar in its objective and in the arrangement of its material to that published in 1938, is, in many respects, a new work.

The material available for the study of conditions in Africa has vastly increased in volume since the publication of the original Survey, and the preparation of the present work has in consequence been protracted beyond the date originally contemplated. Assistance for the expenditure involved has again been generously provided by the Carnegie Corporation of New York, and additional aid has been given by the Rhodes Trustees and the Leverhulme Trustees. The Council of the Royal Institute of International Affairs has again made the facilities of Chatham House available for the Survey.

An effort has been made to render the record of political or other developments complete up to the end of 1955, but there is great variety in the dates on which the different governments concerned publish their statistical material, and in some cases the figures quoted are necessarily those of earlier years. Owing to the fact that a considerable part of the present volume went to press early in 1956, it has proved impossible to make full use of much valuable material published during that year, such, for example, as the important Report of the Commission for the Socio-Economic Development of the Bantu Areas in the Union of South Africa (the Tomlinson Report), or the record of the views expressed by the East Africa Governments on the recommendations of the East Africa Royal Commission 1953–5, or the debates in the French Parliament on the law of June 1956 making provision for the Constitution of Territorial Assemblies in the Overseas Territories.

The present volume, like its predecessor, owes a major part of its value to those who have contributed the material on which different chapters or sections of chapters have been based, and more particularly those chapters that deal with subjects which demand a specialized knowledge. The names of these contributors will be found in the first Part of the list of Acknowledgements on page viii following. The Survey is especially indebted in this connexion to Miss Phyllis Deane, Dr. Lucy Mair (who has been responsible for the rewriting or revision of a number of the chapters), Mr. G. B. Masefield, Sir Alan Pim, Mr. Kenneth Robinson, and Dr. Charles Wilcocks. Those who have made such contributions will appreciate that it has on occasion been necessary to condense them or to modify them in other respects in order to conform with the general scheme of the Survey. For any modifications made either in the statement of facts or the expression of views, I must accept entire responsibility.

There will be found in the second Part of the list of Acknowledgements the names of those who have given assistance of a general nature in the preparation or in the publication of the present volume. In addition, Professor E. B. Carrington generously undertook to deal with the proofs

of a number of the chapters at a time when I was myself incapacitated
from doing so. Mr. E. H. Lane Poole has collaborated with me for over
a year in the work of the Survey. Mrs. Diana Wynn Jones acted as
Secretary throughout the whole period of the work. To all these I wish
to express my gratitude.

HAILEY

ACKNOWLEDGEMENTS

PART I

Mr. A. Bevens
Mr. H. Scott Booker
Mr. N. V. Brasnett
Dr. R. J. Harrison-Church
The Colonial Geological Surveys, Imperial Institute, London
Mrs. Christine Comber
The Directorate of Colonial Surveys, London
Miss Phyllis Deane
Mr. B. W. Fagg
Sir William Gowers
Mr. J. Grenfell-Williams
The International African Institute
Dr. Stanley P. Jackson
Rev. A. M. Jones

Professor Kenneth Kirkwood
Dr. Hilda Kuper
Dr. Charlotte Leubuscher
Mr. J. Macrae-Simpson
Dr. Lucy Mair
Professor H. J. Mandelbrote
Mr. G. B. Masefield
Mr. J. W. Meldrum
Mr. S. Milburn
Dr. A. Phillips
Sir Alan Pim
Mr. Kenneth Robinson
Dr. Charles Wilcocks
Mr. B. Woods
Dr. E. B. Worthington

PART II

Dr. José d'Almada (Lisbon)
Mr. H. Calvert
The Colonial Office, London; particularly the Library, the African Studies Branch, the Press Section, and the Statistics Department
Dr. Mendes Correa (Lisbon)
Mr. H. Davidson
Miss K. Duff
The London School of Hygiene and Tropical Medicine
Professor G. Malengreau (Belgium)
Professor A. F. G. Marzorati (Belgium)

Ministère des Colonies (Brussels)
Ministère de la France d'Outre-Mer (Paris)
Dr. D. Niddrie
Dr. A. M. Wilson Rae
The Royal Institute of International Affairs, London
Mr. C. W. Scott
Mr. R. J. Simmons
Dr. H. J. Simons
Mr. C. F. Spence (Lourenço Marques)
Dr. B. P. Uvarov
Mons. J. Van Hove (Brussels)

The Index has been compiled by Miss D. E. Marshall

CONTENTS

CONTENTS

CONTENTS

CONTENTS

CONTENTS

MAPS

WEIGHTS, MEASURES, AND CURRENCIES

(a) METRIC WEIGHTS AND MEASURES

Metre	= 39·37 inches (1·093 yards)
Kilometre	= 0·621 mile (approx. ⅝ of a mile)
Hectare	= 2·47 acres
Square kilometre	= 0·386 square mile
Short ton	= 2,000 lb.
Metric ton	= 2204·6 lb.

British Weights and Measures

Yard	= 0·914 metre (36 inches)
Mile	= 1·609 kilometres (1,760 yards)
lb.	= 0·453 kilogramme
Ton	= 1,016 kilogrammes (2,240 lb.)
Acre	= 0·404 hectare
Square mile	= 2,589 square kilometres (640 acres)

South African Weights and Measures

Morgen	= 2·116 acres (0·855 hectare)
Bale of cotton	= 400 lb.
Standard bag of maize or wheat	= 200 lb.

(b) THERMOMETER COMPARISONS

Freezing-point	= 0° Centigrade; 32° Fahrenheit
Boiling-point	= 100° Centigrade; 212° Fahrenheit

° Cent.	° Fah't.
20 =	68
40 =	104
60 =	140
80 =	176
100 =	212

(c) CURRENCIES

(at 1956 *rates of exchange)*

Belgian

140 Belgian francs or Belgian Congo francs = £1 sterling

French

The value of the French African currency (the franc C.F.A.) was fixed at double the value of the metropolitan franc by a *décret* of 17 October 1948.

980 French francs (metropolitan) = £1 sterling

490 French francs C.F.A.   = £1 sterling

Portuguese

80 angolares = £1 sterling (1 angolar = roughly 3*d.*)

80 escudos   = £1 sterling (1 escudo = roughly 3*d.*)

1 conto   = 1,000 escudos = £12. 10*s.*

ABBREVIATIONS AND SHORT TITLES
USED IN FOOTNOTES

Africa	Journal of the International African Institute
African Affairs	Journal of the Royal African Society
Africa Today	C. G. Haines, ed., *Africa Today*, 1955
Africa South of the Sahara	A. Welsh, ed., *Africa South of the Sahara*, 1951
Background to Uganda	Issued by the Government Information Department, Kampala
Bull. A.R.S.C.	*Bulletin des Séances: Académie Royale des Sciences Coloniales*
Bull. I.R.C.B.	*Bulletin des Séances: Institut Royal Colonial Belge* (The *Institut Royal Colonial Belge* changed its title in October 1954 to *Académie Royale des Sciences Coloniales*; abbreviation used is *A.R.S.C.*)
Cd. and Cmd.	British Command Papers
C.S.R. No. —	Southern Rhodesia Government Publication
Enc. A.E.F.	*Encyclopédie de l'Afrique Equatoriale Française*, 1950
Enc. A.O.F.	*Encyclopédie de l'Afrique Occidentale Française*, 1949
Enc. C.B.	*Encylcopédie du Congo Belge*, 1953–4
Enc. C.-T.	*Encyclopédie de l'Afrique Française: Cameroun-Togo*, 1951
F.N.	*Federation of Rhodesia and Nyasaland Newsletter* (issued by the Federal Information Department, London)
Handbook on Race Relations in South Africa	E. Hellmann, ed., *Handbook on Race Relations in South Africa*, 1949
International Affairs	Journal of the Royal Institute of International Affairs
J.A.A.	*Journal of African Administration* (edited by the African Studies Branch of the Colonial Office and published by H.M.S.O.)
J.R.A.I.	*Journal of the Royal Anthropological Institute*
J.R.A.S.	*Journal of the Royal African Society* (superseded by *African Affairs*)
J.R.S.A.	*Journal of the Royal Society of Arts*
Mém. A.R.S.C.	*Académie des Sciences Coloniales: Mémoires*
Mém. I.R.C.B.	*Institut Royal Colonial Belge: Mémoires*
N.A.	Lord Hailey, *Native Administration in the British African Territories*, 5 parts, 1950–3, H.M.S.O.
Overseas Economic Surveys (territory, year)	Great Britain, Board of Trade Commercial Relations and Exports Department, *Overseas Economic Surveys (territory, year)*, London, H.M.S.O.
O.Y.S.A.	*Official Year Book of the Union of South Africa*
O.Y.S.R.	*Official Year Book of Southern Rhodesia*

R.L.I. Papers	*Rhodes-Livingstone Institute Papers*
R.L. Journal	*Journal of the Rhodes–Livingstone Institute*
S.A.S.	*South African Survey* (issued by the South African Government Offices, London)
U.G. No. —	Government Publication of the Union of South Africa

NOTE

British Parliamentary Debates (Hansard) are cited in the footnotes in the following way:

For the House of Commons: H.C. Deb., (date), col. (no.)
For the House of Lords: H.L. Deb., (date), col. (no.)

ABBREVIATIONS
OF MEDICAL PUBLICATIONS
(CHAPTER XVI)

Ann. Parasit. Humaine et Comparée	*Annales de Parasitologie Humaine et Comparée*
Ann. Soc. Belge de Méd. Trop.	*Annales de la Societé Belge de Médecine Tropicale*
Ann. Trop. Med. & Parasit.	*Annals of Tropical Medicine and Parasitology*
Brit. J. Venereal Dis.	*British Journal of Venereal Disease*
Bull. Entom. Res.	*Bulletin of Entomological Research*
Bull. Méd. de l'Afrique Occidental Française	*Bulletin Médical de l'Afrique Occidentale Française*
Bull. Soc. Path. Exot.	*Bulletin de la Société de Pathologie Exotique et de ses Filiales*
C. R. Acad. Sci.	*Comptes Rendus Hebdomadaires des Séances de l'Académie des Sciences*
East African Med. J.	*East African Medical Journal*
Internat. J. Leprosy	*International Journal of Leprosy*
J. Méd. de Bordeaux	*Journal de Médecine de Bordeaux et du Sud-Ouest*
J. Pediatrics, St. Louis	*Journal of Pediatrics, St. Louis*
J. Roy. Med. Corps	*Journal of the Royal Medical Corps*
J. Roy. San. Inst.	*Journal of the Royal Sanitary Institute* (now *Journal of the Royal Society for the Promotion of Health*)
J. Trop. Med. & Hyg.	*Journal of Tropical Medicine and Hygiene*
Proc. Transvaal Mine Med. Officers' Ass.	*Proceedings of the Transvaal Mine Medical Officers' Association*
South African J. Med. Sci.	*South African Journal of Medical Sciences*
South African Med. J.	*South African Medical Journal*
Trans. Roy. Soc. Trop. Med. & Hyg.	*Transactions of the Royal Society of Tropical Medicine and Hygiene*
Trop. Dis. Bull.	*Tropical Diseases Bulletin*

SPELLING OF AFRICAN NAMES

Consistency in the spelling of African names presents many practical difficulties. Ba, Wa, &c., are plural prefixes denoting the people, e.g. Baganda; Mu or M are singular prefixes, e.g. Muganda. The prefixes used to show language are Lu, Si, Se, Chi, Ki, &c., e.g. Luganda. Expert opinion tends to omit the prefix and to aim at a more exact form of the root, e.g. Sotho rather than Suto, or than Ba-suto or Se-suto. In this Survey the policy followed is that recommended in June 1933 by the Council of the International Institute of African Languages and Cultures, which is frankly a compromise. In the chapters dealing with the African peoples and languages in their more technical aspects the latest spelling is generally used, but elsewhere forms familiar through long usage have been retained.

The *Oxford Atlas*, 1951 edition, has been used as a guide to the spelling of geographical names.

CHAPTER I

THE PHYSICAL BACKGROUND

GENERAL DESCRIPTION

The Configuration of Africa

IT has often been claimed that the clue to the history of any large region of the world is to be found in its physical geography, and this is certainly true as regards the earlier periods in the world's history, when the movement of peoples and the spread of civilizations was so largely influenced by the character of the physical features which they encountered. That Africa, for instance, remained for so long 'the dark continent' in the eyes of the rest of the world was largely due to the fact that much of its interior was unusually difficult of access. Between the Mediterranean coastlands and South Africa the Sahara forms a broad and uninhabitable barrier against penetration from the north. It is no doubt true, as Dr. Toynbee has pointed out, that deserts and steppes seem, like the sea, to act also as a means of communication, so that resemblances are found between cultures and languages all round their shores,[1] but this observation applied primarily to the diffusion of languages caused by the migrations of nomadic peoples. The Sahara, indeed, never formed a complete barrier to movement, and both the invasion by armed forces and the penetration by religious influences from Northern Africa have left an enduring mark on the political and social life of West Africa.[2] Nevertheless, the Sahara must always have presented a serious obstacle to the free movement of peoples across it.

It is equally true that the coastline of Africa has furnished few facilities to those who might seek to approach the interior from the sea. The coasts afford little safe anchorage for ships, and the rivers cannot usually be used as routes to the interior; the Congo river, for example, has an estuary of deep water, but farther inland the way is barred by a long succession of rapids. Most other large rivers are blocked by sand bars. The high cost of artificial harbours such as Takoradi and Beira illustrate some of the difficulties which have retarded the penetration of the continent.

The east coast has a larger place in the history of African development than the west; the Muslim cities on the east coast as far south as Sofala and the mouth of the Zambezi were described by Ibn Batuta in the

---

[1] A. J. Toynbee, *A Study of History*, vol. iii, 1934, p. 391.
[2] See D. Forde, in *Transactions of New York Academy of Sciences*, Series II, vol. xv, pp. 206 ff.

thirteenth century, and the penetration into the interior along the Zambezi in the sixteenth century followed closely upon the voyage of Vasco da Gama in 1497. Tribal migrations in the central, eastern, and southern regions of Africa and the lack of permanent land settlement can be attributed, in part at all events, to the relatively poor quality of the soils; owing to their deficiency in certain constituents the tropical and sub-tropical soils of Africa are not generally so fertile as is usually supposed.[1]

Every traveller is impressed by the fact that the population appears very sparse. Figures of density of population must be interpreted with caution when they refer to large areas. In order to compare Africa with other continents it is necessary to bear in mind the considerable proportion of the land surface which is not suitable for human occupation and is therefore practically uninhabited. It would serve no useful purpose to compare the densities of populations of industrialized countries with those of countries which are mainly agricultural and pastoral. In Africa there are some small areas which are well populated, but no region of any size in which the density is near that to be found in Indo-China, Indonesia, or India. The southern part of Nigeria, the Transkei in the Union of South Africa, and parts of Kenya and Uganda in the vicinity of Lake Victoria are probably the most densely populated areas, but their density is still much less than the more sparsely populated countries in Europe.

These facts are not easily explained; it is true that the climates and soils do not offer an easy living and that malnutrition and disease are rife amongst men and domestic animals. But that is not the end of the story. Not all the area south of the Sahara suffers from poverty of soil or an inclement climate. Other peoples, in different parts of the world, have encountered conditions which are not less difficult. There may be other factors, as yet undetermined, which have conditioned what appears to be the inadequate response made by so many African peoples to that 'challenge of environment' which forms the theme of so much of Dr. Toynbee's *Study of History*.

Physical Characteristics

This volume deals only with Africa south of the Sahara. It will be realized, however, that though its scope is thus restricted it will not be possible to give here a full and comprehensive description of its physical features. The chief object of the Survey is to examine the problems which Africa presents, and it has only been felt essential to give so much of the background, whether physical, social, or economic, as is required for a consideration of these problems. The following paragraphs will, however,

[1] See below, p. 819.

serve to describe the physical character of the regions into which this part of Africa may be divided and the climates associated with them.[1]

Physically Africa south of the Sahara consists mainly of a plateau bordered by a coastal belt from which the land rises, in places steeply, to the plateau surface. The general elevation of the plateau is roughly from 3,000 to 6,000 feet, but it rises to a very considerable height in the east, reaching an elevation of 15,000 feet in Ethiopia and yet greater heights in the volcanic peaks on the East African plateau. The escarpment is a well-defined, though not unbroken, feature which can be traced southwards as far as the Union of South Africa, where it forms the precipitous edge of the Basuto Highlands (11,000 feet). In places where hard or horizontal rock formations occur or where its position is defined by recent faults, as in Ethiopia, the escarpment is generally sharp; but where the rock formations are soft, the escarpment slopes gently and is much less important as a climatic influence.[2]

The plateau contains one feature of exceptional interest which also figures prominently in scientific speculations regarding the cosmic or other phenomena which may have determined the configuration of the continent. This is the great Rift Valley system, which has a length of nearly 4,000 miles, and whose course is marked in East Africa by the Great Lakes and by the volcanic mountains for which the forces that created the Rift system seem also to have been responsible. Following a course from the Gulf of Akaba through the Red Sea, the Rift passes through Lake Rudolph, then between Lake Victoria and Mount Kenya and Mount Kilimanjaro, then through Lake Nyasa and down the Shire river, and it is believed to debouch into the sea near Beira. A western Rift has been formed on a line connecting Lakes Albert, Edward, Kivu, and Tanganyika, joining the main Rift north of Lake Nyasa. The Rifts are thought to have been formed in the cretaceous or early tertiary period and to be coeval with the separation of Madagascar from the African continent. The disturbance was accompanied by intense volcanic activity which has not, it is believed, entirely subsided in the western Rift.[3]

The depressions in the plateau surface are also an important feature in the configuration of the continent. The middle Niger basin near the great bend in the river was formerly an area of inland drainage, and in summer the river still floods the extensive area of low-lying lands above Timbuktu. But the lower course of the Niger is steeply graded, for it appears that a coastal stream has cut its way back into the plateau, thus

[1] For fuller details see W. Fitzgerald, *Africa, A Social, Economic and Political Geography of its major Regions*, 5th ed., 1945; and L. D. Stamp, *Africa, A Study in Tropical Development*, 1953.

[2] J. H. Wellington, in *Africa South of the Sahara*, 1951, pp. 25–35.

[3] W. Fitzgerald, op. cit., pp. 4–7, and for particular theories of the Rift formation J. W. Gregory, *The Rift Valleys, and Geology of East Africa*, 1921. A. Wegener, *Origin of Continents and Oceans*, 1922. B. Willis, *Living Africa*, 1930.

capturing the Niger waters. An earlier stage of the same process can be seen farther to the east, where the head-waters of the Benue are cutting back into the low divide which separates them from the Chad basin. Still a third basin lies to the east, and from its northern outlet the waters of the Bahr-el-Ghazal and the Sobat flow into the Nile. The floor of the Congo basin is an alluvial plain intersected by ill-defined drainage channels and scattered lakes and swamp lands. The basin is surrounded by uplands of varying character which rise gradually to the general level of the plateau; they comprise the Malange–Katanga uplands to the south, the Kivu highlands to the east rising to the plateau of East Africa, and the Sangha uplands which form the watershed between the Congo river system and those of the Shari and the Nile.

The uplands of the southern Congo merge into the plateau of southern Africa, of which the middle part is occupied by the sand-covered basin of the Kalahari. Both the Kalahari and the Makarikari depressions, and the basin of the Molopo, are below 3,000 feet in elevation. The northern Kalahari contains the swamps of the Linyanti, Zambezi, and Okovango rivers—a region which may be found to repay planned agricultural development.[1] From the Kalahari basin the land rises gradually to the surface of the South African plateau, averaging between 4,000 and 6,000 feet over most of Southern Rhodesia and the Union of South Africa. The 'highveld' of the Union rises towards the eastern escarpment—the Drakensberg Mountains, which, prominent and imposing in the Transvaal, culminate in the lofty massif of Basutoland.

On the southern side of the plateau in the Union of South Africa the marginal lands between the escarpment and the sea are occupied by parallel ranges of fold mountains which enclose the semi-arid Great Karoo and Little Karoo. In the south-west, where the structure is more complex and the rainfall higher, lies the scenically attractive south-western Cape Province, the Mediterranean region of South Africa. One result of this plateau formation, significant in its effect alike on agriculture, soil structure, and vegetation, is the rapid discharge of water from the rivers to the coast and the interruption of the rivers by waterfalls and rapids, such as the Victoria Falls on the Zambezi, the Aughrabies Falls on the Orange River, or the extensive rapids which mark the lower course of the Congo.

The Climates of Africa

To the student of climate and its effect on the life and economy of the peoples concerned, one of the most important features of the African climates is their symmetrical distribution with regard to the equator. Africa extends from the 35th parallel in the northern hemisphere to the corre-

[1] See below, p. 983, and the references quoted in Lord Hailey, *Native Administration in the British African Territories*, Part V, 1953, pp. 155–8 (hereafter referred to as *N.A.*).

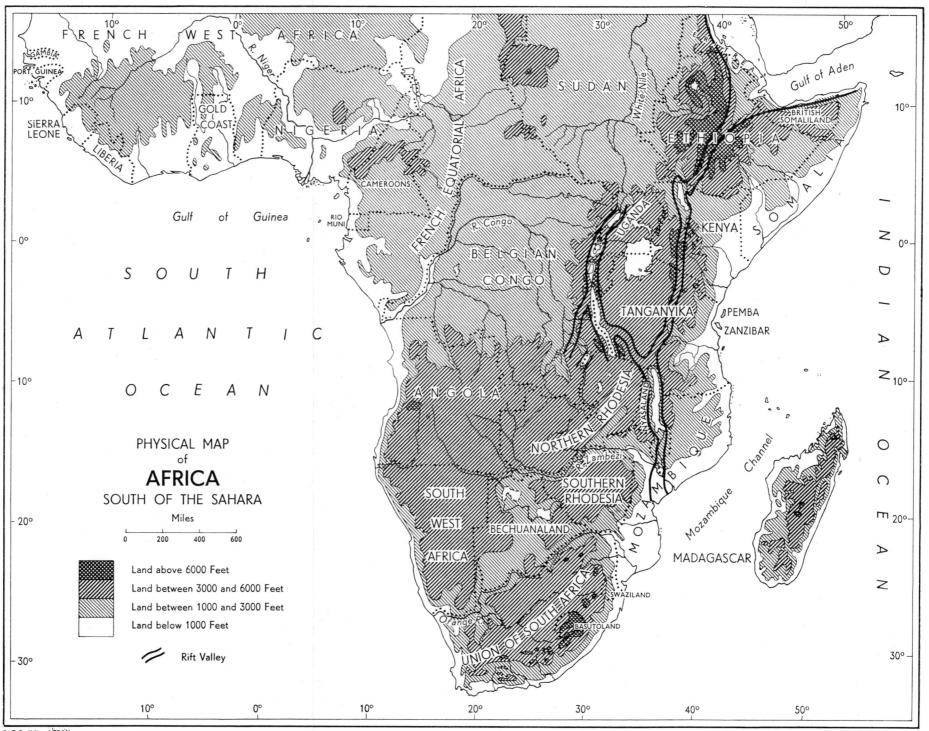

PHYSICAL MAP
of
AFRICA
SOUTH OF THE SAHARA

Miles

0   200   400   600

Land above 6000 Feet
Land between 3000 and 6000 Feet
Land between 1000 and 3000 Feet
Land below 1000 Feet

〰 Rift Valley

D.C.S. (Misc.) 226/1

sponding southern parallel. The interior plateau stretches across the
equator from the southern border of the Sahara almost to the Cape.
Mediterranean climate and vegetation are found on the north African
coastlands and again in the south-western Cape Province; the Sahara also
has a southern counterpart in the smaller and less arid Karoo and Kalahari and again in the rainless Namib, the desert coast of South-West
Africa.

Within the tropics climates are tropical, so far, at least, as regards their
rainfall, and, except in the low-lying basins of the Congo and the Zambezi
and in the coastal margins, the temperatures are moderated by the altitude of the plateau. Europeans have colonized and developed parts of
these areas of relatively temperate climate and will no doubt continue to
play an important part in administering them. It is important to ask,
therefore, how far Europeans have shown capacity to live and work in
tropical climates here and elsewhere in the world. Tropical climates have
hindered settlement and development in two ways; first because high temperature and extreme humidity, especially when they occur together, make
physical exertion not merely uncomfortable but exhausting; and second,
because warm climate is one of the principal factors which favour the
distribution of the micro-organisms of tropical diseases. Recent achievements in tropical medicine have encouraged settlement both by Africans
and Europeans in areas that were thought formerly to have climates which
were gravely prejudicial to health,[1] but there has in the last half century
taken place a remarkable reduction in the amount of sickness and disability among Europeans resident in tropical Africa. That has no doubt been
due not merely to advance in medical science but also to changes in the
general habit of living.

But the general question of the extent to which men can tolerate the
more extreme tropical climates and work efficiently, more especially in
industrial and similar occupations, still remains unanswered.[2] There are
no simple and entirely satisfactory standards by which tolerability of climates can be assessed. Judged by the standards based on experiments into
the effect of human exertion under various conditions of heat,[3] only the
basin of the Congo, the hot, wet forests of the Guinea coast, and the coastal
lowlands of Kenya and Tanganyika appear to be unsuitable for European
occupation in all seasons of the year; even in the warmer parts of East
Africa, Nyasaland, Mozambique, and Northern Rhodesia the uncomfortable season lasts for only about four months of the year. But the physiological factor, important as it may be, is only one of the complex of

[1] See below, p. 1105.

[2] S. P. Jackson, in *Africa South of the Sahara*, 1951, pp. 1–24; and E. B. Worthington, *Science in Africa*, 1938, pp. 120–2.

[3] D. Brunt, 'Climate and Human Comfort', *Proc. Royal Institution of Great Britain*, vol. xxxiii, no. 151. *Proc. Physiological Society*, vol. lix, p. 713.

conditions which have to be considered in assessing the suitability of tropical areas for permanent occupation by Europeans.[1]

The climates of the inter-tropical zone show in general a marked seasonal variation of rainfall and a small seasonal variation of temperature. On the other hand there is usually a marked diurnal range of temperature and also of rainfall. Hot, wet equatorial climates are found on the Guinea coast, in the basin of the Congo, and on the coast of East Africa. The Guinea coast has only a short dry season—November to January—when the warm Harmattan wind blows, filling the air with haze and lowering the relative humidity to about 10 per cent. When the rains begin the prevailing wind changes to south-west; the period of maximum rainfall varies little from place to place, but generally occurs when the sun is overhead. Usually there are two maxima of rainfall—at the equinoxes on the equator, but approaching midsummer in either hemisphere as the distance from the equator increases. The amount of rainfall is high everywhere (60–80 inches), but the hill slopes exposed to the moist winds are exceptionally wet. The Cameroon Peak, 13,400 feet in height, has a mean annual rainfall of not less than 400 inches. The mean annual temperature is near 80° F. and the daily maxima in the hot and relatively dry months are close to 90° F., with a mean diurnal range of about 10° F.

The basin of the Congo is sheltered, and so has a lower rainfall than the coast, averaging about 60 inches. In the short dry seasons between the rains the diurnal range of temperature increases and there are occasional spells of exceptionally low relative humidity; in this season too, fog, mist, and haze sometimes obscure the view for days at a time. In these conditions the natural vegetation is a luxuriant layered rain forest with a close canopy and rich in lianes and epiphytes; this forest continues into the zones of drier climate as 'gallery forests' along the stream courses.

Where the Congo basin rises in the east to the Kivu highlands the climate changes to the more temperate conditions of the East African plateau; it is still equatorial, but is cool because of its altitude. The relief of the land is varied and no short description can treat the climate adequately.[2] East Africa is drier than the Congo—generally the rainfall is 40–45 inches a year except on the exposed mountains and on the north-western shores of Lake Victoria, where it may be 60–100 inches. At the time of the north-east monsoon in the Indian Ocean (corresponding to winter in the northern hemisphere) dry northerly winds prevail in East Africa, but in the summer relatively damp south-westerly to southerly winds take their place. South of the equator 'the south-east trades' bring some rain to the high ground,

[1] A. Grenfell Price, *White Settlers in the Tropics*, American Geographical Society, no. 23, 1939. See also M. Robert, 'La Climatologie congolaise du point de vue de la colonisation européenne', *Encyclopédie du Congo Belge*, vol. i, 1953, pp. 297–300 (hereafter referred to as *Enc. C.B.*).

[2] A. Walter, 'Climate of East Africa', *Quart. Journ. Royal Met. Soc.*, vol. lxiv, 1938, p. 97.

but north of it their direction changes to south-westerly and they tend to blow parallel to the edge of the plateau. Kenya and Uganda, like the Congo basin, normally have two rainy seasons; in Kenya, March to June is the season of 'the long rains'; after a cool season from June to September the 'short rains' come in November and December. On the other hand Tanganyika has a single rainy season in the months of November to April.

In the highlands of Kenya the rainfall is about 40 inches with local variations due to relief, the sheltered Rift Valley getting about 30 inches and the exposed slopes of Mount Kenya over 60 inches. In the warm weather before the rains day temperatures exceed 80° F., but the range is also wide and the temperature may fall by 20° F. to 30° F. after sunset. Uganda, with about the same average rainfall as Kenya, is hotter because of the lower altitude. The climates of the remainder of East Africa are far less attractive than that of Kenya. The fertile and densely populated lowland of Lake Victoria is hot and damp; the rainfall, on the north-western shore, is about 80 inches, and only January and February are relatively dry months. The humidity is usually about 65 per cent.

The Tanganyika plateau is dry and hot; before the summer[1] rains begin temperatures often exceed 90° F. In the northern districts of Kenya and the Karamoja district of Uganda there is a region of arid climate stretching southwards to include the 'Nyika' on the eastern slopes of the plateau.[2] The natural vegetation consists mainly of low semi-desert thorn shrubs and is in striking contrast to the luxuriant growth in the coastal region. The upland equatorial climates support a natural vegetation of non-thorny woodland associated with tall and coarse grass which, as the rainfall diminishes, deteriorates into a drier thorny woodland in which the grasses are short and sparse and coarse.

Passing now from the climates which have been classed as equatorial to those classed as tropical, there is some difficulty in marking clearly the distinction between them. With increasing distance from the equator, the two equatorial rainy seasons merge into one. The summer is the rainy season and winter is dry, the amount of rain depending on distance from the ocean and exposure to the south-westerly winds. The diminishing rainfall from south to north is most marked on the west coast, where it varies from 150 inches on the Gold Coast to 10 inches at the mouth of the Senegal river.

In the dry season the trade wind blows—a moderate wind and cool compared with the summer monsoon. On the coast the Harmattan blows dry and hot during the day, though the nights may be cool. It is mainly due to the Harmattan that the winter months are warm, and midsummer

---

[1] The reference here and in subsequent passages is to the African seasons.

[2] The Nyika is the arid steppe belt widely represented in the Kwale and Kilifi Districts of Kenya.

(the rainy season) is the coolest time of the year. March is the hottest month, with a mean temperature above 80° F., and maxima often above 90° F.

Two important areas of temperate climate are found in this belt—the Bauchi plateau and the Futa Jallon uplands. By contrast the Chad territory, remote from the sea, is at times exceedingly hot. Hot weather occurs just before and after the rains. When the north-east winds blow, the air is hot and dry; the mean daily maximum is over 90° F. and the daily range about 36° F.—a high mean value even for a continental situation. A low relative humidity of about 35 to 40 per cent. makes the heat bearable, but April is an intolerable month; the mean maximum is then 105° F. and the minimum 75° F., and as the rainy season approaches the relative humidity may rise to 75 per cent.

South of the equator the continent is narrower and extreme heat and dryness are restricted to smaller areas. The counterpart of the Sudan occurs in Rhodesia, Angola, and Nyasaland. Apart from the Zambezi Valley the whole area lies above 3,000 feet and some parts of it exceed 6,000 feet. In winter the prevailing winds (dry south-easterly winds) come from the southern hemisphere belt of high pressure, but they are neither so hot nor so dry as their counterparts in North Africa. In Southern Rhodesia the rainfall varies from about 20 inches in the south and west to over 50 inches on the eastern escarpment. Apart from the eastern escarpment the highest rainfall (35 to 40 inches) occurs on the high ground to the east and north-east of Salisbury. The period from May to October is dry, for only about 2 or 3 per cent. of the yearly total falls then. Temperatures vary with altitude, and are highest in the valleys of the Zambezi, Luangwa, and Kafue Rivers. October is the hottest month and in these valleys the mean monthly temperatures are from 77° F. to 85° F. with daily maxima over 90° F. In the higher parts of the plateau, as for example in Salisbury, the mean temperatures for the hottest months vary from 70 to 75° F. Winters are cool with occasional spells of cold weather. Snow was reported for the first time in June 1954 on Mlanje Mountain (10,000 feet high) in Nyasaland.

Northern Rhodesia and most of Angola, with a rainfall of 40 to 50 inches, are wetter than Southern Rhodesia, though winter is still almost rainless. In the hot period from September to November temperatures over 90° F. can be expected on most days. The temperate climate of the Huila plateau in Angola decided the Government to set it aside for the occupation of the original settlers from Portugal. In Mozambique the rainfall varies from about 15 inches in the dry parts of the south to over 60 inches in the western uplands. The rainy season lasts from November to April and the dry season from May to September. The rainy and dry seasons are known in central and southern Mozambique as the seasons of the northern and southern monsoons, the former beginning in late September or early October, and gradually gathering strength till December, when it prevails over the north and middle of the Mozambique channel. The coastal plain between Beira and Pebane has about 50 inches of rain, but the rainfall diminishes towards the south and towards the lowlands in the interior. On the cool misty plateau slopes approaching Lake Nyasa the rainfall increases again to 45–60 inches.

The southern part of Africa, outside the tropics, shows surprising contrasts in climate. The plateau, though it extends into the sub-tropics, has a temperate climate with summer rains. The natural vegetation is grass in the east, but westwards, as the rainfall decreases, it deteriorates into a semi-desert scrub. The west coastal region—the Namib—is a rain-less desert, cloudy and misty on the sea-shore where the Benguela current flows, but hot and dry about 30 miles inland.[1] The south-western Cape Province has a Mediterranean climate and a natural vegetation of sclero-phyllous trees and shrubs.

In the Union of South Africa only a narrow coastal fringe in Natal, extending southwards from Kosi Bay at an altitude below 2,000 feet, can be described as sub-tropical. The northern Natal lowlands are wetter and cooler than Mozambique and there is less contrast between the wet and dry seasons. St. Lucia Bay has a rainfall of 50 inches and the mean maximum temperature in January is close to 90° F., creating a warm, humid climate, uncomfortable during the heat of the day. Yet in the winter this climate is pleasant, for there is a daily mean of about 65° F. and a daily range of 10° F. The sea-breeze blows strongly and affords some relief from the heat.

The slopes by which the land rises from the eastern coast-lands to the plateau surface vary greatly in height and in exposure, and the rainfall and temperature vary in proportion. The river valleys and depressions are dry and liable to extremes of temperature, especially in winter, when 'katabatic' winds blow at night from the intensely dry and thick mountain grasslands high up on the escarpment; the higher land is cooler and sub-ject to low cloud and misty drizzle. In this respect the climate is similar to the plateau slopes in western Mozambique.

The plateau can be divided conveniently into a moist eastern part and a dry western part, which in some areas is semi-arid. The main features of the plateau climate are such as would be expected on an inland plateau in these latitudes; rather low and erratic rainfall, many days of cloudless skies, and large diurnal changes in weather. Summer is warm and rainy and the winter is cool. The mean annual rainfall varies from less than 15 inches in the west to above 60 inches in a narrow zone on the eastern escarpment. In summer the moisture appears to be brought into the

[1] See below, p. 980.

country from the Indian Ocean and much of the rain falls in thunder showers occasionally accompanied by destructive hail. The South African 'highveld' is cool for the latitude. Ermelo, for example, has a mean January maximum temperature of 78° F. and days are unusual when the temperature is above 85° F. In winter the prevailing winds, from the westerly quarter, bring warm dry air which has often subsided from the upper atmosphere. The weather is warm and fine, but the nights are cold. This pleasant weather is interrupted now and then by outbreaks of cold sub-polar air which sweep across the plateau in southerly winds that bring severe frosts and sometimes snow on the mountains.

The climate of the highveld passes gradually through the semi-arid climate of the northern Cape Province, Bechuanaland, and South-West Africa into the true desert of the Namib coast of South-West Africa. This little-known area has an interesting climate. The desert stretches as a narrow, almost rainless zone between the escarpment and the sea from a few miles south of Angola to the north-western Cape Province. Only the coastal zone is cool. Low cloud and fog, the *caçimbo* of Angola, extend for about 30 miles inland on most mornings in the summer season. Towards noon the sea-breeze sets in from the west, beginning gently at first, but in the late afternoon it blows as a strong gusty wind which raises the loose sand of the Namib into clouds of dust. In winter there is an interesting variant—the hot winds from the east (the Berg winds), warm air which has subsided from the upper atmosphere. Temperatures in these dusty east winds rise to 90° F. and over, with the result that the hottest weather occurs in the winter months.

One other region in South Africa is worthy of mention, the south-western Cape Province. In this small region of winter rainfall there are large variations both of precipitation and of temperature due to relief. The year divides into two seasons: a rainy and cool winter and a dry, rather warm, summer. Both seasons are subject to strong winds. In winter they take the form of north-westerly gales and in summer the regular 'Cape south-easter', which often blows with gale force for two or three days at a time.

In the Cape Peninsula and its vicinity the mean annual rainfall is about 25 inches, but the mountains receive as much as 60 to 70 inches in some places. The amount decreases northwards, and at Saldanha Bay, about 100 miles to the north of Cape Town, the rainfall is only about 10 inches. The rains are brought by frontal depressions moving eastwards from the South Atlantic. In these depressions rain is accompanied by strong north-west winds, sometimes developing into the violent gales which were at one time a great danger to ships in Table Bay. The summer is dry and warm; the south-easter does not bring rain though it covers the mountain with thick white clouds. The occasional 'black south-easter' with its dark

AFRICA : CLIMATIC ZONES
(South of the Sahara)

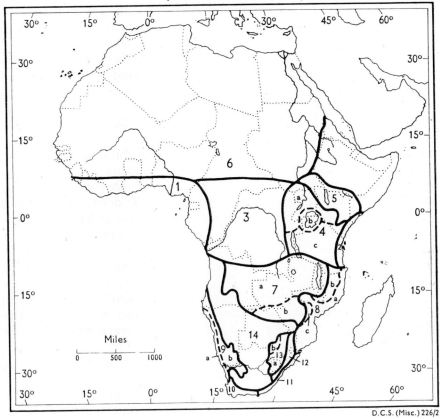

D.C.S. (Misc.) 226/2

1	Guinea Coast
2	East African Coast
3	Basin of the Congo
4	East African Highlands a. West Kenya and Uganda b. Lake Victoria area c. Tanganyika Plateau
5	Northern Regions of Kenya and Uganda
6	Sudan
7	Plateaux of Southern and Northern Rhodesia, Nyasaland and Angola a. Northern Rhodesia, Nyasaland and Eastern Angola b. Southern Rhodesia
8	Mozambique a. Coastal Plain (plus Zambezi Lowlands) b. Plateau towards Lake Nyasa c. Western Uplands bordering Southern Rhodesia
9	South African Deserts a. Western Coastal Region, the Namib b. Interior of the Namib
10	South Western Cape Province
11	Narrow coastal fringe of Natal
12	Eastern slopes of South African Plateau
13	South African Plateau (The Highveld) a. Eastern part b. Western part
14	Semi-arid plateau of the interior

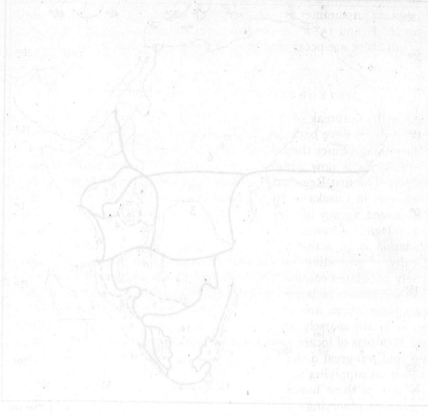

clouds and fine rain is an exception to the rule. At Cape Town the mean temperature in summer is 70° F. and in winter 55° F., and the daily ranges 20° F. and 15° F. Severe frosts are unknown except in the mountains, but there are occasional ground frosts on clear winter nights.

METEOROLOGY AND CLIMATOLOGY

Before the outbreak of the Second World War the African meteorological services were backward and co-operation between them was only just beginning.[1] Since then the situation has materially improved, and no part of Africa is now without a meteorological service under scientific direction. The first Regional Commission of the *Office Météorologique International* met in Lusaka in 1936. This organization has now the status of a specialized agency of the United Nations and has become the World Meteorological Organization of which the existing African Regional Association is an active member.[2] It is unnecessary to enlarge on the difficulty of providing satisfactory meteorological services in a large, sparsely populated continent, with a considerable element of desert belts. There will always be large areas, like Bechuanaland and the Sahara, from which observations are difficult to obtain. It is perhaps inevitable also that, as in any sparsely populated region, the cost should seem relatively high. Members of local Legislatures have, moreover, found reason to complain that too great a share of the provision made for meteorology has to be spent on supplying routine reports to aircraft.

In spite of these handicaps, however, Africa is now reasonably well covered with observing stations which report at standard times for synoptic observations. Collections of observations are broadcast at least twice daily from six sub-continental broadcasting centres: Algiers, Dakar, Kano, Pretoria, Nairobi,[3] and Cairo. So far as is possible, these collected reports include data from neighbouring islands and from ships at sea. Madagascar maintains stations in her island dependencies, the Comoros.

The Union of South Africa has established stations in Tristan da Cunha and Marion islands, and the Weather Bureau (which now has its headquarters at Pretoria) has an active programme of aerological observation and inquiry.[4] Special weather forecasts are issued for ships at sea, with especial regard to the movements of the dangerous tropical cyclones in the western Indian Ocean. Co-operation in these forecast services is now

[1] For the organization at this date see Worthington, op. cit. pp. 88–109.
[2] World Meteorological Organization, *Report of the First Session of the Regional Association for Africa*, Geneva, 1953.
[3] For East Africa, see *Annual Report on the East Africa High Commission, 1953*, Col. no. 305, p. 49. *Background to Uganda*, no. 116, August 1955.
[4] *Official Year Book of the Union of South Africa*, 1950, pp. 37 ff. (hereafter referred to as *O.Y.S.A.*).

organized by the office of the Regional Association in Nairobi. It is recognized that both long-range and medium-range forecasts are needed in the interests of agriculture, but it may be some time before the results will be such as to justify the meteorological services in offering them to the public. In the meantime research into the statistical aspects of this work is being carried on in the Union of South Africa.

The Belgian Congo has devoted special attention to the study of climate, and in particular to eco-climatology.[1] Its Meteorological Service has a network of 775 stations and publishes a monthly bulletin. The *Institut National pour l'Étude Agronomique du Congo Belge* (I.N.E.A.C.) has made a special study of the micro-climate conditions in the Congo which are of especial importance to agriculturalists.[2] The scientific study of climate has also received a good deal of attention in French West Africa.[3] The East African Service recently studied the influence of atmospheric turbulence on the effectiveness of spraying operations against tsetse fly, an intricate theoretical investigation with important practical applications.

Systematic studies of evapo-transpiration are being made at several places, e.g. in the Belgian Congo, on the Gold Coast, and in the Union of South Africa. The *Conseil Scientifique pour l'Afrique au Sud du Sahara* (C.S.A.)[4] recently initiated the production of a climatological atlas of Africa, mainly in order to meet the needs of those who are engaged in agricultural and health problems. It is hoped that the atlas will be completed by the end of 1957. The Regional Commission of the World Meteorological Organization has supported the establishment of a network of solar radiation stations and has agreed on uniform standards for the publication of the readings.

Measures based on the study of synoptic meteorology have recently been applied to the control of the swarms of desert locusts which from time to time cause damage to cultivation over wide areas.[5] The Desert Locust Survey working in collaboration with the East African Meteorological Service has suggested that the movements of swarms are associated with the inter-tropical convergence zone, the relatively narrow zone that separates the trade winds of the two hemispheres. As a contribution to the solution of this problem the meteorological services of certain territories, and notably those of Southern Rhodesia, French West Africa, the Sudan, and East Africa, have undertaken special studies of the inter-tropical convergence zone. Apart from the value of these studies in the destruction of

---

[1] M. Robert, 'La Climatologie de l'Afrique et du Bassin Congolais', *Enc. C.B.*, vol. i, pp. 269–301. *Rapport Annuel du Congo Belge, 1952*, pp. 56 ff.

[2] See below, p. 919.

[3] *Encyclopédie de l'Afrique Occidentale Française*, vol. i, 1949, pp. 217–40 (hereafter referred to as *Enc. A.O.F.*); *Mémento du Service météorologique de l'A.O.F.*, Rufisque, 1942.

[4] See below, p. 21, 1611.

[5] See below, p. 897.

locusts, the results already constitute an important contribution to African meteorology.

There is still much that could be done if the resources could be made available. It is in the first instance essential to free the scientifically trained meteorologists from excessive routine duties in order to give them time to investigate systematically the problems of the circulation of the atmosphere in the tropics. Up to recent years, more attention has been given to the study of meteorology in temperate than in tropical zones, and progress is most likely to be made in the future by scientists who have actually had experience of tropical conditions.

SURVEY AND MAPPING

The Organization of Survey

It is now universally agreed that the orderly development of the land and mineral resources of any territory must be based on accurate topographical surveys and that such surveys must of necessity form the first stage in planning any project of development. There are numerous examples of the unfortunate results which have been due to the lack of adequate topographical knowledge. Some years ago a bridge appears to have been built in Northern Rhodesia eleven miles from its correct site, owing to the use of an inaccurate map, and the railway from Sekondi to Kumasi in the Gold Coast, constructed without an adequate survey, had to be realigned at a cost approaching £2 million. It was estimated in 1921 that the lack of accurate topographical maps had involved the South African farming community in an unnecessary expense of £50,000 a year on farm surveys alone.[1]

However sound may be the basic conception of a scheme for development, it is unwise to attempt to put it into effect without first obtaining full topographical knowledge of the area concerned. This is, in particular, an indispensable preliminary to a geological survey, or for the planning of large-scale projects of irrigation or of railway development. Up to the beginning of the Second World War this does not appear to have been fully appreciated by some of the Governments in Africa, and there are also instances where, though the principle was appreciated, funds could not be made available to carry out extensive topographical surveys or the geodetic operations on which they must be based. Land surveying, although a capital asset which must in due course pay good dividends, was in some cases financed almost entirely from current revenue, and only such moneys were allocated to it as could be spared from other requirements. In many areas precedence was given to cadastral surveys which seemed

[1] *Report of the Survey Commission*, U.G. 39, 1921, para. ii, 5.

to meet more immediate requirements. Expenditure on survey work was often one of the first points of attack during a period of retrenchment.[1] During the Second World War little survey work could be carried out, and when it ended the topographical material available, though sufficient for the more elementary purposes of administration, was frequently inadequate for the purposes of the development that was bound to follow the war.

This was certainly true of most of the British Colonial territories. There, each of the Administrations (with the exception of Gambia) had its own Survey Department whose duties comprised not only triangulation and topographical mapping but cadastral surveying, including the delineation of property boundaries and town planning.[2] These departments were not under any central control, though expert advice on survey policy was tendered by a consultative committee, the Colonial Survey and Geophysics Advisory Committee. The limitations of this system, and the patent deficiencies in the provision of reliable topographical maps, had for many years formed the subject of comment by scientists and at conferences of Survey Officers. It is characteristic that up to about 1944 there were no official topographical maps of Nyasaland, Gambia, Swaziland, or the Bechuanaland Protectorate.[3] Many of the territories were dependent on maps which had been originally published by the War Office but had not been brought up to date; it was stated in 1931 that in some of them even main roads were not shown correctly, and that in others the roads were not shown at all.[4]

The subject was one of the first to occupy the attention of the Colonial Research Committee appointed to advise on the expenditure of the funds provided for research under the British Colonial Development and Welfare Act of 1940.[5] Its recommendations resulted in the establishment in 1945–6 of a Central Directorate of Colonial Surveys, financed from the funds provided under the Act,[6] its function being to co-operate in completing and keeping up to date the geodetic and topographical survey of the Colonies. The Directorate was to have for this purpose an establishment of 73 surveyors of all grades and 146 cartographers. The recruitment of the cadre of surveyors, however, proceeded slowly, and it was still only reaching completion in 1954.[7] It was not intended that this establishment should replace the local survey departments in the Colonies;

[1] *African Regional Scientific Conference, 1949*, vol. ii, p. 11.
[2] Worthington, op. cit., pp. 32 ff.
[3] *Appendix to Central Organization for Geodetic and Topographical Surveys in the Colonial Empire*, Col. no. 200, 1946.
[4] *Proceedings of Geographical Section of the British Association, 1936*; *Proceedings of the Conference of the Empire Survey Officers, 1931 and 1932.*   [5] See below, pp. 202–3.
[6] *Report of Colonial Research Committee for 1945–1946*, Col. no. 208, p. 6.
[7] *Report on Colonial Research 1953–1954*, Cmd. 9303, p. 271. *The Colonial Territories, 1953–54*, Cmd. 9169, p. 135.

these were to continue to function as independent units, but the fact that the central establishment would be available for supplementing the deficiencies in geodetic and topographical survey would leave them an opportunity to devote attention to cadastral survey, which had fallen greatly in arrears during the Second World War. The cartographic section of the central Directorate was made available for the printing of maps.

In the Union of South Africa topographical work has been more advanced than in the British Colonial territories, though the extensive allotment of lands in private right[1] has necessarily led to priority being given to cadastral survey. Each of the four Provinces in the Union maintains its own Survey Department under a Surveyor-General, its primary function being survey 'for the registration of deeds', or, in other words, the cadastral survey. All geodetic surveys are carried out by the Union Trigonometrical Survey, which was instituted in 1897, and to which topographical work was assigned in 1936. The Survey is under a Director who forms part of the Union Department of Lands and Irrigation, and provision for the co-ordination of work exists in the form of a statutory Survey Board which includes the Surveyors-General of the four Provinces.[2] It has been of advantage to the progress of survey work in the Union that triangulation for the Trigonometrical Survey has been financed in part from war funds.

In Southern Rhodesia both trigonometrical and topographical surveys are under charge of a Surveyor-General whose department is a constituent part of the Division of Agriculture and Lands.[3] A large part of the expenditure is met from loan funds, but it is some disadvantage that much of the activity of the department is occupied by the verification of surveys made by professional land surveyors for the purposes of the Deeds Registry.[4]

As will subsequently be shown,[5] the French seem to have attached more importance than the British to geographical studies in general, and the mapping of their African dependencies has been more systematically carried out. The metropolitan *Service Géographique de l'Armée* has in the past been instrumental in co-ordinating and supplementing the work of the local survey departments, and has indeed been responsible for the final preparation of many of the maps issued by the Colonial Ministry. Each Colony and the Trust Territory of the French Cameroons has its own survey service, but technical supervision is now given through the agency of the *Institut Géographique National*, which has its headquarters in Paris. In recent years the work of survey in the Cameroons and Togoland has formed part of the programme financed from Development funds.[6] The

---

[1] See below, p. 694.   [2] Land Survey Act, 1927. *O.Y.S.A., 1950*, p. 753.
[3] Land Survey Act, 1932.
[4] *Official Year Book of Southern Rhodesia, 1952*, pp. 373 ff. (hereafter referred to as *O.Y.S.R.*).
[5] See below, p. 23.
[6] *Rapport Annuel du Cameroun, 1951*, p. 182; *1952*, p. 187. *Rapport Annuel du Togo, 1951*, p. 167; *1952*, p. 140. For the Development Fund, see below, p. 214.

French have published in their *Atlas des colonies françaises* a collection of topographical, geological, and political maps that has no parallel in the British Colonies.[1] An interesting project has been put forward by the *Institut Français d'Afrique Noire* for the preparation of a new International Atlas of West Africa.[2]

In the Belgian Congo the work of survey was originally centralized under a metropolitan organization, the *Service Cartographique et Géodésique de la Colonie*, but since 1949 it has been the function of the *Institut Géographique du Congo Belge* (I.G.C.B.) with its headquarters at Léopoldville.[3] It comprises geodetic topography, aerial photography, and cartography, and its work is indispensable to the ten-year plan envisaged for the development of the country.[4] The survey of the Katanga area has been separately organized by the *Comité Spécial du Katanga*, with its headquarters in Brussels; this has dealt with both geodetic and topographical work. Great importance has been attached by the Administration to topographical survey and to the publication of detailed maps illustrating different aspects of material or cultural development.[5] The *Institut Royal Colonial Belge*[6] has in preparation an atlas of the colony on the lines of the French atlas above referred to.

The organization of survey in the Portuguese territories is in the hands of a department of the Overseas Ministry, the *Junta de Missões Geograficas e de Investigações do Ultramar*, the expenditure on which is borne on the metropolitan budget.[7] It is responsible for geodetic survey, and functions normally through 'missions' dispatched to the overseas territories, but Angola, Mozambique, and Guinea also have small survey establishments of their own (*Repartição de Agrimensura*), which deal with both topographical and cadastral surveys; some of the printing of maps is executed in the territories themselves. Portugal has published a general Colonial Atlas the technical execution of which compares favourably with that of the French Colonial Atlas.[8]

Geodetic Survey

Geodetic survey is primarily concerned with establishing the latitude, longitude, and altitude of a certain series of points, thus establishing the basis of the triangulation on which topographical survey depends for its accuracy. It accordingly provides the foundation of all maps whatever their scale, and all parts of Africa are equally concerned in the provision

---

[1] G. Grandidier, ed., *Atlas des colonies françaises*, 1933.
[2] *African Regional Scientific Conference*, 1949, vol. ii, p. 16.
[3] *Arrêtés* dated 7 December 1949 and 15 May 1950. *Rapport Annuel du Congo Belge, 1952*, p. 60.
[4] *Bulletin des Séances: Institut Royal Colonial Belge*, vol. xxv, no. 1, 1954, p. 396 (hereafter referred to as *Bull. I.R.C.B.*).
[5] See *Enc. C.B.*, vol. iii, pp. 1–12, 793 ff.
[6] See below, p. 21.   [7] Decree 35–638 of 13 May 1946.
[8] *Atlas de Portugal Ultramarino e das Grandes Viagens Portuguesas de Descobrimento e Expansão*, 1948.

of an adequate geodetic basis for the mapping of the continent as a whole, since eventually it will be necessary for the whole to be covered by a framework cutting across all international boundaries. It is held that for this purpose no place should be more than 200–300 miles from the nearest geodetic chain, though this ideal can only be attained in country suitable for triangulation.

In July 1954 the geodetic survey of the arc of the 30th meridian was completed after 70 years of work.[1] The arc extends from Alexandria on the Mediterranean to the southern coast of South Africa at a point close to the boundary between the Cape Province and Natal. The section from the southern coast to the Zambezi was completed at the beginning of the century by Sir David Gill, who had assumed charge of the Cape Town Royal Observatory in 1879. It reached the northern boundary of Northern Rhodesia in 1907, when work was suspended. Between 1931 and 1933 it was taken to Kigoma on the eastern littoral of Lake Tanganyika, and was continued by the Tanganyika Survey Department through the Ruanda Urundi Trust Territory to the Uganda boundary in 1938. Meanwhile the Government of Egypt had undertaken a concurrent triangulation from the north reaching the boundary of the Anglo-Egyptian Sudan in 1930.

The chain was now completed except for a hiatus of 600 miles in the *sudd* region of the Sudan, where normal trigonometrical methods could not be employed. The difficulty was overcome by erecting moveable steel towers, 103 feet high, which supplied the triangulation points in this uniformly flat country. This achievement was due to the co-operation of the United States Map Survey and Coast and Geodetic Survey with the Sudan Administration. The trigonometrical surveys of all territories can now be co-ordinated to the arc of the 30th meridian. Thus in 1954 the triangulation of Nyasaland was connected with it and a chain was begun to complete the connexion of Uganda with the arc.[2]

Before the Second World War the provision of an adequate geodetic framework had been more consistently pursued by the French and Belgian authorities than by the British. This seems to have been partly due to the preoccupation of the British authorities with the cadastral survey required for urgent development projects, and personnel was as a result withdrawn on more than one occasion from unfinished triangulations. The establishment of the British Directorate of Colonial Surveys has now improved the position as far as the British dependencies are concerned, and a geodetic framework for these territories is now being more vigorously pursued. It may be noted that African conditions emphasize the special need for the upkeep of geodetic and topographic work no less than of property surveys; it is noteworthy that the topographical survey of the

[1] See reference as quoted in Worthington, op. cit., pp. 43 ff.
[2] *Colonial Research, 1954–55*, Cmd. 9626, p. 309.

Orange Free State, though excellently carried out, had to be repeated after only 15 years because no provision had been made for the maintenance of beacons or for keeping maps up to date.

Topographical and Cadastral Survey

The extent of detailed topographical and cadastral survey has tended to vary in accordance with the policy followed in regard to land or mineral development. Thus the pursuance of a policy of European settlement in the Union of South Africa, Southern Rhodesia, and Kenya has resulted in attaching particular importance to cadastral survey; it is noteworthy indeed that on one occasion the Kenya Government, when faced with the need for retrenchment, went so far as to state that the only essential surveys were those of the farms and town plots designed for alienation. The grant of quasi-freehold rights on the Mailo lands[1] of Uganda has necessitated a large measure of detailed survey over a considerable area in the Protectorate, and the requirements of the *Union Minière du Haut-Katanga* in the Belgian Congo and of the mining corporations in the neighbouring copperbelt of Northern Rhodesia have led to the completion of two of the most complete topographical surveys of large areas carried out in Africa.

In the British Colonial territories an ordered programme of topographical mapping was envisaged by the Directorate of Colonial Surveys soon after its creation in 1946, but owing to the large number of development projects in different areas for which maps were urgently required, this programme had to be deferred, and mapping has been done as and where it has been demanded. A considerable amount of preliminary mapping (mostly at a scale of 1/50,000) is, however, being carried out, using air survey methods. Owing to the fact that contouring is still the slowest single operation in mapping from the air, the contouring has been confined to the photographs of those areas only where 'heighting' is essential, as for example for hydro-electric schemes and projected railways. This applies to about one-tenth of the total area mapped. Preoccupation with mapping for development projects is, however, an experience that has also been shared by the French and Belgian Administrations.[2]

There will be found in a later chapter some considerations as to the extent to which future developments of land policy may necessitate a cadastral survey in predominantly Native lands.[3] At the moment, it may be said that the chief requirement in regard to the cadastral surveys hitherto completed is the linking up of independent surveys with some common

---

[1] See below, p. 724.
[2] *Rapport Annuel du Congo Belge, 1952*, p. 233.
[3] See below, p. 806.

system of triangulation. The need for accurate cadastral work is, perhaps, more necessary in Africa than in those more developed countries where hedges, dykes, and other prominent landmarks help the surveyor, and where streams are held permanently to one course by artificial means. In Africa, where landmarks may be few, or where tracks constantly change their alignment, a high degree of accuracy is required from the property surveyor.

The need for expanding survey work has recently stimulated the employment of Africans as surveyors. Among the British dependencies Nigeria, the Gold Coast, and Sierra Leone have made the greatest advance in this direction, and the role of the European surveyor is becoming more and more that of supervision, the actual field work being done by African surveyors. Each of these three territories has a survey school where Africans are given their initial training; those chosen for promotion to the higher ranks of the service are now being sent to survey courses in England, with a view to qualifying by taking the examinations of the Royal Institution of Chartered Surveyors. There have already been a number of appointments of Africans to posts of surveyor formerly held by Europeans. All drawing and printing is now done by Africans, at present under European supervision.

Nigeria and the Gold Coast have air survey sections staffed by Africans capable of producing maps from air photographs. Kano in Northern Nigeria possesses an interesting example of a land survey maintained for local purposes by the Native Authority, and now manned entirely by Africans.[1] Only twenty-one students, however, attended the four-year course at the Oyo Survey School between the years 1935 and 1942.[2] Though there is a growing use of Africans in the British dependencies of East and Central Africa, their training is not so advanced. The Survey Department in Uganda has a school in which it trains Africans for field work and also accepts a few students for training from Tanganyika and Kenya. There is also a school in Northern Rhodesia which trains Africans for employment in the local Survey Department and also takes some students from Nyasaland. There are no special survey schools for Africans in the Union of South Africa. In French West Africa instruction in surveying is given at the *École Technique Supérieure* at Bamako, though the number of students is small. In the Belgian Congo there seems to have been some difficulty in securing pupils for the *École de Géomètres-Arpenteurs* at Boma,[3] and there has, in consequence, been an inadequate supply of trained 'auxiliary' surveyors.

[1] C. K. Meek, *Land Law and Custom in the Colonies*, 1946, pp. 155 ff.; *N.A.*, Part III, 1951, p. 77.

[2] *Report of Commission on Higher Education in West Africa* (the Elliot Report), Cmd. 6655, 1945, p. 189.

[3] *Rapport Annuel du Congo Belge, 1952*, p. 145.

Air Survey

Up to the beginning of the Second World War the relative advantages of the use of air survey as compared with ground survey were still in debate.[1] The Tanganyika Administration had established its own air survey section in 1931 for the purpose of mapping its towns and ports, and surveys of a more extensive character had been carried out by air survey companies on behalf of mining undertakings and railways in the Union of South Africa, Northern and Southern Rhodesia, and Kenya. The Northern Rhodesia Government had also used this agency for surveying an area of 72,000 square miles of the Protectorate for general administrative purposes. But the great technical advance made in air survey during the war made it inevitable that it should take the place of ground survey as the normal procedure for topographical mapping, and it was almost universally adopted immediately after the war for producing the maps required by the numerous development schemes then under consideration, especially where the saving of time was a matter of urgency.

In Great Britain the Ordnance Survey is by preference geared to ground survey, but the Directorate of Colonial Surveys has decided to carry out all topographical mapping by the use of air survey. Arrangements were concluded by which a squadron of the Royal Air Force was made available to undertake the major part of the air photography, and in addition a considerable amount of work was given out on contract to commercial air survey companies. As a result some 180,000 square miles were photographed from the air between 1946 and 1953.[2] Not all these photographs have been used for normal topographical mapping, for there has been a growing demand for air photographs from engineers, geologists, and forestry and agricultural officers. It has been decided that owing to the changes in the types of machine used by the Royal Air Force, an increasing amount of the air survey will now be entrusted to commercial companies. Some of the larger of the British Colonial territories are developing their own air units for township surveys and for the mapping of small areas; such units, complete with their own aircraft, already exist in Tanganyika and Nigeria.

In the Union of South Africa practically all topographical mapping is made from air photographs. Until recently the photography was done by the South African Air Force;[3] but here also much of it is now undertaken by commercial companies. The mapping from the air photographs is undertaken by the Directorate of Trigonometrical Surveys in establishments at Pretoria and Cape Town, and special arrangements have been made to make base maps available to the Geological Survey.[4] In Southern

---

[1] See references quoted in Worthington, op. cit. p. 56.
[2] *The Times*, 14 January 1954.
[3] *O.Y.S.A., 1950*, p. 756.   [4] Ibid. p. 950.

Rhodesia 63,000 square miles had been covered by photographic survey up to the end of 1950;[1] the photography was undertaken by commercial companies, but the Surveyor-General has his own mapping section.

In the French, Belgian, and Portuguese dependencies air survey has also largely replaced the ground survey for topographical work. The French depend mainly on the use of the military services. The *Institut Géographique du Congo Belge*[2] has its own aerial establishment, but also employs commercial companies. The *Comité Spécial du Katanga* has made use of the services of the *Institut Géographique Militaire* for the supply of a new series of maps on the scale of 1/500,000.

In spite of the increasing use of air survey, the ground surveyor remains an essential factor in the production of topographical maps, his function being to provide the framework of accurately fixed points on which the map from the air photographs is plotted. As photo-grammetric processes develop, the less the number of control points are required from him, but he will continue for many years to play an important part in the production of the map. Although much progress has been made in air survey, the science is still in its infancy, and techniques are continually changing to keep pace with the improved performances of aircraft and photo-grammetric equipment.

In recent years this has been increased by the development of the airborne profile recorder (which supplements the work of the ground surveyor in contouring), the airborne magnetometer (which utilizes magnetic responses to indicate the presence of oil or minerals), and the scintillometer, which is designed to indicate the presence of uranium and thorium by registering the radio-activity of the earth's surface. The effectiveness of these appliances has admittedly still to be tested, but in one field at least, air survey has performed services that are as undoubted as they were unexpected; both in Europe and in Asia it has proved to be of great value to the archaeologist.[3]

Various systems of projection have been used for mapping in Africa and in some cases local projections have been worked out to suit special needs. The variety of the systems used is perhaps best illustrated by the bulletins issued in 1954 and 1955 by the *Conseil Scientifique pour l'Afrique au Sud du Sahara* (C.S.A.) giving a complete list of the maps, both general and special, published in each of the countries of this part of Africa.[4] As, however, triangulations of the different countries begin to interlock, and as property surveys come into a rigid framework, it becomes desirable to have an agreed system of projection for the continent as a whole, since otherwise

[1] *O.Y.S.R., 1952*, p. 375.   [2] See above, p. 16.
[3] *The Times*, 8 April 1950.
[4] C.S.A. Publication, no. 12, *Mapping and Surveying of Africa South of the Sahara*, 1954; ibid. nos. 15 and 17, 1955.

great inconvenience will be caused when the maps of adjoining territories have to be used in conjunction. A projection system is merely a means of representing the geographical co-ordinates of the curved surface of the earth on the plane surface of a map. It is evident, therefore, that any advantage of a common projection system is nullified unless all surveys concerned are computed in terms of a single origin or datum, but this is impossible unless individual surveys are all connected to the geodetic framework which has itself been adjusted as a single unit on one datum.

There is now general agreement that the best system of projection for Africa is the Transverse Mercator (or Gauss Conformal) in meridional belts, but a difficulty has arisen when various widths of belt (from 2° to 6°) have been adopted in the past for different areas. At the Commonwealth Survey Officers' Conference in 1951 a strong case was put forward in favour of the adoption of belts of 6°. The conference passed a resolution in favour of the adoption of the Universal Transverse Mercator Grid, and it seems likely that this projection will in due course be used at least for all small-scale maps; there would clearly be a great saving of expense if a unified system were to be adopted in the near future. The adoption of the metre as the unit of length by the British Directorate of Colonial Surveys is a step in the direction of greater uniformity in Africa.

GEOGRAPHICAL RESEARCH AND STUDY

Some indication has already been given[1] of the progress made in the mapping of African territories and of the measure in which it has kept pace with the requirements of the geographers, for whom maps are, as has been said, the 'most essential tools'. That observation remains true whether geography be regarded as a branch of the physical or of the 'human' sciences, but in the latter case, geographical research will extend over a much wider field and must involve a range of inquiry in which the activity of the cartographer must be supplemented by that of other scientific workers.

In the last half-century, geography has been increasingly interpreted in this wider sense. It is no longer regarded mainly as the study of the surface features of the earth, or of the climatic and hydrographic factors affecting them, or of the material production which characterizes the different areas concerned. Its scope is now extended to include a comprehensive study of the interaction of social, economic, and political factors with the physical environment. Geography now has a claim to be regarded also as an applied science, in view of the aid which it can give to town planning and to the solution of the many problems connected with the utilization of land.

[1] See above, pp. 14–21.

The study of colonial geography has on the whole received fuller recognition in the universities of Continental countries than in those of Great Britain. In France, for instance, a chair of Colonial Geography was created at the Sorbonne as far back as 1892, and in 1946 chairs were instituted at Strasbourg, Bordeaux, and Aix-en-Provence. The French *École Nationale de la France d'Outre-Mer*, which is now responsible for the training of cadets for the Colonial services, has professorships of Colonial Regional Geography and of Tropical Geography, and there is a similar post at the *Collège de France*. A qualification for the Licentiate in *Études Coloniales* may include among its four certificates one in colonial geography. The names of well-known French geographers who have worked in Africa include those of A. Bernard, E. F. Gautier, C. Robequain, J. Dresch, P. Gourou, L. Papy, Y. Urvoy, and J. Weulersse.[1]

Geographical societies exist in a number of the larger French towns, dating for the most part from the last quarter of the nineteenth century, when French interests in Africa were expanding. These societies have stimulated widespread interest in French Africa and, to a lesser extent, in Africa in general. Apart from the journals of the learned societies, French geographers have published since 1891 the *Annales de Géographie* and more recently the specialized *Cahiers d'Outre-Mer*, published by the *Institut de Géographie de Bordeaux*. Some of the most active research now carried on in French Africa has been undertaken by the geographers attached to the various research institutes to which reference will be found in subsequent chapters of this Survey. Thus the *Institut Français d'Afrique Noire* at Dakar (I.F.A.N.) has five full-time geographers engaged upon research, the *Institut de Recherches du Cameroun* (I.R.C.A.M.) has two and the *Institut d'Études Centrafricaines* (I.E.C.) has one. The *Office de la Recherche Scientifique d'Outre-Mer* (O.R.S.O.M.)[2] also has full-time geographers upon its staff, and has published some remarkable maps by F. Bonnet-Dupeyron, the result of six years' field work with pastoralists in Senegal, Mauritania, and French Sudan.[3]

Among the academic courses provided in Belgium, prominence is given to geographical studies, though there is no specific chair for colonial

[1] A. Bernard, *Afrique Septentrionale et Occidentale*, 1937 and 1939. E. F. Gautier, *L'Afrique Noire Occidentale*, 1935; *L'Afrique Blanche*, 1939. C. Robequain, 'Problèmes de l'Économie rurale en A.O.F.', *Annales de Géographie*, 1937, pp. 137–63. J. Dresch, 'Sur une géographie des investissements de capitaux en Afrique Noire', *Bulletin de l'Association des Géographes français*, 1946, pp. 59–64; 'Villes Congolaises', *Revue de Géographie Humaine et Ethnologie*, 1948, pp. 3–24. P. Gourou, *Géographie des Pays Tropicaux*, 1946, English ed., 1953; 'Géographie du peuplement en Nigeria méridionale', *Bulletin de la Société Belge d'Études Géographiques*, 1947, pp. 58–64. L. Papy, 'La Vallée du Sénégal', *Cahiers d'Outre-Mer*, 1951, pp. 277–324. Y. Urvoy, *Les Bassins du Niger*, *Petit Atlas ethno-démographique du Soudan entre Sénégal et Tchad*, 1942. J. Weulersse, *L'Afrique Noire*, 1934.

[2] See below, p. 64.

[3] I. F. Bonnet-Dupeyron, *Cartes des races et variétés bovines au Sénégal et en Mauritanie*, 1951.

geography. Courses in the geography of the Belgian Congo, physical and human, are given at the Universities of Louvain, Ghent, and Liége, and also at the *Institut Universitaire des Territoires d'Outre-Mer* and the *Institut Supérieur de Commerce* at Antwerp; in the last case these have special reference to the economic geography of the Belgian Congo. The geography of the Colony is a compulsory subject for certain degrees at Louvain, Ghent, and Liége. Among the best known of the studies made of the Colony are those of M. Robert and of Michiels and Laude on its general geography, and of J. Bayens, P. Bernard, H. Buttgenbach, E. Devroey, E. Polinard, and R. Thomas on special aspects of it.[1]

In Portugal the *Sociedade de Geografia*, which deals mainly with the geography of the Overseas Provinces and is responsible for the Colonial Museum, is one of the most active of the cultural societies in Lisbon. There are chairs of Colonial Geography in the *Instituto Superior de Estudos Ultra-marinos* [formerly *Escola Superior Colonial*] at Lisbon, and of African Geography in the *Faculté des Lettres* at Lisbon and Coimbra and also a chair in the history of Portuguese exploration. In the Spanish institutions such as the *Instituto de Estudios Africanos* at Madrid special attention is paid to geographical research on Africa.

There is no chair of Colonial Geography in any of the universities in Great Britain, but a lectureship on the subject was created at Oxford in 1947. Contributions to the study of African geography have been made by the late Professor W. Fitzgerald, Professors L. Dudley Stamp and F. Debenham, Dr. R. Miller, R. W. Steel, Dr. R. J. Harrison Church, W. B. Morgan, A. T. Grove, G. R. Collins, and M. Richardson.[2] A stimulus to work on Africa was given as far back as 1926 by the late Professor A. G. Ogilvie who, as Secretary of a Committee of the British Association on the

---

[1] J. Bayens, *Le sol de l'Afrique Centrale et spécialement du Congo Belge*, vol. i, *Bas-Congo*, 1938. P. Bernard, *Le climat écologique de la Cuvette centrale congolaise*, 1945. H. Buttgenbach, *Les minerais de Belgique et du Congo Belge*, 1942. E. Devroey, *Le Bassin hydrographique congolais*, 1941. Michiels et Laude, *Notre Colonie*, 1951. E. Polinard, 'Quelques aspects physiques du Congo Belge', *Bulletin de la Société Royale de Géographie d'Anvers*, vol. lxi, 1947. R. Thomas, *Les forêts et l'exploitation forestière au Congo*, 1941. M. Robert, *L'Afrique Centrale*, 1934; *Le Congo physique*, 1946; *Le Katanga physique*, 1950.

[2] W. Fitzgerald, *Africa*, 1934. F. Debenham, *The Water Resources of the Bechuanaland Protectorate, Northern Rhodesia, Nyasaland, Tanganyika, Kenya and Uganda*, H.M.S.O., 1949. L. Dudley Stamp, 'Land Utilisation and Soil Erosion in Nigeria', *Geographical Review*, 1938. R. Miller, 'The Climate of Nigeria', *Geography*, November 1952. R. W. Steel, 'The Population of Ashanti—A Geographical Analysis', *Geographical Journal*, vol. cxii, 1947. pp. 64–77; R. W. Steel and E. W. Gilbert, 'Social Geography and its Place in Colonial Studies', ibid., vol. cvi, pp. 118–31. R. J. Harrison Church, *Modern Colonization*, 1951; 'The Case for Colonial Geography', *Transactions of the Institute of British Geographers*, 1948; 'Irrigation in the Inland Niger Delta of the French Sudan', *Geographical Journal*, vol. cxvii, pp. 218–20; 'The Evolution of Railways in French and British West Africa', *Compte Rendu, XVI Congrès International de Géographie*, Lisbon. W. B. Morgan, 'Blantyre—A Scottish Foundation in Nyasaland', *Scot. Geog. Mag.*, 1952, pp. 122–7. A. T. Grove, 'Soil Erosion and Population Problems in South-East Nigeria', *Geographical Journal*, vol. cxvii, pp. 291–306.

Human Geography of Inter-Tropical Africa, collected much material from District Officers.[1]

In addition to the work of professional geographers, noteworthy contributions have been made to geographical study by workers engaged by the African Governments in other professional capacities, as for example by the late Clement Gillman, C. R. Niven, D. Ould, and E. Richardson.[2] A uniform spelling of place names has for some years been under consideration,[3] and was later the subject of the International Conference of Onomastic Sciences held at Uppsala in 1954.

The Use Made of Geographers

Compared with the employment of geographers in French and other research institutes in Africa, it is noticeable that none are regularly so employed in similar British institutes, as for example the Rhodes–Livingstone Institute, the East African Institute of Social Research at Makerere, or the Institute of Social and Economic Research at Ibadan.[4] At the same time, however, a considerable amount of study is being undertaken in the geography departments of the new university colleges in British territories.[5] Thus Professor Garnier at Ibadan has studied the climate of Nigeria, J. C. Puch has worked on the geomorphology of the Jos plateau of Nigeria, and R. M. Prothero and N. C. Mitchell on land usage. In the Gold Coast studies are being made by Professor Varley, whilst E. A. Boateng, an African, and T. E. Hilton have studied the distribution of population and N. Nyarku, also an African, has investigated the development of Kumasi. I. A. Sparkes has studied the population distribution in Sierra Leone, and Dr. H. R. Jarrett in Gambia and at Freetown. Similar work is being done at Makerere University College by Professor S. J. K. Baker and F. J. Birkin, whilst V. C. R. Ford has worked on the economic geography of the Lake Victoria area.[6]

The British authorities have not followed the example set by the French

---

[1] *The Human Geography of Inter-Tropical Africa*, a pamphlet prepared by a committee of the British Association, 1930. A. G. Ogilvie, 'Co-operative Research in Geography, with an African example', *Scottish Geographical Magazine*, 1934, pp. 353–78.

[2] I. C. Gillman, 'A Population Map of Tanganyika Territory', *Geographical Review*, 1936; *A Reconnaissance Survey of the Hydrology of Tanganyika Territory in its Geographical Settings*, 1943. 'Population Problems of Tanganyika', *East African Agricultural Journal*, 1945, pp. 86–93. C. R. Niven, 'Some Nigerian Population Problems', *Geographical Journal*, vol. lxxxv, pp. 54–68. D. Ould and E. Richardson, *Reconnaissance Survey of the Lukanga Swamp, Northern Rhodesia, MS*.

[3] A. N. Tucker, in *Empire Survey Review*, vol. x, no. 77, 1950, pp. 332 ff.

[4] See below, p. 63.   [5] See below, p. 1180–4.

[6] B. J. Garnier, 'Some Comments on Measurements of Potential Evapotranspiration', *Research Notes, University College, Ibadan, Department of Geography*, no. 2, 1950. R. M. Prothero, 'Land use at Soba, Zaria Province', ibid. no. 2, 1953. H. R. Jarrett, 'Population and Settlement in the Gambia', *Geographical Review*, 1948, pp. 633–40; 'The Strange Farmers of the Gambia', ibid. 1949, pp. 649–53. S. J. K. Baker and R. J. White, 'The Distribution of Native Population over South-East Central Africa', *Geographical Journal*, vol. cviii, pp. 198–210.

in the publication of the *Encyclopédie Coloniale et Maritime*, of which the volumes on French West and French Equatorial Africa and on Cameroun-Togo form a valuable contribution not only to the geography of Africa in the more formal sense, but to the knowledge of those factors of environment which now make up so much of the study of the modern geographer. Belgium has made an equally valuable contribution in the recent completion of the three volumes of the *Encyclopédie du Congo Belge*. Great Britain has perhaps been more responsible than any other country for changing the face of Africa, and her scientists and the members of various Colonial Services have made contributions to the knowledge of Africa which are certainly not inferior to those made elsewhere. It is unfortunate that the results of their labours have never been brought together in so useful a form as in the works above mentioned.

The geography departments in the universities of the Union of South Africa have a recognized position in the academic world, and some of them are of relatively old standing. Between 1919 and 1926 Dr. E. H. L. Schwartz, formerly of Rhodes University College, Grahamstown, published much material upon conditions in the Kalahari and on the problems of the Okovango Swamps,[1] and Professor F. E. Plummer, formerly at the University of Pretoria, worked during the same period on problems of rainfall and its significance in farming. Among the present staff Professor J. H. Wellington of Johannesburg has carried out extensive research in geomorphology and its application to water conservation and land reclamation.[2] Professor W. J. Talbot of Cape Town has done similar work on the Cape Province,[3] whilst Dr. S. P. Jackson of Johannesburg has specialized on the question of climate.[4] The South African National Resources Development Council, established in 1947, which is concerned primarily with the planning of new development areas in the Union, employs a number of professional geographers on its staff; they have dealt in particular with the distribution of population in the Union.[5]

It is now agreed that geographers can be usefully employed by African Governments in dealing with a variety of problems, and more particularly such matters as the population density tolerable in planning the resettle-

[1] See below, p. 983.

[2] 'Possibilities of Settlement in Africa', *Limits of Land Settlement, Tenth International Studies Conference*, 1937. 'The Kunene River and the Etosha Plain', *South African Geographical Journal*, 1938. 'A Physiographic Regional Classification of South Africa', ibid. 1946. 'A New Development Scheme for the Okovango Delta, Northern Kalahari', *Geographical Journal*, vol. cxiii, pp. 62–69. *Southern Africa—A Geographical Study*, 1953.

[3] W. J. Talbot, *Swartland and Sandveld—A Study of Land Utilization and Soil Erosion in the Western Lowland of the Cape Province*, 1947.

[4] S. P. Jackson, 'Air Masses and Circulation over the Plateau and Coasts of South Africa', *South African Geographical Journal*, 1947; 'Climates of Southern Africa', ibid. 1952.

[5] T. J. D. Fair, 'Durban—Its Sphere of Influence as a Regional Centre', *South African Geographical Journal*, 1949; 'Agricultural Regions and the European Rural Farm Population of Natal', ibid. 1952.

ment of communities removed from their original holdings, or the regulations to be made for the inter-territorial movement of labour; they can equally be of use in helping to determine the soil and climatic requirements of different types of crop, or the economic range of projected markets. It can be claimed with some reason that the failure of certain development schemes undertaken in recent years might have been avoided if a fuller use had been made of the services of geographers in co-operation with agricultural experts and soil chemists.

CHAPTER II

THE AFRICAN PEOPLES

ETHNIC GROUPING

IT was explained in the preceding chapter that it is beyond the purpose of the present work to give a detailed description of the physical features of the great area of Africa with which it deals. It is equally clear that in dealing with the African peoples it will not be practicable to describe at length the numerous and very diverse communities concerned. For the present purpose it must be enough to discuss the views which have from time to time been held about their ethnic grouping and to indicate the extent of the studies which have been made of their social life and customs.

It was at one time held that the peoples of Africa were descended from three principal stocks—Bushmen, Negro, and Hamite—each of which was associated with a characteristic physical type and with certain cultural features. In only a few parts of the continent, however, have surveys been made which would justify a classification made on the basis of physical traits. The most recent work in physical anthropology tends, moreover, to show that the variability of characters in all human populations is so great that it is not possible to draw any clear inference of a common racial origin from physical character. In present-day Africa we see the results of centuries of migration,[1] intermarriage and conquests; and it is also evident that, except in the least accessible regions (such as parts of Ethiopia, the Kalahari waste, or the Nile swamps), the geographical features of Africa have themselves facilitated the fusion of stocks rather than their segregation. It is inevitable, therefore, that existing classifications should in fact be based on language or culture rather than on physical characteristics.

Dr. Seligman's Classification

For the purpose of a rough preliminary grouping a division made some years ago by Dr. Seligman into Bantu, Negroes, Hamites, Bushmen, and Hottentots[2] is generally accepted, but it should be recognized that, though various criteria were used, the determining factor was actually language.

---

[1] For some of the theories regarding the direction of African migrations, see A. C. Haddon, *The Wanderings of Peoples*, 1911; J. Maes and O. Boone, *Les Peuplades du Congo Belge*, 1935; A. Moeller de Laddersous, 'Les Grandes Lignes des migrations des Bantous de la province orientale du Congo Belge', *Institut Royal Colonial Belge: Mémoires*, hereafter referred to as *Mém. I.R.C.B.*, 1936. [2] C. G. Seligman, *Races of Africa*, 1930.

Of these groups the Bantu (which include roughly all peoples in whose language the root -*ntu*, with its appropriate prefix, means 'man') number about 60 million, and are the predominant population of the territory south of the so-called 'Bantu line'.[1] This runs from the mouth of the Rio del Rey along the frontier of Nigeria and the Cameroons, thence eastwards across French Equatorial Africa and the Belgian Congo, south of the Uele River to the head of Lake Kioga, south of Mount Elgon along the eastern shore of Lake Victoria, thence across Tanganyika and northwards to the hinterland of Mombasa, whence a narrow strip runs north-west to Mount Kenya. West Africa is inhabited by Negroes, who range from the mouth of the Senegal River to the eastern frontier of Nigeria, and number roughly about 45 million.

The languages of the next group, the Hamitic, are found in the purest form in north-east Africa, Hamitic-speaking peoples being strongly represented in Somaliland, Ethiopia, and Eritrea. On the basis of archaeological as well as anthropological evidence the Hamites are believed to have invaded Africa from a cradle-land in the vicinity of southern Arabia or the African Horn, and to have penetrated down the Nile valley to the high ground to the east and west of Lake Victoria. The Iraqu in Northern Tanganyika are considered to be Hamitic.[2] In these latter regions, however, they have mingled with earlier established populations, with the result that within the area covered by the present Survey there are now no peoples classed definitely as Hamites. The pastoral aristocracies which mark the inter-lacustrine kingdoms of south-western Uganda, the Bukoba district of Tanganyika, and the Trust territory of Ruanda Urundi are considered to be of Hamitic origin, but the peoples of all three of these areas now speak Bantu languages.

The inhabitants of the Upper Nile basin, numbering some 3 million, are now specifically known as Nilotes, and the pastoral tribes of the northern parts of Kenya and Uganda, with the Masai of the highlands of Kenya and eastern Tanganyika, who total about 1,300,000, are distinguished as Nilo-Hamites. The last of Seligman's groups, the Bushmen and Hottentots, are numerically insignificant. The former are to be found mainly in the Kalahari wastes, and the latter in South-West Africa north of the Orange River.

The more detailed linguistic classifications which have resulted from recent research are discussed in a later chapter.[3] Attempts have also been made to define culture-areas as such,[4] and some social anthropologists have sought to classify particular institutions, such as political organization

[1] See map, p. 81.

[2] *Journal of African Administration*, October 1953, p. 158 (hereafter referred to as *J.A.A.*).

[3] See below, pp. 84–86.

[4] M. Herskovits, 'The Culture Areas of Africa', *Africa*, vol. iii, no. 1, pp. 59–77. H. Baumann and D. Westermann, *Les Peuples et les Civilisations de l'Afrique*, 1948.

or kinship, according to category or type.[1] It is, however, of interest to note that in the arrangement of the recent Ethnographic Survey of Africa, which was inaugurated in 1944 by the International African Institute,[2] no attempt has been made at general classification. Small groups of neighbouring peoples are taken as units within broad geographical regions, and in many cases these units are culturally similar, but in parts of Central Africa, where much migration has taken place at a relatively recent period, very heterogeneous cultures have had to be treated together. In the present instance also it has seemed simpler to follow the principle of division on a purely geographical basis.

Characteristics of Indigenous Races

Despite the great diversity of communities in Africa, there are certain salient characteristics which have differentiated African traditional institutions from those now associated with Western civilization. The majority of indigenous African peoples are characteristically peasants or herdsmen, whose production is mainly for subsistence rather than for the market. Disparity in individual wealth is not usually great and the possession of wealth has not created so marked a difference of social status as among Western peoples. Possession of wealth is, however, often a source of authority, and where centralized political institutions exist and are maintained partly by the right of the Chief to levy tribute, custom prescribes that he should distribute wealth in various forms of largesse.

Great stress is laid on kinship. In most instances (though not universally) the important kin group is a lineage or body of males tracing descent from a common ancestor for several generations in either the male (patrilineal) or female (matrilineal) line. In some forms of society this group or its subdivisions has joint rights to land and valuable property, such as cattle, and in societies where political authority is little developed, lineage members are commonly accustomed to combine to assert their rights to compensation for injuries. The head of the kin group is responsible for making the appropriate sacrifices to the ancestors on behalf of his group. The importance of kinship ties is emphasized in language by the use of the so-called classificatory terminology, in which the words for father, mother, brother, &c., are used of whole classes of relatives.

A logical consequence of the recognition of the kin group as the land-holding unit is that individual ownership of land (in the modern European sense) is unknown in traditional systems, though the hereditary right of user is fully recognized and respected.[3] Marriage is seen as an institution for securing legitimate descendants for the lineage rather than for regu-

---

[1] M. Fortes and E. E. Evans-Pritchard, eds., *African Political Systems*, 1940. A. R. Radcliffe-Brown, ed., *African Systems of Kinship and Marriage*, 1950.

[2] See below, p. 63.   [3] See below, p. 685.

lating sex relations, and is held to create binding obligations not only between the partners, but between the kin of each of them.[1] It is this principle which explains the common practice of the levirate or 'widow-inheritance', and the less common sororate, in which the wife's kin must supply a substitute for her if she dies young or proves barren.[2] An essential element in the contract of a legal marriage is the transfer of goods or rendering of services by the bridegroom and his kinsmen to the kinsmen of the bride.

Polygamy is universally the social ideal, even though it may often be attainable only by the more fortunate minority. Great importance is attached to seniority as well as to actual age, and the oldest men often have special prestige as being in closest contact with the ancestral spirits. There is nearly everywhere an implicit belief in magic and sorcery. Sorcerers are rarely identified and the activities ascribed to them are in fact often quite impossible of performance. Magicians, however, are known and respected, and are believed to be able to protect the community against sorcerers by the use of the esoteric knowledge which they have learned from their predecessors.[3]

There are a number of communities (particularly in non-Bantu Africa) which have failed to develop a political system wider than the kinship group, and in this case such authority as exists is exercised by the titular head of the group. But over the greater part of the area which may be specifically described as Bantu Africa the system of chieftainship has been fully developed. Its origin is no doubt to be traced to the association of kin groups for defensive or offensive warfare, and its institutions, even in their more fully developed form, bear traces of their origin. In these communities the Chief is often charged with the performance of ritual on a tribal or national scale and is himself frequently believed to have a mystical relationship with the ancestors and the land. If he is described as the 'owner' of the tribal land, it is because he is by tradition the protector of the people and of their lands. If he has become the supreme judicial authority, in the sense that he is the arbiter in disputes which the heads of family groups cannot settle for themselves, that is because the position thus accorded to him constitutes the most convenient method of preserving the internal peace of the community.

Though there are cases of deliberate 'law-making' by African Chiefs and their councillors, they are rare.[4] Above all the indigenous Chief has normally had no executive force at his disposal. It is only rarely (as for example in the case of some of the Zulu kings) that the Chief has been

---

[1] A. Phillips, ed., *Survey of African Marriage and Family Life*, 1953, pp. xiii ff.
[2] Ibid. pp. 3, 168–9.
[3] E. E. Evans-Pritchard, *Witchcraft, Oracles and Magic among the Azande*, 1937.
[4] See typical instances noted in *N.A.*, Part V, pp. 268, 299, 301 ff.

able to maintain a military organization of which he is the absolute head. Usually he has depended on the agreement of his traditional councillors in arriving at a decision on matters affecting the tribe, and has only been able to implement it in action by availing himself of the goodwill of the heads of kin or other groups.

In many regions, particularly in East and South Africa, the local groups inhabit an isolated homestead, or as is frequently the case in Central Africa and the more densely populated parts of West Africa, they join to make up a compact village. It is here that one notices one of the most characteristic differences between Africa and India. In India the village, as such, is a self-contained unit.[1] Even if composed, as is frequently the case, of groups of different descent, it has its own community life and its own servants to serve its common needs; it is the basis for the land survey or the registration of land rights or the record of crop returns. Even where it does not have a regular council of Elders (*panchayat*), it accepts the judgement of informal meetings of the village Elders. It is the one political unit which has remained stable throughout the many changes of authority in India. There is little of this type of formation in Africa. There are instances in West Africa[2] where the village as such forms a unit not unlike that of India, but generally it is the kinship group, or the clan or the tribe that is recognized as the operative unit for administrative or similar purposes.

It is only rarely—as for instance in Bechuanaland or in the Yoruba regions in Nigeria—that it has been customary to form large towns. The character of the town frequently indicates whether the normal life of the people is that of cultivators or pastoralists. With the exception that will be subsequently noticed,[3] there has been very little of that differentiation of individual effort which has in other parts of the world created groups practising handicrafts or industries, or has produced an urbanized population primarily occupied in ministering to the needs of the surrounding rural areas which in turn supply it with its subsistence requirements. The tendency to adopt an urbanized form of life (of which some details will subsequently be given[4]) is a relatively modern development, and has been largely influenced by the expansion of industrial employment.

West Africa

While this picture may serve to describe the main characteristics of African life in general, it is necessary to refer in more detail to the life of

[1] L. S. S. O'Malley, *Modern India and the West*, 1941, pp. 3–4. S. H. Freemantle, 'Village Government in India' in *Journal of the Royal Society of Arts* (hereafter referred to as *J.R.S.A.*), March 1947, pp. 385–400.

[2] See, for instance, the description of the so-called 'towns' of Sierra Leone in *N.A.*, Part III, pp. 296, 322.

[3] See below, p. 33, 301.   [4] See below, pp. 564 ff.

the people in each of the main geographical zones contained in the part of the continent with which this Survey is concerned. It will be convenient to begin with West Africa, that is to say, the area containing the group of Colonies comprised in French West Africa (A.O.F.), those comprised in French Equatorial Africa (A.E.F.), the Portuguese territory of Angola, Liberia, the four British West African territories (Nigeria, the Gold Coast, Sierra Leone, and Gambia), and the Trust territories of Togoland and the Cameroons.

In West Africa the majority of the population are primarily agriculturalists, and the fertile wet coastal plain has a relatively dense peasant population. Cattle exist in some numbers in the savannah regions, and a small short-horn breed which is resistant to trypanosomiasis is kept in the coastal area, but cattle have not the same cultural significance as a rule as in east and southern Africa. It is characteristic of West Africa that economic specialization and trade, both internal and external, had reached a considerable stage of development before the period of European rule. Villages had special sections for potters, dyers, weavers, and other craftsmen, and in different areas cowries, bracelets (*manillas*), brass rods, and arrow-shaped pieces of iron (*umumu*) were accepted as currency. Women played an important part in trade, and in this respect their activities have greatly increased in modern times.

In part of this region the people live in walled compounds in which a number of related families inhabit adjoining houses under the authority of a senior member of the group. Density of population and economic specialization together have led to the growth of a number of large indigenous towns, and the Yoruba are probably the most urban of all African peoples. As shown in the census of the year 1931, almost one-third of an estimated total of 3¼ million Yoruba lived in 15 towns with populations over 20,000.[1]

Some of the peoples of this region are politically loosely organized, as for example the Ibo and Umor of the Eastern Region of Nigeria or the Tallensi and the neighbouring peoples of the Upper Volta basin. Among such communities the largest unit which recognizes a single authority may be very small. With the Ibo it is the group of villagers who have a common meeting-place, called the 'commune'; in 1937 it was estimated that there were 2,000 of these in the Ibo-speaking area, which contains some 4 million people.[2] Amongst the Umor there is a somewhat similar local group. With the Tallensi only the smallest kin group, the joint-family, recognize an authority with the right to command, and outside this group the redress for wrongs was traditionally sought by self-help. In these decentralized

[1] D. Forde, *The Yoruba-Speaking Peoples of South Western Nigeria*, Ethnographic Survey of Africa, 1951; and see *N.A.*, Part III, p. 86.
[2] C. K. Meek, *Law and Authority in a Nigerian Tribe (Ibo)*, 1937.

societies much influence is exercised by priests of the ancestor cult and the cult of the earth. The former are lineage heads and can make their displeasure felt by refusing to accept the offerings of a recalcitrant member of the group. In Taleland certain lineage heads are responsible for rites carried out for the people as a whole, and the annual ceremonies at harvest and sowing are a period during which all the Tallensi are united.[1] It is these ritual heads who now hold office as Native Authorities.[2]

With the Ibo the maintenance of law and order was in great measure one of the functions of the age-sets, into which men everywhere (and in some places women) are organized. They were responsible for seizing suspected criminals and bringing them before the Elders, and for collecting the fines imposed. It is still customary for the Elders to call out members of the younger sets for public work, such as clearing the bush paths or building a village meeting-place.

Police functions were also often exercised in the past by the secret societies which are found among most of the coastal peoples of West Africa, among which those of Sierra Leone and Liberia are the best known. It is not the membership but the ritual of these societies that is secret; they are associated with spirits who are impersonated by masked dancers.[3] Recent study tends to discredit the view held by earlier observers that these bodies merely terrorized the community for their own ends, though it is true that some, such as the Ibo leopard society in West and the Nyao in Central Africa, have resorted to terrorism, possibly in the hope of reasserting an influence which was felt to be diminishing.

While these loosely organized political formations are characteristic of the particular communities above named, there are elsewhere well organized political units. Some of the more important of them were the alliances concluded for war purposes by otherwise independent States, as for example those existing among the Akan-speaking peoples of the Gold Coast. Their most extensive confederacy was that of Ashanti, which was formally recognized by the Gold Coast Government in 1935, though it may be remarked that the result of this recognition was to accord to the leading Chief, the Asantehene, a position of paramountcy which went beyond the authority which he traditionally possessed.[4]

In the Akan States of the Gold Coast, most of which had also a well-established political organization,[5] allegiance is to the authority of a man's birthplace and is not changed through life. Succession to office is in the maternal line, and there is no rule of primogeniture. Commoners are

[1] M. Fortes, *The Dynamics of Clanship among the Tallensi*, 1945.

[2] See below, p. 524.

[3] D. Forde, 'Government in Umor', *Africa*, vol. xii, 1939, pp. 129–61. K. L. Little, *The Mende of Sierra Leone*, 1951. H. C. Luke, *Introduction to Bibliography of Sierra Leone*, 1925.

[4] R. S. Rattray, *Ashanti Law and Constitution*, 1929. *N.A.*, Part III, p. 231.

[5] *N.A.*, Part III, pp. 191, 197.

organized in the 'Young men's Companies' which in the old days were bands of warriors. Their consent is still necessary for the installation of a Chief and there is a recognized procedure of 'destoolment', which entitles them to demand his deposition, a practice which became more frequent under British rule.[1]

The Yoruba kingdoms in Nigeria were somewhat more highly centralized, it being a normal practice for the paramount rulers to place their kinsmen and followers in authority over the towns which recognized their supremacy. The rulers, generally known as Obas, were traditionally sacred persons, but as political authorities they received tribute, and war was organized through their military advisers.[2]

All along the southern edge of the Sahara there existed at an early date a number of African States which built up a considerable wealth by trade across the desert.[3] Islamic influences were introduced from North Africa into this area during the eleventh century, and when the Mohammedan traveller Ibn Batuta of Tangier visited it in the fourteenth century he found a number of well-established Islamic States. At different periods one or other of these kingdoms was politically predominant, as, for example, Ghana, the exact locality of which is uncertain,[4] Mali and Songhay, in what is now the French Sudan, and Bornu in Northern Nigeria. Of these kingdoms Bornu and the seven Hausa Emirates in the North of Nigeria survive today. The Fulani, who appear to have been originally nomadic herdsmen, immigrated into this region from North Africa from the thirteenth century onwards.[5] In the Hausa country they were for long treated as a subject people, but in 1804 a Fulani sheikh, Othman dan Fodio, rebelled against the King of Gobir, and proclaimed a holy war which led to the Fulani conquest of most of the Hausa kingdoms and of some additional territory to the south of them; he subsequently established himself as their suzerain in Sokoto. The Bunduka, or aristocratic Fula in Sierra Leone, were introduced by French slave traders from St. Louis in the second half of the eighteenth century.[6] The Fulani now form the ruling class in the Emirates of Northern Nigeria.

Somewhat similar circumstances have influenced the spread of Islamic political organizations in French West Africa. The Sudanese Empire which developed out of the village of Kangaba spread over all the regions

---

[1] R. Buell, *The Native Problem in Africa*, vol. i, 1928, p. 786. K. A. Busia, *The Position of the Chief in the Modern Political System of Ashanti*, 1951.

[2] D. Forde, *The Yoruba-Speaking Peoples of South Western Nigeria*, 1951.

[3] E. W. Bovill, *Caravans of the Old Sahara*, 1937. J. Greenburg, 'Negro Kingdoms of the Sudan', *Transactions of the N.Y. Academy of Sciences*, 11(4), pp. 126–35. A. Gouilly, *L'Islam dans l'Afrique Occidentale Française*, 1952, pp. 57 ff.

[4] For a tentative identification of Ghana with Koumbi Saleh, see *History and Archaeology in Africa* (School of Oriental and African Studies), 1955, p. 35. See also, below, p. 321.

[5] M. Perham, *Native Administration in Nigeria*, 1937.

[6] *Sierra Leone Studies*, December 1953, p. 14.

of the Sudan, and has been described as a gigantic pyramid, which reproduced at its apex the same arrangement as at its base. It was the village itself which expanded into an empire.[1] In West Africa the Muslims are now estimated to be 33 per cent. of the total population in Nigeria, 11 per cent. in Sierra Leone, 84 per cent. in the Gambia, 50 per cent. in the British Cameroons, 34 per cent. in French West Africa, 30 per cent. in French Equatorial Africa, and 20 per cent. in Liberia.[2]

In most of West Africa descent is patrilineal, but the Akan-speaking peoples form an important matrilineal enclave. There are also some matrilineal peoples among the non-Muslim population of Northern Nigeria. The Yako have an interesting system whereby persons reckon descent for different purposes through both male and female line.[3]

East Africa

East Africa, in terms of territorial organization, includes Kenya, Tanganyika, Uganda, and the Trust territory of Ruanda Urundi. As compared with West Africa, East Africa may be said to be distinguished by a lower density of population, by the predominance of pastoral peoples, by the lack of the economic specialization (in terms both of handicrafts and trade) of which there is evidence in West Africa, and by the relative absence of indigenous towns. In most of this area there are also signs of more recent tribal movement or migration. There is less evidence of the existence of centralized political institutions with a long history behind them, though in this last respect Uganda, the Bukoba District of Tanganyika, and Ruanda Urundi form exceptions.

The majority of the East African peoples agree in regarding cattle[4] as the most desirable form of wealth; they often evince a strong emotional attitude towards them, surrounding them with ritual observances, and it is characteristic that the transfer of cattle is an important factor in marriage contracts. There are, however, some exceptions to this rule. The Kikuyu and Kamba of Kenya, for example, are largely agriculturalists, and goats take the place of cattle in their social observances. The Ganda value the possession of cattle, but attach no ritual or symbolic importance to them.

Most of the tribes cultivate food crops so far as the environment allows, but the Turkana, Karamojong, and Masai are still primarily nomadic herdsmen, while the Nuer and Dinka regard agriculture as a degrading occupation. The Hima aristocracy of the inter-lacustrine kingdoms were

---

[1] R. Delavignette, *Freedom and Authority in French West Africa*, 1950, p. 76.

[2] G. M. Wysner, in *Africa Today*, ed. C. G. Haines, 1955, p. 113. The number of Muslims in East Africa is relatively small.

[3] D. Forde, 'Double Descent among the Yako', in *African Systems of Kinship and Marriage*, ed. A. R. Radcliffe-Brown, 1950.

[4] For the cult of the cattle in Ruanda Urundi, in particular the usage of *ubuhake* and *ubugabire*, see below, p. 558.

accustomed to obtain their vegetable food by barter or tribute from their subjects. In modern conditions, however, there has been in some areas a considerable development of the cultivation of cash crops. Uganda has a large production of cotton, and some of the agricultural tribes of Tanganyika, as for example the Chagga, have a very considerable production of coffee.

There are many types of political organization. The Nilotic peoples are typical examples of a decentralized form of political structure. The Nuer have no judicial institutions; redress for injury is sought by self-help, but feud can be reconciled by a 'Leopard-skin Chief', a ritual specialist with no secular authority. With other Nilotic tribes, as for instance the Anuak and Shilluk, such ritual authorities have rudimentary political powers, which have been enhanced by their recognition under British rule as Native Authorities.[1]

There are, however, more definite evidences of a developed State organization among the inter-lacustrine Bantu. The development of a State organization has in this case (as has often occurred elsewhere in the world) been due to the need for maintaining the dominance of a conquering group among a subject people. There are in this area kings (as for instance the Hima rulers of Buganda) who have been accustomed to maintain their authority through territorial officials charged with keeping internal order, collecting tribute, and organizing manpower for labour or for war.

In some instances, as for example in Ankole and Ruanda, the pastoral (Hima or Tussi) aristocracy still form a class distinct from the peasants (Iru or Hutu).[2] In others, the process of political consolidation has had a different origin, being due to a deliberate effort to acquire strength by union under a single tribal head. In several of the Tanganyika tribes, as for example the Chagga,[3] the Hehe,[4] and the Bena,[5] the process of consolidation under a single ruler was still in progress at the time of the German occupation.

Descent is everywhere patrilineal. Religious practices include the worship both of the ancestors and of a high god believed to live in the sky. The Ganda formerly had an organized national religion, annual ceremonies being performed on behalf of the king by the priests of a number of spirits responsible for giving assistance in different circumstances. Some of the East African tribes, and most notably those of Nilotic or Nilo-Hamitic origin, are characterized by a system of age-grades through which

---

[1] A. Butt, *The Nilotes*, Ethnographic Survey of Africa, 1952.

[2] K. Oberg, 'The Political System of the Ankole', in *African Political Systems*, ed. M. Fortes and E. E. Evans-Pritchard, 1940.

[3] B. Gutmann, *Das Recht der Dschagga*, 1926. F. B. Steiner, in *Africa*, October 1954, pp. 364 ff.

[4] G. Gordon Brown and A. Bruce Hutt, *Anthropology in Action*, 1935.

[5] A. T. and G. M. Culwick, *Ubena of the Rivers*, 1935.

every male member passes, becoming first a warrior and then an Elder
with a judicial and ritual function.[1] Where the age-grade system is fully
developed, as among the Masai, it became a political factor, and the
Elders of the age-grade had a high measure of authority both in military
and civil affairs. The age-grade system is also shared, though in a less
prominent form, by some of the Bantu tribes of Kenya, such as the Kikuyu
and Kamba.[2]

Central Africa

The Central African zone may for the present purpose be taken as
including the Belgian Congo, Northern Rhodesia, and Nyasaland, with
the adjoining parts of Portuguese East Africa. The peoples of this large
region are predominantly Bantu-speaking, and their economic and social
conditions resemble those described above as characterizing East Africa,
but with two differences. There is in the first place less dependence on
cattle as a means of subsistence, and cattle have not usually the same social
significance. In a considerable part of the area (and most notably in the
Belgian Congo and part of the Portuguese territory) tsetse fly or other
conditions make the country unsuitable for the maintenance of domestic
stock. But even where cattle are kept agriculture tends to be the principal
source of subsistence, though in the more tropical parts the crops (finger
millet and cassava) are not of high value.

There is another noticeable feature. A considerable block of land included in this region has a soil which is rapidly exhausted by cropping,
with the consequence that it is necessary to resort to various methods of
shifting cultivation of which a fuller description is given in a subsequent
chapter.[3] There will be found there also a reference to the method of life
of some of the peoples living in the Zambezi flood areas and in the swamp
areas, such as those of the Bangweulu region. There are in the forests of
the Belgian Congo a number of scattered Pygmy tribes, who live by hunting and to some extent also by a crude system of trading with the neighbouring Bantu. There are also small groups of Pygmy or 'Pygmoides' in
the French Cameroons and in French Equatorial Africa.[4]

Almost all the Bantu-speaking tribes of this region have a co-ordinated
tribal structure with a Chief as the central figure, but there is much variety
in their character. Among the Yao of Nyasaland, for example, a large
number of otherwise independent authorities have traditionally recognized

[1] A. C. Hollis, *The Masai*, 1905. G. R. Sandford, *Administration and Political History of the Masai Reserve*, 1918.
[2] J. M. Middleton, *The Kikuyu and Kamba of Kenya*, Ethnographic Survey of Africa, 1953.
S. N. Eisenstadt, 'African Age Groups, a Comparative Study', *Africa*, April 1954, pp. 100–13.
[3] See below, p. 819.
[4] F. Schebesta, *Die Bambuti-Pygmäen von Ituri*, 4 vols., *Mém. I.R.C.B.*, vol. xxvi, 1952. *Enc. C.B.*, vol. i, p. 104.

the ritual superiority of a small group who had a hereditary right to make sacrifices for rain. The Chief of the large Bemba tribe in Northern Rhodesia has a similar position as primarily a ritual leader. Here, however, there was only one Paramount, who appointed subordinate chiefs from the royal clan, but did not control their political activities.

Among the Lozi of Barotseland authority was centralized through the subordination of all members of the tribe on a personal, not a territorial, basis to the authority of specific officials appointed for the purposes of war, the collection of tribute, the employment of labour services, or the settlement of disputes. Among the Ngoni, an offshoot of the Zulu, who migrated into Northern Rhodesia and Nyasaland in the nineteenth century[1] and absorbed a number of groups encountered by them in their passage up country, the Chiefs maintained their hold over conquered tribes by appointing relatives or favoured war leaders to the control of groups of villages. By contrast the Tonga of Mazabuka District of Northern Rhodesia were divided into independent villages which came together only at the shrines where sacrifices were made for rain.[2]

Matrilineal descent is usual in this region; children belong to the mother's lineage, and it is usual for married life to begin at the wife's home where the husband is subject to the authority of her kinsmen. He is generally allowed at a later stage to take his wife away to a home of his own choosing, but the rules on this point differ from one people to another. Patrilineal descent is, however, recognized by the Nkundo of the Equator Province in the Belgian Congo, the Lozi, and the Ngoni. But the Ngoni, having freely intermarried with the matrilineal Chewa in whose country they finally settled, are modifying many of their traditional customs.

Everywhere a belief in ancestral spirits dominates the religion of the people, but the high god Lesa or Mulungu is also recognized and is in some tribes addressed directly. A belief in witches operating through familiar spirits is widespread, and in recent years new organizations of persons claiming to be able to give protection against them have appeared in various localities.[3]

Africa South of the Zambezi

It remains to notice the important area of Africa lying south of the Zambezi. This region is almost entirely inhabited by Bantu-speaking tribes, which in the Union of South Africa alone have a population of over

[1] E. H. Lane Poole, *The Native Tribes of the Eastern Province of Northern Rhodesia*, 1938, pp. 1–10. J. A. Barnes, *Politics in a Changing Society*, 1954.

[2] E. Colson and M. Gluckman, eds., *Seven Tribes of Central Africa*, 1951; Yao, Bemba, Lozi, Ngoni, Tonga, Shona, Nyakyusa.

[3] A. I. Richards, 'A Modern Movement of Witch-finders', *Africa*, October 1935, pp. 448–61. M. G. Marwick, 'The Social Context of Cewa Witch Beliefs', *Africa*, April 1952, pp. 120–35; ibid. July 1954, pp. 215–34.

8 million. The minor African communities, the remains of the Khoisan people (Bushmen and Hottentots), who were once widely distributed over the region, are now confined to limited areas.

The Bushmen are hunters and food-gatherers who wander in small bands from one waterhole to another; they do not recognize any organization superior to that of the family group. When first encountered by Europeans they possessed no cattle and did not know the use of iron. Their naturalistic rock paintings, which are of much artistic merit, give an interesting clue to their earlier mode of life.[1] Their religious rites are directed mainly towards securing rain and increasing the supply of animal food.[2] The Hottentots are by tradition nomadic pastoralists, whose material equipment is more highly developed than that of the Bushmen, though they have no pictorial art. They are organized into patrilineal clans and tribes with chiefs. Their main ritual is concerned with the making of fire.[3]

The Bantu of this region are divided into two main groups, the south-eastern and south-central Bantu. The former are again subdivided into the Nguni cluster in the eastern Cape and Transkei, Natal, Zululand, and Swaziland, and the Thonga cluster in Portuguese East Africa and the eastern Transvaal. The second group are also subdivided into the Venda of the north-eastern Transvaal and the Sotho, who inhabit Bechuanaland, the adjoining parts of the Union, and Basutoland.[4] Owing to the extent to which they have been associated with the European economy, a large proportion of the Bantu tribes of South Africa are now in a phase of transition, but in their own environment they depend for their subsistence both on agriculture and on cattle, these being for some tribes a possession as highly prized as they are by the tribesmen in East Africa. Their principal crops are maize and millets. As compared with the peoples of West Africa, economic specialization was much more limited in the period preceding the European occupation, and trade and exchange had scarcely developed in the traditional culture.

The typical local grouping is the homestead, the residence usually of a man with all his sons and their wives and children. Among the coastal peoples and in Southern Rhodesia the members of this group have their fields and a common pasturage for their herds in the vicinity. In Basutoland and the Transvaal there are small villages of ten to 50 homesteads. In Bechuanaland the majority of the members of the leading tribes are con-

---

[1] See below, p. 73. See also H. Balfour, *Bushmen Paintings*, 1909. I. Schapera, in *South African Journal of Science*, vol. xxii, 1925, pp. 504 ff.

[2] I. Schapera, *The Khoisan Peoples of South Africa, Bushmen and Hottentots*, 1930. D. Bleek, *The Naron*, 1928. P. B. Tobias, 'The Survival of the Bushmen', in *Africa*, April 1956, pp. 174–85.

[3] A. W. Hoernlé, 'Social Organization of the Nama Hottentots of South-West Africa', *American Anthropologist*, vol. xxvii, 1925, pp. 1–24. H. Vedder, *South West Africa in Early Times*, 1938, pp. 128, 170.

[4] I. Schapera, 'The Old Bantu Culture', in *Western Civilization and the Natives of South Africa*, 1934.

centrated in a central town, sometimes with a considerable population, situated near sources of permanent water. Such cultivated lands as exist are generally at some distance from the town, and in the agricultural season each family lives in a crude homestead close to his fields. Cattle are kept at posts often a day's journey or more on foot from the town, and during part of the year the majority of the town population is absent at the cattle posts.[1]

In most of the Bantu tribes of this area the characteristic political system is highly centralized in the sense that it comprises a head Chief who controls his tribal area through a hierarchy of subordinate chiefs or headmen. It is only, however, in rare cases that these represent appointments made by the Chief himself, and they are for the most part hereditary in certain families. In many tribes the organization for war was based on the enrolment of all the young men of the tribe into regiments of age-mates, and in the early nineteenth century several Chiefs built up strong States by conquest, but most of these were broken up by the superior power of Europeans.

At the present time the traditional position of the Chief has been greatly impaired in territories such as the Union or Southern Rhodesia, where he may be said to have retained little effective authority; his position has perhaps been least impaired in the High Commission Territories, where the regiments can still be called out by him for assistance in work of national importance. Succession to the chieftainship is hereditary, usually in the male line; in a few Sotho tribes women may succeed, and among the Swazi the Queen Mother has a titular authority which is in principle parallel to that of the Paramount:[2] her position has some analogy to that of the Mukwae in the Barotse Protectorate, who is always closely related to the royal family, and has her own district and her own Council or Kuta.[3] The selection of the wife who is destined to become the mother of the heir affects the entire tribe; all members contribute to the cattle given at marriage, and tribal councillors and headmen take an active part in the negotiations with her family. Despite the theoretically rigid rules of succession, rival claims are often supported by factions whose opposition lasts for generations; as is illustrated by the dynastic disputes of the Bamangwato tribe in Bechuanaland.

In addition to his military and judicial functions, the Chief may be responsible for the performance of tribal ceremonies, of which the most important is the ritual eating of the first fruits of the country, a rite which is still practised by the Swazi, though fast disappearing elsewhere.[4]

[1] *N.A.*, Part V, pp. 152, 245, 267, 273; *Cambridge History of the British Empire*, vol. viii, 1937, p. 42.
[2] *N.A.*, Part V, p. 355. H. Kuper, *An African Aristocracy*, 1947, pp. 54 ff.
[3] *N.A.*, Part II, p. 97. Kuta is variously spelt Khotla, Kgotla.
[4] Ibid. pp. 86, 197 ff.

Divination, which is performed by specialists, is highly developed. The Sotho, Venda, and Shangaan Tonga most frequently divine by means of ivory dice, which are beginning to be adopted by the Ngoni, together with their own varied techniques.[1] The belief in malevolent magic takes many forms and is active even among completely urbanized Africans. The extent to which the belief in magical practices can survive is shown by the occurrence of the long series of medicine murders in Basutoland,[2] which is the more remarkable in view of the high proportion of the population which practises Christianity.[3]

There is one aspect of African life that has received such wide comment as to need special reference here. The most superficial observer must everywhere be struck by the absence in Africa south of the Sahara of the remains of historical buildings. It is true that the African has in the past shown very little aptitude for building, even where materials have been ready at hand. His comparative shortcoming in this respect adds interest to the speculations which have been so rife among archaeologists regarding the origin of the Zimbabwe buildings in Southern Rhodesia. While Zimbabwe, 'The Great Stones',[4] is by far the largest monument in stone in southern Africa, it is not unique; others, though much less spectacular, have been discovered in Southern Rhodesia and the Union of South Africa. It was known to the Portuguese immigrants in the sixteenth century and first appears in a map of Johannes Leo in 1570. In an atlas published in Venice in 1588, Zimbabwe is described as 'the work not of humans, but the devil', and as having 'an inscription over the doorway written in a language which cannot be recognized by anyone of any nation'.[5] It was rediscovered by Karl Mauch in 1867 and has since been ascribed variously to Arabs, Persians, and Africans.

Since the excavations of 1929, inspired by the British Association and undertaken by Miss Caton-Thompson, the work has been widely held to have been built by Bantu and has been ascribed, largely on the evidence of beads discovered below the surface, to the eighth or ninth centuries.[6] This attribution has, however, been disputed by those who rely upon the evidence of fragments of Persian, Arabian, and Chinese pottery dating from the twelfth century and later, and who find, in the omission of the Persian geographer El Másudi to mention Zimbabwe when he visited Sofala in the tenth century, evidence that it had not been built at that

---

[1] A. W. Hoernlé, 'Magic and Medicine', in *The Bantu-speaking Tribes of South Africa*, ed. I. Schapera, 1937.

[2] G. I. Jones, *Basutoland Medicine Murder*, Cmd. 8209, 1951, pp. 22 ff.

[3] *N.A.*, Part V, p. 2.

[4] The word is derived from *mabwe* meaning 'stones', and the prefix *Zi* meaning 'great'.

[5] *Geographia di Livio Sanuto*; and see E. H. Lane Poole, *The Discovery of Africa from Maps*, Rhodes–Livingstone Institute, 1950, p. 9.

[6] G. Caton-Thompson, *The Zimbabwe Culture*, 1931, pp. 188, 199.

date. The opinion of Miss Caton-Thompson has, however, received some corroboration in recent years when wood taken from a lintel was subjected to radio-active carbon tests which have indicated that the trees from which the wood was cut were between 1,264 and 1,494 years old. The conclusion to be drawn is that Zimbabwe is of Bantu origin and was occupied about the eighth century A.D.[1]

PHYSICAL AND MENTAL CHARACTERISTICS

It has generally been held that if it is possible to make any reliable distinction between the different races of the world, it must take the form of a classification in terms of their inherited physical characteristics. It is true that some authorities would reject altogether the use of the term 'race' as applied to human beings, since they all belong to one species,[2] but the majority of physical anthropologists now agree to use it of populations which are differentiated by the frequency of particular physical traits. They recognize at the same time that the traits which have been selected as criteria constitute only a fraction of the biological heritage common to all human beings, and that if the total number of physical characters is taken into account, the similarities between men are in all cases much greater than the differences.[3]

The earliest work in this field was based on external physical characteristics, in particular the skin, hair, eye colour, form, stature, and the shape of skull, nose, and lips. The use of measurements of these physical characters for comparative purposes has been facilitated by means of various indices. These indices do not, however, provide a basis for the division of humanity into groups all members of which have a number of distinguishing traits in common. If any one criterion is taken, it is possible to show that it has a fairly well-marked geographical distribution; but the distribution of different criteria does not coincide, except in the few areas which are isolated from external contacts. The samples measured are usually taken from populations with a common culture in a limited geographical area, these being correctly described as ethnic groups. The results are expressed in the form of averages, and in all characters which have been so far measured some degree of variation has been found in the averages for different groups. Within each population, however, there is a wide range of variation, so that two individuals of one group often differ more widely than either would differ from some individual of another group. To take an extreme example from Africa, the average height of the Dinka

[1] For a chronology of Zimbabwe see *History and Archaeology in Africa* (School of Oriental and African Studies), 1955, p. 77.

[2] L. S. Penrose, quoted in *The Race Concept*, Unesco, 1953, p. 24.

[3] M. Leiris, *Race and Civilization*, Unesco, 1951.

is among the tallest for any population in the world, but there are some Dinka who are shorter than tall Pygmies.[1]

The Cranial Index

A comparison made in 1931 of the measurements of 120 skulls from the Teita region of Kenya with 600 from other parts of Africa led to the conclusion that no sharp distinction could be drawn on this basis between the population of western, eastern, and southern Africa.[2] In 1932–4 two members of the Kenya Medical Service published certain comparisons between the brains of Europeans and Africans, in which one compared their cranial capacity, and the other the characteristics of the cells of the prefrontal cortex.[3] The results were accepted in some quarters as evidence of the inferior mental capacity of the African, but recent studies of the brain have failed to establish any correlation between cranial capacity and mental intelligence.[4] It is noteworthy in this particular connexion that the Eskimo, Javanese, and some Bantu tribes return higher averages of cranial capacity than the French or English.

Theories based on the shape of the skull have been proved to be equally fallacious. There is for instance no evidence that, as was at one time believed, the long-headed type have greater initiative; the Swede is long headed and so is the Negro, but the Swiss, who are certainly not less distinguished for initiative, are of the round-headed type. Geneticists are not prepared to deny the presence of hereditary differences, but they are unable to point to any one difference in the physical conformation of the brain which can be correlated with a difference in mental characteristics.

Blood Groups

As a means of classifying people according to stocks (that is, the populations from whom they may be supposed to have descended) the use of physical measurements has the limitation that the quantitative expression of most of the characters used is controlled by a number of different genes, and in addition that most of the measurable traits have been affected by environment, and particularly by nutrition in early life.[5] There is, moreover, no ground for assuming that the parent stocks of groups recognized to be of mixed descent were themselves homogeneous.[6]

[1] G. M. Morant, *The Significance of Racial Differences*, Unesco, 1952.
[2] E. Kitson, 'A Study of the Negro Skull, with special reference to the Crania from Kenya', *Biometrika*, vol. xxiii, 1931, pp. 271–314.
[3] H. L. Gordon, 'The Mental Capacity of the African', *Journal of the Royal African Society*, vol. xxxiii, 1934, pp. 226–42 (hereafter referred to as *J.R.A.S.*). F. W. Vint, 'A Preliminary Note on the Cell Content of the Pre-frontal Cortex of the East African Native', *East African Medical Journal*, vol. ix, 1932, pp. 30–55.   [4] G. Walter, *The Living Brain*, 1953.
[5] A. E. Mourant, 'The Use of Blood Groups in Anthropology', *Journal of the Royal Anthropological Institute*, vol. lxxvii, 1947, pp. 139–44 (hereafter referred to as *J.R.A.I.*).
[6] J. C. Trevor, *Race-crossing in Man*, 1953.

A more satisfactory basis of classification became available with the discovery of blood groups by Landsteiner in 1900. It has been shown that all human beings can be divided into groups in terms of the presence or absence in their red blood corpuscles of certain chemical substances (antigens) which cause the red cells to agglutinate when acted upon by other chemical substances (antibodies) present in the blood serum of other people who lack the antigens. The antigens for which tests are most readily carried out are those originally designated 'A' and 'B' by Land-steiner; he recognized four groups of persons, namely, those with A, with B, with both (AB), or with neither (O). Other antigens were discovered later, the most significant for purposes of classification being the Rh series, discovered in 1940, and so called after the rhesus monkey, the blood of which contains an antigen related to one of the human Rh antigens.

The blood groups are inherited in a known way according to Mendelian principles; they are not affected by environment and are sharply dis-tinguishable. They are believed to have arisen very early in the course of man's evolution, the A, B, and O groups having been found in the higher apes. To a large extent the frequency of different groups in man is corre-lated with geographical areas, and the frequencies of the A, B, and O groups for most of the principal peoples of the world were determined by 1939. It was discovered that Negroes have a high frequency of O, but that the frequency of A is less common in Africa than in Europe; the distribu-tion of B is similar to that found in Eastern as opposed to Western Europe.

In 1939 the blood types of a number of African tribes were examined, and it was considered probable that an important component of the original population of Africa was similar in blood-group frequency to the modern Egyptian and the modern Congo Pygmies.[1] It has since been indicated that Africa south of the Sahara shows a uniform preponderance of a chromosome (cDe) of the Rh group, which is, as far as is known, unique.[2] 'There is no overlap, nor any approach to an overlap, between the Rh frequencies of any known population in Africa south of the Sahara and any known population whatsoever.'[3]

The conclusion reached from this distribution is that no substantial component of Rh blood group extends from Egypt or the Mediterranean southwards beyond Abyssinia. This conclusion, while rejecting contact with the north, suggests that the Pygmies may constitute one of the main components of many African tribes.[4] Though some of the results obtained so far are suggestive, they do not as yet provide material for a complete

---

[1] R. Elsdon-Dew, 'Blood Groups in Africa', *Publications of South African Institute of Medical Research*, vol. ix, 1939, pp. 29–94.

[2] A. E. Mourant, *Distribution of Human Blood Groups*, 1954, p. 16.

[3] Ibid. p. 87.

[4] Ibid. p. 97. See also J. A. Donegani, K. A. Ibrahim, E. W. Ikin, and A. E. Mourant, 'The Blood Groups of the People of Egypt', *Heredity*, vol. iv, 1950, pp. 377–82.

classification of the indigenous peoples of Africa on the basis of their blood groups.

Sickle Frequency

A hereditary trait which was first identified among American Negroes in 1910 consists of a condition of the red corpuscles in which they assume a sickle shape when deprived of oxygen. The first case known to have been observed in Africa was that of an African from Angola working in the Luanshya copper mine in Northern Rhodesia. Surveys were made of the incidence of this trait among all labourers employed at that mine and elsewhere in Northern Rhodesia,[1] but no general conclusions have been drawn from these surveys.

In Uganda 5,000 persons coming from all the tribes of the Protectorate were examined. Among five groups classed as Hamite (four on the basis of language, the fifth being the Hima of the inter-lacustrine region), four had a very low incidence of this trait; the exception were the Teso, who did not show the Caucasoid features regarded as characteristic of the Hamites and have also, in becoming settled agriculturalists, adopted an important element of Bantu culture. The Nilotes are homogenous in having a high incidence. Among the Bantu the incidence varies widely and appears to be inversely proportional to the degree of their contact with Hamitic invaders.[2] It is, however, safe to say that the sickle cell occurs with greater frequency in the east than in the west, and the high frequency in East Africa may be related to the high frequency among the Veddahs in India, suggesting an origin from Asia. On the other hand, a predisposition to the sickle gene may occur in populations exposed to malaria.[3]

Intelligence Tests

The assumption that there are innate differences in mental capacity between persons belonging to different ethnic groups is widely held, and various attempts have been made to draw conclusions on this point from the results of the application of intelligence tests. In the United States such a test was given to all army recruits in 1917 and in every State resulted in higher scores for Whites than for Negroes. The fact that the Negroes of the northern States did better than those of the south seems to

---

[1] W. B. English, in *South African Medical Journal*, vol. xvii, 1943, p. 389. R. W. Evans, in *Transactions of the Royal Society of Tropical Medicine*, vol. xxviii, 1944, pp. 281–6. E. A. Beet, 'Sickle Cell Disease in the Balovale District', *East African Medical Journal*, vol. xxiii, pp. 75–86, and 'Sickle Cell Disease in Northern Rhodesia', ibid. vol. xxiv, pp. 212–22.

[2] H. Lehmann and A. B. Raper, 'Distribution of the Sickle Cell Trait in Uganda', *Nature*, vol. clxiv, 1949, pp. 494–5. See also H. Lehmann, 'Distribution of the Sickle Cell Gene', *Eugenics Review*, vol. xlvi, July 1954.

[3] A. E. Mourant, *Distribution of the Human Blood Groups*, 1954, p. 97.

be an indication of the importance of environmental conditions in producing the type of intelligence that was the subject of the tests.

At one time hopes were entertained that important conclusions regarding racial abilities could be drawn from tests of this kind, but as the methods used came to be studied more critically it was realized that they were not so devised as to eliminate the effects of differences in environment and upbringing. More recently it has been shown that nutritional conditions, and in particular the lack of certain vitamins, directly affect the development of intelligence. An investigation made in Jamaica of samples of the White, Negro, and mixed populations had the advantage that the differences in social environment are not in this case great. In this experiment little difference could be found between the aggregate performances of the different groups; some excelled in one type of test and some in another.[1]

A definition of intelligence has been propounded in which the most important element is the ability to educe relationships.[2] It is held that in seeking to determine the potentialities of African intelligence, in the sense of its power to learn, whether from a teacher or from experience, this is the quality which must be measured, and the possible methods of measurement would be by problems which normally arise in the environment of the person tested or by devising non-verbal tests involving the recognition of relationships. The first method is of course open to the criticism that the results achieved would not be comparable with those attained in other tests; the second method would obviate this difficulty, but up to now few such tests have been found satisfactory as bases for comparison.[3]

A general intelligence test for Africans, representing an adaptation to local conditions of the technique most widely used in Europe, was the subject of an investigation made in 1932 on behalf of the Carnegie Corporation.[4] The test requires an elementary degree of education and is advocated for the limited object of determining how far schoolchildren at a given stage can profitably proceed to further education. This test was not devised with a view to drawing comparisons between African and European intelligence, and the author himself expressed the view that none of the grounds of comparison so far used yields valid or decisive data. No existing mental test can in his view be used as a standard of comparison between populations which differ widely in culture. Nevertheless, the results of its application to 93 African and 124 European secondary schoolboys in Kenya have a certain interest. The average mark of the

[1] S. F. Nadel, 'The Application of Intelligence Tests in the Anthropological Field', in *The Study of Society*, ed. F. C. Bartlett, 1939.
[2] C. E. Spearman, *The Abilities of Man*, 1927.   [3] Nadel, op. cit.
[4] R. A. C. Oliver, 'Mental Tests in the Study of the African', *Africa*, vol. vii, no. 1, 1934, pp. 40–46.

Africans was approximately 85 per cent. of that of the Europeans, but some 14 per cent. of the Africans, in spite of the group's undoubtedly lower level of environment and education, gained marks as high as, or higher than, the European average.

Standardized tests were used on a large scale by the Interdepartmental Committee on Native Education of the Union during 1935–6,[1] having been applied to some 12,000 African pupils, comprising practically all those in Standard VI and above in all four Provinces of the Union. The tests used were those which had previously been standardized in connexion with nearly 30,000 pupils in European schools, and were tests of knowledge gained in school rather than intelligence tests as that term is usually understood. They consisted of arithmetical questions and problems, and of tests of familiarity with English words, both simple and difficult. It is obvious, however, that the comparisons between European and African children which were based upon such tests refer to the quality of the instruction received rather than to natural intelligence.

At the South African Bureau for Educational and Social Research a number of examinations with different non-verbal tests have been made. A sample of 637 African school pupils between the ages of 12 and 19 were examined and the conclusion was reached that 'around the ages of 13 and 14, Native children are from 4 to 5 years inferior to European children in educability'.[2] These findings have, however, been criticized on the ground that some of the tests used are not regarded by their inventors as intelligence tests, and that they were not in fact so chosen as to eliminate the influences of environment and culture. Some involved employing pictures of objects that are not familiar to African children, others depended on speed of performance, a quality which is valued in European but not in African culture. It was further argued that conclusions regarding innate mental abilities cannot be drawn from comparisons between children whose home environment and state of nutrition differs as widely as do those of the African and European children tested in the Union.[3] The same conclusion was reached in a comparison of Negro and White populations in the United States by the Swedish sociologist Gunnar Myrdal.[4]

A body of eight anthropologists and sociologists, convened from all parts of the world by Unesco, arrived at the following conclusions. They agreed that the only characteristics that could be used as a basis for classification were physical and physiological; that there was no proof that groups of mankind differ in their innate mental characteristics, whether of intelligence or temperament; that genetic differences were not

[1] *Report*, U.G. 29, 1936, paras. 502–12.
[2] M. L. Fick, *The Educability of the South African Native*, South African Council for Educational and Social Research, Research Series no. 8, 1939.
[3] S. Biesheuvel, *African Intelligence*, 1943.
[4] Gunnar Myrdal, *An American Dilemma*, vol. i, 1944, p. 152.

of importance in determining social and cultural differences between different groups; and that there was no evidence that race mixture had bad results from a biological aspect.[1]

It will be observed that all the experiments referred to in the preceding paragraphs have been concerned with the testing of a single characteristic, namely, proficiency in those mental processes which the European system of education seeks to develop. They do not in themselves afford evidence in support of the assumption that the mental capacity of Africans is in general inferior to that of Europeans, even if judged by standards primarily devised with reference to European conditions. A more extended use of intelligence tests, on a basis suited to African environment, may give results of value to the educationalist; but it is doubtful if any investigation into the comparative mental capacity of the African can yield conclusions which will form a safe basis for the determination of general administrative policy. It has been said with truth that the history of the mental testing of ethnic groups has resulted so far in a progressive disillusionment with tests as measures of native ability and a gradually increasing realization of the many complex environmental factors which must influence the result.[2]

Some psychologists and anthropologists, particularly in America, have sought to correlate differences in culture with differences in personality type. Some have held that the characteristic personality is determined very early in life and have concentrated their attention on differences in the treatment of infants in different societies.[3] Others consider that all social institutions play their part in encouraging the emergence of one personality type rather than another.[4] Such studies as have been made in Africa of the influence exercised by social institutions on the development of personality have not always been the work of scientific observers.

To take one example, it has been argued that the long period of suckling habitual in most parts of Africa creates a state of emotional dependence which makes it difficult for Africans to adapt themselves to the competitive conditions of modern economic life.[5] It appears, however, that an equally long period of suckling is characteristic of the Chinese.[6] A French writer, dealing with the nationalist movement in Madagascar, compared it to the familiar effort of the adolescents who seek freedom from the control of their parents while still remaining dependent on them.[7] The subject-matter of studies of this kind, however, is not really the development of psychological

[1] *UNESCO and its Programme III, The Race Question*, Unesco Publication, 791, p. 9.
[2] O. Klineberg, *Race Differences*, 1935.
[3] G. Gorer and J. Rickman, *The People of Great Russia*, 1949.
[4] A. Kardiner and R. Linton, *The Individual and His Society*, 1944.
[5] J. F. Ritchie, *The African as Suckling and as Adult, Rhodes–Livingstone Institute Papers*, no. 19 (hereafter referred to as *R.L.I. Papers*).
[6] F. Hsu, *Under the Ancestor's Shadow: Chinese Culture and Personality*, 1949. H. T. Fei, *Peasant Life in China*, 1949.   [7] O. Mannoni, *Psychologie de la colonisation*, 1950.

states, still less of characteristic types of personality, but is really concerned with the changes in values which accompany changes in social structure. The treatment of historical processes in terms of analogies with the individual life-cycle can be very misleading.

It does not seem in short that either biology or analytical psychology can provide any definite evidence of the existence in different ethnic groups of innate characteristics which connote superiority in mind or character as compared with other groups. That need not, however, impair our recognition of the fact that in the world's history certain groups have given evidence of greater initiative than others in the use of the mechanical arts or the many other developments which have conduced to the improvement of their physical conditions or social standards.

Whether or not this fact can be justly interpreted as reflecting any difference in innate characteristics, it is clear that as a whole the African peoples south of the Sudan have not in this respect shown the same activity as many other ethnic groups in Europe or in Asia. It is only possible to speculate as to the explanation of this phenomenon. One cannot accept as completely adequate the explanation that the physical geography of this part of Africa has resulted in the isolation of its peoples from outside influences, for such segregation was by no means complete. Many of them had, for instance, contacts with peoples in the Nile Valley and with immigrant communities on the east coast.[1] It may be that, as has been observed, stimuli from abroad reached the interior in thin streams and with many interruptions. It is certainly true that until the arrival of Europeans the peoples south of the Sahara were not as a whole subject to the widespread impact of a more highly developed form of culture.

But it is by no means the case that ethnic groups in other parts of the world have been dependent on an outside stimulus before making improvements in their technique of cultivation or in the social arts. It is possible that the explanation is to be found partly in the circumstances which predisposed so many of the African tribes to a nomadic form of life, and partly in the prevalence of deficiencies of soil and climate which resulted in impairing their health and vitality. But this explanation is at best speculative, and speculation about the past life history of Africans is of less immediate concern than an attempt to estimate their competence to adjust themselves to the changed circumstances of the present time.

STUDIES OF AFRICAN SOCIAL LIFE

Towards the end of the nineteenth century Mary Kingsley emphasized the need for a wider knowledge of the facts of African life. In colonial rule, as she justly remarked, goodwill is no substitute for the knowledge

[1] See below, pp. 380–1.

'which will help to prevent us from engineering our good intentions in such a manner as to make them appear tyrannies and hateful to those whom we wish to benefit by them'.[1] It would be possible to point to many errors into which Administrations have fallen owing to the misinterpretation of African custom. Perhaps the most typical example is the attack made at an early period by the missionary societies on certain institutions connected with the African marriage system, and in particular the practice of 'bride-price'. One result of this misunderstanding was seen in official declarations of policy, such as the demand made by Sir Harry Smith in 1848 that the Natives of Kaffraria should 'abolish the sin of buying wives',[2] and in the practice by which courts in some parts of South Africa refused to take cognizance of marriage contracts based on the delivery of cattle.[3] It was not until 1927 that the Native Administration Act of the Union laid down that the payment of cattle should not be deemed to be repugnant to natural justice, thus finally recognizing the true character of this institution[4] as a guarantee of the validity of a marriage. In effect, the *lobolo* (or *lowola*), as the payment of cattle was called among the Bantu, enabled the bridegroom to remove the bride from the village of her kin to the village of his own family and to recompense the bride's parents for the loss of her services.

The attempt of the Gold Coast Administration in 1899 to take possession of the Golden Stool of Ashanti has often been quoted as an instance of similar misunderstanding, though it was perhaps evidence of a flagrant disregard of popular feeling rather than of ignorance of indigenous custom.[5] On the other hand, there is no doubt that numerous difficulties have been caused by official declarations which have recognized as Chiefs persons who have held no traditional authority. On more than one occasion Governments have been constrained to admit mistakes which have been due to their failure to appreciate the nature of African land tenures. The verdict of the official inquiry into the disturbances of 1929 in south-eastern Nigeria, which condemned the introduction of taxation until further knowledge had been gained of the social institutions of the people,[6] is one of many instances of a formal recognition of the need for fuller information on which to base administrative action.

It has been suggested that the introduction of the system of Indirect Rule in the British territories without a preparatory anthropological study

[1] S. Gwynn, *Life of Mary Kingsley*, 1933, p. 238.

[2] *Cambridge History of the British Empire*, vol. viii, p. 821.

[3] See below, p. 419; also I. Schapera, ed., *The Bantu-Speaking Tribes of South Africa*, 1937, p. 381; A. Phillips, ed., *Survey of African Marriage and Family Life*, 1953, pp. 360 ff.

[4] *Report of the Native Economic Commission*, U.G. 22, South Africa, 1932, pp. 102–4. E. H. Brookes, *The Colour Problems of South Africa*, 1934, p. 145. Phillips, op. cit. p. 195.

[5] R. S. Rattray, *Ashanti*, 1923, p. 292. E. W. Smith, *The Golden Stool*, 1926, but see also *Man*, vol. xliv (5), pp. 10 ff.

[6] Sessional Papers of the Nigerian Legislative Council, nos. 12 and 28, 1930.

of the peoples to whom it was applied was the boldest of experiments and that its success in the absence of that knowledge was little short of miraculous.[1] This view hardly does justice to the first authors of the system and their knowledge of African institutions, nor of the intensive work afterwards devoted to it by Administrative Officers. But there is, nevertheless, a fundamental truth in the proposition that in order to carry out any reform it is necessary to have a competent knowledge of the institutions which are being reformed.

Early Anthropologists

Such information regarding indigenous African custom as was available in the past was derived from a variety of sources. Earlier Administrations relied largely on the observations of travellers, the personal knowledge acquired by such of their officials as had left permanent records of custom in District Notebooks, or the writings of missionaries. If the value of the last source was sometimes liable to be diminished by the prejudices of the observer, it had on the other hand the advantage that the observation of custom was often closely associated with the study of the vernacular languages which, as will subsequently be shown,[2] owes so much to missionary effort. In more recent years, moreover, these studies have gained value from the fact that many missionaries have received a training in anthropology which has enabled them to see more clearly the place held by any one feature of indigenous custom in relation to the whole social life of the community. It was only at a comparatively late date that the information gained from these sources was amplified and at the same time given a more systematic form as the result of studies made by trained anthropologists.

There was towards the end of the nineteenth century a very marked increase in the general interest shown in anthropological studies. For this there were various reasons, but prominent among them was the influence exercised by Sir James Frazer. His *Golden Bough*, first published in 1890, made a profound impression not only upon scholars but also upon the layman. Recent research has shown his argument from comparative analogy to have often been fallacious, and his conclusions to be open to attack. But the interest which he aroused in anthropological study is largely responsible for attracting to it the scholars whose work has in subsequent years contributed so materially to our knowledge of the life of African society and its indigenous institutions.

A number of the Administrations have sought the aid of anthropologists to supplement the information received by them from their own official agencies or other local sources, though generally speaking action in this direction has been taken at a somewhat late date in their history. The early Administrations in Africa exhibited far less interest in investiga-

[1] F. H. Melland and Cullen Young, *African Dilemma*, 1937, p. 51.   [2] See below, p. 79.

tions of this nature than was shown by the Dutch in Indonesia. There was, however, a special reason for the interest shown by the Dutch; they had from the outset determined to exercise local rule entirely through indigenous authorities, and they were anxious as a matter of policy to protect Native custom from any form of foreign encroachment.[1]

That the British Government in India did not at an early period show any marked interest in sponsoring systematic inquiries regarding the custom of the country may be attributed to the fact that the laws and social customs of Hindus and Muslims were felt to be already well documented. The best administrators in India, it has been said, 'have all been anthropologists, even if they did not know it'.[2] When the East India Company purchased in 1807 the original manuscript of the work of the Abbé Dubois on Hindu customs,[3] it spoke of this purchase as 'an arrangement of great public importance'. Moreover, the Indian Administration always had available to it the services of competent Indians who could supply the information required on any doubtful point of indigenous custom. It was not until 1891 that an official survey was undertaken of the tribes and castes of Bengal, to be followed between the years 1896 and 1916 by a number of similar surveys made in other Provinces, and still later by special studies of the areas administered as 'backward' tracts.

There were, however, some exceptions to the general lack of interest shown by the earlier African Governments in inquiries of this nature. As early as 1668 the Government of the Cape arranged for some studies to be made of the customs of the Hottentots, and these were followed in 1679, 1696, and 1719 by further studies of special aspects of their customs. A study of the customs of the Xhosa by an officer of the South African Government was published in 1810.[4] At a later date the report of the Natal Native Affairs Commission of 1852, and the Compendium of Kaffir Laws and Customs, issued in 1858, contained much information on local custom, and in 1873, following on the incorporation of Basutoland into Cape Colony, a commission inquired into the laws and customs of the Southern Sotho. In 1880 a similar commission was appointed to investigate the customs of other territories annexed to the Cape. At a later date studies extending over the whole Union were made by the Native Affairs Commission of 1905.

Growth of Social Anthropology since 1900

Though financial support was given at an early date to the publication of studies of African custom by officers in the British Colonies, no formal

[1] R. Kennedy, 'Acculturation and Administration in Indonesia', *American Anthropologist*, vol. xlv, no. 2, 1943.   [2] Sir G. Grierson, in *Man*, vol. xiv (35), p. 61.
[3] J. A. Dubois, trans. H. Beauchamp, *Hindu Manners, Customs and Ceremonies*, 1899, p. xv.
[4] I. Schapera, 'Ethnographical Research in South Africa', *Bantu Studies*, vol. viii, no. 3, pp. 221 ff.

inquiry was instituted into any important aspect of African institutions until the West African Lands Committee was appointed in 1912.[1] One advantage of inquiries undertaken by this and subsequent bodies (as for example the Kenya Land Commission of 1933)[2] was that they frequently resulted in the preservation of information in the possession of Administrative Officers which might otherwise have been lost.

In more recent years the process of inquiry into African custom may be said to have entered on a third phase in which investigations have been both more systematic and more comprehensive. This has been due to two causes. In the first place a number of the Governments have realized the necessity for widening the scope of their existing knowledge and have utilized for this purpose the services either of their own officers who have shown an interest in anthropological study or of anthropologists specially engaged for the purpose. Action in this direction was stimulated in the British Colonies by the progressive adoption of the policy which has employed the Native Authorities as agencies of local rule, a policy which made it imperative to acquire a closer knowledge of the traditional institutions of the people.[3] In the second place there has been a general increase in the interest taken by European countries in anthropological study, whether as an academic discipline or as a branch of general knowledge. This has resulted in a growing volume of studies of African custom, partly undertaken by research workers on their own initiative, and partly sponsored by cultural societies or similar bodies.

It is only possible to notice some of the incidents that have marked this later phase. In 1908 the Administration of Southern Nigeria, faced by the difficulty of adjusting to the conditions prevailing in the Western and South-Eastern Provinces a system of local administration which had been instituted in the north in 1900, appointed an anthropologist as Government Ethnologist, though this measure was not repeated when his appointment expired. The Government of the Sudan made a more definite use of a trained anthropologist when in 1909 it appointed Dr. C. G. Seligman (who had already conducted a study of the Veddah for the Government of Ceylon) to carry out an ethnographic survey of the territory,[4] thus creating a branch of its administration which continued to exist up to very recent years.[5] In 1919 the Union Government, yielding to the approaches made to it by a number of European scientific bodies and by its own universities, appointed a commission to investigate the need for research in African languages and customs. As a result, the University of Cape Town instituted Chairs of Anthropology and of Bantu Ethnology, and both the Cape

---

[1] See below, p. 735.
[2] *Report of the Kenya Land Commission*, Cmd. 4556, 1934.   [3] See below, p. 195.
[4] C. G. and B. Z. Seligman, *The Veddahs*, 1911; *Pagan Tribes of the Nilotic Sudan*, 1932.
[5] E. E. Evans-Pritchard, *The Nuer*, 1940; *The Political System of the Anuak of the Anglo-Egyptian Sudan*, 1940. S. F. Nadel, *The Nuba*, 1947.

Town and other South African universities established courses in Bantu Studies. An Ethnological Section of the Union Native Affairs Department was instituted in 1925, with a trained ethnologist in charge,[1] an appointment which has also been retained up to the time of writing.

Meanwhile the Gold Coast Government had in 1920 created a post of Government Anthropologist, and appointed to it an Administrative Officer, R. S. Rattray, whose researches into Ashanti custom were to have an important influence on the official policy of the territory.[2] In 1921 Nigeria decided that the census of that year should include as wide a measure as possible of ethnographical material,[3] and appointed as the Census Commissioner in the Northern Provinces Dr. C. K. Meek, an Administrative Officer who had had some anthropological training. The ensuing census report of Northern Nigeria took largely the character of an ethnographic survey, and the experience thus gained was turned to account in 1927, when the system of local administration in Southern Nigeria having broken down, an extensive series of inquiries into the social institutions of the region was organized under the leadership of Dr. Meek, as a basis for the revision of the procedure of local rule.[4] The report made by P. Talbot on the census of the Southern Provinces was also largely of the nature of an ethnographic survey.[5]

In 1954, when the report of the parliamentary delegation visiting Kenya exposed the depravity of the Mau Mau oaths, a psychologist made an interesting analysis of the circumstances which led to the outbreaks, although his purely psycho-analytic approach to the problem failed to find general acceptance.[6] An independent study of the social aspects of Mau Mau has also been made by a scholar who has already written other authorative works on the Kikuyu.[7] An anthropologist was engaged to examine the causes underlying the long series of medicine murders which had occurred in Basutoland.[8]

When the International African Institute, which had for its objective the promotion of cultural as well as linguistic studies, was established in 1926, it received the financial support of a number of British as well as foreign Governments, and the series of field studies which it initiated[9]

[1] I. Schapera, 'Anthropology and the Native Problem', *South African Journal of Science*, vol. xxxv, 1939. H. Rogers, *Native Administration in the Union of South Africa*, 1933, p. 250.

[2] R. S. Rattray, *Religion and Art in Ashanti*, 1927; *Ashanti Law and Constitution*, 1929; *The Tribes of the Ashanti Hinterland*, 1932.

[3] Sir H. Clifford, in C. K. Meek, *Northern Tribes of Nigeria*, 1925, pp. 5-6.

[4] M. Perham, *Native Administration in Nigeria*, 1937, pp. 221 ff. C. K. Meek, *Law and Authority in a Nigerian Tribe*, 1937. M. M. Green, *Ibo Village Affairs*, 1947, pp. 3 ff.

[5] P. Talbot, *The Peoples of Southern Nigeria*, 1926.

[6] J. C. Carothers, *The Psychology of Mau Mau*; and see C. J. M. Alport, 'Kenya's Answer to the Mau Mau Challenge', in *African Affairs*, July 1954, p. 241.

[7] L. S. B. Leakey, *Mau Mau and the Kikuyu*, 1952; *Defeating Mau Mau*, 1954.

[8] G. I. Jones, *Basutoland Medicine Murder*, Cmd. 8209, 1951.

[9] Lord Lugard, 'The International Institute of African Languages and Cultures', *Africa*,

served to stimulate the growing interest shown by African Administrations in this branch of inquiry.[1] There was a direct connexion between these field studies and the interesting experiment supported by the Tanganyika Government for a joint report by an Administrative Officer and an anthropologist on the Hehe tribe in the Southern Highlands Province.[2] To these researches may be attributed the creation of appointments such as those made for the study of social conditions in the High Commission Territories of South Africa,[3] or the inquiries into the effects of migrant labour in Nyasaland,[4] or into the problems of land and diet in Northern Rhodesia.[5] Kenya has made a full use of the services of its own officers, as is shown by the informative report on the system of Native tribunals by A. Phillips and the studies of land systems by H. F. Lambert,[6] but it has also on several occasions reinforced such inquiries by engaging the services of trained anthropologists.[7]

The Government of Nigeria has also commissioned a number of investigations by its own officers, the most notable being a study of Yoruba land tenure and a report on the organization of the Tiv.[8] It is interesting to note that the Government of the Eastern Region appointed in 1954 a Committee to investigate the system of Bride Price and its social effects.[9] In 1937 the Governments of the two Rhodesias and Uganda joined with a number of industrial and commercial companies in supporting the establishment of the Rhodes–Livingstone Institute in Northern Rhodesia, which has subsequently carried out numerous inquiries on the social conditions of Central Africa.[10]

Lastly, the British Government authorized in 1944 the formation of the Colonial Social Science Research Council to deal with the problems of

January 1928. D. Forde, 'The Work of the International African Institute', *J.R.A.S.*, vol. xciii, no. 4682, 1944. 'The Outlook for Anthropology', *Africa*, April 1947, p. 137.

[1] International Institute of African Languages and Cultures, *Report to Rockefeller Foundation*, July 1931 to July 1939.

[2] G. Brown and B. Hutt, *Anthropology in Action*, 1935. On the merits of this system of inquiry, see A. Richards, in *Africa*, July 1935, pp. 388 ff. G. Baker, ibid. pp. 304 ff. M. M. Edel, in *American Anthropologist*, vol. xxxix, p. 152.

[3] I. Schapera, *Handbook of Tswana Law and Custom*, 1935; *Native Land Tenure in the Bechuanaland Protectorate*, 1943; *Migrant Labour and Tribal Life*, 1947.

[4] *Report of Nyasaland Committee on Emigrant Labour*, 1935. See M. Read, 'Migrant Labour in Nyasaland', *International Labour Review*, vol. xlv, no. 6, 1942, p. 7.

[5] A. Richards, *Land, Labour and Diet in Northern Rhodesia*, 1939.

[6] A. Phillips, *Report on Native Tribunals*, 1945. H. E. Lambert and Wyn Harris, *Memorandum on Policy in regard to Land Tenure in the Native Lands*, 1945.

[7] J. G. Peristiany, *The Social Institutions of the Kipsigis*, 1939. P. H. Gulliver, *A Preliminary Survey of the Turkana*, 1951. P. Mayer, *Two Studies in Applied Anthropology*, Colonial Research Studies no. 3, 1951.

[8] H. L. Ward Price, *Land Tenure in the Yoruba Provinces*, 1933. R. C. Abraham, *The Tiv People*, 1933.

[9] *Report of the Committee on Bride Price, Eastern Region of Nigeria*, 1955.

[10] M. Gluckman, in *Rhodes–Livingstone Journal*, no. 1, 1944, pp. 4 ff. (hereafter referred to as *R.L. Journal*). G. Wilson, 'Anthropology as a Public Service', *Africa*, January 1940, pp. 43 ff.

social research arising in the British Colonies.[1] Under its auspices support has been given from funds provided by the Colonial Development and Welfare Acts to a number of projects of inquiry in the African dependencies,[2] including the comprehensive Ethnographic and Linguistic Surveys elsewhere referred to.[3] The case for granting a full measure of support to studies of indigenous custom was emphasized by an important commission—the Scarbrough Commission—which reported on this and similar cultural activities of the British Government in 1947.[4] It will, however, be convenient to leave for a subsequent section of this chapter a reference to various institutions for the conduct of research which have now been developed in the countries with which this Survey deals.[5]

METHODS OF SOCIAL ANTHROPOLOGY

The enhanced interest which the Governments and industrial and commercial bodies have taken in these inquiries has been materially influenced by the change during the last half century in the direction followed in anthropological studies. In Great Britain and some other of the European countries the early interest in the study of Native custom had been stimulated by the humanitarian movement which secured the abolition of the slave trade in 1807 and the passing of the Emancipation Act of 1833.[6] When the interest inspired by this movement ceased to operate, there succeeded a period in which the study of indigenous institutions occupied the attention principally of academic anthropologists concerned to find evidence bearing on the origin and relationship of different groups of mankind.

A new phase may be said to have dated from the dispatch of the Cambridge expeditions to the Torres Straits in 1898 and 1899, when a number of anthropologists made a personal investigation of the structure and social custom of a Native community. There gradually emerged a school which at first distinguished its studies by the designation of Practical, Functional, or Applied Anthropology.[7] They are now comprehended in the generic term Social Anthropology, though there is still some argument as to the precise range and objective of this branch of study. For the present purpose, however, it is sufficient to say that anthropologists of this school are concerned less with the origin of the communities they study than with

[1] *Report of Colonial Research Committee, 1943–44*, Cmd. 6535, p. 5.
[2] *Report on Colonial Research*, 1953–4, Cmd. 9303, pp. 47–85.
[3] See above, p. 30, and below, p. 85.
[4] *Report of the Interdepartmental Commission of Enquiry into the Facilities for Oriental, Slavonic, East European and African Studies* (the Scarbrough Commission), 1947.
[5] See below, pp. 62–66.   [6] *Man*, vol. xliv, pp. 10 ff.
[7] C. G. Seligman, 'Applied Anthropology', *Encyclopaedia Britannica*, 14th ed., 1945. See also the articles on the Applied Anthropology Committee of the Royal Anthropological Institute, in *Man*, vol. xxxvii (139), p. 115, and A. Richards, in *Man*, vol. lxiii (1), p. 1.

their functioning as social organisms; it is regarded as essential to examine not only the structure of such societies but the factors and forces which condition the behaviour of their members.

In the second place they attach primary importance to field studies which will give them first-hand knowledge of the lives of the peoples concerned and, as far as possible, of their languages.[1] It is significant that the increased support given by the Governments and by private bodies to studies of this nature has greatly increased the number of openings for anthropological work and has led to a corresponding enlargement in the body of persons who seek to qualify themselves to take part in it. The range now available for field study has in particular proved attractive to students from America. There is some difference of approach by British and American social anthropologists, though this does not constitute any real point of divergence as to the general purpose of social anthropology.

If the earlier field studies of anthropologists were made in the islands of the Pacific rather than in Africa, it was because scholars were at that period still strongly influenced by evolutionary theories, and research consequently tended to be concentrated on those societies in which institutions familiar to the modern world might be supposed to appear in their most rudimentary form. Such societies were to be found most characteristically in the isolated islands of the South Pacific. The change of direction in anthropological study, with its new emphasis on the analysis of observable social processes, naturally brought research workers into contact with the problems of Administrations and of commercial bodies which had practical interests in Africa. As has already been indicated, their studies gained increased significance during the earlier part of the century, when the policy of utilizing African institutions as an integral part of the administrative organization became the accepted policy of most of the British dependencies.

Progress in the new type of study owed much to the establishment by the University of Cape Town of its School of African Life and Languages,[2] and to the provision made by the International African Institute in 1926 for implementing its programme of research in Africa,[3] and in particular to the prominence assumed by its studies on the problems of culture contact.[4] It owed something also to the publication in 1926 of *The Golden Stool*, which appealed for understanding of institutions which were in danger of destruction and difficult to replace.[5] Similar arguments were

---

[1] B. Malinowski, 'Practical Anthropology', *Africa*, vol. ii, 1929, p. 23; 'The Rationalization of Anthropology and Administration', ibid. vol. iii, 1930, pp. 405 ff.; 'Applied Anthropology', *Man*, vol. xxxvii (139), p. 115.

[2] See above, pp. 54-55.   [3] See above, p. 55.

[4] B. Malinowski and others, *Methods of Study of Culture Contact*, International African Institute, Memorandum XV, 1938; also 'The Present State of Culture Contact Studies', *Africa*, January 1939, pp. 27 ff.   [5] E. W. Smith, *The Golden Stool*, 1926.

advanced in France and in Belgium by writers who called attention to instances in which policy had failed to make due allowance for indigenous custom.[1]

Social anthropologists do not now consider that their field is limited to societies which have been described as 'primitive', 'peasant', or 'small-scale'. They tend, however, even when working in highly complex societies, to study the interaction of institutions upon each other rather than particular institutions in isolation. Reaction against a past school of thought which sought to explain existing institutions as part of an evolutionary process from hypothetical origins led anthropologists at one stage to deny any value to evidence relating to the past conditions of the societies they examined. This position, however, became untenable when they began to look on the process of social change as one of the central points for their study, and it is now recognized that all reliable historical evidence should be taken into account.[2]

On the other hand, their not unnatural concern at the growing evidence of the disintegration of traditional institutions has led to their studies being identified, particularly by African nationalists, with a 'reactionary' interest, concerned to support the conservative elements in African society and opposed to the aspirations of those who have adopted European culture.[3] There are indeed many Africans who feel that the only purpose of making studies of the lives of their less sophisticated compatriots must be to provide evidence of the 'backwardness' of Africa. But this attitude betrays some confusion of thought. Regret for the passing away of traditional social controls is not incompatible with the realization that they cannot be preserved by giving artificial support to institutions that are inadequate to meet the demands of modern life.[4]

Practical Value of Anthropological Studies

It is more difficult to find an answer to the question which so often confronts the social anthropologist as to the practical value of the studies which he makes. To some extent the answer depends on the attitude of the Administrations towards the policy of maintaining traditional institutions as part of the machinery of rule. If the Governments which have hitherto attached importance to this policy[5] were now to abandon it, one of the most obvious contributions of anthropology would appear to

[1] L. Vignon, *Programme de Politique Coloniale*, 1919. H. Labouret, *À la Recherche d'une Politique Indigène*, 1935. G. van der Kerken, *Les Sociétés Bantoues du Congo Belge*, 1920.

[2] E. E. Evans-Pritchard, *Social Anthropology*, 1951, pp. 58 ff.

[3] W. M. Macmillan, *Africa Emergent*, 1938. E. H. Brookes, *The Colour Problems of South Africa*, 1934, pp. 131 ff. R. Oliver, *The Missionary Factor in East Africa*, 1953. M. Fortes, in *Fabian Colonial Essays*, 1945, p. 215.

[4] A. W. Hoernlé, 'Social Organization', *Bantu-Speaking Tribes of South Africa*, 1937. E. Hellman, 'Native Life in a Johannesburg Slum Yard', *Africa*, January 1935, pp. 34 ff.

[5] See below, p. 416.

be eliminated. Nor can it be said that the claims of anthropologists to provide a solution to specific administrative problems have often been borne out in practice. They can sometimes indicate where a policy which promises clear material advantages (as, for example, in the improvement of public health or of soil fertility) may meet with unexpected resistance, but they are less often able to suggest means of overcoming this resistance.

The problem of the maladjustments in African society created by the extension to it of Western economic or political institutions is no more amenable to treatment by the anthropologist than by anyone else. The most conspicuous field where his studies still have a direct application is in the elucidation of the customary rules of law regulating marriage, succession, and land tenure. Here they have a definite use, and their value is not limited to the field in which they can be immediately applied, for it is probably even greater in its illumination of the context of African custom and values within which all administrative action must work. It is of interest that the French authorities are coming to attach importance to similar studies for just this reason: 'On n'agit pas utilement sur des hommes que l'on ignore'.[1]

It has already been remarked that the change in the objective of anthropological studies has also involved a substantial change in techniques. In the early years of this century the method usually pursued was a survey, in which the observer travelled over a wide area recording for each tribe the broad characteristics of physical type, social organization, and material culture. In the Torres Straits expedition of 1898,[2] for instance, the method followed was to spend a short time with each tribe, questioning perhaps only one informant. Dr. J. Roscoe, who spent 25 years among the Ganda, states that he obtained much of his information from Africans who were brought to his home from various parts of the country.[3] Modern anthropologists can find in the material thus collected a useful starting-point for making more detailed inquiries in the areas which their predecessors have covered. But a modern research worker is expected to spend at least a year, and preferably two, among the people whom he is studying, and to be able to speak to them in their own language. In a population of any considerable size he should also be able to apply the principles of statistical sampling.[4] The technique of co-operation with teams of locally trained African inquirers is now being developed. Techniques are also being evolved to make censuses and to estimate rates of marriage, divorce, and infant mortality among pre-literate people.[5]

[1] Office Scientifique des Recherches d'Outre-Mer, *Courrier des Chercheurs,* no. iv, 1951, p. 61.
[2] See above, p. 57.   [3] J. Roscoe, *The Baganda,* 1911.
[4] Royal Anthropological Institute, *Notes and Queries in Anthropology,* 6th ed., 1951, pp. 36–62.
[5] See, for example, J. A. Barnes, 'Measures of Divorce Frequency in Simple Societies', *Journal of the Royal Anthropological Institute,* vol. lxxix, 1949, pp. 37–62. J. C. Mitchell, 'An Estimate of Fertility in some Yao Hamlets', *Africa,* October 1949, pp. 293–308.

But over and above the necessary special techniques much depends on the personality of the anthropologist and his ability to appreciate a different way of life. Government officers who have spent many years of their lives in Africa are apt to question the value of an anthropological inquiry carried out in a relatively short period of time. They are inclined to add, moreover, that inquiry by a professional anthropologist is frequently directed to elucidate points which may be of academic interest but are of little significance in the practical work of administration.

On the other hand, it is clear that the Administrative Officer himself works under certain disadvantages in making inquiries of this character. His relations with Africans are apt to be coloured by the fact that he represents the Government. In certain areas (as for instance in West Africa) the tour of service is so short that there are few officers who have a long knowledge of any one locality. In some districts the present conditions involve a pressure of work which leaves little leisure for detached study; even therefore if an officer has had training in anthropological methods, he is not likely to prove a successful investigator unless he is permitted to devote sufficient time for the purpose.

Appointment of Government Anthropologists

The preceding pages have given a number of illustrations of the extent to which various Administrations have in the past employed the services of anthropologists or have alternatively commissioned inquiries to be made by their own officers. There is an equal variety of practice at the present day. The Government Anthropologist of the Union of South Africa[1] has now a staff of five Europeans and seven Africans, four of the former having been trained as anthropologists, and the Municipality of Johannesburg also has a research division with a trained anthropologist in charge. Tanganyika has since 1949 had a staff of three full-time anthropologists, who are officially described as sociologists. Kenya, as already shown, has made use of both procedures.[2] Nigeria continues to show some preference for the use of the services of its own officers, especially in regard to inquiries into indigenous systems of land tenure.[3]

If it were necessary to express a view as to the relative merits of these two forms of procedure, it may be suggested that Governments are likely to derive the greatest advantage from inquiries undertaken by anthropologists in close association with their own technical or Administrative Officers. This form of collaboration should not debar the anthropologist from expressing his views on the effect which Government measures may

[1] For official statement of the creation of this section, see H. Rogers, *Native Administration in the Union of South Africa*, 1949, p. 232, and also *Report of Department of Native Affairs, 1950*, U.G. 51, p. 32; ibid. 1951, p. 15. [2] See above, p. 56.

[3] See reference to the studies of C. W. Cole, L. T. Chubb, and C. W. Rowling cited below, pp. 790–1, 813.

have on those indigenous institutions that provide the framework of African social life, for this is a point on which his assistance can be of special value.[1]

As regards the French territories, though there have in the past been notable studies made by Administrative Officers, especially in respect of customary law,[2] the Government appears to rely now mainly on the researches done by members of the institutions devoted to research in social subjects, such as the *Institut Français d'Afrique Noire*, or in French Equatorial Africa the *Institut d'Études Centrafricaines*.[3] There does not, however, exist in the French territories the same reason for a special study of indigenous law and custom as was created in the British territories by the policy of utilizing the Native Authorities as an agency of local rule.[4] In the Belgian Congo studies of some six different tribes were made by Government officers between 1909 and 1913 at the instance of the *Société Belge de Sociologie*,[5] and valuable contributions to the study of African law in the Katanga have been made by A. Sohier.[6] But it would seem that, as in the French territories, the chief agency of research in the future is likely to be *Institut pour la Recherche Scientifique en Afrique Centrale* to which subsequent reference will be made.[7]

INSTITUTIONS FOR RESEARCH

Research in British Territories

The Royal Geographical Society of Great Britain has since its foundation in 1830 made Africa its special concern and has placed all its resources at the disposal of those who have explored the continent or investigated its content. The contribution it has made to our knowledge of Africa is invaluable. The Royal Anthropological Institute provides facilities to untrained observers by putting at their disposal its accumulation of anthropological information. It has also issued publications for the assistance of missionaries, administrators, and travellers.

In the inter-war period the institution which took the chief initiative in social research in Africa was the International African Institute, the formation of which has already been referred to.[8] That the Fellows of the

[1] See on the subject generally, I. Schapera, in *J.A.A.*, vol. iii, no. 3, 1951, and also J. P. Moffett and H. A. Fosbrooke in vol. iv, no. 3, 1952. L. Mair in *Principles and Methods of Colonial Administration* (Colston Research Society), 1950, p. 178.

[2] M. Delafosse, *Haut-Sénégal-Niger*, 1912. G. Geismar, *Recueil des coutumes civiles des races du Sénégal*, 1933. H. Labouret, *Les Manding et leur langue*, 1934.

[3] See above, p. 23, and below, p. 65.   [4] See above, p. 52.

[5] E. van der Kerken, *Sociétés Bantoues du Congo Belge*, 1920. J. van Wing, *Études Bakongo*, 1921. E. Verhulpen, *Baluba et Balubaïsés du Katanga*, 1936.

[6] A. Sohier, *Pratique des Jurisdictions Indigènes*, 1932.   [7] See below, p. 65.

[8] See above, pp. 55–56. For the researches conducted by the Institute in linguistics, see below, p. 113. See also B. Wyatt, in *Civilisations*, vol. iv, no. 2, 1954, pp. 213–17.

Institute were enabled to undertake during the period 1932 to 1939 a series of field investigations extending over the Union of South Africa, French West Africa, the Belgian Congo, and the majority of the British Colonial territories was due to a grant made for this purpose by the Rockefeller Foundation of New York. The Institute has recently published, with the assistance of Unesco, a comparative study of African kinship systems,[1] and with the aid of the Carnegie Corporation and the British Colonial Office, has issued a survey of our existing knowledge on African family life and the marriage system.[2] It has undertaken for Unesco a study of industrialization in Africa.[3] The Ethnographic Survey initiated by it in 1944[4] and financed by the Colonial Office (as far as the British territories are concerned) aims at collating all available material on the subject of tribal ethnology. By 1955 some 29 volumes had appeared out of the 52 projected.

A reference has also been made to the foundation of the Rhodes–Livingstone Institute, an independent institution governed by a Board of Trustees.[5] It is now situated at Lusaka in Northern Rhodesia. It has been enabled to undertake a long-term programme of research on Central Africa by an allocation of funds provided under the Colonial Development and Welfare Act of 1940[6] and has also received assistance from the Beit Trustees. It has published a large number of monographs and a volume dealing with the social organization of seven tribes in the area.[7] An allocation from the British Colonial Development and Welfare Vote assisted in the foundation in 1943 of the West African Institute of Arts, Industries, and Social Sciences, situated at Achimota in the Gold Coast. It has initiated a social survey of Ashanti.[8]

The Colonial Social Science Research Council, which, as already shown, was established in London in 1944,[9] has been instrumental in securing funds for the foundation of two institutions, the East African Institute of Social Research, in connexion with the new University College at Makerere, and the West African Institute of Social and Economic Research, in connexion with the new University at Ibadan. The former, which was opened in 1948, is at present engaged on a series of comparative studies of land tenure in East Africa;[10] and at the suggestion of Unesco it has co-operated in a survey of two areas of unusually low fertility in the

[1] A. R. Radcliffe-Brown, ed., *African Systems of Kinship and Marriage*, 1950.
[2] A. Phillips, ed., *A Survey of African Marriage and Family Life*, 1953.
[3] *Industrialization in Africa* (mimeographed), 1953.
[4] See above, p. 30.   [5] See above, p. 56.
[6] M. Gluckman, 'The Seven Year Research Plan of the Rhodes–Livingstone Institute', *R.L. Journal*, no. 4, 1945.
[7] E. Colson and M. Gluckman, eds., *Seven Tribes of Central Africa*, 1951.
[8] K. A. Busia, *The Position of the Chief in the Modern Political System of Ashanti*, 1951.
[9] See above, p. 56.
[10] East African Institute of Social Research, *A Report on Three Years Work*, 1953.

Buganda Province of Uganda and the Bukoba District of Tanganyika.[1] The West African Institute, which commenced work in 1951, has made a study of the economic as well as the social organization in the Yoruba area and in the Cameroons.

As has been seen, the Rockefeller Foundation and the Carnegie Corporation of the United States have given generous assistance in aid of social research in Africa, and in addition the Fulbright Foundation, the Social Science Research Council, the Wenner-Gren, and Guggenheim Foundations have on occasion provided fellowships for research work. In Great Britain, University College, London, offers two studentships for field study, and other sources of support, though on a less regular scale, are the Goldsmiths' Travelling scholarships, the Horniman, Leverhulme, and Nuffield Trusts, and the Simon Fellowships of Manchester University. Grants under the Colonial Development and Welfare Acts have on occasion been made to supplement these sources, and in 1947 twelve postgraduate studentships were offered by the Secretary of State for field research in the Colonies.

Mention has already been made of the courses of Bantu Studies established in various universities of the Union of South Africa,[2] and though those who take the courses do not necessarily take a part in research, the holders of the University Chairs have made a notable addition to inquiry in this field. The South African Institute of Race Relations, established in 1929, promotes investigations on matters bearing on the relations between various sections and races in South Africa,[3] but these are normally more of a sociological than an anthropological character.

Research in French Territories

In metropolitan France the body which is primarily charged with advising the Ministry on the co-ordination of overseas research is the *Conseil Supérieur de la Recherche Scientifique et Technique d'Outre-Mer*, which has a panel comprising representatives of all bodies which can be considered as dealing with *les sciences humaines*. Its main executive organ is the *Office de la Recherche Scientifique d'Outre-Mer* (O.R.S.O.M.) founded in the year 1943, when the whole system of overseas research came under reorganization. The *Office* has two principal functions, namely, the recruitment and training of candidates for employment as research workers, and the establishment of local research centres in the Colonies. Its budget is separately voted by Parliament, but it also receives assistance from the *Fonds d'Investissement pour le Développement Économique et Social* (F.I.D.E.S.).[4]

[1] A. I. Richards, ed., *Economic Development and Tribal change—a study of Immigrant Labour in Buganda*, 1954.
[2] See above, pp. 54–55.
[3] *O.Y.S.A.*, *1949*, p. 255; ibid., *1950*, p. 261.
[4] See below, pp. 214, 329–30.

As regards the training of research workers, it would seem that the *Office* has so far confined itself to the training of *chercheurs* in the natural sciences, and save in two specific instances it does not appear to have directly supported sociological inquiry in Africa, one such instance being a study of the position of women in French West Africa generally,[1] and the other an ethnographical study of the Dogon and Bambara in the Niger Valley. The *Institut d'Ethnologie*, attached to the University of Paris, but supported by a separate grant from the *Ministère de la France d'Outre-Mer*, has a course of African ethnography, but does not itself carry out field study.

The senior of the two local centres of research in the French African Colonies is the *Institut Français d'Afrique Noire* (I.F.A.N.) founded in 1938, with headquarters at Dakar, but with a local branch in each of the territories of French West Africa.[2] Though it would appear to have previously devoted most of its activity to the study of problems arising in the field of the physical sciences or economic development, it has now a section for ethnology, which publishes its own journal and memoirs. This has organized research on the results of urbanization in Dakar, St. Louis, and Cotonou, on migrant labour in the Mossi region of the Haute-Volta, on the development of modern cults in the Ivory Coast and in northern Dahomey, and on the problems arising from the relations between the nomadic Fulani and the sedentary peoples through whose country they move.[3]

In French Equatorial Africa, the *Institut d'Études Centrafricaines* (I.E.C.) situated at Brazzaville, which was established in 1947,[4] has similar functions and publishes its own journal. The section on sociology and demography has only recently commenced its operations, but has made three surveys in urban areas and a study of labour incentives. Its activity has been restricted by shortage of staff, but it proposes to organize a series of demographic surveys in different environments. The finances of both these institutions are borne partly by the *Office de la Recherche Scientifique d'Outre-Mer* and partly by the local budget.[5]

Research in Belgian Territories

In the Belgian Congo and Ruanda Urundi the principal organ of research is the *Institut pour la Recherche Scientifique en Afrique Centrale* (I.R.S.A.C.) which has its local headquarters at Bukavu (Costermans-

---

[1] Sœur Marie-André du Sacré Cœur, *La Femme Noire en Afrique*, 1939.
[2] *Arrêté* of 16 October 1938.
[3] *Office de la Recherche Scientifique d'Outre-Mer*, Exposé, 1948–50, p. 25; and *Courrier des Chercheurs*, no. v, 1952.
[4] Décret of 18 June 1946. See *Encyclopédie de l'Afrique Équatoriale Française*, 1950, p. 245 (hereafter referred to as *Enc. A.E.F.*).
[5] H. Deschamps, *Recherches de Sciences Humaines dans les pays de l'Union Française*, 1953.

ville). It was established by *arrêté royal* in 1947, when it received a capital grant of 200 million francs. Its *Conseil d'Administration* is assisted by specialist panels in Belgium and by locally constituted consultative panels. The panel concerned with the social sciences (*Commission de Science de l'Homme*) has arranged for a programme of training for its *chercheurs*, and in 1952 four anthropologists were at work in this field, research in social science being conducted mainly at the Uvira centre in the Belgian Congo and the Astrida centre in Ruanda Urundi. The section on social science at Astrida has interested itself in inquiries regarding the political organization of Ruanda at the beginning of the century, and in the cultural conceptions of the Bangarwanda. A special study has been made of the demographic statistics of the country, following suggestions made by Unesco.[1]

The *Institut pour la Recherche Scientifique* financed the journey made by Father Schebesta[2] in 1949–50 in order to complete his study of the Pygmies, and also the publication of his most recent work, in which he has summarized his conclusions as to their social structure and customs.[3] In addition the Administration of the Congo assists in maintaining a local institution at Elisabethville, the *Centre d'Études des Problèmes Sociaux Indigènes* (C.E.P.S.I.). It was formed in 1946, its members being drawn mainly from the local Catholic missions and the labour department of the *Comité du Katanga*, which provides a greater part of its funds. It is interested chiefly in welfare questions, but has made some studies of social change.

Research in Portuguese and Spanish Territories

In the Portuguese territories there are the *Sociedade de Estudos de Moçambique* at Lourenço Marques and the *Centro de Estudos da Guiné Portuguesa* at Bissau, the latter founded in 1945. The *Museu de Angola*, Luanda, also publishes studies on various topics including the history of the Colony. In Portugal itself the *Agencia Geral do Ultramar* publishes articles on African affairs.

There is no local institute in the Spanish colonies, but an Institute for African Studies was founded in 1945 and was placed under the direction of the Minister for Colonies in the following year. It publishes a monthly review, *África*, and a quarterly, *Estudios*.

Bibliographies of African Studies

The volume of published material on social anthropology in Africa is now so considerable that it would be impossible to notice every item. The following recent bibliographies may, however, be mentioned: I. Schapera, *A Select Bibliography of South African Native Life and Problems*, 1941 (this

[1] *Rapport à l'Assemblée Générale des Nations Unies de l'Administration du Ruanda-Urundi*, 1951, p. 192. *Rapport sur l'Administration Belge du Ruanda-Urundi*, 1952, p. 226.   [2] See below, p. 107.
[3] P. Schebesta, trans. Henri Plard, *Les Pygmées du Congo Belge*, Mém. I.R.C.B., vol. xxvi, no. 2, 1952.

includes Southern Rhodesia); A. Holden and A. Jacoby, supplement to the above, 1950; O. Boone, *Bibliographie Ethnographique du Congo Belge et des Régions Avoisinantes*, 1952; H. A. Wieschoff, *Anthropological Bibliography of Negro Africa*, 1948; Helen F. Conover, *Introduction to Africa, a selective guide to Background Reading*, 1952; E. Joucla, *Bibliographie de l'Afrique Occidentale Française*, 1937; P. Sanner, *Bibliographie de l'Afrique Équatoriale Française, 1914–1948*, 1949. A number of periodicals publish bibliographies of current publications, the most interesting being *Africa* (London), *Zaïre* (Brussels), *Journal de la Société des Africanistes* (Paris), *Sudan Notes and Records* (Khartoum).

AFRICAN MUSIC

The growing body of literature devoted to African music is unanimous in pointing to the exceptional position which it occupies in the life of the African people. Music infuses all the activities of the African from the cradle to the grave:[1] 'whatever the occasion, music will be there, not as an embellishment, but as a functional part of his activity; it is the only constant factor which permeates the very fibre of African social and personal life'. There are, it is true, authorities who have claimed a somewhat similar position for the dance as a spontaneous and intuitive expression of every form of feeling, and particularly of any feeling which is shared with others or in which it is desired that they should participate. The African, it is claimed, stands out among all others as the man who expresses every emotion with rhythmical bodily movement.

There are indeed those who have held that dancing has always held first place for the African as a form of expression, and that music or the decorative arts have been evolved to supplement the dance, to which they are (except for sculpture in certain cases) still subsidiary.[2] There is no need to attempt here to resolve the question of precedence between dancing and music; it is sufficient to agree that both music and the dance serve to a singular degree as modes of expression of African feeling or as an accompaniment to social or religious activity. In the African village singing, clapping, dancing, and drumming are not separate entities, but may be said to constitute one homogeneous art form.

The position thus accorded to music may not be equally applicable today in respect of the more sophisticated members of the urban communities, but it remains true of the great mass of the Bantu, who maintain their attachment to the traditional form of music-making, the folk music of the

[1] P. R. Kirby, in *Western Civilization and the Natives of South Africa*, ed. I. Schapera, 1934, p. 131. See also E. Hellmann, ed., *Handbook on Race Relations in South Africa*, 1949, pp. 619 ff. H. Tracey, 'The Social Role of African Music', *African Affairs*, July 1954, pp. 234 ff.; 'The State of Folk Music in Bantu Africa', in *African Music*, vol. i, no. 1, 1954.
[2] G. Gorer, *Africa Dances*, 1935, p. 303.

village.[1] It is advisable accordingly to distinguish this from what may be termed the neo-folk music, which is of growing usage among the Africans who have come under the influence of European music.

Traditional Folk Music

This is for the African the standard and normal form of music-making, exhibiting the characteristic quality of spontaneous creation and the predominantly social character of his music. But he has at the same time a prolific supply of both vocal and instrumental music of a relatively restricted nature for use in more limited contexts, as for example on ceremonial occasions. Ceremonial music is sanctified by tradition and ritual, and thus stands outside and above the daily round of song and dance. It is a powerful factor in the preservation of tribal loyalties and beliefs. Every Murozi, for example, would be deeply stirred by the sound of the royal drums of the Paramount Chief of Barotseland, which can be beaten by none but the royal drummers and then only to the prescribed rhythms. In time of drought a rain-making ceremony could not be held without the proper songs. At birth, at puberty, at marriage, in sickness, at death, the song must be used which is associated by immemorial custom with these events, and the details of the music are as integral a part of the occasion as the details of the prescribed ritual.

Social music on the other hand embraces all the music-making associated with the multifarious activities of village life and recreation. 'The African', it has been said, 'sings about work, about hunting, about money, about women, about canoeing, about planting, about war—in short about all the things that men dwell naturally upon in their minds.'[2] Singing is for the most part essentially communal; in his music the African is normally anything but an individualist. Such songs do more than lighten toil, they serve to stimulate the workers both to sustained and to precise rhythmic movement. The women pounding grain in a mortar or grinding it on a stone will sing to their work; paddling canoes, hoeing, threshing, and even walking will all have their songs. This characteristic vocalization of repeated muscular action is sometimes carried from the village into the new context of the European farm or mine; the continuous tap of the hammer on a rock-drill must have a song, and all adjacent workers will tap in synchrony.

As distinct from work-songs, music also provides the basis of nearly all recreation. It is part of the education of an African boy or girl to learn to take part in community music-making and dancing—this includes (in some tribes at least) a repertoire of personal songs made by the owner for use on general social occasions. New dances and drummings are continu-

[1] A. M. Jones, *African Music in Northern Rhodesia and Some Other Places*, 1949.
[2] *Report of the Commission on Higher Education in West Africa*, Cmd. 6655, 1945, p. 18.

ally appearing in the usual manner of folk music, thus providing a virtually limitless body of folk music, always accepting new material and employed for the pleasure of the community generally. The essence of African social recreative music is that everyone takes part. There are no rehearsals, the whole community appears to burst into song and dance. Viewed as a popular form of recreation this must surely be of a higher value than the Western concert with a passive audience or the modern European dances, which an Indian author has not inappropriately described as 'stylized animality'. The words sung are, like the music, variable. They are often comments on happenings in the village, on personalities, or at times on the Government and its institutions. They are thus of some importance for appraising the African's attitude to life in general. 'Sly digs at the pompous; condemnation of those who neglect their duties . . . outcries against social injustices as well as philosophy in the face of difficulties are all to be found in these songs.'[1]

Neo-Folk Music

Contact with Europeans has made its mark on African music and Africans in towns have assimilated modern American music, though they have not swallowed it entirely. Four-part singing, whether of hymns or of secular songs in school, has given to the Africans' powerful sense of harmony a new sequence of chords, a sequence which can now be heard in almost any musical assembly of urban Africans. The combination of these two forces has produced a neo-folk music, Western in basic time and harmony, but characteristically African in rhythmic treatment and in melodic outline.[2] Described as 'High Life Music' in West Africa, and 'Makwaya' or 'Saba-saba' in Central and South Africa, this form of music is spreading from the towns to the villages, and though it was at the outset purely recreative in its use, it has begun to invade the entrenched realm of ceremonial music. At least one of the Funeral Song recordings sent to the British Broadcasting Corporation for use at the death of King George VI was a 'Makwaya' song.

It has, however, taken over from European practice some features which conflict with African tradition and which make it fundamentally unsuitable for village social recreation. It is a sophisticated form of music, performed by a small number of skilled people, and it thus tends to be an exhibition which needs listeners or spectators. If it invades a village it tends to kill the spirit of corporate social participation and to this extent impoverishes village social life. With its fixed four-square rhythm it curbs the spontaneous creation and use of improvisation which is a central feature of the drumming, singing, and dancing of the real folk music. Its

[1] H. Tracey, *Chopi Musicians*, International African Institute, 1948.
[2] The more technical aspects of this process are described by Kirby, op. cit. pp. 132 ff.

growth in popularity is undoubted, but this must inevitably involve a corresponding loss to the cultural heritage of the African.[1] It is unfortunate that the social ambitions of many literate Africans lead them to express active hostility to the culture of their own folk and to despise both their art and their music.[2]

We have here a problem which has its analogy in many other aspects of African cultural or social life. Is it possible to save what is valuable in African usage or tradition from being overwhelmed by the dynamism of Western civilization? It may be that some African musical genius may arise who may be able to utilize the old African folk music as the foundation of a new type of creative art, thus achieving a development comparable to that in the Western world, where the old dance forms have been the basis of many orchestral masterpieces. Even though there would be a loss of *naïveté* and an increase of sophistication, something might thus be retained.

Meanwhile, it is important in this connexion to note the current attitude of educational authorities in regard to the teaching of music. In general there is today no lack of appreciation either of the value of music as an element in education, or of the special appeal which it can make to Africans, as shown by the proficiency which they readily attain in certain aspects of its exercise. There is today little to justify the charge, which could once be levelled against the missions, that they treated African music either as barbaric or as serving the purpose of dancing, in itself regarded as an immoral practice. There is a general recognition of the existence among Africans of a natural, as opposed to an artistic, sense of harmony and a highly developed sense of rhythm.

But the recognition given to indigenous music by schools and missions extends chiefly to vocal and especially choral, not to instrumental music. Songs in the vernacular sung to original African melodies are encouraged, even though there may exist at the same time a tendency to teach African children either European music or African-composed music constructed after European models. The position is also affected by the fact that in South Africa, as in most of the other territories, music is now printed for school use in the Tonic Sol-Fa notation, in which little real African music is available. Those who are interested in the survival of indigenous music naturally deplore that school and mission education has failed to pay adequate regard to it. But the difficulties in the way must also be recognized, for it is not easy to adopt for educational purposes a form of art which owes some of its chief value to its spontaneity, has little in the way of

---

[1] H. P. Junod, *Bantu Heritage,* 1938, p. 85. H. Tracey, in *African Music Society Newsletter,* vol. i, no. 6, 1953, p. 41.

[2] H. Tracey in *Problèmes d'Afrique Centrale,* no. 26, 1954 (Bulletin de l'Association des Anciens Étudiants de l'Institut Universitaire des Territoires d'Outre-Mer), Brussels.

standardized instruments, and which is difficult to record in recognized methods of notation.

Some General Observations

The present neo-folk craze, discarding true African rhythmic technique and appropriating elementary European 4/4 dance time together with certain European chordal progressions, is not sufficiently developed to merit consideration from the purely musical point of view. It remains an open question whether it will take sufficient nourishment from African tradition to become in time a characteristic African contribution to world music. But the true folk music of Africa exhibits a virility and a spontaneity of creation which entitles it to a place of esteem. It offers to the world three special musical principles, two of which are unusual if not unique: first, the remarkable structure of its melodies which, though seemingly free and liable to spontaneous variation, are yet strictly metrical; second, the principle, fundamental to African rhythm-combination, which demands that in an ensemble there must be a series of differing rhythm-patterns played simultaneously, and which must overlap, and which therefore are not conterminous. In its simplest form this principle may be enunciated thus: 'If two drums are playing in 3/8 time and at the same speed, the main beat of the second drum must fall on either the second or third beats of the bar of the first drum. The main beats of the bars of the two drums can never coincide.'[1] To Western music this is a novel conception, but it is at the root of the whole African musical system.

The third principle is that of spontaneity of creation. It is part of the art of singing to be able to make subtle variations and innovations in both words and melody. The art of a dancer consists in his ability to make a personal contribution of his own creation whenever he dances, provided he keeps within the main framework of the dance, and it is the business of the master drummer to improvise a sequence of rhythms which, though co-ordinated with the other drums, shall yet be a spontaneous comment, in rhythm, on the style of each dancer. African music must be different every time it is performed yet still true in essential outline to the particular song or dance.

The use of the drum for sending messages has widely attracted the interest of travellers, but its use for this purpose belongs to a different branch of study and has a literature of its own.[2]

[1] For a fuller treatment of the technique of rhythm in African music, see A. M. Jones, 'African Music', no. 2, 1943, *R.L.I. Papers*; and *Africa*, vol. xxiv, pp. 26 ff. See also E. Jokl, in *Handbook on Race Relations in South Africa*, 1949, p. 451, and the previous reference to the treatment of the technical aspects of African music by P. R. Kirby.

[2] R. St. B. Baker, *Africa Drums*, 1942. J. F. Carrington, *Talking Drums of Africa*, 1949. H. Labouret, 'Langage tambouriné et sifflé', *Bulletin du Comité d'Études historiques et scientifiques de l'A.O.F.*, 1921, pp. 120–58. A. Verbeken, 'Le tambour téléphone chez les indigènes de l'Afrique

Research

Though much has been written on the subject of African musical instruments or the technique of drumming and singing,[1] there has been relatively little in the nature of the fundamental research which will ultimately enable musical Africans to analyse and critically appreciate their own music and its possibilities. The only institution which is devoted solely to the study of African music is the African Music Society which has its headquarters in Johannesburg. The Society lacks the funds to engage a permanent staff for research, but has a large library of recorded African music, which is of especial value in view of the fact that it is difficult to reduce the music to print. The first number of the Society's journal, *African Music*, to be published annually, appeared in 1954.[2] In the United Kingdom the London School of Oriental and African Studies has a temporary post of lecturer in African music.[3]

AFRICAN ART

In the immediately preceding part of this chapter it has been necessary to adopt a somewhat restrictive definition of African music in order to confine discussion as far as possible to African music of an indigenous type, as distinguished from the type of music which shows the effect of European or other external influences. It will be necessary to apply the same principle in dealing with African art. For the present purpose it may be defined as that type of visual art which has been produced by Africans within the framework of their own system of values and social organization. But there is a further limitation to be imposed. Artistic expression in a visual form may be manifested in a variety of ways, such, for instance, as architecture, textile design, the production of articles of domestic use, or the creation and use of ornaments. Consideration here will be confined to the two visual arts of painting and sculpture, for in them will be found some of the most typical forms in which African artistic impulses have found expression.

Painting and Engraving

The geographical fields of these forms of African art may be defined in reasonably broad terms, and are to some extent mutually exclusive.

Centrale', *Congo*, vol. i, 1920, pp. 253–84. R. S. Rattray, 'The Drum Language of West Africa', in *J.R.A.S.*, vol. xxii, 1923, pp. 226–36, 302–16.

[1] See, for example, E. M. Hornbostel in *Africa*, April 1933, pp. 129–57, 277–311; H. Pepper, *Enc. A.E.F.*, pp. 552–65; S. Chauvet, *La Musique Nègre*, Éditions Géographiques, Maritimes et Coloniales, 1929; *Enc. C.B.*, vol. i, p. 200.

[2] See *African Music* (Journal of the African Music Society), vol. i, no. 1, pp. 71 ff.

[3] For a bibliography on African music, see A. Merriam, 'Annotated Bibliography of African and African-Derived Music since 1936', *Africa*, October 1951, pp. 319 ff.

Within the area dealt with in this survey traditional painting or engraving in a developed form is found chiefly in South Africa, the Rhodesias, and the Kondoa District of Tanganyika;[1] it has recently been identified for the first time near Kano in Northern Nigeria. Elsewhere it exists in Ethiopia and in parts of northern Africa. The techniques of painting are indeed widely known throughout Negro Africa, and are used freely in the enhancement of masks and other wood-carvings and in the decoration of the human body and of houses, but the painting of representational pictures is largely confined to areas now or in recent centuries inhabited by the Bushmen and to some of the neighbouring Bantu areas. In its most interesting and most artistic form it is revealed in rock paintings. The finest of these rock paintings are conceived in a kind of 'Japanese naturalism' and sometimes exceed in realistic detail the best Magdalenian work of palaeolithic Europe. The depicting of the movement of animals is clearly the result of close observation. The human figure is commonly stylized (often with marked steatopygy) in a way which recalls the European upper palaeolithic paintings, but the possibility of a common origin remains hypothetical.

A theory[2] has been advanced that prehistoric cave art flourished as early as 50,000 years ago. According to this view cave art originated with African hunters at a very early epoch, and was subsequently modified by influences from the Mediterranean and the Nile Valley; at a still later date it was subjected to influences emanating from the eastern and southeastern coasts, which in turn were superseded by those introduced by relatively recent migrations of Bantu into southern Africa. But the theory that African cave paintings are of an antiquity comparable with those in Europe has been received with considerable scepticism.[3] Radio-carbon tests applied to charcoal from hearths associated with paintings at Solwezi in Northern Rhodesia ascribe a probable date of about 4500 B.C. Further research is required before an earlier attribution can be made.

The subjects depicted in the African cave paintings are often of a narrative character, including lively scenes of warfare and the chase, but narrative art is otherwise rare in Africa, being practically confined to a few of the bronze reliefs of Benin (perhaps under European influence) and to carved doors in the north-east Yoruba region. It seems to be agreed that some of the southern Bantu have until recently practised this type of

[1] H. P. Fosbrooke and others, *Tanganyika Rock Paintings: A Guide and a Record*, 1950, Dar-es-Salaam. This contains a useful bibliography on the subject of rock paintings.

[2] H. Breuil, 'Les Roches peintes d'Afrique australe — leurs auteurs et leur âge', *L'Anthropologie*, 53, 5/6, 1950, pp. 377–406.

[3] C. van Riet Lowe, 'L'Âge et l'origine des peintures rupestres d'Afrique du Sud', *L'Anthropologie*, 54, 1950, pp. 421–31. E. Rosenthal and A. J. H. Goodwin, *Cave Artists of South Africa*, Cape Town, 1953. B. J. Craig, 'Rockpaintings and Petroglyphs of South and Central Africa', *Bibliography of Prehistoric Art*, Cape Town, 1947.

painting, but generally speaking rock painting and engraving are almost everywhere an obsolete art. The aptitude for painting often shown by African pupils in the schools of south and South-East Africa is not to be regarded as the continuance of an unbroken tradition, and is in fact found as often among tribes that have never known visual art at all.

West African Sculpture

In West Africa sculpture is the African art *par excellence*. Its distribution is largely confined to the basins of the Niger and Congo. The reasons for the absence of sculptural art—or its failure to survive—east of the Great Lakes and south of the Zambezi are not clear, but it is noteworthy that the art area corresponds roughly with that of heavy rainfall and of the predominance of agriculture, as opposed to pastoralism in the east and south. It is characteristic also of this area that its inhabitants have for the most part been settled for a relatively long period in their present homes. It may be that tribal factions and disturbances have diverted the creative energy of the eastern and southern peoples into other forms of expression, such as music.

Attempts have been made to classify the numerous styles and sub-styles of African sculpture in terms of supposed layers of culture dating from different periods. It has, for instance, been suggested that the occurrence of abstraction in some Congo tribes may connote an historical connexion with tribes of the western Sudan, but the variety of styles all over the area is so striking that such similarities are often more likely to be due to coincidence than to any former association. With few exceptions, our present knowledge of styles is not yet wide enough to do more than arrange them in simple geographical groups for convenience of study. Even the distinction sometimes drawn between the forest and savannah cultures of West Africa, though it has a certain broad validity, is not easy to apply in detail.

The following is a summary classification of the most important styles (exclusive of East and Central Africa), but it does not imply that greater stylistic similarity will necessarily be found within the groups than between them:[1]

1. the western Sudan tribes, of which the most important in sculpture are the Bambara, the Dogon, and the Mossi;

2. the Guinea Coast tribes from Senegal to Dahomey, notably the Baga of French Guinea, the Mende of Sierra Leone, the Dan-Ngere tribes about the frontiers of Liberia, French Guinea, and the Ivory Coast; the Guro, Baule, and Senufo of the Ivory Coast; the Ashanti, Ewe, and Fon of the Gold Coast and Dahomey;

3. Nigeria, with a greater profusion of style than any other region,

[1] See for further details M. Trowell, *Classical African Sculpture*, 1954, pp. 41 ff.; also the Bibliography on p. 99.

including the Yoruba and Bini in the west, the Nupe and various pagan tribes in the north (more closely related to the Sudan than to the peoples in the south), and the Ijo, Ibo, Ibibio, and Ekoi to the east;

4. the Cameroons and French Equatorial Africa, the most important tribes being those of the Cameroons grasslands and the Bakota, Fang, and Bateke of the French Congo;

5. the northern, and for the most part heavily forested, region of the Belgian Congo, including the riverain tribes loosely described as Bangala, the Kundo-Mongo peoples (with a rather sparse and little-known art), the Azande-Mangbetu area in the north-east, and the Balega or Warega near the northern end of Lake Tanganyika;

6. the southern Belgian Congo with northern Angola and the north-western region of Northern Rhodesia, with the following principal art-producing tribes: Bakongo, Bayaka, Bapende, Bushongo, Bena Lulua, Basonge, Baluba, Lunda-Bajokwe, and Barotse.

It would be unprofitable to consider here the relative aesthetic merits of these styles, but all those mentioned have produced at least some works which have been thought fit by competent judges to stand for Africa in representative collections of the world's most characteristic works of art.

African and European Traditions

The European is for the most part ill equipped by his own aesthetic tradition to appreciate the real nature of African art, and he does not easily avoid forming the naïve misconceptions about it which have determined the attitudes of most Europeans in Africa. Yet he must so equip himself if he is (for example) to make a contribution of value to the teaching of art in African schools, and the facts of history and philosophy which the teacher needs to learn would also help to save many Europeans from forming false stereotypes of African character and intelligence. The form taken by artistic expression must have been influenced by many different historical trends in the various tribes concerned, but the observer is made conscious of one circumstance, which is reflected everywhere in the art of the Negro peoples of Africa. The fundamental principles of industrial civilization, which became the basis on which the whole edifice of our modern culture was built, are only now beginning to spread into Negro Africa.

These principles appeared first in Egypt and Sumeria and spread thence to Greece, accompanied by the new invention of writing. The most obvious principle is mensuration and the idea of precision work, without which (to take one example) the construction of large buildings was impossible. In Greece the development of mathematics and the growth of rationalism went hand in hand and they revolutionized art itself by introducing the principle of visual representation of the subject. This principle,

leading to the pursuit of precision as an end in itself, has been dominant in
the European tradition during most of the ensuing 2,500 years, never being
wholly submerged even in the Middle Ages. In Negro Africa, however,
a regard for precision has never been among the essential values accepted
by society; the straight line, for example, is avoided rather than sought
after. This trait is not, as is often supposed, evidence of a failure of intellect
on the part of Africans, but may rather be connected with deep differences
between the two ways of life. A bias towards the dynamic rather than
towards the static conceptions implicit in the growth of mathematical
science would account for the way in which the African art forms, far from
developing along a single line based more or less closely on realism, have
left far more to the imagination. Thus metaphor rather than description
is their artistic language, and this taste informs not only African art but
many other aspects of indigenous life.

The undiscerned conflict between these concepts of industrial and pre-
industrial society has doubtless been at the base of many misunderstand-
ings. In the field of art its results have often proved to be regrettable. Thus
it is widely believed that while certain African works may have great
aesthetic value for Europeans, they had none for their African carvers or
for those for whom they were carved, being wholly conditioned by ritual
considerations to the exclusion of all conscious artistic effort. Such a conclusion would be misleading. It is true that African artists are in some
respects more closely governed by tradition than their European counterparts have usually been; but this is to view African art from one aspect
only, and the ideas of conformity and of creative individuality are in fact
conceptions between which there is a continuous and well-balanced inter-
play. This tension is perhaps responsible more than anything else for the
excellence of the best Negro sculpture; the works of different individual
artists can be as readily distinguished in Africa as in Europe, and essentially
by the same methods.

Development of Local Styles

Study of the historical development of African sculpture is hampered
by the fact that wood, its normal medium in most areas, seldom survives
as long as a hundred years, which is hardly long enough to discern historical trends. Bronzes and terra-cottas which have survived from ancient
times bear no necessary relation to the woodcarving of the same times.
Apart from African cave paintings, the earliest datable Negro art, namely,
the terra-cotta figures found in the tin-fields round Nok and southwards
to the middle Benue valley, seems to show that in the last centuries
before Christ there was already flourishing a substantial culture whose
art was highly developed. Iron was in occasional use along with neolithic
stone tools. The art of this period encompassed so remarkable a range of

stylizations within a common tradition that we must postulate a still greater antiquity for the origins of the aesthetic conceptions which subsist in Africa to this day.

It is not yet clear whether the Nok culture played any part in the ancestry of the famous art style of Ife, the ancient centre of the Yoruba people, with its extraordinary naturalism which has led many to associate it, though too readily, with Greece, Rome, or Renaissance Italy. The social milieu of the city state of Ife a thousand years ago may well have been as favourable to the emergence of an indigenous humanistic naturalism in art as was that of post-Homeric Athens. In that case the 'archaic' culture of the Benue valley (between which and Yoruba culture other links have been discerned) could have been the forerunner of the Ife style as we know it. Excavation may be able to reconstruct in coming years at least part of these great historical processes. About the fourteenth century Ife seems to have handed on its art of bronze-casting to the more barbaric Bini, but the slow fusion of the two tribal styles eventually produced at Benin a hybrid which lacked both the sensuous beauty of the early work and the vigour of the work of surrounding peoples. Unfortunately Bini culture, of which alone we have some historical knowledge, is so unrepresentative as to throw little light on the development of African art in general.

In so far as it is ancillary to pagan religious practice, African art is inevitably vulnerable to the spread of Christianity and Islam, and even where, as in the country of the Yoruba, there is a tradition of secular art, it is often undermined by the infiltration of Western culture. The preservation of representative examples of traditional art in museums, though a most necessary task (only now being seriously undertaken),[1] cannot arrest the decline in the practice of art. European teaching methods have been unsuccessful both in fostering the traditional African skills and in implanting any real substitute when they have disappeared.

The school system of teaching art is in any case alien to the African tradition, which is based, as in medieval Europe, on apprenticeship. The imparting of European standards and principles, especially perspective, often does actual harm not only by destroying the natural 'vision' of the pupils, but by causing them to despise it. It is, moreover, unnatural, at least in West Africa, to emphasize painting instead of sculpture. There is here a serious dilemma which educationists have so far been unable to resolve. Given that it is not now possible to re-create the conditions which inspired the traditional art of Africa, as shown especially in its wood carvings, is it nevertheless possible to hope for the appearance in Africa of a live art, in keeping with modern social and economic developments, instead of the weak, second-rate, derivative art without

[1] The first local Museum, that at Jos in Nigeria, was opened in 1952. *Annual Report of the Antiquities Service*, Nigeria, 1952–3, p. 4.

background or support in its homeland' which seems likely to emerge from the teaching now given in African schools?[1] Not the least of the problems of the educationist appears to be the difficulty of securing teachers with the necessary appreciation of pre-literate forms of art and with the requisite adaptability and breadth of outlook.

[1] K. C. Murray, 'Art Courses for Africans', *Overseas Education*, vol. xxi, no. 2, 1950, p. 1020.

CHAPTER III

THE AFRICAN LANGUAGES

THE LINGUISTIC FIELD

SCHOLARS have differed in their estimate of the number of the languages spoken in Africa. While some have held that out of a possible total of 2,000 languages in the world, Africa is responsible for 700, others are inclined to put this figure at nearly 1,000,[1] though such estimates will remain largely speculative, until it is decided how far the distinction between some of these tongues classed as languages is really fundamental. One thing is, however, clear. Africa has in proportion to its population an unusual number of languages, a fact which seems natural enough, when one reflects that it is mainly in those parts of the world which have a high density of population and a relatively advanced social structure that neighbouring peoples have united in evolving a common language.

There is another point of interest in this connexion. It is a widely accepted theory that a written alphabet was first employed at some period between 1300 and 1200 B.C. by a Semitic people (possibly the Phoenicians), and that the alphabetic systems now used in a large part of the world can be traced back to this source.[2] Though, however, an alphabet was employed at an early stage in parts of northern Africa, its use does not seem to have penetrated to the south until the establishment of the trans-Saharan Kingdoms[3] introduced the use of the Arabic script into the Islamized areas of West Africa. In the part of Africa with which this Survey deals, only the Vai tribe (who are found partly in Sierra Leone and partly in Liberia) and the Bamum tribe in the French Cameroons are known to have evolved their own written script, and this at a comparatively recent date.

The first attempts to study the indigenous African languages and to reduce them to writing were made by missionaries, who needed a medium both for preaching and for translating the Scriptures. They encountered the difficulties which must be inherent in any study of the tongue of illiterate peoples. There was no documentary material, and it became necessary to devise a script and an orthography which would convey pronunciation and structure to persons to whom the language was unfamiliar, while proving at the same time to be capable of manipulation by

[1] I. Ward, in *Fabian Colonial Essays*, 1945, p. 131.
[2] D. Forde, in *Progress*, vol. xliii, no. 237, 1952, p. 44.
[3] See above, p. 35.

Africans who were to be taught to read and write their own tongue. In spite of these difficulties, however, much work of scientific value was done by the missions and a considerable number of languages were reduced to writing by them. The British and Foreign Bible Society, for example, has stated that 36 complete Bibles and 82 New Testaments have been published through its agency in the African tongues, while portions of the Bible have been published in a further 18 languages.[1] In the early years of this century, moreover, many vocabularies and grammars were compiled by Administrative Officers in British and other colonies throughout Africa.

The second stage began with the acceptance by missionaries and later by the Governments of an increasing measure of responsibility for education, and with the assignment to African languages of a definite place, either as a medium or a subject, in schemes of popular instruction. A period of intensive philological study, associated with the work of scholars such as Alice Werner, Krapf, Bleek, Meinhof, and Westermann, linked the two stages, and their labours laid the foundations upon which the scientific study of African languages could be based. Among British linguists Sir Harry Johnston accumulated vocabularies from 276 Bantu languages in a volume which is still of much importance.[2]

But this development created a further series of problems both in linguistic study and educational policy. It was impossible to provide education in every one of the numerous vernaculars, and it became necessary to decide which of them should be selected for this purpose and consequently in which language school books should be prepared and the production of original literature encouraged. In some cases the early translation of the Bible in one dialect gave it the prestige of a literary language. Other areas adopted a current African lingua franca; others have selected for school use the languages understood over the widest practicable area, while in a few cases 'Union' languages have been constructed for dialect groups, using where possible the forms common to a predominant majority among the peoples concerned.[3]

The standardization of language clusters has often been attempted, but seldom with success, and the attempt to unify dialects has as a rule also failed, the most notable example being the attempted union of Fante and Twi into a single Akan language of the Gold Coast. National jealousy and difficulties of orthography were in this case the main causes of the miscarriage of what appeared to be a feasible union of two not dissimilar dialects.[4] While the need for a language more universal than local dialects

[1] Report of British and Foreign Bible Society, 1950.
[2] H. H. Johnston, A Comparative Study of the Bantu and semi-Bantu Languages, 1919.
[3] G. P. Lestrade, 'Some Reflections on the Future of South African Bantu Languages', The Critic, vol. iii, 1934, p. 137.
[4] The Use of Vernacular Languages in Education, Unesco, 1953, pp. 115 ff.

AFRICA : LANGUAGE GROUPS

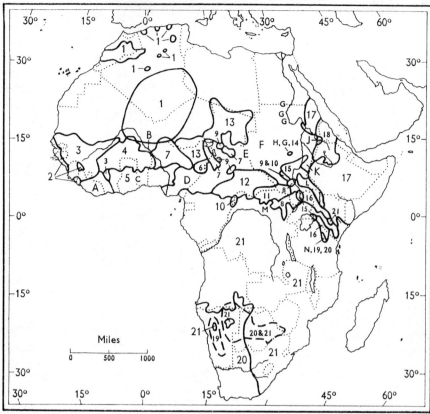

D.C.S. (Misc.) 226/4

LARGER UNITS

1	Berber	11	Zande
2	West Atlantic (including Fulani)	12	Banda-Gbaya
3	Mande	13	East Saharan
4	Gur	14	Koalib-Tagoi
5	Kwa	15	Nilotic
6	Chadic	16	Nilo-Hamitic
7	Chado-Hamitic (including Hausa)	17	Cushitic
8	Moru-Mangbetu	18	Semitic
9	Bongo-Bagirmi	19	Sandawe-Hottentot
10	Sere-Mundu	20	Bushman-Hadza

21   Bantu

OTHER LANGUAGES AND GROUPS

A	Kru	G	Nubian
B	Songhai	H	Other languages of the Nuba Hills
C	Togo Languages	J	Barea and Kunama
D	Ijo, Ibibio, Tiv and other	K	Berta, etc.
	Isolated languages and Groups	L	Didinga-Murle, etc.
E	Maba, Tama, etc.	M	Mba
F	Fur	N	Iraqw

Drawn from information supplied by the
International African Institute

is generally recognized, experience seems to show that it is more practical to select and standardize one dialect from a group than to attempt an artificial unification of the dialects composing the group.

The rapid expansion in the numbers of pupils in the vernacular classes of the schools has required the provision on an increasing scale of grammars and textbooks, and the production of general literature has become an essential requirement if the habit of reading is to be maintained after the pupil has left school. This need was met in the first instance by translations from European works, but there is now a growing body of original vernacular literature, though African pioneers in this new method of expression still require assistance and encouragement. This was at the outset provided, among other measures, by competitions such as those organized by the International African Institute, the Interterritorial Swahili Committee, and similar organizations, but a number of African authors have now achieved literary reputations which justify the publication of their work on its own merits. The demand for vernacular newspapers was met in the first instance by the publication of Government newspapers which formed at the same time a convenient agency for the promulgation of Government notices or regulations and of the rules made by Native Administrations. There is, however, now a growing number of independent vernacular newspapers, especially in West Africa.[1]

The distribution of vernacular literature was at first mainly in the hands of missionary bodies, who set up printing presses, publishing organizations, and book-shops. These are still active, but in addition the literature committees and bureaux established in various territories, and usually financed either wholly or in part by the Government, are now producing an increasing volume of reading matter. Nigeria, for example, has the subsidized Gaskiya Corporation at Zaria, which deals with Hausa and other vernaculars of the Northern Provinces; the Gold Coast has a Bureau of Vernacular Literature at Accra; Sierra Leone has a Protectorate Literature Bureau at Bo. In East and Central Africa there exist the Literature Committee at Nairobi, the African Literature Committee in Uganda, and the Northern Rhodesian and Nyasaland Joint Publications Bureau at Lusaka.

The Literature Bureau of the East Africa High Commission has been active and progressive. It publishes the African magazine *Tazama*, which has reached a sale of 14,000 copies per issue. It has extended its African library service, giving special attention to prisons and detention camps during the emergency conditions occasioned by the Mau Mau outbreak in Kenya.[2] There is an increasing demand for special material for use in

[1] See below, p. 1239.
[2] *Annual Report on the East Africa High Commission 1953*, Colonial no. 305, pp. 16–17.

mass education or community development schemes,[1] and much of this is supplied by official agencies. Certain commercial publishers in Europe and in the Union of South Africa are now issuing books in the African languages.[2] The *Commissie Voor Afrikaanse Taalkunde* has published a number of texts, together with Dutch translations. In the Belgian Congo the *Librairie Évangélique du Congo*, a commercial publishing house supported by the *Conseil Protestant du Congo*, has published a considerable body of vernacular literature.

CLASSIFICATION OF AFRICAN LANGUAGES

The earliest attempts at classification of the languages of Africa were based on vocabulary resemblances, this being the only material then available for comparison over a wide area. As early as 1854 Koelle gave in his *Polyglotta Africana* a comparative word list of over 100 West African languages, which he classified into a number of groups. The importance of such vocabulary correspondence is shown by the fact that much of Koelle's classification is still regarded as valid today. Later scholars, however, extended their studies to a comparison of the structure of languages as well as their vocabulary, and with the increase of knowledge of African linguistics, older classifications have now been materially modified.[3]

Lepsius, in his work *Nubische Grammatik*, divided African languages into three main groups: Semitic, Hamitic, and Primitive African, the last being in turn divided into two sub-groups, namely, the Bantu and the mixed Negro.[4] He placed Hottentot-Bushman in the Hamitic group and regarded the Negro languages as the diversified product of the mixture of Hamitic and Bantu. F. W. Müller proposed a division into six groups:[5] Semitic, Hamitic, Nuba-Fula, Negro, Bantu, and Hottentot-Bushman, a classification also adopted by R. N. Cust.[6] A later classification by A. Werner[7] divided the languages into five groups, namely, Sudanian, Bantu, Hamitic (including Hausa, Fulani, Masai, and Hottentot), Bushman, and Semitic. In 1935 Dr. D. Westermann grouped them into three main families, namely, Khoisan (Bushman and Hottentot), Negro (including Sudanic, Bantu, and Nilotic), and Hamito-Semitic.[8]

---

[1] M. Read, 'Some Aspects of Adult Education', *Community Development Bulletin*, vol. iii, 1952, pp. 62–82.

[2] References to these publications will be found in the current issues of *Africa* (the Journal of the International African Institute), and in *Books for Africa*, the bulletin of the International Committee on Christian Literature for Africa, which was set up by the International Missionary Council in 1929.

[3] For a history of this change, see E. W. Smith, *J.R.A.I.*, vol. lxv, 1935, pp. 44 ff.

[4] R. Lepsius, *Nubische Grammatik mit einer Einleitung über die Völker und Sprachen Afrikas*, Berlin, 1880. [5] F. W. Müller, *Grundriß der Sprachwissenschaft*, 1858.

[6] R. N. Cust, *The Modern Languages of Africa*, 1883.

[7] A. Werner, *Language Families of Africa*, 1915.

[8] D. Westermann, 'Charakter und Einteilung der Sudansprachen', *Africa*, April 1935,

No major attempt at classification followed for some years, though several scholars have worked on classification within particular fields, notably Drs. Doke, Guthrie, Van Bulck, and Hulstaert in respect of the Bantu languages; Tucker in respect of languages of the southern Anglo-Egyptian Sudan; Lukas (Chado-Hamitic and Chadic languages); and Cerulli, Conti Rossini, and Moreno (Cushitic languages). With the increased study of African languages the importance of tone has been realized, and Miss M. Green[1] has proposed that tone should be admitted as one of the criteria of classification.

In 1949–50 J. H. Greenberg[2] put forward a reclassification of all the languages of Africa into the following families: (a) Niger-Congo, which with 15 sub-divisions would include almost all the languages of West Africa, but would also include Bantu as a 'Central Branch', together with most of the so-called 'semi-Bantu' languages, (b) Songhai (not yet related to any other family), (c) Central Sudanic, comprising the Moru-Madi and Bongo-Bagirmi of Tucker,[3] (d) Central Saharan (Kanuri, &c.), (e) Eastern Sudanic, with seven sub-divisions, including Nubian, Didinga, &c., and, as a 'Southern Branch', the languages usually known as Nilotic and Nilo-Hamitic, (f) Afroasiatic or Hamito-Semitic, in five sub-divisions, including under the heading 'Chad languages' both the Chado-Hamitic (including Hausa) and Chadic of Lukas, (g) Click languages, in three sub-divisions, namely, Khoisan (Bushman, and Hottentot), Sandawe, and Hadza, (h) a number of small and as yet unallocated 'families', as, for example, 'Kordofanian', Berta, and Fur.

The chief difficulty has resulted from the attempt to build up a classification from material that is still inadequate and is often inaccurate. In the course of carrying out the Linguistic Survey embodied in the *Handbook of African Languages*, to which reference will be made subsequently,[4] the International African Institute has sought a classification on a more authoritative and a more comprehensive foundation. It will be based as far as possible on phonetic, morphological, and syntactic criteria as well as on vocabulary correspondence.[5] The term 'Language Family' has been abandoned, and the basic unit of classification will be the individual

pp. 129–48. He has, however, modified this classification, see 'African Linguistic Classification', ibid. xxii, vol. 1952, pp. 250–6, and D. Westermann and M. A. Bryan, *The Languages of West Africa; Handbook of African Languages*, Part II, International African Institute, 1952.

[1] 'The Classification of West African Tone-languages, Igbo and Efik', *Africa*, July 1949, pp. 215–19.

[2] 'Studies in African Linguistic Classification I–VI', *South-western Journal of Anthropology*, vol. v, 1949, vol. vi, 1950. See also I. Ward, *Fabian Colonial Essays*, 1945, p. 133.

[3] A. N. Tucker, *Eastern Sudanic Languages*, vol. i, 1940.

[4] See below, p. 113.

[5] See the Introduction to Westermann and Bryan, *The Languages of West Africa; Handbook of African Languages*, Part II, International African Institute, 1952. See also D. Forde, 'The Cultural Map of West Africa', in *Transactions of the New York Academy of Sciences*, Series II, vol. xv, pp. 206–19, April 1953.

Language or Dialect Cluster. Languages which are demonstrably closely related are arranged in Language Groups, and wherever possible groups regarding whose interrelation there can be no doubt are classed together in certain Larger Language Units. These Units, arranged roughly from west to east and from north to south, are as follows: West Atlantic (including Fulani); Mande; Gur; Kwa; Chadic; Chado-Hamitic (including Hausa); Central Saharan, class languages of the Nuba Hills; Banda-Gbaya; Sere-Mundu; Bongo-Bagirmi; Moru-Mangbetu; Nilotic; Nilo-Hamitic; Cushitic and Berber; Semitic; Sandawe-Hottentot; Bushman-Hadza and Bantu.

From this list are omitted all languages which are known not to be attached to any of the above Units (e.g. Songhai) or are insufficiently documented. Such languages are termed 'Isolated Language Groups' or 'Isolated Units' and the large number which have to be treated in this manner shows how great is the need for further research before any complete classification can be attempted.

Those responsible for the *Handbook* did not feel that any broader classification could then be made, although it was recognized that there are strong affiliations between, for example, the Nilotic and Nilo-Hamitic Larger Units, as also between Bongo-Bagirmi and Moru-Mangbetu; a less obvious one between Banda-Gbaya, Sere-Mundu, and the Isolated Groups Mba and Zande, and possibly even between these and Bantu. All these latter were included by Greenberg in the 'Niger-Congo' family.[1] The so-called Khoisan or Click languages cannot be classed in one Larger Unit, in spite of strong vocabulary and phonetic resemblances, owing to the fundamental differences of their grammatical structure. They are therefore divided into two Larger Units: Nama (Hottentot)-Sandawe (including Naron) and Bushman-Hadza (including Hiechware). The last grouping is still tentative.

THE PROBLEM OF ORTHOGRAPHY

The early missionaries generally represented the sounds of African tongues by the nearest symbols for sounds in their own language, with the result that, where a language area was divided by a political boundary, or where missionaries of two nationalities were at work among the same tribe, rival orthographies were adopted. Sometimes different methods were devised even by investigators of the same nationality for representing the same sounds. The disadvantages of this procedure were early recognized, but it has not been easy to secure agreement on the adoption of a uniform system of orthography. A system intended to be of general application was designed by Lepsius in 1850 at the request of various Pro-

[1] See above, p. 85.

testant missions.[1] A second edition of his work was published in 1863, and further improvements were made by Meinhof and by Pater Schmidt in his 'Anthropos' alphabet. The accuracy of representation given by the Lepsius system, as modified by Meinhof, makes it an admirable instrument for scientific research, but there are practical difficulties in the way of its wider use. It is constructed by the addition of diacritical marks to the letters of the ordinary Roman alphabet, but the use of these marks has certain practical disadvantages, not the least of which lies in the fact that such type is expensive, since it is more fragile than ordinary type and requires more frequent renewal.

For these reasons the International African Institute sought in 1928 to lay down principles on which a simpler system of orthography could be based. It was clearly impossible to secure absolute uniformity of practice throughout Africa, but it was considered imperative both to clear up the confusion resulting from the use of different spellings for the same or closely related languages, and at the same time to ensure that the sounds of the spoken word should be represented in writing in a manner that would be intelligible to the African reader. Exact phonetic representation for the foreign student was regarded as being less important. The new system, which soon acquired the name of the 'Africa' orthography, is based in the main on the alphabet of the *Association Phonétique Internationale*. It avoids the use of diacritical marks or diagraphs, and the sounds for which the Roman alphabet provides no symbols are represented by new letter forms, taken from the alphabet of the *Association Phonétique*, as for example the symbols ɛ, ɔ, ʒ.[2] The Memorandum of the Institute states that its aim has been to show how existing orthographies may be modified and improved, rather than to provide a ready-made alphabet for every African language.[3]

The introduction of a new orthography necessarily encounters certain initial difficulties, such as the provision of new symbols in printing or the adaptation of lettering on typewriters. Some of these difficulties have now been overcome, and a Morse code for the new symbols has been devised, though not yet adopted.[4] The psychological obstacles have been more serious, and although in several areas representative committees have accepted the new form of orthography, the decision has not always been implemented in practice, and it has sometimes been decided later to revert to the old style of writing. Since Governments still leave to the missions a large share of education in schools, they have not always been able to insist upon the adoption in practice of official decisions on

[1] D. Westermann, *Proceedings of the Rejaf Conference*, 1928, p. 15.
[2] i.e. open e; open o; and *ng* as in sing.
[3] *A Practical Orthography of African Languages*, International African Institute, 1930, pp. 4 and 6.
[4] A. N. Tucker, 'African Alphabets and the Telegraph Problem', *Bantu Studies*, vol. x, 1936, pp. 67–73.

orthography, and in many cases have not pressed such decisions against opposition. It is characteristic that objections have sometimes come from African nationalist leaders, notably in Nigeria and the Gold Coast, where the non-Roman letters have been described as 'something unnatural forced upon the people'.[1] The objection, curiously enough, does not seem to extend to the use of the Roman alphabets as introduced in the original script.

Dr. Westermann visited the Gold Coast in 1927, the southern Sudan in 1928, and Nigeria and Sierra Leone in 1929, in order to investigate local languages and explain the method of their representation by the 'Africa' script. All these territories officially adopted the orthography agreed upon with him; the Sudan appointed Dr. A. N. Tucker as linguistic adviser, and under his auspices a considerable amount of useful literature has been produced. In 1946 Dr. Tucker also advised on the standardization of orthography in the countries of Uganda and Unyoro, and the non-Bantu languages of Kenya and Uganda. Dr. I. Ward made in 1944 a further investigation for the Gold Coast Government. The principles of the 'Africa' script are now officially in use for over 60 vernaculars, and unofficially for many more. There is, however, still little agreement on the principles of word division. This has been discussed by various authors in relation to particular languages, and studies of the general principles involved have been made by Drs. M. Guthrie[2] and C. M. Doke.[3]

There have been relatively few purely African attempts at devising an orthography. Among the Somali, however, a new alphabet, known to the Italians as the 'Osmania' alphabet, has come into prominence during the last 30 years.[4] It has features of Arabic, Amharic, and even Hebrew cursive, and is phonetically and grammatically of high accuracy. After being banned under the Italian Administration it was adopted in 1945 by the 'Somali Youth League', which now produces manuals and school books in it, and there seems to be no doubt of its popularity. The only African alphabets which have had any importance are those of the Vai in Liberia and Sierra Leone and the Bamum in the French Cameroons. The Vai alphabet (or rather syllabary, for it had 200 characters, each denoting a syllable) is said to have been developed by a local chieftain, Dualu Bukere, and perfected in 1832; in 1849 some manuscripts in the Vai script were printed in England. It is not now in general use.[5] Doubts

---

[1] I. Ward, *Report on the Investigation of Some Gold Coast Language Problems*, 1945.

[2] *Bantu Word Division*, International African Institute Memorandum 22, 1948.

[3] *Phonetics of the Zulu Language*, 1926; *Bantu Linguistic Terminology*, 1935.

[4] M. Maino, 'L'Alphabeto "Osmania" in Somalia', *Rassegna di Studi Etiopici*, vol. x, 1951, pp. 108–21.

[5] S. W. Koelle, *Narrative of an Expedition into the Vy Country and the Discovery of a System of Writing Recently invented by the Native*, vol. vi, 1849. A. Klingenhaben, 'The Vai Script', *Africa*, April 1933, pp. 158–71. O. G. S. Crawford, 'The Writing of Njoya (Sultan Njoya's Ideographic Script for the Bamum Language)', *Antiquity*, 1936. B. Davidson and A. Ademola, *The New West Africa*,

have been expressed about the truth of the claim that the Bassa of Sierra Leone had at one time their own script.[1]

There is now a general agreement by educationists as to the necessity for taking more decisive action for the standardization of orthographies. The latest of the reports dealing with the progress of education in the British African territories suggests that when once an orthography has been settled by a majority decision of the Departments of Education concerned, its teaching in schools should be enforced if necessary by financial sanctions.[2] In 1954 the Shona Orthography Committee of Southern Rhodesia evolved a standard system of Shona spelling, which has been accepted by the Government and is being introduced into African schools. Textbooks using the new spelling have already been prepared.

The divergence between the standard orthographies now in use and the spelling of place-names in maps creates a problem of special difficulty, for the recording of place-names by cartographers who are unfamiliar with the languages concerned has led to some unfortunate results.[3] Proposals for dealing with this problem were made by the International African Institute in 1948 and considered by a committee of the Royal Geographical Society of Great Britain,[4] which advised that where there was an official orthography it should be used for recording local names. This procedure has not, however, been fully adopted even in the British Colonial territories, and there is little uniformity in practice. The Union of South Africa established in 1939 a place-name committee under the Department of Education; Kenya formed a standing committee on geographical names in 1948, and Southern Rhodesia a similar committee in 1952. The Third International Congress on Toponymy and Anthroponymy, which met in Brussels in 1949, expressed the view that the spelling of African place-names was of such importance as to merit international treatment.

ADMINISTRATIVE PROBLEMS AND POLICIES

The multiplicity of languages creates many serious problems for those charged with the administration or the development of the African territories; there is, indeed, hardly any aspect of governmental activity which has not linguistic implications requiring careful study. One of the most prominent of these problems arises in respect of the use to be made of the African vernaculars for official purposes, and most notably by officers

1953, p. 21, quote also an article by A. Hamilton in *Journal of Royal Geographical Society*, vol. xx, and an account by H. Rowley in *Africa Unveiled*, 1876.

[1] R. Buell, *The Native Problem in Africa*, vol. ii, 1928, p. 705.

[2] *African Education, A Study of Educational Policy and Practice in British Tropical Africa*, 1953, p. 80.

[3] A. N. Tucker, 'The Spelling of African Place-names on Maps', *Bulletin of the School of Oriental and African Studies*, vol. xii, 1948, pp. 824–30, and *Empire Survey Review*, vol. x, no. 77, 1950. See also M. Robert and E. J. Devroey in the *Bull. I.R.C.B.*, vol. xxiv, 1953, p. 211.

[4] Leaflets No. 6, October 1950, and 6a, July 1952.

discharging administrative or judicial functions or responsible for the agricultural or educational services. Singularly enough, there has been some difference of view in regard to the value to be attached to the study of the vernacular by such officers. To those who are aware of the practice which was followed in British India or in the Netherlands Indies,[1] it would seem impossible that an administrative or judicial officer should be expected to carry out his duties to the satisfaction of the people unless he had a working knowledge of the vernacular. In British India, for example, the existence of an official interpreter was unknown, except in the Supreme Courts of Justice, where his presence was justified by the fact that a certain proportion of the judges were usually recruited direct from the English Bar.

In Africa, however, there is great divergence of practice in regard to the obligation laid on public servants for acquiring a knowledge of the vernacular. In the Union of South Africa recruits for the public service are not required to give any proof of knowledge of an African language, and no preference is given to those candidates for the Native Affairs Department who may have taken the course of Bantu Studies at one of the universities. At one period the Union Government could usually rely on obtaining a number of recruits from families who had acquired an adequate colloquial knowledge of a Bantu language, but with the increase in the proportion of Europeans resident in urban centres this has now become more difficult. In Southern Rhodesia knowledge of the vernacular is not a condition for appointment in the Native Department, but officers are not considered to have qualified for selection as Assistant Native Commissioner unless they have passed the Civil Service examination in the language either of the Mashona or the Matabele.

In the British Colonial territories, on the other hand, tuition in a vernacular language forms a regular part of the course given to cadets in the Administrative Service, and a colloquial knowledge of the language studied is one of the necessary qualifications before they are confirmed in the service.[2] The results are, however, somewhat unequal.[3] There are some territories in which administrative and judicial officers show a mastery of the vernacular, especially in those areas which have a widely used indigenous language, such as Hausa, or a lingua franca, such as Swahili, but there are many other areas in which far too great reliance is placed on the use of an interpreter. That is no doubt due in part to the existence of a number of areas in which, as it has been said, 'languages jostle

---

[1] A. de Kat Angelino, trans. G. J. Renier, *Colonial Policy*, 1931, pp. 75, 100, 660. E. Blunt, *The Indian Civil Service*, 1937, pp. 193, 196. W. Huendu, 'Training Courses for Service in the Netherlands East Indies', *Africa*, July 1943, p. 136.

[2] C. Jeffries, *The Colonial Empire and its Civil Service*, 1938, p. 107.

[3] J. T. Saunders, R. L. Turner, D. Veale, *Report to the Nuffield Foundation on a Visit to Nigeria*, 1946, pp. 22, 33, 41, 50, 52.

each other', but as Lord Lugard emphasized, the use of an interpreter is always to be deprecated, and should be avoided if possible.[1]

In the early days of the Colonial Administrations little use was made of interpreters, and indeed there were few Africans who knew sufficient English to act as such. Many officers became fluent linguists and some published vocabularies and grammars in the local dialects, but as Africans assumed a larger share in the functions of local government, opportunities to cultivate an idiomatic usage became fewer. The substitution of the procedure of indirect for direct rule[2] relegated to the Native Tribunals a variety of litigation previously heard by Administrative Officers, and the Native Authority also disposed of a large number of the multifarious matters hitherto dealt with by them.

Exigencies of the service have, moreover, involved more frequent transfers, not only from district to district, but often from one territory to another. To these causes, among other, may be attributed the disturbing statement that the Administration in Kenya recently found itself seriously embarrassed in dealing with the Mau Mau emergency by the lack of officials with a working knowledge of the Kikuyu language. That Administrative Officers should acquire a basic language at the Colonial Course in the United Kingdom rather than a local dialect in the area to which they are posted in Africa has for some years been an accepted policy, and no Administrative Officer can gain promotion until he has passed the higher language examination, an equivalent of the language test that was applied in British India. But the languages of the East offer as a rule a greater incentive both to study and to current use than do many of the languages of Africa; there are fewer instances in the African administrative services of that complete mastery of the vernacular which distinguished many officers in British India.

The course provided for candidates for the French Colonial Service in the *École Nationale de la France d'Outre-Mer* comprises tuition in African languages, and an examination in vernacular languages forms part of the test for selection of those of the candidates who are already in some form of Government service (*stagiaires*).[3] There has been considerable interest shown in the study of certain languages of French West Africa, though this is largely confined to the researches of French linguistic scholars,[4] and it does not appear that the local Administrations attach in practice any great importance to a knowledge of the vernacular by their officers. It is characteristic that a recent authoritative study of the Sociology of Colonies, written mainly for the benefit of French Colonial cadets,[5] makes no

[1] Lord Lugard, *The Dual Mandate in British Tropical Africa*, 1926, p. 133.
[2] See below, p. 452.
[3] For the system of selection and training, see below, p. 373.
[4] See below, p. 110.
[5] R. Maunier, *The Sociology of Colonies, A Study in Race Contact*, Eng. ed., 1949.

reference to the need for the study of the vernaculars, and one of the best known of the books written by officers of the French Colonial Administration speaks of the knowledge of an indigenous language as being a convenience rather than a necessity.[1]

In the Belgian system, on the other hand, far greater importance is attached to the study of indigenous languages by officers entering the Colonial Administration, and a considerable degree of knowledge is in fact common among them. This is particularly in evidence on the part of officers presiding over the Native Tribunals.[2] In Portugal courses in Mbundu and Ronga are provided for cadets at the *Sociedade de Geografia de Lisboa* (formerly the *Escola Superior Colonial*), and it is proposed to institute also a course in Swahili. More significance appears, however, to be attached to the phonetic principles in the formation of these languages than to the acquisition of a colloquial knowledge of them. There are no language tests applied for promotion in the administrative or other services.

INDIGENOUS LANGUAGES AND EDUCATION

The General Principle Adopted

It is, in the second place, important to note the attitude taken by the various Administrations towards the use of indigenous languages in the system of education, and the action taken by them to promote the production of vernacular literature. The question of the use of the indigenous languages in school instruction is nowhere viewed entirely as an educational problem, and the policy observed in practice is largely determined by current conceptions as to the place which the African may be expected to fill in the future government of the country or the measure in which it is designed that he shall share in the more important of its institutions. There is no doubt some general measure of agreement that instruction is, if only as a matter of convenience, most easily imparted at the very early stages of school education through the medium of the mother tongue. One of the best known of the commissions which examined the system of education in British India went farther, and spoke of the matter in terms which seem, at all events from the British standpoint, to have an application also to conditions in Africa: 'Only through the wise use of the mother tongue can clearness of thought, independence of judgement, and sense of individual responsibility be developed at the start.'[3]

[1] R. Delavignette, *Service Africain*, 1946; see the English edition published under the title of *Freedom and Authority in French West Africa*, 1950, p. 42.
[2] *Rapport à l'Assemblée Générale des Nations Unies de l'Administration du Ruanda-Urundi*, 1951, p. 30. *Rapport sur l'Administration Belge du Ruanda-Urundi*, 1952, p. 26. See below, pp. 557 ff.
[3] *Report of the Calcutta University Commission*, 1919.

That view has in general commended itself in practice to the British Administrations in Africa.[1] They have in some cases had unusual difficulty in deciding which language was in fact to be treated as the mother tongue for this purpose, and there have at times been doubts whether the use of the vernacular as a medium should not be restricted, in order to allow for the earliest opportunity of introducing the study either of English or of a generally used lingua franca; but this does not detract from the general preference shown for the use of the vernacular as a medium of instruction at all events during the more elementary stage of school courses. But for the British the argument in favour of the use of the vernacular is not merely one of expediency, for its use has also been an accepted part of the philosophy of indirect rule, which saw in the regard paid to indigenous institutions one of the safeguards against the premature disruption of African society.

To a large measure the use of the vernacular in primary education has also commended itself to the Administration of the Belgian Congo. On the other hand, the French and Portuguese Administrations have tended to hold that their mission as agents of civilization demands that the instruction of Africans should, as far as possible, be conducted throughout in a European language. They have, for the same reason, shown far less interest in the production of vernacular literature.

South Africa

In the Union of South Africa the great majority of the African population are Bantu-speaking. In an exhaustive survey made of the linguistic situation in 1932 Dr. Doke classified the languages of southern Africa into geographical zones, which can be sub-divided into groups of languages that have 'a high degree of mutual intelligibility as well as an extreme sharing of grammatical, phonetical, and lexicographical phenomena'. The languages fall into four such groups: Nguni (comprising Xhosa, Zulu, and Swazi), Sotho (Northern and Southern, and Tswana), Venda, and Tsonga (Thonga), which is spoken mainly in Portuguese East Africa. Under Zulu may be included Ndebele (both Rhodesian and Transvaal) and Transvaal Sotho-Ndebele, a mixed Sotho-Zulu dialect.[2]

Throughout the Union it is the general practice to use the vernacular as the medium of instruction in the primary course of African schools, and one vernacular language is also required as a subject in the secondary classes. As elsewhere in Africa there is frequently some difficulty in deciding what is the 'mother tongue', for purposes of primary instruction, and

---

[1] *African Education, a Study of Educational Policy and Practice in British Tropical Africa,* 1953, pp. 21, 79, 171. *Report of the Commission on Higher Education in the Colonies,* 1945, Cmd. 6647, pp. 91 ff. *Report of the Commission on Higher Education in West Africa,* 1945, Cmd. 6655, pp. 11–12.
[2] See note on Bantu Prefixes, p. xxvi.

this is a matter of such exceptional difficulty in urban areas that there is a growing tendency to substitute English or Afrikaans at the earliest possible stage. Northern Sotho (Pedi) is used as the medium in primary education in the northern part of the Transvaal; Tsonga and Venda are also used in the Transvaal; Tswana in Northern Cape Province and Western Transvaal; and Southern Sotho in the Orange Free State. Zulu is used in Natal, and Xhosa in the Cape Province.

The use of English and Afrikaans in the educational curriculum of schools in the Union of South Africa is discussed in a later chapter.[1] While no recent figures have been published, in 1946 roughly 69 per cent. of the European population were shown as bilingual, 17 per cent. as speaking only English, and 13 per cent. only Afrikaans.[2] Until the end of the nineteenth century Afrikaans was regarded only as a dialect (popularly known as the Taal) and at that time it was not thought that it would survive in competition with High Dutch, which was used by the Dutch Reformed Church and was the medium of education. It did not become a written language in common usage until the end of the nineteenth century, but became an official language in 1925 when an amendment of the Union Act of 1909 recognized Afrikaans as legally equivalent to Dutch. It now has a well established literature and a recognized place in journalism; it enjoys the advantage that it is the chosen vehicle of Nationalist and Republican aspirations. It appears to be steadily gaining on English in ordinary colloquial use. Dutch is now seldom used; a speech made in the House of Assembly in March 1955 was said to be the first made in Dutch for 25 years.[3]

The languages of South Africa have been the subject of much detailed study, and dictionaries and grammars of the principal tongues are now available.[4] Consideration has also been given to the question of the unification of dialects with a view to developing literary media.[5] A comprehensive programme of research prepared by Dr. Doke in 1948[6] included proposals for the phonetical and grammatical studies of the various languages and for a systematic study of the tone systems of each language. A uniform system of orthography is now in use for Northern Sotho and Tswana, but there is still no uniformity between these and Southern Sotho, or between

[1] See below, pp. 1137-9.

[2] O.Y.S.A., 1950, p. 1165.

[3] The Times, 23 March 1955.

[4] C. M. Doke, Bantu: Modern Grammatical, Phonetical and Lexicographical Studies since 1860, International African Institute, 1945, pp. 73-97.

[5] C. M. Doke, 'The Linguistic Situation in South Africa', Africa, October 1928, pp. 478-85; and 'Native Languages of South Africa', African Studies, vol. i, 1942, pp. 135-41.

[6] Suggestions for a Programme of Linguistic Research in Bantu and other Native Languages of South Africa, National Council for Social Research, Union Education Department, Pretoria, 1948.

the Sotho and Nguni groups, or even between such closely related groups as Zulu and Xhosa.[1] Insufficient attention has so far been given to the languages of South-West Africa, and a general survey is needed; some work is, however, being done, including the translation of parts of the Bible into Herero and Ndonga (Ambo).

The development of vernacular literature has been greatly stimulated by some of the authorities in charge of Native Education, and missionary enterprise has also done much to encourage its production.[2] There is now a very considerable body of literature in the Sotho and Nguni groups of languages, particularly Southern Sotho, including folk-lore, history, fiction, poetry, and drama.[3] The works of Mofolo in Sotho, and in particular his life of Chaka, are well known, and the Xhosa author, S. E. K. Mqhayi, has enjoyed a wide reputation. Henderson Soga has made a valuable contribution to history. In Zulu the outstanding name is that of Dr. Vilikazi, who, in addition to collaborating in the preparation of a Zulu dictionary, wrote novels, poetry, and literary criticism.[4] The translation of some of Shakespeare's plays by Sol. P. Plaatje are of high merit. The *Bantu Treasury* series, published by the Witwatersrand University, includes original works by Africans in Zulu, Sotho, and other languages; bibliographies relating to vernacular literature are included from time to time in the series of African Studies published by the University.

The Lovedale Press, the Morija Sesuto Press in Basutoland, and the Witwatersrand University Press are still the chief agencies which finance the publication of vernacular literature, but commercial publishers are increasingly entering this field.[5] A considerable number of vernacular newspapers are now published in South Africa.[6] The most influential agency in this field is the Bantu Press Limited, which controls 15 newspapers and links 22 vernacular publications throughout the Union of South Africa, the High Commission Territories, and Southern Rhodesia. The editors of its papers are Africans. Of the periodicals one of the best known is the Zulu *Natal Sun*, edited by R. C. Dholomo, himself a poet and novelist. Most of these papers are issued weekly; there are as yet no Bantu daily papers.

[1] J. Nhlapo, *Bantu Babel*, 1944; *Nguni and Sotho*, 1945; 'The Orthography of South Bantu Languages', *South African Outlook*, 1946, pp. 15–16. A. N. Tucker, 'Sotho-Nguni, Orthography and Tone Marking', *Bulletin of the School of Oriental and African Studies*, vol. xiii, 1949, pp. 200–24.

[2] See *Books for Africa*, January 1938.

[3] 'Bibliography of existing Literature in Northern Sotho', *South African Outlook*, no. 76, 1946, p. 907. See also G. H. Franz, 'The Literature of Lesotho', *Bantu Studies*, September 1930; and G. L. Lestrade, *African Studies*, December 1944.

[4] D. MeK. Malcolm, 'Zulu Literature', *Africa*, vol. xix, 1949, pp. 33–39.

[5] For this subject generally see *Handbook on Race Relations in South Africa*, 1949, pp. 499 ff.

[6] *O.Y.S.A.*, *1952–53*, gives 54 as the number which have been registered in order to qualify for postal rates. Further details are given in the *Handbook on Race Relations in South Africa*, pp. 484–500.

The High Commission Territories

In the High Commission Territories of South Africa the local languages are the medium of instruction in the primary schools. Thus in Basutoland the prevailing vernacular, Southern Sotho, is the medium of instruction up to Standard VI, English being taught as a subject. There is a fair volume of local literature, hitherto mainly issued from the Paris Evangelical Mission Press at Morija, though the Roman Catholic Press at Roma is now publishing a considerable amount of similar material.[1] Local literature includes a number of works by African authors dealing with Bantu folk-lore and history, and also works of poetry and fiction.

In Bechuanaland the sole medium is Tswana, though other languages are spoken by the numerous tribes in the Protectorate.[2] In Swaziland the medium of instruction in the lower primary schools is the Swazi language,[3] but Zulu (to which Swazi is closely allied) is the accepted literary medium, and is taught as a subject in the middle and higher classes. There is little vernacular literature in Swazi, and it would seem probable that African authors are likely to favour Zulu in preference to Swazi as a vehicle of expression. Vernacular newspapers are issued both in Southern Sotho and Tswana. The poem by A. S. Mopeli-Paulus on the sinking of the ship *Mendi* during the First World War is a notable contribution to vernacular literature by an indigenous author.

Central Africa

In Southern Rhodesia two vernacular languages are recognized for educational and administrative purposes, namely, Ndebele and Shona, both of which are used as media of instruction in primary education. Zulu is, however, also studied. The medium of secondary education is English, but some of the vernaculars can be taken as examination subjects. A linguistic survey made in 1931 by Dr. Doke recommended the unification of the Shona group of languages (Korekore, Zezura, Manyika, Ndau),[4] but there has been acute controversy on the subject, and the proposals made for a unified form and a standard orthography have not been universally accepted.

The Shona language has been extensively studied by linguists both in the territory and in South Africa, the most notable works, being those of Father B. H. Barnes and Dr. Doke. A number of Shona texts have been published in the *Native Affairs Department Annual*. The Karanga language, which is spoken in the western area of the territory, has received some attention, and collections of proverbs and phrases have been published in the journal *Nada*. Part of the Bible has been translated into

---

[1] *N.A.*, Part V, 122.   [2] Ibid. pp. 168 ff.   [3] Ibid. pp. 349, 408.
[4] C. M. Doke, *Report on the Unification of the Shona Dialects*, 1931.

'Union' Shona. Four weekly papers are published by the Rhodesian extension of the Bantu Press,[1] and a monthly paper, the *Bantu Mirror*, is published in English, Shona, and Ndebele.

In Northern Rhodesia some 40 different tongues are spoken, but five main languages are recognized for educational and administrative purposes: Bemba, Lozi, Luvale, Tonga, and Nyanja. Primary education is given in other vernaculars also when reading material can be provided. Bemba, with its various dialects, is widely spoken in the northern part of the territory and has become the lingua franca in the Copperbelt. In addition to serving as the medium of instruction in primary education, it can be studied throughout the school course, and it is one of the two languages in which School Certificate papers are set. The Ila and Tonga languages predominate in the Southern Provinces. Proposals for their unification which were considered in 1928 have not been pursued, but Tonga has been developed as a literary language and a medium of instruction.

The Nyanja language, which emanates from Nyasaland, is widely used as a lingua franca and in education. Attempts have been made to bring the orthography of Nyanja, Lozi, Tonga, and Bemba into line, but without success. In Nyanja itself the existing dictionaries give inconsistent spellings, and proposals for reform have been made.[2] Linguistic studies have been made in many of the local languages, notably Bemba, Nyanja, Luvale, Lozi, Lamba, Ila, Tonga, Bisa, Lala, Tumbuka, and Nsenga, and an increasing volume of literature is being produced, the chief agency for which is the Publications Bureau of Northern Rhodesia and Nyasaland. This was set up in 1948 and took over the work previously undertaken by the Nyasaland Education Department and the African Literature Committee of Northern Rhodesia.[3] Though officially subsidized, the Bureau works in co-operation with commercial publishers, one of its objects being the encouragement of African authorship. The editorial staff includes a number of Africans, and there is a wide measure of African and European collaboration. In 1951 twenty-four new titles were published in seven different languages.[4]

Nyanja is the lingua franca throughout Nyasaland and is the language of education, though Tumbuka has also been recently recognized as the medium in the Northern Province, and Yao in the Yao-speaking areas. Vernacular literature is being produced in all these languages by the

[1] See above, p. 95.
[2] G. Atkins, *Suggestions for an Amended Spelling and Word Division of Nyanja*, International African Institute, Memorandum 25, 1950.
[3] G. H. Wilson, 'The Northern Rhodesia–Nyasaland Joint Publications Bureau', *Africa*, January 1950, pp. 60–69.
[4] *Publications Bureau of Northern Rhodesia and Nyasaland, Annual Report for the Year 1951*, Lusaka, 1952.

Bureau just referred to. The whole Bible has been translated into Yao. A news-sheet in Nyanja is issued by the Government Information Office; periodical and other literature is published by mission presses.

East Africa

Swahili is the lingua franca throughout Tanganyika and is the language of the peoples of the coastal belt. It is recognized as the official language for administrative purposes and for schools, except for 'bush' and village schools, where the local vernacular may be used. English is both the medium of instruction and a subject of study in secondary schools. Vernacular literature and translations of the Bible, or parts of it, have been produced in certain other local vernaculars, namely, Sukuma, Sagala, Gogo, and Taveta, mainly by missionary bodies. Vernacular literature is also produced by the East African Literature Bureau.

In Kenya Swahili has been recognized for many years as the official language and a knowledge of it is required of all Administrative Officers. It has been the language of instruction in primary schools generally from Standard III upwards, though in the earliest stages teaching might be given in the local vernacular. In 1950, however, it was recommended that though Swahili should continue to be used for primary education in the towns, arrangements should be made for the provision of textbooks in 20 of the principal vernacular languages for use in rural areas.[1]

There are language committees concerned with the Kikuyu and Luo languages and an increasing volume of vernacular literature is being produced, including the Bible. There is also a Nandi-Kipsigis Language Committee, but the vernacular literature in these languages and in Masai is not extensive. In all these languages there still exist unsolved problems of orthography. The East African Literature Bureau, which also serves the purposes of Tanganyika and Uganda, produces textbooks and general literature in a number of local vernaculars.

Swahili has a wide use as a lingua franca throughout East Africa, and is, as has been shown, recognized as the official language of Kenya and Tanganyika. Two views have been held regarding the origin of the language. Some scholars assert that it was originally the tongue of one of the tribes occupying a small region on the Lamu coast of East Africa opposite Zanzibar.[2] Others have held that it is not based upon the tongue of any one tribe, but grew up as a commercial language in Arab settlements along the coast as a result of the fusion of many different Bantu languages with Arabic. It seems to have owed its expansion in the first instance to its

---

[1] *Proposals for the Implementation of the Recommendations of the Report on African Education in Kenya*, Sessional Paper no. 1, 1950.

[2] D. Westermann, 'Swahili as the Lingua Franca of East Africa', *The Church Overseas*, vol. vi, 1933, pp. 1–11. See also W. H. Whiteley in *Africa*, October 1956, pp. 341 ff.

adoption by the Arab traders who at one time had the monopoly of trade (and above all of the slave trade) from the coast into the Congo. They were joined by others, such as Persians and Indians, and by the descendants of slaves from the interior, who formed the composite people known today by the name of Swahili, and whose language became the common tongue not only of the trade routes, but of the coastal areas in Kenya and Tanganyika.[1] Speakers of Swahili, including the relatively small number whose mother tongue it is, are now estimated to number over 7 million. It has long been a literary language and a considerable literature, mainly in verse, exists in classical Swahili.[2]

Swahili as now used contains a number of Arabic loan-words, and English words are increasingly being absorbed,[3] but these are incorporated into its structure in such a way as to lose their foreign character. It is not, in a grammatical sense, a mixed language, but is of a pure Bantu type, and has the further advantage in that while it is closely related to most of the languages of East Africa, it has lost the distinctions of tone which make some of them difficult to master.[4] It has been described as a linguistic alloy, with an African base and an Arabic infusion.[5] It has extended from East Africa into the Belgian Congo. There are two important dialects, that of Mombasa (Kimvita) and that of Zanzibar (Kiunguja), the former being now confined to the littoral region of Kenya, while the latter is widely dispersed in East Africa. Farther west, on both sides of the Belgian Congo border, the language, though changed considerably from its original form, is known as Kingwana. On the east coast the Arabic script, formerly the accepted script for writing Swahili, is still in use, though it is now tending to disappear.

An Inter-territorial Swahili Language Committee[6] was set up in 1932 for the purpose of establishing a standard orthography and of encouraging African authors. In 1948 it was reorganized and placed under the authority of the East Africa High Commission. The literary competitions formerly organized by the committee are now carried out by the East African Literature Bureau. There is today a considerable literature in modern Swahili, including books on agriculture and medicine, together with some original verse and prose.

The language has during recent years become a crucial issue in the argument whether it would not be preferable to substitute English from the earliest stage of school instruction in those areas where recourse is had

---

[1] The word 'Swahili' is derived from an Arabic word meaning 'the coast people'.
[2] L. Harries, 'Popular Verse of the Swahili Tradition', *Africa*, April 1952, pp. 158-64.
[3] R. H. Gower, 'Swahili Borrowings from English', *Africa*, April 1952, pp. 154-7.
[4] For the advantage of Swahili from this point of view see *African Education, a Study of Educational Policy and Practice in British Tropical Africa*, 1953.
[5] A. J. Toynbee, *A Study of History*, abridgement of vols. i–vi, by D. C. Somervell, p. 473.
[6] See also above, p. 83.

to a lingua franca or a 'Union language'. There is no question but that
the use of Swahili is entirely suitable in those coastal areas of Kenya and
Tanganyika where it is the mother tongue of the people. But in other
parts of the territories its use in school teaching has been criticized as an
unjustifiable intrusion, detrimental both to the teaching of the vernacular
and the teaching of English. Those who hold this view claim that Swahili
is, as a lingua franca, already being superseded by the use of English, and
urge that it should be gradually eliminated from the school curriculum.[1]
The East Africa Royal Commission 1953–5 has expressed the view that
the teaching of Swahili as a second language is a waste of time and effort;
it would substitute the teaching of English at the earliest possible stage.[2]

In Uganda three of the Bantu languages spoken locally, namely, Ganda,
Nkore, and Nyoro, are officially recognized as languages of administration
and education. Luo, a Nilotic language, Teso (Nilo-Hamitic), and Lug-
bara (Eastern Sudanic) are also recognized. All these are used in primary
education, and in all of them a standardized orthography has been agreed
on. Examinations in these languages are held for European officials and
their wives. A number of modern school textbooks, as well as other literature, have been produced in Ganda, Nyoro, Luo, and Swahili.

Original verse in Ganda by African authors has also been published,[3]
and Africans have collaborated in the preparation of Ganda dictionaries
and grammars. Recent studies of importance include the work of Father
Crazzolara on the Luo and Acholi languages, and of Dr. Tucker on the
orthography of Ganda; several studies of the languages of Uganda have
also been published by the White Fathers. The Uganda African Literature Committee has produced a large body of material for use in connexion with the literacy campaigns which have been actively carried out
with the co-operation of African teachers. The East African Institute of
Social Research affiliated to the new University College of Makerere has
recently begun research in linguistics.[4]

West Africa

Turning to West Africa, the most widely spoken language in the
Northern territories of Nigeria is Hausa, which is also spoken and understood in many other West African territories; it is used as a medium of
instruction in primary education over very large areas, Kanuri being
substituted in the Bornu and Dikwa Emirates and Fulani in the Bauchi
and Adamawa Provinces. The Nupe Language Group (including Gbari

[1] On the general question see *African Education*, op. cit. pp. 21, 79, 81–83. See also the debate
on the subject in the Kenya Legislature reported in *The Times*, 24 July 1953.
[2] Cmd. 9475, p. 184.
[3] *Africa*, October 1948, p. 45.
[4] 'Report of East African Institute of Social Research', in *Colonial Research, 1953–1954*, Cmd.
9303, 1954.

and Igbira) is spoken by about 600,000 people, and the languages of the Tiv group are largely used in mass literacy schemes in the Benue Province.

Hausa was a literary language before the advent of Europeans (being then written in an adaptation of Arabic script), and it now possesses a very considerable vernacular literature[1] and some notable linguistic studies.[2] Mention should also be made of Mr. W. Miller's translation of the Bible, and the language has been studied by numerous French and German scholars. Studies of Fulani (which is also spoken over large areas of French West Africa and Gambia) have been published by Mr. F. W. Taylor, Mr. de St. Croix, Mrs. Leith Ross, and by a number of French linguists; some selections of Fulani verse have also been published.[3] Studies have been made by Dr. R. C. Abraham of Tiv and Idoma dialects[4] as well as vocabularies of dialects of the former group of languages.[5] Kanuri and the neighbouring languages have been studied by Dr. J. Lukas. An acquaintance with Arabic is considered an essential part of the religious education of Muslims, but though the study is seriously pursued by certain classes, and especially by those qualifying for judicial posts in the Muslim Emirates, the knowledge acquired by the people generally is very elementary. A proposal has, however, been accepted for the establishment of a higher school of Arabic studies.

The Literature Bureau at Zaria, founded in 1930 by the Education Department, produced a number of Hausa textbooks for schools as well as general literature; it has now been reorganized as the Gaskiya Corporation, and its activities have been extended to include other vernaculars.[6] It publishes a weekly paper in Hausa and Tiv as well as news-sheets in several languages, and a considerable volume of booklets and other material has been produced for use in mass literacy campaigns.[7] Publications in Hausa, Tiv, and Nupe have been issued by various missionary organizations. The Gaskiya Corporation uses the 'Africa' script in all its publications, and this is in general use for Hausa, but other orthographies are still employed by missionary presses for Fulani, Tiv, and Idoma.

In southern Nigeria no one language, with the exception of Yoruba in the Western Region, has a dominance equal to that of Hausa in the north.

[1] R. M. East, *A Vernacular Bibliography for the Languages of Nigeria*, 1942.
[2] G. P. Bargery, *A Hausa–English Dictionary and English–Hausa Vocabulary*, 1953. R. C. Abraham, *Dictionary of the Hausa Language*, 1949.
[3] S. Leith Ross, *Grammar of the Fulani Language*, 1921. G. Vieillard, 'Poèmes Peuls du Fouta Djallon', *Bulletin du Comité d'études historiques et scientifiques de l'A.O.F.*, vol. xx, no. 3, 1937, pp. 225–311; *Récits Peuls du Maçina*, 1931. M. D. W. Jeffreys, 'Speculative Origin of the Fulani Language', *Africa*, January 1943, p. 4.
[4] R. C. Abraham, *The Idoma Language*, 1935, and *Dictionary of the Tiv Language*, 1940.
[5] C. K. Meek, *Tribal Studies in Northern Nigeria*, 1931.
[6] R. M. East, 'Recent Activities of the Literature Bureau, Zaria, Northern Nigeria', *Africa*, April 1943, pp. 71–77.
[7] United Nations, *Non-self-governing Territories*, vol. iii, 1951.

There is a great variety of languages and in some coastal areas there is no common tongue except 'pidgin' English, which has almost achieved the status of a local vernacular.[1] Wherever possible the vernacular is used as the medium of instruction in primary education, but where the diversity of languages is very great and no lingua franca exists, the language of instruction is usually English. English is also the medium of secondary education.

Yoruba, spoken in the Western Region, particularly in the Oyo, Abeo-kuta, Ijebu, and Ondo Provinces, is used as a medium of primary educa-tion and taught as a subject in the higher standards, School Certificate papers being set in it. There is a considerable vernacular literature, and the Yoruba show in other ways an exceptionally strong interest in their own language. In 1929 it was suggested[2] that Yoruba should become the school language for the area which now constitutes the Western Region, but that books for infants and religious literature might still be necessary in some other languages, notably in the Edo group. Bini (also known as Edo), Sobo, and Kukuruku, which are spoken in Benin and Warri Pro-vinces, are used to some extent in primary education. Although the orthography devised by the International African Institute for the Efik, Ibo, and Yoruba languages was officially adopted by the Education Board at Lagos in 1929, it has not been implemented in the case of Yoruba. A standard orthography is, however, in general use. A number of recent grammatical studies of Yoruba by African authors have been published in Lagos, and there are several works by French and British scholars.[3]

In the Ibo-speaking areas the linguistic situation is very confused. An attempt was at one time made to unify the dialects of Ibo (Igbo), and to promote the use of 'Union Ibo', the language which was used for a transla-tion of the Bible in 1915. This attempt met with little success, and further recommendations were made by Dr. Westermann during his visit to Nigeria in 1929. The difficulties arising from the failure to agree on language policy were much debated in 1936,[4] and no great advance has been made since that date, the production of vernacular literature being hampered by a policy of rigid dialectal standardization. The Ibo of Onitsha, Owerri, Rivers, and Ogoja Provinces is used in primary educa-tion, and may be offered in the General Certificate of Education. It has a considerable educational and religious literature. Ibo is also used in pre-primary education in bilingual Ibibio areas and to some extent in the

[1] *Report of the Commission on Higher Education in West Africa*, Cmd. 6655, 1945, p. 10.
[2] D. Westermann, 'The Linguistic Situation and Vernacular Literature in British West Africa', *Africa*, October 1929, pp. 337–51.
[3] I. Ward, *Introduction to the Yoruba Language*, 1952.
[4] M. M. Green, 'The Present Linguistic Situation in Ibo Country', *Africa*, October 1936, pp. 508–23.

Niger Delta areas. The standard works on the Ibo language are those of R. F. G. Adams, N. W. Thomas, and Dr. Ida Ward.[1]

Recent studies have emphasized the significance of tone in West African languages, particularly Ibo and Efik.[2] In the Ibibio-speaking area (mainly Calabar Province) the Efik dialect has become the 'literary' language, and its use is spreading among speakers of other dialects. Ibo and Ibibio, as well as Efik, are used in primary education; English is, however, taught as a subject during the primary course and is the medium of instruction in all secondary education. The most authoritative studies of Efik have been those of Dr. I. Ward, 1933, and H. Goldie, who compiled an Efik dictionary. There is a considerable literature in Efik, including the whole Bible.

The language problems of Nigeria were discussed by a Nigerian author in an article published in 1948,[3] in which, after indicating the obstacles presented by the diversity of languages, he proposed the compulsory elimination of 'pidgin' and the adoption of Basic English in all schools. Mass literacy campaigns have been organized in Nigeria since 1947,[4] and in connexion with these large supplies of primers and other material have been produced in Hausa, Tiv, Yoruba, Ibo, and Efik.

In the British Cameroons, owing to the great number of vernacular languages, 'pidgin' English is becoming a lingua franca and has to be used in the early stages of primary education. English is, however, taught as a subject and becomes the medium of instruction at the earliest possible stage. Duala is also used in the south of the Cameroons in primary education, and an attempt has been made to use Bali, but it is unpopular and is being replaced by 'pidgin'.

In the southern part of the Gold Coast (including part of Togoland) the four main languages are Twi, Fante, Ga, and Ewe; they are media of instruction in all primary schools and are taught as subjects in secondary schools. The Asante dialect of Twi, and, in the west, Nzima and Sefwi, are used in primary education. Twi and Fante are closely connected, and linguistically Fante may be classified as a dialect of Twi, but it has attained the status of a literary language and has produced a considerable literature. A weekly paper is published in Fante and the Bible has been translated into both Twi (Asante) and Fante.

A number of dialects are included in the term Ewe, and three of these are used for literary purposes. There is a large volume of literature, and the Bible has been translated into two of the Ewe dialects. The 'Africa'

[1] I. Ward, *An Introduction to the Ibo Language*, 1936, and *Ibo Dialects and the development of a Common Language*, 1941.

[2] M. M. Green, 'The Classification of West African Tone-languages; Igbo and Efik', *Africa*, July 1949, pp. 213-19.

[3] Eleazar Obiakonwa Enemo, 'The Social Problems of Nigeria', *Africa*, July 1948, pp. 190-9.

[4] E. R. Chadwick, 'Mass Literacy in Udi Division', *African Affairs*, January 1948, pp. 31-41.

script is now in use for Ewe. Vernacular literature is produced by the Gold Coast Bureau of Vernacular Literature, and the Scottish and Methodist missions have established committees to arrange for the provision of educational books, the Scottish mission (in co-operation with the Presbyterian Training College at Akropong) having given special attention to Twi, and the Methodist mission to Fante. Ewe had been the concern of the Ewe Presbyterian Church, and a Ga Society publishes books in Ga. Mass literacy projects have been launched in most of the main vernaculars. Many of the earliest studies of Twi, Ewe, and other Gold Coast languages were the work of German scholars and missionaries, and several of these, in particular those of Christaller, Westermann, and Spieth, are still standard works. Work is being done at present by Dr. W. J. Berry of the School of Oriental and African Studies, and by African students. In the Northern Territories of the Gold Coast the only vernacular used in official primary education is Dagomba. The orthography has been standardized, and a small printing press at Tamale, under the direction of the Dagomba Native Authority, publishes vernacular literature.

The Colony area of Sierra Leone makes considerable use of the Creole 'patois', a tongue peculiar to this community. Though it is of English origin it is so puzzling to an Englishman at first hearing that it is necessary for the Supreme Court to employ an interpreter in it. Freetown has also its own 'pidgin' type of English, the use of which is extending to the Protectorate.[1] English is, however, the ordinary language of instruction in the schools of the Colony.

In the Protectorate Mende is the language generally used in education, but Temne and the Kono dialect of Vai are used in mission schools. There is some vernacular literature, including translations of the New Testament, in all three languages, and the Sierra Leone Protectorate Literature Bureau encourages the production of literature, especially in Mende. There is, however, as yet no standard literary form. Some studies of local dialects of Mende have been made, the most comprehensive being that of the late K. H. Crosby in 1944.

In Gambia the language most widely used is Mandingo (Malinke), and Wolof is also spoken, both these languages being also predominant over a wide area in French territory. The language of instruction is for the most part English, though local vernaculars are used in some of the schools in the Protectorate. A mass education scheme was initiated in 1948 and broadsheets were issued in Mandingo, which has a small body of vernacular literature including translations of the Gospels. Some short studies of the Mandingo language as used in Gambia have been published locally, but the principal studies of the language have been made by French scholars.

---

[1] *Report of the Commission on Higher Education in West Africa*, Cmd. 6655, 1945, p. 10.

French Territories

In dealing with the languages of French West Africa (generally stated as over 126 in number) we may for the present purpose neglect those spoken by the Islamized people of Mauretania or the language of the Touareg, which is largely Berber in origin.[1] Contemporary French authorities divide the other languages, largely on a geographical basis, into five main groups, of which three run from west to east, and two are mainly in the south. Of the three groups running from west to east, the first, the *Groupe Sénégal-Guinéen*, includes Fulani[2] (Peul, Fula, Fulbe) and Wolof, which together are spoken by a population roughly estimated at about 3 million; while a sub-group, including Sérère, Dyold, Baga, Sherbro, and Kissi, are spoken by about half a million people. There is some division of opinion regarding the interrelation of these languages and their connexion with the Bantu tongues. Very different sources have in particular been assigned to the language of the Fulani, and the diversity of views expressed has been increased by the migrations of the tribe and the intermarriage of certain sections with Hausa-speaking peoples.[3]

The second group, the *Groupe Nigéro-Sénégalais*, is probably the largest linguistic group in the territory; it comprises over 30 languages and has a population estimated roughly at four million. It is divided into two sub-groups, of which the southern contains a number of languages, including Susu and Dyalouke, each spoken by comparatively small populations. The northern, which is by far the largest, contains the different dialects of Mandingo,[4] the most widely spoken being Malinke (about 1 million speakers), Bambara (about the same), Sarakole or Marka (about half a million), and Dyula (about one-quarter of a million). These languages are traditionally associated with the past empire of the Mali, and both Bambara and Dyula (Dioula) have in consequence acquired some of the character of a lingua franca. The languages of this sub-group, and in particular Malinke, Bambara, and Dyula, have been the subject of special study by French scholars.[5]

The languages of the third group, the *Groupe Voltaïque* or Gur (of which the chief is Mossi, with about 2 million speakers) and the various Dahomey dialects have been less carefully studied. There is also an unclassified linguistic group in which Hausa is spoken by some 500,000 and Kanuri by about 100,000 Africans. The remaining languages of French West Africa (i.e. the Kwa languages of the Ivory Coast and Dahomey) have

[1] J. Richard-Molard, *Afrique Occidentale Française*, 1949, p. 73. *Enc. A.O.F.*, vol. i, p. 146.

[2] See above, p. 101.

[3] O. Temple, *Notes on the Tribes, Provinces, Emirates and States of the Northern Provinces of Nigeria*, 1922. A. Gouilly, *L'Islam dans l'Afrique Occidentale Française*, 1952, pp. 17, 66.

[4] H. Labouret, *Les Manding et leur langue*, 1934. C. G. Seligman, *The Races of Africa*, 1939. *Enc. A.O.F.*, pp. 117 ff.

[5] M. Delafosse, *La Langue Mandingue et ses dialectes (Malinke, Mambara, Dioula)*, 1929.

been little studied. The language of the Anyi and the Baule has acquired something of the character of a lingua franca. The language of the Fon of lower Dahomey is usually associated with this group. There appears to have been a considerable extension of the use of a French 'pidgin' in the coastal area of French Guinea.

The languages of French Equatorial Africa have not been subjected to a generally accepted classification.[1] A large part of the people speak Bantu languages,[2] the most notable being Kongo, Yombé, Lingala (which is shared with the people of the Belgian Congo), Fang, Benga, and Nyong (used in the Gabon and Middle Congo territory).

As is more fully explained elsewhere,[3] it is the policy throughout the French territories in Africa to rely on the use of French, both as a medium and subject of instruction, rather than the use of a vernacular. Even in the earliest stages the approach is as far as possible through the use of French, for it has been felt not merely that French 'is the key language of initiation to French civilization',[4] but also that the development of French as a lingua franca may help to bridge over the differences which divide Africa into so many separate communities.[5] But it has been recognized that there are certain needs which cannot wait to be implemented until the French language is understood, so that instruction in such matters as better farming and sanitation is allowed to be given in the local vernacular for strictly limited periods. It is noteworthy, however, that the Brazzaville Conference of 1944,[6] while favouring the general decentralization of authority, nevertheless opposed the impetus which might be given to local nationalistic sentiment by the teaching of 'local dialects'.[7]

Belgian Territories

In the Belgian Congo there are four languages which form the chief means of communication between Europeans and Africans: Kongo, Luba, Lingala, and Swahili (Kingwana).[8] There is a tendency to regard some of these tongues as official languages, but they are not as yet definitely recognized as such. Lingala is generally used among the armed forces as their only common language. Four other languages—Luba-Katanga, Rwanda and Rundi, Mongo (Nkundo), and Ngombe—are widely used as the medium in primary education, while Ngbandi, Ngbaka, and Shi

---

[1] *Enc. A.E.F.*, pp. 112 ff.

[2] H. Baumann et D. Westermann, *Peuples et Civilisations de l'Afrique*, 1948.

[3] See below, pp. 1197 ff.

[4] W. B. Mumford and G. St. J. Orde Browne, *Africans Learn to be French*, 1937, p. 106.

[5] G. Hardy, *Une Conquête Morale*, 1917.   [6] See below, p. 209.

[7] H. Deschamps, *L'Union Française*, 1952, p. 42.

[8] Dr. G. van Bulck, 'Les deux Cartes Linguistiques du Congo Belge', *Bull. I.R.C.B.*, vol xxv, no. 2, 1952. G. van der Kerken, 'Le Swahili — langue de grande expansion', *Bull. I.R.C.B.*, vol. xv, no. 2, 1944, pp. 234 ff.

are also used in some localities. A standard form of Luba has been adopted, and the standardization of Kongo and Lingala is in progress. The late Dr. Edouard de Jonghe put forward in 1935[1] a proposal for the development of Luba as a single language for the whole territory, but the proposal did not gain general acceptance. All questions of the choice of languages for official use and of the unification and standardization of languages are now considered by a *Commission Linguistique Africaine* in Brussels.

Belgian scholars have devoted much attention to the languages of the Colony, and there is a very considerable volume of published studies on them. Kongo has been the subject of valuable work by Bittremieux, Laman, Declercq, and Van Bulck, and a number of manuals, dictionaries, and grammars have been published by the Jesuit Fathers, as well as collections of texts. In Luba the outstanding studies are those of Dr. Burssens and Dr. Meeussen.

Father Schebesta has now completed the four volumes of his work, *Die Bambuti-Pygmäen von Ituri*, dealing with the Pygmies and their language.[2] Dr. Guthrie has compiled a grammar of Lingala, and Fathers de Boeck and Hulstaert have also published a number of valuable studies of the language. A large proportion of the published vernacular literature consists of translations of the Bible or religious works issued by the missions. There are also a number of periodical publications, most of which are published in the four main languages, but some are multilingual, and 15 are issued in different vernaculars. *La Voix du Congolais* is in French, but is edited and written by Africans, and other original literary work by African authors has also been published in French.

In Ruanda Urundi the two prevailing tongues, Rundi and Rwanda, which are the common medium of school instruction, have so many points of resemblance that measures have been considered for their formal unification. Their orthography and pronunciation have been regularized, but a philologist appointed in 1950 to inquire into the possibility of their unification encountered difficulties arising from the political relations of the Barundi with the Ruanda people, and so far it has only been possible to achieve unification in some minor details.[3]

The Belgian system gives to the vernacular a place in school instruction similar to that which it occupies in the system followed in British territories, though with an earlier concentration on the teaching of French. French is taught as a compulsory subject in the third year of the primary course, and in most cases forms the medium of instruction in the *écoles du second degré*. It is the sole language recognized in the 'superior' schools.

[1] E. de Jonghe, 'Vers une langue nationale congolaise', ibid., vol. vi, 1935, pp. 340–51.
[2] See above, p. 66.
[3] *Rapport Annuel du Ruanda-Urundi, 1951*, p. 185.

Liberia

In Liberia the official language is English and this is the only tongue recognized in the upper classes of such schools as exist in Monrovia or the hinterland. But there is outside Monrovia a growing use of 'pidgin' which in this case includes a considerable number of foreign words introduced during the period of the slave trade; it has also many interesting formations of its own.[1] It seems likely to become a lingua franca.

Among the indigenous tribes there are a variety of tongues—said to amount to over 40 in all—but in the more prominent of them, such as Mano, Bussi, or Kpessi, there is now a certain amount of reading material, mainly due to the efforts of missionary societies. Reference has already been made to the Vai script invented about 1840 by Dualu Bukere and his colleagues;[2] it has a considerable circulation, and folk tales have been printed in it.

Portuguese Territories

In the Portuguese territories Thonga (Tsonga) is the most important vernacular language of Mozambique, though other languages (Chopi, Lenge, Ronga, Sena, and Tswa) are spoken, and have been studied by French, German, English, and some Portuguese linguists. In Angola there is a marked variety of tongues, Chokwe, Mbundu, Ganguella, and Kwanyama being extensively spoken. Most of these languages are used by the missions in the very early stages of school instruction, and religious literature published by mission organizations exists in Thonga, Chopi, Chokwe, Mbundu, and Tswa. Among the Chopi of Mozambique, verses, some of which have been transcribed, are composed by the leaders of their orchestras and are sung to the accompaniment of music and dancing.[3]

The policy of the Administration has hitherto been to insist on the use of Portuguese as the sole language of education and administration,[4] but there are some signs that this policy may be modified. An increasing interest in the study of African vernacular languages is now developing among Portuguese scholars.[5] It is of interest that the first translation of the Bible into an African tongue was made by the Portuguese, and that the first book in a Bantu language was produced in 1642 by Padre Francisco Paccionio. The Administration has, however, hitherto discountenanced the publication of vernacular literature without a concurrent Portuguese translation, a regulation which adds greatly to the cost of publication by missionary bodies. The languages of Portuguese Guinea (Balanta, Man-

---

[1] C. M. Wilson, *Liberia 1847–1947*, 1947, pp. 60–62.
[2] See above, p. 88.   [3] H. Tracey, *Chopi Musicians*, 1948.
[4] A. Durieux, *Essai sur le statut des indigènes portugais de la Guinée, de l'Angola et du Mozambique*, *Mém. A.R.S.C.*, vol. v, 1955, p. 14.
[5] *Africa*, October 1951, pp. 330–1.

dyak) have been studied by Portuguese scholars, but so far as is known no literature has been published in the vernacular.

INSTITUTIONS FOR STUDY AND RESEARCH

There are few institutions devoted exclusively to the study of the African languages, for the study of language is normally treated as part of a wider field of knowledge which embraces both the history and the social institutions of the peoples concerned. But this is fully in accord with the modern conception of the principles which should regulate linguistic study, as it is now generally accepted that language cannot be profitably studied save in close relation to social facts.

Recent advances in phonetics and in the elaboration of methods for distinguishing and reproducing speech-sounds have greatly improved the technical efficiency of linguistic study, but this covers only part of the task of the investigator or teacher. Speech must be seen as functioning in action. Words descriptive of social institutions peculiar to one people cannot be adequately rendered by merely selecting the nearest available equivalent in another language. 'Context of situation must be more than linguistic: it must include an analysis of the general conditions under which a language is spoken.'[1] The sociological approach is, moreover, of definite importance if the result of study is to be appreciated by Africans themselves and is to assist in the production of vernacular literature. It is necessary, as has been said, 'to look on the grammar of a Bantu language from the Bantu point of view, instead of pressing it into the frame of an Indo-European language'.[2]

In enumerating the existing institutions which include the study of language or provide for research,[3] it will be convenient to consider the different territories in alphabetical order.

Austria still maintains at the Vienna University an Institute devoted to Egyptian and African culture, but this has only a minor interest in African linguistic problems.

In Belgium a Royal Decree of 1947 established the *Institut pour la Recherche Scientifique en Afrique Centrale* (I.R.S.A.C.), which includes linguistic studies among its other activities.[4] It has awarded a number of bursaries for the training of linguists and has made grants for projects of field research; it has, for example, lately provided the team of linguists who are studying the problem of the unification of the languages of Ruanda

---

[1] B. Malinowski, 'The Problem of Meaning of Primitive Languages', in supplement to C K. Ogden and I. A. Richards, *The Meaning of Meaning*, 1927.

[2] E. W. Smith in *J.R.A.I.*, vol. lxv, 1935, p. 47.

[3] See also above, pp. 55–66.

[4] See also above, p. 65.

Urundi. The publication of linguistic studies is a regular feature of the Proceedings of the *Institut Royal Colonial Belge*[1] (now the *Académie Royale des Sciences Coloniales*).

The University of Louvain has an *Institut Africaniste*, and the University of Ghent has a seminar for Bantu and Sudanic languages. The *Institut Universitaire des Territoires d'Outre-Mer* has two professorships in African languages, and some of these languages are also taught at the *Musée du Congo Belge* at Tervuren. A permanent body, the *Commission Linguistique Africaine*, has been established to advise the Colonial Ministry on linguistic problems, including that of orthography and the recognition of languages for use in education.[2] Mention has already been made of the work of some of the more distinguished scholars who have studied the languages of the Belgian Congo, and to these must be added the name of the Rev. Alexis Kagame, a native of Ruanda Urundi, who has lately published some interesting studies of the traditional poetry of Ruanda, as well as a long original poem in Rwanda.

In France two official organizations, the *Office de la Recherche Scientifique d'Outre-Mer* (O.R.S.O.M.)[3] and the *Centre National de Recherche*, now sponsor ethnographic and linguistic research in the French African territories, the workers being usually attached to one of the local research centres. The best known of these centres is the *Institut Français d'Afrique Noire* (I.F.A.N.) established at Dakar in 1938, which has local centres in Guinea, Dahomey, Ivory Coast, Haute-Volta, Togo, and the Cameroons.[4] The more recently founded *Institut d'Études Centrafricaines* at Brazzaville (I.E.C.) occupies a similar position in French Equatorial Africa.[5] Another of the French metropolitan institutions, the *Centre des Hautes Études d'Administration Musulmane*, founded in 1936, shows a special interest in the Islamic languages of the Orient and Africa, but has no definite organization for research. One of the most important centres for linguistic research is the *École Nationale des Langues Orientales Vivantes*, and at the Sorbonne is established the *Groupe Linguistique Chado-Hamitique*. The *Institut d'Ethnologie* at Paris has a course on African languages.

Germany still maintains two institutions, the *Afrikanistisches Seminar* of Berlin University and the *Seminar für Afrikanistische Sprachen* at the University of Hamburg, which had a distinguished position in African linguistic studies during the period when Germany still had Colonial possessions in Africa. The work carried on in these institutions by Drs. Köhler, Klingenheben, Lukas, and Emmi Kähler-Mayer reflects the distinguished tradition established by Dr. Meinhof and Dr. Dietrich Westermann.

---

[1] See below, p. 1605.   [2] See above, pp. 106–7.
[3] See above, p. 64, and below, p. 1604.
[4] *Enc. A.O.F.*, vol. i, p. 326. See also above, p. 65, and below, p. 1608.
[5] *Enc. A.E.F.*, p. 245.

In Great Britain the principal academic institution concerned with African languages and cultures is the School of Oriental and African Studies, University of London. Established in 1916 as a School of Oriental Studies it began to give instruction in African languages (mainly Swahili) in 1917 under Dr. A. Werner. A combined Department of African Languages and Phonetics was instituted in 1932, and a separate African Department was established in 1937 under Dr. I. Ward. The title of the School was changed in 1938 in order to indicate the importance of the part it had begun to take in African Studies.[1] From 1948 the School has shared in the benefit of the substantial provision which the British Government has made for the promotion of Oriental and African Studies as the result of the recommendations of the important Scarbrough Commission appointed to examine the subject in 1945.[2] This Commission, after expressing its view that the provision made for African studies was 'unworthy of our country and our people', made recommendations for appropriate teaching and research. The establishment of the School now includes two professorships in the languages of Africa, and a staff of eleven lecturers in these languages, with a considerable number of African Assistants. Members of the staff of the School have been enabled to carry out a number of field researches in Africa, and they have been able to render direct assistance to the Colonial Governments on questions of orthography.

In addition to the work of the Phonetics Department of the School, the Department of Phonetics at University College, London, has also carried out research in African languages.[3] The recently established department of Oriental Studies at St. Andrew's University in Scotland is concerned mainly with the Semitic tongues, but there is now a Department of African Studies at the University of Glasgow. Courses in certain of the Bantu languages are given at Oxford and Cambridge Universities, in addition to those provided by the London School of Oriental and African Studies, for the benefit of probationers in the Colonial Services.

The Colonial Social Science Research Council, which has been established as part of the organization for research from resources granted under the Colonial Development and Welfare Acts,[4] has made a considerable number of grants for linguistic research in Africa,[5] as well as providing a large part of the finance required for the linguistic handbook to which subsequent reference will be made.[6] Finally it is contemplated

---

[1] *Calendar of the School of Oriental and African Studies*, 1954–5, p. 35.
[2] *Report to the Interdepartmental Commission of Enquiry into the Facilities for Oriental, Slavonic, East European and African Studies* (the Scarbrough Commission), 1947.
[3] D. Jones and S. T. Plaatje, *A Sechuana Reader*, 1917. D. Jones, *The Tones of Sechuana Nouns*, 1928. L. Armstrong, *The Phonetic and Tonal Structure of Kikuyu*, 1940.
[4] See above, p. 57.
[5] *Colonial Research 1954–1955*, Cmd. 9626, 1955, pp. 51 ff.
[6] See below, p. 113.

that the new university institutions in Africa will not merely provide advanced courses of instruction in the indigenous African languages but will constitute a regular agency for linguistic research.[1]

Holland is now diverting to African studies some of the activity which formerly made such notable contributions to linguistic and other studies in the Netherlands Indies. A Chair of Bantu Studies has recently been founded at Leyden University, under the auspices of the *Nederlandsch Afrika Instituut*, the first holder being the Swahili scholar, Dr. Blok.

In Italy the *Istituto Orientale* at Naples and the *Istituto per l'Oriente* in Rome have carried out numerous studies in African languages, the more recent of which, associated with the names of Drs. Moreno and Cerulli, have been concerned with the languages of Ethiopia and Somalia. The African missions of the Verona Fathers have been responsible for a valuable series of linguistic studies.

In Portugal there is no institution specifically devoted to the study of African languages, but the *Instituto Superior de Estudos Ultramarinos* in Lisbon had professorships in Kimbundu and Ronga, and the holder of the former has carried out linguistic research in Angola. The *Sociedade de Geografia de Lisboa* has sponsored the publication of grammars of the Lomwe and Chopi languages.

In the United States of America the Summer Institute of Linguistics, founded in 1934, which holds its principal academic sessions in association with the University of Oklahoma, is largely concerned with the training of missionaries for Central and South America, but it also organizes summer programmes of research into linguistics in collaboration with the Linguistic Society of America.

Some study of the Ethiopic and other Semitic languages has been carried out under the auspices of the former *Cercle Linguistique* of the *École Libre des Hautes Études* (now known as the Linguistic Circle of New York), but the most serious contribution to the study of African linguistics is that of Dr. Greenberg of Columbia University, to which reference has already been made.[2] The centre for African studies at North-Western University, Illinois, under the direction of Dr. M. Herskovits, is concerned with sociological studies rather than with purely linguistic research.

In the Union of South Africa the University of the Witwatersrand has a Department, and the Universities of Stellenbosch, Pretoria, and Potchefstroom and the University College of Fort Hare all have courses of Bantu Studies. The University of Cape Town has a School of African Studies. Most of these have been established as the result of a survey made in 1930 by the Inter-University Committee for African Studies.[3] Since 1921 the

---

[1] *Report of the Commission on Higher Education in the Colonies*, Cmd. 6647, 1945. *Report of the Commission on Higher Education in West Africa*, Cmd. 6655, 1945, pp. 11, 55.
[2] See above, p. 85. [3] *Bantu Studies*, March 1933.

University of Witwatersrand has been responsible for the quarterly journal *Bantu Studies* (now named *African Studies*) in which much linguistic material has been published, and it has also sponsored the publication of the *Bantu Treasury* and of a standard Zulu dictionary. Proposals have been under discussion for the establishment of an Academy of Bantu Language and Literature, which would deal with all cognate matters, such as orthography, standardization of grammar, and linguistic terminology.[1]

The Universities of Witwatersrand and Cape Town have professorships of Bantu languages, and the studies made by Dr. C. M. Doke of the Zulu, Shona, and Lamba languages, and by Dr. G. M. Lestrade of Tswana and Venda have given them high rank among scholars in African linguistics. Valuable work has also been done by Dr. A. N. Tucker in Sotho, Tswana, and Pedi, and in Shona by Father Fortune. Important contributions have also been made by Africans, particularly the late Dr. Vilikazi in Zulu and the late G. Letele in Southern Sotho.

Among the international organizations the International African Institute (which has its headquarters in London) has, as already pointed out, a special position in African cultural studies; the field studies which it has been enabled to organize have embraced not only sociological but linguistic problems.[2] It has taken the initiative in the inquiries necessary to establish uniform systems of orthography,[3] and has issued a number of works designed as guides for those engaged in linguistic research in Africa.[4] In more recent years it has undertaken, by the aid of a grant from the British Government, the preparation of a comprehensive *Handbook of African Languages*,[5] constituting a general survey of the languages of Africa, and has organized an international study in which Belgian, French, and British scholars have co-operated, with the object of determining the classification of a number of little-known languages distributed along what is known to linguists as the 'Bantu line' in Central Africa.[6] Reference has already been made to the Ethnographic Survey undertaken by the Institute, which will in one sense be complementary to the Linguistic Survey.[7] *Africa*, the quarterly journal of the Institute, provides what is probably the most widely read organ for contributions on linguistic research both from British and foreign scholars.

[1] *Handbook on Race Relations in South Africa*, 1949, p. 605.
[2] See also above, pp. 55–56.
[3] See above, p. 87.
[4] I. Ward and D. Estermann, *Practical Phonetics for Students of African Languages*, 1933. I. Ward, *Practical Suggestions for Learning an African Language in the Field*, 1937. *Short Guide to the Recording of African Languages*, 1933.
[5] *Colonial Research 1953–1954*, Cmd. 9303, p. 54; ibid. *1954–1955*, Cmd. 9626, p. 57.
[6] G. van Bulck, 'Les deux Cartes Linguistiques du Congo Belge', *Bull. I.R.C.B.*, vol. xxv, no. 2, 1952. I. Richardson, in *Africa*, April 1955, pp. 161 ff.
[7] See above, p. 63. See also *Colonial Research 1953–1954*, Cmd. 9303, p. 53; ibid. *1954–1955*, Cmd. 9626, p. 57.

The Educational, Scientific, and Cultural Organization of the United Nations (Unesco) has concerned itself with African in common with other vernaculars, particularly in connexion with schemes of 'fundamental education'. A conference held in Paris in 1951 provided the occasion for the expression of a number of views on the use of vernacular languages in education.[1]

[1] UNESCO. Meeting of Experts on the Use of Vernacular Languages, Paris, 1951. See The Use of Vernacular Languages in Education, Unesco Monographs on Fundamental Education, Paris, n.d., probably 1953. See also Educational Studies and Documents, No. 11, June 1953, African Languages and English in Education (Report of a meeting of experts at Jos, Nigeria, November 1952), Unesco Educational Clearing House, Paris. See also The Use of Vernacular Languages as Vehicles of Instruction both in School and out of School, Report presented to Unesco by the International African Institute, 1951.

CHAPTER IV

POPULATION RECORDS

IMPORTANCE OF POPULATION STATISTICS

THE study of population trends is today a matter of more than academic concern, for large numbers of people look to it to throw some light on the much-debated issue whether the increase of the world's population may not within a measurable time overtake the capacity of mankind to maintain itself at a reasonable standard of subsistence. It is true that the position in the African continent has not occupied a prominent place in this discussion largely because of the exceptionally low density of the population in comparison with that of Europe or Asia. But there are nevertheless reasons which have given the study of population statistics a particular interest in some of the countries of Africa. In certain areas of mixed racial composition (as most notably the Union of South Africa) the question of the relative increase of the different communities has been at times a matter of grave domestic concern. In others (of which Kenya may serve as an example) current views regarding the rapid increase of the African population have caused apprehension lest the indigenous methods of cultivation may so exhaust the soil of the Native Trust Units[1] as to throw on the European community the burden of supporting a large part of the African population. The recent East Africa Royal Commission 1953–5, which devoted much attention to the statistics of the growth of population in East Africa, has emphasized the undesirability of allowing policy to be influenced by acceptance of incomplete figures of population trends.[1]

Apart, however, from these special grounds for concern in the study of population statistics, it is obvious that they must form part of the basic material on which a Government depends not merely in the normal operation of its social and economic services, but in the planning of those schemes of development which now form so considerable a part of governmental activities in Africa. Information of this nature is the more essential because so many of these projects do not originate (as they might in Europe) with local bodies which are familiar with their own conditions and needs, but are the outcome of policies initiated by the central departments of the Colonial Administrations, or result from a stimulus applied or help tendered by a metropolitan authority.

Correct information on population movements is indispensable for the

---

[1] *East Africa Royal Commission 1953–1955 Report*, Cmd. 9475, pp. 30–36.

effective discharge of numerous day-to-day functions, such as the regulation of the recruitment of labour or of its migration, the resettlement of the congested population of indigenous areas, or the provision of medical services or educational facilities. It is equally important if Administrations are to be in a position to assess the actual effect of indigenous custom, such for example as the practice of polygamy, which has frequently been the subject of arbitrary and indeed contradictory assumptions.

It is, however, true that until relatively recent years the information available regarding the strength of the population in Africa was very incomplete. There was certainly no statistical material comparable to that available for India, either in respect of population movement or of agricultural production. There is—to take one illustration—no material from which it would be possible to make for Africa such estimates as those which have recently been made by the Census Commissioner for India. He has estimated that the population of the Indian Union, which numbered 357 million in the census of 1951, is likely to number 520 million in 1981, and will require an increase over present subsistence production amounting to about 21 per cent. before 1961, about 37 per cent. before 1971, and 54 per cent. before 1981. It is incidentally of interest to note here the estimated annual rate of population increase in India, the largest geographical unit whose climatic or other conditions can be regarded as in any sense comparable to those of Africa. India has had a regular decennial census from 1881, following an incomplete census made in 1872. For the years 1891–1901 the annual increase was 0·14 per cent., for 1901–11 it was 0·069 per cent., and for the succeeding three decades 0·0867 per cent., 1·06 per cent., and 1·45 per cent. In 1941–51 it was 1·295 per cent.[1] The increase in Burma during the decade 1931–41 was 1·3 annually; that in Ceylon was 2·2 annually, but the statistics for Ceylon are greatly influenced by the seasonal immigration of Indian labour.

Figures of population increase in Europe or America are less useful as a basis of comparison. But it is of interest to note that in both cases there seems to have been since the war an accelerated rate of increase as compared with the pre-war period. The recent growth in the United States of America is about 1¾ per cent. a year. The Russian figures indicate a growth of 2 per cent. These relatively rapid rates of expansion overshadow those of most European countries, where rates of growth range mostly from about ¼ per cent. to 1 per cent. a year, with Great Britain at the lower and Western Germany near the higher end of the range. The rate of increase in France has unexpectedly risen in recent years to ¾ per cent. a year.[2]

---

[1] The figures given in the text refer to all-India, including for this purpose Pakistan but excluding Burma. For more detailed figures, see V. Anstey, *The Economic Development of India*, 1952, p. 605. [2] *The Times*, 4 January 1955.

AFRICA : POPULATION DENSITY
(South of the Sahara)

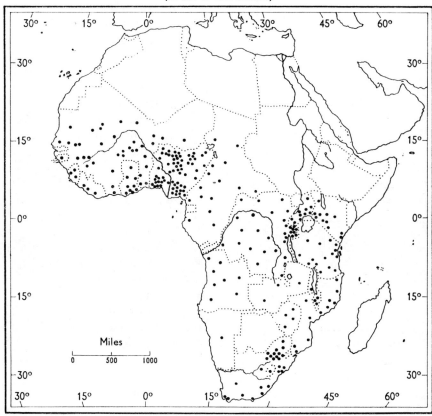

Miles

0   500   1000

D.C.S. (Misc.) 226/5

One dot represents 500,000 people

AFRICA : POPULATION DENSITY
(South of the Sahara)

One dot represents 500,000 people

ESTIMATES OF THE WHOLE OF AFRICA

Although the material for calculating the population of the whole continent is still inadequate, it is nevertheless a considerable advance on that available a generation ago. It was of course inevitable that the early estimates of the population should have been little more than guesses based on insufficient and unreliable data. For the continent as a whole, estimates of 150 million or more appeared during the eighteenth century, but in the early part of the nineteenth century the evidence of explorers as to the relative sparseness of population in the countries they had traversed resulted in the figure being drastically reduced to a range varying between 28 and 41 million. After the middle of the century, however, the publication of the reports of H. M. Stanley's journeys led to a substantial increase in the estimate, figures up to 180 million or more being adopted; that generally accepted in 1882 was indeed as high as 205 million.[1] Estimates made at various times between 1903 and 1936 returned once more to the lower figure, and varied between 126 and 150 million; that given in the *Statistical Yearbook* of the League of Nations for 1934 was 145 million.

In more recent years the Statistical Office of the United Nations has made a special study of the figures of population in the various countries of the world, and has since 1949 published in its *Demographic Yearbook* an annual analysis of the results. The Yearbook for 1952 gave the following series of estimates regarding the African continent, though it was stated at the same time that the figures were subject to a possible error either way of about 10 million in the case of the whole of Africa and of about 6 million for tropical and southern Africa.

Year	All Africa (million)	Tropical and Southern Africa (million)
1920	140	94
1930	155	104
1940	172	115
1951	200	134

Taking these figures purely at their face value, they show in both cases an increase of about 1·2 per cent. annually over the 31-year period ending 1951. The rate of growth, however, is not constant; from 1920 to 1940 the average was 1·0 per cent. a year, whilst from 1940 to 1951 it was 1·4 per cent.; that is to say, there was a rate of increase substantially greater during and after the Second World War than between the wars.[2] The succeeding sections of this chapter will give such details as are available regarding the methods adopted for enumeration in each of the countries

[1] *Encyclopaedia Britannica*, 11th ed., vol. xxii, p. 92.
[2] On the question of the population of the continent generally, see A. M. Carr-Saunders, *World Population*, 1936.

lying south of the Sahara and the results recorded. There has been great disparity in the importance attached by different Administrations to obtaining correct figures of the strength of the African population, and though in a number of cases the statistical material is now reasonably adequate, the differences of method are still such as to leave room for some doubt as to the correctness of impressions drawn regarding the movement of population in the area as a whole.

ESTIMATES OF INDIVIDUAL TERRITORIES

Early Estimates

Some of the earlier estimates of the population of individual African territories have shown fluctuations relatively as great as those which have related to the whole continent. The intensive examination made by the late Dr. R. R. Kuczynski of the population statistics of the British African dependencies contains many illustrations of the wide difference in the estimates which were made from time to time, and shows how often they were falsified when a census was actually taken.[1] In 1854, for instance, Barth estimated the population of Northern Nigeria at 30 to 40 million, and the British Colonial Office List of 1900, the year in which the Protectorate was proclaimed, accepted the figure of 30 million. Lord Lugard, however, writing in 1903, thought that this figure had been reduced since 1854 to 9 million, as the result of slave raids and disease, while another estimate made by a competent authority in 1906 put the total at 7 million.[2] The census of Northern Nigeria held in 1911 (which was, however, admittedly incomplete) showed a total of 8,115,981 and that of 1921 a total of 9,994,515.

The most diverse estimates were also made on different occasions of the population of Uganda. In 1879 a study made by its first missionary visitor put it at 5 million; in 1893 Lord Lugard thought it was $2\frac{1}{2}$ million; the official estimate made in 1900 was roughly 3,800,000. The first enumeration, made in 1911, gave a total of 2,840,469. Sir A. Hardinge put the population of Kenya in 1897 at $2\frac{1}{2}$ million; the *Statistical Abstract for the British Empire* placed it shortly afterwards at 4 million; and in 1911 it was officially stated to be 3 million.[3]

At one time the population of the Belgian Congo was assumed to be about 40 million,[4] but shortly before 1910 official estimates reduced this figure to $15\frac{1}{2}$ million. In 1933 the Belgian Government adopted the figure of $9\frac{1}{4}$ million, and in 1935 that of 11 million. Estimates regarding French

[1] R. R. Kuczynski, *Demographic Survey of the British Colonial Empire*, vols. i and ii, 1948 and 1949.
[2] C. K. Meek, *The Northern Tribes of Nigeria*, vol. ii, p. 169, 1925.
[3] Kuczynski, op. cit. vol. ii, pp. 144, 235.
[4] E. W. Smith, *The Golden Stool*, 1930, p. 141.

Equatorial Africa have shown equally significant variations. In 1911 it was believed that the country had 20 million inhabitants; in 1921 they were stated to be only $7\frac{1}{2}$ million, and in 1931 about $2\frac{1}{2}$ million.[1] The figure officially adopted in 1936 was 3,423,000. In both Belgium and France the difference between these figures and the original estimates became a prominent topic in public discussions on Colonial policy.

In the case of the Belgian Congo, the difference between the first estimate of 40 million and the figure of $15\frac{1}{2}$ million recognized in 1910 was attributed by critics to the depopulation caused by the exploitation of the country during the régime of the Free State. Partisans of the Free State on the other hand attributed it to the introduction of disease by Europeans; others were content to find the cause simply in the existence of European occupation—'la pénétration européenne, telle quelle, par elle-même'.[2]

The debate thus raised had, however, one beneficial result. The National Colonial Congress held in Brussels in 1924 concluded that there was a danger that the African population of the Congo might 'collapse or disappear',[3] and the influence of this view has been seen in the special regard paid in later years to health questions and to the effect produced on the population by labour recruitment.[4] The assumption of a progressive depopulation of French Equatorial Africa was used at one time to support attacks by domestic critics on the Colonial policy of France in general, but it was also alleged in particular that the abuses of the concessionaire system[5] and of conscription had led to a wholesale migration into British territories. The extent of the alleged emigration, sometimes put as high as 2–3 million, has not been supported by the census figures of the neighbouring British territories, and it is also significant that the concessionaire system was in full operation for only a limited period, namely, between the years 1901 and 1912. Nevertheless, the assumption undoubtedly provided an important argument in the campaign waged in France against the continuation of the system of concessions.[6]

It is of interest to recall one other instance where an estimate regarding population trends had an influence on national policy. In 1921 the Report of the Director of Census in the Union anticipated that after the next 50 years there was likely to be in the Union a population of 4 million Europeans faced by 19 if not $24\frac{1}{2}$ million non-Europeans. The experience of the last 30 years has not justified this assumption regarding the ratio of non-European increase, but the anticipation undoubtedly influenced for

[1] *L'Intransigeant*, 17 August 1934, quoted in G. Gorer, *Africa Dances*, 1935, p. 132.
[2] *Bulletin Officiel*, 1920, pp. 654, 656. J. Schwetz, 'Contribution à l'étude de la démographie congolaise', *Congo*, March 1923, p. 297.
[3] *La Question sociale au Congo*, 1924, p. 101.
[4] See below, p. 1001.   [5] See below, pp. 1391, 1402.
[6] G. M. Vassal, *Life in French Congo*, 1925, pp. 126 ff. A. Girault, *Principes de Colonisation et de Législation Coloniale*, vol. i, 1927, pp. 405, 456.

some years the outlook of the European community on Native policy.[1] Here, however, the deduction was based on census figures, not, as in the cases previously referred to, on estimates or assumptions supported by no process of enumeration. When once the stage is entered at which actual enumerations have been made, the range of error has been sensibly reduced, and, if error occurs, it is due either to faults in the system of enumeration or to a misreading of the population trends shown by its results.

Present-day Census Figures

It will be convenient to refer at this stage to Table I at the end of the chapter,[2] which shows the total population of the countries lying south of the Sahara. In this table is shown the population as recorded in the latest census taken in the respective territories; earlier figures must be regarded as tentative. A supplementary table[3] gives the number of Africans, Europeans, and 'others' (Asians, Arabs, Syrians, Coloured, &c.) in each territory according to the latest available information.

In most cases the figures for the minority communities, Europeans and others, are the result of specific enumeration and are subject to a smaller margin of error than the accompanying figures for Africans. If certain of the Administrations (and most notably those of the Belgian Congo and French West and Equatorial Africa) have not yet taken a complete census, it is partly because they are convinced that in present circumstances an adequate system of sampling can give sufficiently reliable results, and especially so when it is based, as in the Belgian Congo, on the maintenance of a card index system covering a large part of the territory. There is a somewhat similar reason for the fact that Southern and Northern Rhodesia have relied on sampling rather than on the attempt to make a complete enumeration of their African population.[4]

The respective merits of complete enumeration and of sample survey have been the subject of debate by statisticians representing the different Colonial Governments, and it has been generally agreed that where details of the population of relatively small geographical areas are required for administrative purposes there is no alternative to complete enumeration, but that where the needs of the Administration are not so detailed, a well-organized sample survey can provide a sufficiently reliable alternative.[5] In any case, it is now felt that an adequate use of the method of sampling can afford a very valuable check on the results of enumeration, and is also the

[1] W. Macmillan, *Africa Emergent*, 1938, pp. 50–65.
[2] See below, p. 143.
[3] See below, p. 144.
[4] See below, p. 128.
[5] *Report of Conference of Statisticians of Countries in Africa South of the Sahara*, Salisbury, 1951, para. 17; *Report of the Second Conference of Colonial Government Statisticians*, 1953, pp. 5 ff.

best means of securing a record of certain additional data which a census in African conditions is not able to supply.

Only those who have actual experience of carrying out the census of a population such as is to be found in large parts of Africa can have any conception of the difficulties involved. In certain areas there still survives the traditional suspicion that the making of a count is a preliminary to imposing taxation. In others the population may be largely nomadic, and even when this is not the case, opinions may be divided between the advisability of pursuing the system of a *de facto* count, which may omit the large numbers of wage earners absent from their territories in employment elsewhere at the time of census, or a *de jure* system, which will record those domiciled, whether or not they are resident at the time of the census. Above all, there is the prevailing difficulty of finding a sufficient number of reliable enumerators to allow of a census being carried out simultaneously over a sufficiently large area. It is not surprising therefore to find that Colonial Administrations were at one period driven either to the use of rough-and-ready expedients for calculating the African population, or else to make a count which at the best could only be partial.

Africa has possibly no parallel to the crudity of the expedient on which the Government of Hong Kong once relied for calculating the size of its population; 'the amount of night-soil now being collected approximates to nearly 4 million taels, which at three taels per head gives a population of over 1,300,000 without allowing for wastage'.[1] But in many cases it was considered adequate to rely on inquiries made from Chiefs or Headmen, who with the best will in the world had no head for figures, or, where the procedure for the levy of a poll-tax had been put into force, to use the tax register as a basis for calculating the strength of the groups concerned. There was no doubt some scriptural warrant for this procedure, in the sense that the first census in the Christian era resulted from the decree of Augustus that 'all the world be taxed'. The statistical accuracy of the results shown by the use of the poll-tax register depended, however, largely on the assumptions made as to the average number of persons dependent on the taxpayers shown in it. Experience shows that these assumptions might in practice vary widely according to the individual views held from time to time by the Administrative Officers responsible for reporting the result;[2] multiples have been recorded varying as far apart as $2\frac{1}{2}$ and $4\frac{1}{2}$ in different areas.

Where a hut tax was imposed the tax register was sometimes elaborated to include the names, not only of the taxpayers, but also their wives and

[1] *Report on Census of the Colony of Hongkong*, 1931, quoted by R. R. Kuczynski, *Colonial Populations*, 1937, p. vii.

[2] See R. R. Kuczynski, *Demographic Survey of the British Colonial Empire*, vol. ii, 1949, pp. 135, 404. E. B. Worthington, *Science in Africa*, p. 558.

children, and consequently came to be called a census. When, in course
of time, a poll tax was substituted for the more primitive hut tax, the tax
register lost some of its value as an estimate of the population. Resort was
had in other instances to the use of the records of 'registered Natives' as a
basis of calculation, as for instance in Kenya, though this method was
perhaps even more fallible than the use of the tax register.[1] Where the
system of the poll tax or hut tax was not in force (as notably in the Gold
Coast)[2] there was no alternative to attempting an enumeration, even
though the machinery for this was defective or was entirely lacking.

It was seldom that the work of enumeration was at this period entrusted
to a specially qualified authority, and there were instances in which an
Administrative Officer, placed in charge of the operation, was given no
additional establishment for the purpose. In one case it was apparently
deemed sufficient to provide the Director of Census with one lady clerk
(who did not, however, join his office until five months later) and one
African office boy.[3] It was a further disadvantage that censuses were in
some territories taken at irregular intervals, and that no uniformity was
observed as to the type of entries to be recorded or as to the method of
their presentation.[4] When one reflects that India had taken a census at
regular intervals and on a uniform system since 1881, one can appreciate
the relative disadvantages encountered by students of demographic data
in Africa.[5]

It adds to the difficulty of such a study that in the past the Administrations frequently felt it to be incumbent on them to explain the reasons for
the changes in the number of the population which the statistics as published by them seemed from time to time to reveal. Thus when they were
confronted in early days with the difference between previous assumptions
as to the strength of the population and the figures of their own census or
its equivalent, it was common to have recourse to hypotheses based on the
past effects of the slave trade or of tribal warfare.

No basis exists, however, for calculating with any accuracy the losses
caused directly or indirectly to Africa by the slave trade. One of the older
estimates put the number of Africans landed in North America and the
West Indies between 1680 and 1786 at 2 million; the Abbé Raynal on the
other hand estimated in 1780 that 9 million Natives had been exported
from Africa. In 1933 a spokesman of the British Anti-Slavery Society
expressed the view that in 1841 there were 6¼ million slaves in Christian
countries alone, apart from those in other areas. Dr. Kuczynski lent some
support to an estimate which put the number transported from Africa in the

---

[1] Kuczynski, op. cit. vol. ii, pp. 139 ff.
[2] See below, p. 666.
[3] *Northern Rhodesia, Report of Director of the Census of 1931*, p. 5.
[4] R. R. Kuczynski, *Colonial Populations*, 1937, pp. 13 ff.
[5] A. M. Carr-Saunders, *World Population*, 1936, p. 303.

course of the last four centuries as high as 15 million.[1] An official estimate, given in a memorandum annexed to a report of a Select Committee of the House of Commons in 1848, gave the figure of $5\frac{1}{2}$ million slaves exported in the 60-year period 1788–1848. The export of slaves would seem to have reached its peak between 1835 and 1840, when in each year an average of 135,800 were transported from Africa, but it has been stated that in the previous 25 years the number seldom fell below 100,000 annually.[2] Whatever the value of these figures, it must be realized that the direct losses by the export of slaves and the indirect losses incurred through slave raids, grave as they certainly were, were nevertheless spread over a long period of time.

It is even more difficult to make any estimate of the number of lives which Africa may have lost through the tribal wars that occurred before the period of European occupation. Early administrators, looking for reasons to account for an apparent increase in the population, no doubt found an easy explanation in the cessation of tribal wars, following on the introduction of a régime of law and order.[3] But the actual damage done by such fighting may well have been exaggerated,[4] for the object of the tribal war was primarily plunder of cattle or grain, and the casualties were not as a rule heavy, save perhaps in such exceptional devastation as was caused by Chaka (Shaka).[5]

At a later stage the Administrations expended much effort in analysing the presumed loss or gain of population as shown by their enumerations, though in fact many of these changes were actually the result of defective methods of counting or were even due to arithmetical errors.[6] In the natural order of things these elaborate explanations could make little constructive contribution to the study of the population problems of Africa, and they served in fact chiefly to give publicity to impressions formed about such matters as infant mortality, the ratio of fertility, or the incidence of disease. It was possible to speak with the greater assurance of such matters because there was no means of testing the conclusions to which they seemed to point.

While there is some cause to complain that the earlier Colonial Administrations failed to appreciate the need to overcome the difficulties inherent in the organization of a reliable census, there are a number which can claim credit for the fact that within some 20 years of their occupation they had evolved statistics sufficiently approximate for practical purposes. It will be realized, moreover, that the comprehensive census, as we know

[1] See reference quoted in W. Macmillan, op. cit. 1938, p. 48; also H. M. Stevens, *The Slave in History*, 1904, p. 109; Sir John Harris, *A Century of Emancipation*, 1933, p. 94; R. Coupland, *East Africa and its Invaders*, 1938, pp. 208, 500; *The Exploitation of East Africa, 1939*, pp. 232 ff.

[2] Quoted in *The Nigeria Handbook, 1953*, pp. 30–31.

[3] W. Macmillan, op. cit. pp. 47 ff.

[4] On the demographic effects of slave raiding and tribal wars, see Kuczynski, *Demographic Survey*, op. cit. vol. i, p. 13; vol. ii, pp. 119, 121, 193, 314, 533, 630.

[5] I. Schapera, ed., *The Bantu-speaking Tribes of South Africa*, 1937, p. 49.

[6] Kuczynski, *Colonial Populations*, p. 13.

it today, is even in Europe a relatively recent development of the original purpose of a census.

The interest of Administrators has lately been stimulated by the work of the statistical bureaux of various international bodies, and by institutions such as the World Health Organization.[1] Many of the Governments have also seen the need of more accurate information on which to base their development programmes. The British Colonial areas in particular have effected since the Second World War not merely a substantial improvement in the process of enumeration, but a far greater uniformity in the presentation of the resulting data. It is not possible to make here a detailed survey of the material on which earlier estimates were based, but some indication of their value will appear in the following notes.

Union of South Africa

South Africa has been covered by regular censuses which began at an earlier date than in any other area of Africa. In the Cape the Dutch took a yearly census as far back as the seventeenth century and the British adopted the same practice for several decades, but interest subsequently declined, and a census was afterwards taken at irregular periods and often in an incomplete form. Thus the Cape had a census in 1865 and 1875, but the next was not taken until 1891. Natal has more or less reliable records of the White population from 1840 onwards, but the first complete census of the whole population was not taken until 1891. In the Free State the earliest enumeration of the White population was recorded in 1855, and the first census of the total population was made in 1880. In the Transvaal an incomplete record was made in 1876, followed by a general though unreliable census in 1890.[2] The first complete census for the whole area of the Union was made in 1904, followed by censuses made in 1911, 1921, 1936, 1946, and 1951. The results are shown in the following table.[3]

Year	Africans 000	Africans incr. per cent.	Europeans 000	Europeans incr. per cent.	Asians 000	Asians incr. per cent.	Coloured 000	Coloured incr. per cent.	Total 000	Total incr. per cent.
1904	3,491	..	1,117	..	123	..	445	..	5,176	..
1911	4,019	2·0	1,276	1·9	152	3·1	526	2·4	5,973	1·7
1921	4,698	1·6	1,519	1·8	166	0·9	546	0·4	6,929	1·5
1936	6,597	2·3	2,004	1·9	220	1·9	770	2·3	9,590	2·2
1946	7,832	1·7	2,373	1·7	285	2·6	928	1·9	11,418	1·8
1951	8,537	1·7	2,644	2·2	366	5·1	1,103	3·6	12,650	2·1

[1] 'Report of First International Conference of National Committees on Vital and Health Statistics', *Chronicle of World Health Organization*, January 1954, p. 7.

[2] A. Roberts, 'A Statistical Enquiry into the Population Problem in South Africa', *Transactions of the Royal Society of South Africa*, 1926.

[3] The rates of increase are stated as average per cent. increase per year between the censuses.

The census records (which are supplemented by the annual records of migration) can claim accuracy as regards the European population, but are much less reliable in respect of Africans. The results for 1911 and 1921 are in particular open to doubt, and the accuracy of the figure of Africans as recorded in 1951 has also been questioned.[1] The statistics relating to the European community throw an interesting light on the change in the character of White settlement, in so far that the disparity between the sexes has tended to disappear; there were 132 males to 100 females in 1904, but only 101 to 100 in 1946. Among non-Europeans the ratio of the sexes has approximated to equality throughout, except in the Transvaal, where (as might be expected owing to the conditions of employment in the Rand mines) there have normally been 30 per cent. more males than females.

It is again noticeable that the proportion of the population living in urban areas has increased from 33 per cent. in 1936 to 43 per cent. in 1951. In that year 78 per cent. of the Europeans were living in urban areas; the proportion of Africans had increased from 19 per cent. in 1936 to 27 per cent. in 1951, the increase being especially noticeable in the case of towns with a population over 20,000. Out of the African population as recorded in 1946, when it numbered 7,832,000, there were 1,328,000 living in municipal locations and other urban areas, 2,187,000, living on European farms, 600,000 in mine, industrial, or municipal compounds, 2,758,000 on Native Trust lands, and 864,000 on other Native lands.

High Commission Territories

In the High Commission Territories the first regular census was taken in 1904, followed by a census in 1911, 1921, 1936, and 1946. Greater attention was clearly paid to the operation in 1946 than on previous occasions, the census of 1921, in particular, being open to criticism. Difficulty has, however, been created from the first by the large volume of migratory labour, especially in Basutoland. In that territory no less than 101,273 out of a total African population of 562,311 were recorded in the census of 1936 as 'absentees at labour centres', and in 1946 the total of these 'absentees' was 70,778 out of a total of 561,289. There was, it will be seen, a small decline in the total population of the territory during the ten years ending 1946. In Bechuanaland the exodus was less marked, being in 1946 only 14,119 out of a total of 296,310.[2]

Federation of Rhodesia and Nyasaland

The Government of Southern Rhodesia has shown itself to be impressed by the consideration that a modern census depends for its value not merely

[1] J. D. Rheinallt Jones, in *Africa South of the Sahara*, 1951, pp. 50 ff.
[2] The details are given in *N.A.*, Part V, pp. 2, 149, 335. The statistics of migration in the High Commission Territories are discussed by R. R. Kuczynski, *Demographic Survey of the British Colonial Empire*, vol. ii, 1949, pp. 21, 24, 26.

on the counting of heads, but on a reliable record of other data, such as the tribal, the sex, and the age distribution. The ordinary African, even when he is not suspicious of questions on some of these matters, is notoriously lacking in ability to date events, and it needs special qualities on the part of the enumerator if these data, and especially those relating to the age of his dependants, are to be correctly ascertained and recorded. It was largely the difficulty of securing a qualified personnel for these purposes that influenced the authorities in charge of the Southern Rhodesian census of 1948[1] in their choice of the procedure to be adopted. Such personnel, they felt, could not be secured without a considerable period of training, and they decided therefore to rely largely on the use of sampling by trained field officers. A similar decision was made in respect of the census of Northern Rhodesia in 1950.[2]

Some reference will be made subsequently to the value which can be claimed for the use of this method in recording information about age distribution and the like,[3] and it will be sufficient to say here that though accuracy can be claimed for the enumeration of Europeans, no complete count has so far been made of the Africans in the two Rhodesias. The sample censuses of 1948 and 1950 covered only about 10 per cent. of the rural areas in Southern and 5 per cent. in Northern Rhodesia. In Southern Rhodesia the census of 1948 gave the number of Africans as 1,262,000 in Native areas, 325,000 in European areas, and 32,000 absent in other territories, a total of 1,619,000, but it is noticeable that an official estimate issued in 1951 suggested that the total number of Africans should be taken as 2 million, against 1 million in 1928 and half a million in 1901.[4] As regards Northern Rhodesia Dr. Kuczynski characterized the position of the population estimates in 1934 as chaotic, and it was clear that at that date the Administration itself had no confidence in them.[5] Should it be possible to make a complete enumeration in 1960, it will be interesting to see how far the sample census of 1950 gave a reliable estimate of the total African population.

The position in regard to Nyasaland is of unusual interest partly because the social consequences of the large emigration of Nyasaland labour to other parts of Africa have for many years been a special cause of concern,[6] and partly because the large influx of Nguru, the immigrant settlers from

[1] J. R. Shaul and C. A. Myburgh, in *Population Studies*, December 1948 and 1949; *O.Y.S.R.*, *1952*, pp. 128 ff.

[2] *Economic and Statistical Bulletin of Northern Rhodesia*, no. 10 of vol. iii and no. 3 of vol. iv, 1951.

[3] See below, p. 139.

[4] *O.Y.S.R.*, *1952*, pp. 130, 161 ff. See also *Southern Rhodesia Census of Population, 1951*, 1954. The Central African Statistical Office stated in December 1955 that the number of Africans at that date was 2,220,000; the number of Europeans was stated to be 166,000.

[5] Kuczynski, *Demographic Survey*, vol. ii, pp. 408, 409. See also *Report of the Commission to Enquire into the Financial and Economic Position of Northern Rhodesia*, Col. no. 145, 1938, p. 7.

[6] *N.A.*, Part II, p. 21. Kuczynski, op. cit., vol. ii, pp. 537 ff. See also below, p. 1381.

Portuguese East Africa, has given rise to a political problem of some importance.[1] The first census was taken in 1911, and owing to the special circumstances of the Protectorate arrangements were subsequently made for a five-yearly enumeration, the first being held in 1921 and repeated in 1926 and 1931. That for 1936 was deferred on grounds of economy and again deferred in 1941 on account of the Second World War. A special organization was created for the census held in 1945, but the supply of competent enumerators was inadequate, and the census actually lasted from March to July.[2]

The enumeration seems, however, to have been far more reliable than that of 1931. That it did not provide convincing results regarding population trends was due largely to the preponderance of the figures of immigration from Portuguese territories, which some authorities hold to have extended to some hundreds of thousands in the 50 years of British administration.[3] In a memorandum submitted by representative organizations of the settlers and landowners of the Southern Province of Nyasaland in May 1954, it was pointed out that out of a total population of a little over 2 million, roughly 1 million were living in the Southern Province, of whom it was asserted that 688,000 were not indigenous but immigrant, and that the density of population in that province was brought up by their presence to 111 persons to the square mile.[4] The density of population in Nyasaland as a whole is double that of any territory in Eastern or Central Africa. The Director of the Central African Statistical Office estimated in 1954 that the total African population of the three territories constituting the Federation was 6,630,000 and expected that in ten years time it would increase to about 9 million.[5]

British East African Territories

The demographic statistics of the British East African territories are of special importance, for the ratio of growth of the population (and in particular that of Kenya and Uganda) has of recent years been a matter of some controversy. As regards Kenya a full census was not taken before that made in 1948. The figures returned in the 'census' of 1931 were the result of a complete enumeration of Europeans, but represented merely an estimate of the number of Africans, except of those living in the towns and on European farms, that is to say, about 2 or 3 per cent. of the whole. The estimate was based on the poll-tax registers, the assumption being made that poll-tax payers represented 37 per cent. of the total population;

[1] N.A., Part II, pp. 24, 48. See also below, p. 137.
[2] Report on the Census of Nyasaland Protectorate for 1945.
[3] Kuczynski, op. cit. vol. ii, pp. 537–42.
[4] Africa Digest, vol. ii, no. 2, May 1954, p. 3.
[5] Press reports stated in December 1955 that the population of the Federation had then reached a total of 7,007,000, the Europeans being 234,000 and the Africans 6,810,000.

but these registers were not in fact up to date, for there were some districts in which only one-quarter of them were brought up to date in any one year. It is noteworthy that prior to 1916 the total African population had been officially accepted as amounting to about 4 million. In 1917 the estimated figure fell to 2,848,700, and according to official estimates it continued to fall each year until 1923, when it was given as under 2,530,000. Independent opinion concurred in believing that the African population was diminishing,[1] but as will be seen from the figures given in the table at the end of this chapter the census of 1948 has restored the total to over the 5 million mark.

In Tanganyika the 'census' of 1931 was officially described as being the result of 'bringing up to date the poll-tax records in certain areas and the compilation of new statistics in other areas'.[2] In effect the number of poll-tax payers was multiplied by a factor (usually $4\frac{1}{2}$) in order to arrive at the total population. A more serious effort had, however, been made in 1931 in Uganda, where information was obtained by counts of small administrative units of up to 500 persons controlled by a Headman. This provided a more reliable basis of information, even though the result was affected by the fact that the census was not taken in a single day, and that a number of relatively untrained schoolchildren had to be used as enumerators.[3]

It is regrettable that measures could not have been taken in 1931 to provide a more complete count in these three territories, since there is reason to believe that the population was decreasing from 1895 to 1920; up to 1910 at all events 'famine and epidemic disease had more than offset the beneficial effects of the abolition of inter-tribal warfare'.[4] If a more reliable census had been taken in 1931 it might have provided material for judging of the extent to which this process had actually been reversed.

The three territories had to wait till 1948 for the next census, which was organized under the direction of the East Africa High Commission.[5] It was conducted by the Director of the newly created East Africa Statistical Department and took the form of a complete enumeration of the whole population. It consisted of two parts, the first part being a count of the population which recorded tribe, sex, and age group, and the second part comprising a sample (like that of Southern Rhodesia) taken over about 10 per cent. of the population, this being designed both as a check on the enumeration and as a means of securing data about fertility and similar details. The services of some 25,000 persons were employed, and where schoolchildren were used, guides were provided to take them round the huts and to put the necessary questions. Some of the staff had

---

[1] Norman Leys, *Kenya*, 1925, pp. 281 ff.
[2] *Report to United Nations Organization for 1952*, p. 230.
[3] C. J. Martin, 'The East African Population Census, 1948', *Population Studies*, December 1949.
[4] Kuczynski, op. cit. vol. ii, pp. 120–5, 215–27, 313–22, 345–9.
[5] *Report of East Africa Royal Commission, 1953–1955*, Cmd. 9475, pp. 30–34.

a preliminary period of training. The actual count followed the process of 'group' enumeration: that is to say, that the enumeration form normally embraced a household, and showed the number of males and females in it, together with the distribution of age groups.

The material provided by the census of 1931 for Tanganyika and Kenya had not been sufficiently accurate to allow of a reliable estimate being made of the rate of annual increase in the 17-year period that terminated in 1948, though Uganda provides somewhat better material for the purpose. The East Africa Royal Commission 1953–5 quotes with approval the view held by the Director of the East Africa Statistical Department that the annual rate of natural increase over the 17 years from 1931 to 1948 was 1 per cent. in Tanganyika, 1·4 per cent. in Uganda, and 1·9 per cent. in Kenya. In general terms he thought that the annual rate of natural increase in East Africa for this period had been between 1 per cent. and 1·75 per cent. It is of interest to note that the Commission discounted the view, so frequently expressed in East Africa, that the growth of the African population has exceeded the overall ability of the economy of the three territories to support it.[1]

Zanzibar has a somewhat better census record than many other territories. There was a census of the whole population in 1910; separate counts of non-Natives in 1921 and Natives in 1924; a census of the whole population in 1931 and again in 1948. It was an advantage that circumstances permitted of the last census being taken on a single night;[2] and the material available seems to justify the conclusion that there had been a modest increase of 0·05 per cent. annually between 1931 and 1945.

British West African Territories

In the British West African dependencies there was in theory a decennial census from 1871 onwards, but this was in practice only a partial count, often referring only to special areas. Taking the territories in detail, the Gold Coast has a record of counts of varying value which began in 1891 and were made in whole or in part every ten years until 1931; after that there was no census until 1948. There was in the Gold Coast no system of poll-tax registers such as furnished the Administrations of East Africa with a rough-and-ready system of enumeration; the earlier counts were described as the result of 'inquiries made from Chiefs and Elders of the Quarters and Companies', but the census of 1921 was an attempt at complete enumeration.

It was, however, admitted that in the relatively backward Northern Territories the enumeration took on occasion the form of receiving from the Chiefs' messengers 'a number of calabashes filled with beans, ground-

---

[1] Ibid. p. 30.   [2] *Notes on the Census of the Zanzibar Protectorate*, 1948.

nuts, and stones representing the number of males, females, and children'.[1]
In 1931 the census was more fully organized; there were a number of paid
enumerators, and the Chief Census Officer was able to congratulate himself that he had been able to dispense with the method of counting by
'cowries, stones, or similar convenient articles'.

The enumeration effected was probably more complete than in most of
the counts carried out at that date, though it was not possible to secure
accuracy in the data regarding age distribution, occupation, or the like.[2]
Dr. Kuczynski formed the opinion that the African population of the Gold
Coast and Togoland, which was shown in this census as 3,160,386, might
have been any figure between 2,950,000 and 3,400,000.[3] The census of
1948 was organized on a comprehensive scale; 39 Census Districts were
formed, and the Census Officer in charge of each was empowered to engage
supervisors and enumerators. It was decided (as in the Rhodesias) to
leave the collection of subsidiary data (as for example those bearing on
fertility) to a separate sampling census, thus enabling the questions asked
to be reduced to a minimum. The result of the two censuses of 1931 and
1948 would seem to provide a sufficiently reliable basis for an estimate of
the growth of the population of the Gold Coast; the total increase of roughly
30 per cent. during the intervening period of 16 years does not seem unreasonable in view of the fact that it includes a considerable element of
labour immigration from French territories employed on the mines and
the cocoa farms.

Nigeria has a somewhat longer record of counts or 'censuses' than the
Gold Coast, for they began in 1866 and from 1871 onwards were taken
every ten years till 1931; there was then no census till 1952–3.[4] Before
1911, however, actual enumeration was practically confined to Lagos, and
so far at all events as concerns the Northern Region, there was only a
rough estimate based on the tax register. The census of 1921 took a more
regular form, in so far that it attempted a house-to-house enumeration in
rural areas and a more intensive count in the larger towns.[5]

The census of 1931 was designed to include a full count in the towns,
but the enumeration was in effect confined to Lagos and a part of the
Northern Region, so that for 95 per cent. of the total area the only figures
were those obtained from existing records, brought where possible up to
date. This gave a total of 21,902,000 for all Nigeria, but its deficiencies
were obvious, and expert opinion was only able to conclude that the
population in 1931 was probably not much under 18½ million and probably

---

[1] *Census Report of Gold Coast*, 1921.
[2] A. W. Cardinall, *The Gold Coast, 1931*, vols. i and ii, 1932.
[3] Kuczynski, op. cit. vol. i, p. 2.
[4] Northern Region, July 1952; Western Region, December 1952; Eastern Region, June
1953.
[5] C. K. Meek, *The Northern Tribes of Nigeria*, vol. ii, 1925, p. 169.

not much over 22 million.[1] The census of 1952 was on a more comprehensive scale than any hitherto attempted in Nigeria and involved the employment of an extensive organization. It gave a total population of 31,171,383, comprising 15,354 non-Africans and 31,156,029 Africans. On the basis of the expert view held of the census of 1931 Nigeria has therefore had an increase of population amounting to some figure between 12½ and 9 million during the 21 years intervening between the two census periods.

Sierra Leone has had 'censuses' of various kinds from 1802 onwards, but the earlier of these comprised only the small Colony area, and the first to include the Protectorate as well as the Colony was that of 1911. The Protectorate, it should be observed, comprises about 94 per cent. of the total population of the territory. But even the 'census' of 1911 was not a real count of the population of the Protectorate; it was officially described as an estimate 'based on such information as could by approximation be furnished by District Officers'; these had a tax register as basis, and employed various expedients for estimating the total population. One Commissioner, clearly a man of precise temperament, estimated that for every three houses there were 2·1 boys, 2·8 girls, 4·2 men, and 5·6 women; other authorities adopted more general percentages, as, for instance, that there were in each tribe 20 per cent. men, 30 per cent. women, and 50 per cent. children.[2]

The succeeding 'census' of 1921 followed the same procedure in the Protectorate. Plans were made for a complete enumeration in 1931, but in the event they were so far modified that actual enumeration was on a very small scale, possibly not exceeding 6 per cent. of the total population of the Protectorate. The census of 1947–8 was also incomplete; a full count was taken in the Colony area in 1947, but only 'test counts' were made in the Protectorate in the following year. No special establishment was employed, and it is not claimed that the result did more than give some guide to the distribution of the population.[3]

In Gambia censuses were taken in 1851 and 1871, and thereafter every ten years up to 1931, but it was not until 1901 that they included the Protectorate (which had been proclaimed in 1889) as well as the Colony. The Protectorate was not, however, at this time under active administration, and though the estimate made in 1911 was probably an improvement on that of 1901, it was admitted at the time to be little more than a rough approximation. The censuses of 1921 and of 1931 were closer estimates, based partly on tax registers, but there was a large margin for error in making any estimate on the basis of those figures, owing to the fluctuation in the seasonal influx of the large body of 'Strange Farmers'[4] from French

[1] *Census of Nigeria*, vol. i, 1931, p. 2; Kuczynski, op. cit. vol. i, pp. 2, 572.
[2] *Census Report of Sierra Leone*, 1911, pp. 3, 4, 35.
[3] *Colonial Reports: Sierra Leone*, 1951, pp. 9–10.   [4] *N.A.*, Part III, p. 347.

territory. The total African population of Gambia as shown in the count of 1931 was 199,246, and it was considered in 1948 that the correct figure was probably not less than 180,000 and not more than 230,000.

Belgian Territories

Belgium has, as already stated, had special reason for interest in the population trends of the Belgian Congo, but she has not so far followed the procedure of territorial enumeration which has been common in most of the British dependencies. The Government has apparently attached less importance to obtaining a record of total figures as shown by such an enumeration than to securing the statistical material needed for the improvement of its health organization or the regulation of supplies of labour for industry. This material cannot in its view be obtained by a general census, owing to the lack of machinery for eliciting the required information. Since about 1922, however, the Administration has maintained in a large part of the Colony a card-index containing an individual record (*fiche*) of each member of the population, and this is linked with the regulation which requires each adult male to possess a *livret d'identité*.[1] The *fiches* are prepared and periodically brought up to date by European District Assistants, who conduct their inquiries on the spot. Though initiated primarily as a basis for payment of the poll tax, the *fiche* now contains not only the name of the taxpayer, but the names and ages of his dependants.

The system has obvious advantages for the purpose above mentioned,[2] but for demographic purposes its use has been limited by the fact that it has not yet been extended to the whole territory; it was stated in fact in 1945 that it applied only to 82 per cent. of the whole.[3] It is clear, moreover, that if it is to be effective it must be kept regularly up to date, and it is noteworthy that the system was in abeyance for some years of the Second World War.

On the other hand, the study of population movements has been assisted by careful 'check' counts, made every year in sample areas. In 1951, for instance, a check was made of 251 groups, involving some 375,000 individuals. The continuous process of the *enquêtes démographiques* has further been augmented by the intensive investigations made regarding health conditions, such, for example, as that conducted in the Lower Congo by the *Fondation Reine Élisabeth pour l'Assistance Médicale aux Indigènes* (Foréami).[4] The careful studies made of population statistics for a number of years seem to justify a large measure of confidence in the correctness of the figures for the Belgian Congo shown in Table I.[5]

---

[1] *Ordonnance* no. 30 of 14 March 1935, Article 3; amended by nos. 21–75 of 25 February 1948.
[2] *Bull. I.R.C.B.*, vol. xvii, 1946, pp. 875 ff.
[3] *Rapport Annuel du Congo Belge, 1951*, p. 71; 1952, pp. 64–77.
[4] See below, p. 1091. See also Worthington, op. cit. p. 565.   [5] See below, p. 143.

Ruanda Urundi has an exceptionally dense population; the Belgian Congo with 40 times its area has only three times its population;[1] the density of population in the Congo is only 12·2 to the square mile, in Ruanda Urundi it is 184.[2] The enumeration has presented unusual difficulties. The rough estimates made before 1914 gave totals that varied from 3 to 5 million, but no explanation was given of the basis of calculation. The estimates subsequently made were based, in the first instance, on a registration of all able-bodied adult males, and afterwards on a registration of all adult males and their families, the record being maintained on a card-index system similar to that used in the Belgian Congo.

It is clear that great importance was attached by the Administration to this record and to the correct maintenance of the *fiches*.[3] During the Second World War, however, the system was handed over to the Chiefs and sub-Chiefs for keeping up to date, and the resulting records varied greatly in accuracy. Special field studies have subsequently been made by medical and other officers, which have covered roughly 4 per cent. of the population; these suggest an annual population growth of about 2 per cent., but this figure admittedly has the value of only an estimate. A study of possible methods for obtaining more reliable statistics was undertaken in 1952 by the Central African Scientific Research Institute (I.R.S.A.C.),[4] which arranged for a sample census to be made, covering about 9 per cent. of the population. As a result steps are now being taken to re-establish the system of card-index registration on a more reliable basis.

French Territories

No census in the ordinary sense of the term has been taken of the population in the French West African territories, save in the case of Europeans (or in some cases Europeans and *assimilés*),[5] of whom censuses were made in 1946 and 1951. For the large African population it has only been found possible to proceed 'par sondages, approximations et extrapolations en attendant des données plus estimables'.[6] One of the major purposes has been to assess the degree of density in the different parts of the territory as a guide to schemes of development. Though a number of medical studies have also been made of factors such as fertility, infant mortality and the implications of the sex ratio, these have had only a limited value for demographic purposes. The local records of population are stated to be brought up to date every three years, but being based partly on tax collection they are clearly only estimates.[7]

[1] United Nations, Department of Social Affairs, *Population Division—Study No. 15.*
[2] *The Times*, 28 November 1955.
[3] *Rapport Annuel du Ruanda-Urundi, 1950*, p. 158; ibid. *1952*, p. 239.
[4] *Civilisations*, vol. iii, 1953, p. 391. See also Pierre Gourou, *La Densité de la Population au Ruanda-Urundi*, 1953.   [5] See below, p. 207.
[6] J. Richard-Molard, in *Enc. A.O.F.*, pp. 125–32.   [7] Worthington, op. cit. p. 566.

Much the same observations apply to the estimates made of the population of French Equatorial Africa. Here also the figures are described only as 'approximations, indiquant un simple ordre de grandeur; le taux de l'erreur même échappe au calcul'.[1] The population was given as between 8 and 10 million in 1909, and under 5 million in 1913. These figures do not necessarily reveal a decrease in the population; they indicate rather that the explorer or traveller making the first computation calculated the density of the whole territory as the result of observation of a limited and populous section of it. 'Ils se laissaient guider de village en village, très souvent le long des cours d'eau—glissant, en somme, le long d'une façade de vitalité et de prospérité.'[2]

The most recent estimate suggests a population of the range of $4\frac{1}{4}$ to $4\frac{1}{2}$ million. A regular census has, however, been taken of the Europeans and *assimilés*. The process of estimating Africans is complicated by the fact that a large part of the population is nomadic. Medical studies have been made of factors affecting population trends, but these are founded on an even smaller range of observations than in French West Africa. On the whole, official opinion in French Equatorial Africa seems doubtful whether the facts actually point to an increase of the African population or the reverse.[3]

Portuguese Territories

Angola is one of those countries where the population was at an early stage the subject of a great variety of estimates; they ranged, indeed, from a total of 4 to 12 million. The European community first came under a regular census in 1925, when it was relatively small; but there has since that period been a considerable growth of the European community, stimulated by the effort made by the Government to promote emigration from Portugal to the Colony, where the Huila plateau has been commended both by the Government and by unofficial bodies as specially well adapted for settlement. Since 1945 the Colonization Fund has assisted 12,000 persons to emigrate from Portugal, or an average of 2,000 a year, but though they are provided with an equipped farm, a house and stock, they have not readily adapted themselves to the vocation of peasant farmers, and few remain as permanent settlers.[4] There is at the same time a considerable influx of European traders and others, so that the total White population has grown rapidly.

In accordance with the doctrine of assimilation favoured by Portugal, recent census operations have embraced the whole of that section of the population which is classed as *civilizada*. In Angola the figures for 1950

---

[1] Henri Ziéglé, *Afrique Équatoriale Française*, 1952, p. 51.
[2] Ibid. p. 52.   [3] *Enc. A.E.F.*, p. 103.
[4] Speech of Dr. Mendes Correa in National Assembly, 12 March 1952.

gave a total of 135,355 for the section of *civilizada*, which included 78,826 White, 26,355 Half-caste, and 30,089 African *assimilados*.[1] The number of the *não-civilizada* section of the population, shown as 4,009,911 in 1950, represents an estimate based on the poll-tax registers.

Under the Native tax system now in force a taxation booklet (*caderneta*) is issued to all adult males; the responsibility for the issue of the booklets rests on the District Intendants, who act on the information supplied by Headmen. Besides providing space for the record of tax payments, the booklet contains also space for the names of the wife or wives of the tax-payer and his children, with dates of birth. The information provided by these statements may not have the same value as that of a regular census, but it is claimed by Portuguese authorities that the total figures of population can be accepted as reliable.

The population statistics of Mozambique are prepared on the same basis. In 1950 the *população civilizada* numbered 92,619, of which 48,813 were Whites, 1,615 Yellow (*amarelos*), who are Chinese, 12,673 Asians (Indian), 25,165 half-caste (*mestiços*), and 4,353 *negros*. The *não-civilizada* section, predominantly of course African, were shown as numbering 5,640,363,[2] the total population according to the 1950 census being 5,732,982.

The compilation of a census in Mozambique has been complicated by two factors. The first is the continuous efflux of Africans into Nyasaland and to a lesser extent into Northern Rhodesia. Something has already been said of the large number of Nguru settlers in Nyasaland,[3] but there are also numerous cases where the movement is not a genuine migration, for it often happens that by polygamous marriage the labourer supports a domicile and cultivates crops in either territory. The second factor is the migration of Africans to the labour markets in the Union of South Africa in pursuance of the Convention between the two Governments to which reference will subsequently be made in the chapter dealing with labour problems.[4] The total number of Africans working outside their own territory was in 1954 estimated to be at least 200,000.

Liberia

The number of the population of Liberia is a purely conjectural figure; it has been put as low as 1 million and as high as 2½ million. It is composed chiefly of the indigenous tribes who inhabit the hinterland; the number of the dominant ruling class has been put at various figures from 12,000 to 20,000. It is descended from the so-called 'founding families', but their blood has become so diluted by intermarriage with the indigenous tribes

[1] *Anuário Estatístico do Ultramar, 1952*, p. 26.
[2] *Anuário Estatístico do Ultramar, 1952*, p. 27.
[3] See above, p. 128.   [4] See below, pp. 1378, 1385.

that their designation as America-Liberians is ceasing to be strictly accurate.[1]

PROVISION OF VITAL STATISTICS

It is the more necessary for the Administrations in Africa to consider the improvement of the organization of census operations because a periodic census is in practice the sole means at present available for ascertaining the increase or decrease in the number of the African population. There is generally speaking no such system of vital statistics in force as would afford reliable assistance in checking calculations of population trends. The maintenance of vital statistics is indispensable for many of the social activities of the modern State; it has been compared to commercial book-keeping without which no business enterprise can hope to succeed.[2] But the consistent recording of vital statistics has so far been confined mainly to the European section of the population; where it has been extended to Africans it has for the most part been limited to the urban areas.

In the Union of South Africa, for instance, legislation provides for the compulsory registration of births and deaths of Europeans, Asians, Coloured persons, and Natives in urban areas.[3] The registration of African births and deaths in urban areas is, however, so incomplete at present that it cannot properly be used for calculating the figures of natural increase.[4] The record of African marriages is even less reliable, partly owing to the diversity of practice observed in the Union in regard to the recognition of marriages concluded under African custom.[5] The law of Southern Rhodesia regarding the registration of vital statistics is similar to that of South Africa;[6] though the registration of deaths among urban Africans is sufficiently accurate, that of births is very defective.[7]

The position in regard to the High Commission Territories and the British Dependencies in East and West Africa has been described at length in Dr. Kuczynski's two volumes already referred to. In the majority of these territories there is at present no system of registration of births and deaths among Africans. In some others, as in Northern Rhodesia, Kenya, and the Gold Coast, the law provides for their registration in townships or 'special areas', and for some years Native Authority Ordinances have provided for the issue of rules for the compulsory registration of births and deaths.

[1] T. Hodgkin, 'Education and Social Change in Liberia', *West Africa*, 12 September 1954, p. 847.   [2] P. G. Edge, *Vital Records in the Tropics*, 1932, p. 1.

[3] Act no. 17 of 1923 amended by no. 7 of 1934 and no. 5 of 1943.

[4] *O.Y.S.A., 1949*, pp. 1134, 1137, 1146. Ibid. *1950*, p. 1200. See also *Handbook on Race Relations in South Africa*, 1949, op. 26, 411.

[5] A. Phillips, ed., *Survey of African Marriage and Family Life*, 1953, pp. 178 ff.

[6] Births and Deaths Registration Act, Chapter 149 of the Statute Law.

[7] *O.Y.S.R., 1952*, pp. 278, 302.

But though provision for registration has been made in these various ways, there is in the majority of cases the same result; either the regulation is neglected, or the figures are so incomplete as to have no statistical value. Only in Uganda is a regular record kept by Native Authorities in rural areas; in this case the results have been described as useful in some *sazas* (counties), though entirely inadequate in others.[1]

LIMITATIONS OF PRESENT-DAY TECHNIQUES

It will be recognized that in the present circumstances of Africa a census, however carefully organized, must have definite limitations. The usual methods of enumeration can record certain simple facts about the African population, such as their number, sex, tribe, or religion, though the last category can only be described in standardized terms more familiar to Europeans than to Africans themselves. But the returns obtained in a census cannot in most cases be trusted to provide dependable figures of marital condition or age distribution or literacy among Africans. Though efforts have been made to overcome the lack of age-sense in the African by 'grouping' ages for census purposes (as for example, infants, children, active adults, &c.), the grouping adopted for use must in practice have such variable limits as to deprive the results of any accuracy. The greater part of the elaborate statistics of age distribution among Africans which are now published for many areas are without any real value.[2]

Statistics showing the ratio between births and deaths of Africans are as a rule equally unreliable. The difficulty of depending on census returns for statistics of literacy is illustrated by the case of Nyasaland. On the strength of the census of 1931 it was generally considered that Nyasaland, where over 50 per cent. of Africans were shown as literate in the vernacular, had attained an outstanding measure of literacy. The census of 1945, however, which adopted a different test of literacy, reduced this figure at once to a mere 6½ per cent. of the *de facto* population.[3]

Technique of Sampling

Modern experience, and in particular that of some of the censuses made from 1948 onwards,[4] goes to show the advisability of leaving details of this character (and particularly information as to the factor of fertility)

[1] Kuczynski, op. cit. vol. ii, pp. 271 ff.

[2] See, for example, the *Colonial Reports, Uganda*, 1951, p. 18, and *Swaziland*, 1952, p. 15, or the statistics of age distribution published for Nyasaland, Portuguese Guinea, Zanzibar, or the Union of South Africa in the *Demographic Yearbook* of the United Nations Organization for 1952.

[3] *N.A.*, Part II, p. 22.

[4] C. J. Martin, 'The East African Population Census, 1948', *Population Studies*, December 1949, J. R. Shaul and C. A. Myburgh, 'Census of Southern Rhodesia', *Population Studies*, December 1948 and 1949. *Statistical Bulletin of Northern Rhodesia*, January and June 1951.

to a separate sampling census. It must be admitted that there is still much to be learnt of the technique of sampling in African conditions,[1] and it must, moreover, be recognized that whatever the advance made in technique, there will remain the problem of securing enumerators who can elicit the information required and make an intelligent use of it. For the success of the sampling system, it is advisable that the process should be continuous, thus allowing the persons engaged in it to acquire experience in its practice; it is essential, among other things, to acquire the local knowledge which will ensure that the sections chosen for sampling are representative of the whole population.

The use of a well-organized system of sampling will help in some measure to supply the material for which authorities holding charge of census operations have in the past depended on the studies made by medical men. Though directed primarily to serving the needs of the health organizations, many of these inquiries have made a close study of demographic factors.[2] They have in particular provided material relating to problems such as fertility or infantile mortality, which has proved a corrective to some of the generalizations previously current on these subjects. In a sense these inquiries can be regarded as 'sampling' on a small scale by patient and intelligent observers, though their range has sometimes been so small as to reduce their value for demographic studies on a more extended scale.

CONCLUSIONS ON THE GROWTH OF POPULATION

There is nothing unusual in the fact that most of the Governments in Africa failed for many years to recognize the need for a census or for improving the methods of enumeration. The decennial census was first taken in Great Britain in 1801, but neither then nor in 1811, when the country was engaged in the Napoleonic wars, were the figures regarded as precise, and it was not until peace had been restored that the census of 1821 reached even approximate accuracy. The case of early censuses in Africa was not very different. The census was at first regarded with suspicion by Africans themselves as a prelude to some innovation to increase taxation or to produce more labour and accordingly to be avoided at all costs. If some concession be now made for the difficulties due to the lack of enumerators and the illiteracy of those enumerated, the population statistics which have become available of recent years in Africa

[1] H. Sonnabend, 'Demographic Samples in the Study of Primitive and Backward Populations', *South African Journal of Economics*, vol. ii, no. 3. See also *Report on the 1950 Demographic Sample Survey of the African Population of Northern Rhodesia*.

[2] See references in Worthington, op. cit. pp. 557–90, and Kuczynski, op. cit. vols. i and ii, *passim*.

probably compare not unfavourably with those available in the Great Britain of 1821.

But what concerns Administrations in Africa is not so much the imperfections of the census in the past as the trends of population increase or decrease in the future. The underlying assumption of the policies with regard to soil and water conservation, land apportionment, irrigation or forestry protection which are considered in subsequent chapters is that there is likely to be an accelerated increase in the number of the indigenous population. It has even been held in some quarters that what is held to be an alarming increase can only be kept in check by the inculcation in the African community of modern methods of birth control. A progressive increase in the population is the assumption of all long-term development plans. It is, therefore, pertinent to inquire how far this prediction is borne out by statistics.

The part of Africa which lies south of the Sahara does not of course represent a definite geographic or ethnic unit; it is indeed composed of countries situated in different climatic zones and with diverse economies and interests. No special significance attaches therefore to any estimate that may be made of the population trends in the area south of the Sahara as a whole, but any verifiable trends may be of great importance to the individual countries concerned, and in particular to those which, like the Union of South Africa or the Rhodesias or Kenya, have a permanent settlement of Europeans, or to others, like the Belgian Congo, where the supply of labour is a problem of increasing difficulty.

The evidence available does not reveal an abnormal or even an unusual rate of increase in those countries where the taking of a census has been most systematic. In the Union of South Africa the annual rate of growth of the African population in the period 1904–11 has been calculated at 2·03 per cent.; for the period 1911 to 1921 it was 1·57 per cent., for 1921 to 1936 it was 2·29 per cent., but for the period 1936 to 1946 it fell to 1·73 per cent.[1] Taking again the Gold Coast as an instance of an area in West Africa in which the censuses appear to have received more attention over a series of years than in many other territories, the annual rate of increase for the period 1921 to 1931 was recorded as 3·3 per cent., but from 1931 to 1948 it was only 1·6 per cent. It should be noted, moreover, that though the figures of 1931 and 1948 have been held to be fairly reliable (within the limits applying to most censuses taken in Africa) the figures of 1921 were regarded with some suspicion by the Census Officer of 1931.[2]

In most other territories the early estimates suffered from so many imperfections as to fail to provide any reliable data from which a valid

[1] *Handbook on Race Relations in South Africa*, 1949, p. 13; see also above, p. 126.
[2] A. W. Cardinall, *The Gold Coast, 1931*, vols. i and ii.

conclusion of the rate of increase or decrease of the African population can be drawn. In this connexion particular interest attaches to the examination made by the East Africa Royal Commission 1953–5 of the older census results in East Africa.[1] Since the Second World War, however, much progress has been made in establishing statistical departments and in the collection of statistics. Censuses taken since the war have made so marked an improvement that they may be generally regarded as recording an approximately accurate figure of the population; but it will be necessary to await a second post-war census before it will be possible to calculate with any confidence the direction of population trends. So far as any conclusion can be based on data collected year by year since the most recent census, it would appear that the present rate of increase in British Colonial territories and the Union of South Africa may be assumed to be between $1\frac{1}{2}$ and 2 per cent. per annum.[2]

[1] See above, p. 131.
[2] For comparative population trends for Europe and America, see above, p. 116.

TABLE I

Country	Area (sq. miles)	Most recent census figure	Density per sq. mile
Angola	481,351	4,145,266 (1950)	8·6
Basutoland	11,716	561,000 (1946)	47·9
Bechuanaland	275,000	296,310 (1946)	1·1
Belgian Congo	904,756	11,660,798 (1951)	12·9
Cameroons, British	34,081	1,455,000 (1953)	4·3
Cameroons, French	166,489	3,077,000 (1952)	18·5
French Equatorial Africa . . .	968,860	4,434,800 (1951)[1]	4·6
French West Africa . . .	1,815,768	17,361,700 (1951)[1]	9·6
Gambia	4,003	289,405 (1951)	72·3
Gold Coast	78,802	4,118,450 (1948)	52·3
Kenya	224,960	5,405,966 (1948)	24·0
Liberia[2]	43,000	..	35·1
Mozambique	297,654	5,732,982 (1950)	19·3
Nigeria	338,919	31,171,383 (1952)	92·0
Nyasaland	37,374	2,049,914 (1945)	54·8
Portuguese Guinea	13,948	510,777 (1950)	36·6
Rhodesia, Northern	287,640	1,816,000 (1950)	6·3
Rhodesia, Southern	150,330	2,146,000 (1951)[3]	14·3
Ruanda Urundi	20,900	4,110,932 (1952)	196·7
Sierra Leone	27,925	1,858,275 (1948)[4]	66·5
South-West Africa . . .	317,725	417,948 (1951)	1·3
Spanish Guinea	10,852	198,669 (1950)	18·3
Swaziland	6,704	185,215 (1946)	27·6
Tanganyika Territory . . .	362,000	7,477,677 (1948)	20·7
Togoland, British	13,041	382,768 (1948)	29·4
Togoland, French	21,893	1,029,945 (1952)	47·0
Uganda	93,981	4,958,520 (1948)	52·8
Union of South Africa . . .	472,491	12,648,123 (1951)	26·8
Zanzibar (incl. Pemba) . . .	1,020	264,162 (1948)	259·0

[1] European census only in this year, African figures are estimates.

[2] The estimate of 1,510,000 (1937), given by U.N. *Demographic Yearbook, 1954,* is used to calculate the density per sq. mile.

[3] The statistics for Natives included in this figure are based upon extrapolations from the 1948 'Sample Survey' and upon the number of migrant Natives employed in 1951.

[4] A census was made in the Colony, but was only partial in the Protectorate.

TABLE II. Latest Population Returns

Year	Country	African	European	Others	
1950 Census	Angola	4,036,687	78,826	29,648	(Asian and Coloured)
1946 Census	Basutoland	561,289	1,689	876	(Asian and Coloured)
1946 Census	Bechuanaland	292,755	2,379	1,176	
1952 Estimated	Belgian Congo	11,788,711	76,764	*	(mainly European)
1952–3 Census	Cameroons, British	1,439,800	758	*	
1952 Estimated	Cameroons, French	3,063,827	13,173	...	
1953 Estimated	French Equatorial Africa	4,413,100	21,885[1]	...	
1953 Estimated	French West Africa	17,299,500	62,236[1]	...	
1953 Estimated	Gambia	288,317[2]	544	*	(half are European: majority of the remainder Syrian and Lebanese)
Mid-1953 Est.	Gold Coast	4,468,970	7,100	1,930	(Lebanese and Syrian)
1948 Census	Kenya	5,251,120	42,200[3]	164,800[3]	(about ⅔ Indian and Goan; ⅓ Arab and others)
Estimated	Liberia	2,500,000[4]	c.1,000	...	
1950 Census	Mozambique	5,644,716	48,813	39,453	(Hindus, 12,673; Mestiços, 25,165; Chinese, 1,615)
1952–3 Census	Nigeria	31,115,000	15,339	*	(mainly European)
1953 Estimated	Nyasaland	2,501,010	4,387	6,178	(Asian)
1950 Census	Portuguese Guinea	503,935	2,263	4,568	(Mestiços)
1953 Estimated	Rhodesia, Northern	1,960,000	50,000	5,000	(Asian and Coloured)
1953 Estimated	Rhodesia, Southern	2,070,000	160,000	10,900	(Asian and Coloured)
1952 Census	Ruanda Urundi	4,102,486	5,121	3,325	(1,997 Asian; 1,328 Mulâtres)
1947–8 Est.	Sierra Leone	1,855,237[5]	964	2,074	(Asian)
1951 Census	South-West Africa	368,333[6]	49,612	...	
1953 Estimated	Spanish Guinea	194,227	4,436	...	
1946 Census	Swaziland	181,269	3,201	745	(Coloured)
1953 Estimated	Tanganyika	7,965,000	20,300	84,000	(mainly Asian)
1953 Estimated	Togoland, British	416,000	less than 100	...	
1952 Estimated	Togoland, French	1,028,519	1,427	...	
1953 Estimated	Uganda	5,300,000	7,000	50,000	(Asian)
1951 Census	Union of South Africa	8,535,341[7]	2,642,713	1,470,069	(1,103,405 Coloured, remainder Asian)
1948 Census	Zanzibar	199,860	296	64,006	(44,560 Arab; 15,211 Asian and others)
Totals	Africa south of the Sahara	131,939,869	3,324,526	1,938,748	

TOTAL ALL RACES 137,203,143

* Included in the European total.
[1] Includes assimilés.
[2] 1951 Census in Colony area.
[3] 1953 Estimates.
[4] There is no census and no reliable estimate of the population, which has been given as between 1 and 2½ million.
[5] Of whom 30,447 are classed without explanation as 'non-Natives'.
[6] Including 'Coloured'.
[7] Figure for Africans provisional.

CHAPTER V

POLITICAL AND SOCIAL OBJECTIVES

CONCEPTS UNDERLYING THE OBJECTIVES OF
STATE POLICY

IT is the singular fate of Africa that so many of its countries should be subject to the political control of one or other of the European Powers; in the area south of the Sahara there are indeed only two countries, the Union of South Africa and Liberia, which have full autonomy in their internal and external affairs. A discussion of the objectives indicated by the systems now in force in the various dependencies in Africa would, if it were to be complete, involve a comprehensive examination of the Colonial policies of the Powers concerned; but it would clearly be beyond the scope of this Survey to explore the full range of factors which have in the past determined the direction of these policies. Such factors are to be found partly in the inherent character and the domestic history of the metropolitan peoples, and partly in the events which have shaped the general course of international affairs. The influence of the French Revolution or of the movement for the abolition of the slave trade is written into the Colonial policies of the European Powers no less effectively than the consequences of the economic upheaval that succeeded the First World War or the manifestation of international interest in the future of the dependent peoples which at one period found expression at Geneva and later in the Organization of the United Nations. It will be possible here to do little more than discuss the objectives of the policies now followed in the different units of government as they appear today, whether these be autonomous States or dependencies of Colonial Powers.

It is admittedly difficult to epitomize policies which have been subject to influences coming from so many sources; but, if we take in the first instance the objective of current policy in the Union of South Africa, this has been expressed by its Government with an exceptional degree of clarity. Its basis is the determination to maintain the state of civilization as established in the Union by the European community, and it is held that this cannot be adequately safeguarded if non-Europeans are allowed to intrude into the social or economic field occupied by Europeans. Non-Europeans can be allowed (and are indeed to be encouraged and assisted) to progress to the full extent of their capacity in their own social or economic field of action; but this is to remain a separate field, and it is implicit that, though they are to be permitted a considerable measure of control over

their own affairs, they will not be allowed to share in the political government of the country as a whole. This must remain in the hands of the
European community.

The policy which now holds the field in Southern Rhodesia, though
equally insistent on the maintenance of a civilization of European pattern,
does not contemplate so complete a separation of the European and non-
European fields of social and economic activity, nor would it entirely
debar the non-European from a share in the government of the country.
He is to receive from the State all possible help in improving his standard
of living, and when he attains a position in which he is qualified to take
part in the political life of the country he is to be allowed to do so; but it
must be the European community which will decide both the time and
the measure of the part that he is to play in it.

In point of constitutional form, the Union of South Africa remains a
member of the British Commonwealth of Nations as recognized in the
Statute of Westminster of 1931,[1] but its Government has in recent years
laid an increasing emphasis on its right to opt for itself the status of a
Republic and to stand either within or without the Commonwealth as it
may decide. Southern Rhodesia, now a member of the newly constituted
Federation of Rhodesia and Nyasaland, foresees the future of the Federation in a status equivalent to that of the Dominions which joined in
acknowledging membership of the British Commonwealth of Nations as
constituted in 1931.[2]

As regards the position of the other territories lying south of the Sahara
which are now under British control, it is for the present purpose im-
material whether they bear the designation of Colonies, Protectorates, or
Protected States. The status of different areas has often been determined
rather by historical accident than by legal theory.[3] As regards all these
constitutional entities alike the British Government has made it clear in
a series of authoritative statements which have been consistently repeated
for many years that they can look forward to achieving a status of
self-government.[4] But unlike the terms 'Responsible Government' or
'Dominion Status',[5] the term 'self-government' has no precise connotation in British constitutional practice.

[1] K. C. Wheare, *The Statute of Westminster and Dominion Status*, 4th ed., 1949, pp. 139–40.

[2] *East Africa and Rhodesia*, 9 December 1954, p. 450.

[3] A. Berriedale Keith, *The Government of the British Empire*, 1935, p. 463. For the distinction
between political units under these various designations see the following: O. Hood Phillips,
The Constitutional Law of Great Britain and the Commonwealth, 1952, p. 676; M. Wight, *British
Colonial Constitutions, 1947*, 1952, pp. 5–14. M. F. Lindley, *The Acquisition and Government of
Backward Territories in International Law*, 1926, p. 183. *Current Legal Problems*, 1954, ed. G. W.
Keeton and G. Schwarzenberger, 1954, p. 177.

[4] *Problems of Parliamentary Government in Colonies* (Hansard Society), 1953, pp. 116–31.

[5] For an illustration of the difference between the terms 'self-government' and 'responsible
government', see Lord Ronaldshay, *Life of Lord Curzon*, vol. iii, 1928, pp. 168–70.

So far as the dependencies are concerned, it has never been defined in any authoritative statement of policy.[1] That is not merely a concession to the tradition of elasticity which has for so long been favoured by the British in constitutional matters. There is a more practical reason. The dependencies comprise a large number of units at very different stages of political progress. They include some which have a considerable settled European community, though with a numerically predominant Native population. There are others which have practically no settled European community, but contain indigenous elements that are advancing rapidly in political aspirations and experience. There are again others which have no such elements and in which indigenous African society is still at a tribal stage. It would therefore have been premature to attempt any determination of the content of self-government which would cover all the possibilities involved.

At an early stage, however, one qualification was normally added; the objective was announced as 'self-government within the Empire', a phrase which has in later years been modified to that of 'self-government within the Commonwealth'. This qualification has represented a legitimate aspiration entertained by the Government and people of the United Kingdom, but its significance has in other respects been only notional. If self-government is to amount to political autonomy, it clearly cannot bind a dependency to any final decision as to the nature of its external ties; if it is not to amount to autonomy, then it will be something less than the Colonial peoples have been encouraged to expect. It has never been suggested that force would be or could be used to prevent a self-governing unit from moving out of the orbit of the Commonwealth should it desire to do so.

The objective of French Colonial policy has differed in one material respect from that of the British. There has existed from the first a basic conception of the unity between metropolitan France and her dependencies, and this has in recent years taken concrete form in the Constitution of the *Union Française*.[2] There are two facets to this conception of union. On the one hand, it involves a very wide extension of French citizenship in favour of the non-European inhabitants of the dependencies, together with a considerable measure of direct representation in the metropolitan parliamentary institutions; on the other, it contemplates the maintenance of a definite measure of legislative and executive control from the metropolis, though it is intended that this shall be combined with an extension of the powers enjoyed by the institutions of Local Government within the Colonies.

The measure of self-government which the French people is at present

[1] Wight, op. cit. p. 18.
[2] See below, pp. 211–14.

pledged to introduce must be understood in this sense. It has been said that one must not in this respect interpret the refusal of self-government as the refusal of all ideas of liberation; the attitude of the French on this question 'involves the fullest equality in marriage, but no divorce'.[1] But that attitude leaves open a problem of which only the future can reveal the solution. It lies in the possibility that the movement directed towards a formal measure of political integration with the metropolis may encounter a sentiment of African nationalism or self-determination which may demand a new interpretation of the French concept of union.

It is less easy to categorize the Belgian outlook on the constitutional future of the Belgian Congo, for as a former Belgian Colonial Minister has said, 'Belgians are reluctant to define their colonial policy; but they are proud of their first realizations and sure of the rightness of their intentions'.[2] In political matters the approach has, in the words of another Belgian authority, been one of 'cautious empiricism'.[3] Belgium had no colonial history before its Government took over the administration of the territory from the Congo Free State. In the period of a little under 50 years which has since elapsed, it has concentrated its attention on the economic development of the country and the improvement of the standards of life of its inhabitants, rather than on the development of political institutions. The institutions of government to which it admits both the European community (which at the last census numbered over 70,000) and the non-European population are still only of a consultative character. The most significant indication of the future trend of policy lies in the recent legislation giving formal recognition to the existence of a class of African *immatriculés* who are to have a status approaching that of Belgians.[4] This may prove to be the first stage in a policy based on the recognition of a culture bar, as distinct from a colour bar, as the basis of the division of the population into two sections in respect of the grant of political rights.

There is not an equal difficulty in characterizing the current objective of Portuguese policy. From an early date there has been a marked emphasis on the unity of Portugal and its dependencies. The former Colonies are now formally designated as provinces of Portugal; they have representatives in the metropolitan Legislature; and the recent Development Plans of the Government embody schemes which apply jointly to the metropolitan and the African provinces.[5] But there is a significant difference between the application of the

---

[1] J. H. Huizinga, in *Manchester Guardian*, 11 March 1949.

[2] Pierre Wigny, 'Methods of Government of the Belgian Congo', *African Affairs*, vol. l, October 1951, pp. 310–17. See also R. Goddard in *Progress*, winter 1953–4, p. 198.

[3] G. Malengreau in *Africa Today*, 1955, pp. 337 ff.   [4] See below, p. 224.

[5] See below, pp. 230–1. See also M. Gaetano, *Colonizing Traditions, Principles and Methods of the Portuguese*, 1951. A. Durieux, *Essai sur le statut des indigènes portugais de la Guinée, de l'Angola et du Mozambique*, Mém. A.R.S.C., vol. v, no. 3, 1955, p. 4.

French doctrine of unity and that adopted by Portugal. The French principle of common citizenship derives from the equalitarian philosophy of the First Republic; the Portuguese principle of common citizenship is of earlier date and had its origin in the sentiment that an equal political status should be extended to all those subjects of the country, whatever their race or colour, who had embraced the Christian religion. The result is represented today by the definite line drawn between those who have achieved a culture entitling them to enjoy the same status as the Portuguese (the *assimilado*) and those who are still classed as 'Natives'.[1]

The Colonial policy of Spain is less clearly defined, partly no doubt because the overseas territories now remaining to her are of relatively small importance. There is, however, no question of the strength of the Spanish feeling that the African Colonies must be closely integrated with the metropolis for all economic purposes. Their political future is not so obvious, but it must be realized that the Spanish community in the Colonies is small, and that the more important section of the African population consists of immigrant labour from other territories.[2] There is, however, one significant feature in the present position. The Spanish have taken the first step in the establishment of a system which will make a formal discrimination between the 'civilized' and the 'tribal' sections of the African population, on much the same principle as has been adopted by Portugal.[3]

The Republic of Liberia stands in one sense by itself, for its major problem has not been, as elsewhere, the need for adjustment between the interests of a European Administration and those of the indigenous inhabitants of the country, but the issues arising out of the rule of a small African governing class (the Americo-Liberians) over a large indigenous community which is still mainly in the tribal stage. As will be shown in the following pages,[4] the objective of rule of the Government of Liberia has in the past been well marked; it has reflected the determination to maintain the freedom of Liberia from external control or from any such intervention (even on the part of an international body such as the League of Nations) as would curtail the authority of the governing class.

There can be no question that rule was in the past exercised by this class in its own interest, with little consideration either of the needs or the rights of the indigenous inhabitants of the country. But the position is changing, as the result of two factors. In the first place, the wide admixture of the Americo-Liberian community with the indigenous people is now tending to rob the ruling class of some of its individuality; secondly, the expansion of the economy of the country (mainly due to developments initiated by external enterprise) is making possible the extension of

[1] See below, p. 231. [2] See below, p. 234.
[3] See below, p. 234. [4] See below, pp. 235-7.

communications and of educational and health facilities to an extent which must eventually affect the balance of authority in its Government. How far the indigenous inhabitants are likely to exercise an influence over its constitutional development still remains to be seen; and the field for conjecture is the more interesting, because the gradual absorption of the more progressive members of the 'tribal' communities into the ranks of the governing class tends to deprive these communities of their natural leaders.

Principles of 'Identity' and 'Differentiation'

Whatever factors may in the past have influenced the direction taken by Colonial policies, it is clear that the conceptions held about the part which Africans can or should play in the social and political life of the country are now coming to the front as a matter of primary concern. There are some parts of the continent where this issue has been complicated by the existence of non-European communities, notably the Cape Coloured and the Asian in South Africa and the Asian in East Africa, but the major question remains that of the future relationship between Europeans and Africans. Views held on this issue have varied greatly at different times and in different places, but the two poles round which they arrange themselves may be conveniently characterized as those of 'identity' and 'differentiation'.[1] The doctrine of identity conceives the future social and political institutions of Africans as destined to be basically similar to those of Europeans; the doctrine of differentiation aims at the evolution of separate institutions appropriate to African conditions and differing both in spirit and in form from those of Europeans.

The factors which have most strongly influenced the choice between one or other of these doctrines have been, firstly, the existence in some territories (but not in others) of immigrant European communities which have made their permanent homes there, and secondly, the range of variation in the extent to which African social structures have been penetrated by influences derived from Western European civilization. It will be necessary in the ensuing paragraphs to lay special emphasis on the measure to which the political objectives now current in the different territories reflect the influence of one or another of these conflicting doctrines concerning the future status of Africans and their position in the political and social life of the country.

[1] For these terms see M. Perham's Introduction (p. vii) to J. Wheare, *The Nigerian Legislative Council*, 1950.

UNION OF SOUTH AFRICA

Nowhere can these conflicting attitudes be observed more clearly than in the Union of South Africa. It is conveniently typified by the contrast between Cecil Rhodes's phrase—'Equal rights for all civilized men south of the Zambezi'—and the well-known clause from the original Constitution of the Transvaal—'There shall be no equality between Black and White, either in Church or State'. But it is not possible to deal with this aspect of South African life without some reference also to another of its characteristic features. It is true that throughout the history of South Africa the problem of the relations between the European and the non-European communities (Bantu, Coloured, or Asian as the case may be) has been at the background of all thought given to questions of domestic policy. But since the establishment of the Union in 1910, the problem of its external relations, and more especially of its status in relation to Great Britain, has forced itself prominently on the attention of the politically minded section of Europeans. The thought given to the former of these two problems has expressed itself in the formulation of the doctrine of segregation (*apartheid*). The outcome of the concern felt in the latter problem is to be seen in the achievement by the Union of a fully autonomous status within the Commonwealth. It will be convenient to deal here in the first instance with the developments which have led to the latter result.

Sovereign Status

The Union is the first country of the African Continent to have advanced from Colonial to full sovereign status. When the new Constitution of South Africa came into force in 1910, its status was technically that of a non-sovereign but self-governing State under the Crown.[1] It was limited in the legislative sphere by the doctrine of repugnancy whereby its laws could not be in conflict with a British Act extending to it.[2] In theory, though not in practice, the British Parliament was in a position to legislate for it, particularly in matters affecting the Empire as a whole. In the executive sphere, all treaties and the issues of war and peace and foreign affairs generally were determined by the Royal Prerogative, the King acting ultimately on the advice of his Ministers in the United Kingdom. The Union had no direct diplomatic relations with foreign States. In judicial matters appeals lay, under certain conditions, from the decisions of the Supreme Court of South Africa to the Judicial Committee of the Privy Council.[3] It thus had a position which came to be generally known as that of Dominion Status.

[1] Preamble to the South Africa Act of 1909.
[2] Colonial Laws Validity Act, 1865, section 2.
[3] A. V. Dicey, *Law of the Constitution*, 9th ed. 1939, Chapter 2.

It is, however, of importance to note one characteristic of the States then constituting the Dominions of the British Empire which seems to be of greater significance than the detail of their purely constitutional relations. In the body of the Dominions the predominant influence has been the expression of certain types of European thought and manner of life. The ruling communities in them are predominantly of European stock. These conditions have prevailed also in the Union of South Africa, and the non-European communities have had no voice in the government or in the constitutional development of the country.

There is thus a characteristic difference between the position of the Union and that of the present British dependencies in Africa. In Southern Rhodesia, for example, which presents the nearest analogy to the Union, the process of constitutional development is now likely to be increasingly influenced by a Federal Legislature in which Africans are represented.[1] In other countries, as typically in West Africa, the non-European element has even now an important part in politics. It cannot be assumed therefore that the precise course followed by the Union in its access to full sovereignty will necessarily be followed by dependencies in Africa where the non-European element is prominently represented in the Government, and which have an entirely different social and political tradition.[2]

The main lines of the process by which the Union moved towards its present status are, however, sufficiently clear. The legal dependence of the Dominions in general had over a course of years been modified through the non-use by Great Britain of its overriding powers, by the obsolescence of such prerogative usages as 'disallowances', and by the policy of formal consultation at Imperial Conferences on matters of common concern. The process was uniform for all Dominions. 'Whenever any Dominion obtained a concession or right, the concession was automatically extended to all the other Dominions.'[3] The earlier history of South Africa, and in particular of the Transvaal and the Orange Free State, had created in the Union at large an exceptional concern for a formal recognition of the independent status at which it had arrived as the result of the general prevalence of such practices.

General Hertzog as Prime Minister of the Union took a leading part in the discussions of the Imperial Conference of 1926[4] which defined the status of the Dominions; it will be recalled that it was the substance of this definition which was subsequently embodied in the Statute of Westminster of 1931, the instrument which gave legal existence to the entity of the British Commonwealth of Nations. 'Great Britain and the

[1] See below, p. 279.
[2] Lord Simon, *Crown and Commonwealth*, The Romanes Lecture, May 1953, pp. 14–15.
[3] W. P. M. Kennedy and H. J. Schlosborg, *The Law and Customs of the South African Constitution*, 1935, p. 479.
[4] General Hertzog was Prime Minister from June 1924 to September 1939.

Dominions are autonomous communities within the British Empire, equal in status, in no way subordinate one to another in any aspect of their domestic or external affairs, though united by a common allegiance to the Crown and freely associated as members of the British Commonwealth of Nations.'[1]

The Statute had the effect of enhancing the status of the Dominion Parliaments in three ways.[2] It freed their laws from the restrictions imposed upon them by the Colonial Laws Validity Act; it gave them extra-territorial validity; and it embodied the principle that no future Act of the British Parliament should form part of the law of a Dominion except at the request and with the consent of its Legislature. There was general agreement in the Union Parliament for the subsequent enactment of two Acts, the Status of Union Act and the Seals Act of 1954, which made the necessary modification in the Constitution of 1909 in order to give effect to the new status of the Union.[3]

These Acts declared the Union to be a 'Sovereign Independent State', with the addition that no future British Act should form part of the law of the Union 'unless extended thereto by an Act of Parliament of the Union'. The procedure by which enactments of the Union Legislature could be 'reserved for the signification of the pleasure of the Crown' was abolished, as was also the procedure of 'reservation' generally, save as regards appeals to the Privy Council, but it should be noted that appeals to the Privy Council were also subsequently abolished in 1950. Finally a far-reaching clause was inserted to make it possible for the Governor-General to exercise all the Royal Prerogatives on behalf of the King.[4] It was by virtue of this power that the Union became the first Dominion that declared war in 1939 independently of Great Britain.[5] Consultation and co-operation remained the basis of Commonwealth relations, but since the Second World War there has been far less formality about the procedure followed.[6]

The term 'Dominion' and the description 'British' as applied to the Commonwealth were dropped on the attainment by India of full membership in 1947. Two years afterwards allegiance to the Crown ceased to be a condition of membership when the conference of Commonwealth Prime Ministers agreed to India's proposal that though constituted by her own Legislature as a Republic she should remain a member of the Commonwealth as long as she continued to recognize the King as 'Head of the

---

[1] *Imperial Conference 1926*, Summary of Proceedings, Cmd. 2768, 1926.

[2] Statute of Westminster, 1931, sections 2, 3, 4.

[3] Status of Union Act 69 of 1934. Royal Executive Functions and Seals Act 70 of 1934.

[4] Section 6 of the Royal Executive Functions and Seals Act 70 of 1934.

[5] H. J. May, *The South African Constitution*, 1949, p. 51, gives the text of the Proclamation declaring a state of war between the Union and Germany, 6 September 1939.

[6] H. Harvey, *Consultation and Co-operation in the Commonwealth*, 1952.

Commonwealth'.[1] On the accession of Queen Elizabeth II in 1952 each of the Commonwealth countries adopted its own version of the Royal title,[2] and as a result the formal designation 'British Dominions beyond the Seas' was eliminated from use as part of it. The Commonwealth countries have continued the practice, which originated in 1924, of nominating their own diplomatic representatives.

It is not necessary to explore here some of the purely legalistic issues raised in regard to the Constitution of the Commonwealth, such as the question of the divisibility of the Crown. There are, however, three points of practice which are in particular indicative of the status now enjoyed by the Union of South Africa. There is full acceptance of the principle that members of the Commonwealth have the option of secession, for which the Union House of Assembly had stipulated in 1930.[3] Eire, for example, exercised this right in 1949. Secondly, the convention of neutrality is also well established. Eire's declared policy of neutrality during the Second World War was in effect respected by all belligerents.

The position in regard to the status of citizenship in the Commonwealth is somewhat more complicated. Up to 1946 common allegiance to the Crown still implied the existence of a common status of British subject, but a conference on nationality which was held in 1947 recommended that each member of the Commonwealth should have a distinctive nationality, but should also recognize a common status, following the lines of the Canadian Citizenship Act of the previous year.[4] The British, Australian, and New Zealand Acts of 1948 conformed to these proposals, but South Africa in its Citizenship Act of 1949 made provision only for a single South African citizenship. The Minister who introduced the Bill in the Assembly maintained that there could no longer be a Commonwealth subject or citizen; 'since common allegiance is no longer a condition of membership, there cannot be a common subjecthood to circumscribe the common status'.[5] Under the South African Act the citizens of Commonwealth countries may become South African citizens by registration after five years' residence, whereas aliens can be naturalized only after six years' residence; in other respects the conditions are substantially the same.[6]

Political Parties

It was natural that in South Africa the division of the European population between elements of Dutch and British stock should be reflected in

---

[1] Pakistan announced in February 1955 its intention to follow the same course as India.

[2] The title adopted by the Union was 'Elizabeth II Queen of South Africa and her other Realms and Territories, Head of the Commonwealth'. Royal Style and Titles Act 6 of 1953.

[3] *Round Table*, vol. xx, 1929–30, p. 882.   [4] Harvey, op. cit. p. 65.

[5] *Union House of Assembly Debates*, 1949, col. 7579.

[6] South Africa Citizenship Act, 44 of 1949, section 8. For the full terms prescribed as qualifications for citizenship, see *O.Y.S.A. 1952–3*, pp. 1113–21.

the formation of political parties to whom the relation of the Union with Great Britain should constitute a matter of major concern. But the present formation of the two major parties does not in fact represent a definite alignment of the members of the communities of Dutch or British stock. A noticeable proportion of the European residents of the Union are of neither British nor Dutch origin. There has been of recent years a marked growth of bilingualism; in the census of 1946 it was estimated that nearly 70 per cent. of the European population was bilingual. The 'home language' of $39\frac{1}{2}$ per cent. was recorded as English and $57\frac{1}{2}$ per cent. as Afrikaans; about $1\frac{1}{4}$ per cent. came from homes speaking both languages.[2]

But the division of parties does not closely follow linguistic lines; all that can be said with certainty is that the Afrikaner element has on the whole been the more active in the political world; none of the five Prime Ministers since the formation of the Union has been of British stock.[3] It is the members of the Afrikaner community who have pressed most strongly for a clear enunciation of the sovereign status of the Union, and it is they who have constituted the force behind the demand for the recognition of the right of the Union to opt for the status of a republic, thus recalling the tradition of republicanism of the Boers of the Transvaal in earlier days.

The South African Party, of which General Botha was the first and General Smuts the most famous leader, favoured in general a policy which accepted the Imperial connexion. This Party had a majority in the first Administration of the Union, which was formed by General Botha in May 1910. The Nationalist Party was formed in 1915 by General Hertzog, who had been Minister of Justice in the first Botha Government; it was pledged to 'freedom from Imperial control', to 'redress the wrongs done in 1902', and to secure 'a truly free South Africa'.[4] As already explained, it fell to General Hertzog as Prime Minister to attend the Imperial Conference in 1926 at which the equality of status of the Dominions with the United Kingdom was explicitly recognized; on his return he expressed himself as fully satisfied with this position.[5] On the acceptance by the Union Parliament of the Statute of Westminster he stated that 'we have now come to finality with regard to our constitutional freedom'.[6]

In 1933 a United Party was formed by the fusion of the parties under the joint leadership of General Hertzog and General Smuts, and shortly afterwards Dr. Malan, who had been Minister of Education in General Hertzog's Cabinet, left him in order to become the leader of the 'Purified' Nationalists, who were committed to a republic, 'but not necessarily in our

[1] S. G. Millin, *The South Africans*, 1934. *Union of South Africa Census Report*, 1926, Part IV.
[2] *O.Y.S.A., 1950*, pp. 1165–6.   [3] *The Times*, 13 January 1955.
[4] *Round Table*, vol. x, 1919–20, pp. 191, 203.
[5] Ibid., vol. xvii, 1926–7, p. 394.   [6] Ibid. vol. xxi, 1930–1, p. 914.

time'. The United Party passed in 1934 the Status of Union and Seals Acts to which reference has already been made. The Nationalist Party had frequently asserted the right of South Africa to remain neutral in the event of a war in which Great Britain was engaged; this had indeed been described by General Hertzog while in opposition as 'an unassailable right' which 'must necessarily be so of any country which possesses the right of self-government'.[1] The claim was not actually tested in 1939, since a Nationalist Party motion in favour of 'benevolent neutrality' was defeated and a new Administration was formed under General Smuts. It was under his leadership that the Union entered the Second World War.

A Defence Act of 1912 had provided for the military defence of the Union.[2] At the time this law was enacted it was assumed that naval defence must depend primarily on the maintenance of the sea-power by the British Navy,[3] and under an agreement of 1922, the terms of which were not published, the Union was given access to the British naval base at Simonstown. The Nationalist Party at one time proposed that, in order to safeguard South Africa's neutrality, Simonstown should be ceded outright 'as another Gibraltar'. Dr. Malan, however, when he became leader of the Party, spoke of Union control of the ports as a 'basis for negotiation with the British Government for the cession of the High Commission Territories'.[4] In 1955 Simonstown was transferred to the Union under the Anglo-South African Defence Agreements.[5]

Since 1935 the Nationalist Party had, as already shown, set before itself the ideal of making South Africa a Republic.[6] The reconstituted Nationalist Party which came into power under Dr. Malan's leadership in 1948 included in its statement of aims the assertion that a republican government outside the Commonwealth was best suited to South Africa. In October 1953 the House of Assembly adopted a resolution providing that a republican constitution would be introduced 'only . . . as the result of a special and definite mandate from the European electorate'. It stated further that in the light of the London Declaration of 1949, which showed that such a constitution is not incompatible with Commonwealth membership, the proclamation of a Republic and the withdrawal from the Commonwealth need not be considered simultaneously. This is in effect the attitude also taken by Mr. Strijdom, who succeeded Dr. Malan as Prime Minister in 1954; there must in his view be clear proof of such a

[1] Address at Stellenbosch University, 1917, quoted in *Round Table*, vol. vii, 1916–17, p. 285.

[2] South Africa Defence Act, no. 13 of 1912.

[3] *Round Table*, vol. ii, 1911–12, p. 377.

[4] *The Times*, 24 September 1952.

[5] *Exchanges of Letters on Defence Matters between the Governments of the United Kingdom and the Union of South Africa*, June 1955, Cmd. 9520, p. 10.

[6] Dr. Malan, Address to Cape Nationalist Party at George, 20 October 1954, quoted in *South African Survey*, 15 November 1954 (hereafter referred to as *S.A.S.*).

desire, as given by a plebiscite among Europeans or by a special election fought on this definite issue.[1]

The future status of the Union remains therefore an open question. The signs of the former 'Imperial connexion' are now few; perhaps the only effective reminder of its existence is provided by the fact that the Act of Union of 1909 was enacted by the British Parliament. But that was not a measure which was in any way forced on South Africa, and the 'entrenched clauses'[2] which have created the legal stumbling block so greatly resented in recent years by the Nationalist Party were introduced in order to secure general acceptance of the scheme of government proposed for embodiment in the Constitution.[3]

Doctrine of Segregation

As was observed earlier in this chapter, South African policy has had a double objective: in external affairs, the achievement of a status of constitutional autonomy; in internal affairs, the maintenance intact of a European pattern of civilization, the assurance for which has been held to lie in the practical application of the doctrine of segregation. The concern felt in the latter of these objectives goes back to the earliest days of European settlement in South Africa. The Great Trek northward of the Boer farmers which began in 1836, and which led ultimately to the creation of the Transvaal Republic and the Orange Free State, had its origin partly in a determination to acquire rights over lands which the British Government of the day hesitated to annex, and partly in dissatisfaction with the economic policy of that Government. But it was also a protest against the principle involved in the British recognition of a legal equality between all sections of the population and the emancipation of the slaves, for though this measure had in fact involved only a minor material hardship to the Afrikaners, it had outraged their sense of what was fitting in the relations between White and Black.

Opinion in Great Britain has always looked on the grant of the franchise to Africans in Cape Colony as the symbol of a policy by which opportunities equalling those of the White man were offered to any Africans who could attain his standards of civilization. But it would be wrong to suppose that any clear-cut distinction of outlook on this point has in fact existed between the English-speaking and Afrikaner communities in South Africa. Some of the most distinguished proponents of the 'Cape Policy' have been Afrikaners, while the dominantly English-speaking community of Natal has shown no anxiety to support the application there of a policy similar to that of the Cape. So far as concerns the attitude maintained towards the admission of Africans to a share in the government

[1] S.A.S., no. 98, 15 February 1955, p. 5.   [2] See below, p. 161.
[3] See the authorities quoted by E. A. Walker in *The Times*, 26 May 1955.

of the country, the major difference between the Afrikaner and the Briton resident in South Africa lies in the fact that the deep-seated Afrikaner conception of racial separatism has been strongly reinforced by the other strands in Afrikaner nationalism.

It was the Labour Party in the Union, at that time an essentially English-speaking group, which in 1912 first gave formal expression to the doctrine of 'segregation'. That doctrine assumed the permanent maintenance of the White community in a position of political and economic supremacy and held that the standards of European civilization must be preserved by reducing to the minimum the contacts of the two races.[1] In 1924 the Nationalist Party made an electoral alliance with the Labour Party and came into power on a programme which committed it to giving practical support to this doctrine. General Hertzog's internal policy was designed to complete a process, initiated by the Land Act of 1913, under which the Union would be divided into 'Native' and 'Non-Native' areas, and he sought to establish the principle that the residence of Africans outside the areas reserved to them could only be justified if they were in European employment.

One of the admitted obstacles to implementing this principle was the fact that the area which previous land policy had left to Africans was inadequate for their support.[2] In 1933 a coalition was effected between General Hertzog's Nationalist Party and the United Party under General Smuts, with General Hertzog as Prime Minister, and in 1936 his Native Trust and Land Act set up the South African Native Trust, which was authorized to purchase up to 15,345,000 acres of land for the settlement of Africans. This was to be a 'final settlement' of the distribution of land between Europeans and Africans.[3]

At this stage the policy of 'separatism' was also finding a significant expression in legislation affecting labour conditions. The general aim of the 'civilized labour policy' was to assign to the African his place in unskilled labour, reserving skilled employment for Europeans. Under the Mines and Works Act of 1911 a legal colour bar was in effect introduced into the mining industry and the employment of Africans as skilled workers in that industry was prevented; under an amendment of 1926 certain mining employments were restricted to 'Europeans, Cape Coloured and Mauritius Creoles, or persons from Saint Helena'. The definition of employee in the Industrial Conciliation Act of 1937 had the result of rendering Africans ineligible for membership of trade unions registered under the Act.[4] The policy was also exemplified in the Native Urban Areas Act of 1923, which aimed at the rigorous control of the number of Africans permitted to

---

[1] For a more detailed study of the development of the policy of segregation, see W. K. Hancock, *Survey of British Commonwealth Affairs*, vol. ii, Part II, 1942, pp. 11 ff.

[2] See below, p. 692.   [3] *O.Y.S.A., 1949*, p. 487.   [4] See below, p. 1440.

reside in urban areas and sought to effect the permanent separation of African 'Locations' from the areas in which Europeans reside.[1] Even at this stage, however, some of the difficulties involved in carrying this policy into complete effect became apparent when the census of 1936 showed that out of a total African population of 6,596,900, only 3,396,550 were living in areas which could be regarded as 'Native' in strict terms of the law.[2] The remainder were residing in areas described in the census as European, such as European-owned farms, mining or municipal compounds, and the like.

Non-Europeans and the Franchise

In the constitutional field the endeavour to give definite expression to the principle of separatism had at an early stage manifested itself in the attitude maintained on the question of the admission of non-Europeans to the franchise. In the discussions of the National Convention which paved the way for the establishment of the Union, there was no issue which stood more obstinately in the way of unity than that of the electoral franchise.[3] The Republics of the Transvaal and Orange Free State had never extended the franchise to any but their European population, whereas the Cape, and to a minor extent Natal, had non-Europeans on their electoral roll. The policy which had thus distinguished the Cape from the Voortrekker republics was first embodied in the Fifth Ordinance of 1828, which cancelled all Cape laws differentiating against the Hottentot population.[4] The Constitution granted to the Cape in 1853 extended the franchise on equal terms to all male British subjects, taking the ground that 'all Her Majesty's subjects, without distinction of class or colour, should be united by one bond of loyalty and a common interest'.[5]

At the time of the adoption of the policy of 1853 the Cape had only a small non-European population, but when its territory was extended by the annexation of lands largely inhabited by Bantu, fears began to be entertained that the electorate would be swamped by the African vote. The registration of African voters in appreciable numbers began in 1884. The introduction of an education qualification in 1892,[6] though of general application, was intended to keep 'blanket kaffirs' off the register.[7] At the same time the general qualification was raised to the possession of property worth £75 or an income of £50. When the Glen Grey Act of

[1] See below, pp. 167-9.
[2] Hancock, op. cit. p. 16. The Native areas referred to were the Native Areas (Rural) plus the Native Urban Locations, Rural Suburbs, and Native and Rural Townships.
[3] L. M. Thompson, *The Cape Coloured Franchise*, 1949. *Cambridge History of the British Empire*, vol. viii, p. 633. C. W. de Kiewiet, *A History of South Africa, Social and Economic*, 1941, pp. 144 ff.
[4] E. A. Walker, *A History of South Africa*, 1947, p. 177.
[5] Walker, op. cit. p. 252.
[6] Franchise and Ballot Act, no. 9 of 1892.   [7] Walker, op. cit. p. 438.

1894[1] provided for the allotment of individual land holdings to Africans, it laid down at the same time that occupation of land under its terms did not qualify for the franchise. The National Convention was informed that during the 53 years in which the franchise had been open to the Coloured and African communities, no member of them had ever been elected to the Parliament.

In Natal a representative form of government was established in 1856, and full Responsible Government in 1893.[2] Africans were not explicitly debarred from the franchise, but the Native Franchise Act of 1865, while imposing the same property qualifications on all sections of the community, set up a restrictive procedure for the registration of African and Asian voters. At a later date persons not of European origin were disqualified from voting if they were descended from persons who had come from a country which had not hitherto possessed parliamentary institutions, thus effectively excluding Asians.[3] In 1909 there were in Natal only 186 non-European voters, while of the Africans only three ever acquired the vote.[4]

When the British Government annexed the Republics of the Transvaal and Orange Free State in 1902, the terms offered to them included not only the promise of self-government, but an assurance that no Native franchise would be given before self-government had been attained.[5] It was recognized, however, that control by the Crown implied the application of a uniform Native policy, and the Native Affairs Commission appointed in 1903 to formulate such a policy gave particular attention to the franchise. They found that in the Cape there were 8,117 registered African voters out of a total electorate of 135,168, and that in seven out of 46 constituencies the African vote was strong enough to determine the issue of an election.[6] They held that a 'franchise which makes the organized Native vote the arbiter in any acute electoral struggle . . . is an unwise and dangerous thing', and they proposed the creation in each Colony of constituencies in which Africans should vote separately.

The National Convention of 1908–9 fully realized that the line taken on the franchise would be of crucial importance for the future of Native policy in South Africa. The Cape delegation, supported by the High Commissioner, Lord Selborne, proposed a uniform franchise dependent on the possession of a 'civilized' standard of life, which would have admitted some Africans while excluding some 'poor Whites'. Other delegations preferred the abolition of any Native franchise.

No agreement could be reached, and the South Africa Act of 1909

[1] See below, p. 761.   [2] Act no. 14 of 1893.
[3] Natal Act no. 8 of 1896.
[4] E. H. Brookes, *History of Native Policy in South Africa*, 1927, p. 284. Thompson, op. cit. pp. 11, 15.
[5] Walker, op. cit. p. 505.   [6] Brookes, op. cit. pp. 280–1.

accordingly provided that the Parliament of the Union should be empowered to prescribe the qualifications required for the franchise.[1] But it
provided at the same time a safeguard for the African and Coloured voters
in the Cape which came afterwards to be widely known as an 'entrenched
clause'.[2] This laid down that 'no such law shall disqualify any person in
the Province of the Cape . . . from being so registered by reason of his race
or colour only, unless the Bill be passed by both Houses of Parliament
sitting together, and the third reading be agreed to by not less than two-
thirds of the total number of members of both Houses'.[3] The right of non-
Europeans to sit in Parliament, which had been implicitly theirs in the
Cape, was not explicitly withdrawn.

General Hertzog's Policy

When General Hertzog formed the first Nationalist Government in
1924, he announced a policy of segregation for Africans but of integration
for the Coloured people 'industrially, economically, and politically'.[4] He
introduced in 1926 two Bills, the first of which provided for the abolition
of the Cape franchise for Africans and the substitution of a limited parliamentary representation of Africans throughout the Union, voting on a
separate roll; the second Bill provided that the Coloured population in the
Cape should retain their existing rights and that those outside the Cape
should also be represented by one European member. As the first of these
Bills failed to secure the necessary majority of both Houses sitting together,
the second was withdrawn. The African electorate in the Cape attained
its maximum of 16,480 in 1927. Between 1930 and 1933 some 6,000
African voters were disqualified as the result of applying a strict interpretation to the clause contained in the Franchise Act of 1892 under
which the qualifying income must have been earned during the twelve
months preceding registration.[5] In 1930 the franchise was extended to all
European women over 21, and Act 41 of 1931 removed the property
qualifications previously imposed for Europeans in the Cape and Natal.
The effect was to establish a system of universal adult suffrage for the
European population.

It was not until 1933 that General Hertzog obtained through his alliance
with General Smuts and the South African Party a sufficient majority in
Parliament to allow him to proceed with the comprehensive electoral
plan he had put forward in 1926. The Representation of Natives Act of
1936 removed the Africans of the Cape Province from the common
electoral roll. The passing of this enactment, however, involved some
compromise, since the African voters in the Cape were permitted to

[1] de Kiewiet, op. cit. p. 144.   [2] See above, p. 157.
[3] South Africa Act, 1909, section 35.
[4] L. M. Thompson, *The Cape Coloured Franchise*, 1949, p. 22.
[5] *Race Relations*, vol. ii, no. 4, 1935, p. 22.

continue to elect three members to the House of Assembly, albeit as a separate electorate,[1] registered on a Cape Native Voters' Roll. At the same time Africans throughout the Union were given the right to elect, through electoral colleges, four Senators who, like the members of the House of Assembly elected by the new Cape Native Voters' Roll, were required to be Europeans.[2]

The Act established at the same time a Natives Representative Council. This consisted of twelve elected and four nominated African members, together with the Secretary for Native Affairs as Chairman and the six Chief Native Commissioners, but these had no vote. The powers of the Council were purely advisory; it was to be summoned before the opening of every session of Parliament in order to report upon the estimates of moneys to be applied for Native purposes; it was to report also on proposed legislation in so far as it might affect the African population, and it could recommend legislation in the interests of Africans. Despite its purely advisory status, it exercised a considerable influence upon parliamentary deliberations and the decisions of the Government, though its advice on major issues tended to be disregarded. As will subsequently appear, it adopted in 1945 a resolution to adjourn and not to reconvene until the Government had abolished discriminatory legislation.[3] It was itself abolished in 1951 by the Bantu Authorities Act enacted by the Nationalist Government.

In spite of the enactment of the various measures designed to give effect to the declared policy of segregation, it would seem that General Smuts himself became doubtful whether it was practicable to carry out the principle to its logical conclusion. He had become Prime Minister in 1939, and in a speech made in 1942 he declared that the policy of segregation had not so far been fruitful of result; 'the high expectation that we entertained of that policy has been sadly disappointed'.[4] Some support was later provided to this judgement by the report of the Native Laws Inquiry Commission, presided over by Mr. Justice Fagan, which pointed out that more than half the African population were living in European areas, and that it was impossible for the whole of the African population to be adequately supported in the Native Reserves. The urbanization of Africans in the European areas was not a process which could now be reversed, nor was it now possible to confine the employment of Natives in South Africa to the migratory type of labour.[5]

---

[1] Representation of Natives Act, no. 12 of 1936. Africans were allowed to elect also two members of the Provincial Council, *O.Y.S.A., 1952–53*, p. 465.

[2] *O.Y.S.A., 1952–53*, p. 465.

[3] See below, p. 429. See also E. H. Brookes, 'Government and Administration', *Handbook on Race Relations in South Africa*, 1949.

[4] J. C. Smuts, *The Basis of Trusteeship*, South African Institute of Race Relations, 1942, pp. 9–10.   [5] *Report of the Native Laws Commission 1946–8*, U.G. no. 28, 1948.

On the other hand the reconstituted Nationalist Party of 1948 urged that if this policy had failed of success it was because its practical application had been only half-hearted, and it decided to press the doctrine of segregation (*apartheid*) as a major item of its programme. The Party had originally been composed of the uncompromising advocates of Afrikanerdom who had seceded from General Hertzog's leadership when he formed his alliance with General Smuts in 1933, but its strength grew steadily after the split between Hertzog and Smuts in 1939 on the question of South African participation in the war.

A Party pamphlet published in 1948[1] pointed out that there were two sections of thought in South Africa in regard to the policy to be adopted concerning the non-European community:

> On the one hand, there is the policy of equality which advocates equal rights within the same political structure for all civilized and educated persons, irrespective of race or colour, and the gradual granting of the franchise to non-Europeans as they become qualified to make use of democratic rights. On the other hand, there is the policy of separation, which has grown up from the experience of the established European population of the country, and which is based on the Christian principles of justice and reasonableness. . . . We can act only in one of two directions. Either we must follow the course of equality, which must eventually mean national suicide for the White race, or we must take the course of separation (*apartheid*), through which the character and the future of every race will be protected and safeguarded, with full opportunities for development and self-maintenance in their own ideas, without the interests of one clashing with the interests of the other.

Dr. Malan and Policy of 'Apartheid'

The statement that to 'follow the course of equality' would mean suicide for the White race was in effect a repetition of the case which General Hertzog had put before the Union Parliament in 1926. Dr. Malan, who became Prime Minister in 1948 as leader of the reconstituted Nationalist Party, emphasized that *apartheid* was not a new policy; it was only the policy of separatism expressed in terms which experience had shown to be better adapted to the actual facts of the situation as it now stood. 'Total territorial separation', he said in 1950, 'is impracticable under present circumstances . . . where our whole economic structure is to a large extent based on Native labour.'[2] There was, he repeated in 1953, no difference in meaning between 'segregation' and *apartheid*. They differed only in the fact that the objective of separation would now be pursued by a Nationalist Party which was, unlike the United Party in

---

[1] The National Party's Colour Policy, quoted in *Report of the U.N. Commission on the Racial Situation in the Union of South Africa* (U.N. Document), A/2505, p. 140.
[2] *Union of South Africa, House of Assembly, Debates*, vol. 71, p. 4142.

previous Parliaments, wholly united and determined to implement the policy as rapidly as possible, at any rate in the political and social sphere.[1]

The policy of *apartheid* was thus to be comprehensive, and it involved racial separation in the electoral as well as in every other sphere. In the Separate Representation of Voters Act of 1951[2] an attempt was made to apply to the Coloured electors of Cape Province a procedure similar to that by which the African electors had been removed from the common roll under the Representation of Natives Act of 1936. The Act of 1951 was passed by Parliament by the ordinary procedure, the Government having claimed that the 'entrenched clauses' of the South Africa Act had lost their legal effect when the Union adopted the Statute of Westminster. Under the provisions of the Act of 1951 the Coloured electors were placed on a separate roll and were to elect four European members to the House of Assembly.

The Act was, however, declared by the Supreme Court to be invalid, and an attempt made by the Government to establish a High Court of Parliament which would have power to overrule the Appellate Division of the Supreme Court[3] was also declared to be invalid. The attempt made by the Government to secure a two-thirds majority of both Houses of Parliament sitting together was also unsuccessful. But the dominant position acquired by the Nationalist Party in the election of April 1953 made it obvious that it would not fail to pursue other legislative measures for effecting its purpose. The result was seen in the legislation undertaken in 1955 for effecting a change in the composition of the Senate and for increasing the membership of the Appeal Court.[4]

A civil disobedience campaign directed against discriminatory laws was organized by the African Congress in 1952; a few Europeans and a number of Asians associated themselves with the African 'defiers', about 8,000 of whom were arrested. The Suppression of Communism Act, no. 44 of 1950, which includes in the definition of Communism actions which promote hostility between Europeans and non-Europeans, was invoked against the leaders. During the session of 1953 an Act was passed enabling the Governor-General to proclaim a state of emergency for twelve months;[5] when this Act is applied, it has the effect of suspending without discussion any of the common law and statutory civil rights at present recognized. An Act passed in the same year increased the penalties for engaging in civil disobedience or encouraging or giving financial aid to movements of this character.[6] Not merely the legislation but the manner in which the law has been applied, and in particular the use made of the

[1] *S.A.S.*, no. 55, 15 March 1953.
[2] Separate Representation of Voters Act, no. 46 of 1951.
[3] High Court of Parliament Act, no. 35 of 1952.
[4] See below, p. 166.   [5] Public Safety Act, no. 3 of 1953.
[6] The Criminal Law Amendment Act, no. 8 of 1953.

Suppression of Communism Act, have gone very far in the application of repressive procedure; it has been justly urged that the measures taken for the suppression of political views by non-Europeans go far beyond the practice observed in peace-time by most European countries.[1]

The action taken to implement the policy of *apartheid* has been carried also into the sphere of social and industrial legislation. The Prohibition of Mixed Marriages Act, 1949, provided that no marriage might in future be solemnized between a European and a non-European, while the Immorality (Amendment) Act of 1950 penalized irregular carnal intercourse between Europeans and non-Europeans. The industrial colour bar was extended by the Native Building Workers Act of 1951, which made it illegal to employ Natives to perform skilled work in the building industry in urban areas. The Native Labour (Settlement of Disputes) Act of 1953 constituted a separate category for Native labour disputes, and while providing for the establishment of purely Native trade unions made special provision for their regulation and control.[2] But the cornerstone of the *apartheid* policy has been the Group Areas Act passed in 1950,[3] the object of which is to lay down for each of the racial groups defined in the Act the areas in which only members of the specified group may occupy or own immovable property. The groups specified in the Act are Whites, Coloureds, and Natives. A Bill for the amendment of the Urban Areas Act put forward in April 1956 embodied a summary procedure for the compulsory removal of Africans from any urban area.

The earliest effect of this legislation was seen in the measures taken in Natal for the removal of Asians to areas where their competition would not affect European traders.[4] The removal of large numbers of Africans in the Western Areas of Johannesburg, which had such reverberations in Europe, was a measure which was fully in the spirit of the Act, but it could also be justified as an essential measure of slum clearance.[5] The most recent, and to some extent the most conspicuous, of the measures contemplated under the Act, is the scheme envisaged for the removal of all Africans from the Western Province of the Cape, in the interests of White and Coloured labour. There has, however, been an opposition to this measure by industrialists and other European interests which makes it doubtful whether it can be carried into effect.[6] An attempt has also been made to substitute, under the Natives (Abolition of Passes and Co-ordination of Documents) Act, 1952, a single 'reference book' for the whole series of passes and similar documents which Natives were required to carry.[7] Difficulty has, however, been encountered in carrying out this

---

[1] For an analysis of these measures see J. Lewin in *The Forum*, December 1954. See also *The Times*, 24 March 1954.   [2] No. 48 of 1953.
[3] No. 41 of 1950.   [4] See below, p. 395.   [5] See below, p. 570.
[6] *Round Table*, June 1955, pp. 293–5.   [7] See below, p. 432.

Act, since the reference book in effect constitutes a new 'pass' which would be required of thousands of Africans who had not previously been obliged to carry documents producible on the spot.

A significant insight into the philosophy which underlines the doctrine of *apartheid* is also to be found in the passing of the Bantu Education Act of 1954, which has caused even graver reverberations in Europe than the movement of Africans from the Western Areas of Johannesburg. The Act is based on the assumption that African education must in the future be adjusted to the needs of the Bantu world of ideas and not to that of Europeans, and the steps contemplated in order to give effect to this concept will affect the whole course of Native education, both in the school stage and in more advanced courses. The subject will be further referred to in the chapter dealing with education;[1] it is of great importance, for it affords evidence of an intention to effect a fundamental change in the outlook of the more advanced Bantu towards European civilization and the share which he may hope to take in its benefits.

It would not have been unnatural if the Government of the Union had adopted as a matter of expediency a procedure of education which is felt to be more consonant with Bantu custom than a procedure framed on a European pattern. But the Act goes far beyond this. The advocates of the principle of separatism clearly hold that the gulf between the European and the Bantu is so deep that it would be unprofitable, even if it were not politically inadvisable, to attempt to bridge it. There had already been some indication of this trend of thought in the enactment of the Bantu Authorities Act of 1951, which discountenanced the extension of the use of the electoral system in African Local Government institutions and preferred recourse to the use of Bantu tribal institutions as being more representative of African opinion.[2] But the Bantu Education Act, and the action subsequently taken to implement its provisions is by far the more significant of the two enactments. It amounted to a decision that education on European lines would be no good to an African in the sphere which he was now destined to fill, and it might even be dangerous, as encouraging him to trespass into that occupied by the European.

Nationalist Party and Entrenched Clauses

As was remarked in a previous paragraph, it was inevitable that the Nationalist Party should, in view of its victory at the polls in 1953, seek new measures to overcome the legal obstacles created for it by the 'entrenched clauses' in the Union Act of 1909. The result was seen in two measures enacted in May and June 1955. The Appellate Division Quorum Act[3] took power to create such number of judicial posts as would ensure that on any disputed point of constitutional law the quorum of

---

[1] See below, pp. 1149–52.   [2] See below, p. 430.   [3] No. 27 of 1955.

Judges (which had previously been five) should be raised to eleven.[1] The ground put forward in support of this measure was that the Appellate Division had, when dealing with the competence of the South African Legislature to enact measures modifying the Union Act of 1909, given two contradictory decisions in 1937 and 1952. The Quorum Act was strongly opposed by the Unionist Party, on the ground that the obvious intention of the Government was to 'pack' the Bench with its own partisans, in order to secure a judgement favourable to it on the question of the continued validity of the 'entrenched clauses'. That was, however, a charge which could only be substantiated if and when events showed that Judges could be found in the Union who would allow their partisan feelings to override their loyalty to their judicial traditions.

The second Act was more far-reaching, and its purpose was unmistakable. The Constitution of the Senate Act[2] raised the membership of the Senate from 48 to 89,[3] and did so in such a manner that the Nationalist Party would be assured of a majority. The representation of the Transvaal in the Senate was raised from eight to 27 and that of the Cape from eight to 22; the nominations made by the Governor-General were increased from eight to 16. It was at the same time provided that the Senate would have no power to reject a financial Bill passed by the Assembly, and that a motion by the Senate which would have the effect of overriding any other measure framed by the lower House should (like similar motions passed in the British House of Lords) cease to have effect if the lower House re-enacted the law at the end of two years. It was clear that this measure would (unless declared invalid by the Courts) give the Government the two-thirds majority necessary to secure the valid enactment of a measure placing the Cape Coloured on a separate register. In February 1956 the Union Parliament thus reconstituted, re-enacted the separate Representation of Voters Act of 1951. In November 1956 the Appeal Court gave judgment for the Government in a case brought to contest the validity of the Senate Act.[4]

A Further Note on the Doctrine of Separatism

It may be asked why the doctrine of separatism, which has been an old-standing feature in the outlook of large numbers of Europeans in South Africa, has of recent years been pressed with so much insistence. The explanation lies partly in the appeal which it makes to Afrikaner tradition. It has become, like the concept of a republican Constitution, one of the symbols of Afrikaner nationalism, and its principle has the support of the Dutch Reformed Church. The Dutch Reformed Church would indeed go farther, and seems to hold that on both ethical and

[1] *Round Table*, June 1955, pp. 293 ff.   [2] No. 53 of 1955.
[3] For the previous composition of the Senate, see below, p. 265
[4] *The Times*, 10 November 1956.

logical grounds the doctrine would seem to demand a complete physical separation of White and Black areas, with all the consequences that this must involve.[1] But the recent insistence on the doctrine of separatism is also due to a general realization of the improved economic and social standing of Africans as a result of the part taken by them in the modern expansion of industrial production in the Union.[2] There has, in particular, been a significant invasion by Africans of the ranks of semi-skilled labour.

The 'maintenance of the standards of European civilization' is a conception which makes an appeal extending far beyond the boundaries of the Union, but for the European in the Union itself this is something more vital than merely a cultural ideal. Rightly or wrongly, it is assumed that its realization demands the continuance of an unchallenged predominance by Europeans in the political life of the country. It is, indeed, this conception which underlies the exposition of the doctrine of *apartheid* as set out by the South African Bureau of Racial Affairs (S.A.B.R.A.). This institution was established in 1949 by the Nationalist Party as an organ for expressing its views on racial relations.

The final judgement on the merits of the doctrine of separatism will not necessarily depend on the success of the methods now being used to implement it. But regarded from a purely objective standpoint, *apartheid* has as yet produced little in the way of material results.[3] The Native Reserves stand much as they did in 1948. The great growth of secondary industries has made the factories more than ever dependent on African labour. *Apartheid* has not reversed the trend of the movement of Africans from the rural to the urban centres. White labour has not been attracted to the Union to take the place of the many Bantu who in theory should be sent back to the Native Reserves. There is no indication that the Bantu in general are giving a welcome to a procedure of education or to the formation of types of local government institutions which will reflect Bantu traditions rather than those of Europe, for though the Transkeian General Council has passed a resolution accepting the Bantu Education Act this seems to be clearly contrary to the opinion held by the large section of the community which is in closer contact with industrial employment. There is no indication that the European community is prepared to accept the radical changes in its manner of life that the logical application of the theory of *apartheid* would demand, at all events on the lines of 'total *apartheid*' as set out in the resolution of the Dutch Reformed Church.[4]

[1] *Round Table*, March 1954, pp. 161 ff. *South African Survey*, 31 August 1954, p. 12. See also the Proceedings of Conference of Dutch Reformed Churches, Bloemfontein, 1950, quoted by P. Mason, *An Essay on Racial Tension*, 1954, pp. 103–5.

[2] *Overseas Economic Surveys, Union of South Africa*, 1953, pp. 52 ff.

[3] *The Times*, 15 January 1955.   [4] Ibid., 5 December 1955.

The doctrine of separatism has still to face the crucial question whether the economy of a modern industrialized State will permit the maintenance of a crude form of differentiation against a major part of the manpower on which it is dependent. As has been observed by an unusually well-qualified authority:

The greater industrial areas are in fact engaged in an active process of economic integration between the races. This process is dictated by the inescapable needs of industry for a constant supply of labour. It is becoming yearly more imperative that such labour be more dependable, more experienced, more adjusted to the habits of a modern industrial society. In consequence there is a fundamental quarrel between the natural integration of urban life and the unhistorical effort to impose 'disintegration' upon the vital centres of South African economic prosperity.[1]

In no country south of the Sahara is there any such stark insistence on the principle of differentiation as in the Union of South Africa. Almost everywhere, as will subsequently be seen, there are signs of the closing of the gap which once seemed to separate African institutions and usages from those prevailing in the Western world; almost everywhere there are in consequence signs of changes in the conceptions held about the principles which should determine the future relations of the European and non-European communities.

Nowhere has the concept of separatism as held in the Union been illustrated more clearly than in the lengthy debate on the Report of the important Commission on the Socio-Economic Development of the Bantu (the Tomlinson Commission) in 1956.[2] From time to time Europeans who have settled in other territories have shown an inclination to look to South Africa for countenance in their effort to maintain policies based on separatist ideas, while to those who look forward to a greater measure of integration, the régime of the Union has become a natural target for attack. But there is here something more than a contrast of philosophies. Both sides realize that the essence of the matter lies in the fact that the doctrine of *apartheid* implies that the European community must continue to hold a position of control over the non-European communities. It is actually on this basic issue, and not because of any argument about the maintenance of a European pattern of civilization, that the two schools of thought tend to range themselves so decisively in opposite camps.

SOUTH-WEST AFRICA

The acceptance of the Statute of Westminster by the Union Government had, as already shown, gone far to satisfy public opinion in South

---

[1] C. W. de Kiewiet, 'Fears and Pressures in the Union of South Africa', *Africa Today*, 1955.
[2] Union of South Africa, House of Assembly Debates (Hansard), 14 May to 18 May 1956. See also below, p. 763.

Africa regarding one much canvassed feature of its external policy, namely, the claim for a recognition of its sovereign status. In the post-war period another feature of its external policy, the position of the Union as Administering Authority of South-West Africa, became an issue of much interest, though the concern which it actually aroused was of a different order. The Government of the Cape had at an early date held strong views in regard to the status of this territory; in point of geography it seemed to be naturally a part of the Union, and large areas of it were held by half-breed Hottentots who had migrated from the Cape Province. The 'hesitant and evasive policy' of British statesmanship[1] during the latter part of the nineteenth century had allowed Germany to make an intrusion into the Cape sphere of interest of which the significance was only to become fully apparent at the outbreak of the First World War.

In the discussions at Versailles which led up to the creation of the mandatory system in 1920, the representatives of the Union made it clear that there were important considerations, both economic and strategic, which distinguished the territory from a number of the other areas to which it was proposed to apply the system of Mandates; they could truthfully claim that the course followed in its administration must vitally affect the domestic affairs of the Union itself. They urged that it should be incorporated in the Union, and though they had to yield on this point, the territory was regarded as falling within the special terms of Article 22 of the Covenant of the League of Nations, and the Mandate for its administration authorized its being administered as an integral portion of the Union.[2]

The Union and the Mandatory System

Throughout the inter-war period the Union Government continued to co-operate fully with the Permanent Mandates Commission of the League. There will be given in the following chapter an account of the constitutional provision made for the day-to-day administration of the territory, but it is convenient to give here some outline of the facts which have made its international status so controversial a topic. In 1923 the Union Government took a decision of policy which afterwards had important consequences in the history of the territory. When it had accepted the Mandate for its administration the White population of German origin were stated to number 11,500, but this number was rapidly reduced by the departure of officials and others; as many as 6,000 were repatriated shortly before 1921. But early in the twenties South-West Africa began

---

[1] C. W. de Kiewiet, *A History of South Africa, Social and Economic,* 1941, pp. 109, 143. *Round Table,* September 1946, pp. 337–8. For the declaration of the German Protectorate over Namaqua-Damaraland in 1884, see *Cambridge History of the British Empire,* vol. viii, 1936, pp. 513–17.

[2] Article 2 of the Mandate of 12 December 1920, *O.Y.S.A., 1952–53,* pp. 1148–9.

to figure prominently in the campaign for the restoration of the German Colonies which became so disturbing a feature of European politics *J.R.A.S.* in the years preceding the outbreak of the Second World War.[1]

In 1923 the Union entered into negotiations with German representatives in London regarding the status of the remaining German settlers in the territory. An agreement was concluded in which the representative of the German Government undertook that it would use its influence to persuade its nationals to accept Union citizenship under a 'general naturalization' in South Africa, and the Union Government agreed to give them the same position and privileges as its other citizens.[2] In 1924 the Union enacted a law for the automatic naturalization of all German nationals in South-West Africa who did not make a written declaration of their wish to be excepted.[3] Out of the 3,489 heads of families or other persons then eligible to make the declaration, only 262 refused naturalization.

If the Union believed that the action taken by it in 1924 had ensured the abandonment by the Germans of all claim to recover possession of South-West Africa, it was undeceived when a vigorous movement was organized by the Nazi party in Germany for the revival of the German influence in the territory. The party leaders in Germany impressed on their nationals in South-West Africa that the terms on which they had accepted naturalization in the Union were compatible with the retention of their allegiance to Germany, and the provocative action taken by the Nazi section among them rapidly became a menace to local peace and order in the territory.[4] It was partly in order to meet this menace to public order that the Legislative Assembly of the territory passed in 1934 a resolution asking that it be administered hereafter 'as a fifth province of the Union, subject to the provisions of the Mandate'. There were at the same time other causes which accounted for this recommendation, the most notable being the complaint that the uncertainty involved by the status of the territory was an obstacle to the investment of private capital in it. As a result the Union Government appointed in 1935 a commission (the Van Zyl Commission) to inquire into the affairs of the territory, including its financial position.

Its report was a document of first-class importance, though it unfortunately revealed the existence of divided views within the Com-

---

[1] General Ritter von Epp, 'The Question of Colonies from the German Standpoint', *J.R.A.S.*, January 1937. L. S. Amery, *The German Colonial Claim*, 1939, pp. 127 ff. F. S. Joelson, *Germany's Claims to Colonies*, 1939, pp. 235 ff. Barbara Ward, *The International Shareout*, 1938, pp. 138 ff.

[2] United Kingdom White Paper, Cmd. 2220, 1924.

[3] South-West Africa Naturalization of Aliens Act, 1924.

[4] R. Hardinge, *South African Cinderella*, 1937, pp. 187–96, 291–312. *Report of Commission to Enquire into the Situation in South-West Africa*, U.G. no. 26, 1936, paragraphs 253–309. C. Dundas, *South-West Africa, the Factual Background*, 1946, pp. 18–19. Joelson, op. cit, pp. 285–6.

mission.[1] Its members joined in agreeing that there were many defects in the system of administration of the territory as well as difficulties arising from the assumed instability of the mandatory status and from the position occupied by the German section of the population. Its financial difficulties in particular could only be cured by some form of closer association with the Union. They also agreed that there was no legal obstacle to its 'incorporation', but they differed as to the form which this should take. There seems to have been an equal division of opinion in the Union itself, for its Government, while agreeing that incorporation in the Union was not incompatible with the terms of the Mandate, expressed in 1936 the view that no sufficient ground had actually been put forward for the incorporation of the territory as a fifth Province of the Union.

The part taken by the Union in the Second World War and its growing appreciation of its position as a sovereign State combined to argue the need for securing a more complete integration of the territory with the Union and at the same time to strengthen the confidence which the Government felt in its ability to secure this result. But the legal position was obscure. The authority which the Union exercised over the territory had been received from the Allied and Associated States when they created the mandatory system in 1920, and it was these States which had authorized the League of Nations to exercise supervision over the manner in which the terms of the Mandates were being observed.[2] The League of Nations expired at the end of the Second World War.

The Allied Nations who were victorious in 1945 were not the same as the Allied and Associated States who had created the mandatory system in 1920, but when they instituted the Organization of the United Nations in 1945–6, they set up at the same time a Trusteeship system comparable with the system of Mandates. The Powers who had held Mandates were asked to transfer to the Trusteeship Council of the United Nations the rights and corresponding obligations arising in their mandated territories, and at an early date the British, French, and Belgian Governments complied with this request.

The Union's Appeal to the United Nations

Instead of accepting the course thus indicated General Smuts, then head of the Union Government, preferred in 1946 to approach the Assembly of the United Nations with a proposal that it should assent to the formal annexation of South-West Africa by the Union. Various of the mandated territories (as for example Togoland or the Cameroons) had been administered as provinces of the neighbouring Colonies; some mandated territories (as for instance Iraq) had achieved a status of

---

[1] U.G. no. 26, 1936.   [2] See below, p. 241.

self-government with the assent of the League of Nations;[1] but there was no precedent for the acquisition by a mandatory Administration of a status over a mandated area which would imply the total cancellation of its mandatory obligations. General Smuts was conscious of this, and was prepared, if he were successful, to continue to administer the territory subject to the submission of reports to the Assembly of the United Nations. He was not, however, willing to accept the status of Trustee under the United Nations Organization,[2] for he foresaw that the activities of the Trusteeship Council might involve in practice a direct intervention in the domestic policy of the Union. In putting the case for annexation he relied on a Resolution passed by the Legislative Assembly of the territory as expressing the assent of the European population to this course, and also on the result of inquiries which had been made early in 1946 from the African inhabitants for an expression of their own views. The numbers given to the Assembly showed that 208,850 were in favour of annexation and 33,520 against it, while the views of 56,000 could not be ascertained.[3]

These figures could not be said to be of any substantial value, for it was difficult to explain to illiterate Africans the difference which might be made by the supersession of the Mandate; at the best, their opinions could only serve as an expression of preference for or against a change in the existing régime. The views actually expressed by the African inhabitants against the proposal were mainly those of the Herero, but for them the issue did not actually lie between annexation and the acceptance of Trusteeship. A domineering and predatory tribe, they had before their conquest by the Germans held control over a number of the other tribes in the territory, and their vote expressed their dissatisfaction that after conquering the Germans the Union Government had not restored their tribe to the position it had once occupied, particularly in respect of the control exercised over tribal lands.

Subsequent Action by the Union

The Assembly of the United Nations rejected the proposal made by General Smuts and accepted a motion urging that the territory should be placed under Trusteeship.[4] This result might perhaps have been foreseen, but the actual course taken by the discussion on this occasion was such as to cause acute resentment in the Union. To the large number of the Member States in the United Nations Assembly which are not of White stock the prestige of the non-European peoples has throughout been the uppermost concern, and for them the annexation of the territory meant the continued subordination of its African inhabitants to the political

[1] *Statesman's Year-Book, 1954*, p. 1134.   [2] *Round Table*, September 1946, pp. 337 ff.
[3] Ibid., March 1947, pp. 134–5. Slightly different numbers were given to the Assembly in 1947.   [4] Resolution 65 (I), 14 December 1946.

control of a White minority. Further, the issue was utilized by Indian representatives for ventilating their dissatisfaction with the disabilities which the Indian community felt that it had suffered within the Union itself.[1]

It is not astonishing that in the following year the Union Government refused the request proferred by the Assembly of the United Nations that it should submit for consideration its own proposals for a Trusteeship Agreement. It formally expressed, however, its willingness to continue its former practice of submitting annual reports regarding its discharge of the obligations which had been imposed by the Mandate. But in 1948 with the accession to power of the reorganized Nationalist Party, the Union Government showed its increased resentment of the attitude taken by the Assembly, and in 1949 it categorically refused to continue to submit annual reports to it. The only course now open to the Assembly was to refer the matter to the International Court of Justice for an advisory opinion on the status of the territory and on the obligations due by the Union.[2] That, as the result showed, was a course which might with advantage have been taken much earlier.

As had been obvious from the first, there was only one answer open to the International Court of Justice. Its advice was that South-West Africa was still a territory held under the Mandate of 1920; that the Union could not modify the international status of the territory without the consent of the United Nations; that the Union continued to have the international obligations stated in Article 22 of the Covenant of the League;[3] but that on the other hand the Charter of the United Nations imposed on the Union no obligation to place the territory under Trusteeship. In effect, therefore, the Union was in the view of the Court still under the obligation to submit an annual report to the Assembly of the United Nations.

The Government of the Union has since continued to refuse to submit such a report, claiming that the case for this refusal has been strengthened by the inclination of the Assembly to allow discussion regarding South-West Africa to be used as an occasion for a general attack on the attitude adopted towards non-Europeans within the Union itself.[4] The Committee of the Nationalist Party has recently gone further, and has maintained that 'in effect no Mandate now exists; South-West Africa has become one territory and one people with that of the Union so far as the outside world is concerned'.[5] The Assembly of the United Nations has on its part created a special committee which has admitted representations put

---

[1] See below, p. 397.
[2] Resolutions 141 (II), 1 November 1947; 227 (III), 26 November 1948; 337 and 338 (IV), 6 December 1949.   [3] Resolution 449 (V) A.
[4] *Round Table*, June 1948, p. 666; June 1949, p. 292; March 1950, p. 186.
[5] *The Times*, 25 December 1954. *Africa Digest*, September–October 1954, p. 10; September–October 1955, p. 15.

forward on behalf of Natives of South-West Africa by outside advocates whose good faith is undoubted but whose credentials are open to question. In November 1955 the Union recalled its delegation and its permanent representative from the Session of the General Assembly as a protest against its interference with the domestic affairs of the Union.[1] This, it will be recalled, followed the withdrawal of the French delegation in September 1955 for much the same reason.[2]

Whatever the arguments used, it seems clear that the Union will continue to pursue its policy for the closer integration of South-West Africa with its own political and administrative organization, and reference will be made in the following chapter to the legislative measures (and notably the South-West Africa Affairs Amendment Act, no. 23 of 1949) which have been taken to this end.[3] But there has never been any doubt as to the legal right of the Union to adopt measures of administrative integration, nor has this been in fact the matter at issue between the Union and the Assembly of the United Nations. The real issue concerns the liberty which the Assembly has allowed itself in debating the policy followed by the Union in respect of the non-Europeans within its own territory. A further reference to the International Court in 1956 elicited the reply that the Assembly of the United Nations was competent to accept representations and discuss issues relating to policy in South-West Africa. But the issue which vitally affected the Union was the admission of discussions which affected the domestic policy of the Union itself.

HIGH COMMISSION TERRITORIES

It was usual at one period to refer to these Territories as the South African Protectorates,[4] but this designation was not strictly accurate. Basutoland was annexed in 1868 and was soon afterwards incorporated in Cape Colony, being administered as part of it until 1884, when its direct administration was resumed by the Imperial Government.[5] Bechuanaland was proclaimed a Protectorate in 1885, but within a year the southern part of the country was detached and was annexed as the Crown Colony of British Bechuanaland, being finally incorporated in Cape Colony in 1895. It is the extensive northern portion which now constitutes the Bechuanaland Protectorate.[6] For a number of years Swaziland was treated by the British and Transvaal Governments as a form of condominium, but in 1894 a Convention between the two Governments led to its being controlled entirely by the Transvaal, though not

[1] *The Times*, 10 November 1955.
[2] The Union revised this decision in June 1956.   [3] See below, p. 270.
[4] M. Perham and L. Curtis, *The Protectorates of South Africa*, 1935.
[5] *N.A.*, Part V, pp. 47–55. *Basutoland, the Bechuanaland Protectorate, and Swaziland, History of Discussions with the Union of South Africa 1909–1939*, Cmd. 8707, 1952, p. 104.
[6] *N.A.*, Part V, pp. 192–4. Cmd. 8707, p. 105.

formally incorporated in it. Its administration was taken over by Great
Britain in 1903, following on the annexation of the Transvaal as a result
of the South African War.[1]

On the establishment of the Union in 1909 a section was included in
the South Africa Act prescribing the conditions in which new provinces
might be incorporated in it,[2] and official pronouncements made it clear
both to the Parliament of the United Kingdom and to the people of the
three Territories that this section was intended to make provision for their
incorporation in the Union if and when the Governments of the United
Kingdom and the Union should agree that it was opportune that this
measure should be taken. The history of the inclusion of this provision
in the South Africa Act and of the subsequent negotiations regarding the
proposals made for the transfer of these Territories has so close a bearing
on the relations existing between the United Kingdom and the Union that
it will be convenient to refer to it here, leaving for the following chapter
a reference to the system of administration prevailing in the three Territories. The two Governments published in 1952–3 the correspondence
which has taken place between them on the subject of transfer.[3]

Negotiations on Transfer to the Union

When the National Convention of the four South African Colonies met
at Durban in 1908–9 to consider proposals for their federation, it was
generally assumed that the Act of Union would provide also for the
inclusion of the three Territories, which were then being directly administered by the Imperial Government.[4] The Native Authorities of all
three Territories took early steps to protest against the proposal;[5] the
Basuto, who had had the experience of being administered between the
years 1871 and 1883 by the Government of Cape Colony, felt so strongly
on the subject that they sent a deputation to London to represent their
views.[6] As already shown, there were certain crucial issues on which the
different delegations to the National Convention were unable to agree,
and in particular the question of the extension to the Transvaal and the
Free State of the Native franchise exercised in Cape Colony and Natal.
The issue in regard to the transfer of the Territories became closely linked

---

[1] *N.A.*, Part V, pp. 367–70. Cmd. 8707, 1952, p. 108.

[2] South Africa Act 1909, Section 151 and Schedule.

[3] *Basutoland, the Bechuanaland Protectorate, and Swaziland, History of Discussions with the Union of South Africa, 1909–1939*, Cmd. 8707, 1952. *Negotiations Regarding the Transfer to the Union of South Africa of the Government of Basutoland, the Bechuanaland Protectorate and Swaziland, 1910–1939*, Pretoria, 1952–3.

[4] E. H. Walton, *The Inner History of the National Convention of South Africa*, 1912, pp. 295–302. R. H. Brand, *The Union of South Africa*, 1909, pp. 97–109.

[5] Cmd. 8707, p. 5. *N.A.*, Part V, p. 207.

[6] *Cambridge History of the British Empire*, vol. viii, pp. 631 ff. *N.A.*, Part V, p. 64. G. Lagden, *The Basuto*, 1909, vol. ii, pp. 623 ff.

up with that of the extension of the franchise, and it was so treated not only in the debates in the Convention, but in the subsequent discussions on the draft Act of Union in the United Kingdom Parliament.[1]

The National Convention was in consequence unable to make any definite recommendation on the proposal for transfer of the Territories, and limited itself to making detailed provision in the draft South Africa Act for the terms on which transfer should be made, if and when the occasion arose. These conditions embodied substantial safeguards for the maintenance of the rights of the Natives of the Territories in the event of transfer, and in particular as regards the question of rights in their land. The terms and conditions as drafted by the Convention[2] were eventually embodied with only small modifications in Section 151 and the Schedule to the Act as passed by the United Kingdom Parliament.[3] The matter was debated at some length there and an assurance was given that Parliament would have the fullest opportunity of discussing and, if its members so wished, of disapproving any proposed transfer of the Territories; it was also emphasized that the wishes of the inhabitants would be ascertained and considered before any transfer took place.[4]

In Great Britain the official view was at the time clearly in favour of the transfer and it saw no reason to doubt that this would take place in due course. The deputation of Basuto were told by the Secretary of State in 1909 that there would be no immediate change, but that if South Africa were to be united, then it would be desirable as well as necessary that the Basuto people should come under the same Government as the rest of South Africa.[5] In 1910 the High Commissioner, Lord Selborne, informed the Bechuana Chiefs that it was not possible to say how long it would be before Bechuanaland was handed over to the Union, but that in the natural course of things this would take place some day.[6] In 1913 certain references made at a meeting of the British South Africa Company to the subsistence of the rights which it claimed in Bechuanaland[7] called forth from General Botha a request that the transfer of Bechuanaland and Swaziland should be expedited; he was informed in reply that it would be impossible to justify to Parliament in the near future the transfer of Bechuanaland, but the terms of the reply left it to be assumed that the transfer of Swaziland might be considered.[8]

At the end of the First World War, Generals Botha and Smuts put

[1] M. Perham and L. Curtis, op. cit. pp. 12–14. [2] Issued as Cmd. 4525, 1909.

[3] Cmd. 8707, Appendixes IV and V, pp. 118–24. For the grounds for the inclusion of these clauses, see E. A. Walker, *Lord de Villiers and His Times, South Africa, 1842–1914*, 1925, pp. 445 ff.

[4] Ibid. pp. 6, 115–17, 131. [5] *N.A.*, Part V, p. 64.

[6] *Colonial Reports, Bechuanaland Protectorate*, 1909–10, p. 12.

[7] For the connexion between the Chartered Company and Bechuanaland, see *N.A.*, Part V, pp. 197–200; and *Report of Rhodesia-Nyasaland Royal Commission*, Cmd. 5949, 1938, pp. 240–2. See also the correspondence with the Government of Southern Rhodesia printed as Appendix VII, Cmd. 8707, p. 127. [8] Cmd. 8707, pp. 6, 12–13.

forward a strong plea that consideration should be given to the immediate transfer of Swaziland, while agreeing that there was no special urgency about the other two Territories. They stated that the Union was prepared to provide at once full political rights to the European inhabitants of Swaziland.[1] The matter was, however, dropped for a time owing to the death of General Botha. Informal discussions which took place in 1922 between General Smuts and members of the European Advisory Council in Swaziland caused such concern to the Swazi Native Authorities that they sent a deputation on the subject to London; they were reminded by the Secretary of State of the safeguards for Native rights which were provided in the Schedule to the Act, and they were assured that these provisions would necessarily come into operation if and when the transfer should be approved by the King.[2]

In 1924 a number of European residents in Swaziland and Bechuanaland approached the Prime Minister of the Union with the request that he would take active steps to secure the early incorporation of their territories with the Union; the movement made on behalf of Swaziland was admittedly due to the desire of those Europeans who held land rights to secure the extension of the Union railway into the Territory. It is noteworthy that while the Prime Minister urged the British Government to take the question into early consideration, he at the same time told the European deputation that his Party was not prepared to incorporate in the Union any territory 'unless the inhabitants of the country themselves were prepared to come in'.[3]

In the course of these discussions no direct reference had so far been made to Basutoland. There were in Basutoland no European settlers whose views could be cited in regard to the proposal for transfer, and the Native Authorities had shown in 1909 that they were strongly opposed to it. As regards the other Territories, the approach made by the Union to the British Government had so far been confined to a ministerial *pourparler*, and no formal request had been made in the manner contemplated by Section 151 of the Act. The Union Ministers clearly appreciated the force of the argument used by the Secretary of State in 1927, that it would be unfortunate if the question of transfer were definitely raised and could not be carried through. There was a full exchange of correspondence in the years 1926 and 1927, and the Secretary of State pointed out that a personal visit lately paid by him to the Territories had convinced him of the strength of African feeling against the transfer; even an attempt to ascertain the African view on the subject of transfer would in his view be likely to lead to serious unrest.[4]

---

[1] Cmd. 8707, pp. 14–15. For the European population of Swaziland see *N.A.*, Part V, pp. 335, 377, 402–5. [2] Cmd. 8707, p. 125.
[3] Ibid. pp. 15–17. [4] Ibid., p. 36.

In the following years it was becoming increasingly clear to the authorities in Great Britain that the application of the policy of segregation on which General Hertzog's Government was now entering, and which was to culminate in the enactment of the Representation of Natives Act of 1936,[1] was likely to make it increasingly difficult for any British Minister to sponsor in Parliament a proposal for the transfer of the Territories to the Union. On the other hand, the spirit which inspired the policy of segregation was increasingly urging its exponents in the Union to secure the transfer of the Territories to its charge, if only because the principle on which they were then being administered under British auspices manifested an outlook on African relations so entirely different from that which was implicit in the doctrine of segregation.

British Ministers had at one time undoubtedly gone to some lengths in encouraging the Union to believe that the transfer would take place in due course; but the Union Ministers could not complain that there had been a breach of a definite undertaking to transfer the Territories. The declarations made to the British Parliament at the passing of the South Africa Act made it clear that the Crown would concede the transfer only after Parliament had had an opportunity of discussing its merits. The stipulation for the previous consultation of Natives did not imply that their assent to the transfer was essential; but Parliament was obviously entitled to take their views into account in judging of the merits of the scheme. Realizing no doubt their inability to argue that there had been a clear breach of contract, the Union Ministers turned for a time to arguments based on the embarrassment caused to the Union by the fact that it had no hand in the administrative control over areas which were so largely an *enclave* within its boundaries. For a time the correspondence was full of allegations and replications about east coast fever, locust invasions, sheep scab, fugitive offenders, and lung sickness.[2] But while the need for the adjustment of such matters might call for a more satisfactory measure of administrative co-operation, it did not advance the case for a transfer of political control.

Aide-mémoire of 1935

Negotiations entered on a new phase when the Secretary of State handed to General Smuts in 1933 a Memorandum which was subsequently to form the basis of an *aide-mémoire* formally agreed with Generals Smuts and Hertzog in 1935.[3] Its gist was an agreement, first, that certain of the provisions of the Schedule to the Act required to be re-examined in the light of the constitutional developments which had taken place since it

[1] See above, p. 164.
[2] Cmd. 8707, pp. 45–52.
[3] Published as Cmd. 4948, 1935. See also Cmd. 8707, pp. 53 ff.

was passed,[1] and secondly, that the policy of the two Governments should in future be directed 'to bringing about a situation in which, if transfer were to become a matter of practical politics, it could be effected with the full acquiescence of the populations concerned'. The terms were precise. They did not, as General Hertzog was unfortunately led to suggest in 1936,[2] imply that the British Ministers had for the first time declared that they were ready to hand over the Territories and that Swaziland at least would be handed over within two or three years. The *aide-mémoire* went no farther than to urge a measure of co-operation between the two Governments in order to secure the goodwill of the people of the Territories towards the scheme of transfer.

But co-operation did not prove to mean the same to the Union Ministers as to the British Authorities. The former clearly hoped that Union officials might be invited to join in the work of administration and that British officials in the Territories would openly impress on the Native Authorities a policy of goodwill to the Union. The British on their part proceeded to draw up a scheme of material improvements needed in the three Territories, for which the Union was invited to provide half the cost. Its Government agreed to do so, and included in its Estimates a sum of £35,000 for expenditure during the year 1936; but the attitude taken by the Native Authorities in the Territories towards the grant was such that the question of the Union contribution was by common agreement allowed to remain in abeyance.[3]

The Territories had as a group received in the past little direct assistance from the Imperial Exchequer for the improvement of their local conditions,[4] and the attention now directed to their needs was of benefit in securing them more aid from this source; but it was not to be expected that the offer of a contribution by the Union should start a tide of goodwill in its favour. Nor did much more in the nature of goodwill accrue from the appointment in 1938 of a Joint Advisory Conference on Co-operation between the British and the Union authorities.[5] It made a useful study of possible schemes of improvement, but during and after the war most of these came within the scope of the greatly increased grants which followed the passing of the British Colonial Development and Welfare Act of 1940.[6]

It is at this stage that the negotiations on the question of transfer may be said to have rested. The Government of the United Kingdom has continued to reiterate its pledge that no decision will be taken till the inhabitants have been consulted and Parliament has been given an opportunity to express its views.[7] The European inhabitants of Swaziland and

---

[1] See below, p. 263.
[2] Cmd. 8707, pp. 65–69.
[3] Ibid., p. 69.
[4] *N.A.*, Part V, pp. 20, 298.
[5] Cmd. 8707, pp. 90–96.
[6] *N.A.*, Part V, pp. 20, 166, 347.
[7] Statement by Prime Minister in House of Commons, 22 November 1951.

Bechuanaland now appear to show much less interest in securing the transfer; the Native Authorities in all three Territories seem to be even more opposed to it than before.

The Territories continue to be economically dependent on the export of their labour and of their local produce to the Union,[1] though the opening of a market for the export of beef from Bechuanaland to Southern Rhodesia and the Belgian Congo has rendered the Protectorate somewhat less dependent than previously upon export to the Union. By an Agreement of 1910 the Territories are treated as part of the Union for customs purposes, each receiving a proportion of the revenues collected. Union currency is used in all three Territories, and communications, including postal services, are to a large extent provided by the Union. It can indeed be urged with justice that the inhabitants of the Territories are in an economic sense more in need of South Africa than South Africa is in need of them, and that if the Union treated them as inhabitants of foreign territories the economic consequences to them might be very serious.[2]

The Union's Policy

Within the Union there has been increasing pressure from the Nationalist Party and press in favour of transfer. But no formal demand has yet been made, supported by addresses from the Houses of Parliament in the Union, as seems to be required by Section 151 of the South Africa Act. The Nationalist Party urges that the recent development of its policy, which will in the future rely on the use of indigenous institutions as the agencies of Local Government and will remodel the procedure of Native education in the spirit of Bantu tradition,[3] should assure the African population of the Territories that their customary institutions will continue to be respected after transfer. Africans in the Territories are apt to reply that the movement for the adoption of a republican status for the Union gives them cause to fear that transfer may remove them entirely from the orbit of the British Crown, which has hitherto stood as sponsor for the maintenance of their institutions and the possession of their lands.

Meanwhile there are certain doubts regarding the position created by the constitutional developments of the early thirties which still require to be resolved. In 1934 a British parliamentary committee appointed to study the question pointed out that the position had changed widely in respect of the safeguards which the South Africa Act had provided for regulating the administration of the Territories in the event of the transfer taking place.[4] The enactment of the Statute of Westminster and of the

[1] N.A., Part V, pp. 14, 333, 428.
[2] Prime Minister of the Union, as reported in *The Times*, 15 May 1952.
[3] See above, p. 166.
[4] Cmd. 8707, Appendix IX, p. 131.

Status of the Union Act of 1934[1] had explicitly repealed those general sections of the South Africa Act of 1909 which had made provision for the reservation of legislation for the pleasure of the King and for the possibility of the disallowance by him of any measure passed by the Union Parliament.[2] The latter is accordingly free to repeal or alter section 151 of the Act or any of the 25 Articles of its Schedule which prescribed special safeguards for the protection of the people of the Territories; it will be recalled that Article 20 of the Schedule specifically reserved to the King the right to disallow any legislation referring to a transferred Territory and Article 25 required that any Bill of the Union Parliament which sought to amend the Schedule should be referred for the King's pleasure.

Moreover, the whole constitutional position against the background of which section 151 was framed has radically altered.[3] In 1909 the King was advised in all matters, including Dominion affairs, by his Ministers in the United Kingdom. The Queen on the other hand is now advised on South African affairs by her Ministers in South Africa. Should, therefore, these Ministers, acting with the support of the Union Legislature, make a formal demand for the transfer of the Territories to the Union, it would be possible for the Crown to receive divergent advice on the merits of the transfer from two sources, both having equal constitutional authority. Failing any solution by mutual agreement, it would appear that a refusal by the United Kingdom to hand over possession of the Territories must, from a practical standpoint, be regarded as decisive. It would be of no advantage to speculate here either on the reaction which such a decision might entail on Union policy regarding its economic relations with the High Commission Territories, or on the influence which it might have on the attitude of the Union towards matters such as the maintenance of its membership of the Commonwealth.[4]

FEDERATION OF RHODESIA AND NYASALAND

When Southern Rhodesia was created a 'self-governing colony' in 1923 its Constitution reproduced from the Charter of the British South Africa Company the provision under which Africans who possessed the general electoral qualifications had the same right of franchise as Europeans.[5] At the same time provisions were incorporated in its Constitution which sought to safeguard the interests of the African population by making the assent of the Government of the United Kingdom necessary for the enactment of any legislation of a discriminatory character.[6] In fact, however,

[1] See above, p. 153.   [2] South Africa Act 1909, Sections 64, 65, 66.
[3] Cmd. 8707, paragraphs 29–31, p. 10.
[4] See above, p. 157.   [5] *O.Y.S.R., 1952*, p. 61.
[6] Letters Patent (Constitution) 1923. The Charter is given at length in the *Official Year Book* above quoted.

legislation was enacted, particularly at an early stage in the history of the new Government, which recalled some aspects of the differential legislation of the Union of South Africa. From the first there was strong pressure exerted by the local European community for the delimitation of separate European and African areas, on lines similar to those followed by the creation of Native Reserves in the Union, and this course was duly recommended by the Land Commission which reported in 1925; it was given effect in the Land Apportionment Act of 1930.[1]

While, however, the general tendency has been to separate the areas held by the two communities, it is also true that the legislation has resulted in leaving for the African community a proportion of the total area of the Colony which is far more favourable than that which has resulted from the legislation undertaken at various times in the Union. On the other hand, the pass system for Africans, which was consolidated by the Natives Registration Act of 1936, has followed the pattern of that of the Union, and the legislation designed to control the admission of Africans to residence in the urban areas was of the same character.[2] The Industrial Conciliation Act of 1934 had in practice the effect of establishing an industrial colour bar comparable (at all events as regards employment in the scheduled areas) with that in force in the Union.[3] The procedure followed in the system of Native Administration, like that of the Union, has paid little regard to the traditional position of the Chiefs, and it has shown the same disinclination to allow the Native Tribunals to exercise the power of criminal jurisdiction.[4]

The European community in Southern Rhodesia had at the outset close associations with South Africa, and it is not unnatural that the policy adopted towards Africans should in the first instance have been modelled on the legislation of the Union. There have, however, been certain factors which have tended in later years to differentiate the policy of Southern Rhodesia from that followed in South Africa. The attitude adopted towards Africans has in general been that which has characterized the Europeans of Cape Colony rather than those of the Transvaal and the Orange Free State. Secondly, the economy of Southern Rhodesia has until recent years been largely rural and did not give rise to the problems created in the Union by large aggregations of Africans in industrial centres. Nor was the position complicated by the existence of large communities of Indians and Coloured people.

At the period when General Hertzog and his Party were giving practical expression in the Union to a policy of segregation, the leaders of opinion in Southern Rhodesia were evolving a conception of the relations between the communities which they themselves described as 'parallel development'.

[1] See below, p. 703.
[3] See below, pp. 1440-2.
[2] See below, pp. 572-3.
[4] See below, p. 567.

In 1935 the objective sought in this conception was set forth by the Prime Minister of Southern Rhodesia in a passage which was quoted at length in the report of the Rhodesia-Nyasaland Royal Commission appointed in 1938. The country should, he said, be divided into two areas, European and African, and the two communities should develop side by side, though there could be no question that the European must remain in control of the country and must supervise the development of the African area. At the same time he urged that Rhodesia should exhibit a liberal outlook on the progress which might be achieved by the African within his own field of activity.[1]

During the Second World War and in the years immediately following the war, the views of the European leaders seemed to be moving away from the conception of parallelism as thus defined. When the Land Apportionment Act was amended in 1941, the Prime Minister expressed a doubt whether a mere separation of the country into two areas could be a final solution; the task of the future was rather to make the African a counterpart of the European in mind and vigour. The number of Africans in urban and industrial employment continued to increase, and the amendment to the Land Act put forward in 1945, together with the Natives (Urban Areas) Accommodation and Registration Act of 1946, recognized this development by making provision for the establishment of Native Urban Areas and by rendering it compulsory for employers to provide accommodation for African workers and their wives.[2] Views on the relative position to be assigned to Europeans and Africans seemed indeed to be in a state of transition, and there was a growing tendency to reject the rigid differentiation implied in the South African doctrine of *apartheid*.

This tendency was strengthened in the course of the long series of debates which preceded the establishment of the Federation of Rhodesia and Nyasaland.[3] It was clear that if the scheme of federation was to secure a general acceptance, some measure of adjustment would have to be found between the views which had originally inspired the conception of 'parallelism' in Southern Rhodesia and those officially sponsored in Great Britain, which had held out to Africans in Northern Rhodesia and Nyasaland the prospect of taking their part in the self-governing régime to be extended to those dependencies. There was, moreover, an instinctive repugnance in Southern Rhodesia to the prospect of racial friction which seemed to be the inevitable consequence of the application of the doctrine of *apartheid* in South Africa.

At the same time there was a division of opinion in the European community as to the wisdom of any change which might endanger the

---

[1] *Report of the Rhodesia-Nyasaland Royal Commission*, Cmd. 5949, p. 170.
[2] See below, p. 573.   [3] See below, pp. 278 ff.

maintenance of what appeared to be the core of the doctrine of 'parallelism', namely, the concept that the control of the government of the country must rest permanently with their community. There was no disposition to advocate the abolition of the system which admitted Africans to the electoral franchise, but Europeans in general were not ready to contemplate that the balance of voting power might pass into the hands of Africans. Already in 1951 measures had been taken to safeguard against any serious increase in the number of African voters. The original franchise qualification had included both an educational and an income test, and by Act 27 of 1951 the income qualification was doubled, on the ground that there had been a comparable decline in the value of money since the qualification was originally determined.[1] By 1953 only 481 Africans had been registered as voters, though a very much larger number were said to be eligible for the vote. So far there has been no elected African member in the Southern Rhodesia Legislature.

'Partnership' as the Basis of Race Relations

The range of divergence between Europeans and Africans in the new Federation is thus less than in the Union of South Africa, and it should not be so difficult for them to find a common meeting-ground. Attempts have been made by the majority party of Europeans in the Federation to find such ground in the conception that the relations of European and non-Europeans in a multi-racial State should be regarded as those of 'partnership'. The term appears to have been first used in this particular connexion in 1950,[2] though it had (as will subsequently be seen) already begun to come into use in political discussions in Great Britain in a somewhat different relation.[3] One of the objectives set out in the preamble of the Constitution of the Federation is to 'foster partnership and co-operation' between its inhabitants.[4]

But like the term 'trusteeship', that of 'partnership' has in fact a moral rather than a political connotation. No one can question the great influence which can be exercised both in politics and in social life by moral conceptions of this character; the principle of trusteeship, for example, was a 'word of power' in British Colonial policy long before it was adopted by the League of Nations as expressing the standard which should be universally adopted in dealing with undeveloped peoples.[5] But the value attaching to a principle of this character lies in the authority it can exercise in the discussion of issues where the interests of Europeans and Africans are openly at variance, and the proceedings of the Federation

---

[1] Sir G. Huggins, *African Affairs*, vol. li, April 1952, p. 144.
[2] Ibid.   [3] See below, p. 193.
[4] Annex to Rhodesia and Nyasaland Order in Council, no. 1199, 1953, p. 15.
[5] See below, p. 247.

have not yet provided an issue which will show whether it can comply with this test.

Meanwhile the implications of 'partnership' as used in Rhodesian political circles have been subject to a variety of interpretation by parties which hold divergent views regarding the principles which should determine the relations of European and African. The Federal Party Congress of Southern Rhodesia, meeting in 1952, contemplated the 'gradual extension of political rights and privileges to those who conform to civilized standards of behaviour and culture'. On the other hand, the rival Confederation Party appeared to hold that the conception of partnership might cover the complete social separation of Europeans and Africans and the limitation of African political representation to 'a few Africans on the common roll'.[1] A more liberal outlook was reflected in a resolution accepted by the Legislative Council of Northern Rhodesia in 1954 which dealt specifically with the principle of 'partnership'. It looked forward to the termination of the existing system of racial representation in the Legislature of the Protectorate, holding that 'every lawful inhabitant of Northern Rhodesia has the right to progress according to his character and qualifications without distinction of race, colour, or creed'.[2]

While, however, there has been a lively debate among Europeans in the Rhodesias regarding the implications of the principle of partnership, it is not always realized that it will have no value as a solution of the problems of a multi-racial society unless it can commend itself also to Africans. It has been described by one critic as 'a sophisticated and Western-centred concept which can never appeal to Africans, and is therefore at the best only a desperate line of defence against the dangers perceived as a consequence of nationalism'.[3] How far this will prove to be true will depend on the temper in which the European community in the Rhodesias approaches the concrete problems presented by the scheme of Federation, and not least those of an economic and social character.

BRITISH EAST AFRICAN TERRITORIES

Schemes for Closer Union

After the British occupation of Tanganyika during the First World War, there were many aspirations expressed for the creation of a 'New Dominion' in East Africa, which should, in the view of its sponsors, include Kenya, Uganda, Tanganyika, Nyasaland, Northern Rhodesia, and Zanzibar.[4]

[1] *Commonwealth Survey*, 25 September 1953, no. 131, p. 3.
[2] Resolutions known as the Moffat Resolutions, Northern Rhodesia Hansard, 29 July 1954, col. 616.
[3] N. Steven-Hubbard, in *Africa Today*, 1955, pp. 256 ff.
[4] *The Times*, 12 June 1926.

The suggestion met, however, with little official support.[1] Among other things, it was considered doubtful whether the creation of a self-governing Dominion would be compatible with the maintenance of the mandatory obligations undertaken by Great Britain for the administration of Tanganyika. The Mandate had authorized the administrative union of a mandated area with a neighbouring territory, provided that measures adopted to that end did not otherwise infringe the provisions of the Mandate, but the Permanent Mandates Commission showed itself doubtful of the legal propriety even of a customs union between the three East African dependencies.[2] The proposal to include Tanganyika in a self-governing Dominion clearly had political implications which went far beyond those of a customs union.

In 1924, following a motion in the British Parliament for the appointment of a commission to report on the co-ordination of policy in East and Central African dependencies, the East Africa Commission made some local inquiries on the views held about federation,[3] and reported that they found little support for the idea and some definite hostility. It recommended, however, the holding at regular intervals of inter-territorial conferences in which all six dependencies should be represented; matters of general policy should be discussed at a conference of Governors, and the heads of technical services should meet to discuss other matters, such as education and agriculture. The first Governors' conference was held at Nairobi in 1926.

The question of union was again examined by the Commission on the Closer Union of the Dependencies in Eastern and Central Africa (the Hilton-Young Commission) which reported in 1929.[4] It recommended a series of steps to be taken towards an ultimate administrative union of the East African territories under a Governor-General.[5] Following on this recommendation a proposal was considered in 1929 for the appointment of a High Commissioner exercising control over certain major services, all other matters, including Native policy, being left to the local Legislatures.[6] In 1930–1 the Joint Select Committee of both Houses of Parliament, to which the proposals of the Commission on Closer Union had been referred, expressed the view that any far-reaching step in the direction of closer union in East Africa would be inopportune, but recommended that there should be regular conferences of the Governors of Kenya, Uganda, and Tanganyika, with periodical extraordinary conferences including

---

[1] For more recent proposals for the creation of an East African Dominion see *The Times*, 21 November 1953, and *Africa Digest*, March–April 1955, p. 18.

[2] C. Leubuscher, *Tanganyika Territory, a Study of Economic Policy under Mandate*, 1944, pp. 101–20.

[3] *Report of the East Africa Commission* (the Ormsby-Gore Commission), Cmd. 2387, 1925.

[4] See also below, p. 276.

[5] Cmd. 3234, 1929, pp. 142–5. See also Cmd. 3574, 1930.

[6] *Report of Sir S. Wilson on his visit to East Africa*, Cmd. 3378, 1929.

the Governors of Northern Rhodesia and Nyasaland, and the Resident, Zanzibar. It added that a Joint Secretariat should be created which would serve also for inter-territorial conferences on technical subjects.[1] When in 1934 and 1935 representatives of European unofficial opinion again urged an early union of Kenya and Tanganyika, the Secretary of State replied that the reasons which had led the Joint Select Committee to regard such a step as premature still held good.

During the Second World War the East African Production Supply Council and a number of other bodies were set up to co-ordinate the economy and manpower of the East African territories, and as the result of this experience it was proposed in 1945 to attempt some practicable measure for dealing with the services common to the three territories without reopening the question of their political union.[2] It became clear, however, that if the scheme was to work successfully, some forum of public discussion, in the nature of a Legislative Chamber, would be an indispensable feature of the machinery. Tentative proposals were put forward at the end of 1945 as a basis of discussion,[3] but it was not until 1947 that the somewhat contentious issues regarding its composition were finally settled, and a revised scheme sanctioned by the British Government.[4]

East Africa High Commission

The High Commission, consisting of the Governors of Kenya, Tanganyika, and Uganda, held its first meeting at Nairobi in February 1948. The East African Central Assembly, the legislative organ of the High Commission, was established by Order in Council for a period of four years from 1948, but this was subsequently extended to the end of 1955. The Central Assembly is presided over by a Speaker, and consists of seven *ex officio* members who are officers in the service of the High Commission, three nominated official members (one from each territory), and 13 unofficial members, who are appointed in the manner explained below.[5]

The High Commission has power to legislate, with the consent of the Assembly, in respect of a defined range of inter-territorial services, and, with the consent of the Legislatures of the three territories, on any matter concerned with the order and good government of the territories. The Commission has been responsible for the administration of the railway, harbour, post and telegraph, and customs and excise services, together with the research and scientific services dealing with agriculture, forestry, health, and fisheries, and also the organizations for dealing with tsetse

[1] *Report of the Joint Select Committee on Closer Union in East Africa*, 1931, pp. 14–15.
[2] *Annual Report of the East Africa High Commission 1953*, pp. 91–92.
[3] Colonial no. 191, 1945.
[4] Inter-Colonial Organization in East Africa, Revised Proposals, Colonial no. 210, 1947. East Africa (High Commission) Order in Council 1947, cf. Cmd. 7423, paras. 123–4.
[5] See below, p. 196.

and locust control. It is, indeed, in the expansion of the scientific and research services that the influence of the Commission has been most strongly felt.[1]

The major services undertaken, such as the administration of the railways or of the customs and excise, are self supporting in point of finance; the range of the activities concerned with services of other kinds is best shown by the extent of the contributions made by the three territories to the Commission to defray the expenditure which they involve.[2] In 1953 revenue was provided for these operations to the extent of £3,310,816, the major contributors being Kenya (£968,949), Tanganyika (£651,672), and Uganda (£537,003). The United Kingdom contributed £784,639, mainly for the financing of certain schemes supported by funds provided by the Colonial Development and Welfare Act.

The Commission is thus an institution of a somewhat unusual character; it does not deal with political issues nor control domestic policies; it can be effective only with the co-operation of the Legislatures and Executive Governments of the three territories. But the fact that it is so largely functional in its operations seems so far to have saved it from the tension in the political field which was forecast in the discussions that (as will be subsequently shown) took place in 1946 and 1947 regarding the composition of the Central Assembly.[3]

Multi-Racial Problems: Kenya

It would be difficult to find in the other British territories of Africa any views regarding the two concepts of 'identity' and 'differentiation' as definite as those to be found in the Union or (to a lesser degree) in the Rhodesias. The eventual achievement of self-government has for long been the declared objective of British Colonial policy,[4] and the political institutions which have been created in a number of dependencies as a first step towards that end have demonstrated clearly the intention of the British Government that all the major communities should as far as possible be represented in the local Legislatures which will be the organs of self-government. In practice, therefore, the crucial issue has resolved itself into the question of the weightage to be given to European and non-European interests respectively in the political structure of the country. The most typical instance of the part played by this issue is afforded by Kenya, and it provides an instructive chapter in the record of the British endeavour to solve the problems involved in the development of dependencies with a multi-racial population.

[1] See below, pp. 901–2, 915–16, 970.
[2] *Annual Report on the East Africa High Commission 1953*, Colonial no. 305.
[3] See below, pp. 195–6.
[4] See above, p. 146.

In Kenya this problem was at an early date responsible for a conflict
of view between the British Government and members of the local
European community. They had maintained that the principle of devolution culminating in full Responsible Government, which had been
followed by Great Britain in her relations with other British settlements
in Africa and elsewhere, was applicable also to their case. There was
reasonable precedent for this claim. Cape Colony had acquired a status
of Responsible Government in 1872 and Natal in 1893.[1] Southern
Rhodesia achieved Responsible Government in 1923, when its European
population only numbered 32,600.

But the definite issue created by the claims of the non-European communities in Kenya had not been openly faced in Southern Rhodesia;
there the choice presented to the vote of the European community in 1923
had only lain between incorporation with the Union and a régime of
Responsible Government. When confronted with the demand put forward
by the European community in Kenya the British Government showed
that it was no longer prepared to accept as a rule of practice the procedure
which had been followed in Cape Colony, Natal, or Southern Rhodesia,
and which had left the European community in each case in a position to
control the share to be taken by other communities in the future government of the country. The decision of the British Government was expressed in a declaration which, though made with special reference to the
position of Indians in Kenya, was widely understood to reflect a statement
of general policy. The Devonshire White Paper of 1923[2] declared that:

Primarily Kenya is an African territory, and His Majesty's Government think
it necessary definitely to record their considered opinion that the interests of the
African Natives must be paramount, and that if and when those interests and
the interests of the immigrant races should conflict, the former should prevail.
. . . In the administration of Kenya His Majesty's Government regard themselves as exercising a trust on behalf of the African population, and they are
unable to delegate or share this trust, the object of which may be defined as the
protection and advancement of the Native races.

The issue of this statement was, however, followed next year by the
visit of the East Africa Commission to Kenya and by its reminder of the
fact that the European settlers in Kenya had been responsible for providing the stimulus to such economic progress as the Colony had shown.[3]
In 1926 there took place a conference of the Governors of the British East
Africa dependencies which, though dealing primarily with what came to
be known in East Africa as the 'dual policy' (namely, the complementary
development of non-Native and Native production), followed the example

[1] *Cambridge History of the British Empire*, vol. viii, pp. 487, 542.
[2] *Indians in Kenya*, Cmd. 1922, 1923, p. 9.
[3] *Report of the East Africa Commission*, Cmd. 2387, 1925.

of the East Africa Commission in emphasizing the importance of the part that was being played by Europeans in the development of the territory.

It was largely as the result of this conference that the British Government issued in 1927 a White Paper of which one object clearly was to assuage some of the feelings aroused by the categorical assertion of the paramountcy of Native interests contained in the declaration of 1923. The responsibilities of trusteeship must, it asserted, rest for some considerable time mainly on the agents of the Imperial Government, but the Government desired 'to associate more closely in this high and honourable task those who as colonists or residents have identified their interests with the prosperity of the country'.[1]

Kenya and the Commission on Closer Union

There followed in 1929 the report made by the important Commission on Closer Union in the East African Territories. The conception of the position of the Imperial Government as the impartial arbiter between communities whose interests might be in conflict formed an essential feature of the constitution which the Commission outlined for a possible federation of the three East African territories.[2] That the British community in Kenya showed itself unwilling to accept the scheme put forward by the Commission was partly due to their apprehension lest the large Indian community in the Colony[3] should acquire an undue share of representation in the Legislature, but it was due in part also to the persistence of the feelings aroused by the original declaration regarding the paramountcy of African interests.

A White Paper of 1930 made a further attempt to allay this feeling. It agreed that the creation of a field for the full development of Native life was (as the Commission on Closer Union had represented) the first charge on any territory; but this was not incompatible with the common duty of any government to promote the prosperity of all the inhabitants, including the immigrant communities within it. Dominion status was the ultimate goal of Kenya, but this could not be attained until the Native community were able to participate in self-governing institutions.[4]

The sentiment thus expressed was unexceptionable, but it was not sufficient to reassure the European settlers. It required the authority of the Joint Select Committee of Parliament, which was appointed to deal specifically with the Report of the Commission on Closer Union in East Africa, to provide a final statement of policy on the issue. The principle of paramountcy, as it pointed out, had been enunciated in relation to

---

[1] *Future Policy in regard to Eastern Africa*, Cmd. 2904, 1927.
[2] *Report of the Commission on Closer Union of the Dependencies in Eastern and Central Africa*, Cmd. 3234, 1929.   [3] See below, p. 408.
[4] *Memorandum on Native Policy in East Africa* (the Passfield White Paper), Cmd. 3573, 1930.

specific points (particularly in connexion with land and labour questions) on which a direct conflict of Native and non-Native interests might arise, and it added that 'the doctrine of paramountcy means no more than that the interests of the overwhelming majority of the indigenous population should not be subordinated to those of a minority belonging to another race, however important in itself'.[1] Here, as was afterwards officially agreed,[2] was a supersession rather than an interpretation of the terms of the declaration made in 1923 on the subject of paramountcy, and if that declaration remained an uncomfortable memory with the Europeans in East Africa, it now ceased to be the object of active attack by them. In Kenya their demand was now for an elected non-official majority in the local Legislature rather than for an early grant of Responsible Government on the model of Southern Rhodesia.

In its detailed recommendations the Joint Select Committee had not gone farther than to propose an increase in the number of members of the Legislature nominated to represent African interests, but without prejudice to the power of the Governor to nominate persons of African descent for inclusion among them. The Europeans in Kenya have never wholly abandoned their contention that the control of the Colony's affairs should rest in their hands, and some of their leaders have shown a doubt whether this can be sufficiently secured by means of an unofficial European elected majority in the Legislature. They have sought accordingly to secure greater influence in the field of executive government. The inclusion of unofficial (and especially European) members in the Executive Council,[3] the creation of Statutory Boards under unofficial (and especially European) control, the reorganization of the Executive Council in such manner that each member would be directly responsible for the affairs of a Department or of a group of Departments—all these measures were designed to increase the effective influence of the European settled community without openly claiming a guarantee for the permanence of European control.[4]

But if European unofficial influence in the executive conduct of affairs was thus increasing throughout this period, changes were also occurring in the representation of Africans in the Legislative Council. The first African member was appointed in 1944,[5] taking the place of a European nominated to represent African interests; the second European member

[1] *Report of the Joint Select Committee on Closer Union in East Africa*, H.C. 156, 1931, paras. 67, 73, 101.

[2] Secretary of State in H.C. Deb., 22 September 1948, col. 872.

[3] In 1937 the Executive Council was reconstituted to include four officials and four unofficials (two Europeans normally chosen from the elected members of the Legislature, one Indian, and one member representing African interests).

[4] *Proposals for the Reorganization of the Administration of Kenya* (Sessional Paper no. 3 of 1945).

[5] Kenya Legislative Council, *Debates*, 9 June 1944, cols. 241–2.

representing African interests was replaced by an African member in 1947; in 1948 two more nominated unofficial African members were added.[1] In 1952 the unofficial member of the Executive Council representing African interests, who had hitherto been a European, was replaced by an African.

'Partnership' as the Aim of British Policy

It was in these circumstances that the word 'partnership' began to be widely employed to describe the relations between members of the European and other communities which it was the aim of British policy to establish in East Africa. Something has already been said regarding the use of this term in the particular conditions of the Federation of Rhodesia and Nyasaland.[2] As then remarked, its use in Great Britain had an earlier history. It had originally been employed there with a general connotation designed to indicate the relationship which should exist between the United Kingdom and those dependent territories which were emerging to self-government. It was thus designed to mark an advance over the concept of Trusteeship, the term hitherto accepted as signalizing the nature of the responsibilities of the United Kingdom towards its dependencies.[3] 'Some of us feel now', the Secretary of State said in 1943, 'that the word "trustee" is rather too static in its connotation, and that we should prefer to combine with the status of trustee the position also of partner.'[4]

This specific use of the word was, however, relatively short-lived, and it soon came to be used to describe rather the character of the relationship which British policy sought to promote between the various communities in multi-racial territories such as Kenya or Tanganyika. As such it was rather an aspiration than a policy, and it was to be defined as much by what it did not demand as by any positive desiderata. If it did not require universal suffrage or even the common roll, it seemed at least to require that each community should have some voice in the political process; there was, in short, an underlying assumption that it was possible to achieve such measure of accommodation between the various communities as would justify the British Government in handing over its responsibilities to an Administration which represented the outcome of such a process. So far as concerned East Africa, partnership seemed to depend partly on the feasibility of arranging for an adequate measure of African (as well as

[1] Additional Royal Instructions, 27 April 1948.   [2] See above, p. 186.
[3] E. A. Walker, *The British Empire, Its Structure and Spirit*, 1943, pp. 50, 163–4. E. Barker, *Ideas and Ideals of British Empire*, 1946, pp. 54, 61–71. Lord Hailey, *The Future of Colonial Peoples*, 1944, pp. 8–9. H. D. Hall, 'The British Commonwealth and Trusteeship', *Journal of International Affairs*, 8 November 1945.
[4] H.C. Deb., 24 June 1942, coll. 2017–18; 13 July 1943, col. 48. Cf. H.L. Deb., 20 May 1942, coll. 1094–5. See also *The Times*, 2 June 1942 and 11 July 1943. *Journal of the Royal Empire Society*, April 1944, pp. 255–63. B. Bourdillon, 'Partnership in Nigeria', *British Commonwealth Objectives*, ed. H. Lindsay, 1946, p. 260.

Asian) representation in the Legislatures, but partly also on the United Kingdom being willing to surrender a substantial measure of political influence to the European unofficial residents.

A statement made by the Secretary of State for the Colonies in 1950 may be regarded as the most recent attempt to define the assumptions made by official policy in regard to territories in which a number of different racial groups are established. He emphasized that the objective continued to be the achievement of self-government by the territory concerned, but indicated that self-government must include 'proper provision for all the main communities which have made their home in East Africa'. He added that it was essential that the United Kingdom should maintain its control until the assistance given to the indigenous people in developing their resources had set them so far on the path of progress that they could take their full part, together with other sections of the community, in the political and economic life of the territory.[1] The terms used were thus general, and they avoided any attempt to meet the practical problems involved in the interpretation of partnership, such as the definition of what constituted a community, the procedure for the representation of the communities and the relative weightage, if any, to be accorded to them. It did not attempt to face the crucial problem of finding a method of providing within a multi-racial unit approaching the stage of self-government any substitute for the role of the Imperial Power as an 'impartial arbiter'.

It is one of the consequences of systems of communal representation that they tend to emphasize the separateness of the communities and not infrequently result in new demands for the separate representation of smaller groups. In Kenya, for example, the Muslim Indians demanded separate representation in 1946, and after an initial attempt had been made to meet their claims by the reservation to them of two of the Indian elected seats they were granted in 1952 separate representation with a separate electoral roll. In Tanganyika, where it had been decided to introduce a system in which each of the 'major communities' would be accorded an equal number of members, this involved treating both Indians and Arabs, as well as some smaller communities, as one 'major community' to be designated as 'Asian'. The political unrealities concealed in this arrangement were brought out in the report of the Commission appointed in 1952 to make detailed proposals to implement the scheme of 'equal representation'.[2] Indians number about two-thirds of the Asian population, and electoral success will always depend on the support of the other 'Asian' communities, who have no real affinity with the Indian.

But similar problems arise also in regard to other 'major communities'.

---

[1] H.C. Deb., 13 December 1950, col. 1167.
[2] *Constitutional Development Commission*, 1951, p. 67.

The Tanganyika Commission, while recognizing that there was already a section of the African population which did not 'think tribally', held that it would be some time before the general sentiment of one tribe could be truly represented by a member of another tribe. If an electoral system were introduced the largest tribe would almost always win.[1] It is implicit in policies of partnership that some provision should be made for the representation of all the 'communities' deemed 'major', and although this might theoretically be secured by the device of reserving seats or by some system of proportional representation combined with common roll elections, such a device could not be introduced in present circumstances unless the qualifications for the franchise were such as would exclude the great majority of the African population. It seems inevitable therefore that for some time to come there should be some measure of representation on a communal basis.

'Balanced' and 'Equal' Representation

But it has been the third major issue, that of the relative representation to be accorded to the communities, which has been most debated in East Africa. Two rival arrangements have been advanced which may conveniently be contrasted in the phrases 'balanced representation' and 'equal representation'. 'Balanced representation' involves assigning to one community which is considered to have predominant claims a measure of representation equal to that accorded to all other communities taken together. 'Equal representation' would, on the other hand, accord the same numerical representation to each community. The principle of 'balanced representation' has been exemplified in Uganda, where African unofficial representation has equalled that accorded to Europeans and Asians together.

In Kenya, however, 'balanced representation' has taken the form of granting to Europeans, who are numerically the smallest of the major communities, a representation, both in the Legislature and since 1954 in the Council of Ministers, which equals that accorded to Asians, Arabs, and Africans taken together. The European leaders made the maintenance of this arrangement a condition of their acquiescence in the increase in the number of African unofficial members of the Legislature in 1951,[2] and the principle was maintained in the constitution of the Council of Ministers[3] in 1953. This was also the basis of the multi-racial Constitution which came to be known as the Lyttelton settlement.[4]

The issue of 'balanced representation' as opposed to 'equal representa-

---

[1] *Constitutional Development Commission*, 1953, Dar es Salaam, p. 61.

[2] *East African Standard*, 25 May 1951. H.C. Deb., 31 May 1951, col. 409.

[3] *Kenya: Proposals for a Reconstruction of the Government*, Cmd. 9103, 1954. H.C. Deb., 22 March 1954, col. 881.   [4] See below, p. 300.

tion' had first been clearly focused when the scheme for the creation of the East Africa High Commission came under discussion.[1] In their original form the proposals provided for the establishment of a Central Legislative Assembly comprising, in addition to twelve official members, a body of 18 unofficial members, six of whom would be Europeans and six Asian (both being elected by the territorial Legislatures), together with six members to be nominated by the Governors of the three territories; as many as possible of the last-named group were to be Africans; and two of them were to represent Arab interests.[2] It was claimed that this scheme had been designed as a practical embodiment of the principle of equitable racial representation, but though it was welcomed by the leaders of the Asian and African communities it was strongly opposed by the European. The Government eventually substituted a more complicated measure, which was accepted by the Europeans, though opposed by the Asians and Africans. Official sources repudiated the suggestion that the principle of 'equal representation' had been abandoned, but the fact remains that the European leaders felt able to assure their followers that the European unofficial numbers in the Legislative Assembly would in practice be found to equal in number the representatives of other races. Their position would thus resemble that existing in the Kenya Legislature.[3]

It was not till after the Second World War that there developed in the European community of Tanganyika an outlook on the relative parts to be played by the various communities which could more correctly be expressed by the word 'partnership' than by that of 'paramountcy'. This attitude was crystallized in the report of a Committee on Constitutional Development which was issued in 1951. The Committee stated that the responsible opinion of all races agreed that for the next few years the Legislative Council should continue to have a majority of official members. Accepting the principle of partnership as that which should regulate the relations between the different communities, it held that the most practical method of giving effect to it would be to divide the seats allocated to unofficial members equally among the three races.[4]

These proposals were accepted by the Government in spite of the opposition from a section of the Europeans in the territory. Tanganyika does not yet appear to consider that self-government is attainable in the immediate future, and this fact both helps to explain its readiness to accept the continuance of the official majority and reduces the present difficulty of reconciling the claims of the various communities. But a solution on

---

[1] See above, pp. 188–9.

[2] *Inter-Territorial Organization in East Africa*, Col. no. 191, 1945.

[3] *East Africa and Rhodesia*, 17 January 1946. Cf. H.C. Deb., 1 February 1946, col. 1340. *Inter-Territorial Organization in East Africa, Revised Proposals*, Col. no. 210, 1947.

[4] *Tanganyika Government: Committee on Constitutional Development*, 1951, paras. 29 and 30.

the basis of 'equal representation' may not prove to be equally acceptable in the future.

Both in Kenya and Uganda, in which the principle of 'balanced representation' has been adopted and the official majority retained,[1] an attempt has been made to create a form of official majority more acceptable to local opinion than one wholly composed of civil servants. This has been effected by including among the nominated members a number who need not be civil servants and who are free to speak or vote against the Government 'except on matters of confidence'.[2] During the transition from Colonial rule to self-government this expedient might afford a partial substitute for the balancing role of the Imperial Government, provided that it is possible to devise an acceptable method of choosing such members on grounds of their detachment from strong communal interests; but the value of the expedient must vary with every change in the personality and local standing of the members so selected.

Britain's Role as 'Impartial Arbiter'

It remains to examine the degree to which subsequent events have shown it possible to expect the emergence of any alternative provision for the role of 'impartial arbiter' assigned to the Government of the United Kingdom by the Commission on Closer Union of 1929.[3] In view of the change in current opinion regarding the future of the Colonial status, it would seem that the retention by the United Kingdom of its present role is likely to be acceptable only so long as it is recognized as a temporary expedient. If so, it becomes increasingly important to find some alternative within the structure of a self-governing political unit, and to secure it from the attack of interested groups by attaching local loyalties to it. So long as some measure of external control is maintained (even in the attenuated form of the provision in the Southern Rhodesian Constitution which requires United Kingdom assent to any discriminatory legislation),[4] there must be a tendency to look outside the territory for the 'impartial arbiter' rather than to attempt to develop a local substitute.

The African Affairs Board projected in the original scheme of the Central African Federation was designed to provide a body independent of both the Federal and the Territorial Legislatures,[5] but in the Constitution ultimately adopted this was replaced by a Standing Committee of the Federal Assembly to be composed of members specially selected for the

---

[1] In Kenya there was an unofficial majority from 1948 to 1952.
[2] For Kenya, see H.C. Deb., 31 May 1951, col. 410. *Colonial Reports, Kenya*, 1953, p. 151. For Uganda, see *Correspondence relating to the Composition of the Legislative Council*, Entebbe, 1953, p. 7.
[3] See above, p. 191.
[4] See below, p. 281.
[5] *Draft Federal Scheme*, Cmd. 8573, 1952, p. 5.

purpose.[1] It thus became a political rather than a judicial body; but in any case it had no final authority to intervene in order to protect the interests of the African community; at the best its function was to secure (whether by reservation of Bills or otherwise) that the views of Africans were fully represented to the Government of the United Kingdom before effect was given to any Federal measure affecting their interests.

When the problem of the provision of an impartial arbiter has arisen elsewhere, suggestions have sometimes been made that it might be met by an internal partition of the country on a community basis. Neither in Central nor East Africa, however, does partition into European and non-European areas seem to be practicable.[2] It must further be realized that the security which the existence of an impartial arbiter can provide is not necessarily limited to safeguarding the right of political representation, but may in practice extend over a wide range of administrative activities—a field which may well appear to some of the less dynamic communities to be more important than representation in a legislative body.

In some instances which have arisen in other parts of the world it has been sought to secure the rights of different communities by 'entrenching' them in the law of the Constitution, as for example in statements of 'Human Rights'. Such an expedient has, for instance, been adopted in the recently enacted Constitution of the Republic of India. Hitherto, however, British practice has shown a characteristic distrust of such devices,[3] which are at the best negative in their operation, and are calculated to act only as a restraint on a more powerful community. They do not necessarily help to bring the communities closer together.

It is inevitable that in the preceding paragraphs the treatment of the major issues involved should have largely assumed the character of a discussion of a series of expedients. But the questions involved permit of no doctrinaire answer. To develop a degree of political consensus which will make it possible to hand over the full responsibilities of administration where communities are so ill-balanced numerically but are so interdependent economically, and to do so without handing over final control to any one community—that is a problem for which it is not easy to find a ready solution. The recent partition of British India between India and Pakistan is a reminder of the difficulties which may occur even where the major communities concerned show no outstanding difference in origin and in social conditions. When they are as far apart as those which exist

---

[1] For the details, see below, p. 281, and see also M. Beloff, 'The Federal Solution in its Application to Europe, Asia, and Africa', *Political Studies*, vol. i, no. 2, 1953, p. 122.

[2] See, for example, *Report of Commission on Closer Union of the Dependencies in Eastern and Central Africa*, Cmd. 3234, 1929, pp. 96–98, pp. 284–5.

[3] *Report of Committee of Houses of Parliament on Indian Constitutional Reform*, vol. i, Part I, 1934, pp. 215–17.

in East Africa no constitutional device can supply the place of the one fundamental condition of a successful transfer of power—the previous establishment of a working system based on goodwill between the communities concerned.

BRITISH WEST AFRICAN TERRITORIES

Though Central and East Africa have been most fruitful in schemes for a federal grouping of the dependent territories now under British control, there has for many years been a strong sentiment in favour of some form of inter-territorial organization in British West Africa. But the obstacles in the way of implementing the project are considerable. There was a period of history when the Administrations of the different territories in West Africa were temporarily united, as for example when the Colonies of Lagos and of the Gold Coast were placed under the orders of the Governor of West African Settlements resident at Sierra Leone, or later when Lagos was controlled by the Governor of the Gold Coast.

But the areas concerned in those arrangements were relatively small; they consisted in fact of little more than coastal ports and the country immediately surrounding them. The present British West African territories, with their large areas of hinterland, are not contiguous; they are in fact enclaves in the great expanse of the French Empire. Sierra Leone is the only country which is not entirely surrounded on land by the French territory.[1] The four Administrations concerned lack therefore what has often furnished the most pressing incentive to some form of international organization, namely, the need for concerting road or rail communications or for framing a Customs Union.

West African Inter-Territorial Conference

Following, however, the practice adopted in East Africa, a conference of the Governors of the British West African territories was inaugurated in August 1939. It set up a permanent office organization in 1940, but the system was superseded in 1942 by the creation of a post expressly designed to meet requirements created by the war, namely, the appointment of a Resident Minister in West Africa, with his headquarters on the Gold Coast.[2] In 1945 both these institutions were replaced by a West African Council composed of the Secretary of State as chairman and the four Governors as members; its functions were mainly consultative and aimed at co-ordinating as far as possible the policies of the four Colonial Governments.[3] It was equipped with a permanent Secretariat. The Secretary

[1] M. Wight, *British Colonial Constitutions*, 1947, p. 84.
[2] *The Colonial Empire (1939–1947)*, Cmd. 7167, 1947, p. 17.
[3] H.C. Deb., 17 October 1945, coll. 1143–5.

of State presided at meetings held in 1947 and 1948; soon afterwards, however, the formal meetings ceased, but the Secretariat of the Council continued to arrange meetings of heads of the Departments in the four territories to discuss matters of common concern.[1]

The Council was formally dissolved in 1951, and was replaced by the West African Inter-Territorial Conference, consisting of two Ministers or Members of the Executive Council from each territory concerned; the Governor of Nigeria normally presides. The West African Inter-Territorial Secretariat continues to carry on the functions discharged by the Secretariat of the former Governors' Conference, and has in addition taken part in the administrative control of the Research Institutes concerned with cocoa, trypanosomiasis, oil palms, or fisheries.[2] In view of the growing measure of self-government in the major West African territories it seems unlikely that any move will now be made towards the establishment of any constitutional form of closer union.

Evolution of Indigenous Self-Government

The British West African territories have not had to face the difficulty in reconciling the interests of the indigenous population with those of the immigrant communities which has formed so large a part of the history of East and Central Africa. In British West Africa the original extension of sovereignty had a twofold motive; it sought to assist in the suppression of the slave trade and at the same time to safeguard the sphere of British commercial interests. The resident immigrant population (whether of Europeans or other non-Natives) was always small, and it did not aspire to take over from the Government the responsibilities of administration. There was not therefore the same scope for a conflict of view between the principles of 'identity' and 'differentiation' as occurred in South or Central Africa, and for our present purpose the interest lies rather in the process by which a system of indigenous self-government is being evolved under British auspices.

In that process there have been three phases. The earliest phase had as its guiding principle the policy of minimum interference with the indigenous political authority, whether this took the form of a Native State or a tribal system headed by a Chief. The British asked little more of such authority than that it should observe a satisfactory attitude regarding the slave trade and should maintain suitable conditions for the expansion of import and export trading. This phase is most fully illustrated in the early history of the Gold Coast.[3] The second phase was marked by the gradual extension of executive and judicial administration in Native areas, in the

---

[1] *The Colonial Territories, 1950–1951*, Cmd. 8243, 1951, p. 34.
[2] *The Colonial Territories, 1951–1952*, Cmd. 8583, 1952, p. 19. Ibid. *1952–1953*, Cmd. 8856, 1953, p. 94.   [3] *N.A.*, Part III, pp. 194–9.

course of which the use of that procedure of indirect rule which was based on the use of the traditional Native Authorities as agencies of rule became of continually increasing significance.

The methods adopted in that system and the results achieved are discussed in detail in the subsequent chapter dealing with systems of Native Administration;[1] here we are concerned chiefly with the objective at which it aimed. It has often been described as a preparatory stage to self-government, but this is only true in a limited measure. Those who first evolved the use of the system in Northern Nigeria hoped that the traditional institutions of which it availed itself might be developed into a series of Native Administrations which could eventually constitute the government of the country under British guidance and control. They believed that Africa would gain more from such a development than from one in which administration was based on some form of representative government of the modern pattern.

Few of them could then have envisaged the final goal of Colonial policy as consisting in the achievement of self-government in the form which it is now adopting. For the most part their eyes were fixed on the immediate and tangible benefits which the Native Authority system seemed to promise: the grant to Africa of the benefits of Western civilization without disrupting the social institutions of the African people; the growth of indigenous responsibility for the management of local affairs and for the improvement of local conditions; and the possibility that under this system indigenous Africa might be able to develop for itself the type of political institutions best suited to its own environment. It was only at a later date that one of the most convinced supporters of the system, Sir Donald Cameron, held that the obligation of a Mandatory Administration to encourage the political evolution of peoples 'not yet able to stand by themselves' could not be achieved by any other method than by adopting the procedure of indirect rule. But though, as Governor of Tanganyika, he advocated the establishment of local councils for the discussion of their common interests by the Chiefs,[2] there is nothing to show that he looked forward to this as a first step towards self-government in the form in which we now know it. The expression of opinion through the ballot box he dismissed as inconceivable.[3]

Though, however, the early exponents of the system did not themselves look on it as the first step in the evolution of a system of political self-government, there was a gradual change of emphasis in the manner in which the system was applied. Among such innate empiricists as the British, the actual policies inspired by the philosophy of Indirect Rule

---

[1] See below, p. 452.
[2] D. Cameron, *My Tanganyika Service and some Nigeria*, 1939, p. 115.
[3] Circular of July 1925, quoted in R. L. Buell, *The Native Problem in Africa*, vol. i, p. 453.

became greatly diversified. There were areas in which the preservation of traditional institutions soon ceased to rank as an object of importance; more and more emphasis came to be laid on the utilization of the traditional authorities as agencies for the supply of local Government services,[1] a function which formed no part of indigenous custom as these Authorities had known it. It is an even more important fact that circumstances were creating outside the orbit of the Native Authority system a number of elements which were either inimical to it on principle or were intolerant of the use it made of the powers entrusted to it.[2]

The existence of what have been conventionally described as 'detribalized' Africans had always posed a problem for which Indirect Rule had no satisfactory solution, and as Western education became more widespread and as more and more Africans entered the money economy there emerged a class of 'new men' who felt themselves excluded from a share in political authority owing to the operation of the Native Authority system. Their number was increased by the growth of urbanization[3] which inevitably accompanies economic development, even where (as in West Africa) it may take other forms than the expansion of manufacturing industry. Attempts to adopt the machinery of Indirect Rule so as to make possible some accommodation of these growing pressures might have taken place earlier had not the war compelled the Administrations to concentrate on more insistent tasks.[4]

New Influences on Britain's Colonial Policy

These changes found support in Great Britain from the altered climate of ideas which had begun to show itself even before the outbreak of the war. The assumptions of Trusteeship,[5] though admittedly possessing a moral influence, had been basically negative in so far that they failed to place on a Colonial Power any direct obligation to assist in the material or social development of the indigenous population. It was taken for granted that the Colonial relationship would endure for a long time; the task of an Administration was to provide the political stability and the economic and social equipment which were the pre-conditions of such measure of development as the resources of a territory might make possible.

The financial backing necessary for the development of resources was to be supplied by private enterprise. The public expenditure involved in the development of the administrative and social services was to be met from the revenues of the Colony; it was only in the early years of Colonial administration, or as a consequence of such natural disasters as hurricanes

---

[1] R. E. Robinson, 'Why Indirect Rule has been Replaced by "Local Government" in the Nomenclature of British Native Administration', *J.A.A.*, July 1950, pp. 12–15.

[2] See below, p. 526.   [3] See below, p. 564.

[4] M. Fortes, 'The Impact of the War on British West Africa', *International Affairs*, vol. xxi, 1945, pp. 206–19.   [5] See above, p. 185.

or earthquakes, that a Colony could expect to receive financial assistance from the United Kingdom, and then only subject to stringent Treasury control. This attitude, the translation into the Colonial sphere of the *laissez-faire* principles of the Victorian era, was after the turn of the century challenged by a new concept which had come to be increasingly accepted in domestic politics, the doctrine, namely, that active State intervention was a necessary lever to the amelioration of social conditions. The new doctrine was given legislative expression in the Colonial Development and Welfare Act of 1940 and its successive amendments.[1]

The greater importance thus attached to the provision of the fullest possible range of social services as a justification of Colonial rule would no doubt have involved by itself some change in the attitude towards the Native Authority system, inasmuch as the value of that system would now be assessed not by the measure in which it found general acceptance or by its success in the maintenance of social peace but by its suitability as an agency for the provision of 'Western' social services such as those of health and education. But to these new impulses was added another, which came in the immediate post-war years to occupy a dominant role; the conception, namely, that Colonial rule could be justified only by its success in preparing the way for its early supersession by political self-government. The attainment of independence by India, Burma, Ceylon, Pakistan, the Philippines, and Indonesia powerfully enforced this approach, and to this was added the fact that the United States of America and the Soviet Union, which had emerged from the war with a greatly enhanced influence in world politics, were both strongly 'anti-colonial' in their dominant ideologies.[2] The aim of good Colonial administration thus came to be defined positively as the promotion of economic and social advance in order to provide the essential basis for political self-rule.

Post-War Constitutional Changes

The earliest reactions to these new influences were to be found partly in the increase of unofficial (and more especially African) membership in the Legislative Councils, partly in a greater emphasis on the need to link these bodies with the system of Native Administration (usually by the creation of Provincial or Regional Councils from whose membership African members of the Legislative Councils might be selected), and partly in attempts to promote changes in the constitution of the traditional Native Authorities by finding room for some of the 'new men' in their organization. The attitude generally current in the immediate post-war years might thus have been described as one of modified 'differentiation', in so much that it attempted to incorporate in the system of Native

---

[1] See *Statement of Policy on Colonial Development and Welfare*, Cmd. 6175, 1940, p. 4. See also below, pp. 1323 ff. [2] See H.C. Deb., 13 July 1943, coll. 47 ff.

Administration some of the adaptations deemed necessary as a result of Western penetration and the emergence of educated Africans.

As was suggested in the 'Proposals for the Revision of the Constitution of Nigeria' in 1945,[1] it was hoped that political advance on the lines embodied in it would provide a type of representation 'which would be in accordance with custom, would fit in naturally with existing institutions, and would be readily intelligible to the people themselves. . . '. The Constitutions ordained for the Gold Coast and Nigeria in 1946 were the most typical expressions of this attempt to effect a reconciliation between the underlying principles of Indirect Rule and that growing body of African opinion in West Africa which saw the attainment of self-government based on parliamentary institutions as the objective of Colonial rule. To this end, the authority of the Legislatures was extended to include Ashanti and the Northern Territories in the Gold Coast and the Northern Provinces in Nigeria, while the majority of the unofficial members were in each case chosen by electoral colleges created from the Native Authorities.

A Colonial Office Conference on African Administration held in 1947 expressed views which seemed to point to the progressive replacement of the Native Authority system by institutions following the pattern of the Local Government bodies in Great Britain.[2] The result of the impulse thus given varied according to local circumstances. In Eastern Nigeria it assisted to ensure a complete break with the tradition of the Native Authority system;[3] in Tanganyika on the other hand it fostered the increased adaptation of the system by measures designed to ensure greater popular participation in it.[4]

In so far as West Africa was concerned, it soon became clear that the attempted reconciliation of the principles of 'differentiation' and 'identity' had come too late to secure the support of that section of Africans which had been most affected by Westernization. The policy of reconciliation received, it is true, some measure of support in one of the most remarkable of the series of State papers in which the problems of government in British African territories have been discussed, namely, the report of the Committee on Constitutional Reform in the Gold Coast, which was composed wholly of African members.[5] They affirmed that they had 'chosen the British model', but that they had at the same time 'sought to blend it with our traditional institutions'. But it was the Westminster model to which the Constitutions enacted for the various West African territories gave the

---

[1] Cmd. 6599, para. 4. [2] *J.A.A.*, January 1949, p. 6.
[3] Nigeria, Eastern Region House of Assembly, *Report of Select Committee set up to review the Existing System of Local Government*, Lagos, 1948.
[4] *Development of African Local Government in Tanganyika*, Col. no. 277, 1951.
[5] *Report by the Committee on Constitutional Reform* (the Coussey Committee), Gold Coast, 1949, Col. no. 248.

decisive preference, and it was the Africans who demanded the fullest realization of that model who were able to command the largest measure of support among their own people.

After 1950, the year in which the Gold Coast was given a form of 'semi-Responsible' government,[1] the tide turned definitely in this direction. Save in the Northern Region of Nigeria, the traditional Native Authorities began to fade into the background of the political picture. It was claimed at the time in the British Parliament that all parties represented in it were ready to assist the Colonies along the path to self-government. But in West Africa the decisive voices in pressing that self-rule should take the form of parliamentary government based on universal suffrage were after 1950 those of Africans, rather than those of political interests in the United Kingdom.

There is a school of thought in Great Britain which does not agree that traditionalism is so definitely in retreat in indigenous Africa as the preceding paragraphs would seem to imply. That school sees on the contrary strong evidence of a renascence of tribalism. 'The peoples of Africa', it has been said, 'are being subjected in varying degrees to a formidable pressure through the impact of Western ideas and techniques, which they view with fascinated repulsion. Their instinctive response is to close their ranks against these alien forces, and the only ranks they know are those of the tribe'.

The recent uprising of the Mau Mau is, in the view of this school, an outstanding proof of the elemental force of tribalism among the Kikuyu. In Tanganyika the Chagga, hitherto composed of a number of separate groups, are now seeking permission to elect a Paramount Tribal Chief; elsewhere in Tanganyika the four districts comprised in Sukumaland are drawing together in a close tribal federation.[2] The constitutional developments in Uganda show the importance attached by the Buganda people to the maintenance of their own tribe as a separate entity. Tribalism, it is contended, is still the mainspring of African life, and any government that hopes to develop Africans as balanced human beings must be based on indigenous African custom, which is that of the homogeneous tribe.[3]

It must be agreed that in East Africa (from which the majority of the evidence of the revival of tribalism is taken) the tribe is still a factor of great significance. That is true also of areas such as the High Commission Territories and some parts of Central Africa. But it would be difficult to find in the Union of South Africa, in the British West African territories or in the French, Belgian, or Portuguese dependencies any clear evidence

[1] See below, p. 319.

[2] V. Harlow, 'Tribalism in Africa', in *Manchester Guardian*, 26 October 1954. P. Henry, in *New Commonwealth*, 7 March 1955, pp. 215 ff.

[3] E. Huxley in *Time and Tide*, 10 December 1955, reviewing Lord Altrincham, *Kenya's Opportunity*, 1955.

of a renascent spirit of tribalism, in the sense in which that term is now being used.[1]

Such leaders of popular opinion as are now emerging are not traditionalists; if at times they may call on tribal sentiment in order to aid their own campaign of nationalism, their vision of a political future has little place for tribal organization or for tribal leaders. No one could deny the value of the use which was made of the tribal organization and of the traditional authorities under the system of Indirect Rule, and no Administration would now be wise to neglect these agencies where they can still command a popular support. But, experience has shown that they now have only a limited value as agencies of development.

The succeeding chapter describes the further stage of advance which has guaranteed a full status of Responsible Government to the Gold Coast.[2]

FRENCH TERRITORIES

The problems and the perplexities arising from the conflict of the conceptions of 'identity' and 'differentiation' are simplified, though they are not entirely avoided, in the French philosophy of Colonial rule. It has never included any counterpart to that vision of a progressive local autonomy for overseas territories which has come to be characteristic of British policy. The permanence of the association between metropolitan France and her overseas dependencies has never been doubted, and its expression in the clear-cut legal form appropriate to a single political entity has been not so much an objective of French policy as its unquestioned starting-point. This conception of a juridical and administrative integration of dependencies with the metropole has not, it is true, invariably been accompanied by an assumption of the practicability of the full measure of social and cultural assimilation which it is so commonly taken to imply.[3] It could not be said that it has always attained the ideal which was succinctly expressed in the phrase of Schoelcher, the great abolitionist: 'the French Republic does not intend to make distinctions in the human family'.[4] The actual institutions of the French system of overseas rule have indeed frequently taken forms that have reflected the practical realities which have led elsewhere to theories of 'differentiation'. But it has been to the concept of identity inherent in their universalist thinking that the French have invariably returned at moments of difficulty or crisis. In this respect

[1] Lord Hemingford, *Nationalism in Africa*, The Ramsay Muir Memorial Lecture, Cambridge, 1 August 1954, pp. 9–10. *Round Table*, September 1955, pp. 329 ff.
[2] See below, pp. 320 ff.
[3] For an analysis of the French conception of assimilation see R. Maunier, *The Sociology of Colonies* (*Translation by E. O. Lorimer*), 1949, vol. i, pp. 37–45 and 184–9.
[4] Quoted by K. Robinson, at p. 88 of *Annals of American Academy of Political and Social Science*, March 1955, to which this section of the Survey is much indebted.

the French can claim with some justice that they are the true heirs of the Roman tradition:

Haec est in gremio victos quae sola recepit,
Humanumque genus communi nomine fovit.[1]

If the French have appreciated the difficulties of realizing this ideal it is because in modern times the grant of a title of common citizenship carries more exacting implications than it did when Claudian paid his tribute to the genius of Rome. Moreover, though the French genius has been described by one of its best exponents[2] as marked above all by its faith in 'the virtue of doctrines and the logic of principles', it has frequently been forced by circumstances to adopt courses which might well seem to have been dictated by British empiricism.

Policy of Assimilation

The policy of identity was strikingly exemplified by the grant of citizenship and the franchise to the Senegalese of the coastal towns as long ago as 1848,[3] a measure which was reaffirmed in the early days of the Third Republic. But the extension of French sovereignty late in the nineteenth century to great areas which were hitherto practically unknown resulted in the evolution of a new system of administration under the stress of practical needs. At first, indeed, it might have been thought that when they were faced with the difficult problems involved in the pacification of these extensive new territories, French administrators were arriving at much the same philosophy of Colonial rule as their British contemporaries. Under the impulse of such men as de Lanessan,[4] Galliéni,[5] or Lyautey, the 'politique de protectorat' was defined in terms which might well have been used by Lugard. Writing from Tananarive in 1902, Lyautey thus described it:

maintenir le plus possible dans leur intégrité les rouages indigènes, les institutions, les usages à utiliser, les chefs traditionnels, leur laisser l'exercice direct de la police, de l'administration, de la justice même, de la perception de l'impôt, sous le simple contrôle d'un seul agent résidant auprès du chef. C'est par cet agent, en contact permanent avec le chef indigène, que s'ouvrira progressivement l'horizon de ce dernier et, par lui, celui de son peuple.[6]

This phase of the French Colonial philosophy was in substance anti-assimilationist, and the principle of rule which it embodied found its most complete expression in the work of Jules Harmand.[7] He distinguished

---

[1] Claudian, *In Secundum Consulatum Stilichonis*, ii, 150–2.
[2] M. Sarraut, *J.R.A.S.*, June 1933.   [3] See below, p. 332.
[4] J. L. de Lanessan, *L'Expansion coloniale de la France*, 1886; *Principes de Colonisation*, 1897.
[5] P. J. Galliéni, *Rapport d'ensemble sur la pacification, l'organisation et la colonisation de Madagascar*, 1900.   [6] *Lettres du Sud de Madagascar*, Paris, 1935, pp. 295–6.
[7] *Domination et Colonisation*, Paris, 1910.

colonies of settlement from those *dominations* in which European rule was exercised over a large indigenous population, and where 'the true *colon* was the Native and the great colonizer the State'. The social standards of the Native inhabitants were too remote from those of France for assimilation to be practicable, and there should accordingly be substituted a 'policy of association' which would involve some measure of indirect administration and a general respect for indigenous institutions.

In the form in which it was later defined by M. Sarraut[1] the policy of 'association' placed major emphasis on the functional collaboration between the French rulers and the Native *élite* who had accepted the standards of Western civilization. The philosophy of Colonial development formulated by him in 1922 contemplated a planned economy in which each Colony should contribute its quota of the product for which it was best suited, while at the same time the means of transport were to be improved on an extensive scale. The policy of association, as thus developed, was closely bound up with his scheme for the expansion of Colonial production. The Native *élite*, for example, had its own definite part in this development. Although conditions in France itself made the full execution of this programme throughout its Colonial Empire impracticable, a planned system on a smaller scale was introduced in which each territory adopted an expanded programme of cultivation and the resulting production was assured entry to the French market, usually by means of a preferential tariff.

Some of the disadvantages of political assimilation were thus recognized, and considerable recourse was had to systems of indirect administration for territories which were in the process of being brought under effective European control. But the French outlook did not readily accept the inefficiency and injustice, which, as it appeared to them, were almost inevitably involved in a procedure of rule under which their own role was confined to supervision.[2] As Galliéni had noted, few of them 'savent se limiter à ce rôle de contrôleur supérieur et deviennent tracassiers, formalistes, s'ingérant dans tout, à propos de tout'.[3]

The development of the *politique de protectorat*, combined with the practical difficulty of applying in the French African territories the political integration implied by the policy of assimilation, resulted in fact in the arrest of any further assimilative measures of the kind which had been exemplified in the grant of citizenship to the Senegalese of the coastal towns. It resulted also in the development of a French version of a policy of 'differentiation' or, more specifically, administrative separatism. The features which characterized this phase of rule in French overseas terri-

---

[1] A. Sarraut, *La mise en valeur des colonies françaises*, 1923; *Grandeur et servitude coloniales*, 1931.
[2] See below, pp. 211 ff.
[3] Cited by H. Deschamps and P. Chauvet, *Galliéni Pacificateur*, 1949, p. 279.

tories were most notably the separate régime of law applied to them as compared with metropolitan France; the absence of any attempt either to consolidate existing indigenous institutions or to develop new ones as the basis of an African local government; the admission only of specially qualified Africans to the privileges of citizenship; and the slow development of local advisory councils with small and largely nominated membership.

Nevertheless the underlying assumption remained that, on a long view, the future of the overseas territories must be one of eventual integration with France in a larger political unit. Though the general framework remained that of administrative differentiation, many of the activities of French administrators implied a more active pursuit of the concept of integration than was compatible with a policy of continued political subordination and of differential treatment for the African peoples. The pursuit of the concept of integration was in particular a marked feature of educational policy.[1] There was indeed a period in which the combination of this underlying assimilationist ideology with the practical acceptance of an *élite* as partners (albeit junior partners) in *la mission civilisatrice* of France appeared to provide a more satisfactory outlet for the Westernized inhabitants of French territories than the British policies dominated by the procedure of Indirect Rule.

Though this was the case, it was at the same time natural that such aspects of French administrative practice as continued to discriminate between the *citoyens* and the *sujets* should be increasingly challenged by the *élite* when their numbers grew and as they found themselves in a position to claim that they should be accorded the position of equality implicit in the assimilationist terms of proclaimed French policy. Up to 1939, however, economic and social development in the French tropical African territories was on the whole insufficient to produce challenges in the overt form which they took both in Indo-China and in North Africa, where the policy of 'association' had been increasingly challenged as a mere pretext for the refusal of the rights of 'assimilation'. Although the fall of France and the eventual establishment of a provisional Government in Algiers led naturally to a greater preoccupation with the problems of Colonial policy, it did not result in the emergence of any fundamentally different conceptions; the two tendencies of 'assimilation' and 'association', the French variants of 'identity' and 'differentiation', continued to hold the field, and the post-war Constitution as framed in 1946 proved to include something of each of them.

Brazzaville Conference, January 1944

The extent of their intermixture was well shown in the recommendations of the Brazzaville Conference which was convoked by the Provisional

---

[1] See below, pp. 1197–8.

Government in January 1944.[1] It represented essentially the point of view of the Colonial administrators concerned with tropical African territories, and it stood on the whole for the maintenance of assimilation as the goal of policy, so far as political rights and status were concerned. It made at the same time some concessions to the actual situation, most notably in its recognition of the value to be attached to the traditional institutions of African society. But it was definitely against assimilation in the sense of executive centralization, and it advocated greater administrative freedom in the individual territories, combined with the maintenance of political unity by some type of federal constitution.[2]

On one important point it expressed itself strongly. 'Les fins de l'œuvre de civilisation accompli par la France dans les colonies écartent toute idée d'autonomie, toute possibilité d'évolution hors du bloc français de l'Empire; la constitution éventuelle, même lointaine, de *self-government* dans les colonies est à écarter.'[3] Though, however, it was opposed to any conception of autonomy for the French dependencies, it was emphatic that these should make their voice heard in the reconstruction of the French political system after the war. They should accordingly be represented in the Constituent Assembly which would deal with the framing of the new Constitution.

The Constitution of 1848 had provided for the election by the then existing Colonies of twelve Colonial Deputies in the metropolitan Parliament, and in 1875 provision was added for the election of Senators from certain of the Colonies subsequently acquired. Tropical Africa was represented by one Deputy, elected from the old *commune* of Senegal.[4] The Brazzaville Conference did not, however, consider that an extension of Colonial representation in the French Parliament was the appropriate way of arranging for the permanent participation of the Colonies in the political life of France. This should be secured by a new body, a Colonial Parliament, or preferably a Federal Assembly, working in a definite relation to local Assemblies to be established in each territory. Such local Assemblies should be representative both of Europeans and Africans, elected where possible but, failing that, representative of the traditional *élite*. They should have considerable powers of decision in economic and financial matters, subject only to the approval of the Colonial Ministry.

In the sphere of economics, the conference urged the abolition of all forms of forced labour; in the social sphere it advocated the rapid extension of education to the masses, though instruction was invariably to be in French.[5] The *indigénat*, the special legal régime to which non-citizens were

---

[1] *La Conférence Africaine Française, Brazzaville, 30 January–8 February 1944*, Paris, 1945. See also *Enc. A.E.F.*, pp. 183–6.

[2] K. Robinson, *The Public Law of Overseas France*, 2nd ed., 1954.

[3] *La Conférence Africaine Française*, op. cit. p. 33.

[4] See below, p. 338.   [5] See below, p. 1197.

subject,[1] should be abolished, and although customary law should continue to regulate commercial and civil cases among Africans, a common African penal code should be drawn up, on the basis of that lately put in force in French West Africa.[2] Traditional political institutions should be maintained, not as an end in themselves, but in order to promote a vigorous local and municipal life.

In this latter part of their recommendations the conference endorsed the principles of a circular letter on Native Policy which had been issued in 1941 by Governor-General Éboué.[3] This remarkable man was a resident of Guadaloupe and of African descent; it was under his inspiration that French Equatorial Africa and the Cameroons adhered to the Allied cause in 1940. His Circular Letter of 1941, while emphasizing the importance of maintaining traditional African institutions, had also recognized the emergence of a 'true African *bourgeoisie*' in urban areas, and had proposed the creation for its members of a *statut des notables évolués*. That was to be a form of Colonial citizenship which, unlike full French citizenship, was compatible with the adherence of Africans to their customary law as opposed to the French civil code. It was thus to be analogous to the citizenship accorded to the Senegalese of the coastal towns, but was not to be granted, as that status had been, to a whole population *en bloc*, but was to be accorded to individuals.

Both Éboué's circular and the Brazzaville Conference were thus inspired by conceptions of a modified type of differentiation which were not fundamentally dissimilar to those which marked the contemporary development of ideas among British West African administrators. In the event, however, political developments in France during the post-liberation period resulted in decisions on policy which differed materially from the form favoured by the Brazzaville Conference. Something of the traditional 'centralist and unitarian character' of French administration[4] reasserted itself in the discussions which took place in the Constituent Assembly, and it is clear that its final decisions were viewed with disappointment by many who had hoped for the emergence of a Constitution which would correspond more closely with the principles set out at Brazzaville.[5]

Constitution of 1946

The Constitution as it finally emerged in 1946 laid far greater emphasis on assimilationist ideas, though in fact both the main tendencies of policy

[1] See below, p. 338. [2] See below, p. 616.
[3] F. Éboué, *Politique indigène de l'Afrique Équatoriale Française*, Brazzaville, 1941; Eng. trans., *French Colonial Policy in Africa, Free France* (Special Issue No. 2), New York, September, 1944, pp. 13–39. See also *Sudan Notes and Records*, vol. xxv, Part II, 1943. See also below, p. 546.
[4] J. Coleman, 'The Emergence of African Political Parties', in *Africa Today*, 1955, pp. 225 ff.
[5] R. Pleven, 'Evolution of the French Empire towards a French Union', *Journal of the Anti-Slavery Society*, 21 July 1949. H. Laurentie, *Colonial Administration by European Powers*, 1947, p. 19. See also an interesting assessment in H. Deschamps, *Peuples et Nations d'Outre-Mer*, 1954, p. 146.

found expression in the political structure actually created. The Brazza-ville Conference had pointed to the creation of a federal system, and during the ensuing debates on Colonial policy this line of thought found expression in the frequent substitution of terms like 'Federation' for the older word 'Empire'. The overall pattern of the structure which actually emerged was, however, on more traditional French lines, and was typified by the choice of the word 'Union' to describe it. The Constitution of the Third Republic had contained no special reference to the French Empire; that of the Fourth Republic[1] devoted to the French Union, which it formally created, a substantial part of its Preamble. The Union is described as made up of 'Nations' and 'Peoples', and France is described as forming with the Overseas countries a 'Union founded on equality of rights and duties'.

But the working structure thus created is not actually of a federal character. The Union is composed,[2] on the one hand, of the French Re-public (comprising metropolitan France and the Overseas Departments and Territories) and, on the other, of the Associated Territories and Asso-ciated States. The Overseas Departments are the old Colonies of Mar-tinique, Guadaloupe, Guiana, and Réunion.[3] The Overseas Territories are all the remaining Colonies of the pre-war Empire, except Cochin China, which became part of the Associated State of Viet Nam in 1950. The concept of the Associated Territory and Associated State was intended to provide for the parts of the Empire which had not been formally an-nexed to France: that is to say, the Mandated Territories and the Protec-torates of Indo-China, Morocco, and Tunisia. Togo and the Cameroons under French Trusteeship are thus Associated Territories, the position of which is assimilated to that of Associated States. It is difficult to fit Algeria into these constitutional categories, and it is really a class by itself; its three Departments of Alger, Oran, and Constantine are not normally considered as Overseas Departments but as parts of metropolitan France.

New organs were established for the French Union, a President (the President of the French Republic, *ex officio*), a High Council[4] (composed of representatives of the Government of the French Republic and of the Associated States), and an Assembly of the French Union, in which equal representation was accorded to Metropolitan France, on the one hand, and to all the Overseas areas, taken together, on the other. The number

---

[1] The Constitution was confirmed by the Referendum of 13 October 1946 and came into force on 24 December 1946 (*Statesman's Year-Book, 1954*, pp. 967–70).

[2] K. E. Robinson, 'The Public Law of Overseas France since the War', *Journal of Comparative Legislation*, vol. xxxii, Parts III and IV, pp. 36–57. P. Lampué, 'L'Union Française d'après la Constitution', *Revue Juridique et Politique de l'Union Française*, 1947. G. Catroux, 'The French Union', *International Conciliation*, no. 495, November 1953.

[3] *Loi*, 19 March 1946; Articles 73–82, Constitution of 1946.

[4] R. de Lacharrière, 'La Fonction du Haut Conseil de l'Union Française', *Revue Juridique et Politique de l'Union Française*, vol. iii, pp. 1–24.

of its members is 204, of whom 47 represent the Overseas Territories and the Associated Territories; of these, 39 represent the African territories included in this Survey. The Assembly of the French Union was, however, only the ghost of the 'Colonial Parliament' or 'Federal Assembly' suggested by the Brazzaville Conference. Its powers were in effect confined to the right to be consulted on the text of decrees relating to the countries now formally designated as the Overseas Territories. But if the conception of a true federal or even quasi-federal association between metropolitan France and the Overseas areas as a whole failed to be carried into effect in the new Constitution, it also stopped short of the complete political incorporation of any of them, except the four old Colonies above mentioned.[1] Algeria was by the law of 20 September 1947 accorded a special position in which political integration was tempered by a degree of regional autonomy.[2]

Within the Overseas Territories a political structure was established which might be described as one of modified identity rather than modified differentiation, since the direction proposed for these countries seemed clearly to point towards an eventual goal of political integration. They were granted substantial representation in the metropolitan National Assembly and in the Council of the Republic. Out of the 627 Deputies in the National Assembly, the Overseas Departments and Territories have a total of 41; of these, 32 come from the territories included in this Survey. The Council of the Republic has 320 Senators of whom 50 are elected by the Overseas Departments and Territories; of these 34 come from the Survey territories. Citizenship was extended to all the inhabitants, though it did not necessarily carry with it the franchise, nor, on the other hand, the obligation to accept French private law.

In all the Overseas Territories there were established Territorial Assemblies,[3] but their powers and functioning were modelled closely on those of the *Conseil Général* of a Department of metropolitan France, that is to say, they were not given independent legislative powers, although it was provided that metropolitan laws would not apply to the Overseas Territories except when expressly so stated. The most usual form of legislation for these Territories had been by ministerial decree issued on the authority of the metropolitan Government, and it seems to have been assumed that this would continue to be the standard practice. In all the Territorial Assemblies in tropical Africa, except that of Senegal (where a common electoral roll was established), the electoral arrangements ensured that although the representatives of Africans were in a majority, Europeans

[1] K. E. Robinson, 'The End of Empire: Another View', *International Affairs*, vol. xxx, pp. 186–95.
[2] P. Lampué, 'Le Statut de l'Algérie', *Revue Juridique et Politique de l'Union Française*, vol. i, pp. 477–525.
[3] See below, p. 337.

were substantially represented, while in the elections for the metropolitan parliamentary institutions (except in the elections for the National Assembly held in French West Africa and Togo) Europeans were assured of separate representation.

As regards the administrative and juridical régime, the *indigénat* and forced labour were abolished, and all the inhabitants, European or African, were subjected to the French Courts in penal cases.[1] In economic matters, while the powers accorded to the Territorial Assemblies implied some relaxation of the assimilation of customs tariffs, these were in the post-war years a less important instrument of economic integration than the currency control, which rested with the metropolitan authorities.

The management of the main instrument for economic development, the Fund for Economic and Social Development established in 1946, also rested in Paris. The Fund was commonly referred to as F.I.D.E.S., from the initial letters of its French title.[2] Its establishment was inspired by motives similar to those which had led in Great Britain to the passing of the Colonial Development and Welfare Acts,[3] and the changed emphasis in the current objective of economic development was expressed in the requirement that Development Programmes should seek *par priorité* to meet the needs of the indigenous peoples, though they should also assist in developing the economy of the French Union as a whole. The Act was passed shortly before the enactment of the new Constitution, and some adjustment of the procedures it envisaged was necessitated by the subsequent establishment of the Territorial Assemblies, to whom a somewhat greater voice had to be given in settling the details of Development Plans.

Efforts to Secure Racial Equality

Under the impulse of these changes African leadership in the French tropical African territories was for some time preoccupied with efforts to secure a more complete identity of political rights and social benefits with those of metropolitan France. Demands were, for example, made for the extension of the franchise and the abolition of the system of separate electoral rolls and of separate representation for Europeans and Africans;[4] for the abolition of salary differences between Europeans and Africans; and for the extension to the African territories of the metropolitan labour legislation. In each case some measure of success was achieved. The franchise was extended more widely by the Electoral Law of 1951; the proportion of members of the Territorial Assemblies elected by the African

---

[1] See below, p. 616.

[2] *Décret*, 6 January 1946, *Loi*, 30 April 1946. See also below, pp. 329–30.

[3] See above, p. 203.

[4] It is not strictly true that seats are assigned to Europeans as such, though in practice the system of separate electorates for 'metropolitan status' citizens and 'local status' citizens has the same effect. See below, p. 339.

electorate as opposed to the European was increased by the Representative Assemblies Law of 1952. The new Labour Code went some way towards extending to the Overseas Territories the principles of metropolitan labour legislation.

These demands were, however, prompted less by any positive acceptance of the policy of political integration with metropolitan France than by that passion to achieve equality with the European which in the British territories has found expression in the consistent demand for self-government on British parliamentary lines.[1] This was well expressed by a spokesman of French Africa in the National Assembly; Africans had at the moment (he said) the *mystique de l'égalité*, 'They wanted the same principles to be established for the metropole and for the Overseas Territories in the first place; when that had been done, they were ready to take account of realities'.[2] 'La réclamation essentielle des Africains tient en un mot: Égalité.'[3]

It is this urge to secure acceptance as equals which underlies the demands made for improving the status of the Overseas Territories by the grant of a greater measure of political autonomy and for the development of a more truly federal relationship with metropolitan France. The Territories should not, it is urged, be treated as States associated within a French Union, but as fully integrated States within the Republic.[4] Such an adjustment of the structure of power might indeed effect a reconciliation between the integrating tendency so long accepted in French policy and the new awareness of the distinctive values of African life noticeable among French African leaders since the war. It might make it possible to realize the aim expressed by one of the most notable of them in the phrase 'assimiler, non être assimilés'.[5]

The practical steps by which such an adjustment might be achieved have not yet been defined, nor has the objective itself been formally accepted by the French Government. In 1954, however, the Minister of Overseas France envisaged the possibility of considerable changes in this direction.[6] If effect were given to them, the powers of the National Assembly in regard to the Overseas Territories would be confined to major issues affecting the Republic as a whole, while those of the Assembly of the French Union would be increased in order to permit that body to pass Ordinances on specified subjects. The Territorial Assemblies would enjoy legislative powers on all matters not expressly reserved to the metropolitan

---

[1] See above, p. 204.

[2] *Journal Officiel*, Débats Parlementaires: Assemblée Nationale, 22 November 1952, p. 5503.

[3] *Marchés Coloniaux du Monde*, 14 July 1951, p. 1863.

[4] L. Senghor, 'L'Avenir de la France dans l'Outre-Mer', *Politique Étrangère*, 1954, pp. 419–26.

[5] L. Senghor, *La Communauté Impériale Française*, 1945. For L. Senghor, see R. Delavignette, *Freedom and Authority in French West Africa*, 1950, p. 148.

[6] *Journal Officiel*, Débats Parlementaires: Assemblée Nationale, 3e Séance, 9 April 1954, pp. 2025–6. See also H. Deschamps, 'Les Assemblées locales dans les territoires d'Outre-Mer', *Politique Étrangère*, 1954, pp. 427–36.

Parliament or to the Assembly of the French Union. The advisory *Conseils de Gouvernement* in each territory[1] would be given a more important role as a kind of Executive Council, linking the executive Head of the territory with the Assembly, by which some of the members of the *Conseil* would be appointed. The development of a more representative system of Local Government not only in the urban municipalities, but also in rural areas, has already begun in the Cameroons,[2] where elected *conseils de circonscription* have been created.

The future of the structure created for the Overseas Territories by the Constitution of 1946 is, however, still a matter of uncertainty, and there may be changes impending which will extend far beyond those suggested by the Minister in 1954. For the moment, the measure of participation in the work of the metropolitan institutions accorded to the representatives of the Overseas Territories has proved to be attractive to a certain section of the *élite*, and the representatives themselves have become keen adherents of the different political parties in the French National Assembly. But it is unlikely that the future will lie entirely in the hands of the *élite* of these territories. To judge by the developments taking place elsewhere in Africa it is likely to be decided by the growing 'middle' class, and it remains to be seen how far this class will be affected by the doctrine of self-determination now so much in evidence in Western Africa.

It would be wrong to conclude these considerations without allusion to the legislation regarding the Overseas Territories which was enacted in June 1956.[4] This points to changes of the nature of those envisaged by the Minister of Overseas France in 1954 and in particular to the enhancement of the status of the Territorial Assemblies and the closer assimilation between 'citizens' of African and of French origin in the matter of voting. But the law as enacted is permissive only and does not actually bring these changes into effect. The passing of the law, however, may constitute a crucial point in the development of French Colonial policy.

BELGIAN CONGO

As has already been observed, it is difficult to find any authoritative statement of the objective of policy in regard to the Belgian Congo.[5] When Belgium annexed the territory of the Congo Free State in 1908,[6] she had behind her no long history of Colonial rule or indeed any experience of

---

[1] See below, p. 337.

[2] *Arrêté* 537, 21 August 1952, of the High Commissioner for the French Cameroons. *Rapport Annuel du Gouvernement Français à l'Assemblée Générale des Nations Unies sur l'Administration du Cameroun*, 1952, pp. 492–6.

[3] K. E. Robinson, 'French Africa and French Union', *Africa Today*, 1955, pp. 321 ff.

[4] See below, p. 343. [5] See above, p. 148.

[6] *Loi*, 18 October 1908, approving the treaty concluded on 28 November 1907 between the Government of Belgium and the Congo Free State.

the government of overseas territories. The policy which she now adopted was shaped less by any views held as to the political future of the Colony than by consideration of the more immediate problems of its administration and its economic development. The basic law of the Colony, the *Charte Coloniale*, makes little reference to its political status; it merely states that the Congo is a territory under the sovereignty of Belgium, but possesses a separate legal personality from Belgium; Belgian legislation does not apply to it, as it is governed by a separate code of law (*par des lois particuliers*).[1]

It is not difficult, however, to realize the practical considerations which for the time being determined the main lines of Belgian policy in respect of the Colony. The responsibility for its rule had been forced on the Belgian Government by the pressure of international opinion, following on the revelations made by the commission appointed in 1904 to inquire into the affairs of the Congo Free State.[2] If Belgium was to avoid further international pressure and the possibility of intervention by more powerful neighbouring Powers,[3] then clearly it was necessary for her to establish an administrative and judicial régime in the Congo which would obviate occurrences such as those which had brought the Free State under such hostile criticism. Secondly, if she was to be in a position to prove that she was duly discharging her responsibilities in charge of this great area of Africa, she must give early evidence of substantial activity in its development.

It was realized by this time that the most readily available asset of the Colony lay in its minerals.[4] The finance for their exploitation could best be secured by an appeal to private investment, though policy also dictated that the appeal made to private capital should be framed in terms which would allow the State some part in directing the course of exploitation and an adequate share in its returns.[5] For a country of the size of Belgium the amount of the capital that has since been invested in the Colony has been remarkable.[6] The investment was not at first profitable, but of recent years its returns have come to form an important item in the metropolitan economy of Belgium, and many critics have in consequence drawn the conclusion that the Administration has been so preoccupied with the

[1] *Codes et Lois du Congo Belge*, 1954, pp. 5–16.
[2] R. L. Buell, *The Native Problem in Africa*, vol. ii, 1928, pp. 438–50. See also E. D. Morel, *Affairs of West Africa*, 1902, pp. 312–43.
[3] R. L. Buell, op. cit. p. 473.
[4] See below, p. 1514.
[5] P. Wigny, 'Methods of Government in the Belgian Congo', *African Affairs*, vol. l, October 1951, pp. 310–37. R. Godding, 'The Belgian Congo Before, During and After the War', *Progress*, winter 1953–4, p. 198.
[6] S. H. Frankel, *Capital Investment in Africa*, 1938, pp. 165–7. R. Godding, 'Administration of the Belgian Congo', in *Colonial Administration by Colonial Powers*, 1947, p. 56. He estimated the investment from all sources between 1885 and 1939 as equivalent to £770 million.

economic development of the country that it has failed to devote any consideration to the question of its political future.

But it would not be just to accept this judgement as final. The adverse impressions which were formed in the outside world during the régime of the Congo Free State have proved to be long lived, and there are still those who have in their minds a picture of the Belgian Congo as a country of which the Administration lives on an iniquitous traffic in ivory and rubber. The exponents of present-day Belgian policy are apt accordingly to start by emphasizing the achievements of the Administration in the expansion of the material resources of the country, in the improvement of transport, and the provision of economic services. But all impartial observers join in agreeing that the concern of the Administration has not in fact been merely material; there has been a real element of goodwill towards the African population and its welfare.

When they proceed to quote the many opinions which have been recorded to this effect, the exponents of Belgian policy are on sound ground. Some of them have, however, gone farther, and have spoken of the political objective in terms for which it is difficult to find a warranty in any authoritative declaration of policy. A former Colonial Minister has, for example, claimed that the aim of Belgium is 'to create a democracy wherein governmental power and the form of the State is decided by common consent of the people'. 'Political separation', he has added, 'is a possibility; if people want it, they will get it, though such an outcome is not a necessity.'[1] That is no doubt a genuine expression of a personal view, but it does not carry the same weight of authority as the affirmation that political self-government is the objective of British Colonial policy, or that the French have in view the political integration of the Overseas Territories in the French Union. It may prove more profitable therefore to inquire now how far the existing institutions of the Colony do actually convey an indication of the objectives of current policy.

The *Charte Coloniale* of 1908 embodied provisions designed first and foremost to ensure that the Government of the Colony should vest in an Administration which was definitely responsible to metropolitan supervision and control. While the Parliament was to be legislatively supreme, it was envisaged that most of the laws of the territory should be enacted by Royal Decree. The King acts on the advice of His Ministers, and the Royal Decrees would therefore constitute in fact orders issued on the authority of the Government of the day. Explicit parliamentary assent was, however, required for certain major decisions of policy. Thus its approval was to be given to the annual budget of the Colony, and was required also for the grant of concessions and for the contracting of loans, while an annual report on the activities of the Administration was to be

---

[1] Wigny, op. cit. Cf. J. M. Jadot in *Civilisations*, vol. iv, 1954, no. 4, p. 620.

laid before it. Close touch with the Ministry was to be assured through the employment of a colonial inspectorate.

The legislative power of the Governor-General of the Belgian Congo was to be limited to the issue of a local *ordonnance-loi* which would cease to be valid if not confirmed by a decree within six months. Special bodies were to be established to ensure the protection of Colonial interests; a *Conseil Colonial*, sitting in Brussels, was to examine and advise on all draft decrees and its reports on them were to be published. A special commission for the Protection of Native Interests was to be set up in the Colony itself. The form subsequently taken by those institutions of government will be discussed in the succeeding chapter;[1] it will be convenient to proceed here with a discussion of those administrative and economic developments in the Belgian Congo which seem to throw some light on the objective underlying current policy.

Economic Development

The vast size and relatively small population of the Colony, coupled with the limitations initially placed on its capacity to raise revenue by customs tariffs,[2] tended at the outset to increase the concentration of interest on the possibilities of industrial or other forms of economic development. Concern on this head remained the prevailing characteristic of Belgian policy until the end of the Second World War, when the success of the measures taken, accelerated as elsewhere by the pressures of the war period and the growing evidence of the changes being made in the political structure of other territories, began to result in a somewhat more active interest being taken in political problems. Economic policy has been greatly influenced by the legacy of the concessions régime pursued in the Free State period, as a result of which important interests were handed over to companies in which the Government had a large interest. Large-scale enterprise has accordingly occupied a predominant place in economic development; it was stated in 1952, for instance, that 51 per cent. of the wage-earning population was employed in a little over 3 per cent. of the commercial undertakings,[3] and it has been estimated that these undertakings hold roughly 86 per cent. of the total capital investment. The part taken by the present Government in the actual promotion of industrial undertakings has been more prominent than in most other territories. The shares held by the Colony in mining enterprises alone were stated to amount in 1953 to a total value of 19,000 million francs (roughly £125 million). The receipts of its 'portfolio' of investments were 762 million francs[4] (roughly £5 million).

---

[1] See below, pp. 345 ff. [2] R. L. Buell, op. cit. vol. ii, pp. 425 ff.
[3] *Congo Belge, Conseil du Gouvernement*, 1952; Discours du Gouverneur Général Pétillon, p. 21.
[4] P. Ryckmans, quoted in *East Africa and Rhodesia*, 2 June 1954.

As will be shown subsequently the sparseness of the population has resulted in the formulation of a system designed to regulate the outflow of labour from the rural areas to mining and other enterprises, with the double object of avoiding excessive depletion of manpower in the rural areas while promoting the creation of a stabilized labour force in the industrial centres.[1] No industrial colour bar has been recognized in industry and the Belgian system is conspicuous in the remarkable degree to which skilled African technicians have been used in forms of employment which in other parts of Africa have been reserved to Europeans.[2]

The 'stabilized labour' policy was for a time successful in checking the exodus from the rural to the urban areas; but since the Second World War there has been a spectacular increase in the African population of the towns.[3] On the other hand the policy pursued has been successful in providing for the establishment of wives and families in the towns, as opposed to the use of migrant labour which prevails so widely elsewhere; it is generally agreed that the conditions in which Africans are now domiciled in the urban areas of the Belgian Congo are much superior to those which have hitherto prevailed in the Union of South Africa and many of the British dependencies.[4] Nor can there be any question of the relatively high standards attained by the large industrial organizations in the provision of housing and medical and educational facilities for their employees. There can be no better evidence of the interest shown by Belgium in the improvement of the social conditions of Africans than the large sums now being devoted to this object by the Ten-year Development Programme.[5]

Agriculture, Health, and Education

In African conditions the attitude of the Administration in matters relating to land policy affords one of the most significant indications of the relations which it seeks to establish with the African population. The Belgian Government has on the whole been chary of taking advantage of its position in order to secure an extension of the area of European settlement. As many observers have noted,[6] it has seemed nervous of the prospect of creating a European 'settler' problem such as exists in parts of East Africa, and it has in recent years avoided making any considerable addition to the list of concessions held by companies interested in purely agrarian development.

[1] V. Charles, 'Le Problème des Centres Extra-Coutumiers au Congo', *Compte Rendu de l'Institut Colonial International*, 1936.

[2] For some recent illustrations of the development, see *New Statesman and Nation*, 10 April 1954, and *Daily Telegraph*, 6 April 1954.   [3] See below, p. 345.

[4] For details of the system followed in these urban centres, see F. Grevisse, *Le Centre Extra-Coutumier d'Élisabethville*, Brussels, 1951. E. Capelle, *La Cité Indigène de Léopoldville*, Brussels, 1947.

[5] *Plan Décennal du Congo Belge*, vol. i, 1949.

[6] See below, p. 345.

There has been a marked preference for the extension of African peasant cultivation. During the First World War a policy was adopted aiming at the extension of African production by making obligatory the cultivation of a fixed area or of a particular crop.[1] More recently an extensive series of controlled settlement schemes have been put into operation with the object of increasing African agricultural output.[2] Reference will be found in a subsequent chapter to the procedure employed,[3] but it may be observed that by 1953 some 140,000 divided plots had been organized.

Reference will also be found in succeeding chapters to the extensive operations undertaken to improve the health conditions of the African population, and it is noticeable, as illustrating the general attitude of the people of metropolitan Belgium, how considerable a part of the medical facilities now available has been contributed by non-official agencies.[4] There has been a similar movement for the provision of non-official assistance in measures taken for the improvement of methods of cultivation.[5] The provision of educational facilities has also been described at length in a later chapter.[6] In the Colonial world the procedure adopted in public instruction often provides significant evidence of the views held in regard to the conflicting conceptions of 'identity' and 'differentiation', and the more so because the type of education initially adopted is likely to be determined by the general outlook of the ruling race regarding African affairs rather than by any rationalized ideology.

There has in recent years been a liberal provision made for the primary and middle standards in school education, and from the first the instruction at these stages has been given to Africans in the vernacular; the 'assimilationist' principle which led the French to insist on the use of their own language as a medium of instruction[7] has had no place in the Belgian system. In the second place, effort has until recent years been directed mainly to the provision of school instruction of a 'practical' type, rather than higher education of an academic standard.[8] The Government has sought in fact to create a body of useful craftsmen or agriculturists, or at the most a well-equipped middle class, rather than an *élite* fitted to occupy the higher administrative posts or to take a part in political activities. Advanced academic courses only began to be provided in 1954. Thirdly, there has until recently been a practical though not a formal colour bar in the admission to schools; the University Colleges which were being inaugurated in 1954 were the first educational institutions to be established

[1] See below, p. 841.

[2] G. Malengreau, 'Vers un paysannat indigène: les lotissements agricoles au Congo Belge', *I.R.C.B. Mém.*, vol. xix, no. 2, 1949.

[3] See below, pp. 798–800.   [4] See below, pp. 1091–4.

[5] See below, pp. 1206–14.   [6] See below, p. 1206.

[7] See below, p. 1197.   [8] See below, p. 1210.

on a full multi-racial basis.[1] This development is significant because in social relations the attitude of Belgians resembles that observable in the British rather than in the French or Portuguese dependencies.

Local Administration

In approaching the problem of local administration the Belgian Government had to choose between the desirability of direct rule by European officials and an attempt to develop indigenous institutions as part of the agency of rule. Here Belgian policy has exemplified once again its essentially pragmatic approach. Although the apparent disintegration of African society might have seemed to justify a system of direct rule,[2] official opinion inclined at an early date to the view that an attempt should be made to develop and where necessary to reconstruct African social and political institutions. The procedure of Native Administration which was gradually evolved during the earlier years of the new régime was finally embodied in the Decree of 5 December 1933 which prescribed the constitution of the *circonscriptions indigènes*. It reflected ideas similar to those of the contemporary exponents of the Native Authority system in British territories.

Provision was made for the recognition of customary Chiefs and for the assignment to them of a certain range of administrative duties as distinct from their customary functions. But it also made provision for the continuance of the policy, initiated in earlier years, by virtue of which small chiefdoms were grouped into a larger unit, a *secteur*, with a Council representing all the Native Authorities in the area, headed by a Chief selected from among them by the Administration.[3] Similarly, the Decree of 23 November 1931, one of the most original initiatives of the Belgian Administration, provided for the creation of *centres extra-coutumiers* in areas (and particularly urban areas) where the population includes members of a number of different ethnic groups. In these *centres* provision was made for a Council composed of members of the different groups and for the appointment of a Chief, to whom considerable administrative tasks might be assigned.[4]

Experience showed, however, the difficulty of finding Chiefs capable of carrying out the duties envisaged for them. More and more of the chiefdoms were grouped in *secteurs*, while in the *centres extra-coutumiers* recourse was had to a provision which allowed officers of the Administration to assume the functions assigned to the appointed Chiefs. Both tendencies were accentuated by the Second World War, and indeed the creation of *centres extra-coutumiers* virtually ceased. The larger urban areas, once considered as the most appropriate areas for the establishment of these *centres*,

---

[1] See below, p. 1211.
[3] See below, p. 553.
[2] See below, p. 552.
[4] See below, p. 556.

are now administered under the direct control of European officers, in accordance with the provisions of the legislative *Ordonnance* of 20 July 1945 dealing with the *cités indigènes*.[1] The position was expressed by the Governor-General, M. Pétillon, in an illuminating passage. 'Notre ancienne conception de l'administration indirecte . . . aussi timide et mitigée qu'elle ait été dès le départ, n'a cessé de s'atténuer. Sous la pression des circonstances économiques et des situations de guerre, avec le souci louable de faire plus vite et mieux, nous avons voulu tout prendre en main et diriger la masse congolaise, bon gré mal gré, vers un bonheur conforme à nos concepts.'[2]

To remedy this situation Belgian policy has more recently envisaged the development of a new structure of Local Authorities which will incorporate the traditional Chiefs, wherever it is found possible to do so, together with representatives of the more Westernized elements of the population. It is hoped that these elements will thus be enabled to play their proper part in the political education of the masses. This policy was brought into effect in the Trust Territory of Ruanda Urundi in the Decree of 14 July 1952,[3] but no similar legislation had up to the end of 1954 been promulgated in respect of the Belgian Congo.

In one respect the political system in the Belgian Congo stands by itself. No rights of the nature of a franchise have been given either to European residents or to Africans; the *Conseil de Gouvernement* is, for example, a wholly consultative body.[4] On the other hand the Colony, unlike the French Overseas Territories, has no representative in the Belgian Parliament.

The merits of a system of paternalistic control responsible to a metropolitan Ministry is, however, increasingly questioned by a number of the Europeans who have more recently settled in the Colony. During the Second World War the Belgian Congo was completely isolated from Belgium and its only contact was with those members of the Belgian Ministry who had taken refuge in London. Such resources as the latter could command were derived from the credits provided by the Allied Powers in return for exports from the Colony required for war or similar purposes.[5] The major industries and commercial undertakings, hitherto rigidly controlled from Brussels, were during the war carried on by the local managers on their own responsibility. There inevitably grew up among the European residents a feeling that the Colony should have some greater measure of independence in the control of its own affairs, and this feeling persists,

[1] See below, p. 557.
[2] *Congo Belge, Conseil de Gouvernement, 1952*, Discours du Gouverneur Général Pétillon, p. 37. See also A. Maron, 'Le Décret du 5 Décembre 1933, Son esprit et son application', *Bull. du C.E.P.S.I.* no. 6, 1948, pp. 109–29.
[3] See below, p. 560.
[4] See below, p. 352.
[5] R. Godding in *Progress* (Magazine of Unilever), winter 1953–4, pp. 200 ff.

though it has not so far crystallized into a demand for any definite measure of political self-government.

There is at present little evidence of organized political movement among the African population. Progressive opinion is in their case largely concerned with the status of the better educated and more advanced Africans—the *évolués*. The rapid economic development of the territory and the growing volume of skilled employment open to Africans have resulted in the emergence of numbers whose aspirations are towards a European way of life and European social values. They are, however, virtually excluded from positions of higher responsibility in the Administration, and so far there has been no clear decision of policy as to the measures to be taken to distinguish their juridical or political status from that of Africans who continue to live in their traditional *milieu*. The history of the steps hitherto taken in this direction is of importance and must be explained in some detail.

Process of Immatriculation

As early as 1892 provision was made by the Congo Free State for the registration (*immatriculation*) of Africans who were prepared to be regulated by the terms of the Belgian civil code, but as no conditions were laid down for registration, this did not in effect separate Europeanized Africans from those who were living according to indigenous custom, nor were those who were registered exempted from any of the special conditions applicable in law to Africans. They remained subject to the jurisdiction of Native Courts and to the Native labour laws, and were required to live in the African quarters in the towns. The process of *immatriculation* was in consequence little used and fell into abeyance. In 1938 the Commission for the Protection of Native Interests recommended that *immatriculation* should be available only to those Africans who were capable of taking their place in European society on a basis of complete equality and that the conditions should in consequence be precisely defined and strictly applied.[1]

The number of Africans living wholly or partly outside tribal society was considerably increased by the development of industry during the Second World War, but the post-war discussions on the subject revealed two different schools of thought in respect of *immatriculation*. One school urged that a charge of racial discrimination could not be rebutted unless the small number of Africans who were completely Westernized could secure a civil status identical with that of European residents in the Colony. This, it was claimed, implied the need for a meticulous definition of the criteria of Westernization. The second school of thought refused to accept the implication that legislation of this type must necessarily involve

[1] L. Guebels, 'Relation complète des Travaux de la Commission Permanente pour la Protection des Indigènes, 1911–51', *Bulletin du C.E.P.S.I.* no. 22, 1953, pp. 534–9.

acceptance of the concept of complete Westernization as the objective of Belgian policy.[1] It emphasized that there were many Africans who, though remaining attached to their own social custom, had abandoned 'uncivilized' practices. *Immatriculation* was, it was claimed, unsuited to the needs of this class, but so also was their treatment in the same way as Africans in tribal society; a special status, intermediate between the two, seemed to be required.[2]

In 1949 the Minister for Colonies appointed a commission to make recommendations for conferring an appropriate legal status on Africans who had adopted a European mode of life. The result was the enactment of the revised decree on *immatriculation* of 17 May 1952.[3] It instituted a process not unlike that of naturalization. Requests for registration are examined by a magistrate with four assessors, who must include officials and, as soon as practicable, one 'registered' African. The applicant must satisfy them of his capacity to profit by the rights and to fulfil the obligations provided by statutory law. *Immatriculation* does not give exemption from all regulations applicable to Africans; the *immatriculés* are, however, subject to the European Courts, have all rights under the Civil code, and have similar treatment with Europeans on public transport vehicles.[4]

The measure has not satisfied those who had looked forward to the enactment of a measure which would give the advanced African exactly the same status as the Belgian resident in the Colony. It represented a concession to those who followed the school of thought which held that the grant of *immatriculation* need not necessarily depend on proof of a complete state of Westernization. The essential condition was, in short, only that the candidate should be able 'justifier par sa formation et sa manière de vivre d'un état de civilisation impliquant l'aptitude à jouir des droits et à remplir les devoirs prévus par la législation écrite'.

It is this attitude which for the present seems to carry most weight in the direction of public policy. It emphasizes that there are now numerous Africans who, though they have abandoned many aspects of African custom, may yet not wish to be assimilated for all purposes to Europeans, more especially in regard to the personal law relating to marriage, succession, and the like. Some attempt had already been made in 1948 to meet the requirements of this class by the institution of the *Carte du Mérite Civique*.[5]

---

[1] *Congo Belge, Conseil de Gouvernement, 1952*, Discours du Gouverneur Général Pétillon, p. 34.
[2] A. Sohier, 'Le Statut Personnel des Autochtones au Congo Belge', *Civilisations*, vol. iii, pp. 179–87.
[3] *Décret modifiant les dispositions du Code civil sur l'immatriculation des Congolais*, 17 May 1952. *Code et Lois du Congo Belge*, 1954, pp. 48, 156. See also J. J. Maquet, 'The Modern Evolution of African Populations in the Belgian Congo', *Africa*, October 1949, p. 271. The discussions in the Conseil Colonial on the subject of *immatriculation* in January 1952 are reproduced in a pamphlet *Immatriculation des Congolais*, Brussels, 1952.
[4] G. Malengreau, 'Recent Developments in Belgian Africa', in *Africa Today*, 1955, p. 348.
[5] *Ordonnances*, 12 July 1948, 24 June 1950.

This is a special form of identity card obtainable by anyone who is literate, is not a polygamist, and has not within the previous five years been convicted of any of certain specified offences. Illiterates may also obtain the card if they can show evidence of qualification as artisans or of long service in the employ of Europeans or of any African authority.

The process by which access to the *Carte du Mérite Civique* is acquired is somewhat similar to that applying to requests for *immatriculation*. It entitles the possessor to such rights as may from time to time be specified as appropriate to Africans belonging to this category, and holders of the card may at their request be judged in the *tribunaux de territoire*, not in the Native Courts; they have a special position in regard to the acquisition of real property. It has been described as intended to afford recognition of 'les meilleurs de nos pupilles, ceux dont le standing de vie s'apparente le mieux au nôtre et dont l'éducation et le mode de vie personnel, familial, et social témoignent d'une évolution réelle'.[1] The conception of an intermediate status involved in the grant of the *Carte du Mérite* has been criticized in some quarters as involving a form of discrimination, and preference has been expressed for a system which would avoid the creation of a special civil status, but would merely make applicable to those Africans who deserved it the régime applicable to Europeans in certain defined matters, such as the acquisition of real property.[2] It appears that only some 452 Africans had received the privileges of the *Carte* by the end of 1952.

General Trends of Belgian Policy

On a broad view, the present trend of Belgian thought seems to be towards a policy of 'modified differentiation'. Nor is there anything which would show that policy is likely to incline towards that measure of assimilation which would seem to be implied in a scheme of complete political integration with metropolitan Belgium. If, however, there exists a strong argument on cultural grounds against any advanced measure of assimilation, there are equally strong arguments on economic grounds against a complete political separation. Further speculation on this point would be out of place until local opinion in the Colony has declared itself more fully.

Belgian officials are often said to be equally nervous on the subject of Belgian settlers and of African *évolués*. There are now well over 70,000 Europeans in the country, but the actual number of settlers holding land is relatively small; it is noteworthy that under existing regulations no settler is allowed to take up more than 500 hectares of land.[3] It appears that

[1] Governor-General's Circular, 10 August 1948.
[2] G. Malengreau, 'L'Accession des Indigènes à la Propriété foncière individuelle', *Zaïre*, 1953, pp. 607–9; 'Recent Developments in Belgian Africa', in *Africa Today*, 1955, pp. 348 ff.
[3] *The Times*, 5 July 1955. See also *Africa Digest*, vol. ii, no. 5, September–October 1954, p. 11.

some of the newer type of European *colons*, notably those settled in Bukavu (Costermansville), have lately shown some tendency to claim a share in political rights, but they can only make their views felt by organizing pressure in Belgium itself. In the Colony the Governor-General can constitutionally override them, and is usually prepared to do so.

As regards the expression of African opinion, this has not (as has already been observed) taken so definite a form as in the British or French territories. But the Colony has not had so entirely uneventful a political history as has been represented in some quarters. It is true that some of the movements which have caused disturbance in the past have been of religious origin, such as that associated with Simon Kimbangu in 1921 and the following years, or the Kitiwala rising which took place in the Manyema area in 1940–1.[1] They have usually been led by prophets offering their own version of the Christian religion, claiming to perform miracles, and promising a millennium when all Europeans will be removed from Africa. The Administration has had no difficulty in dealing with these outbreaks, but it exhibits some degree of anxiety regarding combinations formed for political purposes; there were some 3,818 persons described as deportees (*relégués*) in 1952,[2] and there are not the same opportunities permitted for the public expression of opinion as in the British and French territories.

The apparent absorption of the Africans of the Belgian Congo in the economic life of the country by no means precludes the possibility of the development of a strong sentiment of political nationalism such as has made its appearance elsewhere in Africa. It is no doubt an overstatement to describe the policy of the Belgian Government as one of 'paternalism combining the uplift of the African with political suppression',[3] but there is a substratum of truth in the criticism. The conception of the metropolitan Power as the impartial arbiter between the races, which must not relinquish authority until Africans are in a position to carry their full political weight, is carried by the Belgians to what seems to them to be its logical conclusion. Political rights, they claim, should not precede the raising of the African standard of living.[4] The logic of this attitude is not open to question. But the claim of Belgium to exercise the position of an impartial arbiter is vulnerable, owing to the exceptional measure of its material interest in the economic development of the Colony.

---

[1] G. Balandier, in *Encyclopédie Coloniale et Maritime Mensuelle*, Paris, vol. i, fascicule 12, 1951, pp. 218–20. R. L. Buell, *The Native Problem in Africa*, vol. ii, pp. 601 ff. J. Comhaire, 'Sociétés secrètes et mouvements prophétiques au Congo Belge', *Africa*, January 1955, p. 54. Kitiwala or Chitiwala is a phase of the Watch Tower or Jehovah's Witnesses which also caused trouble in Northern Rhodesia during the early twenties. Its basic tenet is that all forms of authority are evil.

[2] *New Statesman and Nation*, 24 April 1954.

[3] A. Campbell, *The Heart of Africa*, 1954.

[4] R. Godding, 'The Belgian Congo', *Progress*, winter 1953–4, pp. 195 ff.

PORTUGUESE TERRITORIES

The Concept of Identity

Of the States which come within the scope of this Survey there is none which can rival Portugal in its insistence on the concept of 'identity' in preference to that of 'differentiation'. This is, indeed, an old-standing feature of Portuguese policy. A Royal Ordinance of 1755 laid down that in the American possessions of Portugal any Portuguese subject who married a Native woman should be 'treated with dignity', and that reference to their offspring as 'half-breeds or any similar insulting term' should be punished as a criminal offence. Royal Orders of 1761 and 1763 declared that inhabitants of Mozambique, whether White, Half-caste, or Negro, should all enjoy equal privileges before the law 'if enfranchised and free and instructed in the arts and sciences'.[1] From the frequent reference to baptism in these and similar laws it would seem that 'enfranchisement' referred in particular to baptism; the profession of Christianity was regarded as a sufficient qualification for equal political and judicial rights, if accompanied by a certain measure of education.

It has been suggested that the lack of colour prejudice shown by the Portuguese is to be attributed to their long contact with the Moors, who at the period when they conquered the Iberian Peninsula had a civilization which was by no means inferior to that of the peoples who then occupied it.[2] But the attitude of the Portuguese goes farther than the toleration of racial admixture which this explanation might suggest. From an early period they were accustomed to think of their overseas territories as part of Portugal. Early in the nineteenth century the Colonies were commonly spoken of as 'overseas provinces', and their inhabitants were declared to be Portuguese citizens and endowed with the vote.

But this policy achieved little reality outside the pages of the Official Gazette, and early in the twentieth century a contrary trend set in, inspired by the concept of Colonial autonomy. In 1907 Mozambique received a Colonial Charter which, though stillborn, pointed clearly towards the ultimate attainment of an autonomous status. With the advent of the Portuguese Republic in 1910 this trend was accentuated. Control was transferred largely into the hands of the Colonial Governors, supported by a semblance of elected Parliaments. Angola was permitted to vote its own organic Charter. One of the earliest measures of the Republic, the 'Law of Separation of Church and State' (1911), which withdrew all State support from the Portuguese missions, was an additional obstacle to the maintenance of the ties which had formerly bound the Colonies to the public of the metropolis.

[1] A. A. Andrade, *Many Races, One Nation*, 1954, pp. 23–27, 43–47.
[2] L. Kraft, 'Rival Colonial Policies in Africa', *Listener*, 1 July 1954.

This phase ended with the new régime initiated in 1926. Apart from other grounds, the financial chaos which had for many years reigned in the Colonies was a powerful argument against a policy which would allow them to raise their own loans and might at the same time deprive Portugal of any economic support she could derive from them. In Angola public debt charges were absorbing as much as 25 per cent. of the total revenue. There was now a studied and purposeful resurgence of the doctrine of Colonial integration with metropolitan Portugal. The main lines of Colonial policy in the 'New State' were laid down in a series of measures of which the more important were the Colonial Act of 1930, the Organic Charter of the Empire, and the Act of Overseas Administrative Reform of 1933. In 1935 the Colonies were declared to be part of the territory of Portugal and to stand together in solidarity with each other and with the mother country.[1]

Current policy has shown a strong tendency in favour of a return to the earlier designation of the Colonies as 'overseas provinces'. It is agreed that solidarity must admit of some differentiation of treatment and of a measure of administrative decentralization in the light of local conditions,[2] but there has at the same time been insistence on the retention of ultimate authority in Lisbon as a safeguard against any possibility of either financial deterioration or political disintegration. One corollary of this was the replacement of the earlier Colonial Parliaments (which were held to be potential seed-beds of dissension and of separatism) by 'Advisory Councils of Government'.

It was in accordance with this line of approach that an Act of 1951[3] altered the designation of the Colonies to that of 'overseas provinces', a change which was subsequently embodied in the organic law of the Overseas Territories.[4] The title of the Ministry of the Colonies was altered accordingly to that of the Ministry for Overseas Provinces (*Ministério do Ultramar*). The solidarity of the overseas territories is now expressed by a form of political union which gives to all the inhabitants of the former Colonies the titular status of Portuguese citizens; as such they are in theory entitled to take part, for example, in the election of the President of the Republic.

It should be explained that in the 'unitary and corporative Republic' the President is elected every seven years by universal adult suffrage. The Executive administration is vested in the Council of State and the Ministers, whose function it is to 'advise' the President of the Republic, much in the same way that the Ministers in Great Britain may 'advise' the Crown in

---

[1] A. J. Peaslee, *Constitutions of Nations*, 1950, vol. iii, p. 26.
[2] M. Caetano, *Colonizing Traditions, Principles and Methods of the Portuguese*, 1951.
[3] *Lei*, no. 2048 of 11 June 1951.
[4] *Lei*, no. 2066 of June 1953, in *Nova Legislação Ultramarina*, vol. i, Lisbon, 1953.

the discharge of its constitutional functions. The Council of State is a small body consisting partly of *ex officio* members and partly of members nominated by the President of the Republic: the President of the Council is nominated by him.

The legislative power is vested in the National Assembly, now consisting of 120 Deputies, elected by all adult citizens of Portugal for a fixed period of four years. Each of the two African provinces, Angola and Mozambique, elects three Deputies; Portuguese Guinea elects one Deputy and Sao Tomé and Principe jointly elect one. But these are not necessarily local residents; they need in fact have no definite connexion with Africa. Two of the present delegates for Angola are a Governor of the Bank of Angola and a former Governor-General of Angola. It will, of course, be realized that the Assembly is in practice, though not in principle, constituted on a 'one-party' basis. There is no recognized Opposition party. The Ministers are not responsible to the National Assembly, though they must secure legislation from it, and must also secure its sanction for their financial measures. The National Assembly receives the advice of another organ of the Corporative State, namely, the Corporative Chamber, which discusses all motions or Bills or International Conventions before they are brought before the National Assembly. The Corporative Chamber is composed of representatives of local autonomous corporative bodies and of certain 'social interests'; its sessions are held in private.[1]

Referring now to those provisions of the Portuguese Constitution which regulate the administrative and legislative control of the Overseas Provinces, it will be seen from the details given in the succeeding chapter[2] that they involve a large measure of that centralized control which is characteristic of the systems that point to the integration of overseas territories with the political and economic régime of the metropolis. It is easy to understand the influences which account for the emphasis laid on the maintenance of this control. For a prolonged period Portugal itself had suffered from a continuous series of financial crises. That it has since 1928 contracted no external loan, and that it succeeded in extinguishing all its floating debt in 1934, is due largely to the control exercised over its domestic finances and to the measures taken to improve the productive capacity of the country and of its overseas territories.

If this unified control has some economic aspects which seem to be unfavourable to the Colonies there are on the other hand two features which have been definitely favourable to them. There has been an end of the series of unbalanced Colonial budgets of the twenties; since 1935 all the Colonial budgets have been balanced. Secondly, the National Development Plan put forward in 1953[3] includes measures which affect both

[1] For the character of these bodies, see S. G. West, *The New Corporative State of Portugal*, 1937.
[2] See below, pp. 353 ff.   [3] *O Plano de Fomento no Ultramar*, Lisbon, 1953.

Portugal and its Overseas Provinces, and the improvements to be undertaken in the latter will account for nearly half the total expenditure envisaged by the Plan.[1] It is an important feature of present policy that the subsidies to the Portuguese Catholic missions, which were withdrawn in 1911, have been resumed, and that in 1930 the Colonial Act recognized Portuguese Catholic missions overseas as 'an instrument of civilization and national influence'. The Missionary Agreement appended to the Concordat of 1940 and implemented by the Bull *Solemnibus Conventionibus* of the same year, together with the Missionary Statute of 1941, have completed the return to an earlier policy. The Portuguese Catholic missions have now an important position in the control of State schools for African education.[2]

Limits to Application of the Principle of 'Identity'

While there can be no question of the strength of the sentiment attaching in Portuguese policy to the concept of 'identity', there are nevertheless well-marked limits to its application in practice. There is a definite line of demarcation between those who are entitled to exercise the full rights of citizens of the Republic and those who do not yet qualify for the exercise of these rights. In the African Provinces Europeans fall automatically into the former category, which is classed as that of the *população civilizada*; the Coloured and African inhabitants come within it only if they fulfil the necessary qualifications. These are, firstly, the definite adoption of the European manner of life and the abandonment of certain Native customs, such as polygamy; secondly, the ability to speak fluently and to write Portuguese; thirdly, the possession of some trade, profession, or calling giving a recognized financial status; fourthly, the applicant must have completed his military service.[3]

The emphasis placed on the first of these qualifications makes it difficult for anyone who is not a professing Christian to gain recognition as an *assimilado*. Given proof of the necessary qualifications, the Coloured or African inhabitant is entitled to a certificate by which he ranks as *assimilado*. He then acquires responsibility for paying the European scale of taxation, thus escaping the Native Tax and certain contingent disabilities, such as those subsequently to be described in dealing with the labour régime.[4] He comes within the jurisdiction of Courts administering the civil and criminal law based on that of metropolitan Portugal. All observers agree that the *assimilado* does actually acquire the status accorded to a Portuguese citizen of European birth. It is the European and the

---

[1] *The Times*, 21 June 1954.   [2] See below, pp. 1214 ff.
[3] C. F. Spence, *The Portuguese Colony of Mozambique*, 1951, pp. 28–30. The qualification of completion of military service was emphasized in Law No. 39666 of May 1954, see *The Times*, 8 June 1954. Service is performed in the Colonial Guard, beginning at the age of 20, see *Civilizations*, vol. v, no. 1, 1955, p. 129.   [4] See below, p. 1372.

assimilado who actually take part in the elections for the President of the Republic or for the membership of the National Assembly, though on the last occasion of the election of a President a number of selected local notables, not necessarily 'assimilated', were also invited to join in the voting.

The number of the *assimilados* is, however, at present limited, partly because the facilities for higher education are such that the possibility of achieving assimilation is practically confined to the urban areas. The figures recorded in the census of 1950 will be most readily appreciated in the following table.[1]

	Total Population	População Civilizada	White	Half-caste	Indian	Negro
Guinea . . .	510,777	8,320	2,263	4,568	11	1,478
Sao Tomé and Principe	60,159	4,501	1,424	2,245	11	821
Angola . . .	4,145,266	135,355	78,826	26,335	..	30,039
Mozambique .	5,782,982	92,619	48,813	25,165	12,673	4,353

If the ratio now existing between the categories of *civilizada* and *não-civilizada* is maintained for any length of time, it would go far to constitute a denial of the reality of the concept of 'identity', so far as this concept purports to confer equal rights of citizenship on Europeans and Africans, for in effect the population is divided sharply between 'Portuguese Citizens' and 'Portuguese Natives'.[2] The differentiation is not limited to the denial to Natives of a share in political privileges; there is a very real difference both in judicial and administrative status between the two categories of inhabitants.[3] This illustrates the paradox which is always liable to arise in the actual implication of the concept of 'identity'. Insistence on a cultural qualification can in practice create a more restrictive barrier than that of colour. In the Overseas Provinces of Portugal it has been possible for these Africans who stand outside the barrier of culture to be treated with less consideration than would be accorded to the indigenous peoples by some of those Governments which prefer to adopt the concept of 'differentiation'.

It has been suggested that in the case of the Portuguese Overseas Provinces the distinction now observed is an unavoidable expedient which in any case is only temporary. It is difficult, however, to assess the probability of a substantial change in this respect. Although recent legislation has re-emphasized the politically integrative aspects of Portuguese policy, no change of substance seems to have been made in its attitude towards the indigenous institutions of African society. It is not irrelevant to recall that

---

[1] *Anuário Estatístico do Ultramar*, 1952, pp. 26–27.   [2] Caetano, op. cit. p. 43.
[3] A. Durieux, *Essai sur le statut des indigènes portugais de la Guinée, de l'Angola et du Mozambique*, Mém. A.R.S.C., vol. v, no. 3, 1955, p. 9.

the Portuguese territories were the only major areas in Africa which were unaffected by the acceleration of social and economic change that was elsewhere the most important result of participation in the Second World War. In the Portuguese areas economic development is now beginning to make some progress, but any great change in the rate of development, especially in respect of the tribal areas, may be expected to reproduce the tension which exists elsewhere between European residents and the increasing number of Africans who seek admission to the privileges of European status.

At present there are many obstacles to any great increase in the number of Africans qualified for citizenship, especially (as has been pointed out) in the limited facilities for higher education which are at present open to Africans. The strict age limit for admission to the State high schools means that Africans are not often qualified for admission, while the fees charged by private secondary schools preclude the entry of many African children. The Decree of 1954 which restated the qualifications for admission to the category of *assimilado* appears to have been intended to narrow rather than to enlarge the avenue of approach to this status; it is indeed possible that this measure is in effect a corollary to the recent campaign for an increase in the number of Portuguese colonists in the African Provinces. The increase of the number of persons admitted to this category during the years 1935 to 1950 was by no means dramatic. Against the 75,728 persons (including 8,357 Half-castes) recorded as *civilizada* in Mozambique in 1935, there were only 92,619, including 25,165 Half-castes, so recorded in 1950. The census of 1950 recorded only 4,353 Negroes as included in this category.

SPANISH TERRITORIES

The area of the Spanish territories south of the Sahara is relatively small, but the most important of them, the volcanic island of Fernando Po,[1] has a position of some importance in the modern history of West Africa. It is not only the reputed source from which cocoa was brought to the Gold Coast in 1870,[2] but it was the market for the 'forced' labour, the recruitment of which formed the subject of the more serious of the charges brought against the Government of Liberia in the early thirties.[3] The mainland area (Rio Muni or Continental Guinea) was originally occupied from Fernando Po. It is, in an economic sense, of minor importance, and is now administered by sub-governors stationed at Bata and Elobey, subject to the control of the Governor of Fernando Po.[4]

[1] More correctly spelt, Fernando Pôo, the African equivalent of 'the land of Ferdinand'.
[2] See below, p. 828.
[3] See below, p. 236. See on this point R. L. Buell, *The Native Problem in Africa*, vol. ii, 1928, pp. 777 ff., and *Liberia, A Century of Survival*, 1947, pp. 34 ff. R. E. Anderson, *Liberia, America's African Friend*, 1952, pp. 101–6. [4] *Real Decretos*, 11 July 1904, 16 April 1935.

Fernando Po was at the outset held by the Portuguese, and Europeans are still known there as 'Portos'; it was ceded to Spain in 1777–8 in return for concessions made to Portugal in America. It was occupied by the British from 1827–44, but was then restored to Spain. The British head-quarters, Port Clarence, was renamed Santa Isabel by the Spanish, and is now the headquarters of the Governor of the island. Effective Spanish administration did not, however, begin till 1858, and little importance was attached to the Colony; up to 1883, indeed, it was utilized mainly as a residence for political deportees, and only acquired importance with the extension of the cultivation of cocoa. The Spanish occupation of Rio Muni was recognized by Germany in 1885 and by France in 1900; it was agreed that if Spain desired at any time to give up its possession, France should have the right of pre-emption.

Throughout their occupation of these areas[1] the Spanish have treated them as an appanage of Spain, both for administrative and for economic purposes.[2] Legislation is effected by decree from the metropolitan Ministry, the *Dirección General de Marruecos y Colonias*; the local budget is approved by the *Cortes*.[3] There is no local institution possessing legislative powers, but the Governor has two Advisory Councils (*junte*), one composed of the civil and military heads of local services, and the other of repre-sentatives of the Chambers of Commerce and certain nominated officials. It is claimed that some of the Local Government institutions possess powers which have an element of autonomy, but it is clear that they are still very loosely organized, and are in practice subject to a close official control.

There are at the same time indications that in regard to the African population the Spanish are prepared to adopt a system of differentiation on a basis of culture somewhat similar to that followed in the Portuguese territories.[4] A number of European residents have settled in the Moka Highlands of the island. The original inhabitants, mainly of the Bubi tribe, are small in number, and the bulk of the African population consists of immigrant labourers, who are largely Ibo from Eastern Nigeria, to-gether with some immigrants of an earlier date from Liberia or the Gold Coast who have settled in the island. There are estimated to be between 15,000 and 20,000 of this type of immigrant, and they are reputed to have a much higher degree of literacy than the local population. In the main-land area of Rio Muni, which is very little developed, the Natives still live in tribal conditions.

The Spanish now recognize two classes of 'assimilated' Africans, namely

[1] For a general description of existing conditions, see R. J. Harrison Church, 'Spain's West African Territories', *West Africa*, 8 March, 5, 12, and 19 April 1952.

[2] G. Héraud, 'Aperçu sur l'Organisation des Territoires Espagnols d'Outre-Mer', *Revue Juridique et Politique de l'Union Française*, July 1954, pp. 316–20.

[3] *Ley*, 11 November 1935.   [4] See above, p. 232.

those fully assimilated (*emancipados*), and those who have had the benefit only of *emancipacion limitada*. The first class has the same civil status as Europeans and is subject to the metropolitan Penal Code.[1] Those who have 'limited emancipation' have restricted civil rights and come under the jurisdiction of Native Tribunals.[2] The number of *emancipados* has been stated to be roughly 15,000 out of a total Native population returned as 194,726 in the census of 1950. The grant of the status of *emancipado* is regulated by a board of twelve members nominated by the Governor, of whom two are 'emancipated' Africans, but a certificate of full emancipation requires the approval of the Ministry. The effect of emancipation seems to be largely juridical, and there are as yet no political bodies for the election of which 'emancipation' could confer the right of a vote.

LIBERIA

There is some similarity in the earlier history of Liberia and of Sierra Leone, for both owed their origin to a philanthropic effort to establish a home in Africa for liberated African slaves. But there the resemblance ends. The 'Creoles' of the Sierra Leone Colony have never sought to establish control over the indigenous tribes of what is now the Protectorate, and though their community has shown much political activity, especially in regard to the achievement of a type of self-government of the British pattern, their influence has extended very little beyond Freetown and its vicinity.[3] The Americo-Liberians, on the other hand, have succeeded in gaining administrative control over the Natives of the coastal region, where the principal tribes are the Kru, the Bassa, and the Grebo, and also (though in this case the control exercised has been much looser) over the tribes of Northern Liberia—such as the Mandingo (who are chiefly Muslim), the Gissi, and Kpwesi. There has been no census held in Liberia, but the Americo-Liberians are now usually stated to number between 12,000 and 20,000, and the rest of the population have been estimated at various figures between 1 and $2\frac{1}{2}$ million.[4]

It is unnecessary to discuss at length here the methods by which the Americo-Liberian governing class maintained this measure of control,

[1] *Leyes*, 22 December 1944 and 6 June 1945.

[2] The Criminal Law as applied to Natives is described in a work by F. Munido, *Derecho Penal aplicable a indigenas en los territorios españoles del Golfo de Guinea*, 1953.

[3] *N.A.*, Part III, p. 285.

[4] See above, p. 137. The United Nations *Demographic Yearbook of 1952* gives a figure of 1,150,000, but quotes as its authority the figures of 1937, though the total given by the League of Nations for that year was $2\frac{1}{2}$ million. The *Statesman's Year-Book, 1954*, gives $2\frac{1}{2}$ million. Other estimates have been $2\frac{1}{2}$ million (N. Azikiwe, *Liberia in World Politics*, 1934); about 1 million (R. L. Buell, *Liberia, A Century of Survival*, 1947); 1,015,000 (F. J. Pedler, *West Africa*, 1951); between $1\frac{1}{2}$ and 2 million (R. E. Anderson, *Liberia, America's African Friend*, 1952, p. 4). See also G. W. Brown, *The Economic History of Liberia*, 1941, p. 41.

though it is of interest to note the explicit statement made in 1947 by Dr. R. L. Buell that this was only rendered possible by the receipt of periodic assistance from American sources. This was sometimes indirect, in the form of the dispatch of a warship to Liberian waters at times when its Government was in difficulties either with its indigenous tribes or with its British or French neighbours. At other times the aid given was more tangible, in the form of the loan of personnel. Nor is it necessary to detail here the series of financial crises from which Liberia suffered from 1906 onwards, or the charges regarding the use of forced labour and other abuses which culminated in the appointment by the League of Nations of the International Commission of Inquiry of 1930.[1] This was followed by the creation of a 'Liberia Committee' nominated by members of the League, charged with the function of considering plans for the guidance or assistance to be given to the Republic. The committee appointed three experts to examine the local position, and subsequently made a number of recommendations for administrative and financial reforms in the country.[2]

The rejection by Liberia of these recommendations, combined with the publication of the story of the methods used to suppress a recent outbreak of trouble on the Kru coast, led to diplomatic relations with Liberia being broken off by Great Britain and the United States; the two nations actually discussed proposals for recommending its expulsion from the League of Nations.[3] It has been suggested that the attitude of Great Britain represented a deliberate attempt 'to end the independence of the Republic of Liberia through the intervention of the League of Nations'.[4] If that were true, the United States must share in the guilt, for the condemnation of Liberian maladministration by the United States Government of the period was much more emphatic than that of the British. The proposal for expulsion was not, however, pursued further when Liberia agreed to adopt a three-year programme of reform, the chief feature of which was the appointment of eight 'emergency' advisers dealing with different aspects of administration. They were given no executive powers, but their appointment tided over the trouble for the time being.

A number of complaints against the Liberian Government had referred to the abuse of power, and it was mainly these which the British Government had in mind when its dispatches to the United States Government spoke of the misdeeds of the 'corrupt and inefficient oligarchy of Mon-

---

[1] R. L. Buell, *The Native Problem in Africa*, 1928, vol. ii, pp. 714 ff., and *Liberia, A Century of Survival*, 1947, pp. 20–27. The report of the Commission (the Christy Commission) was published as League Paper, no. C. 658, M. 272, 1930.

[2] These recommendations, and the report of the experts on which they are based (the Brunot Report), were reproduced in a British Blue Book, *Liberia No. 1*, Cmd. 4614, 1934.

[3] League of Nations, *Official Journal*, 1934, p. 511. For an account of these proceedings as seen from the standpoint of Liberia see R. E. Anderson, *Liberia, America's African Friend*, 1952, pp. 110–25.

[4] Anderson, op. cit. p. 124.

rovia'. But there were other charges also, based on the failure of the Government to make provision for services of health and education. Here it was obvious that there was (apart from anything else) a serious lack of the finance required for such purposes. The Administration had shown itself incapable of developing the resources of the country, and the fear of outside interference had made it unwilling to accept any form of foreign assistance other than that of the missionary societies which had provided practically the only means of education in the country.

In 1926, however, it acquiesced in the proposal of the Firestone Corporation of America to take up a 90-year lease of a large area of land for the establishment of a rubber plantation,[1] and from this point onwards the questions involved in the development of this project and the terms of the Loan Agreement which accompanied it began to exercise a growing influence on the attitude adopted by the Government of the United States towards Liberia.[2] It is partly to this project and partly to the interest of other American enterprises in Liberia (some of which resulted from the contacts established during the Second World War) that the country owes the recent improvement in its economic condition. This has not only been notable in itself but has had a marked reaction on the political and administrative conditions in the country.

The Firestone Plantations, some 100,000 acres in extent, now produce a yearly average of 80 million pounds of rubber and employ 25,000 workers. In 1943 the United States agreed to build a port for Monrovia with 'lend-lease' funds, at an estimated cost of over $19 million; this was opened to commerce as a 'free port' in 1948.[3] Between 1944 and 1946 a number of missions from the United States dealing with public health and economic, educational, geological, and agricultural conditions, visited the country and studied its requirements. The American Foundation for Tropical Medicine initiated in Monrovia an Institute of Medicine which has had the support of a liberal grant from the Firestone Company.

In 1950 a General Agreement for Technical Assistance and Co-operation was concluded with the United States. The America-owned Liberia Mining Company (in which the Republic Steel Company is interested) completed in 1953 the first stage of the development of the iron-ore deposits on the Bomi Hills; the annual export to the States amounts roughly to 1 million tons of high-grade iron-ore.[4] Cocoa is being produced by the Liberia Company, founded by the late E. R. Stettinius, and timber is being exploited by the interest known as the Letourneau group. The

[1] See below, p. 964.
[2] Buell, *Liberia, A Century of Survival*, 1947, pp. 32 ff. G. W. Brown, *The Economic History of Liberia*, 1941, pp. 160, 211, 262–82. C. M. Wilson, *Liberia*, 1947, pp. 99–136. F. J. Pedler, *West Africa*, 1951, pp. 127–34. Anderson, op. cit. pp. 116–18, 126 ff., 276.
[3] Anderson, op. cit. pp. 164 ff.
[4] See Anderson, op. cit. pp. 179 ff.

financial position of the country now seems to be secure. When the Brunot Committee[1] reported in 1932 they looked forward to securing an increase of the public revenue to $650,000 a year. In the years 1951 to 1953, however, the revenue, which was derived mainly from the tax on iron and rubber undertakings,[2] amounted to a little over an average of $10 million a year.[3] All floating debts had been paid off. The Five-year Development programme of Liberia drawn up in 1950, which embodies the result of the Agreement for Technical Co-operation above referred to, envisaged the expenditure of $32½ million, towards which the Export-Import Bank had agreed to provide a loan of $6½ million.

The achievement of financial independence by Liberia has now made irrelevant the variety of phraseology which the political world had in the past employed in order to describe its status.[4] Liberia is in fact today, as it asserted in its original Constitution of 1847, a 'free, sovereign and independent republic'.[5] The Constitution reproduces many of the characteristic institutions of the United States of America, such as the elected President, an Executive independent of the Legislature, the nomination of Ministers by the President, and the existence of two Houses of Legislature, namely, the Senate and the House of Representatives.

If one seeks a statement of the objective of its national policy this is to be found, in a formal sense, in the Article of the Constitution which declares that the purpose of the State is 'to provide a home for the dispersed and oppressed Children of Africa, and to regenerate and enlighten this benighted Continent'. In order to implement this purpose the Constitution laid down that none but Negroes or persons of Negro descent should be admitted to citizenship, that none but citizens should be entitled to hold real property, and that only property holders should be entitled to vote or to hold elective office.[6] In a less formal sense it is obvious that for many years the most engrossing objective of policy has been to maintain the independence of the Republic, free from any form of outside intervention, and one must pay a tribute to the tenacity with which this policy was pursued in practice. But it must also be realized that what was so strenuously claimed to be a determination to uphold the inviolability of Liberian independence was in effect only a resolution to preserve intact the authority of the small governing class of Americo-Liberians and their associates.

---

[1] See above, p. 236, note 2.

[2] For the contribution made by the Firestone Company see Buell, op. cit. pp. 48–54. Anderson, op. cit. pp. 126 ff. The State now takes half the net profit of the Liberia Mining Company.

[3] *Statesman's Year-Book, 1954*, p. 1206; and *Liberia, A Diplomatic Press Survey*, December 1953.

[4] See Azikiwe, op. cit. pp. 17–19, 59–65.

[5] A. J. Peaslee, *Constitutions of Nations*, vol. ii, p. 362.

[6] Article I, Section 2; Article II, Sections 2 and 5; Article III, Section 7; Article V, Sections 12 and 13.

That is not the less true because it has now become increasingly difficult to draw a clear distinction between the America-Liberians and the indigenous peoples of the country. There is a less clearly marked difference between them today than between the Creoles of Freetown and the indigenous tribes of the Sierra Leone Protectorate. The America-Liberians of Monrovia have perhaps a closer connexion with the Natives of the coastal area than with the Natives of the Northern area, for contact with the latter has until recent years been rendered difficult by an almost entire absence of communications.[1] It is commonly estimated that there are now between 40,000 and 50,000 of the indigenous population who now have some measure of education, and though there is not in Liberia any such formal recognition of 'assimilation' as exists in the Portuguese territories,[2] it is naturally to the America-Liberians of Monrovia that the educated classes are most closely affiliated. Any assessment of the present objective of policy in Liberia must therefore involve consideration of the extent to which political privileges have been extended outside the direct field of America-Liberian interests. This development will be discussed in the succeeding chapter regarding the system of government and of administration in the country.[3]

INTERNATIONAL INTEREST IN COLONIES

Up to a few years ago, it was usual to employ this term in a specific sense connoting the interest shown in the material and social progress of those Colonial peoples who had come within the sphere of the Mandatory system of the League of Nations or the Trusteeship of the Organization of the United Nations. As will be seen, however, attempts have since been made to give the term a more extended meaning, as reflecting the interest shown by the Organization of the United Nations in the welfare of all non-self-governing peoples, not merely of those who have come under the system of Trusteeship.

Historical research has revealed little evidence of any international movement in the more distant past directed explicitly to the improvement of the welfare of the peoples of the Colonies.[4] At the outset international law limited itself to clarifying the principles regulating the relation between States which were regarded as civilized. Even the General Acts of the Berlin and Brussels conferences of 1885 and 1890, which are usually regarded as responsible for the first of the international conventions dealing

---

[1] See below, p. 1590.   [2] See above, p. 231.
[3] See below, p. 357.
[4] *The Mandates System, Origin, Principles, Application*, Geneva, 1945, pp. 8 ff. See also H. Duncan Hall, 'The International Franchise', in *American Journal of International Law*, vol. xlii, no. 1, January 1948. F. M. van Asbeck, 'International Law and Colonial Administration', in *Transactions of Grotius Society*, vol. xxxix, 1953, p. 7.

with the welfare of Native peoples,[1] did little more than to embody the embryo of some of the principles which were to be subsequently enunciated in the mandatory system. Article 6 of the General Act of 1885 included, among its other objectives, 'the furthering of the moral and material well-being of the Native population', but the major purpose of the conferences was directed to finding some means of settling the inter-State disputes that had arisen from the occupation of Native areas in Africa by different European Powers.[2] Their most tangible result in the sphere of international relations was the establishment of the principle of the 'open door' in the conventional Congo Basin,[3] but the primary beneficiaries of this measure were not the African people so much as the European nations which were concerned in trade in Africa. The declared objective of the conferences was the suppression of the slave trade, but though there was still some internal raiding by Arab slave dealers, the export of slaves to countries outside the African continent had ceased many years before the conferences were convoked.

Mandatory System

The international interest in the Colonies, in the more specific sense in which that term has been used, refers back to the decision of the Principal Allied and Associated Powers in 1919 to adopt the mandatory system as a solution of the complex problems which arose in consequence of the disposal of the Turkish territories and the German Colonies held by these Powers at the end of the First World War. There were conflicting inter-State interests involved in regard to the Ottoman possessions, and though there seemed likely to be less difficulty in regard to the German Colonies in Africa, the Allied Powers which had occupied them were inhibited from exercising the normal rights of conquest by their own announcement that the Peace Settlement would not be accompanied by annexation.[4] The basis for the application to the ex-enemy territories of the principle then described as 'internationalization' is to be found in declarations of the type of those put forward in the National Congress of the British Labour Party in 1917, in the Fifth Point of President Wilson's Fourteen Points enunciated in January 1918,[5] and in the proposal for the establishment of a League of Nations made by General Smuts in December 1918.[6] The

[1] E. A. Walker, *The British Empire, Its Structure and Spirit*, 1943, p. 163. H. W. Temperley, *History of the Peace Conference of Paris*, vol. vi, 1924, p. 502.

[2] S. E. Crowe, *The Berlin West African Conference 1884–1885*, 1942, pp. 11–34.

[3] See below, p. 1347.

[4] D. H. Miller, *The Drafting of the Covenant*, vol. i, 1928, pp. 104 ff.

[5] The conception of a League of Nations began to be mentioned in 1917, partly as the result of a conference held in Philadelphia in March of that year. It had been preceded by conceptions such as 'the League to Enforce Peace', 'the Council of Powers', and 'the Concert of Nations'. See *Round Table*, June 1915, p. 609; December 1915, p. 20; March 1917, p. 290; March 1918, p. 221.   [6] General Smuts, *The League of Nations, A Practical Suggestion*, 1918.

project put forward by him included a definite scheme for the initiation
of a Mandatory system for the control of the ex-Turkish territories: it
would seem that he confined his proposal to those areas owing to his belief
that the mandatory procedure was a temporary expedient, chiefly useful
as a stepping-stone to self-government. He regarded it as impracticable to
apply any idea of political self-determination to the African colonies.[1]

President Wilson, however, expanded the mandatory conception to
embrace the African Colonies, and the Allied Powers embodied the provision of a mandatory system in Article 22 of the Covenant concluded in
May 1919; the formal inauguration of the League of Nations took place
in January 1920. Article 22 of the Covenant laid down that those Administrations which exercised a Mandate should render to the Council of
the League an annual report of the proceedings in the territory committed
to their charge, and that a commission (afterwards designated as the Permanent Mandates Commission) should examine the reports and advise
the Council of the League 'on matters relating to the observance of the
Mandate'.[2] The Allied Powers themselves decided which of the States
concerned should receive Mandates, but they proposed to leave to the
Council of the League the actual drafting of the Mandatory Instrument
applicable to each case. Owing, however, to disagreements as to the procedure to be followed, they themselves submitted to the Council a number
of draft Mandates, which it finally adopted.

Up to this point the main lines of action had thus remained in the hands
of the Allied Powers themselves, not in those of the Council of the League.
It was the Allied Powers which included in Article 22 of the Covenant the
well-known declaration that the well-being and development of peoples
'not yet able to stand by themselves in the strenuous conditions of the
modern world' should form a sacred trust of civilization. But at the same
time they also sought to achieve a more material purpose, namely, to
ensure equitable treatment by the Mandatory Administrations for the
commerce of the Members of the League'[3] or in other words the maintenance of the 'open door' and the principle of non-discrimination as between
the nationals of the Administering Power and the nationals of other constituent States.

The draft Instruments were of three types, A, B, and C. The A class
Mandates were intended for the Near Eastern territories which were provisionally recognized as independent, though needing the temporary
assistance of a Mandatory Administration. The B and C Mandates were intended for those territories for which autonomy was not in view. Since the
C Mandates provided that the mandated territory should be administered

---

[1] Duncan Hall, op. cit. p. 51.
[2] Sections 7, 8, 9 of Article 22 of the Covenant of the League of Nations.
[3] Sections 1 and 9 (g) of Article 22 of Covenant.

as an integral part of the territory of the Administering Government, its obvious destiny seemed to lie in some form of incorporation with it, not in any form of self-rule.[1] The C Mandate, it should be noted, also differed in form from the B Mandate to the extent that it did not stipulate that the Administering Government should give to the nationals of other Members of the League an equality of economic treatment with its own nationals. As regards both B and C Mandates the Mandatory Instruments included a number of salutary provisions prescribing the respect to be paid to Native custom, the prevention of forced labour, the restriction of traffic in drugs and drink, and the provision of safeguards for the preservation of Native lands. The Instruments contained no indication of the political future intended for people of the Mandated area.

The Permanent Mandates Commission consisted of persons nominated by the Council of the League, who must not be in the employment of any Government and were not technically Government representatives. Its constitution provided that the majority of its members must be nationals of non-Mandatory Powers and that one must be a woman; in practice it had an original composition of nine members. The specific role assigned to it was to advise on matters relating to the observance of the Mandates, and it is not surprising therefore that much of its attention should have been absorbed by a close (and often legalistic) examination of anything that appeared to be an infringement of the principle of the 'open door' or to savour of economic discrimination against the nationals of other Members of the League.

In dealing with issues relating to the welfare of the Native peoples the Commission did not fail to call attention to any evidence of what seemed to be an abuse of authority (as for example the measures taken for the suppression of the Bondelzwarts trouble[2] in South-West Africa in 1922), and it scrutinized studiously the material relating to the progress made in the provision of medical and educational facilities. In all such matters the advice of the Commission was carefully weighed and was tendered without bias; its work was educative, in the sense that it obliged Mandatory Administrations to examine for themselves the principles on which they were acting, and it led to the publication of a large body of material about the conduct of Native Affairs that would not otherwise have been made available to the public.

It was, however, a common criticism that the Commission interpreted the terms of its mission too narrowly, and that its approach failed in consequence to be sufficiently constructive. It admittedly had the value that it gave publicity to the affairs of the Mandated areas, but it did not, as might

[1] See, for example, pp. 170 ff.
[2] 'Report on the Bondelzwarts Rebellion', *Annexes to the Minutes of the Third Session, Permanent Mandates Commission*, p. 296.

perhaps have been hoped when it was first set up, lay down positive standards to which Mandatories must conform. Its critics deplored in particular that the Commission, when consulted on the suggestion that it should receive authority to conduct investigations on the spot in order to supplement information received from the Mandatory Authority, showed itself opposed to the proposal.[1] There can be no doubt, however, that the work of the Commission made its contribution to general thought on Colonial questions.[2] But it will be appreciated that the Colonies held under Mandate constituted only a small proportion of the total Colonial area, and that there was no method by which questions relating to Colonial problems as a whole could be brought before the Council of the League.

That the international interest in the Colonies has since that period taken a new and more incisive form is due to influences for which the merits or defects of the Mandatory system were a matter of relatively minor concern. There have been three phases in the subsequent history of the course taken by this interest. The first phase was largely a by-product of the campaign conducted in Germany for the restitution of her Colonies which (as already observed) formed so significant an incident in the inter-war period.[3] There were then many who believed that this claim could be forestalled by allowing Germany to administer her former Colonies under some form of international control; an intimation had been given in the Locarno Conference of 1926 that if Germany joined the League she might be considered 'as a possible candidate for a Colonial Mandate'. The suggestion was strongly opposed by sections of British, French, and Belgian opinion who saw in it a veiled undertaking to restore to Germany the control of her former Colonies. It was in any case rejected out of hand by the German Government as a measure that would not satisfy Germany's claims for the restitution of her Colonies.

It was argued in other quarters that since the German demand was partly based on the plea that her Colonies furnished the source of the raw materials required for the revival of her domestic industry, some solution of the problem might be found if all Colonies were brought under a form of international control which would guarantee a fair distribution of Colonial raw materials. Support for this proposal was stimulated by a conciliatory speech made to the League Assembly by the British Foreign Secretary in September 1935,[4] but much of the interest taken in the proposal evaporated when it was demonstrated that the world's Colonies provided (if rubber be excluded) a very small proportion of the total raw material required by world industry.[5]

[1] *The Mandates System, Origin, Principles, Application,* op. cit. pp. 39–40.
[2] Van Asbeck, op. cit. pp. 11–15.
[3] See references quoted above, p. 171.
[4] *The Times,* 12 September 1935.
[5] Royal Institute of International Affairs, *Raw Materials and Colonies,* 1936, p. 51.

Scheme for Internationalization

It was also argued, taking a broader ground, that since the possession of Colonies had in itself been one of the causes of friction in the world, one of the menaces to world peace might be removed if all Colonies were 'internationalized'.[1] Most of the advocates of this view had to agree that (as General Smuts had pointed out in 1919) it was difficult to cite a case in which joint international administration had been successful; 'the general result', he said, 'has been paralysis tempered by intrigue'.[2] Nevertheless it was hoped that some form of Mandatory or similar procedure would emerge which might be effective in eliminating the possession of Colonies as a possible source of world friction. It is fair to assume that the support which this view secured reflected the urgency of the general desire to fend off a menace to world peace rather than a considered belief in the efficacy of the measure proposed; but there is no question of the widespread following it attracted in Great Britain.[3] It did not secure the same measure of support in France or Belgium,[4] and it is significant that it was strongly opposed in the vernacular press of a number of the African dependencies. The reason was clear; in the case of dependencies which might expect some form of self-rule in the relatively near future the Mandated status might well represent a setback rather than an advance.

Anti-Imperialist Campaign

It has subsequently been asserted that the movement above described failed of its effect because it reflected a philosophy in which peace was seen merely as the avoidance of warfare, not as a positive achievement in itself. However this may be, this particular phase in the endeavour to secure the 'internationalization' of Colonies lost most of its interest with the outbreak of war in 1939. It was followed by a second phase, which had its origin in a different source. In the early days of the Second World War public opinion in the United States of America was strongly moved by a wave of anti-imperialist feeling, which found its most pointed expression in an attack on the possession of Colonies; it was indeed hardly distin-

[1] For an analysis of the extent to which Colonial disputes have actually endangered peace, see Royal Institute of International Affairs, *The Colonial Problem*, 1937, pp. 23–27.

[2] General Smuts, *The League of Nations, A Practical Suggestion*, 1918.

[3] See references quoted in Royal Institute of International Affairs, *The Colonial Problem*, 1937, pp. 77–78, and in *Germany's Claim to Colonies*, 1938, pp. 57–67. F. S. Joelson, *Germany's Claims to Colonies*, 1939, pp. 210 ff. See also the following pamphlets: The League of Nations Union, *The Demand for Colonies*, 1936; Pacifist Research Bureau, *War and the Colonies*, 1939; Advisory Committee of National Executive of Labour Party, *Demand for Colonial Territories and Equality of Economic Opportunity*, 1936; G. D. H. Cole, *War Aims*, 1939, p. 45; N. Bentwich, *The Colonial Problem and the Federal Solution*, 1941; H. van Zeeland, *Report on Reduction of Obstacles to International Trade*, 1938, Cmd. 5648; Q. Wright, *Mandates under the League of Nations*, 1930, p. 64.

[4] O. Louwers, *Le Problème Colonial du point de Vue International*, 1936.

guishable from the 'anti-colonialism' of a later date.[1] Its basis was an emotional rather than a logical feeling, but so far as it was an expression of the conviction that no people should be held subject to external authority against their will, it was fully in line with the emphasis laid by President Wilson in 1918 on the principle of self-determination, a principle which had been restated with a very definite emphasis in the Atlantic Charter of August 1941. It is significant that early in 1942 there were already studies being published in America of the implications of the Second and Third Points of the Atlantic Charter in regard to the future of the African Colonies.[2]

The fact that the anti-imperialist feeling received at this period so much support in the United States was no doubt due in large measure to the attacks made from some quarters on the motives of the Allies in seeking for aid in the war. Events such as the loss of Malaya or the Netherlands East Indies no less than the collapse of the French Empire made a strong impression on American opinion. 'Great Britain', said one journal, 'had better decide to part with her Empire, for the United States is not prepared to fight in order to enable her to keep it.'[3] It was incidentally the view thus expressed which elicited the masterly exposition which General Smuts gave to America of the true meaning of the British Empire in modern conditions.[4]

The initial outcome of the anti-imperialist campaign was seen in the support given to a demand for the 'immediate liberation' of all dependencies or at all events the assignment of a term of years within which they would be given independence;[5] the ultimate result was a demand, repeated in many responsible quarters, that all Colonial Powers should accept the 'principle of accountability' in respect of their conduct of Colonial rule. It must, however, be realized that this attitude represented only one facet of the serious thought which was now being given in America to the problem of securing world peace. In the American philosophy of the day it was not enough to provide a means of settling quarrels when they arose; some way should be found of removing those great disparities in the standards of life and in political status which were held to provide the fuel on which the spirit of conflict is fed. There was here a constructive addition to world thought on the problems of peace; and if the ideals then expressed sometimes seemed to be unrealistic, it remains the fact that the people of the United States have shown their faith in their

---

[1] The classical exposition of anti-colonialism (as indeed of Imperialism itself) is that of J. A. Hobson, *Imperialism*, first published in 1902. See edition of 1938, p. 3.

[2] The Committee on Africa, the War, and Peace Aims, *The Atlantic Charter and Africa from an American Standpoint*, 1942.

[3] *Life*, 10 October 1942.   [4] Ibid., 28 December 1942.

[5] K. Robinson, 'World Opinion and Colonial Status', *International Organization*, vol. viii, no. 4, 1954, p. 471.

convictions by the practical help they have since provided for some of the more backward and undeveloped parts of the world.

International Trusteeship and the United Nations

We are, however, concerned here only with that aspect of the post-war settlement which related to the position of the Colonial dependencies. When this question was being canvassed towards the end of the war, the most immediate task of the Allies was to find a successor body to discharge the functions of the League of Nations in respect of the Mandated territories. The broad lines of this problem were settled at Yalta early in 1945 when it was agreed that there should be a system of international trusteeship which might be applied to the mandated countries and also to certain other ex-enemy territories, and 'to any dependent territory which the responsible Powers might wish to put under trusteeship'.

The addition of this provision seems to have been suggested by the British authorities for a specific purpose. Trusteeship had, as has previously been observed,[1] for long been regarded by the British as indicating the moral principle which should guide a Colonial Power in the administration of its dependencies, rather than as implying any particular form of political relationship or administrative system. The existence of a Mandatory system applying only to a small number of Colonial territories seemed to them to blur this fact. They hoped that the conflict of views regarding the possession of Colonies might be resolved by a Convention accepting on behalf of all Colonial Powers the obligation to administer all Colonies alike as trusts. But no such solution was possible in the atmosphere prevailing in the conference which drew up the Charter of the United Nations later in 1945.[2] There had, it is true, been differences of standpoint and conflicts of interest between the Allied and Associated Powers at the Peace Conference of 1919. But there were in 1945 differences of ideology of a far more fundamental character. It was indeed only possible to secure agreement on the three chapters of the Charter which were devoted to the treatment of the Colonial question by purposely providing for certain ambiguities and loopholes in them.[3]

Chapter XI of the Charter of 1945 contains a general declaration made by the States responsible for the administration of those territories 'whose peoples have not yet attained a full measure of self-government'. The phrase used gives the keynote of the approach of the San Francisco Conference to the Colonial question, and it is at the same time a revealing example of the ambiguities to which it was necessary to resort. The States which

---

[1] See above, p. 193.

[2] For the discussions on this subject, see the British White Papers Cmds. 6560, 6571, and 6666.

[3] V. McKay, 'The Impact of the United Nations on Africa', in *Africa Today*, 1955, pp. 366 ff. For an analysis of some of the ambiguities referred to see Van Asbeck, op. cit.

joined in this general declaration included all those holding dependencies in Africa south of the Sahara except Portugal and Spain. The chapter proceeds to spell out the broad principles which the States concerned joined in regarding as their objective in the fulfilment of their obligation to promote the well-being of the inhabitants of their dependencies. Borrowing the language which Article 22 of the Covenant of the League had applied to the Mandated territories, they accepted as a 'sacred trust' their obligation towards the inhabitants of the non-self-governing countries for which they were responsible.

The most significant feature of the chapter is, however, the declaration that their object is to develop self-government and to assist the people in the progressive development of their free political institutions, 'according to the particular circumstances of each territory'. This statement of objective is a material modification of the 'independence' which had at one time been prescribed as the goal, and to that extent is a withdrawal from the one-time ideal of multiplying sovereignties as a measure of world peace. It was already perceived that the 'Balkanization' of these territories might have effects far other than those intended.[1]

Chapter XI does not in terms give the organization of the United Nations any authority to intervene in the control of these territories.[2] Any measure of control or supervision to be exercised by the organization was confined to the former Mandated territories or to other territories now to be brought under Trusteeship. The extent to which some members of the United Nations organization have since then sought to assert a right to exercise a measure of supervision over the administration of the Colonial dependencies lying outside the range of Trusteeship will be subsequently discussed.[3]

The organ exercising control in the Trusteeship system is primarily the Trusteeship Council, though when the Trust Territory is a strategic area, the Security Council operates with the assistance of the Trusteeship Council.[4] The principles laid down for the guidance of the Trusteeship Council or other agencies exercising the functions of Trusteeship correspond in the main to those of Article 22 of the Covenant of the League, though phrased more flexibly. There are, however, two important modifications. The first is economic: the so-called 'open-door' clause is subject to a qualification which had no counterpart in the Covenant, namely, that this provision shall not prejudice the advancement of the inhabitants or be detrimental to international peace and security. In the second place the Administering Authority is given wider scope in matters of defence. Forces

[1] See on this point, Lord Samuel, 'The British Colonial System and its Future', *Address to Anti-Slavery and Aborigines Protection Society*, 10 June 1943, p. 4.

[2] *Commentary on the Charter of the United Nations*, Cmd. 6666, 1945, para. 53.

[3] See below, p. 250.

[4] Chapter XII, Articles 75–85.

raised in the territory can be used to carry out the obligations of the Administering Power in respect of the maintainance of international peace as well as for local defence or the maintenance of law and order.

The functions of the Trusteeship Council are laid down in Chapter XIII. The Council has a supervisory position analogous to that of the former Permanent Mandates Commission of the League of Nations. Action is taken on its reports by the General Assembly, working through its Fourth Committee, a larger and much more diffuse body than the Council of the League of Nations.[1] But the major difference lies in the composition of the Trusteeship Council itself. Unlike the Permanent Mandates Commission, which was composed of members appointed for their individual qualifications, the Trusteeship Council consists of appointed representatives of the Member States. The Administering Authorities hold half the seats. Although Article 86 of the Charter of the United Nations provides for the representation of Member States by 'specially qualified persons', the non-administering Member States have not usually been able to nominate such persons, and the proceedings of the Trusteeship Council were, at all events in its early years, influenced more by extraneous political considerations than by any kind of acquaintance with the special problems of the territories held under Trust.

The Trusteeship Council receives petitions relating to the Trust Territories and discusses the annual reports on them submitted by the Administering Authorities. The Council's Rules provide that in the examination of annual reports the Administering Authority concerned shall be entitled to have present a special representative who should be well informed on the territory involved. In practice these Special Representatives have invariably been experienced serving officers in the Territorial Administration. The Council has dispatched a visiting mission to each Trust Territory every three years.

It was left to the Administering Authorities of the former Mandated areas to apply that these Territories should be recognized as Trust Territories, and application was at an early stage made in respect of all such areas lying south of the Sahara except in the case of South-West Africa. Reference has been made earlier in this chapter[2] to the circumstances in which the Union of South Africa refused to take this step. No Colonial territories have as yet been placed voluntarily under Trusteeship. The Agreements reserve to the Administering Authorities 'full powers of legislation, administration and jurisdiction', and the Authorities have insisted that these powers cannot be qualified. They have on occasion asserted their freedom to follow their own judgement in interpreting their duty, and they have refused to admit the right which has been claimed at times

[1] McKay, 'The Impact of the United Nations on Africa', loc. cit. pp. 366 ff.
[2] See above, p. 172.

by the Assembly that it should be consulted before policy decisions are taken.

The first visiting missions to the various Trust Territories seem to have devoted much of their time to a genuine effort to acquaint themselves with the local conditions,[1] and such criticisms as they made could not be regarded as unreasonable by the Administering Authorities. Some of the later reports, and notably those regarding Tanganyika and Ruanda Urundi, have contained less carefully considered recommendations which have, as will be shown, been much criticized by the Authorities concerned.[2] It was very obvious that some of these recommendations came from persons who not only had no acquaintance with African conditions, but who belonged to nations which have never had experience of Colonial responsibilities.

But the action taken by the visiting missions of the Trusteeship Council has proved to be of less concern to the Powers possessing Colonies than the efforts made by a section of the General Assembly to extend its range of supervision over all 'non-self-governing territories'. Article 73 (e) of Chapter XI provided only for the regular transmission to the Secretary-General, for information purposes, of statistical and other information of a technical nature relating to economic, social, and educational conditions in the territories for which Powers are respectively responsible. The section was carefully phrased. Information of this character had been habitually published in the past in the annual reports issued by a number of the Colonial Powers and there could therefore be no mistake as to the intention of the Article in question. In 1946 the Secretary-General was requested by the General Assembly to summarize for its benefit such information as had been received from the Administering Powers.[3] In 1947 a committee set up by the General Assembly was empowered to make substantive recommendations relating to the functional fields concerned, though not with respect to individual territories. The committee has since been renewed at intervals, although the Administering Powers have never conceded the legality of its existence, and have insisted on the fact that the Article provides explicitly that material should be submitted by them 'for information only'.

The General Assembly has, however, shown a tendency to regard any matter dealt with in the transmissions as proper for discussion in the Assembly itself, and it is for this reason that some of the Administering Powers have persisted in refusing its invitation to include political information in their transmissions. Such information is made available by them to the public in published form elsewhere, but its inclusion in the

---

[1] For a summary of their reports, see *United Nations Bulletin*, vol. xvi, no. 7, April 1954.

[2] See below, pp. 304, 352.

[3] Appendix III to United Nations, *Summaries of Information on Non-Self-Governing Territories submitted in 1946*, pp. 147–9.

transmissions would in practice open the way to discussion by the General Assembly of the internal political affairs of the Administering Powers as well as those of the Colonial territories under their administration. It has been argued that since the Powers administering Colonies have accepted the principle of trusteeship, they must be held to have acknowledged also the principle of accountability. But as the wording of Article 73 shows, their acceptance of the principle of trusteeship was accompanied by a clear indication of the limits to which they were prepared to render themselves liable to supervision or control.

Critics of the United Nations Organization have not failed to point out the illogicality involved in its claim to interest itself in the welfare of peoples belonging to 'non-self-governing States' while there are numerous people within the orbit of the 'self-governing States' of the world who are clearly deserving of a far greater measure of international interest and attention. Representatives of Belgium, who have shown themselves especially critical of the position taken in this respect by a section of the General Assembly[1] have developed one aspect in particular of this argument, which is now generally known as *La Thèse Belge*. They emphasize the special needs of aborigines and primitive peoples for the attention of all welfare organizations, and they point to the complete neglect by the United Nations of the needs of these people when they form part of the population of 'self-governing States'.[2]

The reluctance of the Colonial Powers to admit the right of intervention by the General Assembly in this respect is understandable when it is realized that the ultimate power of supervision is now entrusted to a body consisting of more than 70 governmental delegates of whom only eight are representatives of Colonial Powers. This is a political not an expert body, and many of its members carry to the discussion of Colonial affairs not only ignorance of Colonial affairs but a background of national prepossessions and prejudices based on considerations that have no bearing on such affairs. The United Nations are at present deeply divided by political issues which are clearly of greater immediate concern to themselves than the problems of the Colonial peoples. The Administering Powers have cause to complain that it is actually with reference to these other issues that sides are taken in debates on Colonial matters. So long as this situation continues, it would be hard to show that the modern form of 'international accountability' has improved on the limited achievements of the Permanent Mandates Commission.

[1] P. Orts, 'Un tournant de la Colonisation', *La Revue Coloniale Belge*, 1 June 1946. P. Ryckmans, quoted in *East Africa and Rhodesia*, 21 April 1953, pp. 1122–3.

[2] F. van Langenhove, at Plenary Session of the United Nations General Assembly, 27 November 1953. Idem, *The Question of the Aborigines before the United Nations*, Royal Colonial Institute, Belgium, vol. xxxvii, no. 4, 1954. 'The Sacred Mission of Civilization', *Belgian Government Information Centre*, New York, 1953. *The Times*, 15 August 1955.

The difficulty experienced by the United Nations in exercising an effective influence in Colonial policy is partly due to its composition. Against a handful of Western European States there are 20 Latin-American members, with an equal number of African and Asiatic countries. The attention of representatives of the majority of such States is for the most part directed to the effort of detecting evidences of what, not without American encouragement, they call in a derogatory way 'colonialism'.[1] But it is possible that the real trouble lies deeper. The approach to the Colonial problems which underlies Chapters XI–XIII of the Charter is largely irrelevant to most of the vital issues. 'It assumes a clear-cut distinction between dependence and independence, and takes as its major problem the achievement of formal independence, the chief impediment to which is assumed to be the imperialist egotism of the Colonial Powers.'[2] But the real problem does not lie there. It lies in the improvement of the material and social conditions of the peoples of the territories themselves. Were these adequately improved, the civilized world could rest assured that they might safely be left to secure for themselves what changes they felt to be needed in their political status.

THE RISING SPIRIT OF AFRICANISM

Africanism and Nationalism

It seems advisable on this occasion to give prominence to the use of the term 'Africanism' rather than 'nationalism'. In Europe nationalism is a readily recognizable force, even though it may not be easily definable, but as a concept it has associations which make it difficult of application in the conditions of Africa. As has so often been emphasized in the literature on the subject, the population of most of the countries of Africa south of the Sahara consists of peoples who have been brought together under one form of government by the accidents of history;[3] they have for the most part no tradition of a common origin nor common outlook on their political future. It is true to say, in general terms, that whatever may have been the other influences that have shaped the destinies of these countries, the majority have in the past missed the dynamic influence of the concept of territorial nationalism.

To this generalization there are admittedly some exceptions. It is, for instance, obvious that the concept of nationalism played its part in assisting the fusion into one country of the four territories which now form the

---

[1] Dr. van Kleffens, Address to Association of International Law, quoted in *The Times*, 29 March 1955.

[2] K. Robinson, 'World Opinion and Colonial Status', *International Organization*, vol. viii, no. 4, 1954, pp. 482 ff.

[3] See, for example, the references by G. Balandier, in *Zaïre*, April 1951, p. 379.

Union of South Africa. At a later date it played its part in setting before the two White communities of the Union the common goal of a sovereign status. The outstanding feature in the past history of Liberia (or at all events of the ruling caste in the country) has been its determination to preserve its national identity, even to the extent of refusing to accept foreign aid in the development of its resources.[1] The Basuto, welded into one people by their founder, Moshesh, have a long history of struggle for the maintenance of their identity, and they continue today to display a strong feeling of pride in their national life.[2] The Gold Coast has developed a conception of nationhood which though artificial in its origin now has something of the quality of a genuine national ideal.

But taking the African peoples at large, the term 'Africanism' seems to describe most nearly the movement which is now so much in evidence in many of the countries dealt with in this Survey. It is indeed the manifestation of the spirit of Africanism which is one of the most distinctive features in the picture of post-war Africa. A generation ago, studies such as those which are contained in this volume were largely concerned with the diverse policies of Colonial Powers or with the position of the settled European communities in Africa. Today attention centres in increasing measure on the reaction of Africans to these policies and on the manner in which they are in consequence being modified or readjusted.

The development of a spirit of Africanism has not involved the emergence in Africa of a concept of pan-Africanism any more than the latter-day manifestation of the spirit of Asianism has involved the emergence of a concept of pan-Asianism in the East.[3] The spirit of Africanism varies greatly in force and in objective from one country to another and from one community to another. But as has occurred also in Asia, it has two characteristic phases, of which one is more definite and in a sense more constructive than the other. Its more constructive phase envisages the attainment (at all events in those countries where its manifestation is strongest) of a government dominated by Africans and expressing in its institutions the characteristic spirit of Africa as interpreted by the modern African. That vision is not, however, a purely indigenous product; it emanates as a rule from Europeanized groups of Africans, who apply to the conditions of Africa the ideal of self-determination which was born not in Africa but in the Western world.

In its less constructive phase Africanism does not necessarily express itself in any one vision of the political or social future of the African. It may indeed at times show itself as nothing more definite than a reaction against the dominance of Europeans in political and economic affairs. On

---

[1] See above, p. 236.   [2] See below, p. 273.
[3] *Nationalism*, Royal Institute of International Affairs, 1939, pp. 144 ff.

other occasions it may be said to reflect an irredentism inspired by a revolt against modern influences which threaten traditional institutions and social habits.

It would carry this study too far to examine in detail the reasons why this movement, in one phase or another, has now become so prominent a factor in African affairs. In one aspect it reflects a reaction against the manner in which the doctrine of *apartheid* is now being pressed home in the Union of South Africa. In another aspect, it has been stimulated during recent years by the encouragement which has been given in international circles to the doctrine of self-determination and to the claims made for the achievement of political independence. Where the policy of a Colonial Power has, like that of the British, resulted in the progressive creation of the institutions of a 'responsible' form of government, the stimulus has been all the greater, because prominent political figures can begin to see themselves as the heirs of the authority which is now being exercised by the agents of the Colonial Power.

That they should see themselves in this light is neither unnatural nor unreasonable. But in circumstances where, as is the case in most parts of Africa, there exists a wide gap between the more advanced political elements and the great mass of the population, movements fathered by the former only acquire an operative force when they receive a substantial measure of support from among the people at large. The most significant features of the present situation are to be found in the changes which have influenced the growth among the population at large of an interest in the views voiced by the relatively small groups of advanced or progressive Africans. Among those influences it must be realized that the Second World War brought to large numbers of Africans a direct experience of affairs in the outside world. During the course of the War the British enlisted a total of 372,000 Africans, of whom about 166,000 served outside their own territories. Between 1939 and 1940 French West Africa dispatched 65,000 men to destinations outside the territory and 76,000 between 1940 and 1945.

There have at the same time been influences derived from a variety of other sources. In South Africa and in the Belgian Congo there has since the War been a rapid expansion of industrialization which has brought African workers widely into the ranks of semi-skilled employment and has created among them a new interest in improved standards of living. There has been a spectacular increase in the urban population, with a consequent alteration in the traditional structure of African society. The greatly increased prices of tropical produce in the world market have reacted strongly on rural economy, and in some areas, as notably in West Africa, the handling of export production has resulted in the creation of a middle class possessing both access to advanced education and leisure to pursue a political career. Almost everywhere the great extension of motor traffic has spread to the countryside the influences which were formerly associated with the life of the towns. It is hardly necessary to add the influence exercised by a great increase in the number of schools and in the growth of the vernacular press. If ever it was true that the population of Africa consisted of a small educated class at the top and an inert mass below, that is no longer the case.

It is at the same time true, however, that the circumstances of Africa are such that the movement of Africanism has so far shown little coherence, and that to all appearances it lacks any one pattern or any common objective. Even where its tenor is definitely anti-European there seems to be no general agreement throughout Africa as to the part which Europeans can continue to play in developing its social and economic life. There are equally wide differences in the estimate formed by Africans of the competence of their own people to fill the place which has hitherto been taken by Europeans in developing the resources of the continent.

Africanism in the Union

Looking in detail at the position in some of the countries south of the Sahara it is especially difficult to estimate the actual force of Africanism in the Union. There can be no question of the strength of the resentment aroused in the African population by the activity shown during recent years in the application of the doctrine of *apartheid*. But it is difficult to assess the extent of the following secured by that section of the intelligentsia which looks forward to the achievement by Africans of an effective share in the government of the Union. To very many Africans the obstacles in the way of the attainment of such an ideal must appear to be insuperable. It is true that the sponsors of the doctrine of *apartheid* have held out to Africans the prospect of a future in which they may in their own sphere of action live under a régime of institutions inspired by Bantu tradition. But there has been no pledge that this will secure for the Bantu any measure of political autonomy, whole or partial, in any defined area of the Union.

It is not unnatural therefore to find that at the moment there should be some division among Africans themselves as to their place in the future of the Union. There is a group which, looking largely to the support it hopes to receive from world opinion, continues to base its hopes on the development of an inter-racial form of government in which Africans will have a share. On the other hand, large numbers of Africans seem to be impressed by the extent to which their social standards (which are now higher than those of most of their indigenous neighbours) depend on the White economy to which they minister. They are engrossed in the effort to win a larger share in its benefits, but they lack both the cohesion and the leadership necessary to secure their purpose. In this confused picture, full of the possibilities of discord and trouble, the observer will find only one feature clear. The African concept of nationalism is very seldom inspired by visions of a return to a traditional régime; whatever may be the terms in which the African of the Union envisages the future, he does not see it in terms of Bantu irredentism.

The High Commission Territories

In the High Commission Territories the position is simpler. Africanism is seen there mainly in terms of the maintenance of the national identity of the indigenous community concerned. Africans, following the spirit of the times, are ready to press the British Government for a greater measure of self-rule, but they also seem to be very alive to the threat which absorption in the Union might bring to the maintenance of their national identity. That is a consideration which sets limits to the lengths to which they might be prepared to carry the concept of nationalism.

The Federation of Rhodesia and Nyasaland

In Central Africa the scheme for the establishment of the Federation of Rhodesia and Nyasaland energized a phase of Africanism which had hitherto lain dormant or was confined to a limited objective. Nyasaland had for some years had an African Congress whose most important activity had been devoted to the support of the claims of the resident tenants on European estates in the Protectorate.[1] The European community of Nyasaland is relatively small, and the local African leaders anticipated a time when, with the expanding application of the British principle of self-rule, the Government of Nyasaland might assume a predominantly African character. It was not unnatural therefore that the African Congress should have taken the lead in combating against a scheme of Federation which seemed likely to give to the European element in the Rhodesias the opportunity to exploit their position to the disadvantage of the African elements in the two Protectorates, as they were held to have already done in Southern Rhodesia. The campaign thus initiated against the scheme of Federation secured a considerable measure of support in Northern Rhodesia and to some degree also in Southern Rhodesia.

How far the movement will develop a militant phase of Africanism will depend on the progress made by the Federation in the evolution of a working system of multi-racial government. For the moment there appear to exist within the Federation two different nationalistic ideals. To the majority of Europeans the future of the Federation is that of a Dominion

[1] See below, p. 709.

whose basic laws will provide a place for all its component communities. On the other hand, a large body of Africans in Nyasaland and possibly also in Northern Rhodesia continues to hope for a change of policy which may give them a greater prospect of a predominantly African form of self-rule.

The East African Territories

In the three British East African Territories there is no common factor in the African outlook on the future, save that in all three of them Africans have begun to show fear lest Asians may succeed in winning a share in political control which will affect the position of their own community. Uganda has a special position, in that there is a very small European element in the country, and the people of the Protectorate have been officially assured that they can look forward to 'an African form of government'. With its tradition of Hima leadership in the past, Uganda provides a favourable field for the development of a concept of territorial nationalism, and the thoughts of progressive Africans had already begun to envisage the future in these terms. For the moment, however, the horizon has been obscured by dissensions arising regarding the position of the Kingdom of Buganda in relation to other parts of the Protectorate.

In Tanganyika the African community, perhaps because of the dispersed character of the population, has not so far given evidence of the same political activity as in Uganda.

On the other hand, the Mau Mau episode seems likely to result in Kenya being quoted as an outstanding example of militant Africanism. But the Mau Mau episode is rather a reminder of the latent possibilities of trouble in Africa than a manifestation of the spirit of African nationalism. It furnishes a proof of the ability of a group of malcontents to secure adherents to a revolutionary anti-European programme, and to compel obedience by resort to a form of terrorism which takes full advantage of African superstition and fear of magic. But the Mau Mau movement has been practically confined to the Kikuyu tribe, and this tribe comprises only about one-fifth of the African population of Kenya. The adherents of Mau Mau are only a part of the Kikuyu tribe.[1] By far the greatest number of acts of violence have been committed against other members of the tribe, not against Europeans. The eventual suppression of Mau Mau will owe much to the loyalty of a large number of Kikuyu, and particularly those members of the tribe who have formed part of the Kikuyu Home Guard.[2]

There clearly remains in Kenya a large block of African opinion which is neither revolutionary nor anti-European in its outlook, and which is prepared to share the government of the country with Europeans and

[1] L. S. B. Leakey, *Mau Mau and the Kikuyu*, 1952.
[2] P. Mitchell, 'Mau Mau', in *Africa Today*, 1955, pp. 485-93.

Asians. Circumstances have forced the Europeans to abate much of their one-time vision of a national future in which they would control the administration, and their leaders are now engaged in the effort to settle the terms on which they will be prepared to share with Asians and Africans a régime of Responsible Government.

British West Africa

It is in British West Africa that current manifestations of Africanism have reflected most strongly the influence of the principle of self-determination. This movement, however, owes little to the stimulus which organs of international opinion have sought to give it, for nationalistic movements have been long in gestation.[1] The urge for the attainment of self-rule originated in the teachings of an early phase of British Liberalism. That they made so ready an appeal to local African sentiment was due to the deeply engrained passion for achieving equality with Europeans which is characteristic of West Africa, probably because the West Coast had the closest contact with the slave trade. Self-rule for the Gold Coast was to be the European act of reparation for the slave trade.

But it was not enough merely to concede to Africans an equality of status with the small resident European community. African sentiment demanded the satisfaction of the concept of territorial nationalism on a scale which would impress the outer world. In the struggle for party supremacy in the Gold Coast the leadership went to those whose demands for the creation of an autonomous African State made the widest appeal and who could engender the maximum of emotion by the extravagance of their attack on the British Government.

It is still to be seen whether the emotion thus generated will be adequate to bridge over the fissures which are already beginning to appear in the constitutional structure of the Gold Coast. They could perhaps be prevented from widening, were it not that there are defects in the administrative régime of the new semi-Responsible Government which offer obvious points of attack against the party now in power. These defects are not due merely to want of experience; they seem to reveal a lack of moral stability which may prove to be an even greater danger to the maintenance of the structure of the new State.

The course followed by the constitutional development of Nigeria differs in some respects from that of the Gold Coast, but there is a close analogy between the course taken by the development of the spirit of nationalism in the Gold Coast and in Southern Nigeria. It is Southern Nigeria that has provided the chief impulse behind the local movement for territorial nationalism. The obvious artificiality of the present constitutional structure

[1] J. S. Coleman, in *The Annals of the American Academy of Political and Social Science*, April 1955, pp. 105 ff.

is due to the fundamental difference of outlook between the Northern and Southern Provinces. The principle of self-rule based on popular representation did not readily commend itself to the more aristocratic societies of the North, and if in addition self-rule was to be achieved at the price of giving the South a voice in the affairs of the North, this was a further drawback to any form of closer union.

The amalgamation of the Northern and Southern Provinces in 1914 was fully justified on purely administrative grounds, but Lord Lugard could not anticipate in 1914 that Great Britain would so soon decide to establish a régime of self-government in Nigeria. Here as elsewhere the prospect of an approaching surrender of its authority by the Colonial Power has brought into action underlying hostilities which might otherwise have rested for a prolonged period below the surface.[1] The existing constitution of Nigeria has brought together in what may prove an unfruitful union two political units each of which might otherwise have formed the basis of a nation exhibiting a fruitful type of nationalism.

The French Territories

The French policy of overseas rule, with its traditional emphasis on the principle of integration with metropolitan France, has been far less favourable to the development of the spirit of territorial nationalism than has that of Great Britain. There have admittedly been shortcomings in the implementation of the process of integration initiated in the Constitution of 1946, most notably in the maintenance in tropical Africa of a system of separate electoral rolls for the new African citizens and the French citizens of metropolitan status. It has been pointed out, for instance, that the Frenchmen in tropical Africa, who cannot number more than 150,000 out of a total population of some 30 million, return no less than six out of the total number of 37 deputies in the National Assembly.[2]

We may assume, however, that there will be a progressive measure of integration in this and similar respects. So far as the spirit of territorial nationalism exists, it is intended that it shall find its outlet mainly in the development of the Territorial Assemblies which form part of the new organization of the overseas countries. They are at present only consultative, and at this stage the energies of the indigenous African elements are largely occupied in two directions, first, in securing for the Assemblies an effective part in the legislative and administrative organization of rule; and second, the further implementation of the concept of 'parity' in the details of current legislation, such as the Labour Code and similar laws.[3]

At present, such political activity as is displayed by Africans has little

---

[1] *The Round Table*, December 1955, p. 19.
[2] K. Robinson, in *The Annals of the American Academy of Political and Social Sciences*, March 1955, p. 91.   [3] See above, pp. 214–15.

local outlet, and it has been found more profitable to establish a connexion with the political parties in metropolitan France. The *Rassemblement Démocratique Africain*, for instance, which is a pan-African political movement having very considerable strength in the Ivory Coast, Guinea, Niger, and Chad, started as an affiliation of the metropolitan *Rassemblement du Peuple Français*. To take another instance, there exists in Senegal the *Bloc Démocratique sénégalais*, which is an affiliation of the *Section française de l'Internationale Ouvrière*, the formal designation of the French Socialist Party. So far these and similar African organizations have not developed a separatist programme (save to the limited extent that the parties formed in Togo and the Cameroons could be considered as separatist) but form pressure groups which use their metropolitan affiliation to secure a greater devolution of power to the Territorial Assemblies in Africa, or to the African territorial governments.

We are left therefore to speculate how far indigenous opinion in tropical Africa is likely to develop a definite sentiment of territorial nationalism. There is at the moment no evidence of separatist tendencies. The position in North Africa offers little direct guidance in this respect. The two Protectorates, Tunisia and Morocco, have had a tradition of hostility to French domination which goes back to the outset of French penetration into the region. There has never been here any real measure of integration with metropolitan France. Algeria, with a population of 1 million Europeans against 2½ million Muslims, has no close parallel in the tropical African territories, where the settled French population is relatively small.

The Belgian Congo

Belgian policy has been no more favourable than that of France to the development of a spirit of territorial nationalism. But the reason differs. France has led its African population to look for a progressive measure of integration, both political and cultural, in the metropolitan régime. Belgium has sought to divert the attention of its African population from political activities to those which may win for it a fuller participation in the economic life of the country. There is little evidence of any political movement which reflects African opinion throughout the whole of the Territory. It is, indeed, significant that the movements which have hitherto attracted most attention are those 'Messianic' or religious movements (as, for example, Kibanguism or Kitiwala) which seldom have more than a local following.[1] They acquire a political significance only because the removal of Europeans is considered a prerequisite for the realization of the good life. If the pressure of African opinion has had any effect in modifying official

[1] See above, p. 227.

policy, it is to be seen chiefly in the attempt to satisfy indigenous middle-class opinion by the creation of the *Carte du Mérite Civique*. The new type of European *colons* who have come to the Colony since the Second World War are said to show signs of dissatisfaction with the present administrative régime, but this does not amount to a display of territorial nationalism. The missions from the United Nations that visited Ruanda Urundi in 1951 and 1954 remarked on the lack of an organized African opinion capable of making itself felt.

The Portuguese Territories

There is little opportunity in the present circumstances for the exhibition in Portuguese territories of the spirit of Africanism, for there is a severe measure of restriction on the expression of public opinion. But apart from this, it is characteristic of those countries that are divided by a culture-bar into two classes, the privileged and the under-privileged, that the former attracts to itself the more progressive and politically minded elements who might otherwise constitute the leaders of the under-privileged and the champions of their cause. The exponents of the difficulties experienced by the indigenous population are to be found for the most part among certain outspoken religious personalities, both Catholic and Protestant.

CHAPTER VI

SYSTEMS OF GOVERNMENT

THE SIGNIFICANCE OF THE FORM TAKEN BY
COLONIAL INSTITUTIONS

THE preceding chapter has given some indication of the political and social objectives to which the existing systems of government in the African territories appear to point. It is proposed to add in this chapter some indication of the form taken by their legislative and executive institutions, and it will be appropriate also to consider certain connected topics, such as the procedure adopted in the organization of the administrative establishments. This is a subject of some significance, since it throws much light on the principles on which the system of government is conducted.

It will be apparent that the form of such legislative institutions as exist in the Colonial areas has been influenced by a variety of causes, partly arising out of historical developments and partly of recent origin. In the British dependencies, for example, the African territories of today are the heirs of a tradition that first began when the British settlers in Virginia were granted a Council in 1606.[1] Throughout the long period which has since elapsed there has been a continuous process of devolution of authority on to the local Legislatures. The original Legislative Council, largely official in composition, has developed first into a representative body with a growing elected element, then into the organ of a semi-Responsible and subsequently of a fully Responsible form of government.[2] Its final destination is that of the legislature of an autonomous State.

The French preference for a centralized system of rule has, on the other hand, led to the relative concentration of legislative authority in the hands of the metropolitan Ministry, and it is only of recent years that consideration has been given to the possibility of the formation of local Colonial Legislatures with some measure of independent power.[3] In the Belgian Congo the retention of the power of legislation in the hands of a metropolitan Ministry directly responsible to the national Parliament was the fruit of the conviction that it was essential to prevent the recurrence of situations such as those which had laid the Congo Free State open to the

---

[1] M. Wight, *The Development of the Legislative Council 1606–1945*, 1946, pp. 26–29; *British Colonial Constitutions, 1947*, 1952, pp. 18–20.

[2] For the definition of semi-responsible and responsible forms of Government, see Wight, op. cit. 1952, pp. 38, 39, 58–62.

[3] See above, p. 215.

criticism of other nations.[1] If Portugal does not now delegate to any overseas province an effective power of legislation, its chief object has been to emphasize the status of its Overseas Possessions as an integral part of the home country.[2]

There is the same story of a diversity of influences in determining the form of the executive organization of rule, though in this case it is less easy to point to any leading principles underlying the actual course which has been taken in the territories of different Powers. In general, however, the form of the executive organization has been largely determined by the procedure adopted for the administration of Native affairs, to which reference is made in a succeeding chapter.[3] In this respect the Union of South Africa has retained the tradition of 'magisterial rule' which originated under the Dutch Administration and was retained by the British in the loosely knit period of Civil rule which characterized the era of the Kaffir Wars. This tradition was carried by the Chartered Company into the British Central African areas. In British West Africa the form of executive organization was determined by the fact that jurisdiction was only gradually extended from the small coastal trading settlements into a hinterland over which the British Government long hesitated to undertake control, until it was forced into action by its local officers. The position of administrative officers was deliberately viewed as that of political agents; they were, indeed, definitely so termed in Northern Nigeria.

In French tropical Africa, the original form of the executive administration was due to the influence of the military authorities who were responsible for the extension of French rule; it will be realized that there is a history of military activity behind the expansion of French rule in West Africa which is not shared by the other Powers now holding territory in Africa. In the Belgian Congo the objective which at the outset regulated the formation of the executive administration was largely economic—a fact which is still reflected in the strength of the economic organization employed at the headquarters of the Government and in the larger provinces.

For our present purpose, however, the matter of major significance is not so much the influences which have guided the original shape of the legislative and executive organization but its present form. Here it is essential to make one initial observation. Throughout this study it will be necessary to call attention to evidence of the growing importance of the African in the political and administrative life of most of the countries with which this Survey deals. The most interesting and to some extent the most suggestive feature of recent history has been the record of the instances in which the institutions of government have been adjusted to meet the needs or the claims of the indigenous communities. This is,

---

[1] See above, p. 217. [2] See above, p. 218. [3] See below, p. 414.

indeed, the development which more than any other distinguishes the record of the post-war years from that of any pre-war period.

UNION OF SOUTH AFRICA

The Union is to a certain extent an exception to this rule, since the most conspicuous feature of its recent history has not been the adjustment of its governmental system to secure an appropriate measure of African participation in its political or administrative institutions, but rather the attempt to implement the policy which would keep the Bantu, the Coloured people, or the Asian from invading the political and social field occupied by Europeans. But there are some features in its constitutional development which are important to note in the present connexion. The form taken by the Constitution of the Union followed the lines of the recommendations made by the National Convention which assembled in 1908–9 to discuss the terms on which the four Colonies (the Cape, Natal, Transvaal, and Orange Free State) would accept a scheme of political union.[1] The result represented a measure of compromise between the advocates of a federal form of union and those who were in favour of a unitary form of government.

At the time of Union each of the four Colonies had its own representative government with a full measure of responsibility in internal affairs. The Colonies became Provinces of the Union, but with a measure of local autonomy which they exercise as of right and not by delegation. Each Province has a unicameral Legislature in the form of a Provincial Council whose membership equals in number that of the provincial representatives in the Union Parliament; they are elected on the parliamentary franchise and hold office for three years. Each Provincial Council elects by proportional representation an Executive Committee, though not necessarily from among its own members; the President of the Executive Committee is the Administrator of the Province, who is appointed by the Union Government and is the Chief Executive Officer of the Province.[2] He has a casting vote in the deliberations of the Committee.

Provincial Councils

The Provincial Councils are empowered to impose direct taxation, to raise loans, and to legislate on education (other than higher education),[3] agriculture, hospitals, public health, and Local Government institutions. They can in addition legislate on such matters as are, in the opinion of the Governor-General in Council, of a merely local or private nature in the

---

[1] See above, p. 160.
[2] South Africa Act 1909, Section 142. See for further details *O.Y.S.A.*, *1952–53*, pp. 101 ff.
[3] For the recent legislation regarding Bantu education, see below, pp. 1148 ff.

Province.[1] It is noteworthy that Native Affairs constitutes a central, not a provincial subject. Provincial Ordinances have effect only in so far as they are not repugnant to Union legislation. Ordinances are submitted by the Administrator for the approval of the Governor-General, and the Central Government may refuse assent to provincial legislation or may pass laws overriding it,[2] but there are certain statutory safeguards to protect the Provinces from Central legislation which may directly affect their existence.[3]

In practice measures contemplated by the Central Government which are likely to affect the Provinces are discussed in advance by an Advisory Council which was set up in 1935. Financial policy is subject to control by the Union Government through the fact that the Administrator is President of the Provincial Executive Committee and that no financial legislation can be introduced in the local Legislature without the approval of the Committee. The dependence of the Provinces on the Union Parliament for financial subventions has, moreover, given the latter body a considerable measure of direct influence in their affairs.[4] The Provincial Legislature has no direct control over the Executive Council of the Province which when once elected holds office for a term of years, nor is the Administrator responsible to it. On the other hand, there is a well-established convention that the Central Government should, if possible, avoid withholding assent from Provincial Ordinances.

Central Government

The Central Government consists of an elected House of Assembly, with a Senate partly elected and partly nominated. Until the change effected by the Act of 1955, to which reference has been made in the previous chapter,[5] the Senate had 48 members. Eight members were elected from each of the four Provinces by members of the House of Assembly for the Province voting together with the members of the Provincial Councils; eight Senators were nominated from the Union by the Governor-General in Council; four of these were selected for their knowledge of 'the reasonable wants and wishes of the Coloured races'.[6] In addition, the Native Representation Act of 1936[7] provided for the election of four Senators (who under an express provision of the Act must be White persons) by the Natives of the Union.[8] When South-West Africa

[1] South Africa Act, 1909, Section 85.
[2] In 1953 the Union Government refused to assent to a clause in an Education Ordinance of the Cape Province, no. 16 of 1952.
[3] Section 149 of the South Africa Act, as amended by Act 45 of 1934.
[4] See below, p. 266.   [5] See above, p. 167.
[6] South Africa Act, 1909, Section 24.
[7] See above, p. 164. See also *Handbook on Race Relations in South Africa*, 1949, p. 28.
[8] See below, p. 265.

was given representation in the Union Legislature in 1949 it was empowered to elect two Senators; there are also two nominated Senators from the Territory, one of them being selected on account of his knowledge of the wants and wishes of the Coloured races.[1]

The normal duration of the Senate is ten years; the four elected representatives of Africans hold their seats for a term of five years, but are not affected by the dissolution of the Senate. An elaborate machinery was created for the election of these four members. The four electoral units are the Transkeian Territories, the rest of the Cape Province, the Province of Natal, and the Provinces of the Transvaal and Orange Free State taken together. In each unit there is an electoral college consisting of specified voting units; in the Transkeian Territories these are the African members of the General Council,[2] at present about 80 in number; elsewhere the electoral colleges are Local Councils or Chiefs or Headmen where there are no Local Councils, or Native Advisory Boards in urban areas. Where no authority of any of these types exists, an electoral committee is elected by the resident taxpayers.[3]

It was the number of Senators who were to be elected by the four Provinces which was affected by the legislation of 1955, and also the number of nominations made by the Governor-General. The former was raised to 71, the latter to 18; the total number of Senators was thus raised to 89. The new Senate was elected in November 1955; as already stated, the Appeal Court rejected in November 1956 a suit which challenged the validity of the Senate Act of 1955.[5]

The House of Assembly consists of 159 members of whom three are elected by Africans in the Cape Province on a communal roll,[4] and 150 by Europeans in the Union. Six are elected from South-West Africa as the result of the enactment of the legislation of 1949. The original distribution of 150 seats between the Provinces of the Union was not determined in proportion to population nor to the number of electors, special representation being given to Natal and the Free State in order to allay the apprehensions with which they entered the Union. In 1931, however, provision was made for a readjustment on the basis of the quinquennial censuses, and in 1952 the allocation was made dependent on the number of registered European voters.[6] The present allocation of the 150 seats is 54 seats to the Cape, 15 to Natal, 68 to the Transvaal, 13 to the Orange Free State.[7] It should be added that within each Province the electoral divisions are required by the South Africa Act to be so delimited as to

[1] South West Africa Affairs Amendment Act, no. 23 of 1949.   [2] See below, p. 426.
[3] *O.Y.S.A. 1950*, p. 473. *Handbook on Race Relations in South Africa*, 1949, p. 28.
[4] See above, p. 161. For the procedure of election of members of the House of Assembly, see *O.Y.S.A. 1950*, pp. 90, 91, 472.   [5] See above, p. 167.
[6] Electoral Laws Amendment Act, no. 55 of 1952.
[7] *O.Y.S.A., 1952–53*, p. 95.

make the number of voters in each 'as near as may be' equal,[1] but the effect of the present delimitation is that the representation has been weighted in favour of the rural areas (*platteland*); in the elections of 1948 and 1953 this had the effect of giving a majority of seats to the Nationalist and Afrikaner Parties (which drew their chief support from the rural areas) although they received a minority of the total votes cast.

It is significant that the Union of South Africa has never been formally known as a Federation; the South Africa Act describes it as a 'Legislative Union under one Government'. It was hoped at the time that the component Provinces would retain under the Union the individuality which had formerly characterized them as Colonies, and to some extent this result has been achieved. But though they exercise original, not delegated powers of legislation, the tendency has been to limit their activities in any direction which may be felt to trench on national issues. Their administrative authority is in practice largely confined to matters which would in most countries be described as of the nature of Local Government activities.[2] The control of the judiciary is entirely in the hands of the Central Government.

It is really only in regard to the conduct of the health and sanitary services and the conduct of the lower range of educational institutions that they may be said to discharge distinctive functions.[3] This is not merely the result of legislative restrictions; it is partly due also to the circumstances which make the Provinces so largely dependent on the Central Government for finance. When the Union came into existence the whole of the expenditure of the Provinces was at first met from central finances. By a series of Acts beginning in 1913[4] and ending with the important Financial Act of 1945[5] the relations have been so adjusted that, while the Provinces collected in 1951–2 a total revenue of roughly £29¾ million from local taxation and similar sources, subsidies or grants made to them from the Union Government amounted to over £33 million. The total revenue of £29¾ million collected by them compares with a total of a little over £207 million collected by the Union Government. The major part of the provincial expenditure has been incurred on education and public health; in 1951–2 the Provincial expenditure on education was just over £33 million, and on health a little under £15½ million. The position in regard to education has been, however, materially affected by the passing of the Bantu Education Act of 1954.[6]

---

[1] South Africa Act, Section 40.

[2] For Provincial Ordinances enacted in the years 1951–3, see *O.Y.S.A.*, *1952–53*, pp. 103–5.

[3] See below, p. 1146. For a general discussion of the allocation of functions between the Centre and the Provinces, see E. H. Brookes, in *Handbook on Race Relations in South Africa*, 1949, pp. 27 ff.

[4] Financial Relations Act, 1913.

[5] Financial Relations and Consolidation and Amendment Act, no. 38 of 1945. See *O.Y.S.A.*, *1952–53*, pp. 597 ff., 637 ff.   [6] See below, p. 1148.

Ministerial System

In the Central Government the Ministerial system follows the pattern usually associated with a parliamentary form of government. The number of Ministers in charge of Departments of State is limited by the South Africa Act to 14, and as there are at the present time 19 separate Departments this means that in some cases two and in one case three Departments are held by one Minister. Some indication of the extent of the field of administration occupied by the Central and Provincial Governments respectively is given by the number of public servants employed. Those employed by the Central Government in 1952–3 numbered 102,007, while those employed in the Provinces numbered 9,259, but the latter figure was exclusive of teachers, nurses, and hospital board officials. Of the 102,007 public servants mentioned above, 75,316 were classed as White and 26,691 as non-White, the majority of the latter being employed in the Police (9,238), Postal (3,631), Health (3,498), and Native Affairs (2,455) Departments. As a general rule the non-Europeans are employed in the lower ranks of service; in the Police Force, for instance, the highest grade for non-Europeans is that of sergeant. The Department of Native Affairs employs a number of African clerks and interpreters and African agricultural demonstrators; there is a special branch of African departmental police.[1]

In general the practice follows that which from 1924 onwards has required preference to be given in Government employment to 'civilized labour', and failing any formal definition of this term, 'civilized labour' was generally taken to mean European labour. In 1944, however, the subject came under review, and it was laid down that 'opportunities should be given to Coloured persons for service within their own community'. It seems to be taken for granted that a situation should not be permitted to arise in which non-Europeans would be placed in authority over Europeans in the public service.[2]

Public Services Commission

The public servants of the Central and Provincial Governments are selected by the Public Services Commission, for which provision was made in Section 142 of the South Africa Act. The Commission had for some years a somewhat chequered career, owing to the effect of enactments which curtailed its powers,[3] but as the result of later legislation[4] it now has an important place in the administrative organization of South Africa. It is the co-ordinating authority for all the public services and makes recommendations to the Government not merely on the subject of pay and

---

[1] *Handbook on Race Relations in South Africa*, 1949, pp. 33, 123.

[2] *Fifth Report of Public Service Enquiry Commission*, U.G. 53–46, 1947, pp. 39–42. This gives a history of Government Orders passed in this connexion.

[3] *Fifth Report of Public Service Enquiry Commission*, pp. 2–14.

[4] Act no. 27 of 1923 as amended by Act no. 36 of 1936.

service conditions but also as to the number and grading of the staff required in the different Departments of State.[1] It has a standing in this respect which is similar to that of the Public Service Commissions in Canada, Australia, New Zealand, and India. It will, moreover, be realized that a body of this nature has an especial position in conditions such as those of South Africa, where public servants are drawn from two different European communities, which for the most part use two different home languages. It was laid down in the South Africa Act of 1909 that both English and Dutch should be treated as official languages in the Union, and Dutch has since been held to include Afrikaans.[2]

SOUTH-WEST AFRICA

As will be gathered from the preceding chapter,[3] the legislative and administrative institutions of the Territory may now be regarded as in a stage of transition, and it is probable that they will in future be brought into still closer conformity with those existing in the four Provinces of the Union. There will remain, however, one issue which has from the first been a matter of much local concern, the question, namely, of the measure to which the inhabitants of the Territory will be allowed control over its domestic policy. In the days of the Mandatory Administration the concern on this point was most marked among the German community which, though it had received the benefit of 'automatic naturalization' as British subjects, still retained memories of former German rule.[4] The German community continued to form an important part of the 'settler' population,[5] and it remains strongly interested in the question of the maintenance by the Territory of some measure of political independence.[6]

At the outset the powers vested in the Governor-General were exercised by Proclamation; the responsible local authority was an Administrator appointed by him, and as in the Provinces of the Union the Administrator was regarded as the Chief Executive Officer of the Territory. Following on recommendations made in 1920 by the de Wet Commission, the Administrator established a nominated Advisory Council of nine members representing different sections of the European community.[7] In 1925 a Constitution was created for the Territory which was described at the time as conferring 'a limited measure of self-government'. This was analagous to that of a South African Province, but it was in some respects of

---

[1] For details see *O.Y.S.A.*, *1952–53*, pp. 88–90.

[2] South Africa Act, Section 137, as amended by Act no. 8 of 1925. On the use of Afrikaans see above, p. 94.   [3] See above, p. 175.   [4] *Round Table*, June 1948, p. 667.

[5] In the 1937 Report to the Mandates Commission the European population was shown as 18,128 Afrikaans-speaking, 2,395 English-speaking, and 9,632 as German-speaking. The total European population was shown in the census of 1951 as numbering 48,588, an increase of some 18,000.

[6] *Africa Digest*, March–April 1955, p. 10.   [7] Proclamation no. 1 of 1921.

a more representative composition.[1] It provided for a Legislative Assembly, an Advisory Council, and an Executive Committee. The Executive Committee consisted of the Administrator, with four members chosen by the Legislative Assembly in the same manner as for the Executive Committee of a Province of the Union; they held office for the duration of the Assembly. The Advisory Council consisted of the members of the Executive Committee, with three additional nominees to advise on matters over which the Legislative Assembly had no competence; one was to be selected for his knowledge of Native affairs.

The Legislative Assembly consisted of twelve elected and six nominated members. All adults of European origin who were British subjects had a vote for the election of the twelve members. Unlike the legislative bodies of the Provinces of the Union, which had enumerated powers, the South-West African Assembly had general powers, with a number of specified limitations, among these being Native Affairs, Courts of Justice, and Customs and Excise.[2] The Union reserved the right to legislate for the Territory on all matters, either by Statute or by Proclamation.

The Van Zyl Commission Report

Reference has already been made to the circumstances which caused the working of the Constitution to be examined by the Van Zyl Commission of 1935.[3] Besides the local tension caused by the provocative action of the Nazi section of the German population, there had for many years been a serious budget deficit; in 1935 the Territory was in debt to the South African Government (including its Railway Department) to the extent of nearly £2¾ million. It was largely this fact that moved the Commissioners to recommend that the Act of 1925 should be repealed, and that the Territory should be incorporated in the Union, though they differed both as to the constitutional and the financial measures which should take the place of the existing arrangement.[4]

Within the next few years the growing solvency of the Territory and the result of the control exercised over the Nazi section by action taken under the Criminal Law Amendment Ordinance of 1933 combined to remove the need for taking immediate action on the report of the Van Zyl Commission. But the constitutional position remained open to criticism, on the grounds that the Legislature had no jurisdiction in a number of subjects that were essentially domestic and that the Administrator was responisble neither to the local Legislature nor to the Parliament of the Union.

---

[1] South-West Africa Constitution Act 42 of 1925, Proclamation 57, 19 March 1926.
[2] Sections 26, 27, and 44 of Constitution Act of 1925.
[3] U.G., no. 26, 1936. For a discussion of its Report see C. Dundas, *South-West Africa, The Factual Background*, 1946, pp. 22–30.
[4] See above, p. 172.

South-West Africa Affairs (Amendment) Act, 1949

A significant change was brought about in 1949 by the enactment of the South-West Africa Affairs (Amendment) Act,[1] though this does not seem to have been primarily designed to remedy the deficiencies of the Constitution of 1925. The Prime Minister, Dr. Malan, pressed it on the Union Parliament as a measure which, by achieving closer incorporation of the Territory with the Union, would help to limit the field of attack on the Union available to the United Nations; his opponents claimed that his motive was to secure for his Party the votes of the members whom the new Constitution would add to the Parliament in the Union.[2] The German residents were, in particular, thought to be well disposed to the Nationalist Party.[3]

As has already been indicated, the Act of 1949 provided for the election of six members to represent the Territory in the Union House of Assembly, and for the addition of four members to the Senate, two being elected by the Legislative Assembly in South-West Africa, and two nominated by the Governor-General.[4] The provision of this number of seats somewhat over-represented the European population of the Territory as compared with that of the Union, the quota for membership of the House of Assembly being only 4,400 in South-West Africa against 9,600 in the Union. In the Territory itself the Advisory Council was abolished; the Legislative Assembly was to be composed as before of 18 members, but it became fully elective.[5] Its language was to be English and Afrikaans, but any member could if he desired address it in German.

Its legislative powers were enlarged; it can now legislate for education, for mines and minerals, and for land questions, subjects which were previously reserved from its purview. Native Affairs continue to be reserved from the Legislature, but it now has full powers for raising taxation, save as regards customs and excise duties. The Union Parliament retains the right to legislate for the Territory, and some Union Acts, such as the Citizenship Act and the Act for the Suppression of Communism, have been extended to it.[6] Legislation will, however, cease in the future to be by Proclamation, and will take the form of enactment of law. On the whole, the present Constitution has in practice given to the Territory a somewhat larger measure of self-government than it previously enjoyed, its status in this respect being superior to that of the Provinces of the Union.

The administrative organization is of the same pattern as that of the Provinces of the Union. Where the subject is outside the purview of the

[1] South-West Africa Affairs (Amendment) Act, no. 23 of 1949. For details see *O.Y.S.A.*, *1952–53*, p. 1152.
[2] *Round Table*, June 1949, p. 292.   [3] *Africa Digest*, January–February 1955, p. 8.
[4] See above, p. 265.   [5] *O.Y.S.A.*, *1952–53*, p. 1152.
[6] South African Citizenship Act, no. 44 of 1949. Suppression of Communism Act, no. 44 of 1950.

Legislature of the Territory, as, for example, Native Affairs, the Ministry in the Union has final executive authority, and it is alleged that the Department has recently exercised a more direct form of control than previously in order to ensure the application to the Territory of the current policy in regard to the Bantu Education Act and the like. The greater part of the official personnel are members of the public services in the Union, placed either permanently or temporarily at the disposal of the Administration of the Territory.[1]

THE HIGH COMMISSION TERRITORIES

Something has been already said of the period at which these Territories came formally under British jurisdiction.[2] They were from the first regarded in a different light from the Colonial dependencies in Central, East, and West Africa. The British Government had shown marked reluctance to extend jurisdiction over them, and it had only agreed to this course because it seemed essential to prevent action being taken by the Transvaal Republic or the Orange Free State which might menace the peace of Cape Colony or Natal.[3] For many years such control as was exercised over the three Territories appeared to be the concern of the authorities in the Cape or Natal rather than of Great Britain herself. Up to the year 1931 they remained under the charge of the Governor-General of South Africa, by virtue of his appointment as High Commissioner for the Territories, but there is no evidence of any consideration being given by the British Government at this stage to the policy to be observed in regard to their development or their political future.

The Territories were administered by officers who were locally recruited, and who as a rule therefore had the advantage of previous knowledge of the South African environment, but who, with some rare exceptions, had no acquaintance with the policy or procedure of rule prevailing in the British Colonial dependencies elsewhere in Africa. For all the earlier period of British rule very little guidance was given to them in regard to the policy to be followed in the matter of Native Administration, though it was this aspect of rule which was of primary importance in areas such as Basutoland, where there has from the first been practically no European settled community, or in Bechuanaland, where it was relatively small. Each Territory was administered as a separate unit, and no effort was made to develop a common policy. It was not until 1927 that the Imperial Government began to give any sign of a practical interest in the means necessary to improve the local economic and social services.[4]

---

[1] See also below, p. 435, for note on Officers of the Native Affairs Department in South-West Africa.
[2] See above, p. 175.
[3] *N.A.*, Part V, pp. 41-43, 187-93, 361-8.
[4] Ibid. pp. 382-3.

'Parallel Rule'

The system locally observed in the direction of African Affairs has been not inaptly described as aiming at a form of 'parallel rule'.[1] It showed the maximum regard for the customary authority of the Chiefs, and it restricted intervention to such measures as were necessary to satisfy the more simple requirements of local rule, such as the collection of tax or the preservation of order. This procedure had its convenience, but it failed to take account of the unprogressive character of the rule of Chiefs as established by Native custom, and it had to face the consequences of the low standard of responsibility shown by some of them. A growing local demand for the improvement of the procedure of the Native Courts combined with a tardy recognition by the British Government of its responsibilities for the expansion of the social and economic services led in the early thirties to the introduction of a series of reforms which followed the model of the Native Authority system then holding the field in most of the British dependencies.

Reform of this character was first introduced in Bechuanaland in 1934, though it did not come into full operation till 1943.[2] It was introduced in Basutoland in 1938,[3] and finally in Swaziland in 1944, but in this case also there was a delay in bringing it into effect which ended only in 1950.[4] The result was to bring the procedure of Native Administration into conformity with that prevailing in other dependencies which had adopted the Native Authority system.

Each territory is controlled by a Resident Commissioner under the direction of the High Commissioner for the United Kingdom in the Union of South Africa, who is also High Commissioner for the three Territories. The post of High Commissioner was separated from that of Governor-General in 1931; the final control rests with the Commonwealth Relations Office in the United Kingdom, not with its Colonial Office. The administrative personnel employed in the three Territories constitute a special establishment under the High Commissioner. The effort to increase the proportion of African personnel in the public service has resulted in the employment of what is, compared to the Union of South Africa, a relatively small European staff. Thus, taking the Police Force as a typical case, the establishment in Basutoland consisted in 1953 of 17 Europeans and 398 Africans; in Bechuanaland the numbers were 59 and 332; in Swaziland 30 and 162.

Consultative Councils

Legislation takes the form of Proclamation issued by the High Commissioner,[5] but the Administration makes full use of certain of the local

---

[1] *N.A.*, Part V, pp. 133, 217–18, 324. See also below, p. 497.   [2] Ibid. pp. 212–28.
[3] Ibid. pp. 79–85.   [4] Ibid. pp. 383–93, 423–4.
[5] M. Wight, *British Colonial Constitutions, 1947*, pp. 21, 78; see also below, p. 500.

institutions for purposes of prior consultation. The Basuto National Council has a history dating from 1903, but its actual beginnings can be traced farther back;[1] it has indeed something of the character of a national institution with a considerable tradition behind it, differing in this respect from the position of the Legislative Councils of most of the dependencies, which have had no roots in indigenous tradition. The nearest analogy to it is the Lukiko of Buganda.[2] Though at one time consisting mainly of members of the Chiefly class, its composition has in recent years been broadened, and it is, moreover, now linked up with a number of ancillary District Councils elected on something of a popular basis. It was in the past a source of law-making, in the sense that it issued rules which were implicitly accepted as codifying Basuto custom on a variety of matters, including the allocation and holding of land.

There are in Bechuanaland two institutions used for consultative purposes, the Native Advisory Council instituted in 1919 and the European Advisory Council instituted in 1920.[3] The former cannot claim the status of a national institution in the same sense as the Basuto Council, but it has proved to be of acknowledged value for purpose of official consultation. The two bodies agreed in 1951 that each should send eight members to form a Joint Advisory Council, and this has since met regularly. The Libandhla, the traditional organ of the Swazi, has had a different position, and has not in the past acted to the same extent as an agency for the consultation of African opinion.[4] Approach has in this case been made direct to the Paramount Chief and his personal Advisers. A European Advisory Council was instituted in 1921[5] and has been regularly consulted by the Administration.

The Problem of Dual Rule

The reforms made in the system of Native Administration in the three Territories had the effect of assigning to the Native Authorities a defined position within the executive organization of the country, and to this extent they have provided a salutary modification of the conception of 'parallel rule' previously referred to.[6] But there still survives, especially in Basutoland and Swaziland, something of the atmosphere of dual rule as between the Government organization and the Native Authorities.[7] It is a feature far less marked in Bechuanaland, where there is no single Paramount Chief and where authority is exercised by a number of Chiefs, each having independent control in his own area. The atmosphere of dualism does not consort well with the modern concept of a central

[1] *N.A.*, Part V, pp. 46, 61–66, 91, 101–2.
[2] See below, pp. 293 ff.
[3] *N.A.*, Part V, pp. 209, 318–21.
[4] Ibid., pp. 356–8, 395.
[5] Ibid. pp. 377–8, 429.
[6] See above, p. 272.
[7] *N.A.*, Part V, pp. 133–4.

organization of government which can shape schemes of social policy and delegate their execution to local authorities exercising a defined range of powers. It was primarily the problems created by the existence of a pronounced form of dualism in Basutoland which led to the appointment of the Administrative Reforms Committee which reported in 1954;[1] its recommendations were still under discussion in 1955.

But this problem creates a less difficult issue than that of devising a means by which the Territories can make a definite advance in political self-government. When the reforms of 1934 onwards were debated with the Chiefs and the peoples concerned they were put to them partly as measures of administrative reform and partly as evidence of the desire of the British Government to promote institutions which would give the African people a better means of organizing their own affairs; they were not specifically advocated as measures preparatory to the introduction of a system of political self-government.[2] Declarations have, as already shown, been made regarding the intention of the British Government to introduce a system of self-rule throughout the Colonial dependencies generally, but a specific declaration of this character in respect of the High Commission Territories has presumably been felt to be out of place so long as the question of their transfer to the Union remained open.[3]

That consideration still retains its force. Even, however, should the decision be against transfer of the Territories to the Union, there are considerations arising from their geographical position and from the extent of their economic dependence on the Union[4] which must effectively limit the measure of autonomy which could suitably be granted to them. This consideration should not, however, be regarded as incompatible with the extension to them of a considerable measure of self-government in the control of their internal affairs. Nor should the problem of political advance be complicated in this case, as it is in the Union, by considerations based on the necessity of providing by legislative or constitutional measures for the maintenance of a European pattern of civilization or way of life.

Basutoland is to all intents a Native State with practically no settled European community.[5] In Bechuanaland there are European mining interests in the Tati area and the small European community owns farms in some of the eastern districts,[6] but there seems no immediate prospect of any considerable increase in its number. Though Europeans still hold a large proportion of the land in Swaziland, a number of the owners are non-resident.[7] The part which Europeans have played in the development

---

[1] *Basutoland, Report of the Administrative Reforms Committee*, April–July 1954. See *Africa Digest*, March–April 1955, p. 3.

[2] *N.A.*, Part V, p. 139.   [3] See above, p. 182.

[4] *N.A.*, Part V, pp. 9–11, 13, 16, 20–21, 160–5, 341, 345, 428.

[5] Ibid. p. 1.   [6] Ibid. pp. 149, 231–2, 322–3.

[7] Ibid. pp. 335, 339–44, 414–15.

of the mining and other enterprises of this Territory undoubtedly gives them a claim to an adequate share in its future government, but such a claim would be of a different order from that on which the European community in the Union bases its position. The most immediate of the problems of the three Territories lies in the need for assigning to the Paramount and other Chiefs a position that would be compatible with African tradition, but which would at the same time permit of the development of a representative form of legislature endowed with a reasonable measure of executive responsibility.[1]

SOUTHERN RHODESIA AND FEDERATION

The somewhat unusual structure of the Federation reflects the fact that it constitutes a union of two types of territory of different political status. Southern Rhodesia is a self-governing Colony which has since 1923 enjoyed the status of full Responsible Government; its Administration is responsible to a Legislature elected by the European section of the population; though Africans are entitled to a vote, the Legislature has at present no African member. The country has so much the aspect of a Dominion that it is treated as lying within the sphere of interests dealt with by the Commonwealth Relations Office in the United Kingdom, the successor to the former Dominions Office. On the other hand, Northern Rhodesia and Nyasaland are Protectorates which remain under the control of the British Colonial Office; the former has a Legislature in which there is a majority of elected Europeans, with a smaller number of nominated Europeans and Africans and European officials; Nyasaland has a Legislature in which ex officio or nominated Europeans have hitherto predominated, with a smaller number of nominated Africans.

The combination of these units of different status has, however, had a background in history. The two Rhodesias were originally linked together through their connexion with the British South Africa Company. The territory which is now included in Northern Rhodesia was before 1899 vaguely included in the Company's Charter, but in 1899 and 1900 the Barotseland–North-Western Rhodesia Order in Council and the Northern Rhodesia Order in Council placed the administration on a definite basis; the two areas were amalgamated in 1911 under the designation of Northern Rhodesia. The control of the Company continued till 1924, when its administration was assumed by the Crown.[2] A part of the present north-eastern Territory of Northern Rhodesia was from 1891 administered from Nyasaland, but in 1909 control was handed

[1] Ibid. pp. 429 ff. See also Tshekedi Khama, *Bechuanaland and South Africa*, the Africa Bureau, 1951, p. 9.
[2] *Rhodesia-Nyasaland Royal Commission Report* (the Bledisloe Report), Cmd. 5949, 1939, pp. 5–7.

over to the Chartered Company, which continued to administer it until 1924.

Early Schemes for Closer Union

As early as 1915 a movement was set on foot by Sir Starr Jameson for the amalgamation of Southern and Northern Rhodesia under one adminis-tration. At that time, however, the small White population of Northern Rhodesia was reluctant to accept the control of the larger European com-munity in the Southern territory, while the latter was apprehensive of the burden on its resources that would result from amalgamation with a Terri-tory which was at the time entirely undeveloped. In 1929 the Commission appointed to report on schemes for the Closer Union of the Dependen-cies in Eastern and Central Africa[1] took the view that Northern Rhodesia and Nyasaland, even taken together, formed too small an economic unit to justify the establishment of a unified form of government such as was recommended for Tanganyika, Kenya, and Uganda. The Commission discussed a number of alternative possibilities, including the amalgama-tion of Northern and Southern Rhodesia. On the publication of its report the Prime Minister of Southern Rhodesia issued a memorandum which laid stress on the close connexion between the two Rhodesias, and protested against the adoption of policies likely to lead to the eventual absorption of Northern Rhodesia into an East African system.

The discussions which arose from the issue of the White Papers of 1923 and 1930 and the reference made to the paramountcy of Native interests[2] created much anxiety among the European population of Northern Rhodesia and Nyasaland, and stimulated a movement in favour of amal-gamation with Southern Rhodesia as likely to provide the only means by which Northern Rhodesia could hope to achieve the status of Responsible Government. In 1931 joint representations were made by the Southern Rhodesian Government and the elected members of the Northern Rhodesian Legislature, asking that a conference be held to discuss the possibility of amalgamation. They were informed that the British Government, while considering that amalgamation was not practicable now or in the near future, did not wish to reject the idea in principle.[3]

Proposals of the 1937 Royal Commission

In 1936 the demand for amalgamation had the support of all the Southern Rhodesian political parties and of the majority of the elected members in Northern Rhodesia; a conference held at Victoria Falls agreed on the terms of amalgamation to be submitted to the Government of the

---

[1] *Report of the Commission on Closer Union of the Dependencies in Eastern and Central Africa* (the Hilton Young Commission), Cmd. 3234, 1929, pp. 281–5, 295–7.

[2] See above, p. 190. [3] H.C. Deb., 2 July 1931, col. 1472.

United Kingdom.[1] They were told that there had not been such a change in conditions as to justify reconsideration of the decision of 1931. In 1937, however, a Royal Commission was appointed to inquire into the possibility of some form of 'closer co-operation or association' between the Rhodesias and Nyasaland. It expressed the belief that the three Territories would in the course of things become more and more closely interdependent, but it was not in favour of Federation at that stage because of the difference in their constitutional status. Amalgamation was regarded as the ultimate objective, but there were for the moment differences, particularly in Native policy, which stood in the way of amalgamation.[2] In view, however, of the desirability of keeping this objective in view, the Commission recommended the establishment of an inter-territorial council to co-ordinate the existing Government services.

Partly because of the outbreak of war this recommendation was not immediately put into effect, but in 1945 the Central African Council was established in order to promote the co-ordination of policy between the three Territories. The Council, which was purely consultative, consisted of the Governor of Southern Rhodesia as chairman and four members from each of the three Territories, including the Governors of the two northern Territories. The Council succeeded in arranging for the extension of a number of Southern Rhodesian services to cover the northern Territories,[3] but its activities were hampered by the fact that it had no machinery for eliciting the public support necessary to ensure that its recommendations would be carried into effect.

So far the movement for closer union, which was at that period almost invariably viewed in the form of amalgamation, had come mainly from Southern Rhodesia where the major incentive appeared to have lain in the prospect that the two Rhodesias might acquire by union a political stature which might entitle them to the full status of a Dominion. If the Europeans of Northern Rhodesia joined in the movement it was chiefly because they saw in it the means of escape from the control of the Colonial Office, for since the issue of the Devonshire declaration of 1923[4] they continued to regard it as determined to support the interests of Africans against those of Europeans. The Nyasaland Europeans were, for reasons connected with the migration of local labour, divided on the subject of closer union with Southern Rhodesia.

There is no question that such organized African opinion as then existed in Northern Rhodesia and Nyasaland was opposed to closer union on the ground that it would involve the political predominance of the Europeans of Southern Rhodesia. That view was in particular voiced by the African

---

[1] Cmd. 5949, 1939, pp. 108 ff.   [2] Ibid. pp. 213–18.
[3] *Central African Territories, Report on Conference on Closer Associa ion*, Cmd. 8233, 1951.
[4] See above, p. 190.

Congress in Nyasaland, whose leaders (like the leaders of advanced opinion in Uganda) were looking forward to seeing in Nyasaland a self-governing territory with a predominantly African government.

After the Second World War, however, an additional factor supervened to stimulate the interest shown by Southern Rhodesia in the cause of union. The Colony now had a rapidly growing European population, but it had a large public debt[1] and was faced with a full programme of schemes of development for which it had inadequate capital resources. It saw the great advantage which closer union with Northern Rhodesia would give it in its approach to the investment market. When the Commission on Closer Union had issued its report in 1929, the public revenue of Northern Rhodesia had stood roughly at an average of £500,000 a year, and its exports at approximately the same figure.[2] In 1953 the revenue of the Protectorate was estimated at £30¼ million and the exports were valued at £94¾ million. Other less material considerations undoubtedly existed, to which some reference has been made in the preceding chapter;[3] but the economic factor remained throughout as a very pertinent argument for union.

Results of the 1951 Conference

Towards the end of 1950 the British Government agreed that there should be a fresh examination of the possibility of the closer association of the three Territories. A conference held in London in 1951 was announced as being purely exploratory, but after rejecting projects for the complete amalgamation of the three Territories or for a league under which they could delegate powers to a central body, the conference decided to recommend their federation under the designation of 'British Central Africa'.[4] In order to meet the objections put forward on behalf of Africans in the two Protectorates, it was laid down that matters affecting the day-to-day life of the inhabitants, and more particularly that of the African inhabitants, should remain under the control of the three territorial Governments.

There followed a prolonged period of discussion and conference, both in Central Africa and the United Kingdom.[5] A minority of Europeans in Southern Rhodesia were opposed to the project, fearing lest close political association with territories controlled by the Colonial Office might result in impairing the dominant position which, they held, Europeans were

[1] In July 1954 the public debt of Southern Rhodesia was stated as £133 million, that of Northern Rhodesia as £21 million, and that of Nyasaland as £6 million.
[2] Cmd. 3234, 1929, pp. 318–19.
[3] See above, p. 186.   [4] Cmd. 8233, 1951.
[5] The history of these discussions is contained in the White Papers: *Geographical, Historical and Economic Survey*, Cmd. 8234, 1951; *Comparative Survey of Native Policy*, Cmd. 8235, 1951; *Draft Federal Scheme*, Cmd. 8573, 1952; *Draft Federal Scheme, Report of the Fiscal Commission*, Cmd. 8672, 1952; *Draft Federal Scheme, Report of the Civil Service Preparatory Commission*, Cmd. 8673, 1952; *Report by the Conference on Federation*, Cmd. 8753, 1953; *The Federal Scheme*, Cmd. 8754, 1953.

entitled to claim in Southern Rhodesia. Africans, so far as their views could be said to be voiced by their existing organizations, were opposed to the scheme of federation, and it was in consequence much criticized in the United Kingdom by those who felt scruples against imposing on the Protectorates a form of Constitution to which the more advanced Africans were hostile. This sentiment was reinforced by a genuine desire to avoid creating in Central Africa that alienation of feeling between Europeans and Africans which the application of the doctrine of *apartheid* appeared to be arousing in the Union of South Africa. The scheme was, however, accepted by the three Legislatures concerned and by a referendum held in Southern Rhodesia.[1] After considerable debate it was approved by the British Parliament in July 1953.[2]

There has since arisen in Southern Rhodesia a minority party among Europeans which has revived a previous proposal for the creation of a Dominion comprising Southern Rhodesia and that part of Northern Rhodesia where European interests predominate; it would hand back the more distinctly Native areas, and in particular Barotseland and Nyasaland, to be administered as Protectorates. The suggestion has, however, been strongly opposed by the party representing the majority of Europeans. Though Africans cannot be said to be reconciled to the concept of federation, there has been little active opposition shown by them, save on the part of the African Congress in Nyasaland, which stands for the achievement of self-government by Nyasaland as a separate unit.[3]

The 1953 Constitution

The Constitution as finally enacted makes it clear that the two Protectorates are to retain their right to enjoy separate Governments for as long as their respective peoples desire, these Governments remaining responsible (subject to the ultimate authority of the Government of the United Kingdom) for the control of land in their Territories 'and for the local and territorial political advancement of their peoples'.[4] Legislative powers are divided between the Federal and Territorial Legislatures, which within their own spheres of legislation are in no respect subordinate to one another. There is a considerable range of subjects reserved for the Federal Legislature (the Exclusive List), and there are others (the Concurrent List) with which both the Federal and Territorial Legislatures can deal subject to certain restrictions.

[1] The referendum was confined to registered voters who, as subsequently explained below, p. 283, were predominantly European.

[2] Rhodesia and Nyasaland Federation Act, 1953. The Federation of Rhodesia and Nyasaland (Constitution) Order in Council (Statutory Instruments, no. 1199) 1953.

[3] *Africa Digest*, vol. ii, no. 7, January 1955, pp. 19, 22.

[4] Preamble to the Constitution as given in the Annex to Federation of Rhodesia and Nyasaland Order in Council, no. 1199, 1953, p. 15.

All subjects not included in the Exclusive or Concurrent Lists remain the responsibility of the Territorial Legislatures. The Exclusive List comprises matters such as external affairs, defence, migration into the Federation, customs, currency, railways, inter-territorial roads, posts, major irrigation works, higher education, and primary and secondary education of persons other than Africans. The Concurrent List includes subjects such as migration between the territories, the development of industries, electricity, scientific research, health, and broadcasting. As a result, subjects which are normally regarded as being of special concern to Africans, such as the system of land rights or the procedure of Native Administration or of Local Government institutions, remain entirely within the sphere of territorial legislation.

The Federal Assembly consists of 35 members, namely, 17 from Southern Rhodesia, eleven from Northern Rhodesia, and seven from Nyasaland. Twenty-six of these are to be elected from ordinary constituencies and will therefore be entirely European (14 from Southern Rhodesia, eight from Northern Rhodesia, and four from Nyasaland). Six will be specially elected African members (two from each territory), and three will be European members charged with special responsibilities for African interests (one being specially elected in the case of Southern Rhodesia and one to be nominated by the Governor from each of the two Protectorates). The six specially elected African members are to be elected in accordance with regulations made by the Governor of the territory concerned, as is also the specially elected European member from Southern Rhodesia.

In Northern Rhodesia African candidates are indirectly elected through the agency of the Northern Rhodesia African Representative Council,[1] and in Nyasaland through an electoral college consisting of the District and Provincial African Representative Councils.[2] The Crown is represented in the Federation by a Governor-General, who acts on the advice of the Federal Ministers, except in the exercise of those powers which are stated in the Constitution to be exercisable by him at his discretion. These powers include the giving or withholding the assent to Bills, or the decision to reserve them for the pleasure of the Crown.[3] The Prime Minister and other Ministers are appointed in accordance with British constitutional conventions.

Some indication of the relative scale of revenue and expenditure which was expected to ensue from the operation of the Federation and from the transfer to it of certain of the major services which had been conducted by the three territories is provided by the estimates framed in the report of the Fiscal Commission issued in 1952. It estimated that out of a total revenue of £52,054,000 the Federal Budget would account for £27,624,000

---

[1] See below, p. 491. [2] See below, p. 495.
[3] Article 24 of Constitution.

and the three Territorial Budgets for £24,430,000 (Southern Rhodesia £12,977,000, Northern Rhodesia £8,567,000, and Nyasaland £2,886,000). The major items of Federal expenditure would be public works £4,151,000, public debt £3,613,000, development projects £3,000,000, non-African education £2,646,000, health £2,967,000, and defence £2,337,000.

Safeguarding of African Interests

Though matters usually held to be of major concern to Africans remain within the territorial field of legislation, the Constitution contains a special provision for safeguarding African interests where measures are taken by the Federation within its own field of action. The African Affairs Board designed to fulfil this purpose was originally planned as an independent body consisting of persons who were neither members of any Legislature nor public officers.[1] Its function was to make to the Prime Minister or Executive Council of the Federation such representations regarding any matter within the authority of the Federation as it considered to be desirable in the interests of Africans. Bills were to be sent to the Board before introduction in the Federal Assembly; the Board might make formal objection to the Prime Minister if it considered the Bill to constitute a 'differentiating measure'. If the Bill were passed, the Governor-General was (save in certain special circumstances) to reserve it for the signification of the pleasure of the Crown.

Much importance was attached to this provision by that section of public opinion which felt that the Federation was being imposed on Africans against their wishes. Before the Bill was passed, however, the character of the Board was altered by a change made in its composition.[2] It now takes the form of a Standing Committee of the Federal Assembly and consists of the three European members of the Federal Assembly specially elected or appointed to represent African interests, and one African member from each of the territories, selected by the specially elected African members.[3] Its functions remain the same. The provision is in its present form more in accord with normal parliamentary procedure, but it remains to be seen how far it will serve the purpose originally aimed at.

The structure of the Federation is thus essentially a compromise. Southern Rhodesia has gained the financial advantage which federation seemed to open to it, and the influence of this fact has since been seen in the activity shown in planning large-scale schemes of development,[4] as, for instance, in the form of railway extensions[5] or far-reaching hydro-electric projects.[6] On the other hand the formal association now established with

---

[1] Cmd. 8573, 1952, pp. 23–25.   [2] Cmd. 8753, 1953, pp. 6–7.
[3] Articles 67–76 of the Constitution.
[4] G. Rennie, 'The First Year of Federation', *African Affairs*, January 1955, pp. 18 ff.
[5] See below, pp. 1552 ff.   [6] See below, p. 985.

the two Protectorates seems likely to constrain the European community of Southern Rhodesia to make larger (or at all events earlier) concessions to African claims than would otherwise have been the case. Evidence of this is already to be seen in the acceptance of the principle that in the new University of Rhodesia there shall be no discrimination on racial grounds between different categories of students.[1]

Responsible Government in Southern Rhodesia

For many years Southern Rhodesia has stood politically in a position intermediate between that of an autonomous member State of the Commonwealth and a Colony in which the Administration has been in principle and in practice responsible to the Government of the United Kingdom. As has already been indicated, both Southern and Northern Rhodesia owed their origin to the operations of the British South Africa Company, which received its Charter in 1889. At the outset the two main scenes of its operations were known as Northern and Southern Zambezia; they acquired the title of Rhodesia by Proclamation in May 1895. Southern Rhodesia was constituted by uniting Mashonaland and Matabeleland, which had been brought under the Company's administration in 1894 and 1898 respectively.

The aim of Cecil Rhodes had been the early establishment of a system of full Responsible Government, but the Constitution which was granted to Southern Rhodesia by the Order in Council of 1898[2] provided for a Legislature with a minority of elected members, five of the nine members being nominated by the Company and four being elected by registered voters in the territory; the Order in Council, moreover, expressly reserved control over Native Affairs to the Imperial Government. In 1914 the number of elected members was increased to twelve as against six nominated members. The term of the Charter had been fixed at 25 years from 1889, and on its expiry in 1914 the only alternative to its renewal appeared to be the incorporation of Southern Rhodesia in the Union, an eventuality which the predominantly British electorate did not regard with favour.

The Charter of the Company was accordingly prolonged for ten years. In 1922 a referendum was held in which two alternatives were offered to the electorate: Responsible Government or incorporation with the Union. As a result, 8,774 voters chose the first alternative and 5,989 the second. In September 1923, therefore, Southern Rhodesia was formally annexed to the British Crown, and under Letters Patent issued on 1 October the Colony was given Responsible Government, but certain matters, of which the principal were projects of legislation differentiating between Africans

---

[1] See below, p. 1160.
[2] For the Orders in Council which apply to Southern Rhodesia, see *O.T.S.R.*, *1952*, pp. 40–42.

and Europeans or those affecting the Rhodesia Railways, were to be reserved for the decision of the Secretary of State. Eventually only the
reservation referring to Native interests was retained.[1] The supervision of
the British Government over Native Affairs was exercised through the
High Commissioner in South Africa until 1937, when his functions in this
respect were transferred to the Secretary of State.[2]

The system of Responsible Government embodied in the Letters Patent
of 1923 was based on a draft scheme prepared by a Committee which had
sat in 1921 under the chairmanship of Lord Buxton.[3] This scheme was
placed before the electors when they were called upon to make their choice
of alternatives in 1923.[4] Its general effect was to transfer the executive
power, which had previously been exercised by officials nominated by the
Chartered Company, to Ministers responsible to the Legislative Assembly.
It provided for the creation of a Second Chamber when the Assembly
should have passed a law to this effect; the Buxton Commission had held
that the numbers of the European population from whom legislators could
be drawn were too small to warrant the immediate establishment of an
Upper House. The franchise for the Assembly is open to all British subjects, male and female, including non-Europeans, subject to the possession
of certain property and income qualifications. In 1953 the franchise
qualification comprised the holding or occupation of property of a minimum value of £500 or receipt of salary or wages of not less than £240 a
year; in addition, electors must have a speaking and writing knowledge of
the English language. In 1953 the number of Europeans registered as
voters was 47,533, and there were 535 Asiatic, 535 Coloured, and 429
African voters on the roll.[5]

The Legislative Assembly consists of 30 members elected by 30 electoral
districts; the average voting strength of the districts is therefore small, and
at the election of 1948 varied from a minimum of 939 to a maximum of
2,683. Until 1948 the Cabinet comprised six Ministers, including the
Prime Minister, but in that year the Constitution was amended to permit
of the appointment of a seventh. The number was reduced to five in 1953
in consequence of the reduction of functions allotted to the Territorial
Administration following on the establishment of the Federation.

Reference will be made in subsequent chapters to the policy followed
in Southern Rhodesia in regard to Native Administration and to the

[1] For the reservation in regard to Native interests, see p. 440.

[2] Southern Rhodesia Constitution Amendment Act, no. 22 of 1937. Southern Rhodesia
Letters Patent, 1937.

[3] *South Africa, First Report of a Committee Appointed by the Secretary of State for the Colonies to Consider
Certain Questions Relating to Rhodesia*, Cmd. 1273, 1921.

[4] The terms of the Constitution, as amended by subsequent Letters Patent, are given in the
O.Y.S.R., 1952, pp. 43–58. Since the year 1937 amendments have been effected by Acts of the
Southern Rhodesia Legislature, pursuant to the provisions of the Constitution Amendment Act,
1937.   [5] *Year Book and Guide to Southern Africa, 1954*, p. 343.

participation by Africans in industrial and other employment.[1] For our present purpose the point of major importance relates to the current views held regarding the part they are to be entitled to take in the political institutions of the country, and to the means they are to possess for pressing in the Legislature for an adjustment of any disabilities to which they may feel that they are subject. It has been stated that there are some 2,000 Africans now qualified for the vote, though in 1953 there were in fact only 429 who had sought to have their names on the electoral roll. The efforts being made by the Government during recent years to encourage European immigration doubtless have in view not only the economic result but the possibility of securing extra weightage for Europeans in point of voting power. But apart from any possible increase in the proportion of Europeans on the electoral roll, it would seem that if the present qualifications for the franchise are maintained it must be long before the African vote can seriously affect the composition of the Legislature as now constituted. There appears therefore to be a valid case for the establishment of a Second Chamber in which Africans can secure a place through a system of indirect election or a similar procedure.

OTHER BRITISH TERRITORIES

There are many local variations in the structure of the legislative and executive organization of the other African territories controlled by Great Britain, but it nevertheless follows a general pattern which is clearly distinguishable from that of the dependencies of the other Colonial Powers to which reference is made in this chapter. Its general outlook on policy is centrifugal, in so far that it exhibits a well-marked tendency to the devolution of legislative and, by implication, also of executive power to locally constituted Legislatures based on a gradually widening franchise. This delegation of authority forms in effect (as has already been observed) part of the progressive evolution of a system of political self-government.[2]

Legislative Councils

In this process the most typical feature has been that of the Legislative Council, and the most characteristic chapters in its history are those which record its development from a purely consultative body into a fully powered Legislature whose representatives, in the persons of Ministers responsible to it, are empowered to take over the executive control of the Administration.[3] In the course of that development the composition of the Legislature

---

[1] See below, pp. 1444 ff.

[2] For some remarks on the changes in Administrative procedure necessitated by this process, see below, p. 526.

[3] Wight, *British Colonial Constitutions, 1947*, pp. 17–39; *The Development of the Legislative Council, 1606–1945*, pp. 66–90.

undergoes a continuous process of change. The first phase of its evolution from a purely official body is marked by the inclusion in it of a small proportion of unofficial members. Such members may be appointed either by nomination or election, but there is a progressive increase of the unofficial over the official element, and of the elected over nominated unofficials, until the official element either disappears or is in a complete minority, and the unofficial membership becomes mainly if not wholly elective. It is during this stage, when the Council has become increasingly representative,[1] that the withdrawal of metropolitan control over the Government of the Territory begins to become more apparent. But this does not represent merely a decrease in the use of the Imperial Parliament as a source of legislation in Colonial affairs, for as a matter of fact metropolitan legislation has never been a prominent feature of Colonial rule as practised by Great Britain. The withdrawal of metropolitan control represents in fact rather a relaxation in the use of such administrative or executive controls as the Constitution permits to the Imperial Power.

In order to avoid subsequent explanations, it may be convenient at this point to describe the British practice in the matter of legislation for the Colonial dependencies. In the British constitutional system, Parliament legislates only for the subjects of the Crown. It does not therefore legislate directly for territories under the foreign jurisdiction of the Crown, such as the Protectorates or the Trust Territories. Jurisdiction is in their case normally exercised under powers vested in the Crown by virtue of the Foreign Jurisdiction Acts.[2] These Acts, which date from 1874, originally authorized jurisdiction only over British subjects in foreign territories or over foreign persons in respect of whom their own Governments had granted jurisdiction to the British Government.

In effect, this amounted to the grant of a right of consular jurisdiction over those classes of persons, and was usually the result of an agreement made by the British Crown with the ruler of a country possessing a settled Government. But when it became necessary to extend authority over the people of countries with no settled Government competent to make a grant of authority to the British Crown, it was assumed that there had been a legitimate acquisition of jurisdiction by 'usage, sufferance, or other lawful means'. Thus the effect of the law is not to create authority for the Crown but to make legal the exercise by it of authority either actually acquired by agreement or assumed to be acquired by these means, and to do so 'in as ample a manner as if such authority had been acquired by the cession or conquest of territory'.[3]

By a liberal and perhaps inevitable interpretation of the terms of the

---

[1] 'The term Representative Legislature shall signify any Colonial Legislature of which one half are elected by the inhabitants of the Colony', Colonial Laws Validity Act, 1865, section 1.
[2] Foreign Jurisdiction Act, 1890, as amended in 1913. [3] Ibid. section 1.

law, the authority thus acquired was in time held to extend to the exercise of every aspect of administration, and this became in effect the source of jurisdiction in the Protectorates or in Mandated Territories. If a question arises in any Court within the dominions of the Crown as to the existence of this jurisdiction, a certificate by a Secretary of State that such jurisdiction does in fact exist is to be accepted by the Court as conclusive evidence of its existence.[1] 'The jurisdiction of the Crown in a protected country is thus indistinguishable in legal effect from what might be acquired by conquest.'[2] It appears to be an accepted principle of law that the validity of Orders in Council issued by virtue of the Foreign Jurisdiction Act cannot be challenged in the Courts of a British Protectorate, and in a well-known Swaziland case the British Privy Council ruled also that Orders in Council made under that Act could not be questioned on the ground that they were inconsistent with previous Agreements or previous Orders in Council.[3]

The legislation enacted by virtue of the Foreign Jurisdiction Act is normally embodied in Instruments issued as from the Crown, either by use of its prerogative power or more frequently by availing itself of general or special authority granted for the purpose by Act of Parliament. In modern practice if Parliament is legislating for the dependencies generally the enactment usually embodies also a provision that in those territories which lie outside the range of parliamentary legislation, but where the Crown has jurisdiction, legislation shall be applied by an Instrument issued from the Crown. This may take the form either of Letters Patent or of an Order in Council.[4] There is in actual practice little difference between the authority inherent in legislation emanating directly from Parliament and that which comes to the Colonies or dependencies by way of the Crown Instruments just referred to. Legislation conveyed by Instrument is in British constitutional practice equivalent to action taken by the Government of the day, since the Queen acts 'on the advice of Her Ministers'.

In the relatively few instances where Parliament has legislated directly for the Colonies this has (apart from Acts of general application such as the Colonial Laws Validity Act of 1865 or the British Settlements Acts of 1887 and 1945) normally been confined to purely constitutional matters, as most typically the legislation dealing with the uniting, federating, or dividing of Colonies. Legislation by way of Crown Instrument has a wider range, but here also there are in practice certain definite limits to its scope.

[1] Foreign Jurisdiction Act, 1890, as amended in 1913, section 4.

[2] See authorities quoted by M. Wight, *British Colonial Constitutions, 1947*, 1952, p. 8.

[3] Privy Council Appeal 158 of 1924, Sobhuza II versus A. M. Miller and others; see *N.A.*, Part V, pp. 379–80.

[4] The difference between Orders in Council and Letters Patent is largely one of form. Letters Patent are, however, normally issued in prescribing the Constitution of a Colony rather than a dependency where jurisdiction is exercised by virtue of the Foreign Jurisdiction Act. Wight, op. cit. 1952, pp. 94–98. This passage explains also the position occupied by another form of Instrument, namely, the Royal Instructions issued under the Sign Manual and Signet.

It is normally confined to issues of policy which though arising in a particular dependency are of Imperial importance in their application; examples may be seen in the Orders in Council relating to the Crown Lands and Native Reserves in East Africa or the institution of the East Africa High Commission.[1] Crown Instruments may in the same way be issued on currency regulations or on reciprocal arrangements between Britain and the dependencies regarding legal and financial matters, such as the recognition of probates or the relief from Estate duties.[2] What may be described as purely domestic legislation is almost invariably left to the local Legislative Councils.

In the case of legislation by the local Councils, such metropolitan control as has been exercised has in the past been secured by the application of a variety of provisions. Where an official majority in the Legislature has existed, it has often been deliberately used for the purpose of exercising metropolitan control. Again, the Governor's assent being necessary to validate an Act, it might be refused in pursuance of instructions from the Colonial Office. Certain classes of Bills might under Royal Instructions be reserved by the Governor for signification of the assent of the Crown,[3] and the Crown retains the power of disallowing Ordinances even when already passed. Annual estimates of the revenue and expenditure of a territory were at one period submitted to the Secretary of State before being presented to the Legislature. Again, where a dependency had been in receipt of an Imperial grant-in-aid, its estimates were subject to the control of the British Treasury.

The modern trend towards the evolution of a system of political self–government has meant that many of these provisions have now been abrogated or allowed to fall into disuse. In modern practice the Governor retains the power of withholding assent to legislation (otherwise called 'the veto'), and the Crown may still disallow a law passed by a local Legislature even after the Governor has assented to it; but the use of this power is very exceptional. A Governor is still required to reserve for the pleasure of the Crown any legislation which may make amendments to the Constitution of a territory. In some cases, especially where an official majority has been withdrawn, a Governor has a 'reserve power' to legislate for matters on which a Legislature has refused its assent or on which it has refused its assent beyond a reasonable time;[4] but the occasions for the exercise of this

---

[1] East Africa (Lands) Order, 1901; Northern Rhodesia (Crown Lands and Native Reserves) Order, 1939; Kenya (Highlands) Order, 1939; East Africa High Commission Order, 1947.

[2] Wight, op. cit., 1946, p. 140.

[3] For an example of such Instructions see Article XVI of Royal Instructions to the Governor of Nigeria, 2 August 1946. For further examples see Wight, op. cit., 1946, pp. 152–3.

[4] See, for instance, Nigeria Legislative Order in Council, 1946, Section 26, and the more recent instances in which the Governor of Eastern Nigeria intervened to 'restore' the expatriate allowances attached to certain posts in the Region. See *West Africa*, 14 May 1955.

power (which is sometimes termed the power of 'certification') are in practice of very exceptional occurrence.

Financial control has of recent years been greatly relaxed. Annual estimates are still sent to the Colonial Ministry, but only for information, and they do not now require previous sanction; formal control is in practice confined to cases where payments made by the United Kingdom Government are involved. Sanction for loan expenditure is no longer required, though proposals for raising loans require the previous agreement of the Colonial Ministry. In general, a process of discussion has been substituted for the requirement of formal approval; it is customary to send to the Colonial Office a memorandum giving in broad outline the expected budget position and proposals, but this is mainly in order to allow of advice being given to the financial authorities in the Colony.

Executive Councils

Though the Legislative Council has everywhere been the most conspicuous feature in the progress of the British dependencies towards the stage of Responsible Government, there has been a second institution, the Executive Council, which has at different periods also occupied a formative position in this development. It may be said indeed to have provided the bridge over which the Legislative Council passes on its way to gain control of the executive agencies of rule. In some of the earlier British Colonies the Executive Council had a history of vicissitudes,[1] but in Africa its course has followed a relatively simple line. It had its origin in a body of official advisers whom the Governor was obliged to consult in executive matters, though he could overrule them, so that the 'Governor in Council' came to indicate only that the Governor had consulted his Council, even though he had not in fact accepted its advice. In modern practice the trend has been to prescribe in constitutional Instruments that the Executive Council shall be 'the principal instrument of policy' whose advice the Governor is required both to seek and to follow, save in a few matters, as, for example, the power of assent to Bills or the use of the prerogative of mercy, which are explicitly left to his discretion.

In a few cases the establishment of an Executive Council has preceded the formation of a Legislature, but usually it has existed side by side with it, and members of the Executive Council have normally been at the same time ex officio or nominated members of the Legislature. It has, however, been increasingly used as a means of associating unofficial members of the Legislature with the decisions of the Government on matters of policy. In recent years it has discharged an even more important function, for by appointing unofficial members of an Executive Council to act as Heads of

[1] Wight, *Colonial Constitutions*, pp. 126–35, 149–51; *Legislative Council*, pp. 16, 21, 43.

Departments, it has been possible to initiate them into the responsibilities of executive administration and thus to provide a stepping-stone to the subsequent introduction of a 'Ministerial' system. The unofficial member of a Legislature who has been appointed to the Executive Council and as such has held charge of a Department is more than half-way to achieving the status of Minister.[1]

It was said of the British Empire of the past that constitutionally speaking it might be described as a procession, for it consisted of a variety of communities at a number of different stages in their advance towards self-government.[2] Africa, as the succeeding paragraphs will show, has today many illustrations of this process. The present-day Constitutions of the British dependencies comprise a number of Legislatures which are still organs of an officially controlled régime in so far that their membership contains a majority of officials; but there are also Legislatures which have an elected majority and in other respects also have become the organs of a semi-Responsible form of Government.[3] There is, on the other hand, less evidence in Africa of a process which should normally accompany the transfer of authority into the hands of the elected representatives of a Colonial people, namely, the substitution of an indigenous agency for the European-recruited official services which have been maintained by the controlling Power.

In this respect those African dependencies which are now nearing the attainment of self-government occupy a less favourable position than did British India when the transfer of power took place in 1947, for by that date the superior posts in most of the official establishments had been largely Indianized. Since the matter is of special importance it may be of interest to give the following figures showing the progress of Indianization of two of the major services between 1922 and 1946.

	1922			1932			1946		
	European	Indian	Total	European	Indian	Total	European	Indian	Total
Indian Civil Service	1,179	208	1,387	843	465	1,308	504	623	1,127
Indian Police	627	66	693	528	152	680	329	215	544

Whatever may be the merits of a policy which has in recent years conceded so large a measure of political advance to the British dependencies in Africa, it is obvious that the transfer of power is finding some of them without an indigenous machinery which is adequately equipped for their

[1] For the development of the 'Minister' system, see Sir A. Pim, *Report on the Economic and Financial Position of Northern Rhodesia*, 1938, col. 145, paras. 286-7. Also *J.A.A.*, April 1949, pp. 51-59.

[2] A. Zimmern, *The Third British Empire*, 1934, p. 8.

[3] For the definition of semi-Responsible Government see Wight, *Colonial Constitutions*, 1952, pp. 38-39, 58-62.

L

administration.[1] This may prove to be a very serious obstacle to the smooth working of the new Constitutions.

Northern Rhodesia and Nyasaland

Northern Rhodesia, as already indicated, was up to 1924 administered by the British South Africa Company. In 1918 an Advisory Council to the Administrator was appointed; it consisted of five unofficial members representing the various communities.[2] The Constitution promulgated on the assumption of Administration by the Crown in 1924 provided for both a Legislative and an Executive Council.[3] The latter consisted of officials only; the Legislative Council comprised originally nine official members (including the members of the Executive Council) and five elected unofficial members; the number of the latter was increased to seven in 1929. In 1938 the unofficial members were made equal in number with the official by reducing the nominated official members from four to three and adding a nominated unofficial member to represent African interests. The membership of the Council was revised in 1945 to provide for the first time for an unofficial majority; as against nine officials there were 13 unofficials, of whom five were nominated and eight elected. Three of the five nominated unofficials represented African interests.

The position at the time when the Federation was established in 1953 was that the Legislative Council, sitting under the presidency of a Speaker, consisted of ten European elected members, two European nominated unofficial members representing African interests, two African unofficial members nominated by the Governor (who in practice nominates two Africans selected by the African Representative Council from among its own members),[4] and nine official members.

The Executive Council consisted in 1953 of the Governor, seven official members, and four unofficial members, three being appointed by the Governor from among the elected members of the Legislative Council and one a nominated member of the Council representing African interests. The portfolio system had been introduced in 1947 when two unofficial members of the Executive Council were given responsibility for a group of Departments while retaining their seats as elected members of the Legislative Council; they were not, accordingly, treated as officials. The franchise is restricted to British subjects over 21 years of age, with certain other qualifications based on literacy, length of residence, and property or income. This provision appears to envisage the acquisition of the franchise by

[1] *Round Table*, March 1953, p. 150.
[2] For the first stages of Northern Rhodesian history, see *Report of Commission Appointed to Enquire into the Financial and Economic Position of Northern Rhodesia*, Col. no. 145, 1938, pp. 148–9. *Rhodesia-Nyasaland Royal Commission Report*, Cmd. 5949, 1938, p. 18.
[3] Northern Rhodesia Order in Council, 1924.
[4] For the African Representative Council, see below, p. 492.

educated Africans, but for this purpose a revision of the existing qualifications would be required, since Northern Rhodesia is a Protectorate and the African inhabitants are accordingly classed as British Protected Persons. As such they do not at present qualify for a vote, and only a few have become British subjects by naturalization.

The Constitution was amended in December 1953, after the establishment of the Federation. There are 18 unofficial members, namely, two nominated to represent African interests, twelve elected European members, and four African members nominated in the manner described above. There are eight official members. The Executive Council consists of five official members and four unofficial members, one of whom is an unofficial member of the Legislative Council representing African interests and three are elected European members of the Legislative Council. All members of the Executive Council now hold portfolios.

The preceding facts have been given in some detail in order to illustrate the difficulty experienced in attempting to meet the political claims of different communities in a multi-racial society, and especially one where, as in Northern Rhodesia, the Europeans represent activities which contribute so large a proportion of the finances of the State. The Africans in Northern Rhodesia have lately pressed for the extension of the franchise to British protected persons with an income of £50 a year and ability to read and write their mother tongue. The present qualification is £240 a year and the ability to read and write English.[1]

The Constitution of Nyasaland dates from 1907 when Executive and Legislative Councils were set up,[2] the former with five official members and one nominated unofficial member, and the latter with six official and six nominated unofficial members, one of whom was selected from the missionary organizations in order to represent African interests. No material change was made until 1946, but this was followed by other changes in 1949. In 1953 the Legislative Council comprised 21 members (including the Governor), namely, three *ex officio* members, seven other official members, and ten unofficial members. Five of the unofficial members were Europeans selected from nominations made by public bodies representing European interests; one European was appointed by the Governor on other grounds; three African members were selected from nominations made by the African Protectorate Council[3] set up in 1946, and one Asian member from nominations made by an Asian public body.

In June 1955 a scheme was accepted which provided for a Legislative Council of 23 members, namely, twelve official members including the Governor, six non-African unofficials (shared between Europeans and Asians), and five African unofficials.[4] The scheme had been opposed by

---

[1] *The Times*, 22 December 1955.   [2] Nyasaland Order in Council, 1907.
[3] See below, p. 496.   [4] Ordinance no. 25 of 1955.

Europeans as constituting too rapid an advance, by Asians because they were not prepared to share seats with Europeans, and by the Africans because they claimed parity with the other races.[1] The African members were to be elected by the African Provincial Councils instead of being selected by the Governor from a panel nominated by them; the non-African members were to be elected on a non-African electoral roll, including both Europeans and Asians. The roll was expected to be completed in December 1955, but it should be noted that a number of Asians were precluded from the franchise as they were 'protected persons', not British subjects. It was decided that the time was not appropriate for the addition of an African to the Executive Council. It will be seen that the scheme was so framed as to avoid giving actual parity between the non-African and the African sections of the population.

Uganda

In Uganda the first Order in Council which definitely extended jurisdiction over the country was issued in 1902,[2] and from 1902 to 1920 the Protectorate was administered by the Governor without formally constituted advisers. An Order in Council of 1920 established both Executive and Legislative Councils;[3] the membership of the former was purely official; the latter consisted of four members of the Executive Council together with two nominated unofficial members. All were Europeans. The number of unofficials was increased to four in 1926, two then being European and two Asian.

The first change in the Legislature was made in 1934, as the result of which the total unofficial membership was brought up to nine (three European, three Asian, and three African). In the first years of this arrangement the convention was established that the African member from Buganda should be one of the Kabaka's three Ministers,[4] the Western Province should be represented in rotation by the Katikiro (senior Minister) of each of the three Agreement States of Toro, Ankole, and Bunyoro, and the Eastern Province similarly represented in rotation by the Secretaries-General of the four Native Administrations.[5] In 1947 the Northern Province was constituted as a separate province, and a fourth African unofficial member was appointed to the Council, another official being added to maintain the balance. In 1948 African Provincial Councils, consisting of representatives of all the Native Administration Councils in the Province,[6]

---

[1] *The Times*, 27 April and 16 June 1955. *Africa Digest*, May–June 1955, p. 13.
[2] H. B. Thomas and R. Scott, *Uganda*, 1935, pp. 33, 41–42, 66.
[3] Uganda Order in Council, 17 May 1920.
[4] For the constitutional position of Buganda and its Agreement States see below, pp. 479–83.
[5] *N.A.*, Part I, pp. 33–35, 51–52, 63–65.
[6] For the system of Native Administration Councils, see below, p. 482. See also *N.A.*, Part I, pp. 39, 54.

were created in the Eastern and Northern Provinces; these Councils submitted names for nomination to the Legislative Council. The official membership was now ten, and the ten unofficial members comprised four Africans, three Europeans, and three Asians.

In 1950 the membership of the Legislative Council was further expanded to 16 official and 16 nominated unofficial members, the latter being eight Africans (two from each Province), four Europeans, and four Asians,[1] thus maintaining the established convention of 'parity'. In the case of the Western Province one member was recommended by the Provincial Council, and the other by the Rulers of the three Agreement States in turn. In the case of Buganda one member was to be nominated by the Kabaka and the other elected by the Great Lukiko. This body, however, was unwilling to elect its representative as it now held that the Agreement of 1900 had placed Buganda in a special position and that the appropriate link between the Buganda and Protectorate Governments should be consultation between the Kabaka and the Governor.

A further change took place in 1954 when the total membership was increased from 32 to 56.[2] The new Council consisted of the Governor as President, 28 'representative members' (14 Africans, seven Europeans, and seven Asians), and 28 'Government members', consisting of nine *ex officio* and 19 nominated members. Of the latter eleven were unofficials, forming a cross bench, free to vote as they liked except on issues of confidence. This cross bench consisted of six African members (making 20 African members in all) and five others;[3] one of these was an Asian, the other four were Europeans.

The Executive Council continued until 1946 to consist only of officials. From 1946 to 1952 it included two unofficial members, an Asian and a European. The unofficial membership was then increased to six, comprising two Europeans, two Asians, and two Africans, this being the first time that Africans had been appointed to the Council. In 1953 the *ex officio* membership was increased to eight.

The Crisis in Buganda, 1953–5

There had thus been from 1945 onwards a rapid series of changes, but further projects of change ensued during the period of local ferment which followed the banishment of the Kabaka of Buganda in December 1953. To some extent this incident was linked up with the question of constitutional advance in the Protectorate. The history of the Kingdom of Buganda had from the first given it a position of pre-eminence in the country,[4] and,

---

[1] *The Colonial Territories, 1950–1*, Cmd. 8243, p. 29.

[2] Ibid., *1953–4*, Cmd. 9169, p. 18.

[3] For this extension of the Legislature see Appendix B of the White Paper, *Uganda Protectorate, Buganda*, Cmd. 9320, 1954.   [4] *N.A.*, Part I, pp. 5–8.

as has been shown, its representative Assembly, the Great Lukiko, had claimed for it a special relationship with the Protectorate Government. It is hardly possible that the more serious of the Baganda could have entertained the ambition of acquiring for Buganda the position of an independent sovereign State, for its future was irrevocably fixed as an integral part of Uganda by the so-called Treaty of 1893 and by the Agreement of 1900.[1] It nevertheless seems to be true that certain sections of the Baganda actually entertain this aspiration, and it was presumably the somewhat equivocal attitude taken up by the young Kabaka on this point that led to his banishment in 1953.[2] However that may be, his banishment speedily became an issue which for the time being overshadowed the question of constitutional reform.

Though however, there was from the first little likelihood that Buganda could ever hope to gain recognition as an independent sovereign State, there was nothing in the Agreement of 1900 which would prevent the State from exercising the hegemony in a Uganda which was (as had been officially stated) destined to become 'an African government'. But those among the Baganda who looked to this development foresaw two possible impediments. Much had been said both locally and in Great Britain about the possibility of the establishment of an East African Federation,[3] and it was felt that if this should ever happen, the status of Uganda might be prejudiced by the dominant position of Europeans in Kenya. Secondly, Africans in Buganda saw in the Asian community a menace to African leadership; local Africans had, indeed, from the first been opposed to any scheme of multi-racial government.[4]

The discussions which ensued terminated in a conference (the Namirembe Conference) presided over by Sir Keith Hancock. Here the Baganda leaders wisely refrained from pressing the case for separatism. There appeared to be reasonable ground for modifying the constitutional position as laid down in the Agreement of 1900, and conditions now seemed to justify the British Government in undertaking to reconsider its decision regarding the banishment of the Kabaka. Meanwhile it was announced that the Protectorate Government would be remodelled on a ministerial system.[5]

The new Agreement, which made some adjustment in the position of the Kabaka, was signed in August 1955[6] and the Kabaka returned to

---

[1] For the 'Treaty' of 1893 see E. Hertslet, *Map of Africa by Treaty*, vol. iii, pp. 975, 1016, 1023. For the Agreement of 1900, see H. B. Thomas and R. Scott, *Uganda*, 1935, pp. 40, 82, 100 ff.

[2] *Uganda Protectorate, Withdrawal of Recognition from Kabaka Mutesa II of Buganda*, Cmd. 9028, 1953; Cmd. 9320, 1954. See also *Round Table*, December 1954, pp. 36–43.

[3] See above, p. 187.

[4] *The Times*, 10 May 1955. J. S. Coleman, 'The Emergence of African Political Parties', *Africa Today*, 1955, pp. 225 ff.   [5] *The Times*, 27 April 1955.

[6] For the new Agreement see *African Digest*, October 1955, p. 3.

Uganda in October. The new ministerial system was introduced at the same time, together with changes in the composition of the Legislature.

The Legislative Council now has 60 members, divided into a Government side containing 30 members and a representative side of equal strength. The Government side consists of eleven Ministers (Africans three, Europeans seven, Asians one), two Parliamentary Secretaries (African); four official members (Europeans) and 13 back-benchers (African seven, European four, Asian two). The back bench is free to vote as it likes, save on a question of confidence. The representative side consists of 18 Africans, six Europeans, and six Asians. Thus of the total of 60 members 30 are Africans, 21 are Europeans, and nine are Asians. Most of the African representative members are elected; in the case of Buganda, election is by an electoral college made up of representatives from the different counties (*sazas*), and in other provinces by representation of the District Councils.[1] The European and Asian members are nominated by the Governor.

The 'parity' established by this system has a certain air of artificiality, and can only be maintained so long as an external Power is prepared to act as an impartial arbiter.[2] But the system may in any case come under modification if, as suggested by the Governor in 1956, arrangements are made for the election in 1961 of members of the Legislative Council on a common roll. If this should prove to be the case, it is difficult to see how the previous system of 'parity' can be maintained.

Kenya

Kenya, like some of the British West African dependencies, comprises both a Colony and a Protectorate area. In one respect, however, there is a difference; in Nigeria, Sierra Leone, and Gambia the Protectorate occupies by far the major area, whereas in Kenya the Colony area is in every respect the more important. The whole area now comprised in Kenya was originally known as the East Africa Protectorate;[3] the Colony area was constituted a Crown Colony in 1920; the 'ten-mile strip' of coastal area which now constitutes the Protectorate was formally leased from the Sultan of Zanzibar by virtue of an Order in Council issued in the same year.[4] The Protectorate is administered as an integral part of the Colony; the Legislative Council of the Colony legislates also for the Protectorate, and the electoral divisions take no account of the boundaries between the Colony and the Protectorate. As the Arabs are mainly concentrated on the

---

[1] See below, p. 483. [2] See above, p. 194.

[3] For the early history of the Protectorate and for the part played by the Imperial British East Africa Company, see R. L. Buell, *The Native Problem in Africa*, vol. i, 1928, pp. 263–85; also the references given in H. B. Thomas and R. Scott, *Uganda*, 1935, pp. 482–3.

[4] Kenya Protectorate Order in Council, 1920, as amended by Clause II of the Amending Order of 1948. The terms of the lease are given in the *Report of the Kenya Land Commission, Evidence and Memoranda*, Col. no. 91, 1934, vol. iii.

coastal strip their communal representation in the Council is in effect a degree of specifically Protectorate representation.[1]

If the development of political institutions has had a somewhat more complicated history in Kenya than in Uganda it is not because of the combination of a Colony and Protectorate in one legislative area; Kenya's somewhat tangled story has been due to the efforts made to secure an adjustment of claims made first by Asians and subsequently by Africans to a share in institutions in which the European community had at an early date secured precedence. Some reference has already been made in the previous chapter to the attempts made by Europeans to secure a Constitution of Responsible Government which would effectually confirm the dominant position occupied by them in the Administration.[2] The claim for self-government for Kenya was put forward by them as early as 1913.[3] An Order in Council of 1906[4] had established both an Executive and a Legislative Council; the latter had six official and two nominated unofficial European members, these being later increased to four. The claim made in 1913 included an initial demand for elective representation in the Legislature. The principle of election was formally accepted by the British Government in 1916, and was embodied in an Ordinance of 1919;[5] the number of elected European members was fixed at eleven, and the official membership of the Legislative Council was at the same time increased in order to preserve the official majority on it. The electoral franchise was confined to British subjects of European descent.

This proved to be the first move in a controversy regarding the political rights of Asians which was for long to disturb the atmosphere in Kenya. The Government of India became a party to the controversy, which had an unexpected outcome when the British Government, anxious to find a means of escape from the immediate embarrassment caused by the Asian claim, took the occasion to issue its now famous declaration regarding the paramountcy of African interests.[6] In 1920 the Secretary of State issued an instruction that the Council should, in addition to the eleven elected Europeans, provide seats for two Asians who were to be elected on an Asian communal franchise.[7] The Asians, who then numbered 23,000, responded by claiming equal representation with that of the Europeans, whose total number was then roughly 10,000.[8]

[1] M. Wight, *British Colonial Constitutions 1947*, p. 82.
[2] See above, p. 192.   [3] E. Huxley, *White Man's Country*, vol. i, p. 279.
[4] Kenya Order in Council, 22 October 1906.
[5] Kenya Legislative Council Ordinance no. 22, 1919. Constitutional provisions were embodied in Letters Patent, 11 September 1920. Wight, op. cit. pp. 272 ff. R. L. Buell, op. cit. vol. i, pp. 292 ff.
[6] See above, p. 190.   [7] Government Notice no. 281, 18 August 1920.
[8] At the most recent census (1948) the European population numbered 30,000, the Indian 91,000, the Arab 24,000, and the African about 5,251,000.

It is unnecessary to enlarge here on the reaction of Europeans to this claim or to the subsequent proposal made by the Wood–Winterton Committee of 1921 that the franchise should be based on a common roll, with appropriate property or educational qualifications.[1] If the European community was intransigent the British Government of the day proved itself to be singularly lacking in any definite policy. The final result was the adoption by it of the principle of separate communal rolls for the European and Asian electorates, but accompanied by an increase of the Asian members to five. As the Asians were still recalcitrant, they were at the outset represented by nomination, but in 1927 they accepted the principle of the system of communal elections.[2]

A new constitution of the Legislative Council became operative in 1927.[3] It provided for a small official majority, the official membership consisting of eleven *ex officio* members and nine nominated members, of whom one was to represent Arab interests. The unofficial membership of 18 members comprised eleven Europeans, five elected Asians, one elected Arab, and one nominated European to represent African interests. The Asian community, dissatisfied with the quota of elected members assigned to them, again boycotted the elections, and only began to co-operate fully in 1934. Kenya was actually the first East African territory to include an African unofficial member in its Legislative Council; this appointment was made in 1944, and in 1946 a second African was appointed as a temporary measure, this second seat being made permanent in 1947.

After the election of European and Asian members in April 1948 the Legislative Council was reorganized so as to create an unofficial majority. Reference has been made to the fact that a number of senior officials were transferred from the three Legislative Councils in East Africa to the East African Central Assembly,[4] and the four Kenya officials thus transferred were not replaced in the Kenya Legislative Council. African representation was increased from two members to four, these being nominated by the Governor from a panel of names submitted by African Local Government bodies;[5] the Arab official member was replaced by a nominated unofficial; a Speaker was appointed to preside as Vice-President of the Council. As thus reorganized the Council had 16 official and 22 unofficial members, comprising eleven elected Europeans, five elected Asians (of whom two must be Muslims),[6] four nominated Africans, and one elected and one nominated Arab.

The earlier history of Kenya had been characterized by recurrent periods of political ferment, sometimes arising in protests made by the

---

[1] *Indians in Kenya*, Cmd. 1922, 1923, p. 7.
[2] Details of the history of these years will be found in R. L. Buell, op. cit. vol. i, pp. 292–7.
[3] Royal Instructions, 28 March 1927.
[4] See above, p. 188.   [5] *N.A.*, Part I, p. 208.
[6] *Colonial Reports, Kenya*, 1948, p. 1.

settler community against action taken by the Government, sometimes the result of tension between the European and Asian communities. That there has in recent years been less open tension on the latter account has been due to the fact that the European community has shown itself readier to admit the claim of other communities to a share in representation in the Legislature. It was now easier for it to do so because unofficial Europeans had, as already shown in the preceding chapter,[1] secured a strong position in the administrative organization of the Government. This was to be seen in particular in the composition of the Executive Council. As originally constituted in 1906 the Council was entirely official. When the elective principle was introduced for the Legislative Council in 1919 provision was made for the inclusion of two of its unofficial members to be members of the Executive Council, and this number was later increased to three by the addition of a European to represent African interests. An Asian member was at the same time added to the Council.

It subsequently became the practice to nominate to it the leader of the European elected members in the Legislative Council and one of the European members for Nairobi. The situation thus created was anomalous, since the leader of the elected Europeans might on occasion also be the leader of a party in the Legislature which was directly opposed to the Government programme.[2] The Executive Council was not, it is true, a ministerial Cabinet jointly responsible for that programme, but the unofficial European members must have occupied an equivocal position when, as members of the Executive Council, they were invited to share in the inner counsels of the Administration. In 1945 the responsibilities of the Chief Secretary were distributed among a number of senior officers who were in consequence described as members for the Departments in their charge,[3] and were treated as *ex officio* members of the Executive Council, thus involving an increase of its *ex officio* membership to seven. At first one, and afterwards two, of the unofficial members of the Executive Council were given charge of Departments.

In 1951 the constitutional structure of the Colony came under review owing to an unusual combination of circumstances. The Governor had in 1947 called attention to the need of agrarian reform in a pamphlet which raised important issues regarding the land policy of the Colony,[4] and this had been followed by suggestions which seemed to point to the need for a new political and social structure which might be evolved jointly by all the three communities.[5] The Asian community was, on its

[1] See above, p. 192.

[2] See also Wight, *Colonial Constitutions*, p. 30; Wight, *Legislative Council*, pp. 116–17, 132.

[3] See the recommendations which had been made on this subject in the *Report of the Commission Appointed to Enquire into and Report on the Financial Position and System of Taxation in Kenya*, Col. no. 116, pp. 58–62.　　　　[4] Sir P. Mitchell, *The Agrarian Problem of Kenya*, 1947.

[5] *The Times*, 24 and 25 September 1952.

part, showing signs of apprehension regarding its own position in view of the growing political activity among Africans. Europeans were impressed with the increasing signs of lawlessness in the Colony. The Mau Mau disorders, which were subsequently to have so serious an effect on the life of the Colony, had not yet become a matter of deep concern, but early in April 1950 an outbreak by a fanatical religious sect, the *Dini ya Msambwa*, had caused a serious affray in the Baringo District, and later the precaution was taken of proscribing the Mau Mau as a subversive secret society.[1]

On the constitutional plane the problems seemed to be threefold. There was now a feeling that the time had arrived for appointing an African to the Executive Council, and for increasing the number of Africans on the Legislative Council. But the Europeans held strongly to the view that if this were done steps should be taken to preserve the existing numerical parity of European elected members with the representatives of the two other communities put together.[2] A further problem concerned the adjustment of the ratio between official and unofficial members, a point to which the European community had from the first attached great significance.[3]

A visit by the Secretary of State early in 1951 failed to bring complete agreement between the communities,[4] but their leaders arranged to meet subsequently in an endeavour to reach agreed proposals on the subject. It was accepted meanwhile that certain interim adjustments should be made in the Constitution, and these were brought into effect in 1952.[5] The unofficial side of the Legislature was increased to 28, namely 14 European and six Asian elected members,[6] one Arab elected member, six African 'representative' members, and one Arab 'representative' member. The African representative members were appointed from among the three names submitted by each of the electoral colleges set up in six areas of the Colony. The official side now consisted of 26 members, namely eight *ex officio* members and 18 nominated members, each of whom accepted the Government Whip on major issues of policy. The Executive Council comprised twelve members, of whom eight held portfolios; of the four who did not hold portfolios two were Europeans, one an Asian, and one an African, this last appointment being made in 1952.

Kenya—Constitutional Changes, 1954

It was inevitable that the work both of the Legislature and the Administration should be overshadowed by the necessity for conducting operations

[1] *Colonial Report, Kenya*, 1949, p. 84; 1950, pp. 2, 65; 1951, pp. 3, 97; 1952, pp. 3, 108; 1953, pp. 3, 104–9. See also L. Leakey, *Mau Mau*, 1952. Sir P. Mitchell, 'Mau Mau', *Africa Today*, 1955, pp. 485–95. *Report of the Parliamentary Delegation to Kenya*, Cmd. 9081, 1954. 'Reconstruction in Kenya: the Prospect beyond Mau Mau', *Round Table*, June 1954, pp. 251–8.

[2] See above, p. 195.

[3] *The Times*, 17 May and 1 June 1951.   [4] H.C. Deb., 31 May 1951, coll. 405–10.

[5] Legislative Council (Temporary Provisions), Ordinance 1951.

[6] Four of the Asian members were to be non-Muslim and two Muslim.

against the terrorist campaign of the Mau Mau. A State of Emergency was declared in October 1952[1] when the Government assumed special powers for the maintenance of law and order. Nevertheless, some thought was given to the proposals for the reconstruction of the Constitution in pursuance of the understanding arrived at in 1951, and in March 1954 the Secretary of State, in the course of a visit to Kenya, announced changes which were designed with the declared purpose of establishing a multi-racial system of government in the Colony.[2]

There was to be set up a Council of Ministers, composed of the Governor and a Deputy Governor, six official members, two nominated members, and six unofficial members. Of the unofficial members three would be Europeans, two Asians, one being Hindu and the other Muslim, and one African. The Executive Council would continue in existence and comprise the members of the Council of Ministers, together with one Arab and two Africans; it would continue to exercise functions such as the review of death sentences and the approval of draft legislation. In addition to the Ministers there would be created a number of Parliamentary Secretaries who are not necessarily members of the Executive Council; at the end of 1955 these comprised three Africans, one Arab, and one Asian. These arrangements were brought into effect in April 1954.

The reconstruction thus left the Legislative Council untouched for the time being, it being understood that an inquiry would be undertaken in order to ascertain the means of providing for African representation by other means than nomination. As will be shown in a subsequent chapter,[3] Kenya had many years previously taken the lead in the regular use of the elective system to secure representation on its African Local Government bodies, and there was a clear indication of an intention to use the method of election, either direct or indirect, in order to secure African representation in the Legislature. Detailed proposals for extending the system of voting to Africans were put forward late in 1955 and were accepted by the Legislative Council in 1956.[4]

The achievement of a permanent solution of the political quandary of Kenya is bound to be difficult. From the point of view of a section of Europeans the only logical answer is the division of the Colony into European and non-European areas, thus making it feasible to grant a status of Responsible Government to the former,[5] but as the Commission on Closer

[1] *Colonial Reports, Kenya, 1952*, p. 2. For a summary of the operations conducted against Mau Mau in 1952 and 1953, see *The Times*, 20 October 1954.
[2] *Kenya: Proposals for a Reconstruction of the Government*, Cmd. 9103, 1954. The changes described in the text are commonly known as the Lyttelton settlement.
[3] See below, pp. 447 ff.
[4] Sessional Paper no. 39, 1955. See also *The Times*, 28 February 1956.
[5] Those who favour this course have lately formed a Federal Independence Party. This policy has recently been advocated in Lord Altrincham, *Kenya's Opportunity*, 1955.

Union in East Africa found in 1929, the partition of Kenya on geographical lines would encounter very serious economic and administrative obstacles.[1] In other quarters it is felt that the solution might be found in establishing a general electorate on a common roll, but with appropriate qualifications for the franchise. If, however, the qualifications are acceptable to Europeans, they are likely to be strongly opposed by both Africans and Asians, and in any case this will hardly mean the achievement of a full Responsible status of government, since it will imply the retention of some form of Imperial rule as an 'impartial arbiter' between the three communities.

Tanganyika

The Constitution of the Trust Territory of Tanganyika[2] differs from that of a Protectorate only in so far that in international law its administration has been subject to the degree of international supervision formerly exercised by the League of Nations through the agency of the Permanent Mandates Commission, and more recently exercised by the General Assembly of the United Nations through the agency of the Trusteeship Council.[3] In domestic law the Administration is, as in the case of the Protectorates, based on Crown Instruments issued under the terms of the United Kingdom Foreign Jurisdiction Act, 1890.[4] The power of the Crown itself in issuing such Instruments is by implication subject to respect for international obligations, and it is doubtless for this reason that the Order in Council[5] relating to legislation in Tanganyika contains no specific provision that local legislation will be void for repugnancy to the Trusteeship Agreement.[6] It is assumed that on proof of such repugnancy, the Crown itself will arrange for the issue of amending legislation.

It does not appear that in the case of Tanganyika the form of constitutional development has been seriously affected by the fact that the Territory was administered under Mandate between the years 1920 and 1946 and under Trusteeship after 1946.[7] The Permanent Mandates Commission devoted at one time some discussion to the question whether the scheme for Closer Union in East Africa referred to in the preceding chapter[8] was compatible with the terms of the Mandate, but such discussion

[1] *Report of the Commission on Closer Union of the Dependencies in Eastern and Central Africa*, Cmd. 3234, 1929, p. 96.
[2] This term is now in current use, see East Africa (High Commission) Order in Council 1947.
[3] *Trusteeship Agreements approved by the General Assembly of the United Nations*, Cmd. 7081, 1946.
[4] For the operation of the Foreign Jurisdiction Act, see above, p. 285.
[5] Tanganyika Order in Council 1920, Royal Instruments, 31 August 1920.
[6] Such a provision was, however, included in the Togoland under British Mandate Order in Council 1923, sections 5 and 6.
[7] The United Kingdom agreed to the application of the Mandatory System to the Territory in 1920; the Mandatory Instrument was formally agreed in 1922.
[8] See above, p. 191.

was mainly on a theoretical and legalistic basis.[1] Save for this, nothing occurred during the Mandatory period which had a direct influence on the course of constitutional development. The Trustee Agreement, which was based on Articles 73 to 91 of the Charter of the United Nations, differed chiefly from the Mandatory Instrument in so far that it placed on the Administering Authority a definite obligation to promote 'the development of free political institutions in Tanganyika, and to that end to . . . develop the participation of its inhabitants in advisory and legislative bodies and in the government of the Territory, both central and local, as may be appropriate to the circumstances of the Territory'.[2] But so far as Tanganyika was concerned, there was nothing novel in the acceptance of this obligation; it amounted in effect to the endorsement of a principle of policy that was in practical operation elsewhere in the British African dependencies.

In the early history of the Mandatory Administration attention was directed less to purely constitutional developments than to the procedure of Native Administration, which (as will be explained in a subsequent chapter) showed a marked difference both in spirit and form from that which had characterized the German régime.[3] At a later period, when political issues began to occupy a more important place in the Territory, they never provided the same occasion for inter-racial discord as in Kenya. That was no doubt partly due to the difference between the character of the European and Asian communities in Kenya and Tanganyika. In Tanganyika the Europeans formed a far less homogeneous group; they represented a number of different nationalities, and they had not the advantage of occupying a compact block of country such as the Highlands in which most of the Europeans of Kenya were concentrated.[4] The Asian community of Tanganyika was smaller in number than that of Kenya, and it was also more scattered and was less efficiently organized.

Evolution of Tanganyika Legislative Council

The Tanganyika Order in Council and Royal Instructions of 1920 established an Executive Council which was wholly official in composition. A Legislative Council was established in 1926; this consisted of 13 official and ten nominated unofficial members;[5] it was the practice that two of the latter should represent the Indian community and that one of the European members should be selected to represent African interests. The effect of the usual provision that members of the Legislative Council must

---

[1] C. Leubuscher, *Tanganyika Territory, A Study of Economic Policy under Mandate*, 1944, pp. 115–17.
[2] Wight, *Colonial Constitutions*, p. 558.   [3] See below, p. 472.
[4] For the distribution of Europeans between the Provinces of Tanganyika, see *Report of Committee on Constitutional Development*, 1951, p. 2. The 1952 census recorded 499 Germans, 12,154 British, and 4,944 other Europeans; there were 77,609 Asians.
[5] Tanganyika (Legislative Council) Order in Council, 1926.

take the oath of allegiance to the King was to disqualify from membership the considerable German population of the Territory, and the question was raised whether this was consistent with the principle of non-discrimination imposed on a Mandated Territory. In 1945 an amendment to the Constitution provided for an enlarged membership consisting of 15 officials and 14 nominated unofficials.[1] Of the unofficial seats, seven were allotted to Europeans, including a European representative of African interests, three to Asians, and four to Africans. Only two of the African members were appointed at once, the other two taking their seats in 1947 and 1948.

The composition of the Council in 1945 was thus an example of the 'balanced' type of representation to which reference has been made in the preceding chapter.[2] In 1949 it was decided to appoint a Committee of the Legislature, partly to consider a reorganization of the constitutional structure and partly to give a more effective and at the same time more popular form to the institutions of Local Government.[3] The Committee, which reported in 1951, recommended the retention of an official majority in the Legislature, but there was a divergence of opinion as regards the maintenance of the previous ratio of European representation. The Government finally accepted the view that the only solid foundation for the political development of the Territory lay in the equal distribution of the unofficial seats between the three communities. There were also important recommendations regarding the establishment of Local Government institutions on a basis which would permit all three communities to take part in their working.[4]

A Special Commissioner was appointed in 1952 to consider, among other things, the most appropriate system for election to the Legislative Council. His conclusions[5] were that the ultimate goal should be a system of common roll elections with safeguards for minority representation, but that such a system was not practicable in the greater part of Tanganyika in the near future; he thought, however, that such elections, with an educational qualification and safeguards for minorities, might be tried as an experiment in two three-member constituencies. Meanwhile, European and Asian representation should be chosen by communal election, or, where this was not feasible, by nomination. Africans would if possible be represented through some form of indirect election. Though these proposals were accepted in principle by the British Government,[6] there

---

[1] Tanganyika (Legislative Council) Amendment Order in Council, 1945.

[2] See above, p. 195. See also Sir E. Twining, in *African Affairs*, October 1951, p. 297.

[3] *Report of the Committee on Constitutional Development 1951*, Tanganyika Government, 1951, pp. 18–20.   [4] See below, p. 474.

[5] *Report of the Special Commission Appointed to Examine Matters arising out of the Report of the Committee on Constitutional Development*, Tanganyika Government, 1953.

[6] H.C. Deb., 25 June 1952, coll. 2239 ff.

continued to be a long process of discussion regarding the procedure for putting them into effect,[1] and the new Constitution did not come into being until April 1955.[2]

It gave effect to the principle of racial parity. The number of members of the Legislative Council was raised to 61, of whom 31 were official members, namely, 19 officials and twelve nominated unofficials, these latter being divided equally between Europeans, Africans, and Asians. The 30 Representative members on the unofficial side are also divided equally between the three communities. The system of appointment has been by nomination, but in 1956 the Government was studying the possibility of the adoption of a system of elections in certain districts in 1958.[3] The Executive Council, which in 1938 comprised eight officials, was extended in 1939 to include four unofficials (three Europeans and one Asian). Further changes were made in 1953 and 1955, and the Council in the latter year comprised eight official members (all European), and six unofficial members, divided equally between Europeans, Asians, and Africans. In 1948 the working of the Executive Council was reorganized by allocating the responsibility for different departments among the eight official members.

The report of the Mission of the United Nations which visited the Territory in 1951 was generally accepted as containing useful suggestions for the guidance of the Administration. The report of the Mission which visited the Territory in 1954 had a different reception. The chairman of the Mission dissented from the recommendation of his colleagues that a date should be fixed for the grant of self-government to Tanganyika and that this should in any case be within the next 20 years.[4] A unanimous resolution was passed by the Tanganyika Legislative Council condemning the report, and it was described by the British Government as so vitiated by errors as to have no claim to authority.[5] In the event, the United Nations Trusteeship Council did not endorse its Mission's recommendations that the Territory should attain self-government in 20 years.

If the present Constitution of Tanganyika has an air of artificiality which is somewhat less striking than that of the Constitutions of Uganda and Kenya, it is only because communal differences are at present less marked a feature of political life in Tanganyika than is the case elsewhere in East Africa. The existing Constitution provides no basis for forecasting the shape which would be assumed by the Constitution of the Territory

---

[1] See in this connexion *The Colonial Territories, 1951–1952*, Cmd. 8553, p. 20; *1952–1953*, Cmd. 8856, p. 16; *1953–1954*, Cmd. 9169, p. 17.

[2] Tanganyika Amendment Order in Council, no. 430, 17 March 1955.

[3] *The Times*, 5 September 1956.

[4] Ibid. 11 February 1955; 26 February 1955; and 22 March 1955. See United Nations Trusteeship Council, 15th Session, 1955, Meetings 584–96, 606–7.

[5] H.C. Deb., 9 March 1955, coll. 417–22. *The Times*, 22 February 1955.

under any system of self-rule which left the representation of the different communities to the natural play of political forces.

Zanzibar

Zanzibar is usually referred to as a Protectorate,[1] though it seems to fall rather within the definition of a Protected State, since there is some element of division of sovereignty based on a treaty agreement between Great Britain and the Sovereign of the State.[2] But the degree of control over Protected States varies widely, and in actual practice the control exercised over Zanzibar does not differ greatly from that which normally characterizes a Protectorate. Zanzibar retains, however, one distinguishing mark of the status of a Protected State; British authority in the island is represented by a Resident, not by a Governor.

The original Agreement by which the Sultan formally accepted the protection of Great Britain was made on 14 June 1890.[3] The jurisdiction to be exercised and the classes of persons who were to be subject to that jurisdiction were laid down in 1924 and 1925 by the Zanzibar Order-in-Council issued under the British Foreign Jurisdiction Act of 1890. They comprised at the outset all British subjects and 'protected persons', and also all subjects of those foreign nations whose consular tribunals were closed down as the result of agreements with the nations concerned which provided that jurisdiction should be exercised by a British court. Jurisdiction was subsequently extended to cover also certain classes of offences committed by the Sultan's subjects.[4]

Laws passed by the Legislative Council of Zanzibar and assented to by the Sultan issue as Decrees of the Sultan, but if they affect interests other than those of the Sultan's subjects, they require to be countersigned by the British Resident, under the provision of Article 42 of the Zanzibar Order-in-Council of 1924. It was in pursuance of this procedure that the Sultan established in 1926[5] an Executive and Legislative Council. The Executive Council is presided over by the Sultan, with the British Resident as Vice-President, and consists of the Heir Apparent to the Throne, four *ex officio* members, and three nominated officials, all these being British members of the Administrative or Departmental services.

The Legislative Council is presided over by the British Resident and comprises four *ex officio* members (namely, the four *ex officio* members of the Executive Council), five nominated officials, and eight unofficials. These last are nominated by the Sultan with the advice of the British Resident and include three Arabs, two Africans, two Asians, and one European.

[1] *Colonial Reports, Zanzibar, 1951–1952*, p. 3.
[2] Wight, *Colonial Constitutions*, p. 9.
[3] *Zanzibar Treaties (Foreign Office)*, 1910, p. 82. See *N.A.*, Part II, pp. 5–7.
[4] Ibid. pp. 9–10. J. H. Vaughan, *The Dual Jurisdiction in Zanzibar*, 1935.
[5] *Zanzibar Councils Decrees*, 1926 (Laws of Zanzibar Protectorate, 1934, chapter 28).

The practicability of introducing elections for the Arab and Asian un-official members of the Legislative Council was examined in 1949 and the following years, but a decision was postponed pending the consideration of the constitutional amendments which might be necessary before any electoral system could be introduced.[1]

The administrative and judicial systems are so organized as to maintain the tradition that Zanzibar is an Arab State under British protection, while retaining in the background a definite element of British control. It is interesting to note, for example, that though the judicature comprises two categories of Courts, namely, Her Britannic Majesty's Courts and those of the Sultan, a conflict of jurisdiction is avoided by the arrangement that in practice the two series of Courts have the same personnel.[2]

The representatives of the Arab Association have claimed that circum-stances in the islands justify the creation of an advanced form of self-government under the sovereignty of the Sultan but based on a Legisla-ture elected on a common roll. There has hitherto been no marked display of communal feeling in Zanzibar, but it is doubtful how far the majority of the Arab and African populations would in fact favour this solution, in view of the prominent part played by the immigrant Asian community in the economic and business life of the country. Even the memorandum put forward by the Association suggests certain safeguards, as for example the reservation of seats for each community. Meanwhile the British Government announced in October 1955 its decision to modify the exist-ing governmental institutions on lines which, it is stated, will enable Zanzibar to attain by appropriate stages a status of 'internal self-govern-ment within the Commonwealth'.[3]

A Privy Council will be established, to be presided over by the Sultan. It will consist of the British Resident, two other British officials and three other persons to be nominated by the Sultan. The Executive Council will continue in existence, with the British Resident as President, four *ex officio* official members, three other official members to be nominated by the Sultan on the advice of the Resident, and three unofficial nominated members (one Arab, one African, and one Asian). The Legislative Council will now have 26 members, namely, the British Resident as President, four *ex officio* members (being the *ex officio* members of the Executive Council), nine official members, and twelve unofficial members. Half of the twelve seats will be filled by election on a common roll, but voting will be confined to persons who are subjects of His Highness. The remaining half will be nominated by the Sultan on the advice of the Resident from among candidates who can prove that they have the support of 100

---

[1] *The Colonial Territories, 1948–1949*, Cmd. 7715, p. 24; *1949–1950*, Cmd. 7958, p. 28; *1951–1952*, Cmd. 8553, p. 28.　　　　　　　　　　　　　　　　[2] *N.A.*, Part II, p. 9.
　Statement by British Resident, 3 October 1955; *The Times*, 21 October 1955.

registered electors. It is hoped by this means to secure some balance of
representation between the different communities.

The Privy Council is to have a purely advisory function, and appears
to have been devised as being a body more suitable for the presidency of
the Sultan than the Executive Council. The Executive Council will continue to be the chief instrument of policy; an African now becomes for the
first time a member of it. So far, therefore, the constitution will continue
to have a predominantly official element.

Nigeria

Nigeria[1] is in technical terms a 'multiple Dependency' since it comprises
for constitutional purposes the small Colony area of Nigeria,[2] the extensive area of the Protectorate, and the Trust Territory of the British
Cameroons.[3] But though it thus forms one constitutional unit its more
recent history reveals a continuous effort on the part of some of its peoples
to secure freedom from the limitations of a unitary form of government
and to find constitutional means for the expression of separate territorial
interests and social outlook. It is the conflict between this effort and that
of those sections of opinion which have been mainly interested in securing
an early achievement of self-government by the Dependency which has
been responsible for the difficulty experienced during recent years in
securing an agreed readjustment of the constitutional framework.

The problem is fundamental, and is typical of the obstacles that beset
the rising tide of nationalism in so many of the countries of Africa. As a
unit of government Nigeria is an artificial creation; it is perhaps the most
artificial of the many administrative units created in the course of the
European occupation of Africa. But there is more. In Nigeria the British
Administration has in the past recognized three Regional units which
have hitherto been accepted as representing natural divisions of the territory for governmental purposes, and which have accordingly been regarded as the appropriate constituents of a Federal system, should the
Constitution take that form. But it has become doubtful whether this
assumption is fully justified.[4] The Northern Region is, for example, usually
regarded as a homogeneous unit, mainly owing to the predominance of
the Muslim Emirates. But there is a large area in Northern Nigeria which
is neither Muslim nor part of the Emirate system. The Yoruba Chiefdoms
constitute something like a natural core in the Western Region, but the
Benin and Delta Provinces are essentially different in their character. In

---

[1] Nigeria takes its name from the river Niger. The word 'Niger' is said to be a corruption of
Nigeir, of which the root *ni* (found also in the word Nile) indicates a waterway, the whole word
being equivalent to 'big river'; *The Nigeria Handbook*, 1953, p. 2.

[2] Formerly the Colony of Lagos.   [3] Wight, op. cit. 1952, p. 82.

[4] Okoi Arikpo, 'The Future of Nigerian Federation', *West Africa*, 28 May and 4, 11, 18, 25
June 1955.

the Eastern Region the Ibo constitute not one but two natural groups, and the Efik-Ibibio contribute a third group.

Events may eventually prove that a more radical system of division is essential, and the solution of the constitutional dilemma may be found to lie in a centralized form of government which will preside over a large number of local units with expanded Local Government powers. It would at all events be wrong to assume at this stage that the solution must necessarily lie between the stereotyped form of a Federal or a unitary system of government.

Taking, however, the history of the development of the Nigerian Constitution in its present form, it will be seen from a subsequent chapter that the Territory occupies a special position in the development of the system of Native Administration in the British African Colonies,[1] and it is not unnatural that in the first quarter of the present century the evolution of the Native Authority system should have seemed of greater concern to the Government of the day than issues of political procedure. It was indeed believed at one period that the development of the Native Administrations as organs of local rule might in time form the basis on which to build up the organization of government in Nigeria.[2] That constitutional development did not finally take this direction was due not merely to the fact that there were important areas (such as the present Eastern Region or the Lagos Colony) where the recognized Native Administrations had little foundation in indigenous custom,[3] but also to the growth among the educated middle class of political ideals which predicated the progressive development of institutions of a parliamentary pattern.[4] These ideals have received some encouragement from the official policy which, though at the outset distrustful of the use of the procedure of election, has latterly lent its weight to the establishment of legislative institutions based on that principle.

A small nominated Legislative Council established in Lagos soon after its annexation in 1862 had a competence which extended only to the Lagos Colony. It continued, however, to exist in a reconstructed form when a larger body, the Nigerian Council, was set up after the amalgamation of Northern and Southern Nigeria in 1913–14. But this larger body was advisory only, and it failed to secure any measure of general interest.[5] There was a growing demand by the more progressive part of the population of Lagos Colony and of the south-eastern provinces for a Legislature which would include an element of the elective principle, and, in

---

[1] See below, pp. 453 ff.

[2] M. Perham, *Native Administration in Nigeria*, 1937, pp. 386–7; also Introduction (pp. vi–viii) to J. Wheare, *The Nigerian Legislative Council*, 1950.

[3] See below, p. 465.   [4] See above, p. 204.

[5] Nigerian Order in Council, 22 November 1913; see for this body R. L. Buell, *The Native Problem in Africa*, vol. i, 1928, pp. 739–40.

spite of the mistrust with which this demand was then viewed by official opinion,[1] a Legislative Council was instituted in 1922 which made some concession to the principle of election.

Its competence was confined to the Colony and the Southern Provinces of the Protectorate; the Governor legislated for the Northern Provinces, save in so far as the expenditure of money was concerned.[2] The Legislative Council had a majority of officials, who were 27 in number; the unofficial minority of 19 members comprised four elected members, namely three for Lagos Town and one for Calabar Town; the 15 nominated seats had by convention a regular distribution, four being allocated to represent the Chambers of Commerce, three to other communal interests, and eight to the representation of eight territorial Divisions. The four elected members representing Lagos and Calabar towns were Africans, the first elected Africans in the Legislatures of British Tropical Africa; the great majority of the other 19 nominated members were likewise Africans. The Constitution of 1922 provided also for an Executive Council. Up to 1942 its composition remained entirely official, but three unofficial members were then added, one European and two Africans. These members had, however, no departmental responsibilities.[3]

It is somewhat astonishing that this Constitution remained practically unaltered for so many years. It became clear, however, during the inter-war period that the Legislative Council was viewed by a growing body of moderate opinion in Nigeria as out of touch with the feeling in the country, and it was in particular impressed on the Government that the Council comprised no representation of opinion in the great Northern Provinces. In September 1942 the then Governor, Sir B. Bourdillon, put forward a scheme of reform which provided for three Regional Councils and would thus bring the Northern Provinces into the legislative field for the first time. He proposed to assign a proportion of the membership of these Councils to representatives of the numerous Native Administrations, but would elsewhere substitute gradually the system of election for that of nomination. A study made of this and similar schemes by his successor, Sir A. Richards,[4] led to the enactment in 1946 of the first of the 'reformed' Constitutions of Nigeria.[5]

The general effect of the reform of 1946[6] was to give the Legislative Council a substantial majority of unofficials, namely 28, as against 17

---

[1] Lord Lugard's criticism is contained in *Report on the Amalgamation of Northern and Southern Nigeria and Administration, 1912–1920*, Cmd. 468, 1920, p. 19.

[2] J. Wheare, *The Nigerian Legislative Council*, 1950, pp. 33 ff. Wight, op. cit. 1952, p. 50.

[3] Wheare, op. cit. pp. 161–7.

[4] Afterwards Lord Milverton.

[5] Sessional Paper, no. 4 of 1945, embodying Dispatch dated 6 December 1944. See also *Proposals for the Revision of the Constitutions of Nigeria*, Cmd. 6599, 1945.

[6] Nigeria (Protectorate and Cameroons) Order in Council, 1946. For the various Constitutional Instruments involved, see Wight, op. cit. 1952, pp. 83, 220–63.

officials; this implied that the total number of Africans would exceed the total number of Europeans in the Legislature. Of the 28 unofficials, however, only four were directly elected, a point much criticized by those who condemned the reform as inadequate. It should, however, be realized that 18 of the other unofficial members were actually selected by the vote of the Regional House of Chiefs or the Regional Houses of Assembly, which themselves had unofficial majorities consisting of members selected by the Native Authorities. Regarded from this point of view, the Legislative Council had at least 22 members whose appointment was due to some form of election, as against 23 non-elected, and this gave it a relatively high standing among the more representative of the legislative bodies of that period. The Constitution established Regional Houses of Assembly for the North, Western, and Eastern Regions, and in addition a House of Chiefs for the Northern Region; all these had large unofficial majorities, but they had no legislative capacity and were in practice confined to discussion only.[1] They were given some financial powers, but these left them with little liberty of action. No change was made in the Executive Council or in its relation to the Governor.

It was intended that the Constitution should be reviewed after it had been in force for nine years. But it had been much criticized locally, partly on the ground that it did not provide for an adequate measure of popular election, and partly for its failure to give legislative competence to the Regional Houses of Assembly.[2] It could be claimed on the other hand that the new Constitution had been successful in integrating the Native Administrations into the political system of the country, and that it had created a central Legislature which for the first time represented the whole Territory.

It is not easy therefore to appreciate the real ground for the announcement made in 1948 which pointed to the necessity for the early revision of the Constitution. Discussions were now undertaken at a variety of levels, and a general conference was held at Ibadan in 1950. The final proposals were there approved in principle, and a new Constitution was promulgated by an Order in Council of June 1951.[3] It went much farther in achieving what seems to have been the main objective of those who were pressing for a revision of the Order of 1946; that is to say, it gave the Constitution a more distinctly federal form, and it introduced in Nigeria a ministerial system, this being locally regarded as the essential pre-condition of the attainment of a régime of self-government.

The Executive Council, now described as the 'principal instrument of

---

[1] The composition and function of the Councils are analysed in Wheare, op. cit. pp. 168–82.
[2] Memorandum of the National Council of Nigeria and the Cameroons on the New Constitution of Nigeria, 27 March 1945.
[3] Nigeria (Constitution) Order in Council, 29 June 1951; Statutory Instruments no. 1172, 1951.

policy in and for Nigeria', was transformed into a Council of Ministers, presided over by the Governor and consisting of six *ex officio* members and twelve Ministers (four from each Region, including in the Eastern Region one representative of the Southern Cameroons under United Kingdom trusteeship). Nine of the twelve Ministers had portfolios, but in the allocation of functions the responsibility for Defence and External Affairs, the Public Service, Finance, and Justice continued to be exercised by the *ex officio* members of the Council, who held posts in the Administration. The Regional Executive Councils, which formed the principal instruments of policy in Regional matters, were presided over by the Lieutenant-Governor of the Region, and comprised from six to nine Regional Ministers, three *ex officio* members of the Council, and not more than two other officials.

The Central Legislature—the House of Representatives—was much enlarged, and now had a large majority of elected members. It comprised the President, six *ex officio* members, 136 'Representative' members, and not more than six 'Special' members, representing interests which in the Governor's opinion would not otherwise be represented. Of the 136 Representative members, 68 were chosen by the Joint Council of the Northern Region, 31 by the Western House of Assembly, three by the Western House of Chiefs, and 34 by the Eastern House of Assembly. In the Regions there were, as before, two Houses in the Northern Region, the House of Chiefs and the House of Assembly. A House of Chiefs was now added to the House of Assembly in the Western Region; the Eastern Region continued to have only a House of Assembly. In all the Regional Assemblies the great majority of the members were elected by local electoral colleges; in each House of Assembly the official members numbered only from three to a maximum of five.[1]

The first meetings of the Legislature under the new Constitution were held in 1952. But it soon appeared that the Constitution presented great difficulties in operation. The leaders of progressive opinion had in effect fallen between two stools. They had been absorbed in their campaign for the achievement of early self-government, a campaign which demanded the single-minded effort of a strong party. But they did not represent a united Nigeria; there were other parties less interested in the immediate attainment of self-government than in making good the position of the Regions which they represented. Opposition to British control had previously furnished the common link between the parties and interests concerned, and with the approaching prospect of its removal the spirit of regional particularism, if not of separatism, grew all the more rapidly.[2] It was impossible to secure unity among Ministers in the Central Government, or to carry out any common policy.

[1] *Colonial Reports, Nigeria, 1952*, pp. 142–3, 151–6.
[2] M. Perham in *The Times*, 17 and 19 March 1955.

The British Government arranged[1] accordingly for a conference of the leaders of the different parties in London in the summer of 1953,[2] and this was resumed early the following year in Lagos.[3] It was difficult to achieve agreement between the main political parties represented, namely, the National Council of Nigeria and the Cameroons (largely based on the Ibo country and on Lagos), the Action Group (representing mainly Western and more especially Yoruba interests), and the Northern People's Congress. The position to be assigned to Lagos was in particular a very critical and controversial point. The result of the two conferences was, however, embodied in a 'revised' Constitution which was promulgated in an Order in Council issued in August 1954.[4]

The representatives of the Northern and Western Regions have made their point good in so far as the new Constitution formally establishes a Federation of Nigeria, under a Governor-General; the Lieutenant-Governors of the Regions now bear the title Governor. The Regions receive a greater measure of autonomy, and two of them have earned a considerable measure of internal self-government. Certain defined subjects have now been allocated to the Federal Government at the centre, leaving all others (except 'concurrent' matters on which both the Federal and Regional Legislatures can make laws) in the control of the Regions. The town of Lagos becomes the capital of the new Federation of Nigeria and is constituted a Federal Territory independent of the Western Region. The Southern Cameroons, while continuing to be administered as part of Nigeria, becomes a quasi-Federal Territory with its own Legislature and Executive, which will deal with matters that would normally be within the competence of a Region.[5] The Northern Cameroons continue to be administered as part of the Northern Region, but a Consultative Committee will be set up for advising on the interests of the public in this area.

A Commissioner was appointed to make recommendations for the reallocation of revenue necessitated by these changes.[6] Provision has been made for separate elections to the House of Representatives, which, in its enlarged form, consists of a Speaker, three *ex officio* members (who will also be members of the Federal Council of Ministers), special members up to six in number to be appointed by the Governor-General to represent interests not otherwise adequately represented, 92 elected members from the Northern Region, 42 elected members from the Eastern and Western Regions respectively, six elected members from the Southern Cameroons,

---

[1] H.C. Deb., 21 May 1953, coll. 2263–4.
[2] *Report by the Conference on the Nigerian Constitution held in London, 1953*, Cmd. 8934, 1953.
[3] *Report by the Resumed Conference on the Nigerian Constitution (held in Lagos), 1954*, Cmd. 9059, 1954.
[4] Nigeria (Constitution) Order in Council, no. 1146, 30 August 1954.
[5] See further below, p. 470.
[6] *Nigeria, Report of the Fiscal Commissioner on the Financial Effects of the Proposed New Constitutional Arrangements*, Cmd. 9026, 1953.

and two elected members from Lagos. The total number is thus 194. The election of representatives will now be by universal adult suffrage except in the Northern Region, where the vote will as before be confined to men. The system of adult suffrage will also be extended to elections for Local Government bodies. The Council of Ministers is composed of ten Ministers (three from each Region and one from the Southern Cameroons), three *ex officio* members (who are also members of the Federal House), and the Governor-General as President.

The working of the new Constitution is to be reviewed at a further conference in Nigeria in 1957. The British Government has also declared that it will be prepared at that time to grant full self-government to any Region that may wish it in respect of those subjects which are a Regional responsibility, subject to the condition that Regional Governments do not act in such a way as to prejudice the performance by the Federal Government of its functions. What has been promised to them is therefore a form of diarchy rather than full self-government in the normal sense of the term.[1]

The campaign for the grant of immediate independence for Nigeria still continues. There is, however, an obvious obstacle to its attainment in the disinclination of the Northern Region to trust its future to the political leaders of the Western and Eastern Regions. The achievement of a Federal system of Government may in consequence prove to have created for the time being an obstacle in the path of those whose ambition it is to secure an immediate grant of political self-government to Nigeria. It seems in any case to be doubtful whether the machinery provided for the creation of a Council of Ministers will achieve its purpose. Nor is it easy to foresee the degree to which the enactment of a Federal Constitution will suffice to maintain a lasting political union between the conservative elements in the North and the more radical elements in the South. The differences between them are of old standing,[2] and at the end of 1954 it seemed as though the desire for self-expression by the North was likely to prove a far stronger force than the call by the South to form a single front in the interests of the early attainment of Nigerian independence.

In the spring of 1955 it was already clear there were going to be great difficulties in forming a central Cabinet as the instrument of a common Federal policy. Of all forms of political union, the least effective is likely to be a Federation of which the constituent States have no link that compels them to a sense of cohesion. If there is anywhere a real tie between the North and the South it lies in a geography which makes the North dependent on the South for its line of communications and the South dependent on the North for some part of its subsistence and a large part of its export. It still remains to be seen if this will in fact form an

[1] Wight, op. cit. 1952, pp. 35–38.
[2] For a recent analysis, see M. Perham in *The Times*, 17 and 19 March 1955.

adequate ground for the maintenance of the form of Federation in an autonomous Nigeria. Already there are beginning to appear signs of a serious danger to the efficiency of the Administration as a whole owing to the growing insistence, especially in the Eastern Region, on a rapid process of Africanization of the superior administrative and departmental posts. This was a not unnatural outcome of the campaign for self-government; but it is clear that there is at the present time no indigenous personnel available to replace the former occupants of these offices.[1] It is unfortunate also that the Governor-General should, towards the end of 1955, have found it necessary to refer publicly to widely circulated complaints of bribery and corruption in the Administration. In January 1956 a Commission was appointed under the direction of the Secretary of State to report on the investments made by the Government of Eastern Nigeria in the African Continental Bank.[2]

The British Cameroons

Some reference has been made in a previous paragraph to the constitutional position of that part of the Cameroons which is under British Trusteeship.[3] The Northern section is divided from the Southern by a 45-mile-wide strip of land belonging to the Northern Region of Nigeria; the population of the Northern section, which will continue to be administered as part of Nigeria,[4] is roughly the same in number as that of the Southern section. While the people of the Northern Cameroons maintain close relations with the Nigerian tribes of which they are a part, the people of the South, who are more advanced in education, are becoming a separate social and political entity. The plantations, particularly those of the Cameroons Development Corporation,[5] now occupy a dominant position in the economy of the Southern area.

Under the 1954 Constitution of Nigeria the population of the Northern section shares in the election of four members to the Federal House and seven to the Northern House of Assembly. The Southern section became a separate quasi-Federal Region with the right to elect six members to the Federal House of Representatives, one of whom will be a member of the Federal Council of Ministers. It has an Executive Council comprising four *ex officio* members (including the Commissioner of the Cameroons) and four members selected from among the 21 members of the Legislature after consultation with the leader of the majority party.

With the growing movement towards the achievement of a status of full Responsible Government in Nigeria, the future both of the Northern and Southern sections of the British Cameroons has presented a problem which

[1] See below, p. 466.
[2] H.C. Deb., 23 July 1956, col. 215.
[3] See above, pp. 307, 312.
[4] Nigeria (Constitution) Order in Council, 1954.
[5] See below, p. 909.

has (like that created by the future of British Togoland)[1] already engaged the attention of the Trusteeship Council of the United Nations. It is in one sense a more difficult problem than that of British Togoland, owing to the relatively greater size and economic importance of the Trust Territory of the Cameroons administered by France.

Gold Coast

The Gold Coast is the most complex of the 'multiple Dependencies',[2] for it comprises the Gold Coast (a 'settled' Colony transferred to the Crown by Act of Parliament in 1821), Ashanti (annexed as a Colony in 1901), the Northern Territories (declared a Protectorate in 1901),[3] and the former Mandated Territory of British Togoland, which is now a Trust Territory.[4] There has in the past been some difficulty in distinguishing the exact source of legislation for the Northern Territories and British Togoland, but the points involved were largely technical, and these areas attained full legislative integration with the Gold Coast by the enactment of the Constitution of 1950–1.[5]

The constitutional history of the Gold Coast presents in one respect a significant contrast to that of Nigeria. As has been explained, the Government in Nigeria was for many years so much impressed with the importance of developing the procedure of the Native Authority system that it was inclined to pay less attention to political developments, and it had some justification for this course in the evidence of the growing strength and competence of the Nigerian Native Administrations, at all events in Northern Nigeria and part of the Western Provinces.[6]

The Gold Coast, on the other hand, preoccupied with its political problems, neglected for many years any attempt to integrate into the machinery of government the organizations headed by the traditional Native Authorities, and was by comparison with many other territories, noticeably backward in the expansion of the local economic and social services. At a later date it set itself to make up some of the leeway in this respect, and sought, among other things, to build up a system of Indirect Rule, based on the use of the indigenous authorities on lines similar to those adopted in other British territories.[7] But it was too late. The indigenous authorities had lost much of their prestige, and the inefficiency of some of their institutions (and in particular their Tribunals) had brought them into disrepute.[8] When therefore the dominant political party in the Gold Coast threatened to sweep the Native Authorities aside in the

---

[1] See below, p. 322.   [2] Wight, op. cit. 1952, pp. 80, 81, 89.
[3] M. Wight, *The Gold Coast Legislative Council*, 1946, pp. 15–21.
[4] Togoland under British Mandate Order in Council, 1923; Togoland under United Kingdom Trusteeship Order in Council, 1949.
[5] See below, p. 319.   [6] See below, pp. 455–61.
[7] *N.A.*, Part III, pp. 200–1.   [8] Ibid. pp. 211–13.

reconstruction of the constitutional system, the Chiefs had no effective answer to make and in the result they were largely jettisoned.

The Gold Coast now stands out most prominently among the British African Dependencies in the progress made towards the attainment of political self-government. A number of causes have contributed to this result. In the early history of the Gold Coast Colony it was for long the tradition of the Government to respect the political independence of the Akan and Fanti States,[1] while from 1889 onwards the Constitutions of the municipal bodies in the coastal towns had made the local public familiar with the use of the system of electorates.[2] But the major cause is to be found in the emergence of an African middle class, relatively prosperous, accustomed to incur considerable expenditure on higher education and possessing an independent social outlook. This class, which was something of a new phenomenon in the African territories south of the Sahara, was largely the outcome of the economic conditions created by the cocoa industry, which began to give large money returns both to cultivators and to middlemen in the first years of the present century.[3] These 'new men' rapidly became prominent both in the legal and other professions.

Executive and Legislative Councils, composed at the outset of officials, were established as early as 1850, when the Gold Coast Territory, which had hitherto been administered from Sierra Leone, was declared a separate Colony. In 1865 it reverted for a time to control by Sierra Leone, but it was again given an independent existence in 1874, when the Colony of the Gold Coast and Lagos was constituted. Lagos was separated from the Gold Coast in 1886. The Legislative Council still comprised only official members, but it received an unofficial African member in 1888. In 1901 it contained four unofficial members, and in 1916 a convention was established of nominating to it three unofficial Europeans, three Paramount Chiefs, and three representatives from among educated Africans.[4]

But there was now a growing pressure for a more representative form of Legislature, and it was in answer to this movement that the British Government sanctioned the Constitution of 1925, which embodied a considerable advance in the direction of elected representation.[5] Though by this time the Gold Coast Colony and Ashanti were unified economically and administratively, the Legislative Council still had competence only for the Gold Coast, and Ordinances passed by the Gold Coast Legislature were applied to Ashanti and the Northern Territories by 'enactment' by the Governor. The Gold Coast Council now had 15 official and 14 unofficial members; the latter comprised nine elected African members, of

[1] Wight, *Legislative Council*, 1946, pp. 21–32. *N.A.*, Part III, pp. 195–7.
[2] Ibid. pp. 216–17.
[3] See below, p. 828.   [4] Wight, op. cit. 1946, p. 26.
[5] Gold Coast Colony (Legislative Council Order in Council), 1925. For the accompanying Constitutional Instruments, see Wight, op. cit. 1946, p. 39.

whom six were representatives of the provinces and three of municipalities. There were five European members, of whom two were elected
by commercial or other bodies and three nominated. But though this
Constitution was hailed at the time as an unusual step forward in the
application of the procedure of election, the field of election was actually
limited, for the six 'provincial' members were elected by the newly created
Provincial Councils, which were bodies composed entirely of Head and
other Chiefs.[1]

The Chiefs occupied at the time an unusual position. They included
many men of good education and ability who were prominent in the
debates of the Legislature and to some extent also in business affairs.[2]
As a class, they had at one period united with members of the legal
profession and with other progressive Africans to form the Gold Coast
Aborigines' Rights Protection Society; its primary object was to oppose
the Lands Bill introduced into the Legislature in 1897,[3] thus originating
the influential Opposition party which became a standing feature in the
Gold Coast Legislature.[4] This party succeeded in defeating or delaying
a number of Government measures, including not only the original Lands
Bill and a Forests Bill, but also measures designed to improve the system
of Native Tribunals and to prevent the misuse of 'stool' property.[5] It
held up for some time any attempt to enact measures designed to introduce
the Native Authority system. Though, however, the Chiefs as a class
actually used their alliance with progressive Africans largely in order to
protect their own interests, they were nevertheless accepted for the time
as representative of popular (or at all events anti-official) interests. The
influence which they then exercised in the country at large was amply
illustrated in the course of the 'Cocoa hold-up' of 1937-8.[6]

The Constitution of 1925 remained practically unaltered up to 1942.
Though the opposition to the Gold Coast Government in the Legislature
continued and the local press was constant in its attacks on it (particularly in regard to shortcomings in dealing with the twin issues of education and the Africanization of the Services), circumstances combined to
strengthen its position, and it was able to carry through a considerable
number of measures for improving the system of Native Administration.[7] In this it now secured the support of some of the more far-sighted
Chiefs. The character of the opposition was in fact changing; the Chiefs

[1] Wight, op. cit. pp. 45-51.
[2] G. R. Cartland, *African Affairs*, April 1947.
[3] See below, p. 738.
[4] Wight, op. cit. 1946, pp. 25-27, 74-75, 94-95, 184-7, 196. R. L. Buell, *The Native Problem in Africa*, vol. i, 1928, pp. 808, 818, 830-2.
[5] *N.A.*, Part III, pp. 200-2, 221-2.
[6] See below, p. 520. See also *Report of the Commission on the Marketing of West African Cocoa*, Cmd. 5845, 1938. Wight, op. cit. 1946, pp. 70, 105-9. F. M. Bourret, *The Gold Coast*, 1949, pp. 70-73, 85.   [7] *N.A.*, Part III, pp. 202 ff.

as a class were losing popular support, owing to the feeling aroused by the misuse made of 'stool' property in a number of Chiefdoms, and they could now no longer count on the support of the lawyers and other progressive Africans, from whom they had parted company on political grounds.

On the other hand, there was continued pressure for the concession of a further measure of self-government.[1] In 1934 a deputation to the Secretary of State made specific claims for reform both of the Executive and Legislative Councils. In 1939 a significant step forward was taken when non-Chiefs were made eligible for election as Provincial members.[2] In 1942 two unofficial Africans were appointed to the Executive Council, hitherto purely official in composition, and in 1942-3[3] the movement for a revision of the Constitution received fresh impetus from a demand made by the Confederacy Council at Kumasi that Ashanti should be admitted to representation in the Gold Coast Legislature. In 1944 the British Government accepted proposals for a reformed Constitution, which was now to embrace the representation of Ashanti.[4]

The new Constitution, which took effect in 1946,[5] created an African unofficial majority in the Legislature. It now comprised six *ex officio* members and 24 unofficial members of whom 18 were elected, namely, nine Provincial members from the Gold Coast and four from Ashanti, with five Municipal members. There were in addition six nominated members, and it was indicated that these should be mainly Africans. In the Gold Coast Colony the Provincial members were elected by the Joint Provincial Council whose close connexion with the Chiefs has already been described; the Ashanti members were elected by the Confederacy Council.[6] With the disappearance of the official majority the Governor was given 'reserve' powers enabling him to legislate, if an exceptional need arose, over the heads of the Legislative Council.[7] The Gold Coast was thus in 1946 the first Colony in tropical Africa to have an elected unofficial majority. Provision was made in 1949 for the addition to the Council of an elected member in order to represent Southern Togoland.[8] In 1946 an additional African member was appointed to the Executive Council, thus bringing its membership to eight official members and three African unofficial members.

It should now have been possible for the Gold Coast and Ashanti to

[1] Wight, op. cit. 1946, p. 197.
[2] Legislative Council (Amendment) Order in Council, 1939.
[3] Governor's Announcement in Legislative Council, 29 November 1942.
[4] H.C. Deb., 5 October 1944, coll. 1161-2; ibid. 11 October 1944, coll. 1759-60; H.L. Deb., 20 December 1944, coll. 461-77. Cmd. 6599, 1945, para. 2.
[5] Gold Coast Colony and Ashanti (Legislative Council) Order in Council, 1946.
[6] For the Ashanti Confederacy Council, see below, p. 522.
[7] For the use of 'reserve powers', see above, p. 287.
[8] Gold Coast Colony and Ashanti (Legislative Council) Amendment Order in Council, 1949.

settle down to the period of administrative reform which they clearly needed, but in 1948 local rioting broke out in the southern part of the Gold Coast, and the circumstances were considered to justify the appointment of a Commission of Inquiry into its origin. The Commission, though not definitely charged to deal with constitutional issues, made a number of recommendations[1] for radical changes which the British Government of the time announced that it was willing to accept in principle, subject to their being submitted for consideration to the Gold Coast people.[2] An all-African Committee under Mr. Justice Coussey issued in 1949 a moderate and well-written Report[3] which was accepted as providing a framework within which constitutional development might proceed.[4] Its main proposals were for the conversion of the Executive Council into a body discharging ministerial functions and for an enlarged Legislative Council which was to be wholly elected, directly or indirectly, by popular vote. The proposals were accepted by the Gold Coast Legislative Council in 1949, the Constitution was published in 1950, and elections were held early in 1951.[5]

The Executive Council, as now reconstituted, comprised three *ex officio* members (who were British officials)[6] and eight African Ministers appointed from within the Legislature; the three *ex officio* members and six of the Ministers held portfolios, the Ministers being held to be answerable to the Legislature for the departments under their control. There were two competing parties at the election, the United Gold Coast Convention (U.G.C.C.) which was of relatively old standing, and the Convention People's Party (C.P.P.) which had recently broken away from the former. The C.P.P. won the election by a large majority, and its leader, Dr. Kwame N'Krumah, was appointed Leader of Government Business; in 1952 he was accorded the title of Prime Minister.

The Legislative Council now consisted of the three British officials who were *ex officio* members of the Executive Council, six 'special members' representing European commercial and mining interests (but only two having votes), and 75 African elected members. The Council now legislated for the Northern Territories as well as for Ashanti; of the African elected members 37 came from the Gold Coast Colony, 19 from Ashanti, and the same number from the Northern Territories. The Governor retained his 'reserve powers' of enacting legislation.

Only three years later the British Government sanctioned a further

---

[1] *Report of the Commission of Enquiry into Disturbances in the Gold Coast, 1948*, Col. no. 231, 1948.
[2] *Statement by His Majesty's Government on the Report of Commission of Enquiry into Disturbances in the Gold Coast, 1948*, Col. no. 232, 1948.
[3] *Report to H.E. the Governor by the Committee on Constitutional Reform, 1949*, Col. no. 248, 1949.
[4] *Statement by His Majesty's Government on the Report of the Constitutional Committee*, Col. no. 250, 1949.   [5] Gold Coast Ordinance no. 2, 1951.
[6] The Attorney General, Colonial Secretary, and Financial Secretary.

revision of the Constitution, chiefly framed with a view to dispensing with the three *ex officio* members of the Executive Council and of the nominated 'special members'. The proposals were contained in a White Paper issued by the Gold Coast Government[1] in 1953 and later in the year they were accepted, subject to some small modifications.[2] The Executive Council thus became a Cabinet of Ministers presided over by the Prime Minister; the portfolios of Finance and Justice were taken over by the African Ministers, while the charge of Togoland and of the reserved subjects of Defence and External Affairs remained the responsibility of the Governor. This last measure was facilitated by the creation of the appointment of a Deputy Governor with his own secretariat.[3] The Legislature now consisted of 104 members directly elected from single-member constituencies on a basis of adult franchise; there were no *ex officio* or nominated members.

The Gold Coast has thus been the first African Colony to have a wholly elected Legislature with an all-African Cabinet of Ministers chosen from its members. Its first meeting was held in July 1954. The constitution may be said to represent at this stage a semi-Responsible form of government, and so far it has operated with a reasonable measure of success. The Governor has made no use of his 'reserve powers'. The Prime Minister, as leader of the C.P.P., has a majority of votes that has made it easier for him to take a definite line in regard to the most urgent of his administrative problems—that of the cutting out of trees affected by the swollen-shoot disease.[4] The emotional excitability that had characterized the political atmosphere during the last few years still prevails, but perhaps in a less marked form.[5] The Administration has had the advantage of being able to finance a number of development projects owing to the large receipts from the cocoa export duty and to the surplus funds accumulated by the Cocoa Marketing Board.[6]

It has been fortunate for the new Government that it was able at the outset to depend on the assistance of a large proportion of the British Administrative Service, since the progress of Africanization of the higher posts has been slow. Some observations will be made on this point in a subsequent part of this chapter; it is clear that the Government may at a later stage have to face serious difficulties from this source.[7] There is in particular a great lack of experience of the working of Local Government institutions; many members of the Legislature have had no experience of Local Government, even in a village, for the new institutions now being

[1] *The Government's Proposals for Constitutional Reform*, Accra, 1953.
[2] H.C. Deb., 21 October 1953, coll. 1943–4.
[3] *Round Table*, March 1955, pp. 149 ff.   [4] See below, p. 828.
[5] Lord Hemingford, address to the Anti-Slavery Society, 3 September 1953.
[6] See below, p. 1314. The Cocoa Duty in 1952–3 amounted to £16¼ million; the estimate for 1953–4 was £15⅞ million. The assets of the Cocoa Marketing Board in 1953 amounted to £78 million. *Colonial Reports, Gold Coast*, 1953, pp. 25, 51.   [7] See below, p. 368.

introduced by the semi-Responsible Government have only just begun to function. There have been numerous charges of corruption, particularly in regard to the organization for the marketing of cocoa. The management of the Cocoa Purchasing Company Limited, which had been established by the leaders of the Convention People's Party, was the subject of severe comment by a Commission of Inquiry which reported in 1956.[1] The working of the parliamentary system requires the corrective of a regularly organized opposition, and the Gold Coast suffers seriously from the lack of such an opposition.

It is true that there has lately arisen a new party, the National Liberation Movement (N.L.M.), the main purpose of which has been to press for a more federal form of Constitution, particularly in the interests of Ashanti; one prominent item in its programme is the establishment of a Second Chamber. At one time this movement seemed to cause much anxiety to the Administration and to the dominant C.P.P., but it is difficult to estimate the strength of the support which it has actually secured, for a conference of the Chiefs in the Colony area has voted against the scheme for a federal Constitution. The Government accepted in April 1955 a demand for a Select Committee to examine the case for a Second Chamber. Later in the year the Legislative Council supported the views expressed by the Committee against the institution of a Second Chamber, at all events until after the status of self-government had been achieved.[2] This has not, however, lessened the strength of the demand from Ashanti and some other quarters for a revision of the constitution and for the introduction of a federal system. At the request of the Gold Coast Government Sir F. Bourne was appointed as Constitutional Adviser to examine this issue, but the National Liberation Movement and its allies refused to meet him for the purpose of consultation, and have announced their opposition to the suggestions made by him for the establishment of Regional Assemblies with consultative powers. They have continued to demand the appointment of a Constituent Assembly to determine the issue of Federation.[3]

In the election held in 1956 the Convention People's Party won a decisive victory in the country as a whole, though in Ashanti they won only eight seats out of twenty-one. The British Government has accepted this as evidence of the general desire of the country for the grant of the demand made for 'immediate self-Government', and by virtue of legislation embodied in the Ghana Independence Act, the Gold Coast will achieve independence in the course of 1957. It should be explained that association with the traditional Kingdom of Ghana has for some years been the symbol

---

[1] *Report of the Commission of Enquiry into the Affairs of the Cocoa Purchasing Company Limited*, Accra, 1956.   [2] *Africa Digest*, March–April 1955, p. 22; May–June 1955, p. 2; September 1955, p. 20.
[3] *Report of the Constitutional Adviser, Gold Coast, 1955. The Times*, 23 January 1956.

of the Akan aspiration for independence. Ghana was capital of a legendary Kingdom of which Arab travellers told fabulous stories in the eleventh and twelfth centuries; the Ghana Kingdom actually known to history was founded about the eighth century A.D. and destroyed about the thirteenth.[1] The evidence of the connexion of the Akan people with Ghana is very slender, and is completely denied by some authorities.[2]

British Togoland and the Ewe People

The position described above, in which British Togoland was integrated for administrative purposes with the Gold Coast, had now to be reconsidered. When the Gold Coast attained a fuller independent status, it would no longer be possible for the United Kingdom to utilize the Gold Coast Administration as its agent for the exercise of its authority over any part of the Trust Territory. Again, the present connexion with the Gold Coast would have to be modified if Togoland as a whole (including French Togo) became an autonomous unit free from Trusteeship. Both possibilities had since 1954 been under the consideration of the United Nations Organization, but the issue which it had to face is of a very complicated nature.

The problem had its origin in the movement among the Ewe people for their unification under one form of government. The partition of Togoland between France and Great Britain after the First World War aroused from the outset strong protests from the Ewe people of Togoland, and especially those in the neighbourhood of the capital town, Lomé.[3] But it is chiefly as the result of the Second World War that there arose a specific movement for the unification of the Ewe.[4] In 1940 the French Government directed from Vichy closed the frontier between French and British Togoland and thus effectively shut off the Ewe in the French territory from their kindred living in the Gold Coast. A demand for the unification of the tribe was expressed forcibly in an all-Ewe conference held at Accra in 1946. Representations on the subject were first sent to the Trusteeship Council in 1947, and since then the matter has often engaged its attention, but the divergence of views was so great that it was difficult for it to arrive at any definite recommendation.

Various associations in British Togoland (such as the Ewe Union or the Ewe Unionist Association) and other associations in French Togo (such as the *Comité de l'Unité Togolaise*) have been active in demanding from the United Nations the unification of the different parts of Togoland into

---

[1] See above, p. 35.

[2] E. W. Bovill, *Caravans of Old Sahara*, 1933. A. Meyerowitz, 'A Note on the Origins of Ghana', *African Affairs*, October 1952, pp. 319 ff. R. A. Mauny, 'The Question of Ghana', *Africa*, July 1954, pp. 200–13. W. E. F. Ward, *A History of the Gold Coast*, 1948, pp. 41–45.

[3] R. L. Buell, op. cit. vol. ii, pp. 361–3.

[4] F. M. Bourret. *The Gold Coast*, 1952, pp. 115–18.

one independent State. This demand has, however, been opposed by another Association in French Togo (the *Parti Togolais du Progrès*) which does not desire to see the creation of a separate Ewe State, but looks forward on the contrary to a unified Togoland under French administration.

The problem is therefore not merely one of the unification of the Ewe people. There are wider interests concerned. The area of British Togoland is 13,041 square miles, and of this 7,196 square miles, forming the Northern Section, is administered with the Northern Territories of the Gold Coast; the 5,845 square miles of the Southern Section form the Trans-Volta–Togoland Region in conjunction with those parts of the Gold Coast which lie east of the Volta River. The peoples of the Northern Section, including the dominant Dagomba, Mamprusi, and Gonja tribes, form part of the peoples that inhabit the Northern Territories of the Gold Coast and have only a slight connexion with the inhabitants of French Togo on their eastern border. They have from the first made it clear that they desire integration with the Northern Territories of the Gold Coast and are averse from any measure which would separate them from it. The representatives of all the eight constituencies of the Gold Coast Legislative Assembly which cover the Northern Section have expressed themselves as in favour of full integration with the Gold Coast.

In the Southern Section of British Togoland about two-thirds of the present population of 227,000 belong to the Ewe tribe; about 400,000 Ewe live in the neighbouring north-eastern corner of the Gold Coast Colony, and about 175,000 Ewe live in the part of Togoland under French Trusteeship. It is to be assumed that the scheme of Ewe unification would not include the Northern Section of British Trust Territory or the corresponding part of the French Trust Territory, since these are not Ewe country. But assuming that Ewe unification were feasible, it would still remain to decide whether the Ewe now living under British or French Trusteeship should, when united, form part of British or of French Trust Territory, or whether they should form a new independent Ewe territory. The unification of the two Togolands into one State would not embrace the numerous Ewe living in the Gold Coast, but it would include a number of non-Ewe people who have no interest in Ewe unification. There are now in the Gold Coast Assembly six seats which cover Southern Togoland, and its representatives are strongly divided on the merits of the alternative policies of integration and unification.

The British and French Governments have both addressed memoranda on the subject to the United Nations, but the only concrete action which the Organization was able to undertake was the establishment in 1948 of a Joint Standing Consultative Commission for Togoland, in which representatives of the two Territories have sat under the joint chairmanship of the Governor of the Gold Coast and the *Commissaire de la République* for

French Togo, in order to facilitate the discussion of common affairs. The difficulty which has been encountered in arranging a suitable membership of this consultative body is an indication of the depth of the differences between the parties concerned. In June 1954 it was pointed out on behalf of the Government of the United Kingdom that as the Gold Coast was now 'in its last stage before assuming full responsibility for its own affairs', the future of the British part of the Trust Territory as a self-governing entity could best be assured if it became part of a self-governing Gold Coast.[1]

The Visiting Mission of the United Nations recommended in 1955 that the question of the future of British Togoland should be referred to the decision of a plebiscite to be held in the following year. Early in 1956 the French Government promulgated a statute whereby French Togo was declared to be an autonomous republic within the French Union. The plebiscite held in British Togoland in 1956 showed a majority in favour of integration with an autonomous Gold Coast, though there was also a considerable vote in favour of the continuation of Trusteeship in the hands of the United Kingdom. The Trusteeship Council has recommended that action should be taken in accordance with the majority vote. Reference is made subsequently[2] to the position which was created in French Togo as the result of the enactment of the statute above-mentioned.

Sierra Leone

Sierra Leone is, like the Gold Coast, a 'multiple dependency', in so far as it comprises both a Colony and a Protectorate. The Colony owed its origin to a philanthropic effort to find a home for the African slaves who had obtained legal freedom in England as the result of Lord Mansfield's judgment of 1772. It was transferred to the Crown by the Sierra Leone Company in 1807,[3] and was subsequently classed as a 'settled Colony' under the British Settlement Act of 1843. In 1888 it was declared a separate Colony,[4] having previously shared its administration at various periods with the Gold Coast or Lagos or Gambia. The hinterland, which greatly exceeds both the area and population of the Colony itself, was declared a Protectorate in 1895.[5] There is now in Sierra Leone a plural society of a somewhat unusual character. The dominant community in the Colony is that of the Creoles or Sierra Leoneans, who are mainly descendants of the liberated African slaves in whose interest the settlement was originally founded, or of the Negroes discharged from the army and navy at the close of the American War of Independence. On the other

---

[1] *The Times*, 22 June 1954. The *Manchester Guardian*, 22 June 1954. *Africa Digest*, June 1954, pp. 1–2; March–April 1955, p. 25. See also V. McKay, 'The Impact of the United Nations on Africa', *Africa Today*, 1955, p. 379.　　　　　　　　　　　　　　　　　[2] See below, p. 334.

[3] For the foundation of the Colony, see *N.A.*, Part III, pp. 284–5, for the Protectorate, pp. 298–9.　　　　　　　　　　　　　　　　　　　　　　　[4] Letters Patent, 28 November 1888.

[5] Sierra Leone (Protectorate) Order in Council, 24 August 1895.

hand the inhabitants of the Protectorate are indigenous Africans, made up partly of autochthonous tribes and partly of descendants of invading tribes from the Upper Niger country, in what is now French Guinea.

The two communities have marked differences, not merely of a racial but of a social and cultural character.[1] The Creole community of Freetown, with their advanced standards of education and their passion for adopting British political institutions, have been mainly responsible for the constitutional developments in the Colony. At one time Freetown and its affairs went far to monopolize the attention of the Government;[2] the Protectorate seemed to be only a secondary consideration. But though the Colony still derives a certain precedence from the superior education of the Creoles and the importance attaching to the port of Freetown, the Protectorate is gaining in position owing to the contribution it makes to the revenues of the Territory as a whole, following on the recent development of the iron and diamond industries.[3]

Unlike some other of the 'multiple dependencies' Sierra Leone forms a single constitutional unit in the sense that since 1924 the Legislative Council has legislated both for the Colony and the Protectorate.[4] The development of its political institutions antedates that of most other British territories in West Africa, reflecting the history of a period when Freetown was the centre of the activities which were conducted by the British Navy for the suppression of the export of slaves from West Africa. At that period it was for some years the centre at which the Court of Vice-Admiralty and the Court of Mixed Commission heard slave cases, and it then produced a number of Africans of distinction both in the practise of law and in politics.

In 1811 an unofficial member was appointed to the Governor's Advisory Council, which was replaced in 1863 by a Legislative Council.[5] At the same time an Executive Council was created, consisting of officials nominated by the Governor. In 1923 the nominated unofficial members of the Legislative Council were increased to five; in the following year provision was made for the inclusion of three elected members from the Colony area, though the electorate numbered only a few hundreds. The Council then consisted of eleven official and ten unofficial members. The three elected members were invariably Creoles from Freetown; but it was laid down that three were to be Paramount Chiefs of the Protectorate.[6] In 1943 two unofficial Africans were appointed to the Executive Council.

[1] J. D. Hargreaves, 'Western Democracy and African Society', *International Affairs*, July 1955, pp. 327 ff.

[2] G. Beresford-Stoke, 'Sierra Leone Today', *United Empire*, November–December 1953, pp. 243–7.

[3] See below, p. 1572.   [4] M. Wight, *Colonial Constitutions*, p. 84.

[5] M. Wight, *The Development of the Legislative Council, 1606–1945*, 1946, pp. 69, 73, 170.

[6] Sierra Leone (Legislative Council) Order in Council 1924, Article 4, as amended by Amendment Order in Council, 1939. For some account of the proceedings of the Council see Hargreaves, op. cit. p. 330.

Schemes made in 1947 and 1948 for the revision of the composition of the Legislative Council gave rise to a prolonged controversy owing to the opposition offered by the Creoles to the official proposal to add substantially to the representation of the Protectorate. This controversy was only ended when an Order in Council of 1951 laid down the new constitution of the Legislature.[1] It was now to consist of seven *ex officio* members (that is, British officials), 21 elected members (seven representing the seven Districts of the Colony, elected on a low property franchise, and twelve being elected from among the members of the District Councils of the Protectorate, with the addition of two elected by the unofficial members of the Protectorate Assembly),[2] and two unofficial members nominated by the Governor to represent trade and commerce. Eight of the group elected from the District Councils of the Protectorate are Paramount Chiefs. There was thus a large African majority. The Governor continued to preside, but he now had neither an original nor a casting vote; certain powers were, however, reserved to him.

At the same time the Executive Council, which previously consisted of five official and three unofficial members, was reconstituted with four *ex officio* members and four members appointed by the Governor from among the elected members of the Legislative Council.[3] In 1952 the Legislative Council adopted a motion urging the allocation of portfolios to members of the Executive Council, and the necessary amendments to the constitutional Instruments came into force in April 1953. Portfolios were subsequently allotted to five unofficial members, and one became Minister without Portfolio.

In August 1953 the Legislative Council debated a motion for the extension to the Protectorate of the system of direct election which was already in force in the Colony. In 1954 the whole of the electoral system was reviewed by a Commission appointed for this purpose.[4] As a result the British Government has accepted proposals for an enlarged Legislature of 57 members. This would comprise four *ex officio* members; 14 members directly elected from the Colony; 24 members directly elected from the Protectorate; twelve Paramount Chiefs (selected by each of the twelve District Councils in the Protectorate); one member elected by the Bo urban area; and two members without voting rights nominated to represent special interests. Elections will be based on a franchise recommended by the Commission above referred to. Thus the Protectorate will be represented in the Central Legislature for the first time by direct election.

[1] *The Colonial Empire, 1947–48*, Cmd. 7433, 1948, p. 21. Sierra Leone (Legislative Council) Order in Council 9 April 1951 as amended by Amendment Order in Council 1 April 1953. [2] For the Protectorate Assembly see below, p. 536.

[3] Instructions under Royal Sign Manual dated 9 April 1951 and 5 April 1953.

[4] *Report of Electoral Reform Commission* (the Keith-Lucas Commission), Freetown, 1954.

Gambia

In Gambia the form taken by constitutional development has been affected by the existence of a difficult geography. The Protectorate contains over 90 per cent. of the population, but such parts as lie away from the Gambia River have in the past been difficult of access; the people cling to their indigenous customs,[1] and the area itself was considered of so slight an importance in comparison with the Colony that it was not consolidated into one unit until the issue of the Protectorate Ordinance of 1935.[2] The small population of the Colony, mainly resident in Bathurst, are of mixed origin, and have now no close affinity with the people of the Protectorate; for them, as for the people of Freetown and of some other of the West African coastal towns, interest has centred on the composition of their Town Council.

The Colony, which had been transferred to the Crown in 1821,[3] was declared a separate Colony with its own Legislature in 1888.[4] This body legislated in practice for the Protectorate also, though there was no Protectorate representative on it; the Governor exercised administrative authority over the Protectorate by virtue of the fact that the Foreign Jurisdiction Act of 1890 was extended to it in 1893.[5] This system came under review with the revision of the Constitution of 1946, when Gambia was defined as consisting of the Colony and Protectorate together, and provision was made for representation of the Protectorate on the Legislative Council.[6]

The Constitution of 1946 provided for a Legislative Council consisting of the Governor as President, three *ex officio* and three nominated officials, and six nominated unofficial members, one of them representing Muslim interests, one commercial interests, and four the Protectorate; there was in addition one elected member, who represented the town of Bathurst and Kombo St. Mary Division. Together with these changes in the Legislative Council African unofficial members were nominated for the first time to the Executive Council. Its membership now comprised the Governor, five officials, and three of the unofficial members of the Legislative Council. An amendment made in 1951[7] increased the number of elected members on the Legislative Council to three. The Executive Council was increased by one official and one unofficial member, the three elected members of the Legislative Council being appointed to it. Two of the unofficial members were appointed members of the Government

[1] See *N.A.*, Part III, pp. 333 ff.   [2] Laws of Gambia, 1942, cap. 99.
[3] Wight, op. cit. 1952, p. 89.
[4] Letters Patent, 28 November 1888.
[5] For the Foreign Jurisdiction Act, see above, p. 285.
[6] Gambia (Legislative Council) Order in Council, 1946; Gambia Protectorate Order in Council, 1946.
[7] Gambia (Legislative Council) Order in Council, 1951.

without portfolio, and a number of subjects were allotted to each on which their advice was sought in the formulation of policy.

Proposals for the further amendment of the Constitution were submitted in 1953 by a Consultative Committee which had a large African unofficial majority.[1] They recommended the creation of an Executive Council of five official and six unofficial members, and an enlarged Legislative Council of five official and 16 unofficial members, of whom 14 would be elected. Special responsibilities would be assigned to not less than two or more than three of the unofficial members of the Executive Council, who would be styled Ministers. Thus the Executive Council would for the first time have an unofficial majority, while the Legislative Council would have an elected majority.

An unusual method of election was proposed to meet Gambia's peculiarities of geography. As most Protectorate members resided at too great a distance from the capital to make frequent journeys to it, the effective unofficial representation on the Executive Council was limited to the elected members for Bathurst and the Colony. It was accordingly necessary for the Protectorate not only to have representatives from up the river but also to have a voice in the election of persons residing in or near the capital. It was proposed therefore that of the 14 elected members seven should be elected from the Protectorate and four from Bathurst and Kombo, while the remaining three should be elected by these eleven members from a panel of nine names submitted by the Bathurst Town Council and the Kombo Rural Authority. In this way the Protectorate would have the main voice in the election of the three members.

In the Colony there was to be universal suffrage for British subjects or British-protected persons over 25 who complied with certain residential qualifications. In the Protectorate an indirect system was proposed. Four of the seven members who would directly represent the Protectorate on the Legislative Council would be elected by the four Divisional Councils,[2] on which the Native Authorities of the area are represented; the other three would be elected by the Chiefs of Gambia. The new Constitution based on these recommendations came into force in September 1954. It may well be doubted whether in this case, as also in the case of Sierra Leone, the proposed wide extension of the electoral system may not prove to be premature.

FRENCH TERRITORIES

Relations between France and her African Territories

The assumption that local autonomies are not only natural but indeed inevitable has been the constant if often unconscious postulate of British

---

[1] *The Times*, 3 August 1953.   [2] See below, p. 538.

Colonial policy. This assumption, however, finds no true parallel in French philosophy, and it is accordingly not surprising that the devolution of legislative authority to local Legislatures has been little exemplified in French practice.[1] Since the Second World War some not inconsiderable developments have taken place in French territories in the direction of greater political as opposed to merely administrative autonomy, but the theory remains that all legislation formally emanates from France. If such legislation takes the form of a statute it requires the assent of the French Parliament, while even if it is effected by the *décret* of the Head of the State it must, before formal enactment, be considered by the Assembly of the French Union. The territories of Overseas France are represented on both these bodies, but their representatives are by no means in a majority on them.[2]

In the Overseas Territories legislation relating to the criminal law or to political and administrative organization must be by parliamentary statute, but no metropolitan law applies to them unless expressly so stated. The Executive Government has power to legislate for them by *décret*, subject to the condition above stated. Each of the Overseas and Associated Territories has a separate budget, distinct from that of the metropolitan Government. In French West and Equatorial Africa there are also general budgets for the group as a whole in the form of the budget of the *Gouvernement Général*. The principle of the 'budgetary autonomy' of the Colonies was established by a Finance Act of 1900, which provided that all civil expenditure and the cost of the *gendarmerie* was in principle a charge on the budget of the Colony concerned; a Colony might receive grants from the metropolitan Government and could be called upon to meet, wholly or partly, any military expenditure incurred by the Government in respect of the Colony.[3] Parliamentary approval was required for the raising of a loan if it was guaranteed by the metropolitan Government.

Before the Second World War, metropolitan grants were, as in British dependencies, restricted in practice to those cases where they were unavoidable, and they carried with them liability to close metropolitan control of the Colony's finances. The need for the provision of external financial aid to underdeveloped dependencies which led in Britain to the enactment of the Colonial Development and Welfare Acts of 1940 and 1945[4] resulted in France in the establishment of the *Fonds d'Investissement*

---

[1] The nearest approach to legislative power in a local Assembly is the right of the Algerian Assembly to apply to Algeria, with or without modification, such French metropolitan legislation as does not apply *proprio motu*; Article 15, 20 September 1947.

[2] See above, p. 213.

[3] *Loi*, 13 April 1900, *Article 33*. See C. M. Merly and B. Sol, *Le Régime Financier des Territoires d'Outre-Mer*, Paris, 1952. J. C. Haumont, *Initiation aux Finances Publiques des Territoires d'Outre-Mer*, Paris, 1952. Also 'Note sur l'évolution du rôle du Trésor public dans les finances et dans l'économie des territoires d'Outre-Mer', *Annales des Finances Publiques VIII–IX*, 1949, pp. 114–38.

[4] See above, p. 214.

pour le Développement Économique et Social de la France d'Outre-Mer (usually referred to as F.I.D.E.S.), of which an account has already been given in the preceding chapter.[1]

The Ministry of Overseas France was required to draw up ten-year Development Plans for each of the Territories with which it was concerned, and was authorized to establish public corporations (*Sociétés d'État*) or joint undertakings (*Sociétés mixtes*) for this purpose. The Fund was provided in part by annual subventions in the metropolitan budget and in part by contributions from the Territories themselves, either by the use of surplus revenues or by long-term loans provided by the Central Bank of Overseas France. The Fund is controlled by a Managing Committee, presided over by the Minister of Overseas France; it includes both senior officials and also representatives of the Council of the Republic and of the Assembly of the French Union.[2] Contributions from the Overseas Territories must be voted by the Territorial Assemblies.[3]

Direct contributions by the Territories have not in practice formed any considerable proportion of the total sums available, but the service of loans from the Central Bank of Overseas France has since become an important charge on the local budgets. The Bank was also empowered to provide capital for development projects which are part of approved programmes but are to be carried out by private enterprise. In 1949 the ten-year plans were in effect replaced by four-year programmes, divided into a General Section, drawn up by the Ministry of Overseas France, and Territorial Sections; the latter are drawn up by the local Administrations and settled in French West and French Equatorial Africa by the *Grands Conseils* and elsewhere by the Territorial Assembly.[4] At the end of 1952 the total value of approved projects for French West and French Equatorial Africa, the French Cameroons and Togo, was approximately £280 million, of which some £140 million had actually been spent.[5] The establishment of F.I.D.E.S. is not the only way in which the principle of budgetary autonomy has been modified since 1945. Expenditure on the salaries of Governors-General, Governors, *Administrateurs*, and Judges, together with that on the *gendarmerie* in Overseas Territories, is now provided on the metropolitan budget.[6]

A French institution which has no parallel in the British dependencies is the Inspectorate of Overseas France, a service recruited by examination

---

[1] *Loi*, 30 April 1946. See above, p. 214.

[2] Composition as amended by *Loi*, 24 May 1951.

[3] See below, p. 332.

[4] *Réglementation financière concernant la réalisation des plans d'équipement et de développement des territoires d'Outre-Mer*, Paris 1950. For the *Grands Conseils* see below, pp. 333–5.

[5] *Bulletin Mensuel de Statistique de la France d'Outre-Mer*, no. 5, 1953, p. 63.

[6] *Loi*, 21 March 1948. For an examination of the financial role of the metropolitan Government in Overseas Territories, see P. M. Sanner, 'Budgets et Fiscalité des Territoires d'Outre-Mer', in *L'Économie de l'Union Française d'Outre-Mer*, ed. G. Leduc, Paris, 1952, pp. 293 ff.

from officers who are already members of certain services of the metropolitan Government or of the Overseas Administrative service.[1] The Inspectorate is responsible for the financial supervision of the operations of the Ministry, as well as for carrying out inspections overseas. An Inspector may normally expect that in every two years he will spend some eight to ten months overseas, and about a year in the central office of the Ministry.

The Inspectorate does not now examine technical services except from the financial point of view; technical experts are, however, sometimes associated with a *mission d'inspection*. The Inspectors have no power to issue orders, and they may not be appointed to any administrative position unless they are specially released in order to take up employment in the Ministry itself or a post of similar standing. To some extent the Inspectorate carries out special investigations which would in British territories be entrusted to a commission of inquiry. Its reports are not, however, made public.

The principal official source[2] of published information on the French Overseas Territories in Africa is the *Journal Officiel* of the French Republic, and each Territory or group of Territories also publishes its own *Journal Officiel*. Records of the proceedings of the Assemblies of the component Territories of French West and French Equatorial Africa are generally only available in mimeographed form. The annual reports made to the United Nations Trusteeship Council on the Trust Territories of the French Cameroons and Togo are published; but there is nothing equivalent to the annual reports of the British dependencies issued by the Colonial Office in the United Kingdom. An *Annuaire Statistique*, comprising information for the period 1939–51, has been published for French Equatorial Africa, and similar volumes for 1938–45 for the French Cameroons and for 1937–49 for French West Africa.

French West Africa

French West Africa consists of a group of eight Overseas Territories, each with its own Governor, and, since 1946, an elected Territorial Assembly. Each territory is subject to the general direction of the Governor-General, High Commissioner of France, whose headquarters are at Dakar. The eight Territories are Mauretania, Senegal, Sudan, French Guinea, Ivory Coast, Dahomey, Upper Volta, and Niger. Senegal has its capital at St. Louis, Sudan at Bamako, French Guinea at Conakry, Ivory Coast at Abidjan, Dahomey at Porto Novo, Upper Volta at

---

[1] *Décret*, 1 April 1921, amended by *Décret*, 16 January 1946. There are at present nine Inspectors-General (plus eight on secondment) and 21 Inspectors (plus three on secondment). See Haumont, op. cit. pp. 104–6. L. Rolland et P. Lampué, *Précis de Législation des Pays d'Outre-Mer*, 2nd ed., Paris, 1952, pp. 138–9.

[2] K. Robinson in *American Political Science Review*, no. 4, March 1956.

Ouagadougou, and Niger at Niamey. First formed into a group under the Governor of Senegal in 1895, the present organization of the eight Territories dates from 1904.[1] The Upper Volta Territory was suppressed as a separate administrative unit in 1932, but was re-established in 1947.[2] Each Territory is divided into *Cercles*, under an Administrator, usually referred to as a *Commandant de Cercle*;[3] within a *Cercle* there may be created *Subdivisions*, each under a *Chef de Subdivision*. In 1950 there were 105 *Cercles* in French West Africa with 173 *Subdivisions*.[4]

Senegal has returned representatives to the French Parliament since 1870. The Constitution of 1848 made provision for the election of a total of twelve Colonial Deputies, and though this system was annulled under the Second Empire, it was reintroduced in 1870. Until 1946 the election was confined to the *citoyens français*.[5] Since 1946 all the Territories have returned members to both the upper and lower Houses of the metropolitan Parliament, as well as to the Assembly of the French Union.[6] It is noteworthy that a Deputy from Upper Volta was appointed Secretary to the Ministry of the Interior in the Government of 1954.

In Senegal and Mauretania there is a single electoral roll (*collège unique*). In the remaining Territories the Deputies in the National Assembly are elected on a single roll, but for the elections to the Council of the Republic (the former Senate) some members are returned by the members of the Territorial Assembly elected by the *citoyens de statut français* (*premier collège*), others by those members of the Territorial Assembly who are elected by the *citoyens de statut local* (*deuxième collège*). The eight Territories of French West Africa return 20 representatives to the National Assembly (voting by the *collège unique*), 20 to the Council of the Republic (of whom six are voted by the *collège de citoyens de statut français*, ten by the *collège de citoyens de statut local*, and four by the *collège unique*), and 27 to the Assembly of the French Union (voted by the *collège unique*).

As has been explained, Territorial Assemblies were established in each Territory in 1946.[7] In all the Territories except Senegal, where there is a single electoral roll, *citoyens de statut français* and *citoyens de statut local* vote separately. The number of members of the Territorial Assemblies varies, but in all Territories except Senegal the *citoyens de statut français* return a smaller number of members than the *citoyens de statut local*, though

---

[1] *Décret*, 18 October 1904, amended 4 December 1920; 30 March 1925; 22 December 1946. See R. L. Buell, *The Native Problem in Africa*, vol. ii, pp. 115–30.

[2] *Décret*, 5 September 1932. *Loi*, 4 September 1947.

[3] The pre-war position and duties of a *Commandant de Cercle* are discussed by R. Delavignette in *Service Africain*, Paris, 1946, Eng. trans., *Freedom and Authority in French West Africa*, London, 1950.　　　　[4] *L'Afrique Occidentale Française* (*Les Carnets d'Outre-Mer*), Paris, 1951, p. 40.

[5] Buell, op. cit. pp. 99 ff.

[6] See above, p. 212.

[7] *Loi*, 7 October 1946; *Décret*, 25 October 1946; *Loi*, 6 February 1952. For the powers of these Assemblies, see below, p. 342.

many more than in proportion to the relative strength of their community. The membership is as follows:

Territoire	Premier Collège	Deuxième Collège	Total
Mauretania . .	8	16	24
Sudan . .	20	40	60
Ivory Coast . .	18	32	50
French Guinea .	18	32	50
Upper Volta .	10	40	50
Niger . . .	15	35	50
Dahomey . .	18	32	50
	Collège Unique		
Senegal . .	50		50

In 1947 a *Grand Conseil* was established which exercises for French West Africa, as a whole, powers similar to those exercised by the Territorial Assemblies in regard to matters within the competence of the Territorial Governments. The *Grand Conseil* of French West Africa has 40 members, five elected from each Territorial Assembly by all the members voting together.[1]

Trust Territory of French Togo

The régime applied to the Trust Territory of French Togo differs in an important respect from that applied to the Trust Territory of British Togoland. Togo consists of a narrow strip between British Togoland and Dahomey.[2] Unlike British Togoland, which is administered as part of the Gold Coast,[3] it is not linked up for administrative purposes with Dahomey but is constitutionally an Associated Territory, forming a separate administrative unit, with a Commissioner of the Republic at its head.[4] It has a Territorial Assembly, established in 1946, and elected since 1952 on a single roll; it is composed of 30 members.[5] Between 1933 and 1946 Togo was brought into closer administrative association with French West Africa, but its autonomy was restored in 1946.[6] It was in 1952 divided into nine *Cercles* in some of which there are subdivisions.[7] Togo is represented in the metropolitan National Assembly by one Deputy, in the Council of the Republic by two Senators (one elected by the *premier*

[1] *Loi*, 29 August 1947.
[2] *Rapport Annuel sur l'Administration du Togo placé sous la tutelle de la France, 1952*, p. 9.
[3] See above, p. 322.
[4] For the history of Togo previous to the acceptance of the Mandate by France, see R. L. Buell, *The Native Problem in Africa*, vol. ii, pp. 316 ff.
[5] *Loi*, 6 February 1952.
[6] *Décret*, 3 January 1946. *Rapport Annuel, 1947*, p. 21.
[7] *Rapport Annuel, 1952*, p. 270.

collège and one by the *deuxième collège*), and by one member in the Assembly of the French Union.

French Togo has shared with the British Trust Territory the differences originating from the demand of the Ewe for their unification under a single administration, and, as already explained, the matter has been continuously before the organization of the United Nations since 1947.[1] The position has been modified by the statute of 1956 which, as above explained, declared French Togo to be an autonomous republic within the French Union, providing at the same time for a new Constitution for the territory. There was to be a Legislature elected by universal suffrage. The Executive Government was to be conducted by Ministers responsible to the Legislature. It was to have full control over all internal affairs, but the defence of the country and its foreign relations were to remain the responsibility of the metropolitan Government. The declaration of the new status of the territory had been made without a previous reference to the Assembly of the United Nations, and was therefore subject to its approval. The new Constitution was, however, submitted to a referendum of the inhabitants of the territory in the autumn of 1956, and a majority of voters expressed approval of it.[2]

French Equatorial Africa

French Equatorial Africa, once known as French Congo, is a group of four Overseas Territories: Gabon (capital, Libreville), Middle Congo (capital, Pointe Noire), Oubangui Chari (capital, Bangui), and Chad (capital, Fort Lamy). The early history of the Territories was marked by much confusion and instability[3] until they were reconstituted in 1910 on the model of French West Africa.[4] Each Territory is administered by a Governor, under the direction of the Governor-General at Brazzaville. Each is divided into *Régions* under a *Chef de Région*, and *Régions* may be subdivided into *Districts*. In 1950 there were 34 *Régions* and 128 *Districts*.[5]

The representation assigned to French Equatorial Africa in the different metropolitan parliamentary institutions is 23, distributed as follows: seven representatives in the National Assembly (of whom two are voted by the *premier collège* and five by the *deuxième collège*), nine in the Council of the Republic (of whom four are voted by the *premier collège* and five by the *deuxième collège*), and seven in the Assembly of the French Union.

---

[1] See above, p. 322.

[2] *West Africa*, 27 November 1954, p. 1110; 9 April 1955, p. 318. *Africa Digest*, January–February 1955, p. 13. *The Times*, 11 September and 30 October 1956.

[3] Buell, op. cit. vol. ii, pp. 221 ff.

[4] *Décret*, 24 January 1910; *Décret*, 16 October 1946, amended 6 November and 30 December 1946 and 28 February 1950.

[5] *Annuaire Statistique de l'Afrique Équatoriale Française*, vol. i, Brazzaville, 1936–50, p. 30.

The Territorial Assemblies have the same powers as those in French West Africa. Their composition as remodelled in 1952[1] is:

Territoire	Premier Collège	Deuxième Collège	Total
Chad . . .	15	30	45
Middle Congo .	13	24	37
Oubangui Chari .	14	26	40
Gabon . . .	13	24	37

As in French West Africa, there is a *Grand Conseil* for the group as a whole, consisting of 20 members, five elected from each Territorial Assembly by all the members as a single electoral body.[2]

The French Cameroons

The Cameroons under French Trusteeship was originally attached to French Equatorial Africa for purposes of administration,[3] but when France was entrusted with a Mandate, the Territory was organized as a separate unit under a Commissioner of the Republic. It has since retained its separate status and is now constitutionally an Associated Territory under a High Commissioner, with headquarters at Yaoundé. It was in 1952 divided into 18 *Régions* and 52 *Subdivisions*.[4] It is represented in the National Assembly by two Deputies elected by the *citoyens de statut français* and two by the *citoyens de statut local*. In the Council of the Republic it is represented by one Senator elected by the *premier collège* and two by the *deuxième collège*, and by five members of the Assembly of the French Union. In 1942 it was given a Consultative Economic and Social Council which had 34 members. This was succeeded in 1945 by a Territorial Assembly;[5] under an amending law of 1952 it has now 50 members, of whom 18 are elected by the *premier collège* and the remainder by the *deuxième collège*. The Constitution of the Cameroons is, however, likely to be one of the earliest to be reformed under the important *loi cadre* of 1956.[6]

Powers of High Commissioners

The powers of the High Commissioners in French West Africa and French Equatorial Africa have not been comprehensively defined, but as Governors-General they are the representatives of the French Government in their Territories and the *dépositaires* of the powers of the Republic, charged to ensure the general co-ordination of the public services and to exercise the supervisory powers of the metropolitan Government over

---

[1] *Loi*, 6 February 1952.   [2] *Loi*, 29 August 1947.
[3] Buell, op. cit. vol. ii, p. 279.   [4] *Rapport Annuel, 1952*, p. 12.
[5] *Décret*, 9 October 1945.   [6] See above, p. 216.

subordinate local bodies (e.g. municipalities).[1] They are responsible for the defence and the internal security of their Territories and are in particular empowered to declare a 'state of siege';[2] this power is exercisable in metropolitan France only by Parliament or, if it is not sitting, by the President of the Republic.

In 1948 a Central African Strategic Area was established which was divided in 1951 into 'defence areas', namely, French West Africa with Togo, and French Equatorial Africa with the French Cameroons, for which the two High Commissioners are respectively responsible under the Ministers for National Defence and Overseas France. Subject to certain special provisions for defence,[3] the High Commissioner for the French Cameroons and the Commissioner for Togo have powers in their respective Territories similar to those of the Governor-General in French West and French Equatorial Africa.

Although the High Commissioners and the Commissioner for Togo possess no legislative powers in the ordinary sense, they are entitled to issue subordinate legislation in the form of *arrêtés*. They are given this authority by various enactments which empower them to regulate administrative and police matters and to organize public services,[4] but on many subjects *arrêtés* must now be submitted to the Territorial Assemblies or the *Grands Conseils* for an *avis* before enactment. Enactments of the metropolitan Government, other than statutes which are applicable overseas *de plein droit* by virtue of their subject-matter, do not enter into force until promulgated by the Governor-General or Governor in the local *Journal Officiel*. No period within which this must be done is prescribed, so that the local authorities can delay the coming into force of any such enactment, except those applicable *de plein droit*. The only sanction is a direct order from the Minister.[5]

There is no comprehensive statement of the respective powers and responsibilities[6] of the *Gouvernements-Généraux* of the two groups of Territories of French West and French Equatorial Africa *vis-à-vis* the *Gouvernements* of the individual Territories comprised in them. While the creation of these two large units has effected a considerable measure of decentralization in relation to the metropolitan Government the general result has been to leave a relatively small field to the initiative of the Territorial Governments. The two main factors which have operated in this direction have been, first, the division of executive powers between the Governors-

[1] *Décret*, 26 April 1951.
[2] *Loi*, 9 August 1849. *Loi*, 3 April 1878. *Décret*, 30 December 1916.
[3] *Décret*, 5 July 1951.
[4] P. Lampué, 'Le pouvoir règlementaire des représentants du Gouvernement dans les territoires d'Outre-Mer', *Revue Juridique et Politique de l'Union Française*, 1949, pp. 257 ff.
[5] L. Rolland et P. Lampué, *Précis de Législation*, 1952, pp. 188–92.
[6] B. Aurillac, *Régime Politique et Administratif de l'A.O.F.*, Dakar, 1949.

General and Governors of the individual Territories, and, secondly, the division of the revenue between the Territorial budgets and those of the *Gouvernements-Généraux*. More recently these factors have had a parallel in the division of powers between the Territorial Assemblies and the *Grands Conseils*. The Governors-General organize public services and appoint all officials with the exception of those posts which are expressly reserved to metropolitan control; they alone have the right to correspond directly with the Ministry of Overseas France; and it is explicitly stated that the Governors of the Territories administer them 'under the authority' of the Governor-General.[1]

The major sources of revenue for the budgets of the *Gouvernements-Généraux* are customs and export duties, while those of the Territorial budgets are the capitation and similar direct taxes and the tax on corporate income. The effect is to place the most readily expansible sources of revenue at the disposal of the *Gouvernements-Généraux* and to make the Territories dependent on them for substantial assistance by way of rebates and grants. In 1950, for example, the estimates for the general budget in French Equatorial Africa were some £7½ million, compared with a total of £6 million for the four Territorial budgets, but of this latter sum more than £2 million was provided by grants from the general budget. In French West Africa the general budget totalled £43 million. The total of the eight Territorial budgets amounted to £22 million, but of this some £10 million was provided by rebates and grants from the general budget.[2]

The subordination of the Territories to the *Gouvernements-Généraux* is also reflected in the powers of the Territorial Assemblies *vis-à-vis* those of the *Grands Conseils*. The latter decide the general budget and the basis of assessment of all taxes, including those which are paid into territorial budgets, while the Territorial Assemblies decide the actual rate at which these latter taxes are levied. The *Grands Conseils*, moreover, have powers in all matters otherwise within the competence of Territorial Assemblies if these involve issues of general concern to the group as a whole. Although the more extreme centralizing tendencies of the years immediately preceding the Second World War were temporarily arrested by the post-war reforms and in particular by the establishment of the Territorial Assemblies, the relative importance of the *Gouvernements-Généraux* has also been enhanced by the fact that it is the *Grands Conseils* which must be consulted on development programmes financed by the *Fonds d'Investissement pour le Développement Économique et Social des Territoires d'Outre-Mer*[3] (F.I.D.E.S.)

[1] French West Africa *Décret* of 18 October 1904, amended 4 December 1920, 13 October 1922, 27 November 1924, 5 September 1932, 22 December 1946. French Equatorial Africa *Décret* of 16 October 1946, amended 6 November 1946, 30 December 1946, and 28 February 1950.

[2] R. Bargues, *Problèmes Financiers en A.O.F.*, Dakar, 1949. *Annuaire Statistique de l'Afrique Occidentale Française*, vol. ii, Paris, 1951.

[3] See above, pp. 329–30.

and it is the *Gouvernement-Général* which is responsible for their elaboration and execution.[1]

Citizenship and the Franchise

Before the enactment of the Constitution of 1946, citizenship, which was not merely a question of national status but involved also the exercise of political rights, was closely associated with the attainment of a certain degree of cultural assimilation and the acceptance of French private law.[2] Throughout French Africa a distinction was made between persons subject to Native custom (*sujets*) and those assimilated to European law (*citoyens*), the latter having identical civil and political rights with persons of French origin.

The *sujets* in these Territories could become *citoyens* by a process analogous to naturalization if they satisfied the qualifications prescribed by law; the general effect of these provisions was to require evidence either in the form of educational qualifications or of character of employment that the candidate had adopted a European mode of life. *Citoyens* were exempt from the obligation of compulsory labour and also from the *régime de l'indigénat*, or 'disciplinary penalties', which could be summarily imposed by an Administrative Officer.[3] There were, however, relatively few applications for citizenship; in 1936 only 2,136 of the total number of *indigènes citoyens français* in French West Africa came from Territories other than Senegal,[4] where, as will be seen from what immediately follows, citizenship was in certain cases acquired automatically.

In Senegal the 'four *communes*' of St. Louis, Dakar, Gorée, and Rufisque[5] represented the four coastal towns from which the French extended their hold over the hinterland; they were at an early stage described as the 'territory under direct administration', the remainder of Senegal being regarded as a 'protectorate'. A law of 1833 provided that all free persons should enjoy equal civil and political rights on conditions determined by law, but this latter phrase was held from the outset to permit of exceptions being made to the principle which prescribed the complete assimilation of Africans to French law. The impracticability of such a step was, indeed, recognized in 1848 by the establishment in St. Louis of a Muslim tribunal.

Following the enactment of the Constitution of 1848 Senegal was, in accordance with the assimilationist theories of the day, endowed with the same adult male suffrage as was introduced in France. It received, moreover, the right to return one of the twelve Colonial Deputies in the metro-

---

[1] *Décret*, 3 June 1949.

[2] K. Robinson, 'The Public Law of Overseas France since the War', *Journal of Comparative Legislation*, Ser. III, vol. xxxii, Parts III and IV, p. 37.   [3] See below, p. 544.

[4] *Annuaire Statistique de l'Afrique Occidentale Française 1934–1935*, 1936, p. 19. The legislation on the subject was embodied in *Décrets* of 1912, 1932, 1935, and 1937.

[5] Now three, Gorée having been combined with Dakar in 1929.

politan Parliament. In 1916 a law passed with the object of defining the liability of the *citoyens indigènes français* to conscription declared that all persons born within the four *communes* and their descendants were citizens;[1] a prolonged controversy on the question whether this made them subject to French civil law was finally decided in the negative by the *Conseil d'État* in 1936.[2] In 1936 the number of Africans having the status of citizens in Senegal was 78,373, out of a total African population of about $1\frac{3}{4}$ million.[3] African citizens were entitled to the franchise on the same basis as Frenchmen in respect not only of the election of the Deputy for Senegal but also in elections for the Communal Councils of St. Louis, Rufisque, and Dakar, and for the *Conseil Colonial* which was established for the whole of Senegal in 1920.[4]

It was appropriately the Senegalese Deputy who as member of the post-war Constituent Assembly secured in May 1946 the passage of a law usually known after its author as the *Loi Lamine Gueye*, which conferred citizenship rights on all Colonial peoples. Article 80 of the Constitution of October 1946 provided that all inhabitants of the Overseas Territories of France should be *citoyens*, but that the conditions on which they would exercise their rights would be determined by separate laws. There was some apparent conflict between this Article and Article 82, which made it doubtful how far the extension of citizenship affected the personal status of Africans under Muslim law or Native customary law, but it is clear that it was not intended that the fact of possessing such a personal status should debar them from exercising the rights of citizenship.[5] As inhabitants of the Trust Territories of Togo and the French Cameroons are not legally French nationals, the right to elect representatives to the National Assembly now conferred on the inhabitants of Overseas Territories was extended by special enactment to those of the two Trust Territories.[6]

The procedure for the exercise of electoral rights by the new citizens and by the *administrés français* of Togo and the French Cameroons was prescribed in the same enactment. In French West Africa, French Equatorial Africa, the French Cameroons, and Togo, the conditions of the franchise were identical. In addition to those who had previously enjoyed electoral rights, the law conferred such rights on *nationaux et ressortissants français* of either sex who were 21 years old and belonged to any one of a large number of categories, which was subsequently extended in 1951;[7] the general effect of this extension was to admit as a voting qualification practically any document which afforded evidence of the voter's identity.

[1] *Loi*, 29 September 1916.
[2] *Conseil d'État*, 4 December 1936. M'Bodje Habibou, *Recueil*, p. 1060.
[3] *Annuaire Statistique*, op. cit. p. 14.
[4] For the *Conseil Colonial* of Senegal, see below, p. 340.
[5] Robinson, op. cit. p. 47. [6] *Loi*, 5 October 1946, *Article* 40.
[7] *Loi*, 23 May 1951, *Article* 3.

The total number[1] of registered voters in the French Territories south of the Sahara at the parliamentary election of 1946 was 1,096,534, and at the election of 1951 this stood at 4,176,914, namely, French West Africa, 3,062,594; French Equatorial Africa, 564,798; Togo, 32,496; and the French Cameroons, 517,026.

Departmental and Advisory Councils

Senegal, as already indicated, stood for many years on a different basis from the rest of French West Africa. A *Conseil Général du Sénégal*, corresponding to the Departmental Councils of metropolitan France, was introduced in 1879. It consisted of 20 members elected by *citoyens français*; as these included all persons born in the 'four *communes*'[2] they nearly always elected African representatives who were, however, required to be able to speak and write French. Its powers included the imposition of taxation and the approval of the budget.[3] When French jurisdiction was extended to the hinterland the scope of the Council was still confined to the 'four *communes*', but this limitation was regarded with some local resentment, and in 1920 the demand for a representative body for the whole Colony was met by its transformation into a *Conseil Colonial* which included, in addition to the members elected by the French citizens, a total of 18 others elected by Chiefs from among their own number.

The power of the *Conseil Colonial* to vote the budget, which was in practice its most important function, was restricted by the standing distinction between obligatory and optional expenditure. It would appear that the Chiefs, as paid agents of the Government, tended to form an official opposition to the citizen members. In 1939 the Council was reorganized to include, in addition to the 26 members elected by citizens and 18 by Chiefs, a further 18 members who were non-citizens born in or descended from persons born in Senegal. These were elected by all non-citizens who fulfilled the same conditions.[4] This Council was suppressed under the Vichy régime in 1940.[5]

The Governor-General of French West Africa had the advice of a *Conseil de Gouvernement*, composed of the Lieutenant-Governors of the component Territories, the Commissioner for Togo, and seven other official members together with the Deputy for Senegal, the four members of the *Conseil Supérieur de la France d'Outre-Mer* (a metropolitan advisory body) elected by the French citizens in French West Africa, four non-citizens also elected from French West Africa, and four members elected by the Chambers of Commerce and the Municipal Council of Dakar. This body

---

[1] Figures for 1946 compiled from *Journal Officiel*, 1946–7, those for 1951 from *Les Élections Législatives de Juin 1951*, Paris, 1953. [2] See above, p. 338.

[3] A. Girault, *Principes de Colonisation et de Législation Coloniale*, vol. ii, 1927, p. 613.

[4] *Décret*, 8 April 1939.

[5] A. Villard, *Histoire du Sénégal*, Dakar, 1943, p. 180.

met annually and after hearing an exposition of policy from the Governor-General considered the general budget and those of the individual Territories.

In each of the component Territories of French West Africa, except Senegal, the Lieutenant-Governor was assisted by a *Conseil d'Administration*, which he was required to consult regarding the territorial budget and similar administrative matters. In Dahomey, Ivory Coast, French Sudan, and French Guinea, these bodies contained three official members, two French citizens elected by the Chambers of Agriculture and Commerce respectively, and three non-citizens elected by non-citizens, who had various special qualifications and included a number of senior Chiefs. This experiment in the creation of an African electorate afterwards formed the basis of the Electoral Law of 1946.[1] The *Conseil d'Administration* in Equatorial Africa had a somewhat similar composition,[2] but the *Conseils* in Niger and Mauretania included, besides official members, only unofficial members nominated by the Lieutenant-Governor. Bodies similar to that in French Equatorial Africa existed in the French Cameroons and Togo.[3]

The conference held at Brazzaville in 1944[4] declared itself in favour of the creation in all the African Territories of local Assemblies composed partly of Europeans and partly of Africans, elected so far as possible but, where election was difficult, representative of the traditional African *élite*.[5] The Constitution of 1946[6] provided for the creation in each Territory of elected Assemblies which have since 1952 been known as Territorial Assemblies, and for *Assemblées de Groupe* or *Grands Conseils* for the two groups of Territories, French West Africa and French Equatorial Africa. The Territorial Assemblies were brought into existence by a series of decrees of October 1946;[7] the *Assemblées de Groupe* or *Grands Conseils* were set up in 1947.[8] The membership and method of election of the Territorial Assemblies and the *Grands Conseils* have already been briefly described.[9] Except in Senegal, where the law established a single electoral roll, the Territorial Assemblies were each divided into a section elected by the *citoyens de statut français* who had acquired French citizenship on the conditions prescribed by earlier legislation,[10] and another section elected by those *citoyens de statut local* on whom the franchise had been conferred by the law of October 1946.

---

[1] See above, pp. 332–3. [2] *Décret*, 31 December 1937.
[3] *Décrets*, 6 March 1923, 13 April 1923, 3 November 1928, 23 November 1934.
[4] See above, p. 209.
[5] *La Conférence Africaine Française, Brazzaville, 30 Janvier–8 Février 1944*, Paris, 1945.
[6] Articles 77–78.
[7] J. Ravanel, 'Le Conseil d'État et les Assemblées des Territoires d'Outre-Mer', *Conseil d'État, Études et Documents*, no. 4, 1950, pp. 49–62.
[8] *Loi*, 29 August 1947. [9] See above, pp. 332–3. [10] See above, p. 338.

This arrangement was criticized as savouring of racial discrimination, and indeed as denying to the *citoyens de statut local* one of the civil liberties which the Constitution had guaranteed to them. It was nevertheless maintained by the law of February 1952, except in Togo, where the single electoral roll was then conceded; by this law, however, the total membership of the Territorial Assemblies and the proportion elected by the *citoyens de statut local* was generally increased, especially in the Territories where metropolitan interests were less important.[1] Pressure for the introduction of the single electoral roll elsewhere may, however, be expected to continue. In principle the *Cercle* in French West Africa (except Dakar), the *Région* in French Equatorial Africa and the Cameroons, and the *Subdivision* in Togo are the electoral *circonscriptions*, but for the elections by the *citoyens de statut français* several units may be combined, while for the elections by the *citoyens de statut local* an administrative area having more than 450,000 inhabitants may be divided.[2] In general the electoral arrangements are similar to those in metropolitan France. There is no provision for electoral symbols for the candidates or for similar devices sometimes employed in elections where many electors may be illiterate.[3]

Powers of Territorial Assemblies

The powers of an Assembly in Territories such as Togo and the Cameroons, which do not form part of the grouped Territories of French West or French Equatorial Africa, may conveniently be described first. They have powers of decision (*délibération*) on economic and fiscal matters, subject to the limitation that decisions on rates of tax, loans, and guarantees require the approval of the *Conseil d'État*; if, however, this is not given within 90 days of the notification of a decision to the Minister, the decision comes into effect as though approved. They must be consulted by the Administration on all proposed regulations concerning the disposal of public lands, labour conditions, or the execution of development programmes. They are entitled to pass resolutions (*vœux*) for submission to the Minister on matters of Territorial interest other than political questions.[4]

The territorial budget is prepared by the Administration. It alone has authority to propose expenditure in respect of the public services; on other matters the Assembly may also initiate proposals. Provision must be made for 'obligatory expenditure', as for example the service of public loans or any expenditure imposed by express legislative enactment. If any such expenditure is struck out by the Territorial Assembly the Ad-

---

[1] P. F. Gonidec, 'Les Assemblées Locales des territoires d'outre-mer', *Revue Juridique et Politique de l'Union Française*, vol. vi, 1952, p. 337.

[2] *Loi*, 6 February 1952, *Article* 3. For the detailed arrangements, see *Décrets*, 28 February 1952.

[3] Gonidec, op. cit. p. 354. [4] Ravanel, op. cit. p. 52.

ministration may provisionally make the necessary allocation in the budget and the amended votes are then included in it by a decree of the *Conseil d'État*. The Territorial Assemblies of Togo and the French Cameroons have somewhat larger powers than other Assemblies inasmuch as, under the respective Trusteeship Agreements, their consent is required if the administering authority wishes to create fiscal monopolies or to establish public enterprises which may involve a departure from the régime of equal economic treatment of the nationals of all member States of the United Nations.[1]

In the two 'groups of Territories', on the other hand, the powers of the Territorial Assemblies are inevitably somewhat more restricted. A number of fiscal regulations are reserved for decision by the *Grands Conseils* and it is these bodies, not the Territorial Assemblies, which must be consulted regarding the execution of development programmes or the organization of credit. Moreover, any matter otherwise within the competence of a Territorial Assembly which affects more than one of the component Territories thereby becomes the concern of the *Grands Conseils*. Finally, grants to the general budget of the group for which provision has been made by legislation are included in the obligatory expenditure which the Territorial budget must meet.

Territorial Assemblies and *Grands Conseils* normally meet twice a year in ordinary session, but extraordinary sessions may be held. Both Territorial Assemblies and *Grands Conseils* annually elect a Standing or Permanent Committee; the Permanent Committees of the *Grands Conseils* have one member for each component Territory; they meet once a month.[2] The Assemblies also appoint a number of specialist committees, as, for example, for dealing with financial questions, and much of their work is done in these committees.[3] It was natural that to much of the outside world the most striking result of the reforms of 1946 should seem to be the great extension of the representation of the Overseas Territories in the parliamentary institutions of metropolitan France. History is, however, likely to regard the establishment of the local Assemblies as a development which is potentially of far greater importance. It is here that will lie the test of the reality of the intention of the French to share with the people of the Overseas Territories the power which they have hitherto kept in their own hands.

It is this consideration which gives special importance to the 'framework'

[1] Trusteeship Agreement for the French Cameroons, Articles 4 and 9, U.N. Document T/8 1947. For the French Cameroons Assembly, see 'Les Débuts d'une Assemblée Locale d'Outre-Mer', *Conseil d'État: Études et Documents*, no. 3, 1949, pp. 123–8.

[2] The Permanent Committees are subject to the rules applicable to the *Commissions Départementales* in metropolitan France and the jurisprudence of the *Conseil d'État* restricts such delegation within narrow limits; see Ravanel, op. cit. p. 56.

[3] C. Corby, 'Le Grand Conseil de l'A.O.F.', *L'Afrique et l'Asie*, no. 22, 1953, p. 46.

law (*loi cadre*) passed by the French Parliament in June 1956, to which reference has been made in the preceding chapter.[1] If this is fully implemented it will create Territorial Assemblies which will have much the same powers in internal affairs as the Legislatures in the British Colonies. It also provides that the chief organs of policy, the Executive Councils, will be responsible to the Assemblies.[2] The Assemblies will be elected by universal suffrage on a single 'electoral college'. It has been claimed in France, and with some justice, that the enactment of this law may initiate a new phase in French Colonial policy.[3]

BELGIAN TERRITORIES

Belgian Congo

The present system of government in the Belgian Congo shows no marked change from the pattern which was laid down in the *Charte Coloniale* of 1908.[4] As has already been observed the form taken by these institutions was influenced by a desire to guard against the recurrence of administrative practices which appeared at one time likely to involve the intervention of neighbouring Powers in the affairs of the Congo Free State.[5] It is, however, opportune to refer here to some of the subsequent changes in the conditions of the Colony which have had a bearing on the operation of these institutions. It is not necessary to describe the many material changes which have occurred in the improvement of communications,[6] or in the development of industrial enterprise in the country.[7] They have had an important influence on the resources available for improvement of the social and economic services, but material progress is less calculated to exert a direct influence on constitutional development than an alteration in the relative strength of the European and African communities or in the character of indigenous society.

There has in the first place been a marked growth in the number of Europeans in the Colony. In 1908 they numbered only about 3,000, of whom 1,700 were Belgians.[8] An estimate made in 1952 put the total at over 76,000.[9] Only a small proportion of this population, however, amounting perhaps to not more than 10 per cent. of the whole, consists of *colons* of a landholding or similar class which can be regarded as

[1] See above, p. 216.
[2] For a debate on the transfer of power, see *Journal Officiel de l'Assemblée Nationale*, 9 April 1954, pp. 1908–38.
[3] *The Times*, 21 June 1956.
[4] *Codes et Lois du Congo Belge*, 1954, p. 9.
[5] See above, p. 217. See also R. L. Buell, op. cit. vol. ii, p. 473.
[6] See below, p. 1341.
[7] See below, p. 1298.
[8] F. Masoin, *Histoire de l'État Indépendant du Congo*, 1912–13, vol. i, p. 103.
[9] For the most recent census figures, see p. 143.

permanently settled in the country.[1] The Belgian conception of a *colon* is in the main that of a professional man or one who has a guaranteed employment of some kind; no immigration is countenanced of persons who are merely seeking employment or whose interest is that of 'settling' in the country in the sense that this term might be used in Rhodesia.[2] This fact has hitherto gone some way to assist the Government to avoid the creation of political institutions in the Belgian Congo which would involve the grant of a franchise to Europeans and by implication also to Africans.

As regards changes which have taken place in the position of the African population during the last half-century, there can be no question of the great improvement which has been made in its standard of living and in the provision of educational and health services for its benefit. There have in consequence been changes in its character which would be viewed with some astonishment by the members of the Legislature which enacted the *Charte Coloniale* of 1908. One striking result can be seen in the growth of urbanization. In 1938 the urban population was estimated at only 8·33 per cent. of the whole; in 1946 this was stated to be nearly 15 per cent., and in 1954 it stood at 21½ per cent., a figure which is roughly equivalent to 32 per cent. of the adult males. But there has been a change also in the character of the rural population. In earlier days the activity on which the rural people depended for satisfying their money needs was the practice of what is best summed up in the word, *la cueillette*,[3] or the collection of forestal or similar produce. That is no longer the case; there has been in this respect a noticeable alteration, owing partly to the growth in the cultivation of cash crops (as most notably cotton), and partly to the extension of the system of settlement usually known under the title of the *paysannat indigène*.[4] This has been accompanied by a considerable development of the system of African Co-operative Societies.[5]

Provisions of the Charte Coloniale

By the provisions of the *Charte Coloniale* the power of legislation for the Colony was delegated from Parliament to the King,[6] who exercises it by royal decree; Parliament, however, retains certain powers, particularly in connexion with financial matters and the grant of concessions. Both the budget estimates submitted by the Governor-General and the budgetary accounts of the Colony (which are audited in Brussels by the *Cour des Comptes*) must be approved by Parliament, and its authorization is also required for Colonial loans or for agreements with commercial companies

---

[1] G. Malengreau, 'Recent Developments in Belgian Africa', in *Africa Today*, 1955, p. 337. It has been stated elsewhere that only 1,200 are actually farmers; see H. D. Ziman in *Daily Telegraph*, 6 April 1954.　　　　　　　　　　　　　　　　　　　　　　　　[2] *The Times*, 3 July 1954.

[3] Sir A. Pim, *Colonial Agricultural Production*, 1946, pp. 128 ff.

[4] Malengreau, op. cit. p. 344. See below, p. 799.

[5] See below, p. 1480.　　　　　　　　　　　　　　　　　　　　[6] *Charte Coloniale, Article 5.*

which guarantee them a prescribed rate of interest on their capital investment. The grant of concessions is made by decree, but Article 15 of the *Charte* specifies certain types of large-scale concessions which must be laid on the tables of both Houses for a period of 30 days[2] before the grant can become effective.

If the Legislature has not passed the budget five days before the opening of the period to which it applies, it may be provisionally approved by *arrêté royal* for three months at a time, and in urgent cases supplementary expenditure may be sanctioned by *arrêté*, subject to the retrospective approval of Parliament. In addition to his function as adviser to the King on Colonial legislation, the Minister for the Colonies issues to the Governor-General instructions on the main lines of policy to be observed, and he is largely responsible for the appointment and dismissal of administrative officials. Appointments to the post of Governor-General, Vice-Governor-General, and certain superior officers are made by royal *arrêté* on the advice of the Minister; all other appointments of European personnel are made by *arrêté ministériel*.

The *Charte* created an advisory body to the Minister for the Colonies in the shape of the *Conseil Colonial*. The Council has 14 members; eight are nominated by the King, three elected by the Senate, and three by the *Chambre*. Neither the elected nor the nominated Councillors may be members of either House of Parliament or officials engaged in the service of the Administration or employees of any of the commercial concerns in the Belgian Congo in which the Colonial Government has direct financial interest. This body must be consulted on all decrees before their issue. It gives its opinion in the form of a reasoned report which must indicate the number of members who oppose the decree and their reasons; these reports are published along with the legislation to which they refer and are a valuable source of information on Colonial policy. The Minister has power to override the Council, but he must publish his reasons for doing so; it has been stated that in practice this power is never exercised.[1] In case of urgency, decrees may be issued by the Minister without consultation with the Council, but it is still necessary for them to be submitted to it for consideration and report. The Council has also the right to recommend legislative or administrative measures.

A number of expert commissions have been appointed either to investigate conditions on the spot or to advise on general lines of policy; the number is smaller than is the case in the British territories, though it has increased in recent years. Examples of the first type are the two Labour Commissions which visited the Colony in 1925 and 1931,[2] and the Mission of Inquiry into measures for the development of agricultural production

---

[1] M. Halewyck de Heusch, *Les institutions politiques et administratives des pays africains soumis à l'autorité de la Belgique*, Institut Colonial International, 1934, p. 12.   [2] See below, pp. 1391, 1413.

with which the Duke of Brabant (afterwards King Leopold III) was entrusted in 1933.[1] Examples of committees set up to deal with specific subjects are the Native Labour Committee which in 1928 drew up a scheme for the restriction of grants of concessions,[2] a Committee on the reform of the administrative system which reported in 1930, and a Commission on the status of Europeanized Africans set up in 1949. There are also permanent commissions concerned with hygiene, education, the administration of Africans in urban areas, and the conditions of transport.

An institution peculiar to the Belgian system is the Commission for the Protection of Natives. A body of this character was originally created under the Free State régime by a Royal Decree of 1896. It then consisted of six members nominated by the King from 'representatives of philanthropic and religious Associations', and was charged to indicate measures to be taken against the slave trade, the liquor traffic, or barbarous customs. But the original nominations were for only two years, and no provision was made for their renewal; the Commission therefore ceased to exist after having made some proposals, among other things, for the education of orphans and children abandoned by their parents.[3]

The organization of the present Commission was laid down in a Royal arrêté of 1925. Its constitution makes it independent of the Governor-General; its President is the Procurator-General of the Appeal Court at Leopoldville, and there are 18 members nominated by the King from residents in the Colony who are qualified to judge of Native interests. It is required to meet annually and to report on the measures which it recommends in the interests of Native welfare; its members are expressly empowered to report abuses or the illegal treatment of Africans. It actually met in the years 1911, 1913, 1919, 1923, 1928, 1931, 1947, 1951, and 1954.[4]

The Belgian Government has devoted more attention than some of the other European Powers to the publication of material on Colonial conditions. It issues the Annual Report on the Administration of the Belgian Congo submitted by the Governor-General, and also an Annual Report on economic conditions. A Colonial Congress was first organized in 1920; it was originally intended to meet every five years, but now meets annually. In 1929 a Royal Colonial Institute was founded with the object of encouraging the study of colonial questions; this became in 1955 the Royal Academy of Colonial Science, and its proceedings have become a valuable agency for the discussion of matters relating to the Colony.

A periodical, *Congo*, devoted partly to studies in social anthropology and partly to the discussion of administrative questions, was founded in

---

[1] *Rapport Annuel du Congo Belge, 1933*, p. 5.   [2] See below, p. 752.
[3] L. Guebels, *Aperçu rétrospectif des travaux de la Commission permanente pour la Protection des Indigènes*, 1949, pp. 7, 21.   [4] See below, p. 348.

1926 with a senior official of the Colonial Ministry as editor. Publication was suspended when Belgium entered the War in 1940, and in 1947 the paper was replaced by the journal *Zaïre*, which covers the same type of subjects, but is independent of the Government both editorially and financially. Both journals have on occasion carried articles critical of Government policy. The recent completion of the three volumes of the *Encyclopédie du Congo Belge* provides a source of authoritative information on all aspects of the economy and political organization of the Colony to which it is difficult to find a parallel elsewhere in Africa.

As has been indicated it was one of the objects of the *Charte Coloniale* to reproduce in the Colony the fundamental law of human rights which formed part of the Belgian Constitution, and to make it possible for the full force of public opinion to be brought to bear on colonial affairs. The provision that the budget of the Colony should be approved by Parliament, a measure found neither in Britain nor France, was directed to this purpose; but it is doubtful if it was the method best calculated to achieve it. It invariably involves great delays and it has frequently happened that the budget has not been discussed till half the financial year to which it refers has elapsed. In 1923 the two Chambers sought a remedy by enacting that the budget should be voted biennially instead of annually, and this procedure was followed in 1924 and 1926, but was then found impracticable, and the Act became a dead letter. It has been found in Great Britain that parliamentary interest in Colonial finances can best be met by making provision for a debate on the vote for the maintenance of the Colonial Office.

The provision made in the *Charte Coloniale* for the establishment of the *Conseil Colonial* has proved a more effective measure. It may be true, as its critics have contended, that the sphere of work of the Council is limited since it deals only with legislative proposals, not with executive proceedings, and that where it has been critical it has dealt with the details rather than with the principles of decrees placed before it. Even so, however, it has certainly succeeded in bringing an informed and to a large extent independent opinion to bear on Colonial policy. The Commission for the Protection of Natives has had a career of somewhat sporadic activity. It owed its origin largely to the suggestion of Roman Catholic missionaries, and has at times ventilated matters in which the Church was much interested; its opportunity for useful work must, however, vary with the need for pressing that due considerations should be given to African interests, and the Administration has not of late years shown itself at all deficient in this respect. The Commission has today a function of relatively minor importance.

Despite the existence of these formal institutions for the discussion of policy, affairs in the Belgian Congo rarely occupy the attention of political elements in Belgium to the same extent as in the periods immediately preceding or following the annexation of the Colony. The dominant influence in Colonial affairs is that of a small group of officials and businessmen. From time to time specific projects of legislation may be inspired from outside this circle, as for example the project for granting individual titles to land in African occupation.[1] But the intervention in Colonial affairs of persons representing political ideologies is discountenanced and it is in practice kept within narrow limits. Committees of inquiry, for example, are usually composed of experts and do not normally include politicians.

It is, however, possible that this situation may change when the Belgians who have come to the Colony in recent years have organized a more systematic measure of political support for their interests. Their demands have begun to include a claim for increased governmental assistance as well as for an effective voice in a form of Colonial government endowed with a much greater measure of autonomy than is now the case.[2] Their interests are at present represented by a Colonization Consultative Committee established in Brussels,[3] but this so far exercises only a limited influence.

Functions of Governors-General and Governors

Whatever the exact nature of the constitutional procedure provided, it is clear that the Ministry has a predominant voice in regulating Colonial policy. The extent to which this can be said to be initiated locally or to be controlled in detail from Brussels would appear to depend largely on the personality of the Minister and of the Governor-General at any given time. An *arrêté royal* of July 1947, which reorganized the Administration of the Belgian Congo, maintained the provision of 1922 that the Governor-General must be consulted on all decrees before they are submitted to the Colonial Council; in practice they are also normally circulated for comments to the *Gouverneurs de Province*.

The right of the Governor-General himself to exercise legislative powers is, however, limited by the terms of the *Charte* to cases of emergency. In such cases he may suspend the application of decrees in force or may introduce new legislation by *ordonnance-loi*; but in either case his legislative actions cease to be valid if they are not confirmed by decree within six months. In the early days of the Colony the heads of the different Provinces (then known as Vice-Governors-General) were authorized to make an *ordonnance-loi* on the same conditions as the Governor-General, but when in 1933 the Vice-Governors-General were replaced by Provincial

[1] See below, p. 799.
[2] G. Malengreau, 'Recent Developments in Belgian Africa', in *Africa Today*, 1955, p. 341.
[3] *West Africa*, 6 November 1954, p. 1038.

Commissioners (now known as Governors of Provinces), the latter were not given the same powers. Certain executive actions of the local Administration also require the sanction of a decree, in particular the grant of land concessions and the annual programme of recruitment for the militia (*force publique*).

Under the administrative reorganization of 1947 there was created the post of Vice-Governor-General, who has no specific administrative functions, but collaborates with the Governor-General and replaces him in his absence. The services at the Governor-General's headquarters comprise seven *Directeurs Généraux*, who are responsible to him for the general policy of the various technical Departments. The Central Service of Inspection, formerly part of the headquarters establishment of the Colony, has been abolished, and the Provincial Governors, each with his own staff, are now responsible for the control of the technical Services in each Province. Members of the Land, Agriculture, Public Works, and Veterinary Services are allocated as itinerant Advisers to the *Commissaires de district*, and this measure represents a certain degree of decentralization, since the *Directeurs Généraux* previously had their headquarters in the Ministry of the Colonies.

In 1914 Councils were attached to the posts of Governor-General and to those of the then Vice-Governors-General, but their functions were strictly advisory, and the inclusion in them of unofficial members was left to the discretion of the Governor-General and Provincial authorities. The metropolitan Colonial Council expressed in 1945 the opinion that they were not sufficiently representative,[1] and in 1947 they were reorganized so as to increase the unofficial element, but their function remained advisory. The *Conseil de Gouvernement* at Leopoldville now consists of the Governor-General and Vice-Governor-General, the Secretary-General, the Procurator-General, the six Provincial Governors, the Commander-in-Chief of the *force publique*; up to six unofficial *notables* nominated by the Governor-General at his discretion; 16 persons representing various groups, such as Chambers of Commerce or Settlers' or Employers' Associations, and chosen from names put forward by them; and eight persons representing African interests. Since 1951 all eight of these persons have been Africans. There is a Standing Committee (*Députation Permanente*) of the Council which as a rule holds quarterly sessions.

There are now six fully constituted Provinces, each under the charge of a Governor: Leopoldville, with its headquarters at Leopoldville; Kivu (with headquarters at Bukavu, formerly Costermansville); Kasai (Luluabourg); Equator (Coquilhatville); Katanga (Elisabethville); and Eastern (Stanleyville). The Governor of the Province now has the assistance of a *Commissaire provincial* who officiates for him in his absence or in case of

[1] Report quoted in *Codes et Lois du Congo Belge*, 1954, p. 490.

illness, and also a *Secrétaire provincial* who has administrative charge of the provincial establishments.[1] The Provincial Services now include the Provincial Secretariat and Provincial Departments of Justice, Native Affairs, Labour, Education, Finance, Economics, Land, Agriculture and Animal Husbandry, Public Works, Posts and Telegraphs, and Health.

The Conseils de Province include the *Gouverneur* as President, the *Commissaire provincial*, the *Secrétaire provincial*, the *Procureur du Roi*, the *Commissaires de District*, the *Commandant* of the local forces, four unofficial *notables* chosen by the Governor, twelve persons representing the groups mentioned above, and six members representing African interests. Like the *Conseil de Gouvernement*, these Councils have as yet only advisory functions. The Provinces are divided into Districts (of which there are now 20 in all), each under a *Commissaire de District*, and the Districts into *Territoires* of which there are now a total of 128; the cities form separate *Territoires*.[2]

The scale on which the establishments in the provinces are now organized would seem to point to a policy involving a progressive devolution of executive authority on their Administrations. To this extent they seem to be following the same course as the 'Provinces' of British India, which achieved in the course of time the status of Governments with an increasing measure of autonomy in their domestic affairs, leaving a defined range of subjects (such as defence, external relations, customs and excise, and railways) as the exclusive sphere for the Central Government. But it still remains to be seen how far the Belgian Government is likely to follow the same course in regard to the devolution of legislative authority on the Provinces. It will not, indeed, be possible to anticipate the course of events in this direction until there is evidence of an intention to delegate legislative authority to a representative legislature at Leopoldville.

Ruanda Urundi

The Trust Territory of Ruanda Urundi is in large measure administered on the same principle as the Belgian Congo. It will be recalled that the Mandate for South-West Africa as accepted by the Union of South Africa provided that the Mandated Territory should be administered as an integral part of the Union.[3] In the case of Ruanda Urundi the terms of the Mandate left it open for the Mandatory Administration to constitute the Territory into 'a customs, fiscal or administrative union or federation with the adjacent territory'. The Belgian Government accordingly enacted in 1925 a law which provided that the Territory should be united for the purpose of administration with the Belgian Congo, of which it should constitute a Vice-Governor-General's Province; but it also

---

[1] *Enc. C.B.*, vol. iii, p. 531.
[2] See below, p. 557.   [3] See above, p. 170.

provided that its Government should have a separate *personalité juridique* and a separate budget.[1] The position 'was explained to the Permanent Mandates Commission, and was accepted as being within the terms of the Mandate.[2] Belgium accepted the charge of Ruanda Urundi as a Trust Territory under the organization of the United Nations in 1946, this being confirmed by legislation passed in 1949.[3]

The constitutional effect of these provisions is that the Vice-Governor-General has the same limited power of legislation in local matters as is exercised by the Governor-General for the Belgian Congo. An advisory *Conseil de Vice-Gouvernement Général* was created in 1947.[4] Its composition resembles that of the provincial *conseils* in the Belgian Congo and includes three persons representing the interests of Africans. The Territory retains its separate identity as provided by the provisions in the law of 1925 regarding finance and legislation. Measures applied to the Belgian Congo do not become operative in the Trust Territory unless specially applied thereto by the Vice-Governor-General.

The estimates for Ruanda Urundi are compiled separately from those of the Colony and no transfers may be made between the funds of the Territory and those of the Colony. The Vice-Governor-General is not a member of the *Conseil de Gouvernement* at Leopoldville. His headquarters are at Usumbura. The Territory is divided for administrative purposes into two 'Residencies' and 17 *Territoires*. The term 'Residency' is a relic of the German occupation, when a Resident was appointed to each of the two 'Sultans', the Mwami of Urundi and the Mwami of Ruanda.[5]

It is clear that for the time being the most insistent problem of Ruanda Urundi is not that of political or constitutional development so much as that of over-population, for which no effective solution is yet forthcoming.[6] The large annual migration of labour to Uganda is hardly even a partial remedy.[7] The Mission of the Trusteeship Council which visited Ruanda Urundi in 1954 made a recommendation, similar to that contained in its Report on Tanganyika Territory,[8] which indicated its view that the Trust Territory should be guaranteed self-government within a fixed period not exceeding 20 years. As in the case of Tanganyika the chairman of the Mission dissented from the view expressed by his colleagues; and also as in that case the recommendation was vigorously opposed by the representative of the Belgian Government with the United

[1] *Lois*, 20 October 1924, 21 August 1925. *Arrêté Royal*, 11 January 1926.
[2] R. L. Buell, op. cit. vol. ii, pp. 462–3.
[3] *Arrêtés*, 4 March 1947 and 11 April 1949.
[4] *Arrêtés Royaux*, 4 March 1947 and 11 April 1949.
[5] See chart in *Rapport Annuel, Ruanda-Urundi, 1952*, p. 16. See below, p. 558.
[6] P. Gourou, *La Densité de la Population au Ruanda-Urundi*, 1953. *Africa*, July 1954, p. 276. *The Times*, 28 November 1955. See also above, p. 135.
[7] See below, p. 1383.   [8] See above, p. 304.

Nations organization. The opposition was the more emphatic because the recommendation seemed to carry an implication that if Ruanda Urundi was approaching the stage when it could be granted self-government, then the Belgian Congo, admittedly much more advanced in its social and educational standards, must be even more ready for this measure. The recommendation made by the Mission was not, however, supported by the Assembly of the United Nations.

PORTUGUESE TERRITORIES

Importance of Executive

It is characteristic of the Constitution of the Corporative State of Portugal that it assigns a much higher range of authority to the executive than to the legislative institutions of the government.[1] As applied to colonial affairs the effect of this principle is to be seen in three directions. In the first place, policy is not determined to the same extent as in Great Britain, France, or Belgium by the views expressed by different political parties in the Legislature, and though in those countries the criticism expressed regarding colonial policy may sometimes be only the reflection of differences existing in the field of domestic policy, there are also occasions when it represents the result of an informed and constructive interest in colonial affairs. The Corporative State must inevitably lack some of the benefit of such expressions of view.

In the second place, the operation of the corporative principle ensures that the economic life of the overseas Provinces, like that of metropolitan Portugal, should be closely integrated through legally constituted bodies which act under the guidance and supervision of the Government. Thus the Executive Government will be found to play an active part in the life of both Mozambique and Angola, acting through various bodies such as the Import, Export, Cotton and Rice Boards, the Exchange Council, and similar organizations. Under the National Labour statutes employers and employees are encouraged to establish collective bodies, that of the employers being designated as a 'guild' and that of the employees as a 'syndicate'. There are, for example, two 'guilds' in Mozambique and five 'syndicates'; the latter are described as 'working under the guidance of the Government'.[2]

In the third place, the dominance of the executive side of the Government in the Corporative State is seen conspicuously in the actual organization of colonial administration. The range of legislation specifically reserved for the National Assembly is relatively limited; it embraces only the modification of Colonial Constitutions, the conclusion of Agreements

---

[1] See above, p. 230.
[2] *Overseas Economic Survey; Portuguese East Africa (Mozambique)*, 1952, p. 44.

with foreign Powers, the authorization of loans requiring a special guarantee, and the delimitation of the respective powers of the metropolitan and the different overseas Governments in regard to the grant of concessions.[1] The Minister has therefore a considerable field of legislation by decree, in addition to the wide range of executive powers which experience shows to be the normal corollary of a policy of centralization in administrative affairs.

In the exercise of these powers the Ministry of Overseas Provinces[2] has the advice of two consultative bodies, the Council of Empire (now designated as the Council of Overseas Provinces) and the Conference of Overseas Governors.[3] The Council of Overseas Provinces consists of members nominated by the Minister, co-opted members (who must not exceed half the number of nominated members), and all Colonial Governors who may be in Lisbon, together with certain acting or retired officials who are appointed as experts.[4] The Council is at the same time the final administrative and judicial Tribunal for the Overseas Provinces. The Governors' Conference is normally held in Lisbon every three years; delegations of officials or colonists nominated by the Governors may take part in it.

In principle, the Minister must consult the Council of Overseas Provinces or the Conference of Governors on all projects of legislation, except in cases of urgency; both bodies may make recommendations to him, but only on matters put before them by him. The Ministry also has the advice of a number of Conferences or Standing Committees which deal with different aspects of the economic interests of the Overseas Provinces.

The executive control of the Minister over the conduct of affairs in the Provinces is assured through the maintenance of a body of Inspectors, who (like those serving the French Overseas Ministry)[5] have no administrative functions, but report to the local Administration and to the metropolitan Ministry.[6] The Provinces of Mozambique and Angola are in charge of Governors-General, who are appointed by the Council of Ministers; Sao Tomé and Principe are in charge of a Governor. Both classes hold office for four years. Subject to the general control of the Minister of Overseas Provinces, the Governors-General have in principle the power to legislate by decree on any matter not falling within the field of legislation by the National Assembly or the Ministry, but in practice only a limited use has been made of this authority.

[1] A. J. Peaslee, *Constitutions of Nations*, vol. iii, 1950, p. 29.

[2] The organization of the Ministry was laid down by the *Lei* of 7 January 1936.

[3] *Lei* 2066, 27 June 1953, in *Nova Legislação Ultramarina*, 1953, p. 20.

[4] J. de Penha-Garcia, *Organisation politique et administrative de l'empire colonial portugais*, Institut Colonial International, 1936, pp. 261–3. The Council was instituted under *Lei*, no. 26,180, 7 January 1936.   [5] See above, pp. 330–1.

[6] The Law of Overseas Administrative Reform, 1933, Article 22.

The Governors-General and Governors have since 1926 had Councils of Government, which have hitherto had only a consultative capacity. In Angola and Mozambique these consultative bodies have consisted of five officials (of whom three were *ex officio*) and five nominated unofficials chosen from Portuguese citizens resident for more than three years in the Province.[1] Four of the members (of whom two are *ex officio*) constitute a Permanent Section of the Council whose approval the Governor-General has been obliged to obtain on a certain number of specialized matters.

The executive authority of the Governors-General is in practice much wider than the legislative, though, since the inauguration of the revised régime of 1928 and the following years, it has been closely restricted in all financial matters. The range of executive authority is widest in all matters relating to Native Affairs. The Colonial Act lays down certain general principles regarding Native policy, to which reference will be made in a subsequent chapter,[2] but it has been the Governor-General or Governor who has been specifically charged to implement these provisions and to protect Native interests.[3]

Recent Legislative Changes

Some of the institutions described above must now be regarded as in a state of transition owing to the change of policy during recent years.[4] Effect was given in the autumn of 1955 to the new Organic Law of the Overseas Provinces[5] which provided for the constitution of Legislative Councils in Angola and Mozambique. Guinea and Sao Tomé will not for the present have Legislative Councils. In Angola the Council will have 18 elected and eight nominated members, while the figures for Mozambique are 16 and eight. The nominated members in Angola consist of six officials and two members chosen to represent the interests of the African population. The elected members are: one each from Portuguese citizens, trade corporations, and workmen's corporations; two each from (1) moral and cultural organizations, (2) public administration; and eleven by direct vote from the electoral districts of Angola. The same applies to Mozambique, except that there are only nine electoral districts sending one member each. The functions of the Legislative Councils are confined to the expression of opinion on legislative decrees and on such subjects as the Minister and the Governor-General may submit to them. Measures which will increase expenditure are expressly excluded.

The Council of Government will include an elected member from each

---

[1] A. J. A. Cardoso, *Angola, Your Neighbour*, 1950, p. 58.   [2] See below, p. 562.
[3] Article 36 of Colonial Act.   [4] See above, p. 229.
[5] No. 2066 of 27 January 1953 in *Nova Legislação Ultramarina*, Lisbon, 1953, Articles 24–30.

of the Districts of the Province, together with the head of each District and the Military Commander. The Council will remain a consultative body, but the Governor-General must inform the Ministry when he refuses to accept its advice on any matter on which he is bound to consult it. Some change is also contemplated in the staff of the major Provinces. There will be two Provincial Secretaries, of whom the General Secretary will have the rank of a Superior Inspector of Overseas Administration; the Governor-General will be able to delegate to him the general control of administrative work.

Recent Administrative Changes

In dealing with the present organization of local Administration it should be noted that considerable changes have taken place in Mozambique since the termination of the Charter held by two undertakings, the Moçambique and Niassa Companies, which at one time exercised powers of administration within the areas held by them. Their position resembled in some respects that of the Chartered Companies in the British system. The Niassa Company administered a large area to the extreme north of the Colony, but in 1929 its concession was ended and the area shortly afterwards incorporated in the general Administration of the Colony. The *Companhia do Moçambique*, which held the present district of Manica and Sofala, was in large measure independent of the Government of the Colony; it had a Governor, resident at Beira, and maintained 15 departments of its own. The Government retained in its own hands only the administration of justice, defence, and foreign policy. The 50 years' concession of the Company expired in 1941 and it was wound up in 1942. Both companies exercised at one time the right of imposing taxation.[1] Other companies, such as the *Companhia da Zambezia* or the *Companhia Colonial do Buzi*, had rights in large areas (including the exercise of rights over land) under what was known as the *prazo* system,[2] but they did not have the same rights of administration.

Under the system established in 1946[3] Mozambique is divided into four districts, Manica-Sofala (which comprises the *intendências* of Beira and Tete), Sul do Save (which comprises the *intendências* of Gaza and Inhambane), Zambezia (consisting of the *intendência* of Quelimane), and Niassa (comprising the *intendências* of Nampula, Lago, and Cape Delgado). Angola is divided by the same decree into five districts with 16 *intendências*.[4] The different administrative grades are described as those of *Administrador* (of whom there are three grades), *Secretário*, *Chefe do Posto*, and *Aspirante*. The primary unit of administration is the *Circunscrição*, each of which is in charge of an officer of the rank of *Administrador*. Each *Administrador* has a

---

[1] L. Mair, *Native Policies in Africa*, 1936, p. 250.   [2] Ibid. p. 252.
[3] Decree, 4 July 1946.   [4] *Statesman's Year-Book*, 1954, p. 1337.

Secretário under him. The *Circunscrição* is divided into a number of *postos* which may vary from two to six; each *posto* is in charge of a *Chefe do posto*. The work of the *Administradors* is co-ordinated by an officer holding the title of *Intendente*, usually in the senior grade of *Administrador*.

The Administrative service is thus more numerous than would be the case in British or other territories. As will be further explained,[1] the upper ranks of the service are recruited mainly from cadets of the *Instituto Superior de Estudos Ultramarinos* at Lisbon; the cadet may be either a Portuguese national or an *assimilado* from one of the overseas provinces. The lower ranks, up to the grade of *Administrador*, are normally recruited locally and are not liable to transfer from one overseas area to another. There will be found in a subsequent chapter a reference to the system of administration as applied to Native Affairs.[2]

LIBERIA

As will be clear from what has been said in the preceding chapter[3] the Constitution of Liberia, closely based on the pattern of that of the United States of America, gives to the President and to the Executive a position which is independent of the Legislature, save for the need of obtaining its sanction for legislative enactments or for the provision of finance. The authority conferred by this position is enhanced by the fact that the Legislature has for nearly 80 years been the stronghold of one party (the True Whig Party) which has also been largely instrumental in the election of successive Presidents.[4] Every member of the Legislature belongs in principle to this Party, and it has been stated that all officials of the civil service pay a month's salary into its Party funds. Any opposition remains therefore an affair of cliques rather than of party organization.[5]

The President is elected for a term of eight years, and in 1949 an amendment to the Constitution provided that he might be re-elected for an additional four years. The Cabinet is nominated by him, subject to confirmation by the Senate; the Judges are appointed by him. The Upper Chamber, the Senate, is a small body of ten members, two from each of the five 'Counties' into which the coastal area is divided. The lower Chamber, the House of Representatives, has 31 members, 12 of whom have from an early date been elected by the five Counties of the coastal area;[6] since 1945 the inhabitants of the interior have also provided three representative members. The interior or hinterland is divided into three Provinces, Western, Central, and Eastern.

[1] See below, p. 378.   [2] See below, p. 563.
[3] See above, p. 235.   [4] Peaslee, op. cit. vol. ii, p. 362.
[5] T. Hodgkin, 'Education and Social Change in Liberia', *West Africa*, 12, 19, 26 September and 3, 10 October 1953.
[6] The coastal area also includes the Territory of Marshall, represented in the House of Representatives but not in the Senate.

For administrative purposes the coastal Counties are in charge of Superintendents; each of the hinterland Provinces is in charge of a Provincial Commissioner, and they are divided into eight Districts in charge of District Commissioners. These officials, who are appointed by the President, are normally Americo-Liberian, but, as already indicated, the members of the original 'founding families' have now been so much mixed with members of the indigenous tribes that the name Americo-Liberian is ceasing to be so distinctive as at an earlier stage of Liberian history.[1]

It is clear, indeed, that members of these tribes are gradually being admitted to a place in the political and social life of Liberia. At present their representation in the Legislature is small, but a member of the Grebo tribe has been a Judge of the Supreme Court, and another has been Secretary for War; a member of the Vai tribe has also held ministerial rank. With the growth of the number of schools in the hinterland[2] and the increased opportunities for employment provided by the recent expansion of industrial undertakings,[3] it may be expected that this process will be accelerated. But it is not easy to foresee the relations which are likely to be established in the future between the ruling oligarchy and the indigenous tribes. While on the one hand educated members of the tribes are being progressively admitted to a share in the political institutions of the country, this fact in itself tends to deprive the tribes of their natural leaders, and to that extent serves to maintain the differences between them and the privileged class now holding a dominant position in the politics of the country.

In the administration of the hinterland a wide use is made of the Chiefs, who are in theory elected, but it has been observed that 'in practice the Chiefs appear to reflect the balance of political forces in the country'. In those parts where the Government's authority is strongest, the Chiefs are in fact Government nominees; in the more remote parts there flourish strong tribal Chiefs whom the Government finds it wise to confirm in their position. In the administrative control of the indigenous areas there seems to be in practice no rigid line drawn between the indigenous tribesman and the Americo-Liberian. All cases involving 'civilized men' (that is, those who can read and write English) are held to be within the jurisdiction of the District Commissioner, while others are dealt with by Paramount Chiefs or Clan Chiefs, each having jurisdiction within their own area up to a fixed financial limit.

Any indigenous tribesman who becomes 'civilized' or is able to take up residence in the towns may vote or may hold public office.[4] In view of the charges which were in the past brought against the Government of

---

[1] See above, pp. 235-9.   [2] Hodgkin, op. cit.
[3] See above, pp. 237-8.   [4] F. J. Pedler, *West Africa*, 1951, p. 129.

Liberia,[1] and which were supported by evidence not only of incapacity but of abuse of power, it is not unnatural to regard with suspicion some of the statements now put forward by its friends as to the standards of administration which have been achieved in recent years. But it is at all events clear that a considerable change has been effected, both in the matter of material improvements (such as road communications or the provision of buildings) and in the expansion of the services of health and education. Progress in these respects is bound to be followed by changes both in political structure and administrative organization.

THE ADMINISTRATIVE SERVICES

Important as is the position of the technical and departmental services of the Governments in Africa, it is convenient for the present purpose to confine attention to the Administrative Services, since it is in their composition and character that the most significant indication is to be found of the tendencies of Government policy. It is in a change in the nature of their functions that one observes the first reaction to any constitutional development affecting the relations of the African population and the Government, more especially in those areas which are approaching the status of self-government. It is significant, for instance, that in the semi-Responsible Government of the Gold Coast, the District Officer of the future is to be designated as 'Government Agent'.

So far as the mass of the population is concerned, the reality of constitutional advance towards self-rule is judged not so much by an alteration in the composition of a Legislature as by evidence that the indigenous people are being admitted to posts of executive responsibility. That observation is equally relevant to those types of Colonial Government in which the objective of policy does not envisage self-rule but the political integration of the dependency with the metropolitan Power. The dispatch of representatives to a metropolitan Parliament may appeal strongly to the *élite* or to the limited class of the *évolués* in a Colony, but for the great mass of people the reality of the objective only begins to be appreciated when they see a substantial representation of their own community in posts of administrative or executive responsibility.

Union of South Africa

The Civil Service of the Union is divided under the Public Service Act no. 27 of 1923 into a General Division (which includes the lower-paid clerical grades and artisans, nurses, and the like), a Clerical Division, and an Administrative Division. The personnel of the Administrative Division is

---

[1] See above, p. 236.

largely recruited from the Clerical Division. The minimum qualification for entry to the Clerical Division is the matriculation examination or its equivalent,[1] but it is stated to be the normal practice to appoint only graduates or first-class matriculants. An examination, designed to test general knowledge, accuracy, and ability to use the two official languages, was introduced in 1935,[2] but appointment was not made dependent on the order in which the candidates were placed. Though the improvement of standards of instruction during recent years has resulted in securing for the public services a larger proportion of educated personnel, they have not on the whole been as successful as those of Great Britain in attracting candidates possessing superior educational qualifications, nor do they occupy the same standing in the life of the country.

Appointments to the public services are made through the Public Service Commission for which provision was made, as has already been shown,[3] in the South Africa Act of 1909. The wide range of powers over personnel conferred on the Commission was designed in the first instance to secure impartiality in balancing the claims of the Afrikaner and English communities to appointment or promotion. It has been the practice to appoint both Afrikaans-speaking and English-speaking members of the Commission, and the question as to which side has two members has now become of some importance. At present there are two Afrikaans-speaking members. Under the Act of 1923 recommendations on appointments and promotion which were concurred in by a majority of the Commission could not be disregarded without the sanction of the Governor-General, but instances occurred in which he himself had rejected such recommendations on the advice of a Minister, sometimes in connexion with posts of major importance, and it was also alleged at one period that Ministers often failed to act on the Commission's advice.

An amending Act of 1936 provided that the recommendations of the Commission should come into force automatically unless overruled by the Governor-General within six months.[4] In other respects, however, this Act tended to reduce the scope of the Commission's authority. It had previously been responsible for the investigation of charges of serious misconduct, while cases of misconduct not regarded as serious were to be investigated by an official appointed by the Minister. Since 1936 the latter procedure has applied to all charges, though there is an appeal from the investigating officer to the Commission. Its decision is final.

In the Native Affairs Department,[5] officers are appointed as Native Commissioners in Districts where the population is wholly African and also in those where it is mixed but nevertheless includes a large number

---

[1] Act 36 of 1936.
[2] Government Notice 935 of 1934.
[3] See above, p. 267.
[4] *House of Assembly Debates*, vol. xxvi, 1936, p. 360.
[5] See below, p. 431.

of Africans. In mixed districts where Europeans predominate the Magistrate, who is an officer of the Department of Justice, is appointed also as Native Commissioner and may also be given an officer of the Native Affairs Department as his Assistant. Although some of the Universities offer courses in Native law and administration and also in Bantu studies,[1] the Government does not prescribe special qualifications for entry into the Native Affairs Department, nor does it organize special courses of training.

The Lansdown Commission on Penal Reform, which reported in 1947, commented on the inadequate knowledge of African languages often possessed by both Magistrates and Native Commissioners exercising magisterial functions, and suggested that special allowances for competence in African languages should be granted to judicial officials.[2] The respective numbers of European and non-European employees in the Government service has already been given earlier in this chapter,[3] but, as has been remarked, the employment of non-Europeans is in practice confined to the subordinate grades of service. Some provision is, however, now being made for the employment of non-European graduates in the Native Affairs Department.[4]

Federation of Rhodesia and Nyasaland

The creation of the Federation of Rhodesia and Nyasaland involved the establishment of a Federal public service, which necessarily consisted at the outset of officers already in the services of the three component Territories. About half the posts occupied by Europeans, and about one-third of all posts, were transferred from Territorial services to the Federal service.[5] The terms of service of the European staff in Northern Rhodesia and Nyasaland are those of the United Kingdom Overseas Services, and differ from those offered in Southern Rhodesia, particularly in regard to such matters as free medical attention, housing, and passages when going on overseas leave. The scales for the Federal service were so arranged as to compensate officers transferring to it from the United Kingdom Service;[6] at the end of five years they will be given the option of choosing between the Federal and the Territorial services.

The Federal Constitution provides that, until the subject is regulated by Federal legislation, authority over the public service is vested in the Governor-General, with the advice of an Interim Public Service Commission. It includes a provision that no British subject or British Protected

[1] See below, p. 1140.
[2] *Report of Penal and Prison Reform Commission,* U.G. 47, 1947, para. 293.
[3] See above, p. 267.
[4] *Handbook on Race Relations in South Africa,* 1949, pp. 33, 123.
[5] *Report of the Civil Service Preparatory Commission,* Cmd. 8673, p. 3.
[6] *Federation of Rhodesia and Nyasaland, Basic Conditions of Service for Europeans in the Federal Public Service,* 1954.

Person shall be ineligible for Government employment on the grounds of race alone.[1]

In Southern Rhodesia the organization of the Civil Service is defined by the Public Services Act[2] which is based on Act 29 of 1931. It has four divisions: administrative and clerical; professional and technical; schools; and general. Preference in recruitment is given to applicants from the Territory, the minimum educational qualification being a four-year secondary course approved by the Public Services Board. Before appointment to the permanent staff candidates must, if not graduates, have passed a prescribed examination; for officers of the Native Affairs Department this is an examination in Native languages and customs. A Commission of Inquiry on the Public Services which reported in 1945 recommended the provision of systematic training courses within the Service, the establishment of specialist courses such as those given for the United Kingdom Oversea Administrative Service, and the exchange of officers with the services of other Commonwealth territories.[3]

A Public Service Board was constituted in 1927,[4] the field within which it was entitled to make recommendations being the same as that of the Public Service Commission in South Africa, but its functions were advisory only. A Commission which reported in 1938 suggested various measures to improve its status, and proposed also that the Public Service Act should be so amended as to give the recommendations of the Board the same authority as those of the South African Public Service Commission.[5] Although this was not done, it became the normal practice to follow the Board's recommendations. In 1943, however, the rejection by a Minister of a recommendation for promotion made by the Board caused a crisis in the Public Service, and the measure which had been recommended in 1938 was then introduced by Act 18 of 1944. In 1946 the standing of the Board was further improved by the provision that all three of its members should hold full-time appointments.

The Native Affairs Department occupies a special position in that it has been regulated by the Constitution of the Colony. This provided that no officer of the Department should be removed from office without the approval of the Governor in Council, and that the Chief Native Commissioner should not be removed from office without the approval of the Secretary of State.[6] In the procedure now in force Native Commissioners are appointed to predominantly African districts, where they exercise

---

[1] *Federation of Rhodesia and Nyasaland (Constitution) Order in Council*, S.I. 1199, 1953, sections 6 and 40.   [2] Chapter 68 of Laws of Southern Rhodesia.

[3] *Report of the Public Services Inquiry Commission* (the Plewman Commission), 1945, para. 195.

[4] For its history and constitution, see *O.Y.S.R.*, *1952*, pp. 71, 80.

[5] *Report of the Commission of Enquiry into Promotions in the Civil Service*, C.S.R. 2, 1939, pp. 8–9.

[6] Constitution of Southern Rhodesia, section 39, as amended by Letters Patent of 25 March 1937.

judicial functions in respect of Africans and are sometimes also appointed as Assistant Magistrates. In the European areas Magistrates, who are officers of the Department of Justice, are also styled Civil Commissioners, and have certain administrative duties by virtue of that office.

This duality has been the subject of comment by various commissions. An officer of the United Kingdom Treasury who investigated the Public Service in 1935 observed that the amalgamation of the two Departments would both effect economies and would broaden the outlook of the officials in each.[1] The Commission of 1945 above referred to recommended the creation of a combined Department of Justice and Native Administration which should be responsible for all forms of district administration. This change might, however, have required an amendment of the Constitution, and a further obstacle has now been created by the fact that under the Federal Constitution Justice is a federal and Native Affairs a territorial subject.

It would seem that Southern Rhodesia has met with difficulty in securing candidates of the necessary qualifications for the Public Services. Between 1937 and 1944 only 13 graduates entered them; the Administrative Division, which has an establishment of 779 male posts, had 157 vacancies at the end of 1954. The Public Services Board has recommended that more funds should be provided for recruitment overseas, in order to remedy the existing unsatisfactory staff position.[2] Though, however, Southern Rhodesia cannot claim that its Administrative cadre has the same academic qualifications as the members of the British Colonial Service or that it has had any special training for the work on which it is employed, the Government is justified in holding that its officers have one advantage over the members of the British Service in that they have a far greater continuity in the tenure of district posts, and are consequently able to acquire a greater acquaintance with local conditions and personalities.

British Colonial Services

The British Colonial system differs in one material feature from the practice followed by most other Colonial Powers; the personnel of the administrative section in the Colonial Office is drawn from a different source than that which discharges administrative duties overseas. The establishment of the Colonial Office is part of the general body of the Home Civil Service, which is recruited for service in the various Departments of the Central Government. As part of the Home Civil Service, it is in principle liable to transfer between the various Departments of the Central Government, but is not liable to transfer to service in the Colonies.

[1] *Report of the Commissioner appointed to enquire into the Administrative system and methods of the Government of Southern Rhodesia*, C.S.R.I., 1936, paras. 41–43.
[2] *Report of Public Services Board of Southern Rhodesia*, 1954.

As a body, therefore, the administrative personnel of the Colonial Office has in the past been without direct experience of Colonial conditions or administration. The deficiencies of this system have, however, been recognized, and of late years a practice has grown up under which personnel appointed to the Colonial Office have accepted a liability to serve overseas in a junior capacity for two or three years. A large proportion of those who join the Colonial Office establishment as junior officers now proceed on service of this nature. Instances have also occurred in which the Colonial Office has brought home an experienced officer from the overseas establishment to serve for a time in one of the senior posts in the Office.[1]

It nevertheless remains the fact that overseas experience is not treated as essential for promotion to the higher posts in the Office, and instances have, indeed, occurred when the official head of the Office, the Permanent Under-Secretary of State, has not merely been without personal experience of the Colonies but has been transferred to the Colonial Office from another Department of State which has had no direct concern with them. It is this fact that has given force to the suggestion made in some quarters that the Secretary of State should have the advice of a standing Colonial Council, consisting of persons with an adequate experience of service in the dependencies. It is pointed out that the tenure of office of the Secretary of State has seldom lasted long enough to give him any length of personal experience of Colonial affairs. In 1794 the Colonial and War Departments were placed under one Secretary of State, and from that date till 1854 there were 23 holders of the office. The two Departments were separated in 1854, and from that year till 1955 there were 50 Secretaries of State for the Colonies.

It was at one time considered that the 'Council of India', which was part of the establishment of the India Office in Great Britain from the year 1858 up to the year 1937, might afford a suitable precedent for the institution of a Council of the type suggested. But the Council of India was created in exceptional circumstances, and it had a statutory function as a safeguard against the possibility that Indian revenue might be utilized for Imperial purposes.[2] A more relevant analogy in modern conditions might be afforded by the *Conseil Colonial* of Belgium to which some reference has already been made in this Survey.[3] But the chief function of the *Conseil Colonial* is to offer advice on projects of legislation. Not only is direct legislation on Colonial subjects a relatively minor function of the Parliament in Great Britain[4] but in Colonial affairs generally legislation

---

[1] C. J. Jeffries, *The Colonial Empire and its Civil Service*, 1938, pp. 137, 220–1. C. Parkinson, *The Colonial Office from Within 1909–1945*, 1947, pp. 100–26. See also *Appointments in Her Majesty's Oversea Civil Service*, 1955, p. 18.

[2] For the history of the Council of India, see *Cambridge History of India*, vol. v, 1932, chapter xi; also *Report of Joint Committee on Indian Constitutional Reform*, 1933–4, p. 225.

[3] See above, p. 346.   [4] See above, p. 285.

is a less important feature of governmental activity than that of administration. Projects of legislation may provide an important indication of
administrative policy, and the discussion to which they give rise in a
Legislature can be of great value. But much that is embodied in legislation
is in fact only an affirmation of previous decisions arrived at by the Administration; a Legislature can modify policy, but it seldom initiates it.

The proposal for the creation of a Colonial Council has during recent
years received support from individual thinkers in Great Britain,[1] but it
has not become an issue of practical politics. There is a general feeling
that the existence of a standing body of this nature might prejudice the
responsibility which the Secretary of State for the Colonies owes to Parliament, and that on the whole more is to be gained by encouraging members
of the Legislature to acquire an interest in Colonial affairs by personal
visits to the Colonies. There is now considerable activity of this nature
in Great Britain, and it has been reinforced by the support of influential
organizations such as the Commonwealth Parliamentary Association.

The Administrative Branch of the Colonial Services engaged in service
overseas has since 1930 formed one of the 'unified' Colonial Services,
which are recruited and regulated by the Secretary of State and are
allocated to the different overseas dependencies for service in them.[2] In
principle its members can be transferred or promoted from one dependency to another, but in practice transfers have usually taken place only on
promotion, as in the case of Colonial Secretaries or Governors, or occasionally in the case of senior members of a local Secretariat. Members of
the Colonial Service are public servants of the territory in which they are
serving, and their salaries and pensions are paid from local revenue;[3] they
are under the disciplinary control of the Colonial Government, subject to their having a right to appeal to the Secretary of State against
its decisions. Officers are not compelled to accept transfer to a territory
offering less favourable terms than those on which they were engaged
to serve.

The total number of administrative appointments in the 'unified'
Colonial Service is roughly 2,000. It is significant that owing to the
decline in the number of candidates the Kenya Government decided in
1956 to appoint a new cadre of District Assistants from other sources than
the 'unified' Service.[4] Unlike the procedure for recruitment to the Home
Civil Service or the former Indian Civil Service, entry to the administrative section of the Colonial Service is by selection, not by competitive

---

[1] H.C. Deb., 13 July 1943, 20 July 1944. H.L. Deb., 25 July 1950, 27 February 1946, 3
December 1942. *The New Commonwealth*, May 1943.
[2] For these 'unified' Services, see C. J. Jeffries, *The Colonial Empire and its Civil Service*, 1938,
pp. 101–4. *Appointments in Her Majesty's Oversea Civil Service*, Colonial Office, 1955, pp. 1–6.
[3] There is an exception to this rule in respect of the pensions of Colonial Governors.
[4] *Appointments in Her Majesty's Overseas Civil Service*, 1955, p. 15. *The Times*, 26 May 1956.

examination, appointments being made on the advice of the Overseas Civil Service Appointments Board. No educational qualification is prescribed for appointment, but the candidates selected are almost all University graduates, exceptions being made only in the case of persons with special experience, such as service with a Colonial Force.

After selection the cadets follow a course of training, the content and organization of which was reorganized as the result of recommendations made by the Committee on Post-War Training which sat in 1945.[1] Successful candidates are allocated to their respective territories before taking the course. Those going to African territories spend one academic year at Oxford or Cambridge Universities, and during vacations receive practical instruction in the procedure followed in Local Government institutions. The subjects covered by the University courses include Colonial Administration, land use, tropical agriculture, sociology, languages, and law. The Committee on Post-War Training also recommended that all officers should take a second course after their first term of service, but it has never been found possible to release for the purpose more than a small number of officers of this standing. In the result, however, a number of officers at a higher stage of seniority have been sent each year for courses of two or three terms to the three Universities of Oxford, Cambridge, and London. After a few years' experience of following a prescribed course, it was found preferable to allow each individual to work out a course for himself, so that the second course now approximates to what used to be called 'study leave'.

The normal age of retirement in the British African dependencies is 55, but in most territories officers may be called upon to retire or elect to retire voluntarily at the age of 50. In certain of the East and West African territories an arrangement is in force whereby officers may retire at 45 at the option either of the officer himself or of the Government. The length of the 'tour of service' which qualifies for leave varies very widely; at one end of the scale, the West African territories prescribe a tour of twelve months for officers with more than 20 years' service and 18 to 24 months for officers with less than ten years' service; at the other end of the scale, the High Commission Territories, which have a climate similar to that of the Union, have fixed the length of tour at from three to four years' service.

It is partly (though not entirely) the brevity of the 'tour of service' in some of the British territories, and the frequency of transfer which this entails, that accounts for the lack of continuity of local experience which has been so frequent a source of complaint in regard to the Colonial Service. The complaint is not, however, limited to the West African

[1] *Report of Committee on Post-War Training for the Colonial Service* (the Devonshire Committee), Col. no. 198, 1946.

territories, where the 'tour' is shortest; it has been the subject of adverse comment in Central Africa also, as for example in the Report of the Rhodesia-Nyasaland Royal Commission of 1938.[1]

It is open to question whether there can be any justification for the system under which officers of the rank of Colonial Secretary or Governor are appointed to posts in Africa in spite of the fact that their experience has lain entirely in other parts of the Commonwealth; but, however this may be, it is certain that the frequency of transfer in District and Provincial posts is detrimental to the proper conduct of public business, especially in conditions where the chief attention of District Officers is normally absorbed by problems of Native Administration. It is not surprising that the difficulties due to the lack of continuity in the administrative cadres should so frequently be quoted as an argument for substituting some system of local recruitment.[2]

Africanization of Services

During recent years there have been two developments which have a critical bearing on the recruitment and employment of members of the British Colonial Administrative Service. The first of these developments is the progress made in the Africanization of the Higher Civil Service of the Colonies; the second is the effect of the extension of political self-rule on the scale of employment of European personnel generally. Something has already been said on the first point.[3] It is characteristic of the Public Service in the West African Territories that it is staffed by Africans at all levels except in the higher administrative grade; in this respect the Public Service differs from that of some parts of East Africa, where clerical posts are often held by Asians.

The administrative grades in West Africa have until recently been divided into a 'Senior' and 'Junior' Service, but the classification of posts as 'Senior' and 'Junior' has now been abandoned, and the Gold Coast in 1952 created a Local Civil Service to include all Africans, whatever their grade, who might be appointed after that date. African officers already appointed to 'Senior Service' posts had the option of transferring to the Local Service, and about half the 500 Africans in this position did so. In order to accelerate the process of Africanization the Gold Coast in 1952 adopted the principle that 'expatriate' officers would in future be appointed only on contract for limited periods, unless it proved impossible to fill a post except by appointment on pensionable terms. In Nigeria a Committee on Nigerianization of the Service[4] further recommended that

[1] *The Rhodesia-Nyasaland Royal Commission Report*, Cmd. 5949, 1939, paras. 371–5. See also Northern Rhodesia, Legislative Council Debates, 31 May 1938.
[2] See above, p. 363.   [3] See above, p. 289.
[4] S. Phillipson and S. O. Adebo, *The Nigerianization of the Civil Service*, 1954, p. 51.

non-Nigerian officers on secondment or contract should not be eligible for promotion, but this proposal was not accepted by the Council of Ministers.[1] All the West African Governments have sought to increase the number of qualified Africans available for recruitment by the grant of scholarships on a liberal scale.

In the Gold Coast the number of Africans holding posts in a variety of Civil Services which were formerly classified as 'Senior' and were held by Europeans rose from 171 in 1949 to 916 in 1954, but as the total number of posts had increased, the percentage of Africans had risen only from 10 to 36.[2] In 1953, however, the Prime Minister of the Gold Coast stated that there would still be an urgent need for the experience of overseas officers in a fully self-governing Gold Coast and that Africanization would not be accelerated at the expense of efficiency. A similar statement was repeated in 1954.[3] In Nigeria, with a total authorized 'Senior Service' staff of 5,400 in 1954, some 2,000 posts were held by Nigerians, as against 245 in 1948 out of a total of 2,541.[4] About 25 per cent. of the expatriate officers were on contract.[5]

In Sierra Leone, 'Senior Service' posts increased from 235 in 1939 to 708 in 1952. A Commission which reported in 1953 doubted whether the resources of this relatively undeveloped territory could continue to support the financial burden involved, and there were also complaints that the qualifications of the new staff were inadequate. In this dependency the percentage of Africans in 'Senior Service' posts rose from 11·0 in 1939 to 20·9 in 1952.[6] It was stated in 1955 that the Government of Northern Rhodesia had proposed to create posts for Africans in the Administrative Services, but that no candidate had as yet come forward with the necessary qualifications.

The structure of the Public Services in the three Territories of the East African High Commission and in Zanzibar was examined by Commissions in 1947–8,[7] and 1953–4.[8] In the three High Commission Territories the situation differs from that in West Africa in that the locally domiciled population includes Asians and Europeans as well as Africans, and a

---

[1] As regards the definition of 'expatriate', see the *Report of the Commission on the Civil Service of Sierra Leone*, 1953, p. 4.

[2] *Gold Coast Government, A Statement on the Programme of the Africanisation of the Public Service*, 1954, p. 10.

[3] Debates in Gold Coast Legislative Council, 23 March 1954.

[4] Phillipson and Adebo, op. cit. p. 108. Statement by Chief Secretary in House of Representatives, quoted in *West Africa*, 16 April 1955.

[5] Phillipson and Adebo, op. cit. p. 46.

[6] *Report of the Commission on the Civil Service of Sierra Leone*, 1953, pp. 7–8.

[7] *Report of the Commission on the Civil Services of Kenya, Tanganyika, Uganda and Zanzibar, 1947–48* (the Holmes Report), Col. no. 223, 1948.

[8] *Report of the Commission on the Civil Services of the East African Territories and the East African High Commission* (the Lidbury Report), 1954.

locally recruited Civil Service may be expected to draw its members from all three groups. At present Africans provide almost the whole of the subordinate services and of those grades of the clerical service for which the Cambridge School Certificate is not required as a qualification. The qualifications obtainable at the University College of Makerere[1] did not up to the end of 1953 attain to the minimum required for the professional and administrative services, though they qualified for the 'middle grade' technical posts for which full professional status is not necessary.[2] Asians hold a large share of the clerical posts for which the School Certificate is required, and also a considerable number of 'middle grade' posts. Europeans are recruited locally for many of the 'middle' and a few of the administrative and professional posts. Locally recruited women are employed extensively in the higher clerical or executive grades.[3] The majority of the administrative posts are, however, still filled by members of the unified Overseas Civil Service.

The 1953–4 Commission to which reference has already been made (the Lidbury Commission) proposed to meet the problems of the salary position of the public servant recruited overseas not by adding an expatriation allowance to the basic salary but by recommending that the pay of a locally recruited official should be three-fifths that of one coming from overseas. In view of the opposition offered by local officers to this 'three-fifths' rule, the Commission decided to substitute the addition of 'inducement pay' to a basic salary. Difficulties have, however, arisen regarding the scale of 'inducement pay' to be given to candidates of local origin recruited by the Secretary of State to the unified services.[4]

In Zanzibar a higher-grade Local Civil Service, known as His Highness's Zanzibar Service, was inaugurated in 1947. This is normally filled by the promotion from the junior professional grade of men who have had secondary schooling in Zanzibar, followed by a course at the Makerere University College; at present most of the local men with these qualifications are Arabs. The Zanzibar Government announced in 1954 that in future it would recruit from overseas only when no suitable local candidate was available.[5]

The Employment of Expatriates

As regards the effect which the extension of constitutional self-rule has had on the employment of Europeans or other expatriates in the higher Civil Services of the British dependencies in West Africa there has been

---

[1] See below, p. 1183.
[2] *Report of the Commission on the Civil Services of the East African Territories*, vol. i, 1954, p. 21.
[3] Ibid., p. 22.
[4] Ibid. pp. 31, 34, 35–36.
[5] *Zanzibar Protectorate, Papers laid before the Legislative Council during the year 1954*, p. 25.

no lack of recognition by their Governments of the need of a specialist staff which cannot at present be found locally. But they show great anxiety to build up their own public services as quickly as possible, particularly in the field of general administration. The recruiting of Administrative Officers from outside the Territory was suspended by the Gold Coast in 1951. In Nigeria, although the Constitution of 1951 brought Higher Civil Service appointments under Federal control, the Western Region Government attempted to exercise a veto on appointments of Europeans by refusing to authorize the payment of the expatriation allowance which European officers receive in addition to the salary of the post. In Eastern Nigeria a subsequent effort of the same kind led to a minor constitutional crisis in 1955 when the Governor used his 'reserve' powers to 'certify' a budget grant for certain expatriate officers whose posts the Regional Government was seeking to retrench.[1]

The situation in Nigeria has been complicated by the constitutional changes which came into being on 1 October 1954. A Public Service hitherto unitary was now divided into one Federal and three Regional Services; the Federal Public Service has, moreover, territorial responsibility in the Colony area of Lagos and also in the Southern Cameroons, which no longer shares in the administrative organization of the Eastern Region. While the Commission appointed in 1954[2] to report on the Public Services of the Federation of Nigeria found it impracticable to administer the Federal and Regional services from a joint staff list, it recommended as free an interchange as possible and the maintenance of uniformity in the conditions of service.[3]

The 'Nigerianization' of the Public Service had been the settled policy of the Administration for several years. It was, however, embarrassed by the fact that there were still an inadequate number of qualified Nigerians to fill posts on the senior staff. In the middle of 1954 there were only 824 Nigerians on the senior staff out of an establishment of 5,127 (exclusive of the Railways).[4] That there were even so many Nigerians qualified for this grade of service is largely due to the award of 385 scholarships by the Nigerian Government during 1948 and the following years and to the measures taken to raise the College at Ibadan to the status of a University College. There were at the same date 2,389 pensionable Overseas Officers serving in 'Senior Service' grades, of whom 25 per cent. were on contract,[5] and it is relevant that the Mission of the International Bank reported in 1954 that 2,000 additional recruits from overseas were required to imple-

---

[1] *Africa Digest*, May–June 1955, pp. 2–3.
[2] *Report of the Commission on the Public Services of the Governments in the Federation of Nigeria, 1954–55* (the Gorsuch Report).
[3] Ibid. p. 27, para. 50.
[4] Ibid. p. 32, para. 65.
[5] S. Phillipson and S. O. Adebo, *The Nigerianization of the Civil Service*, 1954, p. 46.

ment the Territory's Development Plans.[1] There were 1,028 vacancies which Nigerians were either unwilling or lacked the qualifications to fill.

A further obstacle to Nigerianization has been the attitude adopted by the Northern Region, and to a less degree by the Southern Cameroons. The former, recognizing its own inability to fill posts in the Public Service from within the Region, has preferred to employ staff from overseas rather than Nigerians from other Regions. In the Southern Cameroons opposition has been expressed to the employment in the 'Senior Service' of personnel recruited elsewhere than locally. The dilemma therefore is the reconciliation of a policy of Nigerianization with the necessary retention of a qualified overseas staff. The Commission hoped that it might be resolved by the abolition of the terms 'Senior' and 'Junior' in the Public Service,[2] by the revision of salary scales, and by attracting overseas recruits by the offer of an 'inducement addition' to the salary.[3]

In the Gold Coast, members of the Colonial Civil Service have had, with effect from July 1955, the option of transferring to the new Local Service or of retiring with compensation. One hundred and fifty European officers of different branches of the Oversea Services, representing nearly a fifth of the total, were expected to retire.[4]

It has been announced that when any dependent territory attains a status of self-government the United Kingdom proposes to secure by formal agreement certain guarantees regarding the terms of service of those officers of the Colonial Service serving overseas who have been appointed by the Secretary of State. The officers now in the Colonial Service to whom these principles will be applied will then constitute a service to be known as Her Majesty's Overseas Civil Service.[5] Proposals have been made in some quarters for the creation of a Commonwealth Civil Service directly employed by the United Kingdom Government,[6] but while not excluding such a development the present Government has stated that it is not ready to reach any conclusions upon the proposal.

French Territories

In one respect the French system presents an appearance of greater uniformity than the British, for a considerable part of the personnel of the *Administration centrale* of the Ministry of Overseas France is supplied by members of the Colonial Administrative Service. There is, as will be seen, a regular procedure of transfer between the metropolitan and the Colonial

---

[1] The Economic Development of Nigeria, *Report of a Mission organized by the International Bank for Reconstruction and Development*, 1954, p. 59.

[2] *Gorsuch Report*, op. cit. p. 37, para. 79.

[3] Ibid. p. 76, para. 206.   [4] *West Africa*, 14 May 1955.

[5] H.C. Deb., 2 April 1954, coll. 2499–506. *Reorganization of the Colonial Service*, Col. 306, 1954. *Appointments in Her Majesty's Oversea Civil Service*, 1955.

[6] *The Times*, 7 September 1953, 18 June 1954, 1 May 1956.

establishments, and a number of the *Directeurs* dealing with the civil work of the Ministry are officers holding the rank of *Administrateur en chef*.

The personnel of the Administrative Service falls into three categories, the *corps des administrateurs*, the *cadre d'administration générale*, and the local service. The first two categories are unified services whose members are transferable between different Colonies and between the Colonies and the Ministry for Overseas France. The local service is divided into a *cadre supérieur*, which is transferable between the territories of a 'group' (as, for example, the component territories of French West Africa), and the *cadre local*, which is confined to a single territory. The terms of service of the first two categories are fixed by ministerial decree; that of the third is determined by local *arrêté*. Since 1948 the cost of the salaries and allowances for *Administrateurs* and also for Magistrates has been borne on the metropolitan budget, unless they are expressly seconded to the service of a central or local government in an overseas territory.[1] The cost of their travel within the territory is, however, met by the local budget. A law of 1950 abolished all discrimination in pay and conditions based on race or place of recruitment, but introduced two kinds of special allowance for overseas service. The first is a percentage increase on all salaries, fixed separately for each territory or group of territories; the second an *indemnité de dépaysement* payable to anyone serving away from the country where he normally resides.[2]

The category of *Administrateurs* is divided into (1) *Administrateurs adjoints*, (2) *Administrateurs*, and (3) *Administrateurs en chef*; this last rank includes a special grade (*classe exceptionelle*). The duties of Secretaries-General are, for example, usually performed by *Administrateurs* of the *classe exceptionelle*. The *Administrateurs adjoints* begin their service in a district, but may be transferred to a secretariat after 18 months, or to the Ministry at the end of three years' service, two of which must have been in a district. There are four grades of *Administrateurs adjoints* and three grades of *Administrateurs*; the period normally spent in each grade is two years, except that *Administrateurs adjoints* of the highest grade may be promoted after one year to the division of *Administrateurs*. Promotions are made by ministerial decree.

Admission to the category of *Administrateur* and of Magistrate is gained by examination. Candidates must have the *baccalauréat* or an equivalent diploma, or have been employed in the Ministry of Overseas France for two years. The candidates have normally studied the group of subjects bearing on Colonial affairs which are specially taught at three of the *Lycées* in Paris, at a *Lycée* in Bordeaux, and at one in Nancy. Successful candidates have an option as to which group of Colonies they will enter, and during their training they are divided into 'groups' on this basis. A

---

[1] *Loi*, 21 March 1948.   [2] *Loi*, 30 June 1950.

special examination is also held in order to regulate the admission of a limited number of officials who have been serving in a lower grade in the Colonies or have served in the armed forces. These candidates must have had four years' service and have passed the first-year examination of the *Licence en Droit* or the *Licence d'Études des Populations d'Outre-Mer*. In their case the examination is of a special form and may include tests in the knowledge of a Native language or local Colonial law. The successful candidates of this class have a two-years' course of training as compared with the three-years' course of the ordinary candidates for the category of *Administrateur*.

The training for *Administrateurs* and Magistrates is now given at the *École Nationale de la France d'Outre-Mer* (E.N.F.O.M.). This succeeded in 1934 the former *École Coloniale* founded in 1889. The present institution was reorganized in 1950[1] on a plan analogous to that of the *École Nationale d'Administration* which was founded in 1945 for the training of members of the metropolitan Civil Services in general. In both of these institutions a greatly increased emphasis is now laid on practical training.

The course of studies for *Administrateurs* begins with four months' lectures on the political and economic organization of the Colonies, followed by eight months' service in a Colony overseas, at the end of which cadets must have a favourable report from the Governor of the Colony before they are allowed to continue their course. In the second year they study law or social or economic questions arising in the Colonies; there is an examination at the end of the year, as the result of which cadets may be rejected or may be assigned to a lower category of service. In the third year their studies are of a more strictly professional character; it does not appear, however, that the study of any Native language is compulsory. Those who complete successfully the course of three years (or of two years in the case of the special entrants) are entitled to the *brevet* of the *École*.

Paris has also a *Centre des Hautes Études d'Administration Musulmane*, which receives a State subvention but is under the administration of the University of Paris. Here members of the Colonial Service or of the armed forces with four years' overseas service are admitted by a competitive examination which involves knowledge of an Oriental or African language. Successful candidates spend three months at the *centre* and then work by themselves for two years on a thesis. If this is approved and if they also pass an oral examination they receive the *Brevet des Hautes Études d'Administration Musulmane*. The *centre* has a special section on *Islam en Afrique Noire*, and officials from West Africa as well as North Africa attend it. The theses, which might form a valuable source of first-hand information, are not as a rule published.

The normal tour of service for *Administrateurs* and Magistrates is two

---

[1] *Décret*, 30 October 1950.

years, followed by six months' leave. A law of 1924 established two classes for pension purposes,[1] one retiring at the age of 60 after 30 years' service, and one at 55 after 25 years. At one time it was the rule in French West Africa that no Administrative Officer should serve two consecutive tours in the same Colony; this rule was, it is understood, originally intended to prevent corruption. But it is now long out of date, and the present policy is directed to securing greater continuity of service in the areas of which Administrative Officers have gained experience. This is, however, as hard to achieve in the French territories as elsewhere,[2] though it would seem that a greater measure of continuity has been achieved in the Cameroons than elsewhere in French Africa. When M. Mandel was Minister for Overseas France, a scheme was discussed under which *commandants de cercle* should be appointed for a tenure of five years, but this project did not pass into law.

The *cadre d'administration générale* is divided into the following grades: *commis, adjoints, adjoints-principaux, sous-chefs,* and *chefs de bureau*; officials in each grade act as auxiliaries to the *administrateurs* of the corresponding grade. They are employed both in the Administrative and Judicial Services, and, as has been mentioned, selected members of this *cadre* can qualify by a competitive examination for appointment in the category of *administrateurs*. Three-quarters of the posts in the *cadre local* are reserved for ex-non-commissioned officers; the remainder are recruited from candidates under the age of 30 who have had a secondary schooling or have passed an examination which is uniform throughout the colonies.

The members of the *cadre*, who serve in numerous subordinate posts in the educational and many other departments, are now beginning to include an increasing proportion of Africans. It remains, however, the fact that as compared with the British dependencies, a relatively large proportion of the subordinate posts in all the services, including the Administrative Services, continues to be held by what may be described generally as the class of French non-commissioned officer. It is largely to the competence of this large body of auxiliaries that the various services owe their efficiency. They have in particular proved to be indispensable in the expansion of the system of education.[3]

The higher personnel is, as has been shown, the product of a process of competitive selection and of systematic training. There is no question that the French Administrative Officer of the present day exhibits the valuable qualities which such a procedure is calculated to secure. In one sense his range of duties is wider than that of officers holding similar posts in the British territories, since the French officer has the responsibility for executing or supervising a number of activities (including the operation of the

---

[1] *Décret*, 14 April 1924.
[2] See above, p. 366.   [3] See below, p. 1201.

important development plans) which in the British dependencies would fall on officers of the technical or professional departments. If there is any ground for criticism at all, it lies in the fact that the French Administrative Officer is to a marked degree the devotee of the French doctrine of rule and finds it difficult to see beyond the concept of the African as the potential heir of a specifically Western form of civilization. With many of them, the indigenous culture or custom is significant only in so far as it can be moulded to this purpose.

It is part of the implication of the constitutional changes embodied in the *loi cadre* of June 1956 referred to above that there shall be a material increase in the recruitment of Africans in the higher Administrative and other Services. So far there has been a certain number of Africans in the higher grades of the Administrative as well as of the technical Services, but they have frequently been residents of the West Indies; most noteworthy of them has been M. Félix Éboué, to whom reference has been made in a preceding chapter.[1] The French have the great advantage that their refusal to admit differences based on colour has enabled them to stand consistently by the principle that Africanization of the services must not be merely a concession to political considerations; merit must remain the determining factor in recruitment; and candidates for the superior services must comply fully with the same test of competitive selection as that which regulates entry into the metropolitan services. If in this matter there is no rejection on the ground of race or colour, there is equally no concession to it.

Belgian Congo

The administrative system in the Belgian Congo was reorganized in 1947 at the same time as that of the metropolitan Civil Service, the purpose being to bring it into line with the latter in such a way as to facilitate transfer from employment overseas to service in the Colonial Ministry.[2] All public servants are described as *agents*, but both Administrative and Technical Services are divided into four grades, the first three known as *fonctionnaires*, while the members of the lowest grade are described as *agents de la quatrième catégorie*.[3] Appointments to the grade of *fonctionnaire* are made by royal *arrêté*; the appointments to the fourth grade are made by ministerial *arrêté* or by the Governor-General, according as to whether recruitment is made in Belgium or in the Colony. Since 1947 all candidates have been required to have Belgian or Luxembourg nationality.

Candidates for the category of *fonctionnaire* must have a university degree

[1] See above, p. 211.
[2] *Arrêté du Régent*, 1 July 1947, with subsequent amendments.
[3] *Arrêté Royal*, 27 February 1952.

and must have completed at least four years at a university. Though it is not obligatory to have the diploma of the Colonial University at Antwerp, the course which it gives is the most frequent channel of entry to the Administrative Service. Candidates for appointment as *agent de la quatrième catégorie* must have a teacher's diploma or one of the various certificates obtainable on the completion of a year's study at a university.

The Colonial University at Antwerp was established by a royal *arrêté* in 1923. It gives a four-year course, instruction being provided in both French and Flemish. At the end of the first-year course, which includes Colonial geography and an introduction to ethnology, a competitive examination is held; the number who may go farther is limited to those for whom there are expected to be posts when they have completed their course. The rest of the course is much more closely concentrated on the Belgian Congo, and involves an intensive study of its constitution, law, administrative organization, and ethnography; courses in Lingala and Swahili are also given throughout these three years. Courses for persons who have not attended the Colonial University are given at the *École Coloniale* in Brussels, the curricula of which are fixed by regulation of the Minister for Colonies. Persons originally appointed to the fourth category above referred to can qualify for a higher grade after a period of Colonial service, the length of which varies with their educational qualifications, the maximum being three years. An official who has been ranked 'very good' in three successive annual reports may apply to return to Belgium for a shortened course at the Colonial University and thus qualify for promotion through an examination taken at the end of this period.

The tour of service in the Colony is three years, at the end of which six months' leave is due. The full term of service was increased in 1934 from 18 to 23 years, exclusive of leave periods. Officers with 15 years' completed service may retire or be asked to retire, but in this case they are entitled to pension. An age-limit of 60 was introduced in 1953.[1] The posting of officials is left to the Governor-General and does not necessarily take into account the language which they have studied in their training course. Continuity of service is, however, maintained as far as possible; transfers are seldom made from one Province to another, and it is the accepted policy that officers should if possible return to the same district after leave. The provision of an assistant to every executive official helps to secure continuity by making it unnecessary to replace every official who goes on leave. There are certain disadvantages, however, following from the extension to the Secretariat of the principle of continuity; it is on the whole a disadvantage that few transfers are made between the Secretariat and the Districts.

[1] *Arrêté Royal*, 23 February 1953.

As has been explained,[1] each Province is administered by a Governor, who has Provincial technical services attached to him; the standing regulations require him to visit each district in his Province at least once a year.[2] The functions of the *commissaire de district* are those of inspection rather than administration; he makes a detailed inspection of every *territoire* in his district at least twice a year and his observations on it are attached to the report submitted to headquarters. Administrative Officers are required to keep in constant touch with Native Authorities and to guide the development of Native institutions, and for this purpose they must spend 20 days of each month in touring. The *agents de la quatrième catégorie* are responsible for census work and for various activities which would elsewhere fall to the technical departments, such as local public works or the supervision of programmes of compulsory cultivation.

Provision was made in 1921[3] for the creation of a grade of African *agents auxiliaires* to be appointed by the Secretary-General. This includes teachers, postal clerks, and assistants in the customs and medical departments. In the actual work of administration Africans are at present employed only as clerks.

At the headquarters of the Governor-General there is a General Secretariat which has six *directions générales*, namely those concerned with (1) political, administrative, and judicial affairs; (2) Native affairs, including education, labour, and social security; (3) finance and customs; (4) economic affairs, land, and mines; (5) agriculture; (6) public works and communications.[4]

Despite the explicit nature of the statutory provisions designed to ensure that African affairs should have the full attention of the local Administrative Services, there is in some quarters a complaint that these are now treated with relative neglect. This was at one time said to be due to shortage of staff: the numbers have, however, increased from under 700 in 1946 to 1,370 in 1954. It seems that here as elsewhere the amount of desk-work required of Administrative Officers has also increased; it has, indeed, been stated that they are able to give no more than 5 per cent. of their time to the problems of Native policy.[5] It is obvious also that senior officials are finding it difficult to find time to train their juniors. This is to be regretted the more because all observers are agreed that, during the régime of the Belgian Government, the Administrative Service has been marked by high standards of conduct and of concern for the problems of Native welfare.

[1] See above, p. 350.
[2] *Arrêté du Regent*, 1 July 1947.
[3] *Ordonnance*, 28 February 1921; now superseded by *Ordonnance*, 22 June 1953.
[4] *Ordonnance*, March 1951. *Codes et Lois du Congo Belge*, 1954, pp. 500–8.
[5] P. Quinet, 'Quelques Considérations sur les Problèmes du service Territorial', *Problèmes d'Afrique Centrale*, no. 27, 1955, pp. 10–14.

Portuguese Territories

In the overseas territories the Services are divided into three categories, namely, central, provincial, and local.[1] The central services are those of Native Affairs, Education, Finance, Justice, Public Health, and Agriculture. Angola adds a special service of Public Works, Industries, and Mines; Mozambique a special service of Railways and Harbours. The provincial services are divided into departments dealing with (1) Civil Administration and (2) Native Affairs. The latter are responsible for the Native Courts, Native Labour, and Native Emigration. Some account has already been given of the different grades in the Administrative service, ranging from the grade of *Aspirante* up to that of *Administrador*.[2]

In point of nationality, this service is recruited both from residents of Portugal itself and from residents in the overseas territories, who are either Portuguese by birth or belong to the category of *assimilado*.[3] In a recent analysis of the civil staff of Portuguese Guinea, numbering 81 in all, 31 came from Portugal, 29 from Cape Verde, nine from Guinea, five from Goa, two from Madeira, one each from Angola, Mozambique, Sao Tomé, Macao, and Brazil. It seems, however, to be a common source of complaint that in the Service preference is given to residents of Portugal; other entrants are, it is said, liable to be relegated to the service of smaller overseas provinces, where the conditions of service and the prospects of pay are much less attractive.

Entry to the service is either through the *Instituto Superior de Estudos Ultramarinos* at Lisbon, or by promotion from a locally recruited service. Entry into the *Instituto* is by competitive examination and cadets who have received its diploma are not required to take a further public examination; they enter with the grade of *Chefe do Posto*, while persons who have entered by promotion from the local services commence with the grade of *Aspirante*. In each case a provisional confirmation is necessary at the end of the first two years; full confirmation is not given until the end of the probationary period of five years.

Entry by approved candidates from local services is secured through a qualifying examination. In the recruitment of these services preference is given where possible to persons who have been born or have lived in the Province, but all entrants are liable to transfer, as the service is a unified one; and for those serving in the smaller Portuguese provinces there is little opportunity of promotion without transfer. Candidates must have had five years' secondary school education. After admission to the class of *Aspirante*, officers of this category must pass a qualifying examination before admission to the grade of *Administrador*.

---

[1] *Decreto-Lei*, 16 November 1933.
[2] See above, p. 356.
[3] See above, pp. 231–3.

It is generally agreed that there has during the last quarter of a century been a marked advance in the qualifications and the character of the members of the Portuguese Administrative Service. By comparison with British standards the pay is low, but the majority of Administrative officers are supplied with furnished houses of a good standard, free of rent, and all officers down to the rank of *Chefe do Posto* have free cars.

CHAPTER VII

THE NON-EUROPEAN IMMIGRANT COMMUNITIES

THE questions to which the existence of the non-European immigrant communities gives rise are of a different class from those which will be dealt with in the following chapter on Native Administration,[1] for they originate not from the need of adjusting administrative methods to an African environment but from the addition which these communities have made to the racial problems of Africa. It is fortunate that this is limited in extent. A small immigrant community such as that of the Syrian or Lebanese traders in West Africa does not create a serious problem, the more so as this particular community readily adjusts itself to local conditions. The existence of an Arab community in the Eastern coastal areas presents questions which require attention but can cause only minor difficulty. The most conspicuous problem is in fact that arising from the existence of the Asian community in the Union of South Africa and in the British East African territories,[2] and it will be necessary to devote this chapter largely to the position now occupied by the community in these areas. Its history has more than once been marked by acute controversy, extending beyond the limits of the territories directly concerned. Since 1947, indeed, the tension existing between the Governments of the Union of South Africa and those of India and Pakistan has become an issue of international significance.

EARLY ASIAN IMMIGRATION IN EAST AFRICA

Arab and Portuguese Conflicts

The importance of the Arab immigration to the East African coastal area belongs largely to the past. Availing themselves of the 'trade winds' which blow from the north-north-west in the winter and from the reverse direction in the summer, Arabs had from a very early date made an annual practice of trading on the coasts of Africa.[3] There is evidence dating from the first century A.D. that the Sabaean kings of South Arabia had long exercised some form of rule over part of the African coast,[4] but permanent

---

[1] See below, p. 414.

[2] It is now convenient to use the term 'Asian' as the term 'Indian' might appear to exclude the residents of Pakistan.   [3] R. Coupland, *East Africa and its Invaders*, 1938, p. 15.

[4] W. H. Schoff, ed. *The Periplus of the Erythraean Sea*, 1921. (The *Periplus* was a guide for navigation and trade, written by a Greek merchant seaman about A.D. 80).

settlement did not apparently take place till the seventh century, when the first settlement was made by a body of refugees from Oman, followed in the eighth century by a number of Shi'ite schismatics known as the Zaidiyah. They in turn were followed in the ninth century by Arabs of the El Harth tribe fleeing from local persecution. These settlements came in time to include Mogadishu, Lamu, Mombasa, Zanzibar, Pemba, and Kilwa, that at Kilwa having been joined by Persians from Shiraz.

It was in the eighth century A.D. that Arabs from Ormuz settled as a trading community on the Malabar coast of South India, where they established friendly relations with the Zamorin of Calicut. It was probably the existence of this colony of 'Moors' which attracted Vasco da Gama to West India, rather than the existence of the old-established Christian community in Malabar now generally known as the 'Syrian' Church.[1]

Arab settlement on the east coast of Africa had by the twelfth century dominated a great length of the *Zinj* (Negro)[2] coast, but there was nothing in the nature of an Arab 'empire', the nearest approach to it being the overlordship exercised for varying periods over other towns by that which for the time happened to be the strongest. The most famous and lasting of these hegemonies seems to have been that of Kilwa, and it is at all events certain that Kilwa attained at this period a high level of material civilization. Chinese coins of the eighth and twelfth centuries testify to the wide range of commerce at these dates. It has been held that it is to Arab or Persian traders that Africa owes the cultivation of rice, sugar-cane,[3] and cotton—cotton being itself an Arabic word. It does not seem, however, that the infusion of Arab blood and civilization ever extended far from the sea. Even at that early date slaves ranked high among the African products which Arabs were exchanging for commodities brought from India, Persia, and Arabia.[4]

This period of Arab domination over the coast came to an end when the Portuguese Admiral, Almeida, following the first visit paid by Vasco da Gama in 1497 to the chief Arab settlements, gained possession of them in a campaign which lasted from 1503 to 1509. In the course of these years the Portuguese sought to secure themselves against reprisals from the Arabian coast by sacking Muscat and occupying Ormuz. Their adventure on the east coast of Africa had two objectives, first, the establishment of footholds on dry land to serve as outposts on the road to India, and second, the seizure of the fabled wealth of the gold-fields of Sofala. They were to be disappointed in the latter purpose, but they still attached importance to the former, though it was in fact only Mozambique that

[1] A. M. Abraham, 'The Christians of Malabar', in *The Eastern World*, January 1956, pp. 30 ff.
[2] *Zinj* is the Arabic word from which Zanquebar (subsequently corrupted to Zanzibar) was derived.
[3] W. Fitzgerald, in *Africa*, January 1945, p. 79.
[4] Coupland, op. cit., p. 18.

they could be said to have actually colonized,[1] for Portuguese authority was far less firmly established north of the Ruvuma. There was nowhere any sustained effort to penetrate into the interior, and Portuguese trading seems to have been less profitable than that of the Arabs.

In the course of time, the growing strength of the Dutch and British fleets was gravely to diminish the capacity of the Portuguese to hold their monopoly of the sea route to India. This helped to make it possible for the Muscat Arabs to renew their attacks on the coast and eventually to force the Portuguese to surrender to them a large part of the authority they had gained in Almeida's campaign early in the previous century.

The Portuguese occupation of the East African coast has been characterized as having left few positive results, political or economic. 'Its chief historical importance lies in the fact that it gave the Portuguese a hold on a section of the coast which they have never since lost.'[2] While, however, it is true that they maintained their African possessions rather as a port of call on the route to Goa than as a colony, the contribution which they made to the exploration of the interior added much to the contemporary knowledge of Africa. Gaspar Bocarro discovered Lake Nyasa in 1616, anticipating Livingstone by two and a half centuries,[3] and their settlements at Sena and Tete added materially to knowledge of the Zambezi and its affluents, giving an entirely new appearance to maps of the interior of Africa.[4] At a later date the transcontinental journey from the Indian to the Atlantic Ocean was made by the Pombeiros in 1810, by Monteiro and Gamitto in 1831, and by Silva Porto in 1852. A river-transport service for 300 miles down the Luangwa to its confluence with the Zambezi was planned in 1798.[5] It stands to their credit that they built the first Christian church and the first hospital at Mozambique in 1508.[6] Although the baptism in 1560 of Monomatapa, the Chief of the Makalanga, was an illusory ceremony, Gonzalo da Silveira was the first missionary to set foot in Africa and the first to suffer martyrdom for his faith.[7]

During the course of their occupation they must have extracted gold worth at least £1½ million from Sofala,[8] and Bocarro described the houses in Tete as being lavishly adorned with silver from the mines at Chikova. The fort at Mozambique, built of stone early in the sixteenth century and said to have been transported from Lisbon, remains as a monument of the great era of Portuguese enterprise. In the succeeding centuries Portuguese

---

[1] R. Coupland, 'Seamen and Crusaders, The Foundation of Portuguese East Africa', *The Times* (Mozambique number), 1 August 1939.

[2] R. Coupland, *East Africa and its Invaders*, 1938, p. 52.

[3] G. M. Theal, *Records of South-Eastern Africa*, vol. iii, 1899, p. 416, quoting the *Decade* of Antonio Bocarro.

[4] See the maps of William Berry, dated 1680, and de Lisle, 1700.

[5] E. H. Lane Poole, 'An Early Portuguese Settlement in Northern Rhodesia', *J.R.A.S.*, April 1931, p. 164.   [6] G. M. Theal, *The Portuguese in South Africa*, 1896, p. 110.

[7] Ibid. p. 163.   [8] Coupland, op. cit. p. 52. Theal, op. cit. p. 284.

influence declined, but north of the Zambezi, as for instance in Nyasaland and Northern Rhodesia, the descendants of the original settlers, mostly of mixed blood and known to the natives of the Zambezi and Luangwa valleys as 'Mambari', carried on a lucrative trade in slaves and ivory until the British occupation put a period to their exploits.[1]

Ormuz was retaken by the Persians in 1622, and in 1650 the Omani Arabs expelled the Portuguese from Muscat and the Arabian seaboard. By a series of sea raids, concluding with that on Mombasa in 1698, the Omani recovered most of the Arab possessions on the coast, and after 1740 the Portuguese had to content themselves with the possession of Mozambique and the small settlements—Quelimane, Sofala, and Tete—which were subject to its control. Though, however, the Arabs had thus regained much of their authority over the coast, they themselves were no longer the people who had surprised da Gama and Almeida by the wealth and beauty of their towns. Their sea power was gone, and the range of their trade was narrowed down to the western section of the Indian Ocean.

Henceforth European visitors were to gaze on the evidence afforded by crumbling walls and ruined mosques that the Arab towns of the coast had once been rich and powerful. The centre of such authority as the Arabs now exercised in Africa was in Zanzibar, and Zanzibar was subject to Oman. How far this implied an active measure of control is doubtful, though in an agreement made in 1822 between the British Government and Seyyid Said, Imam of Muscat, the former recognized him as overlord of all the ports along the African coast. Mombasa at all events succeeded for a number of years in asserting its independence, under the leadership of the Mazrui, one of its leading families.

Oman Arabs in Zanzibar

That the Imam was unable to make his overlordship more effective on the coast was largely due to the weakness of his own position at home. Beset by hostile neighbours such as the Wahabi and the Jawasmi, he was also caught fast in a ferment of family intrigue, and it was this which finally decided him in 1840 to seek in Zanzibar the personal security unobtainable in Muscat.[2] The differences, it may be added, were not primarily of religious origin. The Oman Imamat was of the Ibadi sect, the Ibadis being the surviving representatives of the Khariji section of early Islam. Originally regarded by the Sunnis as heterodox, the differences with the Sunnis had in time ceased to be of any great importance.[3]

[1] Lewis Gann, 'The End of the Slave Trade in British Central Africa, 1889–1912', *R.L. Journal*, no. 16, 1954, p. 32. D. Livingstone, *The Zambezi and its Tributaries*, 1865, pp. 240–1. M. V. Jackson, *European Powers and South East Africa*, 1942, pp. 191 ff.

[2] Coupland, op. cit. p. 293.

[3] J. N. D. Anderson, *Islamic Law in Africa*, 1954, p. 358. S. Vesey Fitzgerald, *Mohammedan Law*, 1931, p. 16.

The advent of the Imam in Zanzibar not only increased the number and power of the Omani immigrants in the island but enabled him to establish a loose system of administration over the coastal areas, exercised through local *Liwalis* and *Akidas*,[1] sometimes Arab but often local Swahili. The authority on which this system rested was, however, tenuous, and in most cases did not extend beyond the collection of a small tribute and the customs dues which formed the major part of Said's revenues. But the name and fame of the Sultan of Zanzibar spread far beyond the coastal area, carried abroad by the caravans of Arab and Somali slave traders, which practically dominated the interior as far west as the Great Lakes.

The reasons for which Seyyid Ali ibn Said, the fourth of Seyyid Said's sons to rule in Zanzibar, sought British protection in 1890 belong to the story of Zanzibar rather than to the present chapter, but it has been necessary to explain here the circumstances which have given the Arab community in East Africa its present character. It might now be better described as a 'domiciled' rather than as an 'immigrant' community. If Oman Arabs still constitute the upper level of Arab society in Zanzibar, the great mass of the community on the mainland is of mixed Arab and African descent.[2] As a result of the local expansion of Islam beyond the limits of the Arab community, their religion no longer provides so conspicuous a point of distinction between them and the African population, nor is it always easy to differentiate the Arab from the Swahili people, that 'mixture of mixtures' to whom some reference has already been made in discussing the origin of the Swahili language.[3] In the past the local Arabs were mainly interested in opening up the trade routes from the coast into the interior and were the leading figures in the slave trade; they are still predominantly traders today, and it is only in Zanzibar and a small part of the coast that they appear as owners of land or of coco-nut groves.

Arabs in Mainland Territories

In the mainland territories Arabs are most prominent in Kenya, where they numbered 24,174 in the census of 1948,[4] the majority (15,272) being residents of Mombasa. Their position has been recognized by the institution of Arab schools and by their representation in the Legislative and Executive Councils. Under the revised Constitution there is one Arab Representative Member and one elected member in the Legislative Council. An Arab sits on the Executive Council; one of the three Parliamentary Secretaries is an Arab. In Tanganyika (where Arabs number

[1] *N.A.*, Part II, p. 7.
[2] For the effects of Arab and African miscegenation, see the references quoted in A. Burns, *Colour Prejudice*, 1948, pp. 35, 121.
[3] See above, p. 98.   [4] In 1954 they were estimated to number 30,000.

13,025) the Tanga Arabs have a nominated member in the Township Authority. There are relatively few Arabs in Uganda (1,475). Both in Kenya and Tanganyika their special form of land tenure has been recognized by the Government,[1] and they have for the most part been brought under the jurisdiction of non-tribal Courts.

But the Arab has neither the political flair nor the unusual aptitude for trading possessed by the Indian, with the consequence that, unlike the latter, he seldom appears in the role of a political or economic competitor to the European. Indeed, the readiness shown by less wealthy Arabs to assimilate with the Bantu seems to show that in the mainland territories the Arabs are likely to occupy in the future a position of diminishing importance as a distinctive community. The position of the Arab community in Zanzibar has been considered in the preceding chapter.[2]

Asian Immigration

The Arabs were not the only adventurers on the Indian Ocean, for the trade winds which proved so useful to them carried Asian traders also to the East African coast and provided them with the same regular means of return from their journey. Whether or not the arrival of the Indian traders preceded that of the Arabs is doubtful, but it is clear that seafaring was common during the Buddhist era of Indian history, for the Sanchi sculptures of the second century B.C. contain many carvings of ships. The Greek navigation manual of A.D. 80 referred to on a previous page[3] makes reference to the arrival of Indian ships in the East African coastal towns. In the thirteenth century Marco Polo wrote of Indian ships 'which visit the island of Madeigascar and that other of Zanghibar'.[4] Some indication of the extent of the export trade from Africa is afforded by the fact that the Muslim King of Gaur in Bengal, who ruled between 1459 and 1474, possessed some 8,000 African slaves.[5]

It was an Asian who in 1498 piloted Vasco da Gama on his voyage from Malindi on the east coast of Africa to the port of Calicut in Malabar. Asian traders do not seem to have established any settlements of their own, but in later days there were frequent references to the existence of 'Banians' at Zanzibar and Mombasa, and it seems that they were content to trade under the protection first of the Arab and then of the Portuguese authorities. Their opportunities for trade must, however, have been severely restricted by the monopoly which the latter exercised at one period in the Indian Ocean.

After the Arabs recovered possession of their settlements in East Africa an increasing number of Asian traders came from India, and Captain

---

[1] See below, p. 783.   [2] See above, p. 383.
[3] See above, p. 380, note 4.   [4] *Travels*, Book III, London, 1818, chapter 26.
[5] *Cambridge History of India*, vol. ii, 1928, p. 268.

Smee, who visited Zanzibar in 1811, reported that they then engrossed the greatest part of the trade.[1] From about 1861 the British Consular Court at Zanzibar, established by virtue of the early treaties of 1822 and 1839 which gave it jurisdiction over British subjects, administered the law of British India, with an appeal to the High Court of Bombay. In 1890 Her Britannic Majesty's High Court was established in Zanzibar. Most of the British subjects over whom it had jurisdiction were Asians from India; in 1863 they were reported to number between 5,000 and 6,000 in Zanzibar and the African mainland, and the greater part of the export trade, valued at over £1½ million, was said to pass through their hands.

Seyyid Said had actively encouraged the immigration of Asians, partly as a means of marketing the clove and coconut production of the two islands (industries which were largely due to his initiative) and partly as an agency for financing the expeditions of slave dealers on the mainland.[2] Of the Asians the Muslims came mostly from Cutch, Surat, or Bombay, and a considerable number were domiciled in Zanzibar; it was said that Hindu traders, who came mainly from Cutch and Jamnagar, usually returned to their own homes.

In view of this long historical connexion it is not surprising that increasing numbers of Asians resorted to the eastern and southern coasts of Africa when the development of sea communications and the expansion of European colonization had its result in stimulating migration in these quarters. Today there are large Asian communities settled in Kenya, Uganda, Tanganyika, Zanzibar, Portuguese East Africa, and the Union of South Africa. They are to be found in smaller numbers trading in the Rhodesias, Nyasaland, and in British Somaliland. There are, however, relatively few in West Africa, where the chief non-European immigrants are Syrians and Lebanese.

UNION OF SOUTH AFRICA

Asian Immigration in the Nineteenth Century

The view held by the Dutch settlers in South Africa on racial questions is illustrated by a petition against Asian immigration addressed to the Government of the Transvaal Republic in 1884. 'Our constitution', it said, 'recognizes only two races of men, white and coloured.'[3] Both English and Dutch settlers, faced by an African problem whose implications had yet to be fully realized, clearly tended to regard the Asian immigrants as an additional embarrassment. The initial cause of offence lay in the competitive advantage which their lower standard of living gave them as traders,

---

[1] *Transactions of the Bombay Geographical Society 1844*, vol. vi, pp. 23–61. See also Coupland, op. cit. p. 179.   [2] Ibid. pp. 314 ff.
[3] *Cambridge History of the British Empire*, vol. viii, 1936, p. 551.

and hostility against them came to be expressed in policies designed to curtail the number of immigrants into the country. It is therefore an irony of history that at a later date action taken by the Government and by European employers of labour was mainly responsible for the large increase of Asian immigrants. The early planters in Natal experienced great difficulty in securing labour.[1] Africans were unused to wage labour and though the Natal Administration had agreed in 1849 to impose a poll tax, largely in order to stimulate Africans to engage in labour, it was unwilling to resort to further measures of compulsion. But labour was essential, especially in the new sugar plantations, and India, which had already supplied labour to Mauritius in 1834 and to British Guiana in 1837 under the indenture system, was the obvious source from which to obtain it.[2]

In 1860 the Crown Colony Government in Natal secured the first Indian labourers by indenture, in order, as was said at the time, 'to fill a dire economic need',[3] although even at that period there seems to have been some opposition from Europeans other than sugar planters. Immigration was suspended between 1866 and 1874 during the economic depression resulting from the American Civil War, but the planters secured its renewal in 1874 and prevailed on the Administration to grant £10,000 a year for a period of 20 years towards the cost of recruiting in India. In the twelve years following 1874 some 30,000 Asian workers entered Natal. In a communication sent in 1875 the British Government made clear its own position regarding the status of these workers. Asian settlers who had completed the terms of their service should, it said, have privileges no whit inferior to any other class of Her Majesty's subjects resident in the Colonies.[4] With the progress of time, however, the position actually occupied by indentured labour and by the 'free' labour which was the result of its settlement in Natal aroused increasing criticism in India. The whole position of indentured labour was reviewed in 1909 by Lord Crewe's Committee on Emigration from India, and in 1911 the public concern shown in India regarding the status accorded to Asians in South Africa led the Indian Government to veto further recruiting for the Union.

The indentured labourers were recruited by agents in India under agreements to serve on terms approved by the Government of India for a period which was originally three, but was later extended to five years. Thereafter they resumed their freedom, and they could either enlist for a further term of indentured service, or could avail themselves of a free return passage to India or remain as settlers in Africa on a small plot of

[1] R. Burrows, *Indian Life and Labour in Natal*, 1952, p. 1.
[2] V. Anstey, *The Economic Development of India*, 1952, pp. 309–11.
[3] *O.Y.S.A.*, *1949*, p. 852.
[4] Lord Salisbury's Statement of 1875 quoted in the *Government of India Memorandum to U.N.O.*, 1946, p. 6.

land which was to be provided by the Government. The European opposition to the presence of Asians grew as the number of ex-indentured labourers electing to stay as 'free settlers' increased. In 1891 the Natal Government ceased to make grants of land to labourers who remained in the country, and it sought, though without success, for permission to recruit labour on terms which would allow of its compulsory repatriation.

In 1893 Natal attained a status of Responsible Government, and the European feeling soon found expression in measures designed to discourage the settlement of Asian labourers. A Bill introduced in 1893 to deprive 'free' Asians of the political franchise was vetoed by the British Government as constituting an affront to India, but by an Act of 1895 every ex-indentured labourer who remained in Natal was required to take out a yearly licence at a fee of £3.[1] Free passages to India were granted to those who returned immediately. All traders were required to obtain licences from the Local Authorities, and it was alleged by the Asians that the Authorities used their powers in order to restrict the number of traders from India. In spite of these measures, however, a large number of ex-indentured Asians remained, and in 1903 pressure on them was intensified by the imposition of a £3 tax on the children of indentured labourers when they attained the age of majority.

Early Legislation on Asian Immigration

In addition to indentured immigration there was a constant flow of unassisted immigration from India and East Africa, and in 1904 the total Asian population of Natal, including some 60,000 'free' labourers settled in the Colony, amounted to 100,918, compared with a European population of 97,109. The hostility of the European community to 'free' immigration had found violent expression in a demonstration at Durban in 1896, when Mr. Gandhi, then a little-known Indian lawyer, narrowly escaped with his life. Asians were disfranchised in 1896, though the few 'free' immigrants who had the vote were not deprived of it. In 1897 the first measure limiting Asian immigration was enacted in Natal, all free immigrants being required to pass a language test in a European language.[2]

In Natal the influx of indentured labour and the subsequent growth in the number of free labourers had given special prominence to the problem of Asian immigration, but in other parts of South Africa opposition was directed against the Asian as trader rather than as labourer. There was no restriction on the entry of Asians to Cape Colony, but the Orange Free State debarred them from trading or farming in its territory.[3] In the Transvaal the Republican Government received as early as 1884 a series

[1] *Cambridge History of the British Empire*, vol. viii, pp. 549–50.
[2] Act 1 of 1897.
[3] *Wetboek van den Oranje Vrijstaat*, vol. xxxiii, 1891, p. 262.

of petitions protesting against Asian immigration and as a result enacted a comprehensive measure, Law 3 of 1885, which deprived Asians of citizenship and the right to own property, and required all Asians who wished to trade in the Transvaal to register for this purpose. The charge for registration was fixed at £3 in the case of new applicants. The Act also empowered the Government 'as a sanitary measure', to set aside streets, wards, and locations for the habitation of Asians, thus introducing for the first time the principle of residential segregation. But as occurred also in the case of much subsequent legislation affecting Asians, the provisions of the law were not fully enforced, and during and after the war of 1899–1902 there was a continued influx of Asians into the Transvaal.

Before the Anglo-Boer War the British Government had protested to the Transvaal Republic against the imposition of disabilities upon its Asian subjects solely on account of race, and these disabilities formed one of the reasons put forward by the United Kingdom for the outbreak of hostilities.[1] But the pressure of public opinion nevertheless constrained the British Administration of the Transvaal in the post-war years to leave the Law of 1885 intact. During the régime of Responsible Government an immigration enactment of 1907 imposed a European-language test, thus in effect excluding a number of Asians who sought entry into the Transvaal for the first time. In order to prevent illicit immigration, the provisions of the Law of 1885, which required a record of finger-prints as part of the procedure of registration, were extended in 1907 to all Asians claiming domicile in the Transvaal.[2]

This legislation became the occasion in 1908 for Mr. Gandhi's first passive resistance campaign. It was claimed that the taking of finger-prints implied a criminal status; but the movement was also a reaction against the various forms of social discrimination exercised by Europeans in the Transvaal towards even educated Asians. Large numbers of Asians went to jail for deliberate breaches of the immigration law, and much sympathy was aroused for their cause both in India and in the United Kingdom. The Government eventually agreed to enact a law which would be applicable to all immigrants, but to make at the same time administrative regulations which would permit of the entry each year of a limited number of educated Asians.

Immigration Act of 1913

With the formation of the Union in 1910 the question of immigration passed into the hands of the Central Government, and in 1913 a general Immigration Act was enacted,[3] which, in addition to imposing a European-

[1] W. K. Hancock, *Survey of British Commonwealth Affairs*, vol. i, 1937, p. 193.
[2] Asiatic Law Amendment Act, 1907.
[3] Immigrants Regulation Act, no. 22 of 1913.

language test, enabled the Administration to exclude any person or class of persons who were deemed on economic grounds or because of their standard and habits of life to be unsuited to the needs of the Union. Under this provision all further immigration was prohibited except for a limited number of educated Asians annually and the wives and children of Asians already domiciled in South Africa. The Act also prohibited the movement of Asians between Provinces of the Union, except in the case of those already lawfully entitled to reside in any Province. These would be permitted to enter Natal and the Cape if they were able to pass the simpler language test prescribed under the Provincial Immigration Acts.

The passage of this Act led to a second and intensified Civil Disobedience campaign, again led by Mr. Gandhi. Its effect, he contended, was not merely to deprive Asians of free entry into the Cape Province but actually to withdraw from indentured labourers in Natal their rights of free settlement. In addition a judgement of the Supreme Court, which declared invalid in South African law the marriages celebrated by the rites of a religion which permitted polygamy, seemed likely to create a bar to the immigration of the wives of Asians.

The wholesale breaches of the immigration restrictions which ensued resulted in numerous convictions of Asians, and strong feelings were aroused in India by their alleged ill-treatment under detention. The campaign of passive resistance was called off in 1914, when an Agreement was reached between General Smuts, then Prime Minister, and Mr. Gandhi, as the result of which all further immigration of Indians to South Africa was to be stopped, in the hope that when once the fear of unlimited Asian immigration was removed it would be possible to secure an improvement in the treatment of Asians already settled in the country. A commission[1] appointed by the South African Government on the suggestion of the Government of India reported that many of the complaints of grievances made by Asians were well founded. Its specific proposals included the abolition of the £3 tax in Natal, the modification of the immigration law, and the creation of machinery to validate Asian marriages in the Union. The Indian Relief Act passed in 1914[2] was designed to implement these recommendations, while at the same time giving to the Union Government new powers to repatriate voluntarily any Asians who had forfeited by reason of their continued residence the right of free passage embodied in the terms of the indenture.

Effects of the First World War

The circumstances created by the First World War tended to frustrate the hopes entertained of a change of attitude by the European population. During the war a number of Asian workers found new occupations in

[1] *The Indian Enquiry Commission*, U.G. 16/14, 1914.   [2] Act no. 22 of 1914.

industry, causing resentment amongst White workers who felt that their place had been usurped. In Natal and the Transvaal some members of the Asian community had become men of considerable wealth, and their investments in property led to an outcry against 'Asian encroachment'. These feelings were intensified in the period of trade depression which succeeded the war.

In the years between 1919 and 1925 further legislative restrictions were laid on the acquisition of property by Asians. Meanwhile India secured from the Imperial Conference of 1921 a resolution to the effect that while each community of the British Commonwealth should enjoy complete control of the composition of its own population by means of the restriction of immigration, it was desirable in the interest of the solidarity of the Commonwealth that the claims to citizenship made by Asians lawfully domiciled in other parts of the Empire should be respected. General Smuts had, however, dissented from this resolution.[1]

In 1925 the Union Government introduced the Areas Reservation and Immigration Restriction Bill, a measure embodying the principle of residential segregation. Its terms were general, but the Minister of the Interior made it clear that it was intended to apply specifically to the Asian community. 'The Bill frankly starts', he said, 'from the supposition that the Indian as a race in this country is an alien element in the population, and that no solution of this question will be acceptable to the country, unless it results in a very considerable reduction of the Indian population.' Municipal authorities supported the Bill on the ground that the occupation of premises by Asians in European areas led to depreciation of the neighbouring property and thus to further Asian penetration. Durban witnesses complained of the difficulty of securing compliance with sanitary regulations by Asians, and stated that nine out of ten prosecutions under the sanitary laws were against members of their community. Opponents of the measure met these arguments by pointing out that the Asian trader in cheap goods was a benefit to the African and to the poorer Europeans, and that in so far as Asians gave trouble in sanitary matters, it was due only to poverty and lack of facilities for education.

Cape Town Agreements, 1926–7

In the years 1926 and 1927 conferences were held between representatives of the Union Government and the Government of India, which resulted in what came to be known as the Cape Town Agreements.[2] The Union Government undertook not to proceed with the Areas Reservation Bill, and the Government of India promised to co-operate in a scheme of assisted emigration for Asians from South Africa. Under this scheme

[1] *Proceedings of Conference of 1921*, Cmd. 1474, p. 8.
[2] *O.Y.S.A.*, *1937*, pp. 1062–3; ibid. *1952–53*, p. 1097.

a bonus of £20 was to be given to every adult Asian who wished to return to India, but only some 17,000 Asians were repatriated during the following five years,[1] and in 1932 the Government of the Union proposed that the possibilities of emigration to other territories should be explored.[2] A commission appointed for the purpose reported in 1934, but the question of increasing the rate of emigration was not again canvassed until the advent to power of the Nationalist Party, when Dr. Malan announced in March 1948 that the basis of his policy was the repatriation of as many Indians as possible.

In 1949 there was some revival of repatriation following a series of anti-Asian riots in Durban, and the Union Government sought to encourage it by offering to double the rate of bonus for a limited period. Between 1948 and 1952, however, only 530 Asians left the Union under this scheme. The Cape Town Agreements of 1926–7 also provided for the appointment of an Agent-General to the Government of India in South Africa. His status was changed in 1941 to that of High Commissioner, but as the result of subsequent deterioration in the relations of the two countries he was recalled in 1946, and the Office was closed when diplomatic relations were broken off in 1954.[3]

Up to the time of the Cape Town Agreements of 1926–7 the problem of the Asian community had, as has been seen, been regarded as one which could be solved by restrictions on immigration or by promoting measures for the repatriation of Asians. From this point onwards, however, it is no longer possible to treat the matter in this light. The situation became complicated partly by the growing recognition that the solution of the problem was not likely to be found merely in varying the factors of immigration or repatriation: it was further complicated by the divergency in the measures affecting the Asian community which were taken by various municipalities or other local bodies in the Union.

Moreover, the problem no longer stood by itself; it became one of the facets in the complex situation which the Union was attempting to solve by the application of the principle of segregation. It will be convenient therefore to proceed now by discussing some of the facts relating to the economic and social standing of the Asian community in the Union, and the extent to which it has in fact been affected by the legislation designed to deal with the complex of social problems of which it is a part.

Statistics of Asian Population

In the first census taken after the establishment of the Union, namely that of 1911, the Asian population was shown as 152,203 as compared with a White population of 1,276,242. In 1951 the community was shown

[1] South Africa, Senate Debates, 1948, vol. ii, col. 1503.
[2] O.Y.S.A., 1952–53, p. 1098.   [3] Africa Digest, June 1954, p. 16.

as numbering 366,664, as compared with a White population of 2,642,713.[1] It increased between 1911 and 1921 at an annual rate of 0·86 per cent., between 1921 and 1936 at 1·90 per cent., between 1936 and 1946 at 2·65 per cent., and between 1946 and 1951 at 5·15 per cent. On the basis of returns compiled in 1951, some 299,491 members of the Asian population lived in Natal, of whom 160,674 were in Durban, where they outnumbered the European population by 9,503. There were only 17,818 in the Cape, 49,342 in the Transvaal, and 13 in the Orange Free State. Of the total number of Asians, 90 per cent. were estimated to have been born in South Africa. The great majority of the Asian residents in Natal are descendants of indentured labourers employed in the coal-mines and on sugar estates, though only a minority are so employed today. They are mainly an urban community, and seven out of ten Asians live in eight of Natal's largest towns. In Natal their total annual income was estimated in 1951 at £12½ million out of a probable total income of £100 million for the Province.[2] The total area of land, urban and rural, held by Asians in the Union as a whole was estimated in 1946 at about 150,000 acres.[3]

There has been a noticeable transition from employment in the mines and on sugar estates to different forms of industrial employment. The 'civilized labour policy' adopted by the Union Government in the period of depression after the First World War aimed at the replacement of Asian and Coloured workers by Europeans in all forms of employment, but the subsequent development of secondary industries and the activity during the Second World War opened increased opportunities to Asians in semi-skilled occupations. Since 1927 they have been admitted to several Natal trade unions, and Asian unions have been legally recognized. Asian commercial establishments, ranging from hawkers' booths to chain stores and cinemas, are to be found in all Provinces except the Orange Free State. The Asian trader has established himself on his ability to trade on a small turnover and a correspondingly small margin of profit. He can justly claim that he has thus rendered a useful service alike to the African and to the less affluent European.

Restrictive Measures directed against Asians

The political and municipal status of the Asian community has varied in the different Provinces. In the Cape anti-Asian feeling was never strong, and Asians were classed with the Coloured population, sharing the same parliamentary and municipal franchise. In the Transvaal Asians never had any franchise. In Natal they were deprived of the provincial franchise in 1897, of the franchise in boroughs in 1924, and of the

[1] *O.Y.S.A.*, 1952–53, pp. 1083–97.
[2] R. Burrows, *Indian Life and Labour in Natal*, 1952.
[3] *Handbook on Race Relations in South Africa*, 1949, p. 217.

townships' franchise in 1925, except for those whose names were already on the rolls. In 1946 the Asiatic Land Tenure and Indian Representation Act[1] granted to Asians a communal franchise which was intended to compensate them for restrictions imposed on their right to own property; the community has, however, rejected the offer of a communal franchise and has demanded recognition for the principle of a common roll with property or similar qualifications. This part of the Act was repealed by the Nationalist Government in 1948. After the passing of the Separate Representation of Voters Act in 1951, Asians were left with no political representation.[2]

The administrative matters in which the Asian community are most concerned are the laws regulating licences to trade and the ownership of immovable property. For many years Asians have contended that the trade licensing system as operated in all the Provinces has discriminated against them. In Natal there is an appeal to the Supreme Court against a refusal by the municipal licensing authorities to renew a licence,[3] but the Licensing Officer for Durban admitted before the Asiatic Inquiry Commissions in 1921 and 1925 that Asian applications for new licences were usually rejected, and that the effect of licensing had been to segregate the Asian traders.[4] It is noticeable that an amending Ordinance of 1935 made the possible depreciation of adjacent property a valid reason for refusing a licence. In the Cape the existing procedure for licensing appears to have given on the whole an adequate protection to legitimate Asian traders. In the Transvaal the Licences Control Ordinance of 1931 gives the Local Authority complete discretion in this matter, thus excluding any appeal to the Courts. It was admitted in 1936 that Municipalities had consistently endeavoured to 'keep the Coloured person separate from the White by refusing to grant trading licences to Indians'.[5]

In regard to the ownership and occupation of property Asians have been subject to a varying measure of discrimination. In the Transvaal the law has since 1885 debarred them from owning property, but up to 1919 they contrived to find a means of doing so through trustees or land-holding companies. In addition there have been special restrictions on the occupation of land by 'Coloured persons' in areas proclaimed as public diggings under the Gold Law and the Townships (Amendment) Act of 1908. These were not, however, strictly enforced, and Asians in illegal occupation of such stands were in 1919 given protection from eviction.[6]

In 1930 it was found that there were still illegal occupants of such land, while many of those who had been protected by the Act of 1919 had since

---

[1] Act no. 28 of 1946.   [2] Act no. 46 of 1951; see also above, p. 164.
[3] Act no. 22 (Natal) of 1909.
[4] Asiatic Inquiry Commission; Minutes of Evidence, 2.1503.
[5] *Report of Select Committee on Transvaal Asiatic Land Tenure Amendment Bill*, 1936, Q.124, p. 109.
[6] Asiatics (Land and Trading) Amendment (Transvaal) Act, no. 37 of 1919.

lost that protection by moving their premises or in other ways. In 1932 the Transvaal Asiatic Land Tenure (Amendment) Act[1] sought to provide for the cases of technically illegal occupation by giving power to the Minister to exempt selected land in the proclaimed areas from the provision of the Gold Law. A commission presided over by Mr. Justice Feetham sat to consider exemptions to be made under this Act, and in 1935 a further Act[2] gave Asians the right of ownership as well as of occupation in 'exempted areas', which were to be proclaimed when the extent of Asian occupation was known. The date was, however, repeatedly postponed, and it is understood that no 'exempted areas' have since been proclaimed.

In Natal Asians were until 1943 under no legal disabilities in the matter of possessing or occupying land, but from about 1939 great anxiety has been expressed by Europeans regarding the penetration of Asians into European residential areas. The Lawrence Committee of 1940 sought to secure an agreement on the basis that there should be no further transfers to Asians in predominantly European areas, but in 1941 the City Council withdrew from the Agreement on the ground that this provision was ineffective. It appears that the number of sites acquired by Asians in 1942 was two and a half times as many as the highest previous annual total.[3]

The Union Government then enacted the Trading and Occupation of Land (Transvaal and Natal) Restriction Act,[4] popularly known as the 'Pegging Act', which prohibited transfers between Europeans and Asians for a period of three years. At the end of that time it enacted the Asiatic Land Tenure and Indian Representation Act,[5] which was likewise applicable only in Natal and the Transvaal. In the Transvaal it did no more than amend the law so as to close the loopholes for illegal occupation; no exempted areas were proclaimed. In Natal it provided for the demarcation of the Province into exempted and unexempted areas. In the former there was to be no restriction on the holding of property by Asians; in the latter they might not buy or occupy property without a permit from the Minister of the Interior. In the Act, premises used solely for licensed trading purposes and not for residence were excepted from this provision, but this exception was removed by an Amendment of 1949.[6]

The series of measures directed against Asians has thus become increasingly restrictive in the last 25 years. But it is doubtful if they have affected the community as gravely as the more recent measure, the Group Areas Act of 1950, which was, as already explained,[7] designed to implement generally the policy of *apartheid* so strongly favoured by the Nationalist

[1] Act no. 35 of 1932.
[2] Transvaal Asiatic Land Tenure (Amendment) Act, no. 30 of 1936.
[3] *Report of Second Indian Penetration (Durban) Commission*, U.G. no. 21, 1943.
[4] Act no. 35 of 1943.   [5] Act no. 28 of 1946.
[6] Act no. 53 of 1949.   [7] See above, p. 165.

Government. Its immediate consequence is likely to be felt most severely by Asians, for not only may it involve their displacement from urban areas in which they have long held house property, but it would restrict the areas in which they can act effectively as tradesmen or craftsmen. The first effect of the Act was seen in the proposals put forward by the Durban City Council in 1952 for the 'zoning' of group areas within the municipality. Asians asserted in 1953 that 146,000 of their community were likely to be evicted from their homes, and property worth some £28 million surrendered in Durban alone.[1] It is not yet possible to say how far this forecast is likely to be accurate.

Indian Government's Reaction

It was inevitable that the increasing stringency of the measures affecting the Asian community should find a response in action taken by the Government of India. Soon after the passing of the 'Pegging' Act of 1943[2] the Indian Government passed a Reciprocity Act designed in general terms to impose on residents of a non-reciprocating country of the Commonwealth the same disabilities as were applied in that country to Indians. After the passing of the Asiatic Land Tenure Act of 1946 India terminated the Trade Agreement between the two countries, and prohibited all exports from India to South Africa and all imports from South Africa to India. These measures are still in force so far as India is concerned, though cancelled in 1950 so far as regards Pakistan. During the years 1940 to 1944 the average yearly imports from India into South Africa had been valued at about £7¼ million. Since 1946 such imports as South Africa receives from India (mainly jute manufactures) come by indirect channels and are not shown as imports from India in the Union trade statistics. The measures taken by India to close indirect channels of export to South Africa have not proved to be fully effective.[3] As already shown, India withdrew her High Commissioner from South Africa in 1946 and closed his office in 1954.[4]

Towards the end of 1946 India decided to bring the question of the treatment of Asians in South Africa before the General Assembly of the United Nations. Throughout the subsequent series of discussions the Union Government has maintained that the matter is a purely domestic one in terms of Article 27 of the Charter, but it has been outvoted, despite the abstention of a number of States (including the United Kingdom) which

[1] *India News*, 24 October 1953. See also *Disabilities of the Non-White Peoples in the Union of South Africa*, Government of India Ministry of External Affairs, 1953, p. 31.

[2] See above, p. 395.

[3] For the history of these transactions see the series of White Papers beginning with that published in vol. iii of Proceedings of Ninth Parliament of the Union, 1946–7, and ending with that published in vol. 3 of First Session of Eleventh Parliament 1953.

[4] See above, p. 392.

have shared the same view. In May 1949 the General Assembly invited the Governments of India, Pakistan, and South Africa to hold a Round Table discussion on the matter at issue. Preliminary talks were held at Cape Town in February 1950, but when the Union refused to defer the passing of the Group Areas Act, the Indian Government declined to take part in the proposed conference.

At subsequent meetings of the General Assembly of the United Nations, resolutions were adopted recommending the appointment of a commission to assist the two Governments to reach a settlement, and urging the Union Government to suspend the operation of its legislation against Asians. On each occasion South Africa has voted against the resolution and no action has been taken on it. A Good Offices Commission sponsored by the organization of the United Nations has failed to persuade the two Governments to come to an agreement on the subject. The insistence of the General Assembly on the discussion of this issue has been one of the reasons which have decided the Union Government to withdraw its deputation to the United Nations organization in 1955. This decision was, as already shown, reversed in the following year.

Housing and Education of Asians

The effect of the constitutional disabilities above referred to has been heightened by the social ostracism to which even well-educated Asians have been subjected by most Europeans in the Union. There are at the same time certain other aspects of the situation which have been of great importance to the Asian community. The Cape Town Agreements, while recognizing the right of the Union to take steps to maintain Western standards of life, held that the conditions of Asians domiciled in South Africa should not be allowed to fall too far behind those of the rest of the community. The Union Government undertook to investigate the housing conditions in the densely populated area in and around Durban and also to examine the provision of facilities for the education of Asians.

As regards housing there have been considerable advances made, particularly in Durban. The worst conditions were in areas outside the municipal boundaries, but these were incorporated in the Borough in 1932 and thus became subject to the Slums Act passed in 1934.[2] Rebuilding under the provisions of this Act and the enforcement of municipal sanitary regulations have resulted in a considerable improvement. Asians have been suspicious of housing schemes designed specifically for them since they may involve racial segregation, but in 1945 the Durban Corporation announced plans for four Asian housing schemes totalling 18,400 houses, and substantial progress has since been made in implementing this scheme.

The Cape Town Agreements have, moreover, resulted in giving

---

[1] See above, p. 175.   [2] Act no. 53 of 1934.

considerable impetus to the extension of Asian education. The community has itself established a number of schools, which have received State aid, but the Development schemes of the Natal Administration have aimed at providing accommodation for all Asian children in the Province. The shortage of trained teachers has so far proved to be a serious handicap to the realization of the programme; by 1948, however, the Administration had launched a scheme designed to meet all Asian primary and secondary educational needs within a period of five years. Primary education was made free in all schools in 1949;[1] the total expenditure on Asian education in Natal rose from £28,430 in 1926–7 to £1,074,936 in 1951. There is, however, still a marked deficiency in facilities for higher or technical education. In Durban two institutions of advanced education were built by Asian subscriptions—the Sastri College, opened in 1929, and the N.L. Sultan Technical College, opened in 1945; both are now State aided.

Relations between Asians and Africans

While Asians complain of discrimination against them in favour of Europeans, Africans, particularly in Durban, have numerous complaints against Asians. Their attitude aroused public attention after the attacks by Africans on Asians in three days of serious rioting in Durban in January 1949. The grounds for ill-feeling cited before the commission[2] which inquired into the circumstances of the riots included profiteering by Asian traders, exploitation by slum landlords, competition by Asians in retail trade in African areas, and the high rate of increase of the Asian population. The commission considered, however, that some of these causes of ill-feeling were greatly exaggerated by Africans.

The oldest organization for the expression of Asian opinion is the South African Indian National Congress, which followed on the extension to the Cape and Transvaal of the Natal Indian Congress formed by Mr. Gandhi in 1894. Asian commercial communities in the Transvaal also organized themselves to defend their own interests at the time of the inquiry made into the question of Asiatic Land Tenures in 1932 and the following years. South African-born Asians began to emerge as political leaders in the decade after 1940, the first important figure being A. I. Kajee, a member of the Lawrence Committee already referred to.[3] He subsequently lost some of his supporters to a new group within the Congress called the Anti-Segregation Council, under the leadership of Dr. Dadoo. This group later took over the Natal and Transvaal branches of the Congress, and in 1951 entered a 'Joint Planning Council' with representatives of the African National Congress in order to organize protests against discriminatory laws. Mr. Kajee became President of the

---

[1] Burrows, op. cit. p. 39.
[2] *Commission of Enquiry into Riots in Durban*, U.G. 36149, 1949.   [3] See above, p. 395.

Natal Indian Organization, which, with its counterpart in the Transvaal, consists largely of merchants and property owners.

The status of Asians has now become one of the most refractory of the problems of racial relations which confront the Union of South Africa, and it has had unfortunate reactions in many parts of the Commonwealth. In its origin it was mainly a local problem, centring on Durban, and the total number of persons then vitally affected by it formed only a small proportion of the population of the Union. Were it not for the existence of this issue, however, the doctrine of *apartheid* might never have found expression in legislation of so challenging a form as that which it has now taken. If the application of the principle of segregation had been limited to Africans, and had not been extended to Asians, it is unlikely that the policy of the Union in racial matters would have become the focus of an attack such as that which has been made on it by certain sections in the United Nations. That attack has not unnaturally encouraged Africans to present a more united front against measures taken to implement the policy of *apartheid*.

Not only is this the case, but there are now indications that, in spite of the causes of differences between Asians and Africans as evidenced in the rioting in Durban,[1] Africans have begun to welcome the co-operation and even leadership of Asians in their opposition to the segregationist measures taken by the Union Government.[2] It is significant in this connexion that there were in 1953 over 100 students from Africa taking courses at Indian Universities,[3] some of which now include a Department of African Studies. It has been stated that over £1 million has been collected in India to finance a resistance movement in Africa.[4] Apart from any question of political disability, the social ostracism to which even the more educated Africans and Asians are subjected by Europeans embitters both of them, so that an anti-European atmosphere tends to emerge out of their association.[5]

There can be little doubt that the movement which has associated Asians as protagonists in the cause of Africans has been encouraged from India itself, for there is among the leaders in Indian politics an almost missionary zeal for the 'liberation' of Coloured races. Had it been possible at an earlier date to foresee that a period might come when African advance might appear to Europeans in South Africa to constitute a menace to their own economic and social life, prudence might have suggested conferring on the Asian community a status which would have secured its support to the interest of Europeans rather than to that of Africans.

---

[1] See above, p. 392.
[2] See speech of the late J. H. Hofmeyr in Union Parliament, 2 June 1939.
[3] *Indian News*, 11 June 1953.
[4] Debates in the Senate of South Africa, 14–18 September 1953, p. 617.
[5] *The Times*, 5 May 1953.

Whether or not such a development would ever have been possible, it is certain that today it would be entirely impracticable.

FEDERATION OF RHODESIA AND NYASALAND

In neither of the Rhodesias does the presence of the Asian community create a problem comparable to that which it constitutes in the Union. In Southern Rhodesia the Asian population was shown in 1954 as only 4,700 (mainly traders resident in Salisbury and Bulawayo) and as 3,500 in Northern Rhodesia. Asians are in Southern Rhodesia eligible for the franchise on the same terms as Europeans, but they share with Africans the social disabilities of a non-European population. In Nyasaland the Asians were shown as numbering 6,000 in 1954.[1]

The establishment of the Federation has, however, had a direct influence on the policy relating to the immigration of Asians. Towards the end of 1954 legislation was introduced prohibiting further immigration of Asians into the Federation, with certain reservations regarding teachers, ministers of religion, and the wives of Asians already residing within the territories.[2] It was announced that the Government would accept in a multi-racial community only those immigrants who were so far imbued with Western ideals that the British pattern of life might not be disturbed. It based its right to this action on the principle accepted at the Imperial Conference in 1921 that self-governing members of the Commonwealth have the right to determine the character of their immigrants.[3] At the same time the Territorial Legislature of Southern Rhodesia passed a law restricting the movement into Southern Rhodesia of Asians and Eurasians from Northern Rhodesia and Nyasaland,[4] a measure which evoked protests from Asian organizations on the ground of racial discrimination.[5]

EAST AFRICAN TERRITORIES

The old-established trading connexion of Asians with the coastal area of East Africa and the part played by them in more recent developments (as for instance in the construction of the Kenya–Uganda Railway) resulted in the settlement in East Africa of an Asian community largely exceeding in number that to be found in Central Africa. The Railway employed at one time a force of as many as 18,000 indentured labourers, largely from the Punjab,[6] of whom many remained after its completion as artisans or traders or in employment on the Railway. The

[1] Figures taken from *The New Federation of Rhodesia and Nyasaland*, 1954, p. 6.
[2] Federal Immigration Act, no. 37 of 1954.   [3] See above, p. 391.
[4] Inter-territorial Movement of Persons (Control) Act, 1954.
[5] *The Times*, 19 August 1954. *Africa Digest*, September–October 1954, p. 2.
[6] V. Anstey, *The Economic Development of India*, 1952, p. 312.

cotton-ginning industry and the sugar plantations of Uganda were largely developed by Asian enterprise, originating in this case mainly from Bombay and Western India. The most recent returns show a total of 168,543 Asians in the three High Commission Territories in East Africa,[1] and though they form only a small proportion of the total population of 17¾ million, there are more than three times as many Asians as Europeans. As the East Africa Royal Commission of 1953–5 points out, the Asian community is in many ways of a more established character than the European.

Tanganyika

The position of Asians in Tanganyika may be said, in one sense, to present the fewest problems, since the terms of the Trusteeship Agreement, like those embodied in the Mandates, secure them against any form of administrative discrimination. The Germans early recognized their value as traders and admitted them freely. In 1921 they numbered 9,411 as against 2,447 Europeans; in 1952 they were shown as numbering 44,248 compared with 17,885 Europeans. Some 29 per cent. of the population of Dar-es-Salaam is Asian. Of the total number included in the community the great majority were shown as employed in commerce or manufacturing; only some 3,000 were shown as craftsmen. It has been stated that Asians control 50 per cent. of the import and 60 per cent. of the export trade.[2] They have bought a considerable proportion of the lands formerly held by Germans,[3] and now possess 420,058 acres as against 2,493,458 acres held by Europeans.

The Constitutional Development Committee which reported in 1951 recommended that the new Legislative Council should have 21 unofficial members, with seven seats for each of the three main communities; in the Constitution as adopted in 1955 this number was increased to ten.[4] In 1955 there were two unofficial Asian members on the Executive Council. The members of all urban local bodies in Tanganyika are nominated; in Dar-es-Salaam the Municipal Council has seven Asians in a total membership of 23. The minor Township Authorities are also inter-racial.

There are two Government secondary schools for Asians, one in Dar-es-Salaam with 1,000 pupils, which teaches up to the Higher School Certificate standard, and one in Tanga, with 2,400 pupils. In 1954–5 the total enrolment in schools of all grades was 18,643. There is an Asian Education Authority, which assists in the administration of an Asian Education Fund financed partly by Government grants-in-aid and partly by the proceeds of an education tax paid by Asians and fees paid in Government schools.

[1] Report of East Africa Royal Commission 1953–1955, Cmd. 9475, para. 20.
[2] C. Kondapi, Indians Overseas, 1838–1949, 1951.
[3] See below, p. 783.   [4] See above, p. 304.

If the Asians in Tanganyika have found any cause of complaint it has for the most part been directed against legislation of general application rather than against any regulation specifically directed against their community. They have, for example, protested against the control exercised over the marketing of African produce, the Land (Restriction of Transfer) Ordinance of 1943, and the restriction imposed in 1941 on private road-transport services working on routes served by the Railway Department's vehicles.[1]

Uganda

In Uganda the Asians (apart from a small number of Goans) were recorded in 1948 as numbering 33,767, having increased from 5,000 in the census of 1921; 60 per cent. are stated to be permanently settled in Uganda; Asians form 45 per cent. of the population of Kampala. The Europeans in the Protectorate were recorded in 1948 as numbering 3,448. The striking increase in the number of Asians since 1921 has caused alarm in both the European and African communities. It has been held in particular that the exemptions to the immigration regulations which permitted the entry of husbands and wives of permanent residents into Uganda would result in a heavy annual increase of the Asian population. A motion to restrict these exemptions was recently adopted in the Legislative Council, being supported by all European and African members.[2]

The majority of the Asians are engaged in commerce, but they were also recorded in 1952 as holding some 62,440 acres of cultivated land. They possess two large sugar plantations, producing some 55,000 tons of white sugar annually. It was calculated as far back as 1928 that 90 per cent. of the total trade of the country was in the hands of Asians, but it is in the development of the cotton industry that they have shown their greatest activity. About 60 per cent. of the lint cotton is on an average shipped to India, about half of this being handled by Asians, and Asians hold by far the largest number of cotton ginneries in the Protectorate.

Incidents connected with this latter development have been one of the major causes of such complaints as Asians have had to make regarding the policy of the Government. The rapid success of the distribution of cotton seed of American Upland varieties in the year 1903–4[3] created opportunities of which Asians took full advantage, whether in marketing, ginning, or exporting cotton, but it also gave occasion for malpractices at the expense of the African cultivator which it was necessary to suppress by administrative control. Legislation, beginning with the Cotton Ordinance no. 11 of 1926, prohibited the sale of cotton except in approved markets,

---

[1] Use of Motor Vehicles (Restriction) Ordinance, Laws Cap. 170.
[2] *Africa Digest*, vol. ii, no. 8, March–April, 1955, p. 20.
[3] G. B. Masefield, *A Short History of Agriculture in the British Colonies*, 1950, pp. 86–87.

and provided for the licensing of buyers and ginners. The licensing of buyers was extended to other African produce by the Native Produce Marketing Ordinance no. 20 of 1932, and the bulk marketing scheme introduced during the Second World War severely restricted the entry of new middlemen into the trade. A Commission[1] which reported in 1948 stated that a number of the ginneries (which then numbered 195) were redundant, and that this fact led to abuses at the expense of the African cultivator. Of the total number of 195 only 12 were held by Europeans and five by Africans; the rest were all in the hands of Asians. The Commission recommended a substantial reduction in the number of ginneries, the progressive participation by African Co-operatives in the ginning industry, and the purchase of existing ginneries by the Government for this purpose.

Legislation was subsequently enacted in order to give effect to these measures.[2] It met with protests from Asians, but if there was any serious display of feeling it was between Asians and Africans, and particularly the more enterprising elements of Africans in Buganda, who have regarded the past monopoly of the cotton trade by Asians as prejudicial to their own interests. Asians have protested that they are now involved in the heavy expenditure of modernizing the ginneries which still remain in their possession. It has, on the other hand, become clear that Africans cannot provide the necessary capital themselves or through their Co-operative Unions, and as a result the Government have enacted the Ginneries (Amendment) Ordinance of 1952 by which it can lease to African Co-operative Unions the ginneries acquired by it.[3]

The question of the representation of Asians caused some discontent between the years 1920–5, when they had only one nominated seat in the Legislature. They then contended for the institution of a franchise based on education and property qualifications which would apply to all communities alike. There is less ground for dissatisfaction with the present system, which as shown in a previous chapter provides for equality of representation with Europeans.[4] It is at the same time significant of the attitude of Africans towards the Asian community that one of the major obstacles to agreement regarding the new Constitution which was under discussion in the years 1954–5 was the strong objection by Africans, and particularly the leaders of opinion in Buganda, to the appointment of an Asian as Minister.[5]

There were in 1953 three Government primary schools and three

[1] *Report of Uganda Cotton Industry Commission*, 1948, p. 11.
[2] Produce Marketing Ordinances of 1952 and 1953. See also *The Colonial Territories, 1952–53,* Cmd. 8856, p. 50.
[3] *The Times*, 21 November 1953. For the policy generally, see *Report of East Africa Royal Commission, 1953–1955,* Cmd. 9475, p. 74.
[4] See above, p. 295.   [5] See above, p. 294. See also *The Times*, 23 May 1955.

Government secondary schools for Asians, with 76 Asian-owned schools, aided from Government funds. Educational facilities were improved when three new primary and two secondary schools were completed in 1954 and 1955. For higher education Asian children are usually sent to India; teaching up to the Cambridge School Certificate Standard is provided at the secondary schools. The cost of Asian education is in part financed from the proceeds of a non-Native Education Tax, its expenditure being supervised by an Advisory Council for Asian Education.

Asian Communities in Kenya

Among the three East African territories it is only in Kenya that issues regarding the status of Asians have given rise to any serious friction, though even there it has been of a very different order from that which has occurred in the Union of South Africa. The Asian community has grown more rapidly in Kenya than in either of the other two territories of East Africa and it now equals the number of Asians in both of them combined. Numbering 10,651 in 1911, as against 3,175 Europeans, it was recorded as 26,759 in 1926 and rose to 90,528 at the census of 1948, compared with a population of 29,660 Europeans;[1] they constituted 34 per cent. of the resident population of Nairobi. The Asians do not belong exclusively to the trading class, and the Colony has depended largely on the Asian community for its clerks, artisans, and craftsmen. In 1948 some 9,498 out of the 27,872 gainfully employed males were shown to be engaged in commerce (including salesmen and shop assistants), and 3,150 as clerks (excluding civil servants). There were 7,156 employed as artisans, craftsmen, or mechanics. Only 292 were engaged in agriculture, of whom 166 were working on their own account, including a group of sugar planters who provide a substantial part of the Colony's production of sugar.

A number of different religious communities are represented, and there is, as in Tanganyika, a strong group of that branch of the Isma'ili Muslims which recognizes the leadership of the Aga Khan. The Isma'ili section of Shi'ite Muslims is divided between those who revere the Aga Khan as the forty-eighth Imam,[2] and those (commonly known as Musta'tis) who follow a number of other Imams. The followers of the Aga Khan are well represented in East Africa, and notably in Tanganyika and Kenya. There is among them one community, that of the Khojas, who are especially prominent in Tanganyika. They come mostly from Sind and Cutch, but

---

[1] Report on the Census of the Non-European Population of Kenya, 1953. The figure in the text excludes Goans and Arabs.

[2] For the position accorded to the Aga Khan as Imam, see J. N. D. Anderson, Islamic Law in Africa, 1954, p. 324.

are said to be descended from Hindus of Northern India who embraced Islam some 500 years ago. They have a long tradition of migration in search of trade, and now include some of the leading business men in East Africa. The various local Khoja communities are organized in a federation with a Supreme Council, which administers the proceeds of the annual tithe contributed by them, and from its revenues maintains a considerable number of schools and medical services.[1] Although no definite figures exist of the numbers of this community, it has been stated that there are some 27,000 in Tanganyika, 17,000 in Kenya, and 6,000 in Uganda.[2]

Up to the time of the separation of Pakistan from India in 1947, there was in East Africa no marked division between Hindus and Muslims, but a certain measure of antagonism has since developed between them. Legislation passed in 1951 gave separate representation to non-Muslims and Muslims in the Legislative Council of Kenya, and the East African National Congress, which claims to represent all Asians, boycotted in consequence the Legislative Council elections of 1952. The principle has been retained in the constitutional changes effected in 1954,[3] where of the two unofficial Asian members of the Council of Ministers one is a Hindu and the other a Muslim.[4] The wisdom of this measure of communal representation is open to question, for it gives recognition in the political field to differences which, whatever may be their social or economic basis elsewhere, tend in East Africa to be of a purely religious character.

There can be no doubt of the value of the contribution made by Asians to the development of the economy of Kenya. It was estimated in 1944 that they paid $27\frac{3}{4}$ per cent. of the indirect taxation as compared with 37 per cent. by Europeans.[5] But, as was pointed out in the Financial Inquiry made by Lord Moyne in 1932,[6] figures such as these do not suffice to indicate the part which has been played by Asians in the development of the country either as traders, or in marketing Native produce, or as artisans and craftsmen. In these directions they have performed a function which Europeans were not prepared and Africans were not qualified to discharge.[7]

[1] *The Times*, 3 August 1953.

[2] Anderson, op. cit. pp. 320, 322, 370. S. Vesey Fitzgerald, *Mohammedan Law*, 1931, pp. 20, 151. The Aga Khan, *Memoirs of the Aga Khan*, 1954. N. Leys, *Kenya*, 1925, pp. 256 ff.

[3] Legislative Council (Amendment) Ordinance 1948, made permanent by Ordinance no. 67 of 1951.

[4] See above, p. 195.

[5] *Report of Taxation Inquiry Committee, Kenya 1947*, East African Pamphlet, no. 238, 1947.

[6] *Report by the Financial Commissioner on Certain Questions in Kenya*, Cmd. 4093, 1932.

[7] See *Report of the Commission on Closer Union of the Dependencies in Eastern and Central Africa*, Cmd. 3234, 1929, p. 26, for an admirable appreciation of the position of the Asian community. See also *East Africa Royal Commission 1953–1955, Report*, Cmd. 9475, p. 65, for the large contribution of the Asian traders to the growth of modern commerce.

Asians and the White Highlands

The differences between the European and Asian communities have centred mainly on three questions: the reservation to Europeans of the lands comprised in the 'White Highlands', the proposal to segregate Asians in urban areas, and the grant of representation to them in the Legislature. An account will be given elsewhere of the decision taken in 1902 to encourage the permanent settlement of Europeans in Kenya and of the steps taken from 1906 onwards to reserve land in the Highland areas for European occupation.[1] Here it will suffice to note that in 1908 Lord Elgin announced the decision that 'while legal restrictions should not be placed on any section of the community, as a matter of administrative convenience grants of land in the uplands should not be made to Asiatics'.[2] It should be explained that the term 'Highlands' is used in a geographical sense to comprise the great central upland plateau of which the greater part is now secured by law for the occupation of various African tribes, while the part known as the 'White Highlands' is reserved for occupation by Europeans. This latter area is now recorded as amounting to 16,173 square miles, of which, however, 3,979 is State forest.[3]

The Crown Lands Ordinance of 1915 did not prohibit Asians from acquiring land anywhere in the Colony, but it has been the practice of the Administration when disposing of lands in the 'White Highlands' to stipulate that the purchaser must be of European extraction, and transfers between persons of different races have required the sanction of the Government. The decision taken in 1908 was strongly resented by Asians. The Government of India, in making remonstrances on their behalf, pointed out that there were already large areas in the Dominions from which they were totally excluded, and claimed that they had a special right to equality of treatment in East Africa by reason of their early association with the country and the part they had played in its development.[4] In addition to reserving this considerable area to Europeans it became the practice from about 1912 to impose as a condition of sale of residential land in certain of the urban areas a covenant that it should not be occupied by any person not a European.

In the years immediately following the First World War there was a marked increase of anti-Asian sentiment among the European community, the result partly of a belief that there had been a disproportionate increase in Asian immigration and partly of a feeling that Asian traders had made excessive profits during the campaign in German East Africa. A local Economic Commission which reported in 1919 made an unfortunate

---

[1] See below, p. 718.

[2] *Tenure of Land in the East Africa Protectorate*, Cd. 4117, 1908, pp. 25, 33. See also Cmd. 9475, pp. 19, 169.

[3] *N.A.*, Part I, pp. 89, 187 ff.   [4] *Indians in Kenya, Memorandum*, Cmd. 1922, 1923.

reference to Asians as people less civilized than Africans in matters of sanitation and as marked by a moral depravity which was inimical to African advancement.[1] It recommended accordingly the limitation of further Asian immigration. This passage in the report was repudiated by Lord Milner, then Secretary of State for the Colonies. He decided that there should be no discrimination against Asians in the application of the immigration regulations, and laid down that an adequate area of land outside the Highlands should be set aside for Asian settlement.[2] He accepted, however, the principle of racial segregation in the residential areas in towns on the ground that this was best suited to the circumstances of both communities.

These decisions led to renewed representations by the Government of India, for events in the Union had now made that Government very sensitive of the reaction shown by Indian opinion to the treatment accorded to Asians in Africa. In 1923 the British Government issued a statement[3] which confirmed the policy laid down in 1908 in regard to the reservation of land in the Highlands, but the policy of residential segregation was now abandoned, and restrictions upon immigration were in future to be only such as were required by economic considerations and the interests of the African population.

Although the restrictive covenants already in force in 1923 in respect of urban properties were maintained, the areas thus reserved to Europeans are in fact relatively small. But the reservation of the White Highlands for European occupation is still a source of resentment to the Asian community, and Asians have also objected to the subsequent Ordinances of 1944 and 1948, which have required the permission of a Land Control Board for all transfers of rights in land elsewhere. It must be noted, however, that though for some years after Lord Milner's dispatch of 1920 a considerable area of Crown land outside the Highlands was kept available for agricultural settlement by Asians, there was apparently no demand for it, and it may be questioned whether there is actually any considerable body of Asians who wish to take up cultivation. The question seems at this stage to have become largely one of status.[4]

Immigration Ordinances of 1949

The resolution of the Imperial Conference in 1921, with its particular reference to Asian immigration, has already been mentioned.[5] Though the Government of the Union dissented from this resolution, the British Government entered into discussions with the Government of India and

[1] *Economic Commission, Final Report*, Part I, 1919, p. 21.

[2] Government Notice no. 281, 18 August 1920.

[3] *Indians in Kenya, Memorandum*, Cmd. 1922, 1923.

[4] For the recent proposals for providing for Asian Agricultural Settlement, see *Land Utilization and Settlement*, Sessional Paper no. 8 of 1945, p. 9.   [5] See above, p. 391.

with the Kenya Government on a number of outstanding issues, including that of immigration. It decided to make no immediate change in the system of immigration control,[1] and the actual position from the years 1923 to 1946 was that any British subject who was not 'undesirable' and who could prove that he had means of support could enter the Colony.

In 1946, however, the Kenya Government proposed to enact an Ordinance requiring intending immigrants to possess capital of amounts varying according to the occupation in which they proposed to engage, and though this proposal was withdrawn in response to representations from India, in 1949 all three East African territories passed identical Ordinances regulating the entry of new immigrants. The new laws put into force part of the legislation proposed in 1946, and were in other ways designed to be of a restrictive character.[2] Although their provisions were not explicitly directed against Asians, yet when they were debated in the Kenya Legislature both the Asian members who opposed them and the African representative who spoke in favour of them made it clear that they were expected to restrict the immigration of Asians.

Asians and the Kenya Legislature

The issues which have arisen in connexion with the representation of Asians in the Legislature have formed an important chapter in the constitutional history of Kenya, and may indeed be said to have a special place in the development of British Colonial policy, for the issue of the much canvassed White Paper of 1923, which proclaimed the paramountcy of African interests, was the result of a controversy which had its origin in an Asian, not an African, claim for franchise rights.[3] The history of the demand made by Asians for an electoral franchise based on a common roll, as opposed to a communal roll, has been told in a previous chapter,[4] and it is only necessary to remark here that subsequent developments have done nothing to weaken the objections felt by Europeans to a common roll. Although both the European and Asian votes continue (as has been shown) to be based on communal rolls, in other respects there has been a marked advance in the position accorded to Asians. In the ministerial system initiated in 1954 there were two Asian Ministers, of whom one held a departmental portfolio.[5] Asians are also assured a definite measure of representation on the various Municipal Councils; they had in 1952 seven elected members on the Councils of Nairobi and Mombasa, five nominated members in Kisumu, three in Kitale and Eldoret, and two elected and one nominated member at Nakuru.

---

[1] *Indians in Kenya, Memorandum*, op. cit. p. 5.

[2] Kenya, Immigration Control (Amendment) Ordinance, no. 20 of 1949. Tanganyika, Laws Cap. 251. Uganda, Immigration Control (Amendment) Ordinance, no. 18, of 1949 (now Cap. 43, revised ed. 1951).   [3] See above, p. 190.

[4] See above, p. 296.   [5] See above, p. 300.

The position of the Asian community reappeared as an important issue in the course of the discussions which preceded the institution of the East Africa High Commission in January 1948.[1] A community so predominantly commercial as the Asians was naturally well disposed to the Customs Union which had in 1927 linked Kenya, Uganda, and Tanganyika into an area of free trade, but the proposal for the creation of the East Africa High Commission involved some disagreement as to the extent of their representation in its Legislature. There was from the first a fear lest this body should be dominated by European representatives in Kenya. The earlier proposals made for an equal numerical representation were subsequently modified, in spite of the opposition of both Asian and African leaders.[2] Though it has been clear that the Asians would still prefer the automatic equality of numbers provided in the original proposal, the type of legislation undertaken has not so far created any issue on which there has been a serious difference between the communities.

The educational system makes separate provision for the education of Asians in the larger centres. In 1954–5 Government and private primary schools for Asian children had 30,871 pupils, and secondary schools had 5,448 pupils. Compulsory primary education for boys was introduced in 1942 in the towns of Nairobi, Mombasa, and Kisumu. Asian children are included in the School Health Service inaugurated in 1949. In 1950 the Asian community decided to make a contribution to add to an increased Government grant for Asian education. The relative cost of European compared with Asian and African education not unnaturally continues to be a matter of standing comment; the cost per enrolled pupil in 1954–5 was roughly £85 for Europeans, £21 for Asians, and £5¾ for Africans.

Race Relations in Kenya

Whatever may have been the relations of the Europeans and Asians of Kenya in the past, it is inevitable that the future outlook of both communities should be affected by a realization of the changes which are now taking place in the position of Africans. It is to be expected that Europeans will maintain their objection to a franchise based on a common roll, and will desire to maintain restrictions on Asian immigration. They are, again, likely to adhere to the principle of the reservation of the 'White Highlands' for European occupation in spite of the growing demand that undeveloped land should be made available to all races without discrimination.[3]

As regards economic matters, however, if there is conflict between Europeans and Asians the issues are of a general nature (such, for instance, as the relative advantage which a protective tariff may have for producers as compared with traders), and do not necessarily raise points of friction

[1] See above, p. 188.   [2] See above, p. 301.   [3] See below, pp. 804–5.

between the communities as such. The procedure for the control of marketing of Native produce introduced in 1925, which has been much resented by Asians in Kenya no less than in Uganda, was designed in the interests of Africans rather than of Europeans. Social differentiation, which at one time virtually amounted to ostracism, is now less marked. Apart, however, from such causes of difference, it must be clear to Europeans that the constitutional claims of Asians, which once seemed to offer the most serious threat to the position of Europeans, are now of less significance than the demand made by Africans, supported as it is by evidence of their growing capacity for political activity.

It has been suggested that Asians have been instrumental in organizing African agitation against Europeans or against the Government, and there has indeed been some evidence of this as, for instance, the leadership of the labour strike in Nairobi in 1950.[1] But though prominent politicians in India have advocated a programme of 'alliance between Indians and Africans',[2] there is no proof that the Asian community in Kenya has interested itself in any major movement affecting law and order in the territory. It would appear that the Isma'ili followers of the Aga Khan have in particular been anxious to stand aloof from any inter-communal movement; they have been warned by their leader that the future of Asians in the East African territories lies in Africa, not in India.[3]

It is clear, moreover, that some sections of the Asian community have found reason to realize the effect of African competition in forms of employment which had at one time been held exclusively by their community, and the evidence of the Mau Mau troubles must suggest that some manifestations of African feeling may have consequences which will be fully as damaging to Asians as to Europeans. The leader of the Asian members of the Legislature has expressed himself strongly in favour of the principle of inter-racial partnership. If this co-operation is to be achieved in practice, it is to be hoped that its first fruits will be shown in a further relaxation of the measure of social discrimination to which Asians are still subjected in Kenya, for persistence in this practice may be more productive of ill will against Europeans than any form of constitutional differentiation.

Zanzibar

Turning now to the position in Zanzibar, some reference has already been made to the important part played by Asians in its past history.[4] In the census of 1948 Asians (other than Goans) were shown as numbering 15,211 in the two islands of Zanzibar and Pemba, as compared with 44,560 Arabs and 199,860 Africans. Asians have an important place in the economic life of the main island, and have a major share in the marketing of the

---

[1] *Colonial Reports, Kenya, 1950*, p. 2.   [2] *The Times*, 5 May 1953.
[3] *The Times*, 3 July 1953.   [4] See above, pp. 305 ff.

clove and copra crops which constitute about 98 per cent. of its exports. Judging by the number of coconut and clove groves held by them, they must own about 10,000 acres of land. The importance of the position held by them in these respects is reflected in some recent protests against the prominence of the part taken by Arabs in the political and administrative life of the island. In the Legislative Council, however, Asians have hitherto had two out of the eight nominated unofficial seats, as against three held by Arabs. Reference has been made in a previous chapter to their position in the reformed constitution.[1]

The claims put forward by their Association, the Indian National Association, do not however deal so much with the question of representation on those bodies as with inadequate recruitment of Asians for the Administrative services. They have complained also of the effect of the land legislation designed to control the alienation of land rights by Arabs and Africans, and have protested against recent proposals for the control of immigration.[2] Most of these representations are of a comparatively recent date, and would seem to be a response to the growth of Arab consciousness in general, and, in particular, the attempts of the younger school of Arabs to emphasize the position of Zanzibar as an Arab State. There has hitherto been little evidence of any real tension between the communities.

SYRIAN COMMUNITY IN WEST AFRICA

The Syrians, as they are generally called in West Africa, are Levantines of diverse origin, the majority being Lebanese. Their community is sometimes represented as the West African counterpart of the Asians in Southern and Eastern Africa, but the analogy is not actually close. They are mainly engaged in commerce, and include some of the leading importers on the west coast, but as a proportion of the total population they are relatively unimportant. Their immigration is of recent origin, dating only from the turn of the century, and the majority arrived in West Africa in the decade 1921–31. Since the latter date immigration has been slight. A considerable number are Muslims, but in distinction to the majority in West Africa who adhere to the Malaki'ite School of Muslim Law, most of the Syrians are Hanafi or Ithna Ashari.[3] In the Gold Coast the community numbers only 1,370 (mainly Lebanese); in Sierra Leone, 1,204 (of whom all but 20 are Lebanese). In Nigeria it numbers 1,509 (of whom 1,360 are Lebanese). There are also a certain number in French West Africa and a few in Liberia.

In the Gold Coast Syrian firms are especially active in the textile and grocery importing trades, and in 1950 they were stated to be responsible

---

[1] See above, p. 307. [2] *N.A.*, Part II, p. 13.
[3] J. N. D. Anderson, *Islamic Law in Africa*, 1954, pp. 322 ff.

for about two-fifths of the territory's total imports.   A few firms combine this business with money-lending; there is also considerable Syrian invest-ment in houses and land.   In Sierra Leone they are mainly engaged in retail trade, much of which they have captured from the Creole popula-tion.   They also tend to replace Africans as middlemen in produce buying, and in 1952 were stated to have been responsible for the export of a major part of the production of kola nuts, piassava, and chillies.   They main-tain a close connexion with African rice farmers, to whom they advance cash in the planting season and recover it in kind at the harvest.

Small as are their numbers, Syrians are the main element in non-Native immigration to West Africa, and it is they who will in consequence feel the effect of the immigration restrictions recently introduced in various territories.   In 1955 a motion was brought before the House of Represen-tatives in Nigeria calling for a commission to inquire into what were described as the activities of 'the grabbing and acquisitive Lebanese and the slick Syrians'.   The Government in rejecting the motion declared that its policy was to exclude aliens from vocations which could be under-taken by Nigerians, but to attract aliens whose presence was of social or economic benefit to the country.   Liberia in 1948 sought to restrict trading in the interior by Syrians, but these restrictions were withdrawn in view of representations made by the Lebanese Government.

EAST AFRICAN AND UNION POLICIES COMPARED

There is, as has been seen, a substantial difference between the present policy of the Union in regard to the Asian community and that now obtain-ing in East Africa.   The insistence shown by the Union in applying the principle of segregation has tended to a progressive alienation of its rela-tions with the Asian community.   In East Africa there has, on the other hand, been a growing recognition by most Europeans of the need for assign-ing to Asians an appropriate place in a multi-racial structure of society. It is significant that this has been accompanied by some indication that Africans are beginning to see in the Asian community a possible source of danger to their own economy.   Both Europeans and Africans appear to be apprehensive of the rate of the natural increase of the Asian population. The report of the East Africa Royal Commission of 1953–5[1] has estimated this at between 2·5 per cent. and 3·5 per cent. per annum, and if this is correct it largely exceeds the natural rate of increase of the African population.   It is not impossible that the Asian population in East Africa may, as suggested, amount to about 425,000 in the year 1970.   That would not be a matter of great importance in proportion to an African population which may then amount to 25 million, but it would produce an increasing disparity

[1] *East Africa Royal Commission, 1953–1955*, Cmd. 9475, pp. 38–40.

between the total strength of the European population and that of the Asian.

It is difficult to forecast the future of the Asian community in the Union. If the policy of the Union Government in this matter has been such as to give rise to much criticism in the outside world, the Asian community has for its part failed to recognize certain weaknesses in its own position. It is now a domiciled rather than an immigrant community. The path of wisdom would seem to lie rather in seeking every means of assimilating its culture and its way of life to that of the dominant community in the Union, than in emphasizing its differences and its reliance on support from India and Pakistan.

There is now a reasonable hope of a growing measure of adjustment in the constitutional relations of the European and Asian communities in East Africa. It is an advantage that material progress in the Asian community does not on the whole offer a threat to the economy of the European; the Asian economy is in fact complementary to that of the European rather than competitive with it.

CHAPTER VIII

THE ADMINISTRATION OF AFRICAN AFFAIRS

THE ORGANIZATION OF A SYSTEM OF LOCAL RULE

THROUGHOUT the course of history, nations that have entered on the administration of a country newly brought under their control, whether by conquest or otherwise, have encountered problems which are fundamentally similar in their character. Where the new sovereign Power has a reasonably close affinity to the subject people in race, language, or social institutions it has been possible for it to find among its own population a body of subordinate agents adequate to carry out most of the functions of local rule. But where the sovereign Power has no such affinity with the people of the country to be administered, the employment of an agency of this type has always been liable to prove a source of friction. The less familiar the type of social institution encountered, the greater the difficulty likely to be met in the organization of a working system of local rule. In most instances, therefore, the new Governments have sought to find in the subject population itself the agencies through which they can administer local affairs. The conditions in which these agencies have been employed have varied widely in accordance with the political philosophy of the sovereign Power and the reactions of the subject people.

In some cases the sovereign Power has been content to leave feudatory rulers in the subject country to enjoy a practical status of autonomy, subject to their acknowledgement of its political paramountcy. The most typical example of this procedure is to be seen in the status accorded by the British to the ruling dynasties of the Indian States. Elsewhere the sovereign Power has recognized the local rulers as constituted by custom, but, like the Dutch in Indonesia, has subjected them to a day-to-day control by way of 'advice' which has deprived them of any real measure of independence. In other cases it has recognized the existence of traditional indigenous authorities (sometimes Chiefs, sometimes tribal Councils, or similar bodies), and has allowed them to exercise a wide range of customary powers, subject to the use of these powers being brought under statutory regulation and administrative supervision. That was the system generally known in the British African dependencies under the title of 'Indirect Rule'.

In other circumstances a sovereign Power has chosen to recognize traditional authorities (more particularly Native Chiefs), but to regard them as subordinate officials exercising derivative powers, as part of its own organization of rule. That is the procedure which has normally been adopted in French West and French Equatorial Africa. To take a final example, a controlling Power has on occasion preferred to neglect the existence of indigenous authorities in the subject community and has created from among the members of that community a hierarchy of appointed officials, controlled by a small body of officers belonging to the ruling race. That was in effect the system used by the Administration in British India.

These instances are quoted mainly to illustrate the diversity of the methods adopted in differing circumstances and at different periods in order to furnish a suitable agency for the conduct of local rule. They do not exhaust the list, for there are numberless gradations between them, nor do they constitute exclusive categories of procedure. There is, for example, no justification for assuming that any such clear distinction exists between systems of Direct and Indirect Rule as might be assumed from the general use of these terms. The suggestion of an underlying antithesis is in fact misleading, and the retention of the terms can be justified only as a convenient way of indicating that the term 'Indirect Rule' as commonly used denotes that the Government concerned has on principle preferred the use of the traditional Native Authorities, as such, for employment as the recognized agencies of Native Administration. To that extent, the procedure adopted in Indirect Rule is specifically and *par excellence* a Native Authority system.[1]

The term 'Native Administration' has acquired in Africa a specific connotation which it will be convenient to explain here. The character of the problems encountered in finding a suitable procedure of local rule in African conditions accounts for the fact that there has been created in a number of African territories a separate branch of governmental activity described as a Department of African Affairs. The outstanding example of this procedure is in the Union of South Africa, where the interests of the European community have been paramount and the position assigned to Africans in the social and economic field has led to the existence of a large body of differential legislation applying specifically to them. The Rhodesias have Departments of Native Affairs or African Affairs for reasons which resemble, but are not identical with, those which exist in the Union of South Africa. There are, however, other British territories where the relatively small range of European interests has made it unnecessary to treat the administration of African affairs as a separate

[1] R. L. Buell, *The Native Problem in Africa*, vol. i, 1928, pp. 717–27. M. Perham, *Native Administration in Nigeria*, 1937, pp. 346 ff. Idem, 'A Restatement of Indirect Rule', *Africa*, July 1934, pp. 321 ff. L. Mair, *Native Policies in Africa*, 1936, pp. 12 ff. *N.A.*, Part IV, pp. 8 ff.

activity, and in cases where this term is used it refers mainly to the procedure by which officers are specially detailed for dealing with certain subjects, such as the selection of the Native Authorities to be employed as agencies of local rule, or the procedure to be followed in the administration of customary law by African tribunals. If these subjects are treated as separate from the general activity of the Government, it is mainly because they are matters which require special study or experience.

It would obviously be out of place to speak now of a separate branch of African affairs in connexion with the semi-Responsible Governments, such as that of the Gold Coast, which are rapidly assuming the status of African Governments. The conception of a special branch of African affairs is less familiar in the French than in the British territories. In the French West African Territories the current doctrine of the assimilation of all races in the *Union Française* would seem to exclude the idea of maintaining a separate branch of government dealing with African affairs. In the Belgian Congo certain aspects of African affairs are officially described under the title of *la politique indigène*; but this does not imply that there is any separate Department of State explicitly devoted to them.

The following pages will deal with the background which lies behind this diversity of practice in the various African territories. But they will also serve a second purpose, for they will trace the course of a more recent development in the same field. In the British dependencies, in particular, the traditional Native Authorities who have been so widely recognized for the purposes of local rule have in the recent past been increasingly utilized as agencies for the provision of what are usually described as Local Government services. This represents an accretion to their functions as originally conceived, for they were viewed in the first instance mainly as agencies for the maintenance of order, the administration of justice, or the collection of tax. The tendency to expand their activity as agencies for the provision of social services has in turn involved the need to expand their financial resources for the purpose and to give them powers to raise a local rate.[1]

The gradual extension of the institutions of political self-government and the increased resort to the use of the electoral system for that purpose have meant that the traditional Native Authorities are now tending to give place to elected bodies in the form of Local Boards largely designed to discharge Local Government functions. In theory this should have left the Native Authorities still in existence as agencies for the discharge of the functions (such as the maintenance of order or the administration of justice) with which they were charged in the first instance, but in practice

---

[1] For a discussion regarding the growth of Local Government institutions in the British Colonies see Royal Institute of Public Administration, *Local Government in the Colonies—1955 Conference Report*, 1955.

the tendency has been to substitute purely official agencies for these purposes also, leaving the traditional Native Authority organization gradually to atrophy or to disappear as part of the machinery of government.

So far this movement has extended only to certain of the more progressive parts of the British dependencies, but it is likely to grow rapidly and the story of the Native Authority system may at some future time retain little more than an historical interest. The major topic of a chapter such as this will in that case be the story of the development of African Local Government institutions. Even so, however, it would be well to realize that those modern institutions will represent an evolution from the system which made use of the traditional Native Authorities, and that this system has played a noteworthy part in preparing the field for their development.

It will be convenient to describe in the first instance the system of Native Administration followed in the Union of South Africa, and subsequently to deal with the British dependencies in an order which will illustrate the evolution of the procedure based on the use of the traditional Native Authorities as an agency of local rule. This will mean that after dealing with Southern Rhodesia and Kenya, where the Native Authority system has never been applied in its entirety, the remaining British dependencies will be dealt with in the order in which that system was developed. They will accordingly be headed by Nigeria, where the procedure was systematized by Lord Lugard soon after the establishment of the Protectorate in the Northern Provinces in 1900. The remainder of the chapter will survey the system of local rule followed in the French, Belgian, and Portuguese territories.

UNION OF SOUTH AFRICA

Early Stages of Native Policy

The procedure now followed in the administration of African affairs had its origin in the relations established between the European and African communities in the early days of the history of the Cape. The first contacts of the Dutch settlers with local Africans were not such as to dispose them to take a liberal outlook on Native institutions. The Bushmen and Hottentots whom they first encountered showed little indication of the existence of an organized system of society, and from the beginning of the nineteenth century the Hottentot was regarded largely as a source from which to obtain labour in order to replace the supply withdrawn by the termination of the slave trade.[1] They were gradually absorbed as wage-earners into the economy created by the expansion of European farming

[1] W. M. Macmillan, *The Cape Colour Question*, 1927, p. 27; idem, *Bantu, Boer and Briton*, 1929, p. 1.

and they retained neither a separate territory nor distinct existence as a community. Subject therefore to the regulation of their position as labourers, they could be brought within the general scope of the administrative and judicial system applicable to Europeans.

The Bantu, however, presented a different problem, not merely by reason of their numbers, but owing to the nature of their early contacts with the European community. They were regarded at the outset as invaders against whom the Colony must be defended. Many of the tribes did not actually come under administrative control until after the opening of the diamond- and gold-mines. The bulk of the 'Kaffirs' and Zulus were ultimately assigned land in Reserves and Locations,[1] where to some extent they retained their tribal organization. Even, however, if circumstances had made it possible to establish in such areas a system under which the tribesmen might continue to be ruled by their own traditional Authorities, this would not have solved the problems which were created by their entry as wage-earners into the field of European agriculture and industry. The conduct of African affairs accordingly assumed a double aspect: first, the determination of the African's position at the point where he entered into the economic life of the European community, and second, the supervision of tribal life in the areas assigned to him for his separate occupation.

In the solution of the first (and in earlier days the more important) of these problems, and in the enactment of the differential legislation which it involved, the needs of the European economy stood out as the dominant consideration. In the solution of the second problem, policy was largely influenced at the outset by views which regarded the institutions of Africans as incompatible with the requirements of a civilized State, even though the Africans concerned might occupy the subordinate position which South Africa was prepared to assign to the Native community. In the absence of formulated theories of differential treatment, social progress seemed to demand that the African habit of life should as far as possible be assimilated to that of civilized societies. On economic grounds the maintenance of tribal institutions appeared to impede the growth of the incentives which might make the tribesman readily available as a wage-earner.

Racial Segregation

At a later stage the definite formulation of the doctrine of racial segregation[2] has exercised a new and for the time being a dominating influence over Native policy. At an early stage attention had concentrated on the problems presented by the African as a factor in the economic life of the European community; the doctrine of racial segregation now concerns

---

[1] For the history of the Reserve policy, see below, p. 690.
[2] See above, pp. 157 ff., 167 ff.

itself also with the position which he is to be assigned in its social and political life. It continues to assume that as regards the European economy Africans will be restricted as before to the ranks of unskilled (or at the most of semi-skilled) labour in industry or on the farms. For the rest, Africans will not be allowed to practise within the sphere of the European social organization any of the professions which may bring them into close contact or competition with the European, nor will they be allowed any such political rights as will give them a direct share in the government of the country. On the other hand, no restriction will be placed on their capacity to improve their social or material conditions in the Reserves or other lands assigned to them; they will indeed be afforded from the general revenue of the country such aid as is required to improve their education and their health and the production of their lands.

Today the differential legislation which regulates the position of the African in his relations with the European community covers almost every aspect of social and economic life. Its operation in the sphere of political representation has been described in a previous chapter.[1] As will be shown later in the present chapter, the conditions of the residence of Africans in urban areas are regulated by restrictions administered with the aim of limiting the size of the urban African population to the estimated requirements of the local labour market.[2] The operation of the system in respect of labour,[3] of rights in land,[4] and of State-aided education[5] is discussed in later chapters. In dealing now with the system followed in the organization of the areas specifically reserved for African occupation, it will be convenient to give some account of the development in each Province up to the period when the Union laid the basis for a uniform policy in the Native Affairs Act of 1920 and the Native Administration Act of 1927.

Cape Colony

In Cape Colony the earlier policy in regard to British Kaffraria (subsequently known as the Ciskei) was dominated by the desire to avoid direct relations with the African tribes and to control them through treaties with their Chiefs.[6] The attitude which was taken towards this policy in the Glenelg Dispatch of 1835 has been much debated, but in any case the prospect of operating any such system came to an end with the formal renunciation of the treaty policy by Sir Harry Smith in 1847.[7] Henceforth British Kaffraria was treated as a Crown dependency.[8] In 1848 the Chiefs

---

[1] See above, pp. 161 ff. [2] See below, pp. 566 ff.
[3] See below, pp. 1439 ff. [4] See below, p. 691. [5] See below, p. 1142.
[6] E. H. Brookes, *The History of Native Policy in South Africa*, 1927, p. 13.
[7] *Cambridge History of the British Empire*, vol. viii, 1936, pp. 368 ff.
[8] It was formally declared a Crown Colony in 1853 and incorporated in the Cape Colony in 1865.

were allowed the 'reasonable exercise of their authority' under the super-vision of the Magistrate; but in 1855, though still allowed to hear cases, they were 'assisted' by the Magistrates in doing so, and they were given an annual stipend in place of the revenues which they formerly enjoyed from fines and confiscations. The inevitable sequel followed. The Magistrates were given sole authority to decide cases; the Chiefs were reduced to the position of Assessors; administrative control passed into the hands of the Magistrates, and the Chief tended to disappear as the recognized authority over the tribe.

Some details have already been given regarding the reluctance shown in the earlier days of South African history to give any formal recognition to African customary law as the basis for the decision of disputed issues.[1] In 1835, it is true, Resident Agents between the Keiskama and Great Kei rivers were ordered to take into their Courts only major criminal charges, leaving minor offences and civil causes to be disposed of by Chiefs. After the war of 1850 the Grey system, under which Magistrates heard cases jointly with Chiefs, was applied to Kaffraria; the Colonial Courts were now ordered to decide cases according to equity and good conscience, deviating from African custom only so far as might be necessary to attain this end.

After Kaffraria was incorporated in the Cape in 1865, colonial law was in theory applied throughout and no mention was made of customary law except for specified matters, such as intestate succession. The practice of the previous régime, however, forced the Magistrates to admit expedients such as the establishment of an extra-legal Court at King William's Town, which settled disputes under customary law on the understanding that the parties would submit to its decisions.[2] There arose an embarrassing uncertainty as to the law applicable to any given case; the prevailing practice was that in purely African matters custom should prevail, but if this clashed with colonial law, the latter applied.[3] 'Bride-price' (*lobolo*) contracts were not recognized by colonial law,[4] but some Magistrates admitted them, while others refused.

Though this system showed an inadequate regard for African institutions it was, on the other hand, associated also with the Cape political doctrine of 'equal rights for all men' which received its most notable expression in Ordinance 50 of 1828, and in 1853 manifested itself in the grant of franchise rights to non-Europeans. When British Bechuanaland was annexed in 1884, the lack of administrative personnel indicated a different policy. By Proclamation no. 2 of 1885 the operation of Native law was

---

[1] See above, p. 418.
[2] H. Rogers, *Native Administration in the Union of South Africa*, 1933, p. 220.
[3] Brookes, op. cit., p. 96. *Cambridge History of the British Empire*, vol. viii, 1936, p. 825.
[4] See below, p. 594.

recognized to the extent that Chiefs were given exclusive jurisdiction in civil cases between members of their own tribes and were allowed to retain criminal jurisdiction except as regards serious crimes. These powers were subsequently preserved to them by the Native Administration Act of 1927.

Transkeian Territories

The Transkeian Territories had a different history. From the first they were viewed as a purely African area to which there might suitably be relegated those tribes whose presence within the Colony was embarrassing. The process of annexation began with Fingoland and Griqualand East in 1879, and was completed by the incorporation of Pondoland in 1894. The annexation laws recognized that the Africans were 'not sufficiently advanced to be admitted to the full responsibility granted and imposed respectively by the ordinary laws of the Colony'. While, therefore, magisterial rule was extended to them, thus reducing the Chiefs to the position of stipendiaries, customary law was to be administered. It was not, however, until the Cape Native Laws and Customs Commission made its report in 1883 that a uniform system was adopted throughout the Transkei. The colonial criminal law was introduced in the form of the Transkeian Penal Code,[1] which was designed as suitable for Africans, but was made applicable also to the few Europeans resident in the Territories.[2] Native civil law was recognized in the magisterial Courts, but no attempt was made either then or at any subsequent date to codify it.

The Commission of 1883 did not, however, stop at regularizing the legal position; it recognized the need for the creation of institutions of Local Government, and recommended the establishment of an informally elected Native Council. An example of a Native area with its own revenues had existed since the Fingo District of Victoria East had been surveyed in individual holdings the rents of which were administered by the Magistrate. A Fingoland District Fund was established, into which Fingo men paid a small voluntary levy, the proceeds being used to maintain a hospital and for public works.[3] In 1882 Captain Matthew Blyth, the first Chief Magistrate of the Transkei, recommended that 'a sort of Municipal Council be formed in each District'; and in his evidence before the 1883 Commission Sir T. Shepstone suggested the creation of a Council of Chiefs. The recommendation of the Commission for the creation of a Native Council did not bear fruit until the passing of the Glen Grey Act of 1894, but meanwhile the parliamentary franchise was extended to the Transkei by Act 30 of 1887.

[1] Act 24 of 1886.
[2] Brookes, op. cit., p. 306. *Cambridge History of the British Empire*, vol. viii, 1936, p. 506.
[3] F. Brownlee, 'Administration of the Transkeian Native Territories', *J.R.A.S.*, vol. xxxvi, no. 144, 1937, pp. 337–46.

The Glen Grey Act, introduced by Rhodes, referred to a district in the Ciskei, but its significance in the history of Local Administration is due mainly to its subsequent application to the Transkeian Territories. It had a dual purpose; first, the introduction of an individual form of land tenure, and second, the initiation of a practical system of Local Government in Native areas. The first of these purposes will be separately discussed in the chapter dealing with land problems,[1] but the second may appropriately find a place here. Two separate types of local authority were to be created. There were to be subsidiary bodies known as Location Boards for the control of individual Locations, while a higher body, the District Council, was to be responsible for the administration of local affairs in the district as a whole.

In the Transkeian Territories the District Council was from the first the only form adopted. The Transkeian Proclamation 352 of 1894 established four District Councils, each of which sent representatives to a General Council (Bunga). By 1903 Councils had been established in 13 Transkei districts;[2] by 1920 Councils had been constituted in the rest of the Transkeian districts, excepting Xalanga and Mount Currie, which are predominantly European. All the District Councils sent their representatives to the Bunga. In 1911 a General Council was established for the three districts of Western Pondoland.[3] The later history of the Transkeian General Council and the Pondoland Council will be subsequently narrated in dealing with the development of African Local Government institutions after the establishment of the Union.[4]

In the Ciskei the form of institution adopted under the Glen Grey Act was the Location Board. Its functions were confined to such matters as the care of water-courses,[5] control of grass-burning, and the regulation of stock-grazing; the maintenance of soil conservation works was added in 1940.[6] These Boards had therefore only a minor range of functions and appear to have operated with little effect. Their chief value was indeed to provide a useful source of advice to the Magistrate in land administration. The Glen Grey District Council for which provision was made in the Act was established in 1895; the Location Boards were made subordinate to the Council by the Glen Grey Amendment Act of 1905.

Natal

In Natal Native policy was dictated by circumstances rather than by choice. The Blood River battle of 1838 appeared to have given to a White community of some 6,000 persons the command of a territory then largely depopulated as the result of Zulu raiding. The first proposal of the Volks-

---

[1] See below, p. 776.
[3] Proclamation no. 169 of 1911.
[5] Government Notice 956 of 1919.
[2] Proclamation no. 152 of 1903.
[4] See below, pp. 426 ff.
[6] Proclamation no. 43 of 1940.

raad was to limit the size of the African population in the European area with strict reference to the number required for farm labour. But Africans continued to pour in from Zululand, and by 1845 the Administration found that it had some 100,000 to deal with. Wholesale removal was clearly impossible, and the Natal Native Commission of 1846–7 recommended that the refugees should be placed in 'Locations',[1] an operation which Sir T. Shepstone was able to complete with very little opposition.

Of the mass of Africans for whom provision had now to be made, more than two-thirds were, as the result of Zulu rule, without Chiefs or tribal organization, but the Government could not find funds for the appointment of Superintendents to take charge of the Locations, and Shepstone's only resource was to attempt the re-establishment of the tribal system. In some cases he was able to gather the scattered members of tribes together under a scion of the old 'royal house'; in others, newly appointed Chiefs had to be given jurisdiction. He succeeded in overcoming the Cape influences which would have made the Native subject to Roman-Dutch law, and Ordinance no. 3 of 1849 formally recognized customary law, subject to the normal clause of 'repugnancy'. It is noteworthy that Magistrates were at a later date officially styled as 'Administrators of Native Law'. The Chiefs exercised judicial powers, but they were in this respect subject to the general control of the Magistrates. In 1850 the Lieutenant-Governor of Natal was proclaimed Supreme Chief of the Native population, a measure intended to mark that he now stood in the place of the Zulu monarch. As Supreme Chief he had authority to remove or appoint Chiefs, and in all Court cases he was the final appellate authority.

To a large extent, therefore, Shepstone's policy had prevailed, but it was to meet with many obstacles. The Natal Commission of 1852–3[2] found that the Locations were so large as to dry up the source from which a supply of Kaffir wage labour might have been procured, and stated its preference for a system involving the direct rule of Magistrates appointed for each Location. The real obstacle in Shepstone's way lay, however, in the lack of funds for the improvement of the Locations, and though his system established a traditional type of control over the tribesmen, it could do little to advance their welfare.[3] He himself was opposed to the Europeanization of the African people; but he recognized that the procedure of customary law was not universally applicable, and he made provision for more advanced Africans by a system of exemptions.[4]

His patriarchal administration came to an end in 1875, and was followed

---

[1] For the Reserve policy in Natal, see below. p. 690.
[2] *Report of the Natal Commission, 1852–3*, p. 4.
[3] *Native Affairs Commission 1903–5, Evidence*, vol. ii, p. 398.
[4] Law 11 of 1864, replaced by Law 28 of 1865.

by a period of transition lasting until 1893, in which some important aspects of his policy were modified. In Zululand, which had remained outside the Natal system, the war of 1879 resulted in the final destruction of the Zulu military power; the Paramount Cetewayo was banished, and though he was subsequently restored, local disorder led to the annexation of Zululand in 1887. In 1897 it was brought under the system of Native Administration followed elsewhere in Natal, as it was felt to be dangerous to leave so large a Bantu population under the almost unrestricted power of the Chiefs who had been created after the banishment of Cetewayo.

In 1875 a Board was appointed to codify the Bantu customary law; crimes committed by Natives were to be tried before the ordinary Courts, but the Chiefs were given power to decide disputes between them; a Native High Court was instituted for hearing appeals from the Courts of the Administrators and for trying certain crimes excluded from the jurisdiction of the ordinary Courts, such as faction fights. The institution of this Court was an interesting and significant development. Appeals from it were to lie to a Court of Appeal, a branch of the Supreme Court, consisting of the Secretary for Native Affairs and Judges selected from the Supreme and Native High Courts.[1] The reference to the Supreme Court now brought Natives in the final resort under a non-Native system of law.

The first Natal Code promulgated in 1878 was little more than a guide to Bantu customary law, but a statutory Native Code having legal force was enacted as Law 19 of 1891. This could only be revised by Act of Parliament, a defect which was criticized with good reason by the Natal Native Affairs Commission of 1906–7. While maintaining the civil jurisdiction of the Chiefs in all cases except divorce, it allowed them no criminal powers; they were, however, made responsible for the maintenance of order and for the apprehension of criminals.[2]

The period from 1893 up to the Zulu rising of 1906 was marked by an increasing departure from the system which Shepstone had introduced. In 1908 the Government claimed that in Natal 'all the efficient machinery of the Native form of government had been brought into play, adapted and made available'.[3] But there was little justification for this claim. The Chiefs were allowed only subordinate judicial powers; Magistrates grew increasingly out of touch with African affairs; and, though the Native Reserves were protected by the creation of the Native Land Trust,[4] little was done to improve their condition. The Commission of 1906–7 recommended certain administrative adjustments, including the appointment of Native Commissioners as executive officers, but its proposals did not suggest any radical change in a system that now seemed to halt between two very different concepts of African development.

---

[1] Law 26 of 1875.
[3] Natal Government Notice 39 of 20 January 1908.
[2] Natal Native Code, 1891.
[4] See below p. 692.

Transvaal

The early conduct of African affairs in the Transvaal requires a less detailed record. At the outset the treatment to be accorded to Natives was regarded by the authorities chiefly as a military problem,[1] with the result that the tribes, either expelled from their lands or settled under the control of Boer farmers, were broken up and disorganized. The course taken in regard to the land is described elsewhere.[2] Only Roman-Dutch law was recognized, and it was administered by Magistrates; the Chiefs were given no jurisdiction, though they continued to regulate disputes between tribesmen. After the annexation in 1877 the British Government set up a Department of Native Affairs; this was retained after the retrocession and its existence had some influence on Native policy.

A memorandum[3] issued in 1879, which seemed to be inspired by Natal influences, stated that experience had shown that the government of the Native could not be carried on under the ordinary law of the country, and shortly before retrocession an Ordinance, no. 11 of 1881, was issued by which the Administrator was designated as Supreme Chief and the Land-rosts as Administrators of Native law. Customary law was now formally recognized in regard to civil issues coming before the Courts. This Ordinance was repudiated by the Government of the restored South African Republic, but many of its provisions were later embodied in Law 4 of 1885. It is noticeable that this law did not set up a Native High Court, but left the right of appeal with the President as Paramount Chief, while a new system was initiated by the appointment of Native Commissioners distinct from the Magistrates and exercising both executive and judicial powers.

It does not appear, however, that the Supreme Court ever relinquished jurisdiction in civil cases, and the effect of the recognition of customary law was undermined by the use which was made of the repugnancy clause; the Court refused, for instance, to acknowledge the legality of customary marriages. It is doubtful how far this ruling was actually applied in the subordinate Courts, but when Law 3 of 1897 definitely gave recognition only to Christian and civil marriages, these Courts decided to refuse recognition to *lobolo* marriages.[4] The law of 1885 provided for the grant to Chiefs of petty civil jurisdiction within their own tribes, but they were given no power of enforcing the execution of their decisions.

Orange Free State

In the Orange Free State the general policy of the Government was to make Magistrates responsible for the control of the Native population, and at the outset no general recognition was given to customary law,

---

[1] *Cambridge History of the British Empire*, vol. viii, 1936, p. 398.   [2] See below, p. 690.
[3] Quoted by Brookes, op. cit., p. 125.   [4] See below, p. 594.

though a special enactment[1] acknowledged the legality of Native marriages in the Thaba 'Nchu Reserve. Elsewhere they received no recognition until Law 26 of 1899 provided that the children of such marriages were to be regarded as legitimate for purposes of inheritance. A system of intestate succession, derived from Roman-Dutch law and repugnant to Bantu conceptions, was introduced, but it was not operated outside the Thaba 'Nchu Reserve. A Native Reserve Board was created in each of the Reserves under Ordinance no. 6 of 1907. The Free State had at one time a Department of Native Affairs, but this was abolished in 1908.

Extension of System of Councils

The Constitution of the Union by the South Africa Act of 1909 did not for some years affect the system of Native Administration in the four Provinces as described in the preceding paragraphs. But in 1920 the Union Government decided on the general extension of the system of Local Councils which had, as shown above, originally been initiated in the Transkei and Ciskei. The Native Affairs Act 23 of 1920 provided that the membership of such Councils might be either elective or appointed. It gave them a wide range of powers, including the right to levy a local rate and the responsibility for the provision of medical and educational facilities.

In the Transkei the four District Councils of Eastern Pondoland were combined in 1927 in the Pondoland General Council,[2] and the General Councils of the Transkei and Pondoland were federated in 1931 under the name of the United Transkeian Territories General Council.[3] This continued to be known generally as the Bunga. Under the procedure now in force, each District Council contains two members appointed by the Government and four members who are chosen by different methods in the Transkei and Pondoland. A concession to tradition has been made by the recognition of the right of the two Paramount Chiefs in Pondoland and the Chiefs of Tembuland and Galekaland to act as additional members of the Councils in the districts where they reside.

In essence, however, the Council system, while providing for a measure of Local Government, has been largely a projection of the system of magisterial rule. The District Magistrate is chairman ex officio of the District Council, though in 1954 the Government appointed Natives as chairmen in four District Councils, an innovation which was warmly welcomed.[4] The Chief Magistrate is chairman and chief executive officer of the General Council. This Council (the Bunga) consists of the chairman, the Magistrates of the districts in which there are District Councils, and three members of each District Council; the Chiefs of Eastern and Western

---

[1] *Wetboek van die Oranje Vrijstaat*, Hoofdstuk, iv i.   [2] Proclamation no. 166 of 1927.
[3] Proclamation no. 279 of 1930.   [4] *S.A.S.*, 30 June 1954, p. 11.

Pondoland and Tembuland are *ex officio* members of the Bunga. The District Councils meet six times a year; the General Council meets annually.

In 1932[1] the powers of the General Council were extended to include the consideration of any matter relating to the condition of the Native population of the Union, in so far as this might affect the people of the Transkei. At the close of its meetings its resolutions are reviewed by a conference of the official members before they are submitted to the Governor-General. The Constitution of 1932 contained another innovation. Hitherto the competence of the General Council had been limited to offering advice to the Chief Magistrate; a Standing Executive Committee was now created, consisting of the Chief Magistrate with three other Magistrates and four of the African members of the Council.[2] This was made responsible for the appointment and dismissal of staff, the establishment of agricultural institutions, and the consideration of tenders for public works.

The Treasurer is a European official appointed by the Government. The Councils originally derived their revenue from an annual head tax of 10s., but the Native Taxation and Development Act of 1925 allocated to them the rents payable for land held on quit-rent, together with the proceeds of a local tax of 10s. levied in respect of every hut or dwelling in a Native Location occupied by a person who is not a quit-rent payer. The District Councils are executive organs of the Bunga; they have no separate revenue, but initiate proposals for expenditure which are laid before the General Council; the estimates, as passed by the Council and the official conference, require the approval of the Governor-General.

Though it is not possible to regard the General Council as a fully autonomous Local Government body, the scale of its activities is considerable. It is responsible for an annual expenditure of approximately £300,000; its total expenditure since its inception up to June 1949 amounted to £7,176,266. It has established three agricultural schools, a sheep farm, and three small experimental farms; it employs 174 agricultural demonstrators, and is responsible for maintaining some 4,500 miles of road. Considerable sums have been spent on measures to combat soil erosion, on the supply of domestic water, and on the fencing of arable land.

In the Ciskei the eight Local Councils were in 1934 federated in the Ciskeian General Council.[3] Its functions are similar to those of the Transkeian General Council, but there is one important difference. The District Councils are on a federal instead of a Union basis, and the revenues (which are derived from the same source as the revenue of the Councils

---

[1] Proclamation no. 191 of 1932.
[2] *Handbook on Race Relations in South Africa*, 1949, p. 35.
[3] Proclamation no. 34 of 1934.

in the Transkei) are paid direct to each Council and expended by it according to estimates approved by the Governor-General. The relatively small funds of the General Council are derived mainly from a percentage contribution from the subordinate Councils; in 1950 its expenditure amounted only to £8,017. On more than one ground, therefore, the Ciskei General Council occupies a far less important position than that of the Transkei.

Three Local Councils under Act no. 23 of 1920 have been set up in Natal, 14 in the Transvaal, and eleven in the Cape Province.[1] In the Orange Free State, Proclamation no. 164 of 1940 altered the constitution of the Reserve Boards so as to give them four elected as against two nominated members, but the posts of chairman and vice-chairman continue to be filled by the Native Commissioner and his Assistant. These Boards draw their revenues from the local tax imposed by the Act of 1925, their functions being somewhat wider than those of the Location Boards in the Cape.

The important Native Administration Act 38 of 1927 was not confined to the extension of the system of Councils, for it made also some concession to the Shepstone principle of using Native Authorities as part of the machinery of rule. It not only provided for the appointment of Chiefs and Headmen but gave them some measure of executive authority. In principle, persons having traditional claims are appointed as Chiefs; their administrative functions,[2] however, do not go beyond a general responsibility for the prevention of crime, the giving of help in the registration of taxpayers, and the collection of taxes. Under the Act of 1927 the Chiefs had no judicial powers unless these were expressly conferred, and it was mainly in Natal that such powers were given. As has already been pointed out, the Act provided for the recognition of customary law in matters of marriage and succession, and permitted the revision by Proclamation of the Natal Native Code. A revised code was promulgated in 1932.

In the prevailing philosophy of South Africa the Native in the urban areas is a transitory resident who in the words used in the Transvaal 'should depart therefrom when he ceases to minister to the needs of the White man'.[3] There was accordingly no development of Local Councils in the Native Locations which are attached to practically every municipality. A limited measure of consultation of Native opinion was provided through the creation of Native Advisory Boards consisting of not less than three African members, who might be either elected or nominated, but it is noteworthy that their chairman was usually the Location Superintendent. The Advisory Boards take part in the election of the four Senators

[1] H. Rogers, *Native Administration in the Union*, 1933, pp. 79–84.
[2] Government Notice 2251 of 1928.
[3] *Transvaal Local Government Commission*, T.P. 1, 1922, para. 42.

referred to in a previous chapter[1] as chosen to represent African interests. The Commission of Inquiry on Laws applicable to Natives in urban areas[2] found in 1948 that little interest was taken in the elections to these Boards or in their working, owing to the fact that their status was purely advisory.

Though the measures above described were undoubtedly designed to make an advance in the extension of Local Government institutions for the Native community, at all events in rural areas, they made in practice only a limited concession to the principle of Native self-government in local affairs. The Transkei General Council is frequently quoted as a progressive step in this direction, and some observers have been impressed by the scale of the works undertaken by it. But the large resources available to it have been derived from a general tax imposed by the Government, not from a rate raised by the Council, and the major responsibility for expenditure has remained in official hands. The test of the system must lie in the evidence which it can afford of the capacity of the African members of the Council to undertake a more independent control of the interests committed to it, and of their ability to secure local support in raising fresh resources where necessary.

It is all in favour of this development that the history of the Transkei Territories has given their inhabitants a common sentiment and some sense of independence; the Bunga has, moreover, had the guidance of a succession of officers who have closely identified themselves with Native interests. All who have had experience of its proceedings agree that the African members have shown a strong sense of responsibility in debating the issues which have been laid before them. Membership of the Council has undoubtedly had an educative influence, but it will only be possible to judge whether it constitutes a real organ of local self-government if the present measure of official control is materially relaxed.

The deficiencies of the Local Councils in this respect were appreciated by the Government of General Smuts, and in 1946, after the Natives Representative Council had adjourned as a protest against the laws which discriminate against Natives,[3] proposals were made to reconstitute it and to confer on it some authority for local legislation. The Local Councils were to be made more representative, in that they would consist wholly of elected Africans; Tribal Councils consisting of Chiefs with a small number of additional members were to be set up in those areas where the people preferred administration by their traditional rulers. It was left to the Native Laws Commission to make proposals for the development of urban Advisory Boards. It was held that the existence of a permanent urban population should be recognized; elected 'Village Boards' (this term being considered preferable to Location Boards) should be made responsible,

[1] See above, p. 264.
[2] *Report of Native Laws Commission*, U.G. no. 28, 1948, p. 21.   [3] See above, p. 162.

among other things, for the expenditure of a share of the funds allotted by
municipalities to the Native areas and for the allocation of housing.

There were here proposals which, though modest in their scope, nevertheless contemplated a definite advance towards the development of
African Local Government institutions. But more recent years have seen
the emergence of a new phase of policy, inspired by the determination of
the Nationalist Party to give full effect to what it has regarded as the logical
outcome of the doctrine of segregation as applied to the Native population.
Some reference has been made in a previous chapter to the measures taken
(most specifically in the field of education) in order to give effect to the
concept that Native development must be adjusted to the needs of the
Bantu world of ideas, not to that of Europeans.[1] This concept has now
inspired a policy in respect of Local Government institutions which might
not have been out of place if advocated in the days of Shepstone, but has
some air of unreality in the existing constitution of Native society.

In the view set out by the Party, the existing Councils lack authority
because they have no background of traditional institutions.[2] The Bantu
Authorities Act, no. 68 of 1951, has assigned to the Chiefs a role which,
though familiar enough in the British dependencies, had not previously
been regarded in the Union as appropriate to them—namely, as chairmen
of Native Councils entrusted with the expenditure of funds for local services. The Act incidentally abolishes the Natives Representative Council
and substitutes provision for the summoning of *ad hoc* conferences by the
Minister for Native Affairs. It authorizes the creation of Tribal Councils
consisting of Chiefs with Councillors officially nominated, who will, it is
understood, be mainly persons with traditional claims to the position. No
officials will be members of the Councils, though the official responsible
for their supervision (normally a Native Commissioner) will have the
right to take part in their discussions, but without a vote.

The Tribal Councils are to have Treasuries, to which will be paid all
Court fines and fees, the proceeds of tribal levies, and moneys assigned
from Trust Funds or from general revenue. Tribal Councils may be combined in Regional and Territorial Councils with rating powers. In the
course of the year 1953 nine Tribal Councils were set up in three of the
Transvaal districts. An amendment to the Native Administration Act in
1955 increased the judicial powers of Chiefs and Headmen. The original
Act had authorized Chiefs to try only offences under Native law and
custom; the amendment now permitted them to hear cases under common
law as well, except a certain number of offences which include homicide,
witchcraft, and stock-theft. Their powers of punishment are limited to

[1] See above, p. 166.
[2] Address of Secretary for Native Affairs, quoted in *The Times*, 13 December 1951. See also
statement of Minister in Senate, 7 June 1954.

fines, but they are increased from £5 to £20 or two head of cattle or ten of small stock. Chiefs have as yet no authority to pass a sentence of imprisonment.[1] Jurisdiction, it need not be said, extends only to Natives.

Central Control of Native Affairs

The South Africa Act of 1909 laid down in its section 147 that the control of Native Affairs should vest in the Governor-General in Council, who should exercise all special powers previously exercised by the Governors of the several Colonies. From the first, Native Affairs had been reserved in greater or less measure from the normal field of legislation. When the various territories of the Transkei were annexed to the Cape Province, the Governor was given power of legislation by proclamation. In Natal the Governor had been declared Supreme Chief in 1850,[2] and exercised wide authority in regard to the appointment or control of Chiefs. Proclamations issued under his authority had the force of law. The Transvaal Law 4 of 1885 which constituted the President as Paramount Chief gave him power to frame regulations, and the Letters Patent issued upon the grant of Responsible Government to the Orange River Colony in 1907 conferred a similar authority on the Governor of that Colony. On the establishment of the Union, the Native Affairs Department became the executive authority for the purpose of the powers transferred by the Union Act to the Governor-General in Council.

The authority of the Native Affairs Department thus depended partly on statute and partly on the powers which it derived as successor to the Governors as Supreme Chiefs. These latter powers, however, were undefined, save in Natal, where they were embodied in the Natal Code; elsewhere they were based on an interpretation of Bantu customary law which was, as has frequently been pointed out, of very questionable validity.[3] They could not in any case be logically exercised in the same manner over Natives living in tribal conditions and over those who had become permanently resident in European areas. In a number of matters, therefore, the authority of the Native Affairs Department stood for some years on an indefinite basis and the need of a clearer legal basis was more than once emphasized by the Courts.

The first step taken, however, was not in this direction, but in the establishment of a body to advise on Native affairs. Act 23 of 1920 established a permanent Native Affairs Commission which was given a consultative but influential position in regard to the conduct of Native affairs. If the Minister did not accept its advice, it might require that the papers should be laid before both Houses of Parliament. In certain matters it

---

[1] S.A.S., no. 99, 28 February 1955, p. 11.
[2] See above, p. 423.
[3] E. H. Brookes, The Colour Problems of South Africa, 1934, p. 107.

was incumbent on the Minister to seek its advice, and the Native Trust and Land Act of 1936 required that the Minister, in administering the affairs of the Native Trust Fund, must act in consultation with it.[1] The influence which such a body could exercise obviously depended largely on the independence of its members. In January 1951, however, it was reorganized, and its four members—a Senator and three Members of Parliament—were given sub-ministerial responsibilities for certain phases of the work of the Native Lands Branch. The provision made in the Act of 1920 for holding Native conferences had its effect in the summoning of annual conferences for a few years after 1922, but the attitude taken by the conference in regard to the Native Land and Franchise Bills was viewed with disfavour, and after 1927 it was convened only once.

Some of the provisions of the Native Administration Act of 1927 were also designed to clarify the legal position of the Government in its control of Native affairs. The general effect was to give to the Governor-General a practically unfettered power of legislation in African matters by proclamation.[2] It further gave explicit powers to create 'pass' areas and issue 'pass' regulations, and to restrict entry into Native areas or to order removal from them. The only limitation on this edictal legislation lay in the provision that Proclamations must be laid on the table of both Houses of Parliament, which could by resolution move for their repeal.

The maintenance of this wide range of powers in the hands of the Executive has been much criticized. It is admitted that there are a number of administrative matters in which the Executive must have in the Union, as it has elsewhere, a rule-making power, but it has been argued that in normal practice the limits of this power are defined in the substantive law and that it is not usual to permit it to make restrictions on individual liberty or the rights of property. But powers of a somewhat similar character have been exercised by the Executive in many of the British dependencies, and even where legislation normally takes the form of law passed by a Legislature, the Crown still retains the power to make laws in the form of an Order in Council.[3] Again, in the French Colonies, legislation is largely by ministerial decree, and the same is true of the Belgian Congo.[4]

If therefore there is any anomaly in a system such as that created in the Union by the Act of 1927, it lies largely in the measure of discrimination which it represents. The power of making rules which may vitally affect personal rights is exercised almost exclusively in connexion with Native affairs; measures affecting the personal rights of Europeans are normally embodied in legislation. The use to which the power has been put is perhaps a better criterion than any theory of constitutional law. Pro-

---

[1] Native Trust and Land Act of 1936, subsection 3 of section 4.
[2] Interpretation of Laws Act 5 of 1910.
[3] See above, p. 329.   [4] See above, p. 345.

clamation no. 165 of 1932, which applies to Natal, contains a provision for the summary arrest and detention of any Native judged to be dangerous to the public peace. Proclamation no. 252 of 1928, which applies to the three northern Provinces, prohibits the holding in any Native area of gatherings of more than ten persons for other than religious or domestic purposes without the previous approval of the Magistrate of the district. Both these provisions are of a type which would normally have been made the subject of substantive legislation, and the extent of the discrimination involved is emphasized by the severity with which they are sometimes applied in practice.[1]

Reference has been made in a previous chapter to the administrative personnel engaged in dealing with Native affairs in the Union, and to the extent of the special training given to it for this purpose.[2] The relevance of the facts there given is apparent when one recalls the wide range of differential legislation applicable to Africans in the Union and the corresponding range of the activities of the Native Affairs Department. The Native Labour Regulation Act of 1911 vested in it the supervision of the recruiting of Native labour. It administers the Natives (Urban Areas) Amendment Act of 1945[3] and is responsible for the purchase and management of lands in 'released' areas under the Land Act of 1936.[4] From 1925 it became concerned with African education through its control of the Native Development Fund, and since 1953 it has been wholly responsible for this subject.[5] The increased attention given to the improvement of the Native Reserves has involved the addition of Agricultural and Engineering sections to the Department, functioning under an officer known as the Controller of Native Settlements.

The Native Affairs Department thus discharges in regard to Natives a number of functions which in relation to Europeans are carried out by separate Departments of State. It was proposed in 1951 to reorganize the Department in such a way as to bring within its scope the whole of the activities of the technical Departments in African areas,[6] but so far this scheme has not been carried into effect.

Recent Changes in Native Policy

As has been made clear in a previous chapter, the insistence during the last few years on the application of the doctrine of *apartheid* has resulted in increasing emphasis on various aspects of differential legislation. In this respect the Union may be said to occupy the position at one end of the scale which British India once occupied at the other. In the latter the

---

[1] For a list of the Proclamations issued, see Rogers, op. cit. pp. 26–29.
[2] See above, p. 267.   [3] See below, p. 567.
[4] See below, p. 692.   [5] See below, p. 1149.
[6] *Report of Commission on Native Education*, U.G. 53, 1951, p. 135.

only legislation which could be described as differential was that which gave to Europeans, as also to Muslims and Sikhs, the right to exercise a communal vote. The criminal law at one time secured to Europeans a certain privilege in regard to the composition of the jury in criminal cases, but later legislation extended the same privilege to Indians who were involved in cases in which Europeans were also concerned.[1] With these exceptions, it would be difficult to find any instance of discrimination, for the existence of a legal provision securing to each group in the community the right of maintaining its personal law of marriage or succession does not, of course, come within this description.

But the matter must be viewed with a due sense of proportion. The circumstances in which a régime of White civilization was established in South Africa and the great disparity in the social and economic development of the European and Bantu made it inevitable that some measure of differentiation should become a recognized feature of public policy. The difficulty does not lie there. It lies in the assumption that discrimination is not merely an act of expediency but a law of nature. Its most refractory aspect is the inability of the European to admit that there can ever exist within the social and political structure of the Union any place for the African who has passed outside the traditional life of his own group.

The effects of insistence on the segregationist doctrine are not entirely one-sided. It has been accompanied by a more realistic appreciation by Europeans of the needs of Africans in the sphere which policy assigns to them. That is to be seen in the greatly increased provision made for African education,[2] for the development of medical facilities, and for the improvement of agriculture in the Native Reserves. Very large sums of money are now being provided for the improvement of African housing in the urban areas.[3] But the recent decision to improve the status of Chiefs or to base the institutions of Local Government on Tribal Councils rather than on electoral bodies belongs to a different category. It is an attempt to divert the attention of the African from institutions of a pattern which is favoured by Europeans, and in which he might desire to have a share. The change of policy embodied in this decision has been made at a time when in most of the British and French dependencies the African is being given increasing access to institutions of a European pattern. The forces of traditionalism are still strong in Africa, and it is possible that the change may have attractions for some part of the African population in the Union; it is not likely to appeal to the growing body of more progressive Africans or to the great mass of those who now live in urban conditions. For them it can have little or no meaning, and it is to this class that African society now looks for its leaders.

---

[1] W. H. Moreland and A. C. Chatterjee, *A Short History of India*, 1936, pp. 434–5.
[2] See below, p. 1147. [3] See below, p. 569.

SOUTH-WEST AFRICA

Circumstances have not yet called for any such public debate on Native policy in South-West Africa as marked the course of the discussion on the Native Trust and Land Bill and the Representation of Natives Bill in the Union Parliament. It must nevertheless be assumed that the general interest in the development of European settlement will result in the same outlook on African affairs in South-West Africa as in the Union itself. It must be realized, however, that the interest of the Union in the Tribal territories (Ovamboland, Okovangoland, the Western Caprivi Zipfel, and the Kaokoveld) is of a different order from that which is felt in the administration of the area designated by the Germans as the 'Police Zone', the area, namely, to which European settlement has so far been confined. The Tribal territories are isolated from the Police Zone by a broad belt of waste land, maintained as a Game Reserve. Their population was estimated in 1951 at 205,337, as compared to 153,631 in the Police Zone.[1]

Native affairs are included in the subjects which are reserved from the authority of the Legislative Assembly of the territory, and fall therefore under the executive control of the Union Government.[2] A recent enactment, the South-West Africa Native Affairs Administration Act of 1954, made a significant alteration of procedure by bringing the administration of Native affairs in the territory under the control of the Native Affairs Department of the Union. All land in the territory set apart for the use of Natives has been transferred to the Native Trust, which is controlled by the Native Affairs Department.[3] The Union Government has taken charge of the subject of immigration; but it is not yet clear how far Native policy, and in particular the policy in regard to labour recruitment, will be affected by the change.[4]

The local control over Native affairs is exercised, under the Administrator, through an Additional Native Commissioner who travels throughout the Territory. There are full-time Native Commissioners in Ovamboland, Okovangoland, and the Kaokoveld, and Assistant Native Commissioners at Windhoek and Tsumeb in the Police Zone; these are officers who belong to the cadre of the Native Affairs Department of the Union. In the 16 districts of the Police Zone,[5] Native affairs are administered by Magistrates from the Union Department of Justice who hold also the position of Native Commissioner. There are 17 Native Reserves in the Police Zone,[6] and in each of the major Reserves there is a Welfare Officer; these

[1] *Statesman's Year-book, 1954,* p. 277.

[2] South-West Africa Affairs (Amendment) Act, no. 25 of 1945.

[3] *O.Y.S.A., 1952–3,* p. 467.   [4] *Africa Digest,* June 1954, p. 16.

[5] The Eastern part of the Caprivi Zipfel is administered by the Union Minister of Native Affairs. Eastern Caprivi Administration Proclamation, no. 147 of 1939.

[6] *O.Y.S.A., 1950,* p. 1256.

officers are engaged on rates of pay which reflect the fact that they do not possess the academic qualifications in law required for appointment to the Native Affairs Department.

In dealing with the relations of the European and African communities the Administration has taken over from the Union much of its differential legislation. Native labour regulations have been adopted for the control of conditions of employment;[1] there are in force a Masters and Servants Law,[2] a Vagrancy Law,[3] and Pass regulations modelled on those of the Union.[4] Proclamation no. 34 of 1924, which regulates the conditions of urban Natives, includes the main provisions of the Union Natives (Urban Areas) Act of 1923. The actual application of differential legislation is, however, of a less extensive order than in the Union, largely owing to the fact that the rural economy is mainly pastoral and that industrial activity is on a very minor scale.

The general organization of local rule in the African areas is regulated by the Native Administration Proclamation of 1928, which applies the main provisions of the Union Native Administration Act of 1927. Customary law is formally recognized, and the Chiefs have similar functions to those described in connexion with the Act of 1927 in the Union. In this respect, however, conditions have led to the adoption of a considerable difference of practice as between the Tribal territories and those included in the Police Zone.

Organization in the Tribal Territories

Under German rule the Tribal territories were left to the operation of their own tribal organization, and this area still represents today the one part of South-West Africa where this organization now survives in any strength. Though the Chiefs have not been given any defined judicial powers, they and their traditional Councils are in practice allowed to dispose of the major part of civil and criminal cases, only the more serious crimes being taken to the Native Commissioner's Court, where they are either tried as offences against customary law or (more rarely) are transferred to the Court of a Magistrate in the Police Zone. The institution of a Reserve Trust Fund,[5] into which are paid all Reserve Fund Fees (mainly derived from grazing fees) and also the proceeds of tribal levies, affords some measure of Local Government, in so far that, while the responsibility for expenditure lies with the Native Commissioner, he is advised by a Board consisting of the Headman and six other Native members, selected at a representative meeting. The main service rendered by this Fund lies

---

[1] Proclamation no. 3 of 1917, amended by Proclamation no. 6 of 1924, no. 6 of 1925, and no. 27 of 1931.

[2] Proclamation no. 34 of 1920, amended by Proclamation no. 19 of 1923.

[3] Proclamation no. 25 of 1920.   [4] Proclamation no. 11 of 1922 and no. 20 of 1935.

[5] Proclamation no. 9 of 1924 and Government Notice 157 of 1924.

in the systematic provision of village food and seed reserves as a precaution against crop failure.

In three of the tribes the Chiefs constitute the recognized Native Authorities; the other three are governed by a Council of Headmen. If this system does not qualify for the designation of a full Native Authority régime as understood in the British dependencies, it is at the same time true that the Tribal territories occupy an exceptional position in the Native areas administered by the Union, if judged by the extent to which a conscious effort has been made to utilize the tribal institutions.

There is nowhere in the Union where the African is more self-sufficient in his way of life and less affected by contact with Europeans. The only lands held by Europeans are those occupied by missions; the number of European shops is reduced to a minimum. There is no poll tax.[1] European visitors require a permit to enter the territories. Looking at the situation of these territories as a whole, the Native Commissioners appear to have achieved with success an unobtrusive system of personal rule. If there is a weakness in the system, it is in the fact that the resources available for expenditure allow little provision for the extension of the social and economic services. Proposals for increased Native taxation were made as far back as 1935, but have not since been renewed.

Organization in the Police Zone

The situation in the Police Zone offers a marked contrast to that of the Tribal territories. The Union succeeded to a situation in which large areas of land had already been alienated; just before war broke out in 1914 roughly one-third of the total area of the Zone was in the hands of European settlers. In 1951 the area occupied by European farms, either in freehold or on rent from the Government, was roughly 86 million acres; the Native Reserves had a total area of 51 million acres. The German régime had resulted in the complete disorganization of the Bantu tribal institutions; indeed, some tribes, such as the Herero, had for military reasons been deliberately dispersed.[2]

For some years, therefore, the primary concern of the Administration was the resettlement of the African population in the 17 Native Reserves provided for their occupation in the Police Zone.[3] Settlement was, however, largely haphazard, and in consequence very few of the Reserves are held on a true tribal basis. They seem to have been regarded at the time mainly as a source of labour supply for the European farms or for local

---

[1] This applies also to the Police Zone, where, however, there is a wheel tax; see *O.Y.S.A.*, *1952–3*, p. 1173.

[2] *Report on the Outbreak of the Rebellion and the Policy of the Government with regard to its suppression,* U.G. no. 10, 1915. *Report of South-West Africa Commission,* U.G. no. 26, 1936, p. 23. C. Dundas, *South-West Africa,* South African Institute of International Affairs, 1946, p. 8.

[3] *O.Y.S.A.*, *1952–3*, p. 1175.

industries, such as the copper-mine at Tsumeb and the diamond-mines near Luderitz. The rainfall is, especially in the southern part of the territory, exceptionally low; the land of the Reserves is as a rule poor, and the standard of life is much inferior to that prevailing in many parts of the Union. Where a Chief and Council can be found to function, they are allowed much the same powers to dispose of Native cases and the same part in the management of the Reserve Trust Fund as in Ovamboland; where, however, no such organization is active, as among the Damara and Nama,[1] cases go direct to the Magistrate.

The Bastards of mixed European, Malay, and African descent, having been evicted from the banks of the Orange River in 1865, settled on the pasture-lands of the Rehoboth Gebiet, where they held their land from the Hottentot Chief for an annual payment of one horse.[2]

They claimed before the Inquiry Commission of 1921[3] that they should be administered as a separate unit by their own Council. This Council was recognized in 1923 by the Administration,[4] but was suspended in 1924 owing to internal dissensions. Its functions were then vested in the Magistrate, who is assisted by an Advisory Council which has since 1935 been elected by the community.[5]

The creation in 1947 of a Territorial Development and Reserve Fund for South-West Africa[6] has enabled considerable sums to be provided for expenditure on improvements in the Native Reserves, more especially in the provision of dams and bore-holes and other water-supplies; some of these services have extended also to Ovamboland, Okovangoland, and the Kaokoveld. The total sum expended on the Native Areas Account for the period 1947 to 1953 was £327,138.

SOUTHERN RHODESIA

The nature of the control to be exercised over the conduct of Native affairs formed a prominent issue when Southern Rhodesia received its Constitution in 1923.[7] The Charter granted to the British South Africa Company in 1889 had prescribed respect for Native religion and for the customary law regarding the holding of land and other personal rights.[8] The Order in Council of 1898, which created a Legislative Council, was more definite in that it reserved to the High Commissioner special powers to regulate the settlement of Africans on the land and to safeguard their rights in other respects. The Order prohibited the Company from imposing without the sanction of the Secretary of State any disabilities on

---

[1] *Native Tribes of South-West Africa*, Windhoek, 1928.
[2] *O.Y.S.A., 1950*, p. 1255. Dundas, op. cit. p. 4.   [3] *Report*, U.G. 24, 1921.
[4] Proclamation no. 28 of 1923.   [5] Proclamation no. 9 of 1928 and no. 5 of 1935.
[6] Ordinance no. 8 of 1947.   [7] See above, p. 182.
[8] E. Hertslet, *The Map of Africa by Treaty*, vol. i, 3rd ed. 1909, pp. 271–7.

Africans which did not apply equally to Europeans, save in respect of the supply of arms, ammunition, and liquor. The intention was clearly to control differential legislation of the type which had already become a feature of South African policy.

When the terms of the Constitution of 1923 were being debated the question of the control to be exercised over Africans, then estimated to number 800,000, by a Responsible Government which at the time represented a European population of only 34,000, was referred to a committee presided over by Lord Buxton.[1] In the result, those provisions of the Order in Council of 1898 which related to Native affairs were maintained, and the Governor was required to forward to the High Commissioner any information he might require for the exercise of his authority in respect of Native affairs.[2] It was added that a Chief Native Commissioner should be appointed who was not to be removed from office without the sanction of the Secretary of State. The policy which dictated these provisions also resulted in the decision, to which reference has already been made, to keep open the right of Africans to the exercise of the franchise.

Projects for Racial Separation

At the outset the policy of the Responsible Government tended towards the adoption of the system of territorial segregation which had been developed in South Africa. Inquiries made by the Land Commission of 1925 were largely directed to finding means for achieving a territorial separation of the European and African communities. The Land Apportionment Acts of 1930, 1941, and 1950 have had the effect of confining the holding of land by Europeans and Africans to separate areas;[3] the movements of Africans are regulated by a pass system, similar to that in the Union, though less drastic in its application;[4] the Native Urban Locations Ordinance of 1906, with its subsequent amendments, controls the entry of Africans to urban areas, and its provisions have been reinforced by the Natives (Urban Areas) Accommodation and Registration Act of 1946; the Industrial Conciliation Act of 1934, which regulates the operation of the trade unions, excludes Africans from its scope; the Maize Control Amendment Act of 1934 provides different marketing systems for African and European producers.

There is thus a considerable body of differential legislation,[5] though there are several factors (as for example the absence of any considerable

---

[1] *Report of a Committee Appointed by the Secretary of State for the Colonies to consider certain questions relating to Rhodesia*, Cmd. 1273, 1921.

[2] For the position of the High Commissioner in regard to Native affairs, see above, p. 283.

[3] See below, p. 703.

[4] Native Pass Consolidation Ordinance no. 14 of 1933.

[5] A. Burbridge, *A Review of Five Years' Native Legislation*, 1935. *Central African Territories; Comparative Study of Native Policy, 1951*, Cmd. 8235, pp. 8–22.

number of 'poor Whites') which have resulted in less political importance being attached to some of its provisions than is now the case in the Union. Nor has Southern Rhodesia gone to the same lengths as has the Union in the application of the doctrine of segregation to the conduct of Native affairs. For this there are a variety of reasons. The early contact of Europeans with the Bantu of Mashonaland and Matabeleland was of a different order from those of the pioneer settlers in the Union. The size of the African population in Southern Rhodesia has not been such as to suggest what the European element may have to contend with the same preponderance of Bantu; the relatively large provision of lands for African occupation has in itself made a significant distinction between the circumstances prevailing in Southern Rhodesia and those of the Union.[1]

Certain aspects of Native policy, and in particular those which were felt to show the influence of political elements in the Union, were actively debated in the discussions which preceded the establishment of the Federation of Rhodesia and Nyasaland in 1953,[2] but it was not suggested that European opinion in Southern Rhodesia was likely to follow the doctrine of *apartheid* to the extent of advocating the permanent exclusion of Africans from the government of the country. To judge by statements made on behalf of the European community, its policy has not gone farther in this respect than is represented by the statement that 'in order to fit the African to take his place in the community as full partner with citizens of a more ancient civilization, it is first necessary to make him the equal of his future partner in health, material well-being, and education'.[3]

The Organization of Local Rule

As has been shown,[4] the Constitution of the Federation provides that Native Administration shall remain within the field dealt with by the Territorial Legislatures. The African Affairs Board for which provision is made in the Constitution deals only with matters arising within the legislative or executive authority of the Federation itself, not within that of the constituent Legislatures.[5] It remains to be seen, therefore, how far the current procedure of Native Administration in Southern Rhodesia will be modified by contact with the systems in force in the two other member territories of the Federation. In both these territories the procedure followed is (as will be seen) that which is associated with the use of the traditional Native Authorities as part of the machinery of rule. In

---

[1] See below, p. 705.   [2] See above, pp. 278 ff.

[3] Cmd. 8235, p. 9. See also, *Report of the Rhodesia-Nyasaland Royal Commission of 1938*, Cmd. 5949, pp. 164–92, 215. *Report of the Conference on Federation, 1953*, Cmd. 8753, para. 15. H.C. Deb., 24 July 1952, coll. 773–882; 24 March 1953, coll. 658–796; H.L. Deb., 1 April 1953, coll. 457–572; 2 April 1953, coll. 573–660.

[4] See above, p. 283.   [5] See above, pp. 281 ff.

Southern Rhodesia, however, the circumstances which at the outset determined the policy of the Administration did not favour the employment of the Native Authorities in this manner. The disintegration of the Shona tribes after their subjugation by the Matabele and the subsequent breakdown of authority among the Matabele following the defeat of Lobengula produced an impression of widespread tribal disorganization. The Matabele rebellion created a positive argument against attempts to restore the position of the Chiefs and their status was not clearly defined till the Native Affairs Ordinance of 1910 granted them powers in terms resembling those embodied in the Natal Code; they were required to assist in the collection of tax and had the rank of constables responsible for law and order.

The Native Affairs Act of 1927 slightly increased these obligations, but a number of powers normally exercised by Chiefs under customary law, such as the allocation of land, were specifically reserved to the Native Commissioners. In the present practice the use made of Chiefs varies widely, but is largely of an informal character. They are paid salaries, but on a significantly small scale. Customary law has not been recognized in criminal matters; but the Order in Council of 1898 laid down that in civil cases Courts should be guided by Native law, subject to the usual condition of repugnancy. The possibility that difficulty might arise in regard to the recognition of customary marriages was obviated by a declaration that polygamous African marriages might be regarded as valid.

While these provisions have prevented some of the anomalies which in the Union of South Africa marked the earlier treatment of African domestic law,[1] in Southern Rhodesia this law has also been directly modified in important respects by statute. Thus legislation has made an attempt[2] to prevent the practice of child-marriage; the law forbids the pledging of children in marriage and penalizes the use of compulsion to force African females into an unwilling marriage.[3] The Courts have held that bride-price is only incidental to and not an essential element in Native marriages.[4] Up to 1937 the only Courts administering Native law were those of the Native Commissioners; the Chiefs had no judicial powers, though they acted informally as arbitrators in minor civil disputes. In 1937, however, an Act was passed which allowed Native Courts to hear civil cases between Natives in matters capable of being decided according to Native law and custom.[5] There were in 1952 some 180 recognized Native Courts, but they had no criminal jurisdiction.

[1] See above, p. 420.
[2] C. Bullock, *The Mashona*, 1927, p. 330.
[3] Native Marriages Ordinance, 1917, as amended by Act no. 16 of 1929.
[4] *Muchenje* v. *Kunaka* (1912), S.R. 207.   [5] Act no. 33 of 1937.

The System of Councils

The general reluctance to rely on the re-establishment of the status of traditional Native Authorities has led to the adoption of a system of Councils of the pattern of that existing in the Union. In 1930 the initial step was taken of creating Advisory Boards with an equal number of elected members and of Chiefs or Headmen; the Native Commissioner was in each case chairman. These Boards were, however, given no legal status, and their lack of positive functions inevitably meant that they had little vitality.[1] In 1936 a fresh effort was made to develop the Council system; a course of training for Chiefs was started at the school at Domboshawa,[2] and the Native Councils Act, no. 38 of 1937, provided for the establishment of Councils in the Native Reserves which were to consist of Chiefs or Headmen, with other Africans approved by the Governor; the Native Commissioner was to be chairman.

Up to 1943 their revenues consisted of local fees, together with grants from central revenue, but in that year an amending Act, no. 25, made it possible for them to be given taxing powers, and by 1951 there were 57 Councils, of which 45 imposed local taxes, receiving grants from central revenue on a £ for £ basis. The total sum expended by the Councils in 1951 was £36,547. The contribution made to the development of social services is not therefore considerable, and in the few cases where Councils have made any substantial use of their powers this has been largely due to the stimulus given them by Native Commissioners.

The Natives (Urban Areas) Act of 1946 has provided for the creation of Native Advisory Boards in the Native Locations attached to the European urban centres; their members were to be elected from the Location residents and a chairman nominated by the Local Authority; he may be a European or an African, but he is normally the chairman of the Municipal Native Affairs Committee.

As has been seen the Administration started with a mistrust of the ability of the Native Authorities of the period to prove of any value as agencies of local rule. The position is today substantially the same; with few exceptions the Chiefs and their Advisers have not succeeded in winning the confidence of the Administration in this respect. For this the lack of official encouragement is in part responsible, but this is not the whole story. Modern African history can show a number of instances where tribes, broken up and disorganized in various ways, have reorganized themselves under a Chief who has been able to win their allegiance. His authority is then the greater, because it flows not merely from tradition but from something like a public suffrage. But such a revival of a tribal organization has seldom occurred where economic and social changes have

---

[1] *Report of the Chief Native Commissioner*, 1935, p. 10.   [2] See below, p. 1164.

so seriously affected the whole of African society as has been the case in Southern Rhodesia. If there is to be any use made now of African institutions they must, it would seem, be institutions of a new form, and not those which centre on the authority to be accorded to the Chiefdom. In 1951 Provincial Assemblies of Chiefs were established. They were to meet twice a year and discuss questions affecting African interests; but it is doubtful how far the Chiefs can in present circumstances be considered as having a value as representatives of public opinion.

Health and Education

The procedure to be adopted in Native Administration would seem to have been a matter of less importance to the Government of Southern Rhodesia than consideration of the measures needed to improve the standards of life of the African population. It has in this respect shown a considerable measure of liberality. Out of a total expenditure of a little over £22½ million in 1950, the Government spent roughly £2½ million on education, health, and agricultural services for Africans, together with another £383,231 from the Native Production and Marketing Fund and the Native Reserve Fund.[1] As against this, it has shown an equally marked measure of hesitation in encouraging the employment of those institutions of Local Government which might give the African some confidence in his ability to manage his own affairs. It is especially noteworthy that it has hitherto been unwilling to trust African Courts to administer any process of criminal justice.

From the grant of Responsible Government up to the year 1949 the Prime Minister was also Minister for Native Affairs. In that year a separate Minister for Native Affairs was appointed, but this portfolio was subsequently combined with that of Health, and this is still the position. In 1927 a Department of Native Education was created, but Native education has recently become a branch of the Native Affairs Department, with its own Director of Native Education. The Native Affairs Department now also includes branches dealing with agriculture, Native lands, labour, and engineering. An Advisory Council on Native Affairs, consisting of the Chief Native Commissioner and three other members appointed by the Governor, was created in 1930,[2] but in 1949 there was substituted for this a Native Affairs Advisory Board consisting of the Minister as chairman sitting with the senior members of the Native Affairs Department.

KENYA

Although political and social developments in Kenya have for so many years furnished occasion for debate and indeed for controversy in the

[1] *Central African Territories; Comparative Survey of Native Policy*, Cmd. 8235, 1951, p. 38.
[2] Government Notice, 13 February 1930.

outside world, this has not turned primarily on the procedure adopted for the administration of African affairs. It has been suggested that but for the interest created by the political claims of Asians in Kenya, the issues which concern the status of the African population might have attracted less attention outside the Colony, and it is at all events probable that the controversies first aroused by Asian claims have actually stimulated a more general concern in a number of matters concerning the non-European population generally.[1] Some of these questions are referred to elsewhere in this Survey, and discussion must be confined here to those which primarily concern the African population, and in particular the system of local administration applicable to it.

During the early thirties the distribution of State expenditure between the European settled area and the purely African areas was a prominent topic of debate in connexion with the schemes then being considered for the closer union of the East African territories.[2] At that period items which were primarily of concern to Europeans undoubtedly absorbed the major part of public expenditure, and Lord Moyne, who made in 1932 a study of the finances of the Colony, recommended the institution of a Native Betterment Fund which would be earmarked for expenditure in the African areas.[3] For various reasons this proposal was not accepted, but in later years the position has been substantially altered by the increasing interest shown in those projects of social and economic development which primarily affect Africans. In the Ten-year Development Programme which was adopted in 1946 a noteworthy proportion of the estimated expenditure was provided for projects designed for this purpose. Out of a total expenditure of a little over £17 million, a sum of £3 million was allocated for the reconditioning of African areas and the resettlement of congested populations, £806,000 for African education, £1,025,000 for the provision of water-supplies in African areas, and £600,000 for a loan for municipal housing for Africans.[4]

As there has been relatively little industrial development in Kenya there has been no occasion for the same conflict of interest between Europeans and Africans as has arisen in the Union regarding the admission of Africans to skilled employment, and so far as this issue is concerned, the European community has chiefly shown an interest in promoting the replacement of Asians by Africans.[5] It is in the matter of land distribution

[1] *Report of the Commission on Closer Union of the Dependencies in Eastern and Central Africa*, Cmd. 3234, 1929, pp. 35 ff.   [2] Ibid., p. 62.

[3] *Report of the Financial Commissioner on Certain Questions in Kenya*, Cmd. 4093, 1932, p. 38. *East Africa Commission Report*, Cmd. 2387, 1925, pp. 47 ff. *Report of Financial Position and System of Taxation in Kenya*, Col. 116, 1936, p. 44.

[4] *Report of Kenya Development Committee*, 1946. For subsequent variations in the Development Schemes, the total estimate of which was raised to £35 million in 1951, see *Colonial Reports, Kenya, 1952*, p. 7; *Kenya, African Affairs Department Report*, 1952, pp. 40 ff., 76 ff., 103 ff.

[5] E. Huxley, *White Man's Country*, vol. ii, 1935, p. 180.

that the most acute differences have arisen,[1] and such differential legislation
as is applicable to Africans is to a large extent the corollary of the policy
under which certain areas have been assigned by legislation for the exclusive occupation of Europeans. The history of this policy is given in a later
chapter, in which also the restrictive provisions governing the residence of
Africans in the European farming areas are discussed.[2]

The section of Europeans which has displayed the greatest interest in
questions of African administration is that which is represented in the
Farming Associations, and it is clear that these organizations were at one
time able to exercise an influence over the formation of policy hardly less
than that which they would have possessed had they been the dominant
party under a fully developed form of Responsible Government. At the
same time it was by no means unreasonable that the views of the European
farming community should carry due weight, in view of the part it had
played in building up the economy of the Colony. A calculation made in
1935 showed that the European areas accounted at that period for 68 per
cent. of the total agricultural exports, the African areas for 13 per cent.,
and mixed European and African production for 19 per cent.[3] In 1945
the purely European contribution was estimated at 72 per cent. of the
total production.

An examination will be found in Chapter XX of the system followed in
regard to the employment of labour and in particular of the use of the
kipande, or labour pass, which up to 1947 was a subject of some resentment
by leaders of African opinion.[4] The regulations for the control of Africans
in urban areas are described in the last part of the present chapter;[5] they
are in general far less restrictive than in the Union or Southern Rhodesia.
The marketing of Native produce has been the subject of special legislation,[6] but though this is differential in form, its main object has been to
improve marketing facilities for African crops, and its terms do not differ
materially from those of Ordinances passed in Uganda and Tanganyika.

The range of differential treatment has not, however, been confined to
legislation of this character. The influence of the European farming
interest has in the past been seen in the measures taken to support it by
the reduction in railway freights on exports, and by the liberal assistance
given in the form of agricultural loans. At one period the Administration
was induced to assist the European coffee industry by placing obstacles
on the production of coffee by Africans, and an account of this development will be found in the chapter dealing with agricultural developments.
But the matter has now ceased to be one of active concern to Africans.[7]

[1] L. S. B. Leakey, *Mau Mau and the Kikuyu,* 1952, pp. 8, 86 ff. Colonel O. Lyttleton, 'Kenya',
United Empire, March–April 1953.
[2] See below, p. 722. [3] Col. no. 116, 1936, p. 8.
[4] See below, p. 1423. [5] See below, p. 578.
[6] The Marketing of Native Produces Ordinance no. 28 of 1935. [7] See below, p. 834.

Administrative Procedures

Turning now to the actual procedure followed in the system of Native Administration, it may be premised that Kenya, though making wider use of Native agencies than the Union or Southern Rhodesia, has not in principle relied for this purpose mainly on the use of the traditional organization of Chiefs or Chiefs in Council. In a memorandum dealing with its policy in this respect,[1] the indigenous organization of rule as it existed before the British occupation was described as being of 'a nebulous character'. The authority of such Chiefs as existed was precarious; 'nowhere', it was added, 'was there any Chief who could command the respect accorded to the Kabaka of Uganda, nowhere was there any ready-made organization which could be converted into an administrative machine'.[2] The failure to make use of traditional Native Authorities seems to have been a concession to circumstances rather than a decision of principle. As will be shown in a later part of this chapter, there was from the first a strong feeling that the Councils of Elders should, where possible, be utilized as agencies in the sphere with which they were familiar, namely the Native Tribunals, and it is only in recent years that there has begun to be a departure from this principle. On the executive side there has not been the same tendency to rely on the use of traditional institutions. The Village Headmen Ordinance of 1902 provided for the appointment of 'Official Headmen' charged with the responsibility for maintaining order and keeping public roads in repair; but though in their case the law did not require the appointment of traditional authorities it was usual to utilize them where it was possible to do so. It became usual to refer to all the 'Official Headmen' as Chiefs, though only in a few cases did they actually hold this position in African custom. Their powers were extended by the Native Authority Ordinances of 1912 and 1937; they now became responsible for the execution of official policy in such matters as the control of grazing, the cutting of timber, and the manufacture of liquor; they were at the same time the principal agents for the collection of tax in the Native Land Units. The area under a Headman is now known as a Location. Some Locations correspond to tribal or clan divisions, but in a large number of other cases the boundaries have been determined mainly by administrative convenience.[3] The Headmen have from the first been regarded as Government employees, in the sense that their salaries are paid from central revenues and not from the Local Native Treasuries.

---

[1] Quoted in *Report of the Commission Appointed to Enquire into and Report on the Financial Position and System of Taxation of Kenya*, Col. no. 116, 1936, p. 102.

[2] See also on this point *N.A.*, Part I, p. 92. It should be said that the phrase 'Chief and Council' does not necessarily denote a regularly constituted body of advisers; the Council may consist of Elders, relations, place-holders, or persons performing ritual functions.

[3] *N.A.*, Part I, pp. 92 ff.

Local Native Councils

But the most characteristic feature of Kenya policy in the administration of African affairs has been the development of the system of Local Native Councils. In this respect Kenya anticipated the movement made in the same direction by the British dependencies dealt with in the ensuing pages of this chapter. An amendment of 1924 to the Native Authority Ordinance provided for the establishment of Local Councils, with the District Commissioner as chairman and chief executive authority,[1] and an African as his deputy. Some more progressive Councils have since suggested that the presidency should be given to an African, but the Government has not yet accepted this measure.[2] The Councils were to be composed by 'such Headmen and other Natives as the Governor may appoint', but before any other person than an Official Headman was appointed, the people of the area were to be given the opportunity to nominate persons to represent their interests.

In some districts there was at first a separate Council for each tribe, but there is now a single Council for each district. There has also been a marked increase in the proportion of elected members as compared with those 'appointed'; taking the Councils as a whole, there were in 1950 a total of 227 nominated members (of whom 132 were Chiefs or Headmen) as compared with 358 elected members. There have of recent years been instances in which the elections to the Local Native Councils have aroused much popular interest and have been keenly contested.

The Councils are authorized to levy rates and to pass resolutions in respect of any matters affecting purely local Native administration; such resolutions, if approved by the Governor, have the legal effect of by-laws. Generally speaking, the constitutional position resembles that of some of the local Native Councils in the Union—whose function is to advise the Administrative Officer on the expenditure to be incurred out of funds available for the provision of local services—rather than that of the Native Authorities as existing in most of the British Colonial territories subsequently referred to in this chapter. These latter authorities are empowered to act on their own initiative, subject to the sanction of the Administration. A further contrast with this latter system lies in the fact that up to 1944 the Local Native Councils in Kenya received no share of the direct Native tax levied by the Government, but were dependent mainly on their local rates or on Government grants.[3]

There is no doubt as to the importance which the Councils had by this period acquired in the life of some of the more advanced districts. The matters at issue were freely and keenly debated, and there was a growing

---

[1] The provision in respect of the establishment of Local Native Councils was further amended in the Native Authority Ordinances of 1933 and 1937.

[2] *J.A.A.*, July 1955, p. 124.   [3] See below, p. 680.

tendency to discuss issues from a political standpoint. On the more practical side of their work, however, the Local Native Councils suffered from
the defect that up to 1949 there was no clear division of functions as
between them and the Government. Subordinate technical staff, for
example, might be carried on either budget; there might be a number of
agricultural demonstrators paid from Council funds and others in the
same class paid from Central revenues.[1] In 1948–9, however, a division
was made on a more logical basis; the Local Councils became responsible
for the construction and maintenance of dispensaries, markets, and cattle
dips, the upkeep of minor roads, and all primary education. The Government agreed to contribute 2s. for every local rate collected.

Since then the expenditure of the Councils has increased steadily. In
1949 it totalled £626,000, of which 35 per cent. came from local rates.[2]
The Government grant based on the local rate collected totalled £74,000,
and the grant in reimbursement of certain agricultural services amounted
to £33,000. Expenditure on education, which chiefly takes the form of
grants to the District Education Boards,[3] accounted for 24 per cent. of the
total expenditure; in many cases the local rate included a special levy
earmarked for this purpose.[4] In 1952 the total expenditure of all Local
Native Councils had risen to £1,042,283, their revenues having been
increased by the cesses imposed under emergency legislation on exported
produce, notably maize and wattle-bark.[5]

African District Councils

A further change took place in 1950, the relevant sections of the Native
Authority Ordinance being superseded by the African District Councils
Ordinance 12 of 1950. This gave formal recognition to the Local Native
Councils (now designated as African District Councils) as ranking with
the Municipalities and District Councils in the European areas as organs
of the Kenya Local Government Board. The Ordinance prescribes, as
before, that a Council shall consist of the District Commissioner as chairman with 'such Africans as the Provincial Commissioner may determine',
but it is the intention that all the members shall be elected whenever
possible. In practice it has become usual for the District Commissioner
to preside only over the formal meetings of the Councils, while an African
Vice-President conducts their routine discussions. Delegates from the
Councils meet in regional groups to recommend to the Governor the
names of Africans to be appointed to the Kenya Legislative Council.

[1] *Report of Taxation Enquiry Committee* (the Plewman Report), 1947, p. 24.
[2] For the incidence of local rates, see below, p. 660.
[3] See below, p. 1173.   [4] *N.A.*, Part I, pp. 96–98.
[5] T. C. Colchester, 'The Kenya Local Native Council Budgets for 1949', *J.A.A.*, July 1949,
pp. 106–13. 'Survey of Development of Local Government in the African Territories since 1947',
Supplement to *J.A.A.*, October 1952, p. 38.

A considerable number of by-laws have been enacted by the Councils, usually at the instance of Administrative Officers; many of them deal with such matters as soil conservation, tsetse clearance, or the control of plant pests, and they are frequently in a standard form with small local variations. The enforcement of these by-laws tends, however, to be left to the Chiefs or Headmen, on the principle that they are the agents of the District Commissioner as chief executive officer of the Council. This dependence on the services of the official organization clearly weakens the status of the Councils, and the more important of them are now seeking to employ a qualified staff of their own; there is, however, a dearth of candidates with the necessary qualifications.[1] As will subsequently be seen, the question whether the Councils are the appropriate bodies to deal with changes in customary land tenure has been the subject of some debate.[2]

There is a further development which may affect the future of the African District Councils as agencies of Local Government. In so far as tribal or clan divisions can be said to have been recognized for purposes of Local Government, this is mainly at the level of the Location. In the Nyanza Province, Locational Advisory Councils were created some years ago in order to act as advisers to the Chiefs or Headmen, but it is now the intention of the Government to develop Locational Councils in other areas, as subsidiary bodies to the African District Councils.

Somewhat special considerations apply to two sections of the African population of Kenya; first, the considerable urban community to be found in the larger towns, such as Nairobi and Mombasa, and second, the section of Africans normally resident in the settled area of the European Highlands. A reference to the provision made for the first section will be found in the subsequent part of this chapter which deals with the position of Africans in urban areas.[3] As regards the Africans in the European Highlands, roughly 200,000 in number, they have up to recent years had no representation on the District Councils serving the European areas. These bodies had until 1952 only rudimentary functions, but in that year the Local Government (County Councils) Ordinance provided for their replacement by County Councils with powers modelled on those exercised by similar bodies in Great Britain. The Member for Local Government is empowered to nominate three members of each County Council, and has undertaken to nominate non-Europeans if they do not receive adequate representation through the electoral system.[4] As has been shown in a previous chapter, a scheme was put forward towards the end of 1955 for

[1] *Colonial Reports, Kenya, 1952*, p. 141.
[2] *N.A.*, Part I, pp. 99, 130, 156, 193; and see below, p. 785.
[3] See below, pp. 578-80.
[4] 'A Survey of the Development of Local Government in the African Territories since 1947', Supplement to *J.A.A.*, July 1952, p. 40. See also *N.A.*, Part I, pp. 179-83.

the organization of African voting on a separate communal roll. This scheme would, if accepted, apply also to the election of Africans to local bodies.[1]

Native Tribunals

It has been convenient to reserve for separate mention the development of the system of Native Tribunals to which reference was made in a previous paragraph. It will be recalled that from the first there was a strong feeling in favour of making use of the Councils of Elders who by custom discharged a judicial or at all events an arbitral function. Under the Native Courts Regulations of 1897 all cases arising within a radius of 15 miles from a Government station were to be tried by Administrative Officers, but outside this radius certain Tribal Authorities were given concurrent jurisdiction, and were required to administer Native law and custom subject to reasonable supervision; the Administrative Officers were, however, instructed not to interfere with their decisions unless these were 'essentially inhuman or unjust'. The purport of the Courts Ordinance of 1907 and the Tribunal Rules of 1911 was that judicial powers were to be exercised by Councils of Elders constituted under Native law and custom, and though Regulations made in 1913 permitted of a departure from Native custom so far as concerned the membership of the Courts, such departure was held to be desirable only in exceptional cases.

There have, however, been later developments which, though not amounting to a change of principle, have nevertheless involved important changes in actual practice. A noteworthy feature of the working of the Native Tribunals in Kenya has been the measure to which they have become responsible for the administration of the statutory law. In 1945[2] there were 27 Ordinances triable in whole or in part by Native Tribunals generally, but in the Nyanza and Central Provinces a number of others have since been added to the list. In these Provinces in particular, the majority of criminal cases are not tried in the Native Courts as offences against customary law, but as breaches of the Penal Code or of some specific Ordinance.[3]

It is natural therefore that a reasonable standard of education should now be considered a more important qualification for the Bench of the Courts than the prestige of old age or local standing in the community, and the general trend in the composition of the Tribunals in recent years has been to reduce the number of members, and wherever possible to appoint permanent presidents who have had some education. It is now accepted as a principle that the Chiefs or Official Headmen should not be members of the Courts. The declared objective is now the evolution of a modernized

---

[1] See above, pp. 300–1.
[2] Government Notice no. 891, 1945.
[3] See below, p. 615.

system of law and justice.[1] An increasing number of the presiding officers are now likely to be Africans with a university degree.

The Native Tribunals Ordinance of 1930 provided for the constitution of Appeal Courts; appeals were henceforth to be to the District Commissioner and Provincial Commissioner, and not as previously through a Magisterial Court to the Supreme Court.[2] The change was not in itself of great importance, and it is more significant that in 1945 there was created the post of Judicial Adviser with responsibility for the supervision of the working of the Native Courts.[3] He was subsequently designated as Native Courts Adviser, and Provincial Native Courts Advisers were also appointed to two of the Provinces. The Native Tribunals Ordinance was replaced in 1951 by an African Courts Ordinance,[4] but the principal change made was the creation of a Court of Review,[5] which will hear appeals in cases in which the Provincial Commissioner certifies that an important point in law is involved.

The Departmental Charge of African Affairs

There is now in Kenya no separate branch of the Administration which deals specifically with African affairs. The post of Chief Native Commissioner was created in 1918 and, until the late twenties, he was the head of a Native Affairs Department. His position in this capacity was that of an adviser to Government, but he was *ex officio* a member of the Executive Council. In the reorganization of 1945, under which groups of Departments were allocated to certain members of the Executive Council, he became Member for African Affairs. As such he could issue 'directives' on matters affecting Native Administration; but in a considerable field of governmental activity (including since 1951 the supervision of the District African Councils) the responsibility rests with members of the Executive Council holding other portfolios.

African Associations

Africans are now represented on a large number of bodies which have been created to advise different governmental Departments on current issues of policy or administration.[6] Numerous African Associations have been organized for various purposes, but they are not all primarily political, and it is particularly among the Kikuyu that organizations with specifically political aims have been developed.[7] The Kikuyu Central Association was founded in 1922, when one of the most prominent of its

[1] A. Phillips, *Report on Native Tribunals in Kenya*, 1945, pp. 7–15, 320.
[2] For the appellate system generally, see below, pp. 635–6.
[3] For these posts, see below, p. 634.
[4] Ordinance 65 of 1951.   [5] See below, p. 635.
[6] For a list of 30 such bodies, see *N.A.*, Part I, p. 209.
[7] L. S. B. Leakey, *Mau Mau and the Kikuyu*, 1952, pp. 86–94.

expressed aims was the recovery of the legendary 'lost lands' of the tribe; it had a considerable membership and published its own newspaper. It was suppressed in 1940 under War Emergency legislation, but its place was taken in 1944 by the Kenya African Union, which, though proclaiming itself as the mouthpiece of African opinion throughout the Colony, concentrated its attention on matters of interest primarily to Kikuyu. At different times it organized opposition to the inoculation of cattle, to soil conservation measures, and to land settlement schemes; it acted, in other words, as the spearhead of African attack on official policies, without particular regard for their merits. Jomo Kenyatta, a former official of the Kikuyu Central Association, became its president in 1945; he organized a training college for teachers in the Kikuyu 'independent schools', which were alleged to have been the chief impulse behind what subsequently became the Mau Mau movement. A meeting at Nyeri, convened by the Kenya African Union in July 1952, is generally regarded as the first overt demonstration of Mau Mau intentions, and three months later, in October 1952, a State of Emergency was proclaimed.[1] The Association was proscribed under the Emergency Regulations in June 1953.[2]

NIGERIA

Both Southern Rhodesia and Kenya have (as has been seen) made some use of the traditional African institutions as agencies of local rule, but they have done so on different grounds from those which have influenced the Governments, now to be noticed, which have adopted the Native Authority system as the guiding principle in their administration of African affairs. The distinctive concepts which have determined the use of that system are shortly as follows. It has in the first place avoided as far as possible the employment of any local authority which has not held a recognized position of influence derived from indigenous custom or tradition. Second, it has contemplated that the entities so employed (whether they have been Chiefs, Chiefs in Council, Councils of Headmen, or groups of Elders) should rely mainly on the authority they derive from indigenous custom when giving their aid in the furtherance of schemes of social or economic welfare promoted by the Administration.

It has, in the third place, realized that for this purpose the recognized authorities should be allowed a considerable measure of initiative and freedom of action within the framework of statutory regulations and administrative supervision to which they have been subjected. Fourth, it has shown itself aware that the progressive departure from the character of their traditional activities which the discharge of their new functions

---

[1] *Kenya, African Affairs Department Annual Report, 1952*, p. 21.
[2] *The Colonial Territories, 1953–54*, Cmd. 9169, p. vi.

involved, implied that the Native Authorities must come to depend more and more on the support received from the Government, with a corresponding diminution of their dependence on the influence derived from traditional sources. The traditional Authorities would in short be used as agencies of change; but they must themselves suffer a radical change in the process.

Early Administration in Northern Nigeria

It is proper that Nigeria should be given the precedence among the large group of British territories which have adopted the use of this system as part of the machinery of local rule. As has already been explained, it was in Northern Nigeria that this procedure was first given a systematic form by Lord Lugard during the years which followed the declaration of the Protectorate in 1900. The area which was thus brought under British protection was the scene of one of the most effectively organized systems of indigenous rule to be found south of the Sahara. Most of the old-established Hausa Kingdoms had embraced the Islamic faith, and under its influence they had by the early sixteenth century developed a well-organized fiscal system, a definite code of land tenure, a regular scheme of local rule through appointed District Heads,[1] and a trained judiciary administering the tenets of Mohammedan law.[2] The Fulani, who gained the ascendancy in the greater part of the Hausa country as the result of the Holy War launched by Othman dan Fodio in 1804, had formed part of this organized system of rule, and they subsequently showed as a ruling caste an ability which enabled them to retain their leadership for nearly a hundred years.[3]

Some of the rulers of these States accepted the British Protectorate without resistance, a few only after military defeat, and those who refused to submit were replaced by other members of the ruling families. They were given Letters of Appointment which made clear their dependence on the Protectorate Government, with authority to exercise only such jurisdiction as might be conferred upon them by law. In effect therefore the rulers could now make no claim to exercise 'inherent' authority, but Lugard's policy was to allow them the widest possible measure of responsibility in their own field of rule. When Northern Nigeria was divided into 14 provinces in 1903, the Residents appointed to administer them were described as 'political officers', and they were instructed that their functions in relation to the Native Authorities were to be essentially advisory.

The Emirs and Chiefs continued to collect the taxes prescribed in the

[1] N.A., Part III, pp. 47–50.

[2] For the Maliki school of Mohammedan law followed in Nigeria, see J. N. D. Anderson, *Islamic Law in Africa*, 1954, pp. 7–8.

[3] L. Mair, *Native Policies in Africa*, 1936, pp. 118 ff. M. Perham, *Native Administration in Nigeria*, 1937, pp. 37 ff.

previous fiscal system, but from 1904 they were required to pay one-fourth of this revenue to the Government. Between 1906 and 1911 they agreed that the remaining three-fourths of the tax should be divided between a fixed amount representing their personal income and a further amount representing provision for expenditure on public purposes. It was thus that the Treasury system came into being, though strangely enough no legal provision was made for it until the Native Authority Ordinance was amended in 1948.[1]

The Fulani system of rule did not, however, extend throughout Northern Nigeria; on the Bauchi plateau and south of the Benue River there were large areas where the 'pagan' tribes had never fully acquiesced in it. Though it would have been convenient to treat those areas as falling within the Fulani system, this was not thought to be justified. At an early stage, therefore, Political Officers were required to undertake a direct responsibility in such areas,[2] in the course of which they normally made use of appointed District Heads similar to those employed by the Fulani. At a later date, however, investigations were made with a view to locating the seat of indigenous authority in the 'pagan' areas, with the view of conferring upon the persons holding it such powers as their capacity seemed to justify. It was in pursuance of this policy that the term 'Native Authority' was redefined in 1933 so as to include not only a Chief appointed in his personal capacity, but a Chief with a Council, or even a customary form of Council no one member of which could be recognized as pre-eminent.[3]

Effects of the Amalgamation of Northern and Southern Nigeria

The procedure of Native Administration thus described had been introduced in Northern Nigeria by a series of Proclamations and administrative Orders, but after the amalgamation of the two Protectorates of Northern and Southern Nigeria in 1914, its principles were embodied in Native Authority Ordinance 19 of 1916 which applied to the whole of the areas thus amalgamated; this was later consolidated in Ordinance 17 of 1943. Under these provisions a Native Authority is constituted solely by appointment from the Governor, who may appoint a Chief, or a Chief associated with a Council, or a Council, or any group of persons, and may either prescribe the membership of a Council or of a group, or may simply direct that it be constituted in accordance with Native law and custom. In spite of the width of the powers which these provisions seemed to confer, the Government has in actual practice sought consistently to confine recognition to the Native Authority indicated by tradition or custom.

[1] Native Authority (Amendment) Ordinance, no. 4 of 1948.
[2] F. D. Lugard, *Instructions to Political and other Officers on Subjects chiefly Political and Administrative*, 1906; and *Political Memoranda*, 1918.
[3] D. Cameron, *Nigeria: Principles of Native Administration and their Application*, 1934.

The recognized Native Authorities have the primary duty of maintaining law and order, and are also empowered to issue legal Orders on a wide schedule of matters bearing on the welfare of the community. The Resident may revoke or suspend an Order, or may require the Native Authority to issue an Order, or may issue it himself in default. Subject to the sanction of the Governor, the Native Authority may also make Rules, under 26 different heads, for the good order and welfare of the persons within the area of its authority, and penalties are provided under law for the breach of such Rules or Orders. The scope of the rule-making power of Native Authorities was extended in 1945 to embrace the definition and modification of Native law and custom. In the same year they were also given special power to deal with matters relating to the tenure of land, the significance of which is discussed in a later chapter.[1]

On the amalgamation in 1914 of the two Protectorates of Northern and Southern Nigeria, the Native Authority system as it was then in operation in the north was extended by Lord Lugard to the Yoruba kingdoms of the south-west and subsequently by his successors to the Ibo and related peoples in the south-east. Its development encountered very different problems according to the social structure of the peoples who were brought under it, and it will be convenient to deal in turn with the position in each of the three Regions, Northern, Western, and Eastern, into which Nigeria was subsequently divided by the political reorganization of 1946.[2]

The Northern Region

In the Northern Region the most noteworthy feature has been the development made in the procedure for the assessment of taxation, and in the application of the system of Native Treasuries. The facts regarding the procedure of direct taxation in the form of a poll tax are given in a subsequent chapter;[3] here it is sufficient to point out that Northern Nigeria stands out as the area which from the first sought to find an alternative to the imposition of a flat rate of poll tax. If the attempt did not attain complete success, it nevertheless led the way in achieving a certain measure of flexibility by variation of the rate imposed in different localities.

The success achieved in the evolution of the system of Native Treasuries has been most pronounced in the North, and it has had a marked influence on the extension of the Native Authority system elsewhere. The 116 Native Authorities in the Northern Region have 59 Treasuries, a number of the smaller units being united for this purpose. The scale of their operations may be deduced from the extent of their revenues. In the estimates for 1953–4 their total revenue amounted to a little over £5¾ million; 14 Treasuries had amounts above £100,000, the most important

[1] See below, pp. 788–90. See also *N.A.*, Part III, pp. 11–13.
[2] See above, pp. 309–10.
[3] See below, pp. 662–3.

being that of Kano £797,723, Sokoto £513,324, Katsina £437,243, and Bornu £381,610.

The management of these large sums has required a measure of supervision which has inevitably gone beyond the 'tender of advice' envisaged by Lord Lugard as the function of the Resident. Supervision was made effective through the provision that estimates of expenditure must have official sanction, and must be drawn up in accordance with detailed instructions.[1] The larger Native Authorities have their own Treasury staff, by whom the estimates are prepared for submission to a Finance Committee of the Native Authority Council, of which the Resident or the District Officer is usually a co-opted member. In many of the smaller organizations, however, the District Officer has still to prepare and explain the estimates. The Financial Instructions were revised in 1951 so as to relax the control exercised over those Treasuries which could be classed as 'financially sound', in the sense that they have a 15 per cent. surplus of revenue over expenditure. In the year 1952 there were 42 Treasuries so classified.

The approved emoluments of the Rulers, their Councillors, and their official establishments (such as the District Heads) are borne on the Treasury Estimates. In the major Emirates, such as Kano, Sokoto, and Bornu, the Ruler has an allowance of £6,000 a year, together with certain fixed establishment expenses (£3,000 in the case of Kano, £1,500 in the case of Sokoto and Bornu). Others have smaller amounts, and the salaries of their Councillors vary accordingly; some of the more important Councillors in the larger Emirates receive as much as £1,200 a year, but there are many others on a comparatively low scale. The District Heads receive salaries which range from £840 downwards.[2]

The provision made for the supply of public services in the capital towns of some of the Emirates is impressive; the Kano Native Authority, for example, supports a modern hospital with over 300 beds. The Native Authority has its own electricity and water-supply installations. These are managed by officers deputed to the Native Authority from the Government Departments. It has also a School of Arabic Studies, and a Survey and Printing Department staffed by African employees. Other important Emirates can parallel these developments, though on a smaller scale. The larger Native Authorities also carry out extensive public works in their areas on an agency basis for the Central Government. They take full responsibility for the policing of their areas and maintain their own prisons.[3] Their administrative activities are usually organized into Departments corresponding to those of the Central Government, and some of the Rulers

---

[1] *Financial Memoranda for Use in Native Treasuries*, Zaria, 1951.
[2] *N.A.*, Part III, pp. 50–63.
[3] M. Perham, op. cit. pp. 97–98.

have allocated the responsibility for different Departments to individual members of their Councils.

The members of the Native Authority Councils are personally appointed by the Ruler; they were at one time composed largely of men of the leading local families or holding a traditional position, but there has of late years been a growing practice of appointing men who have earned the position by experience in the official service of the Authority, generally as the District Heads through whom the local administration has normally been conducted. In their case also appointments have in recent years been increasingly made on merit rather than on the basis of family position.

The capitals of the major Emirates are also administered through District Heads, the area assigned for occupation as the Government Station being excised from their jurisdiction and constituted as a Township under the District Officer as Local Authority. The Sabon Garis, or 'stranger cities', in which traders from other parts and other immigrant Africans normally live,[1] were at first made subject to this Township Authority, but from 1940 have in most cases been placed under the control of the Native Authorities.[2] The rule-making powers of these Authorities include specific provision for matters arising primarily in urban conditions, such as the control of building lines or the regulation of traffic.

The traditional organization characteristic of the Emirates was exceptionally well adapted to the purposes for which the Government sought in earlier days to utilize it. So much was this the case that many of the Administrative Officers in the Northern Provinces were convinced that its intrinsically African character would render it at all times more acceptable to Africans than any form of representative institutions; some indeed hoped that a largely self-governing Nigeria might ultimately emerge from a union of Native Authorities.[3] But it is doubtful if those who shared this view could have seriously considered the difficulty of extending to other parts of Nigeria a Native Authority system which was so peculiarly identified with the character of the indigenous institutions of the North. Nor could they have foreseen the influence likely to be exercised in the North itself by political forces which were, as shown in the preceding chapter, pressing for the extension throughout Nigeria of representative institutions framed on a 'popular' basis.

Unfavourable as was the atmosphere of the North at one time to these influences, the Region now has its own political Association, the Northern People's Congress, which has sought among other things to curtail the personal authority exercised by the Ruling Chiefs, and it is noteworthy that this body now numbers among its members a number of the leading

---

[1] M. Perham, op. cit. pp. 101–3.
[2] Regulation 30 of 1940 under Land and Native Rights Ordinance, Laws Cap. 85; see *N.A.*, Part III, pp. 86–88.   [3] See above, p. 308.

Native Authority officials. In 1952 the Northern House of Assembly passed an amendment to the Native Authority Ordinance which had the effect of abolishing the status of sole Native Authority, hitherto enjoyed by a considerable number of the Emirs, with the result that some 86 Superior Native Authorities became Chiefs-in-Council, and were as such obliged to consult their Councils, though not legally bound by their advice. This amendment was subsequently incorporated in the Northern Region Native Authority Law of 1954, which at the same time authorized the Lieutenant-Governor so to prescribe the membership of the Council of a Native Authority as to require the inclusion of elected members or even to make membership wholly elected. It further prescribed that a Chief who is associated with a Council as 'Chief-in-Council' must abide by the decision of the majority of its members.

There had for some years been signs of a popular movement in the Emirates against the authority of the Emirs, but it seems to have derived its force not so much from antagonism to their personal position as from a desire to make the District Heads more responsive to popular opinion. From 1945 onwards the Government sought to promote the creation of a system of District and Village Councils[1] as a means of arousing interest in schemes of local welfare, and the law of 1954 authorized the Lieutenant-Governor to require the appointment of such Councils. Up to the present, however, the Northern Provinces have shown relatively little popular interest in the creation of District and Village Councils, and such work as has been undertaken by these Councils seems to have been on a negligible scale.

The influence of the movement for giving a more popular form to the Native Authority system in the North has also been seen in the effort to secure the broadening of the membership of the Emirs' and Chiefs' Councils by the inclusion not merely of educated members but also of representatives of non-Fulani and also of 'pagan' communities. In addition, the creation of Native Authority Advisory Councils, composed partly of District Heads and partly of representatives of the District Councils, has opened an avenue for direct contact between the Ruling Chiefs and local opinion.[2] In the Emirate capitals a series of Advisory Councils have been created, consisting of elected representatives of the different Wards, and in some of the newer towns these bodies have been given the status of Subordinate Native Authorities. The Sabon Garis have their own elected Councils; that of Kano had in 1953 a revenue of £14,031, derived largely from the proceeds of fees and licences.

In Nigeria, as elsewhere in the territories which have adopted the Native Authority system, the organization of Native justice has formed an integral feature of that system. In view of the nature of the relation

[1] N.A., Part III, pp. 68, 69, 96.
[2] D. A. Pott, *Progress Report on Local Government in the Northern Region*, Kaduna, 1953.

between the executive and judicial functions of indigenous authorities in Africa, it would have indeed been difficult to envisage the evolution of an effective Native Authority organization had it not been so closely associated with the formation of Native Tribunals. In a large part of the Northern Provinces of Nigeria, however, the Native Tribunal has occupied an unusual position in relation to the Native Authorities, for in the Muslim Emirates there has been a considerable measure of separation of executive and judicial functions.

In these Emirates the Courts, except that of the Emir himself, are presided over by specially trained officers, the Alkalai.[1] The Alkali sits with a number of clerks (Mallams) trained in the law, but he is the sole judge. The Alkalai and Mallams are now trained at the School of Arabic Studies in Kano, and their Courts continue to follow Muslim procedure and rules of evidence.[2] Lord Lugard had held that all cases involving Africans should remain within the jurisdiction of administrative officials, and he established Provincial Courts, sitting under the presidency of the Residents, to hear appeals from the Native Tribunals. After 1939, however, these were replaced by Magistrates' Courts subordinate to the Protectorate High Court, which in 1945 was merged with the Supreme Court. The Northern Region consequently shares in the general provision under which there is now an avenue of appeal to the Supreme Court.[3]

In those 'pagan' areas which were not brought under the system prevailing in the Emirates, the membership of the Native Court is generally the same as that of the Native Authority, and there is often a large Bench of no defined composition and with no permanent president. In the urban areas provision is made for the immigrant elements by the creation of special 'Mixed Courts', of which the members are, as far as possible, familiar with the custom of the principal tribes represented in the area.[4] The system of Alkalai Courts, with their judges detached from any executive functions, has continued to be well accepted by the Muslim community in the Hausa States, but members of other communities are inclined to resent the application to them of the procedure of Muslim law followed in these Courts. Reference will be found in a subsequent chapter to the inquiry into the Court system of the Northern Region carried out in 1950 by Mr. Justice Brooke.[5] He recommended the gradual development in the non-Muslim areas (including the towns) of a Judiciary with some training in legal procedure, sitting as sole Judge, but with Assessors to advise on points of customary law. He held that this type of Court should gradually replace the Alkalai Courts for dealing with matters not covered by Muslim law.[6]

[1] Proclamation no. 1 of 1906.
[2] Anderson, op. cit. pp. 171 ff., 191 ff.   [3] See below, pp. 611–12.
[4] N.A., Part III, pp. 79–85.   [5] See below, pp. 638–9.
[6] *Report of the Native Courts (Northern Provinces) Commission of Enquiry*, 1952.

Whatever may be the political future of the Native Authorities in the Northern Region, no one could fail to be impressed by the personality of a number of the Emirs and Chiefs, or the dignity and sense of order which marks their conduct of affairs. There are among them a growing number of men of good education, and there are many of their Councillors who have given proof of notable competence as heads of executive Departments. The Native Authorities of this type represent an older school of thought and a manner of life that is now passing away, but they should not be overlooked in any estimate one may make of the inherent qualities of the African character and its capacity for the conduct of affairs. Their type of rule was well suited to the circumstances of the time, and if it is now seen to require some modification, it is mainly because the authoritarian character of the Emirate rule has with the changing times had to face a popular demand of increasing strength for a larger voice in the management of local affairs.

The Western Region

The conditions for the introduction of the Native Authority system were less favourable in the areas which are now comprised in the Western Region. Though the leadership of the Yoruba Chiefs (Obas) was well accepted both in ritual matters and in time of war, they did not as a class possess the measure of personal command which the Fulani rulers had acquired and had made effective through the agency of the District Heads who were their direct representatives throughout their territory. The sub-divisions of the Yoruba kingdoms possessed a large measure of autonomy under the leadership of hereditary office holders or heads of aristocratic families. The Royal Niger Company had in 1892 and 1893 concluded agreements for the suppression of the slave trade with the more important of the Yoruba Chiefs, and by so doing had recognized them as the local representatives of indigenous authority; but at this stage little attempt was made by the Government to find a definite place for them within the frame-work of its own organization of rule. There was at that period no pro-cedure of direct taxation in force, and there was therefore no possibility of the establishment of Native Treasuries on the basis of shared revenues.[1]

Such intervention as was made in Native affairs was mainly directed to the improvement of the judicial system in the interests of public order. Proclamation no. 9 of 1900 created Councils consisting of nominated African members, with the District Commissioner as chairman, in order to discharge functions which were primarily judicial in character, though they were also endowed with Rule-making powers.[2] It was not till 1916 that the Obas were persuaded to surrender their quasi-independent status,

[1] See below, p. 664.
[2] M. Perham, op. cit. pp. 61 ff.; *N.A.*, Part III, pp. 108–13.

and the Native Authority system prevailing in the North was formally extended to Yorubaland by an Ordinance of that year. In 1918 the Native Revenue Ordinance of 1917, originally enacted for application to the Northern Provinces, was also extended to the Southern areas.

The formal appointment of the Obas as Native Authorities appeared in the first instance to confer on them a somewhat larger measure of authority than that actually accorded to them by local custom. It is not astonishing therefore to find that there succeeded an uneasy period in which the traditional office holders and other Local Authorities endeavoured to secure such readjustment of their relations with the Obas as was feasible within the framework of the Native Authority Ordinances. There was a process of reorganization which in many cases took the form of creating Subordinate Native Authorities which managed their own Treasuries, subject to the approval of their estimates by a Superior Native Authority. Readjustments of this kind were still being debated up to the time of the introduction of the measures to be shortly described which provided for the replacement of the existing Native Authorities by local bodies modelled on the pattern of British Local Government institutions.[1]

Outside Yorubaland, and notably in the Warri Province, the indigenous social structure was of a type more characteristic of the Eastern Region,[2] where no common authority is recognized over any unit wider than a clan or village group, and where the authority acknowledged by such groups is not that of an individual but of a Council of Elders. Here Group Councils, which were often large bodies of indeterminate and fluctuating composition, had to be appointed as Native Authorities, but their individual resources were so small that it became necessary to federate them into unions in order to constitute Treasuries with adequate working revenues. In 1947 the policy was adopted whenever possible of amalgamating all Treasuries situated within the same administrative division; in this case the constituent units usually retained the status of Subordinate Native Authorities and elected their representatives to a combined Council.

The effect of this policy was to be seen in the reduction of the number of Superior Native Authorities from 137 in 1945 to 53 in 1951. As in the Northern Region, the urban centres were normally left under the control of the Native Authorities within whose jurisdiction they lay, the Government stations being excised from their jurisdiction and regulated under the Townships Ordinance. Some of the larger African towns were given the status of Subordinate Native Authorities and possessed their own Treasuries. Two townships, Warri and Sapele, had Advisory Boards consisting of three official members together with one appointed and one elected member from each Ward.

The contribution made to the provision of Local Government services

[1] See below, pp. 465–70.   [2] *N.A.*, Part III, pp. 132–3.

by the Native Authority Treasuries in the Western Region has been much less impressive than that made by the organizations in the Northern Region. In the estimates for 1953-4 the total ordinary expenditure of the Western Region Treasuries was a little short of £2 million. Eleven had a revenue of under £5,000; only ten had more than £50,000, but out of these there were three (Ibadan, £278,484, Benin, £216,870, and Egba, £159,667) which can rank with the leading Treasuries of the north. Every Treasury had a Finance Committee; some of these actually prepared the estimates, but there were a number where the preparation of the estimates still lay wholly in the hands of the District Officer. The only really important Local Government institution, the Adeoyo hospital, which was formerly maintained by the Ibadan Native Authority, was taken over as a teaching hospital by the West African University College in 1952. In the large Yoruba towns electricity and water have been supplied by the Native Authority on a 'conjoint' system similar to that in the Northern Region, in which the Government has provided the superior technical officers and the Native Authority the subordinate staff and labour.

The system in the Western Region, as described above, has recently undergone a definite change. This may be said to date back to a Circular Dispatch issued from the Colonial Office in 1948 urging the Colonial Governors to encourage the development of a system of 'efficient democratic Local Government'. As a result the status of 'sole Native Authority' was shortly afterwards abolished in the Western Region, and all Native Authorities were gazetted as consisting of Councils, with a traditional Chief as president where this was appropriate.[1] A further stage was marked by the enactment in 1953 of a Local Government law,[2] which authorized the establishment of a system of Local, District (urban or rural), and Divisional Councils based on the model of British Local Government bodies, including powers of rating.

Up to one-fourth of the membership of these Councils may be 'traditional members', the rest being elected; there is provision for a Chief to be appointed as the ceremonial President of a Council, and the members may make him chairman if they wish. Financial control is to be exercised mainly through the procedure of audit and surcharge, with the result that Residents and District Officers will cease to have the right of intervening in the activities of the Councils. There are, however, to be Inspectors of Local Government bodies, and for the immediate present these Inspectors must clearly be the Administrative Officers. A beginning was made in implementing these provisions when Divisional and Local Councils were set up in two divisions of Ijebu Province during 1953.

It is convenient to add here a reference to the position of the Native Courts in the Western Region. While the legislation regulating the

[1] O. Awolowo, *The Path to Nigerian Freedom*, 1947, pp. 77 ff.   [2] Law no. 1 of 1953.

Native Courts has been uniform in all three Regions,[1] their composition in the Western Region has necessarily differed from that in the Northern. In the Yoruba divisions the Native Courts are those of the Obas and their Councils; elsewhere they are those of the Councils which have been recognized as Native Authorities. In the large Yoruba chiefdoms the Chief selects the Court members, but does not himself sit on the bench. In the areas where an entire Clan or Group Council (which often comprises a very large body of individuals) has been gazetted as a Court (as in parts of Warri and Benin), it has been usual to appoint panels from which sitting Benches are made up.

Though the Native Courts of the higher grade have not such wide powers as those of a corresponding grade in the Northern Region, they have as a whole been accustomed to deal with the great majority of all civil and criminal cases affecting Africans. The Commissioner appointed in 1950–1 to make recommendations for their improvement pointed out that the Magisterial Courts were already so overburdened that it would be impracticable to transfer to them the work now being carried out by the Native Courts. He recommended that Native Courts should be constituted consisting of a single Judge sitting with Assessors, and that Provincial or Divisional Courts should be established with Administrative Officers or other suitable persons as Judges.[2]

The principal political Association in the Western Region is the Action Group led by Mr. O. Awolowo. This originated as the Egbe Omo Oduduwa, an organization created to further the interests of Yoruba students in the United Kingdom; it adopted its new name on the occasion of the first general election in the Western Region under the Constitution of 1951. There are also in this Region some adherents of the older National Council of Nigeria and the Cameroons, a body whose membership is predominantly Ibo, and whose main strength is accordingly in the Eastern Region.

As has been previously explained, Lagos and the Colony area were under the Constitution of 1951 administered as part of the Western Region. Though this arrangement has now been modified, so that Lagos will be treated as falling within the administration of the Federal Government,[3] it will be convenient to deal at this point with the system of Native Administration hitherto in force in the Colony. It is divided into three districts. Up to 1938 there was in these districts no regular organization of local rule, but there were Chiefs who, though they held the titles characteristic of Yoruba chieftainship, were in status little more than village headmen, and were paid stipends in return for their services in tax collection.[4] In 1938,

---

[1] For the history of the judicial system in the Southern Protectorate, previous to the amalgamation of 1914, see *N.A.*, Part III, pp. 110–13.

[2] See below, p. 637, and *Native Courts Commission of Enquiry, Western Provinces of Nigeria*, 1952.

[3] See above, p. 312.

[4] *N.A.*, Part III, pp. 28 ff.

however, it was decided to introduce into the Colony area a Native Authority system on the same lines as in the Western Provinces, and by 1950 there had been created a series of Local Councils which in this instance had a predominantly elected membership. They comprised in that year a total of 26 traditional and 743 elected members; the latter included a considerable number of educated men engaged in business or professional work in Lagos.

In 1952–3 the total ordinary revenue of the twelve Native Treasuries was £33,492. Only one Native Authority, that of Ikeja, could be said to have made any noteworthy contribution to the provision of local services. Up to 1937 there were only Magistrates' Courts in the Colony districts, but in that year Native Courts were established, and in 1952 there were 19 such Courts, but no Native Court of Appeal. In many of them the whole body of Native Authority members constitute the Court, but a smaller number selected from among them is impanelled for a month at a time to serve as a Bench.[1] Efforts are now being made to reduce the number of Court members to a President and three or four others.[2]

The town of Lagos was administered up to 1919 by a Board of Health which had been established some 50 years earlier. This was replaced in 1919 by a Township Council with a small number of elected members, and after a number of changes this body was finally reconstituted in 1950 as the Lagos Town Council. The Council was composed of 24 members elected by universal franchise; it elected its own Mayor and had the normal powers of a municipality.[3] Its experiences in its new form were, however, unfortunate. The Councillors were partisans of two opposing political parties and expressed their differences largely in the form of controversy over the appointment of the Council's executive officers. In 1952 Mr. B. Storey, Town Clerk of Norwich, was invited by the Government to inquire into the allegations of corruption which were being freely made; his report indicated that these charges were well grounded, and that the Council in general had seriously neglected its duties.[4]

The Regional Authority dissolved the Council, and substituted for it a Committee of Management consisting of twelve members. This was reconstituted in 1953[5] as the Town Council with the head of one of the Houses of the former titular 'Kings of Lagos'[6] as its president, but exercising only ceremonial functions. Eight other 'traditional' members were to be elected by the Lagos Chiefs from among themselves for a period of six years: the remainder of the Council were to consist of elected representatives of the Wards. The creation of this body seems to have repre-

[1] *N.A.*, Part III, pp. 31–33.
[2] *Report of the Native Courts (Colony) Commission of Inquiry*, 1949.
[3] Lagos Local Government Ordinance, no. 7 of 1950.
[4] B. Storey, *Report of the Commission of Inquiry into Administration of the Lagos Town Council*, 1953.
[5] Lagos Local Government Law, 1953.   [6] *N.A.*, Part III, pp. 24, 25.

sented a compromise, for the Lagos Chiefs had for many years ceased to hold a position of any importance in the life of the town.

The Eastern Region

The position in the Eastern Region of Nigeria has presented in many ways a marked contrast to that in the Northern and Western Regions. Circumstances favoured the evolution of the Native Authority system in a large part of the Northern Region, and from the first it met with a considerable measure of success. If circumstances were not equally favourable to its introduction in the Western Region, this does not mean that the decision to adopt it there must be regretted. It was clearly better to take this course rather than to allow a continuance of the previous situation, which made some use of the traditional institutions of the Yoruba, but assigned to them no definite place in the organization of local rule. The adoption of the Native Authority system in 1916 allowed to the various elements concerned, the Chiefs, the titled office holders, and the people, a breathing space in which they could adjust their relations without an undue upheaval of local society.

In the Eastern Region circumstances were, as will be seen, even less favourable than those of the Western to the introduction of a Native Authority system based on the Northern model; but in the end the judgement must be much the same. The operation of the system has, if nothing more, provided an experience of great value in the political education of the population concerned. In the Southern Provinces of the Region the social structure was marked by the absence not only of hereditary Chiefs, but of any personalities who could claim an inherent right to the allegiance of any large group of people. Authority was usually distributed among kinship heads and the members of title-holding societies, and the group of people who were accustomed to look to a common source of authority was very often no wider than that inhabiting a small village.[1]

During the régime of the Southern Nigeria Protectorate the first Ordinance dealing with the system of Native Administration (no. 7 of 1906), provided for the establishment of Councils or Courts consisting of nominated African members with the District Commissioner as chairman; they had both civil and criminal jurisdiction and also the right to make rules for the preservation of peace. The members of these Councils, who came to be known as Warrant Chiefs, were selected from villages within the Council or Court area. In default of any other available agency, they became the executive agents of the Government, each in his own village. In many cases care was taken to choose for this purpose men of good local standing; in others, however, more consideration was given to purely

[1] M. M. Green, *Ibo Village Affairs*, 1947.

personal qualifications, such as an experience of service under the Administration.[1]

At this stage no direct taxation had been levied. During the years 1925–6, however, it was proposed to extend the Native Authority system in this area, and to introduce direct taxation in order to finance the proposed Native Treasuries. Taxable capacity was to be assessed by the methods already in use in the North,[2] and the inquiries made for this purpose aroused much suspicion. The first year's tax was collected without undue difficulty, largely by the aid of the Warrant Chiefs. In the following year there were in the Calabar and Owerri Provinces a series of serious disturbances which were remarkable in that the actual rioting was almost entirely confined to women. A commission of inquiry[3] into the origin of the disturbances found that discontent with the Warrant Chiefs was a contributing factor, and as a result investigations were made throughout the area in order to discover the real seat of traditional authority, with the object of providing a more secure basis for the introduction of the Native Authority system.

The peculiar nature of the structure of local society was reflected in the form of organization which ensued. A diversity of Native Authority units was organized, the majority of which took the form of Clan or Group or Village Councils. Many of these bodies were in fact of the nature of village moots, as all the family heads or other leading members of the relatively small groups had equal claims to be included. There were at one time in the Owerri Province alone as many as 245 Native and Subordinate Native Authorities. In spite of efforts made to reduce the number by various types of federation, there were in 1948 still as many as 217 Native Authorities and 300 Subordinate Native Authorities in the whole Region.

For obvious reasons the policy was adopted of combining the smaller units into a unified Native Authority with a Treasury, the component Councils being classed as Subordinate Native Authorities with executive and judicial but no financial powers. There was at the same time a development which became of great significance in the subsequent history of the system; an increasing proportion of the members of the Councils were drawn from the 'Progressive Unions' of educated men which had by this time become a characteristic feature of Ibo and Ibibio society. About 1940 the practice began of forming Provincial and Divisional Councils representing all Native Authorities, but though such Councils were effective as a means of expressing popular opinion they proved of little value as an agency for furthering measures of social welfare. The basic difficulty lay in the fact that the organization of the Native Authorities made no provision

---

[1] R. L. Buell, *The Native Problem in Africa*, vol. i, 1928, p. 715. L. Mair, *Native Policies in Africa*, pp. 128 ff. M. Perham, op. cit. pp. 201 ff. *N.A.*, Part III, pp. 158 ff.

[2] See above, p. 455, and see below, pp. 662–3.

[3] Sessional Papers of the Nigerian Legislative Council, nos. 12 and 28 of 1930.

for an executive machinery, and the functions normally falling on Local Government bodies were perforce carried out by the District or other Administrative Officers.

From a practical point of view the system was clearly ineffective, and its dependence on the activity of the Administrative Officers was an invitation to the criticism of the more politically minded members of the Progressive Unions. The Native Authority system in this Region had from the first been viewed with suspicion by the progressive element; it was decried as a reactionary policy designed to strengthen the position of Chiefs and hereditary title-holders at the expense of educated African opinion. With every advance made towards the attainment of political self-rule the expression given to this argument was intensified. The system was now described as a symbol of the Imperialism from which every true African must seek release. The logic of this particular charge was far from obvious, but it helps to account for the fact that the substitution of a system of purely elective Councils has formed so prominent a feature of the programme of a body such as the National Council for Nigeria and the Cameroons or of the numerous Improvement and Progressive Unions on whose support it has relied.

Proposals for a radical reform of the system were discussed by the Government of the Eastern Region in 1947,[1] and in 1948 and 1950 legislative provision was made for the creation of County Councils, Urban or Rural District Councils, and Local Councils on an elective basis. As a general rule the Local Councils were to cover the areas of the existing Subordinate Native Authorities; the District Councils were to become the rating authority and to have the widest range of functions. In form this constituted a 'three-tier' system of Councils, but it was the District Council which was to form the focal point in it. The Ordinance did not create any supervisory body comparable to the Local Government Inspectorate of the Western Region; Councils were to be directly responsible to the Regional Authority, and the function of Administrative Officers was limited to keeping the Regional Authority in touch with the proceedings of local bodies.[2]

Here then was a scheme of reform which had a double purpose. It replaced by a series of elected bodies so much of the former Native Authority system as was based on the employment of traditional institutions for Local Government purposes, and at the same time it removed the new bodies from the control of the local Administrative Officers. The change was the more significant because in fact it was the Administrative Officers who had hitherto been responsible for any effective action in the provision

[1] *Memorandum on Report of Select Committee appointed to Review the Existing System of Local Government in the Eastern Provinces*, 16 July 1949.

[2] Eastern Region Local Government Ordinance no. 16, 1950, amended by no. 33 of 1950.

of Local Government services. The enactment of the Local Government Ordinance of 1950 preceded the entry into force of the semi-Responsible Constitution of the Eastern Region,[1] and its implementation had been envisaged by the Government as a long-term programme which could not in any case be completed before 1962. In 1953, however, the Regional Government, now operating under new auspices, announced an accelerated programme. There were at that time four County Councils, each with four District Councils; in 1954 elections were held for seven more.

From the first the formation of these bodies has been hampered by the lack of a competent staff, though an effort has been made to train men either in the United Kingdom or at the West African University College for service as secretaries or Executive Officers. In the case of the four District Councils of Niger County, Government officials were seconded to them as secretaries. It would seem that when the formation of the new Councils is completed there is likely to be a considerable reduction in the number of Treasuries. The very large number previously in existence had been reduced in 1947 to 107; by 1953 they had been reduced to 68. In the estimates for 1953–4 the total ordinary revenue amounted to £950,794, and the Treasuries had an accumulated surplus of £548,987. It has become apparent that in the Eastern Region the shortage of finance is likely to prove an obstacle as grave as the lack of adequate staff. The ambitious schemes now in view for the expansion of education will, in particular, prove to be impossible of achievement without a drastic change in the system of local taxation.[2]

While the majority of the urban areas had been left under the jurisdiction of the Native Authorities, a small number were administered as second-class Townships under a Local Authority consisting of the District Commissioner with an Advisory Council, the members of which were at first nominated but were later elected as representatives of Wards. Of these bodies Calabar and Enugu have now been constituted as Urban District Councils, and the same course was contemplated in the case of Aba. On the Urban District Councils the District Commissioner usually represents the Government station, which forms one electoral ward. The other towns will be constituted Urban District Councils as the application of the Ordinance is extended. Port Harcourt, however, is in a special position. As an artificial creation laid out in 1914 on land leased by the Government, it was never under the management of a Native Authority, and was administered as a second-class Township until 1949, when it became a first-class Township with a Council which had an elected majority.

The composition of the Native Courts remained unchanged after the amalgamation of Northern and Southern Nigeria in 1914, save that the

[1] For the semi-Responsible Government in the Eastern Region, see above, pp. 310 ff.
[2] See below, p. 1175.

District Officers were withdrawn from them. In 1934, however, they were reorganized on the same principle as the Native Authorities. There were thus created a great number of Courts, sometimes even exceeding the number of Native Authorities, and most of them had a large but indeterminate membership. They clearly gave greater general satisfaction than the Courts of the Warrant Chiefs had done at an earlier date, but their methods were informal, and the fact that their membership was not continuous (for like many of the Councils they had much the character of a village moot) tended to affect gravely the consistency of their judgements. The number of the Courts was, however, considerably reduced at a later date, and Native Appeal Courts were created. The composition of the Benches was reorganized on what is known as the 'best-man' system; that is, a fixed number of persons were chosen by popular acclaim at mass meetings, and were appointed by the Resident as Court members. It now appears probable that these Courts will, like those of the Western Region, be reconstituted with 'professional' presidents working with Assessors.[1]

The history of the recent developments in the Eastern Region reveals the existence of two separate influences. The first is that of the section of thought which has genuinely distrusted on personal grounds the position accorded to Chiefs and other traditional authorities under the Native Authority system. The second influence was of that section whose chief concern was for the early attainment of self-government. Their objective has been expressed in words which, if they have some element of hyperbole, nevertheless have a certain basis of realism. 'The object is to repeat on the lower levels of government the reforms which have come with such a rush at the top, or to dismantle the lesser imperialisms simultaneously with the dismantling of the central imperialism from which they draw their authority and to which they look for protection.'[2] There was a belief that the British Government was attempting to preoccupy the educated elements with questions of Local Government 'in order to divert them from their national aspirations'.[3]

It still remains to be seen how far the reform will be justified by the results attained. Reform was sought for other reasons than the attainment of a greater measure of efficiency in Local Government services. Moreover, the test which will have to be applied will go beyond the achievement of improvements in the field of Local Government as usually defined. The reforms have not provided for the performance of the more general functions which were discharged by the traditional Native Authorities, such, for example, as the part played in the maintenance of law and order

---

[1] See above, p. 463.

[2] H. Cooper, 'The Gold Coast and Nigeria on the Road to Self-Government', in *Africa Today*, 1955, p. 308.

[3] J. Coleman, 'The Emergence of African Political Parties', in *Africa Today*, 1955, p. 240.

or the provision of an acceptable system of Native justice. The divorce between the officers of the Administrative service and the organization for the supply of local welfare services has created a hiatus over which there is at present no sign of a bridge.

BRITISH CAMEROONS

In the Cameroons under United Kingdom trusteeship the system of local administration follows closely that of the neighbouring districts of Nigeria.[1] The British Trust area, which occupies roughly 34,000 square miles out of the 200,725 square miles of the former German Colony of Kamerun,[2] is divided into two distinct sections. The Northern section is for administrative purposes integrated with the Northern Region of Nigeria; the Southern section formed until 1954 the Cameroons and Bamenda Provinces of the Eastern Region, but is now constituted as a separate quasi-federal territory.[3]

The Northern section is divided between the three Northern Region provinces of Bornu, Adamawa, and Benue. The Trust area lying within the Bornu Province constitutes the division of Dikwa. The present Emirate of Dikwa once formed part of the ancient Empire of Bornu, but it is now an independent Emirate, of which the Emir is a member of the Bornu ruling family. Bornu itself under its Kanuri rulers maintained its independence of the Fulani, though it practised the Fulani system of rule.[4] The Emir of Dikwa, following the precedent set by the Fulani, controls the Emirate through appointed District Heads. He has a Council of six members, one of whom represents the 'pagan' part of the population. A series of Village Councils is being formed, and when this is completed representatives will be sent from the Trust Territory to what was formerly known as the Outer Council of the Emirate, but is now termed the Advisory Council.[5]

The Trust area which forms part of the Adamawa Province is largely populated by 'pagans', who remain subject to the District Heads appointed by the Lamido of Adamawa. Of recent years, however, there has been a breakaway from the previous oligarchic tradition of Adamawa; the Lamido Council has been enlarged in order to include representatives of the 'pagan' population; Village and District Councils are in process of being formed, and under the Constitution of 1953 they send representatives to an 'Outer' or Advisory Council. In the Benue Province the Trust area is a part of the Wukari Division; it comprises a Chief and Council (the

[1] For the constitutional relations with Nigeria, see above, p. 314. *Annual Report of Cameroons under United Kingdom Trusteeship, 1953*, pp. 8, 9, 25.

[2] The name seems to be derived from the Portuguese Rio dos Camarões (or Camarones in Spanish), the River of Shrimps.   [3] See above, p. 313.

[4] *N.A.*, Part III, p. 44. *The Nigeria Handbook*, 1953, pp. 43 ff.

[5] *Cameroons under United Kingdom Trusteeship, Report for the year 1953*, Col. no. 309. pp. 22–25.

Chiefdom having been a German creation) and two tribal Councils. Here the reorganization of the previous system is not so far advanced as in Adamawa.

The position in the Southern section of the Trust Territory is more complex. The social institutions of this area were carefully surveyed before the extension to the Cameroons of the Nigerian Ordinance of 1943,[1] and as a result a number of Native Authorities of various types were recognized. Five Chiefs in the Bamenda Division and one in the Kumba Division have in the past been gazetted as sole Native Authorities, but they have Councils of Elders whom they consult. There are also 17 Clan Councils and 22 other Councils, including one Town Council at Kumba, and 64 Subordinate Native Authorities. The Councils consist of 'village' or 'quarter' heads appointed by public assent. Literate members nowhere form more than 40 per cent. of a Council, and in Bamenda they are in some cases only 10 per cent. Divisional and Provincial meetings are held in the same manner as in the Eastern Region of Nigeria.

The Government of the Eastern Region has recently held that the introduction of elected local authorities would be feasible only in the Victoria Division, but it is not unlikely that the indigenous population of the Division may oppose the grant of representation to the numerous immigrants from French territory. In general the replacement of the existing Native Authority system by what is now usually designated as the Local Government system is clearly destined to be less rapid than in the more advanced parts of the Eastern Region. The total revenues of the Native Authorities in the Trust Territory for 1953–4 were estimated at £374,300. The highest salaries are those paid to the Lamido of Adamawa (£2,500), the Emir of Dikwa (£1,800), and the President of the Federated Council of Victoria in the Cameroons Province (£300). Finance committees have not yet been set up, and the preparation of the estimates devolves largely upon the District Commissioner.

The judicial system follows so closely that in force in the Northern and Eastern Regions of Nigeria as to call for no comment.

TANGANYIKA

Sir Donald Cameron's Reforms

The present system of local administration in Tanganyika owes its form largely to the influence of Sir Donald Cameron, who brought to the governorship of the Territory in 1925 the traditions he had formed during a service of some 16 years in Nigeria. In Bukoba the Germans had found Chiefs (termed by them Sultans) whom they confirmed in their authority, subject to control by the Residents. The rest of the Territory was divided

---

[1] See above, p. 454.

into 17 civil districts under District Officers, who carried on their administration through the agency of subordinate officials of the type of those who had been employed by the Sultan of Zanzibar in the mainland areas under his suzerainty.[1]

The Sultan's representatives were known as Liwali and Akida and the Germans retained these titles for them; they were normally of Arab or Swahili extraction. The more influential village Headmen were appointed to the post of Jumbe, which carried the same magisterial powers as that of the Akida, though it was in other respects subordinate. Some of the Akidas were educated men of considerable ability though, being learned only in Muslim law, they tended to disregard local custom; others have been described as having been overbearing and corrupt. As will be seen, some of the best of them were subsequently employed by the British in areas where it was found impracticable to re-establish any indigenous authority.

The British Mandatory Administration made little use of the indigenous authorities as administrative agencies until the enactment of the Native Authority Ordinance of 1926,[2] which was based on the legislation of a similar type enacted in Nigeria. Sir Donald Cameron had described the principles of the system in a Circular of July 1925,[3] and it is noteworthy that he held that, apart from its value for the purpose of local administration, it was the best way of training the African population for a full place in the political structure of the country. Just as Administrative Officers of an early date in Northern Nigeria had believed that a federation of Native Authorities might eventually become the governing body of Nigeria,[4] so Cameron envisaged for Tanganyika the development of two Central Councils, Native and non-Native, each of which would send delegates to a combined Legislature. These anticipations are perhaps now chiefly of historical interest, but it is in any case clear that the introduction of the Native Authority system in 1926 signalized an almost revolutionary change in the official outlook on Native policy in the Territory.

Native Authorities since 1926

It will be sufficient to deal with the principles rather than the details of the various Native Authority Ordinances from 1926 onwards.[5] As in Nigeria the Native Authorities are defined as 'Chiefs or other Natives or any Native Council or groups of Natives declared as such by the Govern-

[1] R. L. Buell, op. cit. vol. i, pp. 271, 449. *N.A.*, Part II, p. 7.
[2] Laws of Tanganyika, 1928, cap. 47.
[3] Buell, op. cit., pp. 451 ff.   [4] See above, p. 457.
[5] *N.A.*, Part I, pp. 217–19. See also the following: C. Winnington-Ingram, 'Reforming Local Government in Tanganyika and District', *J.A.A.*, April 1950, pp. 10–15. F. Montague and F. Page-Jones, 'Some difficulties in the Democratization of Native Authorities in Tanganyika', ibid. January 1951, pp. 21–27. 'Recommendations for the Development of Local Government', ibid. January 1952, pp. 29–31. 'A Survey of the Development of Local Government in the African Territories since 1947', Supplement to *J.A.A.*, April 1952, pp. 13–32.

ment'. Usually, however, Chiefs and Headmen were appointed as Native Authorities in their personal capacity, Councils being recognized as Native Authorities only where there was no Chief. There were some areas, however, in which it was found impracticable to appoint as Native Authority any person who had traditional claims to fill this position. A typical case was the area of mixed population in Ujiji, on the shores of Lake Tanganyika, where an Arab Liwali was made Native Authority in 1934.

In the coastal districts, which had been under Arab rule for many years before the declaration of the German Protectorate, attempts were made to revive such of the traditional authorities as still existed, but it was found that they no longer had the standing which could make their influence effective, and they were replaced by nominated officials bearing the titles of Wakili, Liwali, or Akida. These were appointed after consultation with the people, and were usually local men, many of whom had previous experience of employment under Government or a Native Authority; they were all literate in Swahili.

Tanganyika has adopted from Nigeria a procedure which has proved of great value in establishing a working system of administration. Native Authorities with limited resources have been freely combined in federations which operate joint Treasuries. The Federal Council has in such cases become the Superior Native Authority, while the constituent Authorities have retained the status of Subordinate Native Authorities, with their own judicial and executive powers. The largest Federation, that of Sukumaland, now includes 51 Native Authorities belonging to five administrative districts and embraces a population of over a million. This policy has helped to break down the isolation of small Chiefdoms and has enabled agreement to be reached over reasonably wide areas regarding the introduction of Native Authority rules, particularly those modifying indigenous custom. It has not on the other hand been equally effective in improving the standard of efficiency of the individual Chiefs, and the functioning of the Treasuries has tended to be left largely in the hands of the District Commissioners.

There has not been so far the same political impulse as has produced in Nigeria the movement for replacing the traditional Native Authorities by Local Government bodies on an elective basis. But proposals for the introduction of elective bodies have been under discussion from the year 1945, and a statement of policy which was issued in 1949 envisaged the eventual development of a system of Village, Area (sometimes described as Divisional), and District Councils, which would normally be based on the existing Native Authorities, but in which the proportion of elected members would be steadily increased.[1]

[1] 'A Survey of the Development of Local Government in the African Territories since 1947', Supplement to *J.A.A.*, April 1952, p. 15.

An analysis made in 1951 revealed the diversity of the types of Council which have been developed in the Territory. The Councils in the Tanga District consisting of the Chiefs or Headmen, together with commoners nominated by themselves, seem to typify the process of transition from the purely traditional to the partly elected Council. Another type is to be found in Sukumaland, where separate elected Councils of commoners meet the Confederacy of Chiefs for discussion. The type of Council evolved in Kisarawe is characteristic of the districts where the Native Authorities are Liwalis appointed by the Government. It consists of the Liwali of each district with one Village Headman elected from the Headmen of each division and one commoner elected from the members of the Divisional Council; in addition the District Commissioner may nominate members for their personal qualifications. In Usambara, where there are hereditary authorities, the District Council includes both Chiefs and sub-Chiefs along with their nominees and other persons popularly chosen. Among the Chagga the sub-Chiefs are excluded, leaving the Superior Chiefs as the only executive authorities who are members of the Council. A special system has been devised for the Masai, whose social structure is based on a division of the whole population into age-grades with different functions, the young men, for example, being warriors who are independent of the control of the Elders.[1] It has been arranged that Area Councils, the members of which are elected by age-grades and kinship units, should put forward representatives to a Masai Federal Council.

The Native Treasuries

The total number of Native Authority units in 1952 was 386, which were combined for financial purposes in 51 Treasuries.[2] Until recent years the revenues of the Treasuries were barely sufficient to meet the emoluments of the Chiefs, the cost of Tribunals, and the like. The position has since been improved by legislation which allows the Treasuries to levy a local rate, and in 1954 their total revenue amounted to £1,247,316. Of their total expenditure some 20 per cent. was spent on education, and 11 per cent. on medical and sanitary services.

Local Councils

Tanganyika has recently made an attempt of a novel type in East Africa to provide that Europeans and Asians should take common part with Africans in the activities of the rural institutions of Local Government; hitherto efforts made in this direction had been limited to the management of urban affairs. A Constitutional Development Committee which was appointed in 1949 proposed the creation of County Councils

[1] N.A., Part I, pp. 169, 282.
[2] Tanganyika, Report for the year 1952, Col. no. 293, p. 32.

in which Africans, Asians, and Europeans should be represented.[1] A Special Commissioner, appointed to consider matters arising from this report, recommended the immediate formation of Councils in eight areas, including more especially the Meru and Kilimanjaro areas, which contain a number of European settlers. The Councils in these areas would have a majority of African unofficial members. A Local Government Ordinance (no. 35) enacted in 1953 has since provided for the constitution of County and Local Councils (Urban and Rural) of which the Local Councils are intended to represent the same units as the existing Native Authorities or Federations.[2] They are to be composed of nominated or elected members or a combination of them; no specific reference is made to traditional status as a qualification for membership, nor is membership limited to Africans. The African Chiefs Ordinance (no. 27) of the same year seems to imply that outside the field of custom the status of Chiefs is to be confined to that of executive agents. These Ordinances have still to be implemented in detail.

Native Courts

As has been observed, the use made of the traditional authorities as judicial agencies preceded their formal recognition by the Mandatory Government as organs of local administration. Native Courts presided over by Chiefs and Headmen were established by Ordinance no. 6 of 1920, which made them subordinate to the High Court, though they in fact remained under the supervision of Political Officers acting in their capacity of Subordinate Magistrates. The Native Courts Ordinance of 1929, following the lines of that in force in Nigeria, made a substantial change in procedure; it had for its object the institution of a self-contained system of Native Courts under Administrative control, thus removing them from the control of the Supreme Court and making the Administrative authorities the sole avenue of appeal. The Courts of the Liwali[3] were excepted from this provision until 1941, when they were reclassed as Native Courts constituted under the provisions of the Ordinance of 1929.

Up to this time no provision had been made for the separation of the judicial and executive powers combined in the person of the Chiefs. Later policy was, however, directed to securing that, while the Chief might continue to preside over his Court, the Elders constituting its Bench should be persons holding no executive position, and where it was the custom for the Chief to have a deputy, the latter was appointed as Court President. Under the Ordinance of 1929 the same provision as in Nigeria was made for the review of decisions by Administrative Officers, and sentences of

---

[1] *Report of Committee on Constitutional Development in Tanganyika*, 1951.
[2] W. J. Mackenzie, 'Changes in Local Government in Tanganyika', *J.A.A.*, July 1954, pp. 123–8.   [3] See above, p. 471.

corporal punishment required their confirmation. Appeal lay from Native Appeal Courts, of which a large number were created, to the District Officer, and thence to the Provincial Commissioner and the Governor; but the latter's appellate powers were in 1940 devolved on a Board of which the Attorney-General was a member. A Native Courts Adviser was first appointed in 1948.

There were altogether some 800 Native Courts in 1951. In that year the 1929 Ordinance was replaced by the Local Courts Ordinance (no. 14 of 1951). While the existing Native Courts were now recognized as Local Courts, it was no longer stipulated that Native custom should be followed in their constitution or procedure; only matters not expressly prescribed in the Warrant were to be regulated by customary law. It is now intended that there should be only two classes of Court, differing in the extent of their civil and criminal jurisdiction. A Central Court of Appeal, presided over by a High Court Judge, has been substituted for the Governor's Appeal Board. Statutory provision was made for the appointment of a Local Courts Adviser and for Provincial Local Courts Advisers; they are to exercise a general supervision over the local Courts.

Municipal and Provincial Councils

Of the urban areas only Dar-es-Salaam has the status of a Municipality, having been so constituted in 1949. The members of the Municipal Council are all nominated; but the original number of four members each from the three major communities, European, Asian, and African, was increased in 1950 to seven from each community. In addition there are two European official members.[1] Members serve for a period of three years under a mayor who is elected annually. The Council has an African Affairs Committee and employs an African Affairs Officer. The African Location is divided into three wards, each under a Wakili; a Liwali working under the African Affairs Officer has authority over the whole area. Ward Councils consist of twelve to 16 elected members from whom one is chosen to represent the Ward on the Municipal Council.[2] A number of the 30 Township Authorities regulating the affairs of the minor towns include nominated African members, and in twelve there are African Advisory Councils or African Ward Councils, who represent the views of Africans to the Township Authority.

Provincial Councils, which have, however, only deliberative functions, were set up in the Lake Province in 1949 and the Southern Highlands Province in 1950. These have nine official and nine unofficial members, five of the latter being Africans. There is also African representation on a large number of the Advisory Boards or Committees attached to different Government Departments.[3] There is no separate Department of African

---

[1] *N.A.*, Part 1, p. 338.   [2] Col. no. 293, p. 35.   [3] *N.A.*, Part I, p. 358.

Affairs. Associations for the representation of African interests are less numerous and less active than in some other African territories, many being concerned primarily with local interests. The African Association, with headquarters at Dar-es-Salaam, now has a number of local branches, and has shown a tendency to absorb the local Associations; it contains a large number of Government and Native Authority employees as well as some traders and farmers.

ZANZIBAR

Under Sultan Seyyid Ali Bin Said,[1] Zanzibar was administered by a hierarchy of officials with the titles of Liwali, Akida, and Sheha, the last being Africans appointed as Headmen but responsible only for the control of other Africans.[2] Muslim law was administered by Courts presided over by Kadhi. When Zanzibar was brought under the Colonial Office in 1914 the Liwali were gradually replaced by British District officers, the last Liwali retiring in 1923. In the Native Administration and Authority Decree no. 15 of 1922, the jurisdiction of the Kadhi was limited to civil cases arising under Muslim law. The Zanzibar Courts (Amendment) Order of 1929 provided for the creation of Courts with members drawn from the Arab, Asian, and African communities; but owing to lack of local interest these Courts ceased to function, and were replaced in 1947 by Courts in which the Mudir (as the Liwali was now called) sits alone, with the civil and criminal powers of a Third Class Magistrate. In cases where questions of customary law arise the Mudir must sit with two qualified Assessors.[3]

There are now six Mudir and 84 Masheha in the island of Zanzibar and five Mudir and 53 Masheha in the island of Pemba. The areas for which they are responsible do not correspond to tribal or ethnic boundaries, and are delimited mainly with a view to administrative convenience. The Mudir are members of His Highness's Zanzibar Service, but are appointed by the British Resident; they are mainly Arabs of local families, and are for the most part well educated. The Masheha are selected by public acclaim, subject to the approval of the District Commissioner, but in practice their office is frequently treated as hereditary.

Provision was made in 1947 for the creation of Mudirial and Local Councils,[4] with nominated members; the Local Councils are, however, intended to include any tribal Elders who may have natural authority. The Masheha are both *ex officio* members and executive officers of these Councils, which are empowered to raise rates and make by-laws. Nine

---

[1] See above, p. 384.　　　　　　　　　　　　　　　[2] *N.A.*, Part II, p. 5.

[3] District (Mudirial) Proclamation, 1947.

[4] District Administration and Rural Local Government Decree no. 14 of 1947, and amendment no. 14 of 1949.

Local Councils had been constituted by 1953, three in Zanzibar and six in Pemba. As there is at present no direct tax in the Protectorate, the scope of their activities depends largely upon the willingness of the population to accept taxation in the form of local rates. The rural Local Councils in Pemba have imposed rates, but those of Zanzibar have not so far been willing to do so. The limited scope of the activities of the Councils may be seen from the fact that their estimated revenues of 1951 ranged only from £70 to £281. The projected Mudirial Councils, which were intended to be advisory only, have not so far been established.

Some 45,000 persons, roughly one-sixth of the population of the Protectorate, live in Zanzibar Town, which was administered from 1934 onwards by a Town Board. This was replaced in 1944 by two Town Councils, one for the business area and one for that inhabited mainly by Africans, but these two bodies were amalgamated in 1949.[1] The Zanzibar Township Council as constituted in 1950 had a membership of four Africans, four Arabs, four Asians, one Comorian, one European, one Goan, and four officials of whom one was President. All members were nominated by the British Resident, the Arabs and Asians being selected after consultation with their representative Associations. The functions of the Council are largely advisory, but the question of increasing its sphere of responsibility was under discussion in 1953.

UGANDA

In the history of the development of systems of local administration there is in one respect an analogy between Northern Nigeria and Uganda. In the Emirates of Nigeria and in the Buganda Kingdom of Uganda there existed a well-established political organization of a type that was not unfamiliar to Europeans, and in both instances the British used it as the basis of a type of local rule which had some notably successful results. The circumstances attending the conclusion of the Buganda Agreement of 1900 have already been explained, as also those which produced the Agreements with the rulers of Ankole, Toro, and Bunyoro;[2] it is therefore sufficient to add here that the result has been to create in the Protectorate a procedure of local administration of three different types, first, that existing in the Buganda State, constituting the Province of Buganda, with a population of a little over $1\frac{1}{4}$ million; second, that of the three Agreement States of Ankole, Toro, and Bunyoro in the Western Province, with a population of about three-quarters of a million; and third, that existing in the remaining eight districts of the Protectorate, which have a population of roughly $2\frac{3}{4}$ million.

[1] Townships (Amendment) Decree, no. 24 of 1949.
[2] For details, see N.A., Part I, pp. 5, 44–45.

Buganda Province

In Buganda and in the kingdoms which were developed as the result of the invasions of the Hima, the conquerors had exercised their authority through the appointment of subordinate territorial officers who held a position comparable to that of the District Heads in the Nigerian Emirates. From this origin there grew up a cadre of officials who though described as Chiefs, actually owed their position to appointment by superior authority and not to the possession of an hereditary status in local society. In Buganda the practice eventually involved the maintenance of a hierarchy of various grades, having something of the aspect of a Civil Service; its members might be promoted from grade to grade, and the higher ranks were entitled to a pension. In this respect the system followed in Buganda was clearly distinguishable from those Native Authority systems which have relied almost entirely on the use of agencies of traditional origin and generally of hereditary status.

Under the indigenous system of rule in Buganda the Kabaka, acting through his Ministers, and subject to certain conditions prescribed in the 1900 Agreement, exercises what is officially described as direct rule over the Native population of his State.[1] The terms of the Agreement conferred on him, acting with his Council (the Lukiko), the right, subject to the approval of the Governor, to make laws to that end, though the laws of the Protectorate were also to apply to Buganda unless they conflicted with the terms of the Agreement. As in Nigeria, the Kabaka and his officers were made responsible for the collection of the tax imposed by the Protectorate Government,[2] and a proportion—in this case 25 per cent.—was returned for expenditure in the Buganda state. The three Ministers of the Kabaka were to be appointed by him subject to the approval of the Governor. The Lukiko was to consist of 89 members, namely, the three Ministers above referred to (the Prime Minister, Chief Justice, and Treasurer); the 20 Chiefs of saza or 'counties' (the largest administrative divisions), three notables from each 'county', and six other persons, all to be nominated by the Kabaka. The Lukiko was therefore to be predominantly official in character.

The 20 counties (saza) are subdivided into 135 sub-counties (gombolola), each with a population ranging from 1,000 to 4,000, and these again into 1,328 parishes (miluka, *singular* muluka), which are villages or groups of villages. Only the appointment of the county (saza) Chiefs requires the approval of the Governor. All the Chiefs have Councils (nkiko, the plural of lukiko) which until about 1939 consisted of the Chiefs of their subdivisions. The muluka Council was composed of local landowners, who by custom have the courtesy status of Chiefs. The nominated members of the

---

[1] *Colonial Reports, Uganda, 1953*, p. 121.   [2] See below, p. 660.

Central Lukiko were in practice drawn almost exclusively from among this class.

From 1939 onwards, however, steps were taken to introduce a certain proportion of unofficial and elected elements into all these Councils. The Kabaka agreed in 1939 to include among his nominees one unofficial member from every county, and in 1945 provision was made for a proportion of the members in all Councils to be filled by election. At the muluka level all adult residents were entitled to vote, and the elected members of each muluka Council chose from among themselves representatives to sit in the next superior Council. A total of 36 members were elected by this process to the Central Lukiko, which it has now become usual to distinguish as the Great Lukiko. As it was found that business men were not willing to stand for election at the muluka level, the system was modified in 1950 so that 20 unofficial members were elected from the muluka Councils and 20 others were chosen by the county Councils, officials and unofficials voting together. In 1953 the number to be elected by muluka Councils was increased to 40, thus giving the Great Lukiko a total elected membership of 60 out of 89. At the same time the Kabaka agreed to consult the Lukiko on the appointment of the Ministers.

It was originally envisaged that the relationship between the local officers of the Protectorate Government and the Chiefs or other officers of the Buganda Government should be largely advisory, on the lines which Lord Lugard had sought to establish with the Nigerian Emirs. In practice, however, the Administrative Officers stationed in Buganda Province came to exercise much the same type of intervention as has been usual in areas where Native Authorities have been treated in practice as the subordinate agents of the Administration. More recently it became the declared intention of the Protectorate Government that the functions of its officers in the Buganda Province should become in reality advisory, and this was expressed in 1935 by a change in their designation to Resident, Assistant Resident, or Protectorate Agent. The practical effect of this policy was first seen in the judicial field, where the powers of revision once exercised by Administrative Officers were withdrawn and were assigned to the Judicial Adviser to the Buganda Government, a post which was created in 1940 as part of this change of system.

The Ganda system of rule, exercised through what is in effect an official hierarchy, has resulted in the development of units of local administration both larger and more uniform in size than those which it has usually been possible to establish in countries where a separate Native Authority has been recognized for each tribal or clan group. It has in consequence avoided the dissipation of effort which often results from the latter system. It is true that Chiefs appointed in this manner cannot hope to command the same loyalty as is given in most African communities to hereditary

Chiefs, but there can be no question of the relative degree of efficiency which the Buganda Chiefs have shown. Many of the senior Chiefs have been men of long experience and of high repute in the community. The system had, however, some definite limitations.

In the first place, it made little provision for the expression of popular opinion in the conduct of local affairs, a defect which is now, as shown above, being repaired by the extension to Buganda of a series of Local Councils largely dependent on a system of popular election. In the second place, this system, while it was effective for such purposes as the maintenance of law and order or the collection of tax, made comparatively little provision for the expansion of the social services. Up to 1953 it would have been roughly true that, while the Buganda Government took the greater part of the responsibility for the maintenance of order, the administration of justice, and the upkeep of police and prisons within the Buganda Province, the greater part of the provision of social or of economic services came from the departments of the Protectorate Government. In that year, however, the decision was taken, after an inquiry into the development of the institutions of Local Government throughout Uganda,[1] to hand over to the Buganda Government the responsibility at provincial level for the primary and the junior secondary schools, rural hospitals, dispensaries, and agricultural and veterinary extension work.

This decision will involve a material readjustment of the financial relations of the Buganda Government with the Protectorate Government.[2] Buganda has an efficient Treasury staff; its estimates were debated in the Central Lukiko for the first time in 1951. The Buganda budget contributes at present about £88,000 a year to the cost of the services which it is now to take over from the Protectorate Government; the transfer will involve it in additional expenditure rising from about £422,000 in the first year to £500,000 in the third. In the course of the following years arrangements were to be made (partly through the introduction of a graduated personal tax) for Buganda to have the benefit of a revenue equal to an agreed percentage of their cost.

The Eastern, Western and Northern Provinces

The other three Hima States, Toro, Ankole, and Bunyoro,[3] have not the same standing as Buganda, nor do their Agreements confer on their Rulers[4] and their Councils the same measure of executive and legislative authority. That of Bunyoro was under revision in the autumn of 1955.[5]

[1] C. A. G. Wallis, *Report of an Inquiry into African Local Government in Uganda*, 1953.
[2] See below, p. 660.
[3] The technical designations used are: the Native Government of Bunyoro-Kitara; the Native Administrations of Toro and Ankole. *N.A.*, Part I, pp. 44–52.
[4] The Mukama of Bunyoro, the Kabaka of Toro, the Mugabe of Ankole.
[5] *N.A.*, Part I, p. 46. *The Times*, 16 August 1955.

Each of the Rulers presides over a Lukiko which was formerly of entirely official composition, as was that of Buganda, but is now reorganized in the manner which will shortly be described. Their own position is best described as that of titular heads of the Native Administrations which have been established in these three States,[1] which are, however, in other respects similar to those instituted in the other eight districts of Uganda.

The subordinate executive officers of the three States consist of a hierarchy of Chiefs of the same pattern as in Buganda. Each of these Chiefs has a Council (Lukiko) which is now organized on the model adopted in the eight Protectorate districts. In these districts the procedure was in the first instance regulated by the Native Authority Ordinance no. 17 of 1919. This provided for the establishment in each district of a Native Administration of which the District Commissioner was to be the head. Each district is divided into county, gombolola, and muluka areas on the Buganda model, with a similar range of Chiefs, though these are known by different names outside the Bantu-speaking areas.[2] As in Buganda they derive their authority from their appointment, not from the recognition of a traditional status. It is noteworthy that in the Eastern Province a number of the more important county Chiefs were at an earlier stage brought over from Buganda.

As head of the Native Administration the District Commissioner presided over a District Council and each Chief also presided over a Council which is in the Bantu-speaking areas described also as a Lukiko. The Councils were purely official in composition, but in 1936 these, together with the District Councils, were reorganized so as to comprise a large proportion of unofficials. The unofficials in the lower grade of Councils included the heads of kinship groups, together with a number of persons elected by all adult males and the co-opted representatives of various religious denominations. A further stage in the movement for giving a more representative form to the Native Administrations was taken when Ordinance no. 2 of 1949 provided for the establishment in each district of an African Local Government, which was to consist of a District Council and subsidiary Councils, comprising ex officio, nominated, and elected members. No provision was now made for the District Commissioner to preside, but all the Committees of the Council were to be nominated by him, and he was to be the chairman of the Standing Committee. The ex officio members of the African Local Governments included Ministers in each of the Agreement States, and in the Busoga District three executive officials known as the Secretary-General, the Cashier, and the Chief Judge.

Reference will be found in a subsequent chapter to the tax and other sources from which the District Administrations have drawn their

---

[1] Protectorate Native Authority Ordinance no. 17, 1919.
[2] N.A., Part I, pp. 61–62.

revenues.[1] A considerable proportion of the expenditure has been devoted to the payment of personal emoluments, which have amounted to as high as 70 per cent. in some districts; apart from this, the major expenditure has been incurred on public works such as Native Administration buildings, including the residences for Chiefs. Generally speaking, services such as those of education, health, or agricultural extension have hitherto been provided by the Central Government, not by the local bodies.

Local Government Ordinance, 1953

As already shown, an investigation was carried out in 1953 of the working of the system of Local Government throughout the Protectorate. While allowing for the inclusion in the Councils of nominated members (some of whom will at the outset no doubt be Chiefs) the report rejected the principle of *ex officio* membership.[2] It proposed that Chiefs should be appointed by the Councils—an innovation of a questionable character, since it overlooked the fact that the Chiefs have functions outside the range of the agencies which provide Local Government services. The District Commissioners were to be entitled to be present at all meetings of Councils, but not to preside at any. It was at first proposed that the responsibility for primary education and a number of similar services should be transferred to Local Authorities within a period of five years, but it was found that the shortage of trained staff would make this impossible. Impressive as had been the work of the Councils in some respects, it was premature to assume that they could take over operations of a character so different from those to which they were accustomed, especially if they were to be deprived of the day-to-day guidance of the Administrative Officers on whom they had hitherto depended.

The decisions taken on the report were embodied in a revised Ordinance of 1955.[3] The recent interest in the further development of the conciliar system may have a reaction of some significance in the political field. The frequent use of the term 'Local Government'[4] appears to have encouraged certain sections of Africans outside the Buganda Province to hope that their District Councils might attain the status claimed for the Great Lukiko of Buganda as the organ of an African Government in some measure independent of the Protectorate Government. For some years a section in Busoga District has sought to gain recognition of the post of Secretary-General as hereditary, with the view to securing for Busoga an Agreement comparable with those in operation in the States of the Western Province. A similar project appears to be gaining support in other parts of Uganda.

[1] See below, p. 661. [2] Wallis, op. cit. p. 48.
[3] District Administration (District Councils) Ordinance, 1955.
[4] Proceedings of Uganda Legislative Council, 23 November 1953.

Native Courts

In Uganda, as elsewhere, the administration of justice by Native Courts has from the first formed an integral part of the system of Native Administration. The existing constitution of the Native Courts throughout the Protectorate is defined in Ordinances enacted in 1940.[1] A Court is attached to each county or gombolola Chief (and the Chiefs of the corresponding grade where the local nomenclature is different); there is a superior Court representing the major territorial unit which is known as the Principal or Lukiko Court in Buganda, the Central Court in the other Agreement States, and the District Court elsewhere. The Principal or Lukiko Court in Buganda consists nominally of the Kabaka and various of his Ministers, but in practice the Bench is composed of the Chief Justice and other legal officers of the Buganda Government. It has unlimited powers except in criminal cases where the charge is of an offence alleged to have caused death, or in certain civil cases, such as those arising under the Protectorate marriage laws. The procedure for appeal from the superior Native Court in Buganda differs from that in force elsewhere; in criminal cases, where the sentence exceeds imprisonment for five years or a fine of £100, and in civil cases where the subject-matter exceeds £100, there is a right of appeal to the High Court, but in all other cases appeal lies to the Judicial Adviser (who was first appointed in 1940), and from him to the High Court on a point of law only.[2]

In Buganda the Protectorate Administrative Officers ceased in 1940 to exercise direct powers of revision, but if a sentence appears to them improper, they may forward the proceedings to the Court to which an appeal would lie. The Judicial Adviser may revise or amend any sentence or direct retrial. The Kabaka's Chief Justice has the same powers in regard to the county and gombolola Courts. The Chiefs' Courts in Buganda consist at present of the Chief of the unit concerned, with a Bench consisting of a number of Chiefs of the next junior grade. To this extent, therefore, they maintain their original character as tribunals of a predominantly official composition.

In this respect the Courts in the rest of the Protectorate now differ from those of Buganda. Until recently they had a Bench consisting of Chiefs of a junior grade,[3] but there is now a movement for associating unofficials in the composition of the Benches. These are taken from a panel nominated by the Provincial Commissioner for the purpose. The superior Native Courts in the three Agreement States (the Central

---

[1] Buganda Courts Ordinance no. 2 of 1940, amended by no. 10 of 1945 and no. 28 of 1946. Native Courts Ordinance no. 3 of 1940, amended by no. 29 of 1948, and no. 7 of 1947.

[2] Supplement to *J.A.A.*, October 1953, p. 42.

[3] For the history of the Judicial system, see *N.A.*, Part I, pp. 40, 56, 69, and *Colonial Reports, Uganda Protectorate, 1952*, p. 46.

Courts) are presided over by the Chief Minister (Katikiro); the superior Courts elsewhere (the District Courts) are presided over by the senior Chief. These Courts and the gombolola Courts have somewhat lower powers than in Buganda. The appeal from the superior Native Court lies to the District Commissioner in his capacity of Magistrate and thence to the High Court. The Buganda Government controls its own prisons, to which condemned persons may be committed without an order from a Protectorate officer; in 1952 some 1,201 prisoners were committed. Convicts with sentences over two years are, however, as a rule transferred to the Protectorate prisons. Elsewhere the prisons are maintained by the Protectorate Government. In both Buganda and the Eastern Province the Courts maintain unusually complete records. There is general agreement that substantial justice is administered in the Native Courts, though there has been criticism of the practice of dealing with statutory offences by a charge of disobeying the lawful order of a Chief.[1]

The only municipality in Uganda is Kampala, which attained this status in 1948. It has a wholly nominated Municipal Council with five official members and 13 unofficials, the latter comprising four Europeans, four Asians, one Goan, three Africans, and a woman nominated as such. The Mayor is an unofficial, at present an Asian. In most of the Townships the nominated members include an African, usually the gombolola Chief responsible for African affairs in the area.

Outside Buganda there are a number of tribal Associations, but with the exception of the Young Busoga Association, whose political aspirations have already been referred to,[2] their activities are social rather than political. In Buganda the Association known as that of the Butaka has for some years organized active criticism of both the Buganda and Protectorate Governments; its activities led to rioting in 1949, as a result of which it was proscribed. The term Butaka signifies 'landowners', and the existence of the Association dates back to the claim that the clan heads were deprived of their rights in land by the distribution of freehold estates under the Uganda Agreement of 1900.[3] The leading political Association in Buganda at the present time is the African National Congress, which claims as its members a majority of the representatives elected to the Lukiko in 1953. A new political party claiming to represent and promote progressive interests among the Buganda was formed as the 'Progressive Party' in 1955,[4] but this has not so far gained any general recognition.

---

[1] Wallis, op. cit., p. 45.
[2] See above, p. 483.
[3] See below, p. 787. See also C. K. Meek, *Land Law and Custom in the Colonies*, 1946, pp. 132–3. L. Mair, *Native Policies in Africa*, 1936, p. 176. R. L. Buell, *The Native Problem in Africa*, vol. i, 1928, p. 590.
[4] *The Times*, 31 January 1955, 30 August 1955.

NORTHERN RHODESIA

There are two factors which have strongly influenced the course taken
by the administration of Native Affairs in Northern Rhodesia. The first
is the dominance of the mining industry, which has thrown out of balance
the indigenous economy of the African population. In 1948 it was estimated that less than 16 per cent. of the cash income of Africans was earned
by the sale of crops, the rest being provided by wage-labour. As shown in
a subsequent chapter,[1] the average proportion of men absent from their
homes on wage-labour is unusually high. The significance of these facts is
obvious. On the one hand the normal development of the rural areas is
hampered by the absence of most of the younger men, and, on the other,
the Administration has to make provision for urban populations in the
industrial areas which number between 140,000 and 160,000 and are,
moreover, of mixed tribal origin.

The second factor arises from the character of the tribal distribution in
the Protectorate. There are in all some 73 tribes; they speak 30 different
dialects, and they are intermingled in such a way that it is often difficult
to distinguish tribal boundaries. With the exception of the Lozi, the
dominant tribe in the Barotse Province, and the Bemba of the Northern
Province, few of these have ever had a centralized form of political structure. There are again sections of tribes in the Protectorate which owe
a traditional allegiance to Paramount Chiefs resident in other territories.
There is in short throughout the greater part of the Protectorate an
unusual lack of tribal cohesion.

During the régime of the British South Africa Company it was usual to
appoint Chiefs as Government agents and in practice their authority was
upheld in so far as this was compatible with the rule of the Company.
The Administration of Natives Proclamation issued in 1916 provided for
the appointment and dismissal of Chiefs; they were liable to punishment
for failure to carry out the lawful orders of Administrative Officers; they
were paid small subsidies, and were responsible for recruiting paid labour
for Government service. They themselves retained the customary right to
command labour of kin subjects for the cultivation of their 'gardens'.[2]

The administration of the Protectorate was taken over by the Crown
in 1924, and in 1927 a conference of Administrative Officers recommended
that the Native Authority system then in force in Tanganyika should be
adopted, but the Government of the day felt some hesitation in conferring
on the Chiefs any of the powers necessary to establish a system of Native
Treasuries. Native Authorities and Native Court Ordinances were en-

---

[1] See below, p. 1381. See also *N.A.*, Part II, pp. 78 ff. *Report of the Financial Relationship Committee*, Lusaka, 1949, para. 23. *Northern Rhodesia, Annual Report on African Affairs, 1952.*

[2] *Report of the Commission Appointed to Enquire into the Financial and Economic Position of Northern
Rhodesia*, Col. no. 145, 1938, pp. 179–81.

acted in 1929, their most significant effect being the formal recognition of the judicial authority of the Chiefs. These laws were replaced in 1936 by enactments modelled more closely on those in force in Tanganyika; in particular they made provision for the establishment of Native Treasuries.[1] The laws of 1936, though amended in various details, have since continued to regulate the constitution of the Native Authority system.

In practice nearly every Native Authority constituted under these Ordinances was a Chief and Council, the Council having the membership prescribed by local custom. The desirability of encouraging Chiefs to appoint representatives of the more progressive elements as Council members was emphasized in an Administrative Circular of 1939, but this has presented peculiar difficulty in the circumstances of Northern Rhodesia, where the more enterprising of the people tend to migrate to the industrial areas. A partial solution was found in 1948, when the practice was introduced of including in the Councils a small number of paid members with executive responsibility for particular aspects of their work. Some success was achieved by this innovation, especially in the more fully organized Native Authorities; in the Northern Province, however, it has been found expedient to put the Councillors in charge of areas rather than of departments, in order to avoid personal jealousies.[2]

Native Treasuries

The Treasuries began to function in 1938. In many cases the area of a Superior Native Authority included a number of Subordinate Native Authorities, and each was given its own Treasury, but experience showed that the smaller authorities were unable to engage an efficient staff. From about 1947 policy was therefore directed to the reduction of the number of Treasuries by the amalgamation of the Superior and the abolition of the Subordinate Native Authorities. In 1953 there remained 42 Superior Native Authorities, including the Paramount Chief of Barotseland, and 87 Subordinate Native Authorities. From an early date, however, the progress of the Native Authority system was hampered by the lack of resources available to them. In 1953, for example, the total revenue of the Native Treasuries, inclusive of grants from the Central Government, was only £303,212. From the outset special grants had been made to the poorer Treasuries to enable them to balance their budgets, and in 1944 a sum of £25,000 was voted by the Legislature to enable the Native Authorities to build up adequate Reserve Funds. A Central Native Treasury Board was set up to advise on the disbursement of this sum, and on its recommendations there was created a permanent Native Treasury Fund, into which was paid a sum equal to 1*s*. from every Native taxed.

[1] Native Authority Ordinances 9 and 25 of 1936. Native Courts Ordinances nos. 10 and 26 of 1936. [2] *Northern Rhodesia, Annual Report on African Affairs, 1952*, pp. 30, 52.

A Financial Relationship Committee appointed in 1949 made detailed recommendations on the distribution both of responsibilities and of revenues as between the Central Government and the Native Authorities.[1] As a result, a change was made in the proportion of the tax payable to Central revenues and that retained by the Treasuries. The Central Native Treasury Fund was abolished and replaced by Provincial Funds, into which is now paid the balance of the tax collected when the share allocated to Government revenue and to the Native Treasuries has been deducted. The imposition of local rates began in 1945, and all Native Authorities now impose local taxation varying from 2s. 6d. to 10s. per annum.

As regards the administration of justice, provision for the constitution of Native Courts was first made in Ordinance no. 10 of 1936. The composition of the Courts is normally of the same pattern as that of the Native Authorities; the Superior Native Authorities both exercise original powers and also act as Courts of Appeal from the Subordinate Native Authorities.[2] As a rule the Chief or his deputy presides over the Court, and the Bench is composed of the persons who by local custom habitually attend on such occasions. The Courts are normally divided into three classes; appeals from a Native Court of Appeal lie to the District Commissioner and Provincial Commissioner, and thence to the High Court. A Native Courts Adviser was appointed in 1948. The delegation to Native Courts of the power to try cases under the Native Tax Ordinance was made in Northern Rhodesia later than elsewhere, but the more efficient Native Courts in all Provinces are now specially authorized to do so. The system of urban Native Courts will be separately described.[3]

Barotseland

Barotseland has from the first occupied a special position in the Protectorate. At the outset its position was regulated by an Agreement concluded in 1900 with the British South Africa Company and later recognized by the Secretary of State as having the force of a treaty.[4] This instrument differed from the Uganda Agreement of the same year in various respects, as it was primarily concerned with the regulation of matters in which the Company was interested, rather than with matters of concern to the Barotse. The Company received a monopoly of trading and mineral rights and agreed to make an annual payment of £850 to the Paramount Chief, who was to retain his customary authority and to have the sole right to adjudicate in cases arising between Africans. Cases in which both Africans and Europeans were concerned were to be dealt with

---

[1] *Report of the Financial Relationship Committee*, 1949.
[2] *N.A.*, Part II, pp. 85–6, 109, 118, 126, 134, 145.   [3] See below, p. 492.
[4] *N.A.*, Part II, pp. 88–90.

by the Company. An area covering about three-fifths of the territory of Barotseland was reserved from prospecting and from the grant of land concessions.

The Barotse people possessed a well-established system of centralized rule. Political power was in the hands of the dominant tribe, the Lozi, whose Paramount Chief was recognized as holding ultimate ownership of the lands both of the Lozi and of their feudatory tribes. His authority was made effective, not by the appointment of subordinate Chiefs on a territorial basis, as was the usual practice of the Bantu tribes,[1] but by the allocation of divisions of the population to the control of relatives or of different members of his Council residing at his capital. This system applied both to the Lozi and to members of the other tribes brought under Lozi rule. It was, however, one of the standing problems created by this system that the section of the people allocated to a particular Councillor was not necessarily confined to one area of the country, but might live in different parts of it. In addition certain members of the Royal Family were stationed in outlying districts where they had their own capitals on a smaller scale.

Attached to the Paramount Chief was a Council known as the Kgotla or Kuta, which by custom consisted partly of office holders (Induna) and partly of members of the Royal Family. It was divided into three sections, Katengo, Saa, and Sikalo, which deliberated separately on all questions of importance. The Katengo was the most numerous, and the first to discuss any matter; it reported its decisions to the Saa, over which the Paramount's Chief Minister (a commoner) presided. The Saa reported to the Sikalo, which consisted of the near relatives of the Paramount Chief. All three sections were expected to reach agreement, but if they could not do so the Sikalo carried the greater weight.[2]

It had been agreed in 1905 that 10 per cent. of the tax collected in north-western Rhodesia should be paid into a fund for use in works to benefit the African inhabitants of Barotseland, and that the Paramount Chief should receive from this fund a subsidy of £1,200 a year in lieu of his previous claim to tribute. In the same year he had agreed that the British Courts should have the power to decide civil and criminal cases between Natives, except in a reserved area, where they would have jurisdiction only over cases of murder and of any other offence against the law of England, such as witchcraft.

By further Agreements,[3] the Chief and his Kuta were recognized as possessing in the greater part of the Barotse Province full powers in civil proceedings affecting Natives only, and full powers in criminal proceedings affecting Natives except when the offence was punishable with death

---

[1] M. Fortes and E. E. Evans-Pritchard, *African Political Systems*, 1940, p. 10.

[2] *N.A.*, Part II, p. 94.   [3] Proclamations 2 and 3 of 1913.

or imprisonment exceeding six months. It is noteworthy that no provision was made at this stage for any supervision of the proceedings of the Barotse Courts, nor for any right of appeal. In 1924 the Paramount Chief agreed that he should abandon the previous system by which he could exact twelve days' compulsory unpaid labour from his subjects, and he received in return an annual allowance of £2,500, of which £2,000 was paid to the Chiefs and Induna who had shared this privilege. In 1925 a Barotse Trust Fund was established. It received a sum representing 30 per cent. of the tax collected from the Natives of Barotse Province.[1] The Fund was administered by a Board on which the Paramount and his Kuta were represented.

The system thus developed involved little friction between the British and the Barotse Authority, but it occasioned some difficulties in working until the enactment of the Barotse Native Authority and Native Courts Ordinances nos. 25 and 26 of 1936. The former resembles closely that in force in the rest of the Protectorate, save that it requires that the Paramount should be consulted on certain matters, such as the removal of Subordinate Chiefs. The Barotse Trust Fund was taken over in 1936 by a Barotse Native Treasury, with sub-Treasuries in each of the five districts of the Province. Its share of the Central Government tax was increased to 50 per cent. in 1946 and to 75 per cent. in 1947. A large proportion of expenditure is devoted to payment of administrative charges; in 1951 they accounted for no less than £30,000 out of an estimated recurrent expenditure of £47,000.[2]

The Barotse Native Courts Ordinance differs from that in force in the rest of the Protectorate only in so far that the power of review by Administrative Officers is limited to criminal cases. The Courts are still constituted in accordance with local custom. That of the Paramount Chief, which is also an Appeal Court, consists of all members of the Saa–Sikalo Council, though normally only about ten attend. Appeals from the Higher Native Appeal Court (the Court of the Paramount Chief) lie in criminal cases to the Court of the Resident in his magisterial capacity, and thence to the High Court. Civil appeals lie direct to the High Court.

While these changes have occurred in the systems of Native Administration as applied to Barotseland, certain changes have also occurred in the organization of its traditional system of rule. After the enactment of the Native Authority Ordinance of 1936 the Katengo practically ceased to function in its original form, but a new body bearing the same name was created in 1946. This consists of five commoners from each district,

---

[1] Ordinance no. 18 of 1925.
[2] *Northern Rhodesia, Annual Report on African Affairs, 1951*, p. 81. The estimate for 1953 was an expenditure of £31,520 on personal emoluments out of a total recurrent expenditure of £50,000; op. cit. *1952*, p. 87.

together with ten members of the traditional Katengo, five being office-holders and five members of the Royal Family; the commoner members are now chosen by a process of election. The Council so constituted submits its resolutions to a National Council consisting of members selected from the Saa and Sikalo Councils sitting with six representatives of the new Katengo.

In 1941 the area controlled by the Paramount was materially reduced, when the greater part of the Baluvale District (which is inhabited mainly by the Lunda, Luvale, and Luchaze tribes) was excised from Barotseland and transferred to the Western Province.[1] This was largely as the result of a strong separatist movement by those tribes, and though the decision was accepted by the Paramount of the day and his Council, there remained a strong feeling of uneasiness in the minds of the Lozi. Evidence of this was manifest when the discussions were taking place which led to the establishment of the Federation of the Rhodesias and Nyasaland. Fears as to its possible effect on their status led to consultation between Lozi leaders and the Protectorate Administration, the result of which was the issue of an Order in Council which formally confirmed the position of Barotseland as a Protectorate.[2] The designation of the Provincial Commissioner of Barotseland was at the same time changed to that of Resident, presumably following in this respect the practice adopted in Buganda.[3]

Problem of Urban Communities

It remains to note the special problem in Native Administration created by the growth of the urban communities in the Copperbelt mining area or along the line of the Railway. While a considerable proportion of the labourers on the mines (stated in 1953 to average 46,000[4]) are resident in the Mine Compounds,[5] there is also a large African population living in the Locations attached to the two Municipalities and 13 Townships in the Protectorate, while others live in the five new 'African Towns' for which sites have been provided by the Administration and which are now being constructed under official supervision.[6]

The African population in the mines, in the Locations, and in the new African towns is of mixed tribal origin, and contains a large element of temporary residents. As a rule the District Commissioner represents their interests on the Councils or the Management Boards of the Town Authorities

[1] P. MacDonell, *Report of Commission of Inquiry relating to Baluvale District*, 1939. Northern Rhodesia Government Gazette, 9 July 1941. Ordinance 12 of 1941.
[2] Northern Rhodesia Order in Council, 30 April 1953.
[3] See above, p. 480.   [4] *Colonial Reports, Northern Rhodesia, 1953*, p. 12.
[5] For the system under which tribal representatives are utilized in the Mine Compounds, see *N.A.*, Part II, p. 147; for the new African towns, see ibid. pp. 146, 150.
[6] *J.A.A.*, July 1951, p. 113.

which control the Municipalities and Townships, and from 1938 onwards a number of African Urban Advisory Councils have been set up to keep him in touch with African Affairs. The members of the Advisory Councils have normally been representative of tribes, wards, or occupations, or a combination of all three. In 1948 the principle was accepted that they should be elected.[1]

There were originally in the urban areas eleven Native Courts consisting of Elders from the major tribes represented in the population; the members were nominated by their respective Native Authorities. These Courts handle a large number of cases and have in the past had a good reputation for efficiency. Some dissatisfaction with them has, however, been expressed of recent years, partly on the ground that individual members are apt to regard themselves as tribal representatives rather than judges, and that the Benches as a whole find difficulty in reconciling the conflicting customs of different tribes. It has been suggested that it would be desirable to abandon the present mode of selection and to appoint the members of the Courts solely on the basis of their personal qualifications.[2] But although a Court President with professional qualifications, sitting with assessors, is likely to be the final solution to the problem of the urban Courts, an attempt to improve the existing practice has been made by dividing the territory into so-called 'law areas'. Representatives from each 'law area' form the Bench and have power to co-opt a fifth member from an area not already represented.[3]

Regional Councils, consisting of representatives of the Native Authorities, the Urban Advisory Councils, and of African Associations existing in those urban areas where no such Councils exist, have been developed since the year 1942. These Associations are as a rule small local groups, in a number of which the leading members are Government employees. In 1945 the meetings of the Regional Councils were formally designated as Provincial Councils; the Provincial Commissioners usually preside at their meetings, and officials of the technical departments also attend them. In 1946 an African Representative Council was created, consisting of members elected by the Provincial Councils, together with four members nominated from Barotseland. This Council meets annually under the presidency of the Secretary for Native Affairs; two members are elected from it to represent African interests in the Legislature.[4] The Secretary for Native Affairs is an *ex officio* member of the Executive Council of the Protectorate, but there is no separate Department of Native Affairs.

[1] G. C. Clay, 'African Urban Advisory Councils in the Northern Rhodesia Copperbelt', *J.A.A.*, January 1949, pp. 33–38. F. M. N. Heath, 'The Growth of African Councils on the Copperbelt of Northern Rhodesia', ibid. July 1953, pp. 123–32.

[2] A. L. Epstein, *The Administration of Justice and the Urban Africans*, 1953.

[3] *Judicial Advisers' Conference*, Supplement to *J.A.A.*, October 1953, p. 16.

[4] See above, p. 290.

NYASALAND PROTECTORATE

Early Relations with Chiefs

The early records of the Nyasaland Protectorate, like those of Kenya, make pointed reference to the difficulty of finding Native Authorities suitable for employment as agencies of local rule. The Administration of the British Central African Protectorate had so far recognized the position of the Chiefs with whom it had made treaties[1] as to assign them a subsidy of 10 per cent. of the hut tax in lieu of their former tribute, and a few were also given annual allowances in compensation for the abrogation of their right to levy tolls on passing caravans. The subsequent introduction of a system of direct collection of tax by the District Officers and the withdrawal of the allowances on the death of the original recipients left the Chiefs and Headmen without a fixed income, and their status suffered a general decline. In 1904 it was remarked that although the tribal leaders still arbitrated in disputes between their followers, the customary institutions had in other respects largely broken down.[2]

Another factor combined to create an obstacle to the employment of the traditional Native Authorities. Considerable areas of land had been alienated to Europeans, and in some districts, notably Zomba and Blantyre, a large proportion of the population were resident on European estates.[3] Though, therefore, the Government continued to look for agents who could assist in the work of administration, it sought other means for satisfying this need than the restoration of traditional authority. When it enacted the District Administration (Native) Ordinance of 1912, which recognized as its agents official Headman appointed by it, it stated that their position was to be in no way 'similar to the archaic one of Chief', though in fact the Headmen were frequently chosen from among Chiefs or local leaders.

The districts were divided into administrative sections under Principal Headmen, each section having what was designated a Council consisting of the Principal Headman and two village Headmen.[4] Principal Headmen and village Headmen were paid, though on a low scale; the Headmen were allowed no judicial authority, though they were used as assessors in Native cases; their administrative functions were mainly confined to carrying out police and sanitary regulations and the improvement of village communications. An Ordinance of 1924[5] constituted a series of Village, Section, and District Councils, consisting of nominated Headmen and others, though their functions were to be purely advisory. At a later date Native Courts were instituted under the title of Section Courts; they were presided over by a Principal Headman.[6]

[1] H. H. Johnston, *British Central Africa*, 1897, pp. 50 ff. Buell, op. cit. pp. 245 ff.
[2] *Annual Reports on the Protectorate, 1903–4, 1911–12*, and *1912–13*.
[3] See below, pp. 708–12.
[4] *N.A.*, Part II, pp. 25–27.
[5] District Administration (Native) Ordinance, 1924.
[6] Courts Ordinance, 1929.

Up to this point official opinion was still opposed in principle to measures which would, in the phrase used by the Governor in 1924, 'tend to revivify or perpetuate governance by Native Chiefs'. But the stimulus which the enactment of the Tanganyika Ordinances of 1926 gave to the extension of the Native Authority system in East Africa was already beginning to make itself felt. It will be recalled that in 1927 a conference of Administrative Officers recommended the adoption of this system in Northern Rhodesia, and in 1930 the recommendation was repeated by a similar conference held in Nyasaland. The effect was seen in the issue of the Nyasaland Native Authority and Courts Ordinances of 1933, which were modelled on those which had come into force in Tanganyika.

The majority of the Native Authorities who were now recognized under these Ordinances had previously been appointed as Principal Headmen. Though the Ordinances followed their model in defining a Native Authority in such a way as to recognize Councils as well as Chiefs, it was at the outset the almost invariable practice in Nyasaland to appoint Chiefs as sole Native Authorities. More recently, however, it has become the practice that when a Chief dies his successor should be gazetted as Chief-in-Council. In this and other respects the procedure adopted has followed the course taken elsewhere in the development of the Native Authority system. There was, however, one feature in the social structure of Nyasaland which has in some measure militated against its success. Inter-tribal warfare and the upheaval caused by the persistence of the slave trade had caused a great intermixture of tribes, and few Native Authority areas are inhabited by populations that are tribally homogeneous. The loss of authority which this may involve is accentuated in the Southern Province by the presence of large numbers of Nguru, the immigrant tribe from the neighbouring districts of Portuguese East Africa.[1]

Native Treasuries

The Native Treasuries instituted under the Ordinance of 1933 were credited with a small percentage of the poll tax collected, this sum being in the first instance allocated for the payment of Chiefs; as will be seen in a following chapter, the rate of tax was in the first instance low, and it was not indeed till 1948 and 1949 that it approached the incidence of the tax in neighbouring territories. The Native Authorities were authorized to levy rates, but none did so until 1949, when a small 'education rate' was imposed by the Authorities throughout the Protectorate. Grants in aid of approved objects of expenditure have been made from a Native Development and Welfare Fund, in which the reserves of two small previous funds were combined in 1944. A share of the profits made in the marketing of African cotton and tobacco are now also paid into this Fund.[2]

[1] See above, p. 128, and below, p. 676.   [2] N.A., Part II, p. 60.

The total resources of many of the individual Native Authorities are small, and nearly everywhere the practice has been adopted of combining all the Treasuries of an administrative district in a Federal Treasury under the formal control of a Council of the Chiefs concerned. Some Councils have Finance Committees, but their duties are apt to be performed in practice by the District Commissioners.[1] The total estimated revenues of all Native Treasuries in 1952 was £196,499, of which the greater part was represented by the Treasuries in the Southern Province; the total from the Northern Province was only £22,888. Of the receipts roughly three-fifths came from the share of the Central Government tax.[2]

In general, the local interest taken in the working of the Native Authorities has been small, and many Chiefs have shown themselves lacking in activity and a sense of responsibility. An effort was made in 1949 to stimulate interest in local affairs by the creation of 'Local' or 'Group' Councils. They were composed of the Headmen of groups of villages, with other representatives chosen by popular acclaim; one of the Headmen was selected as Group Headman and presided over the meetings. This innovation was, however, regarded with suspicion by some Chiefs, and the Councils themselves showed little initiative, though there was an exception in the case of the Domasi Community Development Scheme in the Zomba District, which was under close administrative supervision. This scheme, initiated in 1950, extends over a wide field of rural activity, including health and education, and has made full use of the system of Group Councils.[3] It was recently decided not to press for the creation of Local or Group Councils where there was no demand for them.

District Councils

Rather earlier, namely from 1944 onwards, the policy was adopted of holding periodical meetings which became known as District Councils, and included all Chiefs in the area, together with some of their Advisers or Councillors and in addition a selection of educated persons who were not members of the Native Authority bodies. As the result of an inquiry into the working of these Councils,[4] it was decided in 1953 to legislate in order to give statutory recognition to them.[5] It was intended that they should be representative of all communities including Europeans, but that the form of their constitution should be adjusted to suit the circumstances of each area concerned. It was the intention that they should in time take over all the Local Government functions of the previous Native Authorities.[6] The

[1] *Annual Report on Native Administration, 1951*, p. 3.
[2] *Colonial Reports, Nyasaland, 1952*, pp. 38–40.
[3] Ibid., pp. 118–19.
[4] R. S. Hudson, *Report on Development of Local Government in Nyasaland*, Colonial Office, 1951, unpublished.   [5] Local Government (District Councils) Ordinance no. 48 of 1953.
[6] *J.A.A.*, July 1954, p. 110.

first of the District Councils was established on a tentative basis in Cholo District in 1954.[1] In 1955 Councils were functioning in five other districts and three others were in process of formation.[2] A few contained a considerable non-African element.

There are in the Protectorate four townships, but the largest, Limbe, has a population of only 6,000. There is no specific provision for the representation of African interests on the Township Councils, but there have since 1951 been African Urban Advisory Committees nominated in order to assist the Township Councils with advice on African interests. There is one nominated African on the Zomba Township Council.

The Native Courts established under Ordinance no. 17 of 1933 have relatively restricted powers, compared to those of some neighbouring territories. An amending Ordinance, no. 17 of 1947, created the post of Native Courts Adviser, and under its provision an appeal from a Native Court of Appeal now goes to the High Court only by way of case stated by him.[3]

Provincial Councils and the Protectorate Council

The system of Provincial Councils inaugurated in 1944 and 1945 forms part of the measures taken in the political field rather than in that of Native Administration. These Councils consisted originally of Chiefs elected by District meetings of Chiefs, with a small number of nominated members, but the number of unofficial members has now been increased. They meet twice a year with the Provincial Commissioner as president, and it is usual to seek their views on any outstanding question of policy affecting African interests. The three Provincial Councils elect from among themselves representatives to form a Protectorate Council which also meets twice a year and has similar consultative functions. When in 1949 two African members were appointed to the Legislative Council, it was this body which was invited to submit a panel of names.[4]

Political Associations

The principal political Association representing African views is the Nyasaland African Congress founded in 1943; it was recognized by the Government in 1946 as representing the various African Associations in Nyasaland. It has a wide membership, including both Chiefs and Government servants, as well as a number of educated Africans; it has been the mouthpiece of the Africans resident on the private estates in their demand for recognition of land rights,[5] and it took the chief part in the local opposition to the proposal for the creation of the Federation of Rhodesia

---

[1] Government Notices, nos. 55, 56, 57 of 1954. See *Africa Digest*, July–August 1954, p. 11 for account of the first meeting.

[2] *East Africa and Rhodesia*, 8 December 1955.   [3] *N.A.*, Part II, p. 29.

[4] See above, p. 291.   [5] See below, p. 712.

and Nyasaland.[1] On this occasion it was able to organize a campaign which led to the resignation of a number of Chiefs, particularly in the Southern Province, where its chief strength lies. The agitation threatened at one time to produce a breach of public order, and had to be controlled by police drafted into the Province from the Rhodesias. For the time being, the machinery of Native Administration appeared to have broken down.

The more militant aspect of this opposition abated after the formal enactment of the Federation, but there has remained a considerable section of the Association which supports an alternative scheme of a Federation of Northern Rhodesia, Nyasaland, and Tanganyika. The incident was one of the numerous reminders which recent experience has provided of the relative weakness of traditional Native Authorities in the face of a demonstration of public feeling organized by politically minded elements.

THE HIGH COMMISSION TERRITORIES

If the High Commission Territories come low in the list of the British dependencies which have followed the procedure of the Native Authority system it is because the system was not definitely adopted until 1934 in Bechuanaland, 1938 in Basutoland, and 1944 in Swaziland. Before that period the administration of Native affairs had followed what has been described in a previous chapter as a form of 'parallel rule'.[2] Its aim was to leave the Paramount Chiefs in Basutoland and Swaziland and the eight ruling Chiefs in the Tribal Reserves of Bechuanaland to control the course of affairs in the areas under their charge subject to the minimum of official intervention.

It has recently been said that 'the power of the Chiefs was built up to an excessive extent, owing to the faithfulness with which the conception of a Protectorate as opposed to a Colonial status was preserved'.[3] But the adoption of this principle was not without some justification during the period which immediately followed the extension of British jurisdiction, for in the case of Basutoland and Bechuanaland, and to a minor extent also in the case of Swaziland, the primary object of the British in extending their jurisdiction over the country was to protect it from encroachment by the Transvaal or the Free State.[4] But there arrived in due course a period when the Government had to view itself not merely as a protecting Power but as an Administration responsible for the improvement of the standards of life of the African population.[5] The extension of jurisdiction had been accompanied by an understanding (and in one case at least by a definite

[1] See above, p. 275.
[2] See above, p. 272. For the term used, see *N.A.*, Part V, pp. 218, 222, 324.
[3] *The Times*, 12 July 1953.   [4] *N.A.* Part V, pp. 37-41, 189-91, 361-5.
[5] Compare M. Perham, *Native Administration in Nigeria*, 1937, p. 355.

undertaking) that the Chiefs were 'to continue to rule their country as before'.[1] But the issue was sooner or later bound to arise whether the obligation to respect the status of the Chiefs was in fact compatible with the discharge of the obligations of a sovereign Power towards the people for whose welfare it had become responsible.

In surveying the development of the system of Native Administration in the three Territories, it is important to observe the differences which exist between them in regard to the strength of the European community which they contain. The position in Basutoland is of special interest because though the Territory is in a geographical sense an enclave of the Union of South Africa, it contains no Europeans other than a small body of Government officials, traders, or missionaries, and also because no part of the country as now constituted has been permanently alienated for the purpose of European settlement. The Bechuanaland Protectorate has a small European settlement, though Europeans have taken a less important part in the development of the country than in Swaziland, where Europeans hold a large proportion of its lands as well as being responsible for the development of its industries. It will be convenient to deal here with the three Territories in an order determined by the dates at which the Native Authority system was formally adopted by them.

Bechuanaland Protectorate

The most significant difference between Bechuanaland and the other High Commission Territories lies in the fact that its African population presents no such evidence of the possession of a national sentiment as do those of Basutoland and Swaziland. The peoples now known as the Tswana (Bechuana) derive from a common stock, and it is the Tswana who now hold the dominant position in each of the eight Native Reserves. But each section is politically independent of the others; there is no Paramount Chief of the Tswana nor any evidence of a feeling of national unity. Moreover, the Reserves are not inhabited by single tribes but by sections of a variety of tribes, among which the Tswana do not always represent the majority of the population. Thus the Ngwato, perhaps the most conspicuous of the Tswana tribes in the Protectorate, only comprise about one-fifth of the population of the large Ngwato Reserve.[2]

The fact that many sections of other tribes have within a comparatively short period of time become incorporated with the ruling Tswana tribe is evidence of the flexible nature of the African tribal organization, but the cohesion is not always complete, and there is frequently a difference in status between the members of the ruling tribe and the other 'allied tribes' as they are now frequently termed. There are in addition a considerable number of indigenous inhabitants, whose occupation of the country pre-

---

[1] *N.A.*, Part V, pp. 44, 199, 365-70.   [2] *N.A.*, Part V, p. 274.

ceded the arrival of the Tswana, and who have in some cases been treated not merely as subordinate but as of servile status. The Sarwa, the descendants of the Bushmen, and the Kgalagedi, about whose origin there is some difference of opinion, are the best known of this class.[1]

As will be seen, there was some opposition to the introduction of the Native Authority system in 1934, but it was not the opposition of a people apprehensive lest the recognition given by this system to tribal differences should militate against the recognition of their national status. It represented the resistance shown by certain more prominent Chiefs to the proposal to regulate by statute the authority they had exercised under custom, and there was also some fear by the dominant sections lest there might be a loss of their control over the less powerful communities. The more crucial problems of administration may be said therefore to have arisen from the manner in which the Chiefs exercised their authority, and from the differences which arose when it was proposed to subject it to control.

As early as 1876 Khama, the Ngwato Chief, had asked for protection from the Transvaal Boers, and in the following years it became obvious that, partly on account of the incursion of Boer 'freebooters' and partly owing to the conflicts between some of the local Chiefs, southern Bechuanaland was in a state of anarchy.[2] In 1884 the British Government concluded treaties with the Chiefs of two southern tribes, the Thlaping and the Rolong, which gave it jurisdiction to enact laws and appoint magistrates in their area; and when in 1885 it extended British jurisdiction over Bechuanaland,[3] it made a distinction between the territories of these Chiefs and the rest of the country. Within a few months of the extension of jurisdiction their territories were constituted a Crown Colony,[4] and in 1895 they were incorporated in Cape Colony as British Bechuanaland.[5] In the remainder of Bechuanaland jurisdiction was in the first instance assumed only over British subjects.

The interests of the British lay mainly in ending the state of anarchy on the frontiers of the Cape, and in preventing the Boers from closing the 'road to the North' through Bechuanaland. They were less interested in administering the country, most of which was pronounced as 'unsuitable for European colonization'.[6] The first Assistant Commissioner sent to the Bechuanaland Protectorate was instructed in 1887 that he was 'not to interfere with Native Administration; the Chiefs are understood not to be desirous to part with their rights of sovereignty, nor are her Majesty's Government by any means anxious to assume the responsibilities of it'.

The legal conception which at this period underlay the theory of a protectorate depended for its operation on the protecting Power finding a

---

[1] *N.A.*, Part V, pp. 168, 169, 290–3.
[2] Op. cit. pp. 188 ff.
[3] Order in Council, 21 January 1885.
[4] Order in Council, 30 September 1885.
[5] Order in Council, 3 October 1895.
[6] *N.A.*, Part V, pp. 194–6.

working political organization in existence, and here, as elsewhere, the theory tended to break down when such conditions were not encountered. It is this fact which has accounted for the development of the modern conception of the 'colonial protectorate'[1] as a means of providing a legal cover for the extension of administration over a 'protected' area. In May 1891, following on the enactment of the Foreign Jurisdiction Act of 1890, an Order in Council issued authorizing the High Commissioner to provide 'for the administration of justice, the raising of revenue, and generally for the order and good government of all persons'. In issuing his Proclamations, however, he was to respect Native custom, so far as it was compatible with the 'due exercise of Her Majesty's power and jurisdiction'.[2]

Following the current policy of the day, a caution was added regarding the obligations which such a measure might involve, together with the habitual warning that these obligations should as far as possible be avoided. A dispatch of 15 May 1891, which accompanied the Order, directed that jurisdiction should be confined so far as possible to Europeans, leaving the Native Chiefs and persons living under their tribal authority almost entirely alone. A proclamation of June of the same year provided for the appointment of magistrates whose jurisdiction was to be confined to Europeans or to cases involving Natives of different Reserves, though it might also be exercised 'in the interests of peace' in matters concerning the inhabitants of the same Reserve.[3]

The Order in Council of 1891 is still the authority upon which the High Commissioner acts in issuing proclamations. In view of the doubts subsequently cast on the competence of the Crown to exercise jurisdiction over all the inhabitants of the Protectorate, it is sufficient to say that legal decisions, and most notably that recorded in the case filed by the Ngwato and Ngwaketse Chiefs in 1935, have placed beyond doubt its legal competence to exercise the fullest legislative authority in this respect.[4]

A protecting Power may, however, find itself limited by treaty or other form of commitment as to the manner in which it can with propriety exercise a legislative authority which may not be open to challenge on purely legal grounds. It could not be said that there was in the earlier history of the relations of the British Crown with the Bechuanaland Chiefs any agreement or other commitment which would prevent its intervening to control the manner in which the Chiefs exercised their own authority. It was not until 1895 that it committed itself to a statement which seemed to imply a definite engagement to them.

The facts form an outstanding incident in the history of the Protectorate. In 1894 the Government had declared itself in favour of handing over

[1] A. B. Keith, *The Governments of the British Empire*, 1935, pp. 497 ff.
[2] Order in Council, 9 May 1891. Laws of Bechuanaland Protectorate, vol. i, p. 5.
[3] Proclamation of 10 June 1891.   [4] See below, p. 502.

its administration to the British South Africa Company.[1] Khama, the Ngwato Chief,[2] and two other of the major Chiefs made the journey to England in order to protest against this policy, and they secured an agreement that, if they gave up the strip of land needed for the construction of the Rhodesian Railway, they should remain under the administration of the British Crown. They were, moreover, assured that they would 'continue to rule their own peoples much as at present'.[3] This settlement was the first occasion on which the character of the powers assumed by the Crown had been explicitly discussed with any of the Chiefs, and though its terms referred only to the particular Chiefs who had approached the Secretary of State, it has not unnaturally been treated as of general application to the whole body of Chiefs.

It is of interest, therefore, to examine the extent to which Crown rule since 1895 can be said to have conflicted with any commitment then made. It has not anywhere been claimed that the tribes have since then been deprived of land in the interests of European colonization. The judicial system in force up to the issue of the 'reform' proclamations[4] encroached only to a minor extent upon the jurisdiction of the Chiefs. In 1896 provision was made for the transfer to the Crown Courts of all charges of murder; in 1919 it was provided that appeals against the decisions of Chiefs were to be heard by a combined Court composed of the Magistrate of the District and the Chief. The Chiefs were made responsible for the collection of taxes, but they were remunerated by a commission of up to 10 per cent. of the proceeds. They retained other sources of income in the form of receipts from mining concessions and trading sites; they also had the right under Native custom to unpaid labour organized through the regimental system.[5] Estimates have placed the incomes of different Chiefs at various stages between £2,750 and £7,000, but these figures are of doubtful value, and a large part of the revenues referred to were in any case earmarked for tribal purposes.

The system of rule as it was developed after 1896 gave to the officers of the Administration a limited jurisdiction in criminal issues, and an influence (though not a direct control) in executive matters. The Chiefs retained a very large measure of authority in tribal affairs. The normal exercise of their powers could not be termed autocratic, because in all matters affecting the tribe it was the invariable habit to allow for full discussion in the

[1] For the history of this incident, see *N.A.*, Part V, pp. 197–201.

[2] More correctly described as Kgama III. For the question of Tswana orthography, see A. Sillery, *Sechele*, 1954, p. 10.

[3] For the full terms, see Colonial Office letter 7 November 1895, quoted in the *Explanatory Memorandum on the Bechuanaland Protectorate Native Administration and Native Tribunals Proclamations*, 1934, p. 2.

[4] Native Administration Proclamation no. 74 of 1934, and Native Tribunals Proclamation no. 75 of 1934. See below, p. 502.

[5] I. Schapera, *A Handbook of Tswana Law and Custom*, 1938, pp. 21, 80–85.

Kuta (Kgotla), which has been well described as 'a sort of parliamentary *levée en masse* of the tribe'.[1] The Kuta was largely and regularly attended; debate was often keen, and opinions frankly expressed. It gained also in importance from the fact that it was the ordinary tribunal for the trial of cases, and that it was regarded as one of the regular duties of the Chief to preside over its meetings, both for judicial and other purposes.

There was thus much truth in the Tswana axiom that a 'Chief is Chief by grace of his tribe'. Nevertheless, there were Chiefs who could on occasion be arbitrary, and it seems to have been the action taken in 1926 by Tshekedi Khama, then acting Chief of the Ngwato, in pursuance of a family feud, that caused the British Government to decide in 1930 that the position and powers of the Tribal Courts ought to be more carefully defined.[2] It should be added that much concern was also felt at the time regarding the 'servile' status assigned to the aboriginal Sarwa.[3]

Proclamations of 1934, 1938, and 1943

A lengthy period of discussion followed at the end of which there were issued two Proclamations, no. 74 of 1934, dealing with Native Administration, and no. 75 of 1934, dealing with the Native Tribunals. An explanatory Memorandum which was issued at the same time claimed that the Administration in the Protectorate had since 1895 consistently followed a principle 'known nowadays as Indirect Rule'. The general terms of the two Proclamations were clearly influenced by the legislation which had been enacted in Nigeria and Tanganyika,[4] though their authors hardly seem to have appreciated the full implications of the principle adopted in those territories. The most important result of the two Proclamations was to replace the Kuta as a judicial body by a tribunal with a fixed membership, and as a consultative organ by a Tribal Council with formally nominated Councillors.

There was here a definite departure from a custom to which the Tswana attached the highest importance, and two of the Chiefs challenged in the Courts the competence of the Crown to legislate in this sense. They took the ground that this constituted a violation of the basic Order in Council of May 1891, which had prescribed that legislation undertaken in pursuance of the Order must 'respect Native Custom'. In a decision announced in November 1936 the Court decided that the Crown had satisfied this condition by allowing for a full period of discussion of the draft Proclamations, and it added that there was no treaty or other commitment which

---

[1] *The Times*, 12 July 1954.

[2] *N.A.*, Part V, pp. 212 ff., 290 ff.

[3] Proclamation no. 20 of 1931, ordering a commission of inquiry into the position of the Sarwa.

[4] *Explanatory Memorandum on the Native Administration and Native Tribunal Proclamations*, 28 December 1934.

would limit the 'unfettered and unlimited power of the Crown to legislate for the Government of the Protectorate'.[1]

The legal validity of this decision was incontestable, but it became clear that the scheme of reforms embodied in the Proclamations had overlooked two important considerations. The procedure of Native Administration embodied in them differed so widely from Tswana custom (especially in regard to the position assigned to the Kuta) as to be unworkable in practice, and no provision was made for the creation of Native Treasuries, though in other territories such Treasuries were now recognized as the keystone of the Native Authority system. The next nine years saw a number of modifications of the original scheme, and the legislation in which they were embodied met with a far readier acceptance by the leading men among the Tswana.

In 1938 provision was made for the establishment of Native Treasuries in each of the Native Reserves,[2] and in 1943 there followed two Proclamations, no. 32 (Native Administration) and no. 33 (Native Courts), which reproduced more closely the spirit and the form of the Native Authority system as in force elsewhere. The result was to allow of the reinstatement of the Kuta in its traditional form as the consultative body of the tribe, and the 'trial by Kuta', as the normal form of Native tribunal.[3] The revisionary powers of the Administrative Officers were at the same time increased.

The acceptance thus given to the Proclamation of 1943 has been due in part to the success achieved in the working of the nine Treasuries established in the Native Reserves under Proclamation no. 35 of 1938. A Fund for expenditure on education and similar purposes (the Bechuanaland Native Fund) had been created in 1919; it was financed by a special levy, this being additional to the Government tax, which then took the form of a poll tax. In 1938 the levy was merged in the Government tax and 35 per cent. of the total amount collected was made payable to the Native Treasuries. From this date the Chiefs were given a fixed stipend from the Treasuries and ceased to draw a commission on the tax collected.

In the estimates of 1955–6, the revenue of the Treasuries amounted to a total of £140,904; the receipts derived from the share of Native tax amounted to 29 per cent. of the total revenue, while approximately the same proportion came from a graded tax, based on the taxable capacity of persons in different classes of occupation (including cattle-owners) which was introduced in 1949.[4] All the Treasuries now have Finance Committees, which attain a level of competence a good deal higher than is to be seen in many other African territories. In the majority of the Reserves the annual

[1] N.A., Part V, p. 217. The decision is printed in Colonial Reports, Bechuanaland Protectorate, 1936, p. 35.   [2] Proclamation no. 35 of 1938.
[3] N.A., Part V, pp. 220–8, 293–5.   [4] For the Native tax, see below, pp. 654 ff.

estimates are referred to a meeting of the Kuta, but discussion is usually confined to the members of the Finance Committees.[1] The expenditure has been largely devoted to education, but the Treasuries have also spent considerable sums on the maintenance of bore-holes and dams.[2]

The Chief's Representatives and Rule-making Powers

While in general the procedure of administration is now similar to that followed elsewhere in the territories which have adopted the Native Authority system, it has one special feature, due to the relations existing in the major Reserves between the ruling tribes and the 'allied' or other constituent tribes. The larger Reserves are divided into areas under the charge of authorities who are formally described as 'Chief's Representatives'; in some cases these are members of the ruling tribe and in others are selected from the tribe most strongly represented in the locality.[3] A demand has recently been made that local opinion should be consulted in filling these posts; it has also been suggested that a type of Local Council should be developed in which the 'allied tribes' should be assured of adequate representation. The problem is of importance, for while most of the internal troubles of Bechuanaland have in the past arisen from dynastic troubles (as most characteristically the recent upheavals in the Ngwato tribe which led to the banishment of Seretse Khama),[4] there is a wide field of potential discord arising from the increasing sentiment of independence among the 'allied tribes'. The most obvious remedy seems to lie in the creation of some form of representative Local Council.

There is another feature of tribal practice in Bechuanaland which deserves some notice. Though the current practice of conferring rule-making powers on Native Authorities has usually been regarded as no more than the legal recognition of a power inherent in their traditional position, it has not actually been usual in African practice for a Chief or Chief and Council to modify existing custom by formally proclaiming new 'laws'. In Bechuanaland, however, a procedure of 'law-making' came into existence in the early days of contact with Europeans, these 'laws' being almost invariably debated in the Kuta. It later became the practice to encourage the Chiefs to enact 'laws' on such matters as the burning of the veld or the sale of intoxicating liquor, rather than to deal with these practices by official legislation. A considerable volume of local law has thus accumulated,[5] which in some cases has the form of a published code, and the Chiefs continue to follow the traditional practice in this respect, rather than make Rules under the Native Administration Proclamation.

---

[1] *N.A.*, Part V, pp. 229–81, 295–9, 304.   [2] See below, p. 984.
[3] I. Schapera, *Handbook of Tswana Law and Custom*, 1938, pp. 9, 97–101. *N.A.*, Part V, pp. 282–4, 328–30.
[4] *Colonial Reports, Bechuanaland, 1944, 1950, 1951, 1952.*
[5] I. Schapera, *Tribal Legislation among the Tswana*, 1943.

A Native Advisory Council was first established in Bechuanaland at the time of the institution of the Native Fund in 1919. At the outset it consisted of the Chief and up to four other representatives from each of the six southern Tribal Areas. The Tawana Tribal Area was added in 1931, but the Ngwato did not send representatives till 1940, though the acting Chief Tshekedi Khama had attended as an observer when the reforms embodied in the Proclamations of 1934 were under discussion. In 1940 the title of the Council was changed to that of the African Advisory Council, and representatives of the three non-tribal districts of the Protectorate were subsequently added. In 1953 the Council had 38 members. It met once a year with the Resident Commissioner as President, and it has in its yearly meetings taken a full part in the discussion of the more important measures affecting Native Administration. The representatives of the Tribal Areas, in addition to the Chief, are normally Headmen or men of influence at the tribal headquarters. Though it is not strictly an organ of popular representation, it has afforded a useful link between the Administration and the African public of the Protectorate.

The European population, which numbered 2,379 in the census of 1946, also has an Advisory Council, instituted in 1920, which normally meets twice a year. The Protectorate is divided for this purpose into eight electoral areas, from each of which one member is elected. In 1951 a Joint Advisory Council was created, in which eight representatives from the Native Advisory Council meet eight members of the European Advisory Council, together with four official members.

Basutoland

When the British Government resumed control of Basutoland from the Government of Cape Colony in 1884,[1] it recognized the difficulty which had been encountered by that Government in the attempt to bring the Basuto under the régime of 'magisterial jurisdiction' which was the current administrative practice in the Cape. It is true that the Basuto were no longer the people who had so long withstood the attacks of the Boers of the Orange Free State, but they had shown in the course of the Gun War of 1880–1 their determination to resist any invasion of what they held to be their custom and their traditional rights. It was not without reason that the High Commissioner decided that order could best be ensured by administering the country through its Paramount Chief and his subordinate Chiefs. The most prominent of these were members of the family of Moshesh, the founder of the Basuto nation, and as a body they represented a well-established tradition of rule.[2]

[1] For the developments up to this period, see A. Pim, *Report on the Financial and Economic Position of Basutoland*, Cmd. 4907, 1935, pp. 7–20. *N.A.*, Part V, pp. 44–78. G. Tylden, *The Rise of the Basuto*, 1950, pp. 53 ff. *Basutoland, Report of Administrative Reforms Committee*, 1954, pp. 3–4.

[2] *N.A.*, Part V, pp. 45, 57–59.

The Basutoland Proclamations of 1884 and 1889 accordingly recognized the authority of the Paramount Chief and his subordinate Chiefs; they were authorized to adjudicate on any case in which Natives only were concerned, and they were accepted as the agency for the collection of tax. The years which followed, though at first marred by violent quarrels among some of the Chiefs, saw nevertheless a progressive consolidation of the position of the Paramount Chief, and it was at the motion of Lerotholi, the then Paramount Chief, that a Basutoland National Council was established in 1903. The Council received official recognition in 1910 as the mouthpiece of the Basuto people,[1] and one of its earliest functions was to issue a code of rules, known as the Laws of Lerotholi, based on what was held to be the custom of the Basuto.

Reorganization of Native Authorities and Courts

The dissensions of the leading Chiefs had by this time ceased to take a violent form, and the ensuing era of order led to a substantial improvement in the economy of the people. There was, however, a disturbing feature in the popular discontent shown during 1922 and the following years, arising out of the conduct of justice in the Courts of the Chiefs; it was notorious that these were in many cases utilized for the personal advantage of the presiding Chiefs, who found a source of income in the fines imposed by them. There were also many complaints by District Officers of the lack of help given to them by the Chiefs in measures of local improvement, such as those taken for the conservation of the soil.[2] Some of the reasons for this growing dissatisfaction with the policy observed in Native affairs were exposed in the Inquiry which Sir Alan Pim made in 1935 into the economic position of the Territory.[3] In his view no attempt had been made to combine the governmental and the Native organizations into one administrative system, nor to adapt them to modern conditions. It was mainly on his recommendation that a reorganization was undertaken in the year immediately following, based on the model of the Native Authority system then in operation in Nigeria and in Tanganyika.

Proclamations nos. 61 and 62, designed to give effect to this reform, were issued in 1938.[4] They had been fully accepted by the then Paramount Chief, but had not been discussed by the Basutoland National Council. They started from the basic position that Chiefs and Headmen were to be appointed and tribunals to be recognized by the High Commissioner in consultation with the Paramount Chief. The process of reorganization was, however, faced at an early stage by the results of the

---

[1] Proclamation no. 10 of 1910.
[2] *N.A.*, Part V, pp. 79–86.   [3] Cmd. 4907, 1935, pp. 49, 76.
[4] Native Administration Proclamation, no. 61 of 1938. Native Courts Proclamation, no. 62 of 1938.

practice followed by successive Paramounts of 'placing' their relatives in posts of territorial authority,[1] with the consequence that in the course of years the number of Chiefs and Headmen had gradually reached extravagant proportions. After an inquiry made in 1938, a total of 1,340 such authorities were gazetted, but it was said that they represented in fact only about half the number of those who were at the time exercising some form of authority. In 1950 their designations were reclassified as Principal Chiefs, Ward Chiefs, Chiefs, and Headmen.[2] The Wards, it should be explained, represent the areas controlled by those Chiefs who are themselves directly subordinate to the Paramount. In spite of the efforts made in the interval to bring the numbers under control, the total of gazetted Native Authorities stood in 1953 at 1,146, namely, ten Principal Chiefs, eleven Ward Chiefs, 281 Chiefs, and 844 Headmen.[3]

The process of reduction had not been easy. It is significant that when an inquiry was made in order to discover the underlying causes of the outbreak in 1947 and 1948 of 'Medicine murders' (that is to say, murders committed with the aim of using portions of the victims' bodies for magical purposes) it was held that they were in large measure due to Chiefs or Headmen who were anxious to recover by recourse to magic the position which they had lost or feared to lose as the result of these reforms.[4] It should be added that some change in the position of the traditional authorities had been made in 1948 by the commutation of the right to unpaid labour claimed by Principal Chiefs and Ward Chiefs. They were entitled by custom to call up their subjects as a body to work on the tribal fields of which they received the produce, and in subsequent years labour was also called up for works which were held to be of general benefit to the locality. It was agreed that in lieu of this obligation each taxpayer should pay an additional shilling in taxation; this was to be known as the local rate and the Chiefs were to receive one-third of it.[5]

A further effort was made in 1954 to effect a reduction in what was clearly an excessive number of local authorities. The Report of an Administrative Reform Committee which was issued in that year found that there was in existence a cadre of what were designated as 'Ineffective Chiefs', who continued to enjoy the perquisites of office in various ways, even when they might have secured more remunerative employment elsewhere.[6] The Committee prepared two schemes, of which the more drastic would make a reduction of 1,025 in the number of Chiefs and Headmen recognized by

---

[1] For the process of 'placing', see *Basutoland, Report of the Administrative Reforms Committee*, 1954, pp. 2–3. G. I. Jones, *Report on Medicine Murder in Basutoland*, Cmd. 8209, 1951, pp. 35–38.

[2] Proclamation no. 37 of 1950.

[3] *Basutoland, Report of Administrative Reforms Committee*, 1954, pp. 62–65.

[4] Jones, op. cit. p. 39.

[5] See below, p. 653.

[6] *Basutoland, Report of Administrative Reforms Committee*, 1954, pp. 8–11.

the High Commissioner. The second scheme would make an immediate reduction of 144, with a long-term reduction of a further 380. The matter was still under discussion in 1955.

The problems created by the use of the system of 'placing' were aggravated by the fact that all Chiefs were by custom entitled to try cases, so that there must at one period have been some 2,000 persons who were in principle entitled to hold a Court; the holding of a Court was indeed the main source of income of some of the minor Chiefs. The Native Courts Proclamation no. 62 of 1938 gave the Native Courts for the first time the statutory right to impose a sentence of imprisonment; but this measure was naturally followed by continued official pressure to secure a reduction in their number. The efforts made in this direction were, however, pursued independently of those directed towards the reduction in the number of Chiefdoms, a fact which throws light on the lack of considered policy which marked at one period the conduct of the affairs of the High Commission Territories. By 1944, however, the number of Courts had been reduced from 1,340, at which it stood in 1938, to a total of 134.

Up to this time litigants paid no fees, and the Chiefs had continued to reimburse themselves from fines imposed. The need for a further reduction in the number of Courts was again considered in 1946 when the National Treasury became responsible for the salaries of the Presidents of the Courts. In 1946 provision was made for the appointment of a salaried 'Assessor' to each Court President; these were not, as in some other territories where the term is used, specialist advisers on local custom, but were regarded as the equivalent of the kinsmen or subordinate Chiefs who were formerly associated with the Chief in judging cases. It now became usual for the Chiefs to appoint the presiding officers over Courts instead of presiding over them in person. It is noteworthy, however, that many of the Chiefs who had lost their Court warrants continued to adjudicate on cases by virtue of their administrative authority, so much so that it became usual to speak of the existence of 'Administrative Courts'.

A committee appointed in 1950 on the advice of the Basuto National Council[1] proposed that the Presidents of Courts of first instance should be appointed by local committees under the chairmanship of the District Commissioner, vacancies in higher Courts being filled by promotion from the lower Courts. The number of tribunals was to be reduced, and the 'Administrative Courts' were to be declared illegal. The number of Courts was as a result reduced to 63.[2] Of the 63 Courts four are Central Appeal Courts, twelve are 'A' Courts which have appellate as well as original jurisdiction, and 47 are 'B' Courts of which 30 are peripatetic between two Court sites. Salaried Presidents have been substituted for the Chiefs who

---

[1] Proceedings of 40th Session of Basutoland National Council, 1950, Appendix A.
[2] *Colonial Reports, Basutoland, 1953.*

previously presided over the Tribunals; their emoluments range from £130 in the 'B' Courts to £210 and £300 a year in the Appeal Courts.

As regards the procedure of the Courts, Administrative Officers have power to revise the findings of tribunals or to transfer a case to a Magisterial Court. The appeal from the Chiefs' Courts lies to the Court of the Paramount, and since 1944 it has been arranged that the appeal from the Paramount's Court shall lie in the first instance to the Court of the Judicial Commissioner, and thence by his leave to the High Court of Basutoland.[1] The post of Judicial Commissioner was created in 1928 and a second Judicial Commissioner's Court was created in 1950.[2]

The National Council and District Councils

It has been convenient to survey developments at the level of the chieftainship and of the Native Court before proceeding to deal with the higher structure of the indigenous organization. It was intended by the Paramount Chief Lerotholi that the Council, instituted by him in 1903,[3] should provide an alternative to the consultations which Moshesh had been accustomed to hold with members of his own family and other members of the feudal aristocracy of Chiefs. When the Council was given recognition in 1910 it was agreed that it should consist of 100 members, of whom 94 would be nominated by the Paramount, and five by the Resident Commissioner, with the Paramount himself as Chief Councillor.

At this stage it was therefore almost wholly representative of the class known currently as the 'sons of Moshesh', and it appeared to consider that its primary function was to defend their prerogatives against invasion by the Government. But the discontent caused by the defects in the administration of Native justice which found expression in 1922 and the following years called into being a body of commoners known as the Progressive Association, who urged that a proportion of the members of the National Council should be elected. Though this was not accepted at the time, the Paramount's nominations ceased to be entirely confined to Chiefs or Headmen. When the projects of reform previously mentioned were under debate in 1937, the National Council already contained 22 commoners in addition to the five Government nominees.

In 1943 progressive opinion within the National Council was able to secure from the High Commissioner an undertaking that he would refer to it all draft Proclamations affecting Basuto welfare; the Paramount Chief agreed at the same time to consult it on the issue of any Rules or Orders issued by him under the Native Administration Proclamation. Its representative character was increased by the provision that there should be set up in each administrative district a District Council with the right to elect

[1] For the High Court of Basutoland, see *Colonial Reports, Basutoland, 1953*, p. 57.
[2] Proclamation no. 25 of 1950.   [3] See above, p. 506.

from its own body certain representatives on the National Council; at
first one was to be elected from each district, but this number was increased
in 1950 to four. In 1950 provision was also made that the Government
should nominate six representatives of various local Associations, such as
the Teachers' Association or the Ex-Servicemen's Union.

As a result of these changes the Council in 1950 contained 36 Chiefs, 32
Headmen, and 31 commoners. It was apparent that a number of the last
group shared the views sponsored by the Progressive Association. The
Council has recently been able to insist on being formally associated in
certain of the measures taken by the Paramount Chief. In 1948, when the
personal credit of the Paramount (the Regent 'Mantsebo Seeiso, widow of
the preceding Paramount) had suffered from the scandal caused by the
'Medicine murders', the Council secured the appointment of three of its
members to be attached as Advisers to the Native Administration headquarters at Matsieng. Their number was subsequently increased to four.
In 1950 the Paramount agreed not to impose any levy or local rate without
the concurrence of the Council.

The District Councils received statutory recognition in 1948.[1] They are
composed of those Chiefs and Headmen in the district who are members of
the Basutoland Council, together with persons nominated at pitsos (public
meetings) held in each Ward. In 1950 there were in the nine District
Councils a total of 45 Chiefs, 49 Headmen, and 180 commoners; a number
of the last group are members of the families of Chiefs and Headmen, but
the group includes also representatives of various small local Associations.
The chief function of the Councils has been the discussion of resolutions to
be submitted to the National Council, but they also advise on the expenditure of that part of the local rate (a relatively small sum) which is allocated
to the districts. Little or no public interest was at first taken in the Councils,
no doubt because their functions were only consultative. In 1949 the
Paramount issued an order requiring Ward Chiefs to arrange for the
calling of regular Ward and Village pitsos as a means of restoring the contact of Chiefs with the people. Up to the present, however, there has been
no indication of the establishment of a regular system of Village Councils;
even the District Councils hardly seem as yet to have a position of any
importance.

National Treasury

The National Treasury now receives 36 per cent. of the Native tax.[2] In
1954 its revenue was £180,111, of which £110,527 represented its share
of the Native tax. It has, however, as yet contributed little to the development of the social services. In 1926 a special levy of 3s. per taxpayer

[1] Proclamation no. 48 of 1948. See N.A., Part V, pp. 96-98.
[2] For the Native tax, see below, pp. 653 ff.

had been imposed in order to finance a National Education Fund, but by 1946 the reserves of the Fund had been exhausted and the Government took over the responsibilty for financing education, the special levy being merged in the Native tax. The Treasury has itself allocated no funds to education or to the medical services, but in 1950–1 it provided a small sum for the pay of ten soil conservation supervisors and another small sum to be expended on afforestation by the District Councils. It has become responsible for the assessment and collection of the Native tax, and for this purpose the Paramount Chief maintains a representative in every District as an adjunct to the staff of the District Office.

The Principal and Ward Chiefs are now paid salaries, which range from £130 to £1,238 a year; other Chiefs and Headmen receive an annual gratuity made up of 5 per cent. of the tax collected plus an additional sum of £3,584, based on a proportion of the salaries of the Principal and Ward Chiefs. There is no fixed basis for the allocation of this sum, and Chiefs are dependent on the receipt of allocations from the Treasury Office at Matsieng.

From the days of Moshesh the Paramount Chief had always held a special position in Basutoland, but the measure in which he could exercise his control depended largely on his personal qualities. He now, however, has the support of the Government in the exercise of his authority, and has enjoyed the benefit of the legal sanctions applying to his orders. The effect of this has been seen in the development of one particular aspect of Native Administration which has already become the cause of some embarrassment to the Government. The High Commissioner has final authority over the procedure of the Treasury, and no expenditure may be incurred against the estimates until his approval has been given. But the Treasury is situated at Matsieng, the residence of the Paramount Chief, not at Maseru, the headquarters of the Government. It works under the control of the Paramount Chief, who is advised by a Finance Committee which in its present form consists of one representative of the Paramount Chief and one representative elected from each district by the Basutoland Council. The position in regard to the Treasury has served to add to that atmosphere of 'dualism' which has never been entirely absent in the relations between the Government of the Territory and the organization of the Native Authority.

The appointment by the Government of an Administrative Reforms Committee of 1954 was largely designed in order to suggest a remedy for this situation. It advised the institution of a permanent Advisory Committee to the Resident, sitting not at the Paramount Chief's town of Matsieng, but at the Government headquarters at Maseru. The Paramount Chief would have no power to issue orders save on the advice of that Committee. Advisers of the Paramount Chief, since they would be members of the Advisory Committee, would also reside at Maseru. There would be a wide measure of delegation of executive powers to the District Councils presided over by District Commissioners. These recommendations were unfavourably received in Basutoland[1] as involving a serious reduction in the authority of the Paramount Chief and loss of prestige to the representatives of the house of Moshesh. The matter was still under discussion in 1956.

To the people of Basutoland, no less than to the outside observer, it must seem that most of their indigenous institutions are now in a stage of rapid transition. There is a growing element of the type represented in the Progressive Association which is impatient of the position exercised by the traditional Native Authorities. But there is at the same time a strong national feeling, which at one period asserted itself against any measure which appeared to threaten an invasion of the traditional institutions of the Basuto by the British Government. Today it seems to be more seriously concerned to protect Basutoland from influences originating in the Union of South Africa. If this section of the community now demands respect for its indigenous institutions, including its Native Authorities, it is largely because it regards them as linked with the independence of Basutoland in the past and in some measure also as a symbol of its national life in the future.

Swaziland

The Swazi people have, like the Basuto, shown that they possess a strong national feeling. But they do not possess the same advantage as the Basuto in the effort which they make to maintain it. They cannot look back on a military history that has won the respect of their European neighbours.[2] They cannot claim that Swaziland is a purely African territory, for roughly one-half of its lands are today owned by Europeans. Like the Basuto, they are united under the authority of one Paramount Chief, but they do not occupy a self-contained block of country; Swaziland shows on the map as a patchwork of European and African lands. It is a misfortune also for the Swazi that memories of the process by which so large an area of land had been alienated should have engendered a mistrust of European intentions which for a considerable period hampered the attempts made by the Government to develop an effective system of local administration.[3]

The European population is small; in 1946 it numbered only 3,201, as a considerable number of the European landowners are resident in the

---

[1] *Africa Digest*, March–April 1955, p. 3.
[2] E. Walker, *History of South Africa*, 1940, pp. 429 ff. *N.A.*, Part V, pp. 349–53, 360–9.
[3] A. Pim, *Report on the Financial and Economic Situation of Swaziland*, Cmd. 4114, 1932, p. 18.

Transvaal and use their lands only for seasonal sheepgrazing. Since 1921 there has been a European Advisory Council. It was reconstituted in 1949, the territory being divided for this purpose into ten electoral divisions, each returning one member. There are in addition eight official members on the Council, who have, however, no power to vote. European enterprise has made an important contribution to the economic development of the territory in mining and farming, and during recent years also in the promotion of schemes of reafforestation and irrigation. The history of British administration dates from 1903, and for some considerable time the attention of the Administration was largely devoted to matters of concern to the European community, so much so that in 1932 Sir Alan Pim could remark that the contact of the District Officers with Africans had tended to be confined to the work of the Courts and to tax-collecting tours.[1]

During most of this period, however, the revenues of the territory were small; there was little encouragement to formulate policies of African development, and questions relating to the organization of the economic life of the Territory or the improvement of the social services received relatively minor attention. The growth of revenue in later years and the assistance given from the United Kingdom Treasury from 1929 onwards have provided larger resources for schemes designed to minister to the needs of the African population,[2] and have at the same time resulted in a marked change of outlook on the part of the Administration. The desire to secure a more active collaboration of the indigenous authorities in the development of these schemes was one of the major reasons which prompted the measures taken in 1941 to modify the system of Native Administration. In the years immediately preceding the enactment of this measure, the Government had already started to undertake certain improvements in the social services and in the work of the agricultural and veterinary departments. But there had remained a singular air of detachment in its attitude towards the control of purely Native affairs.

The African population of Swaziland traces its traditional origin back to about 70 clans, of which some 25 clans are regarded as forming the Bomdzabuko, the group of 'true Swazi' which originally settled in Swaziland under the leadership of the Dlamini clan. There was a titular hierarchy of clans, led by the Dlamini, to which the ruling lineage and many of the leading Chiefs belonged, but there was in other respects little difference in status between the different sections of the people. In the indigenous organization the Paramount Chief had the advice of two Councils, the Liqoqo and the Libandhla, to which reference will be made in a later part of this chapter.[3] There was under the Paramount a body of hereditary Chiefs, numbering some 172 in all; of these there were in 1949 a total of 119 classed as Bomdzabuko, and out of the 119 there were 75 of

---

[1] Cmd. 4114, p. 40.   [2] *N.A.*, Part V, pp. 382 ff.   [3] See below, p. 516.

the Dlamini clan. The Chiefs held charge of areas of varying size and were subject to a complicated system of control from Swazi headquarters, control being in practice exercised through the agency of the 'governors' of the Royal Villages.[1]

The only definite function laid on the Chiefs by the Government itself was to bring to the Tax Camps which were held by District Officers the taxpayers living within their area of control.[2] In the basic law of the Territory, both the Paramount and the Chiefs were prohibited from exercising criminal jurisdiction,[3] but it was notorious that many Chiefs used the authority conferred on them for the adjudication of civil disputes in order to impose fines for a variety of offences, including disobedience to their own orders. It is clear that in the field of general administration the services of the Chiefs were very seldom available to District Officers for the purpose of carrying out schemes designed for the public benefit.

Introduction of the Native Authority System

It was the general complaint regarding the misuse by the Chiefs of their powers of adjudication which provided the immediate ground for proposals put forward by the Administration in 1940 for the introduction of the Native Authority system. But the Paramount and the Chiefs proved to be unusually tenacious in their opposition to a procedure which, as they saw it, would subject them to the type of control characteristic of the procedure developed in Nigeria and Tanganyika. They quoted the terms of the Anglo-Boer Convention of 1894 which had made Swaziland a dependency of the Transvaal and of the Order in Council of 1903 which established British jurisdiction over the territory.[4] The first of these instruments provided that 'Native laws and custom shall be administered by the Native Chiefs entitled to administer the same'. The second, like the Order in Council of 1891 which had provided for the extension of jurisdiction over Bechuanaland,[5] provided that the Government 'should respect any Native laws by which the civil relations of any Native Chief, tribes, or populations are now regulated'. When, however, the Swazi stated their case in a Memorial sent to the British Crown in 1941 they seem to have recognized the inadequacy of this line of argument, for they devoted the greater part of their plea to explaining the disabilities from which they had suffered as a result of the alienation of their lands.

On this point, as will subsequently be seen,[6] they succeeded in obtaining some relief, but the officers in charge of the local Administration were instructed to proceed with the scheme for the introduction of the Native

---

[1] H. Kuper, *An African Aristocracy*, 1947, pp. 65–71.
[2] High Commission Notice, no. 50, 1909.
[3] Swaziland Administration Proclamation no. 3, 1904. *N.A.*, Part V, pp. 371–3.
[4] *N.A.*, Part V, pp. 367, 370.
[5] See above, p. 500.   [6] See below, p. 698.

Authority system. The Proclamations which gave effect to this decision did not, however, issue until 1944, after three years' further discussion with the Swazi leaders, and even then the system was not brought into full force until 1950. In that year a series of revised Proclamations were issued in a form which was designed to meet some of the objections brought by the Swazi against the laws originally promulgated.[1]

The revised Native Administration Proclamation of 1950 has the same general effect as the Native Authority Ordinances in force in East and Central Africa, but it has certain provisions which represent concessions made to the Paramount Chief and his Council. It has been usual elsewhere for the law to provide that the Native Authorities should be such persons or bodies as may be recognized as such by the Government, and the Proclamation of 1944 had been expressed in these terms, but the law of 1950 refers specifically to the Paramount Chief in Council as the sole Native Authority,[2] and the Chiefs under his control are referred to as such, instead of being termed Subordinate Native Authorities, since this might carry the implication that their power is derived from recognition by the Government. The appointment of Chiefs is not stated to require the previous assent of the Administration. The Paramount Chief in Council is the authority for the issue of Orders enforceable by the Native Courts and also for revoking Orders issued by Chiefs. In the matter of the revoking of Native Authority Orders the Resident Commissioner may act only after consultation with the Paramount Chief; but he may in the last resort issue an Order in default of appropriate action by the latter, and may revoke an Order if it is clearly injurious to the welfare of the Natives concerned.

In the terms of the law of 1950 it is also the Paramount Chief in Council who makes Rules for the 'good order and welfare' of the Natives of Swaziland, and who may impose a local rate in money or in kind, though in each of these cases the approval of the Resident Commissioner is required. The Chiefs cannot issue Orders at their own discretion, but only subject to the direction of the Paramount in Council. They are required to take action for the prevention of crime, but they still have no responsibility for the collection of taxes. If the Proclamation be strictly interpreted, its general effect would thus appear to be that officers representing the Government have a right of veto in certain cases, but have less power than elsewhere to originate or guide policy in local affairs.

Recent Judicial and Financial Changes

The extension of official control over the Native Courts met with particular opposition from the Swazi leaders, and it was eventually agreed that

[1] Native Administration (Consolidation) Proclamation no. 79 of 1950; Native Courts Proclamation no. 80 of 1950; National Treasury Proclamation no. 81 of 1950.

[2] For a somewhat similar provision, see Basutoland Native Administration Proclamation no. 61 of 1938.

the authority for the establishment of Courts should vest in the Paramount Chief in Council, subject to the approval of the Resident Commissioner; the latter may, however, exercise this power in default of action by the Paramount, provided that it is exercised with respect for Native law and custom. The powers of review or revision by Administrative Officers are limited to criminal cases; the appeal in civil cases is from a Native Court of Appeal to a Higher Native Court of Appeal and thence to the High Court of Swaziland,[1] while criminal appeals go first to the Judicial Commissioner, an officer of the Administration specially appointed for this purpose. The Presidents of Courts may be either Chiefs or commoners. Fourteen Courts were constituted in 1951, and a second Court of Appeal was added in 1953. The Presidents of the Courts receive from the National Treasury a salary of £150 a year; each Court has four 'Assessors' who receive sitting fees. The President of the Higher Native Court of Appeal has a salary of £240 a year. The system is still being worked out, but it can hardly fail to prove superior to the unregulated procedure of the past.

The raising of funds for expenditure on common purposes has been familiar to the Swazi from the time of the Chief Regent Gwamile, who in 1913 encouraged her subjects to go to the Transvaal mines in order to earn money to be applied to the repurchase of alienated lands. The Lifa Fund, created in 1946 for this purpose, is proof of the ability of the Swazi to combine for objects of national interest.[2] The Chiefs agreed in 1911 to impose an annual 'special' levy of 2s. per adult male which was to be devoted partly to measures against the cattle disease (East Coast Fever), but partly also to education. In 1916 the 'special levy' was discontinued,[3] and 2s. from each tax paid was allocated to a Swazi National Fund. From 1931 onwards the bulk of this Fund was expended on the Swazi National School, founded in that year at Mathapha.

Resources for expenditure of this type have now been provided by the establishment of the Swazi National Treasury under the terms of the Treasury Proclamation of 1950. It is under the control of the Paramount Chief, subject to the approval of the Resident Commissioner. The main source of the revenue of the Treasury is its one-third share of the Native tax. The estimated ordinary revenue for 1955–6 was £54,788. With a few notable exceptions, the Chiefs have so far shown little interest in such matters as measures designed for soil conservation, and the Administration has been obliged to enlist the support of progressive commoners by the creation of Rural Development Committees.

Reference has already been made to the two Swazi Councils, the Liqoqo and the Libandhla, as the traditional source of advice of the Paramount

---

[1] For High Court, see *Colonial Reports, Swaziland, 1953*, p. 40.
[2] See below, p. 698.
[3] See below, p. 655.

Chief. In the past, the Liqoqo constituted a type of 'Inner Council' consisting of the Paramount's close kinsmen and other leading Chiefs, while the Libandhla included not only the members of the Liqoqo but all other Chiefs with their leading Councillors; its meetings were indeed in theory open to all men of the tribe. Today, however, the Liqoqo rarely meets as a body, since the Paramount Chief prefers to seek the advice of a small number of its more progressive members. It is the Libandhla which has been formally recognized as the Council of the Paramount Chief in the terms of the Native Administration Proclamations. This body meets once a year and sits for about a week; the number of commoners who attend has increased of late years, and many of them are members of the Swazi Progressive Association founded in 1929. In 1950 the Libandhla instituted a Standing Committee consisting of a senior Chief as chairman, with one member from each of the six administrative districts; this body seems to have a majority of progressive elements. A Finance Committee of eleven members has been made responsible for the management of the Swazi National Treasury; seven are commoners, including the Chairman. It seems likely that power will pass progressively into the hands of these committees.

The acceptance given to changes thus made in the administration of Native affairs in Swaziland has to some extent been assisted by the recent quickening of the economic life of the country, due to the expansion of mining activity and development of projects of reafforestation, irrigation, and the like.[1] But it is doubtful how far they can be said to have achieved that integration of Native institutions with the governmental organization which formed one of the objectives sought in the introduction of the Native Authority system. Nor is it yet clear how far recent economic progress will influence the public attitude towards the Native Authorities themselves. Of the place which will be accorded to the Paramount Chief himself there can be no doubt; he is the symbol of the national life of the Swazi, and is bound to the people by a potent mystical tie.[2] But there is likely to be a progressive decline in the position of the Chiefs, and a growing movement for the popularization of the local administrative and judicial institutions.

GOLD COAST

It was not until 1944 that a procedure similar to that followed in the Native Authority system was formally adopted in the Gold Coast Colony and Ashanti, and it had only been in practice for a short period when it began to give place to a series of institutions of Local Government which were largely based on the principle of popular election. In the Northern Territories of the Gold Coast the Native Authority system had been

[1] *N.A.*, Part V, pp. 338–44. [2] Ibid. p. 354.

introduced somewhat earlier, but there also it is now giving place to Local Government institutions based on the same principle.

The Akan and Fanti States

The majority of the inhabitants of the Gold Coast Colony and Ashanti belong to the Akan and Fanti-speaking peoples. Both had a well-developed political organization, so that in the early days of British contact it became customary to refer to a unit controlled by a Head[1] Chief as a State, and this term is still current as a convenient designation of such units, though it may have ceased to possess other constitutional significance. The different States had within certain limits a common origin and Constitution. Villages, each of which had its own Council of Village Heads chosen from Elders of different groups, were combined into Divisions; each Division had its Divisional Chief with a Council representing the Councils of Village Heads. The Divisions were combined into States under a Head Chief, with a Council of Divisional Chiefs. Among the Ashanti the Divisions corresponded to the sections of the military forces which composed the army of the Ashanti Confederacy, and the Divisional Chiefs were by tradition the war leaders of these sections. Authority was symbolized by the possession of a sacred stool, and the lands held by the Chief and his Council on behalf of the group were accordingly known as 'stool' lands, while the Council was known alternatively as the Stool Council.[2]

At every level the Chief or Headman was chosen from a number of possible candidates belonging to his predecessor's lineage, and he could be 'destooled' if he acted in a manner contrary to accepted tradition. This was a provision which came at times into very active practice,[3] and there tended to be a continual widening of the grounds which were held to justify destoolment. The largest unit of this type was the Ashanti Confederacy, which embraced the greater part of the population of Ashanti as it exists today. In the early days of the British connexion the Fanti States of the coastal area were treated as allies who shared in the defence against the attacks of the Ashanti, and as such they were held to remain outside the range of British jurisdiction. But there were some aspects of this jurisdiction which appealed to the Fanti Chiefs themselves. In the Agreement known as the 'Bond' of 1844, a number of the Fanti Chiefs agreed that certain criminal offences should be tried by British magistrates and that the Fanti customs should be moulded 'to the general principles of British law'. Though the 'Bond' was of this restricted character, it was subsequently claimed on behalf of the Chiefs that it defined by implication

[1] 'Head Chief' was the term originally used. The term 'Paramount Chief' was introduced by the Gold Coast (Legislative Council) Order in Council of 1925 and the Native Administration (Colony) Ordinance no. 18 of 1927.　　[2] *N.A.*, Part III, pp. 190–4, 230–8.

[3] F. M. Bourret, *The Gold Coast*, 1952, p. 48. *N.A.*, Part III, p. 192. J. B. Danquah, *The Akim Abuokwa Handbook*, 1928.

the extent of British jurisdiction, beyond which it could not legitimately
be extended.

Relations with the British Government

The relation of the British to the people of this part of the Gold Coast
was officially described as that of a Protectorate, but this term had not at
that stage acquired the juridical implications which afterwards became
attached to it. Moreover, in 1842 and again in 1863 Select Committees
of Parliament expressed a reluctance to undertake any definite responsibilities in regard to it; the second of these committees recommended in
fact that the Protectorate should only be retained in order that the Chiefs
might as speedily as possible 'learn to do without it'.[1] The Fanti Chiefs on
their part promulgated in 1871 a Constitution, the so-called Mankesim
Constitution, which would have formally bound the British Government
to acknowledge a marked degree of independence in the Fanti Confederation which it purported to constitute. There appeared to the British
Government of the day to be no middle course between accepting the
Mankesim Constitution, thus abandoning all claim to exercise authority
over the Fanti States, and assuming a fuller measure of responsibility for
their control. It chose the second course, and in 1874 it created the Gold
Coast Colony by Order in Council,[2] though no formal act of annexation
was made till 1901.

The position of the Chiefs was defined by the Native Jurisdiction Ordinance of 1878, which remained substantially in force till 1927. The Ordinance of 1878 empowered Chiefs 'with their Councillors authorized by
Native law' to enact by-laws and to form tribunals to try breaches of those
laws, and to exercise minor civil and criminal jurisdiction. Provision was
made for an appeal in judicial matters to an Administrative Officer and
thence to a Divisional Court of the Supreme Court. Administrative
Officers had, however, no supervisory powers over the Native Tribunals,
nor could they in administrative matters issue regulations in default of
action by a Chief, with the result that local regulations (such for example
as those dealing with the control of the cocoa disease) had to be enacted by
Government Ordinance. Since no direct taxation was imposed in the
Gold Coast, either then or for long afterwards,[3] there could be no question
of organizing Native Treasuries to be financed by a share of the tax. The
Ordinance of 1878, like the 'Bond' of 1844, was interpreted locally as a
recognition of the inherent rights possessed by the Chiefs, and the Chiefs
themselves quoted it as legal warranty for their claim that no further
limitations of their authority could be imposed without their assent.

[1] *Cambridge History of the British Empire*, 1936, vol. ii, pp. 672 ff.
[2] Letters Patent, 24 July 1874; Orders in Council, 6 August 1874.
[3] See below, p. 666.

Defects of Administrative System

The defects in this system, and in particular those arising from the irregularities of the Native Tribunals, were fully recognized by the Colonial Government. The fact that the Courts were by custom entitled to appropriate all fees and fines gave a material value to the right to hold a tribunal, and numbers of minor Chiefs instituted their own Courts, where business was so conducted as to derive the maximum income from this source.[1] Between 1894 and 1922 no less than five Bills were introduced with the view of effecting a reform in the judicial system, but they were abandoned in face of the argument that they invaded the inherent rights of the Chiefs. This contention had for a time the support of those African lawyers who were associated with the leading Chiefs in the West African Aborigines Rights Society, a body which had been founded in 1897 to oppose the Public Lands Bill introduced in that year.[2] But the interests of the lawyers and the Chiefs began to diverge after the Provincial Councils (the statutory bodies into which the Chiefs were organized) were constituted as electoral colleges for the choice of six African members of the Legislative Council. As has been explained in a previous chapter,[3] the Chiefs now came to be seen as rivals in the competition for political authority. Less was heard of their inherent rights and more of their responsibilities as Chiefs. A Chief, it was urged, was expected to act in consultation with his Councillors and Elders; he had not only to be elected by his Council, but he was liable in certain circumstances to be destooled by it.

It is in this connexion noteworthy that under British rule destoolments had become so frequent, and were so often followed by long periods of controversy during which there was no recognized Chief, as to create in official circles some doubt whether the Native Authority system could in fact be profitably adopted in the Gold Coast for the purpose of carrying out the functions of Local Government. On their part the lawyers were by no means anxious to see the introduction of the Native Authority system in the form in which they saw it practised in Nigeria; it was decried by them as likely to give to the Chiefs something of the character of autocrats rather than of constitutional rulers.

There existed at the same time a moderate school of African opinion which held that the conduct of the affairs of the 'stools' by the Chiefs, and in particular their use of funds derived from 'stool' lands should be supervised by some statutory body, preferably composed of Africans, and that their tribunals should be subject to supervision by the Magistrates' Courts. In the face of these currents of opinion some of the more influential Chiefs

---

[1] *N.A.*, Part III, p. 201. J. B. Danquah, *Akan Law and Customs*, 1928, pp. 69–83. *Report of the Committee of Enquiry into Native Tribunals in the Gold Coast* (the Blackall Committee), 1943.

[2] See below, p. 738.   [3] See above, p. 317.

themselves introduced into the Legislature the measure subsequently enacted as the Administration (Colony) Ordinance of 1927. In some degree this was a measure of reform. It defined the position of the State Councils, and laid down a procedure for the election and destoolment of Chiefs. It regularized the procedure of the Native Tribunals, while at the same time enlarging their powers. But in many ways it fell short of the measure which the situation demanded. The authority enjoyed by the Chiefs remained independent of their recognition by the Government; there was no provision for the creation of Native Treasuries; and the control exercised over the Native Tribunals went little farther than to empower the Provincial Commissioner to transfer a case to a Magistrate's Court.

In 1932, when the Government revenue (which was mainly derived from indirect taxation)[1] had suffered from the depression in world prices, a proposal was made to impose a direct tax which would be divided between the Government and the States; but even when the whole proceeds of the tax were afterwards offered to the States for expenditure on public purposes the opposition of the Chiefs secured the withdrawal of the proposal. The Native Authority (Amendment) Ordinance of 1931, however, empowered the States to establish Treasuries into which would be paid the proceeds of Court fees and of the rents for stool lands; a subsequent amendment legalized the imposition of 'levies' by those States which had instituted Treasuries. But there were still no means of securing that all revenues received should be brought to account in a State Treasury, nor was there provision for control over the expenditure incurred.

It was not until 1939 that the dissatisfaction with the conduct of 'stool' affairs enabled the Government to enact the Native Administration Treasuries Ordinance,[2] which empowered it to compel a State to establish a Native Treasury and to submit its operations to supervision. The position of the Native Tribunals was shortly to receive an even more positive measure of reform. In 1942 a committee of inquiry was appointed with a majority of African members, and in the course of the following year it made a report which amounted to a forthright condemnation both of the composition of the Tribunals and of their administration of justice.[3]

Native Authority and Native Courts Ordinance, 1944

As a result a comprehensive measure of reform was embodied in the Native Authority and Native Courts Ordinances of 1944.[4] The former made it clear that the organs of Local Government were to be only those Native Authorities who were duly recognized as such by the Government.

[1] See below, p. 666.   [2] No. 16 of 1939.

[3] *Report of Native Tribunals Committee of Enquiry*, 1943.

[4] Native Authority (Colony) Ordinance no. 21 of 1944, amended by nos. 24 of 1945 and 13 of 1947; Native Courts (Colony) Ordinance no. 22 of 1944, amended by nos. 76 of 1945 and 44 of 1947.

An Administrative Officer might, if necessary, be appointed to discharge the functions of a Native Authority. The State Councils thus ceased to possess authority as of right, though they retained their ceremonial and ritual functions and were authorized to determine matters such as the contested elections or the destoolments of Chiefs. Native Authorities were made subject to the usual measure of administrative control; they were empowered to levy an annual rate, and from 1946 they received a grant from central revenues equal to the amount raised by such rates.

As regards the Native Tribunals, the Native Courts Ordinance of 1944 laid down that Native Courts must be constituted by order of the Governor in Council, and could exercise only such jurisdiction as was conferred on them by that order. By 1951 the number of Courts had been reduced from 324 to 135. The Native Authorities were to be consulted as to the constitution of the Courts and were to appoint their Presidents; by 1951 the number of Presidents who held the rank of Chief had fallen to 55 per cent. of the total.[1] Courts were created of four grades; appeals lay to the Magistrates' Courts, and review by Administrative Officers, which had at an earlier date been introduced for criminal cases, was now extended also to civil cases. A Judicial Adviser was appointed with powers of review and revision.

Ashanti—Administrative Ordinances of 1935

The British connexion with the Ashanti began at a relatively late period, and their approach to the problems of Native Administration was determined by special circumstances. After the declaration of the Protectorate in 1896 the major preoccupation of the Government was to prevent the resurgence of Ashanti power, and in order to break the authority of the Confederacy the Asantehene and the leading Chiefs were deported, while a number of minor Chiefs were treated as autonomous. A reversal of this policy began in 1921, when, recognizing the strength of Ashanti sentiment,[2] the Government took a series of measures which in 1935 culminated in the recognition of the Ashanti Confederacy. This event was the occasion for the enactment of a Native Authority Ordinance (no. 1 of 1935) which, as amended by no. 21 of 1939, regulated for some years the system of local rule.

In practice, Chiefs with their traditional Councillors were almost invariably gazetted as Native Authorities.[3] The Confederacy Council (Asanteman Council), with the Asantehene as President, was recognized as the Native Authority for Ashanti, save for the three small territorial Divisions which were not members of the Confederacy. The Council exercised

---

[1] *Gold Coast, Report of the Commission on Native Courts*, 1951, pp. 11–12.
[2] E. W. Smith, *The Golden Stool*, 1926.
[3] For the special position of the Kumasi Clan Chiefs, see *N.A.*, Part III, pp. 237–8.

rule-making powers, but the executive responsibilities rested with the Native Authorities of the Divisions which composed the Confederacy. Their Chiefs were members of the Asanteman Council[1] and acknowledged the political ascendancy of the Asantehene as its President.

The Native Authority Ordinance of 1935 empowered the Governor to require the recognized Native Authorities to establish Native Treasuries, but for some years it proved impracticable to ensure that all revenues received were brought to account, and it was not until 1940 that legislation was enacted to regulate the power of Chiefs to deal with 'stool' property, thus bringing the Treasuries' resources under effective administrative control.[2] Hitherto there had been no direct tax in Ashanti, but in 1942 the Asanteman Council gained assent to the imposition of an Ashanti National Fund Levy: two-thirds of the proceeds were retained by the Division in which they were raised and the remaining third was paid to the Confederacy Council, which utilized the sum realized mainly for educational purposes. The separate Treasuries subsequently imposed Development Levies which were regarded as the equivalent of the *ad hoc* levies previously raised by Chiefs. Government grants were made from 1946 on the basis of £1 for every £1 raised locally for expenditure on development. The Asanteman Council became in 1946 the electoral college for the representatives of Ashanti in the Legislative Council of the Gold Coast, and under the Constitution of 1950[3] it became entitled to elect six members to the Legislative Assembly.

The Native Courts Ordinance enacted in 1935 created Native Courts of four grades in Ashanti, of which only that of the Asanteman Council is an 'A' Court; it also sits as a Court with criminal jurisdiction in 'constitutional' offences against custom, which it can punish by fine, imprisonment, or banishment. There is a widely extended system of Native Appeal Courts, from which appeals lie to a Magistrate's Court, thence to the Chief Commissioner's Court, and thence to the West African Court of Appeal.[4] There is no provision for the composition of these Courts other than that prescribed by tradition, and the Asanteman Council refused to agree to the appointment of others than Chiefs as members of its own Court. The Asantehene and some of the Divisional Chiefs, however, have now ceased to preside over their Courts.[5] A Judicial Adviser for Ashanti was appointed in 1948.

The Northern Territories

As has already been indicated, the Northern Territories of the Gold Coast have a history which differs materially from that of the Gold Coast

---

[1] *N.A.*, Part III, pp. 238–9.
[2] The Stool Property Protection Ordinances nos. 22 of 1940 and 25 of 1941.
[3] See above, p. 319. [4] *N.A.*, Part III, pp. 243–5.
[5] *Gold Coast, Report of the Commission on Native Courts*, 1951, p. 11.

Colony or Ashanti. Here a number of kingdoms had been established at intervals from the twelfth century onwards as the result of invasion by tribes residing beyond the present boundaries of the Northern Territories. The country thus invaded was by local custom divided into areas (tengani) which were defined by their common recognition of a shrine to the Earth God and a common veneration for its priests (tendana). The invaders appointed subordinate authorities to take charge of the different tengani areas so defined, and many of them succeeded in gaining a position of independence.

Although a large proportion of the invaders professed the Islamic faith, the Chiefs who were in power at the time of the declaration of the British Protectorate in 1901 did not exercise the authority normally character-istic of Muslim rulers, but were regarded primarily as religious not as secular heads.[1] The Administration Ordinance of 1902 simply em-powered Chiefs to exercise jurisdiction 'in the same measure as such juris-diction has heretofore been exercised'. No steps were taken to define its extent, and the support which the Government gave to the Chiefs enabled them to exercise powers much in excess of those enjoyed by them under previous custom. These powers were alleged to have been frequently abused for purposes of private gain.

A number of inquiries into the social organization of the people were initiated in 1929, and as a result Ordinances were enacted in 1932 which provided for the introduction of a Native Authority system which followed in a simplified form the pattern of legislation then in force in Northern Nigeria and Tanganyika.[2] The Northern Territories were thus brought under the Native Authority system before either the Gold Coast Colony or Ashanti. At this time no direct taxation had yet been imposed in Ashanti or the Gold Coast. In 1934, however, the Native Authorities as constituted in the Northern Territories agreed to accept the imposition of a local tax, which became known as the tribute tax, since it was regarded as a commutation of the customary tribute and labour which had been claimed by the Chiefs. The general acquiescence in the imposition of this tax was doubtless aided by the fact that the entire proceeds were credited to the new Native Treasuries. From 1946 the Treasuries, like those which had by that time been set up in the Colony and Ashanti, received grants from the Central Government equivalent to the total sum raised by the local taxation.

The Native Authority Councils were usually composed of the traditional Chiefs and Elders, but from 1948 the co-opted members of the local

[1] R. S. Rattray, *Tribes of the Ashanti Hinterland*, 1932. E. F. Tamakloe, *Brief History of the Dagamba People*, Accra, 1931. A. W. Cardinall, *Natives of the Northern Territories of the Gold Coast*, 1920, p. 15. W. E. F. Ward, *A History of the Gold Coast*, 1948, pp. 120–6.

[2] Native Courts Ordinance no. 1 of 1932; Native Authority (Northern Territories) Ordinance no. 2 of 1932; Native Treasuries Ordinance no. 10 of 1932.

Finance Committees were given rank as full members. A Territorial Council representing all the Native Authorities met annually from 1946; its functions were consultative, but under the Gold Coast Constitution of 1950 it became the nucleus of the electoral college for the Northern Territories.[1] Looking back on the history of the introduction of the Native Authority system in the country as a whole, one cannot fail to be struck by the difference between the Northern Territories and the Gold Coast in this respect. The peoples of the North are in some ways less advanced than those of the Gold Coast, but the readiness with which they accepted the new administrative institutions formed a pleasing contrast to the obstruction which so long stood in the way of the development of a system of Local Government in the areas lying farther south.

The Native Courts Ordinance of 1932 was superseded in 1935 by a more comprehensive measure which provided for the establishment of three grades of Native Courts, the highest grade of Courts being generally also Courts of Appeal from the decisions of Courts of lower grade. The composition of the Courts followed closely that of the Native Authorities.[2]

Establishment of Town Councils

Throughout the period referred to in the preceding paragraphs the form taken by the institutions of Local Government in the towns of the Gold Coast and Ashanti became a factor of much importance, for these towns are the home of the middle class which has of late years dominated the politics of the territory. As early as 1858 an attempt was made to establish at Cape Coast and Accra Municipal Corporations of a type which would have been regarded as highly advanced even in the Europe of the period,[3] but after this had proved to be abortive, nothing more was attempted in the same direction until 1894. Town Councils were then established in these two towns and in Sekondi.[4] These had official chairmen, with an equal number of nominated and elected members, but they commanded so little interest that in 1922 only about 4 per cent. of the registered electors in Accra seem to have voted and fewer still elsewhere. The Government sought in 1929 to revive an interest in urban affairs by creating municipalities with elected majorities, but the Chiefs of the States in which the towns are situated demanded the inclusion of direct representation for their States, and the scheme was not carried into effect.

In the years 1943–5, however, three Ordinances were enacted establishing Town Councils in Accra, Cape Coast, and Sekondi-Takoradi which had an official president but an elected majority; they now included nominees of the local Native Authority. These Town Councils were replaced in 1953 by Municipal Councils composed of a large majority of

---

[1] See above, p. 319.
[3] Ibid. pp. 215–19.
[2] N.A., Part III, pp. 269–72.
[4] Town Councils Ordinance no. 17 of 1894.

elected over traditional members.[1] They choose their own presidents. In Ashanti the town of Kumasi was administered from 1925 by a Public Health Board, which under its constitution as revised in 1937 consisted of five officials and five nominated unofficials of whom a majority were Africans. In 1943 this was replaced by a Town Council having an official president with six elected Africans and six nominated members, of whom two are nominees of the Asantehene. The remaining towns were controlled by the Native Authorities within whose jurisdiction they are situated, with the exception of the mining town of Obuasi, where in 1935 a Sanitary Board replaced a Sanitary Committee set up in 1909. The members of the Board consisted of two officials, three nominees of the Ashanti Goldfields Corporation, and two of the Adansi Native Authority,[2] with three members elected from each of the three Wards into which Obuasi is divided.

The short life of the Native Authority System

The developments in the field of local administration in the Gold Coast Colony and Ashanti which have been recorded in the preceding paragraphs fell into two stages. In the earliest of these stages the Colonial Government, standing by the tradition that it was dealing with States to which it was bound to allow a high measure of independence in domestic matters, refrained from exercising administrative control over them, in spite of the patent evidence of their deficiencies. It was a period of rising public revenue, owing to the growing profits made by the cocoa industry, and the official attention seems to have been concentrated on the creation of certain of its central institutions, such as the Achimota College or the Central Hospitals at the larger towns. The second stage was marked by the progressive extension of measures of control in local affairs, most notably through the introduction of the Native Authority system.

But this reform came too late, and was not pressed home. Apart from the opposition which was allowed to delay the full introduction of the system, its working was prejudiced by the maintenance in existence of the State Councils, exercising an influence and possessing resources over which it was difficult to exercise statutory control. There has now arrived a third stage, reflecting the predominance of a political element which, while seeking an early release for the Gold Coast from any vestige of external control, is also opposed to sharing political power with the traditional authorities as such. It would substitute everywhere a range of Local Government institutions based on the extension of the system of popular election, and would confine the Chiefs or other traditional

[1] Municipal Councils' Ordinance no. 9 of 1953, amended by nos. 34 of 1953 and 140 of 1954
[2] Ordinances nos. 36 of 1935, 18 of 1943, 20 of 1944, 34 of 1946, and 51 of 1950.

authorities to the exercise of the ceremonial or ritual functions dictated by custom.[1]

Establishment of Local and District Councils

Though, however, the influence of this movement in the field of constitutional change can be stated with some accuracy, the actual results achieved in the field of Local Government are less easily described, for the process is not yet complete. The movement received a strong stimulus when the Commission appointed to inquire into the disturbances which took place in 1948[2] recommended that the existing Native Authorities should be superseded by local authorities of a more representative type, with functions corresponding to those of Rural District Councils.[3] The local committee which in the following year drew out a scheme for constitutional reform took a less radical view, and was prepared to allow the traditional authorities to retain some share in Local Government institutions, in so far at all events that the States or Stool Councils should be empowered to nominate up to one-third of the membership of the projected District, Urban, or Local Councils.[4]

A Special Commissioner appointed in 1950 to make proposals regarding the activities appropriate to this series of new bodies reported in 1951,[5] but before action could be taken on his recommendations, the revised Constitution which had been envisaged in the report of the Committee of 1949 had been brought into being and the new semi-Responsible Government had fixed April 1952 as the date for the first Local Government elections. Public interest was consequently focused on the establishment of the 280 new Councils which it had been decided to set up.[6]

Of the total number of these Councils, 229 were designated as Local, 14 as Urban, and 37 as District Councils. All but 20 of the total number of 280 had been established by the end of 1954. One-third of the membership of all Councils is reserved for Councillors appointed by State or Stool Councils or by other 'chiefly' bodies; the rest are elected on a popular franchise, though a small number may be nominated to represent particular interests.[7] It was accepted as the normal rule that every Local Authority should have a Chief as its President; but except in the Northern Territories the post was to be only of ceremonial significance, the conduct of business being in the hands of an elected chairman. In the Gold Coast

[1] See above, p. 315. [2] See above, p. 319.
[3] *Report of the Commission of Enquiry into Disturbances in the Gold Coast*, Col. 231, 1948, pp. 25–28.
[4] *Report of the Committee on Constitutional Reform* (the Coussey Committee), Col. 248, 1949, pp. 21–32.
[5] S. Phillipson, *Gold Coast: Report of Regional Administrations*, 1951.
[6] Local Government Ordinance no. 29 of 1951, amended by nos. 16 and 17 of 1953, nos. 15, 29, and 38 of 1954.
[7] *Colonial Reports, Gold Coast, 1952*, pp. 108–10, 121–4; ibid. *1953*, p. 131. *Local Government Reform in outline*, Accra, 1951.

Colony the Paramount Chiefs are debarred from actual membership of the Councils.

It still remains to determine such matters as the precise function and powers of the Local and District Councils, the extent to which the Minister will delegate his statutory control to the Regional Officer and Government Agents (as the former Chief Commissioners and District Commissioners are now termed), and the exact position to be occupied by the former State Councils. The existing legislation restricts the latter to 'constitutional and customary matters', of which the most important are contested elections to Chiefdoms or destoolments. Government Agents are expressly debarred from intervention in these matters. It is significant that under this law the new Local Councils are responsible for the collection of revenues accruing from stool lands, which are to be divided between the Local Councils and the Stool Authorities in agreed proportions.[1] The latter may not dispose of stool lands without the concurrence of the Local Councils. The issues involved are of much local importance and were the subject of debate during the latter part of the year 1955.[2]

Native Courts

As regards the Native Courts, the Committee on Constitutional Reform of 1949 recommended that they should be dissociated from the Native Authorities.[3] A commission appointed in 1950 to deal with judicial administration recommended the creation of a system of 'Area' and 'District' Courts to be under the control of the Chief Justice. District Courts were to be presided over by professional justices, save in the Northern Territories, where District Magistrates forming part of the cadre of the Legal Department would be in charge of them. Area Courts would consist either of a stipendiary lay Justice or of two or three honorary Justices, who would generally be laymen; except in the Northern Territories, Chiefs should be barred from membership.[4] Here also it appears probable that the future will see a material departure from the previous type of Native Court, which, as has been shown, reproduced much of the traditional character of the State Council.

There has been a disposition in some quarters to describe the recent course of events in the Gold Coast as evidence of the failure of the Native Authority system. It would be more correct to say that they reflect the failure of the Gold Coast Government to realize in time the potentialities of that system and to put it into force. It is in particular difficult to excuse the omission of that Government to attempt an earlier reform of the

[1] Local Government Amendment Ordinance no. 35 of 1953.
[2] A. St. J. J. Hannigan, 'Local Government in the Gold Coast', *J.A.A.*, July 1955, p. 121.
[3] *Report of the Committee on Constitutional Reform*, Col. no. 248, 1949, pp. 32–33.
[4] *Gold Coast, Report of Commission on Native Courts* (the Korsah Commission), 1951.

administration of Native justice which it had itself admitted to be a matter of grave reproach.[1] There is no question of the determination shown by the present leaders of the Convention People's Party to deprive the Chiefs of any effective power in the political structure.[2] They have admittedly made a provision guaranteeing to all Paramount Chiefs a grant of a minimum of £50 a month from the Local Councils; but this appears to be a concession made on grounds of political expediency. It is significant that they have opposed the proposal for a Second Chamber, now favoured by the Ashanti Confederacy.[3]

It must be admitted that the conduct of the Chiefs themselves has contributed to the disfavour in which they stand with advanced political elements, for a considerable number of them have shown little interest in anything save the maintenance of their own privileges. Sooner or later, therefore, they would have had to face radical measures of reform which would have gravely affected their position, but it remains to be seen whether the new institutions of Local Government will prove a successful solution. It is a grave disadvantage that the Ministers who now regulate their course have themselves little direct experience of the working of such institutions, and that they can hope for little aid from a population which has itself had no knowledge of them.

BRITISH TOGOLAND

The circumstances which brought part of Togoland under the trusteeship of the United Kingdom have been described elsewhere, as also have the suggestions recently made for the constitutional future of this area if and when the Gold Coast attains a status of self-rule.[4] Reference has also been made to the views regarding closer association which have been put forward by the Ewe community in the areas at present under the trusteeship of the United Kingdom and France respectively.[5] The present paragraphs will therefore deal mainly with those activities of the Administration of British Togoland which affect the development of its Local Government institutions.

As has been explained, the British portion of the Trust area of Togoland is divided for administrative purposes into two sections. The northern section is treated as part of the Northern Territories of the Gold Coast; the southern was up to 1952 administered with the Eastern Province of the Gold Coast Colony. In that year effect was given to the proposals made by the Gold Coast Committee on Constitutional Reform[6] for the

---

[1] *N.A.*, Part III, p. 202.

[2] H. Cooper, 'The Gold Coast and Nigeria on the road to Self-Government', *Africa Today*, 1955, p. 308.   [3] See above, p. 321.

[4] *Gold Coast, Report by the Committee on Constitutional Reform* (the Coussey Report), 1949, pp. 42–44. *Gold Coast, the Government's Proposals for Constitutional Reform*, Accra, 1953, p. 9.

[5] See above, p. 322.   [6] Col. no. 248, 1949.

creation of a new Region consisting of the former southern section of Togoland together with the three Ewe-speaking areas of the Gold Coast Colony; the new Region is designated the Trans–Volta–Togoland Region.[1]

Under German rule the authority of Chiefs had been recognized in so far as they could be utilized by the Government, and they were authorized to maintain tribunals, though with severely restricted civil and criminal jurisdiction. During the period of British Mandatory rule different systems were introduced in the northern and southern sections, reflecting the difference in the procedure of local administration followed in the Northern Territories and the Colony Area of the Gold Coast. In the northern section the Native Authority, Native Courts, and Native Treasuries Ordinances of the Northern Territories were applied, but in practice more emphasis was laid on the executive authority of the Chiefs than on their judicial powers.

Chiefs are by local custom chosen from the members of certain 'chiefly' families and are selected by the Elders if there is more than one candidate, though it was only on appointment by the Governor that they became Native Authorities and presided over the Native Courts. The recognition thus accorded to them afforded them a greater security in the tenure of their office than tribal custom might otherwise have allowed, with the result that their rule became in some respects more authoritarian, though it was in practice subject to the control of the local Administrative Officers. Direct taxation was introduced at the same time as in the Northern Territories of the Gold Coast.[2]

In the southern section there was no indigenous organization comparable with that of the Fanti States in the Gold Coast, and under German rule any tendency shown by different groups to combine for political purposes was actively discouraged. In 1931, however, the Mandatory Authority decided to encourage the amalgamation of the independent Divisions (of which there were then no less than 69) in order to form 'States' of a size which would allow of the establishment of local rule on a more systematic basis. To this end those Chiefs who joined one or other of the amalgamations were granted authority to hold tribunals, whereas in other areas all cases continued to be dealt with by Administrative Officers or by District Magistrates. A Native Administration Ordinance was enacted in 1932 with special application to the southern section of Togoland. In its general form this resembled the Native Administration Ordinance of the Gold Coast Colony, but with a significant difference; it was based on the principle that the right of jurisdiction flows from the Crown and is not inherent in the Chiefs by virtue of their selection by the people. Sixty-seven tribunals were subsequently recognized under this Ordinance; an

[1] *Togoland under United Kingdom Trusteeship*, 1952, Col. no. 296, pp. iv–v, 29.
[2] See below, p. 667.

Order of 1933 prescribed that not less than three or more than seven members should form the bench.

Native Treasuries

The Gold Coast Treasuries Ordinance of 1939, providing for the compulsory establishment of Native Treasuries,[1] was made applicable to Southern Togoland, but the revised Native Authority Ordinance and Native Courts Ordinance of 1944[2] were not extended to it till 1949. The result of these provisions was briefly as follows. In 1951 there were seven Native Authorities (consisting of Chiefs and their Councils) in the southern section; there was also one Division (Anfoega) which was not included in the area of a Native Authority. The Native Authority Councils were in the main of traditional composition, but they included a non-traditional element, averaging as a rule one-third of the total number of members and embracing representatives of the 'stranger' communities.

The Councils had Finance Committees which were made up largely of the non-traditional members. In 1952-3 there were 14 Native Treasuries, with a total revenue of £124,378, but of this amount no less than £36,372 was derived from Government grants-in-aid.[3] The largest item of expenditure was on education, and the contributions to other social services were on a relatively small scale. Under the provisions of the revised Native Courts Ordinance a number of the existing tribunals had been amalgamated, the total being reduced to 22. No 'A' Court had been constituted; the 'B' Courts had a relatively low range of jurisdiction.

Reorganization of Local Government, 1951

The system of Local Government as constituted by the Ordinances of 1944 came under a radical reorganization as the result of the enactment of the Gold Coast Local Government Ordinance of 1951.[4] In Togoland its general effect was to replace the traditional element, so far as it was reflected in the existence of the Native Authorities, by representative institutions based on the system of popular election. These institutions were to take the form of a structure of District, Local, and Urban Councils as part of the new Regional organization. In the northern section one District Council and 14 Local Councils with jurisdiction wholly within the Trust Territory, and four District Councils and five Local Councils, with a jurisdiction lying partly within and partly without the Trust Territory, had been established by the end of 1952. In the southern section, 14 out of an eventual 15 Local Councils had been established, one of which has

[1] See above, p. 521.   [2] See above, p. 522.
[3] *Togoland under United Kingdom Trusteeship, 1951*, p. 19; ibid. *1952*, p. 180; ibid. *1953*, p. 126.   [4] See above, p. 527.

an area partly within and partly without the Territory. One Local Council and three District Councils were constituted in the following year.[1] No Urban Councils are at present contemplated.

As in the Gold Coast, one-third of the membership of the Councils is reserved for nomination by State Councils or other traditional bodies, and here also the District or Local Councils will have Chiefs as Presidents, though in the southern section their functions will be purely of a ceremonial nature. The State Councils established by local custom will continue in existence, but Ordinances enacted in 1952[2] made it clear that their activities were to be confined to 'customary and constitutional functions', including the settlement of questions regarding the succession and abdication of Chiefs. In the southern section the Local Councils will collect and take a share of the revenues from stool lands.

The Native Authority Ordinance of 1949 had provided for the creation of a Southern Togoland Council, but when the Trans–Volta–Togoland Region was constituted in 1952[3] provision was made for the establishment of a Regional Council, consisting of representatives elected by members of the District and Local Councils. One of the chief purposes of this Council was to provide the Ewe in the Gold Coast and in the Trust Territory with an opportunity for deliberating together on matters of common concern within the Region. The District and Local Councils, which have replaced the former Native Authority organization, are constituted as to two-thirds by representatives elected by universal adult suffrage. One-third is composed of representatives of traditional authorities. They are to be independent bodies, whose connexion with the Regional Council will lie mainly in the fact that they will provide an electorate for its membership.

SIERRA LEONE

There is a marked difference in the measure to which the development of the institutions of Local Government in the Colony and in the Protectorate areas respectively has engaged the attention of the Government of Sierra Leone. In the Colony area Freetown was constituted a Municipality with a City Council in 1893. In the Protectorate, which came under jurisdiction in 1895, it was not until 1932 that consideration was given to the establishment of an organized system of Native Administration. It will be necessary therefore to deal with the two areas separately.

Freetown Municipal Council

In the total population of the Colony area (124,657) as recorded in 1948 there were included 28,050 African-non-Natives. This is the community

---

[1] *West Africa*, 28 August 1954.

[2] The State Councils (Colony and Southern Togoland) Ordinance, the State Councils (Northern Territories) Ordinance, 1952.   [3] See above, p. 529.

usually described as Creoles or Sierra Leoneans; they are mainly the descendants of the liberated slaves who formed the major part of the population of the Colony as originally constituted.[1] They are a relatively well-educated community, of which 60 per cent. are resident in Freetown, and their political activity accounts for the establishment in 1893 of a Municipality and a Municipal Council with an elected majority composed almost entirely of members of their own community. The career of this body was, however, unfortunate, and as the result of the report made by a commission of inquiry[2] in 1926 the Council was replaced by a Board with an *ex officio* President and a majority of official Councillors. The justice of this decision long remained an outstanding issue of local politics, and Creole opinion pressed strongly for a return to a more representative form of institution. The elected unofficial majority was restored in 1948, together with the right to elect a Mayor.[3] The functions of the Council remain, however, of a limited range, since the services of education, health, and major communications are provided by the Government Departments. The income of the Municipality in 1952–3 was £94,778.

The Council is in practice the preserve of the Sierra Leonean community, and no specific provision has been made for the needs of the other African residents of Freetown, though they are far superior in number. A certain measure of authority was at one time given to the Headmen (Alimani) representing the members of 14 of the indigenous tribes of the Protectorate who are resident in Freetown, but in 1932 they lost such judicial powers as they then enjoyed,[4] and suffered otherwise in status. Though proposals have recently been made to appoint Ward Headmen on an elective basis, this solution has not been acceptable to the communities concerned, who prefer an organization of a traditional character. As a result the facilities provided for the indigenous Africans in Freetown are far inferior to those enjoyed by the Native community in many of the other urban centres of Africa.[5]

An outlying suburb of Freetown, the Sherbro Judicial District, was administered by a Board under the presidency of the District Commissioner till 1952, when the provisions of the Sherbro Urban District Council Ordinance[6] were put into effect. These provided for a Council of six elected, one nominated, and one *ex officio* member. In the Rural Areas of the Colony, 115 villages were at various times grouped in units for Local

[1] *N.A.*, Part III, pp. 284 ff.
[2] *Report of Commission of Enquiry into the Affairs of the Freetown Municipality*, 1926. See R. L. Buell, *The Native Problem in Africa*, vol. i, 1928, pp. 882–9.
[3] Ordinance no. 19 of 1947.
[4] Tribal Administration Colony Ordinance no. 48 of 1932.
[5] A. B. Matthews, *Report on Tribal Administration in Freetown*, Sessional Paper no. 4 of 1940. M. P. Banton, 'Tribal Headmen in Freetown', *J.A.A.*, July 1954, pp. 140 ff.
[6] Sherbro Urban District Council Ordinance no. 22 of 1950.

Government purposes,[1] but under a revised procedure introduced in 1949 there are now 28 Village Area Committees, each electing its representatives to one of six District Councils.[2] Each District Council elects a member to a Rural Area Council, of which the District Commissioner is the chairman. The Rural Area Council is empowered to impose a local rate, and the Village Committees to levy improvement cesses. Their activity is, however, on a very minor scale. The Rural Area Council had a revenue of £15,825, mainly provided by Government grants-in-aid. The system introduced in 1949 has so far failed to attract any active interest.

Native Administration in the Protectorate

In the Protectorate, as has been explained, the organization of a system of Native Administration first received considered attention in 1932. Previous Ordinances of 1896, 1901, and 1905 had imposed a hut tax,[3] but they had not gone farther than to lay down the general principle that local administration should be carried on through the Chiefs. There were at one time as many as 216 Chiefdoms, each headed by a Paramount Chief, with a Council of the form recognized by local custom. The Chiefs held Courts, the powers of which were subject only to the general prescription that they should not inflict any punishment involving death, mutilation, or grievous bodily harm.[4] The term Paramount is in Sierra Leone applied generally to all independent Chiefs[5] and is not limited, as in most other territories, to those Chiefs who have subordinate Chiefs under their control. The membership of the Councils depended in practice partly on selection by the Chief, but they were seldom a formally constituted body, and often consisted only of members of the Chief's family, increased on occasion by the attendance of Headmen interested in some issue of importance.

Administrative Reorganization, 1932–6

The reorganization effected during the years 1932–6 followed in general the procedure of the Native Authority legislation of Nigeria and Tanganyika, and was finally embodied in three Ordinances enacted in 1937, the Tribal Authorities (no. 8), Chiefdom Tax (no. 10), and Chiefdom Treasuries (no. 11). The Tribal Authority was defined as meaning the Paramount Chief, Chiefs, Councillors, and men of note as recognized by custom, if and when they were appointed by the Governor to act as Tribal Authority for any specified area. The Authority was held responsible for law and order and had rule-making powers, but it was not empowered to levy a local rate, nor was it held responsible for the collection of the

---

[1] N.A., Part III, pp. 291–2.   [2] Rural Area Ordinance no. 11 of 1949.
[3] For the hut tax, see below, p. 668.   [4] N.A., Part III, pp. 296–300, 311.
[5] Protectorate Ordinance no. 33 of 1901.

Government tax (house tax), this being retained, for no very obvious reason, as the separate function of Chiefs and Headmen. The Chiefdom Treasuries established under Ordinance no. 10 were financed from a 'Chiefdom tax' (this tax being held to represent the customary payments formerly made to the Chiefs) and from Government grants representing a varying proportion of the Chiefdom tax.[1]

The new organization was not introduced at once to all the Chiefdoms, for attention was directed in the first instance to an effort to reduce their number by amalgamation or similar means. By 1949 they had been reduced to 191, and by the end of 1955 to 144, but there still remain a number of Chiefdoms with small areas and resources. As the result of this progressive introduction of the Native Authority system the Chiefdoms fell into two categories, the 'reformed' and the 'unreformed' Chiefdoms. Those classed as 'reformed' (otherwise designated as 'Native Administrations') numbered 136 in 1946 and had increased to 141 in 1955.[2] The major point of difference between the two categories lies in the fact that as the 'unreformed' Chiefdoms have no Treasury, the Chiefs do not draw fixed salaries, but depend on the receipt of tribute or on the fines and fees of the Courts, nor do the people within their jurisdiction have the benefit of such services as are made available from the Treasuries of 'reformed' Chiefdoms. The total estimated revenue of the 'reformed' Treasuries for 1953 was £405,800. There seems to be no definite reason for the delay which occurred in making the Native Authority system applicable throughout the Protectorate.

There has not as yet been a general movement, such as characterized the Gold Coast, for the replacement of the traditional Native Administrations by electoral institutions. Measures were, however, taken in 1945 to give some unity to the Native Authority system by the creation of District Councils consisting of representatives from each Tribal Authority in the District. The District Councils are large bodies, which meet only at considerable intervals, and most of their work is done by their Standing Committees; they are mainly consultative, and though they have been responsible for certain works—such as the provision of roads—their finances have depended partly on grants made by the Government[3] and partly on sums voted by the local Chiefdom Treasuries. Their estimated total revenue for 1952 was £208,504, mainly derived from Government grants in various forms; the contribution of the Chiefdom Treasuries towards this total was only £31,684.

Their position has hitherto been unsatisfactory in another respect: they have had no power to raise revenue and have been responsible only for

---

[1] See below, p. 669.
[2] *Sierra Leone, Annual Report on the Administration of the Provinces for the Year 1955*, p. 17.
[3] Ordinance no. 17 of 1950.

making provision for capital works, not for their maintenance. The question of their future has been under debate for some years,[1] but it was decided in 1953 to legislate in order to enable them to raise a new District tax for their own purposes, and to take over control of primary education. In the political field they at present provide the agency for the nomination of a large part of the membership of the consultative body, the Protectorate Assembly, referred to in a previous chapter;[2] the representatives of the Councils comprised in this body number 24 out of a total official and unofficial membership of 40.

The revised Courts Ordinance which formed part of the reorganization effected in 1932[3] applies only in the 'reformed' Chiefdoms. There the Chiefs' Courts now consist normally of the Paramount Chief with three or four members of the Tribal Authority sitting in rotation.[4] There are, however, still vestiges of the former system, in so far that the members of the Courts, including the President, receive a percentage of the Court fees. Appeals from these Native Courts go to the District Commissioners in their administrative capacity and thence to the Supreme Court. In the 'unreformed' Chiefdoms sub-Chiefs and village Headmen may hold Courts, and fees and fines are distributed among the members.

The future of the system of Native Administration in the Protectorate has now become one of the issues in the debate on constitutional reform in the territory to which some reference has been made in a previous chapter.[5] In the past there has been little sign of political movement in the Protectorate area, and the recent emergence of the Sierra Leone People's Party (S.L.P.P.) is perhaps evidence rather of a growing feeling of resentment in the Protectorate against the political predominance of the Freetown Creoles than of the growth of a nationalist sentiment such as has been seen in other parts of West Africa.[6] So far as the problem of Native Administration is concerned, the Commission appointed in 1954 to consider the question of electoral reform confined itself to recommendations regarding the part to be played by Chiefs in the elections.

GAMBIA

There is not in Gambia the same disparity of conditions existing between the Colony and the Protectorate as has been described in the case of Sierra Leone. It is, however, convenient to deal with these areas

---

[1] H. W. Davidson, *Report on the Functions and Finances of District Councils in Sierra Leone*, 1953. O. H. Morris, *District Councils and the Davidson Proposals*, April 1953.

[2] See above, p. 326.

[3] Protectorate Courts Jurisdiction Ordinance no. 32 of 1932.

[4] *Colonial Reports, Sierra Leone, 1952*, p. 59.

[5] See above, p. 325.

[6] J. S. Coleman, 'The Emergence of African Political Parties', in *Africa Today*, 1955, p. 237.

separately. The problems of the Colony are almost entirely those which arise in connexion with two Local Government institutions, the Town Council of Bathurst and the adjacent Rural Authority of Kombo St. Mary; those of the Protectorate are created by the difficulty of making the normal use of traditional institutions in a society which has been so widely disorganized by the intermingling of tribal elements.

Bathurst Town Council

Bathurst, which was at one time administered by the Commissioner with a nominated advisory Town Council, was given in 1946 a Town Council under an *ex officio* chairman, but with an elected majority of members.[1] All the elected members are Africans. The Council has, however, a very limited range of functions, the major services of the town, including the provision of water, electricity, education, and hospitals, being supplied by the Government Departments. In the last census the town population was only a little over 21,000, and the opportunity for the exhibition of municipal activity is therefore small. There was a minor extension of the Council's activities in 1951, when certain parts of the sanitary services were handed over to it, but the change was not such as to make any noticeable difference in its status. Its revenue in 1953–4 was £32,400. The Kombo St. Mary Rural Authority takes an even lower rank as a Local Government body; it has an official chairman, and comprises 21 village representatives, who were originally nominated from among village Headmen but have since 1951 been elected.[2]

Local Rule in Protectorate Area

The Protectorate area, as already indicated, is marked by a great fusion of tribal elements, due to past internal conflicts and to the constant process of infiltration across the Gambia River. The most stable political unit that has survived is the 'yard', consisting sometimes of a village and sometimes of part of a village, and usually divided into 'quarters'. The greater part of the population is Muslim. Owing to the intermingling of tribal elements neither the four Administrative Divisions of the Protectorate nor the 35 'Districts' into which they are divided correspond to tribal or clan boundaries. Each 'District' is under a District Head or Head Chief (Seyfu).[3] A few of these belong to former 'kingly families', but the majority are senior Alkalolu or village Headmen who have been promoted to the ranks of the Seyfolu. There is usually a process of consultation with the village Heads of the area before any appointment of Seyfu is made, but there has been a growing tendency to regard the post as hereditary or confined to

[1] The Local Government (Bathurst) Ordinance, 1946.
[2] Kombo St. Mary Division Ordinance no. 15 of 1946.
[3] *N.A.*, Part III, pp. 335–40.

members of families of standing in their community. An Alkali is sometimes (as in the small 'wharf towns' along the Gambia River) selected by
the Administration for his personal qualifications, but otherwise the
Alkalolu represent selections made or confirmed by the 'yard heads' or
'quarter heads' in the villages.

The present organization of local rule dates from 1933,[1] when legislation
of that year introduced a system which was expressed as based on the
principles embodied in the Native Authority law of Tanganyika.[2] But
though this Ordinance provided formally for the creation of Native
Authorities who were authorized to maintain the peace and to issue Rules
for the welfare of the people, progress made in the working of the system
was in other respects slow. In 1944 and 1945, however, revised Ordinances
were enacted which made a material change, providing for the creation
of District Councils with the Seyfu as President, and having the power
to impose a Local Rate and to establish Treasuries.[3] The local rate (under
the name of the District tax) was to constitute an addition to the Government tax (the Yard tax), the collection of which had been one of the
functions of the District Heads.[4]

The District Councils are informally constituted, and consist as a rule
of a number of representatives of all the villages in the district, these being
normally the Alkalolu or persons deputizing for them. They are thus often
bodies of considerable size but of variable attendance. The total revenue
of the Councils for 1951–2 was £62,816.[5] The proportion expended on
salaries is high, but it is now laid down that it must not exceed 50 per cent.
of the total; the contribution made to local services is, however, still inconsiderable. The District Councils have in addition a function which it has
hitherto been unusual to attach to bodies of this character; they are
charged with the administration of African lands in their area, and are
thus responsible for the granting of leases both to Africans and non-
Africans.[6]

The unusual degree of tribal intermixture has created conditions which
have not been favourable to the normal operation of the Native Authority
system, and the procedure now in force will clearly require further adjustment before it succeeds in eliciting the general interest of the people. It
has not so far provided a basis for the formation of more advanced political
institutions. Divisional Councils, consisting of District Heads with three
or four representatives of their District Councils, meet two or three times

[1] Native Authority Ordinance no. 2 of 1933.
[2] *Political Memoranda for the Guidance of Commissioners and other Government Officers working in the Gambia Protectorate*, 1933.
[3] Native Authority (Amendment) Ordinance no. 19 of 1944.
[4] Protectorate Treasuries Ordinance no. 13 of 1945.
[5] *Colonial Reports, Gambia, 1950–1*, p. 50.
[6] Supplement to *J.A.A.*, October 1952, pp. 10–12; see also below, p. 741.

a year under the presidency of the Divisional Commissioner. Their functions are, however, purely advisory. Since 1944 a conference of all Head Chiefs in the Protectorate has also been held annually, and this would appear to have attained greater importance than the Divisional Councils.[1]

Native Tribunals

The present constitution of the Native Tribunals was laid down in 1933. It is noteworthy that they are explicitly empowered to administer Muslim law in matters concerning marriage or succession, in addition to the local customary law.[2] There are two grades of tribunals. The District Tribunal has criminal powers up to six months' imprisonment or £10 fine and civil jurisdiction up to £25; there is one such tribunal in each of the 35 Districts, with the District Head as President. The members of the Benches are not chosen on a tribal basis, and there seem in fact to be only three tribunals in which all members are of one tribe. The higher Court, the Group Tribunal, may impose sentences up to 12 months or a fine of £25; its civil jurisdiction extends to £50 suit value. No Native Tribunal may pass a sentence of corporal punishment on anyone over 16 years of age. There is no formal provision for appeal, but District Commissioners have wide powers of revision, and a monthly return of all criminal cases is made to the High Court. This operates as an appeal and thus brings into operation the revisional powers of the High Court.

Bathurst has no Native Court. Criminal cases are dealt with by the Bathurst Police Court or by the Magistrate or by the Justices of the Peace, these being both European and African; minor civil cases are dealt with by a 'Court of Requests' consisting of Justices of the Peace. There is a Muslim Court presided over by a Kadhi, which deals with civil cases between Muslims concerning such matters as marriage and succession.[3]

REVIEW OF THE NATIVE AUTHORITY SYSTEM

As the preceding pages show, the Native Authority system has during the first half of this century held the field as the procedure of local rule adopted by a large number of the British dependencies in Africa. That it is now being replaced in certain of those areas (and most notably in West Africa) by the establishment of elective Boards does not necessarily reflect a radical defect in the conception of the system; it is due to the changes in African society that have of late years brought to the front political elements which hold that traditional institutions can no longer be regarded

[1] *Colonial Reports, Gambia, 1950–1*, p. 50.
[2] Native Tribunals Ordinance no. 4 of 1933. J. N. D. Anderson, *Islamic Law in Africa*, 1954, p. 227.
[3] Mohammedan Law Recognition Ordinance, 1905. See Anderson, op. cit. p. 226.

as an adequate foundation on which to build up social and economic progress. As will be gathered, the distinctive feature of the Native Authority system did not lie merely in its use of the traditional authorities as subordinate agencies of rule, nor in their integration into the machinery of government. It lay in the endeavour to encourage them to utilize the influence derived from their traditional position as a means of promoting objects such as the maintenance of order, the administration of justice, or the provision of local services for the benefit of those who by custom fell within the range of their authority. It deliberately preferred that they should depend on the influence derived from this source rather than on the support they might receive from statutory enactment or from their connexion with the official machinery of government.

At the outset, the use of this procedure may have been dictated by considerations of expediency, but it speedily acquired the support of a philosophy which accorded fully with the British tendency to adopt an empirical rather than a theoretical approach to novel problems of administration. 'The British', said M. Sarraut in 1933, 'build day by day on what already exists; the French dream of new and rectilinear architectures.'[1] Given a genuine desire that the extension of jurisdiction should bring in its train the advantages following from the introduction of the social and political institutions of Western civilization, it was reasonable to hold that such a use of indigenous institutions would not only provide the readiest vehicle for this purpose, but would secure the most lasting results. The original authors of the system went farther. They felt that any other method might lead to the progressive disintegration of indigenous institutions, leaving the African a prey to the unsettlement which must inevitably follow from the undermining of his customary code of social behaviour.

In the circumstances this was a valid argument. A number of critics, both European and African, were at an early period gravely concerned with one possible source of weakness; the Native Authorities, the central figures in the indigenous institutions which it was intended to utilize, were usually conservative and were often reactionary, and as such they seemed likely to stand in the way of any form of progress. In practice, however, this has created less difficulty than the fact that in process of time the system came to demand from these Authorities a type of service which their experience ill fitted them to provide. They could without great difficulty adjust themselves to requirements such as the preservation of order or the administration of a simple form of justice. Here they were on not unfamiliar ground. But the conduct of Treasuries and the organization of social services were novel functions, so foreign to previous custom as to present to many of them obstacles which they found it difficult to surmount.

[1] Quoted in L. Mair, *Native Policies in Africa*, 1936, p. 189.

Here was the most obvious source of weakness. It did not lie in the refractory character of African custom, for though great value is attached in Africa to tradition in ritual or in religious observances, in many other matters custom is eminently flexible. A change that is acceptable on general grounds readily acquires the sanction of custom; the test is not the provenance of the change, but the measure of acceptance it can secure. In the customary law as administered by the Native Courts there are a number of observances of which the breach is, with general assent, punished as an offence against custom, though the observances are themselves of demonstrably recent origin. The flexibility of African custom and its readiness to adapt itself to a change of circumstances is especially noticeable in the field of political or administrative organization. It is mainly where change involves an open break with a ritual or religious tradition that any serious difficulty is apt to occur.

In a certain number of cases the Native Authorities have succeeded in surmounting the difficulty presented by the novelty of the duties laid on them. In others they have succeeded largely through the assistance afforded to them by their Administrative Officers. There are admittedly some in which the record has been one of failure.[1] But taking the position as a whole, it is not open to question that the use of the system has been justified by the results. It was from the first obvious that the official support given to the Chiefs, whether in the form of statutory sanctions or otherwise, must enhance the personal power previously enjoyed by them, even though safeguards might be adopted for preventing its misuse. But this has very seldom had the result of rendering them autocratic, for the Chief is in African custom dependent to a marked degree on the support of his 'councillors', and he has no machinery at his own disposal for enforcing decisions taken against their wishes. The sub-Chiefs and the Headmen who form his executives (if indeed that term is appropriate in this connexion) are seldom appointed by him; nearly everywhere they owe their position to inherited status or selection by the community of which they are in charge. It is literally true therefore that a Chief is, in the Tswana phrase already quoted, 'a Chief only by grace of his tribe'.[2]

The use of the Native Authority system has unquestionably made a great contribution to the maintenance of order and the administration of justice; in some of the more progressive areas it has made a useful contribution to the provision of local services; to numerous communities it has provided an education, not easy to secure by other means, in the practice of managing their own affairs in the changing conditions of modern Africa. To this extent it has materially assisted in preparing them to take part in the working of the new Local Government institutions indicated by the changed political outlook at the present day.

[1] *N.A.*, Part IV, pp. 36–45.   [2] See above, p. 542.

To this survey of the working of the system it is only necessary to add one consideration. It should be realized that the preservation of indigenous institutions (and in particular the Chiefdom) was never an end in itself. Save among a few enthusiasts, there has been in British Administrative circles a general acquiescence in the axiom attributed to Lord Cromer,[1] that it is a delusion to suppose that Native society can be reconstituted on an improved Native model. There is no evidence that there was ever a conscious effort to preserve Native institutions from change. Almost every advance achieved in the employment of the Native Authority system has in fact involved changes in the form of the indigenous institutions which were its instruments. It is not possible to forecast now the ultimate destiny of the Chiefdom as an institution, but it may well be that in some areas it will retain little more than a ceremonial or ritual significance in local society. If that should prove to be the case, there would be nothing in the result which would be alien to the spirit in which the system was first envisaged or subsequently employed.

It might seem reasonable to inquire why, if the system could ensure the benefits thus claimed for it, its use did not commend itself more widely to the Governments of other Colonial Powers? But such a question is in fact out of place. Colonial policy is, as has so often been said, the result of the projection into overseas areas of certain domestic characteristics and philosophies of life. It would have been as difficult for some other Colonial Administrations to operate to their satisfaction the Native Authority system adopted in the British dependencies as it would have been for the British to implement in their own areas the characteristic ideals of French or Portuguese rule.

THE FRENCH TERRITORIES

The observation made in the last paragraph is not without relevance to the study of the procedure of local rule adopted in the French territories. The day to day procedure of Native Administration adopted in different colonial territories would often seem to have been due less to any deliberate determination of policy than to the manner in which the official personnel of an Administration have sought to solve the problems that have formed their own immediate task. But the result must none the less have been influenced by their national philosophy or the traditions derived from their domestic history. That is conspicuously the case in respect of the procedure adopted in the French dependencies in West Africa. As will be seen, recent influences are now tending to diminish the difference between the British and French systems of local rule, but for

---

[1] F. Melland and C. Young, *African Dilemma*, 1937, pp. 16, 40.

many years they presented a notable contrast, due in large measure to a fundamental divergence in the approach adopted by the personnel of the two Administrations.

It was difficult for the French colonial officer to conceive of any better destiny for the African people than that they should absorb the culture and adopt the institutions of France, which had for him not a comparative but a positive value.[1] He showed therefore a natural preference for those methods of local rule which seemed most suited to serve that purpose. The British administrator is not less deeply attached to the culture and institutions of his own country, but he is not convinced that they are equally well suited to peoples of an origin and a tradition different from his own. He has at all events been more ready to admit of experiments which may reveal the institutions likely to be best adapted to local circumstances.

Again, the French official brought with him from his home country the well-established tradition of a centralized system which, though it might admit of the wide delegation of powers to a local institution such as the *commune*, never failed at the same time to predicate the existence of a central control. It is said that the most distinguished teacher in the *École Coloniale* from 1889 to 1932, M. Paul Dislère, used to insist that the primary object to be attained in the Colonies was the creation of real French Administrative Departments.[2] On the other hand, the central control now exercised over Local Government institutions in Great Britain is not a long-established principle, but is a relatively late innovation, which was alien to earlier British tradition.[3]

The Three 'Communes' of Senegal

The effect of these influences, of which the evidence is to be seen in many directions, is most typically illustrated by the use made of the Chiefdom as an agency in local rule. But before dealing with this aspect of Native Administration it is convenient to refer first to the exceptional situation existing in the three *Communes de plein exercice* of Senegal, for though their area is small, they have an important place in the history of French rule in West Africa. Their area corresponds roughly to that of the original French trading posts on the coast, and their Constitution had its origin in the decision of 1833 to grant to their population the same civil rights as were enjoyed by the citizens of metropolitan France.

Reference has been made in a previous chapter to the questions which have arisen in regard to the grant of the full rights of citizenship to the

[1] H. A. R. Gibb, 'Middle Eastern Perplexities', *International Affairs*, October 1945, p. 465.
[2] Quoted by R. Delavignette, *Freedom and Authority in French West Africa*, 1950, p. 50.
[3] H. Tinker, *The Foundations of Local Self-Government in India, Pakistan and Burma*, 1954, pp. x–xi.

originaires of these areas.[1] Here it is only necessary to note that the two *communes* of Saint Louis and Gorée were formally endowed with the institutions of local self-government in 1872, and that this measure was later extended to Dakar and Rufisque.[2] Their constitution corresponds therefore very closely with that of the *communes* of France, the mayor (who is the chief executive officer of the *commune*) being elected by the *conseil municipal*, which is itself elected on a popular franchise.[3] The majority of the members have been Africans and the elected mayor has normally been an African. Though, however, these *communes* have in principle a large measure of autonomy, the proceedings of the *conseil municipal* are in practice strictly controlled by the Administration. The urban organization of Dakar stands on a special footing, as the Government services (on which the city now largely depends) are controlled by an official Administrator, and the Port of Dakar, which is in charge of a special Commissioner, has its own budget and forms an important section of the city. In regard to the administration of justice, the population of the three *Communes de plein exercice* are subject to the jurisdiction of the French Courts, as distinct from that of the Native Courts.

The influence exercised by the introduction of this system was subsequently seen in the provision made in 1920 for the creation in the rest of French West Africa of *communes* of two types, the Native and the Mixed, but this development formed for some years a relatively minor feature in the system of Native Administration, and it is advisable to return here to the major feature of the picture, namely, the use made of indigenous institutions (and in particular the Chiefdoms) as executive agencies.

Chiefdoms as Agencies of Local Rule

At an early stage the French, like the British, made treaties with a number of major Chiefs; the occupation of Senegal, for example, is stated to have involved the making of as many as 130 treaties between 1785 and 1891. In compliance with the terms of these treaties the rural areas of Senegal were for a considerable period controlled much on the lines of a Protectorate, in contrast to the coastal towns, which were from the first treated as appropriate subjects for a system of direct rule.[4] But the original conception of a protectorate status changed with the growing demands for improvement in the standards of administration. It seemed to the French improper that when Chiefs were accused by their people of the misuse of power they should be able to shelter themselves behind official authority, and official authority reacted by reducing their status to that of subordinate

---

[1] See above, p. 338. See also R. L. Buell, *The Native Problem in Africa*, vol. i, 1928, pp. 946 ff.

[2] *Décrets* of 10 August 1872, 12 June 1880, 17 June 1887. The *communes* of Gorée and Dakar were amalgamated by *Décret* of 3 January 1946 (*Enc. A.O.F.*, vol. i, p. 252).

[3] B. Chapman, *Introduction to French Local Government*, 1953.

[4] Buell, op. cit. pp. 901 ff.

agents liable to an increasing measure of control. In some cases the Administration refused to appoint successors to former Paramount Chiefs, as for instance the Paramount Chief of the Allarda *cercle* of Dahomey, the Ardo of the Peuls (Fula) of Dagana, the Chief of the Wolof (Ouolof) in Ziguinchor, or the Bur of Sine. The administrative *cercles* were purposely constituted without regard to tribal boundaries, on the ground that any other course might encourage 'separatist traditions'.

There were three classes of Chiefs recognized; first, the *chefs de province* or *chefs supérieurs*,[1] the successors of the 'feudal' Chiefs of former times; second, the *chefs de canton*, who may be said to have been the creation of the Administration, at all events in the sense that the *canton* itself was an artificial unit created by it; and third, the *chefs de village*, or Chiefs assimilated to that status, such as Chiefs of independent divisions who had no *chef de canton* over them. Some indication of the numbers involved is given by the fact that in 1937 French West Africa had 52 *chefs de province*, 2,206 *chefs de canton* (including auxiliary Chiefs), and 48,049 *chefs de village*. As has been explained, the *chef de canton* was in some sense an administrative creation. The *chef de village*, however, was a real representative of the indigenous system, having the intrinsic authority derived from his customary status;[2] in the words used by Renan regarding the old Breton Chiefs, he was 'the keystone of the social structure of the people'.

It was perhaps in Senegal that the official status of these 'auxiliaries of the Administration' was most clearly marked. At one stage they were classified in 20 grades, within which they might be promoted or reduced. Though at an early period it had been usual to treat as *chefs* only those Chiefs who were so recognized by local custom, it became the practice to make appointments on qualifications such as army service or service as interpreter. It is significant that the Schools for Sons of Chiefs[3] became in time Schools for Sons of Chiefs and Interpreters, and the courses given there were described as 'designed to produce French civil servants'. The Chiefs received a rebate which might vary between $3\frac{1}{2}$ to 10 per cent. of the tax collected by them. In addition they had a salary varying according to grade; it was usually low, but in the case of an important Chief, such as the Mogho-Naba of Ouagadougou in the Mossi country, it might amount to 20,000 francs a year, a considerable sum in view of the purchasing power of the franc at that period.

There was, therefore, a system of what is generally, though not very accurately, described as 'direct rule'; the function of the Chief was simply to carry out the instructions of the *Commandant de cercle*, or those of the more immediate executive officer, the *chef de territoire*. In one sense the Chiefs formed a hierarchy, but the authority exercised by the *chef de canton* over

---

[1] In some instances referred to as *Chef d'état*.　　[2] Delavignette, op. cit. pp. 73, 77.
[3] See Buell, op. cit. vol. i, pp. 992–5.

the *chef de village* could only in a few instances have been based on a traditional relationship; its real nature was in fact that of authority exercised by
an official superior.

There arrived, however, a second phase, in which the Government
itself showed doubt whether the system had not overlooked forces inherent
in the African social system which might be used to greater advantage.
In 1909 the Governor-General W. Ponty expressed the view that more
regard should be paid to the *politique de races*. In 1917 M. van Vollenhoven
was more precise. It was useless to employ intermediaries who did not enjoy
the confidence of the Native population, and he held that greater reliance
should be placed on those Chiefs who owed their position to established
custom.[1] There was something of the same tenor in the admirable administrative instructions issued by a later Governor-General, M. Brévié;[2] he
emphasized the importance of popular consent in the appointment of
Chiefs and urged the introduction of a system of Councils to be associated
with Chiefs of all grades.

More recently still the late M. Éboué, as Governor-General of French
Equatorial Africa, insisted on the need to restore the prestige of traditional
political institutions.[3] Nowhere in the literature describing the British
Native Authority system is there any plea for the maintenance of indigenous
institutions more effective than that which is embodied in M. Éboué's circular of 8 November 1942 on Native Policy.[4] It is noteworthy that in 1951 a
statement was issued which showed that there were still some 30 tribes in
the French territories whose Chiefs could be regarded as the successors of
the powerful African rulers of the past.[5]

Though, however, there has been a tendency to see the merit of paying
fuller regard to the traditional institutions of African society, there has not
been in fact any such change in administrative policy as would result in
giving to Native Authorities the powers (and in particular the financial
powers) which they have exercised under the British Native Authority
system. There has been a constant reluctance to admit of anything that might
seem to trench on the executive supremacy of the Administration and its
officers. M. van Vollenhoven had himself insisted that there could not, as
he expressed it, be two authorities in the *cercle*, the French Authority and
the Native Authority; there was only one. 'The Native Chief never speaks
or acts in his own name, but always in the name of the *Commandant de Cercle*
and by express or tacit delegation from him.' The position of the Chiefs
has in fact remained that which has recently been summed up by M. Deschamps in the phrase 'les chefs gardaient leur autorité traditionnelle tout

[1] J. van Vollenhoven, *Une Âme de Chef*, 1920.
[2] J. Brévié, *La Politique et l'Administration Indigènes en A.O.F.*, 1931–5.
[3] See above, p. 211.
[4] *French Colonial Policy in Africa* (*Free France*, Special Issue no. 2), September 1944, pp. 17–26.
[5] Assemblée de l'Union Française, *Annexe au procès-verbal*, no. 275, 1951, pp. 18–19.

en devenant des fonctionnaires'.[1] M. Delavignette has added a characteristic expression of the modern French view of the position of the Chiefs. 'What is needed is not to re-establish them in a social structure that is dying, but to establish them in a modern Africa that is being born.'[2]

The status of the Chiefs has been regulated by a series of local *arrêtés* enacted from 1929 onwards in the different territories of West Africa, and in one enacted in 1936 in Equatorial Africa.[3] The principle that local opinion should be consulted before appointments are made was formally recognized in the Cameroons in 1928,[4] and in 1932 a model *arrêté* by M. Brévié laid down that *chefs de village* should be chosen by the heads of families by a majority vote. It was stated in 1951, however, that Chiefs are in practice nominated by the Governor from the customary families.[5] Villages are normally grouped into *cantons* under a *chef de canton*, though in a few cases, as for instance in the Yoko subdivision of the Cameroons, there are no Native Authorities superior to the *chefs de village*.

The village Chiefs are normally responsible for tax collection and receive the rebate referred to above; they are also formally responsible for the maintenance of order and the arrest of criminals. They are expected to organize measures to meet crises such as floods or the invasions of locusts, to arrange for the storage of food reserves and the upkeep of roads in their areas. The *chef de canton* keeps the register of taxpayers, and is the agent of the Government as regards military conscription. He allots the proportion of taxes, and formerly allotted that of *prestation* labour[6] between the constituent villages. The *chefs de canton* receive fixed salaries, since they are not responsible for tax collection. Up to 1946, when the distinction between 'citizen' and 'subject' status was abolished,[7] Chiefs were liable like other 'subjects' to the *régime de l'indigénat*; they are now subject to the disciplinary measures applicable to subordinate officials.

Native Councils and 'Communes'

A model *arrêté* circulated by M. Brévié[8] in 1932 was designed to give effect to his recommendation that each Chief should be assisted by an Advisory Council. The Village Council was to be constituted in accordance with local custom, but it should in principle consist of all heads of families; its proceedings were to be subject to the supervision of the *chef de*

[1] H. Deschamps, *Peuples et Nations d'Outre-Mer*, 1954, p. 167.
[2] Delavignette, op. cit. p. 81.
[3] Senegal, 4 May 1929, Mauretania, 20 August 1936; Sudan, 30 March 1935; Guinea, 15 November 1934; Ivory Coast, 10 October 1934; Dahomey, 10 November 1934 and 12 October 1935; Niger, 11 January 1936; A.E.F., 28 December 1936.
[4] H. Labouret, *Le Cameroun*, 1937, p. 20.
[5] *Assemblée de l'Union Française, annexe au procès-verbal*, no. 275, 1951, p. 16.
[6] See below, p. 671.   [7] See above, p. 338.
[8] Annex to *Circulaire générale*, no. 421, 28 September 1932.

canton. The *conseil de canton* was also to be constituted according to Native custom, but should in principle include all village Chiefs. This provision presupposed, however, a degree of political unity which has often been lacking in the *cantons* as they have been constituted. It is indeed open to doubt how far the system of Councils thus indicated has actually fulfilled any useful purpose; it is at all events clear that the proceedings of the *conseils de notables*, shortly to be described, have now far more influence than those of the *canton* Councils.

The *conseils de notables* are one of the fruits of the measures referred to above[1] as having been undertaken in 1920 with the design of extending the system of *communes* throughout the rural areas of French West Africa. A decree of 2 December 1920 provided for the creation of two types of *commune*, the Native and the Mixed. The former are described as *commissions de notables*; the actual membership of each is laid down in the instrument which creates it, but in principle it should conform to local custom. The members of the 'Mixed' *communes* are nominated by the Governor of the territory, irrespective of any question of traditional status.[2] Both types of *commune* have as president an Administrative Officer nominated by the Governor, who is called the 'administrator-mayor'.

A more recent decree of 26 November 1947 provided for the establishment of *communes de moyen exercice* in localities with resources from which they could be expected to derive adequate revenues. Their members are elected by universal suffrage, but they have a nominated official as mayor. The creation of Mixed *communes* in French Equatorial Africa was prescribed in a decree of 19 March 1921, and that of Native *communes* by a decree of 29 July 1942. Similar provisions were made for Togo by a decree of 6 November 1929, while in the French Cameroons a decree of 19 November 1947 provided for the creation of *communes* with either elected or nominated membership.

The establishment of these bodies has proceeded slowly,[3] though there has of recent years been a certain acceleration, which owes its inspiration partly to the demand put forward in the Territorial Assemblies[4] and the Assembly of the French Union for the development of some measure of Local Government on a representative basis. In 1953 there were in French West Africa (apart from the original *communes de plein exercice*) 16 Mixed *communes* of the first degree and 33 of the third degree, these being mainly elected urban bodies. In French Equatorial Africa there were seven *communes* of the first degree, all being nominated municipal bodies. There were

---

[1] See above, p. 544.

[2] In Algiers the system distinguishes the *communes mixtes* (in which wide powers are exercised by a French Administrator) and *communes de plein exercice* which have full municipal self-government. *The Times*, 10 and 11 November 1954.

[3] *Assemblée de l'Union Française, annexe au procès-verbal*, no. 275, 1951, p. 22.

[4] See above, p. 341.

six also in Togo. In the French Cameroons there were nine urban and twelve rural *communes*, the latter being elected. The *communes* derive their revenues from licences and fees, particularly market fees;[1] they may impose for local purposes a rate which is in effect an increase on the amount of certain taxes collected in the locality by the Territorial Government. They receive from the Territorial Government a proportion of all direct taxes levied by it in their area.

It is obvious that the creation of *communes* has for the most part been confined to the urban centres, and is only beginning to reach the rural areas. In these areas more importance attaches at present to the advisory *conseils de notables* above referred to.[2] These have for the most part a nominated membership.[3] In the territories of Niger, Sudan, and French Guinea a special *taxe de cercle*, additional to the personal tax levied throughout West Africa,[4] was introduced in 1950 and 1951, and its proceeds are allocated to the *cercle* for expenditure on local works. The *Commandant de Cercle* is advised on the disposal of this fund by a Council consisting of the local representatives on the Central Assembly of the territory, with an equal number of 'notables'.[5]

In Togo the Councils of notables have been replaced by *conseils de circonscription*, elected indirectly, with universal suffrage at the primary stage. These Councils elect their own President and Standing Committee. They must be consulted on all financial matters affecting their area; if they reject a proposal referred to them they may be asked to reconsider it; after a second rejection the Commissioner of the Republic decides the point at issue. There are some 140 of these Councils, covering the whole of Togoland outside the area of the Mixed *communes*.[6]

The *conseils de notables* would, however, seem to perform their most practical service by the part taken by them in the conduct of the *sociétés de prévoyance*, of which a fuller account is given in a subsequent chapter.[7] In a sense, they perform something of the same function as the Native Treasuries of those British territories which have adopted the Native Authority system, and they undoubtedly make a useful contribution to the needs of rural society. How far they are likely to continue in their present form is doubtful, for they have already come under attack by African political leaders as too obviously a part of the machinery of European administration.

[1] G. Gayet, 'Autonomies financières territoriales en A.O.F.', *Civilisations*, vol. iii, 1953, p. 345.

[2] See above, p. 548.

[3] A.O.F., *Décret*, 21 May 1919; A.E.F., *Décret*, 4 July 1936; Togo, *Décret*, 17 February 1922; French Cameroons, *Décret*, 7 July 1936.

[4] See below, p. 670.

[5] Sudan, *Arrêté*, 11 March 1950; Niger, *Arrêté*, 11 December 1950; French Guinea, *Arrêté*, 6 April 1951.

[6] *Rapport annuel à l'Assemblée Générale des Nations Unies sur l'administration du Togo, 1951*, pp. 339–42. See also ibid. *1952*, pp. 47 ff.   [7] See below, p. 1477.

Status of Native Authorities

In some of the more populous of the British dependencies in West Africa there has been (as has been shown) a growing pressure for the creation of Local Government institutions on an elective basis, in place of the traditional Native Authorities. In the French territories there does not appear to have been as yet an equally pronounced movement in this direction, partly perhaps because there has not yet arisen a middle class similar to that which has in the British territories led the movement against the grant of privilege to traditional authorities.

In the French territories neither the Chiefs nor their partisans among educated Africans appear to have suggested that they should play any other part than that of consultation with the officials responsible for the administration of their area. Their interest seems to have been directed mainly to securing a modification of the prevailing tendency to assimilate their status closely to that of civil servants. In 1947 the *chefs de canton* of French Guinea drew up a manifesto demanding a legal definition of their status and some guarantee of their future position as guardians of traditional custom.[1] A draft Bill was submitted to the Assembly of the French Union in 1949. The measure which it was finally agreed in 1953 to recommend to the National Assembly is described as 'dealing with the status of customary Chiefs who are auxiliaries of the Administration'.

It is concerned more with the clarification of their rights as Chiefs than with the statement of their functions. It provides that appointments of Chiefs should be made solely by the appropriate customary body, this being described as a Council which will examine candidates; its choice will be confirmed by a notice in the *Journal Officiel*. Chiefdoms are to be classed in suitable categories, and there will be an appropriate remuneration for Chiefs in each category. The sanctions to be applicable to Chiefs resemble those applicable to civil servants and appeals against their orders or complaints of their actions will go before a body analogous to the *conseil de contentieux* established for French officials.

THE BELGIAN CONGO

It is unnecessary to dwell at any length on the policy observed in regard to Native affairs during the 23 years of the régime of the Congo Free State, for in this as in many other matters there occurred a material change in policy when the Belgian Government took over the country in 1908. For the greater part of the Free State régime, policy was dominated by the demands of the State or of the *concessionnaire* companies for labour or for the collection of wild produce, and the record of the methods employed to

---

[1] *Assemblée de l'Union Française, annexe au procès-verbal*, no. 275, 1951, p. 2.

secure compliance with these demands provides a clearer indication of the character of the rule exercised over the African population than would be afforded by a recital of the enactments regulating the administrative procedure of the Free State.[1]

It is sufficient to explain that the part to be played by the indigenous Authorities was first recognized by the Free State in the measure which prescribed the limits within which Chiefs might exercise judicial functions. Cases between Africans which fell within the range of the customary law were to be dealt with by them, though if a case was also covered by statutory law the Chief could not deal with it unless the European authorities had referred it to him.[2] Such Africans as were employed at the outset as executive agents of the Administration were in many instances alien to the peoples over whom they were set and one of their major functions seems to have been the supervision of the collection of wild rubber.

In 1891, however, traditional Chiefs were formally confirmed in the exercise of their customary authority, and were made responsible for the execution of official orders for the supply of labour for public works or the delivery of the produce required from their subjects.[3] A circular Order of 18 April 1904 pointed out that recognition accorded by the Government not only affirmed the customary authority of the Chiefs, but made them 'delegates of the sovereign Power, in order to assure by means of the exercise of this authority the execution of Government orders'.[4] But there was in fact little chance of making this principle good without a change in the attitude of the Administration in other respects; it is at all events stated that the position it was sought to create for the Chiefs was so unpopular that a traditional Chief would often put forward a man of straw for Government recognition, while he himself continued to exercise his purely customary powers.[5]

Administrative Reforms, 1904–6

The Commission of Inquiry of 1904, whose report impelled the Free State Government to undertake a certain number of administrative reforms, emphasized the need for recognizing hereditary rather than 'artificial' Chiefs. It claimed that there would thus be created a body of authorities who, 'appuyés par l'État, formeraient une classe extrêmement utile, intéressée au maintien d'une ordre de choses qui consacre leur prestige et

[1] Buell, op. cit. vol. ii, pp. 426 ff. L. Mair, *Native Policies in Africa*, pp. 218 ff. G. Hostelet, *L'Œuvre Civilisatrice de la Belgique au Congo, de 1885 à 1953*, 1954, pp. 12, 13. R. Godding in *Colonial Administrations by European Powers*, 1947, p. 41.

[2] *Ordonnance*, 14 May 1886; *Décrets du Roi-Souverain*, 7 January 1886, 27 April 1889, 11 January 1891, 3 June 1906.

[3] *Décret*, 6 October 1891.   [4] *Arrêté*, 10 November 1894.

[5] A. Gille, 'La Politique Indigène du Congo Belge et du Ruanda-Urundi', *Enc. C.B.*, vol. iii, 1954, p. 712.

leur autorité'. A decree of 1906, which was designed to give effect to this recommendation,[1] indicated that Chiefs should be formally invested by the Government, and should receive a salary. The decree seems to have envisaged the formation of a regular organization of *chefferies indigènes*, since it laid down that all Natives should belong to a *chefferie*, and that any person who wished to leave his tribal area must have the express permission of his Chief.

A circular accompanying this decree energetically combated the prevalent view that the Chiefs could never acquire the necessary sense of responsibility. The destruction of the power of the Chiefs, it asserted, must lead to the disintegration of African communities and must leave the State face to face with a population emancipated from every social bond and without attachment to the land. More care must be taken to define the boundaries of Chiefdoms in accordance with tradition. The policy thus inaugurated has been described by a well-known authority on Belgian Colonial policy as 'le régime de l'administration indirecte, si atténué qu'il soit'.[2]

These recommendations seemed to point to the intention to adopt a procedure of the same character as that which had been inaugurated in the Northern Provinces of Nigeria, but conditions had already been created which seriously diminished the chance of an equal success in the Belgian Congo. The long series of internecine wars and the ravages of the slave trade which preceded the introduction of the Free State régime, no less than the attitude towards Native affairs which had characterized the earlier years of that régime, had resulted in the disintegration of most of the powerful Chiefdoms which at one time dominated large parts of the country. There still existed some Chiefdoms in the Kivu and Manyema regions and among the Nilotic groups in Ubangi, but elsewhere there were few vestiges of strong political organizations.

The earlier regulations enacted after the annexation of the Congo by the Belgian Government in 1908 were of much the same tenor as the legislation of 1906. The judicial competence of the Chiefs was now extended to cover certain minor criminal offences, though their power of punishment was limited to 15 days' imprisonment.[3] On the other hand, their authority was materially enhanced by the provision that Natives wishing to leave their own *chefferie* for more than 30 days were required to have a written *passeport de mutation*, which was to be issued by the *Administrateur de territoire* after consulting the local Chief. The *passeport* was inscribed on the *carte d'identité* maintained by Natives, and this system of official 'movement

[1] *Décret*, 3 June 1906; *Arrêté*, 16 August 1906.
[2] M. Halewyck de Heusch, 'Organisation Politique et Administrative des Colonies', *Bibliothèque Coloniale Internationale*, 1936, p. 37.
[3] For this period see official statement of policy in *J.A.A.*, April 1956, p. 88.

'control' became a feature of major importance in the administration of Native affairs.

The System of 'Secteurs'

In the period immediately following the enactment of the decree of 1910 a large number of Chiefs were formally recognized, but in spite of the policy as announced in 1906 they included a number who had no traditional claim to an independent status.[1] The number of *chefferies* increased from 1,068 in the year 1909 to no less than 6,095 in 1917, but many of these were small; some indeed had fewer than 50 taxpayers. A movement in favour of their reduction to a more manageable number was initiated as part of the administrative reforms inagurated by M. Louis Franck as Minister for the Colonies in 1920. He recommended the grouping of small units into *secteurs* controlled by a Council representing all the traditional authorities in the area, one authority being selected from among them for appointment as Chief of the *secteur*. There should on an average be three to five *secteurs* in an administrative district; the *secteur* headquarters should also be the site of the Native Court, and of the school or dispensary, or any similar institution.

There was thus initiated a process of reorganization which continued to exercise an influence over the procedure of Native Administration for some 30 years. During this period, however, a new factor was introduced into the structure of African society by the gradual movement of population from rural to urban areas, a factor which was to be intensified by the Second World War and the period of industrial activity that followed it. It is this movement which has been responsible for the creation of the *centres extra-coutumiers*, an interesting development in the Belgian system of administration which will be subsequently described.[2]

In one sense the creation of the system of *secteurs* may be said to correspond with the movement in many of the British territories—and particularly in Tanganyika[3]—which resulted in the federation of a considerable number of the smaller Chiefdoms.[4] But the procedure adopted in the Belgian Congo was less flexible, nor does it seem to have been inspired by an equal faith in the potential virtue of traditional institutions as agencies for the development of African society. Be that as it may, the procedure for the formation of *secteurs* was consistently pursued, and the annual report of 1951 stated that in this respect the political reorganization was virtually complete.[5] In 1938 there had been 1,212 *chefferies* and 340 *secteurs*; in 1953 there were 460 *chefferies* and 519 *secteurs*. The evolution in the Eastern

---

[1] Gille, op. cit. p. 716.
[2] See below, p. 555.   [3] See above, p. 473.
[4] G. Malengreau, 'Political Evolution in the Belgian Congo', *J.A.A.*, October 1954, pp. 161 ff.
[5] *Rapport sur l'administration de la Colonie du Congo Belge, 1951*, pp. 84 ff.

Province and in the north of the Kivu Province had been less rapid than in the Provinces of Leopoldville, Equator, or Kasaï, where the breakdown of traditional institutions was far advanced.[1]

Formal recognition of the *secteur* as an administrative unit had been given in a decree of 8 December 1933, which for the first time authorized Chiefs to issue Orders for the protection of public health and the maintenance of order. Every *chefferie* or *secteur* had now a 'Council of *Notables*' whom the Chief as head of the *chefferie* or the *secteur* was required to consult in such matters as finance. In the *chefferies* these Councils are composed of heads of kinship groups; in the *secteurs* they are composed of the Chiefs of the constituent units, the members of *secteur* tribunals and other persons nominated by the *Commissaire de District*. He himself is entitled to preside at their meetings. The salary of Chiefs is composed of a basic rate which varies with the size of the *chefferie* or *secteur*, and a bonus on tax collected, which again varies according to the classification of their merits as 'mediocre', 'good', or 'very good'.

Native Treasuries

Up to a certain point therefore the system has developed on lines that bear some resemblance to those followed in the procedure of the Native Authority system in the British territories. As is now the prevailing practice in those territories, the Chief is a 'Chief in Council'. There has been created in addition a further point of resemblance. Since 1933 the Belgian Congo has adopted the system of Native Treasuries, in the form of *caisses de circonscription,* the term *circonscription* being the general term denoting a unit of Native Administration, thus including both *chefferies* and *secteurs*.[2] The customary revenues of Chiefs, if the *Commissaire de district* so directs, are paid into these Treasuries; in return, the Chief receives an emolument for which provision is made in the budget of the Treasury. The main income of the Treasuries is derived from a supplement to the poll tax which may amount up to 20 per cent., the rate being fixed for each district after consultation with the Councils of *notables*. In 1951 the addition made to the poll tax accounted for 22 per cent. of the total income of the Treasuries. Other resources include local levies, rents of land, market dues, and Court fees and fines.

From the year 1953 special Controllers of Native Treasuries have been appointed to supervise their working. Their total revenue amounted in 1952 to a sum of 717 million francs.[3] In 1951 a high proportion of expenditure—26 per cent.—was devoted to road construction and maintenance; other objects were the purchase of implements, the provision and control

---

[1] Malengreau, op. cit. p. 164.
[2] *Rapport sur l'administration de la Colonie du Congo Belge, 1952*, p. 86.
[3] Ibid. *1952*, p. 92.

of markets, and subsidies to educational and medical work carried on by voluntary bodies.[1] The budget is drawn up under the supervision of the *Administrateur de territoire*, who usually keeps the accounts; the Administration has power to insist on expenditure which is considered necessary. Unpaid labour for works designed for purely local welfare has been made available through the obligation imposed on all able-bodied males of giving up to 60 days unpaid labour in a year for work of public importance. Each year's programme is drawn up in advance by the *Commissaire de province*, with a view to ensuring that the limit of 60 days' work is not exceeded. For work on main roads labour can be called up, but wages must be paid by the Central Government.

A large number of Chiefs and members of their Councils appear to be illiterate. This has been described as a cause of great difficulty in the local administration of many areas,[2] and it is clear that for this and similar reasons there has been a tendency on the part of many Administrative Officers to disregard the existence of the purely traditional Chiefs as possible auxiliaries in the work of Local Government. As has already been explained, in the Belgian Congo the emphasis has from the first been laid on the increase of production rather than on the achievement of political advance.[3]

In a series of discussions on the means to be adopted for furthering political advance which were sponsored by the Colonial University of Antwerp, it was held that the measure which promised most success lay in the development of the Councils of the Chiefdoms. Some authorities suggested that their members should be elected; others that they should be given rule-making powers. It is, however, noteworthy that the feeling prevailed that they could not for some time be given any financial responsibility. There was a general consensus on the need for education of the Chiefs.[4] It has also been suggested that the whole personal tax should be credited to the Native Treasuries, and that such of the revenues of the *Fonds du bien-être indigène* as are allocated for local works should be paid to them. Schools for the training of Court clerks and treasurers were opened at a number of centres in 1952.[5]

The 'centres extra-coutumiers'

Mention has already been made of a characteristic institution of Native Administration in the Belgian Congo, namely, the *centre extra-coutumier*.[6]

[1] Ibid. *1951*, p. 89. [2] Ibid. *1949*, p. 90.

[3] See above, p. 216. See also G. Malengreau, 'La formation politique des Indigènes', *Problèmes d'Afrique Centrale*, no. 14, 1951, p. 86; idem, 'Political Evolution in the Belgian Congo', *J.A.A.*, October 1954, p. 163.

[4] A. Sohier, G. Moulaert, G. van der Kerken, P. Coppens, F. Nisot, H. Depage, G. Malengreau, J. M. Habig, 'La Formation politique des indigènes congolais', in *Problèmes d'Afrique Centrale*, 1951, pp. 132, 135, 169, 185, 260, 289, and 1952, pp. 11–23, 92–101.

[5] *Rapport sur l'administration de la Colonie du Congo Belge, 1952*, p. 86. [6] See above, p. 222.

This indeed at one time appeared likely to become of increasing importance with the growth of industry and the tendency to the formation of urban communities. The *centre extra-coutumier* was originally introduced in 1931 in order to provide for the needs of populations of mixed tribal origin in the neighbourhood of centres of employment.[1] In the *centre*, the local authority is a Chief appointed for two years, with a Council of from five to twelve persons. The judges of the Native tribunal are *ex officio* members of the Council, the other members being nominated from residents in the *centre* by the *commissaire de district*. It is laid down that he must take into account both their personal qualifications and the wishes of the inhabitants. The Chief and sub-Chief must be chosen from the Councillors and by preference from those judges of the Native Tribunal who are members of the Council; there is provision for the appointment of an official as Chief if no agreement can be reached on a suitable African.

The constitution of the *centre* is therefore non-traditional, and in fact resembles to some extent that of the 'mixed' *commune* in French West Africa. The Chief is responsible for the maintenance of order, and with the Council may make Rules on all matters of local interest not regulated by general legislation; he may impose a penalty of seven days' imprisonment for offences against them. The Council may levy taxes for local purposes. As an example of these sources of revenue, the Stanleyville *centre extra-coutumier* may be quoted where, in addition to the supplementary tax normally levied by the Native Authorities, there are taxes on plots of land allotted by the Council, on shops, and on palm wine, and a hut tax is levied on unmarried women. The constitution of the *centres* provides that they may receive subsidies from general revenue, but these do not make a significant contribution to their resources; in 1951, for example, they amounted to less than 1 per cent. of the receipts of the *centre* Treasuries. Their total receipts amounted in 1952 to 90 million francs.[2]

All *centres* in a Province are subject to the supervision of a *comité protecteur* nominated by the Governor-General and consisting of official and unofficial Europeans; it is required to supervise the moral and social conditions of the inhabitants. The local *agent territorial* attends all meetings of the Council of the *centre* and may preside; he may veto their proceedings; he also advises the Council on the recommendations made by the *comité protecteur*. It is evident that in practice he exerts an influence which differs little from control.

As has been explained, the system was introduced in 1931, and 21 *centres* had been set up by 1935. It might have been expected that with the

---

[1] *Décret*, 23 November 1931, amended by *décrets*, 6 and 22 June 1934, 20 January 1939, *ordonnance-loi*, 17 April 1942, *décret*, 16 October 1942, *ordonnances-lois*, 20 July 1945, 11 February 1947, October 1947, *décret*, 28 March 1949.

[2] *Rapport sur l'administration du Congo Belge, 1952*, p. 94. See also *J.A.A.*, April 1956, p. 92.

general development of urbanization the number would increase rapidly. But by 1952 it had only risen to 35 with a population of 431,261 in all.[1] It was stated in that year that the delay in the creation of new *centres* was due to the difficulty of finding Africans capable of exercising the functions of Chief or of acting effectively as members of a *conseil*.[2] Meantime, however, urban populations were increasing at a rate which was accelerated during the Second World War. It has been estimated that in 1938 Africans living outside the 'traditional' areas amounted to 8·33 per cent. of the whole; in 1946 the number was estimated as 14·9 per cent.; in 1953 at 20·57 per cent., or roughly 37 per cent. of the adult male population. The need to bring the African population in the larger *centres* under a suitable form of control led to the enactment of the *ordonnance législative* of 20 July 1945, which empowered the Governor of a Province to declare any such population to be a *cité indigène*.

The type of administration applied to the *cité indigène* is itself significant. There was a period when outside attention was much attracted to the *centres extra-coutumiers* as a possible solution of the problem of a suitable form of administration for Africans who were passing out of their traditional surroundings. But Belgians themselves now seem to have lost faith in this type of organization, and the *cité indigène* has been brought under a form of direct official rule. There were ten such *cités* in 1952. They had a total population of 259,248; but the great majority were in Leopoldville, which had a total population of 244,152. The residence of Africans in a *cité indigène* is controlled by a permit system, and an unemployed person may have his permit withdrawn. The *cité* at Leopoldville is controlled by an Administrative Officer, with African Assistants; he has a small Advisory Council, but it is a nominated not an elected body. It is divided into quarters, each under a Chief whose position is that of a subordinate agent of the Administration. There is a Native Tribunal of three judges nominated by the *Commissaire de district*; they are usually taken from the three tribes most strongly represented in the population. Three of the towns (Leopoldville, Elizabethville, and Jadotville) have a special status as *villes*, referred to later in this chapter.[3]

RUANDA URUNDI

In the Trust Territory of Ruanda Urundi the Belgian Government has adopted a pattern of Native Administration similar to that evolved by it in the Belgian Congo. There are, however, some points of difference, particularly those arising from the survival of the representatives of the two Tutsi (Watutsi) Kingdoms in Ruanda Urundi. While events to which

[1] This included large centres such as Leopoldville, Stanleyville and Elisabethville.
[2] G. Malengreau in *Compte Rendu des Journées Interuniversitaires d'Études Coloniales*, 1952, p. 28. See also *J.A.A.*, April 1956, p. 93.   [3] See below, p. 584.

previous reference has been made had resulted in the disintegration of most of the former great Chiefdoms in the Belgian Congo,[1] these two kingdoms had continued in existence, and the Germans had recognized the authority exercised by the Mwami of Ruanda and the Mwami of Urundi, to whom they gave the designation of 'sultans'.

The Watutsi, probably of Nilotic origin,[2] occupied as a conquering tribe a position not unlike that of the Hima in Uganda. By tradition they arrived from the north-east some 500 years back and were then a pastoral people, with a prevailing cult of their long-horned cattle. They appear to have intermingled less with the Bantu (Bahutu) than the Hima have done in Uganda, and have retained in greater measure their physical character-istics of an exceptionally tall and slender people, of marked intelligence, and of an aristocratic social constitution. The cult of the cattle is reflected in the persistence of the usage (known as *ubuhake* in Ruanda and as *ubuga-bire* in Urundi) by which the owner of cattle hands them over to a caretaker, who as a consequence stands in a general relation of vassalage or even personal servitude to the owner (*shebuja*). A large part of the country seems to be covered by the prevalence of this contractual relationship,[3] the effect of which is the more marked because the Bahutu have not an alternative occupation, such as the cultivation of cotton which has now made so important an addition to the economy of Uganda.

In the days of the German occupation, the Mwami of Ruanda was a quasi-feudal ruler of a State organized on something of the same pattern as the Hima States in Uganda;[4] the Mwami of Urundi, though the head of a State which had not an equal element of centralization, was treated in the same way as the Mwami of Ruanda by the Germans, and the practice has been continued by the Belgians. Under the Mandatory Administration these two Bami[5] were placed in a position to exercise their traditional authority, subject to instructions conveyed to them through the medium of Residents acting as their Advisers. Subordinate Chiefs have been appointed by the Mwami with the approval of the Resident, the policy pursued being to combine small units wherever possible. Cus-tomary tributes have been maintained, but were made commutable for cash in 1931, and a decree of 19 July 1952 made the substitution of a cash payment obligatory. It empowered the Mwami in Council to fix the amount of the emoluments of Chiefs; this varied in 1951 from 1,000 to 1,200 francs a month; plus a sum of three francs for each tax collected.[6]

---

[1] See above, p. 552.

[2] *Enc. C.B.* vol. i, p. 190. J. J. Maquet, 'Le Problème de la domination tuse', *Zaïre*, October 1952, pp. 1011–16.

[3] *Bulletin of the United Nations Organization*, vol. xvi, no. 7, April 1954.

[4] See above, p. 479.   [5] Plural of Mwami.

[6] *Rapport soumis par le Gouvernement Belge a l'Assemblée Générale des Nations Unies au sujet de l'ad-ministration du Ruanda-Urundi, 1951*, p. 61.

There were in 1952 a total number of 89 Chiefs and 1,127 sub-Chiefs. Though there has been a tendency to recognize hereditary rights in the appointment of Chiefs, there has nevertheless been a process of selection in which education is now taken into account. The Chiefs are not taken entirely from the Watutsi ruling class; there have been cases where the Bami have appointed members of the Bahutu on account of their special qualifications.[1] The duties of the Chiefs were defined by an Ordinance of 4 October 1943 in the same terms as apply in the Belgian Congo. Every Chief has a Council and a separate Treasury for each *chefferie* was established in 1951, the Councils being required to decide on the amount of the local addition to the head tax and to approve the budget. The total revenue of all the *circonscriptions indigènes* amounted in 1953 to 261 million francs. At the outset African treasurers were appointed after being given a short training in accounting, but at the end of the first year's trial it was reported that the entire responsibility for the Treasuries still rested with the Administrative Officers.[2]

An effort has been made to secure a greater measure of efficiency in the conduct of the *chefferies* by the introduction of an elected element into the Councils.[3] At the lowest level, that of the *souschefferie*, a list of *notables*, including at least twice as many as are to be elected, is drawn up by the sub-Chief after some form of popular consultation, and is approved by the Administrator of the district. This body elects the Councillors from among its members. The *conseils de territoire* are composed of all Chiefs in the area, with an equal number of members of the subordinate Councils. The Mwami has a Council (*conseil du pays*) consisting of the elected presidents of District Councils, six Chiefs elected by the whole body of Chiefs, and one elected member from each District Council. These members co-opt four persons having knowledge of social and economic problems in the country, and four Africans who are either *immatriculés* or hold the *Carte du Mérite Civique*.[4]

The Mwami and Chiefs are now formally authorized to appoint an administrative staff. They are also empowered, with the consent of their Councils, to make Rules (*arrêtés*) and Orders which have the force of law; these Rules may also modify Native custom. The right to impose compulsory labour[5] for educational cultivation or for *travaux collectifs* is now delegated to the Mwami in Council, but the maximum period is reduced to 40 days, and the obligation may be commuted for a cash payment. The lower authorities also have power to compel labour to work up to 15 days in a year for the upkeep of certain buildings for which they are made responsible. The Mwami's Council has a Standing Committee of five, three

[1] *Rapport sur l'administration belge du Ruanda-Urundi, 1952*, pp. 18 ff.
[2] Ibid. *1951*, p. 24.   [3] *Décret*, 14 July 1952.
[4] See above, p. 224.   [5] See below, p. 1370.

of whom are elected by the Council and the other two nominated by him; the Committee is responsible for preparing the budget estimates, and also examines the records of lower Councils and reports on them to the full *conseil du pays*.

In some respects, therefore, the position of the Councils is in advance of that of the *secteur* and *chefferie* Councils in the Belgian Congo. There has been little activity shown in the Trust Territory in respect of the creation of *centres extra-coutumiers*; there were in 1953 only four. The *Ordonnance* of 20 July 1945 has been applied to the Trust Territory and as a result five relatively small urban communities have been placed in the category of *cités indigènes*.[1]

A GENERAL NOTE ON THE BELGIAN TERRITORIES

It has been observed that in some of the British dependencies and in those of French West Africa the procedure of Native Administration is now in a stage of transition. That is also the position in the Belgian Congo and Ruanda Urundi, but the circumstances differ. In the British and French territories the pressure for change has come largely from popular, or, to be more precise, from political sources. In the Belgian territories it proceeds mainly from official dissatisfaction with the quality of unofficial personnel available for undertaking the conduct of services in the sphere of Local Government. The Administration may in the circumstances defer further change until its educational activity has produced a more reliable form of African unofficial agency. But this may prove a lengthy process, and it seems more likely that it may prefer to train a purely official agency, mainly manned by Africans, to replace such of the indigenous unofficial agencies (whether traditional or otherwise) as it has hitherto employed.

It has been pertinently observed that traditional institutions cannot be re-created but that traditional attitudes of mind must be respected.[2] The Belgians can claim that though they have not relied to the same extent as the British on the use of indigenous institutions as part of the machinery of government, they have made a more consistent effort than the French to turn them to good account. If they have now to make use of a procedure which assigns to these institutions a lower place in the system of rule, it is largely because they have found that they are inadequate as organs of Local Government. It will be recalled that there has been much in the history of some of the British territories (as for example in that of Tanganyika)[3] which reflects a somewhat similar experience.

The preceding account admittedly deals rather with the machinery of Native Administration than with the spirit in which it is conducted. It is

[1] See above, p. 557.
[2] G. Malengreau, 'Political Evolution in the Belgian Congo', *J.A.A.*, October 1954, p. 160.
[3] See above, p. 472.

usual to speak of the Belgian system as 'paternalistic', though the word has a connotation for Belgians which differs from that given to it by those who are critical of their attitude towards African advance in the political field. It is more correct to say that the Belgian Government has purposely postponed a decision on the question of political concessions until it has made further progress with the economic and social developments affecting Africans which have hitherto monopolized its attention. That is a logical policy, when carried out with goodwill and sincerity.

At the same time, one may sometimes doubt whether the Belgian Government shows itself sufficiently alive to the fact that in Africa no policy can be pursued in isolation; the efforts of the most well-intentioned Administration are liable to be overtaken by the force of African opinion in other territories. In the British and French territories political developments are proceeding along a road that is at least recognizable, and even familiar, though it is true that its end lies below the horizon, and there may be many surprises still awaiting both the Governments and the people concerned. But in the Belgian territories neither the Government nor the European community nor the African people seem as yet to have any clear conception of the direction along which they intend to move. It is not, for instance, sufficient for the Government to give a half-hearted reception to a few educated Africans in the upper range of its political institutions, while attempting to satisfy other advanced elements by a superficial concession such as that of the *Carte du Mérite Civique*.[1]

At the same time there can be no question of the goodwill shown by Belgium in the promotion of the services designed for African welfare. It is true that no great importance attaches now to the institution which the Colonial Charter of 1908 provided as a safeguard for African welfare, the *Commission pour la Protection des Indigènes*,[2] which was to meet annually, but had no executive authority. There is, however, a definite indication of the interest in African social welfare to be seen in the creation of the numerous institutions for assistance to Africans, of the type of the *Foréami* or the *Fomulac*,[3] directly operating from Belgium itself.

It is noteworthy also that soon after the end of the Second World War there was inaugurated a Fund for the betterment of Native conditions, the *Fonds du bien-être indigène* (F.B.E.I.), referred to later,[4] which has a capital of a little more than 2,000 million francs.[5] Of this 1,780 million francs was paid from the Belgian Treasury as compensation for the extraordinary expenditure borne by the Belgian Congo while Belgium was under German occupation; 100 million was a free gift from Belgium; and 220 million represented the profits of the Colonial Lottery, all subsequent profits of

---

[1] W. Ugeux, in *Africa Today*, 1955, p. 360.   [2] See above, p. 347.
[3] See below, p. 1091.   [4] See below, p. 1340.
[5] *Arrêté*, 1 July 1947. *Codes et Lois du Congo Belge*, 1953, pp. 770-1.

which have also been paid into the Fund. It is controlled by an autonomous Board, which has interpreted its wide terms of reference so as to concentrate on 'the struggle against poverty, sickness and ignorance'. Since its inception the Fund has expended rather over 1,696 million francs, of which 775 million have been devoted to medico-social activity among Africans, 219 million to water supply, and 313 to education. Three areas, the Kasongo and Befale districts in the Bas Congo and one district of Urundi, have been selected for intensive assistance in the first instance. Reference will be made elsewhere to the progress of the scheme for peasant settlement,[1] and to the large grants made for Native housing in the *cités indigènes*.[2]

THE PORTUGUESE TERRITORIES

In dealing with the system of administration of African Affairs in the Portuguese overseas territories it is well to recall one relevant fact in the history of their acquisition. In Africa and in the far East, Portugal did not set out to colonize in the sense in which that term could be used in regard to some other Colonial powers. She established trading stations either in islands or at points on the coast, and did not at the outset seek to exercise any jurisdiction over the interior. Her real colonizing effort was directed towards Brazil. It was only after Brazil had won its independence that Portugal sought to establish effective control over the African hinterland, being compelled to do this when effective occupation was held internationally to be a legal qualification for the recognition of sovereignty.[3] This fact helps to explain the apparent inconsistency between the conception of the integration of all Portuguese subjects overseas with metropolitan Portugal and the fact that the law regulating the status of the inhabitants of the overseas territories differentiates between two legal entities, the Portuguese Citizen and the Portuguese Native.[4] The Portuguese Citizens include of course those *civilizados* who have achieved the full status of citizenship; the Portuguese Natives comprise all the inhabitants of the territory who have not reached that status.[5] To the Portuguese there is no real inconsistency here, since they conceive of Portuguese Natives as being in the position of minors who may become full citizens of Portugal when they reach the cultural maturity which entitles them to that standing.

From the legal and juridical standpoint the difference lies mainly in the fact that for the purposes of the civil law the affairs of Portuguese Natives are regulated by custom and customary law, in so far as this is not incompatible with the standards of humanity and public morality. For admini-

---

[1] See below, p. 799.   [2] See below, p. 585.

[3] *The Times Portugal Supplement*, 25 October 1955.

[4] The Law of the Constitution, no. 2048 of 11 June 1951. The Organic Law of Overseas Portugal, no. 2066 of 26 June 1953. *Decreto Lei*, no. 39666 of 20 May 1954. *Estatuto dos Indígenas Portugueses das Provincias da Guiné, Angola e Moçambique*, 20 May 1954.

[5] See above, p. 231.

strative purposes, they fall under the control of the Native Authorities, subject to the overriding authority of the Administrative Officers of the Government. In the matter of labour Portuguese Natives come under a special régime, namely the Labour Code, which regulates the conditions of the labour contract. In regard to rights over land, their rights and tenures are regulated by the customary law and not by the 'common law'.[1] The Native as such has no direct representation in the legislative organs of Government. Until he arrives at the full status of citizen he is compelled to carry the identification book, *caderneta*, to which reference has been made in a succeeding chapter,[2] and to be prepared to exhibit it on demand. He cannot move from one locality to another unless he obtains an authorization, which is duly entered in his identification book.

The Portuguese overseas Province is divided into a number of areas (*circunscrição*), which may be compared with the French *cercle*. Each such area is controlled by an *Administrador* directly responsible to the Governor. Each *circunscrição* contains a number of *postos* administered by a *Chefe do Posto*, and the *posto* is again divided into areas which might be said to correspond to the French *canton*. Where the area contains not merely Natives but a number of *assimilados* or Portuguese colonists it is known as a *concelho* and comes under a slightly different régime. Each of the areas is under charge of either a *regedor*, who is an appointed local authority, usually an *assimilado*, or of a *régulo*, who is not an appointed officer of the Government but is a recognized Native Chief.

As a rule the *régulo* is chosen from a ruling family though there is now some tendency to appoint old soldiers or former officials; he receives a small pay, averaging £4 a month, and also an annual gratuity; he exercises judicial authority as an arbitrator, but not in the capacity of a judge. It is his function to maintain public order, to report any extraordinary occurrence, to prevent the sale of spirits to Natives, to use his influence to see that Natives work either on their own land or accept contracts to labour in European areas or industry. The Village Head is subordinate to the *régulo*; he is not paid, but receives a gratuity at the end of the year which is based on the collection of taxes in his area; he has little definite function except to maintain the village roads or to carry out the orders of the *régulo*. At times he has a council of Elders to help him but this is not the universal rule.

There are no Native Courts. Portuguese law is generally applied in the Courts, but when cases concerning Natives only are involved the *Chefe do Posto* is said to summon African Chiefs or councillors in order to inform himself what is the African custom in any particular case, and in giving judgement he attempts to mediate between the two systems. There are two classes of tribunals, namely the ordinary and the special (*especiais*)

[1] *J.A.A.*, January 1957, p. 16, see also below, p. 801.　　[2] See below, p. 675.

tribunals; the latter act also as a court of appeal against judgements delivered in the first category of tribunals. The final appeal is to the metropolitan High Court in Lisbon.

AFRICAN AFFAIRS IN THE TOWNS

The report of the East Africa Royal Commission 1953–5 has devoted a chapter of some length to the study of the conditions created by urban developments in Africa.[1] It holds that the towns now have a significance which does not depend merely on the number of their inhabitants. They are 'the centres of social and intellectual life, of economic enterprise, and of political activity. It is essential to break down the barriers which prevent Africans from full participation in the life of the towns. The African must come to regard them as places which fully provide him with an outlet for his courage, ability and initiative.' The proposals which the Commission have made for achieving this result are of especial interest, but a comprehensive treatment of the subject would involve an examination of the conditions prevailing not merely in the African sections of the larger European centres but in the purely African towns, such for instance as the large indigenous cities of West Africa.[2] Everywhere the change from a life on the land to a life in the town must bring with it a material break with previous social habits. The urban resident has moved from a world where ties are largely personal to one in which his obligations are to an increasing extent impersonal. There must in particular be a weakening of those associations which form the basis of the organization of the Native Authority system, and it is for this reason that in the West African towns (with the exception of those of Northern Nigeria) the Governments tend to withdraw the responsibility for the management of African affairs from the traditional authorities.

The survey of the whole field of African urbanization would, however, carry this chapter into a discussion of problems extending far beyond its original scope.[3] It will be convenient therefore to discuss here only the special problems created by the growth of the urban populations which

---

[1] *East Africa Royal Commission Report, 1953–5*, Cmd. 9475, 1955, pp. 200 ff.

[2] See above, p. 33.

[3] On the conditions in these centres, see J. D. Rheinallt Jones, 'The Effects of Urbanization in South and Central Africa', *African Affairs*, January 1953, p. 40. G. Wilson, 'An Essay on the Economics of Detribalization in Northern Rhodesia', *R.L.I. Papers*, nos. 5 and 6, 1941. J. Clyde Mitchell, 'A Note on the Urbanization of Africans on the Copperbelt', *R.L. Journal*, no. 12, 1951, and 'African Urbanization in Ndola and Luanshya', *R.L. Communication*, no. 6, 1954. J. Ghilain, 'La Naissance d'une classe moyenne noire dans les centres extra-coutumiers', *Bull. I.R.C.B.*, 1952, p. 294. M. F. Grevisse, 'Les Centres extra-coutumiers d'Élisabethville', ibid., 1950, pp. 576, 687, and 1951, pp. 675–87. E. Hellmann, 'Urban Areas', in *Handbook on Race Relations in South Africa*, 1949, pp. 229 ff. S. H. Frankel, *The Economic Impact on Underdeveloped Societies*, 1953, pp. 173 ff. Sir P. Mitchell, *African Afterthoughts*, 1954, p. 236.

have come into being as the result of the activities of Europeans, or (as in East Africa) of the activities of the European and Asian communities.[1]

In the past the attitude taken by Europeans towards the African communities thus created was largely influenced by two conceptions. In the earlier stages of colonization the African working in one of the European centres was in the main viewed as a temporary visitor; his home was in the Reserves created for his protection; the scale of his wage was that which would be appropriate to a single man, since his family would be earning their subsistence in the Native areas. If accommodation had to be provided, its character was regulated by a similar consideration. The obvious convenience of such a conception caused it to be cherished long after it ceased to have any relation to the actual facts of the situation.

The second conception which helped to determine the attitude taken towards the African urban communities derived from a different source. The rigidity of the attitude taken in the Union on this question is only partly a by-product of the doctrine of segregation, for there were also practical considerations arising from the need for maintaining sanitary conditions and town-planning amenities. The site value of properties reserved for Europeans is markedly different from that of those where the residence of Natives is also admitted. Practical considerations of this character have often been decisive, even where there is no evidence of the vitality of the principle of segregation.

In so far as the majority of the African communities now resident in or near European centres may consist of the employees of single large enterprises, the immediate responsibility for their welfare falls largely on the employer and where, as in the case of the Rand Mines, the employees are men who come for fixed periods without their families, the day-to-day control is also largely left to him. Where the employees are established in such centres with their families, as most characteristically in the Belgian Katanga copper-mines and to an increasing measure in the mines of the Northern Rhodesia Copperbelt, further social needs have to be met, but these are relatively easy to deal with if the residents are under the industrial control of a single employer.

There is a far greater complexity in the problems created by an African population which has grown up within or close to a large European centre, and follows a considerable variety of employment. Here are to be found shop assistants, unskilled labourers, persons making a livelihood from the new trades created by the needs of a large body of Africans in regular employment, together with that margin of unemployed Africans which the conditions of modern industry seem inevitably to involve. Adequate housing, education, and medical services are regarded in Europe as social

[1] For a more general review of the position see International African Institute, *Social Implications of Industrialization and Urbanization in Africa South of the Sahara*, 1956.

requirements falling within the responsibility of public authorities in every urban centre, but not all African Local Administrations have been equally ready to accept responsibility for them. The only solution offered by some consists in an effort to restrict the movements of Africans within the urban centre, and they have sometimes carried this measure to a length which seems incompatible with the exercise of civil liberties as recognized in a modern State. The situation that has been created varies widely in different territories and, as will be seen, it has in some cases features which have brought the Administration under severe criticism.

Union of South Africa

It is not necessary to dwell here on the situation created by the large number of Africans, amounting now to over 300,000, who live in the compounds of the Rand mining area, nor the large number for whom provision is being made in the African Locations attached to the new gold-fields of the Orange Free State. It is, however, characteristic that the South African Department of Native Affairs has allowed the undertakings concerned with the Free State gold-fields to provide married quarters for only 3 per cent. of their employees, not for 10 per cent. as originally proposed.[1] Our immediate concern is rather with the problems arising from the growth of African populations as part of, or in the neighbourhood of, the European residential or industrial towns. Problems of this nature have inevitably assumed increased importance as the result of the measures which began to be taken in 1936 to implement the policy of territorial segregation.[2] This policy implies in principle that no Africans will reside outside the Native Reserves or the other areas scheduled for Native occupation except those Africans who are actually in the employment of Europeans, or the handicraft or other workers essential to the needs of Africans so employed. Although, however, the growth of a resident African population within the town areas or in their neighbourhood has always been regarded as undesirable, it has proved to be inevitable and the present aim of South African policy is to devise means for restricting the numbers as closely as possible.[3]

The insanitary conditions in which such populations lived in the African Locations attached to some of the larger towns of the Union were the subject of adverse comment by successive commissions of inquiry from 1903 onwards, though little action was taken till public opinion was attracted to the high death-rate caused by the influenza epidemic of 1918. The Native population classed as urban, which at the census of 1921 was estimated as 508,000 or 13 per cent. of the total African population, had by 1951 risen

[1] *The Times*, 13 December 1954. [2] See above, pp. 159, 163, 168.
[3] In February 1956 it was announced that plans were being made for the planning of 35 purely African towns in the Native Areas.

to 2,312,000, or a little over 27·1 per cent. of the total. In 1946 the number of Africans in the city and suburbs of Johannesburg alone—some 357,175 in all—greatly exceeded the total number of the Africans resident in urban centres in the whole of the Union in 1904.[1] It is significant that throughout this period the number of women increased much more rapidly than that of men. In Johannesburg the female population increased by 245 per cent. between 1911 and 1936, and by a further 127 per cent. between 1936 and 1946. It is in such figures as these that the best indication is to be found of the extent of permanent urbanization, as opposed to temporary migration in the towns of the Union.

The aim of the Natives (Urban Areas) Act passed in 1923 was to make provision for the accommodation of urban African populations in separate areas and at the same time to limit the numbers resident there. Under the law as consolidated in 1945[2] every municipality has been required to set aside land, known either as a Location or Native Village, for African occupation, and to provide housing on a plan approved by the Minister. When suitable accommodation has been provided, proclamations made under the Act may prohibit the residence elsewhere of all Africans not belonging to certain categories explicitly exempted, such as domestic servants residing on their employer's premises.

In urban areas specially proclaimed for this purpose the entry of Africans is prohibited except in accordance with prescribed conditions. By April 1947 a total of 279 such proclamations had been issued, the majority in the Cape Province. Those issued in regard to the Transvaal included the whole Rand area from Randfontein to Heidelberg; in the areas so proclaimed no African coming from outside the Union or the High Commission Territories may reside without the written permission of a higher authority. Every male African entering such an area must obtain a document certifying that he has permission to be there, and permits may be refused if there is already a surplus of labour. Employers must obtain permission before introducing Africans into the area, and must undertake to repatriate them on the termination of their employment. Local Authorities were to render reports every two years showing the numbers and place of origin of all Africans within their areas, the numbers necessary for reasonable requirements and the surplus which they might desire to have removed. Reports of this kind were, however, submitted only in 1938, and they were not renewed after the Second World War.

Much of the legislation of this character was obviously intended largely as an indication of policy; it can never have been thought possible that it should be fully implemented in practice. A further attempt to restrict the entry of Africans to the towns was made by regulations made in 1946, as

[1] Frankel, op. cit. p. 173.
[2] Natives (Urban Areas) Consolidated Act no. 25 of 1945.

the result of which they could purchase railway tickets only on production of a certificate showing that employment was awaiting them. That regulation could also have been intended mainly as an indication of policy.

The Commission usually known as the Fagan Commission which was appointed to investigate the operation of the Natives (Urban Areas) Act expressed in 1948 the view that the existence of a permanent African urban population must be accepted, and the development of a permanent labour force encouraged.[1] There is an indication that the main lines of this recommendation commended themselves to the Government headed by General Smuts,[2] but the Nationalist Party, committed to a more extreme form of the policy of segregation, has enacted legislation which has imposed increased restriction on the entry and residence of Africans in urban areas.[3] The period during which an African may be in a proclaimed area without having either a contract of employment or a permit to seek work is restricted to 72 hours. Those who are held to be undesirable (a term which includes persons who are held to be surplus to labour requirements) may be sent to a 'work colony' or removed elsewhere. There is, however, no indication that these powers are actually used on any extensive scale.

The expenditure on the maintenance of a Native Location is provided by a Local Authority out of a separate Native Account, into which all income derived from the Location is paid.[4] This includes rents and fines and a fee, not exceeding 2s. a month, paid by employers for each service contract, a charge which can in certain circumstances be shifted to the employee.

A more important source of revenue has been provided by the sale of 'kaffir beer' under municipal monopoly. This system was first introduced in Natal by a law enacted in 1908, but was not widely adopted elsewhere in the Union till some years later. Under the provisions of the Natives (Urban Areas) Act of 1923, as amended in 1937, a total of 48 towns have now adopted the system of monopoly supply by their own agencies. Port Elizabeth, which has in other respects also a progressive Native policy, is an exception in this respect. The receipts from the beer monopoly have led to a marked increase in the Location revenue of most municipalities, and to a tendency to regard the Native Revenue Account as one which should be self-supporting. A report which was published in 1943 remarked that beer-hall profits had been used to finance expenditure which should more properly be borne by the general account.[5] An inter-departmental committee of the same year considered that in view of the low standard of

[1] *Report of Native Laws Commission 1946–8*, U.G. no. 28, 1948.
[2] *Handbook on Race Relations in South Africa*, 1949, p. 230.
[3] Native Laws Amendment Act, no. 54, 1952.
[4] For the details of legislation on this subject see, *O.T.S.A., 1950*, pp. 507–10; ibid. *1952–53*, pp. 499 ff.
[5] *Native Affairs Commission: Report on Kaffir Beer*, 1943, para. 93.

services in the Native Locations, Local Authorities should be prepared to supplement the Native Revenue Account from general revenue.[1] Little has, however, been done to implement this recommendation. From the year 1944 municipalities were required to keep a separate Kaffir Beer Account, to which might be charged only expenditure certified as calculated to improve the social or recreational facilities available to African residents. The interest on loans for housing was added in 1945,[2] and in 1952 all expenditure on housing was made chargeable to the Account.[3] The Native Revenue Accounts in 1950–1 totalled approximately £4½ million; the contribution to them from the general revenue of the municipalities amounted to £435,000 only.[4]

No direct measures seem to have been taken by the Central Government to enforce the provision of the original Act of 1923 which laid on Local Authorities the obligation to supply adequate accommodation for those Africans whose residence in the urban centres was held to be desirable. A considerable measure of assistance has, however, been offered by the Government to municipalities which have undertaken housing schemes. The Housing Act (no. 35 of 1920) set up a Central Housing Board to administer loans to Local Authorities for this purpose, and in 1934 the Board was authorized to recommend loans for housing schemes undertaken as measures of slum clearance. By the end of 1939 a total sum of nearly £5¼ million had been approved in respect of loan applications for housing for non-Europeans; of this just over £4 million was classed as sub-economic. In addition some municipalities had financed their own housing schemes.

In 1940, however, it was estimated that about one-third of the urban African population were still living outside recognized Locations, while a high percentage of those in the Locations were housed in unsatisfactory conditions.[5] The latter fact was obvious, and became the subject of very adverse comment by visitors to the Union. War conditions accentuated the shortage of housing, and in 1944 the Central Housing Board was replaced by a National Housing and Planning Commission. Loan funds were now made available at 3¼ per cent. interest, and the Government undertook to meet a proportion of the losses on housing up to a maximum of 75 per cent., though when costs rose further the State contribution was limited to £30 per house in schemes for housing for Africans. By the end of 1950 approval had been given to loan applications for African housing which amounted to a little over £14¼ million, and 33,076 dwellings had

---

[1] *Report of the Inter-departmental Committee on the Social, Health and Economic Conditions of Urban Natives*, 1943, para. 202. See also *Handbook on Race Relations in South Africa*, 1949, pp. 258 ff.

[2] Natives (Urban Areas) Amendment Act no. 43, 1945.

[3] Native Laws Amendment Act no. 54, 1952.

[4] *Annual Report of Departments of Native Affairs, 1950–1*, p. 22.

[5] *Report of the Committee to consider the Administration of areas which are becoming urbanized but which are not under local Government control*, U.G. no. 85, 1940, para. 155.

been built.[1] In 1949 it was estimated that the annual losses borne by the State and municipalities on 71,500 houses built under the various subsidy schemes were £1,400,000 and £565,000 respectively.

The National Housing and Planning Commission, whose personnel had been largely changed under political auspices in 1948, now took the view that the formula of 1944 had encouraged extravagance in the municipalities; direct assistance from the Central Government could appropriately be given for the capital cost of streets, lighting, water-supplies, and sewerage, but not for house-building. This should, as far as possible, be provided on an economic basis by the employment of African labour and by encouraging Africans to build their own houses, which they would hold on renewable 30-year leases. An Act to permit Africans to do skilled building work in their own areas was passed in 1953.

The municipal authorities were then invited to submit five-year schemes, and the total number of new houses required was estimated by them at 119,280, though other estimates have varied between 200,000 and 350,000. In June 1953 the total number of houses built since the Second World War was officially given as 37,587 and the amount advanced as over £13 million.[2] An additional source of revenue for the provision of services in new housing areas was made available by the Native Services Levy imposed by an Act of 1953. This obliged employers of labour to contribute 2s. 6d. for every six man-days worked by Africans; of this 6d. was earmarked for the provision of transport facilities. The levy has actually been imposed in 22 towns; it brought in £1,600,000 in the first full year. It is an offence to make any deduction from wages to offset this contribution.

Although a policy of retrenchment has led to some curtailment of funds for the housing schemes already planned by municipalities, this has not prevented the promotion of schemes for the concentration of scattered Native Locations into single areas, in accordance with the principles of the Group Areas Act of 1950.[3] The first of these, the Meadowlands resettlement plan, entailed the removal of some 70,000 Africans from the Western Areas of Johannesburg (embracing the Native Locations of Sophiatown, Martinclare, and Newclare), at a cost of approximately £5 million spread over five years.[4] The new site is seven miles farther from the city; it is, however, within half a mile of a station served by an electric-train service to Johannesburg. The move began in March 1955, under the authority of the Natives Resettlement Act passed in 1954.[5]

[1] *National Housing and Planning Commission, Annual Report*, 1950, Annexure C. 3.
[2] *S.A.S.*, no. 62, 30 June 1953. [3] See above, p. 165.
[4] *The Western Area, Mass Removal*, South African Institute of Race Relations, 1953. *The Times*, 8 October 1954 and 7 December 1954.
[5] *The Times*, 7 December 1954. See also *Africa Digest*, March–April 1955, pp. 5 ff. Also *S.A.S.*, no. 99, 28 February 1955, p. 14. The Resettlement Board acts directly under the Minister and is thus independent of the Johannesburg City Council.

The policy which dictated this removal became for a time a topic of acute controversy, which had wide repercussions in Great Britain. It was pointed out that it involved the removal of a number of Africans who had acquired freehold rights in the Western areas before the Land Act of 1913; on the other hand, it was claimed that only a few hundred Africans had actually held freehold property and that those who had occupied their houses had received in compensation a price 40 per cent. above the municipal valuation. It was asserted at the time that the majority were ready to move to the better accommodation and other amenities now offered, a claim which received some confirmation from the large number of those who made applications for the new houses. A second scheme of resettlement involved the transference of 40,000 Africans from a 'squatter' camp at Benoni to the new urban Native Township at Daveyton. The new Township is to be built on model lines at a cost of £7 million.[1]

On various occasions since 1944 Africans who were living as sub-tenants in urban Locations have moved out in bodies and have encamped themselves on vacant land, building shelters of any materials that they could find. The impossibility of providing adequate housing for them has been so far acknowledged that a number of municipalities have officially proclaimed areas as 'squatters' camps' and have restricted camping to those areas. There are issues of great difficulty involved in such operations as the removal of the Western Area Locations or in the steps taken elsewhere to replace 'shanty towns' by less undesirable forms of accommodation. The responsibility for the existence of slum conditions does not rest on the municipalities alone, but must be shared with the Government, which for many years paid no regard to the growth of slum areas and 'shanty towns' in the vicinity of the cities. The supply of loan funds has of late years admittedly done much to ameliorate conditions, though the extension of accommodation seems to lag behind the continual growth of the African population. There still appears to be in some areas an unfortunate reluctance to supply the Locations with amenities in the form of roads, sewerage, and lighting, so that they present a striking contrast with the provision of such services made in the adjoining European town areas.

Inadequate attention has also been given by the Government Departments to the provision made for travel to and from the African Locations to work in the towns. The police arrangements made to secure the observance of Government or municipal regulations in the African quarters are of a character which it is unusual to find in a civilized community. 'The constant raiding of Locations to enforce taxation, pass, and liquor laws, the invasion of private homes, and the use of force must have a brutalizing

---

[1] *S.A.S.*, no. 101, 30 March 1955, p. 12.

effect on the police.'[1] If the attitude of the police can thus be described, there is little wonder that the attitude of the urban African in the Union should be distrustful and resentful.

Not all the changes made in the readjustment of the sites of Locations have been unwelcome to the Africans concerned. There have been many applicants for transfer from Locations near Pretoria to the new areas opened near Vlakfontein, where Africans may purchase their houses by instalments, though they may only rent the sites.[2] An important feature of some of these new towns is the ethnical grouping of their inhabitants. It is a significant outcome of the policy of separatism that the Government has announced its decision to abolish the Advisory Boards hitherto existing in the various Native Locations in the Union. Their place is to be filled by some form of appointed Native Authority.[3]

South-West Africa

In South-West Africa the procedure adopted follows that of the Union, though with far less rigidity. Proclamation no. 34 of 1924 provided for the establishment of Native Locations attached to the urban areas; this regulation has been applied in twelve of the 16 municipalities in the Police Zone[4] of the territory, no one of which is, however, of any considerable size. Revenue derived from the Locations is spent on local improvements; the sale of Kaffir beer is controlled, and profits from this source are also devoted to these improvements. In 1953 the urban African population was estimated at 31,000, of whom 9,000 were at Windhoek. The Location there is of very inferior type,[5] but in that year the Administration made available £50,000 for loans to the local authorities for African housing.

Southern Rhodesia

The earlier practice of Southern Rhodesia followed that of the Union. The Native Urban Locations Ordinance of 1906 empowered the Administration to establish Native Locations and to introduce in them a registration and pass system. The Private Locations Act of 1908 authorized the grant of licences to owners of land to lease it to Africans for residential purposes, and it also enabled a number of urban employers to erect barracks for the housing of their employees on their property. But the result of these measures proved to be unsatisfactory and the Land Apportionment Act of 1930[6] provided for two alternatives: one was the creation

[1] *Report of Police Commission of Inquiry*, 1937, U.G. no. 50, 1937. See also the further references quoted in *Handbook on Race Relations in South Africa*, 1949, pp. 75 ff.

[2] *S.A.S.*, no. 85, 30 June 1954.

[3] *The Times*, 19 September 1954.

[4] See above, p. 435.

[5] R. Gardiner in *African Affairs*, July 1955, p. 206.

[6] See below, p. 703.

by the Government of Native Village Settlements outside municipal boundaries, the other the establishment of 'Native Urban Areas' by local Town Authorities. A Registration of Natives Act passed in the same year[1] provided for a control of the entry of Africans into urban areas in terms which closely resembled those of contemporary legislation in the Union. So far, however, little real attention had been given to the question of policy, and there ensued a period during which the Central Government and the local authorities each left action to the other.

It became obvious during the Second World War that the abuses due to the neglect of the needs of the growing urban population of Africans which had marked the history of the Union were being repeated, even though on a less conspicuous scale, in the towns of Southern Rhodesia. The Land Apportionment Act was amended in 1945 in order to empower the Government to proclaim Native Urban Locations, and in the following year there was enacted the comprehensive Native (Urban Areas) Accommodation and Registration Act no. 6 of 1946. This embodied what was in one sense a new principle in that it placed on employers the obligation to provide accommodation for their employees, either on their own premises or in a 'Native residential area'.

The situation arising under this legislation is somewhat complicated as the two Acts apply in practice to different areas. The large statutory undertakings, such as the Railways and Iron and Steel Commissions, now house their own employees. The Wankie Colliery has now a labour force of nearly 9,000 and a total population of roughly 17,000. It has long had a reputation for its well-laid-out and well-managed labour estate; electric light is in the course of being supplied to all houses and the health services seem to be on an exceptionally liberal scale.

In the case of other undertakings the majority of African employees are in practice required to be accommodated in a Native Urban Location provided by the local Town Authorities.[2] In this case the employer must pay rental to the Local Authority. The rising cost of construction has created a difficult problem in the adjustment of an 'economic' scale of rentals, and a certain proportion of the housing now remains 'sub-economic'. In some Locations, where the demand has exceeded the supply of houses, Africans were at one time permitted to build their own huts, but the practice has since been discontinued.

Apart therefore from the provision made by the large statutory undertakings, the great bulk of accommodation for employed Africans is provided by the Local Authorities, who thus have a definite interest in exercising control over the number of Africans admitted to residence under the

[1] No. 32 of 1936.
[2] G. W. Noble, 'African Housing in the Urban Areas of Southern Rhodesia', *J.A.A.*, July 1951, p. 124.

current residential and pass legislation. The direct contribution made to the housing problem by the Government itself comprises, in the first place, the establishment of the Native Village Settlements for which provision was made in the Land Apportionment Act of 1941. Four have been established, the best known being that at Highfield near Salisbury. More recent regulations have given permission to Africans to buy their houses or to acquire ground leases of 30 years on which to build their own houses. The type of accommodation in these Settlements is good, but they can go only part of the way to meet the demand for the housing of Africans with superior standards of life.

The second direct contribution made by the Government consists of the creation of the African Townships for which provision is made by the Native Land Husbandry Act.[1] These are designed to give security of tenure to craftsmen, traders, and the like resident in the Native areas. The Townships may be either urban or rural. At present there are only two of the former, Seki near Salisbury and Ntabazinduna near Bulawayo, but sites have also been selected at Umtali and Gwelo. The four rural African Townships are situated near the boundaries of the Reserves, where they are most accessible to the neighbouring towns in which the inhabitants work. Townships are also being constructed to provide accommodation for workers engaged in the erection of the hydro-electric installation at Kariba Gorge.[2]

As has been shown, there was a stage in which the Government failed to recognize the importance of the provision of accommodation for Africans in the towns, but of recent years the matter has engaged more serious attention, and it has been approached in a spirit which shows greater consideration for the position of Africans than does that of the Government of the Union. The main burden of providing housing has fallen on the Local Authorities, and here the major problem has been one of finance. So far, African housing has been financed almost entirely by loan, and between 1946 and 1953 the expenditure amounted to £3¾ million. A loan projected in 1954 was intended mainly for the expansion of the accommodation provided for Africans and though the loan was not fully subscribed, it was announced in October 1955 that £1½ million has been made available for this purpose.[3] In 1955 Salisbury had 64,000 working males. Altogether 95,292 persons (men, women and children) had been accommodated either by the Council, Government departments, or private employers.[4] Houses can now be purchased in the Government Settlements by payments extending over 20 years.

---

[1] The Southern Rhodesia Native Land Husbandry Act no. 52 of 1951.

[2] See below, p. 986.

[3] It was stated in February 1956 that during the years 1945–55 Southern Rhodesia, including the Local Authorities, had spent a total of nearly £8 million in providing accommodation for more than 134,000 Africans.

[4] *Annual Report of Director of Native Administration, City of Salisbury, 1955.*

It is now realized that the provision of accommodation has an important bearing on the question of stabilizing the labour force, which has from the first formed one of the major problems of Southern Rhodesia. The earlier policy which considered it enough to supply quarters for single men overlooked the fact that, taking even the narrowest point of view, 'labour cannot be efficient while it is unstable and is precluded from sharing in a full family life'. The ill-balanced ratio of African males to females in the majority of urban areas has been the cause of many social evils, and it is significant that the two major Local Authorities, Salisbury and Bulawayo, have now fixed the ratio of accommodation to be provided at one married house to 3·5 or 3·7 unmarried quarters.

Northern Rhodesia

In Northern Rhodesia the problems of African urbanization are relatively new, but they have become increasingly important owing to the expansion of activity in the Copperbelt. The principal urban area is that formed by the five Townships of the Copperbelt, with a total African population which was estimated in 1952 at 215,860.[1] Other important centres are Livingstone and Broken Hill, with respectively 17,000 and 13,000 Africans in employment in 1951.[2] Lusaka, though it is not itself a mining centre, has an African population which has increased from 17,000 in 1945 to 55,000 in 1953.[3] A considerable part of the Africans employed in Northern Rhodesia are immigrants from other territories, but the proportion both of married men and of the families which have decided to make their home in the Protectorate is steadily increasing.[4] A sample survey made at Luanshya in the Copperbelt indicated that 4 per cent. of the population there had known no other home; a further 27 per cent. intended to stay there permanently, while 27 per cent. expected to remain on the Copperbelt till the end of their working lives.[5]

The number of African workers actually employed in the mines of Northern Rhodesia in 1954 was 40,026,[6] of whom about four-fifths lived in the compounds attached to the mines. The character of the housing provided in some of these compounds was a matter of adverse comment in the reports of the commissions which inquired into the industrial disturbances that occurred in 1935 and 1940;[7] the general standard was also at one time criticized in other quarters as inferior to that provided in some other parts

---

[1] *Annual Report on African Affairs, 1952*, p. 6.

[2] *Northern Rhodesia, Employment Census, 1951. Local Government and African Housing Department Annual Report, 1952*, p. 7.

[3] *Report of Committee to Enquire into African and European Housing in Lusaka, 1953.*

[4] *N.A.*, Part II, pp. 146–7.   [5] *R.L. Journal*, no. 12, 1951, p. 26.

[6] *Annual Report of the Department of Labour, Northern Rhodesia, 1954*, p. 28.

[7] *Report of the Commission Appointed to Inquire into the Disturbances in the Copperbelt, Northern Rhodesia, 1935*, Cmd. 5009, 1935; ibid. *July 1940*, Lusaka, 1940.

of Africa.[1] While the provision of health and welfare services had been fully satisfactory, less regard had been paid to the higher standards of accommodation which were bound to develop in an African population living in close contact with the notably high scale of amenities provided for European employees.

In the newer housing schemes, however, the conditions are now greatly improved. It was stated in 1952 that provision was now being made for married quarters at a ratio of 60 per cent. of the total. 'Special type' houses are now being built which compare favourably with the lower-class European housing in southern Africa; these are available to workers of the 'inclusive wage group' at a reasonable rent.[2] All other workers are housed free. The major mining companies concerned decided in 1954 to set aside a sum of £2 million to be expended during the next five years on the improvement of housing and on the provision of amenities for African workers. Electric light was to be installed in all the houses.[3]

The conditions in the Native Locations which are attached to the Townships, or in the Settlements maintained by the Government or by the Local Authorities, give rise to problems of a different type. The Municipalities and the Townships both erect houses and also lease plots on which the occupier builds his own house. These Locations have taken the place of the former 'shanty' villages erected in the vicinity of the Townships or on 'private Locations', the conditions of which were for some time a matter of public scandal.[4] Though, however, the new Locations represent a marked improvement, the inadequacy of the accommodation thus provided remained a matter of serious complaint, and on the recommendation of a commission appointed in 1943,[5] a Local Government and African Housing Department was set up in 1946. A sum of £1 million was voted for loans for African housing, and £500,000 allocated for Government housing for African civil servants.

The post-war Development Plans subsequently provided a sum of £3¾ million for Local Authority housing and £710,000 for African civil servants' houses.[6] By the end of 1952 some 13,560 houses had been built. In the programme for 1953 and the following years provision was made for a further sum of £6 million, and it was anticipated that when the programme had been completed about 17,650 houses would have been built by or for the Local Authorities and 5,530 for the Government.[7] Even so, it has been difficult to keep pace with the increase in the population. In Lusaka alone,

---

[1] W. W. Jameson, *Report on African Housing in Urban and Rural Areas*, 1945.

[2] *The Times*, 30 September 1953.

[3] *Report of the Board of Inquiry on the Advancement of Africans in the Copper Mining Industry of Northern Rhodesia*, 1954, p. 15.   [4] *N.A.*, Part II, p. 148.

[5] *Report of a Commission appointed to Enquire into the Administration and Finances of Native Locations in Urban Areas*, Lusaka, 1944.   [6] *Colonial Reports, Northern Rhodesia, 1952*, p. 58.

[7] *Report of the Development Authority for 1953*, Lusaka, 1954.

where in 1953 the number considered to be satisfactorily housed was 24,000, it was estimated that the total requiring accommodation in the next few years might be likely to rise to 80,000.[1]

Northern Rhodesia has now, like Southern Rhodesia, invoked the aid of legislation which places on the employer the obligation to provide living accommodation for his employees. Under the terms of the Urban African Housing Ordinance of 1948, employers (including Local Authorities) are made responsible for providing accommodation at their own expense for every African employee, and, if requested, for such employee's legal wife also. Employers of more than 25 Africans may be required to build accommodation for them. Representative Africans have, however, opposed the 'tied cottage system' as giving the employer an undue measure of control over labour.

In 1936 the Government embarked experimentally on the creation a few miles outside Lusaka of an 'African Town' (Chilenje), laid out on the lines of a village, in which Africans could lease building sites and plots. Separate provision has also been made for Africans who are working on their own account (for example as hawkers, artisans, or traders), in the form of five small 'African Towns', one in the neighbourhood of each of the major Copperbelt Townships. They are making some progress, and their total population amounted in 1951 to about 4,000.[2]

In Northern Rhodesia the Local Authorities are not required to keep a separate Native Revenue account, but they must devote the profits from municipal beer halls to welfare schemes; the schemes so defined were indeed wholly dependent on beer-hall profits up to 1952 when the Government began to make some grants for this purpose. The attitude of the Local Authorities of some of the Townships has from the first been illiberal and lacking in foresight; they have, for example, refused to make provision from their general revenue for the amenities of Africans in the neighbouring Locations on the ground that they do not contribute to the Township rates.

Nyasaland

In Nyasaland the urban African population is small and consists of civil and domestic servants, and the like, with a relatively negligible element of industrial labour. The practice regarding the residence of Africans in the existing small European townships is not uniform. Blantyre and Limbe prohibit it in principle to those who are not in employment; Port Herald excludes in theory all who are not domestic servants; Fort Johnston provides for the issue of special permits to others than domestic servants but in 1935 its Town Council passed by-laws taking power to order their

---

[1] *Report of Committee to Enquire into African and European Housing in Lusaka*, 1953, pp. 2–3.
[2] *N.A.*, Part II, pp. 146–9. *J.A.A.*, July 1951, p. 113.

exclusion. Near Zomba a model village is being constructed by the Government to accommodate Africans employed in the Township who are not housed on their employer's premises. The village is to be provided with electricity, water-supply, and a recreation hall; plots are to be available for leasing to employers or to individual Africans. The proposed amalgamation of Blantyre and Limbe under a united town council will exclude the small African town at Soche, which will continue under the management of its own authority. It is intended to lease individual plots to Africans or to employers who will build their own houses. Ultimately the area will be served with water and water-borne sewerage.

Kenya

The Royal Commission on East Africa, 1953–5 has dealt so fully with the question of urban development in these territories[1] that it will be sufficient to refer here to certain special features of town administration which affect the position of Africans. There is, of course, a wide difference between the circumstances of Africans living within the periphery of a European township such as Nairobi and of those who inhabit cities such as Mombasa or Dar-es-Salaam, with their large Asian, Arab, and indigenous populations. To anyone prepared to recognize the trend of affairs elsewhere it must have been obvious from an early period that permanent provision must be made in Nairobi for the accommodation of a considerable African population. But it was not until the late thirties that any serious attention was paid to the problem.

Some improvement was effected between 1940 and 1947 when the small amount of existing accommodation was roughly doubled; but it was estimated in the latter year that provision for an additional 11,363 adults was required in order to relieve overcrowding. A total of £288,500 was provided from the Colonial Development and Welfare Vote towards the cost of housing schemes, half as a free grant and half as a loan. In 1947 the African population of Nairobi was estimated to have risen to no less than 77,032; the shortage of housing was repeatedly described in Government reports as constituting a most serious problem, and in 1953 it was stated that 20,000 Africans were in urgent need of housing.[2]

The existing legislation makes provision for the establishment of a Location in which only Africans may reside; except in the case of those who are housed by their employers, they may live outside the Location only if they obtain a special permit. Africans may build their own houses, in conformity with municipal regulations, on plots rented from the

---

[1] *East Africa Royal Commission, 1953–5*, Cmd. 9475, pp. 200 ff.
[2] *Kenya Land Commission Report*, Cmd. 4556, 1934, para. 582. J. Huxley, *Africa View*, 1932, p. 217. T. Askwith, 'African Housing in Nairobi', *J.A.A.*, July 1950, pp. 37–39. *Colonial Reports, Kenya, 1952*, p. 5; ibid. *1953*, p. 8.

municipality, or they may rent single-roomed or two-roomed quarters erected by it. Provision exists for eviction in case of failure to pay rent, or of more than one conviction under the Liquor Licensing Laws. Africans not in employment are prohibited from residence for more than 36 hours without a permit, but this measure had never been given full effect in practice, and the attempt to enforce it in 1930 resulted in the temporary expulsion of more than a thousand persons from the town.[1] The regulation is now generally admitted to be ineffective as a measure for day-to-day use. The slum village of Maparani outside Nairobi, which was estimated to house 7,000 persons, was destroyed in 1953 on the ground that it was used as a base by Mau Mau terrorists.

While, however, there continues to be a grave problem of overcrowding in Nairobi, there has of late years been a marked improvement both in the amount and in the type of accommodation provided and in the provision of social amenities; the houses erected in the Makongeni Settlement, for instance, compare favourably with any in Africa. The amenities now include a maternity home, ante-natal and child-welfare clinics, a stadium, and two community centres at Kaloleni and Makongeni. Among the latest schemes of the Kenya Government is a plan to build at Nairobi houses sufficient to accommodate 25,000 Africans at a cost of over £2 million.

The principal source of Location revenue in Nairobi (as in the Locations of other Kenya municipalities) has been the municipal beer monopoly. The towns in Kenya are also eligible for grants from an African Trust Fund, financed by half of the proceeds of the tax of 2s. which is paid by African urban residents,[2] the other half of each payment being credited to the African Local Council of the taxpayer's home area. This is in addition to the normal poll tax and takes the place of a local rate payable to the Local Council. Altogether the Administration and Local Authorities of various municipalities provided houses for 16,000 Africans in 1953 at an approximate cost of £950,000.[3]

Mombasa differs in character from Nairobi, for its African and Arab communities are of much longer standing than the European, while the commercial element is mainly Asian. Africans are not restricted to Locations reserved for them, nor is control exercised over the residence of Africans in the town. Up to 1943 they lived chiefly in 'villages' laid out on land owned by Arabs and Asians, and though the construction of new villages was prohibited from 1934, on account of the highly unsatisfactory character of the housing, no effective steps were taken to increase the provision of African accommodation. There has in fact been a persistent history of overcrowding and insanitary conditions. Some improvement began in 1943 when the Government, the Railway Administration, and

---

[1] *Kenya Local Government Report*, 1933, p. 22.
[2] See below, p. 660.
[3] *Africa Digest*, December 1954, p. 11.

the municipality began to provide quarters for their employees, and the municipality also built a small number of houses for leasing to the public. A sum of £350,000 was made available from the Colonial Development and Welfare Vote for housing schemes, and an estate was purchased which was expected to house 8,000 persons. But the shortage of African housing was still officially described in 1952 as a serious problem;[1] it was indeed admitted in the following year that there were 27,000 persons in urgent need of accommodation.

At the instance of the Minister for Health and Local Government a study was made of the conditions prevailing in the Union and the Rhodesias by two officers deputed from Kenya. This was published in 1950[2] and the subject was further discussed in memoranda dealing with the general problem of land and population in East Africa.[3] A pilot African Housing Scheme was started in Thika in 1951. The study made in 1950 had called special attention to the need for the increase of African-owned housing in the towns as a measure likely to promote a stable urban population, and the Thika experiment was largely directed to encouraging the construction of houses by Africans. The housing issue came again under consideration in 1952-3 by the Committee on African Wages,[4] which pointed to the deficiencies existing both in Nairobi and Mombasa, and emphasized that the greater part of the existing accommodation was for single men.

In Kenya the Locations attached to the European townships are administered by the municipal or other urban authorities in charge of the towns. Nairobi has now a City Council; Mombasa and four other towns have Municipal Boards, and smaller townships are administered by the District Commissioners with nominated Advisory Committees. Since 1946 African representatives have been nominated as members of all these bodies. Where there are municipalities there are in addition African Advisory Councils or Committees, the members of which are elected either by Wards or by tribal, occupational, or religious organizations. Names for nomination to the Municipal Boards are put forward by these Councils, and in Nairobi and Mombasa, where there are Municipal African Affairs Officers, they are advisory also to these officials.

Tanganyika

In Tanganyika the position of the capital town of Dar-es-Salaam resembles that of Mombasa. The European population is largely transitory;

---

[1] *Colonial Reports, Kenya, 1952*, p. 5; ibid. *1954*, p. 79.
[2] Report of F. W. Carpenter and T. C. Colchester, Appendix A to E. A. Vasey, *Report on African Housing in Townships and Trading Centres*, April 1950.
[3] *Land and Population in East Africa*, Col. no. 290, 1952, p. 18.
[4] *Report of the Committee on African Wages*, Nairobi, 1954, pp. 93-105.

Asians comprise 29 per cent. of the inhabitants. There is no legislation designed to separate the residence of Africans from that of Europeans and Asians, but there is a marked degree of congestion of the African population,[1] and the Asian and Arab householders charge rents out of all proportion to the inadequate accommodation provided. The municipality had up to 1954 taken no effective steps to solve the housing problem, but plans are now being considered for using the site of the former aerodrome for a housing scheme. Up to date, such increase of accommodation as has been made is on a relatively small scale.[2]

Uganda

Uganda has not attempted to establish separate residential areas for the different communities,[3] and such problems as have arisen are those normally encountered in the provision of urban housing. A number of small housing estates have been developed from 1948 onwards, the sum of nearly £1 million having been contributed for this purpose up to the end of 1953. Towards the end of the year an African Housing Department was established with a staff working under a Director of African Housing. Its chief activity has up to the present been devoted to the creation of housing estates for the higher and lower groups of wage-earners,[4] both estates—Naguru and Nakawa—being in the vicinity of Kampala. Another estate is growing up at Ntinda (also near Kampala) where Africans are being encouraged to build their own houses, and are being given facilities by loans from the Uganda Credit and Savings Bank. A sum of £40,000 was allocated for capital development on housing in 1954–5.[5]

There must be a wide agreement with the recommendations of the East Africa Royal Commission regarding the need for the increase of accommodation for Africans and with their view that encouragement should be given to schemes which will allow Africans to build and own their own houses. But the problem at issue is not limited to the provision of more living accommodation or more amenities for an African urban population. The Commission seek to promote a new conception of the town as the centre of the intellectual and political life of African society. If, however, it is the objective that the town should acquire a status akin to that which it has acquired in Europe it must be realized that it is unlikely to do so if it is an artificial creation owing its form to alien influences. Its growth must be organic; its houses must reflect the way of life of its people; its institutions must be the result of a natural growth. In this development the Administration can assist by helping to provide some of the material

[1] *N.A.*, Part I, p. 339.   [2] *Tanganyika, Report for the Year 1954*, Col. no. 317, pp. 78–79.
[3] For the history of the Uganda towns, see *The Times, British Colonies Review*, Winter, 1955.
[4] *Statement of Policy on African Urban Housing*, 1954.
[5] *Background to Uganda*, no. 71, September 1954; no. 93, March 1955.

conditions, but that will be the limit of the functions it can perform. If the town seems likely, for obvious reasons, to be the centre of intellectual activity in Africa, it is none the less possible that the manner of its creation and development will continue to give it a relation with the rural areas which differs materially from that which determines the relation of the town and the country in the Western world.

British West African Territories

There is in British West Africa no instance of the legal segregation of the African from the European town areas or of legislative restrictions on the residence of Africans in the latter. In many cases the 'Government quarter' has been constructed at a short distance from the Native Town, and it is common to find that a different régime applies to it, in the sense that the Local Authority takes the form of a Board of official members not of a Native Authority. If Africans do not construct houses in the Government quarter, it is not because of any legal restriction but generally because the land on which the 'Government quarter' stands has been secured purely for official purposes. In some of the larger towns the representatives of European trading firms have, as a matter of convenience, been permitted to construct residences in the 'Government quarter', but this does not mean that African officials or persons of similar standing are in practice debarred from residence in it. The most characteristic feature of towns such as Lagos and Accra is not the separation of European and Native residential areas but the fact that the African areas contain slum quarters not materially better than those to be seen in the 'shanty towns' of the Union.

French Territories

The rapid growth of urbanization in French West Africa appears remarkable in view of the relative lack of large-scale industrial enterprise. Out of the estimated total number of 370,000 workers in French West Africa in 1952, only 27,000 were engaged in industry of any kind, including 11,000 engaged in mining. Nevertheless the population of Dakar, which was stated to be 90,000 in 1936, is now estimated at roughly 300,000; the population of Bamako and Abidjan are recorded as having exceeded 100,000; that of Conakry and of Porto Novo now stands at roughly 60,000.[1] After the Second World War the European population of Dakar has risen to 42,000. Part, at all events, of this increase can be attributed to the decision of the Government to emphasize the importance of the town both as a naval base and a commercial port.[2]

The French have paid much attention to the planning and layout of

---

[1] T. Hodgkin, in *West Africa*, 13 January 1954, p. 127.
[2] *Enc. A.O.F.*, vol. i, pp. 273 ff.

their Colonial towns, and in some cases the African area, the *ville indigène*, is separated from the European area. This appears, however, to be a matter of expediency rather than of principle. There is no formal separation of this kind in the greater part of French West Africa. Only Senegal and the Upper Volta appear to have made formal provision for the reservation of certain areas as urban centres for African occupation;[1] in the Sudan, however, it has been the practice to set aside such areas, separated by an open space from the European quarter.[2]

At Bamako the African quarters are separate from the European town, but they are only a very short distance apart. Pointe Noire is laid out on a circular plan, with roads radiating from an open space in the centre and linked by concentric avenues. In Abidjan the *ville indigène* has grown up on the Little Bassam island opposite the peninsula of Abidjan, where the main town is occupied by the Europeans and the African *évolués*. This arrangement reflects the difference between the European and indigenous way of life rather than a racial discrimination such as that which has dictated the existence of the African Locations in South Africa. Though the African population in Dakar is congested, and though part of the areas in the neighbourhood of the port are overcrowded and ill kept, there are other instances where the *villes indigènes* are well laid out and the African houses are reasonably well built. There are few of the slum areas such as are to be found in the towns of British West Africa.

Belgian Congo

As has been shown, the growth of African urbanization was unusually rapid in the Belgian Congo during and after the Second World War. It represents, however, a movement of older standing, since it is one outcome of the policy directed to the stabilization of labour which was originally adopted in the mines in the Katanga, and has since been widely followed by other European undertakings.[3] The growth in certain areas during recent years has been spectacular. Leopoldville, which had rather over 46,500 African inhabitants in 1939, had in 1953 a total estimated at about 300,000;[4] Elisabethville has increased from a total of just under 27,000 to one of roughly 120,000[5] in the same period; Stanleyville has increased from just over 17,000 to nearly 46,000. A proportion of this urbanized population is admittedly only temporary, depending on the

---

[1] E. Maguet, *Concessions domaniales dans les colonies françaises*, 1930, pp. 159, 191.

[2] *Congrès soudanais de technique et colonisation agricole africaines*, vol. i, 1936, p. 94.

[3] L. Mottoule, *Déterminisme fonctionnel de l'industrie dans l'éducation de l'indigène congolais*, 1934, p. 18. R. L. Buell, *The Native Problem in Africa*, vol. ii, 1928, pp. 553–63.

[4] *The Times*, 5 July 1955. It is not, however, clear whether this total also includes the new industrial centre at Limete containing 45,000 Africans. The population of Leopoldville was given as 244,000 in 1953.

[5] *The Times*, 19 January 1956.

economic situation from time to time,[1] but there is nevertheless a marked and to all appearances a permanent increase in the resident African population of these towns.

Reference has already been made to the current system of administration in the *cités indigènes*, and to the fact that three major towns have the special standing of *villes*.[2] They come under a system of direct control, being governed by an *Administrateur de territoire*. He presides over an urban committee composed of eight members, who must be of Belgian nationality.[3] These eight members are appointed by the Governor-General. Their position is advisory only, and the matters to be referred to them are determined by the Governor. They may, however, impose local taxation, subject to his approval. As already explained, the *Administrateur de territoire* exercises control over the *cité indigène*, with the assistance of a European *chef de cité* and Africans appointed as *chefs de quartier*.

Under the provisions of an earlier law[4] the Administration is empowered to require all 'persons of colour' to live in areas set apart for them, and in practice this regulation is used to require all Africans who are not housed by their employers to take up their residence in the *cité indigène*. As a consequence there are only a small number of Africans actually resident in those areas of the *ville* which are inhabited by European residents or by commercial undertakings. The police have powers to enforce this provision, and in fact the residence of Africans in the *cité indigène* is as carefully regulated (especially in the Katanga) as in South Africa. Permanent residence is restricted to persons in recognized employment.[5]

The *cité indigène* is as a rule situated at a short distance from the *ville* or other European town; in the Katanga there is a neutral zone between them which is occupied as a park or by public buildings, such as hospitals or schools. In Leopoldville the house plots were originally allotted to Africans on leasehold, and they were assisted by loans to build their own houses to approved designs. The results were for the most part satisfactory, but the great influx of Africans during and after the Second World War created a problem which it has only been possible to meet by public housing schemes.

A commission appointed in 1948 recommended the creation of Housing Officers whose activities would be co-ordinated by a Central Council, but after a trial period of three years the functions of the Council were transferred to the institution known as the *Office des cités indigènes*, which has a

---

[1] J. Ghilain, in *Bull. I.R.C.B.*, 1952, p. 294.

[2] See above, pp. 557 ff.

[3] *Enc. C.B.*, vol. iii, 1953, pp. 534, 734–7. For the relevant legislation see *Codes et Lois du Congo Belge*, 1954, pp. 518–24, 552–62. See also *J.A.A.*, April 1956, p. 93.

[4] *Arrêté*, 14 September 1898, and *Ordonnance*, 19 May 1932. *Codes et Lois du Congo Belge*, 1954, p. 552.

[5] *The Times*, 19 January 1956.

series of local agencies throughout the Belgian Congo.[1] Each of the latter has an Advisory Committee with African members. The *Office* is responsible for the construction of houses for lease or sale to Africans in the towns of the Belgian Congo, and may also make loans to them for building. It is financed by a revolving fund of 750 million francs, and a loan of 1,000 million francs from the Belgian Treasury; its losses are to be borne by the Colonial budget. It has undertaken to build a total of 33,000 houses; 2,875 had been built by June 1953.[2] It is significant that in Elisabethville Africans have built and own the proprietary rights in no less than 8,000 houses.

No one could fail to be struck by the contrast between the well-ordered appearance of the African houses in the *cités indigènes* of Leopoldville or Elisabethville and the sordid African settlements which have sprung up in the neighbourhood of Johannesburg. There is an equal impression of contrast in the lives of the residents. They are purely African; Europeans are not allowed to stay in the *cité indigène* without special authority from the Administration.[3] There is a general appearance of order and well-being among them. The public services appear to be well maintained; electric light is available to occupants who can pay for it. Critics remark on the large number of *brasseries* and on the large proportion of *femmes libres* or *femmes célibataires* in the population, but similar phenomena seem to be universal in urban Africa.

One gains generally a favourable impression also from the housing arrangements made for the employees of the majority of the large industrial undertakings in the Belgian Congo. These are of two types. The former is best illustrated by the villages established by the *Forminière* (the *Société internationale forestière et minière du Congo*) which has induced considerable groups of tribesmen to migrate to the neighbourhood of its mines, where they continue to live in accordance with Native custom, selling their surplus foodstuffs to the Company. The *Huileries Congo Belge* has followed a similar policy in order to provide a permanent supply of labour for its oil-palm plantations.

The *Union minière* of Katanga, on the other hand, when it adopted its 'stabilization of labour' policy in 1927,[4] had to look for its labour much farther afield, and had to establish it in an area of poor soil and in a climate unfavourable for agriculture. Although the type of accommodation provided for its employees is that typical of the African village, it has something of an urban character. The huts are of good pattern and well built; they are laid out on carefully planned lines; social services are

---

[1] *Décret*, 30 March 1952; *Arreté Royal*, 14 April 1952. *Codes et Lois du Congo Belge*, 1953, pp. 781–3.

[2] F. Peigneux, 'Le logement du travailleur urbain au Congo Belge et au Ruanda-Urundi et l'office des cités africaines', *Problèmes d'Afrique Centrale*, no. 21, pp. 175–89.

[3] *Codes et Lois du Congo Belge*, 1953, p. 552.   [4] See below, p. 1391.

provided on a generous scale and medical treatment is exceptionally well organized. A bonus is paid to every mother who is confined in a maternity ward; the proper feeding of the young children is ensured through a common refectory at which they have two meals a day. Education is compulsory for children from five to twelve years old; a medical examination of all school children is made once a month.[1] A similar system is observed in the villages attached to the Kilo-Moto mines.[2]

[1] P. Charles, 'Le Problème des centres extra-coutumiers', *Record of 23rd Session of International Colonial Institute*, Annex II, 1936, pp. 33–180. Buell, op. cit. p. 56.

[2] See also Basil Davidson, 'In the Belgian Congo', *New Statesman and Nation*, 10 and 24 April 1954. H. D. Ziman, 'Belgium's Untroubled African', *Daily Telegraph*, 6 April 1954; 'The Congo's Way Ahead', ibid. 8 April 1954.

CHAPTER IX

LAW AND JUSTICE

THE INTRODUCTION OF A SYSTEM OF LAW

THE introduction into Africa of a system of law, based in the main on European concepts, has not only presented to the student of law an interesting series of problems in comparative jurisprudence, but has brought to light difficulties of adjustment which have forced themselves on the attention of the social psychologist. The problems are not entirely new; they have occurred in some form whenever conquering or colonizing nations have faced the need for integrating into their legal system the law of peoples with different habits or standards of social behaviour. There is, for example, much in the history of the evolution of the system of law in the Roman Empire and in British India that is suggestive to the student of its development in Africa, and it may be useful to refer briefly to the subject here.

As Lord Bryce showed,[1] Rome attempted at the outset to confine the operation of her legal system to those indigenous peoples who had the status of 'citizens'; the 'subjects' were left to the operation of their own Courts where such existed, as in Sicily or Greece, or to regulation by tribal custom in the less-advanced areas. Gradually, however, Rome had to face the results of the political forces she was bringing into play. In more civilized areas there was a continuous growth of the numbers admitted to citizenship, and an increasing tendency for the activities of the Administration to pervade the whole public life of the province; in the more backward areas some remedy had to be found for the conflict between tribal observances and civilized concepts. In the metropolis the law had from about the third century B.C. been gradually modified by praetorian edicts to meet the needs of an expanding society; in the provinces the Governor began to regulate the law by his own edict in 'mixed' cases between citizens and aliens and to issue orders regarding the procedure of criminal law in the alien Courts.

During the three formative centuries, 150 B.C. to A.D. 150, the metropolitan law gradually expanded until it became more suitable to the needs of the Empire at large and the provincial law began by a process of absorption to draw nearer to that of the metropolis. The law of property and contract, the penal law, and the system of legal procedure became nearly identical throughout the Empire, but family relations and

---

[1] J. Bryce, *The Roman and the British Empires*, 1914, Essay II.

inheritance were still regulated by customary law. In the third century A.D. the legal distinction between citizens and aliens vanished with the grant of full citizenship to all subjects of the Empire. But the effect was not at first to supersede the customary law peculiar to certain provinces. Even when Imperial legislation took a new and vigorous form under the unifying influence of Christianity, local variations persisted. That remained true even when codification was completed in the reign of Justinian.

The evolution of a system of law in British India moved in another direction, determined as much by diversity of environment as by difference of objective. In India the British had no large body of their own citizens to consider; on the other hand, they encountered an indigenous civilization, shared by a great mass of people, which was probably more tenacious of its customs than any with which the Romans had to reckon. To the British in the days of Clive and Warren Hastings, India appeared to be already regulated by Hindu and Muslim law, which they viewed as developed systems. In effect, however, the law in use consisted of mixed elements. There was an elaborate procedure of inheritance and family law, the Muslim uniform, the Hindu much diversified, but both of them based on writings and textbooks having religious authority. There was a body of well-defined and readily ascertainable custom relating to land; and there were finally certain penal rules drawn from Muslim law and generally enforced throughout what then remained of the Mogul Empire.

To these conditions it was impossible to apply forthwith the English common law of the day, and the early administrators carried on with what they found, applying English law to the English and Indian law to the Indians. Gradually, however, it was found necessary to regularize the law of judicial procedure and the law of crimes; in particular, the penal law of the Muslim Courts had provided for punishments of a type which the British were not prepared to enforce.

The tentative beginnings of a more regular system of legal procedure were extended during the first part of the nineteenth century, a period when the spirit of legal reform inspired by Bentham was in vogue in England. There were two noticeable features in this process. The Administration preferred to issue local regulations suited to Indian conditions, rather than to reproduce in India the forms of English law. The course which it took presented, moreover, definite advantages, since only a small part of the ordinary law of England had been codified. Secondly, all law, including Indian customary law, was administered through the regular tribunals, a process rendered easier by the fact that the subordinate personnel of the judiciary was Indian; no special Courts were instituted or recognized for administering Indian law.

The Indian Law Commissions of 1833, 1853, and 1861 laid the foundations of a uniform system of codified law, including the law of crimes, of criminal and civil procedure, of evidence and of contract. In drawing up these codes the conceptions of English law prevailed, though the form was adapted to Indian conditions; but this process left untouched the body of family law and the law of inheritance, while the law of land tenures, being subject only to Provincial legislation, retained its local characteristics. If the customary law dealing with matrimonial issues or the procedure of succession has in any sense been regularized it is mainly owing to the study which has been given to it in Indian textbooks, or to the fact that it has been administered by the same Courts as the statutory law.

Expressed in the briefest terms, the chief problem of Rome was one of assimilation, and in this respect the Latin mind tended to regard identity of legal rights as a more important element than equality of political powers. The problem of the British in India was primarily to find a system of law which would avoid emphasizing to Indians the fact that the country was passing under the dominion of a Power professing an alien faith. Strongly, therefore, as the British were impressed with the value of a uniform system of law, they were equally strongly moved by the need for maintaining a customary law based on the social and religious life of India.

The student of jurisprudence who may seek to add to the history of the evolution of law in the Roman and the British Indian Empires a chapter tracing its development in Africa will enjoy the advantage that he will have before his eyes a living process. In his approach to this study, however, he will meet one initial difficulty. He will find little evidence that there was in indigenous Africa the conception of law as an organ of authority to be deliberately employed for the purpose of preserving social order or safeguarding private rights.

Such a conception of law was, however, well established in India. Long before the Mogul Empire set up its organization of rule the pillar edicts of the Mauryan Emperor, Asoka, carried an unquestioned authority throughout the greater part of India. In the Mogul régime, the current law was supported by the sanctions of an organized judicial system. It may be that the formulation of law was often irregular and arbitrary, or that the quality of justice administered by the Courts was often doubtful. But the conception of law as one of the organs of rule and of the Courts as its instrument was always there. It is not, of course, the fact that the indigenous Africa of the past had no method by which it could give effect to the will of the community, or could safeguard social order as it understood it. It was not without means of determining the character of private rights. But the method used did not until a relatively late period involve a definite formulation of law.[1] It was a régime of accepted custom,

---

[1] For some examples of indigenous law-making under European influences, see below, p. 609.

variable as circumstances required, but custom was not usually adjusted by a deliberate process of law-making.

Basic Aspects of African Customary Law

There was a period when the study of African customary law seemed to have little contribution to make to those who had to undertake legislation in Africa, for the systems observed were thought to be so alien to European concepts as to disclose little of what, on the Austinian analysis then in vogue, seemed to be the essential characteristics of law. Later students have realized that in this respect the indigenous Africa which first came under the observation of Europeans was at a stage that must have been traversed by many of the earlier civilizations known to history. The laws of the ancient Babylonians, Hebrews, Romans, and Saxons present many analogies to what is to be seen among the African peoples of the present era.[1] If there is any peculiarity in the institutions encountered in a study of prevailing African custom, it does not flow from their intrinsic character. They may differ from the codes familiar to us today, but they exhibit to the modern world some of the scenes in a story which must have been enacted in a distant past in parts of the Middle East and at later eras in Rome, Germany, or Britain.

Scholars who have sought to define the objective of African customary law have described it as primarily designed to maintain the social equilibrium,[2] and they have held that the remedies applied for the punishment of offences or the righting of wrongs were normally seen as a means to restore that equilibrium. The apparent deficiency of a penal or deterrent sanction on the one hand, and on the other hand the prominence given to compensation for wrongs done, are, they consider, sufficiently explained by this view.

But in one respect this conception of the position needs to be amplified. While all African societies have held a clear conception of mutual obligations not all had evolved judicial institutions in which a sentence was passed and executed. In societies where a judicial machinery was lacking recourse was necessarily had to some measure of 'self-help'. Loss of life or the commission of less serious offences were compounded by the payment of compensation by the kinsmen on one side which was apportioned among the kinsmen on the other side. It was usual for an injured party to employ a friend who acted for him much as a solicitor, in order to mediate and obtain the best compensation obtainable; often he might use methods

[1] A. S. Diamond, *Primitive Law*, 1935, p. 174.

[2] J. H. Driberg, 'The African Conception of Law', *Journal of Comparative Legislation and International Law*, 3rd series, vol. xvi, Part IV, November 1934, pp. 230–45. A. R. Radcliffe-Brown, 'Primitive Law', *Structure and Function in Primitive Society*, 1952. B. Malinowski, *Crime and Custom in Savage Society*, 1926, and Introduction to H. I. Hogbin's *Law and Order in Polynesia*, 1934. W. Seagle, *The Quest for Law*, 1941. G. W. Paton, *A Textbook of Jurisprudence*, 1946, Chapter II.

which would now be termed as 'third degree'. In such circumstances political authorities might have no function other than that of performing a rite at the reconciliation of the parties to a feud. Only in the more highly centralized polities was the execution of decisions carried out by an agent responsible to the ruler; more often, even where he pronounced judgement, it was left to the aggrieved party or their friends to carry it out.

The conception of a crime as an offence against an impersonal community was rare, but the germ of the idea was present when an offender paid compensation to his Chief or Headman as well as to the injured party. A murderer, for instance, might be called upon to compensate a Chief because he had shed blood in his country in addition to making payment to the relatives of the deceased. The settlement of disputes, whether by making arrangements for mediation or by the exercise of judicial powers, was universally regarded as an essential and indeed a most important function of political authority. As Sir H. Maine observed, 'In primitive conditions, that which lies most in the background is the legislative power; that which is most distinctly conceived is judicial power.'[1] The persistence of this conception is seen today in objections that are sometimes raised against projects for the reorganization of the system of Native Tribunals; 'A Chief', it is urged, 'is not a Chief if he has no Court.' Where law derives its validity from custom (as opposed to enactment) the conception implicit in the theory of a separation of the powers of a ruler as law-giver and as Judge cannot arise. The authority of the traditional ruler was such that he could secure enforcement of his orders without the intervention of an independent Judge.

Introduction of European Legal Conceptions

For the African the most conspicuous changes caused by the introduction of European legal conceptions were first, that recognized breaches of the law were now settled not by redress for the aggrieved but by punishment of the transgressor, and second, that a large number of actions which had not hitherto been regarded as wrong now became offences punishable in law. Thus he found, for example, that where the doctrine of self-help resulted in violence, violence was an offence against the law. So also was the strangulation at birth of twins, in spite of the fact that in some tribal areas the birth of twins was firmly held to threaten misfortune to the whole community. He found in more recent times that a growing number of minor omissions and commissions, such as riding a bicycle without a light or failing to comply with an agricultural regulation, came within the same category. Each of these experiences demanded an effort of adjustment, though in the great diversity of conditions in Africa the degree of effort required must also have differed widely.

[1] Sir H. Maine, *Lectures on the Early History of Institutions*, 1875, pp. 388–9.

But perhaps the greatest effort involved was caused by the introduction to Africa of European methods of procedure for the trial of offenders against the law, whether in its capacity as the protector of private rights or as the guardian of public order. It was here that the African must have experienced the greatest sense of change. He no doubt realized that the procedure adopted was intended to secure an equitable decision, and he was not slow to appreciate the value of this intention. But he must often have reflected on its shortcomings in this respect, due to the form of judicial machinery employed for ascertaining the truth. Whatever the merits of this procedure may have been in the conditions of contemporary Europe, they were not readily recognized by the African in the early days of European administration. It was fortunate that in so many areas of European rule the majority of civil issues, including those arising in the field of personal law, as also the less important criminal cases, continued to be tried by Native Tribunals which followed their own traditional procedure.

The difficulties of adjustment created by the introduction to Africa of European law have been increased by a factor which only assumed significance in the later stages of the development of law in the Roman Empire and in British India. In most parts of the world legislation has now become the instrument for giving definite form to the changes which a community deems best suited to minister to its social and material advance. In Africa the system of law introduced by the European Powers is passing beyond the rudimentary purpose of maintaining order, and it has already entered on a more extended phase requiring the promulgation of a wide range of enactment designed to effect improvement in the economic and social conditions of the country.

Such an enlargement of the scope of legislation has brought into prominence the question of its relation to public opinion and to the general social background. Even when the chief purpose of legislation is only to implement the more elementary requirements of social order, the lawgiver has to ask himself whether the law he is introducing is not so far alien to all the African associations which regulate the behaviour of the people as to be unlikely to secure an instinctive respect from them. It is implicit in the modern conception of the function of law that its process cannot be purely authoritarian; it obtains its most effective sanctions not from imposed obedience, but by evoking some answering contribution from those to whom it is applied. There are, moreover, many thinkers who hold that we ought not to limit ourselves to this obvious precaution against maladjustment; it is not merely a question of making it easier for the lawgiver to secure obedience for his law. Whatever the relative value of African conceptions, they must have for the law-giver a positive value as the expression of the forces which regulate African conduct, and it has been held that we ought to begin by inquiring how far we can use them as part of the foundation on which new African institutions can be built up. The principle which underlies this view is closely akin to that which has inspired the use of traditional Native Authorities as part of the machinery of executive administration.[1]

THE SOURCES OF LAW

It is at this stage important to consider the actual source of the law now in force in the different African countries, since this may in itself afford some indication of the measure to which there has been a conscious adjustment of legal conceptions to the needs of the African environment. It will be seen that there is a diversity in the sources of law which reflects the differences in political and social objectives of which some account has been given in the two preceding chapters.

Union of South Africa

Since 1934, when the Union enacted the Status of the Union Act and Seals Act, it has exercised the full powers of legislation enjoyed by a sovereign State. There was a period of South African history when the course of domestic legislation was influenced, though it was not controlled, by views held in the British Parliament on Colonial policy, as for instance in respect of the extension of the franchise to Africans. But as seen today, the main body of law is largely the product of legislation enacted by a territorial Parliament composed entirely of Europeans and strongly concerned with the promotion of European interests. In recent years legislation has, under the influence of the current policy of segregation, tended to emphasize more sharply the line of demarcation between the status of the European and non-European communities. If there has been any restriction in this process, it is only as the result of judicial decisions which have pointed to the need for compliance with the procedure laid down in the Act of Union for enacting legislation which may affect certain of the constitutional provisions contained in that Act. The needs arising from the existence of a large African population have been met by the enactment of special laws relating to them, rather than by a modification of the general body of law, and there is in consequence a considerable body of differential legislation which directly affects non-Europeans and Africans.

The recognition of the Native customary law has (except in Natal and the Transkeian Territories) come late and hesitatingly, for the early law-givers in the Cape showed marked reluctance to face the legal consequences of the absorption of the Native people in their economy. In theory the civil law of the Cape was applied to them, but in practice

[1] See above, p. 539.

Magistrates were driven to disregard the law and to apply Bantu custom, and the extra-legal Native Court at King William's Town became a notable, if an anomalous, feature of the Cape system.[1] It was only the special circumstances of the Transkeian Territories which compelled the Cape Parliament to make provision between 1879 and 1894 for the application of Bantu law to them.[2] In Natal, on the other hand, the recognition of Bantu law, which was an essential element of the Shepstone policy,[3] was formally accepted in an Ordinance of 1847. A codification of the Native law of Natal was made in 1878 and was issued as a schedule to Law 19 of 1891.[4]

The recognition given to African customary law in the Transvaal and in the Orange Free State was strictly limited, and as a result the most difficult legal situations were liable to arise. In numerous reported cases, for example, the Courts refused to recognize the validity of a customary union or the status accorded to women by Native law, on the ground of 'inconsistency with the general principles of civilization'.[5]

It was therefore a definite advance on the previous position when section 11 of the Native Administration Act of 1927 gave statutory recognition to Native law in all Provinces of the Union to the extent of authorizing its application by certain special Courts. It must be noted at the same time that this measure was directed less to the maintenance of African customary law than to differentiating its field. Though it enabled some provision to be made for dealing on uniform lines with cases involving questions of Native custom, it still left indefinite the position which African law was to occupy. Doubts have arisen, for example, as to the manner in which Native Commissioners should exercise their discretionary powers of applying Native law and, in particular, whether priority is to be accorded to Native or to European law.

It is unfortunate that on such questions the Higher Courts have not always given clear guidance.[6] Moreover, while it may be argued that the ordinary Courts have discretion to apply Native law in civil cases wherever such law satisfies the tests required under English and Roman–Dutch law for the recognition of local custom,[7] its effective application seems in practice to be confined mainly to those areas in which special Courts for Africans have been established. These special Courts comprise not only

---

[1] See above, p. 420.

[2] H. Rogers, *Native Administration in the Union of South Africa*, 2nd ed., 1949, p. 200.

[3] See above, p. 423.   [4] Reproduced in *African Studies*, 1943, pp. 1–26.

[5] G. M. Whitfield, *South African Native Law*, 2nd ed., 1929, p. 8. A. Phillips, ed., *Survey of African Marriage and Family Life*, 1953, pp. 176–89.

[6] H. J. Simons, 'The Law and its Administration', in *Handbook on Race Relations in South Africa*, 1949, p. 51.

[7] J. Lewin, 'The Recognition of Native Law and Custom in British Africa', *Journal of Comparative Legislation and International Law*, 3rd ser., vol. xx, 1938, pp. 16–23. S. M. Seymour, *Native Law in South Africa*, 1953, pp. 1–2.

those conducted by Native Chiefs and Headmen and by Native Commissioners,[1] but also Native Appeal Courts. The activity of these Appeal Courts since 1929 has resulted in the accumulation of a growing body of case-law, contained in published Law Reports.

In the purely juristic field South African law has a special characteristic which it shares with that of Southern Rhodesia. It is an heir to the tradition of Roman law. The Roman–Dutch law which the first colonists brought with them was however largely modified at a later date by the English common law. As early as 1827 the Charter of Justice introduced the jury system and brought the law of evidence into harmony with English law. Henceforth the law in its procedural aspect became largely English, a fact of major importance, for experience shows that it is the procedure of the tribunals rather than the principles of the law that gives it its distinctive character in the eyes of the population at large.

Southern Rhodesia

When Southern Rhodesia achieved the status of Responsible Government in 1923 it acquired full power to legislate for its internal affairs, subject to two conditions, first, that the Governor should reserve for the signification of the pleasure of the Crown any Act relating to alterations in the constitution of the Legislative Council, and second, that the sanction of the Secretary of State should be required for any law imposing differential treatment on Natives, save in respect of the sale or supply to them of arms or liquor.[2] Legislation has from the first been in the hands of a Legislature composed entirely of Europeans, for though non-Natives share in the franchise their number on the roll has not hitherto been large enough to ensure the election of a non-European member.[3] Some mention has already been made of the extent to which legislation has been directed to establish the political and social position of Europeans; it is sufficient to note here that its tendency has in this respect been less marked than in the Union of South Africa.

The Colony has also occupied a different position from the Union in regard to the recognition of African law. The need for recognizing the customary law was acknowledged from the outset; the Charter of the British South Africa Company required that careful regard should always be had to Native customs and laws, especially with respect to property (including land), succession, and family relations. The Order in Council of 1898 directed that in civil cases between Natives the Courts should be guided by Native law, so far as it was not repugnant to natural justice or morality or to any enactment in force. In practice Africans are subject to the criminal law applying also to Europeans. In regard to the civil law

---

[1] See above, p. 360.   [2] See above, p. 182. See also *O.T.S.R.*, *1952*, pp. 49–50.
[3] See above, pp. 283–4.

regulating matrimony, succession, and the like, the customary law has been maintained, though affected in some respects by enactments intended to eliminate what was thought undesirable.

The Roman–Dutch system of law was introduced in the Colony by the Southern Rhodesia Order in Council, 1898, which laid down that the law to be administered by the Courts should be the same as that in force in the Cape Colony in 1891. Here, however, even greater inroads have been made upon the Roman–Dutch system by local legislation and by the adoption of English legal principles. The English law, it has been said, 'is a rich mine to which legislators and judges are constantly turning to supplement the common law, particularly in the direction of mercantile law, and in criminal and adjective law'.

The adherence of Southern Rhodesia to the Federation of Rhodesia and Nyasaland has not materially affected the position of its Legislature in respect of domestic legislation. As already shown the Federal Legislature has exclusive powers only in respect of certain defined matters, such as the law relating to income-tax, customs, railways, and the like, which are of interest to all three constituent territories.[1] Since matters which are primarily of interest to Africans remain as subjects of territorial legislation, the scope for Federal legislation is limited in this respect, but as already observed the Constitution also provides a special machinery, in the form of a Standing Committee of the Federal Assembly, as a safeguard for African interests.[2]

The Federal Supreme Court has exclusive jurisdiction in certain matters, such as differences arising between the Federation and its constituent territories or the interpretation of the Federal Constitution, and it has also exclusive appellate jurisdiction from the territorial High Courts on questions relating to the interpretation of the Federal or territorial Constitutions.[3] The Supreme Court was established in July 1955. The recognition given to Roman–Dutch law in Southern Rhodesia had involved the necessity of recognizing the Appellate Division of the judicature in the Union as the final Court of Appeal from the decisions of the High Court of Southern Rhodesia in matters of law.[4] Steps were, however, taken in 1955 to change the law in this respect, and to recognize the Supreme Court as the final appellate authority.

Other British Territories

As regard the two other constituent members of the Federation of Rhodesia and Nyasaland, Northern Rhodesia and Nyasaland, their position in respect of the formation of Colonial law does not differ materially

---

[1] See above, p. 279.   [2] See above, p. 281.
[3] Rhodesia and Nyasaland Federation, Order in Council no. 1199 of 1953, Article 55, p. 35.
[4] *O.Y.S.R. 1952*, p. 336.

from that of the large group of British dependencies of which the status falls short of Responsible Government. As has been made clear in a previous chapter, there is from the standpoint of constitutional development little practical difference between those dependencies which are designated as Colonies, Protectorates, Protected States, or Trust Territories.[1] The Colony is in a full sense part of the possessions of the Crown, and its inhabitants are British subjects; inhabitants of a Protectorate are not British subjects, but British protected persons. As such they are not aliens, but are 'foreign subjects of the Crown'.[2] For the inhabitant of a dependency the distinction normally becomes apparent only when he travels outside it, but the distinction has a definite bearing on the political system in Northern Rhodesia, where the franchise is at present confined to British subjects. Until existing legislation is modified, it will be necessary for an African or other protected person to apply for naturalization as a citizen of the United Kingdom and Colonies before he can qualify for the vote as a British subject.[3]

Reference has also been made in a previous chapter to the juristic basis of the right claimed by Great Britain to exercise authority in the different classes of dependencies, and also to the procedure by which various forms of Regulation or Ordinance having the force of law have been enacted for them.[4] We are concerned here, however, mainly with the exercise of that aspect of jurisdiction which is responsible for the introduction of a system of law and the organization of justice. In these dependencies the source of law is twofold. In principle, the original or basic law has consisted of English law as applied to the territory by the relevant enactment in which jurisdiction over it was asserted. Section 38 of the Courts Ordinance of the Colony of Sierra Leone may be taken as a typical instance: 'Subject to the provisions of this or any other Ordinance, the common law, the doctrines of equity, and the statutes of general application in force in England on the 1st day of January, 1880, shall be in force in Sierra Leone.'

Almost from the first, however, there has been a tendency to meet the expanding needs of the Colonies and Protectorates not by the further extension to them of Imperial legislation, but by the issue of local regulations, which as the dependencies came to be endowed with Legislatures, took increasingly the form of enactment of local legislation. Thus the great body of existing law in the British dependencies has been secured by local legislation; what has been described above as original or basic law has tended to assume the character only of a residual law, still operative within certain limited fields (as for example the law of contract and of

---

[1] See references given above, p. 146.

[2] See the Privy Council Judgement in the case *Sobhuza II* v. *Miller*, 1926, A.C. p. 518. See also G. W. Keeton and G. Schwarzenberger, eds., *Current Legal Problems 1954*, p. 177.

[3] *Central African Territories, Report of Conference on Closer Association*, Cmd. 8233, 1951, p. 43.

[4] See above, pp. 285–7.

torts), but providing elsewhere guiding principles rather than substantive law.

The local Legislatures have themselves derived their authority from the United Kingdom, either by virtue of direct legislation by Parliament or by issue of a Crown Instrument,[1] but within the limits imposed by their status as subordinate Legislatures they have full power to legislate 'for the peace, order and good government' of the territories concerned. As has been explained, it is now very unusual for Parliament in the United Kingdom or for the Crown to enact laws directly applicable to the dependencies. It is equally rare for Crown Instruments to be employed as a means of legislation, save for the purpose of modifying the Constitution of the dependency or for regulating matters that concern more than one territory. Control over the proceedings of a Colonial Legislature is effected mainly by previous consultation between the Colonial Office and the Government of a dependency, but on occasion also by the use of the 'reserve' powers of the executive head of the Colonial Government. The instances of the use of this power are however very rare.

Apart from the adaptation of some part of the English substantive law or its procedure, the Colonial law has certain characteristics, due largely to the influence of British legal conceptions. Thus the 'rule of law' is maintained in the sense that the Executive is assumed to have no powers, prerogative or otherwise, which entitle it to take action against personal liberties or individual property, otherwise than in strict accordance with statute or common law.[2] Though the Colonial law may give a certain limited protection to officials in discharge of their duties, there is a uniform rule that administrative actions are held to be justiciable in the ordinary Courts.[3] It is also very rare to give to the Executive Authority any power to fine or imprison without resort to judicial process. There is a second distinctive feature of the British system which deserves mention. It admits of the creation of a body of subordinate legislation by Native Authorities, who have been given by statute the power of making rules to the breach of which legal penalties are attached. The nature of these rules is more fully explained elsewhere;[4] but they must be regarded as creating an additional source which has added largely to the general body of Colonial law.

The fact that so large a part of the body of law is the result of enactment by local legislation adds significance to the information given in the preceding chapter regarding the composition of the Legislatures,[5] particularly

---

[1] For the practice in regard to Crown Instruments, see above, p. 286.

[2] To this rule the possibility of pleading the defence of 'act of State' for torts committed in Protectorates must apparently be admitted as an exception. Cf. *The King* v. *Crewe, ex parte Sekgome*, 1910. 2 K.B. 576, in E. C. S. Wade and G. G. Phillips, *Constitutional Law*, 4th ed., 1946, p. 409.

[3] For the Administrative Court in French territories, see below, pp. 603 ff.

[4] See above, pp. 455 ff.   [5] See above, pp. 290 ff.

in respect of the progressive increase in the number of unofficial members, including in some cases a large proportion of Africans. In some instances it has only been possible for the Government of the day to secure the enactment of a law by the use of the official majority; there are instances, as in the Gold Coast, where unofficial opposition has compelled it to abandon a number of projects of legislation which were regarded by it as being for the express benefit of the African public.[1]

But it would not be correct to conclude that the general body of law resulting from local legislation has as yet been definitely coloured by the influence of the growing African membership on the Legislatures; its influence is perhaps best seen in what the law omits rather than what it includes. Nor is it possible to say that the result has gone far to produce a common body of law covering both non-Africans and Africans. In some of the multi-racial dependencies, as most conspicuously in Kenya, there are instances of discriminatory law, referring only to Africans, but this is a feature which is much less prominent in areas (such as the West African dependencies) where European interests command less influence in the Legislature.

There is a further point. We still have to await a time when the Colonial law will embrace any substantial body of legislation on the 'personal' law of Africans, in the sense of law which regulates the system of inheritance, marriage, and similar relationships of Africans living under their own customs. The earlier Orders in Council contemplated (to quote one example) that the Colonial Courts should decide cases in which Natives were parties 'according to substantial justice, without undue regard to technicalities of procedure and without undue delay'. Elsewhere it was provided that 'in all cases, civil and criminal, to which Natives are parties, every Court shall be guided by Native law so far as it is applicable, and is not repugnant to justice and morality or inconsistent with any Order in Council or Ordinance'.[2] That general prescription reappeared in a more definite form in many of the laws defining the jurisdiction of the Colonial Courts; thus the Courts Ordinance of the Gold Coast provided that 'nothing in this Ordinance . . . shall deprive any person of the benefit of any Native law or custom . . . such law or custom not being repugnant to natural justice, equity, and good conscience'.[3] These provisions, however, left a wide field of uncertainty as to the exact law which might be applied in any particular case.

In a few instances, as in the Gold Coast, the trial by the Colonial Courts of certain prominent types of cases led to the growth of a case law based on Native law, but elsewhere Native law has remained for the most part outside the system of law as administered by the Colonial Courts.

[1] See above, p. 318.　　[2] See, for example, Uganda Order in Council, 1902, Article 20.
[3] Gold Coast, Laws, cap. 4, section 74.

This hiatus has to a large extent been filled by the formal organization of the system of Native Tribunals or Native Courts to which detailed reference has been made in Chapter VIII. But the addition of these Courts to the hierarchy of Colonial Courts has created certain new problems in the administration of justice. At an early stage it was appreciated that the Native Courts might develop along two different lines. They might on the one hand remain entirely independent of the system of justice as administered by the Colonial Courts, and they might to that extent be described as proceeding along a parallel course to that followed by those Courts, subject to the qualification that certain major civil issues and the more serious type of criminal cases were normally reserved by law for cognizance by the Colonial Court. On the other hand they might at some point make contact with the system of Colonial Courts, and become to that extent integrated with them.

The comparative merits of these two developments were at an early stage a matter of some controversy among those who were concerned with the evolution of the system of Native Administration in the British areas.[1] It is sufficient to say here that the more recent tendency has been towards maintaining at some point a link between the Colonial Court and the Native Court systems, and the instances in which the 'parallel' system have been retained are now comparatively rare.[2] But there is considerable diversity in the practice which prescribes the nature of this link. The well-known Report on the Kenya Tribunals published in 1945 expressed the view that it was desirable to retain 'at least a token link with the Supreme Court',[3] but the point of contact in this Territory is in fact remote and is reached only at the ultimate Appeal tribunal. In Tanganyika the dual system inaugurated during the governorship of Sir Donald Cameron is such as to provide only a tenuous link with the High Court, and the system may properly be classed in the same category as Kenya. Elsewhere, and especially in West Africa, the Native Court structure is definitely integrated with that of the Colonial Court, and the process will be intensified if the more recent recommendations made for the Gold Coast are adopted.[4]

From the details which have been given in Chapter VIII regarding the actual operation of the system of Native Courts in the British dependencies it will be appreciated that they dispose of a very large body of litigation, applying everywhere the Native customary law, subject to the condition of repugnancy. The effect is to bring into the general body of Civil law as administered by judicial processes those phases of unwritten Native law

---

[1] See, for example, Lord Lugard, *The Dual Mandate in Tropical Africa*, 1926, pp. 540 ff.
[2] Judicial Advisers' Conference, 1953, supplement to *J.A.A.*, October 1953, p. 5.
[3] A. Phillips, *Report on Native Tribunals, Kenya*, 1945, p. 318.
[4] *Gold Coast, Report of the Commission on Native Courts*, 1951.

which deal with land, inheritance, or marital relations. The operation of the Native Court system also adds to the Criminal law a certain number of offences, in the shape of actions violating tribal custom, which would not necessarily be classed as offences under the statutory law.

So far therefore as the British dependencies are concerned the position may be summarized as follows. By far the greater part of the statute law is derived from enactments of local Legislatures, over which metropolitan control is now being increasingly relaxed, and in which the proportion of African membership is progressively increasing. The statutory law is normally administered by the Colonial Courts. There is, second, a considerable body of subsidiary statute law, in the form of Rules made by Native Authorities acting under statutory sanction. This subsidiary law is administered by the Native Courts. There is, third, a body of unwritten customary law, embodying for the most part the personal law of the various indigenous communities. This is administered by the Native Courts, which are supervised by officers of the Administration, but are in the majority of the dependencies linked with the Colonial Courts through the process of appeal.

The French Territories

In the French dependencies of tropical Africa we have to deal only with Colonies and Trust Territories; there is not the added complication of the Protectorate status such as exists in the British dependencies. In the French Colonies the basis of jurisdiction is to be found in the position within the *Union Française* which has been accorded to them under the Constitution of 1946;[1] in the Trust Territories the right of jurisdiction is held to flow from *décrets* of January 1948 which were based on the acceptance by France of the Trust Agreements of December 1946. Legislation is in these areas of a more uniform type than in the British dependencies in the sense that it has either emanated directly from the metropolitan Parliament or where it takes the form of *décret*, has been closely controlled by metropolitan influences.

To some extent the position is liable to change in this respect owing to the tendency shown in the new Constitution to give greater power of legislation to the local *conseils*,[2] but it still remains to be seen how far this movement will in practice withstand the force of the tradition of centralization which has hitherto dominated French thinking on Colonial developments. At the present time the evolution of law is being influenced by certain contrasting though not necessarily conflicting principles. On the one hand, the content of legislation is being influenced by the existence of a number of indigenous representatives from the Colonies in the metropolitan parliamentary institutions.[3] On the other hand, the overriding

[1] See above, pp. 211–14.   [2] See above, p. 340.   [3] See above, p. 213.

concept of uniformity in the *Union Française* has produced a tendency to extend throughout it a considerable body of metropolitan legislation, such for instance as the Penal or Labour Codes.

The feeling that the formation of a body of Colonial law is in a stage of transition is increased by the operation of other features of the Constitution of 1946. The wide extension of French citizenship has meant that the distinction between 'citizen' and 'subject' is no longer the basis for the determination of legal status. The significant distinction is now between *citoyens de statut français* and *citoyens de statut local*.[1] Furthermore, not only has the differentiation of legal status been placed on a new basis but its scope has been restricted, in so far that its relevance is now confined to the field of civil and commercial law; in the sphere of criminal jurisdiction there is no such differentiation, since all persons, whatever their degree of citizenship, are now subject to the French *code pénal*, as applied with certain modifications to the overseas territories. Such recognition as was formerly accorded to African law and custom in this particular sphere has now been withdrawn.[2]

French thought regarding the basis of law emphasizes that in any country the laws of Public Order must be regarded as fundamental and applicable to all its inhabitants alike; the interests of the State demand that such laws must on occasion override ancient custom or practices sanctified by religion.[3] It is also held that there must exist a right for any group or section of persons to opt, subject to the overriding force of the laws of Public Order, for the adoption of French law instead of the customary or other law regulating issues such as those of inheritance, succession, or the like.

As the consequence of the division between *citoyens de statut français* and those of the *statut local*, there is now a dual system of Courts, comprising *tribunaux de droit français* and *tribunaux de droit local*. Those in the former category have exclusive jurisdiction in criminal matters; in addition, they are responsible for the administration of the *code civil*, the *code de commerce*, and similar metropolitan laws. They are constituted on the metropolitan model as nearly as local circumstances permit, the most significant difference being first, the substitution of Assessors for the jury system and, second, the admission of Administrative Officers instead of professional lawyers to act as *justices de paix*.[4] The enactments which define the constitution and powers of the *tribunaux de droit local* declare that in civil and commercial matters they are to apply Native customs in so far as these are not 'contraires aux principes de la civilisation française'. This repugnancy

---

[1] L. Rolland and P. Lampué, *Précis de Droit des Pays d'Outre-Mer*, 1952, pp. 239 ff.
[2] Ibid. p. 296.
[3] R. Maunier, trans. E. O. Lorimer, *The Sociology of Colonies*, vol. ii, 1949, pp. 563–5.
[4] Rolland and Lampué, op. cit. pp. 492 ff.

clause is in practice interpreted in accordance with a conception of *ordre public territorial* which is designed to express the ideal of civilization subject to overseas conditions.[1]

The Colonial law shares with the metropolitan law the principle of the *droit administratif*; that is to say, that executive and administrative actions as such are justiciable not in the ordinary Courts but in a special Administrative Court.[2] In actual practice the *droit administratif*, in the form it has assumed in modern French law, is surrounded by safeguards which make its exercise less noteworthy as an invasion of private rights than is often assumed. It may be added that the *régime disciplinaire de l'indigénat*, under which Administrative authorities formerly possessed the summary power of inflicting extra-judicial punishment on Natives who were not of the status of *citoyens*, has been abolished.[3]

The application of this régime of 'summary justice' was admittedly a deviation from French law,[4] and had features which brought it under frequent criticism in practice. It was difficult for the higher authorities in a dependency to apply safeguards against its abuse, for there was no trial held and no appeal was possible against the decision of the Administrative Officer who inflicted the punishment; indeed the greater part of a sentence (the maximum penalty being two weeks) would often have been served before notice of appeal could reach higher authority. Protests against the system were made at different periods in the *Conseil Colonial*, and in 1924 a decree was issued which exempted from the *indigénat* eight classes of Africans.[5] Exemption from the *indigénat* became in effect a certificate that an African had attained recognition as a member of the *élite*. It will be recalled that the abolition of this system had a prominent place among the recommendations made by the Brazzaville Conference of 1944.[6]

The Belgian Territories

Compared with the position in the dependencies of Great Britain and France the determination of the source of law in the Belgian Congo presents far less difficulty. Its basis is the *Charte Coloniale* of 1908 and the supplementary metropolitan legislation, enacted in the form either of parliamentary statute or Royal Decree; there is in the Colony no local institution having legislative competence, and an *ordonnance-loi* of the Governor-General has validity for only six months unless confirmed by a Decree. The whole

---

[1] Rolland and Lampué, op. cit. p. 287.
[2] P. Dareste, *Traité de droit colonial*, vol. i, 1931, p. 522.
[3] *Décrets*, 22 December 1945, 20 February 1946. See Rolland and Lampué, op. cit. p. 296.
[4] R. Maunier, *The Sociology of Colonies*, vol. ii, 1949, p. 708.
[5] For the terms of the relevant *décret*, see R. L. Buell, *The Native Problem in Africa*, vol. ii, 1928, pp. 378–92.
[6] See above, p. 210.

body of declared law is to be found in the useful publication, *Codes et Lois du Congo Belge*, which has periodically been brought up to date.[1]

The circumstances which determined the framing of the Constitution combined to give it from the outset a more comprehensive form than that of any other Colonial dependency included within the scope of this Survey, and it is of interest to consider how far its authors anticipated that the *Charte* would actually form the basis of a uniform body of law for all the communities in the country. At the beginning the view seems to have been held that the statutory law, based on the Belgian model, could become the prevailing Colonial law regulating the civil rights of Belgians, stranger Europeans, and *immatriculés*. Africans would be regulated by the Native customary law, so far as it was not inconsistent with the statutory law or *l'ordre public*,[2] but it was considered that the process of *immatriculation* would provide an avenue by which an increasing number of Africans would in due time be absorbed within the range of 'civilized' law.

The process of *immatriculation* was, in its original design, automatically operative in the case of some categories of Africans, as for example those who had been employed for more than two years as resident workers by a European enterprise; in other cases it was conditional on the observance of certain formalities; in all cases it entailed the abandonment of Native law as the personal law of the individual concerned. But, as has already been shown,[3] the extension of the process of *immatriculation* was slow, nor indeed is there evidence of any enthusiasm for quickening it. Neither on political nor on social grounds are the Belgians as ready as the French to welcome association with an educated African *élite*, and it is characteristic that as the European population of the Belgian Congo increased there was a growing tendency to raise the standard of the qualifications which were required of the candidate for *immatriculation*. The African, on his part, also appeared unwilling to abandon his own social custom as the price of admission to the ranks of the *immatriculés*. Meanwhile there was a growing appreciation by Europeans of the value to be gained from organizing a system of Native Administration which would utilize the African traditional institutions, and from constituting the Native Tribunals as supplements to the Courts administering the statutory law.[4] The present tendency appears to point to the gradual assimilation of the African customary law to 'civilized' conceptions and practice, rather than to aim at an increased absorption of Africans within the range of the Belgian law.

In the Belgian Congo, as elsewhere, the institution of Native Courts, properly so called, gave a more clearly recognized position to African customary law. For civil purposes the great majority of Africans come

---

[1] P. Piron et J. Devos, *Codes et Lois du Congo Belge*, 1954.
[2] Piron and Devos, op. cit. p. 873.   [3] See above, pp. 224–6.
[4] For Native Administration in the Belgian Congo, see above, p. 550.

under their own law, and this may now be said to constitute part of the general law, in so far that the decisions of the Native Courts form part of a recognized judicial process. The Native law applied remains of course subject to the condition of repugnancy to *l'ordre public* which, as in the case of French law, is a term of wide significance. For criminal purposes Africans are regulated by the Penal Code and the Code of Criminal Procedure, as administered by the Belgian Courts in the Colony. Native Courts are, as far as possible, restrained from trying cases which come under the Penal Code, but as the distinction between civil and criminal matters is not always clear to the Native Courts, a considerable number of cases are disposed of by them which might otherwise have been held to come under the Penal Code.

The recognition given to the Native Courts had, moreover, the effect of extending the scope of the criminal law where Africans are concerned in as much as the Courts are allowed to take cognizance of offences against Native customary law which are not within the scope of the written law; but offences against the State, breaches of Administrative Regulations, and the more serious criminal offences always come for trial under the Penal Code. There is, however, one limitation to the acceptance given by Africans themselves to the use of the Native Court and the customary law. Here as elsewhere the customary system of law has not proved to be adequate to the needs of the new generation of *évolués*; and, as shown in a previous chapter, provision was made in a decree of 1952 for a revised procedure of *immatriculation*.[1]

The Portuguese Territories

As has been shown in previous chapters, the only source of legislation for the overseas Provinces of Portugal has hitherto been the enactment of metropolitan law or ministerial decree. Recent constitutional changes envisage the grant of legislative powers to the Councils of the Governors-General of Angola and Mozambique,[2] but it is not clear from the terms of the law of the Constitution how far the actual range of legislation will extend. The law-making capacity of the Councils will be restricted to matters which do not fall within the range of functions of the National Assembly and the measures enacted will be subject to close control of the Ministry of Overseas Provinces.[3] The only law at present recognized in the Provinces is the common law, so termed, which proceeds from the metropolitan sources above referred to, and it is this law which is administered by the Courts of Justice. This body of law has been primarily framed to regulate the legal relations of Europeans, but the *assimilados*,

---

[1] See above, p. 354.   [2] See above, pp. 355–6.
[3] A. Durieux, 'Essai sur le statut des indigènes portugais de la Guinée, de l'Angola et du Mozambique', *Mém. A.R.S.C.*, vol. v, no. 3, 1955, p. 26.

who correspond to the *immatriculés* of the Belgian Congo system, share fully in the legal régime which it establishes and come for all purposes within the jurisdiction of the Courts referred to.

Though there is no formal recognition of the African customary law, the Constitution recognizes in general terms the existence of certain Native rights, as more particularly their rights in land. It would appear, however, that the intention of the law is to define the position of the State in regard to the acquisition of rights over land held or claimed by Natives, rather than to define the rights of Natives *inter se*.[1]

Since there is no formal recognition given to African customary law there are no Native Courts, but as explained in a previous chapter,[2] efforts are made by the officers presiding over the ordinary Courts to take account of the customary law of the parties in cases where both parties are Africans.

THE ADMINISTRATION OF JUSTICE

The problem of building up a régime of law in Africa has thus been approached from a number of different standpoints, and it is difficult to attempt any objective assessment of the results, for each system is part of a different philosophy of rule. It may be claimed on behalf of the British system that the procedure whereby the bulk of legislation is enacted after discussion in a local Legislature at least ensures that the law-giver must take account of the sentiments of the people most closely concerned. On the other hand—though this is perhaps a matter of relatively less concern —it has led to a noticeable lack of uniformity in the law as between territories similarly placed.[3] Certain efforts have, however, been made to introduce something in the nature of common form. At the outset the East African dependencies secured a measure of uniformity by adopting certain of the Indian codes, and though these have since been replaced by local Ordinances, the latter follow the form of models drawn up by the legal Advisers at the British Colonial Office. The French and Belgian system of legislating by Decree has the advantage of elasticity and dispatch; but French authorities have themselves criticized the present system as something of an anachronism in modern conditions.[4] Belgian writers have also criticized the system now applied to the Belgian Congo, on the ground that it withdraws initiative from the Colonial authorities;[5] it seems at all events to make initiative depend to an undue measure on the personal relations between the Ministry and the Governor-General.

---

[1] Durieux, op. cit. pp. 41 ff.   [2] See above, p. 563.

[3] M. Wight, *The Development of the Legislative Council, 1606–1945*, 1946, pp. 140–1.

[4] P. Leroy-Beaulieu, *De la colonisation chez les peuples modernes*, vol. ii, 1908, p. 670. S. H. Roberts, *History of French Colonial Policy, 1870–1925*, vol. i, 1929, p. 153.

[5] P. Ryckmans, *La politique coloniale*, 1933, pp. 21–22.

It is perhaps true, however, that in the present circumstances of Africa, the procedure actually adopted in the application of the law and in the administration of justice are matters of greater concern to the mass of the population than the source of law or the processes adopted for legislation. There is throughout the different territories a great variety of practice in this respect which it would be impossible to describe in detail; but it is necessary to summarize its main features.

The Union of South Africa

In the Union of South Africa the machinery for the administration of justice comprises a co-ordinated system of superior Courts, which has as its apex an Appellate Division to which lie appeals in civil cases, with the leave of a Provincial Division Court, and since 1948 also in criminal cases, with leave of the trial Court.[1] There is a Provincial Division for each of the four Provinces, and Local Divisions which have local jurisdiction within the areas of the Provincial Divisions. They have original jurisdiction both in criminal and civil matters, and the Provincial Divisions and the Eastern Districts and Griqualand West Local Divisions (but not other Local Divisions) have appellate criminal jurisdiction from Magistrates Courts, and also have appellate civil jurisdiction. The Natal Court has original criminal jurisdiction which is restricted to offences committed by Africans in Natal.[2] All these Courts have a well-established tradition of judicial independence and are strongly professional in character.

Magistrates have civil jurisdiction and also criminal jurisdiction over offences committed within their area, except treason, murder, and rape,[3] but their powers of punishment are limited to a maximum of six months' imprisonment or a fine of £50 and twelve strokes with a cane; their competence in civil cases is confined to those where the claim does not exceed £200. Magistrates are members of the Civil Service of the Union, and discharge both administrative and judicial functions; the arrangement is discussed elsewhere[4] whereby magisterial functions are exercised by officers of the Departments of Justice or of Native Affairs according to whether the population is predominantly African or non-African.

Native Commissioners' Courts are established for civil cases where both parties are Africans;[5] they are authorized to apply African law and custom, provided they are not opposed to the principles of public policy or natural justice. An appeal lies from the Native Commissioners' Courts to one of three Native Appeal Courts situated respectively at King William's Town, Pretoria, and Johannesburg.[6] These Courts are composed of a President who is a permanent official and two members selected from

---

[1] Act no. 37 of 1948.
[2] Act no. 49 of 1878.
[3] Act no. 32 of 1944.
[4] See above, p. 360.
[5] Act no. 38 of 1927.
[6] Act no. 38 of 1927, Section 13.

a panel of Magistrates or other qualified persons. Normally their decisions are final, but on a case stated leave to appeal may be allowed to the Appellate Division. Three Native Divorce Courts have also been established with jurisdiction conterminous with that of the Native Appeal Courts.[1]

As regards criminal justice the African population is regulated by the ordinary criminal law of the Union, except in the Courts of Chiefs and Headmen. But the jurisdiction of the Chiefs' Courts is of very limited range. At a comparatively early date the Government of Cape Colony accepted a policy which allowed for the retention of judicial powers in the hands of the Chiefs of British Bechuanaland,[2] and the same principle was followed in Natal, but there was no general recognition of the principle of according judicial powers to Native Authorities until the enactment of the Native Administration Act of 1927. This provided for the grant both of civil and criminal jurisdiction to Chiefs and Headmen.

In that Act the civil jurisdiction in cases arising out of Native law and custom was expressed to be without limit, subject to appeal to the Native Commissioner; the criminal jurisdiction, which was confined to offences punishable under Native law and custom, was limited to the imposition of a fine up to £5 or two head of cattle. The use made of the power to grant such jurisdiction has, however, been unequal; there has, for example, been a greater readiness to confer judicial powers on Chiefs and Headmen in Natal and Zululand than in the Transkeian or Ciskeian Territories of the Cape Province, and the power is very little used in the Transvaal or Orange Free State.[3] For various reasons, including the ban on the employment of lawyers in the Chiefs' Courts, there now seems to be a general tendency for Africans to have recourse to the Court of the Native Commissioner as a tribunal. Though some proposals have been made for the extension of the jurisdiction of Native Courts,[4] it remains the fact that official policy has so far shown a marked lack of confidence in their capacity.

The customary law applicable in Natal is contained in Proclamation 168 of 1932, which was based on the Natal Code of 1878 and the subsequent law of 1891. Elsewhere in the Union it is the unwritten Native law, as discovered from assessors, reported cases, textbooks, and the like. The Code of Native Law introduced in Natal gave recognition to certain customs which had previously been challenged by some missionaries and

---

[1] Act no. 38 of 1927, Section 10 as amended by Act no. 9 of 1929.

[2] H. Rogers, *Native Administration in the Union of South Africa*, 1933, p. 225. For the incorporation of British Bechuanaland in Cape Colony in 1885, see *N.A.*, Part V, p. 192.

[3] H. J. Simons, 'The Law and its Administration', *Handbook on Race Relations in South Africa*, 1949, pp. 54–55.

[4] See *Report of the Native Economic Commission 1930–32*, U.G. 22, 1932, para. 225. See also Simons, loc. cit.

disparaged by many Administrators, but at the same time it made its own modifications in such matters as *lobolo* or the payment of cattle at marriage.[1] A considerable measure of Europeanization has been introduced in other respects, notably in such matters as testamentary disposition.

Though the policy of racial separation has tended to keep African customary law in a field of its own, the separation is not in practice complete. In civil cases arising under Native law both the Native Commissioners' Courts and the Native Appeal Court may sit with African assessors; but when doubt arises as to the correctness of a decision given by a Native Appeal Court on a question of law, the Minister of Native Affairs may obtain a ruling from the Appellate Division of the Supreme Court.[2] The line of distinction is more clearly marked in the case of the criminal law. The African comes under Native law only when he commits an offence which is triable in a Chief's Court having criminal jurisdiction. This has at times the effect of enlarging the range of the criminal law. Thus in Natal the Code of 1932 penalizes breaches of orders issued by Chiefs, as also the seduction of unmarried women, which would not in either case constitute offences against statutory law.

In spite of the reputation for ability and independence enjoyed by the superior judiciary of the Union there are features in the administration of the criminal law which have received much adverse criticism. Attention has already been drawn to the unusual extent to which authority is given to the executive authorities to bring numerous classes of persons within the provision of the penal law by administrative order, against which there is as a rule no appeal to the Courts.[3] The arbitrary use of their powers by the Police was condemned by the Police Commission of Inquiry of 1937[4] as responsible for the creation of an 'attitude of mutual distrust, suspicion, and dislike' between the Force and the non-European population. This is largely due to the manner of their enforcement of discriminatory laws.

It is characteristic of the Union that there is a notable predominance of the class of crimes described as 'statutory offences', such, for example, as breaches of the Native Pass laws, or laws regulating the possession of Native liquor, or prohibiting Natives from entering or living in certain areas, or punishing the breach of labour contracts. Offences falling within these categories account for at least 70 per cent. of all non-European convictions;[5] there is also a very high proportion of African offenders

---

[1] *Lobolo* has usually been translated as 'bride-price', see above, p. 51.

[2] Act 38 of 1927, Section 14.

[3] See above, p. 432.

[4] U.G. no. 50, 1937. See in this connexion N. N. Franklin, *Natives and the Administration of Justice*, South African Institute of Race Relations, 1936, pp. 6–10.

[5] H. J. Simons, 'The Law and its Administration', *Handbook on Race Relations in South Africa*, 1949, p. 86.

against the law of taxation. In 1952 some 956,500 Africans out of a total population of 8½ million were the subject of criminal prosecutions.[1]

There are in addition a number of points in the procedure of criminal trials which call for comment. Africans are not eligible to serve on juries. Since 1917 accused persons have had the option of trial without a jury, and the Minister of Justice has power, in cases of alleged offences by non-Europeans, to direct that the trial shall be by a Judge without a jury.[2] But the use of this power is cumbrous and may involve much delay. The report of a Committee appointed in 1945 expressed a strong suspicion that a European jury is not a satisfactory tribunal for the trial of a case in which a European is charged with an offence against the person of a non-European or vice versa.[3] The Committee was not prepared to recommend the abolition of the jury system, but it proposed that trial by a Judge sitting alone or by a Judge with assessors (the procedure already adopted in 75 per cent. of cases) should be the universal rule, unless the accused expressly demanded a trial by jury. Considerable public comment was caused by a case which arose in 1954 in which a non-African was charged with the murder of an African convict, and the Jury found the accused guilty of common assault only, although the presiding Judge condemned his action as brutal in the extreme and as the most serious case of common assault in his experience.

The Committee also emphasized the importance of an adequate knowledge of African languages on the part of Magistrates and Police and of an adequate standard of competency on the part of Court interpreters. It is again obvious that Magistrates trying certain classes of cases, notably stock theft, are at times exposed to considerable pressure from the local European public. There is much to be said for a change of system which would provide a cadre of Magistrates who would have no administrative or executive functions, and who would in consequence be responsible to the Supreme Court and not to a Department of State for their conduct of judicial proceedings.

High Commission Territories

It is characteristic of these Territories, which have had by tradition something of the character of Native States, that full recognition has been given to the customary law not merely as providing the source of the personal law of Africans, but as applying the procedure followed in local custom to the trial of civil issues and a considerable proportion of criminal cases. This system has been regularized by the adoption from 1934 onwards of the series of reforms which have in effect reproduced in the

[1] *O.Y.S.A. 1952–53*, p. 444.
[2] Simons, op. cit. p. 67.
[3] *Report of Penal and Prison Reform Commission*, U.G. 47, 1947, paras. 354–63.

High Commission Territories most of the features of the Native Authority system in force in the British dependencies.[1]

Other British Territories

The study made of the sources of law reveals evidence of a spirit of dualism in the British territories which contrasts sharply with the French concept of unity. The statute law, as has been shown, derives partly from Imperial sources, but the great body of it is the product of local legislation. In the administration of justice the sense of dualism is even more strongly pronounced. Colonial law as administered by the Colonial Courts is derived from the legislative process above referred to, but in the majority of the dependencies formal recognition is also given to the system of customary law administered by Native Courts. These are duly constituted by statute and deal not merely with the personal law of Africans but with a wide range of civil and criminal issues, which includes in some territories a number of offences against the statutory law.

Taking the statistics of civil and criminal cases as a whole, the actual number disposed of by the Native Courts far exceeds those disposed of by the Colonial Courts. For example, in Nyasaland the High Court and Subordinate Courts disposed in 1953 of 1,359 civil cases and 12,439 criminal cases, whereas the Native Courts dealt with 16,022 civil cases and 26,626 criminal cases.[2] In the same year the Magistrates' Courts, Supreme Court, and West African Court of Appeal in the Gold Coast heard 5,585 civil cases and 42,111 criminal cases, while the Native Courts in the financial year 1952–3 disposed of 36,818 civil and 48,753 criminal cases.[3] In Tanganyika the High Court and its Subordinate Courts heard 38,704 criminal charges: the Local Courts on the other hand heard nearly 66,000 criminal cases and 56,552 civil suits.[4]

Though, however, recognition is thus given to the use of the customary law, it is nevertheless the Colonial Law which constitutes the major sanction; the Colonial Courts deal with the most important civil issues and the graver criminal charges; and though the judicial supervision of the Native Courts is vested in Administrative Officers, there is in the majority of the territories a point at which the Native Court becomes subsidiary to the Colonial Court, in the sense that the latter becomes the appellate or revisionary authority for the Native Courts.

Though there are many differences of detail in the machinery adopted for the administration of justice, there is one feature common throughout the British dependencies. Each territory has its own Supreme or High

---

[1] See above, p. 502.
[2] *Colonial Reports, Nyasaland, 1953*, pp. 103–6.
[3] *Colonial Reports, Gold Coast, 1953*, pp. 88–89; the figures for the Native Courts include Togoland.
[4] *Tanganyika, Report for the year 1953*, Col. 307, pp. 118–19.

Court,[1] which serves as a Court of Appeal, as well as exercising original jurisdiction in certain classes of cases—comprising, in general, the most important cases, both civil and criminal. It has in addition the power to issue prerogative writs of *habeas corpus* and the like. Some measure of co-ordination has been effected by the creation of Regional Appellate Courts, such as the Court of Appeal for Eastern Africa and the West African Court of Appeal, and there was also, before the creation of the Federation of Rhodesia and Nyasaland, a Central African Court of Appeal for the hearing of appeals from the decisions of the local High or Supreme Courts.[2] From these Courts of Appeal a further appeal lies in certain cases to the Judicial Committee of the Privy Council in Great Britain.

The appointments to the High and Supreme Courts and to the Regional Courts of Appeal are made predominantly from the ranks of practising lawyers, and the Judges are eligible for transfer to and from other British Colonial territories. The same principle has been followed in the most recent of the Supreme Courts to have been created in the British areas in Africa, the Supreme Court of the Federation of Rhodesia and Nyasaland. In that instance the qualifications for the appointment of the Federal Justices require that they are or have been Judges of a Court having unlimited jurisdiction, or that they are or have been an advocate practising in such Courts for not less than ten years.[3] To ensure that the Bench is in this instance equipped with a knowledge of Roman-Dutch as well as English law, one of the Judges so appointed has been selected from the Transvaal Divisional Court.

On the other hand, except in the larger towns, the officers exercising subordinate (that is to say magisterial) jurisdiction still belong mainly to the administrative cadre; the policy of substituting a class of 'professional' Magistrates has been much discussed, but so far without decision.[4] Normally a Magistrate makes the preliminary inquiry in certain scheduled charges, such as homicide, rape, and other serious offences, and either dismisses the case or commits it for trial before a Circuit Judge of the High or Supreme Court. Cases not falling into the scheduled class are disposed of within the limits of the Magistrate's own jurisdiction. Here the variations of competence are considerable; a common provision is a maximum of six months' imprisonment; but in some cases it extends to two years, in others up to the full limits imposed by law on any class of offence; in Northern

---

[1] The term Supreme Court is generally used in regard to the highest Court in a Colony and that of High Court in a Protectorate. There is no difference in status.

[2] There is one High Court for the three High Commission Territories; appeals from this Court go direct to the Judicial Committee of the Privy Council. *Colonial Reports, Basutoland*, 1953, p. 57.

[3] Rhodesia and Nyasaland Federation Order in Council no. 1199 of 1953, p. 33.

[4] A measure has been introduced in Kenya to provide that temporary District Officers should not *ex-officio* exercise magisterial powers. *The Times*, 19 October 1955.

Rhodesia the law admits the possibility (which has more than once occurred) that even cases of treason and murder may be tried by Magistrates.

This variety of competence is to some extent adjusted by the general existence of a rule that a return of all criminal cases tried by Magistrates shall be submitted to the High or Supreme Court. Those cases in which the punishment exceeds a certain period of imprisonment (for which six months may be taken as typical) require confirmation by the High or Supreme Court, and all others are liable to the exercise by it of the power of revision. There exists as a rule a liberal right of appeal, but where the exercise of the power of revision operates as a bar to appeal (as is the case in a number of territories) it seems probable that there will be an increasing tendency to substitute appeal for revision.[1]

The Emergency declared in Kenya owing to the outbreak of the Mau Mau disorders necessitated the enactment of legislation designed to accelerate the administration of justice. Among the measures enacted was the abolition of the Preliminary Inquiry which normally preceded a trial before the Supreme Court, but not before a trial in a Magistrate's Court. There is some discrimination as between races in the conditions regulating the trial of an accused person before the Supreme Court. A European must by a section of the Penal Code of Kenya stand his trial before the Supreme Court sitting with a jury, should his offence be punishable by a sentence of more than six months' imprisonment. An African has the right to a trial in the Supreme Court only if the offence is punishable by death or life imprisonment. In African cases the trial is held without a jury; the Judge sits with Assessors only, and he is not bound by their opinion. It has been argued that the Africans accused in Kenya in certain well-known cases were prejudiced by the existence of the Emergency Regulations for, if they had been Europeans, their trial would have been before the Supreme Court and a jury; they would, moreover, have benefited from the holding of a Preliminary Inquiry.[2]

This general outline of the Colonial Court system holds good for the greater part of the British dependencies in Africa. In the form in which the system has been developed the jurisdiction exercised by the Supreme Court and its subordinate Colonial Courts provides for the disposal of all cases involving non-Africans and of those cases involving Africans which are held to be unsuitable for trial by the Native Courts. Thus the categories of cases with which the Colonial Courts deal to the exclusion of the Native Courts, may include not only cases of serious crime and inter-racial cases (that is to say, Master and Servant disputes), but certain other matters involving special considerations of an administrative character, such as prosecutions for witchcraft or serious charges of stock theft. In

[1] See below, p. 636.　　　　　　[2] *Current Legal Problems*, vol. vii, 1954, pp. 181 ff.

Northern Nigeria the Colonial Court system has a diminished function owing to the more extended jurisdiction given to the Emirate tribunals,[1] and similarly in Buganda, where the Lukiko Court[2] exercises wide powers subject to the appellate and revisory jurisdiction of the High Court and the Judicial Adviser. Even in its fullest and most complete form, however, the Colonial Court system has been so constituted as to leave to the Native Courts the disposal of the bulk of Native civil disputes, the lesser criminal offences between one Native and another, and breaches of the customary law.

The chapter dealing with Native Administration has given some account of the historical development of the Native Court system in the British dependencies.[3] The recognition of Native Courts as part of the judicial system has been an essential feature of the British policy which looks to the maintenance of indigenous institutions as a factor in the social and political development of the African people. It is inevitable that these Courts should be of great diversity, alike in their composition as tribunals and in the competence assigned to them; the local circumstances which have produced an almost endless variety of Native Authorities for executive purposes have also produced a corresponding variety of Native Tribunals.

The warrant recognizing or creating a Native Court appoints in some cases the Chief to function as a Court, in others a Chief and his councillors, in others a federation of Chiefs, in others a body of Headmen; there are even cases, as in Eastern Nigeria, where the Court has had no designated personnel, but has been somewhat of the nature of a 'village moot'. There have been instances where the Chief did not under the indigenous system actually hear cases, for he has often been a sacred personage not easily approachable and has thus been far removed from the modern conception of a local Native Authority or President of a Court. Where Africans are living in non-Native areas outside tribal conditions, it has been necessary for the Administration to create special 'urban' tribunals which have no basis in tradition, though accepted by Africans as adequate exponents of customary law and procedure.

The appointment of Courts as such has introduced a principle not previously recognized in African society, which did not usually make a clear separation between judicial and executive functions. Nor indeed is this separation always clear under the present system in which the same person may often act in two capacities; thus the Chief who makes Rules in the exercise of the powers conferred by the Native Authority Ordinance[4] may under the Native Courts Ordinance sit in judgement on offenders against

---

[1] *Nigeria (Northern Provinces), Native Courts Commission of Inquiry, 1949–1952*, pp. 73 ff.
[2] Buganda Courts Ordinance, 1940.
[3] See above, Chapter VIII, *passim*.   [4] See above, pp. 455 ff.

those Rules. The competence of the Native Courts also varies widely. It is usually adjusted to local conditions by the terms of the warrant establishing the Court, and may be limited, for example, to sentences of one month's imprisonment or a fine up to £5 for a Subordinate Native Court, or three months' imprisonment and a fine of £10 in the Superior Native Court. On the other hand, the Courts of certain of the major Emirates in the Northern Region of Nigeria may impose capital punishment, subject to confirmation by the Governor.[1]

There was a period when the Native Courts generally (with the exception of those which were on a special basis, such as those of Buganda or the Emirates in Northern Nigeria or the Court of the Paramount Chief of the Barotse)[2] were envisaged primarily as dealing with matters relating to indigenous law and custom, and it was generally understood that they would treat as offences against Native law mainly such crimes as theft, assault, and the like. For the most part the Administrations encouraged this development, while reserving to the Colonial Courts the trial of graver criminal charges and of breaches of administrative laws, such as those concerned with the collection of tax, Master and Servant relations, and the like. There has grown up, however, in most of the British territories a tendency to bring within the jurisdiction of the Native Courts a certain number of the offences arising from breaches of administrative laws. In most territories, for example, the more efficient Native Courts are now permitted to try cases of default in the payment of Native tax, and there are territories in which the statistics of Native Court cases show a continuous increase in the number of such 'statutory' offences. In such areas the work of the Native Courts is not merely supplementary to that of the Colonial Courts, but is tending to replace it in the disposal of this class of case.

This picture of the relative position occupied by the Colonial Courts and the Native Courts would not be complete without some mention of the changes now observable in the public attitude towards the Native Court system. In parts of West Africa in particular the Native Court has of recent years come to be regarded by progressive Africans as so closely associated with the Native Authority system that, like the latter, it needs now to be replaced by a judicial institution of a more modern order. There is thus a growing tendency to advocate the replacement of the typical Native Court by a Court presided over by a stipendiary officer, if possible a professional lawyer, and thus gradually to bring such Courts into line with the position occupied by the Subordinate Courts in the hierarchy of Colonial Courts.[3]

---

[1] Further details regarding the constitution of Native Courts in the different territories have been given in Chapter VIII.

[2] *N.A.*, Part I, pp. 19 ff.; Part II, p. 100; Part III, pp. 79–85.   [3] See above, p. 611.

This development would have one important consequence. The Native Court, including the now well-organized system of Native Appeal Courts, lies at present within the régime of the Administration in the sense that the work of the Native Court is supervised by Administrative Officers, who exercise certain powers of revision and review or of transferring cases. This has indeed from the first been considered to be an essential feature of the Native Court system. The reformed Native Court, as now envisaged, would pass out of the administrative into the judicial régime. In a sense this may be regarded as part of the same 'modernist' tendency as the movement which would convert the position of the Administrative Officer from that of the controller (subject to certain limitations) of a variety of traditional Native Authorities, into that of the adviser of a series of independent Local Government bodies constituted on an electoral basis.[1]

Those who now deprecate this change as a break with what has proved a useful and salutary form of procedure, should reflect that the Administrative Officer of the future will be the agent of Ministerial rule, subject (unlike his predecessor) to party pressures and influences. These are influences which should not be allowed to trespass on the field of justice.

The French Territories

There can have been few aspects of administration in the African dependencies of France where the impact of the Constitution of 1946[2] has been seen so dramatically as in the field of law and in the organization of the system of justice. As a result of the recommendations of the Brazzaville Conference of 1944,[3] measures were taken for the revision of some aspects of the criminal law applicable to Africans, a number of the provisions of the metropolitan Penal Code being adopted for the purpose.[4] But in 1946 the universal extension of French citizenship meant that the whole population, whether *citoyens* or *sujets*, became justiciable under the French Penal Code, which was practically identical with that of metropolitan France.[5] This had previously applied only to French *citoyens* and *assimilés*, a small proportion of the entire population; the effect of the new law was to bring within the range of those French Courts which exercised criminal jurisdiction many millions of people who had in point of the penal law been previously subject to *la justice indigène*. The immediate consequence was a demand for a great increase in the number of *magistrats* who were concerned with the administration of penal justice;[6] the administration of civil justice was not similarly affected by the constitutional change of 1946.

---

[1] See above, p. 527.   [2] See above, p. 211.   [3] See above, p. 209.
[4] See, for instance, *Décret* of 17 July 1944, instituting a *Code pénal indigène* for French Equatorial Africa.
[5] *Décret*, 30 April 1946.   [6] H. Laborde, 'La Justice', *Enc. A.O.F.*, vol. i, pp. 261 ff.

In these dependencies there is now a clear line of distinction between the organization of the system of *justice de droit français* and the system of *justice de droit local*. The former is served by Courts based as nearly as circumstances permit on the French model. Thus French West Africa has a *Cour d'Appel* at Dakar whose decisions are appealable in certain circumstances to the metropolitan *Cour de Cassation*. A *Cour d'Assises* sits at the capital of each of the component territories of French West Africa.[1] In these Courts there are two *assesseurs* who take the place of the jury provided by metropolitan practice. There are eight *tribunaux de première instance*, one for each component territory, and four *justices de paix à compétence étendue*, with jurisdiction roughly equivalent to that of the *tribunal de première instance*. Owing to the demand created by the constitutional change of 1946 for an addition to the ranks of *magistrats*, the Governor-General was authorized to make temporary appointments of *justices de paix* to deal with criminal charges of minor importance; it was intended, however, that these appointments should be replaced as soon as possible by *magistrats* of the normal cadre.

Notwithstanding the fact that criminal jurisdiction is now reserved entirely to the *tribunaux de droit français*, there remains a considerable body of judicial work which falls to be dealt with by the system of *justice de droit local*. While there are some differences between the judicial organization of French Equatorial Africa and that of French West Africa the latter may be taken as representing the system of *justice de droit local* in its present form. The term *tribunaux indigènes* has in French usage a connotation different from that of the Native Courts in the British territories. It has reference not so much to the composition of the Courts as to the range of their jurisdiction; for many years indeed the *tribunaux indigènes* included no purely African personnel, and although provision is now made also for *juridictions coutumières*, the powers of these tribunals are very limited, even within the sphere of Native law and custom.

They are, for example, normally debarred from adjudicating on such matters as marriage, divorce, custody of children, and the like. The greater part of the civil judicial work, which in the British dependencies is commonly dealt with by the Native Courts, constituted for the most part on a traditional basis, is reserved under the French system to the higher grade of *tribunaux indigènes*, which are entirely non-traditional in character.[2] Their function is to deal with the civil issues arising between Natives and it is laid down that in deciding these issues they are to apply exclusively the customary law of the parties involved.[3]

The *tribunal du premier degré* and the *tribunal du second degré* correspond to

---

[1] See above, p. 332. There is, however, a combined *Cour d'Assises* for Senegal and Mauretania.
[2] *Décret*, 3 December 1931.
[3] Laborde, op. cit. p. 265.

the administrative area of the local *subdivision* and *cercle*. Each of these Courts is presided over by an Administrative Officer of appropriate rank, who sits with two African Assessors, chosen from a panel representative of the customs of the parties concerned. The *tribunal du second degré* has both original and appellate jurisdiction. At the headquarters of each component territory there is a *tribunal territorial d'appel*, composed of a lawyer as President, two Administrative Officers, and two selected African *notables*. There is finally at Dakar the *chambre d'annulation* for French West Africa, also composed of professional lawyers, Administrative Officers, and African *notables*. At Dakar, Saint Louis, and Rufisque there are also Courts of Cadis dealing with cases arising under Islamic law; they represent the survival of Courts specially created in 1857 to deal with cases arising among Muslim residents of the four *communes de plein exercice* of Senegal.[1] They were reorganized in 1932,[2] but the system has not been extended elsewhere in French West Africa or in the other French tropical dependencies.

The system of *tribunaux indigènes* thus described prevails also in French Equatorial Africa and in the Trust Territories of the French Cameroons and Togo. There are no such material differences as to call for separate notice here.

The system thus differs widely from the system of Native Courts in British territories. The most important of the *tribunaux indigènes* are institutions framed on a European rather than an African model; they draw no support from traditional sources, save in so far as the African Assessors may command local respect. Nor do they follow the traditional methods of procedure, such as the public discussions of evidence and findings, which in large measure preserve the indigenous character of the British Native Courts. They are in fact 'Native' mainly to the extent that they are not charged with the administration of the statutory law.

It would seem further that the system must tend to leave a large body of cases to be settled by conciliation or by some similar process outside the regular jurisdiction of the Courts. It need hardly be pointed out that there is here a significant difference of objective. It has been the British tradition to maintain African social and political institutions in being until such time as they merge into a modified series of institutions reflecting the adjustment of the usages of Africa to the purposes of Western civilization. The French do not attach the same value as the British to indigenous institutions as such; they are in fact more ready to use the administrative machinery of the State in order to mould African institutions as rapidly as possible into conformity with the pattern of the institutions of metropolitan France.

[1] See above, p. 338.
[2] *Décret*, 20 November 1932.

The Belgian Congo

As has been shown, the Constitution framed for the Belgian Congo in 1908 was less the reflection of a national philosophy than of a determination to avoid the practices which had brought the Government of the Congo Free State under criticism.[1] It was as part of that policy that the principles originally embodied in the *Charte Coloniale* contemplated a definite separation of the executive and judicial functions, and looked forward to the general use of a system of tribunals presided over by professional lawyers who would form no part of the administrative system. The incompatibility of such a system with the existing needs of the country, quite as much as the lack of trained European personnel, showed at an early date that this was not a practicable ideal, and the pressure of facts produced the reorganization of 1923, which gave a certain range of judicial powers to Administrative Officers.[2] This was followed by a Decree of April 1926, which assigned to the Native Tribunals a recognized place in the judicial system.

There still remains, however, enough of the original tradition of the *Charte Coloniale* to give 'professional justice' a prominent place in the judicial organization, so that Magistrates who discharge no administrative functions are proportionately more numerous than elsewhere. A Decree of 1934, which made it necessary that all non-African cases should come before a Court presided over by lawyers, represented in fact something of a definite swing back in favour of 'professional' justice.

Before describing the hierarchy of Courts in the Belgian Congo it will be convenient to explain the system of the *Parquet*, which plays an important part in the judicial organization of the Colony. The *Parquet* is a body which in some measure corresponds to the Attorney-General's Department in a British dependency, though its functions are in fact much wider. Its personnel are mainly professional lawyers, but the Governor-General also appoints Administrative Officers to assist the *Parquet* in the discharge of its functions. Officers of the *Parquet* act as prosecutors in the criminal Courts; they are also charged with the duty of conducting inquiries concerning the behaviour of Magistrates and also into alleged abuses. But the function of the Department does not end with legal administration; it also exercises judicial functions. Thus the revision of judgements given in the *tribunaux de police* is entrusted to it. Its officers sit as Courts (*tribunaux du parquet*), which are the regular Courts of First Instance for civil suits involving non-Africans. On the criminal side officers of the *Parquet* may also exercise jurisdiction over Africans in cases arising in areas more than 25 kilometres distant from the nearest regular criminal Court.

[1] See above, p. 216.
[2] J. M. Jadot, 'La Justice répressive au Congo Belge', *L'Afrique française*, 1936, pp. 387 ff.

The system of regular criminal Courts begins with the *tribunal de police*.[1] This exercises jurisdiction in a *territoire* or a *ville*.[2] It is presided over by an Administrator and its jurisdiction extends to all offences committed by Africans in which the maximum legal penalty does not exceed two months' imprisonment or where the maximum penalty is up to five years' imprisonment but the Court considers two months' to be an adequate punishment. For petty offences the Police Court may sit without an officer of the *Parquet* but, as already explained, its decisions are subject to revision by the *Parquet*. The *Parquet* receives the record and can use its revisory power either on its own motion or at the request of the parties.

The next higher criminal Court is the District Court, presided over by an Administrative Officer, which has jurisdiction over all offences committed by Africans. Over this system of Police and District Courts there is the *tribunal de première instance* for each Province,[3] the personnel of which consists of professional lawyers. In addition to unlimited civil jurisdiction the Tribunal has appellate criminal jurisdiction in regard to first-instance decisions of the District Courts and revisionary decisions by the *Parquet*. It also has original criminal jurisdiction for offences committed by non-Africans.

Above this again there are two Courts of Appeal for the whole of the Belgian Congo, one at Leopoldville and one at Elisabethville, both professional in constitution. These are subject in civil matters to the overriding jurisdiction of the *Cour de Cassation* in Brussels.

In addition to this system of 'European' Courts, however, the Belgian Congo has a system of Native Courts. Its development had a double source. It was primarily designed to fill the gap caused by the insufficiency of the original system of European Courts, but the principle of the Native Court has received additional support from the school of thought which shares the view that African institutions have their own intrinsic value, in so far that their employment may form an appropriate bridge between African social life and that of Europe. The *tribunaux indigènes* comprise, first, the *tribunaux de chefferie* (graded as principal and secondary), which are in effect the customary Courts of Chiefs; second, the *tribunaux de secteur*, which are 'created' institutions in the sense that they do not correspond to any pre-existing traditional institutions;[4] third, the *tribunaux de centre*, which are also Courts created to provide for the needs of the mixed African populations in the *centres extra-coutumiers*;[5] and finally, at a higher level, the *tribunaux de territoire*. The last are composed of an Administrator as President, with two or more African Judges nominated from the *chefferie*

[1] A. Durieux, 'Le Pouvoir Judiciaire', *Enc. C.B.*, vol. iii, pp. 536 ff.
[2] For the position of the *ville* in the system of urban administration, see above, p. 584.
[3] For the Provinces, see above, p. 350.
[4] For the system of *secteurs* in the Belgian Congo, see above, pp. 553 ff.
[5] See above, p. 222.

Courts or other Courts in the *territoire*. They are mainly designed to act as revisionary Courts.

The *tribunaux indigènes* exercise jurisdiction over Africans in all civil matters which do not involve the application of the *droit écrit*; their criminal jurisdiction is normally confined to offences against customary law, but it may be extended by express authorization of law to specified statutory offences. The punishments which they may impose are limited to one month's imprisonment and a fine of 1,000 francs, or two months' imprisonment and a fine of 2,000 francs if the Court is sitting under the presidency of an Administrative Officer. Revision on questions of fact lies with the *tribunal de territoire*; but the supervision of the proceedings of the Native Courts lies with the *Parquet*, which has certain administrative powers over them and sees their records. It can annul their decisions on grounds of law, or can order retrial.

The statistics for the year 1950 included the following figures of cases disposed of by Native Courts; *tribunaux de chefferie*, 140,990; *tribunaux de secteur*, 186,133; *tribunaux de centre*, 42,026; *tribunaux de territoire*, 12,536; making a total of approximately 370,000.

The judicial system in Ruanda Urundi is broadly similar, but a distinction is made between *tribunaux coutumiers* (which include the Courts of the Mwami)[1] and *tribunaux extra-coutumiers*. In the latter category provision is made for the establishment of *tribunaux de revision*. The *Parquet* has here the same powers and functions in relation to Native Courts as in the Belgian Congo proper.

The Portuguese Territories

In the Portuguese territories the only law formally recognized is the 'common' law, which largely reproduces the civil and criminal codes of metropolitan Portugal. There are accordingly no Native Courts in the sense in which this term is used in either the British or Belgian territories. There are two classes of Colonial Courts, the Ordinary Courts (*tribunais ordinários*) and the Special Courts (*tribunais especiais*)[2] which act partly as higher Courts of First Instance and partly as Courts of Appeal. The final appeal lies to the metropolitan High Court at Lisbon. The system also comprises the existence of an Administrative Court dealing with offences committed by officials and with the investigation of complaints made against them.

Though, as shown in the preceding chapter, there are no Native Courts, an attempt is made to take account of African custom in suits where only

---

[1] See above, p. 589.

[2] *Nova Legislacão Ultramarina*, vol. i, 1953, pp. 55 ff. For an examination of the position of the Portuguese Native in law, see A. Durieux, *Essai sur le statut des indigènes portugais de la Guinée, de l'Angola et du Mozambique*, Mém. A.R.S.C., 1955.

Africans are concerned.[1] But any such procedure, however faithfully pursued, must clearly give unsatisfactory results from the point of view of those who are interested in securing a systematic adaptation of the principles embodied in the customary law. It is admitted that some careful studies have been made of the customary law of Mozambique, both criminal and civil,[2] but it is obvious that under the existing system there must remain a wide field of issues in which no provision is made for any form of adjudication, or where, if any adjudication exists, the result must necessarily depend on the extent of the interest shown by the Administrative Officer and his personal experience of African custom. A great deal must depend on the competence of, and the extent of, the authority allowed to the recognized Native Chief (*régulo*).

The Spanish Territories

There are two 'District' Courts which deal with cases in which Europeans and those Africans who have secured *emancipación plena* are concerned,[3] and there is a Court of First Instance at Santa Isabel. There is also a system of 'Native Courts'. These are divided into Canton and District Tribunals, presided over by Administrative Officers; in the former case there are two Village Chiefs as Assessors, and in the latter case six Chiefs as Assessors in Rio Muni and two in Fernando Po. In civil matters these Courts have competence over all 'non-emancipated' Natives; in criminal matters they have competence where the accused is either 'non-emancipated' or has only *emancipación limitada*.[4] The basis of the penal law applicable to Natives (*indígenas non emancipados*) was laid down in a Decree of 10 November 1938.[5]

RECONCILIATION OF EUROPEAN AND AFRICAN LEGAL CONCEPTS

It was inevitable, as has already been suggested, that the law-giver should encounter unusual difficulty in introducing to Africa a system of law based on the principles accepted in Europe. That was not due merely to differences in the respective concepts of law. There were obstacles which were in some respects more fundamental, since they reflected a difference of outlook on the nature of justice and the part to be played by the machinery of justice in maintaining social order. An African found no

---

[1] See above, p. 563.

[2] J. Cotta, *Codigo Penal dos Indigenas* and *Estatuto do Direito Privado dos Indigenas da Colonia de Moçambique*, Lourenço Marques, 1946.   [3] See above, p. 234.

[4] G. Héraud, in *Revue juridique et politique de L'Union Française*, no. 3, July–September 1954, p. 319.

[5] F. F. O. Munido, *Derecho Penal Aplicable a Indígenas en los Territorios Espanoles del Golfo de Guinea*, 1953, p. 101.

difficulty in appreciating the idea that the State should punish crimes which are reprehensible in his own eyes as well as in those of Europeans, but he did not readily accept the idea that it is necessary for Society to apply penal sanctions to police rules regulating public conduct or to laws dealing with matters such as tax, pass, or labour conditions.

On the civil side the African's inexperience of all the complex of contractual relations arising from the usage of a money economy made him a stranger to the legal methods in which modern society has expressed its needs. How far is it possible to adjust European conceptions of justice to these conditions? The answer does not lie merely in the possibility of effecting changes in the law; it depends fundamentally on the manner and the tempo in which Administrations seek to impress their own conceptions of behaviour on Africa.

We must be clear, in the first place, as to the limits of the field in which it is possible for the law-giver to make wider concessions to the difficulties felt by the African. There are certain questions on which it is not possible to find any compromise. No Administration could allow the perpetuation of a system of trial by ordeal, or the forcible elimination of persons who have become involved, however involuntarily, in actions which are traditionally believed to be a danger to the health or welfare of society. Nor is it possible to suggest that Governments should deprive themselves of the power to implement their administrative ordinances (such as those regulating health conditions or the preservation of forests or the conservation of the soil) by attaching penal clauses to them. To take an even more crucial example, one of the outstanding problems of the law-giver in Africa is the treatment of witchcraft in the criminal law.

Here there are clearly limits beyond which it would be impossible for an Administration to go in meeting African sentiment. The operations of both protective and harmful magic are continually in the mind of the African, and although the spiritual forces of African religion may be diminished by contact with European influences, the belief in magic persists no less in the urban and industrial areas than in rural districts.[1] An element of fear of occult forces seems to be inherent in the minds of vast numbers of Africans. In the majority of the countries lying south of the Sahara, the practice of magic and witchcraft is now prohibited by a variety of laws which are not readily appreciated by people of whom large numbers regard the operations of magic as normal events of everyday life. In this case part at least of the trouble arises from the failure of most of the legislation to draw a clear line of demarcation between the so-called witch, the sorcerer, and the witch-finder.

The reason for bringing any of these practitioners within the scope of

---

[1] D. Westermann, *Africa and Christianity*, 1937, p. 133. G. I. Jones, *Report on Medicine Murder in Basutoland*, Cmd. 8209, 1950. M. Hunter, *Reaction to Conquest*, 1936.

the criminal law is that the practice of witchcraft and of witch-finding do actually cause death or injury. In ordinary Native practice it was usual for a group of individuals to state their conviction that witchcraft had been at work but to avoid naming an individual person as a witch,[1] and in such cases the procedure was to summon a witch-finder to detect the witch by using one of several methods of divination. Often, but not invariably, the witch (and sometimes the accuser also) was subjected to one of the recognized ordeals, such as that by boiling water, in order to put to the test the single issue of innocence or guilt. A witch found guilty was usually put to death, but was sometimes banished and settled down in other communities. Chiefs readily resorted to the use of a witch-finder, because this enabled them to escape from a dilemma and relieved them of the onus of pronouncing judgement.

Africans find it difficult to reconcile their own view of witch-finders as being the protectors of society, owing to their ability to detect witches, with the European judgement of them as fraudulent charlatans.[2] It would, however, be impossible in the public interest to abandon the sanctions applied by the criminal law against the witch-finders, though something could clearly be done to clarify the actual provisions of the law. The gravamen of the charge against them is not that they are charlatans, but that they have been the means of causing the death of thousands of persons who were certainly not guilty of witchcraft and probably of no crime whatsoever. Movements have arisen from time to time of persons professing to have discovered new methods of detection and more efficacious protective measures, but they have inevitably come into conflict with a law on which no compromise can be made.[3]

There is one further consideration. Africa is no longer divided between non-Africans and primitives; the law must be such as is suitable also to the rapidly increasing section of the population which has ceased to be primitive but is not fully Europeanized. There is thus no clear-cut solution of the difficulties arising out of the divergence of European and African concepts of justice; it is not possible to do more than to attempt to secure the utmost acceptance for the law in the course of discussion before it is made and by a careful study in advance of its probable reactions on African society.

Penal Sanctions

As will have been gathered, it is in the Law of Public Order (to use a convenient French expression) rather than in the field of civil law that

---

[1] M. Wilson, *Good Company*, 1951. G. Lienhardt, 'Some Notions of Witchcraft among the Dinka', *Africa*, October 1951, pp. 303 ff. W. P. Mayer, *Witches*, 1954.

[2] F. H. Melland, *In Witchbound Africa*, 1923. E. E. Evans-Pritchard, *Witchcraft, Oracles and Magic among the Azande*, 1937.

[3] A. I. Richards, 'A Modern Movement of Witchfinders', *Africa*, October 1935, pp. 448 ff. M. G. Marwick, 'Another Modern Anti-witchcraft Movement', ibid. April 1950, pp. 100 ff.

there is the greatest divergence between the European and African concepts of justice. The difficulty of securing from the African a ready acceptance of the European system of criminal law is increased by the apparent incompatibility of European ideas of penology with African traditional usage. The African practice was to compensate the injured party in such a way as to leave him no worse off than he was before; it did not embrace, except in special circumstances, the idea that an offence was committed against the State. The Bantu had no prisons, though sometimes an offender might be incarcerated in a slave-stick or a murderer confined in a hut with the corpse, until his relatives produced adequate compensation. They had no system of fines, though the Chief trying the case might sometimes exact payment to himself in addition to the compensation awarded. They had no public executioner; the relatives of the injured party were usually permitted to execute a murderer in whatever way they thought best.

European methods of fine and imprisonment were thus alien to African ideas, and their imposition as the sanction by which justice is enforced was an innovation. Doubts have been entertained as to the deterrent value of long sentences of imprisonment which carry no social stigma.[1] The social stigma attached to a term of imprisonment appears in fact to vary inversely with the number of persons committed. When so large a proportion of the African population is sentenced to short terms for 'statutory' offences, as is habitual in the Union of South Africa,[2] no stigma follows: but when committal to prison is confined to the few who perpetrate serious crime and are severely punished, the convict is likely to be stigmatized as the enemy of society. But as those who have examined the question at various times have realized, it is easier to find reasons for doubting the effect of imprisonment on the African than it is to find an alternative method of dealing with offenders which is suitable for adoption in modern conditions.

Reforms in Treatment of Offenders

European penal methods are now being gradually applied to African prisons. The conception of punishment is giving way to the idea of rehabilitating the offender and of training him to useful employment. In the British territories more attention is now being given to the classification of offenders and to their accommodation in separate institutions, Central Prisons, Reformatories, Borstal establishments, and the like.[3] Formerly the only classification of prisoners was by sex, the females being

[1] See on the subject generally, Lord Lugard, *The Dual Mandate in British Tropical Africa*, 1926, pp. 558 ff.   [2] See above, p. 609.
[3] *Colonial Office Advisory Committee on Treatment of Offenders in the Colonies*, Memorandum, June 1954.

separated from the males and often confined in very unsatisfactory accommodation. The quarters for females are still usually a semi-detached part of the men's prison, but an advance has been made in Tanganyika, where a large prison for women has been built. In the Gold Coast there is also a large central prison for women. In a number of areas, first offenders sentenced for trivial offences are put on probation or in Reformatories where the atmosphere of a recidivist prison is absent; schooling is part of the curriculum, and instruction is given in manual skills.[1] A Borstal Institution is part of the penal system of Kenya and the Gold Coast, and there is a Broadmoor for criminal lunatics in Tanganyika.[2]

Prison farms have been a success almost everywhere. The best known in British territories is the Prison farm at Kingolwira in Tanganyika, where there is accommodation for 1,000 prisoners; it has an elaborate system of training for different trades.[3] Farms are now an adjunct of most large prisons, rendering them largely self-supporting in foodstuffs; they also serve in some instances as demonstration centres in crop rotation or soil conservation. Training in useful vocations is beginning to be a standing feature of African prisons.[4] In the Union of South Africa, farm prisons have been recently established mainly in order to relieve congestion in the urban prisons. Under this policy the Department of Prisons contracts with a local Association of Farmers that, in consideration of their providing the building, it will supply them with prisoners for employment on a fixed rate of hire. The system is apparently appreciated both by farmers and by prisoners in rural areas, but has proved to be open to abuse.[5]

Legislation for the establishment of Juvenile Courts has been passed in a number of territories, and in some instances women sit on the bench.[6] The problem of increasing hooliganism and juvenile delinquency is now the subject of frequent comment in the annual reports of the Colonial Administrations. To meet this problem in Kenya, where juvenile delinquency is especially prevalent in Nairobi, a Remand Home has recently been established. In certain territories Welfare Officers and Discharged Prisoners' Aid Societies have been formed to assist the rehabilitation of prisoners after discharge, and they claim to have been successful in Northern Rhodesia, Kenya, and Sierra Leone.

While most of the preceding details refer to conditions in the British dependencies or in the Union of South Africa, there is evidence of the growing extension in other territories also of reforms in the treatment of offenders. In many instances, however, their introduction has been too recent to make it possible to assess their results. The Juvenile Court, for

[1] Northern Rhodesia, *Prison Service Annual Report, 1953*, p. 16.
[2] *Tanganyika, Annual Reports of Provincial Commissioners, 1953*, p. 14.
[3] *Tanganyika, Report for the year 1952*, Col. no. 293, p. 180.
[4] *Colonial Reports, Uganda, 1953*, p. 93.   [5] *O.Y.S.A., 1952–53*, p. 452.
[6] *Colonial Reports, Gold Coast, 1953*, p. 82.

instance, is still at the experimental stage, and it is clear that the establish-ments necessary for the proper operation of this and some others of these reforms are at present lacking. The efforts to provide a probation system in particular are clearly only tentative, and at the best its operation must at present be confined to the larger towns.[1]

Corporal punishment was at one time inflicted with a whip of hippo-hide, an instrument with which Africans had been made familiar by slave traders, and it was often applied with great severity. It was in general use in all British territories and with certain limitations also in French and Belgian possessions. In British territories it has now been altogether abolished,[2] and has been replaced by a rattan cane. Since 1950 there has been a general movement in the British dependencies in favour of the abolition of corporal punishment, but there are at the moment marked differences in practice. In Sierra Leone it may not be inflicted upon adults (except adult prisoners), but it may be awarded to juveniles for any offence not punishable by death. In Nyasaland, on the other hand, it has been abolished as a punishment for juveniles, but retained as a punishment for adults convicted of prescribed offences. The value of corporal punishment as a deterrent to adult delinquents has long been debated, but in so far as it is an alternative to imprisonment it has some advantage as a punish-ment for juveniles.

Though the greatest number of sentences of corporal punishment passed by the Colonial Courts are imposed on juveniles, the power to impose it also on adults is still exercised and in some territories, as notably Tanga-nyika and Kenya, such sentences have increased in recent years. It has for some years been the declared policy of Tanganyika to abolish this form of punishment, but the question has been left in abeyance in view of expressions of opinion by an inter-racial committee appointed to consider the question in 1952 and of the unanimous vote of the unofficial members of the Legislative Council against abolition.[3] In the Native Courts sen-tences of corporal punishment may be awarded, but they are usually subject to confirmation by an Administrative Officer. The merit claimed for its use is that as it follows quickly upon conviction it does not involve detention in prison; but some of this advantage disappears when it is necessary to await confirmation, and the use of this form of punishment appears in consequence to be declining.

Principles of Compensation and Collective Responsibility

The substitution of fines for the compensation which was the commonest feature of African custom has doubtless been one of the changes which the

---

[1] M. Fry, 'Treatment of Offenders', *The Anti-Slavery Reporter*, May 1955, pp. 24-26.
[2] See, for example, Tanganyika Corporal Punishment Ordinance, 1930.
[3] *Tanganyika, Report for the year 1953*, Col. no. 307, p. 21.

African mind has found most difficult to accept. To some extent the position has been relieved in the British dependencies by the wide extension of the system of Native Courts, since these have continued to make use of the system of compensation. It is understood that the French *tribunal indigène* also makes use of the system. The British Colonial Courts have not found it easy to give it the place which the African has assigned to it. It is true that East African codes allow for compensation being given in addition to or in substitution for any other punishment, and that Magistrates are advised to use it in all suitable cases; it is also the fact that the Supreme Court Ordinance of Nigeria allows a Court to stay proceedings in any case falling short of felony on payment of compensation.[1] But in practice the procedure is little used; the attitude of some High Courts shows that they tend to the unpractical view that the injured party ought to resort to civil action to get compensation. There is, of course, a growing field of offences in which compensation is in any case inapplicable, namely, the breach of health, sanitary, and other administrative Ordinances.

The use of collective punishment, which is sometimes advocated as a logical corollary to the African conception of collective responsibility, is recognized by British Colonial law, and at an early period the Collective Punishment Ordinances were not infrequently invoked. The procedure had the merit of being readily understood, since it was a process analogous to traditional custom, but for many years it has been reserved only for use in emergency conditions. In recent years, for example, it has been employed in Kenya as a means of suppressing the Mau Mau; in under two years more than 10,000 cattle, 12,000 sheep, and 5,000 goats, were confiscated by collective punishments involving 3,514 Africans. Although rarely used it is clearly advisable to retain it on the Statute Book. The Transkei Spoor Law[2] was the application of an executive rather than a judicial process. The authorization of collective punishment must indeed always be an administrative rather than a judicial proceeding.

Procedures for Trial of Criminal and Civil Cases

Considerable as is the obstacle created by differing concepts of the function of law, it has been less grave than that which has arisen from differences in the procedure adopted in the trial of criminal and civil cases. As has already been suggested the procedure followed by the Courts of Justice is everywhere liable to be regarded as more significant of the spirit in which justice is administered than the substance of the law itself. It would be a mistake to assume that primitive Africa made no provision for the decision of contentions issues; there existed everywhere a recognized means of securing decisions on them, beginning with the arbitrament of

---

[1] Laws of Nigeria, cap. 3.
[2] E. H. Brookes, *The Colour Problems of South Africa*, 1934, pp. 188 ff.

family heads or of heads of kin groups and ending with the more formal adjudication by a Chief, or a Chief and his Council, or some form of clan or tribal moot.

If these tribunals had their limitations, they nevertheless seem to have been accepted as dispensing justice to the general satisfaction of those who sought their decisions. But the procedure of trial differed widely from that practised in the present Colonial Courts. Africans do not seem to have had any clear concept of relevancy, and no limits were set to the relevancy of the evidence given; not only were the antecedents of the case often traced back for several generations, but every aspect of the relations in which the parties stood towards each other was held to be relevant to the case in issue.[1] Where writing was unknown, documentary evidence was necessarily excluded and hearsay evidence was entirely unrestricted. Spectators were permitted to address the Court on the facts and freely discussed the merits of the case; the decision often appeared to be the result of these discussions rather than a judgement pronounced by those who presided over the proceedings. Africans are therefore understandably perplexed at the rigid relevancy required by the procedure of the European Courts.

In more than one instance the law of the territory has recognized the difficulty arising from the formal nature of trial in the Colonial Courts and has made some effort to obviate it. As already mentioned, some of the earlier British Orders in Council provided that the Courts should decide cases where Natives were parties 'according to substantial justice, without undue regard to technicalities of procedure and without undue delay'. But though Courts of First Instance might have been able to proceed with some degree of informality, the elaboration of a system of Appellate Courts has involved the formulation of rules of evidence, a procedure which has inevitably occasioned exceptional difficulties for Africans.

In various instances concessions have been made by the Colonial Courts to meet these difficulties. It is generally acknowledged, for instance, that the truth is more easily ascertainable by allowing African witnesses to tell their story in their own way than by eliciting the facts by examination,[2] and this principle is generally adhered to. At one time it was the practice to allow affirmation to be made by traditional oath, but the practice is now becoming obsolete in the Colonial Courts, largely because no penal consequences ensued to a witness affirming falsely. In serious cases such as homicide, where the accused may be confused by an elaborate procedure, Administrations sometimes provide a District Officer, with a

---

[1] M. Gluckman, *Judicial Process among the Barotse of Northern Rhodesia*, 1955.

[2] *Report of the Commission of Inquiry into the Administration of Justice in Kenya, Uganda and Tanganyika in Criminal Matters* (the Bushe Report), Cmd. 4623, 1934.

knowledge of the language of the accused, to act as his adviser and advocate.

In the British Colonial Courts presided over by an Administrative Officer in his judicial capacity, procedure is sometimes modified to suit Native custom; but here again the difficulty arises that these are also Courts of Record, in which evidence must be taken according to prescribed rules in view of the possibility of appeal. The growth of a technical procedure seems to be inevitable where a European system for the administration of justice has been introduced, though it is conceded that the technicality involved offends against the fundamental principle, frequently affirmed in the British Orders in Council, that in issues to which Natives are parties the Courts shall be guided by Native law and custom, so long as they are not repugnant to justice and morality.[1]

It is partly in order to control the growth of technical procedure that in the British dependencies the employment of professional advocates has been barred from certain of the Subordinate Colonial Courts. They are universally excluded from practice in the Native Courts, a measure which has also been supported on the ground that it will reduce the cost of litigation.[2] Where, however, a case goes from a Native Court to a Supreme or High Court no bar has been placed on the appearance of an advocate.

In Kenya advocates may appear in the Court of Review, by leave granted by that Court.[3] In the Gold Coast, which envisages a professional judiciary as gradually replacing the former lay Magistrates, a recommendation has been made that advocates should be allowed to appear in all Courts, except those presided over by Honorary Justices.[4] In Nigeria, also, opinion favours a relaxation of the general rule, and though advocates are still to be excluded from Native Courts, it is proposed to permit them to practise in appeals to the higher Colonial Courts.[5] The more advanced development of West Africa appears to justify a greater latitude for the employment of advocates, but it seems obvious that for some years to come the general provision excluding them from the Native Courts must prevail, more especially in East and Central Africa.

FUNCTIONS OF NATIVE COURTS

It has been convenient to retain here the term Native Court, though it actually bears a different connotation in the British, French, or Belgian

---

[1] A. Phillips, *Report on Native Tribunals*, Kenya, 1945, paras. 561 ff.

[2] See, for example, Nigeria, Native Courts Ordinance, no. 12 of 1930, Section 20. Tanganyika, Local Courts Ordinance, no. 20 of 1951. Kenya, African Courts Ordinance, no. 65 of 1951, Section 29. [3] *J.A.A.*, October 1952, p. 137.

[4] *Gold Coast, Report of Commission on Native Courts*, 1951, p. 34.

[5] *J.A.A.*, April 1953, p. 86.

usage. In the Union of South Africa use is made, though on a relatively small scale, of the customary tribunals held by Chiefs, but their range of jurisdiction is small, and it is not improbable that they will before long cease to retain any place in the judicial organization of the country.[1] The *tribunaux indigènes* in the French dependencies as now constituted have no basis in African custom, as they consist of an Administrative Officer and two African Assessors. They have now no jurisdiction in criminal matters; they are, however, empowered to apply the customary law in civil issues in which the parties are Africans.[2] In the Belgian Congo the *tribunaux de chefferie* are the customary Courts of Chiefs, but sitting usually with an Administrative Officer as 'Adviser'. They apply the local customary law. The *tribunaux de secteur* and the *tribunaux de territoire* have no traditional basis, but they apply the local customary law and have jurisdiction in all civil matters which do not involve a resort to the statutory law and in criminal matters they deal with offences against the customary law.[3]

It is the Native Court in the British territories which may be described as the Native Court *par excellence*, since it is most nearly indigenous in its composition; it makes use of the customary procedure for trial of issues and, until its functions were extended in comparatively recent years, dealt only with offences against Native custom and with civil issues falling within the field of customary law.

As shown more fully in Chapter VIII, the Native Court forms an important element in the system of Native Administration followed in the British dependencies. In African usage, as indeed in that of most primitive peoples, the sources of executive and judicial authority are not separable, and the Native Court has from the first been an integral feature of the Native Authority system; it can indeed be claimed that much of the benefit that has accrued from the use of this system could not have been realized had not the Native Court been a recognized part of its organization. On the one hand the loyalty given to the Native Authorities was in large part due to their close connexion with the Native Court; on the other, the discharge of judicial functions assisted both to inculcate in the Native Authority a sense of responsibility in executive matters and to keep it in close touch with the people. The wide extension of the powers of the Native Authorities which has enabled them to make Rules and Orders on matters vital to the welfare of the people (such as the conservation of the soil or measures for protection against famine) was rendered possible by the fact that breaches of such Rules or Orders were brought to trial in the Native Courts.

Looked at from the purely functional standpoint, the Native Courts in these dependencies have disposed of a great volume of both civil and criminal cases which, if referred to any type of adjudication at all, would

[1] See above, p. 430.　　　[2] See above, p. 617.　　　[3] See above, p. 620.

have fallen on the Colonial Courts.[1] They afford in this respect a contrast
to the *tribunaux indigènes* of the French dependencies which, owing to their
small number (which is regulated by the number of Administrative
Officers available to preside over them), can only provide for the adjudication of a relatively small number of cases, leaving large numbers to
be settled by informal arbitrament in the villages. In the second place,
the organization of the Native Court system in the British dependencies
provides that the decision of the Courts should be subject to appeal to
a higher Native Court; it is subsequently subject to revision in the first
instance by Administrative Officers, and ultimately (in most territories
at all events) by the higher Colonial Courts. In the third place, though
the Native Courts are to a growing extent Courts of Record, yet since
they follow the indigenous usage of trial, their procedure is free from most
of the technicalities which create one of the impediments to the full use
of the Colonial Courts.

But the Native Court of this type can also claim an importance which
extends beyond its functional use. If we can look forward to any measure
of reconciliation between the European and African concepts of law, the
bridge may actually be provided by experience of the use of the Native
Court system. This may show that the scope for adjustment between the
two systems will be found most readily in the field of procedure. It is less
likely to be found in the field of criminal law, for it is possible that the
future may see in the British territories, as in the French, a resort to the
use of a uniform Penal Code which will cover the whole field of criminal
law. There will, however, remain that aspect of civil law which relates to
matters such as matrimony, succession, or land tenure, for which some
regular means of adjudication must be provided.

This personal law will not necessarily take the form of a body of customary law in its present form, for customary law is far from static, and
is constantly being modified under the impact of economic and social
changes. But it is the Native Court which now provides the agency by
which the customary law is given form and definition. It is its records
that supply the most reliable authority for recording the modifications
produced by the changing conditions of African society. Under the
French system of *tribunaux indigènes* there is a probability that the customary
law will be consciously remodelled to meet the prevailing concepts of
French law. But the British system of Native Courts seems to provide for
a more natural and more organic procedure for its adjustment.

Changes in Scope and Jurisdiction of the Native Courts

There has for some years been a process of change in the Native Court
system as employed in the British territories which seems likely to have

---

[1] See above, p. 611.

a bearing on the place which the institution may ultimately occupy in the administration of justice. There has in the first place been a definite movement towards the separation of the judicial from the executive element in the personnel of the Courts. At the outset Chiefs, with or without their councillors, were naturally chosen to preside over the Native Courts, for Chiefs and their councillors were throughout large areas the only persons capable of exacting obedience. But the question of the separation of judicial from executive authority has from an early date exercised the mind of a number of the Governments. In Kenya, for example, the Chiefs have been excluded from the personnel of the Native Tribunals.[1] In the Gold Coast it was recommended some years ago that Chiefs *qua* Chiefs should not be appointed to Native Courts, and the majority of the personnel constituting the Courts now hold no hereditary post.[2] Judicial Assistants have been appointed in some areas of Uganda as a first step towards separating the judicial from the executive element,[3] and the Chiefs' judicial powers are in some areas now wholly delegated to the Assistants.

A similar development is occurring in Tanganyika, where the experiment has been successfully tried of appointing stipendiary Benches and Chiefs' delegates.[4] The Basutoland Native Courts Reform Committee of 1950 recommended that no Chief should be president of a Court in an area where he had administrative functions,[5] and this recommendation has since been carried out. In Northern Nigeria there had long been a separate judiciary, in the form of the Alkali Courts, though it should be noted that the separation from the Executive was not fully complete, as the Emir's Courts still retained some judicial functions.[6] While it may be premature to express an opinion upon the success of the Kenya and Basutoland decisions to exclude Chiefs altogether from the personnel of the bench, these decisions would appear to be in harmony with existing tendencies in many areas. In the more backward territories, however, the policy is clearly one to be approached with caution, for no alternative source for constituting the personnel of the Tribunals is at present in sight.[7]

It is noteworthy that in a number of areas steps are being taken to overcome the difficulty created by the inferior education of some of the Chiefs. In the Northern Province of Uganda, for example, a law course is being provided for members of Court Benches.[8] There has been in many territories the definite exercise of administrative influence to secure the inclusion of 'new men' and non-traditional elements in the composition of the sitting Benches.

[1] *N.A.*, Part I, p. 100.   [2] *N.A.*, Part III, p. 213.
[3] *Colonial Reports, Uganda, 1952*, p. 46; ibid. *1953*, p. 85.
[4] *Tanganyika, Annual Reports of Provincial Commissioners, 1953*, p. 124.
[5] *N.A.*, Part V, p. 109.   [6] *N.A.*, Part III, pp. 83–84.
[7] See on this subject generally, N. J. Brooke, 'The Changing Character of Customary Courts', *J.A.A.*, April 1954, pp. 67 ff.   [8] *Colonial Reports, Uganda, 1952*, p. 145.

Attention has already been drawn to the tendency shown towards the increase of the scope of the jurisdiction of the Native Courts. In a considerable measure this extension of jurisdiction is due to administrative considerations; it has been a convenience that regulations regarding measures of local welfare should issue as Native Authority Rules, the infringement of which has been logically dealt with by the Native Courts. It was logical also that default of payment of the Native tax should be tried in the Native Courts, since a portion of the tax is now in most territories credited to the Native Treasuries.[1] But there are instances in which the Native Courts have been given jurisdiction to deal with offences under Statutory Ordinances,[2] and this is less logical, for the issues raised are at times too technical to be properly understood by a Native Court.[3]

Reference has also been made to the significance now attached in the British territories to the provision of a link between the Native Court system and that of the Colonial Courts.[4] In British Administrative circles there seems to have prevailed at one period a conception of the Native Court as a separate system,[5] supervised entirely by Administrative Officers, and provided with an avenue of appeal which terminated in some purely Administrative authority. There was a suspicion that Judges of a Supreme or High Court, recruited from the ranks of European practising lawyers, would not only lack the knowledge to deal with issues arising under the customary law of Africans, but would prove to be out of sympathy with the procedure of Courts which followed methods so alien to those with which they were themselves familiar. Some of the suspicions felt at one time in British circles regarding the effect of linking the Native Court system with that of the Supreme or High Court have now been allayed. There has nevertheless been less emphasis laid on strengthening that connexion than on devising means for the improvement of the procedure of the Native Courts, partly by making provision for their supervision, and partly by creating suitable avenues of appeal within the Native Court system itself.

Supervision of Courts

Supervision is in the British territories carried on primarily through the inspection of records by Administrative Officers and the consequent exercise by them of the power of revision or of transfer to the revising officer's own Court. This may be done either on his own motion or on application from a dissatisfied party. It has, however, become evident that the increasing volume of litigation in the Native Courts does not allow the Administrative Officer to carry out the same measure of supervision of records as

[1] See below, p. 654.   [2] See, for example, *N.A.*, Part I, p. 162.
[3] *J.A.A.*, October 1953, Supplement, p. 21.
[4] See above, p. 611.   [5] *N.A.*, Part IV, p. 40.

formerly. This duty is now being entrusted in many territories to a special officer, bearing the title of Judicial Adviser or an equivalent designation, the appointment of these officers having followed a precedent set in Uganda in 1940.[1]

The functions of the African Courts Adviser as envisaged in Kenya were stated to comprise a general supervision of Native Tribunals and a revision of the judgements given in criminal cases by Native Tribunals.[2] But in other territories the duties and status of these officers have been less clearly defined, and the intention seems to have been to allow individual territories to utilize their services to the best advantage in the light of their special circumstances. This officer sits as an Appellate Court in Buganda, Swaziland, and Basutoland, and as a member of the Court of Review in Kenya. In the Gold Coast he has a statutory duty to revise cases concurrent with that of Administrative Officers.[3] In Kenya he exercises revisionary jurisdiction in criminal cases only.[4]

Courts of Appeal

While in some territories the greater number of appeals still lies to the Administrative staff, there has been a progressive development of the system of Native Courts of Appeal. Until recently the normal course of appeal lay from the original Native Court to the Native Appeal Court, thence to the Courts of the District and Provincial Commissioner respectively, and finally to a High or Supreme Court, but in some instances the procedure has been modified with a view to eliminating some of the intermediate stages of appeal. Thus in Nigeria appeal to the District Commissioner lies only when there is no Native Court of Appeal. In Kenya appeal normally lies only upon a 'case stated'.[5] Subject to certain limitations, the appellant may now proceed in Kenya to a new Court, the Court of Review, whose president must have held high judicial office. Tanganyika[6] and Sierra Leone[7] have also adopted methods for abbreviating the course of appeal. In Basutoland both criminal and civil appeals lie to the Judicial Commissioner's Court,[8] but in Swaziland he hears appeals from the Higher Native Appeal Court only in criminal cases. In Nyasaland the Native Courts Adviser may revise any decision of a Native Court or Native

---

[1] In Kenya the officer is known as African Courts Adviser, in Tanganyika as Local Courts Adviser, in Northern Rhodesia as Native Courts Adviser, in Basutoland and Swaziland as Judicial Commissioner, in Uganda, the Gold Coast, and some other territories as Judicial Adviser.

[2] A. Phillips, *Report on Native Tribunals*, 1945, para. 669.

[3] *J.A.A.*, October 1953, Supplement, p. 11.

[4] Loc. cit.

[5] *Kenya, African Affairs Annual Report, 1952*, p. 35.

[6] *Tanganyika, Annual Reports of Provincial Commissioners, 1953*, p. 51.

[7] *Report on the Native Court System in Sierra Leone, 1953*, p. 61.

[8] *Colonial Reports, Basutoland, 1953*, p. 59.

Appeal Court;[1] in Buganda also the Judicial Adviser has qualified appellate jurisdiction.[2]

A number of changes have also occurred in the procedure regulating the exercise of the power of revision or review by Administrative Officers. In their hands it has been regarded less as a judicial than as an executive function for which they were especially qualified by their knowledge of local custom. But the tendency is now to place emphasis on resort to the normal course of appeal rather than on the exercise of review or revision; it has, for example, been recommended in the Gold Coast that cases sent to the Judicial Commissioner on review should be referred by him to the Court to which an appeal would normally lie.[3]

While there are likely to be many areas where the Native Courts have not reached the stage at which revision by an Administrative Officer or Judicial Adviser can be dispensed with, the advantage clearly lies in so improving the character of the Native Appeal Courts that they can become the normal remedy available to an aggrieved litigant.[4] The exercise by an Administrative Officer of the power to transfer cases from a Native Court to a Colonial Court may reasonably be held to be an essential feature of a dual system of Courts and of law,[5] and it is certainly advisable in certain classes of cases, such as those which may have political consequences. But it is an emergency power which is now more sparingly used.

Though there can be no question of the value of the part played by the Native Court in the British dependencies, it will be realized that the Native Court system is not based on the employment of a uniform type of Court, capable of general adoption. It is based on the recognition given to a large number of strictly local Courts, each of which can only operate successfully in its own environment. A Native Court which can successfully cater for the needs of its own tribe or group would fail as an instrument of justice in a different tribal or local setting. The Colonial Court on the other hand is a tribunal of general use which, if it has its own drawbacks, nevertheless has the advantage that it employs a uniform type of procedure and administers a uniform body of law.

The limitation imposed on the Native Court by the fact that it can operate only in its own local setting has made it necessary to devise a special form of tribunal for the growing number of aggregations of groups of Africans of different tribal origin. The problem has become increasingly urgent with the modern growth of urbanization,[6] and a number of different

[1] Ordinance no. 17 of 1947. See also *N.A.*, Part II, p. 29.

[2] *J.A.A.*, October 1953, Supplement, pp. 11, 42.

[3] *Gold Coast, Report of Commission on Native Courts*, 1951, p. 33. See also *Report on the Native Court system in Sierra Leone*, 1953, p. 61.

[4] On the question of review, see P. C. Hodgson, in *J.A.A.*, July 1955, p. 131.

[5] *J.A.A.*, April 1953, p. 93.   [6] See above, pp. 564–86.

solutions have been attempted. In the Copperbelt towns of Northern Rhodesia, Urban Courts were at one time composed of members appointed by the Native Authorities of those tribes whose workers in the Copperbelt were the most numerous. Under the most recent arrangement the territory has been divided into four so-called 'law areas', the Native Authority in each of these areas being invited to nominate a member to sit on an urban Bench.[1] In Kenya members of Urban Courts are appointed after consultation with the African Advisory Councils. In Nyasaland a panel is kept of suitable persons from whom three are called at each session of the Court.

The solution most favoured by those who have studied the problem in West Africa is the appointment of a single African Judge having professional qualifications, sitting with Assessors.[2] There such an appointment may prove to be feasible, but it must be some time before professional African Judges can be found in the Eastern and Central African territories. There have been some interesting attempts made by the members of the Urban Courts to adapt Bantu law to meet the exigencies of local conditions, as for example the problem created by the recognition given to 'temporary marriages' in the copper-mining areas of Northern Rhodesia.

Inquiries and Recommendations of Various Commissions

Looking to the history of the Native Court system in the British territories during the last 50 years, there can be no question of the improved standing it has acquired as the result of the measures above referred to. That is a fact on which both Administrative Officers and the professional lawyers constituting the higher judiciary are agreed, and it is probable that its standing will be further improved by the recent appointment of Judicial Advisers, many of whom have been practising lawyers. It would, however, seem that there are now some parts of these territories in which the Native Court is to be regarded as having reached the limit of its value as part of the judicial organization. It is in origin an integral part of the Native Authority system, and the influences which have pressed for the replacement of that system by Local Government institutions of a non-traditional character are also pressing for the replacement of the Native Court by judicial institutions which also owe nothing to tradition. That is especially the case in the Gold Coast and the Eastern Region of Nigeria.

It is of interest to note the changing attitude observed towards the Native Court system by the commissions which have from time to time dealt with the question of judicial organization in the British African territories. The earliest of these, the Commission of 1933 which reported

---

[1] A. L. Epstein, *The Administration of Justice and the Urban African*, 1953, p. 23. See also *J.A.A.*, October 1953, Supplement, p. 16.

[2] *J.A.A.*, April 1953, p. 86.

on conditions in East Africa,[1] dealt only with the subject of criminal justice and did not include a review of the position of the Native Courts. The Report on the Native Tribunals of Kenya,[2] while supporting the policy of excluding Chiefs from membership of the tribunals, nevertheless favoured the retention in other respects of a link with traditional institutions; but its most important recommendation was for the appointment of selected 'permanent' Presidents of Native Courts,[3] who would gradually give place to African judicial officers educated at a university level. It proposed the establishment of the new Court of Appeal which has, as already shown, emerged as the Court of Review.

In the Gold Coast the grave inefficiency which up to 1942 characterized its Native tribunals[4] led to the appointment of two commissions, whose chief recommendations referred to the steps needed for the removal of existing abuses, and were responsible for the reforms embodied in the Native Courts Ordinance of 1944.[5] A further commission on the Native Courts appointed in 1950 had a more fundamental objective as it was a corollary of the constitutional inquiry which led to the issue of the important report of 1949 on constitutional changes in the Gold Coast referred to in a previous chapter.[6] The commission recommended the replacement of the existing Native Courts by Local Courts (in the form of Area Courts and District Courts) whose jurisdiction would coincide with the boundaries of the newly created Local Government areas.[7] The new Courts were to consist of either 'lay' honorary Justices or of a single stipendiary Justice of professional qualifications.

In Nigeria five Inquiries were held between 1950 and 1952.[8] They proposed to substitute 'Customary Courts' for the existing Native Courts, but the composition of the new Courts was not to differ materially from that of the existing Courts. Their jurisdiction was, however, to be more strictly confined to dealing with cases falling within the field of custom, and they were in particular to be the original Courts dealing with land cases. It is noteworthy that this series of Nigerian Reports is emphatic in asserting that the ordinary Colonial Courts (including the Supreme Court) are not well equipped to try land issues; indeed, the reports quote

---

[1] *Report of Commission of Inquiry into the Administration of Justice in Kenya, Uganda and Tanganyika in Criminal Matters*, 1934, Cmd. 4623.

[2] A. Phillips, *Report on Native Tribunals*, Kenya, 1945, pp. 318–26.

[3] On this point, see *N.A.*, Part I, pp. 205–6.

[4] *N.A.*, Part III, pp. 203–4, 211–14.

[5] *Report of Native Tribunals Committee of Enquiry* (the Blackall Report), 1943. *Report of a Commission of Enquiry into Expenses incurred by Litigants in the Courts of the Gold Coast and Indebtedness caused thereby* (the Havers Report), 1945. For the reforms of 1944, see above, p. 521.

[6] See above, p. 319. [7] *Report of Commission on Native Courts, Gold Coast*, 1951.

[8] Reports on the Colony and Northern Region, 1951; Eastern and Western Regions and Cameroons, 1952 (the Brooke Reports). See *J.A.A.*, April 1953, pp. 80–84; July 1953, pp. 140–3. See also *Native Courts Commissions of Enquiry, 1949–1952, Summary of Conclusions and Recommendations*, Zaria, 1953.

admissions made by the Supreme Court Judges that land issues require special knowledge which the ordinary Courts do not possess.[1]

In 1953 the system existing in Sierra Leone was also examined by a Commission.[2] It would retain for the present the system of Chiefdom Courts, and would also keep supervision and control in the hands of Administrative Officers; but it foresaw that the new District Councils might arrive at a stage when they could take over this function.[3] There is an air of realism about the proposals made for Nigeria and Sierra Leone which is much less marked in those which originate from the Gold Coast.

RESEARCH ON CUSTOMARY LAW

Reference has already been made to early studies carried out in the Union of South Africa regarding Bantu law.[4] The result of the codification of Native law in Natal has not been altogether fortunate, and it has been held to have 'frozen' its development; the experiment has not been repeated in the Union. The law and custom of the Tswana of Bechuanaland has been the subject of a comprehensive study.[5] The collection of the Laws of Lerotholi issued by the Basutoland National Council is an interesting attempt to bring together the main points of Basuto custom, but it is not a complete code of law.[6] A study of the customary law of the Haya has had the advantage of collaboration by African Assessors,[7] and a more recent investigation into that of the Sukuma[8] illustrates the special interest taken in this subject in Tanganyika. The Law Panel in Kenya has compiled memoranda on Bukusi-Tachoni land law and is studying the influence of case law on customary law.[9]

There have in addition been a considerable number of studies of different aspects of African customary law, such as witchcraft, and some aspect of the customary law has usually formed part of the more general studies made of tribal custom.[10] A study of African marriage law forms an important part of the *Survey of African Marriage and Family Life*,[11] concluded in 1953, and the question of the impact of Islamic law on African customary

---

[1] See in particular *Report of the Native Courts (Eastern Region) Commission of Enquiry*, 1952, pp. 23–24. *Report on Western Provinces*, 1952, pp. 20–21.

[2] N. J. Brooke, *Report on the Native Court System in Sierra Leone*, Freetown, 1953.

[3] See above, p. 533.

[4] See above, p. 424. See also W. G. Stafford, *Native Law as practised in Natal*, 1935.

[5] I. Schapera, *A Handbook of Tswana Law and Custom*, 1938.

[6] *N.A.*, Part V, p. 92.

[7] H. Cory and M. M. Hartnoll, *Customary Law of the Haya Tribe*, 1945.

[8] H. Cory, *Sukuma Law and Custom*, 1953.

[9] *Kenya, African Affairs Annual Report*, 1952, p. 2.

[10] For a list of such studies, see C. K. Meek, *Colonial Law, A Bibliography with special reference to Native African systems of law and land tenure*, 1948, pp. 21–36.

[11] A. Phillips, ed., *A Survey of African Marriage and Family Life*, 1953, pp. 173–328.

law has been included in a work on Islamic law in Africa published in 1954.[1]

In the French territories a collection has been made of the customary law of the constituent territories of French West Africa,[2] and a special study of the customary law of Senegal.[3] The Belgian Congo has given an unusual measure of attention to this subject. The *Société d'études juridiques du Katanga* publishes two periodical journals, the *Bulletin des juridictions indigènes et du droit coutumier congolais*, and the *Revue juridique du Congo Belge*. A conference on the future of African customary law was organized by the Afrika-Instituut, Leiden, in 1956. It published a useful bibliography.[4]

The Formation of a Single Body of Law

It is a matter of speculation whether it is possible to expect the formation in any of the African territories of a comprehensive corpus of law which will serve the purpose of the whole of its population. At one period both French and Belgian policy seemed to look forward to a period when the African would adapt himself to a single system of law of a predominantly European pattern. Events have shown, however, the strength of the preference of Africans in those territories for retaining at least so much of their personal law as will allow them to maintain their customary procedure in matrimonial relations, or in the succession to property, or in the tenure of land. Whatever may have been their reaction to the European concepts of criminal law or of the civil law regulating commercial or economic relations, their adherence to their personal law has accounted for much of the unwillingness shown even by progressive Africans to avail themselves of the benefits offered to them by schemes of *immatriculation* and the like.[5]

Both the French and Belgian Administrations have (as has been seen) been compelled to recognize this fact, and to adjust both their legal system and their organization of justice accordingly. The effort made by the Administration of the Belgian Congo to proscribe the practice of polygamy[6] provides a typical example of the standing difficulty which must at present be encountered by any attempt to formulate a homogeneous body of law applicable to all sections of a mixed population. It has been justly observed that when a dominant people is dealing with the customs of a different civilization and of different religions, the tests of reasonableness, morality, and public policy must be looked at from a very different angle from that which would be appropriate in the conditions of European

---

[1] J. N. D. Anderson, *Islamic Law in Africa*, 1954, pp. 58–287.

[2] *Coutumiers juridiques de l'Afrique occidentale française*, 3 vols., 1939.

[3] L. Geismar, *Recueil des coutumes civiles des races du Sénégal*, 1933.

[4] *L'Avenir du Droit Coutumier en Afrique*, Symposium-Colloque, Amsterdam 1955, Leiden, 1956. See also *Africa*, January 1940, pp. 25–42.

[5] See above, p. 224.

[6] *Décret*, 4 April 1950. See Phillips, op. cit. pp. 190–3.

society.[1] The British, always less definite in objective, have characteristically given first place to what appeared to them to be the immediate needs of African society, and have provided the mechanism for this in an extended use of purely Native Tribunals administering the customary law. The Portuguese, unwilling to appear to countenance the existence of 'uncivilized' practices such as polygamy, seem to have preferred to leave the greater part of the population of their territories without any recognized tribunals for adjusting the differences arising within the field of Native custom.

Legal Dualism

There thus prevails in practice a system of legal dualism, and it is not easy to foresee clearly the course which the two elements of law, European and African, will ultimately take. One point is obvious. Native customary law is continually adjusting itself to meet the new economic and social conditions with which African society is being faced. Much has been said of the unwisdom of any attempt by a Colonial Power to impose its own concepts of law on peoples who are at a different stage of civilization; but it must also be realized that the economic and social institutions of European civilization have a dynamic quality which leads Africans (particularly those of a 'progressive' character) almost automatically to adjust their own custom to that which is characteristic of Europe. The dynamic force of European civilization is the more impressive because it does not encounter the opposition of a unified form of custom reinforced by religion, such as exists among some Asian peoples, and which regulates the social life of vast masses of the population.

If it is possible to venture a forecast in this matter, the future is likely to see (as already suggested) the progressive adoption of a uniform penal law, which will be mainly of a European pattern. Much the same prospect may be forecast for the civil law relating to commercial and similar relations. The personal law of Africans, modified in various respects to meet changing circumstances, is likely to remain as a special field of the civil law, as it does for example in India, but it is likely to be administered in due course by the ordinary Courts, not by any special branch of the judiciary.[2] It is here, and not in the modification of the law itself, that will be found the practical measure of integration. This will mean the continuation of the process, already begun in some territories, by which the 'traditional' Court will be replaced by a normal 'professional' Court.

It is at the same time not unlikely that while the law may in time prescribe a uniform procedure, based on a European pattern, for all the

---

[1] C. K. Allen, *Laws in the Making*, 1946, pp. 502–3.

[2] For this subject generally see also A. Phillips, 'The Future of Customary Law', *J.A.A.*, October 1955, p. 151.

normal Courts, the Administrations may decide to recognize a special class of subordinate Court, of the type of a village Court with a strictly restricted jurisdiction but following its own form of procedure for the trial of cases. There can be no doubt that the strong popular support due to the revival of the *panchayat* system in India is (apart from any political or ideological reasons) largely due to the fact that it affords a means of deciding minor issues, both civil and criminal, without the formality of normal judicial procedure.[1] In 1953 there were in India some 150,000 villages served by *sabhas* or *panchayats*, either singly or joined in small groups.

Some further considerations on this subject will be found in the papers presented to the conference on the future of African customary law held by the Afrika-Instituut, Leiden, to which previous reference has been made in this chapter.[2]

[1] *J.A.A.*, January 1953, pp. 2 ff.
[2] See above, p. 640. See also S. F. Nadel in *Africa*, April 1956, p. 162. J. Sohier, 'Essai sur les transformations des coutumes', *Mém A.R.S.C.*, vol. v, no. 8, 1956.

CHAPTER X

DIRECT TAXATION

THE study of the procedure of taxation in Africa has an interest extending beyond its bearing on fiscal policy, for the methods adopted provide one of the most significant examples of differentiation between the non-African and the African communities. Indirect taxation is seldom discriminatory in its form, though customs duties may be specifically designed to favour the interests of one community or of one section of a community rather than another—as for example the agricultural producer in the Union of South Africa or the European farmers in Kenya. But in the case of direct taxation there is in many territories a basic difference in the procedure applied to non-Africans and Africans. The non-African is subject to the payment of a direct tax in the form of an income tax (or some variety of income tax) which is assessed on his individual resources. On the other hand, the most typical form of tax applying to the African is the flat-rate tax, in the form of a hut or poll tax, which does not vary with the extent of the resources of the individual or his income. It might almost be said that the African begins to be recognized as a member of civilized society when he becomes subject to the payment of income tax instead of poll tax, and much of the interest of the following pages lies in the record of the stages in which different Administrations have succeeded in applying the basic principle of the income tax to the taxation of Africans.

But a study of the methods pursued in taxation has an interest also in other directions. The imposition of direct taxation on Africans has in the past been urged on Administrations, more especially in South and East Africa, as the most effective means of stimulating the supply of labour for plantation or industrial undertakings. It has, again, been claimed that where there are mixed communities of non-Africans and Africans, the amount contributed to the general revenue by the taxation of Africans should determine the limit to which the social services (and most typically that of education) should be provided for them by the State.[1] Both these somewhat medieval forms of argument are, however, now passing out of use, save perhaps among the more extreme sections of opinion in the European communities.

At the present day one of the most interesting chapters in the history of African taxation deals with the part it has played in the development of institutions of Local Government. In Africa the delegation of powers

---

[1] See, for instance, above, pp. 568, 577, 648, 651, 1147.

from a Central Government to local bodies must normally amount to a devolution of authority into the hands of the African community, and the measure to which such a devolution of authority has been accompanied by the concession of the power of taxation is one of the most significant proofs of the progress made in the extension of institutions designed to minister to the principle of self-rule.

The present chapter is primarily concerned with an examination of the systems employed in the direct taxation of Africans, but, as a preface, it may be convenient to consider briefly the methods applied to the taxation of non-Africans.

DIRECT TAXATION OF NON-AFRICANS

Union of South Africa

Throughout Africa the principal direct tax on non-Africans takes the form of a general income tax, which in most cases covers also the taxation of companies. In the Union of South Africa the legislation imposing a direct tax on non-Africans varied in the different Provinces until 1925, when Act 40 of that year brought them under a uniform system. The procedure regulating the imposition of the income tax is now governed by Act 31 of 1941, which has been modified in various details by subsequent amendments[1] but continues to form the basis of direct taxation both of individuals and companies. Individuals are liable to normal tax and to super-tax, on both of which surcharges, varying from year to year, have been levied since 1946, except in 1948. During recent years concessions have been made which considerably reduce the incidence of direct taxation.[2] The income at which liability to normal tax begins has been lowered from £406 to £276 for unmarried and from £600 to £400 for married persons; there are large allowances for married persons, children, and dependants, and the maximum tax rate has been reduced from 15s. to 10s. in the £, or 12s. 6d. including the Provincial tax.

Each of the four Provinces levies for the purpose of its own budget a surcharge in addition to the normal tax and super tax. The surcharge is calculated in percentages of the sum payable to the Union Government. Thus in the Cape the addition to both normal and super tax is 30 per cent., and companies pay 9d. in the £ on their taxable income in so far as it is derived from sources within the Province. The rates in the other Provinces vary, but have generally an incidence comparable to that in the Cape. In addition to this surcharge the Provinces have levied a graduated personal tax on all non-Africans resident in the Province, the whole of which accrues

---

[1] *O.Y.S.A., 1952–53*, pp. 605 ff.
[2] *The Times*, 25 March 1955.

to the Province. The income below which this tax is not levied in the Cape Province and the Transvaal is £150 for unmarried and £250 for married persons, and in Natal £250 for unmarried and £150 for married persons. The Orange Free State has adopted the figure at which taxable income is assessed for normal tax in the Union. The maximum amount paid in the Cape is £10 for unmarried and £5 for married persons; the corresponding rates in the other Provinces are £5 and £3. 10s. in Natal, £9. 7s. 6d. and £6. 5s in the Orange Free State, and £12. 10s. and £7. 10s. in the Transvaal.[1]

The income-tax system of the Union is so devised as to relieve the poorer European of taxation, and the greater part of the revenue derived from direct taxation is paid by companies. Thus in the fiscal year 1950–1 out of a total revenue from income tax (normal and super tax) amounting to £65¾ million, companies contributed £43¼ million and individuals £22¼ million. Farmers, besides receiving much special assistance in other ways, are treated lightly for income-tax purposes, being allowed liberal rebates for expenditure; thus in 1950–1, out of a total taxable income of £283½ million, farming accounted for a little short of £9 million.

South-West Africa and the High Commission Territories

In South-West Africa direct taxation on non-Africans consists of an income tax and a personal tax. Married persons become liable to income tax at an income exceeding £1,067 and unmarried persons at an income above £755. Personal tax (with rebates for children and other dependants) is payable by married persons with an income over £500 and by single persons of over £300; the tax is graduated, starting at £2 and £4 for married and single respectively and rising to £10 for both. These taxes apply both to the European and Coloured communities, but not to Africans.

In the High Commission Territories the income both of individuals and of companies is taxed on the same lines as in the Union. In addition, all non-African males over 21 are liable to a poll tax of £3 per annum.

The British Territories in Central, East, and West Africa

In the Federation of Rhodesia and Nyasaland income tax was graduated in the 1954 budget at different rates for married and unmarried persons; for the former the rate ranged from 9d. in the £ for the first £500 to 6s. 3d on the last £500 of income below £3,000; above £3,000 super tax was charged at a rate which began at 9d. in the £ and rose to a maximum rate of 3s. 3d. Single persons paid a slightly higher rate of income tax;

[1] See *Income Taxes in the Commonwealth*, vol. i, 1951, pp. 379 ff. *O.Y.S.A., 1952–53*, pp. 613, 635–6.

super tax was payable on the same scale as by married persons. The company tax was 6s. 3d. in the £.

In Southern Rhodesia income tax was first introduced in 1918 and was, until 1955, levied under the Tax Consolidation Act of 1948. This Act had close analogies with the legislation in the Union, and has been used as the basis of the Federal tax law.[1] In terms of Article 82 of the Constitution of the Federation of Rhodesia and Nyasaland each of the constituent territories is entitled to levy a surcharge on individuals resident in the territory and upon the taxable income derived by companies from such territory. In the case of Southern Rhodesia, the surcharge for individuals has, since March 1955, been fixed at 20 per cent. of the amount payable as basic tax (income tax and supertax), and for companies 1s. 3d. in the £ of taxable income derived from the territory. The same surcharge is levied in Nyasaland. In Northern Rhodesia no surcharge is levied in the case of individuals; the surcharge on companies is, however, at the same rate as in Southern Rhodesia.[2]

The Federation has in addition an undistributed profits tax of 1s. 6d. on the first £2,000, and 3s. on the undistributed profits of companies (other than private companies) which are registered within the Federation.

Whereas before the Second World War the only British dependencies other than Southern Rhodesia to impose income tax were Northern Rhodesia (1921), Nyasaland (1921), Nigeria (1927), and Kenya (1937), all British dependencies in Africa now do so. With a few exceptions, income tax applies irrespective of race, but in practice it is paid almost exclusively by non-Africans, partly because of the administrative difficulty of applying it to Africans, and partly because few Africans are in receipt of an income high enough to fall within the taxable category. Africans are, however, explicitly exempt from income tax in Nyasaland, Northern Rhodesia, and Nigeria, except in Lagos and the area surrounding it. There are no statistics available to show the number of Africans who pay income tax in those territories where they are liable to it, but it is known that the total number is much higher in West than in East Africa.[3]

The principles governing the taxation of incomes are much the same in all the territories; the scale is in all cases progressive, but rates vary between the different countries. The following table shows the amount of tax payable in 1950 on a gross income of £1,000 by a single man (I), a married man without children (II), and a married man with two children (III) respectively.[4]

---

[1] *Report of the Fiscal Commission on Draft Federal Scheme*, Cmd. 8672, 1952, p. 15.

[2] Federation of Rhodesia and Nyasaland, Income Tax Act of 1956.

[3] 'Methods of Direct Taxation in British Tropical Africa', *J.A.A.*, October 1950, p. 10.

[4] Ibid. An informative table of the rates of income taxes in Colonies, African and non-African, is given in H.C. Deb., 23 April 1952, col. 398.

Territory	I	II	III
	£	£	£
Kenya ⎫			
Tanganyika ⎬	112	59	44
Uganda ⎭			
Nyasaland	88	46	18
Nigeria	67	37	31
Sierra Leone	30	17	15
Gold Coast	25	17	15
Gambia	65	42	27

In Kenya the introduction of an income tax was preceded by an interesting history. When the Kenya Administration raised the African poll tax to 8 rupees per adult in order to meet the crisis caused by the financial depression of 1920–1, the British Government stipulated that the non-African tax be increased at the same time. Hitherto Europeans and Asians had paid only a poll tax of 30s. a year.[1] An Income Tax Ordinance became law in 1920, but met with resistance by the European community, with the result that of the estimated yield of £328,413 for 1921 only £95,073 was actually collected,[2] and of this sum the greater proportion was paid by Government servants and other employed persons. The opposition to the tax was supported by a number of arguments, though only one of them was actually valid—it was certainly the fact that Europeans themselves had been hard hit by the depression. This plea served to bring about the abolition of the income tax in 1922, but it did not secure any equivalent concession in the direct tax paid by Africans. Up to 1927 the non-African community continued to pay only the poll tax of 30s.; in that year a special levy of 30s. from Europeans and 20s. from Asians was sanctioned in order to cover the cost of European and Asian education.

The financial difficulties of 1931 again brought to the front the question of increasing non-African taxation. A levy on official salaries was imposed in 1932; shortly afterwards a proposal for the imposition of income tax was accepted by the Government in Great Britain, but the protests of the European community again succeeded in securing its withdrawal. A number of minor financial measures were substituted, many of which were from the first unremunerative. The poll tax, which in 1930 had brought in £43,702, yielded an average of £64,805 a year in the years 1932–41, and meanwhile the levy on official salaries was bringing in sums varying in the same years between £48,188 and £53,815.

The comprehensive inquiry made into the financial position of Kenya in 1935–6[3] recommended that an income tax be substituted for the various

[1] Non-Native Poll Tax Ordinance, 1912.

[2] *Report by the Financial Commissioner (Lord Moyne) on Certain Questions in Kenya*, Cmd. 4093, 1932, p. 59.

[3] *Report of the Commission appointed to Enquire into and Report on the Financial Position and System of Taxation in Kenya* (the Pim Report), Col. no. 116, 1936, pp. 233 ff.

duties imposed in 1933, and an Income Tax Ordinance accordingly became law with effect from 1937. Its acceptance by the non-African elected members of the Legislature was, however, conditional upon an assurance being given that the financing of services for Africans should not be a burden on the non-African communities. Though the tax had been accepted by the European members of the Legislature a Taxpayers' Protection League was formed to obtain its repeal. The rates remained unaltered during the Second World War, but reliefs for taxpayers with children were increased. A local taxation inquiry committee which reported in 1947 held that the incidence in the higher ranges of income might prove a deterrent to development, and recommended a reduction of rates throughout.[1] These recommendations have not, however, been adopted. Liability now begins at £200 for single persons and at £350 for married persons; the child allowance is £120 for the first child and £60 for each child after the first, up to a maximum of £300.

There have been no similar incidents in the development of the income-tax system in other British territories. The income tax has been everywhere extended to include the taxation of companies. As a general rule companies pay income tax at a flat rate which varies from territory to territory; in 1954 it was 4s. in the £ in Uganda, 5s. in Kenya, Tanganyika, and Zanzibar, 7s. 6d. in Northern Rhodesia and Nyasaland, 9s. in Nigeria, the Gold Coast, and Sierra Leone, and 10s. 3d. in Gambia.

In addition to income tax a non-African poll tax is levied in Nyasaland, Tanganyika, Kenya, Uganda, and Sierra Leone, its main function being to ensure some contribution from those non-Africans who do not pay income tax. In Kenya, where it is designated a personal tax, the rates are £1 on incomes under £60, £2 on incomes between £60 and £120, and £3 on all incomes over £120.[2] Uganda charges, under the head of non-African poll tax, £5 on incomes above and £3 on incomes below £200; women with an income of less than £150 are exempted. In Tanganyika the tax, applicable only to adult males, is graduated from an initial £1, levied on incomes up to £100, to £2. 10s. on incomes exceeding £200. In Nyasaland and Sierra Leone a flat rate of £4 is levied on males over 18.

The non-African poll tax is generally allowed as a deduction from income tax. Where persons are liable to income tax, it would appear rational to incorporate this tax in income tax, but up to now this has been done only in Northern Rhodesia. Though the retention of a personal tax (or non-African poll tax) involves a certain measure of complication, it is a convenient form of taxing those persons (especially Asian, Syrian, or European traders) who keep no regular accounts.

---

[1] *Report of Taxation Enquiry Committee, Kenya* (the Plewman Report), 1947.
[2] *Kenya, Report of the Committee of Enquiry on Graduated African Taxation* (the Marchant Report), 1950.

Besides income tax and poll or personal tax the four East African territories impose on non-Africans a certain number of contributions in support
of special services. In Kenya, for instance, Europeans pay a hospital
contribution, graduated according to income, ranging from 10s. to 2,000s.
Uganda and Tanganyika charge all male non-Africans, including Asians,
an education tax graduated according to income. Zanzibar also levies
a European education tax. The maximum rate of surtax payable by individuals is 9s. in the £ in Tanganyika, but 11s. in the £ in other East African
territories.

The French Territories

The Governments of the groups of Colonies constituting French West
Africa and French Equatorial Africa derive their main revenue from
indirect taxation, but the constituent territorial Governments levy direct
taxation for their own budgetary purposes. This division of financial
resources is a recent development, dating in French West Africa from 1942
and in French Equatorial Africa from 1946. The tax system is structurally
the same throughout the French territories. In principle no distinction
is drawn between non-Africans and Africans, but in practice income tax
is paid almost exclusively by the former.

As in France income taxation is divided in two parts; the first part comprises taxes levied proportionally on income derived from particular
sources (*impôts cédulaires*) such as industrial and commercial undertakings,
professional work, and (up to 1952) wages and salaries. The second part
comprises a general income tax, *impôt général sur le revenu*, based on the
taxpayer's total income irrespective of source and levied at progressive
rates. By far the more important of the two is the tax on income derived
from particular sources. In the budget for French West Africa for 1950,
revenue from this source was estimated at rather over 787 million francs,
compared with only 113 million francs from the general income tax.[1]
Furthermore, all persons over 14 (but only males in Togo) are subject to
a personal tax, graduated by classifying taxpayers in three or four categories according to their economic position. As the personal tax is the
principal direct tax paid by Africans it will be treated more fully in the
section dealing with the taxation of Africans.[2] Besides income and personal
taxes, taxes on house and land values are levied at varying rates in the
different territories.

The Belgian Territories

In the Belgian Congo income tax was introduced in 1920, but in its
present form it is based on a Decree of 10 September 1951 which

[1] Pierre Doublet, *Traité de Législation fiscale dans les Territoires d'Outre-Mer*, vol. ii: *Régimes fiscaux
de l'Afrique Occidentale Française et du Togo*, 1952, p. 245.   [2] See below, p. 670.

consolidated the regulations passed during and since the Second World War.[1] Taxation on income takes the form of several taxes varying according to the sources from which income is derived, as, for instance, the rent of house property, professional work, and the like. These rates range from 1 to 25 per cent. of taxable income, the highest rate being reached at an income level of 650,000 francs. Companies are taxed on a progressive scale according to their capital at rates ranging from 10 to 25 per cent. of the net revenue; companies domiciled outside the Belgian Congo pay in tax 25 per cent. of the revenue originating in the Colony.

In addition to income tax, a personal tax was imposed by a Decree of 16 March 1950. In practice, however, it has little of the character of a normal personal tax, since it is assessed according to certain economic criteria, such for example as the number of labourers or domestic servants or motor vehicles employed. Of the two kinds of taxes, the income taxes are financially the more important; in the budget for 1951 they were estimated to yield 1,480 million francs, while it was expected to obtain only 115 million francs by the personal tax.[2] Taxation of income in the Trust Territory of Ruanda Urundi follows the lines obtaining in the Belgian Colony.

The Portuguese Territories

Non-Africans in Angola are not liable to a uniform income tax, but are subject to taxation classified according to the source of their income.[3] Thus an industrial tax of 10 per cent. is levied upon incomes derived from industrial and commercial enterprises and a professional tax, graduated from 1 per cent. on incomes of 20 *contos* to 20 per cent. on incomes exceeding 100 *contos*, is levied upon employees or members of joint stock concerns. The technical professions are taxed at a fixed rate. A complementary tax is imposed upon individuals and companies not included in the above categories; for the former it varies from 3 to 20 per cent., and for the latter from 1 to 8 per cent. A predial tax of 10 per cent. is levied upon undeveloped land in urban areas.

In Mozambique an income tax at rates graduated from 2 to 18 per cent. upon incomes of 60 *contos* or more was introduced in 1945.[4] A supplementary tax, a survival of war legislation, is levied upon incomes of 200 *contos* and over. Industrial and professional taxes are imposed as in Angola, but are collected by a 'licence' which is subject to a 20 per cent. surcharge. The predial tax is extended to cover rural as well as urban undeveloped land. There is also a defence tax of 1 per cent. on high incomes and a profits tax of 15 per cent. The nominal rate of taxation on non-Africans is thus relatively high.

---

[1] *Codes et lois du Congo Belge*, 1954, pp. 1383 ff.
[2] *Rapport sur l'administration de la colonie du Congo Belge, 1951*, pp. 49, 51.
[3] Decree, 16 December 1948.   [4] Decree, 8 December 1945.

DIRECT TAXATION OF AFRICANS

Direct taxation is a conception foreign to the ideas of the indigenous peoples of Africa. Except in the Emirates of Northern Nigeria, where Muslim influences introduced into the old Hausa Kingdoms a system of organized rule derived from the Muslim Empires of Northern Africa,[1] direct taxation has been due to the initiative of European Administrations during relatively recent times. Africans were formerly accustomed to the payment of tribute and to the performance of services to their Chief, but these exactions were levied rather on the community than on the individual; some, like the Chiefdom tax in Sierra Leone[2] or the *Luwalo* in Uganda,[3] have been continued in a modernized form. But the course taken in the imposition of a direct tax on Africans will best be seen from a survey of the position in the major groups of territories, beginning with the Union of South Africa.

Union of South Africa

Up to 1925 the direct tax on Africans varied with each Province, but by the Native Taxation and Development Act no. 41 of 1925, the power of imposing direct taxation was withdrawn from the Provincial Councils and a unified method of taxation was introduced throughout the Union. This law, as amended, still remains the basis of the taxation of Africans. The principal tax levied under it, now called the General Tax, is a poll tax, and is payable at the rate of £1 by every male African between the ages of 18 and 65, except by the few whose income brings them into categories liable to income tax. In addition, a local tax of 10s. per hut, up to a maximum of £2, is levied from Africans living in a Native location;[4] Africans over 65 and those holding land on quit-rent tenure are exempt. The proceeds from local tax and quit-rent tenure are now paid to African Local Councils or Location Boards, and are mainly used for the improvement of local agriculture and animal husbandry.[5]

Though the taxation of Africans was designed in the first instance mainly with the object of increasing the supply of labour, especially in the mines,[6] this object is now no longer of importance. It is significant that the rate of the tax has not been increased in the 30 years that have since elapsed, and today the major contribution of Africans to the general revenue is through indirect taxation.

The Act of 1925 was based on the principle that services for the benefit of Africans must be met from African taxation and that an extension of African education, in particular, must be financed from that source. The

---

[1] *N.A.*, Part III, pp. 75 ff.   [2] Ibid. pp. 302 ff.   [3] See below, p. 661.
[4] *O.Y.S.A.*, *1950*, pp. 510, 652.   [5] See above, p. 427.
[6] W. M. Macmillan, *Bantu, Boer and Briton*, 1929, pp. 66–67, 268.

measure to which the proceeds of the General Tax on Africans has actually been earmarked for expenditure on African education is discussed in a subsequent chapter.[1] It is noticeable that though South Africa long held to the principle that services provided for Africans should be paid for by African taxation, the argument did not actually lead to an increase in the rate of the General tax. A further noteworthy feature of the taxation of Africans in the Union is the omission of any system of graduation of the tax. Neither the method of varying the rate of poll tax according to the economic development of different localities, which has for many years obtained in most other African countries, nor the attempt to adjust the tax to the assumed taxable capacity of different strata of society, finds a place in the legislation of the Union.

Although the rate may not appear excessive, having regard to the reduced value of money in the years following the Second World War, a tax at a uniform rate inevitably tends to weigh most heavily on the poorest members of African society and is felt least by those who are capable of paying a higher rate.[2] Moreover, a tax which takes no account of varying capacity to pay is liable to prove unremunerative, since the uniform rate must be low enough to enable the poorer members to pay it. In 1952–3 the revenue from direct taxes on Africans was as follows: from the General tax £1,855,375; from local tax, £274,067; from quit-rents and farm taxes £60,078.[3] As compared with non-Africans on the lower income level, Africans appear to be heavily taxed, as is evident from a comparison of the exemption limits of the non-African personal tax with the rates and exemption limits of the African General and local taxes.

The method of collection increases the burden. The tax is paid in a lump sum and payment has often to be made at distant places, involving the taxpayer in loss of time and earnings. Until 1939 default by Africans was treated as a criminal offence, punishable by either a fine or imprisonment up to three months. An Act passed in that year introduced a method by which defaulters can pay arrears of tax by a deduction from wages.[4] Africans can, however, still be sentenced to detention in a labour camp for failure to pay taxes.

South-West Africa

Direct taxation of Africans has been little developed in South-West Africa. Although the South-West Africa Commission of 1936[5] reported that the Hereros expressed a desire that a uniform poll tax should be

---

[1] See below, p. 1146. For a fuller discussion of this issue see *Handbook on Race Relations in South Africa*, 1949, pp. 299–300.
[2] Ibid., p. 295. W. M. Macmillan, *Africa Emergent*, 1938, pp. 285 ff.
[3] *O. Y. S. A., 1952–53*, pp. 502 ff.
[4] *Handbook on Race Relations in South Africa*, 1949, p. 302.
[5] *Report of the South-West Africa Commission*, U.G. no. 26, 1936.

substituted for the levy of grazing fees, no such substitute for grazing fees has been introduced. The only direct taxes imposed on them in the Police Zone[1] are dog and wheel taxes; of these the dog tax accrues to the Trust Funds of the various Reserves in so far as they are collected there. The main revenue of the Reserves in the Police Zone is derived from grazing fees, which are fixed at varying rates for different classes of stock; the receipts are credited to the Trust Funds of the Reserves.

In the tribal areas—Ovamboland, Okovango, the Kaokoveld, and the Caprivi Strip—Tribal Trust Funds have been constituted under Proclamations issued in 1929 and 1937; their main function is to provide a stock of grain reserves against times of scarcity. All males between 18 and 60 years old contribute in cash or kind a sum of 7s. 6d. per annum (5s. in the Kaokoveld). At their present level these levies do not provide any surplus for extending the services required by the Tribal Areas. In 1936 the Legislative Assembly expressed the view that 'it would be inequitable further to tax the European population for services conceived entirely in the interests of the Natives, who hardly contribute to the revenue at all'.[2] That view apparently still prevails, but at the same time little effort seems to be made to increase the taxable capacity of the Africans in the tribal area.

High Commission Territories

Basutoland, like the other High Commission Territories, has its own system of African taxation. In Basutoland the declaration of British rule in 1869[3] was followed in 1870 by the imposition of a hut tax of 10s., payable in cash, grain, or stock. An increase to £1, imposed by the Cape Government in 1880, was one of the causes which resulted in the Gun War of that year, and the old rate was restored on the assumption of direct control by the British Government in 1884. In 1898 the rate was again raised to £1. In 1911 a poll tax was substituted for the hut tax, thus for the first time extending taxation to unmarried men, but the principle of the hut tax was retained by the imposition of an additional £1 for each wife after the first up to a maximum of £3.

The basic tax was increased by 5s. in 1920, and an additional levy of 3s. for educational purposes was imposed in 1927, making the minimum tax £1. 8s. 0d. This rate was maintained until 1946, when the poll tax was raised to 34s. and the tax on plural wives to 25s. with a maximum payment of 90s. for any one taxpayer.[4] An attempt to introduce some measure of graduation was made by providing that all Chiefs, Sub-Chiefs, and

[1] See above, p. 535.
[2] *Report of the South-West Africa Commission*, U.G. no, 26, para. 384.
[3] *N.A.*, Part V, pp. 42–44.
[4] Ibid. pp. 78, 90, 95.

Headmen, and all male Africans with incomes of over £5 a month, should pay poll tax at the rate of 40s. a year. The estimated total Native tax collection for 1954 was £285,000.

A proportion—at present 36 per cent.—of the revenue from Native tax is paid into the Basutoland National Treasury, which first began to function in 1946.[1] At the outset the Chiefs collected the tax, and up to 1899 they appear to have carried out this task without assistance from the Administrative Officers. The Administration subsequently took a more direct share in both assessment and collection, but the system has at various periods been found to be defective, partly owing to the fact that so large a number of the adult male population migrates for considerable periods to employment in the Union.[2] After the establishment of the National Treasury assessment and collection became largely the function of the Treasury staff maintained at the headquarters of each District, but the maintenance of the registers of those assessed still appears to require a much closer measure of supervision.

In Bechuanaland a hut tax of 10s. payable in cash, grain, or stock, was introduced in 1899, but was converted into a poll tax by Proclamations of 1900 and 1904, and was raised to 20s. in 1907. In addition from 1903 onwards several of the Chiefs began to collect a levy of 3s. from every taxpayer for the development of the social and agricultural services in their Reserves. In 1919 these levies were made universal and constituted the basis of a Native Fund which served mainly to finance African education. In 1930 the rate of the levy was raised to 5s. and in 1938 it was embodied in the poll tax, which thus became 25s. with an additional 25s. for each wife in excess of one, up to a maximum sum of £3. 15s. The plural wives tax was finally abolished in 1950, and in 1951 the Government poll tax (as it was now called) stood at the rate of 28s., this being raised to 30s. from the beginning of 1956. When Tribal Treasuries were set up in 1938, they assumed responsibility for services hitherto financed by the Native Fund and this was then dissolved.[3] The Treasuries were allocated 35 per cent. of the revenue from the basic tax.

In 1949 a graded personal tax was added to the basic Government poll tax.[4] This new tax grew out of a special levy imposed by the Native Authorities during the war. There are now ten categories of taxpayers. The lowest comprises cattle-owners possessing up to nine head of stock and wage-earners receiving a salary not exceeding £48 per annum. These pay 5s. In the highest category are included owners of over 300 head of stock and wage-earners drawing a salary exceeding £500 a year, who pay

[1] N.A., Part V, pp. 93, 111.
[2] A. Pim, *Report on the Financial and Economic Position of Basutoland*, Cmd. 4907, 1935, pp. 57–58. N.A., Part V, pp. 78, 146.
[3] See above, p. 503. For the history of tax in Bechuanaland, see N.A., Part V, p. 223.
[4] Proclamation no. 16 of 1949, amended by Proclamation no. 85 of 1953.

£10. The graded tax is levied entirely for the purpose of the Native Authority Treasuries, which continue to receive 35 per cent. of the proceeds of the basic Native tax. The system of taxation introduced in 1949 is of particular interest, since it represents one of the few experiments in the graduation of a personal tax payable by Africans.[1]

From the outset the collection of taxes has been in the hands of the Chiefs, who have attached great importance to their position in this respect.[2] Until 1938 they received a commission on collections. Though Administrative Officers exercised a general supervision over assessments, there were clearly many defects in the system, and in some instances it became necessary to resort to a procedure of direct collection.[3] After the establishment of the Tribal Treasuries in 1938 the Chiefs received fixed stipends in lieu of a commission. The system depends for its efficiency on the personality of the Chief, and there are inevitably great differences in the standard attained in different Reserves. The success of the new graded tax will depend on the equity of the assessment and some effective measure of supervision by the Administration appears to be indispensable.

In Swaziland a Native tax was introduced in 1897. The present rates were fixed as far back as 1920, namely, a basic tax of £1. 15s. 0d. payable by every adult male African, with a further tax of £1. 10s. 0d. for each wife above one, with a maximum liability of £4. 10s. The basic tax is thus higher than in Basutoland or Bechuanaland, and it is also higher than the direct Native tax in the Union if land-rent be disregarded. It is, however, apparent that very few Swazi actually pay the tax for additional wives. Up to the date of the establishment of the Swazi National Treasury,[4] 2s. of each tax was credited to the Swazi National Fund, which was originally set up in 1911 to combat East Coast fever, but has been used in the last two decades mainly for educational purposes.[5]

The Chiefs were until 1950 under a general obligation to assist the Administration in the collection of tax, but received no remuneration for their services[6] and thus had not the same interest in effective collection as the Chiefs in the two other High Commission Territories. There were each year large arrears. The system was, however, materially modified by the establishment of the Swazi National Treasury in 1950. The Chiefs now receive a fixed remuneration for their services in general, and their duties have been more clearly defined. The estimated recurrent revenue of the Treasury for 1955–6 was £54,788.[7]

[1] Details of the special levy and of the graded tax are given in *J.A.A.*, January 1951, pp. 39–40.
[2] *N.A.*, Part V, p. 199.
[3] Ibid. p. 306.
[4] See above, p. 516.
[5] *N.A.*, Part V, pp. 376–7, 420.
[6] Ibid. p. 419.
[7] *Swazi National Treasury: Estimates of Revenue and Expenditure 1955–6.*

Federation of Rhodesia and Nyasaland

In Southern Rhodesia a poll tax at the flat rate of £1, with an additional 10s. for each wife after the first, was imposed in 1904; it is noteworthy that it has since remained unaltered. It is assessed and collected by officials of the Native Affairs Department. A large proportion of the revenue derived from the poll tax (£152,000 out of a total of £479,000 in 1950) is paid by Natives of Northern Rhodesia and Nyasaland who are employed in work in Southern Rhodesia and half of the sum so collected is remitted to the countries of origin.[1]

The local African Councils, of which some 57 have been established since 1943,[2] are authorized to impose direct taxes and licence fees for services provided in their respective areas. In 1951 a poll tax ranging from 2s. to 30s. per annum was levied by 43 of the Councils.[3] The collection of these local taxes is the responsibility of the Native Commissioners in their capacity as Chairmen of the Native Councils. The Councils have thus had less direct responsibility in financial matters than the Native Authorities in many other territories, for instance in Northern Rhodesia and in Nyasaland.

In Northern Rhodesia the Tax Proclamation of 1905 imposed a hut tax of 3s. in what was then known as North-Eastern Rhodesia and a poll tax of 10s. on every adult male over the age of 18 in North-Western Rhodesia and Barotseland. There was an equivalent tax on plural wives. The two territories were amalgamated in 1911 and their tax legislation was consolidated in 1914, the hut tax in the former North-Eastern territory being superseded by a poll tax and increased by stages to 10s. In 1929 the tax on plural wives was repealed, but the rates, with one exception, were increased by 2s. 6d. By an Ordinance of 1935 the tax was graduated on a regional basis, and a further change was made in 1953 when the territory was divided into Rural and Urban areas for taxation purposes.[4]

In the former rates ranged from 6s. to 10s., the major part of which is paid to the Native Authority. In Urban areas the rates varied from 12s. 6d. to 17s. 6d. In every case 6s. 6d. was paid to the Native Authority and the Provincial Treasury Fund received a varying proportion of the remainder. A small sum, namely 1s. in Rural and 2s. in Urban areas, was retained by the Government. These rates were increased from the beginning of 1956, the 6s. and 7s. 6d. rates being raised to 10s., the 10s. and 12s. 6d. rates to 15s., and the 15s. and 17s. 6d. rates to £1. The whole of the ensuing increase will go to the credit of the Native Treasuries.

At various times Administrative Officers have availed themselves of the terms of the tax law to accept payment in kind instead of cash. This has,

---

[1] *O.Y.S.R., 1952*, p. 114.   [2] See above, p. 442.
[3] *Central African Territories, Comparative Survey of Native Policy*, Cmd. 8235, 1951, p. 33.
[4] Northern Rhodesia, Laws, cap. 161.

however, been on a small scale, though in 1933 advantage was taken of the high price of beeswax to pay the tax with a small quantity of this portable commodity. Practice has varied in regard to the punishment inflicted for default in payment of tax. Though it has by law been punishable by fine or imprisonment, defaulters were given the option of taking work on public undertakings or with private employers if this was available. In 1929 procedure by distress for the recovery of arrears tax was substituted for criminal proceedings, but this proved to be too cumbersome for general use. In 1936 tax-relief labour schemes were introduced by which arrears were liquidated by 23 days' labour on roads or air landing grounds, but this proved to be so popular that it had to be withdrawn. The penalty for default is now a fine up to £15 or three months' imprisonment, in addition to payment of tax due.[1]

Up to 1936 Administrative Officers were assisted in the collection of tax by Chiefs and Headmen, but in that year a departure was made by the appointment of African clerks whose sole function was to make tax-collecting tours through the districts. An immediate increase in collection was the result. Before the institution of the Native Authority system, Chiefs had as a rule no direct interest in the proceeds from taxation, as they were not paid the commission on the collection of tax which was the practice in some other territories. Since the general establishment of Native Treasuries throughout the Protectorate, there has been a marked increase in the interest taken both in the assessment and collection of tax. Exemption from payment of tax, which as elsewhere is granted in cases of old age, disease, or infirmity, is high in the Protectorate.

Nyasaland had for many years an unusually low scale of taxation. Up to 1938 the normal rate of the hut and poll tax was 6s. and though an increase began to be made in 1940, the poll tax, which took the place of the hut and poll tax, still ranged between 7s. and 9s. in 1947. It was graduated according to the presumed taxable capacity of different areas; even so, however, there was a high ratio of exemptions.[2] In 1948 a uniform rate of 10s. was introduced, and this was increased three years later to 17s. 6d., partly as the result of the higher prices realized by the production of Native tobacco and partly in order to meet the need for a larger provision of funds for the Native Authority Treasuries.

The allocation to the Native Authority Treasuries was raised from 2s. to 5s., a local education rate of 1s., which had been levied by Native Authorities since 1949, being now included in the allocation. Statistics of tax collections have been held to justify the assumption that a poll tax of 17s. 6d. leaves sufficient taxable capacity available for the imposition of a local rate, and measures were undertaken in 1953 to this end.[3] A land

[1] *J.A.A.*, January 1951, p. 34.   [2] *N.A.*, Part II, p. 21.
[3] *Colonial Reports, Nyasaland, 1952*, p. 41.

tax is chargeable on the owner or occupier at the rate of ½*d.* per acre of all occupied land other than Crown land.[1]

Tanganyika

In Tanganyika Territory a direct tax was first introduced by the German Administration in 1897, but in its present form the tax was imposed by the Mandatory Government in 1922.[2] The Administration took from the first a firm stand against pressure brought on it to increase taxation in order to secure labour for the sisal and other plantations.[3] In contrast to many other British African territories the hut tax (here called house tax) has survived to the present day,[4] but a poll tax is levied on those Africans above the age of 16 who do not own huts. The house tax is payable in respect of every occupied dwelling, but over the greater part of the territory, a dwelling is interpreted as 'a series of dwellings housing one family'.[5] It is claimed for this provision that it puts no restriction upon the building of new huts and thus affords no excuse for the overcrowding of a single hut. In a few areas, however, as for instance in the Moshi District, the tax is graduated from 10s. to 16s. according to the number of houses owned. The rates of the house and poll tax are fixed annually and vary according to districts; the range is fairly wide, varying from 13s. in the poorer districts to 50s. in the Masai country.

An amended Native Tax Ordinance of 1934 made provision for the introduction of a graduated personal tax calculated on the assessed taxable resources of individuals in specified districts. Much attention has been attracted to the attempt made in 1942 to implement this provision in the Pare District. At the outset provision was made for 14 categories of taxpayers, thus introducing a complication which made it difficult to operate the scheme. But even when their number was reduced to four, active opposition resulted, particularly from the higher-rated taxpayers. The experiment had, therefore, to be abandoned, and the graduated method was replaced in 1947 by a flat-rate tax of 12s.[6]

Until 1951 taxpayers unable to meet the demand could discharge their liability by work on Government undertakings, and during the depression period of the thirties a large use was made of this provision, the number employed rising on occasion to 59,000 a year. Of late years only a few thousand have paid their tax in this manner. The tax is collected by the Native Authorities and an average allocation of 40 per cent. of the collection is paid into the Native Treasuries; the actual shares vary, however,

---

[1] *J.A.A.*, January 1951, p. 37.
[2] C. Leubuscher, *Tanganyika Territory: A Study of Economic Policy under Mandate*, 1944, pp. 133 ff.
[3] R. L. Buell, *The Native Problem in Africa*, vol. i, 1928, pp. 499–507, 509–10.
[4] It survives also in Swaziland and Sierra Leone.   [5] *J.A.A.*, January 1951, p. 31.
[6] For the Pare experiment, see *N.A.*, Part I, p. 334; and *Development of African Local Government in Tanganyika*, Col. no. 277, 1951, p. 40.

between 27 and 88 per cent. (1951). The accepted policy aims at parity of revenue between the Central Government and the Native Treasuries. In the Moshi District the rebate was replaced in 1947 by a local rate graduated from 9s. to 18s. and at the same time the Government tax was increased to a range of 10s. to 16s.

A cattle tax, imposed by the Native Authorities, was first introduced in 1941 as a war-time measure and has since been extended to all Provinces. It was originally imposed at rates which varied widely in different localities,[1] but under an Ordinance of 1942 it is now levied at a uniform rate on every head of cattle sold on the public markets.[2] In some districts, other sources of income besides cattle, such as receipts from trade and wages, furnish the basis of the graduation of the local rate, and it is likely that this system will be more widely adopted when local bodies generally decide to make a fuller use of the authority to levy rates conferred on them by an Ordinance of 1942. By 1951 only 19 out of the 54 districts[3] had levied rates under this Ordinance.

Kenya

In Kenya, as in Tanganyika, the question whether taxation should be utilized in order to stimulate the supply of Native labour formed at one period a prominent issue of local politics.[4] In the case of Kenya, however, the Administration did not oppose the demand made by the European interests concerned as strongly as did the Government of Tanganyika and for some years the policy of taxation was influenced by pressure from this source. With the progress of time the point lost its importance, for here as elsewhere the obligation to pay a poll tax now ranks as only one of the various incentives which impel Africans to have recourse to the earning of wages.

A hut tax first introduced in 1901 was transformed in 1910 into a hut and poll tax[5] at a uniform rate of 3 rupees, except that the Masai, because of their wealth in cattle, have from 1920 onwards paid a higher rate than Africans in other parts of the Colony. Women were made liable in 1934 to hut tax, a measure much criticized in subsequent years on the ground that ownership of a hut was not necessarily a sign of wealth. The present taxation of the great majority of Africans is based on the Native Tax Ordinance of 1942. A poll tax is levied on male Africans of 18 and over; in 1952 the rate ranged between 17s. and 23s., the bulk of the population paying 17s., the Masai 19s., the Northern Frontier 20s., and the six municipal areas between 21s. and 23s.

---

[1] N.A., Part I, pp. 252, 262, 291.   [2] J.A.A., January 1951, p. 38.
[3] Col. no. 277, 1951, p 41.   [4] N. Leys, Kenya, 1925, p. 186. Buell, op. cit., vol. i, pp. 331 ff.
[5] Report of the Commission appointed to Enquire into and Report on the Financial Position and System of Taxation in Kenya (the Pim Report), Col. no. 116, 1936, pp. 33 ff. W. Wood, Fiscal Survey of Kenya, Uganda and Tanganyika, 1946, pp. 85 ff.

Kenya differs from most other territories in that the Local Authorities do not take a share of the Native poll tax, except in the case of municipalities, where the Central Government retains 16s. of each tax, while the balance is divided between the Municipal Authorities, the African District Council,[1] and the African Trust Fund. In the rural areas the African District Councils levy local rates which vary according to the services undertaken by them, the highest rate of 14s. being levied by the Masai Council.

Since 1947 the Government has paid the Councils 2s. for every rate collected, this being treated as its own contribution to the cost of primary education.[2] Where no local rate is levied by the local body the poll tax is increased by 2s.[3] In most areas the African District Councils collect the poll tax, but the Revenue Officers who now form part of the District Administration are responsible for the collection in remote and backward as well as in urban areas.[4]

The absence of any real graduation in the taxation of Africans has more than once been criticized as a serious defect in the prevailing system,[5] and the matter was given renewed consideration by both the Plewman committee of 1947 and by a subsequent committee appointed in 1950 to examine specific proposals for the graduation of the taxation imposed on Africans.[6] The first of these committees recommended the incorporation of the African poll tax in a general non-racial personal tax to be levied below the level at which income tax becomes payable. The second committee held, however, that the assessment of such a tax would be impracticable in present conditions, when many of the wealthier Africans, such as traders, contractors, lorry-owners, or the like, are not yet capable of keeping accounts. It recommended assessment in two grades; incomes between £120 and £240 were to pay 30s., and incomes above £240 were to pay 40s. These proposals admittedly failed to reflect the difference which separates the wealthier from the poorer Africans, but the committee deferred to the opinion of their African witnesses who were in general opposed to the graduated taxation of individuals. By 1955, however, there had been no attempt to establish a graduated taxation system.

Uganda

In Uganda direct taxation at the outset took the form of a hut tax of 3 rupees; in 1910 it became a poll tax of 10s. and in 1925 a poll tax of 15s. graduated according to districts, with a minimum of 5s. in the poorer

---

[1] For the African District Councils, see above, pp. 447 ff.
[2] See above, p. 448, and below, p. 1173   [3] *J.A.A.*, January 1951, p. 35.
[4] *Report of the Taxation Enquiry Committee* (the Plewman Report), 1947.
[5] *Report of Financial Commissioner on Certain Questions in Kenya*, Cmd. 4093, 1932. Col. no. 116, 1936.
[6] *Kenya, Committee of Enquiry into Graduated African Taxation*, 1950.

areas. By 1948 the rate of poll tax ranged from 8s. to 20s. in different districts; there was no tax on plural wives. The position at this stage became complicated owing to changes in the system by which the Buganda Government, the other Native Governments, and the District Native Administrations[1] received an allocation at varying rates (under the name 'rebate') out of the proceeds of the Protectorate poll tax.

It is sufficient to say that from 1949 these authorities (with the exception of Buganda) received a flat rate of 6s. instead of the differential rates formerly allocated to them, but in compensation for this loss of revenue it was agreed that an increase should be made in the Native Administration tax, of which the entire proceeds were credited to them, though the tax was actually imposed by the Protectorate Government.[2] Buganda retained the system in force previous to 1949 under which it received a 'rebate' of 20 per cent. of the Protectorate poll tax. Proposals have, however, been made for a substantial change in this system, as part of the readjustment of constitutional relations to which reference has been made in a preceding chapter.[3]

The Native Administration tax was imposed in 1938 in the Northern, Eastern, and Western Provinces, but not in Buganda. In those Provinces it replaced the former *Luwalo*, or annual liability to perform work for one month on public undertakings, which had been traditional before the British occupation.[4] It is a flat-rate tax, the actual rate being determined each year in consultation with the Native Governments and the District Native Administrations concerned. It may be said accordingly to serve the same purpose as does a local rate in other territories.[5] In the majority of districts the rate is now 8s. In Buganda, however, the *Luwalo* tax has been retained, and the Native Administration tax is consequently not applied. The rate is by tradition directly correlated to the cash value of one month's labour.

The Buganda Government levies also a land tax which is based on the quasi-freehold tenure (*mailo*) by which landlords hold property in Buganda.[6] This tax is graduated according to the size of holdings and the number of tenants. Thus a landlord with fewer than five tenants pays 5s. or more according to the district, and one holding more than ten acres pays 15s. to 25s.[7] The Buganda land tax is one of the few graduated taxes on property in tropical Africa.

These various taxes have made the incidence of taxation in some parts

---

[1] For these terms, see above, pp. 479–83. For fuller details, see *N.A.*, Part I, pp. 11, 29, 50, 60.

[2] Native Authority Ordinance no. 17 of 1919, as amended by various laws ending with no. 3 of 1949; Native Administration Tax Ordinance no. 16 of 1938.

[3] See above, pp. 481 ff. See *Uganda Protectorate, Buganda*, Cmd. 9320, 1954.

[4] Buell, op. cit., vol. i, pp. 584 ff. L. Mair, *Native Policies in Africa*, 1936, p. 174. See also below, p. 1368.   [5] *J.A.A.*, January 1951, p. 37.

[6] See below, pp. 786–8.   [7] *J.A.A.*, loc. cit.

of Uganda higher than in neighbouring territories, but owing to the high prices obtained since the Second World War for the two main export crops, cotton and coffee, the weight of taxation does not appear to have had a depressing effect on the general standard of living. The modifications introduced in 1949 have shifted on to the Local Government bodies the burden of the taxation specifically imposed for providing for local requirements. There has been a general agreement that the development of the Protectorate has reached a stage where a definite measure of graduation in the direct taxation of Africans is called for. Proposals were made to this effect in 1953,[1] and it was decided in 1954 to impose a graduated tax in 1955.[2]

Zanzibar

Zanzibar has no hut or poll tax; it depends for its revenue on income tax, the clove duty, and duties on copra, coconut oil, and soap.[3]

Nigeria

Nigeria, and more particularly Northern Nigeria, has a special place in the history of the evolution of systems of direct taxation on Africans. Writing in 1918 Lord Lugard observed that in Nigeria as a whole, systematic taxation had not been contemplated until Northern and Southern Nigeria had been amalgamated in 1914.[4] He had himself initiated at an earlier date in Northern Nigeria a procedure of taxation which for some years remained the only considered attempt to adjust tax demand to the individual resources of the African taxpayer. In the Northern Provinces there was, as has already been observed, a precedent for direct taxation in the practice adopted by the Muslim Emirates,[5] and in effect the tax imposed by the new British Administration was a continuation of the revenue previously collected in the name of the Emirs or the Hausa Chiefs.

At the outset it was considered sufficient to require these authorities to hand over to the Protectorate Administration a portion (usually one-fourth) of the total amount collected. When this revenue subsequently came under more definite regulation, the form taken by the direct tax became known under the name of the 'lump-sum assessment'. The unit was the village or group of villages, and their resources were examined and assessed by an Administrative Officer, who from an estimate of the average yield of the area under cultivation, and the yield from other sources (such

---

[1] C. A. G. Wallis, *Report of an Inquiry into African Local Government in the Protectorate of Uganda*, pp. 24 ff. *Government Memorandum on the Report by C. A. G. Wallis*, 1953.

[2] *The Times*, 14 December 1954.

[3] *Colonial Reports, Zanzibar, 1951–52*, p. 11.

[4] *Nigerian Political Memoranda*, 1918, p. 167.

[5] See above, p. 453. For the pre-British system of taxes, see *N.A.*, Part III, pp. 75 ff. See also Lord Lugard, *The Dual Mandate in Tropical Africa*, p. 296. A. Burns, *History of Nigeria*, 1948, p. 48.

as livestock or wage earning), assigned a cash value to the gross resources of the unit. A percentage not exceeding 10 per cent. of the total gross value was taken to be the 'lump sum' payable in form of tax, and this was apportioned among the inhabitants by the Headman according to their capacity to pay.[1] Safeguards for this apportionment were provided by the publicity given to the whole process. In some measure therefore the method resembled that which was used by the Settlement Officers in British India for determining the land revenue demand, though in their case the procedure was more elaborate, for they had at their disposal far more complete material (notably in the form of a field-to-field survey and a continuous system of crop records) than was available to the Administrative Officers in Northern Nigeria.[2]

This system of assessment has evoked both interest and criticism. It has aroused interest, because it was a pioneer attempt to adjust taxation to the resources of the community. It has met with criticism because in fact the revision of the original assessments has not been systematically undertaken, and also because of the obvious difficulty of assessing the 'gross value' of the income of the group concerned, in view of the fluctuation of market prices.[3] These criticisms do not apply in full force to the more advanced Native Authority areas, where revision is more up to date, but they hold good with regard to the less advanced areas, and in particular to the more primitive 'pagan' areas. In these areas the 'lump-sum assessment' has hardly been applied, and a poll tax at a flat rate has usually been imposed.

The Northern Region of Nigeria has also made some progress in the application of the procedure of taxation of individual incomes among the African population. Africans in receipt of 'ascertainable' incomes—in practice largely the salaried staff of Government Departments or of Native Authorities—are taxed on a graduated scale. In 1951 the rates were 4d. in the £ on incomes up to £72 p.a., and 6d. in the £ on incomes over £72 p.a. The more prosperous class of traders, whose incomes are not so easy to ascertain, are assessed individually on the basis of inquiries made by local Assessment Committees. A graduated mine-labour tax on wages paid in the mining areas is deducted at source.[4]

In the closely populated farming areas round Kano a land-revenue tax is imposed; it is assessed on the average productivity per acre of different types of soil, but amounts generally to about 10 per cent. of the value of the crops. The assessment is made by agents maintained by the Local

[1] *N.A.*, Part III, p. 76. M. Perham, *Native Administration in Nigeria*, 1937, p. 105. L. Mair, op. cit. p. 122. *J.A.A.*, April 1951, p. 84.
[2] L. S. S. O'Malley, *Modern India and the West*, 1941, pp. 282 ff. E. Dowson and V. L. O. Sheppard, *Land Registration*, 1952, Colonial Research Publications, no. 13, pp. 33–35. L. Curtis, *Dyarchy*, 1920, pp. 239–90. [3] *Report of the Commission on Revenue Allocation*, 1951, p. 122.
[4] *J.A.A.*, April 1951, p. 85, for detailed rates.

Authority.[1] In the semi-nomadic pastoral areas of the Northern Region, the *jangali*, a cattle tax, is levied at a fixed rate per animal. Although many animals escape taxation, *jangali* is one of the main sources of revenue to the Native Treasuries of that area.

The preceding observations apply almost entirely to the evolution of the system of Native taxation in the Northern Region of Nigeria. Recent developments, both constitutional and economic, have led to a considerable diversity of procedure in the other two Regions. The Direct Taxation Ordinance no. 4 of 1940 was applicable to the whole territory,[2] but its terms were sufficiently flexible to permit of a number of methods being employed. In the Western Region the two principal taxes are now a flat-rate tax and an income-tax rate.[3] The flat-rate tax is paid by adult males with an income below a certain maximum, the rate varying between 7s. and 15s. according to provinces. Graduation is effected in this Region mainly by variations designed to reflect the assumed resources of different areas.

The income-tax rate is payable by adult persons of both sexes (save in Bornu and Warri Provinces, where females are exempted) whose income exceeds the maximum at which the flat rate applies. The rates of the tax vary, as the Native Authorities are entitled to impose a surcharge on the standard flat-rate tax; these surcharges vary from $12\frac{1}{2}$ to $37\frac{1}{2}$ per cent. Assessments are based on taxpayers' returns supplemented by inquiries made by local Assessment Committees.[4] Two Provinces, Oyo and Ijebu, impose special taxes on certain tradesmen, such as blacksmiths, goldsmiths, and cattle dealers: these are additional to the flat-rate tax. They also levy a tax on 'unearned income', that is to say, on earnings from rents, securities, and other investments at a rate which varies from $2\frac{1}{2}$ to 5 per cent.

In the Eastern Region taxation also takes the form of a flat-rate tax and an income-tax rate. The great majority of the population pays a flat-rate tax, in which the rates ranged in 1950 from 4s. to 12s. according to locality. In recent years, however, a procedure for the individual assessment of 'ascertainable incomes' exceeding the upper limit of flat-rate tax has been brought into use. Local Assessment Committees of the Native Authorities communicate to the Divisional Officer a list of persons who are held to be liable to income-tax rate. The tax is collected (as is also the flat-rate tax) by local Tax Collectors on demand notes signed by the Divisional Officer. A simple graduation is applied which begins at a somewhat higher level than in the Western Region.[5] As in the Northern

---

[1] *N.A.*, Part III, p. 77.

[2] Amended by Ordinances no. 10 of 1941, no. 2 of 1943, no. 2 of 1948.

[3] A. R. Prest and I. G. Stewart, *The National Income of Nigeria*, Colonial Research Studies, no. 11, 1953, p. 92.   [4] *N.A.*, Part III, p. 131.

[5] A comparison of the differences in methods applied by the three Regions is drawn by Professor Hicks in *Report of the Commission on Revenue Allocation*, 1951, pp. 125 ff.

Region the *jangali* cattle tax is levied, but is in this case much less productive.

Income tax, properly so called,[1] is paid by Africans only in the township of Lagos. A tax of 18s. is charged on African incomes up to £50, 4½d. in the £ on incomes up to £150, and thereafter on a progressive scale, with substantial personal reliefs. In the rural areas adjoining Lagos, taxation is usually at a flat rate, the proceeds being retained by the Native Treasuries, except for a deduction of 3d. per taxpayer, which is surrendered to the Government.

The deduction thus referred to has an interesting history. In Nigeria the General tax (the name given to the various forms of tax collected under the terms of the Direct Taxation Ordinance no. 4 of 1940) was in its origin essentially a Native Authority tax, from which until 1948 the Central Government received only a proportion.[2] In 1948 a fixed quota calculated on a capitation basis was substituted for the variable proportion, and under the Nigerian Constitution of 1947 this 'capitation share' was allocated to the Regional instead of the Central Government.

Looking at the system of taxation in Nigeria as a whole, it may be said that if the 'lump-sum assessment' had no other merit it certainly possessed the virtue of bringing the Admininistrative Officer into close contact with the people who pay the tax, and of giving them an opportunity to discuss the incidence of the assessment. But the effect of this and of similar measures must not be overrated. 'Lump-sum' assessment and the procedure of individual assessments above described apply now only to a minority of tax-payers, at all events so far as the Western and Eastern Regions are concerned. A recent investigation found that there is a gap between the living standards of various classes of Africans, on which the present structure of taxation 'makes little or no impression'.[3] It is also a significant feature of the Nigerian system that the General tax, whatever its form, is largely operated by the Native Authorities. The incidence of taxation is in consequence liable to be gravely affected by the competence shown in the assessment of incomes.[4]

British Cameroons

In the area of the Cameroons under United Kingdom Trusteeship taxation is generally similar to that in Nigeria. In the Northern Section of the Trust Territory which has the same historical background of Muslim rule as the Northern Region of Nigeria, 'lump-sum' assessment on villages is the most typical form of taxation. Here, as in the Northern Region of

---

[1] Income Tax Ordinances of 1940 as revised in 1943.
[2] *N.A.*, Part III, pp. 8–11. See also *Report of Fiscal Commission on Financial Effects of Proposed New Constitutional Arrangements*, Cmd. 9026, 1953.
[3] Prest and Stewart, op. cit. p. 82.
[4] Ibid. p. 83.

Nigeria, the value of the system depends largely on the ability of the Administration to keep the assessments under a process of periodical revision. In the more backward areas a flat rate is levied. As in the Northern Region of Nigeria individual assessment has also been introduced for the taxation of persons with 'ascertainable' incomes and of wealthy traders. Fulani and other nomad herdsmen pay the *jangali* tax. In the areas administered as a part of Adamawa Province the average incidence per adult male ranges from 7s. to 18s. 6d. according to district;[1] in the Dikwa Division of Bornu Province it varies between 11s. 2d. and 18s. 2d. About one-third of the total tax collection in Adamawa is derived from *jangali*, and nearly one-half in Bornu.

In the Southern Section of the Trust Territory, taxation now takes the same form as in the adjoining Eastern Region of Nigeria. The majority of the population pays a flat rate varying according to district; it ranges from 8s. to 12s. per adult male in Cameroons Province, and from 6s. to 10s. in Bamenda Province. An 'income-tax' rate on 'ascertainable incomes' is levied on the same scale as in the Eastern Region. In Bamenda Province the *jangali* brings in over 40 per cent. of the total sum raised by direct taxation. As in Nigeria a capitation share, varying between $2\frac{1}{2}$ and 10 per cent. of the tax, is transmitted to the Regional Governments concerned.

Gold Coast

The Gold Coast has an unusual record in respect of Native taxation. In the earlier history of the Colony the relations with the Akan and Fanti States, to which reference has been made in a preceding chapter,[2] were held to preclude the imposition of a direct tax. At a later date local political influences proved to be strongly opposed to any form of direct taxation; it was urged that a duty on export products (such as cocoa) was a preferable source of revenue, since part at least of the burden might be presumed to fall on the foreign purchaser. The income tax, which was finally introduced in 1943, and which was at that period the lowest, with one exception, in the entire British Empire, fell almost entirely on non-African sources of revenue.[3] The imposition of direct taxation specifically affecting Africans came into effect only as part of the movement for the organization of the Local Government institutions of which the story has already been told.[4]

The Northern Territories led the way in this respect. There the tribute which had formerly been rendered to the Chiefs in kind was in 1932 consolidated in a tribute tax.[5] It was, in effect, a Native Authority tax,

[1] See *Cameroons under United Kingdom Trusteeship, Report for 1952*, Col. no. 299, p. 227, from which these and other figures are taken.   [2] See above, pp. 518–21.
[3] F. M. Bourret, *The Gold Coast*, 1952, pp. 59–60, 158.   [4] See above, p. 520.
[5] Native Authority Ordinance, no. 1 of 1932.

collected and wholly retained by the Treasuries of these Authorities. The tax was imposed at a flat rate varying from 2*s*. to 6*s*. on adult males, except in a few districts where females also were liable. In some areas, however, a community assessment was adopted similar to the 'lump assessment' in operation in the Northern Region of Nigeria. The 'lump sum' was apportioned to villages by the Native Authorities and collected in each village by the Headman. In the six small Municipalities local rates on property were also levied by the Local Authorities.

In the Gold Coast Colony and in Ashanti direct taxation in the form of an annual rate was also a consequence of the establishment of Native Treasuries and was imposed in principle in 1935, but it was some years before the system could be made to function even with moderate efficiency.[1] Only in 1944 was it found possible to introduce an annual rate and thus to provide the Native Treasuries with a regular income from direct taxation. Until 1951, when the Local Government Ordinance altered the structure of local administration, the Native Authorities levied a rate on all able-bodied Africans between the ages of 16 and 70 who were resident or owned property in their district. Rates were variable: Chiefs and Elders were taxed at a higher rate than the rest of the population and women at half the rate of men. For example, an Omanhene Chief paid £5 and an Elder 10*s*., while other males paid 4*s*. and females 2*s*. only. The rates in the districts fluctuated from 2*s*. to 10*s*. for males, and from 1*s*. to 5*s*. for females.[2]

Under the Local Government Ordinance of 1951 the Native Authorities were (as shown in a previous chapter) superseded by Local and Urban Councils in the Southern areas and by District Councils in the Northern Territories.[3] The basic rate, levied *per capita*, is the minimum contribution made by all sections of the community. In addition the rating authorities may impose either a graduated personal tax or a property tax calculated on the assessed value of immovable property or possessions.[4] All persons, including non-Africans, above the age of 18 years resident in an area are liable, but in the Northern Territories women may be exempted. The basic rates varied in 1952 from 2*s*. to 10*s*. in the Colony, from 5*s*. to 46*s*. in Ashanti, and from 6*s*. to 8*s*. per adult male in the Northern Territories. In the Northern Territories a beginning was made in the introduction of a cattle tax.

British Togoland

In British Togoland, although the former German Administration had imposed a direct tax,[5] the United Kingdom Administration has in the

---

[1] *N.A.*, Part III, p. 240.   [2] *J.A.A.*, April 1951, p. 83.
[3] See above, p. 527.   [4] *Colonial Reports, Gold Coast, 1952*, pp. 18, 123.
[5] Bourret, op. cit. p. 108.

past (as in the Gold Coast) relied largely upon indirect forms of taxation. The only direct tax levied is an income tax under the Income Tax Ordinance of 1944. Taxation for local purposes has been imposed as the result of the institution of Native Treasuries. In the Northern Section of Togoland a tribute tax (applying to males only) was first collected in 1936; in the Southern Section taxation was at the same rate as in the Gold Coast. The whole proceeds accrued to the Native Authority Treasuries.

The Local Government Ordinance of 1951 applied also to Togoland, and in the following year Native Authorities were replaced by Local and Urban Councils in the South and by District Councils in the North.[1] The basic rates now imposed in the Southern Section, which are levied equally on men and women, have varied between 2s. and 10s., with an additional graduated tax on men only. Special rates are payable in certain centres of the Council areas, ranging from £4 to 5s. for men and from £1 to 2s. for women. In the Northern Section the basic rates of 6s., 8s., or 9s. according to districts, apply only to males; two District Councils levy in addition a cattle tax. Certain modifications in the system are now under consideration, the main object of the proposed changes being to allow for greater flexibility in rating methods, and for the exemption of women in the Southern areas.[2]

Sierra Leone

In Sierra Leone there are two different systems of direct taxation applicable to the Protectorate area. As few Africans pay income tax the only direct tax levied there by the Government is the house tax. It has a history of some interest. The Ordinance which established a protectorate over the hinterland in 1896 required every Chief to collect a tax of 10s. a year for each house with three or four rooms and 5s. for each house with less. The attempt to collect this tax led in 1898 to serious disturbances in which a number of Creole traders and some European missionaries were murdered. The Inquiry subsequently made by a Special Commissioner condemned the tax as obnoxious to the customs of the people[3] and Mary Kingsley, who had consistently supported the policy of indirect in preference to direct taxation, headed a movement in Great Britain which pressed for the abolition of the tax. The Government, however, decided to retain it, but reduced the rate to 5s., and it is still levied at this rate. Though applicable to both Africans and non-Africans (a term which includes the 'Creoles' of the Colony area), it is paid mainly by Africans; there is, however,

---

[1] *Togoland under United Kingdom Trusteeship, Report for 1952*, Col. no. 296, pp. 187 ff.
[2] Ibid. p. 40.
[3] Sir D. Chalmers, *Report on the Subject of the Insurrection in the Sierra Leone Protectorate, 1898*, Cd. 9388, p. 73. See also *N.A.*, Part III, p. 299, and Buell, op. cit., vol. i, p. 863. E. D. Morel, *Affairs of West Africa*, 1902, pp. 281–2.

a distinction in the incidence: in the case of non-Africans the tax is levied on the individual householder, in the case of Africans on the family. The house tax has thus a close similarity to the tax levied under the same name in Tanganyika.[1]

The tax is assessed locally by the Chief or Headman under the direction of a Paramount Chief.[2] The efficiency of the system of assessment and collection leaves much to be desired, largely owing to the fact that official receipts are given to the Headmen and not to the taxpayers.[3] Evasion is believed to be considerable. In the Sierra Leone budget of 1954 only £91,116 accrued from the house tax out of a total ordinary revenue of £6,930,131.

The second form of taxation in the Protectorate is the Chiefdom tax, which is in effect a local rate. It is a commutation of the traditional communal services formerly rendered to the Paramounts or other Chiefs, and the entire proceeds are credited to the Native Treasuries. The rate remained for many years at 4s., but now varies between 10s. and 15s. The tax contributes from one-third to one-half of the income of the Native Treasuries, but, as has been explained, there are still some Chiefdoms in which Treasuries have not yet been organized.[4] Matters arising in connexion with the incidence and collection of tax occasioned serious disturbances in the Protectorate at the end of 1955, involving some loss of life. A formal inquiry on the subject of the tax was to be made early in 1956.

In the Colony areas lying outside the municipality of Freetown a house tax was until recently levied in the form of a local rate on property. In the Freetown municipal area a system of local rating by the Municipal Council had long been in use, and this was extended to the rural area of the Colony by Ordinance 11 of 1949 and to the Sherbro District by Ordinance 22 of 1950. The rates, which are levied in these areas by the Urban District Council, are calculated on the assessed valuation of premises. In addition, the Village Area Committees have levied village improvement cesses at rates from 5d. to 1s. 8d. in the £.

Gambia

In the Protectorate area the tax (termed the yard tax) which was originally levied by the Government has for practical purposes been replaced by the district rate levied by the Local Authorities. The term 'yard' is defined in the law as 'every parcel, lot, or enclosure of land, other than farm lands, containing one or more huts or houses'.[5] The tax was a charge upon all adult male owners or occupiers of a yard, and the

[1] See above, p. 658.
[2] See J.A.A., April 1951, p. 78, for further details of the procedure.
[3] N.A., Part III, p. 308.
[4] See above, p. 535. See also N.A., Part III, p. 303.   [5] Ibid. pp. 291 ff.

amount payable varied with the number of huts, being 4*s.* for a yard of up to four huts and 2*s.* 6*d.* for each further hut. Persons who were not members of the family, such as servants, paid a lodgers' tax of 5*s.* There was also a Strange Farmers' tax at a flat rate of 10*s.* imposed on peasants immigrating for the ground-nut season from another district of Gambia or from French West Africa.[1] The proceeds from these taxes were paid into general revenue.

When Native Treasuries were instituted in 1946 the Native Authorities were empowered to levy a district rate applicable to the Protectorate, and the proceeds were wholly retained by them for expenditure within their areas. Where this rate is paid, Africans are exempted from the yard tax. The rate is limited to a maximum of twice the rate of the yard tax.[2]

In the Colony of Gambia, which consists of Bathurst and the small Kombo Rural Area, a local rate on property is levied by the Town Council and the Rural Authority respectively.

The French Territories

In French West Africa a personal tax (*impôt personnel*) is imposed without discrimination of race.[3] The principle applies to all the eight territories of the 'group', but methods of application vary. All inhabitants over 14 years of age, irrespective of sex, are liable, but exemptions are allowed to soldiers and their families, students, monogamous mothers of four or more children, or indigent and aged persons. Most Africans pay the *minimum fiscal* of the *impôt personnel*, but nomads, usually found in the three northern territories, are taxed at a rate above the general rate. The lowest rates for the permanent residents range from 50 francs in the Niger to 250 francs in Guinea, and the highest from 175 francs in Mauretania to 410 francs in Dahomey. The lowest rate imposed on the floating population has been 175 francs in Mauretania, and the highest 1,500 francs in Dahomey and Upper Volta.[4]

So far as there exists any system of taxation equivalent to the rate levied for local purposes in the British territories, it has its origin in the local levy which has taken the place of the system of *prestation*. The system of *prestation* was in origin, as explained in a subsequent chapter,[5] an obligation to perform labour for a definite period and was redeemable by a cash payment of 1 to 3 francs a day according to district. It was, however, repealed in 1944, and a road tax (*taxe vicinale*) of 25 francs, payable by all persons liable for the *minimum fiscal*, was introduced in its place. Since 1950 the

---

[1] *N.A.*, Part III, p. 347.   [2] *J.A.A.*, April 1951, p. 82.

[3] For further details see Pierre Doublet, *Traité de Législation fiscale dans les Territoires d'Outre Mer: Régimes fiscaux de l'A.O.F. et du Togo*, 1952.

[4] The value of the French African currency—the franc C.F.A.—has been fixed at double the value of the metropolitan franc by a *décret* of 17 October 1948.   [5] See below, p. 1369.

three territories of Sudan, Niger, and Guinea have substituted a *taxe du cercle* for the *taxe vicinale*. This is a capitation tax, the revenue from which is allocated to sub-districts in order to finance approved public works; in the Sudan the tax is 25 francs and in Niger 20 francs.

In Dahomey and Ivory Coast the assessment is made in five categories. The first four categories are based on information contained in nominal registers, the relevant rates being 3,000, 2,000, 1,500, and 500 francs, the last comprising African employees and assimilated persons. In the fifth category, which is assessed on registers compiled by families or villages, the rate ranges from 75 francs to 260 francs. The rate applicable to the floating population is 1,000 francs. The impact of graduation, however, has as yet been almost negligible; out of a total of 1,331,455 taxpayers in Ivory Coast in 1950 no less than 1,261,533 were included in the fifth category and liable therefore to the *minimum fiscal*.

The *pacage* or tax on livestock, similar to the *jangali* in Nigeria,[1] has been abolished everywhere except in Niger, where the rate has been appreciably reduced. In Mauretania the ancient Muslim tax, *zakkat*, assessed on the value of the animals owned, has been retained and takes the place of the *impôt personnel*. The *achour* tax, another survival of the Muslim régime and in effect a tithe of all cultivated products (*ushur*), was abolished in 1946. In Mauretania those who are not liable to *zakkat* pay the personal tax and in addition a capitation fee on every animal. The capitation fee on animals is levied in all territories except the Ivory Coast, but in Guinea it is restricted to horses.

An examination of the 1950 Estimates for the territories of French West Africa, excluding Senegal, shows that the contribution made by the *minimum fiscal* makes up 85 per cent. of the total revenue derived from personal taxes including income tax. In Senegal the *minimum fiscal* contributes only 36 per cent. The position in French West Africa contrasts noticeably with that in most British territories, where the income tax on individuals and companies has in recent years contributed considerably more to Government revenue than African direct taxation.

In French Togo no departure has been made from the general pattern of taxation in vogue in the territories of French West Africa, except that females are not liable to the personal tax. The assessment falls into three categories, incomes of less than 36,000 francs, those between 36,000 and 48,000 francs, and those in excess of 48,000 francs. In 1951 the revenue derived from the two higher categories was insignificant and the bulk of the African population is included in the lowest income category. The rate of this tax is proclaimed each year, but in 1952 it varied from 45 to 180 francs. As in other French overseas possessions the *prestation* has been superseded by a road tax (*taxe vicinale*) imposed at rates ranging from 65

---

[1] See above, p. 664.

to 200 francs. Personal tax in the 'ordinary' category is assessed on numerical registers, but a nominal register was in 1952 introduced in the municipality of Lomé.[1]

In the Cameroons under French trusteeship, taxation had in German times been limited to the imposition of a labour tax which was restricted to 30 days in the year and commutable into cash. The French Mandatory Administration substituted a *prestation*, and also introduced a capitation tax. After the Second World War, the capitation tax was embodied in a non-racial personal tax and the *prestation*, or its cash commutation, was replaced by a *taxe vicinale*. The bulk of the African population pay personal tax in the lowest grade. The basic rates are fixed annually and in 1952 varied between 100 to 200 francs[2] in different areas. The basic rate may either be reduced or increased for particular categories of taxpayers; thus labourers pay only half the rate, while certain groups, such as those of small planters or traders, are charged double or even treble the rate. The aim of the Administration is to apply the individual assessment to an increased number of taxpayers, but shortage of qualified staff has so far prevented this. Both men and women between 14 and 60 years of age are liable to personal tax. A cattle tax is levied in the pastoral northern area of the Territory.

The system of taxation in French Equatorial Africa does not differ materially from that in French West Africa. Up to 1909 a tax in kind was imposed, consisting of delivery of goods, usually rubber, to the value of 3 francs per person, designed mainly for the benefit of the *concessionnaire* companies.[3] In that year, however, it was superseded by a capitation tax which in its turn has become a general personal tax. Graduation by grouping taxpayers into categories is here adopted as in other French territories. The rates are fixed separately in each of the four territories and in 1951 ranged from 70 to 2,500 francs, the latter being the highest rate payable on incomes assessed individually. The majority, however, pay the flat rate fixed for the territory. Both sexes are liable to the tax, but in contrast to French West Africa liability begins at 18 instead of 14 and mothers of three or more children are exempted. In the Chad area a tax of 1,000 francs is imposed on temporary immigrants and a tax is also levied on animals.

As regards the part played by the direct tax in the total public revenue it was estimated in 1953 to be 11·2 per cent. from personal tax and 8·1 per cent. from income tax, compared with 55 per cent. from export and import duties. In view of the low yield from taxation, the separate territories in French Equatorial Africa rely to a large extent on a subvention from the

---

[1] *Rapport annuel à l'Assemblé Générale des Nations Unies sur l'administration du Togo, 1952*, pp. 76 ff.
[2] *Cameroun sous la Tutelle de la France: Rapport pour 1952*, p. 64.
[3] Buell, op. cit. vol. ii, pp. 232–3.

Central Government which is normally calculated at 75 per cent. of the revenue from export duties.[1]

The Belgian Territories

The early history of taxation in the Belgian Congo resembles in many respects that of French Equatorial Africa. The labour tax imposed by the Congo Free State, though restricted in theory to 40 hours a month, was in practice unlimited in duration. It took the form of an *impôt de cueillette* or in other words a compulsory collection of wild rubber delivered either to *concessionnaire* companies or to State agents. The abuses to which this tax gave rise formed one of the major articles of the impeachment of the Administration of the Congo Free State.[2]

When the Belgian Government assumed control it passed in 1910 a decree[3] requiring the payment of taxes in cash only, and a capitation tax was imposed on adult males with a supplementary tax for each additional wife after the first. These methods still continue with certain modifications, but a decree of November 1940 prepared for the gradual abolition of the plural wives tax, which had become financially insignificant. It applies now only to polygamous marriages contracted prior to 1 January 1951; polygamous unions entered into after that date have been deprived of legal status.[4]

The rates of the capitation tax, to which all adult males are liable, are fixed annually by the Governor within the range of 10 to 300 francs and vary in different districts.[5] Higher or lower rates may be fixed for particular groups of taxpayers, but the rate of the supplementary tax may not be fixed at a rate higher than that of the capitation tax. Certain groups, such as Chiefs and sub-Chiefs, persons who have done military or police service during the tax year, fathers of four or more children who are the progeny of a single wife, and teachers and missionaries, are exempted. Defaulters may be detained for a period of up to two months for labour on public works, but few taxpayers have defaulted in recent years; in 1951 the figure was 4,930 or 2·75 per cent. of all taxpayers.[6]

The average incidence of the capitation tax in 1951 was 83·37 francs, ranging from 91·15 francs in Katanga Province to 79·52 francs in the Equatorial Province. The average incidence of the supplementary tax was 81·75 francs. The proceeds of the taxes are paid into the general revenue, but the Authorities of the *circonscriptions indigènes* may levy

[1] *Annuaire Statistique de l'A.E.F. 1936–50*, vol. i, p. 181.
[2] Buell, op. cit. vol. ii, pp. 235, 429–32. E. D. Morel, *Affairs of West Africa*, 1902, pp. 329 ff. G. Hostelet, *L'Œuvre Civilisatrice de la Belgique au Congo de 1885 à 1945*, 1954, p. 13.
[3] *Décret*, 2 May 1910.
[4] A. Phillips, ed., *Survey of African Marriage and Family Life*, 1953, pp. 192–3.
[5] In 1956 140 Belgian Congo francs were equivalent to £1 sterling.
[6] *Rapport sur l'administration de la colonie du Congo Belge 1951*, p. 44.

surcharges up to 40 per cent. of the Government tax. The taxes were at
one stage collected by official Tax Collectors, but the Native Authorities
are now increasingly entrusted with this task; in 1951 they were responsible
for the collection of approximately 75 per cent. of the tax.

The contribution made by African tax revenue is small compared with
that accruing from other sources; in 1951 it accounted for little more than
4 per cent. of the total revenue, as against 18½ per cent. from non-African
income and personal tax, and about 60 per cent. from customs and excise
duties.[1] Africans are liable to personal tax if they carry on a commercial
or industrial business with at least one employee,[2] and to income tax if their
income falls within the limit of tax liability. If they pay income tax or
personal tax they are exempted from the capitation tax, but the number
of Africans so exempted is relatively insignificant.[3]

Taxation in the Trust Territory of Ruanda Urundi follows closely that
in the Belgian Congo; there are, however, some features peculiar to this
territory. Capitation tax becomes due only at the age of 19, and a deduction of 50 per cent. is allowed to Africans with one wife or to unmarried
men who have entered into a labour contract for at least 300 days with
a non-African employer. The rates of the capitation tax and the supplementary tax on additional wives vary between districts; the range of both
taxes was from 75 to 150 francs in 1951. In addition a cattle tax of 35
francs per animal is levied. A system of traditional *prestations*, formerly
rendered in kind or in labour to Chiefs and sub-Chiefs, has now been
generally commuted into cash payment, 3 to 4 francs being regarded as
the equivalent of one day's labour. The Native Authorities are, moreover,
entitled to levy surcharges up to 40 per cent. on the capitation and supplementary taxes and on the cattle tax.

The Portuguese Territories

A direct tax of the nature of income tax is levied on income derived
from commercial or agricultural enterprises, professional occupations,
urban or landed property, and is paid by non-Africans and also by a small
number of Africans.[4] Such Africans are relieved from payment of the
capitation tax to which the bulk of the African population in all Portuguese
territories (except Cape Verde) are liable.

Under the title of the annual personal tax in Angola and the individual
Native tax in Mozambique, Sao Tomé, and Principe, this tax is levied on
all adult males over the age of 16 (Angola and Guinea) or 18 (Mozambique, Sao Tomé, and Principe) and under the age of 60 (55 in Sao

---

[1] *Rapport sur l'administration de la colonie du Congo Belge 1951*, p. 35.
[2] *Codes et Lois du Congo Belge*, 1954, pp. 1385 ff.
[3] Y. van Delhaye, 'Le Régime fiscal au Congo Belge', *Enc. C.B.*, vol. iii, pp. 568 ff.
[4] Decrees no. 37, and 215, 16 December 1948, as subsequently amended.

Tomé and Principe). The rate is fixed annually by the Governor of each of the territories and differentiates between regions, but in recent years the tax has ranged from escudos 80.00 to escudos 250.00 in Mozambique and from angolares[1] 20.00 in the rural areas of Angola to angolares 230.00 in towns near the coast.

The proportion borne by the Native tax to the total revenue has declined since the Second World War in all territories, except Guinea. In Mozambique it contributed only 8 per cent. and in Angola only 6·5 per cent. of the whole, though in Guinea it accounted for one-fifth of the total revenue. Exemptions are granted to numerous classes of persons: the aged and infirm; administrative officials; soldiers, sailors, and policemen; Chiefs and sub-Chiefs; catechists, teachers of Catholic missions speaking Portuguese and the pupils of such missions; and the fathers of four living children, begotten of one wife. In Mozambique there was formerly a social tax levied on farmers 'in return for the gratuitous help they receive from all branches of the public administration'.[2] It has now been replaced by obligatory labour for five days on road or other public works and is known as *Contribuição braçal*.

The tax on plural wives has been abolished in all Portuguese Provinces except Guinea, where the rate is escudos 50 for additional wives up to a maximum sum of escudos 400. The Native tax may be discharged by work for the Government or a municipality and, in Angola, for private employers. Employers of indentured labour are under an obligation to deduct the tax from wages. The Administrative Officer or *Chefe do Posto* is responsible for the collection of tax, with the assistance of Headmen; the Headmen receive 2 per cent. of the collection if 70 per cent. of it is paid up to date. A booklet (*caderneta*) containing particulars of the taxpayer is issued; this includes a photograph and finger-prints, and serves the purpose of a passport to Africans emigrating in search of work.[3] A peculiarity of the Portuguese law is that the family is responsible for the payment of tax until proof is produced of the taxpayer's death.

In the Portuguese system the procedure of taxation plays an important part in emphasizing the line drawn between the *civilizada* and the *não-civilizada* section of the African population.[4] It is clear that the law is so applied as to relieve the *civilizada* section of many of the disabilities imposed by the tax laws, such as the liability to 'correctional arrest', for default or delay in payment of tax. Secondly, a certain number of observers have asserted that the application of the tax laws is utilized by officers of the Administration for securing the labour required by the

---

[1] The value both of the *escudo* and of the *angolar* is roughly 3*d*.
[2] Decree no. 919, 5 August 1944, and no. 6408, 6 April 1946.
[3] For the use of this booklet as part of the record of vital statistics, see above, p. 137.
[4] See above, p. 231.

European cocoa, coffee, or sisal plantations or enterprises such as the diamond mines. Further reference is made to this matter in that section of the chapter dealing with labour problems which discusses the position in regard to 'contract' labour in the Portuguese Overseas Provinces.[1] A common ground for inflicting penalties is delay in payment, it being laid down that payment must be made within three months of the end of the financial year. It will be recalled that the rigour of tax collection in Portuguese East Africa has been alleged to be one of the causes which have in the past accounted for the large influx into Nyasaland of Nguru tribesmen from the neighbouring Portuguese districts.[2]

A GENERAL NOTE ON TAXATION OF AFRICANS

Evolution of Methods of Direct Taxation

It was inevitable that the diversity of economic and social conditions in different territories should be reflected in a considerable variety of procedure for the direct taxation of Africans. But if we exclude the 'labour tax' or *impôt de cueillette* imposed during the régime of the Congo Free State[3] (which falls indeed into the category of exploitation rather than of taxation), the procedure of taxation is shown to have been evolved in the majority of territories through a well-marked cycle. Starting from a hut tax it becomes a poll or capitation tax, usually graduated according to regions. It eventually develops into a personal tax graduated according to categories of taxpayers, though only in a few instances has it yet attained to the final stage of this process.

In the passage through this cycle, territories have discarded a number of out-of-date or unproductive taxes in favour of more remunerative methods. Thus the hut tax was either elaborated into a 'house' tax, conforming closely to traditional custom (as in Tanganyika or Sierra Leone), or a 'yard' tax (as in Gambia), or it has been altogether superseded. *Prestation*, although justified by precedents both in Europe and Africa, has acquired a disagreeable flavour of compulsory labour, and has in most cases been replaced by a 'road' tax. The tax on plural wives has proved difficult to defend. It ignored the fact that many polygamous wives were inherited under the dictates of a custom which left the 'inheritor' no choice in the matter. It was subversive of the salutary custom which enjoined that each wife should occupy a separate hut, since it impelled the husband to crowd them all into a single hut; and it tended to encourage indulgence in irregular relationships. It is doubtful whether the tax ever really did much to discourage polygamy.[4] It is now retained only in Swaziland,

---

[1] See below, p. 1372.   [2] *N.A.*, Part II, p. 48.   [3] See above, p. 673.
[4] For the retention of the tax as an incentive to monogamy, see A. Phillips, ed., loc. cit. p. 673.

Southern Rhodesia, Portuguese Guinea, and the Belgian Congo, but in the last case it now applies only to polygamous marriages contracted prior to 1951. Marriages contracted since that date are no longer 'recognized'.

Fiscal ideas were at an early stage regulated by the concept that an annual tax should, where the African was concerned, be roughly equivalent to the wage for one month's work. Circumstances have put this concept out of date. General economic advance and increases in the sale price of cash crops and in the scale of wages, have deprived it of any value it might once have possessed. At the best, it now serves to provide a convenient formula to be used in the graduation of direct tax in those cases where taxation is related to the rate of wages. There have admittedly been instances, more particularly in the history of South and East Africa, where the major consideration in the levy of the direct tax has proceeded not only from fiscal motives but from a desire to force Africans into employment in European enterprises.[1] But here also circumstances have changed. The liability for payment of the tax remains as a general incentive, but is only one among a number of economic and other incentives which bring Africans into the labour market.[2]

Circumstances have also tended to modify the system under which direct taxation originally took the form of a simple flat-rate tax. A flat-rate tax is admittedly the form most appropriate to backward rural areas, and for that reason it must be retained in many territories. But even the more backward areas now contain increasing numbers of relatively prosperous traders or farmers. The flat-rate tax, which must be fixed at a rate which can be paid without hardship by persons on the lowest economic scale, is likely to be unduly favourable to the well-to-do.

Methods of Graduating Direct Taxes

This survey of methods of direct taxation has postulated problems to which a solution must be found if improvements are to be effected. It may be asked in the first place how far existing methods of graduation are successful and how far their development is practicable. A regional graduation, which reflects the scale of local resources or the extent of the opportunities for earning a wage, is now adopted in a majority of territories, and it is noteworthy that it has been used on occasion (as for example during the depression period of the early thirties) in order to reduce no less than to increase the pitch of taxation. If neither the Union of South Africa nor Southern Rhodesia, where the rate of tax has remained unaltered over a long period of years, has found it advisable to adopt the

[1] See above, p. 651.
[2] See I. Schapera, *Migrant Labour and Tribal Life*, 1947, p. 134. *N.A.*, Part II, pp. 15, 163, 377. W. M. Macmillan, *Africa Emergent*, 1938, pp. 241 ff.

device of graduation, it is because this is felt to be a makeshift which may retard the application of a more comprehensive system for adjusting tax demand to personal income. Provided that legislation is sufficiently flexible to admit of forms of graduation which will react alike to prosperity and depression, they may serve to adapt the tax to the capacity of different groups or different sections of the community. They will, however, be less effective in adjusting the tax demand to the circumstances of the individual taxpayer.

Where wealth consists in the possession of animals, as pre-eminently in the territories of nomadic pastoralists but also in other areas where an agricultural is supplemented by a pastoral economy, three systems of graduation have been employed. Either a flat rate is imposed for each species, graded from sheep to camels and horses (as in Nigeria under the title of *jangali*), or the tax is graduated according to the size of the herd (as in Bechuanaland), or it is levied on the selling price in the open market (as in Tanganyika). An advantage of this type of tax is that it is easily understood and put into practice. The high yield from *jangali* in the Northern Region of Nigeria suggests that it is, on the whole, a well-accepted form of taxation. Elsewhere, however, as in Basutoland, there are complaints that the assessment of the tax leaves too much power in the hands of the Headmen concerned. It is a form of taxation over which it is exceptionally difficult to exercise an effective supervision.

While considerable progress has thus been made in graduating the original flat-rate tax to the circumstances of different localities or different groups in the African population, less progress has been made in the development of a procedure which will distinguish individuals whose income is above that of the flat rate and will relate the tax to their income. Experiments on these lines have been made in Bechuanaland, Nigeria, and the French territories and though relatively few Africans are at present affected, their number must rapidly increase in future years. The production of cash crops by Africans may seldom bring them within the province of income tax, but it frequently removes them by a wide margin from the level appropriate to the poll tax. But the failure of the Pare experiment in Tanganyika[1] and the opposition shown in Nigeria and Kenya to the principle of individual assessment seem to show that African opinion is not yet ready for this further development in graduation.

Opposition is the stronger because it is likely to be the more influential members of African society who will be affected by the taxation of 'ascertainable income'. African reluctance to declare income is well illustrated in Southern Rhodesia, where the franchise is based on an income qualification, with the result that only a small proportion of those entitled to exercise a vote have claimed it.[2] In the 1954 session of the Legislature of

[1] See above, p. 658. [2] See above, p. 283.

the Western Region of Nigeria, the leader of the House admitted that 'the majority of our people never declare their true incomes; rather they strive their mighty best to evade paying tax on their real income'. At present the taxation of 'ascertainable incomes' is practically confined to the raising of revenue for Local Government bodies, and the operation of assessment is carried out by Native Authorities. Their efficiency has often been impugned, but it is doubtful whether any other agency is better equipped to discharge this function.

Land Tax: African and Indian Procedures Contrasted

It would not have been unreasonable if the Administrations concerned had attempted to find a more suitable type of taxation in some form of tax based on the land, for in a rural economy an appropriately framed tax on land or its products should provide automatically for an adjustment of tax demand to the resources available to the group or the individual. In British India the 'land revenue' (which represented the cash equivalent of that part of the produce of the land which was assigned by tradition as the share of the ruler) constituted the major source of the revenue of the Empires or States which had preceded British rule.[1] Under British rule it continued to fill the same role until the receipts from income tax and from indirect taxation became the dominant items in the budget.

Africa can show very few instances in which land has been adopted as the basis of African taxation; they are confined to cases such as the tax imposed on the farm lands near Kano in Northern Nigeria,[2] or that imposed on the *mailo* lands in Buganda.[3] The system of 'lump assessment' practised in the Northern Region of Nigeria had some features resembling the procedure followed in assessing the Indian 'land revenue', but for reasons already explained it never constituted in the same sense a scientifically assessed tax on the land or its produce.[4] Apart from the difficulties created in Africa by the traditional system of land-holding, there has nowhere existed in the Native land areas that authoritative record of land titles or that system of crop returns which made taxation in the form of 'land revenue' possible in British India.

Financial Relations between Local and Central Government Bodies

An issue to which this review of taxation has not supplied any clear answer concerns the future financial relations between the Local Government bodies and the central Governments in regard to the administration and control of direct Native tax. There are at present two conflicting policies. In British West Africa the central Governments have largely

[1] L. S. S. O'Malley, *Modern India and the West*, 1941, pp. 279 ff.
[2] See above, p. 663.　　　　[3] See above, p. 661.　　　　[4] See above, p. 603.

dissociated themselves from the direct taxation of Africans and have either delegated this function to the Native Authorities or have surrendered the tax in its entirety to Local Government bodies. It is argued in favour of this policy that it stimulates in Africans a greater interest in the development of their areas, as the transfer of tax has been accompanied by the transfer to Local Authorities of many services ministering to local welfare. In the British Central and East African territories, on the other hand, the policy has been followed of retaining the central control of the direct Native tax but allocating a percentage of the proceeds to the Native Treasuries. Both policies admit of the allocations from the central Government being augmented by local rates which are often graduated.

The second of the two policies above described has the advantage that the allocations made to the treasuries of local bodies may be increased or reduced, stabilized or withheld according to circumstances, and grants in aid adjusted to the needs of poorer and richer areas. The decision between these conflicting policies cannot, however, depend on purely fiscal considerations. The promotion of local self-governing institutions is now part of the accepted policy of the majority of the Governments concerned, and practice in the problems connected with the incidence and assessment of a local rate provides the readiest field for imparting to Africans those lessons of financial responsibility which are so essential to the success of such institutions.

Effect of Improvement in Economic Conditions

There is a final consideration. Unquestionably a time existed when the direct Native tax was viewed as oppressive by a large section of Africans, not merely because of its novelty, but because of the serious hardship often involved in finding the means of paying the tax. At that period the task of collection absorbed an undue part of the activity of Administrative Officers, and the methods sometimes employed by them threatened to cause a permanent alienation of African feeling. That there has been in most territories so marked an improvement in this position is due partly to the economic changes which have made the Governments less dependent on the contribution made by the direct taxation of Africans and partly to causes which have made it far easier for the African taxpayer to secure the money needed to meet the annual demand.

But in the succeeding years most Administrations have also recognized the need for caution in increasing the rate of tax as originally fixed. Some have seen the wisdom of maintaining it unchanged over prolonged periods. Where the Governments have decided to allot to the Treasuries of the Native Authorities or of Local Government bodies either the exclusive benefit or a considerable part of the proceeds of the direct tax, local African opinion has acquiesced far more readily in proposals to increase its incidence. There must always be sections of the African community on whom a general tax of this character, which is basically related to an assumed earning capacity rather than to actual income or resources, must inflict some measure of hardship. This is especially the case during the periodical 'scarcity times' which climatic conditions create in certain parts of Africa. But broadly speaking the direct Native tax has ceased to present the number of unpleasant problems which half a century ago were so obvious to observers of African affairs.

The direct tax imposed on Africans now forms an item of constantly declining significance in the budgets of the majority of the countries lying south of the Sahara. This fact is fully illustrated by the details given in the tables on the pages immediately following, and it is the subject of further comment in the course of the study made of the financial position of the different Goverments in chapter XVIII.[1]

[1] See below, pp. 1311 ff.

BRITISH AFRICAN TERRITORIES

Country	Year	Total Revenue £'000	Income Tax £'000	Percentage of Total Revenue	Direct Taxes on Africans £'000	Percentage of Total Revenue	Total Direct Taxes £'000	Percentage of Total Revenue	Indirect Taxes £'000	Percentage of Total Revenue
West Africa										
Gold Coast	1938	3,566	53	1·5	..[1]	..	53	1·5	3,513	98·5
	1951	15,148	4,241	28·0	..	..	4,241	28·0	10,907	72·0
Nigeria	1938	5,741	37	0·6	816	14·2	853	14·8	4,889	85·2
	1951	26,186	4,000	15·3	369	1·4	4,369	16·7	21,817	83·3
Sierra Leone	1938	805	159	19·8	80	9·9	239	29·7	566	70·3
	1951	3,261	955	29·3	98	3·0	1,053	32·3	2,208	67·7
Gambia	1938	162	..[2]	..	14	8·6	14	8·6	148	91·4
	1951	764	170	22·3	..[1]	..	170	22·3	594	77·7
East Africa										
Kenya	1938	3,776	172	4·5	532	14·1	704	18·6	3,072	81·4
	1951	13,134	3,455	26·3	839	6·4	4,294	32·7	8,840	67·3
Uganda	1938	1,848	34	1·8	571	30·9	605	32·7	1,243	67·3
	1951	12,013	639	5·3	437	3·6	1,076	8·9	10,937	91·1
Tanganyika	1938	2,027	48	2·4	643	31·7	691	34·1	1,336	65·9
	1951	9,936	1,694	17·1	1,050	10·6	2,744	27·7	7,192	72·3
Zanzibar and Pemba	1938	465	2	0·4	..[1]	..	2	0·4	463	99·6
	1951	1,151	36	3·1	..[1]	..	36	3·1	1,115	96·9

[1] There are no direct taxes on Africans.   [2] Income tax was not introduced until 1940.

BRITISH AFRICAN TERRITORIES AND THE UNION

Country	Year	Total Revenue £'000	Income Tax £'000	Percentage of Total Revenue	Direct Taxes on Africans £'000	Percentage of Total Revenue	Total Direct Taxes £'000	Percentage of Total Revenue	Indirect Taxes £'000	Percentage of Total Revenue
CENTRAL AFRICA N. Rhodesia	1938	1,581	764	48·3	134	8·5	898	56·8	683	43·2
	1951	14,418	9,755	67·7	171	1·2	9,926	68·9	4,492	31·1
S. Rhodesia	1938	3,515	947	26·9	413	11·7	1,360	38·6	2,155	61·4
	1951	21,236	10,923	51·4	528	2·5	11,452	53·9	9,784	46·1
Nyasaland	1938	591	47	8·0	145	24·5	192	32·5	399	67·5
	1951	3,013	773	25·7	400	13·3	1,173	39·0	1,840	61·0
SOUTHERN AFRICA Union of S.A.	1938	51,853	18,215	35·2	567	1·1	18,782	36·3	33,070	63·7
	1951	187,942	92,032	49·1	1,326	0·6	93,358	49·7	94,043	50·3
Basutoland	1938	394	7	1·8	174	44·1	181	45·9	213	54·1
	1951	1,237	251	20·3	292	23·6	543	43·9	694	56·1
Bechuanaland	1938	188	36	19·1	62	33·0	98	52·1	90	47·9
	1951	772	142	18·3	105	13·6	247	31·9	525	68·1
Swaziland	1938	116	5	4·4	44	38·4	49	42·8	67	57·2
	1951	657	323	49·2	58	8·8	381	58·0	276	42·0

FOREIGN TERRITORIES

Country	Year	Total Revenue	Income Tax	Percentage of Total Revenue	Direct Taxes on Africans	Percentage of Total Revenue	Total Direct Taxes	Percentage of Total Revenue	Indirect Taxes	Percentage of Total Revenue
BELGIAN AFRICA										
Congo[1]	1938	489·9	149	30·5	119·6	24·4	268·6	54·5	221·3	45·5
	1951	8,012	2,196	274·4	272	3·4	2,468	30·8	5,544	69·2
Ruanda Urundi	1938	42·5	9·6	22·5	20·8	48·9	30·4	71·4	12·1	28·6
	1951	559	74	13·2	84	15·0	158	28·2	401	71·8
FRENCH AFRICA[2]										
Equatorial Africa	1938	122	36·9	30·2	..	..	41·7	34·2	80·2	65·8
	1951	6,069	1,168	19·2	..	..	1,331	21·9	4,738	78·1
West Africa	1938	876·5	201	22·9	..	..	271·7	31·0	604·8	69·0
	1951	38,511	..	..	..	..	6,270	16·3	32,241	83·7
Cameroons	1938	121·4	39·1	32·2	..	..	44·1	36·3	77·3	63·7
	1951	6,207	1,241	20·0	..	..	1,386	22·3	4,821	77·7
Togo	1938	39·7	7·1	17·9	..	..	7·9	19·9	31·8	80·1
	1951	1,292	141	10·9	..	..	158	12·2	1,134	87·8
PORTUGUESE AFRICA[3]										
Angola	1938	1,964	142	7·2	431	21·9	573	29·1	814	70·9
	1951	8,810	482·3	5·5	934	10·6	1,416·3	16·1	6,867	83·9
Mozambique	1938	3,680	?	?	?	?	1,290	35·0	2,390	65·0
	1951	8,175	777·4	9·5	1,425·9	15·2	2,203·2	24·7	5,775	75·3

[1] Figures in million francs: income tax is the sum of 'Impôt sur les revenus' + 'Impositions personnelles'.

[2] Million francs C.F.A. In the French budget it is impossible to distinguish between African and non-African direct taxation, hence the omissions in the column headed Direct Taxes on Africans.

[3] Figures in hundred contos. One conto = 1,000 escudos.

CHAPTER XI

THE LAND

PART I. THE STATE AND THE LAND

THE POLITICAL SIGNIFICANCE OF LAND POLICY

IT is not easy for those who know only the industrialized countries of the Western world to realize the significance of the position occupied by the land in the eyes of most of the peoples of Africa. Anthropologists have described the mystic bond which unites the African to the home of those ancestral spirits who continue, as he believes, to play an active part in his daily life.[1] Jurists point out that the tribal Chief derives his authority largely from the fact that he is in war the traditional defender of the lands of the tribe and in peace the arbiter of the differences which arise regarding their use. Viewed from a material standpoint, the land still provides for the great majority of Africans the sole means of subsistence. If for any reason this fails the peasant, his only alternative is to join the ranks of migrant labour, at the cost of a journey which may often run to hundreds of miles and of entry into a form of life to which he and his kind have hitherto been strangers.

But there is also another point of contrast between the position of land as seen by the African and as seen by the inhabitant of the modern world. It lies in a fundamental difference in the conception of the place of land in the life of a community. To the citizen of the Western world the land represents an aggregate of physical units over each of which some member of the community has individual rights of occupation, use, or disposal. To the African the dominant conception is that of communal, not of individual, rights over the land. By traditional African custom the individual and his family can claim an undisturbed tenure of a holding so long as they need to use it but, when they cease to do so, it reverts to the community and may be apportioned to others. Where the usual practice is that of shifting cultivation, every member of the group can claim by right the use of the necessary portion of the unoccupied waste; but the land remains from first to last the land of the community.[2]

It is this all-pervading sense of a communal right over the land which seems to have made the African exceptionally sensitive about the attitude of Colonial Powers in respect of the appropriation of Native lands in the interests of non-Natives. The feeling is general and is by no means

[1] G. Howard Jones, *The Earth Goddess*, 1936, pp. 3 ff.
[2] For modern changes in the African tradition of landholding, see Part II of this chapter.

confined to those communities whose land has been taken for this purpose.[1]
There is certainly no one feature of Colonial policy which has had an equal
influence in determining the character of the relations between the indigenous people and a Colonial Administration. Whatever other reasons
may exist for the estimate made by Africans of the character of a Government, the fact that a considerable area of Native lands has passed permanently into the hands of non-Natives will always tend to colour any
judgement that is formed of it. Nor will the emotion which this fact
arouses permit of an objective assessment of the value which the use of the
land by non-Natives has brought to the African community, however
obvious this may be to the outside world. There will be no place for
recognition of the difference between the appropriation of lands that
have been at any time in actual occupation by a Native community and
lands over which it has at one time or another merely asserted a claim.

Governments have acquired control over lands and land rights in a
great variety of ways. In some cases they have simply availed themselves
of rights based on conquest. Elsewhere they have taken advantage of
treaties or agreements with Chiefs which have purported to be cessions of
land, but they have also in many instances taken their stand on agreements
that have been interpreted by them in that sense, though with little or no
justification. In some instances they have availed themselves of the juristic
principle that a Government is entitled to the ownership (including the
right of disposal) over all 'vacant' or unoccupied lands. Various juridical
considerations have been put forward both in attack and in defence of the
policies adopted in this matter by Colonial Governments. But the extent
of the appropriation of indigenous lands has depended more on factors
of climate or soil than on juridical arguments. It is considerations of
climate and soil which have directed the stream of European settlement
to southern and eastern rather than to western Africa.

It is these factors also that were responsible for the fact that the British
decided that in India their activity should be directed towards trading
rather than to the introduction of European settlement. In British
India the claim of the Crown to ownership over lands was confined
to the exercise of rights over the forest lands which had in pre-British
India been recognized as reserved for State purposes, or those small areas
in which the elaborate process of cadastral survey conducted under
British rule revealed no private rights. In one respect this turned to the
advantage of the British Administration. The long period during which it
enjoyed the benefit of the general acquiescence of Indians in its rule might
have been appreciably shortened if Indian opinion, with its unusual talent
for exploiting any instance of the misuse of power, had been able to point

[1] See, for instance, below, p. 732. See also *East Africa Royal Commission 1953–1955, Report*, Cmd
9475, 1955, pp. 51 ff.

AFRICA : ALIENATED LAND
(South of the Sahara)

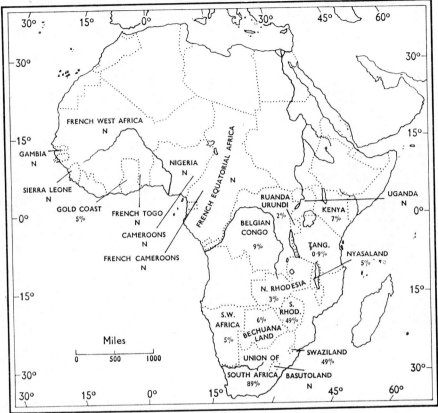

D.C.S. (Misc.) 226/6

Percentage of Areas of African Territories Alienated or Reserved for European Occupation

N = 0·5% or below

The 5% shown in Gold Coast (including Togoland) consists mainly of mining concessions

No precise information is available for Portuguese or Spanish Territories, or for Liberia

to a large-scale appropriation of Indian lands for the benefit of European colonists.

If this particular feature of the policy of the various African Administrations occupies so prominent a place in the ensuing paragraphs, the justification lies in the influence which it has exercised in determining the relations of the African people towards the Colonial Governments. Save in certain conspicuous cases, as most notably in the Union of South Africa, the Rhodesias, and parts of East Africa, the area alienated is only a small proportion of the total area of the country. There are instances where the proportion is negligible. It is no doubt true that as a rule the alienated lands have been selected for their advantage in point of soil, but nowhere could it be said that they have monopolized the whole of the best area available. There are in the Union of South Africa some areas held by Africans which are equal to the best lands held by Europeans. If in Kenya the 'White Highlands' offer unusual advantages both for agricultural and pastoral purposes, there are other large areas of good soil (including much of the highland plateau) which are held by the indigenous tribes.[1] The areas held by *colons* in the French territories are not distinguishable in quality from those held by African peasants. In the Belgian Congo there is no marked difference between the lands in the Concession areas and those in Native hands.

Although, however, the story of the alienation of African lands occupies, for various reasons, an important chapter in African history, the period of alienation has for all practical purposes come to an end. It is not likely that there will now be any substantial additions to the total of alienated lands in the countries south of the Sahara. For the future, interest will be focused on the changes in systems of landholding and in the procedures of land tenure which will form the principal topic of Part II of the present chapter of the Survey.

The Union of South Africa

In the early history of Cape Colony circumstances did not seem to call for any definition of the legal position in regard to rights over the land. At the outset, when only Hottentots and nomad Bushmen were encountered, the available areas were so large and signs of settlement so far wanting that, had the question arisen, the land would no doubt have been described, in the phraseology of international law then current, as *territorium nullius*. When towards the end of the eighteenth century the Boers advancing northwards first met the southward movement of the Bantu, neither Boer nor Bantu could justly claim to have any superior title to the land. The question of right, however, was not one which occupied the Government of the time; its first problem was to establish a frontier

[1] *N.A.*, Part I, pp. 89, 187–9.

behind which it could contain its own difficult and unruly colonists, and thus avoid the military consequences which each forward thrust involved.

As it was, each extension of the frontier could mean only the assumption by the Colony of full rights over the newly occupied land. There was a time (1835–47) when the adoption of the Glenelg policy of separation might have obviated the need for making any definition of Native land rights, for the system of treaties on which that policy was based would have left Bantu tribes in independent possession of their lands, reduced in area no doubt, but under their own control. But the forward thrust of farmers made this policy impracticable. Lands were allotted to meet the needs of farmers until, with successive extensions of territory, it was found that the Kaffirs were too numerous or too strongly settled to permit of fresh expropriations.

In British Kaffraria, now known as the Ciskei, the abandonment of the 'treaty' policy resulted in the confiscation of land from rebellious tribes and the interspersing of Europeans among the Natives both as a military measure and a financial expedient;[1] in other parts of the country the system of Native Reserves was adopted. The Reserve system may be traced to an early stage of Cape history, when some effort had been made to provide for dispossessed Hottentots in the small settlements established under missionary influence at Bethelsdorp and elsewhere.[2] At a later date certain Locations in the Ciskei were recognized as Native areas, in which Europeans could not purchase land. A more important step was taken when, in 1864, it was decided to treat the Transkeian Territories in general as areas in which land was not available for Europeans, a position which was maintained in principle in spite of the annexations which took place at various stages between 1879 and 1894.

The Reserve policy was most fully recognized in Natal, where Shepstone's influence with the Natal Native Land Commission of 1846–7 resulted in considerable areas being left to Natives on terms which protected them from further reduction by alienation. In 1864 the Crown regularized the position by vesting the lands in a Native Trust.[3] When Zululand was annexed in 1897, a Lands Commission was instructed to provide liberally for the Natives with regard to both their present and future requirements. About three-fifths of Zululand was formed into Reserves and placed under the Zululand Native Trust.

In the Transvaal African land requirements received from the first less consideration than elsewhere. Under the Volksraad Resolution of November 1853 the Commandants were instructed to grant land for occupation by Natives conditional on their good behaviour but, as a matter of

[1] W. M. Macmillan, *Bantu, Boer, and Briton*, 1929, pp. 129, 267, 299.
[2] *Idem. The Cape Colour Question*, 1927, pp. 148, 271.
[3] Letters Patent, dated 27 April 1864.
[4] H. Rogers, *Native Administration in the Union of South Africa*, 1933, p. 118.

fact, Boer farmers occupied land at their own option, without any regard to the needs of the African population.[1] The terms of the Pretoria Convention of 1881, which recognized the independence of the Transvaal, stipulated for the appointment of a Standing Native Location Commission, whose main duty was to assign to Natives such Locations as they might be equitably entitled to. Its recommendations appear generally to have been accepted by the Transvaal Government, but the work was not completed before the Anglo-Boer war; after the war the Crown Colony Government appointed a new Commission in 1905, and its reports were finally adopted in 1907. Some 2 million acres were thus allocated as Native Locations.

In the Orange Free State immigrant farmers found few Natives, the country having been depopulated as the result of the upheaval caused by the wars of Chaka in Natal. There are only three small Reserves. The first, Witzieshoek, comprises the lands assigned to the tribe of Mopeli, a Basuto Chief who submitted to the Republic during the Basuto war of 1865-6; the others comprise the remainder of the lands which the Basuto assigned in 1829 to a section of the Barolong after it had been driven south by invading tribes. The Barolong, under their Chief Moroka, subsequently assisted the Voortrekkers against the Basuto, and the former did not disturb them in the possession of their lands. When the 'Moroka Ward' was annexed in 1884, considerable areas were found to have been already alienated to Europeans and to other Natives. The grants made were recognized by the Government, and the Seliba and Thaba Nchu Reserves were in 1885 set aside for the accommodation of landless Africans.

These various measures had the effect of reserving for African occupation an area which, at the time of the establishment of the Union, amounted to 23½ million acres, or roughly 7·13 per cent. of the total area of the country. The constitution of a Reserve meant only that the State refrained from making grants in the area so delimited and did not allow Europeans to purchase land in it. It is true that where Trusts were created, as in Natal and Zululand, land could not be alienated without the sanction of the Secretary of State and was therefore fully protected for African use, but, in point of law, the Reserves continued to be classed as Crown property. Up to 1913 lands held by Europeans could, save in the Orange Free State, be purchased from them by Africans and considerable areas were so acquired, particularly in the Cape Province. In the Reserves land was held in customary Native tenure and not under any title which could be defined in terms of European law, except in the Mission Reserves in Natal. There allotments of land had been made in freehold before the institution of the Trust.

As part of the reconstruction which followed the Anglo-Boer war, a

---

[1] *The Cambridge History of the British Empire*, vol. viii, 1936, pp. 399, 816.

Native Affairs Commission was appointed in 1903 to consider the policy to be applied to Natives throughout South Africa.[1] Hitherto the Reserve policy had had two objectives; it acted as a measure of protection to Natives and, in so doing, it secured a reservoir of cheap labour available for employment on the farms. With a growing interest in policies pointing to a complete segregation of the European and Native communities, the question of the relative proportion in the distribution of available land between them became a matter of increasing concern. The Commission itself was less interested in the question of the adequacy of the areas occupied by Natives than in the need for their strict delimitation, with the corollary that thereafter European interests should be protected by a provision that the right of purchase by Natives should be strictly confined to prescribed areas. Effect was given to that policy in 1913[2] but General Botha, in sponsoring the Bill, was careful to emphasize that the African had as much right to the country as the European, and he repudiated the idea that such legislation was aimed at providing a labour reservoir.

The Act scheduled the areas already occupied by Africans and restricted their purchase outside, save in Cape Province, where this prohibition was restrained by a judicial decision.[3] It provided for a commission charged to recommend a permanent division of the land into African and non-African areas. The Beaumont Commission, appointed for this purpose, proposed to set aside an area of 17,700,000 acres where Natives could purchase land, thus bringing the African areas to roughly $38\frac{1}{2}$ million acres in all, or 13·3 per cent. of the area of the Union. Their proposals were submitted to committees in each Province, and all of these, except that in the Cape, reduced the areas proposed for allocation to Natives. No action was taken to implement these proposals till 1936. An Act passed in that year was explicitly put forward as a measure of racial segregation.[4] It provided for the acquisition of a maximum of $14\frac{1}{2}$ million acres on behalf of Natives, to be added to that already scheduled for Native occupation.

A sum of £10 million was to be expended during the next ten years on the acquisition of this land, but it was expected that this expenditure would eventually be recouped out of the payments made by Africans for its occupation. A South African Native Trust, with the Governor-General as Trustee, was made responsible for purchasing and controlling any lands acquired under the Act. Native Trust land might be resumed for public purposes with the consent of both Houses of Parliament, and subject to compensation; it could only be sold or leased to non-Africans if this was to the advantage of the African community. Up to 30 June

---

[1] See above, p. 160.   [2] Native Land Act no. 27 of 1913.
[3] *Thompson and Stilwell* v. *Kama*, 1917, A.C. 209.
[4] Native Trust and Land Act no. 18 of 1936. See above, p. 158.

1952 a sum of £7,798,734 had been expended in the acquisition of 4,535,636 acres.[1] The term 'African lands' now comprises (a) Scheduled areas (under the provisions of the Act of 1913), (b) Released areas (released for acquisition under the Act of 1936), and (c) Trust areas actually acquired by the Native Trust.

TABLE

Allocation of Native Areas in Acres (000's omitted)

Province	1 Areas scheduled by Act 27 of 1913	2 Scheduled areas as extended by subsequent Acts	3 Additional areas recommended by Beaumont Commission 1916	4 The revised areas recommended by the local committees of 1918	5 Maximum areas to be 'released' under the Act of 1936	6 Total of scheduled and released areas (cols. 2 and 5)	7 Percentage of col. 6 to total area of Province
Cape	12,791	12,925	2,779	3,404	3,420	16,345	9.2
Natal	5,880	6,343	3,940	911	1,113	7,456	33·0
Transvaal	2,256	2,608	10,673	9,921 (Alternative suggestions)	10,642	13,250	18·7
O.F.S.	157	157	314		169	326	1·0

By June 1954, the latest date for which figures are available, the Trust had acquired altogether 10,053,261 acres, namely, 5,764,963 acres by purchase and 4,288,298 acres by the transfer of Crown Land or by purchases effected by African tribes or individuals. Together with the areas scheduled in 1936 and later additions to them, the Reserves amounted then to just under 32 million acres, or to about 11 per cent. of the total area of the Union.[3] In the year ending March 1955, the Native Trust spent a further £435,168 on land purchases, but the area thus acquired has not been made known.[4] It was 19 years since the Native Trust and Land Act had been passed, but the area which it proposed to add to the Native Reserves was still very far from complete.

The land acquired by the Trust is not a net addition to the land previously occupied by Africans because, first, the Crown Land handed over to the Trust carried a large African population and is thus not available for further settlement; and second, at the same time as the area reserved for African occupation is being extended, land is being lost to Africans,

---

[1] *Report of the Department of Native Affairs, 1951–2,* U.G. no. 37, 1955, p. 29.
[2] *Handbook on Race Relations in South Africa,* 1949, p. 174.
[3] M. Horrell, *A Survey of Race Relations in South Africa, 1953–54,* South African Institute of Race Relations, 1954, p. 87.
[4] Union of South Africa, *Government Gazette,* 14 October 1955, p. 26.

even though on a much smaller scale. The loss occurs mainly in respect of unallocated Crown Land which is largely occupied by Africans legally considered as squatters.[1] From time to time land in these areas is handed over for European settlement, and the Africans have to quit without any claim to compensation. Usually the Native Trust finds land for Natives thus dispossessed, but it is under no obligation to do so.

It must at the same time be noted that Africans hold in individual title some 1,393,000 acres in 'released' areas and 646,000 acres in European areas, which are additional to the acreage shown in column 6 of the preceding table. The area owned by Africans in the European areas may be sold to Europeans and may not then revert to African ownership. Apart from this contingency, and if the Trust acquires land to the full extent contemplated by the Act, the total available for Native occupation will amount to 39,417,000 acres, or roughly 13 per cent. of the area of the Union. The purchased land is either added to existing tribal Locations or is used to accommodate tribes and communities to which Locations have never been assigned.

There is a further feature of land policy to be considered. From a very early date attempts have been made to restrict the practice known as 'Kaffir farming' by which lands in the areas reserved for European occupation were leased to Natives for cash or a share of the produce. There has been a progressive increase in the legal disabilities imposed on the 'squatter'. On Crown Land in the Transvaal and Natal high rents were charged. As regards alienated lands, earlier Acts were supplemented by the more drastic Native Service Contract Act of 1932, but the enforcement of this measure would have led to the displacement of large numbers of 'squatters' for whom no land was available and its provisions were superseded by those of chapter iv of the Native Trust and Land Act of 1936. This chapter, which operates only in proclaimed districts, prohibits a Native from living on land in any such district unless he is the registered owner, or a servant of the owner, or a registered tenant or a registered 'squatter', that is to say, neither a servant nor a 'registered tenant'. The Act empowers the police to remove under warrant an African who has been convicted of unlawful residence. No new 'squatters' are allowed to be registered after the application of the Act, while the owner is required to pay an annual licence fee, increasing from 10s. in the first two years to £5 in the tenth and subsequent years, for every 'squatter' resident on his land.

Labour Control Boards may be appointed with power to determine the number of labour tenants required by any landowner for his bona fide activities, and to reduce the number if it is considered excessive. In making the determination, the Board is obliged to presume, until the contrary is proved, that five labour tenants are required and that each is engaged to

[1] For the latest estimates of land available to Africans, see U.G. no. 61, 1955, pp. 45, 74.

work at least six months a year. The owner may not keep on his land more labour tenants than the number fixed by the Board. The Administration is charged with the duty of providing adequate accommodation for ejected Africans in a scheduled or 'released' area, but it has not hitherto been found practicable to apply this part of the Act. More lately the Native Trust and Land Amendment Act, no. 18 of 1954, has applied further stringent measures to reduce the number of 'squatters', and the number affected is likely to be considerable.

South-West Africa

The basis of the German Protectorate of South-West Africa was a series of so-called land purchases made from African Chiefs by Lüderitz on behalf of the German Government. These usually covered the entire territory of the Chiefs, and it is mainly on the strength of these agreements that the Germans alienated the land required for their colonists. It is of interest to note that the treaty concluded with the Rehoboth Bastards, who were not treated on the same lines as Africans, recognized the joint right of this community to their land. The German settlement was confined to the central and southern part of the territory, now known as the Police Zone; the tribal areas of Ovamboland and Okovangoland in the north were practically unadministered,[1] and no land was taken up for colonists. Imperial Proclamations of 1898 and 1903 provided for the establishment of Reserves, and for the expropriation by the State of land which was formerly African property in order to provide for the settlement of landless Africans, but these provisions do not seem to have been implemented.

The discontent of various tribes at the expropriation of their lands as the result of transactions with Chiefs, the implications of which the tribesmen had not understood, was one of the causes of the Herero and Namaqua rebellions, which were punished by the general confiscation of their tribal lands. The Decree of 1905 authorizing this action explicitly permitted the expropriation of these lands and also of the lands of tribes whose organization had been broken up; it further empowered the Governor to reduce the extent of unduly large tribal areas. The German Government actively encouraged colonization by its nationals and allotted expropriated lands for this purpose. The area of the Police Zone left in the possession of African communities amounted to about $2\frac{1}{2}$ million acres. A reversal of policy shortly before 1914 led to the issue of orders that Reserves were to be allocated for African occupation, but no steps had been taken for this purpose when war broke out in 1914.

The Mandatory Government proceeded on the assumption that it held the same wide powers as the Germans in regard to the appropriation of

[1] See above, p. 436.

tribal lands for the use of colonists, and it pursued a vigorous policy of settlement. In particular, the Union Government found land for the settlement of 301 families of Boers who had at an early period trekked to Angola and were now repatriated. By 1936 Europeans in South-West Africa numbered 30,677, as against some 10,000 in 1914. A Commission appointed in 1935 to make a general investigation into the situation of the territory did not take an optimistic view of the possibility of further settlement;[1] nevertheless the European population had increased by 1950 to 49,612, and the total area of land alienated in farms from 62,930,000 acres to 84,938,000 acres, or 39 per cent. of the area of the Police Zone. This comprised 3,415 farms in private ownership, 1,102 leased to settlers, and 39 to companies. A further 485 Government farms, covering an area of 9,010,000 acres, had been surveyed.[2]

Upon the assumption by South Africa of the mandate for the territory, Proclamation no. 13 of 1920 extended to it the provisions of the Union Land Settlement Act of 1912 and the Transvaal Crown Land Disposal Ordinance of 1903, which had the effect of defining as Crown Lands all unalienated land that was the property of the German Government, or in other words, all land not held in separate title. The same definition was contained in the Land Settlement Consolidation Proclamation no. 310 of 1927, which superseded the 1912 Land Settlement Act. But while assuming these general powers, the Administration also decided to give effect to the policy of creating Native Reserves, which the Germans had initiated but had not implemented.

A Commission was appointed in 1921 to make recommendations regarding areas to be set aside as Native Reserves. Some difficulty arose from the hopes entertained by the Herero and Hottentot that the Administration would confiscate the German farms and return to the tribes the areas which they claimed originally to have held. There was much resentment when this hope was not realized and there was also delay owing to the prevalence of drought and the necessity of boring for water. Provisional Reserves were, however, set apart in six districts. The total area eventually reserved for African occupation in the Police Zone and the Kaokoveld was 8,738,000 acres, including a temporary Reserve at Hoachana. In all, 15 reserves have been created in the Police Zone. In addition the Ovambo and Okovango tribal territories of 10,477,000 and 10 million acres respectively, were declared to be Native Reserves; the Kaokoveld, with an area of 13,803,000 acres, was also proclaimed a Reserve in 1948.[3]

The Reserves in the Police Zone have been declared to be set aside for

[1] *Report of South-West Africa Commission*, U.G. no. 26, 1936, para. 168.
[2] *O.Y.S.A.*, 1952–53, p. 1176.
[3] Ibid. p. 1175.

the sole and exclusive occupation of Natives,[1] and under the provisions of the South-West Africa Mandate Act no. 49 of 1919 they cannot be alienated without the consent of both Houses of the Union Parliament. The Reserves, however, are not in the true sense tribal Reserves. They have not been proclaimed in the name of particular tribes and their residents are still on occasion moved from one Reserve to another. Moreover, an African tribesman previously resident outside a Reserve cannot take up residence in it by right; he needs the sanction of the officer in charge.

Some reference has already been made to the procedure by which all receipts from grazing and other fees in a Reserve are paid into a Reserve Trust Fund.[2]

The High Commission Territories

The position of the British Government in regard to land in Basutoland has from the first been clear. The main object of the Proclamation of March 1868, declaring the country to be British territory, was to secure it against further attack by the Orange Free State.[3] The Treaty of Aliwal North in 1869 regained for the Basuto a large portion of the corn lands which would have been lost to them had the Treaty of Thaba Bosigo of 1866 remained in force. The Basuto had already, however, lost some of their most fertile lands in earlier wars with the Free State. There was from the first no question of appropriating any of the Basuto lands for settlement by colonists.

In the Regulations of 1870 the right of allotting land for occupation by members of the tribes was vested in the High Commissioner. In practice, however, this power has been left in the hands of the Paramount Chiefs, and its exercise is regulated by customary law as recognized in the Code of Lerotholi;[4] but it is subject to the statutory restriction of Proclamation no. 65 of 1922, that any Concession or grant made by the Paramount Chief is invalid unless approved by the British Government. The Basuto authorities have, however, shown themselves to be very tenacious of their rights over their lands, and the only land grants made are of small plots for Missions, schools, or trading-stands. Such grants are usually restricted as to the right of transfer. There has hitherto been some difficulty in securing even the right of prospecting for minerals;[5] there have been no Concessions of land to mining enterprises.

In Swaziland the position has been complicated by the grant of land Concessions on the widest scale by the Paramount Chiefs ruling between 1878 and 1890; it was, indeed, at one time calculated that they had 'conceded' rights of various kinds over an area exceeding the whole area

---

[1] Native Administration Proclamations no. 11 of 1922 and no. 15 of 1928.
[2] See above, p. 653.   [3] *N.A.*, Part. V, pp. 42 ff.
[4] Ibid. p. 62.   [5] See below, p. 1526.

of the country.[1] When the British Government took over the territory from the Transvaal in 1903 its most immediate concern was the problem thus created. By the Swaziland Crown Lands Order in Council, 1907, and the Concessions Partition Proclamation of the same year, the British Government assumed the right, first, to adjudicate on the validity of Concessions already made, second, to set aside such land as was needed for the exclusive use of the Swazi people, and, third, to treat the remainder as Crown Land available for grants to non-Natives. The legality of these measures was upheld by the Privy Council[2] in a judgement which, though of much general interest, did not deal with the question whether the Chief had the right to make Concessions of tribal land, nor did it discuss whether the Crown was entitled to claim rights over the unalienated land.

The proceedings following on the legislation of 1907 left the total area of Swaziland divided roughly into a Native area of 1,638,000 acres (about one-third of the total area of the territory) and a Crown area of 1,115,000 acres, the rest being in the hands of European Concession holders, who now received freehold title from the Crown. In order to defray the expenditure of the Administration the latter alienated some further part of the Crown area but, at the same time, the Swazi, by a national effort headed by their Regent Paramount, purchased back from European holders certain farm areas held by them. As a result, the position in 1952 stood as follows. About 49 per cent. of the total area of Swaziland was in the possession of Europeans, but this figure included an area of roughly 213,000 acres held by the Colonial Development Corporation for the development of forest and irrigation projects.[3] A little over 50 per cent. was held by the Swazi or was reserved for their exclusive use.[4] This area included a total of 346,000 acres under the Native Land Settlement Scheme, comprising 229,160 acres purchased for the purpose by a grant made under the Colonial Development and Welfare Act, and 134,932 acres set aside for the purpose from lands previously included in the area of Crown Lands. It also comprised certain further purchases made by the Swazi for 'national' purposes. The Crown Lands now stood at only about 1 per cent. of the whole territory.

Money collected by the Swazi for the purchase of lands for national purposes is included in the Lifa Fund, instituted in 1946, of which some account is given in an earlier chapter of the Survey.[5] A considerable part of the alienated land is occupied by Transvaal sheep farmers, whose activities contribute little to the resources of the territory but do consider-

[1] *N.A.*, Part V, pp. 373–5, 414–16.
[2] *Sobhuza II* v. *Miller*, 1926, A.C. 518. *N.A.*, Part V, pp. 379–81.
[3] See below, pp. 940, 981.   [4] *N.A.*, Part V, pp. 374–88, 414–78.
[5] See above, p. 516.

able damage, as the burning of the pasture reduces the 'sponge' on which the water supplies of the country depend.

The position in regard to land in the Bechuanaland Protectorate presents a far simpler picture. In the past the British Government had on at least two occasions disclaimed any desire to use their powers in order to expropriate tribal lands in the interest of European settlement. The first occasion occurred in 1885, at the time of the declaration of the Protectorate, when the Government stated that the waste lands not required by the Chiefs were vested in the Chiefs themselves and not in the Crown. In 1895, when it was proposed to cede the administration of the country to the British South Africa Company, the protests made by the Chiefs related largely to the possibility that the cession would involve a change in African land rights.[1] The Government then contented itself with arranging that the 'Railway Strip' required by the Company should be acquired by it by direct arrangement with the Chiefs concerned.[2] The decision was no doubt made the easier by the fact that, with the exception of a small area on its eastern border, the greater part of the Protectorate was ill-suited for European settlement. Mineral Concessions had, however, already been granted by various Chiefs and control over this process was imposed by the Proclamation of 10 June 1891, which declared that such transactions should be valid only with Government approval. A number of such grants which had been made before 1891 were validated by the Concessions Commission of 1893.

In 1896 it was announced that claims to land made by any tribe would be recognized only if based on occupation which had taken place before the declaration of the Protectorate, or, if subsequent to that date, then with the assent of the High Commissioner. There are now eight delimited tribal areas, officially termed as Tribal Reserves.[3] The Kwena, Tawana, Kgatla, Ngwaketse, and Ngwato Reserves were delimited by proclamation in 1899, and the Malete Reserve similarly in 1909. Lands outside the boundaries of these Reserves were vested in the Crown by Orders in Council of 1904 and 1910. In 1933 the Crown acquired an area of land from the Chartered Company for the creation of the Tlôkwa Reserve. Land for the Tati Reserve was obtained by the Government on lease from the holders of the Tati Concession granted by Lobengula in 1870.[4]

The rights of the Africans in these tribal Reserves have never been expressly defined in legislation, though the Government has consistently maintained that 'all land in Native tribal areas belongs to the Chief and the tribe occupying the areas',[5] and it is clearly the intention that this principle should apply to the Tlôkwa tribe as well as to the tribes which may be said to have had original or inherent rights in the lands of their

[1] *N.A.*, Part V, pp. 191-4, 197-9.   [2] See above, p. 500.   [3] *N.A.*, Part V, p. 151, 235 ff.
[4] Ibid. p. 231.   [5] *Colonial Reports, Bechuanaland, 1927-8*, p. 20.

tribal Reserves. In the case of the Tati Reserve the ultimate right to the land remains with the Tati Company.

The total area of Bechuanaland is 275,000 square miles, now divided as follows: Reserve areas, 102,000 square miles; old alienated areas, 7,500 square miles; Crown Land, 165,500 square miles. The bulk of the Native population is concentrated in the tribal Reserves; the European settlements are largely confined to a narrow strip along the eastern border (including the Tati District), Ghanzi on the western frontier, and the Gaberones and Lobatsi Blocks held by the British South Africa Company. An area of 16,000 square miles (since reduced to 9,000 square miles) in the Chobe area was leased to the Colonial Development Corporation for a ranching project in 1950.

Southern Rhodesia

In Southern Rhodesia the legal position in regard to the rights to be exercised over land received no definite consideration till the period when the British South Africa Company and the British Government were engaged in discussions on the terms on which the charter of the Company should be wound up. The original Concessions given by Lobengula were for mining rights; and in 1888 the agents dispatched by Rhodes had secured the grant (usually known as the Rudd Concession) of all mineral rights. It was this grant which formed the basis on which the Royal Charter was secured for the Company in 1889. In granting the charter, the Crown did not itself assume sovereign rights over lands in the territories included within its scope, but authorized the Company to hold and administer rights obtained under the 1888 agreement or under any subsequent agreements; it was, however, a condition of the validity of such agreements that they should be approved by the Secretary of State. It was provided that in exercising the general powers of administration which the charter conferred, the Company was to have regard to the laws and customs of the people, especially those concerning the holding and disposition of lands. Subject to these conditions the Company could make grants of land or mineral rights either on freehold or on leasehold right.

In 1890 Édouard Lippert secured a Concession from Lobengula empowering the holder to grant, lease, or rent land in his (Lobengula's) name, and this Concession was subsequently acquired by the Chartered Company. In granting mineral rights the Company acted on the strength of the Rudd Concession and they made also considerable grants of land, both to colonists and companies, on the authority which they obtained through the Lippert Concession. In the latter operation their action was subject to some measure of control by the British Government. Thus the Mashonaland Order in Council, 1891, declared that land titles should not be valid without the assent of the High Commissioner, and the concern at the scale on which alienations of land were being made led in 1894 to the appointment of a Land Commission which was directed to assign an adequate area of land to the Natives of Matabeleland. The Southern Rhodesia Order in Council of 1898, which created an administration with legislative capacity, varied the original terms of the Company's charter to the extent of requiring it to assign to Africans an area of land sufficient for their occupation.

The question of the Company's right to dispose of land has an important history. In 1908 settlers' representatives claimed in the Legislative Council that money received from the sale of the land still unallotted should be credited to the budget of the territory and not to the Company. This point became an issue in the discussions regarding the financial adjustments to be made on winding up the charter, and the question of ownership of the land was referred by the Crown to the Judicial Committee of the Privy Council. Its report, delivered on 29 July 1918,[1] stands as one of the classic pronouncements on land rights in British Colonial territories. It is of especial value because the rights of Africans in these lands were made a definite issue. On the other hand, the scope of the report was limited by the fact that it referred only to the unallotted lands. Neither the sale of mineral rights nor the validity of the land titles which had already been given by the Company was in issue.

The Privy Council advised that the Lippert Concession did not convey any authority over the unallotted lands; it conferred only certain rights to act as Lobengula's agent in the disposal of lands, and this right ceased with the conquest of the country in the Matabele campaign of 1893. In the campaign the Company had acted only as agent of the Crown, and sovereign rights thus passed to the Crown by virtue of conquest. The Crown could have exercised its sovereign powers in 1893 to declare itself owner of all lands not held in private right and, had it done so, the question as between the Company and the Crown regarding the unalienated lands could not have arisen.

The Court had, however, still to consider whether such rights as were possessed by the Natives of the country constituted private rights which the Crown could be required to recognize, in view of the acknowledged principle of law regulating the position of the sovereign power towards private rights in conquered territory.[2] The Privy Council found that such rights as the Natives of Southern Rhodesia possessed at the time of conquest could not be described as falling into the category of rights of private property which the sovereign power would be required to recognize; and the unalienated land, which included the Reserves, was, therefore, held to be the property of the Crown. As has been stated above, the mineral

[1] *In re Southern Rhodesia*, 1919, A.C. 211.
[2] See below, p. 731.

rights were not in question. They remained with the Company, and were acquired by the Southern Rhodesian Government for £2 million in 1933.

The establishment of Responsible Government in 1923 would normally have left the new Government with full powers to deal with unalienated lands including the Reserves. But an Order in Council of 1920 had already vested the Reserves in the High Commissioner in South Africa, and section 42 of the Letters Patent of 1923 expressly stated that those lands should not be alienated save for the purposes laid down in the Order of 1920, and then only in exchange for other suitable lands. The provisions of section 26 of the Letters Patent prohibit the local Legislature from altering the terms of section 42, which can be modified or revoked only by Order in Council. An amendment of 1949 to section 26 authorized alterations in the schedule of reserved lands which would have the effect of enlarging their area.

The determination of rights in the land has, therefore, followed the same course as in the Union, in so far that all land has been assumed to be Crown Land until alienated in individual title. In Southern Rhodesia, however, the Charter of 1898, following in this respect the old Cape Colony rule, had stipulated that, outside the Reserves, Africans and Europeans should have equal rights to acquire land.[1] Under this provision Africans had by 1923 purchased about 100,000 acres in the European farming area. This provision was maintained by section 43 of the Letters Patent.

As early as 1894 the Chartered Company had made a rough allocation of the land at its disposal; one purpose of this was to set apart the area required by Natives for their occupation, but the lines of the allocation were ill-considered. The attempt made to confine the African population to two large Reserves was never practicable, and the failure to make suitable provision for their needs is admitted to have been one of the causes of the Matabele rebellion. A further Commission which the Company was required to appoint in 1914 resulted in the creation of 104 Reserves having a total area of some 21,600,000 acres; there was then a population of about 834,000 Africans, of whom some 500,000 were resident in the reserved areas. These were finally gazetted in 1920. Even allowing for the fact that about 3 million acres of this area were not suitable for settlement, the provision was much more generous than that made for Africans in the Union.[2] Before long, however, a reconsideration of the system of allocation was prompted by a demand from settlers for a final separation of the areas available for European and African occupation.

With the assent of the British Government which expressed unwillingness to modify the long-accepted principle of equal rights of purchase, a Commission was appointed in 1925 to consider whether any change was justi-

---

[1] Order in Council, 20 October 1898, section 83.
[2] See above, p. 693.

fied in those provisions of the charter which related to Native lands, with particular reference to the proposal to restrict African purchase to areas set aside for the purpose.

The Commission[1] held that from both the European and the African standpoint it was desirable to separate as far as possible the areas held by the two communities; 'until the Native has advanced much further on the paths of civilization, it is better that the points of contact in this respect between the two races should be reduced'. The detailed proposals made to secure this end seemed to the British Government to justify them in holding that it would be permissible within the terms of the provision made in 1898 to reserve separate areas for purchase by Europeans and Africans respectively. The allocations which had been made in 1914 prevented any such radical readjustment as would effect complete territorial separation and though the Land Apportionment Act of 1930 which gave effect to the Commission's views made provision for some considerable interchange of areas, the lands of the two communities still remain much intermingled. Nor was it possible to form the Reserves into large homogeneous blocks; they are still 83 in number and often divided by European lands.

The main features of the scheme now put into effect were, first, the provision for each community of an area into which it could expand by purchase, while neither could invade the area left for the expansion of the other, and second, the designation of a large 'unassigned' area for allocation at some future date. A total of 49 million acres, including 32,100,000 acres already alienated, was assigned for European occupation. The Native area totalled $28\frac{1}{2}$ million acres, including $7\frac{1}{2}$ million acres scheduled for purchase on individual tenure. The unassigned area was 17,793,000 acres, of which all but 2,300,000 acres were later stated to be deficient in water or infested with tsetse.[2] A number of minor readjustments were made in the next two decades. With regard to the Native Purchase Area it was stated in 1955 that 3,618 farms were occupied, averaging in size 207 acres. Out of £5,581 advanced to African farmers to enable them to purchase, over £2,000 had been repaid. In 1949 an area of approximately 3,257,000 acres was proclaimed under the National Parks Act as the Wankie Game Reserve, but was not formally excised from the unassigned area.[3]

When the original apportionment was made no time limit was set for the movement of Africans from the European area but, when land was alienated for farms, the African occupants were given notice to leave. This process began soon after 1930, but it was only after 1945, when an active settlement policy was instituted, that the removal of Africans began to be regarded as urgent. At the same time the African population was

---

[1] *Report of the Land Commission*, C.S.R.3, 1926, para. 63.
[2] Secretary for Native Affairs in Legislative Assembly, 18 May 1953.
[3] See below, p. 930.

increasing. From 995,000 in 1931 it rose to an estimated 1,684,000 in 1948, when there were 158,000 living on European land and another 112,000 on unalienated land in the European area.

In order to effect the removal of Africans from the areas most urgently required for development, a total of 1,135,930 acres from the European area and 2,205,617 from the Native Purchase Area were transferred in 1950 to the Native area,[1] it being understood that in each case an acreage equivalent to that lost would be provided from the unassigned area. In addition 250,000 acres from the unassigned area were allocated for African occupation. The land so transferred was not classed as Reserve land, but was given a new status as a 'Special Native Area' in which occupation would be dependent on the observance of such farming standards as the Administration should impose. In 1951 a further 367,500 acres were added to the 'Special Native Area' when it was discovered that the spread of tsetse had rendered useless a total of over 1,785,000 acres.

A Select Committee was appointed in 1950 to make the adjustments consequential on the passing of the amended Land Apportionment Act and, having done so, to make a final allocation of all the land in the Colony. It reported in February 1953. It did not, in fact, assign all the land to defined categories, as there was an area of $2\frac{1}{2}$ million acres in the Sebungwe and Wankie districts which had not been fully explored. It proposed to increase the European area by about a million acres above the amount due in compensation, and the 'Special Native Area' by some $6\frac{1}{2}$ million. About a million acres in each category were expected to be irrigated from the projected Kariba Dam.

There followed a prolonged discussion in the Legislature, due partly to the proposal made by the Committee that about half a million acres required for the resettlement of Natives moved from Crown Land should be excised from the Wankie Game Reserve.[2] The final settlement of the question maintained the area of the Game Reserve and reduced the area proposed by the Committee for allocation to Natives. There is reason to doubt whether the arrangement as accepted does actually provide adequate accommodation for the displaced Natives and the question appears likely to be reopened.

There were further differences in the Legislature owing to the proposal to establish Native Purchase Areas in the neighbourhood of industrial centres where Africans might acquire a freehold plot on which to build their own houses. It was urged that this might give occasion to claims by Africans to participate in City and Municipal Councils and might in other ways also create a precedent for the encroachment of Africans into European areas.[3] The discussions showed a certain hardening of the European

---

[1] Land Apportionment Amendment Act no. 25 of 1950.   [2] See below, p. 930.
[3] *Africa Digest*, June 1954, p. 11; December 1954, p. 18.

attitude towards Africans, and revealed a sentiment which by no means accorded with the professed acceptance of the doctrine of 'partnership'.[1] It was stated in these discussions that in the last five years about 64,000 Africans had been moved from Crown Land in European areas to new land but that there remained 47,000 still to be transferred.

The accompanying table shows the distribution of land after the Land Apportionment Acts of 1930 and 1950 (with subsequent adjustments), and gives also the proposals of the Select Committee as amended by the Legislature.

LAND APPORTIONMENT

	1930	1953	Proposal by Select Committee as amended by Parliament
	Acres	Acres	Acres
European Area . . .	49,149,174	47,407,792	48,722,000
Native Reserves . . .	21,127,040	20,859,350	20,737,000
Native Purchase Area . .	7,464,566	5,657,135	8,042,000
Special Native Area . . .	..	4,135,427	7,782,000
⎰ Unassigned Area . . .	17,793,300	17,105,918	5,292,000
⎱ Wankie Game Reserve .	..	*(2,898,000)	2,898,000
Forest Area	590,500	987,745	3,129,000
Undetermined Area . . .	88,540	59,753	60,000
Total Area of Colony . .	96,213,120	96,213,120	96,662,000

* Included in Unassigned Area.

The important changes which will be effected in the usage of the Native Areas by the operation of the Native Land Husbandry Act are discussed in a subsequent section of this chapter.[2]

Northern Rhodesia

In Northern Rhodesia also the history of land rights is bound up with that of the British South Africa Company. In 1890 it obtained from Lewanika, the Paramount Chief of the Barotse, a Concession of mineral and commercial rights and, in 1899, an Order in Council gave the Company statutory powers of administration in the territory west of the Kafue River. In 1900 an agreement known as the 'Barotse Concession' was made[3] by which the Company obtained exclusive mineral and commercial rights over North-Western Rhodesia, excepting the Barotse Valley proper

---

[1] See above, p. 185.   [2] See below, p. 780.
[3] *Rhodesia–Nyasaland Royal Commission Report*, Cmd. 5949, 1939, pp. 6–7 (the Bledisloe Report).

which was reserved from prospecting and alienation. The original Barotse Concession, together with further Concessions made by the Barotse in 1900 and 1909 were affirmed in the agreement of 1923 between the Chartered Company and the United Kingdom Government at the time when the Administration of Northern Rhodesia was transferred to the Crown.[1] In 1953, before the Order in Council establishing the Federation of Rhodesia and Nyasaland, the territory immediately under the Paramount Chief of Barotseland was formally proclaimed as a Protectorate. The provisions of the Concessions were confirmed in the Order in Council establishing the Federation.[2]

After the Charter had been extended to North-Eastern Rhodesia in 1891 the Chartered Company acquired 2,758,000 acres, known as the 'Tanganyika Estate' (in what is now the Northern Province), from the African Lakes Corporation whose title had been confirmed by certificates of claim issued by the Commissioner and Consul-General of British Central Africa. This transaction was recognized by the Northern Rhodesia (Crown Lands and Native Reserves) Order in Council of 1928.[3] The area covered by the Concession was surrendered to the Government in 1938 under covenants whereby 947,500 acres were made a free gift and the balance was acquired by purchase.

In 1891 a Concession of 10,000 square miles, known as the 'Wiese Concession', situated immediately north of the Anglo-Portuguese boundary in North-Eastern Rhodesia, was reported to have been made by Mpezeni, the Paramount Chief of the Ngoni, to a German, Carl Wiese.[4] It was made over to the Mozambique Company, which was under an obligation to form a subsidiary body, the North Charterland Exploration Company, in which the British South Africa Company held a large block of shares. The formation of this Company had the effect of extinguishing any rights held by Carl Wiese.

In 1900 the North-Eastern Rhodesia Order in Council required the British South Africa Company to set aside sufficient land for the occupation of the Native inhabitants suitable for their requirements,[5] and this clause was recapitulated when North-Western and North-Eastern Rhodesia were amalgamated in 1911.[6] The British South Africa Company was thus

---

[1] Agreement between the Secretary of State for the Colonies and the British South Africa Company for the settlement of outstanding questions relating to Southern and Northern Rhodesia, 1923, (3) (G).

[2] Order in Council no. 1199 of 1953, Rhodesia and Nyasaland Federation, Article 33 (2).

[3] Agreement for settlement of outstanding questions, quoted above (3) (D). Northern Rhodesia (Crown Lands and Native Reserves) Order in Council, 1928, 3 (1).

[4] *North Charterland Concession Inquiry, Report to the Governor of Northern Rhodesia by the Commissioner, Mr. Justice Maugham*, Col. no. 73, 1932, Appendix, pp. 6–17.

[5] North-Eastern Rhodesia Order in Council, 1900, Part V, clause 40.

[6] Northern Rhodesia Order in Council, 1911, clause 40.

committed to the obligation to set apart Native Reserves. When the Charter of the Company terminated in 1924, the Colonial Office, in pursuance of these Orders in Council, appointed a Commission to demarcate Native Reserves within the North Charterland Concession. The Northern Rhodesia (Crown Lands and Native Reserves) Order in Council of 1928, to which the North Charterland Exploration Company took strong exception, reaffirmed the right of the Crown to demarcate Native Reserves.[1]

Litigation initiated by the Company followed[2] and in 1932 an Inquiry held before Mr. Justice Maugham (afterwards Lord Maugham) established that, immediately before the transfer of administration from the British South Africa Company to the Crown, the title to the Concession was vested in the North Charterland Exploration Company and that the Crown had the right to set apart Native Reserves without compensation. In 1941 the Government purchased the unalienated portions of the Concession, which embraced 3,800,000 acres. The Crown, therefore, has full control over all unalienated land in Northern Rhodesia, with the exception of Barotseland. The British South Africa Company receives half the proceeds of the sale or lease of land in North-Western Rhodesia until 1965 and has assigned 20 per cent. of the income accruing from royalties to the Government of Northern Rhodesia until 1986, after which date it will surrender them altogether.[3]

The first Native Reserve of 225,400 acres was demarcated in the North Charterland Concession area for the Ngoni tribe in 1904. After 1924 Native Reserves were set aside in all provinces.[4] In 1938 the total area set apart as Native Reserves amounted to 34,532,000 acres; the area of Barotseland, also classed as a Reserve, was then shown as 37 million acres.[5]

The proposal to proclaim the unalienated lands to be Native Trust Land, on the analogy of legislation obtaining in Nyasaland, originated with the Commission appointed in 1938 to inquire into the financial and economic position of the Protectorate.[6] Circumstances such as the occurrence of large mineral deposits demanded some departure from the Nyasaland model, and it was recommended that unalienated areas shown by the Ecological Survey to be unsuited to Native cultivation and areas known to contain workable minerals should be retained as Crown Land. This recommendation was not, however, implemented until 1947[7] when

---

[1] Northern Rhodesia (Crown Lands and Native Reserves) Order in Council, 1928, Preamble (C).

[2] Col. no. 73, 1932, Appendix, p. 163.

[3] *Agreement with the British South Africa Company on the Mineral Rights: Transfer of those Rights to the Northern Rhodesian Government*, Col. no. 272, 1951. See also below, p. 1521.

[4] *Report of the Commission appointed to enquire into the Financial and Economic position of Northern Rhodesia*, Col. no. 145, 1938, pp. 56 ff.

[5] Cmd. 5949, p. 37.

[6] Col. no. 145, 1938, p. 75.

[7] Native Trust Land Ordinance, 1947.

the unalienated land was classified according to these principles. The resulting distribution of land is:[1]

	Square miles
Barotseland	57,364
Other Native Reserves.	54,239
Native Trust Land	159,766
Forest Reserves and Protected areas	1,806
Land alienated to Europeans (Freehold and Leasehold)	7,258
Township areas	319
Unalienated Crown Land (Railway Belt, Abercorn, Fort Jameson, and Mkushi)	7,377
	288,129

The clause introduced into the Charter of the British South Africa Company providing for the right of Africans to acquire land on the same terms as Europeans was retained in the 1947 Order in Council.

Some apprehension has been expressed in the African Representative Council regarding the power vested in the Government to alienate Native Trust Land and a demand has been made that these lands should be safeguarded in the same way as the Reserves. The claim thus put forward is based on the fact that the Native Trust Land Order in Council, 1947, contains the proviso that 'the Governor may, when it appears to him to be in the general interests of the community as a whole, grant rights of occupancy to Natives and non-Natives, after consultations with the Native Authority'.[2]

In some measure the apprehensions expressed seem to be due to fear lest European interests within the Federation may exercise, over land policy, an influence opposed to the interests of the African community. The establishment of the Federation has not, however, modified the position in regard to the control of the lands in Northern Rhodesia. The Administration is, in this respect, subject to the control of the Secretary of State for the Colonies and any legislation on the subject of land is explicitly reserved to the Territorial Legislature. The Federal Government cannot acquire land, except for public purposes.[3] The first occasion for the exercise of this power in respect of Northern Rhodesia appears to be in connexion with the riparian land at the Kariba Gorge, to which reference is made in Part II of this chapter.[4]

Nyasaland

In Nyasaland climatic and other conditions seemed at one time to point to the country as a suitable area for European settlement and, about 1884, both companies and individuals began to acquire land by purchase

---

[1] *An Economic Survey of the Colonial Territories*, Col. no. 281, vol. i, 1952, p. 7.
[2] *Central African Territories: Comparative Survey of Native Policy*, Cmd. 8235, 1951, p. 14.
[3] The Federation of Rhodesia and Nyasaland (Constitution) Order in Council no. 1199 of 1953, Article 33.   [4] See below, p. 781.

from local Chiefs. Some of the Concessions were of considerable extent; that held by the British South Africa Company, for instance, included a large part of the present Northern Province, and there were others of very considerable size. When a Protectorate was declared in 1891 the Crown took power to regularize these transactions, issuing 'certificates of claim' to those who could prove lengthy occupation together with development of the land or authentic purchase from recognized Chiefs on reasonable terms. It was, however, a usual condition that such titles were held subject to the rights of the African inhabitants living in the alienated areas.[1] The Concessions covered over 15 per cent. of the total area of the Protectorate and their validity has been vigorously contested by the successors of the Chiefs who made them.[2] Sir Harry Johnston, when issuing the certificates of claim,[3] admitted that it was doubtful if the Chiefs could be said to have power to alienate tribal lands.

When the claims to title had been settled, agreements were made by the Administration with all the Chiefs in the Protectorate, securing the control over the remaining lands, henceforth known as Crown Lands, and withdrawing from the Chiefs the power of further alienation. The area in which claims were held to be good and for which certificates were granted stood originally at nearly $3\frac{3}{4}$ million acres, including the British South Africa Freehold of $2\frac{3}{4}$ million acres in the Northern Province. Subsequent acquisitions by the Government, fresh alienations in the southern districts, and the withdrawal of the British South Africa Company from its surface rights in northern Nyasa, in substitution for mineral rights, have now left a total of 1,003,219 acres alienated, or approximately 5 per cent. of the area of the territory. Of the alienated area 72·3 per cent. is in the hands of eleven large estate-holders.

Certain further alienations were made by the Crown in the southern districts under the terms of Ordinance no. 18 of 1912, though the area involved was small in comparison with that held under the certificates of claim. The presence on the alienated estates of large numbers of African residents created a problem similar to that which, as has just been seen, had arisen also in regard to the Chartered Company's lands in Northern Rhodesia. Some of the estate-holders in the Nyasaland highlands claimed that as successors to the African Chiefs they had the right to demand the customary compulsory labour both from the original tenants and from later immigrants from Portuguese territory. The latter category, it may be noted, amounted in 1945 to 18·6 per cent. of the African population of the Southern Province.[4] The situation was reported on by a local

---

[1] *Nyasaland Protectorate, Report of a Commission to enquire into and report upon Certain Matters connected with the Occupation of Land in the Nyasaland Protectorate*, Zomba, 1921.

[2] *Report of the East Africa Commission*, Cmd. 2387, 1925.

[3] H. H. Johnston, *British Central Africa*, 1897, p. 113.

[4] *N.A.*, Part II, pp. 25, 48–50.

Commission in 1921.[1] This body was opposed to the delimitation of European and African areas on the lines which have been followed elsewhere in pursuance of the Native Reserve policy; it held that any restriction of the land in African occupation would seriously prejudice the welfare of communities who are obliged, owing to shortage of water and other local circumstances, to live in scattered villages. It preferred to recommend the assignment of limited areas for European settlement, after the fullest provision had been made for Africans.

The East Africa Commission of 1924–5[2] suggested that blocks of the alienated estates should be redeemed by the Government from a fund formed by a tax on freeholds. Impressed, as it had also been in Kenya, with the feeling of insecurity among Africans regarding the tenure of their lands, it recommended the constitution of a Native Lands Trust Board, and an Ordinance for this purpose was enacted in 1927. At the same time certain areas were gazetted as 'Crown Lands required for the settlement of Natives', and excluded from alienation under the authority of the Ordinance of 1912. It would seem, however, that policy was as yet undecided, for opinions continued to be expressed against the Reserve system, towards which the proceedings of 1926–7 seemed to tend.

A solution was ultimately found which seems to have been inspired by the policy of Nigeria or Tanganyika rather than by the principle of segregation favoured farther south. A Native Trust Land Order in Council of 1936 divided the territory into Crown Lands (limited to those acquired for strictly public purposes), Reserved lands (that is, lands included in townships, forest Reserves, and lands already alienated), and Native Trust land, which included the great bulk of what was previously classed as Crown Land.

The Native Trust lands are vested in the Secretary of State 'to be administered for the benefit of the Native inhabitants'. With no intention of subordinating the interests of the African majority to those of the European minority, it was nevertheless felt that a certain amount of European development benefited the African population and the law made provision for alienations for this purpose, to be made after consulting Native Authorities and limited to leases of 99 years. The policy embodied in the law was clearly one to which the reduction in the demand for land by Europeans, due to the depression in world prices, had largely contributed.[3]

There remained, however, the problem of the rights of Africans on alienated lands. This arose mainly in the Blantyre and Zomba Districts. In 1921 half the population of the former and one-quarter of that of the

---

[1] *Report of a Commission on the Occupation of Land*, 1921, p. 5. See also R. L. Buell, *The Native Problem in Africa*, vol. i, 1928, pp. 249 ff. C. K. Meek, *Land Law and Custom in the Colonies*, 1946, pp. 115–59.

[2] Cmd. 2387, p. 110.   [3] *N.A.*, Part II, p. 18.

latter were living on European-owned estates, and a system known as *thangata*[1] prevailed whereby the African tenant worked for the landowner or grew crops over which the landowner had a right of purchase, instead of paying a cash rent. Under the terms of the certificates of claim, villages which existed when the title was granted could not be required to move; but difficulties arose both in deciding which were the villages to which these rights applied and in defining the terms on which residents were entitled to cultivate land for their own subsistence. At an earlier stage landlords had pressed for the payment of rent though, in a decision in 1903,[2] the High Court decided that rent could not legally be exacted from original residents, and the Chilembwe rising of 1915 was held to be partly due to the levy of rent on their lands.[3]

As tobacco cultivation extended, the position of the landlords changed. They now preferred to obtain labour from the resident 'rightholders' rather than to receive rent. Legislation passed in 1904 and again in 1917[4] did not seem to supply a remedy, and the Land Commission of 1921 and the East Africa Commission of 1924–5 both made recommendations on the subject. Fresh efforts were made to find a solution in the Natives on Private Estates Ordinance of 1928, a complicated measure which in effect embodied the *thangata* system. It gave the African tenant on European lands the right to work for wages in abatement of rent or, if work were not available, to receive facilities for growing economic crops, of which the estate-holder had to purchase sufficient at current market prices to entitle the tenant to a rebate of rent.

Tenants could be evicted from land required by the owner, but only at intervals of five years and only if alternative land were available. In the period of depression after 1930 there were few evictions but, when agricultural prices rose during the Second World War, estate owners were anxious to develop their lands, and in 1943 notice was served on a large number of Africans. Large numbers of these, however, refused to leave.

An Inquiry conducted in 1946 by Sir Sidney Abrahams held that the existing legislation was too complicated to be operated effectively by either landlords or tenants.[5] The tenants complained that it was applied unfairly, the landlords that African farming practices were destroying the land. The report recommended that land preferably already under African occupation should be purchased by the Government and reserved for controlled settlement by Africans. Where this was not practicable African residents should be given the option of leaving the European estates or of remaining as labour tenants.

---

[1] The spelling *tangata* is also in use.
[2] *The Supervisor of Native Affairs* v. *The Blantyre and East Africa Company*.
[3] Buell, op. cit. vol. i, pp. 247–9.
[4] Lands Ordinance (Native Locations), 1904. Native Rents (Private Estates) Ordinance, 1917.   [5] *Land Commission, 1946, Report by The Rt. Hon. Sir Sidney Abrahams.*

The legal position was redefined by the Africans on Private Estates Ordinance no. 8 of 1952. This makes the right of Africans to reside on alienated land dependent on the consent of the owner and so extinguishes any claims that might be based on descent from the original occupants. 'Resident Africans' are liable to pay a standard rent, but if they are not offered work in lieu or in abatement, they pay only two-thirds of this amount; an additional one-third must be paid by or on behalf of unmarried women or plural wives. They are entitled to land for subsistence crops, but may not grow cash crops without the owner's consent. They may be moved from one part of an estate to another but must be compensated for disturbance. They may not be evicted without an order from an Arbitration Board which is to include three Africans appointed by the Governor. The grounds for eviction are defined in the law.

The cause of the tenants has been actively supported by the Nyasaland African Congress and the campaign initiated in their favour led to widespread disturbances in the Cholo district in 1953. In 1954 the Congress claimed that all land for which no documentary proof of sale could be produced should be 'returned to the original inhabitants as African Trust Land for occupation by Africans' and that no further alienations be made.[1]

It was announced in 1954 that the Government considered that the *thangata* system should be brought to an end and that steps were being taken to acquire land for the resettlement of *thangata* tenants.[2] An area of nearly 300,000 acres in the Cholo district had been acquired by agreement with the owners in 1952. In 1954 it was stated that 100,000 acres were under estate crops, 500,000 acres were leased to Africans, and 887,000 acres were held by Africans under the *thangata* system of labour rents. In 1955 an area of 48,000 acres in the Southern Province was acquired from the British Central Africa Company by the Nyasaland Government.[3] Part of the land acquired is to be devoted to the residential settlement of industrial workers but about two-thirds is suitable for agricultural settlement.[4] In the Northern Province 52,000 acres were acquired in 1955 from the Church of Scotland Mission and added to the African Trust Land. The terms of the resettlement of *thangata* tenants have not been finally decided, but it is stated that land will be held on conditions of good husbandry.

Kenya

The history of land rights in Kenya has its origin in the days when the Imperial British East Africa Company, which received its charter in 1888, was extending its hold over the mainland on the strength of the grant

[1] *Africa Digest*, May 1954, p. 2.
[2] Ibid. July–August 1954, p. 10. H.C. Deb., 24 May 1954, col. 26.
[3] *The Times*, 13 August 1955.   [4] *Colonial Reports, Nyasaland, 1954*, p. 14.

obtained during the previous year from the Sultan of Zanzibar. The Company's charter was in all material points in the same terms as that granted to the British South Africa Company. Settlers had already acquired some lands either by purchase from Chiefs or from the British East Africa Company before the East Africa Protectorate was declared in 1895, in which year also the charter of the Company was terminated.

There had been at a previous period much discussion in Great Britain as to the nature of the rights over land which the Crown could assume, in virtue of the general provisions of the Foreign Jurisdiction Act, following on the declaration of a Protectorate.[1] In 1899, however, the British Government accepted the view of its legal advisers that the declaration of a Protectorate enabled the Crown to claim sovereign rights over land, subject to the recognition of any private rights then existing; in general terms, this was considered to give the right to dispose of 'unoccupied' lands. It was clear from the first that the Government had been anxious to avoid encroachment on Native lands. All the available evidence tended, however, to show that there were very large areas which were not in any kind of Native occupation. Travellers had joined in commenting on the great untenanted spaces through which they had passed; as the East Africa Royal Commission (1953–5) points out, the prevailing belief was that 'there was land and to spare for all'.[2]

Regulations had been issued in 1897 which provided that a certificate might be given for the occupation of land up to a maximum period of 21 years, but further stipulated that a certificate would not be granted in respect of any land cultivated or regularly used by any Native or Native tribe. These regulations were in terms similar to those issued in Uganda[3] and were intended to meet the same situation; it should be realized that what is now the Nyanza Province and the greater part of the present Turkana District were at that period included in Uganda.

Fortified by the legal advice of 1899 the Government was now able to plan the introduction of European settlement under conditions more suited to local circumstances, though it was intended to defer the allotment of land on any large scale until the railway to Uganda, which was sanctioned in 1895, had been completed. The railway was ready for traffic in 1901. It at once created a new problem for the Administration, for the maintenance of a line running along difficult gradients through 580 miles of empty country put a severe strain on the resources of the Protectorate.[4] It was this, combined with a growing feeling that the Highlands of Kenya were (as Lord Lugard had represented as far back as 1893)[5]

---

[1] For the Foreign Jurisdiction Act, see above, pp. 285 ff.   [2] Cmd. 9475, p. 19.
[3] See below, p. 724.   [4] See below, p. 1556.
[5] F. D. Lugard, *The Rise of our East African Empire*, vol. ii, 1893, p. 656. See also H. H. Johnston, *The Uganda Protectorate*, vol. i, 1902, p. 299.

well suited for European settlement, that induced the British Government to endorse the policy of European settlement put forward in 1901 by the then High Commissioner, Sir Charles Eliot.[1]

The great pasture lands of the high plateau of Kenya appeared to be almost free of inhabitants, for the predatory raids of the semi-nomad Masai had kept most of them free from occupation for agricultural purposes. The Kikuyu, then and for many years afterwards mainly a forest people, had been largely pinned down to the wooded slopes of the Highlands.[2] But when the prospect of European occupation first presented itself, the Masai no longer appeared to constitute the same danger; the great cattle epidemics of 1883 and 1889 and a very severe epidemic of smallpox had reduced them to a condition which prevented them from being the obstacle they had once seemed to present.[3]

There was a further reason for giving support to the policy of European settlement. The British Government desired to anticipate the possibility of Indian settlement on the vacant lands opened up by the railway, in the construction of which Indians had taken so considerable a part. The growing immigration from Asia was already forcing itself on the attention of the Administration.[4] It is well to emphasize here that the schemes of settlement then contemplated affected only the Highland areas, roughly about one-thirteenth of the whole territory of the Colony. The most crucial aspect of the land problem is confined to this region and its neighbourhood. The rest of the country has been affected only in a very minor degree.

The need for a more definite control over land for the purpose of colonization was met by the issue of the East Africa (Lands) Order in Council of 1901. This measure proceeded on the assumption that land required for disposal must first be brought into the category of Crown property, and it proceeded to characterize as Crown property all 'public lands' which for the time being were subject to the control of the Crown. The terms used were unfortunately vague. In the use of the strange and inappropriate term 'public' as applied to land, the Order in Council seems to have referred by implication to those unoccupied lands over which it was now accepted that the Protectorate had powers of control. The Order in Council failed to add such provisions as would have guided the Administration in the interpretation to be placed on the extent of its authority over 'occupied' or 'unoccupied' lands.

The terms on which 'Crown Lands' could be granted were laid down in the East Africa Order in Council, 1902, followed by the Crown Lands

---

[1] *Report on the East Africa Protectorate*, Cd 1626, 1903, pp. 18–30.

[2] P. Mitchell, in *Africa Today*, 1955, p. 486.

[3] L. S. B. Leakey, *Mau Mau and the Kikuyu*, 1952, p. 9.

[4] Cmd. 9475, pp. 18–19. For the subsequent history of Indian protests against their exclusion from the area reserved for Europeans, see above, pp. 406 ff.

Ordinance of that year, which made, however, no further definition of the 'Crown Lands' in question. There has been some tendency to hold that the intransigence of the European settlers was responsible for the fact that the subsequent history of colonization in Kenya was marked by an increasing series of difficulties between the Administration, the European community, and the Natives. The responsibility for these incidents rests, however, primarily with the British Government. It proved itself to be unable to plan ahead for the control of the operations involved in the policy of colonization, or to take a firm stand on the decisions at which it arrived.

The Ordinance of 1902 was intended to offer terms more attractive to settlers than those of the Regulation of 1897. The sale as well as the lease of Crown Lands was allowed and provision was now made for the grant of areas up to 640 acres. The Ordinance took, however, the precaution of repeating the condition made in 1897, namely, that 'in all dealings with Crown Land, regard shall be had to the rights and requirements of the Natives and, in particular, the Commissioner shall not sell or lease any land in the actual occupation of the Natives'. Though he could grant leases of land containing African villages, land in occupation by Africans was deemed to be excluded from the lease so long as actually occupied. The land grants increased rapidly in 1903 and it soon appeared that the Administration had underestimated the extent to which Africans could assert claims to the apparently empty lands of the Highland area. It was at all events clear that, by recognizing only agricultural cultivation as constituting occupation, Europeans were being permitted to acquire land in a manner that caused hardship to the tribes concerned in pastoral husbandry. To quote an expression subsequently used, the process of alienation 'got out of hand'.

A local Committee appointed in 1904 recommended that, in view of the difficulties arising from the dispossession of Africans, the establishment of Reserves for them should precede the further opening up of the country for European settlement. It suggested in effect that there should be Reserves both for Europeans and Africans.[1] Though, however, various areas were soon afterwards indicated as reserved for Native occupation and were so proclaimed, the limits set were not strictly observed in practice. There were constant complaints of refusal to allow Native cattle-owners access to their pasture lands, and in certain cases 'proclaimed' lands were actually alienated.[2] Administrative officers of the period clearly knew too little about the circumstances in which land was used by the Native population, nor were they strong enough at the time to resist the demands for conveniently situated lands which were made by European settlers. Had the limits proposed for European occupation been clearly indicated from

---

[1] Cmd. 9475, p. 19.   [2] L. P. Mair, *Native Policies in Africa*, 1936, p. 82.

the first, much of the trouble which arose both then and afterwards might
have been avoided.

An incident which arose in connexion with lands allotted to the Masai
directed public attention to the insecurity of tenure in the 'proclaimed'
areas. An agreement was made with the Masai in 1904 regarding the lands
they were to occupy but, as it was subsequently desired to move them
from part of this area (the Laikipia), a fresh agreement was made in 1911.
In 1912 dissatisfaction with the transfer resulted in an action being brought
against the Government by a section of the tribe; its main purpose, however, was not to contest the right assumed by the Crown over land, but
to prove that the 1911 agreement was improperly obtained. It was decided by the East Africa Court of Appeal on the technical point of jurisdiction. The Court held that the agreement was not a contract but a
treaty and that treaties entered into by foreign subjects (the technical
status which the Masai then held as residents in a Protectorate) were not
cognizable in municipal courts.[1]

The action of the Government in disposing of lands was now coming
under attack from two different points of view. Those interested in advancing the programme of colonization held that the conditions prescribed
in the Order in Council of 1902 impeded the development of the country.
The Colonial Office was, on the other hand, becoming impressed with
the need for preventing land speculation and the accumulation of large
areas not subject to stipulations regarding their beneficial use.[2] The controversy turned mainly on the terms on which leases were granted; the
local Land Board (which had been constituted in 1904) demanded perpetual leases without reassessment of rent; the Colonial Office, which had
at first stipulated for 21-year leases, subsequently agreed to a term of
99 years with periodical revision of rents. But there was growing pressure
by the settlers and, in 1915, the Colonial Office yielded to it and agreed
to increase the period of lease to 999 years. It also agreed to extend the
control of the Governor to cover transfers between members of different
races, a measure designed to prevent the sale of land to Asians. The history
of the measures taken to exclude Asians from acquiring possession of lands
in the Highlands has already been told in a preceding chapter.[3]

The second line of attack came from other quarters which were increasingly impressed with the need for protecting Native interests. They
pointed out that the declarations reserving lands for Native occupation
had so far received no statutory recognition and that Natives had in fact
no real security of tenure. The Crown Lands Ordinance of 1915 was
designed to meet this point also. It sought to effect its purpose by declaring

[1] *Ol Le Njogo* v. *The Attorney-General*, E.A.L.R., vol. v, 1913, p. 70.
[2] *Tenure of Land in the East Africa Protectorate*, Cd. 4117, 1908, p. 30.
[3] See above, p. 406.

that Crown Lands were to be held to include 'all lands reserved for the use of any Native tribe', and this provision would not have been open to objection had the Administration been able to treat the reserved areas as inviolable. But the settlers had never accepted the previous regulations as finally debarring Europeans from obtaining grants in the reserved areas, and it is clear that in one area at least (that reserved for the Lumbwa) lands were subsequently alienated for the settlement of ex-soldiers.

So far the boundaries of the reserved areas had never been formally gazetted. Official circles, however, now showed a growing recognition of the undesirability of a position which left the Administration itself with no statutory provision on which it could rely in withstanding the pressure of those who sought to extend the area of European settlement. A Land Tenure Commission of 1920 admitted that the allocation of the lands reserved for Native occupation had followed no fixed principle and advocated a formal delimitation, with the further suggestion that this should now be made on a basis which would provide Africans with sufficient land also for the next generation.

The position of the land in Native occupation again came under discussion in the Courts in 1921. In a case between two Kikuyu, one of whom claimed to have acquired land in individual tenure by purchase from a member of another tribe, it was held that all private rights had disappeared by virtue of the Declaration of 1915. The Court added that the legal position of the Native in the Reserves was that of a tenant-at-will of the Crown, an unfortunate instance of the application of terms of English law to a situation which had no real parallel with that law.[1] Whatever the legal propriety of the language used, it added to the prevailing sense of insecurity with regard to the rights by which Natives held their lands. It served to throw into clearer relief a situation which should never have arisen had the Colonial Office been better equipped for dealing with issues so vital as those of land policy.

There were no alienations of any considerable extent after 1919, but the feeling of insecurity among Africans regarding their rights in their lands impressed the East Africa Commission of 1924–5 and, as a result of its recommendations,[2] the Reserves were formally gazetted in 1926. In 1929 the Commission on Closer Union in East Africa[3] urged the necessity for giving Africans some effective guarantee of the security of their tenure of the Reserves. A draft Ordinance of 1928 had proposed to create a local Lands Trust Board in which the Reserves should be vested, but this was now felt to be inadequate. In a revised Ordinance which was issued in 1930 the Reserves were declared to be 'set aside for the benefit of the Native tribes for ever' and were placed under a Native Lands Trust Board,

---

[1] *Gathomo* v. *Indangara*, E.A.L.R., 129, 1920.
[2] Cmd. 2387.
[3] Cmd. 3234, pp. 43–44.

which consisted of Government officials, with two unofficial members of the Legislative Council, one of whom would represent African interests.

The question of the sufficiency of the area in the Reserves had hitherto been in some measure subordinated to the question of the security of their tenure. The Joint Select Committee of Parliament, which dealt with the Report of the Commission on Closer Union, required in 1931 that an authoritative Inquiry should now be made, not only into the adequacy of the security afforded by the Lands Trust Ordinance of 1930, but into the present and prospective needs of Africans in the matter of land. The Commission which undertook the Inquiry was also to be assigned the task of delimiting the area in which the European was to enjoy a privileged position.

The Land Commission appointed in 1933 to carry out this recommendation was presided over by Sir Morris Carter. Its Report, issued in 1934, made an important contribution to the study of the land question in Kenya,[1] but, before proceeding to discuss its terms, it is proper to point to certain limitations which affected the character of its recommendations. As has subsequently been pointed out, it did not consider the requirements of the population as a whole. It considered primarily the needs of tribes which had directly or indirectly been affected by European settlement. The issues which it was charged to consider arose mainly from the claim that the Concessions made to European settlers had trespassed on areas which were by rights 'tribal' property and had indeed been in some cases declared as such.[2]

As the position stood when the Commission began its sittings, the area set apart for European settlement was about 16,000 square miles, while that of the Native Reserves was roughly 43,000 square miles. The whole area of the Colony is roughly 224,960 square miles. The Commission made a conscientious and painstaking investigation of the extent to which alienation had affected the area of the tribal lands. As a result, it proposed an addition to the existing Native Reserves of 2,629 square miles, of which 1,474 were allotted in satisfaction of claims of right, 896 on grounds of economic need, and 259 as temporary Reserves to be held on lease terminable by the Government. An area of 939 square miles was also allocated for leasing by Africans on individual tenure. The total area specifically reserved for African occupation was thus about 50,000 square miles.

The Commission had, in addition, been required to define the limits of the Highlands in which Europeans 'were to have a privileged position in accordance with the White Paper of 1923'.[3] It recommended the demarcation of certain boundary lines to embrace an area of 16,700 square miles, of which, however, 3,950 square miles were Forest Reserve. In order to

---

[1] *Report of the Kenya Land Commission*, Cmd. 4556, 1934.
[2] Cmd. 9475, pp. 53 ff.
[3] See above, pp. 190, 407.

provide the European community with a guarantee that the area would
not be invaded by non-Europeans, it proposed that the boundaries should
be laid down by Order in Council, which, as has been pointed out, would
carry the same validity as an Act of Parliament.[1]

There has been much criticism both by the African and the European
communities of the conclusions of the Commission regarding the extent
to which tribal lands had been affected by the reservation of the White
Highlands for use by Europeans. Subsequent examination of the question
has, however, done little to modify the picture presented by their report.
Alienation was shown to have affected directly only a relatively small part
of the country actually lying within the tribal boundaries. The Kikuyu,
for example, who have been most vocal in complaints of the loss of tribal
territory, were shown by the Commission to have lost not more than
106¾ square miles allotted to settlers.[2] On the other hand, the reservation
of the White Highlands for Europeans prevented the process of expansion
by which the more populous tribes would normally have found relief from
congestion. One may readily presume, for instance, that the Kikuyu,
whose rate of increase has been exceptional, would certainly have over-
flowed into the lands made available to them by the decline in the strength
of the Masai, had not European colonization supervened at the moment
when the Masai were at their weakest.

In dealing with the area reserved for European occupation, the Land
Commission appears to have proceeded on the assumption that the occupation of the White Highlands by Europeans was an accepted principle
and that the only question at issue was one of boundaries. At the time
when the Commission reported the area actually held in European
occupation was 10,345 square miles, of which 11·8 per cent. was cultivated, 40·7 per cent. used for stock, 20 per cent. occupied by Native
squatters, and 27·5 per cent. not in use. The margin between the 16,700
square miles which were eventually defined by the Commission as reserved for European occupation and that already beneficially occupied
by settlers was therefore considerable, even allowing for the fact that a
portion of the unalienated land is designed as a Forest Reserve.

In approaching the problem of the security of tenure of the tribal Reserves, the Commission was at an early stage faced with the trouble arising
from the appropriation of the land required for the development of the
Kakamega Gold Mine in the well-populated Kavirondo Reserve. The
area involved was small, but the action taken by the Administration
under the Native Land Trust Ordinance of 1930, followed by the issue
of an amending Ordinance in 1932,[3] gave rise to a controversy which
reflected the importance of the principle involved rather than the extent

---

[1] See above, p. 286.   [2] P. Mitchell, in *Africa Today*, 1955, p. 485.
[3] Native Lands Trust Amendment Ordinance, 1932.

of the disturbance caused to the land rights of the Kavirondo.[1] The facts
at issue in the case are now of small importance, but they had a considerable influence on the recommendations eventually made by the Commission for giving the tribes concerned a firmer guarantee for the preservation
of their rights over the lands in the Reserves.

The Commission recommended that lands gazetted as Reserves should
be termed 'Native', not 'Crown' Lands and should be expressly declared
to be held in accordance with Native custom. They should be vested in
a Native Lands Trust Board which had no administrative but only protective functions; it should not therefore contain officials.[2] It considered
that the enactment of the necessary regulations for the creation of a Native
Lands Trust by an Order in Council would afford a greater guarantee
than the passing of an Ordinance by the local Legislature. It further
recommended that local questions regarding the Reserve lands should be
dealt with in the first instance by local Land Boards consisting of Africans
with the District Officer as president. As regards the grant of leases in the
Native Reserves, the Commission considered that any lease exceeding ten
acres should be approved by the Trust Board, after consulting the local
Land Boards; in the proposed Native Leasehold areas leases should be
allowed to non-Natives for any purpose which would assist Native development.[3]

When land was needed for public purposes, or for mining, or industrial
requirements, the Commission advised that the usual procedure should
not take the form of excluding the area from the Reserve, but that it
should be 'set apart' and an annual payment for it made to the Local
Native Council. The Lands Trust Board would have power to veto any
proposal to 'set apart' an area over ten acres. Exclusion of the area from
the Reserve would remain a possibility, but should be resorted to only if,
in the opinion of the Governor, it was essential in the public interest.

The main recommendations of the Commission were implemented by
Orders in Council of 1938-9,[4] except as regards the composition of the
Native Lands Trust Board. This now consists of unofficials, but sits with
the Chief Native Commissioner as president. The Native Lands Trust
Ordinance defines as Native lands the original Reserves with such modifications of their boundaries as the Commission had recommended in
satisfaction of claims of right. Nine 'Land Units' were formed by the
amalgamation of existing Reserves and allocated to the principal tribes;
the term 'Reserve' is now applied only to the land which was allocated to the
African area on grounds of economic need and to the communal Reserves

---

[1] Mair, op. cit. p. 86.   [2] Cmd. 4556, paras. 1693, 1793, 1817.
[3] Ibid. paras. 1467, 1541.
[4] Kenya (Highlands) Order in Council, 1939; Kenya (Native Areas) Order in Council, 1939;
Crown Lands (Amendment) Ordinance no. 27 of 1938; Native Lands Trust Ordinance no. 28
of 1938. See also N.A., Part I, p. 189.

allocated on the coast to Arabs and Africans jointly. The Ordinance authorizes the forfeiture of land for treason or rebellion.

The Crown Lands (Amendment) Ordinance covers the Native Reserves, as the term is now used, temporary Native Reserves, and Native Leasehold areas. It empowers the Governor to set aside additional areas of Crown Land for Reserves. It also defines the boundaries of the Northern Frontier and Turkana Districts, which are not included within the scheduled Native Lands and Reserves, but are defined as areas wherein the African tribes at present residing there 'shall have a prior interest'. The Highlands Order in Council provided for the creation of a Board to advise the Governor on matters relating to land in the Highlands. This Board was constituted by the Land Control Ordinance (no. 22) of 1944. All transactions in land must have its approval and, when giving its consent to a transfer, it may require the new holder to effect specified improvements.

The Commission recognized that, among the Africans living on European farms, there were some who had been in occupation long before the land was alienated, but it considered that it was in the general interest that their rights should be expunged and other land be found for them, within the African area. Provision was made for this in 1940. A more intractable problem is created by the residence in the White Highland area of African farm labourers who can claim no rights there, the class locally known as 'squatters'.[1] In 1948 there were 149,351 Africans on European farms and 32,452 in the Forest Reserve; the majority of these (114,505) were Kikuyu. It has been estimated that the area occupied by them for cultivation and grazing is nearly 1 million acres.[2] As regards the farms, the Resident Natives Ordinance of 1918 made it illegal for an African to live on a farm unless he and every adult male member of his family is bound by a contract to work for the owner for not less than 180 days in the year; contracts must be for not more than three years. A revised Ordinance (no. 30 of 1937) with amendments (nos. 18 of 1939 and 38 of 1941) required the employer to pay a stipulated wage and to provide land for the cultivation of food crops and grazing for a specified number of cattle.[3]

These latter details are fixed for different areas by the District Councils, which consist of representatives of local European residents.[4] The details of the regulations made by the Councils vary widely,[5] but in general they represent the prevailing feeling among European settlers against what in the Union of South Africa would be termed 'Kaffir farming'. There has been a tendency to increase the number of working days required and to

[1] Ibid. 'The Squatter Problem', pp. 198–202.
[2] P. Mitchell, *The Agrarian Problem in Kenya*, 1947, p. 20.   [3] Meek, op. cit. pp. 82–84.
[4] For the District (now County) Councils, see above, p. 449.   [5] Cmd. 9475, pp. 162–72.

reduce the permissible acreage for cultivation and also the number of stock. A Government Order of 1952 limited to two acres the area of land which an individual might be allowed to cultivate. The general feeling among the settler community is against the admission of any more 'squatters', and there has lately been a demand for the removal of all African-owned stock. But the future of the 'squatter' continues to constitute an issue for which the uncoordinated efforts of the District Councils can provide no solution. The problem of the provision of labour for the European farms is deep-seated and its solution requires a broader approach.

In 1945 the Government expressed the opinion that the resident labourers 'must now be regarded as having become a permanent and indispensable part of the population of the Highlands'.[1] The East Africa Royal Commission of 1953–5 has recommended that the existing 'farming-contract' system of obtaining resident farm labour be ended, and that Government should acquire land for Rural Labourers' Villages. This would make it possible for farm workers to rent plots on which they could erect their own houses and cultivate 'allotments' for the subsistence of their families.[2] There would thus be created the basis of a permanent force of agricultural labourers, looking to this type of employment as its main source of livelihood. The labour would be free in the sense that it would not be bound by contract. Official agencies in Kenya had previously put forward a somewhat similar programme for dealing with the problem of labour on European farms.[3]

A Bill to make further provision for European agricultural settlement in the White Highlands passed its first reading in the summer of 1955. An important provision transfers from the Minister of Agriculture to the European Agricultural Settlement Board land which is subject to settlement and the granting of titles. The Board thus acts as the agent for the Government Departments concerned.[4]

One chapter in the contentious history of land policy in Kenya has closed with the legislation which has given to Europeans in the Highlands and to Africans in the Native Land Units a guarantee against the reduction of the areas assigned to them. It remains to be seen how far a new chapter will be opened as the result of the Report of the East Africa Royal Commission 1953–5.[5] The Kenya Government has published its views regarding three recommendations which bear directly on the matters discussed in the preceding paragraphs, namely, the proposals for the general extension of the principle of individual ownership, the registration of titles, and the removal of restrictions on the transfer of landholdings as between members of different communities. On the first two points it has

---

[1] *Land Utilization and Settlement*, Sessional Paper no. 8 of 1945.
[2] Cmd. 9475, p. 169.   [3] *N.A.*, Part I, pp. 200–1.
[4] *Africa Digest*, July–August 1955, p. 4.   [5] Cmd. 9475, 1955, pp. 346 ff.

expressed a qualified approval. The third, however, raises a point which is likely to be contentious. The Government is in favour of retaining the right now vested in the Governor of controlling transfers of the Highland lands held by Europeans. As regards African lands it would not go farther than to allow the grant of leaseholds.[1] The subject will be further discussed in Part II of this chapter.[2]

Uganda

The question of land rights in Uganda has not been influenced to the same extent as in Kenya by a policy of colonization, though the country was originally regarded as well suited for European enterprise.[3] But the early treatment of the land question is of interest, since it reveals the gradual steps by which the British Government came to a definite view as to its legal powers over land in areas held under a Protectorate. The agreement made by the British East Africa Company with the Kabaka of Buganda in 1892 bound the latter not to alienate rights over land to Europeans without its consent.[4] In 1894 the Crown still held, as in the case of Bechuanaland,[5] that the declaration of a Protectorate gave it no legal powers over the control of land; and it was not until 1899 that the British Government finally decided that it could claim control over waste or unoccupied land in those Protectorates where there was no settled form of government, and where land had not been appropriated either by the Sovereign or by individuals. This view did not give to the Crown all the powers which, as the Privy Council report in the Southern Rhodesia case[6] subsequently showed, it might legally have claimed, but it appeared at the time to meet the needs of a somewhat complicated situation. It will be seen from what is said subsequently that restrictions which legal advice then placed on the powers of the Crown have disappeared. The theory of law on which the land statutes of Nigeria or Tanganyika are based gives the Crown full rights over land, restricted only by its obligations to the African population.

The terms of the Uganda Agreement of 1900 reflect the view taken in 1899; it was held that, more than any tract between the coast and the Congo, Buganda fell within the category of a 'settled government', and the agreement was negotiated on the assumption, which was in principle correct, that all the unoccupied land of Buganda was in the gift of the

---

[1] *Despatches commenting on the East Africa Royal Commission 1953–1955 Report*, Cmd. 9801, 1956, pp. 93 ff.   [2] See below, p. 786.

[3] M. T. Dawe, *Report on Botanical Mission in Uganda*, 1906. For the history of non-African 'plantations' in Uganda, see Cmd. 9475, pp. 15–18. For the system of land tenure generally see Meek, op. cit. pp. 131 ff.

[4] H. B. Thomas and R. Scott, *Uganda*, 1935, p. 31. For the history of the subsequent treatment of land rights, see ibid. pp. 98 ff.

[5] See above, p. 699. With regard to Kenya, see above, p. 713.   [6] See above, p. 701.

Kabaka. A few months later Agreements were made with the Mukama
and Chiefs of Toro, and in 1901 with the Mugabe of Ankole; but it was
not felt that there was in these territories a settled Government holding
the same position as the Kabaka of Buganda.

The Uganda Agreement reserved an area, subsequently surveyed as
9,003 square miles, for the benefit of the Ruler and his Chiefs, numbering
in all about 3,700 persons. The land was not considered as a grant, but
as property to which the Crown had no claim; it constituted the Buganda
mailo lands subsequently to be referred to,[1] their distribution being left
to the Kabaka and his Chiefs.[2] The Agreement explicitly vested all the
remaining Buganda lands and forests in the Uganda Administration.
The Toro and Ankole Agreements merely stated that all 'waste and uncultivated lands' would belong to the British Government; in their case only
small areas were granted to the Rulers and a few prominent Chiefs.

In 1902 the British Government took a larger view of its powers and
defined its position in regard to land in the Uganda Order in Council of
that year. This Order was in the same terms as the East Africa Order of
the same year, and contained the same definition of Crown Lands[3] as that
Order, with the same implication that the 'public' lands comprised all
unoccupied lands. The Crown Lands Ordinance of 1903 detailed the
terms upon which the rights conferred by the 1902 Order would be
exercised, and an amending Ordinance of 1910 was enacted to pave the
way for grants of land to European enterprise; it was laid down that the
Administration could sell or lease Crown Lands on which there were
Natives, but that Natives actually in occupation could continue there as
of right until arrangements had been made for their removal or for the
payment of compensation to them. After this their status would be that
of tenants-at-will.

That the use of the powers thus asserted over all Uganda lands, other
than those reserved under the Agreements, did not involve difficulties to
the same extent as in Kenya, is due to the fact that the areas best suited
for colonization had been withdrawn from Uganda and transferred to
Kenya in 1902.[4] Freehold alienations in other areas, which proceeded
slowly till 1916, were then suspended, it being announced that future
Concessions would be in leasehold. The decision was largely influenced
by the fact that with the expansion in the growth of cotton, economic
development was being increasingly based on indigenous peasant cultivation.

The total area of Uganda is 80,371 square miles exclusive of open water.
An area of 731 square miles has been alienated to non-Africans. Of this,

---

[1] For the *mailo* lands, see below, pp. 785–6. The term *mailo* is an adaptation of the English
'square mile'.   [2] Native Land Law of 1908.
[3] See above, p. 714.   [4] See above, p. 713.

101 square miles have been sold and 39 square miles given on lease by Africans in Buganda; 263 square miles have been granted in freehold and 333 square miles on lease by the Government in other parts of the Protectorate. There is acute local congestion in parts of the Protectorate, for example in Buganda where the population density is 200 per square mile, and in Teso, where five out of eight 'counties' (sazas) have a density of over 100 per square mile.

All land not held on documentary title is defined as Crown Land, by virtue of the Crown Lands Declaration of 1922, which was based on the Ordinance of 1903. This Declaration was understood to be a preliminary to the enactment of legislation which would finally define the respective rights of the Crown and of Africans in these areas. No such enactment was, however, made but in 1950 there was an explicit announcement[1] that it was not the intention of the Authorities to develop Uganda as a country of non-African settlement. It was stated that Crown Land, outside that in townships and trading centres and in Buganda, is regarded as being held in trust for the benefit of the African population. No land would be appropriated for public purposes without full consultation with the African Local Government concerned.[2] Alienations to non-Africans, apart from small areas for residential purposes, would not be made except for undertakings which would promote the welfare of the inhabitants of the territory.

Since that time it has been customary in official publications to describe as 'African Trust Land' the area which still has the legal status of 'Crown Land'. Ordinance no. 8 of 1949, which lays down that in townships and trading centres, and in Buganda, land may not be occupied without a lease or a licence from the Government, expressly states that elsewhere Africans require no lease or licence, and that if the Crown takes possession of land in African occupation the Governor in his discretion may award compensation to African occupants.

Following the example of the holders of the *mailo* lands in Buganda, holders of the Crown Lands in the rest of the Protectorate had made numerous transactions in the nature of sale or lease. They had thus created a series of titles which could have no basis in law, since their own status was merely that of tenants-at-will of the Crown. The situation thus created was anomalous. Early in 1956, however, the Government announced its intention to undertake legislation which would declare all lands hitherto held as Crown Lands (except those in gazetted townships) to be 'African lands' and would make provision for granting a registrable title to all holders of land who desired it. It subsequently recorded its agreement with the proposals of the East Africa Royal Commission 1953–5 for the general

[1] Government Notice no. 551 of 1950. See Cmd. 9475, p. 17.
[2] For the African Local Government bodies, see above, pp. 479–83.

extension of a system of individual ownership of land.[1] It felt, however, some hesitation as to the possibility of granting full freedom for the transfer of registered holdings to members of other tribes or other communities. That was a matter which it preferred to leave to the decision of local Land Boards to be created for this and sinilar purposes.[2]

Tanganyika

At the outset of the German régime the Administration clearly had in view a wide extension of the system of European colonization. An Imperial Decree of 26 November 1895 declared that all land in the German East Africa Protectorate was Crown Land, but added that the right of the Crown was subject to the rights of private individuals and corporate bodies[3] or of Chiefs and Native communities. In taking possession of Crown Land in the vicinity of Native communities areas were to be reserved which would secure to the Natives enough land for cultivation, taking into consideration future population increases. Land Commissions were to be appointed to determine the area which should be set aside, and a local Ordinance required them to reserve for the Natives at least four times the amount of land under cultivation.[4]

The provision contemplated was thus more systematic than any scheme of colonization organized by the Kenya Administration, but the precautions for the protection of Native rights seem to have been neglected in practice. Very little delimitation of Native lands was carried out and, in the north-eastern highlands, dispossession took place to an extent that dangerously reduced the areas cultivated by the local tribes. That more land had been alienated in this locality than was desirable was indeed admitted by the Administration and steps were taken to prevent further allotment.

The Mandatory Instrument under which the British Government took charge of the Administration in 1920 was noticeably vague in its references to the policy to be observed in respect of rights in the Native lands. It confined itself to prescribing that no rights were to be enacted in favour of non-Natives without the previous consent of the public authorities. The Mandatory Administration, however, adopted from the first a cautious policy in regard to the extension of European settlement in the territory. It referred to it indeed as being chiefly of an experimental character, and subject in any case to observance of the prior rights of Natives in the land.[5]

The Tanganyika Order in Council, 1920, vests the land of the territory

---

[1] Cmd. 9475, 1955, pp. 346–67.
[2] *Despatches commenting of the East African Royal Commission 1953–1955 Report*, Cmd. 9801, 1956, pp. 149 ff.　　　　　　　　　　　　　　　　　　　　　　　　　[3] *Juristische Person.*
[4] Ordinance of 4 December 1896, *Landesgesetzgebung.*
[5] C. Leubuscher, *Tanganyika Territory; a Study of Economic Policy under Mandate*, 1944, pp. 30, 31.

in the Governor, and the Land Ordinance, cap. 68 of the Laws, originally enacted in 1923, followed the model which, as will be seen, had been adopted in Northern Nigeria.[1] It declared the whole of the lands of the territory, with the exception of lands over which title had already been acquired, to be public lands to be administered for the common benefit of the inhabitants of the territory. No title to the occupation and use of any such lands was to be valid without the consent of the Governor. Title would henceforth take the form of a certificate granting a right of occupancy for not more than 99 years; such titles could be granted to both Africans and non-Africans and could be revoked under certain conditions defined in the Ordinance. The practice of consulting the Native Authority concerned before granting such rights was subsequently made mandatory by an amendment of 1950 to the Ordinance.[2]

The form of the Land Ordinance was clearly dictated by the desire to acquire a control which, while recognizing African customary rights, would enable the Government to intervene in order to prevent undue alienation to non-Africans. The fact that it did not specifically require that the Crown, when making alienations, should respect African occupation caused it to be compared unfavourably in some quarters with the German decree above quoted; and some difficulty was also felt in the fact that the Ordinance made the validity of a title depend on its grant or recognition by the Government. This, it was felt, might prejudice rights depending on occupation under Native custom. In its reference to titles the Ordinance clearly had in view titles acquired by non-Africans, and in 1928 a subsequent Ordinance so defined a right of occupancy as to meet this point.[3]

A further apprehension was expressed as to the possibility that the powers given to the Governor to revoke a title to occupancy might be used to interfere with rights obtained from customary occupation. This was met by a declaration that the conditions regarding the revocability of rights of occupancy did not apply to customary rights.[4] It may be added here that a public notice issued in 1953 stated expressly that Africans lawfully using or occupying land according to custom had rights of occupancy even though no document had been issued.[5]

Of the alienations made by the German Government the titles over a total area of 1,922,700 acres were recognized by the Mandatory Government, but the estates, with the exception of a few which were taken over for return to African occupation, were sold by auction in the course of war liquidation. There followed a period when Tanganyika shared with

---

[1] See below, p. 734.
[2] No. 5 of 1950. See also the directions in Government Circular no. 4 of 1950.
[3] Ordinance no. 7 of 1928. See also Laws, cap. 68, section ii.
[4] *Annual Report to the League of Nations on Tanganyika Territory, 1932*, p. 146.
[5] Government Circular no. 4 of 1953.

Kenya the considerable measure of public attention directed to the question of the alienation of land for European settlement. The East Africa Commission of 1924–5, while holding that the greater part of Tanganyika was best suited for development by peasant cultivation, pointed out nevertheless that the highlands of the north-east and south-west of the territory had areas which were well suited for non-Native enterprise. Settlers who had purchased the ex-German estates pressed the Government to encourage the investment of capital by expanding European settlement throughout East Africa. In 1923, however, the Administration closed certain districts to further alienation, apart from exceptional cases. These districts were situated in the Central, Northern, Tanga, and Lake Provinces, but it was prepared to encourage a limited non-Native settlement in areas affected by the German alienations and, in 1924, it disposed of some 17,000 acres in the southern part of the territory.

In 1926 the Governor of Tanganyika made it clear at the Conference of East African Governors that he was not prepared to adopt the policy of 'Reserves' as accepted in Kenya, but his Government agreed in the same year to the offer of 40,000 acres for occupation by non-Natives in the Iringa District. Policy was, however, now turning more definitely towards recognition of the need for making a fuller study of the actual situation in the matter of land, and in 1927 a Land Development Survey was instituted in order to make an investigation both of African needs and of the economic possibilities of European settlement. It is noteworthy, however, that the satisfaction of African requirements was postulated as a condition of the release of land for other purposes.

In 1930 the Lindi, Tabora, Mwanza, and Bukoba Districts were closed to non-Natives for agricultural purposes unless applicants could prove that they were in command of sufficient capital to undertake operations on an adequate scale, especially in connexion with water supplies. It was accepted that, in the closed areas, no alienation of land in excess of ten acres should be made without the consent of the Secretary of State.[1] It may be noted that the blocks of land subsequently leased to the Overseas Food Corporation for the mechanized cultivation of groundnuts were included in the closed area.[2]

With the passing of the period of economic depression of the thirties there was a renewal of interest in non-African settlement. A Development Committee appointed in 1938, while not advocating the extension of plantation agriculture, favoured the encouragement of 'homestead' settlement of both Europeans and Asians, the aim being in the latter case to establish on the land persons already resident in the territory. It proposed the creation of a Land Bank and the throwing open of part of the areas set aside for African use on the recommendation of the Land Development

[1] Mair, op. cit. pp. 140 ff. Leubuscher, op. cit. p. 32.   [2] See below, p. 844.

Survey. A Land Utilization Board, constituted in 1950, was instructed to make recommendations on rational land utilization, the selection of areas for allocation under rights of occupancy, and the development of a suitable system of land tenure for Africans.

The grant of rights of occupancy for 33 years with the possibility of renewal was resumed in 1948 and, in 1950, grants for 99 years were again permitted, except in the congested part of the Moshi and Arusha districts. This was made the subject of a special Inquiry. The realienation of former enemy estates was completed in 1951. By this date an additional area of 1,045,721 acres had been allocated, so that the total area alienated now amounted to 2,315,726 acres, representing approximately 1 per cent. of the total area of the territory. Of this area, 1,341,151 acres were held in lease-hold and 974,575 in freehold. The area permanently alienated has been estimated as roughly 0·9 per cent. of the area of the territory.[1]

Africans living on land over which occupancy rights have been given to non-Africans are entitled, if they wish to remain, to have a part of the land set aside for their use. This is excluded from the right of occupancy. They cannot be required to pay rent and are secured from disturbance as long as they continue in occupation. If they prefer to move they must be compensated by the lessee.[2] Africans whose land is absorbed into a township must be provided with alternative holdings before being dispossessed, and are entitled to compensation for improvements on the land.[3]

The present policy of the Government regarding non-African settlement and land utilization in general was set out in a circular issued in 1953. It is now emphasized that land should not be allocated for non-African settlement unless it is not likely to be required for African occupation in the foreseeable future. There must be no question of allocating the best land for non-African settlement to the detriment of the African population. Subject to these stipulations, non-African settlement by suitably selected persons and under conditions of proper Government control should be encouraged.[3] Such land as is held not to be essential for the natural increase of the African agricultural population should be allocated for whatever mode of utilization is held to be in the best interests of the territory as a whole.

Since a large part of Tanganyika is very sparsely populated owing to the lack of surface water or infestation by tsetse, there is a tendency to congestion in the habitable areas. Though the average density is only 22 to the square mile, there are five districts with over 100, namely, Moshi (136), Kwimba (128), Rungwa (126), Arusha (109), and Ngara (100). In Moshi and Arusha the congestion has since German days been accentuated by

[1] Sir E. Twining, in *African Affairs*, October 1951, p. 297.
[2] Government Circular no. 12 of 1941.
[3] Government Circular no. 4 of 1953.

alienation to Europeans. On the recommendations of a special Commission appointed in 1949, a total of 11,190 acres of alienated land was resumed for African occupation, a new area of 150,000 acres adjoining the Meru tribal lands was opened up for settlement, and minor adjustments were made which involved exchanges of land in European occupation and the moving of some 350 African families.[1] The majority of these, however, refused the offer of holdings in the new area. Reference will be made in Part II of this chapter to the views held by the Government on those recommendations of the East Africa Royal Commission 1953–5 which relate to the extension of the principle of individual ownership and to the registration of title.

Zanzibar

In Zanzibar, with its constitutional position as an Arab State under the protection of the British Government,[2] there is no question of any claim by the Crown to the disposal of land. By the Public Land Decree of 1921,[3] all waste and unoccupied land and all land occupied in accordance with local or tribal custom is vested in the Sultan. No document purporting to dispose of such land is valid unless countersigned by a District Commissioner. The British Resident may take possession of any such land on behalf of the Sultan, subject to compensation for dispossession.

Nigeria

In passing to the British West African Colonies and Protectorates, it is at once apparent that policy has been far less influenced than in Central or East Africa by demands for land for European settlement. The chief problem before the Administrations has been the regulation of concessions for the exploitation of mineral or forest products. Taking Nigeria in the first place, it is necessary to draw a distinction between the Colony and the Protectorate, and within the latter to discriminate between the Southern and Northern Provinces.[4]

The small area in the Colony justifies mention only on account of the position it has occupied in the judicial history of Colonial land law. Extensive grants of land, under titles stamped by the British Consul, were made by the local King Docemo before the cession of Lagos in 1861. In 1863 the British Government regularized the situation by calling in these titles and issuing Crown grants to Africans claiming land. Transactions between persons holding rights under these grants have caused much difficulty, since they have sometimes been regulated by Native custom and sometimes by the terms of English law.

---

[1] *Tanganyika Territory: Report of the Arusha–Moshi Lands Commission*, 1947 (the Wilson Report).
[2] See above, p. 305.   [3] Laws, cap. 106.
[4] For land rights in Nigeria, see Meek, *Land Law and Custom*, pp. 145 ff.

As regards the lands not subject to the Crown grants, the Privy Council[1] decided in 1915 that they had been ceded to the Crown in 1861, subject to the condition that all rights existing in the inhabitants by grant or otherwise from King Docemo or his predecessors would have to be respected. The nature of these rights was determined in the Apapa case of 1921,[2] in which the Privy Council arrived at a decision which is noteworthy in that it discriminates in an important respect between the private rights found to exist in the Lagos Colony and those which formed the subject of adjudication in the Southern Rhodesian case.[3] In both instances the Council proceeded on the principle that rights of ownership are not to be regarded as affected by a change of sovereignty; but in the case of Lagos (unlike that of Southern Rhodesia) the Court found that a customary right of the nature of that existing locally, though a right of a communal nature, could be recognized as a private right to be respected and upheld. The Crown has in consequence only a negligible interest in the lands in the Colony.

In the areas comprised in the former Southern Nigeria Protectorate, now the Eastern and Western Regions, the Government has taken the view that the authority derived from the treaties made with Chiefs did not extend to the cession of rights over land. The Royal Niger Company had acquired land rights by various treaties made in the area it controlled, and these were taken over by the Crown when the Company's charter was terminated in 1900. The Government, while maintaining the freehold of the Company in certain areas occupied by its trading stations[4] and also recognizing the validity of the Concessions obtained by it over mineral rights,[5] did not assert any claim over African lands, holding that these were in effective Native occupation.[6]

It is noteworthy that, after the occupation of Benin in 1897, the Crown treated rights in the land as having passed to itself and issued leases on it, but after the restoration of the Oba in 1914 he was allowed to resume control over land occupied by his people. In effect the Crown has in Southern Nigeria limited itself to measures designed to control the alienation of land by Africans to non-Africans; the Proclamations of 1900 and 1903, as modified in Ordinance no. 32 of 1917, provide that no alien shall acquire any interest in land from an African except under an instrument approved by the Governor. A certain number of such sales have been so authorized, mainly in urban centres for trading purposes, but they have been far from numerous.

The Crown Lands Ordinance no. 7 of 1918[7] defined Crown Lands as

[1] *Attorney-General of Southern Nigeria and John Holt & Co., Liverpool, Ltd.*, A.C. 599, 1915.
[2] *Amodu Tijani v. The Secretary, Southern Nigeria*, 2 A.C. 399, 1921.
[3] See above, p. 701.
[4] Niger Lands Transfer Ordinance, 1916. [5] See below, p. 1522.
[6] *N.A.*, Part III, pp. 139-41. [7] Laws, cap. 84.

all public lands subject to the control of His Majesty, but in 1945 the Government took powers by the Niger Lands Transfer (Amendment) Ordinances (nos. 2 and 22) to divest itself of land acquired from the Royal Niger Company on which the African occupants had remained in undisturbed possession. At the same time the Crown Lands Ordinance was amended so as to exclude from the definition of Crown Lands the lands which were subject to the Land and Native Rights Ordinance.[1]

The full recognition given to Native rights in Southern Nigeria formed an issue of some importance in discussions which originated soon after the First World War regarding the development of Colonial resources. The attempts made by the Leverhulme and other interests to secure a freehold area for oil-palm plantations attracted much public attention between 1920 and 1926,[2] and the discussions held on the subject in England found their echo in the expression by Africans of fears lest the Government should adopt in West Africa what was termed the 'Kenya system of expropriating Native lands'. As far back as 1911 alarm had been shown at the appointment of a Committee to inquire into land rights in West Africa. Mr. W. Ormsby-Gore, afterwards Secretary of State for the Colonies, in his report on a visit to West Africa in 1926,[3] expressed himself as opposed to any system of compulsory acquisition of land, but held the view that the Protectorate would have much to gain from the introduction of scientific palm cultivation on a large scale. He believed that Africans could have no objection if vacant lands were given on leasehold, since their chief objection was to the grant of permanent rights in the land.

In the attitude which the Government of Nigeria then adopted it was perhaps influenced by doubt as to the superior value of the plantation as opposed to the peasant method of development[4] but, in rejecting the application of the Leverhulme interests, it maintained that even a lease could not be obtained without invading fully acknowledged African rights. Since then, however, the United Africa Company has obtained long leases for some 12,400 acres for experiments in rubber and oil-palm plantations, and in other cases Concessions for exploitation of timber have been given.[5] These are, however, mainly in the form of leases of land reserved under the Forest Act or secured by agreement with the Native Authorities.

In Northern Nigeria historical developments gave a different direction to land policy. The treaties made by the Royal Niger Company with the Emirs between 1885 and 1890 gave it no general rights over land,[6] and

[1] See below, p. 734.   [2] Buell, op. cit. vol. i, p. 769.

[3] *Report by The Hon. W. G. A. Ormsby-Gore, on his visit to West Africa*, Cmd. 2744, 1926, pp. 108–9.

[4] 'Correspondence relating to the Policy to be adopted with regard to projected Commercial Enterprises for Cotton-growing on a large scale in the Tropical African Colonies and Protectorates', *Sessional Paper*, no. 1, Nigerian Council, 1920.

[5] A. Pim, *Colonial Agricultural Products*, 1946, p. 135.

[6] E. Hertslet, *The Map of Africa by Treaty*, vol. i, 1909, pp. 128–30.

when its charter was terminated in 1900 the Crown took early steps to issue a declaration of its attitude on the subject of land rights. General policy indicated the maintenance of the institutions embodied in the Emirate system, and these comprised a sufficiently well-defined practice in regard to land.[1] Under a strict application of the Maliki system of Islamic law which was followed by the Fulani, all cultivated lands are on conquest treated as 'Wakf'; they may be retained by their owners on conversion to Islam, but are otherwise assigned to Muslims; land not under cultivation, including sites in cities, is at the disposal of the ruler. But this theory was not followed in practice, and under the Fulani rule there remained a strong residuum of customary tenures. The Emirs granted fiefs to favoured followers, but their control over occupied land normally took the form (as in India) of levying a tax based on cultivation. In this case it was fixed at one-tenth of the produce, corresponding to the Koranic 'ushur'.

The Letter of Appointment given to the Emirs[2] stated that such rights in land as were enjoyed by the Fulani dynasty as conquerors now belonged to the Crown. The first law on the subject, Proclamation no. 8 of 1900, provided that no person other than an African of the Protectorate should acquire land from an African without the consent of the Government. Proclamation no. 13 of 1902 permitted the High Commissioner to declare as public lands all lands which were the property of conquered or deposed rulers or which were not occupied by persons having an original or derivative title under any law or custom. No grants of freehold were to be made. Such lands as were held by the Royal Niger Company, with the exception of one or two minor freeholds, were taken over in full title under Proclamation no. 16 of 1902, but these proved to be small in area.[3]

The subsequent course of land legislation in Northern Nigeria is linked up with the history of the discussions leading to the appointment of the Northern Nigeria Land Committee, whose report was issued in 1910.[4] The connexion which had always existed between land tenure and taxation under the Emirate system directed attention to the possibility of introducing in Northern Nigeria a tax based on land which would be similar to the Land Revenue levied in India,[5] but the course of the discussions was at the same time influenced by theories largely based on the contemporary writings of Henry George.[6] They advocated the principle that the State, as ultimate owner of the land, should be entitled to recover as 'economic rent' the increment represented by any increase in land values, whether this was due to development by the State itself or to individual enterprise.

On the question of land rights the Committee held that the 'ultimate ownership' of the land was vested in the Chiefs and had been acquired by

---

[1] *N.A.*, Part III, pp. 89 ff.   [2] F. D. Lugard, *Political Memoranda*, 1918, p. 344.
[3] Ibid. p. 348.   [4] *Report of the Northern Nigeria Land Committee*, Cds. 5102, 5103, 1910.
[5] See above, p. 662.   [6] Buell, op. cit. vol. i, p. 752.

the British by conquest, but rights so acquired should be exercised for the use and common benefit of Africans and in accordance with Native custom. As regards revenue, they could find in the circumstances of the territory no theoretical basis on which 'economic rent' could be assessed; it was contrary to custom for the State to take rent for land. Their preference was for taking a tax of the type already introduced by the Native Revenue Proclamation, 1906—namely, one which was in principle an income tax. This, as it will be realized, is not fundamentally a tax based on the ultimate right of the State to dispose of land.

The action taken, as embodied in the Land and Native Rights Proclamation no. 9 of 1910, now standing in a modified form as Chapter 85 of the Laws of Nigeria, was largely influenced by this recommendation. Whereas the intention of the previous law had been to claim for the State only the right to dispose of land not in actual occupation and to control leases to aliens, the new law declared that all lands, whether occupied or unoccupied, were Native lands subject to the disposition of the Governor, to be held and administered for the use and common benefit of the Natives of Northern Nigeria. No title to the occupation and use of such lands would be valid without the consent of the Governor who, in exercising his control, was to have regard to Native law and custom. He was empowered, when granting a right of occupancy to Africans or non-Africans, to fix a rent and revise it periodically. Rights of occupancy could be accorded for a definite or indefinite term; but no single right of occupancy granted to a non-African could exceed 1,200 acres if granted for agricultural purposes, or 12,500 if granted for grazing purposes.

The distinction between Crown and public lands thus disappeared. The assumption by the State of the 'ultimate ownership' of the land was much criticized at the time;[1] it was described in some quarters as expropriation;[2] others, pointing to the provision that no title to the occupation of land would be valid without the Governor's assent, urged that this would have the effect of rendering customary occupation invalid or, alternatively, would place on the Administration the impossible burden of defining and registering some millions of African titles. Reference has already been made to the similar criticisms directed against the land law of Tanganyika, which was based on the model of that of Northern Nigeria.[3] The provision by which rent could be demanded on a right of occupancy was also strongly attacked as contrary to African custom. It is clear, however, that the intention underlying the assertion of 'ultimate ownership' by the State was mainly to secure full control over alienations.

Experience has shown that the manner in which the provision has been applied in practice is actually of greater importance than the legal form in which it is expressed.

[1] Mair, op. cit. p. 133.   [2] Lugard, op. cit. pp. 347, 348.   [3] See above, p. 727.

The Government has used its powers to make only a very limited number of alienations, mainly connected with the development of the tin mines on the Bauchi Plateau.[1] The security of customary rights has been maintained by leaving the settlement of land disputes in the hands of the Native Authorities and their Courts; in practice, their control is complete, subject to the power of revision exercised over all decisions of the Native Courts. The Native Authorities also deal with land transactions between Africans.[2] There is in practice no restriction on sale, transfer, or bequest to a blood relation, but the approval of the Administration is needed for the transfer of land to an African not resident in the district.

No rent is taken by the Government in respect of Native lands, nor is the imposition of any such charge by Native Authorities contemplated in the regulations. It would not appear therefore that the actual working of the law has tended in any sense to invalidate customary rights, while it provides a machinery for the evolution of Native tenures in response to altered economic conditions. As will subsequently be shown, the decision that the form of title, whether on Native or non-Native lands, should be one of occupancy and not freehold is of far-reaching importance in the development of African land tenures.[3]

It is significant that in 1912 the Government was invited to consider the extension of the Northern Nigerian land law to the Southern Provinces of Nigeria, with the aim of legalizing the rights of Natives in the occupancy and use of the soil 'and of reserving the value of the land and freedom of access to it for future generations'.[4] It was a period when there was much discussion of the difficulties and abuses created by large-scale concessions of land and the monopolistic use of its products, and it was against this practice that the movement for the extension of the Northern Nigerian land law (which originated from Liberal circles) was in the main directed.

The appointment of a West African Land Committee, as the result of this movement, caused much public feeling among the people of Lagos and the Southern Provinces, for it was widely asserted that the references to the grant of rights of occupancy implied that the Government did not recognize the African ownership of land and was preparing to grant concessions on a large scale to European enterprises.[5] There were some differences of view in the Committee and it did not issue a report, though its minutes provide valuable material for the study of land rights in West Africa.[6] This is one of the many typical instances of the sensitiveness of African opinion in regard to the alienation of land to non-Africans.

[1] See below, p. 1509.
[2] Regulations in Schedule 3 of Ordinance no. 1 of 1916. *N.A.*, Part III, p. 93.
[3] See below, pp. 808–10.
[4] Meek, op. cit. p. 149.
[5] Buell, op. cit. vol. i, pp. 770, 823.
[6] Meek, op. cit. pp. 172–86.

The British Cameroons

In the Cameroons the German Administration made a number of alienations before the enactment of the Imperial Decree of 15 June 1896 which defined the rights claimed by the State. This laid down that, except in the case of property or other realty to which private or legal persons, Chiefs, or Native communities could substantiate a claim, all ownerless land should be considered as Crown Land. In theory this assumed that Crown Land as such would eventually be demarcated, but this was never done. In practice, when Europeans made a request for land, a local Land Commission invited persons affected to state their claims; if these were established, they were bought out by the Government, and a Crown lease was then issued to the applicants. This procedure had the effect of placing the onus of proof on the African, and its operation may be illustrated by the case of the extensive North-West Cameroon Concession, which conferred rights over all land which might at any time become Crown Land— a contingent grant which the British Government was not prepared to regard as constituting a valid title. At the same time Land Commissioners were appointed to delimit appropriate areas as *Reservate*, not liable to alienation.[1]

At the time of the First World War there were in the Cameroons a total of 56 German-owned estates, covering some 258,000 acres.[2] As in Tanganyika these estates were auctioned after the war; a large number were repurchased in 1925 by their former holders. After the Second World War, however, they were bought by the Nigerian Government, classed as 'Native lands', and leased to the Cameroons Development Corporation, a statutory body established in 1947 which is required to devote any surplus profits to the benefit of the peoples of the Cameroons.[3] The Corporation holds in all some 495 square miles. The land law of Northern Nigeria was extended to the Cameroons by the British Cameroons Administration Ordinance no. 1 of 1925.

In order to relieve congestion among the Bakweri of Victoria Division, the Nigerian Government repurchased in 1931 some 5,000 acres with the aim of securing to the Bakweri an area of nine acres per adult male. This was regarded as a final and adequate settlement. In 1948, however, a new investigation showed that the Bakweri lands were again congested, largely as a result of immigration, and 25,000 acres were excised from the Corporation's holding and offered for occupation in 15-acre plots as part of a scheme of controlled tenancies.[4]

---

[1] E. W. Ardener, 'The Origins of Modern Sociological Problems connected with the Plantation System in the Victoria Division of the Cameroons', in *West African Institute of Social and Economic Research Annual Conference Report, 1953*, pp. 89–106.

[2] Mair, op. cit. p. 134. *N.A.*, Part III, p. 177. [3] Ibid. p. 178.

[4] *Cameroons under United Kingdom Trusteeship, Report for 1951*, Col. no. 299, pp. 106 ff.; *1953*, p. 7.

In general, therefore, the treatment of land in the British Trusteeship area has followed the procedure adopted in the Northern Region of Nigeria. The main object of this procedure in the British Cameroons has been (as in the Northern Region of Nigeria) to obtain power to control the alienation of land by Africans to non-Africans. The Government has made practically no use of its power to grant certificates of occupancy to non-Natives, and where it has required land for public purposes, such as aerodromes or school buildings, it has preferred to obtain it by paying compensation to its occupants for unexhausted improvements or disturbance.[1]

The Gold Coast and Togoland

In the Gold Coast different conditions apply to the Colony, Ashanti, and the Northern Territories. In view of the manner in which jurisdiction was extended over the Colony area,[2] it is natural to find that no definite policy was evolved regarding the position of the Government in relation to the land.[3] The coastal tradition led the Administration to dissociate itself from Native affairs in its hinterland; the Crown was not assumed to have any rights over the land, and it is characteristic that in this case the Government did not for some time even take powers (as it had done elsewhere) to control alienation to non-Natives. It made its position clear by enacting provisions such, for instance, as that which laid down that the lands of an African who died intestate were to be distributed according to Native law instead of reverting to the Crown.[4] This position was fully accepted in judgements of the local Supreme Court, which proceeded on the principle that all unoccupied land which was in the control of a Paramount Stool belonged to such Stool.[5] The needs of the Government for land for public use were met by Ordinances such as no. 8 of 1876, which provided for purchase on full consideration.

The failure to exercise an earlier control over the Chiefs in their disposal of Stool land or of mineral rights had unfortunate results.[6] The possibilities of the gold-fields began to attract attention about 1880, and Chiefs proceeded to give out mining Concessions on a wide scale. In the absence of any control by the Administration and of any land survey which would indicate the boundaries of Stool areas, great confusion ensued, and it is clear that the Concessions made by the Chiefs paid no respect to the rights of individual occupiers. The need for some form of control was obvious, and in 1894 an Ordinance was proposed, similar to the Crown Lands

---

[1] *Annual Report to the General Assembly of the United Nations on the Administration of the Cameroons under United Kingdom Trusteeship for the year 1948*, Col. no. 244, 1949.

[2] See above, pp. 518 ff.

[3] On this point, see Meek, op. cit. pp. 169 ff.

[4] Laws, cap. 96, section 47. See H. C. Belfield, *Report on the Legislation Governing the Alienation of Native Lands in the Gold Coast Colony and Ashanti*, Cd. 6278, 1912, para. 23.

[5] *Wiapa v. Solomon*, 1905. *Renner's Gold Coast Reports*, vol. i, Part II, 1915, p. 410.

[6] W. K. Hancock, *Survey of British Commonwealth Affairs*, vol. ii, 1942, p. 182.

Ordinances of other dependencies, which aimed at vesting in the Crown all waste lands, forests, and mineral rights. The Bill met with a vigorous opposition and was not pressed.

In the following year the Government endeavoured to strengthen its case by an investigation into African land rights. This, however, produced an inconclusive report.[1] A further measure (The Public Lands Bill) was put forward in 1897, but the Secretary of State, yielding to the representations of a deputation claiming to represent the majority of the Chiefs, decided that it should not be proceeded with. The primary object of the Bill was to encourage permanent settlement by recognizing a right of proprietorship over land which had been held in continuous occupation for a number of years. Opposition to the Bill came mainly from the Chiefs, but they now secured the political support of the growing body of African lawyers. It was this Bill which provided the occasion for the foundation of the Gold Coast Aborigines' Rights Protection Society to which reference has been made in a previous chapter.[2]

Failing in legislation of a wider scope, the Government contented itself with an attempt to regulate the conditions of Concessions by means of the Concessions Ordinance of 1900. By this measure all Concessions were required to be validated by the Supreme Court, which could modify their terms if conditions appeared to justify it. But the machinery thus set up proved to be inadequate even for the limited purpose of sifting and validating claims, while it was no part of its purpose to provide means of control over the action of Chiefs in disposing of communal property.[3]

The Supreme Court was charged primarily with the duty of trying issues arising between grantor and grantee, and it did not possess the requisite knowledge for safeguarding the interests of other people affected or for fixing terms which would ensure that the public derived reasonable benefit from the grant of a Concession. Nevertheless, some value attaches to the provision that concessions of mining rights must be limited to five square miles and rights over agricultural or forest products to 20 square miles, and that reasonable protection must be given to customary rights existing over the land. The effects of the existing legislation were investigated by a Commission which reported in 1912, but though it expressed concern at the extent of alienations in the Colony, no further steps were taken. Not the least significant of the effects of this system has been the widespread growth of indebtedness owing to litigation over rights based on Concessions.[4]

When Ashanti was annexed in 1901 the opportunity was not taken to assert rights for the Crown which would give to the Administration some

---

[1] *Report upon the Customs Relating to the Tenure of Land in the Gold Coast*, 1895.
[2] See above, pp. 317, 520.   [3] Cd. 6278, para. 67.
[4] Cmd. 2744, p. 147. *Address by the Governor at the Opening of the 1932–33 Session of the Legislative Council*, 1932, p. 71. C. R. Havers, *Report of Commission of Inquiry into Expenses incurred by Litigants in the Courts of the Gold Coast and Indebtedness caused thereby*, Accra, 1945.

means of control over the disposal of lands. The system prevailing in the Gold Coast Colony was maintained, save that the Kumasi town lands were reserved to the Crown. The Ashanti Concessions Ordinance gave the Government powers to regulate the procedure in the acquisition of Concessions, and it took advantage of this provision in order to require negotiations to be carried out through the District Commissioner.[1] Provision for lands required for public use was secured by Ashanti Ordinances nos. 1 and 2 of 1902, which reproduced the Colony Ordinance of 1876. In 1943 the Kumasi town lands were, as a concession to Ashanti sentiment, vested in the Asantehene 'for the support of the dignity of the Golden Stool', the rentals of leases formerly granted by the Crown being paid to him.[2] More recently the Local Government Ordinance, no. 29 of 1951, prohibits the Stool Authorities, both in the Colony and Ashanti, from disposing of land without the consent of the representative Local Authority.[3]

It is not easy to give complete figures of alienations to non-Africans in the Gold Coast Colony and Ashanti. Concessions for agricultural purposes have been few, and it has been stated that only one European company interested in cultivation of the land survived the inter-war period of depression. The total Concessions validated by the High Court up to 1951 covered in all some 137 square miles out of 23,937 square miles in the Colony, and 2,395 square miles in Ashanti out of a total area of 24,379 square miles. The great majority were mining Concessions. Alienations of some extent seem to have been made to Africans for cocoa gardens and the like, but no record exists of the amount.

Circumstances gave the Administration a freer hand in framing its land policy in the Northern Territories. Exposed to the attacks of Muslim forces from the countries south of the Sahara, the tribes in the Northern Territories of the Gold Coast nevertheless escaped absorption in strong States such as were built up in Northern Nigeria. They had, however, been subjected to the full force of slave raiding and, as a result, the population was for the most part sparse and disorganized. There were no strong political authorities such as were encountered in the Colony and Ashanti. In its administrative policy the Government was, as already shown,[4] able to adopt a system which recognized local Native Authorities as its agents, following the pattern adopted in Northern Nigeria and Tanganyika, and its land policy was on the same model. There was no pressure from outside for Concessions of land, either for mining or for agricultural purposes. The Government found no difficulty in asserting the Crown ownership of mining rights and the control of prospecting or of the right of exploitation.[5]

[1] Concessions Ordinance, 1903, section 4(3), and Schedule B, Laws of Ashanti, 1928, cap. 5.
[2] Kumasi Lands Ordinances nos. 17 of 1943 and 14 of 1945. *N.A.*, Part III, pp. 247–8.
[3] See above, p. 528.   [4] See above, pp. 523–5.
[5] Minerals Ordinance no. 20 of 1936.

Legislation on the subject of land rights in general had preceded by some years that relating to mineral rights. The linking up of communications with the south in the early twenties seemed to make it desirable to introduce a definite measure of control over the land. In doing so the Government was influenced both by the recommendations of the Belfield Report of 1912, which had emphasized the mischief of unregulated alienation, and by other investigations referred to in the previous paragraphs relating to Nigeria and the Gold Coast Colony. In 1927 it enacted the Northern Territories Land and Native Rights Ordinance, which, following the lines adopted in Nigeria,[1] declared all lands to be public lands, with the qualification that the validity of existing titles would be recognized if proved within three years. This provision was intended, as in Nigeria, to safeguard titles, if any, previously granted by the Administration. The provisions for the grant of a certificate of title of occupancy also follow the Nigerian precedent. The power of the Governor to levy rent was now limited to the towns; rights of occupancy were to confer no rights to minerals, and it was declared unlawful for an African to alienate his rights to a non-African without the consent of the Governor.

The Ordinance met with the typical Gold Coast criticism that it was a confiscatory measure, but criticism served on this occasion merely to secure, in the revised Ordinance no. 8 of 1931, the substitution of the term 'Native' for 'public' lands, with the added declaration that they were to be at the disposal of the Governor 'for the use and common benefit' of the African people. Rights of occupancy might be granted for periods not exceeding 99 years.

Further, the rent clauses were modified by withdrawing the provision which made it permissible for the Governor to levy rent only in urban areas; but a proportion, not less than one-half, of all urban rents and of rents received from non-Natives in rural areas, was to be paid to the recognized Native Authority. Since 1936 an amendment[2] to the Ordinance stipulates that one-sixth of the balance of all rents received shall be paid into a Benefits Trust Fund[3] which has as its object the provision of assistance for the poorer Native Administrations. The Crown has so far used its powers only to grant rights over 5 square miles of land.

This Ordinance has been extended to the northern section of Togoland under British Trusteeship.[4] It does not appear that use has been made of it to alienate land to non-Africans, there being no demand from them for the acquisition of land rights. In the southern section of Togoland the same system prevails as that described in the Gold Coast Colony and Ashanti; its application has been the easier in that there has been no

[1] See above, p. 731.   [2] Ordinance no. 27 of 1936.
[3] The Benefits Trust Fund Ordinance no. 26 of 1936.
[4] Lands and Native Rights Ordinance 1931, (Application) Ordinance no. 2 of 1933.

demand for mining Concessions. On the other hand, there has been some sale to Africans other than local residents, and it is a question how far failure to control such sales is technically in accordance with the obligations of the Trusteeship Agreement.[1]

Sierra Leone and Gambia

Both in Gambia and Sierra Leone the small Colony areas may for the present purpose be neglected.

In Gambia the definition of Crown rights given in the Protectorate Ordinance of 1896 was ambiguous, but as no action was taken to assert these rights the fact is of little significance.[2] In 1945 this measure was replaced by the Protectorate Lands Ordinance no. 16. This declares that all lands are vested in the Native Authorities of the districts in which they are situated, to be held for the common benefit of the communities concerned. The Governor may acquire any Protectorate land for a term of years, on payment of compensation, and the Crown Lands are now limited to those which have been acquired under the provisions of this Ordinance.

The occupation and use of land held by 'indigenes' is declared to be subject to the customary law. No 'non-indigene' may occupy land without the consent of the Native Authority concerned; tenancy agreements must also have the approval of the District Commissioner. Rents are paid to the Native Authority and are subject to revision every seven years. It is to be noted that the body thus recognized as exercising authority in the matter of land is defined in terms of the Native Authority Ordinance of 1933, that is to say, it is a body which, as at present constituted, does not necessarily consist of persons with traditional rights over the allocation of land.

In the Sierra Leone Protectorate the principle of African ownership has likewise been fully recognized.[3] The Protectorate Lands Ordinance of 1927, as extended by Ordinance no. 32 of 1933, states that 'all land in the Protectorate is vested in the Tribal Authorities, who hold such land for and on behalf of the Native communities concerned'. Two measures of control have, however, been adopted. The grant of Concessions was dealt with in a series of Ordinances, consolidated in Ordinance no. 29 of 1931, which regulated alienations by the Tribal Authorities. The assent of the Governor is required for such alienations; he may sanction Concessions to non-Africans of not more than 1,000 acres if they are for the benefit of the Chiefdom and of larger areas, if for the benefit of the country as a whole, subject to the sanction of the Secretary of State when the area exceeds 5,000 acres.[4] A Concessions Court, constituted as a Division of the

[1] Article VIII, para. 1.
[2] *N.A.*, Part III, p. 345.   [3] Meek, op. cit. pp. 195 ff.
[4] Concessions Amendment Ordinance no. 29 of 1906. Concessions Ordinance no. 29 of 1931.

Supreme Court, is charged with examining the validating Concessions recognized by the Governor.

As in Southern Nigeria, European commercial interests have shown some desire to acquire land rights in Sierra Leone which would allow them to develop the palm-oil industry. In the years immediately preceding the First World War the British Government showed anxiety lest the competition of companies operating under Concessions granted in foreign dependencies, and notably the Belgian Congo, should gain an advantage over the production of British West African Colonies,[1] though it felt at the same time bound to protect the African from the expropriation of Native lands. After lengthy negotiations,[2] it agreed to the passing of the Palm Oil Ordinance no. 7 of 1913, which empowered the Governor, with the assent of the Tribal Authority, to grant for a period not exceeding 21 years in the first instance, certain rights over areas of not more than 10 square miles. These rights would enable the concessionaire to erect oil mills to the exclusion of other enterprises; the Ordinance did not, however, give any rights over land, nor did it give an exclusive right to purchase produce.[3]

The measure was not fruitful of results, for the African was unwilling to sell his produce at prices which at times compared unfavourably with those he could earn by extracting the oil himself. A committee appointed in 1924 considered that the oil companies could not be left entirely dependent on the willingness of the Africans to sell their palm fruit, but should have their own plantations.[4] The Concessions Ordinance had been amended in 1922, so as to legalize Concessions not exceeding 5,000 acres if made for the sole purpose of cultivating the oil palm on scientific lines, but the leases were to be granted by the Tribal Authority, and not more than 1,000 acres could be obtained from any one Chiefdom. This provision was repealed by the Concessions Ordinance of 1931, which provided moreover that a Concession granted by the Governor for this purpose need not be submitted to the Concessions Court. It does not appear, however, that any Concession has so far been authorized under this Ordinance for the cultivation of the oil palm.

A second measure of control relates to the regulation of the terms of tenancy rights held by 'stranger Natives'. The Protectorate Lands Ordinance of 1927 provided that such persons require the assent of the Tribal Authority before taking up land, but their occupation would be temporary unless covered by a lease, when it might extend to a maximum of 50 years.

[1] H.C. Deb., 7 April 1913, col. 786.
[2] *Correspondence respecting the Grant of Exclusive Rights for the Extraction of Oil from Palm Fruits*, Cd. 6561, 1912–13.
[3] Buell, op. cit. vol. i, p. 686. For the Lever Concession in Sierra Leone, see also C. Wilson, *The History of Unilever*, 1954, pp. 166 ff.
[4] *West Africa, Palm Oil and Palm Kernels*, Col. no. 10, 1925, p. 9.

The French Territories

The course taken in regard to land rights in French West Africa was in some degree influenced by experiences in Algeria. There the demand by *colons* for land in the occupation of the Algerian Muslims had been mainly responsible for the conflicts which for long made Colonial expansion an unpopular cause in France. The history of land policy in Algiers has chapters reminiscent of the Union of South Africa; the early policy of *refoulement*[1] or 'driving back' of the Natives and the confiscation of their lands was followed by a policy of *cantonnement*, which presented some of the features characteristic of the South African system of Native Reserves.[2] The next stage saw one of those reversals of policy not unknown in French Colonial history; the tribes were to be declared proprietors of the lands of which they had 'permanent and traditional enjoyment'.[3]

But that step came too late as a measure of protection, since tribal lands were not closed to European purchase. On the contrary, a law of 1873 applied to Native lands the principle of French law which recognizes only individual rights and not communal ownership; co-sharers in tribal lands were to apply for the partition of their shares and these were to be alienable.[4] Caught in a maze of litigation, the Arabs had lost by 1889 nearly 40 per cent. of their lands,[5] largely through executions for debt, and further legislation was necessary in 1897 to check this process and give some stability to tribal conditions.

The circumstances in French West Africa differed in one important respect from those in Algeria. There was little pressure to secure land for colonists. An attempt to start a plantation system in Senegal early in the nineteenth century had proved abortive, and henceforward economic policy was directed mainly to the development of a peasant economy assisted by the State.

In French Equatorial Africa circumstances led to the adoption of a policy which differed materially from that of French West Africa. The reduction of the home subsidy for development had left the Colony without resources, and the fact that a relatively greater outlay was required to overcome climatic and transport difficulties indicated a policy of development through European *entrepreneurs* similar to that which was being followed in the Congo Free State. This involved the concession of a monopolistic control over forest produce, with the guarantee of an ultimate freehold over selected areas of land proportionate to the development effected. Already in 1893 certain monopoly Concessions of this type had

---

[1] L. Vignon, *La France dans l'Afrique du nord*, 1888, p. 32.
[2] See the Franck–Chauveau Report, 'Propriété foncière', *Journal Officiel*, 1893, pp. 262 ff.; and S. H. Roberts, *History of French Colonial Policy*, vol. i, 1929, p. 197.
[3] *Sénatus-Consulte* of April 1863.   [4] Buell, op. cit. vol. i, pp. 1022 ff.
[5] V. Piquet, *La Colonisation française dans l'Afrique du nord*, 1912, p. 207.

been given by the Ministry, but the agitation which followed caused the Government to revoke them in 1895. Demands made by commercial interests led, however, to the appointment in 1898 of a Commission on Colonial Concessions, which recommended the introduction of legislation defining the terms on which they could be granted. The Decrees issued in 1899, as a result of the proposals of the Commission, represented the first definite statement of the nature of the rights claimed by France in the land of her tropical African territories.

In a number of treaties which had been previously concluded with African Chiefs the French Government had guaranteed their rights over the land, and Decrees issued in February and March 1899 showed a desire to recognize the existence of these rights. In claiming for the State only the ownership of the *terres vacantes et sans maître* they followed the principles of the metropolitan French Code, but its application to Colonial territory was criticized by well-known French authorities on the ground that there is not, even in the less thickly populated Sudan, 'an inch of land without a master'.[1] That is of course a point of view which has also received practical recognition in some of the British West African territories. The consequences in which the Decrees of 1899 involved the African population depended on the interpretation given in practice to the term 'vacant lands'.

Those who supported the system of monopolistic Concessions in French Equatorial Africa pointed out that the Decrees contemplated the grant of freehold areas only at a secondary stage, the initial stage involving merely the grant of rights over the collection of forest produce. The form of the Decree would, they urged, enable areas to be selected for alienation after further investigation had shown where rights were non-existent or so tenuous as to be easily compensated, as for example, rights of hunting or of occasional grazing.

In the application of these Decrees the two territories have adopted methods so different that it is well to treat them separately. In French West Africa the framing of the land decrees has shown evidence of a definite concern for African rights, an attitude that was natural to an Administration which had experience of the close-knit organization of the tribes in Senegal or the Sudan. When, on the formation of the 'federation' of French West Africa,[2] the legislation enacted by its constituent Colonies was consolidated in the Decree of 23 October 1904, the basic principle that the State is the owner of 'vacant lands' was maintained, but it was laid down that lands forming the collective property of Natives could be ceded to individuals only after approval by an *arrêté* of the Lieutenant-Governor.

---

[1] M. Delafosse, *Haut-Sénégal–Niger*, vol. iii, 1912, p. 14. P. Dareste, *Le Régime de la propriét française en A.O.F.*, 1908. Buell, op. cit. vol. i, pp. 1022–5.   [2] See above, p. 332.

There are some differences in detail as between the various Colonies which formed the French West Africa 'group'. In Niger an *arrêté* of 12 August 1924 prescribed that Natives could not be evicted without their consent, but in the Sudan, under the *arrêté* of 24 April 1920, Natives were held to be entitled only to compensation for removal. In Guinea, by the *arrêté* of 13 April 1912, land required for Native cultivation was to be reserved from Concession, but removal of Natives to other lands could be effected by agreement or payment of compensation.

In French West Africa the position taken by the State in regard to 'vacant lands' has created less difficulty than in some other territories, since there has been little demand for land for colonization. But the legal position has not always been easy. In 1907 the West African Court of Appeal held that in succeeding to the rights of a Chief over territory in which no individual property was recognized, the French Government acquired absolute rights over all land not held under title. That was a decision dictated by the inability of French law to recognize any right in land other than that of the individual, with the result that in principle a communal tenure can have no status at law.[1] The Government at one time accepted this position so far as to agree that the State was legally proprietor of all lands other than those on which Africans had acquired title by administrative concession or by prescription. But the Courts, in their turn, denied that the principle of prescription could be extended from French to African conditions. The position taken up by the Courts was thus at variance with the intentions of the Decree of 1904, and a Land Commission was appointed in 1915 to consider a solution. This Commission did not report owing to the conditions created by the First World War; but there has been no evidence that the Government has sought to take undue advantage of the position which the legal decisions seemed to create for it.

The various Decrees on the subject of land were consolidated in that of 15 November 1935. This, while repeating that the State is owner of lands which are vacant and *sans maître*, added that it has control also of any land not used or occupied for ten years. The law of 29 August 1947, constituting elected Councils in the Colonial territories,[2] gives these bodies a voice in the disposal of State lands. No Concessions may be granted without consulting the Council concerned or the *Grands Counseils*, if the grant affects more than one Colony. If their view is in conflict with that of the Governor or Governor-General, the matter is referred to the Council of Ministers in Paris, who must consult the Assembly of the French Union. This applies to all Concessions, whatever the area.

The terms of a Concession must indicate the areas which are occupied by or reserved for Africans; land under cultivation cannot be taken up

---

[1] Dareste, op. cit. pp. 16, 20.   [2] See above, p. 341.

without compensation to the occupier, which must be arranged by the Administration. Concessions in rural areas are given in the first instance provisionally, the title being confirmed on compliance with stipulated development conditions. In 1938 a total of 57 Concessions with an area of 13,035 acres were recorded as held on 'definitive' tenure, and 693, with an area of 197,500 acres, on 'provisional' tenure. By 1949 the number held on definitive tenure had fallen to 20, with an area of 3,120 acres. Those held on provisional tenure had increased to 993, but the total area had fallen to 114,317 acres. The majority of Concessions are in the Ivory Coast and French Guinea, and are used for the plantation of bananas, rice, and coffee.

In French Equatorial Africa the first rush of Concessions, which began in 1899, resulted in the grant of monopoly rights over about two-thirds of the whole territory.[1] They were divided between some 40 companies, and carried a monopoly over all forest produce for 30 years, subject to Native rights in areas to be defined by the Government. The Concessions involved the payment of a low annual rent and of 15 per cent. of the profits to the State. Freehold was ultimately to be given over all 'developed' areas, of which there was a somewhat complicated definition, including the planting of 150 rubber-trees for each ton produced. The first protests against the system came from English traders affected by the operation of the monopoly, and pressure from the British Government resulted in their receiving a considerable measure of compensation. An indirect result of their complaints was a decision of the French Court at Loango in 1900 that, until the African lands were delimited, the entire area of the Concessions must be taken as subject to the rights of the concessionaires.

It is unnecessary to recall here the reign of anarchy which these monopolies introduced or the hardships which they inflicted on the Native population. In regard to the land, it is sufficient to say that, while they did not in the first instance actually deprive Africans of its possession, its use was gravely restricted. In the treaties made with Chiefs during the original occupation of the French Congo the Government had agreed to respect their rights over land; but Native lands were defined in the ministerial instructions of 1899 as comprising only the areas necessary for the cultivation of foodstuffs. The Colonial Ministry ordered in 1901 and again in 1902 that an attempt should be made to delimit Native Reserves, but the opposition of the concessionaire Companies prevented any effective steps being taken in this direction. The local Administration contented itself with issuing an *arrêté* in 1903, declaring that in principle Reserves should extend over one-tenth of the conceded territory. This provision could, however, have had no effect in the absence of a survey which would allow of the delimitation of the areas affected.

---

[1] For a criticism of the operation of these *Concessions congolaises*, see E. D. Morel, *Affairs of West Africa*, 1902, pp. 285 ff.

The revulsion of feeling in France against the abuses produced by the monopolies, and the growing evidence of the economic failure of the Companies, combined to force the Government in 1910–12 to consider a revision of the system. A long series of negotiations resulted in the abandonment by a number of the Companies of their rights under the Concessions of 1899 in return for a reduced grant of land, a monopoly of rubber collections for ten years in the original areas, freehold over the area under cultivation at the end of that time, and after that a rubber monopoly over ten times the freehold area during a further ten years. The additional area brought under cultivation at the end of the second period was likewise to become the property of the Companies. This arrangement provided for a return to the State of 78,750,000 acres out of the 217,500,000 acres which were in theory alienated in 1899. At various times after 1912 other Companies came into the agreement: in some cases a fixed area was at once given in freehold as compensation, while the Concessions of a certain number of Companies which had stood out of the arrangement expired in 1929.

The commitments of 1899–1900 were thus liquidated at a heavy loss to the African inhabitants, while the financial gain of the monopoly system to the Colony was comparatively small. An *arrêté* of 1926 provided that the power to grant Concessions up to 25,000 acres, conferred by the legislation of 1899, should be subject to the condition that land over which Africans hold rights can be alienated only on payment of compensation at rates fixed by the Administration. Between 1938 and 1945 the grant of Concessions of areas over 50 acres was suspended owing to the difficulty of obtaining labour. The law of 29 August 1947[1] applies to Equatorial as well as to West Africa. The total remaining area covered by Concessions in 1951 was stated as 330,000 acres.

The French Cameroons

The land law which the Germans introduced in the Cameroons has been described in dealing with the British Cameroons.[2] At the outset of their rule they made Concessions, of the type of those granted by the Congo Free State and by the French Congo, mainly with a view to the collection of rubber. That made to the *Süd-Kamerun-Gesellschaft* in 1898 comprised an area of 18 million acres, but it was stated to be subject to Native land rights. In the following year rights over 11,750,000 acres were given to the *Nordwest-Kamerun-Gesellschaft*, which had the right to choose Crown Land within this area, but in occupying such land it was to respect existing Native rights. Difficulties which arose with the *Süd-Kamerun-Gesellschaft* led to the application of the process of 'cantonment' to its grant and in 1905

---

[1] See above, p. 745.   [2] See above, p. 736.

the area was reduced to 3,750,000 acres and the conditions were revised. The *Nordwest-Gesellschaft* failed to meet its obligations and its grant terminated in 1913.

Meanwhile a considerable number of Concessions had been made to individual grantees, mainly in the south-west of the territory, for cocoa, rubber, and oil-palm plantations. In the liquidation of ex-enemy property at the close of the First World War the estates held on a recognized title were auctioned by a Commission appointed for the purpose, subject to the right of the State to exercise pre-emption at prices fixed by the Commission. By 1925 some 362 properties had been dealt with, of which 219 were auctioned and 107 were taken in pre-emption, while some 40 sites occupied by the Germans for administrative purposes were held to have passed to the new Administration under Article 120 of the Treaty of Versailles. The former German owners did not succeed in regaining their holdings to the same extent as in the British Cameroons, and the area in their hands in the inter-war period was relatively small. A number of the pre-empted properties were resold to French subjects.

The provisions of the French West African legislation of 1904 were extended to the Cameroons by a Decree of 11 August 1920, thus giving the State a claim to the ownership of 'vacant lands'. In 1950, partly as a result of the discussion on petitions to the Trusteeship Council which protested against this claim, the French Government appointed a Commission to redefine the State *domaine* after consulting local opinion in all its African dependencies. In the Cameroons a committee consisting partly of officials and partly of members of the local Assembly agreed that it would be desirable to recognize three types of Native rights—individual (over land used for cash crops), family (over land used for food crops), and collective (over bush land, subject to rights of hunting and collecting wild produce). This last category could be regarded as *domaine communal* and should be administered by regional administrative officers in consultation with local Councils.

'Vacant land' is alienated by the State under different rules for urban and rural lands. A proposal to alienate must be published in the *Journal Officiel*, with a local notice to the Africans concerned, who have a right to object; but it is stipulated that if claims which are heard by the administrative authorities are proved to be baseless, the claimant is liable to a fine. As in French West Africa, a provisional title is first given, and is completed only on proof of compliance with the conditions laid down regarding beneficial use. Grants of over 500 acres cannot be made without consulting the local Assembly created by the Decree of 9 October 1945.[1] In case of disagreement they are referred to the Minister for Overseas France if less than 3,750 acres in extent, and to the Council of Ministers,

[1] See above, p. 335.

with the advice of the Assembly of the French Union, if in excess of that amount. The same legislation is applicable to French Togoland.

Under existing legislation[1] lands in the neighbourhood of villages are defined as Reserves. These are considered to be held in usufruct and the occupants cannot dispose of them, though they may be alienated by the State, subject to the grant of compensation to the occupiers. There has been no regular delimitation of these Reserves. The German Government had set aside certain *Reservate* in districts such as Dschang, where they regarded Native occupation as too dense to allow of any alienation. These were maintained by the French Administration, which added certain other areas to this class.

While the explicit recognition that land in actual occupation is to be regarded as reserved may represent an advance on previous legislation, rights in such land are in fact inadequately safeguarded in the absence of a survey or other means of delimitation. Colonization was at first encouraged, and loans were given to colonists by the local *caisse de crédit agricole*. For climatic and other reasons, however, alienations were not extensive and were suspended between 1938 and 1945. Such grants as have been made are of small areas, mainly for growing coffee and bananas. They totalled 259,040 acres in 1951.

The Belgian Congo

The history of the Belgian Congo reflected at one time the results of the pursuit of the Concession policy in an even more extreme form than that which had characterized French Equatorial Africa. In the earlier days of the Free State King Leopold II had no method of securing capital for railway or similar developments other than by the grant of large areas of land or of monopolies for the marketing of forestal and other produce. The Matadi–Stanley Pool Railway owed its inception in 1886 to the agreement to concede to the Company an extensive grant of land, and the railways connecting the Upper Congo with the Lakes were similarly financed in 1902. This principle was afterwards extended in order to obtain revenue which neither the customs receipts, limited in their range by the Berlin Act of 1885, nor direct taxation was able to supply.

The first formal declaration of the rights claimed by the State over land was made when the Concession was given for the Matadi Railway. It took the same form as that which, as has been shown, was adopted in 1899 by the basic Decree regarding lands in the French African Colonies— namely, a statement claiming all 'vacant' lands as the property of the State.[2] 'Vacant' lands could be alienated by the Administration, and sales

---

[1] *Arrêté* of 15 September 1931.

[2] *Ordonnance*, 1 July 1885. *Décret*, 14 September 1886. *Codes et Lois du Congo Belge*, 1954, p. 1560.

of land made by Africans were to be recognized only if confirmed by the State. In Belgium, as in France, this measure was criticized on the ground that all land is in fact claimed by some tribe and that, in particular, palm-trees always have a potential owner.[1]

The first occasion for the formal discussion of the nature of African rights in land arose after the introduction in 1885 of a State monopoly over the collection of rubber and ivory, when it became necessary to decide whether any African rights could be held to exist in the forest areas. A circular of 1891 recognized the right of Africans to collect rubber in those woods which were deemed to form an integral part of their villages, but the woods were to be so regarded only if they were 'occupied, that is to say, continuously exploited'. A Decree of 1892 required that an Inquiry should be held into the extent of African rights over forest produce, and these rights were to be duly recorded; the issue actually examined, however, was whether Africans had exploited the wild rubber commercially before 1885. The conclusion arrived at went to show that practically the whole area of Native land was 'unoccupied'.[2] The Free State Government then proceeded to utilize its rights over the forests in order to give Concessions of the monopoly of purchase to rubber companies (such as those subsequently merged in the *Compagnie du Kasaï*), and also to make direct collections itself through the rubber tax.[3]

The protests of foreign traders against this monopoly and the widespread feeling against the abuses produced by the use of forced labour for the collection of rubber were largely responsible for the appointment of the Commission of Inquiry in 1904[4] and for a material modification of the system of collection, together with a change in the land law. A Decree of 3 June 1906[5] recognized that land inhabited, cultivated, or exploited in any manner was 'occupied', and indicated that steps were to be taken to demarcate Native Reserves, which were to be at least three times as large in area as that of the 'occupied' land. Such lands could be sold by Africans, subject to the sanction of the Administration. The delimitation was, however, effected only within the territory of two large Concessions, the Bus-Bloc (the areas owned by the *Compagnie du Congo* and its subsidiaries) and the Katanga. Owing partly to the difficulty of allowing for the practice of shifting cultivation and partly to the cost involved, the attempt to complete the delimitation of Reserves was abandoned in 1922.

The abuses of the Free State monopoly system belong so much to past history that they need not be enlarged upon here. But it is important to note the remarkable extent of the Concessions granted. They were of

[1] A. Vermeersch, *La Question congolaise*, 1906, p. 175. H. Vanderyst, 'Les Concessions de forêts secondaires et de palmeraies congolaises', *Congo*, vol. ii, 1925, pp. 731–7.

[2] E. Boelaert, 'Législation foncière de l'État indepéndant et droit naturel', in *Aequatoria*, vol. xvii, no. 2, 1954, pp. 41–50.   [3] See above, p. 673.

[4] Buell, op. cit. vol. ii, pp. 415 ff.   [5] *Codes et Lois du Congo Belge*, 1954, p. 183.

three kinds. The grants to the Railway Companies covered over $22\frac{1}{2}$ million acres. The terms of the Katanga Concession were more comparable to those of the charters in which Great Britain had entrusted administrative functions to the British South Africa or similar companies, but they also included the grant of freehold property in one-third of the territory which the Company brought under control. In the end no delimitation was made, the whole area of the Katanga being placed under the administration of a joint body, the *Comité spécial du Katanga*. Two-thirds of its members represented the Government and one-third the Company, the latter receiving one-third of the revenues. The total area subject to the administration of this body was estimated at $112\frac{1}{2}$ million acres.

The third type of Concession was that to which reference has already been made, the monopoly of marketing of forest produce. These monopolies, in their original form, covered an immense extent of territory, but as they did not confer freehold rights their area was not calculated. The total area covered by grants of freehold when the Congo Free State was annexed by Belgium in 1908 has been calculated as $67\frac{3}{4}$ million acres.[1] The Belgian Government concluded a series of negotiations with the concessionaires, other than the Katanga Company, as a result of which they abandoned certain of their monopoly rights in exchange for the right to receive freehold areas to be selected within the boundaries of their Concessions. Some of the original freehold areas were also reduced. A total of some $25\frac{1}{2}$ million acres reverted to the State.[2]

The Government continued to encourage European enterprise, but it now alienated land under Concessions of a different type. Under this form the grantee had at the end of a preliminary period the right to choose blocks of land up to a fixed maximum within an area from which other claimants had been excluded during this period, the area to be acquired depending on the fulfilment of certain development conditions. The most important grant of this type was that made in 1911 to the *Huileries du Congo Belge*, which was associated with the Lever interests.[3] This Company obtained the right to lease a maximum of 1,875,000 acres, divided between five circles, each with a radius of 60 kilometres, the amount leased in each circle being dependent on the erection of oil mills of a given capacity. It was to become entitled in 1945 to freehold rights in an area of 375,000 acres, not more than 100,000 acres being included in one circle but, if in the five years preceding 1945 it had exported 30,000 tons of oil, it would be entitled to ownership of the whole 1,875,000 acres.

It proved impossible to find land free of Native rights up to the stipulated

---

[1] T. Heyse and H. Leonard, *Régime des cessions et concessions*, 1932, p. 186.
[2] T. Heyse, *Grandes lignes du régime des terres du Congo Belge*, 1947, p. 35.
[3] Wilson, op. cit. pp. 167 ff. Buell, op. cit. vol. ii, pp. 511, 516.

area within the zones as laid down, and a new agreement was made in 1938. By its terms the maximum obtainable in freehold in the five zones was reduced to 325,000 acres, and the Company was authorized to select a further 250,000 acres anywhere in the Belgian Congo, which it would receive in freehold in 1956 provided 30 per cent. of the area had been developed by that time. The selection was completed in 1944. It is estimated that about 90,000 acres will be surrendered in 1956 on account of failure to comply with the conditions regarding development. The land is held on payment of a nominal quit-rent. In 1952 the Company received a new Concession of 247,500 acres for ranching. This was divided between two areas, one in Kwango District and the other at Bosobolo in the bend of the Ubangui River.

On the recommendation of the Advisory Committee on Labour it was announced in 1929 that no further mining Concessions were to be granted, and only one-third of the territory was to be open to large-scale, and one-third to small-scale agricultural Concessions.

A special arrangement has applied since 1928 to the Kivu region, which is the only area of the Belgian Congo proper whose climate appears to be suitable for European settlement. Here the *Compagnie des Chemins de Fer des Grands Lacs* had a Concession which, as revised in 1921, gave it an option over 900,000 acres to be selected by 1936. In order to resume its control, the Government reconstructed this Company on the lines adopted for the Katanga. The *Comité National du Kivu*, created in 1928, in which the Government holds a controlling interest, is charged with the development of an area of 14 million acres.

The Concessions to the *Huileries du Congo Belge* may be said to mark the close of the era of large-scale Concessions of land by the Belgian Government, and since that period land Concessions have been on a relatively minor scale. A policy which involved the active encouragement of colonization by small farmers was inaugurated early in 1940 and was pursued by the Belgian Government in exile during the Second World War. Special facilities were offered to ex-soldiers and to persons deported during the German occupation, and also to former officials of the Belgian Congo Government or of the two great *Comités*. Such Concessions, however, involved a comparatively small area.[1]

Looking to the history of land Concessions in the Belgian Congo as a whole, it is noteworthy that even after the Concession policy had been brought under a definite measure of control, no general delimitation of African lands was made. The procedure adopted was to go over the ground when a Concession was applied for and to mark off the areas over which Africans held rights; these had to remain untouched unless the concessionaire could come to terms with the African right-holders. A

[1] Heyse, op. cit. pp. 7 ff.

Decree of July 1938 prohibited the sale of African lands to anyone but the Government. An Ordinance of October 1930 had provided that before sanction was given to such sales, there should be an Inquiry on the spot by a Commission consisting of a member of the judiciary as chairman, a missionary, and either an official or a leading local non-official European. Their report had to include an opinion as to the fairness of the price and indicate the persons to whom it should be paid. An amendment of 31 May 1934 substituted for the Commission a special delegate of the Governor-General, and set a limit of two years during which the evidence recorded in the Inquiry might be contested.[1]

While this procedure has apparently proved adequate to provide against any serious invasion of private rights in the later Concessions, it seems that considerable difficulty has arisen in regard to Native rights held within the territory of the older grantees, particularly the oil-palm Concessions of the Lomami Company and of the *Huileries du Congo Belge*. The absence of a defined boundary between Native and Company land led at one time to constant complaints of trespass against Africans when collecting fruit. By an arrangement made in the Lomami Concession the whole land was left *en indivision* until a demarcation could be made as between the Company and the inhabitants, the latter being meanwhile free to collect fruit anywhere, but under an obligation to sell it all to the Company.

The agreement concluded with the *Huileries du Congo Belge* is more complicated. In each of the five blocks chosen by the Company an area not greater than the total estimated to be free of Native rights was left *en indivision*. In this area the people could move freely and establish habitations where they chose until any land was appropriated by the Company for plantation, when it was marked off and fenced. Natives were then excluded from it. Within the rest of the area they could gather palm fruit as they pleased, but must sell it to the Company.

Both here and in the Lomami Concession the price of the fruit is fixed by the Government. It was originally arranged that the final delimitation of land was to begin in May 1936, when the Natives were to receive a total area equivalent to that calculated as requisite for their needs at the time the contract was concluded. In 1934, however, it was decided that the operation could not be carried out within the prescribed period, and demarcation was deferred until 1944 when the Company made its final selection of freehold land.

It was stated in 1955 that there were in occupation by Africans about 120 million acres of land, and that there were in addition 500,000 acres of vacant *domaine* land upon which the indigenous population could settle without hindrance. The area alienated to non-Africans amounted to a

[1] *Codes et Lois du Congo Belge,* 1954, p. 1561.

total of 51 million acres.[1] The statement did not, however, make clear how much of the area over which rights of ownership had been alienated was actually in use by Africans, whether for the collection of forest produce or for agricultural or pastoral purposes.

Ruanda Urundi

In what is now the Trust Territory of Ruanda Urundi the German Imperial Decree of 26 November 1895 claimed for the Crown complete ownership of the land. A local Land Commission was to decide what lands were unoccupied and therefore available for grant by the State to Europeans. Direct grant from the State was the only means by which freehold could be obtained; land might be leased from Africans, but the period was limited to five years. At the same time Europeans could themselves arrange directly with Africans to vacate their land on payment of compensation, and when the State was satisfied that this had been paid it was prepared to give a grant of freehold. In the event, the area alienated was actually small and, when the Belgian Government first examined the matter, it admitted titles in only 3,896 acres.

The Belgian Government was for some time chary of allowing any alienation of land to non-Africans. At the outset it made provision only for leases up to five and then ten years, increasing this to 20 years in 1925, the chief demands for land up to this time being for mission stations. In 1927 it put in force a Belgian Congo Decree of 14 September 1886, which made the validity of sales by Africans dependent on the sanction of the Administration, and forbade any measure which would result in their expulsion from land in their occupation or deprive them directly or indirectly of means of subsistence. The Decree of 3 June 1906, above referred to,[2] has not been extended to this area, but the Decree of 6 October 1930, which regulates the inquiry to be made before land is alienated, is in force. There has been no encouragement of a policy of colonization. Out of the total area of roughly 13,300,000 acres, the State had by 1938 taken over for its own purposes 93,750 acres, of which 87,250 formed part of the *Parc National Albert*.[3] Much of the remainder was used for seed farms. It has reserved 467,500 acres for a *Parc National de la Kagéra*. The Decree constituting National Parks preserves the rights of Africans living within the Park areas.[4] The areas alienated by the State (including the recognition given to German titles) amounted in 1951 to 348,800 acres, of which 201,600 acres are still on lease; 68,480 acres are occupied by missions.[5]

---

[1] M. Ryckmans' Address to the Fourth Committee of United Nations, quoted in *East Africa and Rhodesia*, 2 June 1955, p. 1345. [2] See above, p. 750.
[3] See below, p. 929. [4] *Décret*, 26 November 1934, *article* 4.
[5] *Rapport soumis par le Gouvernement Belge à l'Assemblée Générale des Nations Unies au sujet de l'Administration du Ruanda-Urundi, 1951*, p. 67.

The Portuguese Territories

In the Portuguese Overseas Provinces the legal position regarding land is regulated by a Law of 9 May 1901 which laid down that all land which did not at that date constitute private property in accordance with Portuguese law was State domain. Decrees of 1918 for Mozambique and 1919 for Angola provide for the reservation of certain areas for the exclusive use of the African population, and these lands may not be alienated. Africans are not obliged to reside in these reserved areas, but may occupy unalienated land outside them; land in their actual occupation must not be included in grants to Europeans.

In Angola a Decree of 1927 provided that the area over which Africans were to retain rights was to be calculated as four times that in actual occupation. Africans cannot be required to leave these lands except on payment of compensation and on a guarantee that an equal area of land will be made available for them in the Reserves. Land left uncultivated for more than a year is regarded as vacant. No individual rights are recognized on the Native lands. The total area of Angola amounts roughly to 481,351 square miles or about 30,806,464 acres. The Survey Department of the territory stated in 1933 that an area of 401,180 acres was in the hands of Natives, 386,390 acres being tribal Reserves and 9,795 acres held in individual title. The figures clearly need some further clarification and it is in particular doubtful how far the land which was to be reserved for Natives has been actually demarcated. Statistics are not available regarding the Native area in Mozambique.

The normal method of land alienation is by Concessions similar to those given in French West Africa—that is to say, temporary grants which are confirmed on the execution of stipulated development conditions. The maximum area of a single Concession is 125,000 acres, but in specified districts the limit is fixed at 25,000 acres. The approval of the Minister of Overseas Provinces is required for Concessions above an area which varies in different territories from 2,500 acres to 12,500 acres.[1] In order to obtain confirmation of title, the concessionaire must spend on improvements 200 times the price of the land. Concessionaires are exempt from land tax for the first eleven years if the Concession is beneficially used, otherwise an additional tax may be imposed. At the end of ten years the State may revoke the whole or part of the Concession because of their failure to develop it.

In Portugal the traditional field for European settlement has been Brazil, and up to a recent date settlement in Angola or Mozambique was of a sporadic nature. In Angola a project for colonization on a considerable scale was adopted in 1928. Collective colonies were to be formed by

[1] Comte de Penha-Garcia, ed., *Les Colonies portugaises*, 1931, pp. 345 ff.

the emigration of whole villages to selected sites which were to be surveyed and prepared for them in advance. The State was also to provide assistance to the colonists in the form of seed, stock, and implements. Owing partly to the fact that the economic depression began to be felt almost as soon as the scheme had been put into operation, it was found to be unduly costly and its abandonment was recommended in 1933.[1]

The Benguela Railway Company[2] was authorized by a decree of 9 February 1935 to undertake a colonization scheme on land adjoining the railway. This, too, involved considerable assistance to the colonists; each one on arrival found awaiting him a house and stock, and 35 acres of land already planted. The cost was to be repaid to the Company after eleven years, and the holding would then become the settler's property. The size of a holding was increased to 70 acres in 1937, but it is now considered that the economic minimum is 125 acres. Only nine farms were said to remain in occupation under this scheme in 1947.[3]

In Mozambique rights over a considerable part of the Zambezi region were allotted in the early seventeenth century to individuals who were held to exercise over the African population such powers as had previously been vested in their own Chiefs. Various measures increasing the control of the State over these *prazos*, some of which are hundreds of square miles in extent, were introduced in the course of the nineteenth century, and they are now held as concessions for 25 years.[4] The holder is obliged to cultivate a stipulated area, and is responsible for the administration of justice and the collection of taxes. Conditions on the *prazos* are subject to inspection on behalf of the Administration. A number of them are administered by the Zambezia and Mozambique Companies, who may alienate them subject to Government approval. The proportion of its lands alienated by the Mozambique Company is given as 6 per cent.; for the rest of the province no statistics are published.

The colonization of the Limpopo River area in Mozambique by immigrant families from Portugal has been for some years a favourite project of the Portuguese Government. Several schemes started in the past have proved abortive, owing, it is said, to the selection of the wrong type of settler; they easily became discouraged and emigrated to the Union of South Africa in search of more congenial conditions. It has been stated that in 1949 some 500 Portuguese *Colonatos* were ordered to be removed from the country.[5]

The Six-year Development Plan adopted by the Portuguese Government in 1953, to which reference has been made in a previous chapter,[6] com-

---

[1] *Relatório de Repartição dos Serviços de Cadastro e Colonização*, 1933.
[2] See below, p. 1571.   [3] *Revue Coloniale Belge*, July 1953, pp. 488–91.
[4] Mair, op. cit. pp. 252 ff.
[5] E. Mondlane, in *Africa in the Modern World*, ed. C. W. Stillman, 1955, p. 240.
[6] See above, pp. 230–1, and below, p. 1341.

prised new schemes of colonization in both Angola and Mozambique.[1] In the latter territory the Limpopo River Scheme provides for the eventual settlement of 6,000 Portuguese and 3,000 African families. It involves an area of 500,000 acres, of which 75,000 acres will be irrigated. Each European family will be allotted 70 acres, of which ten acres will be irrigated.[2]

The colonization scheme proposed for the area on the Cunene River in Angola differed in some respects from that of the Limpopo Valley. It was open to both races, Europeans and Africans. The underlying purpose of the European farms was to establish a 'Sanitary Zone' along the frontier; that of the African settlement to stabilize Africans in agricultural production and so to prevent them from emigrating to the adjoining territories. A report on the scheme published in 1953 estimated that if one-third of the proposed numbers were established on the land in six years the result would be satisfactory.

In 1955 there were already five villages inhabited by 155 families or about 1,000 people in all, and it was hoped that by the end of that year there would be 300 families established in twelve villages. About 1,250,000 acres have been set aside for this project, which is intended to support 8,000 colonists. Each holding consists of 152½ acres, made up of 15 acres of irrigated and 30 acres of non-irrigated land, 100 acres of grazing, five for coffee production, and 2½ acres of orchard. The land is given free, but the house, stock, and agricultural equipment is on loan, averaging about £2,000 in value, and repayable over 25 years, when full title is acquired. The scheme will admittedly involve some disturbance of the African population, which is being resettled elsewhere.[3]

Spanish Guinea

In Spanish Guinea the rights claimed by the State over land were first defined by a Royal Decree of 1904, which followed the same principles as had been applied in the Spanish American colonies. The 'private domain' of the State was to consist of all land not subject either to Native or to individual rights. Native lands were to be demarcated, and their alienation by the occupants was to be subject to official approval. More detailed provisions as to the demarcation of land of different categories were contained in a Ministerial Decree of the same year. Concessions up to 250 acres could be granted by the Governor and up to 25,000 by the Minister, for not more than 50 years; larger areas required the approval of the Council of Ministers.

The rights of the State and of Africans respectively were redefined by

[1] *Ministérios da Economia e do Ultramar, Plano de Fomento*, vol. i, 1953, p. 409.
[2] *Overseas Economic Surveys, Portuguese East Africa*, 1955, p. 21. See also below, p. 1009.
[3] *The Times*, 22 September 1955.

a law of 4 March 1948 which excluded from the category of State property all 'lands which had been or might be demarcated as the property of Native tribes, peoples, or family groups'. An Ordinance of 23 December 1949 laid down that State land on which Africans were actually living should be regarded as Native land. Information is not available as to the extent to which Native lands have actually been demarcated.

From the time of the loss of her American Empire, Spain tended to look on her West African possessions as possible colonies of settlement, but projects initiated in the nineteenth century met with little success. After 1904 a special section of the Ministry was made responsible for the furtherance of Colonial settlement, and in 1907 a subsidy of half a million *pesetas* was granted to the *Sociedad General Hispano-Africana* for the development of Spanish interests in Africa. This Company, however, concentrated its attention on Morocco. In the same year the Governor of Spanish Guinea initiated a scheme to encourage Spanish immigration by the creation of local recruiting committees in Spain. Immigrants were offered a ten-acre lot with building material and the opportunity of acquiring full possession, together with seven years' exemption from taxation and military service. They were settled in villages, each with a local council which administered an area of communal land.

In 1930 the work in the Concessions was suspended on account of the difficulty in obtaining labour. It was recommenced in 1944. In 1945 Europeans and 'assimilated Africans' were stated to hold rights over 154,000 acres.[1]

Liberia

The land on which the American Colonization Society planted its first settlement in Liberia was obtained by treaty from local Chiefs. The President of the Liberian Republic in his inaugural address in 1904 stated that these agreements included either express or implied reservations to Native use of land which was in actual occupation. Later in the same year, however, a number of Chiefs presented an address to him complaining that they had been 'deprived of all their lands and now practically possessed none'. While this statement may have involved some exaggeration, there is evidence that in the coastal lands aboriginal tribes were frequently dispossessed of land in the interests of American Liberians. There has on various occasions been much trouble caused owing to complaints by the Kru tribe and in the Maryland County that Native lands have been alienated for the benefit of this class. It will be recalled that persons who are not citizens of Liberia are excluded by the Constitution from the possession of land.

[1] J. M. Cordero Torres, 'The Spanish Territories in Africa, 1940–50', *Civilisations*, vol. ii, 1952, pp. 272, 275.

It was apparently the intention at one time to demarcate tribal Reserves for the protection of the lands of aboriginal tribes,[1] but no effective steps appear to have been taken with this purpose. There is a procedure by which so-called 'tribal Reserves' are created by the grant of deeds to Native villages; land is then allocated to them at the rate of 25 acres per family. This appears to lie within the competence of the Land Commissioners, of whom there is one in each of the five Counties. They may lease or sell land to Liberian citizens, and make free 'Bounty grants' to soldiers of the Liberian militia. It has, however, been alleged that the Commissioners have no regular system of records of these grants of 'Reserves'.

The Firestone Concession of 1925,[2] extending in the first instance to an area of 1 million acres, involved the dispossession of a large number of indigenous occupiers, though in theory 'tribal Reserves' were excluded from the Concession area. The Firestone Company announced, however, that it was prepared to allow the Chiefs, as an act of grace, to select land for the occupation of their people.[3]

It would appear that a number of Concessions of land have been given since 1950, and there has been some indication of the intention of the Liberian Government to enact a new land law, on the ground that the existing legislation is now out of date.

THE NATIVE RESERVE POLICY

The merits and demerits of the Native Reserve policy formed at one time a prominent topic in discussions on the land problems of Africa. At the present time, however, the question no longer holds the same importance. There has of late years been no tendency to extend the use of the system, and its operation is in effect confined to the Union of South Africa, the Federation of Rhodesia and Nyasaland, and certain parts of the British East African territories. It has not been adopted in the British West African territories. Some suggestions have from time to time been made for its adoption in the Belgian Congo,[4] but the suggestions were never actually followed in practice. Proposals for its adoption in the Portuguese Overseas Provinces have not apparently proceeded beyond the stage of discussion.[5] For this position there are a number of reasons which will become clear from the following account of the operation of the system in those territories where it is now in practice.

At the outset the policy was adopted in the Union of South Africa with two purposes in view. In the first place it was designed as a means of providing certain tribes or groups of tribes with a settled and defined area for their occupation, which would be protected from alienation by statutory provisions that would make it illegal for Natives to alienate land to

---

[1] C. M. Wilson, *Liberia*, 1947, p. 38.   [2] See above, p. 237.
[3] Buell, op. cit. vol. ii, p. 832.   [4] See above, p. 750.   [5] See above, p. 755.

non-Natives. There had been cases in which certain tribes (as, for instance, the Griquas) had been dispossessed of all their lands as the result of sales or similar transactions. As a secondary object the system was designed to set up separate spheres of European and African occupation of the country, for from an early date the separation of the two races was envisaged as an objective of general policy. This implied the eventual exclusion of Africans from European lands save as wage-earners or tenant labourers.

If at one period the policy appeared to serve also as a means of securing labour for farmers and others, this was perhaps rather a by-product of the Reserve policy than part of its major objective. There is no doubt, however, that the system received considerable support at the outset from farmers and later from industrial employers, on the ground that it would increase the labour supply. It must have given employers a larger body of labour on lower terms than would have been possible had Africans been allowed to retain large areas for their subsistence. Further, there was from the employers' point of view the substantial advantage that the Reserve served as a 'shock absorber', in the sense that it provided for the unemployed, the infirm, and the aged without any charge on the State.

While allowing this to be true, it is not easy to measure the degree to which the curtailment of the area available for African occupation is responsible in modern conditions for increasing the supply of labour. In a later chapter figures are given showing the extent of the exodus of wage-earners from the Reserves,[1] but it is clear, as shown there, that factors other than the restriction of African lands are now responsible for a greater part of this movement. The most striking illustration is to be found in Bechuanaland where there is a considerable annual exodus, though the areas of land in African occupation have not been curtailed. The migration to the Union from Northern Rhodesia and Nyasaland is also due to general economic conditions rather than to shortage of Native lands.

It is something of a paradox that, at a period when some at least of the original objectives of the Native Reserve system seemed to have become progressively less important, the policy should have acquired a new significance owing to the prominence of the part played by the Reserves of the Union in the application of the doctrine of *apartheid*. The vision of the Bantu confined to the Native Reserves and leading there a tribal form of life has appealed strongly to advocates of segregation, though it can be only the most idealistic of them who can believe that a total severance of contact between Europeans and Natives is practicable. That is, however, a point which has been discussed at some length in previous chapters; here it is merely necessary to remark on certain physical aspects of the

[1] See below, pp. 1378 ff.

separation of the two races. It is only the Transkeian Territories and part of Zululand which can be said to constitute homogeneous Native blocks; in most other areas the holdings of the two communities are intermingled.

In the second place it is generally recognized that the Native Reserves could not support an indefinitely increasing population of Bantu. Whatever improvements in farming might be introduced, the subsistence provided would still be inadequate. But whereas the committee on postwar planning appointed by General Smuts in 1941 regarded further migration to the European centres as inevitable, and the development there of a permanently settled labour force as economically desirable,[1] the more convinced advocates of the doctrine of *apartheid* now believe that the remedy can be found in the industrialization of the Reserves themselves.

It is relevant to ask how far the Government of the Union has directed its attention to improving the economic condition of the population actually resident in the various Native Reserves. In all of them there is marked congestion. Estimates made in 1944 on the basis of the census of 1936 gave a density of 79·5 per square mile in the Transkeian Territories as a whole and 95·4 in the Ciskei. The density in Zululand was 41·6, and in the rest of Natal 83·3 per square mile, as against 21 per square mile for the Union as a whole. Figures of density are, however, of limited value as evidence; their relevance depends on the type of rural economy practised in the area as well as on the potentialities of the land.

It was estimated in 1941 that, in the Transkei, 2,563,000 acres of land were under cultivation and 6,067,000 under stock,[2] a considerable proportion of the Territories being fit only for grazing. In the course of the inquiries which followed the Land Act of 1913 the Eastern Transvaal Local Committee calculated that a minimum of 38½ acres per family was required; the Glen Grey Act of 1894 allowed 8 acres per holding for arable apart from provision for grazing, the proportion assigned to grazing being 70 per cent. of the whole Location. According to a report of the Social and Economic Planning Council the typical holding in 1944 was of 10 to 12 acres.[3]

Large numbers of families, however, have no arable land. The estimated number in June 1943 was 19,690 in the Transkei and 12,814 in the Ciskei.[4] At this time the proportion of the total area under cultivation varied between one-seventh and one-fourth in different Reserves. In all regions except the North Western Cape and Northern Zululand the cattle population was in excess of the estimated carrying capacity of the land.

---

[1] Social and Economic Planning Council, *The Native Reserves and their Place in the Economy of South Africa*, U.G. no. 32, 1946, paras. 189–91.

[2] Committee on Overstocking in the Transkei, quoted in *Witwatersrand Mine Natives' Wages Commission, Report*, U.G. no. 21, 1944, para. 126.

[3] Report of the Social Security Committee, *Social Security, Social Services and the National Income*, U.G. no. 14, 1944, p. 87. [4] U.G. no. 21, 1944, para. 150.

Yet 30 to 35 per cent. of taxpayers in the Ciskei, 44 per cent. in the Transkei, and 26 per cent. in Natal owned no cattle at all.[1]

The Native Economic Commission of 1932 stated that in point of rainfall and quality of land the Reserves were not inferior to the average land in the Union. Nevertheless, their report stated that in the reserved areas, 'with few exceptions, the carrying capacity of the soil for both human beings and animals is definitely on the down-grade, a state of affairs which, unless soon remedied, will within one or at the outside two decades create in the Union an appalling problem of Native poverty'.[2] Fourteen years later the Social and Economic Planning Council remarked: 'Not only is the deterioration of the Reserves affecting the European areas through the drying up of watersheds, the spreading of soil erosion and so forth, but the general debility of the Reserve population means that the major portion of the Union's labour force is attaining only a very low degree of efficiency.'[3]

It was estimated as early as 1933 that the African population as a whole (including those in the towns) consumed 8 million more bags of maize than they produced,[4] and in 1945 the Reserves were said to be producing 'less food than 20 or 25 years ago'.[5]

The cost of agricultural education, dipping, fencing, and soil conservation was for some time borne largely on the budgets of the local Native Councils,[6] but as a result of the attention directed to the condition of the Reserves by the Native Economic Commission, grants were made for this purpose from the Native Development Fund. Between 1934 (when it first undertook expenditure on measures against erosion) and 1944 the Fund provided £330,000 for such works.[7] After the passing of the Land Act of 1936 the Native Affairs Department initiated a detailed survey on which rehabilitation measures were to be based. The first step taken was the establishment under Proclamation no. 31 of 1939 of a number of 'betterment areas' in which, when the local inhabitants had voluntarily agreed to limit the numbers of their stock, the Local Councils bore the cost of fencing the arable areas. By 1945 a total of 170 such areas had been proclaimed.

No action involving expenditure on any considerable scale was taken by the Union Government till 1944, when the Minister for Native Affairs forecast the operation of a twelve-year scheme which was to employ large

---

[1] U.G. no. 32, 1946, paras. 77–78, 211.
[2] *Report of Native Economic Commission, 1930–1932*, U.G. no. 22, 1932, paras. 69, 250–349.
[3] U.G. no. 32, 1946, para. 98.
[4] J. F. W. Grosskopf, 'Die Plek van die Bantoe-bevolking in die Suid-Afrikaanse Volkshuishouding', *South African Journal of Economics*, vol. i, 1933, p. 459. W. M. Macmillan, *Complex South Africa*, 1932, Chapter xi.
[5] Social and Economic Planning Council Report no. 4, *The Future of Farming in South Africa, 1944*, U.G. no. 10, 1945, para. 32.
[6] See above, pp. 426–8.
[7] U.G. no. 32, 1946, Annexure XXI, p. 81.

numbers of African ex-soldiers on soil-reclamation works, fencing, and the building of dams.[1] The estimated cost was first given in 1948 as £40 million.[2] The Social and Economic Planning Council considered that the scheme should be broadened so as to cover all measures calculated to improve the standard of living in the Reserves, including the development of a diversified economy and the building up of urban centres.[3]

In the first years after the Plan was announced there were difficulties in securing trained staff and fencing materials, but, by 1953, a total of 251 European agricultural officers, 249 European engineers, and 466 trained African assistants were employed in the development branch of the Native Affairs Department.[4] The whole question of the measures to be taken to improve the 'African lands' was reopened as the result of the Report of the Commission for the Socio-Economic Development of the Bantu areas (the Tomlinson Commission) in 1955.[5] This body was appointed by the Nationalist Government in 1950 to consider 'the rehabilitation of the Native Areas with a view to developing within them a social structure in keeping with the culture of the Native'. The material provided by its Report is of unusual value, not the least because it has stimulated, for the first time since 1936, an open debate between the three schools of thought which stand respectively for the policies of 'integration', 'separation', or a 'middle-of-the-road' course in regard to African affairs.[6]

In regard to the African lands it estimated that by 1952 measures taken for the conservation of the soil had stabilized conditions in 23 per cent. of the Released but only in 3·8 per cent. of the Scheduled areas. The total cost had been £3,800,000. More important than these estimates, however, was the conclusion that the existing land policy would bring no alleviation of the agricultural poverty of the Bantu, and that it would remain essential for a considerable proportion of them to sell their labour outside the Reserves in order to provide for their needs. The provision of funds made as the result of the Report will be discussed in Chapter XIX.[7]

Something has already been said regarding the Native Reserves in South-West Africa. Though the Tribal Territories of Ovamboland and Okovangoland have been formally declared as Reserves they differ from Native Reserves in the sense that this term has been used in the Union of South Africa and elsewhere. If they have been declared as Reserves, it is mainly for certain administrative reasons, such for instance as the exercise of control over Europeans travelling in or attempting to trade in

[1] House of Assembly Debates, vol. 50, 1944, cols. 9203–5.

[2] Statement by Minister for Native Affairs, quoted in *Johannesburg Star*, 1 December 1948.

[3] U.G. no. 32, 1946, paras. 192–239.

[4] *S.A.S.*, 30 August 1953, p. 10.

[5] *Summary of the Report of the Commission for the Socio-Economic Development of the Bantu areas*, U.G. no. 61, 1955.

[6] Union House of Assembly Debates, 14–18 May 1956.   [7] See below, p. 1334.

them. From the first there has been no question of alienating lands in these Territories to non-Natives.

The Native Reserves in the Police Zone of South-West Africa have been created out of land previously classed as Crown Land.[1] They were declared to be set aside 'for the sole and exclusive occupation of Natives',[2] and, under the terms of section 4(3) of the South-West Africa Mandate Act of 1919, no land set apart as a Reserve for Natives or Coloured persons can be alienated without the authority of the Union Parliament. It will be recalled, however, that they have not been proclaimed in the name of particular tribes or sections of tribes; many of them indeed contain a considerable variety of tribes. Herero are to be found in at least six of the Reserves; in several of them there is almost an equal number of Hottentot and Berg-dama, together with a slightly larger number of Herero. Observation shows that on the whole the conditions of soil and grazing in the Reserves are not inferior to those in the farming areas of the Police Zone.

It is noteworthy that, in making its recommendations, the Commission which had been appointed to make proposals for the areas to be set aside for Native Reserves spoke of the contemplated Reserves as 'the beginning of a policy of segregation'. It is likely therefore that they will continue, for the same reason as the Native Reserves in the Union, to form for many years a part of the land system of the territory. But it is when one contemplates the poverty of soil and low agricultural possibilities of these Reserves that one realizes the difficulty of assuming that the Native can ever achieve a really adequate standard of living in the areas set aside for his occupation.

In the High Commission Territories Basutoland may be said to constitute in effect a Native Reserve, though it has never been formally declared as such. The designation of Reserve is in this case given to the small area held by the British Government by agreement with the Basuto and utilized as the headquarters of the territory and of those of the eight districts. The conditions regarding the grant of shop sites or similar purposes within these areas are regulated by Proclamation no. 32 of 1938.[3] For the rest it is recognized that the lands in Basutoland are the property of the Basuto people and are inalienable. By the customary law of the Basuto, non-Natives may be allowed to occupy the land allotted to them for shops or as mission stations, but not to acquire rights which would allow of the sale of this land to others.

In Bechuanaland the tribal Reserves occupy an exceptional position. As has been seen,[4] the British Government, when taking the measures which led up to the declaration of the Protectorate in 1885, did not assume

---

[1] See above, pp. 696-7.
[2] Native Administration Proclamation no. 11 of 1922, and no. 15 of 1928.
[3] *N.A.*, Part V, pp. 113-15.   [4] See above, pp. 699-700.

that the exercise of protection over the Bechuana tribes would give it any rights over their lands. It did not even claim the right of disposing of those waste or vacant lands over which no rights had been exercised by private persons. By a series of agreements with the Bechuanaland Chiefs the Government acquired rights over certain lands which were then proclaimed as Crown Lands in the Order in Council of 16 May 1904, but the Order expressly excludes from the definition of Crown Lands those areas which had been declared or might in the future be declared as Reserves. The Reserves, or more appropriately the Native Tribal Areas, were originally declared as such by a Proclamation of 1899, and it has from the first been recognized that the ownership of the land is vested in the constituted Native Authorities. The term Native Reserve is in fact somewhat of a misnomer.[1] In Swaziland there has not from the first been any question of the establishment of Reserves.[2]

As has been indicated, it seems likely that the Reserve policy will, if only for political reasons, continue for many years to be a feature of the general policy of the Government of the Union of South Africa. It would also seem probable that, for somewhat similar, though not identical reasons, Southern Rhodesia will continue to maintain its system of Native Reserves. Whatever progress may be made within the Federation in pursuance of the principle of 'partnership',[3] the Reserves are likely to be retained in Southern Rhodesia in pursuance of the long-standing tradition which indicates the advisability of separating African and non-African spheres of economic interest.

As has been remarked, the provision of land made for African occupation in Southern Rhodesia is more liberal than in the Union.[4] But it has also been shown that there is an increasing movement for the exclusion of Africans from occupation of the areas now set apart for European use. The situation in the Native areas is therefore still in a state of transition, and it is not possible at the moment to say how far they are in fact adequate for the support of their population. The Native population, which numbered 530,000 in 1902, was estimated at 1,683,659 in 1948, of whom 1,261,800 were living in the Native Reserves and Native Purchase areas.[5] Calculations made in 1951 led to the conclusion that only ten of the 96 Native areas were not fully populated. In 28 Reserves there were said to be more than 1,000 surplus families; in the Gutu Reserve the estimated surplus was 4,352 families and in the Mtoko Reserve 7,713.

In the early thirties the state of the Native Reserves began to cause grave concern to the Administration. Evidence of over-grazing and loss of topsoil were apparent over wide areas, and far-reaching measures of

[1] N.A., Part V, pp. 309–13.
[2] Ibid. pp. 414 ff.
[3] See above, p. 185.
[4] See above, pp. 693, 702, 705.
[5] O.Y.S.R., 1952, pp. 107, 165.

rehabilitation had clearly become necessary. It was then that the Agricultural Department introduced the policy of 'centralization', which involved the separation of arable from grazing lands, the regrouping of the scattered Native homesteads into central positions, and the allocation of fixed holdings in the arable area. The measure was somewhat drastic and was far from popular; but the Agricultural Department had already succeeded in acquiring the confidence of the people of most of the Reserves and the early results of the changes which it now introduced secured increasing support for further development. By 1950 about 9 million acres, or over half the cultivable land in the Reserves, had been brought under the new system.[1] In the 'Special Native Area' the right of occupation was made directly dependent on the adoption of the methods prescribed by the Department. Where these methods have been followed, yields have undoubtedly been greatly increased, and reference is made in a subsequent chapter to the high rates of yield of maize realized by some of the more successful of the Native farmers.[2] The total area of cultivation was stated to amount in 1951 to over $2\frac{1}{2}$ million acres.

But though the sums allocated under the Native Affairs vote for development in the Reserves had amounted to over £3 million, and nearly £1 million had been spent by the Irrigation Branch of the Department on dams and bore-holes, it was stated that only $14\frac{1}{2}$ per cent. of the necessary conservation work had been completed. It was felt that a new and, in some sense, a more fundamental approach to the problem was required. In 1944 the Native Production and Trade Commission had expressed the view that the full adoption of the practices inculcated by the Agricultural Department was not likely to be seen 'within three generations'. It emphasized the urgency for adequate registration to enforce good husbandry, pointing out that it was impracticable to expect that the provisions of the Natural Resources Act could be enforced in regard to so large a number of land users scattered about the Colony. It urged that grave damage was being done to natural resources owing to the fragmentation of arable land and the overstocking of much of the grazing.

The Native Department first turned its attention to the task of reducing the stock held in overstocked areas and, by use of the provisions of the Natural Resources Act, it succeeded in introducing a measure of compulsory destocking of those areas. Within the next eight years it brought this aspect of the problem under reasonable control. Following on this, the Government enacted in 1951 the Native Land Husbandry Act in order, it was stated, to provide the means to cope with the problems created by the communal system of Native landholding and the consequent misuse of the land. Of its many important features the most outstanding are the provisions for the registration of land rights in the names of individual

---

[1] *Report of the Secretary for Native Affairs, 1951*, C.S.R. 36, pp. 105–7.   [2] See below, p. 848.

holders and the recognition given to the fact that ownership will carry with it the power of alienation.[1]

Some further reference will be made to this aspect of the Act in Part II of the present chapter, but meanwhile it may be noted that considerable expenditure will be involved during the next five years in completion of the Development Plan for the Native areas. From 1949 until 1954 a total sum of £2¾ million had been expended under the provisions of the Native Development Fund Act. The revenues of the Fund were made up partly of produce levies and partly of rents, but the major part was contributed by Government grants. It is estimated that the total expenditure to be incurred up to 1959 in speeding up the implementation of the Native Land Husbandry Act is approximately £6½ million.[2] A large part of this expenditure will consist of schemes of water development, including boreholes, dams, and wells, together with some development of irrigation.

As regards Northern Rhodesia, reference has been made in the earlier part of this chapter to the Order in Council of 1900 which required the British South Africa Company to set aside sufficient land for Native occupation in the territory. That measure was clearly designed to protect Native interests from the wide range of alienations which it was understood that the Company had in view. The first small Reserve, the Angoni Reserve, was delimited in 1907, and by 1938 the position as described in the Report of the Commission on the Financial and Economic Position of Northern Rhodesia showed that the Native Reserves outside Barotseland, some 38 in number, occupied a little over 34½ million acres.[3] The position in the Reserves was for some time very unsatisfactory. Some tribes had been moved into the Reserves allocated to them, in other cases they still occupied Crown Lands, and some of the Reserves created at an earlier date had proved to be altogether inadequate in area.[4]

The system of reservation of lands for Natives underwent a radical change when the Northern Rhodesia Native Trust Land Act Order of October 1947 was issued. The order did not affect the existing Reserves but set apart, in the form of Native Trust lands, a considerable area of what had hitherto been described as Crown Lands. These Native Trust lands amounted in all to roughly 109¼ million acres. (This figure did not include the Barotseland area, which amounted roughly to 29½ million acres.) The Native Trust areas differ from the older Reserves in an important respect in that they will not technically constitute Reserves set apart for the sole occupation of particular tribes or groups of tribes. There has been a continual process of movement from the older Native Reserves into lands allotted for the purpose out of the Native Trust area, a process which is still in active operation.

---

[1] *What the Native Husbandry Act means to the Rural African and Southern Rhodesia*, Salisbury, 1955.
[2] See below, p. 780. [3] Col. no. 145, 1938. [4] *N.A.*, Part II, pp. 76–77.

The steps which were taken for the constitution of the Native Trust lands in Northern Rhodesia followed on the model of the system adopted in the Native Trust Land Order in Council of Nyasaland in 1936.[1] This was deliberately adopted as an alternative to the creation of Native Reserves. In the early thirties there was little demand for land on the part of Europeans, for the depression in world prices had destroyed for the time being any interest in this type of enterprise. There appeared therefore to be no definite benefit in any attempt to divide off the lands of the territory into areas allocated to Natives and non-Natives.

It was realized that the protection of Native lands from alienation, which had elsewhere been secured by a system of Native Reserves, could now be adequately guaranteed by the creation of a system of Native Trust lands vested in the Secretary of State, since rights in such lands could be secured in the future only by grant from him or from local authorities acting under his instructions. It was foreseen also that there would be a further advantage in the fact that the Native Trust lands need not be definitely allotted to the occupation of specified tribes. Native society in the Southern Province of Nyasaland was in a state of transition, for local conditions were still unsettled as the result of the intermixture of tribes which had been occasioned by the Yao and Angoni invasions, and at the same time large numbers of immigrants were moving into the Protectorate from Portuguese territory.[2]

The history of the development of the Native Reserve system in Kenya followed an unusual course. Unlike the position in South Africa and Southern Rhodesia, there was at the outset no underlying conception of the division of the Colony into separate areas, to be held respectively by Europeans and Africans. The issue had a purely local origin. The European community sought to secure for itself a defined area of settlement (the White Highlands) which would be free of African claims and also protected against the possibility that Asians might acquire rights in it.[3] The resulting interference in the lands of tribes neighbouring on this area drove the Administration to the necessity of treating them as Native Reserves, the lands in which could not be alienated. But neither its resolution nor its administrative competence was equal to the occasion, and the prevailing feeling of insecurity among the tribes resulted in the development of the system, initiated by the Land Commission of 1933, by which the tribal lands became Native Trust lands, protected by a special organization of Local and Central Trust Boards.[4]

The Native Reserves, while still protected under the Native Lands Trust Ordinance of 1938 and Native Areas Order in Council of 1939, have now been merged in the larger organization of Native Land Units,[5] and thus

---

[1] Meek, op. cit. pp. 116–19.　[2] N.A., Part II, pp. 23–25.　[3] See above, pp. 406–7, 713–23.
[4] See above, pp. 718–21.　[5] For the Native Land Units, see N.A., Part I, pp. 186–9.

their problems have become part of the overriding problem created by the need to improve the productive capacity of the Native areas in the Colony. That problem has been affected only to a minor extent by the reservation of the area of the White Highlands for European use. It is true that there exists a relatively high congestion of population in the vicinity of the White Highlands, but congestion of population is not confined to this particular area and, where it exists, is due to more general causes.

It is probable that the greater part of the population of the territory must always have been concentrated in the area near Lake Victoria now held by the Kavirondo and in the central regions occupied by the Kikuyu and tribes such as the Kamba. These groups today number roughly $3\frac{1}{2}$ million in all and the balance of the population, roughly 2 million, is distributed over a large number of tribes, some of which have a remarkably low density of population. The reports of the Agricultural Commission of 1929, presided over by Sir Daniel Hall, and of the Land Commission of 1933 made it clear that in certain areas there was already a dangerous degree of soil deterioration. The latter Commission held that unless this process were stayed some of the Reserves would be irretrievably ruined. Although more stock are put on the land than the supply of grazing warrants, the Commission considered that in many cases the unsatisfactory conditions were the result of maldistribution rather than of shortage of land.

Later investigations have tended to show that, while in the Colony as a whole there are areas of local congestion, the greater part of the region is both underpopulated and underdeveloped. Some of the unoccupied land cannot be made habitable without the expenditure of capital on the eradication of tsetse or the provision of water supplies, but there are areas of empty or thinly populated land which could be brought into fuller use to relieve congestion elsewhere. The problem for the Administration therefore is not so much the extension of the areas open to African occupation as that of adapting the system of African agriculture to the needs of a rapidly growing population.[1]

The Agricultural Department in Kenya enlarged its organization between 1923 and 1929, and a number of Reconditioning Officers were appointed in 1930 and in 1935. Grants were made from the Colonial Development Fund in 1937 for a reconditioning campaign in the Ukamba land unit and in 1936 for water-boring in the African areas generally. Under the Ten-year Development Plan adopted in 1946 a total sum of £3 million was provided for betterment schemes. Some 50 of these schemes were in operation in 1950 and involved the control of grazing, measures

---

[1] *Report of the Kenya Agricultural Commission, 1929. Report of the Kenya Land Commission,* Cmd. 4556, 1934, Part III, Chapters I and X. *Native Production and Trade Commission, Report 1944,* p. 27. *Land and Population in East Africa,* Col. 290, 1952, p. 2. *Select Committee on Native Production and Marketing, Development Fund Estimates Report, 1954.* Cmd. 9475, p. 2.

for the conservation of water and soil, and for the opening up of hitherto unused lands for settlement. Four new settlements are now in existence, of which the largest, at Makueni in Ukamba, may be regarded as a satisfactory example of what can be done in waterless and tsetse-infested land. It is expected that 1,200 families will be settled there by the end of 1957. In addition a ten-year scheme of soil conservation and general agricultural development costing £1,025,000 was approved under the Colonial Development and Welfare Act, and in 1953 an additional grant of £5 million from the Colonial Development and Welfare Vote was made for a five-year plan for the improvement of African agriculture.

The British West African territories have not made use of the Native Reserve system. Apart from the fact that there has been in these territories no pressure for the alienation of Native lands for European settlement, it has now been appreciated that, in order to exercise control over the alienation of Native lands to non-Natives, it is not necessary for the Government either to assume rights of ownership in the land (as, for example, by legislation creating a category of Crown Lands) or to establish a system of Native Reserves. It is sufficient for the Administration to take legal power to control the alienation of Native lands to non-Natives by laws which declare any such transaction invalid unless it has obtained the sanction of the Government.

In the French and Belgian territories the Governments have, as has been explained, assumed that all vacant and unoccupied lands fall into the State *domaine*, thus giving the Administration full power to control alienation. Even outside the State *domaine*, however, it has been usual for the Government to take legal power to exercise control over the alienation to non-Natives of lands occupied by Natives. Though, therefore, the Administrations have decided that certain areas should for various reasons be excluded from alienation, it has not been thought necessary to create a formal system of Native Reserves for this purpose.

Looking to the history of the development of the Native Reserve system as a whole, it would seem likely that the Union of South Africa will retain the system in being for some considerable period to come, owing to the part it can play in the service of the doctrine of *apartheid*. Elsewhere we may look to see a gradual merging of the existing Native Reserves into areas which may variously be described as Native Land Units or Native-Occupied Areas, in which the major problem will not be so much the need for controlling their alienation as the need for improving their production. There will no doubt also be a growing recognition of some of the inconveniences of the Native Reserve system, in which the Reserve is set apart for the occupation or use of a particular tribe or group of tribes. Reservation of this character was fully in accord with the outlook of a period which regarded the tribe as an essential unit of Native life and the

Tribal Authority as an integral factor in the machinery of administration. As, however, will be subsequently explained in Part II of this Chapter when dealing with the question of African land tenures, it may prejudice the development of the economy of the territory as a whole if various sections of its agricultural population are subjected to the artificial restraints in the holding and use of land which result from the existence of a system of tribal Reserves.

THE EUROPEAN SETTLEMENTS

There appear to be two views held regarding the value of the contribution made to the population as a whole by the settlement of Europeans on the land. One school holds that, in such countries as Northern Rhodesia or Kenya, results of equal value could have been achieved if the Administration had paid adequate attention to the extension of African cultivation and the improvement of its production. The other school is inclined to hold that the European has been the mainstay of the agricultural production of the countries in which he has settled, and has in particular been responsible for providing the necessary supplies of food for the African in times of scarcity.

This is an issue on which it is difficult to express any definite judgement. It is a matter of speculation how far the African would in fact have succeeded in maintaining an adequate level of subsistence production, apart from any contribution to the export market. Because the African in Uganda has succeeded in the production of cotton, we cannot assume that the African would in the very different conditions of Kenya or Northern Rhodesia have been equally successful in the production of maize and wheat. There are no reliable statistics regarding the proportion borne by European and African production respectively to the total production of those countries where there is a considerable settlement of Europeans. In the Union of South Africa such figures as are quoted are based on Police reports and are of doubtful value where they refer to the production of the Native Reserves.[1] In Southern Rhodesia the volume of maize produced by Africans is stated to have greatly increased in recent years, but the published figures of production represent only estimates where the Native Reserves are concerned.[2] The figures for Northern Rhodesia seem to refer only to maize or other crops which have been brought to market and do not include the amounts produced for subsistence purposes.[3] Here, as elsewhere, one encounters the standing difficulty of

[1] O.Y.S.A., 1952–53, pp. 745 ff.

[2] Federation of Rhodesia and Nyasaland, *Monthly Digest of Statistics*, February 1956, p. 50. *Report of the Secretary for Native Affairs for 1954*, Salisbury, 1955, p. 61.

[3] *Report of Commission of Enquiry into the Out-turn of the European Farming Industry of Northern Rhodesia*, 1954. *Colonial Reports, Northern Rhodesia, 1954*, p. 30.

estimating African agricultural production, both subsistence and market-able.[1]

It would be equally difficult to assess in any definite form the value of the general contribution which the European farmer has made to the economy or the social progress of the country, for any estimate made is liable to be influenced by racial or political prepossessions. There are, however, certain facts, relating in particular to the nature of the assistance given to the European settler, which are matters of record. The scale of such assistance has been considerable.

In South Africa it was part of the policy of Lord Milner after the Anglo-Boer War to attract settlers from outside Africa. Grants were offered to new settlers for development purposes, and farmers returning to land which had been abandoned during the war were assisted by a Land Bank created mainly for this purpose. At a later date steps were taken, on the recommendations of the Transvaal Indigency Commission, to provide for the increasing number of Europeans of South African origin, many of whom were of the Poor White class, who had been deprived of employment on the land by the subdivision of holdings or by changes in methods of agriculture. For this purpose areas of alienated land were repurchased by the State, and special assistance was given to those settling on it.

The expenditure on the provision for land settlement was considerable. By a series of amendments to the original legislation the amount advanced by the Union Government for the purchase of land was increased to nine-tenths of the price, the obligations in regard to beneficial occupation were gradually reduced, and the arrears of debt owed to the State by settlers were twice capitalized, with a substantial write-off on each occasion. From the date of Union to 1949 a total of nearly £22 million had been advanced to farmers by the Land and Agricultural Bank, and of this amount £4½ million had been recovered. Other advances to farmers totalled £23¼ million, of which £16½ million had been recovered.[2]

The cost of the settlement policy has been increased by the fact that land was frequently purchased by the State at an uneconomic figure, and remissions of arrears were necessitated by unusual conditions, such as drought or locust invasions. But there is perhaps no State in the world which has been able to allow purely economic considerations to outweigh the claims of social schemes which have strong political support, and the land policy of the Union is pre-eminently of this nature.

In Southern Rhodesia land settlement schemes were first organized in 1919 for ex-soldiers, a small number of whom were enabled to acquire farms on special terms. The Government also took advantage of the terms offered by the Empire Settlement Act of 1922, and introduced various

---

[1] P. Deane, *Colonial Social Accounting*, 1953, pp. 41, 89, 262, 318.

[2] *O.Y.S.A., 1949*, p. 679.

assisted schemes, half the cost of which was borne by the British Government. New provisions for land settlement were made by the Land Settlement Act of 1944 and specially favourable conditions were offered to Rhodesian ex-servicemen. At the end of 1950 the total amount expended on the settlement of ex-servicemen was £236,536 from general revenue and £1,412,936 from loan funds. The number of ex-service settlers still on their farms was 496, and 210 applications from the general public had also been accepted.

The Rhodesia Land Bank was originally formed by the British South Africa Company in 1912. Loans amounting to £155,288 in respect of farm mortgages were described in 1933 as being to a considerable extent 'frozen' capital, which would be realized only when conditions improved in the industry. Soon after the grant of Responsible Government, a State Land and Agricultural Bank was established under the Land Bank Act, 1924, with an initial capital of £300,000, subsequently increased to £970,000. The assets of the Bank were taken over in 1947 by a new Bank with wider powers created by the Land Bank Act of that year. Its capital at the end of 1950 was £4½ million. In the 20 years from 1930 the Bank had lent to farmers a total of £2,732,000, and the amount outstanding had risen from £872,000 to £1,371,000.[1] Advances are made for the purchase, development, and improvement of land and for the purchase of cattle and machinery.

In Northern Rhodesia an Agricultural Loans Board with a capital of £24,000 was formed in 1934; the largest amount on loan at any time was £21,000 at the end of 1941. In 1949 its losses were written off and the one loan remaining on its books was handed over to a Land Board which had been constituted in 1946 to administer loans to new settlers. By the end of 1952 the Board had issued loans totalling £476,813, of which £342,194 was outstanding. This included, in addition to loans for new settlement, a total of £14,049 for drought relief and £82,506 for flood relief. The activities of the Board were taken over by the Land Bank which commenced operations in 1953.

In Kenya, State assistance to agriculture has taken a variety of forms, including protective duties, favourable railway rates for exports, and exemption of agricultural machinery from customs duty. At an early stage the indebtedness incurred by settlers on the security of their lands became a serious problem; at the end of 1932 the total agricultural debt of the Colony was estimated by the Agricultural Department to be between £4 and £5 million.[2] After the depression period of 1929 a number of special measures were introduced. In 1929–30 reduction of railway rates on cereals was made to a total of £98,000, and rebates on maize

---

[1] *O.Y.S.R.*, *1952*, p. 642.
[2] *Kenya Land Commission, Evidence and Memoranda*, vol. iii, Col. no. 91, 1934, p. 3075.

amounted to £15,071. A special loan to maize exporters was authorized by Ordinance no. 17 of 1930.

In the same year an Agricultural Advances Board was created for the purpose of making advances to farmers in difficulties; its functions were taken over in 1934 by the Land and Agricultural Bank established in 1931. In 1936 the amounts originally fixed as the limits of advances were raised; the maximum advance for the discharge of an onerous mortgage was increased to £3,500, and the maximum for general purposes to £5,000. The rate of interest charged by the Bank was 6½ per cent. till 1946, when it was reduced to 4½ per cent. By the end of 1951 the Bank had advanced £2,383,712 in long-term and £135,011 in short-term loans. Of this total £738,663 was devoted to the discharge of existing mortgages. A total of £1,428,884 had been recovered, and £19,853 written off.

Grants under the Agricultural Advances Scheme were discontinued in 1941. The total advanced was £155,406, of which £26,066 was written off. On the recommendations of a Committee on Agricultural Indebtedness appointed in 1935, a Farmers' Conciliation Board was empowered to make advances to farmers threatened with bankruptcy. When this scheme was wound up in 1950 a total of £66,659 had been advanced to 20 farmers, all but four of whom repaid the advances in full. A Second World War measure, the Increased Production of Crops Ordinance (no. 7 of 1942), empowered the Government to compel farmers to plant certain crops subject to the guarantee of a minimum price, and to make special payments to farmers breaking new ground. By 1951 a total of £1,771,779 had been advanced, of which £1,308,061 had been recovered. A total of £95,926 was paid out in claims for the guaranteed minimum. Grants to farmers breaking new ground totalled £207,658, and special grants to farmers planting maize £86,394. In 1951 the Legislature voted £200,000 for an Agricultural Land Rehabilitation Fund in order to assist farmers to change from single-crop to mixed farming; a total of £116,140 was granted during the year.

From 1939 financial assistance has been offered to intending settlers, mainly in the form of loans to enable them to purchase privately owned land. In 1939 the Government offered to advance up to 90 per cent. of the price of £1,800. A Committee on Land Settlement Schemes recommended in 1944 that not more than 75 per cent. should be advanced except in special cases, but that the maximum sum should be increased to £2,500. Interest was at 4 per cent., and payment of interest was deferred for the first four years.

PART II. CHANGES IN THE INDIGENOUS
SYSTEM OF LANDHOLDING

The most potent influence making for change has hitherto been due to economic circumstances, as, for example, the increasing density of population, the introduction of new types of cultivation, the replacement of a subsistence economy by the growth of marketable crops, or the substitution of fixed holdings for shifting cultivation. Instances of change due to such causes are general, and are not confined to any one type of territory. Changes in the system of landholding due to measures taken to implement State policy have been less marked. They are best seen in instances such as the Glen Grey Act in the Union of South Africa, the operation of the system of Native Land Purchase Areas in the Rhodesias, the wide extension of freehold in the *mailo* lands of Buganda, the operation of the system known as the *paysannat indigène*[1] in the Belgian Congo, or the introduction of individual holdings on the irrigated lands of the Niger scheme in French West Africa. Finally, there are instances in which Africans have consciously adopted forms of tenure modelled on the pattern of European systems of landholding, but they are relatively rare, and are confined to special areas. One of the most prominent examples is to be found in the Colony area of the Gold Coast. The effect of these different influences can best be seen by reference to the position as shown in the following paragraphs.

South Africa

In the Union the greater part of the land in the Native Reserves is still held under customary tenure as modified by a series of Proclamations.[2] Their general effect has been to make the allocation of land by Chiefs and Headmen subject to the approval of the Chief Native Commissioner and to render its occupation subject to prescribed conditions. Village registers may be kept by Native Commissioners and they may fix the maximum area of a holding. An allotment of land may be cancelled for failure to cultivate, or failure to pay the local tax, or for conviction of stock theft or arson. It may also be cancelled if it is required for public purposes, or is held to interfere with the interests or convenience of other persons.

The Natal Commission of 1881–2 recommended that Africans should be allowed to purchase land to hold on individual freehold tenure,[3] and the Commission of 1903–5 considered that they should be given an oppor-

---

[1] See below, p. 798.

[2] Cape Province, Ciskei, no. 302 of 1928; Transkei, no. 26 of 1936; Natal, no. 123 of 1931; Orange Free State, Government Notice no. 1049 of 1916 and Proclamation no. 186 of 1941.

[3] E. H. Brookes, *The History of Native Policy in South Africa*, 1927, p. 70.

tunity of owning land in individual tenure, but in demarcated areas only.[1]
It is, however, only in the Cape Province that the movement for the
introduction of individual title has attained real significance. The earliest
instance in this Province was the settlement in 1849 of the 'loyal Fingoes'
in the Smith–Calderwood Locations of Victoria East, where individual
holdings were allotted on an annual quit-rent.[2] The Cape Natives Locations Act of 1879 further extended this principle, and the Native Laws and
Customs Commission of 1883 recommended that where Africans desired
to acquire individual titles in place of their customary rights, these should
be conceded.

These measures prepared the way for the Glen Grey Act of 1894. Its
objective was wider than the regulation of land settlement, and to many
at least of its supporters it represented a genuine contribution to the
civilization of the Bantu by extending to him the benefits of individual
property.[3] It provided for the survey of allotments of a standard size of
eight acres, the spare land in each Location being treated as grazing
commonage. The allotments were to be held on a perpetual quit-rent,
the grant of freehold being avoided in order that the tenure might be
subjected to prescribed conditions.

The conditions imposed were similar to those applied to holdings under
customary tenure by the Proclamations above referred to. The Native
Administration Act of 1927 authorized the appointment of Commissioners
to investigate the occupation of allotments in 'surveyed Locations' and to
register the owners. A Native Deeds Registry was established by Proclamation no. 119 of 1931. Transfers are endorsed on the title by the
Chief Native Commissioner, and formal conveyancing is not required.
The Chief Native Commissioner thus has control over the disposal of land,
and can exercise it to prevent the acquisition of holdings in excess of the
maximum, the alienation of the holdings, or the allocation of land to
persons considered undesirable. Under the Native Administration Act
(no. 38 of 1927) a table of succession was drawn up which is followed when
land passes at the death of the holder; only one male heir is recognized,
though a widow is allowed to occupy land during her lifetime.

The Glen Grey Act was extended to the Transkeian Territories by a
series of Proclamations from 1898, but in only seven of their 27 districts
have lands been surveyed into allotments on the lines contemplated in the
original Act. The condition of the 'surveyed districts' has not proved to
be so superior to that of other districts as to furnish a strong argument for
a general extension of the system. It appears indeed that the success of the
Act as an experiment in individualization has been prejudiced by circum-

---

[1] *Cambridge History of the British Empire*, vol. viii, 1936, p. 628.
[2] Brookes, op. cit. 1924 ed., pp. 84–89.
[3] *Report of the South African Native Affairs Commission, 1903–1905*, vol. i, Cape Town, pp. 88–89.

stances. Though undue subdivision is nominally prevented, the density of population is such as to deprive the regulation of most of its effect, since the landless members of the family continue to squat on the allotment. As far back as 1929 there were in the Glen Grey district 4,000 adults paying tax for whom allotments were not available. In the seven 'surveyed districts' it was estimated that 11,000 married hut-owners had no arable plots.

It is doubtful whether with their present methods of cultivation the holders can in fact support themselves on their allotments. The rural economy is largely dependent on the keeping of stock, and the numbers maintained are such that pasture is rapidly exhausted and the soil in consequence eroded. It has not been possible for the allotment-holder to become in any real sense a farmer; the Native Economic Commission, indeed, recommended that the restriction on the size of holdings should be relaxed, the maximum suggested being 105 acres.[1] The conditions in the Transkei have not been such as to demonstrate clearly that more intensive cultivation would yield an enhanced return as compared with stock-raising, and there is little incentive to acquire an allotment so long as the common grazing is open to all members of the community whether or not they are allotment-holders. Numerous allotments have been cancelled for failure of beneficial occupation.[2]

The Commission for the Socio-Economic Development of the Bantu (the Tomlinson Commission),[3] after making an informative survey of the working of the Glen Grey Act, has recommended that all land in the Bantu area be sold to the Bantu. The tenure of land would, however, be subject to the condition that land must be beneficially used. A simple form of land survey should be introduced, but registration of individual title should be optional, except where a majority of right-holders favour the change.[4]

It is important, however, to note the extent to which Africans have acquired lands by purchase, since by so doing they pass out of the régime of land tenure regulated by Native custom into that of tenures regulated by European systems of law. It has been explained that purchase of land from Europeans was permitted under various local conditions, except in the Free State, up to 1913; between that year and 1936 it was restricted, except in the Cape Province. The Land Act of 1913 laid down that lands could not be acquired by Africans anywhere outside Native areas, except with the Governor-General's approval. As this approval is in practice given only in exceptional circumstances, they are virtually debarred from acquiring land outside the 'released' areas. Transfers of land already held by Africans in freehold title outside scheduled and released areas are regulated by Roman–Dutch law. The areas of land owned by Africans

---

[1] *Report of Native Economic Commission, 1930–1932*, U.G. no. 22, 1932, Addendum, paras. 140–52.
[2] W. M. Macmillan, *Complex South Africa*, 1932, p. 189.
[3] See above, p. 763.   [4] U.G. no. 61, 1955, pp. 195 ff.

outside Native Locations in 1949 were 573,939 acres in the Cape, 510,055 acres in Natal, 86,834 acres in the Orange Free State, and 2,596,000 acres in the Transvaal.[1] These areas include land which has been purchased from the South Africa Native Trust, in the circumstances explained in a following paragraph.

Regulations for the administration of the 'released' lands held by the South Africa Native Trust for leasing or renting to Natives were issued in 1945 and 1949.[2] They provide for the payment by every holder of Trust Land of a rental of £1 per annum for an arable allotment, with an additional 5s. for every *morgen* in excess of five, and 10s. for a building lot, unless the holder pays the local tax. The rental for arable land includes a grazing fee for five cattle, and extra payment must be made for stock in excess of this number. Trust Land can be forfeited for failure to cultivate according to administrative instructions. An allotment is cancelled on the death of the holder, but his widow or heir has full claim to the re-allocation. One consequence of the difficulty that has been found in obtaining additional land for African occupation is that the average area of holdings allotted by the Trust is smaller than that of land held under any other form of tenure. In an area of the Ciskei where an intensive survey was carried out, the average was 5·6 acres on quit-rent land, 8·7 on freehold, 5·01 on customary tenure, and 3·5 on Trust Land.[3]

There is provision in exceptional cases for Africans to purchase land in individual title from the Trust. By 1950 they had bought 696,739 acres. The Native Laws Amendment Act of 1948 provides for the control of sub-division of these holdings, which were being resold in small plots.

The High Commission Territories

In Basutoland and Bechuanaland the reversionary right of the community to unoccupied land is still recognized, and land is normally allocated by Chiefs and Headmen. In Bechuanaland[4] the total area to be occupied by a Ward (or political subdivision) is defined by the Chiefs, who may transfer a whole Ward to a new locality. The right of Chiefs and Headmen to evict a landholder for political disloyalty is also recognized. In Basutoland[5] these rules are embodied in a written code, the Laws of Lerotholi, compiled in 1922 and revised in 1946.[6] They are appropriate to the traditional system, in which the land that is cultivated in the summer is open to common grazing in the winter.

[1] H. Rogers, *Native Administration in the Union of South Africa*, 2nd ed. 1949, pp. 126–8.
[2] Proclamations no. 12 of 1945 and no. 92 of 1949.
[3] M. E. Elton Mills and M. (Hunter) Wilson, *Land Tenure*, vol. iv of *Keiskammahoek Rural Survey*, 1952, p. 128.
[4] I. Schapera, *Native Land Tenure in the Bechuanaland Protectorate*, 1943.
[5] V. G. Sheddick, *Land Tenure in Basutoland*, Colonial Research Studies no. 13, 1954.
[6] *N.A.*, Part V, pp. 46, 62.

Winter cropping is now becoming increasingly common, as is the cultivation of cash crops. Although this development necessarily encroaches
on the land available for grazing, it does not appear to have been impeded
in Basutoland by the assertion of common grazing rights; in Bechuanaland
this has been a matter of some controversy. Individuals may lend surplus
fields, but cash transactions are still held to be illegal. In Basutoland the
practice has arisen of contracting with the owner of a plough to break up
new ground in return for the full use of the land for two years. The shortage of draught oxen is a more serious obstacle to the extension of cultivation than the difficulty of obtaining land. Nevertheless, some young men
are beginning to demand a form of tenure which will not depend upon
their tribal affiliation.

In Swaziland some 12,000 acres are owned in individual title by Africans
who have bought their holdings from Europeans. It has been mentioned
that a Settlement Scheme was inaugurated in 1946 by the Administration,
which made 346,000 acres available for the purpose.[1] Three Settlement
Areas were opened. One of these, at Piggs Peak, was resumed in 1950 for
afforestation, and a rather larger area was made available in its place,
settlers already established being compensated for disturbance. By the
end of 1952 some 1,742 families had been established on these Settlements.
Allotments are of six acres per family unit. Allocation is on 'permanent
lease'; no rent is charged, but holders can be evicted for failure to cultivate
to approved standards. Holdings are not heritable but are usually renewed
in favour of members of the holder's family. The land has been classified
as belonging to the Native area under the administration of the Paramount
Chief in Council, subject to supervision of the Director of Land Settlement.

Southern Rhodesia

In Southern Rhodesia there seems to have been little spontaneous
change in African land custom, but it is noteworthy that the powers of
allocation normally exercised by Chiefs or Headmen have been withdrawn
in favour of Native Commissioners.[2] New forms of land tenure have been
introduced on a considerable scale by administrative action. The 'Cape
Clause' reproduced in the Charter of the British South Africa Company
had given Africans the right to acquire and hold land on the same terms
as Europeans,[3] and though the Administration did not allow them to
make purchases from Crown Lands, they acquired from Europeans an
area estimated in 1923 at about 100,000 acres.[4]

The Land Apportionment Act, no. 30 of 1930, provided for the purchase

---

[1] See above, p. 698.
[2] Native Affairs Act, 1927, section 42.   [3] See above, p. 702.
[4] A. C. Jennings, 'Land Apportionment in Southern Rhodesia', *J.R.A.S.*, July 1935,
pp. 296–312.

by Africans through the Native Land Board of individual holdings any-where in an area of 7,464,600 acres, increased in 1941 to 7,860,000 acres. An amending Act, no. 25 of 1950, declared 2,205,617 acres of this, which was already closely settled by Africans, to be part of a 'Special Native Area' for occupation on communal tenure. The total open to purchase was thus 5,654,000 acres. Title in the Land Purchase Area is not in the form of fee simple, but can be forfeited if the land is not beneficially occupied. Transfer and mortgage are invalid without the consent of the Board, and in order to prevent undue subdivision, both testamentary and intestate succession have also been subjected to its control. By December 1950 Africans had taken up 2,637 holdings, with a total area of 669,174 acres. The original allocations were of 400 to 600 acres: the average holding is now 220 acres.[1]

Reference has been made in an earlier part of this chapter to the impor-tant measures of reform of land usage embodied in the Native Land Hus-bandry Act of 1951, and in particular to the fact that they are designed to result in the individualization of African landholding.[2] African farmers are required under the Act to have a permit to cultivate, known as a 'farming right'. A farming right is granted in the first instance in respect of land which was being cultivated by the applicant at the time that the Act came into force, but as the aim of the measure is to rationalize the system of landholding, the Native Commissioner is authorized to allot to each farmer an area equal to that over which he holds a right and to require him to cultivate this area. The farmer is also required to build his house on a site designated by the Native Commissioner.

A farming right is transferable subject to the consent of the Native Commissioner after consultation with the local Chief or Council, but it may not be given as security for debt. It expires on the death of the holder, but he may 'recommend' his successor. Farming rights can be forfeited for breach of the regulations prescribing the use to which land may be put. A standard acreage is fixed for each district, the minimum being six acres on non-irrigated land; polygamists are entitled to an additional allotment of one-third of the standard area for each wife after the first.[3]

The Act was first applied experimentally to two Reserves in the Goro-monzi District. The reallocation of holdings is proceeding in the rest of the African areas, where its compulsory provisions have not yet been brought into force. It appears that both arable and pastoral land will be allocated. It is intended to apply to the Reserves and the Special Native Areas the system which already obtains in the Native Purchase Areas, by

---

[1] *Report of Committee on Additional Land for Natives*, 1949 (unpublished), p. 44.

[2] See above, p. 766.

[3] For a study of the clauses of the Native Land Husbandry Act, see *J.A.A.*, July 1955, p. 99; and for the method of aerial photographic survey and registration of land, see R. E. Tanner, 'Sur-vey and Registration of African Land Units in Southern Rhodesia', *J.A.A.*, October 1955, p. 165.

demarcating the land into personally owned farming units on the European pattern. Grazing rights will be controlled on the English commonage principles. In considering applications for land in the Native Purchase Area the Native Land Board decided in 1953 to insist upon the standards of 'Master Farmer',[1] and it seems probable that this qualification will be required for the acquisition of farming rights in the Reserves and Special Native Areas.

The magnitude of the operation can be judged by the fact that it involves 26¼ million acres of land. As already observed, the implementation of the Act will involve an expenditure of £6 million.

Northern Rhodesia

In Northern Rhodesia changes in customary practice seem for the most part to take the form of the closer demarcation of family holdings in the more congested Reserves. In the Southern Province a number of Tonga farmers cultivate fairly extensive areas with ploughs and wage-labour, with the result that some of their fellow-tribesmen cannot obtain holdings large enough to allow of the necessary fallowing. Native Authorities have made a number of rules affecting the use, but none affecting the tenure of land. Representatives of African opinion expressed to the Land Commission of 1946 a desire for the extension of opportunities to acquire holdings on individual tenure, and small allotments of Crown Land are now leased to Africans near townships. At Broken Hill they hold some 900 five-acre lots on lands lying within the Mining Concession.

Near Livingstone about 20 plots of 15 to 20 acres on Crown Land are leased at £3 a year, but not all these are always taken up. There are a certain number of plots of five to ten acres leased to Africans near the Chunga river, about eight miles from Lusaka, plots of this type being in demand mainly for market gardening. Only about 20 Africans hold farms on individual tenure in rural areas; the size of these varies from 20 to 1,385 acres. In Chinsali District Native Authorities have allotted over 20 farms, and in Mporokoso District also a few 40-acre farms have been leased, some of them to returned soldiers.[2]

A 'peasant farming scheme' designed to encourage permanent settlement of groups of at least ten farmers with improved methods of cultivation was approved in principle by an administrative conference in 1949. A revolving fund of £260,000 has been appropriated for their expansion in 1953 and there are now such farms in most Provinces.[3] The disturbance of some 25,000 Tonga Natives living on the north bank of the Zambezi will be necessitated by the construction of the dam at the Kariba Gorge

[1] *Report of the Secretary for Native Affairs, the Chief Native Commissioner, and the Director of Native Development for the year 1953*, C.S.R. 27, p. 58.   [2] *N.A.*, Part II, pp. 156 ff.
[3] *Northern Rhodesia, Report of the Development Authority for 1953*, Lusaka, p. 11.

hydro-electric station and the consequential inundation of the country by the lake, 200 miles in length, which will be thus created.[1] The tribe concerned, which must be resettled by 1959 when their land will be inundated, is amenable to the transfer to new country. It is assumed that the tenure of land thus assigned to it will follow the customary forms in which its original land is held.

Nyasaland

In Nyasaland the Land Commission of 1920 found that a practice of transfer existed in the old Marimba and West Nyasa Districts, and that there was a desire among Africans for individual ownership, but in 1953 only 47 Africans held freehold properties. Their total area was 4,600 acres.

There are no special areas assigned for acquisition on individual title. A small number of African tobacco-growers have acquired holdings above the average by applying to the Chiefs in the customary manner. They do not claim the right to dispose of this land, but in some cases Chiefs have sought to resume it on the ground that it was needed for landless fellow-tribesmen. This action is apt to be resisted, and sometimes with success. The Land Commission of 1946[2] recommended that Africans who wish to cultivate on a commercial scale should be required to obtain certificates of occupancy on the same terms as non-Natives.

Tanganyika

In many parts of Tanganyika customary systems of land tenure have as yet been little modified. The cultivation of marketable crops has, however, led to new developments in a number of areas. The sale of land is practised among the Arusha, Sambaa, Haya, and Chagga. In most of the Sambaa Chiefdoms the seller is not required to obtain the consent of his kinsmen or of any superior authority. The right of pre-emption by the kin group is still recognized in Arusha, but is frequently disregarded among the Haya.

The system prevalent among the Haya and Hangaza has peculiar features due to the grant of large estates by the former rulers to Tusi fief-holders, who, like the landlords in Buganda, collect rent in cash and kind from the peasants living on the land. The Haya Native Authority has forbidden the making of new grants, but in Hangaza they continue to be made. The maximum area of these estates and the maximum rent have been fixed by rules of the Haya Native Authority. Other rules regulate succession, require the consent of the Native Authority for the eviction of a tenant, and authorize the Native Court to direct a tenant who neglects his holding to cultivate it properly. A register of transactions is main-

[1] See below, p. 987.   [2] See above, p. 711.

tained, and registration fees charged. Other land carrying permanent crops is allotted by the Native Authority on payment of a fee.[1]

Land rules intended to protect the peasant have been more recently introduced among the Hangaza. The Chagga formally recognize the relationship of landlord and tenant, but the Native Authorities have refused to take responsibility for registering transactions. The other peoples who practise the sale of land (the Arusha and the Sambaa) do not recognize the landlord and tenant system of tenure.[2] In the Sukuma-land Federation land custom has been defined in a set of detailed rules drawn up by an anthropologist in consultation with a body of representative Africans as part of a general record of Sukuma customary law. These rules do not recognize any commercial transactions. In addition the Native Authorities have set up a committee with the District Commissioner as chairman, and a number of local joint committees, to regulate the distribution of holdings and stock.[3]

In the coastal areas of the Southern, Eastern, and Tanga Provinces a large area of land is held under Muslim law. A confused situation has arisen, partly as a result of the issue of documents of title under the German Administration. There is also conflict between those, including the Native Authorities, who desire to maintain group rights over land and those who seek to extend the area regarded as private property.[4]

As has already been indicated[5] an individual title can under the Land Ordinance be secured only by the grant of a right of occupancy. A wide concession of such titles over African lands, even if accepted as desirable in point of policy, could not be made effective without a land survey and the provision of machinery for registration of title. So far Africans appear to have applied for rights of occupancy only in small parcels of Crown Land in the vicinity of townships, on which rent becomes payable. A registration scheme was proposed in connexion with the resettlement of Chagga from congested areas, but met with general opposition from the people. The new holdings are, however, allotted for occupancy on customary tenure by local Boards consisting entirely of Africans, and a record is kept of them.[6] A Land Utilization Board, upon which all races are represented, was set up in 1950. It was instructed to make recommendations on 'the measures to be adopted to encourage and develop a suitable system of agricultural land tenure for Africans giving the stability and continuity required by modern conditions'.

---

[1] C. K. Meek, *Land Law and Custom in the Colonies*, 1946, pp. 108–9, 113–14.

[2] E. B. Dobson, 'Comparative Land Tenure of Ten Tanganyika Tribes', *J.A.A.*, April 1954, p. 81.

[3] See H. Cory, *Sukuma Law and Custom*, 1953, pp. 111–34, and D. W. Malcolm, *Sukumaland*, 1953.   [4] *N.A.*, Part I, pp. 342–50.   [5] See above, p. 727.

[6] *Report to the General Assembly of the United Nations on the Administration of Tanganyika under United Kingdom Trusteeship for the year 1950*, Col. no. 278, p. 68; ibid. *1951*, Col. no. 287, p. 62.

Zanzibar

The customary land tenure of the African tribes of Zanzibar has been recently described in terms which imply that alienation is still not recognized.[1] During the last 150 years, however, Arabs have become possessed of large estates by purchase and also by grants from the Sultan or by simple occupation. The rights in these areas are equivalent to freehold, although they have not been defined in law.[2] Registration of transactions is compulsory, but there has been no cadastral survey and there is no system of record of titles. A Bill to establish this was introduced in 1937, but has not yet been passed.

A number of estates passed into the hands of Indians in the depression years after 1928, and in 1934 a moratorium was declared and the alienation of Arab and African lands to persons of other races was forbidden.[3] A Decree of 1939 prohibited the attachment for debt of Arab or African lands or their produce and made all alienation subject to the control of a Board appointed by the British Resident.[4] Subsequent inquiries seemed, however, to indicate that the scale of alienation was less than had been estimated. The Agricultural Indebtedness Commission of 1940 found that the total debt secured on land was only £213,000; the number of owners affected was 904, but of these, 540 owed a sum of only £8,300.

Kenya

It is not surprising to find that some of the Kenya tribes who have come most closely in contact with Europeans have now substantially modified their traditional procedure of landholding, more especially in admitting the validity of the transfer of land rights, whether by sale or otherwise. This implies in principle an assertion of individual against group rights over land. Though the movement has gone farther in the densely populated Central Province, there is some indication of it also among the Nandi-speaking tribes of the Nyanza Province, who not long ago were more interested in cattle than in cultivation.[5]

Both the Kikuyu and the Kamba now recognize the sale of land, subject to certain limitations. In one Kikuyu district it is still held that the sale of group land requires the consent of all members, but this is frequently evaded. Some Kiambu Kikuyu invoke the tradition that their forefathers 'bought' their land from the original Dorobo inhabitants as evidence that individual rights in the European sense were in existence before the British occupation, and they claim that on this ground they ought to

---

[1] *Review of the Systems of Land Tenure in the Islands of Zanzibar and Pemba by the District Commissioners (W. R. McGeagh and W. Addis) 1934*, Zanzibar, 1945. R. H. W. Pakenham, *Land Tenure among the Wahadimu at Chwaka*, 1947.

[2] Meek, op. cit. p. 72.   [3] The Alienation of Land Decree no. 1 of 1934.

[4] The Land Alienation Decree no. 9 of 1939.   [5] *N.A.*, Part I, pp. 190–5.

receive title deeds similar to those granted by the Crown to non-Native settlers.[1] It is claimed among the Kamba that the individual farmer has full right to dispose of his land as he wishes, provided he does not sell it outside the tribe. The Committee on Kikuyu Land Tenures in 1929 recommended that a register of land boundaries should be opened, and the South Nyeri Local District Council instituted in 1942 a register of transactions which is regularly maintained.[2]

A guide to land cases has been drawn up by Administrative Officers for the benefit of Native Tribunals in the Central Province. This deals in detail with the procedure in cases involving the redemption of pledges, outright sales, and the relations of landlord and tenant, in particular as regards compensation for improvements. The Local Native Councils in both Fort Hall and Kiambu Districts have passed resolutions advocating the registration of transactions, though Fort Hall would not register sales and so admit their legality. The Fort Hall Council have proposed that all pledges dating from before 1899 should be regarded as irredeemable. Kiambu District has passed a resolution that land should not be attached for debt. These resolutions have not, however, been confirmed by the Government of Kenya, which has hesitated to make these Councils the agents of its policy in land matters.

The enclosure of grazing grounds or arable holdings has begun on a small scale in the Rift Valley Province, and pledging is already common in the Elgeyo-Marakwet District. Among the Bantu of Nyanza Province pledging and renting are common, and pledges are often admitted to be irredeemable. Among both Nandi and Kipsigis some individuals now plough areas up to 150 acres; in the case of the latter the legality of claims to exclusive possession is not undisputed, and the community sometimes asserts its rights by breaking down fences or pasturing cattle on growing crops. The Luo Native Tribunals still usually insist that all pledges are redeemable, but their decisions are not consistent. In the Teita District of the Coast Province land is regarded as fully transferable.

The position in the coastal districts is exceptional, since here, as in the corresponding areas of Tanganyika, the customary law came under Arab influences, and individual rights are well recognized. But the titles to land are in a state of some confusion. In 1908 a Land Titles Ordinance was enacted, and from that date till 1922 inquiries into titles were carried out by a special Recorder. Some 21,700 claims were examined and 10,000 titles issued giving an indefeasible title, subject to an appeal to the Supreme Court. About 4,000 of these cases were never taken up, mainly because the cost would have been more than the claims were worth. The question formed the subject of a special inquiry by Sir Ernest Dowson in 1938. He

---

[1] L. S. B. Leakey, *Mau Mau and the Kikuyu*, 1952, p. 68. P. Mitchell, 'Mau Mau', in *Africa Today*, 1955, pp. 486–7.   [2] *N.A.*, Part I, pp. 190–4.

recommended a survey of the area block by block, and the issue of a possessory as distinct from an absolute title, as was the normal practice in India. The matter still awaited a decision at the end of 1955. In 1946 there were 4,000 land disputes awaiting adjudication.[1]

The Crown Lands (Amendment) Ordinance of 1938, following the recommendations of the 1932 Land Commission, provides for the reservation of 939 square miles as Native Leasehold areas. In these areas leases may be granted to either groups or individuals. Title is indivisible on succession, and no disposal or encumbrance is valid without the sanction of the Administration. An amendment in 1942 provided for the creation of Native Settlement Areas in which Settlement licences for a term up to 999 years may be granted to groups or individuals. A number of such Settlements have been opened, but no licences have yet been issued.

Proposals for the grant of title in the Native Land Units, as the Reserves are now termed,[2] were made by the African Affairs Committee in 1950.[3] They recommended the issue of rights of occupancy in specially selected areas to applicants whose right over their land was undisputed, provided they were approved by the Agricultural Department as good farmers and the land to which title was sought was an economic area. The grant of a right of occupancy would be considered a special privilege for farmers whose methods were such that they might reasonably be expected to improve land to which they had secure title. A survey of these areas began in 1952 in the Nyeri and Kipsigis Districts. In the former the issue of titles began in 1954.

Uganda

In Uganda the most conspicuous developments have been seen in the results of the grant of proprietary rights in the Buganda *mailo* lands under the Uganda Agreement of 1900.[4] The Buganda *Mailo* Law of 1908 accorded to 'Chiefs and private landowners' a right approximating to freehold, though transfers to non-Africans required the prior consent of the Governor and the Buganda Government. This allocation of land seems to have been viewed at the time as the confirmation of existing quasi-feudal rights. Later, however, it was alleged that the measure had taken no account of the position of the peasants (Bakopi) or of the clan heads (Bataka) who held certain lands as burial grounds for all members of the clan.[5]

The complaints of the Bataka were vigorously canvassed in a controversy which occupied a prominent place in local politics between 1921 and 1925, but it was not considered feasible to modify the provisions of the

[1] *N.A.*, Part I, pp. 191–7.
[2] See above, p. 720.
[3] *J.A.A.*, April 1950, pp. 19–24.
[4] See above, p. 724.
[5] R. L. Buell, *The Native Problem in Africa*, 1928, vol. i, pp. 594 ff.

1900 Agreement. More recently, alleged injustices in the allocation of land have become the rallying ground for all Ganda who are dissatisfied with official policy. The Ganda political organization which took a prominent part in the rioting of 1949 was called the Bataka, though its members did not claim to be themselves clan heads. The Buganda Land Succession Law of 1912 and the Law to Safeguard Bataka Rights of 1925 recognized the position of clan heads in that it is now their function to advise the Kabaka on the confirmation of an heir in his succession to land rights. This is still required by Native custom.

More significant, however, is the effect of the *Mailo* Law on the relations between Chiefs and peasants. The holding of land has in effect been divorced from the exercise of those political functions on which the control over land had previously depended, so that the relation of landlord and tenant is now purely commercial. The interests of the resident tenant have been protected by the Buganda Busulu and Envujo Law of 1927,[1] which limits the dues chargeable by landlords and permits eviction only if the land is abandoned, so that in practice a tenancy can become hereditary. High rents are charged for the hire of a plot to cultivate for one season to a tenant who does not wish to build on the land; such tenants are often immigrants from neighbouring territories. The custom of charging entry money to an incoming tenant is also widespread. Nevertheless, Ganda tenants regard the system as giving them adequate security, and immigrant Africans state that they prefer it to the customary tenure of their own countries.[2] The East Africa Royal Commission recommended that the Busulu and Envujo Law should cease to apply on any estate on which landlord and tenants agree to substitute for these statutory provisions a contractual form of tenancy.[3]

A considerable area of land has changed hands by sale in small plots. Where originally there were 3,700 allottees of *mailo* land, in 1952 there were 52,000 registered properties and approximately 8,000 whose claims had not yet been investigated.[4] A Registration of Titles Ordinance was introduced in 1923, but the procedure was so costly that it was little used. In 1939 the Buganda Government enacted a law providing that no transaction in *mailo* land should be valid unless it was registered, and making it an offence for anyone not a registered proprietor to purport to sell land.[5] There is, however, a marked degree of congestion in the *mailo* registry, which is responsible for the actual preparation of the transfer agreements.

The establishment of the *mailo* system in Buganda was followed by requests for its extension to the Toro, Ankole, Bunyoro, and Busoga

[1] V. Liversage, *Land Tenure in the Colonies*, 1945, p. 47.
[2] See A. I. Richards, ed., *Economic Development and Tribal Change*, 1954, pp. 126–31.
[3] Cmd. 9475, p. 360.
[4] *Colonial Reports, Uganda, 1952*, p. 33.
[5] Buganda Land (Agreements) Law of 1939.

districts, but the Government confined itself to the grant to the Ruler and a few leading Chiefs in Toro and Ankole of a limited area, to which they were entitled by the agreements of 1900 and 1901 respectively. These grants were made as freeholds under the Crown Lands Ordinance of 1903. The question of the right to be granted to peasant cultivators in these districts was investigated by a committee whose inquiries lasted from 1911 till 1920, but its recommendations were not accepted by the Administration. It has been explained in an earlier part of this chapter[1] that in 1956 the Government decided to legislate in order to declare Crown Land to be 'African land', and to make provision for the registration of a title of ownership for those occupants of such land as desired it.

Pending legislation in this form, however, there remains in force in certain districts the system initiated in 1926 under which certificates of occupancy can be granted to cultivators, while reserving the proprietary right to the Crown. These certificates give to the cultivator an undisturbed tenure so long as he occupies the land. He has, moreover, the right of testamentary disposition and the right to dispose of trees, buildings, and crops when the occupancy is terminated. Certificates are issued by the Native Authority, now termed the African Local Government.

In Bunyoro the issue of these certificates has in many cases been regarded as equivalent to the traditional grant of fiefs, while at the same time the fee paid for the certificate is interpreted as a purchase price giving full control of the land, except that rent may not be required of tenants. It is estimated that about 1,500 holders of occupancy rights (out of a total of 5,000) have obtained these certificates over areas on which other cultivators are living. These latter have no security of tenure and are prevented by the rightholders from planting trees or even building houses lest this should lead to their claiming rights over the land. The scheme of general legislation put forward in 1955 may assist to provide a solution for these and other difficulties into which the people of these districts have been led by the previous failure of the Administration to clarify the character of the tenure of the Crown Lands.

Nigeria

In the Northern Region of Nigeria the political authority of the Emirs is manifested chiefly in their claim to ultimate control over the land and in the exercise of seigneurial rights. The fiefs they granted were in effect administrative areas, and the right of the fief-holder to take a share of the tax collected was a reward for political or military services. To this extent the system resembled that of the Mogul empire in India. Under British rule a fixed salary has been substituted for these taxes; but it was

---

[1] See above, p. 725.

recently found that they were still being collected in at least one Emirate (Bida).

The principal effect of economic developments has been seen in the increasing tendency to delimit individual holdings, both in Muslim and pagan areas. The application of Islamic law, which results in the sub-division and fragmentation of holdings, has reinforced this tendency. The conferences of Chiefs which were held at one period in the Northern Provinces discussed the possibility of fixing a minimum limit for the sub-division of land under Islamic law, but reached no decision.[1]

In the area of dense population around Kano, 782 square miles have been surveyed by the staff of the Native Administration as a basis for the assessment of a tax based on the land. The survey is said to be only 80 per cent. accurate, but it is nevertheless the only instance in West Africa of the compilation of a record of land holdings. Although the Emir of Kano and his Council insist that land cannot be sold, this practice appears to be common, while leasing is judicially recognized.[2] In other rural areas pledging is on the increase and it may be equivalent to sale if the terms are such as to make redemption difficult. On these and other matters, such as rights of succession, there is often an open divergence between current practice and the tenets of Muslim law. In the Jos Division of the Plateau Province, where there is considerable pressure on the land as the result of the immigration of Africans employed at the tin-mines, land is leased on cash rents, but local opinion still does not countenance sale.

The Native Authority (Control of Alienation of Farmland to Strangers) Rules, 1948, require 'strangers' to obtain a licence to farm from the Native Authority. Licences are to prescribe the rules of cultivation to be observed, and are not to be transferable. Regulations under the Land and Native Rights Ordinance (no. 1 of 1950) empower Native Authorities to declare 'Settlement Areas' within which zones may be reserved for agriculture or grazing, to issue rights of occupancy, and to control the alienation and devolution of rights. These regulations are in force in the Northern Region, and have been applied to various schemes for improved farming, such as the Anchau Settlement Scheme in Zaria Province.[3]

In the 'stranger settlements' attached to the large towns, Kano, Kaduna, Lokoja, Zaria, and Jos, land is leased in surveyed plots. Up to 1940 these settlements were administered by European local officers, but in that year they were placed under the Native Authorities,[4] and a regulation (no. 18 of 1940) was introduced to govern the issue of titles and the control of transfers.

The Native Authorities have shown little interest in the enforcement of these regulations, for which they have no adequately trained staff. Transfers

[1] Meek, op. cit. p. 241.
[3] See below, p. 908.
[2] See above, p. 663. Meek, op. cit. pp. 155–6.
[4] N.A., Part III, p. 87.

are rarely reported and applications for transfer are frequently left un-answered. The Native Authority normally refuses to grant more than one plot to any person, but this rule is evaded by such devices as registration in false names. For all these reasons there is considerable uncertainty as to title. In the neighbourhood of Jos, plots are allocated by Native Authorities, but no written titles are issued. A register of allocations is kept at Kafanchan, and at Bukuru such transactions as are reported are recorded. Not only buildings but also vacant sites are sold.[1]

In the Western Region commercial dealings in land have long been common. The question how far the Yoruba Chiefs were entitled to control such transactions was first raised in 1903, when the Bale and Council of Ibadan claimed that all land should be treated as vested in them. This was, however, a claim which went beyond any authority which they possessed in Native custom. It is also of some importance to note that the Native Authority system in the Western Region had developed by about 1948 to a point where the Chief was in most cases only a presiding figure in a body with a majority of elected members.[2] The Ibadan Native Authority issues leases and imposes rent; it maintains a Lands Officer and a standing Lands Committee. The right to lease plots in Benin City has for many years been exercised by the Benin Native Authority. Plans are issued by the surveyor of the Native Administration and are treated as documents of title which authorize the occupier to dispose of the land. In one or two other towns of the Benin Division holdings are allocated on documentary title. Benin has sought to organize a survey and charge rents in proportion to acreage, but has not had adequate technical staff for the purpose. The creation of a Land Registry for Abeokuta (Egba Native Authority) has been under discussion at intervals since 1929.

The position of the Native Authorities as the bodies controlling the use and disposal of land was formally recognized by the Native Authority (Control of Lands) (Amendment) Ordinance no. 73 of 1945, which confers on Native Authorities more extensive powers than they have in any other British dependency. They may make rules for the control of alienation and mortgaging, for prescribing that purchase at sale shall be subject to their approval, for regulating the allocation of 'communal or family land' and for controlling its use. Action has already been taken under this Ordinance by a considerable number of Native Authorities, and such Authorities (or the Local Authorities which are to replace them) will probably make increasing use of these rules in urban areas, where rents are becoming a matter of concern to them. In Benin Province the position of 'stranger' immigrants on farmland has been considered by a number of Native Authorities; some have expressed a desire to exclude or even expel

---

[1] C. W. Rowling, *Report on Land Tenure in the Kano Province*, Kaduna, 1949; idem, *Plateau Province*, Kaduna, 1949.   [2] See above, p. 462.

them; others have been somewhat reckless in raising revenue by the grant of rights, particularly forest rights.[1]

In the Eastern Region leasing of farming land for a season is now a common practice. A cash rent is usually charged, and long-term leases for a fixed rental are on the increase. Land transfers, which are in practice permanent although they are not recognized as sales, occur in the Onitsha, Owerri, and Rivers Provinces. Mortgaging appears to be still unknown in rural areas, but is common in the large townships, where it has long been permissible to mortgage land to an alien, though subject to official consent.[2] Some Ibo have expressed a desire that Native Authorities should make rules clarifying the accepted custom regarding the persons entitled to be consulted on the transfer of land, but others are suspicious of any intervention which might seem to be prompted by the Government. In the town of Onitsha land is openly sold, conveyancing being done by a solicitor.[3]

In Lagos itself much confusion has resulted from the fact that the nature of the rights over land acquired by the Crown at the cession of the island in 1861 was only finally determined by the Apapa case of 1921.[4] As has been explained, a number of 'Crown grants' were issued in early days, most of them being to persons who were already in occupation of the land concerned. About 2,500 such grants were made up to 1878 and about 750 between that date and 1914, after which the practice was discontinued.

A number of Ordinances designed to validate these grants were passed in 1947.[5] Such grants were treated as titles under English law, and land covered by them was freely disposed of. A number of decisions, however, have upheld customary law to the extent of requiring the consent of the family to an outright sale.[6] The Privy Council recommended in 1936 that the nature of the title to land in Lagos should be clarified by legislation, but apart from the validation of the Crown grants no such action has yet been taken.

A system of registration was, however, introduced for the Colony area by Ordinance in 1935.[7] Titles are registered after the Registrar has made a full investigation of the nature of the rights claimed. An absolute title in fee simple can now be acquired only by purchase from a registered owner. Where land is shown to be family land under Native law and

---

[1] *N.A.*, Part III, pp. 142–5. C. W. Rowling, *Report on Land Tenure in the Benin Province*, Kaduna, 1949.

[2] Regulations under Native Lands Acquisition Ordinance no. 32 of 1917.

[3] *N.A.*, Part III, pp. 180–2.   [4] See above, p. 730.

[5] Crown Grants (Township of Lagos) Ordinance no. 18 of 1947. Arotas (Crown Grants) Ordinance no. 19 of 1947. Epetedo Lands Ordinance no. 20 of 1947. Glover Settlement Ordinance no. 21 of 1947.

[6] Cf. *Oshodi* v. *Balogun and others*, W.A.A.C. 1, 1936. See cases quoted by Meek, op. cit. p. 297; T. O. Elias, *Nigerian Land Law and Custom*, 1951, pp. 144 ff.

[7] Registration of Titles Ordinance no. 13 of 1935, as amended by nos. 8 of 1936 and 46 of 1943.

custom a transfer in fee simple is not registered unless the family consent. Registration is compulsory in the case of sales and of leases or assignments of land for 40 years or more, otherwise it is voluntary. There is, therefore, no complete register of titles, but 1,974 freehold and 353 leasehold titles had been registered up to March 1954.[1]

In the parts of the Colony area adjoining Lagos land is coming to be more and more regarded as individual property; it is now being transferred by conveyances following the forms of English law. This applies particularly to the area around Ikeja, where it is estimated that half the land is now recognized as the absolute property of individuals. It applies also to that part of the Awori area near Lagos which is in demand for building sites. Elsewhere in the Awori area the position of the Oba of Irewe as ultimate owner is still recognized, and some 600 'stranger' farmers pay rent to him; he receives this in his personal capacity and it is not paid to the Native Treasury.[2]

In the southern part of the Cameroons under United Kingdom Trusteeship the development of cocoa farming has had results similar to those created in the Yoruba provinces. It is common for land to be leased, either for a cash rent or a share of the crop. Though sale is not recognized as legal, in the eastern districts of Mamfe land is sold publicly in the market place. In other areas right-holders are coming to regard their land as primarily a source of cash income.

In some areas Native Courts refuse to recognize the right of redemption of pledged land if it is not exercised within what they consider a reasonable period, thus implicitly accepting the doctrine of prescription. Conflicts arise in such matters as the claims of tenants to crops planted on land which is transferred over their heads. The judgements of the Native Courts on these matters do not follow any common principle. The majority of tenants or purchasers are 'strangers'. In the Victoria Division many of these immigrants are said to be 'squatters' who have taken up land without receiving permission from resident right-holders.

The Gold Coast and Togoland

In the Northern Territories of the Gold Coast there seems to be little evidence of mortgage or sale, though pledging is said to be common. Here the most significant change in the customary system arises from the fact that the Chiefs who have been appointed as Native Authorities are not by local custom authorized to allocate land.[3] This is the function of the Tendana, the priest of the Earth God.[4] Proposals have been made that the

[1] Federation of Nigeria, *Annual Report of Land Department for Year ending 31 March 1954.*
[2] *N.A.*, Part III, pp. 36–37.
[3] M. Fortes, *The Dynamics of Clanship among the Tallensi*, 1945, pp. 177–87.
[4] *N.A.*, Part III, pp. 260, 276.

Tendana should be associated with the Native Authority or Native Court when these are dealing with land matters. It seems unlikely, however, that the Gold Coast Ministers, whose policy is to europeanize all institutions as rapidly as possible, will act on this suggestion.

In the Colony area and Ashanti commercial transactions in land are even more common than in the corresponding parts of Nigeria. In the Colony particularly the wide use made by the Chiefs of their powers to grant Concessions[1] over 'stool' lands, the increase in land values resulting from the expansion of the cocoa industry, added to the widespread adoption of English documentary forms of transfer, were described as long ago as 1931 as having virtually destroyed the customary system.[2]

The volume of litigation regarding land is said to be greater in the Gold Coast than in any other African territory. This is largely concerned with disputed claims to 'stool' lands, namely, the unallocated areas which are a potential source of revenue from Concessions, or from the 'tribute' paid by 'stranger' cocoa planters. The cost of this litigation is well illustrated by the history of the Asamangkese Division, where, after about £100,000 had been spent by each of the parties on a single dispute, a special Ordinance had to be passed in 1935 controlling the finances of all stools in the Division.[3] Another example of the tenacity of litigants is the Himang case, which was opened in 1872 and was still being fought in 1948.[4]

These disputes have involved two separate issues, the ownership of particular areas of land and the extent of the jurisdiction of the States. An Ordinance of 1950 (no. 49) authorized the Governor to appoint State Boundary Committees, and the first was set up in 1953. But while such bodies can determine the limits of jurisdiction, they do not dispose of disputes concerning ownership of land. The only satisfactory solution would appear to be the appointment of a Statutory Commission with final powers to deal with both issues. It remains to be seen whether African Ministers will be willing or able to take the necessary action. Meanwhile the management though not the 'ownership' of stool lands has been transferred by the Local Government Ordinance (no. 29 of 1951) to the new local authorities,[5] in which elected members are in the majority.

The problems created by the uncertainty of individual titles increase in proportion as more farmers take up land in areas to which they are 'strangers', and they have been intensified by the search for new cocoa land to replace that on which trees have been destroyed as a means of combating Swollen Shoot disease.[6] Cocoa farms are sometimes held on the *abusa* system whereby the owner of the land receives from the 'stranger'

[1] Meek, op. cit. pp. 169 ff.   [2] A. W. Cardinall, *The Gold Coast*, 1931, p. 68.
[3] Asamangkese Division Regulation Ordinance, Laws, cap. 78.
[4] C. R. Havers, *Report of Commission of Inquiry into Expenses incurred by Litigants in the Courts of the Gold Coast, and Indebtedness caused thereby*, Accra, 1945.
[5] See above, p. 527.   [6] See below, p. 828.

one-third of the crops; others are sold according to the forms of English conveyancing.[1] About half the population of Manya Krobo State, for instance, are now farming in the Akwamu and Akim Abuakwa States, and whole tracts of Akim Abuakwa land have also been acquired by Akwapims. There are many similar instances.

The remedy can only be found in the organization of a system of registration of titles; but this will not serve its purpose unless registration (which must be accompanied by an adequate cadastral survey) is compulsory and is universal. The situation has passed the stage when a partial or an optional system of registration will be of any avail. In Ashanti, where the traditional system is similar to that in the Colony, there is less evidence of the practice of sale of land or of the use of documents which purport to transfer freehold rights. Here too, however, there is litigation over boundaries, which could be reduced by the institution of a survey.[2]

In the northern section of Togoland under United Kingdom Trusteeship certificates of occupancy may be obtained on the same terms as in the Northern Territories of the Gold Coast. No indigenous African has applied for such a certificate, but immigrant cocoa farmers from the Gold Coast Colony, French Togoland, and the southern section of British Togoland have been given leases extending over a considerable area.[3] Rent is paid to the Gold Coast Government and two-thirds of the amount received is allocated to the Native Authorities concerned.

A remarkable example of the use of these certificates occurred in 1950, when after an investigation of the claims of 31 'stranger' farmers in the Kete Krachi district, titles were issued declaring them to have 'an absolute perpetual hereditable and alienable right' to their lands 'subject to the ultimate reversion being vested in the Stool'.[4] There could be no clearer evidence of the need for an authoritative registration of titles, based on a clear definition of the legal implication of the nature of the title registered and carrying an accurate indication of the position and area of the parcel of land to which the title refers.

Sierra Leone and Gambia

The laws of the Sierra Leone Protectorate accord to the constituted Native Authorities (here known as Tribal Authorities)[5] powers over the control of land which elsewhere have more usually been left in the hands of the Chiefs or Headmen traditionally responsible in such matters. Since, however, most Tribal Authorities now consist of the heads of the principal land-owning families in the Chiefdom, they appear to constitute an appropriate body to determine the policy of land usage, and this position seems

---

[1] Meek, op. cit. pp. 295 ff.   [2] N.A., Part III, pp. 252-4.
[3] Annual Report to the General Assembly of the United Nations on Togoland, 1949, Col. no. 259, p. 61.
[4] Ibid. 1950, Col. no. 274, p. 149.   [5] See above, p. 534.

to be well accepted.[1] It is mainly in Mende country that customary tenures are undergoing change, as a consequence of the expansion of rice cultivation and the reclamation of swamp land for this purpose.

Pledging of land is common, and money-lenders are advancing considerable sums on the security of pledges.[2] Though redemption is theoretically possible at any time, the land may be pledged again to a third party, so that the original ownership becomes obscure. This is a fruitful source of litigation. Other difficulties arise from the claims made by Tribal Authorities to collect rent on swamp lands which have been cleared at the expense of the Native Treasuries, since family groups sometimes assert rights over these lands. Tribal Authorities and Native Courts require guidance in clarifying the customary law on these points. A report on soil conservation prepared by members of the Department of Agriculture in 1951 expressed the opinion that the demarcation of holdings had gone far enough to warrant a system of registration.[3]

In Gambia, village Elders are recognized as the effective land authorities, while District Heads and Alkalis are concerned only with the grant of rights to 'non-indigenes', that is, persons not belonging to tribes indigenous to the Protectorate.[4] Most of these are immigrants from French territory. Local right-holders allot land to them in return for help with their own farm work.[5]

The French Territories

In the French territories changes in customary law seem to have been less extensive than in the British West African colonies.[6] There are, however, recognizable instances of developments in the direction of individual ownership. Thus in Senegal there is an established system of rental, which appears to be based on an original recognition of seigniory, the payment being on a scale fixed by custom similar to that of the *zakkat* or Islamic tithe. This has a parallel in the similar rentals taken by Arab holders of land in Dikwa in the British Cameroons. In the well-populated lands of Dschang in the French Cameroons, holdings are marked off with permanent boundaries,[7] and on the lower Sanaga river there have occurred cases where men of tribes living in the delta islands have purchased lands on the mainland, which they now claim to hold in individual right.[8]

In urban areas, such as Douala, Yaoundé, and Kribi, sales are common,

---

[1] 'Land Tenure in Sierra Leone Protectorate', *J.A.A.*, July 1949, pp. 119–22.
[2] *N.A.*, Part III, pp. 322–4.
[3] *Soil Conservation and Land Use in Sierra Leone*, Sessional Paper no. 1, Freetown, 1951.
[4] *N.A.*, Part III, pp. 345–7.
[5] J. H. Palmer, ed., *Notes on Strange Farmers*, Sessional Paper no. 15, Bathurst, 1946.
[6] L. Geismar, *Recueil des coutumes civiles des races du Sénégal*, 1933.
[7] *Rapport annuel au Conseil de la Société des Nations sur l'administration du Cameroun, 1922*, p. 46.
[8] Ibid. *1923*, p. 50.

including sales to non-Africans; these require to be sanctioned by the *Conseil d'Administration*, and are registered. Approval is given only if the seller has other land for his own occupation.[1] In French Togoland the leasing of land is a well-established practice, and it would seem that this is also the case in Dahomey and the Ivory Coast.

In their land system the French recognize two classes of rights—namely, the full title of proprietorship, and the customary rights existing under Native law. The full title is obtained by the *immatriculation* of lands acquired by the process of grant, concession, or purchase from the State, or by purchase from Natives. As the title when registered by the State is indefeasible, in the sense that it is certified by the State against all third-party claims, it is granted only after full notice to other claimants and the examination of their claims by the Conservator of Property. Contested cases are referred to the Courts. The registered holder has then full rights of disposal in transactions of all kinds.

In French West Africa the system was introduced by a Decree of 24 July 1906; registration was made compulsory in cases of alienation by the State or purchase of rights from Natives by Europeans or *assimilés*. It was open to Natives to seek *immatriculation* for property held or acquired by them. In Equatorial Africa the privilege of *immatriculation* of land was at first confined to Europeans and *assimilés* but was extended to Africans, with some limitations, by a Decree of 12 December 1920. It was introduced in French Togoland by a Decree of 23 December 1922 and in the French Cameroons by a Decree of 22 July 1932.[2] It is an important fact that the *immatriculation* of land renders it subject to the French Civil Code, as modified for use in the Colony, in so far as concerns transfer, mortgage, or encumbrance, though it is still subject to Native law in regard to succession.

The provision for the *immatriculation* of African property is part of a general policy which attaches great importance to processes tending to encourage the recognition of individual title in land of Africans. Some reference has already been made to the influence of the judicial conception of property as an individual right, but individualization has been advocated equally on economic grounds. Not only have writers such as P. P. Leroy-Beaulieu[3] emphasized this policy, but official reports have consistently put it forward as the objective of the Government.

As the Report of the Colonial Budget of 1910 put it, 'the system of individual ownership is incontestably the one which is most favourable to production'.[4] Its advantages as affording a basis of credit have been freely

---

[1] *Rapport annuel à l'Assemblée Générale des Nations Unies sur l'administration du Cameroun, 1951*, p. 88.

[2] A. Girault, *Principes de colonisation et de législation coloniale*, vol. iii, 1930, chapter xvi. P. Dareste, *Traité de droit colonial*, vol. ii, 1932, pp. 216–17. *Rapport annuel au Conseil de la Société des Nations sur l'administration du Cameroun, 1934*, pp. 91, 187.

[3] *De la colonisation chez les peuples modernes*, 1908 ed.

[4] Quoted in F. D. Lugard, *The Dual Mandate in British Tropical Africa*, 4th ed. 1929.

pointed out to African leaders. Thus the Governor of Togoland, speaking to the Lomé Council of Notables in 1924, stated: 'Si vous désirez avoir de l'argent, il faut immatriculer vos terrains; vous pourrez ainsi obtenir des avances de la Banque.'[1] The opening to Africans of the right of registering their lands by *immatriculation* was regarded as a step to 'voluntary individualization'. The progress made under the procedure of the Decree of 1906, was, however, disappointing; a Commission appointed to investigate the matter in 1915 found that the total number of titles then issued was 1,267, the majority being for urban property.

As a result of the recommendations of the Commission a simpler process, that of the *constatation des droits fonciers des indigènes*, was introduced in French West Africa in a Decree of 8 October 1925, in French Togoland by that of 24 August 1926, amended on 15 August 1934, and in the Cameroons by that of 21 July 1932. This last Decree supplemented in turn an earlier Decree of 20 August 1927, providing for the issue by District Officers of *actes de notoriété*. The same system was introduced in French Equatorial Africa by a Decree of 10 February 1938. Persons who seek a record of *constatation* approach the *Chef de Circonscription*, who, after publishing the demand locally, makes an inquiry from Chiefs and Notables, referring contested cases to the Native Tribunal. He finally delivers to the claimants a *livret foncier* describing the nature of their rights. This can be applied to family and collective as well as to individual rights. Unlike *immatriculation* it does not create an indefeasible proprietary title, but is intended to secure the holder from dispossession by anything but judicial process, and it has the advantage of leaving the land subject to Native law.

In the Trust Territories the production of this document is required before the alienation to a non-Native of land registered under this procedure can receive administrative sanction. Applications for *constatation* have so far been confined mainly to areas such as the cocoa lands of the Ivory Coast and to urban properties. Elsewhere it has not yet become widely popular. In Togoland Africans desiring title appear to belong mainly to the urban class, and prefer the process of full *immatriculation*. Applications under the simplified procedure are so rare that the Administration has ceased to publish figures. In the Cameroons, however, land speculation in urban areas appears to have stimulated demands for the *livret foncier*, and 235 were issued in the course of 1951. By the end of that year this procedure had been applied in a total of 1,224 cases, covering 1,027 acres in urban and 15,877 acres in rural areas.

The process of *immatriculation* is devised for the recognition of a system of proprietorship rather than one of usufruct, nor is it adapted to the record of family or collective rights. The procedure is expensive, and from the Native standpoint it has the defect that the prescribed method of

[1] Minutes of Session, 1924.

publication in the *Journal Officiel* does not give adequate notice to other possible claimants. The latter fact furnished the grounds for the protests which were from time to time put forward against the system by the *Conseil Général* in Senegal. In the view of some Africans it has the further disadvantage that it subjects property rights to French law, and thus takes them out of the cognizance of the Native Courts.

At one time its general application was opposed in some Colonies by the authorities themselves, who hesitated to encourage the acquisition of clear title by Africans in areas where the State might be likely to require land for public purposes or for alienation to Europeans. They urged that in that case property might have to be purchased which could otherwise have simply been treated as *terre vacante*.[1] It is, however, correct to say that less importance now seems to be attached to this consideration. Local policy appears to recognize that resort to *immatriculation* on any considerable scale must await an expansion in the use of the powers of *constatation* as a method of establishing individual rights in holdings.[2]

The movement towards individualization has been to some extent assisted by another process—namely, the grant of Concessions to Africans from State lands. In urban areas in Senegal, Sudan, and Upper Volta, where locations have specially been reserved for Native occupation, the title granted is subject to the condition that there is no right of disposal to non-Africans. In most cases the grant depends on the completion of development conditions.[3] Again, in the irrigated area of the Niger delta[4] special arrangements for the grant of title to peasant cultivators have been made by an *arrêté* of 16 July 1937. After ten years' continuous occupation a farmer who is approved as a person of good character by the Director-General of the *Office du Niger* may obtain a *permis d'occuper* conferring rights of usufruct which can be transmitted to his heir.[5] In French Equatorial Africa the plans set on foot in 1951 for the concentration of scattered groups of cultivators into villages do not appear to have involved the offer of documentary titles.[6]

The Belgian Congo

In the Belgian Congo there is for the most part little pressure of population, and though a few individuals have bought land from the *Comité Spécial* in the Katanga, many tribes still practise the type of shifting cultivation which involves the movement of large groups, and sometimes in-

---

[1] *Journal Officiel*, 1922, p. 102.
[2] *Rapport annuel à l'Assemblée Générale des Nations Unies sur l'administration du Togo, 1951*, p. 87.
[3] *Arrêtés*, 8 October 1924, Senegal; 24 April 1920, Sudan; 22 December 1928, Haute Volta.
[4] See below, pp. 1003 ff.
[5] G. Spitz, *Sansanding, les irrigations du Niger*, 1949, pp. 111–35.
[6] 'Le Regroupement des villages au Gabon', *Bull. A.E.F.*, 2 August 1951.

deed of whole villages. There is, however, in Belgium a school of thought which holds that economic advancement could best be secured by a system of peasant proprietorship; 'L'établissement du paysannat sous la forme la plus intégrale' was one of the policies recommended by King Leopold III in addressing the Senate in 1933, after his visit to the Colony.

A draft Decree which was circulated in 1934 proposed that Africans should be allowed to reach proprietorship by a series of stages. A man who had farmed the same land by approved methods for three years would be entitled to a *droit individuel d'occupation* which would lapse if he abandoned the land for more than two years. After another ten years' continuous occupation he could obtain a certificate of *propriété agraire* which again would lapse if the land were abandoned for three years. Only those Africans who by the procedure of *immatriculation* had been made subject to the Belgian *code civil* in all respects could obtain full legal titles.

By a Decree of 10 February 1953, however, the right to obtain titles of any kind recognized by the statutory law was thrown open to all Africans. Succession to land held on documentary title is to be in the direct line according to the principles of European law, though customary succession among most of the Congo tribes is matrilineal. Other provisions are designed to prevent subdivision on the death of the holder. Africans who are not *immatriculés* may not mortgage their land except to approved persons and with the authorization of a tribunal.[1] Meanwhile the Government of the Belgian Congo had adopted a procedure which appears to aim at development in a somewhat different direction. It envisaged an extensive policy of village settlement. Instead of waiting for individuals to qualify for the status of peasant proprietors or making this a reward for efficient farming, the Government decided to allocate demarcated holdings to family groups—the system of *paysannat indigène*.

The ten-year plan adopted in 1948 envisaged the settlement on this basis of 385,000 families by the end of the period. Demarcated plots consisted sometimes of holdings in land which the farmers were already occupying, sometimes of entirely new settlements. Documentary titles are not issued. In carrying out this policy officials were instructed to respect existing rights of occupation, though the possibility was envisaged that communities with surplus land might be asked to cede a part of it for the settlement of 'strangers'.

Most of the original allocations were made by officers of the Agricultural Service without the assistance of Administrative Officers as these could not be spared from other work. While in some cases existing rights were scrupulously respected, in others it was assumed that no valid rights

---

[1] G. Malengreau, 'De l'accession des indigènes à la propriété foncière individuelle du code civil', *Zaïre*, vol. i, 1947, pp. 235-70, 399-434; vol. vii, 1953, pp. 607-12.

existed over unoccupied land, or that representatives of right-holding communities had agreed to cede or exchange their land. Sometimes a whole Chiefdom was taken as the right-holding unit and sometimes a large kin group. Exclusive rights claimed by smaller subdivisions were often disregarded.

As a result, some populations were settled on land to which the original holders still laid claim, and they were so conscious of the insecurity of the position that they could not be induced to improve their holdings. A report made by Professor Guy Malengreau[1] urged that no further allocations should be made without investigation of existing rights, that movement to the new settlements should be entirely voluntary, and that wherever possible each settlement should have some unallocated land available for an expanding population. It was also urged that houses should be grouped in villages instead of scattered on the separate allotments. Most of these recommendations have been followed, though the shortage of staff still makes adequate investigation difficult. The total number of holdings allocated under this scheme at the end of 1954 was 158,825; it appears that they cover over $7\frac{1}{2}$ million acres. Of these holdings, over 126,000 were in occupation.[2]

Tribal lands are now held to be conterminous with the *chefferies* recognized by the Administration. People cultivating land in a *chefferie* other than their own are required by a Decree of 12 June 1951 to pay a tax, half of which goes to the local Treasury. It appears that these 'strangers' are usually not individuals, as in British West Africa, but village groups which move as units.

The Belgian Congo law attaches legal validity only to titles which have been secured by *enregistrement*, and Native land rights not so secured remain subject to Native law and custom.[3] Registration is effected by the *Conservateur des Titres Fonciers*, and is compulsory for all lands alienated by the State, or acquired by non-Natives from Natives. In the latter case the grant of title has to be approved by the Administration. *Enregistrement*, though not carrying on its face the same guarantee as the French *immatriculation*, has much the same effect; in certain circumstances the State would appear to become responsible for a defect in the registration of encumbrances.[4] It will be seen that the procedure applies only to proprietary titles acquired by non-Africans. There appears to be no provision, such as that existing in the French Colonies, for enabling land in African occupation to be registered in proprietary title.

[1] G. Malengreau, 'Vers un paysannat indigène: les lotissements agricoles au Congo Belge', *Mém. I.R.C.B.*, vol. xix, no. 2, 1949.

[2] *Rapport sur l'administration de la colonie du Congo Belge, 1954*, p. 254. See also G. Malengreau, 'Recent Developments in Belgian Africa', in *Africa Today*, 1955, p. 344.

[3] *Décret*, 14 September 1886; *Arrêté*, 8 November 1886.

[4] *Décret*, 5 January 1923.

The Portuguese Territories

In the Portuguese Overseas provinces there is, as has been observed, a clear line of distinction between Africans who have adopted the régime of the 'common law' (or in other words have been accepted as *assimilado*) and those who are living under the customary law. As regards the former, they acquire, with some small exceptions, all the rights attached to individual property under the civil law of Portugal.[1]

The Native has been able to acquire 'real' rights in land or to have the benefit of the process of inheritance, legacy, or purchase, only if he opted for the régime of the 'common law' in respect of land tenure. It is true that under Article 38 of the Statute of Indigenous Peoples he could acquire rights over an 'empty or abandoned plot', and that plots of Native lands could be set apart by a Governor's order for individual appropriation as the basis of the formation of villages or plantations. But the rights thus acquired were those of 'stable usage' only.

In June 1953, however, the Organic Law of the Overseas Territories envisaged the enactment of special statutes under which ownership 'Susceptible to registraton of title' could be conceded to individual Natives. Such title would be transferable only between Natives and in accordance with Native custom. It was hoped that the concept of individual ownership might thus gradually be implanted in Native custom.[2] It does not appear that any such special statutes have as yet been enacted.

Spanish Guinea

In Spanish Guinea a committee was appointed in 1907 'to delimit the properties of Native tribes and notables'. Each tribal area was to be divided between groups of 20 individuals, and further demarcation between families appears to have been contemplated. The Law of 4 May 1948, which now regulates land rights, states that Native peoples, tribes, or family groups, farmers' co-operatives, and other Native associations, syndicates, or agricultural colonies, may own their property collectively. Certificates of occupancy are issued for holding collective property, which may not be subdivided, alienated, or encumbered.

Special provision is made for the allocation to Christians of family holdings; these are under the supervision of the *Patronato de Indígenas* or of organizations which may be created to manage settlement schemes, and the supervising body may reallocate holdings. An Ordinance of 23 December 1949 provides for the grouping of holdings in 'colonies'. 'Emancipated' Africans may obtain individual titles. About 90 per cent. of African land in Fernando Po is stated to be held under title. The grant to Africans

---

[1] A. Durieux, 'Essai sur le statut des indigènes portugais de la Guinée, de l'Angola et du Mozambique', *Mém. A.R.S.C.*, vol. v, no. 3, 1955, pp. 43–44.

[2] A. de Sousa Franklin, in *J.A.A.*, January, 1957, pp. 16 ff.

of Concessions for the production of palm oil had been authorized by a
Decree of 24 May 1928; the register of Concessions does not distinguish
between Africans and other holders.[1]

THE FUTURE OF THE INDIGENOUS SYSTEM OF
LANDHOLDING

There is nothing exceptional in the system of landholding followed in
African custom. Throughout the world it must have been the method
commonly followed by communities which had a background of pastoral
or semi-nomadic life. In such circumstances the keeping of flocks and herds
is normally the work of families or kin groups, not of individuals, and the
group concept which thus originated during the pastoral stage was in the
natural course extended to the holding of land. In pastoral conditions,
moreover, ownership was essentially functional, for the possession of flocks
and herds necessarily connoted their care and protection. When the
community settled down to cultivation, its holding of land was similarly
functional, and ownership came to be interpreted strictly in terms of
beneficial use.

It has been shown in the preceding paragraphs how reluctantly the
concept of the holding of land which originated in this manner has yielded
place to the concept of individual possession. It is characteristic that in the
Gold Coast, where the process of individualization has perhaps made its
way more widely than in any other indigenous area, the ownership over
a holding, even though it may have been acquired by a personal purchase,
nevertheless still tends to be interpreted by the Courts in terms of a family
right.[2] This reluctance to break with the traditional concept of landholding is no doubt due largely to the unusual vitality of the family or kin
tie in the social and religious life of Africans. But it is also due to the fact
that the collective or group system of landholding has a practical value.[3]
It had, and indeed still has, its use in conditions which are to be found both
in East and Central Africa, where the cultivation of the arable is combined
with the keeping of cattle. It possesses an especial value where shifting
cultivation provides the main source of subsistence. The type of shifting
cultivation which involves the felling of woodland or scrub and its
burning to make a seed-bed involves in particular the combined labour
of a number of individuals.[4]

But the individualization of rights in the land is only the first stage in the
modern departure from the customary system of landholding. There has
been a more pronounced reluctance to face the further stage, described

[1] J. M. Cordero Torres, *Tratado elemental de derecho colonial español*, 1941, pp. 207–8.
Civilisations, vol. ii, 1952, pp. 272, 275.   [2] See above, p. 791.
[3] *Communal Land Tenure*, F.A.O. Agricultural Study no. 17, 1953.
[4] See below, pp. 819–20.

comprehensively as the commercialization of land rights, where land is sold, mortgaged, leased, or given out on rent. It is common to find, even in some of the relatively progressive communities, a categorical statement that the sale of land rights is not recognized, though the transfer of rights may in fact be publicly practised. 'Pledging' of land is in the same way described as always redeemable however long a period may have elapsed since the pledging was made, though it is well known that in practice terms are sometimes arranged which are designed to make redemption impossible. It is only rarely admitted that adverse possession, however long it has continued, can give rise to a right which will override that of the original occupants of a holding.[1] The letting out of land is discountenanced, though this practice is considered to be less objectionable to established custom if the rent takes the form of a share of the produce, thus bringing the transaction within the convention of a partnership in cultivation.

In almost every area in which subsistence cultivation has given place to the cultivation of marketable crops there can now be found instances of the commercialization of land rights, with the result that the conflict between the customary law of land tenure and the practices actually coming into force has become one of the chief problems of the Native Courts. Hitherto the modifications made in traditional procedure have followed, as it were automatically, on changes in economic circumstances, but it is probable that the process will now be definitely stimulated by measures taken to implement official policy. The individualization of land tenures has from the first been a principle of policy with the French and Belgian Governments,[2] though the measures they have so far taken have been designed to remove individual Africans from a régime of customary law into one of European law, rather than to modify the customary system of African land tenure. It is for this reason that the law of *immatriculation* has had only a limited extension in the African community. In the Union of South Africa the Glen Grey Act was based on a conviction of the inherent superiority of the individual form of tenure, though the law had only a partial effect because the physical circumstances in the 'surveyed' districts have been such as to hinder the attempt to introduce a real measure of individualization.[3]

In the British territories a régime of individual holdings has for long been the ideal of the official Agricultural Departments. They have never failed to impress on the Administrations the implications of the classic observation made by Arthur Young when he studied the results of the cultivation of the seemingly barren sand dunes near Dunkirk. 'The magic of property has turned sand into gold.' Hitherto, however, there has been little in the way of direct legislation on the subject, though the individual

[1] For some indication to the contrary, see Cmd. 9475, pp. 347–8.
[2] See above, pp. 796, 799.   [3] See above, p. 776.

holding has been the practice followed in establishing some of the projects of agricultural settlement. Perhaps the most noticeable of these is the important Land Settlement lately initiated in Swaziland.[1] The individual holding has also formed a feature of the provision made for the acquisition of holdings in Native Purchase Areas, as for example in Northern Rhodesia and Kenya. Where, however, schemes of resettlement covering large blocks of country have been involved, as for instance in the settlement of the areas cleared of tsetse fly in Tanganyika, the new areas thus made available are normally occupied by the tribes or groups concerned in accordance with their own traditional custom. A similar course is being followed in the resettlement of the considerable number of tribesmen displaced by the construction of the hydro-electric installation at the Kariba Gorge in Rhodesia.[2]

The position has recently been affected in a practical sense by the measure of individualization undertaken in Southern Rhodesia under the provisions of the Native Land Husbandry Act.[3] The significance of this measure lies in the wide scale of its operations, for it will affect all the occupants of the Native Reserves in the Colony. It will be realized that in this instance individualization will not extend to the grant of a freehold title. The African in the Reserves will in fact have the status of a tenant of a heritable holding, unlimited as to the period of tenancy, but subject to administrative control in the matter of beneficial use and terminable on proof of failure to comply with the regulations made for the purpose. Nevertheless, the measure now enacted will clearly have a wide influence on the land policy to be followed in the British Dependencies.

The recommendations of the East Africa Royal Commission 1953–5 on land policy will have an influence extending beyond the territories to which they directly referred.[4] Early in 1956 they were considered by a conference on African land policy held at Arusha. Later in the year the Colonial Office published dispatches setting out the views held on them by the three East African Governments.[5] While there was some hesitation on their part in accepting the opinions of the Commission regarding the removal of restrictions on the transferability of land between members of different communities, there was general accord as to the desirability of the extension of a system of individual landholding. These two issues constituted a closely linked feature of the recommendations of the Commission for the improvement of African production, but from the standpoint of land policy they are not necessarily interdependent.

Up to a recent period of their history, African tribes moved freely about the relatively empty lands of East and Central Africa, but this situation

---

[1] See above, pp. 698, 779.   [2] See below, p. 987.   [3] See above, pp. 766–7, 780–1.
[4] For an analysis of the recommendations, see *J.A.A.*, April 1956, pp. 69–74.
[5] See above, pp. 722, 725, 730.

changed radically with the advent of the European. He did not in general dispossess the African of land, but he wrought a revolutionary change by fixing and stabilizing its tenure. Where the Reserve policy was put into force, Africans were confined to, but also protected in, their Tribal Reserves.[1] The first objective of the Royal Commission has been to break down this régime of rigid stabilization. The Report does not deal with the racial or political aspects of the situation, but takes its stand on economic grounds. It holds that land can only attain its full productive value if holdings are individualized and if right-holders are free to negotiate the sale or lease of their land without restrictions imposed on either tribal or racial considerations. The African must be free to acquire rights in what are now other tribal areas. In Kenya a European or Asian must be free to acquire rights in areas hitherto reserved for African occupation, and an African or Asian to acquire rights in the White Highlands. On no other terms would it be possible, in the view of the Commission, to bring about that modernization of the methods of cultivation which is essential if the standards of life of the indigenous population of East Africa are to be substantially improved.

Whatever the prospect of economic advantage held out by these recommendations, it is obvious that they must meet with opposition from members of two at least of the three communities concerned. It has from the first been a cardinal article of policy with the Europeans in Kenya that non-Europeans must not be allowed to acquire a foothold in the White Highlands area, a restriction directed in the first place against Asians. Africans are not likely to oppose strongly the principle of individualization of landholdings, for there has already been a well-marked trend in this direction among the more advanced African communities in Kenya and Uganda, though this has been less marked in Tanganyika. But tribal sentiment is still strong, and the more conservative of the tribal elements are bound to feel strongly about any measure which may involve not merely a loss of tribal lands to Europeans or Asians, but may also allow of the infiltration of members of other tribes into their own areas. Long before the days of Mau Mau, for instance, there had been many signs of the unpopularity of Kikuyu 'immigrants' in other tribal areas. It is clear therefore that in any case some of the economic changes advocated by the Commission could only come into effect over a considerable period of time.

Apart from these considerations there are also other grounds for exercising some measure of caution in giving effect to these proposals. Social stability is an important factor in the furtherance of economic advance, and any hurried measure of reform in respect of indigenous land tenures might defeat its own purpose. A notable warning of the need of caution in this respect is afforded by the history of Algeria, where the effort made

[1] *The Round Table*, September 1955, pp. 123 ff.

to bring indigenous systems of landholding within the régime of French civil law was for many years a cause of grave differences between the Administration and the Muslim population.

It must be recognized also that nature has created certain obstacles to the extension of the system of individual holdings. It is not readily applicable to pasture lands, save where the holdings of individuals are of wide extent (as, for instance, the characteristic Boer farm of South Africa or some of the European holdings in Northern Rhodesia or Kenya), or where the climate provides for a more or less continuous renewal of the grazing. There are, therefore, likely to remain large areas of commonage. It is true that the commonage may have to be divided between different units on a family or group basis, and this operation will not be as easy as, for instance, it proved to be in India, where villages (or sections of villages) had for many centuries been recognized as holding rights over defined areas of commonage. There is no inherent difficulty in breaking up commonage in this way, but in that case the commonage as such will remain under a collective not under an individual system of holding.

Again, the system of individual holdings is not readily applicable to conditions where shifting cultivation or bush fallowing is habitual. There it would be unwise to seek to introduce a system of individualization until the local economy had passed beyond the stage in which the practice of bush fallowing is a necessary part of the routine of cultivation.

There are, moreover, matters arising within the general framework of a policy of individualization which demand a much closer consideration by the Governments concerned. Hitherto most of them seem to have been content to stand aside while customary tenures adjusted themselves to changes in economic circumstances. They have failed to realize that they had a direct responsibility for guiding the direction of change. In the British territories, for instance, there is a striking contrast between the extent of the consideration given during a series of years to the case for excluding non-Europeans from the White Highlands of Kenya and the fact that it was not until early in 1956 that a conference was convened to discuss the problems arising from the modernization of African land tenures. It is of interest to reflect that in British India provisions regulating the relations of landlord and tenant were initated as far back as the Bengal Land Act of 1859, and that the subject of land tenures continued thereafter to form one of the most fruitful topics of debate both in the Imperial and Provincial Legislatures.[1]

It will be obvious that the process of individualization of holdings will involve in the first place some form of physical survey, and in the second place the creation of an organization for the registration of title. Where climatic and soil conditions are suitable, the process of individualization

[1] L. S. S. O'Malley, *Modern India and the West*, 1941, pp. 282 ff.

may be said to commence automatically with the construction of field boundaries which as they become consolidated can supply the place of documentary evidence if any question arises regarding the position or area of the holding. In the conditions of Africa, however, it would be unwise to attempt any formal recognition of the individualization of holdings without a preliminary survey. But this need not be of the elaborate type of the cadastral surveys usually carried out where parcels of Crown or 'public' lands are made the subject of grant or sale by the State, conferring a title the accuracy of which the State is under an obligation to protect. An initial process of triangulation is of course indispensable,[1] but given this, an adequate field survey can (as the procedure followed in British India has shown) be carried out by a non-professional and relatively inexpensive establishment.

The process of registration has sometimes been viewed as a simple operation of which the purpose will be satisfied if the register indicates the identity of the occupant of a holding. But as soon as the procedure of land-holding begins to become commercialized, the registration inevitably acquires the status of a record of land titles and thus assumes an importance far beyond its original scope. It will not, therefore, be sufficient to provide for a voluntary system of registration; it must be compulsory and universal, and it must be preceded by a process of authoritative inquiry which will provide an adequate presumption of the correctness of the entry.

It is claimed that one of the strongest reasons for the individualization of holdings is that it will give to the cultivator an adequate security of title. But African customary procedure already secures to him a right of occupation in which he is protected from disturbance not merely by the custom of the tribe or group, but by the action of the Native Courts. If there is any feeling of insecurity in his right of occupation it arises not so much in fear of interference by members of his own community but from the apprehension that the Government may, for its own purposes (such as the need of land for public use or for alienation to colonists), disturb him in the possession of his holding. It would be no benefit to him if under the new procedure he were given a title which was liable to attack because of a failure in the manner of registration. Much may be lost by failure to recognize the necessity for creating an organization which will both ensure the accuracy of the initial entry and also provide for keeping the register up to date in respect of the entry of successions to title, transfers, or encumbrances by way of mortgage or the like.

It may be assumed that the title recorded will not be absolute or indefeasible, but will be presumptive, in the sense that if it is challenged the onus of proof will lie on the party who attacks its accuracy. That is the

[1] See above, pp. 16–18.

procedure adopted in the Indian record of land titles. It has been applied over the course of about a century to the registration of many millions of titles, and has proved to be fully adequate for its purpose.[1] An entry of presumptive title, made after due inquiry and readily available for public inspection, acquires with the progress of time a standing which, if not indefeasible in a legal sense, is for practical purposes unchallengeable.

But the title recorded, though presumptive, must be sufficient in itself. Whether or not it has been defined by statute, it must be such as to carry a definite legal connotation in the law administered by the Courts of the territory. To express a title in terms of European law may carry legal implications peculiar to that law, many of which will be inapplicable to African conditions. But a series of issues will arise which are of cardinal importance to the African population concerned. Will the title be recorded in the name of an individual or is the right of the family to be recognized? If the name recorded is that of an individual, will it be in a personal or a representative capacity? Should it recognize, directly or by implication, the right of a Chief or any other traditional authority to intervene in the disposal or in the use of the holding?

Whatever the form or the phraseology used, it is the actual content connoted by the title registered which is all-important. In the legislation referred to in previous pages describing the grant of rights over holdings which are in the British dependencies described as Crown Lands, the title granted has normally been that of a Right of Occupancy. Though this has had its convenience in so far that it has permitted of maintaining restrictions over alienation to non-Natives, it does not offer the same security (particularly in respect of any action to be taken by the Government) as a title of freehold. Moreover, there are large areas, particularly in West Africa, where the Crown has never claimed superior rights over the Native lands, and where the registration of individual title will accordingly be extended over lands which have been in full Native proprietorship, though subject to the terms of Native customary law in respect of succession, transfer, &c. For such areas the registration of land rights in the form of an Occupancy Tenancy would be inappropriate.

It is indeed doubtful whether the title of Occupancy Tenancy should really be considered as appropriate even in the case of holders of lands classed as Crown Lands. It is apparently assumed that in Crown Lands the State has a superior proprietary status which enables it to impose on the actual cultivators of these lands the restricted title of Occupancy Tenancy or to insist on compliance with conditions of beneficial occupation. But the unsubstantial nature of the rights conferred on the Adminis-

[1] E. Dowson and V. L. O. Sheppard, *Land Registration*, Colonial Research Publication no. 13, 1952, p. 42. See also for the subject generally, Meek, op. cit. Introduction p. xii, and pp. 272–88; and Supplement to *J.A.A.*, October 1952.

tration by classifying lands as Crown Lands is best seen in the fact that these lands are now in many areas being reclassified under the more appropriate designation of 'public' or 'Native' lands.[1] If therefore it is intended to impose restrictions on the power of transfer or alienation, or any conditions regarding beneficial usage, these should properly be embodied in specific legislation, and cannot be made part of the process of registration of title. This observation applies both to lands formerly designated as Crown Lands, and to those designated as Native lands over which the Crown has never assumed any proprietary or over-proprietary rights. The proper basis for the imposition of such conditions is not an assumed right of Crown or State proprietorship; it must be based on legislation enacted in the interests of public policy.

It is likely accordingly that there will be a general demand for the registration of individual holdings under a title equivalent to that of freehold. But as the East Africa Royal Commission has pointed out, the recognition of freehold involves the danger that an inexperienced peasantry may take advantage of the fact to incur a chronic burden of unproductive debt based on the security of land.[2] The danger is real. It is unfortunate that the Government in British India did not perceive in time the danger involved in the general recognition of a right equivalent to freehold in the absence of any legislative restriction over the power of encumbrance or transfer. Reference will be made elsewhere to the disastrous consequences which ensued.[3] They did not end with the social mischief resulting from the fact that so large a part of the rural population of India lived in a position of servitude to the moneylender. The economic results were equally unfortunate. The cultivator lost any incentive to increase the production of his land, since any surplus earned by him over a bare subsistence was at once impounded by his creditors. The remedy for this danger does not, however, lie in a qualification of the freehold title; it must be the subject of specific legislation. The East Africa Royal Commission recommended, for instance, that statutory restrictions should be placed on the mortgaging of land, though they would not apply this restriction in the case of the Land Banks whose establishment they propose.[4]

Somewhat similar considerations apply to the danger (also referred to by the Royal Commission) that a few persons may accumulate large holdings of land. The social danger involved in this possibility is perhaps more obvious than the economic disadvantages; a certain measure of accumulation of holdings may indeed assist in the furtherance of a system of good husbandry.[5] But this matter also is a subject for specific legislation, as also is provision for making the tenure of a holding subject to the obser-

---

[1] C. K. Meek, in *The Journal of Comparative Legislation and International Law*, 1946, vol. xxviii, p. 90.   [2] Cmd. 9475, p. 355.   [3] See below, pp. 1456-7.
[4] Cmd. 9475, p. 356.   [5] Ibid. p. 357.

vance of an adequate measure of good land use. It is noteworthy that under the current legislation in Southern Rhodesia the holder of a farming right who fails to comply with the condition of good land use may be compelled to sell it.[1] The East Africa Royal Commission concur in holding that the remedy does not lie in a deprivation of title but in enforcing an obligation to sell or lease a holding. In either case, it does not seem right that this condition should be embodied in a qualification of the title registered; it should form the subject of separate legislation.

It will be realized that the preceding observations apply in the main to rural conditions. The holding of land in urban areas is in the nature of things individualized, though in the customary law the tendency may have been to recognize ownership as inherent in the family rather than in the individual. The general registration of title in urban areas may prove to be a complicated and expensive process, and there will no doubt be a tendency to consider it sufficient to provide an organization for the registration of deeds recording sale or lease of property. But in African conditions there exists a special case for organizing such a measure of registration of urban titles as will make it easy for owners of urban property to take full advantage of its negotiable value. As the East Africa Royal Commission has pointed out, it is essential to the economic progress of the African population that the urban communities should be encouraged to own their own houses. Both Northern and Southern Rhodesia have recognized the need for making provision for this purpose.[2] There has also been a general recognition of this principle in both the French and the Belgian territories. So far the only provision made in the British dependencies for the full registration of urban titles is in Lagos,[3] but the matter is now likely to assume a general importance.

It is not easy to forecast the course likely to be taken in the French and Belgian territories in respect of the adjustment of African customary land tenures to modern requirements. As has been remarked, there is in the French territory a well-marked tendency towards adopting measures for the individualization of landholdings; the concept of collective rights seems indeed to be alien to the spirit of the French civil code. But the association of projects of individualization with the procedure of *immatriculation* seems likely to continue to hinder any active progress in this direction. The Belgian Congo retains the individualization of holdings as its ideal,[4] and the system is applied in practice to the numerous holdings organized during recent years under the system of the *paysannat indigène*.[5] But it does not seem likely that the Administration will readily adopt any procedure which will by the recognition of a title equivalent to freehold make it more

---

[1] See above, p. 780.   [2] See above, pp. 574, 576.
[3] See above, pp. 791–2.   [4] See above, pp. 799–800.
[5] See above, p. 799.

difficult to insist on the observance of regulations regarding the use of improved methods of cultivation.

THE STUDY OF AFRICAN SYSTEMS OF LAND TENURE

Whether modification in the traditional systems of land-tenure holding be due to the influence of economic change or to action taken to implement State policy, there will remain with the Administration the obligation to make itself fully acquainted with the indigenous methods of land tenure. The obligation will indeed be the stronger if change is due to the determination of official policy, since it is only knowledge of the existing indigenous practice which can secure that the change shall be evolutionary and command the acceptance of the people most closely affected. There will remain, moreover, a wide field for study of land custom in order to provide guidance for the tribunals which have to deal with land issues. There are few matters which are more likely to inspire confidence in the goodwill of an Administration than the knowledge that it is determined to give serious regard to a matter of such vital concern to the interests of the great majority of the indigenous population.

Governments have in the past admittedly made serious errors for lack of such special knowledge. The reservation of a large area of land for the Buganda King and his Chiefs in 1900[1] was an act of political expediency, but the decision that the rights granted over it should take a form which was practically that of freehold produced unfortunate consequences, not merely by overlooking the existence of clan rights in the soil, but, even more important, by neglecting to realize its inevitable effect on the traditional relationship of the peasants to the Chiefs. In commenting on a study made of the Yoruba land systems, the Governor of Nigeria[2] admitted that the failure to study existing land tenures had led to grave mistakes in the past; a similar admission was made in the official report on the North Kavirondo tenures in Kenya.[3]

The mistakes of the past have arisen mainly in connexion with rights over land of which the Administration desired to take possession or with measures conferring upon African landholders titles implying rights not recognized by custom. There are now other spheres of action in which difficulties may arise through the absence of adequate information. Examples readily suggest themselves, as for instance measures designed for the creation of model holdings of an economic size, schemes for the colonization of irrigated areas, or the resettlement of Africans moved from over-populated or tsetse-infested land. All such measures, if introduced

[1] See above, pp. 724, 725–6, 786–8.
[2] D. Cameron, *A Note on Land Tenure in the Yoruba Provinces*, 1933, para. 15.
[3] *Report of Committee on Native Land in the North Kavirondo Reserve*, Nairobi, 1931, p. 18.

without full knowledge of the rights existing over the land to which they are applied, may create such resentment as would seriously prejudice the proposed improvements.

In the Union of South Africa the Government has initiated no specific inquiry on this subject. The reports of the Natal Native Commission of 1881–2, the Cape Native Laws and Customs Commission of 1883–5, and the South African Native Affairs Commission of 1903–5 all contain sections referring to land custom, but they are not based on investigations made specifically for the purpose. Many of the studies made by anthropologists in the Union bear on the subject, but in general may be said to have paid more attention to economic conditions than to details of land tenure.[1] There is, however, a careful study of the subject in relation to Pondoland by M. Hunter,[2] and the report of the Keiskammahoek Rural Survey initiated in 1947 includes a volume in which the systems of tenure in four villages in this district are described in detail.[3] I. Schapera has made a comprehensive study of land tenure in the Bechuanaland Protectorate,[4] and V. G. Sheddick in Basutoland.[5] The subject is also dealt with, though in more general terms, in E. H. Ashton's study of the Basuto,[6] and in the report of an Agricultural Survey conducted in 1949–50.[7] For Swaziland some information has been given by H. Kuper.[8]

In the United Kingdom the Secretary of State for the Colonies addressed in 1939 a dispatch to the Governments of all British dependencies in Africa indicating the necessity of making a systematic study of the principles of customary tenure as a basis for the registration of titles if and when this was considered opportune. His suggestion was developed by an informal committee which met at the Colonial Office during 1943. This body recommended the establishment in London of a formal committee to advise the Secretary of State on land questions, and a panel of advisers was set up in 1945. It included among its functions the provision to Colonial Governments of information on land problems and policies, and among its more immediate objectives arranged for the preparation of a bibliography of existing studies.

A detailed study of land tenures in the British territories was embodied in the work of Dr. C. K. Meek, *Land Law and Custom in the Colonies*, published in 1946. The bibliography above mentioned was published in 1950,[9]

---

[1] G. P. Lestrade, 'Some Aspects of the Economic Life of the South African Bantu', *South African Journal of Economics*, vol. ii, no. 4, 1934, pp. 429–30.

[2] M. Hunter, *Reaction to Conquest*, 1936.

[3] M. E. Elton Mills and M. (Hunter) Wilson, *Land Tenure*, 1952.

[4] I. Schapera, *Native Land Tenure in the Bechuanaland Protectorate*, 1943.

[5] V. G. Sheddick, *Land Tenure in Basutoland*, Colonial Research Studies no. 13, 1954.

[6] H Ashton, *The Basuto*, 1952.

[7] A. J. A. Douglas and R. K. Tennant, *Basutoland Agricultural Survey*, Maseru, 1952.

[8] H. Kuper, *An African Aristocracy*, 1947; idem, *The Uniform of Colour*, 1947.

[9] *Bibliography of Published Sources relating to African Land Tenure*, Col. no. 258, 1950.

and it is only necessary here to supplement it by reference to work which has appeared more recently. This includes studies of the Lala of the Serenje Plateau in Northern Rhodesia;[1] of the Machinga Yao in Nyasaland;[2] of the Sukuma in Tanganyika;[3] of the Kikuyu and Kamba in Kenya.[4] The effects of the introduction of proprietary rights in Buganda have been described by A. B. Mukwaya.[5] In Nigeria an investigation of the situation in every province was initiated in 1946, and for the Northern Region reports have appeared on the Kano, Zaria, Niger, and Plateau Provinces.[6] Similar studies have been made of the Benin, Kukuruku, Ishan, and Asaba Divisions of Benin Province and the Ondo Province.[7] For the Eastern Region there are recent studies of the Ibo by G. I. Jones[8] and L. T. Chubb.[9] A volume by T. O. Elias gives much information on changes introduced in the land laws of the Eastern and Western Regions as the result of decisions by the superior judicial Courts.[10]

For the Cameroons under British Trusteeship there is an account of Nsaw land tenure by P. M. Kaberry[11] and a report of the Cameroons Province by C. W. Rowling.[12] The available information on the Trust Territory has been summarized by C. K. Meek.[13] For the Mende of Sierra Leone some information on land tenure is given by K. L. Little.[14] It may be added that the *Journal of African Administration*, published quarterly by the Colonial Office, issued in October 1952 a special supplement on land tenure.

In the French territories the inquiry made by the Commission of 1915[15] appears to have been directed mainly to questions bearing on proposals for modifying the law relating to the alienation of land. The general characteristics of African land rights were discussed by M. D. Delafosse in a memorandum of 1911,[16] and are further dealt with in his study of

[1] D. U. Peters, 'Land Usage in Serenje District', *R.L.I. Papers*, no. 19, 1950.

[2] J. C. Mitchell, 'Preliminary notes on Land Tenure and Agriculture among the Machinga Yao', *R.L. Journal*, vol. x, 1950, pp. 1–13.

[3] H. Cory, *Sukuma Law and Custom*, 1953. D. W. Malcolm, *Sukumaland*, 1953.

[4] H. E. Lambert, *Systems of Land Tenure in the Kikuyu Land Unit*, 1950. D. J. Penwill, *Kamba Customary Law*, 1951.

[5] *Land Tenure in Buganda*, East African Studies no. 1, Nairobi, 1953.

[6] C. W. Rowling, *Report on Land Tenure in the Kano Province*, Kaduna, 1949; idem, *Report . . . Plateau Province*, Kaduna, 1949. C. W. Cole, *Report on Land Tenure in the Niger Province*, Kaduna, 1949; idem, *Report . . . Zaria Province*, Kaduna, 1949.

[7] C. W. Rowling, *Notes on Land Tenure in the Benin, Kukuruku, Ishan and Asaba Divisions of Benin Province*, Lagos, 1949; idem, *Report on Land Tenure in Ondo Province*, Sessional Paper no. 5, Lagos, 1952.   [8] 'Ibo Land Tenure', *Africa*, October 1949, pp. 309–23.

[9] *Ibo Land Tenure*, 1948.   [10] *Nigerian Land Law and Custom*, 1951.

[11] 'Land Tenure among the Nsaw of the British Cameroons', in *Africa*, October 1950, pp. 307–23.

[12] *A Study of Land Tenure in the Cameroons Province* (pamphlet, roneoed), Colonial Office Land Tenure Panel, 1948.   [13] Unpublished.

[14] *The Mende of Sierra Leone*, 1951.   [15] See above, p. 797.

[16] 'Memorandum on Land Tenure in French West Africa' (trans. by F. H. Ruxton), *J.R.A.S.*, April 1911, pp. 258–73.

family law and property;[1] the land customs of the Agni were described by him with R. Villamur in 1906.[2] This tribe is also discussed in two articles by F. J. Clozel, published in 1901 and 1906. Land custom in the Cameroons is referred to in G. Tessmann's *Die Pangwe*, 1912.

The preparation of manuals of customary law for the guidance of the tribunals was initiated in French West Africa by the Governor-General M. Brévié in 1931, and out of 123 studies submitted 28 were considered worthy of publication.[3] The majority of these studies, however, deal only briefly with land under the general heading 'Property'. The more detailed studies are those by F. de Coutouly on the Marka-Sarakollé of Nioro in the French Sudan,[4] G. Vieillard on the Hausa and Beriberi of Zinder,[5] and E. Dunglas on the Bete of Issia in the Ivory Coast.[6] Some articles have been published on land rights in Senegal.[7]

For the Belgian Congo the most substantial source of information is a study by Guy Malengreau of the general principles of customary tenure throughout the Colony.[8] The *Bulletin des jurisdictions indigènes*, a legal review which has been published in the territory since 1933, contains a number of brief accounts of the customary law of different tribes. They usually include some references to land rights.[9]

Experience has shown that one of the most effective methods for the study of land custom is that which takes a sufficient number of plots as the basis of inquiry, and by recording all the ascertainable changes in the use of each plot gradually builds up a knowledge of the law which determines the local system of tenures.[10] That approach has the further advantage that it enables tenures to be described in terms which express African conceptions of land custom and avoids the danger, which appears to be inherent in the questionnaire method, of forcing the facts into the categories of European law. An outline scheme for an investigation of this type was drawn up by Dr. C. K. Meek for the guidance of administrative officials in 1951.[11] It is possible that this method of inquiry increases the difficulty of making a logical analysis of principles, such as seems to be desired in some of the French studies on the subject; but this is a difficulty which must be recognized as inevitable in all inquiries into African custom. The infor-

---

[1] Dr. Poutrin and M. Delafosse, *Enquête sur la famille, la propriété et la justice chez les indigènes des colonies françaises d'Afrique*, 1914.   [2] *Les Coutumes Agni*, 1906.

[3] *Coutumiers juridiques de l'Afrique occidentale française*, 3 vols., 1939.

[4] Ibid. vol. ii, pp. 228–35.

[5] Ibid. vol. iii, pp. 142–52.   [6] Ibid. pp. 412–24.

[7] H. Gaden, Abdou Salam Kane, and M. Vidal, in *Bulletin du Comité d'Études historiques et scientifiques de l'A.O.F.*, vol. xviii, no. 4, 1935.

[8] *Les Droits fonciers coutumiers chez les indigènes du Congo Belge*, 1947.

[9] See, for example, R. Marchal on the Bazela, Balomotwa, and Banwenshi, and F. Grévisse on the Bayeke, 1937. E. Simons on the Barundi, 1944, and H. A. Guillaume on the people of the Ruzizi plain, 1950.

[10] C. K. Meek, *Law and Authority in a Nigerian Tribe*, 1937, p. 344.

[11] *J.A.A.*, January 1951, pp. 9–13.

mation which can be gained from a study of judicial decisions, though by no means without its use, has a limited value in any comprehensive inquiry into land custom; the decision of a Native Court will no doubt reflect correctly the prevailing sentiment as to the custom by which the issue before it should be decided, but the Court is seldom equipped to give a statement of principle. The European Court, on the other hand, is largely dependent upon the evidence produced by the parties and the opinion of a selected body of assessors. It would, perhaps, be true to say that judicial proceedings are calculated to afford useful evidence as to the application of custom, rather than the material on which a comprehensive statement of its character can be built up.

CHAPTER XII

AGRICULTURE AND ANIMAL HUSBANDRY

PART I. AGRICULTURAL AND PASTORAL PRODUCTION

THE title of this chapter suggests so extensive a range of topics that it may be convenient to state at once the subjects with which it will be concerned. The economic questions arising out of the industries of agricultural and animal husbandry will be dealt with in chapters XVIII and XIX, which also deal with the controls exercised over marketing.[1] Certain specific aspects of the system of land tenure which may affect agricultural production have been dealt with in chapter XI; the problems of irrigation and water supply will be discussed in chapter XIV, and those of soil conservation and erosion in chapter XV. The present chapter is confined, therefore, to discussion of the main features of the crops cultivated and the herds maintained by Europeans or Africans and the measures taken for their improvement.

It is not possible to draw any clear line of distinction between the crops produced by Europeans and Africans respectively, for certain crops are cultivated by both communities. As a general rule, however, it may be said that the African rural economy is typically that of the small peasant cultivator, while that of the European or non-Native is that of the farmer employing paid labour or of the company which possesses adequate capital not merely for cultivation but for processing commodities for consumption or for use in industry. The African was in the first instance interested mainly in subsistence cropping, and if he has in modern conditions extended his activities to embrace certain marketable crops, his own methods are still largely those dictated by the needs of subsistence cultivation. The interest of the majority of Europeans has from the first been in the development of 'commercialized' agriculture. The measure in which this type of agriculture has been practised in the past and in which it will continue to be practised will depend on the availability of a supply of relatively cheap African man-power or the possibility of substituting mechanization for this source of labour.

The policies of the various Governments with regard to the settlement of non-Natives on the land and the extent to which land has been

---

[1] Statistics quoted in the text, unless otherwise stated, are taken from the United Nations, Food and Agriculture Organization, *Year Book of Food and Agricultural Statistics: Production, 1953*, vol. vii, Part I, 1954, or from the same authority's *Trade, 1953*, vol. vii, Part II, 1954.

alienated to them have already been discussed in the preceding chapter. But it will be convenient to give here some general indication of European activity in the different areas with which this Survey deals.

NON-NATIVE AGRICULTURE

In the Union of South Africa there were in 1952 a total of 119,556 European farms, covering an area of some 205½ million acres.[1] Only 15 per cent. of the land area of the Union can be classed as arable land capable of being cultivated, and only 5 per cent. is so utilized. Most of the remainder of the country is, however, classed as suited for pasturage of some kind, though parts are undeniably of low quality. It is estimated, for instance, that in the Karroo 6½ acres are required for the maintenance of one sheep.[2] The main products of European farming are maize, wheat, fruit, sugar, and tobacco; there has, moreover, been a noticeable expansion in groundnut production since 1945. The Union is not, however, self-supporting in the production of wheat, and in most years imports a considerable quantity. In South-West Africa agriculture is of small importance compared with stock-farming in different forms, including the important *Karakul* industry.[3] In Swaziland about half of the land is under European ownership and is utilized for stock-raising, supplemented to a small extent by tobacco and maize. The few European farms in Bechuanaland are occupied almost entirely in stock-raising.

In Southern Rhodesia Europeans actively engaged in agriculture numbered in the census of 1946 roughly 14 per cent. of the total number of persons gainfully employed, but there has since that time been increased immigration and industrial activity. In 1951 about 12 per cent. of the employed Europeans in the country were stated to be engaged in agriculture.[4] The crops grown are maize, tobacco, and to a relatively minor extent cotton and groundnuts. The value of European agricultural production was estimated as £33¼ million in 1953–4. Of the 17,000 Europeans classed as 'occupied' in Northern Rhodesia comparatively few are engaged in agriculture; they are occupied principally in the production of maize, tobacco, coffee, and wheat, but there are some stock-breeders. In Nyasaland the area held by Europeans is relatively small, the principal crops produced being tobacco and tea. Tung, which showed signs of becoming an important subsidiary industry, has declined in acreage and yield, owing to a fall in price.

In Tanganyika the major European plantation crop is sisal, but there is some farm production also of coffee, tea, maize, and tobacco. In Kenya

---

[1] *O.Y.S.A., 1952–53,* p. 852.
[2] *S.A.S.,* no. 98, February 1955.   [3] See below, p. 884.
[4] *Southern Rhodesia: Census of Population 1951,* 1954, p. 19.

the value of the agricultural production of Europeans greatly exceeds that of Africans, the principal products being coffee, sisal, and tea, with smaller quantities of maize, wheat, pyrethrum, and wattle extract. The pyrethrum crop is valuable, but it can be grown only at altitudes of 7,000 feet and over. Efforts have been made to promote the production of essential oils with the aid of grants under the Colonial Development Act. The export of essential oils amounted in 1951 to 1,420 cwt.

In Uganda the lands held by European interests are relatively small in area. They have a sisal estate, and share also in the production of coffee. Most of the tea and rubber plantations are in their hands, but the exports of rubber have for many years been inconsiderable. Tea on the other hand is an important interest. Cotton production is chiefly in the hands of Africans, but the great majority of ginneries are owned by Asians.[1] Nigeria has three European-owned rubber plantations and there are several in the British Cameroons, in addition to plantations of cacao, oil palms, and bananas. In the Gold Coast there is one European rubber plantation, but little purely European production of other commodities.

In Sierra Leone a European company has taken over an oil-palm plantation originally established by the Government, but otherwise there is very little European agricultural activity.

In French West Africa there are considerable banana plantations and some smaller areas cultivated by Europeans with coffee and rice, mainly in the Ivory Coast and Dahomey. In French Equatorial Africa European agriculture is on a smaller scale, and is represented by a few coffee plantations and two sisal estates in the Oubangui Chari region. In the French Cameroons there are a number of company-owned plantations dating originally from the German occupation and now producing important exports of bananas and some cacao, coffee, and a small amount of rubber.

In the Belgian Congo the *Huileries du Congo Belge* has a large land Concession in which important oil-palm plantations have been developed.[2] The Company obtains raw materials partly from wild fruit collected by Natives and partly from its own plantations. It has lately obtained a further Concession of land for the development of ranching. Some detailed reference will subsequently be made to the part taken by Europeans and Africans respectively, in the production of palm oil and palm kernels.[3] Private settlers are engaged mainly in mixed farming (including stock-raising) in the Eastern Province, or in the cultivation of coffee, pyrethrum, and cereal crops in the highlands round Lake Kivu.

As regards the Portuguese colonies the area cultivated by Europeans in Mozambique amounted only to 1,078 square miles in 1951; but it is intended to increase it by various settlement schemes of which that on the

[1] See above, p. 403.
[2] See above, p. 751.   [3] See below, pp. 852 ff..

Limpopo River is the most important.[1] The principal products of European agriculture are sugar-cane, sisal, tea, copra, maize, tobacco, fruit, and vegetables. In Angola the foremost export products—coffee, sisal, and sugar-cane—are cultivated mainly on large plantations, while some 2,700 European farmers concentrate on the growing of foodstuffs such as cereals, beans, potatoes, fruit, and sometimes tobacco.[2] The rubber plantations of the Firestone Company in Liberia occupy about 110,000 acres and are of considerable importance to the country's economy.

AFRICAN CULTIVATION

The characteristic facts about African cultivation require a more detailed treatment. As has been observed, African rural economy remains today predominantly that of peasant cultivation. But there is another fact of outstanding significance. Over a large part of Africa south of the Sudan, the basic method of African agriculture has been the 'shifting' cultivation of subsistence crops, and the problems which arise are mainly due to the changes produced in this system by the stabilization and increase of the population, the absence of large sections of the male workers for long periods in order to earn wages, and the extension of cultivation in order to produce crops for sale.

Shifting cultivation has sometimes been described as a relic of barbarism, but it is in fact rather of the nature of a concession to the character of the soil.[3] It is an error to suppose that tropical conditions in Africa imply the existence of exuberant vegetation and rich soil.[4] With some exceptions, limited in area, the soil in Africa south of the Sudan is generally poor, and in the arid and semi-arid regions, which make up perhaps half the total area of the continent, it has little humus. In addition to this, one or more of the elements essential for plant growth, notably calcium and phosphorus, are insufficient over wide areas, and in arid conditions 'brak' or 'alkali' (usually sodium salts) form layers which are toxic to plant growth.

The continuance of shifting cultivation, or its replacement by a stabilized form of peasant farming, thus depends on the introduction of systems of husbandry which will both maintain fertility and also suit African conditions of life and labour. The existing system is in many areas admittedly unsuited to the conditions of African life as it has now developed, and one of the first requirements for its improvement is the intensive study of African methods of cultivation and an appreciation of the effect of such methods on soil productivity. In Africa the value of soil surveys lies not

[1] See above, p. 756.
[2] *Angola* (Institute Edition), Luanda, 1953, p. 76.
[3] G. B. Masefield, *A Short History of Agriculture in the British Colonies*, 1950, pp. 76 ff. P. Ady, 'Africa's Economic Potentialities', in *Africa Today*, 1955, p. 400.
[4] E. B. Worthington, *Science in Africa*, 1938, pp. 123-43.

so much in their immediate practical application as in the collection of data on some of the more fundamental problems of African agriculture.

Shifting cultivation is in essence a system of bush fallowing. It operates on the principle that the ground should be used for as many years as it remains fertile, usually three or four years, and then allowed to revert to bush until it has regained its fertility. The use of the system was only made possible by the superabundance of land. It is not peculiar to Africa, but was practised all over the world where soil or climatic conditions militated against a more intensive land usage. There is an early reference to it in the first century A.D., when Tacitus, describing the agricultural system in Germany, wrote that they 'changed their fields every year, but there was always land left over'.[1]

The actual procedure followed in forest areas differs somewhat from that followed in the 'savannah' type of country.[2] Where forest land is available it is usually preferred for cultivation to secondary bush. In some parts of Northern Rhodesia, for example, the branches are lopped, laid in piles, and burnt, in order to form thick patches of ash. A newly burnt garden has been shown to contain more phosphate than an unburnt one; the amount of potash is also increased, and the reaction of the soil is changed from slightly acid to slightly alkaline.[3] The effect of the burn soon wears off and a move to another forest area is then made. This type of cultivation, known as *chitemene*, is the most wasteful, but as burnt forest land has proved to be particularly suited to the staple crop of small millets, it is practised throughout the woodland areas of Africa, a fact which has undoubtedly contributed to the progressive disappearance of the high forest.[4]

In non-forest areas shifting cultivation may best be described as a system of rotational 'bush fallows'.[5] Cultivation often takes the form of 'mounding', in which weeds and trash are laid as a foundation, a method which appears to be based on sound principles. These systems require large operating areas, and it is estimated that as much as 20 years is sometimes necessary for the woodlands to regenerate. Shifting cultivation, which involves at intervals the movement of whole villages to a new site, has given rise to claims to exercise rights over wide areas. To these claims inadequate recognition has been given in some territories. The Lozi living in the inundated plain of the upper Zambezi occupy permanent village sites on mounds above flood level with farming land attached to them,[6] and the

---

[1] Tacitus, *Germania*, 26: 'Arva mutant per annos et superest ager.'

[2] See below, p. 936.

[3] *Report on the Commission Appointed to Enquire into the Financial and Economic Position of Northern Rhodesia*, Col. no. 145, 1938, p. 221. See also below, p. 943.

[4] See below, p. 935.

[5] O. T. Faulkner and J. R. Mackie, *West African Agriculture*, 1933, p. 44.

[6] M. Gluckman, 'Economy of the Central Barotse Plain', *R.L. Papers*, no. 7, 1941.

Bisa inhabiting the swamps surrounding Lake Bangweulu build villages and cultivate land on ant-hills protruding above the water level.[1]

Native agriculture varies in method and type of crop according to the nature of the country, the possession of stock, and the custom in regard to consumption of food; but everywhere it is based on a simple economy in which groups of persons co-operate in a system of mutual obligation to produce the necessities of life. The duties of collaboration are divided among the members of the household, recognized tasks being assigned to men, women, and children. The African tradition of cultivation, although empiric, recognizes a system of rotation of crops, the usage of soils, and the means of fertilization; it sometimes even combines anti-erosion measures, which are often well adapted to the prevailing conditions of labour and climate.[2]

The implements of cultivation are the hoe and axe. The months are marked by a routine of clearing bush or tree cutting, fertilizing, sowing of crops, fencing, and harvesting. The character of the marriage relationship in various tribes and the general status of women in the community are closely related to the share which they take in the provision of food. In purely pastoral tribes women exercise relatively less influence than among agricultural peoples, where the heavy work they perform is a measure of their importance in the economic system, and where they are often able to acquire property of their own by marketing crops.[3]

The agricultural system is also closely linked with the position of the political authority from which in principle every member of the community derives his right to land cultivation. In many cases the Chief is responsible for carrying out regular ceremonies on which the success of cultivation is believed to depend, and is sometimes required to perform a special ritual to produce rain in times of drought. His own fields are usually cultivated with the assistance of his domestic circle, but to enable him to carry out the duties of chiefly hospitality, his grain bins are filled by offerings of grain from his subjects' gardens or by communal labour in special gardens at his capital. When the village is moved, the Chief or Headman is the first to cultivate his ground on the new site, and the success or failure of his crops determines whether others will follow.

In some areas shifting cultivation necessitates the continual removal of villages, which consequently assume a temporary character. If they are more permanent, the population moves to its gardens at suitable seasons and lives there in shelters erected for the purpose. The building of huts and grain bins is closely associated with agricultural work, and the problem

[1] V. Brelsford, 'Fishermen of the Bangweulu Swamps', *R.L. Papers*, no. 12, 1946.

[2] C. G. Trapnell and J. N. Clothier, *The Soils, Vegetation and Agricultural Systems of North Western Rhodesia: Report of the Ecological Survey*, 1937. See also C. G. Trapnell, *The Soils, Vegetation and Agriculture of North Eastern Rhodesia: Report of the Ecological Survey*, 1943.

[3] A. Phillips, ed., *Survey of African Marriage and Family Life*, 1953, pp. 92-95, 137-9.

of improving conditions in the villages is to a great extent connected with the stabilization of agriculture.

Certain of the cattle-owning tribes, such as the Masai, Nandi, and Turkana tribes in Kenya, the Hima aristocracies of Uganda, or the Herero of South-West Africa, pay little attention to cultivation. Among other cattle-owning tribes, whether in East, West, or South Africa, the care of herds is combined with cultivation. In their case, however, cultivation is left largely to the women, the men being absent at cattle posts or being left free to protect the herds against wild beasts or to indulge in hunting. The system of herding at distant cattle posts or in the open has militated against the use of animal manure. Thus in Northern Nigeria, where mixed farming is more developed than elsewhere, it is estimated that over two-thirds of the manure is wasted in the bush. The East African and Rhodesian tribes have only of recent years begun to realize the use of manure for fertilizing the soil. On the other hand, some tribes, like the Barotse in Northern Rhodesia, tether cattle to posts in their gardens in order to conserve their manure.

The African bush provides a variety of edible roots, indigenous fruits, wild honey, and the meat of wild game. It is conjectured, for example, that the wild yams of the rain forests formed the diet of the original tribes in West Africa. But it is agreed that in Africa generally very many of the foodstuffs and domestic animals which are common today have been introduced either by migrants from the north, by the Arab and Indian traders from the East, by the Portuguese, or, in more modern times, by other European settlers. The truly indigenous cereals are confined mainly to the sorghums and the bulrush millets. The African oxen, except the Hamitic long-horn cattle and sheep, came from Asia. Bananas, rice, wheat, and sugar-cane were, it is agreed, introduced by Arabs who settled on the East Coast about the seventh century and traded with India. The Portuguese enriched African agriculture with groundnuts, the sweet potato, cassava, and maize, which were introduced from their American colonies.[1]

These early introductions were incorporated with the system of shifting cultivation, and the staple diet of Africans became a form of porridge made from one or other of the grains or from the cassava root, ground by hand between stones or pounded in a mortar. This is supplemented by a relish of vegetables, meat, or milk. Among a few tribes bananas still form the usual food, and in parts of West Africa, yam flour and groundnuts are popular. The introduction of cassava and sweet potatoes by the Portuguese conferred a great boon on many tribes by providing them with a crop which flourishes under conditions unfavourable to grain crops and thus furnishes a valuable stand-by in times of famine or scarcity.

In 1822 the Portuguese introduced cacao from South America to Sao

[1] Worthington, op. cit. p. 340.

Tomé. The cultivation of cloves in Zanzibar was due to Sultan Seyyid Said, who is said to have obtained them from the Île de France or Bourbon, where the French had brought them from the Moluccas.[1] At a later date European enterprise introduced the plantation type of rubber from America, which was also the original source of the types of cotton now grown for commercial purposes. On the other hand, the cultivated species of coffee are indigenous.[2] Sisal was introduced from Mexico by a German, Dr. Hindorf, in 1893.

In areas where cash crops are now grown, such as cotton in Uganda or cacao on the West Coast, the peasant or garden farmer usually began by growing them on a small scale alongside his subsistence crop, or sometimes combined his own efforts with a system of metayage, allowing kinsmen or other co-partners to cultivate part of his holding and providing them with the means of cultivation in return for a share of the produce. The extension of this system has contributed to the great reduction of shifting cultivation, primarily in West Africa,[3] but later in the more fertile areas of East Africa, as most notably in Uganda. It has led also to the development of the new conceptions of land tenure, such as the system of cash rentals, to which reference has been made in the preceding chapter.

Cultivation of this type is becoming more and more general, but the intensive cropping which results from the stimulation of production for sale or export has increased the strain on the fertility of the land. There is also evidence that in some areas, as notably in Gambia, concentration on the cultivation of export crops has resulted in a dangerous decline in the cultivation of food crops, with the result that the provision of food has become increasingly dependent on the farming of marketable crops.[4] There are again some instances, notably in the cacao-producing areas of the Gold Coast and French West Africa, where the peasant system of mixed cultivation has been abandoned and African farmers have extended production to what is practically a plantation scale.

In other areas the European occupation and the introduction of a money economy have induced cultivators to grow a surplus of subsistence crops, but to achieve this they have been obliged to vary their traditional routine of cultivation. This change in the rural economy has naturally been greater near centres of European enterprise, where money can often be earned as easily from cultivation as by wage labour. As, however, the basic methods of agriculture remain those of shifting cultivation, the available soil becomes rapidly exhausted. A system which may prove useful when an area of 200 acres or more of woodland is available for the

[1] R. Coupland, *East Africa and its Invaders*, 1938, p. 314.
[2] See below, pp. 832 ff.
[3] G. Howard Jones, *The Earth Goddess*, 1936, pp. 96–97.
[4] *Economic Advisory Council, Committee on Nutrition, First Report, Part II, Nutrition in the Colonial Empire*, Cmd. 6051, 1939, pp. 34–36.

use of each family cannot endure indefinitely where the population is increasing and woodlands decreasing.[1]

The effect of European occupation on the cattle-owning tribes has also been far-reaching. More stable conditions and the application of veterinary science have resulted in a rapid increase of African livestock, particularly cattle. The great rinderpest epidemic of 1895 provided a temporary check, and the movements of the tsetse fly have eliminated cattle in some areas. There have also been occasions when large herds have been decimated by pleuro-pneumonia, as, for instance, in the Barotse country. Nevertheless, over-concentration of stock has in many areas led to widespread soil exhaustion and erosion.[2] Some of the problems connected with overstocking are further discussed in another chapter dealing with the problems of soil conservation and erosion.[3]

The conception of agriculture as a profitable industry is new to the Africans, many of whom have been accustomed to look on cultivation largely as part of the struggle to win enough food to keep themselves and their families alive. Systems of shifting cultivation have seldom resulted in producing plenty, and the records of travellers and early administrators show how frequent have been the famines or 'hunger periods' in the history of African tribes. Though, however, the cultivator is traditionally conservative, he is not so conservative as to cling to methods which experience has shown to be unfruitful, nor does he resist the introduction of new crops.[4]

Instances of a change in the methods of cultivation were by no means unknown in the period before European influences acquired their present force. Thus the staple food has been changed to cassava where the cultivation of millet has become impossible owing to the deforestation of the woodlands.[5] The production of cacao in the Gold Coast and of groundnuts in Northern Nigeria are examples of the ready development of new industries where the African has been satisfied that production is within his capacity. The wide adoption of maize and other crops, which are comparatively recent introductions, is further evidence of his capacity for adaptation, and the extensive growth of cotton in East Africa is another case in point. What some of these innovations have brought to the cultivator in the way of money-returns is shown by the fact that the income accruing from the cotton and coffee production in Uganda was stated to be £24 million in 1954.

Though the scientific study of tropical agriculture is still in its infancy, it is clear that the European agronomist, by a careful observation of Native methods and social conditions, can do much to assist African agriculture

---

[1] J. M. Davis, *Modern Industry and the African*, 1933, p. 190.

[2] For a discussion of veterinary control in relation to overstocking, see Worthington, op. cit. pp. 434–40.

[3] See below, pp. 1020 ff.

[4] Faulkner and Mackie, op. cit. p. 6.   [5] Davis, op. cit. p. 191.

in a period of transition, and can when necessary intervene to advise against an unwise extension of the cultivation of cash crops. Some reference has already been made in the preceding chapter to the measures being taken to introduce changes in the indigenous system of land tenure which should create an incentive to the further increase of agricultural production. It has been stated that the reaction of Africans to such measures, lately introduced in Southern Rhodesia, has been by no means unfavourable.[1]

In the following pages some account is given of the extent to which the more important crops have been cultivated and developed for sale and export; but it must be remembered that millets and most root crops, and in some areas maize, are grown in gardens of no great size for home consumption and that the relatively small amount grown for sale by Africans is generally the surplus of the crop grown for food. Crops such as beans and peas are primarily grown for use as relish, to be salted and eaten with the porridge; this in some areas is true also of groundnuts. Native gardens contain a variety of other subsidiary crops, such as pumpkins and cucumbers, and in the neighbourhood of villages wild spinach, tomatoes, peppers, and occasionally sugar-cane are also to be found.

Where maize is not the staple cereal it is grown in the early rain season as an extra crop, usually for eating in the cob before it hardens. Where the staple crop is millet, such as the fine bulrush variety, it is grown in small patches. Subsidiary crops are numerous, and a survey in one limited and comparatively primitive area in Northern Rhodesia identified over 100 varieties.[2] In a number of gardens examined in Southern Nigeria, where yams are the staple crop, it was found that in 93 per cent. corn was also grown, in 99 per cent. pumpkins, in 24 per cent. cassava, in 92 per cent. groundnuts, in over 80 per cent. some variety of beans, and in 90 per cent. peppers. The woman cultivator has a peculiar interest in these subsidiary crops;[3] most are planted to provide the relish dishes into which the mush or porridge is dipped, and her success as a wife and housekeeper depends on her skill in varying the diet from her garden. There is, in the African bush, a variety of edible wild plants, roots, mushrooms, and fruits, and a familiar sight is that of parties of women collecting these in the appropriate seasons.

Another general article of diet is the sweet potato, which grows freely over a wide range of tropical country. It is easily propagated by vine cuttings and has a long period of growth; its trailing habit and dense foliage serve to prevent erosion. The cultivation of European potatoes is

---

[1] *Africa Digest*, March–April 1955, p. 15.

[2] *Report on the Financial and Economic Position of Northern Rhodesia*, Col. no. 145, 1938, pp. 217 ff. See also, Trapnell and Clothier, op. cit. pp. 26–30.

[3] C. Daryll Forde, 'Land and Labour in a Cross River Village', *Geographical Journal*, vol. xc, no. 1, 1937.

unimportant except in Kenya and the eastern parts of the Belgian Congo, where they are said to be gaining favour as an ingredient of African diet. The sweet potato is, however, more nourishing, and it would be unfortunate if it should pass out of use.

THE CHIEF CROPS GROWN

There will be found in the following pages some details regarding the crops which form the major part of the agricultural production, whether grown by Africans or Europeans. They are arranged in alphabetical order. It will be realized that where crops are grown in mixed gardens by very numerous individuals, as in the African system of agriculture, it would be difficult to give any precise indication of the amount grown annually in each territory, even were the machinery for estimating agricultural production far better organized than is at present the case. In general the temperate-climate cereals, such as wheat, oats, or barley, are grown by Africans only in restricted areas, and are less important than the warm-season rainfall crops, of which maize and millets are the most important.

Cassava (Manioc)

Cassava is grown almost entirely by Africans. It is a staple food in many of the tropical and sub-tropical areas of Africa[1] and its cultivation is widely encouraged as a reserve crop in case of scarcity. In various British territories cultivation of a minimum acreage of cassava for this purpose has been made obligatory by the Native Administrations.[2] It is not universally popular and some tribes dislike it as a food, for the starchy porridge made from cassava flour is said to be more filling than nourishing. There are two distinct varieties, the bitter and the sweet; the root of the bitter variety contains cyanogenetic glucoside which develops hydrocyanic acid;[3] in the sweet variety the glucoside is confined to the skin. Cassava is comparatively free from pests, but is subject to a virus disease known as mosaic, which has increased in recent years. Resistant varieties bred at the Amani Research Station in Tanganyika are beginning to be put into cultivation.

In West Africa cassava, which is commonly grown in the rain forest area, is generally planted on ridges as the final crop before the farm is abandoned. It is then left to fend for itself. In Liberia the crop is estimated at about 460,000 short tons.[4] In French West Africa the average

---

[1] For botanical details, see *Enc. C.B.*, vol. i, pp. 461–70.

[2] For instance, Rules made under the Agricultural Law, 1946, of the Buganda Kingdom. See also *N.A.*, Part I, pp. 38, 68.

[3] Worthington, op. cit. p. 361, and *Enc. C.B.*, vol. i, pp. 335–76.

[4] U.S. Department of Agriculture, *Foreign Agriculture*, May 1950, p. 110.

annual crop is computed to be between 1 and 1½ million metric tons. The production from French Equatorial Africa is also on a large scale, being estimated at 1,240,000 metric tons in 1951.[1] There has been some export from French Togoland of tapioca made from the cassava root. In the Cameroons cassava is grown as a foodstuff in the forest and savannah zone, and in the north has been encouraged as a precaution against famine caused by locust invasions. In the Belgian Congo manioc is described as the basic food of a large part of the African population, the cultivated area in 1952 being about 1 million acres. Cuttings of mosaic-resistant varieties have been distributed in Ruanda Urundi.

Cloves

Cloves are the principal export of Zanzibar accounting, with clove oil and clove-stem oil, for approximately 80 per cent. of the Protectorate's domestic exports. Two-thirds to four-fifths of the cloves entering world trade originate in Zanzibar, the only other important source being Madagascar.

Cloves are the unopened dried flower-bud of *Eugenia carophyllus*, a tree which was introduced into the islands of Zanzibar and Pemba between 1820 and 1830 from the Moluccas. It reaches full production between the fifteenth and twentieth year, when the yield is from 3 to 8 lb. per annum. Production is seriously threatened by two diseases. For over 50 years trees in the two islands have been affected by a virus disease known as Sudden Death, which, however, became menacing only by about 1935. Since then it has destroyed over half the mature trees of Zanzibar. It has not spread to the same extent in Pemba, and about four-fifths of the clove crop is now produced in that island.

A Clove Research Scheme, which was financed partly from Colonial Development grants and partly by the Zanzibar Clove Growers' Association, operated from 1947 to 1952, and indicated that a fungus—*Valsa eugeniae*—is the most likely cause of the disease. The spores of this fungus attack the tree roots and cause the whole tree to die within a short time.[2] So far no device has been found to control this disease. Field experiments are mainly directed towards investigating whether soils can be made innocuous for saplings by being treated with lime.

Another serious disease which affects clove trees is Dieback. This is caused by one of two fungi—either the *Valsa eugeniae* or the *Cryptosporella*—which infect any open wounds in the branches. Some success has been achieved by cutting out the diseased tissues and covering the exposed parts with a protective paint.

[1] United Nations, Food and Agriculture Organization, *Year Book of Food and Agricultural Statistics: Production, 1953*, vol. vii, Part I, 1954.
[2] *Colonial Research, 1952–1953*, Cmd. 8971, 1953, p. 128.

Cocoa (Cacao)

The cacao tree, *Theobroma cacao*, originally indigenous to the tropical forests of Central and South America, requires a high temperature with a humid atmosphere and flourishes under West African conditions. In 1952, in fact, West Africa produced 70 per cent. of the total world production of cacao.[1] The tree was first brought from America to Sao Tomé by the Portuguese, and afterwards established on the mainland, first in the Gold Coast and later in Nigeria.[2] These two countries at present are the largest producers, but the Ivory Coast of French West Africa and the French Cameroons are now exporting increasing quantities. Cacao is predominantly African-grown, except in the Belgian Congo, Fernando Po, Sao Tomé, and also the Cameroons, where large plantations, some of which continue to be under European control, were established under the German administration.

The cacao crop of the Gold Coast is produced from the forest belt, where it occupies about 950,000 acres, and the development of the industry has been so rapid as to overshadow other agricultural activities, to the prejudice of subsistence cultivation. The cultivation is almost exclusively in the hands of peasant farmers, and it is estimated that there must be over a quarter of a million cacao farms, varying in size from about $2\frac{1}{2}$ to $6\frac{1}{2}$ acres, with a number of larger farms held by the growing monied class in the Gold Coast. The labour is usually provided by the peasant's family, but labourers, generally from the Northern Territories of the Gold Coast, are employed on the larger farms.

The Gold Coast crop has been threatened with extinction by a virus disease known as 'swollen shoot' which was first reported in 1936.[3] The only remedy so far known to science is the cutting out of infected trees. Attempts to enforce the destruction of trees which are still capable of some yield have aroused a resentment among the growers which has at times assumed a political complexion, and faced with this attitude official policy has alternated between compulsory and voluntary cutting out.[4] Compensation on a liberal scale is paid to growers from funds provided by the operations of the Cocoa Marketing Board.[5] By the end of 1952 some 16 million trees had been cut out and African farmers have now come to realize that the future of the cocoa industry depends upon effective

---

[1] United Nations, Food and Agriculture Organization, *Year Book of Food and Agricultural Statistics: Trade, 1953*, vol. vii, Part II, 1954, p. 150.

[2] Masefield, op. cit. pp. 54–55.

[3] It has been estimated that some 200,000 tons of cacao may be lost yearly by the swollen shoot disease and by the attacks of capsid bugs; *The Times*, 18 September 1952.

[4] *Report of the Commission of Enquiry into the Swollen Shoot Disease of Cacao in the Gold Coast*, Col. no. 236, 1948. See also *An Economic Survey of the Colonial Territories, 1951: vol. vii, The Products of the Colonial Territories*, Col. nos. 281–7, 1952, p. 15.

[5] See below, p. 1349.

control of the disease.[1] Swollen shoot is also present in Nigeria and to a minor extent in the Ivory Coast.

The type of plant cultivated in the Gold Coast, the yellow-podded *Amelonado*,[2] yields well over 500 to 600 lb. of dried cacao per acre. The crop is harvested at two seasons, the main season from August to January and the mid-season (which is far less important) in May and June. The standard Gold Coast product is not of as high a quality as the *Criollo* of Venezuela and Trinidad, but it is in good demand as the basis of cacao mixtures.

Beginning with an experimental shipment of 80 lb. of beans in 1891, the average export from the Gold Coast in the three years 1949–51 was 253,509 tons, and in 1953 the figure was 236,634 tons, as against an average world consumption of between 750,000 and 780,000 tons. The overall annual value of the export during these years has been £56 million. The price actually paid to the cultivator is best illustrated by the figures paid per head-load (60 lb.). During the four years 1928–9 to 1931–2 the average price paid was 13s. 1d. Cacao was during these years purchased by the trade in the open market. From 1939 onwards the price has been officially fixed under the system of purchase to be subsequently described.[3] During the years 1938–9 to 1941–2 the average price paid was 6s. 3d. During the four years 1948–9 to 1951–2 the average price paid rose to 65s., equivalent to £121. 10s. a ton. It was 70s. in 1952–3 and 72s. in 1953–4,[4] when the price was a much-debated political issue. The world price of cocoa was £359. 10s. 0d. a ton in 1954, having attained a peak of £556 a ton in May of that year. An agitation in 1955, although conducted against the Cocoa Marketing Board[5] rather than against the price of cocoa, nevertheless succeeded in increasing the fixed price from 72s. to 80s. per head-load. But the world price had already fallen to £270 per ton.

Cocoa is the major item in the domestic economy of the Gold Coast and dominates the financial position of its Government. The control over production, the management of marketing, and the determination of the price to be paid to the producer have become the outstanding issues of Gold Coast politics. The operation of the Cocoa Marketing Board in particular seems likely to form one of the classical illustrations in the history of the use of this type of economic organization in Colonial territories.

The cocoa industry in Nigeria has not been developed to the same extent as in the Gold Coast, as climatic and soil conditions are suitable only in the areas lying to the west of the territory. The original exports

[1] *Colonial Reports, Gold Coast, 1953,* p. 46.
[2] See *Enc. A.O.F.,* vol. ii, pp. 98–105. *Enc. C.B.,* vol. i, pp. 540–9, for a description of local types. [3] See below, pp. 1349 ff.
[4] The figures relate to the trade year 1 October to 30 September.
[5] For the development of Marketing Boards in the British Colonies, see below, pp. 1473 ff.

were of poor quality, but an improvement was made when in 1922 the Department of Agriculture organized fermentation centres and promoted the formation of a series of Cocoa Co-operative Societies.[1] The export of cocoa from Nigeria has since shown a steady increase, and in 1952 amounted to 114,731 tons, valued at over £28½ million. In 1955, however, exports showed a decline owing to the damage inflicted by black pod disease. The Co-operative Supply Association of Western Nigeria has imported over £250,000 worth of sprayers and chemicals for fighting this disease.

Before the Second World War the purchase of cacao for export from the Gold Coast and Nigeria was in the hands of private firms. An agreement between them which was designed to prevent uneconomic competition and which had, in practice, the effect of imposing a fixed price led in 1937 to a boycott by growers which received direct support from the politically minded elements in the country.[2] During the Second World War bulk purchase and export sale of the crop were undertaken by the United Kingdom Government, and after the war the profits made in the war period were transferred to Cocoa Marketing Boards which were set up in the Gold Coast and Nigeria in 1947.[3] These Boards are now the sole buyers, and have power to devote their profits primarily to the maintenance of a price stabilization fund but also to the furtherance of any purpose which will assist the cacao industry.

The profits have in some years been very considerable, and at the end of 1954–5 the Marketing Board of the Gold Coast had assets of just under £87 million.[4] The Cocoa Marketing Board has employed the Cocoa Purchasing Company as its agent and licensed buyer. There has recently been some criticism in the press as to the use to which the Company has put its funds and assets, and the Marketing Board has had to complain that it has received no Certificate of Audit of the Company's accounts. Early in 1956 the Government, yielding to popular criticism, appointed a Committee to inquire into the charges made against the management of the affairs of the Company. There appears, however, to be no substantiation of the suggestion that the funds had been used for political purposes. The Cocoa Marketing Board of Nigeria had in September 1954 a General Reserve of £29·1 million, and a special Research Reserve of £2·9 million.[5]

The cultivation of cacao in the Ivory Coast of French West Africa was first seriously pursued in 1912,[6] when the Administration decided to

---

[1] Colonial Reports, Nigeria, 1951, pp. 49 ff.

[2] Report of the Commission on the Marketing of West African Cocoa (the Nowell Report), Cmd. 5845, 1938. W. K. Hancock, Survey of British Commonwealth Affairs, vol. ii, 1942, pp. 210 ff. Report on Cocoa Control in West Africa, 1939–1943, Cmd. 6554, 1944.

[3] See below, pp. 1349 ff.

[4] The Gold Coast Cocoa Marketing Board, 8th Annual Report and Accounts for the year ended 30th September 1955, p. 1.

[5] Seventh Annual Report of the Nigeria Cocoa Marketing Board, 1953–54, p. 30.

[6] Enc. A.O.F., vol. ii, p. 98.

promote its growth by the application of the procedure of *culture obligatoire*.[1] There was a progressive increase of production up to 1938, when 52,720 metric tons were exported, but there was a decline during the Second World War; the farms were neglected and drastic measures had to be taken by the Administration to secure the replanting of areas invaded by parasitic disease. The position has been so far restored that exports amounted in 1953 to 63,000 and in 1954 to 50,200 metric tons.

Cacao has become an important export from the French Cameroons also.[2] The plantations originally established by the Germans fell into disuse as the result of the First World War, and the bulk of the production, both in these areas and in other parts of the Trust territory, now comes from African gardens. As a result of the control extended since 1920 by the Agricultural Service the export figure, which in 1920 was only 2,500 metric tons, was raised to 51,100 metric tons in 1952. The Cameroons has so far been free of swollen shoot disease. In both the Ivory Coast and the French Cameroons the sale is controlled in the sense that the price is officially fixed and purchase is restricted to authorized centres. Measures for improving production are met from a fund which is financed by a levy on the difference between the purchase price as officially fixed and the market price realized.

The production from French Togoland is relatively small; exports have fallen from an average figure of 8,600 metric tons over the period 1934–8 to 4,500 metric tons in 1952.[3] The export from French Equatorial Africa is small; it amounted to 2,700 tons in 1952.

In the Belgian Congo the cultivation of cacao is practically confined to European planters,[4] but the total export in 1954 amounted only to 2,936 metric tons. There is no noteworthy production in Angola, but Sao Tomé and Principe exported 8,400 tons in 1952, the cultivation being mainly in the hands of European estate-holders. There was a larger average export (13,700 tons) from Spanish Guinea. In Liberia it is planned to expand the 10,000 acres already planted under cacao to 150,000, and it is hoped to achieve an annual export of 15,000 tons.[5]

Coco-nuts (Cocotier) and Copra

The coco-nut palm (a near relative of the oil palm) has a wide distribution throughout Africa. In many areas the coco-nut is an article of food; the copra (the dried fruit of the nut), once an important source of vegetable oil, now takes a much less prominent place in the world's markets. Africa, moreover, only makes a small contribution to the export of coco-

[1] See below, p. 1370.   [2] *Enc. C.-T.*, pp. 198–203.
[3] See United Nations, Food and Agriculture Organization, *Year Book of Food and Agricultural Statistics: Trade, 1953*, vol. vii, Part II, 1954, p. 166.
[4] *Enc. C.B.*, vol. i, p. 540.
[5] U.S. Department of Agriculture, *Foreign Agriculture*, February 1951, p. 29.

nut oil; it exported in the three years ending 1952 an average of only 9,333 tons, compared with 248,333 tons from Asia.

The coco-nut palm thrives best near the sea, but will grow well inland at elevations up to about 1,500 feet. It is subject to a number of pests (such as scale and coco-nut beetle) which may at times assume serious proportions, and there appears to be no cure for the disease of bud-root which kills the tree. Coco-nut palms in Africa are cultivated only when grown in plantations, and even then the cultivation consists mainly in keeping down grass and undergrowth. In Tanganyika efforts are being made to improve the production of copra by the introduction of simple drying kilns. Zanzibar has for long been the chief source of production in this part of Africa and in 1952 it exported 5,359 metric tons.

In West Africa the copra industry is making some progress in the coastal area of the Gold Coast; the exports were 5,000 metric tons in 1952. The use of drying kilns is essential in this area of high humidity, and the Department of Agriculture is giving technical assistance to the industry. Nigeria in 1953 exported 5,767 tons of copra. In French West Africa Dahomey is the main producer,[1] but export did not exceed 800 metric tons in 1951, and fell to 400 in 1952. In French Togoland coastal plantations of coco-nut extend between the sea and the lagoons, and the cultivation of the palm has been stimulated since 1922 by the distribution of seedlings from Government nurseries.[2] Copra exports showed a gradual increase until 1951, when they reached 6,200 metric tons, but they decreased the next year to 2,300 tons. There is practically no export from French Equatorial Africa.

The Belgian Congo takes little interest in the commercial production of copra.[3] Mozambique, on the other hand, has for some years given much attention to the production of copra from its coastal area, and it has the largest export of any country in Africa. During the four years 1948 to 1951 it exported an average of 41,675 metric tons a year. At Gurué in the Zambezia Province there is said to be the largest plantation in the world, with a total of 2 million palm trees.

Coffee

Coffee is indigenous to Ethiopia and first reached South America, now the world's largest producer, through the Dutch settlement of Surinam about the year 1718.[4] It is as yet scarcely used by Africans as a beverage. Though some use is made of it in Uganda, this is confined to chewing the berries, which have a certain ceremonial importance and are offered to guests by persons of standing. The three principal varieties, *arabica*, *robusta*, and *liberica*, are native to Africa; *arabica* originated in the mountains

[1] *Enc. A.O.F.*, vol. ii, pp. 61–64.
[2] *Enc. C.-T.*, p. 484.
[3] *Enc. C.B.*, vol. i, p. 518.
[4] Masefield, op. cit. p. 18.

of Abyssinia, *robusta* (or more correctly *canephora*) in the Belgian Congo, French West Africa, and North West Angola, and *liberica* in Liberia. A lesser variety, *stenophylla*, belongs to the highlands of Sierra Leone.[1]

The *arabica* coffee is classed for trade purposes as the superior quality and is the variety which is most widely cultivated by Europeans, thriving best at heights above 2,000 feet. It needs better soil and more careful cultivation than the other varieties, which are hardier and grow best from 2,000 feet down to sea-level. It is the sole type now produced in Brazil and Colombia. *Robusta* is in turn superior to *liberica*, which thrives in humid climates. Its production is now declining in face of the competition of *arabica* and *robusta*.

Coffee is grown both by Europeans and Africans, and it is noteworthy that the production by Africans has shown a steady increase in recent years, partly as the result of the encouragement given by the different Administrations in both East and West Africa. The attempts made to grow coffee in the Union of South Africa have not been successful, nor has there been any production in Southern Rhodesia. In Northern Rhodesia planters in the Abercorn district have experimented with coffee, but no permanent production of any importance has been established. In Nyasaland coffee planting by Europeans dates from 1878, and a peak was reached in 1900 with an export of roughly 1,000 tons, but other crops have since proved to be more profitable to the European estate-holders. It is held that the long dry season will prevent its development by African farmers.

In Tanganyika African production amounted to 11,250 tons and European production to 3,550 tons in 1953;[2] and there was much the same proportion in 1954. Both in the Bukoba District and the Moshi area, from which most of the coffee comes, the crop is largely African-grown, though there is also some production (mainly of the *arabica* type) by European planters in Moshi. In this district Native growers are organized in the Kilimanjaro Native Co-operative Union;[3] it is noteworthy that the coffee from the Chagga area on Kilimanjaro was valued at £2¾ million in 1953. The Bukoba crop has greatly deteriorated since the Second World War and efforts are now being made to restore its quality. In the Moshi area the expansion of the African production of coffee has been due largely to the direct assistance given by the Government.[4]

In Uganda interest in the growth of coffee began about 1922 and was encouraged by the wide distribution of seedlings by the Agriculture

---

[1] Worthington, op. cit. pp. 362–4. The varieties of coffee and the systems of cultivation are described in detail in Col. nos. 281–7, 1952, pp. 17 ff. *Enc. C.B.*, vol. i, pp. 523–40. *Enc. A.O.F.*, vol. ii, pp. 92–97.

[2] *Tanganyika, Report for the Year 1953*, Col. no. 307, p. 31.

[3] See below, p. 1468.

[4] R. L. Buell, *The Native Problem in Africa*, vol. i, 1928, p. 474.

Department, both *arabica* and *robusta* varieties being grown according to the suitability of climate. It was stated in 1955 that about one-eighth of the total production of 67,000 tons came from non-Native estates, and the remainder (known as *kiboko* coffee) from African peasant holdings.[1] About 9 per cent. of the output was *arabica*. The total export (35,280 metric tons in 1954) now exceeds that of any other British territory in Africa. The control of diseases has been the subject of much experimental work and is taught to African growers by Agricultural Instructors. The control of marketing was until 1953 the subject of a variety of legislation, but this was consolidated in the Coffee Industry Ordinance of that year. Though the price is fixed for a whole season, growers now receive more or less the full world price of coffee.

In Kenya coffee was at the outset grown entirely by Europeans, and it is clear that at one stage their opposition to its cultivation by Africans was such as to induce the Administration to discourage its growth by them, as notably by the Coffee Plantation Registration Act of 1918. After this even *robusta* coffee could not be grown without a licence, which was liable to be refused.[2] This policy was ostensibly dictated by the fear that disease would spread from African to European plantations, but experience in Tanganyika showed that it could be prevented if African production was adequately supervised by Agricultural Officers. The subsequent Coffee Rules of 1934, as amended in 1949, permitted African cultivation of *arabica* coffee under licence in specified areas, and the number of African growers has steadily increased. In 1953 there were 15,019 licensed African growers on about 3,867 acres. It was estimated that by the end of 1955 the number would be increased to 20,000 and the acreage to 8,500. The coffee produced is reported to be of high quality.[3] No similar restrictions have been placed on the growing of other export crops. The total export of coffee, which had begun with an export of 8 tons in 1909, rose to 14,970 tons in 1953.[4] The commercial side of the industry is controlled by the Kenya Coffee Board, and coffee curing and cleaning factories have been established at Nairobi, Kitale, and Mombasa. Research is carried on at the Jacaranda Experimental Station.

The production in British West Africa is confined to Sierra Leone and the Gold Coast; the former exports a few hundred tons, the latter has so far consumed its production locally. The variety grown is *robusta*, and culti-vation is in the hands of Africans.

[1] *Colonial Reports, Uganda, 1955*, p. 41.

[2] *Report of the Kenya Agricultural Commission*, 1929, para. 144. J. Huxley, *Africa View*, 1932, pp. 54 ff. *Report of the Commission on Closer Union of the Dependencies in Eastern and Central Africa*, Cmd. 3234, 1929, p. 62. For similar difficulties raised in Tanganyika, see Buell, op. cit. vol. i, pp. 393, 493; and Masefield, op. cit. p. 102.   [3] *Colonial Reports, Kenya, 1952*, p. 43.

[4] *Kenya, Annual Report of the Department of Agriculture, 1953*, pp. 12 ff. The total crop for the season 1954–5 was 12,385 tons, valued at over £4½ million.

In French West Africa the Ivory Coast is the chief centre for coffee. Guinea and Dahomey provide relatively smaller quantities. About two-thirds of the crop is produced by African peasants.[1] The prevailing type is *robusta*, but as the result of a severe attack by a parasitic disease in 1926 some attention was paid to the substitution of a local variety of *canephora* known as *assikasso*. A certain measure of control over cultivation and export has been exercised by virtue of regulations issued in a decree of July 1948. The export amounted in 1952 to 71,400 metric tons, a figure which far exceeded that of any British territory.

In French Togoland there was very little coffee grown until 1929, and it was much subject to parasitic disease.[2] Efforts made to control this have, however, met with some success, and exports have risen from 24 metric tons in 1929 to 2,600 tons in 1952, almost entirely of the *robusta* type.

Coffee has not the same importance in French Equatorial Africa. Efforts were made between 1925 and 1939 to promote its production by Africans, but had little result. European planters, however, mainly in the Oubangui Chari area, have begun to grow coffee, and the total export amounted in 1952 to 5,000 metric tons. The prevailing type was *robusta*.[3] The French Cameroons has proved more favourable to its growth, and the *arabica* type has been established in the higher plateaux, such as Bamiléké and Bamoun. The initial attempts to promote the growth of the crop were made in 1925, a very large number of trees being planted under administrative supervision. Export amounted in 1952 to 9,200 metric tons. About one-half was produced by Africans and the rest by planters; roughly one-fourth of the total export was of *arabica*.

The Administration of the Belgian Congo has for some years sought to promote the cultivation of cash crops by those Africans who have no opportunity of taking part in the production of palm oil or in industrial labour. The stimulation of cotton-growing was part of the result of this policy, and it has extended also to the growth of coffee. It has resulted in increasing the export from a yearly average of 17,000 metric tons in 1934–8 to a figure of 30,900 metric tons in 1952. But in this case the increase in production has been due mainly to European planters, for though the African production has been brought under the system of obligatory 'educative' cultivation, Africans were credited in 1951 with only about 6 per cent. of the total.[4] There has been little substantial advance in the last five years and production has remained uniform at an estimated average of 20,902 tons. About one-third of the total production is *arabica*.[5]

Coffee was introduced into Ruanda Urundi in 1931, and by 1936 a large

[1] *Enc. A.O.F.*, vol. i, pp. 91 ff.
[2] *Enc. C.-T.*, pp. 204–10, 486, 506.   [3] *Enc. A.E.F.*, p. 319.
[4] For 'educative' cultivation see below, pp. 840, 850.
[5] *Enc. C.B.*, vol. i, p. 523.

number of trees had been planted under official supervision. The chief type grown is *arabica*, the banana groves with their accumulated humus having been found to provide suitable sites. Production had risen to 13,109 metric tons in 1952.[1] In Liberia efforts are being made to resuscitate coffee production, which has declined in recent years. An annual export of 7,000 tons is aimed at.

The statistics published by the Food and Agriculture Organization show that Angola has today an export of coffee which actually exceeds that of any other country in Africa except French West Africa. From a yearly average of 16,400 metric tons in 1934–8, the export rose in 1952 to 47,700 metric tons. It is produced mainly on the slopes of the coastal hill range, and the bulk of the production is by European enterprises employing African labour; about one-fifth is, however, stated to be produced by African peasants.[2] There is a small export from Mozambique, but in 1951 this amounted only to 728 tons.

Cotton

Indigenous African cottons existed and cotton textiles were being woven in West Africa when European traders first arrived.[3] But the cotton of modern commerce has been derived from American long-stapled varieties introduced at various times since the beginning of the twentieth century. The climatic conditions required by cotton are moderate rainfall during the growing period and dry weather for the setting of the bolls; if the rains last too long or stop too early, yields are seriously affected. Cotton is grown in some areas as a mixed crop and is often planted in the same gardens as the staple food crops; its development by Africans is indeed largely due to the ease with which cultivation can be combined with that of subsistence agriculture. It may be said that in general cotton has not proved to be a remunerative crop for 'plantation' cultivation by Europeans, partly no doubt because the cost of picking seed cotton has proved to be out of proportion to the market price, especially during periods of price depression. Cotton has, moreover, shown itself to be very susceptible in Africa to attacks of pest and disease, such as boll-worm, stainer, jassid, and capsid.

In South Africa cotton-growing has been tried by European farmers for many years, but production has remained on a comparatively small scale. Since the Second World War, however, it has received some impetus from the high prices prevailing and from the creation of a local market by the new textile factories in the Union. Production in 1955 had risen to 41,000

[1] *Rapport sur l'administration belge du Ruanda-Urundi, 1952,* p. 330.

[2] *Overseas Economic Surveys, Angola, 1949,* p. 5.

[3] Masefield, op. cit. p. 9. *Ethiopia Orientale* (1609) quoted by G. McC. Theal, *Records of S.E. Africa,* vol. vii, states that indigenous cotton was found on the banks of the Zambezi by Dos Santos, a Dominican friar, at the end of the sixteenth century.

bales.[1] The most suitable country for cotton lies in the northern and eastern parts of Natal, northern Transvaal, and in Zululand. It is noteworthy that the Empire Cotton Growing Corporation, which was founded in 1921, at first established its experimental station at Barberton in the Union, where it bred the various strains which have proved of such value in the promotion of the growth of cotton in Uganda and elsewhere. In view, however, of the comparative failure to expand the growth of cotton in the Union, it was decided in 1939 to transfer the station to Namulonge in Uganda. The Corporation received a grant for this purpose under the Colonial Development and Welfare Acts, and the new station was opened in 1950.

In Southern Rhodesia cotton-growing showed an early expansion in 1924–6, but after a fall in prices most European farmers stopped growing it. It was decided in 1935 to stimulate the cultivation by Africans, and in 1950 the output of African-grown seed cotton exceeded for the first time European production. After reaching a peak of 9,500 bales in 1952, the total production has since fallen steeply and was only 400 bales in 1955.[2] The crop is purchased on behalf of the Cotton Research and Industry Board and sent to the Gatooma ginnery. Varieties resistant to jassid insects are grown and, though the boll-worm remains a limiting factor to cultivation, it has been proved that cotton fits well into a rotation with maize.

In Northern Rhodesia cotton-growing by Europeans has had a varied history. The attempts made to cultivate it in the early twenties failed, and its production is at present very limited. Only about 2,000 acres were planted in 1951–2. Experiments with cotton as an African crop have been under trial since 1932, and in the Eastern Province output had reached 45 tons of seed cotton in 1953. It is also planted near the railway line, especially in the Mazabuka District, but in the season 1953–4 only 90 bales were produced.

In Nyasaland cotton was at one period the crop most favoured by European estate-holders, but its cultivation was subsequently abandoned as unremunerative. The Government began to encourage its growth by Africans about 1922.[3] The Egyptian seed originally used was later replaced by American Upland; the type now grown is derived from the American strain, U4, introduced from Barberton. In 1950 some 10,700 bales of cotton were marketed. Early planting, newly introduced in 1951, appears to afford some control over red boll-worm, and 15,400 bales were produced in 1955, most of which came from African cultivation.[4]

In Tanganyika cotton is grown almost entirely by African peasants and is

---

[1] A bale of cotton weighs 400 lb.

[2] *The British Cotton Growing Association, Fifty-first Annual Report and Statement of Accounts, 1955,* no. 183, April 1956.   [3] Buell, op. cit. vol. i, p. 252.

[4] *The British Cotton Growing Association, Fifty-first Annual Report and Statement of Accounts, 1955,* no. 183, April 1956.

an important export, reaching a record figure of 120,600 bales in 1955.[1] Yields are not, however, equal to those in Uganda, and improved strains are being developed by the Empire Cotton Growing Corporation at an experimental station at Ukiriguru. The cotton produced by Kenya is now almost entirely an African crop. The lint has been exported in small quantities for many years, but not until 1930 was there a definite increase in cultivation. In 1950 7,973 bales were produced mainly from the Nyanza and Coast provinces, strains from Uganda having been successfully introduced. In 1955 production amounted to 14,000 bales. In some areas cotton has been satisfactorily worked in with food crops, but in others it is causing overcropping, and where it is grown on hill slopes it is said to be responsible for adding to the extent of soil erosion.

The spectacular development of the cotton industry in Uganda has been assisted by the extension of the railway and by the development of roads, but as already remarked it affords evidence of the capacity of the African peasant to adopt new types of cultivation where he finds them profitable. There appears to be no evidence of indigenous cotton in Uganda, its cultivation having been introduced by Arabs. The strain known as Gallini was introduced by Sir Samuel Baker at Bunyoro in 1872,[2] but there is no trace of further types being used until 1903 when Egyptian and American Upland varieties were tried as an experiment, largely on the initiative of missionary societies. It was decided in 1907 to restrict importation to American types. In 1929–30 there were introduced the varieties U4 and U4/4/2 bred by the Empire Cotton Growing Corporation at Barberton in South Africa. The latter strain is the parent of many selections now being cultivated.

Cotton is grown mostly in the Buganda, Eastern, and Northern Provinces, where there is a rainfall of about 50 inches. Its cultivation has led in some districts to a degree of soil exhaustion which at one time threatened general yield levels, though it is now coming under better control. The dressing of cotton seed with cuprous oxide against blackarm disease has lately given promise of increased yield. It is significant, however, that though production has increased at the expense of more land being put under cultivation, yields per acre have not. For a crop which takes so much out of the soil as cotton, an appropriate fertilizer may do more to restore fertility than a ley fallow.[3] Uganda cotton is of longer staple than the indigenous cotton of India and it enjoys a premium over American middling, but this may be lost if the standard is allowed to deteriorate through the mixing of strains.

[1] *The British Cotton Growing Association, Fifty-first Annual Report and Statement of Accounts, 1955,* no. 183, April, 1956.
[2] J. D. Tothill, ed., *Agriculture in Uganda,* 1940, pp. 183 ff. Masefield, op. cit. p. 86.
[3] *East Africa Royal Commission 1953–1955, Report,* Cmd. 9475, 1955, p. 333.

The progressive increase of production has been remarkable. It was not until 1906 that there was an appreciable export (500 bales), but from that time development was rapid, reaching 418,000 bales in 1937–8. The crop of that year was, however, a record which has not since been equalled, though production in 1953–4 reached 398,252 bales.[1] In 1952 the export from Uganda exceeded that of the Sudan, though it was far less than that of Egypt.[2] The total income to growers in 1954 is said to have amounted to £12¾ million,[3] of which nearly £4½ million accrued to those in Buganda.[4] Large quantities of cotton seed are exported to the United Kingdom, but more is crushed locally, much of the resulting oil and oil-cake being exported to Kenya.

The Uganda Government issued in 1928 a Cotton Ordinance (amended and enlarged in 1933) as the result of which the purchase of seed cotton is limited to gazetted centres where both buying operations and the quality of cotton are under official inspection. The minimum price and the variety of cotton to be grown are fixed by regulation and the right to erect and operate ginneries is controlled. The first power gin was established at Kampala in 1906. In 1954–5 there were 130 ginneries in operation. The majority are owned by Asians, but as a result of arrangements made by the Government eight ginneries are at present operated by the African growers' cooperative societies.[5] An export tax was imposed in 1919, its proceeds at first being devoted to the development of the industry but now forming part of the general revenue; the total contributed by the tax in 1953 was £2,526,000, about one-seventh of the total revenue of the Protectorate. Of the exports in 1954–5 about 73 per cent. went to India and 13 per cent. to Germany; only 2 per cent. went to Great Britain.

Passing to West Africa it would appear that cotton has been grown from a very early period in Nigeria, in order to supply the demands of the indigenous spinning and weaving industry, but the bulk of the modern export production now comes from the Zaria and Sokoto Provinces in the north, where American cotton has practically replaced the indigenous variety. In the Southern Provinces an improved indigenous type known as Ishan is favoured, but the total yield is small. There was an exceptional crop in 1940–1, when all previous production records were broken. This total was exceeded in 1955, when a new all-time record crop of 187,741 bales was produced.[6] It is of some interest that in the local markets the price of raw cotton to be used for spinning or weaving is often higher than the export price.

---

[1] *Empire Cotton Growing Corporation, Annual Report 1953–1954.*

[2] United Nations, Food and Agriculture Organization, *Year Book of Food and Agricultural Statistics: Trade, 1953*, vol. vii, Part II, 1954, p. 185.   [3] *Background to Uganda*, no. 62, June 1954.

[4] Ibid. no. 88, February 1955.   [5] See above, p. 403, and below, p. 1467.

[6] *The British Cotton Growing Association, Fifty-first Annual Report and Statement of Accounts, 1955*, no. 183, April 1956.

After the First World War the production of cotton in her African Colonies became a matter of much concern to France, as the cost of the import of cotton lint accounted on an average for 7 per cent. of the value of her total imports. In Equatorial Africa the local authorities undertook in 1924 to secure from African cultivators a production sufficient to guarantee the operation of four cotton companies, which were given the monopoly of purchase over defined zones. The price was to be regulated by the Administration, and the companies were to supply improved types of seed, supervise cultivation, and undertake transport, ginning, and exportation.[1] Cotton-growing, which is conducted largely on a family basis, was promoted by an extensive and, to all appearances, a somewhat drastic use of the process of 'educative' cultivation,[2] but it has since been accepted as a factor of primary importance in the local African economy. Cotton exports in 1952 amounted to 29,400 metric tons; this figure represented about 40 per cent. of the country's total exports. A type of American Upland was at one time commonly used, but other varieties have recently been adopted as the result of experiments made through the *Institut de Recherches du Coton et des Textiles Exotiques*, the institution which in 1945 took the place of the *Union Cotonnière de l'Empire Français*. Cultivation is mainly carried on in a wide belt of cotton country running through Oubangui Chari and extending into Chad.[3]

The production of cotton is of less importance to French West Africa and is practically confined to the irrigated lands in the Niger basin.[4] A Concession was given in 1919 to the Diré Cotton Company, but development began only in 1930. The progress made in the growth of cotton in the Niger Delta area has been slow, and the average production has been only 1,500 metric tons of seed cotton a year, though hopes were at one time expressed of an ultimate annual production of 70,000 tons of lint cotton from this source.[5] A ginnery is owned by a local Co-operative Society, membership of which is compulsory for cotton-growers. The type grown is derived from an improved American seed from Nigeria.[6] The total production from French West Africa in 1952 was estimated at 7,000 metric tons of cotton lint, with an export of 2,100 metric tons. In French Togoland cotton is grown in association with yams in the Central Plateau area, but the average exports of lint do not exceed a figure of between 1,500 and 2,000 metric tons.

Though the Government of the Belgian Congo has not been under the same pressure as the French to promote the growth of cotton, the matter has nevertheless been regarded as one of much importance, and cotton

---

[1] *Arrêté*, 17 February 1927.   [2] See below, p. 1370.
[3] *Enc. A.E.F.*, pp. 21, 308 ff.
[4] See below, p. 1003.   See also *Enc. A.O.F.*, vol. i, p. 35.
[5] See below, p. 1005.
                                                          [6] *Enc. A.O.F.*, vol. i, p. 351.

was the first crop to which the procedure of obligatory 'educative' cultivation was applied about the year 1917.[1] This, however, presented difficulties in view of the great fluctuation in price, and in 1921 a system was
adopted under which the monopoly of purchase was given to cotton
companies operating within zones allotted to them. These were originally
eleven in number, but some have since been absorbed by the major company, the *Compagnie Cotonnière Congolaise*. The companies discharge much
the same function as those in French Equatorial Africa in so far that they
provide seed and encourage the expansion of cultivation. The price to be
paid to the cultivator is fixed by regulation, and the companies pay part
of the difference between the purchase and the market price to a fund
which enables a stable producer-price to be maintained over a course of
years. This procedure proved its value during the depression period of
the thirties.

At the outset there were complaints both locally and in Belgium that
undue pressure was being exercised on the cultivators by local officials in
order to meet the demands of the influential cotton companies, but
though there was undoubtedly some justification for this complaint, there
can be no doubt that the peasants appreciate the value of the cash resources
made available to them. The area under cultivation was estimated in 1950
at an average of 750,000 to 875,000 acres, and the number of cultivators
at about 700,000.[2] If there is now some criticism of the system, it is mainly
because the use of the obligatory form of cultivation has resulted in maintaining the use for this purpose of certain areas which for reasons of climate
or soil yield an inadequate return to the cultivator.

The most productive areas are in the valleys of the rivers Uele and
Oubangui in the north and Sankuru and Kasai in the south. The type of
cotton sown is American Upland, and the variety U4 from Barberton[3] is
becoming increasingly popular. Part of the production is absorbed by the
local textile mills in Leopoldville and Albertville. The export in 1952 was
45,700 metric tons. In the Trust area of Ruanda Urundi cotton-growing
was a compulsory 'educative' process until 1943, when the law permitting
this form of compulsion was revoked. In 1952 the production of seed
cotton amounted to 5,003 metric tons.

In Mozambique cotton is now the most important export. In 1952 the
export figure rose to 30,100 metric tons, nearly all of this being grown by
African peasants. It is a valuable cash crop to the peasants, and it is stated
that they receive from it more than they earn from work in the Transvaal
mines. In Angola the production is less valuable, only 6,200 metric tons
being exported in 1952. An attempt is being made to secure from the two

[1] L. Banneux, *Quelques données économiques sur le coton au Congo Belge*, 1938.
[2] *Enc. C.B.*, vol. i, p. 485.
[3] See above, p. 837.

territories a larger proportion of the 300,000 tons which is estimated to be the total requirement of cotton lint in the textile industries of Portugal.

Fruit

The cultivation of fruit, and particularly of fruit for the export market, has in the past been mainly in European hands. The tropical areas contain a large number of trees bearing wild fruit, but little interest has been taken by Africans in trees of the type which may need continuous care. In Central Africa the system of shifting cultivation, involving the frequent removal of villages, discourages the planting of the more permanent type of fruit tree. Cashew nuts, picked by peasants from semi-wild trees, are an important export from Mozambique, and in 1950 some 68,000 metric tons were exported, nearly all to India and Pakistan. The nuts are mainly undecorticated, though an increasing proportion is being decorticated before export. Tanganyika produced 16,000 tons in 1954, with a value of a little over £500,000, and a nut-processing factory was established at Mtwara in the same year.[1] Encouragement has been given in recent years to the planting of cashew trees in Southern Nigeria; they are useful soil stabilizers for eroded areas, and a demand has, moreover, arisen from the plastics industry for the phenol which can be extracted from the fruit.

Kola nuts are chewed in West Africa on account of their stimulating and sustaining properties. In former years Nigeria imported kola nuts from the Gold Coast and Sierra Leone, but internal production has increased and there is now an export surplus. Cultivation of kola has been recommended in order to replace the cacao tree in districts where it has ceased to be economically profitable, and seed and plants of the better varieties have been distributed. Both Nigeria and Sierra Leone have an export of kola nuts, mainly to the United States.

In the Gold Coast an export industry in lime products began in 1929 when two factories were established near Cape Coast by a well-known company, using fruit from African gardens, but in 1940 the trees were attacked by the 'tristeza' virus disease. When it was found that limes budded on rough lemon stocks showed tolerance to the disease, rehabilitation of the industry began, and from 1947 to 1951 some 150,000 budded lime trees were issued. Exports in 1950 included 139,000 gallons of lime-juice (about a third of the 1936 export), 403 tons of fresh limes, and 13,816 gallons of grape-fruit juice. Only 600 tons of fruit, however, were exported in 1953. Internal demand for citrus fruits is slowly growing in West Africa. In Nigeria there is a plant for bottling citrus juices at Abeokuta and another operated by a Farmers' Co-operative near Lagos, both of

---

[1] *Report of the East African Commissioner for the Year 1954*, East African Office, London, p. 20.

which use fruit grown by Africans. In 1949 an overseas firm opened a factory at Umuahia with a view to the extraction of orange juice.

An officially encouraged industry in French Guinea produced 238 metric tons of essential oil from oranges in 1938, approximately equal to the total world consumption. This trade suffered during the Second World War, and in 1946 exports were only 93 tons, but there are, nevertheless, important possibilities of citrus development in this territory. A number of citrus plantations have been established in the Bas-Congo region of the Belgian Congo, mostly in the hands of European planters.[1] There was a small export in 1950.

The citrus industry has been the basis of the Union export trade in fruit, which now has a recognized place in the economy of the country. Oranges were introduced from St. Helena soon after the occupation of the Cape in 1652, but exports were small until after the First World War. Expansion began in 1918, when a large number of trees were planted, but many of these proved worthless. With improved cultivation, however, there was a rapid increase, and in 1954 the export of citrus fruit from the Union amounted to 194,000 tons.[2] The principal areas of production are around Port Elizabeth and in north and east Transvaal. Citrus-growing is carried out on estates of varying size and in all cases irrigation is necessary. After 1926 several citrus-fruit marketing associations united to form the South African Co-operative Citrus Exchange Limited, which was financed from a levy on the exported fruit. In 1939 this was replaced by the Citrus Board, which became the sole exporter and has control over sale in local markets.[3]

There has been a similar development in the production of deciduous fruits. South Africa became known as a grape and wine producer two centuries ago, when Cape Town was a port of call for ships bound for the Indies, but it was not until refrigeration in ships was improved in the early part of this century that the export of deciduous fruit became of importance. Rapid expansion began after 1926. In 1951 over 49,000 tons of grapes were produced for consumption as grapes, 29,000 tons for drying into raisins, and 217,000 tons for wine-making. All three products are in part exported. The principal grape-growing district is near Cape Town, where rainfall is sufficient and irrigation unnecessary.

The expansion in vine culture is largely due to the enactment of the Wine and Spirit Control Act of 1924, which gave the Co-operative Wine Growers' Association of South Africa control over the making or disposal of wine. The principal areas for other deciduous fruits lie inland from Cape Town and along the south coast, and there are two important irrigated areas north of Port Elizabeth. The Deciduous Fruit Board performs functions similar to those of the Citrus Board. The total export

---

[1] Enc. C.B., vol. i, pp. 623–32.
[2] Commonwealth Economic Committee, Fruit, 1955, p. 5.
[3] O.Y.S.A., 1950, p. 822.

of deciduous fruits amounted in 1954 to 38,000 tons, together with nearly 50,000 tons of canned and dried fruit.[1]

In Southern Rhodesia the citrus industry is mainly in the hands of the British South Africa Company. In 1954 some 274,000 cases of citrus fruit were sold, mostly to the local market. Plans for building up an export trade in citrus fruit have, however, been adopted following the completion of the rail link between Southern Rhodesia and the coast at Lourenço Marques, and an area of 40,000 acres has been surveyed for this purpose by the Government. In Kenya the passion-fruit industry is growing in importance; 9,449 gallons of juice were exported in 1952, but in other respects conditions in East Africa are not favourable to the development of the export of citrus or other fruits.

Groundnuts (Arachides)

The groundnut (peanut) is indigenous to Brazil. It is believed that it was introduced to Africa by the Portuguese. It can be grown as an annual crop on light soils in almost any tropical or sub-tropical country, and cultivation extends from Gambia all along the West Coast, across Central to East Africa, and down to the Union. The nut is valued by Africans as a foodstuff and its oil is used for domestic purposes; it is probable that a more extended use of it would remedy some of the deficiencies in the African dietary. The plant acts as a soil renovator, and the haulms are a valuable addition to the fodder supply in mixed farming.

In Central, East, and West Africa its cultivation is carried on mainly by African peasants, but it is noteworthy that the increase in the consumption of edible oils (due largely to the movement of the population from rural to urban areas) has stimulated its production by European farmers in the Union of South Africa. Here production is mainly on European farms, and in 1953–4 amounted to 96,900 tons. Both Southern and Northern Rhodesia are dependent on the African for 90 per cent. of their production, which at the 1953–4 harvest amounted to 48,427 metric tons in Southern Rhodesia, and a little over 5,000 metric tons in Northern Rhodesia. Both the pilot schemes of mechanized production in the Eastern and Central Provinces of Northern Rhodesia proved abortive.[2]

Tanganyika and Uganda for many years produced small export surpluses, varying with the season, but of late years these have declined owing to increasing internal consumption; in some years Tanganyika had to import groundnuts in order to fill the needs of the local oil mills. The growth of the groundnut in Tanganyika has, however, come prominently into the history of Colonial agriculture owing to the failure of the East African Groundnut Scheme undertaken by the British Overseas Food

---

[1] *Commonwealth Economic Committee, Fruit, 1955*; pp. 5, 8.   [2] See below, pp. 906 ff.

Corporation in 1946.[1] It would be out of place to dwell here on the controversies which have grown out of the failure of this unfortunate project. Its sponsors envisaged that it could produce by 1948 some 56,000 tons of groundnuts, rising to 609,000 tons in 1951. It actually produced up to the end of 1951 a total of 9,162 tons of shelled nuts, together with some small quantities of maize and millets. The expenditure involved during the period was of the range of £35 million.[2]

The ground for undertaking this enterprise lay in the fact that in 1945 the Ministry responsible during the Second World War for the control of foodstuffs anticipated that there might be a serious shortage in the supply of edible oils owing to the decline in the export of groundnuts from India, China, and Indonesia, partly as a result of the war, and partly because India had begun to consume her own production of groundnuts.[3] This situation would be the more serious as owing to war conditions there was a grave deficiency of animal fats. The British Government consequently entered on the groundnut scheme in much the same spirit as had dictated the financing of war operations. But it is not possible to find any justification for many of the measures actually taken in the execution of the project, and in particular for the hasty assumption that mechanization would overcome the climatic and other defects of the notoriously unsuitable area selected for the operation of the major part of the scheme.

With the virtual abandonment of the project in 1951 the work of the Overseas Food Corporation in Tanganyika was restricted to investigations, partly designed to establish the value of mechanized agriculture in tropical conditions, and partly to test the potentialities of peasant farming. One of the most interesting of these investigations is that known as the African Tenant Scheme at Nachingwea (Southern Province).[4] The investigations extend also into the local potentialities of stock-raising. The Overseas Food Corporation were finally given rights of occupancy over 354,000 acres. In March 1955 these were transferred to the Tanganyika Agricultural Corporation which will be assisted by a grant under the Colonial Development and Welfare Act until September 1957. The capital

[1] Masefield, op. cit. pp. 168 ff. See also the White Papers: Cmd. 7030, February 1947; Cmd. 7314, January 1948; Cmd. 8125, January 1951; Cmd. 9158, May 1954; and *Overseas Food Corporation, Report and Accounts for 1951–52; 1952–53; 1953–54; 1954–55.* A. Wood, *The Groundnut Affair*, 1950, and the analysis of the economics of the schemes by S. H. Frankel, *The Economic Impact on Underdeveloped Societies*, 1953, pp. 141 ff.

[2] The balance of advances which, under the Overseas Resources Development Act, 1951, the Corporation is not required to repay. This sum was, however, liable to subsequent adjustment.

[3] Between 1934 and 1938 India (including Pakistan) had exported a yearly average of 715,500 metric tons of shelled and unshelled nuts, China 195,900, and Indonesia 18,600. In the period 1948–51 the yearly average from all three countries combined was 151,300 metric tons. In 1952 India exported only 17,800 metric tons.

[4] See below, p. 907.

advances which had been made towards the construction of the Port of Mtwara and the Southern Province Railway have been written off.[1]

Though there is no reason to suppose that the production of groundnuts cannot be to some measure increased in East Africa, it is actually West Africa which has hitherto been responsible for the major volume of export and would seem likely to remain the principal source of supply so far as Africa south of the Sahara is concerned. In Nigeria production is entirely in the hands of peasants, and the groundnut is the main agricultural product of the Northern Region. During and since the Second World War rising prices have resulted in a considerable expansion of the acreage, and this has also made possible a beginning in the purchase and use of super-phosphate fertilizer, which has proved to be very beneficial to the crop.

The average export from Nigeria during the years 1946 to 1954 was 283,000 tons, though this period included one season of unusually short rainfall (1950–1). In 1953 exports totalled 326,700 tons. The increased production has, however, been achieved only at the expense of a heavy strain on the railway system, which in some years has become so choked that there has been great delay in evacuating the crop.[2] Groundnuts have long been the main export of Gambia; in 1952 61,700 metric tons were exported. In 1954 a deterioration of quality gave rise to anxiety, and it is considered that seed stocks have degenerated. They are grown largely by 'strange farmers', or immigrants from the adjacent French territories who each year migrate, to the number of some 15,000, to grow and harvest groundnuts.[3]

The West African Oilseeds Mission of 1948 considered that the limit of productivity had been reached by the use of the primitive implements available to the African cultivators.[4] It recommended that experiments be made in the use of mechanized tillage and of fertilizers. The report indicated various areas as suitable for investigation by a pilot scheme; it considered that, if these schemes were successful, developments involving an expenditure of approximately £25 million might result in an increase of production of the range of 225,000 tons a year.[5] The progress made in the operation of some of the pilot schemes will be referred to in a subsequent section.[6]

French West Africa was for many years the leading exporter of groundnuts in Africa, though in the years 1948 to 1950 the average figure (218,600 metric tons) fell short of that of Nigeria.[7] Senegal is the principal source,

---

[1] See below, p. 1296. Also Foreword to *Overseas Food Corporation, Report and Accounts for 1954–55.*   [2] See below, p. 1562.

[3] *Colonial Reports, The Gambia, 1951,* p. 16. For the 'strange farmers', see *N.A.,* Part III, pp. 347–9.   [4] *Report of West African Oilseeds Mission, 1948,* Col. no. 224.

[5] The average yearly value of the exports for the years 1948–52 was nearly £15 million.

[6] See below, p. 910.

[7] The figures for 1952 were: French West Africa 201,800 and Nigeria 264,600 metric tons.

and the impoverishment of the soil in the Rufisque district through over-production has led to active experiments with the use of fertilizers. There is some production in the French Sudan and the Niger Province, but that in the Haute Volta is declining, also on account of over-production and soil deterioration.

A research station at M'Bambey is supported by the *Fonds d'Investisse-ment pour le Développement Économique et Social* (F.I.D.E.S.),[1] as is also an experimental area for mechanized production of the crop at Kaffrine. The production of groundnuts is also one of the objects of the scheme for mechanized cultivation in Casamance, the area initially investigated amounting to 75,000 acres.[2] In French Equatorial Africa exports are relatively small and fell to 400 metric tons in 1952, but the expansion of groundnuts as a food crop is now being actively encouraged. The French Cameroons exported 8,500 metric tons and Togoland 3,700 in 1952.

In the Belgian Congo the crop has hitherto been valued rather for local consumption than for export, though during and since the Second World War there has been some export of groundnut oil. During the years 1948–51 the average export of decorticated groundnuts was only a little over 1,000 metric tons, but efforts are being made at the experimental station at Yangambi to improve the species now grown.[3] Portugal derives small supplies of groundnuts from both Angola and Mozambique, but in neither case is production at all large, although exceeding that in the Belgian Congo.

Maize

Maize is one of the crops most widely grown in Africa south of the Sahara. On the figures provided by the Food and Agriculture Organization the total annual production of this region is estimated at about $3\frac{1}{2}$ to 4 million metric tons, of which the quantity grown by Africans forms a very high proportion. The successful growth of maize requires a fertile soil and a timely rainfall. In many areas, however, where maize porridge is the main diet of the people, the crop is grown continuously on the same land whether the soil is suitable or not, and usually without any attempt at rotation with a legume or root crop. As may be expected, the return in these circumstances is low, and the average may not be more than 2 to $2\frac{1}{2}$ bags an acre, as against the 6 or 7 bags which similar land might yield under better methods of cultivation.[4] As will be seen, however, there are instances where crops produced by African peasants using improved methods have largely exceeded these figures.[5]

The history of the maize trade in the great maize-growing areas of

[1] See below, p. 1339. [2] W. V. Blewett, in *J.R.S.A.*, August 1950, p. 795.
[3] *Enc. C.B.*, vol. i, pp. 454 ff.
[4] The standard weight of a bag of maize is 200 lb. [5] See below, p. 848.

southern and eastern Africa has in recent years run on parallel lines. Before 1939 the Union of South Africa and, in lesser degree, Northern and Southern Rhodesia and Kenya were all exporters of maize, much of this export having been grown on European farms. During and after the Second World War, however, the exports declined materially owing to the increase in internal consumption, while in poor years (as for example in the years 1945–7) some of the countries concerned became importers of maize.

In the Union production had increased considerably after the Anglo-Boer War, when the depleted animal population caused the farmer to turn to the cultivation of grain. The output of the Union, which was estimated at 361,000 tons in 1904, was stimulated by high prices and in the early thirties it reached an estimated total of $2\frac{3}{4}$ million tons. But with the ensuing fall in prices maize for export had to be subsidized in order to be profitable to the producer. Export subsidies were provided under the Act of 1931, and when they were discontinued from 1937 the export, which in 1935 had been about half a million tons, fell gradually to less than 200,000 tons in 1941. Since then diminishing quantities of maize have been available for export, and they fell to 23,000 tons in 1953. The 1953–4 crop was the heaviest ever harvested, reaching the record total of 3,513,000 tons.[1] On such figures as are available it would seem that European production was responsible for roughly 80 per cent. of this total. The general story, therefore, has been one of growing production, but also of rapidly increasing domestic consumption and falling export.

In Southern Rhodesia yields per acre are generally higher than in the Union. In the season 1949–50, some 341,000 acres of maize on European farms produced 162,767 tons of grain. From a third to a half of this maize is retained for farm use, the remainder being delivered to the Grain Marketing Board at an annually fixed price. The export, which in 1938 had been 61,700 metric tons, had fallen by 1952 to 29,900 metric tons. It is estimated that in 1948–9 African farmers produced 166,499 metric tons of maize, of which 71,803 metric tons were delivered to the Grain Marketing Board after retaining the amounts needed for home consumption.

The average yield on the European farms has been stated as varying between $4\frac{1}{2}$ and 6 bags per acre during the years 1947–50.[2] The general average on African lands is much lower, but some remarkable instances have been quoted of yields reaped in 1951–2 on the holdings of African Master Farmers, under the system of supervision and control initiated by the Agricultural Department. Considerable blocks yielded $8\frac{1}{2}$ bags an

---

[1] *Commonwealth Economic Committee, Grain Crops, 1955.*
[2] *O.Y.S.R., 1952*, pp. 76, 392, 454.

acre, and there were quoted in the press instances of groups reaping 15 bags an acre in one district and 12 in another. The 1954 crop in Southern Rhodesia was expected to yield 272,000 tons, and the territory seems now to be self-supporting in the production of maize.

In both the Union and Southern Rhodesia the more progressive maize-growers are now attempting to keep abreast of modern developments. The production and use of 'hybrid' maize seed on the American pattern is leading to increased yields; in Southern Rhodesia, for instance, hybrid maize planted in 1949–50 on 22 per cent. of the sown area produced 32 per cent. of the total crop. With the introduction of maize-picking machines in recent years, complete mechanization of the crop on the European farms may be in sight.

In Northern Rhodesia the local production of maize has usually made a substantial contribution to feeding workers on the Copperbelt, but unfavourable local conditions necessitated a small importation in 1950. In 1953 over 90,720 metric tons were produced, practically equalling consumer requirements,[1] and at the end of the season of 1954–5 the surplus was estimated at 75,000 tons. Cultivation has become largely mechanized on European farms, except for harvesting. The seed in general use is hybrid maize, introduced from Southern Rhodesia; this is said to respond well to a dressing of sulphate of ammonia.[2] Maize is extensively cultivated by Africans, but mainly for home consumption, except near the railway line, where ploughs are now in general use by Africans and a considerable surplus is grown for sale. In 1953 some 39,463 metric tons were thus disposed of, and 11,715 tons were also marketed from the Eastern Province. This grain is bought at fixed prices by the Maize Control Board, a small part of the price being withheld from the producers and credited to the African Farming Improvement Fund.

Northern Rhodesia has a system of Improved African Farmers somewhat similar to that of the Master Farmers of Southern Rhodesia. Under a scheme introduced in 1947 two criteria of farming standards were adopted, the higher qualifying for a bonus of 21s. an acre, the lower for one of 12s. an acre. In 1952 over 1,000 farmers were registered in the Southern Province and others in the Central Province. The yield obtained by these is said to be double that of less advanced farmers.

In Tanganyika the production of maize on European farms rose from 400 tons in 1936 to 26,635 tons in 1950, and the total export in 1952 was 8,500 metric tons. There is a large but very variable production on African lands, mainly for home consumption, but in 1950 Africans marketed 37,829 tons surplus to their own requirements. In Kenya maize grows

---

[1] *Northern Rhodesia, Annual Report of the Department of Agriculture, 1954.*
[2] L. G. Troup, *Report of the Commission of Inquiry into the Future of the European Farming Industry in Northern Rhodesia—Tenure of Agricultural Land,* 1954, p. 19.

readily from the coastal belt to the highlands, provided that the rainfall is sufficient. European production was estimated at 100,646 metric tons in 1952. Much of the output of the farms goes to fill up the deficiency in African production, but in the past there usually remained a surplus for export; this, indeed, rose in 1952 to 69,300 metric tons.

Maize is the most important African foodstuff, the consumption of which is rapidly rising. It is one of the most satisfactory crops in suitable areas because it not only meets the home food demand but also yields a cash return.[1] On the European farms the use of early maturing Muratha seed and of South African and American varieties has largely superseded the lower-yielding local types. In Uganda maize is only a subsidiary food in the rural areas, but it is also grown to feed the increasing urban population and for export. In 1950 the Protectorate marketed 33,150 tons, of which 9,740 were exported to other East African territories, and in 1953 there was a heavy export to Kenya during the emergency caused by Mau Mau disturbances.[2]

In the coastal regions of Nigeria and the Gold Coast maize is a valuable foodstuff, but the extensive growth of more profitable crops has reduced its importance as a cash crop. Attempts to introduce new varieties have generally failed as the indigenous type is considered more palatable. Recently rust disease, which made its appearance in 1950, has become a serious problem.

In French West Africa maize is a less important food crop than millet,[3] though in 1952 the gross production was estimated at 492,000 metric tons. The crop is most important in Dahomey, which exported 35,736 metric tons in 1938, but after the Second World War exports fell off and were finally prohibited because the decline in rice imports made it necessary to keep the maize in the country. In French Equatorial Africa maize is grown only in the neighbourhood of Lake Chad and there on a relatively minor scale.[4]

In the Belgian Congo maize is a staple food in the savannah regions, and its cultivation has been extended under the 'educative' system,[5] primarily with a view to increasing the food supply. Whereas at one time it was necessary to import a considerable amount of maize for consumption at the industrial centres, the territory is now self-supporting. The total production in 1950 was estimated at 337,000 metric tons. It is almost entirely an African crop.

Angola, where maize is the chief peasant crop of the uplands, has maintained a more continuous record of export than most African territories.

---

[1] R. J. M. Swynnerton, *A Plan to Intensify the Development of African Agriculture in Kenya*, Nairobi, 1954, p. 22.

[2] *Colonial Reports, Uganda, 1953*, p. 44.   [3] *Enc. A.O.F.*, vol. ii, pp. 29 ff.

[4] *Enc. A.E.F.*, pp. 306 ff.   [5] See below, p. 1370.

In 1951 export was recorded as 136,800 metric tons, which exceeded that of any other territory in Africa; in 1952 it amounted to 91,100 metric tons. No separate figures of production were recorded for Mozambique, but the area of millets and maize together was returned at 67,000 acres.

Millets

Millets of various species were the principal cereal grown in tropical Africa before the introduction of maize,[1] and the total area under this crop still amounts to almost three times that of maize. The yield per acre is seldom large, but the crop has the advantage of requiring a less fertile soil than maize and some varieties can be matured on less rainfall. In general it is less liable to total failure when climate conditions are unfavourable. Owing to their exceptional keeping qualities the millets are often stored in granaries as reserves against famine, and in some British Colonial territories the Native Authority rules require the cultivator to make an annual contribution of millet to communal granaries for this purpose.[2]

Millet flour provides a staple food for large sections of the African population in South Africa, the Rhodesias, the East African territories, and the interior of West Africa. Production is almost entirely in the hands of Africans. The great millet or sorghum (*Sorghum vulgare*), also known as Kaffir corn or Guinea corn, is the most usual variety, but in drier areas the lesser millets, such as *pennisetum* (the bulrush millet) and *Eleusine coracana* (the finger millet), are widely grown, both as pure or mixed crops.

Sorghum is an important crop in the Union of South Africa and the High Commission Territories. Nyasaland and Northern Rhodesia also depend very largely on millet as an alternative or supplement to maize. When it is grown in addition to maize, the maize is usually used for food and the millet for beer. In Tanganyika millets are the staple crops for food and for the brewing of beer; it is estimated that 2 million acres are under cultivation and produce annually about half a million tons. Sorghum is grown extensively for food in Kenya, and in the drier parts of Uganda the finger millet is the staple cereal; it is estimated that over a million acres are so planted.

In Northern Nigeria the principal grain crops are sorghum and bulrush millet (*gero*). The latter is quick-growing and requires little pre-cultivation. It is accordingly the first crop to be planted in fields where other crops are grown as well. *Gero* is also resistant to drought and adaptable to different soils. In 1950 it was estimated that Nigeria produced 1,862,000 metric tons of sorghum and 973,000 metric tons of millets of other kinds. Every part of sorghum is used; the flour for human food, the bran for feeding stock, the leaves for fodder, and the stalks for building houses and fences.

---

[1] Masefield, op. cit. p. 9. *Enc. C.B.*, vol. i, pp. 452–3.   [2] *N.A.*, Part I, pp. 68, 263.

In French West Africa millets are the staple food throughout the drier northern areas and also in the palm belt in Dahomey. In 1952 the crop was estimated to yield 2,614,000 metric tons. In the French Cameroons millet is the staple food of the northern population, and exports have been made to Nigeria and French Equatorial Africa. Millets are important as a Native food crop in Ruanda Urundi and are grown, though not on an extensive scale, in some parts of the Belgian Congo, where they are also used for making beer. The average production in the Belgian Congo is given as about 55,000 tons.[1]

Palm Oil and Palm Kernels

Palm oil and palm kernels (*palmistes*) are derived from the fruit of the oil palm (*Elaeis guineensis*), whose natural habitat is West and Central Africa. A fibrous pericarp contains the oil and covers the shell, which is cracked to obtain the palm kernel of commerce. The edible pericarp oil is extracted by crude methods and the nuts are cracked by women and children; the kernels are not, however, used by the Africans and are exported to Europe for crushing and processing.[2] Palm oil, as extracted from the pericarp, is utilized for a great variety of purposes, including processes employed in the mining and steel industries; the oil derived from the palm kernels is used mainly in the manufacture of margarine and soap.

Though even before the Second World War Asia competed with Africa in the export of palm oil, West Africa remains the principal source of the export of palm kernels. In 1953 Africa exported 736,000 tons of palm kernels to the world's markets, while Asia contributed only 54,000 tons. Of the exports from Africa in that year, Nigeria was responsible for no less than 352,600 tons, smaller quantities coming from Sierra Leone, the Belgian Congo, French West Africa, and the French Cameroons.

The first export of palm oil to Europe was made from Nigeria in 1790, and the export of palm kernels followed in 1822. The *Elaeis* palm was introduced from Africa into the Far East during the nineteenth century, but it was not till the beginning of the twentieth century that it was extensively cultivated on a plantation scale, first in Sumatra and then in Malaya. Some years later palm oil produced in the Far East on the plantation system began to appear in the world's markets in competition with the product from West Africa. In the years 1934–8 Indonesia and Malaya were exporting on average approximately 205,000 metric tons of plantation palm oil, against 243,000 metric tons from Africa, but by this time a certain proportion of the African export (notably that of the Belgian Congo) was being supplied from European estates or plantations.

[1] *Enc. C.B.*, vol. i, p. 452, where the varieties of millet are described at length.

[2] See *Statistical and Economic Review*, United Africa Company Ltd., March 1954, for a detailed account of the trade.

The success of the competition from the plantation palm oil was due to the fact that it had a lower percentage of free fatty acid.[1] But there also seems to have been an advantage in the actual production of nuts; an acre of oil palms on the best estates in Malaya is said to produce 30 cwt. of nuts, against 3 to 5 cwt. per acre of oil palms grown by Africans, and 12 cwt. per acre grown by Europeans in West Africa.[2] The situation produced by the Second World War has gravely affected the export from the Far East, and particularly from Indonesia, but in 1952 Asia nevertheless exported 167,000 metric tons against 350,000 metric tons from Africa. Since then competition from the Far East has reasserted itself, and the price of oil which stood at £130 a ton in 1951 fell to £85 in 1952 and £67. 10s. in 1953. The price of palm kernels has not been equally affected.

Nigeria, as has been explained, has a secure position in regard to the export of palm kernels and in 1952 still headed the list of African exporters of palm oil[3] with a total of 169,965 metric tons, against a total of 146,073 metric tons from the Belgian Congo. Save for the plantations owned by the United Africa Company,[4] practically the whole of the palm oil of Nigeria is produced by peasant farmers from fruit collected from wild trees. That Nigeria has been able to meet the competition of plantation oil from the Far East is partly due to the fact that Nigerian oil has continued to command a market, on account of its value for industrial purposes, and partly due to a remarkable improvement in the average quality of Nigerian palm oil in recent years.

The Oil Palm Research Station near Benin was brought into full operation shortly after the Second World War.[5] Plans have been drawn up for the establishment of an experimental plantation of 10,000 acres in Calabar and schemes have been put in force for the improvement of existing palm groves by planting selected types. The Agricultural Department has introduced the use of hand-power presses to improve the quantity and quality of the oil. It has been difficult, however, to persuade the Africans to depart from their old-established methods, and more difficult still to make them realize the menace of outside competition. They are averse to felling old trees, and according to custom this can be done only with the consent of the group owning them.

Extraction plants known as 'Pioneer' oil mills have since 1946 been erected at strategic centres, and in 1952 there were in the Eastern Region

---

[1] Worthington, op. cit. pp. 349–52. Masefield, op. cit. p. 95. A. Pim, *Colonial Agricultural Production*, 1946, pp. 135–40. H. C. Sampson and E. M. Crowther, *Report of Leverhulme Trust, West African Commission, 1938–9.*

[2] W. V. Blewett, in *J.R.S.A.*, August 1950, p. 797.

[3] The average yearly value of the Nigerian export of palm kernels for 1948–52 was £17,543,000, and of palm oil £12,619,000.

[4] The total area is 35,000 acres, of which roughly half are under oil palms.

[5] See below, p. 917.

46 such mills under the management of the Eastern Regional Production Development Board. It has been proposed that Nigeria shall have some 300 of these mills at a cost of £1½ million. The extraction by the mills appears to increase the amount of oil by as much as 25 to 30 per cent. The marketing of oil-palm products has since the Second World War been a monopoly of the Oil Palm Produce Marketing Board, which in 1953 arranged to maintain the price of oil at £75 a ton, as against a market price of £67. 10s., at an expenditure of about £3 million. Incentives are being given to improve the quality of the oil and have been so successful that the share of the two highest grades in the oil purchased by the Marketing Board has risen steadily from 61 per cent. in 1950 to over 88 per cent. in 1953.[1]

In the Gold Coast the palm-oil industry is entirely in African hands. Its products formed at an early date the staple agricultural export, but the superior attractions of cacao resulted in the decline of the palm-oil industry. In the 1953 season exports were only 239 metric tons of oil and 6,441 of kernels. The sale of palm oil for domestic consumption in those parts of the country which do not carry the oil palm is probably of greater importance than the export trade, for palm oil has a high dietetic value for the African population.[2]

The importance of the oil palm to Sierra Leone is reflected in the export of 77,900 metric tons of palm kernels in 1952, in addition to 849 metric tons of palm oil. The fruit of the indigenous Sierra Leone oil palm yields relatively little oil; breeding is therefore now confined to imported varieties, of which a large number of seedlings were issued for planting in 1950. The Sierra Leone Produce Marketing Board performs the same functions as the similar Marketing Board in Nigeria. It has provided a considerable number of 'Pioneer' oil mills of the same type as those established in Nigeria.[3]

In French West Africa[4] the principal producing areas are the Ivory Coast, Guinea, and Dahomey, conditions being most favourable in the southern parts of the Ivory Coast. The export in 1952 was 9,492 metric tons of oil and 64,200 of kernels. The oil is admittedly of low quality, but attempts are now being made to improve the palm groves, in pursuance of researches made by the *Institut de Recherches pour les Huiles de Palme et les Oléagineux* (I.R.H.O.) at La Mé in the Ivory Coast and Pobé in Dahomey. It is also the subject of research at Adiopodoumé in the Ivory Coast, which may in future become the chief centre of French agricultural studies. The indigenous palm, like that of Sierra Leone, is poor in oil content, but the primitive method of extracting oil from the pericarp is

[1] *Fifth Annual Report of the Nigeria Oil Palm Produce Marketing Board, 1953*, p. 14.
[2] See below, p. 1070. [3] *Colonial Reports, Sierra Leone, 1951*, pp. 17 ff.
[4] *Enc. A.O.F.*, vol. ii, pp. 49–60.

being improved by the use of a simple apparatus furnished by the *Sociétés de Prévoyance*,[1] and machines for cracking the nut (*concasseurs*) have also been distributed. Eight factories for treating the oil have been erected in Dahomey and the Ivory Coast.

In French Togoland the oil palm is an important source of income in the southern section.[2] Palm kernels were the most valuable export in 1950 at 12,700 metric tons, plus 820 tons of oil, but there was a marked fall in both commodities in 1951. Compared with earlier years production seems to be declining. Mechanical crushers have now been provided by the local *Sociétés de Prévoyance*, and a modern processing factory was built near Lomé in 1950.

French Equatorial Africa has been less prolific than French West Africa in the production of palm oil. Exports have in recent years been in the range of 2,600 to 3,900 metric tons of oil and 7,900 to 8,500 metric tons of kernels. So far the production has been almost entirely the result of African collection of fruit from wild palm trees, but an effort is now being made to encourage plantations in the Moyen Congo and Oubangui Chari Provinces. This will be controlled by companies of the type of the *Compagnie Générale des Oléagineux Tropicaux*.[3]

In the French Cameroons the source is again the wild palm; and here also assistance is being provided by the local *Sociétés de Prévoyance* in the form of mechanical crushers and presses.[4] Exports in 1952 totalled 19,600 metric tons of palm kernels and 1,112 tons of oil. The chief area of production is in the coastal region to the south-west of Yaoundé. There still remain a few plantations originally established by the Germans, but the greater part of the production is African. The measures being taken to improve production have included researches at the Agricultural Station at Ebolowa, the construction of a processing factory at Dibombari, and another at Edéa for the extraction of oil.

In the Belgian Congo the oil palm is found in the greatest number in the equatorial regions of Mayumbe and Kwango-Kasai.[5] It is to palm oil that the Colony first turned as an alternative to the exploitation of wild rubber at the period when the rubber plantations of the Far East began to take precedence in the world market.[6] The world supplies of plantation rubber exceeded for the first time those of wild rubber in 1914. The Belgian Congo was then exporting an average of about 2,440 tons of palm oil. The production from the wild palm was, however, of low quality, and the Belgian Government was well advised to accept the offer made by the Leverhulme interests in 1911-12 to establish plantations on a large scale

---

[1] See below, p. 1476. [2] *Enc. C.-T.*, p. 485.

[3] *Enc. A.E.F.*, p. 313. F. J. Pedler, *West Africa*, 1951, p. 125.

[4] *Enc. C.-T.*, pp. 192 ff. *Rapport annuel à l'Assemblée Générale des Nations Unies sur l'administration du Cameroun, 1951*, p. 158.

[5] *Enc. C.B.*, vol. i, pp. 500-18. [6] See below, p. 964.

and to assist in the organization of the local palm-oil industry.[1] These interests are now represented by the *Huileries du Congo Belge*. Between 1919 and 1925 the Government gave six other Concessions (though not on such a considerable scale) to companies formed either to establish plantations or to organize the processing of palm oil. By 1952 the Belgian Congo was exporting 146,073 metric tons of palm oil and 93,500 tons of kernels.

In the plantations of the *Huileries du Congo Belge* the wild trees are now being replaced by the variety known as *Deli*, which is common in Sumatra, or by a more recently favoured variety of *tenera*. An analysis made of the figures of 1952 showed that Africans sold in the market some 7,876 tons of oil and 43,161 tons of palm kernels, and sold to European extraction factories (including those of the *Huileries du Congo Belge*) about 103,199 tons of oil-palm fruit. European concerns produced 59,288 tons of oil from their own plantations and 103,199 tons from purchased fruit, together with 19,191 tons of palm kernels from their own plantations and 47,156 tons from purchased fruit. The area of the European plantations was stated to be 267,300 acres, with an additional area of 145,400 acres under their control; the area of African plantations was stated to be 153,000 acres.[2]

The chief centre of research into the oil palm is at Yangambi (roughly 100 miles west of Stanleyville) which is the headquarters of the *Institut National pour l'Étude Agronomique du Congo Belge* (I.N.E.A.C.). One of its main objectives is the substitution of the type of oil palm developed in the Far East for the local West African 'wild' oil palm. Yangambi is also an important centre for the study of the 'corridor' system of cultivation.[3]

Of the Portuguese territories Angola had in 1952 an export of 13,500 metric tons of palm kernels and 11,451 tons of oil; all the oil and half the palm kernels are produced in properties under European management.[4] In Mozambique about 125,000 acres have been planted under oil palms. Liberia in 1952 exported 23,800 metric tons of kernels and a small quantity of oil, all from African plantations. Spanish Guinea had in 1951 an export of oil which amounted to a little over 2,800 metric tons.

Plantains and Bananas

Plantains and bananas are cultivated very extensively in tropical Africa. They thrive best in areas of high rainfall, but will grow where the rainfall is as low as 20 to 30 inches. For the purposes of this chapter, the term 'banana' may be taken to refer to the sweet fruit and 'plantain' to the

[1] Masefield, op. cit. pp. 94–96. R. L. Buell, *The Native Problem in Africa*, 1928, vol. i, p. 869, and vol. ii, pp. 511–17. For the area now held by the *Huileries du Congo Belge*, see above, p. 751. See also C. Wilson, *The History of Unilever*, 1954, pp. 167 ff.

[2] *Rapport sur l'administration de la colonie du Congo Belge, 1952*, pp. 248–9.

[3] See below, p. 904. Also W. V. Blewett, in *J.R.S.A.*, August 1950, p. 809.

[4] *Overseas Economic Surveys, Angola, 1949*, p. 8.

variety which requires cooking. For African consumption the plantain is the more widely cultivated, and in some parts constitutes the staple food crop; thus in Uganda over a million acres are estimated to be under plantains,[1] and in Tanganyika the African production of plantains and bananas was estimated in 1952 at 1,320,000 tons. Farther south the conditions are generally too dry for successful cultivation, but there is a small export of bananas from the coastal belt of Natal, principally from European-owned plantations. In West Africa, especially in the southern regions of the Gold Coast, Nigeria, and the Cameroons, there is a big consumption of plantains, often as a supplementary diet to yams.

Bananas and plantains are sometimes interplanted with permanent crops and used for shade purposes. The stools are allowed to multiply almost indefinitely, and the result is often a veritable forest of plants. In some areas a flour used for bread-making is prepared from dried plantains, and liquor is extensively brewed or distilled from them, but there is no commercial preparation of banana fibre in Africa.

Before 1914 German merchants from Hamburg had organized an export trade in fresh bananas from the Cameroons, but it was not until after 1918 that other west-coast countries considered the possibilities of this trade. Some of the fruit companies which operate in the West Indies studied the trade in the west coast, but found that conditions in the British areas were not suitable for trade on the large scale which they desired. In 1933 the Gold Coast Government arranged some trial shipments, but the export then hoped for did not develop. On the other hand, the plantations established by Germans in the Cameroons and now leased by the Nigerian Government to the Cameroons Development Corporation,[2] together with a few plantations held by private firms, have been responsible for an export of bananas amounting in 1952 to no less than 74,200 metric tons.

The export of bananas has long been a feature of the trade of French West Africa, and in 1952 the total amounted to 79,900 metric tons, the greater part coming from French Guinea, but some also from the Ivory Coast. In the French Cameroons there is in the Mbangé area a belt of country largely occupied by banana plantations, which are almost exclusively in the hands of European planters.[3] They have joined in a syndicate which sells its produce to a single exporting firm. The total export of the Cameroons amounted in 1952 to 51,400 metric tons. The growing banana exports of these countries have hitherto been absorbed by the French market, but this, it is believed, has already been saturated.

In the Belgian Congo plantains are an important African food crop, but the production of bananas for export (22,400 metric tons in 1952) has been left to Europeans.

[1] For varieties grown in Uganda, see J. D. Tothill, ed., *Agriculture in Uganda*, 1940, pp. 111 ff.
[2] See below, p. 1327. See also *N.A.*, Part III, p. 178.   [3] *Enc. C.-T.*, p. 161.

Pulses

Pulses such as beans and peas include a very large class of leguminous crops which are widely cultivated for consumption, with occasional small surpluses for export. The favourite cowpea (*Vigna unguiculata*) is to be found growing throughout tropical Africa, and the tall pigeon pea (*Cajanus cajan*) is common. In the Union beans are increasingly grown by Natives as a subsistence crop in the high veld districts and also in the coastal areas of Natal and the Ciskei. Pulses are among the few cereal exports from Bechuanaland, and beans and peas have now for some years exceeded in value the export of wheat and other cereals from Basutoland.[1] In Swaziland the chief legume is the *nhlubu* bean,[2] which, like the groundnut, ripens its grain in the ground. Throughout East Africa beans and peas of all sorts are consumed locally; the Indian community provides a ready market for grams, chick peas, and *dhall*.

The East African territories generally have a small export of pulse crops which varies from year to year; in 1950 it amounted to 8,078 tons from Tanganyika, 6,685 from Uganda, and 4,492 from Kenya. These figures include also some production of seed beans of pure strains produced by European farmers in Kenya and Tanganyika. In West Africa local diets include more groundnuts and less pulses than in East Africa; cowpeas are here relatively more important, and *phaseolus* beans less so. Export surpluses have never appeared in more than trifling amounts.

The soya bean, originally indigenous to Asia, has been widely introduced by European agronomists into southern and eastern Africa, and varieties have now been found which give a reliable yield. It might form a valuable addition to African diets, but the African housewife finds the beans difficult to cook, and is not disposed to adopt them as a food.[3] In 1952 Uganda exported some 200 tons of soya beans, Nyasaland 700 tons, and French West Africa 100 tons, but other cash crops give a better return, and at present prices the export of soya beans is unlikely to increase.

Rice

Rice, as already noted, was probably introduced to Africa by the Arabs. Today such cultivation as is carried on is almost entirely in African hands, but rice is less used as a food than either maize or millets. Little is grown in the Union, though it is produced as a subsidiary crop in a few areas of Nyasaland where recently there have been larger yields, especially from the lake shore at Kota Kota and Karonga. In these areas the crop is marketed by African Trading Societies.[4] In the East African territories it has not yet passed from the status of a subsidiary to a staple food, except

---

[1] *Colonial Reports, Bechuanaland, 1951*, p. 25. Ibid. *Basutoland, 1952*, p. 31.
[2] A. Pim, *Report on the Financial and Economic Situation of Swaziland*, Cmd. 4114, 1932, p. 145.
[3] *Enc. C.B.*, vol. i, p. 460.   [4] *Colonial Reports, Nyasaland, 1952*, p. 54.

in some small coastal communities, though as the population increases the crop tends to expand. In Tanganyika it is mostly grown in the Eastern and Lake Provinces, but the methods used are primitive and the yields very low in comparison with the standards attained in Asia. With increasing internal consumption, exports to other East African territories have declined from a peak of 17,965 tons in 1941 to negligible amounts in recent years.

The British Government has been impressed with the potential field for increased production in Africa, in order to offset the deficit in the Commonwealth and the Far East, and measures are now being taken to implement some of the recommendations of the East African Rice Mission of 1949 for the expansion of cultivation.[1] The major scheme in hand is that in the Rufiji area of Tanganyika.[2] Pilot schemes have also been initiated as a result of an aerial survey in Kilangali in the District of Kilosa, and in the Kilombero Valley. Rice shares in the scheme of investigation at Urambo and Nachingwea, which formed part of the area held by the Overseas Food Corporation.[3]

Kenya, though it has some cultivation in the Nyanza Province and on the coastal belt, still imports rice. Recently, however, it has been introduced in the Kikuyu country and is being cultivated on the Mwea Plains south of Mount Kenya as part of the scheme for the resettlement of thousands of Kikuyu families with no land of their own. It is hoped, eventually, to cover 40,000 or even 50,000 acres with high-quality rice.[4] Uganda had about 10,000 acres under rice cultivation in 1952, but is not self-sufficient.

In West Africa rice is a staple food for some of the coastal populations, especially in French West Africa and Sierra Leone, and there is an increasing consumption by the labour force in mining areas. In pursuance of the recommendations made by the British West African Rice Mission,[5] the Government of Nigeria has erected rice mills to help the growers. The total production in Nigeria was estimated in 1950 at 250,000 metric tons of paddy (unhusked rice).

There was a somewhat smaller production in Sierra Leone, where Upland rice has been a regular feature of cultivation since the sixteenth century; the Upland crop is, however, precarious and both the yield and the quality are poor. There have in the past been a number of years in which Sierra Leone has had to import rice, but the country is now self-sufficient.

[1] *East African Rice Mission Report*, Col. no. 246, 1949.
[2] See below, p. 907.
[3] See above, p. 845.
[4] R. J. M. Swynnerton, *A Plan to Intensify the Development of African Agriculture in Kenya*, Nairobi, 1954, p. 22. Alastair Matheson, 'Kenya's Experiment in Kikuyu Resettlement', *New Commonwealth*, 30 April 1956.
[5] W. N. Clark and S. H. Hutchinson, *British West African Rice Mission Report*, 1948.

Increased attention is being directed to the cultivation of swamp rice on the Scarcies river.[1] A rice research station has been established at Rokupr and one of its principal problems is to find a means of dealing with the toxic elements in the soil, which form an obstacle to the expansion of the industry.[2] Altogether grants of roughly £3 million have been given under the Colonial Development and Welfare Acts to develop rice cultivation in the British dependencies.

In French West Africa rice production is one of the main objectives of the Sansanding irrigation scheme on the middle Niger.[3] In 1951 production in the Niger area was at the rate of 25,000 tons of paddy annually, but the yield is low and does not exceed about 2,000 lb. per acre. A cultivation of as much as 2 million acres is, however, envisaged for the future, and it is hoped to raise the yield per acre to 3,000 lb. The total production in French West Africa from all sources is estimated at between 530,000 and 545,000 metric tons of paddy. Little rice is produced in French Equatorial Africa.

In the Belgian Congo dry-land rice is an important food crop throughout the more humid area of the central Congo Basin. Here production has received considerable official encouragement; it was estimated at about 140,000 metric tons in 1950 and 1951. The Belgian Congo has for some years had a small rice export; it amounted to 8,536 metric tons in 1950, but has since fallen.

The practice in the Portuguese territories is for private corporations to supply seed to African cultivators, who sell back the produce to the corporations at a price fixed by the Government. The practice is reported to be very unpopular with cultivators. Rice is a staple article of food in Liberia, but in the past it has often had to be imported.

Rubber

Though there is some cultivation in Uganda, Nigeria, the Gold Coast, the Belgian Congo, and Liberia, it seems convenient to deal with rubber, including the collection of wild rubber, in the following chapter.[4]

Sesame (Benniseed)

Sesame (*Sesamum orientale*), also known as *simsim* and benniseed, is cultivated by Africans in both East and West Africa. It grows freely in areas of moderate rainfall. The seed contains oil which is used commercially as a substitute for olive-oil, and it is much appreciated as a relish in African food. In East Africa oil is processed in Indian-owned crushing mills, the residual oil-cake being sold to European and African stock-owners.

[1] See below, pp. 1054 ff.
[2] Sierra Leone Sessional Papers nos. 8 of 1924, 4 of 1925, and 7 of 1938.
[3] See below, p. 1003.   [4] See below, p. 964.

In Tanganyika, where in some areas *simsim* is the staple crop, steps are taken to ensure supplies of pure white seed, which commands a premium over coloured varieties. In Kenya and Uganda the crop is utilized chiefly as an article of diet, and the exports which used to be made before 1939 have come to an end as the result of increasing internal consumption and the competition of more rewarding cash crops.

In Nigeria the establishment of an agricultural station in the Benue Province in 1924 gave an opportunity for the combined efforts of trading firms and the Department of Agriculture to encourage the cultivation of benniseed, which is the money crop of the local Tiv farmers.[1] As this area has no other cash crop cultivation has steadily expanded. The Nigerian exports rose to 13,700 metric tons in 1952, and the quality has been improved by the distribution of pure seed. In French West and Equatorial Africa, as in East Africa, export surpluses have now fallen to negligible amounts. In the Belgian Congo it was estimated in 1950 that out of 6,199 metric tons produced only 1,967 metric tons were sent by growers to the local markets.

Sisal

Sisal, which is obtained from the leaves of *Agave sisalana*, is mainly the product of non-Native enterprise, and cultivation is generally conducted by companies which have their own decorticating plant. Tanganyika is now by far the largest producer of sisal. The industry survived a difficult period during the thirties as a result of the general depression in world prices, but it recovered when the Allied navies were cut off from supplies of Philippine hemp in 1942, and relatively high prices after the Second World War led to a marked expansion of production.

Sisal grows well at a low altitude in moist conditions and it thrives on the sandy soils of the coastal areas. In Tanganyika more than half the area under plantation (some 1,529 square miles in all) is situated along the Tanga railway line. In 1954 the out-turn was 170,250 tons, produced mainly from European but also partly from Asian estates. It reached the record value of nearly £24 million in 1951, but owing to the decline in world markets the export value of the sisal crop in 1955 had fallen to £10 million.[2] Labour supply has at times been a limiting factor, and attacks by the sisal weevil have caused anxiety in some areas. A Sisal Experimental Station was opened at Mlingano in 1934 with support from the Government and the sisal industry; in 1950 its ownership was vested in the Tanganyika Sisal Growers' Association.

It was not until 1915 that exports from Kenya, where cultivation was first developed on a commercial scale, reached the moderate level of 1,652

---

[1] O. T. Faulkner and J. R. Mackie, *West African Agriculture*, 1933, pp. 127 ff.
[2] *Annual Report of the Tanganyika Sisal Growers' Association, 1955.*

tons, but the post-war demand brought them to 35,334 tons in 1953. In contrast with the position in Tanganyika, the greater part of the acreage in Kenya is situated in the Highlands. The investigation of systems of planting and of the improvement of fibre extraction is carried out on the estates by the operating companies. It would appear that the Kenya crop is relatively free from pests and disease. In Uganda a sisal estate of 5,000 acres in Bunyoro was responsible for an export of 1,190 tons of fibre in 1951.

Mozambique has climatic and soil conditions which resemble those of the coastal region of Tanganyika and are well suited for the growth of sisal. There was an export of 18,000 metric tons in 1952. In West Africa Angola is the only territory which has any large export of sisal; the operating companies exported 25,100 metric tons in 1952. French Equatorial Africa had a small export of 1,300 tons in the same year. Attempts have been made to establish a sisal industry in the Belgian Congo, but with little success; there was an export of only 100 tons in 1952.

Sugar

It is doubtful if sugar is indigenous to Africa, though it has been cultivated there for some centuries. It is frequently found in African gardens, among other supplementary crops, and chewing is one of its domestic uses. It is seldom that the juices are expressed by crushing and boiled to produce molasses or 'jaggery', though this process is carried out by Asians.[1] The manufacture of white or crystallized sugar is confined to non-African undertakings, which use cane from their own plantations or purchase it from farms which are for the most part maintained by Europeans or Asians.

In the Union of South Africa the cultivation of sugar-cane is confined to a narrow strip along the coast of Natal Province, about 235 miles long and 10 to 15 miles wide.[2] Nearly half of the crop is produced by companies owning large estates, and most of the remainder by about 670 independent planters on estates averaging 300 to 400 acres but sometimes extending to as much as 1,600 acres. The industry dates from 1847 when a European settler obtained a consignment of cane from Bourbon (Réunion); in 1860 the need for labour was responsible for the introduction of the indentured labour from India.[3]

At the outset the industry was threatened by subsidized imports, and in spite of protection in the form of an import duty (imposed in 1867) it was found difficult to meet the competition of sugar produced in Mauritius. Demand increased, however, with the opening of the diamond and gold mines, and by 1905 the case for the consolidation of the industry became a matter of Government policy. Zululand was opened for development

---

[1] Tothill, op. cit. pp. 386 ff.
[2] O.Y.S.A., 1950, pp. 886 ff.   [3] See above, p. 387.

by the sugar interests and the protective tariff increased. In the season 1954 production reached 702,505 metric tons and export 182,535 tons.[1]

The price and distribution of sugar is controlled under the Sugar Act of 1936. A Sugar Experimental Station at Mount Edgcumbe, established in 1927, is maintained by the South Africa Sugar Association. The African production of cane is relatively small, the area under cultivation amounting only to 4,500 acres.[2]

In Southern Rhodesia the Government initiated in 1937 a scheme for the extension of the growth of sugar-cane and in 1944 purchased an estate for this purpose. Part of this has been leased to a Natal syndicate. Its yield was expected to reach 5,500 tons of sugar in 1957. The enterprise has involved the erection of a dam at a cost of nearly £2 million on the Mtilikwe river,[3] and it is hoped that production will justify a connexion, 35 miles in length, with the newly opened railway line to Lourenço Marques.[4]

The Rhodesia Sugar Refinery Limited has cleared 3,000 acres at Chirundu, in the Zambezi Valley, and planted a large portion of it with sugar-cane. The estate is expected to yield about 7,000 tons annually. A sugar mill has been transported from Natal and re-erected near by. The balance of Southern Rhodesia's requirements is imported from Mozambique.

Tanganyika has one large European-owned sugar estate, at Arusha Cheni, which produced 10,708 tons of sugar, mainly for local consumption, in 1953. In Kenya there are estates owned by both Europeans and Asians; production in 1951 was 13,724 tons, nearly all of which was consumed locally. Uganda has two large Asian estates with factories situated at Lugazi (started in 1924) and Jinja (started in 1929). In 1952 production was 54,000 tons of sugar, of which 800 tons were exported, nearly all to the other East African territories. The Uba type of cane, common in Natal, was grown at the outset but has been replaced by one of the POJ varieties grown in America.

The Belgian Congo has a single estate (Moerbeke-Kwilu in the Lower Congo). It produces a yearly average of roughly 16,000 tons of sugar, which is consumed locally. Angola and Mozambique both have factories which utilize the production of cane grown on neighbouring planters' estates. The out-turn is large, the former having an export of 38,900 metric tons during the season 1951–2 and the latter an export of 66,600 metric tons.

Tea

The production of tea is almost entirely in the hands of Europeans and is for the most part carried out by tea companies (a number of which also

---

[1] *Statistical Bulletin of the International Sugar Council*, January 1956.
[2] *O.Y.S.A.*, *1950*, p. 479.   [3] See below, p. 985.   [4] *The Times*, 21 October 1955.

have tea estates in Asia) rather than by individual planters. There is practically no production in the Union; planting was begun in Natal in 1878, but never attained any considerable dimensions. In 1947–8 some 600,000 lb. of tea were produced, but the high cost made production unprofitable and in the following year the plantations were ploughed up. There has been since 1948 a small export from Southern Rhodesia, but it amounted in 1951 to only 200,000 lb.

Nyasaland now produces tea on a considerable scale. The crop was established about 1868 and has proved most successful in the districts of Mlanje and Cholo, where the rainfall is above the general average of the country. In 1954 tea exports were valued at over £2 million. A cess on exported tea is imposed, the proceeds of which are used by the Nyasaland Tea Association for the benefit of the industry. In Tanganyika tea development has been mainly in the Southern Highlands; in 1952 the value of the export was stated to be £300,000. Kenya has a larger area under cultivation (21,753 acres in 1953) and in that year produced nearly 13 million lb. of tea, of which more than half was consumed locally and the rest exported. In 1954 the value of exported tea was £2 million.[1] In Uganda production in 1952 amounted to just under 4 million lb.

In the three East African High Commission Territories, together with Nyasaland, production forms 4 per cent. of the world's consumption. In these four territories 62,000 acres are now under tea. The agricultural plan for Kenya aims at increasing the African acreage, which is at present only an experimental estate of 35 acres, to 12,000 acres in 15 years.[2]

The production of tea in Mozambique is of older standing and has been on a large scale; the export in 1952 amounted to over 6 million lb.

The Belgian Congo has not made any special effort in the production of tea. Cultivation was, however, started in Kivu Province in 1948, mainly with a view to supplying local needs;[3] an area of some 3,680 acres was under the crop in 1951.

Tobacco

The use of tobacco of the type grown in America was apparently introduced to Africans by Portuguese traders in the last half of the sixteenth century, and it became so popular that tobacco from Brazil or the West Indies formed the greater part of the cargo of the ships which visited the West African ports in quest of slaves.[4] The tobacco plant has now a wide range of cultivation in Africa from temperate to tropical climates, but the successful production of tobacco for export is restricted by its sensitiveness

[1] *Report of the East African Commissioner for the Year 1954*, East African Office, London, p. 71.
[2] Swynnerton, op. cit. p. 19.
[3] *Enc. C.B.*, vol. i, p. 551.
[4] R. P. Dieud-Rinchon, *La Traite et l'esclavage des Congolais*, 1929.

to soil and climate.[1] Coarse Native tobacco is, however, grown on the outskirts of most villages throughout Africa, the leaves being dried and rolled into balls or ground into snuff. In some localities, such as in the mining areas of the Belgian Congo and Northern Rhodesia, there is considerable traffic in this product.

In the Union the cultivation of tobacco by Europeans dates back to the early colonial days; the original product was the well-known Boer tobacco prepared by fermenting and rolling the leaf. Most of the crop now produced is sold for consumption in the Union. Until recently the greater portion was air-cured; flue-curing was not adopted to any extent till 1930. Production has varied; it has reached a peak in recent years, and was estimated at over 53 million lb. in 1950–1, but in 1952 fell to a little short of 38 million lb. The principal area of production is the Western Transvaal, and a considerable part of the crop is grown on irrigated land. Swaziland has a small export of tobacco, sold mainly for consumption by Africans in the Union; it was valued at £45,000 in 1950. A Co-operative Company has been formed in the Hlatikulu district, membership of which is compulsory for tobacco-growers, who are almost entirely European.

In the Rhodesias nearly all the production of tobacco for export has been in European hands. A great stimulus to the tobacco industry occurred after the First World War, and again after the Second World War, when dollar shortage had severely restricted Great Britain's imports of American tobacco. The greatest expansion has been shown in Southern Rhodesia, where tobacco-growing was begun by the pioneer settlers in 1895. The industry has owed much to the measure in which it was fostered in its early years by the Southern Rhodesian Government.[2] It is of interest to note that in 1938 the export of tobacco was valued at only about £1 million. In the ten years following 1939 production increased from 23 million to roughly 107 million lb. Some 2,122 European growers participated in the industry in 1950. In 1955 a little over 120½ million lb. were sold for £20¼ million after an unpropitious season. One-eighth of the world's tobacco export now comes from the Federation of Rhodesia and Nyasaland.[3] Nearly the whole is flue-cured Virginian, which is classed by the trade as the best quality of African tobacco. It has been pointed out, however, that the type of one-crop farming involved by concentration on the growth of tobacco has both economic and agricultural weaknesses.[4]

In Northern Rhodesia also a considerable expansion has taken place, though the total production does not equal that of Southern Rhodesia.

[1] S. S. Murray, *Report on Tobacco, East and Central Africa*, Colonial Research Publication no. 4, 1949, pp. 10 ff.
[2] Masefield, op. cit. p. 109.
[3] *The Times*, 20 October 1955.
[4] F. Engledow, *Report on the Agricultural Development of Southern Rhodesia*, Salisbury, 1950.

In 1953 production was almost 10½ million lb. Auctions are held at Fort Jameson for tobacco coming from that area, but leaf from north-western Rhodesia goes to the auction floor at Salisbury in Southern Rhodesia.

In Nyasaland tobacco was first planted in 1889 and exported in 1893. There is considerable variation in the figures of annual production: in 1951 the total was estimated at 36 million lb.; in 1952 it slightly exceeded 20 million lb.;[1] in 1953 over 36 million lb. of all types of tobacco were sold over the auction floors.[2] At the outset the production was largely in the hands of Europeans, but there has been a remarkable increase in African-grown tobacco, which is now five or six times greater in quantity than that produced from the European estates.

The European product is mainly flue-cured, and Native tobacco is largely fire-cured, with a corresponding difference in value. The market was originally the Union of South Africa, but tariffs enforced a change to a European market, chiefly the United Kingdom; Africans have also produced a quantity of dark fire-cured leaf which is in demand in the West African market. The Imperial Tobacco Company established a factory at Limbe in 1908; the sale and markets for African tobacco are organized by the Native Tobacco Board. The growth of small crops of tobacco is easily combined with work in food gardens, and this, in addition to the action taken by the Native Tobacco Board, accounts for the rapid increase in Native production during the last 30 years. The Kasungu Tobacco Estates, a pilot enterprise financed by the Colonial Development Corporation, harvested their first crop in 1951, but neither the yield nor the quality was good. They have been continued on a reduced acreage and under more intensive cultivation.[3]

There has been some expansion of the tobacco trade in Tanganyika also. Non-Native tobacco is produced in the Southern Highlands Province and is controlled by a non-Native Tobacco Board instituted under an Ordinance of 1952. The yield of non-Native (flue-cured) tobacco in 1953 was a little short of 2 million lb. African-grown tobacco is produced in Songea and Biharamulo Districts and is subject to the control of the Songea and Nyamirembe Native Tobacco Boards respectively. At Urambo, where 45,000 acres were transferred in 1955 from the Overseas Food Corporation to the Tanganyika Agricultural Corporation, flue-cured tobacco has replaced groundnuts as the principal cash crop within the framework of an African tenant scheme. Although much of the tobacco goes to the local market, an appreciable amount goes abroad; some 1,970 tons were exported in 1955.

[1] *Colonial Reports, Nyasaland, 1952*, p. 6.

[2] *Nyasaland, Annual Report of the Department of Agriculture, 1953*, p. 6. See also *An Economic Survey of the Colonial Territories, 1951: vol. vii, The Products of the Colonial Territories*, Col. no. 281–7, 1952, pp. 84 ff.

[3] *Colonial Development Corporation, Report and Accounts for 1954*, p. 41.

The competition of other cash crops in Kenya has militated against the expansion of tobacco in African areas, but the development of such areas as are suitable for fire or flue-cured tobacco is under examination.[1] In Uganda serious consideration was not given to the cultivation of tobacco until 1925, but in 1927 a small quantity was produced from the Bunyoro area, and cultivation was extended to the West Nile District in 1931 and to Mubende in 1948. It is grown almost entirely by Africans. The total production in Uganda in 1953 was: flue-cured tobacco, 4,316,000 lb.; fire-cured, 2,424,000 lb.; and air-cured, 338,000 lb. An outlet for most of the local crop is found in the manufacture of cigarettes for Uganda and for export to Kenya, Tanganyika, and the Belgian Congo. Seed is issued from the Tobacco Experimental Station at Bulindi. There is a Government reconditioning plant at Masindi and factories at Jinja and Kampala. The yield is estimated at 100 to 500 lb. per acre.

In West Africa, as elsewhere, coarse tobacco is grown for local use, and in the Gold Coast peasants are assisted in producing black leaf tobacco to meet a local demand. In Nigeria, where there is a system of marketing, small quantities of leaf are purchased in Zaria Province; there is also a small but growing cultivation in Sokoto and in Oyo Provinces. The estimated production in 1953 was 5 million lb. The tobacco is sold mostly for local consumption.

In French West Africa coarse tobacco is grown by Africans for their own use, but in 1910 a Commission considered measures for promoting the local production of tobacco of a type which would reduce the expenditure incurred on its import. It was not, however, till some years later that European planters could produce a small amount for the local manufacture of cigarettes. Attempts to grow tobacco for export were renewed in 1942, but in spite of some encouraging results in Dahomey and Guinea, export has not exceeded 300 metric tons. The growth of the crop for export has been almost entirely in the hands of European planters.

Local authorities hold out more hopes of success from the Cameroons where cultivation of 'Maryland' tobacco was started as early as 1907.[2] A concession, originally German, was taken over by the *Régie Française des Tabacs* in 1944 and a private undertaking, the *Société Bastos*, has been operating since 1947. The results are described as encouraging, and there was an export of 500 metric tons in 1952. Very little of this could, however, be described as African production. Small quantities of tobacco have been produced in the Belgian Congo, but mainly by European agencies; the product is consumed by local cigarette and cigar factories.[3]

---

[1] Swynnerton, op. cit. p. 23.

[2] *Enc. C.-T.*, pp. 210 ff.

[3] For details of cultivation, &c., see *Enc. C.B.*, vol. i, pp. 560–5; *Enc. A.O.F.*, vol. ii, pp. 114–18.

Wheat

With few exceptions the wheat grown in Africa is the product of European farms. In the Union its cultivation was introduced towards the end of the seventeenth century. During the present century efforts have been made to increase its cultivation by the grant of subsidies, and in 1931–2, as the result of a protective tariff on imported wheat imposed in the previous year, production was brought up to the level of consumption. By 1935 production was in excess of consumption; but more recently the Union has again become an importer of wheat, the total import being 215,700 metric tons in 1952. Of the domestic production, which was 552,000 metric tons in 1952, about 60 per cent. comes from the Cape Province. The Wheat Industry Control Board fixes prices, controls marketing, and imposes a levy to cover its costs. Some wheat is grown by Africans in the Transkeian territories, where the General Council has provided threshers. In Basutoland the high valleys now produce a variety of hard wheat which is valued for milling purposes; 3,320 metric tons of wheat and wheatmeal were exported in 1952.[1]

Neither of the two Rhodesias is well adapted to the growth of wheat. In Southern Rhodesia local production was valued in 1952 at only £18,000. Seed imported from Kenya is now being used for trial planting. Encouragement is being given to irrigation-cropping and planting in moisture-retaining soils.[2] Northern Rhodesia is also far from self-supporting. In spite of assistance from a subsidy on production, the crop showed a steady decline from 2,550 tons in 1945 to 113 in 1952. There has for some years been a steady increase in importation of wheat; in 1953 imports amounted to 18,000 tons. Wheat and maize subsidies in Northern Rhodesia have during recent years cost an average of £1¾ million.

Before 1939 Kenya was a net importer of wheat, but since the Second World War production has remained at a high level, and in 1952 the total harvest was 115,130 metric tons. Exports have fluctuated widely; in 1951 they were 21,362 tons and in 1952 fell to 7,500 tons; no wheat was exported in 1953. Varieties of wheat have been locally bred to resist the different forms of rust disease which are prevalent. Both here and in Tanganyika production is confined to the higher altitudes; in Kenya, for instance, the bulk of wheat is grown at altitudes of 7,000 to 8,000 feet, though suitable varieties can be grown at lower levels. In Tanganyika nearly 5,000 tons were marketed in 1953; this was consumed locally.

Elsewhere the cultivation of wheat is restricted by climatic conditions. No wheat is grown in British West Africa. In French West Africa and in the Costermansville Province of the Belgian Congo some wheat is grown,

---

[1] *N.A.*, Part V, p. 7. The standard bag of wheat, like that of maize, weighs 200 lb.
[2] *Southern Rhodesia, Report of the Division of Agriculture and Lands, 1953*, 1954, p. 4.

but generally speaking it is not consumed by Africans and is grown under European encouragement for local use.

Production of other grain crops in the African territories is on a comparatively small scale. In the 1952–3 season the Union of South Africa produced 57,000 tons of barley and 80,000 tons of oats. Kenya produced small crops of barley and oats, amounting to 15,000 tons and 10,000 tons respectively, in the 1953–4 season.[1]

Yams (*Igname*)

The term 'yams' is sometimes used to include all the tropical tubers, but it should strictly speaking be applied only to varieties of *Dioscerea*, the big yam, which is cultivated in tropical Africa, principally in the coastal regions and middle belt of West Africa, where it is a staple food crop.[2] In South Africa and most parts of East Africa the rainfall is inadequate for yam cultivation. In typical yam-growing areas only good land is used and cultivation is carried out carefully, a usual practice being to plant on mounds of soil or in well-made ridges; in some cases the mounds are about four or five feet high and correspondingly broad. Under good cultivation huge tubers weighing 50 or 60 lb. can be produced. In all yam fields other crops are inter-planted on the sides of the mounds or ridges, and it is seldom that two crops of yams are taken off the same land in succession.

Coco-yams (*Colocasia antiquorum*) are widely cultivated in the wetter areas of tropical Africa, but are usually regarded as of secondary importance; they do not occupy any specific place in systems of cultivation, often being planted in odd pieces of land and under the shade of trees where few other crops will thrive. Their tolerance of shade allows them to be grown as ground cover under permanent crops, but in the forest areas of southeastern Nigeria and the British Cameroons they form an important food crop, as they do also in Ruanda Urundi.

In many areas figures of the production of yams are combined with those of sweet potatoes, and if the two are taken together the estimated total production of the two crops in Africa south of the Sahara is very large; it was shown in 1950 as amounting to more than 16 million metric tons, and, even if the figure is speculative, it is evidence of the wide diffusion of these tubers. It has been stated that one acre planted to yams can feed a family of five for one year, whereas the produce of African-grown cereals from one acre is usually insufficient to sustain two people

---

[1] *Commonwealth Economic Committee, Grain Crops, 1955*, pp. 69, 84.

[2] For the significance attaching to the distribution of yams and similar West African crops, see D. Forde, 'The Cultural Map of Africa', *Transactions of New York Academy of Sciences*, April 1953, pp. 206–19.

for the same period.[1] Its value therefore as a subsistence crop is important, especially since it is less susceptible to climatic conditions.

Miscellaneous Products

There are a variety of minor commodities for the production of which Africans are almost entirely responsible. They are, however, often of local rather than general importance. In Tanganyika, where the industry has been encouraged by the provision of technical instruction, the collection of beeswax is of some value. Angola also exports certain quantities of beeswax. It is regrettable, however, that the collection of honey and wax is some-times accompanied by extensive burning of the woodlands.

The collection of the shea nut (*karité*) from wild trees is of importance in parts of West Africa, and the extraction of shea butter from the nuts is a useful local industry.[2] It is unfortunate that the process of refining shea butter for commercial use involves difficulties which have militated against its fuller entry into the export market for vegetable oils. Shea butter is also used as a lubricant, for lighting, and for anointing the body.

Among other commodities piassava fibre, obtained from the raphia palm, provides a not unimportant product from Sierra Leone,[3] which has in recent years exported quantities varying from 5,348 to 6,118 tons. An improvement in the quality of the fibre marketed has been effected by means of a system of inspection introduced under the Sierra Leone Native Produce Ordinance.[4] Nigeria exported 2,164 tons in 1950; the Second World War gave an impetus to the production of the fibre, and the Belgian Congo exported 640 tons in 1942. The Belgian Congo also found a demand for a fibre derived from the plant *Urena lobata*, which it was at one time hoped would come into use as a substitute for jute.[5] A total of 18,355 metric tons was produced in 1952.

Ginger thrives in West Africa, usually being planted on patches of rich soil near villages, where it can conveniently be manured. It is not of high quality, though this has recently been improved. Exports from Nigeria rose to 434 tons in 1950.

ANIMAL HUSBANDRY

The cult of the cattle plays so conspicuous a part in the social custom of many African tribes[6] that it might well be assumed that the pastoral interest is of dominant concern in African economy. Though, however, this may have been true at one period in the history of Africa, and more

---

[1] W. V. Blewett, 'Agricultural Development in Tropical Africa', *J.R.S.A.*, August 1950, pp. 791 ff.

[2] *Enc. A.O.F.*, vol. ii, pp. 65–68.

[3] Col. no. 281–7, 1952, p. 90.

[4] No. 16 of 1928.   [5] *Enc. C.B.*, vol. i, pp. 496 ff.   [6] See above, p. 36.

particularly of East and Southern Africa, it is not today equally true even of those regions. It is no doubt a fact that there are certain tribes, as for example the Masai, who still depend entirely on their cattle for their subsistence and who themselves eschew cultivation. Again, the 'cow' Fulani of Northern Nigeria are nomadic pastoralists. Elsewhere, as for instance in the Bechuanaland Protectorate, physical conditions make stock-raising the most reliable means of winning subsistence, and the same is true of that part of South-West Africa where the chief asset is the *Karakul*. But elsewhere even those tribes which still maintain a strong pastoral tradition now show some tendency to look to cultivation in order to supply their subsistence needs, and regard their cattle rather in the light of a capital asset which can provide a reserve available for expenditure on other needs. A number of tribes holding large herds will kill cattle for food only on ritual or ceremonial occasions.

It might reasonably have been expected that the subsistence needs of a growing population, together with the incentive of earning money by the cultivation of marketable crops, would have secured the substitution of an agricultural for a pastoral economy; but this has not actually happened. The pastoral peoples are by no means oblivious of the monetary value of livestock and of products such as skins and hides. It is noteworthy that in 1953 there were roughly 800,000 head of cattle sold for slaughter in Nigeria, and that hides and skins to the value of nearly £6 million were exported. But there is a strong vein of conservatism among the African pastoralists, more especially in East and Central Africa. Agronomists still have cause to deplore the persistence of the tendency to multiply livestock without regard to their quality or their disposal value.

It is conceded that the herds and their progeny furnish the only form of interest-bearing investment known to indigenous Africa. But even so, the results of stock-raising cannot be said to justify the use of so large an area of land as pasturage now occupies. The production of milk is often negligible, even for domestic purposes, and it is still exceptional to encounter the regular provision of a marketable product such as butter or ghee. Worst of all, the overstocking, or rather the over-concentration of cattle, is in large measure responsible for the erosion which is becoming so marked a feature of the pasture lands.[1] There is here, the agronomist would urge, an obvious case of maladjustment, which might be all the graver were it not for two factors: that infestation by tsetse fly has hitherto placed a limit on the areas in which it is possible to maintain cattle, and that epidemic disease, such as rinderpest, has on occasion taken a heavy toll of cattle.

To part at least of this charge there is, of course, an answer. One cannot argue as though land in Africa can, like so much of the land in Europe or America, be utilized alternatively either for cultivation or pasture.

[1] See below, Chapter XV.

Something has already been said of the inherent deficiencies of some of the African soils from the point of view of the agriculturalist,[1] and there are, moreover, large areas where the seasonal distribution of the rainfall (which is more important than its actual volume) makes cultivation much less practicable than stock-raising. Experience of Asia has demonstrated the difficulty of converting to the practice of agriculture those peoples who have had a long pastoral tradition, and this difficulty is all the greater in Africa, where old-established custom has in so many cases caused cultivation to be regarded as the proper function of the women of the tribe.

There can clearly be no royal road to be followed in effecting such a conversion. Action is, however, likely to be more successful if it has complied with three conditions. In the first place the African must be given such facilities for disposing of his stock as will convince him of the value of breeding for quality rather than for numbers. He must be shown that the cattle have a place as an essential part of 'mixed' farming. Finally, cultivation must be assisted by the provision of drinking-water supplies and of means of ready access to markets. Compulsory culling may on occasion become imperative in the interests of soil conservation, but it will not necessarily convert the pastoralist into a cultivator. It is at present rarely practised except under regulations made by the Native Authorities, though there is a notable exception in the general measure of culling undertaken by the Agricultural Department of Southern Rhodesia.[2] What is now required is to achieve a better balance between cultivation and the keeping of livestock and a greater appreciation of the economic principles regulating the maintenance of pasture lands. If this can be attained it may ultimately be found that the regions referred to may have room for at least as many cattle as at present.

Some of the African tribes own sheep and goats, the latter in greater numbers than cattle. In many cases goats may also play their part in marriage and other social customs; with the Kikuyu, for example, they take the place of cattle in this respect. In some areas also, as for example in Basutoland, the mohair of the goat has become a valuable product.[3] Sheep are normally maintained by Africans for their meat rather than for their wool, though the Union and Basutoland form an important exception in this respect.

Both in South and East Africa the European colonists relied at the outset mainly on stock-rearing, and in the Union this still remains a feature of great importance in the economy of the country. The Union agricultural census of 1948–9 showed that Europeans had at the time over 7 million cattle, $22\frac{1}{4}$ million woolled and $5\frac{1}{2}$ million non-woolled sheep, and $1\frac{3}{4}$ million goats. Apart from the profits of the meat and dairying industries, South Africa takes fourth place among the wool-exporting countries of the world.

---

[1] See above, p. 819.   [2] See above, p. 766.   [3] *N.A.*, Part V, p. 12.

In 1951 its total exports of wool were valued at £75 million.[1] During the following four years the annual export averaged £60 million.

Some authorities have indeed expressed the opinion that the country, with the exception of small areas where special crops such as citrus can be grown with profit, is better suited for animal husbandry than for cultivation. It is claimed that more than four-fifths of the total area of the Union can be used only for grazing, and that animal husbandry has the further advantage to a country with predominantly poor soil that it can produce the manure necessary for enriching the grasslands or assisting in mixed farming. As already indicated, the same consideration applies, in an even more marked degree, to South-West Africa. While it is not possible to give any precise figures of the areas involved, it is nevertheless clear that throughout South, Central, and East Africa there are certain areas which are primarily suited for stock-raising rather than for agriculture, either because of the character of the climate and soil or on account of difficulties of transport. Unlike other agricultural produce, cattle have the merit that they can 'convey themselves to their market'.

The Domestic Animals

As regards the domestic animals now found in Africa, the indigenous African cattle appear to be derived from three original stocks, the longhorn, the shorthorn, and the zebu. The Hamitic longhorn is possibly descended from the giant-horned wild ox of the Nile valley (*Bos primigenius*) and it is possible that the surviving strain nearest to the original type is the N'Dama cattle, widely distributed in West Africa. The *Brachyceros* or shorthorn, is conjectured to have come originally to Africa from Asia at the end of the neolithic era, and general fusion with the Hamitic longhorn resulted. The dwarf cattle of the regions near the Gulf of Guinea do not constitute a distinct breed, but are a survival of the older form. It may be remarked also that the term 'West African shorthorn' (*maturu*) does not denote a breed, but is used to describe the unhumped shorthorned cattle of West Africa which are a mixture of the Hamitic longhorn, the shorthorn, and the zebu. The zebu are, broadly speaking, humped cattle, and are more recent arrivals in Africa; they have not the same resistance to trypanosomiasis, but have better resistance to rinderpest.[2] The Afrikander cattle of South Africa are the nearest to the pure zebu.

Indigenous sheep are of many types; the majority are hairy and fat-tailed. Merino sheep were successfully introduced in Cape Colony in 1812, and the number in South Africa is now second only to that in Australia. Blackhead Persians, which can thrive on land too poor for merinos, were

[1] *Annual Statement of the Trade and Shipping of the Union of South Africa, 1951*, 1954, pp. 522 ff.
[2] S. L. Stewart, *The Cattle of the Gold Coast*, 1937. I. L. Mason, *The Classification of West African Livestock*, 1951.

introduced later. Mutton-breed rams such as Dorset Horn, Southdown, Leicester, and Romney Marsh have been imported for crossing with local varieties. The indigenous sheep industry of Basutoland is based on the merino introduced from the Cape, and wool is the principal export of the territory. Blackhead Persian and *Karakul* have been introduced in South-West Africa, and have provided a very profitable export of pelts known to the trade as Persian Lamb. There are some merino herds in the drier parts of Kenya, such as Naivasha; in the wetter areas Romney Marsh are crossed with indigenous sheep. Attempts to introduce merinos in Northern Nigeria have not been successful.

No very sustained effort has been made to improve the breed of sheep in French West Africa, though the Diré Company had at one time a flock of merinos.[1] In the Belgian Congo attempts have been made to naturalize merinos and Romney Marsh at the Government farm at Nioka in Ituri, but so far with no definite result.[2] Improvement work has been concentrated on the pastoral areas in the north-east and south-east. In Angola Portuguese and French merino strains and Rambouillet rams have been imported for breeding wool sheep, and Blackhead Persians from South Africa for mutton.

African goats are remarkable for their resistance to trypanosomiasis, their apparent immunity to tuberculosis, and their ability to obtain food in difficult conditions. Angora goats have been successfully introduced both in the Union of South Africa and Basutoland.

Animal Diseases

The prevalence of animal disease, often in an epidemic form, has formed a serious obstacle to the development of an animal industry in Africa,[3] particularly in view of the restriction of markets frequently imposed by quarantine regulations. By far the most serious of these diseases is trypanosomiasis, spread by the tsetse fly. While the *Glossina palpalis*, the riverine tsetse, is largely responsible for spreading the *Trypanosoma gambiense* in man,[4] the bush or scrub type of tsetse is responsible for most of the disease (*Nagana*) in animals, and *G. morsitans*, *G. Swynnertoni*, and *G. palidipes* are the most important members of this type. Tsetse is prevalent in an area bounded roughly on the north by a line from the mouth of the Senegal river through Lakes Chad and Rudolf to the coast of Italian Somaliland, and on the south by one which bisects Angola and runs southward along the boundary between that territory and Northern Rhodesia and then eastwards across Southern Rhodesia and Portuguese East Africa.[5]

It is estimated that 65 to 75 per cent. of this area is infested in greater or

---

[1] *Enc. A.O.F.*, vol. i, p. 361.   [2] *Enc. C.B.*, vol. ii, p. 436.
[3] For animal diseases, see E. B. Worthington, *Science in Africa*, 1938, pp. 441 ff.
[4] See below, p. 1124.   [5] See maps on pp. 875, 877.

AFRICA : TSETSE FLY
(South of the Sahara)

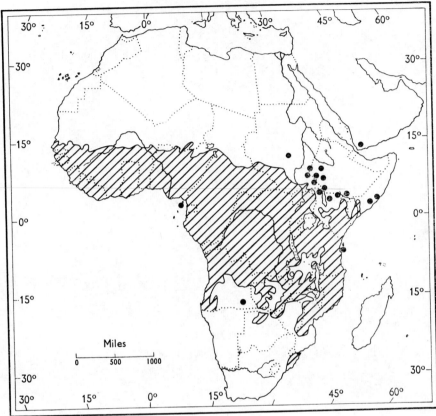

D.C.S. (Misc.) 226/7

Distribution of the Genus Glossina

 Genus Glossina

● Small areas or isolated records

Reproduced from Professor P.A. Buxton's, The Natural History of Tsetse Flies,
London School of Hygiene and Tropical Medicine, Memoir No. 10, 1955.

AFRICA : TSETSE FLY
(South of the Sahara)

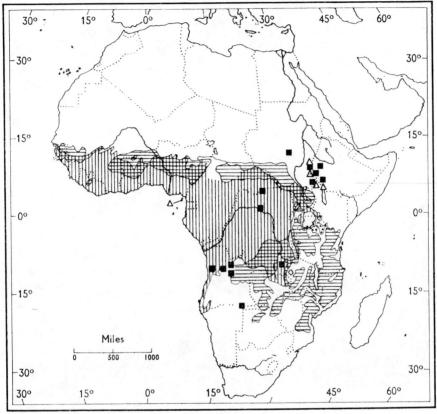

D.C.S. (Misc.) 226/8

Distribution of Glossina Morsitans,
Glossina Palpalis and Glossina Swynnertoni

G. Morsitans

G. Palpalis

G. Swynnertoni

■ G. Morsitans small or isolated areas
△ G Palpalis   „   „   „   „

Reproduced from Transactions of the Royal Society of Tropical Medicine
and Hygiene, Vol. XLVII, No 1, 1953 (H.S. Leeson)

less measure by fly; the infested area has been put as high as 4 million square miles.[1] It has recently been estimated that in Northern Rhodesia 85,000 square miles were infested by *G. morsitans*, and an area twice as large was affected by the fly's movements. Three-quarters of Uganda, two-thirds of Tanganyika, and one-fifth of Kenya are estimated to be infested by the fly; in Southern Rhodesia it has encroached on areas which were freed from it by the destruction of game in the great rinderpest epidemic of 1896. The rate of this encroachment was estimated some years ago at 1,000 square miles a year. Over half the Special Native Area and four-fifths of the forest area are infested by tsetse. The policy initiated some years ago led to the organized destruction over a broad belt of country of all forms of animal life, large and small, with a view to establishing a zone over which the infected tsetse could not be transported by animals. This involved for some years the destruction of game at a rate of over 3,000 a month. The local Trypanosomiasis Committee, in a report at the end of 1954, expressed itself convinced that there was no alternative to a policy of game destruction in conjunction with close settlement of the population.

With the formation of the Federation of Rhodesia and Nyasaland in 1953, tsetse control and trypanosomiasis became a Federal responsibility; a Commission of Inquiry was appointed to make recommendations regarding the position in Southern Rhodesia. The Commission's Report, published in 1955,[2] contained a recommendation that the destruction of game should continue for at least a few years. It also suggested the setting up of a Department of Tsetse and Trypanosomiasis Control and Reclamation, together with stricter control and co-ordination of every form of development proposed in a tsetse-infested area.

In Bechuanaland the encroachment of fly in the Tawana Reserve was countered by the same method, though on a much smaller scale.[3] Trapping of flies has been carried out in Tanganyika, Zululand, and parts of the Belgian Congo, but its chief value appears to be that of helping to clear up isolated patches of fly which have been attacked by more wholesale methods. It is generally recognized that tsetse fly can be eliminated by the felling of forest trees and scrub which afford it cover, but it is a method very destructive of timber. The East African Tsetse and Trypanosomiasis Research Organization has held the view that destruction on such a scale is not necessary. By locating the habitat of the fly, and by the exercise of 'discriminative clearing', the felling of about 10 per cent. of the area infested has been found to be effective in the Ankole region of Uganda.[4]

[1] P. A. Buxton, *Trypanosomiasis in Eastern Africa, 1947*, 1948. H. E. Hornby, *Animal Trypanosomiasis in Eastern Africa, 1949*, 1952. P. A. Buxton, *The Natural History of Tsetse Flies*, London School of Hygiene and Tropical Medicine, Memoir no. 10, 1955.

[2] *Report of the Commission of Inquiry on Human and Animal Trypanosomiasis in Southern Rhodesia*, Salisbury, November 1955.

[3] *N.A.*, Part V, p. 260.   [4] *Background to Uganda*, no. 125, October 1955.

Of the various drugs used for treatment of animal trypanosomiasis[1] the greatest claims have been made for the phenanthridinium series (particularly dimidium bromide) and antrycide, recently developed by British chemists. The former was used in controlling large epizootics of trypanosomiasis in Zululand and the Southern Sudan in 1947–8. But neither drug can yet be said to be perfect; it may indeed be doubted whether drug therapy can at present be fully effective in the presence of tsetse fly.[2] The East African Tsetse and Trypanosomiasis Research and Reclamation Organization has also established that the *T. congolense* could be transmitted by biting flies.[3] In Northern Rhodesia importance is now attached to the development of resistance by satisfactory feeding. In West Africa it has been suggested that there are many local strains of trypanosome, resistance to one of which does not imply resistance to others, but the N'Dama cattle appear to have the most general resistance.[4]

The question of importing cattle for breeding purposes is bound up with that of resistance to disease; exotic cattle are more susceptible, and the African pasture is not generally of a quality to build up such resistance. For Native stock the better course at present would appear to be the improvement of indigenous breeds, in order to develop the useful dual-purpose animal needed for mixed farming.

Rinderpest entered Africa by way of the Nile towards the end of the last century. In 1896 a widespread epidemic of great virulence devastated the cattle areas of eastern and southern Africa, and the disease penetrated also into West Africa. Over large areas not only cattle but wild game were almost exterminated. Methods of immunization were first discovered in South Africa, and the disease has now been brought under control there and in the British Central African Territories. At present it is being held back by preventive inoculations to the north of the Central Railway line in Tanganyika. Research has produced a continuous improvement in the types of vaccine used; the goat-attenuated virus which is now in standard use is being supplemented by an adjuvant spleen vaccine, both of which are supplied by the Kenya laboratories, and by lapinized vaccine, flown by air from Nigeria. Production of rinderpest vaccines to serve all tropical Africa is being concentrated, by international agreement, at Kabete in Kenya, Vom in Nigeria, and Bamako in French West Africa.[5] In Northern Nigeria inoculations are carried out at immunization camps, to which both the Fulani and Hausa readily bring their herds.

It is at the same time claimed that the most effective remedy may be to break the contact between wild and domestic animals, if necessary by

[1] For measures taken with regard to human trypanosomiasis (sleeping sickness), see below, pp. 1124–5.
[2] *Report of Director of Veterinary Services, Southern Rhodesia*, 1953, p. 23.
[3] *Annual Report on the East Africa High Commission, 1953*, Col. no. 305, 1954, p. 39.
[4] T. H. Davey, *Trypanosomiasis in British West Africa*, 1948.   [5] See below, p. 915.

completely segregating the former in National Parks.[1] In the 1942 epizootic in Uganda prevention of contact was attempted by immunizing
cattle in front of the advance of rinderpest, but infected wild game penetrated the immunized belt which proved to be lacking in depth. In the
1954 epizootic the shooting of game served as a useful interim measure
which retarded the advance long enough to allow a more thorough immunization to be carried out.[2]

East Coast Fever (*piroplasmosis*) was at one period the most dreaded
disease of cattle in South Africa. It is to be found in all regions between
Natal and the southern part of Italian Somaliland and extends westward
into the Belgian Congo. It is not found in West Africa.[3] The discovery
that the fever is a parasitic disease carried by ticks was made by Sir Arnold
Theiler in 1904 at the Onderstepoort Veterinary Laboratory in South
Africa. No satisfactory method of immunization has been found, and the
usual method of control is the dipping or spraying of stock with arsenic or
gammexane at frequent intervals, in order to remove the ticks. Spraying
has now been found to be more effective than dipping; this is a routine
operation in large parts of East Africa, and is readily practised by Africans.

Contagious pleuropneumonia is controlled by quarantine and by vaccination both in East and West Africa. Much work has been done in
Kenya on the preparation of vaccines, and the disease has been eradicated
from most European herds. In Northern Rhodesia it was for long enzootic
in the Barotse Province, to which it was confined by a police cordon, but
has now been brought under control with a resultant increase in the cattle
population. In Tanganyika the disease is confined by quarantine measures
to certain areas, but outbreaks still occur particularly in the Masai
District. In Uganda an intensive campaign in 1926 brought the disease
under control over a large area, but it is still enzootic in Karamoja, where
the inhabitants have been singularly unco-operative in enforcing measures
to combat animal diseases. In Kenya control is rendered difficult by the
fact that some tribes set a high value on cattle which have recovered from
the disease (lungers) and they are not readily persuaded to slaughter
infected animals. In the Gold Coast the disease is spread by the smuggling
of infected cattle over the French frontier. In Nigeria the triple prophylactic vaccination carried out over a period of two to three months is
unpopular with the nomadic owners, and vaccination campaigns can be
carried out only when outbreaks occur.

Foot-and-mouth disease is usually less virulent in Africa than in Europe,
though it has attained serious proportions in Southern Rhodesia. Anthrax
is widespread in Native areas in the Union; it is a most destructive disease

---

[1] E. B. Worthington, 'Geography and the Development of East Africa', in *Geographical Journal*,
July–September 1950, p. 41.   [2] *Background to Uganda*, no. 97, April 1955.
[2] E. B. Worthington, *Science in Africa*, 1938, pp. 295, 442 ff.

in Bechuanaland and is prevalent in Northern Rhodesia in the Zambezi and Kafue Valleys. In Tanganyika the disease occurs sporadically and is rarely reported except when cases of human infection occur; vaccination and the burning of carcasses in pits are carried out as preventive measures. It is also serious in Ankole and in the Masaka District of Buganda. In Kenya annual vaccination is carried out in the settled areas.

Recent studies in Uganda indicate that bovine tuberculosis is more common than was previously supposed, and in Nigeria this disease is found in the Eastern Region and the Cameroons. The white zebu cattle owned by the Fulani in the Northern Provinces are apparently resistant to it.

Quarantine restrictions on the movement of cattle have had an important influence on the development of animal husbandry. The Cape Colony was closed to imports of cattle early in the present century owing to an outbreak of East Coast Fever in the Rhodesias and the Transvaal, and the Union continued the restriction after 1909. In 1923 the quarantine regulations were relaxed, but they were reintroduced between 1932 and 1935 as the result of an outbreak of foot-and-mouth disease in Southern Rhodesia. At present these precautions have been lifted to the extent that Bechuanaland, the main exporter of cattle in this region, is able to market cattle in both countries.

The Products of Animal Husbandry

Throughout tropical and southern Africa the picture is one of rapidly expanding local consumption of meat, due partly to the increased European population but in general also to greater consumption by Africans. In many areas the supply coming forward is not enough to satisfy local demand, and most of the territories which were formerly exporters no longer have any surplus available. In 1952 the total export of beef made by the countries south of the Sahara was only 6,100 metric tons. The Union of South Africa is a net importer of beef.[1] Bechuanaland in 1952 exported over 70,000 head of cattle, of which over 50 per cent. went to the Union,[2] 37 per cent. to Northern Rhodesia (45 per cent. of that territory's consumption), 12 per cent. to the Belgian Congo, and 1 per cent. to Southern Rhodesia. It is now one of the few territories south of the Sahara which have a regular surplus available for outside sale, and the Colonial Development Corporation is engaged in developing its potential ranching resources.

In Southern Rhodesia (as in certain parts of the Union) particular attention has been paid to the improvement of the local breed of cattle by

---

[1] *O.T.S.A.*, *1952–53*, pp. 1041, 1048.
[2] For the measures taken by the Colonial Development Corporation for improving the cattle export from Bechuanaland, see below, p. 890.

importation of selected stock. In 1952 the number of European-owned cattle was a little under 2 million, of which over 24,000 were pure-bred, and nearly 500,000 were 'grade' cattle. The local market is the principal outlet and in 1952 absorbed 164,000 cattle of which a high proportion were African-bred. Exports were only 2,902 head. In Northern Rhodesia cattle of predominantly low quality are slaughtered entirely for a local market. A recent inquiry in the Federation has estimated that by 1960 there will be an annual shortage of 123,000 head of cattle. Assuming that 33,000 head would be available annually from Bechuanaland, the cattle population of the Federation would require to be increased by 80,000 head per year above the increases in production already planned.

Nyasaland shows a typical history of increased slaughtering and local shortages. In order to supply the demand for meat in the Southern Province a scheme was promoted for transporting cattle from the Northern Province by a specially converted barge down Lake Nyasa. Experiment has shown that it is not impracticable.[1] In the East African territories the picture is similar. Selectively bred African cattle are being increasingly used by European farmers in Kenya for meat production, the Boran type being particularly suitable. In the thirties it was repeatedly urged that a meat-products factory would provide an outlet for stock then regarded as surplus to local demands, and in 1937 one was opened by Messrs. Liebig in the Masai Reserve.

The large demand for meat during the Second World War resulted in a Livestock Control being set up. It was replaced after the war by the Meat Marketing Board, the effect of which was to reduce the surplus of stock and raise purchasing power in the pastoral areas. In 1950, however, the Government wound up the Meat Marketing Board[2] and substituted the Kenya Meat Commission with a monopoly in the trade. The Commission proved unsuccessful in disposing of surplus stock, and in 1952 it was supplemented by the African Livestock Marketing Organization. In 1953 this Organization was offered more beasts than it could dispose of,[3] and an experimental field abattoir was established by it in the Samburu country. This has met with such success that three more abattoirs of the same type have now been recommended; but the facilities for dealing with the normal annual surplus of stock are still insufficient. It has been calculated that out of the 6 million head of cattle in the territory, the annual reduction should be in the order of 650,000.

In Tanganyika the Government has a controlling interest in the meat factory of Tanganyika Packers Limited; exports of meat and meat products

[1] *Colonial Reports, Nyasaland, 1952*, p. 63.
[2] *East Africa Royal Commission 1953–55, Report*, Cmd. 9475, 1955, pp. 303–4.
[3] R. J. M. Swynnerton, *A Plan to Intensify the Development of African Agriculture in Kenya*, Nairobi, 1954, pp. 33–34.

rose to 28,820 cwt. in 1951, in which year some 200,000 African cattle were slaughtered in the territory.

In Nigeria meat has long been a regular article of Native diet, and there is a large movement of cattle from the Northern Provinces to the markets of the Southern towns. In the year 1951–2 recorded slaughterings were about 1 million head of Nigerian cattle and 6 million sheep and goats,[1] together with 160,381 head imported from French territory.[2] In the Gold Coast recorded slaughterings in 1949–50 included 12,915 cattle of local origin and 55,959 from French territory.

African hides and skins are playing an increasingly important part in the world market. In the past their quality was poor,[3] but most of the major producing countries have now passed legislation which has led to a marked improvement. South Africa has had an Inspectorate since 1930. The British Colonial territories which have Ordinances on this subject include Kenya, Tanganyika, Uganda, Nyasaland, and Nigeria. Exports from the Union in 1951 were valued at over £8½ million,[4] and were the most valuable agricultural export after wool and fruit; over half of these were sheepskins. The export of sheepskins (including *Karakul* from South-West Africa) was valued in 1952 at over £5½ million. Southern Rhodesia in 1950 exported hides to the value of nearly £1½ million. In Tanganyika hides and skins exported through Dar-es-Salaam were worth over £1½ million in 1953, about two-thirds of the hides being suspension-dried. Kenya exports in 1953 were worth £1½ million, more than half being skins; some hides and skins are also absorbed by the local tanning and shoe-making industry. At a training centre on the Athi river Africans are being taught curing and tanning. Uganda's exports of hides and skins were valued at nearly £1 million in 1951.

In Nigeria the exports of hides and skins were valued in 1952 at £3¼ million. The most valuable skin produced in Nigeria is that of the red Sokoto goat, and the breeding of flocks of pure red goats is being actively encouraged. The tanning of the skins of goats and sheep is an ancient industry in Northern Nigeria, and Kano is said to have been the original home of 'Morocco' leather. The remaining territories of Western Africa are relatively small exporters, retaining most of their hides and skins for home use. In French Equatorial Africa there are tanneries at Brazzaville and Dolisie. The export of hides from the Belgian Congo in 1954 amounted to 1,326 tons.

The Union of South Africa is the fifth largest producer of wool in the world. The number of sheep is about 36 million, of which 3½ million are

---

[1] *Colonial Reports, Nigeria, 1952*, p. 47.
[2] T. Shaw and G. Colville, *Report of Nigerian Livestock Mission*, 1950.
[3] I. Mann, *A Handbook on Hides and Skins*, Nairobi, 1951.
[4] *O.Y.S.A., 1952–53*, p. 798.

wool sheep. The tendency is now to breed for wool rather than for mutton, and it is estimated that in 1954 wool sheep increased by about a million. The annual average value of the wool clip in the 30 years from 1910 to 1940 was about £10 million, but in the years from 1950 to 1954 it had increased to the order of some £70 million annually.[1] Its export value is second only to gold. About 23 per cent. was merino.

Wool is the most valuable export from Basutoland. Marketing in poor condition had given it a bad reputation in the past, but measures for grading have now been taken, and the introduction of merino rams from recognized breeders in the Union has also improved the quality.[2] Basutoland mohair is said to be of exceptional value for blending.[3] The export of wool was $8\frac{3}{4}$ million lb. in 1952, and of mohair $1\frac{1}{4}$ million lb. In Kenya wool is a product of European farming with sheep of the merino–Masai cross; the export in 1953 was nearly $1\frac{1}{2}$ million lb. Exports of wool from French West Africa in 1952 amounted only to 104 metric tons.

In most African territories the manufacture of ghee (clarified butter) has been the principal dairy industry developed among African stockowners, but butter and cheese production have attained some importance in areas of European settlement. In the Union dairying is organized under the Dairy Industry Control Board, which controls the erection of creameries and cheese factories. African creameries are supervised by the Native Agricultural Department. The total production in 1947–8 was about 56 million lb. of butter and $20\frac{1}{4}$ million lb. of cheese. Exports from the Union are small, and it has for some years been importing increasing quantities of butter. A State-aided scheme for the supply of milk and cheese to schools was inaugurated in 1935. In South-West Africa efforts are being made to expand the dairy industry by means of creameries; in 1950 about $10\frac{1}{2}$ million lb. of butter were exported to the Union. Swaziland has a butter factory at Bremersdorp which produced 454,966 lb. in 1953. In Bechuanaland there is a combined cheese and butter factory; 227,000 lb. of butter were exported in 1952. In Southern Rhodesia cheese production rose in 1953 to 566,000 lb., but this was inadequate for local needs.

In Tanganyika the chief attention is given to the production of ghee, for which there is a market in India. It is made at numerous creameries owned by Native Authorities, by the Central Province Creameries Board, or by private African operators, especially in Musoma and North Mara Districts. The total production in 1950 was 45,420 tins of 36 lb. each. In Kenya butter and cheese are produced in the European areas; the Second World War provided a great stimulus to production, which rose from 2,800,000 lb. of butter in 1938 to 5,725,724 lb. in 1948. Ghee is

[1] *S.A.S.*, no. 98, 15 February 1955, p. 8.   [2] *N.A.*, Part V, p. 12.
[3] Basutoland, *Annual Report of the Department of Agriculture, 1953*, p. 44.

produced in Native Reserves, the principal source being South Nyanza. In the purely pastoral areas with their low rainfall there is rarely a milk surplus, but encouragement is given to its production by means of 'dairy units' established (chiefly by local Native Councils) during the short periods of abundant rainfall when milk is plentiful. The number of dairies is, however, limited.

In Nigeria a creamery at Vom produced a considerable supply of butter in 1952, but prices were too high for export. In the Belgian Congo about 1¼ million lb. of butter and rather over 150,000 lb. of cheese were produced in 1952. Ruanda Urundi, a land rich in cattle, has creameries which in 1951 produced 650,000 lb. of butter and 450 metric tons of ghee (*samli*).

Improvement of Systems of Animal Husbandry

To prevent the exhaustion of the nutritive grasses and the injury done to the soil by constant trampling, it has been held in the Union of South Africa to be necessary to introduce some system of rotational grazing by which areas can be kept free of stock until the pasture has had time to recover. The length of time required for recuperation may vary according to local conditions from six months to a year, and success depends on the prohibition of grazing during the resting period. In some Native areas this has been enforced by fencing, financed from the Soil Erosion Vote, and recovery of the natural grasses has been found to be very rapid.[1] There are some notable instances of this in the Transkei, where the process has been assisted by grants made from the Transkeian General Council. In the six years up to 1954 £67,000 was expended on fencing in South-West Africa. In Southern Rhodesia the system of 'centralization' in the Native Reserves has had the effect of demarcating the lands into arable and grazing areas;[2] the procedure has now been completed in the most populated Reserves, with much benefit to the grazing.

In the majority of the British dependencies it has been found of advantage to enlist the co-operation of the Native Authorities in the measures taken for the protection of grasslands. In Basutoland the Paramount Chief, at an early stage in the campaign for soil conservation, ordered that areas contoured to prevent erosion should be excluded from grazing.[3] In the Sukuma District of Tanganyika dams have been built for the storage of rain-water in grasslands lying at a distance from the villages, and as many cattle as possible are sent to pasture there during the rainy season, thus resting the grass around the permanent sources of water near the villages. In Kenya some individual Africans in the Kiambu District have made paddocks, and more recently members of the Nandi and Kipsigis tribes have been enclosing communal grazing land by fences.[4]

---

[1] *Union of South Africa, Report on Native Affairs, 1935–6*, p. 44.   [2] See above, p. 766.
[3] *N.A.*, Part V, pp. 128, 412.   [4] Ibid. Part I, pp. 192, 194.

In Uganda an Ordinance of 1945, which was applied to four districts, gave powers to the Native Administrations to prohibit grazing in any area where pastures were eroded or overstocked. In the Bamenda District of the British Cameroons the grazing control exercised through the Native Authority has given very useful results.

The improvement which can be effected in stock is limited by the nutrition available to keep animals in good condition; 'the degree of improvement must always be dictated by the plane of nutrition'.[1] The natural pasture is frequently found to have mineral deficiencies which can be supplied only by hand feeding. It is usual to assess the value of pasture lands in relation to the number of acres required for the maintenance of one head of cattle, and it is noteworthy that in some of the less favoured areas the estimate may be as low as 40 to 50 acres per head.[2]

The most extensive pasture research work has been done in the Union of South Africa and in Kenya. In the Union the study of the grasslands has reached a point where it is possible to recommend with a fair degree of certainty the type of pasture suited to different areas; large numbers of indigenous and other grasses have been tested by the Division of Plant Industry at Pretoria under the direction of Dr. Pole-Evans.[3] In Kenya there is a main grassland Research Station at Kitale, and sub-stations at Molo, Naro Moru, and Kabete, representing different climatic conditions. Tanganyika has a Pasture Officer and staff at Mpwapwa. Grasses, such for instance as Rhodes grass or molasses grass, which were found useful in the past, are now being supplemented by newer grasses, such as *Cenchrus ciliaris* and *Panicum makarikariense*. Phosphatic and nitrogenous fertilizers are beginning to be used on grasslands in Kenya and are also being tested at Entebbe in Uganda.

The value of a policy of compulsory culling in order to prevent erosion forms one of the most debatable topics in the field of agricultural policy. Apart, however, from the possibilities it may present for this purpose,[4] culling practised on a voluntary basis forms one of the most obvious of the measures which can be taken for the improvement of the quality of indigenous stock. Culling may be said to begin with the castration of inferior male animals; but as this is not a common indigenous practice Veterinary Departments have preferred to keep it in their own hands. In Kenya 41,600 cattle were recorded as castrated in Native areas in 1948; in Uganda 75, 296 in 1951; and in the Northern Provinces of Nigeria 81,848 animals of all kinds in 1949–50. In the intensive Livestock Improvement Areas of Uganda advice on culling is combined with the provision

[1] F. Fraser Darling, *Animal Breeding in the British Empire*, 1934.
[2] *Report of Mission to Bechuanaland Protectorate (Western Kalahari) 1952*, 1953.
[3] Worthington, op. cit. p. 311. *O.Y.S.A., 1950*, pp. 868, 922.
[4] J. D. Tothill, ed., *Agriculture in Uganda*, 1940, pp. 80, 496–510. See also below, p. 1044.

of selected sires. In Kenya, where the annual increase of stock is between 5 and 25 per cent., it is held that the proportion culled should be at least 10 per cent. In Tanganyika the culling ratio is 5 per cent., and this is regarded as satisfactory.

In many territories improved facilities for marketing stock, including auction markets and the establishment of meat factories, encourage the African to sell surplus animals. In Kenya and Tanganyika some thousands of inferior animals have been brought in for slaughter.[1] De-stocking operations may also be combined with selective culling. An early example of this was given in the Glen Grey District of South Africa by a Proclamation under which inferior cattle were branded by the authorities and had then to be disposed of within six months. The compulsory measure of de-stocking undertaken in Southern Rhodesia as a preliminary to the passing of the National Resources Act (no. 9 of 1941) was accompanied by a process of voluntary culling.[2] Similar provisions are made in Nyasaland under the De-stocking Rules, 1947.

There is an interesting example of the use by Africans of the principle of selective disposal of stock in the operation of the Lifa Fund in Swaziland, by which money is provided to enable the Swazi people to repurchase lands previously alienated to Europeans.[3] Once in three years herds are compulsorily culled in a fixed proportion according to the size of the herd, and a percentage of the proceeds of their sale is applied to the Fund. In Basutoland 'bastard' rams are being gradually eliminated and merinos introduced.[4] In general, however, de-stocking regulations have been quantitative rather than selective; it may be said indeed that the culling of the flocks and herds of indigenous Africa on a really adequate scale has as yet barely begun.

Disease and pests are in Africa as great or, it may be, even a greater menace to the pastoralist than to the cultivator. One of the most important measures to prevent the spread of certain tick-borne diseases, more particularly East Coast Fever, has been dipping and fencing.[5] In the Union of South Africa dipping is now general among European farmers. It was first introduced in the Transkei during the serious outbreak of East Coast Fever in 1900, and by 1932 nearly £1 million had been spent on tank construction and dipping operations. Regular dipping is compulsory in Swaziland, in a large part of Nyasaland, and in Southern Rhodesia in the wet season. Northern Rhodesia and Kenya have laws providing that dipping may be made compulsory in areas where the inhabitants request it; this has been applied in some highland districts of Kenya. In Tanganyika similar laws have been applied to four areas,

---

[1] See above, p. 883.   [2] See above, p. 766.
[3] See above, p. 516, and also N.A., Part V, p. 415.
[4] Ibid. p. 12.   [5] See above, p. 881.

including part of Mafia Island. A cheaper alternative is the spraying of animals with organic insecticides to kill ticks, and in Uganda African stock-owners are beginning to buy spray pumps.

Much progress has been made in the Union in the paddocking of the lands of European farmers, and State assistance has been provided for this purpose. In the Transkeian Territories the General Council contributes on a pound-for-pound basis to the cost of fencing schemes undertaken by ten or more contiguous farmers. Kenya and Northern Rhodesia have enacted Ordinances making fencing compulsory in areas to which they apply, and in Northern Rhodesia two European areas were scheduled for this purpose in 1950. Here it is regarded as of such importance as to justify a recommendation for a State grant towards the cost.[1] On the other hand an Association of European stock-owners in the Belgian Congo has protested that fencing is too expensive to be economic.[2]

The Introduction of Imported Stock

It is a much debated point whether the grading up of indigenous stock can best be effected by the selective breeding of indigenous strains or by their admixture with imported stock. In the Union of South Africa there has as yet been no definite policy adopted. The Afrikander strain has many qualities, including that of resistance to scarcity conditions, but over a large part of South Africa it has already ceased to be a pure strain. Some authorities hold the view that, if more than 50 per cent. of European blood is introduced into the African stock, there will be a retrogression, due to the inability of the progeny to adapt itself to difficult environmental conditions. In Southern Rhodesia, however, seven-eighths pure-bred stock are said to have done well.[3] A second indigenous breed, the Drakensberger, has received recognition in the Union; it is a dual-purpose type, best suited to the higher and colder regions. The Administration adopted in 1932 the 'bull and ram camp' schemes, under which the service of improved sires is provided free for the herds and flocks of African owners. In the Transkei the Tsolo School of Agriculture has concentrated on the breeding of rams for sale to African farmers. The Afrikander breed of cattle is regarded as the most satisfactory, owing to its ability to forage under difficult conditions.

In Swaziland the cattle appear to represent every variety of breed,[4] but efforts have recently been made at the cattle farm at Mpisi to grade up indigenous stock without resort to cross-breeding. In Bechuanaland the cattle are superior, being mainly of the Afrikander type, but with some

[1] L. G. Troup, *Report of the Commission of Enquiry into the Future of the European Farming Industry in Northern Rhodesia—Tenure of Agricultural Land*, 1954, para. 301.

[2] *Comptes rendus de la conférence africaine des sols*, Goma, 1948, vol. ii, p. 1873.

[3] Worthington, op. cit. p. 418.

[4] A. Pim, *Report on the Financial and Economic Situation of Swaziland*, Cmd. 4114, 1932, p. 142.

intermixture in the north with cattle from Angola. Their number was estimated in 1954 to be over 1 million. Exports amount normally to about 75,000 head, to the value of £1½ million. In 1950 the Colonial Development Corporation entered on an undertaking which had three complementary projects. The plan was designed to facilitate the slaughter and marketing of surplus cattle in Bechuanaland, to provide a central abattoir at Lobatsi where cattle might be slaughtered, and to build a cold-storage plant there. This would obviate the loss attending the movement of cattle on the hoof. Agreements were made with the Union of South Africa, Northern Rhodesia, and the Belgian Congo to purchase the output.

Owing to structural defects the Lobatsi abattoir was not completed until September 1954, but in a few months it was treating the 300 beasts a day as originally estimated.[1] Ancillary to the abattoir was a holding ranch at the Molopo river, 600,000 acres in extent, intended to regulate the flow to the abattoir of an estimated 55,000 beasts a year.[2] In 1953 a revised scheme was accepted, whereby only the easternmost 200,000 acres were utilized and the function of the holding ranch became the improvement of breeding.[3] The residue of the ranch was transferred to the Government.

One of the sources from which cattle were to be drafted was the Bechuanaland Cattle Ranch, with an area of 16,000 square miles of Crown Lands in Northern Bechuanaland taken over on lease by the Corporation. The intention was to form a herd of 350,000 beasts and at the same time to put 300,000 acres under fodder crops.[4] In 1952 the scheme underwent a revision which resulted in the projected agricultural operations being greatly restricted. A flock of Persian sheep was also introduced.[5] In 1953 the herd of cattle had increased to 17,000, but the percentage of loss proved to be high. The ranch was as a consequence reduced to an area of 200,000 acres near the headquarters at Panda-ma-Tenga, where it is intended to maintain a herd of 3,000 ranch-bred cattle and to adapt it as a 'holding' ranch for cattle bought from the Ngamiland Cattle Exporters' Association, to which the outlying ranch at Bushman's Pits has been transferred.[6] In spite of the reduction in the scope of the scheme it has been stated that financial loss must be expected for some years. In Basutoland Afrikander cattle were introduced by the Government in the late thirties, but the major interest of the Native Administration has been in measures taken for the improvement of the sheep and goat stock by eliminating half-breed or 'bastard' rams. Some 4,338 pedigree merino rams were purchased between 1935 and 1943, and Angora stock is now being introduced for the production of mohair.[7]

[1] *Colonial Development Corporation, Report and Accounts for 1954*, p. 44.
[2] Ibid. *1950*, p. 8.   [3] Ibid. *1954*, p. 44.   [4] Ibid. *1950*, p. 9.
[5] Ibid. *1952*, p. 48.   [6] Ibid. *1954*, p. 43.   [7] *N.A.*, Part V, p. 12.

In Southern Rhodesia both Ayrshire and Friesian cattle have been successfully acclimatized, and by crossing with Afrikander have produced good carcass beef for the market. Three local types of indigenous cattle have been evolved by crossing with Herefords, Aberdeen Angus, and to a smaller extent with Devons and Shorthorns. For artificial insemination Friesian semen is most in demand.[1] In Northern Rhodesia the improvement of indigenous herds has not hitherto met with much success.[2] In Tanganyika indigenous stock has been crossed with Friesian and Ayrshire cows to increase the milk yield. A cattle-breeding scheme which was started by the Overseas Food Corporation in 1950 at Kongwa, with beef production as its main object, is being continued by the Tanganyika Agricultural Corporation.[3] In Kenya there has been a considerable import of high-grade dairy cattle, mostly for farms in the highlands. The local Boran breed is popular both with European and African farmers, and is considered by some to be a superior animal to the Afrikander.[4] The experiment is being tried of crossing Nandi cattle with the Sahiwal breed of Indian zebu, which have proved the most suitable stock in marginal areas.

In Nigeria experiments are in progress at Shika, near Zaria, for the improvement of three types of Native zebu (the White Fulani, Godali, and Shuwa) in order to evolve dual-purpose cattle for the mixed-farming areas. Work was begun in 1936 at Ilorin stock farm on the breeding of cattle resistant to trypanosomiasis; it was based on the indigenous West African shorthorn and the imported N'Dama breed, both of which have some resistance to trypanosomiasis. The former is very small, and the problem is to increase size while retaining disease-resistance. In the Northern Territories of the Gold Coast the Government livestock farm at Pong-Tamale has made similar experiments.

In French West Africa more attention has been given to the breeding of sheep than of cattle. In the wool-producing districts half-bred merino rams are distributed free to African breeders. The Diré Company has found on its farm at Goundam that half-bred merinos are more resistant to disease than animals with a larger proportion of merino blood. The grading up of indigenous breeds of cattle and sheep is carried out at the Government farm at El-Oualadji in the Sudan. Charollaise, Normande, and Tarentaise cattle have been used for crossing with local N'Dama or Zebu herds.

In the Belgian Congo the Government farm at Nioka in Ituri is breeding cattle suitable for both milking and beef. Many strains have been

[1] Report of Director of Veterinary Services, Southern Rhodesia, 1953, p. 22.
[2] Troup, op. cit. p. 33.
[3] Overseas Food Corporation, Report and Accounts for 1954-55, p. 85.
[4] R. H. Bisschop, The Improvement of Livestock in Kenya, 1949.

tried for crossing, including Herefords, Devons, Ayrshires, Friesians, Bretons, and Brown Swiss. The European herds numbered 350,000 and cattle rearing is now firmly established in all Provinces of the territory. About 50,000 were made available for slaughter in 1953. Angola cattle have been imported for many years and crossed with European types, but the resultant animals have not the stamina of local breeds and attention has more recently been directed to the selective breeding of indigenous stock. In Coquilhatville Province African cattle have been introduced from Dahomey and Conakry.

EDUCATION IN AGRICULTURE AND ANIMAL HUSBANDRY

In the sections of this Survey which deal with certain of the other technical departments, such as those of health and forestry, it is emphasized that expansion of their activity must necessarily depend on the success achieved in the training of African assistants qualified to undertake posts of responsibility. In regard to agriculture and animal husbandry, however, the need for qualified Africans is not confined to the subordinate staff, but extends also to the superior ranks, for there can be few other departments of work where so salutary an influence can be exercised by a cadre of officers who, in addition to their scientific qualifications, are intimately conversant with the life and customs of the people.[1]

The academic facilities which now exist for the training of this class are not at present extensive. In the Union of South Africa the Native College at Fort Hare, affiliated since 1951 to Rhodes University, offers a degree course in agriculture. The newly established University Colleges of Makerere, Ibadan, and Achimota[2] have Agricultural Faculties and prepare candidates for diplomas or for the external degree of London University. It is regrettable that very few Africans have as yet shown interest in agricultural research. There is also a serious shortage in all British territories of trained laboratory workers. This can be repaired only if there is a further provision of secondary education in science.

Hitherto the chief attention has been given to the training of a subordinate, and frequently of a lower subordinate, grade of agricultural assistant. In the Union of South Africa the officially organized agricultural education of Africans began with the creation in 1929 of the separate Agriculture Section of the Native Affairs Department.[3] The Director of Agriculture estimated in 1932 that a minimum of 400 demonstrators

---

[1] *Report of the Commission on Higher Education in the Colonies*, Cmd. 6647, 1945, p. 69.

[2] See below, p. 1180.

[3] In 1925 the Department of Education instituted agricultural post-primary schools and in 1938 these were transferred to Provincial Administrations. The Bantu Education Act of 1954, however, has relegated African agricultural education to the Department of Education of the Central Government.

would be necessary to make any real impression on Native systems of cultivation, and the Native Economic Commission of 1932 regarded this as a conservative estimate.[1] In 1950 the number of Government posts was 339, of which 49 were vacant, but there were also some 160 employed under the United Transkeian Territories General Council.[2]

There are two well-equipped schools of agriculture in the Transkeian Territories (Teko and Tsolo) and one in the Ciskei (Fort Cox), offering a two-year diploma course, besides shorter courses. A number of demonstrators trained in these schools are employed in Swaziland and Basutoland.[3]

Southern Rhodesia had in 1950 an African staff of nine instructors, 298 agricultural demonstrators, and 76 community demonstrators, mostly trained at the African Training School at Domboshawa.[4] In East Africa the school of Agriculture at Makerere provides diploma and degree courses and from it students proceed to the posts of Assistant Agricultural and Veterinary Officers. Their number is however inadequate, and to supplement them the Education Department in Uganda intends to establish a Senior Secondary School offering agricultural science as a subject for the school certificate.

In the evolution of agricultural methods training in field work is essential,[5] and there is need for an extension of the school at Makerere. Farm Institutes, of which the first was built in Uganda in 1955, are intended to train staff, Chiefs, and private farmers in field operations.[6] Most of the British dependencies arrange for the training of agricultural subordinates at the main experimental stations, these establishments sometimes being designated schools and, as in Nigeria, allotted a whole-time Principal. Some territories have different centres for each ecological region, as at Ibadan and Samaru in Nigeria, or at Bukalasa and Serere in Uganda; others have relied on a single main station, as at Bukura in Kenya.

In French West Africa 'Apprenticeship Centres' give instruction up to a standard qualifying for entrance to the lowest grade of the Agricultural Service. Agricultural Technical Colleges, of which that at Katibougou is an example, provide a four-year course up to the standard of *Lycée premier cycle*. A Bachelor's degree may be taken after three years at a Higher Technical School and may be followed by specialization.[7] The Agricultural Service employs about 520 African *moniteurs* and 200 *conducteurs de travaux agricoles*.

In the Belgian Congo the development of African agriculture is pro-

---

[1] *Report of the Native Economic Commission, 1930–1932*, U.G. no. 22, 1932.
[2] *Report of the Department of Native Affairs, 1950–1951*, U.G. no. 30, 1953, p. 8.
[3] *Handbook on Race Relations in South Africa*, 1949, p. 185.   [4] *O.Y.S.R., 1952*, p. 449.
[5] On the importance of Field Officers, see Cmd. 9475, pp. 375–7.
[6] *Report of the Agricultural Productivity Committee*, Uganda, 1954, p. 70.
[7] *Enc. A.O.F.*, vol. i, p. 276.

moted, under the auspices of I.N.E.A.C., by a system of local field stations (*sous-stations d'essai locales*). By 1952 over 6,700 *moniteurs*, 650 of whom had diplomas, had been trained at centres for agricultural extension work. There are also schools for agricultural assistants, of whom there were more than 180 in 1952, and facilities for higher studies in agriculture are to be provided at the new University centre of Lovanium at Kimuenza.[1]

In the use of these trained subordinates for agricultural extension work there is a clear bifurcation of method in the different territories concerned. Under one system, which is in force in most of the British dependencies, they work as agricultural instructors, under the title of 'overseers' or 'agricultural assistants' or similar forms. Their duty is to endeavour to improve the level of farming by advice and demonstration. A recent development is the employment of a female staff; in Uganda a few agricultural instructresses have been employed since about 1942, and in Kenya there were in 1952 some 48 in employment.

The other system, as practised in the Union of South Africa, the High Commission Territories, and Southern Rhodesia, consists in the use of agricultural demonstrators in a more practical sense. In Southern Rhodesia, for example, there were in 1952 some 519 demonstrators; each demonstrates on the land of not more than 16 farmers, who have undertaken to carry out an agreed rotation and programme of manuring. The demonstrator assists with his own hands. An African farmer who carries on the programme after the demonstrator has worked with him for four years may receive a certificate as a Master Farmer. There were in 1950 some 1,665 Master Farmers and also a substantial number of others who, though they had co-operated with the demonstrators, had not yet reached the stage of qualifying for the Masters' certificate.[2] Neither of these two methods in the use of demonstrators has been pursued far enough to warrant a judgement on its respective merits, though high claims have been made for the system followed in Southern Rhodesia. Some figures have already been quoted of the remarkable results attained by a number of the Master Farmers.[3]

But agricultural extension work clearly demands much besides the employment of a staff of demonstrators or the like. It is now generally accepted that agriculture should be included in the school syllabus of rural schools, though the Education Mission to East Africa in 1951–2 considered that it was still not enough merely to supply an agricultural background to education.[4] Most schools of any size have a school garden, though not all are well managed. Many Agricultural Departments assist in the training of teachers in agriculture. In French West Africa the

---

[1] See below, p. 1211.   [2] *O.Y.S.R., 1952*, p. 449.   [3] See above, p. 848.
[4] Nuffield Foundation and Colonial Office, *African Education: A Study of Educational Policy and Practice in British Tropical Africa*, 1953.

training of teachers for rural schools is given at two centres in the Sudan and Guinea, which have been selected as typical of the dry steppe land and the forest belt respectively.

The use of other publicity methods in agricultural extension in Africa has received increasing attention in recent years.[1] In most of the African territories articles in the vernacular press, broadcasts, films shown by the mobile cinema, and agricultural shows are all in wide use. In Uganda 'demonstration teams', which visit the villages and combine entertainment with instructional items, have also dramatized agricultural improvements. Agricultural extension is an accepted part of what has come to be known as 'community development'.[2]

No courses leading to full veterinary qualifications have in the past been available in Africa for Africans, but those now being given in some of the territories should in time produce candidates for the superior cadres of the Veterinary Service. The University College of Makerere has its Veterinary School at Kabete in Kenya, where it is near to the East African Veterinary Research Organization,[3] and a veterinary course is commencing at the University College of Ibadan. Facilities for training veterinary assistants are more widespread. In the Union of South Africa courses in Animal Husbandry form part of the curriculum at Fort Cox Agricultural School.[4] There are veterinary schools at Mazabuka in Northern Rhodesia, Mpwapwa in Tanganyika, Entebbe in Uganda, and Vom in Nigeria, and another is to be developed at Mpemba in Nyasaland. In Uganda the Veterinary Department has organized short courses for schoolmasters at one of its stock farms.

The results of agricultural and veterinary education of this type may be seen in the figures of the departmental staffs employed in different territories. Nyasaland, for example, employs 1,112 Africans, 124 Europeans, and seven Asians on its agricultural staff; of these, 12 Europeans and 85 Africans were attached to the research stations. In Tanganyika, out of a staff of 1,820, only 220 were European and 73 Asian; the Africans numbered 1,527. Although most of the Africans are engaged in field work, or in other subordinate posts, a proportion are now being trained in laboratory work or in similar agencies of research.

CONTROL OF PLANT PESTS AND DISEASES

Under primitive conditions of agriculture the relative isolation of the areas under cultivation served to provide a measure of protection against the spread of pests and diseases, but the wider extension of agriculture in modern conditions has necessitated a general introduction of measures

[1] C. W. Lynn, *Agricultural Extension and Advisory Work with Special Reference to the Colonies*, 1949.
[2] See below, p. 1191.   [3] See below, p. 1183.   [4] See above, p. 893.

of official control. These measures have in particular been advocated where African and European cultivation exist in the same area and African crops are in consequence considered to be potential sources of infection.[1] It has, for example, been shown that in Kenya the cultivation of *arabica* coffee, once definitely restricted, is now permitted only in scheduled areas, and subject to a licensing system which permits of inspections of the health of the trees.[2] Restrictions of a similar character were once strongly pressed on the Administration of Tanganyika. While these form somewhat special cases, most of the territories now have regulations providing for the inspection and quarantining of imported plants and seeds.[3] The four British West African territories constitute a 'plant interchange schedule' and each permits some relaxation for plants coming from any of the others.

Crop sanitation is also implemented by the imposition of close seasons for certain crops as a means of preventing the carry-over of diseases from one season to another. In the Union of South Africa a close season for cotton may be adopted by local option for any magisterial area, and was first so applied in the Barberton District. In the cotton-growing areas of most British dependencies a date by which cotton plants must be uprooted and burned is usually proclaimed annually, and the enforcement of this regulation is normally entrusted to the Native Administrations. In Southern Rhodesia a close season for tobacco was adopted in 1933 in order to meet the menace of leaf-curl disease, and similar provisions have been made in Nyasaland and the Songea District of Tanganyika. In Kenya close seasons have been imposed in certain districts for maize and sorghum, with the aim of eradicating the stem-borer and other insect pests.

Measures for the control of the swollen shoot disease of cacao in the Gold Coast have already been mentioned.[4] It has also been stated that a considerable proportion (sometimes estimated as high as 20 per cent.) of the West African cacao crop is lost annually by capsid bug damage; this can be controlled in young trees if an insecticide is painted on the affected parts, but it remains a difficult problem on older trees. Some African territories have laws under which certain plants are scheduled as noxious weeds, and farmers are required to destroy them. There is a very long list of such noxious weeds in the Union of South Africa.[5] In a number of British dependencies the Native Authorities have been a recognized agency for administering regulations for the control of noxious weeds.[6] In the East African territories the lists include species of *Datura* (thornapple) and *Lolium* (darnel), whose seeds can be dangerous impurities in

---

[1] Worthington, op. cit. pp. 280 ff.   [2] See above, p. 834.
[3] See the regulations issued in the Union of South Africa under the South Africa Customs Act no. 35 of 1944.
[4] See above, p. 828.   [5] *O.Y.S.A.*, *1949*, pp. 774–8; *1950*, pp. 804–9.
[6] See, for example, *N.A.*, Part I, p. 306; Part III, p. 79.

wheat or rye. The parasitic *Striga* (witch weed), which can cause heavy losses in cereal crops, has now been found to be subject to control by the new organic herbicides. The latter are beginning to be used in a few parts of Africa.

Organization of Locust Control

Though invasions by locusts are intermittent, and some parts of the continent may escape them entirely, yet when they occur the devastation is so great that locusts must be regarded as one of the major pests of Africa. It is impossible to make any reliable estimate of the total losses caused by locust invasions in the past, but some idea of the order of damage caused in certain territories is available. Kenya estimated that in the period 1928–34 crops valued at £800,000 were lost. In Sierra Leone 50 per cent. of crops in the invaded areas were lost in 1930. In Nigeria the losses in 1925–34 were valued at £300,000.[1] It has been recently stated that an uncontrolled invasion of East Africa by the Desert Locust might result in a loss of about £3 million in a single year.[2] The areas under cultivation in Africa are growing rapidly, and the further expansion of agriculture would increase the chances of locust swarms descending on crops rather than on wild vegetation. An example of the order of damage that can be caused in a relatively well-developed country season is offered by Morocco, where locust swarms caused in a single (1954–5) damage assessed at £4½ million.

It was believed in the past that plagues of locusts were a feature of undeveloped countries, and that the advance of civilization would automatically solve the locust problem. It is, however, now recognized that their activities are furthered rather than reduced by agricultural development,[3] a fact which underlines the need for a long-term approach to the locust problem. This was realized as early as 1929 by the British Committee of Civil Research, which established a special Committee on Locust Control charged primarily with the organization of inquiries into the reasons for the periodic swarming of locusts. The investigations were from the beginning planned to cover all territories affected, and this required their extension to south-western Asia. The British initiative received a ready support from other countries, and an International Locust Conference, which met in Rome in 1931, recommended that all reports on locust movements should be centralized in a special branch of the Imperial (now Commonwealth) Institute of Entomology in London. This became in 1946 an independent Anti-Locust Research Centre under

[1] B. P. Uvarov, *Locust Research and Control, 1929–1950*, Colonial Research Publication no. 10, 1951.
[2] East Africa High Commission, *Report of the Commission on the Desert Locust Control Organization*, 1955.
[3] *Fourth International Locust Conference*, Cairo, 1936.

Dr. Uvarov; it was financed from funds provided by the Colonial Development and Welfare Acts.[1] International co-operation was further developed at conferences held in Paris (1932), London (1934), Cairo (1936), and Brussels (1938).

The results of centralizing locust information in one research institution soon became apparent. It was established that the tropical African territories are subject to invasions by three different kinds of locust, the Desert, the Red, and the African Migratory Locust. Each of these three species has its own area of distribution, different habits, and different areas in which swarms can arise from scattered and economically unimportant locust populations. Thus the drier parts of northern, western, and equatorial Africa, the Sudan, Ethiopia, the Somalilands, and eastern Africa suffer mainly from the Desert Locust, the ravages of which extend also to Arabia, the Middle East, Pakistan, and India. The Migratory Locust infests somewhat less dry grassland areas of almost the whole continent, partly overlapping with the Desert Locust. The Red Locust presents greatest danger to the territories south of the Equator, but its swarms may also invade Uganda and Kenya.

The invasions of the Red and the Migratory Locust, widespread though they were in the years 1930–40, had their sources of origin in relatively restricted localities which have been designated as outbreak areas.[2] Thus the swarms of the Migratory Locust are known to originate from a single area of flood plains of the Middle Niger in the French Sudan. From that area, less than 10,000 square miles in extent, there arose in 1926–8 an invasion which gradually spread over nearly 10 million square miles and lasted 14 years, causing great devastation in West, Central, and East Africa. Similarly, the origin of invasions of the Red Locust has been traced to two outbreak areas in the marshy plains surrounding Lake Rukwa in Tanganyika and in those round Lake Mweru in Northern Rhodesia. The last plague of the Red Locust began there about 1927, reached its maximum extension of about 3 million square miles by 1935, and continued, though on a reduced scale, for another ten years. Great losses of crops were caused during that period, particularly in sugar-cane areas.

The discovery of the outbreak areas of the Migratory and the Red Locust made it possible to envisage measures for the suppression of locust invasions in their early stages. The Locust Conference at Brussels in 1938 adopted a scheme for a permanent international organization for the control of the Niger outbreak area of the Migratory Locust. Owing to the war, this organization was at first established by the French authorities alone, but in 1947 an International Convention between France, Belgium,

---

[1] *Colonial Research, 1944–1945*, Cmd. 6663, 1945, p. 8; ibid. *1945–1946*, Col. no. 208, 1947, p. 9.
[2] See map on p. 899.

AFRICA : LOCUST AREAS

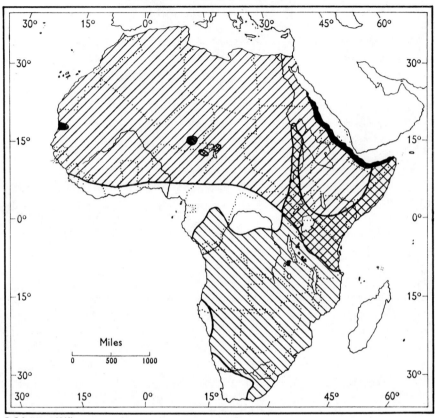

D.C.S. (Misc.) 226/9

Invasion Areas in Africa of the Desert Locust and Red Locust

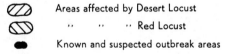

▨   Areas affected by Desert Locust

▧   ,,   ,,   ,, Red Locust

●   Known and suspected outbreak areas

Drawn from information supplied by the Anti-Locust Research Centre
and the International Red Locust Control Service

and the United Kingdom was concluded, and the organization became internationally financed and administered.[1] The Red Locust problem has been met by the establishment of the International Red Locust Control Organization under a Convention in which the United Kingdom, Belgium, Southern Rhodesia, and the Union of South Africa participate.[2]

Both these organizations have their own personnel and equipment in the actual outbreak areas. Continuous scouting is being carried out and any concentrations of locusts are attacked by insecticides. It is significant that since the establishment of these services no serious swarms have been permitted to escape from the outbreak areas, although in some years strenuous efforts were required to suppress incipient swarming in them. It is clear that the discovery of outbreak areas and the possibility of keeping locusts in them under control has resulted in protecting large parts of Africa from the ravages of the Red and the Migratory Locust.

It was not possible to achieve the same result in the case of the Desert Locust. Studies of that species have so far failed to indicate the existence of geographically localized outbreak areas, although many parts of the desert zone in Africa and Asia are suspected to be able to produce swarms when climatic conditions are favourable.[3] The Desert Locust, therefore, continues to constitute a serious menace to African economy. Investigation has indicated considerable regularity in the seasonal breeding and migrations of swarms, thus rendering it easier to forecast invasions and to organize control campaigns. The extent of swarm migrations of this species is, however, prodigious and control operations can be effective only if they are carried out with the same vigour in a number of countries. This fact led the British Government to organize between 1942 and 1947 a series of anti-locust campaigns in Arabia, Persia, East Africa, the Somalilands, and Libya. These campaigns were run on semi-military lines, at a cost of about £1 million per annum, and as a result only minor crop losses were caused in the more fertile areas to which swarms move after breeding in deserts and semi-deserts.

The Desert Locust plague showed some signs of recession about 1948 when the East African Governments established the Desert Locust Survey, which was charged with watching developments in those desert areas of Eastern Africa and Arabia considered to be the main sources of swarms invading East Africa.[4] It was hoped that a sufficiently long interval between invasions would make it possible to organize preventive control, but new swarms appeared in 1950 and the forces at the disposal of the Desert Locust Survey proved to be inadequate. A larger organization,

[1] B. Zolotarevsky, 'History of the International Organization for Control of the African Migratory Locust', *Locusta*, no. 1, Paris, 1954.
[2] D. L. Gunn, 'The Red Locust', *J.R.S.A.*, March 1952.   [3] Uvarov, op. cit.
[4] P. R. Stephenson, *Report of the Desert Locust Survey and Control, 1 October 1948–30 September 1950*, Nairobi, 1951. Ibid. *1 October 1950–31 December 1952*.

Desert Locust Control, had to be created, and it has been waging a continuous series of campaigns since then. The cost of these operations to the East African Governments has averaged over £1 million per annum and, although they are successful in preventing heavy damage to crops, the financial difficulties involved are serious.

More recently the problem of the Desert Locust has attracted the attention of the Food and Agriculture Organization of the United Nations, which succeeded in promoting internationally financed anti-locust campaigns in the Arabian peninsula. These campaigns commenced in 1953 and at the same time there has been a gradual improvement of the anti-locust services in the countries concerned, so that the Desert Locust is now less of a menace than in the past. New insecticides and the use of spraying aircraft have made possible a more extensive protection of cropped areas. The financial problem, however, remains acute even in the case of the Red and the Migratory Locust, since some Governments which contribute to the upkeep of preventive organizations have begun to show concern regarding the annual expense involved. The annual cost of the International Red Locust Control Organization reached in 1956 the figure of £283,000.[1]

The virtual absence of devastations during the recent decades is undoubtedly due to the control exercised; but, nevertheless, the heavy expense involved suggests to a layman some doubt as to whether it is justified. It would seem that the ultimate aim of the anti-locust organizations should be not merely to control invasions or suppress swarms in their early stages but to prevent their formation. Expert opinion suggests that outbreak areas must have some peculiar features in their ecology which favour the production of the initial swarms.[2] Research on locust ecology in the outbreak areas carried out systematically may indicate the conditions leading to swarm formation and suggest ways of preventing swarming.

The international campaign against the Desert Locust suffered a severe set-back early in 1956 when the Saudi Arabian authorities withdrew facilities from the British teams operating there, an action which was criticized by the Rome headquarters of the Food and Agriculture Organization.

THE IMPROVEMENT OF SYSTEMS OF AGRICULTURE

It is not unnatural that the efforts made to secure an increase in agricultural production should at the outset have been directed mainly to

[1] International Red Locust Control Service, Ordinary Session of the Council held at Pretoria, 26–30 September 1955.

[2] B. P. Uvarov, *Locusts and Grasshoppers: Report of the Fifth Commonwealth Entomological Conference*, 1948.

the improvement of cash crops and especially to those grown for the export market. Concern for improved production of this type still continues, and, as has been shown, it is reflected in the promotion of numerous institutions engaged both in research and field work on particular crops. But the need for a general improvement of subsistence cultivation is also recognized and is now receiving attention. The expansion of industrial enterprise has increased the need for providing foodstuffs for a growing urban population. Even more noteworthy is the conclusion drawn by medical science that much of the 'backwardness' of indigenous Africa is due to the shortage of food or the lack of nutritional values in its diet.[1] In some territories, such as the Gold Coast or Gambia, or in the coffee areas of Tanganyika, the cultivation of commercial crops has led to the neglect of food crops, with the result that farmers are beginning to depend on bought food. Over all hangs the shadow of population increase. If there is an upward trend in the African population figures, as anticipated,[2] agriculture will be hard pressed to provide food for these extra people at even the present standards of diet; to improve standards of living will be still more difficult.

There is one consideration which is common to the growth of both subsistence and cash crops, though doubly imperative in the case of the former, namely, the need for improving soil fertility without recourse to shifting cultivation. If, however, new methods of fertilization are to win their way, they must be adapted to the financial and labour resources of the African farmer. Though the use of artificial fertilizers must have its place in this operation, there is an obvious advantage in basing improved fertilization as far as possible on the use of natural processes. An examination of the present methods used by Africans reveals in some instances a planned effort, the balance of which may easily be upset by ill-considered innovations. Cotton production in Southern Nigeria, for example, is combined with the cultivation of yams, maize, and beans; the crops are planted at varying times and are not necessarily harvested in the order in which they were planted, so that the variation in the times of maturity allows a suitable distribution of labour. The soil is generally well weeded and cultivated, and full use is made of the available soil fertility. Such a system, which is of proved value in African eyes and is peculiarly adapted to African conditions of life, requires careful consideration before changes can be recommended.

Much can be done to improve types of seed. The usual practice has been for seed to be set aside for use without any special method of collection. In most territories seed farms are now maintained in connexion with marketable crops, and in some cases they are managed by the Native

---

[1] *Economic Advisory Council, Committee on Nutrition, First Report, Parts I and II, Nutrition in the Colonial Empire*, Cmds. 6050 and 6051, 1939.　　　　　　[2] See above, pp. 140 ff.

Authorities. If a continuous supply of planting material is to be maintained, an extension of this method of supply is necessary.

Perhaps the most helpful alternative to shifting cultivation lies in the planting of grass after a cropping period, in order to replace the natural succession of weeds and bush. The modern advocacy of this method is based on experiments in Uganda which showed that three-year cropping periods alternating with three years under elephant grass fully maintained the fertility of the soil. Elephant grass is, however, laborious both to plant from cuttings and to clear, so that other species, such as Rhodes grass and molasses grass, have more commonly been used. The value of these perennial grasses appears to lie largely in the restoration of crumb structure to overworked soils, permitting air and water to enter the soil and promote crop growth. While many agronomists are in favour of this system it cannot be said that it is being readily adopted by African cultivators; its labour requirements, among other things, stand in its way.

A variant of the system, where population is sparse, is the replacement of the short grass fallow by a long forest fallow. A rotation, in which five years' cultivation is followed by 15 years' forest regrowth, is the basis of many settlement schemes in the forested central areas of the Belgian Congo, where the system originated. It has come to be known as the 'corridor' system, and is founded on the principle that tropical cultivation must be protected from the sun without excluding light. These conditions are fulfilled by clearing 'corridors' 800 metres wide by 2,000 metres long, running east and west to ensure exposure to sun, but planted with mixed crops to afford soil cover and shade. The usual rotation is a cereal crop followed by beans, cassava, or bananas. Contiguous with the cultivation 'corridor' is a forest belt, and adjacent to that another cultivation 'corridor'. The yields are good. The period of cultivation is three or four years, by the end of which the next 'corridor' is cultivated. After a lapse of 15 years the forest has regenerated, and cultivation is resumed on the original 'corridor'.[1] Under the Ten-year Development Plan this system is to be extended to the savannah region and it is hoped to accommodate ultimately one-fifth of all African farmers in the Belgian Congo.[2]

This method is, however, only suitable in conditions which will allow of a close supervision over its operation. The grass fallow system shows its maximum value on heavy soils; on light sandy soils it may be of little use. These conditions are found in much of the Rhodesias and Northern Nigeria. An alternative lies in the application of farmyard manure, to which many of these soils give an exceptional response. In Southern Rhodesia it has been claimed, perhaps optimistically, that one-third of the

[1] W. V. Blewett, in *J.R.S.A.*, August 1950, p. 809.
[2] G. Malengreau, 'Vers un paysannat indigène: les lotissements agricoles au Congo Belge', *Mém. I.R.C.B.*, vol. xiv, no. 2, 1949.

African cultivators are now using it. In order to produce any quantity of manure, however, it is necessary to persuade cultivators to keep a few oxen on their holdings, a rare practice in many parts of Africa. On the other hand, it has been suggested that if the plant food content of manure is not sufficiently high, it can be economically replaced by a small dressing of artificial fertilizer.[1] It is mainly in regard to the use of manure that the origin of the campaigns for 'mixed farming' is to be found. The most notable is that now being conducted in Northern Nigeria. The Native Administrations of this region make advances for the purchase of ploughs and plough bullocks, and the number of 'mixed farmers' had risen to 9,000 in 1952. Their farms are in general larger and more productive than those of their neighbours.

Cattle cannot, however, be kept in tsetse-infected areas, and it is where a light soil is combined with the prevalence of tsetse that the problem of maintaining soil fertility is perhaps most intractable. Green manuring has given disappointing results in the Belgian Congo and Uganda, but has been more successful in the experiments made in Nigeria, where the *Mucuna* bean is the chief crop used. This is not, however, suited to all soils, and it has not been widely adopted by cultivators. If the green manure crop is burned and the ash is incorporated in the soil the results are as good as obtained by digging in the fresh crop, and labour is saved. Compost manures are useful where suitable materials are available; township and slaughter-house wastes have, for example, been composted at Kano, Kampala, and Nairobi.

The use of artificial fertilizers was restricted before 1939 by their high cost, but it has now become more economic to use them. Superphosphate has been shown to be particularly valuable for groundnuts on Northern Nigerian soils, and from 1950 the Government has distributed annually 1,000 tons free of cost in order to demonstrate its value to cultivators. Imports of chemical fertilizers increased from 267 tons in 1943 to 7,791 tons in 1953. The rock phosphate from deposits near Tororo in Uganda, when treated with Kenya soda, produces a 'soda-phosphate' fertilizer which is useful on many East African soils, though not so good as superphosphate. The schemes for development of hydro-electric power at Jinja in Uganda and in the Kariba Gorge in Southern Rhodesia[2] open up a prospect of the production of sulphate of ammonia and also of superphosphate in the former. However, it should be noted that the present demand for artificial fertilizers in East Africa alone is about 35,000 tons annually, which is too small to justify a factory.[3] Experiment has shown that groundnuts, maize, sorghum, rice, yams, cotton, tobacco, and wheat respond well to the application of artificial fertilizer.

Though mechanization is usually viewed as a means of increasing the

[1] Blewett, op. cit. pp. 802 ff.   [2] See below, p. 986.   [3] Cmd. 9475, p. 319.

production of marketable crops, it may have its uses also in developing subsistence production. African cultivation is at present hampered by the fact that the peasant has to wait for the rainy season before he can prepare his land for seeding; the use of the tractor might not only extend the area he could sow but might also greatly improve its preparation. It is, however, still a matter of debate how far the use of mechanized cultivation can be regarded as of value as a means of increasing African production, given the extra cost involved in its purchase and maintenance.

In Nigeria it has been stated that there is still no evidence to prove that tractor cultivation can be economically employed in upland farming.[1] But the same report testifies to its value in dealing with the swamp areas of Sokoto and Kano. Often when mechanization is condemned the wrong type of tractor has been used.[2] The Agricultural Departments have shown much activity in conducting experiments in the use of different types of machinery. The successful employment of mechanized cultivation at Sokoto, Nachingwea, and elsewhere has afforded evidence that the tractor is likely to play an increasingly important part in any large-scale agricultural development. It is not at present suited to the small peasant farm, but it is an important factor in making corporation or group farming possible[3] in so far that it assists in effecting deeper cultivation and in preparing the soil for plantation at the most suitable date. For the clearance of bush it is likely to prove less economical than manual labour.[4] A representative Committee which examined its possibilities also laid emphasis upon the necessity of improving hand tools and animal-drawn machines for the peasant farmer.[5] It is of some interest that a School of Farm Mechanization was established in Lagos in 1954.

Development and Resettlement Schemes

If the failure of the Tanganyika groundnut scheme was expensive,[6] its lessons have not been entirely wasted, and practically every project since initiated in tropical Africa has been exploratory, or—to adopt the term now in common use—a 'pilot scheme'.

In the British Colonial territories some 31 projects were in 1953 being financed either from the funds provided under the Colonial Development and Welfare Acts or from the revenues of the Administrations concerned.[7] Some of these projects are designed primarily for the extension of particular crops, and reference has been made to them in previous sections of this

[1] *Colonial Reports, Nigeria, 1952*, p. 42.
[2] *Report of a Conference of Directors of Agriculture held at Wye College, Kent, September 1953*, Misc. 519, unpublished, p. 59.
[3] *Report of Survey of Problems in Mechanization of Native Agriculture in Tropical African Colonies*, 1950.
[4] *Mechanisation of Agriculture, Inter-African Conference, Entebbe* (C.C.T.A.) Report, no. A. 3, 1955, p. 31.
[5] Ibid. pp. 33, 43.   [6] See above, p. 845.
[7] *Notes on Some Agricultural Development Schemes in Africa and Aden*, Colonial Office, 1953.

chapter. A typical example of a scheme of this character is in operation in the Rufiji valley in Tanganyika,[1] where by mechanized cultivation undertaken by the Tanganyika Agricultural Corporation some 7,600 acres of rice have been planted. The cost of ploughing is recovered in advance from the cultivator. A similar scheme, also initiated with the object of producing rice, is in progress in the Sokoto Province of Nigeria. Here 25,000 acres of seasonally inundated land has been mechanically ploughed at the low cost of 30s. per acre, and planted to rice; the Regional Production Development Board has furnished the capital.[2] Another interesting project has been started at Damongo in the Gold Coast by the Gonja Development Company for the production of groundnuts and other foodstuffs, and for a group settlement of peasant farmers, to whom the use of mechanical equipment is made available.[3]

Other schemes designated as pilot schemes are designed mainly to test the use of mechanization in African conditions. Some 15 of the schemes above mentioned are of this class. Others again are schemes for the 'resettlement' of communities removed from congested areas or for similar reasons.

It is not easy to draw any clear line of distinction between these various schemes, for it is frequently found desirable to utilize a 'settlement' scheme as the occasion for securing the use of improved methods of cultivation. Again, the 'centralization' of the Native Reserves in Southern Rhodesia has assumed importance as the keystone on which both community development and the policy of soil conservation are centred.[4] The Land Settlement Scheme in Swaziland, extending to over 346,000 acres, is, as already explained, the result of a decision to purchase for occupation by the Swazi a part of the large area previously alienated to Europeans.[5] It will provide up to 1,800 arable holdings together with a large area of common pasture land. A scheme involving 3,000 acres at Kingolwira in the Eastern Province of Tanganyika received its first 25 settlers in 1936,[6] and, though the ideal peasant holdings then contemplated did not prove a success, something was learned from the scheme about the economics of smallholding production. At Urambo, on land transferred in 1955 from the Overseas Food Corporation to the Tanganyika Agricultural Corporation, an African Tenant Farmers' Scheme, adjacent to an experimental farm, has been established, while at Nachingwea selected African tenants partake under supervision in an experiment of mechanized farming.[7]

A Five-year Plan[8] evolved for the development of African agriculture

---

[1] See below, p. 991. [2] Colonial Reports, Nigeria, 1952, p. 43.
[3] Colonial Reports, Gold Coast, 1954, p. 60.
[4] See above, p. 766. [5] See above, pp. 698, 779.
[6] C. Leubuscher, Tanganyika Territory; a Study of Economic Policy under Mandate, 1944, p. 47.
[7] Overseas Food Corporation, Report and Accounts for 1954–55, pp. 33 ff., 159 ff.
[8] R. J. M. Swynnerton, A Plan to Intensify the Development of African Agriculture in Kenya, Nairobi, 1954.

in Kenya has a dual purpose in that it combines agricultural improvement according to modern principles of land usage with the resettlement of Africans displaced for security reasons during the Mau Mau emergency. The Plan is financed from a loan of £5 million from the United Kingdom, of which £1 million is allocated to the development of the coffee, tea, and sisal areas, and another £1 million to African District Councils for promoting the production of cash crops, especially coffee, pyrethrum, and pineapples. A further £1¾ million is allotted to irrigation, the provision of water supplies, and a hydraulic survey.[1]

At Anchau in Northern Nigeria, where 600 square miles had been cleared of tsetse fly, about 5,000 people had been moved and housed by 1948; this scheme is now affording a useful lesson in community development.[2] One of the most noteworthy of the schemes of resettlement necessitated by local over-population is that in the Kigezi District of Uganda, where over 16,500 people from the congested hill areas were resettled in the years 1947–50.[3] Their farming is not regulated in detail, but they have brought with them the practice of strip-cropping which had already been inculcated on their old lands. A small scheme at Usambara in Tanganyika is designed mainly to afford local experience in cultivating hill lands.

In Kenya the purpose of the Makueni resettlement project first adumbrated in 1938 was to relieve the pressure of population in the tribal lands of the Kamba. It entailed the clearance of over 400 square miles of dense and fly-infested bush, during the course of which a hundred elephants and nearly a thousand rhinoceroses had to be killed. By 1953 some 994 families had been settled upon holdings of 20 to 30 acres; the cost of resettlement was £230 a family. In Nigeria the Shendam and Jema'a schemes provide supervised holdings on the plains for the overflow of farmers from the congested Jos Plateau. In the first of these projects some 300 settlers from five different tribes have been successfully established. In each of the last three instances there has been some provision of mechanical aids to cultivation.

The Kontagora scheme in the Niger Province of Nigeria is on a different basis, since it is a test of measures of social and economic planning in an area where there is much empty land. Holdings are of 30 to 35 acres, and the emphasis is on teaching mixed farming and ploughing with oxen. A larger scheme, with a somewhat similar objective (the Niger Agricultural Project), was initiated in 1950 near Mokwa in the Northern Provinces of Nigeria; this is further referred to later in this chapter.[4]

It was usual in the past to speak of agricultural production in Africa

---

[1] *Colonial Development* (Colonial Development Corporation), Winter 1954, p. 34.
[2] See below, pp. 1191 ff.
[3] *N.A.*, Part I, p. 45.   [4] See below, p. 911.

as falling into two classes, suited respectively to 'peasant' and to 'plantation' forms of economy. The latter were characterized especially by the need for capital for planting crops of a type which might be slow to come into bearing, or by the necessity for an estate factory for processing the produce on the spot.[1] But during the first 40 years of the century the distinction became increasingly blurred by the encroachment of peasant producers on what had been regarded as the normal sphere of plantation production. Products such as coffee and rubber, long regarded as typical plantation crops, came to be produced by peasants in increasing volume, until only tea and sisal remained among the major crops as almost entirely plantation products. Even in this sphere Africans have now begun to encroach. The co-operative tea factory at Nyeri, in Kenya, was designed in association with European tea interests, and a peasant plantation of sisal at Machakos, also in Kenya, is managed by the local African District Council.[2]

The Administrations have had to face something of a dilemma. On the one hand, the contributions made to agriculture by mechanization or by the use of fertilizers have combined to give an increasing advantage to the farmer with skill and capital. On the other hand, social and political opinion has hardened against the alienation of further large tracts of land to capitalist undertakings. In the circumstances the Administrations have tended to give their support to two new developments, namely, farming by public corporations, and group farming by peasants under scientific advice or supervision.

One of the earliest examples of corporation farming is provided by the Cameroons Development Corporation, which was founded after the Second World War to take over the estates in the British Cameroons which had been originally established by German settlers.[3] The Corporation farms its land on ordinary plantation lines. Its policy, however, is to delegate progressively more responsibility to the people of the territory,[4] and agreements for the marketing of produce have been entered into with local co-operative farming associations.[5] In 1953 it was decided to institute a Research Section to be concerned with soil science, fertilizers, and plant pathology. A beginning has also been made with the laying-out of a tea plantation.

Of the various schemes undertaken by the Colonial Development Corporation of Great Britain the most enterprising are those which it has conducted directly through its own officers.[6] Schemes of direct farming

[1] A. Pim, *Colonial Agricultural Production*, 1946, pp. 4–12.
[2] Cmd. 9475, pp. 320–1.
[3] See above, p. 736. See also *N.A.*, Part III, p. 178.
[4] *Cameroons under United Kingdom Trusteeship, Report for the Year 1952*, Col, no. 299, p. 77.
[5] *Annual Report of the Cameroons Development Corporation, 1953*, pp. 5–6.
[6] *Colonial Development Corporation, Report and Accounts for 1954*, p. 7.

initiated by the Corporation include the growing of wattle in the Njombe District of Tanganyika, an extensive cattle ranch in Bechuanaland,[1] tung and tobacco estates in Nyasaland, and an irrigation scheme and the Usutu Forests Scheme in Swaziland.[2] It is early yet to assess the final prospects of any of these schemes, but so far the original plans have often proved too optimistic, and operations have had to be reduced accordingly. The scheme for production of tung oil in Nyasaland had a special interest, as it was an attempt to extend an industry that had hitherto existed on little more than an experimental scale. The area of the large-scale plantations on the Vipya Plateau was substantially reduced in 1952. By the beginning of 1956 it covered 4,200 acres only, but it was planned to add another 700 acres during 1956.[3] The future of this plantation is, however, rendered doubtful by movements that have occurred in the world price of tung.

Apart from the operations of these two major corporations several British Administrations have since the Second World War undertaken schemes on somewhat similar lines. In Uganda the Busoga Farms were designed largely to produce food for the growing industrial population around Jinja, and the management was vested in a Board appointed by the Government. The cost of clearing the land was, however, high[4] and by the end of 1953 the scheme showed an accumulated loss of £63,000. The Uganda Government has sponsored a tenancy system in Bunyoro, in partnership with the Bunyoro Agricultural Company, the Bunyoro African Local Government, and two commercial firms. The Nyasaland Maize Farms are Government food farms initiated in order to relieve local food shortage. The Northern Rhodesia Government undertook a pilot groundnut scheme on 1,400 acres at Mumbwa which, however, was not considered sufficiently fruitful to be continued.

In the same category are some of the pilot schemes undertaken by the Regional Production Development Boards of Nigeria.[5] In the Western Region these include the Ijebu farming projects with oil palms, citrus, and cacao; in the Eastern Region oil-palm estates in under-populated areas and the Obudu cattle ranch, to which cattle of the Montbéliard breed have been introduced from the French Cameroons. A common feature of nearly all these schemes is the experimental use of mechanized cultivation.

In non-British territories the two chief examples of corporation farming are to be found in French West Africa. A groundnut scheme in the Casamance area of Senegal is in the hands of the *Compagnie Générale des*

[1] See above, p. 890.
[2] See below, pp. 940, 981.
[3] *Colonial Development Corporation, Report and Accounts for 1955*, p. 46.
[4] Cmd. 9475, p. 327. *Report of the Agricultural Productivity Committee*, Uganda, 1954, p. 89.
[5] *Colonial Reports, Nigeria, 1952*, pp. 40 ff.

Oléagineux Tropicaux, in which the French Government holds a majority interest. Heavy tractors have been used for bush-clearing, and the scheme has other features suggestive of the East African groundnut scheme, though on much more cautious lines. Work was begun in 1949; the objective is reported to be an annual output of 40,000 tons of groundnuts from this and other schemes yet to be developed. At Richard-Toll, near the mouth of the Senegal river, a scheme for irrigated rice has been undertaken by the *Mission d'Aménagement du Sénégal*. This involves damming the Senegal river and irrigating a million acres for the production of cotton and rice by mechanical cultivation.[1]

'Group farming' is a term of convenience rather than of precision, for the cultivators engaged in undertakings of this type do not necessarily act as a collective group. Corporation farming normally operates with paid labour, much as does a plantation company; group farming aims either at settling independent cultivators in supervised groups, or providing group services (usually in the form of machinery) to farmers already in occupation of land. The modern development of agricultural machinery, too expensive for individual farmers, now puts the Administration into a position in which it becomes essential for it to take a lead in the provision of mechanized equipment if some of its major schemes of development are to bear fruit. That is especially the case where the development of the productive capacity of major irrigation schemes is involved, as has been shown, for example, in the operation of the Gezira scheme in the Sudan or the Niger Basin scheme in French West Africa.[2]

There are some interesting schemes of group farming on unirrigated land to be found in French Equatorial Africa. In 1949 some 2,150 acres in the Niari valley of the Middle Congo Province were tractor-ploughed and planted to rice by the Aubeville Agricultural Co-operative, and there is also some groundnut production on similar lines. In the Belgian Congo group farming is associated with the 'corridor' system which has already been described.[3] In Ruanda Urundi a resettlement scheme is in progress in the Southern Kivu Province. About 14,000 families, which it is hoped to increase to 30,000, have been assigned pasture and arable land.[4]

In the British dependencies the value of systems of group farming has been much canvassed in recent years and, as has already been shown, a number of experiments are being made. The Niger Agricultural Project at Mokwa in Nigeria was financed in equal shares by the Government of Nigeria and the Colonial Development Corporation, but the latter withdrew in 1954 and transferred its assets to the Northern Regional Government. The original project comprised an area of about 65,000

[1] See below, p. 1005.
[2] See below, pp. 1003 ff.
[3] See above, p. 904.
[4] *Civilisations*, vol. iii, no. 3, 1953, p. 392.

acres, of which at the beginning of 1955 some 12,000 acres had been wholly or partially cleared. The land is leased to peasant farmers. A three-year rotational course is followed in which a fundamental principle is that one-third of the holding shall always lie fallow. Besides being an experiment in group settlement the scheme has been a test of mechanization in cultivation, especially of oil seed,[1] but the future of the scheme is by no means assured.

The Gold Coast Agricultural Development Corporation has undertaken the Gonja Development Scheme for group farming. Settlers are to be placed on the mechanically cleared land in villages, each with a communal herd of cattle. In some other cases Governments have directly organized schemes of group farming. In the Nyanza Province of Kenya group farmers in Kericho and Nyanera have accepted some readjustment of their landholdings and housing sites, and have adopted the use of mechanical equipment. In the Bamenda–Cross River–Calabar scheme in Nigeria, designed to relieve the congestion of an over-populated area, difficulty was at one period experienced in getting settlers who would work their holdings according to the provisions of the scheme, which is based on a mixed oil-palm and subsistence land use. The procedure followed in the African Tenant Farming Scheme at Urambo and Nachingwea, already referred to,[2] is not unlike that at Mokwa. Clearing and stumping is carried out by manual labour, but ploughing and ridging by mechanical means, for which the tenant pays. All crops are sold by the manager, who, after the deduction of expenses and debts due from the tenant, returns the balance to him.[3]

Most of these schemes of group farming are still experimental, and it will need further experience to show to what extent they can effect a general improvement in the production of African agriculture.

AGRICULTURAL RESEARCH

Research in Great Britain

The expenditure of Government funds on agricultural research in the British Colonies is now the subject of advice tendered by a special body, the Committee for Colonial Agricultural, Animal Health, and Forestry Research, established in 1945 as part of the organization of the Colonial Research Council.[4] The Committee now has three sub-committees, on

---

[1] *Colonial Development*, Autumn 1954, p. 23.   [2] See above, p. 815.
[3] *Report of a Conference of Directors of Agriculture held at Wye College, Kent, September, 1953*, Misc. 519, unpublished.
[4] *Colonial Research Committee, First Annual Report 1943–44*, Cmd. 6535, 1944, p. 5. *Colonial Research, 1953–1954*, Cmd. 9303, 1954, which includes the annual reports of the bodies mentioned in the text.

soils, cocoa, and stored products. Some aspects of agricultural research are also served by the Colonial Products Research Council, established in 1942, the Colonial Insecticides, Fungicides, and Herbicides Committee (1947), the Tsetse Fly and Trypanosomiasis Committee (1943), and the Anti-Locust Research Centre (1946). These bodies advise on the expenditure of that part of the moneys provided under the Colonial Development and Welfare Acts[1] which is allocated to research.

The Royal Botanic Gardens at Kew and the British Museum of Natural History at South Kensington include the study of tropical crop plants among the subjects of their research. The Commonwealth Mycological Institute for the study of plant diseases is also situated at Kew; the Commonwealth Institute of Entomology is at the British Museum of Natural History. The principal centre for general agricultural research in Great Britain is the Rothamsted Experimental Station at Harpenden, where the Soil Science Bureau is stationed; soil science is also studied at the Soil Laboratory at Oxford and at the Macaulay Institute at Aberdeen.

Work on plant genetics for crops, other than herbage, is carried on by the Plant Breeding Institute of the Cambridge School of Agriculture, with which the Bureau of Plant Genetics (Crops) is associated; herbage plants are studied at the Welsh Plant Breeding Station and the Bureau of Plant Genetics (Herbage) at Aberystwyth. The work of the East Malling Research Station in Kent, the Fruit Production Bureau, and the Low Temperature Research Station at Cambridge has been of much importance in connexion with fruit production in South Africa. The Institute of Agricultural Parasitology at St. Albans specializes in the study of plant pests.

There is a Veterinary Research Laboratory at Weybridge, where the Bureau of Animal Health is also stationed. The world centre for research on foot-and-mouth disease at Pirbright, the Animal Health Trust centres, and the Animal Pathology Institute at Cambridge also provide for research. Animal nutrition is studied at the Rowett Research Institute at Aberdeen, and animal genetics at the Institute of the University of Edinburgh, where the Animal Genetics Bureau is established.

The Commonwealth Bureaux[2] publish abstracts of information on agricultural and veterinary research, while the Imperial Institute publishes in its *Journal* the results of research connected with the commercial development of agriculture. The British centre for training in tropical agriculture is the Imperial College at Trinidad, but there are lectureships in Colonial or Tropical Agriculture at the Universities of Oxford, Cambridge, and Edinburgh.

The Empire Cotton Growing Corporation, already referred to,[3] was

---

[1] See below, pp. 1601 ff.　　　　　　　　　　[2] Worthington, op. cit. pp. 308 ff.
[3] See above, p. 837. See also *Report of Empire Cotton Growing Corporation, 1921–1950*, 1951.

established in 1921. In its new headquarters at Namulonge in Uganda it maintains a staff of nine specialists. In Tanganyika it has stations at Ukiriguru in the Lake Province and at Ilonga in the Eastern Province; in Nyasaland it has a station at Domira Bay; in Nigeria it has a seed farm at Daudawa and a station for cotton breeding at Samaru.

The Union of South Africa

In South Africa the Faculty of Agriculture of the University of Stellenbosch was amalgamated in 1926 with the Elsenburg School of Agriculture in order to become the Stellenbosch–Elsenburg College of Agriculture. The Agricultural Research Institute at Pretoria was established in 1940 by incorporating the Faculty of Agriculture of the University of Pretoria (which still, however, retains its teaching identity) in the Government Department of Agriculture. A similar relationship between Government and University exists in the Natal Agricultural Research Institute. The University of the Witwatersrand has since 1932 developed the Frankenwald Estate as a station for pasture research. Pretoria University gives a five-year course in Veterinary Science and a four-year course in Agriculture. Of Government organizations the Veterinary Laboratories at Onderstepoort, founded in 1902, carry out a comprehensive programme of research on stock diseases and in all aspects of animal industry. Onderstepoort is now one of the best-equipped institutions of its kind in the world, and an especial feature of its work is the close touch which it maintains through its field organization with individual stock-breeders throughout the Union.[1]

The Department of Agriculture has a number of sections devoted to research of different types; its main centre is at Pretoria. Grass and pasture research, which involves problems of the highest importance in the Union,[2] is now concentrated on finger grasses, as being specially suited to most conditions. At Rustenburg varieties of tobacco are under trial, and experiments are made in flue-curing. Citrus investigations have been made at Nelspruit and Buffelspoort; there is a special station for pineapples at Bathurst, and viticultural research is conducted at the Paarl Station. The Low Temperature Research Laboratory at Cape Town studies improvements in the methods of storage of fruit for export. The Zebedelia Citrus Estate organizes its own research and, as already mentioned, the Sugar Association has its experimental station at Mount Edgcumbe.[3] Varieties of cane bred in Java and India, and which are resistant to mosaic disease, have been tested there. These varieties are now replacing the thin Uba cane on South African estates. A Wattle

---

[1] Worthington, op. cit. pp. 443–5. *O.T.S.A.*, *1950*, p. 910.
[2] See below, pp. 817, 872.   [3] See above, p. 863.

Research Institute at Pietermaritzburg operates under the University of Natal, with financial assistance from the industry.

Southern Rhodesia and the British Colonial Area

The Veterinary Research Station near Salisbury was founded in 1916, and there is a separate research station at Hillside for the study of trypanosomiasis. There is a separate Dairy Research Institute. An agricultural experimental station was founded at Salisbury in 1909, and later developed a branch at Hillside. Pasture research is carried out at two stations, Marandellas and Matopos. The Trelawney Tobacco Research Station, maintained by contributions from Government and the tobacco industry in equal amounts,[1] has done work on nematode pests, under the guidance of the Tobacco Research Board. The Sabi Experimental Station was established in 1951 to determine the policy to be followed in the development of irrigation in the Sabi area.[2]

In Northern Rhodesia agricultural and veterinary laboratories were opened in 1929 at Mazabuka (where there is now also a Veterinary School), but under a new programme of agricultural research a central station was established in 1951 at Mt. Makulu near Lusaka. There will be three subsidiary stations, one of which (Samfya near Lake Bangweulu) will serve an inter-departmental programme of research in agriculture, forestry, and fisheries. There is a tobacco station at Mochipapa in the Southern Province. In Nyasaland the agricultural research station at Lilongwe carries out work on tobacco and hybrid maize, and there are subsidiary stations for tea at Malange and for tung at Cholo. The Veterinary Department has a research laboratory at Mpemba and three livestock improvement centres provided by a grant made under the Colonial Development and Welfare Act.

In the territories of the East African High Commission research has been co-ordinated in the sense that there are now certain central institutions dealing with basic research, leaving the problems of applied research or field study to be dealt with by the territorial institutions with which they are linked. The oldest station for 'long-term' agricultural research is at Amani in Tanganyika, which was established in 1902 by the German Administration. Here excellent work was done on soil surveys and such problems as the breeding of cassava resistant to virus disease, or the physiology of the coffee plant.[3] Amani has now become a sub-station of the East African Agriculture and Forestry Research Organization whose headquarters was established in 1948 at Muguga near Nairobi, adjacent

---

[1] The Tobacco Research Act no. 24 of 1935.

[2] See below, p. 984.

[3] H. H. Storey, *Basic Research in Agriculture, A Brief History of Research at Amani, 1928–1947*, 1951.

to those of the sister East African Veterinary Research Organization. Both have been designed to undertake basic research in order to support the applied research of the territorial departments in Tanganyika, Kenya, and Uganda. In the same way the East African Tsetse and Trypanosomiasis Research and Reclamation Organization, with headquarters now situated at Sukulu (Tororo) in Uganda, provides backing to the territorial institutions, of which the oldest is the Tsetse Research Organization at Shinyanga in Tanganyika.

The Tanganyika Agricultural Department has its research headquarters at Morogoro. A research station for *arabica* coffee was opened in 1933 at Lyamungu. It was designed to serve all the East African territories,[1] but Kenya and Uganda have actually done most of their own work on this crop. The Veterinary Department has an experimental farm at Mpwapwa, where pasture research has been carried out. In addition to the sisal experimental station at Mlingano, the East African sisal producers have jointly financed a scheme of consumption research which is being carried out from the linen industry research station at Lambeg in Ireland.

In Kenya Colony the main centre for local agricultural research is the Scott Agricultural Laboratory at Kabete, which was first started as an experimental farm in 1907. There is a separate plant-breeding station at Njoro. Coffee has been the subject of extensive research which has been successful in indicating measures for the control of pests, particularly mealy bug and *Antestia lineaticollis*. The types of wheat grown in Kenya have been evolved at the plant-breeding station at Njoro, and hybrid maize and sorghum are now included in the breeding programme. Pyrethrum is studied at a special station at Molo, and sisal at the high-level sisal research station at Thika.

Departmental veterinary research, in addition to the study of rinderpest inoculants, has also been concerned with tsetse research, in co-operation with the East African Research Organization. A Government stock farm was opened at Naivasha in 1935 for work upon nutritional and genetic problems. Breeding experiments are also carried out; a central artificial insemination station for the farming areas has been opened at Kabete.

Uganda has an agricultural laboratory at Kawanda with a subsidiary at Serere. These two stations have taken over for their respective areas the cotton-breeding work begun at Katunguru in 1911. At Namulonge is the central cotton research station of the Empire Cotton Growing Corporation.[2] At Kawanda strains of coffee selected from the indigenous *nganda* type have been put into cultivation through Government nurseries. The veterinary laboratory at Old Entebbe is carrying out experiments on

---

[1] A. Pim, *Report on the Financial Position and System of Taxation in Kenya*, Col. no. 116, 1936.

[2] See above, p. 837; also *Background to Uganda*, no. 129, December 1955.

the effect of drugs used against trypanosomiasis. The stock farm at Mbarara carries out studies of the indigenous types of sheep.

West Africa has three regional research centres, all of which originally started as departmental stations but now serve all the four British West African territories. The West African Institute for Oil Palm Research has a study area of 4,000 acres near Benin and a sub-station in Calabar Province. The West African Cocoa Research Institute is at Tafo in the Gold Coast; it is at present preoccupied with the search for methods of controlling swollen shoot disease other than by cutting out infected trees,[1] but progress has also been made in vegetative propagation for high-yielding strains of cacao. The Rice Research Station at Rokupr in Sierra Leone is on a smaller scale. The West African Institute for Trypanoso-miasis Research, which also started as a regional centre of research, has a laboratory near the veterinary headquarters at Vom in Nigeria and an entomological section at Kaduna.

In Nigeria the Agricultural Department has laboratories at Ibadan for the southern areas and Samaru for the northern. The former has demon-strated the value of green manuring on some local soil types, and the latter has shown the value of farmyard manure and super-phosphate fertilizer on northern soils. A cocoa survey team, formed to study the swollen shoot disease, engaged twelve temporary disease-control officers from the United Kingdom in 1949, but (as also in the Gold Coast) political obstacles have hampered the cutting out campaign. A stock farm at Shika in the Northern Provinces has paid special attention to the breeding of cattle for mixed farming. The veterinary laboratories at Vom on the Jos Plateau are primarily concerned with disease control.

In the Gold Coast the central agricultural laboratories are at Accra; the construction of an Ashanti central agricultural station commenced in 1951. Altogether there are 14 central and district stations, including Kpeve in Togoland. In the Colony area Aiyinasi concentrates on rice and oil palms, Princess Plantation on coconut selection work, and Pokoase on mechanization. A comprehensive soil survey is in progress under a Soil Survey Division set up in 1948. Important veterinary research and study of tsetse clearance has been carried out at the Veterinary Institute at Pong-Tamale in the Northern Territories.

In Sierra Leone the laboratories are at Njala. Research into oil palms has been carried out at Masanki plantation. As has been shown, much work has been done on the reclamation of saline and swampy soils, particularly for rice-growing in riverain areas.[2] In Gambia an experi-mental station is now being developed at Masembe in the central division. A rust research unit is experimenting with varieties of maize introduced from Mexico.

[1] See above, p. 828.   [2] See above, p. 860.

The French Territories

In France the *Musée National d'Histoire Naturelle* has a section devoted to tropical agriculture, and the *École Supérieure d'Application d'Agriculture Tropicale*, which provides for the training of Colonial Agricultural Officers, is expected to develop eventually as a centre for research. Both institutions are situated in Paris. The organization of research in the French African Colonies was at an early period served by the creation of local branches of the *Institut Pasteur* at Paris, as for example the laboratories established at St. Louis in 1896, at Brazzaville in 1910, and Dakar in 1913.[1] Between 1918 and 1930 a series of institutions were created for dealing with special subjects of study, such as those at Bingerville (Ivory Coast), M'Bambey (Senegal), and N'Kongsamba (Cameroons). There was, however, no definite effort to co-ordinate the work of research, and recommendations on the subject were made to the Ministry by a conference of scientists in 1931 and by the Congress which followed the International Exhibition at Paris in 1937.

It was largely as the result of these representations that a *Décret* of October 1943 created the *Office de la Recherche Scientifique Coloniale*, designed primarily to advise the Ministry on the co-ordination of the work of different Colonial research institutions, but also to create a staff of research workers available for work in them.[2] So far as agricultural and veterinary research is concerned, the *chercheurs* for whom provision is thus made receive a two-year post-graduate course, of which the first year is spent at the Institute at Bondy near Paris, and the second at the sister Institute of Adiopodoumé near Abidjan in the Ivory Coast, where work began in 1946. This is now becoming an important centre of work, devoted to both the education of the specialist *chercheurs* and the investigation of the agricultural problems of the 'wet tropics'.[3]

While research of a fundamental or 'long-term' type is, as before, largely organized by visits to the Colonies from specialists of French metropolitan institutions, recent developments have equipped the dependencies with a series of local institutions devoted mainly to field work and 'applied' studies. The most important centre of this type in French West Africa is that maintained since 1932 by the *Office du Niger* at Ségou in connexion with the Niger Basin irrigation schemes, where the staff includes agricultural chemists, an entomologist, and plant-breeders and plant pathologists.[4] There are also agricultural stations at M'Bambey in Senegal, Kindia and Kankan in Guinea, La Mé, Bingerville, and Gagnoa in the Ivory Coast, and Pobé, Niaouli, and Ina in Dahomey. Cacao is studied at Bingerville and Gagnoa, banana cultivation at Gagnoa, rice

---

[1] *Enc. A.O.F.*, vol. i, pp. 326–32.   [2] O.R.S.O.M. See below, p. 1604.
[3] W. V. Blewett, in *J.R.S.A.*, August 1950, p. 795.
[4] See below, p. 1003. See also *Enc. A.O.F.*, vol. i, p. 331.

selection at Kankan, and oil-palm selection at La Mé and Pobé. M'Bambey is a centre for research on groundnuts.[1]

The principal animal-husbandry station is at Sotuba in the French Sudan; in this Colony there are also three minor stations for merino sheep, *Karakul* sheep, and goats, situated at El-Ouladji, Nioro, and Nara. In the Ivory Coast there are stations at Bouaké and Koroko; in Dahomey the Ina station has a veterinary branch, and Mauretania has an experimental sheep farm at Maderdra. The headquarters of research on animal diseases is at Bamako in the French Sudan, which co-operates with the *Institut Pasteur* laboratory at Kindia.

Three developments of general importance have taken place in Senegal since 1945. The agricultural service has a large experimental block for mechanized farming at Kaffrine. The *Mission d'Aménagement du Sénégal* has started irrigated rice-growing at Richard-Toll, near the mouth of the Senegal River, and has now handed over the experimental part of its area to the Agricultural Service. The *Compagnie Générale des Oléagineux Tropicaux* maintains its own research station on the Casamance groundnut scheme.

French Equatorial Africa has four cotton-selection stations and a small coffee experimental station. In the Cameroons cacao and *robusta* coffee selection work is done at Ebolowa,[2] and a station at Dschang specializes in *arabica* coffee. At Dschang there is also an experimental farm which concentrates on the breeding of small stock and poultry.

The Belgian Congo

In Belgium the State Botanical Garden at Brussels has a large collection of tropical plants; the Botanical Department of the *Musée du Congo Belge* at Tervueren was merged with it in 1934. The University of Louvain has an institute for research in soil science, and since 1931 has organized its own research centres in the Belgian Congo for the purpose of improving African agricultural methods. This organization is known as the Cadulac (*Centres Agronomiques de l'Université de Louvain au Congo*). Both agricultural and veterinary research is carried out by the *Institut National pour l'Étude Agronomique du Congo Belge* (I.N.E.A.C.), established in 1933.

The principal experimental stations of the I.N.E.A.C. include one at Yangambi, situated on the Congo River, about 100 miles west of Stanleyville. Here cultural methods for rubber, oil palms, coffee, and African food crops are studied.[3] Other stations are at Gazi, where the work is concentrated on rubber and cacao; at Lula, in connexion with *robusta* coffee; and at Barumba, which has given special attention to the regeneration

---

[1] M. Sagout, 'Exposés des travaux de sélection généalogique de l'arachide et des résultats obtenus à la station expérimentale de M'Bambey', *Bulletin mensuel de l'Agence économique de l'A.O.F.*, 1937, pp. 351–4.   [2] *Enc. C.-T.*, pp. 8, 141.   [3] See below, p. 1606.

of exhausted soils and has plantations of oil palms and cacao. Cotton stations at Bambesa and Gandajika study the control of pests in addition to selection work. Only seed approved by I.N.E.A.C. is distributed to African cultivators.

Much of the investigation carried out in the Belgian Congo has been devoted to the practical task of finding an alternative to the system of shifting cultivation. Particular attention has in this connexion been paid to the development of the 'corridor' system of cultivation, to which some reference is made earlier in this chapter.[1] This is of particular interest in a forest area of light soil, such as that in the neighbourhood of Yangambi; this allows of adequate experiment to be made in the possibilities of combining the growth of food crops with the process of re-afforestation. The study at Yangambi is combined with investigations into the use of artificial fertilizers.

The principal work of the stock farm at Nioka, near Lake Albert, is the improvement of indigenous cattle in connexion with mixed farming; it also carries out research on food crops and coffee.

The Portuguese Territories and Liberia

In Portuguese East Africa a central laboratory for veterinary pathology at Lourenço Marques is conducted in connexion with an experimental farm and a number of subsidiary farms in the principal cattle areas. Angola has a veterinary laboratory in the highlands and stock farms in the Ganda, Humpata, Cuanhama, and Quilengues Districts. With the exception of Humpata, which specializes in the production of wool, milk, and working beasts, these are devoted mainly to the breeding of cattle and sheep for export.

In Liberia the Firestone Plantations Research Laboratory has made experiments with livestock and fruit. A Government-sponsored laboratory was opened in 1953 and the Booker Washington Institute at Kakata undertakes research in crops and the improvement of stock.

Ecological and Land-use Surveys

A special type of field research which has been developed in some British territories is the ecological survey. In the case of Northern Rhodesia the survey was carried out by an ecologist in conjunction with officers of the Agricultural Service. It consisted of an intensive examination of soil conditions, water supplies, population density, existing systems of agriculture, and the possibilities of the development of cash crops.[2] A

---

[1] See above, p. 904.

[2] C. G. Trapnell and J. N. Clothier, *The Soils, Vegetation and Agricultural Systems of North Western Rhodesia: Report of the Ecological Survey*, 1937. C. G. Trapnell, *The Soils, Vegetation and Agriculture of North Eastern Rhodesia: Report of the Ecological Survey*, 1943.

vegetation-types map of Tanganyika has been prepared by a geographer,[1] and one of the natural grasslands of Kenya by pasture research officers.[2] In Uganda the so-called *mutala* surveys were organized by a committee appointed in 1935. *Mutala* is the name for the hill slopes divided by swampy valleys on which the villages and gardens stand. Nineteen surveys have been published, and have provided useful information as to the pressure of population on the land.

In the Gold Coast a land-use survey is now being combined with the soil survey which it is hoped to complete by 1961. It includes a survey of the Kpong irrigation area, the Upper Tako basin, and the Kumasi region.

A vegetation map of Angola was published in 1939.

PART II. FISHERIES

In some of the less-advanced regions of the world fisheries appear to offer relatively cheap opportunities for development compared with agriculture. The processes of preparing the soil, seeding, and tending are dispensed with, so that the whole effort can be concentrated on catching or 'cropping' fish. As an article of diet fish provides animal protein and certain other ingredients which are often deficient in the food of Africans, and presents them in a form most easily assimilable by the human body. Fisheries can be divided in the first place into those of the seas and those of inland waters; a further division of both categories may be made into natural fisheries—which depend on the fertility of the oceans, lakes, and rivers—and fish-farming in waters made artificially for the purpose.

The marine fisheries of tropical Africa are in general less abundant than those farther north or south, the waters being rich in variety of fish but relatively poor in quantity of the economic kinds. As a further generalization, the oceans bordering the western seaboard are richer than those of the east. The prevalent seasonal winds produce surface currents from east to west over the great oceans of the inter-tropical belt with generally an upwelling, along the western seaboards, of deep water which is comparatively productive. Thus, in the Indian Ocean, by the time the surface water has reached the East African coast its capacity for maintenance of life is partly exhausted. It happens that the purity of sea-water, caused by this exhaustion of its nutrients, favours the life of reef-building corals, so that the abundance of marine life around coral

---

[1] C. Gillman, 'A Vegetation-Types Map of Tanganyika', *Geographical Review*, vol. xxxix, no. 1, 1949, p. 7.
[2] D. C. Edwards and A. V. Bogdan, *Important Grassland Plants of Kenya*, 1951.

reefs is more noticeable along the eastern seaboard than the western, and may give a deceptive appearance concerning the potentiality of economic fisheries. Much remains to be learned about the basic factors of oceanography which provide the background for the development of fisheries. One of the least-known areas is that of the Mozambique Channel and the oceans immediately to the north, and it is significant that this is the region where coelacanth fishes have recently been discovered, after they had been thought to have been extinct for some 300 million years.

Outside the inter-tropical belt, that is, in the seas surrounding the coasts of the Union of South Africa, South-West Africa, and parts of Mozambique, the oceanic conditions are more favourable for the large-scale production of fish. The Union of South Africa indeed has fisheries of high economic importance. There is an example in the well-known Cape crawfish, for the processing of which numerous factories have been established. There are, moreover, substantial areas of shallower water within reach of the fishing ports of the Union, notably the Agulhas Bank. This has permitted the development of trawling on a large scale from the neighbourhood of Walvis Bay in the west, around the Cape, and up the east coast as far as Durban. Farther north in the Natal waters the nature of the bottom generally precludes trawling, but line-fishing is practised on a substantial scale. In order to conduct research on these fisheries a Division of Fisheries was established by the Union Government, and recently a Fishing Industry Research Association has been established at Cape Town. This has greatly assisted the industry, more particularly in the processing and marketing of fish.

In other countries the establishment of marine research institutes did not start so early, but there is now a series of centres which, when fully equipped, should be adequate for nearly all the exploratory work required. Thus in the British territories there is an East African Marine Fisheries Research Organization centred at Zanzibar. A West African Fisheries Research Organization has been based on Freetown in Sierra Leone, with a sea-going research vessel capable of operating from Gambia in the north to the waters off the Niger delta in the east. Both of these have been established by grants made since the Second World War under the Colonial Development and Welfare Acts.[1] With few exceptions, each territorial Government has also established its own group of fishery officers.

The system in the French territories is somewhat similar. Fisheries based on Port Étienne north of Dakar were developed many years ago; those along the other coasts as far as the Belgian Congo border have received increased attention during recent years. The *Institut Français d'Afrique Noire* has studied some of the scientific problems in the waters

[1] *Colonial Research, 1952–1953*, Cmd. 8971, 1953, pp. 254 ff.

of French West Africa and has a marine laboratory on the island of Gorée off Dakar, and another at Abidjan, concerned especially with the sea-water lagoons of the Ivory Coast. The *Institut d'Études Centrafricaines* has recently established a fishery research centre at Pointe Noire to serve the needs of French Equatorial Africa. The *Institut de Recherche Scientifique de Madagascar* has a laboratory at Nosy Bé near the northern end of Madagascar; it is this institute which has been responsible for most of the existing knowledge concerning coelacanth fishes.

The Belgian Congo seaboard is limited in extent, but the possibility of establishing marine fisheries has been examined by a specially equipped expedition working off the coast. The Portuguese territories have fisheries of long standing. A small marine laboratory has been built on an island off Lourenço Marques, with the co-operation of the Witwatersrand University, whose staff uses it as a field station. Angola has conducted a fully equipped fishery and oceanographical survey.

The possibilities of marine fish-farming in tropical Africa, particularly where mangrove swamps predominate, has begun to attract attention in recent years. The pattern for this development may be seen in the Far East, where marine fish farms around Java and Sumatra produce large crops of fish. A few fishponds have been built for experimental purposes by private enterprise in some of the mangrove swamps along the Tanganyika coast.

Turning to the fisheries of inland waters, we find that their total production is perhaps less than that of the ocean fisheries, but, being closer to the major centres of population, they have an importance out of proportion to their size. The extent of inland waters is considerable; they amount indeed to more than 50,000 square miles in the British territories alone. The productive capacity of fresh water is usually higher than that of the sea, particularly in extensive shallow-water lakes, where conditions may approximate to those of fish ponds. It has been stated that 20,000 tons of fish were landed in Uganda in 1954, the industry giving employment to 15,000 Africans. A fishery recently opened in Lake George in Uganda produces an average of 35 tons per square mile per annum. A more extreme case is that of Lake Nakivali in the same country, where a fishery was created by introducing appropriate fishes. It now produces 60 tons per square mile per annum. Lake Victoria, by contrast, produces only about 1 ton per square mile on average of its whole area. The catch is in this case from a relatively small part of the lake, accessible to canoes. Such figures may be compared with 4 tons per square mile per annum, which is the average for the North Sea, where fishery is exploited to the maximum by the most modern methods.

In Africa attention to the inland fisheries originated with the interest taken in sporting fish, and even today the organization of the fishery administration in the Union devotes much of its attention to the problems of introduced trout. In the British territories a number of surveys of indigenous fishery resources had been conducted before the Second World War, and since the war an East African Fisheries Research Organization has been established at Jinja on the northern shore of Lake Victoria. This has been followed by a similar unit for Northern Rhodesia and Nyasaland, at present working on Lake Nyasa. Several of the other territorial Governments have been active independently and have appointed officers for fishery research. This applies to Nigeria and the Gold Coast as well as to the East and Central African territories. The French also have been concerned with their rivers and lakes and have established a research centre on the upper Niger, under the *Institut Français d'Afrique Noire*.

Interesting new possibilities for inland fisheries are arising in connexion with major hydroelectric schemes. Thus plans for the Volta River Project in the Gold Coast[1] indicate the creation of a lake of 2,500 square miles, which might, at a conservative estimate, produce an annual crop of about 15,000 tons of fish, more than the present total fish production of the Gold Coast. A similar possibility may arise in connexion with the Kariba Gorge hydroelectric scheme on the Zambezi River.[2]

The demand for fish in accessible waters is sometimes greater than the natural productivity can stand, and overfishing has become a local problem. In the Kavirondo Gulf of Lake Victoria, the return of fish per unit effort, which was about 30 fish per net per night early in the century, fell to five in 1927 and is now only about two. This indicates the need for a progressive system of Government control if these natural resources are to be maintained.

There has since the Second World War been a development of great importance in the form of the adaptation to African conditions of the fish-farming techniques which have been worked out during many centuries in parts of Europe and the Far East. In this the Belgian authorities have been prominent and have undertaken a campaign for establishing fish farms in every Province of the Belgian Congo. The number of fish ponds had by 1952 reached 18,000, covering an area of about 3,750 acres. This industry is based on a species of *Tilapia*, a genus of fish which has proved itself to be remarkably adaptable under conditions of domestication. Very large crops can be obtained, amounting to a ton or more of fish per annum per acre of water. Fish farming raises problems in relation both to bilharziasis and malaria, but there is no reason to suppose that these questions cannot be solved. Experimental fish farms are now established in nearly every British territory and in several of the French territories.

The fisheries of Africa, both marine and inland, have a considerable

[1] See below, p. 1001.   [2] See below, p. 966.

potential value when the continent's food supply is considered, and there is clearly much scope for developing the natural fisheries to produce a maximum sustained yield. There is, however, some danger of over-optimism when calculating the possible returns. The records of the Colonial Development Corporation, for example, show that a substantial capital investment on fishery development in the Seychelles Islands and a smaller investment in a fishery on Lake Nyasa was lost because the return per unit effort on a commercial scale proved to be materially less than that calculated from experimental trials. The factors limiting development today include the inadequacy of scientific and technical knowledge, but perhaps more important are the inevitable delays in applying modern technology to an old indigenous industry and introducing improved methods of marketing.

Inter-African co-operation concerning the problems of inland fisheries has been arranged at an Anglo-Belgian Fishery Conference held in 1949 at Elisabethville, followed by another held in 1952 at Entebbe, under the auspices of the Scientific Council for Africa South of the Sahara. Similar conferences are likely to be arranged by the Scientific Council during the next few years.[1]

PART III. NATIONAL PARKS AND GAME
RESERVES

The profusion of wild animal life has from the first played a prominent part in the ecology of Africa. At an early stage of African history the subsistence readily provided by wild game must have determined the wide dispersal through Central and Southern Africa of the aboriginal 'brown' peoples, of whom the survivors, the Bushmen of South-West Africa and the Kalahari wastes, still live almost entirely on the flesh of wild animals. There can be little doubt that the prevalence of game influenced the direction taken by the incursion of the Nilotic tribes into East Africa, and also decided the course of the movement which brought the Southern Bantu into the areas which they now occupy. It must again have been in some part responsible for the traditional preference shown in many of these areas for the nomadic and pastoral life as compared with the more settled life of agriculture.

At a later date the great rinderpest epizootic of 1896,[2] which was conveyed from the wild fauna to domestic animals, had reactions of great importance on the tribal history of peoples living as far apart as the Masai of Kenya and the Matabele of Southern Rhodesia. The relative abun-

---

[1] See below, p. 1611.
[2] Worthington, op. cit. pp. 226, 271.

dance of wild fauna is no longer a factor of the same importance in the economic life of Africa, but it is still of some considerable significance. There are many areas, and particularly those in which the prevalence of the tsetse fly precludes the keeping of cattle, where game meat is regarded as a necessary addition to diet.[1] From another standpoint also the existence of the wild fauna has a special significance, since it provides the health and veterinary services with one of their most difficult problems owing to the part played by wild animals as carriers of human and animal disease.

The question of the survival of wild fauna has of late years received much attention from scientists and others who are interested in the protection of fauna generally or in the preservation of certain of the rarer species from destruction. A century ago the reports of hunters and explorers seemed to suggest that the stock of wild animals was practically inexhaustible.[2] A half century later, however, it was estimated that their number had been reduced by as much as 75 per cent., and during recent years a number of species have, according to some observers, been reduced to 10 per cent. of the number which existed in the time of Dr. Livingstone. This has been partly due to the use by Europeans of the modern high-velocity rifle, but the main factor has been the use of firearms, from an early date, by Africans. The earlier methods of hunting by game-drives did no doubt result in some cases in wholesale slaughter, but the drives were carried out during certain seasons only. The weapons used were primitive, in addition to which tribal warfare in the past denied access to considerable areas which virtually became game reserves.

It is reasonable to conclude, therefore, that earlier methods of hunting were not so wasteful to game life as the type of hunting which now takes place by Natives armed with muzzle-loading or other guns. There has been a great difference in the practice observed by different Governments in respect of the sale of firearms to Africans; it may, for example, be recalled that the sale of guns was at one period encouraged as an inducement to workers to come forward for employment on the Kimberley diamond field.[3]

Various Colonial Administrations began at a relatively early date to recognize the need for measures restricting the indiscriminate destruction of wild animals. The Transvaal Republic passed a law on the subject as early as 1846, and the scope of this measure was enlarged in 1858. In 1870 it appointed a number of Game Rangers, and in 1898 President Kruger passed orders establishing a Game Reserve (the Sabie Reserve) in the Eastern Transvaal. Before the end of the century a number of other

[1] *Report on a Faunal Survey of Northern Rhodesia*, 1934. P. Offerman, 'Le Gibier dans l'économie rurale de la colonie', *Économie rurale indigène au Congo Belge*, Brussels, 1952.

[2] See, however, on this point, D. Foster-Vesey-FitzGerald in *Oryx* (Journal of the Fauna Preservation Society), August 1954, p. 286.

[3] G. Tylden, *The Rise of the Basuto*, 1950, p. 117.

Governments had made regulations for the protection of fauna,[1] but the value of legislation of this type, which ran strongly counter to African custom, was admittedly impaired by the lack of any machinery for making it effective.

In 1900 a number of the Governments accepted a proposal made by Great Britain for a conference to be held in London in order to discuss measures for the preservation of various forms of animal life in Africa 'which are either useful to man or harmless'. Those who attended the Conference were undoubtedly influenced by the evidence of the virtual extermination of the American bison, which had existed a few decades earlier in almost unbelievable numbers. They drew up four schedules of animals deserving protection in various degrees, and for the rest they agreed on the desirability of establishing a system of licences for the shooting of game and also accepted the need for imposing closed seasons for hunting. But, more important, they advocated the establishment of 'Game Reserves of sufficient area to provide for the maintenance of wild animals throughout the year as regards food, water and, if possible, salt'.

Though the Convention agreed by the Conference was not ratified by the Governments concerned, its terms were generally accepted as a guide for action. A number of the Administrations in East and Central Africa instituted Game Departments, Kenya being the first to take this step. Besides dealing with the observance of regulations designed for the protection of game, these Departments have exercised an important function in reducing the number of game responsible for depredations on crops of the African peoples. Thus the Game Department of Uganda was obliged to destroy in one year (1935) no less than 1,546 elephants, and in 1952 the destruction of 477 was noted as the lowest number ever recorded. There are other instances where the extensive destruction of animals has been necessary. The clearance of bush for the African settlement at Makueni in the Machakos district of Kenya involved the killing of nearly a thousand rhinoceroses,[2] and from 150 to 200 elephants are killed monthly in the neighbourhood of the Gorongoza National Park in Mozambique.[3] In an effort to protect the sisal plantations in Kenya from the depredations of elephants the Game Warden has tried in turn shooting, electric fencing, and the use of chemicals alleged to be repellent to animals. But all these devices have failed to repel the intruding herds.[4]

In the Belgian Congo the operations of the *Section Chasse et Pêche*[5] (which

---

[1] C. W. Hobley, 'The London Convention of 1930', *Journal of the Society for the Preservation of the Fauna of the Empire*, no. 20, 1933, pp. 33–49.   [2] See above, p. 908.

[3] *Hunting in Mozambique* (a monograph presented by the Mozambique Hunting Committee), 1952, p. 43.

[4] Report of the Director of National Parks, Kenya, quoted in *East Africa and Rhodesia*, 21 April 1955.

[5] *Rapport sur l'administration de la colonie du Congo Belge, 1952*, p. 277.

in 1952 employed 13 permanent and four temporary European officers)
have also resulted in the destruction of considerable numbers of game,
with the object of protecting crops. The measures taken in West Africa
do not involve so wide a range of operations. The French West African
territories have an *Inspecteur Général des Chasses*, but have not a separate
cadre of Game Wardens. In Nigeria and the Gold Coast also the application of the laws relating to wild fauna has been left to the local Administrative Officers.

Not only, however, have circumstances made it difficult to give full
effect to laws passed for regulating the hunting of game, but it is inevitable that there should from the first have prevailed some conflict of view
between those who have been interested in the preservation of wild fauna
and those who have claimed prior consideration for the agricultural and
pastoral production of the African population. A Pan-African Conference
held in Pretoria in 1929 and the International Conference held in London
in 1933 discussed the problem of game protection at some length, and
saw the solution largely in the extension of the system of Game Reserves,
on the lines advocated by the Conference of 1900, and in the establishment of National Parks which would serve these purposes, as well as
others. This conclusion was subsequently reaffirmed in a further Conference held in London in 1938.[1]

The conception of the National Park has spread from the United States,
where the first of such Parks—the Yellowstone National Park—was
created in 1872 at a time when bison were on the point of being exterminated. A National Parks Service was set up by Congress in 1916. The
characteristic feature of the National Park is that it is normally established
by legislation and that its boundaries and inviolate character can consequently be modified only by legislative action. The establishment of a
Game Reserve on the other hand has usually been a purely administrative
act.[2] It need not be said that the purposes of a National Park may extend
beyond the preservation of fauna or flora, and there are several instances
in Africa of National Parks being created for other reasons, as, for example,
the Zimbabwe National Park in Southern Rhodesia or the Royal Gedi
and the Royal Olorgesailie National Parks of Kenya, which are mainly
of archaeological interest.[3] But the protection given to fauna in the
National Parks is normally complete, and in Africa in particular this has
been accepted as one of their more important functions.

The number of Game Reserves increased considerably between 1900
and 1933, but by the latter year the only National Parks which had been

[1] Treasury Publication, Code no. 63–87, May 1938.

[2] J. Huxley, *Africa View*, 1936, pp. 233–4.

[3] *Year Book and Guide to East Africa, 1953*, p. 63. For the scientific value of National Parks, see
Worthington, op. cit. pp. 176, 217. *Proceedings of the African Regional Scientific Conference*, vol. ii,
Johannesburg, 1949, p. 216. Huxley, op. cit. p. 358.

established as such were the *Parc National Albert* in the Belgian Congo (1925) and the Kruger National Park in the Union of South Africa (1926), which was a development of President Kruger's Sabie Game Reserve. The Nairobi National Park was proclaimed in 1946, and recently the Bunyoro and Gulu Game Reserves have been added to the Murchison Falls National Park, where there are some 2,000 to 3,000 elephants. In Tanganyika the former Game Reserve in the Serengeti Plains has been declared a National Park. There will be found at the end of this section a table giving the areas at present set aside either as National Parks or Game Reserves. No distinction can be drawn between them for the present purpose, as the classification to be adopted is in some territories still under consideration.

There is, moreover, no accepted standard by which it is possible to discriminate between the two categories. The Kruger National Park[1] (roughly 8,000 square miles in extent) is administered by an organization which ensures the complete protection of game. It is visited annually by 35,000 to 40,000 visitors. On the other hand, the Kalahari National Park (roughly 3,729 square miles) in the Cape Province of the Union is a National Park in name only, and is indeed inadequately organized even as a Game Reserve. The *Parc National Albert* (roughly 1,562 square miles) does not receive the same number of visitors as the Kruger Park, but it is administered by an expert staff and is pre-eminent in Africa for its scenic and structural variety and beauty.[2] Both to the north and south of Lake Edward it is contiguous to the Queen Elizabeth National Park in Uganda, and the value of both parks as agencies for the preservation of fauna is enhanced by this fact.

The *Parc National Albert* is controlled by an Administrative Commission which contains representatives of a number of other countries, and the studies of which it has been the subject, made under the auspices of the *Institut des Parcs Nationaux du Congo Belge* and the *Fondation pour Favoriser l'Étude Scientifique des Parcs Nationaux du Congo Belge,* have made a valuable contribution to zoological and botanical science. The Belgian Congo and Ruanda Urundi have four other National Parks under the same system of control. Although the station established at Gangala na Bodio for the domestication of elephants is situated outside the Garamba National Park, the elephants are captured within it. Their capture seems incompatible with the purposes of a National Park.[3]

---

[1] For details regarding the Kruger National Park and other National Parks and Reserves in the Union, see *O.Y.S.A., 1950,* pp. 42 ff.

[2] For the National Parks and Reserves in the Belgian Congo and Ruanda Urundi, see the *Rapport quinquennal de l'Institut des Parcs Nationaux du Congo Belge,* Brussels, 1941 and *The National Parks of the Belgian Congo,* Brussels, 1949. See also Huxley, op. cit. p. 366, and H.-G. Maurice, *Parle à la terre,* 1946.

[3] H. Hediger, 'La Capture des éléphants', in *Bull. I.R.C.B.,* vol. xxi, no. 1, 1950, p. 223.

The Kafue National Park in Northern Rhodesia, which was established in 1953, rivals the Kruger Park in the extent of its area (8,650 square miles) and the range of its fauna. It is under the control of the Federal Parliament.[1]

In French West Africa there was in 1952 one National Park, known as the *Parc National de W*, but it had by that year been only provisionally delimited.[2] There are a number of forest areas (roughly 2,344 square miles in extent) which have been classed as Game Reserves, but, with the exception of the *Réserve des Monts Nimbas*, these are admittedly treated only as 'partial Reserves'. In French Equatorial Africa there existed in 1950 the National Parks of St. Floris and Bamingui in Oubangui and the *Parc d'Odzala* in the Middle Congo Province. There was a Game Reserve at Vassaka Bolo in Oubangui, and the establishment of other Game Reserves is being considered.[3] In Angola there are seven areas described as Game Reserves, but in some of them the restriction on hunting applies only to certain species.[4] Of the areas classed as Reserves in Mozambique, only the Gorongoza National Park (1,150 square miles) appears to be a true Game Reserve, in the sense that no licences are issued for shooting. There are three Game Reserves in South-West Africa, all of which have a very considerable area.

The total area shown as 'protected' in the attached schedule is considerable,[5] and amounts to 3½ per cent. of the whole area of the part of Africa lying south of the Sahara. In some territories the proportion is noticeably larger, amounting, for example, to 8·3 per cent. of the whole territory in the case of Tanganyika, 7·7 per cent. in Kenya, and 6·8 in Northern Rhodesia. Should it prove possible to maintain this 'protected' area effectively in the form of Game Reserves or National Parks, there should be an adequate guarantee for the preservation of most of those species of African fauna which appear to be threatened with extinction. But the permanent retention of so large an area for the protection of wild animals will have to meet the opposition which must inevitably be encountered from those who are interested in extending the areas available for African cultivation, and the pressure exercised by those who hold this view will doubtless increase with the attainment by Africans of a larger share in the government of the territories concerned. It has been mentioned that already in 1953 a somewhat contentious debate took place in the Legislature of Southern Rhodesia on a motion for excising a considerable area from the Wankie National Park.[6] This measure was designed to provide for Africans who were being moved from Crown Land

---

[1] Rhodesia and Nyasaland Order in Council no. 1199 of 1953, Schedule II.
[2] *Enc. A.O.F.*, vol. ii, p. 352.   [3] *Enc. A.E.F.*, p. 530.
[4] *Oryx* (Journal of the Fauna Preservation Society), November 1952, p. 344.
[5] See below, p. 933.   [6] See above, p. 704.

in pursuance of the current policy determining the allocation of land between the European and African communities. The Kenya Government has been compelled to refuse proposals which have been made for the inclusion of a salient in the Tsavo National Park and for a corridor leading to the Mount Kenya National Park.

It is clearly not sufficient to set aside as Game Reserves only those areas which may be unsuited for cultivation or for pastoral use, since the land best suited for these purposes is often that preferred by wild animals. Since, moreover, National Parks should provide facilities for the study of fauna under entirely natural conditions, room should also exist in them for a seasonal change of habitat for animals. On the other hand, it seems that even the largest animals will, when assured of their safety, be content to confine themselves to a relatively restricted area. The Addo Bush National Park in the Union, which occupies only about 26 square miles,[1] has become the permanent home of a small herd of elephants, a relic of the great herds which existed in South Africa when the Dutch first settled there. The care given to safeguarding natural life in a Reserve and in providing the wild fauna with water and other facilities (which are now very deficient in some of the Reserves) may perhaps prove to be of greater importance than the extent of the area reserved.

The issue whether Game Reserves are to be maintained in their present strength is therefore likely to be a matter of future controversy in several of the countries of South, Central, and East Africa. Though there are some parts of Africa—as for instance the Union of South Africa—in which it is now rare to find any of the major fauna outside the Game Reserves or National Parks, it is true that there are still many areas in which they exist in some profusion. The annual reports of the Game Departments continue to record the need for destroying large numbers in order to protect African cultivation. An official pamphlet issued in Mozambique advertises as available for hunting a number of areas in which 'the profusion of game is a cause for frequent, though not always reasonable, complaints'.[2] It has been officially stated that in spite of the destruction of animal life in the operations for combating the advance of tsetse[3] there are still 10,000 elephants in Southern Rhodesia and that they are increasing at a rate of about 700 a year.[4]

Apart from the arguments which are based on the need for safeguarding or expanding African cultivation, the maintenance of a protective régime has, as has already been mentioned, been held to be objectionable on the ground that certain wild fauna act as vectors of human or animal disease.

---

[1] *O.Y.S.A.*, *1950*, p. 48.

[2] *Hunting in Mozambique* (a monograph presented by the Mozambique Hunting Committee), 1952, p. 45.

[3] See above, p. 879.   [4] *F.N.*, 21 October 1955.

This applies pre-eminently to the connexion which has been proved to exist between certain types of fauna and the tsetse fly.[1] Not only does game supply the mammalian blood without which most species of tsetse cannot exist (though a few species may feed partly on avian or reptilian blood), but game harbours in its blood the trypanosomes which, after going through a cycle of development in the fly, cause human or cattle trypanosomiasis. When the first Conference on the Protection of Wild Fauna met in 1900, scientific research was not sufficiently advanced to take account of the existence of this source of danger, but it has been the subject of active discussion in the subsequent conferences.

The matter has also aroused much public interest on account of the steps which have been taken, as shown in an earlier part of this chapter, to establish a tsetse-free cordon in Southern Rhodesia.[2] The cordon thus maintained is stated to have involved the destruction in 30 years of over half a million head of animals of various kinds, and it is of interest to note that even in the years 1949–51 it was necessary to kill as many as 102,025 head.[3] As has already been indicated, the authorities in Southern Rhodesia have hitherto held that no alternative existed to this procedure for dealing with the menace of invasion by the tsetse, but a formal inquiry has lately been opened in order to reassess the position.[4]

Any judgement passed in this matter must also take account of the fact that wild fauna can convey diseases other than trypanosomiasis. A game-fence and a game-free belt were established in 1943 between Lakes Tanganyika and Nyasa as a precaution against the introduction of rinderpest by game. In five years 2,266 head of game were shot, of which more than half were *duiker*. Though danger in this latter direction has been reduced by the success of the measures taken to give immunity to cattle by inoculation,[5] science has not as yet produced prophylactic agencies which will safeguard domestic animals from all disease communicated through the agency of the wild fauna. The advocates of the policy of extermination of wild fauna will no doubt continue to point to the lesson which nature has provided in this connexion. The destruction of wild game by the great epizootic of rinderpest 60 years ago seems to have held back for a full generation the menace of tsetse infestation which Southern Rhodesia is now called upon to combat.

The interest in the protection of wild life has led to the establishment of numerous organizations devoted to this object. In the United States of America a number of such societies joined in 1930 in supporting the

---

[1] See above, pp. 874 ff.   [2] See above, pp. 879 ff.
[3] *Oryx*, November 1952, p. 354. See also the references given by C. Wilcocks, J. F. Corson, and R. L. Shepherd in *A Survey of Recent Work on Trypanosomiasis*, 1946, p. 62. See also *The Times*, 11 May 1954; 22 July 1954.   [4] See above, p. 879.
[5] See above, p. 880. See also *Proceedings of the African Regional Scientific Conference*, vol. ii, Johannesburg, 1949, p. 218.

establishment of the American Committee for International Wild Life Protection, and a subsequent organization, the International Union for the Protection of Nature and Conservation of Natural Resources, established in 1948 with headquarters in Brussels, has secured the active support of the United Nations Educational, Scientific, and Cultural Organization.[1] In Great Britain the leading Society is the Fauna Preservation Society, originally created in 1903, under the title of the Society for the Preservation of the Fauna of the Empire. Reference has already been made to the position occupied by the *Institut des Parcs Nationaux du Congo Belge*. In France the leading institution devoted to this purpose is the *Société d'Acclimatation et de Protection de la Nature*.

Territory	Total Area in sq. miles	Protected Area	
		In sq. miles	As percentage of Total Area
Angola	481,351	24,000	5·0
Basutoland	11,716	none	
Bechuanaland	275,000	3,750	1·4
Belgian Congo	904,756 ⎫	11,000	1·2
Ruanda Urundi	20,900 ⎬		
Cameroons, French . . .	166,489 ⎫	35,600	3·1
French Equatorial Africa . .	968,860 ⎬		
French West Africa . . .	1,815,768 ⎫	28,000	1·5
Togoland, French . . .	21,893 ⎬		
Gambia	4,003	none	
Gold Coast	78,802 ⎫	4,616	5.0
Togoland, British . . .	13,041 ⎬	none	
Kenya	224,960	17,240	7·7
Liberia	43,000	none	
Mozambique	297,654	23,807	8·0
Nigeria	338,919 ⎫	5,322	1·4
Cameroons, British . . .	34,081 ⎬		
Nyasaland	37,374	1,250	3·3
Portuguese Guinea . . .	13,948	not known	
Rhodesia, Northern . . .	287,640	19,500	6·8
Rhodesia, Southern . . .	150,330	7,280	4·8
Sierra Leone	27,925	none	
South-West Africa . . .	317,725	34,000	10·7
Spanish Guinea	10,852	not known	
Swaziland	6,704	none	
Tanganyika	362,000	30,000	8·3
Uganda	93,981	3,000	3·2
Union of S. Africa . . .	472,491	12,500	2·6
Zanzibar	1,020	none	
Total	7,483,183	260,865	3·5

[1] *Proceedings of the International Union for the Protection of Nature*, Fontainebleau, 1948; Lake Success, 1949; Brussels, 1950; The Hague, 1951; and Caracas, 1952. These have been published by the United Nations Educational, Scientific, and Cultural Organization.

The area of land protected (whether in the form of National Park or Game Reserve) in the territories south of the Sahara is tabulated on the preceding page. The table has been compiled from such information as is available, but it is not complete and, since there is no standard definition of either a National Park or a Game Reserve, it is open to doubt whether some of the areas included properly fall into either category.

CHAPTER XIII

FORESTS

THE IMPORTANCE OF FORESTRY

THE importance which attaches in Africa to an organized forestry régime does not lie merely in the extent to which timber can be exploited for export or for home consumption. There are, it is true, some territories, and more particularly those situated on the west coast, in which the forests represent a valuable commercial asset. But there are many others in which they have little such value, and their importance lies in the protection they can afford to the sources of water supply or in their influence on climatic conditions, both of which are matters of vital importance to the livelihood of the African population. Reference will be made in the course of a subsequent chapter to the equally vital function which can be performed by a permanent or semi-permanent vegetal covering in preventing erosion or soil deterioration,[1] a factor which has a special significance in areas where, as in a large part of Africa, production is already handicapped by deficiences in the constituents of the soil.[2] The value of a State Forest Department as an agency for serving these purposes was not fully recognized a generation ago, but there has since been a material change in this respect. The justification for instituting such a Department is not to be found in its ability to pay its own way, for the community can derive an indirect value from its operations which is of far greater importance than its direct contribution to the public revenues.

A recent publication of the United Nations Organization describes Africa (excluding North Africa) as containing roughly 2 million square miles of forest area in a total of nearly 9 million square miles. About half of the forest area is said to consist of tropical rain forest, including belts of mangrove, and half of hardwood forest.[3] Such figures have, however, little actual value, owing to the difference of the system of classification adopted in various territories. Perhaps the only conclusion which can be drawn with any certainty is that there has been within a recognizable period a vast reduction of the extent of 'high forest' in the continent. It is generally accepted that the greater part of Central Africa was at one time covered by high forest, but today the surviving belt is estimated to comprise only about 8 per cent. of the total land area, and is in fact only

---

[1] See below, pp. 1015 ff.   [2] See above, p. 829.

[3] United Nations, Food and Agriculture Organization, *Forests and Forest Products, World Situation, 1937–1946.*

a 'relic of itself'.[1] This progressive deforestation has in many quarters been attributed to the indigenous method of shifting cultivation, but it remains a matter of conjecture whether the action of man accounts entirely for the rapidity of the disappearance of the equatorial forest, for it may well be in part due to changes in climatic conditions.

The tropical evergreen forests of West and Central Africa are practically the only areas at present capable of providing an important export trade in timber to Europe and America, those of the Gold Coast, Nigeria, Gabon, the Ivory Coast, the Cameroons, and the Belgian Congo being the most important. The tropical evergreen forests in East Africa are much smaller in extent. Fast-growing, artificial forests of exotic conifers are, however, assuming considerable importance in South and East Africa for local supply, and it is from such forests that Kenya hopes to maintain her timber exports. Although the natural tropical forests are luxuriant in vegetation, they are usually composed of a large variety of tree species, of which the luxury timbers, such as mahogany, are scattered and comprise only a small percentage. Exploitation had a long start over replacement and is still proceeding more rapidly. At first only the finest trees of a few high-grade species were acceptable on the world markets, but the increased demand for timber of all kinds has now made it possible to sell a considerable number of woods which were not used a few years ago. The increasing number of saw-mills and plywood factories in Africa also enables timber which would not be acceptable in the round to be cut from logs and exported. Techniques have now been evolved for the replacement of most of the useful species, though it is unlikely that they will ever be grown again to the size of the trees which are still being cut. These techniques are not, however, being used as yet on a big enough scale, and a large proportion of the tropical evergreen forest is not yet being managed on the basis of a sustained yield.

In the greater part of Africa the prevailing type of woodland is that known as savannah. This extensive area of hardy trees, of indifferent shape and often swept annually by grass fires, has two important functions. It is now realized that large areas ought to be maintained permanently under trees as protective forest, particularly on hill-sides, catchments, and watersheds. Many savannah soils are of low fertility, easily eroded if their cover is removed; they are perhaps more a source of danger if abused than a source of direct revenue if well cared for. In parts of Central Africa and Tanganyika, however, savannah woodland does provide some valuable timbers, such as *muninga* (*Pterocarpus angolensis*), which are in demand both locally and in Europe. Once forests of the savannah type have been declared as protection forests and closed to cultivation,

---

[1] L. Lavauden, 'The Equatorial Forest of Africa', *J.R.A.S.*, Supplement, vol. xxxvi, no. 143, 1937, p. 7.

their chief need is safeguarding from fire, and methods are being success-fully evolved of 'early firing', in which the fierce grass fires of the dry season are anticipated by a deliberate burning earlier in the year.

The second function of savannah forest, namely, as a basis for African shifting cultivation, has perhaps been less appreciated. It may be many years before agricultural research discovers means of reducing the long period of bush fallow which so much of Africa requires between short spells of agricultural cropping.[1] Until this is done, it is not easy to see in what manner the savannah can be protected from the invasion of shifting cultivation. Where the practice follows its traditional course and allows an adequate time for regeneration between periods of burning or cut-ting, the injury done to the savannah is not serious; mischief arises when the 'rest' periods are curtailed under the influence of causes which are largely connected with the introduction of modern economic conditions. Although therefore shifting cultivation has undoubtedly done much to reduce the high forest belt and has caused the substitution of degraded growths for the original timber, it is possible to exaggerate the harm it may have caused in the past or is now capable of causing to the savannah growth.[2] Certainly no observer can fail to be struck by the enormous areas of savannah still remaining in the Belgian Congo, Tanganyika, Northern Rhodesia, or Nyasaland.

Most Governments have now begun to demarcate areas containing their best timber forests, to put them under legal protection, and to regulate their management. Less advance has been made in the estab-lishment of protection forests, partly because they are less directly re-munerative, and partly also because they cannot be adequately maintained until African public opinion has been educated to appreciate their value. Speaking generally, forestry work in Africa may not unjustly be described as being in its initial stages. In many areas it is still necessary to decide how much of the existing forest or woodlands needs to be maintained for watershed conservation and the prevention of erosion, for African sub-sistence agriculture, for local fuel supplies, or for timber required for use in local industries. Occasion will be taken to discuss at a later stage in this chapter the factors which an Administration must consider in arriving at a decision on these points.

FORESTRY WORK IN VARIOUS TERRITORIES

The Union of South Africa

The indigenous high forests of the Union are estimated to occupy now only 2,028 square miles, and are confined to the region of constant rainfall

---

[1] See above, p. 830.

[2] C. G. Trapnell and J. N. Clothier, *The Soils, Vegetation and Agricultural Systems of North Western Rhodesia: Report of the Ecological Survey*, 1937, para. 199.

in the south and to the seaward slopes and deep kloofs of the southern and eastern escarpments. The need for afforestation has been felt from the earliest period of settlement, and it is noteworthy that in 1690 the Governor of the Cape of Good Hope ordered that 100 young oaks should be planted by every agriculturist. South Africa also owes to early Dutch settlers the stone pine, cluster pine, and a species of poplar; the last proved of much use during the Second World War for the match factories of the Union. The modern policy of afforestation dates from 1876 when a small grant was made towards the renewal of the Crown forests, which were placed under the direction of Conservators.[1] In 1887 the system whereby trees are planted among crops, known in Burma as *taungya*,[2] was introduced, burnt forest land being given out to cultivators for planting. Some pine plantations were also formed at Knysna. From these unpretentious beginnings plantation work has so far advanced that the State today owns 661 square miles of plantations, and has reclaimed upwards of 500 square miles of drift sand, much of which is now under trees.

The latest step taken in this direction is the large-scale planting of Caribbean pine on the sandy Zululand coast, at the rate of about 10,000 acres a year. Public bodies and private individuals now maintain some 1,890 square miles of plantations. The periodic recurrence of drought conditions and the attention which has been directed to the problem of water and soil conservation by recommendations, such as those of the Drought Commission of 1923,[3] have given public importance to the plantation policy, to which the activity of the Forest Service is now largely directed. Since 1934 the Forest Department has been combined with the Department of Agriculture and a Division of Forestry is presided over by a technical officer termed the Director of Forestry. Forests, consisting of demarcated and undemarcated Reserves, are controlled by a Forest Act,[4] which also deals with the protection to be afforded to private forests.

The area of Crown Lands reserved for forestal purposes amounted in 1952 to 6,000 square miles[5] or rather more than 1 per cent. of the total area of the Union; 931 square miles consisted of indigenous forest, and 675 square miles were under plantation. The remainder was scrub forest and land held for protective purposes. These figures do not include Game Reserves or the National Parks.[6] In addition about 2,000 square miles under the control of the Department of Forestry are privately owned.

The policy of the Forestry Division is, first, the protection of indigenous forests so as to increase their future productivity, and second, to increase the production of timber by plantations of exotic trees. Numerous species,

[1] *Division of Forestry, Annual Report, 1937*, U.G. no. 53, p. 5.
[2] G. V. Jacks and R. O. Whyte, 'Erosion and Soil Conservation', *Imperial Bureau of Soil Science, Technical Communication*, no. 36, 1938, p. 34.
[3] See below, p. 1017.   [4] No. 13 of 1941, amended by no. 10 of 1948.
[5] *Overseas Economic Surveys, Union of South Africa, 1953*, p. 24.   [6] See above, p. 925.

yielding the ordinary softwoods or durable softwoods of the cedar and cypress classes, or durable hardwoods such as eucalyptus, are planted for this purpose. The Division has aimed at increasing the pre-war programme of planting 15,000 acres a year with softwoods to a total of 35,000 acres a year, but shortage of trained staff has prevented this achievement, only 14,300 acres being planted in 1950–1. The afforestation by private land-owners has increased rapidly, the most extensive planting being that carried out with wattle for the production of tan-bark. This now covers 894 square miles, and the value of bark and its extract exported in 1952 was over £6½ million. South Africa is now one of the chief exporters of wattle extract in the world's markets.[1] During recent years much atten-tion has been given to the control of water catchment areas, in conjunction with the Division of Soil Conservation and Extension,[2] and considerable areas of Crown Land have been reserved for this purpose. All forests on Crown Land in Native areas which have not already been demarcated under the Forest Act are vested by law in the Native Trust.

The total expenditure of the Forestry Division amounted in 1951–2 to rather more than £2¾ million and the revenue derived from Govern-ment areas to £2 million. The European staff consists of 90 officers, including research workers, and 271 European Foresters. The higher branches of the Division are recruited from students who have completed a four years' course at the Institute of Forestry and Wood Technology of the University of Stellenbosch; the Saasveld Forest School near George provides a two years' course for Foresters. Many Africans are employed in subordinate capacities by the Department, but no provision appears to be made for special training for them. Research is carried out at the Forest Products Institute at Pretoria and at the Silvicultural Research Stations in Pretoria, Knysna, and Pietermaritzburg. There are two Re-search Stations at Jonkershoek and Cathedral Peak for the study of the effects of different types of vegetation on stream flow. The latter is con-trolled by a Hydrological Research Officer, whose headquarters are at Stellenbosch University. There is also a Wattle Research Institute at Natal University, financed jointly by the State and by the Wattle Growers' Association. In 1951–2 the total output, including firewood, from Depart-mental Plantations was 30,556,615 cubic feet, of which 19,954,716 cubic feet were softwood logs from the exotic plantations. The total consump-tion of wood in 1950 expressed as the equivalent of round timber was 141,600,000 cubic feet, of which 41,100,000 cubic feet were imported.

The High Commission Territories

Basutoland is characterized by an almost entire absence of indigenous trees, and with the exception of sporadic efforts to plant poplars the Basuto

---

[1] *S.A.S.*, 30 January 1955.   [2] See below, p. 1020.

have done very little tree planting. Measures taken for the prevention of erosion have been successful in many respects; but the efforts made to encourage tree planting have so far had little effect, partly because the system of land tenure discourages individual tree growing.[1]

By far the greater part of Bechuanaland is for climatic reasons unsuited for growing trees, though there is a forest growth of some dimensions in the comparatively well-watered part of the Chobe District, adjacent to some of the forests of Northern Rhodesia. Here a concession to fell *mukusi* or Rhodesian teak (*Baikiaea plurijuga*) and *mukwa* or bloodwood (*Pterocarpus Angolensis*) has been granted over an area of 200 square miles, and in 1951 some 576,300 cubic feet of logs were converted into sleepers and parquet strips for export to Livingstone. As complete fire protection of the exploited *coupes* is practically impossible, they are burnt early in the dry season in order to save the natural regeneration from destruction by late fires. Replanting does not appear to be economically practicable. Efforts made to interest the Native Authorities of the southern part of the Protectorate in tree planting have been unsuccessful. A tract of Rhodesian teak and bloodwood near to the border of Southern Rhodesia has been surveyed, and if this is worked it may provide funds for the establishment of a Forestry Department.

In Swaziland the 'low veld' is heavily bushed, and isolated forests also exist in the Drakensberg Range. There are, however, few indigenous timbers of any value, but in 1943 a private company experimented in planting pines on part of the high veld not suitable for pasture or farming. The results were promising, and four forestry companies, of which the largest is controlled by the Colonial Development Corporation,[2] have now acquired between them some 200,000 acres of grassland. By the end of 1954 over 122,000 acres had been successfully afforested. If the rate of tree growth fulfils early promises it is quite possible that an integrated industry producing marketable timber, boxboards, and paper may be developed within 30 years. There is one State Forest Officer, and the companies employ nine professional Foresters, and eight other technicians, recruited in South Africa. Part of the Usutu forest plantation controlled by the Colonial Development Corporation is being developed in the interests of the Swaziland Native Authority.

Southern Rhodesia

In contrast with the Union the territory is relatively well wooded, about 80 per cent. of its area being covered with woodland, but as a rule

[1] *N.A.*, Part V, pp. 129, 230.
[2] *Colonial Development Corporation, Report and Accounts for 1954*, p. 46. *N.A.*, Part V, p. 340. The Usutu Forest project of the Colonial Development Corporation was described at length in the issue of its journal *Colonial Development*, Winter 1951.

trees of large dimensions are found only in the mountain forests and in woods bordering the rivers. Indigenous forests have played a useful part in the development of the country, supplying fuel and timber to the mines, and, until coal was discovered, to the railways. In the early stages of occupation free cutting was permitted to miners and prospectors on un-alienated land and in Native Reserves, but certain measures of control were subsequently instituted. A Forestry Adviser was appointed in 1912; in 1922 the small Mtao Forest Reserve in the Chilimanzi district was formed, and in 1925 measures were taken for protecting the indigenous savannah forests on Crown Lands in three of the administrative districts.

In 1927 the Stapleford Forest Reserve of 7,771 acres was formed in the mountainous eastern border area where softwoods, including pines and cypresses, can be grown, and in 1929 about 1,223 square miles of tree veld in Matabeleland were taken over.[1] By 1954 the area of demar-cated forest amounted to 1,718 square miles. In addition, 1,485 square miles of communal forest in Native Reserves were controlled by the Native Department, and private landowners had dedicated 131 square miles to forestry. These three categories of land make up together a forest estate comprising a little over 4 per cent. of the total land area. Afforestation with exotic conifers is becoming increasingly important, and in 1950 nearly 100 square miles had been planted. In 1950 the total consumption in terms of roundwood was 87 million cubic feet (mainly firewood and rough poles), the excess of timber imports over exports being about 2 million cubic feet. The Forestry Department was part of the Division of Agri-culture and Lands, and employed 13 Forest Officers educated at United Kingdom universities or at Stellenbosch, and 19 European Foresters. By legislation passed in 1953 the Forestry Department was replaced by a Forestry Commission.

There is a school for the European Forestry Service, but men are also recruited from British Forestry Commission Schools. There is no trained African staff. For the present the Department is concerned chiefly with the building up of commercial forests, the bulk of the main catchment areas being privately owned. Protection work is in the hands of the Natural Resources Board and the Sub-Department of Conservation and Extension. The work of conservation and protection is now recognized to be of increasing importance owing to the heavy losses incurred by veld fires, but no adequate measures for dealing with them have yet become available.

Training Schemes for British Dependencies

Before the First World War there existed no organized system for training officers for the Forest Services of the British African dependencies,

[1] *O.Y.S.R., 1952*, p. 478.

although Forestry Schools existed at the Universities of Oxford, Cambridge, and Edinburgh, nor was the local organization of forest work such as to make any material impression on the problems which had to be faced. A proposal to establish a Forest Research Institute was made at the Empire Forestry Conference held in London in 1920, and the opening of the Imperial Forestry Institute at Oxford followed in 1924. Candidates for the Colonial Forestry Service are now required to possess a degree in forestry, which is obtainable at the Universities of Oxford, Edinburgh, Aberdeen, and the University College of Bangor, but after a two-year tour of service overseas they must complete a post-graduate course of one year at the Imperial Forestry Institute before they are confirmed in their appointments.

The vast areas of thinly populated woodlands in East and Central Africa provide problems different from those of the southern territories, where forest lands are less extensive but better defined, and also from those of the tropical rain forest belt of West Africa. Trees of special value are rarely found in any considerable numbers in the savannah woodlands. Such trees are, moreover, liable to be felled by any person desiring timber for any purpose, and little can be done for their preservation unless the interest of the Native Authorities and the people themselves is aroused. Little success has so far been achieved in forestry organization in the tribal areas, though extensive schemes are being considered in various quarters for improving the situation. Meanwhile there is clearly need for a comprehensive reconnaissance of the forestal position on lines similar to those of the Ecological Survey carried out in Northern Rhodesia.[1]

Northern Rhodesia

In Northern Rhodesia the only forest area, correctly so called, is that in the Zambezi valley to which reference will subsequently be made, but some 40 per cent. of the Protectorate is covered by deciduous woodlands, containing many trees which are large enough for sawn timber. In these woodlands exploiting agencies have been developed which provide 85 per cent. of all the timber used locally, including that consumed by the copper mines, and are responsible also for the export of sleepers and mining timbers. The latter were valued at £254,750 in 1951. Local supplies of timber do not, however, meet the requirements of the territory, which in 1953 had to import wood to the value of £1,400,000 and round logs to the value of over £65,000 from the Belgian Congo.[2] Nearly 250 Europeans and 11,000 Africans and Asians earn their living in wood industries of this class.

[1] Trapnell and Clothier, op. cit., and C. G. Trapnell, J. D. Martin, W. Allan, and others, *Vegetation-Soil Map of Northern Rhodesia*, Lusaka, 1948.
[2] *Northern Rhodesia, Forestry Department, Annual Report, 1953*, p. 9.

When there is a shortage of coal the mines are dependent on wood fuel, and it is stated that 200,000 tons a month were at one time consumed in the furnaces of the Copperbelt, the cost being materially higher than that of coal. The wooded areas which lie within economic range of the centres of consumption are, however, being used up rapidly, and plantations must now be made near those centres if the high cost of supply from more remote districts is to be avoided. So far the total area of production Reserves is 4,858 square miles only; but it is important to recall that Northern Rhodesia controls the catchments of the Zambezi and Kafue river systems and that the former will shortly be utilized for the development of hydro-electric power.[1] Up to 1953 the area of protection Reserves was 3,159 square miles, making with the production Reserves a forest estate of 8,017 square miles, or a little over $2\frac{1}{2}$ per cent. of the total land area.

The first Forest Officer was posted to the Protectorate in 1928, but a Forestry Department was not established until 1947. It is only just beginning to make progress with schemes for regenerating the Reserves. In 1926 a concession to cut timber was granted over part of the valuable Rhodesian teak woodland of the Zambezi valley, and when the licence expires in 1957 more than 80 per cent. of the accessible portions of the 500 square miles of the forest will have been worked out. After 1957 cutting will be possible only on a small scale for the next 90 years or so. If the management had been organized from the first by an expert Forest Service a steady yield of timber, even though of smaller dimensions, might well have been assured in perpetuity.

In the Copperbelt an intensive technique of repeated patch-burning in the early part of the dry season has been developed in order to bring on root-shoots and coppice regeneration in cut-over areas. There is a Forest School for Africans at Mwekera, in which Rangers and Guards are trained for departmental employment. In 1953 there were 17 professional officers in the Forest Service, 28 European Foresters, and 64 African Rangers. Expenditure was estimated at £147,900, and revenue at approximately the same figure.

Nyasaland

Nyasaland is comparatively well wooded, the forest occupying about $24\frac{1}{2}$ per cent. of its area, but, as in other territories where shifting cultivation is practised, there has been much degradation of the original woodland. The State Forest Reserves now number 64, with an approximate area of 3,085 square miles, which is equivalent to $10\frac{1}{2}$ per cent. of the land area of the Protectorate. Protection of stream banks, hill slopes, and catchment areas is provided for by legislation,[2] but much further control

[1] See below, p. 966.　　　　　　　　　　[2] Forest Ordinance no. 2, 1942.

is required to ensure the preservation of natural vegetation on the poorer soils and to provide sufficient belts of woodland to form wind breaks for the conservation of soil moisture. Since 1926 a scheme has been in operation for the formation of Village Forests, with the object of providing local supplies of firewood,[1] but although there are some 5,800 Village Forest areas, totalling nearly 297,000 acres, little interest is taken in the majority of them, and little effort is made by Village Headmen to make them successful. On the other hand, an order issued to every registered tobacco grower in the Lilongwe District of the Central Province to plant a certain number of trees as a measure of reafforestation is said to have been well received.

Nyasaland possesses about 6,000 acres of indigenous softwood, *mupande* or *mlanje* cedar (*Widdringtonia whytei*), and it is proposed to establish 1,000 acres of conifers a year. A syndicate, partially financed by the Colonial Development Corporation, was formed in 1952 to investigate the afforestation of the Nyika Plateau by planting conifers, and the growth has been reported to be satisfactory.[2] Short courses of instruction in forestry have been given to Africans, and a school for more comprehensive training has been built at Dedza. In 1950 there were three professional officers, eight European Foresters, of whom four had been trained at the Saasveld School in South Africa, and 41 African Rangers. The requirements of the tobacco industry have been met by the establishment of five saw-mills with an output of over 30,000 cubic feet a year, and by several enterprises which provide staves for tobacco hogsheads. In 1953 the production of softwood was 211,600 cubic feet and of hardwood 288,000 cubic feet.[3]

Tanganyika

The original forests of Tanganyika had been seriously reduced long before the European occupation. Climatic and soil conditions indicate the existence at one period of large areas of evergreen forest which is now represented only by some 4,000 square miles of closed high forest, though well over half of the rest of the 334,400 square miles of land surface carries woodland and bush of varying densities. By 1953 Government Forest Reserves amounted to 11,330 square miles, about $3\frac{1}{3}$ per cent. of the area of the country. There were also 654 square miles of Native Authority forest, constituted under by-laws, and 317 square miles of privately owned forest. In a recent statement on forest policy,[4] the Government declared as its immediate aim the reservation of 27,400 square miles (8 per cent. of land area) by 1962. A German Forest Department was in exis-

[1] *Nyasaland, Forestry Department, Annual Report, 1936*, paras. 48 ff.
[2] *Colonial Development Corporation, Report and Accounts for 1954*, p. 42.
[3] *Colonial Reports, Nyasaland, 1953*, p. 74.   [4] Sessional Paper no. 1, 1953.

tence from 1896 to 1914, and a British establishment was set up in 1921, but until 1947 it existed in little more than name.[1] Exploitation was stimulated by the Second World War, and in 1953 there were 77 mills which extracted over $2\frac{1}{2}$ million cubic feet of roundwood from State forests and public land. Natural regeneration has so far been successful only for East African camphorwood (*Ocotea usambarensis*), and there are some 19,000 acres of plantation, about half of which is owned by Native Authorities.

There appear to be wide opportunities for planting both softwoods and hardwoods, but developments of this nature are preferably undertaken by private enterprise or as special schemes with their own personnel and funds. The Colonial Development Corporation initiated one such project in 1950 by leasing 69 square miles of grassland for growing wattle (*Acacia mollissima*) and had by 1954 established 22,500 acres of wattle from which tanning extraction should begin in 1958.[2] The departmental establishment sanctioned is 32 professional officers and 33 European Foresters. There are only 22 African Rangers, but it is hoped to overcome the shortage of Africans of this class by enlarging a small pre-war school in order to provide two-year courses.

Kenya

In Kenya there was at one period an unusually large area of high forest, but its rapid destruction was already in progress when European occupation began in the late years of the last century. Though some measures of reservation were undertaken as early as 1901, the process of deforestation, particularly of the forests which clothed the sides of Mount Kenya, continued actively until demarcation reached a sufficiently advanced stage about 1911. It has been estimated that the Kikuyu tribe alone had destroyed at least 1,000 square miles of forest before demarcation.

There are no exact figures of the area of forest now remaining, but that reserved under the Forest Ordinance[3] was stated in 1953 to be 5,334 square miles, or about $2\frac{1}{2}$ per cent. of the total land area. This includes most of the remaining high forest in the highlands and on the coastal strip, except for some 700 square miles of valuable timber in the south of the Colony held by the Masai, who have been unwilling to agree to reservation. African Local Government bodies hold 888 square miles of the total reserved, these areas being managed directly by the Forestry Department, which pays over to them any profits made. In addition there are 100 square miles managed directly by the District Native

---

[1] *Forestry in Tanganyika, 1946–50, Statement to the British Commonwealth Forestry Conference, Canada, 1952*, Dar-es-Salaam, 1951.

[2] *Colonial Development Corporation, Report and Accounts for 1954*, p. 38.

[3] Ordinance no. 26, 1941. Cap. 176 of Laws, as amended by Ordinance no. 1, 1949.

Councils. A Forest Boundary Commission, appointed in 1946, recommended changes which should lead to some increase in the area of the Reserves.

All the accessible forests have been heavily overcut and little has been done to assist natural regeneration in them, mainly because this is considered to be too slow a policy to be economic. Replacement of the timber supplies has mainly taken the form of plantation of exotic conifers and is for the most part effected with the assistance of resident Kikuyu cultivators under the *taungya* system.[1] By 1955 120,000 acres had been planted, the aim being to increase the area of softwoods to 210,000 acres at the rate of 6,000 acres a year. It is hoped that this may provide the basis of a paper industry. There are also considerable plantations, mainly of wattle and eucalyptus, on European estates and in some of the African Reserves. In 1950 the total cut in roundwood from Reserved forests was 22 million cubic feet. Exports, about half of which consisted of slats of African pencil cedar (*Juniperus procera*), exceeded imports by the equivalent of about 1 million cubic feet of roundwood.

The staff of the Forestry Department consisted of 22 professional officers, including specialists, 40 European and seven Asian Foresters, and 55 African Assistant Foresters. European Foresters, some of whom are local nominees, are now being trained in the Forestry Commission Schools in Great Britain. There are as yet no facilities for the formal training of Africans. The large population living in the forests, estimated to amount to 45,000 persons in all, has created a special problem in the provision of African welfare. Two European and 54 African officers have been employed on welfare work and by the end of 1952 the operations had included the building of 22 schools, five markets, and 14 dispensaries.

Uganda

In Uganda little is left of the original flora of the large forests which once covered much of the country, except for some remnants along the western escarpment and on the mountains; there are also some patches of secondary high forest along the north-western shores of Lake Victoria. Destruction of the more heavily covered areas, such as the slopes of Mount Elgon and Ruwenzori, was in progress when the country was first occupied in 1896. In the lower areas the clearing of woodland was accelerated by the introduction of cotton cultivation, particularly in the Eastern Province, but there are still considerable tracts of woody growth of varying densities. A Forestry Department was first constituted in 1917, though at first with a strength of only one senior officer.

In 1954 the Central or Crown Forest Reserves amounted to 5,365

[1] See above, p. 938. The system is described in *East Africa Royal Commission 1953–1955, Report*, Cmd. 9475, 1955, p. 170.

square miles, of which 2,850 square miles were savannah woodland and 788 square miles were held by African Local Government bodies as Local Forest Reserves. The work of reservation is still being continued, except in five districts which have an average of 15½ per cent. of their total area reserved, and have now been declared to have adequate forest estates. Private forests, mostly situated in the *mailo* lands,[1] are estimated at 100 square miles, and there are 130 square miles of unreserved forests in the country as a whole. All accessible tracts were worked heavily during the Second World War, and the export of any timber for which there may be a local use has now been prohibited. The output of timber, poles, and firewood from Crown forests and lands amounted in 1952 to 128,651 cubic feet of round timber.[2] Imports of timber were negligible.

Working plans have been prepared on a basis of sustained yield for 1,784 square miles of Reserve. The species planted for timber replacement are the indigenous mahoganies (*Khaya nyasica* and *Entandrophragma* spp.) and *iroko* (*Chlorophora excelsa*), but exotic softwoods have also been recently planted in the Western Highlands, at the rate of about 150 acres a year. The total area of all plantations is about 24,000 acres. The staff consisted in 1953 of 22 Europeans and 150 African Guards and Rangers. A Forest School for Africans was started at Nyabyeya in 1932 and has trained a number of the Assistant Foresters, who had started their service as Rangers, but it has not as yet been found possible to attract candidates with the necessary education to read for degrees in forestry in Great Britain.

Nigeria

Nigeria is predominantly a savannah woodland country with a narrow coastal belt of closed high forest, but a great deal of the woodland country is the bush fallow of peasant agriculture and will never be available for permanent forestry. It was estimated in 1938 that the high forest itself is being reduced by shifting cultivation on its northern and eastern boundaries at the rate of 1,000 square miles a year.[3] It was stated in 1953 that 119,431 square miles of forest and woodland remain, of which 29,114, about 7½ per cent. of the total land area of the territory, had been reserved. Except, however, for 5,200 square miles of State forest, the Reserves have been constituted as 'African-owned forest' under Native Authorities, and are managed by these bodies. Now that Nigeria has been divided into three Regions, each with its own Forest Department, with a Federal Inspector-General, the uneven distribution of the forest estate has become more apparent. In the Western Region the permanent estate is 15·6 per cent. of the total land area, in the Eastern 10·4 per cent., and in the

[1] See above, p. 725, and also *N.A.*, Part I, pp. 6, 75.
[2] *Colonial Reports, Uganda, 1953*, p. 53.
[3] E. B. Worthington, *Science in Africa*, 1938, p. 194.

Northern 6·1 per cent. These figures are partly a reflection of the fact that in the past more attention was paid to the rich forests of the south, where the bulk of the Forest Staff were concentrated.

The main obstacle to further reservation in the Eastern and Western Regions lies in the fragmentation of land ownership and the continuing disputes regarding it. Efforts are now being made to increase the area of the woodland estate in the Northern Region, where the same problem of land rights does not arise, but the need for the control of tsetse fly creates obstacles to large-scale reservation. The grazing of stock in savannah Reserves has to be accepted as one of the necessities of the situation, and indeed the improvement of fodder in these areas will probably be the most important argument for their reservation. It will however be necessary to control the larger gregarious antelopes which carry the trypanosome of sleeping sickness and cattle disease, and this can best be done in comparatively small Reserves isolated by farmlands. A provisional limit of 100 square miles and a minimum distance of five miles between Reserves have been accepted as most suitable.

Exploitation has so far had no serious effect on the permanent forests, chiefly because the bulk of the cutting of timber has been in the nature of salvage fellings from land cleared for agriculture. Working plans have now been drawn up for the controlled exploitation of 5,217 square miles of Reserves, and 160 square miles are under natural regeneration. A *taungya* system of regeneration has also been introduced, mainly in the Benin area, and 8,800 acres of valuable indigenous species have been established. Land directly afforested amounts to a further 15,616 acres, part of which is planted with indigenous species, and part with exotics, such as teak (*Tectona grandis*), *Gmelina*, eucalyptus, and, in the north, neem (*Azadirachta*). The recorded output in 1952 was 32,648,500 cubic feet of roundwood, of which 8,655,000 cubic feet were exported, partly in the form of sawn timber. The growth of mills and the export of sawn timber is a fairly recent development, as is the completion of a veneer and ply-wood factory, from which products to the value of over £500,000 were shipped in 1953. Imports are negligible.

The Forest Staff consists of 67 senior officers and 108 Forest Assistants. Rangers in Nigeria are a higher grade of Forest Guard and do not perform technical duties (as do many so designated in most Colonies). There is a Forestry School for the training of Africans at Ibadan, and some of the Forest Assistants trained there have been selected for a special course of one year at the Imperial Forestry Institute, Oxford. They have since been promoted to the post of Assistant Conservator. This step was taken in order to speed up the Africanization of the Department, but a number of men have now begun to study at University College, Ibadan, with a view to qualifying for the Forestry Schools in British Universities.

Two plantations of rubber were established about 1914 near Sapele and in 1952 produced 41 million lb. from 2,000 acres. Much, however, was reported to be of low quality.

The Gold Coast and British Togoland

The Gold Coast (including Togoland) is divided ecologically into a high forest zone of some 30,385 square miles in the south west, and a savannah woodland zone of 61,450 square miles. About half of the former is estimated to be covered by forest, of which 5,790 square miles are reserved; this represents a substantial increase above the 1,712 square miles which was recorded as reserved just before the beginning of the Second World War. Before that date the balance was being cleared for farming at the rate of a little over 250 square miles a year; in 1953 it was reported as being cleared at the rate of 780 square miles, owing to the stimulus given by the high price of cocoa.[1] In the savannah zone there are believed to be 42,600 square miles of woodland, of which 1,567 square miles are reserved.

The present forest estate amounts to some $7\frac{1}{2}$ per cent. of the total land area, and is regarded as virtually complete in the high forest zone, though requiring considerable expansion in the north. But the Gold Coast has had an exceptionally difficult history from the point of view of its Forestry Department, and the present result has been achieved only after many years of patient work. The process has been rendered more difficult than elsewhere by the prevailing system of land tenure,[2] and there are only 63·7 square miles of Government Forest Reserve. In 1911 a Forest Ordinance providing for the establishment of Government Reserves was withdrawn after much opposition based on the ground that this would be an invasion of 'stool' rights.[3] In 1920 the Chiefs were urged to establish 'stool' Reserves, but by 1926 only 307 square miles had been reserved out of the 6,000 square miles which had been considered necessary.[4]

In 1927 a Forestry Ordinance was passed which provided that the Government should constitute Reserves, but that these should continue to be the property of the stools. In many cases, however, rather than see these powers used by the Government, Chiefs preferred to constitute 'stool' forests, and this secured some measure of reservation of the main catchment and other vital areas. Of the present forest estate some 4,923 square miles have been constituted under the by-laws, and only 2,102 square miles under the Forest Ordinance. As has been explained the high price of cocoa after the Second World War stimulated further

[1] *Gold Coast, Report of the Forestry Department, 1952-3.*   [2] See above, pp. 737 ff.
[3] See above, p. 738. See also *N.A.*, Part III, p. 221.
[4] Sir F. G. Guggisberg, *The Gold Coast, A Review of the Events of 1920-6, and the Prospects for 1927-8*, 1927, p. 61.

destruction of unreserved forest, and in 1946 the Chief Conservator was granted powers under the Concessions Ordinance to control Concessions for timber cutting. He was thus able to concentrate logging operations on those parts of timber Concessions which appeared likely to be cleared for agriculture during the next ten years.

The present policy of the Government is to retain a series of permanent shelter belts of high forest for the protection of cocoa, in conjunction with a belt along the watershed between the Pra and Volta river systems, which is also the north-eastern edge of the high forest zone. As the permanent forests are opened for exploitation working plans are prepared for them on a basis of sustained yield by natural regeneration. About 16,700 acres of plantation have been established, some by *taungya*, in order to provide fuel and poles for townships or mines. In the Northern Territories the Department is co-operating in the establishment of Land Planning Areas, the development of which is being combined with measures for soil and water conservation. This policy has superseded an earlier scheme for establishing a protective belt against the assumed southern encroachment of the Sahara.[1]

An export trade from the Gold Coast started many years ago, and in 1952 over 3,400,000 cubic feet of mill-sawn timber were exported, together with 5,900,000 cubic feet of logs. African mahogany (*Khaya*) made up 37 per cent. of the exports. One rotary peeler started production in 1948, and another peeler and two veneer-slicers were erected in 1950. It was estimated that the production of forest produce from areas outside the Reserves was equivalent to over 181,000 cubic feet of roundwood.

There is a school for Forest Rangers, the entrants numbering 40 in 1951, and scholarships are available to Africans to enable them to proceed overseas to read for degrees in forestry, though so far very few have done so. The staff in 1952 consisted of 38 senior officers, 181 technical subordinates, and 312 Forest Guards.

Sierra Leone

The greater part of Sierra Leone, which has an average rainfall ranging between 90 and 130 inches, must at one time have been covered by forest, but shifting cultivation has converted this into secondary forest, savannah woodland, or farm bush. Indeed the degradation to bush and savannah has, in the opinion of some observers, proceeded farther in Sierra Leone than in any other part of West Africa.[2] The light lateritic soil seems to be particularly liable to erosion when stripped of its natural cover. In the Colony area there are now 67 square miles of State Forest Reserves, but they are protection forests on steep water catchments with little productive

[1] See below, p. 1050.
[2] E. P. Stebbing, *The Forest of West Africa and the Sahara*, 1937, p. 3.

value, except for firewood. In the Protectorate area forests can, owing to the existing system of land tenure,[1] be safeguarded only if the Tribal Authorities request the Government to do so. The total area of Forest Reserves and Protected forests was 1,024 square miles in 1953, or $3\frac{3}{4}$ per cent. of the land area; besides the small area of Crown forests in the Colony, this includes 860 square miles of Reserved forests and 97 square miles of Protected forests in the Protectorate. The Forest Reserves are managed by the Forestry Department at State expense, the gross revenue being divided equally between the State and the Chiefdoms. The revenue accruing from Protected forests, which are small areas managed directly by the Local Authorities under State supervision, accrues to the Local Authority Treasuries.

The Forestry Department, which was established in 1911, had little staff until after the Second World War, but now has twelve professional officers. Under the Tribal Authorities Ordinance of 1937 the Authorities can be empowered to declare Soil Conservation Areas,[2] in which cultivation or cutting and burning of vegetation can be regulated, and it is intended that the forest estate shall be constituted as an integral part of the general scheme of land utilization.[3] As this will be a slow process the reservation of hill areas, a matter of urgency, is being pushed forward in advance. The existing subordinate staff of five Africans is inadequate, but it is difficult to obtain suitable candidates for entry to the Ibadan Forest School in Nigeria; the first two Africans from Sierra Leone to read for degrees in forestry started their studies in the United Kingdom in 1950.

Gambia

Gambia has so far nothing in the form of a forest régime. In 1950 a grant was made under the Colonial Development and Welfare Act to provide for an inquiry into the possibility of establishing small Forest Reserves as a contribution to the solution of the problem of preserving soil fertility. The Protectorate Land Ordinance of 1945[4] was amended to enable Reserves to be constituted, but it was decided that they should be called Forest Parks to avoid possible confusion with other forms of Reserve. By the end of 1953 some 83,500 acres had been demarcated, of which 46,600 acres had been gazetted. A number of men have been selected for training for forest work, but they are of poor education, and progress in this direction has not been encouraging.

French West Africa

Of the French territories south of the Sahara French West Africa possesses in the two territories of Senegal and French Sudan a large expanse

[1] *N.A.*, Part III, p. 319.   [2] See below, p. 1055.
[3] *Report on Soil Conservation and Land Use*, Sessional Paper no. 1, 1951.
[4] *N.A.*, Part III, p. 345.

of country which is for climatic reasons likely to remain devoid of any natural woodlands. On the other hand, the Ivory Coast has a rather higher proportion of commercially exploitable forest than any other portion of Africa, amounting in fact to no less than $11\frac{1}{2}$ per cent. of the total area of the territory. The degradation of the savannah woodland, especially in the Niger and Haute-Volta area, has not proceeded as far as in many of the British territories, for there is a relatively low pressure of population on the soil and less development of marketable crops of the type of cotton or coffee. The savannah contains in consequence a larger proportion of scattered old trees, and these are protected under regulation.[1] The classification of the woodlands follows different lines from those adopted in the British system, but the definition of a forest is wide enough to include nearly all uncultivated land except grass savannah. On lands classified by decree as State Forest Lands the Africans' rights of user are limited, and in the case of reafforestation zones such rights are annulled. French authorities estimate the total woodland area of French West Africa at 656,000 square miles (out of a total land area of 1,798,374 square miles), of which 192,000 are described as productive or partially productive areas.

Up to the present 27,170 square miles have been scheduled as *forêt classée*, but the process of scheduling is not yet completed. The term *forêt classée* or *domaine classé* is applied mainly to selected forests in which exploitation is organized. In general, all forest lands are held to be the property of the State, as having been *terres vacantes et sans maître*,[2] but the application of this principle to land held by African communities has been the source of much legal dispute, which has delayed the process of scheduling the woodland areas. In French West Africa there are also about 1,000 square miles of privately owned forest lands.

Active interest in the forests of French West Africa may be said to have been awakened by the realization of their commercial value in the Ivory Coast. The exploitation of these forests by *concessionnaires*, which commenced about 1884, proceeded so rapidly that it produced a labour crisis in the Colony. Owing largely to the lack of communications, living conditions were bad and there was high mortality among the workers. Recruits were only obtained by severe administrative pressure. The scale of exploitation permitted was, however, gradually reduced and the labour situation brought under some measure of control. Forest management was regulated by a Decree of 1912,[3] and a Forest Service created in 1925. Meanwhile the *concessionnaires* had stripped the rain forests of a considerable part of their more valuable trees.

---

[1] *Enc. A.O.F.*, vol. i, pp. 371 ff. *Annuaire statistique de l'Afrique occidentale française, 1951*, pp. 127 ff.

[2] See above, p. 744.

[3] *Décret*, 18 June 1912.

It is perhaps largely on account of the devastation thus caused that the French, who have in Europe been firm exponents of the principle of natural regeneration of woodlands, were led to adopt in the Ivory Coast a system of restocking by the planting of commercial species in lines cut through the forest. More recently the planting of indigenous species by *taungya* has been practised where cultivators have been available. There has also been a considerable increase in saw-milling, the territory of the Ivory Coast alone having as many as 20 mills in 1950, and a growing proportion of the export is now in the form of sawn timber instead of logs. There is a veneer and plywood factory near Abidjan, and a pilot paper-pulp factory at Bimbresso. If this factory succeeds it may create a new problem regarding the methods to be followed for the large-scale regeneration of mixed tropical hardwoods.

In the evergreen and deciduous forests of the rest of French West Africa increasing attention is now being given to the replacement of the woodland by regeneration, while in the drier tracts the rehabilitation of water catchments and eroded areas is being pursued mainly by measures designed for the protection of natural vegetation. Schemes for the formation of village plantations supervised by the Forest Service have met with some success. Fire protection plays an important part in the drier areas of French Guinea, Dahomey, and the Sudan, where 'early burning' is carried out over much of the savannah zone. In 1950 French West Africa exported 3,813,000 cubic feet of logs and 106,000 cubic feet of sawn timber, made up of 15 species of woods. Of these the more important were *Khaya* (African mahogany) and *Entandrophragma* spp., *obechi* (*Triplochiton*), and *makore* (*Mimusops heckelii*).

French Equatorial Africa

In French Equatorial Africa the woodland area is estimated by French authorities at 588,540 square miles, out of a land area of 913,800 square miles, but only 104,400 square miles are reckoned to be productive forest. So far the scheduled forest estate (*domaine classé*) amounts to roughly 4,000 square miles, but its extension is considered to be of much importance, if only for climatic reasons. The extreme scarcity of wood near the capital, Brazzaville, is being met by a large scheme of afforestation. The Gabon, however, has conditions which somewhat resemble those of the Ivory Coast. The *okoumé* or *gaboon* (*Aucoumea klaineana*), now much sought after, springs up gregariously in the secondary forest which follows shifting cultivation, but only occurs as scattered trees in the mature forest. It is found in 10,000 square miles of accessible forest in Gabon, over about half of which concessions to cut timber have been granted. In the Middle Congo half the timber cut is *limba* (*Terminalia superba*), and in Oubangui Chari about half is *ayous* or *obechi* (*Triplochiton*). There are now 38 saw-mills in the territory and two veneer plants. In 1952 the export, which plays a very important part in the economy of the group of territories in French Equatorial Africa, amounted to 5,093,261 cubic feet of logs, 934,952 cubic feet of sawn timber, and 334,572 cubic feet of veneer and plywood.

The French Cameroons

The French Cameroons, with a total area of 166,489 square miles, has an estimated woodland area of 111,200 square miles, of which 72,500 are classed as potentially productive. There has been a good deal of afforestation here with *Cassia siamea*, neem (*Azadirachta*), and eucalyptus. In 1950 there was an export of 2,436,000 cubic feet of logs and 424,000 cubic feet of sawn timber, there having been of recent years a considerable increase of saw-mills, which now number 30. The practice here is to allow the saw-mills the monopoly of a zone proportional to their capacity. The principal species exported was *azobé* or *ekki* (*Lophira alata*).

The French Forestry Services

The Forest Service for the African Colonies (the *Service Forestier* or *Service des Eaux et Forêts*) was organized under a Decree of July 1923. This provided that Forest Officers were to be recruited from the metropolitan service or from candidates who had passed through the *École Nationale des Eaux et Forêts* at Nancy. A lower grade (*Contrôleur*) was established by a local decree of 1932, under which candidates were to be trained at an Agricultural College for two years, and then for a year in France at the Forest School at Barre. The majority of the territories comprising French West and French Equatorial Africa now have their own Forest Services, the total number in the former being shown in 1950 as 36 Forest Officers, 44 *Contrôleurs*, and 36 African Assistants. In French Equatorial Africa there were 28 and in the French Cameroons eleven Forest Officers, and this remained the average establishment in 1952. All Forest Officers were graduates of the national school at Nancy.

There is a Forest Research Station in the Ivory Coast, and also in the French Cameroons, with a school which provides a two-year course for African Forest Assistants. Most of the territories have local schools for training Forest Guards. In both French West and French Equatorial Africa there is an Inspector-General of Forests, and there is, at the *Ministère de la France d'Outre-Mer*, a Technical Adviser, the *Chef du Service Central des Eaux et Forêts*.

The Belgian Congo

The Belgian Congo is by repute the country *par excellence* of equatorial forests, and this reputation, based as it is on the reports of many early travellers, has a substantial measure of truth. There is, in the first place, the vast equatorial forest of the central Congo, stretching some 750 miles along the equator and in places extending to 250 miles on either side of it. There are the 2,000 square miles of the Mayumbe forest near the western coast, and there is a large belt of open woodland in the south east of the Katanga region. Finally there are widely extended savannah lands to the north and the south of the equatorial belt, and it is noteworthy that the savannah of the Belgian Congo, with its relatively high rainfall, has a greater proportion of useful woodland than most of the neighbouring territories. The Belgian authorities have estimated that in the total land area of 925,656 square miles in the Belgian Congo and Ruanda Urundi there are 463,000 square miles which contain productive or potentially productive woodlands. It is, however, only within the last 30 years that serious attention has been given to the problem of the exploitation or the protection of the forest areas. In the early history of the Colony, interest was focused on the woodlands as a source of rubber,[1] and it was only when the indigenous wild rubber ceased to command an export market that attention was given by the Administration to its other forest property. About a quarter of the Mayumbe forest has a sufficient stocking of *limba* (*Terminalia superba*) to make exploitation profitable, and it is here that production of marketable timber began in 1920. The great central equatorial forest contains some hundreds of different species of trees, but most of these are not marketable, and such stands of valuable timber as exist are scattered over considerable distances.[2]

Reservation was first attempted in 1910 when a decree declared 2,300 square miles to be Reserved forest. This reservation was, however, only theoretical, and it was not until 1924 that measures for reservation took a practical form. Commercial exploitation was regulated by decree in 1934;[3] a forest policy was adopted by the Government and a Forest Service set up in 1936. Forest Officers were appointed to most of the provincial headquarters to act as technical advisers to the companies holding concessions to exploit the forests, as well as acting as Conservators of the woodlands in the Native areas. In 1949 a more comprehensive decree was issued for the regulation of all woodlands,[4] which were divided into two classes, Scheduled and Protected. Scheduled forests (*forêts classées*) can only be exploited under working plans providing for sustained yields, while the regulation of Protected forest aims mainly at preventing waste of timber and damage to the soil by exposure. Customary rights may be exercised in Scheduled forests only with special permission, but may be exercised freely in Protected forests, subject to a few restrictions.

[1] See below, p. 964.   [2] *Enc. C.B.*, vol. i, pp. 377 ff.
[3] *Décret*, 4 April 1934.
[4] *Décret*, 11 April 1949. *Ordonnance* 52/214, 7 July 1951.

In the absence of local sources of coal and oil, large quantities of wood are consumed by industry and by railways and river steamers. As in Northern Rhodesia,[1] these sources of fuel are exploited by wood-cutting companies. A certain proportion of the work of regeneration is now left to these companies under an arrangement by which they carry out this operation instead of paying an annual fee for the Concession and a re-generation tax.[2] Thus two firms, cutting in the Mayumbe forest, plant *limba* in lines after exploitation, and in the Kasai Province two companies plant teak (*Tectona grandis*) and other exotics. There are also privately owned plantations of cypress, wattle, and eucalyptus in the Kibali-Ituri, Kivu, and Elisabethville areas.

The open forest of the Katanga region is used as a source of pitwood and fuel for the mines, and is regenerated naturally from coppice and suckers. An interesting experiment was made recently in the use of forest-fallow for communal farming in the high-forest area. This 'corridor system', which is fully described elsewhere,[3] permits of the natural re-generation at five-year intervals of the secondary forest, which consists mainly of *Musanga cecropioides* (umbrella trees). Village plantations are encouraged, though they have not made much progress, and a scheme has been put forward to give forestal cover to some 500,000 acres of deteriorated grazing land.

There was in 1952 a Forest Service (*Service des Eaux et Forêts*) consisting of a Director, 19 *Ingénieurs Forestiers*, 50 *Agents Forestiers*, and 205 *Agents Indigènes*. The Katanga has its own Service working under the *Comité Spécial*.[4] The European officers are trained either at one of the two national Institutes maintained by Belgium, the *Instituts Agronomiques de l'État* at Gembloux and at Ghent, or at the *Institut Agronomique* of the University of Louvain. In 1953 the *Université Libre* of Brussels began to give a two-year course for candidates for the post of *Ingénieur Agronome*. The full course qualifying for the position of *Ingénieur Forestier* is of five years' duration, namely two years as *Agronome* and three as *Ingénieur*.[5] The African personnel receives its training at the *Écoles Professionnelles Agricoles*, but this training is general, not specialized, and it is now pro-posed to create special sections in those schools for training in forestry.

As regards Forest Research the *Institut National pour l'Étude Agronomique du Congo Belge* (I.N.E.A.C.)[6] has a Forestry Division with a Research Centre at Yangambi, and Research Stations in the Mayumbe, Katanga, Ituri, and Lower-Congo areas. The Administration has instituted a *Mission anti-érosive* for the study of the general problems of land and water use,

---

[1] See above, p. 913.

[2] The Forestry Decrees are dealt with in *Enc. C.B.*, vol. iii, pp. 649 ff. See also *Codes et Lois du Congo Belge*, 1954, pp. 1146 ff.   [3] See above, p. 904.

[4] René J. Cornet, *Terre katangère*, 1951, pp. 240 ff.

[5] *Loi*, 27 June 1947.   [6] See above, p. 919.

irrigation, and protective afforestation. The Chief of the Mission is a Forest Officer.

In 1950 the output of logs was stated to be 17,027,000 cubic feet. Of these, 3,603,000 cubic feet were exported in log form, with 974,000 cubic feet of sawn timber and 37,600 cubic feet of veneer. The quality of exports is regulated by an Ordinance of 1948 which makes inspection prior to shipment compulsory. Of the timber exported 83 per cent. was *limba*, and the balance was made up of a number of other species. It would seem that in the Belgian Congo, as elsewhere, market demands have of recent years stimulated *concessionnaires* to place on the market a variety of other hardwoods which were not formerly recognized as marketable. The proportion of *limba* was in consequence reduced in 1951 to 72 per cent.[1] In 1952 exports fell to 909,585 cubic feet of logs and 217,400 cubic feet of sawn timber.[2]

The Spanish Territories

Spanish Guinea shares with the Gabon region of French Equatorial Africa a monopoly of *okoumé* wood (*Aucoumea klaineana*). Forests are classified in three grades corresponding to their proximity to the coast, and are leased to some seven Concession Companies. Out of 292,000 acres so conceded about 85 per cent. is being exploited. Some 60,800 tons are exported annually. Before the Second World War approximately half of this went to Germany, but now the total export is shipped to Spain. The headquarters of the Forest Service is situated at Benito.

The Portuguese Territories

The distribution of rainfall in Angola varies from a negligible quantity at Mossâmedes, where the country borders on the rainless desert of the Namib, to the typical precipitation on the plateau, where an annual rainfall of 52 inches is the average at Nova Lisboa. The territory is as a whole well wooded, especially along the border of the Belgian Congo and the upper waters of the Zambezi, but the principal location of its most valuable timbers is the Cabinda enclave to the north of the estuary of the Congo river.

The protection of the natural forests rests with a Forestry Department whose work is divided over 13 zones, together containing 156 square miles of forest.[3] In 1942 Forestry Experimental Stations were established at Ganda, Cabinda, and Chela Mountain; there is at Chela a branch of sylvicultural research whose special function is the study of the species constituting the Mayumbe forest in the Cabinda enclave. It is staffed by three engineers, a botanist, and an entomologist. The Angola forests

[1] *Rapport sur l'administration de la colonie du Congo Belge, 1951*, p. 272.
[2] Ibid. *1952*, p. 276.
[3] Angola Institute Edition, *Angola*, Luanda, 1953, p. 111.

produce about 200,000 cubic metres of timber annually, chiefly for domestic use in the form of railway sleepers and plywood, but 37,500 tons were exported in 1951, and the industry is capable of greater expansion.

The principal forest in Mozambique extends in a belt, some 40 miles in depth, situated between the Pungwe valley and the Zambezi river, being densest in the Inhaminga district near the Zambezi. This belt contains a variety of hardwoods such as the *kiaat* (*Pterocarpus angolensis*) and the *iroko* (*Chlorophora excelsa*), but only those which approach nearest to the true African teak command the high market prices which make exploitation commercially profitable. Before the Second World War production was confined to railway sleepers, but a great impetus was given to the industry by the interruption of supplies to the Union of South Africa from Australia and Scandinavia. The export of timber by *concessionnaires* was, however, carried out unsystematically until the Government made the issue of a licence conditional upon the timber being properly sawn. Saw-mills were erected at Lourenço Marques, Beira, and elsewhere. Timber has now become one of the territory's principal exports, having risen to 126,000 tons in 1953.

Liberia

It has been estimated that between 90 and 95 per cent. of the total area of Liberia was at one time under high or close-canopied forest. Today a little over $37\frac{1}{2}$ per cent. of the whole territory is so classified. Broken bush constitutes about $20\frac{1}{2}$ per cent. of the total.[1] From an aerophotographic survey undertaken by the United States Air Force in 1945 it was deduced that Liberia offered forestal prospects comparable with any territory on the west coast, though these have been very little exploited. The forest belts correspond closely with the amount of rainfall. Near the coast, where the annual rainfall is between 100 and 200 inches, there is a fairly deep belt of evergreen rain forest; in the centre, which has an annual rainfall of 75 to 125 inches, the forest is deciduous, but in the northern areas, with a much lower average, the country is mainly savannah.

The chief problem of the future lies in the question whether, assuming the continuance of the present system of bush fallow cultivation, there is a possibility of the present balance of growth and drain on the forests being disturbed to a dangerous extent. It is estimated that at the present time some 50,000 acres are being converted annually from high forest or broken bush to farm clearings. Such losses of woodland are somewhat less than the corresponding rates in adjacent territories, but shifting agriculture, unless it is controlled, would eventually cause a dangerous reduction in

[1] K. R. Mayer, *Forest Resources of Liberia*, U.S. Department of Agriculture, Bulletin no. 67, p. 1.

the total forest area. The danger point for Liberia would not, however, be reached for 35 to 40 years, if it is assumed, in the light of West African experience, that it would be to the advantage of Liberia that half its total area should remain under forest.[1]

Reference will be made subsequently to the export of rubber which now forms the most profitable asset in the forest estates of Liberia.[2]

ECOLOGY AND STOCK-MAPPING

Botanical knowledge of most of the African forest areas is now well advanced. In the British territories the Imperial Forestry Institute at Oxford has compiled check-lists of forest species for Uganda (1935), Nyasaland (1937), Gold Coast (1937), Tanganyika (1940 and 1949), and Bechuanaland (1948). The one for Northern Rhodesia is now being completed. The Royal Botanic Gardens, Kew, published a *Flora of West Africa* between the years 1931 and 1936,[3] and has recently issued the first part of a *Flora of Tropical East Africa*. They are also collaborating with the *Instituto Botánico de Coimbra* in the production of a *Conspectus Florae Angolensis*.

Local ecological studies which have a bearing on forest work have received some attention in certain areas. C. G. Trapnell and others have embodied the results of many years of work in a *Vegetation-Soil Map of Northern Rhodesia*, 1948. The late C. C. Gillman published a *Vegetation-Type Map of Tanganyika Territory* in 1949, and in the same year R. W. J. Keay produced *An Outline of Nigerian Vegetation*. There is, however, a great deal of work still to be done in this respect on both sides of the continent.

In the British territories the stock-mapping of forests has been assisted by the recent aerial surveys carried out by the Colonial Survey Directorate,[4] and a number of maps have been prepared of several previously unsurveyed forests, while the distribution of different types of vegetation in others has been determined. The enumeration of forest growing stocks has been in hand for many years, but in such vast areas it is a protracted operation, and, since the Second World War, increased attention has been paid to the improvement of methods of sampling as applied to forest conditions. At the Commonwealth Forestry Conference of 1952, the representatives of the British African territories stated that reliable estimates of growing stock had been made for 12,600 square miles of forest, of which nearly two-thirds was in West Africa. It had been necessary to write off a great deal of earlier work done in this connexion, but more

---

[1] Ibid. p. 14.
[3] J. M. Bulcial, *The Useful Plants of West Africa*, 1937.
[2] See below, p. 964.
[4] See above, p. 14.

rapid progress is now being made. A 'working plan' cannot be concisely defined, but it usually includes a description of a forest area, a definition of the long-term objects of management, and a general scheme for their attainment within a reasonable period of time. Working plans such as this have been drawn up for some 5,500 square miles in the British Colonial areas of Africa. In this sphere also considerable advance can be expected in the next few years.

Silvicultural studies have been undertaken in all the British territories, but it cannot be said that satisfactory techniques for regenerating either the tropical high forest or the savannah woodlands have yet been developed. The largest experiment undertaken in this direction is the regeneration of high forest in Nigeria by the so-called Tropical Shelterwood system, which was started in 1944 and had by 1951 covered 160 square miles, mainly in the Benin and Ondo forests. Nowhere, however, is the regeneration yet old enough to be classed as completely established new high forest. Mention has already been made of the use of the *taungya* method of regeneration, and of afforestation by planting, in which considerable progress has been made, particularly in South Africa.

Botanical information about the forests of the French African colonies has been published from 1919 onwards. The most recent works are *La Flore forestière de la Côte d'Ivoire* by A. Aubréville, 1936 (3 volumes), and *La Flore forestière Soudane-Guinéenne—A.O.F.—Cameroun—A.E.F.* by the same author, 1950. Also *Flore vivante de l'Afrique Occidentale Française*, by A. Chevalier, and *La Forêt du Gabon*, by H. Heitz, 1943.[1] Information about areas under working plans and areas which have been subjected to various systems of treatment is not, however, so readily available. The method of regeneration which has been used most widely is that of enrichment planting in lines cut through exploited forest.[2]

In the Belgian Congo extensive studies have been made by various Forest Officers, notably A. Delevoy in Katanga. A flora for the Belgian Congo and Ruanda Urundi was published in Brussels in 1948, and a useful *Monographie des principales essences forestières* was issued by the Information Office in Brussels in 1952. P. Humblet has discussed the regeneration of the Mayumbe forest,[3] which, like that of the French territories, is mainly by enrichment planting.

THE INTRODUCTION OF EXOTIC TREES

The early introduction of exotic trees in the Union of South Africa has already been referred to, and in the Rhodesias and parts of East Africa

---

[1] For a further bibliography see *Enc. A.O.F.*, vol. i, p. 390.   [2] See above, p. 953.
[3] P. Humblet in *Bulletin agricole du Congo Belge*, vols. xxxv, 1944, pp. 137–65, and xlv, 1954, pp. 1277–88.

the planting of fast-growing exotics, particularly pines and eucalyptus, has of recent years formed an important part of the activities of the Forest Departments. In both the British and French Colonies of West Africa the principal exotics are teak, *Cassia siamea*, *Gmelina arborea*, *Cedrela mexicana*, *Dalbergia sissoo*, and neem (*Azadirachta indica*). Teak usually does well, and both *Cassia* and *Gmelina* flourish in their earlier stages, though liable to deteriorate later.

The question of the planting of exotics was considered to be of sufficient importance by the British Empire Forestry Conference of 1928 to call for a special inquiry.[1] The case for exotics is that in many African territories the indigenous species are slow-growing and difficult to establish in high concentrations. A eucalyptus from Australia will often produce ten times as much firewood per acre as any local species, and where wood is the only fuel available, this may be very important. In suitable sites in South, Central, and East Africa, pine from Mexico or the West Indies will provide in a relatively few years much more timber per acre than the local coniferous species would supply after a very prolonged period.

There are, however, many difficulties attending the introduction of non-native species. Their rapid growth may wear out African soils more quickly than the slow-growing indigenous species, and many of the exotics appear to succeed when grown as pure crops, but not as mixtures. This means that a concentrated population of one species is made liable to fungi and insect pests, which, while they may do little harm in the natural mixed forests, can reach epidemic proportions in the pure plantations. On poor sites exotics are particularly susceptible to disease, which then spreads to crops on good sites also. Experienced foresters, therefore, use exotics with discretion and only where they offer advantages which outweigh the possible risks. In some of the dry areas it has now been found better to regenerate and protect the local bush for fuel rather than to plant exotics. In poor soils greater success can be achieved by planting some of the local species of acacia or the like than was at one time thought possible.

In the Union of South Africa some alarm was caused about 20 years ago by the belief that exotic pine and eucalyptus plantations brought about drier conditions of the soil and might endanger water supplies.[2] Hydrological research has not, however, indicated the truth of this belief, and it appears that there is no cause for the fears expressed.

[1] R. S. Troup, *Exotic Forest Trees in the British Empire*, 1932.
[2] Empire Forestry Conference, South Africa, 1935, *Report of Committee on Forests in Relation to Climate, Water Conservation, and Erosion*, p. 12.

SPECIAL TIMBERS AND OTHER FOREST PRODUCTS

West Coast Timbers

The largest and finest timber from African forests comes from the territories on the west coast. At one time African mahogany or *Acajou d'Afrique* (*Khaya* spp.) and the timbers of *Entandrophragma* spp. (*sapele, sapelli, tiama, sipo,* &c.) were the most sought after, but now woods of the utility class, *gaboon* (*Aucoumea*), *obechi* or *ayous* (*Triplochiton*), *abura* or *bahia* (*Mitragyna*), and *limba* or *afara* (*Terminalia superba*) provide the bulk of the timber. Before 1939 only 15 to 20 of the 300 species growing to timber size had been marketable abroad, but between 30 and 40 species can now be exported, and many more have been found to be of use locally. At the same time it is true to say that a very few species still make up the bulk of the trade in most territories.

The demand for sawn timber has grown rapidly. The Gold Coast and the Belgian Congo have increased the proportion of sawn timber in their total exports more noticeably than other West African territories in recent years, but large mills have been installed in all these territories. Many, such as Nigeria and Gabon, have gone farther, and are developing integrated industries in which the best logs are peeled or sliced locally and the rest are sawn. The most ambitious venture is that in the Ivory Coast, where experiments in the manufacture of paper pulp from the mixture of local hardwoods are being carried out. If this should prove economic, it may, as already pointed out, involve a great extension of forest operations. It is reported to be successful to the extent that it now provides Kraft paper for banana packing.

Central and East African Exports

Exports from Central and East Africa have been on a much smaller scale than those of West Africa, and are almost entirely in the form of sawn timber. The so-called Rhodesian teak has been exported for many years, but the main source of supply in Northern Rhodesia is nearly exhausted.[1] The conifers *Podocarpus* and *Juniperus procera* (the latter in the form of pencil slats) are shipped in small quantities from Kenya and Tanganyika. The main hardwood exports are *iroko* (*Chlorophora excelsa*), *muninga* (*Pterocarpus angolensis*, the *kiaat* of South Africa), and East Africa camphorwood (*Ocotea usambarensis*), but these also are on a small scale. Exotic softwoods now provide two-thirds of all the timber sawn in South Africa and are beginning to be important in Kenya, where 10 per cent. of the mill intake in 1950 consisted of plantation logs.

[1] See above, p. 913.

Minor Forest Products

A number of important minor products come from the African forests. Some of these are true forest products, for example tans, fibres, gum arabic, and resins. Amongst those which pertain in some measure to the character of agricultural products are rubber, the oil-seeds of the oil palm, shea nuts, and kola nuts.

An important supply of tan stuffs is obtained from the introduced wattle, now largely grown in the Union and East Africa. Mangroves also produce a tan; the extract is known as 'cutch' (originally identified with the extract from an Asiatic tree, the *Acacia catecha*), and is used for tanning fishing-nets and sails. The export trade in mangrove bark is now smaller than formerly, as tests of bark from West Africa have shown that the tannin content of the local mangrove is somewhat low for commercial use. Fibres are not uncommon in the forests, but though serviceable for local purposes they cannot compete with fibres grown as agricultural crops. In times of high prices for sisal, however, *sansevieria* (or bowstring hemp) fibre is exported from Tanganyika. Several species of the raphia palm are found in the rain forests and yield a tough fibre from the young unopened leaves.[1] *R. vinifera* and *R. gaertnerii* are found in West Africa and *R. munbuttorum* in tropical East Africa. The product is exported as *piassava* or African hemp from West Africa, notably Sierra Leone.

Flosses or 'silk cottons' are produced in considerable quantities from the covering of the seeds of certain species of trees, notably the *bombax*; the 'silk cotton' is, however, too brittle to spin. Another floss, kapok, is yielded by the *Ceiba pentandra*, and exports from Nigeria were of some considerable value in 1951. In the savannah lands of the Ivory Coast all isolated trees of this species are marked for reservation.

The gum arabic of Africa is well known, owing to the fact that a considerable part of the world's supply comes from the Sudan.[2] It is obtained from various species of acacia, the *verek* (*Acacia senegal*) being the most important. In Tanganyika, where the production has been taken over by the Agricultural Department, exports were valued at £113,400 in 1951, and in Nigeria they brought in £218,000 in 1952. It is, however, difficult to secure a steady supply, collection as a rule being made only at times when crop failures have reduced the possibility of obtaining cash by other means. The kinds of resins used for making varnishes are known either as damars from the Malay States or copals from West Africa, where they are obtained from species of *Copaifera*, *Trachylobium*, and *Daniella*. The best quality comes from the Belgian Congo,[3] medium quality from

[1] See above, p. 870.
[2] D. W. Malcolm, *Report on Gum and Gum Arabic*, 1936, p. 59.
[3] E. Mertens, 'Recherches sur le Copal du Congo', *Bull. I.R.C.B.*, vol. iv, 1933, pp. 268 ff.

the Gold Coast and Sierra Leone, and the poorest from Nigeria. In East Africa the chief copal tree is *Trachylobium hornemannianum*.

The most important indigenous rubber tree of Africa is the West African or Lagos rubber (*Funtumia elastica*) which is found in the evergreen forest from Uganda westwards. There are in addition various rubber vines (*Landolphia* spp.). At one time the collection of wild rubber was the most profitable product of the African tropical forests; it furnished as much as 80 per cent. of the exports of both the Congo Free State and French Equatorial Africa, and also figured in the trade of the British West African territories and of Uganda. Like many other wild products, however, it could not withstand the competition from the products of a plantation system, and when the 'Para' rubber (*Hevea brasiliensis*) was introduced into Asia from South America it speedily drove the indigenous African rubber from the market. *Hevea* was also introduced as a plantation product into Africa, but it has had no great success save in Liberia, where it constitutes about 88 per cent. of the total exports. The Firestone Company[1] has plantations of 110,000 acres, and there are also some 600 independent planters. During the Second World War Liberia supplied the United States of America with about one-fifth of its requirements of rubber. Production on a smaller scale is to be found in the Belgian Congo (where it was first introduced in 1896) and in Nigeria, the Cameroons, and Uganda.

Other species of trees or plants producing rubber, such as *Ceara* and *Castilloa*, have also been tried, but have proved to be unsuitable. Wild rubber is now uneconomic in Africa, though in both the World Wars, and particularly during the Second, intensive tapping of *Funtumia* and rubber vines was organized and valuable quantities were obtained. This was, however, achieved at considerable expense and it caused heavy mortality among the plants. The well-known 'red rubber' is not the product of the vines *Landolphia* or *Funtumia*, but is extracted from the roots of *Carpodinus chylorrhiza* which thrives on the sandy Angola plateau. Collection of red or root rubber was first organized there in 1886 and by 1891 the value of exports exceeded $1 million.

The possibility of making paper pulp from forest trees or plants has attracted attention for many years. Bamboo, the *Arundinaria alpina* of the eastern highlands, papyrus, and elephant grass from Uganda and elsewhere have been found to be suitable, but economic considerations have prevented commercial production. The French experiments have shown that mixed tropical hardwoods can provide pulp suitable for Kraft paper, but they have not yet proved that its production can be economic. There can be little doubt that conifers planted in South, Central, and East Africa will produce woods suitable for the manufacture of pulp, and, given

[1] See above, p. 759.

a large enough supply of these woods surplus to timber requirements and sufficient water, manufacture may prove to be economic. In that case integrated industries producing lumber, boxboards, and pulp are likely to develop, as for instance in Swaziland.[1]

The oil palm (*Elaeis guineensis*) is indigenous to West Africa and just reaches into the western fringe of Uganda. For commercial purposes it is now becoming an agricultural rather than a forestal species,[2] but the collection of fruits from wild palms is the predominant form of production in British, French, and Portuguese Africa.

PESTS AND DISEASES

The insect and fungal pests of African forests are not of great importance until the constitution of the natural forests is changed by favouring selected species of trees, and particularly by the establishment of large pure plantations. Such pests may then become controlling factors. It is not surprising, therefore, that most of the investigations carried out into insect and fungal activities in Africa have so far been in South Africa, where plantations of exotics were first established. The *Pinus insignis*, for instance, has proved to be susceptible to disease where there is a summer rainfall, but not in the Western Cape Province, where there is a good winter rainfall. One of the most dramatic successes achieved by scientific investigations in recent years has been the control of the attacks made by the eucalyptus snout beetle on timber in the Rhodesias and East Africa, this having been effected through the introduction of an egg-parasite from Australia.

The Division of Entomology, Pretoria, has done much work in respect of the ravages of termites and powder-post and furniture beetles, which cause serious loss throughout Africa. The protection of wood against these pests and against pinhole borers (*Ambrosia* beetles) would be equivalent to increasing the area of the productive forests of Africa by thousands of square miles. One of the recommendations of the sixth British Commonwealth Forestry Conference, 1951, was that a team of entomologists should work intensively in West Africa on the problem of preventing damage by pinhole borers.

The East African Agriculture and Forestry Research Organization[3] in Kenya is now commencing investigations into timber pests throughout East Africa. Its most immediate tasks are to control the canker disease of cypress (*Monochaetia unicornis*) and the attacks of the longicorn beetle (*Oenida gahani*), which was previously a deadwood borer only but is now attacking healthy cypress trees, with the result that in afforestation in East Africa pines have been preferred to cypresses.

[1] See above, p. 940.   [2] See above, p. 852.   [3] See above, p. 915.

THE ORGANIZATION OF TRAINING

The preceding pages have shown how belated has been the interest taken by many of the African Administrations in the conservation and betterment of their woodlands. It is worthwhile in this connexion to compare the development of a forest policy in British India, for in one respect at all events—the progressive Indianization of the Forest Service—it suggests a lesson which some of the African Administrations would do well to appreciate. At one time India had dense forests in the Gangetic plain, but most of those had disappeared long before the introduction of British rule.[1] The remaining forests, situated mostly in the hill areas of India or Burma and Assam, were estimated in 1947 (the year of the passing of the Indian Independence Act) to cover rather more than 20 per cent. of the whole of India and Burma, or $7\frac{3}{4}$ per cent. if Burma and Assam were excluded. The danger of their destruction was perceived as early as the middle of the nineteenth century, and in 1855 a general policy of forest conservation was inaugurated by Lord Dalhousie.[2]

At the outset the purpose was to preserve to the State a valuable source of revenue, but it was subsequently realized that the control of fellings in the Himalayan and other mountain forests was essential in order to conserve the sources which supplied India with its great schemes of irrigation. The first Forest Act was passed in 1865. In default of British-trained personnel it was necessary to seek at the outset the aid of experienced continental foresters and to utilize the French and German forestry organizations in order to give some practical experience to candidates for an Indian Forest Service.[3] A Forestry School was opened at Dehra Dun in 1878 for the training of Indians as Forest Rangers, and the School was subsequently raised to the status of a College. In 1906 a Forest Research Institute was formed, also at Dehra Dun. Shortly before the outbreak of the Second World War India had a senior staff of 427 Forest Officers, 42 per cent. of whom were Indian nationals, and, in addition, it had a large number of trained Forest Rangers, who could justly be described as the backbone of the Service.[4] There thus existed in India a competent organization not merely for administration but for making systematic investigation into the problems of a great forest estate. When power was transferred in 1947, the organization was no doubt put to some temporary strain, but it was not crippled by the withdrawal of those European officers who still formed part of its establishment.

It is characteristic of the history of forest organization in the British

[1] *Statement exhibiting the Moral and Material Progress and Condition of India, 1924–5*, p. 203.
[2] *Imperial Gazetteer of India*, vol. iii, p. 107.
[3] *Empire Forestry Review*, vol. xxxi, 1952, p. 20.
[4] R. S. Troup, *Colonial Forest Administration*, 1940, p. 294.

Colonies that up to 1915 only twelve university-trained Forest Officers were sent to all the Colonies, including those of Africa.[1] The increased importance attached to the development of a trained Forest Establishment is shown by the fact that the senior staff in the British African dependencies alone numbered 116 in 1938 and 228 in 1954. The Oxford School of Forestry founded in 1905 became the Imperial Forestry Institute in 1924.[2] The post of Forest Adviser to the Secretary of State for the Colonies was created in 1941. Though, however, the senior staff has been substantially increased in these territories, there remains a serious deficiency in the cadre of African Rangers. Not only can men of the Ranger class set free a scientifically trained higher staff for research or similar work, but it is the Ranger who also forms the essential link between the Forest Department and the local peasant or farmer. There has, as has been shown, been also a significant increase in the superior Forest Staff of the French and Belgian dependencies, and their Administrations seem hitherto to have been much more successful in attracting qualified Africans for training as Rangers or the equivalent category of officers.

RESERVATION OF FORESTS AND WOODLANDS

While there is general agreement as to the advisability of extending the area of forest reservation in order to preserve the remainder of the high forest as a State asset, there is considerable difference both in the theory and practice applied to the conservation of other woodlands. There is no one formula which can determine the extent to which reservation of woodland areas is required in order to protect water supplies or otherwise assist in conserving the productivity of the soil. For some years the accepted policy in Nigeria sought to secure on general grounds a reserved area of woodland equal to 25 per cent. of the total land area. Elsewhere, as for example in the French Cameroons, the target has been placed at from one-quarter to one-third of the savannah.

Experience shows, however, that the question of reservation cannot be approached in the abstract, and it is, in particular, necessary to take into account the requirements of Africans for subsistence production under the system of shifting cultivation. Until science finds some method which will be equally effective as a means of dealing with a soil so liable to rapid exhaustion as that of Africa, no Administration engaged in planning the reservation of permanent woodland areas will be able to overlook the requirements of shifting cultivation. It will be necessary also to pay regard to the needs of graziers, though it is to be hoped that time may bring a change in the African habit, common at all events in East Africa, of

---

[1] *Empire Forestry Review*, vol. xxxi, 1952, pp. 21–22.
[2] *Handbook of the University of Oxford*, 1947, p. 226.

maintaining an uneconomic number of cattle. It is noteworthy that in India the Reserved forests have been regarded as of great value in supplementing the normal grazing areas in times of drought,[1] but in this respect they are likely to have a more limited use in Africa.

The question of the conservation of a suitable extent of existing woodlands and (in certain localities) the creation or re-creation of tree-bearing areas is clearly one which should occupy an important place in the development programme of most Administrations. But it is not necessarily the function of a scientifically trained Forest Service. It is for the Administration to educate the African in the need for this measure and to secure his co-operation—a point of increasing importance in view of the rapid extension of schemes of African self-government. It must have also the assistance of Agricultural Officers, for the growth of trees by peasants on their holdings is almost as important as the increase of Reserved woodlands.

The land rights possessed by the Governments of different territories in respect of the reservation of forest areas have been referred to elsewhere when discussing the powers of the different Administrations in relation to land.[2] In the British dependencies the major difficulty arises in areas such as the Gold Coast Colony and Ashanti, the southern parts of Nigeria, or the Protectorate area of Sierra Leone, where the Crown has not asserted a claim to exercise superior rights over the great bulk of the lands. In the French and Belgian systems the operation of reservation is, from the purely legal standpoint, one of relative ease, since the state has legislated in order to establish its right over all *terres vacantes*.[3]

In actual practice, however, the most difficult of the problems to which reservation may give rise is that of devising a machinery for the management of the Reserved lands which will give them the necessary measure of protection, but will do so with as little friction as possible. It is easy to imagine the resentment felt by cattle-owners who see their herds, hard hit by seasonal drought or by the exhaustion of pasture lands, excluded from lands which are no less tempting because the Administration has reserved them for other purposes. It is largely this consideration which has led various Administrations to supplement State reservation by confiding the task of protecting communal woodland areas to Native Authorities, or by attempting the development of small Village Forests, as in Nyasaland.[4] The management of such areas under either the 'village' or the Native Authority systems is admittedly likely to be less efficient than if carried out by an official establishment; but some falling off in the standards of management may be justified if general good will can be secured for measures designed for the preservation of the woodlands.

---

[1] V. Anstey, *Economic Development of India*, 1952, p. 175.
[2] See above, pp. 731, 738, 741.   [3] See above, pp. 745, 749.   [4] See above, p. 944.

Administrations are always likely to find it difficult to carry the African public with them in this matter, for, as experience elsewhere shows, the doctrine of forest conservation is likely to encounter opposition even among people who readily accept modern practice in most other respects. The need for education in the proper attitude towards forest conservation adds point to what has been said in previous paragraphs regarding the training of an African Forest Staff.

INTERNATIONAL CO-OPERATION

Reference is found elsewhere to the effort made in recent years to break down the isolation existing between the professional and scientific workers belonging to different African territories.[1] This is especially necessary in the case of those concerned with problems of forest research or adminis-tration, for the issues with which they have to deal differ little from one part of Africa to another. The five-yearly meetings of the Empire (now Commonwealth) Forestry Conferences (of which the latest was in 1952) have made a useful link between Forest Officers working in the British areas, but it was not until 1941 that the first Inter-African Forestry Con-ference assembled at Abidjan in the Ivory Coast. Many Forest Officers also attended the African Soil Conference held in 1948 at Goma in the Belgian Congo and the African Regional Scientific Conference held at Johannesburg in 1949. The establishment of the Agricultural and Forestry Research Organization in East Africa[2] will provide fresh facilities for intercolonial consultation on the technical problems of forestry in Africa.

FORESTRY RESEARCH

The research work which can be undertaken in Europe for the assistance of African forestry is in the main confined to systematic botany, to the study of wood structure, and to an appraisal of the commercial possi-bilities of forest products. In Great Britain the Imperial Forestry Institute at Oxford provides a centre for advanced study and training of research workers,[3] and in this respect it collaborates closely with the Common-wealth Forestry Bureau and with the Forest Products Research Laboratory at Princes Risborough. The latter is a branch establishment of the De-partment of Scientific and Industrial Research concerned with wood and wood products, and has carried out tests of timbers for all British African territories. Several African timbers, now in common use, were unmarket-able before the laboratory demonstrated how they should be treated or used.

The Union of South Africa, which has for many years been self-con-

---

[1] See below, Chapter XXIV.   [2] See below, p. 970.
[3] *The Imperial Forestry Institute, Oxford, Annual Report, 1953-4.*

tained in such matters, maintains a Forest Products Research Institute at Pretoria,[1] which has, in particular, carried out important work on the relationship between density, age, and strength of coniferous timber. The Institute has also assisted various Central and East African territories by carrying out tests on their timbers for them. The Botanical Department of Stellenbosch University and the pathological section of the Division of Plant Industry co-operate in the study of tree diseases.

In the British African territories research has been assisted by the recent addition of specialist officers (as, for example, silviculturalists and Utilization Officers) in the course of the reorganization of local Forestry Services. An important step has also been taken by the establishment, under the auspices of the East Africa High Commission, of an East African Agriculture and Forestry Research Organization with headquarters at Muguga near Nairobi. This is designed to serve Kenya, Tanganyika, and Uganda.[2] The Organization includes bureaux of silviculture, of utilization of forest products, and of forest entomology; the Research Officers in charge work in close contact with the territorial Research Officers.

In metropolitan France an organization was established in 1917 entitled the *Section des Bois Coloniaux*, but after undergoing various changes it was reconstituted in 1949 as the *Centre Technique Forestier Tropical* at Nogent-sur-Marne near Paris. It has an establishment of a Director and twelve research scientists. The *Comité National des Bois Tropicaux*, a private organization, undertakes the dissemination of the results of research and their application to commerce. The *Régie Industrielle de la Cellulose Coloniale* originally carried out the research which led to the building of the pilot plant for paper pulp at Bimbresso in the Ivory Coast.[3] In the French Colonies local forest research is under the general direction of the *Inspecteur-Général des Eaux et Forêts* at Dakar. There are local research stations in the Ivory Coast and the French Cameroons.

In Belgium a Laboratory of Wood Technology was founded in 1948 as part of the State Agricultural College of Ghent, its main activities being the study of the anatomy of Belgian Congo woods and their identification. There is also a *Commission d'Étude des Bois Congolais* in Brussels; it has a membership representative of both forest institutions and the timber trade, and is concerned mainly with the study of timber uses and marketing. In 1947 the *Institut pour la Recherche Scientifique en Afrique Centrale* (I.R.S.A.C.) was set up to co-ordinate all scientific work in the Belgian Congo. Reference has already been made to the work done in the Colony itself by the *Institut National pour l'Étude Agronomique du Congo Belge* (I.N.E.A.C.).[4]

---

[1] *O.Y.S.A., 1949*, pp. 885–96.

[2] *Colonial Research, 1950–1951*, Cmd. 8303, 1951, p. 144. For the Organization's achievements in 1954–5, see its *Annual Report, 1955, Record of Research for the Period 1st January 1954 to 30th June 1955*, Nairobi. See also below, p. 1607.

[3] See above, p. 953.   [4] See above, p. 99, and below, p. 1606.

CHAPTER XIV

WATER SUPPLY AND IRRIGATION

As has been seen in the first chapter of this Survey, there are certain parts of Africa south of the Sahara in which the problem of water supply is not a matter of real concern, though in the arid or semi-arid areas the problem is one of vital importance.[1] The figures of total annual rainfall relating to some of these areas can be deceptive, for its distribution over the months of the year can prove to be an even more important factor in agricultural production. A heavy rainfall spread over a comparatively short period and falling on a soil made friable by long exposure to the sun can leach out some of its most valuable constituents and thus become a potent source of soil deterioration.

It is interesting to recall, when dealing with the figures of the average rainfall in different parts of Africa, that the annual rainfall in London during the ten years ending 1951 averaged only 23½ inches, but that there was an average of 150 'rain days', and 463 'rain hours'. The average given is, moreover, fairly constant over a series of years; the records show that the mean average rainfall is reached in nine out of ten years. There is thus an entirely different factor of soil-saturation from that found in many parts of Africa where the annual precipitation may be far heavier but the duration of rainfall much shorter. In the more arid parts of Africa there is thus a double problem—that caused by the low volume of rainfall and that due to the actual seasonal distribution of such rainfall. Maldistribution, among other evils, accounts largely for the lack of vegetal cover, the main cause of 'sheet' erosion,[2] which is seldom seen in countries with a well-distributed rainfall and a reasonable standard of humidity.

The existence of large arid or semi-arid areas in Africa has not un-naturally attracted attention to the success attained by some of the countries of Asia in meeting the problem of aridity by the extension of irrigation. 'A special peculiarity of Indian agriculture', it was once observed, 'is the ingenious and assiduous manner in which water is applied to increase the produce of the soil.'[3] The great irrigation systems of India, now the most extensive in the world, have a long history behind them; the earliest of the major irrigation canals constructed by the British in Northern India, the Lower Ganges canal, was actually opened three years before the Sepoy Mutiny of 1857. The major proportion of the cultivation of the Indian sub-continent of today is dependent on rainfall, but it

---

[1] For the 'zones of aridity', see J. H. Wellington, in *Africa South of the Sahara*, 1951, pp. 35–39.
[2] See below, p. 1016.   [3] *Report of Indian Farming Commission*, Part II, 1880, p. 82.

is noteworthy that in 1936–7 India and Pakistan had no less than 20 million acres irrigated by State or private canals, apart from 28 million acres irrigated from wells, tanks, or other sources. The area irrigated was roughly one-fifth of the total area sown. In 1947 India and Pakistan had a length of 80,000 miles of canals, and the area irrigated amounted to 72 million acres, or nearly twelve times the area under irrigation in Egypt.[1] This proportion of irrigated acres will be materially increased after the completion of the great irrigation undertakings which form part of the present development plans. Under the programme of the Indian Republic it is proposed to expend £421 million on irrigation and power schemes.[2] In the Punjab Province of Pakistan, which is, for the most part, a typically arid area, 52 per cent. of the total sown area in 1949–50 was irrigated from State canals, and another 13 per cent. from wells.

The total cultivable area of Egypt is usually stated to be about 9 million acres and, of this, about $5\frac{1}{4}$ million acres are under cultivation; the whole of this area is cultivated under irrigation, roughly $4\frac{1}{4}$ million acres from waters controlled by the barrages, and 1 million under the traditional 'basin' system. But the development of great works on the scale of those now existing in India or in Egypt is due to conditions which have sometimes been overlooked by those who have urged the wide expansion of irrigation in Africa. The most successful undertakings in India have been those constructed in the areas where the surface gradients have provided an extensive field of 'command' for a canal based on a relatively low (and therefore relatively inexpensive) form of headwork. Again, the most successful irrigation projects have been able to reimburse to the State their capital and maintenance costs because, as a rule, comparatively high-priced crops have been grown and have had a ready access to market. Though there may be instances in Africa where it may be advisable for the State to undertake schemes of irrigation which are designed mainly to support subsistence cultivation, plans for 'productive' works are likely to find a ready support only where conditions favour the intensive cultivation of marketable crops. There are relatively few areas in Africa where the surface contours or the 'régime' of the rivers are as favourable as they have proved to be in India or Egypt.[3] Irrigation in Northern India is particularly favoured by the fact that the surface contours give the canals a very extensive 'command', and that the diminished winter flow of the rivers is reinforced in the spring by the melting of the Himalayan snows, thus bridging the critical period before the advent of the monsoon rains.

It is in the circumstances likely that, in Africa, the future will see an

---

[1] G. Lacey, in *Irrigation*, published for the British Council, 1950, p. 67.

[2] *India, 1952, An Anniversary Review*, 1953.

[3] See on this point generally, *East Africa Royal Commission 1953–55, Report*, Cmd. 9475, 1955, pp. 270–1.

increasing importance attached to small-scale irrigation projects,[1] where conditions make them possible, and to the development of measures for the storage of surface water by the use of dams, or the provision of wells or bore-holes for utilizing subsoil supplies. It has been pointed out that, as sources of water, wells are cheaper than dams[2] and though, as a rule, they provide water for irrigation purposes only on a minor scale, they are of primary importance for the provision of domestic supplies or for watering stock. In some of the more arid areas, therefore, the development of the use of subsoil water may prove to be the key to the improvement of the rural economy.

The succeeding paragraphs will contain a short survey of the use now made of water supplies in each of the more important territories. It will be convenient to refer at the same time to the use made of rivers for the production of hydroelectric power, a matter to which the shortage in the supply of coal or mineral oil has given increasing importance of recent years.[3] Various calculations have been made of the potential water-power of Africa. One estimate has stated it to be equivalent to 190 million horse-power, or three times the estimated potential horse-power of Europe.[4] But such a calculation does not pretend to be based on a detailed survey, nor is it reasonable to include those potential sources which are so situated that the power thus developed could not expect to find a consumer. It is, for example, significant that the above-mentioned estimate credits the French Congo with a possible 35 million horse-power and the French Cameroons with 13 million, but the Union of South Africa, where there is the chief demand for power, with only 1·6 million. Another authority has estimated the water potential of Africa as two-fifths of the world's potential, and four times greater than that of North America: according to this authority, only one-tenth of 1 per cent. is now utilized.[5] It has again been stated that 44 per cent. of the world's potential of hydroelectric power resides in Africa, and 25 per cent. in the basin of the Congo.[6] But global figures of this character must be accepted with due reservation.

The Union of South Africa

Aridity is certainly the characteristic feature of a considerable part of the Union of South Africa, and one of its best-known authorities has recently estimated that 46 per cent. of its 302 million acres must be classified as

[1] K. Busia and F. Debenham, in *The Development of Tropical and Sub-tropical Countries with Particular Reference to Africa*, ed. A. L. Banks, 1954, p. 78.

[2] C. Clark, 'The Economics of Irrigation', *New Commonwealth*, 25 November and 9 December 1954.   [3] See below, pp. 984 ff.

[4] A. W. Postel, 'The Mineral Resources of Africa', *African Handbooks*, no. 2 (University of Pennsylvania), 1943, p. 78. See also Wellington, op. cit. pp. 181–6.

[5] F. Osborn, *The Limits of the Earth*, 1954, p. 66.

[6] Busia and Debenham, op. cit. p. 70.

arid or, at the best, semi-arid.[1] The Union Department of Irrigation estimates the whole annual mean run-off throughout the Union at approximately 40 million acre-feet, but holds that, owing to lack of storage sites and other factors, considerably less than 12 million acre-feet are available to meet all requirements.[2] With an average population density of nearly 27 per square mile, drought in the Union does not carry the same danger of famine as in South and South-East Asia, where population densities are far higher. Nevertheless, the recurrence of drought has gravely retarded economic progress. The Drought Commission of 1923 assessed at £16 million the direct losses from the drought of 1919, and the drought of 1933 is calculated to have resulted in the loss of 8¼ million animals. The Union has since then suffered severe losses in periodic droughts, that of 1949, for instance, causing the loss of over 2¼ million animals.

The direct effects of drought, however, are seen more in the areas devoted to animal husbandry than in the agricultural districts, and measures to protect the stock-raiser are of a somewhat different class from those intended for the protection of cultivation. They will be discussed separately, and it is proposed to deal here, in the first instance, with irrigation designed as an aid to agriculture.

The Union may for this purpose be divided into three zones: first, that in which irrigation is not required for the majority of crops, as in the coastal belt of Natal and in portions of the south coast; second, that in which no crops can be grown without irrigation—namely, the greater part of the Karroo and part of the south-western Free State; and third, that in which irrigation is necessary for certain crops at certain periods of the year. This last zone includes the south-western corner and eastern portions of the Cape, the northern and eastern regions of the Orange Free State, and the greater part of the Transvaal. Here the need for irrigation arises from conditions attending the seasonal distribution of rainfall rather than from a deficiency in the total volume. During the most critical periods of the year the lack of precipitation coincides with rising temperature, hot winds, and low humidity. There is a certain amount of summer rainfall in the northern part of this zone, but it is irregular and may produce extensive flooding. While, however, nature has created conditions which make irrigation essential for successful agriculture in the second zone and of considerable value in the third, she has at the same time created other conditions which limit the extent to which it can be successfully employed.

South Africa has a relatively low proportion of cultivable soil. Apart from the considerable proportion of hilly or mountainous country, much

[1] F. E. Kanthack, *Industrial Development in the Union of South Africa in Relation to Water Reserves* (Presidential Address to the Associated Scientific and Technical Societies of South Africa), 1946.
[2] *Report of the Commission of Enquiry concerning the Water Laws of the Union*, 1951.

of the plateau consists of shallow soils overlaying either original rock or thick beds of secondary formations, and it is thus unsuited for the more intensive cultivation which will repay the outlay on irrigation. A calculation first made in 1922 that the total area in the Union suitable for irrigation was 4 million acres was, in consequence of data since accumulated, considerably modified in 1941, and one authority then held that the total was not more than 1 million acres.[1] In the following year another authority, approaching the problem from the angle of the availability of water, was of the opinion that an area of 3 million acres could be supplied with adequate irrigation.[2] It was estimated in 1951 that there were 1 million acres under irrigation in the Union, of which 572,000 acres were, however, irrigated only under flood-water conservation schemes.[3]

The flood-water system, originally developed to meet the needs of lucerne-growing on ostrich farms, was the chief means of irrigation in the Union prior to 1910 and was in the main confined to Cape Colony. The system entailed the rapid leading of a large volume of water from the streams and its distribution over the entire area of irrigable land to a depth of 4 to 6 inches. In the more arid regions of the north-west Cape this system was carried a step farther, flood water being held up by embankments across flat valleys and distributed over the basins thus formed. This had the merit of low initial outlay, being estimated to cost between £2. 10s. and £10 per acre irrigated, but the valley lands are nowhere extensive. In the Transvaal these lands were found to be less suitable for flood irrigation than those in the Cape and this practice was less extensively adopted. As in the Free State, the primary need was for storage works to ensure irrigation during the dry season.

With the possibility that flood-water irrigation in the Cape might be approaching exhaustion, and with storage works the prime necessity in the Transvaal and the Free State, the irrigation policy of the Government came to be directed towards schemes of water conservation, and the greater outlay on storage works as compared with the flood system led it to legislate for the provision of advances to landholders for the purpose of conserving water. From early days, however, the statutory water laws in South Africa have been based on the riparian principle, whereby the right to the use of water is vested in the owners of land riparian to a stream. The consolidating Cape Irrigation Act of 1906 sought to determine the exact nature of these rights, and in 1908 the Transvaal enacted a codifying measure which was particularly concerned with methods for the conservation of water supplies. The period from 1906 to 1914 was one of

[1] F. E. Kanthack, 'Capacity of British South Africa, South of the Zambezi, to absorb and support People of European Descent', *South African Geographical Journal*, April 1941.
[2] D. F. Kokot, in *Proceedings of the South African Society of Civil Engineers*, vol. xl, 1942.
[3] *Report of the Commission of Enquiry concerning the Water Laws of the Union*, 1951.

great activity; many Irrigation Districts were proclaimed and Irrigation Boards formed to which large sums of public money were loaned.[1] Government expenditure on irrigation, including that derived from revenue, amounted to nearly £8 million in 1952–3.[2] Although the irrigation works were comparatively cheap, the cost to the farmers of bringing the land under cultivation was heavy in spite of the fact that farmers were, on the average, seldom able to manage more than 12 acres under irrigation. With the collapse of the ostrich-feather boom the demand for lucerne declined and farmers had to turn to other crops which required larger and more expensive storage works. There were in consequence many failures and it became necessary to write off a considerable proportion of the loans advanced.

In 1926 an Irrigation Commission made recommendations for the coordination of the efforts of the different agencies concerned in irrigation. An Act of 1934 made a significant advance towards a relaxation of the application of the riparian doctrine. While protecting the common law 'right of user' of the riparian owner, it limited that right to one cusec of water[3] for every mile of frontage. In further legislation of the same year the Government provided for the expropriation of lands required for settlement under large national schemes.[4] By 1951 there had been 169 Irrigation and River Districts proclaimed in the Union, and 112 of these had received nearly £6½ million in loans, providing for the development of a total area of over 300,000 acres.[5] The Government had by the same date made itself responsible for some 35 flood-water storage and irrigation schemes at a cost of over £20 million. They varied from minor river storage works at a comparatively low cost to irrigation schemes of some magnitude, involving large expenditure.

The chief of these schemes is the Vaal-Hartz undertaking, which was sanctioned in 1934 and was designed to serve a dual purpose. It provided in the first place for the needs of the Rand Water Board which had by 1950 paid £1¾ million for the right to take 195 million gallons daily from the Vaal Dam, thus making large quantities of water available for industrial purposes, an innovation in the South African water law. The scheme is at the same time calculated to command about 103,000 acres of irrigation. The actual area irrigated in 1951 was over 64,000 acres, including a considerable area in the Taungs Native Reserve inhabited by the Bathlaping tribe. This is the first occasion on which irrigation has been extended to a Native area, and its use in cultivation is being carefully supervised. About 8,000 acres had been brought into use by 1952.[6] In

---

[1] *O.Y.S.A., 1950*, pp. 789–95.   [2] Ibid. *1952–53*, p. 737.
[3] A cusec denotes one cubic foot of water per second.
[4] Acts nos. 38 and 46, 1934.   [5] *Report of the Director of Irrigation, 1950–1*, p. 20.
[6] C. W. Wolvaardt, *Taungs Irrigation Scheme Memorandum*, December 1952.

the European farming area there are some 1,053 irrigators and a water-rate of 10s. per acre is levied, this being the rate generally obtaining in similar schemes throughout the Union. The Union has not yet published any systematic account of its irrigation work which would provide information on such points as the average 'duty' per unit of water or the return on capital outlay, and, accordingly, no comparison is possible between the efficiency of this and similar schemes in other countries. The expenditure on the scheme had by 1952 amounted to roughly £6½ million, the cost having been increased by the fact that the canal at one stage had to be taken through a tunnel over three miles in length.[1]

The area of land commanded by the Vaal-Hartz scheme is thus of no great extent.[2] It would seem also that physical conditions do not favour the development of any large scheme of irrigation in the Union. The Orange river, for example, has been described as 'spasmodic in flow and too deeply embedded'. Attention has, however, recently been directed to a project for constructing a dam on the river, which might provide for the irrigation of roughly 350,000 acres. The site proposed is situated in the Orange Free State and the cost is estimated at about £100 million. The chief obstacle to proceeding with the project is not the cost, but the fact that the source of the river is in Basutoland, and the execution of the scheme might give rise to issues of some complexity with the United Kingdom.[3]

Again, the cost of constructing storage works is heavy; it varies from a minimum of £14 to £160 per acre, and it has been computed that the cost of irrigation per acre may rise to £200 or even more.[4] Water storage in South Africa is made unusually costly by the high percentage of evaporation and by the silting up of reservoirs fed by the debris-laden run-off from denuded mountain ranges; the storage capacity is therefore likely to decrease rapidly unless expensive schemes of head-water reafforestation are undertaken. It is significant that land potentially irrigable has little more value than similar non-irrigable land. The substantial State aid given to water conservation schemes, either indirectly by way of loans to Irrigation Boards or by directly financed State schemes, was the subject of comment by a Commission which reported in 1951.[5] It recommended a much fuller investigation into all aspects of State schemes before the undertakings are put into operation, and, while agreeing that large conservation works

[1] As regards use of rivers for development of electric power, see F. E. Kanthack, *Industrial Development in the Union of South Africa in Relation to Water Reserves* (Presidential Address to the Associated Scientific and Technical Societies of South Africa), 1946.

[2] A substantial raising of the height of the dam (to be completed in 1957) will, however, greatly increase the depth of water and affect accordingly the figures given above.

[3] *S.A.S.*, 30 March 1955, p. 5. *The Times*, 22 December 1955.

[4] D. F. Kokot, 'Irrigation Possibilities in the Union', *Proceedings of South African Society of Civil Engineers*, vol. xl, 1942, pp. 166–220.

[5] *Report of the Commission of Enquiry concerning the Water Laws of the Union*, 1951, pp. 9, 10.

must be financed out of State loans, it held that agricultural interests must be prepared to repay a fair share of the cost.

The high cost of irrigation for intensive agriculture and the limited acreage available for the purpose seems to add force to the view that the Union is essentially a pastoral country, and that the best use of irrigation may lie in the provision of greater security for livestock. It was to this end, indeed, that the recommendations of the Drought Commission of 1922 mainly tended. There is a vast extent of good grazing veld, but its stock-carrying capacity is reduced by uncertain supplies of drinking-water and by the lack of facilities for growing reserves of fodder. There were in 1952 between 11 and 12 million head of cattle in the Union and over 35 million sheep; but in the more arid areas the carrying capacity of the veld might be as low as one sheep on 50 or 60 acres.[1] Although there were thousands of little dams in the country, these were rarely adequate in the more arid areas to serve the needs of livestock throughout the year. Small irrigation schemes might provide for the growth of reserves of fodder and thus help to stabilize the animal industry.

The need for facilities for watering stock was emphasized in the report of the Commission of Inquiry of 1951 when it commented on the results achieved by the grant to farmers of a 50 per cent. subsidy for the construction of dams as part of the measures taken to control erosion.[2] Most of the assistance to stock-raisers will, however, continue to come from the use of subsoil water, and there is some measure of truth in the claim made by one well-known authority that 'more has been achieved towards the general development of the country from the few thousands of pounds spent annually upon State boring than from all the millions expended upon large diversion and storage schemes'.[3]

The Government of the Cape first began boring by State agency in 1904, and a Boring Branch of the Irrigation Department was created in 1910. The Department or an authorized contractor supplies the machinery, while fuel and labour are provided by the farmer. The average cost to the latter has varied from 16s. per foot drilled in 1919–20 to £1. 6s. in 1950–1; the average depth of bore-holes is 150 feet in the Union and over 200 feet in South-West Africa. The investigation of sites for bore-holes is an important function of the State Geological Survey, which has an Underground Water and Geophysics Branch engaged upon this service. Between 1945 and 1951 it had selected sites for 7,246 bore-holes, and 11,010 bore-holes were drilled between 1949 and 1953.[4]

There is a growing use of geophysical methods in investigating the

[1] F. E. Kanthack, in *South African Geographical Journal*, April 1941, p. 12.

[2] *Report of the Commission of Enquiry concerning the Water Laws of the Union*, 1951.

[3] A. L. du Toit, 'Borehole Supplies in the Union of South Africa', *Proceedings of South African Society of Civil Engineers*, vol. xxvi, 1928, p. 74.

[4] *O.Y.S.A., 1952–53*, p. 740.

existence of underground waters.[1] In the Native Reserves expenditure is undertaken by the Native Affairs Department and on an average over 100 bore-holes are being sunk annually in these areas. The report of the Director of Irrigation for 1950–1 refers to the falling 'water-table' of the Union, but it would not seem that there is in fact a general 'water-table'. Supplies are normally maintained by infiltration through pervious strata from the local annual rainfall, and the character of the subsoil beds rather than the amount of rainfall seems therefore to determine the amount of subsoil water available. There is, for instance, less difficulty in obtaining water in the semi-arid Karroo than in the Transvaal or in Natal with a far higher rainfall.[2] By 1951 some 42,844 bore-holes had been completed in the Union, the average supply given by each being between one-thirtieth and one-fortieth of a cubic foot per second. This is, at the most, sufficient for only about seven or eight acres of mixed crops, but it is of value for providing drinking-water and for small fodder reserves.

In certain areas, as in the Transvaal high veld, bore-hole supplies are available in dolomite formations, but the use of these sources by farmers has been controlled in the interests of neighbouring urban populations by the provisions of the Irrigation Act of 1912. Artesian supplies have been found in the Uitenhage district of the Cape, in Namaqualand, and east of Marienthal in South-West Africa. It has been recommended that the use of water from artesian areas should also be controlled[3] and, if this is done, artesian supplies may prove of value for small irrigation schemes.

The possibilities afforded by the existence of subsoil water have led the Government to spend more money on developing the use of underground water supply than on the conservation of surface water.[4] The rain-water dam has its value not merely as an emergency water supply but in assisting to prevent erosion. The embanking of slopes helps to prevent 'sluiting', and an increase of drinking-places facilitates the substitution of fenced paddocks for the kraaling of stock, thus reducing the trampling which is one of the chief causes of erosion.[5] The State has given assistance to farmers for the making of dams as part of the anti-erosion programme, and by 1947 over 700 dams had also been made in the Native Reserves by the Native Affairs Department. Dams have been constructed in those areas at an average rate of 50 a year. There is one other source of assistance to the pastoral industry which might well be further explored, namely, the utilization of the sand rivers common in arid tracts. A simple form of

---

[1] *Proceedings of the African Regional Scientific Conference, Johannesburg*, vol. ii, 1949, pp. 56–64.

[2] A. L. du Toit, *Geology of South Africa*, 1926, p. 420. The water in such wells is, however, frequently saline; see G. W. Bond, 'A Geochemical Survey of Underground Water Supplies in the Union', *Memoir of the Geological Survey Society of South Africa*, vol. xli, 1946.

[3] *Report of the Commission of Enquiry concerning the Water Laws of the Union*, 1951, p. 22.

[4] *Arid Zone Hydrology*, Unesco, 1953, p. 58.

[5] See below, p. 1017.

concrete dam in the bed of these rivers might be of some use in providing water for stock.[1]

South-West Africa

The Tribal Territories situated in the northern part of South-West Africa (Ovamboland and Okovangoland) have only a moderate rainfall and have, on occasion, as for example in 1915 and 1931, suffered severely from scarcity. In certain years they benefit from the fact that a great network of spillways (*oshanas* or *omurambas*), taking the form of broad, sandy watercourses, receive the flood waters which during the season of tropical rainfall pour down from the Angola highlands into the Kunene and Okovango riverain. Exceptional rainfall such as produces these flood waters occurs, however, on an average only once in ten years, and it is said that evaporation may be equal to the normal rainfall.[2] Farther to the south the country grows progressively drier, and the lower part of the so-called Police Zone[3] shares the aridity of the neighbouring Kalahari area of the Union. The Namib, the strip of desert which borders the Atlantic coast, is practically rainless. The water resources of the territory offer therefore very few facilities for irrigation. The streams in its interior flow intermittently, even in the rainy season, and in the east many of them sink out of sight in the Kalahari wastes. Although a small stretch of irrigation is maintained by European farmers on the north bank of the Orange river, there has elsewhere been no systematic development of irrigation on any appreciable scale.

Such water supplies as are at present available are mostly provided by underground sources. By the end of 1952 the Administration had sunk over 4,000 bore-holes and a large number have been sunk by private enterprise. The average cost is between £1. 15s. and £2 a foot, and the average depth is 200 feet; there is however in some localities a noticeably high percentage of failures, for there seems to be no general water-table, and such supplies as are found exist in 'pockets'. A few of these underground supplies come from artesian sources as, for example, in the Auob basin, where 40 major bore-holes give a combined maximum yield of 10 million gallons daily.[4] In the Native Reserves of the Police Zone 322 bore-holes had been sunk by the Administration up to the end of 1952. In some of the Reserves where water is more freely obtainable the policy is to conserve surface flow, and nine new dams have been constructed and four existing dams enlarged since 1948. A small number of suction-pumps has been provided to enable the inhabitants of the Okovango Tribal

[1] F. Debenham, *Report on the Water Resources of the Bechuanaland Protectorate, Northern Rhodesia, the Nyasaland Protectorate, Tanganyika Territory and the Uganda Protectorate*, Colonial Research Publication no. 2, 1948, pp. 82 ff.

[2] *Arid Zone Hydrology*, Unesco, 1953, p. 63.   [3] See above, p. 695.

[4] F. E. Kanthack, in *South African Geographical Journal*, April 1941. *O.Y.S.A., 1949*, p. 1192.

Territory to utilize the waters of the Okovango river for irrigation purposes. A total of £170,000 was expended on the development of water resources between 1947 and 1954.

Basutoland

The major problem of Basutoland is (as shown in a succeeding chapter) concerned with the problems of soil erosion rather than with the development of irrigation.[1] The rainfall is normally adequate, though it is intermittent, and the physiography of the country does not lend itself to agricultural irrigation. The significance of Basutoland in this connexion lies in the fact that the Maluti Mountains contain the greater part of the catchment areas of the Orange and Caledon rivers, whose waters are essential to the Union. Reference has been made to the project by which the waters of the Orange river might become available for use in irrigation in the Union,[2] and in that event might also provide a small amount of irrigation in the valley areas of the territory. There are a few small irrigation works in the lands occupied by the Tlôkwa tribe, and use has also been made of a good natural supply at Bethal, near Thamong. The anti-erosion measures designed to ensure the even distribution of storm water will be subsequently described;[3] they include the provision of local water supplies, for which a sum of £80,000 has been allocated. In addition to the 398 dams already constructed as part of the programme of soil conservation, a number of areas have been provided with domestic water piped from springs and bore-holes.

Swaziland

Though the rainfall of Swaziland is liable to be irregular in distribution over the year, it is normally adequate for agricultural purposes, and the territory is in other respects one of the best-watered areas in southern Africa. The four main streams, the Ingwavuma, the Usutu, the Black Mbuluzi, and the Komati, all offer possibilities of irrigation, but though the Financial Commission of 1932[4] emphasized the advantages to be derived from their use, it is only recently that steps have been taken to put schemes into operation on any noteworthy scale.[5] The most extensive of these is the Swaziland Irrigation Scheme, in the Middle Veld sector, comprising 105,000 acres held by the Colonial Development Corporation. Part of this estate is at present devoted to irrigated cultivation, part to

[1] See below, p. 1024. See also *Report on the Financial and Economic Position of Basutoland*, Cmd. 4907, 1935, p. 143; and *N.A.*, Part V, pp. 12, 127-9.
[2] For the project of a dam at Bethulie, see above, p. 977.
[3] See below, p. 1025. See also *Basutoland, Annual Report of Department of Agriculture, 1953*, p. 55.
[4] *Report on the Financial and Economic Situation of Swaziland*, Cmd. 4114, 1932.
[5] *N.A.*, Part V, p. 344.

rain-grown crops, and the rest to ranching.[1] Water for irrigation is raised by pumps from the Komati river, as part of a pilot irrigation scheme, and 1,200 acres of rice gave an excellent yield in 1953, though there was a falling off in 1954. It is intended to draw water eventually from the Komati by a gravity canal about 40 miles in length.

In the same sector of the country is the Malkerns Irrigation Scheme, operated by an association of European farmers. This scheme draws water from the Great Usutu river to irrigate 8,000 acres of land; of this, 1,200 are owned by the Colonial Development Corporation, which is participating in the scheme.[2] Farther to the north-west is the property of the United Plantations Company, comprising 5,500 acres, which is to be irrigated by water pumped from the Lomati river in the Piggs Peak District. Of this area 600 acres are to be planted to citrus and the rest to rice and other crops. United Plantations also own 1,500 acres in the Stegi District of the Low Veld sector, where rice and cotton are to be grown under irrigation by a gravity canal from the Great Usutu river. A hydrographic survey of the territory is now being financed by a grant made under the Colonial Development and Welfare Act, and may lead to further developments in irrigation.

Bechuanaland

The physiography of the major part of the Bechuanaland Protectorate seems to contain no possibility of irrigation, for it lies in a typically arid zone. Much of it, indeed, is of the Kalahari type of waste. It is only in the north-west of the Protectorate that any such possibility seems to present itself. This area contains an inland river delta in many ways similar to that of the Niger delta which, as will be seen, forms the basis for the important Sansanding Irrigation Scheme in French West Africa.[3] In Bechuanaland the delta is caused by the discharge of the flood waters of the Okovango[4] and Chobe (or Linyanti) rivers into a triangular area of 4,000 square miles of swamp, from which there is no outlet except in years of exceptionally heavy rainfall. In such years the flood waters break through the *sudd* constricting the natural channels of the delta and pass down the Botletle river towards the Makarikari Depression and thence to Lake Ngami.

The theory advanced by Dr. Livingstone for this phenomenon, and later propounded in a modified form by Professor Schwartz,[5] was that the capture of the Linyanti by the Zambezi was one link in a chain of fluvial dislocations which had resulted in the drying up of vast sheets of

[1] *Colonial Development Corporation, Report and Accounts for 1951*, p. 63; ibid. *1952*, pp. 51, 61.
[2] Ibid. *1953*, p. 44. *Colonial Reports, Swaziland, 1952*, pp. 2, 3.   [3] See below, p. 1003.
[4] Shortly before entering Bechuanaland the Okovango river is joined by the Cuito river coming down from Angola. The Chobe is similarly joined by the Kavando river.
[5] E. H. L. Schwartz, *Kalahari or Thirstland Redemption*, 1920.

inland water, of which Lake Ngami and the Makarikari Depression are now the sole remainder. Whatever the value of this speculation it inspired a belief, long cherished in the Cape, that by establishing control over the course of these rivers the two great lakes might be restored to their former state; the results, it was believed, would enhance the humidity and ultimately increase the volume of rainfall in the Cape.

Though scientists no longer lend support to the arguments on which these hopes were based, it is nevertheless true that control of the waters of the Okovango delta and the Chobe (Linyanti) riverain offers the only prospect for large-scale irrigation in the Bechuanaland Protectorate. A number of schemes of different degrees of magnitude have been suggested for the development of this area, including a dam across the Chobe to irrigate the 'Caprivi Strip' and a barrage at Katombora to impound the Zambezi waters. Neither of these would, however, directly promote the development of the Okovango delta. Any proposals affecting the Chobe swamps, which lie partly in the Union of South Africa, would have to be considered jointly by the Union Government and the Administration of Bechuanaland, and the first essential is a joint survey by the two Governments of the potentialities of this area.[1]

Certain measures were taken prior to 1932 to clear the Taoge and Thamalakane channels of the Okovango river, and in 1933 this work was renewed with the aid of a grant made under the Colonial Development and Welfare Act; in subsequent years the channels supplying the Botletle river were also cleared. The further provision in 1949–50 of a considerable grant from this source has enabled the clearance of the Okovango channels to be continued towards Lake Ngami, and this may eventually make a considerable area of swamp land available for cultivation. Although these operations do not form part of any major project of irrigation, they should assist in providing the data on which irrigation in this part of the territory might be based.[2]

The need of the major part of the Protectorate is, however, for the provision of drinking water rather than for irrigation, and the fact that nine-tenths of the African population of nearly 300,000 persons are engaged in stock-raising gives priority to the needs of the pastoral industry.[3] Their requirements can best be met by a development of the supplies obtainable from underground sources and by the construction of small storage dams for watering stock. Considerable progress has been made in this direction with some aid from grants made under the Colonial Development and Welfare Act. Between the years 1937 and 1953 drilling was carried on

[1] Debenham, op. cit. pp. 31–35.

[2] Report on the Financial and Economic Position of the Bechuanaland Protectorate, Cmd. 4368, 1933, pp. 117, 187. L. A. Mackenzie, Report on the Kalahari Expedition of 1945, U.G. no. 28, 1946. J. H. Wellington, in Outspan, August 1946. N.A., Part V, pp. 155–8.

[3] Colonial Reports, Bechuanaland Protectorate, 1951, p. 12; ibid. 1953, p. 49.

continuously, except for the war years 1940–6. In all, 283 operative bore-holes were sunk; in addition some 165 others were sunk, but failed to yield water. A separate unit has been operating in the Ngwato Reserve, which has constructed 54 stock dams, and a few have been built with money provided by other tribal Treasuries.

In the large ranch operated by the Colonial Development Corporation in the north of the territory[1] water supplies are at present assured by 23 bore-holes.[2] In the Corporation's holding ranch at Molopo in the south, 34 bore-holes had been sunk by the end of 1953 and 17 reservoirs constructed. A survey made on behalf of the Corporation in the autumn of 1953 suggested the possibility of a more extended use of the underground supplies in the Ghanzi District, where subsoil water seems to be based on a ridge of limestone formation.[3]

Southern and Northern Rhodesia

The development of large-scale projects of irrigation in the Rhodesias and Nyasaland will now form one of the functions of the Federal Government of the three territories.[4]

As regards Southern Rhodesia the report of a Committee which investigated the matter in 1952 indicated that more reliable hydrographic data are required before a full assessment can be made of the potentialities of irrigation.[5] These investigations are now in the charge of the Hydrographic Branch in the Division of Agriculture and Lands. There are, however, some projects which are engaging immediate attention, such as that on the Sabi river, that in the Triangle Estate, and the Sebakwe regional water scheme. The first is one of the more promising of the schemes of Low Veld irrigation. It is estimated that by using the normal flow of the Sabi river, supplemented by storage supplies from two or three dams, it would be possible to irrigate some 250,000 acres of crops. The total cost of developing this project, excluding provision for communications and health measures, is estimated to be about £45 million.[6] An experimental station, started in 1951 as part of a pilot scheme, is reported to have shown good results in the irrigated cultivation of alfalfa, cotton, and maize. The scheme has been criticized on the ground that the Low Veld is unsuitable for colonization, and it remains to be seen how far this difficulty can be overcome.

---

[1] See above, p. 890.

[2] *Report on Mission to Bechuanaland Protectorate (Western Kalahari) 1952*, 1954.

[3] For Ghanzi District, see *N.A.*, Part V, p. 243. See also *Colonial Reports, Bechuanaland Protectorate, 1953*, p. 50.

[4] The Federation of Rhodesia and Nyasaland (Constitution) Order in Council, 1953, no. 1199, Second Schedule no. 28.

[5] *Report on Large-scale Irrigation Development in Southern Rhodesia*, Salisbury, 1952, pp. 35 ff.

[6] *Overseas Economic Surveys, Southern and Northern Rhodesia and Nyasaland, 1950*, p. 56.

The Triangle Estate Scheme, with considerably less potentialities than the Sabi project, will take off from the Mtilikwe river system (where three dams will be constructed) and provide a supply adequate to irrigate about 15,800 acres.[1] Reference has been made in a preceding chapter[2] to the use to be made of this irrigation as part of the scheme for the local production of sugar.

Another project of some magnitude has been undertaken near Que Que, where a dam constructed across the Sebakwe river will connect three river systems and form the second-largest artificial lake in the territory. Besides supplying water and power to the growing industrial area of the midlands, canals will conduct a water supply to the National Electricity Supply Commission's power-station on the Umniati river and also provide the Rhodesian Iron and Steel Commission (RISCOM) and the Que Que municipality with water and power. The cost will be roughly £1 million, and it is expected that the canal will be completed in 1957.[3]

A number of minor projects of irrigation have already been carried out or are being surveyed by the Irrigation Department. These include the two Umguza Dams near Bulawayo, the Umshandigi Dam near Fort Victoria (irrigating 2,000 acres), the Mazoe Citrus Estates Scheme of the British South Africa Company, commanding 6,000 acres of land, and the Hunyani Poort Dam near Salisbury, which commands nearly 2,000 acres of land. It would seem, however, that the possibilities offered by works of this character, which utilize the normal flow of rivers, are now being exhausted and that it will be necessary to consider the construction of conservation works which will involve the reservation of considerable catchment areas.

Meanwhile, considerable progress has also been made with schemes for using surface water. It was stated in 1956 that during the previous ten years 1,677 dams of varying capacity had been constructed by the Irrigation Department. This figure does not apparently include the numerous small dams made by private persons. An increasing number of bore-holes were sunk, 265 having been drilled in 1950 and 485 in 1951.[4] It is noteworthy that the provision made for expenditure in furtherance of the purposes of the Native Land Husbandry Act[5] involved sums in the range of £200,000 a year during the years 1955 to 1960, the greater part of which is represented by the cost of bore-holes and dams.[6]

Of recent years much of the attention of the Administration has been diverted from the problems of irrigation and water supply to the utilization of sources for the development of hydroelectric power. It will be

---

[1] *Report of Large-scale Irrigation Development in Southern Rhodesia*, 1952, pp. 25, 42.
[2] See above, p. 863. [3] *The Times*, 2 November 1954.
[4] *Southern Rhodesia, Annual Report of the Irrigation Department, 1952*, pp. 10, 24.
[5] See above, p. 766.
[6] *What the Native Land Husbandry Act means to the Rural African*, Salisbury, 1955, p. 27.

convenient to deal here with the hydroelectric project put forward by Northern Rhodesia, based on the use of the Kafue river, at the same time as that put forward by Southern Rhodesia, based on the use of the waters of the Zambezi. The latter project will be sited at the Kariba Gorge, the former was to have been located at the Keshya Gorge, utilizing also the Meshi-Teshi gap upstream for additional storage. In 1949 an Inter-Territorial Commission appointed by the Central African Council[1] reported that the project at the Kariba Gorge could be completed in two ten-year stages at an estimated cost of £75 million. The station on the Kafue was estimated to cost £27½ million, and was capable of being put into operation within five years of commencing the work.[2] A factor of great importance was the urgent need for power in the Northern Rhodesia Copperbelt, where the demands of two new mines had to be met. While the Wankie coal-fields in Southern Rhodesia were capable of supplying sufficient fuel, the Rhodesian railway system was not at the time capable of transporting it to the Copperbelt.[3] The fact that the Kafue scheme could be completed in half the time and at less than half the cost of the Kariba project operated strongly at this stage in favour of the former scheme, more especially as this could at a later date be linked with a power-station at Kariba Gorge. The Governments of Southern and Northern Rhodesia signed an agreement for the construction of the Kafue scheme, subject to certain financial conditions which, however, subsequently proved impossible to fulfil.

In view of the formation of the Federation in 1953 and of differences in the views of members of the two Administrations, it was decided in 1954 to invite the opinions of two French consultants who would be able to examine the merits of the two projects from a detached angle. The consultants expressed the view that the first power could be made available from Kariba in July 1961, a date which compared with July 1959 from the Kafue, but which was none the less earlier than had been envisaged by the previous investigation.[4] But there were numerous other ponderable factors. The annual energy produced at Kariba would be rather more than double the number of units produced at Kafue; the cost per unit delivered at receiving stations in the final stage would also be much less; indeed, that produced at Kariba would compare favourably with that produced at the cheapest known source in the world. The Kariba scheme could be undertaken in two stages, but when it is working to its full capacity (say in 1972) it should provide power at 0·283d. a unit as compared with 0·728d. a unit, the present cost of thermal power at Salisbury.

---

[1] For the Central African Council, see above, p. 277.
[2] *The Times*, 30 January 1954.   [3] See below, p. 1553.
[4] In a final appraisal of the Kariba project this date was brought forward to 1960, *The Times*, 21 May 1955. For the technical features of the scheme see *Optima*, vol vi, no. 2, June 1956.

In the revised estimate the cost of the Kariba scheme was put at £85¾ million; the cost of the first stage of the Kafue scheme was given as £36½ million and the full scheme as £55 million.[1]

Hitherto it had been assumed that the Copperbelt would be the principal consumer of power, but an additional consideration now emerged. Owing to the rapid growth of secondary industry in Southern Rhodesia it appeared that consumption in the Southern might before long equal that in the Northern territory. At the same time serious consideration was being given to the electrification of the railway system. It appeared that the Kafue scheme would become inadequate by 1963 but that the output of power from the Kariba Gorge could always be increased by building additional generating plant. It was pronounced feasible to provide the Copperbelt with current supplied temporarily from the Belgian Congo.[2]

One of the main objections to the Kafue scheme lay in the inadequacy of data. To attain a capacity comparable with that at Kariba, the project would be dependent upon the ancillary storage at the Meshi-Teshi gap. But here the records of river-flow were not sufficiently reliable to be likely to satisfy the International Bank for Reconstruction and Development, from which it was hoped to secure a large part of the money required for the project. On the other hand, the hydrography of the Kariba scheme was accepted as adequate. In March 1955 the Federal Government decided to accept the Kariba scheme, subject to a favourable opinion being received from the International Bank for Reconstruction and Development. In July 1955 it was announced that the Bank would give a loan of £28 million towards the cost of the first stage of the project.

Work on the Kariba Gorge project began in September 1955. It is one of the features of the scheme that the dam will create a lake some 200 miles in length and over 1 million acres in area in the Gwembe Valley. This will displace about 25,000 Africans of the Tonga tribe in Northern Rhodesia, and a similar number in Southern Rhodesia. Steps were being taken in October 1955 to begin their transfer to a new settlement area.[3] Early in 1956 a further revision of the estimated cost of the Kariba Gorge project raised the total from £85¾ to £113¼ million. It was announced that the copper-mining companies and other enterprises in Northern Rhodesia had lent a total amount of £38 million towards the cost of the project.[4] The dam at the Kariba Gorge would provide that the top water level would be 370 feet above the river-bed.

In the north-eastern part of Northern Rhodesia lies Lake Bangweulu and its contiguous swamps, covering some 3,000 square miles, of which

[1] *The Times*, 2 March 1955. [2] See below, p. 1007.
[3] *The Times*, 21 October 1955. See also I. M. Eldridge, 'Resettling Africans at Kariba', *New Commonwealth*, 28 May 1956; H.C. Deb., 15 June 1956, coll. 1012–21.
[4] Proceedings of the Federal Parliament, 22 and 27 February 1956.

one-third is occupied by the shallow waters of the lake. This large lacustrine area, which has been formed by the Chambezi river, is in some
respects similar to the inland delta of the Okovango in Bechuanaland,
already described, but differs from the Okovango swamp-river complex in
having a perennially flowing outlet in the Luapula river. A number of
drainage channels were cut in 1951–2 and are now carrying a large
amount of the discharge of the Chambezi river to the southern side of the
swamps, thus obviating the flooding of the agricultural lands to the north.[1]

Among other developments two are still in their early stages. The
investigation of the large flooded area in the Kafue Flats is being undertaken in order to examine the feasibility of impoldering them to prevent
inundation; this is being financed by the Rhodesian Selection Trust group
of companies.[2] The hydroelectric station at the headwaters of the Lun-
semfwa river near Broken Hill will involve a dam of considerable size,
which is being undertaken by the Anglo-American Corporation of South
Africa. As in Southern Rhodesia much progress has also been made with
small local schemes. In the decade from 1942 to 1952 a large number of
earth dams were constructed, and wells and bore-holes sunk. In 1953
215 bore-holes were drilled at a cost of £65,000.

Nyasaland

The existence of a number of well-established tea plantations in the
southern part of Nyasaland is evidence that the rainfall of that area is
adequate for normal agricultural production, but there are large parts of
the Northern Province where seasonal lack of water has caused much
concern. The matter was the subject of special study by the Geological
Department of Nyasaland in the early thirties,[3] and particular regard was
paid to the provision of wells and bore-holes. A grant of £198,895 for the
development of the water supplies in the Protectorate was made under the
Colonial Development and Welfare Act, and part of this was expended
on the provision of bore-holes, the sites usually being selected by geophysical methods.[4] The cost of boring is high, amounting to over £2. 10s. a foot.
The Native Authority Treasuries make a contribution for each bore-hole
and well sunk in their areas.

The first irrigation scheme on a large scale yet undertaken by the
Nyasaland Government is at Sombani. Its object is to convert 10,000
acres of inundated swamp land round Lake Shirwa into a cultivable area.
The original scheme was restricted to a pilot experiment of 100 acres only,
financed by a grant made under the Colonial Development and Welfare

---

[1] *Northern Rhodesia, Annual Report of the Water Development and Irrigation Department, 1952,* p. 9.
[2] Address by Chairman of Rhodesian Selection Trust, 12 January 1956.
[3] F. Dixey, *A Practical Handbook of Water Supply,* 1932, 2nd ed. 1950.
[4] W. G. Cooper, 'Electrical Aids in Water Finding', *Nyasaland Geological Survey Bulletin,* 1949.

Act. The Blantyre-Limbe power-station generates a supply of electricity for the two townships and the secondary industries that have grown up around them.

The control of the water level in Lake Nyasa and the river Shire has for many years been a problem of concern to the Protectorate. Most of the watershed of the lake (which covers 11,000 square miles) lies within the Protectorate, as does also its outlet, the Shire river, a tributary of the Zambezi. The level of the lake has in recent years receded some 25 feet, thus sharing in that general change in the levels of the great lakes of East Africa, the causes of which have been the subject of much scientific speculation.[1] A preliminary survey carried out soon after the Second World War indicated that control of the water in Lake Nyasa might both provide hydroelectric power and regulate the inundation of the Lower Shire plains in the Southern Province. In 1955 a detailed investigation[2] produced four main recommendations. The stabilization of the water level of the lake was to be effected by the construction of a *bund* at Liwonde and a barrage at Matope. The latter would provide power for a hydro-electric plant with an immediate capacity of 30,000 kW., but capable of expansion to 100,000 kW. The succeeding stages include the reclamation of the marshes in the Lower Shire Valley (400,000 acres in extent and at present valueless) and the cultivation of riparian land as the result of dredging the river.

The total cost is estimated at £77 million, and the first stage of the project will cost £23½ million. Work was started in 1955 and will take ten years to complete. It is hoped that the creation of a source of hydro-electric power will lead to the production of a nitrogenous-fertilizer industry, the economic extraction of aluminium from the bauxite deposits on Mlanje mountain, and the development of jute manufacture. The barrage at Matope would enable shallow-draught steamers to ply between Fort Johnston and Matope (only 40 miles from Blantyre) as they did at the beginning of the century. The urgency of starting the first phase of the work lay in the calculation that in 1956–7 the level of the lake would have further receded by 9½ feet, so that if its progress is not now arrested by the construction of a barrage it may not be possible to carry out the remainder of the project within the present century. The Federal Government has agreed, provided that money to finance the scheme is found outside the ordinary loan vote.[3] Much importance is attached to the hydrographic survey of the lake, which was begun in 1955 and was the first to be under-taken since the lake was surveyed by the Admiralty in 1897.

---

[1] E. B. Worthington, *Science in Africa*, 1938, p. 113. The question of the level of the lake closely concerns Tanganyika as well, and Mozambique also has an interest in it.

[2] W. Halcrow and Partners, *Shire Valley Project; Report on the Development of Lake Nyasa and the Shire River*, 1955.   [3] *F.N.*, 16 July 1955.

Tanganyika

Save for the coastal belt, the plateau edge, and the vicinity of Lake Victoria, Tanganyika is poorly provided with water. The interesting population study made by Mr. C. Gillman in 1936 described 10 per cent. of the country as well watered, about 8 per cent. as fairly well watered, nearly 13 per cent. as poorly watered, and 62 per cent. as lacking water to the extent that though this area may have a fairly good rainfall in the short rainy season it is arid for the rest of the year.[1] Two-thirds of the inhabitants of Tanganyika were, he pointed out, concentrated in the one-tenth of its area which had enough water to support them. The East Africa Royal Commission held that a reliable rainfall of 20 inches is required for satisfactory arable cultivation, and that this quantity of rainfall may be taken as the criterion by which to distinguish the pastoral from the arable lands. It inferred that approximately one-third of Tanganyika and two-thirds of Kenya fell below this criterion.[2]

The immediate needs of Tanganyika lie therefore rather in the development of water supplies for men and cattle than in the construction of irrigation works. In 1931 a programme of water boring was begun, and in 1937 a survey of water resources. More progress was made after a Department of Water Development[3] had been established in 1944 and a succession of grants under the Colonial Development and Welfare Act had been made available; these amounted by the end of 1953 to roughly £900,000. Much had already been done in the investigation of sites for drilling bore-holes or constructing dams or marking cattle-watering points.[4] After 1949, when a technical staff and equipment became available, the work expanded rapidly. Dams and *hafirs* (a type of dam introduced from the Sudan) were constructed by heavy mechanical plant and flood-protection banks were built by African Administrations under technical advice. By 1953 some 58 major earth dams, 200 small dams, 135 bore-holes, and 46 wells had been successfully completed. The costs of boring are comparatively high, being about equal to those in Nyasaland. Where water supplies are provided in communities which are predominantly African, they are owned by the Native Administrations concerned, but are maintained by the Water Development Department from a fund to which the various Native Treasuries contribute annually. The capital cost is borne by the Government, but the Native Administrations normally refund one-third of this sum. No direct charge is made for water consumed.

The possibilities of irrigation from the river systems of Tanganyika have

---

[1] C. Gillman, *A Population Map of Tanganyika*, 1936. See also *American Geographical Review*, July 1946; and *Report to the Council of the League of Nations on Tanganyika Territory, 1935*, Col. no. 113, p. 139.

[2] *East Africa Royal Commission 1935–1955, Report*, Cmd. 9475, 1955, pp. 252–4.

[3] *Tanganyika, Report for the Year 1947*, Col. no. 220, pp. 49–51.

[4] *Tanganyika, Annual Report of the Water Development Department, 1953*, Appendixes.

attracted attention since 1910 when the German Administration investigated a scheme for the canalization of the Kilombero, a tributary of the Rufiji. The subject is of special importance because the development of irrigation appears to offer the readiest means of correcting the present maldistribution of the population. The large-scale projects which are at present receiving attention are those connected with the Pangani, Rufiji, and Kilombero rivers. Much of the Rufiji river and its affluents, the Kilombero and Ruaha, lie in a zone of 'reliable rainfall'.[1] Schemes for the development of these valleys have been under consideration since 1928.[2] It is recognized that extensive works will be necessary not only to control inundation but also to regulate the level of the rivers and to conduct the water to the land. The justification for incurring what must be very heavy expenditure will depend upon the extent of land 'commanded'. On this point opinions have differed in the past, but the latest estimate of 400,000 acres commanded by the Rufiji, 250,000 by the Kilombero, and 150,000 by the Ruaha is higher than earlier computations.[3] By 1953 a little over 7,500 acres had been brought under rice in the Rufiji valley by mechanized cultivation. It remains to be seen whether the financial returns justify an expansion of the scheme.

The chief obstacles to utilizing the waters of the Kilombero river are its excessive seasonal flooding and the malarial nature of the country.[4] Plans involving large engineering works have therefore been postponed pending further examination. The development of the Pangani river[5] (also named Ruvu), which has its source near Mount Kilimanjaro, has been hampered by the existence of an agreement made by the Government with the local electricity supply company guaranteeing a minimum flow of water through the latter's turbines.[6] An aerial survey has recently been made with a view to the selection of other hydroelectric sites at the Pangani Falls and the construction of a high-tension transmission line to Dar-es-Salaam.

An old-established system of irrigation exists on Mounts Meru and Kilimanjaro. Though the process is primitive, the channels are well graded and are led for long distances over difficult ground;[7] the distribution is regulated by long-established Native custom.

Kenya

There are two features of the topography of Kenya which have special interest in connexion with projects for irrigation. The character of the

---

[1] Cmd. 9475, pp. 252 ff.
[2] A. M. Telford, *Report on Development of the Rufiji and Kilombero Valleys*, 1929.
[3] Cmd. 9475, p. 275.   [4] Telford, op. cit.
[5] E. O. Teale and C. Gillman, *Report on the Investigation of the Proper Control of Water and the Reorganization of Water Boards in the Northern Provinces of Tanganyika*, 1934. See also *Tanganyika, Report for the Year 1953*, Col. no. 307, p. 49.   [6] Cmd. 9475, p. 276.
[7] Teale and Gillman, op. cit. J. Huxley, *Africa View*, 1931, p. 65.

large area lying to the east of the Rift Valley (comprising about two-thirds of the Colony in actual area) is such that it must be regarded as only marginal country for either agricultural or pastoral purposes. Secondly, with the exception of the coastal belt, the only regions where heavy rainfall occurs are in the volcanic districts of the Aberdare mountains and Mount Kenya itself,[1] amounting in all to less than 1,000 square miles. It is this relatively small area which provides the water for Kenya's three main rivers, the Uaso Nyiru, the Athi (Galana), and the Tana.

The possibilities of irrigation from the Tana were first indicated in 1911,[2] and a survey was made by Messrs. Harris and Sampson in 1934. They advised that the development of the lower or deltaic Tana was impracticable because the river channel had been so silted up that it was higher than the surrounding land; the cost of an embankment to protect the land from inundation would be prohibitive.[3] The main obstacle to irrigating the basin of the middle Tana is the absence of a suitable site for a barrage. A plan has been put forward whereby 190,000 acres might be irrigated by water conducted from the upper middle Tana through a canal about 200 miles in length,[4] but it has since been estimated that the cost would be upwards of £20 million,[5] and the African Land Utilization and Settlement Board has accepted the view that the development of either of these schemes would be uneconomic. The East Africa Royal Commission (1953–5) examined in some detail the possibilities of irrigation from the Tana, and, while accepting the view that the projects previously put forward were open to objection on various grounds, considered that a detailed topographical and soil survey should be made in the middle Tana with a view to indicating the possibility of irrigation projects of lesser magnitude. But the Commission felt at the same time that the conditions were not favourable to the colonization of the Tana area by tribesmen from other parts of Kenya.[6]

An irrigation scheme for the cultivation of some 7,000 acres in the Taveta Valley is being undertaken by private enterprise. The Taveta Sisal Estates have conducted a canal from the Lumi river to irrigate a further 2,000 acres. The East African Rice Commission recommended in 1948 the further hydrographic survey of the Kano and Kasimu areas of the Nyanza Province, where there appeared a possibility of 16,000 acres being

[1] Debenham, op. cit. pp. 11 ff.

[2] *Report on Irrigation, Water Supplies for Stock, Water Law, &c., in Kenya*, 1925.

[3] *Report of the Tana River Expedition*, 1934.

[4] P. Mitchell, *The Agrarian Problem in Kenya*, 1947. See also Kenya Sessional Paper no. 8, 1945.

[5] R. J. M. Swynnerton, *A Plan to Intensify the Development of African Agriculture in Kenya*, Nairobi, 1954, pp. 38–40.

[6] Cmd. 9475, pp. 271–2.

cultivated under rice. The recommendation has since been endorsed by the East Africa Royal Commission.[1]

The Administration has for some years been seriously concerned with the problems of water supply in the pastoral areas of the rest of the Colony. It is part of the standing policy to introduce a controlled system of grazing in the Native areas, but its feasibility depends on the provision of water supplies for stock. It is estimated that there are $5\frac{1}{2}$ million African-owned cattle in the Colony and the normal annual increase is reckoned to be at least 350,000. In the arid Northern Province the nomad stock-owners have themselves excavated tanks of over 100 yards in length, sunk wells 70 feet deep, and opened water-holes up to 60 feet deep in order to provide sufficient water to keep stock alive until the seasonal rainfall. As regards the more inhabited parts of Kenya the problem is one of particular urgency in the extensive dry areas of the Samburu low country in the Rift Valley Province. Here a solution is being sought on the lines of proposals put forward in 1944[2] which recommended an extensive programme of bore-drilling and tank excavation. Some progress has already been made on this scheme, for which a sum of £485,000 has been allocated from grants made under the Colonial Development and Welfare Act, and a considerable number of bore-holes have been drilled, of which a high proportion have been successful.

In the Machakos District a Betterment Scheme has been introduced and 277 dams have been constructed.[3] Work has begun on the Yatta Furrow Scheme designed to conduct water from the Thika river to a desiccated river-bed in Machakos. It is estimated that the land thus made available will accommodate another 1,000 Kamba families. The Settlement Scheme was estimated to cost £150,000. Water is supplied to the Makueni Settlement by bore-holes and dams with a combined capacity of 18 million gallons; 1,209 families have been settled here and further settlement is limited only by the need for more water supplies. More than 200 bore-holes and over 1,200 dams and tanks have been provided in African areas and it is intended to continue this work at an estimated expenditure of £400,000 to £500,000, towards which a sum of £150,000 has been allocated under the Colonial Development and Welfare Act.

Although the development of the upper Tana river to provide irrigation has been deemed to be unremunerative, its waters have been utilized to supply power to Nairobi. By constructing a barrage across the upper reaches near Fort Hall water has been conducted to the power-station through a tunnel (the Merila tunnel) which is $1\frac{3}{4}$ miles long. The Low

[1] Ibid. p. 273. For the proposed hydrographic survey, see also *Colonial Development*, Winter 1954, p. 36.

[2] F. Dixey, *Hydrographical Report on the Northern Frontier District, Samburu and Turkana*, 1944. See also *Report of Kenya Development Committee*, vol. ii, 1946, pp. 210 and 220.

[3] See above, p. 908, and *N.A.*, Part I, p. 119.

Tana power-station, which is supplementary to the original Tana installation built in 1933, has been constructed at an expenditure of £1¾ million; the Wenjii power-station, situated a few miles distant, is auxiliary to the Low Tana installation. The needs of Nairobi for electric power will now be supplemented by an agreement with the Uganda Electricity Board for the supply of current from the new Owen Falls installation, at a cost of £3½ million.[1]

Provision for water development is organized in Kenya by a Hydraulic Branch of the Department of Public Works. In 1951 a new Water Law was enacted which embodied the principle of vesting all water sources in the Crown; it created a Water Resources Authority to advise on conservation.

Uganda

Uganda has no urgent problem of water development save perhaps in its north-eastern sector; its most important problem may be said to be in the regulation of its drainage.[2] There are some 5,700 square miles of swamp, of which 2,500 square miles are permanent, and as the result of a recent survey steps have been taken to drain certain of the valley swamp regions, thus opening a limited area to cultivation. The Agricultural Productivity Committee in 1954 held that there was at present no such pressure of population on the land as to make it desirable to reclaim the swamps immediately; they should be regarded as a reserve to meet future requirements of land. An exception to this principle was, however, admitted in the case of the Kigezi District, where it is recognized that some congestion exists.[3]

The Protectorate has for some years given much attention to the improvement of domestic water supplies. By the end of 1952 water-supply schemes had been installed or were under construction in all the larger townships. The Department of Rural Water Supplies, organized on lines similar to those followed in Tanganyika, is responsible for the construction of reservoirs and the drilling and maintenance of bore-holes in rural areas. As a result of operations during the period from 1930 to 1953 there were about 1,500 working bore-holes and some 500 reservoirs in the Protectorate, constructed at an estimated cost of over £1 million. It was estimated that these numbers might be doubled by the end of the Uganda Ten-year Development Plan in 1956, at a cost of a further £1 million.[4] The Geological Survey Department and the Local Authorities have built over 400 dams and surface catchment tanks in the stock-producing areas. It is claimed that this has resulted in a more rational distribution of cattle

[1] See below, p. 995.   [2] Debenham, op. cit. pp. 10 ff.
[3] *Background to Uganda*, no. 79, January 1955. See also *N.A.*, Part I, p. 45.
[4] *Uganda, Annual Report of the Geological Survey Department, 1950.*

and consequently better utilization of the pasture lands.[1] The irrigation of the Karamoja District in the Northern Province by conducting the run-off of rain into small basins by means of spillways and dams is a technique introduced from Aden. Ideally suited to the district it has, however, failed to attract the local inhabitants partly, no doubt, because of the hard work entailed.

Uganda has a Department of Hydrological Survey which was in the first instance concerned largely in collecting data regarding the level of the lakes, but now deals with the general problems of water supply. The East Africa Royal Commission of 1953–5 has now recommended that, in order to avoid dissipation of effort, each of the three territories of East Africa should form its own Water Department, divided into a general and an irrigation section. Hydrological research should be a function of the High Commission and form part of the East Africa Agriculture and Forestry Organization.[2]

The Owen Falls Installation and the Nile Waters Agreement

The Protectorate has now an important place in the development of hydroelectric power, but it owes this position to its command over Lake Victoria as a source of the Nile waters, rather than to any measures taken by it to meet a local demand for power for industrial or similar uses. Up to a few years ago there seemed to be little probability that the East African territories would be directly affected by the terms of the Nile Waters Agreement of 1929, in which the United Kingdom agreed that no development likely to affect adversely the supplies of Nile water available to Egypt should take place in the territories under British control without the agreement of the Egyptian Government.[3] The position in respect of these territories has, however, changed of late years, owing to the interest shown by Egypt in measures designed to reduce the loss of water suffered by the Nile during its course between Lake Victoria and Malakal and to the effort being made to arrange for water to reach the irrigated lands of Egypt during the 'timely season' of the year.

The Nile issues from Lake Victoria by the Ripon Falls and, after reaching Namasagali, passes through the papyrus swamps of Lake Kioga (Victoria Nile), then over the Murchison Falls into the northern end of Lake Albert. It then goes through the marshes of the Nimule plain (Albert Nile), and, after entering the Sudan near Rejaf, where it is known as the Bahr el Jebel,[4] it encounters the vast blockage (*sudd*) area of the Bahr el Ghazal, finally emerging as the White Nile at Malakal and Melut. In order to reduce the great losses caused by evaporation during this passage

---

[1] *Uganda, Annual Report of the Veterinary Department, 1951.*
[2] Cmd. 9475, p. 139.   [3] For the terms of the Agreement, see ibid. p. 274.
[4] 'The River of the Mountains'. See plan on p. 997.

a number of works have been projected during recent years: first, a dam below the Ripon Falls; second, a weir near Masindi Port to regulate the discharge from Lake Kioga; and third, a dam near Nimule or Mutir to provide storage capacity in Lake Albert, together with reservoirs to counteract the effects of the torrents encountered between Mutir and Nimule. The most important of these is the river Aswa, the main catchment area of which is in Uganda. The final work contemplated is a diversion canal between Jonglei and the mouth of the Sobat (in the neighbourhood of Malakal) which will allow the main body of water to by-pass the *sudd* swamps of the Bahr el Ghazal. Three-quarters of the Nile's flow at Juba should thus reach Malakal, instead of less than half, as at present.[1]

All these works combine to form the Equatorial Nile Project, and Uganda is intimately concerned with the series from the Ripon Falls at Jinja to the point at which the Nile leaves the Protectorate near Nimule. But, indeed, all the countries having tributaries which flow into this reach of the Nile are also interested, in so far, at all events, as any operations are contemplated which may affect their flow. The most distant source of the White Nile is the Luvironza river, which rises in the Mufumbiro Mountains 30 miles east of Lake Tanganyika and joins the Kagera river. This has its source in Ruanda Urundi and discharges a large volume of water into Lake Victoria. The Semliki, originating from Lake Edward, receives the drainage from the Ruwenzori range and, together with other lesser streams, forms Lake Albert. But the interest of the Uganda Protectorate, as controlling the outlet from Lake Victoria, is of a special order, and it is largely on this account that a grant was made under the Colonial Development and Welfare Act for the establishment of the Hydrological Department now based on Uganda.

The initial stage of the Equatorial Nile Project has taken shape in the completion in 1954 of the Owen Falls Dam, situated about $1\frac{1}{2}$ miles below the Ripon Falls, in the vicinity of Jinja. The scheme first took definite form in 1935 as a project for the supply of electricity. In 1946 it was included in the Uganda Ten-year Development Plan as part of a scheme for controlling the Nile at its source, storing water in Lake Victoria, and supplying electricity. Subsequently the establishment of the Uganda Electricity Board enabled the scheme to be put into effect after its implications had been re-examined in consultation with Egypt, the Sudan, and the three East African territories which converge upon the shores of Lake Victoria.

From the point of view of the Equatorial Nile Project the dam controls

[1] H. E. Hurst, P. Phillips, R. P. Black, *The Nile Basin*, 7 vols, 1931–46. *A Short History of the Nile Basin*, Physical Department Paper, Egypt, no. 45, 1944. J. H. Wellington, in *Geographical Journal*, June 1949, pp. 62–69; J. W. Wright, ibid. December 1949, pp. 173–90; E. B. Worthington, ibid. September 1950, pp. 29–39; P. P. Howell, ibid. March 1953. E. B. Worthington, in *International Affairs*, January 1953.

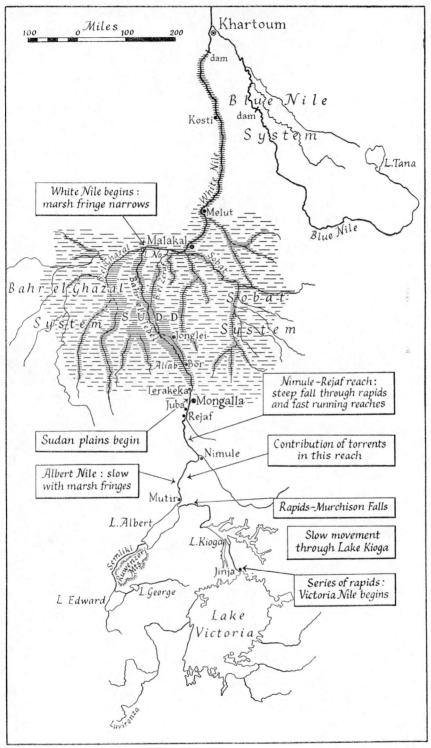

By courtesy of the Royal Geographical Society

the level of Lake Victoria, so that the discharge of the Victoria Nile should be almost constant at its source. The dam will in itself do little to increase the available water supplies to Egypt or the Sudan, but by controlling the Nile at its source will facilitate the subsequent works included in the general project. Egypt is paying the additional cost of raising the dam one metre in order to provide for the extra water storage in Lake Victoria. She is paying compensation to Uganda for the reduction of generating power consequent on the system adopted in controlling the discharge and is also bearing the cost of compensating the occupiers of any submerged lands on the borders of the lake. Egypt is not otherwise contributing towards the cost of the dam.

The dam serves to provide Uganda with a hydroelectric installation designed for an initial capacity of 90,000 kW. and an ultimate capacity of 150,000 kW. In this part of the project Egypt has no share. The total cost to the Protectorate, including the network of transmission lines, is estimated to be approximately £30 million. It was at one time expected that the power produced at Jinja would be used in the development of the Kilembe copper-mine on the Uganda–Congo border,[1] but it now appears likely that the copper concentrates will be railed to Jinja, where an electric smelter will produce blister copper. The smelter will also deal with the products of the Macalder–Nyanza mine in Kenya. The electrification of the main railway line in Kenya is under consideration. A cotton textile factory has been erected at Jinja, at a cost of nearly £2 million. Jinja is also supplying power to the Tororo cement factory, a Uganda Government enterprise.

Nigeria

Nigeria has in its different regions a marked variety of conditions in respect of water supply. In the Northern Region, where the rainless seven months are accompanied by the drying *harmattan* wind, water supply is of vital importance not only as a means of increasing agricultural production but also because it may assist in the redistribution of the population of some of the more congested areas of the northern Emirates. The provision of water-storage dams and wells has been one of the functions assigned to the Native Authorities,[2] but the Administration has for some years been engaged in the exploration of the underground water supplies by geophysical methods. Attention has in particular been paid to the examination of sources of artesian supply in the neighbourhood of Lake Chad.[3] In the Eastern and Western Regions the development of water resources is not

[1] See below, p. 1508.

[2] *N.A.*, Part III, pp. 69 ff. E. B. Worthington, *Science in Africa*, 1938, p. 79.

[3] C. Raeburn and B. Jones, *The Chad Basin: Geology and Water Supply*, 1934. J. H. Wellington, *Africa South of the Sahara*, 1951, p. 37. E. Sargent, *Le Peuplement humain du Sahara*, 1952, pp. 12–14, though this refers rather to the north and central Sahara.

so urgently required in the interests of agriculture or animal husbandry; the chief need is for an improvement of domestic supplies in the interests of health. This applies both to urban and rural areas.

The ten-year plan of development, formulated in 1945, had this as one of its more important objectives. The goal set was the installation of piped water supplies in 180 urban concentrations and the provision of 36,000 water-points in rural areas by the construction of open or tube wells or catchment tanks.[1] The urban water-supply scheme was estimated to cost over £2¾ million; 30 per cent. of this sum was to be met by a grant of £940,500, made under the Colonial Development and Welfare Act, and the balance was to be provided from Nigerian loan funds. By the end of 1952 most of the larger towns had piped supplies installed or under construction. These are in most cases fed from impounding reservoirs, but at Sokoto, Kano, and Maiduguri in the Northern Region the supplies are derived from caissons sunk in the sand-beds of adjacent rivers.

The rural water-supply scheme was estimated to cost approximately £5 million, for which an initial grant of roughly £1¾ million was made under the Colonial Development and Welfare Act. This scheme aimed at securing pure water supplies for rural districts on the basis of one water-point per 500 of population;[2] and, by the first part of 1950, some 4,270 wells had been sunk, of which 2,179 were in the Northern Region, 1,396 (including tanks and minor supplies) in the Western Region, and 695 in the Eastern Region. A grant of £2¼ million was made under the Colonial Development and Welfare Act to the Eastern Region early in 1956 for a combined programme of water supply and road maintenance.

The hydrological investigations made by the Nigerian Government have not so far led to the formation of any large-scale project of irrigation, but several of the schemes which are now being financed as part of the programme of agricultural development[3] involve the control and regulation of flood waters, as, for instance, the Sokoto Mechanized Rice Scheme which involves control of the inundation of the Sokoto and Rima rivers, and the Edozhigi Scheme which contemplates the growing of rice on a plain now flooded by the waters of the Kaduna river.[4] The power-station at the Kurra Falls, which has hitherto supplied electricity to the mines at Jos, was supplemented in 1954 by the hydroelectric plant at Jekko.

Gold Coast

In the Gold Coast, as in Nigeria, it is chiefly the northern areas, with their relatively low rainfall and higher temperatures, which give reason

---

[1] *Colonial Reports, Nigeria, 1952*, p. 104.
[2] *Annual Report on the General Progress of Development and Welfare Schemes, 1951–2*, Lagos.
[3] See above, pp. 906 ff.
[4] *Notes on Some Agricultural Development Schemes in Africa and Aden*, Colonial Office, 1953.

for concern in regard to water supplies, and the Rural Water Development Department, which was established in 1945, has been largely occupied with the construction of village tanks, dams, and wells in the Northern territories. Sites for bore-holes are explored by geophysical methods by the Geological Survey Department which also undertakes the siting of small reservoirs for stock-watering. With the exception of grants amounting altogether to £21,000 the expenditure on rural water development is met from the funds of the Colony. The measure of development can be judged by the fact that, whereas in 1945 a sum of £38,000 was so expended, in 1952 the figure had risen to £337,000.

At the present time the chief preoccupation of the Administration is with the production of aluminium from the deposits of bauxite situated in the neighbourhood of Kumasi. The commercial production of aluminium from bauxite depends upon a close conjunction of the ore with an almost unlimited supply of electricity; it is of importance also, from the standpoint of the British Government, that the metal should be produced within the sterling area. The Government of the United Kingdom has decided to proceed with the construction of a barrage and a hydroelectric power-station near Ajena, about 70 miles from the mouth of the Volta river. The primary purpose of the station is to supply power for smelting the bauxite ore produced at Mpraeso and Yenahin, in the neighbourhood of Kumasi. The aluminium smelter will be erected near Kpong and will have an initial capacity of 80,000 and an ultimate capacity of 210,000 tons of aluminium a year.

Construction has already begun on a new port, Tema (which is estimated to involve an expenditure of £11 million), in order to deal with the production from the power-station and also to provide a more suitable alternative to the open roadstead at Accra.[1] A branch-line connecting the installation with the new port was opened in 1954. The barrage will create a great inland lake of approximately the same size as that which will result from the construction of the dam at the Kariba Gorge on the Zambezi. This, it is understood, can be utilized both for internal transport and for irrigation. Its effect upon the health of the surrounding population, particularly in respect of the dissemination of bilharzia, has been a subject of interest to medical observers. It has also been stated that the area is infested with the organisms of onchocerciasis.[2]

The cost of the scheme as originally estimated was £114 million for a production of 120,000 tons yearly, rising to £144 million for a production of 210,000 tons. The corresponding figures shown in the Report of the

[1] *Togoland, Report for the Year 1952*, Col. no. 296, p. 259; ibid. *1953*, Col no. 308, pp. 187-9. *The Volta River Aluminium Scheme*, Cmd. 8702, 1952.

[2] *Transactions of the Royal Society of Tropical Medicine and Hygiene*, January 1955. See also below, pp. 1110, 1119.

Preparatory Commission on the Volta River project (1956) are £184·9 million and £231·3 million respectively. The cost will be shared by the Gold Coast and United Kingdom Governments and the Canadian and British aluminium companies concerned. The part to be taken by the Gold Coast Government has become a controversial issue in local politics owing to differences of view as to the extent of the finance it can provide and the control it will be entitled to exercise.

Sierra Leone

In Sierra Leone the outstanding problem is rather the control of drainage and the reclamation of swamp land for rice cultivation than the development of irrigation. Reference has been made elsewhere to some of the projects connected with the treatment of the Scarcies swamps and the flooded Bonthe lands.[1] There is a little irrigation in the Binte Chiefdom, where irrigated banana plantations have been established on a system copied from that pursued in French Guinea. Otherwise, the possibilities of small-scale irrigation appear to be limited.[2]

French West Africa

The authorities in French West Africa have been accustomed to divide their territory into five climatic zones running from north to south, the most northern being the Saharan, followed by the Sahel, the Sudan, the Guinea, and the Forest zone in the coastal area. In the Saharan zone both soil and climate appear to exclude any possibility of improving water supplies on an effective scale,[3] while in the Guinea and Forest zones the problem is mainly that of improving supplies for domestic purposes. Here the *sociétés de prévoyance*[4] have made a useful contribution by the sinking of wells, the construction of small dams, and the excavation of irrigation channels, especially in Senegal.[5] In the Sahel zone, however, which lies north of a line drawn roughly between the river Casamance and the centre of Dahomey, water problems have an important bearing not only on agricultural production but on the distribution of population. Over a large area precipitation is small, badly distributed, and often falls in the form of sudden and violent storms resulting in a rapid run-off and wastage of water. Nevertheless some conservation has been achieved, notably in the Brakna river area, by building dams across the river and retaining the water for a few weeks before opening a spillway for its release. In this way considerable areas have been brought under cultivation at Aneikat-

---

[1] See above, p. 860. See also *Notes on Some Agricultural Development Schemes in Africa and Aden*, Colonial Office, 1953, p. 80.

[2] *Soil Conservation and Land Use in Sierra Leone*, Sessional Paper no. 1, 1951.

[3] E. P. Stebbing, 'Africa and its Intermittent Rainfall', Supplement to *J.R.A.S.*, August 1938.

[4] See below, p. 1478.   [5] *J.A.A.*, October 1950, p. 31.

Gaoua, Mokta El Ajar, and elsewhere. In 1951–2 nine such dams were constructed and crops planted which gave a small surplus for export.

The Sahel zone is noteworthy as the site of one of the most important of the irrigation projects in Africa, ranking with the great irrigation canals in India and Pakistan, or with the Gezira Scheme in the Sudan.[1] In French territories the closest analogy is perhaps the damming of the Oued el Abid at Bin el Ouidane, which irrigates 250,000 acres of the Tadla plain in Morocco. The project in the Sahel zone is part of a comprehensive plan for the development of the resources of the Niger Basin. It is an area which presents features of singular interest. In the course of its great northward bend (which is believed to represent the junction of two former river systems), the Niger floods an enormous delta of its own creation. As the result of the deposit of sediment it has raised its bed some feet above the surrounding country, so that when it overflows inundation may extend on occasion to an area of nearly 40,000 square miles. A series of vast but shallow depressions, including Lake Debo, are filled during the flood season and gradually dry up as the river subsides again. These conditions continue as far as the neighbourhood of Timbuktu, where the river resumes a more normal course, but so great is the effect of this dispersal of its flow that water does not arrive in British Nigeria until twelve months after the fall of the rains at the head-waters of the river in the Fouta Djalon Plateau of French Guinea.

The scheme for the development of the Niger lacustrine area was largely due to the initiative of M. Bélime, who began his investigations about 1920.[2] It involved, in the first place, the control of the inundation from the Niger floods, with the purpose of rendering large areas of the flooded depressions available for cultivation, and, in the second place, the provision of permanent irrigation on land (situated in an unusually torrid and rainless area) thus reclaimed. It was hoped that the land brought into cultivation would provide the French markets with a considerable part of their cotton lint. This still remains an objective, though the local production of rice, to meet the needs of the French West African territories, has now become increasingly important, more particularly in view of the reduction of supplies from the Far East. The need of irrigation for the growth of rice in an arid region is shown by the calculation of the International Rice Commission. This estimates that the total water requirement for the successful maturing of a crop of rice in any one season is 60 inches.[3] It was also an attractive feature of the scheme that the Niger barrage might serve as a bridge for the projected Trans-Saharan railway, by which it was at one time hoped to render exports from the West

[1] See below, p. 1011.
[2] F. Bélime, *Les irrigations du Niger, études et projets*, Dakar, 1921.
[3] C. Clark, 'The Economics of Irrigation', *New Commonwealth*, 25 November 1954.

African territories independent of the war-time hazards of an Atlantic voyage.

Although the Timbuktu region had once been well inhabited[1] the present lack of a resident population and the doubt regarding the soil conditions likely to be encountered indicated the need for caution in approaching any major scheme of irrigation. The Government therefore began by utilizing the research station of Niénébalé, 110 miles below Bamako, as an experiment in colonization. A more extended scheme began in 1930 at Baguineda on the Sotuba canal, which had been constructed in 1925 for the provision of hydroelectric power and also to serve as a channel to by-pass the local rapids of the Niger. Since 1932 work on the development of the Niger Basin as a whole has been entrusted to a special State organization, the *Office du Niger*. The barrage at Sansanding, with a total length of 5,981 feet, was begun in 1934; it was practically completed in 1941 and raised the water level in the Niger by 14 feet.[2] The two main channels, the Macina and Sahel canals, were completed by 1938. The scheme for the control of inundation involved the construction of an embankment from Ségou downstream for 73 miles. Owing to the changes in the value of the franc, it is difficult to estimate the exact cost of the work done; part was provided from local sources and the remainder from loan funds.[3]

It has been stated that there are already 500,000 acres under irrigation and planted to cotton and a further 175,000 acres under rice,[4] but it is estimated that ultimately it may be possible to irrigate 2 million acres. There were in 1952 over 21,000 cultivators established in three main areas, some of whom were from the immediate neighbourhood, some from elsewhere in the French Sudan, and some from the over-populated Upper Volta territory. In the most southerly area, Baguineda, 4,342 cultivators holding 13,000 acres had planted over 6,000 acres of rice. The most northerly area, Niono-Molodo, was originally intended for cotton, but rice is now being increasingly cultivated there; completely mechanized rice production was started experimentally in 1949 in Molodo and there are now 14,900 acres under this crop. The more northerly part of the area seems better suited to cotton production and it is intended to develop this in conjunction with the *Compagnie Française pour le Développement des Fibres Textiles*. Altogether some 30,000 acres are under cultivation in the Niono-Molodo area, of which nearly 15,000 acres were under cotton in

---

[1] *Arid Zone Hydrology*, Unesco, 1953, p. 32.

[2] R. J. Harrison Church, 'Rice Cultivation and Irrigation in West Africa', *Indian Geographical Journal*, 1951, p. 44.

[3] G. Peter, *Un Exemple d'assistance technique*, Office du Niger, 1952, MS. R. J. Harrison Church, *Modern Colonization*, 1951, pp. 72–73, and in *Geographical Journal*, June 1951, p. 218. J. Paillard, *Le Périple noir*, 1936, p. 100. G. Spitz, *Sansanding, les irrigations du Niger*, 1949. *Enc. A.O.F.*, vol. i, pp. 341 ff. F. J. Pedler, *West Africa*, 1951, p. 83.

[4] *Arid Zone Hydrology*, Unesco, 1953, p. 32.

1952. The area of Kokry-Kolongotoma, irrigated by the Macina canal, has always been the main rice-producing area; there were in 1953 over 31,000 acres under cultivation by 10,349 peasant farmers, 25,000 acres being under rice.

In 1937 the Government assumed the title to all unoccupied land within the area of the Sansanding Scheme. Land is allocated by the *Office du Niger* to heads of families, the latter being settled in tribal groups. Colonists are required to conform to the prescribed regulation for cultivation and, after ten years of occupation, they may be granted provisional titles of heritable occupation. The colonies are grouped in *associations agricoles indigènes*, which, in addition to responsibility for the maintenance of canal watercourses, are also charged with the distribution of seed and implements; the cultivators market their crops through the co-operatives. The latter collect the water dues and also the handling charges of the *Office du Niger*.

The loan funds for the construction of the works carried a high rate of interest, and the development of cultivation by slow stages has involved an increasing debit for interest charges. The dual purpose for which the scheme was designed would in any case make it difficult to draw up an accurate estimate of the return on the capital expended. The optimistic expectation of cotton production has not been justified, but the French authorities point to the fact that the scheme already produces a useful export of rice, and they are also satisfied that, with its growing settlement of African 'colonists', the canal will make a valuable contribution to the agricultural economy of the territory. But it still has to face a number of difficult problems, and in particular it remains to be seen how the soils of the Niger Basin will react over a longer period of time to continuous cropping.

The attention given to this important project has not prevented the French from pursuing investigations in other directions. There has for some years been a fear lest the continual process of denudation of the forests in the high country of French Guinea, especially the Fouta Djalon plateau, may involve serious damage to the Niger, Senegal, and Gambia rivers which rise in it. The matter is now being studied by the Hydrological Section of the *Office de la Recherche Scientifique d'Outre-Mer* (O.R.S.O.M.).[1] An irrigation scheme, to be situated near Richard-Toll on the Senegal river, has lately been projected. Its main purpose is the mechanized production of rice. A large barrage is to be constructed to regulate the volume of the river and exclude the saline flow from the sea, thus permitting the irrigation of roughly 1 million acres of land. The scheme will enlarge the channel for navigation by ocean-going steamers as far as Matam. Associated with the barrage will be a hydroelectric installation.[2]

---

[1] Office de la Recherche Scientifique d'Outre-Mer, *Courrier des chercheurs*, 1952, pp. 55–58.

[2] W. V. Blewett, 'Agricultural Development in Tropical Africa', *J.R.S.A.*, August 1950, p. 795.

French Equatorial Africa

In French Equatorial Africa a Ten-year Development Plan makes provision for a number of hydroelectric schemes, of which that at Djoué, near Brazzaville, is under construction.[1] Another installation at the Falls on the Loémé river may be built to supply the town of Pointe Noire.

The outstanding water problems in the French Cameroons relate mainly to the improvement of domestic supplies and to the development of hydroelectric power. Until 1948 the only two centres with a public water supply were Douala and Yaoundé, the port and the capital of the territory. Under the provisions of the 1946 Development Plan surveys were extended and by 1951 were completed for eleven centres; new installations were in progress at N'Kongsamba and Edéa and the overtaxed systems of Douala and Yaoundé were being improved. The hydroelectric potential of the territory had previously been neglected in favour of thermal generators, but the increasing development of the European population directed attention towards the use of hydraulic power. Five sites have now been selected as suitable for power-stations. The most important scheme is that which will utilize the Sanaga Falls at Edéa, designed to supply Douala; it is being constructed by the *Énergie Électrique du Cameroun*, a company formed for this purpose in 1948. The plant, estimated to cost over £6 million, is expected to develop an annual output of 60,000 kW.[2]

The Belgian Territories

It will be recalled that, in the global estimates of the world's hydroelectric power, it has been computed that 25 per cent. of the total world potential lies in the Congo Basin;[3] this is said to amount to no less than 90 million horse-power, a larger potential than any country in Africa. The Colony has only very inferior sources of coal and the authorities at an early date turned their attention to the development of hydroelectric power. It has been claimed that the installations in the Katanga were one of the major factors in producing the remarkably rapid development of the copper deposits there.[4] The *Union Minière* erected a power-station on the Lufira river which supplies its own mines and the towns of Elisabethville, Jadotville, and Kolwezi. The Delcommune hydroelectric plant on the Lualaba now supplies additional power to the same towns, where consumption was expected to reach 50 million kW. per annum in 1956. A third, at Le Marinel, also on the Lualaba, is reputed to be the largest in Africa. Its capacity amounts to some 1,400 million kW.

[1] *Enc. A.E.F.*, pp. 426, 481. [2] *Enc. C.-T.*, pp. 319–31.
[3] A. L. Banks, ed. *The Development of Tropical and Sub-Tropical Countries*, 1954, p. 70.
[4] A. Marthoz, *Le Problème de l'énergie électrique au Katanga*, Brussels, 1955, p. 7.

The station at Mpozo, built in 1936, supplies electricity to the port of Matadi. That at Sanga on the Inkisi river, installed by the *Société des Forces Hydroélectriques de Sanga*, provides public services both to Leopold-ville and to Brazzaville in French Equatorial Africa. Since 1933, when it was first installed, its capacity has increased ten times to over 40 million kW.[1] The plant at Zongo, also on the Inkisi, while supplementing the current from Sanga, will also supply power for the electrification of the railway from Leopoldville to Matadi. In the Kasai region two stations at Ishela provide power for the mines at Baceka, and a third was under construction in 1955. Three installations have been erected in the Kivu Province, one supplying Bukavu (Costermansville), and two others the local mines.

The transmission of electric power from the installation at Le Marinel, mentioned above, to Kitwe in the Copperbelt of Northern Rhodesia is of special interest. The necessity for leasing current from the Belgian Congo became evident as more mines were coming into production, and the vulnerability of the existing sources of electric power in the Copperbelt was demonstrated by the failure of the railways to maintain supplies of fuel from the Wankie coal-fields.[2] The critical period was likely to be from 1956 up to the time when the installation at the Kariba Gorge would begin to supply requirements. An agreement was made between the *Union Minière du Haut-Katanga* and the Rhodesia–Congo Border Power Corporation, under which the former was to provide 500 million kW. for a period of five years, to be extended at the option of the latter. The trans-mission line will be the longest and highest-voltage line in Africa.[3]

Among the other projects that have from time to time been entertained in the Belgian Congo, there is one which is of general interest. Some years ago a scheme was put forward for a hydroelectric installation at Inga on the lower Congo river, with a high generative capacity. Its objective was to produce aluminium by means of the almost unlimited water-power available. The scheme involved importing bauxite from Jamaica, British Guiana, or the Gold Coast. Uranium was to be processed at the port of Matadi. It would, however, be necessary to obtain finance for this scheme from external sources, as the Belgian Government did not desire to acquire an interest in it.[4]

In Ruanda Urundi provision is made under the Ten-year Plan for re-search into the hydrology of the country. Hydroelectric power, irrigation, and the resettlement of the indigenous population are being combined in a project in the Ruzizi Valley. The valley has been cleared and drained, and

[1] 'La Centrale hydro-électrique F. Courtoy', extract from the periodical *Énergie*, no. 102, July–August 1950, p. 4.
[2] See above, pp. 986, 1554.
[3] M. Dubois, 'Power for the Copperbelt from the Belgian Congo', *Optima*, June 1955, pp. 39 ff.
[4] *The Times*, 6 July 1955.

the hill-sides terraced; a barrage will provide electric current and irrigation over an area of 16,300 acres. Over 3,000 families have already been established on the settlement. In the Ten-year Plan for the Belgian Congo initiated in 1950 a total of 1,909 million francs were allocated to hydro-electric projects, and 1,052 million francs to the provision of water facilities.[1] The provision thus made includes both the Belgian Congo and Ruanda Urundi.

Angola

Angola, like South-West Africa, has a coastal belt with relatively arid conditions, but there are local streams which supply irrigation to the sugar plantations, nearly all of which are situated in this belt. The plateau which covers the greater part of the country has an altitude varying from 3,500 to 5,000 feet, with a good rainfall and a number of rivers. Of these the Cuanza and Cunene flow into the Atlantic, and the Okovango (Cubango) and Kwando (Cuando) flow into the Zambezi riverain.

In most of this area the major problem has hitherto been that of domestic water supplies during the dry months, but the recent interest in the colonization of the Angola highlands by subsidized emigration from Portugal has given an impulse to the erection of a series of hydroelectric installations. That situated at the Matala Falls on the Cunene river near Sá da Bandeira is designed to supply power to the emigrants from Portugal who, it is hoped, will be attracted there as colonists. It is associated with a scheme to irrigate an area of roughly 7,000 acres; the plant is estimated to cost £2½ million, and the irrigation project a further £6 million. A plan to irrigate several thousands of acres from a power plant at the Duque de Braganza Falls in the Cuanza Valley is under consideration. The town of Luanda is supplied by an installation at Mabubas, which when completed will generate 60 million kW. per annum, and the town of Benguela, together with the city and port of Lobito, will be provided with 38 million kW. per annum, from a plant at Biopio.[2]

A scheme is also under investigation for the supply of power to Malange (the inland terminus of the Luanda railway) from the Cangandala Falls on the Quanza river, which flows into the Congo Basin. In the majority of these cases it is estimated that the construction of a dam or barrage for the purpose of a hydroelectric installation will provide also some measure of irrigation, but the area 'commanded' has not yet been determined. In addition the Development Plan provides for making a number of boreholes in the ranches designed for the breeding of *Karakul* sheep in the neighbourhood of Mossâmedes.

[1] G. Malengreau, 'Recent Developments in Belgian Africa', in *Africa Today*, 1955, p. 342.
[2] *Overseas Economic Surveys, Portuguese West Africa (Angola), 1953*, pp. 21–22.

Mozambique

The major schemes for irrigation in Mozambique are also connected with the current plans for extending the area of European settlement. It is contemplated that lands should be allocated for this purpose in the country between the Maputo and the Incomati rivers, the lower portion of the Limpopo Valley, the highlands of Angónia and upper Niassa, and certain smaller areas, such as the tea-growing districts of Mlanje, Gurè, and Tacuane, and the tobacco country round Malema. The schemes of most immediate importance are those which relate to the lower Limpopo Valley and the highlands of upper Niassa, since they are best suited for the occupation of European smallholders.[1]

The Limpopo Valley Irrigation Scheme, which first came under consideration in 1925, was revised in 1950 and began to come into effect in 1953. The dam, which will create a barrage across the river near the village of Caniçado in the districts of Jinja and Bilene, will support two bridges, one for road traffic, the other for rail traffic on the newly built railway line from Southern Rhodesia to Lourenço Marques.[2] The barrage will irrigate some 72,000 acres. When the project is completed it is intended to settle on the reclaimed area both European and African families; it is hoped that 6,000 of the former will be Portuguese. The Niassa Highlands Settlement would be situated near Vila Cabral on the eastern shores of Lake Nyasa, at an altitude of 4,000 feet. Here the only measures of irrigation required are the harnessing of the local streams for the cultivation of coffee and wheat.

The Development Plans also include an important scheme for the provision of additional water and electric power to Lourenço Marques. This would be effected by making a dam on the small Movene river, about 22 miles west of the city, and by reinforcing the reservoir thus formed by water derived from a barrage to be made on the Incomati river, some two miles from the Transvaal border. This scheme will assure a water supply to Lourenço Marques, which had previously drawn water, though on an inadequate scale, from the Umbeluzi river. It will also, it is estimated, make water available for irrigating part of the flat country between the Little Lebombo mountains and Lourenço Marques. A relatively small scheme for an installation on the Revue river, about 35 miles from Vila Pery, has also been undertaken. This will feed not only the textile works at Vila Pery but the industries situated along the railway line leading to Beira. It is possible that the scheme may in future be extended by the construction of a dam 15 miles south of Bandula.

While the principal schemes have, as has been said, been directed

[1] C. F. Spence, *The Portuguese Colony of Moçambique*, 1951, pp. 116–18. *Overseas Economic Surveys, Portuguese East Africa, 1952*, p. 6. *Year Book and Guide to East Africa, 1953*, p. 125.

[2] See below, p. 1552.

towards meeting the requirements of the European population, a number of smaller projects, mainly taking the form of wells and bore-holes, have been carried out for the improvement of domestic water supplies in African areas.

Liberia

Hitherto little action has been taken to conserve or develop water resources, but in the Five-year Plan now in progress $11 million have been allocated for roads and engineering works. Among the latter is included a hydroelectric plant deriving power from the St. Paul river in order to supply electricity to the capital, Monrovia.

A GENERAL NOTE

There is in the preceding survey nothing which suggests a reason for modifying the view that the physical conditions of Africa south of the Sahara offer little scope for the development of a series of large-scale projects of irrigation such as those which have produced so dramatic a change in the economy of India, Egypt, and the Sudan.[1] In the one scheme that can be said to be comparable with those undertakings, namely, the Niger Basin project, the progress so far made in the extension of cultivation has not been sufficient to justify the hope that it will reach the figure which the *Office du Niger* has set as its objective. There is, however, one comment which is suggested by the record presented in the previous pages. Until recent years inadequate attention has been given to hydrological research and to the possibilities which it might reveal. Considerable attention has, it is true, been paid to this question in the Union of South Africa, and the Department created for this purpose in Uganda is proving of value in connexion with the discussions on measures projected for the regulation of the Nile waters. Both Nigeria and French West Africa have now made a beginning with studies of this kind.

But investigation is in fact only in its initial stage. To take one example, it is very rare to find anywhere a continuous record of 'readings' of the discharge of the rivers, so that engineers lack the material necessary for the efficient planning of irrigation or of hydroelectric works. It is unfortunate, but not surprising, that the plans for the Kafue Hydroelectric Scheme had to be based on only a four-year 'reading' of the discharge of the river.[2] This criticism applies with somewhat less force to the investigations made into the nature of the subsoil water-table or the possibilities of well sinking in different territories, but even in this respect there is great variety in the

---

[1] See also *East Africa Royal Commission 1953–1955, Report*, Cmd. 9475, 1955, p. 13.
[2] *Report on Kafue Hydro-Electric Project* (the Halcrow Report), 1953, para. 9.

measure of study given to a matter which is of such vital importance to the African population.[1]

There is a further point bearing on the development of schemes of irrigation. It has frequently been debated whether such schemes could not be more suitably carried out by a private enterprise, since this may have advantages which are not possessed by a State undertaking. It is clear, however, that there are in Africa certain issues, in particular with regard to land rights, with which it would be inadvisable to allow any private enterprise to deal unless provision existed for a very close measure of administrative control. The control of an irrigation canal involves decisions so vital to those who are dependent on the supply of water that a Government may well share the strong feeling entertained in British India against entrusting it to private management. In conditions where land is of little use without water, the grant of control over the water differs little from granting control over the land. There are, however, many who have been inclined to seek a solution in a third course, by which the development of irrigation projects is shared between the State and private enterprise. The large irrigation undertaking in the Blue Nile Province of the Sudan, known as the Gezira Scheme, may be quoted here as providing an illustration of the successful development of a major enterprise by the State in partnership with private capital.[2]

This project, which began to operate in 1925, has been described as a tripartite partnership, the third partner being the cultivators. The capital cost, amounting to nearly £14 million, was borne by the Sudan Government, which also bore the cost of the annual outlay on the maintenance of the canal. The 'commanded' area is roughly 1 million acres, which, on the system of rotation at present in force,[3] gives an annual area under cotton (the only marketable crop of any importance) amounting roughly to one-quarter of the 'commanded' area. Possession of the necessary land was obtained by the Government under a Land Ordinance by which it compulsorily acquired a long lease of all land rights, subject to a fixed annual payment to the former 'rainland landholders'; the latter had, however, a preferential claim to tenancies on the irrigated lands.[4] The granting of tenancies and the management of cultivation were entrusted to the Sudan Plantations Syndicate, which maintained a large European technical and supervisory staff. The Syndicate undertook mechanized ploughing for the cotton crop and supplied seed to the cultivator; the cost of these operations was recovered from him and he provided at his

---

[1] E. B. Worthington, *Science in Africa*, 1938, pp. 75 ff.

[2] See *The Times*, 3 July 1950. G. B. Masefield, *A Short History of Agriculture in the British Colonies*, 1950, pp. 111–13. A. Gaitskell, in *African Affairs*, October 1952, p. 243. C. W. Beer, in *J.A.A.*, July 1953, pp. 112–17. *First Annual Report, Sudan Gezira Board, 1950–1.*

[3] C. W. Beer, in *J.A.A.*, July 1953, p. 113.

[4] The Gezira Land Ordinances, 1921 and 1927.

own expense the other labour involved, such as the weeding or picking of the cotton and the clearing of watercourses.

The conditions of the tenancy laid down that the tenant must devote a prescribed part of his holding to subsistence crops; the standard holding was 40 acres, of which 10 acres were to be under cotton, 10 under subsistence crops, and 20 to lie fallow. The Syndicate marketed the crop and, after it had deducted its charge for ginning and marketing, the proceeds were divided in the proportion of 20 per cent. to the Syndicate, 40 per cent. to the Government, and 40 per cent. to the cultivators. Of some 29,000 tenants in 1955, about 89 per cent. were local inhabitants or other Sudanese, 8 per cent. came from French Equatorial Africa, and 3 per cent. were *fellata*, or West Africans, including Hausa.

During some of the depression years, the returns to the tenants were poor, and many of them incurred debts to the Syndicate which had ultimately to be written off by it with the assistance of the Government. But cash returns began to improve after 1935, and on the eve of the Second World War the tenants were receiving an average of from £20 to £40 for their share of the cotton. Since then the receipts have risen materially, and in 1949 the estimated income per head was roughly £200. In 1950–1 the average tenant, after repayment of agricultural credit advances and the cost of tools and fertilizers, received about £800 in cash, but this was an exceptional year, when the total cotton crop sold for nearly £54 million. Although in recent years his income has been much less the tenant still receives several hundred pounds yearly and in addition derives his subsistence from the land.[1] The 20 per cent. retained by the Syndicate gave to its shareholders over the course of 25 years an average dividend (including capital appreciation at the time of its final repayment) amounting to about 12 per cent. The 40 per cent. of net divisible profits taken by the Government enabled it to meet the yearly rentals due on the lease of the land and also to repay about half the capital cost of the construction of the canal.

The scheme was nationalized in 1950, at the termination of the 25-year agreement made by the Government with the Syndicate. The Government retained the responsibility for the provision of land and water, and the tenants that for the weeding and picking of the cotton crop and the growing of subsistence crops. The functions of the Syndicate were taken over by a new body, the Sudan Gezira Board,[2] which exercises the functions of management formerly discharged by the Syndicate, though the financial details differ in some minor respects. The division of the joint net profits remains in the same proportion as previously, but it is not intended that

[1] C. W. Beer, 'Social Development in the Gezira Scheme', *United Empire*, January–February 1955, p. 15.
[2] Ordinance no. 16, *Sudan Government Gazette*, no. 818, published 15 July 1950.

the Board should retain more of its profits than will cover its expenses and build up its reserves. The expenses are to include a dividend of 6 per cent. on the capital provided by the Government, which will continue to pay the rental on the land, and it is further provided that the expenses should include a percentage as provision for a Social Development Fund,[1] and a further percentage for agricultural research.

The provision made for a Social Development Fund marks the fact that the Board has a definite obligation to expend money on the social needs of the tenants, including education and the establishment of co-operative societies. It had throughout been a criticism of the original scheme that it did not give the tenants a sufficient sense of personal responsibility or initiative. This, however, could hardly be avoided, for, as one observer has remarked, 'in a highly geared agricultural scheme, dependent on a strictly regulated system of irrigation, it is inevitable that there should be a high degree of regimentation and control'.[2] In order to increase the interest of tenants in the management of their own affairs the Syndicate instituted in 1940 a system of Village Councils, of which there were some 300 in all. As soon as they began to show a greater concern in their own affairs a wider field of social needs became apparent, and it is these needs which the Gezira Board now has to attempt to satisfy. It has carried out its duties in close co-operation with the Gezira Tenants' Association—a representative body elected by the tenants.

Of the value of the Gezira Scheme to the Sudan there can be no question. The remaining half of the capital cost of the undertaking can be paid off within 20 years, and this great undertaking would then be held by the Sudan free of interest charges.[3] The total population figure for the Gezira area amounts to nearly half a million; the irrigation scheme maintains between 90,000 and 100,000 adult males, of whom roughly 29,000 are tenants, with a standard of living far higher than that of most of their neighbours. If there is a less satisfactory side of the picture, it lies in the fact that the tenantry seem to have lacked that sense of ownership which can create so powerful a personal interest in the improvement of the land. The necessity of concentrating on the efficiency of the economic crop has to some extent prevented the emergence of a body of self-reliant peasant farmers with a balanced husbandry.[4]

It was proposed in 1954 to negotiate with Egypt for a share of Nile water sufficient to extend the Gezira Scheme by 1 million acres,[5] but it would be beyond the scope of the present Survey to discuss this topic, or the interesting issue which will arise when the lease of the Gezira lands

[1] On the social aspect, see G. M. Culwick, 'Social Change in the Gezira Scheme', *Civilizations*, vol. v, no. 2, p. 173.   [2] C. W. Beer, in *J.A.A.*, July 1953, p. 114.
[3] *African Affairs*, October 1952, p. 306.
[4] *Notes on Some Agricultural Development Schemes in Africa and Aden*, Colonial Office, 1953.
[5] *The Times*, 14 April 1954.

expires in 1961.[1] It has seemed relevant, however, to give some detail of the scheme, since it illustrates a number of points which may arise should any major project of irrigation be entertained in the area dealt with in this Survey. But it must also be realized that there are a number of more technical issues on which those who plan any such scheme will need more information than is at present available to them. Little accurate knowledge exists as to the behaviour of different types of African soil under permanent irrigation. There are no data for determining the 'duty' which a given measure of water may be expected to perform in varying conditions of African soil and climate. Inquiry is in particular required as to the possibility of the emergence of salinity, which has of recent years caused the deterioration of so great an irrigated area in Pakistan and India.[2] It is now recognized that the presence of salts (usually of the type of sodium sulphate or sodium chloride) is characteristic of all semi-arid regions. In certain conditions a saline soil may become so alkaline under irrigation that its productivity is entirely destroyed. The experience of Egypt also suggests that inquiry is necessary into the data relating to the effect which the raising of the water level may have in propagating bilharzia and certain similar disorders.[3]

---

[1] *Report of the Select Committee on the Future Ownership of Land in the North-West Extension of the Gezira Scheme*, Khartoum, 1949. Mekki Abbas, *The Sudan Question*, 1952, p. 83.

[2] See the study made by M. L. Mehta, 'Land Reclamation', *Indian Central Board of Irrigation*, vol. i, no. 43, 1951, pp. 25 ff.

[3] H. Bloch, *Le Nil* (trans. E. Ludwig), vol. ii, 1937, p. 282.

CHAPTER XV

SOIL CONSERVATION

IT is convenient to draw here a distinction between those measures which are designed to improve the fertility of the soil and those which seek to prevent or repair the damage that may be done to it by natural forces or by human activity. There is a good reason for making this distinction because, in Africa, measures of the latter character have now assumed an exceptional importance. It is sometimes suggested that this has been a modern development in the world, due to pressure caused by the increase of population and by the demand for higher standards of agricultural or pastoral production; but that is not the case. It would, for instance, be of interest to estimate in terms of money the value of the labour expended in the course of centuries on the terracing of the hill slopes of India or of China. They are typical of the many cases in which a congested peasant population has been forced to protect its lands from the effect of a heavy rainfall following a long period during which the soil has been baked by a tropical sun.

A century ago when the population of Africa was half the size it is today land was superabundant and man caused relatively little disturbance to it.[1] Though the structure of African soils must always have rendered them peculiarly liable to damage from natural causes, it is only in the present generation that the endeavour to find a remedy for their degradation has been recognized as one of the essential requirements of public policy.[2] As the following pages will show, it is chiefly in the Union of South Africa and in the British dependencies of Central and East Africa that the more significant attempts have been made to solve the problem. But it cannot be assumed that the interest shown here necessarily implies that these territories are more seriously threatened by erosion than others. There has not been any such comprehensive study of conditions in Africa as would justify this conclusion. Nor are the facts as now known to us sufficient to warrant any definite conclusion as to the respective parts played by natural causes or human agency in soil erosion.

Here, as in so many other instances, current opinion is apt to express itself in a number of generalizations which seldom stand the test of scientific inquiry. We very seldom know what would be the carrying capacity of any given block of pasture land if it were given adequate supplies of water for

[1] L. Dudley Stamp, *Land for Tomorrow*, 1952, p. 34.
[2] For a general discussion on deforestation and desiccation in Africa, south of the Sahara, see H.L. Deb., 31 May 1956, coll. 656–701.

livestock or divided into areas suitable for rotational grazing. There is no standard by which we can judge how long any given area can be successfully cropped without regeneration by bush fallowing or its equivalent. There are many unsolved problems as to the best technique to be adopted in defending arable land against soil-wash or other forms of erosion, and experts are divided as to the relative merits of different forms of terracing or methods of contour cultivation. Some observations have been made in a previous chapter on the fact that engineers are today called upon to prepare schemes for major hydroelectric installations without any adequate record of the discharge of the major rivers.[1] In addition to this, the present state of our knowledge would not enable us to forecast the effect of any major scheme of irrigation in producing waterlogging or other forms of soil degradation.

In the course of the following paragraphs it will be necessary to make use of a variety of terms descriptive of different forms of damage to the soil, as, for example, 'sheet', 'wind', or 'gully' erosion. The terms have no standard connotation, but are sufficiently descriptive to require no closer definition.[2]

The Union of South Africa

The physical features of the Union are of a character which creates an unusual complexity of problems in regard to the conservation of the soil. Some 400,000 square miles have a summer rainfall and a regular six-month winter drought;[3] 50,000 square miles in the south-western Cape Province have a winter rainfall and a six-month summer drought; only some 16,000 square miles in the south have rainfall all the year round. The rainfall decreases from east to west, and only a third of the whole area has an annual rainfall of 25 inches or over. In a large part of the inland plateau of summer rainfall conditions vary from extreme aridity to semi-aridity. Droughts are of frequent occurrence, and a disproportionate percentage of the total fall of rain tends to occur in torrential thunderstorms and this leads to a heavy loss in run-off. The soils of agricultural value are patchy; only 6 per cent. of the available land is under cultivation, and it seems unlikely that more than 15 per cent. will ever be cultivated, the remainder being too arid, stony, or mountainous. The soil is easily pulverized in the dry winter months, and denudation is a perpetual threat as the result of the torrential downpours in summer and the dust storms in winter.

Until about 60 years ago the demands on the land were small, and there was little permanent damage to the vegetation cover of the soil or to the

---

[1] See above, p. 1010.

[2] For a discussion of the use of these terms, see A. D. Hall and G. W. Richardson, *The Soil*, 1945, pp. 31–33.

[3] Throughout this chapter summer and winter rainfall refer to the African seasons.

water supplies. With the growth of the population and of industry the pressure on the soil rapidly increased. Much land that had never been farmed before now came into production, and farms were cut up into smaller units. The dangerous effects of this development on soil conservation were first noticed when there was a serious shrinkage in water supplies due to the formation of gullies and the consequent rapid run-off of rain water. In 1904 the Director of Irrigation drew up a memorandum attributing this in the main to deforestation, overstocking, veld burning, and the kraaling of stock. A Select Committee of the Senate which considered the matter in 1914 received much evidence on the disappearance of vegetal cover and the shrinkage of the subsoil water-table. After the serious drought of 1919 a Drought Investigation Commission was appointed, and its Report[1] made the first general survey of the position as regards desiccation and the growing deterioration of soil conditions in South Africa.

The severe losses of the 1919 drought were, in the opinion of the Commission, caused mainly by faulty veld and stock management. Denudation and erosion were widespread, and the situation was growing rapidly worse. The pastures had deteriorated; the water-table had fallen; rivers had become more seasonal in flow, and their silt loads had increased. A number of remedies were proposed, such as the protection of the catchment areas, the abolition of night kraaling, the control of veld burning, and grazing control to ensure the periodic resting of pastures. The Report was of great value in focusing public attention on the interrelated problems of soil erosion and drought.[2] The first significant result was the calling of a Soil Erosion Conference in 1929, which made it clear that the primary responsibility for taking measures for the conservation of the soil lay with the Department of Agriculture, and emphasized the need for close co-ordination with other State Departments and with public and private bodies. A recommendation to establish a permanent Soil Erosion Advisory Council was implemented in 1930 and proposals made by it resulted in the government's approval in 1933 of a number of schemes for dealing with soil erosion. These provided for subsidies to farmers varying from 25 to 33 per cent. of the costs of anti-erosion works, including dams and reservoirs for watering livestock. Three years later they were supplemented by a Silo and Stockshed Scheme to encourage fodder conservation. The total State expenditure on these schemes up to 1950 amounted to about £2½ million, largely spent on subsidizing the construction of small dams by farmers.

With the passing of the Weeds Act[3] the Central Government assumed responsibility for weed control and eradication and by 1947 had spent several hundred thousand pounds on it. Another part of the State con-

[1] *Final Report, Drought Investigation Commission*, U.G. no. 49, 1923.
[2] J. C. Ross, *Land Utilization and Soil Conservation in the Union of South Africa*, Pretoria, 1947.
[3] No. 42 of 1937.

servation programme dealt with the permanent protection of important hill catchment areas. Over 2 million acres of land were acquired for the protection of water sources and placed in the charge of the Forestry Department. These activities were co-ordinated in 1939 by the creation of a Division of Soil and Veld Conservation in the Agricultural Department. This Division dealt with pasture research, weed eradication, and erosion control. The enactment of the Forest and Veld Conservation Act[1] of 1941, subsequently superseded by the Soil Conservation Act of 1946, embodied the first attempt at comprehensive legislation to deal with soil erosion and related problems. The Act of 1941 authorized the proclamation of Conservation Areas, in which the State might either expropriate the land and reclaim it, or might take possession of the land for the purpose of conservation. Expropriation was in general applied only to the hill catchment areas. In the Conservation Areas the policy was to keep compulsion in the background, and in most cases the full co-operation of the farmers was secured. Five such Conservation Areas were proclaimed under the Act. The total area involved amounted to a little over $3\frac{1}{4}$ million acres.

The Soil Conservation Act of 1946 is claimed to be perhaps the most comprehensive legislation on soil conservation in existence. In addition to amending and consolidating previous legislation, it provides for the establishment of a National Soil Conservation Board advisory to the Minister of Agriculture and Forestry. It provides a legislative basis for full co-operation between the State and the farming community. Landlords may unite to apply for the proclamation of a Soil Conservation District, involving the appointment of a District Committee to manage conservation activities in that District; or any individual may solicit the co-operation of the State in the application of an appropriate conservation scheme to his land. The creation of a new Division of Soil Conservation and Extension provides the machinery for implementing the provisions of the Act.

This legislation came none too soon, as the situation was by then very serious. In 1947 the opinion was expressed that the general position as regards erosion and desiccation had deteriorated since the time of the Drought Investigation Commission.[2] Hardly more than 10 per cent. of the farmers had taken advantage of the facilities offered under the various soil-erosion schemes. Over the country as a whole erosion had destroyed upwards of one-fourth of the original fertility reserves of the soil. As has been pointed out, there are large areas of the Union which are suited only to an extensive system of cattle and sheep farming. But the possibility of maintaining the carrying capacity of the pasture lands has been prejudiced by the continuous increase in the number of livestock. The number of cattle rose from $3\frac{1}{2}$ million in 1904 to a little over $11\frac{1}{2}$ million in 1950. The

---

[1] No. 13 of 1941. [2] Ross, op. cit., p. 29.

number of sheep rose from 12 million in 1904 to 45 million in 1932; it fell to 30,800,000 in 1946, but was estimated at 36 million in 1954. There were then also nearly 5½ million goats.

Overgrazing, trampling, and veld fires had caused a serious deterioration in the pasture lands. It was estimated in 1947 that erosion had caused the deposit of a silt load of 300 million tons in the rivers, apart from other losses of soil.[1] At the session of the South African Society of Civil Engineers in 1942 it was stated that in the arid and semi-arid areas of the north-west Cape thousands of square miles of land had gravely deteriorated and the population both White and Native was steadily decreasing. Over many thousands of acres of pasture land in the Karroo so much soil had been washed away that the crowns of the bushes stood six inches or more above the soil instead of resting on it, and the seeds from the remaining bushes could not establish themselves. The dams, both large and small, were filled with silt.

It is unnecessary to repeat at length the evidence of the widespread damage that had been caused both to pasture and to arable lands. Of the latter the wheat lands in the Cape Province had suffered especially severe damage. Extensive areas which had once been highly productive had been thrown out of cultivation.[2] It was stated that in the Northern Transvaal more than 100,000 acres of formerly productive land had lost practically all of its original topsoil, and only subsoil was left, the latter assuming the hardness of rock during the dry season. It has been estimated that soil erosion has damaged roughly from 211,000 to 422,000 acres of fertile land annually.[3]

There was similar evidence as to the serious deterioration in the sources of water supply, including the dams or other provision for the storage of water for which assistance had been provided by the State. The silting up of the major reservoirs constructed by the Government for irrigation or for municipal use has been a subject of continual concern. It was stated[4] in 1936 that in four large dams constructed between 1920 and 1925 the loss in storage capacity due to the accumulation of silt was in one case 43 per cent. and in the others 14 to 33 per cent. A case was quoted in which a large reservoir supplying water for important farming operations had silted up to 22 per cent. of its capacity within eight years from the completion of the dam.[5] In the Karroo and in the areas just west of the Drakensberg range erosion had reached a most serious stage; most of the larger dams were in danger of being made useless by siltation. These effects were equally manifest in the great number of smaller dams; they are the more

---

[1] Ibid., p. 13.

[2] H. H. Bennett, *Soil Erosion and Land Use in South Africa*, Pretoria, 1945.

[3] *Overseas Economic Surveys, Union of South Africa*, 1953, p. 23.

[4] A. D. Lewis, *Silting of Four Large Reservoirs in South Africa*, Second Congress on Large Dams, Communication no. 5, Washington, 1936, p. 2.   [5] Bennett, op. cit. p. 13.

serious because they aggravate the losses from evaporation which are already extremely high in South Africa.

The enactment of the legislation of the Soil Conservation Act of 1946 was followed by a period of much activity in measures for combating the menace of erosion. By the end of 1951 a total of 441 Conservation Districts had been gazetted, covering an area of some 127,000,600 acres, or nearly 40 per cent. of the total farming area;[1] by 1952 some 456 Districts had been approved for proclamation. In 1948 proclamation was made of the eastern slopes of the Drakensberg range as the Drakensberg Catchment Area. In 1949 the growing danger to the water supplies of King William's Town and East London made it necessary to proclaim the catchment area of the Buffalo river. In the following year danger to the water supplies of Pieter-maritzburg brought about the proclamation of the catchment area of the Henley Dam. This was followed in 1951 by the declaration of the catchment area of Shongweni Dam supplying water to Durban, which had silted up to 31 per cent. of its capacity. The difficulties which may be experienced in restoring Soil Conservation Areas—apart from the engineering problems involved—have been illustrated in the Native Drakensberg Conservation Area of 2 million acres. Here the scheme entailed an extensive resettlement of the Native population.[2]

The activity thus shown, however, cannot be said to have done more than to provide a basis for a campaign against the progress of soil erosion. The effective working of the Act cannot be secured merely by measures taken by the Soil Conservation and Extension Division or by the State grant of subsidies to farmers for fencing of paddocks or the construction of dams; it will be assured only by the active co-operation of landholders in the reform of farming practice or in the management of pasture lands. The reports issued by the Director of the Division give the impression that, from the point of view of the authorities responsible for implementing the policy of the Act, the steps so far taken have only been a beginning; the back of the problem has still to be broken.

It has from the first been held in the Union that the problem in the Native areas differs materially from that presented by the European farm-lands, and requires a different approach. The White Paper on Agricultural Policy issued in 1946 characterized the position in the Native areas as one of exceptional gravity. The factors which caused such serious erosion in the European sector were in fact bound to operate with greater force in the Transkei and in other Native areas because of the much greater density of the rural population and the almost inevitable accompanying overstocking. The Native Economic Commission of 1930–2 reported that all the Reserves were overstocked, and that parts of some of them were

[1] *Overseas Economic Surveys, Union of South Africa, 1953*, p. 23.
[2] *Report of the Soil Conservation Board, 1947–48.*

in danger of reverting to desert conditions. In 1937 the Chief Magistrate of the Transkei stated that though there was little actual erosion near the coast it was very serious in the mountainous belt inland. The grazing was trodden out and seeding rarely took place. Every foot of arable land was used; it was often badly located on steep slopes and was cut up by the numerous gullies, due to the existence of sledge tracks, footpaths, and cattle tracks to the dipping tanks.

The Department of Native Affairs and the South African Native Trust had already taken certain steps before the passing of the Act of 1946 to deal with the special problem created by erosion in the Transkei and the Native Reserves. Between 1932 and 1936 a total of £77,852 was spent on erosion control in Native areas. The measures included the construction of 787 dams and the fencing of 330 springs. Native custom regarding the maintenance of livestock added to the difficulty of reclamation. It was felt that only drastic steps could solve the problem and that these should include a reduction in the number of stock and a definite measure of stock and grazing control. The general picture was no better after the Second World War when the population density had risen to 75·5 per square mile. Meanwhile the number of livestock in the 12,000 square miles of pasture had increased to 1½ million head of cattle, 2½ million sheep, and 130,000 goats.[1]

The first anti-erosion works were undertaken as a famine relief measure in 1933 and were mainly concentrated in the Herschel District of the Cape Province. By the end of the year the Native Affairs Department expanded the original relief scheme to a definite programme of reclamation with the primary aim of combating erosion. A considerable expenditure was incurred, but experience showed that measures for restoring the natural vegetation cover of the veld, including the exclusion of livestock during the growing period of the grasses, were a useful alternative to the construction of expensive dams. The policy of the Department now tended to be based on the principle that veld improvement, including control of grazing and the reduction of overstocking, should take precedence over engineering or other similar work.

During the period 1936 to 1940 a total of over £200,000 was spent on soil conservation in Native areas and £167,000 on reclamation, including fencing and water supplies.[2] Fencing was viewed with suspicion by Natives, and though a Proclamation providing for compulsory fencing had been issued in 1931 it was only applied on a small scale. In Zululand it was estimated that 75 per cent. of the total area had been affected by erosion and that production had been reduced by 10 per cent. Large tracts in the northern and eastern sections were suffering severely from the lack of

---

[1] Agricultural Census, 1948.
[2] Department of Native Affairs, *Betterment for the Bantu*, 1950, p. 12.

a water supply. The Ciskei, with a population density of 69·6 per square mile, had a chronic problem of overstocking. During the Second World War most of the trained staff was withdrawn, and the expenditure incurred on soil conservation was relatively small. Activity was resumed in 1945 and between that year and 1950 a total of £725,000 was spent on soil conservation and £1½ million on reclamation.

So far as the Native areas were concerned, the operations directed towards the conservation of the soil had their legal basis in two different enactments. The first was a Proclamation of 1937,[1] which gave the Minister powers to carry out operations to correct erosion. The second was the Proclamation of 1939, which authorized the declaration of Betterment Areas and also provided for the establishment of the South African Native Trust, to which reference has been made in a previous chapter.[2] As has been shown, the legislation of 1936 gave the Native Trust authority to purchase large areas of land for Native occupation, but the area actually acquired[3] has so far fallen far short of the total which was then considered necessary to establish Native economy on a satisfactory basis. This fact had an important bearing on the problem of soil conservation since many of the soil-conservation schemes involved the extensive resettlement of surplus populations.

After the Second World War the Trust appointed Planning Committees for each of the five rural Native Affairs regions: the Transkei, Ciskei, Natal and Zululand, the Northern area, and the Western area. By 1950 more than a hundred Native Reserves had been surveyed and schemes made for their replanning in accordance with the policy of the Native Affairs Department. This included the demarcation of residential, arable, and grazing areas and the limitation of stock to the grazing capacity of the land. It contemplated also the establishment of rural villages for the families of Natives regularly employed in industries and other services, as it was now realized that there would never be enough land to enable every Native in the Reserves to become a full-time peasant farmer.[4]

In the Betterment Areas a greater measure of control has, it is claimed, brought about substantial improvements in agricultural methods. Arable lands have been largely demarcated, grass contour strips laid out, and many thousand miles of contour banks constructed. Rotational grazing has been introduced in many Locations, and veld burning has been brought under control. There is still, however, much opposition by Natives to carrying out the necessary reductions in the number of stock. In 1950 nearly 500 Locations out of about 1,200 had accepted the application of

[1] No. 199 of 1937, as amended in 1942.
[2] Native Trust and Land Act no. 18 of 1936, as amended by Act no. 17 of 1939. See above, p. 692.
[3] O.Y.S.A., 1952–53, p. 488.
[4] Department of Native Affairs, Betterment for the Bantu, 1950, p. 14.

the Betterment Areas Proclamation, but it had only been possible to cull 7,890 units of stock,[1] The Natives were said to be very suspicious of any effort by Europeans to improve their land; 'they see in betterment schemes a sinister move that may ultimately lead to their losing their precious land and cattle'.[2] Nevertheless, much has been done in the period following the Second World War. In 1950 the Department of Native Affairs controlled 126 minor irrigation schemes, serving in all more than 30,000 acres of land. Much the largest is the scheme at Taungs to which reference has been made in the preceding chapter.[3] The Department has also provided about 1,500 bore-holes and wells equipped with pumping plants, in addition to 1,000 stock dams and 1,680 small dams, while many springs have been fenced and developed.

In the Transkei work has been chiefly concentrated on carrying out the rehabilitation scheme drawn up by the Planning Committees for 19 Locations, though the shortage of technical staff and machinery has hampered operations. The work done has included 986 miles of fencing, 59 miles of training banks and grassed waterways, and the laying down of 542 miles of grass strips. In other areas also the people have co-operated in laying down contour grass strips on a large scale.

The situation in the central belt of the country does not, however, appear to be improving. In 1950 it was showing signs of a continuing erosion of arable land on a large scale and an increase in the area occupied by noxious weeds. The water supplies were very inadequate. In the Ciskei 1950 marked the culmination of as severe a drought as the region had ever known. Slow progress has been made on some Locations in protecting arable areas by contour grass strips. The deterioration of pastures remains a major problem, largely caused by overstocking, and, except in Betterment Areas where grazing camps have been established, little progress has been made towards its solution. In Natal and Zululand, apart from the irrigation schemes mentioned earlier, the most important work has been the reclamation of a badly eroded ward in the Nqutu District of Zululand. The sand drift and wind erosion in the coastal districts have also been dealt with on a considerable scale, Much more, however, remains to be done, particularly in Zululand.

In the Northern region some progress has been made in the Transvaal, especially in the Pietersburg District where heavy equipment has been concentrated. An important flooding scheme, also in Northern Transvaal, is in operation at Moletse.[4] Flood waters are here spread by embankments and graded furrows over a wide area of pasture in Moletse Location.

[1] *Report of the Department of Native Affairs, 1949–50*, U.G. no. 61, 1951.
[2] Department of Native Affairs, *Betterment for the Bantu*, 1950, pp. 11, 28.
[3] See above, p. 976.
[4] Department of Native Affairs, *Betterment for the Bantu*, 1950, pp. 19–20.

In the Western region many of the Native areas are in semi-arid cattle-farming country. Wind erosion is a greater danger than sheet or gully erosion in some of these areas. Veld management and the improvement of grazing are the main problems, and a major obstacle is the shortage of water supply. A number of bore-holes and dams have been constructed, and grazing camps have been organized on Trust farms. Anti-erosion work has been mainly concentrated in the Thaba Nchu, Witsieshoek, and Lichtenburg Districts of the Orange Free State, where some of the older reclamation schemes have also shown good results. Wind erosion on the Trust farms in Lichtenburg is being countered by the planting of tree wind-breaks. Maintenance and repairs in the Thaba Nchu District have been carried out with African co-operation, but in the Witsieshoek District it was reported that the Natives had destroyed plantations and fencing. In the Mafeking District, on the contrary, the Chiefs and their followers have shown exemplary co-operation.

The important Socio-Economic Commission[1] held that by 1952 about 23 per cent. of the Reserved, but only 3·8 per cent. of the Scheduled, areas had been stabilized by measures for soil conservation. The condition of the latter was alarming, but even if funds were available for expediting the work, success would depend on the support given to a social programme which could secure the co-operation of the Bantu peoples concerned.

Basutoland

Three-quarters of Basutoland is mountainous country traversed by offshoots of the main Drakensberg range which unite in the north to form a high plateau at an elevation of 8,000 to 10,000 feet. This plateau includes the watersheds of two of the largest rivers in South Africa, the Orange and the Tugela, as well as the tributaries of the Caledon. Erosion control in this small country has therefore an importance which extends far beyond its borders. The rainfall is variable and is mainly concentrated in the summer months; serious droughts are rare, but long dry winters are often followed by torrential storms, eroding cultivated soils and mostly running to waste. The population is for the most part concentrated in the lowland quarter of the territory, and until recently the mountains were almost entirely reserved for grazing. With increasing pressure on the land in the lowlands, cultivation first extended, some 25 years ago, to the major fertile mountain valleys. When these became inadequate there was a further extension up the mountain slopes.

The natural features of the country must always have tended to the development of gully erosion. With the extension of cultivation this became an increasing menace. In 1935 some 10 per cent. of the arable land

---

[1] *Summary of the Report of the Commission for the Socio-Economic Development of the Bantu Areas within the Union of South Africa* (the Tomlinson Commission), U.G. no. 61, 1955, p. 75.

was said to be threatened. There was a general fall in the water-table and a progressive deterioration of the soil structure and consequent decline in fertility. It was estimated in 1942 that some 300,000 acres mainly of cultivated land had suffered in this way. Similarly on the mountain pastures not only was the grazing area reduced by the spread of cultivation but the edible grasses were replaced by useless scrub which gave little resistance to erosion.[1]

As a result of the recommendations made by Sir Alan Pim in 1935, in the course of his report on the financial and economic position in the territory,[2] a Director of Agriculture was appointed and placed in charge of anti-erosion operations. An interest-free loan of £160,233, made by the United Kingdom Government in 1936, made it possible to operate on a larger scale from 1937. The initial measures taken owed much of their success to the active co-operation of the Paramount Chief. Though work was interrupted by the outbreak of the Second World War substantial progress had been made by 1945, and grants of £282,000 in 1946 and of £122,000 in 1950, under the provisions of the Colonial Development and Welfare Act of 1945, enabled the authorities to increase further the scale of operations. As a result an area of almost 375,000 acres had been terraced in the lowlands region by the end of 1953, 398 dams had been constructed, and over 1,645 miles of watercourses protected.[3] In the foothills and mountains 508,626 acres had been protected by buffer strips and 129,441 acres by division furrows. Thus approximately three-quarters of the arable land in the lowlands and about 90 per cent. of the land in the foothills has been protected.

In the mountains grass buffer-strip work is virtually completed and diversion furrows were to be finished by the end of 1956. There has already been a satisfactory increase in the water level, and there are many signs of the recovery of lands which a few years ago were almost derelict. The first phase of the stabilization of agricultural soils should therefore be completed within a few years, but this will need to be followed by the solution of the equally difficult problem of securing proper maintenance of the work already done. Maintenance will be the responsibility of the Chiefs and Headmen, as the National Treasury will provide funds for only a few 'caretakers'.

The scheme for the restoration of the mountain pastures has also made progress. There was at first some opposition to the introduction of a system of rotational grazing, but in 1947 two major Chiefs offered their co-operation, and in 1949 the acting Paramount Chief requested that her ward should be treated in the same way. In 1953 a denuded mountain site

---

[1] *N.A.*, Part V, pp. 5–12.
[2] *Report on the Financial and Economic Position of Basutoland*, Cmd. 4907, 1935.
[3] *Basutoland, Annual Report of the Department of Agriculture, 1953*, p. 54.

in the Mohales Hoek District was handed over to the Government for reclamation.[1] There has more recently been an increasing demand for rotational grazing; and this practice has now been adopted in all the mountain areas with the exception of one district. The Native Authority has agreed in principle to a reduction of 25 per cent. in the number of goats.

The future progress of soil conservation seems likely to depend upon the attitude of the Basuto towards a pilot scheme in the valley of the Tebetebeng river, initiated in 1953. Its purpose is to protect an area of about 40,000 acres, of which 22,000 acres are arable. Contour furrows are excavated by mechanical aid, but grass stripping and diversion furrows are executed by Africans with their own oxen. A four-year rotation of crops is planned, as well as rotational grazing. In addition the scheme demands from the Basuto a redistribution and a realignment of their arable lands. At the end of the first year a satisfactory beginning had been made and there were indications that it might be possible to limit the number of stock to the carrying capacity of the land.[2]

Swaziland

In a recent socio-economic survey[3] the country is described as divided roughly into four longitudinal strips: the high veld along the Transvaal border, between 2,000 and 6,000 feet in altitude; the middle veld, between 1,000 and 2,000 feet; the low veld, below 1,000 feet; and the Lebombo plateau, with an elevation of 2,000 feet, on the Portuguese border. The high veld is rocky, generally devoid of trees, and covered by a thin soil and sour grass; its arable potentialities in the south and west are largely under the control of Europeans. The middle veld, half of which is owned by Europeans, is a treeless, undulating country. This region is subject to an uncertain rainfall. The low veld—a flat, park-land country—is preeminently suitable for ranching. A large part is held by Europeans.

The effects of erosion are most serious in the parts of the middle and low veld which are occupied by the Swazi. The Report of the Financial Commission[4] of 1932 was confirmed by that of the Agricultural Department in 1944, which laid emphasis on the damage caused by overstocking, indiscriminate grazing, and annual bush fires. An Economic Report of 1948 referred to the deterioration in the previous five years, attributing it to sheet and incipient gully erosion.[5] The fundamental problem was said to be overstocking. The effects of sheet erosion were illustrated in 1947 by

---

[1] *Colonial Reports, Basutoland, 1953*, p. 34.

[2] *Basutoland, Annual Report of the Department of Agriculture, 1953*, pp. 17 ff. *Report of a Conference of Directors of Agriculture, held at Wye College, Kent, September 1953*, Misc. 519, unpublished, pp. 10 ff.

[3] V. Liversage, *Swaziland Development*, 1948.

[4] *Report on the Financial and Economic Situation of Swaziland*, Cmd. 4114, 1932, p. 7.

[5] Liversage, op. cit. p. 6.

experiments carried out on the silt content of the Mzimneni river near Bremersdorp.[1] In one case it was estimated that in two hours the river carried down 3,000 tons of fine silt and clay, representing a loss of soil of a depth of 7 inches from an area of 2 acres. In a similar experiment on the Ingwavuma river in 1948 the river was estimated to have carried over 15,000 tons of silt per hour for at least 20 hours. Erosion on land owned by Europeans did not become obvious until 1947, though it had been remarked in 1944 that much cultivation was being carried out without contour ploughing, and one farm had been so over-grazed that all vegetation, except aloes and thorn, had been destroyed.

Up to 1946 the Agricultural Department directed its attention mainly to the construction of dams to provide increased water supplies in the grazing areas. From 1937 onwards about 70 dams were constructed with grants, made under the Colonial Development and Welfare Act, totalling £21,160; a large proportion, however, became of little use owing to silting up. The position in respect of the conservation of the soil has been materially affected since that date by two measures to which reference has already been made in previous chapters: the operation of the Lifa Fund has helped to reduce the number of surplus 'scrub' cattle; and the Land Settlement Scheme, applying to an area of 346,000 acres,[2] has provided an object lesson in the systematic distribution of arable and pasture land and in the control over the number of livestock. The procedure thus initiated has been strongly supported by the Paramount Chief. The large measures of afforestation carried out in recent years[3] will afford a certain amount of protection to the high veld area.

The herds have been reduced by nearly 70,000 head in the last seven years, and the Reports of the Livestock and Agricultural Department make it clear that the major problem is no longer one of overstocking, but of the distribution of stock.[4] That the number of sheep introduced annually into the territory has declined from 350,000 to 124,000 in 20 years is evidence that redundant stock is being brought within manageable limits.

In the Eight-year Rural Development Scheme[5] some £38,000 were allocated to soil conservation, £3,000 to grass stripping, and £4,500 to water supplies in African areas. A pilot scheme in the Hlatikulu District, originally designed for the diversion of storm water, is now endeavouring to secure the modification of the systems of local cultivation in two stages: first by contour grass stripping, of which 28,600 miles had been completed by 1952; and secondly, by the concentration of widely dispersed plough lands, thus facilitating the introduction of controlled rotational grazing.

[1] Swaziland, Annual Report of the Livestock and Agricultural Department, 1947.
[2] See above, pp. 698, 907.   [3] See above, p. 940.
[4] Swaziland, Annual Report of the Veterinary Department, 1952.
[5] Liversage, op. cit. para. 158.

One of Swaziland's chief assets is her abundant supply of water from rivers.[1] The principal irrigation projects have been described above.[2] but in addition the construction of dams has assisted in the dispersal of stock and the conservation of storm water. Bore-holes have not been uniformly satisfactory and in some the fluorine content has been dangerously high.[3] The cattle tracks leading to the numerous dipping tanks in the territory have hitherto tended to cause gully erosion, but this is being counteracted by increasing the opportunities afforded for the breaking up of the concentration of livestock. The legislation essential to the administration of the Eight-year Development Scheme was provided in 1951 by legislation relating to forests and natural resources.[4] In Native areas the Native Administration Proclamation[5] empowered the Paramount Chief to make all necessary orders for the protection of water supplies, the conservation of the soil, and the regulation of grazing.

Southern Rhodesia

Southern Rhodesia consists of a high central plateau sloping gradually to the Zambezi valley in the north and the Limpopo valley to the south. The rainfall, almost entirely in the summer, varies from 44 inches on the Mozambique border, to from 25 to 35 inches on the north-east of the plateau, the main area of arable cultivation, and decreases south and west to some 15 inches in the Limpopo valley. The tendency of the rainfall to be concentrated in heavy storms materially reduces its efficacy by causing an excessively rapid run-off which results in gully erosion. The soils, derived mainly from granitic and other igneous rocks and from sandstones, appear to be readily erodible.

In the European areas much damage was done to the land during the early phase of colonization when the settlers, assuming that there was an unlimited supply of good land, made no attempt to conserve it. The extent of erosion on the arable lands is not very great, since under 2 per cent. of the area of the European lands is cultivated. But erosion has occurred, mainly in the most fertile regions situated in the north-eastern area of more dependable rainfall. It is estimated that in some of these areas several feet of topsoil has actually been removed. In the less favourable rainfall regions, in which pastoral activities predominate, overstocking and indiscriminate veld burning have led to the destruction of the vegetal cover and have thus caused severe sheet erosion. This is particularly marked in the extreme west, where land which grew good crops of maize 40 years ago is today described as semi-desert.

---

[1] Cmd. 4114, 1932, pp. 6, 136.   [2] See above, p. 981.
[3] *Swaziland, Annual Report of the Veterinary Department, 1951.*
[4] Private Forests Proclamation no. 3 of 1951; Grass Fires Proclamation no. 74 of 1951; Natural Resources Ordinance no. 71 of 1951.   [5] No. 79 of 1950.

In the Native Reserves the very rapid increase in the human and animal population has caused damage on a wide scale both in arable and pastoral land. African stock was estimated at under 50,000 in 1904; it recently stood at a total of $2\frac{3}{4}$ million, including both large and small stock. Gully erosion has been increased by the effect of the rainfall on the tracks made by the ox-drawn sleighs now widely used by Africans for transporting their agricultural produce.

In the European areas the first recorded steps to protect arable land were taken in 1929, and were carried out by the Irrigation Department, then responsible for all protective works. On the advice of the Department a certain number of farmers began to protect their lands by contour ridging. With the growing realization of the gravity of the problem of soil conservation, the Southern Rhodesia Legislative Assembly passed the Natural Resources Act of 1941, which, among other things, authorized local Committees to be set up to control measures designed for the prevention of erosion. A Department under a Director of Conservation and Extension was established in 1948. European farmers are said to be now accepting the fact that the mechanical protection of arable land is an essential part of sound land management. Since 1929 some 740,000 acres of agricultural land have been protected by contour ridging. Extensive gully reclamation has also been carried out and numerous small irrigation projects brought into operation. Less progress has, however, been made in the management of grazing lands in the European areas. Few farmers have so far adopted a system of rotational grazing or attempted to equate the number of stock to the carrying capacity of the pastures. A certain number of pastoral areas have been fenced into paddocks, but a great deal remains to be done in this direction. Some 15 catchment protection schemes are in operation; they are of special importance in areas where high costs make it impossible for the individual farmer to undertake them. The farmer may argue, too, that they are an uneconomic proposition because the direct benefit accrues not to him but to someone else.

In the Native Reserves the first important measure for conserving the soil was the application of the principle of 'centralization' and the separation of arable from pastoral lands.[1] This system, as already shown, has since been applied to over 10 million acres of Native land. The Natural Resources Act of 1941 (also previously referred to) included a special section dealing with conservation and improvement in the Native Reserves. It made provision for the protection of deteriorated areas, the reduction of stock, and the construction of conservation works. A start had already been made in 1936 on the construction of soil conservation works, but at first these were generally confined to contour ridges and

[1] See above, pp. 766, 886.

storm drains. At a later date grass buffer strips were planted, and after 1944 soil-conservation measures included the protection of the grazing lands, the construction of small earth dams in *vleis*, and the fencing of 'sponges'. Two conservation projects were begun in 1949 and a third one started in 1950. These are located in the catchment areas of important river systems and provide for the full protection of extensive areas by the use of heavy mechanical equipment under the control of a Soil Conservation Officer. Soil conservation work has been accepted as an essential part of the duties of Agricultural Officers. There are now five Provincial Conservation Officers and 68 Land Development Officers, assisted by African field staff.

Nevertheless, European opinion in Southern Rhodesia has shown its dissatisfaction with what seems to be the slow progress made in implementing the programme of soil conservation in the Native Reserves. In 1954 a Select Committee dealing with problems of Native production and marketing remarked that only 373,000 out of 2,570,000 acres of arable land had so far been fully protected by contour ridges. Such criticism seemed, however, to be an expression of the current opinion that Native systems of cultivation and production in general were still gravely defective rather than a reflection of the view that the steps taken for the protection of soil in the Native Reserves were inadequate. It was this current feeling which inspired the measures taken for the compulsory reduction of Native livestock under the provisions of the Natural Resources Act, as the result of which 49 of the Reserves were proclaimed as overstocked. It was the same feeling which led to the enactment of the Native Land Husbandry Act of 1951, the operations of which have been described in a previous chapter.[1] The regulation of the procedure of cultivation for which this law now provides may have results of the greatest importance in promoting measures of soil conservation.

Northern Rhodesia

Apart from the flood plains of the Zambezi and Kafue and the large areas of swamp land, the greater part of Northern Rhodesia is under savannah woodland or bush, and only a small part is cultivated. The fact that over 50 per cent. of the country is infested by tsetse fly greatly reduces danger to the land from overstocking. Cattle are kept in large numbers only in the Barotse plains, the southern part of the railway belt, and the Fort Jameson area on the Nyasaland border. On the whole therefore erosion is mainly a local problem, the causes of which are first, the continuous use of the richer soils (such as those found in the maize-growing areas in the southern part of the railway zone and in the Fort Jameson

---

[1] See above, pp. 766–7, 780.

area) without the necessary fallowing, and secondly, the shortening of the period for rotation of shifting cultivation. The latter has become the general and indeed the necessary practice over the great plateau area where the soils are old and leached.

In the Native Reserves of the Mazabuka District of the Southern Province the fertility of the soil combined with the ready access to the large markets of the Copperbelt have led to a concentration of the population in the parts nearest the railway and the replacement of the old system of mixed cropping by the plough cultivation of large fields of maize. The consequence is seen in widespread sheet erosion and in some places the increase of gullies. To a lesser degree similar circumstances have caused losses on the fertile soils of Chisamba and Mumbwa farther north. In the Fort Jameson area the inadequacy of some of the Reserves, or the absence of water supplies, has resulted in local concentration of population and of stock, which has produced serious erosion. In the large areas of shifting cultivation soil fertility is low, and it is estimated that land can be cultivated for only two or three years and must then be rested for some 15 to 25 years in order to allow for the restoration of forest growth. Though the general density of population is low the character of the soils and the distribution of water supplies tend to its being concentrated in small areas, leaving large tracts of land almost uninhabited.

In the Northern, Central, and Western Provinces serious deforestation is occurring, partly for the reasons stated above, partly as a result of differences in the character of the traditional *chitemene*[1] system of cultivation among the various tribes, and partly also because of the demand for wood and fuel by the great mining industries. The latter are said to be consuming timber at a rate of 20,000 tons a month. In the old days *chitemene*, as practised for instance by the Bemba, meant pollarding the trees, in which case they eventually grew up again. Now the practice has developed of chopping them down altogether so that they cannot recover. Large areas have been reduced in this way from forest to poor scrubland and grassland, with consequent soil deterioration.

The other main method of cultivation is the mound system. This is carried on all over the territory on the moist land of the *dambos*. A dry land system of mound cultivation has long been customary in the deforested area of the Mambwe Reserve in the Northern Province without harmful results. In some areas, however, mound cultivation has been found to have led to erosion, and the general policy has been to urge the replacement of mound by ridge cultivation.

Up to the year 1940 little systematic attempt was made by the Government to deal with the increasing menace of soil erosion. There has after that date been a progressive increase in the programme of soil conserva-

[1] See above, p. 820.

tion, commencing with an effort to curtail the damage done by the un-controlled expansion of plough cultivation in the rich maize lands of the Mazabuka area. The use of mechanized equipment after 1945–6 helped to speed up the process of contour ridging and grass stripping. In the Eastern Province the most urgent problem was the rapid deterioration of parts of the former Reserves because of over-concentration of population and of livestock. From 1942 onwards the position was much improved by the resettlement of a part of the population on land formerly included in the North Charterland Concession.[1] In parts of the Eastern Province the rapid increase in the number of ploughs has been checked by restrict-ing permits for their purchase to those farmers who have undertaken to plough on the contour. It was estimated in 1950 that nearly half the arable land in Native occupation was protected by contour ridges. This does not, however, secure the permanent protection of the cultivated area because, under the prevalent system of shifting cultivation, it is necessary to provide every year for the demarcation of a further area of possibly 30,000 acres.

The other main area of over-concentration of population is in the Western Province along the southern and eastern borders of the Copper-belt. From 1943 onwards this has been dealt with by the transfer of a part of the population to unoccupied areas of the Native Trust Land. But in the large area in which some form of *chitemene* cultivation is customary little progress has yet been made in dealing with the problem of the continuing deterioration of the soil due to the shortening of the resting period. In the Northern Province *chitemene* has been taken under control in an area of 3,000 square miles round the sources of the Chambezi river. The spread of hoe cultivation has been encouraged, and the resulting danger of soil erosion has been met by insisting on the protection of all cultivated gardens by contour banks. In the Central Province, where the plateau area of the Serenje District has been described as presenting a typical instance of a Native system of agriculture in an advanced state of decay, protection by mechanical contour has begun in the more fertile regions.

Up to 1949 there was no adequate legal basis for comprehensive action, but in that year a Natural Resources Ordinance was passed, creating powers similar to those provided in the Acts of other territories. A Natural Resources Board was established in 1950 and there has since that date been increased activity both in the European and in the Native areas. In the former provision has been made for loans on favourable terms for conservation work, and there are now three mechanized conservation units operating in them. In the Native areas nearly 5,000 miles of contour ridges and grass strips have been pegged.

[1] See above, pp. 706–7.

Nyasaland

The key to the physiography of the Protectorate is the Great Rift Valley, traversing the country from north to south, Lake Nyasa itself being part of the Rift. East and west of the Rift the country rises steeply; the hills are sometimes precipitous, and include high plateau areas. West of the lake the plateaux are generally at a level of from 3,300 to 4,400 feet, but in the north the Nyika Plateau rises to 8,000 feet. South of the lake the general elevation of the Shire highlands on the west is from 2,000 to 3,500 feet, but Zomba and Mlanje mountains rise to 7,000 and 10,000 feet respectively. The southern part of the Rift Valley is only 200 to 300 feet above sea level. Apart from the shores of the lake, which have a humid climate, the rainfall varies with the altitude from 30 inches to a figure which in certain localities may amount to as much as 70 inches.

Nyasaland has a short summer rainfall of high intensity following on a long dry season. Overstocking is a local and relatively minor problem. Density of population is most marked in the Southern Province, where it amounts in some areas to 300 to the square mile. The position in regard to erosion was reviewed in 1934 in a bulletin of the Agricultural Department.[1] On most forest soils in Nyasaland there is a shallow surface layer of soil, rich in organic materials and plant food elements, but this is underlaid by a red subsoil readily convertible into an almost impervious layer. With the first heavy rains the shallow surface layers tend to move over the subsoil to lower levels. It was computed that much of the highland areas were losing soil at the rate of a quarter inch layer per annum. Measurement of soil loss from a newly cleared 7-acre field of red laterite loams near Zomba showed that nearly 30 tons of soil were removed in a season. The continual loss of soil is accentuated by such factors as the heavy burning which customarily precedes the planting of the widespread finger millet. European farmers must, however, take their share of blame, as erosion has in the past taken a severe toll of tobacco lands. These have in some cases been reduced from a rich loam to a poor sandy loam by the construction of ridges and furrows for tobacco cultivation up and down the slope instead of along the contour. On the other hand, the tea estates have set a good example of contour ridging and of controlled cultivation. There are about 3,100 square miles of Forest Reserve and these are for the most part maintained as protection for the major catchment areas.

In 1933 a Committee of the Department of Agriculture urged that a stop should be put to the destruction of natural vegetation on steep slopes and that cultivation on them should be prohibited unless terracing were first carried out. These proposals received some support from Native

[1] A. J. W. Hornby, Denudation and Soil Erosion in Nyasaland, Bulletin no. 11, 1934.

Authorities in the Northern and Central Provinces, but proved to be unpopular in the Southern Province, which has a much greater density of population. In 1937 a Soil Erosion Branch was established under the control of the Agronomic Development Committee; its functions were largely directed towards co-ordinating the work of soil conservation on which various Departments of Government were now beginning to embark. A Soil Erosion Officer was appointed to deal in particular with the conditions in the Cholo, Zomba, Blantyre, Ncheu, Chiradzulu, and Lower Shire Districts, where there was evidence of an advanced degree of erosion on the steeper slopes. There was also some evidence of erosion due to overstocking in Ncheu, but this was from the first only a local problem in Nyasaland. A census taken in 1953 showed a total of only 273,348 cattle in the Protectorate; the number of goats was nearly 300,000. The danger from this source lay in the number of goats, particularly in the hill areas, rather than in the number of cattle.

On the cultivated lands attention was at first directed to the replacement of the traditional small-mound (*matutu*) system of cultivation by a system of ridging on the contours, with intermediate checks by silt pits. Work continued on these lines up to 1945 with some success so far as contour ridging was concerned, but little progress was made with the heavier work involved in measures for the protection of the steeper slopes,[1] nor was it easy, in the absence of legislative sanction, to enforce measures of soil conservation on private estates. A grant under the Colonial Development Act made it possible to construct an extensive system of storm drains for the protection of the plain south of Port Herald. The appointment of District Fire Boards facilitated progress in fixing dates for the firing of different types of vegetation. In the Northern Province in particular much improvement was reported in the control of fires, and in one district the Native Authority allotted money for fire wardens.

It was nevertheless clear that more comprehensive action was required and that a larger establishment was needed if the advance of soil deterioration was to be checked. In 1946 a Natural Resources Ordinance was enacted, but this was a tentative measure only, and it had to be replaced by the Natural Resources Ordinance of 1949. This was supplemented in 1952 by rules for the control of erosion, the limitation of stock, and the control of bush fires. An important change in the law was the assumption of full powers of control over private estates as regards the conservation of natural resources. The rules prescribe that no person shall cultivate any African Trust Land not subject to a right of occupancy, which has not previously been cultivated or which is covered by natural or regenerated bush, without the permission of the local Native Agricultural Instructor and the local Native Authority. Further that, except in the Northern

[1] T. D. Thomson, 'Soil Conservation—Some Implications', in *J.A.A.*, April 1953, p. 66.

Province, all arable cultivated land shall be cultivated in ridges of a prescribed size and form. As a result of the application of these rules and of an increase in the establishment engaged, considerable progress has been made in measures of soil conservation. The position in the tea estates has continued to improve, and the situation in the tobacco lands is more satisfactory than it was previously, though there is still much destruction of woodlands to provide fuel.

The progress of operations against erosion will be facilitated by the large-scale measures of resettlement undertaken as a result of the report of the Nyasaland Land Commission of 1946, to which reference has been made in a previous chapter.[1] The former tenants of private estates, who so far number over 16,700, will hold their new lands under a controlled system of land usage and pasturage.[2] It seems likely that the programme of resettlement may have to be extended to other groups, as well as the former tenants of private estates, for it may be necessary to provide for the surplus population of districts such as Port Herald or for occupants of areas with dangerously steep slopes, such as those to be found in Cholo.

The Domasi Community Scheme in the Zomba District, which was initiated in 1949, though not primarily concerned with problems of soil conservation,[3] has provided useful examples of the value of check dams in gully erosion and of methods of protecting the verges of streams. But its chief advantage has been in helping to dispel the attitude of suspicion which in many parts of the Protectorate impeded the efforts to check soil erosion.

The physical features of the Protectorate, and the density of population over large tracts, make protection against erosion a very complicated and difficult task. Inadequate financial resources have hampered the development of comprehensive measures, though their necessity has long been recognized. From 1946 onwards there has been an impressive record of progress in legislation, administrative reorganization, and in the extension of efforts to combat erosion. Grants made under the Colonial Development Act have provided for this latter work. Between 1951 and the end of 1954 200,000 acres were protected by soil conservation schemes. Every effort has been made to secure African co-operation, with considerable success, though it is naturally not easy to convert acquiescence into active support of measures which are not in accordance with traditional practices. There remain, however, the equally difficult tasks of securing the maintenance of the works constructed and of organizing methods of land usage promoting the conservation and improvement of the fertility of the soil.

[1] See above, p. 711.
[2] *Colonial Reports, Nyasaland, 1953,* p. 18.
[3] Ibid. pp. 132 ff.; ibid. *1954,* p. 13. *Annual Report of Provincial Commissioners, 1952,* p. 3.

Tanganyika

From the coastal strip, 20 to 30 miles wide, the land rises to the central plateau at an average elevation of some 4,000 feet, falling westwards to the Rift Valley and to Victoria Nyanza. East and west the transition from the plateau to the lower levels is marked by steep and heavily eroded escarpments; north and south it rises to high mountain ranges including Kilimanjaro, Meru, the Usambara and Uluguru mountains, and the Southern Highlands.

The greater part of the country has one rainy season, but a part of the coastal belt and the areas adjacent to Lake Victoria and Lake Nyasa have two. In general, therefore, there is a long dry period, and the rainfall is exceedingly variable. Droughts are frequent and, except at the higher elevations, the climate is mainly of the semi-arid type unfavourable to the conservation of the soil. More than two-thirds of the territory is practically without regular water supplies; as a result there is severe local pressure on the remaining land, particularly the Lake Province and the mountain areas of good rainfall and fertile soil.

A review of the position in 1937[1] showed that erosion was widespread on cultivated land which, however, then occupied only about one-thirtieth of the territory. The Central, Lake, and Northern Provinces were the most seriously affected. In the Central Province gully erosion had reached an advanced stage in many regions; in some areas, such as Kondoa, damage had gone so far as to be practically irreparable. In the mountain ranges the problem was to deal with heavy rainfall on steeply sloping land. Experiments carried out at Mpwapwa (Northern Province) showed that the run-off from a bare uncultivated plot was 55 times that on a grass plot.[2] The extent of the devastation caused by bush fires was incalculable. Each year hundreds of square miles were exposed to irreparable damage, the topsoil being reduced to a fine dust and the land becoming calcined and sterile.[3] In the south-west part of the territory round the Lupa gold-fields land under cultivation 60 years earlier had become barren and uninhabitable.[4] In densely populated Sukumaland adjoining Lake Victoria the problem was one of soil desiccation and wind erosion over the long dry period of the year, as well as of sheet erosion in the heavy rains. In the pastoral areas overstocking was an important contributory cause of erosion. The fact that the greater part of the territory was infested by tsetse fly safeguarded this part from damage by overgrazing, but when, as often happened, the tsetse advanced into cattle

[1] E. Harrison, a Memorandum, *Soil Erosion: Tanganyika Territory*, 1937.
[2] R. R. Staples, 'Vegetation Types and Water Supplies', *East African Agricultura lJournal*, vol. i, no. 6, 1935, pp. 453–5.
[3] P. Mitchell, *African Afterthoughts*, 1954, pp. 139 ff.
[4] D. Grantham, in *Geographical Journal*, vol. lxxxii, no. 2, 1933, p. 147.

country, the resulting concentration of people and cattle in an ever-diminishing area caused serious damage to the soil.

In the early thirties Native Administrations were persuaded to enact rules making compulsory the adoption of anti-erosion measures, and by 1937 the majority of districts had such rules. The Native Administrations in the Kilimanjaro area passed rules regulating coffee cultivation in 1932, following the appointment in the area of 27 African instructors. By the end of the year 1,200 new coffee plots had been planted in the approved way. These Administrations also passed rules prohibiting cultivation near streams and controlling grazing on the sides of valleys. In some areas traditional tribal usages provided a basis for the introduction of conservation methods of cultivation. For example, in the Lake Province, ridge cultivation (not necessarily on the contour) had been the general and traditional practice, and it was therefore not difficult to introduce ridge cultivation on the contour. In Ukara Island in Lake Victoria a system of cultivation had been evolved embodying such modern methods as a rotation of crops and green manuring, and there was a well-developed practice of terracing. In general it was not difficult to introduce sound methods for relatively new crops such as coffee and cassava, but their extension to the great areas carrying traditional crops was far from easy, particularly where shifting cultivation was involved.

It was necessary in particular to adopt a consistent policy in respect of resettlement of the large areas which were cleared of bush in order to combat infestation by tsetse fly. It was, as the East Africa Royal Commission (1953–5) has remarked, of little use to clear more land for occupation if the soil were to be devastated by overgrazing.[1] It was also necessary to take account of the close connexion between the problems of erosion and water supply—problems which had since 1935 occupied much of the attention of the Administration.[2] Though, however, some progress was made at this period, it was rather in the recognition given to the principles of soil conservation than in the actual achievement of results, save in a few local areas, as for example in Sukumaland or the Chagga country. A more active policy was initiated some ten years later when a grant, made under the Colonial Development and Welfare Act, made possible a comprehensive hydrographic survey of the country and the more systematic provision of water supplies by the construction of bore-holes and dams.

A Soil Conservation Service was formed in 1948, as a branch of the Department of Agriculture, with headquarters at Tengeru on the foothills of Mount Meru; in 1951 it had a staff of eleven European officers and 120 trained Africans. Since its first mechanical unit arrived in 1949 the

---

[1] *East Africa Royal Commission 1953–1955, Report,* Cmd. 9475, 1955, p. 295.
[2] See above, p. 990. See also *Report to the Council of the League of Nations on Tanganyika Territory, 1935,* Col. no. 113.

demand for its services has outstripped its capacity to carry out the work required. In the four years up to 1953 nearly 46 miles of the water-ways and cut-off drains required for steeply sloping land had been constructed, and the Service had undertaken the building of numerous *hafirs* and other types of dams. In 1953 dams with a capacity of 60 million gallons were completed. There has been a useful series of experiments in the technique of grass stripping. Strip cropping, with alternate strips of natural grass left between strips of arable, is being tried, but has yet to be proved a practical method of land utilization. Experiments are being carried out with various grasses in the hope of a future closer integration of crop and animal husbandry.

In the Native areas the work of the Service is almost entirely advisory, the extension work being carried on by officers of the Department of Agriculture, and physical works by the Africans themselves. Bench terracing, the ideal to be aimed at in a mountainous country, has not so far proved to be a practical method in most places where it has been tried. Apart from the large amount of labour required experience has shown that there is a persistent 'back terrace' effect, due to exposure of the subsoil which reduces the crop yield, more especially in the case of maize. This 'back terrace' effect may persist for several years. Both in this and in other respects, as for example the adoption in the plain areas of the system of tie ridging, there are still many technical problems to be solved by the combined efforts of research and field workers.

General legislation covering all necessary action was provided by the Natural Resources Ordinance, which became operative in 1949 and followed the lines of similar laws enacted in other territories. Under it a Council has been formed by European farmers on West Kilimanjaro, and another Council is proposed at Oldeani. This Ordinance is supplemented by a Livestock Control Ordinance. Soil-conservation rules have been made in all Provinces under the Native Authority Ordinance. The rules provide that areas can be closed to cultivation, and orders can be imposed for carrying out specified measures of soil conservation and for exacting communal labour for the construction and maintenance of works. Ploughing rules also have been made in the Lake Province. In this region the Government appear to have been very successful in encouraging the growth of scrub and other woodland on the low hills.

In the areas united in the Sukumaland Federation[1] several schemes have been initiated.[2] Here the receipt of mechanical equipment in 1948 expedited operations involving the heavier types of work, and in 1950 a new Land Usage Area policy was introduced. This involved the creation of units which were to be self-contained as regards arable land, pastures,

---

[1] See above, p. 473.
[2] *Tanganyika, Annual Report of the Department of Agriculture, 1953*, Part I, p. 26.

and water supplies. In areas where the principle of stock control and limitation had been accepted these units were to be controlled by local African committees. A temporary relief from overstocking was provided by nature in 1949 when drought was reported to have caused the death of 600,000 cattle.

In the Northern Province the most important developments were the plans for the relief of congestion in the Native areas of the Moshi and Arusha Districts on the slopes of Mounts Kilimanjaro and Meru, and for dealing with the serious position in the Mbulu District, caused mainly by overstocking. On Mount Kilimanjaro the Chagga population had increased from 99,000 in 1933 to 233,000 in 1945. Reference has been made in a previous chapter to the measures taken to relieve congestion by transfer of part of the population to lands which had at one time been alienated to Europeans.[1] The Mbulu District has long been a cause of anxiety, and this was increased by a succession of bad seasons during the Second World War. After the war a rehabilitation scheme was drawn up, and in 1947 a grant of £90,000, made under the Colonial Development and Welfare Act, enabled a five-year programme of stock reduction and general development to be planned. The Central Iraqu area was the core of the problem in the Mbulu District, and it was calculated that 52 per cent. of the stock units would have to be removed from this area. In spite of many initial objections the whole plan of rehabilitation was accepted by the Native Authority at the end of 1949, and in June 1950 the Destocking (Mbulu District) Rules were issued under the Natural Resources Ordinance of 1948. A small compulsory reduction order was enforced in 1950 and full-scale operations began in 1951. There has been a general measure of acquiescence in the rules, and the quotas of sales laid down for 1951 and 1952 were implemented.[2]

In the Central Province the position has continued to be serious in the Kondoa, Singida, and Mpwapwa Districts and especially in the congested Irangi highlands. In parts of Kondoa erosion has gone so far that complete closure for a long period seems to be the only remedy. A thousand families have been moved from the Irangi highlands to cleared lands at a lower level. About 1,300 miles of banking were constructed by communal labour in 1951 and 1952. Ridging is also being extended and rules making it obligatory on the part of every holding have been passed in Dodoma. The Uluguru mountains include the headwaters of some important rivers. In the Usambara a pilot scheme in the Mlalo Basin has been in operation for some years. The measures taken include the retirement from cultivation of very steep land in order to allow of natural regeneration or extensive tree planting.

[1] See above, p. 730.
[2] C. I. Meek, 'Stock Reduction in the Mbulu Highlands', *J.A.A.*, October 1953, pp. 158 ff.

There has unquestionably been considerable progress during the last 20 years in dealing with the menace of soil deterioration. But the physical and climatic conditions of Tanganyika will continue to create special difficulties, and it is doubtful if it will ever be possible to say that the position has been stabilized. In any case the solution, if it is to be found, will demand action over a very wide field, including the clearing of tsetse-infested areas, in order to render possible the wide-scale redistribution of population, and the provision of water supplies and other facilities. There will always remain the necessity for strict control of the number of livestock on the pasture lands, for the latter seem to be peculiarly liable to erosion.

Kenya

Kenya has a great variety of physical features. Of the total land area of 220,000 square miles, 2,000 square miles lie in the narrow coastal belt and have a generally adequate rainfall and no serious problem of erosion. Inland from this belt lies an arid zone of some 150,000 square miles at an altitude of about 2,500 feet. In the north-east it touches the borders of Somalia, and in the south extends to the eastern part of the Masai Reserve.[1] Of this zone some 40,000 square miles consist of almost uninhabitable desert; the remainder is partly arid, with a sparse cover of short annual grasses or stunted perennial grasses which are of little value except in years of favourable rainfall. This vast area is thinly populated, mainly by nomadic tribes owning large herds of cattle, sheep, and goats. Permanent water supplies are few and far apart, and the main problem is to check the overgrazing of the pasture adjacent to these supplies during the long periods of drought.

The agriculturally productive part of the Colony lies for the most part between an altitude of 3,750 feet (the level of Lake Victoria) and an altitude of over 9,000 feet. It enjoys an adequate and, at the higher levels, a heavy rainfall. It includes the European Highlands, the lands of the great agricultural tribes (the Kavirondo and Kikuyu), and, wholly or partly, those of other important tribes, such as the Nandi, Kamba, Kipsigis, Meru, and Embu. Between these two zones lies a semi-arid dry grass belt with a lower and more variable rainfall than there is at the higher levels. It is the home of the Masai and of other mainly pastoral tribes, such as the Kamasia, the Samburu, and the Suk, and of sections of the Kamba, Meru, and Embu. In this belt of country the natural pasture is of medium height and of nutritious quality, but is very susceptible to overgrazing, mainly on account of the short growing period. Intensive grazing or too continuous cultivation leads to soil exhaustion, erosion, and invasion by thorn bush.

[1] See map of Kenya in Cmd. 9475, 1955; for the agricultural position generally, see ibid. pp. 207 ff.

The problem of erosion in Kenya may be summarized as one of sheet erosion in the lower levels, of gully action in the agricultural districts of the highlands, and of the creation of desert conditions in the arid and semi-arid districts used mainly for pasture. The first type of erosion affects both European and African farmers. Realization of the danger from erosion on European farms came with the period of depression in world prices after the First World War, and its effects were aggravated by locust invasions and drought. As a result of propaganda conducted by the Agricultural Department anti-erosion measures such as broad-base terracing, composting, and the withdrawal of steep slopes from cultivation, were undertaken on European farms, but on only a limited scale. Erosion was commonly held to be largely due to the great increase in the number of stock owned by Native 'squatters' on the farms,[1] particularly on those which had been closed down during the period of price depression. Legislation was enacted which made provision for the restriction of the number of livestock of 'squatters' in any district where a majority of the European landowners voted in favour of this course. It had, however, little effect on the problem of overstocking. In 1943 an Ordinance was enacted to consolidate the law relating to the preservation of the land and water resources of the Colony.[2] Action began to be taken on the provisions of the law shortly after the Second World War. A Development and Reconstruction Authority was now established and the Soil Conservation Service was strengthened. So far as the European area was concerned the most important advance was the arrival in 1946 of three mechanized units for the construction of dams. By 1952 an area of nearly 130,000 acres had been protected, and the mechanized units had built 133 dams out of a projected total of 177. Some farmers undertook to build their own terraces under supervision.

Apart from the checking of erosion the general policy of the Agricultural Department has been directed to the encouragement of a gradual change from monoculture to a balanced alternate husbandry. In this they have had the co-operation of a majority of the European farmers. These bear half the operational cost of the conservation service. It has, however, been necessary for the Director of Agriculture to issue a number of orders, under the Land and Water Preservation Ordinance, to an obstructive minority, 136 such orders being issued in 1952. Changes in methods of farming are slow, and monoculture is still the practice on a large proportion of farms. Since 1951 assistance has been given by the Farm Land Rehabilitation Fund, which granted loans totalling nearly £500,000 up to May 1953, including provision for water supplies and for fencing; loans were not, however, permissible for direct soil-conservation work. By 1953 157,000 acres were recorded as being protected under soil

[1] See above, p. 721.   [2] No. 11 of 1943.

conservation schemes[1] out of a total area estimated in 1950 to amount roughly to 600,000 acres.

It is in the Native areas that soil deterioration has from the first created the most crucial problem.[2] Not the least significant of the signs of general deterioration was the fall in the subsoil water-table and the conversion of streams from perennial to seasonal sources of supply.[3] Striking evidence of the loss of topsoil from the cleared slopes of Mount Kenya was afforded by the heavy discharge of silt into the Indian Ocean from the Tana river.[4] In the Rift Valley Province the position was worst in the mainly pastoral Reserves of the Kamasia and the Suk.[5] In the former an arid plain is traversed by a high ridge of hills with a fairly heavy rainfall, where sometimes there was cultivation on slopes of as much as 70 degrees or over. Throughout the Reserve there was a general shortage of water supplies for stock, and as a result dense local concentrations in the dry season. Overgrazing had in some areas stripped the land of all grass or bush cover, and both sheet and gully erosion were almost universal. Over 20,000 acres had been reconditioned up to 1937 at a considerable cost. The results were encouraging, but the total area still requiring reconditioning was estimated at over half a million acres. Experience showed that it was impossible to control grazing in reconditioned areas unless some alternative grazing could be provided. For this purpose two adjacent relief areas have been partially cleared of bush and water supplies provided from bore-holes and dams. A reduction of stock in the district is at present being effected by voluntary means, as for example by giving a bonus on surplus stock sold in the market. Cultivation in the Kamasia hill area is controlled by Native Authority by-laws.

The West Suk Reserve has an area of about 3,300 square miles. The northern portion is mountainous country, falling sharply to the arid desert south of Lake Rudolf; the southern portion is also mountainous. The rest of the area falls into two sections: the northern and eastern portions are covered with desert thorn and scrub; the southern and western sections are of better quality and include forest, park land, and grassland.[6] Already in 1933 the Kenya Land Commission seemed to regard it as hopeless to attempt to rehabilitate an area so devastated by over-concentration of livestock.[7] Some considerable improvement has, however, been

[1] *Kenya, Annual Report of the Department of Agriculture, 1953*, p. 45.

[2] F. Stockdale, 'Soil Erosion in the Colonial Empire', *Empire Journal of Experimental Agriculture*, vol. v, no. 20, 1937, p. 290.

[3] H. C. Sikes, *The Underground Water Resources of Kenya Colony*, 1934, p. 10. A. W. Champion, 'Physiography of the Region to the West and South West of Lake Rudolph', *Geographical Journal*, vol. lxxxix, no. 2, 1937, p. 107.

[4] V. A. Beckley, *Soil Erosion*, Kenya Department of Agriculture Bulletin, no. 1, 1935, p. 8.

[5] For the misuse of pasture land in Kenya, see Cmd. 9475, 1955, p. 281.

[6] I. B. Pole-Evans, *Report on a visit to Kenya*, Nairobi, 1939, p. 17.

[7] *Report of the Kenya Land Commission, September 1933*, Cmd. 4556, 1934, p. 245.

effected by the introduction of rotational grazing, and better grasses are beginning to re-establish themselves. Five new dams have been built and the cultivated area has been protected by terracing. Similar problems of grazing control and of inadequate water supplies characterized the Samburu and Turkana Reserves. In the Samburu low country more than 2,000 bore-holes have been drilled. The East Africa Royal Commission (1953–5) has remarked on the successful use of the system of alternate wet and dry season grazing in the Samburu country.[1] But only the first steps have so far been taken in the rehabilitation of these areas.

In the great arid region of the Northern Province a similar scheme was put into operation in 1947, one of the aims of which was to give resting periods to the grazing areas near the permanent water supplies. In addition a system of rotational closures of sectors, each containing roughly 80,000 acres, was enforced. A similar system of closure introduced in 1951 covers a distance of 28 miles along the Uaso Nyiro river and the Lorian swamp. In the three areas where rainfall is adequate for cultivation, namely, the Moyale escarpment and the Marsabit and Kulal mountains, the cultivated lands have been terraced. On Marsabit mountain five new dams have been built, and weirs in three gorges have been renovated.

Substantial advances have also been made in the Nandi Reserve of the Rift Valley Province where a Betterment Scheme was put into operation in 1946 in order to deal with the problems created by the increase of stock. It began with the fencing off of an area of 27,500 acres in the extreme north, after which came demonstrations of rotational grazing; the Nandi were quick to follow these examples. In addition, bore-holes, dams, and a weir of 10 million gallons capacity were constructed.

In the Central Province the Kamba Reserve (lying partly in the Machakos and partly in the Kitui Districts) has long been notorious for soil deterioration. The Kamba Reserve as a whole has suffered from the double infliction of an over-concentration of livestock and a wasteful use of its cultivable area. A considerable part of the Machakos section has a population density of 200 per square mile. The tops of the hills were formerly forested, but hardly a tree has remained, and the greater fertility and high rainfall have led to increasing cultivation on their slopes. Attention was drawn to the condition of the Reserve by the East African Commission in 1924, the Kenya Land Commission in 1933, and the report made by Sir F. Stockdale in 1937.[2] It was estimated in 1937 that 37 per cent. of the Reserve had been eroded down to the subsoil and beyond.[3]

---

[1] Cmd. 9475, 1955, p. 297.

[2] *Report by Sir Frank Stockdale on his visit to East Africa*, Colonial Office, 1937, p. 95.

[3] C. Maher, *Soil Erosion and Land Utilization in the Ukamba (Machakos) Reserve*, 1937, Appendix A, unpublished.

Much of the land under shifting cultivation was reverting to weed and scrub growth of negligible feeding value.

There have been several determined efforts to rehabilitate the Machakos Reserve, though it is not possible to discuss here in detail the variety of measures adopted. One of the first of these was the appointment of a Reconditioning Officer by the Machakos Local Native Council in 1935. Support was then given to the establishment of the Liebig meat factory on the Athi river in 1937, and subsequently to the efforts made by the Livestock Control Committee to reduce the number of livestock. The steps taken in 1938 for the compulsory culling of cattle were, however, abandoned in view of the opposition of the Kamba. More success has been achieved by the extensive programme for the clearing of scrub and the resettlement of the population of Machakos, to which reference has been made in the Report of the East Africa Royal Commission, 1953–5.[1] By 1952 it was clear that the scheme of regeneration was receiving the support and co-operation of the Akamba people. The Kitui sector of the Reserve is flatter and in general more arid. Here the introduction of the cultivation of cotton has resulted in the widespread expansion of sheet erosion.[2] Reconditioning has taken the form of the wide extension of a system of contouring, by the aid of mechanical equipment, and the construction of numerous dams.[3]

These cases have been referred to at some length because they occupy so conspicuous a place in the record of the measures taken to combat erosion in Kenya. The operations of the Soil Conservation Service and of the Development and Reconstruction Authority—which took over the control of this Service in 1945—have also been extensive. They have included schemes of soil conservation in the Reserves of the Kikuyu, Meru, and Embu tribes and in the Fort Hall and South Nyeri areas. All of these have presented a series of somewhat similar problems, but the important Kavirondo Reserve in Nyanza Province has presented a special problem in that it has the highest density of population in Kenya, amounting in some parts to as much as 1,000 a square mile. Since about 1945 the attention paid by the Kenya Administration to measures for the conservation of the soil has surpassed that displayed in any other territory in Africa. The methods adopted have varied widely, and have embraced not merely the different techniques of contour ridging and the like but also practical lessons in the use of improved systems of cultivation. A considerable part of the operations undertaken were included in the Ten-year Development Plan of 1946–55, which contemplated the allotment of £3 million towards soil conservation, £1½ million towards recon-

[1] Cmd. 9475, 1955, p. 282.
[2] C. Maher, *Soil Erosion and Land Utilization in the Ukamba (Kitui) Reserve*, 1937, unpublished.
[3] *Kenya, Annual Report of the African Land Development Board, 1953.*

ditioning African areas, and £1¼ million for the development of water supplies.

In addition to a grant in 1945 of £139,000, made under the Colonial Development and Welfare Act, there were further grants from the same source of £340,650 in 1947–8 to cover 75 per cent. of the cost of providing additional water in the Northern Province, and of £611,000 in 1948–9 to finance schemes for arresting soil deterioration in some of the more arid districts of the Colony. Some of these schemes were carried out by the Local Native Councils, assisted by funds derived from the African Betterment Fund and the Cotton Sales Fund.

There seem to be increasing signs of readiness by the African population (other than certain sections in the Kikuyu area)[1] to co-operate in measures for the improvement of cultivation and the protection of the soil. It is also important to note that the future of the policy of soil conservation may be affected by the publication in 1954 of the new Five-year Plan for intensified agricultural development,[2] and the decision of the British Government to make a grant of £5 million for expenditure within the framework of the Plan. It has been claimed that as a result of the operation of the former Ten-year Plan large areas of productive land are now reasonably well conserved against erosion. As many as 600,000 families could, it is said, enjoy a much higher standard of living if they were resettled on planned holdings of economic size. The Report embodying the new Plan takes, however, a depressing view of the position in the semi-arid areas, covering three-quarters of the country, where the rainfall is low and the inhabitants are semi-nomadic pastoralists. In these areas there has been a progressive deterioration both of the land and of the livestock. Almost without exception branding censuses have revealed a state of affairs far worse than had been appreciated. One of the few satisfactory aspects of the situation is that, for the first time in the history of Kenya, the idea of selling cattle is now generally acceptable.

The Report seems to accept the view previously expressed by the African Land Development Board that the problem created by the increase in livestock can be solved without recourse to compulsory sales or culling. It would in general rely on the enforcement of grazing control and the establishment of markets for the sale of poor-quality stock. It advocates in addition a larger expenditure on the provision of water supplies, but holds that part of the cost should be recouped by charging watering or grazing fees. For the rest, it advocates increased expenditure on the additional staff and equipment needed to operate the Plan.

[1] *N.A.*, Part I, pp. 205–8.
[2] R. J. M. Swynnerton, *A Plan to Intensify the Development of African Agriculture in Kenya*, Nairobi, 1954.

Uganda

The Protectorate forms part of the Central African tableland at an altitude of 3,500 to 4,500 feet, but it includes parts of two mountain ranges, Elgon on the east and Ruwenzori on the west. It has as a whole a sufficient rainfall, distributed over two rainy seasons, except in the north-east, where in Karamoja the average rainfall is 15 to 20 inches. This is concentrated in one rainy season and is also very variable. In these conditions the soil in most areas has an adequate vegetation cover and a structure which is resistant to erosion.

Before the days of British rule cultivation by the relatively small population was of the subsistence type, scattered in small patches in the bush and elephant grass, and little erosion occurred. In plantain-eating Buganda soil fertility was maintained by mulching with the leaves and split stems of bananas and in the grain-producing areas by growing the crops in mixed stands, so that the soil was seldom without cover. The larger trees were rarely cut down. This position changed with the introduction of economic crops, particularly of cotton, the area under which rose to over $1\frac{1}{2}$ million acres in 1953. The African population increased from a little over 3 million in 1921 to nearly 5 million in 1948; its natural growth having been augmented by immigration from Belgian Ruanda. Of the total land surface of nearly 81,000 square miles it is estimated that over 10,000 square miles are now under regular cultivation.

The progress of erosion was slow in being recognized, and action was not taken by the Government until 1935 when the serious deterioration of the soil in the Teso District came prominently to notice. With a great expansion in the area under cotton the number of ploughs had risen to over 15,000, and ploughing largely superseded hand hoeing. Sheet erosion became widespread. An Agricultural Officer was then posted to the district with the task of organizing such anti-erosion measures as could be carried out without heavy capital expenditure. A general survey of the position in Uganda made soon afterwards found that no area was completely free from soil erosion, but that three districts were seriously affected; Karamoja, in the north-east, and Ankole and West Nile in the north-west. Karamoja occupies a key position between the Turkana desert in Kenya and the more fertile lands in the eastern and northern provinces of Uganda. The water supplies were here particularly deficient, and excessive concentrations of stock were an inevitable result. Sheet erosion was widespread. In Ankole and West Nile Districts both sheet and gully erosion occurred on a large scale as a result of the cutting down of trees and bush. In the West Nile District extensive cultivation of cotton on very shallow soils—'a thin skin over quartz rubble'—and the felling of trees on the savannah had led to a serious loss of fertility. The forests which in the first days of the Protectorate had clothed the slopes of Mount Elgon and the Ruwenzori range had completely disappeared up to an altitude of 7,000 feet.

Later experience has revealed the existence of a serious problem of soil deterioration in other districts also. In Kigezi, for instance, a mountainous district in the south-west corner of the territory, the population increased by 75 per cent. between 1931 and 1948, and more than a third was concentrated in an area of 250 square miles; the most crowded part of this area had a density of over 700 to the square mile. Here the pressure of population led to a serious deterioration of the soil. In Buganda there has been an increasing density of population, and the greater part of the country is now under permanent or semi-permanent cultivation. In Teso the number of ploughs has risen to about 30,000, and the district is also one of the principal stock-raising areas.

To a large extent, however, the growth of erosion has created a local rather than a general problem, and it has been met in various ways. In Kigezi there was a large-scale resettlement of people from the most congested parts to a hitherto unoccupied area. About 10,000 persons had been so far transferred by 1952, with the full agreement of the local Chiefs.[1] The new area has been protected by a widely extended system of terracing, and it appears likely that a further large transfer of the population may take place.[2] In Buganda there has been a general expansion of the system of contour banks planted with permanent grasses. Soil Conservation Rules have been enacted by the Government and, a large part of Teso District has now been protected by grass stripping. This has indeed become the general practice in the cultivation of cotton. It has proved to be more difficult to secure the maintenance of the strips when land is under other crops.

While there has been considerable improvement effected elsewhere the Karamoja and West Nile Districts still present difficult problems. A number of dams have been constructed which have given some relief from the damage done by the over-concentration of livestock. In 1955, however, the Districts could still be described by the East Africa Royal Commission (1953–5) as an area in which 'desert encroachment is taking place'.[3] Desert succulents are conspicuous, the water balance has been affected, and the region appears to be moving towards progressive desiccation. The reclamation of 1,700 square miles of good cattle country between 1948 and 1952 by the expulsion of tsetse fly has reopened to the Karamojong tribesmen their traditional dry-season grazing grounds, but the need for resting and regenerating the eroded areas remains. The

---

[1] *N.A.*, Part I, p. 48.
[2] *Uganda, Annual Report of the Department of Agriculture, 1953.*
[3] *East Africa Royal Commission 1953–1955, Report,* Cmd. 9475, 1955, p. 281.

Five-year Rehabilitation Programme has allotted the sum of £217,000 mainly for this purpose.[1]

Uganda can thus claim to have made definite progress in stabilizing the position in regard to erosion. It is at all events clear that measures designed for the conservation of the soil are securing increasing support from the general population.

Nigeria

Nigeria may be divided roughly into three agricultural zones, with rainfall as the determining factor. The southern zone includes the coastal swamps and mangrove forests and the belt of evergreen rain forest 50 to 100 miles wide. This shades off into the central zone of deciduous forest and bush savannah, with poorer soils and a comparatively sparse population. The northern zone, with a rainfall from under 30 to slightly over 60 inches, has savannah forest or bush in the southern portion, changing gradually to thorn scrub in the dry sandy tracts on the borders of the Sahara. The types of cultivation and the attendant problems of soil deterioration vary with the rainfall and the configuration of the country.

In the greater part of the Southern Provinces, with a rainfall varying from 150 to 90 inches, erosion is to a large extent controlled by the traditional African system of cultivation, based on a definite crop rotation and bush fallowing. The main crops of yams and cassava are grown on mounds. The stumps of trees are not removed and are allowed to be left to bind the soil. Very little land remains bare; the yams are planted on the mounds, but maize or beans are sown between them and speedily form a cover crop. The dangers of soil erosion are also obviated by the fact that each small plot of cultivation is surrounded by bush fallow, and any soil carried off by a rainstorm is arrested in the woodland.[2] The period of fallowing varies; where land is abundant it is from seven to ten years; where a dense population creates pressure it falls to five years or less. The system ceases to be effective when the period is short.

This type of cultivation was in itself some protection against the growth of sheet erosion or of serious soil deterioration, but there were parts of this region, and in particular the densely populated Onitsha and Owerri Provinces, in which erosion reached a serious stage. On the Udi Plateau and in the Awka District sheet erosion was far advanced, mainly because of the drastic shortening of the period of fallow and of indiscriminate burning of vegetation. In the hilly regions there was a marked occurrence of gullies, sometimes a hundred feet deep. The Forestry Department has treated badly gullied areas of the Udi Plateau by checking fires and by building dams at the head of gullies. The attempt to secure the digging

---

[1] *Background to Uganda*, no. 100, April 1955.
[2] L. Dudley Stamp, 'Soil Erosion in Nigeria', *Geographical Review*, January 1938, p. 37.

of staggered trenches along the contour on sloping land or the construction
of terraces failed to secure the support of the African population. Such
rules as were framed by the Native Administrations for control of erosion
had little effect in practice.

The central zone, comprising mainly the Provinces of Ilorin, Kabba,
and Benue, forms a transitional belt between the heavily forest-clad areas
in the south and the drier plains of the north. Here the yam mounds of
the south are replaced by a system of ridges and hollows, in which the
hollows are interrupted at regular intervals by cross ridges. The cultivated land is thus dissected into a series of isolated basins. This system
provides a very considerable protection against gully and sheet erosion.[1]
Serious soil deterioration has, however, been reported in parts of the zone.
A large expanse south of the Niger, formerly heavily wooded, has been
largely cleared of forest, the trees having been replaced by coarse grasses.
As a result a certain area formerly regarded as the granary of the south
was described in 1936 as producing large crops only in favourable seasons.
With the replacement of the forest growth by grasses the fertility was
decreasing, and there was little doubt that the deterioration would be
progressive.[2] An experimental station was established at Ilorin to study
the problem of this area, and as a result it was decided to attempt to
introduce a system of mixed farming. As the country was heavily infested
by tsetse, a small herd of cattle immune to trypanosomiasis was imported
from the Gold Coast, but little progress has as yet been made. In the Tiv
division of Benue Province the position is now serious and is said to be
comparable with that in Onitsha and Owerri.[3] The Tiv system of shifting
cultivation is of a particularly destructive type, and their tribal organization makes it impossible to establish large Forest Reserves or plantation
areas. It is hoped to find a solution by the creation of small plantations.

Practically the whole of Northern Nigeria has been described as a
danger zone of soil erosion, but the area adjoining the Sahara has caused
the most concern. Differing views have been held on the question as to
whether the Sahara is actually advancing into Nigeria. One school holds
that there has been a downward movement of the desert which has
already ousted man from what was once a fertile region with busy towns,
and that the same process is continuing at the present time. It is emphasized that the natural vegetation is dying out and is being replaced by
lower types of growth, owing to the drying up of water supplies. The main
cause, it is held, lies in the destruction of forest by man; even the careful
system of cultivation practised around Kano[4] may be overwhelmed by

---

[1] Ibid. p. 44.

[2] *Report by Sir Frank Stockdale on his Visit to Nigeria, the Gold Coast and Sierra Leone*, Colonial Office,
1936, p. 30.

[3] For the Tiv, see *N.A.*, Part III, p. 53.

[4] See above, p. 789.

the Sahara within 50 years or less if destruction of vegetation continues at its present rate.[1] A Committee of the British Empire Forestry Conference of 1935, referring to the desert area lying beyond the Anglo-French boundary of Northern Nigeria, asserted that 'it has taken only some 200 years to depopulate a country as large as the Union of South Africa'.[2]

In 1936 an Anglo-French Commission was appointed to collect data regarding the progress of desiccation along the Nigerian border. It failed to find evidence which would support the more gloomy of these predictions, but reported that trees had suffered severely from shifting cultivation, and that sand, borne by strong north winds blowing at the beginning of the rains, had frequently destroyed germinating crops. The report was brief, but the evidence has been more fully analysed by a member of the Commission.[3] The available evidence does not in his opinion support the theory of progressive desiccation. Much of the desiccation observable appears to be the natural result of an intermittent rainfall creating a lack of equilibrium between precipitation and evaporation. The fact remains that serious degradation of the vegetation has been taking place on the borders of the Sahara as the result of shifting cultivation, indiscriminate grass burning, and repeated pollarding of trees to provide fodder for goats. The danger comes, in short, not from encroachment by the Sahara so much as from ill-advised human activity.

Since the issue of the Report of the Commission some progress has been made in enforcing measures for the control of grass burning and in demarcating Forest Reserves. South of the Sahara fringe signs of soil exhaustion are apparent in many parts of the Northern Provinces, due to the continuous planting of groundnuts without provision being made for the necessary periods of fallow. The destruction of the savannah woodland by farmers and graziers has reached serious proportions. On the Jos Plateau the overcrowded population, deprived of much of its land by mining operations, has completely deforested a soil particularly susceptible to damage. To prevent further deterioration a considerable programme of forest reservation is being undertaken, mainly by the Emirate Authorities. Sokoto has taken a leading part in this scheme. Early-burning rules have had some measure of success, but Fulani herdsmen are not easy to control, nor (as has been observed) are 5½ million goats amenable to discipline. For dealing with soil depletion reliance is increasingly placed on the development of mixed farming; the number of mixed farmers had increased from 620 in 1935 to 9,000 in 1952, mainly in the Kano Emirate.

[1] E. P. Stebbing, 'The Threat of the Sahara', *J.R.A.S.*, Supplement, May 1937.

[2] Empire Forestry Conference, South Africa, 1935, *Report of Committee on Forests in Relation to Climate, Water Conservation, and Erosion*, p. 25.

[3] Brynmor Jones, 'Desiccation and the West African Colonies', *Geographical Journal*, vol. xci, no. 5, 1938. See also E. P. Stebbing, 'Erosion and Water Supplies', *J.R.S.A.*, May 1945, p. 299.

While there has thus been some local improvement the position in this large territory is such as to give serious cause for anxiety in the future. The danger lies less in the spread of erosion in its most typical form than in a general deterioration of the fertility of the soil and a decline in its production. It is natural to find therefore a growing tendency on the part of the Administration to rely on the results to be expected from the inculcation of improved methods of farming and of soil usage. The resettlement schemes now being promoted by the Government are designed to play an important part in influencing the introduction of improved methods of cultivation. Reference has already been made to some of the most typical of these schemes, such, for instance, as those initiated in the Shendam area and in Kontagora.[1] Another such scheme undertaken at Mokwa by the Niger Agricultural Project Limited, was in its initial stages financed jointly by the Central Government and the Colonial Development Corporation.[2]

Some of the more important Native Administrations have passed simple rules for the protection of the soil, but experience has shown that they have in fact been premature. On the other hand, it has been claimed that the people of the Northern Region are beginning to have a better understanding of the importance of soil conservation. If this is so the fact is of much significance, for hitherto the chief obstacle to the movement for the conservation of the soil in Nigeria has been the apathy and (in some quarters) the opposition of the people. It remains to be seen how the matter will be dealt with by responsible authorities under the new Constitution.

The Gold Coast and British Togoland

Of the total area of 92,000 square miles of the Gold Coast and British Togoland about 30,000 square miles are in the Closed Forest Zone, formerly under rain forest; the remainder consists of savannah. The Closed Forest Zone includes a large part of the Colony and of Ashanti, while the Savannah covers the whole of the Northern Territories, parts of northern and eastern Ashanti, and parts of the eastern Colony. The main danger to the continued fertility of the Closed Forest Zone arises from the felling of the forest for the establishment of cacao farms, on which the prosperity of the territory largely depends.

In 1938 attention was directed to the increase of erosion in the scarp north of Kumasi and the failure of its water supply.[3] It was pointed out also that the failure to preserve shade trees or shelter belts against the *harmattan* wind had accelerated the reduction of humidity in the cacao plantations, and this, combined with the loss of topsoil, was held to be

[1] See above, p. 907.   [2] See above, p. 908.
[3] E. P. Stebbing, 'Man-made Desert in Africa', *J.R.A.S.*, Supplement, January 1938, p. 6.

one of the causes which had contributed to the dying back of cacao trees. Actual erosion has to some extent been held in check by the fact that the stumps of the forest trees have for the most part been left in the ground, thus facilitating absorption of rain water, and by the custom of growing food crops among the cacao trees during the first few years of a plantation. Erosion is more serious where old forest land has been planted with maize, the principal local food crop. Large areas of maize land have been denuded of their topsoil, and the yield has been correspondingly reduced, especially near the coast. The necessity of an active policy of forest conservation has long been recognized, but the remaining area of unreserved forest is now relatively small.

In the Northern Territories the problems are of a different order. Soil erosion has become serious in a large area along the northern border, where the increase in stock and in the density of population are pressing on the resources of the land. The control of epidemics of rinderpest has led to an increase of the cattle population of the Northern Territories from an estimated total of 69,000 in 1921 to 395,000 in 1953, in addition to 464,000 sheep and 428,000 goats. At the last census the density of the human population was 83·3 per square mile in the Mamprusi area, and in some localities round Navrongo it was over 400. In the more congested areas continuous cultivation and overgrazing have led to serious sheet erosion.

Until recent years it seemed doubtful whether the Government of the Gold Coast appreciated the extent of the problem of soil conservation which it had to face, but some progress has now been made in promoting measures to deal with it. It has been claimed that the initial measures taken to meet this situation, namely the encouragement of mixed farming and the control exercised over the customary annual burning of grass, have met with a certain amount of success in areas such as North Mamprusi and Navrongo. The employment of heavy earth-moving machinery by the Gonja Development Company[1] has resulted in the construction of 186 miles of contour terracing. Some progress has also been made in the establishment of demonstration farms: by 1952 there were 838 plough farmers, nearly all in Mamprusi, and in 1956 a beginning was made with the 30,000-acre mechanized farming project in the Damongo area, referred to elsewhere.[2]

Both here and in other demonstration areas (as for instance in a farm laid out near Kumasi and one at Kokoasi in the coastal region) the system of ridge cultivation is demonstrated. Land Planning Committees have been set up,[3] composed of representatives of the main departments concerned and of the local inhabitants. It is intended that they should, when

[1] See above, p. 907.   [2] See above, p. 907.
[3] Land Planning and Soil Conservation Ordinance no. 32 of 1953.

fully developed, become responsible not only for planning anti-erosion measures but for the actual regulation of methods of land usage. An agreement has been made with the Gonja Development Company for the construction of major earth works with the aid of heavy mechanical equipment, and the Company has been engaged on a programme of terrace and dam construction. The chief progress has been in the north-eastern area where some 14 dams now hold water. A total sum of £900,000 has been included in the Gold Coast Development Plan for soil conservation and land planning in the Northern Territories. Two Soil Conservation Officers and three Development Officers are employed exclusively on this work.

Sierra Leone

Sierra Leone may be divided physically into two fairly equal parts by a line running north-north-west from the Liberian border on the south-east to the centre of the French Guinea border on the north-west. North and east of this line the country is generally hilly and the Loma and Tingi mountains rise to a height of 6,000 feet. The southern and western part of the country is flat and low lying, except for a few isolated hills and for the mountainous Colony peninsula, which rises to an altitude of 3,000 feet. The estuaries of the ten major rivers are fringed by large areas of tidal swamps and flood plains. The rainfall in the Protectorate ranges from 130 inches to 90 inches, decreasing with the distance from the coast, but in the Colony peninsula as much as 300 inches has occasionally been registered. The rain falls almost entirely between April and November and is followed by a dry period, intense in the northern and eastern areas owing to the *harmattan* wind from the Sahara desert. The heavy rainfall and the generally undulating character of the country have led to the formation of numerous fresh-water swamps and marshes in the valley bottoms, thus constituting a considerable reserve of land which can be brought into cultivation by suitable provision of drainage.

The alluvial soils in the coastal swamps are inherently fertile, but in the uplands the level of fertility is low. Practically all inland soils are light and very porous, except some of the swamp soils; they are all lateritic and more or less acid and, in general, deficient in potash. Shifting cultivation is universally practised in the uplands, with rice as the principal crop. An initial felling and burning of the bush is an essential preliminary to the short period of cultivation, and eight to ten years of bush fallow are then necessary to restore fertility. Increasing demands for food and cash crops have led to the shortening of the fallow periods and a transformation of the bush, first to savannah woodland and later to grassland. The resultant decrease in productivity is balanced by an increase in the area cultivated.[1]

[1] *Report by Sir Frank Stockdale on his Visit to Nigeria, the Gold Coast and Sierra Leone*, Colonial Office, 1936, p. 109. *Soil Conservation and Land Use in Sierra Leone*, Sessional Paper no. 1 of 1951, pp. 23–27.

The major problem in Sierra Leone is one of sheet erosion in the uplands. It was at one period held that the danger was potential rather than actual,[1] but a Sessional Paper of 1951 pointed out that sheet erosion is taking place over most of the country, particularly on steep slopes, and is increasing in extent and intensity in proportion as the periods of fallowing are reduced in length. It is to a certain degree limited by a natural resistance formed by an 'erosion pavement' of lateritic pebbles on the surface. In the bush areas gully erosion is checked by the presence in the ground of bush roots. In most of the Protectorate the danger lies in the continuation of present methods of upland farming and the consequent deterioration of soil conditions. Other harmful factors are the overgrazing by heavy concentrations of Fulani cattle in some Chiefdoms in the northeast and the annual burning of the greater part of the savannah. The large companies mining ore, chromite, and diamonds have in general taken precautions against the spread of erosion beyond the sphere of their actual operations. On the other hand, when legislation permitted Africans to carry on alluvial gold mining without a lease in 1946, complete villages of 'strangers' sprang up in the mountain area of Lake Sonfon. They have been clearing the forests on steep hill-sides for farming and destroying the vegetation in the watershed of the Pampana river.[2]

The Government has announced its intention to zone areas of production in accordance with their suitability for different types of crops. The western half of the country is considered to be generally adapted to arable farming; the eastern half, being hilly, should, it is held, be devoted mainly to forestal production, as for instance palm kernels, which have been the largest item in the territory's exports.[3] In the savannah areas of the north and north-east the land is chiefly used for cattle farming. An essential part of the programme will be the increasing concentration of rice production in the estimated 500,000 acres of littoral tidal swamps, the adjacent flood grassland, and the numerous inland swamps and seasonal flood plains. The plans for impoldering and draining what appeared to be the large areas available in the Scarcies region have met with a serious difficulty, namely that of the development of toxic salts which are lethal to most plants, including rice.[4] No satisfactory solution has yet been found to this problem.

From 1945 onwards production was accelerated by the activities of the Agricultural Department, especially in the savannah areas of the north.

---

[1] W. C. Lowdermilk, *A Brief Report on General Findings for the Gold Coast and Sierra Leone*, 1949, p. 4.

[2] Sessional Paper no. 1, 1951, p. 79.

[3] *N.A.*, Part III, p. 282.

[4] G. F. Clay, *Report on a Visit to the Belgian Congo and Sierra Leone, 1948*, 1949, p. 16; and see above, p. 860.

Swamp rice has become the staple food of a large part of the Protectorate,[1] and there has been a strong local preference for the consumption of upland rice. It was estimated in 1951 that the annual acreage of the latter was about 700,000 acres, as compared with 80,000 acres of the transplanted swamp rice. The increased production of upland rice has led to a corresponding reduction in the traditional bush fallowing.

There is in consequence an increasing concern for the maintenance of the fertility of the upland soils and for the afforestation or protection of the steeply sloping hill country, especially of the catchment areas of rivers. Up to the present terracing has been negligible and is said to be incompatible with farming systems depending on a bush fallow; in addition no agreement has yet been reached as to the best design for terraces under local conditions. As bush areas diminish, so grass fallows increase, but although research had been conducted since 1944 the most suitable grass for fallows has not yet been ascertained. Afforestation has made little progress. While it is considered that roughly 20 per cent. of the country is the minimum necessary to protect natural vegetation in fact only 3·8 per cent. has been proclaimed. It would, however, seem that the Government has in view the proclamation of further regions embracing some of the main catchment areas.

Local attempts to control annual grass fires have proved to be fruitless, and the Forestry Department has accordingly initiated a system of early burning. It was started on a large scale in the Kono District in 1946–7 and has since been adopted elsewhere; the people are reported to be increasingly co-operative, particularly where cattle are kept in large numbers. Some of the Chiefdoms which have become Soil Conservation Areas have adopted rules regulating early burning and other soil-conservation measures, such as the protection of hill tops and of roadside and streamside vegetation.

Under the Tribal Authorities Ordinance the Authorities have powers for the issue of rules which would, if they could be enforced, be of great assistance in securing the furtherance of a programme of soil conservation. The Water Control Ordinance empowers the Governor to declare an area to be a Water Control Area and to appoint a Water Control Board with wide powers. So far, however, the Administration has preferred to rely on persuasion rather than on the use of legal sanctions in order to carry out a programme of soil conservation. As in the Gold Coast this programme is, in practice, in its initial stage.

The French Territories

The potential danger from erosion and soil deterioration have long been recognized in the French Colonies. In French Equatorial Africa it

[1] Sessional Paper no. 1, 1951, pp. 39–47.

was reported in 1937 that in the dense rain forest of Gabon and of the Middle Congo shifting cultivation and wholesale burning of woodlands had resulted in great clearings 'which could be described as little deserts of sand'. In the tree savannah country of Oubangui Chari the indigenous methods of cultivation were destroying annually the vegetation of hundreds of thousands of acres. Farther north, particularly in the basin of Lake Chad, sheet erosion was severe, and along the middle Logone river it was reported that 'every heavy rainstorm transforms the soil into liquid mud sliding down to lower ground'. In the Cameroons the southern area of high forest was fairly well protected, but the central plateau, more densely populated, had suffered severely as a result of the wholesale destruction of vegetation; in addition to this, heavy rainfall and the hilly character of the country have combined to produce both sheet and gully erosion.[1]

In French West Africa the coastal rain forest belts of the Ivory Coast, Dahomey, and Togo, provide problems similar to those of Southern Nigeria. Increasing population and a rapid extension of plantations of cacao, coffee, rubber, and bananas led to the deforestation of great areas, so that it became impossible to maintain the periods of fallow necessary to safeguard the soil from deterioration. As a result there were signs of a gradual impoverishment of the soil, and both sheet and gully erosion developed on a considerable scale. Farther inland on the north-eastern slopes of the Fouta Djalon mountains the destruction of the forest cover resulted in dangerous flooding and in gully erosion on the Upper Niger and in parts of Senegal. In the French Sudan the threat to cultivation is similar to that confronting Northern Nigeria, though it is to some extent mitigated by the sparseness of the population and by the existence of the great Niger irrigation project.[2] In Senegal the deterioration in areas producing groundnuts has been a cause of acute concern. The Porterès Mission of 1952 traced a gradual transfer of the centre of the groundnut industry from the northern coastal areas to parts of the country farther inland and more to the south. The main cause was the increasing pressure to grow groundnuts on a scale which the traditional system of cultivation could not support.[3]

The measures taken by the French for soil conservation are based on two types of legislation, the first relating primarily to forest administration, and the second to concerted action against erosion by the agricultural and veterinary service. The basis of the first type of legislation is a Decree of July 1935 relating to forest administration in French West Africa. The cultivation of crops on lands cleared for reafforestation is prohibited, and

---

[1] J.-P. Harroy, *Afrique, terre qui meurt*, 1944, pp. 133–5.

[2] Ibid. pp. 138–9. For the Niger Basin project, see above, p. 1004.

[3] *Sols Africains* (quarterly review published by the *Bureau Interafricain des Sols*), vol. ii, no. 1, pp. 15 ff.

in cattle-raising regions the rights of pasture are controlled. In the Sahel region the lopping of branches is forbidden in classified zones. Bush fires are in principle controlled; since their complete prohibition proved to be impracticable early burning was tolerated as the best alternative.

Preventive measures were carried farther in French West Africa by a circular issued in 1949 by the Central Government. It suggested the protection of slopes by the control of clearing and burning, the building of terraces on the contours, the regulation of grazing areas, and the establishment of more water supplies. Under this circular the Governor of the Niger Territory issued Decrees prohibiting new cropping of any kind for 15 years in seven regions of the territory. These were now proclaimed as protective forest belts because of the increasing exhaustion of their soils. It was decided in 1946 to establish Soil Defence Bureaux, consisting of the Heads of all the services concerned, for the various territories. The Bureaux were established between the years 1946 and 1949, and it was intended that they should keep in close touch with the metropolitan Permanent Inter-colonial Commission for Soil Protection. Up to the present, however, these bodies have no executive powers. They have had a number of local conferences to discuss the problems involved and have produced some detailed programmes of research. As a result of their recommendations a pilot scheme for the study of soil conservation was initiated on the upper reaches of the Senegal river in the Fouta Djalon hill plateau. The results of the studies made there may prove to be of value if and when the Administration decides to finance an effective campaign to deal with the menace of soil erosion.

The Belgian Territories

The Belgian Congo is to a large extent protected against dangerous soil erosion by its moist climate, its dense forest cover, and its relatively scattered indigenous population. About 43 per cent. of its total area is in the rain-forest zone, with a rainfall of over 63 inches. Round this equatorial basin there are zones of lower rainfall in which the position is less stable, and the dangers of soil degradation and erosion have been increasingly recognized. In the west the former high forest at Mayumbe has been largely destroyed by excessive fellings, and concern was expressed in 1934 regarding the growing signs of erosion in the cleared areas. In the northern zone of the territory the gradual retreat of the former deciduous forest has been accelerated by shifting cultivation and by fires in the neighbouring high grass savannah. South of the rain forest, and particularly in the area south of Elisabethville, there has been considerable encroachment on the dry savannah woodlands.[1] Here, however, erosion does not appear to be

---

[1] Harroy, op. cit. pp. 118–20.

serious, and the main requirement is the control of grass or bush fires, for which special regulations have been imposed.

In the equatorial-forest region both the high degree of vegetation and moisture and the agricultural methods of the indigenous tribes have assisted in preventing actual erosion. The Africans normally sow several crops of different types together; every crop has a different period of growth, and each plant a different length of root.[1] A superficial clearance of weeds is made in the first year, but after the cassava crop has been lifted the natural forest cover is allowed to grow and the soil is thus protected and conserved.

The chief danger of erosion arises in the mountainous and densely populated eastern sector of the country, comprising Kivu and Ruanda Urundi. Even more important than the felling of forest for cultivation has been the destruction of the vegetation of the pasture lands. Fires, trampling, and overgrazing have caused both sheet and gully erosion and the drying up of water supplies. Wind erosion may, it is suggested, have played a part on the higher plateaux. As regards Ruanda Urundi the arrival of the pastoral tribe of the Batutsi has accounted for many changes during the last 50 years.[2] As the tribe advanced from the east it gradually displaced the earlier inhabitants, and with the growth of human and cattle population the area first occupied suffered increasingly from desiccation and from a fall in the subsoil water-table. Recurring famines were followed by the abandonment of parts of the country and a move westwards in search of better land. The Batutsi first occupied the central plateau; when that deteriorated they went on to invade the mountain forests on the Congo–Nile Divide. The forest was systematically attacked from both sides until the Administration stopped further destruction by establishing the Albert and Kagera National Parks.[3]

In Kivu there has been a similar history of forest destruction and erosion of hill-sides. The difficulty of dealing with the problem of improving pastures in this eastern zone is shown by the returns of the number of indigenous cattle. Out of a total number of 390,000 in the whole of the Belgian Congo, some 170,000 are concentrated in the Kivu Province and 210,000 in the Lake Albert region. There are 930,000 in Ruanda Urundi.[4] A Conference held at Goma in 1948 approved a ten-year plan which, besides recommending various measures for the improvement of pastures, looked forward to reducing the number of cattle in Ruanda Urundi by 45 per cent.

There is in the Belgian Congo no legislation dealing specifically with

[1] F. Jarion and J. Henry, 'Cropping Systems in the Equatorial Forest Region of the Belgian Congo', in *Proceedings of the United Nations Scientific Conference on the Conservation and Utilization of Resources*, vol. vi, 1949, p. 255.

[2] *Rapport sur l'administration belge du Ruanda-Urundi, 1952*, pp. 5–6.

[3] See above, p. 929.   [4] *Enc. C.B.*, vol. ii, p. 427.

conservation of the soil. For the preservation of vegetable soil cover action can, however, be taken under provisions of the forestry law, as for instance the regulations dealing with bush fires which are applicable in Kivu and the Katanga. But the question of policy has received much consideration. In 1937 the Belgian *Ministère des Colonies* published a bulletin on the subject of soil erosion, based largely on experiences in the British territories.[1] In 1945 a special organization was established in Ruanda Urundi under the title of the Anti-Erosion Mission. Its headquarters were transferred to Coster-mansville (Bukavu) in 1947, and in 1950 the *Fonds du Bien-Être Indigène* (F.B.E.I) allotted 14 million francs for its work.[2] The Mission, staffed by Agricultural Officers, works in collaboration with the *Institut National pour l'Étude Agronomique du Congo Belge* (I.N.E.A.C.).[3] The initial purpose of the Mission was to carry out research at experimental stations, and it was planned that the latter should conduct a series of pilot schemes, mainly in Kivu and Ruanda Urundi. Of these, the one dealing with the reclamation of the Ruzizi Valley was the most conspicuous.[4]

Another important step taken in Ruanda Urundi has been the construction of 105,000 miles of ditches or hedges, a measure held to have protected an area of 546,000 acres. Rules issued by the Residents under the Decrees authorizing obligatory cultivation make provisions for the construction of such ditches and hedges and of other forms of protective work declared to be necessary. Other Decrees regulate the practice of grass firing, which is permissible only in the early part of the dry season.

The Portuguese Territories

In Angola the effects of erosion have only lately been recognized. In the coastal belt there is evidence of serious erosion in the north, especially in the black-soil tract where cotton is grown. In the south, wind erosion is the chief problem. On the slopes leading to the inland plateau the soil is said to be adequately protected by vegetation except where the cultivation of coffee has led to damage. The plateau zone, covering the larger part of the territory and including most of the cultivated area, has been seriously affected by both sheet and gully erosion. The study of soil conservation is carried on at the agricultural experimental stations which are responsible for investigations regarding the major crops produced in the territory. The agricultural organization is mainly concerned with the problems of European farmers, advising settlers on matters such as contour ridging or the construction of terraces. Farmers have, however, been slow to adopt the protective measures recommended to them, and in the case of cotton

---

[1] G. Tondeur, *L'Érosion du sol*; this was expanded in a 3rd edition published in 1954 under the title *Érosion du sol spécialement au Congo Belge*, Brussels.

[2] See above, p. 561. [3] See above, p. 919.

[4] See above, p. 1007.

'anti-erosion brigades' are being organized to expedite progress. About one-third of the coffee plantations on sloping ground are reported to have been terraced.

As elsewhere, the traditional African method of bush fallowing is breaking down under the increased pressure on the soil due to the growing density of population and the demand for production both of subsistence and economic crops. The Government has established three pilot schemes, designed to assist in instructing the African farmers in the principles of better cultivation. Practical lessons in soil conservation are included in these schemes. The Forestry Service is charged with making provision for areas liable to erosion by flood action. Under the Forest Laws it has been given powers to deal with steep hill-slopes, gullies, dangerous watercourses, and any hill areas considered to be indispensable for controlling the watersheds of the rivers. It is also the responsibility of the Forestry Service to control bush fires.[1] But it will be realized that the strength of the Service is not in fact adequate for supervision of the large areas involved, nor are the funds placed at its disposal large enough to provide for the construction of the works required for safeguarding the watersheds of the important rivers which take their rise in Angola.

Liberia

Along the coast of Liberia there is a narrow belt of flat land, now mostly cleared of high forest but including mangrove swamps and sparse stands of oil palms, some coconut plantations, and much scrub bush. The immediate surroundings of Monrovia are described as seriously menaced by erosion; the primitive vegetation has been destroyed, and, in the absence of any terracing, the cultivated fields show every evidence of increasing soil deterioration.[2]

The rain-forest zone consists of undulating country intersected by narrow valleys. It contains both the high-forest zone and most of the agricultural region of the country. Farther inland the country is more hilly, but though the rainfall is less than that in the coastal zone it is still relatively high, averaging from 75 to 125 inches. Mountains rise to 4,500 feet in the north of the Western and Central Provinces. Six large rivers traverse the country, running at right angles to the coast; but there are no flood plains or inland swamps.

Two surveys have been undertaken under American auspices, one to study soil conditions and the other to investigate the forest resources. Neither have called attention to evidence of serious erosion, Liberian soils being described as well protected by bush and forest cover. Nevertheless,

---

[1] For Angola, see A. Lobo Azevedo, in *Sols Africains*, vol. ii, nos. 3 and 4, pp. 315 ff. For Mozambique, see Armando Salbany, ibid. p. 321.

[2] J.-P. Harroy, *Afrique, terre qui meurt*, 1944, p. 141.

one of the surveys shows some indication of considerable damage to the soil in the northernmost sections of the country, particularly in the Western Province,[1] and the other survey reports that the physical nature of the soils is conducive to soil erosion.[2] There is no establishment in Liberia specially concerned with measures for the conservation of the soil or the prevention of erosion.

INSTITUTIONS FOR STUDY AND RESEARCH

As has been shown field workers are now engaged on a wide range of practical experiments on the techniques used in the prevention of erosion and in the rehabilitation of eroded soils. Research into the fundamental factors of soil conservation is one of the functions of the various organizations for agricultural study referred to in a previous chapter.[3] Some of these organizations include, or are associated with, institutions specifically devoted to the study of problems of the soil. For instance, the United Kingdom has its large laboratory for soils research at Rothamsted, to which is attached the Commonwealth Bureau of Soil Science. The Union of South Africa has the Division of Soil Conservation and Extension. In East Africa special studies of soil problems are now carried out at Muguga, near Nairobi; this institution has expanded the range of work formerly undertaken at Amani in Tanganyika.[4] The French territories have a series of Soils Defence Bureaux, to which previous mention has been made in this chapter. In the Belgian Congo the Anti-Erosion Mission works in close collaboration with the *Institut National pour l'Étude Agronomique du Congo Belge* (I.N.E.A.C.). Portuguese soil scientists also have done much work recently in Angola and Mozambique, especially in relation to the possibilities of irrigation.

On the inter-Colonial plane the Commission for Technical Co-operation in Africa South of the Sahara and the *Conseil Scientifique pour l'Afrique au Sud du Sahara* (C.S.A.) have been associated with a number of Conferences which have dealt specifically with questions relating to the soil. Following the recommendations of the Inter-African Soils Conference at Goma in 1948 an Inter-African Soils Bureau was established in Paris, and by 1956 four regional soils committees for Southern, Central, Western, and Eastern Africa had been set up. The latest meeting of the Southern African Soils Committee, for example, was held at Mbabane in 1955.[5]

---

[1] K. R. Mayer, *Forest Resources of Liberia*, Bulletin no. 67, U.S.A. Department of Agriculture, October 1951.

[2] W. G. Reed, *Reconnaissance Soil Survey of Liberia*, Bulletin no. 66, U.S.A. Department of Agriculture, June 1951.

[3] See above, pp. 912 ff.   [4] See above, p. 915.

[5] *Southern African Regional Committee for the Conservation and Utilization of the Soil (SARCCUS), Fourth Annual Meeting, Mbabane, November 1955*. For the C.S.A., see below, p. 1611.

During 1954 the second Inter-African Soils Conference was held at Leopoldville under the auspices of the Commission for Technical Co-operation. The work of the International Society of Soil Science, which was founded in 1924 by the fourth International Conference of Pedology at Rome, was interrupted during the Second World War. The Society was, however, reconstituted during the Fourth International Congress of Soil Science in Amsterdam in 1950, and their fifth Congress was held at Leopoldville in 1954.

CHAPTER XVI

HEALTH

HEALTH ORGANIZATION AS A STATE ACTIVITY

THERE are many stages in the process by which nations have adjusted their domestic policy in order to provide the services that minister to the social requirements of the people. Some of these stages have been clearly marked and their achievement has formed part of the current history of the nation concerned; others have been far less noticeable and their achievement can be realized only in retrospect. The stages which have distinguished the extension of the health services in particular have often been of the latter class, and their importance has attracted the attention of only the special interests directly involved.

The part played by the State in the provision of medical facilities has in most countries originated in the grant of aid to voluntary effort or to charitable institutions for the relief of persons suffering from injury or disease. A second stage has been marked by the general application of measures of preventive medicine, and here the action of the State, taken in response to the advances made by scientific discovery, has been more definite and more systematic. The third stage is normally achieved with the recognition of the need for a health organization, co-ordinating all those measures which tend to improve or preserve public health but which often extend far beyond the fields of curative or preventive medicine. It is, indeed, easier to describe the objective of such an organization than to define its activities, for the latter may trench on the sphere of other departments of State work and embrace schemes which, though conducive to the promotion of health, may be primarily designed for other purposes. It is unnecessary to enlarge here on examples of such schemes; but it would be difficult to find a better illustration than the introduction, in the cities of the East, of the water-supply systems which have had so dramatic a result in reducing the appalling ravages of cholera.

In Africa the direct activity of the State is for the most part still confined to the first and second stages above described, that is to say, the application of the curative and preventive uses of medicine. In both respects its activity is (as the following pages will show) of a relatively recent origin. In one sphere of work in particular it can claim a definite measure of success: if the Administrations have not eliminated the great epidemics which at one time took such toll of African life, they have already established a working measure of control over them. As regards curative medicine there has been during recent years a very substantial increase in the provision both of major and minor hospitals and similar institutions, though a really satisfactory coverage has been restricted not merely by lack of finance but in many cases also by the past failure to train a sufficient African agency for extension work. Experience shows that the satisfactory expansion of the institutions of curative medicine can be secured only by the wide provision of such an indigenous agency, both adequately trained and sincerely convinced of the merits of the system it is applying.

It is difficult to speak with any precision of the impact made by the existing health organizations on the general standards of health in Africa. As has been shown in a previous chapter[1] reliable material is lacking on which to base any estimate of the expectation of the duration of life in the different regions of Africa. Even if such information were available, its bearing would have to be determined in the light of other factors pertaining to the health of the inhabitants in each region. This would be necessary in order to attempt some assessment of the extent to which the conditions of health have been affected not merely by the operation of the health organizations but by other factors, such as changes in diet or in the manner of life of the different communities concerned.

THE DEVELOPMENT OF MEDICAL ACTIVITIES

There is no definite record of the date of the first provision of medical aid for the inhabitants of Africa south of the Sahara, but it is clear that, in regard to medical no less than to educational facilities,[2] a great deal is owed to missionary efforts. Mention is made of the existence of a missionary hospital in Mozambique in the year 1518.[3] In 1774 the Franciscan missionaries in Angola discovered the ruins of a hospital built by the Capuchins, who had settled in the territory in 1640. The first qualified medical missionary of the Protestant churches was probably Dr. Vanderkemp, who offered his services to the London Missionary Society in 1795. In 1810 he completed a 'considerable book on midwifery' for the benefit of the Hottentots, among whom he worked at Betheldorp, near Algoa Bay.[4] The Moravian missionaries were also early in the field, and in 1823 they undertook the supervision of a leper colony at Hemel-en-Aarde, in the Cape Province.[5] It is a fact of some interest in this connexion that the value of the Cape to merchant ships voyaging to India lay in its provision of citrus fruits, which even in 1600 were recognized to be a precaution against scurvy.[6]

---

[1] See above, pp. 138 ff.　　　　　　　　　　　　　[2] See below, pp. 1133 ff.

[3] G. McC. Theal, *The Portuguese in South Africa*, 1896, p. 110.

[4] A. D. Martin, *Doctor M. Vanderkemp*, 1931.

[5] J. E. Hutton, *Short History of the Moravian Church*, 1895.

[6] D. McDonald, 'Dr. John Woodall and his Treatment of the Scurvy', *Trans. Roy. Soc. Trop. Med. & Hyg.*, vol. 48, 1954, p. 360.

It was not, however, until David Livingstone had captured the imagination of Europe and America that medical work was widely established as a branch of missionary activity. Livingstone, impelled to devote his life to the 'alleviation of human suffering', insisted on obtaining a medical education before offering himself for work in the missionary field. He sailed for Cape Town in 1840. In his diaries he noted the diseases prevalent among the tribes he visited; he listed 27 medicines employed by the Native doctors and he sent home to London a report on the treatment of malaria, giving the details of many cases, the remedies administered, and their effects.[1]

A year after Livingstone sailed for Africa Dr. John Abercrombie founded the Edinburgh Medical Missionary Society, an institution for training medical students for missionary work after the completion of their medical studies.[2] In South Africa the Lovedale Missionary Institution in Cape Province was founded by the Scottish Presbyterian Mission in 1841, and the Victoria Hospital, which is part of the Institution, was established 'for the treatment of disease and the training of African nurses, hospital attendants, and dispensers'. In 1847 the British Society for the Propagation of the Gospel began medical work at Colesberg. It is noteworthy that in 1849 there were only 40 medical missionaries at work in the whole world.[3] At a later date the American Mission Board in Johannesburg became a pioneer in the establishment of African health centres on the Rand, and also established the Bridgman Memorial Hospital, the first Native maternity hospital in Johannesburg.

Modern medical missions in East Africa appear to have begun when a lay doctor was associated with the work of the Holy Ghost Fathers at Zanzibar in 1863. The Universities Mission to Central Africa began work in the Shire Highlands in Nyasaland at about the same time, but in 1865 moved to Zanzibar, where a hospital was opened in 1887. Many of the missionaries of the United Free Church and of the Established Church of Scotland were at this period fully qualified medical men. These missions considered that a Medical Officer should be appointed to the staff of every station in Africa, both for the benefit of the Europeans and in order to train Africans for medical work among their own people. Work was begun at Livingstonia in Nyasaland in 1875 and in the following year at Blantyre. The year 1875 saw also the beginning of medical work by the Church Missionary Society at Mombasa; in 1893 a hospital with 50 beds was built, and later a leper house was added.[4]

There was a period when West Africa had a very sinister reputation in the matter of health. A large number of the early explorers fell victims

[1] D. Livingstone, *Missionary Travels and Researches in South Africa*, 1857, pp. 647–50.
[2] *A Brief History of Missionary Enterprise*, 1910.
[3] H. O. Dwight, H. A. Tupper, and F. Bliss, *Encyclopaedia of Missions*, 1904.
[4] Church Missionary Society, *Annual Reports*.

to disease.[1] Of the first company of 88 freed slaves and three Europeans which set out for Liberia in 1818, all the Europeans and a large proportion of the Negroes died within a few months. At a later date all the members of a shipload of 105 contracted fever within a month and a large number died.[2] In 1832 three missionaries of the Basle Mission, one of whom was a doctor, reached the Gold Coast, following on an earlier mission of 1828 whose members had all perished. The first medical missionary of the Church Missionary Society arrived in Sierra Leone in 1892.

In the absence of any knowledge as to the cause or cure of tropical diseases the work of the earlier medical missionaries in Africa must often have seemed hopeless. The mortality was very heavy. From 1835 to 1907 the Wesleyan Methodist Missionary Society sent out 225 missionaries to the West Coast, of whom 62 died in the field.[3] Of the Baptist missionaries in the Belgian Congo during the decade 1878–88, half died. It was, indeed, only when it was realized that biological agents were the principal cause of tropical diseases that an improvement was effected in the health of Europeans in tropical Africa. A meeting of doctors convened by the Church Missionary Society in 1893 founded Livingstone College 'for the instruction of foreign missionaries in the elements of practical medicine'. It was decided that those who completed the course should not be entitled to call themselves 'medical missionaries' or assume the positions of qualified medical men. But the course included lectures in elementary physiology and surgery, besides tropical diseases, and also attendance at hospital clinics. The work of missionaries as such, apart from that of medical men attached to the missions, has in many cases been acknowledged by the Administration and some have received State grants towards the cost of drugs and dressings.

In about 1899 the Universities Mission to Central Africa began to organize medical services among Africans in Nyasaland, and the Nyasaland Diocese established in due course a hospital and surgery on almost every one of its stations.[4] A similar principle prompted the dispatch by the Wesleyan Methodist Missionary Society in 1901 of a commission to West Africa to frame regulations for guarding European health and life along the coast. The Society's attention was directed to medical work among the inhabitants of West Africa in 1904, and in 1912 a hospital was built at Ilesha in Nigeria.[5]

[1] S. Gwynn, *Life of Mary Kingsley*, 1933. D. Wellesley and S. Gwynn, *Sir George Goldie*, 1934. Mungo Park, *Travels*, 1799.

[2] R. Gurley, *Life of Jehudi Ashmun*, 1835, p. 382. See also M. D. Mackenzie, *Report on Mission to the Kru Coast*, League of Nations, C. 662, M. 319, 1932.

[3] Methodist Missionary Society, *West African Roll-Call*, 1907.

[4] C. H. Wilson, *The History of the Universities Mission to Central Africa*, 1936.

[5] W. D. Holdsworth and G. G. Findlay, *History of the Wesleyan Methodist Missionary Society*, vol. iv, 1921.

Much medical work has been done by Roman Catholic Missions also. The White Fathers, to whom was entrusted in 1878 the task of evangelizing the area round the Great Lakes, and whose work now extends into the Belgian Congo, Northern Rhodesia, and Tanganyika, receive medical training during their novitiate, and the care of the sick is everywhere a feature of their missionary work.[1] In Uganda the White Sisters also have undertaken health work since 1899. The Franciscans maintain hospitals and dispensaries in Uganda and the Belgian Congo. The Fathers of the Holy Ghost in West Africa, the Jesuits in the Rhodesias, and the Benedictines in Central and East Africa and in the Belgian Congo, to mention only some of the more important Orders, all provide some medical facilities at their stations, maintaining between them over 200 hospitals.[2] The number of fully trained doctors employed by Roman Catholic Missions is, however, small; but much assistance is given to sick persons by a number of members of religious bodies who have taken special courses in medical work in their home countries. In 1936 a Papal Encyclical encouraged the training of nuns in midwifery and child welfare with the aim of combating the high infant mortality in Africa.[3]

As was the case in India also, the Administrations in Africa at first confined the provision of medical services to the needs of their own establishments. Only in a few of the larger centres were these extended sufficiently to make some provision for the African population. Perhaps the greatest single factor in producing a new attitude in the matter of health services for Africans was the impression created in Great Britain by the sleeping-sickness epidemic in Uganda in 1901 and 1902.[4] Various medical missionaries, including the White Fathers and the Church Missionary Society under Dr. (later Sir) Albert Cook, were at work in the affected area, and in March 1902 they reported that there had been a great number of deaths in the neighbourhood of Kyagwe. The Royal Society of Great Britain interested itself in the matter and sent out two Commissions; it was estimated by them that of the 300,000 people living in the infected areas some 200,000 had perished. In 1906 the Uganda Government decided on the evacuation of these areas. The public interest thus created in the health of Uganda was further aroused when the Report of a special inquiry stated in 1908 that in certain areas the incidence of syphilis was as high as 90 per cent. Three officers of the Royal Army Medical Corps were sent to deal with this disease, and the Uganda Government Medical Service was subsequently built up on the nucleus thus formed.[5]

[1] R. L. Buell, *The Native Problem in Africa*, vol. i, 1928, pp. 277, 502, 610.
[2] *Guida delle Missioni Cattoliche*, 1934, pp. 66 ff.
[3] *An Instruction of the Congregation of the Propagation of the Faith to Religious Institutes of Women regarding Assistance of Mothers and Infants in Missionary Lands*, February 1936.
[4] See below, pp. 1124 ff.   [5] H. B. Thomas and R. Scott, *Uganda*, 1935, pp. 299–302.

The part played by sleeping-sickness in bringing the medical needs of Africa to the attention of Europe is further illustrated by the action of the Congo Free State in sending a mission to deal with this disease in 1906. In 1917 news received of the prevalence of sleeping-sickness in French Equatorial Africa moved the Parliament at Paris to sanction a yearly grant of 1 million francs for medical assistance.

In the British West African dependencies medical services were generally neglected in the early days of settlement, and Mary Kingsley complained that 'no trouble is taken to pull the death-rate down by science'.[1] There were, however, a certain number of Medical Officers, and a Committee (appointed after a deputation of merchants had waited on the Colonial Secretary in 1901) recommended the amalgamation of the medical services on the west coast. This was carried out in 1902 when the West African Medical Service came into being.[2] The foundation of Medical Departments in the other British Colonies took place at about the same time; the various East African medical services were amalgamated in 1903, separated in 1908, and again amalgamated in 1920.

As the medical services improved the confidence of the African in European medicine was gradually gained, and hospitals which had originally been built for the use of Government establishments were enlarged to make provision for the African population. The requirements of the Rand for African labour led to growing attention being devoted in Johannesburg to the scientific treatment of health conditions in the mining areas.[3] The Germans showed their sense of the importance of the study of health problems by laying the foundation of a research service in their East African Protectorate. In 1906–7 Dr. Koch spent 18 months in East Africa investigating sleeping-sickness, and his inquiries were largely responsible for the establishment of the Research Institute at Amani.

A beginning was made in French West Africa with the scheme for the medical education of Africans which now centres in the *École de Médecine* at Dakar, though the school itself was not formally opened until 1918.[4] It has now been incorporated in the *Institut des Hautes Études*. The First World War brought a great number of Africans into contact with European medical methods for the first time. Meanwhile, the rejection of large numbers of African recruits on medical grounds called the attention of the Governments to the vast amount of preventable disease.

After the First World War there was everywhere a very substantial expansion in State health services. There was, in particular, a marked development in the Belgian Congo, where the demand for industrial labour revealed a high proportion of physical disabilities in various areas,

[1] *West African Studies*, 1899.
[2] A. Balfour and H. H. Scott, *Health Problems of the Empire*, 1924, pp. 79–80.
[3] See below, p. 1073.   [4] See below, p. 1098.

and the inquiries of the Commissions appointed to investigate the subject resulted not only in a comprehensive planning of the health organization in the gold- and copper-mines but in the foundation of the great organizations for medical relief, the *Fonds Reine Élisabeth pour l'Assistance Médicale aux Indigènes* (Foréami) and the *Fondation Médicale de l'Université de Louvain au Congo* (Fomulac), to which further reference will subsequently be made.[1]

With the extension of the State health services there followed in most African territories a large expansion of the hospital accommodation available for Africans and, in association therewith, the creation of outpatient clinics with satellite dispensaries in the surrounding country. In some British territories this development has been assisted by the activities of the Native Authority Treasuries which have in many cases financed medical and health services in their areas. The hospital system was augmented, especially in the French and Belgian territories, by the creation of mobile units for dealing with outbreaks of epidemic disease or for the application of preventive measures.

THE DISEASES OF AFRICA

The diseases which afflict Africans include most of those which are conventionally regarded as tropical, save that there is an absence of sprue, cholera (though an epidemic of this broke out in Egypt in 1947), *Schistosoma japonicum* infection, and American trypanosomiasis. Less obvious is the absence of arteriosclerosis, with its attendant ills, which has now become a major problem in most countries of Europe.[2] To the tropical diseases must be added many which are prevalent in more temperate countries. All the infectious diseases occur, including the major endemic diseases like tuberculosis, pneumonia, the venereal diseases, the enteric fevers, and trachoma. Some of them, for instance cerebrospinal meningitis, sweep through the country in epidemic form. Smallpox would probably do the same if it were not for the fact that vaccination has now for many years been widely practised.

The replies to questionnaires which have been submitted during recent years to the medical authorities of a number of countries[3] indicate that malaria, helminthic diseases (including hookworm and *Ascaris* infection, schistosomiasis, filariasis, and guinea-worm infection), leprosy, tuberculosis, venereal diseases, trypanosomiasis, and disorders of malnutrition are held to be of major importance. Yaws and tropical ulcer are widespread, and diseases of the respiratory tract and of the bowel are common.

[1] See below, p. 1091.
[2] H. Smith, 'Medicine in Africa as I Have Seen It', *African Affairs*, January 1955, p. 29.
[3] 'First International Symposium on Yaws Control', *Bulletin of the World Health Organization*, vol. viii, 1953, pp. 149 ff.

Of the infectious diseases smallpox is described as a potential cause of epidemics, but it is now more readily controlled than before; cerebro-spinal meningitis seems to be increasing in importance and in recent years serious epidemics have been reported in West Africa, the Sudan, and East Africa. Loss of sight, partial or complete, is very common, and is due to a number of causes. Most of the diseases from which the Africans suffer are either insect-borne or are due to faulty environmental sanitation (including housing and personal cleanliness) or malnutrition.

At the present time the physical disorders and infections dominate the picture, and the extent and character of the mental disturbances from which some of the people undoubtedly suffer have as yet been studied only superficially. Infant mortality is high, although some early estimates were greatly exaggerated,[1] and child mortality remains high after the period of infancy. It has, for example, been estimated, on the basis of the East Africa census of 1948, that over two-fifths of all those born will die before reaching the age of about 14 years. It is noteworthy that in India about one-quarter of the children are said to die before reaching adult life.[2]

Since the expectation of life is much shorter than in Western countries the general pattern of disease is that associated with the earlier stages of life. For this reason alone it would be unlikely that the diseases associated with older people would be a serious problem in Africa. The cancers, the diseases of the heart and arteries, and the degenerative diseases do occur, but they are less common than in populations with different age-group patterns. Some further details regarding the more important of the disorders prevalent in Africa are given in a later part of this chapter.

THE PROBLEMS OF NUTRITION

Gross deficiency of food, or actual famine, has been a common occurrence in Africa, usually as a result of the failure of seasonal rains and therefore of a cereal crop, but sometimes also as the result of invasion by locusts. Famine is less disastrous than it was formerly because information about conditions in remote areas is now more readily obtained and because transport facilities make it easier to organize relief measures. At the same time, however, the situation is being changed by the rapid increase in the populations of certain of the African countries or of certain regions in them. In such areas the general problem of nutrition may have to give place to the immediate need for increasing productivity in order to keep pace with the expanding population.

Even where the total amount of food is sufficient the diet may be

[1] R. R. Kuczynski, *Demographic Survey of the British Colonial Empire*, vol. i, 1948, p. 527.
[2] C. J. Martin, in *Population Studies*, vol. vi, 1953, p. 233; vol. vii, 1953, p. 181.

unbalanced, in the sense that certain essential constituents may be inadequate, notably protein and the vitamins. Protein deficiency is most commonly found in young children, particularly after weaning, when a starchy diet is substituted for breast milk. The condition created by a diet in which carbo-hydrates form too great a proportion and vitamins are short is generally known by the Gold Coast name of *kwashiorkor*, and has been found throughout Africa; it is often fatal.[1] Protein deficiency is accentuated by the various parasitic diseases, in which the parasite not only consumes the host's supplies of protein but in some cases also stimulates the formation of protective antibodies which are themselves protein. A deficiency in iodine which leads to goitre has been observed in parts of West and South Africa; some Governments now issue iodized salt to make good this deficiency.

The attention of Governments throughout the world was first drawn to the problems of malnutrition by the Assembly of the League of Nations in 1935, and the member Governments were invited to institute inquiries into the subject. The reports submitted from the British dependencies were examined by a Committee of the Economic Advisory Council set up in 1937, and on its recommendation the British Medical Research Council appointed in 1939 a Human Nutrition Research Unit to undertake the scientific co-ordination of nutrition surveys.[2] During the early part of the Second World War its work in the colonial field was virtually suspended, but interest in nutrition studies was again aroused by the recommendations of the Hot Springs Conference of 1943. From 1949 onwards a certain amount of work has been done by the Unit in co-operation with the Nutrition Department of the London School of Hygiene and Tropical Medicine. In 1952 an Applied Nutrition Unit of this department was given formal recognition as a technical extension of the Colonial Office, and received a grant made under the Colonial Development and Welfare Act. Dr. B. S. Platt, the Director of the Unit, had in 1939 organized an extensive study of nutrition in Nyasaland, and similar inquiries were made in Gambia in 1945, 1947, and 1949. Members of its staff assisted in the work of the African Labour Efficiency Survey in Nairobi in 1947[3] and in the nutrition survey carried out at Kawambwa in Northern Rhodesia in 1949. Two field-research stations established by the Medical Research Council at Fajara in Gambia and Kampala in Uganda have worked in co-operation with the Unit.

[1] For the use of this and similar vernacular terms for disease, see F. R. Irvine, 'Health and Agriculture in Africa', *African Affairs*, April 1954, pp. 133–42.
[2] *Economic Advisory Council, Committee on Nutrition, First Report, Part I, Nutrition in the Colonial Empire*, Cmd. 6050, 1939, p. 167. See also A. I. Richards, *Land, Labour and Diet in Northern Rhodesia*, 1939, pp. 2 ff.
[3] C. H. Northcott, *African Labour Efficiency Survey*, 1947, Colonial Research Publications, no. 3, 1949, pp. 83–114.

In the British dependencies Committees have been set up representing the various departments whose activities can contribute to the improvement of nutrition, and these are now functioning in the Gold Coast, Gambia, Kenya, Uganda, and Tanganyika. Nutrition surveys have been made by the Nutrition Office in Northern Rhodesia and by local specialists in Northern Nigeria and the Tema area of the Gold Coast.[1]

In French West Africa an organization for the combined study of physical anthropology and nutrition was created in 1945 under the auspices of the Public Health Department. It has made a large number of studies in Dakar, Senegal, the Western Sudan, Western Guinea, and the Upper Volta. A special study of the diet of populations in the Chad territory in French Equatorial Africa was made in 1941,[2] and in the French Cameroons a Hygiene and Nutrition Committee was formed in 1947. In the Belgian Congo a centre for nutrition studies was opened in 1951 at Lwiro under the auspices of the *Institut pour la Recherche Scientifique en Afrique Centrale* (I.R.S.A.C.). The centre maintains liaison with the bio-chemical laboratory of the University of Brussels, and has made a study of the nutrition of Africans in the environs of Lwiro. In addition to this, a physical anthropologist has examined six ethnic groups in the neighbourhood of Astrida under the joint auspices of the centre and of the I.R.S.A.C. Commission for the Social Sciences. It was announced in 1949 that the Portuguese Government proposed to establish a centre for nutrition studies in Lisbon which would have local centres in Angola, Mozambique, and Guinea.

International conferences on the subject of nutrition were organized by the Commission for Technical Co-operation in Africa at Dschang in 1949[3] and Fajara in 1952, the latter being specifically concerned with malnutrition of mothers and infants. The recommendations of the conference of 1952 emphasized the importance of the maximum utilization of existing sources of proteins, both vegetable and animal.[4]

THE ORGANIZATION OF HEALTH SERVICES

The Union of South Africa and South-West Africa

In the Union a separate Department, the Ministry of Public Health, was established in 1919;[5] a Minister of Health, with responsibility for that portfolio alone, was appointed for the first time in 1945. The provision of hospital facilities is mainly the responsibility of the Provincial Administrations, and the increased subsidies to these Administrations made

---

[1] For the results of surveys made by the Nutrition Office in Northern Rhodesia, see B. P. Thomson, 'Two Studies in African Nutrition', *R. L. I. Papers*, no. 24, 1954.

[2] P. V. Créach, *Aliments et alimentation des indigènes du Moyen Tchad*, 1941.

[3] *Conférence interafricaine sur l'alimentation et la nutrition, Dschang 3–9 octobre, 1949.*

[4] *Chronicle of the World Health Organization*, vol. vii, no. 3, 1953, p. 69.

[5] *O.Y.S.A., 1950*, pp. 147–95, gives a full account of the development of medical facilities.

available by the Financial Relations Act of 1945 have resulted in a considerable increase in their activities. For certain purposes, such as the control of sanitation or outbreaks of infectious diseases, most of the Local Authorities have Health Officers and Health Departments, but the scope of these organizations varies widely. In the majority of districts Medical Officers, mostly part-time, known as District Surgeons, are employed by the State for the treatment of indigent persons; in 1952 these posts numbered 436, of which 380 were part-time. The Rand gold-mines employ a large number of doctors and have their own hospitals and dispensaries. In addition there are 73 Mission hospitals.

There is in the Union a total of 570 hospitals (including private nursing homes, maternity homes, and mine and factory hospitals): of these 238 are for Europeans only and 138 for non-Europeans only; there are 17,674 beds available for Europeans and 27,756 for non-Europeans. A National Health Services Commission, which was appointed in 1942, recommended the creation of 400 health centres to be financed by a special tax on incomes.[1] They are to be modelled on the well-known Polela Centre, which was established in 1940. A training establishment for personnel was opened at Clairwood, near Durban, the intention being to develop this into an Institute of Hygiene. In the year 1954 £12·5 million was spent on medical services for Natives, the largest annual sum allocated for this purpose by any territory in Africa.[2]

The principal research centre in the Union is the South African Institute for Medical Research, Johannesburg, where a great variety of investigations have been carried out, particularly (though by no means exclusively) in relation to silicosis, tuberculosis, pneumonia, and the lung diseases to which mine labourers are prone. There are medical schools at the Universities of Cape Town, Witwatersrand, and Pretoria; these give full qualifications in medicine. There are 121 recognized hospital schools of nursing, and 27 hospitals offer training in midwifery. The extent to which these facilities are open to Europeans and non-Europeans respectively is discussed in the following chapter.[3]

The importance attaching to the incidence of silicosis[4] in the mining areas is marked by the creation of a special organization. The Silicosis Medical Bureau is responsible for carrying out research on the disease, as well as for conducting the medical examination of miners.[5] In addition a Silicosis Research Committee is charged with the duty of studying measures to minimize the amount of dust in mines. The Report of the Bureau for 1951 referred to 'the immense technical advances' achieved in

[1] Ibid., pp. 150–5.
[2] S.A.S., no. 89, 15 September 1954.
[3] See below, p. 1139.
[4] See below, p. 1124. See also O.Y.S.A., 1949, pp. 319–24.
[5] Silicosis Act no. 47 of 1946.

this field as one reason for the marked decrease in the disease in the previous 30 years. The principle is accepted that benefits are payable to miners suffering from 'any form of pneumoconiosis due to the inhalation of mineral dust', and in some cases also to the dependants of deceased miners. South African legislation has been taken as a model in other territories where mining is important.

In South-West Africa the headquarters of the Medical Officer to the Administration is at Windhoek; there are also three whole-time Regional Medical Officers: one for the Police Zone, one for Ovamboland, and one for the Okovango Native Territory. In the Police Zone there are 17 part-time District Surgeons, besides a full-time Medical Superintendent at the Windhoek Native Hospital. Registered medical practitioners number 42, most of whom are in private practice, while the rest are attached to the mines.

Hospital Boards have been appointed at eleven centres, and in 1950 nine of these were managing hospitals for Europeans. Two of these hospitals admit Africans also, and there are six other Government hospitals for Africans with a total of 370 beds. Considerable expenditure has lately been undertaken in bringing these hospitals up to date; the Development Programme of the territory contemplates the addition of four new Native hospitals. A large hospital mainly for tuberculosis patients has been erected at Windhoek. Roman Catholic Missions manage seven hospitals, at three of which only Europeans are admitted; the Finnish Missions have three hospitals, and an Anglican Mission one. The German Red Cross Society maintains two institutions. All these institutions receive State aid up to three-fifths of their approved expenditure. There are three leper camps, and seven venereal diseases compounds at various places; in addition, there is a Red Cross maternity clinic at Windhoek. It is note-worthy that there has in the last few years been a very marked increase in the provision made for medical facilities in the Native Reserves.

The High Commission Territories

In Basutoland the first medical work was undertaken in 1844 by members of the Paris Evangelical Mission.[1] The systematic organization of medical facilities by the Administration dates from 1894 when a Principal Medical Officer was appointed. The extension of health centres in rural areas has been assisted by grants made under the Colonial Development and Welfare Act, which has also provided funds to enable Africans to acquire training as medical practitioners by study either in the Union of South Africa or in Europe. There were in 1953 nine Government hospitals, with 13 beds for Europeans and 377 for Africans; one of these hospitals was staffed entirely by Africans. Missions managed

---

[1] *N.A.*, Part V, p. 2.

four hospitals with financial assistance from the Government. Four Mountain Dispensaries were to be built with grants made under the Colonial Development and Welfare Act. The first of these was opened in 1952.

The fully qualified staff of the Medical Department consists of 14 Europeans and three Africans; there are 13 European and 90 African nurses, and eight African leprosy and welfare inspectors. Nearly a quarter of the total State expenditure on medical work goes towards the upkeep of a leper settlement, an old-standing institution to which both the Administration and the Basuto have in the past attached much importance. It treats between 500 and 600 leper patients a year, but since reactions to sulphone therapy are few and mild and recurrences are infrequent,[1] it is doubtful if the same need now exists for its maintenance. In 1955 there was one doctor available to 21,600 persons and one hospital bed to every 1,250 Africans. The increasing number of tuberculosis patients has caused some anxiety, and the new health programme accordingly includes an addition of tuberculosis wards to five existing hospitals and the building of a new hospital at Maseru. A mental hospital to serve all three High Commission Territories is also projected.[2]

In the Bechuanaland Protectorate the staff of the Medical Department included in 1952 a Director of Medical Services and ten other Medical Officers, one of whom was an African. There were three health inspectors, 15 nursing sisters, and 41 locally trained nurses. Mission medical personnel included five fully qualified doctors. There are eight hospitals with 459 beds, and 19 dispensaries (including three maternity and child-welfare clinics and two tuberculosis centres). A total of 35 beds for Europeans and 212 for Africans was provided by Government institutions; the rest were provided by Mission hospitals.[3] The World Health Organization has enabled a survey of tuberculosis throughout the territory to be made, and in 1953 contributed towards a campaign to control treponematosis.[4]

In Swaziland there was little organization of medical work before 1926, when the Nazarene Mission opened a hospital at Bremersdorp and the Wesleyan Mission another at Mahamba. The first State hospital was opened at Mbabane in 1931. The personnel of the Government Medical Department in 1952 comprised a Director of Medical Services and six Medical Officers. The Missions employed five Medical Officers. There were Government hospitals at Mbabane, Hlatikulu, and Mankaiana, with 188 beds, and Mission hospitals at Bremersdorp, Mahamba, and

[1] Basutoland, Annual Report of the Medical Department, 1953, p. 19.
[2] High Commission Territories, Economic Development and Social Services, Cmd. 9580, 1955, p. 10.
[3] Colonial Reports, Bechuanaland Protectorate, 1952, pp. 7, 26–29.
[4] Cmd. 9580, 1955, p. 11.

Stegi, with 140; in addition there were four Government and ten Mission dispensaries acting as health centres. The Nazarene Hospital at Bremersdorp continues to be one of the most important medical institutions in the territory. It has been claimed that malaria has been almost entirely eradicated.[1]

Southern Rhodesia

Public health in the Federation of Rhodesia and Nyasaland was at first a subject upon which both the Federal and Territorial Legislatures were empowered to make laws, but in July 1954 it was transferred entirely to the Federal Government.[2]

The Medical Department of Southern Rhodesia was first constituted in 1897. A Minister for Health was appointed in 1948, when the Department was divided into curative and preventive branches, each under a Director. It had in 1953 a total staff of 112 fully qualified European Medical Officers, of whom 14 were specialists; there were also a large number of private practitioners, who were stated to number over 500. A proportion of these were employed by mining companies and by the Railways. Salisbury and Bulawayo employ full-time Medical Officers of Health, and the other municipalities have part-time officers.

There are 21 Government and 53 Mission hospitals; the latter treat Africans only, and are subsidized. Government hospitals have 904 beds for European, 104 for Coloured or Asiatic, and 2,322 for African patients. Two new hospitals for Africans are being erected at Salisbury and Bulawayo, each containing 650 beds. All African hospitals are said to be overcrowded, with the exception of that at Bulawayo. The main African hospitals are staffed by qualified African women nurses under a minimum of European supervision. The Mission hospitals have 1,267 beds, and a number of hospitals are maintained by mining and industrial companies. In the more remote areas the Department maintains clinics which now constitute a prominent feature in the organization of medical work in the Colony. They are staffed by trained African nursing orderlies and are supervised by visiting doctors; some of the largest of the clinics have a resident doctor. The total number increased from seven in 1930 to 85 in 1953.[3]

An interesting experiment has been carried out in the Mazoe Valley, where teams of Africans were trained to spray dwellings with residual insecticide for the control of malaria in the months from October to April (when mosquitoes are active), and to spray natural waters with

[1] Cmd. 9580, 1955, p. 12.
[2] *Southern Rhodesia, Report on the Public Health, 1953*, C.S.R. 22, 1954, p. 1. *Nyasaland, Annual Report of the Medical Department, 1953*, p. 5.
[3] *O.Y.S.R., 1952*, pp. 261–2. *Southern Rhodesia, Report on the Public Health, 1953*, C.S.R. 22, 1954.

copper-sulphate from May to September. This latter measure aims at the destruction of snails, in order to control schistosomiasis.[1]

The British Colonial Medical Service

The Secretary of State for the Colonies is advised on medical affairs by the Chief Medical Officer and his staff, who have usually been members of the Colonial Medical Service and who make frequent visits to the African territories. He has also the assistance of a Colonial Advisory Medical Committee. The expenditure of the funds made available for medical research from the Colonial Development and Welfare Vote is controlled by the Colonial Medical Research Committee, which was constituted in its present form in 1946.[2] The Secretary of State is further advised by the Tsetse Fly and Trypanosomiasis Committee and the Colonial Insecticides Committee; these bodies are closely connected with the Colonial Research Committee which was originally instituted to deal with the funds made available for research under the Colonial Welfare and Development Act of 1940.[3]

There exist in Great Britain three institutions of special importance for the study and treatment of tropical diseases. There is, first, the Bureau of Hygiene and Tropical Diseases which was formed in 1912 as the successor to the Sleeping-sickness Bureau created in 1908. It publishes two monthly journals, the *Tropical Diseases Bulletin* and the *Bulletin of Hygiene*, which contain abstracts of papers appearing in medical journals throughout the world. There are, secondly, the two great schools of tropical medicine which were founded within a few months of each other in 1899, namely, the London School of Tropical Medicine and the Liverpool School of Tropical Medicine. Each is a centre for post-graduate teaching and research, and each is closely associated with a large teaching hospital.

In the African dependencies the medical personnel usually comprises a Director of Medical Services, and in some instances one or two superior Medical Officers at headquarters, with a body of Provincial and District Medical Officers, who are normally members of the Colonial Medical Service. There are also numerous specialist and laboratory posts. The Colonial Medical Service includes a number of women doctors. Medical Officers of Health and sanitary inspectors are appointed for small towns in some rural areas, though it is more usual for a District Medical Officer to be responsible for the whole of an administrative district. The larger municipalities appoint their own Medical Officers of Health who are usually not members of the Colonial Medical Service.

[1] See below, p. 1120.
[2] *Colonial Research, 1945–1946*, Col. no. 208, 1947, p. 4.
[3] *Colonial Research Committee, Progress Report, 1942–1943*, Cmd. 6486, 1943, p. 5. *Colonial Research, 1952–1953*, Cmd. 8971, 1953, pp. 205–28, 235–50. Ibid. *1953–1954*, Cmd. 9303, 1954, pp. 85–141.

The British Central African Dependencies

Reference has already been made to the health organization in Southern Rhodesia.

In Northern Rhodesia, with its relatively sparse population, the extension of medical services has been difficult, and as late as 1938 it could be stated that over half the territory had no medical facilities.[1] Since that time, however, the marked improvement in the revenues of the Protectorate has made it possible to provide for a large expansion in all health services. In 1938 a grant under the Colonial Development and Welfare Vote was made for the construction of a hospital and training school at Lusaka, and for two other hospitals and 22 dispensaries. The comprehensive Development Plan adopted in 1947 provided for an expenditure on health services during the ten years up to 1956 of a total of £1½ million, of which £500,000 was to come from the Colonial Development and Welfare Vote. The extensions planned aimed at providing services nearly twice as large as they were in 1947 and five times as large as they had been in 1935, and they included the rebuilding of several existing hospitals.[2] Though the rise in cost has made it impossible for the full programme to be carried out, a large hospital for Africans and non-Africans was opened at Broken Hill in 1952; it is said to be one of the most modern in design and equipment in southern Africa. The revision of the Northern Rhodesia Ten-year Plan included the building of two cottage hospitals for Europeans, at Choma and Mazabuka, and four hospitals and 55 rural health centres for Africans.[3]

In 1952 the services provided by the Government included eight hospitals for Europeans with 316 beds, and 14 for Africans with 1,770 beds; four urban clinics for Europeans, 80 rural and 16 urban health centres for Africans, and a leper settlement. Missions, which receive aid for this purpose from the Government, manage 24 hospitals with 990 beds, 79 rural dispensaries, and 16 leper settlements. The copper-mining companies have four hospitals for Africans and Europeans, which admit patients other than their employees, but a new combined Government hospital which has been built at Kitwe will relieve them of this responsibility. A Silicosis Medical Bureau was created in 1950 and in 1952 examined 3,401 Europeans and 23,451 Africans. The European staff of the Medical Department of Northern Rhodesia included in 1952 a total of 49 qualified Medical Officers and 61 nursing sisters.

In Nyasaland, with its smaller area and denser population, the provision of medical services has presented fewer difficulties. From their first entry into the country the Scottish Missions were conspicuous in medical work

---

[1] *Report on the Financial and Economic Position of Northern Rhodesia*, Col. no. 145, 1938, p. 290.
[2] *Ten-year Development Plan for Northern Rhodesia, February 1947*, Lusaka, 1948, pp. 9–10.
[3] *Revision of the Northern Rhodesia Ten-year Development Plan, November 1953*, Lusaka, 1953, p. 3.

and began the training of an African staff; at the outset Asian sub-assistant surgeons were also recruited to supplement the work of Medical Officers. In 1931 a grant of over £40,000, from the Colonial Development and Welfare Vote, was spent on the extension of hospital buildings. There are now 19 Government hospitals for Africans with 1,220 beds; each has a number of satellite rural dispensaries (of which there are 93 in all), and each of the three Government hospitals for Europeans has also a special ward for Africans. Towards the end of 1954 the foundation stone was laid at Blantyre of the Queen Elizabeth Hospital, designed to be the largest central hospital in Nyasaland. It will contain 800 beds and serve people of all races. A new mental hospital has been completed at Zomba. Asian sub-assistant surgeons are in charge of five of the hospitals for Africans, and five of the smaller hospitals are administered by African hospital assistants. Five missions maintain a total of 577 general and 146 maternity beds, with a European staff of nine doctors. The Government opened a midwives' hostel at Zomba in 1953. The first Rural Health Unit was opened in 1951 in Dedza District; this is intended to be both a curative centre for ailments not requiring hospital treatment and also a centre for the application of preventive medicine. Three more such Units are planned. The European medical staff number 56, and there are nine Asian sub-assistant surgeons.[1]

In the Zanzibar Protectorate the staff of the Medical Department comprises eight doctors of the Colonial Medical Service and a number of Asian sub-assistant surgeons and Makerere-trained African doctors. The four hospitals have a total of 303 beds. A new up-to-date hospital has recently been built in Zanzibar, and an isolation hospital was completed in 1952. There is a mental hospital and an institution for the infirm which also admits tuberculosis and leprosy patients. A second leper settlement exists on Pemba, and a school in Zanzibar has recently been converted to a tuberculosis sanatorium. There are some 27 dispensaries at various places on the islands. They are connected with the main hospitals by ambulance.

The East Africa High Commission Territories

In the British East African dependencies the organization of medical research is now one of the wide range of research activities which have been committed to the charge of the East Africa High Commission.[2]

The East African Bureau of Research in Medicine and Hygiene, with headquarters at Nairobi, serves as one of the organs of the Colonial Medical Research Committee above referred to, advising on medical research and its application and providing an information service for

[1] *Colonial Reports, Nyasaland, 1952*, p. 86.
[2] See *Annual Report on the East Africa High Commission, 1952*, Col. no. 297, 1953, pp. 3–6; ibid. *1953*, Col. no. 305, 1954, pp. 52–56.

medical and health workers. The East African Medical Survey was instituted in 1948. Its object is to collect information on all matters affecting the health of selected sections of the African population; in its Report for 1951 three surveys are referred to, namely, in the Mwanza and Bukoba areas of Tanganyika, and in the island of Ukara in Lake Victoria. A survey of schistosomiasis is projected for the Kwimba area of Tanganyika. In the Bukoba area of Tanganyika a special study was made of a reported infant mortality rate of 250 per 1,000.[1] An inter-territorial leprologist was appointed in 1947 and has made extensive surveys.

The East African Malaria Unit, with headquarters at Amani, Tanganyika, came into full operation in 1951. One of its main objectives is to carry out fundamental studies on *Anopheles*[2] in order to provide specialist advice to various Governments on problems of vector control. The Filariasis Research Unit at Mwanza, Tanganyika, has done extensive work on Bancroftian filariasis and on onchocerciasis. The East African Tsetse and Trypanosomiasis Research and Reclamation Organization (E.A.T.T.R.R.O.) has its headquarters at Sukulu (Tororo) in Uganda. Here a laboratory has been established which is concerned mainly with research into the pathogenic trypanosomes. It is staffed by three medical and three veterinary research officers, a biochemist, a protozoologist, and two entomologists. At the other station maintained by E.A.T.T.R.R.O., at Shinyanga in Tanganyika, the staff is composed of entomologists, botanists, and ecologists, and the main subject of research is the tsetse fly itself. The actual putting into operation of the technique advised by E.A.T.T.R.R.O. is delegated to the Tsetse Control Department of the respective territories.[3]

The Virus Research Institute at Entebbe in Uganda has taken over the premises formerly occupied by the Yellow Fever Research Institute. It has been chiefly concerned up to the present with the distribution of yellow fever and its incidence in the forest monkeys of Western Uganda and of other areas. At the suggestion of the World Health Organization a number of samples of human blood from the Belgian Congo, Angola, Tanganyika, Northern Rhodesia, and Nyasaland have been examined with the aim of delineating the southern limit of the disease in Africa.[4]

The East African Standing Committee for Medical Research was formed in 1952. It includes the Directors of Medical Services of the three territories and Zanzibar, and members appointed by the Colonial Medical Research Committee, Makerere College, and the High Commission. Its chief task is to advise on the needs for medical research.

While the general organization of medical research is now mainly the

[1] *East African Medical Survey, Annual Report, 1951*, East Africa High Commission, p. 68.
[2] *East African Malaria Unit, Annual Report, 1951*, East Africa High Commission, p. 2.
[3] *Background to Uganda*, no. 125, October 1955.
[4] *Virus Research Institute, Entebbe, Annual Report*, no. 2, *1951*, pp. 1, 5.

function of the East Africa High Commission the provision and control of the health and medical services remains the function of the territorial Governments.

In Kenya Colony the Medical Department was first organized in 1905. The establishment for 1953 provided for 90 fully qualified European Medical Officers, 140 Asian assistant medical and dental officers, 14 African assistant medical officers, and 144 African nursing sisters and male nurses. Much importance has been attached to the training of an African staff. The training of African girls, who are required to be literate in English, began in 1950.[1] Africans are also trained as hospital assistants, qualified to take charge of small hospitals, and as health inspectors. Schools were opened in 1949 for female health visitors, in 1950 for health assistants, and in 1951 for midwives. Health centres have been established in the Meru, Embu, and Fort Hall districts with the aid of a grant made under the Colonial Development and Welfare Act.

There are altogether 101 hospitals for Africans with 7,270 beds, of which 68 are managed by the Government and 33 by Missions; ten for Asians with 249 beds, of which three are managed by the Government; and 12 for Europeans with 412 beds, of which two are managed by the Government. A leprosy institution has been built at Itesio. African District Councils finance 211 dispensaries and have recently been encouraged to finance health centres where improved methods of treatment are combined with the teaching of hygiene. There are now four such health centres and 12 locational health centres.

The first medical work in Uganda was undertaken by the Church Missionary Society, which opened a hospital at Mengo in 1897. A Government hospital at Kampala is mentioned for the first time in the *Annual Medical Report* for the year 1908. Mulago hospital, which is now the teaching hospital for the Medical School of the East African University College,[2] was opened for the treatment of venereal diseases in 1913, and became a general hospital in 1922. Uganda began to employ trained African medical personnel at a much earlier date than any of its neighbours. Their training was begun at Mengo in 1917; it was taken over in 1923 by a medical tutor attached to the Makerere Training Centre and was brought under the Medical Department in 1928. A six-year course was prescribed for the training of senior African medical assistants, who were in 1931 licensed as medical practitioners; a subsequent Ordinance of 1950 enabled them to be licensed for private practice after a satisfactory period in the Government service. The Medical School is now the Faculty of Medicine of the East African University College at Makerere.[3]

[1] *Colonial Reports, Kenya, 1952*, p. 59.   [2] See below, p. 1100.
[3] See *Uganda Protectorate, Final Report of the Standing Committee on the Recruitment, Training and Promotion of Africans for Admission to the Higher Posts in the Civil Service*, Entebbe, 1955.

The qualification of licentiate in medicine and surgery was attained by 22 graduates of Makerere in 1955, and twelve others with long service in the Government Departments have been approved for local registration. Two of these now hold posts previously occupied by European Medical Officers.[1]

The establishment of the Medical Department provided in 1952 for 75 locally recruited Medical Officers and 52 recruited in Europe; eight specialists who are attached to Mulago and not, as is more usual in Africa, to a European hospital; and 88 expatriate nursing sisters. In 1953 the Government and Local Authorities maintained four hospitals for Europeans, ten for Asians, 24 for Africans (including the mental hospital and the prison hospital), and 113 dispensaries with beds, making a total of 4,741 beds. The Missions maintained nine hospitals and 41 other units, with a total of 1,251 beds.[2] The total number of Government dispensaries and medical-aid posts was 234. There are in addition schools for the training of medical assistants, health inspectors, nursing orderlies, and nurses; the training of midwives remained in the hands of the Missions until 1954 when the Queen Elizabeth Nurses' Hostel was opened at Mulago and 350 women were trained as nurses and midwives. The research carried out on nutrition has already been mentioned.

In Tanganyika the Member for Social Services is responsible for the Medical Department of which the head is the Director of Medical Services. The staff in 1951 included 109 fully qualified Medical Officers (ten being whole-time specialists), 140 sub-assistant surgeons, and six African Medical Officers; there were 101 matrons, nursing sisters, and health visitors, and 94 certificated African nurses. Out of a total of 390 in 1953 there were 223 registered medical practitioners (outside the Government service), of whom 47 were employed by Missions, and 63 licensed medical practitioners with qualifications recognized in East Africa. The Missions employed 206 registered nurses, 57 of whom were African, and 46 medical assistants. The Government maintains a total of 52 hospitals in which there are 214 beds for Europeans, 196 beds for Asians (for whom European beds are also available), and 4,240 beds for Africans. In addition there are 21 Government dispensaries for Africans, with 406 beds.

From the outset the Native Authority Treasuries have incurred a considerable expenditure on the maintenance of small dispensaries for outpatients; the total amount expended on public health by them in 1953 was estimated at £227,138. Missions have 69 hospitals in which there are 57 beds for Europeans, 130 for Asians, and 3,915 for Africans;

---

[1] A. W. Williams, 'The History of Mulago Hospital and the Makerere College Medical School', *East African Med. J.*, vol. 29, 1952, pp. 253–63.

[2] *Uganda, Annual Report of the Medical Department, 1953*, p. 37.

in addition they have 36 dispensaries for Africans, with 518 beds. Various industrial undertakings provide 15 hospitals with 600 beds.[1] A special Sleeping-Sickness Control Unit is administered by a whole-time specialist with his headquarters at Tabora.

The British West African Dependencies

There is in West Africa no regional organization for medical research strictly comparable with that existing in East Africa. There are, however, two institutions which serve the purposes of all four British West African territories. The West African Institute for Trypanosomiasis Research originated as a result of the inquiries made in 1945 by the Colonial Tsetse Fly and Trypanosomiasis Committee.[2] The Institute, which was opened in 1951, comprises two branches, situated respectively at Vom (which is free from tsetse fly) and at Kaduna in Northern Nigeria. Work is organized in four sections. Entomology and epidemiology are studied at Kaduna, and proto-zoology and veterinary trypanosomiasis at Vom. Funds to finance the institute have been provided by a grant, made under the Colonial Development and Welfare Act, and by the four West African Governments. The West African Council for Medical Research was instituted in 1953 to exercise general supervision over the medical-research centres in the area (with the exception of the Fajara nutrition unit);[3] its chief objective is to develop additional research in malaria, yaws, and tuberculosis. The Virus Research Institute at Yaba near Lagos was adopted as the laboratory of the Council.

Of the four British West African territories the medical and health establishment of Nigeria is now by far the most important. As a result of the administrative decentralization of 1947 each of the three Regions has its own Director of Medical Services with executive authority on all aspects of public health within the Region. An Inspector-General of Medical Services retains responsibility throughout Nigeria for specialist and research services, training schools, and recruitment. Under the Constitution of 1951 the Regional Directors became advisers to the Regional Ministers of Health, and the Inspector-General became the adviser to the Central Minister for Social Services. In the Regions the unit of administration is the Medical Area, which usually coincides with one or more of the administrative divisions. It is based on a general hospital in charge of which is a Medical Officer, who is responsible for both medical and health services in the area. The areas are grouped into Medical Divisions, coinciding with one or more Provinces; it is intended

---

[1] *Tanganyika, Report for the Year 1953*, Col. no. 307, pp. 185–97.

[2] *West African Institute for Trypanosomiasis Research, Annual Report for the Year 1951*, p. 1.

[3] *Colonial Research, 1952–1953*, Cmd. 8971, 1953, p. 111. Ibid. *1953–1954*, Cmd. 9303, 1954, p. 95.

to reduce the size of these Divisions so that each will be co-extensive with a Province.

In 1952 the senior staff of the Nigerian Medical Department included 234 Medical Officers, eleven Dental Officers, 121 matrons and nursing sisters, and 125 other officers. There was a large staff of African pharmacists and laboratory assistants, and a total of 1,437 African nurses and midwives. There were a number of African doctors in private practice, and it was estimated that in 1952 there were altogether 500 qualified doctors in Nigeria, or roughly one to every 60,000 of the population.

The published information on institutions for treatment does not give the distribution by Regions. There were in 1952 a total of 76 Government, eight Native Authority, 33 Mission, and 35 private hospitals, with a total of 9,428 beds; 33 Government, 741 Native Authority, 37 Mission, and 13 private dispensaries; and 161 Native Authority, 61 Mission, and 22 private maternity centres. There is in these figures evidence of the important part played in the provision of medical services by the Native Authorities in Nigeria. The hospitals maintained by some of the major Native Administrations (as, for example, that of Kano in Northern Nigeria) are comparable with the largest and best-equipped State hospitals. In the Eastern Region the establishment of small maternity centres is a favourite type of community development project. In the Western Region the hospital at Ibadan, with 500 beds, is now adopted as the teaching hospital for the West African University College.[1] Government rural health centres were opened at Ilaro and Auchi (Western Region) in 1951, and two more at Kankiya and Argungu (Northern Region) in 1952. Eleven mobile field units, all of which are intended eventually to be associated with these centres, carry out mass vaccinations and deal with outbreaks of infectious disease.

There is evidence of much activity by the Government health organizations which deal with certain types of epidemic disease. Thus while in the period 1931–40 the number of people examined by the special staff for sleeping-sickness control was 3,288,236, the number in the period 1946–52 was 5,525,746; and it is satisfactory to note that whereas the cases treated in the first period numbered 395,554, the number in the period 1946–52 had been reduced to 73,585.[2] An outbreak of yellow fever in 1951 was met by the appointment of an emergency staff which vaccinated more than 200,000 persons in the villages affected. There has been increasing activity in popularizing the use of the sulphone drugs for leprosy control, for which there is a special Leprosy Organization under a senior officer. There are in the Northern Region, where the disease is generally of a severe type, 13 provincial settlements and 61 treatment centres. The leprosy research work centred at Uzuakoli is probably the

[1] See below, p. 1182. [2] *Colonial Reports, Nigeria, 1952*, pp. 76–78.

most important now being carried out in any territory in Africa. The West African Virus Research Institute at Lagos studies neurotropic viruses, yellow fever, and rabies; and it has been appointed an influenza research centre for the World Health Organization.[1] There is a laboratory for research on hot-climate physiology at Oshodi and a Loiasis Research Station at Kumba in the Cameroons.

In the Gold Coast the constitutional reforms have led to a number of changes in the departmental organization of the health and medical services. When the Gold Coast attained a semi-Responsible Status a Minister responsible for health and labour was included in the first Executive Council. In 1953 a separate Ministry of Health was constituted. The health services in each of the regions into which the Gold Coast is divided are under a Principal Medical Officer; in the case of the Trans-Volta–Togoland Region his title is that of Senior Medical Officer.

In 1951 the senior staff of the Medical Department comprised 86 Medical Officers (including specialists) and four Dental Surgeons. About half of the senior staff were Africans. Missions and mining organizations maintained 64 Medical Officers. The Government maintained 33 hospitals with 1,983 beds, and there were 26 hospitals managed by Missions, mines, and private persons, with a total of 720 beds. Field units, originally formed for the treatment of yaws and trypanosomiasis, are now organized for the survey and mass treatment of other diseases. A number of ante-natal and child-welfare services and clinics are maintained by the Government, Missions, Local Authorities, and the Gold Coast branch of the British Red Cross Society. In 1952 a Commission of Inquiry on Health[2] pointed in particular to the need for an expansion in the work of the Medical Field Units and recommended the creation of some 40 health centres, which, besides general health work, would treat minor illnesses. Each centre would have six or seven dressing-stations attached to it.

The establishment of the Medical Department for Sierra Leone included in 1952 a total of 40 Medical Officers and three Dental Surgeons. There are 19 Government hospitals with 842 beds; these include one maternity hospital, one mental hospital, one for infectious diseases, and two for the chronically sick. The Government also maintains 28 dispensaries and three health centres. The Missions maintain five hospitals and 13 dispensaries, and the mines have two hospitals and one dispensary. A mobile field unit deals with sleeping-sickness, yaws, and schistosomiasis and other endemic diseases. There is a malarial-control unit in Freetown.

In Gambia the Government maintains two general hospitals (the Victoria Hospital at Bathurst and another at Bansang, 180 miles up the

---

[1] For work on yellow-fever research, see below, p. 1152.
[2] *Report of the Commission of Enquiry into the Health Needs of the Gold Coast*, Accra, 1952.

river), 19 dispensaries, and 22 sub-dispensaries. The Missions maintain
one dispensary, two sub-dispensaries, and a mobile dispensary. There are
also in Bathurst a leper camp, a mental hospital, and a tuberculosis
sanatorium. Charges for treatment were abolished in 1950; although
these had been low the result of this change was a marked increase in the
number of persons coming for treatment. The staff in 1952 included
eight Medical Officers and one Dental Surgeon. In the Bathurst area the
surface drainage works completed in 1951 have greatly reduced the danger
of annual floods and facilitated the control of malaria. Reference has
already been made to the work of the Nutrition Field Research Station.
A trypanosomiasis survey of the Upper River Division was made by the
West African Institute of Trypanosomiasis Research in 1951.

The French Territories

The present organization of health services in the French territories is
described in a report presented to an International Conference in 1953.[1]
There is in France no central institute for dealing with the problems of
tropical medicines which is wholly comparable with the London and
Liverpool Schools of Hygiene and Tropical Medicine, but the *Institut
Pasteur* in Paris exercises similar functions as a research and information
centre. It has local branches at Dakar, Kindia, and Brazzaville, which are
directed from Paris but receive grants from territorial funds. There is a
unified medical service—the *Corps des Médecins de la Santé de la France
d'Outre-mer*—with headquarters at the Ministry for Overseas France.
The majority of its members are military Medical Officers who have
attended a course in tropical medicine at the *École d'Application* at
Marseilles. A number of medical men are also engaged on contract,
and there is a large establishment of Africans trained as auxiliary medical
officers. In each of the two groups of territories, French West Africa and
Equatorial Africa, there is a *Direction Générale* at the capital, with a
Direction Locale in each territory; for this purpose Dakar is treated as a
separate territory.

It is noteworthy that whereas in the British territories hospitals are
regarded mainly as centres for treatment, those in French Africa function
largely as the headquarters of field stations whence curative and preventive
medicine is made available in rural areas. A French writer points out
that the development of preventive medicine in Africa has outstripped
that in France itself. He sees evidence of this in the relatively small number
of centres for fixed treatment in proportion to the total number of agencies
for the treatment of disease.

As early as 1904 the territorial authorities were authorized to declare

---

[1] R. Girard, 'La Situation sanitaire et démographique dans l'Union Française', *Congrès mondial
des médecins pour l'étude des conditions actuelles de vie*, Vienna, 1953.

the existence of a 'state of imminent danger' to public health and to order the immediate execution of the necessary measures. Circulars of 1921 laid stress on the development of a staff of African auxiliaries (whose main function would be public-health propaganda), in preference to increasing the provision for individual curative treatment. Instructions of 1930 emphasized the importance of infant welfare and of safeguarding the conditions of labour; they explicitly stated that the provision for the treatment of individuals, and particularly for curative treatment in hospitals, should be reduced to modest proportions, while hygiene and preventive services should be developed to the maximum. In conformity with these principles it was decided that there should be a single general hospital at the headquarters of each territory, and at the headquarters of every *circonscription* a *dispensaire-maternité*, which is described as the most characteristic feature of the French service. Attached to these centres are 'medical posts' administered by *infirmiers*.

A noteworthy feature of the French medical service in the inter-war period was the mobile *équipe de prospection et de traitement*. This was a team consisting of a European doctor, one or two African auxiliary doctors, and a number of African *infirmiers*, including some trained in the use of the microscope. It selected a small area and examined the entire population; treatment centres were then set up and African auxiliaries put in charge of them. Every person examined received a card with a note of the diseases from which he was found to be suffering and could obtain further treatment from the medical posts or dispensaries. The work of these teams succeeded in bringing medical services to large numbers of people, often in remote areas. From 1934 onwards they concentrated on the eradication of sleeping-sickness, and in French West Africa the work occupied at least a third of the time of all members of the medical service.[1]

In 1944, however, after the increase in sleeping-sickness during the Second World War had been brought to the attention of the Brazzaville Conference, a separate branch of the service was created for mobile work, the *Service Général d'Hygiène Mobile et de Prophylaxie* (S.G.H.M.P.), which is officially described as being responsible for the mass diagnosis, treatment, and control of certain epidemic diseases. It has five sections, dealing with trypanosomiasis, leprosy, malaria, filariasis, and eye diseases. Research is also one of its functions.[2]

In French West Africa there was in 1951 a total of 216 registered physicians, of whom one was employed by a Mission and 30 by business concerns; the returns quoted do not distinguish between Europeans and Africans, but in 1950 all persons included in this category were European.

---

[1] M. Peltier, 'L'Assistance médicale indigène', *Enc. A.O.F.*, vol. i, pp. 279–82. M. Beaudiment, 'Service d'hygiène mobile et de prophylaxie', *Enc. C.-T.*, pp. 131–4.

[2] Girard, op. cit.

There were 376 medical assistants, pharmacists, and midwives; 32 of the midwives were trained in France. The majority in the category of auxiliaries were Africans, as were the majority of the subordinate personnel. Reference is made elsewhere to the distinguished part played by the Medical School at Dakar in training auxiliary medical staff.[1]

In 1951 there were 1,006 institutions for treatment, with 22,449 beds. These included eight fully equipped hospitals, one for Europeans and one for Africans at Dakar and one in each of the territories (with the exception of the Upper Volta and Mauritania), 19 smaller establishments (*ambulances*), 152 medical centres, 232 Government and 23 other dispensaries, and 107 maternity institutions. The headquarters of the *Service Général d'Hygiène Mobile et de Prophylaxie* is at Bobo-Dioulasso in the Upper Volta. In the period from 1950 to May 1952 the service examined 10,366,680 persons, discovered 21,792 new cases of trypanosomiasis, and treated a large number of leprosy patients.

Outpatient treatment is free to Africans; those who wish to pay may consult private practitioners or may pay on a fixed scale in certain institutions. Admission for in-patient treatment, however, is free only to the indigent, though persons on low salaries pay at a lower rate. In dispensaries and maternity clinics admission is free, but patients are expected to provide their own food. This system, which usually means that the patient is accompanied by a relative who cooks the food on the spot, undoubtedly adds to the popularity of the hospital, as missionary bodies which practise it elsewhere have found. But it has been criticized in some quarters as lowering the standards of hygiene and orderliness aimed at in European hospital services.

The Dakar laboratory of the *Institut Pasteur* is the successor of the bacteriological laboratory of Senegal which was founded in 1896. It was transferred to Dakar in 1913, becoming a branch of the *Institut Pasteur* in Paris in 1923. For most of the time, however, the Director carried on the work of the Institute with little other staff.[2] Its present premises were opened in 1937, when its staff was largely increased. The Institute at Kindia (Guinea) was founded in 1922 in order to use anthropoid apes for experimental purposes. Both Institutes are now responsible for the preparation of vaccines and for analyses required by the health or veterinary services. The Laigret yellow-fever vaccine was first produced in the Dakar laboratory in 1927.[3] The Kindia Institute met from 1942 to 1946 the entire needs of French West and Equatorial Africa and the Cameroons for smallpox vaccines which had previously been obtained from France. The *Institut Marchoux* at Bamako, founded in 1934, is the centre for

[1] See below, p. 1098.
[2] C. Durieux, 'Les Instituts Pasteur', *Enc. A.O.F.*, vol. i, pp. 292–6.
[3] See below, p. 1132.

research and treatment of leprosy. There is a psychiatric centre at Thiès and a centre for research and treatment of trachoma at Bamako.

The expenditure on health services in 1951 represented 11·4 per cent. of the total budget; of this sum roughly half was borne on the budget of the Central Government. Credits of a little over 2,000 million francs have been made from the Development Funds for the expansion of health services.[1]

In the French Cameroons the European staff of the health service in 1952 included 52 fully qualified medical men. The African staff included 60 doctors with qualifications from the Dakar School of Medicine. The European staff of Missions included 15 doctors, and there were eight doctors in private practice. The Government provided 40 hospitals of all categories and 61 dispensaries, with a total of 4,150 beds, two sleeping-sickness centres, 32 *leprosaria*, three mental hospitals, and 135 small rural dispensaries. The Missions provided eleven hospitals and five dispensaries, with a total of 1,852 beds, nine *leprosaria*, and 38 dispensaries. Commercial companies provided three hospitals with 165 beds and six dispensaries.[2] The Government centres at the headquarters of the *circonscriptions* are usually in the charge of African doctors. The *Service Général d'Hygiène Mobile et de Prophylaxie* maintains eight mobile groups and plays an important part in the medical system. There is, in addition, a large urban and rural service for maternity and infant welfare, the *Protection Maternelle et Infantile* (P.M.I.). The credits voted from Development Funds for the extension of health services in the Cameroons totalled 500 million francs for the period 1947–52.

In French Togoland there is a large hospital at Lomé and a medical centre at the headquarters of each of the eight *circonscriptions*; these centres are responsible for the urban health services and the rural dispensaries in their area. The staff of the health service in 1952 included eleven European and 21 African doctors. There were three African doctors in private practice. African women, known as *matrones*, who have had a few months' training, conduct normal confinements in the women's homes or at maternity annexes. There are two leprosy villages with about 700 patients.

A training school for male and female nurses was opened at Lomé in 1945, and from 1947 has provided courses for the two auxiliary grades which were created in that year, *agents d'hygiène* and *agents sanitaires*. The former are responsible for the enforcement of sanitary regulations; the latter are recruited by competition from persons who have taken the

---

[1] *United Nations, Non-Self-Governing Territories, Summaries and Analyses of Information transmitted during 1952*, vol. ii, pp. 281–4.

[2] *Rapport annuel à l'Assemblée Générale des Nations Unies sur l'administration du Cameroun, 1952*, pp. 225–40, 438–9.

nurses' training course and are given an additional year's training. Decrees of 18 August 1949 and 31 August 1953 authorized the grant of bursaries to Africans with local qualifications for further study in France. These students are selected by a competitive examination, and in 1952 there were 31 of them studying in France. Expenditure on medical services amounted in 1952 to 24 per cent. of the total expenditure of the territory.[1]

In French Equatorial Africa there is a central hospital at Brazzaville, and there is at each territorial headquarters a hospital with X-ray and dental departments. At the headquarters of each subdivision there are a dispensary, maternity clinic, surgical unit, and hospital blocks forming the medical centre, to which smaller units are subordinate. An *Institut Pasteur*, founded at Brazzaville in 1909, now has three doctors and 32 assistants. A biochemical laboratory was opened in 1952.

In 1952 the Government medical and public-health staff included 119 registered physicians, 189 nurses, and 108 sanitary inspectors, of whom some were European and some African. The African staff included 41 licensed physicians and three public-health assistants. Missions employed two doctors, and private companies had 11 doctors. There were 191 Government institutions giving in-patient treatment, with 7,298 beds, and 84 dispensaries. Non-Government agencies had 53 in-patient institutions, with 1,285 beds, and 80 dispensaries. There were 13 units of the *Service Général d'Hygiène Mobile et de Prophylaxie*, with a staff of 277; the four months' rainy season makes their work particularly difficult. The well-known hospital at Lambaréné is maintained as an independent institution by Dr. Albert Schweitzer.[2]

The Belgian Territories

The first medical installation in the Belgian Congo was a laboratory opened at Leopoldville in 1897. A School of Tropical Medicine was founded at Brussels in 1906, and from this base various specialist missions were sent to the Congo. A local medical service for the Belgian Congo was created in 1909, and local research laboratories were established, the most important being at Elisabethville. A separate public-health service was established in 1922.[3] In 1933 the School of Tropical Medicine in Brussels was superseded by the Institute of Tropical Medicine at Antwerp, and in 1937 the Leopoldville laboratory became the *Institut Princesse Astrid*, now the major institution for local medical research. Medical research is also included among the activities of the *Institut pour la Recherche Scientifique en Afrique Centrale* (I.R.S.A.C.) founded in 1947.

[1] *Rapport annuel à l'Assemblée Générale des Nations Unies sur l'administration du Togo, 1952*, pp. 193–207.

[2] A. Schweitzer, *The Forest Hospital at Lambaréné*, New York, 1931.

[3] *Plan décennal pour le développement économique et social du Congo Belge*, vol. i, 1949, pp. 37 ff.

There has been a greater development of unofficial health organizations in the Belgian Congo than in either the British or the French dependencies. In a sense these organizations are comparable to the preventive health services in Belgium, which are largely in the hands of voluntary associations. In the Colony they function in well-defined areas and are controlled by the State through legal agreements or regulation in the case of mining and similar companies. They are regulated through conventions or the conditions of subsidies in the case of the voluntary Associations and Missions concerned. The Administration has concentrated to a marked degree on medical work in rural districts. The Colony is divided for administrative purposes into provinces and districts, and each district is subdivided into a number of *territoires*. These areas are apportioned between the official organization known as the *Service de l'Assistance Médicale aux Indigènes* (S.A.M.I.) and the unofficial bodies known as the *Service Auxiliaire de l'Assistance Médicale aux Indigènes* (S.A.D.A.M.I.). The former includes the State service, together with a specially endowed organization, the *Fonds Reine Élisabeth pour l'Assistance Médicale aux Indigènes* (Foréami); while the latter includes the numerous medical missions and various other organizations of which the oldest are the *Croix Rouge du Congo* and the *Fondation Médicale de l'Université de Louvain au Congo* (Fomulac).

The operations of the Foréami, which was founded in 1930 with a fund of 150 million francs from the Belgian and Congo Governments and rather over a quarter of a million francs from Queen Elisabeth, were planned on lines comparable with those of the French medical services. The original intention was that a large staff of doctors, *agents sanitaires*, and African assistants should settle in a circumscribed area, examine systematically every person in that area, and, after treating all diseases and instituting appropriate measures of sanitation, should then move on to another area. It was hoped that by this method the major diseases would be eliminated and a foundation would be laid for a satisfactory record of vital statistics. When the diseases susceptible to treatment by mass campaigns, such as sleeping-sickness, yaws, and the venereal diseases, had been brought under control responsibility for the area could then be handed over to the Government medical services.

The task has, however, proved more formidable than was expected, and much of the activity of Foréami has consisted in the treatment of sleeping-sickness. Progress was also hampered by war conditions from 1939 to 1945. Whereas in 1934 there was a staff of 27 European doctors and 20 *agents sanitaires*, Foréami was able to employ in 1945 only ten medical men and 13 *agents sanitaires*.[1] Nevertheless, very valuable work has been done in the Bas-Congo, Moyen-Congo, Lake Leopold II, and

---

[1] *Foréami Annual Report, 1946–7.*

Kwango areas, and in 1952 no less than 6½ million Africans were examined by Foréami and by mobile units of the State service.[1]

Among the unofficial bodies (the *Service Auxiliaire de l'Assistance Médicale aux Indigènes*, or S.A.D.A.M.I.), the *Missions Nationales*[2] maintain 19 health centres and 115 dispensaries, and the foreign Missions maintain 33 and 54 respectively. The *Croix Rouge* began work in the Belgian Congo in 1925, and has concentrated its resources mainly in the Uele region; it has also established clinics and dispensaries in some of the large towns. It employs three European doctors and maintains altogether 39 hospitals or dispensaries, 29 being for lepers with or without other patients. The Fomulac, which was originated in 1931 and is a remarkable tribute to the missionary enthusiasm of the University of Louvain, has similar objects and methods.[3] It operates mainly in the provinces of Leopoldville and Kivu, and in 1951 employed nine doctors. The *Centre Médical de l'Université Libre de Bruxelles au Congo* (C.E.M.U.B.A.C.) concentrates on tuberculosis, and has carried out surveys in Maniema and Kivu, and also in Ruanda Urundi.

Smaller organizations are the *Fonds Social du Kivu* and the *Fonds Social Linéa*, also in the Kivu area. The concessions in favour of European enterprises carry the condition that hospitals and schools must be provided for Africans, but some companies have done much more than was legally required, and the range of their medical services has extended considerably beyond the immediate vicinity of their undertakings. In ten of the 29 urban areas classified as *grands centres* all medical services provided are maintained by these companies, which in 1952 employed a European medical staff totalling 140.[4] The Forminière mine and forestry undertaking and Vicicongo railway are also responsible for four rural hospitals.

The Ten-year Development Plan adopted in 1947 provided for the expenditure of roughly 2,000 million francs on medical and health services, of which 627 million francs were to be spent in urban centres. The total sum was to include the Belgian contribution to the African Bureau for Tsetse and Trypanosomiasis and a grant to the regional office of the World Health Organization. A considerable programme of construction of hospitals and dispensaries was also to be financed. The allocation for rural areas (1,345 million francs) was to cover a number of projects: the construction or the reconstruction of 43 hospitals and the improvement of 50; the construction of 180 dispensaries to supplement those financed from Native Treasury Funds, so as to provide four dispensaries in each *territoire*; the provision of additional centres for the treatment

[1] *Rapport sur l'administration de la colonie du Congo Belge, 1952*, p. 171.

[2] See below, pp. 1206 ff.

[3] E. B. Worthington, *Science in Africa*, 1938, p. 332.

[4] *Plan décennal pour le développement économique et social du Congo Belge*, vol. i, 1949, p. 47. *Rapport sur l'administration de la colonie du Congo Belge, 1952*, p. 160.

of leprosy and tuberculosis; and the allocation of credits to Missions for maternity and child-welfare work.[1]

Reference has been made in a previous chapter to the *Fonds du Bien-Être Indigène* (F.B.E.I.), created in 1947, from which grants might be made for any purpose which would assist the material or moral development of African society.[2] This Fund has, as already explained, concentrated much of its general effort on three areas, Kasongo and Befale in the Bas-Congo and one district of Ruanda Urundi, but it has also assisted in making provision for medical facilities over a wider area. In all, it has financed the construction of 70 maternity centres and has subsidized tuberculosis surveys conducted by the Foréami and C.E.M.U.B.A.C. It has also financed three large-scale experiments in mosquito control, subsidized the construction of *leprosaria*, made a special study of bilharzia, financed the construction of a school for medical assistants at Leopoldville, and provided 152 ambulances for the use of the medical service. In the areas selected for intensive work it has provided for a large hospital at Tongoni in Kasongo, where it has already two treatment centres; in Kasongo and Befale it is conducting studies of the causes of sterility, and both there and in Ruanda Urundi is organizing the mass administration of quinine to young children.[3] In 1952 it made grants totalling nearly 150 million francs for medical and health services in the Belgian Congo.[4]

The European personnel employed by the Belgian Congo Government in 1952 included 286 doctors and 402 medical auxiliaries. Figures for African personnel do not distinguish between those employed by the State, by Foréami, and by the Missions, but in 1952 there were 79 African medical assistants, 642 *infirmiers*, and 2,705 *aides-infirmiers*. There were altogether 92 hospitals for Europeans, with 958 beds; of these, 40 were maintained by the Government, 19 by Missions with Government subsidies, and 33 by companies. For Africans the Government maintained 631 hospitals and dispensaries, with 16,470 beds; State-subsidized Missions 435, with 14,630 beds; and the companies a total of 850, with 14,275 beds.

In Ruanda Urundi there were in 1952 four urban and twelve rural hospitals maintained by the Government, 15 maintained by Missions, and four by companies. The Government maintained 65 dispensaries, the Missions 21, companies nine, and private persons eight. The Government employed 35 medical men, semi-official organizations two, Missions twelve, and companies four. All grades of African subordinate staff are now trained at Usumbura. The expenditure on medical services in 1952 amounted to 21 per cent. of the total expenditure for the territory. The

---

[1] *Plan décennal pour le développement économique et social du Congo Belge*, vol. i, 1949, pp. 46–51.
[2] See above, p. 561.
[3] H. Beckers, 'Le Fonds du Bien-Être Indigène', *Zaïre*, vol. v, 1951, pp. 787–812.
[4] *Rapport sur l'administration de la colonie du Congo Belge, 1952*, p. 164.

Fonds du Bien-Être Indigène made grants totalling a little over 23 million francs for medical and health work.[1]

The Portuguese Territories

The medical and health services in the Portuguese territories are responsible to a branch of the Ministry of Overseas Territories, and the Minister has on this matter the advice of the Institute of Tropical Medicine at Lisbon. Its post-graduate school, which was founded in 1902, is of high standing; the Institute also supervises the work of specialized organizations in the different territories, such as the sleeping-sickness mission in Guinea and the organization for the control of endemic diseases in Angola. It has published from 1943 the *Anais do Instituto de Medicina Tropical*. There is a hospital in Lisbon,[2] mainly devoted to the treatment of tropical diseases.

The overseas health services are regulated by a Decree of 27 February 1945. In each territory the service comprises curative, preventive, and laboratory branches, and various special services (for instance for sleeping-sickness and leprosy). Four grades of medical men are recognized: Chief Medical Officers, Inspectors, and Medical Officers first and second class. In the African territories the establishment in 1952 comprised:

	Angola	Mozambique	Guinea	Sao Tomé and Principe
Chief Medical Officer .	1	1	..	..
Inspectors . .	9	8	1	1
Medical Officers first class . . .	45	45	3	1
Medical Officers second class . .	60	60	7	3
	115	114	11	5

In Guinea there were in 1952 three Government hospitals, ten 'delegations', and 56 'posts', together with a laboratory at Bissau. The sleeping-sickness organization, which is under the technical direction of the Institute of Tropical Medicine at Lisbon, has 31 centres; it also deals with other diseases such as hookworm and guinea-worm infection, filariasis, and leprosy.

The Medical Department of Sao Tomé and Principe in 1952 employed seven medical men;[3] there were two Government hospitals, 50 infirmaries, and one *leprosarium*, with two laboratories. There were also 15 other infirmaries. The bed capacity at the Government hospital on Principe

---

[1] *Rapport sur l'administration belge du Ruanda-Urundi, 1952*, pp. 35, 165, 170–2.
[2] Instituto de Medicina Tropical, *Instruções para o ano académico de 1952, Publicação no. 2*, Lisbon. [3] *Anuário estatístico do Ultramar, 1952*, p. 74.

was 232, with 16 others in one of the infirmaries. In 1950 the plantations had 17 hospitals and dispensaries on Sao Tomé, and four hospitals and dispensaries on Principe.

In Angola the Department of Health in 1952 comprised 148 Government medical men and five Government analysts. In addition there were 36 other medical men and four Government and four other dental surgeons. The Government hospitals numbered 50, other hospitals (maintained by Missions and mining and plantation companies) 30, infirmaries 39, mental hospitals one, and bacteriological laboratories five. There is a special service for sleeping-sickness. The principal Government hospital at Luanda has some 300 beds for Europeans and Africans; other Government hospitals provide from 20 to 150 beds, the total capacity of all hospitals is estimated at about one bed for approximately 2,250 of the population.

The Mozambique Department of Health in 1952 included 168 Government medical men, three analysts, and other staff. There were 67 Government and five other hospitals, one mental hospital, seven leprosy institutions, and a sleeping-sickness unit. There were two bacteriological and four other laboratories. It is not possible to give figures of hospital beds or hospital admissions on a basis comparable to those of other territories. A sleeping-sickness organization, under the joint control of the Health, Veterinary, and Agricultural Services, deals with the control of both human and animal trypanosomiasis, the latter being the more important.[1] In 1950 it employed 13 medical men and seven veterinary surgeons; the persons examined numbered 153,048, and 188 new cases of human sleeping-sickness were found, many of them along the coast south of the Ruvuma river bordering on Tanganyika. Large areas are infested with *Glossina morsitans* near the Southern Rhodesia border and along the river Save. In addition to the sleeping-sickness organization there is a malaria institute, with headquarters in Lourenço Marques.

Spanish Guinea

The health services of Spanish Guinea are responsible to a branch of the *Dirección General de Marruecos y Colonías* in Madrid. Their headquarters are at Santa Isabel on Fernando Po, and there are 14 sanitary districts served by 28 medical men of the Colonial Service. The hospitals are staffed by nursing sisters of religious orders. In 1950 there were four Government hospitals, two on Fernando Po with 230 and 50 beds respectively, and two in Rio Muni on the mainland with 150 and 50 beds respectively. Dispensaries, with a few beds each, are established in the chief towns of each district, and there are two hospitals (one with a village settlement) for

[1] *Província de Moçambique, Missão de combate às tripanossomíases, Relatório anual de 1950*, Lourenço Marques, 1952.

leprosy patients. Small hospitals are maintained by some of the plantation companies. At Santa Isabel there is an Institute of Hygiene, at which laboratory investigations are made; this is being replaced by a modern research laboratory.

The extent of work done in the various hospitals and other institutions[1] may be estimated from the fact that 13,981 Africans and 529 non-Africans were admitted to hospitals in 1951 and 74,308 outpatients were treated. At the two *leprosaria* (Mikomeseng and Ebebiyin) there were 2,480 and 310 resident patients respectively. On Fernando Po there are two Mission hospitals, and there are also two on the mainland.

Liberia

There can be no question of the fact that many of the tropical diseases are endemic in a high degree in Liberia. Some indication of this was given by a survey of malaria made in 1948 by the United States Medical Mission. It revealed a country-wide malarial rate of 30 per cent. Other diseases also appear to be very prevalent, but the problems of control in the sleeping-sickness areas are of unusual importance.

The present organization of medical services is of recent creation and is still very inadequate, especially in the rural areas. It may be said to have originated with the dispatch to the country in 1944 of a mission, from the United States Public Health Department, which was led by two American Negro doctors. Previous to that date there had been only six physicians in the whole of Liberia. There were but few nurses, and half of these had no recognized qualification. The only hospital with really adequate staff and equipment was that maintained on the area held by the Firestone Company. There were some ten clinics in different parts of the country, but only three of these had a qualified doctor in attendance. The programme of expansion was drawn up in 1946–7 in consultation with the Americo-Liberia Foundation, which is referred to later in this chapter.[2] It aimed at the appointment of a physician to every administrative district and the establishment of clinics at a distance of 30 miles apart. The capital and part of the recurrent costs of a public-health centre which was opened at Monrovia in 1945 were contributed by the United States Government; it has X-ray equipment and a pathological laboratory, with a staff of four physicians and a dental surgeon. Attendance averages 2,900 a month.

The general hospital maintained by the Government in Monrovia has recently been equipped with assistance from the United States. The

---

[1] *Resúmenes estadísticos del gobierno general de los territorios españoles del Golfo de Guinea, 1950–51*, Madrid, 1953, pp. 218 ff.

[2] See below, p. 1097. See also *Modernization Programs*, Milbank Memorial Fund, New York, 1950.

mission from the United States above referred to established a school of nursing, which was later expanded to provide sub-professional medical and dental training and also courses for sanitary personnel. It later became the Tubman National Institute of Medical and Applied Arts.[1] A Liberian Institute of the American Foundation for Tropical Medicine was formally opened in 1952.[2] A large grant towards its capital cost was made by Harvey S. Firestone, Jr., and the operating expenses are borne by the American Foundation for Tropical Medicine.

An Act passed by Liberia in 1946 made provision for the construction of seven hospitals, one tuberculosis sanatorium, and a quarantine station. In 1950 the medical personnel in the country was reinforced by the arrival of eight medical men from Germany, and by 1955 there were 28 medical men in the service of the Government, eight in the service of Missions, eleven employed by the Firestone and Liberia Mining companies, and ten in private practice. At the same date there were 14 hospitals, of which six were owned by the Government, three were subsidized by the Government, two were Mission hospitals, two were on the Firestone Company's Estates, and one belonged to the Liberian Mining Company on the Bomi hills. In addition there are 58 clinics and dispensaries, and eight *leprosaria*.[3] A sleeping-sickness team operates in the Western Province. In-patients at Government hospitals are normally charged a dollar a day, but treatment for the indigent is free, and in fact few patients pay fees. A number of Fellowships have been awarded to Liberians by the World Health Organization enabling them to study in the United States.

MEDICAL EDUCATION OF AFRICANS

In the preceding pages describing the organization of the health services in the different territories some mention has been made of institutions for the training of Africans. It will be convenient, however, to give here a more systematic account of these institutions, dealing separately with those designed for the provision of fully qualified medical men and those designed for the training of the auxiliary or subordinate medical staff.

The Graduate or Fully Qualified Staff

In the Union of South Africa a small number of Africans and Coloured students have in the past been admitted to medical courses at the Universities of Cape Town and Witwatersrand. As is shown in the following chapter, however, they are no longer to be admitted to these Universities,

---

[1] R. E. Anderson, *Liberia*, 1952, pp. 268–70.

[2] *The Liberian Institute of the American Foundation for Tropical Medicine, Dedication Ceremonies, Harbel, Liberia, January 1952.*

[3] *Liberia Today* (published by the Liberian Embassy, Washington), vol. iv, no. 5, May 1955, p. 2.

and a special medical school for Africans has recently been established at Wentworth by the University of Durban.[1] The first two African doctors to receive these qualifications in South Africa graduated in 1945. During subsequent years the number has varied from four to seven[2] annually. In 1954 the Rockefeller Foundation gave a considerable grant to the medical school for the specific purpose of training non-European physicians. The intention is to post them to multi-purpose health centres which are in need of doctors familiar with the problems arising from a family practice. The grant is for five years.[3]

The policy of the Government in the United Kingdom is to raise the standard of medical qualifications to the level at which they can be recognized by the General Medical Council.[4] Advanced medical training is now being provided at the East African University College of Makerere and the West African University College at Ibadan. The college at Makerere grants a diploma after a seven years' course. A delegation from the British General Medical Council in 1951 considered that the qualification could fittingly be made locally registrable, though the training given had not yet reached a level at which they could recommend recognition by the Medical Council itself. This latter question was again under active consideration in 1956. The qualification was subsequently made locally registrable, and would confer the right to practise anywhere in East Africa. Local registration is accorded after two years of internship, and doctors are required after registration to remain in the public service for five years. The Ibadan course leads to the Second M.B. examination. This is accepted as sufficient for a local qualification, but in order to obtain a degree registrable with the British General Medical Council the students from Ibadan must take clinical courses overseas.

For the French territories the *École Préparatoire de Médecine et de Pharmacie* at Dakar, which was opened in 1950, was designed to supersede the earlier medical school dating from 1918. It is a branch of the recently constituted *Institut des Hautes Études* at Dakar, but as regards medicine it is still in fact an institution for preliminary studies. The teaching covers the first three years of the same course as is given in metropolitan France, and the examinations are equivalent. For the remaining three years students must go to a metropolitan university, usually Marseilles or Bordeaux; it is not at present contemplated that more advanced training should be given at Dakar. Those who do not complete their training at a metropolitan university will remain as auxiliary medical officers. It should be added, however, that the medical auxiliaries trained at Dakar have a good reputation throughout French West and French

---

[1] *The Durban School of Medicine: A Response to the Challenge of Africa*, Natal University Development Foundation, 1953.   [2] *O.Y.S.A., 1949*, p. 408.
[3] *S.A.S.*, no. 95, 15 December 1954.   [4] H.C. Deb., 8 December 1954, coll. 955–6.

Equatorial Africa on account of the valuable grounding they have obtained.

Hitherto Africans in the Belgian Congo and Ruanda Urundi have been able to obtain only a local qualification at the Government medical institution at Leopoldville[1] or at that conducted by the White Fathers at Astrida in Ruanda Urundi. Policy has not been in favour of making provision for them to continue their medical studies in Europe. The new academic centre, the Lovanium, will, however, give the full medical course as in Belgium.[2]

The Subordinate or Partially Qualified Staff

In the Union of South Africa there are some 120 recognized hospital schools of nursing, 27 of which give instruction in midwifery. African and Coloured women are trained at Mission hospitals up to the same standard as Europeans. It was stated in 1949 that one-sixth of all practising nurses and midwives in the Union were non-European. Mission institutions have also given training to a certain number of Africans as 'medical aides' or hygiene officers and health assistants.[3] In Southern Rhodesia there are schools for male nursing orderlies at Salisbury and Bulawayo, for female nursing assistants at Bulawayo, for maternity assistants at Umtali, and courses for health demonstrators at Domboshawa.

In Northern Rhodesia the African Medical Training School at Lusaka trains hospital, laboratory, and physiotherapy assistants. X-ray orderlies are trained at the Lusaka hospitals, hygiene assistants at Ndola, and nurses at the Government hospital at Livingstone. In Nyasaland there are one Mission and two Government training centres for 'medical aides'; selected students take an additional year and qualify as hospital assistants. The Mission course is a year longer than that given at the Government centres. Sanitary assistants are trained at Zomba; midwives at Zomba and at eight Mission centres. In Tanganyika nurses are trained at Mweka and Moshi and at a number of Government and Mission hospitals; midwives at a Government centre at Dar-es-Salaam and at various Missions; medical assistants at Dar-es-Salaam and a Mission centre (Bumbuli); 'rural medical aides' at Mwanza and a Mission centre at Manaki; malaria assistants at Amani; laboratory, pharmaceutical, and hospital assistants at Dar-es-Salaam; and assistant health inspectors at Kongwa.

In Kenya the Medical Training School at Nairobi trains hospital assistants, Grade I nurses, compounders, and orthopaedic and laboratory assistants. Health inspectors are trained at the Jeanes School at Kabete and also at Siriba, and health visitors and assistant radiographers at Kisumu. Grade II nurses and midwives are trained at a number of

[1] See below, p. 1101.   [2] See below, p. 1211.
[3] *Handbook on Race Relations in South Africa,* 1949, pp. 409–10.

Government and Mission centres. Uganda provides training for medical assistants at Masaka, for nurses at Mulago and at Mission stations, for midwives at Missions, for nursing orderlies at Lira, for dispensers at Mulago, for laboratory assistants at the Kampala Central Laboratories, and for assistant health inspectors at a school of hygiene at Mbale.

In the British West African dependencies Nigeria gives training to nurses at 32 Government or Mission teaching hospitals; to midwives at 33 schools, eight of which give an advanced course for qualified nurses; to sanitary inspectors at Ibadan, Aba, and Kano; to dispensary assistants and dressers at Kano, Zaria, and Makurdi; to X-ray and dental technicians at Lagos; and to pharmacists at schools of pharmacy at Lagos and Zaria. Various leprosy settlements give a one-year course in leprosy control. In the Cameroons nurses are trained at two Government hospitals and two maintained by the Cameroons Development Corporation.[1] In the Gold Coast the nurses' training college at Accra gives a qualification which is now recognized by the General Nursing Council of England and Wales, and five hospitals give a shorter course. The maternity hospital at Accra gives instruction in midwifery to nurses with general training, and two midwifery schools give courses to girls who have no preliminary experience of nursing. Training is also provided for health nurses, sanitary inspectors, and dispensers. In Sierra Leone nurses and midwives are trained at Freetown and Bo, while dispensers, health inspectors, and laboratory and X-ray assistants receive their training at Freetown. Courses are given at Bo for sanitary overseers and dispensary attendants to be employed by the Native Administrations.

In the French dependencies the *École Préparatoire de Médecine et de Pharmacie* at Dakar instructs pharmacists and midwives; the latter, after training, must work at least ten years in the health service. Courses are also provided for male and female nurses and *gardes sanitaires*; the male nurses may proceed to a specialist grade after further training in pharmacy and medical or laboratory work. For specialization in the *Service Général d'Hygiène Mobile et de Prophylaxie* (S.G.H.M.P.) there is the *École Jamot*, which since 1944 has been incorporated in the *Centre d'Études des Trypanosomiases Africaines* at Bobo-Dioulasso. The normal course lasts for nine months. To this centre doctors, *agents sanitaires*, and others also can be sent for courses of from two to three months' duration. Instruction in leprosy work is given at the *Institut Marchoux*, Bamako, under the auspices of the S.G.H.M.P. An International Conference, attended by delegates from French, Belgian, British, and Portuguese territories, was held at Dakar in 1951 to study the problems of medical instruction.[2]

The Belgian Congo has a State school for African medical assistants at

[1] See above, p. 736.
[2] *Les Conférences internationales médicales de Dakar, 16–24 mai, 1951.*

Leopoldville and a subsidized school at Kisantu; four State and three subsidized schools for *infirmiers*, a number of State and two subsidized schools for *aides-infirmiers*; a school at Leopoldville for midwives; and five others for assistant midwives. All the subordinate grades are trained at Usumbura in Ruanda Urundi.

In the Portuguese territories there are schools at Lourenço Marques and Luanda which train medical assistants, nurses, and midwives; that at Luanda also trains sanitary agents and health visitors, while the work of the *Escola Técnica dos Serviços de Saúde* in Mozambique is supplemented by training facilities at the larger hospitals. The *Escola Técnica de Enfermagen* was attached in 1946 to the hospital at Bissau, Portuguese Guinea, for the training of African male nurses for rural dispensaries.

The preceding paragraphs disclose a great variety of subordinate medical posts and of differences in qualifications as well as in designation. In May 1951 the fourth General Assembly of the World Health Organization discussed various aspects of the employment of auxiliary medical personnel. It concluded that adequate health services cannot be provided at the present time in undeveloped areas without the employment of such personnel, but urged that some categories, particularly that of assistant to registered doctors, should be replaced as soon as possible by fully qualified persons. It is hardly astonishing that they should have emphasized the importance of requiring standard qualifications for each grade.

A survey of the existing position in most of the territories of tropical Africa was made by Dr. C. C. Chesterman in 1952.[1] He pointed out that in some territories the class he describes as 'near doctor' is disappearing and is being replaced by the fully qualified African doctor. At the same time, however, new training courses are being organized which are relatively advanced yet do not lead to full qualifications. Examples are the five-year course at the School for Medical Assistants at Kano and the medical assistants' course given in the Belgian Congo, which lasts for four years and is followed by a two-year probationary period (*stage*). In his view persons in this grade tend to resent their subordinate position and do not submit readily to supervision; they are, moreover, unwilling to stay long in rural areas. The medical assistant, who after two or three years' training is placed in charge of a rural dispensary, is in his view at present indispensable. But types of training for this grade vary widely, and some Governments have preferred not to employ auxiliaries of this kind. The Gold Coast, for example, till recently refused to employ any but fully qualified doctors except for the simplest curative medicine. As part of the expansion of health services planned in 1952, however, the Gold Coast is to employ clinical superintendents for its new health centres,

[1] C. C. Chesterman, 'The Training and Employment of Auxiliary Personnel in Medical and Health Services in Tropical Africa', *J. Trop, Med, & Hyg.*, vol. 56, 1953, pp. 123–33.

and their functions seem likely to be in essence those of the medical assistant.

In the Belgian Congo some assistants of this grade follow a training course of four years plus two years' *stage* (probation), and they deserve to be classed with the superior grade of 'near doctor'. Those taking a course of only three years (with two years' *stage*) are called *infirmiers*. Courses similar to these are given in Uganda and Tanganyika. In Northern Rhodesia and Nyasaland persons so trained are called hospital attendants. It is noticeable that a number of territories prefer to give all auxiliaries a basic training in nursing and to select the best for further training of a more specialized type. This has been the practice in Kenya, where hospital assistants are trained at a school controlled by the Kenya Nursing Council.

The 'medical aide' group includes persons with a shorter and more elementary training, who generally serve under medical assistants. Such persons are called dressers in Kenya, Uganda, and Northern Rhodesia, untrained orderlies in Southern Rhodesia, 'medical aides' in Nyasaland, and dispensary attendants in Nigeria, where until recently they have been the only African medical staff other than the Yaba-trained 'near doctor'. The Nigeria dispensary attendants have a one-year course; *aides-infirmiers* in the Belgian Congo six months to one year; and 'rural medical aides' in Tanganyika (who are being substituted for the rural dressers attached to Native Authority dispensaries) have two years of training.

Special training for laboratory assistants is most highly developed in the Gold Coast and Nigeria, where many men after completing a local four-year course take the examination of the Institute of Medical Laboratory Technology. Radiographers are trained in Kenya and Nigeria, and pharmacists in most territories. For all posts of this type or for sanitary officers recruitment is more difficult than it is for the curative services, as boys with the necessary standard of education can often find more lucrative employment as clerks or in one of the fields for which they can qualify in technical schools.

The survey made by Dr. Chesterman serves to emphasize the recommendation of the Assembly of the World Health Organization that some attempt should be made to secure a common policy in regard to the classification of medical subordinates and the qualifications required of them.

INTERNATIONAL CO-OPERATION IN HEALTH WORK

The *Office International d'Hygiène Publique*, established in Paris in 1907, was the first organization which sought to promote international co-operation in the field of public health, though its activities were largely concerned with the promotion of international conventions for preventing the spread of infectious diseases. The organization of the League of Nations included a General Advisory Health Council (which had the same membership as the *Office International d'Hygiène Publique*) and a Standing Health Committee. The work carried out under its auspices on the problems of sleeping-sickness, malaria, tuberculosis, and leprosy was of great value to Africa. The League set up in 1935 a Permanent Commission on Biological Standardization. Its influence contributed to the formation of the Biological Control Laboratory in Cape Town for the standardization of vaccines and sera.

When the League of Nations was superseded by the United Nations, the more elaborate organization of the latter body involved the creation of a number of specialized agencies, including the World Health Organization (W.H.O.) into which the *Office International d'Hygiène Publique* was merged. In addition to carrying on the work of its predecessor it has sponsored projects for the investigation and control of malaria, tuberculosis, and venereal diseases, the promotion of maternal and child health, and the improvement of nutrition. In 1952 it opened a regional office at Brazzaville. Supplies for schemes for the betterment of health conditions carried out by the World Health Organization are made available by the United Nations Children's Emergency Fund (U.N.I.C.E.F.), which has an office in Africa. Assistance is to be provided by these organizations for work in Nigeria on yaws and leprosy. A pilot scheme for malaria control in the savannah country of Northern Nigeria is under consideration, and other activities include a large project for the eradication of malaria in French West Africa. It has an expert committee on yellow fever. In collaboration with the Food and Agriculture Organization it organized in 1952 a series of training courses for African personnel on the problems of nutrition.

There will be found in a later chapter a reference to a number of permanent institutions for scientific and technical co-operation which have, among other activities, sponsored conferences on medical subjects, such for example as that on nutrition at Dschang in 1949 or that on African medical education at Dakar in 1951. Reference will also be found there to the formation of institutions such as the *Bureau Pérmanent Inter-Africain de la Tsé-Tsé et de la Trypanosomiase.*[1]

One of the results of the First World War was to stimulate measures of co-operation between the medical personnel working in the British, French, and Belgian territories, more especially in West Africa. Since 1945 regular meetings have been held of the representatives of all Medical Departments in West Africa. Steps have been taken to accelerate the transmission of information on disease trends, and arrangements have been made for pathological specimens to be sent to the nearest laboratory irrespective of territorial boundaries.

[1] See below, p. 1611.

The voluntary agencies in the field of international health include that of the Friends (Quakers); the International Red Cross; the Rockefeller Foundation (especially its International Health Division); the International Unions against Tuberculosis, Cancer, and Venereal Diseases; the International Leprosy Association; the International Association for the Prevention of Blindness; the World Federation for Mental Health; and the International Union for Child Welfare.[1]

THE PAYMENT OF FEES FOR MEDICAL ASSISTANCE

A State hospital system is liable to fall short in one respect, namely, that it does not provide consultants able to visit patients in their own homes; and a demand inevitably arises either for private practitioners or for the grant of liberty to State doctors to take fees as private consultants. If this be granted, there is likely to arise, either in fact or in the impression conveyed to the public mind, a conflict between the duties for which the State and the patient are respectively paying. It is obviously preferable on many grounds to encourage the growth of an independent medical profession, but it may on occasion be advisable to give to members of a State service (and particularly to specialists) the right of private practice. At the same time the grant of this right may create a number of difficulties. In principle it appears unsuitable for members of the State Medical Service, paid for full-time Government duty, to devote even a small proportion of their time to private work, though it is often difficult to maintain this attitude when no other medical aid is available.

In the case of African patients, the policy regarding payment in return for medical services provided by the Government or Missions varies in different territories. In the French dependencies no payment is asked in return for medical attention, save in exceptional cases where patients can obviously afford it. As has been observed, however, it is usual in the smaller French hospitals for food to be provided by the patients' relatives and not by the State. In the Belgian Congo infectious diseases, including sleeping-sickness and all epidemic and endemic diseases, are treated free. In the case of other diseases and of accidents and most surgical cases, some payment is expected from patients who can afford it, but no private fee may be paid by Africans to a doctor in the State service or working under organizations such as Foréami or the *Croix Rouge du Congo*. Wherever possible the relatives of hospital patients are expected to contribute food to their support. In the British dependencies it is usual for Africans to receive free attention, but in many cases those who can afford to do so are required, both by the Government and Mission institutions, to make small payments for treatment or medicines.

[1] N. M. Goodman, *International Health Organizations and Their Work*, 1952, pp. 287, 300.

In support of the view that treatment should be gratuitous, it is said that in many parts of Africa medical attention is one of the few obvious returns which the African sees for his payment of tax. Furthermore, it is held that free treatment encourages the declaration of diseases which might otherwise be concealed. On the other hand, it is argued that Africans are more likely to appreciate medical aid if the service is not taken entirely for granted. Africans, like some Europeans, are said to appreciate benefits received in proportion to the amount they pay. An expensive injection is thought more effective than one costing less. The policy of elected African Governments in West Africa, however, is to extend free treatment as widely as possible, and there have been cases where a decision not to charge fees has been followed by a rapid increase in the number of persons coming for treatment.

HEALTH POLICIES

Nowhere in the world is it possible to study problems of health in detachment from environment, and it is clear that both physical and social conditions must play a specially important part in the consideration given to questions of disease and sickness in Africa. An understanding of the position regarding nutrition is, in particular, fundamental to the correct appreciation of the medical history of different communities of Africans and their relative liability to disease or power to resist its attacks. But apart from this special consideration the modern realization of the close relationship between environment and health has been reflected in the present-day outlook on medical and health policy in Africa. As in Europe, the recognition of the direct responsibility of environmental conditions for many diseases has emphasized the need for the improvement of working and living conditions and of imparting a knowledge of hygiene. This change of outlook has, moreover, coincided with the very general realization that measures which lead to an improvement in health will have a direct influence on African production, both in agriculture and industry.

It is, indeed, noteworthy that the larger industrial concerns in some areas have anticipated the recognition by the State of the need for the extension of public-health measures. They have realized that, low paid as the African labourer may often be, an ailing employee is expensive and ineffective. The lead given by some of these concerns in investigating the basis of a health dietary and in taking measures for the promotion of health conditions among employees and their dependants has been of direct benefit in the formation of a State health policy in Africa.

In the earlier days of colonial development medical authorities have tended, often perhaps unconsciously, to divide themselves into two schools of thought. The first, anxious for the credit of the European system of medicine, has concentrated its attention on the extension of its hospital work, the standards of which it can ensure by its own supervision. It has shown some suspicion of an expansion of medical facilities which would involve entrusting to inadequately trained hands the application of European methods in medicine and surgery.

The second school does not question the value of hospital work; it acknowledges, in particular, that it would not have been easy to convince the African of the benefits of European medicine if it had not been possible to exhibit to him the achievements of European surgery. But it is impressed with the narrowness of the field which the hospital under strict European supervision can command. It believes that, even if many risks have to be faced, much positive good can still be achieved by a wide extension of dispensaries under partially qualified assistants. That is especially the case if care is taken to see that the assistants in charge of dispensaries can transfer to the major institutions any cases which are beyond their competence. It points out, moreover, that in any case it is necessary to maintain an extensive organization for dealing with epidemic disease, both on the preventive and curative side, and that such an establish-ment must inevitably contain a considerable proportion of partly qualified men. The difference of view is sometimes expressed as a conflict between the advocates of preventive and of curative medicine. That expression, however, overstates the actual facts; often the difference of views is in practice only as to the best manner in which a medical organization can expend the relatively slender resources at its disposal.

It has been seen that the French have been content to maintain relatively few first-class hospitals, and for the rest to rely on the medical centre, with its attached dispensaries, and on mobile detachments for dealing with epidemic diseases. The expenditure on the building and equipment of the less important medical institutions is comparatively low. The food, as already remarked, is often supplied by the family of the patient. This is far from impairing the popularity of the institution with Africans. On the other hand the impression left on the African by the discipline and the isolation from friends which is the rule in many of the British hospitals must be a serious obstacle to their popularity. The French appear to lose, however, by the fact that many of their doctors, being on the military cadre, have little incentive to study African conditions. In addition to this, French policy has at times limited the expansion of medical facilities by refusing to open dispensaries where they cannot be supervised by a French-qualified medical man.

The Belgian system tended at the outset to rely largely on the application of intensive methods to 'clear up' affected areas. In practice this system has, by the force of circumstances, devoted its main efforts to dealing with certain types of epidemic disease, sleeping-sickness in particular. The Belgian Congo has maintained at the same time the normal hospital system, in which it has made an extensive use, as it has done in education also, of the facilities for nursing and the like furnished by the Belgian religious orders. The system has much that is attractive, and, in particular, benefits from the completeness of the studies made of the areas under intensive treatment. There can be no reason to doubt the efficacy of these methods, so long as the areas so treated are subsequently provided with the normal hospital and dispensary facilities.

A comparison between the benefit to public health to be derived from the pursuit of social-welfare schemes and that to be expected from the treatment of disease through the usual agencies of medical science is liable to raise issues which are to a certain extent unrealistic. An improvement in general health can be achieved only by effective co-operation between the various State services which affect the environment of the people. The improvement of nutrition must therefore be recognized as the concern of the Agricultural, Veterinary, and Education Departments as well as that of the health services. The medical authorities can do little more than indicate what deficiencies of diet exist, and it is for other departments to devise the manner in which these deficiencies may be made good or to induce the people to change their dietary. Emphasis on any one aspect of social welfare cannot produce permanent results unless proportionate attention is devoted to the others, and the policy of the medical service requires close co-ordination with that of other State Departments, and also with that of the non-official agencies, such as Missions or commercial companies, which are concerned with the development of the country.

The French and Belgian Administrations have in some instances used a certain measure of compulsion to enforce compliance with medical requirements. The concerted effort to eradicate an epidemic disease from a defined area may often assume the character of a military operation, and there can be no doubt that on occasion this has met with a large measure of success. The question of its general adoption is, however, one of principle, and the decision must depend on the likelihood of its yielding permanent results. It is axiomatic that the efficacy of any health service is dependent in the long run upon the attitude adopted towards the service by the people using it. Although some Governments have considered it necessary to impose compulsion (as, for example, the segregation of lepers, or the enforced attendance of certain groups of people for examination by the mobile units in the French territories) Africans quickly learn to appreciate the value of the curative services and to recognize that European medicine can be more efficacious than the remedies of African practitioners. The almost universal belief that disease is magically caused does not necessarily prevent Africans from accepting the methods indicated by European doctors for its prevention or cure.

Considerable advantage has been taken in Africa of the opportunities which school education affords for teaching the principles of hygiene, and many books in various African languages, as well as in simple English and French, have been prepared for this type of teaching. Instruction is also given at many maternity and other clinics. For the general public lectures, films, articles, and cartoons in African papers have been utilized in an effort to inculcate good health habits. The improvement of sanitation is the first lesson in that type of mass education which is not confined to literacy campaigns. The British Social Hygiene Council has a library of educational films which are lent for exhibition in parts of Africa. It also assists the campaign against venereal diseases by publishing a series of handbooks on biological teaching. Health weeks have been arranged by African local authorities, who work out their own programme and invite officers of the Medical Department to give the instruction. Practical demonstrations have normally been limited to a few elementary points: the main emphasis has, for example, been laid on the disposal of faeces and prevention of contamination of water supplies. There appears to have been in many quarters a significant response to these campaigns, as shown in the protection of water sources and the construction of latrines.

A NOTE ON THE PRINCIPAL DISEASES

There is no accepted standard by which the epidemic or other diseases of Africa can be classed in order of their importance, for both incidence and virulence differ from region to region. It is more convenient, therefore, to arrange them alphabetically.

Blackwater Fever

Blackwater fever is an occasional but serious sequel of *P. falciparum* (malignant tertian) malaria. It occurs particularly in persons brought up in non-malarious areas who go to live in intensely malarious countries and who do not take adequate precautions against infection. It is found especially in those who take quinine irregularly, or take it without proper supervision when an attack of malaria occurs. In the days when quinine was the only or the main drug available, blackwater fever was a very real danger. But since the introduction of the newer drugs—mepacrine, chloroquine, proguanil, and pyrimethamine—which can be successfully used to treat or prevent malaria, there has been a dramatic reduction in its incidence.[1]

---

[1] F. H. K. Green and G. Covell, eds., *History of the Second World War: Medical Research*, United Kingdom Medical Series, 1953, p. 163.

Africans who live from infancy in areas of endemic malaria, where the bite of an infected mosquito is a frequent occurrence, normally acquire considerable immunity to it and are not usually subject to blackwater fever. During the Second World War, however, African troops were often moved to places where malarial-control measures were in force and in consequence lost some degree of immunity. In consequence, on subsequent infection with *P. falciparum*, an increasing proportion of the troops who were not taking suppressive drugs suffered attacks of this disease.

Blindness

Though travellers and missionary workers in the past called attention to the prevalence of blindness in parts of Africa, it is only in recent years that it has been possible to form some estimate of its incidence. Such estimates cannot claim to be complete, but there can be no doubt of the severity of the incidence of blindness in certain regions. In a recent international survey it was stated that in Nigeria the incidence was in some parts 1,736 (possibly up to 2,000) per 100,000; in the Gold Coast it was put at 7,000 per 100,000 in one onchocerciasis area; in Sierra Leone 1,470 and 1,890 per 100,000 in two districts; and in Uganda 1,061 per 100,000. In Kenya 10 per cent. of the adults were said to be blind of one eye. In the Union of South Africa rates were given up to 351 per 100,000 for Africans and in some places probably 2,000.[1]

The incidence of blindness in East Africa is estimated at 0·5 per cent. of the African population taken as a whole.[2] The British Empire Society for the Blind[3] has quoted reliable evidence to show that in Kenya at least 50 per cent. of Africans in that country suffer from trachoma, either active or quiescent. In the Karamoja district of Uganda the figure is 43 per cent., the disease being more prevalent in the dry pastoral areas than in the moister agricultural districts.[4] It is estimated that about 150,000 to 200,000 people are affected in Kenya, Uganda, Tanganyika, and Zanzibar, and the Society, which already has a regional office in West Africa, proposes to set one up in East Africa.

Plans have been made for an East African campaign against blindness, and as part of this campaign a team of three specialists was at work in the Suk, Kamba, and Nyanza areas of Kenya in 1954. River blindness in the Nyanza area is transmitted by a small fly, *Simulium neavei*, and an intensive campaign has been undertaken for its destruction. A principal recommendation of Sir Clutha Mackenzie, who visited East Africa in this connexion, was to train the blind for farming and manual occupations

[1] A. Sorsby, 'The Incidence and Causes of Blindness: An International Survey', *British Journal of Ophthalmology*, Monograph Supplement XIV, 1950.
[2] British Empire Society for the Blind, *Blindness in East Africa*, Reports by Sir Clutha Mackenzie, 1953, p. 10. See also below, p. 1121.   [3] *Annual Report and Accounts, 1953*, p. 11.
[4] Uganda, *Annual Report of the Medical Department, 1953*, p. 11.

and to avoid overemphasis on literacy and academic education.[1] In Northern Rhodesia an analysis of case histories of 1,602 blind persons indicated that in almost all cases the blindness originated from disease which was at some stage preventable.

In West Africa, where an estimate has been made that 10 per cent. of the people of the Northern Territories of the Gold Coast suffer from onchocerciasis, there is a specially high incidence of blindness; in one investigation 293 of 913 outpatients attending general hospitals and clinics were blind. In this area a survey has been arranged to investigate not only the incidence of this filarial blindness (sometimes known as river blindness, owing to the fact that the fly which carries the filarial worm from man to man breeds in the rivers) but also possible methods of controlling the vector.[2]

Societies and organizations for the blind exist in the various countries of West Africa, in East Africa, and in the High Commission Territories of South Africa, under the auspices of the British Empire Society for the Blind.

Cancer

Cancer is probably less common in Africans than among the inhabitants of Europe and North America partly, no doubt, because a smaller proportion of Africans survive to the cancer age. One form, however, is relatively more common in Africans, namely, primary carcinoma of the liver, which is pre-eminently an affection of young adult males.[3] It is usually a sequel of cirrhosis of the liver, which itself may be a result of malnutrition or of infective hepatitis. It has been observed[4] that primary carcinoma of the liver formed 26 per cent. of the malignant tumours found at autopsy in a series of 65 reported from Southern Rhodesia. It was found[5] that 8·1 per cent. of 1,000 tumours examined in Nigeria began in the liver and were associated with cirrhosis; in French West Africa[6] primary cancer of the liver was found in 23 per cent. of 615 tumours, and in most cases it appeared to have been grafted on to long-standing cirrhosis.

In an analysis of reports of primary carcinoma of the liver it has been stated[7] that it varies from 15·3 to 50·9 per cent. in the various countries in which it was observed. There seems reason to hold that the Negro has no racial susceptibility to carcinoma, and that the disease is due to some intrinsic factor, either dietetic or infective.

[1] British Empire Society for the Blind, *Blindness in Africa, Reports by Sir Clutha Mackenzie*, 1953, pp. 18 ff.   [2] *The Times*, 14 July 1954. See also below, p. 1121.
[3] C. Berman, in *South African J. Med. Sci.*, vol. 6, 1941, p. 145.
[4] M. Gelfand, in *South African Med. J.*, vol. 23, 1949, p. 1010.
[5] B. G. T. Elmes and R. B. T. Baldwin, in *Ann. Trop. Med. & Parasit.*, vol. 41, 1947, p. 321.
[6] H. Jonchère, in *Bull. Méd. de l'Afrique Occidentale Française*, vol. 5, 1948, p. 247.
[7] C. Berman, *Primary Carcinoma of the Liver*, 1951.

Of the other malignant tumours, epithelioma of the skin is fairly common, and often arises from chronic tropical ulcer. Skin cancer is relatively more common in Europeans than in Africans; it seems that the European skin has less power than the African to resist exposure to the sun.[1] The other well-known forms of cancer are found, but are not common.

Cerebrospinal Meningitis

This disease has long been endemic in Africa, with occasional epidemic outbursts; the epidemic waves (for instance those in West Africa in 1906–7, 1921–8, 1934–43, 1944–5, and 1950 onwards)[2] seem to be increasing in extent; in 1951 some 11,514 and 7,286 cases were notified in French Equatorial Africa and French West Africa respectively, 9,869 in Nigeria, and 52,068 in the Sudan. The disease is often acute and rapidly fatal. In West Africa the season of maximum incidence is from January to May or June, a period when the climate is hot and extremely dry. At this season the nasal mucosa is adversely affected by the dry air, as well as by the *Harmattan* wind, and nasal discharges become common. Days are hot, but nights are cold, and the people sleep close to each other in their unventilated houses. The bacteria which cause the disease are present in the nasal passages of diseased persons and in a proportion of healthy persons, and are easily spread under these conditions. Epidemics tend to stop abruptly with the onset of the rains.

No satisfactory protective vaccine is yet available and control at present depends on the treatment given by field units or travelling teams. Sulphonamides are very effective if given early.[3] Penicillin is to be tried on a mass scale in the Sudan if another epidemic occurs.

Fevers of the Typhus Group

These fevers are caused by minute organisms of the genus *Rickettsia*, which are smaller than bacteria but larger than viruses; they are transmitted from man to man, or from animals to man, by biting arthropods, or in air or dust which is infectious when inhaled.

In Africa several of these diseases occur. Louse-borne typhus fever is the classical typhus (once known as gaol fever), and associated with bad housing, poverty, and uncleanliness. It is often associated with louse-borne relapsing fever, as in the epidemics which occurred after the potato famine of Ireland in the 1840s, and in those of the early part of the Second World War in North Africa. Louse-borne typhus is reported from West Africa

[1] Gelfand, op. cit.

[2] A. Campourcy and G. Moretti, in *J. Méd. de Bordeaux*, vol. 129, 1952, pp. 976–80.

[3] M. J. Colbourne, in *J. Trop. Med. & Hyg.*, vol. 54, 1951, pp. 3–13. D. W. Horne, in *J. Roy. San. Inst.*, vol. 71, 1951, pp. 573–88.

and South Africa; it can now (as it was in Italy during the Second World War) be controlled by dusting the clothing of louse-infected people with DDT so that this, the most dreaded of the typhus fevers, which has given rise to devastating epidemics in the past, has lost most of its terror. It is, however, relevant to observe that in Korea there are strains of lice which are resistant to DDT, and similar difficulties may arise elsewhere.

Flea-borne typhus is essentially a disease of rats, which occasionally spills over to man, and is found sporadically throughout Africa. Tick-borne typhus (carried by hard ticks very different from the soft ticks which carry tick-borne relapsing fever) is often a disease of dogs which affects man sporadically, as it were by accident. It, too, is found in many parts of Africa. Mite-borne typhus is indigenous to the Far East; there have been reports that it has been found in West Africa, but some doubt exists as to the validity of the diagnosis. Rickettsial pox is a mite-borne infection which was first discovered in the United States; the report that it occurs in French Equatorial Africa awaits confirmation.

Q fever (first described in Australia, where the letter Q indicated the query in the mind of the describer when the cause was not known) is a disease of animals, including cattle, sheep, and goats. It may be transmitted to man in dust infected by discharges from animals and inhaled or swallowed. It is usually a fairly mild infection, showing itself often as a form of pneumonia. It has been found in many parts of Africa.

Infectious Diseases

This section contains a brief note on the less important infectious diseases found in Africa south of the Sahara.

The known incidence of diphtheria is not high, most of the cases being reported in South Africa. There has been a slight increase in the number of notifications in recent years. In 1951 apparent increases in the incidence of whooping cough were observed in several countries of West Africa. Measles occurs sporadically, but no estimate of its true prevalence is yet possible. Epidemics do occur, however, as in Spanish Guinea (especially Fernando Po) in 1951. Scarlet fever is reported to be rare in Africa, and the recorded cases are certainly few.[1]

Intestinal Infections

Typhoid fever and the paratyphoid fevers occur throughout Africa and seem to be due mainly to the contamination of food by bacteria, which multiply in the intestines and give rise to these illnesses. Infections by other organisms (*Salmonella*) allied to the typhoid group are common, and several new members of that group have been found in Africa. The

[1] World Health Organization, *Epidemiological and Vital Statistics Report*, vol. v, 1952, pp. 226, 324, 332, 335, 365.

dysenteries, bacillary and amoebic, are widespread, and as no protective inoculation is available against them prevention is a matter of strict cleanliness in food handling and preparation. These diseases are common in African communities, even in the rural areas. They are, however, particularly fostered in the insanitary conditions of urban slums.

Cholera has not been observed in Africa south of the Sahara for many years, and the epidemic of 1947 which affected Egypt did not spread south.

Leishmaniasis

Leishmaniasis is a disease caused by a minute protozoon of the genus *Leishmania*, and transmitted from man to man, or from certain animals (dogs or field rodents) to man, by sandflies of the genus *Phlebotomus*. It occurs in two main forms, the visceral disease (*kala azar*) and the cutaneous disease (oriental sore).

Kala azar is not common south of the Sahara, though it has been reported from French West Africa[1] and Kenya. In the latter case an outbreak in the Kitui area indicated a disturbing spread from the foci in the Northern Frontier Province which gave rise to extensive infection in African troops during the Second World War. Minor outbreaks still continue at Kitui, which suggests that there may be a vector other than the sandfly.[2]

The cutaneous form has been reported from the French Sudan, where it is fairly widespread,[3] and also from Nigeria.[4]

Leprosy

Leprosy is widespread over all parts of Africa and the incidence is particularly high in those areas where the climate is relatively moist. The infection is not easily transmitted and is usually associated with long and intimate contact with an infected person, such as that of a child with its parent. Recent surveys have suggested the following infection rates: Uganda 33.5 per 1,000; Tanganyika 26.5; Northern Rhodesia 12.6; Nyasaland 14;[5] Kenya 10.2;[6] Belgian Congo 5.5;[7] Nigeria 16 (up to 50–60 in some places); Gambia about 25 per 1,000.

Until recently the only useful treatment of leprosy was by injection of chaulmoogra oil derivatives, which were moderately successful if started early. The discovery of the value of the sulphone drugs (some of which

---

[1] G. Curasson, B. Sissoko, and B. Laurence, in *Bull. Soc. Path. Exot.*, vol. 30, 1937, p. 684; P. Mornet, in ibid. vol. 33, 1940, pp. 253 ff.

[2] N. R. E. Fendall, in *East African Med. J.*, vol. 30, 1953, p. 269.

[3] P. Kervran, in *Ann. Parasit. Humaine et Comparée*, vol. 21, 1946, p. 155.

[4] B. G. T. Elmes and R. N. Hall, in *Trans. Roy. Soc. Trop. Med. & Hyg.*, vol. 37, 1944, p. 437.

[5] J. R. Innes, in *East African Med. J.*, vol. 27, 1950, pp. 459–65; ibid. vol. 28, 1951, pp. 21–28, 168–73. *Internat. J. Leprosy*, vol. 18, 1950, pp. 507–17.

[6] J. R. Innes, in *East African Med. J.*, vol. 26, 1949, pp. 32–35.

[7] A. Dubois, 'Section des sciences naturelles et médicales', *Mém. I.R.C.B.*, vol. x, no. 2, 1940.

can effectively be taken by mouth) has greatly improved the situation. The modern practice is to create leprosy settlements, with hospital accommodation, and outlying leprosy villages served by travelling teams which visit them regularly. Examples of this kind of organization are to be found in the Uzuakoli, Itu, and Oji river institutions of Nigeria, where work of the greatest value has been done for many years and where there are thousands of resident patients. Another instance is at Makate in Tanganyika, staffed by the British Empire Leprosy Relief Association, where there are about 1,000 patients cultivating 3,000 acres of land. An important feature of such an organization is that patients should be encouraged to work and should be paid for their work. Treatment is given according to calculated schedules, and the effects are supervised by visiting or resident medical staffs. The compulsory segregation of leprosy patients is now rarely attempted, since it encourages the concealment of the disease. It is still, however, practised in South Africa, though the law is in this case applied with discretion. Voluntary admissions to leprosy institutions have increased since the results of the sulphone treatment became generally known.

Patients are now encouraged to come for treatment in the early stages, when success is most likely, and leprous patients are encouraged to bring their children. The segregation of infants at birth from leprous mothers is difficult, but is occasionally possible. In the coastal area of Kenya leprosy patients have lately been treated solely as outpatients, returning each week to hospital for a supply of tablets. There are indications that this procedure is successful, and it certainly attracts the patients.

Uganda, where there are said to be 80,000 persons infected with leprosy, now has five 'settlement villages' where patients cultivate their own plots of ground.[1] In the case of leprosy patients the various Mission organizations of Africa have a record of devoted service. It is usually held that one of the most important factors in preventing leprosy is the raising of the general standard of living. If the fear of leprosy can be removed, and if the patients can be induced to come early for treatment, there is no doubt that modern methods may very materially reduce the incidence of the disease. In the Union of South Africa the incidence of leprosy had fallen to 0·7 per 1,000 in 1954 and it is officially claimed that it is now under control.[2] In Southern Rhodesia intensive treatment by sulphone drugs has been so successful that it seems likely that this disease will be eventually eradicated. Discharges from the *leprosaria* in 1953 outnumbered the admissions.

Special mention should be made of the British Empire Leprosy Relief Association (B.E.L.R.A.), which was founded in 1924 'with the aim of

[1] *Background to Uganda*, no 63, July 1954.
[2] *S.A.S.*, no. 93, 15 November 1954, p. 7.

spreading the knowledge that modern science could treat and finally prevent the spread of leprosy'. Though the activities of the Association are not restricted to Africa the major part of its work overseas is done there. It undertakes research, trains doctors, and assists in the building and maintenance of treatment centres.[1] In 1952 the Association made grants for leprosy work amounting to £44,902.

Malaria

Malaria is widespread in Africa except in certain mountainous areas and in the more southerly part of the Union of South Africa.[2] Three main types are found, corresponding to the three common species of malaria parasite which affects man, *Plasmodium vivax*, *P. malariae*, and *P. falciparum*. Malaria due to *P. vivax* is known as benign tertian, and though it causes much ill health is rarely fatal. *P. malariae* causes quartan malaria, which is also rarely fatal and is not common.

P. *falciparum* is the source of malignant tertian malaria, which is a serious infection and if not properly treated is quite frequently fatal to Europeans, though the African populations appear to have acquired a measure of resistance to it. In those areas where it is most prevalent (that is, where the transmission is perennial and frequent) they appear to acquire in childhood enough resistance to be able to live on tolerable terms with the malarial parasites. In places where the transmission is seasonal, however, immunity appears to diminish in the off-season, and when transmission starts again people suffer severely from attacks of fever. The occurrence of epidemics is then possible.

The malaria parasites are transmitted to man by various species of the *Anopheles* mosquito. The African vectors include some of the most dangerous carriers in the world. Of these the principal is *Anopheles gambiae*, which is found throughout tropical Africa and as far south as the Union. *A. gambiae* breeds prolifically in a great variety of pools of water open to the sun—even in seepages and the countless puddles left in the rainy season in ruts and animal hoof-marks. One variety (*A. gambiae melas*) breeds in the brackish water of the mangrove swamps in West Africa and East Africa. Since *A. gambiae* breeds in the rain pools its prevalence is to some extent seasonal. In most parts of its range (except in high country where conditions become too cold for survival during part of the year) there exist permanent collections of water suitable for breeding throughout the year. Since there are (with the possible exception of the chimpanzee)[3] no animal reservoirs of human malaria, transmission takes place by those

---

[1] The British Empire Leprosy Relief Association, *The Story of BELRA*, 1953, p. 4.

[2] The degree of endemicity in different regions has been analysed by F. J. C. Cambournac, in *Malaria Conference in Equatorial Africa*, World Health Organization, Technical Report Series no. 38, 1951, pp. 10–11.

[3] J. Rodhain, in *Ann. Soc. Belge de Méd. Trop.*, vol. 28, 1948, pp. 39–49.

anophelines which seek man; the anthropophilic strains of *A. gambiae* appear to have a remarkable intensity of preference for human blood.

The other principal vector of malaria is *A. funestus*, which breeds in the edges of streams where the water is somewhat shaded by vegetation. *A. funestus* tends to breed throughout the year and is often responsible for the transmission of malaria when *A. gambiae* is least prevalent. It is very strongly attracted to man.

A number of modern drugs have proved to be very effective in the treatment of malaria. Drugs are also used as preventives, especially by Europeans. At present the most popular drugs are proguanil and chloroquine; the action of quinine is less certain. The use of preventive drugs has been applied on an experimental scale among African children with good results. Their regular administration to adolescents and adults, however, except for temporary purposes or in controlled communities such as groups of labourers, would involve obvious practical difficulties.

The control of malaria has been transformed[1] by the discovery of the residual insecticides (DDT, BHC, dieldrin, &c.) which may be deposited in finely divided particles on to a surface, such as the inside wall of a house, on which mosquitoes alight to rest. When the insect comes into contact with the particles, the substance is absorbed through the cuticle and within a few hours proves fatal to the mosquito. The residual insecticides remain lethal to mosquitoes for long periods if applied to materials which do not absorb them, or which are not exposed to wind and rain. The mud walls of African houses, however, are far from ideal surfaces, and insecticides applied to them tend to lose their power relatively quickly, so that repeated application is necessary. The possibility that *Anopheles* mosquitoes may become resistant to insecticides cannot be ruled out, though no evidence that this has occurred with African species has yet been offered. Special consideration is being given to this factor in Southern Rhodesia.[2] DDT is also used as a mosquito larvicide. It is applied in oily solution to the surface of water in which mosquitoes breed and is highly successful. But the application needs to be repeated at intervals of ten days or so.

The question of the resistance to malaria developed in people exposed to it is important in relation to schemes of malarial control in Africa. The subject has become a controversial one. On the one hand it is argued that a very considerable degree of control is now possible by the use of residual insecticides. In rural areas, however, where transmission is normally intense and perennial, the resistance previously developed in the people through repeated infection will largely be lost if these means are

---

[1] For some earlier work in the control of malaria, particularly in Northern Rhodesia, see articles by Sir A. Watson in *The Times*, 1 July 1932, 10 February 1940.

[2] *Southern Rhodesia, Report on the Public Health, 1953*, C.S.R. 22, 1954, pp. 2, 8.

employed. Any unusual conditions which lead to multiplication of the carrier anophelines will then react on a now susceptible population and may cause epidemic malaria with high rates of disabling disease and death.[1] Any relaxation of control measures after they have once been successfully applied would have a like result, and the population might be in a worse state than it was before. The opposing view is that where tolerance of malaria is developed it is only at a high cost of illness and death in young children; and that even when tolerance is achieved the disease is a continual drain on the health of the people. It is also argued that control by anti-mosquito measures and by drugs would result in better health and that if, for any reason, epidemic malaria did occur it could be dealt with rapidly and effectively.

It must, however, be left for experience to decide which of these two considerations should carry greater weight. Meanwhile there can be no question of the strength of the case for pursuing malarial control by the use of insecticides in the towns and in those rural areas where transmission is seasonal. Even there the difficulties are sufficiently formidable. Although control of malaria by anti-mosquito measures has been successful in relatively small areas—islands like Cyprus and Mauritius, for instance—the problem of widespread control in rural tropical Africa is much greater because of the danger of reinvasion. The habits of *A. gambiae*, moreover, render control much more difficult than in the case of some of the American and Asian species.[2] Some useful experience may be gained of control measures in rural areas from the Sokoto Malaria Scheme in Northern Nigeria opened early in 1954. Some 80,000 homes had been sprayed by the end of the year and a marked reduction in mosquitoes was reported.

A Conference, which was held at Kampala in 1950 under the auspices of the World Health Organization and the Commission for Technical Co-operation in Africa South of the Sahara (C.C.T.A.),[3] recognized the difficulties involved but was strongly in favour of pressing forward with measures of control.[4] The success which followed the spraying of limited areas in Southern Rhodesia induced the Government to undertake an intensive spraying campaign in 1955. The intention was to create a malaria-free belt round two-thirds of the colony, using the insecticide BHC. That malaria can be entirely abolished has been shown in the Copperbelt of Northern Rhodesia—a demonstration which has been described as one of the outstanding achievements of modern medicine.[5]

[1] D. B. Wilson, P. C. O. Garnham, and M. H. Swellengrebel, in *Trop. Dis. Bull.*, vol. 47, 1950, pp. 677–98.
[2] M. A. C. Dowling, in *Trans. Roy. Soc. Trop. Med. & Hyg.*, vol. 47, 1953, pp. 177–98.
[3] See below, p. 1611.
[4] World Health Organization, *Malaria Conference in Equatorial Africa*, Technical Report Series no. 38, 1951.
[5] H. Smith, 'Medicine in Africa as I Have Seen It', *African Affairs*, January 1955, p. 28.

Mental Disease in Africans

It was inevitable that the medical organizations in Africa, preoccupied with the insistent need for combating epidemic disease and with the problems arising from the unusually low standards of physical health among the African people, should have given relatively less study to the problems of mental disorder. The field has not, however, been entirely neglected. The most recent and probably the most comprehensive survey of African psychology was published in 1953 by J. C. Carothers.[1] He reached the conclusion that the incidence of insanity among rural Africans is probably much lower than the incidence in Europe and America. Thus he quotes for England and Wales the figure 3·9 per 1,000 of the population notified as insane and under care, and for the parts of Kenya specially studied, having a population of 616,000, the figure given is 0·37 per cent. Figures quoted from other parts of Africa (excluding one of 4 per 1,000 in a very small population in a sleeping-sickness area) reach up to 0·96 per 1,000, but Carothers concludes that 'there is evidence of a disparity between the total incidence of mental derangement in rural Africa, on the one hand, and in western Europe and North America, on the other. . . . In regard to mental deficiency, however, little can be said. . . .' Apart from any question of the relative incidence of insanity in Europe and Africa respectively, there is some ground for holding that the incidence of psychoses in Africans is relatively high in those who have become separated from their tribal communities and have lost their tribal culture.

All degrees of mental deficiency occur. Physical disease is important in the aetiology of mental disturbance, and in this respect sleeping-sickness, syphilis, puerperal fever, malaria, yaws, alcoholism, and various infections, especially pulmonary, have been mentioned.[2] Epilepsy is common, and in a proportion of cases there is some degree of mental derangement, with confusional states, twilight states, and furor; dementia also occurs. 'Schizophrenia is the chronic form of insanity in Africans as in Europeans—a fact reflected in all figures concerning inmates of African mental hospitals.'[3] Persecutory delusions are the rule. There is in rural Africans a strong belief in the intervention of supernatural beings or of occult forces, and the delusional content of schizophrenia is in some parts of Africa almost invariably concerned with the ramifications of the 'fetish system'. But Laubscher (quoted by Carothers) makes the point that schizophrenia is the common psychosis of the rural African; he infers that constitutional factors play the major role, and that the environmental factors have latterly been overemphasized.

[1] J. C. Carothers, *The African Mind in Health and Disease, A Study in Ethnopsychiatry*, World Health Organization, Monograph Series no. 17, 1953. See also above, p. 55.
[2] J. C. Chevenau (1937) and H. Aubin (1939), quoted by Carothers, op. cit.
[3] Ibid. pp. 139, 141.

Of the psychoneuroses, anxiety occurs; it is frequently felt to be an outcome of bewitchment. *Anorexia nervosa,* cardiac neuroses, and sexual neuroses are also mentioned. Hysteria is relatively common, but obsessional neurosis is rare. Among the unclassified cases Carothers mentions temporary insanity in the form of sudden and violent rages which may lead to homicide. In general, he says, 'it seems that the rather clear distinction that exists in Europeans between the "conscious" and "unconscious" elements of mind does not exist in rural Africans. ... Emotion easily dominates the entire mind; and, when it does, the latter's tenuous grip on the world of "things" is loosened, and frank confusion takes the place of misinterpretation.'

Parasitic Worms and Helminthic Diseases

Africans are heavily infected with worms, some of which, like certain trematodes (flukes) and the filarial worms, live in the blood or tissues, and others, like the tape-worms and hookworms, in the intestine. The extent of disability caused by infection with worms is a matter of dispute. They compete with the human host for food, and where the standard of nutrition is low this drain on the resources, and especially the protein resources, of the host may be serious. In the 'hungry season' of villages in Gambia, for example, the obvious signs of malnutrition can sometimes be eliminated by treating with drugs the parasitic diseases from which the patients suffer, while leaving the diet unchanged. On the other hand, anaemia due to hookworm is not commonly found unless the diet of the host is deficient, which means that the elements lost to the worms cannot be replaced. There seems to be evidence, therefore, that these infections represent a drain on health which, though not great in a well-fed community, may be most serious in a population living near subsistence level.

Actually, the relationship between parasites and hosts, in regard to health, is imperfectly understood. Many millions of Africans are infested with the bilharzia worm *Schistosoma haematobium,* but those who are most in contact with labourers infested with it can see little evidence that it reduces their capacity for work, provided they are reasonably well fed. On the other hand, infection with the guinea-worm, *Dracunculus medinensis,*[1] leads to ulceration of the leg and frequently renders the patient unable to work for weeks; but in this case the disability is not due directly to worm infection but to the bacterial invasion to which it leads. Again, infection with the filarial worm *Onchocerca volvulus*[2] often impairs eyesight to the point of blindness. The filarial worm *Wuchereria bancrofti* is the cause of the gross disabling conditions of elephantiasis.[3]

The worms which infect man in Africa may be divided into three groups—the trematodes or flukes, the cestodes or tape worms, and the

---

[1] See below, p. 1121.   [2] Ibid.   [3] Ibid.

nematodes or round worms. As regards the trematodes, the Schistosomes (or bilharzia worms) are widespread. These worms lay their eggs in the human bladder or intestine, and if released or discharged into fresh water the eggs hatch out, liberating an embryo which enters the tissues of certain snails. After a period of development embryos of a different kind are released into the water and may penetrate the skin or mucous membranes of persons who bathe in or drink it. They are most commonly found in the water of irrigation canals, dams, ponds, or slow-flowing streams. In many parts of Africa almost all the people are infected with these worms by the time they reach adult life. Infection rates of 40 to 60 per cent., and in places up to 95 per cent., have been reported. But the true extent of the interference with health is not known. Treatment of schistosomiasis is moderately successful, but it must remain of limited value so long as the opportunities for reinfection are so universal.

In Egypt and Southern Rhodesia copper salts have been used on a large scale to kill the vector snails. Work on different molluscicides is being carried out in various parts of the world, but the enormous extent of infected water to be dealt with presents a most formidable problem. The danger of infection with bilharziasis owing to the expansion of irrigation is fully appreciated in some quarters, as for instance in Southern Rhodesia.[1] Consideration will have to be given to this problem in carrying out projects for hydroelectric installations at the Kariba Gorge in Southern Rhodesia and the Volta river project in the Gold Coast, both of which involve the creation of large inland lakes.[2]

The cestodes, or tapeworms, are common throughout tropical and subtropical Africa. The eggs infect the flesh of pigs or cattle, and if this is eaten without adequate cooking they hatch into adult worms in the human intestine; one of the objects of the inspection of meat is to prevent this occurrence. A serious disease is caused by the cestode *Echinococcus granulosus*, which lays its eggs in the faeces of infected dogs. If the faeces are swallowed the eggs may develop into enormous larvae in the tissues of the animal which swallows them, including man. Treatment is unusually difficult.

The commonest nematode which infects man in Africa is the hookworm. Surveys in tropical Africa have revealed infection rates up to 95 per cent. in Portuguese Guinea, French West Africa, Kenya, and the Rhodesias. Male and female hookworms live in the small intestine, taking blood from the host as nourishment. The microscopic eggs are passed out in the faeces and the larvae enter the human body by penetrating the skin, where they cause the condition known as ground itch. These worms, about half an inch in length, are capable of causing anaemia if present in large

---

[1] *Southern Rhodesia, Report on the Public Health, 1953*, C.S.R. 22, 1954, p. 8.
[2] See above, pp. 987, 1001.

numbers in a person living on a poor diet. Treatment is easy and effective, but reinfection is the rule in the absence of proper care in the disposal of faeces.

The round worm *Ascaris lumbricoides*, which resembles a fairly large earthworm, is common in children throughout Africa, infection rates up to 50 per cent. being quoted in surveys. The children both contaminate the soil and introduce the contamination into their own mouths at play. Treatment is effective, but reinfection is the rule. Prevention is difficult.

The filarial worms have already been mentioned; those which live in the tissues produce embryos that are picked out by mosquitoes or certain biting flies when they feed. The commonest filarial worm is the *Wuchereria bancrofti* which is found throughout West and East Africa, especially along the coasts and round the great lakes. Infection rates up to 40 per cent. are reported in endemic areas. Its embryos are found in the blood in large numbers at night. It is the cause of the gross disabling condition of elephantiasis, though only a few of those infected progress to this stage. The day filaria (*Loa loa*) is found in West Africa; it is transmitted by mangrove flies of the genus *Chrysops*. The Calabar swellings it causes are very troublesome. The Colonial Medical Research Unit working in the British Cameroons is producing interesting findings on the ecology of the vectors.

Onchocerciasis, which is infection with the filarial worm *Onchocerca volvulus*, is much more serious. It is reported from all parts of tropical Africa, but the highest rates are found in villages close to rivers and streams, and in the Belgian Congo it has been found in up to 88 per cent. of the population of such places. The embryos of the adult worms (which live in the skin) are picked out by the black fly *Simulium* when it bites. The effect of this is to cause troublesome skin nodules, and, more important, infections of the eyes which quite often lead to blindness. This filarial blindness is a major medical problem. Treatment with drugs is only partly successful, but a new hope for control has been found in the treatment of the streams in which the vector fly *Simulium* breeds, and by continuous dosing with DDT in small quantities.[1] The application of DDT to the river Nile in 1952 resulted in an appreciable reduction in the number of *Simulium* flies up to the end of 1953.[2] The team working in Kenya on the problem of blindness in 1954 have discovered the larvae or pupae of the *Simulium neavei* on crabs in the streams in Nyanza Province.

Guinea-worm (*Dracunculus medinensis*) is recorded from Uganda and northern Kenya and occasionally elsewhere in East Africa, but it is much more common in West Africa, rates up to 16 per cent. being recorded in Nigeria, and up to 23·5 per cent. in Portuguese Guinea.

[1] P. C. C. Garnham and J. P. McMahon, in *Bull. Entom. Res.*, vol. 37, 1947, pp. 619–28.
[2] *Uganda, Annual Report of the Medical Department, 1953*, p. 16.

Plague

Outbreaks of plague are of relatively minor importance in Africa as compared with the vast and very fatal epidemics of Asia. The disease is due to a bacillus (*Pasteurella pestis*) and is essentially a disease of field rodents and rats which is transmitted by their fleas and conveyed to man when conditions permit. Plague caused the Black Death in the fourteenth century and the Great Plague of London of 1666; it was spread widely by ships at the end of the nineteenth century, and is now found in most tropical countries. It is prevalent in field rodents throughout the greater part of Africa. From time to time, however, they invade the haunts of rodents which live in association with domestic rats or with human habitations, thus conveying the disease to human beings. Outbreaks caused in this way are usually small, but there may be many of them at the same time in areas with similar conditions. In Bechuanaland, for instance, the disease was widespread in 1944–5, when floods drove infected gerbils into contact with semi-domestic mice.[1] In many places this pattern of association between field rodents, domestic rodents, and man leads to periodic outbreaks, the transmitting agents being the rat fleas. There is some evidence that plague can be transmitted from man to man by the human flea *Pulex irritans*, but this is rare, though it has been recorded in Morocco.[2]

Plague normally takes the bubonic form, but it occasionally affects the lungs, causing pneumonia. In this condition the patient's sputum is laden with virulent plague bacilli, which are apt to be scattered into the air when the patient coughs. In such cases there is very serious danger that the attendants of the patient will contract the same disease. This was a most fatal condition until the recent discovery of the sulphonamide drugs and the antibiotics (especially streptomycin).

The use of the new insecticides (especially DDT) can greatly reduce the danger of plague epidemics. To combat outbreaks of the disease immunization of man with killed or live (avirulent) vaccines has been widely practised, especially in Madagascar, but also in South Africa and elsewhere. The presence of plague in rodents is still regarded as a serious potential threat to man, and an energetic campaign is being fought against field rodents and rats in the city of Johannesburg and for many miles round it.

Pneumonia

Pneumonia is one of the commonest causes of death in Africans and has proved a serious problem in industry. Its prevalence among miners on the Rand led to intensive investigation. This work suggested the advis-

[1] D. H. S. Davis, in *South African Med. J.*, vol. 20, 1946, pp. 462–7, 511–15.
[2] G. Blanc and M. Baltazard, in *C. R. Acad. Sci.*, vol. 213, 1941, pp. 813–16.

ability of housing labourers in small cubicles containing only a few men, each having a bunk separated from the others by an effective partition, rather than in rooms accommodating large numbers. There is some evidence that in such barracks the Africans who come from the tropical areas are more susceptible to the disease than those indigenous to South Africa, and it seems possible that the tropical Africans fall ill when on arrival at the mines they encounter the micro-organisms of pneumonia, against which they have little resistance.[1] Deep mines are usually very hot, and sudden emergence into cold air at the end of a shift may be harmful to the miners. Modern drugs—the sulphonamides and the antibiotics—have greatly improved the response to treatment.

Poliomyelitis

Poliomyelitis is reported from most parts of Africa, but the number of verified cases is small; there were, for instance, only 2,760 recorded cases in the whole continent in 1951,[2] though actual incidence must undoubtedly be far greater than this. The disease is caused by a virus, and there is evidence that many persons are infected and overcome the infection without serious illness. Infection is largely spread through faecal contamination from patients or healthy carriers.[3] The virus also gains entry into the mouth through personal contact with an infective person.[4] It may occasionally be spread by flies. Epidemics have occurred in Africa, as in the Belgian Congo and Angola in 1951. In other parts of the world the incidence tends to increase, and epidemics have occurred in many of the more developed countries. The same tendency will probably show itself in Africa.

Relapsing Fever

Two forms of this disease, which is due to a spirochaete, are known in Africa, namely the louse-borne form (common in North Africa and parts of West Africa) and the tick-borne form (found throughout the continent). The former is transmitted from man to man by infected lice and tends to occur in epidemics when for any reason people herd together. It depends to a great extent on the clothing, habits, and cleanliness of the people, and also on styles of hairdressing, some of which favour louse infestation.

Tick-borne relapsing fever is conveyed by soft ticks (*Ornithodorus*) which live in the walls and floors of buildings and which feed on man and other animals but do not remain on their bodies. It is closely associated with the rest houses which are scattered throughout Africa. Africans travelling to

[1] D. Ordman, in *Proc. Transvaal Mine Med. Officers' Ass.*, vol. 28, 1949, p. 75.
[2] World Health Organization, *Epidemiological and Vital Statistics Report*, vol. v, 1952, p. 147.
[3] A. B. Sabin, in *J. Pediatrics, St. Louis*, vol. 39, 1951, p. 519.
[4] W. H. Bradley, in *Medical Officer*, vol. 90, 1953, p. 251.

work in the Union of South Africa from countries farther north, where the disease is more prevalent, carry infected ticks with them and, since these are allowed to bite from time to time, immunity is maintained by the carrier. Relapsing fever may be a severe and fatal disease and may also lead, in a certain proportion of those who recover, to permanent damage to the eye.

Silicosis

Silicosis is a disease due to the deposition of fine dust containing silica (usually in the form of quartz) in the lungs of persons who consistently breathe air containing such dust. It is found in miners and in other persons engaged in certain work such as quarrying, tunnelling, sand-blasting, &c. The penetration of the minute particles of quartz into the lungs causes fibrosis of the tissues. The fibrosis tends to predispose to tuberculosis.

This disease is one of the major health problems of the mining industries of Africa. The gold-bearing rocks of the Witwatersrand are largely composed of quartz, and similar rocks are encountered in the mines of the Gold Coast and the Belgian Congo, and in the copper-mines of Northern Rhodesia. In most parts of Africa silicosis is recognized as an industrial hazard which should be prevented as far as possible by the institution of known measures of dust suppression, and for which compensation should be awarded. Legislation has been introduced in these countries, especially in the Union of South Africa, to enforce the periodic examination of workmen and the employment of protective measures.[1] One of the most recent pieces of legislation bearing on this subject is the Northern Rhodesian Silicosis Ordinance. Legislation of this nature is likely to be adopted by other countries; it covers 'any form of pneumoconiosis due to inhalation of mineral dust'.

Sleeping-sickness (Trypanosomiasis)

Human trypanosomiasis in Africa is of two kinds,[2] caused respectively by *Trypanosoma gambiense* and *T. rhodesiense*. The former infection is widespread in West Africa and Uganda, and is transmitted from man to man by certain types of tsetse fly (*Glossina palpalis*, *G. tachinoides*) which haunt the rivers and lake shores.[3] The severe epidemic which broke out along the shores of Lake Victoria in the early years of the century has already been mentioned;[4] in West Africa the opening of new communications and the development of trading facilities has caused the disease to

---

[1] *O.Y.S.A.*, *1949*, pp. 319–24. Ibid. *1952–53*, pp. 318–22.

[2] The term *Nagana* (a Zulu word) so frequently used in South Africa refers to trypanosomiasis in cattle, not in human beings.

[3] See above, p. 874, and map on p. 877.   [4] See above, p. 1067.

spread very widely. Measures of control include the mass treatment of infected persons by travelling or stationary clinics, and the removal from the watercourses and lake shores of those types of woody vegetation where the flies breed. In addition the French and Belgian authorities have recently used drugs (especially pentamidine and lomidine) on a large scale as prophylactics, giving injections every six months. Pentamidine is a British discovery. These injections give protection for several months, but the effect gradually wears off.

Repeated mass prophylaxis of this kind has undoubtedly led to a great reduction in incidence. It is claimed, for instance, in Ruanda Urundi that the incidence of new cases fell from 1·07 per cent. of the population in 1946 to 0·07 in 1950.[1] In Nigeria the clearing of vegetation to prevent the breeding of tsetse has been combined with large-scale settlement schemes, as for instance in the Anchau corridor, to which reference has been made in a previous chapter.[2] In the Gold Coast, after ten years of anti-tsetse measures, human trypanosomiasis has ceased to be a serious public-health problem. It has, however, been suggested that the creation of the great inland lake involved by the construction of the hydroelectric installation on the Volta river may lead to the spread of trypanosomiasis.[3]

The second type of infection, namely, *Trypanosoma rhodesiense*, is found in East Africa. It is transmitted from man to man (and possibly from wild game to man) by *Glossina morsitans*, *G. swynnertoni*, and (more rarely) by *G. pallidipes*. The first two of these flies feed chiefly on wild game in the fairly open wooded country, and consequently the distribution of the diseases they carry differs greatly from that of *T. gambiense* infection.[4] *T. rhodesiense* infection is found in small human communities within easy reach of the woodland favoured by these flies. It has been dealt with in East Africa by collecting the people into larger settlements which the flies avoid. This policy has met with considerable success. In Southern Rhodesia and Tanganyika control of *G. morsitans* has been attempted by the systematic shooting of the game on which the flies live.[5] In East Africa it is generally accepted that control of the trypanosomiasis of domestic stock is as important to human welfare as that of the trypanosomiasis of man. The trypanosomes which infect cattle, namely *T. brucei*, *T. congolense*, and *T. vivax*, are also transmitted by varieties of the tsetse fly.

On the human side there are a number of drugs in medical use, of which

---

[1] M. Baudart, *Bureau permanent interafricain de la tsé-tsé et de la trypanosomiase*, no. 149/0, Leopold-ville, 1951 (mimeographed report).

[2] T. A. M. Nash, *The Anchau Rural Development and Settlement Scheme*, 1948. See also above, p. 908. J. Huxley, 'Health and Adaptation: Thoughts from West Africa', *Health Horizon*, January 1946.

[3] G. Macdonald, 'Medical Implications of the Volta River Project', *Trans. Roy. Soc. Trop. Med. & Hyg.*, vol. 49, 1955, p. 13.

[4] See above, p. 874.   [5] See above, p. 879.

the German Bayer 205 (now known as antrypol) and the British trypanosomide are the most used. Pentamidine, already referred to, is mainly used as a prophylactic. Antrycide, the most recent discovery, is mainly used for the treatment of cattle.[1]

As regards trypanosomiasis research,[2] reference has already been made to the Tsetse Fly and Trypanosomiasis Committee at the British Colonial Office. The main centres of research in the British dependencies are the East African Tsetse and Trypanosomiasis Research and Reclamation Organization (E.A.T.T.R.R.O.) and the West African Institute for Trypanosomiasis Research (W.A.I.T.R.). The administrative centre for East Africa is at Sukulu (near Tororo) in Uganda. In addition there are laboratories at Shinyanga and Tinde (Tanganyika), Kabete and Mariakani (Kenya), and Entebbe (Uganda).[3] The buildings of the W.A.I.T.R. at Kaduna and Vom in Nigeria were completed in 1951.

In the Portuguese territories, particularly Mozambique and Portuguese Guinea, special trypanosomiasis organizations are responsible for both research and field work. In the Belgian Congo Foréami is particularly active in human trypanosomiasis work, and in the French territories the same is true of the *Service Général d'Hygiène Mobile et de Prophylaxie* (S.G.H.M.P.). Information regarding current research in trypanosomiasis is circulated by the *Bureau Pérmanent Interafricain de le Tsé-Tsé et de la Trypanosomiase* (B.P.I.T.T.) at Leopoldville. This was instituted after the Conference on Trypanosomiasis held at Brazzaville in 1948.[4]

Smallpox

Although the general practice of vaccination against smallpox has helped to control this disease in Africa, there still remain possibilities of epidemic outbreaks. It will be realized that with the establishments at present available there must be large numbers of Africans who escape vaccination.

Cases are recorded every year from most of the countries south of the Sahara, sometimes in large numbers (for example 20,948 cases with 3,420 deaths in Nigeria in 1950).[5] In some African countries the mild form known as *amaas* (or variola minor) is seen. A recent report[6] on world incidence in the period 1936–50 (which in fact contains data relating to cases reported from 1920 onwards) embodies statistics of incidence and

---

[1] See above, p. 880.

[2] See C. Wilcocks, J. F. Carson, and R. L. Sheppard, *A Survey of Recent Work on Trypanosomiasis, 1946*.

[3] *East Africa High Commission, East African Tsetse and Trypanosomiasis Research and Reclamation Organization, Annual Report, 1951*; ibid. *1952*.

[4] *Conférence africaine sur la tsé-tsé et la trypanosomiase, Brazzaville, 2–8 février 1948*, Toulouse, 1950.

[5] World Health Organization, *Epidemiological and Vital Statistics Report*, vol. vi, 1953, p. 45.

[6] Ibid. p. 227.

death-rates, though with the obvious proviso that the reported cases rarely approach the actual figures. For the Belgian Congo the figures given are 19 and 1 per 100,000; Niger (French West Africa) 13½ and 1 per 100,000; and Nigeria 12 and 1¾ per 100,000. Most other territories have returned figures of incidence of about 1 per 100,000, but few of these figures can be accepted as being really reliable. In Southern Rhodesia the epidemic which began in 1946 was not eradicated until 1953 and had a case mortality rate of nearly 16 per cent. There is a danger of smallpox becoming epidemic, once it is introduced, if the 'vaccination protection level' falls below 110 per 1,000 of the population.[1]

Tropical Ulcer

Tropical ulcer, sometimes known as tropical phagedaenic ulcer, is an ulcer of the skin, usually of the legs, which generally originates in a slight puncture or abrasion of the skin. It spreads rapidly, often reaching a diameter of several inches, and sometimes involves the deeper tissues, even down to bone. In the acute stage it is extremely painful and the patient may be incapacitated. Healing is often slow and difficult, and the ulcers (which may be multiple) may persist for months or years. The precise cause of these destructive ulcers is not known, but certain factors are commonly present, namely, injury of the skin, infection by certain bacteria, and a state of poor nutrition. This serious disease is extremely prevalent. In industrial undertakings, especially sisal and other plantations, it is the cause of much economic loss.

Treatment has been improved by the discovery of antibiotics, but it is obvious that prevention is supremely important. In groups of workmen who are under supervision much has been done by ensuring that every injury is treated at once, and by providing a satisfactory diet with adequate protein and vitamins.

Tuberculosis

Tuberculosis is likely to be a problem of increasing gravity in Africa. It is already widespread, and evidence of infection can be found even in remote rural areas. But it usually occurs where population is dense and particularly in the cities and in the shanty towns which have sprung up round them. It is already one of the most common killing diseases. The cause of tuberculosis is a small, slow-growing bacillus (*Mycobacterium tuberculosis*). It is usually spread by the sputum and saliva of patients affected with the disease in the lung. Although the bacilli are soon killed by sunlight, they can live for weeks in dark places.

In a small minority of cases the disease is also contracted through drinking milk from cattle with tuberculosis of the udder. In Africa,

[1] *Southern Rhodesia, Report on the Public Health, 1953*, C.S.R. 22, 1954, p. 10.

however, bovine tuberculosis is not common, though it has been found in the Ankole cattle of Uganda and occasionally in other cattle of West and East Africa. In many parts of Africa, however, the drinking of cows' milk is not a usual practice.

The opportunities for the spread of tuberculosis are greatest in dwellings which are badly ventilated, into which sunlight does not enter, and in which many persons sleep together. Though such dwellings are most commonly found near large towns, the habit of crowding into small huts and of closing all entrances at night is almost universal in villages no less than in cities. At the Mulago hospital in Uganda it has been demonstrated that immigrant labourers predominate among the patients treated for pulmonary tuberculosis, bad nourishment on the journey accentuating their susceptibility. In the rural areas, however, the disease is less prevalent than in the cities. Most of the male population of the urban areas are engaged in heavy work, to which they must often walk considerable distances each day; they usually take a diet grossly deficient in protein and vitamins. In these conditions tuberculosis flourishes and is likely to be of the rapidly developing and fatal type which was at one time known as 'galloping consumption'.

In some industrial towns of South Africa the death-rate from tuberculosis in Africans has almost doubled in eight years, reaching 10 per 1,000 per annum, a rate 30 times as high as that among Europeans in the country.[1] In Southern Rhodesia the number of cases notified has increased progressively since the end of the Second World War, and in 1953 in the Midland region, where most of the mines are situated, reached the ratio of 141 per 100,000 of the population.

The conditions of overcrowding and malnourishment are now less prevalent in the great organized industries of South Africa, such as the Rand mines, but they continue to apply to the less well-organized industries which are now springing up in many parts of Africa.[2] Tests have shown that in urban areas almost every person is infected in early adult life, while in rural areas perhaps only half of the adults have acquired infection. The families of tuberculous persons become infected early. In South Africa men who show very strong reactions to tuberculin are most likely to break down under the stress of physical work. They probably carry a recent and unstable focus—possibly a tuberculous gland related to the lung—which fails under stress to confine the bacilli.

The tuberculin test is much used as a preliminary to vaccination with B.C.G. (the bacillus of Calmette and Guérin). This is an organism

[1] T. J. Wiles, *Tuberculosis in the Commonwealth*, National Association for the Prevention of Tuberculosis, 1947.

[2] B. A. Dormer, in *Proc. Transvaal Mine Med. Officers' Ass.*, vol. 27, 1948, p. 63. C. Wilcocks, in *J. Roy. San. Inst.*, vol. 73, 1953, p. 480.

supposed to be a form of *Myco. tuberculosis* of bovine origin which has been so cultivated on artificial media that it has lost its virulence but retains the power to provoke a modest degree of immunity when injected into man. B.C.G. is being used throughout the world on a very large scale as the only rapid means of protection in countries where housing and sanitation are poor; the protection it affords is, however, only partial. It is possible that treatment with modern drugs and antibiotics may be successful in Africans, but experience has not been sufficient to warrant any conclusion on the subject.

Venereal Diseases

The history of venereal diseases in Africa is obscure. In Central Africa gonorrhoea has existed from the earliest known times, but syphilis is believed to have appeared only after the middle of the nineteenth century.[1] In Uganda an early medical mission found venereal diseases well established; the infection was at that time commonly attributed to the Arabs. The slave trade also contributed largely to its spread. In more recent times the importance of these diseases has been gravely accentuated by the grouping of large numbers of Africans in industrial areas where promiscuous intercourse and prostitution are common. The return of wage labourers to the rural areas further facilitates the spread of infection, particularly of gonorrhoea. Women especially are reluctant to submit themselves for treatment, though they often seek treatment for sterility, and in certain tribes, such as the Masai of East Africa, this is largely due to gonorrhoea.[2]

In 1908 it was estimated that some 90 per cent. of the population in Uganda had at some time or other been affected. This could have been only a conjecture, but the Buganda Government regarded the matter as so serious that in 1913 the Lukiko passed a law to make attendance at hospital compulsory. But the high incidence is not confined to Uganda. In Lagos the incidence of gonorrhoea has been estimated at 110 males per 1,000 per annum, in hospital patients at 200 to 250, and in West African soldiers at 600 per 1,000 per annum, compared with 11 to 50 for British soldiers.[3]

Syphilis is found throughout Africa and all stages of the disease have been observed, though congenital syphilis is rare in Africans.[4] Neurosyphilis is not uncommon, and was found to be the cause of 30 per cent. of cases of insanity at a hospital in Kampala. The disease known as *njovera* is found in Southern Rhodesia. It is regarded as a form of syphilis closely allied to the *bejel* of the Near East, and like *bejel* it is not usually

[1] G. L. M. McElligott, in *Brit. J. Venereal Dis.*, vol. 27, 1951, p. 122.
[2] A. M. Wilson Rae, in ibid. p. 118.   [3] G. H. V. Clarke, in ibid. p. 130.
[4] G. L. M. McElligott, in ibid. p. 122.

transmitted by sexual contact but by close contact, by the use of communal drinking bowls, and possibly also by flies. The incidence of *njovera* in one area surveyed was as high as 26·9 per cent.[1] It is prevalent in rural areas but is diminishing in urban areas where treatment is available. Late lesions may be severe, but the vascular and central nervous systems are rarely affected.

Gonorrhoea and syphilis respond well to penicillin and some other antibiotics, but such treatment demands skill and is not cheap. Moreover, the opportunities for reinfection with gonorrhoea are so numerous that one observer[2] thinks that mass treatment is not likely to be effective until moral and educational standards are raised. Mass treatment of gonorrhoea with the appropriate doses of antibiotics (which are relatively small) entails the risk of suppressing the manifestations of syphilis if (as quite often happens) the two diseases are contracted at the same time. These small doses, however, do not cure the syphilis, which therefore runs a considerable part of its course undetected. The treatment of gonorrhoea with sulphonamides, which do not mask or cure syphilis, though less effective than treatment with antibiotics, is not open to this objection. The treatment of syphilis with arsenical preparations entails a course of several injections, but many African patients fail to attend after the obvious signs of the disease have disappeared. Hence treatment is seldom continued long enough to effect a complete cure.

Venereal diseases remain among the most difficult of the medical problems of Africa. The necessity for action in towns and mine locations is now generally recognized; there are clinics in the more important centres, and treatment is given at a large number of Mission and general hospitals.

Yaws

Yaws is a disease caused by a spirochaete which is closely related to the spirochaete of syphilis. The distinction between the two diseases is not always easy, but most workers regard the two as distinct. Like syphilis, yaws is transmitted by direct contact, but the infective lesions are on the skin and not particularly associated with the genital organs. It may possibly be transmitted by flies also. Yaws is usually contracted in childhood, and infective lesions are infrequent after the age of 30 years.[3] It tends to occur among relatively isolated peasant peoples.[4] In Africa yaws is found south of the Sahara and south of Ethiopia; its southern boundary runs through Angola, Southern Rhodesia, and Mozambique.

[1] R. R. Willcox, in *J. Roy. Army Med. Corps*, vol. 97, 1951, p. 97.
[2] G. H. V. Clarke, in *Brit. J. Venereal Dis.*, vol. 27, 1951, p. 130.
[3] C. J. Hackett, in 'First International Symposium on Yaws Control', *Bulletin of the World Health Organization*, vol. viii, 1953, p. 170.
[4] For the occurrence in Scotland of a disease strongly resembling yaws, see *Trans. Roy. Soc. Trop. Med. & Hyg.*, vol. 47, 1953, p. 431.

Its incidence appears to be correlated with high rainfall and with an average annual temperature above 20° C.[1]

The only way in which incidence rates can be reliably calculated is from the results of surveys. In Sierra Leone in the wet season infective lesions have been found in 4·4 per cent. of the people and active non-infective lesions in 16·4 per cent. In 1954, out of 250,000 people examined in Nigeria by the Medical Field Units of the World Health Organization some 117,150 had signs of yaws. Half of the sum paid from the United Nations through the International Children's Fund is being devoted to the treatment of this disease. It has been estimated that in the whole of the African continent there are possibly 25 million people suffering from yaws. There are certainly some areas where almost every person has probably suffered from the disease. In the endemic area of Africa the total hospital attendances for yaws are about 5 per cent. of all attendances, and about 1 per cent. of the population per annum. Yaws is very amenable to treatment with penicillin and other antibiotics, although relapses occur in a small minority of cases. Though much has been done to relieve sufferers from yaws it remains a difficult and disabling disease, extremely common and widespread.

Yellow Fever

Yellow fever is caused by a virus which in Africa is normally transmitted by the bites of mosquitoes of the genus *Aëdes*. It is in Africa and South America essentially a disease of monkeys, and is contracted by humans either when they enter the wooded area in which monkeys live or when monkeys raid plantations where food is grown and infect the mosquitoes which subsequently bite the cultivators. *Aëdes aegypti* breeds prolifically in pools of water in or near human habitations and may transmit the disease widely, causing an epidemic. The disease occurs throughout West Africa, in the Sudan and Western Uganda, and evidence has been found that cases have occurred as far south as Northern Rhodesia. This evidence is derived from the finding of protective antibodies in the blood of normal persons, which indicates that at some time they had been infected but recovered. The worst epidemic of recent years occurred in 1940 in the Sudan, when it was estimated that some 15,000 cases occurred, with a mortality rate of about 10 per cent.[2] It is not understood how this originated. More recently still, in the winter of 1951, there was an outbreak in the Eastern Region of Nigeria. It was estimated that there were about 5,500 cases with 600 deaths.[3]

[1] 'First International Symposium on Yaws Control', *Bulletin of the World Health Organization*, vol. viii, 1953, pp. 131, 136.

[2] R. Kirk, in *Ann. Trop. Med. & Parasit.*, vol. 35, 1941, pp. 67–112.

[3] J. L. McLetchie, in *Trans. Roy. Soc. Trop. Med. & Hyg.*, vol. 48, 1954, pp. 156–81.

Yellow fever can be prevented by inoculation of a live vaccine, either by injection (as with the American 17D vaccine of reduced virulence) or by scarification of the skin, as with the French *vaccination antiamarile par scarification*. The French had given between 20 and 30 million *vaccinations* by this method up to 1953. It would be a counsel of perfection to suggest that all species of mosquitoes capable of transmitting the disease should be eliminated; the use of residual insecticides, however, could greatly reduce the numbers of *Aëdes aegypti* in towns and villages.

Much of the earlier research work on the disease in Africa was done at the Yellow Fever Research Institutes at Yaba in Nigeria and Entebbe in Uganda. The International Health Division of the Rockefeller Foundation made a very substantial contribution by sending research workers of international repute to both. The Yaba Institute, which was virtually closed after the departure of the Rockefeller Yellow Fever Committee in 1934, was reopened in 1944. The two Institutes are known as Virus Research Institutes, and their scope has been extended beyond the study of yellow fever. The virus from which the American 17D vaccine was derived was isolated in 1927 at Yaba, and proved its value during the Second World War. The French method of scarification was developed at the *Institut Pasteur* at Dakar, which has taken a distinguished part in the study of yellow fever and in the development of prophylactic measures.[1] The subject has also been studied at the *Institut Princesse Astrid* at Leopoldville and at the Laboratory at Stanleyville.[2] In spite of the discovery of systems of preventive treatment, yellow fever remains a great potential danger to Africa.

[1] *Enc. A.O.F.*, vol. i, pp. 291 ff.   [2] *Enc. C.B.*, vol. iii, p. 794.

CHAPTER XVII

EDUCATION AND CULTURAL AGENCIES

A NY description of African social life as seen today, and any attempt to forecast the direction in which it may develop in the future, must inevitably involve an assessment of the reaction of the African people to the forces which have been brought to bear on them by their contact with Western civilization. It is, however, only rarely that those forces can be said to be the outcome of policies framed after a deliberate consideration of the effect which they might have on African society. To this generalization there are two outstanding exceptions. The long sustained endeavours of the Missionary Societies and the continuous expansion of education under official auspices. It would clearly be out of place to attempt here to assess the relative importance of the general influence exerted by missionary effort. But, as will be seen, it is impossible to deal adequately with the development of education without paying tribute to the pioneer efforts of the missionary societies in the introduction and expansion of school and other forms of instruction in Africa.

As in the countries of Western Europe so in their African Colonies popular education was first conceived as a function of the Christian churches. The earliest European schools in Africa were instituted by the Portuguese missionaries in the sixteenth century and, thereafter, the occupation of any part of the African coast-line implied the establishment of a Mission school at which some religious instruction was given, and eventually in the language of the colonizing Power. It was at the Mission schools in all parts of Africa that the problem was posed whether the first steps in education should be taken in a local vernacular, and it was the missionaries who were responsible for the earliest efforts at reducing the vernacular languages to written form.[1] The French and Portuguese Missions, on the whole, adopted the policy of using their own languages as the only medium of instruction, while the British have preferred the use of vernaculars in the early stages. The Belgians have taken an intermediate position.[2]

The situation was different at the Cape where the Dutch settlers occupied an almost empty land, so that the schooling of their own children and dependants, in the Dutch language and the principles of the Dutch Reformed Church, was at first their only educational problem. When British settlers arrived, in 1820, the Evangelical Movement had begun to stimulate the growth of missions to the heathen as well as the growth of

[1] See above, pp. 93 ff.   [2] See above, pp. 106 ff.

popular education. It was, however, neither the Dutch nor the British settlers who were responsible for the penetration of tropical Africa by Christian teachers but the societies established in European countries by several Christian sects. They found the money, they appointed the missionaries, they were responsible for establishing the Mission stations which in many parts of Africa are still the most prominent evidences of Western civilization. Often they are organized as farm colonies, sometimes as medical-aid posts, but always they contain some sort of school however rudimentary. To a large extent these Mission schools are still supported by aid from their parent societies in Europe, especially for reinforcement to the teaching staff, but the emergence of autonomous Christian churches, like the emergence of autonomous political societies, cuts them off from their roots in Europe and throws them upon their own resources. It is only in recent years that the education of the masses has been regarded as an urgent task to be undertaken by the State at the expense of the taxpayer. The administrative problem, harshly limited by the amount of public money available, has been to extend the work begun by the missionary societies or to replace it with a new secular organization. In more than one African territory, as in more than one European country, a struggle between the churches and the State for control of the schools can be observed.

The African has his own methods of education in the form of character training and instruction in crafts, or, in the case of girls, in the duties of domestic life. Initiation ceremonies or 'regimental training' are usually the culminating point, and the system is directed towards fitting the youth to take his place in the traditional life of his group. 'Social obligations', it has been pointed out, 'form the core of all teaching given by tribal elders.'[1] It would be wrong to overlook the value of this indigenous type of education, and there have been some who have sought to adjust its methods to the needs of the more formal type of instruction which modern conditions have seemed to require.[2] It may well be that their chief difficulty has been to reproduce the atmosphere, so essentially African, in which traditional instruction of this type is usually given. But there is of course an even graver obstacle. The environment of the African is being radically modified by influences to which he has hitherto been a stranger, and his education must therefore be designed not only to equip him to deal with his existing environment but to fit him for the new conditions which he will have to face and to assist him to take his own part in shaping those conditions. The method will be new, for it must be institutional, and it cannot follow the traditional form of tribal instruction. Accordingly, the

[1] W. D. Hambly, *Origins of Education among Primitive People*, 1926, p. 412.
[2] H. S. Scott, in *Year Book of Education, 1938*. J. W. C. Dougall, in *Africa*, vol. xi, 1938, pp. 312 ff. E. W. Smith, *Knowing the African*, 1946, pp. 125–44.

African child will be introduced to a world of thought, of achievement, and of conduct which lies outside the experience of his parents. This access to new ideas is bound to make a break in his life, however much the educationist may wish to respect indigenous tradition.

The fact that the field of primary education has in the British dependencies been so largely occupied by missionary bodies[1] has in the past limited the extent of the control which could be exercised over the systems of instruction, though the position has more recently been modified by the wide extension of the principle by which grants-in-aid to schools are given on an approved basis. In the Belgian Congo less difficulty has been found in respect of the schools managed by the 'national missions', which are mostly Roman Catholic, since they are in effect part of a State organization of education. Greater difficulty existed at one time in regard to those non-aided schools which were maintained by Protestant Missions, but this has been modified by the recent change of policy under which these schools also have become eligible for State aid. The French system of education has, in French West Africa at all events, been far less dependent on missionary effort, and it has, as compared with the British, been characterized by a greater precision of objective and unity of method.

In a subject so complex it would seem advisable to begin by giving some account of the course which education is taking in the different territories, and to present sufficient data to explain the conditions which now determine educational policy. Tables giving such statistical material as is available will be found at the end of this chapter.

THE UNION OF SOUTH AFRICA

The Organization of European Education

The organization of European education in the Union illustrates most forcibly some of the still unsolved problems of policy which have beset the path of public instruction in South Africa. The two independent Republics and the two British Colonies which joined to form the Union in 1910 brought with them different systems of education, but each territory showed a strong desire to retain the management of its own schools. The subsequent development of European education in the Union displays a constant effort on the part of the four Provinces to find some measure of accommodation between their individual requirements and the policy which has from time to time carried the approval of the Union Government. The South Africa Act of 1909 laid down in Section 85 that the responsibility for all but higher education was to rest with the Provincial Legislatures until the Union Parliament otherwise decided, but

[1] It was stated in 1945 that 96·4 of the pupils attending schools in British tropical Africa were in Mission schools. H. S. Scott, in *Africa*, October 1945, p. 177.

though this provided what seemed at the time to be an adequate line of demarcation, subsequent changes in the range and the content of education made it impracticable to maintain the balance of responsibility which it was originally sought to establish.

Matriculation was at first taken as the dividing line, but in 1922 the Union Parliament decided to include in the definition of higher education a number of functions which should in its view come under national control. This term is therefore no longer confined in practice to institutions of university rank, but it covers industrial and vocational instruction, including trade and technical schools. The Central Government has moreover taken responsibility not only for these institutions but for certain other aspects of education, as for example child welfare, from the kindergarten onwards. The existence of this dual régime in the field of education is made more obvious by the fact that since 1913 the Provincial Education Departments have received substantial subventions from Central funds, with the result that under the provisions of the Financial Relations Consolidation and Amendment Act no. 38 of 1945 the subventions amounted to 50 per cent. of approved expenditure on education, save in respect of Native education. This, as will be seen, stood on a different basis, and has of late years been subsidized by the Central Government to the full amount of the expenditure annually approved by the Minister.[1]

The system of subventions inevitably involves some separation of financial responsibility from administrative control, though it is true to say that the differences between the Provincial and Central approach to the problems of education are in the main those arising from difference in political outlook or from racial attitudes rather than from any substantial divergence on educational policy. There is an outstanding illustration of this in the conflict of view on the question whether English or Afrikaans should be the medium of instruction in European schools.[2] The Provincial Administrations are still responsible for teachers' training colleges, but in respect of training for secondary-school teachers they are now relieved of some of their responsibilities by the Training Departments attached to the universities. There is a substantial difference in the extent to which the European public is able to share in the actual control of the instruction given. There are local School Boards in all Provinces except Natal, and though their functions are only advisory, they enable parents (particularly in the Transvaal and Free State) to exercise a good deal of personal influence. The local bodies, it should be noted, have no effective share in the raising of funds. There are, again, differences in practice regarding the payment of fees. Education is almost entirely provided out of public funds, 93 per cent. of the European pupils being enrolled in State schools

---

[1] *Report of the Commission on Technical and Vocational Education*, U.G. no. 65, 1948, para. 2108. *O.Y.S.A., 1949*, p. 339.   [2] For further on this point, see below, pp. 1138 ff.

in 1951; it is free and compulsory up to the age of 16 in the Cape and Orange Free State, but only up to 15 in Natal and the Transvaal. Secondary education is free in the Transvaal and the Cape, but not in the other Provinces. The commercial and technical schools are maintained by the Central Government, and in their case fees are charged.

While there is general agreement among teachers and educational authorities that a Central direction of policy is essential, popular feeling is opposed to any surrender of existing Provincial rights in this respect. It would in particular oppose any change which might prevent each Province making its own decision on the controversial question of the language to be used as the teaching medium. In 1928 the Universities and Technical Colleges Commission declared that Union control over technical institutions was essential, since their work would clearly be affected by Union legislation in matters such as the Apprentice Act. In 1935 an Inter-Provincial Consultative Committee was constituted, but agreements reached in principle by this body have not always been implemented. The creation of a National Education Board was unanimously opposed by the Provinces in 1937.

In 1948 a Commission on Technical and Vocational Education, after remarking that it found great difficulty in acquiring a comprehensive picture of European education in the Union because of the complicated organization and divided control, recommended a complete reconstruction of the school system on a uniform national plan.[1] European education, it was proposed, should be free up to the Senior Certificate standard or to the age of 18, whichever was earlier. The increased cost of this provision would be met by raising the subsidy from one-half to two-thirds of the Provincial expenditure, but this increase should be subject to the acceptance by the Provinces of the control of policy by a statutory National Council of Education. Fees for vocational education were abolished in 1952, but the proposals for the establishment of a statutory National Council for Education were rejected by the Transvaal Provincial Council.

The question of the medium of instruction in European schools has been mentioned as typical of the issues which make the Provinces unwilling to surrender to the Centre a full control of the administration of school education. European education in the Union is complicated by the recognition of two official languages, English and Afrikaans, but the question of their use needs to be explained in some detail. Up to 1945 the legislation of all the Provinces except Natal laid down that in State schools primary instruction should be given through the medium of the 'home language'; parents might request that after Standard IV either or both languages should be used as the medium of instruction, but the second

[1] U.G. no. 65, 1948, paras. 228, 2035–41, 2111.

language was to be taught as a subject to all pupils unless their parents expressly objected. In Natal, however, the law allows parents to choose the language of instruction of their children in all forms or standards, and provides that the second language may be taught as a subject if the parents request it.[1] In the Transvaal an Ordinance introduced by the United Party in 1945[2] made the use of the second language as a medium of instruction compulsory in the higher standards.

Since 1948 the question of language of instruction has been closely linked with the educational philosophy of the Institute for Christian National Education, which has the support of Afrikaans-speaking teachers' organizations in all Provinces and also of the Federation of Afrikaans Cultural Societies. Christian national education, as defined in a pamphlet issued by the Institute, is based on the doctrine of the Dutch Reformed Church; its ideal is separate schools for all language groups, in which each will be encouraged to maintain its own culture. In 1949 the Transvaal Education (Language) Ordinance[3] gave effect to a part of this programme by dividing schools into two classes: those which gave instruction only in English and those which gave it only in Afrikaans. It went on to require children to attend the school using their 'home language', whatever the wishes of their parents. A similar proposal was, however, rejected in Natal in 1951, and since the passing of the Transvaal Ordinance a number of Transvaal parents have preferred to send their children to schools in Natal. In 1952 the Government, acting under Section 90 of the South Africa Act, refused assent to a revised Education Ordinance for the Cape Province which allowed parents the right to choose the language of instruction of their children.

The conflict of view on this question is thus largely political in origin, but it also involves a choice between two different methods of school organization. One method (now favoured by the United Party) is that of the 'dual medium system', in which both languages are accorded equal rights, half the subjects being taught in Afrikaans and the rest in English. The other method, preferred by the Nationalist Party, stands for a single-medium school in which either English or Afrikaans may be used, provided that the other is taught as a second language for one hour a day. But the crucial issue really lies in the propriety of denying to parents the option of deciding whether English or Afrikaans shall be the medium of instruction for their children. It is meanwhile of interest to note the figures showing the distribution of European pupils in respect of their use of one or other of the two languages. In all the Provinces except Natal the medium of instruction in the majority of primary schools is Afrikaans;

[1] Ordinances no. 5 of 1921 (Cape), no. 13 of 1916 (Natal), no. 15 of 1930 (Orange Free State), no. 5 of 1911 (Transvaal).

[2] No. 5 of 1945.   [3] No. 19 of 1949.

in Natal the Afrikaans-speaking pupils are a small minority. In the Union as a whole the Afrikaans-speaking percentage of primary pupils was 65 in 1951. In the same year 1·1 per cent. of secondary-school pupils were attending schools teaching in both languages, 36·4 per cent. schools with English as the medium, and 62·5 per cent. schools with Afrikaans.

It is of interest also to note the influence of this issue on institutions of higher education. In this case the language of instruction has not been laid down by law, but the movement for the recognition of Afrikaans has had its effect in the development of the Universities of Stellenbosch and Pretoria as institutions whose primary objective is to make provision for the Afrikaans-speaking population. The exclusive use of Afrikaans at the Universities of Stellenbosch and Pretoria is the direct consequence of the omission to give it an appropriate place at the Universities of Cape Town and the Witwatersrand at their inauguration. The result has been to create a racial and cultural difference between them that has been far from beneficial to the progress of academic education.[1] The incorporation of Pretoria (formerly the Transvaal University College) as a university in 1930 was the occasion for the assertion of its predominantly Afrikaans character, in spite of some protest from those who had hoped that higher education might be a means of providing a meeting-ground between the two sections of the White population. The small University of Potchefstroom, founded in 1866 by one of the Dutch Reformed Churches, was Dutch-speaking from its inception and is now Afrikaans-speaking.

The institutions of higher education are (with the exceptions subsequently to be noted) so exclusively European in character that it is convenient to deal here with the universities, before proceeding to discuss the provision made in the Union for education of the non-European majority. There are in the Union eight residential universities, together with the University of South Africa, which is an examining body, but is also responsible for conducting correspondence courses and evening classes.[2] They depend largely on State grants, some 64 per cent. of their total expenditure being derived from this source. These institutions are impressive both in the scale of their buildings and the extent of their resources, and it would be an interesting study, though one not possible to pursue here, to estimate the influence which they now exert on the life which South Africa is building up for itself. As in many of the more modern universities in Great Britain, a relatively high proportion of teaching is devoted to professional and vocational courses (including the course for the teaching diploma) rather than to general Arts courses. This would

[1] C. W. de Kiewiet, in *Africa Today*, 1955, p. 205.

[2] The dates of the charters were Cape Town, 1916; Stellenbosch, 1916; Witwatersrand (Johannesburg), 1922; Pretoria, 1930; Potchefstroom, 1933; Natal (Durban and Pietermaritzburg), 1949; Orange Free State (Bloemfontein), 1949; Rhodes (Grahamstown), 1951. Many of them were, however, the successors of older foundations; see *O.Y.S.A., 1949*, pp. 344-53.

appear to reflect a situation in which the demand for graduates with specialized training is greater than that for those with a more general education.

Another direction in which it is of special interest to examine the influence exercised by the universities is the public attitude towards the political and social aspirations of the African population.[1] There has been a marked growth of interest in African life and the closer study of African problems. The University of Cape Town (which succeeded to the South Africa College founded in 1829) had in 1916 (the year in which it received its present Charter) established a School of African Life and Languages; a Chair of Bantu Languages was added in 1934, and later a Chair of Social Anthropology. Stellenbosch has a Department of Bantu Studies and has encouraged research in African languages and ethnology. Rhodes University has a Chair of Anthropology. Both Natal and Pretoria have lecturers in anthropology and Native administration, and the University of Witwatersrand has a well-staffed department which includes teachers of social anthropology, Native law and administration, and languages. In a number of the universities there is a 'Bantu Studies Circle' founded under the influence of the National Union of South African Students.

Although entry to the universities is nominally open to non-Europeans, in practice Africans are admitted only to the Universities of Cape Town and Witwatersrand, and to separate classes at the University of Natal. At Pretoria a small separate institution, the *Kolege ya Bana ba Afrika*, managed by a group of religious bodies, had 29 students in 1949, but otherwise the provision for non-European education at the capital of the Union is confined to evening classes and correspondence courses of the University of South Africa. In 1951 there were 149 Africans attending university institutions,[2] a large number of whom were dependent on State bursaries. Since then, however, the Government has reduced the number of grants for medical students in order to ensure that Africans should in future pursue these studies only at the newly established Medical School for Non-Europeans at Wentworth College in Natal. The Government provides 15 bursaries for a seven-year medical course, but half the value must be repaid in instalments by the student. After qualification the practitioner still remains under the control of the Government, which stipulates that he shall enter Government employment for a period, if required, that he shall practise only in areas approved by the Government, and shall restrict his practice solely to non-Europeans. The qualifications prescribed are the same as those laid down for Europeans, and the degree is registered by the independent South African Medical and Dental

[1] M. Perham and L. Curtis, *The Protectorates of South Africa*, 1935, p. 75.
[2] This figure is exclusive of the students in the Fort Hare Native College.

Council. The action taken in this instance is typical of the growing insistence of the Nationalist Party on extending the doctrine of segregation to the field of university education.

The increasing evidence of a desire to exclude Africans from the eight residential universities above referred to gives additional significance to the position occupied by the South African Native College at Fort Hare, now the chief centre for the higher education of Africans. This was created in 1916 as the result of a recommendation of the Native Affairs Commission of 1903–5. In this measure the Union Government had the co-operation of the Transkeian Territories General Council,[1] the Administrations of the High Commission Territories (which have made an annual grant to the College), and the missionary societies. The College has received an annual grant from the Union Government, the amount for the years 1947–50 having been increased from an average of £25,575 to £43,596 in 1952. It gives special attention to Bantu Studies and has a farm of 1,600 acres for instruction in agriculture. A three years' course of training for 'medical aides' has lately been introduced with the assistance of a grant of £75,000 from the Transvaal Chamber of Mines. Apart from the special course for the training of Ministers, all work has since 1938 followed the normal lines of academic studies: in 1949, 31 students were studying theology, 36 education, 11 agriculture, and 25 hygiene (the course for 'medical aides').[2] In March 1951 the College was admitted to temporary affiliation with the newly created Rhodes University, and as a result it remains autonomous in internal organization and finance, but is subject to academic control by the University. It is, however, generally felt that the standard of the courses given at Fort Hare falls below the present-day requirements for higher education, and it was in fact only very recently that a course was established in so useful a subject as economics.

It was largely because of the inadequacy of the academic equipment of the College that the Eiselen Commission in 1951 recommended the foundation of an independent Bantu university, with a view to providing both a general education for African leaders and also the special technical courses required to fit Africans to take a leading part in the economic and social development of their people. In the meantime Africans wishing to study subjects for which their own institutions do not make provision might, in the view of the Commission, be allowed the necessary training facilities in conjunction with European institutions.[3] The College fell into disrepute in 1955 in consequence of allegations of indiscipline and of political activities among the students, and for a time was closed. A Commission of Inquiry recommended the abolition of those 'relics of the

---

[1] See above, p. 422.
[2] *O.Y.S.A., 1950*, pp. 504–5.
[3] *Report of the Commission on Native Education, 1949–50*, U.G. no. 53, 1951, paras. 959–61.

missionary high school past' and its conversion to a modern university with new faculties of law, commerce, and physical education.[1]

The numbers and distribution of non-European students at South African universities in 1953 is recorded as:[2]

	Bantu	Coloured	Asian	Total
University of South Africa (correspondence courses only)	558	98	222	878
Fort Hare	338	33	13	384
Witwatersrand	75	14	131	220
Natal	72	15	201	288
Cape Town	24	147	69	240
Total[3]	1,067	307	636	2,010

Early in 1955 the Report of the Commission on Separate Training Facilities for Non-Europeans at Universities[4] was issued. In addition to describing the provision for non-Europeans at Cape Town and Witwatersrand, at Durban, and at Fort Hare, it also described the new African college, *Kolege ya Bana ba Afrika*, near Pretoria, with an enrolment of 76 students in 1953. On grounds of economy the Commission rejected the proposal for founding a Bantu university at present and recommended the concentration of non-European students at Durban and Fort Hare and of Coloured students at Cape Town. No distinctive recommendation was made for Asians. It is also suggested in the findings of the Commission that the *Kolege ya Bana* might 'be doing work on a modest scale' which would lead to the establishment of a non-European university. In 1956, however, it was announced that the Government would make provision for the foundation of four Universities for Bantu, Indian, and Coloured students, who would not thereafter be admitted to European universities.[5]

Native Education

There has been in the history of the Union a wider divergence than elsewhere between the policy of the Government on Native affairs and the views held by missionary bodies, and this tradition still influences the attitude of a considerable section of Europeans towards mission education. Even in modern times there have been occasions when the official attitude towards missionary bodies has recalled something of the feeling which Dr. Philip provoked among early settlers in the first half of the nineteenth century.[6] This was much in evidence during the controversy on the colour-

[1] *The Times*, 2 September 1955.
[2] The total given for the University of S. Africa includes 53 non-white post-graduate students.
[3] By June 1954 the totals had increased to Bantu 1,600, Coloured 496, Asian 725.
[4] *Report of the Commission of Enquiry on Separate Training Facilities for Non-Europeans at Universities, 1954–1955*, Pretoria.   [5] *Manchester Guardian*, 23 November 1956.
[6] W. M. Macmillan, *Bantu, Boer, and Briton*, 1929, pp. 75–131.

bar legislation of 1926, and has been revived in the course of the more recent discussions on the measures taken to implement the policy of segregation. But the picture as it exists today is complicated also by the fact that African opinion is beginning to show itself impatient of control by missions domiciled in Europe, as is evidenced by the growth of the Christian Separatist Churches. There were said in 1949 to be more than 800 such organizations.[1]

There are wide differences in the extent to which African parents are associated with the management of schools; some missions oppose the formation of local committees, while other denominations regularly establish advisory bodies representative of the African community. The creation of such bodies has been obligatory in connexion with the State schools, and recommended for aided institutions in Natal. In the Cape they might be established under the Education Ordinance, with powers similar to those of a School Board. In the Free State they were a part of the machinery for amalgamated schools, while in the Transvaal they existed for 'rural community schools', but in other respects were not officially recognized. The Interdepartmental Committee on Native Education, reporting in 1936, pointed to the importance of creating a link between the school authority and the parents, and held that local school committees should be established wherever possible.[2]

The proper content of African education has from early times been a topic of active debate in the Union and has occasioned some marked difference of opinion. The teaching given by early missionaries was closely linked with their work of evangelization, but as early as 1854 the case for giving a practical form of instruction was advocated by Sir George Grey as head of the Government of Cape Colony, which in that year promised a subsidy to missions which would give an industrial training. Institutions were subsequently formed at Healdtown, Lovedale, and elsewhere, but these were devoted mainly to the training of artisans; the ordinary school courses for long remained of a literary type and were dominated by the examination standards of the European schools. The nature of the instruction given added point to the arguments of those who opposed the extension of education to Africans. In the words of Rhodes, education as then pursued seemed destined to produce a nation of preachers and editors. It is clear, however, that this controversy reflected something more than divergent conceptions of educational method. To the one side, education of a European type symbolized the grant of equal opportunities to Africans; to the other, it was an article of faith that in the economic structure the African must always occupy a subordinate position.[3]

[1] Handbook on Race Relations in South Africa, 1949, pp. 564–72.
[2] Report of the Interdepartmental Committee on Native Education, U.G. no. 29, 1936, paras. 346–8.
[3] J. E. G. de Montmorency, State Intervention in English Education, 1902, pp. 222–3.

With these considerations in view it is interesting to note, in the first place, that public opinion in the Union now appears to have agreed that education must be extended to the whole of the African population. This development is no doubt due in part to the remarkable extension of the manufacturing industry in recent years,[1] for whatever may have been the preference felt by the farmer or the mine manager for the uneducated African this is hardly likely to be shared by the modern industrialist. There has, in the second place, been some change also in the view held regarding the extension of advanced education to the African. Attention was at one period directed largely to finding reasons against the provision of higher education for him, but it is now directed rather to determining the field in which he can best make use of it. Of the more formal examinations of policy which have been made in recent years four deserve mention: those of the Native Economic Commission (1930–2),[2] the Interdepartmental Committee on Native Education (1936),[3] the Commission on Technical and Vocational Education (1944–8),[4] and the Commission on Native Education (1949–51), known from its chairman, Dr. W. M. M. Eiselen, as the Eiselen Commission.[5]

The Native Economic Commission expressed the view that societies at the African level of development have needs which precede ordinary school education, involving in particular the conquest of those beliefs in supernatural forces which are inimical to progress. 'Education', they wrote, 'must aim at transforming the Native's whole outlook on life. The European bases his education on the three R's. But for the tribal Native there is a great deal that precedes the three R's, and that is definitely more important than the three R's.'

The Interdepartmental Committee insisted on the connexion between the content of education and the environment of adult life. 'The education of the White child', they wrote, 'prepares him for life in a dominant society, the education of the Black child for a subordinate society', and they clearly assumed that this situation would continue. Rejecting the suggestion that any advance could be made without an increase in literacy, they recommended that every African should receive at least an elementary education, and that those who could benefit by further education should be enabled to proceed to it. They recommended in particular the development of agricultural training.

---

[1] See below, p. 1286.

[2] *Report of the Native Economic Commission, 1930–1932*, U.G. no. 22, 1932, paras. 627–30.

[3] U.G. no. 29, 1936, pp. 87–89, 106; paras. 499, 556, 572.

[4] *Report of the Commission on Technical and Vocational Education*, U.G. no. 65, 1948, paras. 1792–1938.

[5] See above, p. 1141. A Summary has been made by K. B. Hartshorne and published by the South African Institute of Race Relations, with the title *Native Education in the Union of South Africa*, 1953.

The Commission on Technical and Vocational Education considered that the system for Africans should be similar in structure to that for Europeans, but that more emphasis should be laid on manual crafts and agriculture during the short period which the majority spend in school. Suitable facilities should be provided for training for all occupations in which a demand exists, including skilled work, the facilities for which should be 'broadly along the lines envisaged for Europeans'. Holding that Africans as well as Europeans should receive some form of education up to the age of 18, they recommended that all boys between 17 and 18 who were not in full-time employment should attend training courses in camps modelled on those of the United States Civilian Conservation Corps.

The Eiselen Commission made a more fundamental approach to the whole question of African education, but one which, while not illiberal in general outlook, nevertheless reflected the influence of the current policy of political and social segregation. They recognized that education must be applicable to the whole population of South Africa, but there must be some differentiation of the content of instruction for each race. They admitted that 'the Bantu child comes to school with a basic physical and psychological endowment which differs . . . so slightly, if at all, from that of the European child that no special provision has to be made in educational theory or basic aims'.[1] But they attached great importance to the preservation of African culture, and recommended accordingly the creation of a separate system of education for Africans, from the nursery school to the university, in order that education might be co-ordinated with other aspects of African development. In a minority report Professor A. H. Murray, while accepting the principle that African and European education should differ in content 'because individuals differ', rejected the view that the function of education is to transmit the culture of a group. Education should, on the contrary, equip the individual to improve his society.[2] Later developments in the form given to Native education, designed to give effect to the policy of segregation (and in particular to the passing of the Bantu Education Act), will be described later in this chapter.[3]

Finance and Administration

Taking the year 1951–2 as a convenient basis the total expenditure of the Union Government, shown as ordinary 'expenditure from revenue', amounted to £193,346,121.[4] The total expenditure on education, both

[1] Ibid. p. 26, para. 773.

[2] Ibid. Annexure, pp. 58–62.

[3] See below, p. 1148. See also A. W. Hoernlé and E. Hellmann, 'An Analysis of Social Change and its bearing on Education', *Race Relations Journal*, vol. iv, 1953, pp. 33–44.

[4] *O.Y.S.A., 1952–53*, pp. 624, 641. Of the Provincial expenditure of £46,603,829, the subsidies from the Union (including the allocation for Native education) accounted for £24,258,876.

Central and Provincial, was £38,568,632, of which £6,637,553 was on Native and £4,671,176 on Coloured and Asian education. Though these sums might appear disproportionate to the total number of pupils for whom this expenditure provided, namely 501,539 European and 1,051,858 non-European,[1] there has nevertheless been a marked increase during recent years in the amounts provided for African education, as the following account will show.

Until the change which was made in January 1954, African education had been exclusively under Provincial control, but up to recent years the actual establishment and maintenance of the schools was left largely in the hands of missions, subsidized by grants-in-aid. The original Constitution Ordinance granting representative government to the Cape in 1855 made a definite provision for the allocation of funds for this purpose. The Royal Charter of Natal followed in 1856 by prescribing that an annual grant should be given for 'Native purposes', a portion of which was to be used for education.[2] A proposal by the Administration of the Transvaal in 1921 to levy an education tax on Africans led to the passing of the Financial Relations Fourth Extension Act (no. 5 of 1922), under which the Provinces were debarred from imposing direct taxation on Africans for Provincial purposes, and were required to expend on African education a sum not less than that which was actually being expended by them at the date of the passing of the Act, this sum being assessed at a total of £340,000.

In 1925 the Union Government assumed the entire responsibility for providing the public finance for African education, while leaving the administration in the hands of the Provinces. The Native Taxation and Development Act of that year abolished all previous forms of taxation on Africans, imposed on them a uniform 'General tax'[3] of £1 per adult male, and created a central Native Development Account, which became in 1936 the Native Trust Fund. The Fund derived its income from one-fifth of the proceeds of the General tax, plus an annual contribution of £340,000 from consolidated revenues, African education being financed thereafter entirely from this source. In 1935 the proportion of General tax to be credited to the Native Trust Fund was raised to seven-twentieths for the current fiscal year and to two-fifths thereafter, and a series of further increases brought it to five-sixths in 1942. The subsequent Finance Act of 1943 allocated the entire proceeds of the General tax to the Native Trust Fund, four-fifths being earmarked for education and one-fifth for general development.

The principles of public finance normally accepted elsewhere do not

---

[1] This figure did not include 19,187 European and about 900 non-European students at Universities and University Colleges, including the South African Native College at Fort Hare.

[2] U.G. no. 29, 1936, paras. 11, 65.   [3] See above, p. 651.

give any support to the contention that the services provided by the State for any one section of the population should be proportionate to that section's contribution to the total body of direct taxation, but European opinion in the Union had for many years clung tenaciously to this principle. It had become clear, however, that the changes of practice above recorded had robbed it of any virtue which it might once have possessed, and the Native Education Finance Act no. 29 of 1945 finally abandoned the principle that the cost of schools for Africans should bear any relation to the taxation levied on their community, and provided that appropriations should be made for the purpose from general revenues.[1] The cost to the revenue of African education was shown in the Provincial budgets of 1935 as £698,665.[2] As has been explained in the preceding paragraph, this amount had risen in 1951–2 to £5,701,544, the remainder of the total sum of £6,637,553 incurred in the Union on Native education being expended directly by the Union Government. The total expenditure in the Estimates for 1952–3 amounted to £6,907,900.[3] The increasing expenditure on the secondary and primary schools, which now falls on Provincial finances, helps to account for the considerable growth in recent years of the Provincial subsidies included in the Central budget.

The cost of the education of Africans was calculated in 1949 at £6·41 per head, compared with £41·99 per head for Europeans and £16·55 for Coloured and Asian.[4] Calculations of this nature must be used with great reserve, if quoted as evidence of the relative expenditure incurred on African education in different territories, for there is a great variety of method observed in calculating the details of cost involved. But the figures may be taken as giving a rough approximation of the relative ratio of State expenditure per pupil in each of the three communities in the Union. In the case of African education there must be added the amount contributed by the missions. No recent material exists on this point, and though it was estimated in 1935 that they provided rather over 13 per cent. of the cost of the education of each African child, this figure would not be appropriate to present conditions. It was estimated in 1950 that 34 per cent. of African children between the ages of seven and 14 were attending school, but this calculation was said to exclude a large number of children who for various reasons did not come under registration.[5]

Until the passing of the Bantu Education Act in 1954[6] the State expenditure on education almost entirely took the form of grants-in-aid to schools under the control of missions. Only in Natal was provision made

[1] O.Y.S.A., 1949, p. 492.   [2] U.G. no. 29, 1936, para. 215.
[3] Report of the Department of Native Affairs, 1950–1951, U.G. no. 30, 1953, p. 18.
[4] M. Horrell, A Survey of Race Relations in South Africa, 1950–1951, South African Institute of Race Relations, 1952.
[5] See references in A. Welsh, ed., Africa South of the Sahara, 1951, p. 69.
[6] See above, p. 166, and below, p. 1148.

on any considerable scale for Government Native schools; this development began in 1918 when the Administration took over some schools
previously managed by the American Mission Board, and by 1954 there
were 165 primary and secondary high schools controlled directly by the
Provincial Education Department. The Cape at an early date made
provision for African education on a more generous scale than the other
Provinces, and in 1954 the Administration supported nine secondary and
high schools for Africans with grants of public money. All primary education in Government and aided schools became free in the Cape in 1920,
and elsewhere in 1941. The general principles on which grants should be
payable were formulated by the Union Advisory Board on Native Education in 1947. The State was to pay teachers' salaries and to make grants
for equipment, for a library, and for school books, together with building
grants. A fund of £21,500 was made available in 1947 for bursaries.[1]

In 1948 the total number of State and State-aided schools for non-
Europeans was 6,593, of which 3,308 were in the Cape; the total enrolment
was 973,470. But here as elsewhere in Africa the most important factor in
African education is not so much the number of pupils in the school or the
relation this bears to the number of children of school-going age. The
important figure is the number who reach the higher classes in the schools.
In this respect the position in the Union is very similar to that which, as
will subsequently be seen, prevails in a large number of the African territories. Of the total African pupils 45 per cent. were in the substandards
in 1951, only 4·2 per cent. in Standard VI, and less than 2 per cent. in
secondary and higher institutions. The corresponding figures for the
European population are 21 per cent. in the substandards, 9 per cent. in
Standard VI, and 20 per cent. in secondary and higher education.

The Bantu Education Act

The Interdepartmental Committee of 1936 had recommended that the
control of Native education should be transferred from the Provinces to
the Union Department of Education, and that a new Department should
be set up under the Minister of Education, advised by a National Board
of Native Education. It appears that this proposal was referred to the
Natives' Representative Council at its first meeting in December 1937,[2]
but was unanimously rejected. In 1945, however, Act no. 29 created a
Union Advisory Board on Native Education, with the Secretary for Native
Affairs as Chairman, but though this seemed to point towards the subsequent transfer of the control of African education from the Provinces to
the Central Government, the Board had only an advisory capacity, and
the control of the Provincial Administrations remained in force. The

---

[1] *Report of the Commission on Native Education, 1949–50*, U.G. no. 53, 1951, paras. 249, 250.
[2] See above, p. 162.

Eiselen Commission of 1951 took a different view from the Interdepartmental Committee of 1936. It recommended a complete reorganization of the administration of African education, involving its divorce from the Education Department and the constitution of a separate Bantu Education Department as one of the branches of a Division of Bantu Affairs which was to be responsible for all aspects of African development.[1] In 1953 the issue was brought to a head by the passing of an Act which definitely transferred the control of Native education from the Provincial Administrations to the Government of the Union.[2]

The Eiselen Commission had made the further suggestion that Bantu Local Authorities should be set up in the Reserves and the urban areas with the intention of eventually taking over the administration of all local services including education. They did not support the view that the Natives should be solely responsible for financing their own services, but proposed that the new Local Authorities should eventually make a financial contribution towards the cost of education on an increasing scale. Until these administrative changes were complete there would still be a place for State-aided Mission schools. A ten-year programme of development was outlined so as to bring the whole Bantu population within reach of literacy in their own languages, and the provision of high schools and higher education in the two European languages of South Africa was contemplated. The number of Bantu pupils in schools of all kinds would rise from 767,170 in 1949 to 1,391,000 in 1959 at a cost increasing in the same period from £4,941,788 to £9,961,400.

The Eiselen Report was studiously moderate in its expression and reasonable in its proposals, whatever may be said of its tendency. When, however, a Bill[3] based upon the Report was introduced into the Union Parliament, the new educational policy was related to the general policy of *apartheid* in the strongest terms. The speech delivered in the Senate on 7 July 1954 by Dr. H. F. Verwoerd, Minister of Native Affairs, made his case quite clear.[4] 'The Bantu teacher', he said, 'must be integrated as an active agent in the process of the development of the Bantu community. He must learn not to feel above his community, with a consequent desire to become integrated into the life of the European community.' The Act transferred the administration of Native education in general from the Provincial Education Boards to the Minister of Native Affairs, and the management of primary schools from the churches and missions to Bantu Boards of Control. Secondary schools, industrial schools, and institutions for training Native teachers were placed immediately under the Native

---

[1] U.G. no. 53, 1951, paras. 800–14.
[2] Bantu Education Act, no. 47, 1953.
[3] Bantu Education Act, no. 44, 1954.
[4] Reprinted by the Information Service of the Department of Native Affairs as *Bantu Education: Policy for the Immediate Future*, Pretoria, 1954.

Department, and it was announced that all European teachers would eventually be replaced by Bantu teachers. Schools were to be reclassified not by their religious denominations but, in the words of Dr. Eiselen, were to be 're-oriented on a new basis of language groups'.[1] No Native school was to be opened after 1 March 1954 unless registered and placed under the control of the Minister for Native Affairs. Churches and missions might retain control of their hostels, but if they wished to retain the schools themselves 'for the time being', it would be only as private institutions with a Government grant reduced in amount by 25 per cent.[2]

It was urged in favour of the Act that it largely followed the unanimous recommendations of the Eiselen Report in respect of administrative reforms and that these reforms had repeatedly been urged by the Natives themselves, even by some religious leaders. When Dr. Eiselen addressed the Ciskeian General Council[3] he emphasized this aspect of the Act, pointing out that it was the Natives who demanded a larger share in the control of schools and who desired schools which would be more closely linked with the life of the community. The former system had been denounced by the Commission for its general lack of method; the persons responsible for administration had no control over policy; the public bodies which made grants-in-aid had no means of ensuring that the money was well spent; and the multiplicity and the mutual rivalry of the religious bodies led to duplication of effort in some areas and to inactivity in others. For the first time, he claimed there was a general policy which followed the characteristic development of education in other parts of Africa by delegating responsibility to Native Authorities.[4] By providing a four-year syllabus of work for all primary schools the Act enabled a larger proportion of pupils to reach Standard VI. The changes would involve no reduction in the number (about 200) of secondary schools, there would be greater facilities for industrial training,[5] and academic education would still be available for Natives, though as a Commission of 1933 had proposed, it would be confined to Durban (University of Natal) and Fort Hare.[6]

It was not seriously argued, at least not by the Protestant Churches, that the Act had hampered or restricted provision for religious instruction. Ministers were to be allowed free access to their congregations, and in fact more time was to be allotted to religious instruction in the new syllabus than in the old. It has, moreover, been pointed out that a large majority of parents are not adherents of the churches controlling the schools which

[1] S.A.S., no. 90, 30 September 1954, p. 12.
[2] Bantu Education: Policy for the Immediate Future, Pretoria, 1954, p. 12.
[3] S.A.S., no. 91, 15 October 1954, p. 11.   [4] See below, p. 1173.
[5] S.A.S., no. 93, 15 November 1954, p. 12.
[6] Report of the Commission of Enquiry on Separate Training Facilities for Non-Europeans at Universities, 1953–1954, Pretoria.

their children attend.[1] Nor has there been much opposition to the assumption by the State of responsibility for training teachers.

The financial arrangements for the reformed policy were subjected to close scrutiny. Under the 1954 Act the State was to appropriate annually £6½ million for education and in addition was to allocate four-fifths of the General tax.[2] The estimated expenditure on education for the year 1954–5 was £8½ million, a larger sum *per capita* than was allotted for African education by any other Government in Africa.[3] It was recognized that the cost of education would rise higher under the new Act, a consideration which implied that additional expenditure must be derived from Native sources. It was suggested, for example, that rents in Native Locations might be raised to pay for school buildings and that the General tax might be increased. At the same time economies were to be effected by substituting female for male teachers.

The Act also applied to schools situated on farms and mines. Objection was taken by some critics to the provision which vested the school in the owner of the land, thus giving him the power to refuse his permission for a school to open. The regulation which limited the pupils of any school (except with Departmental consent) to children of genuine employees or, in the case of farms, to children of approved residents living in the vicinity was also criticized,[4] though only a small proportion of children attending such schools fell within this category. As an instance, out of 1,192 pupils receiving instruction at six farm schools only 52 were children of the farmers' employees.[5]

The gravamen of the criticism of the Act lay in the contention that it provided for an 'inferior' education or, in the words of the Methodist Church at its Annual Conference in 1954, that it aimed 'at conditioning the African people to a predetermined position of subordination to the State'. The justification for this charge appears to be found rather in pronouncements of responsible Ministers than in the Act itself. Resolutions condemning the application of the new principle in education were passed, in much the same terms as those of the Methodist Church, by the General Assembly of the Bantu Presbyterian Church, by the Annual Assembly of the Congregational Union, by the Episcopal Synod of the (Anglican) Church of the Province of South Africa, and by other religious groups, all of whom agreed upon denouncing the policy of keeping particular racial groups in a permanent position of inferiority.[6] The Southern African

---

[1] *Bantu Education: Policy for the Immediate Future*, Pretoria, 1954, p. 12.
[2] *S.A.S.*, no. 99, 28 February 1955, p. 11.
[3] South African Bureau of Racial Affairs, *Bantu Education*, Stellenbosch, 1955, p. 22.
[4] *S.A.S.*, no. 89, 15 September 1954, p. 10.
[5] *Africa Digest*, January–February 1955, p. 3.
[6] Summarized in South African Bureau of Racial Affairs, *Bantu Education*, Stellenbosch, 1955, pp. 36–38.

Bishops' Conference of the Roman Catholic Church, without pronouncing upon the political issue, asserted its determination to provide 'whatever education we can for our children by means of our type of school'. Even the Dutch Reformed Church, which alone among the larger churches gave its general support to the Act, did so expressly on the ground of the administrative changes it authorized.

The churches were now confronted with a dilemma, whether to accept State control with a reduced grant of money or to withdraw from the field of active education. Most of the Protestant bodies reluctantly decided to submit to the new system and to take advantage of a provision in the Act for leasing their school buildings to the new Department. The authorities of the Anglican Church in Johannesburg, where for more than 50 years it had been especially active in the notorious district of Sophiatown, refused to submit. In August 1954 one of the high schools managed by the Community of the Resurrection was closed, and the Bishop gave notice that all the Anglican schools in his diocese would be closed rather than continue their work under the new conditions. This example was not followed in the other Anglican dioceses nor by the other churches. In accordance with the provisions of the Act, the whole work of training teachers was taken out of the hands of the churches, and the year 1955 saw the closing of such celebrated institutions as the Adams Institution in Natal, where 225 students were being trained. Except in Johannesburg and along the Rand, however, the new system was introduced without serious disorder, and the Government could claim that some bodies representing Native opinion welcomed the change.[1] On the Rand there were meetings of protest[2] and the rights and wrongs of the Bantu Education Act became matters of high political importance.

Further plans for the development of Bantu education were put forward in the Report of the Tomlinson Commission, which, as shown above in Chapter XI, issued a summary of its recommendations in 1955, after the passing of the Bantu Education Act. The proposals for primary and secondary education were based upon those of the Eiselen Commission, to which frequent reference was made in the Tomlinson Report. Further points of interest were the insistence upon the necessity of evolving leaders among the Bantu 'trained in the modern technique of a progressive economy', and the relegation of the churches to an advisory status. The representatives of the churches, in the words of the Report, 'can serve on school committees, etc., and can do all sorts of social and enlightenment work'.[3] While recommending the provision of a Bantu university with constituent colleges, the Tomlinson Commission had little to say that was not more

---

[1] *Africa Digest*, December 1954, p. 2.   [2] Ibid. May–June 1955, p. 24.
[3] *Summary of the Report of the Commission for the Socio-Economic Development of the Bantu Area within the Union of South Africa*, U.G. no. 61, 1955, p. 167. See also above, p. 763.

fully treated in the Report on Separate Training for Non-Europeans. In the general section on the financial requirements of the Development Programme it was suggested that £3 million should be made available 'for the erection of three polytechnic schools, at least one agricultural college, one university college, and four development schools'.[1]

The Education of Coloured and Asian Pupils

The Coloured People of South Africa were estimated to number 1,242,000 in 1955. Since 90 per cent. of them live in or near the Cape Peninsula their social problems affect principally the Cape Province. They are town-dwellers rather than country-dwellers and follow a European rather than an African pattern of life, though the policy of *apartheid* has tended to separate them farther from the White South Africans and to group them rather with the Africans.[2] The Asians, estimated to number 410,000 in 1955, live for the most part in Natal.[3] Though the community as a whole is poor it contains some prosperous members who have contributed £310,000 towards the cost of schools for their community. Separate schools are provided for Asian pupils in Natal and there are a few Asian schools in the Transvaal. In the other Provinces Asian and Coloured children attend the same schools, mainly State-aided Mission schools. Primary education is freely provided in all Provinces but it is compulsory for Coloured and Asian children only in Natal, from the age of seven to the age of 15, and in the Cape Province, from seven to 14. Thus it may be said that Coloured education at the Cape and Asian education in Natal are well established, but mainly at the primary level.[4]

After four years' experience of compulsory education for Coloured children in the Cape Province, a Commission was appointed in 1953 to review the financial implications of the system. Before its Report was issued the Superintendent-General of Education for the Cape Province was reported as saying, in January 1955, that 205,047 Coloured children were attending school. Of each hundred children who were in Standard I in 1949, only 61 had reached Standard IV by 1952, and only 31 had reached Standard VI by 1954. Of the total enrolment in 1955 the proportion attending high schools was 3½ per cent. Little provision had been made hitherto for vocational training of Coloured students. The Commission on Technical and Vocational Education recommended the opening of a polytechnic for non-Europeans in the Western Province of the Cape as a means of raising the standard of skill, especially of the Coloured peoples, in the building trade and in commerce.

[1] Ibid. p. 193.
[2] See above, p. 164.   [3] See above, pp. 388 ff.
[4] M. Horrell, *A Survey of Race Relations in South Africa, 1954-1955*, South African Institute of Race Relations, 1955, p. 187.

A report made for the *Teachers' Journal* by Dr. S. Cooppan[1] stated that, in September 1954, there were about 72,000 Asian children attending school, 66,272 of them in primary and 2,729 in secondary schools. There were also 228 Asian teachers in training. The most serious problem was overcrowding in school buildings, so that 15,600 children failed to find places even though double shifts were worked by the teachers. Capital expenditure by the Province of Natal on schools for Asians amounted to £579,995 (to which should be added the private contribution of £310,000 mentioned above). The Provincial expenditure on schools for White children was ten times as great, although the Asians outnumbered the Whites in Natal and although the high Asian birth-rate meant that the proportion of children of school age was higher among the Asians than among the Whites. In the Transvaal, said Dr. Cooppan, the policy of racial zoning had deprived the Indian community of its own high school at Booysens, substituting in exchange a new Government high school at an inaccessible spot.

In order to promote cultural relations with India a plan was inaugurated for the provision of 70 scholarships for Indian students from South Africa at Indian universities.[2] The popularity of this scheme was such that the number of scholarships for the year 1952–3 was raised to 100. The provision of higher education for Coloured and Indian students in South Africa has already been referred to.[3]

SOUTH-WEST AFRICA

Until recently South-West Africa lagged far behind the Provinces of the Union in respect of Native education, and it cannot be said to have yet reached a comparable level, although important reforms were introduced in 1951. The Bantu Education Act was not made applicable to South-West Africa. The total expenditure voted by the Administration for all forms of education in the year 1951–2 amounted to £629,515, of which £496,263 was allotted to the education—free at the primary stage—of 9,953 White children. The system follows the South African model on the whole, with the difference that German has been reintroduced since 1951 as a medium of instruction in certain schools. About one-ninth of the population of South-West Africa is racially distinguished as White. Within the Police Zone[4] the sum of £120,492 was allotted to Native and Coloured education, but only £12,760 to the areas outside the Zone. The enrolment of non-European children in the schools of the whole territory is given as 24,135 for the year 1952–3, out of a total population of 322,179.[5]

---

[1] *Teachers' Journal* (Organ of the Natal Indian Teachers' Society), February and July 1955.
[2] See above, p. 399.   [3] See above, p. 598.
[4] See above, p. 695.   [5] *O.Y.S.A., 1952–53*, pp. 1166–8.

Little information is officially recorded about the schools outside the Police Zone, except that the number of pupils had reached 18,855 and the number of schools had reached 163 by the year 1953.[1] The small subsidy given by the Administration since 1945 has been allotted mainly to boys' and girls' hostels, to four teachers' training schools, with an enrolment of 165 students in 1952, and to a new industrial school with an enrolment of 14. The reorganization of curricula and the modest progress in teacher training since the changes made in 1951, are said to have produced better methods and an increase in the school enrolment. A large majority of the schools are maintained by the Finnish (Protestant) Mission.

Within the Police Zone there were in 1952 six Government schools for Natives, 49 schools conducted by the Rhenish (German Protestant) Mission, and 27 by Roman Catholic Missions, with a total enrolment of 7,296 pupils. The Administration pays the salaries of teachers in Mission schools, supplies furniture, books, and equipment, and, since 1951, has subsidized the cost of school buildings. There were also 30 schools for Coloured children with an enrolment of 2,676. It was estimated that the average annual cost of educating a White pupil was £32. 8s. 11d., of a Coloured pupil £18. 16s. 6d., of a Native in the Police Zone £9. 17s. 1d., and of a Native outside the Police Zone 14s. 8d.[2]

The system introduced by the Education Department in 1951 involved a new syllabus of instruction for all schools up to Standard VI, with a more rigorous scheme of development than the Mission schools had previously attained. An examination held by the Department was introduced at Standard VI and was imposed as the prerequisite for admission to a teachers' training school. The Augustineum Training School had been taken over from the Rhenish Mission in 1944; it was now reorganized with secondary-school classes as well as with classes for training teachers. The Doebra (Roman Catholic) Training School maintained its work in producing teachers according to the new syllabus. Night schools for promoting literacy among adult Natives have also been instituted in three towns.

THE HIGH COMMISSION TERRITORIES

The problems of education are in this case of a very different order from those arising in the Union. The proportion of Europeans in the population of Basutoland (0·3 per cent.) and Bechuanaland (0·8 per cent.) is too small to create any serious problem in the provision of schooling for them. In Swaziland, where the proportion (1·4 per cent.) is somewhat higher, the requirements of the small settled community of Europeans in two of the southern districts, who are mainly Afrikaans speaking, have been met by

[1] Information supplied by the Organizer of Native Education, Grootfontein, 22 September, 1954.　　　　　　　　　　　　　　　　　　　[2] O.Y.S.A., 1952–53, p. 1167.

the establishment of a boarding school at Goedgegun. This has since 1952 had courses up to the matriculation standard. There were in 1953 two high schools, one junior secondary school, and five primary schools, with a total enrolment of 774 pupils. The Government expenditure on White education in that year was £31,912.[1] In Bechuanaland the Administration maintains a primary school for Europeans at Lobatsi, while others are maintained by local communities or by the missions with State aid. A similar procedure is followed in Basutoland. The question of African education has, however, raised issues of particular interest, the chief of which, as will subsequently be seen, arises from the decision taken by the Union Government in 1950 to refuse further admission of non-Europeans of other territories to the institutions of higher education in the Union after 1958. Until then African students were to be admitted to Fort Hare and Durban Medical College at their own expense.

In all the three High Commission Territories, and especially in Basutoland and Swaziland, the Native Authorities have from the first taken an active interest in the provision of facilities for education. The arrival in 1833 of three members of the Paris Evangelical Missionary Society, who had been invited to Basutoland by Moshesh,[2] was followed by the establishment of a number of schools, to which Moshesh and his successors gave full encouragement. The Roman Catholic Mission followed at a later date and founded their first school in 1864. The Anglican Church Mission opened their first school in 1876. From 1871 onwards the Administration of Basutoland began to give financial support to the Mission schools, and a Government high school was established in Maseru in 1939. In 1954 there were 946 schools in Basutoland, of which eight were controlled by the Administration and almost all the rest by the missions. Of these schools, 14 were secondary or 'junior secondary', with a total enrolment of 1,395, and a beginning had been made in the provision of post-secondary courses by the foundation of the Pius XII Catholic University College at Roma.

It is noticeable that of the total of 103,332 pupils enrolled in the schools, no less than 61,304 were girls; but the number of pupils was in itself remarkable in view of the size of the population.[3] It was estimated as early as 1945 that some 75 per cent. of the children in Basutoland were at school, a figure which was said at the time to be without parallel in any territory in Colonial Africa.[4] Subsequent investigations have given an even higher estimate of the proportion borne by pupils at school to the total number of children of school age.[5] The provision made for education

[1] *Colonial Reports, Swaziland, 1953*, p. 28.
[2] *N.A.*, Part V, pp. 2, 29, 122 ff.
[3] *Colonial Reports, Basutoland, 1954*, pp. 47–48.
[4] *Report of the Commission on Education in Basutoland*, 1946.
[5] See references quoted in A. Welsh, ed., *Africa South of the Sahara*, 1951, pp. 68–69.

absorbed rather over 17 per cent. of the total expenditure of the Administration. The fact that the law[1] which eventually gave to the Administration an adequate measure of control over the school system was only enacted in 1948 has admittedly resulted in the lack of a balanced system of instruction, but it has not tended to abate the interest shown by the Basuto in the provision of education.

In 1949 the Basutoland Native Authorities showed a desire to raise a special levy of £100,000 for the furtherance of education of a post-secondary standard, mainly by making provision of bursaries[2] to enable students to proceed to overseas universities. The scheme, which involved a basic levy in cash and a graded tax[3] on cattle or other stock and on wages, came into effect in June 1952 and over £58,000 had been collected in the first financial year. The total expenditure on education for the year 1954 was £259,168, of which £196,432 was drawn from the revenues of the Territory.[4] The Clarke-Eiselen Commission in 1946 formulated a ten-year educational plan towards the cost of which £85,500 was contributed by the Colonial Development and Welfare Vote. By 1954 300 schools had been reconditioned or newly built, the Basuto Training College at Morija was enlarged, and the Lerotholi Technical School built.[5]

In Swaziland also the establishment of schools was at the outset left to the missionary societies, the first school being opened by the Methodist Church in 1880. In 1903 the Administration began to make grants-in-aid on a small scale to the Mission schools, and in 1906 it opened a primary school at the Royal village of the Queen Regent,[6] in order to provide education for the household of the ruling family. In 1931 an important step was taken by the Paramount and Swazi Chiefs in the foundation of a Swazi national school at Mathapha, financed by the Swazi National Fund (a special levy devoted to education and similar purposes) and since that date two national primary schools have also been founded. In 1954 there were 225 schools for Africans, of which three were 'national' and 16 'tribal', with 195 controlled by missions and eleven by the Administration; nine of them provided secondary classes, and three (of which one is the national school at Mathapha) had matriculation courses. The total enrolment in 1953 was 16,452, with a preponderance of girls.[7] The Administration devoted to education about 12 per cent. of its total expenditure of all kinds.[8]

That education should have taken a somewhat different course in Bechuanaland is partly due to the sparse population. Perhaps because of

---

[1] Proclamation no. 28, 1948.   [2] *N.A.*, Part V, p. 124.
[3] Ibid.   [4] *Colonial Reports, Basutoland, 1954*, p. 48.
[5] *High Commission Territories, Economic Development and Social Services*, Cmd. 9580, 1955, p. 9.
[6] *N.A.*, Part V, pp. 408–9.   [7] *Colonial Reports, Swaziland, 1953*.
[8] The figure includes expenditure of grants made under the Colonial Development and Welfare Acts.

the policy of the London Missionary Society in the days of Moffatt and Livingstone, the growth of primary education has been due mainly to tribal effort. The Mission schools are very few, and by far the greater number of the primary schools are managed and financed by the Tribal Treasuries,[1] while the Administration has been responsible for the cost of a teachers' training college at Kanye and for aid to the two secondary and two 'junior-secondary' schools. The total enrolment in 1953 was 19,783. Of these pupils, 12,512 were girls. The reason usually assigned for the disparity between the enrolment of the two sexes is that boys are required for the herding of the cattle, and the conditions in Bechuanaland certainly afford a substantial measure of justification for this explanation. Though the numbers of pupils enrolled are small compared with some other territories, the Native Authorities in most of the Tribal Reserves have shown the interest in education which is characteristic of the High Commission areas. As far back as 1903 a voluntary levy was made in the Ngwaketse Reserve for aid in the upkeep of the local Mission school, an example which was followed in 1910 in the Kwena and Malete Reserves. A more ambitious scheme took shape in 1951 with the opening of the tribal secondary school at Moeng, which was designed to develop into a Bamangwato College. The cost was met by special tribal levy, with the assistance of a small Government grant.[2] The institution has courses working up to the matriculation standard, and has already presented candidates for the Junior Certificate examination of the University of South Africa.

In the three High Commission Territories together expenditure on education has, since 1946, increased from £188,000 to £349,000, and during the same period allotments under the Colonial Development and Welfare Act have amounted to £420,000. The actual sums issued to the three Territories for the period 1946–54 are:

	For Primary and Secondary Schools (£000)	For Higher Education (£000)
Basutoland	69	18
Bechuanaland	57	—
Swaziland	204	8

The programme for the next five years includes the building of six new secondary schools in Basutoland, the enlargement of the Bamangwato College in Bechuanaland, and the improvement of existing schools in Swaziland.[3]

Students from the High Commission Territories have from the first been

---

[1] For the system of Tribal Treasuries, see above, pp. 503, 510, 516.

[2] *N.A.*, Part V, p. 280.

[3] *Colonial Development and Welfare Acts*, Cmd. 9375, 1955.

dependent on the Union for access to post-secondary or academic institutions (of which the most important available to them was the South African Native College at Fort Hare), and there have also been a certain number of private students who, with or without assistance from correspondence courses, have entered for the public examinations conducted by the Union Department of Education or by the University of South Africa.[1] In 1950 the Union Government decided to refuse further admission of non-Europeans to its institutions of higher education, and though in 1951 this ban was lifted for three years in order to enable the neighbouring territories time in which to provide local education for non-Whites, the matter became one of much concern in the Territories.[2] The subsequent decision of the Federation of Rhodesia and Nyasaland to establish an inter-racial university at Salisbury, which was to make provision also for students from the Territories, was therefore opportune.[3] With this object post-matriculation classes were introduced to enable Africans to qualify. It has been estimated that the number of students from the Territories who will qualify for admission to the new university may amount to between 20 and 30 annually. The position was further relieved when in 1953 the Union Government agreed to allow Natives of the Rhodesias and the High Commission Territories to continue for the time being to study at Fort Hare and at the non-European Medical School of Natal University.[4]

THE FEDERATION OF RHODESIA AND NYASALAND

It is inevitable that in territories whose conditions vary so widely as those of the two Rhodesias and Nyasaland there should be a considerable diversity both in educational policy and in methods of instruction. But the point of immediate significance is the place assigned to education generally in the scheme of Federation which came into effect in the latter part of 1953. In that measure the primary and secondary education of Europeans and other non-Africans is declared to be the exclusive concern of the Federal Legislature. Higher education generally, including that of Africans, as conducted in institutions offering courses of a university or technological or professional character, will also be the exclusive concern of the Federal Legislature.[5] By a resolution passed in 1946 by the Southern Rhodesia Legislature a Rhodesia University Foundation Fund was initiated in 1947, and in 1952 provision was made for an Inaugural Board to deal

---

[1] Central African Council, *Report of the Commission on Higher Education for Africans in Central Africa*, 1953, p. 12.

[2] *N.A.*, Part V, p. 125.   [3] See below, p. 1161.

[4] *The Times*, 1 December 1953.

[5] The Rhodesia and Nyasaland Federation Act, 1953, and the Rhodesia and Nyasaland Federation Order in Council no. 1199, 1953 (Second Schedule), p. 52.

with the foundation of a University College, which would eventually become a University of Southern Rhodesia.[1]

Shortly before the Federation was formally constituted, a Commission was appointed to report on the provision which should be made for the proposed University College, and its Report embodied a comprehensive survey of the position of higher education in the organization of the Federal system.[2] So far as Africans were concerned, the question had become one of some urgency because of the decision of the Union Government by which non-European students from outside the Union would be banned from admission to its higher educational institutions. The Report of the Commission was of importance also for another reason. A committee appointed by the Central African Council in 1951 to consider the needs of Africans for higher education had remarked in particular on the paucity of Africans qualified for the Agricultural, Veterinary, or Engineering Services, and had suggested the foundation of a Central African College.[3] The original project of a university, as envisaged locally, had contemplated two separate but co-operating institutions, European and African. The Commission of 1953, however, strongly urged the establishment of a single university institution, open to all races, and this view was finally accepted by the authorities in Southern Rhodesia.

In regard to the constitution proposed for the University College and the academic courses to be followed, the Southern Rhodesia Commission of 1953 was strongly influenced by the recommendations of the Commission appointed in the United Kingdom to advise on higher education in the Colonies generally.[4] Its views had largely influenced the establishment of the new University Colleges in East and West Africa.[5] Following the principles advocated in this Report, the academic standards to be adopted in the new University College in the first instance were to be those of the University of London, and an application to enter into 'special relationship' with the University of London was accepted. The University, which is to be known as the University College of Rhodesia and Nyasaland, has been given an area of 458 acres at Mount Pleasant in Salisbury. A Royal Charter was granted in February 1955 and Queen Elizabeth the Queen Mother accepted the presidency. Teaching and research facilities are to be made available at the projected Botanical Gardens, at a veterinary research station, at an experimental farm of about 1,000 acres, and, for the Medical School, at the new Salisbury African Hospital. In the laying out of the site and the planning of buildings, accommodation, and facilities, it is a fundamental principle that there shall be no discrimination between

---

[1] The University Charter and Inaugural Board (Private) Act, 1952.

[2] Central African Council, *Report of the Commission on Higher Education for Africans in Central Africa*, 1953.   [3] Ibid. Appendix A.

[4] *Report of the Commission on Higher Education in the Colonies* (the Asquith Commission), Cmd. 6647, 1945.   [5] See below, pp. 1180–4.

races. The University will begin with the establishment of a faculty in Arts and Science, followed by faculties in Medicine and Agriculture. The Carnegie Corporation contributed $84,000 towards an Institute of Education which will enable the University to appoint a visiting Professor of Education. The Government in the United Kingdom agreed early in 1954 to make a grant of £1¼ million towards the cost.[1] The decision to throw open admission to the University College to students from the High Commission Territories did not pass without criticism. It was argued that the local population ran the risk of being excluded owing to an influx from beyond the borders.

There was also some criticism when it became known that in the early stages there would be separate accommodation for European and African students. The Principal made it clear, however, that this arrangement was a purely temporary measure until the full academic curriculum could be introduced, when, it was hoped, there would be complete integration. It was further explained that even in some of the older universities separate hostels were sometimes provided for students from different countries. The qualifications for entrance to the University College were described as about the same as for the University of London, that is to say rather higher than the South African standard. Since not many Africans in Rhodesian schools had reached this standard it was unlikely that the College would contain a large proportion of African students in its first years.

A college to train European primary-school teachers for the Federation will be established at Bulawayo in 1956. The Grahamstown Training College which had previously supplied this need has intimated that owing to the local demand it is unable in the future to accept pupils from outside South Africa.

For European education in Rhodesia the Administration relied at the outset mainly on the activities of the missionary societies.[2] The Education Ordinance of 1899 provided for grants on a pound-to-pound basis to Mission-conducted schools for Europeans. In 1908, however, the Administration assumed direct control of all primary education and also established the first State secondary school. Europeans at that period numbered between 13,000 and 15,000, mostly in Southern Rhodesia, but with the increase in the European population (it was estimated in 1954 to number 159,000) the schools have grown in proportion, and in 1953 the total school enrolment was 31,458. Of these pupils, 7,386 were attending secondary schools. In outlying areas grants have been made to 'farm schools', in which parents supply the buildings and furniture while the Government provides the teachers, salaries, and equipment. In 1934 there were 63 such schools, but in 1953 there was a change of policy,

[1] See *Africa*, October 1954, p. 384. [2] *O.Y.S.R., 1952*, pp. 305 ff.

provision being made for hostels at the more efficiently organized schools; there were 90 hostels in 1953, the number of farm schools being reduced to nine, with only 101 pupils. With the recent concentration of European immigrants in the larger centres it has become practicable to open day secondary schools, and the population of boarders has fallen from 31 per cent. in 1945 to 24 per cent. in 1953. In 1953 the total number of Government schools for Europeans was 116; nursery schools in 1953 numbered 40, with 1,305 pupils.[1] A correspondence course for children of primary-school age was inaugurated in 1930, and had over 1,000 pupils in 1953. A technical school was opened in Bulawayo in 1927, and plans for raising it to the level of a technical college were announced in 1951.

Primary education for Europeans was made free and compulsory in 1931,[2] and tuition fees in secondary schools were abolished in 1935. Boarding fees vary from school to school, but the highest fee is £35 per pupil per annum. The secondary-school system was reorganized in 1937, and as a result three types of secondary education were introduced— academic, modern, and technical. For the first type, the Cambridge School Certificate examination was substituted for the South African matriculation, and the second was also made subject to an external examination. Difficulties, however, arose in carrying out the system, especially in respect of the provision of qualified teachers, and the provision of separate schools to teach the 'modern' course was abandoned. In the sphere of primary education the Department, relying on experience in England, has refused to reintroduce any qualifying test for admission to secondary schools, but has acceded to the teachers' demand for the re-introduction of approved syllabuses.

In 1943 some 50 per cent. of the European pupils were not completing the four-year secondary course, but between 1948 and 1953 the number of passes in the Cambridge School Certificate rose from 418 to 653, in the Higher School Certificate from 14 to 39, and in technical examinations of various kinds from 87 to 338. The percentage of post-primary pupils completing the sixth-form course rose from 1 per cent. in 1949 to 8 per cent. in 1951. Nevertheless, serious concern has been felt at the relative lack of interest shown in obtaining an academic type of education, since only one in five of the occupations usually entered by Europeans needs an academic training. When the Federation of Rhodesia and Nyasaland came into existence on 1 August 1953 the subject of European, Asian, and Coloured education was transferred to the new Federal Government.

For Coloured and Asian children primary education is free, but it is compulsory only within a three-mile radius of a school for Coloured children. As the great majority of Coloured and Asian children are at

---

[1] *Report on Education for the Year 1953*, C.S.R. 18, 1954.
[2] Compulsory Education Act, 1930.

school, it has been recommended that education be made compulsory in their case, and that transport and boarding grants be made where necessary. Secondary education for the few Coloured children who have sought it has been provided mainly by the award of bursaries to schools in the Union, particularly in the Cape Province, but a secondary day school was opened in Bulawayo in 1952. In 1951 there were nearly 3,000 Asian and Coloured children at school, two-thirds of them at State and the rest at aided schools. By 1953 the figure had risen to 3,500. It had not then been thought possible to provide vocational training for Coloured and Asian children, owing to the uncertainty regarding the industries in which members of their communities would be acceptable.

When the Federation was founded most teachers for European schools were trained at Rhodes University in the Union, which had the only training college that would accept candidates who did not speak both English and Afrikaans. In 1951 some 72 teachers were recruited from the United Kingdom, 52 from the Union, and 47 were Rhodesians trained abroad. A supplementary means of improving teaching efficiency was provided by the scheme for an annual exchange of six teachers with the United Kingdom. There has been an unusually liberal provision of aid in the form of boarding grants and school scholarships, part of which has come from grants made from the Beit Bequest, from which contributions amounting in all to some £750,000 have been made for the furtherance of education in Rhodesia. As regards higher education, they provide eight bursaries and also two scholarships for engineering; the Government offers six bursaries for university study overseas. Three of the Rhodes Trust scholarships tenable at Oxford are earmarked for Southern Rhodesia. In 1951 there were 478 Southern Rhodesians studying at universities, of whom 415 were in the Union and 53 in the United Kingdom. The total expenditure on European, Asian, and Coloured education in 1953 was £2,070,599.

In Northern Rhodesia, where the European population had in 1951 risen to 37,000, education for Europeans was available in 1952 at 24 Government, two Government-aided, and seven private schools, the total enrolment being 8,223. Of these pupils, 1,400 were in the private schools. While the majority of the schools offered only primary education, there were seven that provided secondary courses, which in some instances worked up to the Cambridge Overseas School Certificate.[1] For children living at a distance from schools hostel accommodation was provided on the same lines as those followed in Southern Rhodesia. No technical-school facilities for Europeans existed in the Protectorate, but bursaries were given for study at institutions in other territories. The only adult education provided by the Government was through classes for apprentices at the

[1] *Colonial Reports, Northern Rhodesia, 1952,* p. 36.

five mining and two other centres in the territory. The sum provided for European, Asian, and Coloured education in 1952 was £484,159 (as compared with £614,561 for Africans),[1] but the amount allocated for Asian and Coloured education was small, as the total enrolment from these races was in 1952 only 391. In Nyasaland, where the European population is relatively small, it had been necessary to make provision for only five primary schools (two of which were conducted by missions with Government aid). Europeans normally resorted to the Union for secondary education.

As regards the education of Africans in the Federation of Rhodesia, the Constitution, as already shown, leaves the three territorial Legislatures responsible for primary and secondary education, while the Federal organization provides for the higher education of all the communities.[2] In Southern Rhodesia African education falls within the sphere of the Minister of Native Affairs. The history leading to this position is of some significance, and has been described elsewhere.[3] The Plewman Commission of 1945 recommended that African education should again be placed under the Education Department. Though this was in accordance with the wishes of Africans the recommendation was not adopted, and the Committee of Inquiry into Native Education which was appointed in 1951 saw no advantage to the African in making this change by itself. It recommended that provision made in the Native Development Act be replaced by an African Education Act, under which a Director of African Education with a Central Advisory Board would take over the functions in relation to education now vested in the Director of Native Development. Thus, though the subject of education would still be divided at Cabinet level between two Ministers, there would be opportunities for consultation on policy.[4]

Southern Rhodesia shared with the Union the system under which the majority of African schools were provided by missions. Grants-in-aid covered between 60 and 70 per cent. of the recurrent costs, and amounted in 1949–50 to £403,772. In 1954 there were about 350,000 pupils attending 2,232 aided and 12 Government schools, in which they were taught by 361 European and 9,000 African teachers. About 65 per cent. of the total child population was estimated to be in school, but half were in the two lowest classes; only 231 received instruction in Standard VI. There were 24 Africans studying at universities. The Government was directly responsible for two boarding schools for boys at Domboshawa and Umzingwane, where post-primary courses in agriculture, carpentry, building, and sanitation qualified pupils for posts as demonstrators or foremen on

[1] This amounted to £744,000 in 1953.
[2] The Rhodesia and Nyasaland Federation Order in Council no. 1199, 1953.
[3] See above, p. 443.
[4] *Southern Rhodesia, Report of the Committee of Enquiry into Native Education*, C.S.R. 6, 1952, para. 340.

farms or as building contractors or teachers. A Government co-educational secondary boarding school was opened at Goromonzi in 1946. By 1953 there were twelve schools giving secondary education for Africans, with an enrolment of 1,078. There were nine Government primary schools in urban areas. Adult education was provided in the form of night schools teaching literacy in the vernacular; the enrolment in 1950 was 4,658. There were three 'homecraft village schools' in Matabeleland and one in Mashonaland, where domestic subjects were taught to married women or girls about to be married.

On 15 March 1956 the Prime Minister of Southern Rhodesia, Mr. Garfield Todd, announced a five-year plan for providing a school course for all African children by 1960.[1] The weakness in the former system, he said, lay in the large proportion of untrained teachers; this was responsible for the fact that most of the pupils never progressed beyond the lowest standard. The Government had begun a campaign to produce 4,000 adequately trained teachers by 1960 and so to double the number of pupils in Standards IV, V, and VI. After 1957 African pupils would not be allowed to remain at school if by the age of 14 they had not reached Standard III. In addition to the one Government secondary school and the 14 Mission secondary schools three more would be opened by 1959 and others thereafter. For these improvements a further sum of £3,800,000 would be provided and the Native Education Vote—£1,600,000 in 1956—would rise to £2,800,000 in 1960. The steadily increasing cost of this and other social services would require an increase of Native taxation by £2 per head.

The provision of African education in Northern Rhodesia and Nyasaland will receive further comment in the following pages, which deal with education in the British Colonial dependencies generally, but the establishment of a University College in Southern Rhodesia has given special importance to the position in regard to the provision of secondary education in the three territories of the Federation. The Report of the Commission on Higher Education for Africans in Central Africa[2] summarized the position as follows:

	Total number of scholars	Number in secondary schools	Average passes in Overseas School Certificate[4]
Southern Rhodesia (1949)	223,918	344[3]	37
Northern Rhodesia (1951)	161,061	248	12
Nyasaland (1950)	219,667	162	6

[1] *The Times*, 16 March 1956.
[2] Central African Council, *Report of the Commission on Higher Education for Africans in Central Africa*, 1953, p. 8. [3] 204 general post-primary; 140 industrial post-primary.
[4] Average passes for three years in Southern Rhodesia, five years in Northern Rhodesia, and two in Nyasaland.

To the number of those who have passed the Overseas School Certificate must be added a certain number of students from the three territories who are known to have sat for the National Senior Certificate of the Union, and for the external examinations of the University of London, but it is difficult to assess the number of successes in these examinations. It is clear, however, that the Administrations of the territories must pay greater attention to the provision of qualified teachers for secondary courses if the new University College at Salisbury is to be ensured an adequate field from which to draw its African students.

THE BRITISH DEPENDENCIES

Education Policy

In education, as in other social services, each of the United Kingdom dependencies has its own local Department, which retains a large measure of initiative and control over policy and administration. Principles of general application have, however, been accepted by successive Secretaries of State on the recommendation of the Advisory Committee on Education in the Colonies, a body set up in 1924, in response to a representation made by the International Missionary Council which urged the Government to take a more active part in the development of education for Africans.[1] The Committee's first declaration of policy in 1925 asserted that 'education should be adapted to the mentality and traditions of the various peoples, conserving as far as possible all healthy elements in the fabric of their social life'. The greatest importance was to be attached to religious teaching and moral instruction. The most effective method of training character was considered to be the residential school. The importance of women's education was emphasized, but stress was laid on the dangers that might attend any action in this matter which did not take account of the social reactions which might follow. At that period education in the African dependencies, with the exception of Northern Nigeria, largely a Muslim area, was still mainly in the hands of various missionary bodies, the official Education Departments having been but recently formed. The British Government announced that it welcomed all voluntary educational effort which conformed to its general policy, but reserved to itself the direction of policy and the supervision of all educational institutions. It suggested that Advisory Boards for education should be set up, and that they should include representatives of the technical Departments, of the unofficial European community, and of Africans.[2]

The next statement of policy was made in 1927 and related to the place

---

[1] A. Mayhew, *Education in the Colonial Empire*, 1938, pp. 40 ff.
[2] *Education Policy in British Tropical Africa*, Cmd. 2374, 1925.

of the vernacular in African education.[1] It was recognized that vernaculars must be used in the first stages of elementary education. English was, however, regarded as essential in all intermediate, secondary, and technical schools, and its inculcation must therefore commence in the higher classes of the elementary schools. In a memorandum on Native policy in East Africa, issued in 1930,[2] the Government declared that education should be made available for adults as well as for children; it should aim not merely at producing efficiency in clerical duties and handicrafts but at effecting a transformation in the daily lives of the whole community. The continued study of the subject by the Advisory Committee led to increasing stress upon the importance of relating education with all other agencies of social improvement. Practical suggestions for the social education of the people, first put forward in 1935,[3] were developed in a memorandum issued in 1943 which envisaged juvenile, adolescent, and adult education as mutually supporting parts of one programme of mass education.[4] Schemes of village betterment should be linked with plans for the extension within a reasonable time of primary education to all children and of literacy to all adults under 50. The Committee referred on various occasions to the growing demand of Africans for higher education. They noted that those able to afford it studied at European or American universities, but held that the results were often undesirable, and they recommended that steps should be taken for the development in Africa of institutions of university standard. The measures subsequently taken to give effect to this recommendation will be narrated in a later part of this chapter.[5]

Material assistance to the expansion of education has been provided by grants made under the Colonial Development and Welfare Acts of 1940 and 1945. The total sums issued for educational development for the period 1 April 1946 to 31 March 1954 to the 15 Colonial territories in Africa were:[6]

	£
For primary and secondary education	5,293,000
For technical and vocational education	3,075,000
For higher education, including scholarships . .	397,000
	£8,765,000

In addition, capital grants have been allotted to the three new University Colleges.[7]

The declarations of policy above referred to have not been intended to produce a uniform system in all the dependencies, and local developments

---

[1] See above, pp. 92 ff.
[2] *Memorandum on Native Policy in East Africa*, Cmd. 3573, 1930.
[3] *Memorandum on the Education of African Communities*, Col. no. 103, 1935.
[4] *Mass Education in African Society*, Col. no. 186, 1943, p. 6.   [5] See below, p. 1179.
[6] *Colonial Development and Welfare Acts*, Cmd. 9375, 1955.   [7] See below, p. 1182.

since 1925 have followed different lines. In Uganda and Nyasaland the Governments have continued to work very largely through missionary bodies, and in most other territories have relied on them at least for all primary teaching, though schools conducted directly by the Government predominate in Zanzibar and on the Tanganyika coast. In the Northern Provinces of Nigeria the local Native Authorities provided in 1951 some 397 out of a total of 1,121 primary schools, and in addition provided funds for eleven Mission schools. In the Northern Territories of the Gold Coast the Native Authority schools far exceed the number of Mission schools, and there is now also a growing number of Native Administration schools in Sierra Leone. There are a considerable number of local Native Council schools in Kenya.[1] In Northern Rhodesia State agencies have direct responsibility for technical education in urban areas only; in the rural areas this is entrusted to missions. In most other territories all technical education is provided by the Government. There are variations in the degree of control exercised over the conduct of schools not managed directly by the Government, such as those of religious denominations or under the management of independent African organizations. It is now usual for the opening of schools to require official approval and for this to be dependent on the ability of the bodies concerned to satisfy the minimum conditions of efficiency. A school may be closed if it fails to satisfy these conditions or is 'conducted in a manner not in the interests of the pupils'.[2]

The control of independent African schools has been a matter of special concern to the Kenya Government since the inception of the Kikuyu independent schools movement about 1930. The Kenya Education Ordinance of 1931 authorized the closing of schools if they were conducted 'in a manner detrimental to the physical, mental, or moral welfare of the pupils' or prejudicial to peace and good government.[3] When the Kenya system was reorganized in 1952 in accordance with the recommendations of the Beecher Report, the more specific provisions then introduced formed the basis for the action taken against those Kikuyu schools that were believed to be centres of recruitment to the Mau Mau movement.[4] Where a school has been closed the Education Department may take over the premises and reopen it.[5] In its Report the East Africa Royal Commission of 1953–5 made some interesting comments upon independent schools. Their emergence was ascribed to the insufficiency of schools rather than to dissatisfaction with existing schools, and a special attraction was the earlier stage at which English was taught. It recommended that independent schools should not be discouraged, but brought under effec-

---

[1] *N.A.*, Part I, pp. 113, 156; Part III, pp. 41, 258, 309.
[2] See Education Ordinance of Nigeria no. 17, 1952.   [3] Laws, Cap. 38.
[4] See above, p. 452.   [5] Education Ordinance no. 58, 1952.

tive inspection and control.[1] By the middle of 1954, 66 of these schools had been reopened, of which 42 were under the management of District Education Boards and 24 under the control of missions.

The Gold Coast law requires only registration as a condition of opening a school, but schools may be closed if they are 'dangerous to the physical or moral well-being of the pupils'. In Tanganyika the propriety of making rules for 'zoning' areas between different missions was at one time the subject of much debate; later, however, schools which only give religious instruction were exempted from control, as they also are in Nyasaland.

Some territories are now coming in sight of a system of universal education. It has been made compulsory for Asian boys in Nairobi, Mombasa, and Kisumu. In Nyasaland and Tanganyika enrolment is optional, but the attendance of children once enrolled is compulsory. Northern Rhodesia in 1943 introduced compulsory education in the Broken Hill, Choma, and Livingstone areas for children from 12 to 16 living within three miles of a school. It will, however, be realized that the efficacy of any such regulation depends on the maintenance of an efficient body of School Attendance Officers, a class that is not readily secured in present conditions in Africa.

The territories containing a mixed population provide in various ways for the needs of their different groups. In Tanganyika special funds created by the non-Native Education Tax Ordinance of 1948 are administered by European and Asian Education Authorities, and there are Advisory Committees on African and other non-Native (including Goan) schools. In Uganda there are separate Advisory Councils for African, Asian, Goan, and European education, and Kenya has similar institutions. The different system regarding European and non-European education in the Federation of Rhodesia and Nyasaland has already been mentioned. There are at present only a small number of primary or secondary schools which are open to members of more than one community, as for example the Royal Technical College at Nairobi or the Institute of Muslim Education at Mombasa. Children of mixed descent are admitted to the State European school in Kampala if their home background is European. The new University Colleges[2] are open to students of all races. Makerere has made a special effort to diversify the composition of its students. In 1955 there were six Arabs, five Asians, and one European, in addition to Africans from 70 different tribes. The East African Indian National Congress announced in 1953 its intention to build a memorial to Mahatma Gandhi in the form of a college at Mwanza, Tanganyika, available for students of all communities.[3] In 1954 it was merged with the Royal Technical College at Nairobi. The combined institution is administered on a multi-racial basis and provides higher

[1] *East Africa Royal Commission 1953–1955, Report*, Cmd. 9475, 1955, pp. 176, 185.
[2] See below, p. 1180. [3] *Africa Digest*, May 1954, p. 13.

education of a technical nature as well as a course in Arts up to a level qualifying candidates to enter a university.

The criticisms levelled against the system now followed in the British dependencies are numerous. They include condemnation of the domination exercised by British external examinations, the failure to provide suitable education for girls, the bookishness of many of the schools, and the disproportionate cost of educating European children. One of the difficulties of meeting some at least of these criticisms lies in the strength of the African opposition to any procedure which would suggest that Africans should receive a different type of education from that given to Europeans. So far as the criticism relates to the slow rate of expansion of educational facilities, a marked quickening of the pace has in recent years been made possible by the grants made under the Colonial Development and Welfare Acts, and yet further increases in the number of schools have been made by the new semi-responsible Governments in West Africa. While, however, criticism is still directed against the inadequacy in actual numbers of schools in these territories, there is at the same time some apprehension expressed lest the rapid increase now envisaged may lead to a serious fall in quality. A mission of experts which visited the Eastern Region of Nigeria in 1951 remarked that in this area the rate of expansion forced upon the Education Department by public demand had resulted in the virtual collapse of all standards.[1]

At the same time there can be little doubt of the earnest desire on the part of Africans for education. 'Even the poorest Africans not only desire education for their children but are willing to make pecuniary sacrifices to secure it.'[2] The chief obstacle to universal education is an insufficiency of teachers. Only 10 per cent. of those who enter primary schools find a place in intermediate schools. As was pointed out by an earlier Committee 'money spent on a child who does not stay four years at school is wasted as completely as if it were burned'.[3] The aim should be universal education at low fees up to the intermediate stage and in the towns to the end of the intermediate stage, and secondary education for those who are prepared to pay for it, assisted by liberal bursaries.

The important part still taken by the missions in the provision of education, particularly in the earlier stages of school instruction, is a matter that has caused much debate of recent years. Missionary apprehensions regarding the increasing measure of State control over education which was envisaged by the Colonial Office memorandum of 1925 were allayed by the prominence which it gave to the value of religion in African education, and the policy which it laid down was welcomed by the Conference of

[1] P. Morris, ed., *African Education*, 1953, p. 35.   [2] Cmd. 9475, 1955, p. 175.
[3] The Binns Committee, whose Report is published in *African Education, A Study of Educational Policy and Practice in British Tropical Africa*, 1953.

Protestant missionary bodies held at Le Zoute in 1926.[1] The Conference agreed that the chief sphere of mission activity must lie in the field of primary and secondary education; higher and technical instruction should ordinarily be conducted by the Government through the agency of governing bodies on which missions are represented. The view of the Conference regarding the use of indigenous languages in education was in the main the same as that embodied in the Colonial Office statement of 1927. The Roman Catholic missionary societies have also welcomed State assistance and supervision in their schools, though they do not regard it as desirable for their adherents to attend State or Native Authority schools.

The official suggestions for guidance in making grants-in-aid to schools indicate that voluntary bodies should expect State aid only if their staffs are as well qualified as the members of the State Education Service.[2] Subject to this proviso it has been recognized that the expenditure on staff should be the basis upon which grants-in-aid of Mission schools should be calculated. More recently, however, Governments have made it their policy to relate their grants to total approved expenditure. The complex problems created by discrepancies between Government and Mission salaries have been solved in some Colonies by the introduction of a unified teaching service and in others by a gradual approximation of teachers' salaries and conditions of service. As the African teaching staff expanded, teachers' associations (which were in some Colonies affiliated to the English National Union of Teachers) not only gained experience in wage negotiations but became concerned to uphold professional standards, a development which has made it easier to accord to them parity of treatment with Government servants. In Northern Rhodesia the Government and mission teachers were paid in 1946 the same salaries, and a unified African teaching service was introduced in 1951. The Kenya Government has taken steps in the same direction. In West Africa and Nyasaland, Northern Rhodesia, Tanganyika, and Kenya teachers' salaries are now equated as nearly as possible with the corresponding posts in the Civil Service, though this is not yet the case in Uganda and Zanzibar. As the number of African graduates increases it will become more difficult to maintain a racial distinction in matters of salary, and it may be necessary to envisage the development of a procedure already introduced in parts of West Africa by which salaries will be equated with qualifications, an expatriation allowance being paid to Europeans.

Since the time of the Le Zoute Conference the position of the religious bodies conducting education has been modified in two important respects. The rise in costs and the standards of teaching have made them increasingly dependent on Government grants, and the proportion of African per-

[1] E. W. Smith, *The Christian Mission in Africa*, 1926, p. 110.
[2] *Memorandum on Educational Grants-in-Aid*, Col. no. 84, 1933, pp. 5, 6, 10.

sonnel has largely increased. It has been pointed out with reference to Uganda[1] in particular that the term 'mission education' is a misnomer if it is taken to imply education conducted by the agents of organizations with headquarters outside Africa. Most Protestant education in the Protectorate is now controlled by the self-supporting Native Anglican Church, one of the Roman Catholic vicariates is under an African Bishop, and the Muslim schools are entirely under African management. A similar situation has prevailed in West Africa from a somewhat earlier date. Most Governments continue to insist on the importance of religion as an element in education, and the Kenya Education Ordinance of 1952 makes religious instruction compulsory, except for pupils expressly excused.

The financial difficulties of the voluntary agencies have been met in part by revising the basis of grants-in-aid. Under the regulations which came into force in Nigeria in 1949 a school which attains the required standards receives an amount equal to all teachers' salaries plus a proportion of other expenses. In Northern Rhodesia voluntary agencies are relieved of all recurrent costs, except for the salaries of the European supervisory staff and one-third of those of the European teaching staff. In Uganda six secondary schools and two teacher-training centres were reorganized in 1942 as self-governing institutions, with their budgets balanced by Government grants. The Church Missionary Society in 1950 surrendered its interest in Fourah Bay College to the Sierra Leone Government.

The group of educational experts who visited East and Central Africa in 1952 recommended that all grant-aided schools should combine the position of State and religious schools, and that as an immediate step every Government or Native Authority school should have a governing body on which missions were represented, and that every Mission school should have an Advisory Committee on which the African local authority was represented.[2] They remarked that some missionaries recruited from outside the Commonwealth are unfamiliar with British institutions and sometimes speak English badly, and urged that those who are to be engaged in education should have adequate training in the speaking of English and in the history and meaning of British institutions. Conditions similar to these are, it will be seen, imposed on non-Belgian missions operating in the Belgian Congo. In Nigeria, on the other hand, it has been asserted that the development of Diocesan Education Councils has given responsibilities to Africans as full as those which they will have as Local Education Authorities. Competition between missionary bodies was the subject of criticism by the group of visiting educational experts in 1952, although they also noted that 'among the missionaries who represent the well-

[1] *Uganda, Annual Report of the Education Department,* 1952, p. 6.
[2] Morris, op. cit., p. 65.

established and venerated religions of the world, we met innumerable examples of mutual respect as well as of active co-operation'.[1] It was clear, however, that in some territories the unwillingness of missions to combine has led to an uneconomic dispersal of resources for teacher training. It should be added that there is not in the British areas any discrimination between 'national' and foreign missions, nor between missions of different denominations.

In every territory Africans are represented on Advisory Committees or Boards of Education, and in some they are in the majority. The constitution of these boards varies. In Nigeria there is a Board of Education for each Region and one Central Board. The Gold Coast has a Board of Education for the Northern Territories, but the advisory functions of the corresponding body for the Colony and Ashanti have been divided between the Ministry of Education and a Central Advisory Committee which was set up in 1952. In Tanganyika the Advisory Committee consists of a mixed body of which three are officials, ten are European missionaries, and seven are Africans. The African Education Advisory Board in Northern Rhodesia similarly consists of a body which has four official members, 16 Europeans representing different religious groups, and five Africans. Most of these bodies, however, meet only once a year. In all territories except Sierra Leone, Gambia, and Zanzibar there are also local boards or committees on which Native Authorities or Local Councils are represented, and which advise on such matters as applications for registration and eligibility for grant aid. Some are given an actual measure of control. Thus under the 1951 Education Ordinance of Northern Rhodesia Local Education Authorities are to be responsible for the general administration of schools and the disbursement of the funds allocated to education by the Central Government and by Native Authorities. The first such authority to be set up was for the Copperbelt and Ndola Urban District; it is responsible for 17 schools.

The Part played by Local Authorities

It has been generally assumed that primary education is one of the services most suitable for transfer to the control of African Local Authorities. This, it may be noted, became the almost universal practice in British India. In Kenya the Local Native Councils have since 1949 borne the financial responsibility for all primary schools in their areas, though control rests with the Department of Education and the Local Education Committees. Recent proposals for the development of Local Government in Uganda envisage the transfer of control over this subject to Local Authorities within five years from 1954.[2] It has been included among the

[1] Ibid. p. 64.
[2] C. A. G. Wallis, *Inquiry into African Local Government in Uganda*, 1953.

functions recommended as suitable for transfer to Local Authorities in Nigeria and Northern Rhodesia;[1] the Government of Northern Rhodesia, however, has preferred the system outlined above, on the ground that something more comprehensive than a Native Authority Council was required to meet the needs of the situation.[2] The Local Government laws enacted in 1951 for the Gold Coast and the different Regions of Nigeria authorize Local Authorities to build and maintain primary schools in order to provide for compulsory education. Elsewhere, as for example in Tanganyika, the development of Native Authority Councils on Local Government lines has included the creation of Education Committees.

The proportion of their total expenditure which has been devoted to education by Local Councils and Native Authorities has varied in recent years from 12 per cent. in Northern Nigeria to 29 per cent. in Kenya. Numerous Native Authorities have imposed 'education rates', though it has been remarked that the description is misleading in those cases where the levies called by this name simply supplement the education expenditure met from general revenue.[3] In Nigeria the Native Authorities were empowered in 1950 to levy special education rates; the first County Council to come into being in the Eastern Region raised a total of £10,000 for this purpose by special precepts, this being equal to a rate of 4s. per adult male. In its plans for providing universal primary education the Government of Eastern Nigeria has proposed to undertake 55 per cent. of the cost and to rely upon Local Authorities for the remainder. In Northern Rhodesia, where the proportion of Native Authority expenditure on education in 1950 was 15·5 per cent. of their total expenditure, the Education Department has stated that the Native Authorities would be required to use their rating powers in order to raise considerably more money for education than they have done in the past.[4] But so great has been the efflux from rural areas to urban centres that in 1955 there were 10,000 vacancies in the schools already established in rural areas.

In the Gold Coast, according to the Development Plan of 1951, the major proportion of teachers' salaries in all schools would be provided by the Central Government, while Local Authorities would be required to meet all other expenditure. Middle schools, in which fees would still be charged, might be provided by Local Authorities, who would receive assistance from the Central Government to the extent that this was possible when the needs of primary education had been met.[5]

---

[1] S. Phillipson, *Financial Relations between the Government of Nigeria and the Native Administrations*, 1946. *Report of the Financial Relationship Committee, Northern Rhodesia*, 1949.

[2] *Northern Rhodesia, African Education, Annual Report, 1951*, p. 19.

[3] Wallis, op. cit.

[4] *Colonial Reports, Northern Rhodesia, 1951*, p. 19. The estimated recurrent expenditure in 1953 was £40,000 (*African Education, Annual Report, 1953*, p. 16).

[5] *Gold Coast, Annual Report of the Education Department, 1951*, pp. 14–15.

The Special Conditions in West Africa

The progress of education in the British West African territories deserves fuller treatment. In each of these territories the Development Plans supported by the Colonial Development and Welfare Acts envisaged a rapid extension of education in all its branches and, especially in the Gold Coast and Nigeria, the advance of self-government has implied a greatly increased allotment of money to educational purposes. In 1951 the Gold Coast adopted an Accelerated Development Plan for Education which, ambitious though it seemed by African standards, was actually surpassed in several respects by the progress made during the succeeding five years. The estimated capital cost was £8 million. The Gold Coast is the wealthiest of the African Colonies and its stability was ensured during those years by the accrued funds of the Marketing Boards[1] from which capital sums were advanced to the Development Plans. For the year 1953–4 the expenditure on education was £4·7 million; in primary and middle schools there were 494,334 pupils, of whom 150,108 were girls; and in secondary schools there were 8,602 pupils, of whom 1,296 were girls. A total of 785 boys and 121 girls obtained the Cambridge School Certificate, and there was notable progress in technical and higher education, which will be referred to later.[2] There were in 1954 3,280 teachers in training at 28 colleges. Enrolment in primary schools had increased by 83 per cent., in middle schools by 66 per cent., and in teachers' training colleges by 100 per cent.[3]

The Ten-Year Plan for Nigeria under the first Colonial Development and Welfare scheme was revised in 1951 and again later as the Nigerian Regions acquired a larger control over their destinies. The total expenditure from public funds on education for the year 1953 was £4,488,710, of which £3,795,180 was derived from grants made under the Colonial Development and Welfare Acts. In that year the enrolment in primary schools was 1,068,789, but of these only 125,989 were at schools in the Northern Region. The secondary-school enrolment was estimated at 22,400.[4] The Minister for Education for the Western Region of Nigeria announced in 1952 a programme designed to enable universal compulsory education to be introduced in 1955. At the beginning of that year there were 400,000 children receiving primary education free. To meet part of the cost the Regional 'capitation share' of the General tax was increased by 10s. in 1953. It has been estimated that in 1952 the Eastern Region of Nigeria spent 30 per cent. of its total budget on education, this being about half the estimated cost of providing free primary education for every child.

In the Colony of Sierra Leone, with its old tradition of missionary

---

[1] See below, pp. 1179 ff.
[2] See below, p. 1182. See also *Colonial Reports, Gold Coast, 1954*, pp. 68–71.
[3] *Africa Digest*, May–June 1955, p. 2.   [4] *Colonial Reports, Nigeria, 1953*, p. 65.

education, 4,009 pupils were in secondary schools in 1953, a high proportion when compared with the 46,853 in primary schools. The total expenditure on education was reported as £622,504, of which grants made under the Colonial Development and Welfare Acts amounted to £218,231. Schooling was still backward in the Protectorate. Though well forward with primary education Gambia has made less progress beyond that stage. There were 359 boys receiving secondary education in 1950.

Secondary Education

The West African territories have for many years enjoyed some facilities for secondary and even for higher education. Grammar schools were opened in Sierra Leone for boys in 1845 and for girls in 1849, and secondary schools appeared in Nigeria and the Gold Coast between 1876 and 1880. An Ordinance enacted for the Colony of Nigeria in 1887 made provision for grants-in-aid for secondary education. In 1937 the Gold Coast had three schools classified as secondary, Gambia had four, Sierra Leone nine, Northern Nigeria twelve, and Southern Nigeria 30, though this did not imply that all of them provided the full secondary course. As regards the provision made at this period in East Africa, a full secondary education could be obtained in Uganda only at the Makerere College. In Kenya there were two Mission schools of junior secondary standard. These, with two others, reached full secondary status in 1940. By 1954, in spite of the disturbed state of the country, Kenya had 1,829 African pupils in secondary schools. In Uganda there were in 1955 some 9,543 boys and girls in secondary schools, of whom 543 entered for the School Certificate examination. In 1954 Tanganyika was providing secondary education for 2,780 pupils, of whom it was estimated that a fifth would reach the Cambridge School Certificate standard. Expansion in this field is now included in the Ten-year Development Programmes of all these territories, and has been assisted by grants made under the Colonial Development and Welfare Acts. Sierra Leone, for example, has received £174,360 for this purpose, Nyasaland £90,600, and Northern Rhodesia £15,000.

In some territories it has long been held to be preferable for the post-primary stage to consist in vocational training rather than in further education of a general type, a tendency which was stimulated by the emphasis placed on vocational training in the 1925 memorandum of the Advisory Committee on Education in the Colonies. In the East African territories there are, in addition to grammar schools, junior-secondary or middle schools, which prepare some pupils for the full secondary course and others for entry to technical training institutions; parallel with them are trade schools taking pupils directly from the primary course. In the Gold Coast, Sierra Leone, and the Northern Region of Nigeria the middle schools are of equal standing with the grammar schools. The De La Warr Commission[1] made the point that technical and general education must be complementary, and this argument gains in force as the level of competence expected of technicians rises.

Vocational and Technical Training

The demand for skilled African craftsmen has been stimulated by the Development Programmes initiated in all the territories from 1945 onwards, by policies of Africanization in Government service and in that of commercial firms, and by the increasing difficulty of recruiting technicians from overseas. Some attempts have been made to meet this demand by organizing short practical courses requiring a minimum of book knowledge, and in several territories ex-service men, who had acquired some knowledge of machinery while in the army, were given such training. A Committee on manpower in Tanganyika has suggested that youths, who need not even be literate, could be taught skilled trades in appropriately designed courses, but experience in East Africa shows that the ability merely to use tools under supervision is not enough to enable an African to hold his own in face of the competition from Indian artisans. The importance of appropriate training in this field has been recognized in most territories, and a number have opened technical institutions giving post-secondary instruction.

In West Africa the Nigerian Government decided in 1950 to establish institutions which would provide education in Arts, Science, and Technology of a non-University character. A College of Technology has its headquarters at Zaria, and other Colleges are in process of formation. The Yaba Higher College, near Lagos, which began in 1931 to train students for employment in the various departments of government, has now become a technical school, and two others are to be opened at Kaduna and Enugu. Three trade centres for training apprentices have been opened, and a secondary technical school commenced work in 1954. In Nigeria the Government collieries provide a five-year course for the training of Africans for promotion to the post of under-manager. In the Gold Coast, Achimota College was boldly conceived as a comprehensive school for both sexes of all ages from the kindergarten to the university stage.[2] As far back as 1929 it began to prepare students for the external examinations of London University in engineering. Step by step, as the educational system of the Gold Coast has developed, Achimota has renounced all but the functions of a secondary school. The University College has grown out of it and finally, in 1951, a College of Technology was opened at Kumasi.[3] In Sierra Leone the

[1] *Report of a Commission on Higher Education in East Africa,* Col. no. 142, 1937.
[2] See further below, pp. 1179 ff.
[3] *Gold Coast, Annual Report of the Education Department, 1951,* pp. 16, 23.

Government Training Centre for artisans at Wilberforce has been developed as a technical institute and will have a branch in the Protectorate. Two existing schools are to be developed as secondary technical schools, and Fourah Bay College is to include a College of Technology.

In East and Central Africa the foundation stone of the Royal Technical College of East Africa in Nairobi was laid in 1952; the Mombasa Institute of Muslim Education, which is also a technical institute, and like the Nairobi College is open to members of all races, was established early in 1951. In Uganda the Kawanda Agricultural School is now a branch of the University College of Makerere and a sum of £2 million was allocated from the Uganda African Development Fund in 1952 for technical education and training. There were in that year five State technical schools; the missionary bodies managed four technical schools with Government assistance, and at Kabale the African Local Government had a trade school which trained carpenters and builders. In Tanganyika the revised ten-year educational plan provided for the establishment of three new trade schools in addition to the one already in existence. Northern Rhodesia's Development Plan provides for a total of 20 trade schools, ten of which will be managed by missions with Government assistance; 16 of these had been opened by 1953. At the school in Barotseland 207 men and women attended the courses for handicrafts, and 201 the course for Local Government. A course on elementary book-keeping attracted 19 Africans. A total of 57 bricklayers and 31 carpenters qualified at Serenje. At Fort Rosebery, besides the usual handicraft courses, Africans are taught cycle-repairing and boat-building.[1] In Nyasaland technical instruction is given at the secondary school at Dedza, and a grant of £76,000 has been made under the Colonial Development and Welfare Acts towards the establishment of a polytechnic. An industrial school was opened in Zanzibar in 1924. In many territories technical and specialist training in departmental workshops or other centres is also given by the Public Works, Forestry, Medical, Veterinary, and Survey Departments, and in railway shops. Many Mission schools give training in carpentry, building, and printing, and most Mission hospitals train male and female assistants and midwives.

The earlier memoranda of the Advisory Committee on Education in the Colonies[2] emphasized the importance of a vocational element in primary education, not in the sense of preparation for specific employment, but as conveying some knowledge of improved methods of agriculture and simple handicrafts. In practice, however, this was generally confined to a perfunctory insistence on a period of work in the 'school garden', often under a teacher who was not qualified to make the exercise

[1] *Report of the Commissioner for Native Development, Northern Rhodesia,* 1954.
[2] See above, p. 1167.

profitable to his pupils. Some territories now make a course at a demonstration farm a regular part of the training of teachers, and in the higher classes of primary schools courses are sometimes designed to bear specifically on the practical problems of rural life. There are, for instance, 'rural industries courses' provided in some Tanganyika Government schools. In Nigeria the curriculum of the middle schools has included agricultural instruction since 1929, and at the middle schools in the Eastern and Western Regions there are school farms under the direction of teachers who have spent a season at the demonstration farms attached to the local Agricultural Experimental Station. In Uganda two farm schools were opened in 1934 by the missions at Namutamba and Gulu, and another was opened at Lira in 1953. Nevertheless the mission of experts which visited East and Central Africa in 1951–2 considered that no satisfactory primary curriculum which related the subjects taught to the environment of the pupil had yet been devised.[1] They made recommendations for improving the system, but the difficulty of giving 'a rural bias' to school education is deep seated.

Higher Education

For generations past Colonial students have been able to obtain higher education in three ways: by enrolling themselves at one of the colleges affiliated to the University of Durham, by entering themselves as candidates for one of the external degrees of the University of London, or by attending some academic institution in the British Isles. In this sphere there has never been racial discrimination, and numerous African students have gained professional qualifications notably at theological colleges, at medical schools, and at the Inns of Court. To a lesser extent they have also used similar facilities at some institutions in the United States. The oldest African institution for higher education is Fourah Bay College, founded in 1827 in Sierra Leone by the Church Missionary Society; since 1875 it has presented candidates for the degrees of the University of Durham. Originally a training school for ministers it has tended to restrict its activity to the Arts subjects. With limited resources it has exercised a considerable influence upon the growth of an educated class not only in Sierra Leone but throughout West Africa.

Between the two World Wars, when systematic plans for Colonial education were much discussed, three new institutions were founded for what may be called post-secondary education. The most ambitious was the Prince of Wales College at Achimota near Accra.[2] Founded in 1925 it was completed in 1929 at a cost of £617,000, a large sum for those days, derived from the revenues of the prosperous Gold Coast. From the beginning it was controlled by an independent council with six African

---

[1] P. Morris, ed., *African Education*, 1953, pp. 99, 170.   [2] See above, p. 1177.

members out of 15. The Higher College at Yaba, near Lagos, opened in 1934, was less ambitious. It provided courses for students who sought scientific appointments under the Nigerian Government and trained teachers and engineers to whom diplomas of proficiency were awarded. Makerere, in Uganda, was founded as a trade school; from 1937 onwards it began to develop as the nucleus of an African University College. In the academic year 1943–4 Fourah Bay had 17 students, Achimota 98, Yaba about 100, and Makerere 128 at post-secondary standards. There were also known to be about 250 African students at institutes of higher education in the United Kingdom.[1]

As part of the programme to be financed under the Colonial Development and Welfare Acts the British Government appointed a Commission (known from its chairman, Mr. Justice Asquith, as the Asquith Commission) 'to consider the principles which should guide the promotion of higher education' in the Colonies. The Report of the Commission was published in June 1945, and has since formed the basis of British Colonial policy in this important subject. It started from the assumption that the formation of universities in the Colonies was 'an inescapable corollary of any policy which aims at the achievement of colonial self-government'; and it rapidly reached the conclusion that 'considerations of finance and policy alike make it essential that the larger a proportion of students shall be locally trained'. While recognizing the tendency of Colonial students to go overseas in order to acquire the prestige belonging to the degree of an ancient university, the Report pointed out that a local university should 'become a focus for the intellectual self-expression of the people' and was therefore a natural concomitant of self-government. It was suggested that study at a university overseas should normally be reserved for postgraduate students or for 'those few who wish to study exceptional subjects for which there is no local provision'. The Commission recommended that universities should be established 'as soon as possible in those areas which are not served by any existing university', and it was stated plainly that this development 'must depend upon the grant of substantial financial aid from Great Britain'.[2]

In order to ensure academic independence a form of constitution based upon the newer universities in Great Britain was proposed. Each institution of this kind in a Colony would be founded, in the first instance, as a University College 'in special relation' with the University of London, which would ensure its academic standards by giving advice and help with syllabuses and examinations. Upon the recommendation of the Commission an advisory body, the Inter-University Council for Higher Education in the Colonies, was brought into existence to supervise the development of

---

[1] *Report of the Commission on Higher Education in the Colonies* (the Asquith Commission), Cmd. 6647, 1945, pp. 8–9, 115–19.   [2] *Ibid.* p. 104.

the new University Colleges, and was given representation on the Colonial University Grants Advisory Committee. As in Great Britain the Treasury makes grants of money directly to universities upon the advice of the University Grants Committee, so also grants were to be made to Colonial universities upon the advice of the Colonial University Grants Committee. The money thus comes directly from grants made under the Colonial Development and Welfare Acts, and is not channelled through particular Colonial Governments.[1]

At the same time, a second Commission, which was subsequently known from its chairman as the Elliot Commission, was examining the particular problems of higher education in West Africa.[2] A majority of the commissioners recommended that three University Colleges should be founded in the three larger West African Colonies and that each should be supported by a college for preliminary studies. A minority report made the alternative proposal that a single university situated in Nigeria would provide for the needs of the whole region. The minority report was accepted in 1946 by the Secretary of State and, accordingly, a University College was founded at Ibadan in 1948. The local pride of the Gold Coast, not yet a self-governing community, took the form of insisting upon a separate institution and this was authorized on the understanding that it should be largely endowed from local resources. A second University College was therefore founded in the same year, at first at Achimota. Plans were at once laid for building on a new site at Legon Hill, near Accra.

In Sierra Leone the decision not to raise Fourah Bay to university status also caused disappointment, and here the limited resources of the country prevented independent action. A temporary arrangement was made in 1948 allowing Fourah Bay to keep its special relation with Durham for the present, while accepting a Colonial Office grant for establishing preliminary courses in science. A Commission which sat at Sierra Leone in 1954 made many proposals for detailed changes, and recommended that 'the aim of Fourah Bay to develop eventually into a full University College should be acknowledged and accepted'.[3] In that year the College had 119 students at the university level, more than half of them drawn from the other West African territories.

In East Africa Makerere passed through the process of development suggested in the Asquith Report. It was recognized by the Inter-University Council as a University College in 1949. The foundation of the Central African University has been described above.[4]

---

[1] Ibid. pp. 107–9.
[2] *Report of the Commission on Higher Education in West Africa*, Cmd. 6655, 1945.
[3] *Report of the Sierra Leone Education Commission*, Freetown, 1954.
[4] See above, p. 1161.

Since the formation of three University Colleges in East and West Africa the demand for higher technical education has become more evident. As in England it is to be met by the provision of technical institutes which prepare candidates for the British professional diplomas and for certificates issued by such bodies as the City and Guilds of London Institute and the Institutions of Civil and Mechanical Engineers. The various institutes founded in recent years are enumerated above.[1] On the analogy of the Inter-University Council, the Secretary of State instituted an Advisory Committee on Colonial Colleges of Arts, Science, and Technology in 1949. The following sums have been issued under the Colonial Development and Welfare Acts towards the capital cost of the various institutions between the years 1945 and 1955:

University College, Ibadan, Nigeria: £1,710,864.
University College, Gold Coast: £400,000.
Makerere College, East Africa: £1,087,223.
Nigerian College of Arts, Science, and Technology: £265,232.
Fourah Bay College, Sierra Leone: £99,853.
Royal Technical College of East Africa: £150,000.[2]

In addition an allocation of £1¼ million had been made for the Central African University.[3]

The cost of establishing the Gold Coast University was borne chiefly by the local revenues in the form of an initial grant of £3,765,000 from the Gold Coast Government and a further £1,897,000 from the reserves of the Gold Coast Marketing Board. Advances were also made towards recurrent expenses at the rate of about £500,000 a year. To this was added in 1954 the promise of £2 million for an endowment fund. The Nigerian Government made a grant of land to Ibadan, allotted £2¼ million as an endowment fund, made capital grants of £1,060,000 to the University College and £3,606,000 to the teaching hospital, and also made grants for recurrent expenditure. Another sum of £1 million was provided by the Nigerian Cocoa Marketing Board. The demand for higher education in Nigeria was so pressing that in 1955 the Government of the Eastern Region voted the sum of £2½ million for the provision of an additional University College, to be situated within that Region.

The East African Governments have contributed £200,000 a year for the recurrent expenses of Makerere and have allotted a sum of £219,000 for a faculty of agriculture. In addition large benefactions have been made by private persons and commercial companies: £61,000 to Ibadan from the United Africa Company and another £50,000 from the Nuffield

[1] See above, p. 1179.
[2] Statement by Secretary of State for the Colonies, H.C. Deb., 6 December 1955, col. 49.
[3] Information from Colonial University Grants Advisory Committee, 13 December 1955.

Foundation, £50,000 to Makerere from Dr. J. Williamson, £150,000 to the Central African University from the two important groups[1] which are developing the Copperbelt of Northern Rhodesia.[2]

The capital cost of founding a university is thus shown to be formidable, especially when related to the small student enrolment which is at first inevitable. In the year 1953-4 there were 527 students at Ibadan, 448 at Makerere, and 349 at the Gold Coast University College.[3] While these Colleges build up their strength an increasing number of African students find their way overseas.

The number of African students from British territories pursuing their education at universities overseas in the year 1953-4 was estimated as follows:[4]

	United States of America	Canada	United Kingdom and Ireland
East Africa			
Kenya . . .	23	1 ⎫	
Tanganyika .	6	.. ⎪	390
Uganda . .	6	.. ⎬	
Zanzibar .	..	.. ⎭	
West Africa			
Nigeria . .	276	34 ⎫	
Gold Coast .	89	8 ⎪	1,036
Sierra Leone.	28	1 ⎬	
Gambia . .	..	.. ⎭	

Students from these Colleges are also to be found at universities in India,[5] where there were said to be 125 in 1954, and in other countries.

All the three University Colleges offer courses for a general degree in Arts and in Science. Makerere has, in addition to Arts courses, Faculties of Medicine (which prepare students for the Licentiate enabling them to practise in East Africa), Agriculture, and Veterinary Science. At Ibadan and the Gold Coast there are also courses for B.A. (Honours), B.Sc. (Special), and B.Sc. (Agriculture); in addition the Gold Coast also offers B.Sc. (Economics). Ibadan offers the Second M.B., though clinical courses are awaiting the completion of a new teaching hospital. The post-graduate Certificate in Education may be taken at the Gold Coast. Extra-mural departments are associated with all the Colleges. There is attached to Makerere a separately constituted Institute of Social Research, and at Ibadan an Institute of Social and Economic Research. It is necessary at

[1] See below, p. 1502.
[2] *Inter-University Council for Higher Education Overseas, 1946-54*, Cmd. 9515, 1955, p. 21.
[3] Ibid. p. 9.
[4] *International Affairs*, October 1956, p. 454. The figure 390 includes also some students from Central Africa.   [5] See above, p. 399.

present, at all the University Colleges, to make an arrangement for an introductory year's work for most students—a requirement that is not only expensive in itself but which may prevent the proper development of sixth-form work in the secondary schools. There is, on the other hand, the danger that as the result of pressure from the universities sixth-form work may be attempted prematurely in schools with inadequate staff.[1]

Teacher Training

Adequate provision for the training of teachers necessitates both an expert staff and well-organized practising schools; it has therefore usually proved to be beyond the means of voluntary agencies, save when they have been able to rely on grants allocated for this purpose from State revenues. Since 1940 grants totalling nearly £4 million have been made for teacher training under the Colonial Development and Welfare Acts. In all the British territories, however, there are still a considerable number of teachers who have had no vocational training, though they may include persons of fair general education. All the Development Plans include provision for a rapid increase in the output of trained teachers.

In Northern Rhodesia teachers are now trained at three Government and 15 Mission centres, but some of the latter have very few students, and in 1952 it was decided to withdraw grants from schools training less than 15 students annually. In Nyasaland training is given at ten Mission centres and by the Government at the Jeanes schools.[2] In Tanganyika one Government and three Mission centres give a two-year course to students who have passed Standard X; the concentration of lower-grade training is being secured by the closing down of smaller Mission training schools. Kenya, in the first five years of the Ten-year Plan initiated in 1946, expended £169,428 on new provision for teacher training,[3] and claims to have trained 10,000 teachers. Teacher training in Uganda has developed more rapidly than elsewhere in East Africa, and in 1952 there were 47 establishments engaged in it, all managed by voluntary agencies and all but two being grant-aided. There is also a small output of graduate students from Makerere University College. The scheme for educational expansion approved in 1952 will, however, involve an annual increase of 1,000 teachers, and for this 22 additional training colleges are now to be provided.

In Uganda a local Committee recommended in 1954 that intensified education for African farmers should be given. They recommended the inclusion of agriculture in the educational curriculum, a special course on agriculture for Chiefs and farmers, and the provision of

---

[1] P. Morris, ed., *African Education*, 1953, pp. 29, 100.   [2] See below, p. 1191.
[3] *Report of the Committee to Inquire into the Scope, Content and Methods of African Education*, Nairobi, 1949.

more highly qualified staff in the superior and subordinate grades.[1] The Ten-year Plan for Zanzibar envisaged the production of 15 male and 20 female teachers each year, the proportion being dictated by the importance officially attached to the education of girls. It was found, however, that there was no demand for this, and that the 23 women teachers who had been trained by 1951 were sufficient for the existing schools. There was, on the other hand, a serious shortage of men teachers, of whom 74 had been trained, and the annual intake is to be increased to 25.

Nigeria has in the Northern Region four teacher-training centres for men, six of which are managed by the Government, and five for women, one being a Government institution at Kano for Muslims. In the Eastern Region the output of trained teachers is about 1,300 a year; a State training centre for women was opened at Enugu in 1951. The Western Region had in 1951 a total of 26 training centres for men, two being managed by the Government, and six centres for women. In Sierra Leone teachers are trained at Fourah Bay and at two Government and two Mission centres in the Protectorate. Up to 1949 Gambia sent students to be trained in Sierra Leone and the Gold Coast, but in that year a Government centre opened with 29 students. The plans for a rapid increase in the number of schools which have been adopted in the Gold Coast and Nigeria must necessarily involve some lowering in the qualifications required of teachers, though it is intended eventually to provide facilities for the full training of all the recruits required. The Gold Coast Six-year Plan adopted in 1951 involves the recruitment of 1,800 new teachers each year. It was calculated that there was a sufficient number of Standard VII pupils available, and these are now being given some training under an emergency scheme, but ten new training colleges are to be built and six others expanded. The Eastern Region of Nigeria expects to increase the annual output of trained teachers to 2,500, mainly by developing the accommodation at existing institutions, but a new centre is to be opened where training will be directed towards the introduction of a school system based on six years' primary and six years' secondary education. The Western Region in 1952 announced an emergency training scheme to be carried out largely by increasing the intake into existing institutions.

Teacher training is usually given at four levels: (1) lower-primary, sometimes called vernacular; (2) senior-primary or intermediate; (3) non-graduate, training being in this case given at Colleges of Technology and University Institutes of Education; and (4) post-graduate. A secondary-school course has been described as the minimum qualification that should be admitted for entry upon teacher training,[2] but in most territories the number of persons with secondary education who seek training

---

[1] *Background to Uganda*, no. 80, January 1955.   [2] Morris, op. cit. p. 37.

as teachers falls far short of requirements, and an increase in the numbers reaching the secondary or middle-school stage of education is a prerequisite for an expansion in the number of trained teachers. That is especially the case in regard to the education of girls.

The Education of Women and Girls

Reference has already been made to the high proportion of girls in the schools of some of the High Commission Territories, but in most of the remaining British territories the education of girls has lagged behind that of boys. In Muslim areas the reason is to be found mainly in the custom which dictates the seclusion of women, but elsewhere it is no doubt influenced by the fact that education is regarded largely as a means of securing paid employment. As the Minister for Education of the Western Region of Nigeria complained, 'It is argued that the place of the women is the home, and any scholastic training is wasted eventually in the kitchen'.[1] The expansion of facilities for the education of girls and women has, however, had a high priority in most Development Programmes; everywhere except in Gambia there is now a Chief Woman Education Officer or an Assistant Director dealing with the education of women and girls. In Nigeria there is one such officer for each Region.

The percentage of girls among the pupils attending primary schools in 1950 was 33 in Northern Rhodesia, 40 in Nyasaland, 27 in Kenya and Tanganyika, 20 in Uganda, 25 in Zanzibar, 22 in Nigeria, 21 in the Gold Coast, and 30 in Sierra Leone. Some territories show a remarkable increase in numbers in recent years: in Nyasaland, for example, the enrolment of girls increased by 15,000 in 1951, and in Tanganyika it increased by 25,000 over the five years from 1946. In Uganda the Native Anglican Church ruled in 1951 that 25 per cent. of places in Class I in every school should be reserved for girls. But it is significant that everywhere only a small proportion of girls entering school stay on to complete the primary course. The proportion in the middle and secondary stage of education is far lower than in the primary. In Northern Rhodesia there are one girls' and two co-educational junior secondary schools, all managed by missions; in Nyasaland six girls in 1952 attended the Government secondary school at Blantyre; in Kenya there are two Mission secondary schools for girls; in Tanganyika one, managed by the Government; and Zanzibar has one Government secondary school for girls. In Kenya the first African girl gained a School Certificate in 1948, but in 1951 there were only 38 girls on the roll of the one full secondary school.

In Uganda the Gayaza High School for Girls was opened as early as 1905. The education of girls is expanding rapidly at the present time. It is proposed to establish junior-secondary boarding schools in every district,

---

[1] *Proposals for an Educational Policy for the Western Region*, Nigeria, 1952.

which will be staffed by women teachers trained at the College for Domestic Science and Technical Teacher Training at Kyambogo near Kampala, opened in 1955. Makerere admitted women in 1945, and there were 32 women students in 1955. Female education owes much to the Community Development Department.[1]

The education of girls is relatively more advanced in West Africa, though the increase is more evident in respect of the total numbers than in the proportion of girls to boys. For example in 1954, of the 494,334 children in primary schools, 150,118 were girls; and of the 8,602 pupils in Government secondary schools, 1,296 were girls. In that year 785 boys and 121 girls passed the examination for the Cambridge School Certificate. There has been during the last seven years a striking increase in the number of African women who have gone to Great Britain for further training, the total having risen from 112 in 1947 to 827 in 1953, of whom 20 were from East and Central Africa and 807 from West Africa. The majority are nursing students. Their number has risen from 36 to 567, that of university students from 35 to 52, and of technical-college students from 41 to 208.[2]

In the plans for community education the instruction given to women in such subjects as housing and child care has an important place. In Uganda special courses in farming for women have been organized by the Agricultural Department. Elsewhere both missions and Education Departments have provided 'marriage-training' courses open to older girls with a minimum of schooling. Such activities, however, fall more naturally within the purview of the Social Welfare Departments, which both in the East and Central African territories have also fostered the growth of Women's Institutes and clubs of a like nature.

The Education of Chiefs

At a period when the traditional Native Authorities were expected to continue to occupy a prominent place as the basis of local administration,[3] some attempts were made to ensure that the boys who were later to become Chiefs should receive an education that would fit them for their duties. Schools for the sons of Chiefs were opened at Georgetown in Gambia, at Bo in Sierra Leone, and at Tabora in Tanganyika;[4] in other territories, however, the view was taken that to segregate the future Chiefs in special schools might cause them to lose touch with their people. The Bo school,[5] which was opened in 1906, soon came to be filled by persons who though nominated by Chiefs were not necessarily marked out as their successors,

---

[1] *Background to Uganda*, no. 109, June 1955.
[2] For the education of girls in the French territories, see below, p. 1199.
[3] See above, p. 541.
[4] For similar institutions in French territories, see below, p. 1200.
[5] R. L. Buell, *The Native Problem in Africa*, vol. i, 1928, pp. 463–4, 867, 932.

and the school was closed, the buildings being eventually taken over for a Government secondary school. The Tabora school after a few years became a central school to which pupils were admitted on educational qualifications alone. The East African territories have preferred the system of organizing adult education courses for Chiefs and Headmen who are already in office; these are conducted at Jeanes schools in Kenya, and in Uganda at agricultural training centres. In proportion as Local Government tends to be increasingly based on elected councils, the importance of educating future Chiefs decreases, and the training of Local Government employees becomes of major interest.

The Influence of External Examination Standards

When African schools began to feel it necessary to enter their pupils for external examinations, they took the obvious course of asking the bodies which set examinations for schools in Great Britain to extend their work to Africa. Two factors accelerated this process: Africans attached the greatest importance to tests which carried a British hallmark; and, secondly, almost all professions to which an African might aspire could be entered only by candidates who had passed a British school-leaving examination or university matriculation. This development, however, imposed upon African secondary schools a curriculum which had been devised for pupils in Great Britain and which was for that reason in many ways unsuitable.[1] Modifications in the syllabus, made in order to adapt it for local needs, were agreed to in the inter-war period by the four British examining bodies, which were represented on the Joint Advisory Board for School Examinations in the British Colonies. It is urged, however, that the Cambridge School Certificate, which is now taken by most secondary schools in the British African territories, tends to dominate the curriculum of the schools far more completely than examinations of this kind ever dominated the English grammar schools, since it is regarded as a 'talisman' ensuring stable employment.[2] It has undoubtedly proved to be one reason for the overweighting of education on the literary side, particularly in private secondary schools.

Provided that standards are maintained, the organization of examinations by autonomous local bodies forms the most satisfactory means of ensuring that curricula are related to the pupils' needs. The De La Warr Commission[3] recommended the institution of an East African school-leaving certificate to be granted by a joint body representing the three mainland territories and Zanzibar; this has not yet come into being, but a West African Examination Council was set up in 1950 to promote the

---

[1] E. W. Smith, *Knowing the African*, 1946, pp. 123, 186.
[2] P. Morris, ed., *African Education*, 1953, p. 27.
[3] *Report of a Commission on Higher Education in East Africa*, Col. no. 142, 1937.

holding of a suitable form of examination in West Africa. In order to make sure that the certificates granted will be recognized outside Africa, the Council will during a transitional period invite suitable outside bodies to conduct the examinations; but it is expected that it will, by maintaining association with the University Colleges, eventually become a body awarding certificates in its own right.

The local preparation of examination syllabuses in chosen subjects is increasing, but a significant influence continues to be exercised by Education Departments through the introduction at their instance of modifications in examinations conducted by external bodies and notably by the Cambridge Local Examinations Syndicate. For example, provision is now made for examination at the School Certificate level of certain agreed vernacular languages, and, if agreement is secured to the proposal of a recent Conference on African Education,[1] that an oral test in English should be compulsory, this might do much to raise the standard of teaching English.

The Language of Instruction

The language to be used as a medium of instruction, and the stage at which the teaching of English should be introduced, have been discussed above. The actual practice varies in different territories. In Northern Rhodesia and most of West Africa, excluding the Northern Region of Nigeria and the Northern Territories of the Gold Coast, English is now introduced as a subject in the fourth year and as a medium in the fifth. In Uganda and Tanganyika it is introduced only in the fifth year and is not used as a medium until the eighth. In Nyasaland the corresponding stages are the third and fourth years. In Tanganyika the vernacular is used in the first year, but thereafter Swahili is used as a medium. The use of Swahili as a lingua franca has created some difficulty.[2] In Kenya the Education Department Report of 1950 announced that its use would be gradually discontinued, a decision taken some years earlier in Uganda. In the urban areas of Kenya an experiment is being made in the use of English from the first year at school. In Northern Nigeria English becomes the medium only at the middle or secondary stage.

The diversity of practice in this respect, and also the difficulty arising from the growing demand for facilities for acquiring English, not unnaturally attracted the comments of the two important expert missions which visited East and West Africa in 1951. Both missions considered that the teaching of English as a language should begin at an early stage. 'All-round proficiency in English', the latter remarked, 'is the most important academic aim of the primary course.' Its Report also raised the

---

[1] Morris, op. cit. p. 172.   [2] See above, p. 98.

question whether there is any value in giving the first stages of instruction in a vernacular which is not the home language of all the children, as is done at present in schools serving a population among whom there is no one dominant language. It was also the opinion of the members of the Royal Commission on East Africa 1953–5 that the teaching of English should begin in as low a class as possible and should thereafter become the medium of instruction. They regarded the teaching of a lingua franca such as Swahili to children whose early education had been in the vernacular as 'a complete waste of time and effort'.[1]

Research on another problem in this field, namely, the relative effectiveness of English and the vernacular languages as a medium for use in school studies, was undertaken by the Gold Coast Institute of Education in 1951. Local opinion in the Gold Coast favours the wider use of the African languages, and the Minister for Education of the Western Region of Nigeria has expressed the view that up to now they have been studied in too 'half-hearted' a manner.[2] The problem is, however, one on which there is likely to be a growing diversity of view when regional aspirations begin to compete with the desire for the recognition of a standardized national language.[3] That is a problem which is now creating much trouble in some of the new national Governments of Asia, where popular sentiment is often at variance with State policy.

Education for Europeans and the Immigrant Communities

Primary education for European children is provided in all the East and Central African territories and is compulsory in Kenya and Northern Rhodesia, where children from seven to 15 must attend school. Grants are available in Uganda for European children to attend primary schools in Kenya, but the pressure on these schools which has resulted from the increase in the European population of Kenya has made it difficult for them to offer places to pupils from outside the Colony. The Tanganyika Education Department provides boarding schools for European children who are unable to reach a school. Secondary education for the East African territories is concentrated in Kenya. In Northern Rhodesia some schools include post-primary courses; the building of the first secondary schools for Europeans, one for boys and one for girls, began at Lusaka in 1952. Pupils for whom places cannot be found in hostels, or who wish to go on to a higher standard than is provided in the Protectorate, are able to obtain grants to attend schools in Southern Rhodesia, the Union, or the United Kingdom. Pupils from Nyasaland have since 1935 had

[1] *East Africa Royal Commission 1953–1955, Report*, Cmd. 9475, 1955, p. 184.
[2] *Proposals for an Educational Policy for the Western Region*, Nigeria, 1952, p. 8.
[3] Unesco, *The Use of Vernacular Languages in Education* (Monographs on Fundamental Education, VIII), pp. 26–30. See also A. N. Tucker, in *Symposium on Popular Education*, Leiden, 1953, p. 74.

the privilege of free secondary tuition in Southern Rhodesia. In 1950 there were 214 pupils from Northern Rhodesia in the non-Government primary schools in Southern Rhodesia, and 107 in the secondary schools.[1]

The only facilities for teacher training for Europeans are in Kenya, where girls are trained as Froebel teachers. In Kenya the Egerton School of Agriculture is at present the only technical-training institution for Europeans, but the Royal Technical College, Nairobi,[2] will provide training for industrial employment. In the Copperbelt of Northern Rhodesia 235 apprentices were receiving part-time instruction in 1951, but most Europeans go to Southern Rhodesia or the Union of South Africa for technical training. In the West African territories provision for European education is not necessary on any considerable scale, but in the larger towns nursery schools are privately organized by European parents.

The educational provision for Asian children has already been described.[3] At Blantyre in Nyasaland there is a primary school open to all non-Africans who are willing to be taught through the medium of English. Its pupils now include Eurafrican, Indo-African, and Indian children.

Community Education

One of the most pregnant conclusions to be drawn from experience of the current system of education has been that radical changes in social life are not likely to be brought about solely through the instruction given to school children. An early attempt to extend the influence of the school to the community at large was made by the opening in East and Central Africa of the Jeanes schools, so called after the founder of a series of institutions of this type in the southern United States. The first of these schools was opened in Africa in 1925.[4] In its present form the Jeanes school is a training centre at which married teachers and their wives take courses together, the men concentrating on such improvements in agriculture and sanitation as are practicable for villagers, the women on the elements of child welfare. They are then expected to use their influence to induce the villagers to adopt the methods they have learnt.

On the other hand, the Advisory Committee on Education have taken the view that a teacher's time should be wholly taken up with his school work, and that adult education should be the responsibility of other persons.[5] The modern movement in favour of 'mass' or 'community' education is a response to the feeling that the extension of education by conventional methods to societies with no tradition of literacy is too slow a process. As

[1] *O.Y.S.R., 1952*, p. 321. [2] See above, p. 1178.
[3] See above, p. 1153.
[4] A. Phelps Stokes, *Report on Education, Native Welfare and Race Relations in East and South Africa*, 1934.
[5] *Mass Education in African Society*, Col. no. 186, 1943, p. 25. See also E. R. Chadwick, 'Community Development in Udi Division', *Oversea Education*, vol. xix, 1948, pp. 627–46.

described by the Advisory Committee, community education involves the teaching of literacy to adults in combination with specific projects for village improvement adopted in consultation with the peoples concerned. Its success depends therefore on securing their active participation in programmes for their social and economic betterment.[1] It thus involves the combined work of teams representing a number of the specialist Departments. Schemes on lines which also involve the teaching of literacy have had the support of the United Nations Educational, Scientific, and Cultural Organization which publishes a periodical under the title of *Fundamental and Adult Education*, devoted to experiments in this field.

In the East African territories the organization of work of this type is now the responsibility of Community Development or Social Development Departments created by the expansion of the personnel of the former Social Welfare Departments. Formal adult education in continuation classes remains under the control of the Education Departments, but the literacy campaigns conducted by Community Development Officers are organized in close co-operation with them. In the Gold Coast the Department of Social Welfare, which is responsible for adult education and community development, is under the Minister for Education. Most territories have a centre for the training of community development and literacy campaign organizers. In Kenya this is the Jeanes school; in Nigeria the training is given in a camp at Man O'War Bay in the Cameroons, where emphasis is laid on physical exercise. Uganda, Tanganyika, Nigeria, and the Gold Coast have made grants from general revenue for community development schemes, and a proportion has been allotted to Administrative Officers for furthering schemes put forward by village committees. Uganda employs eleven supervisors of literacy campaigns who are paid from these public revenues, the instructors being persons of the locality who volunteer to give some of their free time to this work. The Northern Region of Nigeria in 1951 adopted a plan which aimed at producing 1 million literate adults by the end of five years, and by 1953 2,500 classes had been organized.[2] Sierra Leone also has a Five-year Plan for a mass literacy campaign. Northern Rhodesia employs two full-time adult literacy supervisors on the Copperbelt, and seven Development Area schools are being built with a grant of £54,529, designed to serve as the main links between the educational and the general Development Programmes of each area. Four of these were completed by the end of 1953.

Mention should be made of the organizations formed in several territories to foster the publication of reading matter in English and in the vernaculars. The East African Literature Bureau, financed under the

---

[1] 'Community Development in Uganda', *J.A.A.*, April 1953, p. 50.
[2] *Colonial Reports, Nigeria, 1953*, pp. 68–70.

Colonial Development and Welfare Acts with assistance from the British Council, has its own press and by 1953 had published 281 books in 16 languages. It also publishes a magazine with a circulation of 12,000, and arranges exhibitions of books. The Northern Rhodesia and Nyasaland Bureau has had a similar success on a smaller scale. Libraries have been founded in several African towns through the efforts of these and other such bodies. Literature committees have been active in Nigeria, notably in the Northern Region, where reading-sheets in Hausa have had a wide circulation.[1]

THE FRENCH TERRITORIES

French West Africa

In one respect the early history of the educational system of French West Africa resembled that of most of the British territories; policy was at the outset mainly confined to the grant of assistance to missionary effort. St. Louis was restored to the French in 1814 by the Treaty of Paris, after five years' possession by the British, and in 1816 instructions issued by the Ministry in Paris justified the encouragement of Christianity on the ground that its moral basis would make for progress in civilization. It is noteworthy, however, that in the same year the French Government sent out to Senegal a teacher, Jean Dard, who opened at St. Louis an elementary school for Senegalese pupils, in which he endeavoured to introduce the use of Wolof as a medium of instruction. The experiment failed to gain local support, and in 1829 French was formally adopted as the medium of instruction. The progress made in education in Senegal was, however, slow, and in 1854 there were only four schools, situated in the old settlements of Gorée and St. Louis, with a total of 600 students. These schools were managed by the *Frères de Ploërmel*, who had been placed in charge in 1841; from the first the *Frères* made a special feature of instruction in agriculture and handicrafts, taking as their model the *École des Arts et Métiers* at Châlons. A small school for girls was opened at St. Louis by the Sisters of St. Joseph of Cluny.

A substantial change of policy occurred in 1854, when General Faidherbe took over the administration of Senegal, a post which he administered with great vigour till 1860.[2] He instituted 'lay' schools, mainly with the view of extending education to Mohammedans, who had hitherto refused to enter the Mission schools, and he is said to have made it obligatory for pupils at the local Koranic schools to attend evening courses at the schools established by him at St. Louis, Dagana, and Podor. He also

---

[1] Central Office of Information, *Education in the United Kingdom Dependencies*, 1954, p. 57.

[2] For an account of the work done by Faidherbe, see R. Delavignette, *Freedom and Authority in French West Africa*, 1950, pp. 56–66.

founded the *École des Otages* for the sons of Chiefs, of which it has been observed 'le nom indique sans équivoque les conditions de recrutement'.[1] The movement initiated by General Faidherbe was the first step in an educational system which, as will be seen, now depends mainly on the maintenance of State schools in which instruction is entirely secular. During the next 30 years, the establishment of 'lay' schools was extended from Senegal into the Sudan, where Galliéni founded a number of schools, of which the most prominent were those at Bafoulabé and Bamako; Kayes also had its *École des Fils de Chefs*. Guinea had its first 'lay' school at Conakry in 1878, and the Ivory Coast had in 1893 a school at Grand Bassam. Dahomey was annexed only in 1894, but during the next five years had about 20 'lay' schools.

The actual advance in education, however, remained very gradual; there were in 1900 only 70 State schools in French West Africa, with an enrolment of some 2,500 pupils. In 1903 the system of instruction, which had hitherto varied in each Colony of the Federation, was brought into something like uniformity.[2] Under this organization, education was divided into *enseignement primaire élémentaire* and *enseignement primaire supérieure*. For the purpose of *enseignement élémentaire* the country was divided into educational *secteurs*, corresponding usually to administrative subdivisions, and school instruction was carried on either in: (1) the *écoles de village*, almost always with African teachers, and with an emphasis on the teaching of agriculture; or (2) in the *école régionale* of the *secteur*, which was composed of the most promising of the pupils selected from the village schools in each *secteur* (and which often took the form of a boarding school in which the food of pupils was supplied by relatives); or (3) in the *écoles urbaines*, which were similar to the regional schools, but substituted handicrafts for agriculture as a subject of teaching. The *école primaire supérieure* (E.P.S.) was composed of the most advanced pupils from the *écoles élémentaires* (the majority coming from the *écoles urbaines*), and at this period it offered a two-year (or where necessary a three-year) course as a first step in recruitment to subordinate posts in the local Administration.

Schools of this category were divided into: (1) the *écoles supérieures professionnelles*, designed to provide foremen or upper-grade artisans, but they were at the earlier period very poorly equipped as compared with the schools of a similar class in France; and (2) the *écoles normales*, which provided a three-year course to the best pupils of the E.P.S. in order to prepare them for employment in the grade of *Instituteur indigène* in the primary schools, or as interpreters, or as Chiefs. This last development took its most complete form in 1912, when Governor-General W. Ponty created

---

[1] Jean Capelle, in *Enc. A.O.F.*, vol. i, p. 268.
[2] The system was further elaborated in a local *arrêté* of 1918 and a Circular of the Governor-General dated May 1924.

the service of Educational Inspectors and established a *Conseil Supérieur de l'Enseignement Primaire*.[1] The *école normale* at Sebikotane in Senegal occupied a prominent position under the title of the *École William Ponty*, and in addition to the functions mentioned above, provided the preliminary courses for the *École de Médecine* at Dakar, which was responsible for the training of the 'medical aides'.[2] The *École William Ponty* acted also in some sense as a Federal institution, serving the purpose of all the Colonies, though similar institutions were afterwards added at Rufisque and Katibougou, near Bamako. *Écoles primaires supérieures* were in course of time established also in other towns of French West Africa, as for instance in Dakar, Porto Novo, Bamako, Bingerville, and Conakry for boys, and at Bingerville and Dakar for girls.

This remained for some years the general framework of the organization in French West Africa, but special institutions were added as occasion arose, as for instance the *École Normale Rurale* at Dabou near Abidjan, designed to train agricultural *moniteurs*, and the *École Technique Supérieure* at Bamako, which gave a four-year course to recruits for the *Services des Travaux Publics*. There were added also three special institutions of secondary education which provided the same curriculum as the metropolitan secondary institutions, namely, the *Lycée Faidherbe* (opened at St. Louis in 1920), the *Lycée Van Vollenhoven* at Dakar (1940), and the *Lycée Terrasson de Fougères* (opened at Bamako in 1945). The college at Abidjan in the Ivory Coast became a *lycée* in 1953. These *lycées* were primarily intended for Europeans, but they also admitted a certain number of African students.

There followed a third phase in the organization of education, partly as a result of the resolution passed at the Conference held at Brazzaville in 1944, but chiefly as the result of the formal Constitution of the French Union in 1946. The question was not now limited, as it had been in 1903, to the introduction of uniformity in the educational practice of the different Colonies which composed the Federation of West Africa. The problem was now to provide evidence that the integration of the Colonies as members of the French Union was a reality, and educational policy appeared to offer one of the most conspicuous illustrations available for the purpose. M. Jean Capelle, writing in 1949 of the system as it had been developed since 1903, described it as appropriate to the era of the *indigénat*, when the status of French citizenship was confined to Africans who had adopted a European mode of life. He emphasized to the new outlook created by the Constitution of the French Union, in which all its inhabitants are citizens.[3]

[1] See a useful diagram illustrating this system in *Enc. A.O.F.*, vol. i, p. 273.

[2] Subsequently the *École Africaine de Médecine*, a name it bore till it became part of the *Institut des Hautes Études*, when it was renamed the *École Préparatoire de Médecine et de Pharmacie*; see below, p. 1196. [3] *Enc. A.O.F.*, vol. i, p. 272.

Education in French West Africa was not brought within the purview of the metropolitan Ministry of National Education, but it was prescribed that the curricula of the local schools and the standards of examination should as far as possible conform with those of the institutions of metropolitan France. In 1942 the official supervision of education throughout the Federation had been placed in charge of a local Director-General; his title in 1947 became that of *Recteur d'Académie*, following in this respect the practice in the French Provinces, and the five *Inspecteurs d'Enseignement Primaire* became *Inspecteurs d'Académie*, holding office under the Ministry of National Education.[1] Education is now described, as in France, as falling into two categories, *enseignement du premier degré* and *enseignement du second degré*, and the new policy has been signalized by a number of substantial additions to the institutions falling into the latter class. Notable examples are the various *Centres d'Apprentissage* (1946); the *Collèges Techniques d'Industrie* (1947); the *Écoles Techniques Supérieures* (of which there was previously one only, at Bamako); and the *Collège Technique de Commerce* at Dakar (1947).

These measures were taken in preparation for the creation of a *Université de l'Afrique Noire Française*, and as a first step there was established in 1950 the *Institut des Hautes Études* at Dakar.[2] It obtained university status in 1953 and holds a position analogous to that of the University Colleges in the British territories, to which reference has been made. It gives diplomas in science, literature, law, medicine, and geography, the examinations being presided over by professors delegated from the Universities of Paris and Bordeaux.[3] It absorbed in 1950 the *École Africaine de Médecine* at Dakar which had been established in 1918. In the academic year 1953–4, 373 students were in residence, the most popular school being Law. In the years previous to the attainment by the University of its academic status provision had been made for an increase in the grants made to local students for study in France.[4] At the beginning of 1953 there were 471 *boursiers* from French West Africa taking advanced courses, either scientific or technical, in the institutions of metropolitan France. A hostel for overseas students had opened in the *Cité Universitaire* of Paris in 1951.

This recent phase in the evolution of the system of education has tended to confirm the policy which has relied on the State rather than on voluntary agencies for the expansion of the primary schools. The local *arrêtés* of 1903 and 1918 and the circular of the Governor-General of 1924 pre-

---

[1] *Enseignement Outre-Mer*, December 1953, p. 19. The full title is now *Recteur d'Académie, Directeur Général de l'Enseignement et des Sports*. The first *Recteur* was M. Jean Capelle, above quoted.

[2] *Décret*, 6 April 1950. The full title is *Institut des Hautes Études de Dakar, Lettres, Médecine et Pharmacie*.

[3] *Annuaire statistique de l'Afrique Occidentale Française, 1951*, vol. ii, p. 74.

[4] *Décret*, 30 May 1945; and *Arrêté général* no. 5939. T. P., 28 December 1945.

viously referred to had made it clear that while the Government was prepared to grant subsidies to Mission schools, it would only do so if their procedure complied with the practice followed in the State institutions. The respective parts now taken by the *enseignement publique* and the *enseignement privé* (represented predominantly by the Mission schools) are best seen by the following figures. In 1910 the State schools in French West Africa had 11,484 pupils; the Mission and other 'private' schools had 2,962.[1] In 1937–8 the State schools had 56,135 pupils; the Mission schools had 12,281, but there were in addition 64,601 pupils in the Muslim schools.[2] Out of a total of 229,695 pupils enrolled in January 1953, those enrolled in the *écoles privées* numbered 63,734.[3] Though therefore the number of pupils in the Mission schools has materially increased, the relative proportion of the enrolment in State schools has not materially altered. In the budget of 1952–3 the subventions to the *enseignement privé* accounted for only about 3 per cent. of the total expenditure on education. The French Government was a party to the Treaty of St. Germain-en-Laye of 1919, which guaranteed freedom of conscience and the right of missionaries to pursue their calling, but a decree issued in February 1922 stipulated that no private school should be opened without authorization, that education must be given exclusively in French, and that European missionary teachers must have the same certificates as Government teachers.

The most characteristic features of French educational policy have been: first, the universal use of French as the medium of instruction; second, a general policy of relating the provision of the more advanced type of education to the demand which appears to exist for its product; third, the strong emphasis on vocational training as the form which such education should take; and fourth, the progressive assimilation of the curricula and examination standards to those prevailing in metropolitan France. This last feature in particular involves the employment of an increasing proportion of European teachers.[4] The use of French as a medium of instruction from the earliest stage has been supported on the ground that if mastery of a European language is the ultimate aim, it is better to start it as early as possible. The pupils are instructed by the 'word method', that is, by associating the appearance of the whole word with its pronunciation and meaning, rather than by trying to read or write it syllable by syllable. The use of the vernacular should, it has been

---

[1] The *Écoles Protestantes* had 375 and the *Écoles Congréganistes* had 2,587 pupils. *Annuaire Statistique de l'Afrique Occidentale Française, 1951*, vol. ii, pp. 81–85.

[2] These were divided into the *Écoles officielles franco-musulmanes* (190) and the *Écoles coraniques* (64,411).

[3] *Enseignement Outre-Mer*, December 1953, pp. 49–58. This figure does not include the pupils in the Muslim schools.

[4] See below, p. 1201. See also T. Hodgkin, in *West Africa*, 9 January 1954, p. 5.

held, be reserved for 'fundamental education' with adults who do not understand French.[1] The policy of maintaining a relation between demand and supply in the higher branches of education was based originally on the belief that the fuller association of the population in the development of a territory could best be realized through the employment of those whose intelligence qualified them to share the work of civilization. The first object of advanced education was, therefore, to train the specialist cadres needed for this purpose, and education assumed accordingly a dual function which was summed up in 1924 in the well-known phrase of a former Governor-General, M. Carde, as 'instruire la masse et dégager l'élite'.[2]

The resolution on education passed by the Brazzaville Conference of 1944[3] asserted that while instruction must be directed to teaching the mass of the people how to improve their standard of life, its result must also be 'aboutir à une sélection sûre et rapide des élites'. One may well feel, however, that the general change of outlook of which the Conference itself afforded unmistakable evidence, and the subsequent constitutional changes which have so widely enlarged the current conception of citizenship,[4] must have given in effect a new meaning to the interpretation to be placed on the composition of the élite. In the second place the Conference held that the use of 'local dialects' in teaching should be absolutely forbidden. But the emphatic insistence thus placed on the use of French would seem to indicate that there existed at the time a school of thought which would have favoured the use of the home language as a medium of education. It is known indeed that there had been for some years a local movement for the use of Mossi, which is spoken by some 2 million persons.[5] It is significant also that the Government announced in 1951 the formation of a special school in Paris to study and modify for teaching purposes certain of the African languages, for this seems to indicate an intention to modify the existing practice in regard to the use of French as the sole medium of education.

The primary-school system as inaugurated in 1903 contemplated in the first instance an 'initiatory' or 'preparatory' course of two years under an African teacher, concentrating on spoken French, arithmetic, and 'elementary improvements in the technique of cultivation'. The best pupils were to go on to a two-year elementary course, followed by a two-year middle course, at the end of which they could earn a certificate of primary education which was at a somewhat lower level than that offered in France. The curricula were locally devised, with emphasis on agricultural subjects

---

[1] Unesco, *The Use of the Vernacular Languages in Education* (Monographs on Fundamental Education VIII), 1953, pp. 17, 18. But see also G. Balandier, in *Symposium on Popular Education*, Leiden, 1953, pp. 94–109.

[2] See also A. Charton's 'Address on the Social Function of Education in French West Africa', quoted in W. B. Mumford, ed., *Africans learn to be French*, 1937, p. 97.

[3] See above, p. 209.   [4] See above, p. 212.   [5] See above, p. 105.

in rural areas and craftwork in urban schools. Experience showed, however, that the great majority of children who attended school did not go beyond the initial course and retained little of the instruction given them. Expert opinion was, moreover, prepared to acknowledge that spoken French, superficially acquired from African teachers, might in reality be of little value, especially to the large rural population which would subsequently have little chance of maintaining its acquaintance with the language. 'Le français parlé "répandu en surface" n'est autre que du français répandu en pure perte.'[1]

As the result of views expressed at the Brazzaville Conference there was a considerable change in the character of the provision made in the primary course, and by 1949 the number of middle classes in the 'public' schools had largely increased. In the technical phrase, the proportion of *écoles complètes* had largely increased, though there was still a considerable diversity in the number of classes held in each category. But the result of increasing the number of middle classes in the schools was naturally to diminish the distinction between the *école de village* and the *école régionale*. The result of this process is illustrated by an analysis of the enrolment in the 'public' schools in the year 1949. Of the total number of pupils who were enrolled in these schools there were then 57,971 in the preparatory classes, 29,498 in the elementary, and 16,980 in the middle classes.[2]

The Brazzaville Conference also emphasized the special need to encourage the education of girls. They had for many years comprised somewhat less than 13 per cent. of the school attendance in the 'public' schools, though the proportion was higher in the *écoles privées*. There has been a general increase in more recent years. At the beginning of 1953 there were 47,444 girls enrolled in schools of the *premier degré*, and they formed nearly 22 per cent. of the total body of pupils at school.[3] The curriculum in primary schools for girls is designed to be 'a training for the home'.[4] The number receiving education of the *second degré*, including teacher training, was 1,095. A teacher-training college for girls was opened at Rufisque in 1938, and there is a course for midwives at the Dakar Medical School. Most of the primary schools are in the non-Muslim coastal areas.

Evening classes for adults have long been held in some of the village schools. Local education officers at their Annual Conference in 1952 expressed warm interest in community education projects of the type sponsored by Unesco, and three pilot projects have been carried out, at

[1] M. Davesne, quoted in *Enc. A.O.F.*, vol. i, p. 273.
[2] *Annuaire statistique de l'Afrique Occidentale Française, 1951*, vol. ii, p. 98.
[3] *Enseignement Outre-Mer*, December 1953, pp. 43, 50.
[4] A. Charton, 'French Tropical and Equatorial Africa', *Year Book of Education, 1949*, p. 373.

Conakry, in the Fouta Djalon, and at M'Boumba. A training centre for fundamental education was under consideration in 1953.[1]

The education of Chiefs, as has already been shown,[2] received at an early stage the special attention of the Administration, for the Chief was part of that *élite* to which the French looked to supply auxiliary sources of rule. In founding the first Chiefs' school at St. Louis in 1856 General Faidherbe claimed that it was designed to form 'quelques indigènes d'élite pour nous aider dans notre œuvre de civilisation'.[3] Closed for a time, it was revived, and in 1908 became an advanced Muslim school, not confined to Chiefs. It returned to its former status in 1922, entrance being now limited to members of the families of Muslim Chiefs. At a later date three other schools were added; in their four years' course, in which, though Arabic and Koranic law were taught as subjects, French was used throughout as the medium, major stress was laid on the study of administrative methods, including the local law and judicial system. The teaching of agriculture was subsequently added. M. Éboué in 1942 proposed that a special section for sons of Chiefs should be attached to every secondary school, but since the reorganization of the system in 1946 no special training has been provided for them. These schools are designed to produce Civil Servants rather than hereditary Chiefs or Native Authorities. Emphasis is placed on a fluent knowledge of the French language and the French law and administrative system. After a prolonged period of instruction, culminating in a year's course in agriculture, the students are qualified to become the agents of French authority. They may be set in control over tribes to which they themselves do not belong, or transferred from one part of the territory to another, like any other Civil Servant.[4] The curriculum has advanced far beyond what was implied originally in the phrase 'schools for the sons of Chiefs and interpreters'.

As already indicated the most recent figures, relating to the enrolment at the beginning of the year 1953, show that there was then a total of 229,695 pupils enrolled. Of these 80,000 were educated in Koranic schools. There was a total of 216,543 pupils enrolled in institutions classified as *enseignement du premier degré*, namely, 155,192 in 'public' and 61,351 in 'private' schools; the girls included in the total numbered 47,444. There has therefore been a considerable increase, but in relation to the population of the Federation the total enrolment is on a lower scale than in many British territories, particularly in respect of the education of girls.

[1] J. Grandsimon, 'Results achieved in French Fundamental Education Projects', *Fundamental and Adult Education*, Unesco, vol. v, 1953, pp. 131–3. See also *Symposium on Popular Education*, Leiden, 1953, pp. 94–109.

[2] See above, p. 1193.   [3] L. L. C. Faidherbe, *Le Sénégal*, 1889, p. 366.

[4] R. L. Buell, *The Native Problem in Africa*, vol. i, 1928, pp. 992 ff. See also L. P. Mair, *Native Policies in Africa*, 1936, p. 209, who, while agreeing that the Chiefs do not revert to hereditary Chiefdoms, regards their tuition as qualifying them for clerical rather than executive posts.

The ratio of girls to boys attending school is about one to five. It has indeed been estimated (though such estimates have no great statistical value) that school education reaches only 10 per cent. of the children of school-going age. The figures of enrolment in institutions classified as *enseignement du second degré* were 8,996, of whom 7,076 were in 'public' and 1,920 in 'private' institutions. The reorganization of the secondary-school system to conform with the lines adopted in France has resulted in the creation of a number of *collèges* (divided into two classes, 'classical' and 'modern') and *lycées*. The modern *collèges* offer a three-year course leading to teacher training, technical training, or service with a Government Department. The study of French occupies a predominant place in the curriculum.

In 1951 there were 23 public and ten private secondary institutions; of those maintained by the State 17 were modern, and two, the *Lycée Faidherbe* at St. Louis and the *Lycée Van Vollenhoven* at Dakar, gave the full secondary course leading to the *baccalauréat*. *Lycées* were added at Abidjan and Bamako in 1952. In general, however, it would seem that the French have attached chief importance to the institutions which are devoted to specialized or professional education rather than to those giving more general courses. Whatever view may be held of a system which relates the provision of institutions of higher education to the demand likely to be made for the students who have obtained their diplomas, it has at all events had the advantage of enabling the Government to concentrate its resources on this particular objective.[1]

Among the institutions for vocational or professional training the training colleges for teachers are now the most numerous. The earlier training schools—such as the *École William Ponty* or the *écoles normales* of Katibougou or Dabou—had proved inadequate as training centres, and there were many complaints that the number of unqualified and 'haphazard' teachers had increased alarmingly.[2] A number of European teachers are recruited after training at the metropolitan *écoles normales*, and a special course for overseas students and for teachers going overseas was opened in 1951 at the *école normale* at St. Cloud. As regards African staff, two types of four-year course are now offered for their training. French West Africa in 1951 had 23 State training colleges with 1,546 students, and five private institutions with 99 students. It is of interest to note the results produced by the existing training facilities as shown by the current staff list of the State establishment of education. The list of 1951 shows that the official establishment was composed of 3,743 officers, of whom 820 were European.[3] Of these 23 were described as on the *Direction* (the *Recteur* and the *Inspecteurs*), 135 were *Professeurs* or *Licenciés* and *Assimilés* engaged in teaching at

[1] See below, p. 1224.
[2] J. Capelle, 'Education in French West Africa', *Oversea Education*, vol. xxi, 1949–50, pp. 958–66.   [3] The total had risen by 1953 to some 4,968.

institutions of the *second degré*, and 3,470 were *Instituteurs* and *Moniteurs* of different grades in schools of the *premier degré*. Of this number 2,867 held local diplomas.

There were 24 officers engaged in physical education and 91 in technical instruction. As regards technical education there is now a trade training centre and a technical college in each of the component territories of the Federation, and two higher technical schools and a technical college at Dakar. The technical colleges give the metropolitan *certificat d'aptitude professionnelle* at the end of a four-year course; 140 students obtained this in 1952. There is also a two-year course which gives foremen's qualifications, and selected students who have attained this level can go on to the higher technical school. The *Collège de Commerce*, opened at Dakar in 1947, gives a certificate at the end of four years' training on the lines of the corresponding course in France. Agricultural courses are divided into the same three grades as in metropolitan France. It appears that the relation between the numbers who proceed to higher studies in France and the vacancies open for them is not calculated very exactly, as the Conference on Education in 1951 asked for the co-operation of the Ministry of Labour in finding them employment.

As in the British territories, educational expansion has been materially assisted from the metropolitan Exchequer. Under the Ten-year Plan for the social and economic development of Africa a sum of 8,500 million francs has been voted for credits for education in French West Africa.[1]

Togo

The system current in Togo under French trusteeship follows in the main that of French West Africa. Since the provisions of the Mandate required that freedom of access should be granted to all missionaries who were nationals of those States which were members of the League of Nations, mission activity was greater here than in French West Africa, and subsidies to missions amounted in 1951 to 23 per cent. of the total educational expenditure. In 1953 the primary-school population was divided more or less equally between 'public' and 'private' schools, the former having 25,117 pupils and the latter 23,398. There were three State and six Mission secondary schools.[2] Farm schools are conducted in co-operation with the Agricultural Department. Girls' education is largely in the hands of the missions, except in the Muslim area in the north, where there are two State schools. The girls study hygiene and child care instead of natural science, and sewing instead of drawing. In 1953 there were 9,921 girls in primary, 196 in secondary, and 83 in technical schools. In pursuance of a resolution of the Togo Assembly the construction of a college for girls was begun in 1952. A sum of 500 million

---

[1] See below, pp. 1338 ff.   [2] *Enseignement Outre-Mer*, December 1953, p. 92.

francs has been allocated to Togo for education under the plan financed from the *Fonds d'Investissement pour le Développement Économique et Social.*

French Equatorial Africa

The relative lack of resources has left French Equatorial Africa with a less advanced equipment of governmental services than French West Africa, and the difference is especially marked in the organization of education. It is significant that up to 1937 there was no separate Education Service; there were only 7,000 pupils in the 'public' schools, and these were still under the superintendence of Administrative Officers. This 'mise en sommeil de l'enseignement' was the subject of very unfavourable comment by the late M. Félix Éboué in 1941.[1] Such education as the territory possessed up to this time had been due mainly to missionary activity, though the official attitude towards mission work had differed somewhat from that in French West Africa. Before the Treaty of St. Germain-en-Laye was ratified, local *arrêtés* had laid down that only an association incorporated in France might open a school and no school was to be authorized unless teaching was given in French. A subsequent Decree of April 1921, notifying the ratification of the Treaty of St. Germain-en-Laye, did not in terms modify the restrictions placed by previous *arrêtés* on educational institutions, but in practice their application was relaxed, and there appears to have been an understanding that non-State schools might maintain their existence subject to the goodwill of the Administration. Mission schools are subsidized, but may not teach any subject in the vernacular, other than religion, and in order that they may qualify for recognition French must be taught by a teacher with a recognized diploma.

The respective contributions made by the *enseignement publique* and the *enseignement privé* is best illustrated by the fact that in 1939 the former had 9,485 pupils enrolled, as against 12,647 in the latter. Though a considerable change had occurred by 1953, the enrolment in the 'public' schools was then only 68,909, against 60,821 in the 'private'.[2] The number of schools was then 1,068, namely 541 classed as 'public' and 527 as 'private', with a total enrolment of 108,558 boys and 21,172 girls. But the great majority of the pupils were in the primary stage, there being only 2,449 in the secondary schools.

Provision for post-primary courses is made, first, by the centres for teacher training, consisting of two *écoles normales*, with eleven other teacher-training centres managed by the State and 14 managed by missions, and, second, by the one *lycée* and ten other post-primary schools, two of which are managed by missions. The most important of these establishments is

[1] Circular of 8 November 1941, quoted in H. Ziéglé, *Afrique Équatoriale Française*, 1952, p. 183.
[2] *Enseignement Outre-Mer*, December 1953, p. 65.

the *École des Cadres* at Brazzaville, which was founded as the *École Édouard Renard* in 1935, but was reorganized as the *École des Cadres Supérieurs* in 1946. Since 1950 it has had six sections, one of which is devoted to training for the Educational Service and others to training for Administrative, Public Works, and similar establishments.[1] It has a three-year course, and entry is by open competition. The *École Professionnelle* at Brazzaville is a technical school, devoted mainly to the training of mechanics and artisans. There are also 15 *Centres d'Apprentissage*, of which two are managed by the missions. The more advanced of the institutions above mentioned are attended by both Europeans and Africans. It has, however, been realized that it is not yet possible to bring the standards of the educational institutions of French Equatorial Africa into line with those observed in metropolitan France. Though the educational establishment has been extended of late years, there is still a shortage of more advanced staff, both European and African. The credits allocated to education in French Equatorial Africa under the Development Programme amounted to 2,000 million francs.

The Cameroons

The missions have played an important part also in the development of education in the Cameroons under French trusteeship. During the German administration official schools were first established in 1898, but the missions had already opened a number of schools, and in 1913 they had 11,500 pupils as against 1,194 in State institutions. The French Administration introduced in 1921 a system framed on the lines of the one then in force in French West Africa.[2] The subsidies given to the missions have been subject to the same conditions, but it is of interest to note that there has been a more notable increase in the numbers enrolled in the Mission primary schools than in those maintained by the State, with the result that while the State schools had 42,770 pupils in 1953, the Mission schools had 113,381.[3] In 1951 the subsidies given to the missions had risen to a proportion of nearly 25 per cent. of the whole expenditure on education.

There was, however, by this time a difference in the standards attained by the Mission and State schools.[4] In its original form the system had established in the Cameroons, as in French West Africa, a series of *secteurs scolaires*, each of which had a number of village or 'preparatory' schools, with a regional or 'principal' school which gave a 'middle' course, and which took the best of the pupils from the village schools. But as in French West Africa, the tendency here also has been to add a *cours moyen*

[1] *Enc. A.E.F.*, p. 207.   [2] *Arrêté*, 25 July 1921.
[3] *Enseignement Outre-Mer*, December 1953, p. 49.
[4] The organization of State education is regulated by the *arrêté* of 11 July 1950.

to the village schools, thus giving them the character of *écoles complètes* (with five- or six-year courses), and tending accordingly to eliminate the regional school of the *secteur*. This movement has grown more rapidly in the official schools than in those maintained by the missions.

It is noteworthy also that advance has been more rapid in the south than in the north, where progress has been retarded by the poverty of communications and by the predominance of members of the Muslim community. Further, it has been found possible to assimilate the curricula of the State schools more closely than those of the missionary institutions to the standards in force in metropolitan France.

The education of girls has from the first presented difficulties in the northern area; thus, though in the southern area girls now form 18 to 20 per cent. of the enrolment in the primary schools, the proportion among the Bamalike and the Islamized communities of the north is seldom more than 7½ per cent. of the total. Taking the territory as a whole, however, there has been considerable progress. In 1936 there were only 1,536 girls enrolled in the schools, but this had risen by 1951 to 35,697.

In regard to the *enseignement du second degré* the tentative efforts made in 1923 to create institutions for professional and technical instruction secured little popular support, and it was not until 1945 that the subject received serious attention. An *école supérieure* at Yaoundé, hitherto reserved for Europeans, then became a *collège classique et moderne*, open both to Europeans and Africans, and this received in 1950 the title of the *Lycée Général Leclerc*. In 1951 it had 600 students, of whom 450 were African. The *Lycée* gives the full course, working up to the *baccalauréat* on the same model as in metropolitan France. A *collège classique* at Douala and a *collège moderne* for girls also at Douala give a shorter course leading to the *brevet élémentaire*, as also does a *collège* at N'Kongsamba and another at Garoua. This last was designed to meet the needs of students from the north of the territory. There is one State *école normale* for teacher training at Yaoundé, and the missions also maintain four *écoles normales*. There were at the end of 1952 a total of 3,008 students taking post-primary courses.

Technical education is provided at the *École Professionnelle* at Douala, which has a four-year course leading to the *brevet d'enseignement industriel* on the metropolitan model. A first *Centre d'Apprentissage* was opened at N'Kongsamba in 1951 and three others were opened in other centres in 1952. A commercial school was opened at Douala in 1946, sponsored by the Chamber of Commerce. There were in 1953 some 1,137 students taking technical courses. It has, however, been recognized that the local institutions of *enseignement du second degré* are inadequate for the needs of the territory, and a number of *bourses scolaires* have accordingly been provided for both general and professional study in French West Africa and in metropolitan institutions; there were 242 *boursiers* studying in France in 1953. Adult literacy classes were instituted in 1951 and were attended by some 10,000 persons.

The progress of education in the Cameroons has attracted a special measure of support from the funds provided for the Development Programme. The assistance to be provided over the ten years will amount in all to 2,500 million francs.

THE BELGIAN TERRITORIES

Educational Policy in the Belgian Congo

The Belgian Government has relied to a greater extent than either the British or French Governments upon the work of religious bodies as agencies of education. Not only is the close contact between the State and these bodies a striking feature in the administration of the Belgian Congo, but the difference observed by the Government in its relations with Catholic and Protestant Missions respectively has formed a significant incident in its political history. The Berlin Act of 1885 laid down that Christian Missions should be accorded special protection, but the early entry of members of the French Orders caused Leopold II to fear a growth of French influence, and by agreement with the Vatican the Belgian Missionaries of Scheut were substituted for them. The Baptist Missionary Society, under the leadership of George Grenfell, had preceded the Catholics by some years, and in company with other Protestant societies had established a chain of Mission stations along the Congo river; but the Concordat which Leopold II concluded in 1906 with the Vatican established the Catholic Missions in a position of almost exclusive influence, and secured for them subsidies not merely for their educational activities but also for their religious work. In the course of the movement conducted against the Free State régime in the early part of the twentieth century, the Protestant Missions incurred the charge of supporting English and American interests against those of the Free State, and the latter found some of its most vigorous apologists among prominent Catholics.[1] Article 2 of the *Charte Coloniale* of 1908 and the Treaty of St. Germain-en-Laye guaranteed religious liberty in the Congo, but the terms on which subsidies were obtainable tended to favour the Catholic Missions and particularly those of Belgian origin.

After the annexation of the Congo the Belgian Government opened a small number of schools wholly financed from State revenues. They were, however, staffed by members of the Catholic teaching orders, such as the *Frères des Écoles Chrétiennes*, the *Frères Maristes*, and the *Frères Salésiens*. These still retain the designation of *écoles officielles*. But the Concordat of

[1] F. Masoin, *Histoire de l'état indépéndant du Congo*, vol. i, 1913, p. 151.

1906 had also provided that every Catholic Mission established in the country should open a school. A large number of these have since received State grants and they now form the great majority of the class of schools designated as *écoles libres subsidiées*. In 1925–6 a series of 20-year conventions were concluded which defined the terms on which missionary bodies would be eligible for subsidies. Grants were as a result offered only to 'national' missions, defined as those having headquarters in Belgium and administered by a body two-thirds of whom were Belgians. No restriction was laid on the opening of schools by other missions, nor were those who did not receive State grants required to submit to inspection, but Protestant Missions had difficulty in complying with some of the conditions, and accordingly had to carry on their educational activities almost without State assistance, though the work of some of their schools was officially recognized as being of a high order.

It is of interest to note the proportion existing in the inter-war period between the schools of the different categories thus created. In 1938 there were 24 *écoles officielles* maintained for Europeans by the State (2,091 pupils); seven *écoles officielles pour noirs* (4,368 pupils); and 5,156 *écoles libres subsidiées* of different grades (both primary and secondary), with a total of 246,345 pupils. As regards the schools which received no grants, there was an estimated total of 10,000 schools of 'national' (that is, Roman Catholic) Missions, with an estimated total of 200,000 pupils; Protestant Missions, according to the figures supplied by them, had 7,997 schools of various grades, with 266,142 pupils. The number of pupils in schools which received no grants largely exceeded those in the official and subsidized schools. The figures of 1948 were of much the same order. A number of schools which had previously received no grants had meanwhile been brought on to the subsidized list, but the pupils in schools which received no subsidies were still in the majority, and numbered 514,974 against 415,542 in official and subsidized schools. It is a tribute to the work of evangelization carried out by the missions that 40 per cent. of the population are said to have been converted to Christianity, and that they succeeded in attracting to their schools 50 per cent. of the children of school age.[1]

In 1948, however, the previous distinction between 'national' and 'foreign' missions was removed, and grants were offered to all teaching organizations on the same terms. These terms required that all the teaching staff should know French and should have spent at least a year in Belgium attending approved courses of teacher training. The schools were to teach the Government syllabus and the inspectors (who under the Belgian system are employed by the missions but submit reports to the official inspectorate) were required to hold approved teachers'

[1] G. Malengreau, in *Africa Today*, 1955, p. 338.

qualifications.[1] A ten-year period was allowed for teachers already at work to obtain the appropriate qualifications, but during this time the schools were entitled to receive subsidies. In 1951 there were 6,409 pupils in official and 513,146 in the subsidized schools. Unsubsidized schools had 449,789 pupils, of whom 129,348 were in Catholic schools, 272,018 in Protestant, and 50,945 in those provided by commercial and industrial firms for the families of their employees. The Administration could rely on finding among the religious bodies many teachers who had brought not only enthusiasm but professional qualifications to their task. The *Frères des Écoles Chrétiennes*, the *Frères Maristes*, and some of the *Frères Salésiens*, for instance, were trained teachers, and many other teachers in the numerous *écoles congréganistes* were highly qualified.[2] This was the position in 1954, when there occurred the controversy, to which subsequent reference will be made, regarding the extension of the system of 'lay' schools in metropolitan Belgium.[3]

Ruanda Urundi

In Ruanda Urundi the system follows that of the Congo in its general use of the religious bodies, who here also are predominantly Catholic, though the Concordat of 1906 does not apply to the territory. Article 8 of the Mandate of the League of Nations, which is in line with the terms of the Treaty of St. Germain-en-Laye, accorded to all religious bodies an equal right to erect religious buildings and to open schools. There has been in Ruanda Urundi the same difficulty arising from the competition of different denominations for school sites as has been seen in some of the British areas, and there was at one time a complaint that Chiefs, who have the power of vetoing the grant of land for this purpose, had been influenced by their officers to exercise their authority to the prejudice of the Protestant Missions. Local orders issued in 1936 impressed on the Chiefs that there must be equality in this matter, subject to the standing rule that no mission can take up a site within two kilometres of another. Up to 1948 Protestant Missions suffered from the same disability in regard to educational subsidies as those in the Belgian Congo, and only one mission had qualified to receive a subsidy by virtue of the Belgian nationality of its personnel. The legislation of 1948, which removed the previous distinction between 'national' and 'foreign' missions, applied also to Ruanda Urundi.

In 1951 there were 641 Europeans in the five official or subsidized schools of Ruanda Urundi, and 1,140 Africans in official and 142,199 in subsidized schools. Of the pupils at unassisted schools, 245,185 were at

[1] *Gouvernement Général, Organisation de l'enseignement libre subsidié pour indigènes*, 1948, p. 42.
[2] J. Vanhove, 'L'Œuvre d'éducation au Congo Belge et au Ruanda-Urundi', *Enc. C.B.*, vol. iii, p. 753, 768.   [3] See below, p. 1214.

Catholic and 80,367 at Protestant schools. There were also 11 schools for Muslims, with 988 pupils.

The school system was organized on the same lines as in the Congo. Government primary education was concentrated at the Astrida School Centre, which had three official schools, of which one was secondary, and gave a general education. It also gave courses in medical, veterinary, and agricultural studies.

School Organization

The Belgian policy may be said to assign to the African a different cultural future from that envisaged by the French, for it looks less to his association with European civilization than to his fuller development within the range of his own economic and social environment. Nor has education been consciously conceived as a means of producing 'auxiliaries' in the work of administration or for the development of economic or social services. The Colony has a wealth of latent resources, and it has been the outstanding problem of the Government to create among the people of the Congo (to all appearance less advanced than those of French West Africa or Northern Nigeria) an intelligent and competent population which would aid in developing these resources. Some of the first institutions established were a school for clerks and three technical schools, two attached to State workshops and the other to those of the *Compagnie des Chemins de Fer des Grands Lacs* at Stanleyville. The training given in these schools was almost exclusively manual.

After the annexation of the Free State the technical schools were replaced by groups of schools in selected areas, financed by the State but managed by the Catholic Missions, and giving both primary and technical education on a syllabus based on that for Belgian schools. In 1922, however, the field of education was considered in its wider aspects by a Commission which included representatives of the Government and missions and experts from technical schools in Belgium. This laid down principles for the organization of a complete school system which came into force in 1925, but was revised in 1938 and again in 1948.[1] The system thus introduced comprised a two-year lower-primary course in which literary instruction was kept to the minimum, with a three-year higher-primary and middle course, followed in selected cases by a three-year post-primary course with a strongly vocational bias. Special *écoles ménagères agricoles* for girls taught sewing, cooking, and child care. The avowed aim of education as then envisaged was, in the words of an observer, 'to produce better Africans, and not copies of Europeans who could never be more than humans of a third category'.[2]

---

[1] *Gouvernement Général, Organisation de l'enseignement libre subsidié pour indigènes*, 1948.
[2] L. Franck, *Études de colonisation comparée*, 1924, p. 123.

Under the system in force in 1953 a two-year nursery course, which was available mainly in the towns, was preparatory to a primary course which could be completed in four years. This was envisaged as 'the direct preparation of the Native for life in his natural surroundings'. At the end of the second year of the primary course, however, selected children could enter upon a further four-year course intended to lead on to secondary studies. The numbers were limited in relation to the opportunities for employment which were estimated to be open to boys with secondary schooling. In some cases the third and fourth years, or the fourth only, were taken in classes attached to secondary schools. Where possible the work in the fourth year was under a European teacher. Pupils who had completed the ordinary course might enter an *école d'auxiliaires* which trained them for employment as junior clerks in Government or commercial firms, or could take a two-year course qualifying them to teach in village schools.

Secondary schools were divided, as were the French schools, into 'modern' and 'classic' (or Latin) schools. The modern course was common to all pupils for the first three years, after which they specialized for a further three years in one of four fields, namely, administrative and commercial, survey (*géomètres arpenteurs*), science (as preparation for agricultural, veterinary, or medical work), and teacher training. In 1951 there were five Latin schools in existence and an equal number of modern schools was planned.[1] Vocational schools gave courses of two, four, or six years. These included *écoles artisanales* (the primary aim of which was to create a class of craftsmen who could earn an income in the villages), and also institutions designed to produce skilled employees for industrial firms.

Special provision is made for the education of girls.[2] In the first two years of the primary school the courses for boys and girls are identical, but after this girls taking the ordinary course concentrated on practical domestic studies (*études ménagères*). Others proceed to a post-primary course of two or three years in which a more theoretical type of instruction is directed to the improvement of home conditions. While taking this course they can qualify as teachers or assistant midwives. In response to the opinion of educated Africans, it is now intended to open middle schools for girls giving a course of three or four years, combining elements of the home-craft syllabus and of the boys' middle-school syllabus. A four- or five-year teacher-training course is open to girls who have completed the four-year primary course. As in the French territories, education is free at every stage. There is noticeable in this curriculum a selective process that continues throughout the educative period. Only the survivors of the second course of primary education are able to proceed to the fourth- or sixth-year secondary education. Those not so selected, however, continue

---

[1] *Enc. C.B.*, vol. iii, pp. 760–1.   [2] Ibid. p. 763.

in the school of second degree where they are trained for vocational occupations. There are instances in which African children of good character and educational promise are admitted to schools reserved for Europeans.[1]

Advanced vocational education is directly controlled by the Government. There is a school for medical assistants (*École d'Assistants Médicaux Indigènes*) at Kisantu and schools for agricultural assistants (*Écoles d'Assistants Agricoles*) situated at Kisantu and Kamponde. Studies of these and similar subjects will in future terminate at a *centre universitaire*, one of which is the Lovanium at Kimuenza (Kisantu), situated on the heights overlooking Leopoldville. It was formally inaugurated in October 1954, and is affiliated to the Catholic University of Louvain[2] in the same way that British Colonial Colleges are to the University of London. After an introductory course of seven months selected students will have a choice between four lines of study, namely: medicine (seven years), agriculture, engineering, or administration (five years); or they can, as an alternative, take a course qualifying them to teach in secondary schools in the Congo. The foundation stone of the building of the Faculty of Science has been laid, and there were 34 students, mostly African, studying there in 1955. Within a few years it is hoped to increase this number to a thousand. Post-graduate studies will continue to be pursued in the mother country. A collegiate institution, opened at Usumbura in the territory of Ruanda Urundi in 1955, will be devoted mainly to the study of agriculture. This and a somewhat similar institution at Astrida will be subsidiary to the University College at Elisabethville, established by royal decree in November 1955.[3]

A number of commercial firms employ religious and lay teachers, both European and African, at schools maintained for their employees. In 1951 there were as many as 564 such schools, the provision of educational as well as medical facilities being part of the conditions regulating the authorization given to commercial and industrial enterprise in the Congo. These schools follow the official syllabus. Some of the larger companies have also opened technical schools with the object of replacing European by African skilled labour. The Bas-Congo–Katanga Railway established in 1921 four such schools, which draw their pupils from the more promising employees of the company, and all the transport companies now organize similar training. The *Union Minière* has had since 1922 a school with sections for carpentry, ironwork, and engineering. Both the *Union Minière* and the *Forminière*[4] train dispensers for their hospitals.

One of the outstanding impressions left on any observer of the Belgian

---

[1] G. Malengreau, in *Africa Today*, 1955, p. 349.
[2] Idem, 'L'Université congolaise', *Société Belge d'Études et d'Expansion*, 1953.
[3] *The Times*, 9 November 1955.   [4] See above, pp. 585–6.

industrial system must be the wide extent to which Africans are now entrusted with the charge of machinery and are employed in work requiring technical knowledge. On the other hand the Belgians have shown a distrust of the product of a purely literary education, and it is of interest that, although the system will now provide for education up to university level, the subjects taught even at that stage are closely correlated with the fields in which there is likely to be a demand for the employment of specialists. There is a further point of some interest. The wide use of the religious orders at every stage of school and technical instruction has resulted in the existence of an unusual proportion of Europeans in the teaching staff. In the establishments employed in 1951, taking together the assisted and non-assisted schools, there were in all 3,275 Europeans and 37,032 Africans.

The Language of Instruction

The vernacular has been adopted as the sole medium of instruction for pupils who are not going beyond the primary stage. French is taught as a language in the special course in primary schools, and all post-primary education is given solely in French, though Flemish and English are taught as subjects in those secondary schools which prepare boys for employment in business or in the service of the Administration.[1] The exercise of choice among the vernaculars is a difficult problem. Full linguistic studies have been made of 21 languages in the Colony. Work on 34 others is said to be well advanced, and it has been suggested that 20 years hence there will be in the Congo 'a linguistic library based on at least a hundred Congolese tongues of the Bantu, Sudanese, and Negrillo stocks'.[2] For the most part, however, preference is for practical reasons given to the more widely used languages, notably Lingala, Kongo, Luba, or the local form of Swahili.[3] It is understood that courses in African languages and cultures will be given in the new university institutions.

Education for Europeans

The organization for the education of Europeans dates from about the year 1912, but has received increasing attention of late years owing to the large influx of Europeans after the Second World War. As a general rule, the schools for Europeans are not shared by Africans, as they are in the French territories, though some of the more advanced institutions devoted to specialized training are now attended by Africans as well as Europeans.

[1] *Enc. C.B.*, vol. iii, p. 751.
[2] C. Pierre, in *Regional Papers on Vernacular Languages*, no. 10, 1951, quoted in Unesco, *The Use of Vernacular Languages in Education* (Monographs on Fundamental Education, VIII), 1953, p. 18.
[3] See above, p. 106.

The schools for Europeans follow strictly the curriculum prescribed in Belgium, and are largely staffed by the Catholic teaching orders.

The total number of pupils rose from 1,617 in 1938 to 10,111 in 1951; there was then a total of 2,992 pupils in the 13 schools described as *écoles officielles laïques*, 1,720 in the two *écoles officielles congréganistes*, and 4,742 in 29 subsidized schools, mainly conducted by the Catholic Missions. There were in addition 435 pupils in non-subsidized schools. The last group included four schools conducted by industrial firms, as well as the schools for the families of Protestant missionaries, in which the medium of instruction was English. The *écoles officielles laïques* referred to above include the five high schools of Leopoldville, Elisabethville, Costermansville, Jadotville, and Stanleyville, which have middle as well as primary classes; the teaching in the majority is in French, but the schools at Leopoldville and Elisabethville also have courses in Flemish. These schools have been given the name *Athénée Royal*, and their teaching staff is supplied by the religious Orders.

Technical Instruction and Adult Education

A considerable measure of technical instruction is provided in evening classes by industrial undertakings at Elisabethville and Jadotville. Since 1952 the workshop facilities provided by some of these firms have been shared by Europeans and Africans, partly as a measure of economy and partly with the aim of improving industrial relations.[1] There is a School of Art at Elisabethville attended by 70 students, 27 of whom are African. Government assistance is given also to a School of Music. It does not appear that there has so far been any widespread campaign for adult education as such, but in 1950 there were in existence 52 'adult' schools with 4,172 pupils, mainly organized by industrial companies for their adult employees.[2]

The Ten-year Development Programme contemplates an expenditure by the State of 4,876 million Belgian francs on education, of which 3,038 million is shown as provision for recurring expenditure. It has been stated, though only by way of a rough estimate, that if the whole of the educational work carried out by the Mission schools were handed over to State schools, the sum above mentioned might have to be trebled. Bursaries are awarded to pupils who prefer to study agriculture in Belgium rather than to follow a course at a secondary school in the Congo. For education in the territory of Ruanda Urundi a sum of 428 million Belgian francs has been provided, of which 217 million francs are for recurrent expenditure.

---

[1] *Enc. C.B.*, vol. iii, p. 778.
[2] A. Gille, in *Symposium on Popular Education*, Leiden, 1953, pp. 1–17.

Controversy regarding Lay Schools

The system upon which primary schools were organized in these territories was put sharply into reverse when the defeat of the Christian Social Party at the elections of 1954 led to the formation of a new Liberal-Socialist Government in Belgium. In accordance with changes made in the Belgian educational system the new Minister for the Colonies announced his intention to give a vigorous impulse to lay education in the Congo and to make a substantial reduction in the subsidies given to Mission schools. The reaction of the Catholic Missions was prompt. The Vicars-Apostolic of the Congo and Ruanda Urundi declared that if the Government carried out this plan without respect to previous undertakings they would close the whole of the Catholic schools in both territories, and so put a stop to the education of about 70 per cent. of pupils in the Congo and of almost all in Ruanda Urundi.

This firm response compelled the Belgian Government to withdraw its proposal and to be content with developing lay schools while continuing to subsidize Mission schools. The seven *écoles officielles pour noirs* were increased in number to 18 by the end of 1954, and were also increased in size. In December 1955 it was stated that the enrolment of pupils in lay schools had been multiplied four times and that a further large increase was intended. Many new lay teachers had been appointed. The attendance at lay primary schools in 1955 was 1,427 at Leopoldville, 1,039 at Luluabourg, 571 at Stanleyville, and 126 at Elisabethville. As elsewhere in Africa the first reaction of the people was to welcome the provision of new schools of any kind, but the political conflict between the advocates of lay and clerical education inevitably spread from the metropolitan country to the Colonies, with the consequence of a bitter jealousy rather than a healthy rivalry between the two types of school.[1]

THE PORTUGUESE TERRITORIES

The history of education in the Portuguese territories both of East and West Africa has two outstanding characteristics, the insistence on the school as an agency for the spread of the Portuguese language and culture, and the steady discouragement of other than national organizations. This has been specially noticeable in the contribution which the missions have been allowed to make to the expansion of education. In both territories the Catholic Missions are of course of very old standing; a cathedral was built at São Salvador in Angola about 1534, and the first Jesuit Mission arrived in East Africa in 1560. In Mozambique non-Portuguese Protestant Missions established themselves in the middle of the nineteenth

[1] Information from *Ministère des Colonies*, Brussels, 12 March 1955, and from Professor G. Malengreau, 12 December 1955.

century and started a number of schools, and in 1878 the Baptist Missionary Society founded a Mission station at São Salvador in Angola. In Angola the number of Mission schools has been more limited, and they have for the most part been provided by the Catholic Missions.

Under the law of Separation of Church and State the subsidies were withdrawn from all missions in 1911, but resumed again in 1919. In the régime which began in 1926 missions were given a special role in improving the lot of the African. By the Colonial Act of 1930 the Portuguese Catholic Missions were allotted a privileged position and recognized as 'an instrument of civilization and national influence'. The Missionary Agreement of 1940 supplemented by the Missionary Statute of 1941 finally reaffirmed the reversion to an earlier policy and where possible restored all confiscated property, emphasizing the essentially national character of the Portuguese Missions. Where Portuguese missionaries were not available, foreign missions were admitted, but only with Government and Vatican approval and on the condition that they became integrated in the Portuguese Missionary Organization, on the terms for which provision was made in the Statute. One non-Portuguese body, the Swiss Mission, was able to meet the requirements of the law by establishing a consultative body in Lisbon and agreeing to recruit a fixed proportion of missionaries from Portugal, but the decree of 1941 prohibited the grant of subsidies to other than Portuguese Catholic Missions. The Protestant Missions have derived their strength from the *Aliança Evangelica de Angola*, with its headquarters at Luanda, a body representative of all missions except those of the Roman Catholics and Seventh Day Adventists. Their enrolment is said to be over 79,000 pupils.

There is a uniform organization of education in the Portuguese territories of East and West Africa. The schools are divided into three grades, elementary, primary, and secondary. The elementary course is limited to the study of the Portuguese language, reading, writing, arithmetic, and Christian morals.[1] The use of the vernacular is forbidden, except for oral explanations and translations of the Scriptures, where, however, vernacular passages must be accompanied by parallel texts in Portuguese. The Protestant Missions have not failed to point out that it is common experience that children who are first taught to read and write in their own language are likely to learn a foreign language more quickly than others.[2] Though there are some differences between the education given to Africans and non-Africans at the elementary stage, the primary and secondary courses are identical for both Africans and non-Africans; both entrance and promotion examinations are conducted by the State. The primary course is officially stated to include the Portuguese language, the geo-

[1] M. Caetano, *Colonising Traditions, Principles and Methods of the Portuguese*, 1951, p. 45.
[2] R. L. Buell, *The Native Problem in Africa*, vol. ii, 1928, p. 61.

graphy of Portuguese territories, handwork, and agriculture, but it may be mentioned that most elementary schools in Portugal use a *libro unico* which covers all subjects including religion. The primary course leads either to a technical school or a *lycée*, but the technical schools have a very limited scope, and train only shoemakers, carpenters, and the like. For children residing within three kilometres of a school, education is free and compulsory between the ages of seven and twelve years.

In Mozambique since 1938 only the children of Europeans, Asians, and assimilated Africans have been educated in the State schools. In 1952 these had only 258 African pupils. Education of the African population has been officially delegated to the Roman Catholic Missions, which receive a subsidy from the Government, and the controversy regarding the right of Government Inspectors to visit such schools, which has continued over a number of years, still remains unresolved. In 1952 there were 16 State primary schools, having an attendance of 6,669 pupils, one secondary, and ten technical schools. The missions maintained about 1,000 primary schools in which about 150,000 Africans are educated, 44 technical schools, and three teacher-training institutions. The Asian, Chinese, and Greek communities maintain their own schools in the towns of Lourenço Marques and Beira. The Salazar *Liceu* was opened in 1919 with 44 students, a number which increased by 1953 to 941. But in this, as in the other high schools, the number of Africans is negligible owing to the age limit of entry being set at 13, when the African has not yet completed his elementary education. In the technical schools the age limit is waived and, though a fee is charged, they are more popular with Africans. In each district there is a State-managed school of arts and crafts for Africans. In the past these schools produced craftsmen who made European goods and were an asset to the country. In recent years, however, their products have had to suffer the competition of manufactured goods, and the craftsmen are not readily absorbed in factories which offer only the wage of unskilled labour.

In Angola the figures for 1950–1 are much lower, giving a total of 207 primary, 22 secondary, 16 technical, and three teacher-training schools. Of these schools the State maintained 122 primary, two secondary, twelve technical, and two normal schools; the missions managed 48 primary, seven secondary, one technical, and one normal school, and there were 37 primary, 13 secondary, and three technical schools classed as privately managed. There were 13,586 pupils in primary schools, 2,277 in secondary, 1,548 in technical, and 154 in normal schools, not a very noteworthy achievement for an Administration which has in its charge a population of over 4 million people. More attention appears to be given both by the Government and by missions to agricultural education in Angola than in Portuguese East Africa, partly because of the movement in Angola for the expansion of European colonization. There is a *lycée* in Luanda leading from the elementary school to the university stage, its final two years' course being similar to that given in American 'junior colleges'. The Currie Institute in Angola is managed jointly by the United Church of Canada and the American Board of Commissioners for Foreign Missions. It includes a teachers' training school and is approaching collegiate status.

Neither in Mozambique nor in Angola has there been hitherto any reservation of schools for Europeans or Africans, one of the chief objectives of education being to produce the class of *assimilado*. It is therefore of interest to note that in Mozambique the *civilizada* section of the population was given in the census of 1950 as 92,404 (out of a total of 5,732,767), but among these there were 48,910 Europeans, 24,898 Coloured people, and 12,604 Indians; the 'Negroes' only numbered 4,377.[1]

In 1948, however, a decree of the Portuguese Government announced the policy of founding four *Escolas de Preparação* for selected Africans, aged between 14 and 18 years, one for boys and one for girls in each of the two provinces of Angola and Mozambique. The establishment of the first of these schools at Marracuene near Lourenço Marques was authorized in 1950. In addition to a general education, both moral and physical, these schools were to undertake instruction in the rudiments of administration, agriculture, and public health, their declared intention being to train leaders in the ways of European civilization.[2]

In Sao Tomé and Principe there are nine schools conducted by the Government, seven by missions, and two by private agencies. Of these six are primary schools with a total of 1,396 pupils, one a secondary school with 32, and one a craft school with 72. Assistance is given to pupils wishing to take more advanced courses in Portugal.

LIBERIA

In Liberia the organization of education is, like that of a number of its other institutions, in a state of transition as the result of the activity in the development of the social and economic services made possible by the improvement in the financial status of the country. The schools originally had a restricted scope, being designed mainly for the requirements of the relatively small Americo-Liberian community. But education is now being extended to meet the needs of the indigenous tribes which make up nearly 95 per cent. of the population. The first schools were established by the missions: the Methodist Church of America started work in 1832, and its central high school, then designated as the 'College of West Africa', was

---

[1] *Anuário estatístico do Ultramar, 1950–51*, pp. 50–52. The distribution between Europeans and others is not given for Angola.

[2] *Regulamento das Escolas de Preparação das Autoridades Gentílicas*, Lourenço Marques, 1951.

founded in 1839;[1] the Protestant Episcopal Church of America established Cuttington College in 1888; the Lutheran Church, which began work in Liberia in 1866, shortly afterwards built its own training college; and both the National Baptist Convention (an American Negro Church) and the Catholic Church have maintained high schools. All the missions have also had primary schools. The establishment of a primary school was indeed made one of the conditions of permitting their entry into the country.

The only two major institutions in pre-war Liberia which were not mission-controlled were the Booker Washington Institute at Kakata and Liberia College at Monrovia. The former, founded in 1929, concentrated on the training of artisans and agricultural workers. The latter, founded in 1863, was the main Liberian centre of higher education, but up to recent years it seldom had more than what has been described as a 'mere trickle' of graduates. It continually suffered from financial crises, and in other ways also had until recently a troubled and precarious career.[2]

For the most part, as has been indicated, these institutions served the needs of the urban Americo-Liberians, though there were also a small number of primary schools maintained by the State in the hinterland. The Government instituted in 1912 a Department of Public Instruction, and passed in that year a law providing for compulsory education, though this was largely in the nature of a gesture, as very little attempt was made to enforce it. The sum appropriated for education in the budget of 1925 was $18,200, which included $7,000 for Liberia College.[3] There were then stated to be 55 Government schools, but the total enrolment in them was only 1,898. Since then there has been a very substantial increase in the provision made for State schools; the number had by 1952 increased to 227 public elementary schools and five State high schools, with an enrolment of 33,000. Liberia College was raised in 1950 to the status of a university,[4] and had 400 students, though only a small proportion of these were as yet taking full degree courses. There were at this time 112 Liberian students taking courses abroad on scholarships provided by the State or by Unesco. Formerly American universities were most popular with Liberian students, but now an increasing number proceed to English universities. It was reported in 1954 that about 80 students were studying in Great Britain, of whom about 50 were women training for the nursing profession. The total provision for education in the budget was raised in 1951 to nearly $500,000, and it stood in 1952 at nearly $1 million.

All this is evidence of considerable movement forward, though it is noteworthy that of the public elementary schools only 48 are in the hinterland. The plans for expansion put forward in 1952 envisaged an

[1] T. Hodgkin, in *West Africa*, 3 October 1953, p. 919.
[2] R. L. Buell, *The Native Problem in Africa*, vol. ii, 1928, p. 755.   [3] Ibid. p. 757.
[4] *Seventh Annual Message of the President*, 1950, p. 55. *Colonial Review*, vol. ix, no. 2, June 1955, p. 39.

early increase up to an enrolment of 105,000 in the elementary schools, but to reach this figure would have required an expenditure on buildings and on training staff which would have greatly exceeded the appropriation made in that year. Hitherto there has been only one State teacher-training college.[1] Very few pupils have completed the eight years' course given in the elementary schools, while the five State secondary schools have an average enrolment of less than 50, few pupils completing the four years' secondary course. The progress of Liberia College has been hampered by the fact that it can draw from the high schools only a very limited number of students equipped to take university courses. It adds to the difficulties in the way of an expansion of education that there are still a number of different agencies concerned. The Department of Public Instruction is not fully powered, and Unesco, the Technical Co-operative Assistance Mission, and various influential missionary bodies all have their own views on policy. The Mission schools are still far better equipped and staffed than are those of the State and have a far better local standing.

English is the official language of Liberia and is the principal medium of instruction in the schools. The official insistence on English has created difficulties in the way of the 'national literacy campaign' which was initiated in 1950. Literacy material was produced in some 14 vernaculars, but progress was hampered by a departmental order of 1949 which directed that any lesson taught in a dialect must also be taught in English. The campaign has, however, been of importance as part of the effort to abolish the distinction between the 'civilized' and 'uncivilized' sections of the population. That movement has already made some progress, as is evidenced by the fact that two members of the existing Administration are members of the Vai tribe.[2]

Vocational and technical training is now given at some of the larger Mission stations and at the Booker Washington Institute at Kakata, which includes on its staff both American Negroes and Africans from the Gold Coast. It has accommodation for 220 students. At present, however, most of the skilled tradesmen employed in Liberia come from British areas. Girls are trained as nurses at the Government hospital in Monrovia and as midwives at the Samuel Grimes Memorial Maternity Centre at Kakata. A mission consisting of medically qualified American Negroes, which was sent from the United States in response to an appeal from President Tubman, established a school of nursing which was later expanded to train medical and dental assistants.[3] On the advice of an educational mission from Unesco, which was invited to Liberia in 1952, five rural schools with a strong agricultural bias were opened and an emergency teacher-training scheme was started.

[1] W. S. de G. Rankin, *Note on Liberia and its Educational System*, 1952.
[2] See above, p. 239.   [3] R. E. Anderson, *Liberia*, 1952.

THE SPANISH TERRITORIES

In these territories European and African education form separate systems. Schools are provided partly by the State and partly by the missions, but only Catholic Missions are eligible for grants-in-aid. The objective of education for Africans is stated to be 'the spread of patriotism and the Spanish virtues and culture, without uprooting the African, but with the definite purpose of improving his living conditions'.

Education for Europeans is compulsory, and in theory elementary education for Africans is also compulsory. All education provided by the State is free. Schooling for Africans is in three stages. At the lowest (the elementary stage) there are seven courses, the type of schooling being largely practical. Here the teachers are mainly African. In the next or primary stage, where the teachers are preferably Spanish, there are two courses, one of which prepares Africans for the 'activities of the country in general', while the other prepares them for the higher African school, the *Escuela Superior Indígena* at Santa Isabel, which is the avenue to professional and vocational employment. Here the entry is on a selective and competitive basis: one section trains auxiliary teachers, a second trains auxiliaries in health, public works, and other departmental services; a third section gives training for commercial work, the course here being two to three years as against three to four years for the other sections. The courses given in the *Escuela Superior Indígena* are both theoretical and practical. There are also separate schools for office workers and for agricultural employees, and a school of domestic science for women. Emphasis is placed on the fact that the measure of higher education provided is intended for the training of Africans only as 'auxiliaries'. If it should be intended to carry education farther, it is felt that it would be preferable to create local institutions for this purpose rather than to encourage visits to Europe, since Spain does not desire to produce 'Europeanized Negroes'.[1]

DIFFERING CONCEPTS OF OBJECTIVES OF EDUCATION

The Education of Europeans

It was inevitable that in the preceding survey the education of Europeans should have received much less attention than that of Africans. In a large proportion of the territories surveyed there is relatively little permanent settlement of Europeans. In a second but smaller category of territories it is necessary to provide secondary or advanced courses for only a small number of Europeans, and there is in this case a natural tendency

[1] *Cuadernos de estudios africanos*, no. 9, 1950, pp. 227–9, and no. 11, 1950, pp. 35–48.

to frame the curricula as nearly as possible on the model adopted by the metropolitan institutions.

A different situation arises, however, in a third class of territories, of which the Union of South Africa is the most prominent. Here there is a large permanently settled community of Europeans, and one moreover which prides itself on the autonomy of its institutions and their freedom from external influence. Higher education has, in the first place, tended to become mainly vocational or professional, as is not unnatural in a country where current problems of economic development engross so much attention. It is more significant that the content and objective of education should have been so largely influenced by political conceptions. It is understandable that Afrikaans-speaking Europeans should desire to see adequate provision made for their section of the community in the universities, nor does an insistence on bilingualism necessarily create an obstacle to academic progress. But Afrikaans has so limited a range of literature, either original or translated, that any form of original work or of research must present unusual difficulty to those students for whom Afrikaans is the chosen medium for academic teaching.

There is a further problem due to the influence now exercised by politics in the field of education. There was a period when public thought in the Union sought to divide education into two parts, namely, the range of instruction appropriate for Europeans as the dominant race in the country, and the range appropriate for Africans as subordinate figures in its economy. Whatever the ethical value of this distinction, it was at least logical. There is not the same logic in the present-day effort to divide education in terms of European and Bantu culture.[1] It is, of course, proper that education for Africans should take full account of the history and social institutions of the Bantu, but it is illogical to suggest that study of the humanities or of abstract or applied science can be divided into matter appropriate to Europeans as such or Bantu as such. Nor is it likely that any attempt to legislate in this direction will be permanently successful. State regulation may for a time retard the access of the African to certain types of knowledge, but it will not in the end restrain him from efforts to acquire the full range of knowledge which will, in his conception, place him on a level with the European.

Education of Africans: the Diversity of Objectives

This attempt to divide the content of education into two separate cultural fields, European and African, is, however, confined to the Union of South Africa. Elsewhere the difficulty experienced by the student of educational systems lies in the great diversity which prevails in respect both of policy and practice. Lack of uniformity and clarity in defining

[1] See above, pp. 1148 ff.

policy is particularly marked in the British Colonial areas. Policy differs as between French, Belgian, and Portuguese territories, but the policy is more or less clearly expressed, and the school system designed on a consistent plan to give effect to it. Part of this lack of system in the British areas is due to the predominance acquired at an early period by missionary activity in education, but in part also it is due to the projection into the Colonial field of the traditional disinclination of the British to subject education or any other intellectual movement to State control.

The British can no doubt plead that there is always value in an elasticity of method, and that systematization is often most successful when it waits on experience instead of following a rigid logic, but the fact remains that the British Colonial Governments have placed widely different and indeed inconsistent interpretations upon the policy indicated in the memoranda of the Colonial Office Committee. As a consequence there has been no uniformity on such necessary details as, for example, the period at which English should be introduced into the curriculum, or the place to be accorded to handicraft or to practical work of any kind in school instruction. There is no accord as to the extent to which primary courses should be self-contained, or how far they should be designed as preparation for secondary education. The only field of education which seems to reveal a common design is that of academic instruction, due to the influence exercised by the requirements of British qualifying examinations, both at the school-leaving stage and in the new university colleges which are affiliated with the University of London.

The beginnings of education in Africa were laid in an age which assumed the intrinsic value of European civilization. African institutions were judged mainly in terms of their resemblance to those already known, and concern for the improvement of African conditions manifested itself mainly in the effort to make them approximate to those of Europe. To many who held that view the Christian religion was an essential element in the introduction of the African to civilization, and this was reflected in the official encouragement given to Mission schools. As the study of African society developed, however, a more realistic view came to be taken of African institutions. It was at all events seen that they embodied a sense of mutual obligation among members of kinship or similar groups which could not readily be replaced by moral precepts elaborated in a different context. There ensued a movement of opinion in favour of the preservation of those elements of African culture which were not regarded as contrary to the principles of civilization. It was a movement in which many leading representatives of missions also played a part, and it gained force in the British territories from the growing extension of the principle of Indirect Rule. Translated into educational terms, this involved the organization of school curricula in such a way as to relate the matter taught to the background of the pupil's experience and to the problems of his own environment.

The activity of the State Departments of Education and of missionary or other religious bodies is, of course, only one of the influences which have previously been mentioned as modifying African life; and to those influences must now be added the force of the demand for the early achievement of political advance, which itself has a direct bearing on educational policy. The growth of self-government necessarily involves acceleration in the assimilation by Africans of the skills and techniques that up to now have been exercised by Europeans in Africa. In the economic sphere, moreover, it can be seen that the changes which European influences first set in motion have created problems that cannot be solved without still more extensive changes. The most insistent need is perhaps for modification of the traditional farming methods which now threaten to destroy the natural resources of Africa at the same time that an increasing population is demanding a higher standard of living.

But African problems are no longer those only of the peasant farmer. A type of education appropriate to the needs of people who live outside the traditional environment has now become necessary, for we have to meet the requirements of the rising African middle class. The educationist has to devise a curriculum that will remain of significance to those who live in the rural areas while also appealing to those whose interests cover a wider field. This aspect of the educational problem is of peculiar difficulty, because it is clear that the African leaders of the territories which are now approaching self-government (as for example in West Africa) have little interest in a type of education which seems to indicate a separate sphere of development for African culture.

The early concentration on imparting a knowledge of European civilization went at one period to lengths which are now recognized as absurd, such as the use of textbooks designed purely for European schools or teaching the botany of European rather than African plants. It had its parallel in the histories used in early days in the schools of Senegal, which are said to have begun with a reference to 'our ancestors the Gauls'. The change of approach in this respect occurred at the time when the various Governments first began to take an active interest in the organization of educational activity. The Report of the Union Interdepartmental Committee on Native Education of 1936 was the first significant indication of change in South African opinion.[1] As far as the British dependencies are concerned, the change in outlook found concrete expression in the Memoranda of the Colonial Office Advisory Committee, which have not only had their effect on the policies of the Administrations, but have served to give direction also to the activities of missionary bodies. They resulted

[1] See above, p. 1144.

during the inter-war period in an increased use of the vernaculars as the language of instruction, the production of textbooks expressly designed for Africans, the introduction of manual training and of the 'school garden', the opening in a few places of farm schools, the spread of teaching of the type associated with the Jeanes schools, and the introduction, at the secondary stage, of training of a vocational nature as an alternative to literary instruction.

From the time of the Memorandum of 1944 on Mass Education there was a further change, consisting in the extension of the concept of education to cover the adult as well as the child population and to include activities such as the re-siting of villages, the eradication of mosquitoes, the sinking of wells, and all the other projects which are described under the heading of 'mass education', 'fundamental education', or 'community development'. In the British territories some of these activities had a prelude in projects in which literacy was only an incidental feature, as, for instance, some of the Community Development Schemes undertaken in Nigeria.[1] In other cases these activities have been linked with 'literacy campaigns', which have aimed at teaching whole adult populations to read in the vernacular, and have sought to provide them with reading matter calculated to awaken their interest in the practical plans for village betterment. Though this link between the teaching of literacy and projects of betterment is an essential part of the theory of mass education, in practice the two types of activity seem often to have been pursued independently.[2]

The political philosophy underlying the French method makes it difficult to apply the same standards as have been used in examining the British system. The deliberate trend of French thought is towards the creation of a civilization essentially non-African in character. In the initial days of their rule in Senegal they had viewed the African people as composed either of Muslims (who were the dominant community) or of 'fetishists'. Their experiences in Algeria had made them distrust the Muslims as hostile not only to their rule but to Western civilization,[3] while the 'fetishists' appeared to have little to commend them as agencies for the introduction of the ordered form of government which appealed to French thought. If, therefore, the ruling Power had perforce to employ African Local Authorities who were the creation of Native custom, it preferred that they should be clearly recognized as having only the status of agents, and that they should be suitably educated for this purpose. French administrators must have seen with some bewilderment a policy adopted by the British

[1] N.A., Part III, p. 150. See also E. R. Chadwick, 'Community Development in Udi Division', Oversea Education, vol. xix, 1948, pp. 627–46. 'Fundamental Education in Udi Division', Fundamental and Adult Education, Unesco, vol. 1, no. 4, 1949, p. 9.

[2] See M. Read, in Symposium on Popular Education, Leiden, 1953, pp. 60 ff.

[3] R. Delavignette, Freedom and Authority in French West Africa, 1950, p. 102.

in Northern Nigeria which pledged the support of the Government to Native Authorities who had received no form of instruction and who must often have found it difficult to appreciate even the most rudimentary of the functions of Local Government. Their bewilderment must have been increased when they saw the relative neglect by the British of institutions of technical and vocational education to which they themselves looked for the creation of a cadre of qualified subordinates.

For the French, education has thus had a double purpose. It was in the first place viewed as the means for providing an African *élite* inspired by French ideals of civilization, to which they could look for assistance whether in the field of administration or in that of economic development. They have never failed to be mindful of what Renan described as the crime of creating a volume of popular instruction without a serious supply of higher education. In the second place education was seen as the means of providing a popular form of instruction suited to the needs of the masses. But it has also served the purpose of implementing the French policy of 'association'. One cannot overestimate the effect produced on the average African population by a system which, in many of the schools and in most of the institutions of higher education, involves French and African boys sitting side by side and working through the same courses.[1] The Wolof boy of Senegal competes in the same public examinations with his French classmates.[2] The French have made a special effort to meet existing African needs in their system of education for the masses. The rural school aims at improving the African as an agriculturist, and the urban school at assisting him to gain his livelihood in the towns. The fact that education is free at all stages secures a wide measure of equality of opportunity, which cannot happen when the pupil's chances of completing his course depend upon his family's income.

The framework of the French system of education was logically devised for the purpose of securing a class of *élite* as auxiliaries in the task of administration. The best products of the village schools passed by a process of selection, stage by stage, up to the more advanced institutions of cultural or technical instruction. There can be no doubt of the success attained in creating an *élite* which was competent within its own field of activity and proud of its association with the French way of life. But the system had limitations which became apparent when changing circumstances forced the Administration to adopt a new outlook on the scope and purpose of education. Its major premise was the need for drawing a clear distinction between the *élite* and the masses of the people. But a system of education of this restricted scope has become increasingly out of place now that citizenship has been extended to all inhabitants of Overseas France.

[1] W. B. Mumford, ed., *Africans learn to be French*, 1937, pp. 29–31.
[2] F. J. Pedler, in *Listener*, 25 August 1949, p. 307.

Writing in 1949, the *Recteur d'Académie* hoped that the year 1955 would see an educational establishment double that of 1945, and he forecast efforts to secure *la scolarisation totale* of West Africa by 1995.[1] Already the effect of the new outlook has been seen in the change in the character of the village schools, but it will become even more apparent in the eventual multiplication of institutions of secondary and advanced instruction, and it is unlikely that popular feeling will tolerate a situation in which the provision of secondary or advanced courses is regulated by the probable demand for employees in different branches of the Administration. The universal use of the French language as the medium of instruction was bound in any case to stimulate an interest in French culture even in the popular schools and to give their pupils an outlook different only in degree from that of the *élite*.

The adoption of the French language as the medium of instruction at the earliest age and the organization of the educational system on the model of metropolitan France has been criticized on the ground that its effect will be to transform Africans into Frenchmen. It is easy to exaggerate this line of argument. But it may perhaps be justifiably claimed that, thanks to the French method of education, 'African political awakening tends to adapt itself more easily to French modes of thought'. This writer continues: 'In British West Africa everyone who is politically conscious is a nationalist of some kind. In French West Africa there are Catholics and anti-clericals, Communists and Gaullists, Socialists, Syndicalists and Existentialists.'[2]

The two distinctive features of the Belgian system have been a utilitarian outlook and a close association with religious teaching. The Catholic Church is mainly responsible for education and has had a dominant influence in the majority of the schools. Changes of some significance, however, took place in recent years, when the criteria imposed by the State for the grant of assistance were modified so as to enable a number of Protestant missionary bodies to qualify for it, and still later when an anti-clerical tendency appeared. Wherever possible the vernacular is used in the earlier stages of instruction. Manual training is given a prominent place, and almost all post-primary education is vocational. There was no initial attempt to identify and train an *élite*, though more recently some technical education has been directed expressly to the replacement of Belgians by Africans, notably as medical assistants. The educational expansion contemplated in the Ten-year Plan, although providing for studies up to university level, still concentrates attention on vocational subjects to a greater degree than does the education given at the corresponding stages in the British dependencies.

[1] Jean Capelle, in *Enc. A.O.F.*, vol. i, p. 278.
[2] T. Hodgkin, 'The Metropolitan Axis', *West Africa*, 9 January 1954, p. 5.

The Portuguese educational policy has little in common with the British or the Belgian, for it seems to aim definitely at preparing the African to qualify for the status of a European or at all events of a European as conceived by the Portuguese. There seems to be no tendency to see any value in the institutions of African society or to bring them within the range of educational influences. The Portuguese appear to share the feelings of those who hold that to allow an African to study an African rather than a European language is 'to entrap him in a retarded civilization'.[1] The Portuguese practice in regard to the use of the indigenous language in education is akin to that of the French, but the French have had a far more liberal attitude towards other indigenous institutions.

Among the many debatable problems of social science perhaps the last which is likely to achieve an agreed solution is that of the form of education which is most appropriate to any large group of the world's peoples. So far, at all events, as Africa is concerned, the question itself is hardly likely to be discussed on its merits, so long as the content of education is so largely dictated by political views. The time has now come when the African is in a position to take a more positive part in determining the type of education best suited to his circumstances and the genius of his people. But it is difficult at the moment to go farther than to debate the extent to which the existing systems of education are successful in achieving the particular ends they have been designed to serve.

There is, however, one observation of general application, particularly in respect of 'popular' education. There has in the past been too ready a tendency to judge of progress in terms of quantity rather than of quality. The crusade against illiteracy as such has assumed an importance out of proportion to its merits. The great mass of pupils who never go beyond the first few standards of primary education can acquire little that is of value to them or to the society to which they belong. The real test of progress is not so much in the figure of enrolment but in the proportion of pupils who survive into the upper-primary classes.

There is a second observation also of general application. In modern conditions the consistent application of educational policy involves the assumption of a far greater responsibility by the State than in the earlier periods of European education in Africa, if only because of the rise in the cost of education at a time when the resources of voluntary agencies are shrinking. It may well be felt that the time has arrived when the State should show greater discrimination in the support it gives to some of the voluntary agencies, and particularly to the smaller Mission schools. It is true that religion is an important factor in the formation of character, but religious instruction, more than any other type of teaching, demands understanding and personality on the part of the teacher. It cannot be

[1] R. L. Buell, *The Native Problem in Africa*, vol. ii, 1928, p. 61.

claimed that the small 'bush' school, with ill-trained staff and irregular attendance, has much more value for character training than for imparting instruction. Again, the need for a system of scholastic superannuation has now been recognized in some territories, as for example in Nyasaland, where from 1949 an upper age-limit has been enforced for children in primary schools. In many territories these schools are clogged with older children who are unlikely ever to make any progress because they have begun their schooling too late to profit by instruction designed for infants.

There is a further point, arising from the difficulty of assigning to literary and manual instruction their due share in popular education. Manual work can, under suitable conditions, have an educative influence, but its utilitarian value is limited, for it is doubtful if during the short period which general education covers it can be more than a preliminary to instruction in a craft or trade. There is, again, the much-debated question whether the primary stage of education should be complete in itself or designed to afford a preparation for a more advanced course. There is a growing agreement, save in parts of West Africa, that since the majority of pupils can scarcely complete even the primary stage, the instruction given at that stage should be as far as possible complete in itself. Here, however, there is a practical issue involved. Popular education, if complete in itself, cannot provide a sufficient period of instruction in a European language to give the pupil an adequate knowledge of it. The recognition of this fact inevitably produces a demand for a further course, with an inevitable reaction on the whole syllabus of popular education.

The place to be given to the vernacular is thus a crucial problem in those systems (such as the British or the Belgian) which admit of its use. It is clearly the best medium of instruction at the earliest stage and is in practice widely used at that stage. But the question still remains whether further study should be conducted in a vernacular or a European language. Discussions on this question show a marked difference of view. There is no disposition on any side to question that the language of a people is an essential part of their life and is for them the most effective instrument of thought. But we cannot treat every tribe as a people or every dialect as a language; apart from the difficulty of finding teachers for the numerous dialects involved, we should be in danger of creating barriers to that intercommunication of thought which is essential to social progress. The attempt to meet this difficulty by the use of a lingua franca or a 'union' language is open to the argument that we thereby create an artificial medium which is alien to the people, even if less so than a European language. Others would add that it is a waste of effort to teach Africans to read in a language that has no literature, and then to write books for them ourselves in order to satisfy the new demand for reading matter.

There are also many who feel that it is not possible to disregard the desire shown by Africans for a knowledge of a European language not only for its use as a medium of approach to the Administration or in commercial and industrial relations, but as a symbol of a higher status. Experience shows that this may represent a force which is capable in the long run of prevailing over any decisions at which education authorities may arrive. There are, finally, those who urge that even the most convinced advocates of the vernacular do not suggest that higher education can for the present be conducted in any of the African languages. They conclude that, on all these grounds, the claims of a European language as a medium of instruction must outweigh those of any of the vernaculars. But the whole question is one which seems to require that the Administrations should seek the collaboration of sociological inquirers in considering the conflicting issues involved.

As we have seen, schooling is free though by no means universal in the French and Belgian territories, but in both cases the authorities limit the number of pupils who are allowed to attend the higher courses. That is not merely in the interests of economy, it is (at all events in the case of the French) part of a policy of maintaining a distinction between the *élite* and the mass of the people. In the majority of the British areas the policy has been to charge fees for schooling, but the hardships which might result for the children of poor parents are mitigated by the grant of scholarships and bursaries for secondary and higher education. It is now the aim of the semi-responsible Governments in British West Africa to introduce universal free primary education, and the Gold Coast in 1952 remitted all fees for the six-year primary course, at an estimated loss in revenue of £300,000. In the Eastern Region of Nigeria the Administration has decided not to finance free education by an increase in the General tax, but to leave to the Native Councils and Local Authorities the option of doing so through the imposition of a local rate. Elsewhere small fees (or even contributions of food for the maintenance of teachers) are the rule in primary and 'bush' schools managed by voluntary agencies. In the schools financed by Native Administrations there is no uniform policy, but the imposition of small fees is thought to counteract irregularity in attendance, which otherwise is prevalent. It has to be remembered that, except in the form of experiments in limited areas, compulsory education of Africans does not really exist, and that as children assist their parents in the house and 'garden' they are not willingly spared for long periods.

Higher Education of Africans

It is especially in connexion with institutions of higher education that the type of instruction given depends on the view held of the place in society which the educated African may be expected to fill. The result is seen most characteristically in the French territories and in the procedure designed to produce an African *élite*. At present the educated French West African takes an important though usually subordinate part in the Administration, for though persons of African origin are well represented in the administrative and departmental cadres, the majority actually come from the West Indian Colonies, and have qualified for service by completing their education in France. That West Africans are not yet represented in any number is due to the fact that on passing out of the local professional schools they have been at once absorbed into the specific employment for which they have been trained. French policy has not favoured the appearance of the educated African at the local Bar, nor has he yet attained importance in journalism. On the other hand, the relative absence of colour prejudice, and the appreciation shown by the French for men of any race who have acquired the elements of French culture, makes it possible for the educated African to live in some considerable measure on equal terms with the Frenchman. Not only so, but the Constitution of the French Union has opened opportunities for a political career to educated Africans in the metropolitan Government as well as in employment in some of the metropolitan services.

In the British territories no effort has been made to limit the entry into institutions of higher education or to regulate the number of students by reference to the possibilities of their subsequent employment. In all the new University Colleges the greater proportion of the students are in receipt of some financial assistance. All but a few students are in receipt of scholarships or bursaries which cover fees and approved expenses, and it should be noticed that the cost per head has been rising rapidly.

In the British territories no specific statement of principle on the future of the educated African has been made, nor has the educational system been adjusted towards some clearly conceived place which he would be expected to fill. Accepting the general value of an education based on the European model, the British Governments have been content to wait until the product of this type of education have asserted their claim to a position in the political or administrative life of the country. In cases where this position has been accorded, it has more often been in recognition of a claim which has been tacitly encouraged than as the result of a predetermined plan. In West Africa the claim of the educated African to control of the Administration has been asserted earlier than could have been foreseen even a decade ago. In the Gold Coast and in the Western Region of Nigeria the recruitment of expatriate Administrative Officers has already ceased,[1] and the Africanization of the technical services is proceeding at a rapid pace.

The principle is now accepted that only those posts for which no

[1] For the resulting change in the Constitution of the British Colonial Service, see above, p. 367.

qualified African can be found should be filled by recruitment overseas, and, since the elected Ministers have announced policies involving a marked expansion of all social services, the demand for qualified staff is likely to be even greater than that which would be created by the substitution of Africans for Europeans on the existing establishments. In the Gold Coast there are in addition plans for industrialization which will offer opportunities for the employment of technicians of another type. For the present, therefore, there seems to be no ground for the fears which have been felt in the past of the creation of a class of educated unemployed.

The various British Commissions which have made recommendations on the development of higher education in Africa have insisted on its vocational aspect, though only the De La Warr Commission of 1937 stated this point of view without qualification. 'The main purpose of the East African Governments in education . . . must for the present be the improvement of agriculture, animal husbandry, and health.'[1] The Commission on Higher Education in the Colonies of 1945 expressed the contrary view; universities were required which would provide men with the necessary standards of public service and capacity for leadership, and which would produce, in increasing numbers, the professional men required to carry out Development Programmes.[2] The Commission on Higher Education in West Africa referred to the startling shortage of trained personnel in the fields of education, medicine, agriculture, industry, commerce, and administration, but added that 'provision must also be made for those Africans who will find an interest in education for its own sake' and for the training of research workers, particularly in such fields as sociology and linguistics.[3]

It would seem that the Belgian authorities have not envisaged university institutions which would give a general Arts degree. This has not, however, been the position of the authorities either in France or in the United Kingdom, and the latter have in addition encouraged the study of economics and political science. Some Arts subjects, such as geography and history, can be readily brought into relation with local interests and problems, but there is a difficulty in devising suitable syllabuses in economics and politics, since nearly all the existing textbooks in these subjects have been produced by writers familiar with problems entirely different from those of Africa. One of the most urgent tasks awaiting the newly appointed academic staff in the African University Colleges is to acquire such understanding of local problems as may make it possible to relate them to those which are engaging study in the Western world. Until

[1] *Report of a Commission on Higher Education in East Africa*, Col. no. 142, 1937, p. 14.
[2] *Report of the Commission on Higher Education in the Colonies* (The Asquith Commission), Cmd. 6647, 1945, p. 10.
[3] *Report of the Commission on Higher Education in West Africa*, Cmd. 6655, 1945, p. 52.

this has been done it will not be easy to frame a syllabus for the new universities which will pay due regard to the particular requirements of Africa.

As has been explained above, the French authorities have made provision for Arts courses in their new academic institutions, though in practice the major emphasis is laid on the facilities provided for courses of a vocational and professional character. The British, on the other hand, continue to expand the provision for general Arts and Science courses, and have recently increased facilities for the study of economic and political science. From a purely academic standpoint this development presents a difficulty which though not insuperable will require a definite effort if it is to be surmounted.

There is, however, another consideration of graver importance, affecting not merely the pursuit of these particular studies but the provision made for Arts courses generally. The resources available for academic development, in respect both of manpower and of finance, are limited. It is legitimate therefore to ask whether it is proper to devote to general Arts courses any resources which do not assist directly in the production of the graduates in vocational and professional studies for whom Africa has today the greatest need. At this stage of Africa's development the philosophy of those who are planning the new French and Belgian university institutions undoubtedly appears to be more realistic than that of the British. Much has been written in criticism of the direction given under British rule to the organization of public instruction in India. But if this were anywhere at fault, it was not the direct result of what has so often been described as the momentous decision taken in 1835 to adopt English education in the system of public instruction.[1] That decision was in fact confined to the type of 'learned education' which was to be given in the 'higher seminaries',[2] and to that extent it was not open to objection. The error lay in a policy which for long allowed the Arts courses to absorb an attention which should have been devoted to producing the men whose professional services were required for improving the economic resources of India and the standards of living of its people.

THE PRESS

South Africa and the Rhodesias

The European press in the Union of South Africa resembles that of other Commonwealth countries in its organization, make-up, and editorial standards. Several daily newspapers published in the larger cities have a wide circulation throughout whole provinces and exert an important political influence, while local news is provided by popular weekly or

[1] J. Seeley, *The Expansion of England*, 1885, p. 253.
[2] See on this point L. S. S. O'Malley, *Modern India and the West*, 1941, pp. 62–64.

bi-weekly papers published in the country towns. The press is free and in principle is uncensored except by process of law, but the position which it occupies has caused anxiety in recent years both on the part of those who mistrust too much freedom and of those who fear that it is being whittled away. All journals alike depend for their news services upon information supplied by the press agencies, among which Reuters and the South African Press Agency are predominant. In 1955 six of the 14 daily papers were controlled by Argus South African Newspapers Ltd., and these six supported the policy of the United Party, as, generally speaking, did most of the other newspapers published in the English language. The Nationalist Party was supported by the four daily papers published in Afrikaans. There were about 80 local papers, some controlled by the Argus group or some other proprietary organization. Many published their news items both in Afrikaans and in English. In South-West Africa there is a daily paper in the German language.[1]

The widening of the political cleavage in South Africa, due largely to the language question, has affected the press just as it has affected other departments of social life. Many of the English newspapers have a long history, covering a period of more than a century in some instances, while the rise in importance of the Afrikaans press has grown with the enthusiasm for the Afrikaans language during the last 40 years. Allegations have been made that the Nationalist Governments have favoured the Afrikaans press by releasing news to it earlier than to the English press, and by giving it more than its share of Government advertising. At the end of 1955 a survey of 'Government Pressures on the Press'[2] was issued by the International Press Institute at Zurich, and its strictures aroused much comment in South Africa. 'The divorce between Government and Opposition', according to one witness, 'has got so much worse lately that reporters on Opposition newspapers hardly have any normal contacts with Ministers.' Although there was no actual censorship, said another witness, the complexity of other restrictive laws is such that 'editing a newspaper under these conditions is like walking through a minefield blindfold'. It was suggested that the Suppression of Communism Act, 1950, had placed powers in the hands of the Government which might be used to destroy the freedom of the press, as had been shown when a Left-wing newspaper, the *Guardian*, was suppressed in 1952. On the other hand, supporters of the Government attacked the English press on the ground that its association with Reuters and the South African Press Agency gave it a monopoly of internal and external news, with the result that South African affairs were represented to the world in an unfavourable light with a bias against the Nationalist Government.

---

[1] *Willing's Press Guide, 1955*, p. 465.
[2] Summarized in *Johannesburg Star*, 16 January 1956.

The beginnings of a Native African press in South Africa go back to 1884 and 1888 when *Imvo Zabantsundu* and *Um Afrika* were founded respectively by Protestant and Catholic Missions; both are still in circulation. In 1950 there were said to be 26 Native newspapers of various kinds, as well as several weeklies for the Indian population, and the *Cape Standard* which is read by the Cape Coloureds. Some of them make use of the services of the South African Press Association and one or two obtain news items from American or other agencies. The regular issue since 1955 of the *South African Press Digest* provides a further source of news. A new phase in African journalism began with the foundation of the Bantu Press (Pty.) Ltd. in 1931, its object being to develop newspapers, 'in every way possible, to maintain a progressive yet moderate policy on political and economic questions, and to endeavour to mould Native opinion in the best interests of both White and Black in South Africa'. The Bantu Press (Pty.) Ltd. has provided a distribution service throughout South Africa and was, in 1952, associated with 22 journals, including the two missionary journals mentioned above. It is European-owned and controlled, but 44 per cent. of the shares are held by a trust fund which, it is intended, shall eventually become a national trust like that which controls *The Times* of London.[1] Its most important publication has been the bi-weekly *Bantu World*, founded in 1933 and recently renamed the *World*. The circulation was estimated at 40,000 in January 1956, and the policy of the editor, Dr. J. M. Nhlapo, included opposition to Communism and to *apartheid*.[2] The *World* uses the English language and three vernaculars.

Two periodicals of some importance are the monthly illustrated magazines *Drum* and *Zonk*, both produced in Johannesburg for African readers, but edited and owned by Europeans. They carry a high proportion of sporting and social news, and specialize in adapting the advertising techniques of Europe to African tastes. *Drum* has attained much influence by exposing scandals in the Native Administrations without committing itself to any active political line. These journals have been described as fighting for Africans as far as is possible without actually infringing the law.[3] It is noteworthy that their circulation is extending far beyond the Union, thus forming, throughout Africa, a taste for journalism in European style and in the English language. In 1954 their circulation was said to be 75,000 in the Union and 12,000 in West Africa.

In Southern Rhodesia there is no domestic news agency and papers are chiefly dependent upon the services of the South African Press Association. The two European dailies, the *Rhodesia Herald* and the *Chronicle*,[4] are

---

[1] A. Welsh, ed., *Africa South of the Sahara*, 1951, pp. 94–95.

[2] *Johannesburg Star*, 11 January 1956.

[3] *New Commonwealth*, 5 August 1954, pp. 115–17.

[4] Formerly the *Bulawayo Chronicle*. The name was changed in an effort to acquire national status for the paper.

published in Salisbury and Bulawayo respectively, and are owned by the Rhodesian Printing and Publishing Company Ltd., an associate of the Argus Company of the Union. Bantu newspapers under the control of the Bantu Press Group benefit from the information-exchange scheme organized by this enterprise. Both sections of the Southern Rhodesian press receive official news through the Government Public Relations Department.[1] Since the European and vernacular papers are largely controlled by South African interests, key staff may be sent to the Union for training. As a whole the press is small but well established and serves principally the English-speaking population. There are no African dailies, and the three weeklies, two fortnightlies, and one monthly which are published regularly are all controlled by African Newspapers Ltd., a branch of the Bantu Press group previously mentioned. The two main weekly papers, the *African Weekly* and the *Bantu Mirror*, printed in English, Shona, and Nyanja, and English, Shona, and Ndebele, respectively, reached circulations of 15,000 and 10,000 in 1954,[2] the figures having doubled in four years.

In Nyasaland there is one English newspaper, the *Nyasaland Times*, a bi-weekly founded in 1895, which was taken over by African Newspapers Ltd. of Salisbury in 1954. *Msimbi*, a weekly in English and two vernaculars, with a circulation of 8,200,[3] is the official African newspaper, and *Bwalo La Nyasaland*, another vernacular and English weekly with a circulation of 3,500, is also published at Salisbury by African Newspapers Ltd. *Mutende*, originally the official newspaper of Northern Rhodesia, ceased publication in 1952, and was replaced by the *African Eagle*, a weekly with a circulation of 4,000, printed in English and a vernacular by an independent firm, with some Government support. The *Northern News*, controlled by the Argus Press of South Africa, is the only European daily newspaper which has a circulation in Nyasaland.

The Colonial Dependencies: General Position of the Press

The existence of an indigenous African press presupposes a relatively high degree of literacy, and while circulation increases with literacy the newspaper is itself a great stimulus to its expansion. The number of copies of African papers printed is not a true indication of the extent of their circulation since they often reach a much larger public than that which is literate and can read them. It is common for those who cannot read to listen to those who can, so that the effective circulation always exceeds the number of copies distributed. Whatever the degree of development of the

---

[1] Unesco, *Reports on the Facilities of Mass Communication: Press, Film, Radio*, vol. iv, 1950, p. 21.

[2] *O.Y.S.R., 1952*, p. 258; 'An African Press Survey—Southern Africa', *New Commonwealth*, 5 August 1954, pp. 115–16.

[3] The total number of Africans whom it reaches is estimated at 40,000; *Colonial Reports, Nyasaland, 1952*, p. 113.

territory and the corresponding nature of the press, however, the production and distribution of newspapers in Africa present certain constant difficulties. Salient problems are: the provision of an adequate news service, the attainment of a reasonable standard of journalism and reporting (alleged wilful misrepresentation has often been no more than incompetent reporting),[1] the use of efficient machinery and technical staff, and the burdensome question of distribution. Ultimately the solution to all or any of these handicaps lies in adequate financial backing. Since financial interests imply political influence, if not complete control of a paper's policy, the affiliations of African newspapers accordingly depend very much upon whether the source of financial provision is within the territory (private or company ownership) or whether it lies with an external Administration or newspaper company.

A high standard of journalism demands a professional system of training which is not yet available in the Colonial dependencies. While some technical training in typography is obtainable in most territories of Africa south of the Sahara, no general courses in journalism are available in most of the Colonial dependencies for those who aspire to join the staff of a newspaper. Of non-British territories the Belgian Congo is the only exception, and here the course, which consisted of no more than a part-time class in journalism for Congolese newspaper staff, was discontinued in 1951 although it is expected to be resumed. In French West Africa the situation in Senegal is better than in the other territories of this region, for although there are no training courses, all journalists, unless employed on a contract basis, belong to the Union of Journalists of French West Africa, which is a branch of the National Union of French Journalists.[2] In British African territories some provision is now made for training journalists. The London Polytechnic conducts a Diploma Course in Journalism, and in 1951 eight training scholarships were awarded to Colonial working journalists selected by their respective Governments. In 1954, however, there was only one student from Africa.

The recognition of the value of the Native newspaper, and especially of that printed in the vernacular, in consolidating and extending literacy and in fostering interest in general development and progress,[3] has led to the issue by Public Relations Offices and Departments of Information, of the 'official' news-sheets and papers now current in all African Colonies. In meeting the need for the creation of a reliable press, Colonial Govern-

---

[1] I. Coker, *Seventy Years of the Nigerian Press* (published by the *Daily Times*, Nigeria), 1951, p. 42.

[2] See Unesco, *Reports on the Facilities of Mass Communication: Press, Film, Radio*, vol. iv, 1950, and vol. v, 1951.

[3] P. Sanderson, 'Starting a Vernacular Newspaper—Logoiywek', *Community Development Bulletin*, 4 December 1952, pp. 14–18.

ments are presented with three possibilities. They may choose (1) to establish an official newspaper; (2) to encourage a European-sponsored or directed journal; or (3) to grant technical and financial aid towards developing a privately owned Native paper. But in most cases the favourite solution has been to rely upon the Public Relations Office or its French, Belgian, and Portuguese equivalent, and the official newspapers produced from this source often attain large circulations. Typical official newspapers are, in the French Cameroons, *Hygiène et alimentation* (10,000), which appears three times each month; and, in the Belgian Congo, *La Voix du congolais*, which is published weekly and intended primarily for *évolués*, and *Nos Images*, which has a wide circulation among the less literate mass of the population. In French Equatorial Africa five roneoed daily newspapers are produced by the *Service de l'Information* and the *Agence France Presse*.

In Kenya 21 vernacular news-sheets, mostly published monthly, were produced in 1952 in Kikuyu, Swahili, Kamba, Kipsigis, Nandi, and Luo.[1] In Uganda in 1953 *Amut* (News), a Lango monthly and the first paper to be published by an African Local Government, achieved a circulation of 5,000. Up till recently the Public Relations Office of Northern Rhodesia produced *Mutende*, a weekly in English, and four vernaculars which reached a circulation of 12,000; in Tanganyika *Mambo Leo*, the Swahili monthly of the Public Relations Office, has a circulation of 52,000. There is also a weekly Government Gazette in Zanzibar.

One source of material for newspapers and periodicals outside the services of commercial news and feature agencies, which many local publications cannot afford, is that provided by the Government-controlled Central Office of Information in London. In addition to supplying much background reference material through Regional Information and Public Relations Officers in the British territories, the Central Office of Information supplies a reserve of up-to-date news and illustrations daily by wireless, cable, and airmail. Known as the London Press Service, this is distributed free of cost to the newspapers and is widely used by the independent press as well as by Government-sponsored publications. This service is supplementary to, rather than in competition with, the existing commercial agencies.

The service includes six transmissions, in addition to 'Africa', the regional service designed for the African continent, and 'Transmission Zero', a Colonial commentary. The Feature Articles Service consists of feature articles, typed and duplicated, dispatched by air to African Information Offices. In 1951 the greatest use of these services was made by Nigeria, the Gold Coast, Kenya, and Northern Rhodesia. In French Equatorial Africa a Feature Service is relayed from the metropolitan press

[1] Lists of papers and periodicals published in the British territories are to be found in the *Colonial Reports*, published annually.

and a similar scheme is operated for photographs. Regional distribution is effected by the *Service de l'Information*. The *Agence France Presse* has recently developed considerably and publishes a bi-weekly roneoed bulletin of world and local news. Several information centres have been set up throughout the territory. The one at Brazzaville is now furnished with *téléscripteurs* which permit the direct reception of news from the metropolis. In the Belgian Congo the texts of information broadcast by *Radio Congo Belge* are made available to the press, and the *Section de l'Information* maintains a photographic service for newspapers and journalists.

A Note on Individual Territories

Kenya has had a strong press since its earliest days. The *East African Standard*, an English daily presenting the point of view of the White settlers, was founded in 1903. With official encouragement it launched a Swahili newspaper called *Baraza* in 1940 to provide reliable news to the African population. Having the advantage of using the *Standard*'s news service, *Baraza* has attained a circulation of 35,000. The first vernacular journal in Kenya was started by Jomo Kenyatta in 1927; it and several other news-sheets in Kikuyu flourished for some years until the Mau Mau outbreak[1] drew attention to the fact that they were bitterly racial. All were suppressed. In 1952 the new Government Information Department sponsored the formation of the Kenya Vernacular Press Company which has provided technical and financial backing for newspapers in Luo, Kikuyu, and Swahili. Assistance in organizing a vernacular press has also been one of the functions of the East African Literature Bureau,[2] which publishes a weekly magazine, *Tazama*, in Swahili. There is also in Kenya an influential Indian press, largely financed and edited by Indians. At Mombasa the *Kenya Daily Mail*, with a circulation of 12,000, is issued in English and Gujerati.

English journals have been published in Uganda for many years, though it was not until 1955 that an English daily (the *Uganda Argus*) with an effective news service and adequate financial backing was established. The board includes European, Asian, and African directors.[3] The leading vernacular papers in Uganda are the *Matalisi*, with a circulation of 12,000, and the *Uganda Post*, which has the rare distinction of owning its own printing plant. Both are published in Luganda. During the troubles over the Kabaka's exile the *Post* was suspended because of its attacks on the Government.[4]

In Tanganyika there was no independent vernacular press until 1956 when a regular weekly, in Swahili, first appeared at Dar-es-Salaam.[5] Two weekly papers are issued in Zanzibar presenting the views of the

[1] See above, p. 452.　　[2] See above, p. 98.　　[3] *The Times*, 4 January 1955.
[4] See above, p. 294.　　　　　　　　　　　　　[5] *The Times*, 3 March 1956.

Arab community. East Africa appears to be the only great region of Africa where the vernacular press is rapidly gaining strength. Elsewhere the tendency of educated Africans is to turn towards newspapers published in the English language on account of their better editing, production, and news service. In Africa, as elsewhere, the efficiency of the syndicated press overcomes the weak competition of local news-sheets.

The number of weekly or even daily news-sheets in British West Africa, some of them irresponsibly edited and without access to any reliable news agency, has been large for many years. In 1954 there were at least twelve established newspapers on the Gold Coast and at least 25 in Nigeria, all but two of them in English.[1] Dr. Azikiwe was a pioneer of modern newspaper production in Nigeria and his *West African Pilot*, with a circulation of 17,000, has had an important influence on the politics of the country.[2] His organization, the Associated Press, controls several other Nigerian papers. Another group of papers, the Amalgamated Press, supports Dr. Awolowo in the Western Region. Broadcast news, the London Press Service, and the general rise in standards of education have improved the content of the West African press, but nothing has been so effective as the appearance of British newspaper proprietors in this competitive market. The papers with the largest circulation are no longer one-man news-sheets but Fleet Street subsidiaries. The *Daily Graphic* (Gold Coast) and the *Daily Times* (Nigeria), with circulations of between 44,000 and 55,000, demonstrate the advantages accruing from the amalgamation of African papers with European newshouses.[3] Higher standards of journalism resulted, and it has been pointed out how particularly suited the simplified style and presentation of the *Graphic* and *Mirror* Companies are to the West African public.[4]

Distribution still presents many difficulties especially in Nigeria, but the Gold Coast constitutes a practical unit for a daily newspaper and should support a circulation of 100,000 even at its present low rate of literacy. That such figures are not impossible of attainment is shown by the circulation of the Coronation issue of the *Daily Times*, which reached 108,000. The solution to distribution problems lies in the increased pooling of resources.[5] Difficulties of staff recruitment are encountered even by the *Graphic* and *Mirror* Companies. It is stated that in the Gold Coast the most highly paid editor of an African paper earns £550 a year while his equivalent on the *Daily Graphic* receives £1,000; but such terms are not sufficiently attractive to the educated West African whose services are eagerly sought in the new Government establishments.

[1] *New Commonwealth*, 22 July 1954, p. 63.
[2] See above, p. 312.
[3] See *The Times*, July 20 1951; Coker, op. cit.
[4] 'An African Press Survey—West Africa', *New Commonwealth*, 22 July 1954, p. 64.
[5] 'The Gold Coast Press and its Problems', *African World*, May 1952, p. 22.

The real limitations to the growth of the press here, as elsewhere in Africa, continue to be financial; since the news services of locally owned papers are so poor, the Government has stepped in. The Information Services Department of the Gold Coast obtains two daily transmissions from Reuters and distributes these to local papers for a quarterly sub-scription of £5. In Nigeria Dr. Azikiwe's press alone uses Reuters, but several papers have their own London correspondents. Advertisements still occupy a high percentage of space, sometimes as much as 50 per cent. of an issue. Because of the new developments in the two main West African newspapers, Europeans have taken no financial interest in ver-nacular papers. There is no vernacular newspaper published in the Colony or Protectorate of Sierra Leone. In Nigeria there is only the *Gaskiya Ta Fi Kwabo*, a Hausa weekly with a circulation of about 17,500 published by the Gaskiya Corporation.[1] In the Gold Coast the Fante weekly *Amansuon*, which has a circulation of between 3,000 and 4,000, is produced by an African company. The Vernacular Literature Board of the Gold Coast has now discontinued the issue of papers in Fante and Asante to schools and mass literacy classes.

In the Belgian Congo the lack of trained journalists explains why no independent African press yet exists. Of a total of 63 journals published in 1952 for Africans, five were produced under Government auspices, 47 by missionary organizations, and eleven by other unclassified agencies. Only 19 appeared in French, and the remaining 44 were printed in vernacular languages. Apart from Government publications the Congo European press comprised six daily papers (of which *L'Essor du Congo* and *Le Courrier d'Afrique* reached circulations of 10,000), five weeklies and one bi-weekly, and 64 bulletins and reviews.

In French West Africa, where there is little demand for separate papers for Europeans and Africans, Senegal, the Sudan, and Guinea each have a daily newspaper, whereas Dahomey, the Ivory Coast, Niger, and Upper Volta have to rely upon less frequent publications. The Ivory Coast supports two political periodicals directed and edited by Africans, *L'Indé-pendant* and *Le Démocrate*, with a joint circulation of about 4,000. *L'Essor*, the organ of the *Rassemblement Démocratique Africain*, attains a daily circula-tion of 5,000 in the French Sudan. *La Guinée française* has developed from a simple Government news bulletin into a paying daily, half of whose readers are African. *Paris-Dakar*, the only Senegal daily newspaper, serves a public of which 60 per cent. are African. There appear at present to be no special African papers published in French Equatorial Africa, with the exception of a missionary monthly. In Liberia there is no ver-nacular press. The only daily newspaper, the *Listener*, was founded at Monrovia in 1950 and is printed in English. It is an independent com-

[1] See above, p. 101.

mercial concern without political connexions, and has a circulation of only 1,500.

Angola seems as yet to support no Native press and the territory is served by three Portuguese daily newspapers published in the capital, Luanda. Their joint circulation is about 15,000. In addition, there were in 1953, eight other newspapers published in the Province. There were also 13 monthly and one quarterly. Mozambique again has nothing which could be called an African press.[1] There are three dailies, with a total circulation in 1951 of 13,000, and 19 other press publications. The newspapers depend largely upon advertising for their revenue, and approximately 50 per cent. of the total printing space is so utilized. Portuguese Guinea has three journals, only one of which, *Arauto* (a roneoed news bulletin), is published daily, but no African press.

Legislation affecting the Press[2]

In the British African territories registration of newspapers is obligatory except in Uganda, and everywhere the paper must bear an imprint showing generally the name and address of both publisher and printer but sometimes only of the printer. In certain Colonies sureties are further required; in Gambia a bond of £100 with one or more sureties as required by the Legal Adviser must be furnished, except generally in the case of papers published before 1943. Nigeria requires that printer, publisher, and proprietor should each provide a bond for £50 with one or more sureties as required by the Attorney-General, although under certain conditions a bond of £250 may be accepted instead. In Tanganyika the Governor may require the proprietor of a newspaper to furnish a bond for a sum not exceeding 3,000s., with one or more sureties as required by the Attorney-General. A bank or assurance company guarantee can be accepted in place of these.[3] In Uganda a similar regulation obtains, and the amount of the bond exacted is double that in Tanganyika. No provision for sureties is contained in the press legislation of the Gold Coast, Kenya, Northern Rhodesia, Nyasaland, and Sierra Leone.

In 1951 there were no provisions for the licensing of newspapers or printing presses in any British African territory included in this survey. In 1952–3, however, licences for printing presses were required in Kenya.[4] Uganda is the only British Colony in which legislation for the seizure and sequestration of printing machinery on conviction for sedition exists. When a person is convicted of printing seditious material, in addition to any other penalties imposed, the Court may order the printing machinery

---

[1] The Native population is 99 per cent. illiterate.
[2] The information in this section refers to 1951, unless otherwise stated.
[3] Newspaper (Amendment) Ordinance, 1952.
[4] Printing Presses (Temporary Provisions) Ordinance no. 38, 1952.

to be confiscated of a period not exceeding one year, whether or not the person convicted is the owner. Prosecution cannot be initiated without the written consent of the Attorney-General, and a Court may on application from him at any time revoke sequestration. There are further in Uganda, as well as in Kenya, provisions for censorship in time of emergency to the effect that no publication may, without the Governor's permission, print information, comments, or suggestions concerning military affairs connected with the defence of the British Commonwealth and Empire.[1] The Governor may at any time establish by order a rigid press censorship, similarly revocable by him. Uganda is also exceptional in that the Governor can compel the press to publish corrections to any articles or statements which are in his judgement false or distorted.

In South Africa the powers invested in the Governor-General for the suppression of Communism extend to the prohibition of the printing, publication, and dissemination of journals calculated to further Communism. Since this, as defined in the Act,[2] includes action directed towards the encouragement of hostility between the European and non-European populations of the Union, it can be used to impose limits on the freedom of the African press. In Southern Rhodesia the Minister is empowered to prohibit the publication of documentary information in his judgement prejudicial to good feeling among different sections of the community, and similarly to ban the publication of subversive propaganda.[3] No newspaper registered at the G.P.O. prior to the enactment of this legislation can be prohibited except on authorization by Parliament.

Liberia's press is protected by Section 15 of the Bill of Rights of the 1847 Constitution. The only press legislation concerns defamation, and lawsuits on this charge are frequent.

In the Belgian Congo legislation[4] entitles the Governor-General to prohibit the importation and distribution of newspapers or periodicals published outside the colony; no journal can be published without his authorization, and it is an offence to display writing or pictures calculated to undermine the respect due to Belgian authority. In Ruanda Urundi newspapers and periodicals can be printed only after permission has been obtained from the Vice-Governor-General. Offences committed by the press against morals and public order are punishable at law.

The press legislation of the French Cameroons is similar to that obtain-

---

[1] Uganda, Press Censorship and Correction Ordinance, Cap. 231, revised ed., 1951; Kenya, Press Censorship Ordinance, Cap. 311, revised ed., 1948.

[2] Suppression of Communism Act no. 44, 1950, extended by Suppression of Communism Amendment Act no. 50, 1951.

[3] Subversive Activities Act no. 30, 1950.

[4] *Ordonnance-loi*, 13 June 1944.

ing in France except that authorization is required for the publication of newspapers in vernacular or foreign languages. The Administration is entitled to seize vernacular journals attacking the Government or threatening national security.[1] In French Togo similar laws require the preliminary authorization of vernacular newspapers. In French West Africa a legal deposit of all journals printed must be lodged with the *Institut Français d'Afrique Noire* (I.F.A.N.) at Dakar,[2] and the circulation of newspapers and periodicals printed in foreign languages (i.e. other than French or vernaculars) can be forbidden at the discretion of the Governor-General.[3] In French Equatorial Africa the earlier ordinance concerning press legislation in the French African Colonies is still in force.[4]

In Angola and Mozambique, where nothing may be printed in the vernacular unless accompanied by a Portuguese translation, the legislation in force has been unified by a Government decree of the Portuguese Republic, published in 1937. This decree controls the publication and circulation of periodicals written wholly or partly in Native or foreign languages since these may not appear except with the Governor's authorization. The publication of destructive criticism of the Administration or of the Portuguese State is forbidden and, as in Liberia, a considerable portion of legislation deals with defamation, lawsuits for which are common. The Governor is further empowered to maintain a press censorship with a view to preventing the publication of material detrimental to the proper conduct of the territory.

BROADCASTING

It is inevitable that in the circumstances of Africa there should be today, and may continue to be for some considerable time, a limit to the use which can be made of the services of broadcasting. Apart from the difficulties created by the great diversity of languages and dialects, and by the low standard of literacy among Africans, there is also a serious obstacle in their lack of means for the purchase and maintenance of listening sets. In the earlier days the development of the use of radio followed the same pattern as development in other fields in which modern inventions have been introduced to improve industrial or agricultural methods or to add to the amenities of life. It began in those countries where there were communities which could buy listening sets and provide a revenue in licence fees; broadcasting was, in fact, available only to those who could afford to pay for it. There is now, however, general evidence of a growing desire to give broadcasting a more popular form. The stations in the French and Belgian possessions broadcast some programmes

---

[1] *Ordonnance*, 29 July 1939.
[3] *Décret*, 27 September 1946.
[2] See above, p. 65.
[4] *Ordonnance*, 24 November 1944.

in African languages, and the South African Broadcasting Corporation broadcasts programmes in Bantu languages every morning from Durban and on three days a week from Johannesburg.

It is, however, in the British dependencies that the greatest developments have taken place in making use of broadcasting for the benefit of African listeners. In 1936 a formal decision was taken by the Government of the United Kingdom to develop a broadcasting system in the British dependencies as a public service.[1] The Second World War caused a postponement of central planning, but it also provided an opportunity for some territories, such as Northern Rhodesia and Somaliland, to start broadcasting services, and for others, such as the Gold Coast, Sierra Leone, and Nigeria, to extend the local systems which had (as will be shown) been based on the use of wired broadcasting. In 1948, however, the Colonial Office again addressed Colonial Governments, urging the desirability of taking active steps for the development of broadcasting services. The difficulties of finance which had hitherto deterred some of the Governments from committing themselves to a programme of work likely to involve considerable expenditure were overcome by the decision of the Government of the United Kingdom to allocate a sum of £1 million (in 1952 expanded by a further provision of £250,000) from the general reserve of the Colonial Development and Welfare Vote,[2] for the development of broadcasting in the Colonies generally.

The obstacles created by the lack of staff trained in the technical administration of broadcasting or in the provision of programmes have been in large measure met by the deputation of advisers and technical staff from the British Broadcasting Corporation, which has also enabled a number of African members of the local engineering and programme staffs to take part in training courses. Most African Colonial stations also take advantage of the programmes put out by the British Broadcasting Corporation and of its transcription service of recorded programmes. The General Overseas Programme of the B.B.C. was broadcast in 1955 for 147 hours a week. In addition special programmes were broadcast to particular regions with discussions and talks on matters of local interest, often given by visitors to Britain from Africa. The programme hours were: to South Africa and Rhodesia 45 minutes in English and $1\frac{3}{4}$ hours in Afrikaans per week; to West Africa $8\frac{3}{4}$ hours, and to East Africa 45 minutes per week, both in English.[3]

It was natural that the earliest provision for broadcasting should have been made in the Union of South Africa, with a European population which now numbers 2 million. The first radio station was opened in

[1] *Interim Report of a Committee on Broadcasting Services in the Colonies* (the Plymouth Report), Col. no. 139, 1937.   [2] *Handbook on Broadcasting Services in the Colonies*, 1953, p. ii.
[3] *Annual Report of the British Broadcasting Corporation, 1954–55*, Cmd. 9533, 1955, p. 129.

Johannesburg in 1920, followed by others in Cape Town and Durban; but since 1936 all broadcasting has been in the hands of the South African Broadcasting Corporation, which is organized on lines similar to the British Broadcasting Corporation with a Board of Governors responsible to the Minister of Posts and Telegraphs.[1] It broadcasts three programmes in parallel from its transmitters, one in English, one in Afrikaans, while a third, the 'Springbok Radio', carries commercial advertisements. Broadcasts to African listeners are transmitted daily, in the mornings from Durban and three times a week over the national network. In 1952 there were 620,085 effective listeners' licences, mostly held by Europeans. Africans appear to depend for the most part on listening sets being made available to them by their European employers; but a wired-broadcast system has been installed in the Native township of Orlando, near Johannesburg, and some 3,000 subscribers are now paying rentals for loudspeakers. A programme for Indians is broadcast on Sunday mornings in five Indian languages.

Kenya made the next venture into broadcasting in 1927, when a licence was given to the East African Broadcasting Company. This is now held by the Cable and Wireless Company. Though the main programme of the Nairobi station is designed for English-speaking listeners, the transmitters are made available in the afternoons for broadcasts in Kikuyu and Swahili, Arabic, and Hindustani. The periods devoted to broadcasts in these languages are being expanded, but as far as the Africans are concerned the provision of listening facilities remains a major problem. There are as yet few privately owned sets among them. In 1952 there were some 83 community receivers installed at Government expense in African hotels in the main township areas. With the outbreak of the Mau Mau disturbances, efforts were made by means of mobile vans to increase the number of community receivers so as to take the programmes farther afield, but it is clear that broadcasting is still not reaching the vast majority of the African population. A report of a Commission published in August 1954 recommended the establishment of a public broadcasting corporation to operate in September 1956, when the licence held by the Cable and Wireless Company expired. It was to be financed by a grant from the Kenya Government of £440,000, spread over a period of five years. There were to be separate national programmes for European, Asian, and African consumption.[2]

The introduction of broadcasting in Tanganyika, Zanzibar, and Uganda is of more recent date. In Tanganyika a small installation was set up at Dar-es-Salaam in 1951, with the aid of a grant made under the Colonial

---

[1] The Broadcasting Acts, no. 22 of 1936, no. 17 of 1938, and no. 14 of 1949. The last empowered the Corporation to broadcast to South-West Africa.

[2] *The Times*, 28 August 1954.

Development and Welfare Acts; it issues a short programme daily in Swahili. A grant of £55,000 has since been made for erecting an installation which will cover the whole territory, and in 1955 a 20-kW frequency transmitter, the most powerful in East Africa, was erected at Dar-es-Salaam. It is stated that there are some 1,532 private sets in the territory, mostly in the hands of Europeans. In Zanzibar a radio station was established in 1951 at Maruhubi, and is operated by Cable and Wireless Limited. The greater part of the programme is in Swahili, but it also includes readings from the Koran. There are in Zanzibar and Pemba six loudspeakers, two of which are carried on the Information Van. In Uganda a station covering Kampala and the surrounding district was started in 1953 with the aid of a grant made under the Colonial Development and Welfare Acts, but the installation has since been extended with the view of making broadcasting available to the whole Protectorate. The Uganda Broadcasting Service transmitted its first programme to the entire territory on 1 March 1954, using both English and the vernacular.[1]

The Government of Southern Rhodesia started in 1932 a broadcast programme on a small scale from Salisbury, and this was gradually extended to other centres, at first by the employment of land-lines, and subsequently by local transmitters. A fully powered system was installed in 1948–9 and, by arrangement with the Central African Council,[2] Salisbury now provides programmes for European listeners in Southern Rhodesia, Northern Rhodesia, and Nyasaland.[3] There were in 1953 roughly 25,000 listening sets held by Europeans in the three territories. Northern Rhodesia is of special interest, owing to the provision made for the purchase of listening sets by Africans. A small temporary studio was set up at Lusaka in 1941 in order to issue bulletins of war news, and this was extended in 1943. In 1946 an agreement was concluded between the territories which are now included in the Federation of Rhodesia and Nyasaland, making Northern Rhodesia responsible for all African broadcasts in the three territories. The capital cost and half the recurrent expenditure on the African service was met by a grant made under the Colonial Development and Welfare Acts, the remainder of the expenditure on the services being met by Northern Rhodesia and Nyasaland. The contribution made by Southern Rhodesia consisted of the whole cost of the broadcasting service for Europeans. The African programme is now centred at Lusaka, material for it being contributed by officers on the establishment of Southern Rhodesia and Nyasaland. A rediffusion system has been installed in the African Location at Lusaka and has proved very successful. A number of 'community receivers' have also been

---

[1] *Background to Uganda*, no. 73, November 1954.
[2] See above, p. 277.
[3] *O.Y.S.R., 1952*, p. 596.

established in the three territories. The languages used in the African broadcasts from Lusaka are Nyanja, Bemba, Tonga, Lozi, Ndebele, Shona, and English. The number of these languages creates a complexity which can be solved only by adding to the number of transmitters, so that two or three can be used at the same time.

While, however, the difficulty arising from the number of languages still remains to be solved, Northern Rhodesia appears to have gone some way towards meeting the problem imposed upon African broadcasting by the relatively high price of listening sets. It is now possible for Africans to buy certain types of battery sets ranging in price from £6 to £10, a price which is comparable with that of the bicycle or the sewing-machine which have become common possessions of Africans. This has come about largely through the enterprise of the officials in charge of the service at Lusaka, who persuaded a British firm to produce a set at about this price; large numbers of these sets (the so-called 'saucepan special') have been sold, and in 1955 a minimum of 40,000 sets were in use by Africans. In Northern Rhodesia it is estimated that between five and ten Africans listen at each set.

In March 1955 the Federal Government appointed a Commission to advise on the future organization of broadcasting in the Rhodesias and Nyasaland, with an official of the B.B.C. Overseas Service as chairman. The Commission recommended the setting up of a statutory corporation which would be independent of Government control and which would be known as the Rhodesia-Nyasaland Broadcasting Corporation; it would provide broadcasts for both Europeans and Africans.[1] It was estimated that a Government guarantee of £230,000 would be necessary to launch the scheme, which was approved in principle in July 1955.[2]

Sierra Leone can claim to have been the pioneer in broadcasting in West Africa, Freetown having inaugurated in 1934 a wired rediffusion system. The service has proved to be very popular, and there were in 1952 some 2,300 subscribers on the wired-broadcasting system. In 1955 a radio transmitter was installed at Freetown bringing all parts of the territory into direct broadcasting communication. The majority of the wireless sets are held by Europeans; the broadcasts are given in English.

Nigeria adopted a system of wired broadcasting in 1936. The local feeling in the different regions of the territory was met by the use of regional stations, each of which provided its own programmes. It was not, indeed, till 1949 that Nigeria established its own fully powered wireless system. In that year an inquiry was made at the request of the four British West African dependencies into the possibility of a combined service, but it was held that the variety of languages made this impracti-

[1] *The Times*, 10 June 1955.
[2] *Johannesburg Star*, 11 August 1955, 2 February 1956.

cable. It was as a result of this decision that the Nigeria Broadcasting Service came into being in 1951. The size of the territory, its cultural differences, and the clear-cut distribution of the three main linguistic divisions (Yoruba, Ibo, and Hausa) seemed naturally to dictate the adoption of a regional system, with a national headquarters and a powerful transmitter at Lagos, and with regional headquarters at Ibadan for the west, Enugu for the east and the Cameroons, and Kaduna for the north.[1] The whole scheme was estimated to cost a capital sum of £350,000, of which £190,000 was provided from grants made under the Colonial Development and Welfare Acts.

The distribution side of the wired systems was taken over in the Western Region from the Department of Posts and Telegraphs by a new enterprise, the Rediffusion (Nigeria) Company; elsewhere the programme staff was to be taken into the wireless service. With the completion of the first stage of the scheme, there was to be a staff of about 20 Europeans and 250 Africans, many of whom would have been trained in London. In March 1954 it was resolved in the Nigerian House of Representatives to transform the broadcasting service without delay into an independent corporation, expressly in order 'to remove the press criticism that the Nigerian Broadcasting Service is an organ of the Nigerian Government'.[2] The schedule of proposals set forward by the Government estimated the cost at £1¾ million. The Corporation was to be developed according to a three-year plan. Improved rediffusion services would be provided, community receivers would be installed, and cheap receiving sets would be made available to private customers. There would be a large measure of regional autonomy in deciding the contents of the programmes.

The Gold Coast introduced a rediffusion service at Accra in 1935. Here also the service was a success, and in 1939 the Government acquired a short-wave transmitter for general service in the Colony. This, among other activities, enabled a service to be provided during the Second World War for the Free French Movement in West Africa. The wired-broadcasting system was extended to 22 of the towns and larger villages, and has a total of about 10,000 subscribers. There were also in 1953 some 165 loudspeakers in schools and public places, and 27 specially built radio kiosks for community listening, mainly set up in market places. In addition licences for 2,670 listening sets were issued, mainly to Europeans. Programmes originating in Accra were broadcast in the afternoons and early evenings, five vernaculars being employed, as well as English. At night the wired broadcasting usually relayed the General Overseas Programme of the British Broadcasting Corporation.

---

[1] *Handbook on Broadcasting Services in the Colonies*, 1953, p. 77.
[2] *Proposals for the Establishment of a Nigerian Broadcasting Corporation*, Lagos, 1954, p. 1.

In 1954 a Gold Coast Broadcasting Corporation was established, on the basis of recommendations made by a B.B.C. Advisory Commission. Like the Nigerian Corporation its constitution followed the model of the B.B.C.[1] Of the British territories lying south of the Sahara only Gambia is without a permanent broadcasting service. Its geographical position, however, creates an unusual difficulty, for a transmitting station in Bathurst would waste most of its energy outside the territory, and the cost would be out of all proportion to the size of the audience that Gambia could hope to provide.

Considerable use has been made in French West Africa of the system of wireless telegraphy, and a number of stations are connected in this manner,[2] but the broadcasting system is of relatively recent origin. During the Second World War a military equipment operating under the name *Radio Afrique Occidentale Française* used to broadcast news bulletins; after the war a service, *Radio Dakar*, was established by the Administration, at first on a small scale, and after 1949 on a more extended scale, to serve the purposes of the territories within the Federation. The programmes are intended to meet the needs of the whole of French West Africa. There are six daily news bulletins in French (one of which is given at dictation speed for centres in the hinterland), and other broadcasts are given in Baule, Mossi, Fon, Arabic, Wolof, Bambara, Sarakole, and Susu. In addition a station at Abidjan broadcasts a short programme each day. Experiments were made in 1951–2 with a low-power short-wave transmitter at Conakry. It was estimated that there were some 1,600 listening sets in French West Africa, mostly held by Europeans. Fifty-three community listening points in market-places had been established in order to rediffuse the broadcasts from Dakar for about two hours each day.

French Equatorial Africa has also made wide use of the system of wireless telegraphy and telephony,[3] but the broadcasting system dates in practice from the year 1940. A small station had been set up by the Radio Club at Brazzaville in 1935, but it served only local purposes. It was, however, adapted for use by the newly constituted Free French Administration in the autumn of 1940. Its range was gradually extended by a series of clever improvisations, and it became an active organ of the Free French Movement, utilized in particular to counter the broadcasts sent out from Dakar, which was at the time held in the interests associated with Vichy. After the Second World War the installation became part of the French 'international' broadcasting system, its programmes being issued in French and in seven other languages; local needs were met by a new installation, *Radio Afrique Équatoriale Française*, which was inaugurated in 1950. Its broadcasts are mainly in French, but recorded programmes are

---

[1] *Handbook on Broadcasting Services in the Colonies*, 1953.
[2] *Enc. A.O.F.*, vol. ii, p. 300.   [3] *Enc. A.E.F.*, pp. 494–6.

also presented in Lingala and Lari. A station at Fort Lamy issues a programme in Arabic for the Lake Chad region, including news bulletins, readings from the Koran, and Arabic music. There is a low-power station at Douala which serves the French Cameroons, but in view of the great number of local dialects it does not issue broadcasts in a vernacular. There are a number of 'collective listening centres' at Brazzaville, Libreville, and Fort Lamy.

The commencement of broadcasting in the Belgian Congo also dates from about the same period (1936), when the Jesuit College at Leopoldville obtained authority to operate a broadcasting station. This was followed in 1939 by the grant of a licence to a private company, also at Leopoldville. With the outbreak of the Second World War an official broadcasting service, the *Radio Congo Belge*, was inaugurated, and in 1943 the Belgian Government in London arranged to install in the Belgian Congo a service (the Belgian National Broadcasting Service) which would beam programmes to the occupied homeland and to the rest of the world. Its organization was independent of the Administration of the Belgian Congo, but in 1944 an arrangement was made that it should undertake the operation of the *Radio Congo Belge*, pooling staff and equipment for the purpose. After the war the Belgian National Broadcasting Service at Leopoldville was taken over as part of the metropolitan organization, and was assigned the function of broadcasting Belgium's foreign programmes; the Administration of the Belgian Congo resumed contact with the *Radio Congo Belge*, and in 1946 and 1947 two new private stations were set up with transmitters at Elisabethville. The *Radio Congo Belge* has one division responsible for broadcasts to Europeans and another for broadcasts to Africans; the work is centred at Leopoldville, but there are now plans to set up regional stations. The European programmes are in French and Flemish, with daily news bulletins in Portuguese which are heard in neighbouring Portuguese areas. The African programmes are in French, Lingala, Swahili, Luba, and Kongo. But a radio service designed to supply the needs of a large and purely African audience is still lacking. There are also special educational programmes designed for the Colonial Army.

Mozambique began the use of radio in 1933 when the right to operate a broadcasting station (which is prescribed by law as a monopoly of the Portuguese Government) was allotted to two private organizations, the *Radio-Clube de Moçambique* and the *Aero-Clube da Beira*. The former constitutes in a sense a national broadcasting service, as it serves the whole territory and has been officially recognized as being in the public interest. The station of the *Aero-Clube da Beira* operates on a local basis only. The Mozambique radio, like the 'Springbok Radio' of the Union of South Africa, is also utilized for commercial broadcasts in Portuguese, French, and English.[1] The broadcasting stations in Angola are mainly owned by Radio Clubs, of which there were nine in 1953. The *Emissora Oficial de Angola*, operating from Luanda, is the only State-owned station and is under the control of the Post Office; it transmits special programmes from Lisbon on a short wave. In addition there are two others: a privately owned station founded in 1930 and known, after its founder, as the *CR6AA de Alvaro de Carvalho*, which transmits from Lobito; and a smaller one belonging to the Angola Diamond Company. All include advertisements in their programmes except those belonging to the State and the company. The Portuguese language is in universal use, since the vernacular is prohibited.[2]

The arrangements for broadcasting in Liberia, which originated in 1949, are of an unusual type. The installation at Monrovia is the private venture of an American citizen, but the Government collaborates in the enterprise to the extent of giving it an annual subsidy. While the main broadcasts are in English, news announcements are made also in French and Arabic. It would appear that there are a considerable number of listening sets in the country.

If this Survey has directed its attention mainly to services for broadcasting to Africans, it is because a considerable provision has already been made for broadcasting to Europeans, who of course have access not only to bulletins and programmes issuing from local stations but to those of 'international' origin. In the few cases where the language of these broadcasts creates a difficulty, provision is usually made by the local installations, as for example the programme issued in Afrikaans by the broadcasting system of the Union. Vernacular broadcasts from India are also heard by Indians in East Africa.

Although the Administrations are agreed as to the cultural value of broadcasting to Africans, the difficulties of a wide expansion of the use of radio are considerable. In many areas the dialects are so numerous as to demand a large increase in the number of transmitters if broadcasts are to be issued simultaneously. In spite of the success of the experiment made in Northern Rhodesia, there must remain in very many areas a real problem owing to the inability of Africans to purchase listening sets. It was at one time hoped that a solution might be found in 'community listening', but in most African territories the people prefer to listen in small groups, and it is difficult to persuade whole villages to gather regularly for listening. Where they gather naturally, as in a market-place, they have business to do, and a loudspeaker usually fails to attract their attention. There is still a need for much experiment in the type of programme which will attract listeners under these conditions and which will be

---

[1] *Overseas Economic Surveys, Portuguese East Africa, 1951*, p. 39; article in *O Seculo*, Lisbon, 22 October 1954.
[2] *Overseas Economic Surveys, Portuguese West Africa, 1953*, p. 36.

effective. Even when this has been achieved, there may be special problems which may affect community listening in an African community. Tribal custom may sometimes rule that only the Chief shall have the set and at the same time that certain classes of people, as, for instance, women, shall not listen when the men are listening. It is generally agreed that in Africa, as elsewhere, the most effective form of listening is that done in private by the family or by a few friends gathered together. Wired broadcasting, by which the listener can for a relatively small monthly rental receive his local station in his own home, has (as has been shown) been effectively used for many years in the Gold Coast, Nigeria, and Sierra Leone. But this method of broadcasting can be economic only in towns and large villages in which a sufficient concentration of houses can be reached by wires to produce adequate return in rentals for the capital cost involved. The rural areas can be reached only by broadcasting from a transmitter.

There are problems also of an order not directly connected with the technical side of diffusion. There is the complex problem of the relationship between the broadcasting organization, the Government, and the people, a problem which, ideally, can be solved only by setting up an independent organization, but which depends in practice upon the position which any Colony has reached in political and economic development. There is listener research, which in Africa might be expected to take the form of investigations into the actual effects of broadcasts on the life and habits of the people, rather than a mere testing of the opinion of the audience. There are, again, difficulties of recording the music and the folk-lore of Africa, so necessary if broadcasting is to perform its proper function of reflecting the life of the people. But, if broadcasting to Africans has its problems, experience has already shown that it has its advantages also; the African is a born listener and, given the right programmes, he takes to broadcasting with enthusiasm no matter what his standard of living or of education may be.

No study of the use of broadcasting by the Western Powers as a means of educating and informing the African peoples would be complete without reference to the counter-propaganda put out from Egypt and other parts of the Arab world. The Egyptian State Broadcasting Service is used as an instrument of policy by the Egyptian Government so as to influence the views of all Africans whom it can reach. It continually incites them to resist the authority of the administering Powers in spite of repeated protests from their diplomatic representatives. It was reported, early in 1956, that broadcasts from Cairo were regularly received in all the East African territories and even as far south as Angola. The Cairo station was then broadcasting for $24\frac{1}{2}$ hours per week in Sudanese Arabic and for $5\frac{1}{2}$ hours per week in Swahili.[1]

[1] *New York Times*, 1 March 1956; *Daily Telegraph*, 16 March 1956.

THE CINEMA

The organization of the cinema in those parts of Africa where there is a resident population of Europeans is much the same as in their metropolitan countries. Cinema theatres are owned and operated in circuits which import commercial films from America or Europe and thus provide the same form of entertainment as the Europeans would find in their own countries. American films are said to have the advantage of being, generally, cheaper than those from Europe. At least 70 per cent. of commercial films shown in British and Portuguese territories come from the United States; in French and Belgian territories the proportion is about 40 per cent. from the United States and 40 per cent. from France; in Liberia all films of every kind come from the United States.[1] Where there are urban Africans, with some knowledge of the language of the Administration, they are rapidly acquiring the habit of cinema-going, save, of course, in those territories where they are actually excluded by the colour bar.

There are 40 commercial cinemas in Nigeria, 26 in the Gold Coast, and 90 in French West Africa catering largely for Africans and supplying them with American or European entertainment. In those parts of Africa where there is an Asian population some Indian and Egyptian commercial films are also to be seen. The social impact of films upon newly literate Africans is likely to be more pronounced than upon Europeans, and it should be noticed that in all countries anxiety is expressed regarding the tendency of many films to glorify violent crime and erotic passion. But the commercial cinema is a highly sophisticated art, which relies upon such devices as cuts and flash-backs, and expects a high degree of attention if the audience is to follow its 'wise-cracking' dialogue. Not many Africans have sufficient grasp of a European language to follow the dialogue in detail, or sufficient knowledge of European social conditions to follow the whole sequence of events. It is therefore not surprising that the commercial cinema has not, as yet, won much popularity outside the larger centres of population, or that 'comics' and 'westerns' which depend upon rather obvious visual effects are the most popular class of film. Their social consequences can hardly as yet be estimated.

Local censorship exists in most Colonies, though French Equatorial Africa relies on the export visa of the Metropolitan Control Commission in Paris. The Board of Censors of Northern Rhodesia has an *ex officio* African member, a practice recommended as early as 1930 by the Colonial Films Committee.[2] Censorship can weed out obviously unsuitable films

---

[1] Statistics here, and below unless otherwise stated, are from Unesco, *World Communications: Press—Radio—Film—Television*, 3rd ed., 1956.

[2] *Report of the Colonial Films Committee*, Cmd. 3630, 1930, p. 17.

but cannot counteract the cumulative effect of mass-produced entertainment, or prevent Africans from receiving a distorted picture of American and European life. A recent example of its use for more narrowly political purposes is the ban imposed in the Union of South Africa on all films showing the intermingling of races.

The production of documentary and instructional films for illiterate African audiences has now been studied in several territories for many years. An early example was the film produced in Nigeria in 1929 in order to instruct the people how to combat an outbreak of plague. In such early experiments it was soon discovered that the reaction of an audience to whom the cinema is an unknown and amazing phenomenon is not always that which is desired.[1] Often something quite extraneous detracts from the intended result.

Experience has already proved, as might be expected, that European films move too rapidly, and show too much at a sitting for most African village audiences. Even some of the educational films made for Africans may fail in certain places because they aim at standards which are beyond the reach of the audience. Film strips, which can be shown by the cheaper and more easily transported epidiascope, are more easily understood than moving pictures. Locally made commentaries can be most useful; a Disney cartoon on hookworm designed for South America was successfully adapted in this way for showing in Uganda. As there are so many vernaculars, however, it may be more convenient and economical to accompany the silent film with records of African music. If this is done, one of the cinema team explains the film beforehand, illustrating the main points with 'stills'. It is followed up with further commentary and a discussion. Lately a new type of magnetic sound-track has become available on which a succession of commentaries in different vernaculars can be recorded and those not required afterwards erased.

By 1939 sufficient progress had been made to convince the British Government of the importance of the use of films for distributing information, and a central organization, the Colonial Film Unit (C.F.U.), was formed in London, at first as part of the Ministry of Information. Films were to be used as a means of fundamental education and, it was assumed, the responsibility for producing them would eventually be handed over to the Government in each territory. An allotment of £250,000 was made for this work under the Colonial Development and Welfare Act, 1945. A number of production units were dispatched to different parts of Africa to make films on subjects suggested by the Local Governments, to train film producers, and to stimulate production in each territory. After 1951 the work of the C.F.U. had so far progressed that it ceased production on its own account and devoted itself to distribution, technical assistance, and

[1] See L. A. Notcutt and G. C. Latham, eds., *The African and the Cinema*, 1937.

supply. In 1955 the work of the C.F.U. was brought to a close. Courses for training camera-men were held on several occasions, the first in 1948 at Accra. The Gold Coast Film Unit was founded in the following year and by 1953 had produced 25 films, of which several were bought by commercial circuits in England. 'Amenu's Child', a film on child welfare, won an award at the international Venice Festival in 1950. A Nigerian Film Unit, formed about the same time, has produced useful films for agricultural education; it has also been used to explain the new Constitution to the people. In 1951 Nigeria was made the scene of a systematic survey of audience reactions under African conditions.

In Kenya the Film Unit produced documentaries on the Mau Mau outbreak and on the reaction of the African peoples to it. In Tanganyika experiments have been made in films for entertainment as well as for instruction; at the request of the Government two full-length films were made on African life and for African audiences, with the co-operation of a commercial company. A Central African Film Unit was formed before the Federation of the Rhodesias with Nyasaland and has since been taken over by the Federal Government. In addition to films for instructing Africans in economic development, films to promote the tourist industry have also been produced. Some of the films made by this Unit have found a market in the adjacent Belgian Congo and in West Africa. Similar Film Units have been formed in other British territories.[1] The success of the instructional films and newsreels produced by these Units derives from their efforts to reach new audiences in the villages. Mobile cinema vans equipped with power units and radio sets are operated by the Information Department and travel by road or by river-boat all over the territories. Every British territory has at least one such mobile unit; there are as many as 21 in the Gold Coast.

Similar organizations exist in the Belgian Congo, where a notable success has been the full-length picture, 'Bizimana', produced by Father Di Voto, a missionary priest. It was designed to point out the errors of witchcraft. The Ciné Photo Bureau of the Government Information Section produces newsreels which are said to reach audiences of $1\frac{1}{2}$ million persons through cinema circuits and mobile units. There are ten mobile units in French West Africa, two in French Equatorial Africa, and one in the French Cameroons, showing documentaries and newsreels. In Mozambique films on Portugal and instructional films on social welfare are shown by four mobile units, and in Angola by one unit. Documentary films have been produced in both territories. Reports from all Colonial territories in Africa concur in pointing out that many Mission schools possess 16 mm. projectors which show instructional films supplied by Information Departments.

[1] Central Office of Information, *The Instructional Film in the United Kingdom Dependencies*, R. 3161, 1955.

APPENDIXES

I. PUBLIC EXPENDITURE ON EDUCATION IN AFRICAN TERRITORIES

(a) British African Territories
(£'000)

	1947	1952				
		By Central Government				Total Public Expenditure by Central Government
	Total spent on Education	From Colonial Revenue	From Special Development Funds	Other*	Total	
Basutoland . .	165	170	6	26	202	1,147
Bechuanaland† .	51	41‡	11‡	40§	92	765
Gambia . . .	33	n.a.	n.a.	n.a.	59	1,424
Gold Coast . .	1,013	3,780	2,754	830	7,364	36,794
Kenya . . .	898	2,140	1,141	540	3,821	18,859
Nigeria . . .	1,700‖	4,588		2,200‖	6,788	42,041
Nyasaland .	170‖	246	42	119	408	3,904
N. Rhodesia¶ .	320‖	593	187	n.a.	814**	23,438
S. Rhodesia .	1,337	2,969	12††	n.a.	2,982	28,125
Sierra Leone .	118	333	217	75	625	5,487
Swaziland . .	77§§	62	30	25	117	615
Tanganyika .	359**	1,309	211	795	2,315	15,878
Uganda . .	411‖‖	1,540	92	307	1,939	15,950
Zanzibar . .	68	123	75	25	223	1,433

* Including expenditure by Native Administrations and voluntary bodies.

† Figures do not include estimated expenditure by missions amounting to £2,300 in 1947 and £1,500 in 1952.

‡ Includes expenditure on European and African education.

§ Expenditure by Native Administrations.

‖ Estimate.

¶ African education only.

** By Central Government only.

†† From loan funds.

§§ Figure does not include expenditure by missions. This can be only roughly estimated at £10,000.

‖‖ Excluding expenditure by voluntary bodies.

(b) Union of South Africa
(£'000)

1947–8	1951–2			
Total spent on Education	Central Government	Provincial Government	Total	Total Public Expenditure by Central Government
27,515	4,923	33,014	37,937	256,907

(SOURCE: *O.Y.S.A.* for the years 1947–52.)

(c) Foreign Territories
(£'000)

	1948	1951 and 1952				
		By Central Government				
	Total spent on Education	From Colonial Revenue	From Special Development Funds	Other	Total	Total Public Expenditure by Government
Belgian Congo ('000 Congolese francs)	127,000*	(1951) 362,731	(1951) 42,170†	n.a.	(1951) 404,901	(1951) 6,355,519
French Equatorial Africa ('000 francs C.F.A.) .	409,774	(1952) 720,000	(1952) 271,000‡	n.a.	(1952) 991,000	(1952) 9,520,561
French West Africa ('000 francs C.F.A.) . .	942,620	3,710,589	725,000‡	n.a.	4,435,589	51,176,000
Angola ('000 escudos) . .	9,999	n.a.	n.a.	n.a.	(1951) 13,870	(1951) 1,078,862
Mozambique ('000 escudos) . .	15,416	n.a.	n.a.	n.a.	17,642	1,628,906

(SOURCES: United Nations, *Non-self-governing Territories, Summaries and Analyses of Information transmitted during 1950*; ibid. *1952*; *Rapport sur l'administration de la colonie du Congo Belge, 1952*; *République Française: Afrique Équatoriale Française, 1952*, and *République Française: Afrique Occidentale Française, 1952* (issued by the *Direction des Affaires Politiques*, Paris); *Anuário estatístico do Ultramar, 1952*.)

* Expenditure on African education only.
† *Fonds du Bien-Être Indigène.*
‡ *Fonds d'Investissement pour le Développement Économique et Social* (F.I.D.E.S.).

II. ENROLMENT IN AFRICAN SCHOOLS

(a) British African Territories

Territory	Year	Primary Male	Primary Female	Primary Total	Secondary* Male	Secondary* Female	Secondary* Total	Teacher Training†	Other Post-Secondary
Basutoland	1947	31,224	53,213	84,437	647	354	1,001	Nil	Nil
	1952	31,450	61,927	93,377	791	482	1,273	Nil	54
Bechuanaland	1947	6,414	10,920	17,334	42	15	57	Nil	Nil
	1952	6,344	11,398	17,742	87	55	142	Nil	Nil
Gambia	1947	n.a.	n.a.	2,767	n.a.	n.a.	338	6	25
	1952	n.a.	n.a.	3,757	n.a.	n.a.	577	23	43
Gold Coast	1947	n.a.	n.a.	113,816	n.a.	n.a.	4,523	1,043	333
	1952	301,914	117,007	418,924	7,823	968	8,791	2,426	524
Kenya	1947	n.a.	n.a.	246,520	n.a.	n.a.	8,287	845	184
	1952	269,077	84,211	363,288	5,395	2,339	7,734	2,090	292
Nigeria	1947	n.a.	n.a.	611,573	n.a.	n.a.	28,372	2,600	n.a.
	1952	n.a.	n.a.	970,700	n.a.	n.a.	n.a.	6,700	2,200‡
Nyasaland	1947	n.a.	n.a.	22,028	345	17	362	n.a.	§
	1952	135,600	89,000	224,600	208	40	248	706	§
N. Rhodesia‖	1947	114,553	55,281	169,834	846	364	1,210	663	n.a.
	1952	105,350	50,614	156,164	2,925	2,329	5,254	678	33
S. Rhodesia	1947	124,231	97,638	221,869	5,267	3,927	9,194	846	n.a.
	1952	146,967	112,606	259,573	n.a.	n.a.	2,170	986	n.a.
Sierra Leone	1947	n.a.	n.a.	26,124	n.a.	n.a.	3,141	106	19¶
	1952	27,711	11,505	39,216	2,182	945	3,141	390	219
Swaziland	1947	4,872	5,965	10,837	99	102	201	Nil	Nil
	1952	7,160	8,327	15,487	180	152	332	24	Nil
Tanganyika	1947	96,400	35,587	131,987	2,679	607	3,286	452	44
	1952	158,980	68,468	227,468	21,708	5,014	26,802	970	82
Uganda	1947	111,109	32,483	143,592	4,075	671	4,746	1,690	n.a.
	1952	204,290	68,476	272,766	8,169	1,269	9,438	2,575	n.a.
Zanzibar	1947	3,989	842	4,831	370	52	423	58	25‡
	1952	6,314	3,020	9,334	672	148	820	89	25‡

* Including vocational.   † All levels.   ‡ Estimate.   § Technical and vocational other than teacher training included in primary.   ‖ African schools only.   ¶ At Fourah Bay College only.

(b) Union of South Africa

	Primary			Secondary			Teacher Training	Other Post-Secondary
	Male	Female	Total	Male	Female	Total		
1948	189,893*	177,245*	1,315,729†	48,871‡	48,433‡	182,696§	10,230	20,053‖
1951	218,345*	204,307*	1,450,803¶	53,349‡	54,883‡	205,006**	10,291	19,228‖

(SOURCE: *O.Y.S.A.* for the years 1948–52.)

* Figures for White children only.
† Includes 948,591 non-White children engaged in primary and secondary education (undifferentiated).
‡ Figures for White children only. Includes White and non-White technical and vocational education.
§ Omits non-White secondary but includes 29,202 non-White scholars in private schools.
‖ White and non-White students at universities.
¶ Includes 1,028,151 non-White children engaged in primary and secondary education (undifferentiated).
** Includes White and non-White technical and vocational education but omits non-White secondary. Includes 34,727 non-White scholars in private schools.

(c) *Foreign Territories*

		Primary			Secondary*			Teacher Training	Other Post-Secondary
		Male	Female	Total	Male	Female	Total		
Belgian Congo	1948	n.a.	n.a.	875,544	n.a.	n.a.	12,673	2,771	n.a.
	1952	n.a.	n.a.	943,494	10,784	3,010	13,794	5,128	396†
French Equatorial Africa	1948	45,021	6,848	51,869‡	4,440	1,241	5,681	n.a.	n.a.
	1952	93,232	15,556	108,788	3,922	1,942	5,864	n.a.	30§
French West Africa	1948	97,673	23,519	121,192	5,903	710	6,613	1,065	164
	1952	150,250	39,591	189,841	6,919	1,758	8,676	1,697	832‖
Angola	1948	n.a.	n.a.	10,953	n.a.	n.a.	3,022	n.a.	n.a.
	1952	8,368	6,530	14,898	2,343	1,493	3,838	n.a.	n.a.
Mozambique	1948	n.a.	n.a.	153,639	n.a.	n.a.	15,437	n.a.	n.a.
	1952	108,974	65,346	174,320	6,570	2,013	8,583	n.a.	n.a.

(SOURCES: United Nations, *Non-self-governing territories, Summaries and Analyses of Information transmitted during 1950*; ibid. *1952*; *Annuaire statisque de l'Afrique Équatoriale Française, 1952*; *République Française*; *Afrique Occidentale Française, 1952* (issued by the *Direction des Affaires Politiques*, Paris); *Anuário estatístico do Ultramar, 1952*.)

* Includes vocational instruction.   † Of these 79 were preparing for the Lovanium.   ‡ Includes pupils in the *écoles primaires supérieures*.   § Studying in France.   ‖ Of these 547 were in France, the remainder being at the *Institut des Hautes Études* at Dakar.

III. PUBLIC EXPENDITURE ON POST-SECONDARY EDUCATION

(a) British African Territories
(£'ooo)

	1949	1950	1951	1952
BASUTOLAND				
Scholarships	2·9	3·0	2·8	2·4
Grant to Fort Hare University College and other post-secondary	0·8	0·8	1·0	1·0
BECHUANALAND				
Scholarships*	0·5	0·7	0·9	0·4
GAMBIA				
Scholarships	1·8	1·7	1·5	1·9
Teacher training	4·7	2·9	2·6	4·1
GOLD COAST				
Scholarships	71·5	97·8	119·8	189·4
Teacher training	190·5	192·7	234·2	460·8
University education	200·0	146·0	265·5	315·5
Other post-secondary, University College, extra-mural	12·4	29·7	50·6	40·0
Kumasi College of Technology . .	..	204·1	50·0	202·0
KENYA				
Scholarships	12·4	14·5	15·9	15·7
Teacher training	12·9	30·9	47·6	66·9
Other post-secondary	12·9	12·9	50·0	54·8
NIGERIA				
Scholarships†	90·7	125·4	131·8	171·0
Teacher training‡§	224·4	216·2	218·8	107·0
Other post-secondary:				
University College, Ibadan. . .	..	185·0	248·7	16·9
Technical Institute, Yaba . . .	4·0	5·4	7·7	7·5
Nigerian College of Technology . .	..	18·2	69·9	n.a.
NYASALAND				
Scholarships	2·0	2·2	4·4	2·7
Teacher training‖	..	..	..	..
NORTHERN RHODESIA				
African scholarships¶ . . .	2·5	3·0	3·5	3·5
Teacher training** . . .	4·7	6·5	5·0	3·0
Grants to Fort Hare University College .	..	..	0·1	0·1
English scholarships and loans†† .	6·7	7·6	10·9	13·9

* Includes trades training; no post-secondary facilities available in the territories.
† Including secondary.
‡ Financial years for Eastern Region and Central expenditure.
§ Excluding training of primary school teachers.
‖ No post-secondary training.
¶ Post-secondary scholarships from territorial funds.
** The course changed from three-year post-junior Certificate to two-year post-school Certificate.
†† No post-secondary education facilities exist in the territory.

(a) British African Territories (contd.)

	1949	1950	1951	1952
SOUTHERN RHODESIA				
Scholarships, bursaries, &c., tenable at university‡‡	7·1	7·2	7·0	7·3
Teacher training grant	6·8	8·6	9·4	9·0
Other grants tenable at universities and colleges	2·8	4·0	4·8	5·2
SIERRA LEONE				
Scholarships§§	9·5	12·3	13·0	25·5
Teacher training	25·2	36·8	34·2	41·2
Fourah Bay College	1·2	17·4	68·4	75·2
SWAZILAND				
Scholarships	0·9	1·5	1·9	2·1
Teacher training	0·4	0·5	0·5	0·5‖‖
TANGANYIKA				
Scholarships	5·1	12·4	10·3	11·3
Teacher training	44·4	50·0	42·0	91·4
Other post-secondary	9·7	8·1	37·4	54·7
UGANDA				
Scholarships	3·9	3·9	3·9	4·1
Teacher training	46·1	55·8	60·1	89·4
University	101·0	125·0	162·0	229·0
Other post-secondary	n.a.	13·0	10·1	23·1
ZANZIBAR				
Scholarships	2·1	2·1	2·4¶¶	3·4¶¶
Teacher training	2·3	3·0	4·2	3·7
Makerere College	2·4	2·5	7·2	7·4

‡‡ Africans £1,400 annually.
§§ Including secondary.
‖‖ An additional £10,000 was spent on capital expenditure in building the Matapha Teacher Training Centre (from grants made under the Colonial Development and Welfare Acts).
¶¶ Excluding scholarships for craft training.

(b) Union of South Africa
(£'000)

	1949	1950	1951	1952
Grants-in-aid to universities, declared institutions, and courses; bursaries for university education and technical colleges . .	2,074·9	1,967·4	2,174·5	2,766·0
Government grants to universities and colleges	1,162·2	1,344·4	1,465·7	2,034·8
Teacher training* (Provincial) . . .	447·6	484·6	518·5	n.a.

* Does not include expenditure on teacher-training for Native education.

CHAPTER XVIII

ECONOMIC DEVELOPMENT IN AFRICA[1]

THE HISTORICAL BACKGROUND

THE first economic contacts of European countries with Africa south of the Sahara sprang almost entirely from the slave trade and the trade with the East Indies. When Columbus and his successors first discovered the Americas, and when Bartholomew Diaz first rounded the Cape of Storms, Africa south of the northern tropic was virtually unknown. Trade in African slaves had its origins as early as the days of Imperial Rome. It was continued through the period of the Muslim domination of North Africa, and African slaves were common in Arabia, Turkey, Persia, and even India,[2] as well as along the northern coast of the continent. The trade received a new impetus with the sudden demand for labour in the Americas in the early years of the sixteenth century; Spanish, Flemish, and Genoese merchants were all concerned in the traffic, and after 1560 the English began to take their part. At first the slaves came principally from the rivers between Cape Verde and the Niger, but later, as the demand grew, the territories as far south as Angola were exploited. By the time that Vasco da Gama had consolidated the first achievements of Diaz by sailing round the Cape and up the east coast to Mozambique and Malindi, the Portuguese had explored the west coast and had established a series of stations from Cape Verde to the Congo. Once the way to India was known, these stations were quickly extended southwards and up the east coast also. Here the Portuguese interest in African trade received an added stimulus from the search for gold.

During the following three centuries control of the Indian route passed from the Portuguese to the Spanish (following the annexation of Portugal in 1580), to the Dutch in 1620, and, after the vicissitudes of the Napoleonic wars, to the British in 1806.

Throughout this period colonization had been spasmodic and uneven, and limited, in the main, to small areas of cultivation in the immediate neighbourhood of the coastal forts. Only the Dutch settlements in South Africa penetrated inland; they extended by the end of the eighteenth century no more than 150 miles from the southern coast, and were confined to the fertile territories below the Karroo. The relations of these Dutch Colonists with the impecunious administration of the Dutch East India Company at

[1] This chapter and that which follows are based on chapters drafted by Miss Phyllis Deane, Senior Research Officer at the Department of Applied Economics, University of Cambridge.

[2] See above, pp. 381, 385.

the Cape had always been strained. Its supersession by the British increased the friction between the Colonists and the local authorities. Finally, after the emancipation of the slaves in 1833, the first great trek northward took place in 1836, when the large body of voortrekkers determined to remove themselves from the vexations of British rule.

The penetration of other parts of Africa took a more leisurely course. During the last three and a half centuries parts of the interior had been explored and mapped by some few scores of explorers of all nations. In the middle of the nineteenth century there were still large areas of country about which little or nothing was known. Gradually, however, the journeys of explorers and of missionaries filled in these gaps and revealed something of the resources of the country. Among the sources of information some of the most important were those supplied by the missionaries who, from the time of the Jesuits who first accompanied the Portuguese, penetrated farther and stayed longer than all save the most adventurous of the explorers. The activities of Leopold II of Belgium and the conclusions reached by the Berlin West African Conference of 1885 stimulated the European Powers to extend their spheres of influence; but outside the four countries which now form the Union, Africa below the Sahara remained until the last years of the nineteenth century essentially a 'continent of outposts'.

So soon as the partition of Africa was completed, some attempts were made not only at political but also at economic penetration and development. In the initial stages, however, progress was slow. Distances were great and the supply of labour scanty. In such conditions it was not easy to secure from outside sources the capital that was necessary for economic development, or to create a surplus of exports out of which interest payments on that capital could be met. This difficulty was overcome in South Africa by the discovery of diamonds in 1866, which provided a valuable export unaffected by the high cost of transport and requiring relatively little capital for its immediate exploitation. The foreign capital employed in the industry has probably never exceeded £20 million, and the greater part came from the profits of the industry itself. Already by 1882 the annual value of diamond exports had reached approximately £4 million, twice the amount of all other exports before the discovery of diamonds.[1]

The immediate effects were significant. South Africa had hitherto depended primarily on the proceeds of an extensive and casual agriculture. The European community was poor and not very large. In 1865 the total European population of Cape Colony did not exceed 181,000. The taxable resources for internal development were slight, and in bad years virtually disappeared. Moreover, foreign capital could do little to remedy the difficulties of the Colonists. Low-rated agricultural exports and the few im-

[1] See below, pp. 1487 ff.

ports that such a community could afford would serve scarcely to cover the operation and depreciation costs of railways. Indeed, when the diamond discoveries were made, no more than 58 miles of railway existed in Cape Colony. The first extensions, made possible by mineral discoveries, joined Kimberley with the Cape and with Port Elizabeth and East London.[1] Furthermore, when gold began to be mined on the Rand in 1886, the capital for its exploitation could be readily obtained, both from those who had made profits in diamonds and from foreign investors who were already familiar with Africa as a place of investment and with the personalities of the leading figures in the diamond world, now associated also in the gold-mining enterprises.[2] The capital for railway extensions could be borrowed on reasonably easy terms. Finally, the diamond diggings served to demonstrate the field in which African labour could collaborate most profitably with European technique. In an extensive system of agriculture cheap Native labour was of relatively small advantage and did not in Africa suffice to overcome the handicap of distance and the high cost of transport. In mining the close supervision of more routine tasks increased the relative efficiency of Native labour, and transport costs proved less of an impediment.

In the territories economically less fortunate than South Africa, development was slower. In a number of cases it took the form of exploitation by powerful companies, furnished usually with some measure of monopoly power, and sometimes armed with responsibilities also for political administration. Their dual position enabled them, however, to take a wider view than could either a private merchant or a Government Department on the question of what might be regarded as profitable expenditure upon long-range developments. They could set their gain from the expansion of general trade against increased costs of administration, and in later days the profits of mineral exploitation might balance the probable losses of railway operations.

Companies of merchant adventurers to the west coast of Africa had received charters from Queen Elizabeth I, while the Royal Africa Company had enjoyed a charter from Charles II. These earlier monopolies had in most cases been suppressed, or had fallen into abeyance, during the anti-monopolist agitations at the close of the seventeenth century, though powerful associations of merchants in several instances continued to administer the forts and trading stations. The principle of development through the agency of companies was, however, widely revived during the years preceding and following the Berlin Conference. In British territories the Royal Niger Company, the Imperial East Africa Company, and the British South Africa Chartered Company all served to expand British trade and influence, despite the apathy or even, in the earlier years at least, the antagonism of the Government at home. In the Belgian territories the

[1] See below, p. 1547.   [2] S. H. Frankel, *Capital Investment in Africa*, 1938, pp. 75 ff.

Compagnie du Congo pour le Commerce et l'Industrie was founded in 1886, and established a series of subsidiaries for the development of a particular area or activity. In French Equatorial Africa an epoch of Concessions to companies was inaugurated in 1899. In the Portuguese possessions the Mozambique Company and the Company of Mossâmedes, amongst others, possessed almost unlimited powers over a wide area. In the German territories the *Deutsche Ostafrikanische Gesellschaft* and the privileged companies in South-West Africa and in the North and South Cameroons were established upon similar lines.

The companies differed much in size, in the responsibilities imposed upon them, and in the efficiency with which they carried out their varied tasks. Many of them at the end of a comparatively short period found themselves obliged either to cease operations entirely or considerably to curtail their activities. An exaggerated belief in the natural riches of the territories, and an entire misconception of the difficulties of their exploitation, had led in some cases, though not in all, to the loss of a large part of their capital.

In the territories unsuited to European settlement the earliest attempts to develop trade sometimes involved much wastage of the resources of the Colony. Rubber and forest timber were exhausted without proper replacement; accumulations of ivory were for a period obtained by exchange for cheap imports. Such a policy of exploitation could not, however, continue indefinitely. Once the realities of the situation were understood, capital was less easily attracted. But the creation of expensive public works, in particular of harbour works and of railway facilities, was more clearly seen to be an essential condition to the effective *mise-en-valeur* of the various territories. The Niger and the Congo and their tributaries have always provided important roads into the interior, but both required to be supplemented by railways, and the Congo to be connected from a point above the rapids to suitable points below.[1]

As time went on, however, it became increasingly apparent that the development of the African territories required capital formation of a type which seemed likely to yield a return too uncertain to justify commercial investment. Moreover, experience showed the difficulty of reconciling the responsibilities of administration with the interests of shareholders. In consequence the first decade of the twentieth century saw in many territories an attempt to revoke the earlier grants of Concessions and to separate more distinctly the functions of trading and of government. French and Belgian policy early moved in this direction. In the British territories the Administration was transferred from the chartered companies to the Crown by gradual stages, beginning about 1900 when Nigeria became a Protectorate.

[1] See below, p. 1567.

The larger companies continued, however, to perform an important role in the territories in which they operated. On the other hand, as Governments became more strongly established they showed themselves less liable to be dominated by powerful concessionaries and were more insistent on their own responsibilities for the development of the country. At the same time it must be realized that company management could possess certain advantages. The large company can often afford an organization to control the conditions and welfare of its Native employees that would be beyond the reach of the best-intentioned small employer. It can take a longer view of the advantages of training and educating workers and of developing new types of industry or of cultivation; in addition to which, its leaders are ready to grasp the value of planning and applying new methods of economic development. More recently there has been a tendency for Governments in Africa to set up an increasing number of such public corporations in spheres where private enterprise is unlikely to arise spontaneously.

By the third decade of the twentieth century the basic patterns of development had been broadly determined. Over the greater part of Africa the indigenous population was still primarily engaged in cultivating subsistence crops or was able to turn to them when commercial crops ceased to be remunerative or when opportunities for employment failed. The pure subsistence economy, however, was becoming a thing of the past. The need to pay taxes, the desire to buy imports, the opportunity to market a surplus and to sell labour services to the European economy had brought the African people into the orbit of world economy. Although European settlement on any scale was confined to regions which were climatically suitable, European traders, missionaries, and administrators had infiltrated into all parts of the continent and were an important feature of the economic landscape even in the least developed areas. The non-African trader supplied a range of merchandise previously unobtainable but now indispensable. He recruited labour for the mines, he bought surplus grain, and he advanced agricultural credit. The missionary provided educational and medical services where none existed before, and in some cases he gave lessons in husbandry. The administrator maintained the peace, collected taxes, supervised the construction and maintenance of roads and bridges, and organized famine relief and other emergency distress measures.

Where the natural and human resources were favourable to the development of an export crop in areas unattractive to the European settler, the European trader provided the capital and the organization for transporting the products to world markets and, in some areas, he established plantations. This was notably the case in the areas of tropical Africa which produced palm oil, cocoa, groundnuts, rubber, and cotton. Africa was now producing a large proportion of the world's exports of palm and palm-kernel oil, wool, and cocoa, and making a substantial contribution to the export of groundnuts.

It was, however, the minerals which provided the strongest attraction to European capital, and it is largely to the exploitation of mineral resources that Africa owes its railways, ports, and towns. By 1936 it was estimated that about a fifth of the foreign listed capital invested in Africa south of the Sahara went into mines and nearly a third into railways. The greater part of the total investment went to the highly mineralized territories or to those territories whose railways and ports served the mining industries. Where the minerals were found in areas climatically attractive to Europeans, as they were in the Union of South Africa and Southern Rhodesia, a stable European population laid the foundation for the development of local secondary industry. Smaller pockets of European settlement unconnected with the mining developments grew up where the farming conditions were particularly attractive, as in the Kenya Highlands, and served to develop an export crop which required both capital and special skill in processing as, for example, flue-cured tobacco or tea in Central Africa and sisal in East Africa.

The world depression of the thirties and the collapse in world prices for primary products which accompanied it found the African territories largely dependent on primary production. Most of them relied for their export income on a very restricted range of commodities, and not infrequently they produced for a single market. In 1935 Gambia derived the major part of its export revenue from groundnuts,[1] Uganda from cotton, Zanzibar from cloves, the Union of South Africa and Southern Rhodesia from gold, and Northern Rhodesia from copper. Nigeria and Sierra Leone derived nearly half of their export revenue from palm oil and palm kernels. The depression in world prices had produced a sharp decline in the value of exports. Thus Sierra Leone and Nigeria suffered falls of 53 per cent. and 52 per cent. in value respectively between 1929 and the worst of the subsequent five years, Kenya and Uganda a decline of 39 per cent. in value, and Tanganyika and the Gold Coast, despite a growing value of gold production, declines of 56 per cent. and 39 per cent. in value.

Nevertheless, the depression proved to be on the whole less damaging in its effect on Africa than on some more developed areas. The total recorded value of world exports declined by 66 per cent. in the period 1929–34, compared with a decline of 73 per cent. in North America and only 48 per cent. in Africa. The main impact of the decline, moreover, was felt by the European settled communities. European farmers throughout Africa were financially embarrassed and were often forced to depend on Government assistance. The drift of European agricultural labour to the towns in the

---

[1] United Nations, *Special Study on Economic Conditions and Development in Non-self-governing Territories*, 1952.

Union of South Africa produced a serious 'poor White' unemployment problem.[1] But even the wage-earning Africans had never totally abandoned the cultivation of subsistence crops, and they were able to revert to full-time subsistence production when displaced from other employment.

It may be that the indirect results of the depression were a more important influence on the ensuing course of economic development in Africa than the more obvious and direct effects. Experience in the depression showed the severe restrictions under which European farming might have to operate, and to some extent it proved a deterrent to this form of European colonization. Similar doubts were inspired by the fall in Government revenues which was another striking feature of the depression period. Developments in the social services were retarded and the expansionist sentiment which had at one time led to large commitments of loan expenditure gave place to a more cautious view of the financial possibilities of the territories. In the Union of South Africa the White unemployment problem strengthened the movement towards the adoption of the 'civilized labour' policy.[2]

In the Second World War and the years immediately following, the high world prices for primary products led to a recrudescence of the belief that Africa was a continent of enormous resources to which the infallible key was an adequate supply of capital. This more recent history will be discussed in the next chapter; though, as will be noted there, something of the spectre of the great depression lingered on into the post-war period.

PATTERNS OF PRODUCTION

The subsistence economy which characterized the earlier periods of African history was not of a type which demanded any high degree of specialization. In that respect it was in marked contrast to the measure of specialization demanded by the production for export. Some reference has already been made to the extent of the export production in the years immediately preceding the Second World War. Nevertheless, taking the continent as a whole, Africa still presented, at the conclusion of the Second World War, the picture of a great area in which the economy was still predominantly of a simple and rudimentary type.

It is true that to some extent the exchange economy had already made inroads on the old self-sufficient systems of economic activity. In part this was a continuance of trends that had been set in motion before the Second World War. It was conservatively estimated in 1936 that £1,222 million had been invested from abroad in African enterprises south of the Sahara.[3] Much of this had gone into railways and into mines which would enter into

---

[1] See below, pp. 1393 ff.   [2] See below, pp. 1288, 1393.
[3] S. H. Frankel, *Capital Investment in Africa*, 1938, pp. 157-9.

full production only after some lapse of time. Their indirect effects in stimulating auxiliary industries would take still longer to be reflected in the
economy of the territories concerned. There had, however, already been
signs of an increasing trend towards industrialization in a number of areas.
The process had gone farthest in the Union of South Africa. Manufacture,
which accounted for less than 10 per cent. of the national income of the
Union in 1917–18, contributed nearly 18 per cent. in 1937–8.[1] Employment in the mines of the Belgian Congo, the Rhodesias, and the Union was
already the major source of cash income for the African population of a
number of adjacent countries. Fifty-seven per cent. of the Africans employed in the gold-mining industry of the Union in 1947 came from outside its borders.[2] In West Africa the coastal towns, which had grown up in
response to the regular export of cash crops, were becoming increasingly
dependent on outside sources for their livelihood, and both in Nigeria and
in the Gold Coast there was evidence of a growing specialization of particular crops and an expanding internal trade in foodstuffs between one
area and another. The Second World War itself, by creating a large external demand for certain African primary products, and by enforcing self-
sufficiency as the result of breaking off relations with the metropolitan
country, accelerated the processes of specialization and industrialization.
In Southern Rhodesia, for example, the official index of production for
manufacture reached 286 per cent. of the 1938 level by 1948, and had
risen to 437 per cent. by 1952.[3] In the Union, where the process had
gathered momentum before the Second World War, the proportionate rise
in industrial production was less spectacular, but the industrial index,
which stood at 51 in 1938 and 100 in 1948, had reached 127 by 1950.[4]

The speed and the extent of industrialization varied with the size of the
European settled population and the available mineral resources, two conditioning factors which are themselves sometimes independent. It has
proceeded farthest in the Rhodesias and the Union of South Africa where,
as can be seen from Table I on p. 1272, manufacture, mining, and construction account for more than a third of the incomes received or earned in these
countries. Even Nyasaland, which has no mining industry and a very
small European population, obtains roughly 9 per cent. of its 'net geographical production' from the labour of its migrants working in the mines
and factories of adjacent territories. Similarly, for Mozambique it was
estimated that in 1952 more than 260,000 Natives were away at work in
the Union of South Africa or Southern Rhodesia. An even greater
measure of dependence on migration to the industrial or mining centres of

[1] C. G. W. Schumann, 'The Structure of the South African Economy', *Union of South Africa Finance and Trade Review*, vol. i, no. 1, July 1952.

[2] Social and Economic Planning Council, *Economic and Social Conditions of the Racial Groups in South Africa*, U.G. no. 53, 1948.

[3] United Nations, *Statistical Yearbook, 1953*.   [4] Ibid. *1954*.

South Africa characterizes the pattern of output in the High Commission Territories of Bechuanaland, Swaziland, and Basutoland.[1] By June 1953 it was estimated that there were some three-quarters of a million non-indigenous Africans living in the Union of South Africa.

Outside the areas characterized by a specifically European settlement, the most spectacular advance in industrialization has occurred in the Belgian Congo, where the index of manufacturing production (including electricity supply) has increased in value by three-quarters and nearly 90 per cent. in volume in the period 1950–3.[2] The most important industries are the metal and electricity undertakings which depend directly on the mining industry, and enterprises producing textiles, beer, tobacco, and food for local consumption. The main market for consumers' goods is an African urban population of a little over 2 million people living outside their customary environment and hence effectively outside the basic sub-sistence economy. In Kenya, on the other hand, the pattern of production of consumers' goods is largely determined by a non-African population which accounted for more than 75 per cent. of all incomes earned in Kenya in 1951. This demand had produced an expanding manufacturing industry in spite of the relatively small mineral resources of the territory. Manufactures (excluding electricity) accounted in Kenya for 10 per cent. of the geographical product in 1951. It also caused a noticeable tendency towards specialization among the African producers living within reach of the Nairobi market.

In the areas of West and East Africa not characterized either by an important mining industry or by a settled non-African community the scale of industrialization and of specialization consequent on the growth of markets has been much smaller. In Nigeria and Uganda, for example, mining, manufacture, and construction together accounted for barely 10 per cent. of the geographical product by the middle of the century. In Nigeria agriculture, forestry, and fishing account for more than two-thirds of the geographical product, and a similar order of importance is assigned to this industry group in French West Africa and the French Cameroons, where recent inquiries into the national income attribute 68 per cent. of the total to agriculture.[3] For Uganda the share of agriculture, shown in Table I at 54 per cent., would also approach two-thirds of the total if the undistributed profits of the statutory Marketing Boards were allocated to agricultural producers.

In these areas prospects of industrial development seem to be largely confined to industries processing local materials for export or to small-scale production for a predominantly African market. As soon as developments

---

[1] See below, p. 1379.

[2] *Bulletin de la Banque Centrale du Congo Belge et du Ruanda-Urundi*, October 1954.

[3] Luc B. de Carbon, 'L'Afrique noire', *L'Économie de l'Union française d'outre-mer*, 1952, p. 75.

TABLE I. *Geographical Product by Industrial Origin in Selected African Territories*

(in percentages of total product of each country)

	Union of South Africa (1951)	Southern Rhodesia (1950)	Northern Rhodesia (1949)	Nyasaland (1948)	Kenya (1951)	Uganda (1950)	Nigeria (1951-2)	Belgian Congo (1952)
1. Agriculture, forestry, fishing	24·8	23·4	24·2	55·5	46·6	54·4	68·3	35·9
2. Manufacture, mining, construction	36·9	33·4	52·9	6·6	16·6	9·3	9·9	31·6
3. Trade	13·6	13·7	7·7	12·4	15·6	26·5	} 15·1	8·0
4. Transport, communications, public utilities	8·6	5·8	3·2	2·9	6·7	3·2		8·5
5. Government	9·9	7·3	7·3	10·2	7·5	5·4	3·2	7·3
6. All others	16·2	16·4	4·7	12·4	7·0	1·2	3·5	8·7

(SOURCES: United Nations, *Monthly Bulletin of Statistics*, January 1954; idem, *Special Study on Social Conditions in Non-self-governing Territories*, 1953; P. Deane, *Colonial Social Accounting*, 1953; East African Statistical Department, *Estimates of Geographical Income and Net Product, 1947–51*, 1953; idem, *Quarterly Economic and Statistical Bulletin*; A. R. Prest and I. G. Stewart, *The National Income of Nigeria, 1950–51*, Colonial Research Studies no. 11, 1953; *Bulletin de la Banque Centrale du Congo Belge et du Ruanda-Urundi*, November 1953.)

in local industry reach a certain level they will by themselves create a sufficient local demand for producers' goods to permit the establishment of industries providing commodities such as cement, packing materials and containers, and chemicals of various kinds. Hence, even within the restricted range of industrial production open to the tropical African countries (without the broader kind of market which can be created by mineral development or European settlement), there are a variety of possibilities for local initiative on a relatively small scale. Cotton ginning is a well-established industry in the cotton-producing areas of Uganda, the Belgian Congo, and Nyasaland. In French West Africa groundnut oil is now produced and refined together with its by-products—oil-cake, soap, and glycerine. In Angola the most important secondary industry is that producing dried fish, fish cake, and fish oil. Textile, cigarette, and soap factories are found even in the least industrialized areas. Cement factories have been built in French West Africa, French Equatorial Africa, Mozambique, and Uganda, as well as in the Belgian Congo, Kenya, and both the Rhodesias.

In general, however, even the smallest scale of factory industry requires a certain minimum size of market before it is economically justified. In some territories the existence of a well-developed cottage industry may offer greater opportunities of steady economic advance than large-scale industry. In Nigeria, for example, production by factory methods as distinct from Native crafts was estimated to contribute less than £1 million to a gross domestic product of £596·7 million in 1951–2, whereas village rural industries such as spinning and weaving, tailoring, leather-working, illicit gin distilling, wood carving, and other Native crafts were estimated to contribute as much as £8½ million.[1] Even where the village industry is limited to subsistence or semi-subsistence output, the volume of that output may constitute an appreciable part in relation to the gross domestic product.

A very broad index of the levels of total production in African territories and even more broadly of the relative standards of living which these levels permit can be obtained by an examination of the available figures of national income.[2] International comparisons of *per capita* national income estimates can never be more than a very rough method of assessing relative

---

[1] Prest and Stewart, op. cit. pp. 38–39.

[2] For the estimates of national income quoted in these pages see the following reports and journals: Central African Statistical Office, *Monthly Digest of Statistics*; idem, *National Income and Social Accounts of Northern Rhodesia, 1945–53*, 1954; idem, *Economic and Statistical Bulletin of Southern Rhodesia*, February 1954. East African Statistical Department, *Quarterly Economic and Statistical Bulletin*. East Africa Royal Commission 1953–1955, *Report*, Cmd. 9475, 1955, pp. 478–81. Prest and Stewart, op. cit. International Bank for Reconstruction and Development, *The Economic Development of Nigeria*, 1955. D. Seers and C. R. Ross, *Report on Financial and Physical Problems of Development in the Gold Coast*, Accra, 1952. United Nations, *Monthly Bulletin of Statistics*. See also P. Deane, *Colonial Social Accounting*, 1953.

real incomes. Even where methods of estimate are similar (and this is rarely the case except when they are produced by the same agency), the relative variations in price levels prevent precise comparisons from being made.

As might be expected, the overall averages are highest in those territories where the mineral industry is well developed and where the European population is large enough for the characteristically high European averages to have a significant effect on the national average. The Union of South Africa stands well above any of the other territories, with an average in 1953 of about £97 per head. This may be compared with an average of over £290 for the United Kingdom in the same year. Southern Rhodesia, which is next in terms of average national income, had nearly £58 per head, while Northern Rhodesia (the value of whose exports was nearly 60 per cent. greater than those of Southern Rhodesia but whose European population was only one-third the size) had an average income of £43. The Belgian Congo, with a population roughly six times that of Northern Rhodesia, and hence a more predominantly African and rural population, had an average of about £25 in 1953; about 36 per cent. of its national income was attributable to the output of the agricultural industry, compared with under 10 per cent. in the case of Northern Rhodesia.

The other Central and East African territories were even more largely dependent on agriculture for their national income. Kenya had an average in 1953 of approximately £19 per head and Uganda of about £18. The level in Tanganyika was estimated to be in the region of £13 per head, and in Nyasaland it was estimated at only about £7. No figures are available for the Portuguese or French territories in Central and East Africa, but it seems unlikely that the average level of earnings in these territories differs much from that of Nyasaland.

Recent estimates of national income for the British West African territories illustrate the important contribution of a valuable export crop in raising the average level of earnings. For Nigeria the 1952–3 average was estimated to be about £21 per head and in the Gold Coast, where the relative importance of the cocoa crop is appreciably greater, the average income in 1950–1 was estimated at £36, which was nearly twice the estimate made for Nigeria in that year. It might be thought that since the Nigerian estimates were based on a careful and detailed survey, and since they relate to a large proportion of the land and people of West Africa, they should provide an acceptable indication of the order of magnitude of national incomes prevailing in adjacent territories. To some extent this is so; but they also illustrate the limitations of national income averages as indications of productivity or of standards of living. It is significant that an attempt to estimate the division of the national product of Nigeria between its three main regions suggested that when the Nigerian average was £19 per head the average for the West was £29, for the East £19, and for the

North (with about half the total population of the country) only £16. The authors of the Nigerian estimates also found evidence of a marked inequality of incomes as between African and African, and emphasized that 'the recorded figure of mean income may be consistent with the great majority of the population having lower incomes than this mean level'.[1]

In effect, therefore, the differences in average incomes seem to be wide, ranging in 1953 from under £10 per head of total population in the poorer Central and East African dependencies to nearly £100 in the Union of South Africa. Much of this spread, however, can be accounted for by racial and institutional differences which scarcely affect the majority of the populations concerned. In territories where there is a large immigrant population the unequal distribution of incomes between Europeans or Asians and Africans, and the relatively high proportion of corporate enterprises as opposed to individual activities, combine to obscure the real standard of living of the majority. Where there are lucrative African cash crops, standards of living may be obscured to a lesser extent by an unequal distribution of incomes among Africans. In Kenya, for example, the African share in the 'net geographical product' was only 40 per cent. in 1951, and thus for more than 97 per cent. of the population the average income was below £8 per head when the average national income was £18. In Uganda the African average was nearer £9 per head, the higher level being due to a greater volume of trade in African agricultural produce, which was valued at over £25 million in 1951 compared with about £4½ million for the somewhat larger African population of Kenya.

Similar conclusions are suggested by the 1953 estimates for the Rhodesias and the Belgian Congo, in each of which the average income of the African population was in the region of £14, although average national incomes ranged from £25 in the Congo to £58 in Southern Rhodesia. In the Belgian Congo company incomes accounted for approximately 15 per cent. of the national income in 1953 and African incomes for about 56 per cent. In Northern Rhodesia the largest share went to companies, with 35 per cent. of the national income, and in Southern Rhodesia to European individuals, who accounted for about 57 per cent. of the national income compared with about 24 per cent. accruing to Africans.[2]

Hence for the indigenous inhabitants of East and Central Africa average earnings seem to have been at broadly similar levels in all territories and to have been lower on the whole than those prevailing in the west of Africa. Some of the difference may, however, be attributable to relatively lower valuations of subsistence incomes by those making the national income calculations for East and Central African territories. In terms of the average real incomes of the African population the Gold Coast and Nigerian

[1] Prest and Stewart, op. cit. p. 82.
[2] The Southern Rhodesian percentages are for 1952.

estimates suggest a more impressive level of economic achievement than do the corresponding estimates for East and Central Africa. It seems reasonable to conclude that neither industrialization nor European settlement induce an indigenous level of productivity comparable to that engendered by a vigorous development of African cash crops.

Indeed, in the areas which owe most to European settlement and European capital the differential rate of productivity, and hence of earnings as between the races, is artificially maintained. Differential prices are paid for European and African maize in both Northern and Southern Rhodesia. Discriminatory labour legislation exists in Kenya, the Belgian Congo, the Rhodesias, and the Union of South Africa, though its severity is greater in the south than in the north. The legislative provisions, however, are often only a pale reflection of the racial discrimination effectively enforced by the practice of private employers and the pressure of European trade unions. In Kenya new labour legislation is now phrased to avoid reference to distinctions of race, nationality, or origin, and in the newly formed Federation of Rhodesia and Nyasaland salaries in the Federal Civil Service and in the Federal Assembly are the same for Africans and Europeans. But wages and salaries in East and Central Africa are still effectively determined on racial grounds. In the Rhodesias and the Union of South Africa the gap between the earnings of Africans and non-Africans is maintained not only by the operation of different wage scales or price systems for different races but also by the exclusion of Africans from skilled occupations.[1] The process has gone farthest in the Union, where it is a central feature of Government policy.

The policy seems to have been highly effective in maintaining the racial differentials in earnings. The national income estimates in Central Africa show a steady decline in the African share of the national income in recent years. Part of this decline can, however, be attributed to increasing Government income and an increasing volume of undistributed profits. Wage data over a long period from the Union of South Africa tell a more significant tale. Over the second quarter of the twentieth century European earnings from employment have averaged roughly four times as much as the non-European average in railways and factories. In mining the differential has been kept at an even higher level and, before allowing for the value of free food and quarters enjoyed by Africans, the earnings of Europeans in the mines were roughly 14 times as much as the average earnings of non-Europeans.[2]

Restrictive practices of an opposite nature to those prevailing in Central and Southern Africa have been adopted in Nigeria and the Gold Coast in

---

[1] See below, pp. 1396 ff.

[2] S. H. Frankel, *The Economic Impact on Under-developed Societies*, 1953, pp. 111 ff. See also below, pp. 1432 ff.

order to increase the relative share of the African population in the national income. The immigration ordinances adopted in these territories are designed to exclude European personnel from the labour force as far as possible. Expatriate employees are admitted on a strict quota basis and only when the firm applying for the quota can satisfy the immigration authorities that the vacancies could not be filled by Africans. Individual non-African entrepreneurs may also be excluded in certain circumstances. The establishment of new retail enterprises, for example, is now effectively barred to non-Africans.[1] An official statement published in the Gold Coast states that: 'it has long been the policy of the Gold Coast Government to prevent non-African settlement of the Gold Coast. The purpose of this is to ensure that the indigenous population should be allowed to progress without the eventual complications of pressure from powerful and strongly entrenched non-African interests, not only in the political sphere but also in the commercial and economic spheres.'[2]

The restrictive policies practised in some of the British territories may be contrasted with those in the French territories where the principle of non-discrimination established by the Constitution of the French Union is being deliberately applied to the overseas territories. Conditions laid down for Government employment specifically prohibit the fixing of salaries or allowances on the basis of differences in place of origin or in race. In December 1952 the new French Labour Code applied to the French overseas territories a wide range of provisions which are calculated to reduce the differential rates of earnings as between Europeans and Africans.[3]

Although racial restrictions inhibit the occupational movement of labour in Africa, its geographical mobility is unusually high. In such a sparsely populated continent the fact that it has been possible to attract labour over great distances to the more favourably situated regions has been a major factor facilitating the economic development of the African territories. As a result one of the most striking and universal characteristics of the productive systems of Africa is their dependence on migrant labour. As will be explained in a later chapter the causes and incentives for the migration of labour vary greatly. It is, however, convenient to add here some of the implications of migration in the purely economic field.

From the point of view of the employer and of the economy which he represents, the migrant labour system has several advantages. First of all, it provides a large reservoir of unskilled labour from which the employer can select the able-bodied and the fit and reject the aged and infirm. Secondly, the labour force is too unstable to exert an effective collective bargaining power. Thirdly, it has a supplementary source of income in village subsistence production, which can be used to support the worker's

---

[1] P. T. Bauer, *West African Trade*, 1954.
[2] *Gold Coast Gazette Extraordinary*, February 1949.   [3] See below, p. 1437.

family or the labourer himself when unemployed or on holiday, and this may permit the individual to accept less than a full living wage. Fourthly, the tribal connexions provide an independent system of social security which enables the employing economy to avoid direct liability for maintaining the unemployed or retired worker.

Some of these advantages tend to be illusory. The declining fertility of the Native Reserves, due to the withdrawal of the able-bodied males, tends to reduce in the long run the physical quality of the labour they can supply and the food that can be obtained from their cultivation. Even the African who was born in an urban area in the Union of South Africa, and who has worked in it all his life, dare not lose contact with the Reserves, for an unemployed African forfeits his right to live in the town; and an African who has spent too long away from his village or who has no family in the village forfeits his right to a piece of land. The fact that the worker has thus one foot in the Reserves and one in the towns is a source of indifferent attitudes towards work,[1] and is a cause of high labour turnover. A detailed analysis of the work-sheets of 251 firms in the Union showed that one-half of the employment taken by Africans lasted less than six months, three-quarters less than a year, and 90 per cent. less than two years.[2]

The employer must undertake certain obligations in providing food, medical services, and housing for the heterogeneous community he employs. As industrialization progresses the demand for semi-skilled personnel replaces the demand for unskilled labourers, and the attitude of the less responsible class of migrant labourers is liable to reduce their aptitude for even the simplest mechanical tasks. The transient character of labour makes an apprenticeship scheme a precarious investment for the individual employer. There is a perennial shortage of African foremen and charge-hands. In effect, therefore, the direct economic costs imposed by an unstable labour force include permanently low standards of output per head —both in the areas from which the migrants come and in the areas to which they go—and a heavy burden of expensive supervision. The present preponderance of Europeans (or Asians) in supervisory positions is not entirely a result of discriminating labour policies. In many cases and in many areas it is largely due to a lack of responsible African skilled workers capable of exercising effective supervision.

Except in the Union of South Africa, where political factors are opposed to a full integration of the African community into the European economy, there is a growing tendency to permanent urbanization of the industrial labour force, fostered in some cases by deliberate policy among the larger

---

[1] C. H. Northcott, *African Labour Efficiency Survey, 1947*, Colonial Research Publications no. 3, 1949, especially pp. 119–20.

[2] Department of Commerce, Witwatersrand University, *Native Urban Employment, 1936–44*, 1945.

employers. There is significant evidence of this in the Belgian Congo, particularly in the action taken by the *Union Minière du Haut-Katanga*.[1] Whether or not there have been deliberate policies of urbanization, however, the drift of workers to the towns has been universal. In spite of the fact that the vast majority of African labourers continue to belong to the rural areas in the sense that they begin and end their lives there, the growth in the numbers currently resident in urban areas has been one of the most significant concomitants of African industrialization.

In the Union the African population of the towns rose from 587,250 in 1921 to 2,292,228 in 1951, and between 1932 and 1949 the number of Africans employed increased by 356 per cent.[2] A sample survey undertaken in Southern Rhodesia in 1948 revealed the other side of the picture; it showed that by then there was in the rural areas barely one male adult to every two female adults compared with a proportion of three to four in 1921. In Northern Rhodesia the African population in the major towns doubled in three years ending in 1950.[3] In French West Africa the urban population has doubled to about a million since the Second World War, and in French Equatorial Africa the population of the six principal urban centres increased from 86,000 in 1938 to almost 200,000 in 1950. In the Belgian Congo 2·7 million Africans were living in urban areas in 1954, compared with less than a million in 1939.

STANDARDS OF LIVING

If economic development is measured in terms of the growth of industry and of towns and the rise in the money value of the national income, there is abundant evidence during recent years of a remarkable rate of growth in the African territories. It is more difficult, however, to determine whether there has indeed been a corresponding rise in the standard of living or whether changes in the patterns of production and exchange have merely shifted the distribution or altered the content of personal incomes.

There are a number of reasons to account for the inadequacy of information on standards of living. One is that information on consumption is generally more difficult to collect and less frequently required for administrative or fiscal purposes than information on production. Another and less tractable set of problems arises from the heterogeneous nature of the communities. Each African territory contains within its borders not one community but several, each aspiring to a different standard of consumption, each having its characteristic ways of earning a living, and each with its special background of economic and social values. A list of such

[1] See below, p. 1391.
[2] J. D. Rheinallt Jones, 'The Effects of Urbanization in South and Central Africa', *African Affairs*, January 1953. See also *S.A.S.*, no. 95, 15 December 1954.
[3] United Nations, *Special Study on Social Conditions in Non-self-governing Territories*, 1953, p. 76.

communities for the Union of South Africa, for example, would include Africans in urban areas, Africans in the Native Reserves, Europeans, Asians, and Coloured or mixed communities. Similar groups exist in all the African territories with which this survey is concerned, although the relative importance of the different groups may differ significantly from one country to another. There is, of course, some overlap between the groups in respect of consumption, but in some cases the dissimilarities are still very marked.

No system of social accounting has yet been devised which will effectively record aggregate incomes and expenditures for such diverse groups as these, so as to measure changes in their welfare and productivity against a single yard-stick. The evidence, where it exists, is piecemeal and can be analysed only in piecemeal fashion.[1] Figures for what is called 'real national income' are available for Southern Rhodesia and the Union of South Africa. These are calculated by deflating the money national income figures over a period by a price index designed to remove the effect of changes in the value of money. Since the different communities have different patterns of expenditure, however, changes in the value of money affect them in different ways and no light is thrown on the real incomes of a definable group of people by this kind of calculation.

If the level of money earnings is taken as an index of the standard of living, then the communities living in the Union of South Africa could be ranked in the following descending order: Europeans, Coloured persons, Asians, Africans in urban areas, and Africans in rural areas. The Census of Industrial Establishments found averages for secondary industry in 1944-5 as follows: European salaries £540, European wages £341, Coloured wages £149, Asian £145, and Native £91. The rankings would be roughly similar throughout Africa. The margins of overlap and the relative differentials in earnings may, however, differ significantly from one area to another. More important still, if this evidence is considered in terms of relative standards of living, the rates of earnings per head of the population may not show the same relative differentials as the rates of earnings per earner. A survey conducted in Durban by the Economics Department of Natal University College showed that for 1943-4 the percentage of European households living below the poverty datum line was 5·2, of Asian households 70·6, of Coloured households 38·2, and of African households 24·8.[2] The poverty datum line is separately calculated for each group. In terms of these results the poorest community in an urban area in Natal is the Asian community, a result which can be mainly attributed to the large number of dependants attached to each earner. Asian women do not

---

[1] See United Nations, *Monthly Bulletin of Statistics*, December 1953.
[2] Social and Economic Planning Council, *Economic and Social Conditions of the Racial Groups in South Africa*, U.G. no. 53, 1948.

normally add to the family income as do many Coloured women by going out to work, and large families are the rule. The annual percentage increase of the Asian population over the period 1936–46 was 2·65 per cent., larger than that for any other group.

The relatively low proportion of Africans below the poverty line in Durban can be attributed partly to the fact that many employers provide them with free food and housing, but the more significant cause is that a large number of African employees are men who have left their families in the Native Reserves. There is ample evidence to suggest that Africans employed in industrial areas in the Union have shifted their burden of poverty to their home villages, either within the Native Reserves or beyond the Union's borders. Examples of this have been given in the studies of economic conditions in the Reserves, which are referred to in a previous chapter. A recent Report which dealt specifically with the problem of the Reserves concluded that 'they are generally backward areas and the whole atmosphere in them is one of stagnation, of poverty of people and resources'. As the Report points out, however, the burden of poverty cannot be completely shifted to the African villages: 'The general debility of the Reserve population means that the major portion of the Union's labour force is only attaining a very low level of efficiency.'[1]

Outside the Union of South Africa there is no 'poor White' problem of any importance, except possibly in relation to some European farmers in the Portuguese territories. On the other hand not all Europeans have a uniformly high standard of living. There are European missionaries, farmers, and traders in a number of East, Central, and Southern territories whose standard of living is austere in the extreme. In general, however, the standard of living of the European communities in Africa tends to be high, and is indeed higher than that of their metropolitan counterparts. Even in territories where their incomes are not inflated by racial predominance they are such as to offer something more than a compensation for the material disadvantages of being temporary residents. In areas of permanent European settlement taxation is relatively light, and because there is no European 'working class' comparable to that found in Europe itself, the general level of European incomes tends to be on a higher scale. In Southern Rhodesia the results of the income census showed that in 1950 about 20 per cent. of European earners received incomes in excess of £1,000 per annum.[2] Differences in levels and structures of prices and in the availability of social services prohibit a precise comparison with the United Kingdom, but even when allowances are made both for price

[1] Idem. *Summary of the Report of the Commission for the Socio-Economic Development of the Bantu Areas within the Union of South Africa*, U.G. no. 61, 1955, pp. 73 ff.
[2] Central African Statistical Office, *Economic and Statistical Bulletin of Southern Rhodesia*, January 1954.

differences and for differing rates of taxation it is still significant that in the United Kingdom in 1953 less than 5 per cent. of the incomes received by persons were estimated to exceed £1,000 per annum.[1]

The problem of Asian poverty is also less conspicuous outside the Union, partly because the other countries lack the heritage of indentured agricultural labour and partly because there are fewer political and industrial barriers to the development of a non-European artisan or trader class. In general Asian and Syrian traders or artisans have higher standards of efficiency than the indigenous Africans, so that where they can develop without restriction they can achieve relatively high standards of living. This is true, for example, in British East Africa where the part played by the Asian population is influential in both the political and the economic spheres.[2] It is also true in West Africa where Syrian traders operate concerns which can compete effectively with the European companies. On the other hand, the possibilities for Asian advancement vary considerably as between territories. In Nyasaland there is a small Asian professional class of some standing and many of its members hold responsible positions. In Northern Rhodesia, on the other hand, there are no opportunities for Asians outside the trading sphere, and some new townships are closed to Asian traders. Restrictions such as these tend to depress Asian standards of living as a whole. In most areas, however, the fact that the educational standard of the Asian community is higher than that of the African gives Asians an important competitive advantage.[3]

Information is unfortunately not complete enough to provide conclusive evidence that the process of bringing the African peoples into closer contact with the world economy has consistently resulted in an improvement in living standards. There is no doubt that one result of the process has been to widen the range of goods and services available to them. Dietary surveys carried out in four widely separated Bantu areas of the Union of South Africa suggested that most Natives tend to regard sugar, tea, and coffee as 'necessities for their usual diet'.[4] Bicycles, sewing machines, and textile goods are now imported to a greater extent than ever before. Over the three-year period 1949–51, imports of cotton and silk manufactures and other clothing and footwear averaged about 32 per cent. of the total value of imports into Nigeria and 25 per cent. of the value of imports into the Gold Coast.[5] In 1950 imports of cotton piece-goods per head of the population were more than five and a half times the 1938 level in Gambia, nearly two and a half times as much in Sierra Leone and the Gold Coast,

---

[1] Central Statistical Office, *National Income and Expenditure, 1946–1953*, 1954.

[2] *East Africa Royal Commission 1953–1955, Report*, Cmd. 9475, 1955, p. 200.

[3] See above, pp. 404, 1153.

[4] Union Department of Health, Division of Nutrition, 'Dietary Surveys in Rural Bantu Areas', *Journal for Social Research*, December 1952.

[5] P. T. Bauer, *West African Trade*, 1954, p. 48.

and more than 80 per cent. above the 1938 level in Nigeria.[1] New consumers' goods such as radios and gramophones are now imported for the African trade in a number of territories, although the proportion of Africans who can buy these luxuries is limited.

On the other hand, African diets are universally poor in quality, and this is reflected in low standards of health and efficiency. In most areas of Central, East, and South Africa maize (or some alternative such as millet), and in West Africa yams or cassava, are the staple food; meat is scarce and milk is in short supply. Primitive agricultural methods result in low grain yields, and quantity rather than quality is the objective in the production of livestock. The examination of African recruits for the armed forces during the Second World War revealed that in most areas the nutritional state of the population was considerably below normal. In Nigeria, for example, when selected men were medically examined in their own districts with a view to conscription, about 50 per cent. of the so-called able-bodied men were rejected as unfit for heavy manual labour because of physical disability.[2] Experience in recruiting in Uganda 'has proved beyond dispute that a thoroughly fit Native of Uganda is rare. The greater part of the population shows signs of defective nutrition, which is hardly surprising as from birth they are ordinarily sustained on a deficient diet.'[3] Similarly in Kenya an official commission examining the food situation in 1943 concluded that 'there is complete unanimity that both in regard to Natives in the Reserves and those in employment outside the Reserves there is a marked degree of malnutrition resulting from an unbalanced diet; too much emphasis being placed on starch food, particularly maize, with a corresponding deficiency in foods providing the necessary quantities of protein, mineral salts and vitamins'.[4]

Not only are the standards of food consumption low but it has even been argued that they have deteriorated as a consequence of the development of cash crops and European industry.[5] The Kenya Food Shortage Commission concluded that the undue prominence of maize in the Native diet has been a development of the last 30 years or so, and is a result of the common practice of giving rations to employed labour in this form. Although some of the large companies, and particularly the mining companies, provide a scientifically balanced diet for their African employees, this is not so usual among the smaller employers. Another consequence of the development of a market for the sale of agricultural produce in some areas has been a deterioration in the fertility of the soil due to overcropping and overstocking.

[1] United Nations, *Special Study on Social Conditions in Non-self-governing Territories*, 1953, p. 159.
[2] *Report of the Labour Department*, Lagos, 1944.
[3] *Joint Report of Finance Committee and Development and Welfare Committee on Post-war Development*, 2nd ed., Entebbe, 1945, p. 30.
[4] *Report of Food Shortage Commission of Inquiry 1943*, Nairobi, 1943, p. 58.
[5] B. P. Thomson, 'Two Studies in African Nutrition', *R.L.I. Papers*, no. 24, 1954.

A reduction in the area and fertility of the land open to subsistence crops may reduce dietary standards to an extent which the increased cash income derived from more intensive cultivation does not fully compensate. In effect, an agricultural technique appropriate to a primitive system of shifting cultivation generally requires some improvement and adaptation if it is to form the basis of a developing cash-crop economy. A survey carried out in 1945 on the main cash-crop areas of Northern Rhodesia, for example, found that about a third of the families observed retained insufficient grain for their own food needs. Relatively few of them had cash to buy grain when their stocks were exhausted, though the majority were able to rely on free gifts of food from kinsmen who had retained a surplus.[1]

For the African in the urban areas the range of variation in standards of living is wide. The employees of the larger companies enjoy free housing and medical services as well as a balanced food ration. Some companies (particularly some of the mining companies) provide facilities for organized sports and recreation. For a large number of Africans in employment, however, overcrowding, a high cost of living, and all the disadvantages of existing in a relatively impersonal society are the normal features of urban life. The East Africa Royal Commission came to the conclusion that 'conditions of life for the poorer Asian and for the majority of Africans in the towns have been deteriorating over a considerable period'.[2] It must be realized, however, that this judgement applies to the territory surveyed by the East Africa Royal Commission and its terms may need to be qualified in regard to some other urban areas, particularly those in the Rhodesias and the Belgian Congo.

The high cost of living in towns detracts from the apparent value of money wages. The Report of the survey of labour efficiency in Nairobi remarked that: 'Running through all answers received by the investigators, whether they were dealing with diet, wages, housing or family circumstances, ran a murmur of discontent concerning the adequacy of wages to meet the cost of urban life.'[3] In West Africa the town dweller often suffers the additional strain of contributing to a host of unemployed hangers-on who can claim relationship with him and who therefore constitute a severe drain on his limited earnings. Even where recreational and other special amenities exist, they are in large part the expression of a foreign scheme of values. A recent inquiry undertaken on the Northern Rhodesian Copperbelt found that only a small proportion of the population was interested in these facilities, and only about 1 per cent. attended cinemas regularly.

[1] W. Allan, M. Gluckman, D. U. Peters, and C. G. Trapnell, 'Land Holding and Land Usage among the Plateau Tonga of Mazabuka District, A Reconnaissance Survey, 1945', *R.L.I. Papers*, no. 14, 1948.

[2] *East Africa Royal Commission 1953–1955, Report*, Cmd. 9475, 1955, p. 209.

[3] C. H. Northcott, *African Labour Efficiency Survey, 1947*, Colonial Research Publications no. 3, 1949, p. 115.

Finally, it should be noted that the African at work in the towns loses the leisure and the social occupations which are part and parcel of the village way of life. The peasant farmer is to a large extent his own task-master, and within the limits set by his subsistence needs and his processes of production he can plan his own working life. The freedom to take his leisure when he chooses and to co-operate in the social and religious cere-monies of the village community is not a negligible addition to the real in-come of the African villager, although it is not measurable. It is significant that his demand for leisure would seem to take precedence over his demand for material goods. A recent economic survey of the cocoa-producing areas of Nigeria, for example, found that the average amount of time spent at work throughout the year 1951–2 was 209 days for a man and 242 days for a woman.[1] A proportion of the remaining time was spent in funerals, weddings, and other social occasions, and some of the idleness was enforced by the seasonal nature of the agricultural task. But when allowance is made for all these factors there is a substantial residue of voluntary un-employment which was chosen in preference to a gainful occupation.

Though it is not possible to establish precisely the net balance of gain or loss in economic welfare involved in the industrial revolution now taking place in Africa, it is clear that the process of redistribution and revaluation is a complex one. In so far as aggregate rates of economic growth can be defined and measured they are of secondary importance by comparison with the structural changes which are transforming the African economies. These structural changes take different forms in different territories and give rise to a variety of internal problems.

VARYING TYPES OF ECONOMIC GROWTH

The pattern of economic growth which emerges in a given territory may be considered as a consequence of its physical or climatic or human resources, of its political and strategic history, and of its metropolitan at-tachments. Its present economic structure and problems are, indeed, a composite outcome of all these factors and might be classified in terms of any one of them. In trying to consider the joint contribution of these factors we can conveniently group the territories concerned in terms of their position in the African continent.

Southern Africa

The Union of South Africa directly administers the mandated territory of South-West Africa and provides the economic framework within which the three High Commission Territories are obliged to develop. The economy of the Union effectively surrounds these territories and in so far

[1] R. Galletti, K. D. S. Baldwin, and I. O. Dina, *Nigerian Cocoa Farmers*, 1956, p. 294.

as they have developed, they have done so in a state of more or less complete economic dependency. They have not, indeed, advanced far. Their main economic activity is still subsistence agriculture, which absorbs the major energies of the people and provides most of them with their basic livelihood. The value of exports from South-West Africa exceeded £35 million in 1952, but by far the greater part of this represented a return to South African capital and skill in mining and ranching. The money incomes of residents in these territories economically dependent on the Union are largely derived from the sale of livestock or livestock products such as hides and wool, and from the sale of labour services to European enterprise, mainly in South Africa itself.

As far as the exporting areas are concerned the return on this sale of labour services is not large enough to stimulate a local expansion of activity. It was officially estimated, for example, that over 71,000 men from Basutoland were at work outside the territory in 1950. At the rates then prevailing in the gold-mines and excluding the value of their food, housing, and other services in kind, these labourers would have earned a money income in the Union of over £3½ million per annum, a sum more than 50 per cent. above the value of merchandise exports from the territory. Out of the total money value of the labour exported, however, it is estimated that only £600,000 was returned to the territory in cash, including deferred wages, remittances to families, and taxes collected from absentees.[1] The remainder flowed back into the economy of the Union of South Africa.

The agricultural pastoral type of economy, with a strong element of subsistence production and with some leaven of mineral wealth, was indeed the characteristic pattern in Southern Africa before the discoveries of diamonds and gold transformed the situation. Into this moderately prosperous, predominantly rural economy of relatively extensive resources of land and labour and of scanty capital, other than that which could be supplied directly out of personal saving, these two vital discoveries injected new incentives and new forces. They speedily made an impact on the price of agricultural products, on the level of Government revenue, and on the system of communications. By 1895 Johannesburg had been connected by rail to Cape Town, Port Elizabeth, Durban, and Lourenço Marques. By the beginning of the twentieth century the focus of economic life in South Africa had shifted to the rapidly growing cities. The economy was entering into a period of radical structural change.

The essence of this change was the rise in importance, relatively to agriculture, first of mining and then of manufacturing industry. The process of industrialization, already evident at the beginning of the century, became a dominating feature of the economy after the First World War and gathered new momentum in the Second. At the end of the First World

---

[1] Estimate based on information given in *Colonial Reports, Basutoland, 1950*, pp. 18–19.

War the gross value of output of farms, mines, and factories was almost equal, with agriculture highest and manufacture slightly lower than the other two.[1] Before the Second World War the gross value of manufactures was double that of farm products and about a third greater than that of minerals, in spite of the increase in the price of gold which followed the devaluations of 1932. By 1938 the manufacturing and construction industries together accounted for 17·6 per cent. of the net domestic product of the Union of South Africa. By 1953 their share had risen to 23·6 per cent. The rise in the annual gross value of production in these three sectors of the economy between 1917 and 1935 is illustrated in the following table:

Annual Gross Value of Production
(£ million)

	1917–18	1934–5
Agriculture . .	51·52	55·54
Mining . . .	50·49	83·65
Manufacturing . .	50·01	111·22

This transformation was achieved with an amazing speed and was accompanied by a rapid growth in national income. Between 1919 (a year of inflationary boom) and 1951 (also a year of post-war inflation) the money value of the net national income of the Union was multiplied 4½ times. Except during the 1929–32 depression, which South Africa shared with the rest of the world, the growth was almost uninterrupted. The very speed of the advance, however, set up social and economic strains which were to create the characteristic economic problems of modern South Africa. The first of these is the decline of agriculture as a result of the inter-war depression. This necessitated the elaborate system of subsidies, discussed in some detail elsewhere,[2] without which export agriculture would have broken down. The agricultural industry, however, shared in the expansion due to the Second World War. In 1950 the agriculture, forestry, and fishing group of industries accounted for over 17 per cent. of the national income as compared with less than 13 per cent. in 1938. Agricultural incomes increased in money terms from £38·3 million in 1935 to £213 million in 1951; in real terms the increase was of the order of 125 per cent.[3] By 1953–4 agricultural incomes had reached £258 million.[4]

Next is the problem of the 'poor Whites' whose situation is discussed in greater detail in relation to labour policy.[5] They were more exposed than

---

[1] C. G. W. Schumann, *Structural Changes and Business Cycles in South Africa, 1806–1936*, 1938, p. 215.   [2] See above, pp. 848, 868.

[3] C. V. H. du Plessis, 'Agriculture. . . . Some aspects of its importance to the South African Economy', *Union of South Africa Finance and Trade Review*, vol. i, no. 3, July 1953.

[4] United Nations, Department of Economic Affairs, *Review of Economic Activity in Africa 1950 to 1954* (Supplement to *World Economic Report, 1953–54*), 1955.   [5] See below, p. 1393.

the Africans to any kind of economic recession, since the African labourer had a source of subsistence in the Reserves when unemployed. By 1932, when the Carnegie Commission reported on the problem, they were believed to number 220,000.[1] This was more than a ninth of the European population of the Union at that period.

To the European community of South Africa the plight of these people constituted a racial challenge and a warning. Europeans were not prepared to let unskilled White labourers compete for employment with African migrants whose link with the Reserves made them willing to accept low wages. There was a minimum standard below which the European community was not willing to see unskilled fellow Whites fall. They sought to maintain this standard by encouraging the use of European rather than African unskilled labour. Government Departments made it their policy to employ a certain proportion of 'civilized' labourers, and private employers were induced or compelled to do so by direct subsidies, the manipulation of the customs tariff, discrimination by the Government in accepting orders, and the regulation of wages in industries to which the industrial council system was inapplicable.[2]

The third problem is that which arises from the attempt of organized European labour to secure a monopoly of the skilled labour market. In so far as this has been successful, the cost of skilled labour in the Union is unusually high and the range between skilled and unskilled wages unusually wide. A Commission reporting in 1941 stated that:

Skilled wages in the Union are many times higher than the earnings of skilled workers in the main countries from which the Union imports manufacturers' products. Further, the existing classification of skilled workers in the Union is often artificial and does not take cognizance of the fact that the greater mechanization of industry in the Union has provided increased opportunity for the employment of semi-skilled workers in numerous occupations and has reduced the period of training required.[3]

The effects of this rigidity in the labour structure are most marked in the gold-mines where it is traditionally most severe. There African and Coloured workers are limited to the performance of rough and simple manual tasks, and every African worker must be supervised by a White worker. The restrictions which have been placed on the freedom of the industry to introduce flexibility into its labour force have weakened its ability to retain its workers in the face of increased demands from manufacturing industry where there is greater scope for employing Africans in semi-skilled occupations. The full labour requirements of the gold-mines have

[1] *Report of the Carnegie Commission on the Poor White Problem in South Africa*, 1932.
[2] S. T. van der Horst, *Native Labour in South Africa*, 1942, p. 252.
[3] Third Interim Report of the Industrial and Agricultural Requirements Commission, *Fundamentals of Economic Policy in the Union*, U.G. no. 40, 1941, para. 168. See also below, p. 1388.

not been met since 1941, the year of the industry's all-time record output when the monthly average at work was 364,000; the average for 1953 was about 280,000. The burden of rising labour costs is, moreover, particularly serious to an industry the price of whose product is fixed by circumstances beyond its influence. The industry has so far been saved from the necessity of facing this problem by a series of economic windfalls—in 1932 by South Africa's departure from the gold standard, in 1947 by the discovery of the new Orange Free State gold-fields, and in 1952 by the prospects of developing uranium as a by-product. Each time, however, the final reckoning has merely been postponed.

The problem of rising costs is also beginning to be regarded as a threat to some sections of the manufacturing industry. The Second World War introduced an artificial protection for South African industry, which was effectively prolonged by the introduction in 1948 of import licensing as a measure of exchange control. Within this shelter some industries have been able to let costs rise with impunity.

It is reported from Durban that South African manufactured goods have proved so much more expensive than imported articles that the City Council there is considering an approach to the Minister of Economic Affairs to have the issue of special import permits reviewed. The municipality has found that where tenders for South African goods have had to be accepted because no import permits were granted the city had to pay substantially more for local items.[1]

To some extent these increases in the prices of locally manufactured goods, like the increase in the cost of labour, are reflections of the strains put upon the Union economy by an accelerated rate of economic growth to which it has been unable immediately to adapt itself. The demands for labour, food, and urban services have inevitably outstripped the available supplies. The result has been an inflationary rise in prices and incomes which, by encouraging speculative activity, has proved to be cumulative.

The speculative element in the South African economy originated with the diamond and gold booms at the end of the nineteenth century. A writer in 1938 observed that 'South Africa is fast becoming a land of speculators'.[2] In August 1946 the Governor of the South African Reserve Bank remarked in his annual report that 'a mass speculative fever has developed which causes too large a proportion of the public to neglect discretion and discrimination. It appears, for example, that far too little distinction is made between what is investment and what is speculation, or between high-risk and low-risk speculative ventures, or between speculative and purely gambling propositions.'[3] The effect of these speculative ventures

[1] *The Times Review of Trade and Industry*, April 1954.
[2] C. G. W. Schumann, *Structural Changes and Business Cycles in South Africa, 1806–1936*, 1938, p. 380.
[3] C. G. W. Schumann and A. E. Scheurkogel, *Industrial and Commercial Share Price Indices in South Africa*, 1948.

is to divert resources from constructive activities and to create a general feeling of insecurity.

In conclusion it should be noted that the impressive economic growth of the Union of South Africa (whether measured in terms of the rate of increase in national income, or the volume of output of goods and services, or of standards of consumption, or the value of new capital formation) is largely concentrated in three strictly limited areas—the Witwatersrand, Natal (excluding Zululand), and the Cape Peninsula. In these limited areas, which comprise little more than 5 per cent. of the total area of the Union, the process of economic growth has gone farther and has advanced on a broader front than in any other part of the African continent.

Two-thirds of the African population of the Union are employed in these areas, and although, as has been remarked, the opportunities open to them in the older industries are limited, they are entering newer forms of semi-skilled employment to an extent which may ultimately lead to a radical change in their position in the economy of the Union. It will have its own reactions also in the social and political spheres. It has been estimated that in industries which have been investigated by Wage Boards, 40 per cent. of workers classed as semi-skilled were African, 30 per cent. European, 20 per cent. Coloured, and 10 per cent. Asian. In the metal and engineering industries, which employ a quarter of those engaged in manufacturing, more than 20 per cent. of the labour force consists of semi-skilled non-Europeans. In the rapidly expanding textile industry the majority of operatives are African and Coloured, and their numbers are increasing in the production of leather, clothing, and furniture.[1] There is an obvious shortage of skilled workers in these lines of industry, and it appears inevitable that the deficiency must in time be made up from the ranks of semi-skilled African labour.[2]

South Central Africa

North and east of the Union lies a group of territories which can conveniently be regarded as being within its direct sphere of economic influence. They are the three British territories of Northern and Southern Rhodesia and Nyasaland and the Portuguese territory of Mozambique. In some senses they can be regarded as part of the same broad area of economic growth, for there is a considerable flow of productive resources (chiefly of labour, but also of skills, capital, and raw materials) between these territories and the Union of South Africa. Probably nearly half of the 600,000 non-indigenous Africans working in the Union, for example, originate in this area, chiefly in Mozambique and Nyasaland. There is

---

[1] S. T. van der Horst, 'Industrial Development versus Apartheid', *Listener*, 14 June 1956.

[2] See Social and Economic Planning Council, *The Native Reserves and their Place in the Economy of the Union of South Africa*, U.G. no. 32, 1946.

also a flow of European migrants in the other direction. A little over half of the European immigrants into Northern Rhodesia and over 40 per cent. of those entering Southern Rhodesia in the five years 1947–53 were South African born. Many of the European residents in the three British territories take their holidays and educate their children in the Union, which also exerts a direct attraction on other forms of individual expenditure and investment. Conversely, over 40 per cent. of the capital declared by immigrants into Southern Rhodesia in 1951 came from the Union of South Africa.

Statistics of visible merchandise trade also reflect the increasing dependence of these Central African territories on the centres of industrialization to the south. The market for the expanding manufacturing industry of the Union is spreading north, and the Union is providing a market for the raw materials which these territories can supply. Southern Rhodesia took 31 per cent. of its imports from South Africa and sent 15 per cent. of its exports there during the three-year period 1950–2, and Northern Rhodesia found a market in the Union for nearly 10 per cent. of its exports in the same period.[1] Mozambique took 9 per cent. of its imports from the Union and sent to it 14 per cent. of its exports over the five years ending 1951.[2]

The pattern of economic growth emerging in the two Rhodesias shows some broad similarities with that prevailing in the Union. There is the same focus of economic development in the centres of European settlement and industry, in which the African peoples perform predominantly unskilled work. There are the same vast under-developed expanses of territory in which the majority of the population have their homes, with only little evidence of economic progress or opportunity. There is the same dependence on the mining industry to stimulate and finance a spectacular growth in national income and Government revenues.

Within the framework of the money economy there has been a rapid increase in incomes earned in both territories over the post-war period. In Northern Rhodesia money national income measured by constant prices increased more than threefold in the six-year period 1946–52, and in Southern Rhodesia the rise was of the order of 78 per cent.[3] Much of this increase in incomes earned can be attributed to a vigorous influx of European immigrants and capital. Further, by a change in the domicile of all but two of the mining companies, certain undistributed profits which were

[1] Compiled from the monthly publications of the Central African Statistical Office, *Economic and Statistical Bulletin of Southern Rhodesia* and *Economic and Statistical Bulletin of Northern Rhodesia.*

[2] J. Nunes dos Santos, *Commerce between Mozambique and the Other Territories bordering on the Indian Ocean,* paper read at the Pan-Indian Ocean Science Association, 22 December 1953.

[3] See Central African Statistical Office, *Economic and Statistical Bulletin of Northern Rhodesia,* especially January 1954, for information on the national income &c. of Northern Rhodesia. Money national income here is national income exclusive of subsistence incomes, i.e. of goods and services not exchanged for money.

previously attributable to 'foreign' companies accrue now to Northern Rhodesia. The European population of Northern Rhodesia increased nearly $2\frac{1}{2}$ times between 1946 and 1953, and the share of European individuals and European companies in the money national income of the country increased in the same period from less than half to more than 67 per cent. in 1952. Over the same period the contribution of the mining industry to the domestic output of the money economy rose from $55\frac{1}{2}$ to 65 per cent. Thus the trend has been towards an increased specialization. The price of copper is now more than ever the determinant of money national income and Government revenue in Northern Rhodesia.

In Southern Rhodesia the economy has advanced on a somewhat broader front, although the main developments have been in the European economy.[1] European agriculture accounted for about 16·7 per cent. of domestic output in 1952 and about 14·7 per cent. in 1953. The corresponding percentage for Northern Rhodesia in 1952 was only $2\frac{1}{2}$ per cent. A notable tendency towards industrialization has also appeared in Southern Rhodesia, and the industrial output of the territory increased more than fourfold in the 14 years of the Second World War and post-war period. By 1951, when the total domestic output of Southern Rhodesia was estimated at about £100 million, the net value of output from its secondary industries had reached £34·4 million. The mining industry, which was the chief source of incomes earned by residents in the pre-war period, is now outdistanced by manufacturing, by the distributive trades, and by agriculture.

As in the Union, the speed of the advance has been limited by the rate at which auxiliary services, such as those provided by the transport, power, and building industries, could be expanded to carry the increased load placed upon them. Shortages of coal, for example, due primarily to railway-transport problems, have kept copper output in Northern Rhodesia below the capacity of the industry for some years. Exports of chrome from Southern Rhodesia have also been hampered by shortage of rolling-stock. But a more fundamental factor limiting the expansion of industry in the Rhodesias is the shortage of labour. It is possible to attract more labour to the construction and maintenance of new mining and industrial capacity only at the expense of the agricultural industry, which must itself expand if it is to feed the growing urban population. In view of the high cost of imported food, which makes it an uneconomic basis for further industrial expansion, the only alternative is to make better use of the available labour supply.

In the two other Central African territories local opportunities for large-scale investment are less conspicuous, and consequently European immi-

---

[1] *Southern Rhodesia, Annual Statement of Trade with British Countries and Foreign Countries, 1953,* C.S.R. 13, 1954.

grants and European capital play a relatively smaller part in the sum total of their economic activities. Both territories, however, contribute to the expansion of enterprise in the mining or industrial concentrations located elsewhere in Central or Southern Africa by sending to it a substantial labour force. Altogether more than 260,000 Africans from Mozambique and approximately 150,000 from Nyasaland were estimated to be at work outside the borders of their own countries. Most of their earnings are included in the official national income figures of the countries in which they are received and spent.

The share of Mozambique in the industrial and mineral expansion of Southern and Central Africa is, however, greater than the contribution of its migrant labour, for it controls a strategic coastline. The ports of Beira and Lourenço Marques provide an important outlet to the sea for the prosperous mineral industries of the Rhodesias and the Union. Its share in this rich traffic is a major source of finance for its own imports and its own economic development. Over the ten years 1942–51, for example, two-thirds of the value of the traffic passing through Mozambique was transit trade,[1] and it may be inferred from the deficit on visible trade that the invisible items in the balance of trade (transport charges, migrant labour, and tourists) were more than half the value of the visible items.

If the *per capita* value of imports may be regarded as an index of the level of economic advance achieved by the inhabitants of a given area, then Nyasaland, with imports valued in 1952 at less than £4 per head, is the most backward of the four Central African countries, and Southern Rhodesia, with imports of nearly £40 per head, is the most advanced. The difference between the two territories is not, however, as wide as this comparison would suggest. The value of external trade is a less significant indicator of the level of economic development for a country such as Nyasaland, where subsistence production is an important part of total economic activity, than it is for Southern Rhodesia, where a large proportion of the population live in urban conditions. At the same time, the direct share of the Native peoples in the production and proceeds of total economic activity is greater in a country where there has been successful development of African cash crops than in a country where economic initiative is confined to European individuals and companies and is financed largely by foreign capital. In 1952, for example, more than half the exports of Nyasaland were African cash crops. In Southern Rhodesia, by contrast, Native producers contributed a negligible proportion by value even of the cash crops sold within the territory. It is at the same time noteworthy that in the five crop years ended in 1953 Africans supplied nearly a quarter of the quantity of maize sold and nearly 45 per cent. of the cotton crop. They have thus helped to make the territory self-supporting in maize

[1] Nunes dos Santos, op. cit.

and are also making an important contribution to the raw material of the newly established textile industry.

East Africa

The break in the railway communications places the three British territories of Kenya, Uganda, and Tanganyika beyond the direct sphere of influence of the economic developments in Central and Southern Africa. The trade of the East African territories with South Africa in 1951 amounted to only about 3 per cent. of their combined imports and about 4 per cent. of their combined exports. Most of this was sea-borne trade. Trade with the Rhodesias and Nyasaland was negligible. East Africa is, however, generating its own economic expansion, an expansion which dates almost entirely from the post-war years, following a war period characterized by shortages of manpower, capital goods, and materials. The volume of trade increased from under £23 million in 1938 to £72 million in 1947 and again to £219 million in 1954. The monthly consumption of cement, which averaged 4,400 tons in 1938 and stayed below that level throughout the war, had increased fivefold by 1954. The nominal capital of new local companies registered in the three territories was less than £1½ million in 1938; it fell below this level in the early war years, and had not reached £3½ million by 1945, but rose to nearly £15 million by 1954.[1]

The feature which most distinguishes the East African economies from those of the Southern territories is that they are multi-racial economies in which the rapidly increasing non-European communities take a considerable initiative. The European group is still predominant in the higher-paid occupations, in modern farming for the market, and in large-scale enterprise. But there is a substantial Asian group, larger numerically than the European, which supplies a trader and artisan class in the community. There is also in Uganda (and to a lesser extent in Tanganyika and Kenya) an important trade in African cash crops. In Uganda the cash income of African enterprise was estimated to amount to 34 per cent. of the total geographical income of the Protectorate in 1953, and in Kenya the share of African marketed produce alone averaged about 4½ per cent. of geographical income over the five-year period ended in 1953. There is some element of caste rigidity about the East African multi-racial economy, which is reflected in artificially differing wage-scales, but restrictions on the mobility of labour between occupations are to a larger extent traditional and social rather than political and legal. The barriers between

---

[1] East African Statistical Department, *Quarterly Economic and Statistical Bulletin*, March 1955. Unless otherwise stated this *Bulletin* and earlier issues provide the source of the figures quoted in this section.

groups tend therefore to be less rigid under pressure than in the Union, although they are factors of considerable current importance.

The outstanding characteristic of the pattern of growth which has emerged in Kenya in the post-war period has been a trend towards the broadening of the capitalist sectors of the economy and a relative decline in the subsistence sectors. Profits, interest, and rent elements, for example, which accounted for 31·9 per cent. of the geographical income in 1947, had increased to over 42 per cent. in 1951, dropping back to 35 per cent. in 1953. On the other hand, the share of African agriculture fell from 34 per cent. in 1947 to 26 per cent. in 1953. These structural changes took the form of a shift in favour of European agriculture and of industrial activity at the capitalist level. Non-African agriculture increased its share of geographical income over this period from 13·6 per cent. in 1947 to 20·5 per cent. in 1951 and 15·1 per cent. in 1953. It is estimated that some £40 million has been invested in agriculture in the European Highlands where half of the total agricultural labour force is concentrated.[1] The manufacturing and building industries have also expanded since the war, the share of manufacture rising from 8·5 per cent. in 1947 to 11·6 per cent. in 1953. Some indication of the volume of new activity involved can be gained from the fact that the monthly average sales of electricity in Kenya rose from an average of 1·2 million kW hours in 1938 to a monthly average of 14 million kW hours during the third quarter of 1954. The trend towards an increasing industrialization of the territory seems to be well established, although the present rate of growth may not be maintained.

At the same time the relative decline in African agriculture is a serious problem for a territory with an African population of more than 5¼ million. The pressure on the land resources of Kenya was a problem of some magnitude before the Second World War. The war itself, by creating an extraordinary demand for foodstuffs, encouraged the African population to trench on the fertility of the soil at an even greater rate than overcrowding and overstocking had already induced. The Director of Native Agriculture is reported to have expressed the opinion that the productive capacity of the average acre in African areas had fallen by nearly 50 per cent.[2] Although this may be a somewhat hasty generalization, there is no doubt that there had during this period been an unduly accelerated pressure on the soil. In the long run the only solution to this problem is the adoption of improved methods of agriculture and husbandry by the African population. Meanwhile the territory is highly vulnerable to harvest fluctuations and climatic vicissitudes. Its comparatively narrow margin of

[1] L. G. Troup, *Report of an Inquiry into the General Economy of Farming in the Highlands*, Nairobi, 1953. See also *East Africa Royal Commission 1953–1955*, *Report*, Cmd. 9475, 1955, p. 108.
[2] *Kenya, Report on Native Affairs, 1939–43*, Nairobi, 1947.

self-sufficiency must exercise some restraint on the development of a large industrial population.

The post-war pattern of growth in Tanganyika has been largely influenced by the fact that it was selected to take the main impact of the East African Groundnut Scheme.[1] In the event, although the developments which took place were only a fraction of what was originally planned, the scheme did have a marked effect on the pace of progress made in Tanganyika. By March 1952 fixed assets and stocks set up by the scheme had written-down values of over £6½ million, over £19 million had been spent on development and land-clearing, and over £3½ million had been advanced to the East African Railways and Harbours Administration to finance a new port at Mtwara and a new railway line for the purpose of developing the Southern Province. Between January 1947 and March 1951 when the revised scheme was announced large quantities of machinery, vehicles, and skilled European staff were shipped to Tanganyika. Most of the latter subsequently found alternative employment in East Africa. Schools, hospitals, houses, workshops, and stores were built in the territory, electricity and water supplies were established, and roads and air-strips were constructed and maintained. The immediate effect of the heavy expenditure on the scheme was to increase the shortages in scarce capital goods and transport facilities from which the whole of East Africa suffered in the post-war period. It also gave an impetus to inflationary tendencies already present and created difficult problems of readjustment when the scheme was revised. The more permanent effect has been to provide the territory with an improved stock of capital which, though it might have been better utilized from the point of view of the economy as a whole, was a windfall addition to its resources.

The new capital and the new services were, however, designed to support an agricultural expansion, and the scheme reinforced the tendency for Tanganyika to develop as an essentially agricultural country. The majority of the African population is primarily engaged in subsistence cultivation, and there is an important leaven not only of African cash crops but also of large-scale estate agriculture. More than 50 per cent. of the value of exports in 1952 was produced on large estates and a further third emanated originally from African peasant production. About one in five of adult African males were in paid employment in July 1952, about half of them in agriculture, and a further 52,000 women and juveniles also found employment, mainly in agriculture. Their combined wage bill was probably in the region of about £1 million. A small mining industry contributed about 9 per cent. of the total value of exports over the four years 1950–3 and engaged less than 4 per cent. of Africans in employment in 1952. Industry has been largely a by-product of agriculture, and even including electricity

---

[1] See above, pp. 845 ff.

employed only about 5 per cent. of the Africans who were in employment in 1952.

In spite of the fact that Tanganyika's economic development remains orientated towards agriculture there has been some growth in its urban population in the past few years, although by 1948 only 2 per cent. of the total population resided in the urban centres.[1] Twelve main towns had 127,000 Africans at the census of 1948 and the same towns reported 164,000 at the census of 1952, while the total African population was over 7¾ million. The European population increased from 11,000 to 18,000 in the five years ending in 1952, and the Asian population from about 58,000 to 73,000 in the same period. For 1954 population estimates were: Africans 8 million, Europeans 22,500, and Asians 85,000. This expansion of population is exerting a considerable pressure on supplies of housing and other urban services.[2]

A similar tendency for economic growth to be based on agriculture is observable in Uganda with the difference, however, that African agriculture is as much the main basis of the money economy as it is of the subsistence economy. African subsistence income was estimated in 1953 to account for 31 per cent. of the incomes produced in the territory and African cash incomes, exclusive of salaries and wages, for a further 34 per cent. The most important manufacturing industries are those concerned in the processing of agricultural produce—notably cotton, tobacco, sugar, and coffee. For the most part these are owned and operated by Asians, but the trend towards African ownership and control is being fostered by legislative and administrative measures. Legislative provision has also been made to reserve to African enterprise the right to expand capacity in either cotton ginning or coffee hulling up to a certain level of total output and to give preference to African enterprise in permitting further developments when production rises above the prescribed level. It is characteristic of the territory that there is already a very considerable area of land held by Africans on individual proprietary tenure.[3]

Unlike any of the territories to the south of it, therefore, Uganda is being deliberately developed as a territory of small-scale African entrepreneurs united, where possible, in African co-operative organizations. In this type of development the Government must necessarily take a considerable measure of initiative, and a public corporation, the Uganda Development Corporation, has been set up to investigate and promote the industrial development of the Protectorate. It has acquired interests in such widely varying projects as are involved in the fish-marketing and deep-water fishing industries, the Lake Victoria Hotel, the cement industry, the textile factory, and the copper-mining enterprise. Prospects of profitable industrial development in the territory are greatly enhanced by the Owen

[1] Cmd. 9475, 1955, p. 203.   [2] Ibid. pp. 200 ff.   [3] See above, p. 724.

Falls hydroelectric scheme which is designed to have an ultimate capacity of 150,000 kW. The total cost of the project is estimated at approximately £30 million.[1]

The pace of Government-inspired development in Uganda accelerated rapidly in the period following the Second World War. The expenditure on new buildings and roads rose from £364,000 in 1947 to £1,886,000 in 1951. The first section of the new railway, which was to serve the projected copper-mine at Kilembe, was opened in 1953.[2] At the same time the agricultural economy expanded under the influence of high world prices. Between 1947 and 1950 the value of exports had increased by nearly 150 per cent.; between 1950 and 1952 they increased by another 65 per cent., and the geographical income of Uganda went up by 46 per cent. It should be remembered, however, that some of these indexes of development reflect changes in the distribution of the national income and in the value of money rather than an upward movement in national productivity or in real incomes. Thus the main source of finance for Government-inspired development has been high taxation of agricultural producers. It is by no means certain that State expenditure necessarily promotes development of an economy more effectively or more rapidly than expenditure by private enterprise.

The economy of the Belgian Congo is more broadly based than that of any other African Colonial territory. It enjoys mineral wealth and hydroelectric resources comparable to those of the Rhodesias, and Native agricultural resources comparable to those of Uganda. In 1950 the agricultural exports of the Congo and Ruanda Urundi were 24 per cent. of all agricultural exports of Central Africa, and its mineral exports were 41 per cent. of all those emanating from the region.[3] In 1953 nearly 25 per cent. of its gross national product was attributable to African agriculture and more than 21 per cent. to the mining industry.[4] Nearly 56 per cent. of the national income was received by Africans; more than 14 per cent. entered into the profits of companies. The former provide the solid basis of African purchasing power which is essential to a balanced economic development of the country, while the latter create the concentrations of finance which make capitalist development possible and worth while.

A marked expansion of economic activity took place during the Second World War when the loss to the Allies of the products of South-East Asia gave the Belgian Congo a market for almost every commodity it could produce. Its chief products—copper, tin, palm oil, cotton, coffee, and rubber—were in urgent demand. Its strategic and economic importance

---

[1] See above, p. 995.   [2] See below, pp. 1508, 1558.
[3] R. Bertiaux, *Aspects de l'industrialisation en Afrique centrale*, 1953, pp. 34, 73. (Central Africa is defined in this work as including both North Central Africa and South Central Africa).
[4] *Bulletin de la Banque Centrale du Congo Belge et du Ruanda-Urundi*, October 1954.

was henceforth assured. Stimulated by these incentives of world demand, rising African purchasing power, and steadily accumulating company profits, the territory made great economic strides in the post-war period. Between 1950 and 1952 the value of its gross national product increased by nearly 50 per cent. in money terms and by 28 per cent. in real terms. The share of the African population in the national income increased from 52 to nearly 56 per cent. Net investment averaged about a quarter of the national income in the four years 1950–3. Private investment was more than two-thirds of the total gross investment. Industry, including processing of agricultural products, accounted for over 10 per cent. of the gross national product by 1953; industry, excluding the processing of agricultural products (i.e. metal industries, textiles, food, drink and tobacco, and electricity), increased its volume of output by over two-thirds between 1950 and 1952.

The chief limiting factor to this rapid process of expansion is the shortage of labour. The Colony appears to have reached the limit of its available labour force.[1] Any attempt to attract more labour to the centres of growing industry must in present conditions result in a decline in agricultural output. To maintain recent rates of growth it will be necessary to improve the capital equipment of both agriculture and industry and to train labour to higher levels of skill. The Belgian Congo has already made marked progress in the training of Africans in semi-skilled and even skilled employment; but if the increasing demand for labour is to be met this progress must be further accelerated.

The economies of Angola and French Equatorial Africa stand in striking contrast to the economy of their neighbour, the Belgian Congo. They remain among the least developed of African territories. In 1950, for example, the agricultural exports of French Equatorial Africa accounted for over 91 per cent. of the Colony's total exports, but for only about 7 per cent. of the agricultural exports of Central Africa as a whole; the corresponding proportions for Angola were 80 per cent. and 13 per cent.[2]

The post-war rise in the prices of primary products brought some increase in incomes to these underdeveloped territories, but they were not well enough equipped to take permanent advantage of it. Although the history of European settlement in Angola is older than that of any of the other Central African territories, there is little difference between the economic conditions of the settlers and those of the poorer class of peasants in Portugal. By South African standards they fall into the category of 'poor Whites', and in spite of a serious shortage of African labour there has been very little mechanization of European agriculture. It is significant that in 1951, at the height of the prosperity induced by high prices for sisal and coffee,

---

[1] Kredietbank, ed., *La Situation économique de la Belgique et du Congo Belge, 1951–1952*, October 1952.   [2] Bertiaux, op. cit., pp. 34, 62.

imports of agricultural machinery were equal to only 1 per cent. of total imports.[1]

Cotton is grown in Angola by some 57,000 African producers out of a total African population of more than 4 million, and the fisheries occupy about 16,000 fishermen. Smaller numbers are employed in the diamond mines, in estate agriculture, in the few small-scale industries such as fish canning, and in the production of cement, sugar, and textiles. By far the major part of the African population is engaged in subsistence production and finds insufficient incentive within the territory to enter into the activities of the money economy.

A somewhat similar situation exists in French Equatorial Africa. A few industries have been established to process local products in response to the small domestic demand for such commodities as soap, meal, footwear, and cement. They may be able to reduce their costs and extend their market when the various schemes for expansion of electrical power in the Congo Basin come to fruition. But these secondary industries cannot of themselves provide the foundation for a significant development of industrialization. They are merely by-products of a flow of incomes generated at the primary level. Unless new mineral resources are discovered and the agricultural industry receives the stimulus needed to encourage expansion of output (as, for instance, through provision of new transport or the improvement of marketing and processing systems), these territories are unlikely to achieve a rate of development comparable to that of their neighbours.

West Africa

Within this large area, with a total population of roughly 63 million, there exists a wide variety of conditions and stages of development. They range from areas which have barely started to move away from the most primitive subsistence type of economy to the cocoa-growing areas of the Gold Coast where, in a year of good world prices, subsistence incomes may account for as little as 10 per cent. of the incomes of the agricultural community.[2] The characteristic which distinguishes the region as a whole from most of the other areas of Africa south of the Sahara is that European or Asian settlement has, for climatic or similar reasons, been negligible. This factor, combined, in some areas, with the existence of physical resources which have offered a wide scope for African initiative, has materially affected the course of economic progress in West Africa. Its most characteristic feature is the extent of purely African development.

This does not mean that the non-African contribution to development has been unimportant. The role of the important non-African trading enterprises in opening up the channels of intercourse with the world economy

[1] *Overseas Economic Surveys, Portuguese West Africa (Angola), 1954*, p. 27.
[2] R. Galletti, K. D. S. Baldwin, and I. O. Dina, *Nigerian Cocoa Farmers*, 1956, p. 444.

has been a prime mover in the development of peasant cash-crop economies. Again, the European mining companies accounted in 1937 for 59 per cent. of the domestic exports of Sierra Leone, and for 35 and 15 per cent. of those of the Gold Coast and Nigeria respectively. They have thus contributed a flow of incomes to West African peoples and Governments which has been far from negligible. The effect on the development of systems of communications, in particular, has been very marked. Plantation enterprises in the French Cameroons, in Liberia, and in the French irrigation colony in the valley of the Niger, have created expanding economic opportunities where few existed before. In Liberia the output of rubber increased more than tenfold between 1937 and 1949.[1]

In spite of these external stimuli, however, the chief focus of development in West Africa is the indigenous community. The typical entrepreneur, on whose activity the national levels of output depend, and the typical consumer, whose needs determine the factors of consumption and investment, are Africans. This area therefore presents in a significant form those basic problems of African economic development which are relatively obscured in areas where the allocation of resources is determined by settled immigrant communities. The main basis of economic growth in West Africa is the agriculture, forestry, and fishing group of industries. National income inquiries in French West Africa and the French Cameroons have suggested that these industries account for more than two-thirds of the national income.[2] For Nigeria it has been estimated that in 1950–1 farm crops accounted for nearly 50 per cent. of the gross domestic product, and livestock, fishing, and forest products for another 18½ per cent.[3] In the Gold Coast cocoa production alone has been estimated to account for nearly 37 per cent. of the traded output of the territory.[4]

These estimates are, however, inclusive of local transport and distribution costs and partly obscure some of the diversification of the West African economy as it has now developed.[5] The new peasant economies of West Africa have provided the population with many additional sources of income besides the production of cash crops. The picture as seen today includes 'petty traders, women dealers and the hundred and one minor professions' (such as rainmakers, cattle fatteners, sword makers, money changers, Native herbalists, calabash cutters, palm wine tappers, and charm makers—to select only a few).[6] Their incomes are not susceptible

[1] United Nations, Department of Economic Affairs, *Review of Economic Conditions in Africa* (Supplement to *World Economic Report, 1949–50*), 1951.

[2] Luc B. de Carbon, 'L'Afrique noire', *L'Économie de l'Union française d'outre-mer*, 1952.

[3] A. R. Prest and I. G. Stewart, *The National Income of Nigeria, 1950–51*, Colonial Research Studies no. 11, 1953, p. 24.

[4] D. Seers and C. R. Ross, *Report on Financial and Physical Problems of Development in the Gold Coast*, Accra, 1952.

[5] P. T. Bauer and E. S. Yamey, 'Economic Progress and Occupational Distribution', *Economic Journal*, December 1951.   [6] Prest and Stewart, op. cit. p. 54.

of detailed classification, but together produce an output of goods and services estimated at more than 85 per cent. of the gross domestic product of Nigeria. Many of these are subsidiary occupations of the farmer or members of his family. An economic survey of the cocoa-producing areas of Nigeria showed that less than two-thirds of the occupied males gave farming as their only occupation. On the other hand, nearly a third of the occupied females gave trading as their only occupation, and in some areas, as in Ibadan, the figure was more than half. In all areas covered by this survey about three-quarters of the occupied persons (including males and females) were engaged in farming, while half the occupied population was in trade (many persons combining both occupations).[1]

Unlike most of Central and Southern Africa West Africa has developed a remarkable complex of internal trade and of local markets. This is partly a result of the great variety of local resources and partly due to the stimulus provided by the extent of the export crops. A study of the network of interrelationships reveals a widely ranging spirit of initiative and enterprise. Hausa merchants, for example, buy cattle from Fulani herdsmen in the north of Nigeria, drive them south, sell them in the cocoa-producing areas, and use the money to buy kola nuts which are taken back to be sold in Northern Nigeria or the French Sudan. The proceeds are reinvested in cattle to repeat the cycle.[2] Thus the incentive provided by high world prices for West Africa's crops is conveyed deep into the hinterland. In Northern Zaria, for example, where the Hausa depend principally on a grain-farming type of agriculture, a survey undertaken in 1949 showed that the average subsistence ratio (that is, the ratio of goods produced for own consumption to the total value of goods consumed) was only 46 per cent., but the range extended from below 6 to 75 per cent.[3] There is an extensive trade in foodstuffs for local consumption not only between the coastal areas and the inland districts but also within the inland areas.[4]

The effect of such a lively system of internal trade is to spread the influence of a mounting rise in world market prices for West Africa's export crops over a wider area than that actually producing them. This reinforces the tendency for the price realized to be distributed amongst many recipients. In the British West African cocoa trade, for example, the crop passes through a host of middlemen on its way between farmer and Marketing Board; they range from the buyer, who collects an annual average of three or four tons, to the licensed buying agent who buys in thousands of tons and sells in tens of thousands to the final purchaser, the Marketing Board. Each time the crop changes hands it is taken a little farther on its journey and is built up into larger parcels. A similar process

---

[1] Galletti, Baldwin, and Dina, op. cit., p. 201.   [2] Ibid. p. 60.
[3] M. G. Smith, 'A Study of Hausa Domestic Economy in Northern Zaria', *Africa*, October 1952, pp. 333 ff.   [4] Prest and Stewart, op. cit. pp. 96 ff.

in reverse takes place with imports which pass from European or Levantine importing firms to their retail department stores and thence to smaller retailers and market traders and eventually to street traders with a turnover of perhaps only two or three transactions a day. At each stage the goods break bulk until the ultimate transaction may be as small as a single cigarette or ten matches. Thus the character of the economic process is such as to produce what is, by the standards of Central and South Africa, a relative equality in the distribution of incomes. The share of non-African residents and of non-African capital in the gross domestic product of Nigeria has been estimated to amount to less than 2 per cent. of the whole. The share of Africans is split among a multitude of producers and, although this does not preclude the receipt of large incomes by individual Africans, there are social forces at work which tend to reduce the freely disposable incomes of individuals. Foremost among these forces is the traditional obligation on wealthy Africans to support dependent relatives, indigent members of the same tribe, and a large number of professional beggars.[1]

The effect of this fragmentation of incomes is to impede the development of a substantial class of African capitalists. Moreover, by reducing both the means and the incentives for expenditure on durable goods, it retards the rate of capital formation by the small-scale producer. In a survey of the cocoa-producing areas of Nigeria it was found that among the Yoruba the value of clothing possessed was four times as great as the value of farm equipment and household goods together. An inquiry into the banking systems of the Colonies suggested that West Africans were inhibited from making an effective use of banking facilities by the fear that they would thereby expose their wealth to the claims of their relatives.[2] If the personal sector of the economy has a high propensity to consume and the corporate sector controls a negligible proportion of the nation's resources, it may be appropriate to create corporate institutions or to divert a relatively large volume of resources through the Government sector. One solution to this kind of problem is to develop producers' co-operative societies and to facilitate investment by small producers through co-operative channels.[3]

Another solution is to initiate investment at the Governmental level. Since most of the export crops are now marketed through statutory buying agencies it is possible to direct investment by keeping back part of the purchase price and spending it on capital formation. This has been done to some extent in British West Africa where the Marketing Boards have used part of their accumulated surplus to finance Development Schemes for the benefit of the areas in which the crops are produced. It is claimed that impressive results have been achieved by these means in the Nigerian

[1] Ibid. p. 5.
[2] I. Greaves, *Colonial Monetary Conditions*, Colonial Research Studies no. 10, 1953, p. 41.
[3] See below, pp. 1455 ff.

palm-oil industry, but it is arguable that the direct investments of peasant producers who are given an adequate price incentive would be more effective than the investments made on their behalf by a Government agency.[1]

Coupled with price incentives designed to favour the high-quality product, the introduction of simple forms of mechanical processing, such as Pioneer mills and mechanical hand-presses, has helped to bring about a marked improvement in the value of output. Between 1950–1 and 1953–4 the quantity of palm oil purchased in Nigeria increased by more than a third, and the quantity of special-grade oil increased more than tenfold.[2] Between 1950 and 1952 the value of output increased by more than 50 per cent., and the Nigerian industry was in an appreciably better position to compete with the high-grade oil produced under scientific methods of plantation in the Belgian Congo and South East Asia.

It is also possible to use funds, accumulated through taxation or Government-guaranteed borrowing, to finance loans to small producers. In principle this would introduce a greater flexibility into the character of new capital formation than a method which involved direct purchase of capital goods by a statutory authority. In practice this method involves the assumption of extensive responsibilities for direct supervision on the part of the administering authority or its agents, and this of itself will reduce the range of projects which can be so assisted. In a report on industrialization in the Gold Coast emphasis is laid on the fact that 'what potential African industrialists lack is not primarily money; it is rather technical knowledge and experience of factory organization', and reference is made in this connexion to the experience of the Gold Coast Industrial Development Corporation.[3] Technical expertise and managerial capacity are qualities which a specially devised system of training ought, in due course, to provide in sufficient quantity to meet the initial needs of industry. The only immediate solution is to import them from more developed economies.

Another limitation on the ability of the small capitalist to take advantage of the new opportunities for industrialization now appearing in West Africa is the difficulty, under the complex land laws, of obtaining suitable land and buildings. To this must be added the problem of finding the capital to construct buildings. A report on economic development in Nigeria remarked that 'many desirable African enterprises are handicapped by the scarcity of suitable building space for rent. It is difficult enough for the small industrialist to raise capital for machinery and a working reserve; if land must be purchased and a factory built the total investment is often out

[1] See below, pp. 1314 ff.

[2] *Barclays Bank Overseas Review, 1953*, London, 1954. See also United Africa Company, *Statistical and Economic Review*, March 1954, for a description of the contribution of Pioneer mills to the Nigerian industry.

[3] W. A. Lewis, *Report on Industrialization and the Gold Coast*, Accra, 1953, pp. 12 ff.

of reach.'[1] The report went on to advocate the establishment by the Government of industrial estates in suitable urban localities. By providing land and buildings and such other basic amenities as power and water at moderate prices, it may be possible to attract into productive enterprise indigenous resources which would otherwise flow into unproductive channels.

In effect, although the spirit of enterprise is lively among West Africans and although the rising prices of export crops have favoured the development of small-scale indigenous industries, there has been little improvement of industry apart from that which has been centrally inspired. Indeed, as rising farm incomes put imported manufactures within the reach of consumers, output of village industry may well fall. In the towns the inflation produced by the post-war combination of higher incomes and restricted imports has encouraged speculative types of investment as, for example, in distribution and residential building at the expense of more long-term projects.[2]

Meanwhile, although the proportion of national output contributed by agriculture (and the dependent distribution industries) has tended to increase in recent years, there are certain limiting factors to the expansion of the agricultural industry. Most of the West African territories have shown a tendency to concentrate on a narrow range of crops. Gambia, with 97 per cent. of its export income derived from groundnuts, is the classic example of a one-crop economy, and the prominence of cocoa in the economy of the Gold Coast needs no emphasis. In French West Africa in 1950 groundnuts and coffee accounted for two-thirds of exports and in the French Cameroons coffee and cocoa for 62 per cent. It is possible to over-emphasize the vulnerability of these economies since there is also a large element of stability furnished by the growth of subsistence production, but the increasing concentration on a few export crops does actually affect the balance of the West African economies in a number of ways. The high cash returns to be gained from growing these crops have induced an increase in the amount of land and labour devoted to them and a decrease in the resources given to food crops; they have also increased the length of time in which land has been kept under cultivation and decreased the periods of fallowing. In parts of West Africa these developments are reflected in growing land hunger, soil deterioration, and falling crop yields.[3]

For areas which are dependent on cocoa additional sources of uncer-

---

[1] International Bank for Reconstruction and Development, *The Economic Development of Nigeria*, 1955, p. 361.

[2] D. Seers and C. R. Ross, *Report on Financial and Physical Problems of Development in the Gold Coast*, Accra, 1952.

[3] M. Prothero, 'Some Problems of Land Use Survey in Nigeria', *Economic Geography*, January 1954.

tainty are the swollen shoot disease and the marked inelasticity of supply.[1] Although the outbreaks of disease have been less extensive in Nigeria, there may well be some temporary decline in output as a result of the decreased amount of planting which occurred in the depression of the thirties. The level of current output of cocoa depends largely on the age of existing plantations, and the level of future output on the inducements now offered to the farmer to invest in new trees. A cocoa-tree begins to bear five to seven years after planting, and the peak yield seems to be reached when farms are 18 to 22 years old. Thereafter yields tend to decline. Here more than elsewhere it is necessary to frame economic policy in the light of its long-term repercussions.

PROBLEMS OF PUBLIC FINANCE

A notable feature of the history of all the African territories in the past two decades has been an expansion of the economic activity of Governments. In part this is a reflection of a general change in the political climate which emerged very clearly after the depression of the thirties. The duty of Governments actively to intervene in the economic field was no longer seriously in dispute when the Second World War broke out. During the war itself, Government controls became a standing feature of public policy. By the time the war was over the belief that an efficient economic policy demanded planning at the Government level had become an axiom. The Development Plans which were the practical expression of this principle will be considered in the next chapter. Something should be said, however, at this point about the ways in which the ordinary budgets of Public Authorities have been adapted to the needs of the economies which they serve.

It is in the dependent territories that the recent developments have produced the most striking changes in public finance. In the Union of South Africa the line of advance had been well established before the Second World War. The existence of the gold-mining industry had provided the Government with the taxable capacity requisite for its ordinary needs. In 1935–6 special mining taxation was responsible for 27 per cent. of the revenue, and in addition a considerable share of the total was provided by the taxation of incomes derived from mining. In 1951–2 the gold-mining industry was still the principal taxpayer in the Union and direct mining taxation alone accounted for 15 per cent. of the national budget. The total tax revenue of the Union Government and of the provincial Administrations has risen from £9·7 million in 1913 to £36·7 million in 1935 and £187·4 million in 1951.

Probably the most significant change in the budgetary position of the

[1] See above, p. 829.

Union in the post-war period by comparison with pre-war years occurred in the composition of the public debt. The gross public debt increased from £262·6 million in 1937–8 to £648·7 million in 1947–8, but whereas external debt accounted for 38½ per cent. of the total in the earlier year, it supplied only about 2 per cent. in 1947–8. The urgent need to expand the rate of capital formation in the public sector, which lagged far behind the private sector in the immediate post-war years, led to a considerable increase in borrowing abroad in 1949 and 1950, but by the end of March 1953 external debt was still only 5·7 per cent. of a total gross public debt of £842·4 million.[1] No other African territory can at present supply as much as half of its public loan finance from internal sources. Even in Southern Rhodesia national debt interest paid abroad was about half the total interest in 1946 and nearly 60 per cent. in 1952. This increase was due mainly to the purchase by the Government of Rhodesian Railways, which raised the proportion of national debt interest flowing abroad to nearly 70 per cent. in 1948.[2] In the dependent territories the bulk of the interest on national debt still flows abroad.

For most of the African dependent territories the problem of public finance in the inter-war years was a problem of constructing, and then of maintaining, the essential framework of administrative capital equipment in territories which had scarcely begun to finance their own administration. For some of these territories it was a period of deficits, of growing indebtedness, and of lagging revenues. Between 1913 and 1925 the funded debt of the British territories, other than the Union of South Africa, increased from £12·5 million to £63·7 million, and between 1925 and 1932 there was a further increase to £95·9 million. In these circumstances the advent of the years of depression in world prices was a serious setback to development. Between 1929 and 1932, with loan commitments still increasing, revenues were falling. In the dependent British territories they fell from £28 million in 1929 to less than £23 million in 1932. In French Equatorial Africa debt charges still amounted to as much as 40 per cent. of public expenditure in 1937; in the Belgian Congo the proportion was as high as 47 per cent. in 1934. In Liberia revenues fell by 75 per cent. and expenditure by 82 per cent. between 1928 and 1933. By contrast, in the Portuguese territories of Angola and Mozambique where basic development had lagged behind that of the other African dependencies, public debt charges formed a relatively inconsiderable element in total expenditure.

The decade of the thirties therefore began with drastic economies in most territories. Between 1929 and 1932 the European establishment of the Gold Coast was reduced from 1,281 to 437. In Northern Rhodesia, where the end of the period of construction of the copper-mines coincided with a collapse in the world price of copper, a general reduction of activities involved

---

[1] *O.Y.S.A., 1952–53,* p. 646.   [2] *O.Y.S.R., 1952,* p. 610. See also below, p. 1552.

a considerable curtailment of plans for building the new capital at Lusaka. In the French Colonies a programme of retrenchment was launched involving the reduction of Colonial budgets from 3,642 million francs in 1930 to 2,476 million francs in 1934. Schemes for capital development were sharply curtailed.

In the French and Belgian, as in the British dependencies, the metropolitan Government made substantial direct contributions to Colonial budgets in the form of grants and interest-free loans. In 1937 French West Africa received a subvention of 79 million francs—a sum almost equal to the entire debt charges of the territory in that year. In the four years 1934–7 the Belgian Government granted a total of 640 million francs to cover deficits in the budget of the Belgian Congo. British Government aid to the African Colonies went beyond the subvention of unavoidable deficits; in the nine years following the establishment of the Colonial Development Fund in 1929, a total of over £4 million was paid in grants and in interest-free loans to African Colonies, in addition to grants or loans to meet budget deficits in particular territories.[1]

The Second World War changed the financial situation of the dependent territories in a number of ways. The demand for their products, and with it their public revenues, increased and the burden of their public debts lightened as the value of money fell. For most of them the period of financial stringency was over. In the immediate post-war years the limitations on their expenditure were of a physical nature springing from local shortages of manpower and basic equipment and world shortages of capital goods. The effects of these changes can be seen, first, in the greatly increased amounts of the Colonial budgets; second, in the changed pattern of expenditure; and, third, in the reshaping of the sources of revenue. In the 15 years between 1936–7 and 1951–2 ordinary expenditure by the British Colonial Governments rose nearly eight and a half times, whereas the level of costs, as far as can be judged from admittedly inadequate data, has probably not increased more than four times. This increase of expenditure was actually a little greater than the increase in the value of exports from the countries concerned over the same period. Still greater increases took place in the money value of French Colonial budgets, where the fall in the value of the currency was much greater. In French West and Equatorial Africa local budget expenditures multiplied eight times between 1946 and 1951 alone, whereas the cost of living and the amount of money in circulation increased only four times. The ordinary expenditure of the Belgian Congo in 1951 was 4,963 million francs, compared with 686 million francs in 1935, and over the same period the cost of living for Europeans doubled. In Liberia Government expenditures, which only

[1] For a full account of the pre-war financial history of the African territories south of the Sahara, see S. H. Frankel, *Capital Investment in Africa*, 1938.

exceeded $1 million between 1930 and 1942 and fell to under a quarter of a million in 1933, exceeded $10 million in 1951.

The main changes in the pattern of expenditure are illustrated in the following table, which distinguishes a few broad categories of Government expenditure (excluding loan expenditure) in the British dependencies.[1]

TABLE II. *Analysis of Expenditure by British Dependencies 1936–7 and 1951–2*

(in percentage of total expenditure)

	Debt Charges		Defence and Administration		Development and social Services		Non-effective (including Pensions, Transfers to Reserves, &c.)	
	1936–7	*1951–2*	*1936–7*	*1951–2*	*1936–7*	*1951–2*	*1936–7*	*1951–2*
Basutoland . . .	..	0·2	38·0	31·2	57·4	58·4	4·6	10·3
Bechuanaland . .	..	..	43·7	24·4	47·7	63·8	8·6	13·8
Gambia . . .	1·1	0·2	55·6	16·2	33·4	73·4	9·9	10·2
Gold Coast . . .	3·7	2·0	35·4	27·8	44·3	62·6	16·6	7·6
Kenya . . .	9·9	4·5	43·0	28·2	36·5	38·3	10·6	29·0
Nigeria . . .	21·4	3·5	35·9	14·2	29·3	34·7	13·4	47·6
Northern Rhodesia .	16·2	2·9	43·4	18·5	31·3	37·2	9·1	41·4
Nyasaland . . .	15·8	5·1	40·3	17·4	32·2	66·9	11·7	10·6
Sierra Leone . .	7·2	3·3	38·8	15·5	35·3	67·9	18·7	13·3
Swaziland . . .	2·7	0·6	38·9	17·1	54·9	73·8	3·5	8·5
Tanganyika . . .	7·7	1·5	52·3	25·7	31·8	50·4	8·2	22·4
Uganda . . .	8·4	1·7	44·9	14·9	40·9	52·3	5·8	31·1

The most striking change brought out by this comparison of the ordinary expenditure of the Colonial Governments before and after the Second World War is the fall in the proportion allocated to debt charges and to administration and defence. An increase in the non-effective expenditure in some territories is due to transfers to reserves or redemption of debt, which reflect a tendency to use part of the abnormally high revenues of the post-war period to insure against possible future reductions in revenues. For the British group as a whole, however, the proportion of expenditures absorbed by debt charges fell from 11·6 per cent. of total ordinary expenditure in 1936 to a little more than 2 per cent. in 1951; the proportion absorbed by administration and defence fell from nearly 40 per cent. to less than 21 per cent. To some extent these changes reflect an inflationary situation in which salaries and interest charges have risen more slowly than other costs, and to some extent they are the result of an increase in the administrative responsibilities shouldered by Local Authorities; at the same

[1] The 1936–7 figures are derived from the table given in the 1938 edition of the African Survey, p. 1433. The 1951–2 figures are actuals extracted from *Colonial Reports*. The totals of public income and expenditure in the British Colonial territories are given annually in the Report to Parliament of the Secretary of State for the Colonies; see, for example, *The Colonial Territories, 1952–53*, Cmd. 8856, 1953.

time there has occurred a marked widening of the sphere of Government activity.

In effect, therefore, a much larger proportion of public expenditure is now being devoted to nation-building services or to insurance against future depression of prices, and a much smaller proportion is now required for the overhead expenses of pure administration and the service of the public debt. Principles of classification of expenditure vary so much in practice among the different Colonial Governments that a more detailed comparative analysis is impossible without extensive research. Nevertheless a rough allocation of the development expenditures between economic and social services suggests that there is, in the British Colonies at any rate, a tendency for a greater emphasis to be placed on the basic economic services and a correspondingly reduced emphasis on the social services. This shift of emphasis has taken place within expanding budgets and is thus consistent with an increase in the absolute level of expenditure on social services. It does mean, however, that their expansion is now deemed to be less important than an expansion in the economic development services which are expected to have a more direct effect on the improvement of public revenues and which, if they fulfil expectations, will ultimately finance a higher standard of purely welfare services. Allowance should also be made in some territories for a tendency to transfer the responsibility for social services to Local Authorities. In other territories there has been a transfer of responsibility for education from the missions to the Central Government.

Similar trends towards a reduction in the burden of debt and administrative charges are observable in other African dependencies. In the Belgian Congo the expenditure of public authorities on debt charges had fallen to less than 6 per cent. in 1952 from a level of over 40 per cent. in pre-war years. Transfers to a budgetary reserve fund amounted to over 4,200 million francs between 1947 and 1952. In a statement on the ordinary budget estimates for 1952 the Minister for Colonies emphasized the need to provide a budget reserve which would serve to bear the maintenance charges of the Ten-year Development Plan and guarantee financial stability in the event of the recurrence of a period of economic depression.[1]

The partial assimilation of French Colonial finances to the metropolitan budget (which bears the cost of defence and of joint services) renders the individual Colonial budgets incomplete as a reflection of public expenditure. The Colonial budgets themselves make a contribution of about 1 per cent. of their total expenditure to the metropolitan budget for these purposes. It is, nevertheless, significant that general administrative charges (exclusive of defence) still absorb a relatively high proportion of public

---

[1] Quoted by E. Coart, 'Les Budgets du Congo Belge et du Ruanda-Urundi', *Enc. C.B.*, vol. iii, p. 563.

expenditure in the French Colonies. In the 1952 estimates about 33 per cent. was allocated to administration in Equatorial Africa and the Cameroons, and about 30 per cent. in West Africa and Togo. Even more noteworthy is the fact that the social services continue to constitute a relatively important charge on the local budgets. In both French West and French Equatorial Africa the estimated expenditure on social services in 1952 was about 30 per cent. of the total budget, while the former devoted 32 per cent. and the latter 29 per cent. to economic services. In Togo in the same year social services accounted for 42 per cent. and economic services for 24 per cent. of local budgeted expenditure. In the Cameroons the corresponding figures were 33 and 27 per cent.[1] There is thus some danger that the expenditure on social services in the French Colonies may outrun the ability of the Colonial budgets to support them unless the Development Programmes financed out of metropolitan grants and loans bear fruit in the form of permanently increased revenues.

The alteration in the character of Colonial revenues as a result of the Second World War and post-war developments has shown itself in a marked change of emphasis away from the more static types of revenue (such as poll taxes and specific customs duties) in favour of the more dynamic types, such as income taxes and export taxes. In Northern Rhodesia, for example, income and profit taxes accounted in 1951 for more than 67 per cent. of total Government revenue, and royalties added another 8 per cent. Direct taxes and export duties together accounted for as much as 54 per cent of revenue in the Gold Coast in 1953–4. Conversely, direct taxes of a non-progressive type have tended to fall in importance in all areas. In Uganda, where in 1935 the direct Native tax contributed 38 per cent. of the Protectorate's revenue, the proportion had fallen to a little over 3 per cent. in 1955. In Tanganyika it had dropped in 1953 to 12 per cent. from $34\frac{1}{2}$ per cent. in 1935. Even in Basutoland and Nyasaland, where economic development has been far from spectacular in its effect on income distribution or on levels of output, similar reductions have taken place in the proportion derived from direct Native taxation. In the French African territories direct taxation furnished between 15 and 20 per cent. of budget revenue in 1952.[2]

A striking feature of post-war Colonial revenues, however, has been the growing importance of export duties in a number of territories. In Uganda they accounted for nearly 43 per cent. of total Government revenue in 1952 and in the French Cameroons for 28 per cent. The export taxes are derived mainly from a limited range of commodities whose prices are determined in world markets, with the result that the yield of these taxes forms a potentially unstable item in Colonial revenues. In Uganda, for

[1] P. Sanner, 'Budgets et fiscalité des territoires d'outre-mer', *L'Économie de l'Union française d'outre-mer*, 1952, pp. 293 ff.   [2] See also above, p. 681.

example, where about 98 per cent. of the export taxes are derived from cotton and coffee alone, the yield rose from under £3 million in 1949 to over £8 million in 1952 and went back to about £4 million in 1953, to rise again to over £6 million in 1955. Territories such as Uganda and some of the British and French West African Colonies, which have come to rely heavily on export taxes, have simplified their revenue problem in the short run, but they cannot be said to have solved it in the long run. A substantial part of their revenue now depends on the fortunes of a particular group of producers, and while these producers enjoy favourable terms of trade with the rest of the world the public revenues prosper accordingly. If the prices of the commodities concerned return to lower levels, however, the fall in revenues will be phenomenal. These Governments are therefore still faced with the major problem of Colonial finance, namely, that of devising a system of taxation that will adapt itself to the fortunes of the broad mass of the people.

As shown in a previous chapter,[1] direct progressive taxation of individuals engaged mainly in production on their own account is not easy to organize effectively in any country. It raises formidable problems where the general level of money incomes is low and where ordinary standards of commercial accounting are unfamiliar to the producer. In these circumstances everything depends on the quality of the personal contact between tax officials and the people they must tax and on the possibility of devising simple and acceptable criteria of relative wealth which can be generally applied. The varying progress made by the different countries in introducing a measure of graduation into Native taxation has also been discussed previously. In general it may be said that West Africa, especially Nigeria, is more advanced in this respect than East and Central Africa. The cattle tax levied in the High Commission Territories stands out as the only significant experiment of recent times in the graduated taxation of Africans.

It has frequently been found difficult to raise any substantial revenue by taxing the personal incomes of non-Africans. In many cases the numbers concerned are small, and they have sometimes opposed with success the introduction of taxation which would reduce their standard of living below the level they regard as the essential minimum. The main burden of direct taxation consequently tends more and more to be carried by the producers *qua* producers. Often the burden in any given territory is borne by the producer of one type of primary product—cocoa in British West Africa, for example, cotton in Uganda, or minerals in the Rhodesias. As a result, Governments seeking to raise revenues for Development Programmes may find that an increase in taxation has a direct consequence in the reduction of incentives to production.

[1] See above, pp. 677 ff.

The question of incentives has a special significance in connexion with the position of foreign investors. It is true that the rate of taxation is not the only consideration which weighs with an investor who is deciding where to place his capital. But that it is of some importance is clear from the provisions made in the recent legislation of Nigeria and the Gold Coast in respect of the re-equipment of established enterprise. A variety of special tax inducements are also offered to investors in the Belgian Congo, where, however, the tax on company profits is only from 10 to 25 per cent. In French Equatorial Africa, where the direct tax on companies is again relatively light, there is a complicated rate structure designed to discriminate against commercial profits and in favour of industrial profits and of persons engaged in industry. The high level of indirect taxes in the French territories, however, tends to outweigh the effects of a comparatively light system of direct taxes.[1]

In general the budgetary problems of the republic of Liberia approximate in character to those of the dependent African territories, particularly to those of its West African neighbours. Liberia's combination of political independence and economic dependence has had, however, some interesting results. The price of its political independence is reflected in the high proportion of its public expenditure which is devoted to general administration and defence. This is unusually high even by African standards, and it is inflated by items such as the cost of international (consular) representation, which would be borne on the metropolitan budget in the case of a Colony. On the other hand, the price of economic dependence has recently been illustrated by Liberia's experience with its income-tax legislation. The yield of the income tax, which was introduced in Liberia in 1950, has been artificially restricted by the fact that a number of major companies operating in the country secured exemption from tax for themselves and their employees under the terms of their original Concession. Until these Concessions can be revised an important section of the incomes earned in the territory will escape tax.

In conclusion, it may be noted that one effect of the increase in Government activity that has characterized the post-war Colonial economies has been the emergence of problems of fiscal policy of which these areas had little experience before the Second World War. The financial resources at the disposal of public or semi-public authorities in the African dependencies are now so great in relation to the economic activity of the private sector that the direction and timing of their employment have inflationary or deflationary implications of some consequence. It is not simply the fact that the budgets of Colonial Governments have been inflated and strengthened by the prosperity of certain groups of primary producers and supplemented

[1] E. B. Northcliffe, 'Tax Incentives in Under-developed Territories', *Accountant*, February 1954.

by the grants and loans of metropolitan or international agencies concerned in promoting schemes of development. In the fields of local Government, of public corporations, and of other statutory authorities there have also been striking new developments which have added to the fiscal potentiality of the public sector. Municipalities and Native Treasuries now dispose of important revenues, employ considerable staffs, and make appreciable demands on the available stocks of capital goods. More powerful still in the financial sense are the statutory export monopolies which have been set up to purchase certain major export crops in a number of areas. The profits and surpluses of the statutory Marketing Boards of Uganda, for example, accounted for 19 per cent. of the geographical income (excluding export taxes) in 1951. The British West African Marketing Boards handle the great bulk of the agricultural exports of Nigeria, the Gold Coast, Sierra Leone, and Gambia. 'Already their financial resources on both current and capital account exceed those of the West African Governments and the disposal of their vast reserves will be a major influence in the political and economic situation in these territories.'[1]

The importance of semi-public authorities such as these is beyond dispute. Their price decisions are a major determinant of the money values of the national income in the territories in which they operate. But the real, as opposed to the money, effect of their activities is not easily assessed. In all African territories the flow of money incomes takes place within a basic framework of subsistence production. A complex situation is produced by the fact that the boundaries of the subsistence sector and of the exchange sector of the economy are constantly shifting in response to changing conditions of supply and demand. It is always possible for goods that were produced within the subsistence sector to find their way on to the market if prices are attractive. Conversely, it is possible for goods that were produced for sale to be withheld from the market and consumed in the subsistence sector if overall yields are abnormally low or if prices are unattractive.

It is true, on the one hand, that the fluidity of the boundaries between the subsistence and the money economies contributes to the long-term stability of the economy as a whole. A people that continues to produce its own food is less vulnerable to a world depression than a people that is largely dependent on the market for its livelihood. On the other hand, this overlapping of the two sectors of the economy may introduce elements of short-term instability into either. The subsistence sector may suffer hardships, for example, if high prices have attracted to the market the goods that are needed for home consumption. Conversely, the money economy may be contracted if goods that would normally come on to the market are

---

[1] P. T. Bauer, 'Statistics of Statutory Marketing in West Africa, 1939–51', *Journal of the Royal Statistical Society*, Series A, vol. cxvii, Part I, 1954. See also idem, *West African Trade*, 1954.

consumed at home. These effects may result from a redistribution of real incomes rather than an absolute decline in their amount. Those who secure the high prices obtainable by diverting to the market the goods that would otherwise meet the needs of the subsistence economy will gain; their less productive relatives will suffer. Similarly the farmer who decides to convert his surplus grain into beer instead of selling it on urban markets will presumably benefit, while the town-dweller, faced with consequent food shortages, will suffer.

In view of the lack of factual knowledge regarding economic behaviour in this mixed type of environment it is not surprising that there has been considerable uncertainty and, indeed, controversy over the consequences of policies which might be inflationary or deflationary in their effects. This is well illustrated by a series of studies which were published in the course of the years 1952–3 and dealt with the more significant features of the economy of the major British West African territories. An article by D. Seers and C. R. Ross stressed the fragility of the economy of the Gold Coast.[1] On the other hand, A. R. Prest and I. G. Stewart called attention to what in their view was the stability of the Nigerian economy.[2] An article by P. T. Bauer and F. Paish issued in 1952 dealt critically[3] with some of the implications of the price policy of the Marketing Boards.[4]

It is in the power of Governments or of institutions such as the Marketing Boards to produce proportionally large changes in the flow of money incomes. Whether by so doing they produce comparable effects on the overall level of output or consumption is a matter of some uncertainty. It may be that in some territories the effects of fiscal policy are largely diminished by the shift of resources between the subsistence and the money sectors of the economy. It may even be that in some cases a narrowing of the range of fiscal policy will intensify its effects for the particular sector which it reaches. It cannot be doubted that the weapon of fiscal policy is a crude and uncertain tool of economic planning in any country where the subsistence sector is an important element in the total economy. One conclusion is, however, certain. No Colonial Government can afford to overlook the indirect consequences which may flow from its own financial policy or of that of the Local Government or semi-Governmental institutions which it controls.

[1] D. Seers and C. R. Ross, *Report on Financial and Physical Problems of Development in the Gold Coast*, Accra, 1952.

[2] A. R. Prest and I. G. Stewart, *The National Income of Nigeria 1950–51*, Colonial Research Studies no. 11, 1953.

[3] P. T. Bauer and F. Paish, 'The Reduction of Fluctuations in the Incomes of Primary Producers', *Economic Journal*, December 1952.

[4] See further on this subject, C. Leubuscher, *Bulk Buying from the Colonies*, 1956.

CHAPTER XIX

PROJECTS OF ECONOMIC DEVELOPMENT

IN the preceding chapter some account was given of the character of economic development in Africa south of the Sahara in terms of the patterns of production and consumption to which it gives rise. This chapter will deal with the dynamic factors which condition the intensity of economic growth and affect the pace of advance.

In any given area the rate of economic progress depends on the nature of the resources which are at the disposal of the people and on the possibilities of developing them. First of all there are the basic physical resources of the region, such as the character of its climate and of its soil, the extent and location of its mineral deposits and sources of power, its natural communications, and its vulnerability to disease of crops and livestock. Secondly, there are the human resources and the social heritage which determines their skills, their incentives, and their initiative. No less important are such factors as access to external capital or technical skills, the world demand for the products of the region, and the political limitations imposed on production.

The greater part of Africa south of the Sahara lies within the tropics, and the basic land and climatic resources are characteristically poor. The vegetation varies from the luxuriant forests of Central and West Africa to the arid deserts of Southern or East Africa, but the soils are nowhere very fertile. The forests are for the most part secondary woodland, of which the soil is easily exhausted and eroded when the tree cover is cleared. Even where rainfall is adequate in quantity its distribution over the months is such as to make it ineffective for agricultural purposes. A climate which saps the physical and mental energies of human beings provides a breeding-ground for the microbes of disease and germ-carrying insects. Approximately five-eighths of the area of Northern Rhodesia, three-quarters of Uganda, two-thirds of Tanganyika, and one-fifth of Kenya are so infested by tsetse fly that they are closed to most domestic livestock.

Traditional systems of agriculture in such an environment are extremely crude. While the indigenous peoples could roam freely across the continent and their numbers were kept in check by disease, tribal warfare, and periodic famine, the primitive systems sufficed to maintain a relatively stable standard of subsistence. European occupation, however, restricted in many areas the land resources open to shifting cultivation, and reduced the death rate from disease, famine, and war. In some regions the introduction of the plough accelerated soil erosion and in others the attraction of able-bodied men to urban areas reduced the productivity of labour in agriculture; elsewhere, the existence of a market for cash crops increased the vulnerability of the farmer to outside factors such as world crises, or to crop diseases such as 'swollen shoot' of cocoa and 'sudden death' of cloves. These developments have combined in many areas to disturb the already fragile balance of tropical agriculture, with the result that the effective land resources have tended to decline rather than to increase.

The mineral wealth of Africa is still more unevenly distributed than the areas of cultivable soil. Some territories have no mineral resources of any economic consequence. In others, notably the Union of South Africa, the Belgian Congo, and the Rhodesias, the mineral wealth has been a major factor in attracting foreign capital and European immigrants. These are territories where national incomes per head have risen to relatively high levels. The Union of South Africa is the world's largest producer of gold and produces nearly half of the world's diamonds by value. The Belgian Congo is the largest producer of diamonds by weight, and the copper deposits of Northern Rhodesia and the Belgian Congo are among the largest in the world. Most of the minerals needed for heavy industry (notably iron-ore) are located close to the extensive coal deposits of the Union of South Africa. Southern Rhodesia stands out as having immense reserves of coal, much of it near the surface and hence easy to extract. Elsewhere, those territories which are anxious to develop secondary industry must rely on water power.

In spite of the great capital resources which the mineral wealth of Africa has attracted to the continent, and in spite of the great value of the minerals which are annually exported from it, the impact of these developments has been curiously limited. The rural areas of Central and Southern Africa are in general under-developed and where local development exists it is sharply concentrated. Northern Rhodesia provides the most striking example of the geographical limitations of economic development based on mining. The only railway is that joining the Copperbelt in the north to its outlet in the south. The only modern townships and the only macadamized roads of any length lie along the railway line. A narrow belt of country on either side of the railway is the only significant source of African cash crops, and in this area is located the whole of the European farming industry, with the exception of those growers of Virginian tobacco who have been able to find suitable climatic conditions for their crop near the Nyasaland border. Away from the railway belt, in the outer provinces where the bulk of the African population lives and a low subsistence level of production prevails, the pace of development is all the slower because the best of the labour force has been attracted to the centres of industry.

As a result of the poverty of the soil the continent is generally under peopled. Except in West Africa, where there are relatively fertile areas which sometimes carry up to 300 persons to the square mile, and Ruanda Urundi, with a density of nearly 197 to the square mile, the density of population is characteristically low. In Angola, for example, there are only 8·6 persons to the square mile, and French Equatorial Africa has a density of only 4·6. In British East Africa the average density is 32·5, but there are some very densely populated areas such, for example, as the Kikuyu Reserve, with 414 persons to the square mile. Over most of Central and South Africa the country may be said to be over-populated in terms of the carrying capacity of the land under primitive conditions of agriculture, and under-populated in terms of the labour required for mining or industrial enterprise.

To a large extent the shortage of labour is a consequence of technical backwardness and of the unspecialized nature of economic activity under subsistence or semi-subsistence conditions. A great deal of time is necessarily spent on other than purely agricultural activities. Grain must be pounded into flour by pestle and mortar. The crop must be gathered from fields which get progressively farther from the villages as the soil loses its fertility. Storage facilities have to be built. Water has to be brought from distant streams or water-holes. Fuel must be collected from diminishing areas of woodland. An inquiry carried out in the north-east of the Belgian Congo showed that for the people in question cultivation took up only 28 per cent. of the time required in the whole series of operations involved in food preparation; 34 per cent. was spent on harvesting and storing the crop, and 38 per cent. in preparing the food.[1]

In some cases, however, processes involving an expenditure of man-hours which most modern enterprises would not tolerate have been found to have their advantages. An inquiry into grain storage in East and Central Africa, for example, gave evidence that Native storage was better than Government storage.[2] The Native process involves small granaries, frequent spreading of the grain to dry, and frequent examinations after storage. This process is costly in terms of labour and would be prohibitively expensive to finance on a collective scale, but it results in a smaller rate of deterioration and loss of food than the less laborious system of storage in large silos.

It must not be assumed that the indigenous peoples start with no skills of their own. But it is nevertheless true that the skills relevant to primitive self-sufficient systems of agriculture have been rendered largely obsolete by new conditions of production and new demands on the available factors of production. Some of the old-fashioned farming lore is now less

[1] P. de Schlippe, *Bulletin agricole du Congo Belge*, 1949, pp. 361–402.
[2] T. A. Oxley, *Grain Storage in East and Central Africa*, Colonial Research Publications no. 5 1950.

valuable to the African farmer than a knowledge of methods of conserving the land (for example, by contour ridging, manuring, and crop rotation) or of rearing disease-resistant strains of livestock with high yields of meat and milk. The most difficult problem of adaptation is found in those parts of Africa where the traditional practice is for the whole village to move every few years. But in the more common situation where the farmer is permanently settled, difficulties arise from his attachment to the plots inherited from his predecessors, since this leads him to resist such a redistribution of holdings as may be called for in the interests of agricultural improvement. Modern agricultural development schemes are apt to meet with opposition as soon as an attempt is made to group the patchwork of individual plots into blocks suitable for mechanized cultivation.

In some areas the labour shortages have been relieved by immigration. Reference is made elsewhere to the mobility of African labour.[1] In East, Central, and South Africa there is a substantial immigrant population of Europeans and of Asians who have brought with them skills which are the heritage of economically more advanced communities. Thus the urban areas of the Rhodesias and of South Africa are fed largely by an agricultural industry controlled by Europeans which can obtain average yields more than twice as great as those achieved by Native farmers. Over most of East and Central Africa small-scale trade for the African market is mainly conducted by Asians who bring to it a skill which few Africans in these areas can emulate. In all territories European or American technicians and scientists are assisting in development projects and performing essential services of research and instruction. It is through these agents of technological advance that a gradual improvement is now being made.

In sum, the basic resources of Africa south of the Sahara are generally poor. Soils are for the most part infertile, and the climate is usually too difficult to permit the development of a flourishing agricultural industry except where special local conditions provide a suitable environment for certain tropical crops. Mineral resources are varied for the continent as a whole, but they are restricted to particular areas and their exploitation is often limited by inadequate communications. In Uganda, for example, the exploitation of the Kilembe copper deposits has had to await the construction of a railway, and in Northern Rhodesia the limited capacity of Rhodesia Railways has in the past restricted the expansion of copper output. Communications in their turn are hampered by difficulties of terrain, by the vast distances involved, and by labour shortages. Railways have generally had to be financed by the State and have rarely paid their way except where valuable minerals have been an important element in their traffic. Manpower shortages are heightened by technical backwardness

[1] See below, pp. 1376 ff.

and low educational standards, which create a dearth of indigenous skilled and supervisory labour. The migrant labour system, which helps to relieve local shortages, brings with it a high turnover and makes it difficult for the workers to attain even an elementary standard of skill.

In order to develop, from such essentially poor resources as these, standards of productivity which are comparable to those prevailing in European and North American countries, very large amounts of capital may prove to be required. The African economies lag behind those of more developed countries not only because they are late arrivals in the field of production and the capital invested in them is in consequence comparatively small, but also because over the greater part of the field they promise a comparatively low yield per unit of capital invested.[1] Initially, at any rate, a large part of the capital required by an under-developed country must be obtained from sources outside its own borders. Since the more developed countries have a continual internal demand for capital to maintain their equipment at the standards demanded by technological advance, only those enterprises in which an under-developed country can promise an internationally competitive return to investors are likely to attract the capital they need. Ignorance of a country's potentialities will still further restrict the supply of capital, for the developed countries have the advantage of being familiar to investors, who will normally prefer the risks they know to those that are new to them.

Africa's most promising enterprises from the point of view of the foreign investor were at the outset those concerned with the production of scarce minerals such as gold and diamonds. From the end of the nineteenth century onwards, capital flowed spontaneously to projects such as these and to the ancillary services and industries which they brought into being. Further economic penetration of the continent was limited, however, by its physical inaccessibility, and the next stage was the construction of railways. In the main, this type of investment was financed or guaranteed by Governments, for at this level the political urgency outweighed the financial risks. Poor dependencies, such as Nyasaland, had their railway loans guaranteed by the metropolitan Government. Without the railway there could be no trade, but the private investor could not afford to gamble on the prospect that the existence of a railway would create enough trade to pay a return on the capital invested in it.

In the event it has rarely been possible for railways to earn a normal return on their capital, save where a profitable mineral traffic has been available. The profits of the South African railways have been secured largely from the services rendered to the gold-mining community of the Rand. The Rhodesia-Katanga copper-mines, with four outlets to the sea, at Beira and Dar-es-Salaam to the east and at Matadi and Lobito Bay

[1] W. A. Lewis, *The Theory of Economic Growth*, 1955, pp. 203–5.

to the west, have brought from time to time relative prosperity to whichever route was fortunate enough to carry a large volume of output from
the mines. On the other hand, the northern section of the Nyasaland
railway, which joined Blantyre to Lake Nyasa, never created enough traffic
to justify its extension beyond the European Highlands through some 150
miles of territory populated predominantly by Africans.

By 1936, it is estimated, some £1,222 million had been invested in
Africa from abroad. Of this about £546 million took the form of loans
and grants to Governments, and about £581 million was 'private listed
capital' (that is, the public issues of companies); the total of non-listed
capital was estimated roughly at £95 million.[1] Of the total of £1,222
million, about £523 million was the estimated share of the Union of South
Africa. This is 42·81 per cent. of the investment of all territories and
55·54 per cent. of that of the British territories. Of other British Commonwealth territories the most important fields of investment before the
Second World War were: the Rhodesias, which took about £102 million;
Nigeria, £75 million; Tanganyika, £52 million; Kenya and Uganda,
£46 million; the Gold Coast, £35 million; and South-West Africa, £32
million. The Anglo-Egyptian Sudan took £43 million. The total investment in all British Commonwealth territories was estimated to have been
some £941 million to the end of 1936. This was about 77 per cent. of
the whole volume of investment.

In non-British territories the chief investment was in the Belgian Congo
(including Ruanda Urundi), where it was estimated to have been £143
million. In the French territories the estimated total was £70 million,
of which about £30 million was in French West Africa and £21 million
in French Equatorial Africa. The estimated investment in the Portuguese
territories was about £67 million, divided fairly equally between Angola
and Mozambique. Thus the Belgian territories received about 11·73 per
cent., the French 5·76 per cent., and the Portuguese 5·46 per cent. of
the total capital invested.

Some idea of the intensity of capital development implied in these
estimates can be derived by considering them in *per capita* terms. The
foreign investment in the Union amounted to about £55·8 per head of
the total population as it stood in 1936. It was about £38·4 per head in
the Rhodesias and £13·0 in the Belgian Congo. In Angola and Mozambique it was about £9·8 per head, but it should be remembered that the
railway and port developments of both these territories do not serve
exclusively the local populations. It was about £8·1 in British East Africa
and about £4·8 in British West Africa. It was lowest in the French
Colonies at about £3·3; in French West Africa it was no more than £2·1
per head.

[1] S. H. Frankel, *Capital Investment in Africa*, 1938, p. 159.

In considering these figures as a reflection of the level of capital development in the territories concerned it must be remembered that they represent only the foreign investment. In the more highly developed territories —notably the Union of South Africa—there has been a considerable local investment both of private capital and of public money spent upon capital improvements. Most of this represents a ploughing back into the expanding economy of the return on resources originally borrowed abroad for the exploitation of mineral wealth. It should be remembered that, especially in countries where no large-scale capital investment in mining has been justified, the most fruitful form of capital investment may be the expenditure incurred by the small farmer on ploughs or tobacco barns or in planting cocoa-trees or, in pastoral areas, on constructing dams or bore-holes.

Government funds provided an important part of the total investment up to the Second World War. This accounted for about 44·72 per cent. in all the territories south of the Sahara and about 47·68 per cent. for the British territories. The proportion was lowest where there had been extensive borrowing for mining undertakings, and highest where railway construction was almost the only important form of economic development. In the British territories over half the 'public listed capital' had been invested in railways. In the Union of South Africa 'public listed capital' was, according to Professor Frankel's estimate, 42·85 per cent. of the total investment. In the Rhodesias, where Government investment began only after the termination in 1923 of the Charter of the British South Africa Company, public capital constituted 38·68 per cent. of all capital.[1] In the Gold Coast and Nigeria, where large investments have been made by European trading companies, public capital represented 38·13 per cent. and 46·24 per cent. respectively. On the other hand, in Nyasaland it was 84·79 per cent., in Sierra Leone 72·95 per cent., in Kenya and Uganda 68·36 per cent., and in Tanganyika 60·14 per cent. The French territories also fall into the group where the proportion of public investment is high. It was 71·72 per cent. in Equatorial Africa, 60·71 per cent. in Togo and the Cameroons, and 54·15 per cent. in French West Africa. In the Portuguese territories, where British private capital had provided a large part of the whole, it was no more than 27·92 per cent. In the Belgian Congo and Ruanda Urundi the high volume of investment by private capital in mining and in the construction of railways had reduced the share of 'public listed capital' to 25·01 per cent. of the whole. It should, however, be noted that the large financial interest of the State in many of the more important industrial and commercial undertakings in the Belgian Congo is not fully reflected by the figures of 'public listed capital.[2]

[1] S. H. Frankel, *Capital Investment in Africa*, pp. 160–1.　　　　[2] Ibid. p. 168.

By the time the Second World War broke out it was evident that if the pace of development in Africa were to be accelerated there must be some new stimulus that would reach effectively beyond the limited areas in which the mineral deposits lay. A more constructive approach was required from the Public Authorities concerned than that involved in the building and maintenance of lines of communication. In Britain official appreciation of this situation was expressed in a general statement published in February 1940,[1] and in the Colonial Development and Welfare Act which passed into law in the same year.

It had previously been the policy of the British Government to provide grants-in-aid to Colonies which were unable to balance their budgets, and most Colonies availed themselves of this assistance in the early years of their existence. By 1936 the total of such grants-in-aid to British territories in Africa had reached £27 million, of which £10,800,000 had gone to the Anglo-Egyptian Sudan and £5,700,000 to Nigeria. In the latter case this included the sum paid in compensation to the Royal Niger Company. No other Colony had received more than £3 million. In addition to the grants-in-aid to insolvent Colonies there were available from 1929 free grants or loans of up to £1 million per annum for all the British Colonies, these being provided under the terms of the Colonial Development Act of that year. The Act had been designed with the primary object of relieving unemployment in Great Britain, and by the end of 1936 it provided some £3 million in grants to African territories. The Colonial Development and Welfare Act of 1940 greatly expanded the scope and spirit of the Act of 1929 and made available up to £5 million a year for ten years for 'schemes for any purpose likely to promote the development of the resources of any Colony or the welfare of its people', together with a further £500,000 a year for research and inquiry.[2]

The Second World War and its aftermath made substantial changes in the position of Africa in the world economy. The war effort of the African territories early assumed a vital importance. They provided men, money, and scarce raw materials, some of which were of marked strategic significance. The sea and air bases at Dakar, Freetown, and Takoradi were of vital importance to the African campaign. During the crucial years of the war the American forces depended on bases in West Africa for facilities for air transport. Defeats sustained in Asia accentuated the importance of Africa. There were world shortages of such raw materials as fats, rice, rubber, and tin. As mineral resources in the developed areas began to approach exhaustion (for example the iron deposits round Lake Superior) it was natural to look to new potential sources of supply in Africa. Areas where some advance had already been made towards industrialization,

---

[1] *Statement of Policy on Colonial Development and Welfare*, Cmd. 6175, 1940. See also above, p. 203.   [2] For the provision made for research, see below, p. 1602.

such as the Union of South Africa and the Belgian Congo, were encouraged by war-time restrictions on supplies from overseas to produce for themselves and for export much that they had previously bought from abroad. High prices in the post-war period greatly stimulated the production of African cash crops. In Uganda, for example, the coffee acreage trebled between 1938 and 1948.

Possibly the most significant effect of all these developments was a radical modification in the relationship between European Powers and their dependencies. After the war it was believed that the Colonies could assist the metropolitan countries to make good some of the deficiencies created by the war. To a considerable extent also they contributed to European financial resources through their earnings of hard currency. In some of the European countries there actually grew up a popular belief that Africa constituted a vast reservoir of primary products which it needed only adequate capital resources to release for the benefit of the industrial peoples of Europe.

The change in the economic position had marked political reactions. Perhaps the most significant was the formal demand at the Brazzaville Conference of 1944 for the recognition of a new status for the French overseas territories.[1] In the European settled areas also there appeared a new attitude of independence of the home country. The war period had stimulated permanent immigration and severed for a time physical contact with the home country. European settlers in British East and Central Africa, for example, had to take their holidays and educate their children in Africa, and when eventually they were able to resume home contacts with the United Kingdom the British way of life had materially altered. At the same time a substantial tide of South African migrants was flowing into Central and East Africa and for them the home country lay within and not without the continent. Tax differentials gave a more positive incentive for individuals and business men to change from a metropolitan to an African domicile. Since the war Belgian registered companies operating in the Belgian Congo have progressively adopted registration within the Colony, and most new companies operating in it have been locally registered.[2] Similar trends are observable in British East and Central Africa. In Kenya 40 local companies were registered in 1939 and 43 foreign companies; in 1952 the register showed 244 local companies and 33 foreign companies. In 1950 the important copper-mining companies registered in London transferred their registration to Northern Rhodesia. It would seem that their main purpose was administrative, but the move also secured the companies a measure of relief from the tax on profits imposed in the United Kingdom.

[1] See above, p. 209.
[2] R. Bertiaux, *Aspects de l'industrialisation en Afrique centrale*, 1953.

PROGRAMMES OF DEVELOPMENT

To the victorious nations of the Second World War the apparently limitless potentialities of the unexplored resources of Africa and the poverty of its people seemed to constitute both an inspiration and a challenge. It was clear that the African peoples could not provide out of their own low incomes the capital which could break the vicious circle of poverty and low productivity and enable them to make any substantial contribution to world reconstruction. Equally clearly foreign private investors would not provide the capital unless the long-term economic prospects were preceded by well-planned public investment. The conclusion drawn from this situation by a world now accustomed to a high degree of State intervention in economic affairs was that Governments should take the initiative in planning the development of the under-developed areas, and in finding or guaranteeing the funds necessary to start the process. The atmosphere created by international conferences and organizations concerned with economic reconstruction encouraged this conclusion. The result was that in the period immediately following the war, Development Plans covering definite periods of years were drawn up and put into operation in all the African dependencies. Emerging as they did from a more general recognition of the responsibilities of Colonial Powers for their dependencies, these plans had much that was in common. As a whole they tended to take a comprehensive view of the prospects and potentialities of the Colonial areas concerned. In some cases (and most notably in the French and Portuguese territories) plans were not confined to the field of Colonial development, but the metropolitan country and its overseas territories were considered as a single economic unit. To a lesser extent all the recent belligerents were forced to take the Colonial plans into account in considering their own long-term programmes of economic reconstruction. Thus in 1949 when the various countries concerned in the Organization for European Economic Co-operation submitted their programme for 1950–2, these included also a summary of the plans made for their overseas territories.

Another common characteristic of the Development Plans was the definite emphasis placed on schemes designed to promote the welfare of the Colonial peoples themselves. Attention was directed to fields of investment for which the return was measurable in social rather than economic terms, instead of to those fields which might seem appropriate for private investment. Social development was at all events interpreted in a very broad sense and included a substantial expenditure on social services, particularly on education and public health. By 1951 over 43 per cent. of the expenditure included in the Development Plans for the British Colonial territories was allocated to social development. In the Belgian

Congo social projects absorbed 31 per cent. of the estimated expenditure, and in the French territories expenditure of this nature ranged from 14 per cent. to 29 per cent. of the total for the first four years of the plan.[1]

Experience, however, caused some of these plans to be modified during succeeding years. It was found that the capital cost of many of the projects associated with the social services—such as the building of schools and hospitals—far exceeded the original anticipations. It was also found that the recurrent costs of maintaining them—as for instance that of providing immigrant teachers, doctors, and nurses in territories which could supply none of their own—would throw an unduly heavy burden on the local budgets. When it also became obvious that the plans were likely to produce little immediate improvement in the productivity and the revenues of the territories concerned, some revision became essential. The plans for the expansion of the social services in Northern Rhodesia, for instance, were drastically cut in the first review,[2] and in Uganda, where they were originally designed to absorb 29 per cent. of development expenditure, their share was reduced to about 15 per cent. when the plan was revised. This percentage was retained in the plan of capital development which provides for the expenditure of £30 million over the period 1955–60.[3] In the various French African territories the cost of maintaining the public and administrative services provided under the plan, particularly in the field of public health and education, amounted in some instances to between 20 and 25 per cent. of the corresponding capital costs. To meet this position the budgets of the territories would have to be doubled in a decade.[4]

The change of emphasis in favour of the promotion of economic services designed to produce a more immediate impact on the productivity of the areas concerned was accompanied in some instances by official activities which might normally be regarded as lying within the sphere of the private investor. But in general the economic services now provided within the Development Plans were confined to measures involved in such broad objectives as, for instance, the conservation of the basic physical resources, the provision of public utilities, and research (including geological survey). It was felt, however, that there was room for some measure of direct production by Public Authorities in fields where the initial capital expenditure was too heavy and the prospects of a commercial return too remote to attract the private investor. Large schemes of mechanized agriculture came within this category, as also did certain

---

[1] United Nations, *Special Study on Social Conditions in Non-self-governing Territories*, 1953.

[2] *Review of the Ten-year Development Plan of Northern Rhodesia*, Lusaka, 1948.

[3] E. B. Worthington, *A Development Plan for Uganda and the 1948 Revision of the Plan*, Entebbe, 1949. Uganda Protectorate, *A Five-year Capital Development Plan, 1955–1960*, 1954.

[4] 'Aspects financiers et budgétaires du développement économique de l'Union française', *Notes et études documentaires*, no. 1568, 1 February 1952.

kinds of small-scale manufacturing projects. A notable instance of this class was the cement industry, which might begin on an uneconomic scale but could be expected to expand with the general development of the economy of the country.

In a number of territories these State interventions in the field of direct production were designed to be handled by a special form of Government agency—the public corporation. In the British territories, for example, the Overseas Food Corporation was set up to operate the East African Groundnut Scheme in Tanganyika, and the Colonial Development Corporation, which was empowered to borrow £100 million from the Treasury, became the accredited agency for the stimulation of new forms of industrial or rural production. A number of local public corporations have also been created, such as the Cameroons Development Corporation or the Uganda Development Corporation.[1] In Nigeria statutory corporations took over the coal and the electricity industries in 1951, and it is planned to set up both a railway corporation and a ports authority. In the French territories there are separate public corporations concerned with mining, the provision of electric power, and the marketing of a number of export commodities. The list includes the following: *Bureau Minier de la France d'Outre-Mer, Compagnie Générale des Oléagineux Tropicaux, Compagnie Française pour le Développement des Fibres, Énergie Électrique d'Afrique Équatoriale Française,* and *Énergie Électrique d'Afrique Occidentale Française.*

By setting up public corporations the Government can shoulder some of the risks involved in launching new projects which are of significance in the general plan of development but whose prospects are unpredictable. It is not always necessary, however, for the State or its agencies to accept administrative as well as financial responsibility. In some cases there are suitable private entrepreneurs who are willing to risk their own capital, but who are unable to raise the necessary additional funds required to finance the project. To meet this need a number of Governments have set up or encouraged the formation of a variety of credit institutions for agricultural or industrial purposes. Most of the public corporations are empowered to grant credit for the activities which they are established to promote. Co-operative societies provide credit facilities to their members,[2] and in the Northern Region of Nigeria some Native Administrations offer special assistance to farmers. In Nigeria Loan Boards have been set up in the Northern and Western Regions, and corporations authorized to provide loans or grants to public or private enterprise operate in all these Regions.[3] In the territories under French administration Agricultural Credit Banks lend money to farmers through the medium of the *sociétés de prévoyance* at a rate of interest fixed annually by the Governor. In the

---

[1] See above, pp. 736, 909.   [2] See below, p. 1471.
[3] *The Colonial Territories, 1955–56,* Cmd. 9769, 1956.

Belgian Congo the *Fonds Spécial de Crédit Agricole Indigène* finances irrigation and drainage works and provides credit for long-term development projects such as the establishment of rubber and oil-palm plantations. There are industrial development boards in a number of British territories which grant loans to local industries, and the French *Caisse Centrale de la France d'Outre-Mer* gives financial assistance both for the formation and the expansion of private undertakings.

Capital for the Development Programmes has come from four main sources, namely, allocations from Colonial budgets, grants-in-aid from the metropolitan countries, loans made or guaranteed by the metropolitan countries, and loans issued by the Colonial Governments themselves. The line between the loans guaranteed by the Colonial Governments and those guaranteed by the metropolitan Governments is, however, vague in practice. In effect, all Colonial loans are implicitly if not explicitly secured on the credit of the metropolitan rather than of the Colonial country. There are clear and often narrow limits to the volume of capital resources which can be made available for Colonial Development Programmes out of the tax revenue of metropolitan or Colonial Governments. The high post-war prices for some Colonial products (such as cocoa in the Gold Coast and copper in Northern Rhodesia) have permitted some dependencies to command a much larger volume of resources than was available to them before 1939, but the fact that such prices cannot be regarded as permanent has placed some restriction on the freedom with which the Colonial Governments are prepared to commit themselves to large-scale expenditure. The limits to the contribution which can be made through borrowing are, however, more elastic. They are determined in part by the burden of debt service charges which can be carried by the Colonial budgets, in part by the limits, statutory or otherwise, to the obligations which may be incurred by the metropolitan budget, and in part by the nature of the capital resources to which the Governments concerned can obtain access.

Broadly speaking, therefore, the character of the public Development Programmes which any particular dependency can be expected to undertake is determined by its current and anticipated budgetary position. Expenditure on non-revenue-producing services, whether social or economic, may be considered as sound investment only if the net improvement in incomes and productivity resulting from these services is sufficient to outweigh the additional burden of their recurrent cost. Expenditure on revenue-producing activities can be financed by borrowing, but it should be expected to yield in reasonable time a return which covers not only the maintenance costs but also the appropriate debt service charges. These are the true limits to Development Plans, although they may be obscured in practice for some of the more backward areas by the difficulty of forecasting the return from a given project. The return from a new railway running through a hitherto under-developed area cannot be accurately assessed, and the possibilities of borrowing the capital at a rate of interest low enough to be borne by a poor dependency will be correspondingly limited. On the other hand, those economies which have expanded sufficiently to permit a reasoned forecast of the probable speed and direction of their development will find it relatively easy to raise money at reasonably low rates. It is significant, for example, that of a total of £77·7 million borrowed on the London market between 1945 and the end of 1952 by British African dependencies, some £48·6 million or roughly two-thirds went to British East Africa.[1]

While the Development Programmes launched in Africa have for the most part been financed by the territories themselves or by the metropolitan countries, some aid has also been made available through international channels, and some has come directly or indirectly from the United States. The specialized agencies of the United Nations (the Food and Agriculture Organization, the World Health Organization, and the United Nations Economic and Social Council) undertook from their inception a limited programme of technical assistance, but their budgets were restricted. At that stage the initiative lay with the international organizations themselves. In 1950 an expanded programme of technical assistance was approved, but assistance was confined to economically under-developed countries, and the initiative was placed on the receiving country, from which a request must come in the first instance. The total value of technical assistance provided for the whole of Africa by the United Nations up to the end of 1952 was only a little in excess of $2 million.[2]

The International Bank for Reconstruction and Development does not compete with private investors, and, since its loans must be guaranteed by a State or Central Bank, it can in practice only lend to Public Authorities. By 1953 it had approved loans amounting to more than $160 million to African territories, of which $70 million went to the Belgian Congo in support of its Ten-year Development Plan, $14 million to Northern Rhodesia to assist railway expansion, $28 million to Southern Rhodesia as part of its scheme for providing hydroelectric power, and $50 million to the Union of South Africa to finance expansion in railway and power facilities. It should be noted that a loan made in March 1953 to Northern Rhodesia was guaranteed by the United Kingdom and responsibility was shared by Southern Rhodesia. The Bank has lent $24 million to British

---

[1] Central Office of Information, *Economic Development of the United Kingdom Dependencies*, May 1953.
[2] United States Department of State, Office of Intelligence Research, *Postwar Economic Aid to Africa by the US, IBRD, and UN*, Report no. 5970, December 1952.

East Africa to assist railway and harbour development,[1] and has sent missions to British[2] and French West Africa in order to study requests for aid in connexion with programmes of railway expansion.[3]

The financial resources made available to Africa through the agencies of the United Nations and the International Bank emanate to a considerable extent from the United States, for although the capital of the International Bank was subscribed by more than 50 countries, the United States provided 40 per cent. of the total. In addition to this, however, there has been some direct aid from the United States Government to African territories or to European countries on behalf of their African dependencies. Except in Liberia, where the United States had established an economic mission and a public health mission, American Government aid to Africa south of the Sahara up to the end of the Second World War had been negligible in total and largely confined to Lease-Lend operations and other expenditures of a more or less military nature. The events of the war and post-war period, however, impressed on the United States, as on the European Powers with African dependencies, a growing awareness of the strategic importance of Africa. Public expression of the willingness of the American people to undertake some measure of direct responsibility for the provision of technical assistance to under-developed areas was contained in President Truman's inaugural address of January 1949. This embraced the declaration of what came to be known later as the Point Four policy. It was followed in 1950 by the establishment of a Special Reserve Fund for overseas development by the Economic Co-operation Administration, the latter organization being succeeded in 1953 by the Mutual Security Agency.

The object of this Fund was to relieve the restrictions on development projects due to dollar shortages by providing measures to finance the import of essential materials and equipment from the dollar area. The Economic Co-operation Administration (E.C.A.) paid the dollar cost of the goods on condition that a counterpart to the same amount should be set aside in local currency. Until the outbreak of the Korean War the counterpart funds were credited to the metropolitan country. In the case of France they were then allocated to the overseas territories along with some additional amounts drawn from France's own counterpart funds. After the outbreak of the Korean War the Overseas Development Fund could be used to cover general dollar imports, but the counterpart funds (apart from the 5 per cent. required for E.C.A. expenses) had to be used on specific development projects in the territories. Finally the United

---

[1] *The Colonial Territories, 1954–55*, Cmd. 9489, 1955, p. 55.

[2] The International Bank's Report on Nigeria was issued under the title, *The Economic Development of Nigeria*, 1955. See also *African Affairs*, January 1955, p. 14.

[3] International Bank for Reconstruction and Development, *Eighth Annual Report to the Board of Governors, 1952–1953*.

States, acting through the agency of the Export-Import Bank, provided direct loan aid to African territories producing strategic materials. The Bank acts on the recommendation of the Defense Materials Procurement Agency, and may, on the certificate of the Defense Production Administration, make loans on projects which offer less than a reasonable assurance of repayment.

From all these American sources a total of approximately $477 million was made available up to 1952.[1] (This sum does not include American contributions to the United Nations agencies or to the International Bank for Reconstruction and Development.) Approximately $140 million took the form of loans; the remaining $337 million included a sum of $282 million originally granted to France under the European Programme, but subsequently transferred to its overseas territories. If we add to this the amounts made available by the United Nations and the International Bank for Reconstruction and Development, it would seem that from 1945 to 1952 a total of approximately £230 million was invested from public international sources in programmes of development in Africa. In so far as this can be allocated to specific types of investment, the major part has gone to projects in the sphere of communications (mainly railways), power, and mining. Only a small proportion has directly benefited agriculture and that chiefly in the form of technical assistance grants. None has gone to manufacturing industry.

As has been observed, the dominating motive in the African Development Plans has been the recognition that facilities favouring the new investment of private capital must normally be created by the previous investment of public capital on a considerable scale. Since the Second World War the flow of private capital has been predominantly directed to the areas of European settlement and mining enterprise. In the seven-year period from 1946 to 1952 the private capital inflow into the Union of South Africa exceeded £500 million, and of this approximately £30 million came from the United States. In the three years 1950–2 the net balance of immigrant funds accruing to Southern Rhodesia exceeded £6 million and there were similar imports of capital into Northern Rhodesia and Kenya. Of the Government-stimulated loans raised on the London money market in the post-war period up to 1952 by far the largest proportion went to European-settled areas. Even these areas, however, have been affected by the sense of political insecurity which characterizes a large part of Africa today; where European political dominance is less strongly maintained the sense of insecurity is inevitably far greater. A large part of new private investment has been financed by residents or

[1] United States Department of State, Office of Intelligence Research, *Postwar Economic Aid to Africa by the US, IBRD, and UN*, Report no. 5970, December 1952. See also E. W. Moran, in *Africa Today*, 1955, pp. 442 ff.

has been derived from the profits of existing enterprises. In addition there has been in recent years a substantial inflow of private capital through the local subsidiaries of United Kingdom commercial and engineering firms. Where, however, the immigrant population is small there are few enterprises which have surplus capital to invest. There are not many African capitalists even in those areas where the economic opportunities open to them are widest; in West Africa, for example, there is no established capitalist class interested in and capable of financing regular trading.[1]

In addition to the intrinsic characteristics which have made much of Africa unattractive to private investors, an additional deterrent has been created by the existence of currency controls. In this connexion an analysis of recent trends in American investment is of some interest.[2] Its most noticeable feature is a marked preference for direct foreign investments as opposed to the portfolio variety. The latter generally offer a lower rate of interest and leave the investor with only a very indirect control over day-to-day investment policy. Hence they are more vulnerable to the vagaries of exchange-control policy than direct investments. By selection of direct investments the investor is able to concentrate his capital on ventures whose output is sold on a hard-currency market and which thereby generate their own foreign exchange to pay a return on his capital. In 1946 United States direct investments abroad were valued at $8,854 million and portfolio investments at $5,344 million. By 1951 direct investments had reached a value of $14,500 million and portfolio investments had not risen above $6,100 million.[3] United States direct private investments in Africa south of the Sahara amounted in 1952 to only $426 million, nearly half of which was invested in the Union, and the greater part of the remainder in Liberia.[4]

Finally it must be recognized that another—possibly the most important—reason for Africa's failure to attract capital from America lies in the fact that the North American continent is still its major competitor in search of capital. The existence of vast investment opportunities within the United States has been explicitly recognized by American observers. In a report to the President made in July 1953, for instance, it was stated that 'with the exception of the development of petroleum reserves and mineral deposits elsewhere, the opportunities for profitable employment of capital on this continent are too numerous and too great to induce any large outflow on private account into enterprise overseas'.[5]

[1] P. T. Bauer, *West African Trade*, 1954, p. 57.

[2] E. Bloch, 'United States Foreign Investment and Dollar Shortage', *Review of Economics and Statistics*, May 1953.

[3] S. Pizer, 'Recent Developments in United States International Investments', *Foreign Commerce Weekly*, 21 April 1952.

[4] B. Blankenheimer, in *Africa Today*, 1955, p. 467.

[5] United States, *Department of State Bulletin*, 31 August 1953.

The conclusion which emerges from this consideration of the limitations on the flow of private capital into Africa is that the character of African economic development must largely depend upon the action of Governments. Even in the Union of South Africa, with its European population and a prosperous mining industry, the rate of development is largely dependent on State action in expanding public-utility services, and this in turn depends on access to international capital, which is available mainly to the Government. It is of some interest therefore to consider in some detail the character and content of the Development Programmes now in operation in the various countries south of the Sahara.

The Union of South Africa and Southern Rhodesia

The Union of South Africa and Southern Rhodesia occupy a separate position in so far that the reasons which led to the elaboration of special Development Programmes in the territories farther north do not apply to them. The value of domestic production in the Union had by 1952 reached an annual rate of £1,245 million,[1] and it amounted to £1,392 million in 1953. In Southern Rhodesia it rose from £118 million in 1952 to £132 million in 1953.[2] In both countries there were valuable mineral resources to attract foreign capital and a settled European population to supply skill and enterprise for the development of local industry. The war, by restricting imports, had provided an additional stimulus to local enterprise. By the time it ended output was expanding vigorously in mining, in European agriculture, and in secondary industry, a process which of itself created sources of new finance either by attracting foreign capital and immigrants (many of them bringing their own capital) or by producing profits which could be ploughed back into new investment.

The objective of the development planning in both the Union and Southern Rhodesia has been to expand the output of the public utilities, and of coal and steel, food, and housing. But neither country works to a rigid programme. In the Union there has been a major emphasis on the expansion of public utilities. In the five years ended 1954 the railway administration invested £163 million in new works and in the replacement of obsolete rolling-stock and other equipment. An extensive programme of expansion was initiated by the Electricity Supply Commission.[3] The construction programme in operation in 1953 was designed to increase the generating capacity from 1·6 million kW to 3 million kW by 1958. The Union Government Loan Programme for 1954–5 envisaged an expenditure

---

[1] Bureau of Census and Statistics, 'The Net National Income of the Union of South Africa', *South African Journal of Economics*, June 1953. See also *Africa Digest*, March–April 1955, p. 9.

[2] Preliminary figures from Central African Statistical Office, *Economic and Statistical Bulletin of Southern Rhodesia*, March 1954.

[3] International Bank for Reconstruction and Development, *Supplement to Eighth Annual Report to the Board of Governors, 1952–1953*.

of £79·2 million on loan account including provision for a factory to obtain oil from coal. This was estimated to cost £31 million.

The State has also taken steps to assist in the finance of key industries. The earliest State enterprise was the Iron and Steel Industrial Corporation (I.S.C.O.R.), which was established in 1934, and by 1952–3 was supplying 72 per cent. of the local requirements of steel. The Industrial Development Corporation of South Africa was formed in 1940, with an authorized capital of £5 million, which was increased to £22½ million in 1953. The State-financed Fisheries Development Corporation formed in 1944 has invested considerable capital directly in various allied or subsidiary industries and has made available loans at low interest rates for housing, water supplies, and boats.[1]

In one direction, however, the Union has considered a publicly financed Development Programme of a type which is characteristic of the territories farther north. Allusion has been made to the significance of the Socio-Economic Commission for the Development of the Bantu Areas, which was appointed in 1950 (the Tomlinson Commission). It was charged to make recommendations for the development of the Native Areas, so as to implement the policy of *apartheid* by enabling these to support a greatly increased population. Its proposals[2] do not aim at the return of the entire African population to the Native areas, but at slowing the rate of emigration from them in such a manner that at the end of the century the African in the European areas will not greatly outnumber the Europeans. The Tomlinson Commission estimates that by the year 2000 the population of the Union will include 6 million Europeans and 21½ million Africans. The Development Programme aims at enabling 15 million Africans to live in seven large areas to be created by consolidating the existing Reserves and incorporating the High Commission Territories in the Union; the remaining 6½ million would be permanently resident in the European areas.

As an initial step proposals are made for a capital investment of £104 million in development works in the African areas during the next ten years. Of this £37 million would go to soil reclamation, afforestation, and agricultural development generally, £31 million to the establishment of industries, £8 million to roads and railways, £5 million to electric power, £12 million to urban development, and £11 million to education. In addition the plan proposes the creation of a Bantu Development Corporation, with a capital of £30 million, which would be responsible for the construction of 100 new towns. While endorsing its general aims, the

---

[1] W. H. Stoop, 'The South African Fishing Industry', *South African Journal of Economics*, September 1953.

[2] *Summary of the Report of the Commission for the Socio-Economic Development of the Bantu Areas within the Union of South Africa*, U.G. no. 61, 1955. See also above, pp. 169, 763, 1024.

Minister for Native Affairs stated that the Government was not prepared to budget for more than a year at a time. Capital for development was to be made available by allocations from general revenues to the Native Trust Fund. During the debate on the Report it was announced that the amount so allocated for the financial year 1956–7 would be £3½ million.

In the field of private enterprise impressive new developments have been planned in mining. Five mines were in production in the new Orange Free State gold-field by the end of 1953, and it was then predicted that during 1954 the number would rise to nine. Up to the end of 1954 some £130 million had been spent on capital work in this field.[1] The discovery of uranium in association with the gold has improved the prospects of the gold-mining industry in the Rand gold-fields, where rising costs have been a matter of grave concern.

The increase in the amount of capital invested in agriculture since the Second World War has also been impressive. Considerable strides have been made in the mechanization of farming. The number of tractors in use on farms more than doubled between 1947 and 1950, and it has been estimated that farmers spent £27,363,000 on machinery, tools, and equipment in the year 1950–1. According to one observer, 'agriculture in all parts of the country is in an upward spiral of technological progress'.[2]

Foreign capital has made a large contribution to these extensive developments. In the six years ending in 1951 the total gross investment of foreign capital in the Union amounted to nearly £500 million. Over the same period the net full investment amounted to £1,192 million, of which nearly 30 per cent. was public investment (including in this term investment by the Central and Local Governments and railways). This compares with a total net investment for the period 1938–45 of £38 million, of which more than half was public investment.[3] Part, however, of this great increase is due to price inflation. The Klip power-station, for example, cost £15·4 per kW in 1940, whereas the Vierfontein station was estimated in 1951 to cost £55 per kW.

By the beginning of 1954 the demand for capital was beginning to outstrip the supply. Reserves of foreign exchange had been dwindling throughout 1953. The Government was obliged to reduce the loan programme for 1954–5 from the £92 million originally envisaged to £79·2 million, of which three-quarters was to be financed by loan receipts and the remainder by surpluses on revenue account. It also decided not to raise any new public loans in that year, in order to leave the market free

---

[1] See below, p. 1491.

[2] C. V. H. du Plessis, 'Agriculture. . . . Some Aspects of its Importance to the South African Economy', *Union of South Africa Finance and Trade Review*, vol. i, no. 3, July 1953.

[3] H. J. Van Eck, 'Industrial Development in South Africa', in ibid. For regular figures of net investment, see South African Reserve Bank, *Quarterly Bulletin of Statistics*.

to meet the forthcoming demands of the Electricity Supply Commission and the municipal authorities in connexion with the urgent need for the expansion of electric power and water services. It may be added that the International Bank has approved loans to the Union totalling $50 million, largely for railways and electric power.[1]

Southern Rhodesia has drawn up four-year plans covering projects for the improvement of agriculture, irrigation, and communications; the first of these was expected to cost over £48 million from 1949 to 1953. A new railway has been constructed to provide the territory with an outlet at Lourenço Marques.[2] The impressive scheme for the construction of a major hydroelectric installation at the Kariba Gorge has been described in a previous chapter.[3] An active policy of industrialization is being pursued with the State itself undertaking production of key commodities where private capital is slow to venture. A British engineering firm, for example, has been encouraged to open a branch at Que Que as a sequel to the establishment there of the Government steelworks, and the Government-owned Gatooma textile mill now supplies a number of weaving and knitting concerns in the vicinity.[4]

The British Dependent Territories

By the Colonial Development and Welfare Act of 1945 the Parliament of the United Kingdom voted a total of £120 million to be spent on development in the Colonial territories. This amount was extended to £140 million by the Act of 1950. In 1955 the fund thus provided, which was due to close in March 1956, was extended until March 1960. A further £80 million was voted which, added to an unexpended £40 million, brought the total amount available for expenditure during the period 1955–60 to £120 million.[5] There was from the first no conception of the preparation of a regional plan for a group of Colonies. Each Government drafted its own programme, and the plans eventually adopted were evolved from discussions between the authorities in the United Kingdom and the Governments of the individual Colonies. Each Colonial plan was complete in itself and was operated as a separate entity.

The experience gained in the practical application of economic policies both at the British Colonial Office and in the dependencies may have been one of the most valuable results of this process. It is fair to say that most of the early drafts of the Development Plans were little more than a series of departmental estimates inflated above their normal level by anticipation of the receipt of extra-territorial aid. The plans eventually

[1] International Bank for Reconstruction and Development, *The International Bank for Reconstruction and Development, 1946–1953*, 1954, p. 221.
[2] See below, p. 1552.   [3] See above, pp. 986 ff.
[4] A. J. Bruwer, 'Industrial Development', in *Africa South of the Sahara*, 1951.
[5] *The Colonial Territories, 1954–55*, Cmd. 9489, p. 54. See also above, p. 1323.

approved represented the result of a joint attempt to appraise—probably for the first time—the prospects and potentialities of each individual territory, and to devise the most efficient allocation of the resources available for development. The basic appraisal has inevitably remained under constant review in the light of the experience of changing conditions of cost and other factors.

During the Second World War the dependencies had accumulated considerable balances owing to the fact that neither the staff nor the material was available for the normal expansion of the public services. They would, therefore, in any case have undertaken considerable programmes of capital expenditure in the years immediately following the war. The funds made available under the Colonial Development and Welfare Acts served to give a new direction to these programmes, but they represented a relatively small proportion of the total cost. In 1953 the approved Development Plans for the African dependencies provided for a total expenditure of £282·8 million over a ten-year period. Of this, one-half was to be met from local revenues, rather less than one-third from loans secured on these revenues, and about 18 per cent. from grants made under the Colonial Development and Welfare Acts.[1] The expenditure proposed and the relative contribution made from local and United Kingdom resources, however, vary widely between different territories. At one end of the scale British Somaliland proposed an expenditure of under £1 million, to be met wholly from grants made under the Development and Welfare Acts, while at the other the Gold Coast plan involved a total of over £75 million, 96 per cent. of which would be provided from local revenues or loans. The plans envisaging the highest investment per head of population were those of the Gold Coast and Northern Rhodesia; in both cases the figure was between £18 and £19 per head.

By the end of 1952 the total amount borrowed on the London money market by the British African dependencies was approximately £73 million. Loans and grants made to them from United States and international sources amounted by June 1953 to rather under £19 million. In addition to the funds made available to Colonial Governments under the Colonial Development and Welfare Act, certain capital sums were provided under the Overseas Resources Development Act of 1948. As has already been mentioned, the Colonial Development Corporation was given power to borrow up to £100 million from the United Kingdom Treasury for schemes of economic development in the Colonial empire. By the end of 1955 it had received sanction for loans amounting to £31·9 million for African projects.[2] The past operations in Africa of the

[1] *The Colonial Territories, 1952–53*, Cmd. 8856, 1953, p. 141.
[2] *Colonial Development Corporation, Report and Accounts for 1955*, p. 2.

Overseas Food Corporation, and the extent to which they are still being continued, have been described in an earlier chapter.[1]

By the end of 1951, according to a Colonial Office Survey,[2] major capital works to a total value of £122 million were in progress in British Colonial Africa. Of this approximately £94 million represented work undertaken by the Central or Local Governments or by public corporations. Of the remainder, totalling £28 million, at least two-thirds was invested by mining companies in Northern Rhodesia. An analysis of all the major capital works in progress in 1951 (whether undertaken by the Government or by private enterprise) shows that nearly a third of them by value were concerned with railways, roads, harbours, and other forms of communication; a quarter were electricity, drainage, or irrigation projects; 17 per cent. were industrial; 16½ per cent. were concerned with housing, water supplies, or sewerage; and less than 8 per cent. were for the provision of educational or medical facilities. It is, however, difficult to see these large-scale works in their proper perspective unless account is also taken of the private small-scale investment in such directions as housing or farm equipment. No adequate material exists for estimating the amount of this type of investment.

The French Territories

In contrast to the procedure adopted in the British Colonial dependencies the object of French policy has traditionally been to plan the development of the metropolitan country and its overseas territories as a single unit. As early as 1923 M. Albert Sarraut published a master plan of *mise en valeur*, according to which the products particularly suited to each Colonial area were to be determined and measures taken to promote their intensive cultivation, while the increase in production was to be accompanied by a simultaneous development of communications.[3] The tendency towards economic integration was intensified by the political integration of France with its overseas territories in the creation of the French Union in 1946.[4] Early in 1948 the *Commission de Modernisation et d'Équipement des Territoires d'Outre-Mer*[5] produced a statement of the broad directions in which it was hoped to develop the economies of the overseas dependencies and drew up a list of production targets. Meanwhile the Minister for Overseas France was charged with the task of producing provisional schemes for individual territories which would ultimately be brought into line with the metropolitan plans. A law of 1949 provided for a Ten-year Development Programme divided into a general and an

---

[1] See above, p. 845.

[2] *Major Capital Works in the Colonial Territories*, Col. no. 285, 1952.

[3] A. Sarraut, *La Mise en valeur des colonies*, 1923. See also L. P. Mair, *Native Policies in Africa*, 1936, pp. 186–8.

[4] See above, pp. 212 ff.   [5] Created by *décret*, 29 April 1946.

overseas section. The former section was to be financed entirely by the metropolitan Government and was designed in the joint interests of the overseas territory and the metropolis. The latter was to be jointly financed by the Colony and the metropolitan Government and was designed primarily in the interests of the Colony.

As has already been explained,[1] the French equivalent of the provisions made under the Colonial Development and Welfare Acts is the *Fonds d'Investissement pour le Développement Économique et Social* (F.I.D.E.S.), into which are paid allocations from the metropolitan budget as well as the contributions of overseas territories. In practice, however, the French Colonies have been unwilling to contribute out of local revenues to a central fund over which they have no control, and they have fulfilled their obligation in respect of F.I.D.E.S. by borrowing their contributions from the *Caisse Centrale de la France d'Outre-Mer* (C.C.F.O.-M.).[2] The object of this latter organization is to provide credit to assist either Public Authorities or private enterprise to undertake development projects which fall within the framework of the plan. It has attempted to provide for minor as well as for major capital works by creating within the Colonies a number of subsidiary credit societies which make allowances for small-scale enterprises or for house building.

Over the initial stage of planning for the French territories, that is, for the period 1946–52, expenditure of a total of 324 milliard francs was authorized by these Public Authorities. This is the equivalent of £280 million at the official rate of exchange. Of this 50 per cent. comprised expenditure on ports, railways, and roads, 20 per cent. on social equipment (mainly hospitals and schools), 11 per cent. on assistance to mining and industry including hydroelectric power, 12 per cent. on assistance to agriculture, and 7 per cent. on research. Of the total, 42 per cent. was directed to French West Africa, 15 per cent. to the French Cameroons, 15 per cent. to French Equatorial Africa, and the rest to areas outside Africa.

No information is available on the extent of the response by private enterprise, but it is said to have been disappointing.[3] Loans taken up by private undertakings from the *Caisse Centrale* by the end of 1952 did not exceed 20½ milliard francs, and it is probable that this accounted for the major part of the new private investment in French territories over the period of the first four-year plan. There are, moreover, some indications that the expenditure on development has been forced to a pace somewhat faster than that which the Colonial budgets can support. Only a very small proportion of the total development expenditure could be met out of local revenues, and debt service payments constitute a heavy burden

---

[1] See above, pp. 214, 329.

[2] 'Les Plans d'investissement d'outre-mer', *L'Économie de l'Union française d'outre-mer*, 1952, pp. 188 ff.   [3] Ibid.

on the Colonial budgets. In French West Africa public investment under the Development Plan fell from nearly £18 million in 1952–3 to a little over £10 million in 1953–4. Private investment is presumed to have dropped by about £2 million. The consequent decrease in the pace of development has been held responsible in some quarters for the wave of labour unrest and strikes which occurred in 1954–5.[1]

The Belgian Territories

Planning for the Belgian territories has also been conceived in terms of a ten-year period. The plan for the Belgian Congo was published in 1949,[2] and that for Ruanda Urundi in 1952.[3] In both cases the plans have been incorporated in the territorial budgets. The capital required is to be raised entirely by loans; apart from the fact that the interest on the debt of Ruanda Urundi will be met by the metropolitan Government, both territories are expected to meet the full cost of their own development. Part of the loan finance is being raised within the Belgian Congo by the issue of *Bons de Trésor*.

The cost of the Belgian plan was originally estimated at about 25 milliard francs.[4] Since then, however, prices have risen appreciably and the actual cost was stated late in 1956 as 48 milliard (£348 million).[5] The plan for Ruanda Urundi was originally estimated to involve an expenditure of rather more than 3½ milliard francs. These plans resemble other Development Programmes framed in the post-war period in so far that their objective is to create an environment in which private enterprise can develop to the greatest advantage of the community. As in other cases, special attention is given to the needs of the African community. Approximately 50 per cent. of the total development expenditure planned in the Belgian Congo was designed to improve transport and communications (mainly railways and inland waterways). Emphasis is also placed on the one hand on the expansion of the public utilities connected with schemes of urbanization (housing, water supply, and electrification), and on the other hand (particularly in Ruanda Urundi) on schemes of agricultural research and the resettlement of Africans from congested areas.[6] The special welfare fund (*Fonds du Bien-Être Indigène*), which was created after the Second World War in recognition of the contribution made by the peasantry of the Belgian Congo, has already

---

[1] *West Africa*, 26 March 1955, p. 270.

[2] Ministère des Colonies, *Plan décennal pour le développement économique et social du Congo Belge*, 2 vols, 1949.

[3] Idem, *The Handbook of the Ruanda-Urundi Ten Year Plan*, 1952.

[4] In 1956, 140 Belgian Congo francs were equivalent to £1 sterling.

[5] Centre d'Information et de Documentation du Congo Belge et du Ruanda-Urundi, *Aperçu sur le plan décennal pour le développement économique et social du Congo Belge*, Brussels, 1952. See also G. Malengreau, in *Africa Today*, 1955, p. 342.   [6] See above, p. 911.

been described.[1] This fund consists of a capital sum of just over 2,000 million francs contributed by the Belgian Government and has the benefit of the total profits from the Colonial lottery. In its first six years the expenditure from this fund totalled about 1,700 million francs, the major part being devoted to the health services (including hospitals) and to rural development.[2]

A recent study of industrial development in Central Africa gives some interesting figures of the extent of private investment in the Belgian overseas territories. It was estimated that up to the end of 1939 Belgian companies operating in the Congo had invested the equivalent of more than 29 milliard francs (at the 1947 value) and that local companies had invested 7 milliard. Between 1939 and 1948 it was estimated that a further 35 to 40 milliard francs was invested by Belgian companies, 2 milliard by local companies, and ½ milliard by individuals. By 1951 it was estimated that about 50 milliard francs had been invested in Congo companies; of the total new issues of capital over the period 1949–51 in connexion with companies operating in the Belgian Congo those registered in the Colony accounted for 97 per cent. Ruanda Urundi also attracted considerable new private investment in the post-war period, and Congo firms were taking an increased share in this.[3]

The Economic Adviser to the Central Bank of the Belgian Congo has estimated that, in addition to the capital invested by Public Authorities, private investment might be expected to reach 23 milliard francs. It was also believed that it would be possible to attract foreign investment of about 9 milliard francs, of which 7 milliard would be invested in the public Development Plans and 2 milliard in private enterprise.[4] In sum, therefore, it is estimated that over the period 1950–60 private investment equivalent to over £178 million will be made in the Belgian Congo as a corollary of a public Development Programme which may cost up to £285 million.

The Portuguese Territories

Portuguese policy has sought to develop in the overseas territories an economy complementary to that of the mother country, and since 1938 there have been a succession of Development Plans overlapping both in time and content. These plans have been financed from loans from the metropolitan Government, from local surpluses, and from the proceeds of special taxes. During the Second World War shortages of materials and of equipment hindered development, but between 1946 and 1950 the

---

[1] See above, p. 561.   [2] G. Malengreau, in *Africa Today*, 1955, p. 345.
[3] R. Bertiaux, *Aspects de l'industrialisation en Afrique centrale*, 1953.
[4] Estimates made by the Economic Adviser to the *Banque Centrale du Congo Belge*, quoted in *Aperçu sur le plan décennal pour le développement économique et social du Congo Belge*, Brussels, 1952.

sums allocated by Portugal to its African territories have amounted to the equivalent of £15 million.[1] The largest single loan, amounting to £12½ million, was made in 1947 to Mozambique, and was primarily intended for the improvement of communications. Rather more than half of this had been spent by the end of 1951.[2]

The second Development Plan, which covered the period 1951–5, overlaps in time and content with the Portuguese National Development Plan covering the period 1953–8. The latter allocates approximately £36¼ million to Angola and £29¼ million to Mozambique. For Angola nearly 50 per cent. and for Mozambique over 45 per cent. of the expenditure visualized under the National Development Plan is intended for the improvement of railways, ports, and aerodromes. Hydroelectric schemes are expected to absorb 23 per cent. of the expenditure in Mozambique and 14 per cent. in Angola. In Mozambique 20 per cent. of the expenditure is allocated to irrigation in the valley of the Limpopo;[3] the corresponding proportion for Angola is 16 per cent. Agricultural resettlement and assistance schemes account for 18 per cent. of the expenditure in Angola and 9 per cent. of that for Mozambique. In each case between 1 and 2 per cent. is allocated to geological survey.[4]

No information is available on the progress of private investment in the Portuguese territories, but Portugal's own resources for overseas investment are limited and restrictions on foreign entrepreneurs are likely to deter direct investment from international sources. Such difficulties occur also in the territories of other Powers, but they are less acute than those experienced in the case of the Portuguese overseas territories. In industrial undertakings in Mozambique, for instance, it is usually required that 51 per cent. of the shares should be held by Portuguese nationals, while in Angola the purchase of land by aliens must be negotiated through the Foreign Office in Lisbon and the Foreign Office of the country of the intending purchaser.

Liberia

As has been explained in previous chapters[5] the economic development of Liberia has now become in many ways dependent on the relations which have been established either with the Government or with private enterprises in the United States of America. In the year 1951–2, for example, over 93 per cent. of the export trade of Liberia and 75 per cent. of its

---

[1] Organization for European Economic Co-operation, *General Memorandum on the 1950–51 and 1951–52 Programmes, Portugal*, Paris, April 1950.

[2] *Overseas Economic Surveys, Portuguese East Africa, 1952*, p. 5.

[3] See above, p. 1009.

[4] Secretariado Nacional da Informação, 'Les Provinces d'outre-mer et le plan de développe ment économique', *Portugal*, September–October 1952, p. 17.

[5] See above, pp. 237, 759, 1218.

import trade was with the United States.[1] Some details have been given of the substantial contribution which has been made by the Firestone Corporation and the American-owned Liberia Mining Company to the development of the resources of Liberia.[2] Of these two undertakings the Firestone Corporation is the more important, since not only has it received Concession rights over large areas of land but it has also been instrumental in arranging for assistance to the public revenues of Liberia by loans from the United States. In the same way as some of the major concessionaires in other territories, the Corporation has assumed more general responsibilities than those implicit in its operations for producing rubber. In the absence of public utilities, such as are taken for granted in more highly developed countries, the Corporation has had to construct its own hydroelectric plant and telephone system. In addition it operates a bank, and helps to maintain the main aerodrome and many miles of road. It provides two hospitals and seven schools and has assisted in financing research in tropical medicine. Altogether it has invested about $20 million in Liberia.

The Liberian Government's own scheme for development takes the form of a five-year plan which aims at an expenditure of $25 million. Here again American aid is an important constituent of the plan. A development corporation which has recently been formed has been largely financed from United States sources. Under a Point Four Agreement signed in December 1950 some 60 American technicians have been placed at the disposal of Liberia as part of a programme of technical assistance to which the Government has pledged 20 per cent. of its annual revenue. By June 1952 Liberia had received United States Government assistance to the value of over $36 million, of which about $6½ million was in the form of free grants. More than 70 per cent. of this total was designed to provide for the improvement of communications; of the remainder about half was designed to assist mining enterprise and nearly half was allotted to general and social purposes.[3] It is too early to assess the success of this expenditure in stimulating indigenous economic development, but it has been reported that some wholly Liberian trading firms are beginning to make their appearance.[4]

THE FUTURE OF INDIGENOUS DEVELOPMENT

In the course of the Second World War and the post-war period the world demand for primary products remained high, in spite of violent

[1] H.M. Ambassador at Monrovia, 'Liberia, A Dollar Market in Africa', *Board of Trade Journal*, 14 November 1953. [2] See above, p. 237.
[3] United States Department of State, Office of Intelligence Research, *Postwar Economic Aid to Africa by the US, IBRD, and UN*, Report no. 5970, December 1952.
[4] *Board of Trade Journal*, 14 November 1953.

fluctuations in some prices, and ensured more than a decade and a half of relative prosperity for most African producers. By 1954 the volume of production of food in Africa was estimated to be about a third above the average for the years 1934–8.[1] In the Union and in Southern Rhodesia, and to a lesser extent in other territories such as the Belgian Congo and Kenya, there were important developments in local secondary industries. Although the end of the operations in Korea brought some decline in the value of African exports in 1953, it did not destroy the favourable economic prospects.

In some ways, however, the experience of the post-war period has been disappointing. Inflationary conditions have checked the increase of real incomes. In some cases the returns from new capital investment have been disappointing, particularly where attempts have been made by public bodies to stimulate development by investment in fields where private enterprise would not venture. The Colonial Development Corporation had by 1955 achieved a net trading profit in only one of its African enterprises—the Lobatsi abattoir and its Molopo ranch. The Corporation's controlling interest in another profit-yielding undertaking—Chilanga Cement Limited in Northern Rhodesia—had been sold to private enterprise from January 1955. Five other projects had involved the Corporation in a loss of £124,601.[2]

In effect, the result of its seven years of experiment in the possibilities of commercial development in Africa was to force the Corporation into a much more conservative view of these potentialities than had prevailed at the time of its promotion. Since a public enterprise has at its disposal greater facilities for research and experiment than all but the largest of private companies, it should be in a better position to promote successful new ventures, and it seems fair to conclude that its failures must have been due in part to the unusual difficulties inherent in African conditions.

This conclusion is borne out to some extent by more general evidence on capital formation in Africa. It was estimated that in 1952 gross capital formation in all the territories of the British Colonial empire amounted to only about one-fifth of that in the United Kingdom, and that Africa, with over 80 per cent. of the total population of these territories, accounted in the period 1948–52 for only 45 per cent. of their capital formation.[3] The total sum of investment in Africa might be slightly varied by taking into account the value of the type of small-scale investment made by peasant farmers which has been referred to elsewhere. But the fact remains that the short-run return on capital investment in

[1] United Nations, Department of Economic Affairs, *Review of Economic Activity in Africa, 1950 to 1954* (Supplement to *World Economic Report, 1953–54*), 1955, p. 10.
[2] *Colonial Development Corporation, Report and Accounts for 1955*, pp. 6, 18.
[3] *The Colonial Territories, 1953–54*, Cmd. 9169, 1954, paras. 376–80.

Africa is generally low, and that the rate of new capital formation is consequently slow.

There are, however, exceptions to this conclusion. In the mining centres of Central and Southern Africa, for example, the high return on investment in the mines and in their ancillary industries has in the past attracted capital and skill on a large scale, and is now generating a relatively rapid economic growth. But it is significant that this growth has left the large areas of land and population which lie outside its orbit to stagnate and in some respects even to decline. Reference has been made to the deteriorating Native Reserves of the Union of South Africa and to the contrast between the high standards of development in the railway belt of Northern Rhodesia and those in the outer provinces where the majority of the African population still lives. In a sense the development which has taken place in the mining centres and in the European settled areas of Africa is an expansion of the geographical boundaries of European economic growth rather than a process which is organic in the African economies. In so far as this process of growth is reproducing itself within Africa by providing capital and technological skill from internal sources it is doing so most conspicuously within the relatively restricted limits of the transplanted European economy.

History suggests that the high standards of living which have been achieved in some countries during the past century and a half have been due in the main to the growth of the industrial system.[1] This has raised standards of productivity in the industrial countries in which it has occurred and increased the contrast between their wealth and the poverty of the rest of the world, at all events in money terms. The development of world-wide systems of communication and trade has at the same time brought into closer contact peoples of widely different standards of living, and the sense of contrast has become acute. There is consequently an increasing insistence by political leaders in the more backward countries on the need for industrial development.

There are, however, factors which in the past have prevented the growth of industry in Africa and still form obstacles to its rapid development. In most parts of the continent economic specialization has not even now developed to a level comparable with that reached by Europe at the beginning of its industrial revolution. For a long time there was little encouragement of industrialization in this and other backward areas of the world. The traditional role envisaged by the industrialized countries for the peoples of other parts of the world was that of suppliers of raw materials. Now that African territories are anxious to develop their own industries they are handicapped by low standards of education and a lack of ready adaptability to new technical processes. Moreover, Africa lacks a

[1] S. S. Kuznets, in *Economic Change*, 1954, p. 240.

number of advantages which have been enjoyed by Western Europe and North America. The industrial revolution in England took its shape from the close proximity of ample resources of coal and iron. The mass-production methods of the United States have depended for their success on the existence of a large domestic market. The development of a vigorous system of internal markets presupposes the existence of a considerable number of local resources. These conditions do not exist in many African territories.

There are in addition a number of factors which actually militate against a more general industrial development. The apprenticeship system, which spread the skills of the craftsman and artisan through pre-industrial Europe, has so far proved to be a relatively ineffective instrument of progress for communities which must learn their skills from immigrant technicians. This is sometimes due to a definite reluctance on the part of immigrants to share their skill, or more frequently to their inability to reach a satisfactory long-term relationship with the indigenous labourer. Again, the costs of production in many African industries are increased by factors of social rather than economic origin. There are barriers, which at times seem to be perfectly rigid, against the rise of un-skilled labourers to a skilled status. The cost of skilled labour is inflated by the need to import skilled workers and is maintained by their political supremacy, with the result that the cost of the labour force in general is increased by racial or national restrictions on its mobility between occupations. Even in West Africa, where the African is gradually taking his place in skilled occupations, the rates of earnings of the skilled worker tend to be based on the standard established by the immigrant European. The cost of capital is inflated by political uncertainties. Again, the most efficient utilization of land resources may be barred by restrictions on land ownership. Some of these restrictions are socially or politically desirable. Most of them appear to be now politically inevitable. Though any one by itself may be of minor importance, together they involve a serious loss of elasticity for most African economies. It is their cumulative effect, and in some instances the use made of them by modern Governments, which tend to create an impediment to economic progress.

There are also obstacles to development arising from the present character of international finance and trade. Some of these originated in the protective policies adopted during the world depression of the thirties, and others are a result of the Second World War and its sequel. One of the most important is the system of exchange control which was developed during the war, and which divided the world into sharply distinct monetary zones. The result was to set up more effective barriers to trade than had ever existed before and to wipe out most of the advances towards freedom of trade which had been achieved in the nineteenth century and the early part of the twentieth. Tariffs make foreign trade more difficult; exchange control can make it impossible. The effects of such control on the direction of trade have been clearly marked for some African territories. French Equatorial Africa, for example, took 38 per cent. of its imports from the franc zone in 1938, but by 1950 the proportion was 68 per cent. In the French Cameroons French cottons, which accounted for less than 1 per cent. of imports in 1938, represented 63 per cent. in 1951. By contrast, the Belgian Congo, where there is no such control, took less than 40 per cent. of its imports from Belgium and 26 per cent. from the dollar area.

The effects of import control on standards of living are difficult to measure, but there is no doubt that they contribute to a reduction in real incomes. Cotton and hardware goods, which account for about 60 per cent. of the imports of French Africa south of the Sahara, were in 1952 sold at prices 25 and 40 per cent. above the prices at which they could be supplied by foreign countries. Food imported from France was dearer in most cases than foreign products, and French cement cost 20 per cent. more than Belgian or German.[1] For British territories one result of the exchange-control system, at the period during which British goods were not available, was to increase the volume of their sterling assets in London so that, in effect, some of them were obliged to lend to London the funds which they would have spent on imports had they been free to do so. In each of the four years 1951–4 the favourable balances of the British African dependencies with the non-sterling area reached a combined total of over £50 million.[2]

The control of foreign exchange clearly enables the metropolitan Powers to influence the direction of trade with their dependencies to a greater extent than was ever effected by protective tariffs. It will be recalled that in the past history of Africa the possibility of the use of tariffs by the metropolitan Powers in order to secure for themselves exclusive advantages in their dependencies was a matter of much concern. The Powers which took part in the Berlin Congress of 1884 agreed that 'the trade of all nations' should 'enjoy complete freedom' in the Congo Basin.[3] At the Brussels Conference of 1890 the Berlin Act was amended so as to permit the levying by the Congo Free State of duties up to 10 per cent. *ad valorem*, the object being to allow the Free State a regular procedure for raising revenue in order to support the cost of administration. The area covered by the Berlin Act has become known as the Conventional Basin of the Congo, and includes (in addition to the Belgian Congo) Kenya,

---

[1] *L'Économie de l'Union française d'outre-mer*, 1952, p. 78.
[2] *The Colonial Territories, 1954–55*, Cmd. 9489, 1955, p. 183.
[3] General Act of the Congress of Berlin, quoted by R. L. Buell, *The Native Problem in Africa*, vol. i, 1928, p. 892.

Uganda, Tanganyika, Zanzibar, Nyasaland, and parts of Northern Rhodesia, Angola, Mozambique, and French Equatorial Africa. All these areas continue under the general restriction imposed by the Berlin Act on the use of preferential discriminatory tariffs. In West Africa an Anglo-French non-discrimination treaty was in force from 1898 to 1937. At the close of the First World War the general principle of non-discrimination was reasserted in the Convention of St. Germain (1919), and the texts of the League of Nations Mandates for Togoland, the Cameroons, Tanganyika, and Ruanda Urundi elaborated the terms in which equality of commercial opportunity was defined. The same general principles are laid down in the Trusteeship Agreements which replaced the Mandates after the Second World War.

The original motive for the imposition of these provisions was the removal of causes of international tension from the Colonial field, but it was later argued also that the interests of the African populations were best served by the entry of the commerce of all nations on equal terms. Critics of the régime of non-discrimination maintained, however, that it would make it impossible for these territories to protect any industries that they might develop. Under the agreements of 1919 the benefits of equality of commercial access were guaranteed only to the members of the League of Nations, and when Japan left the League the opportunity was taken to impose import quotas on Japanese goods. Such measures were criticized on the ground that they deprived the African consumer of a class of commodities available to him from the low-priced markets of the East, but beyond his means if imported from Europe. At the present moment these controversies are not a matter of international debate, but they might again assume importance if there were to be a return to the free movement of currency.

Some reference has been made in the preceding paragraphs to the growth of the sterling balances of the British East and West African dependencies. This has been a striking characteristic of the post-war period. According to official estimates these balances more than doubled between 1949 and 1954, by which time they had reached a total of £705 million, £488 million for West Africa and £217 million for East Africa (this figure includes Aden).[1] This development is the result of a number of different factors. The financial reserves of these territories are increasing as a normal consequence of their accelerated economic activity, and there are various reasons why they should be invested in London. It is convenient for Colonial Governments and entrepreneurs to keep their reserves in safe sterling investments. Since the African currencies are operated under a system which requires full backing in sterling, all issues

[1] *Memorandum on the Sterling Assets of the British Colonies*, Col. no. 298, 1953. *The Colonial Territories, 1954–55*, Cmd. 9489, 1955, p. 51.

of local currency are secured by the accumulation of sterling funds in London.[1] It is thus inherent in the financial organization of these dependencies that any increase in their Government revenues, in their commercial profits, or in their issues of local currency, should be reflected in an increase in the volume of their sterling balances.

The sterling balances have also been increased, however, as a result of the restrictions placed on Colonial trade by the exchange-control system, and by the accumulation of reserve funds by the various statutory Marketing Boards as an element in their policy of price stabilization. Budgetary surpluses have also been built up in part as a deliberate policy and in part because Development Programmes have had to be postponed owing to the inability of manufacturers in the sterling area to supply the capital goods required. The most important components of the sterling balances are the budgetary surpluses and the reserve funds of the Marketing Boards. Government funds accounted for 40 per cent. of all Colonial sterling assets at the end of 1954;[2] this figure includes all territories under the Colonial Office but does not include the Federation of Rhodesia and Nyasaland. General and development Government reserves held in the United Kingdom at the end of 1952 by the East African group of Colonies amounted to 82 per cent. of their public revenue; for the West African group the percentage was 75.[3] The known sterling securities of the West African Marketing Boards and the Uganda Price Assistance Funds accounted for about a quarter of the sterling assets of British African Colonies (with which Aden is included) at the end of 1951, and at the end of 1954 were one-fifth of those of the East and West African groups. The avowed object of these reserves is to build up funds for price assistance in the years of the depression of prices. By the end of 1954 they had contributed a total of £139 million to Colonial sterling assets, and had made in addition substantial loans to Colonial Governments, apart from deposits of unknown amount with London banks and development agencies.

The accumulation of reserve funds by the Marketing Boards has given rise to considerable controversy. The maintenance of large reserves is considered to be necessary by those who believe that the prices of raw materials since the Second World War have been abnormally high and that they must fall to something nearer their pre-war level. It is not surprising if financial Authorities who recall the experience of the inter-war depression consider it essential to provide against the possibility that extensive commitments undertaken in a period of unprecedentedly high prices may have to be met from greatly reduced public incomes. The

[1] For details, see I. Greaves, *Colonial Monetary Conditions*, Colonial Research Studies no. 10, 1953.

[2] Cmd. 9489, 1955, p. 51.   [3] Col. no. 298, 1953.

retention of a part of the market price is also in their view justified as a means of reducing inflationary pressures, and it is argued that investment from the funds so accumulated is directed to ends more beneficial to the national economy than would be served by allowing farmers to receive the full value of their crops. The latter argument is reinforced by the belief that if a much higher price were paid to African farmers they would be as likely to reduce output and enjoy more leisure as to increase it and raise levels of consumption. Advocates of controlled marketing also assert that the reduction in the number of middlemen has in some cases enabled the actual producer to obtain a better price than he would receive in the absence of control. It is also claimed that one effect of control has been greatly to improve standards of quality. One noteworthy example is the improvement in the quality of palm oil in Nigeria.

On the other side, it is argued that whereas productivity, particularly in cocoa, is actually declining it may well be that demand will continue to be high, and that in such conditions more consideration should be given to the stimulation of output by the incentive of a good price. There are, it is said, cases in which the Marketing Boards have realized lower prices on world markets than independent exporters.[1] It is further argued that the producers of raw materials are in effect subjected, through the control of prices and the imposition of export taxes, to a high rate of discriminatory taxation, the justification for which has never been demonstrated. The critics of the policy of controlled marketing see no reason why prices should fall to a level so low as seriously to dislocate an expanding economy. They believe that if the incomes at the disposal of the African population were increased, expenditure on both consumption and investment would extend into a wider field and create a wider range of economic opportunities. They hold that this process of broadening the domestic economy would most effectively enable it to meet depressions in world prices. P. T. Bauer has calculated the actual contribution to public funds made by producers of raw materials under this system. He shows that over the period 1939–51 some £42 million was paid in export duties in the Gold Coast and Nigeria, and £159 million accumulated as surpluses by the Marketing Boards, as the result of the sale of produce for which the farmers themselves received a gross return of £317 million.[2]

Whatever aspects of this question may be open to controversy, there are two points on which there would be general agreement. On the one hand, the type of social revolution which is precipitated by a rapid change in the value of money would bring with it grave dangers to the stability of the emergent African States. If, therefore, it could be demonstrated

---

[1] P. T. Bauer, 'Statistics of Statutory Marketing in West Africa, 1939–51', *Journal of the Royal Statistical Society*, Series A, vol. cxvii, Part I, 1954. See also C. Leubuscher, *Bulk Buying from the Colonies*, Royal Institute of International Affairs, 1956.   [2] Bauer, op. cit.

that the controls imposed by the Boards did actually prevent inflation, this would go far to justify their existence. On the other hand, there are equally grave dangers in the accumulation of such large sums in the hands of Governments which are subject neither to external control nor to any internal check such as comes in older countries from an organized political opposition. The final judgement on the merits and demerits of the Marketing Boards must depend upon the weight of these practical considerations.

The general circumstances of Africa south of the Sahara are not such as to lead one to expect any rapid or revolutionary economic advance. Limited local developments have occurred where new sources of raw materials, such as uranium, have been discovered. Such technical innovations as have resulted in increased productivity have so far come, even in the wholly African territories, mainly from large-scale European enterprises; an example is the introduction of 'Pioneer' oil mills by the United Africa Company in Nigeria. There are also signs of a considerable industrial development in Uganda as a result of the opening of the hydro-electric installation at the Owen Falls. Another typical example is the introduction of the new system of forest plantations in Swaziland.[1] There does not at present seem to be much prospect of a rapid increase in productivity from purely indigenous enterprise. Whereas the people of India had been long accustomed to the usages of a cash economy and to the accumulation of capital, and readily took advantage of industrial opportunities as they presented themselves, the African has had hitherto little experience of either the accumulation or the utilization of capital resources. As this experience increases we may expect to find a corresponding increase in African enterprise, but the process is likely to be gradual, and rates of development will vary widely from one locality to another. The development of Africa must depend on the mobilization of its human resources and on the removal of any measures restricting the people from attaining a fuller maturity in economic matters. This, it will be recalled, forms also the burden of the recommendations of the Report of the East Africa Royal Commission 1953–5.[2] But whatever the success of Development Programmes may be, the achievement by Africans of standards of living more nearly approaching those of Europeans must be regarded as a long-term prospect.

THE STATISTICAL RECORD OF ECONOMIC GROWTH

When the Second World War broke out there were Statistical Departments in the Union of South Africa and in Southern Rhodesia, but in general the development of such services was regarded as a matter of low priority at a time when the public revenues had been seriously reduced

[1] See above, p. 940.   [2] *East Africa Royal Commission 1953–1955, Report*, Cmd. 9475, 1955.

by the economic depression and administrative staffs generally were being retrenched. Such statistics as were published were incomplete and often misleading. During the war the shortage of administrative staff caused a further deterioration in the position. There were cases where even the regular district counts of taxpayers, on which estimates of African population or manpower were based, fell into arrears. Those countries which were accustomed to publish departmental reports had to suspend them.

There was a considerable improvement in this situation in the post-war period. A strong demand for reliable statistical data now arose from Governments who required accurate material on which to base their Development Plans. It was reinforced by the requests for statistical information which came from the numerous international agencies interested in schemes for financial aid to undeveloped territories. There was accordingly a considerable expansion of statistical staffs. By the beginning of 1953 the establishments of the British dependencies included posts for between 50 and 60 trained statisticians.[1] A Statistics Department which had been set up at the Colonial Office in 1948 held its second conference of Colonial Government statisticians in 1953. African Government statisticians participated to an increasing extent in the numerous world conferences of statisticians which were held in the post-war period, and a number of African territories contributed information for the 1950 World Census of Agriculture compiled by the Food and Agriculture Organization of the United Nations.

The increasing volume of material collected by the new statistical services is now published in a variety of periodical digests emanating from Colonial, metropolitan, and international sources. It is true that there are still many deficiencies in the statistics and pitfalls for the unwary reader.[2] Although a number of the African dependencies now calculate balance-of-payments accounts according to internationally agreed criteria, their basic trade statistics still contain arbitrary valuations for some important commodities. The published accounts of Colonial Governments are rarely set up in a logical and convenient form for use in economic analysis; the distinction between current and capital transactions, for example, is seldom drawn according to consistent and acceptable criteria. Nevertheless, there has been some advance in the majority of the territories.

The problems involved in the calculation of national incomes in the special circumstances of Africa have been considered by many investigators. Various criteria have been suggested for the guidance of the practical statistician by international commissions of inquiry such as those set up by the United Nations. The United Nations have published

---

[1] *Report of the Second Conference of Colonial Government Statisticians, 1953*, Col. no. 301, 1954.
[2] A. R. Prest and I. G. Stewart, *The National Income of Nigeria, 1950–51*, Colonial Research Studies no. 11, 1953, p. 23.

volumes on national accounting and on the definition of capital formation.[1] Other general works on this subject are those of P. Deane, A. R. Prest and I. G. Stewart, and S. H. Frankel.[2] Such conclusions as have been reached from research on economic behaviour in Africa are, however, only tentative, and we are still far from having solved the problem of aggregating heterogeneous activities and evaluating non-monetary activities in monetary terms.

SOME GENERAL CONCLUSIONS

The survey of economic problems in the present and in the preceding chapters shows that in many areas the levels of economic activity and prospects of economic growth have improved appreciably since the pre-war period. Certain of these areas have reached significantly higher standards of living and of productivity, though there are others in which there has been no marked difference; in the Native Reserves in the Union of South Africa and parts of Kenya, for instance, economic progress has been by no means commensurate with what has been achieved in the European areas. Some territories are beginning to develop substantial capital resources within their own borders, and these are being supplemented from metropolitan and international sources. The prospect of the continuance of the world demand for African primary products is still good after more than a decade of high prices.

On the other hand, it must be realized that the average African is still very poor and very unproductive by the standards of the more advanced producers with whom he must trade. As a result of this low productivity the opportunities open to him are narrow and his advance is slow. Moreover, most African economies are still dependent on a small range of exports to an extent that renders them highly vulnerable to fluctuations in world market conditions.

The statistical data do not permit satisfactory estimates of current rates of growth in the different territories, but it is clear that there is considerable variation both as between territories and as between different areas of the same territory. In many territories the rate accelerated sharply during the post-war period, but in some this appears to have been a temporary movement due to abnormally favourable terms of trade for certain commodities and to the removal of some of the restrictions which were a result of the war.[3] A mission which visited Nigeria in 1953 concluded that 'Nigerian *per capita* income has increased in real terms at an

[1] *A System of National Accounts*, 1952. *Concepts and Definitions of Capital Formation*, 1953.

[2] P. Deane, *Colonial Social Accounting*, 1953. Prest and Stewart, op. cit. S. H. Frankel, 'Concepts of Income and Welfare and the Intercomparability of National Income Aggregates', in *The Economic Impact on Under-developed Societies*, 1953, p. 56.

[3] For Kenya and Uganda, see the East African Statistical Office, *Quarterly Economic and Statistical Bulletin*, March 1955, which gives national income data.

annual rate of somewhat below 2 per cent. in the post-war years, while capital formation has run at a level of approximately 10 per cent. of the national product'.[1] In territories where rich mineral resources have attracted a large influx of European capital and European settlers, the average rates of growth appear to have been much greater than this. For the Union of South Africa the evidence suggests that since 1911 real income per head has been increasing at the rate of 24 per cent. per decade, with a marked acceleration since 1940. In the post-war period net capital formation has averaged more than 20 per cent. of the national income. For Northern Rhodesia there is evidence that real income per head of the population has been increasing at a remarkable rate in recent years. Even allowing for a trebling of the price level between 1938 and 1954, average real incomes appear to have nearly trebled, suggesting an average rate of growth of nearly 7 per cent. per annum. Most of the advance took place in the eight years 1945–53, and over this period net investment averaged a quarter of the national income.[2]

Northern Rhodesia presents an extreme case, and the data are subject to various interpretations. One of the most interesting features of the evidence for this, as for some other African territories, is the fact that this rapid economic progress is confined to a very limited sector of the whole population. Often the new economic growth has been achieved by a process that is analogous to an expansion of the territory's geographical boundaries. Immigrants from more developed areas have directly increased the resources of skill and capital embraced by the economy. In some cases—and here again Northern Rhodesia is an extreme example— metropolitan companies operating in Africa have changed their domicile to a local one, and the effect of this change in book-keeping has been to increase national income for statistical purposes by more than the increase in real output or taxable capacity. Even in areas where settlement by immigrants is small in volume (either by natural circumstances or because it is actually discouraged), much of the more notable increase in economic activity has been primarily dependent on the initiative of foreign or metropolitan enterprise and immigrant personnel.

The direction of economic policy has undergone a significant change since the Second World War. The attention of Colonial Governments is now concentrated on measures designed to raise the standard of living of the indigenous population rather than on the export trade and the return on invested capital. The Development Plans which have been described illustrate this point. Even though it was found necessary in some cases to

[1] International Bank for Reconstruction and Development, *The Economic Development of Nigeria*, 1955, p. 30.

[2] Central African Statistical Office, *The National Income and Social Accounts of Northern Rhodesia, 1945–53*, 1954.

revise the original plans in order to meet the immediate need of increasing productivity, the prominence given in them to social improvement in the broadest sense is an indication of the present tendency. The increased interest in the potentialities of internal development in the purely African territories has led to investment on a considerable scale in capital works such as the Owen Falls hydroelectric installation in Uganda. The next stage is likely to be the encouragement of African industries on a small scale, and sometimes even of a domestic character, using the power which has been made available. In Uganda also, the taking over by African co-operatives of a number of cotton ginneries marks the entry of Africans into the field of processing, and may eventually lead, as the same development did in India, to an indigenous investment in textile factories.

Looking now into the future, there are some features about which it is at present difficult to speculate. It is obvious that a serious obstacle to the rapid improvement of economic levels has been created by the numerous restrictions on the direction of economic activities which have been imposed in the war and post-war periods. The growth of income per head which has taken place within the past two centuries in the countries of Western Europe and North America has been closely connected with the removal of restrictions on economic activity.[1] It remains a question for the future how far policies, some of which have been dictated by other than economic considerations, will continue to affect economic development both in Europe and in Africa. Much doubt has also been expressed in some quarters regarding the possible effect of population increases on economic developments. The assumption that African populations are increasing at a rate which is in itself sufficient to outweigh any advantages to be derived from increased productivity has been discussed in an earlier chapter.[2] So far, however, nothing has emerged from the studies quoted there which would lead one to dissent from the contrary view expressed by the East Africa Royal Commission 1953–5 that, given the necessary economic and social changes, an increase in population might actually contribute to a rise in the general standard of life.[3]

We are on firmer ground when we proceed to indicate certain general considerations which must determine our outlook on the future. It is clear, in the first place, that so long as the African population takes only a subsidiary part in economic development, a substantial increase in the general standards of living cannot be expected. Secondly, a rise in the standard of living of Africans must in the first instance be based on the improvement of agricultural techniques, including measures for the

---

[1] P. Mantoux, *The Industrial Revolution in the Eighteenth Century*, 1927. G. N. Clark, *The Idea of the Industrial Revolution*, 1953. W. A. Lewis, *The Theory of Economic Growth*, 1955, p. 78.

[2] See above, p. 131.

[3] *East Africa Royal Commission 1953–1955, Report*, Cmd. 9475, 1955, p. 36.

conservation of the soil. These improvements must extend to animal husbandry and the use of pastoral lands. In the third place, however, it must be recognized that in the world's history a general rise in the standard of living has seldom been achieved only by advance in agricultural productivity; there must be a continuous increase in the part played by the general population in industrial production.

It is unfortunate that in many parts of Africa soil and climatic conditions impose such severe limitations on the possibilities of an economic expansion based on agriculture. As regards industrial activities, one of the earliest stages of advance to an industrial economy may be expected to be seen in the increase of specialization and in the growth of the small domestic industries on which even the simpler societies largely depend for the satisfaction of their day-to-day needs. It is only in West Africa that such specialization had developed to any marked extent before the period of European rule. If at the present time the traditional West African crafts seem to be giving way before the competition of imported goods, their place is being taken by other activities for which there will always be room—those of the carpenter, bricklayer, and mason, the tailor and shoemaker, the repairer of bicycles and lorries, the digger of village wells, the small produce buyer, and the curer of hides and skins. It is this class which grows up most rapidly where there is an excess of population over the needs of subsistence agriculture.

The emergence of a class of small capitalists, which is perhaps most conspicuous in West Africa, is also illustrated by the examples just quoted from Uganda; indeed, there is no territory in which some instances of this could not now be found. It is through the activities of this class, and the accumulation of their small investments, that larger industries may be expected to arise.

There will remain, however, one crucial question to which time alone can supply an answer. It is impossible to predicate what concepts of economy will appeal to the class of Africans who are now acquiring political authority in so many of the African territories. In Europe itself there is now no identity of view on some aspects of economic policy. There are, for instance, strongly divergent schools of thought regarding matters so vital as the respective parts to be played by the State and private enterprise in the promotion of production and the distribution of its proceeds, the direction of exports, or the provision of capital for industrial enterprise. The new African leaders may follow one or other of these schools of thought, or they may evolve another of their own. The African has entered the modern economic drama with a very different background from that of the European, and he may prove to have a rendering of the role of 'economic man' which may differ widely from the versions accepted in the past.

CHAPTER XX

THE PROBLEMS OF LABOUR

To the student of labour conditions in Africa one of the most insistent of the problems which present themselves is that of the shortage of manpower within reach of the major industrial centres and the consequent wide prevalence of the system of 'migrant' labour. He will have to take into consideration the extent to which the emergence of a stabilized labour force is reducing the measure of the dependence on 'migrant' labour. He must attempt to assess the influence of the development of the new type of industrial relationship created by the growth of the trade-union movement and the procedure of collective bargaining. There was a period when it would have been essential to deal also with the facts relating to the employment of compulsion in order to secure labour either for public undertakings or for employment in private industry, for these were matters which at one time figured largely in any discussion of labour problems in Africa. But at the present time the range of compulsion is relatively small, and the subject will require less comprehensive treatment. It is more important to discuss the nature of the incentives which now determine the supply of African labour for industrial or similar purposes, and also such evidence as is forthcoming regarding the relative efficiency of the African as compared with other types of worker. It will not be possible to give adequate consideration to the latter question without dealing at the same time with certain of the factors which affect the efficiency of African labour, and in particular the conditions of employment and remuneration.

THE SHORTAGE OF MANPOWER

Few of the African territories have in the past escaped incidents arising from the effort made to overcome the difficulty once experienced in obtaining manual labour for public or private undertakings. The importation by the Dutch East India Company of convict and other labour from its Far Eastern settlements gave the Cape its Coloured problem, and the use of indentured Indian labour on the sugar plantations of Natal added a new complexity to the population problems of the Union.[1] The use of Chinese labour on the Rand in 1904 had reactions which reached as far as the field of British party politics.[2] Railway construction in the Congo

[1] See above, p. 387.
[2] P. C. Campbell, *Chinese Coolie Emigration*, 1923, Chapter IV.

Free State and in the French Congo attracted international attention to the results of forced recruitment in order to supply the deficiency of voluntary labour.[1] The employment of Asian labour on the construction of the Uganda railway[2] left a legacy which has materially added to the political problems of Kenya. The era characterized by these incidents has now passed, but the local deficiencies in the labour supply still give rise to problems which are of great concern both to employers and to the Administrations.

As the Report of the East Africa Royal Commission 1953–5 points out,[3] the shortage of labour may be attributed in some part to causes connected with the prevailing age structure of the indigenous population. Although their observations refer primarily to East Africa, it would seem to be true that elsewhere also in Africa children form an unusually high proportion of the total population; the Commission had evidence that in East Africa the overall proportion of children exceeded 40 per cent. Moreover (as the Commission also pointed out) the working life of an African adult appears to be shorter than that of adults of many other races. But the basic cause of the shortage of available manpower seems to lie in certain characteristic features of indigenous African society. The demand for wage-earning labour found a population which had hitherto known only a world of subsistence economy, and which had therefore little incentive to improve its condition by wage-earning. Since it was inexperienced in the use of money, it was slow to react to the stimulus of cash inducements. The entry of the African into the new economic field was therefore difficult and hesitant, all the more because those who controlled that field were Europeans or Asiatics.

Native societies had their own systems of economic organization, the obligations of which were well recognized; but the discipline of regular labour, which involved compliance with the orders of employers who had no traditional authority, was unfamiliar to Africans. The practice of slavery had, moreover, left a legacy which not unnaturally created a suspicion of the new relationship of employer and wage-earner. The relationship set up by the practice of wage-earning involved consequences which must at an early stage have been resented by traditional leaders as a threat to the established traditions of indigenous society. Elsewhere in the world the rapid growth of industrial employment has produced its reactions on the social organization, but the conditions have seldom been such as to demand an adjustment so sudden or so radical as in Africa.

In Europe the Industrial Revolution signalized in the main the substitution of large-scale processes for domestic or small-scale industry. This change in the character of industry brought with it the difficulties resulting

---

[1] See below, pp. 1565, 1568.   [2] See below, p. 1556.
[3] *East Africa Royal Commission 1953–1955, Report*, Cmd. 9475, 1955, p. 36.

from the rapid growth of industrial centres and the substitution of urban for rural life, but it did not create a problem of adjustment in the basic conditions of life so marked as that which followed the introduction of industrial conditions in Africa. In Japan, to take another example, the signal capacity of the people for rapid readjustment gave the transition to industrial conditions almost the appearance of a natural evolution. In India the introduction of modern capitalist enterprise caused no radical dislocation in a population which was already experienced in small-scale industries, in the production of marketable crops, and in the employment of wage-earning labour. In Africa, on the other hand, the departure of members of a close-knit indigenous community to distant centres of industry was liable not merely to loosen the tie of tribal loyalties but to exercise a disruptive influence on family relations and the economy of family life. Even where employment did not permanently remove the wage-earner from contact with his own community, it gave him a new economic independence in which he ceased to rely for the essentials of life on close co-operation with his kindred. It is true that opposition by the leaders in the African communities to the migration of wage-earners was not universal, and there were some instances (as, for example, in Bechuanaland and Swaziland) when Chiefs openly welcomed the opportunity of securing resources which could also be drawn upon for the benefit of the tribe at large.[1] Nor is there now any prejudice against it, and in many areas the migration of labour has become a commonplace of modern African life. But some of the problems which it has created have remained, and they have been intensified by the increasing tendency of wage-earners to become permanent residents in urban centres, thus helping to add to the new series of problems arising from the growth of urbanization in Africa.[2]

The Number of African Wage-earners

The difficulty of carrying out a reliable census in Africa has been discussed in an earlier chapter. It is important to emphasize that the figures which now follow can give in most cases no more than a rough indication of the number of persons employed in various occupations. One of the most intractable problems of the demographer is the assessment of the number of migrant workers both within a particular territory or between territories, and in effect the only figures which can claim any accuracy are those based on the returns of recruiting agencies. Figures relating to other migrant labour are estimates only. Some reliance can be placed on figures of employment provided by the Statistical Departments of the Union and of Southern Rhodesia and the Labour Department of Northern Rhodesia; elsewhere the material supplied must be used with caution.

In 1953 there were stated to be in the Union some 2,240,000 Natives in

[1] N.A., Part V, pp. 164, 247, 377.   [2] See above, pp. 564 ff.

wage-earning employment.[1] The numbers employed in different occupations were shown as follows: European farms, 700,000; mines and works, 470,000; secondary industry, 350,000; domestic service, 300,000; State Departments, 100,000; railways and harbours, 100,000; commerce, 100,000; municipal service, 100,000; and others, 20,000. It is noteworthy that in 1951 some 27 per cent. of the African population was classified as urban; 67 per cent. of the semi-skilled and 98½ per cent. of unskilled labour is recorded as having been performed by Natives. The Southern Rhodesia census taken in 1951 gave a total of over 488,450 Natives in employment,[2] of whom rather less than half were indigenous. In Northern Rhodesia the number of Africans employed in 1954 was estimated as 258,340, of whom 36,000 were employed in agriculture and 45,000 in mining.[3] In Nyasaland some 106,900 Africans were shown as employed within the Protectorate.

In the three territories of East Africa it has been estimated that one-quarter of the male African population of working age is engaged in wage-paid employment.[4] In Tanganyika a census of labour taken in 1954 showed that 439,094 were gainfully employed, of whom one-third was engaged in the sisal industry and 5 per cent. in manufacture. In addition between 10,000 and 15,000 Africans were employed outside the territory. In Kenya, according to statistics compiled in 1953, some 359,000 Africans were in employment, of whom a quarter worked in the White Highlands and 42,000 in manufacturing industry. In Uganda the number shown to be in employment was 224,500, but it was estimated that this figure would be raised to 300,000 by the inclusion of many who were not covered by the enumeration. In industry and electricity undertakings 23,600 were employed, making the proportion so employed 13 per cent. of the labour force. This is the highest ratio in the three East African territories.[5] In Zanzibar, according to a census taken in 1948, 107,800 males were in gainful occupation, but this figure may be unduly inflated.

In Nigeria and the British Cameroons the number of Africans in regular employment is believed to be of the order of 500,000. In the Gold Coast 216,300 were reported in 1953 to be in wage-earning occupations. In Sierra Leone 45,500 were estimated in 1952 to be employed in industrial occupations and as many in agriculture. In Gambia some 5,400 were in employment in 1951, excluding casual and dock labourers. This figure does not include those engaged by peasant farmers in growing groundnuts for export.

---

[1] M. Horrell, *A Survey of Race Relations in South Africa, 1952–1953*, South African Institute of Race Relations, 1953, pp. 76–77.
[2] *Census of Population 1951*, Salisbury, 1954, Chapter VII.
[3] *Northern Rhodesia, Annual Report of the Department of Labour, 1954*, p. 28.
[4] Cmd. 9475, 1955, p. 47.
[5] Ibid. p. 107.

The working population of French Equatorial Africa was given as 216,500 in 1951. The latest available figure for French West Africa appears to be that for 1947, when some 232,000 were shown as gainfully employed. The Belgian Congo gave a total of 1,030,900 wage-earners at the end of 1951. In Ruanda Urundi the figure for 1951 was 110,000; some 18,000 workers from Ruanda Urundi were among those employed in the Belgian Congo. The number of Africans in employment in Angola was estimated at nearly 800,000,[1] but the figure is questionable, while the estimate given for Mozambique was 110,000. In Liberia 25,000 Africans are employed on the rubber estates.

The figures which it has been possible to quote refer for the most part to the number in regular employment by companies, individual European or Asian employers, or in Government undertakings. In most cases they exclude the more casual wage-earners and those in the employment of Africans, who in some areas (as in Uganda) employ labourers for cash wages, and elsewhere for other forms of consideration. An example of the latter is to be found in the Gold Coast, where workers are allowed the use of land and a share in the profits realized. The chief defect of these figures is that they fail to provide any reliable basis for calculating the proportion of the population which is dependent on wage-earning. In many types of employment, as most notably in the gold-mines of South Africa, the labourer is not accompanied by his family, which draws its subsistence from its own cultivation. In some cases wage-earning is undertaken only for the sake of paying tax or for personal expenditure, with the result that only a small part of the earning goes to the support of the family. It is interesting to compare the above figures with the estimates given in 1956 by T. Hodgkin in an informative study on the growth of trade unionism in Africa,[2] though it must be realized that all such figures are necessarily somewhat speculative.

On the whole, it may be said with some certainty that the greater part of the indigenous population is engaged in its own subsistence economy. A further but smaller proportion devotes itself mainly to the production of marketable commodities, and only a comparatively small proportion is dependent solely on wage-earning. This last section has, however, increased markedly during the past decade. Calculations made by the United Nations Secretariat regarding the working activity of the African population give the result shown in the table which follows. The figures refer to the percentage of the total male population over 15 years of age in the year 1951,[3] but it must be emphasized that the calculations are

---

[1] *New Statesman and Nation*, 8 May 1954.

[2] T. Hodgkin, *Nationalism in Africa*, 1956, pp. 117 ff.

[3] United Nations Document E/2377, *Aspects of Economic Development in Africa*, 20 March 1953, pp. 26–27.

based on a number of assumptions and can make no claim to any statistical value.

| | Commercialized Production | | | |
	Within Indigenous Economies	In Outside Wage-earning	Total Commercialized Production	Subsistence Production
Belgian Congo . .	29	30	59	41
French Equatorial Africa .	23	15	38	62
French West Africa . .	23	5	28	72
Gold Coast . . .	60	15	75	25
Kenya	13	25	38	62
Nigeria	39	4	43	57
Southern Rhodesia . .	9	40	49	51
Uganda . . .	29	12	41	59
Total	30	12	42	58

THE USE OF FORCED LABOUR

It is true, as has been remarked, that the range of the use of compulsion to secure labour is now very greatly reduced, but one cannot entirely neglect the part which it has played in the past history of African development. Its use by some of the Administrations in order to secure manpower for public purposes has been defended on the ground that it is an adaptation of the indigenous usage by which communal labour is used for making village roads or the like. But the analogy is not convincing, since this traditional use of labour seldom took the peasant far from his home. Its real justification lay in the fact that the construction of railways and major roads was imperative, and that the Administrations had failed to secure labour on voluntary terms.

The British Government was, it is true, successful in securing from India the indentured labour needed for the construction of the Uganda railway; but the French in 1885 had been driven to import Annamites for work on the communications near Brazzaville. At a later stage they brought labour from Cuba, and on at least two occasions attempted the importation of Chinese. For the construction of the lower Congo railway, the Congo Free State employed labour from countries as far apart as China, Barbados, and Liberia. Apart, however, from other considerations, the grave danger to the health of imported labour made it impossible to rely on obtaining workers from this source and the use of impressed African labour appeared to be unavoidable.[1]

[1] R. L. Buell, *The Native Problem in Africa*, 1928, vol. i, p. 1043; vol. ii, pp. 258, 321, 330, 502, 507.

It was in the construction of railways that there occurred the use of impressed labour which has attracted most attention. Besides the instances just mentioned, labour for the Thiès–Niger and the Cotonou and Dahomey railways in French West Africa was secured by an order directed to the Chiefs, and in French Equatorial Africa the demands for the Brazzaville railway were met by the issue of a series of local *arrêtés* which distributed the levy among districts. In the French Cameroons labour for the extension of the railway, which the Germans had constructed as far as Njock, was secured by a system of 'collective contracts' with Chiefs, a procedure which involved a definite form of compulsion; in Togoland labour was conscripted under instructions issued by the district authorities.

It is of interest to note that during the construction of the Leopoldville–Matadi railway in the Belgian Congo, it was proposed to resort to impressment, but this proposal was rejected by the Belgian Government as contrary to the *Charte Coloniale*. Although, however, the Government had thus refused to sanction a formal impressment, the informal levy of labour continued until the completion of the railway. In Nigeria the needs of the Baro–Kano and the Eastern railways were supplied by the use of 'political' labour, a contingent being demanded from each province. An effort to substitute voluntary labour failed in 1924, and it was necessary to resort again to the use of 'political' labour.[1] Compulsory labour was also used on the construction of the Uasin Gishu length of line in Kenya.

It was not, however, merely the use of compulsion which brought the impressment of labour for railway construction under criticism. Its main burden was directed against the lack of organization which in certain notorious cases involved a high rate of sickness and mortality among the workers, and produced much local dislocation of Native life.[2] But the use of impressment for railway construction forms a somewhat exceptional chapter in the record of the attitude taken by the Colonial Administrations towards the supply of labour. In respect of other public works there was in most territories a more definite attempt at legal regulation of the system of compulsion. In the British areas the Natal Native Code permitted compulsory labour, and this was widely used on the roads, but this provision of the Code was abolished in 1906. In Uganda the Native Authority Ordinance of 1919 authorized the use of compulsory paid labour (*kasanvu*) for a term of 60 days in the year, and this was widely applied in the construction of the road system; in Kenya the law allowed the use of compulsory paid labour for the same period, but only if specially sanctioned by the Secretary of State.[3] It was under this Ordinance that labour was

[1] *Report by the Hon. W. G. A. Ormsby-Gore on his Visit to West Africa during the Year 1926*, Cmd. 2744, 1926, p. 123.
[2] See Buell, op. cit. vol. i, p. 1043; vol. ii, p. 262. See also below, p. 1565.
[3] Native Authority Ordinance no. 26, 1922.

secured for the Uasin Gishu railway, and it was also widely used on road work. Nyasaland enacted a similar measure in 1924, but Natives were exempted who had been 'fully employed in any occupation' for three of the preceding twelve months. In the Congo Free State a decree of 1906 authorized the carrying out of public works by the 'second section' of the annual levy of the militia, but a decree of 16 February 1910, passed after annexation, reduced the period of service on such work, and a subsequent decree of 10 May 1919 had the effect of repealing the provision made in 1906. Reference will be made subsequently to the system of *prestation* in the French territories, and to the terms on which it was utilized in the construction and maintenance of the roads.[1]

The decline of activity in railway construction following the period of depression in world prices, and the increase in the supply of voluntary labour made possible by the improvement of motor communications, resulted in the gradual discontinuance of regular resort to the practice of conscripting labour for public works. As will subsequently be shown, resort to compulsion has since then been largely governed by international conventions, and is in the main restricted to emergencies (such as floods or similar catastrophes) or to the use of labour for certain communal purposes. But during the Second World War special circumstances arose which caused a reversion to the use of compulsion in order to secure supplies and services required by the exigencies of war.

Forced Labour in the Second World War

The use of compulsion was in these circumstances made under special regulation and was confined to certain of the Colonial territories. Thus in Kenya 'conscription' was used mainly for securing labour on plantations producing commodities needed in the war.[2] In November 1944 roughly 10 per cent. of the total labour force engaged were 'conscripts'. In Tanganyika at the end of 1943 a little over one-twelfth of the labour force was conscripted. An East African Military Labour Service Unit, compulsorily recruited, was formed in July 1940 to provide unskilled labour under military discipline, originally for military purposes only, but later for other duties also.[3] Northern Rhodesia resorted to compulsion for agricultural purposes, but recruitment to the African Labour Corps, which was set up during the Second World War and continued with a brief interval until 1952, was voluntary. Conscription was used in Nigeria to augment the labour force in the tin-mines for a period of 19 months from October 1942; the average number of 'conscripts' in 1943 was 16,000 out of a total

---

[1] See below, p. 1369.
[2] Defence Regulations, March 1942; Compulsory National Service Ordinance, 1943.
[3] Compulsory Service Ordinance, 1940.

labour force of 71,000 employed at the mines.[1] All these temporary measures were terminated shortly after the end of the war.

In territories other than those of the United Kingdom, war requirements were also met by the use of conscripted labour, but few particulars have been published. In the Belgian Congo the African peasants were obliged to carry out cultivation or harvesting to increase the production of primary materials such as rubber and palm oil.[2] Compulsory recruitment was further extended to provide food for workers at essential undertakings. Here also the special regulations terminated with the end of the war.

THE PRESENT POSITION REGARDING FORCED LABOUR

The International Forced Labour Convention of 1930 defined forced labour as 'work or service exacted from any person under the threat of any penalty and for which the said person has not offered himself voluntarily'.[3] But the exceptions are important: compulsory military service, convict labour, civic obligations, work in any emergency whether in war or peace, and minor communal services performed in the direct interest of the community are excluded from the definition.[4] Applying this definition to African conditions, it would not include as forced labour the summoning of communal labour to destroy tsetse bush, to exterminate locusts, to extinguish bush fires, or to clear village paths. It will be requisite to refer subsequently to the type of legislation which has been enacted to stimulate the production of subsistence crops, partly as a safeguard against scarcity or famine, and partly to combat the danger that the production of economic crops may result in the neglect of subsistence cultivation. But since the product is consumed by the cultivator himself, labour of this character is not held to fall within the definition of 'forced labour'.

No legal powers have been taken in the British Colonies to stimulate the production of marketable crops, but the expansion of the production of cotton and coffee in East Africa was not at the outset left entirely to the operation of the economic incentive. The 'moral pressure' applied to the cultivation of cotton in Uganda and Nyasaland has been officially recognized.[5] In Tanganyika a circular of the Governor of 25 August 1925

---

[1] A. R. Prest, *War Economics of Primary Producing Countries*, 1948, p. 241.

[2] *Ordonnance* no. 68, 10 March 1942, and no. 29, 1 February 1943.

[3] International Forced Labour Convention no. 29, 1930, Article 2.

[4] International Labour Office, *Report of the ad hoc Committee on Forced Labour*, Studies and Reports (New Series) no. 36, 1953. This assembles a great deal of material on the subject, but is not comprehensive.

[5] *Report of the East Africa Commission*, Cmd. 2387, 1925, p. 34. *Report of the Formation of a Native Agricultural Board*, Tanganyika. 1930. *Report of Committee appointed to consider and advise on Questions relating to the Supply and Welfare of Native Labour in the Tanganyika Territory*, Dar-es-Salaam, 1938, p. 14.

declared it the duty of the Administrative Officer 'to use every legitimate means at his command' to induce Native communities to take up the cultivation of economic crops in cases where they had turned a deaf ear to his exhortations to adopt some active form of work. In certain conditions there can be little difference between the giving of advice and the issue of an order; there is, however, a substantial distinction between a general direction to increase production and the issue of an order prescribing a definite task, supported by a threat of penal sanctions.

The Union of South Africa

In the Union of South Africa the use of compulsory labour is prohibited, but the labour of convicts serving sentences in the Prison Outstations is hired out to associations of farmers.[1] The Locust Extermination Act of 1904 in Natal permits an element of compulsion, but this is not of a kind to bring it within the terms of the Convention.

The British Territories

A dispatch from the Secretary of State issued in 1920[2] laid down that Africans might be required to perform work of a public nature, subject to the proviso that no person should be required to perform such work for more than 60 days in any one year, and that any African who was fully employed in any occupation or had been so employed during the preceding twelve months for the period of three months, should be exempted from such labour. A subsequent dispatch of 1921[3] recalled that it had always been recognized that recourse should not be had to compulsory labour for Government purposes, but insisted that the Administration must have the power to call out labour for essential services. For the future, however, the use of compulsion for services other than porterage or transport had to receive the prior sanction of the Secretary of State. It is noteworthy that the Secretary of State refused in 1925 to sanction the further use of compulsory labour for the Uasin Gishu railway in Kenya.[4]

The Joint Committee of Parliament appointed to consider the Report on Closer Union in East Africa[5] noted that forced labour was still sometimes used on Government work, and though this was almost invariably in the interest of Africans themselves the Committee held that the practice should be discontinued. The International Forced Labour Convention of 1930 was ratified by the United Kingdom in 1931, and such compulsory labour as continues to exist in these territories is regulated in accordance with the provisions of the Convention.

[1] *O.Y.S.A., 1952–53*, p. 452. See also above, p. 626.
[2] *Native Labour*, Cmd. 873, 1920. (The Milner Dispatch.)   [3] *Kenya*, no. 1353, 1921.
[4] *Kenya: Compulsory Labour for Government Purposes*, Cmd. 2464, 1925.
[5] See above, p. 191.

In Basutoland and Swaziland the use of compulsion is confined to certain tribal obligations, but Chiefs are in practice expected to provide assistance in such public emergencies as an invasion of locusts. In Bechuanaland resort has up to recent years been made to the system of 'regimental labour', but this is now confined to work required for tribal purposes.[1] In Southern Rhodesia no law authorizes the exaction of forced labour, but co-operation in matters of urgency, such as the extermination of locusts or the extinction of bush fires, is ensured by a provision which requires Africans to comply with lawful requests given by Administrative Officers. Moreover, unemployed Africans may be called upon to work for not more than 90 days, and within their own area, on works of soil conservation or the preservation of natural resources, or in the interests of good husbandry.[2]

In Northern Rhodesia the Native Authority Ordinance authorizes the use of compulsion in an emergency, but in practice Chiefs are required to find labour only for necessary porterage or the upkeep of inter-village roads, both obligations being held to fall within the term 'minor communal services in the direct interest of the community'. In the same category are those Rules made by Native Authorities which enforce communal cultivation to provide against conditions of famine. The right formerly enjoyed by the Paramount Chief of Barotseland to exact twelve days' compulsory and unpaid labour from his subjects was surrendered in 1924.[3]

The use of forced labour in Nyasaland under Rules made by Native Authorities is of the same character as that obtaining in Northern Rhodesia, but the seriousness of soil erosion has necessitated a larger volume of Rules made in aid of the programme for soil conservation. Legal provision exists in the Native Authority Ordinance of Tanganyika for the calling out of labour for essential public works and services, subject to the conditions stipulated in Lord Milner's dispatch of 1920 already referred to. There is also a clause making compulsory the provision of porterage for the transport of goods and persons where there are no adequate all-weather communications, but this regulation is now seldom used. The legal sanction for the discharge of tax obligations by labour was removed by the Native Tax (Amendment) Ordinance of 1951. It is on record that over the period from July 1951 to June 1952, some 4,102 men were requisitioned for porterage (representing a total of 10,656 man-days worked), 10,461 for minor public works (95,203 man-days), and 4,578 for work undertaken by the Native Authorities (104,513 man-days). It is provided that the proportion of men called upon for work from any locality may not exceed 25 per cent. of the able-bodied male population.

Zanzibar was the first of the tropical countries to abandon forced

---

[1] *N.A.*, Part V, pp. 214–15, 247, 253.
[2] Native Land Husbandry Act, 1951.
[3] See above, p. 490.

labour (Decree no. 1 of 1931). In Uganda the Native Authority Ordinance empowers Chiefs to require work (*luwalo*)[1] from able-bodied males for the benefit of the community, the period being limited to 30 days a year. This obligation has now been commuted into a cash payment which in the areas outside Buganda forms a considerable addition to the Native Administration tax.[2] Although the right to discharge the tax by labour remains, it is seldom exercised. Mention is made elsewhere of the extent of the debt owed to *luwalo* labour by the roads in Uganda.[3] A number of the roads maintained in the past by *luwalo* labour are now kept up by immigrant workers paid by the revenue accruing from the commutation of *luwalo* into cash.[4]

In Nigeria and the Cameroons forced labour is prohibited, save that compulsory porterage is authorized, and Native Authorities may require labour to be provided for various specified communal purposes, but only with the agreement of a substantial majority of the inhabitants concerned.[5] Though detailed regulations are made governing compulsory porterage, the power to exact such services is in fact very little exercised. Orders may be issued requiring any person to cultivate adequate crops to ensure a sufficiency of food for himself and those dependent on him.[6]

The laws regulating labour in the Gold Coast and Ashanti are contained in Ordinances which were enacted in 1935. Native Authorities may be required to maintain their roads by the paid labour of adult workers employed for not more than 24 days. Native Authorities are also empowered to issue orders to ensure an adequacy of food.[7] These regulations have been applied to Togoland. In Sierra Leone the Forced Labour Ordinance of 1932 makes provision for personal services to recognized Chiefs, and also for compulsory labour for the construction and maintenance of public highways and Government buildings, the movement of Government stores, and the transport of private persons in cases of urgent necessity.[8] Use of the provision enabling the Chief to require the attendance of labour for his own personal use is now rare. Compulsory labour is prohibited in Gambia except in the case of war or natural calamity and subject to the rights of Native Authorities.[9] Here also Native Authorities are empowered to issue orders to cultivators in order to ensure an adequacy of food.

[1] See above, p. 661.
[2] H. B. Thomas and R. Scott, *Uganda*, 1935, pp. 229, 319.
[3] See below, p. 1583.
[4] *Report of the Committee of Enquiry into the Labour Situation in the Uganda Protectorate, 1938*, Uganda, 1938.
[5] Labour Code Ordinance no. 54, 1945, and Amendment Ordinance no. 34, 1950.
[6] Native Authority Ordinance no. 18, 1943.
[7] Labour Ordinance no. 16, 1948, Articles 106, 107.
[8] Forced Labour Ordinance no. 50, 1932, and no. 11, 1938.
[9] Forced Labour Ordinance no. 8, 1934.

The French Territories

Compulsory labour in the French overseas territories is now prohibited by an Act of 11 April 1946 and by the consolidated Labour Code of 15 December 1952. Despite the comprehensive terms of these laws, reports from French West Africa and the Cameroons continue to imply the existence of various types of labour which contain some element of compulsion. Where labour has been required for public purposes the French Administrations have in the past tended to rely in the first instance on the system of *prestation*; reliance has also been placed, though to a smaller extent, on the use of the *deuxième portion* of the forces conscripted for military purposes and also on tax-default labour. Some use also appears to have been made of the law relating to *vagabondage*.

As has been explained in a previous chapter,[1] *prestation* was a tax payable in the form of a definite amount of labour which was, however, redeemable in certain cases by a cash payment. Theoretically limited to a maximum of ten days, it provided a large amount of labour for public purposes, and the redemption payments also produced an appreciable revenue; there were, indeed, some conditions in which the latter aspect tended to become as important as the former. It was applicable to all inhabitants, with a few exceptions, and was not a tax on Natives only.[2] Much criticism has been directed against the use of *prestation* in Africa, on grounds both of principle and of abuse in practice. It was defended by showing that its prototype had been for many years in operation in France, by citing precedents from African custom, and by quoting analogies in the practice both of the German Administration and that of the Congo Free State.

From the African point of view, however, it resembled the *corvée*, in so far that it appeared to give no direct benefit to the individual called on for his labour. When *prestation* was applied to the maintenance of major roads or the construction of aerodromes this consideration weighed cogently also with some French Administrators, who advocated that its use should be restricted to purposes which would be of direct benefit only to Africans. In practice the system was frequently attended by laxity in observing the rules which regulated the terms of employment, and the Chiefs who were responsible for drawing up the *prestation* lists failed to act impartially unless they were closely supervised. Most of the major roads in French Equatorial Africa appear to have been constructed by labour obtained under this system, but it was at the cost of a considerable dislocation of local Native life. *Prestation* is, however, now almost everywhere commutable for a cash payment, and is rapidly disappearing as a source of compulsory labour.

[1] See above, p. 670.
[2] R. L. Buell, *The Native Problem in Africa*, vol. i, 1928, pp. 1037 ff. L. P. Mair, *Native Policies in Africa*, 1936, pp. 198–200.

The use of military conscripted labour as a labour force for public works—a practice for many years prevalent in French West Africa[1]—has now been abolished. A uniformed but voluntarily recruited 'pioneer corps' has been set up in the Middle Congo, Gabon, and Oubangui Chari. The early law relating to *vagabondage*, dating from the abolition of slavery in 1848, placed vagabonds at the disposal of the State for employment on public works, and they were later treated as falling under the system of the *indigénat*.[2] It does not, however, seem that the vagrancy law was ever utilized to any great extent for securing labour; the present position in the French Cameroons is that 'the meaning of vagrancy is now strictly limited and does not lead to any extensive abuse'.[3]

The Belgian Territories

In the Belgian Congo there is now no law which permits the general requisition of labour for public works, but a decree of December 1922 empowered Administrative Officers to requisition labour on payment as porters or paddlers; the period of employment in such cases was not to exceed 15 days a month or 25 days a year. A decree of March 1925 further defined this authority, and local instructions were issued to prohibit the use of porterage where other means of transport were available or for the carriage of certain classes of heavy goods. In addition, a decree of 5 December 1933 enabled local officers to levy compulsory labour in order to combat infectious diseases or famine or in other emergencies; this authority may also be used for compelling the cultivation of foodstuffs for the exclusive benefit of the inhabitants. The period of employment for this purpose is limited to 60 days in a year.

The decree of 1933 also repeated the provisions of previous legislation which permitted the use of compulsion for the cultivation of marketable crops (*produits d'exportation*), cultivation under such conditions being described as *à titre éducatif*. The principle of 'educative' cultivation was at one period regarded by both the Belgian and the French Administrations as of great importance. The system for the sale of these crops is described elsewhere.[4] When the terms of the International Convention of 1930 proposed to limit the use of compulsion to the growth of subsistence crops both the Belgian and the French Governments made their agreement to the Convention subject to reservation on this point. It must not, however, be assumed that compulsion for the growth of marketable or 'economic' crops had in fact been confined to the Belgian or French territories. The difference between their practice and that of the British Administrations

---

[1] Mair, op. cit. p. 199. Conscription was not applied in French Equatorial Africa.
[2] See above, p. 603.
[3] International Labour Office, *Summary of Reports on Unratified Conventions and Recommendations*, 1950, p. 7.   [4] See above, p. 841.

lay in the fact that the latter did not have legal powers to stimulate the production of marketable crops.

In the Belgian Congo the use of the educative system was first formally sanctioned in 1917, the produce being bought directly by the Government and either exported or sent to the industrial area of Katanga.[1] The decree of 5 December 1933 provided that educative cultivation must be in the exclusive interest of the population and that the power of sale must be unrestricted. When this decree was considered in the *Conseil Colonial* in 1933 it produced an interesting discussion as to the period up to which compulsory cultivation for marketable crops could properly be regarded as educative.[2] In practice the rules laid down the number of acres to be planted by each cultivator; as regards marketable crops, there is no question that the marked growth in the production of cotton has been largely the result of direct compulsion, though here, as in British territories, the normal economic incentive has now largely taken its place. Obligatory cultivation has also been utilized to some extent for expanding the production of coffee. If compulsion were now withdrawn a considerable proportion of the area at present under these crops would no doubt continue to be cultivated. It is, however, noteworthy that as late as 1949 no less than 23,000 persons were sentenced for offences infringing the decree of 1933.

In Ruanda Urundi, according to the Report made to the United Nations in 1950, unremunerated labour for road clearing has been replaced by a tax, with the object of distributing over the population as a whole a burden previously borne entirely by those in the immediate vicinity of the roads. The redemption of the customary contribution of labour by a cash payment was made optional in 1945 and compulsory in 1949. An Ordinance of November 1933, as amended in May 1934 and July 1949, provided that defaulting taxpayers might be employed on such works as the building of roads, porterage, and the construction of State works. In 1951 the number of persons so liable was shown as 1,516.

The Portuguese Territories

There was a period when the treatment of labour in the Portuguese territories aroused criticism almost as severe as that which the Congo Free State faced in its last years. It arose mainly on account of the compulsion used to secure labour for the Portuguese 'Cocoa Islands', Sao Tomé and Principe. Labour for the Islands came at this period chiefly from Angola and was obtained under contract. This was stated to be a voluntary agreement under which the *serviçal* or *contratado* was engaged

---

[1] E. Leplae, 'Méthode suivie pour le développement de l'agriculture au Congo belge', *Congo*, October 1930. See also *Congo*, May 1933.

[2] J. Magotte, *Les Circonscriptions indigènes*, 1934, p. 126.

for agricultural work. It was clear, however, from investigations made in 1906, and repeated in 1909,[1] that labour was not voluntarily recruited, but was obtained by methods which were not very different from those which were often employed by slave traders in the past. As in the case of the slave trade, labour was brought down in caravans to the coast and transported to the Islands. The system originated under a law passed in 1875, and it has been asserted that in the 20 years from 1888 to 1908 alone over 67,000 *contratados* were shipped to the Islands.[2] Inquiries resulted in some doubt being expressed whether 'contract' labour had ever been repatriated.[3]

The reputation of the Islands and the terms of employment there were such that in 1903 British cocoa firms joined in refusing to make further purchases of cocoa from them. In 1909 the facts regarding the treatment of labour sent to the Islands were exposed in a lawsuit which attracted much public attention in Great Britain; The Court expressed the view that the conditions in which 'contract' labour was obtained for service in the Islands differed very little from those of slavery.[4]

The Portuguese Government passed laws in 1906 for Mozambique and in 1921 for Angola which prohibited in general terms the use of forced labour. In the Islands the demand for labour subsequently declined, owing to an outbreak of disease which greatly reduced the production of cocoa. Of recent years labour recruits have been obtained from Mozambique rather than from Angola; contracts signed in Mozambique were originally for four years but have been reduced to one year, and repatriation is insisted upon; the number of labourers repatriated in the years 1947 to 1952 was 33,492, being nearly 7,000 in excess of the number of new immigrants.

There is evidence that diet and medical attention is now reasonably good, and efforts have recently been made to attract whole families to migrate in order to provide a more social atmosphere. Some local disturbances occurred in Sao Tomé in 1953; these were not, however, due to complaints against the conditions of employment, but to a mistaken proclamation which called upon all inhabitants of the Islands, including the indigenous people, to take up contract labour. They were reported to have caused some 200 casualties, and the Governor was subsequently recalled.

[1] H. W. Nevinson, *A Modern Slavery*, 1906. C. A. Swan, *The Slavery of Today*, 1909. J. Bunt, *Slave Labour on Cocoa Plantations*, 1909.

[2] J. Harris, *A Century of Emancipation*, 1933, pp. 179–91.

[3] *Correspondence respecting Contract Labour in Portuguese West Africa, no. 2*, Cd. 6322, 1912. Dispatch no. 47, dated Luanda 27 November 1911 to Sir Edward Grey from Consul F. H. Drummond-Hay.

[4] *Cadbury* v. *The Standard*, see *The Times*, 8 August 1908. See also W. A. Cadbury, 'Angola and San Thomé', *Anti-Slavery Reporter and Aborigines' Friend*, October 1955, p. 43.

It is clear, therefore, that there has been a material improvement in the conditions applying to the employment of labour in the Cocoa Islands, but much criticism has of late years been directed against the use of the methods by which labour is obtained for public works and private employment in Mozambique and Angola.[1] Portugal has acceded to the Slavery Convention of 1926 which limited the use of forced labour to public purposes, but she has not acceded either to the Forced Labour Convention of 1930 or to the Recruitment of Indigenous Workers Convention of 1936. On the other hand, the Labour Code of 1928, which regulates the employment of labour in overseas Provinces and which forms part of the Colonial law of 1933 and the Basic Overseas Law of the same year, restricts the use of forced labour to public purposes; it is provided, moreover, that special sanction for its use for these purposes must be obtained from Lisbon. By an order of 11 April 1930 all such labour must be paid for. It would seem that in practice any labour now requisitioned from local Chiefs is almost entirely employed on the roads, and though Provincial regulations on the subject show a considerable variation, they all provide for the remuneration of compulsory labour on State work at fixed rates and for minimum standards of housing, clothing, and diet.[2]

It is a cardinal feature of Portuguese policy that the obligation to labour is an essential part of the process by which the indigenous population can be raised to the dignity of full Portuguese citizenship.[3] The current legislation, while reaffirming the right of the State to obtain labour for public works subject to the conditions above described, also maintains the right to compel the indigenous population to engage in the production of marketable crops for its own benefit, or in order to discharge tax liabilities.

Present-day critics of the Portuguese system assert that the Administration, while taking a stand on these general principles, nevertheless shows an active interest in promoting the use of 'contract' labour for private employers and in securing recruitment for the diamond industry in Angola.[4] The Administration has also encouraged the supply of labour from Mozambique for the Rand mines, in pursuance of an Agreement made with the Union of South Africa.[5] A similar Agreement was

[1] International Labour Office, *Report of the ad hoc Committee on Forced Labour*, Studies and Reports (New Series) no. 36, 1953. *Anti-Slavery Reporter and Aborigines' Friend*, October 1955, pp. 44–48. B. Davidson, *The African Awakening*, 1955, p. 1.

[2] For the regulations regarding the employment of African labour in Mozambique, see *Regulamento do trabalho dos indígenas na colónia de Moçambique*, 1947. *Província de Moçambique, Regulamento dos acidentes de trabalho dos indígenas*, 1953. *Colónia de Moçambique, Regulamento dos serviçais indígenas*, 1949. For Portuguese Guinea see A. Carreira, 'Problemas do trabalho indígena na colónia da Guiné', *Boletim geral das colónias*, Lisbon, December 1948.

[3] A. Durieux, 'Essai sur le statut des indigènes portugais de la Guinée, de l'Angola et du Mozambique', *Mém. A.R.S.C.*, vol. v, no. 3, 1955, p. 38.

[4] See below, p. 1517.   [5] See below, p. 1378.

concluded in 1934 with Southern Rhodesia in virtue of which 15,000 labourers are sent as recruits annually from Angola. The law explicitly prohibits any official intervention to supply labour for such enterprises.[1] But this has not, it is alleged, prevented the Administration from using pressure to secure 'contract' labour.

It was at one time suggested that this purpose was secured by a liberal interpretation of the law of *vagabondage*, but it would seem that since 1926 the relatively small amount of labour impressed on the grounds of vagrancy is in fact utilized only on public works. It is not clear how far failure to comply with the obligation to work on the production of marketable crops can be used as a ground for bringing pressure on a man to engage as a 'contract' labourer. The regulation seems to be applied more often in Mozambique than in Angola. In 1938, for instance, the Administration, at the instance of the *Junta de Exportação de Algodão* directed that every Native should plant half a hectare of cotton each year. In consequence of the subsequent neglect of the food crops it became necessary in 1946 to order that the normal quantity of food crops should be grown in addition to the requisite cotton crop.[2]

Though it is not easy to ascertain how far official pressure is actually used to compel Africans to engage as 'contract' labour, it would, however, seem that the proportion of *contratado* to 'free' labour is considerable, at all events in Angola. It has been stated that in 1954 there were in Angola as many as 379,000 *contratados*, as against 420,000 classed as *voluntarios*.[3] The Benguela Railway Company[4] had in 1953 a total of 7,055 'contract' workers out of an African labour force of 17,500. The Angola Diamond Company obtained a third of its labour on contract.[5] When the contract is for work outside the labourer's area, it is normally for two years; contracts for work within the labourer's area may be verbal for a period not exceeding one month, but in writing for periods up to a year. Exemption from liability to 'contract' labour can be obtained by showing that the worker has done six months' work in the previous twelve months or that he is actually working, in which case the employer's signature in the work book is required as proof.

It is in regard to the methods employed in recruiting *contratado* labour that criticism is now chiefly directed. It is alleged that an employer who desires to supplement his voluntary labour force is accustomed to apply to the local *Chefe do Posto*, who either himself supplies tax defaulters or submits to the local Chief a quota which he is obliged to fill. Although official intervention in recruiting is forbidden by the Labour Code, there

[1] Articles 145 and 147 of the Constitution as consolidated in the Law no. 2048, 11 June 1951.
[2] C. F. Spence, *The Portuguese Colony of Moçambique*, 1951, pp. 54–55.
[3] *New Statesman and Nation*, 8 May 1954, p. 585; 15 May 1954, p. 621.
[4] See below, p. 1570.
[5] Davidson, op. cit. pp. 199 ff.

is some evidence to substantiate the statement of outside observers that officials are exposed to considerable financial inducements from the large employers of labour. The use of pressure has been officially denied, but the United Nations *ad hoc* Committee on Forced Labour expressed in 1953 the belief that, though forced labour was in principle forbidden, there were certain restrictions and exceptions in the legislation which permit the exaction of forced or compulsory labour.[1]

It is certainly the impression in some of the neighbouring territories that it is the incidence of labour regulations which has been responsible for much of the emigration of peasants from Portuguese territories.[2] The range of the immigration has been specially noticeable in the Southern Province of Nyasaland, in Northern Rhodesia, and the Transvaal. In Nyasaland the total immigration was estimated in 1933 at over 400,000, but the rate has greatly decreased since that period. In 1954 the influx from Portuguese East Africa was estimated at about 7,000 a year, but many of these remained only for short periods.[3] In Northern Rhodesia immigration from Angola has been chiefly experienced in Barotseland.[4] It has been asserted by one critic of the *contratado* system that the total emigration from Angola has amounted to 1 million in all, but though it has clearly been considerable, it is not possible to provide any statistical evidence of its extent; nor has emigration necessarily been entirely due to the incidence of labour regulations.

Liberia

In the early days of this century the export of labour from Liberia to the Spanish island of Fernando Po[5] gave rise to criticism of the Liberian Government which was in some respects similar to that which had been directed against the Administration of Angola in regard to the shipment of labour to the Portuguese 'Cocoa Islands'. Spanish planters in the island began to recruit labour from Liberia in 1900. During the next few years farmers in Liberia persuaded their Government to put a ban on the recruitment of labour for Fernando Po and an Act of 1908 prohibited it so far as the Montserrado and Grand Bassa counties of Liberia were concerned. It continued, however, from other counties, and in 1913 incidents connected with the shipment of Kru labour to Fernando Po formed the subject of comment in the British Parliament.[6] It was alleged that

[1] International Labour Office, *Report of the ad hoc Committee on Forced Labour*, Studies and Reports (New Series) no. 36, 1953, p. 64.

[2] *The Times, Portuguese Supplement*, 25 October 1955.

[3] *N.A.*, Part II, pp. 24, 49. R. R. Kuczynski, *Demographic Survey of the British Colonial Empire*, vol. ii, 1949, p. 546. *Nyasaland, Annual Report of the Labour Department, 1954*, p. 7.

[4] Kuczynski, op. cit. p. 424. For the Transvaal, see International Labour Conference, 37th Session, *Migrant Workers (Underdeveloped Countries)*, Report V (i), Geneva, 1953, p. 34.

[5] See above, p. 233.   [6] H.C. Deb., 14 January 1913, col. 1856.

compulsion had been used by Liberian officials to secure recruits, and that the treatment of labour in the island was inhuman.[1]

In 1914 a Convention was signed by the Spanish and Liberian Governments as the result of which recruitment was organized under the joint supervision of Spanish and Liberian officials, and an arrangement was made that half of the wages due should be paid to the labourer on his return to Monrovia. Recruitment was then resumed, but complaints continued to be made that Liberian officials still used pressure to secure recruits, and that inadequate provision was made in the island for safeguarding the health of the labour employed.[2] By a series of Acts of the Liberian Legislature beginning in 1920 the right of recruitment for Fernando Po was gradually withdrawn, largely, as it would appear, at the instance of Liberian farmers who complained of the shortage of local labour. Recruitment from Liberia practically ceased from 1926 onwards, and it would seem that labour on the Spanish cocoa estates is now largely secured by the engagement of 'free' labour from Nigeria.

Liberia has accepted the terms of the International Forced Labour Convention of 1930. It has, however, been suggested that the greater part of the labour required by the recent programme of road construction in Liberia[3] has been obtained under a form of compulsion and has been unpaid. Accurate information is lacking on this point, but it is noteworthy that even supporters of the Liberian Government have admitted that in the past the services of the Chiefs have been used to secure unpaid labour for public works.[4]

THE MIGRATION OF LABOUR

The migration of labour has become one of the most prominent topics in current discussions on the labour problems of Africa, but the term is often used with some lack of precision. It is natural that where dependence on wage-earning is still an innovation for a great mass of the population, there should be a considerable element of shifting labour, and the more so, because labour is as yet predominantly of an unskilled type. Shifting or seasonal labour is a common phenomenon in a number of other partially developed countries, but such labour is not necessarily migratory.

Thus in India a great proportion of the labour in the coal-mines, the jute mills, and even in the cotton mills is of a shifting type, being largely the product of a peasant population with an agricultural background.[5] Even today the ratio of labour 'turnover' in some of these industries is

---

[1] N. Azikiwe, *Liberia in World Politics*, 1934, p. 170.

[2] H. F. Reeve, *The Black Republic*, 1923. League of Nations, Temporary Slavery Commission, *Minutes of the Second Session*, C. 426, M. 157, 1925, VIB, p. 25.

[3] See below, p. 1591.   [4] Azikiwe, op. cit. p. 180.

[5] See the *Report of the Indian Industrial Commission, 1916–18*, Cmd. 51, 1919. Some of the more recent facts are given in V. Anstey, *The Economic Development of India*, 1952, pp. 123 ff.

high. The duration of the working periods of individuals may depend on a number of factors. Climatic conditions may at one time create the demand for a supplementary means of subsistence, but at another may necessitate a prompt return to field labour. The variable standards of economic demand may also have a decisive bearing; in India the low-class workers in the coal-mines will cease work as soon as their wages have met their demands for clothing or liquor; the higher-standard worker in the Bombay cotton mills may continue to work till he has accumulated enough to satisfy the claims of his family for the means of education. There are equally variable factors which regulate the supply of African manpower and determine the duration of the period which the individual worker is prepared to devote to wage-earning. It has, for instance, been stated that the period during which many Africans are prepared to work away from home coincides with the prolonged lactation period during which a man ordinarily has no connexion with his wife.

Much of the seasonal or more shifting type of African labour is not in the true sense migratory. Nor is it easy to obtain any record of the extent of real migratory movement. African labour moves to and fro from the northern to the southern districts of the Gold Coast, or backwards and forwards to the sisal plantations of Tanganyika, and in and out of the Native Reserves of the Rhodesias and the Union of South Africa. These movements create their own problems and have a definite reaction on the domestic economy of the groups concerned, but since they take place within the same territory they do not normally come within the scope of official statistics.

Many territories provide figures showing the proportion of 'foreign' labour employed; but movement which takes place across a political frontier does not necessarily mean that the journey is longer or that its social consequences are more pronounced than journeys that are made by many Africans to take up work within the boundaries of a single territory. There are instances (as, for example, the Lupa gold-fields in Tanganyika) where employment centres are more accessible to populations across the frontier than to the inhabitants of the territory in which they are situated. Such statistics as it is possible to provide of labour migration must be read subject to these considerations. They can in the circumstances be taken merely as illustrating those movements which are in fact of major consequence, namely, those which take the worker away from his home for considerable periods, and which may place him in an environment alien to his previous traditions and social relations.

The Union of South Africa

Probably the most conspicuous instance of dependence on labour from other territories is the Union of South Africa. In 1946 out of 305,410

African workers employed in the industries represented in the Witwatersrand Native Labour Association only 41¼ per cent. originally came from within the Union. At an earlier stage it had been calculated on the basis of the census of 1936 that half the African labour in the Rand mines came from outside the Union.[1] This labour is recruited from various territories. As will be shown subsequently, there has for many years been an Agreement with the Portuguese Government under which Mozambique supplies labour which is now fixed at a maximum figure of 100,000 Natives.[2] In addition, however, to authorized migration there is a clandestine emigration from Angola and from Mozambique the extent of which it is difficult to estimate. According to a statement made in 1950, there is an average of 100,000 Mozambique workers living continuously in the Transvaal.[3]

But in spite of the large numbers drawn from outside, the effect of the demand made on the indigenous African population is probably more marked in the Union itself than in any other territory. The numbers involved can be estimated only indirectly. A recent study of the conditions in seven territorial divisions of the Union showed that there was a ratio of absentees to total males of all ages amounting on an average to 32 per cent.; if the figures for men absent from their homes could be related to the men of working age only, instead of all males, the ratio might, it was said, reach nearly 100 per cent. in certain districts.[4] Another index of the extent of movement is the increase of the African population in the urban areas of the Union. The African population of the Witwatersrand alone has increased from nearly 300,000 in 1911 to a little over 1 million in 1951. The 1951 census has revealed that out of a Native population of roughly 8½ million, over 2¼ million (or 26·8 per cent.) are now living in urban centres.[5]

It does not appear likely that there will in the future be any substantial reduction in the dependence of the Union on labour from outside the territory or on seasonal labour within it. It is the declared policy of the Administration to discountenance any attempt at the further stabilization of the African population in urban centres. The only exception to the policy of continued dependence on external African labour is likely to be in the Western Province of the Cape, where 72 per cent. of the Native population has been attracted to the towns by industrial expansion. Here the current policy is to exclude foreign migratory labour and to repatriate

[1] *Handbook on Race Relations in South Africa*, 1949, p. 317.
[2] See below, p. 1385.
[3] International Labour Conference, 37th Session, *Migrant Workers (Underdeveloped Countries)*, Report V (1), Geneva, 1953, p. 34.
[4] *Handbook on Race Relations in South Africa*, 1949, p. 313.
[5] M. Horrell, *A Survey of Race Relations in South Africa, 1951–1952*, South African Institute of Race Relations, 1952, p. 24.

Union Natives to the Reserves, with a view to making the Province dependent solely on the labour of the Coloured population.[1]

The explanation of the consistent movement of the Native population
to the industrial centres lies in the great difference between the income
which can be earned by a Native worker on the farms or in the Native
Reserves compared to the income earned by a labourer in the gold-mines
or in industry. As the Report of the Socio-Economic Commission on
the Development of the Bantu Areas points out, life in the Native
Reserves retains many attractions for the Bantu, in so far that residence
with his community is a guarantee of social security, apart from the
opportunities it provides for leisure and for the practice of a traditional
way of life.[2] To these advantages no money value can be attached.
But while the income of a family farming in the Reserves or Trust farms
was estimated in 1949–50 as varying from £43 to £73 a year, the
remuneration of the individual Bantu labourer on a European farm was
estimated at about £83. The earning in mining was put at £90 (including payment in kind), and at £110 in secondary industry. In commerce the average for Bantu males was put between £90 and £100. In
domestic service the remuneration for males was put at £106¾ in 1952.[3]

The High Commission Territories

The effect of migration is also strongly marked in the High Commission
Territories, from which roughly over 100,000 men proceed to the Union
every year, the majority returning to their homes after six or twelve
months' absence.[4] In Basutoland the *Agricultural Survey* published in 1952
estimated the number of persons absent from their villages at any one time
as roughly 77,000 males and 22,000 females. It would seem, therefore,
that the territory is deprived every year of a proportion—generally estimated to be between 50 and 60 per cent.—of its able-bodied men.[5] There
is ground, however, for holding that only a small proportion fail to return
to the territory, though some may stay away for periods of up to ten years.
As a rule the Basuto earn good wages and have in particular acquired
a high reputation as shaft-sinkers. Farm work is not popular with the
younger men because wages are relatively low, but it appeals to a number
of the older men whose health can no longer stand mine work and who
are, moreover, encouraged to bring their families to live on the farms. In
recent years employment in the secondary industries of the Union has

[1] W. W. M. Eiselen, 'The Coloured People and the Natives', *Journal of Racial Affairs*, April
1955, pp. 1–19.
[2] *Summary of Report of Commission on Socio-Economic Development of the Bantu Areas*, 1956, pp.
35 ff., 98 ff.
[3] For earlier figures see *Handbook on Race Relations in South Africa*, 1949, pp. 316–20.
[4] G. N. Burden, 'Labour Migration in Africa', *Corona*, February 1951, p. 55.
[5] *N.A.*, Part V, pp. 13–16. See also H. Ashton, *The Basuto*, 1952, pp. 162 ff.

become increasingly attractive and, as labour in these industries is not organized in the same way as in the mines, the labourer usually stays away longer.

There is not the same ratio of migration from the Bechuanaland Protectorate. The careful investigations made on the basis of figures compiled in 1938–40 showed that some 27½ per cent. of the adult males of the Protectorate were away from home. The tribes on the eastern side of the Protectorate, where there is a greater density of population, migrate more readily than those on the west; some observers have held that one-third to a half of the able-bodied manpower of those districts is normally away at work at one time, while perhaps 70 or 80 per cent. have either been abroad or are still absent.[1] Migration is also a less prominent feature in Swaziland than in Basutoland. Current estimates have placed at 25 or 30 per cent. the proportion of able-bodied men who are away at any one time from their homes.[2]

The Federation of Rhodesia and Nyasaland

According to the census taken in 1951 in Southern Rhodesia, the number of Africans indigenous to the territory then in employment was 271,000. The immigrant labour force in that year numbered nearly 247,000, and comprised roughly 86,000 from Nyasaland, 48,500 from Northern Rhodesia, and nearly 102,000 from Mozambique, the balance being made up from Angola, the Belgian Congo, Bechuanaland, and South-West Africa.[3] It would seem that a considerable proportion of the immigrants from other territories find employment in Salisbury, where the African population was estimated in 1954 at 107,000.[4]

The demand of Southern Rhodesia for immigrant labour and in particular from the neighbouring territories of Northern Rhodesia and Nyasaland has been for many years the subject of negotiation with their Governments, and a series of Tripartite Agreements have, as will be shown, been made to regulate the conditions of immigration. It is of some importance to note in this connexion that while immigration into the Federation is within the sphere of Federal legislation, the control of the voluntary movement of persons between the three territories falls into the category of Concurrent legislation.[5]

In Northern Rhodesia external labour accounts for about 22½ per cent. of the African labour force employed on the mines and other commercial undertakings employing over 300 workers.[6] It is clear that the demand for labour for the Copperbelt and on the European farms leads to an

---

[1] I. Schapera, *Migrant Labour and Tribal Life*, 1947, pp. 33 ff. See also *N.A.*, Part V, pp. 160–2.
[2] Ibid. pp. 344–6.   [3] *Census of the Population, 1951*, Salisbury, 1954, p. 39.
[4] *Annual Report of the Director of Native Administration, City of Salisbury, 1954*, p. 6.
[5] Rhodesia and Nyasaland Federation Order in Council no. 1199, 1953, items 4 and 47.
[6] *Northern Rhodesia Annual Report of the Department of Labour, 1955*, p. 21.

unusually high proportion of absenteeism among the adult male population of the Protectorate. It has been estimated that taking the territory as a whole at least one-third to a half of the able-bodied men are normally away from their villages, the actual proportion varying from as little as 3 per cent. in certain areas near the railway to 70 per cent. or more in certain outlying areas.[1] It is generally agreed that the number of Africans now leaving their villages as wage-earners is such as to be a serious menace to the development of the rural areas.[2] The conditions under which African workers may enter or leave Northern Rhodesia are laid down in the African Migrant Workers Ordinance of 1948.[3] Migrant workers entering the territory in 1953 numbered about 15,000, of whom 5,700 originated from Tanganyika, 3,000 from Angola, and 3,800 from Nyasaland. The number leaving the territory for Southern Rhodesia was recorded in 1954 as 11,219, but in the same year 12,487 returned to it.[4]

The position in Nyasaland is of special interest, since it was the publication of the Report of the Nyasaland Committee on Emigrant Labour in 1935 that first drew general attention in the British dependencies to the social effects of labour migration. It is also of interest because emigration has in this case usually involved a longer period of absenteeism than in most other territories from which migrant labour has been drawn. The social effect of emigration has formed the subject of much subsequent consideration by the Nyasaland Government, notably in connexion with the negotiations which took place in 1942 and 1947 regarding the revision of the Agreements on Migrant Labour concluded in those years with the Northern and Southern Rhodesia Governments.[5] Nyasaland has few industries, and although the production of tea and tobacco now provides a certain field of paid employment, the range of local wages available is far lower than that which can be earned in employment in other territories. The provisions relating to migrant labour are embodied in the Nyasaland Labour Ordinance of 1944. The number of adult males in the Protectorate suited for employment has been put at about 380,000. It was estimated that in 1954 there were about 160,000 Nyasaland workers employed outside the Protectorate, of whom roughly 100,000 were in Southern Rhodesia, 42,000 in the Union of South Africa, 10,000 in Northern Rhodesia, and 8,000 in other territories. Although the proportion which chooses to go out under contract is increasing, the majority still prefer to go without a contract in order to work for an employer of their own choice.

[1] An Economic Survey of the Colonial Territories, 1951: vol. i, The Central African and High Commission Territories, Col. no. 281 (1), 1952, p. 22. N.A., Part II, p. 78.

[2] Northern Rhodesia, Annual Report on African Affairs, 1952, p. 32. See also J. Merle Davis, Modern Industry and the African, 1933, pp. 102–5, 281–2, 286.

[3] Ordinance no. 30, 1948, amended by no. 7, 1951.

[4] Northern Rhodesia, Annual Report of the Department of Labour, 1955, p. 44.

[5] N.A., Part II, p. 19.

In 1954 the proportion of migrants who went out under contract was approximately 37 per cent. of the total.[1]

In the Union of South Africa, Nyasalanders are now classified as 'prohibited' immigrants, unless they enter explicitly as recruits for the Rand gold-mines. Once in the country, however, they are permitted to enter certain areas for work under temporary permits which are valid for six months but which may be renewed. In principle only those who have obtained registration are allowed to work in the proclaimed areas, as, for instance, the towns and their neighbourhood; others can validly accept only work in the mines or in rural areas. Hitherto the number of Nyasalanders actually at work in the Union has been difficult to decide, but the facts will now be accurately established under the operation of the new Registration Act.[2]

Some light is thrown on the reasons for migration by a sample survey conducted in the Southern Province of Nyasaland in 1949. Of the emigrants questioned, nearly 70 per cent. stated that they were emigrating in order to obtain the money needed to buy clothes or other goods; over 72 per cent. said that they would prefer to work in Nyasaland if higher wages were obtainable there. The Administration does not appear to contemplate any restriction on emigration, and its policy is directed mainly to securing such conditions of recruitment as will guarantee the return of emigrant labour within a period of two years and will secure the introduction everywhere of a system of compulsory Deferred Pay and Family Remittances.[3] Up to the date of the Tripartite Agreement referred to above only the recruits of the Witwatersrand Labour Association had been compelled to make such remittances; they amounted in 1945 to £16,476, including a certain number of voluntary remittances. The Family Remittance Scheme under the Migrant Labour Agreement has since been more widely extended. In 1954 the Family Remittances amounted to nearly £38,000 and the Deferred Pay to nearly £34,000. The voluntary remittances sent through the Post Office were far larger in amount, being estimated in 1954 at about £587,000. In addition there were remittances sent through the Salisbury and Johannesburg offices of the Nyasaland Government, amounting in all to £10,800.[4] The remittances of emigrant labour thus form an important element in the economy of Nyasaland.

The British East African Territories

Recruitment to other territories from Tanganyika is on a small scale compared with that of Nyasaland. In 1954 a total of 5,500 persons were

---

[1] *Nyasaland, Annual Report of the Labour Department, 1954*, p. 7.
[2] See above, p. 163.   [3] *N.A.*, Part II, pp. 20–21.
[4] *Nyasaland, Annual Report of the Labour Department, 1954*, p. 24.

recruited for employment in the Union of South Africa or the two Rhodesias, and a few others found employment in Kenya, Zanzibar, and Uganda.[1] On the other hand, nearly 43,000 immigrants from other territories, and most notably Ruanda Urundi and Portuguese East Africa, entered Tanganyika in the same year, and it is probable that on the whole emigration from the territory is more than counterbalanced by immigration.

In Kenya the total number of Africans in employment was estimated in 1952 at 438,700.[2] Three-quarters of these were of the labouring type, consisting of 108,300 unskilled workers in commerce and industry and the public services, and 198,100 agricultural workers. But though there is much movement of labour, a considerable proportion of the force employed seeks work for only relatively short periods and returns to the tribal areas.[3] There is little in the nature of emigration to other territories. The major problems of labour in Kenya are firstly, those connected with the employment of the considerable numbers of Africans in Nairobi and Mombasa, and secondly, those arising from the employment of the large body of 'resident labour' (usually known as 'squatters') on European farms.[4]

The high level of prosperity in Uganda, due to the increased value of the cotton and coffee crops, has created a considerable demand for labour. The total labour force, estimated in 1954 at 280,000 persons, included a number of immigrants from neighbouring countries. A total of 67,000 immigrants (including labourers and their families) entered Uganda by the south-west route;[5] of these immigrants 82 per cent. originated in Ruanda Urundi, 17 per cent. in Tanganyika, and 1 per cent. in the Belgian Congo. The number of immigrants from Ruanda Urundi seems to fluctuate widely; it was stated, for instance, in 1938 that not less than 100,000 Banyaruanda migrate to Uganda from Ruanda Urundi annually. Some 28,000 were recorded in 1954 as entering the Protectorate by the north-western route; of this number 17 per cent. came from the Belgian Congo and the Sudan. There is less precise information regarding the number who followed the eastern route from the Nyanza Province of Kenya, but this number also seems to be very variable.

The majority of migrants from the north-west appear to lease land for cultivating cotton or other cash crops, but whether they come in this capacity or as wage-earners their engagement is usually seasonal.[6] Ruanda

[1] *Tanganyika, Annual Report of the Labour Department, 1954*, pp. 20, 46.

[2] *Kenya, Annual Report of the Labour Department, 1952*, p. 6.

[3] *East Africa Royal Commission 1953–1955, Report*, Cmd. 9475, 1955, p. 146.

[4] Ibid. p. 163. See also *N.A.*, Part I, pp. 198–202; *Kenya, Annual Report of the Labour Department, 1952*, p. 11.

[5] *Colonial Reports, Uganda, 1954*, p. 23. *Uganda, Annual Report of the Labour Department, 1954*, p. 4.

[6] *Report of the Committee of Enquiry into the Labour Situation in the Uganda Protectorate, 1938*, Uganda. 1938, p. 19.

Urundi is the most densely populated rural area in Central Africa; it has been estimated that there are 180,000 families surplus to the land available, and the object of migration is therefore largely to gain subsistence.

The British West African Territories

Save in the Gold Coast and Nigeria the movement of labour in the British West African dependencies is mainly seasonal and for agricultural purposes. In the Gold Coast Colony and Ashanti the majority of unskilled labourers required by commerce and industry are drawn from the Northern Territories and from the French Colonies to the north and west; the migrant worker from these areas usually returns after one or two seasons. There is a considerable intake of migrant labour by the tin-mines of Nigeria.

It was estimated a few years ago that altogether some 100,000 workers are drawn from foreign territories for employment in the mining industries in Sierra Leone, the Gold Coast, and Nigeria.[1] A census taken in 1946 recorded an influx into the Gold Coast Colony and Ashanti of 52,000 Africans from British territories and 121,000 of foreign origin. In 1953 391,500 persons crossed by the ferry on the Volta river travelling south, and 378,400 returned northwards. The replacement rate in the mines in the Gold Coast is unusually high: 100 per cent. of the underground workers were replaced in a single year and 30 per cent. signed contracts for less than six months. There is no organized migratory movement of labour from other territories for service in Nigeria, but men from neighbouring French territories arrive sporadically in search of employment and some of them go to the tin-mines. As shown in a previous paragraph, there is now a regulated recruitment of labour for work in the cocoa and coffee plantations of Fernando Po.

The 'strange farmers' who regularly visit Gambia and to whom more detailed reference is made in a previous chapter,[2] are a special type of immigrant. They come mainly from the French Sudan or French Guinea, and they usually return to their homes after raising and selling a crop of groundnuts, but they may sometimes remain for two or three years. In some cases they are wage-earning labourers, but more often they are temporary tenants. The landlord provides them with land and also with board and lodging, in return for which the 'strange farmer' works a certain number of days for him.[3] In some years the recorded number has been as high as 32,200, but the average over a number of years is about 14,000.

The French Territories

In French West Africa the migration of labour is also mainly seasonal. The principal movements are: first, that of the *navétanes*, who are similar

---

[1] R. Firth, 'Social Problems and Research in British West Africa', Part II, *Africa*, July 1947, p. 172.   [2] See above, p. 846.   [3] *N.A.*, Part III, p. 347.

to the 'strange farmers' in Gambia. In 1951 it was stated that there were some 42,000 who migrate regularly from the Sudan and north French Guinea to cultivate the groundnut in Senegal. Secondly, there are the seasonal workers (numbering about 50,000 in 1951) who migrate from the Upper Volta to the Ivory Coast, signing on for six months at farms and forestry enterprises and then returning to their villages. Thirdly, there is a seasonal migration to neighbouring territories, such as that of the Mossi of the Upper Volta to the Gold Coast (numbering approximately 130,000 persons in 1951) and that of the Songhai and Djerma from the Niger to the Gold Coast, involving about 25,000 persons each year. In French Equatorial Africa the most significant trend has been the migration from the interior to the towns. It has been said that one-fifth of the population of the Middle Congo region is now located in urban centres.[1]

The Belgian Territories

In the Belgian Congo and Ruanda Urundi there is, apart from the migration to Tanganyika and Uganda mentioned above, a marked movement from agricultural areas to industrial centres. Some reference has already been made to the striking increase in the population of Leopoldville and some of the larger towns.[2] Over $2\frac{1}{2}$ million Africans are said to be now living outside their tribal areas.[3] But the main interest in the labour problems in the Belgian Congo lies in the effort made by the Government to introduce the policy of stabilization, which will be discussed later in this chapter.[4]

The Portuguese Territories

As has been shown, various causes have led to a very considerable movement of a more or less permanent character from the Portuguese territories into neighbouring countries. Reference has also been made to the Agreement concluded between the Portuguese and Union Governments by virtue of which workers up to 100,000 in number are annually recruited from Mozambique for the South African mines. In addition to this, there are a large number of unrecruited labourers from Mozambique more or less permanently at work in the Transvaal. An Agreement first made in 1914 and renewed in 1934 provided for the annual recruitment of up to 15,000 labourers from Mozambique to Southern Rhodesia; there is in addition a considerable migration of unrecruited workers from Angola to the Union of South Africa. The total of unrecruited labour from the

[1] International Labour Conference, 37th Session, *Migrant Workers* (*Underdeveloped Countries*), Report V (1), Geneva, 1953, p. 26.
[2] See above, p. 583.
[3] G. Malengreau, 'Recent Developments in Belgian Africa', in *Africa Today*, 1955, p. 343.
[4] See below, p. 1391.

East and West Portuguese territories now working in the Union has been placed as high as 40,000.

The Social Effects of Migration

It would seem from the preceding survey that the most conspicuous effects of labour migration are to be found in South Africa, the High Commission Territories, the Federation of Rhodesia and Nyasaland, Angola, Mozambique, and Ruanda Urundi. The demographic studies made in these areas deal at some length with the effect of migration on the gross figures of population as recorded periodically at the time of census, but there does not appear to be any comprehensive study which deals specifically with the effect of migration on such factors as the reduction in the birth-rate.[1] It is not difficult to visualize the social effect on an indigenous society of the absence of large numbers of its adult males; it is to be seen in the loosening of kindred and tribal ties and the weakening of the influence of the traditional rules regulating social conduct. The effect on the wives remaining behind in the villages may well be imagined. Equally unfortunate has been the growth of prostitution in the urban centres and the consequent spread of venereal disease among migrant workers.

The economic effects are less clearly recognizable. The loss of manpower in the cultivation of subsistence crops is obvious; on the other hand, the receipts from migrant workers can make an important addition to the resources of a rural community.[2] In this respect there is much to be said for the methods adopted in Nyasaland. Here the Government has endeavoured to secure that all labour migration should take place under an Agreement which must include provision for the system of Deferred Payment and of Family Allowances.

It has been suggested that the effect of labour migration in reducing the amount of subsistence cultivation can be over-estimated, since much of the agricultural work is in any case carried on by women.[3] But this view overlooks the fact that in every African community the man has specific tasks which cannot be delegated to women. These are particularly important in areas where the practice of shifting cultivation prevails and trees have to be cut down before the ground can be planted. The substitution of the plough for the hoe has also increased the importance of the male worker in cultivation. A recent study expresses with good reason the view that 'where migrant labour has been drawn from the indigenous agricultural economies in high proportions, this has often had a deleterious

---

[1] See, however, R. R. Kuczynski, *Demographic Survey of the British Colonial Empire*, vol. ii, 1949, p. 494.　　　　　　　　　　　　　　　[2] See above, p. 1382.

[3] J. F. W. Grosskopf, 'Vestiging en Trek Van die Suid-Afrikaanse Naturelle—Bevolking onder Nuwere Ekonomiese Voorwaades', *South African Journal of Economics*, vol. i, 1933, p. 273.

effect on output and on farming practices, giving rise to a vicious circle in which the outflow of labour reduces productivity and falling productivity increases still farther the pressure on workers to seek wage employment'. It is added that 'eventually a stage may be reached at which the system of migrant labour, based on the labourer's retaining his place in a subsistence agricultural community, may break down'.[1] The result of migration on agricultural production still awaits a fully comprehensive study which should include also an examination of its influence on schemes of soil conservation and of land reclamation.

THE STABILIZATION OF LABOUR

It seems inevitable that in the existing circumstances of Africa, the labour market should be in large measure dependent on floating or migrant labour. It is, as the East Africa Royal Commission of 1953–5 has observed, the only system through which a considerable section of the African population can now meet its needs. For many Africans it is not possible to gain a higher income level for the support of their families without wage-earning, and the migrant labour system appears as the most economic choice which they can make, however socially undesirable it may be.[2] The most effective remedy for this situation is to be found in the progressive stabilization of labour.[3] Stabilization does not in itself imply that labour necessarily becomes stationary; there must always be in Africa as elsewhere a certain movement of manpower. In its broader sense stabilization involves the emergence of a type of worker who looks primarily if not exclusively to wage-earning for his own support and for that of his family, and is prepared to face the change in his customary mode of life which this demands.

Labour as it becomes stabilized tends, at all events in the field of industrial employment, to adopt a permanent long-term residence in urban conditions, and to that extent the growth of urbanization is a rough measure of the growth of a stable form of labour. There are, however, limits to its value as an index of stabilization, since the towns tend to contain also a large floating population of unskilled labour, and some discrimination is required to decide how far it actually contains the nucleus of a permanent labour force. That can only be determined as the result of sociological studies made from time to time of the actual conditions of the African residents in the towns.[4]

[1] United Nations Document E/2377, *Aspects of Economic Development in Africa*, 20 March 1953, p. 67. [2] Cmd. 9475, 1955, p. 154.
[3] Ibid. quoting *Report of the Committee on African Wages* (the Carpenter Report), Nairobi, 1954, para. 290.
[4] For some typical instances of such studies, see the references given in *Handbook on Race Relations in South Africa*, 1949, pp. 240 ff.; and in *N.A.*, Part II, pp. 146 ff.

Looking at the question of stabilization of labour as a whole, it would seem that the matter has hitherto been viewed in two different aspects. It has been seen by some mainly as a remedy for the social mischief caused by migration, and by others as a means of improving the character of the manpower available for industry. But the recommendations made by the East Africa Royal Commission[1] have been a useful reminder that stabilization must be viewed in a broader aspect as a factor which will help to promote the all-round improvement of African production. It is here that its true importance lies. Seen in its proper perspective, the increase of production and the consequent improvement in the standards of living are the real remedy for such social maladjustments as have to be faced from the migration of labour.

The Union of South Africa

In a number of the countries of the world, the progress of stabilization has been the natural result of economic forces, though State policy may also have played its part by providing facilities for the training of labour in technical processes. In Africa the process is to a large extent natural, but in certain instances the principle of stabilization has become a controversial issue of State policy. This has been pre-eminently the case in the Union of South Africa. There have been aspects of the policy of segregation which have implied a definite opposition to the creation of a stabilized African labour force. But one must be clear as to the implications of this policy as the advocates of segregation see it. They are not opposed in a general sense to the acquisition of greater skill on the part of the African labour force. This is of great importance in the growing manufacturing industries, if in no other sphere, and it is a relevant fact that in the last few years the manufacturing industry has begun to make a greater contribution to the national income of the Union than the mining industry.

Nor, indeed, is the objection to stabilization primarily directed against the accommodation in or near the larger towns of a certain permanent element of African labour, for that also is recognized as an inescapable condition of the maintenance of the secondary industries. The actual position in regard to stabilization is perhaps best stated in the words used by the Minister of Labour in 1951:

There must be a permanent Native population in the urban areas and non-European labour cannot be withdrawn from secondary industry, but the Native must be allowed to do skilled work only in Native areas if and when industries are established there. The whole crux of the policy of the Government is that we do not want to create a permanent stratum of European unskilled labour and then allow Native labour to advance beyond it.[2]

[1] Cmd. 9475, 1955, pp. 154 ff.   [2] B. J. Schoeman, as quoted in *S.A.S.*, 30 May 1951.

Here a State policy based on racial or social considerations is given priority over principles supported by ordinary economic experience. There is, however, nothing novel in such a phenomenon. In the Western world there are many instances where economic policy has had to give place to considerations based on what is held to be the national interest or the interest of sections of the community who carry major political weight. In all such cases the ultimate test is likely to be that of practicability rather than of economic propriety or ethical principles.

It is of interest to note such evidence as exists of the reaction of Africans in the Union to the policy of stabilization. At present they appear to see it mainly as a factor in extending urbanization, and to this many have in principle been strongly opposed. That is due to the permanently inferior status which is accorded in the towns to the African wage-earner, the unsuitability of the type of accommodation commonly provided for him, and his exclusion from the skilled trades in order to avoid competition with European workers.[1] A survey conducted among factory workers in Durban has shown a surprising degree of hostility to permanent urbanization, based mainly on those grounds.[2]

The Federation of Rhodesia and Nyasaland

As has been shown, Southern Rhodesia has in the past been largely dependent on migrant labour, and in its case attempts at stabilization have largely centred on the endeavour to secure a steady supply of this class of labour through Agreements made with the neighbouring territories. The Report of the Committee of the Central African Council which preceded the Agreement of 1947 suggested, however, that stabilization might be the ultimate though long-term solution of the problem of labour migration.[3] Under the existing Agreement the passes given for entry into Southern Rhodesia are valid for two years, at the end of which labourers are repatriated, except those who are married and are accompanied by their families, who may remain indefinitely. A recent announcement envisaged the possibility of the stabilization of African labourers from Nyasaland within the next 15 years. Hitherto the shortage of housing accommodation has been a standing obstacle to any system of stabilization, but the question of housing is already seriously engaging the attention of the Government[4] and in 1955 it expressed a hope that sufficient progress would have been made by 1960 to permit of attracting a more stable labour force. There is at present a very significant disparity in the number of male and female Africans employed in the principal towns of the

---

[1] G. E. Stent, in *Africa*, July 1948, pp. 161 ff.
[2] University of Natal, Department of Economics, *The African Factory Worker*, 1950, pp. 103 ff.
[3] *Southern Rhodesia, Report of the Central African Council, 1947*, C.S.R. 42, 1947.
[4] See above, pp. 572 ff.

Colony: in 1951 the total number of males was shown as 157,331, against 5,387 women.[1]

In Northern Rhodesia both the Government and the copper-mining companies appear to have entertained at one time some doubts regarding the advisability of adopting the principle of stabilization. The presence of a large force of stabilized African employees might create a serious responsibility for the State if there should again occur a period of depression such as that from which the mines at one time suffered.[2] It is, however, clear that the African population in the Copperbelt now contains an increasing ratio of labour which can be described as stabilized. There is a growing proportion of long-service labour and of families resident in the mines.[3] Reference has already been made to the steps that are now being taken to increase the accommodation available for families in the urbanized areas of the Protectorate; they have been designed to assist the progress of African adjustment to urban social conditions on the Copperbelt, and in particular to assist in the creation of a permanently settled labour force.[4] Inquiries undertaken on the Copperbelt in 1941 and again in 1952–3 provided evidence of a steady increase in the stabilization of the mine employees over the period, although by 1950 only 60 per cent. of the men on the mines had their families with them, compared with 83 per cent. in the Belgian Congo.[5]

The British East African Territories

In the British East African territories there is, as has been explained, a considerable element of shifting labour, but the problem of stabilization takes a somewhat different form from that which it has assumed in the Rhodesias. The major problem in East Africa is to secure a greater productivity of African labour generally and for the most part it is in this light that schemes of stabilization have been discussed. In the examination made of the question by the recent East Africa Royal Commission, the problem of increasing agricultural production takes priority over that of the improvement of the capacity of industrialized labour. The recommendations made by the Commission range over a wide field and include matters such as the regulation of wages, the achievement of permanency

---

[1] *O.Y.S.R., 1952*, p. 198.

[2] Statement dated 18 February 1941. See also J. Merle Davies, *Modern Industry and the African*, 1933, p. 177.

[3] G. Wilson, 'An Essay on the Economics of Detribalization in Northern Rhodesia, Part I', *R.L.I. Papers*, no. 5, 1941, pp. 21, 59. A. Lynn Saffrey, *Report on Some Aspects of African Living Conditions in the Copperbelt of Northern Rhodesia*, 1943.

[4] *Report of the Board of Inquiry into the Advancement of Africans in the Copper Mining Industry in Northern Rhodesia* (The Forster Report), Lusaka, 1954, p. 15.

[5] Wilson, op cit. Unpublished results of the later survey were mentioned by J. D. Rheinallt Jones in 'Urbanisation', *African Affairs*, January 1953, pp. 37 ff.

of residence both in agricultural and urban areas, and the grant of security of tenure on the agricultural holdings of Africans.[1]

In Kenya the problem of the so-called 'squatter', or resident African labourer on European farms, has proved to be of particular urgency. Something like a quarter of a million African resident labourers and their families have been living in the Highlands of Kenya for a number of years, and there is a problem of somewhat similar character created by the resident African population in the Kenya Crown forests. In 1948 their number was estimated at roughly 32,450 persons.[2] The views of the Royal Commission on this subject were discussed by the Government of Kenya in Dispatches published in 1956,[3] but it would be premature to anticipate here the decisions at which it is likely to arrive.

The French Territories

Industrialization, whether in the form of mining or of secondary industries, has not the same importance in the economy of French West Africa as in the Belgian Congo, and less thought appears to have been given to the problem of stabilization of the labour force. At the present time attention seems to have been directed mainly to the problem of improving the quality of agricultural labour, and it is claimed that the poor performances of seasonal labour are to some extent being counteracted by the greater use of mechanization. As regards the position in industry, it is hoped that the general increase of wages will automatically result in an increased measure of stabilization. It is possible that the recent introduction of the French Labour Code in overseas France may result in a more constructive consideration of the advantages of stabilization.

In French Equatorial Africa mechanization has not been developed to any extent except in forestry, but it is claimed that in this case it has afforded some remedy for the difficulties arising from dependence on a shifting labour force. The shortage of labour is also being met by recruitment from Nigeria for Gabon and by the introduction of labour from north-west Africa.

The Belgian Congo

In its approach to the problem of the stabilization of labour the policy of the Belgian Congo stands in some respects at the opposite end of the scale to that of the Union of South Africa. The Belgian Government entered at an early date on a comprehensive study of labour policy, and its approach was much in advance of that of its immediate neighbours. The appointment of the Labour Commission of 1924 had its fruit in various

[1] Cmd. 9475, 1955, pp. 148, 154 ff.
[2] N.A., Part I, pp. 198–201. [3] Cmd. 9801, 1956.

directions, of which perhaps the most important was the attempt to formulate the proportion of labour which could be taken from its habitual
environment and employed on European enterprise.[1] But the result was
also seen in the emergence of a definite policy of stabilization in the mines
and other industries of the Colony.[2]

Something has already been said as to the measures taken in the
Katanga and elsewhere to improve the accommodation in order to provide
for the needs of families of workers and to encourage in them a stable form
of family life.[3] The recruiting conditions now insist upon the labourer
being accompanied if possible by his wife and family, and family allowances are paid to married employees. In 1950 about 46 per cent. of all
workers in the Katanga copper-mines had more than ten years' continuous
service, and only 24 per cent. had worked for less than three years.[4] There
were nine children to each 100 workers in 1927, 56 in 1939, and 146 in
1949.[5]

It has been claimed that the growing stabilization of labour has decreased the ratio of death and sickness.[6] Most observers are agreed as
to the substantial measure to which it has succeeded in raising the standard
of efficiency of the African labour force, which now shows itself capable of
undertaking technical operations of considerable complexity, far surpassing
those so far entrusted to it in the copper-mines of Northern Rhodesia.
The system of stabilization has not been confined to the Katanga copper-
mines; its operation is also to be seen in other mining enterprises, such as
the Kilo Moto gold-mine, and in the industries centred at Leopoldville
and Stanleyville.

THE EFFICIENCY OF LABOUR

The lack of efficiency which is characteristic of a largely migrant labour
force is only one of the causes for the low standards of productivity in
Africa, but it is nevertheless an element of cardinal importance. Here,
however, the discussion cannot be limited merely to the deficiencies of
skill in African labour, for the labour force has to be viewed as a whole,
including both European and Coloured labour. That is more particularly
the case in the Union of South Africa and in the Rhodesias. There can
be no doubt that the general standard of European labour in the Union

---

[1] R. L. Buell, *The Native Problem in Africa*, vol. ii, 1928, pp. 546 ff. See also below, p. 1402.
[2] L. P. Mair, *Native Policies in Africa*, 1936, pp. 231 ff. W. M. Macmillan, *Africa Emergent*,
1938, pp. 255 ff. International Labour Conference, 37th Session, *Migrant Workers (Under-
developed Countries)*, Report V (1), Geneva, 1953, p. 26.   [3] See above, p. 583.
[4] G. Malengreau, 'Recent Developments in Belgian Africa', in *Africa Today*, 1955, p. 346.
[5] R. Bertiaux, *Aspects de l'industrialisation en Afrique centrale*, 1953.
[6] L. Mottoulle, 'Politique sociale de l'Union Minière du Haut-Katanga pour sa main-d'œuvre
indigène', *Mém. I.R.C.B.*, vol. xiv, no. 3, 1946, p. 12.

has much improved since the days when the labour market included so large a number of the class of Europeans known as 'poor Whites', drawn largely from the *bijwoner* class who had once lived on the farms, but had migrated to the towns. The calculations which were made from time to time of the numbers of those who fell within the category of 'poor Whites' varied widely according to the definition adopted. The estimate made in the Report of the Carnegie Commission suggested that they might be considered to represent a population group of 220,000 persons.[1]

The 'poor Whites', who had for the most part been unaccustomed to any form of labour, were for some time supported by the State and were given such employment as they seemed able to perform. For the time being this class exercised an influence both on the economic and on the political outlook of the European community much in excess of its numerical importance. It has now ceased to exist as a definite class, nor does it create the same problem as when the Carnegie Commission reported on it. But it is a matter of some doubt how far the capacity of European labour in the Union compares in general with that of the worker in Europe. It would at all events be useful if the investigations which are from time to time made of the assumed capacity of African labour could also embrace some estimate of the normal capacity of White labour in South Africa. White or 'civilized' labour has as such an entrenched position, and in the determination of wages there is a tendency to accord to it automatically the status of skilled or semi-skilled labour.

It is thus difficult to obtain any objective judgement on the relative capacity of European and African workers, for the capacity of the European is always liable to be coloured by assumptions which are not themselves based on any objective investigation. While, therefore, it may be taken for granted that a great part of African labour, and especially of shifting or seasonal labour, is of low standard, it is advisable to use a certain measure of reserve in accepting some of the current judgements regarding its relative value in terms of European labour. This is the more necessary because it is clear that in some conditions (as, for instance, those which have arisen in the Katanga copper-mines) African labour has shown itself to be readily receptive of training and able to undertake work demanding a sense of responsibility and considerable technical skill. It will be recalled also that there has recently been an increasing tendency in the Union of South Africa to employ non-European labour in semi-skilled work, owing to the shortage of European labour available for the purpose.[2]

Subject to these considerations, it is of interest to note the tenor of some

---

[1] *Report of the Carnegie Commission on the Poor White Problem in South Africa*, 1932, Part I, pp. 163–79. See also W. M. Macmillan, *Africa Emergent*, 1938, pp. 141, 184, 246. L. P. Mair, *Native Policies in Africa*, 1936, p. 38.   [2] *S.A.S.*, no. 93, 15 November 1954, p. 9.

of the assessments made of the relative value of African labour in industry. In Durban numerous tests made in the Dunlop factory on repetition work suggested that the more efficient type of African takes about half as long again to learn a particular job as a European, and that his normal rate of output is about 85 per cent. of that of the European.[1] In French Equatorial Africa a study of the labour force at Douala recorded the opinion that the African's output was about one-quarter that of the European.[2] In the copper-mines of Northern Rhodesia it was stated in 1947 that 'it requires three Africans to undertake completely the work of the European without additional supervision'.[3] Some years later a second Commission of Inquiry concluded that the African was less adaptable in that he could not be switched from one job to another without further training, that his mechanical knowledge was inferior, and that his irresponsibility led him to absent himself for weeks at a time.[4] It has also been pointed out that if a labourer is to attain a high degree of skill it is essential that he must begin to learn while he is young. It is often forgotten that the European child grows up surrounded by mechanical appliances which the African confronts for the first time as an adult in the factory.

It has been said that in the Belgian Congo the productivity of an African craftsman is rated at half that of a European, but that highly skilled Africans may produce 70 per cent. of European production.[5] It was stated in Nigeria (though it seems on very slender evidence) that the average annual output of the African coal-miner in Nigeria appeared to be about half that of a miner in the United Kingdom.[6] In Kenya it was asserted in 1947 (though here also the evidence was slender) that the output ratio between Asian and African masons was five to three.[7] Tests made at Nairobi in 1943–5 suggested that the output of Africans, 'in many cases with poor diet and chronic disease', may not be more than a third of that of a labourer in Europe.[8] It cannot be claimed, however, that such statements have any real value as a basis of comparison.

In examining the causes of apparent inferiority of African labour many observers have held that the cause lies largely in their physical disabilities. In 1941 one expert observer, after studying conditions in the British West

---

[1] University of Natal, Department of Economics, *The African Factory Worker*, 1950, p. 98.

[2] A. M. Lee, in *International Labour Review*, May 1951.

[3] *Report of the Commission appointed to enquire into the Advancement of Africans in Industry* (the Dalgleish Report), Lusaka, 1948, pp. 21 ff., 35 ff.

[4] *Report of the Board of Inquiry into the Advancement of Africans in the Copper Mining Industry in Northern Rhodesia*, Lusaka, 1954, pp. 20 ff.

[5] B. Davidson, *The African Awakening*, 1955, p. 123.

[6] P. Bower, 'The Mining Industry', *Mining, Commerce and Finance in Nigeria*, 1948, p. 28.

[7] C. H. Northcott, *African Labour Efficiency Survey, 1947*, Colonial Research Publications no. 3, 1949, p. 32.

[8] G. B. Masefield, in *United Empire* (Journal of the Royal Empire Society), January–February 1955, p. 24.

African territories, concluded that the African was usually sufficiently well-nourished in his home, where he does not undertake much hard work, but that he showed clear signs of deficiency as soon as he accepted employ-ment involving strenuous exertion.[1] Much the same conclusion was reached in a study of human energy in Gambia, where loss of weight in the 'hungry' season and its increase in the harvest season was analysed.[2] The African Labour Efficiency Survey conducted in Nairobi in 1947[3] found that in a great number of cases there were symptoms of malignant malnutrition, and that this constituted the greatest physical handicap to efficiency.

The East Africa Royal Commission 1953–5, while accepting the medical view that the obvious evidences of malnutrition, under-nourishment, and emaciation which occur in certain other countries are absent, nevertheless found that the inadequacy and monotony of the diets impede efficiency.[4] The Commission observed, however, that most Africans in employment appear to work systematically and well, that they can acquire a satisfactory degree of skill, but that while they work well together in a team, their powers of co-operation need to be fortified by continuous supervision. It has been stated that in the kapok industry on the west coast output in-creased sixfold under good management.[5] Other instances where good management has led to increased productivity have been observed in East Africa, and one possible solution of the problem of supervision has been envisaged as the emergence of a class of African foremen.[6]

It is clear, however, that neither the existence of physical disabilities nor the lack of supervision provide the whole explanation of the relative inefficiency of African labour. No study of the question can be complete unless it examines also the incentives which can stimulate the African to increased efficiency. In general terms low wages and inadequate housing are clearly among the many causes of the rapid turnover of labour, and an improvement in these respects would automatically have some effect on an increase of efficiency. But the major problem lies in ascertaining the range of improvement in wages or in living conditions that will provide the African with an incentive sufficient to induce him to raise himself materi-ally in the scale of efficiency or skill. In the Western world there is in most occupations a recognizable ratio between the remuneration of skilled, semi-skilled, and unskilled labour. The picture which will present itself to the African is not likely to be that of a gradation of remuneration, but

[1] *Labour Conditions in West Africa*, Cmd. 6277, 1941, p. 13.
[2] A. L. Banks, ed., *The Development of Tropical and Sub-Tropical Countries*, 1954, p. 100.
[3] C. H. Northcott, *African Labour Efficiency Survey, 1947*, Colonial Research Publications no. 3, 1949, p. 119.
[4] Cmd. 9475, 1955, p. 153.
[5] F. J. Pedler, *West Africa*, 1951, pp. 96–97.
[6] *Report of the Committee on African Wages* (the Carpenter Report), Nairobi, 1954, pp. 111, 115.

of a gulf which he cannot cross—the gulf between the average rate of pay of a European worker and that available to the African.

In the copper-mines of Northern Rhodesia, for instance, there are normally 6,000 Europeans and 35,000 Africans. There are no Europeans classed as unskilled labour. Europeans working underground drew in December 1954 an average of £112 a month; a European surface worker drew £104 a month. To this must be added a bonus which at that date was 66½ per cent. of basic pay. The average yearly pay of a miner in the Northern Rhodesia Copperbelt approached £2,400, with housing and other benefits.[1] The average monthly wage paid to African underground workers was £7. 0s. 8d. and to surface workers £6. 5s. 6d.; in both the latter cases housing and food were also provided without charge to the worker. The disparity is exceptional, and many other occupations could be quoted in which it is much less marked. It will be realized that when copper first came into production in 1931 it was necessary to secure workers from Europe, South Africa, or America; high rates of pay had to be offered, and these set the standard for the local scale of European labour in the mines. The high prices subsequently realized by copper have enabled the White workers to secure, by way of bonus, a substantial increase of this basic range of wage.

In the Copperbelt the African has claimed that members of his community who have acquired the necessary skill should replace an equivalent European worker and receive the rate of pay enjoyed by him. The issue of the movement which has become known as the 'Advancement of the African in the Copper-Mining Industry' turns therefore on the attainment of a relative degree of efficiency, and it is in this form that it has for ten years involved a continuous process of negotiation and has engaged the attention of no less than six Commissions of Inquiry or similar bodies.[2] From the first, the real focus of difference between the African and European workers has centred on the disposal of the limited number of 'marginal' posts which are now held by European workers and which Africans claim to be able to fill.

The European workers formed a Northern Rhodesia European Mine-

---

[1] *Africa Digest*, October 1955, p. 8. *The Times*, 29 October 1955. The bonus is variable, and depends on the difference between the production price and selling price of copper. In October 1955 it was 101 per cent.

[2] *Report of the Commission appointed to inquire into the Disturbances in the Copperbelt, Northern Rhodesia*, Lusaka, 1940. *Report of the Commission appointed to enquire into the Advancement of Africans in Industry*, Lusaka, 1948. *Report of the Commission appointed to review the Salary Structure, Remuneration and Terms of the Civil Service of Northern Rhodesia, 1952* (the Follows Report), Lusaka, 1952. *Report and Award of the Arbitrator, C. W. Guillebaud, nominated under the Industrial Conciliation Ordinance to arbitrate in a Dispute between the Northern Rhodesia Mineworkers' Trade Union and the Copper Mining Companies, 1953*, unpublished. *Award of A. G. Cowling nominated to arbitrate in a Dispute between the Northern Rhodesian African Shop Assistants' Trade Union and the Associated Chambers of Commerce and Industry, 1953*, unpublished. *Report of the Board of Inquiry into the Advancement of Africans in the Copper Mining Industry in Northern Rhodesia*, Lusaka, 1954.

workers' Union in 1936, and the African workers established an African Mineworkers' Union in 1949. An Agreement drawn up at an early stage between the European Mineworkers' Union and the mining companies contained a clause permitting of the dilution of labour. On its renewal after the Second World War, however, the European Mineworkers' Union succeeded in inserting a new clause which in effect imposed a colour bar in respect of the employment of labour. This clause would in practice prevent the advancement of Africans to any class of work which at the date of the Agreement was being performed by Europeans.

In 1948 a Commission (the Dalgleish Commission) appointed to inquire into the advancement of Africans in industry reported that 28 tasks could be performed by Africans immediately, eleven more after a short course of training, and a further 19 after a more intensive course of training.[1] The European Mineworkers' Union, while it now accepted the general principle of the advancement of Africans in industry, stipulated that their employment in posts formerly occupied by Europeans must be subject to the application of the trade union principle of 'equal pay for equal work'. Though this claim was supported by the General Council of the Trades Union Congress, it was strongly criticized in other quarters, since it would in practice deny to the African any chance of entry into the skilled or semi-skilled posts held by Europeans.[2] It now became clear that no progress could be made so long as the clause which introduced the principle of the colour bar remained in the Agreement. Some difference of opinion arose, however, between the two mining groups, the Rhodesian Selection Trust and the Anglo-American Corporation, as regards the measures to be taken for its revision, the former group being opposed to any revision of its terms which would allow the European Mineworkers' Union the right to veto the appointment of an African to any definite task.

It is unnecessary to follow here all the vicissitudes of the subsequent negotiations. In September 1955 an Agreement was signed between the European Mineworkers' Union and the Northern Rhodesia Chamber of Mines to the effect that 24 categories of jobs formerly held by Europeans should be handed over to Africans after certain preliminaries had been completed. The European Mineworkers' Union withdrew their insistence on the clause which would allow them a veto on the transfer of any particular job to an African. The Africans so selected will receive at once a considerable increase in pay, but it seems implicit in the Agreement that when an African employee has reached the point at which he can assume a European task in its entirety he will become entitled to the appropriate European basic pay, with the same bonus and allowances as are enjoyed

[1] *Report of the Commission appointed to enquire into the Advancement of Africans in Industry*, Lusaka, 1948, pp. 37 ff., paras. 271–6.   [2] *The Times*, 27 July 1954.

by the European.[1] The selection of a number of Africans to fill a proportion of the 24 categories to be given up by Europeans was proceeding in November 1955.

The conclusion of an understanding which has in effect eliminated the maintenance of a colour bar is all to the good.[2] But one feature of it may create a precedent that is likely to affect the future development of industry in the territory. The rate of pay of the Africans who are ultimately to be admitted to the skilled or semi-skilled grades is linked up with that of Europeans. But the original basis of pay of Europeans in the copper-mines was determined by the exceptional considerations previously referred to;[3] the extension of this position to the pay of Africans admitted to the skilled or semi-skilled category of workers might create an obstacle to the future advancement of Africans in the industry of the Protectorate.

The Use of Aptitude Tests

Something has been said in a previous chapter regarding the use of tests to determine the standard of intelligence of Africans,[4] but these were in the main intelligence tests, designed to assess the measure of aptitude for education. Tests of the competence of workers in manual or other forms of labour stand in a special category and must be designed to measure physical as well as mental and psychological aptitudes. There are at present few institutions which are engaged in research of this character. In the Union of South Africa the National Institute for Personnel Research, established under the provisions of the Scientific Research Council Act of 1945, has a division which deals with the problems of labour in certain of the industries, particularly gold-mining, but including also a few of the secondary industries. At present, however, such research as it conducts seems to be directed mainly to formulating systems of selection and classification of labour.[5] It has been stated that in one South African factory the use of such selection tests has resulted in an improvement from less than one-third of the European average of efficiency to nearly one-half, and that a growing proportion of the Africans so selected have proved successful in skilled work.

In the Union two Acts have been passed, namely, the Native Building Workers Act no. 27 of 1951 and the Training of Artisans Act of the same year, which have some bearing on this issue. The first provides for the training of Natives to perform skilled work on the construction of buildings

[1] *The Financial Times*, 12 September 1955.

[2] R. W. Williams, 'Trade Unions in Africa', *United Empire*, September–October 1955, p. 189.

[3] *Report of the Board of Inquiry to consider the Proposed 40-Hour Week in the Copper Mining Industry of Northern Rhodesia*, Lusaka, 1950, p. 14.　　　　　　　　　　[4] See above, pp. 46 ff.

[5] S. Biesheuvel, 'Personnel Selection Tests for Africans', *South African Journal of Science*, vol. xlix, no. 1, August 1952.

for use by Natives; it legislates for the issue of certificates to those who have completed the prescribed course of training. It also provides for the proclamation of areas in which Africans may not be employed in the erection and maintenance of buildings for the use of non-Africans. The second Act provides for the passing by Natives of a trade test of a more general character.

In the French territories two decrees of 1952 provided for the establishment of labour research centres and for the setting up of vocational training centres. One such research and training centre was established at Koto in 1951; it gives two years of theoretical instruction and one year of training.[1] In the Portuguese territories an order of 25 June 1952[2] prescribed that persons employing African manual workers must engage one skilled worker (who may be a European or an African) for every group of five Africans in any trade. Industrial employers must engage foremen who can give guidance to workmen.

THE RECRUITMENT OF LABOUR

Earlier Views on Recruitment

There was undoubtedly a stage in African history when the use of official pressure to secure labour for private employers or companies was far-reaching. It possibly had a greater influence on the relations between the European and the African communities than compulsion used for the purpose of securing labour for public purposes, such as the construction of railways or main roads. Save, however, for some rare exceptions that stage is now largely a matter of historical interest.

In the Union of South Africa the practice had its roots in the traditions attaching to the system of slavery. Though the system was finally abolished by the Act of 1833, its influence continued to be felt in the relations of White colonists and Native labour. Under the system of apprenticeship both Hottentot and Kaffir adults and children were secured in large numbers for farm labour, and the early Masters and Servants Acts were largely designed to secure for employers the means of maintaining control over labour of this class.[3] The supply of farm labour was the issue on which the debate regarding the merits of the policy of creating Native Reserves mainly turned: the Native Reserve, as already explained, was viewed primarily as a reservoir of labour for the farming or mining industries.[4] When fresh demands for the supply of labour arose with the discovery of the diamond and gold-fields, pressure was exercised, through the Chiefs in

[1] *Journal de la République française*, 29–30 December 1952.
[2] *Boletim oficial de Angola*, 25 June 1952, quoted in *Industry and Labour*, 15 October 1952.
[3] W. M. Macmillan, *Bantu, Boer, and Briton*, 1929, pp. 193, 206.
[4] See above, p. 759.

Zululand, Bechuanaland, and Basutoland, in order to secure recruits, and it is clear that the levy of the Native poll tax was regarded as an important factor in stimulating recruitment. It is characteristic that in Natal the hut tax was raised in 1857 from 7s. to 11s. a year on such Natives as were not working for Europeans. The endeavour to secure local labour for the diamond and gold-mines became one of the dominant factors in the policy underlying the Glen Grey Act of 1894.[1] Under this Act any Native not in possession of land under the new system of individual tenure was to pay a tax of 10s. a year, unless he could prove that he had been in employment for three months out of twelve beyond the borders of his district. This clause was, however, repealed in 1905, and from that time no official pressure has been used in the Union to secure labour for the mines or other industrial enterprises.

In most of the British Colonial territories there was less disposition to assist employers of labour by the use of official pressure, and the tendency has been to leave the matter to the operation of the normal economic incentives. But at an early stage the poll tax formed a contributing factor in that incentive.[2] When the tax was originally imposed there were in the majority of the Colonies few European interests which sought the recruitment of labour, and in the instances in which such interests existed official opinion has always expressed itself as opposed to utilizing the tax as a direct means of assisting employers to secure a labour force.[3] Where the question of labour supply has become a current issue of politics, debate has not turned so much on the use of the poll tax or other forms of taxation as on the extent to which it was proper for officials to assist the efforts of agencies engaged in the recruitment of labour. On this point there was at one time a considerable diversity of practice observed by different Governments.

In Southern Rhodesia officers were in 1907 instructed to advise Natives to go to work, but a Native Affairs Committee of 1910 was opposed to officials being allowed to show any interest in recruitment, and this view was officially endorsed by the Governor in 1925. In Kenya the question attracted almost continuous attention between the years 1907 and 1928. There is no doubt that in some cases Official Headmen[4] had forced Natives to seek work, and there was considerable variety of practice observed by officials themselves in regard to the assistance given to

[1] L. C. A. and C. M. Knowles, *The Economic Development of the British Overseas Empire*, vol. iii, 1936, p. 321. For the Glen Grey Act, see above, p. 776.

[2] *Report of Nyasaland Committee on Emigrant Labour*, 1935, p. 131. See also I. Schapera, 'Labour Migration from a Bechuanaland Native Reserve', *J.R.A.S.*, vol. xxxii, 1933, pp. 386 ff.; and idem, *Migrant Labour and Tribal Life*, 1947, pp. 7, 123 ff., 141 ff.

[3] *Kenya, Native Labour Commission Report, 1912–13*, p. 329. See similar views expressed by the Government of Tanganyika in *Report by Major St. J. Orde Browne upon Labour in the Tanganyika Territory, 1926*, Col. no. 19, 1926, p. 10.

[4] For the Official Headmen, see above, p. 446.

recruiting agencies. Pressure from settlers led to the issue of the circulars known as the 'Northey Circulars' in 1919, which directed officers to exercise 'every lawful influence' to secure labour for farmers, but the feeling aroused in England by these orders was one of the causes which led to the issue of Lord Milner's dispatch of 1920 already referred to.[1] It will be recalled that it laid down that while encouragement should be given to Chiefs and Headmen to assist in recruitment, no force or compulsion should be exercised. Settlers continued, however, to inveigh against the policy of neutrality which seemed to be indicated by the attitude of the Government, and local officers continued to apply to its instructions that variety of interpretation which their vagueness seemed designed to encourage.

In 1929 the Commission on Closer Union in East and Central Africa[2] expressed the view that the employment of the Native in non-Native enterprises might justifiably be encouraged so long as it was voluntary. Local officials were, it is clear, far from lacking in sympathy with the Natives' reluctance to engage in wage labour, but there were those who were in favour of the use of some form of pressure since they genuinely believed that no advancement was possible unless Africans accustomed themselves to regular work. In Tanganyika the attitude of the Government was at the outset definitely on the side of neutrality, but in 1926 it issued a Circular which indicated the need for encouraging the Native to work on farms or plantations in areas where his own production was insufficient for his subsistence.[3] In the West African territories there was less demand for labour on farms than in East Africa, but at one time political officers in the Northern Territories of the Gold Coast gave some assistance in securing recruits from their area to the West African goldmines. This was, however, definitely forbidden in 1924.[4] There is no evidence that any such pressure was exercised in Nigeria.

In French West Africa the absence of a large colonizing or mining interest made the question of labour supply one of local rather than of general importance. Up to about 1928 the Administration undoubtedly provided labour for some of the trading and agricultural enterprises and for companies operating Forest Concessions on the Ivory Coast.[5] At a later period, however, the Administration definitely refused to exercise pressure in order to secure labour for any form of private enterprise. In French Equatorial Africa the early concessionaire companies interested in securing the collection of rubber or ivory were able to exercise powers which enabled

[1] *Native Labour*, Cmd. 873, 1920.
[2] *Report of the Commission on Closer Union of the Dependencies in Eastern and Central Africa*, Cmd. 3234, 1929, pp. 63–72.
[3] Tanganyika Government Circular, 5 August 1926.
[4] H.C. Deb., 23 June 1924, col. 8.
[5] Lieutenant Governor's Circular no. 259, 18 January 1925.

them to use an extreme form of pressure, but the legislation of 1895, which was designed to bring the concessionaire system to an end, greatly reduced the power of the concessionaires to secure labour for their own purposes.

It is true that at a later date the Government recognized that it had some obligation to assist private employers, as, for instance, in a Circular issued in October 1911, which acknowledged that there were circumstances when employers were not able to secure the whole of their requirements without resorting to some system of recruitment. After the First World War, however, policy in the French Colonies tended to show concern rather for the protection of labour than for the needs of the employer, and instructions which were issued in 1926 laid down that the first call upon African labour must be for the provision of subsistence and marketable crops; military conscription had the second call, and only after these needs had been supplied could other demands be considered.

In the Belgian Congo the régime of the Free State had, like that of French Equatorial Africa, produced conditions in which the encourage-ment for recruitment for private employment hardly arose as an issue, for the concessionaire companies were already in a position to force local Natives to comply with their requirements. The prevention of the abuses which this situation permitted was one of the first matters to engage the attention of the Belgian Government in 1908, and Article 2 of the *Charte Coloniale* laid down in categorical terms that no one could be compelled to work on account of individuals or of companies.[1] When, however, difficulties subsequently arose in regard to the supply of labour for the mineral industry, the terms used in the *Charte Coloniale* were not deemed to be inconsistent with the use of some measure of pressure in aid of the recruiting organizations. So far as local officers were concerned, the fact that the State had so large an interest in most of the industrial enterprises gave to the recruiters something of the status of an official agency. In certain areas the extent of the recruitment was felt to be responsible for injurious consequences on the family and social life of the local peasantry, and the criticism which the metropolitan Government had to face on this account largely influenced the decision to appoint the well-known Labour Commission of 1924, to which reference has already been made in this chapter.

The Commission directed its attention in the first instance to prescribing the maximum of able-bodied male labour which should be taken from any community for work at a distance from its home. It laid down that a maximum of 5 per cent. of such labour could be taken for work at any considerable distance; a further 5 per cent. could be taken for work within a two days' radius, and a further 15 per cent. might be employed in the vicinity of the labourer's home in the production of foodstuffs or in

---

[1] *Codes et Lois du Congo Belge*, 1954, p. 10.

short porterage or similar activities on behalf of the employer. It contemplated, therefore, a maximum take-off of 25 per cent. of the available adult manpower, but certain districts were at the same time completely closed for recruiters for a series of years. It was obvious that this latter provision was the really operative part of the law for, in the absence of the requisite statistical information, it was unpractical to expect that local officers could secure the observance of the exact percentage prescribed for recruitment.

Protests continued to be made in Belgium against the grant of official aid to recruiters, and in 1925 orders required Administrative Officers to abstain from further direct assistance to recruitment. The difficulty encountered in giving effect to the decisions of 1924 led in 1930 to the appointment of a second Labour Commission. This Commission pronounced definitely against official intervention on behalf of recruiters and introduced various modifications in regard to the percentages of employable labour laid down by the previous Commission. The labour situation in the Belgian Congo changed somewhat rapidly from 1930 onwards owing to the economic depression, and between 1931 and 1933 there was a substantial reduction in the demand for labour on the part of employers. It was no doubt this fact that made it easier for the Government to insist that district officers should for the future be prohibited from accompanying recruiters on their tours. A decree of 5 December 1933 laid down that the gifts which had previously been made to Native Chiefs for aid in recruiting should in future be paid into the Native Authority Treasuries.

The Present Practice in Respect of Recruitment

Policy has thus tended everywhere to move away from reliance on pressure, either direct or indirect, and towards dependence on the normal economic stimulus to secure recruits for industrial or agricultural employment. To this movement various external factors have also made some contributions. The Temporary Slavery Commission of the League of Nations of 1925 urged, for instance, that indirect or moral pressure should not be exercised by officials to secure labour for private employment, since it might in effect be tantamount to compulsion. In Africa itself the effect of the normal incentives to wage-earning was continually making itself felt and, as various observers noted, the shopkeeper was beginning to provide a greater incentive than the tax-gatherer or the Native Chiefs.[1] The extent to which the Native Authorities now exercise an influence on behalf of the recruiting agencies forms a useful index to the extent to which the recruitment of labour can be effected without recourse to pressure. The South Africa Native Labour Regulation Act of 1911 provides that no agreement

[1] G. St. J. Orde Browne, *The African Labourer*, 1933, p. 32. I. Schapera, *Western Civilization and the Natives of South Africa*, 1934, p. 200.

by a Chief or Headman for the supply of labour shall be legally binding. In the High Commission Territories the law provides that no contract by which any Chief binds himself or his people to render labour is valid. In Southern and Northern Rhodesia contracts by Native Chiefs to provide labour are also illegal, and in Kenya and Tanganyika the offer of gifts to Native Chiefs or Headmen with a view to securing labour is punishable by a fine.

In the French territories it is now difficult to find any evidence of pressure exerted by Chiefs in the interests of private recruitment. In the Belgian Congo any bonus given for assistance in recruiting is, as already shown, now paid to the Native Treasury and not to the Chief himself. The policy of the Belgian Government seems to have undergone some change as the result of the revival of industry after the depression period, and in 1934 instructions issued by the Colonial Minister appeared to regard it as reasonable that officials should encourage the recruitment of labour where the conditions were suitable. But it does not appear, however, that the Native Authorities now take any definite part in aid to recruiters. In the Portuguese territories the payment to Chiefs for assistance to recruiters, which was authorized by a decree of 29 November 1922, has been withdrawn, and a decree of July 1930 and the Colonial Law of November 1933 formally prohibit official intervention in aid of recruiting. The law on the subject is clear, but, as already indicated, it is by no means evident how far its spirit is in fact observed in the measures taken to comply with the agreement to supply recruits for the Rand mines or to satisfy the demands for labour made by industrial companies (such as the Diamond Company of Angola) or by owners of plantations or farms.

Generally speaking there is now, in the majority of the territories with which this Survey is concerned, a free flow of voluntary labour, influenced by the normal economic incentives. It is suggested in the Report of the East Africa Royal Commission 1953–5 that there is in East Africa no shortage of labour in industry, and that all large enterprises, and indeed many of the smaller concerns, can secure all the labour that they need under a purely voluntary system.[1] Though there is indication of a shortage of labour in parts of Africa other than those which came within the purview of the Royal Commission, it is nevertheless rare to find any evidence of the use of official pressure to secure it for the benefit of the private employer.

Africa has not, however, yet arrived at the stage when employers are able to secure the whole of their requirements without resorting to some system of recruitment. There is now no territory in which recruitment is carried out as a recognized agency of Government, but unofficial agencies are used on a wide scale, particularly in South and Central Africa.

[1] *East Africa Royal Commission 1953–55, Report*, Cmd. 9475, 1955, p. 146.

The value to the employer of such organizations is that he can rely on securing a better-regulated flow of labour, especially in circumstances where the labour is to be found only at a distance from the place of its employment. It is an advantage to him that the recruiting agency is able to reject any recruit who is clearly physically unfit or over age. It is a further advantage that he can secure labour which is bound by a definite form of contract, the breach of which is in most territories liable to certain legal penalties.[1]

But this form of recruitment has definite advantages also from the standpoint of labour It is part of the function of the recruiting agency to organize means of transport for labour and to provide food and other services during the journey. No one who had witnessed in the past the sight of labour on its long and trying journeys through the great wastes of Bechuanaland or the swamp lands of Northern Rhodesia could fail to recognize the advantage of the organizaion by the major recruiting agencies of journeys by rail, road, or air. In certain circumstances also the recruiting organization can provide the labourer with an advance to meet the immediate needs of his family, such advances being given either directly or through credit at local shops. Almost everywhere, it may be added, shopkeepers continue to act as the main agents of the recruiter.[2] It is even more important that the recruiting organization has made possible the use of the systems of Family Remittances and Deferred Payments for the benefit of migrant labour. That the use of recruitment offers some opportunities of abuse is obvious, however carefully the Administrations may watch its operations. On the whole, however, the balance of advantage lies in the continued use of these organizations so long as the people appear willing to avail themselves of their services.

Looking at the history of employment as a whole, it is obvious that in recent years labour has tended to come forward spontaneously in increasing numbers. The determining factor is now largely one of distance. Where the supply of local labour is insufficient the use of a recruiting organization is still needed, but the more efficiently organized industries, which can attract their own labour, utilize its services largely in the form of a forwarding agency, which assists the worker to overcome the difficulties of the journey. Under the more systematic control now carried out by Governments, a great improvement has taken place also in the methods used. In securing African labour today, a good reputation has become an asset of great importance alike for the employer and the recruiting agency.

The Convention on the Recruiting of Indigenous Workers, which was adopted by the International Labour Conference in 1936, has been ratified only by Belgium and the United Kingdom among the European Governments with territorial interests in Africa. This Convention requires

[1] See below, pp. 1433 ff.   [2] W. M. Macmillan, *Africa Emergent*, 1938, p. 239.

the Authorities to take into consideration the possible effects of the withdrawal of adult males on the social life of the populations concerned, and
to take measures to prevent the risk of pressure being brought to bear
on behalf of employers. It forbids the recruiting of non-adult persons
except for employment on light work under special conditions and requires
Authorities to see that recruited workers should be accompanied by
their families wherever possible. Chiefs and Native Authorities must not
act as recruiting agents or receive presents for assistance in recruiting.
Rules are proposed regarding medical examination and transport.

The Union of South Africa

In the Union of South Africa the most important of the recruiting organizations are the Witwatersrand Native Labour Association (W.N.L.A.)
and the Native Recruiting Corporation (N.R.C.), both of which recruit
for the mines in the Transvaal and in the Orange Free State. The Witwatersrand Native Labour Association engages labour in Portuguese
East Africa south of latitude 22° South (the tropic of Capricorn) under the
terms of the Agreements made by the Governments of the Union and
Mozambique, and also in certain areas lying north of that latitude, namely,
Nyasaland, Bechuanaland, and Barotseland. It should be explained that
recruitment north of that latitude was suspended in 1914 on account of
the presumed liability of Africans resident in the tropics to miners' silicosis.[1] More recent experience showed, however, that there was in fact
little variation in the sickness rate of Africans who were living north and
those south of latitude 22° South, and in 1932 recruitment of labour north
of that latitude was resumed. The demand for labour in the mines had
become so acute that on the recommendation of the Low-Grade Ore
Commission of 1931 an experimental recruitment of 2,000 was made from
Bechuanaland and Northern and Southern Rhodesia. In 1935 permission
to recruit a further 3,000 was granted by the Governments concerned, the
area being at the same time extended to include Nyasaland. The importation of tropical labour was legalized under the Immigrants Regulations
Amendment Act of 1937.

The Witwatersrand Native Labour Association does not recruit in the
strict sense of the term; it is an agency which gives its services to Africans
who offer themselves for employment. It organizes transport, and much
of the labour from Nyasaland and Bechuanaland is now carried by air.
It arranges the labour contract, which is now usually for one year, and
also arranges for Family Remittances, Deferred Pay, and for repatriation.
Recruits are re-engaged if they so desire for a period not longer than six
months, when they are under an obligation to return to their homes. In

---

[1] See above, p. 1124.

the year 1952 the Association was recorded as having engaged 111,500 labourers.[1]

The sphere of activity of the Native Recruiting Corporation lies in the Union itself, together with the High Commission Territories south of latitude 22° South. It employs a number of recruiting agents, who are usually shopkeepers or traders, and has two systems of recruitment. Under the first, the period of contract is usually for 270 shifts or roughly one year. Under the second method, which is now known as the Assisted Voluntary System, the recruit undertakes to accept work at one of the mines selected by himself, and the Corporation provides the expenditure for his journey; the initial period of engagement under this scheme is usually about four months. Neither of these forms of contract provide for compulsory repatriation, but there is a voluntary arrangement by which effect is given to the system of Deferred Pay. In 1952 it was recorded that 167,300 Africans had been engaged by the Corporation, of whom about one-half were engaged under the Assisted Voluntary System.

There are in addition a number of smaller agencies licensed to recruit in the Union. Some of these are private profit-making concerns, and the Native Economic Commission of 1934 recommended that an effort should be made to encourage recruitment through larger units on a co-operative rather than a profit-making basis. It pointed out that the individual recruiter was primarily responsible for a number of abuses, such as the luring away of juveniles. The law in the Union requires the deposit of a substantial guarantee by labour agents and brings their operations under the control of the Director of Native Labour. It prohibits resort to Native Headmen for assistance in recruiting.[2] Keen competition for farm labour has, however, led to certain abuses, especially on the part of groups of farmers who were able to employ persons to engage Native labour on their behalf without labour agents' licences.[3] The existing legislation was amended in 1949 so as to bring recruiting by farmers' groups within the scope of the Act and to make their operations subject to control by the Director of Native Labour.

As has been indicated, recruitment from Portuguese territory has been secured by an Agreement between the Government of the Union and that of Mozambique. In return for the supply of labour from Portuguese territory situated south of latitude 22° South, the Union Government has guaranteed that 47½ per cent. of transit traffic destined for the competitive area in the Transvaal (namely, the area served by Union ports competing with Lourenço Marques) shall be handled by the port of Lourenço Marques and by the railways connecting it with Johannesburg. The original Agreement was made in 1909, but this was denounced by the Union

---

[1] *O.Y.S.A.*, *1952–53*, pp. 505, 915.   [2] Act no. 15 of 1911.
[3] See, for example, a report in the *Johannesburg Star*, 12 April 1949.

Government in 1922, and a new Agreement was not concluded until 1928, this again being revised in 1934. This provided for a complement of 80,000 recruits, the number being raised in 1936 by 10,000, subject to annual review; the revision of 1940 contemplated a maximum limit of 100,000.[1]

Recruitment is limited by the Agreement to a period of twelve months, renewable at the option of the labourer up to a maximum of 18 months, and it is provided that after the first nine months' service one-half of the wages earned shall be deferred and paid through a Portuguese official to the African on his return home. The Government of Mozambique receives an annual capitation fee for each Native recruited. The prosperity of the Province of Sul do Save, from which the bulk of immigrant labour is recruited, is said to be largely due to the receipt of the Deferred Pay of workers recruited under the terms of the Agreement.[2] Though the Agreement has been criticized on the ground that it causes social maladjustment,[3] it does not appear that in this respect recruitment in Mozambique has an effect which differs materially from that produced in other areas.

In South-West Africa recruitment is confined to the Native Territories of Ovamboland and Okovango. In these regions recruitment for labour required by enterprises or farms in the Police Zone[4] is carried out by the Northern and Southern Labour Organization. Relevant legislation makes provision for the return of labour to the places from which it was recruited.[5]

The High Commission Territories

In the Bechuanaland Protectorate the law prescribes the provision of individual contracts specifying wages and the compulsory medical examination of recruits. The usual duration of a contract is nine months.[6] In Swaziland the number of licences to recruiters is strictly limited; contracts may not exceed 360 days, but are usually for shorter periods of from three to nine months, and they must be attested before specially appointed officials in order to ensure that they are perfectly understood.[7]

As has been already noted, there is an especially heavy migration from Basutoland for work in the Union of South Africa. As the Basuto have a reputation as competent workers in difficult and consequently more highly paid tasks, a large number proceed to mines of their own choice without recourse to recruiting organizations. The Chamber of Mines at Johannesburg employs as its agent in Basutoland the Native Recruiting

---

[1] *O.Y.S.A., 1952–53*, pp. 505, 915.

[2] C. F. Spence, *The Portuguese Colony of Moçambique*, 1951, p. 85.

[3] E. Mondlane, 'Mozambique', in *Africa in the Modern World*, ed. C. W. Stillman, 1955, p. 243.

[4] See above, p. 435.

[5] Native Labour Regulation Amendment Proclamation, 1931, and the Extra-Territorial and Northern Natives (Control) Proclamation, 1935.

[6] Proclamation no. 56, 1941.

[7] Native Labour Regulation Proclamation no. 19, 1913, and subsequent amendments.

Corporation, and arrangements are made by it for a system of Deferred Pay and Family Remittances. The amount received through this agency is considerable. In 1954 the sum received on account of deferred wages was £221,136; the amount remitted to families for the same year was £226,252, and it is understood that in addition to this a considerable amount, estimated at not less than £100,000, was remitted from the Union through the Post Offices.[1]

The Rhodesias and Nyasaland

Labour for Southern Rhodesia was at one period secured through the Rhodesia Native Labour Bureau which was established in 1906 and was subsequently assisted by a subsidy from the Government. It supplied, however, only about 10 per cent. of the labour coming to the mines, and owing to differences which developed between the mining and farming interests it suspended operations during the period of depression. Although Southern Rhodesia is still largely dependent upon labour from other territories, an increasing supply of indigenous labour is now coming forward. It provides at present some 45 per cent. of the total labour force, Agriculture employing more than twice as much labour as any other group.

Reference has already been made to the Tripartite Agreement for the supply of labour concluded between Southern Rhodesia, Northern Rhodesia, and Nyasaland, which was the sequel to provisional covenants made in 1938 and 1942.[2] The terms of the 1947 Agreement, which became operative in 1949, included provision for the repatriation of workers after an agreed period and for a system of Family Allowances and their Deferred Pay. An important clause required that each Government should ensure that sufficient able-bodied males remained in its territory to meet the needs of its own economy and to maintain the balance of village society.

In Northern Rhodesia labour contracts are regulated by the Employment of Natives Ordinance,[3] which controls the activities of labour recruiters and embodies many of the provisions of the Recruiting of Indigenous Workers Convention of 1936. The only agency allowed to recruit for work outside the territory is the Witwatersrand Native Labour Association, and it has been found necessary to impose a limit to the number it may recruit. The Agricultural Development Society, which acts in the interests of the Northern Rhodesian farmers, has sought to attract labour from more remote areas, such as Barotseland and Kasama, by transporting it by air to Lusaka; air transport is also used for the conveyance of labourers to Southern Rhodesia.

[1] *Colonial Reports, Basutoland, 1954*, p. 23. See also *N.A.*, Part V, p. 16.
[2] International Labour Conference, 37th Session, *Migrant Workers (Underdeveloped Countries)*, Report V (1), Geneva, 1953, p. 8. [3] Chapter 171, revised 1954.

Labour problems have, as already indicated, been for many years a matter of grave concern in Nyasaland. The Witwatersrand Native Labour Association is the only organization permitted to recruit Nyasaland Africans for the Union; permits to recruit are not issued to individual employers. The recruitment quota allotted to the Association, which stood at 10,000 in 1950, was reduced in 1951 to 8,000 and in 1952 to 7,000. At the same time recruitment in the Southern Province of the Protectorate was prohibited, on the ground that labour was insufficient to meet local demands. In 1953 and 1954 the Rand and Orange Free State mines were allowed a quota of 10,000, which did not, however, represent fresh recruits, but indicated the total number of Nyasaland Africans at work in the mines, including persons who had migrated in previous years and had been re-engaged. The actual total at the end of 1954 was 9,844.

Apart from a tobacco company which is permitted each year to recruit small numbers of Nyasalanders for seasonal employment, the Rhodesia Native Labour Supply Commission is the only agency holding a permit to recruit labour for work in Southern Rhodesia. During 1954 the permit held by it was for 8,000 Nyasaland recruits, of whom 6,400 were actually engaged during the year. Special arrangements were made in 1956 for the recruitment of 5,500 labourers for work on the Kariba dam.

The number recruited through authorized agencies for the two Rhodesias, to which the majority of workers migrate, was only 13,500 in 1953 and slightly over 11,000 in the previous year.[1] Even when allowance is made for those at work in other territories, these figures suggest that a number which may exceed 100,000 must have left Nyasaland as 'free labour' without contracting through a recruiting agency. Two unusual clauses are endorsed on recruiting licences: first, recruiting is prohibited in the planting season, and second, the issue of travel permits is withheld unless the recruit can show that he has fulfilled his obligations under Native Authority Orders requiring him to grow food as a precaution against famine.

The East African Dependencies

Labour legislation in Tanganyika follows the Recruitment of Indigenous Workers Convention, 1936, and Contracts of Employment (Indigenous Workers) Conventions, 1939 and 1947. Recruitment of indigenous labour for work within the territory is undertaken both by professional recruiters and by organizations of employers, the chief operating agencies being the Tanganyika Sisal Growers' Association Labour Bureau and the Northern Province Labour Utilization Board. The former draws part of its recruits from the Belgian Congo and Ruanda Urundi. The Authorities in the Belgian Congo take steps to satisfy themselves as to the conditions of

[1] *Colonial Reports, Nyasaland, 1953*, pp. 24–25.

employment in the Tanganyika sisal estates; contracts are signed for three years and stipulate that the worker shall be accompanied by his wife and family. The renewal of the contract on return after repatriation is becoming a common practice, and part of the labour has now become stabilized. Free transport is arranged, remittances are made to the country of origin, and gratuities are paid in the case of injury or death.

A Tanganyika Committee of 1938[1] advised the maintenance of the recruiting system in the interests both of the employers and of Africans, more particularly in order to mitigate the conditions under which the workers formerly travelled long distances on foot. More recently, it has been the policy to discourage professional recruiting, and many large firms now have permits to recruit their own supplies of labour. The Witwatersrand Native Labour Association and the Rhodesia Native Labour Supply Association have no offices within the territory, but recruit Natives who voluntarily emigrate for work; 4,434 recruits were obtained in 1953 by the former and 734 by the latter.[2]

There is no large industry in Kenya, but secondary industries have developed rapidly in recent years. The worker's home is, however, seldom more distant than a day or two's journey from his place of employment. There are Labour Offices, which direct labour to a place of employment, but there is little organized recruitment of labour such as operates in the territories previously referred to. In the Protectorate of Uganda there is, as has been seen, a considerable seasonal influx of labour from Ruanda Urundi and elsewhere, but it quickly becomes absorbed in employment, and Labour Bureaux exist to direct labour where necessary. The West Nile Recruiting Organization provides about 8,500 workers for the Indian-owned sugar estates and for the sisal estate at Masindi. The Masaka Recruiting Agency operates on the immigrant labour route from Ruanda Urundi, and in 1953 obtained over 7,000 workers. The Kigezi Recruiting Agency obtained over 5,000 workers on contract and forwarded another 2,000 'voluntary' workers to centres of employment.[3]

The British West African Territories

Recruitment is less in evidence in British West Africa than in Central or South Africa. Some mines in the Gold Coast, however, recruit their labour through an agency known as Mines Transit Welfare Centre, and there is said to be also a good deal of illicit recruitment under unsatisfactory conditions. It is reported, for example, that labourers from the French territories who have no money for their fare are 'sold' by the lorry

---

[1] Report of the Committee appointed to consider and advise on the Supply and Welfare of Native Labour, 1938, p. 23.
[2] Tanganyika, Annual Report of the Labour Department, 1954.
[3] Background to Uganda, no. 68, August 1954.

drivers to 'labour collectors', who in turn pass them on to employers (such as cocoa farmers) at a considerable profit.[1]

Reference has already been made to the past history of the recruitment of labour for the plantations in the Spanish island of Fernando Po; as has been there stated the principal source of labour for the island is now the Eastern Region of Nigeria. The Nigerian Labour law of 1929 made regulations to protect recruits for the island, but its propinquity to the Nigerian coastline has facilitated evasion. In 1940 an Administrative Officer was posted to Santa Isabel in the dual capacity of Vice-Consul and Labour Officer, and in 1943 an Agreement known locally as the 'Treaty' was concluded in order to regulate recruitment and repatriation. The Spanish Authorities undertook to allow no one to land or remain on the island without satisfactory documents, and this formed an effective check on illicit recruiting. During the Second World War complaints that the Spanish employers were not carrying out their obligations nearly led the Nigerian Government to repudiate the 'Treaty', but it was renewed in 1950 with some revision. The Anglo-Spanish Employment Agency is now permitted to recruit up to 600 labourers a month, and contracts are attested at Calabar by a Labour Officer. Conditions are now so far improved that a majority of labourers sign on for a second and many for a third term of service. The highest number recruited in any year was 5,100 in 1951–2,[2] but it is believed that as many as 25,000 workers who had originally been obtained in other ways are now at work on the island. A small number of labourers are recruited for service in the timber industry in French Equatorial Africa. The Governor of the Gabon has appointed a committee to be responsible for their welfare. There were 976 recruited Nigerians in the Gabon in 1953. In the Cameroons Messrs. Elders and Fyffes in 1953 obtained a permit to recruit 600 workers for their plantations.[3]

The French Territories

In French West Africa there has been no demand for recruiting agencies. A Labour Regulation of 1952 established an office with the object of guiding and directing labour in the territory. The policy in French Equatorial Africa, which in recent years changed from the recognition of recruitment to the principle of voluntary employment, is again undergoing some modification. In 1949 an Agreement between the Governments of Nigeria and French Equatorial Africa authorized the latter to recruit labour for work in Gabon, but by 1953 not more than 1,000 workers

---

[1] *Report of the Committee of Enquiry into the Working and Living Conditions of Workers in the Mining Industry*, Accra, 1953, p. 6.
[2] *Nigeria, Annual Report of the Department of Labour, 1952–53*, p. 20.
[3] Ibid. pp. 21–23.

had been recruited. The Agreement stipulated that recruits should not be employed in mines, and that the contract should extend to only two years, but might be renewable for a further 18 months. After that period the recruit might not re-engage unless he had returned to Nigeria. A Nigerian Consular Agent is now posted to Gabon.

The Belgian Congo

In respect of the Belgian Congo, reference has been made to the effect of the important recommendations made by the National Colonial Congress of 1924 regarding the regulation of the extent of recruitment of labour in the Colony. As already indicated, only 25 per cent. of the able-bodied population might be engaged at the same time, but it proved quite impracticable to enforce such a limitation. It has been reported that in one area as much as 60 per cent. of the male population were employed 'en dehors du milieu coutumier',[1] and in 1950 34 per cent. of the total manpower of the rural areas, in addition to those permanently settled in the towns, were employed in wage labour.[2] Although, however, recruitment of labour is still practised, the mining industry tends to rely more and more upon employment of 'voluntary' labour. Legislation in 1955 prohibited contracts for more than one year in cases where the worker was separated from his wife and family, and, as has been shown, the direct payment of a bonus to Chiefs for aid to recruitment has now been prohibited.

The Portuguese Territories

Much has been said earlier in this chapter of the methods of recruiting labour employed in Portuguese territories. It has been shown that, although the existing law forbids officials to intervene or to supply police to assist recruiters, there are suggestions that Administrative Officers have not ceased to interest themselves in supporting the efforts of recruiting agencies. This is, however, a matter in which it is difficult to obtain reliable information. At the same time, changes continue to be made regarding the poor conditions in which much *contratado* labour is now employed and of the difficulty encountered in securing equitable treatment for employees.[3]

PENAL SANCTIONS

Of the many debatable topics which have arisen in connexion with the employment of African labour one of the most controversial is that which relates to the application of penal sanctions for breaches of labour contracts or for similar offences. The use of penal sanctions was until 50 years ago

[1] *Zaïre*, vol. vii, 1 May 1953, p. 491.
[2] R. Bertiaux, *Aspects de l'industrialisation en Afrique centrale*, 1953, p. 186.
[3] B. Davidson, *The African Awakening*, 1955, pp. 202 ff.

a conspicuous feature of labour legislation in Great Britain, and it still exists as a recognized article of the law in some parts of Europe and of Asia. In India the Act which penalized breaches of contract by workmen was not repealed until 1926. The question of its general abolition has been approached from two opposite points of view. Those who are acquainted with modern usage in Western Europe are inclined to hold that the remedy for breaches of contract must be found in the application of the civil law or in disciplinary action to be taken by the employer, as for example by dismissal from service. Those who are better acquainted with conditions in Asia and in Africa are inclined to question whether the civil law can afford any redress to an employer for a breach of contract by a migrant worker from a distant territory, who even in his home probably owns no property. The prospect of dismissal, they add, conveys no great threat to an employee whose wage-earning may form only a subsidiary means of subsistence, and who can as an unskilled labourer usually find employment without difficulty elsewhere.

The issues involved in the application of penal sanctions were considered by the International Labour Conferences of 1938 and 1939, and a Convention—the Penal Sanctions (Indigenous Workers) Convention—was adopted which came into force in 1948.[1] The Conference decided not to take cognisance of that group of offences which constitute breaches of health and safety regulations and which in modern times are usually considered a proper subject for criminal action. They confined their consideration to breaches of the obligation to perform the service stipulated or implied in the contract of employment, such as the refusal or failure of the worker to commence or perform the service stipulated in it, neglect of duty, absence without permission or reason, or desertion.[2] Of the countries with which this Survey is concerned only Great Britain has so far accepted the terms of the Convention. Penal sanctions for breach of contract now no longer exist in Gambia, the Gold Coast, Togoland, Nigeria, the British Cameroons, Nyasaland, or Uganda; the situation in the remaining British dependencies and elsewhere in Africa is described in the following paragraphs.

The Union of South Africa

In South Africa the law in force in the Cape Province, from which the laws of the other Provinces of the Union did not differ materially, provided penalties in respect of two classes of offences.[3] The first included failure to commence service, absence without leave, intoxication during working

---

[1] International Labour Conference, 37th Session, *Penal Sanction for Breaches of Contract of Employment*, Report VI (1), Geneva, 1953.

[2] Penal Sanctions (Indigenous Workers) Convention no. 65, 1939, Article 1, para. 2.

[3] Masters and Servants Act of Cape Colony, 1873.

hours, the unauthorized use of an employer's property, brawling, and general neglect of duty. The second, for which the penalty was more severe, included the endangering of property by neglect of duty or drunkenness, omission to account for the loss of animals, assault, and desertion. By a provision of the Native Service Contract Act applying in the Transvaal and Natal corporal punishment might be inflicted on male servants under the age of 18 for any contravention of the original Masters and Servants Acts.[1] All these Acts were originally confined to persons in agricultural employment and domestic service, but the Native Labour Regulation Act of 1911 imposed similar penalties on Native labourers in industry and the mines. Certain clauses of the Masters and Servants Acts refer equally to employers and to servants, and the Acts could therefore be invoked by the servant against the employer. It would seem, however, that the occasions on which the law has been invoked against the employer have been relatively few. From the published statistics of crime it would seem that the convictions of Europeans in 1952 numbered only a very small percentage of the total convictions under the Acts; the convictions of Africans numbered 28,000.[2] The legislation in force in the Union has been extended under Proclamation to South-West Africa.

The British Dependencies

The Cape Act of 1873 was extended to the High Commission Territories, subject to some slight variations. Penal sanctions now exist there only for desertion and for failure to enter upon employment or to carry out the terms of the contract. It is also an offence for a Native who has received an advance from a labour agent and has not completed the service stipulated in his contract to accept an advance from another labour agent. Prosecutions under the existing law are, however, very rare.

In Southern Rhodesia legislation has in the main followed the lines of that in the Union of South Africa; it is embodied in a Masters and Servants Act (Cap. 231 of the Laws) and in the Native Labour Regulations Ordinance of 1911. Though the retention of the penal sanctions in the legislation of Southern Rhodesia has been criticized, it would seem to be the present intention to retain these sanctions until labour conditions have been materially improved. In Northern Rhodesia desertion and a refusal to commence service may involve penal sanctions, but neglect of duty does so only when the employer's property is endangered.[3] The African Labour Advisory Board, on which large employers of labour and farmers are represented, recommended in 1948 the repeal of the provision which

---

[1] The Native Service Contract Act no. 24, 1932.

[2] *O.Y.S.A., 1952–53*, p. 445. For the general operation of labour legislation in the Union, see *Handbook on Race Relations in South Africa*, 1949, pp. 144–57.

[3] Ordinance no. 56, 1929, and subsequent legislation in Cap. 171 of the Laws.

gave power to impose a fine in cases of breach of contract, and it also suggested the possibility that the remaining sanctions might be removed within a reasonable period.

In Kenya the administration of the penal clauses of the Masters and Servants Ordinance of 1910 was once a matter which attracted much criticism, and some aspects of its operation were condemned by the Native Punishment Commission which was appointed in 1923.[1] Since that period legislation has materially modified the provisions of the original Act; the breaches of contract as defined by the International Convention no longer incur penal sanctions, with the exception of desertion in cases where the worker has not repaid a recoverable advance made by the employer, or where there is a written contract.[2] The failure of a cattle herdsman to report the death of stock or breaches of duty causing loss or damage to property also constitute offences subject to penal sanctions. In Tanganyika desertion is a penal offence where it can be shown that there is intent not to fulfil a contract, and an enhanced penalty is imposed where desertion occurs under an advance of wages. Zanzibar retains penal sanctions only in cases of failure to commence work or desertion after having received an advance of wages. As has been noted, penal sanctions for breach of labour regulations have now been abolished in the British territories of West Africa.

The French Territories

In the French territories labour legislation now contains no provision for imposing penal sanctions for infringement of contracts in the terms defined by the Convention of 1939. Legislation does, however, make a distinction between 'justified' and 'unjustified' absence; the former may entail loss of wages and the latter may entail the termination of the contract. The French Labour Code as applied to the overseas territories in 1952 contains no penal provisions, but it has been suggested that the punishment of *vagabondage* has in practice the same effect as a penal sanction for a breach of contract. Indirect sanctions are also implicit in the penalties which can be imposed on workers who neither execute their contract nor repay advances. Since all persons within the overseas territories now have the status of French citizens,[3] there can be no discriminatory legislation, and the law applicable to the African is equally operative in regard to the Frenchman.

The Belgian Territories

In the Belgian Congo a decree of 16 March 1922 provided for penal sanctions for acts considered contrary to the public interest, such as fraudulently obtaining an advance or grave or repeated infringements of

---

[1] R. L. Buell, *The Native Problem in Africa*, vol. i, 1928, p. 358.
[2] Ordinance no. 56, 1948.
[3] See above, p. 338.

labour rules.[1] Under an amendment of 30 July 1945, penalties are also provided for cases where the worker fails to return to his normal place of abode on termination of the contract, unless he secures other work within one month.

The law regulating *les sanctions répressives* applies to employers as well as employees. Critics have, however, suggested that employers are able to rely on the drastic use of the penal sanctions in order to control their labour force which, it is pointed out, still receives a relatively low rate of wage. The point requires further clarification: that a free use is made of the regulation seems clear from the fact that in 1954 there were as many as 32,896 convictions for infringement of the law.[2] The question of the retention of penal sanctions has recently been discussed both in the Council of Government and in some of the Provincial Councils. The discussions have so far resulted in general agreement that it would at present be premature to abolish them. Their impact is, however, lessened to some small extent in so far that the Governor-General is empowered to apply to *évolués* the legal procedure relating to contracts in non-African cases. This does not contain penal provisions.

The Portuguese Territories

The Portuguese Overseas Provinces stand out as giving the most consistent support to the maintenance of penal sanctions for breaches of labour regulations. In Angola and Mozambique imprisonment with hard labour for a period not exceeding one year may be imposed for breach of contract and for disciplinary offences.[3] A person who has entered on a contract but fails to start work must either refund the cost of recruitment, together with any advance received, or become liable to imprisonment for a period up to 180 days. Imprisonment for a period up to twelve months is the penalty for damage done to the employer's property. In addition to the penal sanctions employers are entitled to claim compensation for any expenditure involved, and within certain limitations can recover it by deduction from wages. The law imposing these sanctions applies only to 'uncivilized' Native labour; the category of *assimilados*[4] is exempt from penal sanctions.

Proposals for abolishing Penal Sanctions

The International Labour Organization, in reviewing the results of the adoption of the Convention of 1939, claimed that there had been few

---

[1] *Codes et Lois du Congo Belge*, 1954, p. 936.

[2] *Rapport sur l'administration de la colonie du Congo Belge, 1954*, p. 17. See also V. Devaux, 'Introduction à un échange de vues sur la suppression des sanctions pénales en matière de contrat de travail au Congo', extract from *Bull. I.R.C.B.*, vol. xxiii, no. 2, 1952, pp. 305–47.

[3] International Labour Conference, 37th Session, *Penal Sanctions for Breaches of Contract of Employment*, Report VI (1), Geneva, 1953, p. 10.   [4] See above, p. 231.

serious repercussions in those countries which had abolished penal sanctions. It recommended accordingly that all such sanctions should be
abolished by the end of 1955.[1] It will, however, be noted that, as regards
the British African dependencies at all events, those which have abolished
the use of penal sanctions are for the most part territories in which industrial development has contributed least to the national economy. It may
well be argued that there is a case for abating some of the rigours of the
Masters and Servants Acts of South Africa, where many observers have
claimed that the use of penal sanctions has helped to maintain farm labourers
in circumstances approaching those of serfdom.[2] Moreover, the Native
Service Contract Act no. 24 of 1932 contains an unusual provision in so
far that the contract entered into by a Native is binding also on his children
up to the age of 18 years, so that the penal sanction becomes applicable
to practically all male members of the family. But with every desire to
reduce the possibility of abuse of legislation of this character, whether in
the Union of South Africa or elsewhere, there is clearly need for some
caution in removing from the scope of the penal law such misdemeanours
as the abuse of the system under which advances are now taken by labour;
nor is it reasonable to remove from the régime of penal sanctions the class
of offences which may involve injury to stock. The necessity for the
maintenance of some form of penal sanction in these or similar cases should,
however, be automatically diminished with the development of a stabilized
labour force.

REGULATIONS CONCERNING PASS LAWS

It will be convenient to give here some account of the regulations
generally described under the title of Pass Laws, though they actually
serve a wider range of purpose than control over labour. Thus in the
Union of South Africa, where they are most conspicuous, they were
originally in the nature of police regulations. They were subsequently
utilized to assist in maintaining a supply of labour; but in their final stage,
while still used to safeguard the conditions of labour, they have become
part of the machinery of the policy of segregation, in so far that they are
used to restrict the influx of Natives into urban areas.

Pass Laws in the Union

In point of history, the South African Pass Laws may be said to date from
a Proclamation of 1809, which was designed to give a fixed domicile to
the nomadic Hottentots; persons who had no pass were treated as vagrants,

---

[1] International Labour Conference, 37th Session, *Penal Sanctions for Breaches of Contract of
Employment*, Report VI (1), Geneva, 1953, pp. 3 ff.
[2] *Report of the Native Economic Commission, 1930–1932*, U.G. no. 22, 1932, p. 216.

liable to be contracted out to anyone who needed their services. The regulation thus bore some resemblance to the early English Vagrancy Acts, or to the Statute of Labourers of 1351, which applied a similar system to control the movement of peasants emancipated from *villeinage* or those who sought in other parishes the higher scale of wages which resulted from the scarcity of labour caused by the Black Death. In South Africa a further use was found for the pass in preventing the influx of the Xhosa into the border districts or to confine tribal movement to the Transkeian territories or British Bechuanaland. The control of the movements of Natives living within the Cape Province itself was effected through the operation of the Vagrancy Acts and, as a result, the use of the law relating to the carrying of passes came to be less in evidence in the Cape than elsewhere and to be applied mainly to 'foreign' Natives.

The early use of the system in the Transvaal and Orange Free State had a wider scope; it was directed not only to the control of the vagrant (*land-looper*), but to the stabilization of farm labour. A Native could not travel unless he was in employment or had been authorized to look for fresh work, and in the Transvaal the law added the penalty of flogging to that of imprisonment. The operation of these restrictions became more severe as Natives tended to migrate to the diamond-fields, and the development of the gold-fields saw in turn a new use for the pass regulation. While the diamond-mine protected itself against desertion or theft by the use of the 'closed' compound, the frequent desertions by contract labour on the gold-fields were met by regulations creating 'labour districts' within which any Native found without a pass was liable to arrest.

The Natives (Urban Areas) Act no. 21 of 1923 opened a new chapter in the history of the pass system, in so far that it made use of it in order to control the entry of Natives into the towns. At the same time, legislation subsidiary to that Act (such as the 'curfew' regulations or the provisions made under the Native Taxation and Development Act no. 41 of 1925) helped to control their movements within the urban area. The system was further developed by the Native Laws Amendment Act of 1937, which permitted the removal from urban areas of such labour as was held to be in excess of the requirements of employers. The use of pass regulations in the Union has therefore presented a complicated picture, and it may be convenient to describe the position obtaining in the different Provinces prior to the passing of the Natives (Abolition of Passes and Co-ordination of Documents) Act of 1952.

In the Cape Province passes were, under Act no. 22 of 1867, required by 'foreign' Natives on entering the Colony. In effect, this meant that passes were required by Natives moving into the Cape from South-West Africa or the High Commission Territories, or in and out of British Bechuanaland and in and out of the Transkeian Territories. No pass was required to travel from one part to another within the Transkei.[1] Elsewhere in the Cape no pass was required, but the provision of the Vagrancy Act no. 23 of 1879, as amended in 1881, remained available to check what was technically known as 'vagabondage'. At a later date, however, the system of passes was widely extended for other purposes, such as the pass required for entry into proclaimed areas;[2] the pass for a male permitting him to look for work; a certificate of approval for a Native woman issued by the Urban Local Authority or by the Magistrate or Native Commissioner of the district from which she came; the night pass; and a variety of permits issued under Local Authority regulations, such as lodgers' and visitors' permits in the Locations. In the Cape, however, there was a considerable class of Natives entitled to exemption, such as Chiefs and Headmen, members of various Native administrative and advisory bodies, Ministers of religion, public employees, and persons with an 'exemption certificate'. Coloured persons were also exempt.

In the Transvaal and Orange Free State the use of the pass system proper was more extensive and more rigid. A Native was required to take out a pass to enter or travel anywhere within the two Provinces, except in Native areas scheduled under the Native Lands Act of 1913. The system was to some extent mitigated by the issue of travelling passes by officials and owners of farms, and by the grant of general and special exemptions. Another law[3] utilizing the pass system applied in the mining areas; under this law a Native employed in a 'proclaimed labour district' was required to obtain a permit from his employer if he wished temporarily to absent himself from the property on which he was employed.

The Native Service Contract Act[4] applied to the Transvaal, Natal, and within certain limits also to the Orange Free State, but not to the Cape Province. This Act required a Native resident on a private farm (that is, in effect, all labour tenants) to obtain a document of identification before proceeding to any place other than his home. It prohibited anyone from employing a Native unless his document of identification bore an endorsement authorizing him to seek fresh employment. Further, the Natives Taxation and Development Act provided that any European member of the police, or any Chief or Headman, might demand production of a tax receipt; in default of producing such receipt a Native became liable to arrest.[5]

In Natal the Pass Law[6] provided for only inward and outward passes which thus had the nature of passports; Natives resident within the

---

[1] Proclamation no. 2, 1885 (British Bechuanaland); no. 110, 1879 (Transkei); no. 112, 1879 (Griqualand East); no. 140, 1885 (Tembuland); no. 340, 1894, and no. 497, 1895 (Pondoland); no. 109, 1894 (Transkeian Territories).

[2] Natives (Urban Areas) Consolidation Act no. 25, 1945.

[3] Native Labour Regulation Act no. 15, 1911.

[4] No. 24, 1932.

[5] Act no. 41, 1925.

[6] Act no. 48, 1884.

Province might travel without passes. Urban areas were, however, controlled by the same Acts[1] as applied to the Cape Province and by the enforcement of curfew regulations.[2]

A new feature in the pass system of the Union was introduced in 1952,[3] whereby the Native is required to carry a 'reference book' incorporating an identity card and making provision for noting tax payments and for the receipt of permits from urban Local Authorities or Labour Bureau Officers. The Act also makes it compulsory for all employers to report the engagement or discharge of a Native, and establishes a Native Affairs Central Reference Bureau at which are kept central records, including fingerprints, of those to whom reference books are issued. These reference books relieve the holder from carrying other documents and are issued to all pass-carrying Natives throughout the Union. At the same time the Act repealed many provisions of earlier Pass Laws; in particular, restrictions were removed on the movement of Natives out of Natal and the Transkei, or from one area to another in the Transvaal and the Orange Free State, or movement into an urban area on visits of not more than three days. Restrictions continued, however, to be imposed on Natives entering towns to look for work. Non-indigenous Natives still require permission to move from one district to another, and the control maintained by an urban Local Authority over Natives entering its area remains in force. The curfew regulations in urban areas also remain in force.

Viewed as regulations for the control of industrial labour, the Pass Laws have been in fullest operation in the Transvaal and the Orange Free State. As measures for control of farm labour they have been most fully used in the Transvaal, the Orange Free State, and Natal. As restrictions on the movement to urban areas they have been fully used in all four Provinces. The oppressive nature of some of these regulations, and their liability to misuse, led to the appointment of a Committee of Inquiry in 1914 and again in 1919.[4] It hardly required the evidence which these investigations elicited to demonstrate that the powers conferred by the regulations were liable to wide abuse, or that the ease with which they were evaded by criminals made them ineffectual for some of the police purposes for which they were designed. There was, on the other hand, agreement that some system of identification was required, not merely for occupational but for police purposes. In the words used by Lord Milner in 1902: 'Alike for the protection of the Natives and for the protection of the Whites, it is absolutely essential to have some reasonable arrangement by which the incoming Native can be identified and his movements traced.'[5]

[1] Natives (Urban Areas) Consolidation Act no. 25, 1945.
[2] Act no. 25, 1930.
[3] Natives (Abolition of Passes and Co-ordination of Documents) Act, 1952.
[4] *Report of the Inter-departmental Committee on Native Pass Laws*, U.G. no. 41, 1922.
[5] Ibid. p. 3.

The Native Economic Commission of 1930–2 pointed out that the pass regulations, apart from their generally oppressive nature, had the effect of creating a large volume of technically criminal offences which carried no moral opprobrium.[1] It was significant that, out of 42,000 convictions for offences against the Pass Laws in 1930, no fewer than 39,000 were from the Transvaal alone. In the three years 1939, 1940, and 1941, a total of 273,790 Natives were convicted for pass offences in the Transvaal. In 1942 there was some relaxation in the enforcement of the Pass Laws in certain areas, but in the same year an Inter-departmental Committee on the Conditions of Urban Natives reported that the system gave rise to 'a burning sense of grievance and injustice'. It is too early to discern the practical effect of the legislation of 1952 above referred to which provides for the use of the 'reference books', or how far it will remedy the disadvantages of the pass system. In so far as the new law puts an end to what has been one of the most vexatious features of the previous system—the multiplicity of documents an individual was required to carry and produce on demand—it would appear to be a step forward, even though it may mean that numbers of Africans who did not have to carry passes under the previous system will now have to carry the new 'reference books'.[2]

The Federation of Rhodesia and Nyasaland

The pass system is also in use in the Rhodesias, though in many respects in a less rigid form. In Southern Rhodesia every male African over 16 must obtain a registration certificate, which is both a document of identity and a record of contracts of service. Within towns proclaimed under the Native Registration Act and under the Natives (Urban Areas) Accommodation and Registration Act, every unemployed African male and every unemployed African female and child not accompanied by a husband or parent must carry a pass authorizing him or her to seek employment or to visit the town; those residing in towns must possess a certificate that they are earning their living by employment within the town area. Non-indigenous Africans on first entering the territory must obtain a registration certificate and pass. In certain proclaimed towns every African in employment must possess a certificate of service (town pass) renewable every six months. It is a special feature of the Southern Rhodesian system that the registration certificate shows the rate of wages paid to the African by his employer, and that a medical examination is required before an African enters into a contract of service in a proclaimed municipality or town. Though the pass system in Southern Rhodesia appears complicated, its practical operation is mainly confined to the larger towns and the system is not in fact greatly in evidence in the smaller towns and rural areas.

[1] *Report of the Native Economic Commission, 1930–1932*, U.G. no. 22, 1932, paras. 720–47.
[2] *Round Table*, September 1954, p. 420.

The pass system is less widely applied in Northern Rhodesia. Every male African of taxable age must register, and, if he resides in or visits certain proclaimed districts, must possess a registration certificate. Otherwise his movements are free, but under municipal and township regulations Natives must carry a pass if they are outside their compounds between 10 p.m. and 5 a.m. In the townships Africans not in employment must carry both a registration certificate and a visitor's or resident's permit.

The system has an even narrower range in Nyasaland. Registration is required for taxation purposes, but a registration certificate need not be carried within the territory. In the small township areas a night pass signed by the employer must be carried. Under the Migrant Labour Agreement between the three Central Africa territories made in 1938, an African proceeding from one territory to another in search of work must take with him an identity certificate and work book, but this requirement is waived in respect of Southern Rhodesians proceeding north.

The East African Dependencies

In Kenya the Registration Ordinance of 1915 introduced a procedure under which all Natives were registered and had to carry a certificate of registration (*kipande*). This was subsequently brought into use as a record of employment and discharge.[1] A Native was not called upon to carry his *kipande* in his Reserve, but it came to be treated as a pass when he left it, and more particularly when he visited an urban area. As has been shown in a previous chapter,[2] the necessity for carrying the *kipande* has of late years become a political issue, and recent legislation[3] has extended registration to all communities in the territory, but the certificate of registration now records identity only, not the terms of employment. By-laws in certain municipalities prohibit Africans from remaining more than 36 hours without a permit, but these regulations are difficult to enforce and are admitted to be ineffective.[4]

The Pass System in Other Areas

Elsewhere in the British dependencies the pass system has not been applied. It is not in force in the French dependencies.

In the Belgian Congo there is no general system of passes, but in certain circumstances a Native needs to be furnished with a *permis de circulation*, as for example when carrying on business as an itinerant trader or when visiting the European quarters of a town after nightfall. In certain mining areas, namely those where precious metals are mined, Natives have to obtain a *permis de séjour*; but this requirement does not apply to labourers

[1] R. L. Buell, *The Native Problem in Africa*, vol. i, 1928, p. 357.
[2] See above, p. 445.
[3] Ordinance no. 23, 1947.
[4] *N.A.*, Part III, p. 180.

actually working in the mines.[1] Though the pass system is thus limited in extent the restrictions which it imposes are regularly observed in practice. Certain classes of Africans, however, and in particular those who enjoy the benefit of the *Carte du mérite civique* are excused from the application of the pass system.[2]

In the Portuguese territories the booklet which is issued to Native taxpayers serves also the purpose of a passport to migrant Africans in search of work.[3]

THE ORGANIZATION OF WELFARE

All the territories under review have made provision in greater or lesser measure for safeguarding the welfare of labour and for regulating its working conditions. The legislation varies greatly in character, and it is possible to discuss here only the more important provisions, and in particular those relating to the regulation of working hours or the provision of compensation for accident or disease due to employment. The provision made for housing has been discussed in a previous chapter,[4] and the machinery for the determination of wages will be described in succeeding sections of the present chapter.

The Union of South Africa

In the Union of South Africa the employment of a large number of Europeans and the growing expansion of industrial activity have presented many problems of a type familiar in older countries, though new in the environment of Africa. A Department of Labour and Social Welfare was established in 1924, following the creation of a Ministry of Labour, and this was divided in 1947 into separate Departments of Labour and Social Welfare; the former administers Employment Exchanges for Europeans at the chief urban centres and for Coloured persons at Cape Town and Kimberley, while there are subsidiary Labour Exchanges for Europeans at a number of other centres. The other functions of the two Departments include the training of indigent Europeans for employment, the initiation of schemes for the relief of European and Coloured unemployment, and the development of social work amongst Europeans, for which purpose a Commissioner of Social Welfare and a number of Rural Welfare Officers were appointed in 1935. An Inspection staff supervises the conditions of factory labour, which are regulated by rules under the Factories Act of 1918, as amended in 1931. A 48-hour week is prescribed in mines and factories.[5]

---

[1] *Codes et Lois du Congo Belge*, 1954, pp. 874, 1208, 1455.
[2] See above, p. 225.   [3] See above, p. 675.   [4] See above, pp. 566 ff.
[5] Mines and Works Act no. 12, 1911. Factories (Amendment) Act, 1931.

The regulation of conditions regarding Native labour is largely the responsibility of the Department of Native Affairs. Native Labour Bureaux began to be established in 1952, and had been opened in 30 towns of the Union by the following year. A Central Bureau co-ordinates the activities of the Regional, District, and local Bureaux. Employers must register vacancies and may not employ a Native in an urban area except through a Labour Bureau; Natives seeking work must register, and in principle are not allowed to move from one place to another where employment is not available. The measure is thus designed to operate as part of the control over the influx of Natives into the towns. In 1954 regulations were introduced to control also the 'rural vagrant labour' or 'squatters'. The conditions of health, housing, and diet for Natives employed on mines and works in proclaimed Labour Districts are governed by the Native Labour Regulations Act of 1911, which leaves a wide discretion to the executive in making rules for the purpose; the operation of the Act is now supervised by a Director of Native Labour.

The labour compounds of the Rand mines are open to the objections inherent in a system which brings together a large number of male workers, removed for periods that may last from twelve to 18 months from any contact with domestic life. So far, however, as the arrangements of housing, diet, and other services are concerned, the more important mines have admittedly set a high standard. The Witwatersrand Mines Natives' Wages Commission found in 1944 that the minimum diet laid down by law was usually exceeded.[1] The conditions of farm labour are not, on the other hand, subject to inspection, nor are minimum standards of diet or housing prescribed in farming areas. The grazing and arable rights granted in many cases to farm workers and the fact that the worker leads his own domestic life give some attraction to agricultural employment, though some of the conditions, as for example those relating to housing or rations, compare very unfavourably with conditions in the mining industry.[2]

There has been a number of legislative measures dealing with compensation for injury. The first law to place on a statutory basis the provision of compensation to Native workmen was passed in 1911, but it was limited in its scope. In 1934 employers were required to insure against their liabilities, but in 1941 private insurance was replaced by a mutual insurance fund, which was to be administered under the control of a Workmen's Compensation Officer.[3] An Act of 1951 from which, however, domestic servants and farm workers not engaged in mechanical work are exempt, revised the scale on which benefits are calculated, raising the minimum payment for total disablement to a scale varying from £180 to

---

[1] *Report of the Witwatersrand Mines Natives' Wages Commission*, U.G. no. 21, 1944.
[2] *The Times*, 23 December 1954.
[3] Workmen's Compensation Act no. 30, 1941.

£800, but did not alter the unsatisfactory feature of the previous Acts by which non-Europeans are entitled only to a lump-sum payment.

The special hazards of mining are recognized in the laws concerning compensation for miners' phthisis (silicosis) and tuberculosis. These were consolidated in 1946 in an Act applying to both Europeans and Natives.[1] In this case also a pension is payable to the former, but only a lump sum is payable to the latter. The scale of the provision made for the treatment of sufferers from miners' diseases is impressive. Since the inception of legislation in 1911 up to the year 1952, the expenditure incurred on direct benefits and other forms of assistance amounted to £33½ million, of which £1½ million was expended on non-Europeans and their dependants. In 1952 the investments of accumulated funds for these purposes were valued at over £18¼ million.[2] It is generally held that non-Europeans are less liable than Europeans to suffer from silicosis and similar diseases owing to the fact that a large proportion return home after completion of the term of their contract. There seems, however, reason to doubt the correctness of this assumption.

The Federation of Rhodesia and Nyasaland

In Southern Rhodesia a separate Department of Labour was created from the beginning of 1955. Up to that time labour questions had been dealt with partly in the Division of Internal Affairs, which had been responsible for issues arising under the Industrial Conciliation, Factory, and Workmen's Compensation Acts; but some questions of importance to labour had also been dealt with in the Divisions of Mines and Transport and others in the Division of Trade and Industrial Development. There was at the same time a Department of Native Labour within the Division of Native Affairs; this was created in April 1946 as a result of the recommendations made by the African Railway Strike Commission during the preceding year. The executive head of the Department is the Commissioner of Native Labour; it has a trained staff of Labour Officers operating from the more important centres of the Colony.[3]

There has been of recent years a considerable increase in labour legislation. The Workmen's Compensation Act of 1941 followed closely the legislation in the Union of South Africa. It required employers to cover their liabilities by insurance with an accredited insurance company, but in 1949 an amending Act granted enhanced benefits and, while premiums were as hitherto paid to insurance companies, the Government now assumed the liability for payment of compensation.[4] The growth of secondary industries rendered necessary the passing of the Factories and Works Act which came into force in 1951. Reference has already been

---

[1] Silicosis (Miners' Phthisis) Act no. 47, 1946.　　[2] O.Y.S.A., 1952–53, p. 322.
[3] O.Y.S.R., 1952, p. 215.　　[4] Ibid. p. 211.

made to the special legislation dealing with the accommodation to be provided for Africans in urban centres.[1] An Act of 1951 required the registration of labour contracts in those towns to which it applies; it lays down the standard of accommodation to be provided and the rates payable to Local Authorities. It also provides for compulsory medical examination of the occupants.

Other British Dependencies

In other British territories there has of recent years been much activity in the creation of machinery for the supervision of the conditions under which labour is employed. A Labour Department, the first of its kind in the British dependencies, was established in Tanganyika in 1926, but it was retrenched in 1930 as a result of the economic depression. Since that date Labour Departments have been created in all the British African dependencies except Zanzibar.[2] In nine of these countries officials from the trade-union organization in the United Kingdom have been included in the cadre of Labour Officers. Labour Exchanges have been established in most of the territories either by legislation, as in Nigeria and Sierra Leone,[3] or by administrative action, as in other dependencies. The principle of Workmen's Compensation was introduced by legislation in East Africa in 1934, and factory legislation has been passed both in Kenya and Uganda, though there has been difficulty in putting it into operation owing to a shortage in the Inspectorate staff. In Uganda farther advance in this direction would seem to be a matter of urgency, as there are clearly very low standards of management in the ginning factories, and insufficient attention has been paid to the provision of guards for machinery.[4]

Labour Departments have been operating somewhat longer in West than in East Africa, and in Nigeria and the Gold Coast they have now become part of the establishments controlled by the new Ministries. A considerable body of labour legislation has been enacted, based for the most part on that in force in the United Kingdom; it is designed to regulate contracts, recruitment, the employment of women, and the prohibition of child labour. Factory inspection is carried out in all territories, but there is a marked diversity in the extent to which the Inspectorate has been able to effect improvement in such matters as safety precautions and the like. Perhaps the most striking feature of the labour situation in West Africa is the increase in the rates of pay of unskilled labour during the last

[1] See above, pp. 572 ff.

[2] *Labour Supervision in the Colonial Empire, 1937–43*, Col. no. 185, 1943, p. 1. L. P. Mair, *Welfare in the British Colonies*, 1944, pp. 50–52.

[3] Nigeria, Labour Code Ordinance no. 54, 1945. Sierra Leone, Registration of Employees Ordinance no. 8, 1947.

[4] *Uganda, Annual Report of the Labour Department, 1954*, pp. 41–44.

few years, to which reference will be made in a subsequent section of this chapter.[1]

The French Territories

Legislation in labour matters dates back to the decrees of 1923 in French Equatorial Africa and 1926 in French West Africa. These prescribed a maximum of ten hours' labour both for industrial and farm workers, with an unusual provision in the former case that the hours must not exceed six hours per day in the first and eight in the second month of employment.

Compensation for industrial disablement was provided by a decree of April 1932, which was applied to French West Africa in July 1936.

A comprehensive Labour Code for all overseas territories, consolidating and adding to previous measures, was introduced in 1952.[2] A somewhat elaborate organization is provided to secure the welfare of labour. Advisory committees, including representatives of employers' and workers' associations, are to be attached to the Overseas Ministry and the offices of Governors-General. These committees are to study labour conditions, must be consulted on proposed legislation, and may be asked to advise on any other labour matter. The local committees are expressly charged to obtain the necessary data for fixing minimum wages. There is an *inspection générale* of labour and social laws in the Ministry, and local inspectorates for territories and groups of territories. These Departments are responsible, *inter alia*, for the organization of Employment Exchanges. An unusual Exchange has been established in Paris for persons wishing to go overseas. It is responsible for any special training that may be required.

The Code is based on the principle of the equality of all French citizens, at home or overseas, and it imposes the same standards as in France, with some exceptions to meet local circumstances. Working hours are fixed at 40 per week, but in agriculture the maximum is 2,400 hours in the year, the distribution to be determined by local regulations. Overtime rates are to be paid for all additional work. For work in which the qualifications, conditions, and productivity are equal, payment is to be equal regardless of age, sex, origin, or status, but a special supplement may be paid to persons working far from home or in climatic conditions different from those of their home. Workers have the right to paid holidays with free transport to their homes, and women to maternity benefit in the form of 14 weeks' leave on half pay and free medical treatment. Local regulations may provide for the payment of family allowances. Every enterprise must provide a fixed standard of medical or health services. Each Labour Inspectorate is to be advised by a technical committee on safety and hygiene.

---

[1] See below, pp. 1430 ff.   [2] Law no. 52–1322, 15 December 1952.

The Belgian Congo

Attention has been drawn in previous pages to the close consideration given in the Belgian Congo to the regulation of labour conditions. There is now a very large body of legislation and regulation on the subject.[1] The basic law on labour conditions was that of 16 March 1922, which, among other matters, gave power to the Local Administration to prescribe a statutory scale of diet for workers. Local regulations now lay down balanced scales of diet and require employers to supply all manual workers and also their dependants with an authorized scale of rations in addition to the cash wage. The dietary of labour has received in the Belgian Congo a systematic study to which the nearest African parallel is that made by the Health Organization of the Rand mines of South Africa. The scale embodies a full ration for the male employee, a half ration for his wife, and a quarter ration for each child. Some details have been given in a previous chapter of the provision made for the housing of labour, both in the mining area and in the urban townships occupied by Africans.

Another characteristic feature of the Belgian Congo is the establishment in each Province of an Advisory Council for labour questions; it normally consists of five officials and five unofficials.[2] The supervision of labour conditions is carried out by a special organization, centred in the Labour Office at Leopoldville, which is composed of a Technical Inspectorate staffed by engineers whose function is to organize precautions against industrial accidents, and a Labour Inspectorate which carries out all other non-specialized tasks. There was at the end of 1953 a total number of 16 Labour Inspectors and four Engineer Inspectors (*inspecteurs de la sécurité*). The latest labour regulations restrict the employment of children under 16 years of age to light work and prohibit altogether the employment of children under twelve; they also provide for one week's holiday on full pay to all workers who have completed twelve months' uninterrupted work. A system of Workmen's Compensation was introduced in 1949, and extends to sickness as well as to injury.[3]

The Portuguese Territories

From what has been said earlier regarding the general conditions in Portuguese territories, it will be gathered that while a body of legislation has been enacted to regulate the welfare of workers it is less systematically enforced than in many other territories. There has, for instance, been little attempt to introduce a type of housing accommodation more recent than the barrack dormitory, which is fast becoming obsolete elsewhere. Although employers are required by law to issue a sufficient ration, it has

---

[1] See *Codes et Lois du Congo Belge,* 1954, pp. 928–62.
[2] *Ordonnance Loi,* 11 March 1953.
[3] *Codes et Lois du Congo Belge,* 1954, pp. 918–19.

been stated that the monthly wage has to be largely expended by the worker on the purchase of necessary food. In Mozambique the conditions of labour are regulated by a Code first enacted in 1928; the normal number of hours of work are nine in agriculture and eight in industry. The employer is obliged to provide two meals a day and a third if overtime is worked; overtime may in no case exceed twelve hours a week. A system of Workmen's Compensation has lately been introduced, and was extended to the islands of Sao Tomé and Principe in 1946.

In this field, however, the mere enactment of legislation is not enough. In the history of British labour legislation the most decisive instrument was not the series of Acts passed between 1802 and 1825, which restricted the hours of employment of women and children, but the Act of 1833 which resulted in the appointment of an independent Inspectorate, experienced in its work and interested in the enforcement of the regulations made under the law. It is this essential requirement which still needs to be adequately implemented in the Portuguese territories.

THE SCALE OF WAGES

There is so great a diversity in the conditions of labour in the various territories that it will not be possible to discuss in detail the scale of wages actually paid. It is, however, necessary to refer to certain general factors which have during recent years influenced the changes that have occurred in the scale of wages paid and in the policy followed by different Governments in providing machinery for settling industrial disputes.

Consideration cannot in this connexion be confined to non-European labour, since account has also to be taken of the procedure adopted for the determination of the wages of Europeans. This aspect of the question is at present of importance chiefly in such countries as South Africa and Northern Rhodesia. Though there is a considerable body of European labour in the Belgian Congo, there have been fewer signs of concerted movement on its part to secure changes in the rate of pay or in the conditions of work.

As already indicated, it is everywhere characteristic of European labour that it normally claims to be classified as skilled or semi-skilled, and to be remunerated accordingly, leaving unskilled labour to be carried on by Coloured or African workers. Demands for the improvement of wages or conditions of employment are not as a rule made by an industry as a whole. The two sections, European and non-European, have divergent interests, and the issues are complicated by the fact that the demands made by Europeans imply in principle the maintenance of a pay differential based on a social or racial division between two classes of labour.

The problems which arise are thus of a special order, for the solution of which experience of industrial conditions in Europe and of the machinery employed there to solve industrial disputes is only of limited assistance. It is inevitable that at a certain stage differences between the two sections of labour in some of the major industries should involve the intervention of the Administration. This is not merely in the interests of order or of social peace but also because the productivity of the industries in which such disputes mainly arise is a matter of vital concern to the public revenue.[1]

In regard to the scale of pay of African labour, there is one factor which has had a general influence in determining the wage now available to them. During the last quarter of a century there has been a growing recognition that wages of African labour should no longer be regulated by the older concept of the labourer as a single man whose requirements are limited to his personal needs. In the Union of South Africa, for instance, the pressure on the soil in the Native Reserves has so far reduced the amount of subsistence available that the wage-earner in industry must seek subsistence for his family and not merely remuneration for himself. Both in South Africa and elsewhere there has been an increasing tendency for the migrant worker to be accompanied by his family to the seat of employment. In many cases he settles there for extended periods as part of what is practically an urban community, and as such he requires a scale of wages appropriate to the support of a family in urban conditions.

There is another factor which has had an influence in the same direction. At an early period the demand for indigenous labour came either from a farmer seeking hands for field work or from a mining company seeking hands for work in the mines. In both these cases the wage tended to be standardized, and in both of them it normally consisted partly of payment in kind by way of rations and of housing. The recent growth of secondary industry, more especially in the Union of South Africa, in the Belgian Congo, and in Southern Rhodesia, has made a radical change in this position. In this case wages carry no payment in kind; standardization is much less feasible, and the scale of pay is increasingly determined by the differing degrees of skill attained by workers.

In certain of the areas dealt with in this Survey, and in particular in West Africa, the African worker has become increasingly dependent on the purchase of imported commodities, and the scale of wage has not unnaturally been affected by the rise in the external price of imports of this character. Finally it is necessary to take account of the fact that there has grown up in the ranks of African labour an increasing realization of the value of group action. In many of the British dependencies this has been stimulated by the official encouragement which, as will be shown, has been given to the formation of trade unions. Apart from this factor,

---

[1] For the financial contribution made to public revenues by the mineral industry in particular, see below, pp. 1528 ff.

however, there has been much evidence of a growing sense of solidarity in the ranks of indigenous labour. The operation of the more important of these developments will be illustrated in the course of the following notes regarding the present situation in different territories.

The Union of South Africa

The general policy of the Union of South Africa has been described elsewhere as regulated by the determination to maintain the essentials of European civilization in the interests of its White population. In the economic field this policy has had two objectives: first, the maintenance of the wages of all European employees at standards appropriate to what has been termed as 'civilized labour'; and second, the adoption in European settled areas of measures designed to confine the non-European to unskilled labour, remunerated at rates suitable to African standards. The assumption traditionally made in this connexion was that the African employee was not entirely dependent on wage-earning, since he and his family could, if necessary, draw their subsistence from a holding in the Native Reserves. In South Africa the unusually high ratio of skilled to unskilled wage rates[1] is reflected in the disparity of the average figures of European and non-European incomes. The average annual cash earnings of Europeans in the gold-mining industry was given in 1953 as £712 and those of Natives as £51, but most non-European employees also receive other benefits which are valued at various figures up to 50 per cent. of their cash earnings. The rapid industrial development has altered the situation in which the mining industry occupied a leading place in the payment of wages to African labour. The number of industrial establishments almost doubled between 1930 and 1950,[2] and there was a corresponding change in both the volume and the character of African employment in the Union. Between 1950 and 1951 there was an increase of 260 per cent. in the number of workers employed in manufacturing industry, and the number of Natives employed in those industries rose from 90,500 in 1930 to nearly 395,000 in 1951.[3]

Since the Second World War there has been a marked increase in the rate of cash wages, though the increase in 'real wages' is much less. The average earnings of Natives employed in secondary industry were estimated at roughly £46·3 in 1938–9 and at £110 in 1948–9. During the Second World War the 'civilized labour' policy was largely relaxed, and since then shortage of labour has been a factor of increasing impor-

[1] Social and Economic Planning Council, *The Economic and Social Conditions of the Racial Groups in South Africa*, U.G. no. 53, 1948.

[2] M. Horrell, *Economic Development in South Africa*. See also pp. 1270 ff. and 1280 ff. above.

[3] *Report of the Industrial Legislation Commission*, U.G., no. 62, 1951, p. 18. Union of South Africa, Bureau of Census and Statistics, *Special Report no. 206: Thirty-fifth Industrial Census 1951–2, Preliminary Report*. See also p. 1274 above.

tance. It was reported that, at the end of March 1952, some 12,000 posts on the railways classified as European were in fact filled by non-Europeans. The effects of industrial expansion and of the shortage of labour, combined with a psychological readjustment tending to recognize work as 'semi-skilled' which was once classified as 'skilled', have resulted in non-Europeans being employed in increasing numbers in the semi-skilled occupations.

In spite, however, of these changes in the field of employment, the industrial colour bar continues to operate, based on the ground of social policy rather than on economic considerations. It has indeed been observed that no important South African industry is composed of a labour force graded in point of remuneration, skill, or type of operation wholly in accordance with the technical requirements of the industry or the capacity, output, efficiency, or any other objective criteria of the worker's productivity.[1] Reference is made elsewhere to the important part played by the Industrial Conciliation Act of 1937 in limiting the wage-earning capacity of Africans.[2] In this connexion, the influence exercised by the Departments of Government is significant. The Customs Act[3] contains a clause under which any manufacturer who does not maintain 'satisfactory labour conditions' may be deprived of the right to import free of duty materials and articles required in his business. This provision has been used in practice to enforce the employment of a high ratio of Europeans. The Mines and Works Act[4] contains a provision enabling the Government to make regulations providing for the issue of certificates of competence in mines or works where electrical power is used, and to limit the issue of certificates to European or Coloured persons. The regulations under the Act prescribe that lifts in the mines can be operated only by Europeans. The law provides for the setting up of committees to arrange for the entry of apprentices into various occupations,[5] but since these committees consist of representatives of employers' associations and registered trade unions, the practical result is to exclude non-Europeans from apprenticeship and thus to restrict their entry into the range of more highly paid employment.

The Federation of Rhodesia and Nyasaland

African wages in Southern Rhodesia increased by 25 per cent. during the years 1947 to 1952. In 1950 the average wage for unskilled workers in agriculture was 35s. per month, in mining 47s. 6d. per month, and in domestic service 50s. per month,[6] exclusive of food and fuel. Skilled

---

[1] S. H. Frankel, *The Economic Impact on Underdeveloped Societies*, 1953, p. 121.
[2] See below, p. 1440.   [3] Customs Act no. 35, 1944.
[4] Act no. 12, 1911, as amended.   [5] The Apprenticeship Act no. 37, 1944.
[6] *Central African Territories: Comparative Survey of Native Policy*, Cmd. 8235, 1951, p. 75.

operations might be remunerated by a wage as much as £20 per month, though the average artisan received much less than this figure. The official number of working hours is 48.

In Northern Rhodesia the wage of unskilled African labour ranged between £2 and £5 a month of 26 days in 1954, and in this category were included 79 per cent. of African wage-earners, exclusive of those employed on the copper-mines.[1] Skilled workmen, however, received a monthly wage of from £7 to £15 a month rising, for highly skilled specialists, to a maximum of £45 a month. The usual hours of work were 45 a week. Free housing was provided for all African workers. In the mining industry, as a result of an award made in 1953, the wage scale for African surface workers was fixed at sums varying from £4 to £18. 10s. a month and for underground workers from £4. 10s. to £20. 5s. The majority of these workers receive free food and lodging. Towards the end of the year 1954 the average monthly wage paid to an African surface worker was £6. 5s. 6d. and to an underground worker was £7. 0s. 8d. a month, with free lodging and rations in addition. At the same time the average wage of a European miner was £151 per month.[2]

The prolonged dispute on the Copperbelt in which the major issue was the advancement of Africans in the mining industry, but in which the wage structure occupied a prominent place, has been discussed elsewhere. In the employment of African labour other than in the copper-mines a marked rise has occurred in wages, owing to the keen demand for labour. An Inquiry made by the Department of Labour revealed that whereas in 1953 the highest wage paid to Africans working otherwise than in the mines was £25. 10s. a month, twelve months later the figure was £50. In 1953 only 9 per cent. of agricultural workers received more than £3. 10s. a month, but over 50 per cent. were earning a higher wage in 1954. Many self-employed Africans, such as storekeepers and transport contractors, were stated in the local press to be in receipt of an income of more than £1,000 a year.

In Nyasaland the rates of pay are much lower than in the Rhodesias. A minimum wage order in 1954 prescribed a minimum rate of 1s. per day in rural areas and of 1s. 4d. in townships.[3] A practice has grown up on the farms of offering an incentive bonus of 3d. or 6d. a week in consideration of regular attendance. Skilled labour is now paid at a daily rate varying from 1s. 9d. to 6s. 9d.

The East African Territories

In Tanganyika and Kenya the scale of wages is also lower than in the Federation of Rhodesia and Nyasaland. Minimum Wage Boards have

[1] *Colonial Reports, Northern Rhodesia, 1954*, p. 20.
[2] Ibid. and see above p. 1396.
[3] *Colonial Reports, Nyasaland, 1954*, p. 26.

been set up, but the average wage is stated to exceed in general the minimum prescribed wage, except in the mining industry, which is relatively unimportant in these territories. The minimum rate for unskilled agricultural labour, shown in 1952 as 10s. a month, was increased to 24s. in 1954; these rates were supplemented by rations and housing accommodation.[1] Most labour is, however, employed on the ticket or *kipande* system, and takes the form of task work, completed in five or six hours; where work requires attendance for the whole day, the number of hours is 45 per week. The Government and some larger employers allow their established employees holidays with pay. In Kenya a statutory minimum wage is imposed by regulation only in urban centres, where Wage Councils have fixed rates for particular industries, such as tailoring and road haulage.[2] The statutory minimum wage was based on a formula calculated from what is known as the 'poverty datum line' to which was added the 'human needs requirement' in order to arrive at an effective minimum level. The former comprised the cost of the essential necessities of life; the latter was an arbitrary percentage of the poverty datum line, fixed at $33\frac{1}{3}$ per cent., and a 2s. per month contribution towards the poll tax.[3]

This wage was based on a rate considered to be sufficient to meet the essential living costs of a single worker unaccompanied by his family, but it has been admitted at the same time that one-half of the African workers in urban private industry and one-quarter of those in the public service were remunerated at a rate insufficient to provide for their essential living costs.[4] Since the stabilization of urban labour has been accepted as being a major aim of policy,[5] the Wages Committee of 1954 recommended a transition from a 'bachelor' wage to a 'family' wage. The family wage was to be adequate to support a man, his wife, and two children, and was calculated at the rate of two and a half times a bachelor wage.[6] The transition was to be made in stages by equal percentage additions over a period of ten years from 1956. The Government, while admitting that the family wage was the ideal to aim at, has so far been able to commit itself only to an 'adult' wage sufficient to maintain the worker and his wife (but not his children) and then only when economic circumstances permit.[7] The rigid time-table by which the minimum wage was to be increased was held to be open to many objections.[8]

The effect of the proposals outlined above is that the minimum wage in

[1] Masters and Servants (Proper Feeding) Regulations, 1944.
[2] Regulation of Wages and Conditions of Employment Ordinance no. 1, 1951.
[3] *Report of the Committee on African Wages* (the Carpenter Report), Nairobi, 1954, pp. 50 ff.
[4] Ibid. p. 32.   [5] Kenya Sessional Paper no. 21, 1954, p. 2.
[6] *Report of the Committee on African Wages*, Nairobi, 1954, p. 77.
[7] Kenya Sessional Paper no. 21, 1954, p. 4.
[8] *East Africa Royal Commission 1953–1955, Report*, Cmd. 9475, 1955, p. 159.

Nairobi would be increased from 52*s*. 50 cents to 69*s*. a month—or with housing allowance (which it is proposed should be equated with an economic rent for bed space) from 59*s*. 50 cents to 81*s*. per month.[1] The recommendation that a flat increase of 10*s*. a month should be given to all existing minimum wage rates from January 1955 was accepted and was in operation during the year. Although the proposals of the Wages Committee were limited to Kenya, it has since been recommended that, if adopted, they should be made applicable also to Uganda and Tanganyika.[2]

Whereas the rate of wages for unskilled labour in the urban areas of Kenya is controlled by the statutory minimum wage discussed above, that in rural areas has not so far been controlled by legislation. The Committee on African Wages considered it desirable therefore that a counterpart to the minimum wage should operate also in rural areas. There were a number of objections to imposing statutory minimum wages, and it was recommended that wage rates should be determined by a Rural Wages Advisory Board acting on recommendations from Area Wages Committees.[3] The prevailing wage of the unskilled labourer on farms in 1952 and 1953 was between 20*s*. and 25*s*. a month, plus food; resident labourers or squatters, who were able to grow produce or raise stock on the land of their employers,[4] received in 1953 from 15*s*. to 23*s*. a month, an increase of 7*s*. above the level of the previous year,[5] but to these figures should be added roughly 20*s*. a month to cover the cost of rations and housing accommodation. It was considered by the Committee that in agriculture, other than the plantations, the wages of three-quarters of the workers were not adequate to support a minimum standard of health and efficiency, and that, even allowing for low productivity, the wage bore little relation to the work performed.

The greatest obstacle to the implementation of the proposals regarding urban areas has been the shortage of housing accommodation, which has been referred to above. The wages of domestic servants increased by 12 per cent. in 1954. As a result of a dock strike which took place in Mombasa in 1955 the basic wage for casual labour in the town was fixed at 6*s*. 50 cents, and for stevedore labour at 7*s*. per shift. The Government has accepted as a matter of principle the advisability of paying wages at a shorter interval than a month, in order to minimize the practice by which the employer gives advances of wages and the employee lives in consequence in a state of constant insolvency.

Wages in Uganda increased by 10 per cent. during 1953, and by about 20 per cent. in 1954. Inclusive of allowances the monthly rate of pay of

[1] *Report of the Committee on African Wages*, Nairobi, 1954, p. 69. The standard coin is the East African shilling divided into 100 cents.
[2] Cmd. 9475, 1955, p. 157.
[3] Ibid. p. 163. *Report of the Committee on African Wages*, Nairobi, 1954, p. 144.
[4] See above, p. 1391. [5] *Colonial Reports, Kenya, 1953*, p. 17.

unskilled labour employed by the Government was 45s. 78 cents a month and that of artisans rose in some instances to £12 a month. Most agricultural labour is performed by the task, which is usually completed in under six hours, and it is reported that a 24-hour week is not uncommon, but in industry an eight-hour day is the rule. Employees who have worked more than 280 days in the previous twelve months are entitled to one week's holiday on full pay. The duty of enforcing labour legislation now rests with a Labour Commissioner and his Department.

As has been observed, the system under which agricultural labour is most commonly employed in Central and East Africa is that of the ticket or *kipande*, which requires that 30 working days be completed within a definite period, usually 42 days. The system has certain advantages for both employer and employee, in that the former may not have continuous employment regularly available, and the latter can find time also to work on his own land. Equally it has disadvantages to both. For the employer it is wasteful of labour, and for the employee it in effect deprives him of a paid rest day on Sunday. The Kenya Government has accepted a recommendation that the period within which the ticket must be completed be reduced to 36 days and that ultimately the ticket system be abolished.[1]

The British West African Territories

In the British dependencies of West Africa wages are generally more stable than in East or Central Africa, and they are usually on a considerably higher scale. Unskilled labour is normally paid at rates between 3s. and 4s. 6d. a day; mining workers receive 4s. to 4s. 6d. a day. In Nigeria, however, the question of the minimum daily wage for labour became a political issue. When the Western Region of Nigeria raised the minimum pay for workers on Government undertakings to 5s. a day, the Central Government declined to follow its example. It based its decision on a report of a fact-finding Inquiry which showed that the increased expenditure on workers might involve an increase in taxation and would further augment the cost of the Five-year Development Plan. The minimum wage rate formed a crucial issue in the election of 1954.

The French Territories

The provisions regarding wages introduced in the French territories by the Labour Code of 1952 have been mentioned; it was estimated that they might increase the total cost of labour by 20 to 25 per cent.[2] However, although wages under the new law fluctuate with the cost of living,

[1] *Report of the Committee on African Wages*, Nairobi, 1954, p. 127, para. 335. See also Cmd. 9475, 1955, p. 156.
[2] P. Devinat, in *International Labour Review*, September 1953, p. 249.

it has been stated that in areas where labour is largely dependent on imported goods, the wage is not sufficient to meet minimum requirements.

The Belgian Territories

Mention has been made above of the effort made by the *Union Minière* in the Belgian Congo to stabilize its labour force; its success has been in a large measure due to the fact that during recent years there has been an increasing tendency to fix the pay of the worker at a rate which will enable him to support his wife and family. In general the level of wages is stated to be five times that which it had reached before the Second World War.[1] In the service of the *Union Minière* a casual worker can earn up to 14 francs (2s.) a day, a semi-skilled worker up to 30 francs (4s. 3d.), and a skilled worker up to 133 francs (19s.). A decree of 1954 allowed a worker one week's holiday at full wages after twelve months of continuous service.

It is not easy to estimate how far the rise in cash wages represents a rise in real wages. It is clear that in the Katanga mining area there is a very wide gap between the pay of the skilled and the unskilled worker, and it has been stated that the general rise in wages has not proved to be adequate for the support of a family.[2] Small family allowances are given but these do not appear adequate for family subsistence, and there is some independent evidence to show that it was necessary during the Second World War to resort to some measure of coercion to maintain production. The strain was felt more particularly in the urban areas.

In Ruanda Urundi a Committee on labour and social progress, composed of members of the Government, employers, and employees, advises the Government on labour policy, including the rate of wages. Since 1951 the minimum wage rates have increased appreciably, the lowest being 5 francs (about 9d.) in the rural areas and 7 francs (10d.) in the towns, and it has been stated that 28 per cent. of workers receive benefits in addition to cash wages.[3] The system of family allowances was introduced into Ruanda Urundi in 1953, but was suspended as the result of protests by the employers.

The Portuguese Territories

In the Portuguese Provinces the information available does not permit of a reliable estimate of the scale of wages as a whole, for most of the rates quoted are of local scales. There is evidence of much poverty, and of a low standard of living, especially in the Lunda District of Angola, where most of the diamond-mines are situated.

[1] G. Malengreau, 'Recent Developments in Belgian Africa', in *Africa Today*, 1955, p. 342.
[2] B. Davidson, *The African Awakening*, 1955, pp. 148 ff. See on this question also F. Grevisse, 'Le Centre extra-coutumier d'Elisabethville', *Bulletin du Centre d'Études des Problèmes Sociaux Indigènes* (*C.E.P.S.I.*), no. 15, 1951. J. Van Wing, 'Le Congo déraille', *Bull. I.R.C.B.*, vol. xxii, no. 3, 1951, p. 609. [3] Based on an exchange rate of 140 Belgian francs to £1.

THE MACHINERY FOR ADJUSTING TRADE OR INDUSTRIAL
DISPUTES

In Western countries the trade union is as a rule accepted as an agency of primary importance in settling trade disputes. In most of them (and certainly in the case of Great Britain) the movement originated within the ranks of labour itself, and it was natural that European workers in African territories, such as the Union of South Africa or the Rhodesias, should welcome the trade-union movement for much the same reasons as had secured for it the support of workers in Great Britain.

But the extension of the system to African workers had not the same background. It came at a stage when African labour had not as yet found it possible to combine on any considerable scale for the purpose of collective bargaining with employers. In many cases the labourers were groups of short-term workers from different territories, with no ethnic or social affinities, and they had therefore difficulty in finding a leadership which could win their confidence. The stimulus for the extension of the system came from two different sources. There was in Europe a school of thought which was strongly impressed with the need for the improvement of conditions among African workers, and which saw in the trade union the most effective machinery for achieving it. At the same time, some of the Colonial Administrations had already had experience of the immature attempts of Africans to combine for collective action and they felt that the trade union could provide a more responsible basis for negotiating trade differences. It is difficult, at the present stage, to decide whether the trade union is in the conditions of Africa likely to form the most effective type of machinery for the determination of differences regarding wages or the settlement of trade disputes. Where the movement has shown the greatest vitality, as for instance in the Union of South Africa or in the Rhodesias, it has tended to reflect a division of interest between European and African labour. The European trade union has seen itself as the champion of the cause of European labour against the infiltration of Africans into its own privileged field of employment. The African trade union has secured its greatest support among the workers of its own community because it champions its cause against the interests of European workers. Some of these tendencies will be illustrated by the history of the movement as summarized in the following paragraphs.

The Union of South Africa

In the Union of South Africa organizations of European workers came into existence as early as the 1880s, but it was not until the First World War that they gained any substantial degree of recognition by the

Government or by employers. Such organization as African labour has achieved came at a later date. The first large non-European organization, the Industrial and Commercial Union (I.C.U.) dates from 1919, but this was as much a political as an industrial association. It had for a time an extensive following among Africans, but it ceased to exist in the early thirties,[1] after having served as a training-ground for a number of Native trade-union leaders.[2]

In many countries the interests of skilled and unskilled workers do not in practice coincide, and where this division is identical with that between European and non-European, the sources of tension are multiplied. In the Union of South Africa the recent growth of secondary industry, where both races are sometimes employed on the same kind of work, has resulted in creating a measure of common interest, but the policy of the Government has tended to give legal recognition to those trade unions or similar organizations which are confined to the representation of European labour interests. There is a substantial difference between trade unions which can claim the benefit of the Industrial Conciliation Act, and those associations which, though organized on a trade-union basis, remain outside the scope of that Act.

The main object of the Industrial Conciliation Act no. 36 of 1937 is to provide for the settlement of disputes by conciliation and in certain cases by arbitration; it provides accordingly for the registration and regulation of trade unions and employers' organizations. To this end either Industrial Councils, representative of the two sides of an industry, are set up as permanent bodies, or Conciliation Boards are established *ad hoc* to settle a particular dispute. Any Agreement arrived at by one of these bodies may be declared by the Minister to be binding for a whole industry, with penal sanctions attached to it. Only employers' organizations and trade unions registered under the Act are entitled to make use of its machinery and to be represented on an Industrial Council or a Conciliation Board. The definition of 'employee' laid down in the Act excludes the great majority of Native workers, but the Agreements, or any part of them, may be extended by the Minister of Labour to cover these workers. By this provision employers can be prevented from employing Natives instead of White workers whose wages have been increased or whose working conditions improved by an Agreement arrived at under the Act.[3]

This extension to Native workers of wages and working conditions fixed under the Act without allowing these workers any representation

---

[1] R. L. Buell, *The Native Problem in Africa*, vol. i, 1928, pp. 128–30. *Handbook on Race Relations in South Africa*, 1949, pp. 164–7.

[2] *Report of the Industrial Legislation Commission*, U.G. no. 62, 1951, p. 197.

[3] *Handbook on Race Relations in South Africa*, 1949, p. 148.

on the bodies making the Agreements has proved detrimental to their interests. The Industrial Legislation Commission stated in 1951:[1]

The evidence available to the Commission is sufficient to satisfy it that the interests of Native workers have suffered in the process of collective bargaining between employers and European employees. In some cases it would seem that their interests are deliberately sacrificed by the European employees in order to gain benefits for themselves, while in other cases employers refuse to bargain in regard to Native wages as Natives are not represented on the employees' side. In such cases employers merely stipulate the wage rates they are prepared to concede in respect of occupations in which Natives are employed.

The presence of Department of Labour officials supposed to represent Native interests at meetings of Industrial Councils has proved inadequate as a protection of these interests. On occasion trade unions have included Africans, but a ruling of the Labour Department, reinforced by a Court decision, indicated that a union was liable to be de-registered if it had African members who did not fall within the category of employees as defined in the Industrial Conciliation Act.

Notwithstanding the unfavourable verdict of the Industrial Legislation Commission, the Industrial Conciliation Bill of 1954, which is designed to replace the Act of 1937, further strengthens the Minister's powers in making Agreements of Industrial Councils binding in respect of African workers. The Bill provides further that no 'mixed' trade unions shall be registered under the Act, and that existing 'mixed' unions—at present 60, with 140,000 members—must form separate branches for European and for Coloured, including Asian, members. There will be no obligation for the Coloured unions or branches to be represented on the Councils.[2]

The Bill also provides for the establishment of an Industrial Tribunal 'to conduct an investigation and to recommend whether it is of opinion that employment in that industry or occupation in a stated area should be reserved for members of a specified race'. In this case, Africans are included, although they are not deemed 'employees' under the Act for other purposes.

The provisions of the Bill, most of all that just mentioned, have met with severe criticism from various quarters. The employers regard this provision as an interference with the management's right to select its labour; the trade unions see in it a menace to collective bargaining, but the effectiveness of their action has been reduced by disunity in the movement over the question of the recognition of African trade unions. Even before the publication of the Bill differences on this point led in 1950 to the secession of 23 unions with over 100,000 members from the National Trades

[1] U.G. no. 62, 1951, p. 196.
[2] M. Horrell, *A Survey of Race Relations in South Africa, 1953–1954*, South African Institute of Race Relations, 1954, p. 126.

3 A

and Labour Council, which until then had been the only national co-ordinating body in the South African trade-union movement.[1] The seceding unions, representing mainly the higher wage groups, formed the South African Federation of Trade Unions which, although allowing the affiliation of 'mixed' unions (that is to say unions of Coloured and Asiatic workers), excludes African unions. In October 1954 various trade-union bodies set up a South African Trade Union Council with the object of giving a more unified support to the unions' objections to the Industrial Conciliation Bill. A majority of the Council insisted on the exclusion of African unions. Thereafter the Trades and Labour Council (to which African unions had been affiliated) went into dissolution.

The South African Institute of Race Relations expressed the view that the 'artificial fostering of sectional racial approaches to employment and conditions of work', which it regards as one of the major features of the Bill, will lead to greater racial unrest and be detrimental to economic development.[2]

The Wage Act, first passed in 1925 (no. 27) and revised in 1937 (no. 44), sets up machinery for the fixing of minimum wages and working conditions for unorganized labour. It excludes, however, agriculture and domestic service, both industries where unorganized, mainly Native, labour is predominant. A Wage Board consisting of three appointed members investigates wages and conditions in certain industries at the request of the Minister of Labour, to whom it reports its findings or submits recommendations. On the basis of these latter the Minister may make a wage determination. Most of the industries investigated by the Wage Board employ unskilled African labour, but until 1937 the Board was hampered in making recommendations for Africans by the stipulation that the wages fixed must provide a 'civilized' standard of living. In its revised form the Act prohibits any differentiation or discrimination on the basis of colour in fixing wages and conditions of employment. Since then Wage Boards have been used extensively to improve wages and conditions of African workers. It is stated that 198,324 Natives were covered by the terms of 'determinations'[3] from 1937 to the end of 1948.

Until 1953 the only machinery for the settlement of disputes in which non-Europeans were involved was contained in a Second World War measure, which prohibited strikes and gave the Minister power to appoint arbitrators.[4] The Native Labour (Settlement of Disputes) Act of 1953[5] sets up a separate industrial machinery for Natives. It provides for the establishment of Regional Native Labour Committees consisting of appointed African members under a European chairman, the Native Labour

[1] Horrell, op. cit. p. 129.
[2] Ibid. p. 126.
[3] U.G. no. 62, 1951, p. 196.
[4] Act no. 145, 1942.
[5] Act no. 48, 1953.

Officer of the region, and of a Central Native Board. This is composed of Europeans appointed by the Minister after consultation with the Regional Committees. In addition Works Committees of three to five members may be elected in establishments employing 20 or more Africans.

In a dispute the Regional Committee first tries to mediate; if this is unsuccessful, the dispute is referred to the Central Native Board which, if likewise unsuccessful, reports to the Minister, who may submit the matter to the Wage Board. Representatives of the Central Board and the Chairman of the local Regional Committee are entitled to attend (without voting power) the meetings of Industrial Councils or Conciliation Boards when an Agreement affecting occupations in which Africans are employed is under consideration. If the Central Board is not satisfied that the African workers' interests have been sufficiently taken into account, it may advise the Minister to submit the matter to the Wage Board for a recommendation upon which the Minister can base a 'determination' under the Wage Act.

The prohibition of strikes, embodied in a measure passed in 1942 during the Second World War, has been retained; lock-outs are also prohibited.[1] An African taking part in or instigating a strike is liable to a fine of £500 or three years' imprisonment. Trade unions are not prohibited, but continue to be denied recognition as negotiating bodies, although the Industrial Legislation Commission had advised their recognition in appropriate circumstances. In the Government's view this would not be in the interests either of Africans or of South Africa generally. When the new machinery is operating, the Minister of Labour declared in Parliament, 'Natives will have no interest in trade unions, and trade unions will probably die a natural death'.

Of the African trade unions some are independent and others affiliated to a co-ordinating body. Among the 45 unions (with about 80,000 members) affiliated to the South African Trades and Labour Council were five African unions with 3,750 members. The Transvaal Council of Non-European Trade Unions, with a membership of roughly 70,000, has about 10,000 African members. As already mentioned, the South African Federation of Trade Unions, which is now the largest co-ordinating trade-union body in the country, bars the affiliation of African unions; the same attitude is taken by the Co-ordinating Council of Trade Unions, which is representative mainly of iron and steel workers in Pretoria; some of its affiliated unions have Coloured or Asiatic members, but these have no vote. It is clear that the trend against the recognition of African trade unions has been strengthened by recent developments both in legislation and in the trade-union movement.

[1] Horrell, op. cit. pp. 79 ff.

The High Commission Territories

No active trade unions exist in the High Commission Territories. A measure providing for the establishment of trade unions in Basutoland[1] was enacted in order that the Territory might benefit from a grant from the Colonial Development and Welfare Vote.[2] For the same reason legislation empowers the Government to establish trade unions in Swaziland also.[3]

The Federation of Rhodesia and Nyasaland

Under the constitution of the Federation of Rhodesia and Nyasaland legislation regarding trade unions and industrial conciliation remains a territorial responsibility, and there is a material difference between conditions in Southern and Northern Rhodesia. In Southern Rhodesia African trade unions suffer (as in the Union of South Africa) from the disadvantage that the definition of an employee in the Industrial Conciliation Act excludes Africans.[4] Under the Act Industrial Councils, composed of employers' and workers' representatives, may conclude Agreements which may thereafter be declared by the Minister to be binding both on the parties to the Agreement and also, at the request of the Industrial Council, on other workers and employers. Such an Agreement can then be enforced in the Courts.

The Labour Boards Act of 1947[5] provides for Labour Boards to be set up which may intervene in industrial disputes and make recommendations to the Minister for wages and working conditions of Native workers in many industries excluding, however, farm workers, domestic servants, and employees of the Government and other public bodies. The operation of the Act is, moreover, limited to areas lying within a radius of ten miles of a Local Authority. The Minister may issue a 'determination', on the basis of the recommendations of a Board, which thus becomes legally binding. It may be noted, however, that a high wage prescribed under the Labour Boards Act, like one agreed under the Industrial Conciliation Act and extended to Native workers, can effectively operate against the employment of these latter. Moreover, the strong European trade union can always control the situation by refusing to allow its members to be associated with African labour in any skilled employment. In rural areas, for example, where Agreements made under the Industrial Conciliation Act do not normally apply, it would be useless for an employer to avail himself of relatively cheap African labour in the construction of a house, because the union which controls plumbing or electrical engineering might

---

[1] Proclamation no. 17, 1942.
[2] *Colonial Reports, Basutoland, 1953*, p. 22.   [3] Proclamation no. 31, 1942.
[4] Industrial Conciliation Act, 1934, as consolidated in 1945 (no. 21). See also *O.Y.S.R., 1952*, p. 211.   [5] Act no. 26, 1947, amended by Act no. 52, 1948.

refuse to allow the employment of this labour. The industrial colour bar has in this case been imposed not so much by legislation as by the European trade unions. Both the attitude of the European unions and the legislative framework thus have much in common with what has been described in the Union of South Africa. It is to the strength of the position attained by the European trade unions that one must attribute the fact which has struck so many visitors to Central and East Africa—that whereas in the Rhodesias the railways are operated by Europeans, in the Belgian Congo and East Africa the operating staff is mainly African.

It is, however, significant that with the rise of numerous secondary industries there are now relatively fewer industrial Agreements concluded, and Africans are being more widely employed in machine-operating jobs and on much semi-skilled work in the mines and elsewhere. It is also significant that the number of Africans employed in the manufacturing industry increased by 73 per cent. between 1946 and 1951.

Statutory provision for the registration of a Native trade union was made in the Rhodesia Railways Act, 1949, and a number of other workers' organizations receive *de facto* recognition, in that the Native Labour Department maintains direct contact with them and receives representations from them. It is significant, moreover, that the Minister for Native Affairs acknowledged in 1952 that the time was approaching when full statutory recognition would have to be given to organized Native labour in certain of the industries. In 1956, however, a Select Committee reported against a Bill providing for the recognition of separate African unions and proposed instead to bring Africans within the scope of the Industrial Conciliation Act. Several leaders of European unions have spoken in favour of the admission of Africans, but Africans have expressed the fear that if European wage rates are made applicable to Africans the latter will no longer be able to find employment, and have asked that Africans should first be admitted to apprenticeship.

The law in Northern Rhodesia does not differentiate between unions with a European and those with a non-European membership. If the more powerful groups, such as those of the mineworkers and the railway workers, have formed themselves into European and African unions, that is because their members consider they have divergent interests. The Trade Union and Trade Disputes Ordinance prescribes that trade unions must apply for registration;[1] it provides for the use of machinery for conciliation, for the prohibition of strikes likely to endanger essential services, and for the control of political funds. In 1952 there were 13 unions with a total membership of 50,000, but this figure had increased by 1954 to eight European and 15 African unions; it has been estimated that 25 per cent. of all African adult workers in employment are members

[1] Act no. 23, 1949.

of trade unions. The principal European union is that of the mineworkers, founded in 1936; it has a membership of about 5,100. Another powerful European union in the territory is the Rhodesia Railway Workers' Union, with about 1,000 members. The various African Mineworkers' Unions were amalgamated into one body in 1949, with a membership of over 25,000; the Union of African Shop Assistants and the General Workers' and Railway Workers' Unions are also of importance, though they are inferior in numbers.

Under the Industrial Conciliation Ordinance[1] the Governor may cause a Conciliation Board to be set up for any industry, such a Board to consist of representatives of employers and employees, with a Chairman also appointed by the Governor. If a dispute is expected in any industry, he may take steps to persuade the parties to meet for a settlement or go to arbitration. The differences regarding pay and conditions of work which have occupied so much of the history of the Copperbelt for a number of years, and have caused the appointment of the series of Inquiries to which reference has already been made, have made it essential that the Administration should have some measure of legal authority to intervene when other agencies have failed to find a solution.

It may, however, be said that the experience of Northern Rhodesia conveys on the whole a favourable picture of the potentialities of the trade-union organization, both European and African. That was in particular shown in the course of the strike, already referred to, which was called by the African Mineworkers' Union in 1955. The claims put forward by this body were admittedly ill calculated, but both of the Mineworkers' Unions behaved on the whole with moderation and restraint.[2] It should be added that the Mining Corporations also played a part which reflected credit on them: rather than lay themselves open to the charge of victimizing the African strikers they agreed to support the 8,000 African labourers who had been dismissed in the course of the strike.

Other British Territories

The Rhodesias stand, however, in a special class among the British territories in Africa owing to the importance of the position occupied by Europeans as part of the local labour force. In no other dependency is the problem of trade disputes so complicated by the competitive claims of European and African labour. The emergence of the trade union as an agency for the settlement of disputes has not been to the same extent the result of a natural growth. There has been a large measure of official

[1] Ordinance no. 24, 1949, as amended in 1950.
[2] R. W. Williams, 'Trade Unions in Africa', *United Empire* (Journal of Royal Empire Society), September–October 1955, pp. 186 ff. On the subject generally, see speech of the President of the Rhodesian Selection Trust group of companies, in *East Africa and Rhodesia*, 13 January 1955.

stimulation in the creation of African trade unionism. A circular dispatch issued from the British Colonial Office in 1937 pointed out the desirability of enacting local legislation to deal with the establishment of trade unions, and this was followed by some practical, if limited, results in a number of territories.[1] More definite stimulus was given by the Colonial Development and Welfare Act of 1940, which contained a provision requiring the Secretary of State, when considering a grant of financial assistance, to satisfy himself that the law of the Colony gave reasonable facilities for the formation of trade unions and made provision for fair conditions of labour.[2]

In 1941 the Colonial Office prepared for the assistance of Colonial Governments a model Trade Unions and Trade Disputes Ordinance, and provision for legislation on this subject has since been made in all the British African territories. It varies in detail, but usually provides for the registration of *bona fide* trade unions having a specified minimum number of members, and includes provision for their immunity from actions for tort; it prohibits intimidation, while permitting peaceful picketing. Legislation regulating the settlement of industrial disputes and providing for arbitration tribunals or similar bodies is usually included with the provisions for the establishment of trade unions. The appointment of trade-union organizers from the United Kingdom as Labour Officers in the dependencies, which began experimentally in 1942, is now the general practice, and such men have done much to help the young and often struggling associations.

In Nyasaland trade unions must be registered, and provision is made for the settlement of disputes by conciliation through the Labour Department, and for submission to arbitration.[3] In 1954 there were six registered unions, three African, two European, and one Asian. The Labour Department settled more than 2,000 wage complaints.

In Kenya the registration and administration of trade unions were regulated by a law of 1952,[4] and machinery is also provided whereby the Labour Commissioner may endeavour to effect conciliation between the parties to a trade dispute.[5] Failing a settlement by these means, reference may be made to an arbitration tribunal with the agreement of the parties; if this is not practicable, a Board of Inquiry may be set up to make recommendations to the Member for Labour, who may make an award. In 1954 there were 15 trade unions in the Colony, with a total membership of 33,000. Two are open to Europeans only, three to Asians only, two to Asians and Africans, and eight to Africans only. In 1956 nine African

[1] *Labour Supervision in the Colonial Empire, 1937–43*, Col. no. 185, 1943.
[2] Colonial Development and Welfare Act, 1940, Section 2 (a).
[3] Trade Disputes (Arbitration and Settlement) Ordinance no. 20, 1952, amended by no. 28, 1954.   [4] Trade Unions and Trade Disputes Ordinance no. 23, 1952.
[5] Trade Disputes (Arbitration and Inquiry) Ordinance no. 71, 1948.

trade unions united in a Federation of Labour. Relations between employers and employees are reflected in the material reduction in the number of industrial disputes in 1953 compared with the previous year. A strike in the dockyard at Mombasa in March 1955 involved 10,000 labourers and caused some disturbance, but at the end of a week the employees accepted a moderate wage increase and returned to work.

In Uganda a law passed in 1952 providing for the establishment of trade unions appears to have aroused little local interest.[1] Only four had been registered by the end of 1954, and greater reliance appears to be attached to joint consultative machinery. The position is somewhat similar in Tanganyika, where the three unions registered under the Trade Unions Ordinance[2] had a membership of only 635 in 1952. Special provision is made for the settlement of disputes in essential services and for the maintenance of such services pending a settlement.[3] Six trade unions are registered in Zanzibar, and had a membership of 585 in 1952.

In the three East African territories the formation of unions appears to have involved an expenditure of effort quite disproportionate to the results achieved. Greater success has been attained by the Joint Staff Committees, of which there are some 38 in Uganda. The Trades Disputes (Arbitration and Settlement) Ordinance in Tanganyika, which provides for conciliation by the Department of Labour and, in the event of a failure to agree, for reference to Arbitration Tribunals, has also furnished machinery appropriate to African industrial relations. Its operation was commended by the East Africa Royal Commission 1953-5.[4]

In Nigeria the registration of a trade union includes the right to peaceful picketing and protection against civil actions for breach of contract or for tort in respect of acts done in connexion with a trade dispute.[5] Here also there exists statutory machinery for the settlement of trade disputes by conciliation on lines similar to those noted in the case of Kenya.[6] There has been an exceptionally wide registration of trade unions, but some are of very small membership. Out of the 131 unions registered in 1953 only six have a membership of over 5,000, and it has been acknowledged that the poor organization of the trade unions and the absence of any real understanding of their purpose continue to be matters of serious concern.[7] It is clear also that there has been a certain intrusion of politics into the movement. The report of the Commission of Inquiry into the disorders which occurred in 1949, with special reference to the labour troubles at

---

[1] Trade Unions Ordinance no. 10, 1952. Trade Disputes (Arbitration and Settlement) Ordinance no. 19, 1949.   [2] Trade Unions Ordinance, Cap. 84, 1947.
[3] Trade Disputes (Arbitration and Settlement) Ordinance no. 43, 1950.
[4] *East Africa Royal Commission 1953-1955, Report*, Cmd. 9475, 1955, pp. 161, 162.
[5] Trade Unions Ordinance no. 44, 1938.
[6] Trade Disputes (Arbitration and Inquiry) Ordinance no. 32, 1941.
[7] *Nigeria, Annual Report of the Department of Labour, 1952-53*, pp. 25, 99.

the Enugu collieries, emphasized the importance of separating industrial from political issues particularly in the difficult period of constitutional revision.[1]

In the Gold Coast strikes and lock-outs are illegal if they have any object other than the furtherance of a trade dispute within the trade or industry in which the workers are engaged. They are also illegal if they are designed to coerce the Government either directly or by inflicting hardship on the community.[2] As in other British territories, provision is made for the establishment of an arbitration tribunal and a Board of Inquiry in connexion with trade disputes.[3] In 1953 there were 104 registered trade unions, but many had only a nominal existence; the certificate of registration was cancelled in eleven cases, and not more than 23 were reported to be active. Most of the 42 labour disputes were settled by conciliation.

In Gambia, where legislation was first enacted in 1932,[4] there is no provision for conciliation in labour disputes, but the Labour Ordinance of 1944 provided for voluntary arbitration. The six trade unions registered in 1952 had altogether 1,445 members.

In Sierra Leone the eleven unions existing in 1952 are recorded as having a membership of over 16,000; but, as in some other cases in West Africa, the unions have only a nominal following. They are often the creation of individuals who have sought to make for themselves a personal position; the collection of subscriptions is frequently difficult and the paid-up membership is understood to be rather less than half the total number of members. Wage disputes are actually dealt with by Wages Boards or Joint Industrial Councils. In 1954 the Artisans and Allied Workers' Union combined with the Transport and General Workers' Union and went on strike to obtain a wage increase. The rioting which ensued led to the appointment of a Commission of Inquiry which found that in the Artisans' and Allied Workers' Union 'too much authority had been concentrated in the hands of an ambitious, unscrupulous, and worthless man'.

Looking to the history of trade unionism in the British territories as a whole, it was natural that in circumstances such as those of Northern Rhodesia support should be given to the formation of an African counterpart of the Union of European Mineworkers; but in many other instances the movement has proved to be premature. Better results have actually been achieved by reliance on standing Conciliation Boards or institutions such as the local Joint Staff Committees existing in parts of East Africa. In most of the territories concerned the formation of trade unions might

---

[1] *Report of the Commission of Enquiry into the Disorders in the Eastern Provinces of Nigeria, 1949*, Col. no. 256, 1950.

[2] The Conspiracy and Protection of Property (Trades Disputes) Ordinance no. 12, 1941.

[3] Trades Disputes (Arbitration and Inquiry) Ordinance no. 20, 1941.

[4] Trade Union Ordinance no. 29, 1932.

perhaps with advantage have awaited the development of a more stabilized African labour force and of conditions in which Africans had had more experience of the working of the machinery provided by statute for conciliation and arbitration. At the same time it should be added that a somewhat different view is taken by Thomas Hodgkin in the study to which reference has already been made. He holds that the African movement for the adoption of trade unionism was spontaneous and was a natural result of a widespread desire to acquire more favourable terms of employment. In any case, however, it is clear that now that the trade-union movement has come to be taken for granted by African labour, there can be no question of imposing restrictions upon it.

The French Territories

In the French territories the advance made in the formation of institutions of the type of trade unions has been somewhat less marked. The only condition laid down for the formation of trade unions is notification in advance, and the Labour Code of 1952 provides that no employee shall be dismissed for trade-union membership or activity, but the number of such organizations and their membership appear at present to be decreasing rather than increasing. The number of trade unionists in private employment in French West Africa declined from 52,000 in 1950 to 33,000 in the following year. Under the Labour Code of 1952, trade disputes must first be submitted for conciliation to the local advisory labour committee. If this fails, an expert is appointed to make recommendations. It is illegal to initiate a strike or lock-out before this procedure has been exhausted. Little use seems to have been made of these provisions.

The Belgian Territories

There is in the Belgian Congo a very considerable body of legislation regulating the formation of associations by indigenous labour and the provision of machinery for the determination of trade disputes.[1] Earlier legislation seems to have been of a restrictive character, but the existing law was modified by Ordinances enacted early in 1946. The enactment of this legislation[2] followed a number of strikes or threats of strikes, which in the words of the preamble of the first of these laws revealed 'a lack of contact between indigenous workers and the employers or administrative authorities'. They provided for the creation of regional *comités et commissions du travail* which would keep the Administration in touch with labour

---

[1] *Codes et Lois du Congo Belge*, 1954, pp. 1061–75. See also F. Van der Linden and A. Wauters, 'La Nouvelle Législation sociale congolaise', *Bull. I.R.C.B.*, vol. xix, no. 2, 1948, p. 476.

[2] No. 82, 17 March 1946, as amended by no. 21, 20 January 1948; no. 98, 6 April 1946, as amended on 20 January and 13 October 1948; no. 128, 10 May 1946.

issues; labour disputes or differences regarding wages were to be submitted to Boards of Conciliation or Arbitration nominated by the Governor-General, and there were penal sanctions attached to the action of those whose activities threatened the stoppage of work without awaiting the results of this procedure. It was made obligatory for employers of labour to constitute for each undertaking a *conseil indigène d'entreprise* which would keep them in touch with their own labour force.

The law provided further for the formation of *syndicats professionels indigènes* which would be somewhat in the nature of trade unions. They were to consist either of groups of employees following the same trade or of the body of the employees of one particular undertaking. Their constitution was to receive a 'provisional' authorization from the *Administrateur territorial*, to be converted into a final sanction when the necessary information regarding the membership, the composition of the committee, and the like had been supplied and approved. The conditions laid down are thus somewhat rigid, and the trade-union movement has so far attracted little general interest.[1] In 1952 there were 59 *syndicats* in the Colony, of which 13 were still provisional; the total number of members was 7,067.

The same series of legislative Acts have been extended to Ruanda Urundi, but no *syndicat* had been constituted there up to 1954. Labour in the larger centres was said to have accepted as adequate representation on the officially sponsored *comités du travail*.[2]

The Portuguese Territories

In the 'corporative system' of the Portuguese Republic the employees are encouraged to form collective bodies, but the predominant part played by the executive Government in the regulation of trade and industry, and the fact that strikes are not permitted, seem to distinguish the Portuguese *sindicatos* from trade unions as commonly understood. In Mozambique there were five such bodies in 1951, representing respectively commercial and industrial employees, railway and port employees, bank employees, motor-vehicle drivers and allied workers, and civil construction and allied workers. Under the system developed in accordance with the National Labour Statute, *sindicatos* work under the guidance of the Government, which plays a leading part in the preparation of their rules, fixing hours of work and rates of wages and compensation.[3] The *sindicatos* have powers of investigating grievances or disputes, and provision is made for arbitration; they also try to find employment for members who are out of work.

[1] *Rapport sur l'administration de la colonie du Congo Belge, 1952*, p. 109.
[2] *Rapport sur l'administration belge du Ruanda-Urundi, 1952*, p. 152.
[3] *Overseas Economic Surveys, Portuguese East Africa, 1951*, p. 44.

Affiliation with International Bodies

It is characteristic of the firm hold which the Belgian Government has maintained over labour organization in the Belgian Congo that the formation of any federation of the authorized syndicates within the territory or affiliation with bodies outside the territory is prohibited save with the sanction of the Government. Elsewhere in Africa the trade unions have been freely affiliated with the international organs of trade unionism. These are now grouped round the two chief organizations, namely, the World Federation of Trade Unions and the International Confederation of Free Trade Unions, both of which have shown an active interest in Africa and its labour activities. The former has the reputation of being subject to Communist influences, and it is suggested by its critics that its main interest in Africa lies in the possibility of fermenting industrial unrest. There is no similar doubt about the direction taken by the activities of the International Confederation of Free Trade Unions. It is, however, noteworthy that apart from its attitude in purely industrial matters it gives an influential support to national movements for self-determination; the first and second resolutions in its meeting in 1953 were the condemnation of 'Colonialism' and the recognition of the right of the indigenous peoples to govern the country as they think fit. It exerts therefore a direct influence in political matters in many of the territories of Africa, and especially of South Africa.

The activity of these two bodies has been manifested at various international conferences which have been held in Africa. The World Federation of Trade Unions held a conference at Dakar in April 1947, the International Confederation of Free Trade Unions at Douala in March 1951, and, in addition to these general conferences, the *Confédération Française des Travailleurs Chrétiens* held a conference at Lomé in October 1950, and the *Confédération Générale du Travail* at Bamako in October 1951. At the latter conference two co-ordinating committees were established, one for French West Africa and French Togo, and the other for French Equatorial Africa.

THE INTERNATIONAL LABOUR ORGANIZATION

The International Labour Organization has from its inception in 1919 given particular attention to the problems of Native Labour. Its headquarters Office has a special section concerned with this subject, the director of which is present in his expert capacity at the discussion of labour questions dealt with in the Annual Reports submitted by the Powers administering Trust Territories. Successive conferences of the Organization have adopted a series of Conventions designed to regulate labour conditions in Colonial and comparable territories. The Forced

Labour Convention of 1930 dealt with the conditions under which compulsory labour might be employed. This was followed by Conventions on recruiting (1936), contracts of employment (1939), and penal sanctions (1939).

The International Labour Office was the only organ of the League of Nations to continue in existence throughout the Second World War, and it resumed its annual conferences even before the end of the war, namely in 1944. The Philadelphia Conference of that year adopted a comprehensive recommendation on minimum standards of social policy in dependent territories, the general effect of which was to urge the wider ratification of the special Conventions applicable to indigenous labour and the extension to dependent territories of existing Conventions concerning the employment of women and children, workmen's compensation, and freedom of association.[1] The recommendations also included certain general principles of policy, namely, that economic development should have the raising of standards of living as its prime objective, that all practicable measures should be taken for the improvement of public health, that nutrition and housing should be improved, that co-operative societies should be encouraged, and that discrimination in employment on grounds of colour should be prohibited. The majority of these recommendations were embodied in a Convention adopted in 1947. An additional Convention on contracts of service adopted in the same year aimed at imposing maximum periods of contract, varying in length according to whether labour was employed at, or away, from home and whether or not employees were accompanied by wife or family. Conventions guaranteeing freedom of association and requiring the creation of Labour Inspectorates were also adopted in 1947. None of the 1947 Conventions has yet attained the ratification necessary to bring it into force. As has been shown, however, the principles advocated have been adopted in practice by a number of the countries dealt with in this Survey.

[1] International Labour Office, *Social Policy in Dependent Territories*, Montreal, 1944.

CHAPTER XXI

CO-OPERATIVE INSTITUTIONS

IN the many discussions regarding the aims of the co-operative movement it is not uncommon to find a difference of view regarding the
relative importance of the material and the moral purposes which it
seeks to achieve. In one well-accepted definition of its purposes, co-
operation is stated to be 'a form of organization wherein persons voluntarily associate together as human beings on a basis of equality for the
promotion of the economic interests of themselves'.[1] Other authorities,
however, suggest that it may prejudice the progress of the movement if
stress is laid on the purely economic benefits which it can secure.[2] They
urge that though fundamentally the system may be defined as that of 'self-
help made effective by organization',[3] it may also be claimed that its
object is to achieve conditions of better living in the wider sense of the
term and that its practice has an educative value which can benefit both
the individual and the community of which he is a member. But in a
matter of this nature it is a mistake to attempt any marked distinction
between social and economic objectives, for their lines are constantly
crossing.

The most satisfactory definition seems to lie in the statement that the
end of co-operation is social, though the means used are economic.[4] At
the same time there is inevitably greater difficulty in attempting to
measure the extent of the influence it can actually exert in the moral and
social sphere. The movement is world-wide; there is great variety among
the numerous types of co-operative societies in which its activity is manifested, and the influence which it has exercised on the members of these
societies must vary as widely as the motives which have inspired them to
take part in co-operative activities. It cannot, for instance, be doubted
that the small co-operative society formed by the 28 Rochdale Equitable
Pioneers in 1844 demanded a definite measure of self-denial on their part
and evoked a corresponding spirit of mutual responsibility. But one would
not necessarily draw the same conclusion regarding the $10\frac{1}{4}$ million members of the existing 1,100 co-operative retail trading societies of Great
Britain for whom the chief significance of this form of association lies in
the fact that it provides them with access to an economical form of domestic

[1] H. Calvert, *The Law and Principles of Co-operation in India*, 1926, p. 13.
[2] Fabian Colonial Bureau, *Co-operation in the Colonies*, 1945, p. 161.
[3] H. Plunkett, *Bombay Co-operative Quarterly*, September 1928, p. 7.
[4] M. Dia, 'Contribution à l'étude du mouvement coopératif en Afrique noire', in *Le Mouvement
coopératif en territoires tropicaux arriérés*, Leiden, 1953, pp. 123 ff.

shopping. There is, no doubt, a stronger influence exercised by those forms of producer and marketing societies which impose on their members a joint responsibility for the maintenance of certain standards of production. There are, moreover, some societies of this type which are bound together by the fact that they have enabled their members to secure the raw materials of their craft, and have thus assisted them to liberate themselves from bondage to the money-lender or the capitalist employer. There must again be a strong, though somewhat different, type of influence exercised by membership of the numerous co-operative credit societies both in continental Europe and elsewhere.

These, however, are examples taken from the Western world, and the immediate question concerns the measure to which the co-operative system has been adapted to the needs of Africa. To the European settler or trader in Africa, the procedure of co-operation is familiar and they have made full use of the system in a number of the territories. To the African peoples, on the other hand, it has represented an institution of a novel character, which was evolved in the first instance to meet the needs of the industrialized society of Europe. Two points stand out. The needs of African society at large for associations of the type known generally as consumer trading societies differ widely from those which have accounted for the success of the early societies of this class in Europe. A great part of Africa still lives under a régime of subsistence economy, producing the food which it consumes or obtaining it by what amounts to a system of barter. It is only of recent years that there has grown up a large class of African industrial wage-earners, and the amount of consumer goods which these wage-earners buy is reduced by the fact that for many of them the food ration forms an integral part of their wage. The growth of 'economic' or marketable crops has in some areas provided the African cultivator with a considerable cash surplus for expenditure on consumer goods, but much of this is expended on the relatively less essential commodities.

If consumers in Africa have found it convenient to combine in order to effect economy in their purchases, this has often been influenced by the conviction (particularly in West Africa) that they were being exploited by combines of European importers, or because (as, for instance, in the Union of South Africa or in some parts of East Africa) they felt themselves to be unduly dependent on non-African retailers, whether European or Asian. But even so, there were limits to what could be effected in Africa by the association of consumers, for (as the experience of Europe has shown), the consumers' societies can be most effective when they can entirely eliminate the middleman by direct dealing with manufacturers, or by combining to form wholesalers' societies or consumers' producing societies which can manufacture or arrange for the manufacture of commodities for distribution by the primary societies. The retail trading co-operatives in Great

Britain have, for example, combined to create co-operative wholesale and producer societies whose sales amounted in 1950 to £394 million. A movement in this direction, however, would oblige the African primary societies to combine in organizing a form of enterprise of a type which few have yet been in a position to contemplate.

Development of African Co-operative Societies

There is a second point of contrast between the present needs of Africa and those which have influenced the form taken by the co-operative movement elsewhere. The African peasant has in the past had far less urgent grounds for interest in the creation of co-operative credit societies of the type which have occupied so prominent a place in the co-operative movement in continental Europe. There the rural credit co-operatives have accounted for more than one-third of the total number of agricultural co-operative societies of all types; they had just before the Second World War a membership of over 8¾ million persons.[1] The co-operative credit societies have represented an even larger part of the activities of the movement in India. It is significant that the initial law of 1904, the starting-point of the recognition given to the movement in India, was designated as the Co-operative Credit Societies Act, and it was not until some years later that it was amended in order to bring other activities within the range of registrable co-operative associations.[2] In 1945–6, the last year previous to the separation of Pakistan from India for which figures are available, there were some 171,000 primary societies in the sub-continent, of which 147,000 were classed as agricultural, and, of these, rather over 124,000 were thrift and credit societies. Statistics compiled subsequently show that in India during the period 1946 to 1952 co-operative banks increased from 285 to 495. The increase has been due largely to the interest in co-operative banking shown by the Reserve Bank of India and to the assistance given by it.[3]

But there were special reasons why Indian peasants were ready to welcome the formation of such societies. Over the greater part of the sub-continent there is great pressure of population on the land; holdings are small and are often much 'fragmented', in the sense that a holding, representing the result of a long process of family subdivisions, may also be situated in widely different parts of a village.[4] In some of those areas in which the landlord system prevailed (as most notably in Bengal, Oudh, and part of the United Provinces) the landowners often claimed from the

---

[1] *Co-operative Societies throughout the World: Numerical Data*, Geneva, 1939.

[2] Co-operative Societies Act, 1912. See E. M. Hough, *The Co-operative Movement in India*, 1953, pp. 47–54.   [3] *India, 1953, Annual Review*, p. 97.

[4] *Report of the Royal Commission on Agriculture in India*, Cmd. 3132, 1928, pp. 129–43. *Report of Imperial Conference on Agricultural Co-operation*, 1938, p. 143.

cultivator a share up to one-third of the produce of the land.[1] The periodic years of scarcity due to failure of rain have imposed a far higher strain on the congested population and innumerable smallholdings of the Indian villages than on Africans, who in general have practised a much more extensive form of cultivation. Added to this, a long-established tradition has led the Indian peasant to spend on religious, family, or other social observances an amount out of all proportion to his income. The result has been seen in a widespread practice of borrowing from money-lenders, partly, no doubt, for productive, but even more for unproductive purposes. In a great many parts of India the peasantry were burdened by a crushing load of agricultural indebtedness, a great mass of which was an inherited debt; the peasant was in a perpetual state of economic serfdom to the money-lender, and the moral consequences of his outlook were as unfortunate as were the economic.

It was for this position that the Royal Commission on Agriculture of 1928 saw the best hope of relief in the formation of co-operative credit societies. None of the acts of legislation which had attempted to control usury, to curb the power of the money-lender, or to prevent the landholder from encumbering his holding with debt could provide permanent remedies; the 'greatest hope for the salvation of the rural masses from their crushing burden of debt rests in the growth and spread of a healthy and well-organised co-operative movement, based upon the careful education and systematic training of the villagers themselves'.[2] It is noteworthy that the Indian peasant has come also to see in the Consolidation of Holdings Societies a remedy for the fragmentation of his holdings. By the end of 1946 over $1\frac{1}{2}$ million acres had been 'consolidated' in the Punjab, and 1 million in the Central Provinces; in the United Provinces 177,635 plots had been reduced to 12,342.[3]

The relative absence of similar conditions in Africa helps to account for the fact that the African peasant has not so far shown the same concern in discovering a means of meeting the problems of rural insolvency. It is not because African peasants have no debt problem. In the urban areas both of East and South Africa indebtedness has become a standing difficulty, though in some of the territories the growth of a money-lending industry has been retarded by the obstacles placed by legislation in the way of the shopkeeper (the principal source of credit) from recovering his outstandings. Perhaps the most conspicuous instance of large-scale indebtedness on the east side of Africa is in Zanzibar, where, however, the communities mostly concerned as debtors and creditors are Arabs and

---

[1] L. S. O'Malley, *Modern India and the West*, 1941, pp. 284–8.

[2] *Report of the Royal Commission on Agriculture in India*, Cmd. 3132, 1928, pp. 431–76. See also M. L. Darling, *The Punjab Peasant in Prosperity and Debt*, 1925; and H. Calvert, *The Wealth and Welfare of the Punjab*, 1936, pp. 357–89.

[3] Hough, op. cit. p. 167. *Report of Co-operative Planning Committee*, Bombay, 1946, p. 24.

Asians.[1] In West Africa the mischief has become more general than in the east, because of the growing practice by which cultivators have taken advances from middlemen engaged in the cocoa and palm-oil industries, or have borrowed from money-lenders. But Africa has escaped some of the worst of the experiences of India, owing to the fact that the prevailing system of land tenure (unlike that of India) has not lent itself to the practice of securing credit for goods or money by the pledging or mortgaging of land. In addition to this, African customary law makes no provision for the expropriation of the landholder in order to satisfy the claims of creditors. As will be shown, the tendency in recent times has been for Africans in the rural areas to obtain assistance in the form of credit from the producer or marketing societies of which they are members, instead of forming associations of the nature of a co-operative credit society.

As a result, the producer and marketing societies have become one of the most noteworthy features of the development of co-operative activity in Africa south of the Sahara. It is interesting that here the economic interest has (as in the case of the consumer societies) received an added stimulus from the feeling that the African was being handicapped by the priority acquired by European or Asian interests. The foundation of one of the most successful of the societies in East Africa, the Kilimanjaro Native Co-operative Union,[2] followed on a period of agitation by European settlers against the growing of coffee by Africans. The establishment of co-operative cotton-ginning societies in Uganda was due largely to Government action, but it was stimulated by the desire to gain for Africans an entry into a form of industry from which they had hitherto been excluded by Asians.[3] Again, the formation of the co-operative producer and marketing societies in West Africa was influenced by the belief that the 'export monopoly' held by European firms prevented African cultivators from obtaining a better price for cocoa beans.[4]

Indigenous Institutions and the Co-operative Movement

It has often been asked whether there was no indigenous institution which could have been adapted to the aims of the co-operative movement.[5] African custom is no stranger to the use of joint or communal action to achieve certain purposes. Many of the processes of agriculture are achieved by the collective activity of kinsmen and neighbours. Hunting and fishing are regularly carried on by well-recognized groups. The procedure for the trial of cases in a Native tribunal is itself a signal instance of collective action. But neither these forms of association nor the ties

---

[1] N.A., Part II, p. 13. Fabian Colonial Bureau, *Co-operation in the Colonies*, 1945, p. 81.
[2] See above, p. 833.   [3] See above, p. 403.
[4] *Report of the Commission on the Marketing of West African Cocoa*, Cmd. 5845, 1938, pp. 40 ff.
[5] *Colonial Development* (The Colonial Development Corporation), Autumn 1953, pp. 12 ff.

established by membership of a kinship group formed a workable alternative to the form of association which a co-operative society sets out to establish. Nor was it possible to utilize on any extensive scale the services of traditional Native Authorities in the formation of these associations; experience has indeed shown that there were some instances in which the formation of co-operative societies was at one time opposed by Chiefs as threatening to undermine their own authority.[1] In the traditional organization there is a spirit of solidarity combined with a sense of reciprocity of rights and duties. But the appeal made by the co-operative movement is not primarily directed to the spirit of communal solidarity; its appeal is to the spirit of self-help and the intelligent furtherance of individual interests. Its success lies in the measure to which it can convince the individual that his own interests can best be secured by a disciplined association with others who seek a similar objective. If this demands some self-sacrifice on his part, the primary incentive lies not in the advancement of the welfare of the community but in securing the interests of the individuals concerned. The community will in due course profit in so far as its welfare depends on that of the individuals of which it is composed.

The spirit of self-help and individual initiative is more characteristic of Western civilization than of indigenous African society. It is not surprising to find, therefore, that where there has been in Africa any extensive use of the mechanism provided by the co-operative movement, it has been due to the initiative and support of the Administration. This has been most marked in the British territories, where some of the Administrations followed the precedent set by British India in the earlier years of the present century and appointed Registrars of Co-operative Societies whose function it was to encourage the promotion of such societies and to exercise some measure of supervision over their working.[2] In this latter respect the experience gained in British India was of direct value, for it showed that in the early days of the formation of these societies, inexperience (if nothing worse) can lead to failures which will gravely retard the future progress of the movement. In 1946 the promotion of the movement became a definite feature of British Colonial policy.[3] As will be shown, the official encouragement given to the movement in the French territories was less marked, since the Administrations had from the outset shown a preference for the promotion of the *sociétés de prévoyance*.[4] In the Belgian Congo also little encouragement was given to the co-operative movement until recent years.[5] The following paragraphs will give a more detailed account of the history of the movement in the different areas with which the Survey deals.

---

[1] Fabian Colonial Bureau, *Co-operation in the Colonies*, 1945, p. 77. See also *Report to the Council of the League of Nations on Tanganyika Territory, 1937*, Col. no. 148, pp. 206–13.

[2] See also on these points below, pp. 1485 ff.

[3] *The Co-operative Movement in the Colonies*, Col. no. 199, 1946, pp. 3 ff.

[4] See below, pp. 1477 ff.   [5] See below, p. 1480.

SOUTH AFRICA

The Union of South Africa

The earlier stages of the history of co-operation among Europeans in the Union were closely bound up with that of the system of State aid to the farming community. The agricultural and pastoral industry of South Africa was built up by men who had little personal capital; the internal market open to them was small, and an external market hardly existed until first the wool and then the fruit and wine industries opened up a demand for agricultural exports from the Union. Agriculture could not have attained its present position without a liberal measure of State aid, direct or indirect, and the very considerable assistance given to it was only rendered possible by the revenues derived from taxation of the diamond and the gold industries. Direct assistance was at the outset given through various provincial Land Banks,[1] which were united in 1912 in the Land and Agricultural Bank of South Africa, generally known as the Union Land Bank.[2]

Before this date a small number of European co-operatives or associations had been established. The number increased rapidly when it became a function of the Union Land Bank to promote the growth of co-operatives, in preference to making loans to individuals. The Bank has derived the main part of its capital from the State, and by 1950 it had drawn a sum of just over £20¼ million from this source, on which it has paid interest at rates from 3 to 3½ per cent. It has worked at a net profit amounting in 1950 to a total of £2¾ million. The scale on which it has assisted the co-operative societies or associations is shown by the fact that, while the outstanding loans to individuals amounted in 1950 to £19½ million, the outstanding loans to co-operative organizations of various kinds amounted to £28 million.

The registered European agricultural co-operatives, which numbered 252 in 1952,[3] are of a very wide range, covering almost every form of agricultural or pastoral production, the tendency being to form a separate society or association to deal with each product or group of products.[4] Of these agricultural co-operatives 225 are concerned with marketing. Many societies, however, combine the functions of granting credits, providing farming requisites, milling and other forms of processing, and the grading of products. They had in 1952 a total membership of 231,655, and their

---

[1] Transvaal Act no. 26, 1907; Natal Act no. 27, 1907; Cape Act no. 25, 1907; Orange Free State Act no. 33, 1909.

[2] Union of South Africa Act no. 18, 1912.

[3] Registration originally regulated by the Co-operative Societies Act of 1922 is now regulated by Act no. 29 of 1939, as amended by Sections 27 and 28 of the Finance Act no. 46 of 1944. Of the 243 societies, 229 have limited and 14 have unlimited liability; the former are usually designated 'companies'.   [4] *O.Y.S.A., 1952–53*, pp. 698 ff.

turnover amounted in 1951–2 to £174½ million. Side by side with these agricultural co-operative societies there have grown up many co-operative consumer trading societies; these numbered 171 in 1952 and had a membership of just over 100,000, but they have not attained the same success as the agricultural societies owing, it is said, to the absence of a regular working-class clientele.

There has been relatively little development of co-operative societies among Africans. Some efforts were made by Father Bernard Huss between the years 1920 and 1928 to create co-operative credit societies in the Transkei,[1] and a request for their supervision by the Registrar of Co-operative Societies in the Union was put forward in 1930. This was not, however, granted and a Proclamation—no. 191 of 1934—was issued, providing for the establishment of a committee under the Transkeian General Council[2] to register and supervise them. Some 37 credit societies were thus registered; they had altogether a capital of £25,000. A Commission which dealt with the working of the co-operative movement in the Union in 1934[3] pointed out that the societies were falling into difficulties owing to the fixing of unduly high rates of interest, and held that the further extention of the movement might more usefully take the form of producer and consumer societies. They thought that there was a place for such societies in the Native areas of the Union generally, but a Proclamation which was issued in 1934, providing for the creation of co-operative societies, was in terms limited to the Transkei. This Proclamation was issued in a revised and extended form in 1946. The terms of the Union Co-operative Societies Act of 1922 have been interpreted as excluding African societies.

Such societies as now exist are in the main to be found in the Transkei, but they are on a relatively small scale. There are in that area 17 African credit societies, which in 1954 had a total membership of only 3,444. These have functioned independently of assistance from the Land Bank. There were also 933 Farmers' Associations, and nearly 16,000 women have combined to form sundry organizations which promote shows and competitions. In Natal 36 organizations exist with different objects and functions. Co-operation is even less progressive in the north, where the Letaba Bantu Farmers' Co-operative Society is the most prominent. It has registered 852 members, who cultivate fruit and vegetables on plots of less than one *morgen*; they produced in 1950–1 over 3 million lb. of produce valued at £25,000.[4] But the funds of such bodies stand at a low figure and one, the District Co-operative Society at Potgietersrus, has become insolvent.

[1] B. Huss, *People's Banks*, 1928.
[2] For the Transkeian General Council, see above, pp. 427 ff.
[3] *Report of the Commission to Enquire into Co-operative and Agricultural Credit*, U.G. no 16, 1934.
[4] *Report of the Department of Native Affairs, 1950–1951*, U.G. no. 30, 1953, pp. 38–39.

South-West Africa

In South-West Africa the co-operative movement has so far been confined to Europeans. There are at present ten agricultural co-operatives which are concerned mainly with the acquisition of breeding stock. They are assisted by loans from the Land and Agricultural Bank of South-West Africa.

The High Commission Territories

Of the High Commission Territories Bechuanaland has so far no co-operative society. In Swaziland the only co-operative of any importance is the Tobacco Co-operative Company at Bremersdorp, a European society which deals with the marketing of the locally produced tobacco. Africans are compelled by regulation to sell their tobacco through the Company, though they are not admitted as members. The circumstances are unusual in so far that the sole outlet for the local type of tobacco is through the Union Tobacco Industry Control Board, with which the Tobacco Co-operative is in direct relation. Co-operative activity is far more important in Basutoland. Largely as the result of the recommendations made in the report of the Financial Inquiry of 1935,[1] measures were taken by the Government to secure a better standard for the wool and mohair production of the territory, and for this purpose encouragement was also given to the establishment of marketing societies. The attempt to promote these societies had, however, only a limited success at the time, and it was not until 1948 that the appointment of a Registrar of Co-operative Societies succeeded in stimulating a practical interest in the matter. The three wool and mohair marketing societies registered in 1948–9 were largely the result of this effort,[2] and they had a marked effect in securing a better position for Basutoland wool and mohair in the export markets. In 1953 there were eleven such societies, with a turnover of £79,982. All are in a sound position. It was in some measure due to the success of these bodies that the Basuto have also been moved to establish the present seven agricultural societies, but their agricultural activities are on a minor scale, and they are really a type of small consumer society. In addition there are now eleven consumer and trading societies; they have, however, had a chequered existence, five having been liquidated in 1952, and their total turnover in 1953 was only £6,747.[3] The problems presented by the management of this class of society have obviously been too complex for a small population, purely rural and largely pastoral in character.

[1] *Report on the Financial and Economic Position of Basutoland*, Cmd. 4907, 1935. *N.A.*, Part V, p. 12.

[2] *Annual Report of the Registrar of Co-operative Societies for the Year ending 31st March 1949*.

[3] *Colonial Reports, Basutoland, 1953*, p. 40.

THE BRITISH DEPENDENCIES

Southern and Northern Rhodesia

The European agricultural interests in Southern Rhodesia have followed the example of those in the Union, and have organized themselves into a number of co-operative bodies. There are now ten which deal with special products, and also supply their members with implements and other equipment. There are five of a more general type described as farmers' unions, which are co-operative in name rather than in the form of their activity. In this territory, however, most of the actual purchasing of the local agricultural and pastoral production is in the hands of State organizations, such as the Grain Marketing Board (which takes over and disposes of maize and all other grains) and the Cold Storage Commission, which handles all slaughter cattle and also part of the sheep slaughterings. As in the Union, the co-operative societies are financed from the Land and Agricultural Bank,[1] its outstanding on this account being £284,000 in 1954.

Up to 1954 nothing had been done to assist in organizing co-operative societies for Africans. The current policy concentrated on the development of the official organization for disposal of grain, cattle, &c., which, it was considered, secured for Africans the benefit of good market prices at a stable level. It was held that the stimulation of co-operative activity for other purposes, including the purchase of consumer goods, should follow only when this primary purpose had been achieved. The first step in this direction was taken in 1954 by the appointment of a Registrar with an African Supervisor, who, after studying the legislation in Northern Rhodesia and Nyasaland, was to draft analogous legislation in Southern Rhodesia. Policy is at present directed mainly to the encouragement of the type of producer co-operative which will deal with the marketing of agricultural products.[2]

In Northern Rhodesia there existed for some years a small number of European co-operative societies, mainly of the type of the producer marketing society, but it is only recently that they have attained their present proportions. They now number 15, the more important being the four European producer marketing societies, with a turnover of nearly £1¼ million in 1952. Tobacco is the major commodity dealt with. The Co-operative Creamery Society is also prominent, and is used by the Government as its agent for all imported supplies. There are now also five European consumer and trading societies, which operate largely in the towns of the Copperbelt. They appear to be gaining slowly in popularity, though the Lusaka Co-operative Society has had to close down owing to faults of management.

---

[1] Southern Rhodesia Land Bank Act, 1947.   [2] *F.N.*, 13 May 1954.

The African co-operative societies all owe their existence to the impetus given to the growth of co-operation by the issue of directions from the Colonial Office in 1946. There were in 1952 a total of 84 societies, the more important being the 48 producer marketing societies, which had in 1952[1] a turnover of £160,705. The 21 consumer societies are still small (their turnover in 1952 was only £32,161) and suffer gravely from difficulties of management. Book-keeping is an even more serious problem, and at present it appears impossible to engage locally any African suited for higher employment in the societies. The thrift and loan societies are still in their infancy; they have an average membership of only 30. In 1953 there were, in all, 109 co-operative societies (European and African), with a turnover of £2,167,319. Two building societies had assets of over £2¼ million.[2]

A General Note on Developments in Other Dependencies

As has already been indicated, the development of co-operative organization in the British Colonial dependencies has had two phases. In the first phase various Administrations took steps to promote the formation of societies, largely under the influence of the reports of the expansion of co-operative activity which had taken place in India. It was natural, accordingly, that they should at the time regard co-operation primarily as a means of preventing the growth of indebtedness,[3] and as helping to ensure better standards of living by the inculcation of habits of thrift, for that was the aspect which had appealed most to the advocates of the expansion of the system in India. But they appreciated also the lesson to which Indian experience had pointed, namely, that whatever the emphasis which had been laid in Europe on the voluntary character of the co-operative association, it had owed its growth in India to encouragement from official sources, and it would clearly require the same stimulation in Africa if it were to become a factor which would exercise any widespread influence in African society.

It is doubtful, however, if the Administrations concerned had an adequate appreciation of another lesson which was to be drawn from Indian experience. Large as is now the number of societies in existence in India, progress has not been uniform; there have been considerable areas where the co-operative society has proved a failure, costly alike to the people and to the Administration. Where it has fared best, its success has been due largely to the existence of an active Co-operative Department, with a trained personnel of sufficient strength to carry out on the spot the detailed inspection of the working of the societies and prompt to apply a corrective

---

[1] *Colonial Reports, Northern Rhodesia, 1952*, p. 25.
[2] Ibid. *1953*, p. 24.
[3] Fabian Colonial Bureau, *Co-operation in the Colonies*, 1945, p. 31.

to errors due to inexperience and mismanagement. If the co-operative system were to succeed in Africa, where the standards of education and business experience were far lower than in India, a similar measure of administrative control was clearly essential. During most of this period, however, only Nigeria had a separate Registrar of Co-operative Societies; in other Colonies the Department of Agriculture took charge of the work of co-operative societies, in addition to its other duties.

The second phase was ushered in by directions issued from the British Colonial Office in May 1946,[1] which indicated that the expansion of co-operative activity was now an accepted feature of policy and that its development required the assistance of a staff of the necessary strength. This decision seems to have reflected the influence of the resolutions passed by the United Nations Conference on Food and Agriculture at Hot Springs in 1943, inviting all countries to study the advantages of the co-operative movement, and to furnish information on the subject.[2] By this time, as will be seen, the preference of Africa for the producer marketing type of society was already well established, and it was here that the co-operative system gained its chief impetus. That was partly because of the growing appreciation of the money value of the export crops grown in parts of Africa, but it also gained strength (as already explained) from the feeling that the co-operative system provided a means which would enable the African to bargain on more equal terms with the European or other non-African agencies which appeared to exercise a dominating influence over the price realized for export commodities.[3] In June 1955 the Colonial Office claimed that the policy announced in 1946 had yielded substantial results. In the Colonies as a whole the co-operative movement now embraced about 7,500 registered societies, with over 960,000 members; their paid-up share capital had risen to over £6 million, and total reserved funds to £3½ million. Their deposits amounted to £4 million, and loans to members amounted to £7 million.[4]

Nyasaland

Taking first the Central African territories (other than those already dealt with) Nyasaland had at the end of 1953 some 71 societies, all of which dated from 1946.[5] The new Northern Highlands Coffee Union serves a number of primaries, and a new Rice Growers' Union appears likely to be of benefit to the developing rice industry in the Karonga area.

[1] *The Co-operative Movement in the Colonies*, Col. no. 199, 1946.
[2] *Final Act of the United Nations Conference on Food and Agriculture*, Cmd. 6451, 1943, pp. 27-28.
[3] For developments in the British Colonies generally, see B. J. Surridge, 'Memorandum on Co-operation in the Non-self-governing Territories under United Kingdom Administration', in *Le Mouvement coopératif en territoires tropicaux arriérés*, Leiden, 1953, p. 181. Also W. K. H. Campbell, *Memorandum on Co-operation in the Colonies*, Papers on Colonial Affairs no. 2, 1944.
[4] H.C. Deb., 21 June 1955, coll. 1153-270.   [5] Ordinance no. 20, 1946.

The 33 dairy societies serve a useful function; 13 are found in the Kasitu Valley Ghee Producers' Union, and 16 in the Bulambiya Union. On the other hand the African consumer societies here are in a precarious position, five having been liquidated in 1951. Few have the necessary resources, but the main trouble is lack of skill in management.[1]

Kenya   •

The Report of the Inquiry made in 1936 regarding the finances of Kenya commented on the lack of concern shown by the Government in the promotion of co-operative societies; it condemned the Co-operative Ordinance of 1931 as being better adapted for the needs of Europeans than of Africans.[2] There was, in fact, at this date a complete absence of co-operative organization among African producers.[3] But subsequent legislation,[4] and the creation of a Co-operative Department under its own Registrar in 1945, made a material change in the position.[5] Kenya had in 1954 a total of 320 registered societies, of which ten were European, eleven were Asian, and the remainder African.[6] The major European societies— the Kenya Farmers' Association and Kenya Planters' Co-operative Union —do not in many respects follow co-operative principles, but they have done much for the development of both European and African farming. This group of European societies, which are mostly concerned with marketing, had in 1951 a turnover of £8 million. Like similar societies in the Union, they operate on loans from the Kenya Land Bank. The most successful group of Asian societies is that of the Isma'ili community in Mombasa;[7] these are mainly consumer societies, but include a well-managed credit society.

The African societies increased in number during the Second World War owing to the creation of numerous small egg societies, but the registration of most of these has since been cancelled. The majority of the existing African societies are described as marketing, but there are seven small thrift and ten consumer societies. There has, however, been the same difficulty as elsewhere in regard to the management of the African societies; the members of their committees have no sense of control, and few societies can afford to pay a competent secretary, even if such could be found. An effort is being made to train a co-operative staff at the East African Regional Co-operative Training Centre at Kabete, to which

---

[1] *Colonial Reports, Nyasaland, 1952*, p. 75; ibid. *1953*, p. 82.

[2] A. Pim, *Report on the Financial Position and System of Taxation in Kenya*, Col. no. 116, 1936, p. 175.

[3] Fabian Colonial Bureau, *Co-operation in the Colonies*, 1945, p. 38.

[4] Ordinance no. 38, 1945; also amendment no. 36, 1951.

[5] For the openings for co-operation in Kenya, see W. K. H. Campbell, *Report on an Investigation of Co-operative Possibilities in Kenya*, 1946.

[6] *The Colonial Territories, 1954–55*, Cmd. 9489, 1955.   [7] See above, p. 404.

students have also been sent by Uganda and Tanganyika.[1] It appears likely that for some years there must continue to be a process of weeding out the weaker organizations.

Uganda

In Uganda the record of co-operation goes back to 1913, but the Protectorate had no definite co-operative organization before 1946, a proposal for legislation put forward in 1937 having been dropped in view of local opposition.[2] An Ordinance was, however, passed in 1946, and a Co-operative Department was created.[3] By the end of 1954 there were 1,056 registered societies, with a membership of nearly 100,000.[4] The growth of activity is closely linked with developments in the cotton industry. Although, as explained in a previous chapter, measures had been taken to protect the interests of the cultivator by regulating purchase prices, the inspection of markets, and the like, it remained a common complaint that these measures were insufficient to protect him from exploitation by Asian middlemen.[5] In particular, it was urged that Asians, by purchasing ginneries which were surplus to actual ginning requirements, could gain control of facilities for purchase over relatively extensive areas.[6] As a result the somewhat contentious legislation enacted in 1952 and 1953 provided that the Administration might acquire a certain number of the surplus ginneries, and these were in due course to be handed over to African co-operative societies formed for the purpose of operating them.[7]

There has in recent years been a rapid increase in the number of co-operative societies. These stood in 1954 at a total of 1,036,[8] of which 982, with a membership of 90,918, were agricultural producer marketing societies, 22 were thrift, and seven were consumer societies; among the remainder was one housing society. Nearly 750 of the marketing societies are linked in eleven marketing unions, concerned mainly with the marketing of cotton and coffee. The marketing co-operatives had a turnover of £4¾ million. It is of special interest that, during the year, four rural cattle-marketing societies were registered in the Lango district, and three co-operative farming societies in Bunyoro; the latter now use tractors hired from the Department of Agriculture, and market their crops collectively. The major Cotton Marketing Union was operating two ginneries, with a yield of nearly 12,000 bales of cotton. During the year a Co-operative

[1] *Colonial Development* (Colonial Development Corporation), Autumn 1953.
[2] Fabian Colonial Bureau, *Co-operation in the Colonies*, 1945, p. 76.
[3] Ordinance no. 5, 1946, as amended by no. 39, 1951, and no. 28, 1952.
[4] *The Colonial Territories, 1954–55*, Cmd. 9489, 1955.   [5] See above, p. 839.
[6] *The Colonial Territories, 1952–53*, Cmd. 8856, 1953, p. 50.
[7] See above, pp. 402 ff.
[8] *Annual Report of the Department of Co-operative Development, 1954.*

School was opened at the Local Government and Community Development Training Centre at Entebbe.

Tanganyika

At an earlier period in the history of African co-operative activity, Tanganyika Territory was much in evidence owing to the reputation attained by the Kilimanjaro Native Co-operative Union. This started, largely on African initiative, in 1925 as the Kilimanjaro Native Planters' Association, and its formation was, as has already been observed, stimulated by the opposition of Europeans to the growth of coffee by the Chagga. It was in its earlier stages guided and in a sense controlled by officers of the Administration. It did not become co-operative in character till a Co-operative Societies Ordinance was passed in 1932. The Society owed much at this stage to the fact that it employed a competent European manager. At a later stage it survived a number of difficulties, due at one period to the opposition of local Chiefs, and in 1937 to trouble, culminating in open disorder, resulting partly from the dissatisfaction caused by the fall in prices during the pre-war period of depression, and partly from the operation of a rule passed by the local Native Authorities, which compelled every African cultivator to market his coffee crop through the Union.

These troubles ceased when a Native Coffee Board was created, under the Native Coffee (Control and Marketing) Ordinance of 1937, charged with the supervision of the cultivation and the marketing of coffee on Kilimanjaro. The Union acts for this purpose as the agent of the Board.[1] In 1952 there were 30 societies affiliated to the Union, with 31,000 members; it handled 4,105 tons of coffee, valued at over £1 million, and discharged a number of other functions for its members, including the supply of requisites for cultivation. It holds deposits of over £18,000, and has played a considerable part in promoting educational activity among the Chagga.

Tanganyika had in 1954 a total of 236 co-operative societies, with a total membership of over 157,000.[2] Of the societies 188 are classed as agricultural marketing societies, of which 117 are affiliated in four Unions. Of these the Kilimanjaro Union is the most outstanding. The Ngoni-Matengo Co-operative Marketing Union, which has 17 primary societies, deals with tobacco, but has suffered from trading losses. The Rungwe Union, with eleven primary societies, deals with coffee and rice; it sold in 1951 coffee to the value of £141,000. The Bukoba Union has 51 primary societies and acts as agent of the Bukoba Native Coffee Board. In 1954

---

[1] For fuller details, see *Report to the Council of the League of Nations on Tanganyika Territory, 1937*, Col. no. 148, pp. 206–13. Fabian Colonial Bureau, *Co-operation in the Colonies*, 1945, pp. 20, 77. *N.A.*, Part I, p. 279. *Tanganyika, Report for the Year 1952*, Col. no. 293, p. 70.

[2] *The Colonial Territories, 1954–55*, Cmd. 9489, 1955.

the Lake Province formed for the first time a co-operative society to deal with the marketing of hides and skins, the fourth highest item of export from the territory. The societies are now well established, but have to contend with continued difficulties of management. Though there are three 'non-indigenous' societies, with a total membership of 15,000, only one, the Tanganyika Coffee Growers' Association, has done marketing on any scale. There are five credit societies of Isma'ili Muslims,[1] whose work is supervised by the heads of the local Isma'ili community. There is an interesting development of rural co-operation in the Kilwa Farmers' Co-operative Society in the Pare district, which has secured credit for the ploughing of their rice lands by tractor.

Though co-operative work has thus made considerable progress in the territory, its development owes much to the Government Boards, which exercise supervision over the cultivation and marketing of the more important crops. The staff of the Co-operative Department is now organized under a Commissioner for Co-operative Development. The turnover of all societies in 1953 amounted to nearly £3½ million.

Zanzibar

In 1932 the Administration of Zanzibar, following a recommendation made in the course of the Inquiry into the financial position of the Protectorate,[2] passed a law regulating the establishment of co-operative societies, and appointed a Registrar. Its purpose was partly to provide some means of relieving the standing indebtedness of the Arab and Swahili communities to Asians and partly to provide a means of stabilizing the marketing of cloves. The post was, however, abolished in the following year, and the marketing of cloves handed over to a Clove Growers' Association. This body was accorded in 1938 the sole right to purchase cloves within the Protectorate, and the measure might have been successful in stabilizing the market price if it had not been rendered abortive by the boycott organized against it by Asian traders. The problem of indebtedness in Zanzibar was again made the subject of a Report in 1950,[3] and in 1952 efforts were made to revive interest in co-operative activity. A Registrar was appointed, and some small groups of rice-growers were established as co-operative societies, thus obtaining credit facilities to finance tractor cultivation in their rice lands.[4]

---

[1] See above, p. 404.

[2] A. Pim, *Report on Commission to Report on Financial Position and Policy of the Zanzibar Government in Relation to Economic Resources*, 1932.

[3] A. J. Kerr, *Report on an Investigation into the Possibilities of Co-operative Development in Zanzibar and Ancillary Subjects*, 1950. The first Report on the subject was that by C. F. Strickland, *Report on Co-operation and Certain Aspects of the Economic Conditions of Agriculture in Zanzibar*, 1931.

[4] *Colonial Reports, Zanzibar Protectorate, 1952*, p. 18.

Extension of Co-operative Activity in the West African Territories

Viewed as a field for the extension of co-operative activity, the two major British West African territories have conditions which differ materially from those of East Africa. The relatively small European community is not directly interested in holding land or taking part in agricultural production. Other non-Natives—such as the Syrians[1]—do not exist in sufficient numbers to create an obstacle to the entry of Africans into trade or industry. But the great bulk of the export trade and of the import of consumer goods has hitherto been in the hands of a small number of European merchant firms or companies, and, though the export position is changing with the general extension of the system of purchase by State marketing boards,[2] the firms continue to function in the export market as purchasing agents of the boards, and they still tend to control the import market. On the other hand, the handling of the export crops, notably cocoa and palm kernels, has created a class of African middlemen— 'brokers' and 'sub-brokers'—with considerable experience of trading conditions, and has placed in the hands of cultivators the means of a large expenditure on consumer goods. The general expansion of a cash economy has created conditions in which indebtedness, sometimes in the form of advances on crops, and in certain areas actually based on the 'pledging' of holdings,[3] has become a growing feature of rural life. There is here the first phase in an organized system of money-lending, with the usual exorbitant rates of interest. Finally, there has been a marked growth of those large urban communities which have from early times been a feature of West African social life.[4] The effect of many of these factors is seen in the form taken by the development of co-operative activity, particularly in Nigeria and the Gold Coast.

Nigeria

In Nigeria the formation of co-operative societies was at the outset due to the influence exercised by the Department of Agriculture,[5] but it took a more definite form when a separate Department, with a Registrar and staff, was established in 1936; the staff was enlarged in 1938. The Agricultural Department remained in charge of the work in the Cameroons until 1943. Attention was at first directed to the formation of thrift and credit societies, mainly among salaried workers. This met with a fair measure of success, and the formation of credit societies has been extended in both urban and rural areas. They numbered over 500 in 1952, with a

---

[1] See above, p. 411. [2] See above, pp. 1349 ff.
[3] *N.A.*, Part IV, pp. 36 ff. [4] See above, p. 33.
[5] C. F. Strickland, *Report on the Introduction of Co-operative Societies into Nigeria*, 1934.

considerable working capital;[1] there was a well-established Provincial Union of Credit Societies in Calabar, with 18 less important local unions. It is noteworthy that some of these societies have a purely female membership. On the other hand, the thrift societies, which were at one time important, have lately declined in number. They numbered 276 in 1951, but their management has been poor. The consumer societies also have declined in number, and in 1951 there were only 38. The retail trade is well organized by the importing firms, but it seems to be difficult here, as elsewhere, to establish among Africans the habit of cash payment. The main advantage of the consumer society is that in circumstances such as those in the Northern Provinces it can make some estimate of total requirements and bring in supplies from a distance.

The most important activity of the movement in Nigeria now seems to be the development of the marketing societies, particularly those engaged in dealing with cocoa. There were in 1951 some 310 primary marketing societies, organized in eleven unions, and affiliated to the Association of Nigerian Co-operative Exporters. They dealt with just under 10 per cent. of the Nigerian cocoa crop. The Cocoa Co-operative Marketing Association had a turnover of £2 million in 1953.[2] Much of the success of these societies seems to have been due to the growing practice of granting short-term loans to their members; if they were able to increase their capital by securing larger deposits, they could greatly increase the range of their activity. It is clear, in any case, that the cocoa-grower can no longer exist without taking advances on the crop. There are a few processing societies, including one for fruit products, but the latter has to face keen competition from more experienced sources. There are eight craftsman societies. They are small, however, and are at present operating with varying success. An interesting development is the establishment of co-operative farms, of which seven were registered in 1952.[3] No less than 7,000 women are enrolled in maternity societies, but these have a very precarious existence.

There is in Nigeria a total of some 1,400 societies. All of these were at one time united in support of a Nigerian Co-operative Federation, whose principal function was to supply facilities for audit. There have, however, been a number of changes following on the constitutional reforms which recognized the existence of the three separate Regions in Nigeria.[4] In 1951 a Registrar of Co-operative Societies was appointed for each of the three Regions. The Nigerian Co-operative Federation was dissolved in 1952 and its place was taken by regional organizations: in the Western Region the Co-operative Union of Western Nigeria received a grant from the Regional Government, and in the Eastern Region the Co-operative

---

[1] *Colonial Reports, Nigeria, 1952*, p. 57. See also *The Colonial Territories, 1951–52*, Cmd. 8553, 1952, p. 56.
[2] Ibid. *1953–54*, Cmd. 9169, 1954, p. 81.
[3] Ibid. *1952–53*, Cmd. 8856, 1953, p. 51.
[4] See above, pp. 310 ff.

Union of Eastern Nigeria replaced the Co-operative Federation.[1] There was a similar change in the marketing boards, whose operations now so closely affect the working of the producer marketing primaries and unions in Nigeria. In the Northern Region the specialized marketing boards which dealt exclusively with one product, such as groundnuts, cotton, palm oil, or coffee, have now been amalgamated to form the Northern Regional Marketing Board; this Board arranges for the marketing of all products within the Region.[2]

The definition of 'co-operative associations' given at the beginning of this chapter includes in its widest sense the improvement associations which have in recent years become common in Southern Nigeria. These associations are formed on a lineage, clan, village-group, or tribal basis, and engage in economic, educational, or social activities of many kinds. Some act as credit societies and are open to members of both sexes; the membership of others is restricted to men or women only. An important point in their favour is that they are founded on the traditional social structure and thus serve to bridge the gap between it and the more highly centralized 'co-operative associations' properly so called.[3]

The Cameroons

In the Cameroons under British Trusteeship there were in 1953 a total of 45 societies, of which 32 were classed as marketing, four as thrift, and three as credit. In a few areas, as notably in Mamfe, the marketing societies have operated with some success, but generally there seems to be a marked apathy. An effort is now being made to give greater vitality to these societies by extending their functions to the grant of short-term credit. The Cameroons Co-operative Exporters Limited was formed in 1953 to provide a centralized organization, and has considerably improved the situation. The marketing societies had in that year a turnover of £120,000. The Bekweri Co-operative Farmers' Union marketed bananas valued at £13,410.[4]

The Gold Coast

In the Gold Coast, as in Nigeria, the co-operative movement was in the first instance placed in the charge of the Department of Agriculture. This stage continued from 1929 to 1944, and some considerable progress was made in the formation of societies, which numbered 302 in 1943, the majority (254) being producer societies for marketing cocoa. But the

---

[1] *Colonial Reports, Nigeria, 1952*, p. 58.

[2] *West Africa*, 27 November 1954, p. 1123.

[3] S. Ottenberg, 'Improvement Associations among the Afikpo Ibo', *Africa*, January 1955, pp. 1–27.

[4] *The Colonial Territories, 1953–54*, Cmd. 9169, 1954, p. 81. *Cameroons, Report for the Year 1953*, Col. no. 309, pp. 45, 192.

societies themselves were small, with an average membership of only 261, and in the year of their greatest activity they dealt with only a small proportion (about $2\frac{1}{2}$ per cent.) of the cocoa crop. The West Africa Cocoa Marketing Commission appointed as the result of the cocoa 'hold-up' of 1937, which coincided with a catastrophic fall in the price of cocoa,[1] did not consider that the societies were worth retaining as a means of marketing cocoa, and held that the most suitable employment of co-operative societies was to be found in their provision of credit, a field in which it was held that the existing organizations had already made some progress. The place of the marketing societies was to be taken by statutory associations of producers. It is clear that there was at the time a marked division of opinion regarding the relative merits of the co-operative society and a State-run purchasing organization as the best means of securing the position of the producer.[2] When the Commission made its Report 98 per cent. of the export trade was in the hands of European firms; estimates gave the number of middlemen as 1,500 'brokers' and no less than 37,000 'sub-brokers'. In the official view there was some doubt whether a population of which 98 per cent. was illiterate would be able to combine in societies which could bargain effectively with the existing agencies for the purchase of the crop.

The final decision was to some extent influenced by the experiences of the Second World War, when the whole cocoa crop was purchased by the Government. As a result, the total crop is now purchased by a statutory organization, the Gold Coast Cocoa Marketing Board, to which reference has been made in a previous chapter.[3] But strong support has at the same time been given to the expansion of co-operative societies. A Department under its own Registrar was organized in 1944, and the Gold Coast Co-operative Marketing Association has been utilized as one of the major purchasing agents of the Board. During the season of 1953 the Association marketed some 47,423 tons, which was approximately $19\frac{1}{2}$ per cent. of the total crop of the territory. The amount thus dealt with by the Association was the produce of some 291 co-operative marketing societies, and was valued at approximately £7 million, the export value of the total crop being roughly £56 million. The paid-up capital of the Association was £332,119. There were five other marketing societies dealing with other products, such as fruit, vegetables, and rice, but their operations were on a comparatively small scale. The former Agricultural Produce Marketing Board has been replaced by the new Gold Coast Agricultural Development

[1] See above, p. 1268.
[2] *Report of the Commission on the Marketing of West African Cocoa*, Cmd. 5845, 1938, pp. 168 ff. *Report on Cocoa Control in West Africa, 1939–1943*, Cmd. 6554, 1944. C. Y. Shephard, *Report on Economics of Peasant Agriculture in the Gold Coast*, 1936. W. K. Hancock, *Survey of British Commonwealth Affairs*, vol. ii, 1942, pp. 210, 226. F. J. Pedler, *West Africa*, 1951, p. 109.
[3] See above, p. 1349.

Corporation, which also assumes the functions of the Agriculture and Fisheries Development Corporation.[1]

In addition to the marketing societies there were 82 thrift and credit societies, but in practice the place of the credit societies is being increasingly taken by the marketing societies, which make advances to their members against the value of their crops. The credit societies were grouped under the Gold Coast Co-operative Bank, whose principal function was to finance the operations of the Gold Coast Co-operative Marketing Association and the Gold Coast Co-operative Wholesale Establishment Limited, which is subsequently referred to. The Bank had a working capital of £478,000, of which nearly £26,000 represented shares and £24,000 reserves; the deposits amounted to £135,000. There were 36 consumer societies, with about 13,000 members, grouped under the Co-operative Wholesale Establishment Limited. This institution was established in the hope that it would encourage the formation of consumer primaries and would strengthen their position. It had a Bank guarantee of £250,000 and an interest-free loan from the Government of £100,000. But the consumer society has so far proved to be an unsatisfactory feature of the co-operative organization. The committees of the societies are weak, and have had to obtain their own supplies on credit. In addition to this, the management of the Co-operative Wholesale Establishment Limited has come under grave criticism. Towards the end of 1953 it was the subject of an official inquiry and eventually went into liquidation.

Another example of co-operative activity is to be found in the populous Kusasi area. Here the local agricultural development committee has been registered as a co-operative society. Its purpose is to provide bullocks and ploughs for the promotion of mixed farming and to market the groundnuts produced by the members.[2]

It is unfortunate that the position of the semi-responsible Government of the Gold Coast in relation to the purchase of cocoa has in recent years become an acute political issue. The procedure of the Cocoa Marketing Board, and in particular its power to fix the price paid to the producer at a figure which enables the Board to accumulate such large reserves,[3] renders it very vulnerable to attack. It is freely suggested that the party in power has used for its own purposes funds which were placed at the disposal of the Co-operative Wholesale Establishment Limited, and there have been many unpleasant rumours connected with the history of the Cocoa Purchasing Company, which, though not an official organization, had official support. Reactions from this situation have been seen in the co-operative societies, some of which have demanded a reconstitution of

---

[1] *Colonial Reports, Gold Coast, 1953*, p. 51. *West Africa*, 30 April 1955, p. 403.

[2] Ibid. *1952*, p. 44.

[3] These were valued in 1954 at over £86¼ million. See also above, p. 1350.

the Cocoa Marketing Board in a more popular form, in which they would have some measure of direct representation.[1]

Togoland

The United Kingdom Trust Territory of Togoland reproduces on a small scale the chief features of the co-operative organization in the Gold Coast. The Gold Coast Cocoa Marketing Board is the ultimate purchaser of the whole cocoa crop, and the 30 Togoland Cocoa Marketing Primary Societies supplied in 1953 about 28 per cent. of the cocoa crop of the territory and distributed to their members over £1 million.[2] The sales were made in the first instance through the two marketing unions and next through the Gold Coast Co-operative Marketing Association, which, in Togoland as in the Gold Coast, is the marketing agency for all produce-marketing co-operatives. In 1952 the Association made advances to farmers of roughly three-quarters of the £769,500 paid to them for the cocoa supplied by the primaries.[3] It also acted as the agent of the Gold Coast Co-operative Central Bank for other short-term loans for general purposes; the interest charged does not exceed 10 per cent. and is one of the inducements which attract farmers into membership of the co-operative primaries. The sum so loaned was £34,200. Two consumer societies which drew supplies from the Gold Coast Co-operative Wholesale Establishment Limited had only a small turnover and were liquidated in 1954. The two existing thrift and loan societies, operating mainly among salaried employees, ceased to function and were being wound up in 1952.

Sierra Leone

In Sierra Leone the co-operative movement is still in its infancy, for though an Ordinance was passed in 1939 and a few societies were formed, it was only with the appointment of a Registrar in 1948 that an advance of any importance was made. By the end of 1953 there were 125 societies with a total membership of 5,207 and a turnover of approximately £72,000. Producer marketing societies were the most numerous (96 in 1953) and, of these, 49 dealt with cocoa and 35 with *piassava*. Fluctuations in the world market price of *piassava* affected the marketing societies adversely, but by the end of the year they had achieved a turnover double that of their previous highest total. The cocoa societies have done useful work in improving the quality of the market product. Whereas in 1951–2 most of the cocoa passing through their hands was classified in Grade IV,

[1] *West Africa*, 6 February 1954, p. 100.
[2] *Togoland, Report for the Year 1953*, Col. no. 308, p. 52.
[3] Ibid. *1952*, Col. no. 296, p. 68.

in the following year over 50 per cent. was placed in Grade I; as a consequence, the value of the cocoa marketed was nearly doubled.[1]

There were 20 credit societies described as 'working on sound lines' and, in addition, some of the marketing societies carried out credit work for their members' benefit. The loan system is successful and likely to expand. In spite of these developments the difficulty of recruiting qualified staff continues to be an obstacle to further progress.[2]

THE FRENCH TERRITORIES

French policy regarding the projection of the co-operative system into the Colonial field has differed materially from that of the British. Though there has been in metropolitan France a notable growth of the co-operative organizations which began with the creation of producer societies dealing with wine and wheat and involved in later years a rapid expansion of consumer societies, the movement is, generally speaking, of more recent development than in Great Britain.[3] The French Colonial Administrations were not faced, as were the British, with evidence of the encouragement given by the Governments of British India and Ceylon to the promotion of co-operative organizations.

In the French West African territories the formation of co-operative societies was a sequel to the general use made of an earlier institution, the *société indigène de prévoyance*.[4] This institution was first developed in Algeria, as a contribution to the attempt to remedy the improvidence of the Algerian peasant and, in particular, his habit of disposing of the whole of his crop at harvest-time, thus making it necessary for him either to purchase seed at high cost or to borrow it at exorbitant rates of interest in time for the next season's sowing.[5] The maintenance of reserve seed stores was an essential feature of this system. The legislation needed for the introduction of *sociétés de prévoyance* in Senegal was enacted in 1910.[6] It was then intended that membership of the societies should be voluntary, but the system proved to be of such value, not only for its original purpose but for other allied purposes, that in 1915 membership was made compulsory.[7] The *cotisations* or 'subscriptions' were collected (on the lines of the *centime additionnel* in France) along with the head-tax. The amount of the *cotisation* is fixed by administrative order, but it has usually been a small

---

[1] *Annual Report of the Department of Co-operation. 1953,* See also *West Africa,* 27 November 1954, p. 1111. [2] *Colonial Reports, Sierra Leone, 1953,* pp. 45–46.

[3] M. Digby, *The World Co-operative Movement,* 1948, p. 44.

[4] The full title is *sociétés indigènes de prévoyance, de secours, et de prêts mutuels agricoles;* the usual abbreviation is S.I.P.

[5] Full details are given by K. E. Robinson, 'The Sociétés de Prévoyance in French West Africa', *J.A.A.,* October 1950, pp. 29 ff. See also *Enc. A.O.F.,* vol. i, pp. 321–3.

[6] *Décret,* 29 June 1910.

[7] *Décret,* 8 January 1915. See also *J.A.A.,* October 1950, p. 29.

amount. Each *cercle* now has its society and a number of subdivisions also have societies; the *Commandant du Cercle* (or the *Chef de subdivision*) is *ex officio* President of the Board of Management, the members of which are selected 'in conformity with local custom'. In practice they generally consist of local notables, the *chefs de canton*, and some village Headmen. Each of the eight territories in French West Africa has a supervisory committee, largely official, but including two African notables; the committee manages a Common Fund, to which all societies in the territory make a contribution. This Fund is available for making certain bulk purchases of equipment, and also for loans to individual societies.

The societies have gradually acquired a use which extends far beyond their original purpose. Financed partly by their *cotisations*, and partly by loans from the Common Fund or from the Agricultural Credit Bank, they not only supply seed for sowing but construct dams and wells, supply agricultural equipment, and provide improved transport (such as lorries) for the produce. To that extent they carry out part of the operations which in British territories are the function of a Local Authority operating a Treasury.[1] In addition they have, to a certain extent, assumed the functions of credit societies as sources of short-term loans for the purchase of equipment, and on occasion (though this is much less common) have acted as wholesale vendors of local produce, such as groundnuts. In the past they have in some cases also maintained dispensaries and schools in collaboration with the Health and Education Authorities, and have undertaken the building and management of brick-works and the manufacture of lime. The success achieved in different areas has, it need not be added, varied widely, depending partly on the basic economic conditions or the personal interest shown by officers of the Administration.

The *société de prévoyance* was introduced into French Equatorial Africa in 1937,[2] and in 1950 there existed some 128 societies; there is one society in each subdivision of the territory. The Councils of Management are on the same model as those in French West Africa, and the *cotisation* is also light, amounting in 1947 to an average of only 7 francs.[3] Generally speaking the organization in French Equatorial Africa has had even more of an official character than in French West Africa. In the French Cameroons the system was also inaugurated in 1937, and followed closely the model of the system in force in French West Africa.[4] The societies, of which there is one for each *région administrative*, had received in 1950 loans from the *Fonds Communs*, which amounted in all to 100 million francs. They had to their credit a number of small agricultural stations, that at Dschang, for

---

[1] K. E. Robinson, Address on French West Africa to the Royal Empire Society, 25 January 1954.
[2] *Décret*, 14 January 1937. [3] *Enc. A.E.F.*, pp. 243 ff.
[4] *Décrets*, 7 June 1937. *Arrêtés* 250 and 251, 7 July 1937.

example, dealing primarily with cattle, that at N'Kongsamba with coffee, that at Nanga-Eboko with rice.[1] The system was introduced in the French territory of Togo in 1934,[2] and, though following in general the model of that of French West Africa, differs in the fact that there is no legislative provision permitting the societies to sell local produce. There were in 1951 a total of nine societies; in their case the *cotisation* averaged about $10\frac{1}{2}$ francs. Perhaps the most significant of their services has been the provision of wells for drinking-water, over 500 having been supplied by the end of 1951.

In both French West Africa and Equatorial Africa the *société de prévoyance* has unquestionably been of great benefit to the local peasantry, for it has, apart from other uses, answered the need for some source of revenue substantially under local control and available for small local works.[3] In this aspect it had a close analogy (even down to its method of raising funds by a *centime additionnel*) to the officially controlled District Boards in British India.[4] It proved to be, as in India, a more flexible instrument than could have been supplied by recourse to grants from the Colonial budget. But it has been, in the words of one French observer, 'une organisation para-administrative'.[5] After the First World War an attempt was made in French West Africa to give the organization a less official form by introducing Africans as Presidents of the Boards of Management, but a decree of 1923 reinstated the *Commandant du Cercle* as President.[6] In 1946, however, the *sociétés* came under renewed criticism, partly because of some aspects of their financial management, but mainly because they ran counter to the spirit which was expressed in the creation of the French Union—'révolution politique, mais aussi économique et sociale'. In 1947 the *Conseil de la République* invited the Government to decree the termination of the use of the *sociétés*, both in French West and French Equatorial Africa, and to replace them by agricultural co-operatives[7]—a recommendation which was much criticized at the time by local Administrative Officers as illogical and unrealistic.[8]

The necessary legislation for making this development possible was provided by a law passed in September of the same year,[9] and an Inspector of Co-operative Societies was appointed in the next year. It was subsequently decided that, as the *sociétés de prévoyance* gave place to the new *mutuelles*, the local services for which they had been responsible should be

---

[1] *Enc. C.-T.*, pp. 155–7, 469–72.

[2] *Décret*, 3 November 1934, amended by *décret* of 28 February 1944. *Arrêté*, 7 December 1937.

[3] F. J. Pedler, *West Africa*, 1951, pp. 107 ff. J. Richand-Moland, *Afrique Occidentale Française*, 1949, p. 156. See also M. Dia, in *Le Mouvement coopératif en territoires tropicaux arriérés*, Leiden, 1953, p. 159.

[4] See H. Tinker, *The Foundations of Local Self-Government in India, Pakistan, and Burma*, 1954, pp. 208–14.   [5] Dia, op. cit. p. 131.

[6] *Décrets*, 4 July 1919 and 5 December 1923.   [7] *Résolution*, 22 August 1947.

[8] See, for instance, *Enc. C.-T.*, p. 470.   [9] *Loi* no. 47/1775, 10 September 1947.

supplied by a form of organization now called for short the *Fonds de Génie Rural*.[1] This was designed to make funds available for the support of any local *collectivité* which might be prepared to meet, either in cash or in kind, one-third of the cost of any project for local betterment; such *collectivités* might be either a provident society, a co-operative, or a unit such as a village.

Though there is now a strong sentiment in France to support the change of system, it was not to be expected that there would be rapid progress made in the replacement of the *sociétés de prévoyance* by the new co-operatives or other agencies. In French West Africa the earliest signs of development have been in Senegal; in 1952 there were in Senegal 253 co-operative societies of which 214 related to the marketing of agricultural products. Other territories have not progressed so rapidly, but there were in the same year 50 in the Sudan, four in Mauritania, eight in Upper Volta, 16 in Dahomey, 26 in Niger, and 24 in Guinea.[2] Particular attention has been given in metropolitan France to the marketing of the coffee crop. The French African territories are now the third largest producers of coffee, of which the export in 1954 was estimated at a value of about £20 million. As a precautionary measure to meet a fall in price, and to give assistance to the peasant producer, a decree has been enacted to provide for the creation of a Stabilization Fund controlled by a Board, whose members are in the proportion of one-third each of producers, exporters, and representatives of the local community.[3]

There appears to have been more attention given to the question of co-operation in the French Cameroons than in French Equatorial Africa. The relevant legislation for the Cameroons was passed in 1947.[4] The movement has had some set-backs, notably in the failure of one large society, the *Coopérative des Planteurs Africains*, but in 1951 there were several co-operatives which were operating on a considerable scale, particularly in the export trade: the *Planteurs Bamouns* (dealing with Arabica coffee), the *Planteurs des Manehas* (bananas), the *Coopérative de Bana* (cattle-breeding), and a consumers' co-operative at Yaoundé, are the most prominent.[5] The supervision over these societies is exercised by the *Service de Contrôle des Organismes Coopératifs et des Sociétés de Prévoyance*.[6]

THE BELGIAN TERRITORIES

Until recent years the Administration of the Belgian Congo has shown little concern for the development of co-operative institutions of the normal

---

[1] *Fonds local d'équipement rural et du développement économique et social.*
[2] 'La Situation économique et sociale de l'Afrique Occidentale Française', *Notes et études documentaires*, no. 1834, 9 February 1954, p. 15.
[3] *West Africa*, 30 October 1954, p. 1012.   [4] *Arrêté*, 30 October 1947.
[5] *Rapport annuel à l'Assemblée Générale des Nations Unies sur l'administration du Cameroun, 1951*, pp. 114 ff.   [6] *Arrêté*, 21 January 1949.

type,[1] though it has from an early date recognized the need for providing African peasants with the credit required for the purchase of equipment and the like. This function was in the first instance discharged by the organization known as the *Fonds Spécial de Crédit Agricole Indigène* (F.S.C.A.I.), which was financed partly by the revenues of the Colony and partly by deposits from the Native Treasuries,[2] the *Caisses Administratives des Circonscriptions Indigènes* (C.A.C.I.), but the total transactions were relatively small. More recently the Administration established a Savings Bank, *Caisse d'Épargne du Congo Belge*, which up to 1952 had deposits of roughly 218 million francs, and various missionary bodies had their own Savings Banks, of which those of the Cadulac (the *Centres Agronomiques de l'Université de Louvain au Congo*)[3] were the most important. On the other hand, little official encouragement was given to the formation by Africans of credit societies, or indeed of any other form of co-operative society. A law of 1921[4] provided for the authorization of co-operative societies which 'conformed to the principles of the general law of Belgium', and a small number of European co-operatives were established in pursuance of this provision. A law of 1926 permitted the formation of what were known as *associations professionnelles*,[5] and the subsequent legislation of 1933, which regulated the organization of the Native Authority system, laid down that these Authorities might create, by the sale of produce or by similar means, funds which could be used for the benefit of the *circonscriptions indigènes*.[6]

The most noteworthy approach to the formation of African co-operatives was that of the *Coopérative des Bakongo-Kintuadi ki Bakongo* formed in 1934 under the auspices of the branch of Cadulac at Kisantu. Under the guidance of the local agent of Cadulac this association sold a considerable volume of produce, and maintained its own motor transport. It did not, however, seek authorization under the law of 1921, and in response to pressure from the Government, which was embarrassed by the opposition shown to the undertaking by European traders or colonists, it accepted a formal classification as an *association professionnelle*. It ceased to exist in 1940, when war work made it impossible for the local agent of Cadulac to continue to conduct its operations. Another nominal co-operative, the *Coopérative Agricole des Bena Mitumba*, was maintained between 1936 and 1941 by a mission in Katanga; a third, the *Coopérative de Kirundu*, owed its origin to an official effort to assist the semi-Arab community of Kirundu, but it ceased to exist in 1940.

---

[1] L. O. J. de Wilde, in *Le Mouvement coopératif en territoires tropicaux arriérés*, Leiden, 1953, pp. 43–83.

[2] See above, p. 554.   [3] See above, p. 919.

[4] *Décret*, 23 March 1921, modifying the *décret* of 27 February 1887 on the subject of commercial companies.

[5] *Ordonnance*, 11 February 1926, as amended by the *ordonnance* of 25 September 1937.

[6] *Décret*, 5 December 1933.

Meanwhile there had been established from 1925 onwards a number of undertakings, technically classed as *régies*, conducted by the *Caisses administratives de chefferie*,[1] many of which were described as co-operatives, but were actually maintained under the direction of the local Administrative Officers. These *régies* took various forms. The *agronomats* (which numbered seven) were designed to supply improved seed and tools to local peasants, but they were dissolved after 1936 by the Government, which held that the procedure of trading by which they raised their funds contravened the terms of the law of 1933. Some 21 *laiteries de chefferie* were closed down in 1932, owing, it is said, to the opposition of local colonists; a number of building associations were dissolved in 1936 because they were said to involve unfair competition. Various other societies for promoting local industry, known as co-operatives, suffered the same fate, though a few were allowed to survive in the District of Tanganyika in Ruanda Urundi, as *associations rurales de prévoyance*; 15 remained, however, as agencies of the *circonscriptions indigènes* rather than as co-operative societies of the normal kind.

The Government was clearly faced by a dilemma. Local Administrative Officers were anxious to extend the scope of the activity of the *circonscriptions indigènes*, but any attempt to secure funds by allowing them to deal in produce or to start rural industries was opposed by well-entrenched European trading interests as involving unfair competition, since they were using public money and received the assistance of Officers of the Administration. The official view was, in general, opposed to allowing the free association of Africans for these purposes, foreseeing that the supervision of a large number of autonomous co-operatives was likely to involve the Administration in onerous but thankless responsibilities. During the last few years, however, there has been some change of approach to the question. The Governor-General, in a circular of 1940, questioned whether the existing legislation on co-operative activity could be said to satisfy the needs of the African people. 'Nous sommes dans une impasse; à côté d'entreprises européennes prospères, l'économie indigène végète.' The matter received further consideration in the course of a study of the co-operative system made by a Committee of the *Centre d'Études des Problèmes Sociaux Indigènes* (C.E.P.S.I.) at Elisabethville.[2] The *Conseil Colonial* contemplated in 1947 the experimental formation of co-operatives among the African cotton-growers.[3] There is, it should be added, a strong feeling in favour of the co-operative movement in the ranks of the Labour Party

[1] See above, p. 554.
[2] S. Lauwers, 'Coopératives au Congo Belge', *Bulletin du Centre d'Études des Problèmes Sociaux Indigènes (C.E.P.S.I.)*, no. 4, 1946, pp. 31–50; 'Législation sur les coopératives indigènes', in ibid. no. 7, 1948, pp. 5–16. F. Grévisse, 'Coopérations et coopératives', ibid. pp. 17–44. M. Gerlache, 'Coopératives indigènes et expérience belge', ibid. pp. 45–55.
[3] See Article 37 of the *Décret sur la culture du coton*, 18 June 1947.

in Belgium; co-operative activity is prominent among the industrial workers in the metropolitan coalfields, steelworks, and textile works.

The result of the new approach was seen in legislation enacted in 1949,[1] which was designed to provide a law better suited to the needs of the African peasant. A special service has been created both at headquarters and in the provinces to deal with African co-operatives,[2] and it is noticeable that the law provides for the official appointment of an educative committee to a co-operative society, in order to provide it with advice and guidance. Registered societies must have a 'manager' (*gérant*), assisted by a management board. It remains to be seen how far the new law will succeed in promoting co-operation among Africans in the face of the opposition of European trading interests and the apprehensions felt by Administrative Officers. There had, however, already been considerable progress by the end of 1952. There were then 38 co-operatives registered under the law of 1949, of which 25 were rural producer societies (mainly concerned with cotton), eight trading or artisan, and five consumer societies. Of these societies 19 had European managers. In the course of 1952 loans amounting to nearly 8 million francs were granted to the Native societies.[3] The consumer societies had a membership of 2,040 and the producer societies a membership of 68,537. Of those registered under the 1921 *décret* there remained five of the former with 4,298 members, and five of the latter with a membership of 64. The measures taken must be regarded, to some extent, as tentative.[4] It is noticeable, for instance, that the existence of the producer societies has not been allowed to touch the powerful cotton monopoly interest. The law of 1949 applied also to Ruanda Urundi; seven societies were registered in 1952.[5]

THE PORTUGUESE TERRITORIES

The Portuguese Authorities have shown a noticeable hesitation in regard to the extension of co-operative institutions among the African, or, more correctly, the *não-civilizada* section of the population.[6] Mozambique is described as still being 'in a pre-cooperative phase'. In other words, the Administration is still engaged in experiments which will decide whether Africans can yet be entrusted to form institutions of this type. The most important of the experiments made so far have been in the Chibuto District of the Province of Sul do Save, where, after a preparatory study lasting five years, a multi-purpose society, described as a co-operative,

---

[1] *Décret*, 10 August 1949.
[2] A branch of the *Service des Affaires Indigènes et de la Main-d'œuvre*.
[3] *Rapport sur l'administration de la colonie du Congo Belge, 1952*, pp. 99–100.
[4] G. Malengreau, 'Recent Developments in Belgian Africa', in *Africa Today*, 1955, p. 344.
[5] *Rapport sur l'administration belge du Ruanda-Urundi, 1952*, p. 343.
[6] See above, p. 231.

was formed in 1950. Membership of the society is voluntary, except on the part of the Chiefs; its affairs are conducted by a committee of two members and the respective African Chiefs, under the chairmanship of the District Administrator. The precedent set in Chibuto has been followed in three centres in Manica District and one in the Beira District. These societies are, for the present, mainly concerned in improving local cultivation, in providing ploughs and other equipment, and in marketing production. So far, therefore, the move made towards the introduction of co-operative institutions is only tentative; the hesitation expressed in official declarations on the subject clearly reflects apprehensions lest the formation of societies of the normal character might prejudice the interests of European traders.

Although the extension of the co-operative movement has been advocated by progressive opinion in Angola, it has hitherto made little progress. This is partly due to the conservatism of the European population, who have opposed the adoption of the practice of co-operation among Africans as likely to be detrimental to their own interests; and partly to the fact that the co-operative system as practised elsewhere is not readily reconcilable with the Portuguese ideal of a Corporative State. Angola is more remote from the agricultural developments taking place in other parts of Africa than is Mozambique, and it is to be expected that the success of the experiments being tested in the eastern territory will be carefully studied before being introduced in the western.

CHAPTER XXII

MINERALS AND MINES

MINERALS and the mining industry have an exceptional significance in the history of that part of Africa which lies south of the Sahara. In the remote past it was the quest for precious metals which established the contact of the Arabs with Africa, and in an era of which we have fuller knowledge it was responsible for the Portuguese settlements on both the east and west coasts.[1] Elizabethan England, when it thought of Africa, spoke in Ancient Pistol's phrase of 'golden joys', and the guinea took its name from the coin struck in the seventeenth century by the Company of Royal Adventurers of England trading in Africa. While the slave trade brought nothing but moral and material loss to Africa, it can be claimed for the mineral industry that, in the words of Dr. Frankel, 'The modern economic history of Africa dates from the mineral discoveries in the southern portion of the continent. These inaugurated the investment of foreign resources, and therewith commenced that revolutionary process through which Africa is being incorporated in the income-creating activities of the world.'[2] When once European Powers had committed themselves to establish sovereignty over the vast territories in Africa, capital had to be diverted to them in order to make their rule effective. In the British territories such capital as was forthcoming for development was at the outset derived only from Government loans and grants-in-aid. It was the opportunity offered for the investment in mineral exploitation that subsequently made investment in Africa popular with the European money market, and capital investment of this nature has been largely instrumental in producing the revenues which have enabled so many of the Colonial Governments to extend the scope of their economic and social services for the public benefit. Although a wide range of other commodities has now come on to the export market, yet mineral exports still have a very high place among the total exports from Africa.

The events of recent years have tended to increase the importance of the industry. During the course of the Second World War, Great Britain and her Allies were able to find in Africa a wide range of metals needed as raw material for the weapons of modern warfare. A new factor was the part played in the war by the United States, which with its great economic strength was able to support the extraction of strategic materials in this as well as other parts of the world. This war-time development has continued in the post-war period, for, after the outbreak of the Korean War in 1950,

[1] See above, p. 381. [2] S. H. Frankel, *Capital Investment in Africa*, 1938, pp. 2, 20.

there was a concerted effort to accelerate mineral exploitation. The United States has continued to play an important role in restoring the economic strength of the countries of Western Europe and their Colonial possessions, and, under the European Recovery Programme, the Mutual Security Aid Programme, and the so-called Point Four policy, the material aid afforded has in more than one instance been directed primarily into mineral development in Africa. There have in addition been established a number of new organizations, such as the International Bank for Reconstruction and Development (I.B.R.D.) and the United Nations Technical Assistance Board, which have given direct assistance to the development of schemes of mining or other forms of exploitation of minerals.

It has not seemed desirable to separate in the following pages the position of the precious metals from other minerals, although gold has a special position of its own. As a commodity it has the advantage that the producer is always sure of a market at a relatively stable price. Since the Second World War there has been only one major change in the price of gold when, in September 1949, its price in terms of many currencies, except the dollar, was increased from the equivalent of 172s. 6d. to 248s. per fine ounce. By the end of 1950, however, the gain accruing from the devaluation of sterling was absorbed in increased costs due largely to inflation, and the mines were faced with rising costs and falling profits. Of all commodities only the price of gold remained unchanged.[1] In the Union of South Africa rising costs were to some extent offset by the practice of selling 40 per cent. of the gold production at premium prices in 'processed' form. In 1953, however, the margin between the official price of U.S. $35 per fine ounce and the price of gold on the 'free' market caused the increment obtained by processing to disappear, and the Government abolished the requirement that 40 per cent. of 'premium' gold must be exported in 'processed' form.[2] In 1953 the premium finally disappeared as the result of a combination of circumstances though, when the London gold market was reopened early in 1954, a small premium again developed. Nearly all producers have reopened their pre-war contacts in London and now sell the greater part of their output there. In other instances, for example in Southern Rhodesia, the Governments have introduced special subsidies to relieve the plight of the gold industry.[3]

To some extent the diamond industry also falls into a special category. Enterprises which have incurred heavy outlay in development are always at the risk of a change in demand or of a chance discovery which may flood the market with cheaply produced stones and may thus involve an expensive accumulation of stocks. In fact, however, agreements negotiated

[1] For a discussion of the effects of the stable official gold price, see W. J. Busschau, *The Measure of Gold*, 1949.
[2] *Overseas Economic Surveys, Union of South Africa, 1953*, p. 30.   [3] See below, p. 1498.

between the major suppliers—including in one instance the South African Government—have been successful in keeping excessive supplies of diamonds off the market.[1] Moreover, the extensive use of industrial diamonds, particularly during and after the war, has been a stabilizing factor in the demand.

THE EARLY WORKING OF MINERALS BY AFRICANS

Evidence of the early working of minerals by Africans has something more than an historical interest, for it is clear that the traces of ancient workings have in more than one case afforded a valuable guide to modern prospectors. Long before the Christian era gold deposits in Ethiopia were known to seafaring races trading on the shores of the Indian Ocean, and it was 'the odour of gold', to quote the Portuguese historian, João de Barros, which attracted Arabs to settle on the south-eastern coast.[2] Glowing accounts of mineral wealth stimulated a number of Portuguese expeditions to the coast-lands and to the interior where Monomotapa ruled at Sofala. They found the indigenous peoples extracting gold by primitive methods and carrying off in quills the few grains which they had won. There is no direct evidence to show what was the total value of the gold derived from these expeditions, but one computation has placed it as high as £75 million. In Southern Rhodesia the 'ancient workings' are certainly of remote origin.[3] As recently as the Matabele invasion of Mashonaland, gold was being worked between the Umsweswe and Umfuli rivers, and the tradition that rich ground was to be found in the old diggings acted as a great incentive to the early pioneers in Southern Rhodesia.[4] In Northern Rhodesia the old mine workings scattered over a wide area guided the first prospecting party sent from Bulawayo in 1899 which discovered the Kansanshi mine[5] and located many of the larger copper deposits in the Katanga.

On the west coast the indigenous inhabitants have extracted gold and worked tin-mines for an unknown period. In the fourteenth and fifteenth centuries the gold for the coinage of Portugal, Spain, and Italy is said to have come exclusively from West Africa. The exploitation of the existing West African gold-fields was due to the discovery that deposits at Tarkwa were still being worked by Africans,[6] and the same is true of the tin deposits in Nigeria.

---

[1] See below, p. 1489.
[2] S. R. Welch, *Europe's Discovery of South Africa*, 1935, p. 58.
[3] T. A. Rickard, *Man and Metals*, vol. i, 1932, p. 243.
[4] A. MacGregor, 'Mining and Mineral Resources of Southern Rhodesia', reprinted from *Sands, Clays and Minerals*, vol. ii, no. 4, April 1936, p. 4.
[5] See below, p. 1502.   [6] See below, pp. 1508, 1510.

THE MINERAL INDUSTRY IN DIFFERENT TERRITORIES

The Union of South Africa

In a study of the mineral industry of the African continent, South Africa must occupy the premier place. The Union has played a leading (indeed a pioneer) part in the economic transformation of the continent and, as has been pointed out, it is to its mining industry and to the extent of the external capital which the industry has attracted, that it owes a very substantial measure of its own development. In the history of the mineral industry diamonds led the way and must be given first place.[1]

Dr. Frankel has recalled[2] the prophetic remark of the Colonial Secretary when in 1867 he laid upon the table of the Cape House of Assembly one of the earliest of the diamonds discovered in South Africa. 'This is the rock on which the future success of South Africa will be built.' Though, however, the first diamond was found in that year, it was not until 1870 that there were discoveries which served to attract a considerable number of prospectors to the banks of the Vaal river. The exploitation of the original alluvial diggings or the picking over of dry gravel along the river-beds required little capital, and the same is true of the subsequent 'dry diggings', which continued until about 1885. At first the diamond 'pipes', and notably those of Kimberley, were worked under conditions suited to alluvial diggings, in small and much subdivided claims, but these methods became impossible as the deposits were followed deeper into the earth. In addition the unrestricted sales soon began to depress market values, and it became clear that without capital and an effective organization neither subterranean mining nor the control of production were possible. The claims were therefore consolidated into joint-stock companies, and the five companies which then held most of the properties were subsequently consolidated in 1885 and the following years by Cecil Rhodes, C. D. Rudd and others on behalf of the De Beers Mining Company. The total market value of the properties thus amalgamated was placed at a little below £23½ million. At first the Company under-estimated the richness of the Premier mine near Pretoria, but eventually it acquired a controlling interest in this property also. It is noteworthy that up to the time of this amalgamation financial interests outside South Africa had invested only a negligible sum in diamond mining.

The major problem which the amalgamated Companies had to face at the time was over-production and the consequent effect of widely fluctuating prices. The products of the alluvial diggings did not, however, at first threaten the prosperity of the mines. From the beginning, the diggings scattered along the Vaal river in Griqualand West and extending to Klerksdorp in the Transvaal had provided employment for

---

[1] See above, p. 1485.   [2] Frankel, op. cit. p. 52.

numerous small companies and individuals. In the periodic 'rushes' only a few of these undertakings were successful, and the rest of the individuals engaged drifted back to the towns and the farms. The bulk of the diggers lived in extreme poverty; in 1929 about 45 per cent. of those working the Transvaal were stated to be living on an average of £5 a month or less.[1] Until after the First World War the output of alluvial stones did not exceed 10 per cent. of the total production of the Union, but following the first really scientific attempt to trace the origin of the Vaal alluvial diamonds, rich deposits were found in the Lichtenburg and Rustenburg Districts of the Transvaal. The Government threw open the Lichtenburg fields, and within a year there were stated to be over 180,000 people living there. Between 1925 and 1927 the production of alluvial stones rose steeply, while the average value per carat, which normally was three times that of mined stones, fell from nearly £8 to a little over £2½. In the same period the production of the mines remained roughly constant, and the controlling companies were forced to buy up large quantities of alluvial diamonds to maintain prices.

The next threat to the stability of the industry came from Namaqualand, where the existence of diamonds, though known for many years, had not attracted attention until in 1925–7 Dr. Merensky showed that diamondiferous ground extended for over 100 miles southward from the Orange river mouth and northwards into South-West Africa. Free production in this rich field would obviously have destroyed the market. In 1927 the Precious Stones Act was passed and the Government prohibited prospecting in the Namaqualand area, except for 100 discoverers' claims allocated to the Merensky Syndicate and an area on the Buffels river south of Port Nolloth operated by the Cape Coast Exploration Company. A valuable block of 20 square miles was subsequently reserved as Government diggings, and the State thus acquired a direct interest as a producer and marketer of diamonds. The Act made, at the same time, an important change in the law relating to alluvial diggings. It preserved to private landowners the exclusive prospecting rights on their own land, but enabled regulations to be made which, while allowing for the grant of permits to diggers, in effect excluded all companies and syndicates. A limit could henceforth be fixed on the total amount of alluvial production, and limitations imposed on the number of diggers' permits issued in any area. These measures, together with the exhaustion of the Lichtenburg fields, materially reduced the output of alluvial stones in 1930.

As early as 1893 a syndicate (the London Diamond Buying Syndicate) had been formed to market all the diamonds of the main South African producers, and after the First World War it made agreements also with the South-West African interests. But other countries, as for example

---

[1] *Report of Carnegie Commission on the Poor White Problem in South Africa*, 1932, Part I, p. 153.

the Belgian Congo and Angola, began to assume prominence in the industry, and whereas South Africa had produced 76 per cent. of the world output in 1913, the proportion had in 1925 dropped to 57 per cent. By this time the Syndicate had ceased to be a reliable check, and in 1925 a Diamond Control Act was passed which enabled the Union Government to control the mining and disposal of stones in the absence of an approved producers' agreement. The mines thereupon set up a more influential syndicate, and its operation and the abnormal demand that existed during the 'boom' period in the United States (which took 80 per cent. of world production) helped to protect the market from the shocks caused by the increase in supplies from the Transvaal and Namaqualand alluvial fields, which have been referred to above. But the economic crisis of 1929 again placed the industry in difficulties, and the De Beers interest eventually floated a new organization (the Diamond Corporation Limited) which opened the way for an agreement between De Beers and the Government. Each member of the association now established, including the Government, received a fixed percentage of the trade, and the actual sale of diamonds was entrusted to a subsidiary, the Diamond Trading Company Limited. Further, the Corporation, under agreement with the companies working deposits in the Belgian Congo, Angola, and British West Africa, bought all their stones and marketed them together with the South African diamonds through the same channels. In 1950 the life of the Diamond Producers' Association, as it is now known, was extended for another six years. A crisis was threatened in 1950 when the Williamson interests in Tanganyika[1] declined to come into line with the South African producers, but an amicable settlement was subsequently reached. Satisfactory arrangements have also been made between the Producers' Association and diamond interests in the Portuguese territories.

From the date of the discovery of the diamond fields up to the end of 1954 the value of the diamond production in the Union (excluding South-West Africa) has been estimated at about £490 million. From the establishment of the Union of South Africa in 1908 up to 1936 the State received over £32 million in taxation of, and share of profits from, diamond mining.[2] Since the greater part of the capital invested in the industry has been supplied from within the Union the benefit to its economy has been of a high order. But the indirect benefits have been no less marked. A large part of the profits of the diamond industry went towards the establishment of the Witwatersrand gold-mines, and the experience gained in the 'rationalization' of the diamond industry contributed largely to the success of the subsequent organization of the gold-mines in the Rand.

The modern gold-mining industry of South Africa may be said to date from 1886, when the first mines came into operation on the Witwatersrand.

---

[1] See below, p. 1506.   [2] Frankel, op. cit. p. 53.

But there had been an earlier period when the production of gold had followed a course which in many respects resembled that taken by the diamond industry in its earlier stages. In South Africa the earliest systematic effort to discover minerals had been made by the Dutch East India Company, which introduced miners from Europe in 1669 and succeeded in tracing the source of copper ore which Natives had brought down to Cape Town from Namaqualand in 1681. No steps were, however, taken by the Government to develop this, and subsequent prospecting was left to private enterprise. Almost from the first days of colonization it was believed that the Transvaal was rich in gold deposits, but in spite of the offer of £5,000 for the discovery of a really rich gold occurrence no development actually took place until the German geologist, Karl Mauch, reported gold in Mashonaland in Southern Rhodesia. A stamp-mill was set up as early as 1869 at Tati, now included in the Bechuanaland Protectorate.[1] These discoveries, and the finding of diamonds at Hopetown in 1867,[2] greatly stimulated prospecting, and the next 20 years saw a small gold rush to the alluvial gold-fields of Lydenburg, the opening of the Sheba mine at Barberton, and the beginning of reef-mining on the Witwatersrand in 1884. The first Company registered in England with the purpose of bringing the Rand gold-fields to the attention of the investing public in Great Britain was launched by C. D. Rudd and C. J. Rhodes in 1887.[3] There followed the Rand 'boom' of 1889, which greatly stimulated the interest of the foreign investor in the gold industry of the Union. Henceforth its development lay in the hands of large capitalistic enterprise. But, as has just been observed, the achievement of this stage of development was rendered possible mainly by the efforts of those who had previously been responsible for the organization of the diamond industry and who were thus able to secure the attention of the foreign money markets for the new source of investment in the Rand.

In the Witwatersrand the reefs consist of beds of conglomerate, composed mainly of quartz pebbles bound together by siliceous cement containing iron pyrites, the whole being designated as 'banket'. The occurrence of gold in the sedimentary deposit presented mining engineers with new conditions, for hitherto most of the world's gold output had come from alluvial deposits and quartz veins. While the Rand is the most consistent field yet found, considerable fluctuations in value occur, and in all mines a large proportion of the ore is low-grade.[4] In the early days only the outcrop was worked, but of later years mining at a great depth has been undertaken, though at increased cost of production. Some mines are

[1] E. A. Walker, *A History of South Africa*, 2nd ed., 1940. *N.A.*, Part V, pp. 230–1.
[2] G. F. Williams, *The Diamond Mines of South Africa*, 1902.
[3] Frankel, op. cit. pp. 79 ff.
[4] *Mineral Resources of the Union of South Africa*, Pretoria, 1940.

nearly 10,000 feet deep, and formidable problems of heat and ventilation have to be faced. Individuals and small companies had been able to work the outcrops, but within a few years of the boom of 1889 it had become clear that the development of gold-mining on the Rand demanded a high degree of organization and a large expenditure of capital. Excess of company promotion and speculation had caused a general loss of confidence; in 1893 out of 183 gold-mining companies in the Transvaal 104 had produced no gold. The need to ensure stability in finance and greater working efficiency led by gradual steps to the adoption of a system under which control was placed in the hands of powerful corporations known as groups or houses. Many advantages flow from this system, of which the efficient mobilization of large sums of capital, particularly from overseas investors, is perhaps the principal.[1] Owing to the fact that the general public are less inclined than formerly to subscribe to speculative investment, capital is now provided in the first instance in the form of loans from the groups or houses rather than by the issue of shares to the public. One benefit of this method is that it attracts capital from institutional sources in the United Kingdom and elsewhere; another is the centralization of technical services. There is a further advantage in the system. In order to eliminate competition between the mines for African labour, all the mines belonging to the Transvaal and Orange Free State Chamber of Mines now recruit African labour through two agencies only, the Native Recruiting Corporation and the Witwatersrand Native Labour Association.[2]

Until 1948 the centre of gravity of the gold industry in the Union was unquestionably in the Witwatersrand, but the phenomenal 'strikes' in boreholes sunk near Odendaalsrus in the Orange Free State opened a new era in South African gold-mining.[3] On this discovery there ensued an intense interest in the Orange Free State developments among the large mining houses in Johannesburg. Very large sums of capital were required for development of the new gold-field, and it is evidence of the strength of the group system that the money was forthcoming, largely from overseas investors. By 1954 some £130 million had already been expended on capital works.[4] The four new towns—Virginia, Welkom, Allanridge, and Odendaalsrus—contained a population of 35,000 Europeans and 70,000 Natives in 1954, and were expected ultimately to accommodate 150,000 and 250,000 respectively.[5] There are at present 13 mines, of which the eighth came into production at the end of 1954. Output for that year amounted to $1\frac{1}{4}$ million fine ounces, or roughly $8\frac{1}{2}$ per cent. of the total production of the Union.[6] To some extent, therefore,

[1] On the group system, see Frankel, op. cit. pp. 81 ff. [2] See above, p. 1406.
[3] S.A.S., no. 87, 31 July 1954, p. 12. [4] Ibid.
[5] The Times, 13 December 1954. [6] S.A.S., no. 98, 15 February 1955, p. 10.

the new gold-field has served to stave off the decline in the gold output of
the Union, which appeared to be inevitable owing to the growing cost
of production at continually increasing depths and the rise in the cost of
equipment and labour.

On the Witwatersrand itself development has tended to move south-
westwards. The Blyvooruitzicht mine in this area, which has recently
come into full operation, is now one of the leading producers in the
country. On the Central and East Rand a number of the old producing
mines have already been forced by the pressure of declining profits to
cease operations, and in the Far East Rand the sight of derelict headgear
is testimony to the failure of the search for an eastward extension of the
main reef. Gold is also worked in the Klerksdorp area, and in the Potgietersrus area there has been a continuous series of experimental borings.
In some of the older areas of production, such as Barberton and Lydenburg, gold is no longer of material importance. It is estimated that
throughout the country the present output can be maintained for another
30 to 35 years, but if costs could be sufficiently controlled to allow mining
to be taken to a depth of 13,000 feet, this period could be prolonged for
a further 20 years.[1] The total reserves of profitable ore are computed to
be worth more than £6,636 million at the current price of gold.[2]

There are no reliable figures of the out-turn of gold in the Soviet Union,
but none of the other countries in the world have a production equal to
that of South Africa. On the published figures, it contributed in 1953
nearly half of the world's production, which was valued at £290 million.[3]
Production in the Union increased in 1955 to a value of £182·7 million,
of which the Transvaal mines contributed about £150½ million.[4] Since
the beginning of gold-mining in the Union, rather more than 80 years
ago, the value of the gold produced has exceeded £3,000 million, and it
has been estimated that half the population of the country is directly or
indirectly dependent upon the industry.[5] According to the estimate made
by Dr. Frankel the mean yield to capital invested in the Rand between the
years 1887 and 1932 amounted to 4·1 per cent. per annum,[6] but this low
figure conceals not only a vast range of different returns of varying degrees
of profit, but also the heavy capital costs of a long period of preparation
before a mine can be brought into production. This type of expenditure
was always heavy, but today, it may be noted, a new shaft sunk in the
Orange Free State might cost anything up to £13 million, and a mine
may take up to six years to come into production.[7] It is not easy to state
the total amount of capital that has been invested up to date in the Rand

[1] *Overseas Economic Surveys, Union of South Africa, 1953*, p. 31.
[2] *S.A.S.*, no. 90, 30 September 1954, p. 7.
[3] Ibid. no. 91, 15 October 1954, p. 7.   [4] Ibid. no. 98, 15 February 1955, p. 9.
[5] *Overseas Economic Surveys, Union of South Africa, 1953*, pp. 28–31.
[6] Frankel, op. cit. p. 91.   [7] *The Economist*, 28 August 1954.

mines, but Dr. Frankel estimated that up to the end of 1932 they had absorbed some £200 million of capital, of which roughly £120 million had come from overseas.[1] In May 1955 there were approximately 326,000 Africans employed in the mines.[2]

South Africa's gold is closely associated with uranium, which has become of cardinal importance in the development of atomic energy. The existence of uranium-bearing ores in the conglomerate deposits of the Witwatersrand had been known as long ago as 1923, but it was not until 1945 that serious efforts to exploit the deposits were made. It is now known that this area includes one of the largest accessible deposits of uranium in the world. In November 1950 a Tripartite Agreement between the South African, British, and American Governments resulted in long-term contracts for the production of uranium being made with a number of gold-producers. It is understood that the capital for installing the expensive extraction plant was provided in the first instance by the British and American Governments. The production of uranium can now be undertaken only by agreement with the Minister of Mines. Agreements have been concluded with 27 gold-mines, of which 20 were producing by 1956. It has been authoritatively stated that production is running at the rate of £36 million a year,[3] and it has been forecast that the ultimate yearly value may reach £50 million. In at least two cases the profits from uranium have made it possible for gold-mines to continue in production.

Among other mineral products of South Africa coal is of particular importance, for not only has it been a useful source of foreign exchange either as an export or in bunkers for ships calling at the Union's harbours, but it is of basic importance to the country's rapidly growing secondary industries.[4] There is evidence that the existence of coal in Natal was known to the tribesmen long before the early trekkers arrived in 1839. It was first commercially exploited in 1852, but no serious development occurred until the advent of the railways in Natal in 1881.[5] In the Transvaal, coal-mining began at Bethal in 1868, but it was not until the discovery of the gold-fields 20 years later that it became commercially interesting. As a result of the geological formations which placed the coal deposits in the Union (as elsewhere in Africa) close to the surface, the cost of South African coal bears favourable comparison with that in other countries. Production in 1954 totalled over 32 million tons. An interesting development has been the establishment near Vereeniging of an installation designed to produce petroleum and petroleum products by the gasification of coal; it was financed at a cost of £31 million by the Government. It is, moreover, expected that the South African Coal, Oil, and Gas

[1] Frankel, op. cit. p. 89.
[2] *The Times, Annual Financial Review*, 24 October 1955.
[3] Ibid.   [4] See above, p. 1287.   [5] See below, p. 1547.

Corporation (SASOL) will provide the raw materials for a new chemical industry.

The manganese deposits near Postmasburg in the Cape Province, which were discovered in 1922, occur in two belts extending over 40 miles; most of the ore is of low grade, with only 40 to 48 per cent. manganese. The lack of transport has been a hindrance in its development, but some relief will be afforded when the rail link to Sishen or Kathu is completed. At present two companies work the deposits, and about 90 per cent. of the output is exported. It was estimated in 1943 that assuming a production of 500,000 tons of ore a year, the reserves would last for 30 years.[1] The Union possesses large deposits of low-grade chrome situated in the central Transvaal. The output in 1952 totalled 458,000 tons, most of it being used in the metallurgical and chemical industries.

Copper is not extensively found in the Union, but there are deposits in Namaqualand and at Messina in the Transvaal. The total output in 1953 amounted only to 38,850 tons. There are very large deposits of iron ores. It was estimated in 1928 that the reserves may total 6,000 million tons,[2] and recent prospecting in the Postmasburg area indicates still greater amounts of high-grade ore. The bulk of the ore is at present mined at Thabazimbi in the Rustenburg District of the Transvaal, but a new mine of high-grade ore near Kuruman has already come into production. The existence of large deposits of iron ore, coupled with the presence of easily accessible supplies of coal, have led to a rapid development of the iron and steel industry. The State has taken a major part both in the development of the works of the Iron and Steel Corporation (ISCOR) near Pretoria, and in the recent expansion of the new Vanderbijl Park Steel Works at Vereeniging. New developments are taking place in the use of medium- and low-quality ores at places such as Machadodorp, where the Dominion Iron and Steel Corporation is preparing for an annual output of 70,000 tons, using the Krupp-Renn process of treating the low-grade siliceous ore, and at Witbank, where the object is to produce vanadium slag and pig-iron from the vanadium-titanium-iron ores found at Onderstepoort near Pretoria.

Of other base metals the output of tin is still below the Union's requirements. Rooiberg is the main centre for its production, the smelting being carried out at Zaaiplaats. The search for *galena* (lead) has been stimulated by high prices, but little of real importance has been discovered. Asbestos has, since the war, experienced a chequered history. Until recently production failed to keep pace with the demand, but later the demand fell away and supplies became excessive. The Union's deposits, which include

[1] A. W. Postel, *The Mineral Resources of Africa*, 1943, p. 21.
[2] P. H. Wagner, *The Iron Deposits of the Union of South Africa*, Union of South Africa Geographical Survey Memoir no. 26, 1928.

all five major forms of the mineral, are to be found mainly in the Transvaal near Barberton and in the Cape Province. Output of all varieties has been increasing, and most of it is exported to the United States. Antimony is found in the Murchison Range of the northern Transvaal and, under the stimulus of high prices, output has been greatly expanded. The mineral beryl used in copper smelting is found occasionally, but prospecting is controlled by the Atomic Energy Board. Nickel arises as a by-product in platinum extraction, and an occurrence at Insizwa in East Griqualand is being investigated. The Union is reputed to have the largest known deposits of vermiculite in the world, situated at Palabora in the northern Transvaal. It is used extensively in building and insulating operations. A rich deposit of titanium, which finds extensive use in the aircraft industry, has been found near East London.

Of the precious metals other than gold, the Union is the principal source of platinum in Africa. This is produced by two mines in the Rustenburg District, and developments, including the greater use of electric power, are expected to raise output still farther. Silver is produced mainly as a by-product of gold.

The country has large phosphate deposits, which are now acquiring increasing importance as the source of fertilizers for agriculture. The main centre of production is at Langebaan in the Cape Province. Of particular moment is the acquisition by the State of the deposits at Palabora in the northern Transvaal, and the setting up of a special public corporation (FOSKAR) for developing them. The value of total mineral production in the Union in 1955 was nearly £290 million.

In recent years it has been increasingly realized that South-West Africa is unusually rich in a considerable variety of minerals. Copper has attracted particular attention, and several American companies are actively engaged in mining the deposits at Tsumeb in the Grootfontein District. They were originally worked on a small scale by Natives, but subsequently exploited on a large scale by the Germans. The mine contains a base-metal complex comprising copper, lead, and zinc. The oxidized zone has now been exhausted, revealing proved reserves of concentrates of copper, lead, and zinc, thus ensuring profitable working for a long period. A narrow-gauge railway connecting the mine with Swakopmund was completed by the Germans in 1906, but it has been inadequate to transport the plant required for modern development and has been supplemented by heavy motor traction. Up to 1940 about a million tons of high-grade copper had been exported to Germany, but in 1940 the mine was flooded, and the water was not finally pumped out until 1948. Since then, however, a smelter and floatation plant have been installed. The principal products of the mine are now lead and zinc. The Khad mines near Swakopmund were worked until 1925 and supplied considerable quantities of copper concentrates until flood water inundated the property and the mines were closed down.

There are occasional occurrences of beryl; in 1952 the production was 660 tons. Economic deposits of graphite were developed near Bethanie, but became exhausted in 1952, when production ceased. Tin has been discovered in a large area south-west of the Erongo mountains, but the alluvial deposits are now almost exhausted and future development will depend on quartz bodies. Tungsten exists near Omaruru, where a mine, closed in 1944, was reopened in 1951. The Abenab mine in the Groot-fontein District, once of some importance, now continues to produce a small quantity of vanadium. Two extensive fields of iron ore are reported in the Kaokoveld area, and investigation is now proceeding with a view to removing chemically the impurities in the ore. If the result is favourable, it is proposed to construct a new railway and port at Rocky Point, at a probable cost of £30 million.[1] There are extensive deposits of phosphate, and the large accumulations of sea-bird guano are preserved by the exceptional aridity of the Namib desert. The rich diamond field in the south of the territory has already been referred to. In 1955 diamond production was 802,340 carats, valued at £14·4 million.

The High Commission Territories

Bechuanaland has a considerable variety of mineral occurrences, but for the most part on a scale that does not permit of economic working. It has, however, a place of some distinction in the history of the gold industry since, as previously mentioned, Tati, on the north-east boundary of the Protectorate, was the site of the first gold-mine worked in South Africa. The original Concession obtained from Lobengula in 1869 was renewed in 1880 in favour of the London and Limpopo Company; it subsequently passed into the hands of the Tati Concession Mining and Exploration Company, the predecessor of the present Tati Company Limited. The Concession was explicitly excluded from the area granted by Charter to the British South Africa Company.[2] The mines do not now produce any significant quantity of gold: the total production of the Protectorate declined from 11,297 ounces in 1945 to 1,216 ounces in 1954. Some years ago an unsuccessful effort was made to foster asbestos mining as a village industry at Moshaneng near Kanye; a South African mining house which had taken over the management produced in 1952 a total of 448 tons. Deposits of kyanite are now being worked in the Tati District. The Colonial Development Corporation has provided for a comprehensive geological survey and a large part of the Protectorate has already been examined. An interim Report refers to the probable existence of a 'con-

[1] S.A.S., no. 90, 30 September 1954, p. 9.
[2] See N.A., Part V, pp. 231 ff.

cealed coalfield', which is presumed to be an extension of the Waterberg coalfield in the Transvaal; its economic value has yet to be determined.

In Basutoland the Administration had in the past discouraged prospecting, mainly out of consideration for the apprehensions of the Basuto, who, warned by the fate of Swaziland,[1] feared that extension of mining would involve a threat to their lands. In 1938, however, a reconnaissance geological survey was carried out, and concluded that there was little mineral deposit of commercial value to be found. Thin seams of coal in the Mohales Hoek area have been observed, but do not appear to be of value. There are several deposits of kimberlite, and there have long been local stories of the existence of diamonds. These were not substantiated until 1955 when a pipe of diamonds was discovered at the Kau stream in north-eastern Basutoland by the Basutoland Diamond Corporation, which has the monopoly of prospecting for diamonds in the Protectorate.[2]

Much more is known about the mineral deposits in Swaziland and, indeed, the mining industry plays an important part in the country's economy. Asbestos is the mineral of major importance in the territory; the production in 1954 was over 30,000 short tons, valued at over £2 million. It is a high-grade chrysotile and is mined almost exclusively from the Havelock mine in the north-west of the territory.[3] Production of gold declined steadily after the Second World War and ceased altogether in 1952, due not so much to the exhaustion of the ore as to insufficient capital. Tin production is extremely small, but increasing.

In 1942 funds were provided by a grant made under the Colonial Development and Welfare Act for establishing a Geological Survey Department, and in 1950 a Mining Advisory Board was formed to advise the Administration on mineral development. More than one-third of the country has since been geologically surveyed. Large reserves of barytes have been proved in the Mbabane District, and a small quantity produced. Deposits of coal, diaspore, haematite, and a number of other minerals have also been found. Throughout the three High Commission Territories, and more especially in Swaziland, mineral development has been handicapped by the complications of mineral legislation—a subject to which reference will be made later in this chapter.

The Federation of Rhodesia and Nyasaland

Minerals form a very important part of the export of the Federation; in 1954 their value was £107 million, out of a total export valued at £153 million.[4] Under the Constitution of the Federation minerals are a subject

[1] Ibid. pp. 339, 403–14.
[2] *Africa Digest*, September 1955, p. 9.
[3] *Colonial Reports, Swaziland, 1953*, pp. 23, 63. *N.A.*, Part V, p. 339.
[4] Central African Statistical Office, *Monthly Digest of Statistics*, vol. ii, no. 7, p. 11.

for territorial, not Federal, legislation, and it will be convenient to deal here separately with each territory.

The discovery of gold in Bechuanaland and in South Africa, added to the old-standing tradition of the existence of gold in Matabeleland, gave a great stimulus to the early activities of the British South Africa Company. The grant by Lobengula of the Rudd Concession,[1] which was subsequently acquired by the Company, had given it the sole control of all minerals in his kingdom, and it proceeded in the first instance by the grant of licences to individual prospectors. The pioneers who accompanied the first expedition to Mashonaland began prospecting near ancient workings, without, however, finding a gold-field of any importance. The ore deposits are intermittent, and many, which might in other circumstances have been neglected, were exploited, except in parts of Mashonaland where the relative lack of communications caused some potentially good districts to be overlooked.

Gold occurs in a variety of conditions: as rubble and surface deposits, quartz reefs, and replacement bodies. The deposits are widely scattered, and many are small and easily worked. These conditions favour the individual miner but do not attract the large corporation. The small miner, however, tended to extract such ore as was accessible, and then to pass to another area. Development was also retarded by a shortage of labour, and this could not be overcome by the use of labour-saving devices since the mines were not large enough to warrant the expenditure. The poor results attained by the original prospectors led to a general pessimism regarding the industry, and in 1903 the Chartered Company amended the conditions applying to prospecting. These had at the outset demanded a share in the capital value of a mine, and the new conditions now allowed miners and small syndicates to work for profit. Finally in 1907 royalties were substituted for a share basis in all new claims. The number of producers then steadily increased, and the value of the gold output rose from less than £1 million in 1904 to nearly £4 million in 1916. By 1931, however, the output had fallen again to the 1907 level, but the increase in the price of gold brought about a rapid growth in the number of small properties and at one time, namely in 1937, they contributed as much as 28 per cent. of the total output. During and after the Second World War their problems grew more difficult, and by Acts passed in 1947 and 1948 the Government introduced a general subsidy of £1. 7s. 6d. per fine ounce of gold. This action drew a protest from the International Monetary Fund and, in deference to its views, the subsidy was first revised and then withdrawn altogether when the pound sterling was devalued in September 1949. This brought some relief to the industry, but rising costs have again embarrassed producers and there has been continuous pressure for a new

[1] See above, p. 700.

subsidy. Some assistance was afforded by the decision of the Government
to permit the sale of the Rhodesian gold output in the 'free market', but
when the premium was abolished during 1953 this market also was closed.

The history of the gold industry in Southern Rhodesia has therefore
been chequered and the results disappointing. The shareholders in the
Chartered Company at all events had to wait for many years before the
copper royalties of Northern Rhodesia made up for the failure of their
hopes from the gold-mines of Mashonaland and Matabeleland. The number of 'active' mines has continued to fall: it was reduced from 543 in 1949
to 452 in 1954. In 1953 the total production of gold was a little over
500,000 ounces, valued at rather more than £6½ million. At the same
time, gold still plays a considerable part in the economy of the country;
it provides work for 1,200 European and 25,000 African miners, and
supplies the Federation with a useful source of foreign exchange.

As has been seen, the mining laws have been largely framed with the
purpose of encouraging the individual worker. The small worker has been
able to avail himself of exceptional assistance from the Government in the
way of loans, free testing by the metallurgical laboratory, and advice from
the Mines and Geological Departments; ex-servicemen have also been
afforded special facilities to carry on mining activities. Great hopes have
been based upon the discovery of uranium near the Beit Bridge, though
in 1953 expert investigation did not seem to promise that it would be
found in workable quantities.[1] In 1955, however, the British Atomic
Energy Commission opened an office in Salisbury in order to conduct
prospecting operations. The area of activity is the Lomagundi District.

It was estimated in 1952 that from the outset the total production of
minerals had been to the value of about £292 million, of which gold
contributed 65·4 per cent., asbestos 17·4 per cent., chrome ore 7·1 per
cent., and coal 6·9 per cent. Southern Rhodesia possesses one of the
world's largest deposits of high-grade asbestos, situated in the Districts of
Bulawayo, Victoria, and Lomagundi. Production, which is now more than
twice as large as it was a quarter of a century ago, has generally tended to
rise steadily, though in the years 1952 and 1953 the industry, in keeping with
the asbestos industries of other countries, suffered some set-back. Nevertheless, in 1953 Southern Rhodesia was third in the list of producers in
the world market, and in 1954 the output was nearly 80,000 tons, valued
at nearly £6 million. With the development of the new rail link to
Lourenço Marques, opened in 1955,[2] Rhodesian exports of the lower
grades of asbestos might now become a more important factor in the
country's economy. In the years 1953 and 1954 two new mines were
developed, mainly with Canadian capital, and the production will be

[1] *Report of the Director, Geological Survey, 1953*, C.S.R. 15, 1954, p. 3.
[2] See below, p. 1552.

exported largely to Canada. Chrome ore deposits are widespread, especially in the Lomagundi area, where mechanization has become more
extensively practised in recent years, and at Selukwe. Production totalled
over 400,000 tons in 1954, valued at nearly £2½ million.

Southern Rhodesia has extensive coalfields. They exist over a large
area south of the Zambezi near Shangani and extend from Tuli eastwards
into the territory of Mozambique. The best known is the Wankie colliery,
212 miles north-west of Bulawayo, estimated to contain over 4,000 million
tons of coal; a large area estimated to contain 100 million tons of coal has
been reserved for open-cast working. Wankie is the source from which
the Copperbelt of Northern Rhodesia obtains its solid fuel. The fuel
problem in the Copperbelt will be considered later, though it may be
observed here that the difficulty is not one of the supply of coal but of
transportation along a single line of rail. Reference to this problem is
made in the following chapter.[1] Production had reached a figure of 2¾
million tons in 1953, but the increasing consumption in the Federation
was held to make it imperative to raise the out-turn to a figure of 5 million
tons by 1956. The transfer of management to the Anglo-American Corporation of South Africa was designed to facilitate the attainment of this
objective. The estimated output for 1955 was 4½ million tons. An extensive field of low-grade coal has been confirmed at Makushwe in the Sabi
valley, which is likely to be developed now that the railway to Lourenço
Marques is completed and electric power installed; this field is estimated
to contain 100 million tons of coal. There are further indications in the
Malilongwe coalfield, and the existence of a small deposit has been
proved at Lubimbi.

Of other minerals Southern Rhodesia produces appreciable quantities
of mica, mined in the vicinity of Sinoia and valued in 1952 at a little over
£1¼ million. Tungsten ores were developed extensively during the Second
World War; the output for 1954 was 259 tons. The production of tin has
declined since the alluvial deposits in the Wankie area have been exhausted, but a smelter was erected at Kamativi in 1954, and a new mine
has been developed in the Sabi valley. There are rich haematite ores near
Que Que, which became of some importance to the Rhodesian economy
when their development was taken over by the Rhodesian Iron and Steel
Commission (RISCOM). A blast furnace was erected in 1948, but in
1950 the operations of the Commission began to incur a loss, and it was
on the verge of insolvency when the Government intervened in 1954 with
substantial grants and instituted an Inquiry into the prospects of the
industry. Up to this time the industry had produced 82,000 tons of rolled
steel and 61,000 tons of pig-iron. The Report of the Inquiry recommended
that the accumulated losses of over £1 million should be written off and

[1] See below, p. 1553.

the Board reconstituted. In 1955 it was decided to subsidize the industry at the rate of £150,000 a year in order to reduce the price of steel by £5 a ton. In accordance with its policy of transferring State-owned undertakings to private enterprise, the Government negotiated with a consortium of financial houses in the United Kingdom to subscribe the £6 million necessary to develop the reorganized industry up to the final stage in which production would amount to 40,000 tons of steel. Besides the deposits owned by the Commission at Que Que, there are large deposits at Bukwa, close to the railway line recently opened between Bannockburn and Lourenço Marques.

Copper has not been a profitable mineral in Southern Rhodesia, and in 1954 it was found necessary to close two mines in the Sinoia area. But early in 1955 the Messina (Transvaal) Development Company decided to reopen the Molly mine, which had not been worked since the First World War, and to develop the Unkondo copper-mine in the Sabi valley. The production of lithium ores increased from 20,000 tons in 1953 to 54,000 tons in 1954. Increased production is due to the discovery of lilac-coloured rocks at Bikita containing a large vein of pegmatite. The deposit at Bikita has been described as one of the largest lithium-producing deposits in the world. The total value of all minerals produced in the territory in 1954 was a little over £18¾ million. Minerals contributed 10 per cent. of the territory's total output and gave employment to 63,000 workers.[1]

Northern Rhodesia has few natural resources other than its minerals, but the exploitation of its copper deposits during the last quarter of a century has had a dramatic effect on the improvement of its economy. The Copperbelt of Northern Rhodesia[2] lies in an area situated immediately south of the Katanga field in the Belgian Congo. It contains the second largest copper-producing industry in the world, now yielding precedence only to that of the United States. It produced in 1953 about 93 per cent. of the export revenue of Northern Rhodesia and 80 per cent. of its taxes. Of the £37 million raised by income tax, supertax, and territorial surcharges in the budget of the Federation in 1954, £18 million was contributed by the copper-mines.

Although the Copperbelt of Northern Rhodesia is of the same geological formation as that of the Katanga, the method of extraction of copper differs materially. In the Katanga the copper ores are oxides lying close to the surface; they are, therefore, recovered by open-cast workings, with the single exception of the Kipushi mine, which is mined at depth.[3] In

[1] *Overseas Economic Surveys, The Federation of Rhodesia and Nyasaland, 1954*, p. 101.
[2] R. L. Prain, 'The Copperbelt of Northern Rhodesia', *J.R.S.A.*, February 1955, pp. 196 ff.
[3] Centre d'Information et de Documentation du Congo Belge et du Ruanda-Urundi, *L'Exploitation des richesses minières du Congo Belge et du Ruanda-Urundi*, Brussels, 1955, p. 37.

Northern Rhodesia, on the other hand, the ores are sulphides and are mined at a deep level,[1] with the exception that there is an open pit at the Nchanga mine. This fundamental difference precludes any valid comparison between the two fields. Surface mining permits of a higher degree of mechanization, and of an easier evacuation of the ore. Mining at deep levels involves skilled operations in the extraction of ore, to which Africans are only slowly attaining. On the other hand, while the treatment of oxide ores presents many technical difficulties, sulphide ores can be easily concentrated by the process of floatation.

The presence of copper has been known to Europeans since 1899 when Native workings at Kansanshi were discovered, followed by the discovery of those at Bwana M'Kubwa in 1902. Attention was at first directed to the oxidized ores at Bwana M'Kubwa, in which rich pockets were found. But at that time the state of chemical knowledge precluded extensive treatment of the ores, and it was not until the discovery in 1925 of the sulphide ores that the great era of Copperbelt development began. When the mines now operating the sulphide ore bodies were effectively established, the Bwana M'Kubwa mine was closed.

The subsequent prosperity of the industry was assisted by the owners of the mineral rights—the British South Africa Company—who confined the grant of sole prospecting rights over wide areas to financially powerful companies. From these concessionary companies emerged eventually the two groups, the Rhodesian Selection Trust and the Anglo-American Corporation, which now control the four producing mines and also two mines which are shortly coming into production. The Roan Antelope (originally discovered in 1902), which has an ore body extending for ten miles on the surface, came into production in 1927. Nkana (first discovered in 1910), where there is the second largest smelter in the world, began producing in 1931. Mufulira was opened in 1933. Nchanga, which contains a higher-grade ore than is to be found elsewhere, followed in 1939. A new mine at Chibuluma began producing in 1956 and one at Bancroft is expected to be opened in 1957. In 1955 a sum of £1 million was allocated to establishing a pilot plant to resume mining at Kansanshi; production is expected to start in 1957.[2] The investigation which resulted in the decision to reopen the Kansanshi mine also proved the presence of radioactive minerals, though the grade appears to be low. It was announced in 1956 that a new mine was to be opened at Chambishi.

Ore reserves are conservatively estimated to be 700 million tons, and it is calculated that the life of the copper industry is not less than 50 years.[3] In 1954 the production amounted to 424,000 short tons, of an approximate

---

[1] K. G. Bradley, *Copper Venture*, 1952, p. 71.

[2] *Optima*, September 1955, pp. 102 ff.

[3] R. L. Prain, in *New Commonwealth*, 7 December 1953.

value of £90 million,[1] and it is expected that when both Chibuluma and Bancroft come into production, the total out-turn will be increased to 450,000 tons. An average total of 6,000 Europeans and 35,000 Africans are directly employed, but it is estimated that about a quarter of a million people of both races are indirectly dependent upon the industry.

The position of the two Corporations which now control the industry is one of great financial strength. The total capital invested is of the range of £150 million. The devaluation of sterling in 1949 increased the price of copper by nearly 44 per cent. The headquarters of the companies have recently been transferred from London to the Federation. Although the higher incidence of taxation in the United Kingdom must have been a consideration in favour of this move, it had also become essential for the Boards of Directors to be in closer touch with their problems than was possible in London. Two issues now confront them. The labour dispute has been discussed at length in an earlier chapter.[2] The second difficulty is involved in the transport of coal from the Wankie colliery owing to the shortage of rolling-stock[3] It has been temporarily overcome by burning timber in the furnaces, by leasing current from the Belgian Congo, and by importing coal from America. But early in 1957 electric power will become available from the hydroelectric power-station on the Lualaba in the Belgian Congo and in 1961 by a grid from the power-stations at the Kariba Gorge.[4]

Northern Rhodesia is the second largest producer of cobalt in the world. Cobalt is found in association with copper and its principal source is now the Nkana mine, but in the future the Chibuluma mine is also likely to have a high out-turn. Production of cobalt and other cobalt alloys in 1953 totalled 30,600 cwts., valued at nearly £2 million. A refinery plant is being erected at Nkana. The presence of uranium has been established, and production will commence shortly. Beryllium, which is largely used in aeroplane construction, is also a valuable product of the Copperbelt, and 17,000 tons of manganese ore were produced in 1954.

Lead, which is found in association with zinc and vanadium, is mined at Broken Hill. These deposits were discovered as long ago as 1902, and production began during the First World War; it totalled 11,510 tons in 1953 and was valued at a little over £1 million. The electrolytic extraction of zinc began in 1928, but the exhaustion of the open-cast ores have made it necessary to search for new deposits. A total of 25,330 tons, valued at rather more than £1¾ million, was produced in 1953.

The vanadium deposits at Broken Hill, which occur in association with oxidized lead-zinc, have been described as the second largest in the world. A cement factory at Chilanga was founded jointly by the Government

[1] Central African Statistical Office, *Monthly Digest of Statistics*, vol. ii, no. 7, p. 9.
[2] See above, pp. 1396 ff.   [3] See below, p. 1553.   [4] See above, p. 987.

of Northern Rhodesia and the Colonial Development Corporation. A second kiln is being erected, and will treble the present production of 81,842 tons.[1] It is a serious defect in the Northern Rhodesian mineral economy that no workable deposits of coal have as yet been proved, but in 1956 a promising deposit was found at Kandabwe, in the Gwembe valley.

In comparison with the Rhodesias the economy of Nyasaland owes little to the development of mineral resources.[2] Extensive deposits of bauxite, estimated to exceed 60 million tons in all, were discovered on the Mlanje mountain in 1924. It is, however, of a low quality, and the lack of available power has so far hindered commercial development of the area. But the project of a hydroelectric power-station on the Shire river,[3] which has been sanctioned in principle by the Federal Parliament, might make extraction profitable.

Considerable quantities of coal are known to exist in the Chikwawa area in the Southern Province, only 75 miles west of the bauxite deposits. There are other coal deposits near the railway at Chiromo, the best seams of which lie, however, at some depth, and there are some in the northern part of the Protectorate near Livingstonia, which are now being investigated. A seam of radio-active coal discovered on the Livingstonia plateau was visited by experts of the Atomic Energy Division of the Scientific and Industrial Department. Unless, however, the seam is an indication of a greater body, it is not likely to be exploited. A deposit of vermiculite, claimed to be the best yet discovered in southern Africa outside the Union, was located in the Shire river valley in 1955. The presence of two rare-earth minerals, pyrochlore and monazite, has been reported in the Southern Province and has given rise to intensive prospecting. A geological map is being drawn by the Department of Geological Survey, and a map of the southern half of the Shire valley has been completed. Intensive prospecting in the Central Province was being carried out in 1956 by the British South Africa Company and a South African mining group.

The British East African Territories

The East Africa Royal Commission 1953–5 observed that there is probably no single source from which surplus income for the benefit of a territory can be so readily obtained as from successful mineral exploitation. The amount of such exploitation had, however, been very small in East Africa. The Commission pointed out that while minerals contributed only 6 per cent. of exports in Kenya, 3 per cent. in Tanganyika, and a negligible amount in Uganda, they formed 95 per cent. of the export in

---

[1] *Colonial Development Corporation, Report and Accounts for 1954*, p. 41.

[2] W. G. G. Cooper, 'Geology and Mineral Resources of Nyasaland', *Nyasaland Protectorate Geological Survey*, Bulletin no. 6, Zomba, 1947.   [3] See above, p. 989.

Northern Rhodesia, 60 per cent. in the Belgian Congo, and 24 per cent. in the Gold Coast.[1] It urged that geological survey be expedited, that mineral exploitation be made attractive, and that a single mining authority be created for all three East African territories.

In Tanganyika the German Administration gave prominence to its geological survey and encouraged prospecting for minerals; the results were said to be promising, but there was little in the way of actual exploitation, save at the Sekenke mine, in what is now the Central Province, from which the Germans obtained the gold which they minted into the now rare 'Tabora' sovereigns.[2] Since that time the developments have not been of any considerable importance until the exploitation by Dr. Williamson of the diamond deposits at Mwadui began to show results.[3] The earliest of the metals to figure in the exports of the territory was gold, produced by mines near Mwanza and Sekenke, but in neither case did the output reach a high figure. Prospectors discovered the alluvial deposits in the Lupa gold-fields in the Chunya District in 1922,[4] and they were exploited with varying success by individual workers for some years; the Lupa gold-field provided some means of support to Europeans who had been deprived of their livelihood during the inter-war period of depression in world prices, though the conditions of the workers in it deservedly received much adverse criticism from the Permanent Mandates Commission of the League of Nations.[5] The alluvial deposits in the Lupa gold-field have now been worked out, but gold continues to be produced from reef-working on the New Saza mines, the second largest in the territory. The major production is from the reef-workings in the Saragura gold-field of the Geita District, the Musoma gold-field on the eastern side of Lake Victoria, and the Singida District of the Central Province.[6] Here the difficulties of mining are considerable, and development has been hindered by rising costs. In 1951 the Government gave a temporary stimulus to the industry by permitting the sale of up to 40 per cent. of the gold output on 'free' markets at a premium. The opening of a gold-mine near Musoma by the New Consolidated Gold Fields Limited, in conjunction with the Colonial Development Corporation, was an event of some importance, as it was the first new mine opened for a number of years. It was recommended in 1955 that further development and exploration should be undertaken.[7] In 1954 the total export of gold from the territory amounted to 72,212 fine ounces, valued at £901,000.[8]

---

[1] *East Africa Royal Commission 1953–1955, Report*, Cmd. 9475, 1955, pp. 113–15.

[2] J. P. Moffett, ed., *Tanganyika, A Review of its Resources and Their Development*, 1955, p. 691.

[3] Ibid. p. 684.

[4] C. Leubuscher, *Tanganyika Territory, A Study of Economic Policy under Mandate*, 1944, pp. 54–60.

[5] Ibid. p. 58.   [6] Moffett, op. cit. p. 690.

[7] *Colonial Development Corporation, Report and Accounts for 1955*, p. 43.

[8] *Annual Report on the East Africa High Commission 1954*, Col. no. 316, 1955, p. 77.

The substantial addition made by diamonds to the export of the territory began in the years 1939–40. Diamonds were first found near Mabuki in the Kwimba District, and during the years 1921–31 prospecting and mining met with varying success, the largest production being in 1927, when stones to the value of rather over £100,000 were exported. In 1940 Dr. J. T. Williamson, a Canadian geologist, discovered the now famous Mwadui diamond occurrences about 20 miles north-east of Shinyanga township. The diamonds lie in the gravels near the Kimberlite; whether the Kimberlite itself actually contains diamonds is yet to be discovered. The major producing company is Williamson Diamonds Limited. The value of the export of diamonds had been £12,598 in 1939; with the opening of the operations at Mwadui it rose to £70,236 in 1941, and, though the progressive increase in the export was interrupted in 1950–1 by the difference between the Company and the Diamond Corporation above referred to, during the years 1952–4 the average value of the export of diamonds was £2,980,000 a year.[1] The royalty payable on diamonds is at the rate of 15 per cent. of the value as assessed by a valuer appointed under the Diamond Industry Protection Ordinance.[2]

The most valuable of the other mineral products is now lead. The Uruwira mine at Mpanda, 200 miles south-west of Tabora, is due to a discovery made by a Belgian geologist in 1893. In 1950 the Railway Administration connected the mine to the Central Railway by a branch-line 131 miles long. The plant has been increased as the result of an arrangement made in 1952 by the Defense Materials Procurement Agency of the United States. In return for a loan received from the Agency the mine will send to the United States a proportion equivalent to eleven-sixteenths of its annual output. In 1953 the output was valued at a little short of half a million sterling; but the reserves of ore are estimated to amount to 3 million tons, and the out-turn is being rapidly developed. Two coalfields in the Songea District have been investigated by the Colonial Development Corporation, and it seems clear that there is a large deposit in the Kilewaka and Ngaka areas which would be worth exploitation if the recently constructed railway between Mtwara and Nachingwea[3] were extended to Songea. Prospecting for oil by the Shell–D'Arcy Petroleum Development Company has led to the first deep test well for oil being drilled on Mafia Island, south of Dar-es-Salaam.[4]

Although the contribution made by minerals to the exports of Kenya is relatively small, there has, from the first, been a considerable activity in prospecting. The search for gold has a long history in the Colony. It was worked initially by individual prospectors, and reef gold was sub-

[1] *Tanganyika, Report for the Year 1954*, Col. no. 317, p. 170.
[2] Cap. 129 of Laws.   [3] See below, p. 1559.
[4] *Report of the East African Commissioner for the Year 1954*, East Africa Office, London, pp. 28–30.

sequently mined in the South Kavirondo area. At a later date alluvial finds were made in the Kakamega District of North Kavirondo. The discovery occurred during the period of price depression after the First World War, and it attracted many farmers to the gold-fields, but the out-turn was never considerable, and has since steadily declined. Loans from the Government, which are not to be repayable until the mine is making reasonable profits, have done no more than stabilize output at the present low levels. For many years the individual prospectors were at a disad-vantage compared with concerns possessing some capital resources, and in an attempt to compose their differences certain areas were reserved by the Government to individuals and small companies. The total export of gold was valued in 1953 at only £131,530, a figure considerably below that for 1933.

Other mineral resources are at present of little commercial importance, and a comprehensive geological survey instituted in 1948 with assistance from the Colonial Development Corporation has not yet yielded any substantial results. The most promising of the deposits examined are the copper concentrates at the Macalder mine,[1] which is a complex of copper, gold, silver, zinc, and other metals. Extraction of the copper will even-tually be carried out in a smelter to be erected at Jinja in Uganda, making use of the power provided by the Owen Falls hydroelectric installation.[2] Kyanite occurs in various localities and considerable attention to new plant has recently been given by the one main producer, but output in 1954 was worth only £96,000. In the semi-arid areas of north Kenya the possibilities of oil deposits have long been suspected. In 1937 the Govern-ment took steps to exclude the area from general prospecting, and in 1951 some of the leading petroleum companies sent geologists to re-examine the possibilities. In 1952 two oil exploration licences were issued.

The chief contribution to the mineral output of the Colony (which was valued at a total of £1¾ million in 1954) was made by the production of soda ash from the deposits in Lake Magadi. This was valued at roughly £1¼ million. The surface of the lake is encrusted with practically pure trona which needs only to be freed by draining or washing to yield a high-grade material. The reserves are being continuously renewed from saline springs which feed the lake. It is now worked by a subsidiary of Imperial Chemical Industries Limited. Another natural product is carbon dioxide gas obtained from a bore-hole sunk originally for water at Esageri in the Rift Valley; 582 tons of this unusual product were obtained in 1954.[3]

It has often been said that the relative unimportance of mineral produc-

---

[1] *Colonial Development Corporation, Report and Accounts for 1953*, p. 37.
[2] See above, p. 995.
[3] *Report of the East African Commissioner for the Year 1954*, East Africa Office, London, p. 28.

tion in Uganda has been due to the impediment offered to prospectors by difficulties of transport and by the fact that so large an area of land in the Protectorate is held practically in freehold right by African landowners.[1] Neither explanation seems entirely adequate. A Geological Survey Department was created in 1919, but it has not been able to point to any mineral occurrences of first-class importance. Alluvial gold was discovered in 1931 in the Kigezi District, but so far the production has been insignificant. Wolfram, also found in the Kigezi area, came into prominence during the Second World War, and, following the acquisition of the properties by certain large overseas firms, development proceeded rapidly. In 1953, however, the price of wolfram on the world market declined materially, and the reserves which could be profitably worked were much reduced. Exports in 1954 were valued at only £140,000. The copper and cobalt deposits in the eastern flanks of the Ruwenzori Range, discovered in 1924, promised to be more important. The Colonial Development Corporation and the Uganda Development Corporation joined in extending the small-scale enterprise which had been started at Kilembe. It was proposed to instal a roasting plant at Kasese, near Kilembe, and to utilize the smelter at Jinja which has previously been referred to. Concentrates were to be conveyed to the smelter by rail. The cost of this development was estimated at approximately £6 million, and in 1955 plant construction at the mine was going according to schedule.[2] Cassiterite, also discovered in 1924, has been produced almost entirely from lodes or detritus. Production began in 1927. The value of the export in 1954 was a little over £56,000.[3] The Tororo Exploration Company is investigating the pyrochlore-apatite deposit in the Bukedi District near Tororo and has in view a plant designed to produce chemical fertilizers from apatite concentrates and niobium from pyrochlore concentrates. The Tororo Cement Works produce some 3,500 tons a month, and have gone some way to meet the domestic demand for cement.

The British West African Territories

Nigeria's mineral industry is at present based on three principal products: tin, columbite, and coal.[4] Tin had since very early times been mined by the Hausa within 100 miles of Kano. In 1884 the Royal Niger Company sent an expedition to Badika, then the market for tin, in order to locate the source, but this was not finally ascertained till a force which had been sent to subdue the Emir of Bauchi in 1902 obtained a sample of tin from the Delime river near Naraguta. Large prospecting areas were

---

[1] See above, pp. 723 ff.

[2] *Colonial Development Corporation, Report and Accounts for 1955*, p. 44.

[3] *Annual Report of the East Africa High Commission 1954*, Col. no. 316, 1955, p. 77.

[4] F. Dixey, 'Nigeria—Geology and Mineral Resources', *Bulletin of the Imperial Institute*, vol. xliii, no. 4, 1945.

subsequently taken up by different companies under licence from the
Royal Niger Company, and tin-mining developed into an important
industry in the Provinces of Bauchi, Zaria, Kano, and Ilorin. The richest
of the mines are situated on the Bauchi Plateau, an area of about 2,000
square miles. Here deposits are alluvial, and the ore is won by a variety
of means, ranging from manual washing to steam shovels or bucket
dredges. More than half the tin-bearing ground is still worked by hand
labour, but in other places mechanical excavators and drag-lines are
operated by hydroelectric power developed from the Kurra river. In
1929 a peak output of more than 15,000 tons was produced, but in 1936,
as a result of the scheme of restriction introduced in order to maintain the
price of tin, the output fell to 4,956 tons. In 1944, however, a new peak
of some 17,258 tons was reached, since when it has again tended to decline,
falling to 11,345 long tons in 1953. Reserves are estimated to be of the
range of 112,000 tons, and the working life of the mines appears to be
limited to about ten years, unless new discoveries are made. .The industry
employs more than 52,000 Africans and pays out in wages alone over
£1 million annually. A decline in production would therefore have a
serious effect on the economy of Nigeria. The value of the export in 1953
was £7 million.

More than 85 per cent. of the world's output of columbite[1] comes from
Nigeria, the bulk of it obtained as a by-product of tin-mining. In 20 years
of production over 15,000 tons of columbite, valued at more than £3½
million, have been recovered. The mineral has recently been found to
occur in large masses of graphite, though the quality appears to be too
low to warrant commercial development.[2] Rich primary deposits of the
uranium-bearing mineral pyrochlore were found in 1952, and the United
States Defense Materials Procurement Agency agreed to pay a bonus of
100 per cent. on each ton of columbium sold to the United States Government. Owing, however, to the isolation of the deposits from main roads
and railway lines the future of the mineral is doubtful.

Gold has long been a Native production, though the out-turn has
declined since 1936, when 33,364 fine ounces were produced. It is found
chiefly in the Oyo and Calabar Provinces of southern Nigeria, but is
mainly in scattered alluvial deposits, and the returns have never proved
sufficiently attractive to the larger financial groups. Most of the output is
absorbed inside the country. The value was estimated at £8,500 in 1953.[3]

Both coal and lignite deposits in Nigeria are extensive and known reserves of coal have been put at 28 million tons. Most of it is at present

[1] R. R. E. Jacobson, A. Cawley, and W. N. Macleod, 'The Occurrence of Columbite in
Nigeria', *Geological Survey of Nigeria*, Occasional Paper no. 9, 1951.
[2] 'Recent Discoveries of Columbium (Niobium) in Africa', *Colonial Geology and Mineral Resources*, vol. iii, no. 1, 1952, pp. 76 ff.
[3] *Colonial Reports, Nigeria, 1953*, p. 54.

obtained at Enugu, 151 miles north of Port Harcourt, where some 6,000 Africans are employed. The production, which amounted to 640,000 tons in the year ended September 1954,[1] is consumed chiefly by the Nigerian Railways, though a total of 26,000 tons was exported for the year 1954.[2] Farther north two promising new seams have been discovered and are under investigation. Lead and zinc ores occur in the south-eastern part of the country. Though some investigation has been made on them, their value has not yet been determined.

In the southern part of Nigeria seepages have long suggested the existence of mineral oil. Up to the end of 1954 the Shell–D'Arcy Petroleum Development Company had invested £9 million in its search for oil and eleven wells had been drilled, chiefly in the Owerri District in the Calabar Province. However, though oil has been found, it is not as yet in sufficient quantity to make its production economic.

Although the cocoa industry has so dominant a position in the economy of the Gold Coast, minerals contribute largely to the total value of the country's exports. Gold, manganese, and diamonds all have a major part in the picture. In 1954 the value of the mineral export as a whole was roughly £21½ million, out of a total export valued at £113¼ million.

Gold takes the first place, in respect both of its history and its present value. As early as the fifteenth century Europeans were trading with the Adansi of the coastal area for the locally produced gold. When the Portuguese founded Elmina in 1481, they called it São Jorge da Mina or the Ore da Mina, 'the mouth of the gold river'; it seems that besides the alluvial washings there were actually mines of some kind which were worked at the time on a considerable scale. The interior of the Gold Coast Colony consists of a broad belt of sandstone and marl with an occasional band of auriferous conglomerate. This has been most continuously worked for gold in the Wasaw District of the Western Province. Though the conglomerate bears some resemblance to the 'banket' of South Africa, it is presumably of a more recent origin; the alluvial silts and gravels also carry gold. It was not until after the Ashanti War of 1873 that European enterprise interested itself in efforts to extract gold according to modern methods.[3] The value of the Tarkwa main reef was first discovered by a French trader about 1880. During the period 1880 to 1900 the yearly value of the gold exported ranged from a minimum of £32,000 to a maximum of £103,000. The increasing interest shown in the industry led to the construction of a railway to the gold-fields, and in 1901 and the following years a large number of Concessions were taken

---

[1] Mining Journal, Annual Review, 1955, p. 161.
[2] Nigeria Trade Summary, Lagos, 1955.
[3] N. R. Junner, 'Progress in Geological Investigations and Mineral Developments in the Gold Coast', Bulletin of Imperial Institute, vol. xliv, no. 1, 1946, pp. 44–62.

up. They numbered in the latter year as many as 2,825 and occasioned a boom in the West African market on the London Stock Exchange. Many of them were speedily abandoned, but late in 1902 a company began crushing ore and thus laid the foundation of the present gold industry. The chief mining centres are now at Tarkwa, Prestea, and Obuasi. There are ten companies producing gold from lode, and one from alluvial deposits. The Gold Coast is estimated to have yielded up to 1951 over 30 million ounces of gold.[1] The export in 1954 was valued at a little over £9¾ million. The industry employs a total of 929 Europeans and 37,362 Africans.

Manganese was discovered by the Geological Survey in 1915, and the centre of production is now at Nsuta in the Western Province. The Gold Coast has become the second largest producer in the world. The ore is of high grade and is worked in great open casts; exports amounted in 1953 to 745,990 tons, valued at £8¾ million, but fell in 1954 to 460,000 tons, valued at £5¼ million. Diamonds of the industrial grades are more common than gems, the proportion being 76 per cent. of industrial diamonds; all are from alluvial deposits. They were first discovered by the Geological Survey in 1919. There are four companies operating in the diamond industry, but there is also a large production by Africans working on their own account. The proportion produced by Africans varies greatly; thus in 1950 they accounted for 50 per cent. of the total production by value, compared with less than 7 per cent. in 1946. The diamond field near the river Bonsa, south-west of Tarkwa, is worked by Africans only. The value of diamonds exported in 1954 was a little over £4 million.

It would appear that bauxite is likely to become an important feature in the economy of the Gold Coast. It was discovered by the Geological Survey soon after the finding of the alluvial diamonds. Working began on the deposits near Sefwi Bekwai in the Wiawso District of the Western Province in 1941, and there are large deposits also at Yenahin in Ashanti. A railway has been constructed to link these deposits with the main line running from Takoradi to Kumasi. Export so far has been on a minor scale, amounting in 1953 to only 115,000 tons, of a value of about £200,000. The reserves of ore are, however, estimated at 200 million tons, and when the Volta River Scheme, referred to in a previous chapter,[2] has been completed the extraction of ore will very greatly increase. It is expected that the total production of aluminium from the Volta installation may amount to 210,000 tons a year, and its value to Great Britain is increased by the fact that its source lies within the sterling area.[3]

Minerals have also an important place in the exports of Sierra Leone.

---

[1] *An Economic Survey of the Colonial Territories, 1951: vol. vii, The Products of the Colonial Territories,* Col. nos. 281–7, 1952.

[2] See above, p. 1001.   [3] *The Volta River Aluminium Scheme,* Cmd. 8702, 1952.

In 1953 they accounted for nearly £6¼ million in value, out of a total export valued at £12¼ million. Occurrences of economic value were, however, unknown until the Government geologists discovered important deposits of iron ore and diamonds between the years 1926 and 1931. The most important of the exports has been iron ore. The deposits, which are situated in the Marampa Chiefdom of the Port Lokko District, were first opened up in 1933. The major part of the export consists of hard lateritic haematite, and the ore is transported, for a distance of 50 miles, by a railway constructed by the Sierra Leone Development Company to Pepel, where a modern installation loads it into ocean-going ships. In 1954 a little over 877,000 tons were exported, at a value of £2¾ million. A project is now under consideration for the opening up of further deposits in the Tonkolili District. For this purpose it will be necessary to extend the existing mineral railway by some 90 miles and to make further additions to the port at Pepel.

The export of diamonds was valued at £1¾ million in 1954.[1] The stones, of which 63 per cent. are industrial,[2] are won from alluvial gravels in the Kono District. The gravel is excavated by mechanical equipment and transported to the concentration plants, of which eight have now been erected. The Sierra Leone Selection Trust holds a monopoly for prospecting and marketing of diamonds over the whole of the territory, but of recent years there has been a serious increase of illicit diamond mining. The royalty and income tax paid by the Trust was, up to 1953, fixed at 45 per cent. of the profits, and the illicit diamond mining was estimated to have deprived the Government of an annual revenue of over £1¼ million. Local Chiefs were alleged to be involved; land was unsystematically mined, and a large proportion of stones never recovered. In 1954 the Trust agreed to the royalty and tax being increased to 60 per cent., on condition that the Government would undertake to suppress illicit mining.[3] The failure of the Government to take effective steps for this purpose led to a breach with the Trust, and this at one time became a political issue, but finally led to the conclusion in 1955 of the Sierra Leone Diamond Agreement. Under this the area over which the Sierra Leone Selection Trust was to hold rights was reduced to 450 square miles, which included all existing workings. At the same time the Trust was given the right to prospect for deep diamonds anywhere in the territory for ten years. The Government agreed to pay compensation amounting to £1,570,000, and undertook not to grant prospecting licences to persons not of Sierra Leone nationality without giving the Trust the first option.

---

[1] Sierra Leone, *Monthly Trade Statistics*, vol. xxxiii, no. 392, 1954, p. 197.
[2] *An Economic Survey of the Colonial Territories, 1951: vol. vii, The Products of the Colonial Territories*, Col. nos. 281–7, p. 47.
[3] *Africa Digest*, May–June 1955, p. 5.

In Gambia a geological survey carried out in 1953 disclosed the existence of ilmenite in the littoral area, but it was doubtful if this would repay exploitation.

The French Territories

If the exploitation of minerals has not been so actively pursued in the French as in the British overseas territories, this may be due in part to the fact that French investors have been less ready than the British to invest in enterprises of so speculative a character as mining. They have usually preferred to invest in fixed-interest-bearing shares. France has, moreover, looked to Europe rather than overseas areas as a field of investment.[1] But part of the explanation may lie also in the character of the French law regulating mineral rights. These are held to be separate from rights in the soil and subsoil, and the Local Administrations have a right to exercise their discretion in the issue of prospecting licences. The tendency has been to restrict their grant to parties who can show that they have adequate financial and technical knowledge. Further, there are considerable areas, such as Upper Guinea and the region between Senegal and the Sudan, where mining rights have been reserved to the indigenous peoples. There is still an active African gold-mining industry in Siguiri and in parts of the districts of Dabola, Kouroussa, and Kankan in Guinea, and in Bougouni in Sudan; these areas are closed to prospecting by Europeans.

Since the Second World War, however, and partly as the result of the formation of the French Union, more systematic efforts have been directed to the development of the mineral resources of the overseas areas. Mining stands high in the list of the recent comprehensive Ten-year Development Programme, and some of its provisions are now in operation. In 1948 a special public corporation (the *Bureau Minier de la France d'Outre-Mer*), with a capital of 700 million francs, was set up to promote prospecting and mineral development.

French West Africa had in 1954 an export of minerals valued at 1,555 million C.F.A. francs, or roughly 2·8 per cent. of the total export.[2] Senegal is the third largest producer of titanium in the world; it is present in the form of ilmenite, 6,000 tons having been exported in 1954. The production of calcium phosphate was suspended in 1954, but the export of phosphate of aluminium reached 54,000 tons, and was expected to attain 100,000 tons in 1955. A copper-mine at Akjoujt in Mauritania came into production in 1954; it deals with both sulphide and oxide ores. In 1953 a total of 400,000 tons of iron ore, 300,000 tons of bauxite, and 80,000 carats of diamonds were exported from French Guinea. An important installation

[1] S. H. Frankel, *Capital Investment in Africa*, 1938, p. 19.
[2] *Bulletin de la statistique générale de l'A.O.F.*, no. 4, Dakar, 1954, pp. 29–33.

for the production of aluminium is under construction at Kassa near Conakry which should come into operation in 1957.[1]

The lack of communications has retarded the progress of prospecting in French Equatorial Africa. The territory has, however, an important export of industrial diamonds and of lead, and has large deposits of manganese. The export of minerals was valued at 895½ million francs in 1954, or roughly 0·7 per cent. of the total export.[2] The production of diamonds in the Oubangi area has hitherto lacked the necessary capital for fully mechanized exploitation, but finance has now been secured for this purpose with the aid of a loan from the United States. The discovery of further rich sources at Berbérati in the area of Haute-Sangha led to a total production of 156,705 carats in 1954. The reserves of manganese deposits at Franceville are estimated to amount to 300 million tons, and a company in which the United States has a 49 per cent. interest has been formed to exploit them. The problem of the export of the ore to Pointe Noire presents difficulties which have not yet been solved. The principal source for the production of lead is M'Fouati in the Middle Congo; the export between 1945 and 1948 amounted to some 8,000 tons a year.[3] There are some indications of the presence of oil in the Gabon.

The Belgian Congo

Reference has already been made to the circumstances which at an early date moved the Belgian Government to attach primary importance to the exploitation of the mineral resources of the Colony.[4] For many years this remained one of its chief objectives. It largely determined the direction taken by rail and river transport;[5] it influenced the policy of the regulation of the demands made for African manpower;[6] and from the first it supplied the major avenue for the investment of Belgian capital.[7] Unlike the Governments of the Union of South Africa, the Rhodesias, or the British African dependencies, the Government of the Belgian Congo has itself taken a direct part in the development of mining enterprise. The State has held the mineral rights in the land. Consequently Concessions for prospecting or the extraction of minerals can be obtained only from the State, and its practice has been to retain a substantial holding in the share capital of the companies to which it has granted Concessions. One of the most striking features in the economy of the Colony is the extent to which such shares, and in particular those of the powerful *Société Générale*, figure in the Government 'portfolio'.[8] The continuing importance of mineral and mining development to the Colony is shown by the

[1] *Civilisations*, vol. iv, no. 1, 1954, p. 108.
[2] *Bulletin d'informations économiques et sociales*, Brazzaville, September 1955, p. 2013.
[3] *Enc. A.E.F.*, p. 363.　　　　　　　　　　　　　　[4] See above, p. 217.
[5] See below, p. 1545.　　　　　　　　　　　　　　　　[6] See above, p. 1392.
[7] Frankel, op. cit. pp. 292 ff.　　　　　　　　　　　　[8] Ibid. p. 294.

fact that in 1954 the value of the mineral exports amounted to 12,635 million francs, or nearly 61 per cent. of the value of the total export.[1] Tin has been worked in the north-east of the territory since 1905, copper in the Katanga since 1911, and tin in the Katanga and diamonds in the Kasai since 1913. Progress has been greatly accelerated by the utilization of hydroelectric energy, 95 per cent. of which is consumed by the mines. The mining industry gives employment to over 3,000 Europeans and to about 127,000 Africans, of whom 40,000 work in the Kivu area and 30,000 in the Katanga.

The copper deposits in the Katanga were discovered in 1891, and in 1900 Tanganyika Concessions Limited obtained a grant of prospecting rights in the area known as Sud-Katanga. The major operating company, the *Union Minière du Haut-Katanga*,[2] was formed in 1906 to exploit the minerals over an area of 20,000 square kilometres; it will hold its rights in the Katanga till 1990. In 1912, the first full year of production, some 2,500 tons of copper were produced. In 1954 the out-turn was 224,500 tons. Since its inception up to the end of 1953 the Katanga has produced 4,300,000 tons of copper. Before the Second World War the reserves of ore were calculated to amount to 6 per cent. of the world's total reserves, but prospecting since then has enlarged this figure. The copper deposits are for the most part oxides lying on or close to the surface, but at depth oxide gives place to sulphide ores.[3] The Prince Leopold mine at Kipushi, which was discovered in 1889, is in fact the only subterranean copper-mine in the Katanga.[4] Elsewhere copper is extracted by open-cast working, carried out by intensive mechanization. In the Shinkolobwe mine, situated in the centre of the area, copper was indicated in 1902, but the mine came into prominence with the discovery of uranium in 1915.[5] It was developed in 1931 as an open-cast mine, but the extraction of uranium is now effected by tunnelling. Secrecy has been maintained as to the production of uranium in the Colony. Before the Second World War it was stated that 60 per cent. of uranium ores originated from the Katanga,[6] but this statement has recently been challenged and accurate information is as yet not available. In the western area the best-known mine is that at Kolwezi. First discovered in 1901 from vestiges of ancient indigenous workings, it has been in full production since 1937, and has supplied increasing quantities of sulphide ore. One of the two concentrators in

---

[1] Ministry of Colonies, *Belgian Congo and Ruanda-Urundi Economic Survey, 1954*, 1955, p. 391. In 1956 140 Belgian Congo francs were equivalent to £1 sterling.

[2] *Union Minière du Haut-Katanga, 1906–1956*, Brussels, 1956.

[3] Centre d'Information et de Documentation du Congo Belge et du Ruanda-Urundi, *L'Exploitation des richesses minières du Congo Belge et du Ruanda-Urundi*, Brussels, 1955, p. 16.

[4] Ibid. p. 39.

[5] Ibid. pp. 33, 49.

[6] A. W. Postel, *The Mineral Resources of Africa*, 1943, p. 43.

the Katanga is situated here, the other being at the Kipushi mine; they serve for the treatment by floatation of mixed oxide and sulphide ores.

The production of gold in the Belgian Congo is less important. Its contribution in 1954 amounted to only 11,350 kilograms,[1] or about $1\frac{1}{4}$ per cent. of the total recorded production of the world; its importance to the economy of the territory lies in the part which it plays in the provision of foreign exchange.[2] The main centres of production are the mines in the Kilo-Moto district in the north-east of the territory, which furnished about 65 per cent. of production. The mines were up to 1926 developed by direct State agency, but have since then been managed by the *Société des Mines d'or de Kilo-Moto*. Kimberlite, which is usually associated with the production of diamonds, was discovered in the Katanga in 1908, but the most valuable deposits of diamonds are to be found in the Kasai and the Bakwanga region. The Belgian Congo supplies nine-tenths of the world's requirements of industrial diamonds.[3] Production in 1954 amounted to 12,620 million carats, valued at 1,277 million francs.[4]

Cobalt, found in association with copper, is produced in greater quantity in the Belgian Congo than anywhere else in Africa; the output in 1954 was 8,603 tons,[5] which was 70 per cent. of the world's supply. Under an Agreement made in 1944 between the United States, Belgium, and Britain, 90 per cent. of the uranium produced is bought by a joint purchasing agency of these three countries. The Agreement was extended for a further ten years in 1955. Tin is found in a belt extending from the south-west of the Katanga to the north-east of the Kivu Province and to Ruanda Urundi. The largest mine is situated at Maniema. Production in 1954 amounted to 2,377 metric tons,[6] and exports were valued at $223\frac{1}{4}$ million francs;[7] the reserves are ample to maintain supplies for many years. Zinc, manganese, and cadmium have also been found in association with copper.

There are coalfields situated in the basins of the Lukuga and the Luena rivers, and on account of their proximity to the railway coal has been extracted for the past 40 years. In the Lukuga field, however, the coal is of mediocre quality and extraction is not economic; it was suspended about 1931, when hydro-electric power replaced steam in the mines. The field was mechanized in 1952 and production resumed on a small scale. It is now proposed to install a plant to produce oil from coal

[1] Ministry of Colonies, *Belgian Congo and Ruanda-Urundi Economic Survey, 1954*, 1955, p. 77.
[2] Centre d'Information et de Documentation du Congo Belge et du Ruanda-Urundi, *L'Exploitation des richesses minières du Congo Belge et du Ruanda-Urundi*, Brussels, 1955, p. 107.
[3] Ibid. p. 119.
[4] Ministry of Colonies, *Belgian Congo and Ruanda-Urundi Economic Survey, 1954*, 1955, p. 77.
[5] Ibid. p. 74.
[6] *Bulletin mensuel des statistiques du Congo Belge et du Ruanda-Urundi*, no. 50, Leopoldville, 1954, p. 238.
[7] Ministry of Colonies, *Belgian Congo and Ruanda-Urundi Economic Survey, 1954*, 1955, p. 391.

products.[1] The Luena field has had an uninterrupted production, which has latterly been increased owing to the growth of secondary industry in the country. In 1954 it produced 379,000 metric tons.

The Portuguese Territories

Although mineral development has not so far been extensive in the Portuguese territories, there is evidence of some interesting possibilities. Gold has been mined in Mozambique from very early times, but it appears to occur only in isolated alluvial deposits. Coal is known to exist on an extensive scale near Tete; though it is at present produced in only small quantities, it is easily accessible and of good quality. Belgian financial interests have the largest holding in the chief operating Company, but the State appoints a representative to the Board. By arrangement with the Government the Company supplies free of charge all the coal which is required for use on the Tete railway in order to transport coal from the Dona Ana coalfield; supplies surplus to the needs of the railway are exported to Nyasaland.[2] In the Tete area also there are deposits of radio-active materials; some uranium has been extracted, but the Portuguese Government has restricted the right of uranium prospection throughout the overseas territories. By agreement between the Government and the Mozambique Gulf Oil Company, an American-owned firm, a geological and geophysical survey of the area has been carried out, but so far without conclusive results.

In Angola the occurrence of diamonds has been known for many years, and the Diamonds of Angola Company was promoted in 1917 to exploit them. The diamond industry is now of very considerable importance; in 1954 it exported 724,000 carats, valued at around £4½ million. In the same year exports of manganese amounted to 18,700 metric tons.[3] Drilling for oil near Luanda has yielded promising results, and a trial shipment of nearly 5,000 tons was sent to Portugal late in 1956.

Liberia

No complete geological survey of the mineral resources of Liberia has yet been made. Provision for a survey forms part of the Five-year Plan of Development undertaken under the Point Four Agreement with the United States.[4] Gold has been found in alluvial deposits in the Eastern, Western, and Northern Provinces, but it has been extracted by rudimentary manual methods, and no mining of the original ore lodes has been undertaken. Diamonds are known to occur in the Western Province, and there would appear to be good reason to suppose that Liberia may be as

[1] Ibid p. 129.
[2] C. F. Spence, *The Portuguese Colony of Moçambique*, 1951, pp. 36 ff.
[3] *Boletim mensal de estatística*, no. 12, Luanda, 1954, p. 32.   [4] See above, p. 1343.

rich in this respect as the neighbouring territory of Sierra Leone, but no systematic prospecting has been done. At present the major source of mineral export is iron. High-grade deposits of iron ore exist in the Bomi hills, and with the aid of a loan from the Export-Import Bank they have been developed by the American-owned Liberia Mining Company. Production began in 1951,[1] and in the years 1954–5 provided an average export of roughly 1 million tons to the United States. Geologists have reason to believe that magnesium and corundum may exist in economic quantities, and there are traces of copper, lead, and zinc, but information as to their extent awaits the result of the survey undertaken as part of the Five-year Development Plan.

THE STATE AND MINERAL PRODUCTION

It will have been seen that in only a few instances have the mineral resources of a territory been directly exploited by State agency, and then for exceptional reasons. In several instances the exigencies of the Second World War necessitated participation by the State in the extraction of strategic materials. In general, however, the character of mining operations in Africa has not varied materially in the last half century. The exceptions where the State has intervened in the course of mineral development are few, though important. The Alexander Bay diamond diggings were taken over by the South African Government at a time when overproduction threatened the diamond industry. In the Belgian Congo the development of the Kilo-Moto gold-mines by State agency ended in 1926, but here, as elsewhere in the Colony, the Government has retained a large holding in the stock of the Company which operates them. Since the Second World War the need for large sums of capital in developing the resources of the African territories has everywhere brought the State into closer touch with mineral developments. Practically all the countries holding territories in Africa have since instituted the programmes of overseas development, financed partly from metropolitan and partly from local sources, which have been described in a previous chapter.[2] In all these programmes the development of mineral resources has, directly or indirectly, a recognized part. It is characteristic, for example, that the French programme includes the foundation of the *Bureau Minier de la France d'Outre-Mer*, a public Corporation which is directly concerned in the prospecting for minerals and the development of mines. In the British dependencies the funds made available under the Colonial Development and Welfare Acts of 1940 have directly assisted in the promotion of

[1] E. Anderson, *Liberia*, 1952, pp. 179 ff. U.S. Bureau of Mines, *Minerals Year Book, 1951*, p. 668.
[2] See above, pp. 1333 ff.

geological survey and in the provision of communications designed to aid the mining industry. It seems likely, moreover, that the Government of the United Kingdom may for reasons of policy take a part in the provision of finance required for the Volta project for the production of aluminium in the Gold Coast. The Colonial Development Corporation has already helped to sponsor a number of relatively small-scale mineral enterprises.

The general principle involved in the assumption by the State of a direct responsibility for the exploitation of minerals became an issue of some public interest in Great Britain following the publication by the Government of a Memorandum on mining policy in 1946.[1] While agreeing that there were many advantages in leaving actual exploitation to private agencies, the Memorandum claimed that there were circumstances in which it would be preferable for the State to take on itself the task of development through its own agencies, as for example where strategic interests are involved or where the minerals are consumed mainly within the Colony and it is necessary to protect the interests of the consumer. For the most part, however, it was held that the principal function of the State was to prepare the ground for the development of the mineral industry by the promotion of geological survey, and to protect the public interest by determining the procedure for prospecting or by the due regulation of the share of the proceeds of mining to be taken by public revenues in the form of royalties or taxation. 'Whereas policy in the case of agriculture and animal husbandry aims at the preservation and improvement of the productive powers of the basic natural resources of a territory, mining essentially consists of the removal of valuable natural resources which, once removed, cannot in the nature of things be replaced.' These principles still regulate the policy observed, though in varying measure, by the other Governments concerned, save that the Belgian Government has taken a more direct part than others in the promotion of mining development. But there are some characteristic differences in the practice followed, as for instance in the measures by which the State claims rights over the subsoil and the minerals contained in it, or the regulation of the prospecting for metals. The procedure regulating prospecting is of special importance in Africa. While, on the one hand, it is necessary to have regard to the rights or the susceptibilities of the indigenous peoples, it is, on the other, necessary to secure that there should be no avoidable hindrance to the enterprise of prospectors, for it is the latter who have in the past contributed so much more than official agencies to the discovery of mineral occurrences.

[1] *Memorandum on Mining Policy*, Col. no. 206, 1946.

THE OWNERSHIP OF MINERAL RIGHTS

The law which defines the property in mineral rights has in most cases followed the pattern of the metropolitan law of the Colonial Power concerned. There are, however, cases in which the character of the law has been dictated by circumstances. As will be seen, Southern Rhodesia forms a conspicuous case in point. The Gold Coast, on the other hand, is an instance where circumstances have led to the recognition of a system of rights directly opposed to that prevailing in Southern Rhodesia.

In South Africa ownership of the land is, in accordance with the principles of Roman-Dutch law, held to comprise all values in the land including mineral rights. This principle regulates therefore the rights in the great bulk of the land held by Europeans; the rights in the Native Reserves are held by the State as the proprietor of the land. But the discovery of the Kimberley deposits and the subsequent activity in prospecting first for diamonds and then for gold led to a modification of this principle by laws which, though at first applied to the regulation of mining on public lands, were soon extended to private lands. The result of this measure was that the State asserted the power to restrict the rights of owners over minerals in lands reserved to them by title. As a consequence, the owner could, except in Natal, prospect without licence, whereas other persons required his consent. The land could not be proclaimed a 'public diggings' in the Cape and Natal nor in the other Provinces without the owner's consent. This was subject to the provision in the Transvaal that the Government could in certain circumstances proclaim the land after twelve months' notice. The owner had the entire disposal of mineral rights in the Cape, while in the Transvaal and Orange Free State he was allowed to reserve only part of his land for mining on his own account. In respect of the rest of the land, he received a share of the licence fees paid by claim-holders and stand-holders. All rights to minerals, mineral oils, and precious stones on Crown Lands are reserved to the State, and are retained by it even during the lease of such land; they may, however, be ceded in the case of grants of Crown Land for settlement purposes.

In Bechuanaland the Crown recognized the grant of mineral rights included in the original Concessions to the Tati Company[1] and, by a Proclamation promulgated in 1932,[2] recognized Concessions granted to mining companies by Chiefs holding rights over the lands in the Native Reserves. In Swaziland the Concessions obtained from King Mbandzeni between 1885 and 1889 covered the mineral rights in nearly the whole country, but the Crown has recovered them by purchases extending over nearly half of this area.[3] In Basutoland it has not been questioned that the

---

[1] N.A., Part V, p. 232.
[2] The Minerals Proclamation no. 33, 1932. See also N.A., Part V, p. 311.
[3] Ibid. pp. 362 ff.

rights over minerals rest with the Basuto Native Authorities, and no Concessions of mineral rights have been given by them.[1] In Southern Rhodesia there was, from the first, never any doubt that the treaty rights acquired by the British South Africa Company from Lobengula gave it a claim to rights over the minerals throughout the territory and that the arrangements made on the termination of the Charter left these rights with the Company. In 1933 they were acquired from the Company by the Government of Southern Rhodesia for a payment of £2 million. The investment at one time appeared to be of questionable value, but circumstances have since proved it to be highly remunerative.

In Northern Rhodesia also the termination of the Charter left the mineral rights with the Chartered Company,[2] and this position was formally recognized by the Crown. No question of the Company's right to take royalties on copper produced by the mines of the Copperbelt arose till 1935 when European unofficial members of the Legislature demanded an inquiry into the validity of the title held to have been acquired from Lewanika, the Paramount Chief of Barotseland. At this period the royalties paid to the Company had risen from £7,000 in 1926 to £111,251 in 1935. The British Government, in a dispatch published in 1938,[3] held that the right of the Company was not open to challenge, but the attack on the position of the Company continued. The issue did not depend merely on the character of the rights obtained from Lewanika. The retention by the Company of this potential source of Protectorate revenue constituted a continual cause of tension between it and the public. The Company finally decided in 1950 to accept an arrangement by which it assigned to the Government of Northern Rhodesia 20 per cent. of the income accruing from royalties until the year 1986. After that date royalties would be surrendered in their entirety.[4] In 1951 royalties amounted to £6,655,000, the government share being £1,331,142. The Agreement applied to all mineral rights except diamonds. Diamond rights had been made over by the Company to the De Beers Corporation, but in 1955 an Agreement was concluded with the Corporation by which diamond rights also would be surrendered to the Government in 1986.[5]

In Nyasaland the British South Africa Company holds the mineral rights over a considerable area in North and Central Nyasaland. Over the remaining areas not covered by Certificates of Claim the Crown has retained the mineral rights;[6] so far, however, there has been little mineral

[1] Ibid. p. 116.

[2] *Report on the Financial and Economic Position of Northern Rhodesia*, Col. no. 145, 1938.

[3] No. 574, dated 31 December 1938.

[4] *Agreement with the British South Africa Company on the Mineral Rights owned by the Company in Northern Rhodesia and for the Eventual Transfer of those Rights to the Northern Rhodesia Government*, Col. no. 272, 1951.

[5] *F.N.*, 3 September 1955.   [6] *N.A.*, Part II, pp. 17, 62.

development. In Uganda rights are vested in the Crown, except where they are limited by recognition of title, as for example in the case of the large area of *mailo* lands which are held in a quasi-freehold tenure, or by an express grant from the Crown.[1] Similarly the State has retained these rights in Kenya, save where land has been alienated by the State.[2] But though this implies that the State retains the mineral rights in the large areas included in the category of Crown Lands and in the Native Land Units, the terms of the Kenya (Native Areas) Order in Council, 1939, have placed stringent restrictions on the grant of mining Concessions in the latter.[3] The Crown holds the mineral rights in Tanganyika also.

In Nigeria all mineral rights are vested in the Crown.[4] By an arrangement made in 1899, following the termination of the Charter of the Royal Niger Company, one-half of any royalties collected on a specified area of the territory was paid to the Company, whose rights eventually passed to the present United Africa Company. This arrangement was to last for 99 years. The sums paid on this account were at the outset trivial, but by 1942 they had risen to £156,898. They were redeemed by the Nigerian Government by a payment made to the Company in 1950.[5] In the Gold Coast and Ashanti, on the other hand, rights in minerals have been held to follow land rights, and the Crown has claimed proprietary rights over only the very small areas acquired for public purposes.[6] It has proceeded no farther in regard to the control over mineral rights over other lands than to regulate the procedure for the grant of Concessions by Chiefs and their Councils.[7] It is significant that at one period the mining Concessions granted by the Chiefs to the companies interested in the exploitation of gold exceeded the total area of the Colony and Ashanti.[8] In the northern territories of the Gold Coast the Minerals Ordinance of 1936 vests all mineral rights in the Crown.[9] In Sierra Leone the Crown has followed the practice established in the Gold Coast Colony and Ashanti by which it abstained from asserting proprietary rights over the lands of the Protectorate, but the first Protectorate Ordinance nevertheless vested in the Crown all rights in minerals, metals, and precious stones.[10] The Northern portion of British Togoland follows the Nigerian law, while the Southern follows the Gold Coast precedent.

In the French overseas areas the State has reserved to itself the right to minerals; these are expressly excluded from any Concessions of land.

---

[1] See above, p. 724.   [2] Ordinance no. 29, 1940.
[3] *N.A.*, Part I, pp. 188–9.
[4] Minerals Ordinance no. 10, 1916, and amendments consolidated in 1946.
[5] *The Colonial Territories (1949–50)*, Cmd. 7958, 1950, para. 320.
[6] *N.A.*, Part III, pp. 220, 221.
[7] Concessions Ordinance no. 14, 1900, as amended and re-enacted by Ordinance no. 19, 1939.
[8] *N.A.*, Part III, pp. 224 ff.   [9] Minerals Ordinance, Cap. 131.
[10] Ordinance no. 36, 1927. See *N.A.*, Part III, pp. 319, 320.

Minerals are not, therefore, regarded as the property of the owners of the land, and mineral rights may be granted only by Concession from the State. An exception is made in the case of quarries.

The law in the Belgian Congo, while acknowledging that property in land carries in principle the right to all above it and below it, withholds from the proprietor all rights in 'les substances considérées comme concessibles par la législation minière'.[1] Mineral deposits are the property of the State.[2] Under Article 15 of the *Charte Coloniale* any mineral Concession requires the authorization of the metropolitan Government. The mineral Concessions given to the great corporations, such as the *Comité Spécial du Katanga*, the *Compagnie des Chemins de Fer du Congo Supérieur aux Grands Lacs Africains*, and the *Comité National du Kivu*, entitle them to grant licences and to collect royalties and fees. In Ruanda Urundi mineral rights are also reserved to the State.

In the Portuguese territories rights to minerals are reserved to the State. Under the old *prazo* system prevailing in the Zambezi region of Mozambique the land and rights on it were held to be attached to the *prazo*, and the two Chartered Companies, the Moçambique and Niassa Companies, exercised powers over the land which were similar to those held by the British South Africa Company. As a result of the enactment of the Colonial Charter of 1933 all such rights have since terminated, and the State is the sole authority now holding rights to minerals, save where they are enjoyed by Concessions granted by the Government. These Concessions are at times of very considerable importance. The Diamond Company of Angola, for example, has the sole right for prospecting for diamond deposits in an area comprising almost five-sixths of the land area of Angola. In 1952 there were in existence 103 Concessions, dealing as a rule with prospecting for specially designated classes of minerals.[3] The most extensive of the Concessions granted in Mozambique is that held by the company concerned in prospecting for oil. It is noteworthy that in Concessions for industrial undertakings the Government usually requires that 51 per cent. of the shares should be held by Portuguese nationals.[4]

In Liberia the Government reserves to itself the sole right to grant prospecting and other Concessions. Reference has already been made to the considerable Concession given by Liberia for exploiting the iron deposits in the Bomi hills.

The reasons for the considerable differences in the laws which determine the ownership of mineral rights are now mainly of historical interest. It would be of little value to discuss the theoretical merits of the principle

[1] *Codes et Lois du Congo Belge*, 1954, p. 73, Article 16.
[2] Decree of 24 September 1937.
[3] *Overseas Economic Surveys, Portuguese West Africa, 1953*, p. 15.
[4] *Overseas Economic Surveys, Portuguese East Africa, 1951*, p. 7.

under which the State has asserted its right to ownership as against that under which the owners of surface rights are recognized also as owners of the minerals under the soil.[1] But experience has shown the difficulties which may ensue in practice from the adoption of the latter principle. Where rights of ownership in the land are as ill defined as they are in many parts of Africa, the grant of mineral Concessions by Chiefs and others may lead to a chaotic medley of Concessions, as is shown most conspicuously in the cases of Swaziland and the Gold Coast.[2] It has in every case been necessary for the State to intervene in order to introduce some measure of control which will permit development of the resources available. It has been no less essential for the State to interpose its authority in order to secure that a due share of the royalties or similar receipts shall inure to the benefit of the community immediately concerned, and not merely to that of its Chiefs or other Authorities. The practical disadvantages attending intervention of this nature seem to exceed those which may result from the outright assumption by the State of authority to deal at first hand with the disposal of mineral rights. Experience has shown that it is possible to combine the assertion of State rights in the subsoil with a material recognition of the need for compensation for any damage suffered by the proprietors or occupiers of the surface of the soil.

It is natural that the procedure regulating the grant of the right to prospect and mine for minerals should reflect the difference in the views held regarding the position of the State in respect of mineral rights. In South Africa the early laws of the Transvaal Republic recognized the title of the owner of land to the precious metals in the subsoil, but they also asserted the right of the State to control the usage of these rights in the public interest. The owner and discoverer of precious metals could exercise full rights over a specified area, to be selected by them, but thereafter any member of the public could peg up to 50 claims of 150 by 400 feet.

It was soon realized, however, that this limit retarded development unless the claim happened to contain unusually high-grade reef. In order to avoid both the difficulties of the pegging system and to benefit the general revenue, it was decided that the State should act as vendor. The Transvaal Gold Law of 1908 gave the Government power to establish State mines, or to lease any proclaimed land, and to throw it open for pegging. If it decided to lease it, the claims were allotted by a Mining Leases Board. Applicants for exclusive mining leases were required to pay a percentage of profit to the State in addition to licence fees and taxation. After the constitution of the Union, an Act of 1918[3] permitted

[1] *Memorandum on Mining Policy*, Col. no. 206, 1946.
[2] *N.A.*, Part III, pp. 220–5; ibid. Part V, pp. 373, 403, 421.
[3] Mining Leases Act no. 30, 1918.

the Mining Leases Board to lease undermining rights of small areas which could be exploited profitably only by adjoining companies. Up to 1948 some 44 large gold-mines had operated on areas leased on a basis of participation in profits. The leased mines contributed 50 per cent. of the total tonnage milled on the Witwatersrand. The share of the profits payable to the Government was either a fixed proportion of profits or more commonly varied with the ratio of profit to gold recovery on a sliding scale so calculated that the company obtained fixed proportions of reductions in costs and of increases in recovery.

The law was again amended in 1934 in order to attract capital for the opening of new deep-level mines. This gave the Mining Leases Board wide powers to ensure that mining claims were a workable proposition and that there was no indefinite holding up of mineral areas. These amendments favoured operations by highly capitalized ventures, but South African legislation still contemplates development by small workers. A new phase in the Government's mineral policy was begun by an Act of 1942.[1] This made provision for the prospecting of private land, and, if necessary, for the subsequent exploitation either by private enterprise or by the State of private ground believed to contain minerals in workable quantities. As regards the Native Trust Lands, Act no. 18 of 1936 prohibits prospecting on land in respect of which the Native Trust or a Native is the owner of mineral rights, without the written permission of the Minister. If the land is proclaimed as a 'public diggings', the Trust must impose conditions necessary to preserve surface rights to the Native occupiers.

In Bechuanaland historical developments led to the recognition of a number of large-scale Concessions originally obtained from various Chiefs.[2] The Native Reserves are now closed to prospecting unless the Mining Proclamation[3] has been applied to them. In such cases prospecting is allowed under mineral Concessions granted by the Chiefs, with the approval of the Secretary of State, or by virtue of a Crown grant issued with the owner's consent. The Tati area is excluded from the scope of these provisions.[4] In Swaziland mineral Concessions had, as already explained, been granted by the Swazi King between the years 1885 and 1889 over an aggregate area of 6,000 square miles, the Crown retaining the mineral rights in the remaining 684 square miles. The Crown has gradually acquired a great proportion of the mineral rights, and the Government now owns rights over about 48 per cent. of the country. The unusual complexity of the rights existing on the lands held in private title has militated against independent prospecting,[5] and prospecting or mining

[1] Base Mineral Amendment Act no. 39, 1942.   [2] N.A., Part V, 153–4.
[3] Mines and Minerals Proclamation, 1932.
[4] For the Tati district, see N.A., Part V, p. 235.   [5] Ibid. pp. 340, 421–2.

on Crown Land carrying mineral rights is not generally permitted owing to the inadequacy of legislation at present controlling such operations. A Commission (the Swaziland Mineral Development Commission) was appointed in 1953 with the object of suggesting legislation which will make possible the extension of prospecting and at the same time provide for the share of the profits of mining to be taken by the owners of rights on private lands and by the Native Authorities. Basutoland is, for the time being, closed to prospecting.

The conditions in the territories of the Federation of Rhodesia and Nyasaland have already been referred to. In Northern Rhodesia the Barotseland Province is, in the circumstances already explained, closed to general prospecting.[1] Elsewhere in the Protectorate a licence may be valid for any part of the territory open to prospecting, or may be exclusive in respect of a specified area. It is characteristic of the East African territories that unless the Government specifically closes an area, all African lands are open to prospectors, except the *mailo* lands of Uganda, which are held in individual title. In Kenya, however, the consent of the Natives Land Trust Board is required for prospecting in the Native Land Units. All these territories make provision for the small prospector who, if he finds minerals, can claim an exclusive right in a restricted area, and for the large organization by means of the 'exclusive prospecting licence' which gives sole rights over a specified area. But in commenting upon the small amount of prospecting accomplished in East Africa the East Africa Royal Commission 1953–5 recommended that an East African Prospecting and Mining Leases Board be established, which should advise Governments on mining policy. The Commission was emphatic that the exploration of minerals should be made attractive to the prospector by the provision of geological facilities and by the removal of legal and fiscal impediments.[2]

The British West African dependencies comprise considerable areas (the Gold Coast Colony and Ashanti and the Protectorate area of Sierra Leone) in which the State has not asserted a claim to proprietary rights over the lands, but different systems have been applied to the control of the mineral rights. In Nigeria the legislation regarding prospecting for minerals allows for the grant of prospecting rights valid for a year only, and for licences allowing prospecting in areas not exceeding eight square miles. Mining leases run for a period not exceeding 21 years; they may be renewed for a similar period provided the holder has complied with obligations connected with the employment of labour. There is no limit to the number of rights or leases that may be held by one person or company. The Minerals Ordinance of 1946 contains a clause safeguarding

---

[1] See above, p. 706.
[2] *East Africa Royal Commission 1953–1955, Report*, Cmd. 9475, 1955, p. 115.

the customary extraction of certain minerals by indigenous inhabitants, and provides machinery for the compensation of occupants of the soil who suffer loss or damage from prospecting or mining operations. In the Northern Territories of the Gold Coast mining rights are reserved to the Crown; in the Colony and Ashanti, however, they are vested in the Native landowners. Before undertaking mining operations a lease must be obtained from the indigenous owner of the mineral rights, but the terms of the lease must be validated by the Court under the Concessions Ordinances.[1] The mining laws of Sierra Leone resemble those of the Northern Territories of the Gold Coast; exclusive prospecting licences are granted and mining leases issued by the State. Concession of land rights may be made by the Tribal Authorities subject to validation by the Concessions Ordinance,[2] but such Concessions do not extend to the grant of mineral rights. In 1934 the Sierra Leone Selection Trust obtained from the Government a monopoly in the exploitation of diamonds in the Protectorate; its subsequent history has been referred to in a previous part of this chapter.

In the French territories, where rights in minerals are reserved to the State, it is only in the case of quarries that mining operations can be undertaken without first obtaining a Concession from the Government. Private companies created to undertake mining operations must be formed in accordance with French law and have registered offices either in France or in the French overseas territory. The law permits the State itself to undertake the exploitation of minerals. The Governors-General of the French territories are empowered by special decree to reserve the issue of licences to claimants having adequate financial and technical means. In certain areas of the Upper Guinea and on the borders of Senegal, where the Native inhabitants have traditionally engaged in mining, they have the sole right of prospecting for minerals.

In the Belgian Congo, where not only are mineral rights reserved to the State but Concessions are subject to close scrutiny by the metropolitan Authorities, there is a large body of regulations controlling the issue of the *permis* for prospecting.[3] The *permis de recherches* is of two classes, the *permis général* and the *permis spécial*; the latter gives the holder of a *permis général* the exclusive right of prospecting in a restricted area. The issue of a *permis* is normally confined to inhabitants of the Colony or companies registered or domiciled in it. In the Katanga region of the Belgian Congo special authorization is necessary for prospecting on land in occupation by Africans. In both the Congo and Ruanda Urundi indigenous mining operations are protected by law.

In the Portuguese territories mineral rights are governed by the law of

---

[1] *N.A.*, Part III, pp. 221, 251.   [2] Ibid. p. 320.
[3] *Codes et Lois du Congo Belge*, 1954, pp. 1455 ff.

1906, which was amended slightly in 1942. Prospecting licences are granted only by the headquarters of the Administration. In Angola the *Companhia de Diamantes de Angola* holds exclusive prospecting rights for diamonds throughout most of the Province and has the monopoly of exploitation of all occurrences discovered.

THE CONTRIBUTION MADE TO PUBLIC REVENUES

In a previous part of this chapter mention was made of the British Memorandum on mining policy which referred in particular to one characteristic feature of the mining industry. It essentially consists, it was said, of the removal of valuable natural resources which when once removed cannot be replaced. 'The process is in the nature of the realization of a capital asset, and the general aim of mining policy must therefore be to make the best possible arrangement for realizing such an asset.' The most obvious method of realizing this asset would be by taxation of the agencies which have undertaken the task of exploitation. In all the circumstances the public interest clearly demands that the taxation should be at the highest possible level, subject to paying due regard to certain factors inherent in the nature of the industry itself. The exploitation of minerals often involves a very high amount of capital expenditure, and the capital has in Colonial circumstances normally to be drawn from external sources. Mining is always of a speculative nature, and taxation of the proceeds must also have due regard to the return which the private investor will expect from an investment in what is essentially a wasting asset. The interests of the community demand that the mineral deposits should be thoroughly worked out and the maximum amount of low-grade ore extracted; unduly heavy demands by the State may lead to the wastage of marginal ores. All these factors fall within the field of fiscal policy, and must be studied in relation to the returns which the investment market has normally earned on the capital it has provided.[1]

But their consideration has been complicated by another factor, not strictly of a fiscal character. In certain European countries, and notably in Great Britain, the private owners of mineral rights have availed themselves of the possession of these rights in order to draw considerable sums either by way of initial payment or of annual returns from the agencies engaged in their exploitation. The same procedure has been followed in the Union of South Africa and in territories such as Northern Rhodesia and the Gold Coast. In the Gold Coast, however, the sums received by the indigenous owners of mineral rights have not been considerable, owing to their inexperience at the time when they granted Concessions to exploit these rights. At an early stage the Governments concerned,

[1] 'Capital and Colonies', *J.R.S.A.*, August 1943, pp. 474 ff.

and more particularly those in South Africa, were content to take a share of the 'royalties' paid to the owners of mineral rights. The term 'royalty', it should be explained, owes its origin to the fact that in Great Britain gold and silver procured from the land by mining or similar means were by ancient usage held to be part of the prerogative of the Sovereign. But the Governments of other countries also in which the State, not the landowner, was held to be the owner of mineral rights, sought in turn to take advantage of their legal position by making the payment of royalties a condition of the Concessions they made for the exploitation of the minerals. This development was not unnatural in view of the fact that in many of these countries the principle of direct taxation, in the shape of income tax or its equivalent, did not for some time form a source of raising public revenue.[1] But the position created when the income tax system became fully established was confused by the fact that in realizing for public purposes the value of this mineral asset the State was approaching the matter from two different angles. The complication was increased when the Administrations of certain of the territories adopted the principle of augmenting the revenues available to their Native Authorities by devolving to them a certain part of the taxation of mineral products. It is significant that the Report of the East Africa Royal Commission 1953–5 has held that in East Africa, at all events, such Authorities have no legal title to mineral rights and that it is undesirable that they should be allowed to share in the profits.[2]

The result of these complex factors has been to deprive the mineral industry of the benefit of that comprehensive consideration which should be given to so important a source of revenue. It has also led to the diversion of the revenues thus received to objects other than the replacement of the national asset which is being exhausted by mining operations. Such replacement might suitably have been devoted, in the first instance, to improving the sources of permanent production in the area concerned, as for example by increasing the facilities for the improvement of agriculture or the expansion of communications. The effect of the combination of the system of royalties and of taxation is shown in the ensuing notes on the procedure existing in different parts of Africa.

In the Union of South Africa the contribution to public revenues made by mining in 1951–2 amounted in all to a little over £33 million, out of a total revenue (Central and Provincial combined) of nearly £237 million. The system of royalties which had once prevailed in certain of the constituent Provinces of the Union had by then been abolished, and the major contribution to public revenue took the form of income tax. But there was an important contribution amounting to a little over £2¼ million from the system of lease, some description of which has been given on a previous

---

[1] See above, pp. 647, 666.   [2] Cmd. 9475, 1955, p. 117.

occasion. In addition, there was a contribution of a little over £1 million from the export duty on diamonds, and a further contribution from the diamond industry of about £2 million as the proceeds of State mining, the origin of which has also been previously explained. Very roughly, therefore, the total contribution may be said to be made up of about £27½ million from taxation and about £5½ million from other sources.[1]

Gold-mining was at one period the subject of special discrimination in the matter of taxation. The Mining Taxation Act of 1910 subjected both gold and diamond mines to a profits tax of 10 per cent., which was higher than the rate applicable to base metals. During the First World War the gold-mines were obliged to make, in addition to the tax on profits, a special contribution to the Exchequer. An Act of 1917, however, abolished the discriminatory rates; all companies paid a flat rate of 1s. in the pound, though an element of discrimination still remained in that dividends distributed by gold-mining companies were taxed at a higher ratio than others. In 1925 a consolidation of the income tax laws abandoned the dividend tax, but this was replaced by a profits tax that discriminated against gold- and diamond-mining companies. When the Union went off the gold standard in 1932,[2] the ensuing increase in the price of gold attracted legislation in the form of an excess profits duty and subsequently a surtax designed to absorb the enhanced profits of the gold-mines. A Committee appointed in 1935 recommended a basic tax at a flat rate and a surtax leviable under a formula which would graduate liability according to the ratio of profit to the value of gold recovered. This double form of taxation would, it held, bring to revenue an adequate proportion of profits earned and also stimulate the mining of marginal ore. The 1936 Income Tax Act, which gave effect to these proposals, imposed two taxes on the profits derived from gold-mining: a basic tax of 3s. in the pound, and a 'formula'[3] tax based on the percentage ratio of profits to gold recovered. This tax became effective only when the ratio was 12½ per cent. or more. The Act of 1936 remained in force until 1945.

During the Second World War the gold-mining industry was again called upon to make a special contribution to war funds. This was first at the rate of 11 per cent. of net profits and eventually rose to 22½ per cent.[4] Dissatisfaction with the current policy of taxation led in 1945 to the appointment of another Committee. This recommended that the basic normal tax should be abolished, and that mining companies should be taxed solely on the basis of the 'profits/recovery' formula; that is to say, the ratio should be 5 per cent. or more before any tax became payable,

[1] O.Y.S.A., 1952–53, p. 605.
[2] J. C. Thoms, 'Gold Mining Taxation in South Africa', Optima, June 1954.
[3] For the 'formula' tax, see O.Y.S.A., 1950, p. 640.
[4] Gold Mines Special Contribution and Excess Profits Duty Act no. 25, 1940, repealed in 1946. Report of the Committee on Gold Mining Taxation, U.G. no. 16, 1946.

thereby assisting the working of low-grade ores. It was further suggested that a distinction should be introduced between new and established mines. The new mines were to be exempted from taxation until all capital expenditure had been allowed as a charge against profits. In respect of capital investment by old mines, the Committee recommended that some more favourable basis than the 'life of mine' should be introduced. It is significant, however, that it recommended the maintenance of some element of discrimination against the gold-mining industry; in contrast to the views of its predecessor in 1935, it held that the mines, as a wasting asset, should be treated differently for taxation purposes from those industries which had a more or less indefinite life. Most of these recommendations were adopted, and in 1946 the basic normal tax was repealed so far as gold-mining profits were concerned. In its place was substituted the 'formula' tax, which becomes effective when the ratio of profits to recovery is 6 per cent. and above. Since 1947 additional relief has been given to small mining companies, and new companies have been allowed relief from taxation to the point where capital expenditure incurred in bringing the mine to production has been fully redeemed out of profits.

As regards Southern Rhodesia the contribution made by the mineral industry is best seen by taking the two groups into which the public revenues are divided, namely, 'tax revenue' and 'non-tax revenue' groups. In the 'non-tax revenue' group, which amounted to a total of £2½ million in 1951, mining royalties accounted for nearly £140,000 and mining fees for £57,750.[1] In the 'tax revenue' group, in which the net taxable income amounted in 1949 to £31½ million, gold and other mining together accounted for a net taxable income of roughly £3·7 million.[2] During the Second World War the gold industry paid a special gold premium tax, but this was abolished in 1947. Attempts have been made here to meet the problems occasioned by the imposition of a flat rate on the profits of mining, since this is open to the objection that a light tax enables the richer mines to contribute less to public revenues than they can afford, while a heavy tax discourages the working of low-grade ores. In 1952 Southern Rhodesia introduced the system of a depletion allowance, and this has recently been incorporated into the Tax Code of the Federation of Rhodesia and Nyasaland. In the case of gold-mines this allowance is 10 per cent. of the gross value of annual output; for base minerals it is 2½ per cent. Reference has already been made to the circumstances in which Southern Rhodesia purchased the mineral rights formerly held by the British South Africa Company, thereby avoiding the necessity of dealing specially with the taxation of mineral royalties. Reference has also been made to the circumstances in which the British South Africa Company has surrendered to the Northern Rhodesia Government part of the copper

---

[1] *O.Y.S.R., 1952*, p. 604.   [2] Ibid. pp. 620-1.

royalties enjoyed by it. In this territory the royalty on copper is graduated according to the price realized. The revenue derived by the State from the share of royalties made over to it by the Agreement of 1950 amounted in 1952 to £1·7 million. The mineral industry is by far the largest contributor to the income tax of the Protectorate; in 1952 it paid income tax amounting to £14·3 million, which was 58·8 per cent. of total revenue from this source.

The system of royalties has now been abolished in Kenya, where at one time the royalty on gold was 15 per cent. of the annual profits derived from the undertaking. In Uganda the royalty on precious metals is 5 per cent. and on precious stones 10 per cent. of the gross value, but the miner has the alternative of paying a royalty of 5 per cent. on his production or a 15 per cent. tax on profits. There has been a growing tendency elsewhere in the British dependencies to allow the mining industry a choice of these alternatives. It is, for example, now the rule in Tanganyika. No royalties have so far been taken in Zanzibar. In Nigeria the royalty on the principal product, namely tin, varies according to the sale value of the metal, the rates ranging from 2 per cent. up to 10 per cent. of the value. The royalty on gold is 6 per cent.

In the Gold Coast Colony and Ashanti mineral rights are, as already explained, vested in the owners of the soil, but under the Ordinance of 1939 Concession-holders and mine-owners pay duty of 1s. in the pound on all products. The Ashanti Goldfield Corporation pays a special royalty of 5 per cent. of the value of gold won by it. In the Northern Territories of the Gold Coast, where mining rights are vested in the Crown, minerals pay either 5 per cent. of the current market value of the product or 1s. in the pound of annual profits. The major contribution from mining operations to the public revenues in the Gold Coast is made through the income tax and the operation of the Minerals Duty Ordinance of 1952, which imposes a duty on the value of minerals won, at rates that vary according to the 'yield ratio' of each undertaking. The 'yield ratio' is calculated by deducting from the value of the minerals all expenses necessary to the mining and transporting of the mineral, including allowances for depreciation, and by expressing the resultant figure as a percentage of the value of the minerals won.[1]

In Sierra Leone the royalty on iron was fixed by the Agreement with the Sierra Leone Development Company, the amount varying from 3d. to 6d. a ton according to the price of iron ore when shipped at Pepel. The royalty on diamonds is determined by the Agreement with the Consolidated African Selection Trust. The Trust paid originally a rent of £7,000 per annum and a profits tax of 27½ per cent., together with surface rents and compensation to the Tribal Authorities as assessed under the

---

[1] *Colonial Reports, Gold Coast, 1953*, p. 36.

Minerals Ordinance of 1937. Reference has already been made to the modification of the royalty as the result of negotiations in 1953–4.[1]

In the French Union provision is in many cases made for profit-sharing, in which the State participates on a fixed percentage or on a sliding scale based on net profits after the payment of guaranteed dividends. The share generally amounts to 20 per cent. of the profits distributed. In the Belgian Congo the State has, as already shown, usually preferred the method of retaining an agreed proportion in the shares of the enterprise. It is claimed that under this system the undertaking is not burdened at the outset with fixed charges, and that official control of labour and welfare conditions can be better exercised by representation on the Directorate than by supervision from outside.

GEOLOGICAL AND MINERAL SURVEYS

Although the Colonial Governments have normally preferred to leave to private enterprise the exploitation of the mineral resources in their territories, they have recognized that they have an obligation to support the development of geological and mineral surveys. In South Africa the Geological Commission for the Cape was organized in 1895, and the Geological Survey of the Union came into being in 1910. The Survey then incorporated the Geological Commission of the Cape and the Geological Survey of the Transvaal, which had been reconstituted in 1903. A short-lived geological survey had been initiated in the Orange Free State in 1878, while Natal and Zululand had a geological survey from 1902 to 1906.[2] The Geological Survey, with its headquarters at Pretoria, is now part of the Department of Mines. It is making an extended use of an aerial survey and of magnetic and geophysical methods of surveying.[3] The greater part of the Union has been surveyed in varying degrees of detail, chief attention having been paid to the areas most likely to contain minerals of economic value. The importance of the potential gold-bearing areas of the Orange Free State now gives special value to the use of gravimetric methods, and the use of radio-active methods is also being widely extended as an assistance to the discovery of sources of uranium. In Southern Rhodesia the Department of Geological Survey is part of the Division of Mines and Transport. The Department also acts in an advisory capacity to the mining industry.[4]

In the British dependencies there have from an early date been a number of local geological survey services, but there has until lately been no central organization of survey work. As a result of the recommendations made by the Committee on Colonial Research, which was appointed to

---

[1] *The Colonial Territories, 1953–54*, Cmd. 9169, 1954. See also above, p. 1512.
[2] *Bulletin of the Imperial Institute*, vol. xxxix, no. 3, 1941, pp. 302–7; ibid. vol. xli, no. 4, 1943, pp. 255–86.   [3] *O.Y.S.A., 1952–53*, pp. 906–7.   [4] *O.Y.S.R., 1952*, p. 81.

advise as to the expenditure of the funds provided under the Colonial Development and Welfare Act of 1940, a central organization of Colonial Geological Surveys was instituted with effect from 1947. There was some initial delay in recruiting the necessary staff of trained geologists, but the organization now has its own Directorate and staff.[1] It serves as a means of supplementing the operations of the territorial Geological Surveys maintained in the various Colonies; these exist everywhere except in Gambia, which has, however, been the subject of a report by an officer seconded from the Gold Coast Survey Department. In some instances valuable discoveries have been made by officers of these Departments, as has been shown, for example, by the instances cited in dealing with mining development in West Africa.[2] Their main function, however, has been to provide geological data and a systematic mapping of the country which will indicate where mineralized areas are likely to be situated. The work of locating workable deposits is normally left to private enterprise. It is of interest to note that in Northern Rhodesia the very complete geological survey of the large areas held by the two groups of copper companies has been carried out by their own establishment.

In French West Africa a Geological Service was created in 1930, and attached to the *Service des Mines*. In 1938 it began the publication of a *Bulletin du Service des Mines de l'A.O.F.*, issued at Dakar.[3] A greatly increased provision for geological survey has been made in the Ten-year Plan,[4] and it is intended that this should now be largely devoted to a study of the areas containing indications of mineral resources. In the Belgian Congo much of the geological survey work was originally left to the companies holding mining Concessions; the *Comité Spécial du Katanga*, for instance, has had its own Geographical and Geological Service since 1919, and has published a valuable series of geological maps of the Katanga.[5] The Administration has a considerable Geological Service, which in 1953 comprised 24 European officers and 83 African employees, though this Department devotes only part of its time to actual survey work. Some 25 million francs have been devoted in the Development Plan to the expansion of the geological survey undertaken by the Government. Compared with British territories and the Belgian Congo, the Portuguese territories are still backward in the matter of geological survey, and there are large areas in which little survey work has been attempted. There is, however, a considerable provision made for it in the current Development Programme.[6]

---

[1] Colonial Office, *Report of the Committee on Colonial Geology*, C.M. no. 8, 1944. *Colonial Research, 1947–48*, Cmd. 7493, 1948, p. 12.
[2] *Bulletin of the Imperial Institute*, vol. xxxix, no. 3, 1941, p. 310. See also above, pp. 1511 ff.
[3] *Enc. A.O.F.*, vol. i, p. 197.   [4] See above, p. 1339.   [5] *Enc. C.B.*, vol. iii, p. 793.
[6] *Overseas Economic Surveys, Portuguese West Africa, 1953*, p. 15. *Overseas Economic Surveys, Portuguese East Africa, 1951*, p. 27.

CHAPTER XXIII

TRANSPORT AND COMMUNICATIONS

LEOPOLD II of Belgium is credited with the saying that 'coloniser c'est transporter', and the observation is peculiarly applicable to the history of the modern development of Africa. It is of some interest to contrast the problems of transport which the early Administrations had to face in Africa with those encountered by the British in India. In India the Mogul Emperors had left a number of well-established high-roads between the principal cities; there were milestones (*kôs minâr*) at carefully measured intervals and caravanserais had been built for the use of travellers. There was far less in the way of regular communication away from the main roads,[1] but as early as 1830 the East India Company was metalling the route between Bombay and Poona, and in 1839 it began to convert the road between Calcutta and Delhi into the Grand Trunk Road, 1,000 miles in length, a performance that was probably without parallel in the Europe of that day. Before the transfer of power in 1947, India had roughly 350,000 miles of road, of which about 85,000 were metalled. As compared with India, Africa as seen in the early days of Colonial rule was practically devoid of any provision for regular means of communication. Arabs had cut paths into the interior for their caravans, but they stayed no longer than was required to collect slaves and ivory. The Portuguese, with a maritime tradition, had followed the inland waterways when they left the ocean littoral, but the waterways that could be used as a means of transport were relatively few. Such intercourse as the African peoples had maintained between themselves was usually conducted along narrow tracks that often followed the paths made by the pads of elephants or the hooves of antelope. Indigenous Africans had never evolved the use of the wheel and were singularly slow to adopt it when they saw others employ it. In the large areas, moreover, which were infested by tsetse, domestic animals could not as a rule survive; where they did so, they were not trained to be used as transport.

Navigable waterways were especially deficient in South Africa, and at an early date the European settlers turned their attention to the making of roads. By the Dutch the road was viewed primarily as furnishing a means for the use of ox-wagons, and in this they secured valuable assistance from the employment of Hottentots, who developed a special aptitude for managing trek-oxen. The use of wagons by the Dutch settlers became almost universal, save in such areas as that between Lourenço

---

[1] L. S. S. O'Malley, *Modern India and the West*, 1941, p. 235.

Marques and Lydenburg, where the prevalence of the tsetse fly precluded it. But in the greater part of East, Central, and West Africa the construction of roads served mainly to provide a means for the more systematic organization of human porterage. The use of roads in this manner was a definite advantage, for even if the early roads were no more than well-established tracks, they not only reduced the danger to the life and health of the porters, but provided traders with a more economic use of transport. Head porterage was not necessarily an evil in itself. It indeed caused little hardship until regularly employed by Arabs or Europeans for commercial purposes. The transport of ivory, rubber, or commercial produce might entail long absence from home; it might disseminate disease and cause, in general, much social disturbance. It was in addition, as Lord Lugard observed, 'a most archaic and wasteful form of transport'.[1] During the First World War the transportation of 4,200 tons of foodstuffs by the French was recorded as having involved the employment of no less than 125,000 carriers.[2] In Northern Rhodesia, on the 500-mile journey from the railway line to the German front in East Africa, the carrier, it was said, 'ate nearly all that he carried'. As late as 1924 the transport of Government loads in Tanganyika accounted for 400,000 working days of the porters employed.[3] It is interesting to note that it was calculated in 1926 that in Nigeria the transport of one ton per mile by head porterage cost 2s. 6d., by motor transport 1s.; and by railway 2d.[4] The East Africa Royal Commission of 1953–5 has stated that, whereas the cost of transport by head porterage was 8s. to 12s. per ton mile, it was reduced by the use of the motor lorry to a figure between 3s. 6d. and 5s.[5] It was by the elimination of long-distance porterage that modern systems of transport have made one of their most impressive contributions to progress in Africa.

There were, however, many parts of Africa in which the construction of roads was not at first accepted as an urgent part of the task of administration. In some parts, as most notably in the Belgian Congo, priority was attached to the development of the waterways. In other instances— as for example in French West Africa—the construction of railways actually preceded the systematic extension of the road system. In some other territories also, it was not until the railway programme was well advanced that there arose a demand for the wide expansion of the road system as a feeder to the railways. It needed, at a later date, the great

[1] F. D. Lugard, *The Dual Mandate in British Tropical Africa*, 1926, p. 474.
[2] L. C. A. and C. M. Knowles, *The Economic Development of the British Overseas Empire*, vol. i, 1924, p. 144.
[3] *Report by Major St. J. Orde Browne upon Labour in the Tanganyika Territory, 1926*, Col. no. 19, 1926, p. 37.
[4] *Report by the Hon. W. G. A. Ormsby-Gore on his Visit to West Africa during the Year 1926*, Cmd. 2744, 1926.
[5] *East Africa Royal Commission 1953–1955, Report*, Cmd. 9475, 1955, p. 120.

increase in the use of motors for the transport of passengers and goods to create the imperative demand which exists today for the improvement of the standard of road surfacing.

In Europe the evolution of the railway system formed part of the transition to an industrialized economy. It took shape in an era of new invention and of rapidly expanding trade. In other continents special causes have stimulated the provision of facilities for transport by rail. In the United States, for instance, a large volume of local industry had been created by the use of waterways and roads before the construction of railways; in Canada and Australia the building of trans-continental lines was undertaken in the expectation of attracting European settlers whose activities would provide an adequate return of remunerative traffic. It is frequently said that Africa was first brought clearly within the orbit of European civilization because its minerals and precious stones attracted railway construction. While this may be in some sense true of the Union of South Africa, Northern Rhodesia, or the Katanga area of the Belgian Congo, it does not apply to many other parts of Africa. There have in fact been a variety of motives which have stimulated the construction of railways.

A stimulus was given to railway construction by the Berlin Conference of 1884–5, when it was held that a title to territory could be sustained only by effective occupancy.[1] The construction of a railway was calculated to furnish one of the most obvious proofs of occupancy, and it is noticeable that a number of the railways in Central and part of West Africa were projected in 1885 and the years immediately following. The railways of French West Africa were, in the first instance, designed for strategic purposes. The Kenya–Uganda Railway was approved by Parliament on the ground that, though naval action had been effectual in reducing the scope of the slave trade, it could be completely eradicated only by action taken in the interior of Africa. A similar reason had accounted for the laborious transportation of the first steam launch to Lake Nyasa in 1875. The construction of railways in Nigeria and some other parts of West Africa owed little to the desire to find transport for minerals; the railway system has been built up on the demands made for transport of cocoa, groundnuts, cotton, coffee, and similar tropical products. Though in the Union of South Africa the first stimulus to the construction of railroads was given by the requirements of the diamond and gold industries, the subsequent expansion of the production of economic crops has led to the construction of many branch lines, and the Government has spent at least £14 million on these lines, in the interests of agriculture.

The physical obstacles to the construction of railways were often formidable. Lack of port and harbour facilities sometimes made the unloading

[1] S. E. Crowe, *The Berlin West African Conference*, 1942, pp. 176–82.

of equipment exceedingly hazardous. Maps were often only rudimentary and, as has already been shown,[1] serious mistakes were at times made in the routing of railways owing to inaccuracies of survey. Physical obstacles were considerable along the edges of the Great and Little Karroos, in the Drakensberg mountains, in the Fouta Djalon hills of French Guinea, and between Matadi and Leopoldville in the Belgian Congo, to quote only a few well-known examples. The escarpments of the African plateau, which cause the falls and rapids that obstruct so many rivers, also presented severe problems to railway engineers. A notable instance has been the Rhodesia–Mozambique borderland near Umtali. Some of the rivers have also presented major obstacles. It is reputed that the Zambezi bridge, carrying the Nyasaland–Beira Railway, is the longest railway bridge in the world, and that the Benue bridge, over which the Nigerian Railway passes, is the second longest. There have been other obstacles, even more refractory than those created by nature. The shortage of labour could on occasion be overcome only by expedients such as the importation of immigrant labour, or the undesirable alternative of compulsory recruitment of manpower.

It is a striking feature of the railway system of Africa that so many of the lines have tended to proceed at right-angles to the coastline in order to gain access to the interior. It is rare to find railways running parallel with the coast or connecting one port with another. There is, moreover, a substantial difference between the rail systems in East and West Africa. In the former, the lines may serve several territories; for example, the East African rail system embraces Uganda, Kenya, and Tanganyika, and the Mozambique territory accommodates lines from the Rhodesias, Nyasaland, and the Transvaal. In West Africa, however, each railway is throughout its entire length confined within its own territory. The lines in Senegal, Sierra Leone, the Ivory Coast, the Gold Coast, Togoland, Dahomey, and Nigeria serve at present no territory other than their own. Partly, no doubt, this singular pattern has been due to international jealousy, but it has also been actuated by the propensity of each country to secure for itself the total receipts accruing from railway rates and customs duties. The most outstanding examples of competitive national railways are the Belgian and French lines running parallel on either bank of the Congo river from Leopoldville and Brazzaville respectively to the coast. An opportunity will be taken subsequently of discussing the means of securing greater international co-operation in the designing of railways.

There is another factor which has dictated the routing of railways. The importance assigned to the sea communications to European markets has given a high value to the selection of ports, which thus became the focus from which land communications have radiated. The choice of an inferior

[1] See above, p. 13.

port in the past has therefore not only necessitated its displacement by one superior to it, but has led also to the diversion of inland communications. In the following pages several instances of this will be noted: St. Louis was superseded by Dakar, Accra by Takoradi, Lindi by Mtwara, and Mozambique now seems likely to be replaced by Nacala. One of the best harbours on the west coast—the Gambia river—has never been utilized. This is a difficulty in the organization of transport which it might be possible to obviate by discussions held at conferences such as those which have of late years dealt specially with questions of routing, as for example the Dakar Conference of 1947, and the important Central and South African Transport Conference held at Johannesburg in 1950.[1] Such conferences are also the appropriate means for dealing with differences of gauge. There are at present five different gauges in use on railways south of the Sahara. The adoption of a standard gauge of 3 ft. 6 in. has, however, now been generally accepted as desirable.

The period of greatest activity in the construction of railways occurred between 1895 and 1914. The result has, on the whole, left Africa with a railway mileage similar to that which characterizes many of the underdeveloped regions of the world. It compares unfavourably, for instance, with the 43,000 miles of railway in the relatively small area—somewhat less than that of French West Africa and only about 50 per cent. more than that of the Belgian Congo—of India as it stood before partition. The lack of activity during recent years in the construction of railroads has been due to a variety of reasons, among which the most important is the competitive claim made by the road systems for extension and improvement. That also is a matter which will be more fully discussed in the following pages. The progress of railroad construction has been little affected by the wide expansion in Africa of the most modern of the agencies of transport—the aeroplane. The use of the air has proved to be of great benefit from both an administrative and a commercial standpoint, but travel by air is so far confined to a comparatively small range of passengers.

The following pages will give the chief facts about the use of the waterways, and the development of the road, rail, and air systems of transport in Africa.

THE USE MADE OF NAVIGABLE WATERWAYS

Africa is, as a whole, less well served by waterways than any other continent of comparable size,[2] though, owing to the large extent of waterways in the Congo Basin, West Central Africa is more fortunate in this

[1] H. O. Mance, 'International Transport', *Journal of the Institute of Transport*, November 1949.
[2] C. Lucas, *Partition and Colonization of Africa*, 1922, p. 14.

respect than either South or East Africa. In the Union of South Africa the only navigable river, the Limpopo, can in fact be so utilized for only about 30 miles from its estuary. The Zambezi is navigable for some 400 miles from its delta, but above its confluence with the Luangwa it is interrupted in turn by the Kariba Gorge, the Victoria Falls, and the waterfalls at Gonye, before it again becomes suitable for light draught barges in its course through the Barotse Plain. The rivers in Tanganyika and Kenya carry nothing much larger than canoes. With the exception of the Congo river, the lower and upper reaches of the Zambezi, the Gambia, and the lower Niger, internal transportation by water is practically confined to the Great Lakes—Victoria, Nyasa, Tanganyika, and Albert. Before the construction of railways these were utilized by such craft as Africans were accustomed to employ or European pioneers capable of constructing.

The first steam vessel to cruise up the Zambezi was the *Ma-Robert*, so christened by Africans after Mrs. Livingstone, in 1858. The opening of the railway line from Beira to Chindio, at the confluence of the Shire river with the Zambezi, diverted much of the traffic which had hitherto passed down the river. The construction of the Tete–Moatize line in 1949 also deprived it of the produce—estimated at an annual value of about £250,000—from estates in the interior, and of the coal carried by the colliers belonging to the Trans-Zambezia Railway. Today river traffic is largely confined to steamers of the Sena sugar estates carrying cargo to Chindio.[1]

The incipient desiccation which has now become so characteristic a feature of the Shire river was noticed by missionaries as early as 1889, and by 1912 Port Herald ceased to be a place of embarkation. Although the water level rose again in 1934, and indeed swept away the bridge at Chiromo in 1948, the Shire has never regained its former volume of traffic. Today the Nyasaland Railways maintain a service of paddle-steamers for the transport of cotton and other produce between Chiromo and Chikwawa, and a Portuguese tug towing cargo barges plies between Port Herald and Mgaza. But it was the desiccation of the Shire that accelerated the building of the railway (1922) and of the bridge over the Zambezi (1935), which thus effected a rail connexion between Beira and Lake Nyasa. The first steamer on Lake Nyasa was transported in sections from the coast by a body of 800 porters, and was launched in 1875. Some of the difficulties which have to be faced in the navigation of the lake were shown when the motor vessel *Vipya* was sunk in 1946 with a great loss of life. The Nyasaland Railways now maintain on the lake a motor vessel with cargo capacity of 240 tons and a combined passenger and cargo motor vessel with accommodation for 360 passengers and 100 tons of

[1] *An Economic Survey of the Colonial Territories, 1951 : vol. i, The Central African and High Commission Territories*, Col. no. 281(1), 1952, p. 42.

cargo. The scheme for the construction of a barrier on the Shire river, with the double object of restoring its navigability and of providing power for a hydro-electric plant, may again alter the pattern of communication on Lake Nyasa.[1]

The importance of the harbours in Portuguese East Africa is enhanced by the fact that Northern and Southern Rhodesia, Nyasaland, and the Transvaal are land-locked, and that their nearest route to the sea is to the Portuguese ports of Beira and Lourenço Marques. This was a primary factor in the construction of the Johannesburg–Lourenço Marques, the Salisbury–Umtali–Beira, and the Salisbury–Bannockburn–Lourenço Marques railway lines. Lourenço Marques, which is thus the terminus of two of these lines, possesses one of the best natural harbours on the east coast. Beira, the port of embarkation for minerals and produce from the Central African Federation, is equidistant from London by either the Cape or the Suez Canal routes, but, although many improvements have been made in recent years, there are still complaints of the congestion of both incoming and outgoing freight. Other ports, such as Inhambane, Quelimane, Chinde, Lumbo, and Porto Amélia, have only a local significance, but Nacala, a little north of Mozambique, is a natural harbour, able to afford anchorage to the largest ocean-going vessels. It is now being equipped by the Portuguese Government and is coming into general use.

There are two water routes in Northern Rhodesia which deserve a brief mention. During the First World War a tortuous route through the *sudd* and swamps of Lake Bangweulu was opened to provide an alternative to the head porterage of transport from the railway line to the front in German East Africa. Channels have since been cut and the lake, which is the centre of an organized fish industry, is traversed by the Fisheries Board steamers.[2] Secondly, a scheme put forward in 1954 contemplated the use of a specially designed barge to operate over the 400-mile section of the Zambezi river between Livingstone and Mongu in Barotseland, and ultimately continue service up to the Angola border, north of Balovale. Vessels of this type would replace the cumbrous Barotse barge, propelled by 16 man-handled paddles, and would reduce the period of the journey to Mongu from three weeks to two days. Diesel-driven barges are already employed by a recruiting agency on this route.[3]

Lake Tanganyika, which measures 450 miles in length, serves a considerable tract of country, but the volume of traffic is relatively small. The East African Railways Administration has a regular steamer service, covering 299 miles, from Kigoma to Mpulungu in Northern Rhodesia, and this is

---

[1] See above, p. 989.

[2] F. Debenham, *Report on Water Resources of the Bechuanaland Protectorate, Northern Rhodesia, the Nyasaland Protectorate, Tanganyika Territory and the Uganda Protectorate*, Colonial Research Publication no. 2, 1948, pp. 47 ff.

[3] *Northern Rhodesia, Annual Report on African Affairs, 1952*, p. 17.

supplemented by a tug and lighter service calling at the principal harbours. The lake is connected by motor road with Abercorn and the Northern Rhodesia road system. The Belgian *Compagnie des Chemins de Fer du Congo Supérieur aux Grands Lacs Africains* (the CFL) runs a weekly service from Albertville to Kigoma, to Usumbura in Ruanda Urundi, and to Uvira in the extreme north, and maintains fortnightly communications with Moba in the south and with Nyanza in the north. The volume of traffic passing in and out of Kigoma has, however, declined since the opening of the Benguela Railway, which now takes part of the copper from Katanga to the west coast. Lake Kivu is linked by road to Lake Tanganyika, though a railway line from Uvira runs as far north as Kamanyola. The lake, which is 62 miles long, has a steamer service operated by the *Office d'Exploitation des Transports Coloniaux* (OTRACO), which works in conjunction with the vessels operating on Lake Tanganyika.

Lake Victoria is the largest and, from a commercial standpoint, the most important of the Great Lakes, with a coastline of over 4,000 miles. The first steam launch, brought to the lake in 1895 by Native carriers, was wrecked on being launched, but another vessel was floated in 1896, and there are now three steamers of about 1,200 tons operated by the East African Railways and Harbours Administration. In addition dhows maintain irregular communication between the lake ports. Dhow competition with the Railways craft involved a considerable loss of revenue to the Railways in 1938, and as the result of legislation designed to assist the Railways-operated craft, the total tonnage carried by the dhows was reduced by 1948 to less than half its previous figure. In 1953 the traffic conveyed by vessels managed by the East African Railways amounted to 390,000 tons of freight and 582,000 passengers. The lake is served by rail at three points, namely Kisumu, Port Bell, and Mwanza, the main traffic flowing towards Kisumu. Bukakata serves as an outlet for the south-western areas of Uganda; Bukoba, south of Bukakata, also serves a large area of African-grown coffee; Musoma on the east coast serves the adjacent gold-mining areas. Mwanza Harbour is the terminus of the Tabora–Mwanza branch of the Tanganyika Central line.

Of the other lakes mentioned above, Lake Kyoga is served by a tug with accommodation for passengers; a link is thus provided between Atura on the Victoria Nile and Namasagali, which is connected by rail with the main Uganda line. Masindi Port on the Victoria Nile is linked by road services to Butiaba on Lake Albert. Lake Albert is a waterway of some considerable importance. Three steamers operate a total route of 645 miles, under the control of the East African Railways Administration. A service runs between Butiaba on the eastern shore to Kasenyi in the Belgian Congo, which is connected with the gold-mines at Kilo-Moto by the Belgian Congo motor transport system. To the north another service operates from Butiaba to Mahagi in the Belgian Congo and along the Albert Nile to Pakwach in Uganda. From Pakwach river craft connect with Nimule, on the Sudan frontier; this route is continued by a motor road to Juba, after which the Nile is navigable to Khartoum. On the south side the Semliki river connects Lake Albert to Lake Edward, which in turn is connected by a channel to Lake George, but this line of communication is used chiefly by Native fishing craft.[1] The possibility of canalizing the Katonga river and swamp system in Uganda in order to provide a link westwards from Lake Victoria to the Lake George escarpment has been abandoned in favour of extending the railway line from Kampala westwards to Kasese.[2]

Of the British West African Colonies Gambia, which has no railway, relies for transport on its river, which is navigable for about 150 miles by ocean-going steamers, and for a further 26 miles by vessels of lighter draught. Small Government steamers and local sailing boats maintain a regular service for the export of the large groundnut crop. The Gambia river also provides a natural ocean gateway for the neighbouring French territory, but the flow of Senegal trade through Bathurst has declined since the completion of the Dakar–Niger Railway. In Sierra Leone the lower reaches of the Great and Little Scarcies are navigable for light boats and carry a considerable traffic.

The seaboard of Nigeria has a network of rivers and connecting creeks, which in some areas provide the only means of communication. Commercial interests maintain a large number of self-propelled craft, and much traffic is also carried by Africans in canoes. The upper part of the Niger river is navigable by shallow draught stern-wheelers as far as Jebba, which is 540 miles from the sea. A private company maintains a service between Burutu and Baro, a distance of 407 miles, and also undertakes the transport of goods by steamer on the Niger and Benue rivers. The railway line from Kano to Baro was built to make the Niger accessible to regions in the north, but the bulk of the traffic now goes by direct rail to Lagos. During the months when the Niger is unnavigable above Lokoja, at the confluence of the Benue river with the Niger, the shipping companies transfer their craft to the Benue which is then in flood and navigable up to the French Cameroons. Eastern Nigeria is largely dependent on the traffic on the Benue waterway.

Farther to the east the Cross and Calabar rivers are used largely for transport. Ocean steamers go as far as Calabar, 30 miles from the sea, and a launch service is maintained between the port and stations on the Cross river, extending a distance of 200 miles to Ikom in the high-water

---

[1] S. and E. B. Worthington, *Inland Waters of Africa*, 1933, pp. 153–66.

[2] *The Way to the West, An Economic and Railway Traffic Survey of Certain areas of Western Uganda*, Entebbe, 1951, p. 13.

season. The Imo and Bonny rivers, with their ports of Opobo and Port Harcourt, are the natural outlets for the central southern provinces; the Marine Department maintains regular services on the creeks, and commercial firms also run steam or motor craft in the creeks for trading purposes.

The British Cameroons are served on the western side by the Akwayafe and Meme rivers and the Rio del Rey, which afford a light-draught transport for distances of 30 to 45 miles. On the eastern side the Tiko river is navigable for ocean-going vessels up to the port of Tiko, some 20 miles from the sea. In the northern part of the territory the Benue provides an important artery of communication, on which there is a small fleet of steamers.

In French West Africa the Senegal river was the chief means of access to the interior until the railway was built from Thiès (on the Dakar–St. Louis line) to Kayes and thence to the Niger at Bamako and Koulikoro. Traffic on the Senegal river is now strictly local. Midway between Dakar and Bathurst the Saloum, a tidal estuary, is navigable for ocean-going vessels for 75 miles from the sea to Kaolack. To the south of Gambia, the Casamance river is likewise open as far as Ziguinchor, and to lighter vessels up to 105 miles from the coast. Across the border, Portuguese Guinea is well threaded with navigable waterways, whilst in the Ivory Coast, French Togo, and Dahomey the lagoons are valuable means of communication.

In the French Sudan water transport has been developed farther than in the other French territories in West Africa.[1] Several companies maintain steamers and lighters on the Niger between Bamako and Kouroussa in French Guinea, and from Koulikoro, the terminus of the railway from Dakar, to Ansongo, a distance of 880 miles. The tonnage carried between Bamako and Kouroussa declined between 1925 and 1935, owing to the abandonment of the measures previously taken to maintain the navigation of the river, and also on account of the extension of the Kayes–Niger Railway to Thiès. The introduction of special tariffs for the carriage of low-priced produce over the railway encouraged traffic to go by rail to Dakar, the shipping facilities of which are superior to those of Conakry, the port for the Niger region. On the other hand, traffic has increased on the Middle Niger between Koulikoro and Ansongo.[2] This navigable reach of the Niger forms the logical continuation of the railway from Dakar, and it is indispensable in the economy of the Sudan. The stretch of 318 miles of river from Koulikoro to Mopti serves the rich area of which Ségou is the centre. At Mopti the Niger is joined by the Bani, navigable for 403 miles to Pankourou and passing through the productive district of San. From Mopti to Timbuktu, the Niger flows

[1] *Premier congrès soudanais de technique et colonisation africaine*, vol. ii, 1936, pp. 232–47.
[2] Ibid. pp. 235, 245.

through a series of lakes in an important agricultural region.[1] During the period of the winter rains, from July to January, the Niger is navigable for steamers, but during the remaining months it is practically closed to all craft drawing more water than a barge. The flow of the river is interrupted by rapids, by the *Barrage des Aigrettes* between Bamako and Koulikoro, by the great Sansanding barrage,[2] and by the lakes below Mopti. Through-navigation to Nigeria is also prevented by rapids; it was the rapids at Bussa, near Jebba, that caused the death of Mungo Park in 1805.

The Congo Basin has a special place in respect of the use of waterways in Africa. In a large part of the interior of French Equatorial Africa, and in the north-eastern Belgian Congo, the chief means of communication with the sea is the great river system of the Congo and its affluents.[3] There are two impediments to the 6,000 miles of navigable waterways in the Belgian Congo: first, the course of the Congo river to the ocean is interrupted by the falls at Stanleypool, about 200 miles from the sea, followed by a long series of precipitous rapids, so that access to a seaport can only be obtained by the Brazzaville–Pointe Noire Railway on the French side, and by the Leopoldville–Matadi Railway on the Belgian side. In the second place, the middle and upper courses of the Congo river and its tributaries are also interrupted at critical points by rapids, so that it has been necessary to construct railway links to carry traffic past the un-navigable passages. But for over 1,077 miles of the Middle Congo, traffic by river steamers carrying up to 800 tons is practicable. Steamers of the same size travel as far as Port Francqui on the Kasai, the principal affluent to the left bank of the Congo river. Port Francqui is the terminus of the Bas–Congo Katanga railway system which establishes connexion with Elisabethville, the Katanga, and thence with Southern Rhodesia. On the right bank, French services operate from Brazzaville to the farthest navigable point on the Oubangi river, so providing an important link between the sea and the interior of the Oubangi Chari area. On the upper Oubangi river some 375 miles are navigable, on the tributaries to the right bank of the Congo river about 1,000 miles, on the Logone river 375 miles, and on the Chari river flowing into Lake Chad a further 540 miles.

For the most part of the year the Congo river is thus open to larger craft than those which ply on the section of the Nile above Khartoum. It is noteworthy that the territory of the Belgian Congo has in all some 6,000 miles of navigable river, as compared with 3,125 miles of railway.[4] The freedom of navigation on the Congo river, as on other rivers within the Conventional Congo Basin, was guaranteed by the Berlin Acts of 1885. In the early stages of the development of the territory the organization of

[1] W. Fitzgerald, *Africa*, 1950, pp. 335–6.   [2] See above, p. 1004.
[3] Fitzgerald, op. cit. pp. 291 ff., with map at p. 294.
[4] J. Frederick and G. Gielen, 'Les Transports au Congo Belge et au Ruanda-Urundi', *Enc. C.B.*, vol. iii, pp. 423 ff., with map at p. 432.

river transport was undertaken by the *Marine du Haut-Congo*, which introduced the first steamer in 1881;[1] but in 1925 its services were transferred to an organization entitled the *Union Nationale des Transports Fluviaux*, which was concerned primarily with river transport. In 1936 the *Office d'Exploitation des Transports Coloniaux* (OTRACO) took over the majority of the river and lake services in the territory. It maintains 157,000 tons of Diesel-driven tugs, barges, and stern-wheelers, over 6,300 miles of river. On the upper reaches, the *Compagnie du Chemin de Fer du Congo* (C.C.F.C.) maintains a fleet totalling 9,750 tons for service from Ponthierville up the Lualaba, one of the headstreams of the Congo river, another service of 8,500 tons on Lake Tanganyika, and about 10,000 tons elsewhere. Various commercial companies also maintain their own transport; the *Société des Huileries du Congo Belge*, in particular, has a fleet of some importance, specially equipped for the transport of palm oil.

THE RAILWAY SYSTEMS

The South African Railways

The name of Cecil Rhodes is so intimately associated with the expansion of the railway system in South Africa that it is interesting to note that when he landed in the Cape in 1873 only 300 miles of railway track had been laid. When he died in 1902 over 4,000 miles were open to traffic. Today the total mileage of the railways of the Union and South-West Africa amounts to 13,549. All are owned and operated by the State.[2]

The chief factor which has determined the routes taken by the main lines in the Union and neighbouring countries has been the discovery of rich mineral deposits—diamonds at Kimberley, gold on the Witwatersrand, coal at Wankie, lead and zinc at Broken Hill, and copper in Northern Rhodesia and the Belgian Katanga. The first line opened in South Africa was a two-mile stretch in the neighbourhood of Durban, completed in 1860. At that date a line from Cape Town to Eerste river and on to Wellington was being constructed under guarantee by an English company. The discovery of diamonds at Kimberley gave rise to an urgent demand for a railway for the transportation of stores, but the value of the diamond deposits was still undetermined, and it could not be expected that railway development would be undertaken by private companies unless they received a substantial Concession.[3] But there was an immediate need for speedy construction: ox-wagons took a month or two months to transport goods from Port Elizabeth or Cape Town to Kimberley, at £15 to £30 a

---

[1] Comité Permanent de Co-ordination des Transports au Congo, *L'Organisation actuelle des transports au Congo Belge*, 1930, p. 25.

[2] See also map facing p. 1598 below. S. H. Frankel, *Capital Investment in Africa*, 1938.

[3] See the authorities quoted in Frankel, op. cit. pp. 374 ff.

ton. Coaches or mule carts took seven to nine days for the journey, at a charge of £12 a passenger. The Cape Government was obliged to take construction into its own hands. Acquiring the small private lines to which reference has been made above, it started in 1873 on a standard-gauge railway from the Cape to Kimberley, substituting in 1881 the 3 ft. 6 in. gauge which was subsequently adopted throughout the south. Political pressure from the Eastern Province demanded equality of treatment for all the Cape ports, and a beginning was also made on lines from Port Elizabeth and East London. Natal in 1876 began to build coast lines in order to serve its sugar estates; it subsequently took over the small private line at Durban and began to extend it towards the Free State and the Transvaal.

The 650-mile line from Cape Town to Kimberley was completed in 1885, when the Port Elizabeth and East London lines were nearing Coles-berg and Aliwal North on the Orange Free State border, and the Natal line had been brought as far as Estcourt.[1] But the claims of the gold industry now began to enter the field. The Witwatersrand was pro-claimed a public gold diggings in 1886, and the gold boom of 1889 pro-vided a new objective for the extension of railways in South Africa. The line of advance was obvious, but the policy of railway construction could not be separated from considerations based on the amount of customs duties on goods passing through the ports in transit to the Republics. Up to 1889 the coastal Colonies retained the whole of these duties; but in that year the Cape Colony and the Free State entered into a Customs Union, and agreed that the proposed line to Bloemfontein should be continued by the Cape Government as far as the Vaal river, the border of the Transvaal. Natal, preferring to remain free for a competitive lowering of tariffs, refused to sign the Convention, and pushed on with its own railway to-wards the Transvaal. The Transvaal, for its part, had from the first been anxious to avoid dependence on British ports, and had seen in Delagoa Bay the best exit and entrance for its traffic. In 1875 its Government had signed a protocol with Portugal providing for co-operation between the two States in the building of a railway to the 'centre of trade' in the Trans-vaal.[2] The gold rush at Lydenburg provided a further incentive; the treaty was now ratified and the route surveyed.

So far the negotiations for the railway had presented no great difficulty to the Transvaal; but an obstacle arose when it was unable to find means to finance the project. Pressure from the miners at Lydenburg in 1886 compelled it to approach Cape Colony for a Customs Union and a rail-

---

[1] E. A. Walker, *A History of South Africa*, 2nd ed., 1940, pp. 397, 412. L. C. A. and C. M. Knowles, *The Economic Development of the British Overseas Empire*, vol. iii, 1936, p. 259. *Cambridge History of the British Empire*, vol. viii, 1936, pp. 451, 780.

[2] J. van der Poel, *Railway and Customs Policies in South Africa, 1885–1910*, 1933, p. 5.

way from Kimberley. This the Cape refused, but soon after, when the value of the discovery of gold on the Witwatersrand had been confirmed, the Cape received in its turn a similar rebuff from the Transvaal Republic. The Portuguese Government now arranged to start the construction of a line from Delagoa Bay. The Transvaal then attempted to block the extension into its borders of the railways from Bloemfontein and Kimberley. In 1889 Delagoa Bay was linked to the Transvaal border, and forthwith the Netherlands Railway Company started on the section to Pretoria.

The line from the Cape, strongly backed by Rhodes, thus refused a passage through the Transvaal, continued its way towards Rhodesia through Bechuanaland. In 1890 it was taken from Kimberley to Vryburg, whence the Bechuanaland Railway Company, an offshoot of the British South Africa Company, continued it to Mafeking. The Netherlands Company was now once more in difficulties about finance. The Transvaal Government was driven to buy its shares and to obtain a loan from the Cape, under an Agreement which obliged the Netherlands Company to build a bridge across the Vaal and to construct within the Transvaal a line which would serve to connect the Port Elizabeth line with Johannesburg and Pretoria. This was completed in 1892, and there followed a lowering of rates over the Natal line in order to compete with the Port Elizabeth railway. The latter retained, however, a practical monopoly of the Transvaal carrying trade until the Pretoria–Delagoa Bay line was finally opened in 1894.

In 1895, therefore, the Witwatersrand was connected with the Cape ports and with Durban and Delagoa Bay by lines which competed as far as the Transvaal borders; inside the Transvaal the Netherlands Company controlled all the railways. There followed a period of acute competitive warfare between the interests concerned. Political alliances cut across economic interests, those of the Free State and the Cape Railways competing with those of Natal and the Transvaal. The two latter groups proved the stronger, having the advantage of the prohibitive rates imposed on the terminal section, with the result that in 1897 the Delagoa Bay line carried 60 per cent., and the Natal line 15 per cent. more traffic to the Transvaal than in the previous year, while the Cape lines carried 30 per cent. less.[1] Natal's share then began to decline, falling in 1898 by as much as 17 per cent. When the Anglo-Boer War began, the Delagoa Bay line was depriving the Transvaal of railway and customs revenue that was essential to its financial stability.

After the Anglo-Boer War the lines of the Netherlands Company were expropriated for the sum of £13½ million, and were united with the railways of the Orange River Colony. This did not, however, dispose of the conflict of interest with Natal and Cape Colony, and an Agreement be-

[1] Van der Poel, op. cit. pp. 81, 85.

tween the Colonies was urgently required. But, as the Rand was dependent on Native labour from Portuguese East Africa,[1] the Transvaal entered in 1901 into a *modus vivendi* with the Portuguese Government which preserved to Delagoa Bay its former preference in the matter of railway rates and customs duties. In consequence, the share of the Cape lines in the Rand traffic continued to fall. The major issue in the conflict centred on the system of preferential rates on Colonial produce. To raise these rates to the level of those levied on imported goods would destroy the protection enjoyed by the farmers; to reduce the rates on imported goods would adversely affect the railway revenues. The competitive struggle between the different railway groups led to an inter-State conference in 1908. This dealt not merely with railway issues, but with the broader question of political unification, thus opening the way to the National Convention of the same year. The Portuguese *modus vivendi* of 1901, which secured to Delagoa Bay from 50 to 55 per cent. of the Rand traffic, was renewed in 1928, but a subsequent Agreement in 1934 reduced the proportion to 47·5 per cent.

The mileage of Government lines in South Africa had increased from 4,257 in 1902 to a total of 6,989 at the time of the Union. Much of the new construction had served to correct the longitudinal character which the railway system had assumed as the result of the effort to connect ports and mining centres by the shortest route. In the Cape Province a line was built through the south-western districts to Port Elizabeth, and the sheep country was also opened up to East London. This, and similar lines serving the agricultural districts, formed the second stage in the history of railway development, which continued for a number of years after Union. The South Africa Act of 1909 had embodied in its Section 127 the important provision that the railways and harbours should be 'administered on business principles, due regard being had to agricultural and industrial development within the Union'. The combined effect of the South Africa Act and the Railway Board Act of 1916 was to place the whole of the railway and harbour undertakings under direct State management, though securing the formal separation of railway from general finance.[2] The institution of a separate Railway and Harbours Fund, from which only interest on invested capital can be transferred to Consolidated Revenue, has limited the possibility of using the railways as a method of taxation.

By 1916 the construction of new branch lines into agricultural areas had increased the mileage of the State lines to 9,407. In 1922 the 1,330 miles of railway in South-West Africa were incorporated in the Union system. The building of branch lines continued, and in 1952 the Union and South-West Africa had a total rail mileage of 13,549. The total capital expendi-

---

[1] See above, pp. 1378, 1385, 1407.
[2] S. H. Frankel, *The Railway Policy of South Africa*, 1928, pp. 79 ff.

ture up to March 1951 was recorded as approximately £281¼ million. In the railway budget for the year 1953–4 revenue was estimated at £137 million and expenditure at £138 million.[1] The system was heavily strained during the Second World War, but traffic congestion gradually eased with the delivery of new rolling-stock and locomotives.

Apart from the provision of branch lines to meet local needs, such as those of the newly developed mine-field of the Orange Free State, no major construction is now envisaged in the Union. There is, however, a considerable programme of electrification. Under Act no. 30 of 1922, the South African Railways began to electrify the Natal main line and parts of the Cape peninsular system. The former was chosen because it required high locomotive power to overcome the steep gradients from the coast to the high veld; this line of 323 miles represents the longest single stretch of electrified main line in the British Commonwealth. Electrification has since been concentrated on the two main urban areas, Johannesburg and Cape Town, where the need for the rapid conveyance of daily commuters has become an important transport problem. A total of 50 miles in the Cape Province and more than 150 miles on the Witwatersrand have been electrified. In all about 600 miles have so far been electrified, and it is contemplated that about 9 per cent. of the total network will eventually be converted to electric traction. The Government allocated £63 million to railway development in the year 1955.

The total mileage of railway in South-West Africa is 1,463. The main line runs from Upington in the Cape Province to the capital at Windhoek, from which place there is a connexion with Swakopmund and Walvis Bay on the coast, and also a branch line to Gobabis on the east, which may, it is suggested, ultimately be linked up with the railway system in Southern Rhodesia. There is also a branch line to the sea at Lüderitz farther to the south. A narrow-gauge line runs from Windhoek to Tsumeb and Grootfontein on the north.

The Federation of Rhodesia and Nyasaland

British Central Africa owes the initial construction of its railway system largely to Cecil Rhodes, under whose influence the Chartered Company assumed heavy obligations in the field of railway development. Reference has been made above to the circumstances which caused the extension of the railway north of Kimberley to proceed through Bechuanaland rather than the direct route through the Transvaal. The line reached Vryburg in 1891 and was continued to Mafeking, with the aid of a subsidy and a grant of land from the Chartered Company.[2] In 1902 it reached Bulawayo, was continued to Wankie by the prospect of traffic from the coal-mine, to

[1] *Overseas Economic Surveys, Union of South Africa, 1953*, p. 103.
[2] Van der Poel, op. cit. p. 73.

Victoria Falls by the prospect of tourist traffic, and to Broken Hill in 1906 by the discovery there of lead and zinc deposits. The last section of 132 miles to the Belgian Congo border, to which it was attracted by the exploitation of the copper deposits of Northern Rhodesia, was opened in 1909. A connexion was then effected with the Katanga rail system in the Belgian Congo. Between Bulawayo and the Belgian Congo border construction was shared by three railways, the Rhodesia Railways, the Mashonaland Railways, and the Rhodesia–Katanga Junction Railway Company formed by Sir Robert Williams.[1] The main line from Bulawayo to Salisbury was completed in 1902.

Circumstances had secured to the Portuguese the possession of the land approaches to the Indian Ocean, but the Chartered Company was assured of access to the sea by an Agreement that a railway should be constructed to the port of Beira, and that the duty on British goods in transit should be limited to a maximum of 3 per cent.[2] The Concession for the line, originally held by the Mozambique Company, was acquired from it by the Chartered Company, which proceeded to promote the construction of a line from Umtali to Beira. This was opened for traffic in 1900. Largely with a view to obtaining access to an alternative port, considerable support has for many years been given to a project for the construction of a line which would take off from the Rhodesia Railways, and would terminate at Walvis Bay in South-West Africa. It has been assumed that, starting from Matetsi in Southern Rhodesia, this line would link up with the South-West Africa railway system in the neighbourhood of Gobabis. The increase in the cost of labour and material since the Second World War has put out of date the estimates originally formed of the cost of this project. A new estimate made in 1953 put the total cost at £25 million; a company formed more recently to re-examine the possible route has estimated the cost of the line as far as the border of South-West Africa at £18 million. It is obvious that the scheme could not be carried out without the active co-operation of the three Governments concerned, namely, the Federation of Rhodesia and Nyasaland, the Union (as administering South-West Africa), and the British Government (as administering the Bechuanaland Protectorate). Whatever its attraction from a strategic or political standpoint, it is clear that there would be a lack of wayside traffic on this great length of line. It has been suggested that it might have its use for the export of coal from Wankie or of beef from Bechuanaland. But the production of coal from Wankie is already fully absorbed by local requirements, and it has been estimated that by 1960 the Federation will require 123,000 more cattle than it can itself supply in order to meet the needs of its own increasing population. This requirement must be

[1] F. O. Hammond, *Report on the Railway System of Southern Rhodesia*, C.S.R. 2, 1926, pp. 9 ff.
[2] Van der Poel, op. cit. p. 53.

made good mainly from Bechuanaland, leaving no surplus for export to Europe.

As has been explained, the British South Africa Company took, from the first, a leading part in the creation of the Rhodesian railway system. The capital for its construction was raised largely on debentures guaranteed by the Company, subsequently aided by a grant of £3 million from the Beit Trust. By 1911 the Chartered Company had advanced nearly £1¼ million to meet the deficit on the debentures. The Rhodesian Railways Trust was formed to assume the outstanding debts, and these were gradually liquidated until in 1936 they were reduced to a relatively small figure. Following an inquiry made in 1945,[1] the Southern Rhodesia Government purchased the share capital of Rhodesia Railways for £3,150,000. In 1949 the whole system, including the small lengths of line owned by the Beira Railway Company and the Shabani Railway Company, was nationalized, and was assigned to a statutory authority composed of the Prime Minister of Southern Rhodesia, the Minister of Mines and Transport, the Governor of Northern Rhodesia, and the High Commissioner of Bechuanaland, Basutoland, and Swaziland. In 1953 the system became the responsibility of the Federal Government of Rhodesia and Nyasaland. It now consists of some 2,708 miles of track, of which 1,356 are in Southern and 643 in Northern Rhodesia, 399 in the Bechuanaland Protectorate, 112 in the Union of South Africa, and 198 in Portuguese East Africa. The capital invested in the system was increased by £9 million in the year ending 31 March 1954, and stands at £62,800,000. It was estimated that in the next three years there would be expenditure on capital account of a further £18 million, of which more than a third would be spent on renewals.

Reference has already been made to the project for the extension of the system by a line terminating at Walvis Bay. More immediate importance has, however, attached to a project for a line between the capitals of the two Rhodesias, Salisbury and Lusaka, by a line from Sinoia (north-west of Salisbury) crossing the Zambezi at Chirundu. This line would reduce the journey between the capitals by 514 miles, and, at the same time, reduce that between the Copperbelt and Beira. Even greater urgency was claimed for a line connecting Bulawayo with Lourenço Marques. This involved the construction of about 660 miles of new track, half in Southern Rhodesia and half in Portuguese territory, the cost of the latter being borne by the Portuguese Government. This has been pressed forward as a matter for immediate action, and the line was opened for traffic in August 1955. The cost to the Federation was estimated at about £10 million. The Federation now has access by rail to three ports,

---

[1] H. Howitt, *Communication to the Secretary for Commonwealth Relations*, Dominions Paper no. 3, 1945.

namely Port Elizabeth, Beira, and Lourenço Marques, but the cheapest route remains that to Beira.

A further scheme for shortening the length of railway haulage has taken the form of a projected connexion between West Nicholson in Southern Rhodesia and Beit Bridge on the Limpopo, a distance of only 105 miles. But there was here a conflict of interests. Though the line would pass through Southern Rhodesian territory, the bulk of the revenue would accrue to the South African Railways. The objection to the plan on this ground served in part to divert the attention of the Rhodesian authorities to the Lourenço Marques project just mentioned. The Report of the East African Railways Administration on their survey of a route between Kapiri Mposhi, north of Broken Hill in Northern Rhodesia, to Masimbu, near Morogoro on the Central line in Tanganyika, indicated that a rail link to connect the Rhodesian with the East African system would be practicable from an engineering standpoint.[1] The capital cost would, however, be high; the cost of constructing the two sections in Northern Rhodesia, which would traverse relatively easy ground, was estimated at some £12½ million. Concurrently with the engineering survey, a survey of the prospects of development in the areas which would be served by this 1,100-mile rail link was conducted by an Anglo-American team of consultants. Their Report[2] concluded that there was as yet no evidence of potential industrial development sufficient to warrant railway construction. It was suggested that the correct approach might well be to 'allow road transport to carry the burden hitherto borne by the low-cost railway line'.

There have for many years been complaints of the inadequacy of the Rhodesian railway system in view of the heavy demands now made on it for transport. Part of these complaints have been due to the congestion both of incoming and outgoing traffic at Beira. The Transport Conference which met at Johannesburg in 1950 recommended that relief to the congestion at Beira could best be found by using the spare capacity at Lourenço Marques and Lobito Bay.[3] The connexion now established with Lourenço Marques by the line between Bannockburn and Quinza may be of some assistance in reducing congestion at Beira. The utilization of Lobito Bay has been deferred owing to the failure to reach an agreement on a common freight charge for through traffic. It is noteworthy that, as a result of the recommendations of the Transport Conference, the use of the Benguela Railway for the transport of coal to the Copperbelt was again under consideration in 1956. But only part of the

[1] *East African Railways and Harbours, Report on an Engineering Survey of a Rail Link between the East African and Rhodesian Railway Systems*, Nairobi, June 1952.

[2] *Report on Central African Rail Link Development Survey to the Colonial Secretary by Sir Alexander Gibb & Partners of London and Overseas Consultants Incorporated of New York*, June 1952.

[3] *Central and Southern Africa Transport Conference, Final Act and Related Documents*, Johannesburg, 1950, p. 60.

deficiencies in the system of transport in the Rhodesias has been such as could be remedied by the provision of alternative routes to the ports or to other territories. Although in the five years ending in 1953, £13 million had been spent on locomotives and rolling-stock, the equipment of Rhodesia Railways proved to be inadequate to meet the strain to which they were subjected in the years following the Second World War.

The shortage of facilities for the supply of the Copperbelt with coal from the Wankie colliery has, in particular, formed the subject of much complaint. Though in 1953–4 the railways carried more than $8\frac{1}{2}$ million tons of traffic, as against 4 million tons in 1949 (the year in which they were nationalized), the haulage was still inadequate, and it was stated that as the copper-mines could not get enough coal they were being driven to fall back on the burning of wood. This involved an extra cost of nearly £2 million a year. The re-equipment of the transport system has been one of the chief preoccupations of the new Federal Government; its Four-year Development Programme allocated about £30 million to the improvement of communications generally. In 1953 the International Bank for Reconstruction and Development made a loan to Rhodesia Railways of £5 million; this was devoted to the construction of the line to Lourenço Marques. In 1954 the United States of America made to the Federation a loan of $10 million for railway development.

In 1954 a group of consultants, who had been invited to investigate the organization of Rhodesia Railways, advised that consideration be given to the electrification of the Federal system. Owing to the severe gradients on the Sinoia–Kafue link, electrification appeared here to be inevitable, and there were also other lengths of line where electrification seemed essential. But the cost of electrification is about £100,000 a route mile, and to electrify the whole system of 2,000 miles would involve some £200 million. Meanwhile, attention has been concentrated on the improvement of the rolling-stock on the existing system, and considerable improvement has been effected, in particular, in the delivery of coal from Wankie and in the take-off of copper from the mines of the Copperbelt. In 1956 a new line was opened connecting the new Bancroft mine with the rest of the Copperbelt.

The problems of transport in Nyasaland have now been added to the preoccupations of the Federation with questions of railway development. At the beginning of the century the Nyasaland railway system comprised a length of some 290 miles; the subsequent record of the system has been largely concerned with the establishment of a connexion with the port at Beira, making a total distance of about 497 miles. Exports from the Protectorate were up to 1904 conveyed down the Shire and Zambezi rivers to Chinde, where they were transhipped into lighters and taken to Beira. Reference has already been made to the subsidence of the waters of the Shire river and the stimulus which this gave to the construction of the sector of the Shire Highlands Railway from Blantyre to Port Herald. Increasing difficulties in navigation led to its extension in 1915 from Port Herald to Chindio (on the North bank of the Zambezi) by the Central African Railway Company. In 1919 the Trans-Zambezia Railway built the line from Muraça, on the south bank of the Zambezi opposite Chindio, to join the Beira Railway at Dondo, 18 miles from Beira. This was financed by debentures guaranteed by the Nyasaland Government. The river fleets of the African Lakes Corporation and the British Central Africa Company were then purchased by the Trans-Zambezia Railway, partly in order to ferry traffic across the Zambezi between Chindio and Muraça. This purchase was financed by an issue of ten-year notes guaranteed by the Nyasaland Government.

In 1926 a scheme was put forward for the construction of a bridge to replace the Zambezi ferry, and this was completed in 1935 at a cost of approximately £3 million. Meanwhile the Nyasaland railway system was extended north from Blantyre to Chipoka on Lake Nyasa. With the completion of the Zambezi bridge and of the northern extension of the railway, the more productive parts of Nyasaland were now directly connected with Beira, but the financial provision involved proved a heavy burden to the Nyasaland Government. It had guaranteed debentures issued by the Trans-Zambezia Railway and had made advances to that Railway and the Central African Railway and to a Company, the Nyasaland Railways Limited, which had been formed to assist in financing the construction of the bridge. It had been assisted by a series of interest-free loans from the Imperial Government, but fresh advances were required every year to pay interest on the capital of the Nyasaland Railways Limited. The commitments of the Protectorate Government were so considerable that the Rhodesia-Nyasaland Royal Commission of 1938–9 saw in them an obstacle to closer union with the Rhodesias.[1] A solution was eventually found when the United Kingdom assumed responsibility for the various loans issued, the Government of the Protectorate agreeing, for its part, to hand over to the Treasury of the United Kingdom all amounts which it might receive in respect of its advances to the Railway Companies.[2] Adjustments made at the establishment of the Federation left the Federal Government the possessors of 72 per cent. of the shares in Nyasaland Railways and 25 per cent. of the shares in the Trans-Zambezia Railway. It was stated also that almost all the borrowed capital for the latter and 67 per cent. of the borrowed capital of the former was owned by the Federal Government.

The Nyasaland railway system was heavily overloaded during and

[1] Rhodesia-Nyasaland Royal Commission, Report, Cmd. 5949, 1939, p. 235.
[2] Colonial Reports, Nyasaland, 1946, pp. 6–7.

after the Second World War, and the port of Beira presented for some time a chronic problem of congestion. The total merchandise carried by the Trans-Zambezia and Nyasaland railway systems in 1952 exceeded all previous records, and in 1953 the railways operated 33 million ton miles, more than five times the total for 1939. The completion by the Portuguese in 1951 of the railway connecting Dona Ana with Tete has resulted in the diversion from river transport of a heavy coal traffic from the coal-mines at Moatize. To meet the increased traffic of recent years considerable sums have been expended for additional rolling-stock. Plans for railway extension envisage a connexion with south-west Tanganyika and also with Northern Rhodesia, but in view of the cost involved, it is considered that development of the central and northern provinces of Nyasaland must in the immediate future be effected by road and water transport.

The East Africa High Commission Territories

Under an Order issued by the East Africa High Commission in 1947,[1] the separate systems of the Tanganyika Railways and Port Services and the Kenya and Uganda Railways and Harbours Administration were amalgamated into one transport system, the East African Railways and Harbours Administration. The work of amalgamation was completed with the introduction in 1951 of a railway tariff applicable to the whole system.

The Uganda Railway (afterwards to be known generally as the Kenya–Uganda Railway) has played a notable part in the romance and the controversies of British Colonial policy. A railway into the interior had formed an early ambition of the Imperial British East Africa Company, and it had already built during the years 1885–9 some 65 miles of a light track starting at Mombasa. In 1891 the British Government decided that, so far as its own sphere in Africa was concerned, the most effective means of implementing the resolutions of the Brussels Conference of 1889–90 regarding the suppression of the slave trade would be to construct a railway from Mombasa to Lake Victoria.[2] Whatever the force of this argument (and it is true that the slave market in Zanzibar had at the time been closed for some years), there is no doubt that it was reinforced by the feeling that such a railway would provide the best means of blocking the further encroachment of Germany in East Africa.[3] The case for a railway was strengthened when Lord Lugard and the Missionary Societies succeeded in their campaign against the decision of Mr. Gladstone's Government to

---

[1] East Africa High Commission Order in Council, 1947, para. (c), subsection (1), section 44. Central Legislative Assembly, the East African Railways and Harbours Administration Act, 1950.

[2] H. B. Thomas and R. Scott, *Uganda*, 1935, pp. 32, 234.

[3] A. Pim, *Report on the Financial Position and System of Taxation in Kenya*, Col. no. 116, 1936, p. 240.

abandon Uganda to its fate. A railway was one of the requisites laid down by the Report made by Sir Gerald Portal which led to the declaration of the Protectorate over Uganda in 1894.[1] The construction of the railway began late in 1895, and the line from Mombasa to Kisumu on the northeast shore of Lake Victoria was opened in 1901. The cost of this line, which was defrayed from funds provided by the United Kingdom, was £5½ million. The Treasury waived recovery of the interest charges on this sum,[2] and in 1939 it withdrew any claim to repayment of the capital charge involved.

It is unnecessary to detail here the subsequent additions and extensions, made at the cost of the Uganda and Kenya Governments, which have brought the total length of the line up to 879 miles.[3] At the outset it was taken for granted that the railway, whatever its other uses, would have little commercial value and would not pay for its maintenance. But the growth of the cotton industry in Uganda and the expansion of European settlement in Kenya (to which the railway itself made a most important contribution) have enabled it to earn substantial revenues. For some time, however, it continued to present to the two territories a series of complicated and often controversial problems. The organization was owned jointly by the two countries, and difficulties regarding the extent of their respective interests came to a head in 1918. In that year Kenya placed a surcharge, followed in 1919 by a supercharge, on traffic rates in order to meet a deficit in the general revenue of the Colony.[4] The Advisory Council, which had been officially established in 1925, recommended that the finance of the railway and other transport services be separated from general revenues, and placed to a railway and harbour account. This was accordingly done, and the railway thus ceased to be a means of assisting the general revenue of Kenya.

There were, however, other difficulties. The line had rates which were adjusted to enable the principal crops, such as cotton from Uganda and maize and coffee from Kenya, to be exported as economically as possible. It was therefore the policy to counterbalance the low export rates by high import rates, based on a sliding scale adjusted to the distance travelled. The arrangement was much criticized in Uganda, where it was contended that the Protectorate was subsidizing the export of European-grown maize from Kenya. Preferential rates also existed for crops or commodities of local origin, and this was criticized in Kenya as a form of tariff protection

[1] R. L. Buell, *The Native Problem in Africa*, vol. i, 1928, pp. 281–2. G. Portal, *The British Mission in Uganda*, 1893. E. Huxley, *White Man's Country*, vol. i, 1935, p. 32. R. J. Harrison Church, *Modern Colonization*, 1951, p. 86. [2] Col. no. 116, 1936, p. 242.

[3] The history of the railway has been told in the work of M. F. Hill, *Permanent Way: The Story of the Kenya–Uganda Railway*, 1950.

[4] *Report of the Uganda Development Commission*, 1920, p. 10. See also R. Gibb, *Report on Railway Rates and Finance in Kenya, Uganda, and Tanganyika*, Cmd. 4235, 1933, pp. 43–44.

at the expense of railway finance. Apart, however, from these considerations the high rates charged on the railway were undoubtedly a handicap to the development of Kenya. Save for this consideration the position of the railway was sound, since it was normally able to present a surplus after contributing to sinking as well as to renewal funds.

In 1951, out of a surplus of a little over £2 million, a contribution of £1½ million was made to the Betterment Fund and, in addition to the normal annual contribution to the Renewal Fund of slightly more than £1 million, a special contribution of £469,600 was provided to make good the shortfall brought about by the rising cost of replacements. But the revenue position deteriorated in 1953, when only a comparatively small contribution could be made to the Betterment Fund and nothing to the provision for renewals.[1] From January 1954 a 20 per cent. increase was imposed on all freight traffic rates.[2]

An extension of the Uganda Railway from Kampala to Kasese (on the Belgian Congo border), to connect with the Edward and Albert Lake system, was completed in 1956. The extension is 209 miles in length. This line had been envisaged as far back as 1906, as the result of the discovery of copper deposits in the Ruwenzori mountains. The capital cost (about £4½ million) has been met by a loan from the Uganda Government.[3] Meanwhile the Uganda Development Council has recommended that an extension be constructed to the north, and a survey is being made of the line from Soroti to Lira and Gulu.

The railway system in Tanganyika now comprises three lines running westward from its principal ports. The northernmost line connects the port of Tanga with Arusha, a distance of 273 miles; it was begun by the German Government in 1899 and reached Arusha in 1929. A connexion from Kahe Junction to Voi in Kenya was made during the First World War for military purposes. The second line, namely, the Central line from Dar-es-Salaam to Kigoma on Lake Tanganyika, is 780 miles in length. It was built in 1904 by the German Government, following in the main an old slave caravan route, and was completed in 1914. After the First World War it was relaid, and was reopened in 1928. Besides supplying local needs, this line carries a considerable volume of traffic from Ruanda Urundi and the Belgian Congo. It has now 385 miles of branch lines, the most important being that from Tabora to Mwanza on Lake Victoria, 237 miles in length.

The third of the Tanganyika lines runs from Mtwara, a new port on the coast, to Nachingwea, a distance of 132 miles. Both the new port of Mtwara and the railway were part of the scheme for the production of

[1] *Annual Report on the East Africa High Commission, 1953*, Col. no. 305, 1954, p. 22.
[2] Ibid. *1954*, Col. no. 316, 1955, p. 2.
[3] G. Kirby, *Uganda Today and Tomorrow*, 1954, pp. 46 ff.

groundnuts sponsored by the British Overseas Food Corporation. Though this scheme was abandoned in the circumstances described elsewhere,[1] the Government has persevered with the construction of the port and the railway, owing to the poverty of existing communications in the Southern Province of the territory. The first portion of the new railway, providing a connexion with the port of Mtwara, was completed in 1953; the port was formally opened in 1954, when the dock facilities were withdrawn from the old harbour at Lindi. Mtwara is the only deep-water port in the territory, for both Dar-es-Salaam and Tanga depend on lighterage. An extension of the Mtwara–Nachingwea line to Songea and Lake Nyasa is envisaged, and this may embrace the area of the Ruhuhu coalfields, if these should prove to contain deposits of commercial value.[2] The possibility of a link between the rail systems of Tanganyika and Northern Rhodesia has already been referred to and some of the difficulties of executing it explained. The sections in Tanganyika would traverse a difficult terrain, more particularly in the vicinity of the Kilombero Valley and again between the Usangu Plain and the Northern Rhodesia border. The cost of construction has been estimated at not less than £20 million.

Prior to the amalgamation of the railway system in 1948, the Tanganyika railway lines were owned by the Tanganyika Administration, but the finances were separated from general revenue. They represented a capital charge of only £5 million, for a purely nominal sum was paid to the German Government when the Tanganyika lines were taken over after the First World War.[3] In the earlier stages there were frequent deficits in the annual railway budget. But during the Second World War an increase of traffic brought an improvement in railway finances and at the end of 1948 there was a small surplus. The source from which the railways drew their revenue was, however, limited to local traffic after the year 1931. In that year a considerable part of the copper freight from the Belgian Congo formerly passing over the Tanganyika lines was diverted from Dar-es-Salaam to Lobito Bay. During the war years 1939–45 the Belgian traffic again increased, but it had not in 1948 recovered to the level of the previous years.

The amalgamation of the railway system under the High Commission in 1948 has provided means for the solution of some of the problems of inter-territorial traffic which at one time occupied much of the attention of the two Governments. Thus the extension of the Central line in Tanganyika to Mwanza on the southern shore of Lake Victoria had brought it into competition with the Lake services of the Kenya and Uganda Railways. By a decision of 1932 non-competitive rates were arranged, and by a subsequent agreement the Kenya and Uganda Railways retained all

[1] See above, p. 845.
[2] See above, p. 1506.
[3] C. Leubuscher, *Tanganyika Territory, a Study of Economic Policy under Mandate*, 1944, pp. 14–15.

Lake traffic except that at Mwanza, while the railway rates to Mombasa and Dar-es-Salaam were equalized. The Governments were engaged in 1932 and again in 1935 in the discussion of proposals for the assimilation of rates and the pooling of revenues on the Tanganyika and Kenya–Uganda railway systems, a scheme not unlike that recommended in 1929 by the Commission on Closer Union in Eastern Africa.[1] A provisional settlement of some of these issues was arrived at in 1947. The Tanga line had also brought the two railway systems into competition by its ability to divert to Mombasa part of the traffic of coffee and sisal produced in the Moshi and Kilimanjaro areas of Tanganyika.[2] The amalgamation of the systems has now made it easier to adjust this issue.

In 1955 it was announced that the World Bank had made a loan of £8½ million to the East Africa High Commission for the purpose of modernizing and expanding the railways, roads, and harbours of the three East African territories. The total post-war programme amounts to £60 million, and during the period 1954–7 a sum of £34 million is being spent. This will include the improvement of the handling capacity of Mombasa harbour. The latest review of the Development Programme suggests the need for capital expenditure of a further £34 million to cover the period 1958–61.[3] The loan from the World Bank is guaranteed by the East African territories and the United Kingdom jointly. The completion of hydroelectric schemes in Uganda and Kenya, together with the pressure on the railway system caused by the development of the agricultural and subsidiary industries, have caused consideration to be given to the electrification of the main line from Mombasa as far as Nairobi.[4]

In the view of the East Africa Royal Commission of 1953–5 the Railways Administration had failed to keep pace with the accelerating momentum of post-war traffic.[5] In the previous 20 years the mileage of rail track had increased only from 2,979 to 3,100 miles, in spite of an increase of traffic density of 124 per cent. over roughly the same period. The Commission urged the amendment of the existing law, which stipulates that estimates shall be framed on a non-profit-earning basis, thus making the railways dependent upon loan capital instead of upon profits which can be ploughed back into the undertaking. The clause which enjoins that 'cheap transport shall be provided to assist agriculture, mining, and industrial development' has compelled the Administration to keep rates

---

[1] *Report of the Commission on Closer Union of the Dependencies in Eastern and Central Africa*, Cmd. 3234, 1929, pp. 108 ff., 292–3.

[2] See R. Gibb, *Report on Railway Rates and Finance in Kenya, Uganda, and Tanganyika*, Cmd. 4235, 1933, pp. 49–52. H. O. Mance, *Report on the Co-ordination of Transport in Kenya, Uganda and Tanganyika Territory*, 1937, pp. 49–57.

[3] *East African Railways and Harbours Annual Report, 1955*, Nairobi, 1956.

[4] *Background to Uganda*, no. 82, February 1955.

[5] *East Africa Royal Commission 1953–1955, Report*, Cmd. 9475, 1955, pp. 120–31.

uneconomically low, often under political pressure from the individual territories. It has therefore recommended that the Administration be reconstituted as an autonomous Corporation, with power to operate at a profit, whose share capital shall be owned by the Governments of the three territories, thus making them partners in the undertaking rather than guarantors of the capital in it.

The British West African Dependencies

Though Nigeria claims to possess the second largest railway system in any of the British Colonial dependencies, the territory is markedly deficient in railway facilities in relation to its area and to the size of its population. There was at the outset a conflict of views on railway policy. The Northern Administration advocated the construction of a line from Kano to Lagos in order to provide for the carriage of the groundnut crop of the north. The authorities in the south and south-east pressed for a line traversing the east of the territory, in the hope that this might serve to forestall German designs in the Cameroons.[1] In the result, the development was piecemeal. The first line to be constructed—the short length from Lagos to Ibadan—was completed between 1896 and 1901. It was then decided to build a railway from Kano down to Baro, on the navigable Niger, and to extend the Lagos Railway to join this new railway at Minna. This was the origin of what came to be known as the Western Division main line. The Bauchi Light Railway of 2 ft. 6 in. gauge was opened in 1914 from Zaria in order to serve the Jos tin-fields, and these were in 1927 connected by a direct line of 3 ft. 6 in. gauge with Port Harcourt, thus constituting an Eastern Division main line. The main Lagos–Kano line was extended in 1929 beyond Kano to Nguru, 843 miles from Lagos. This was designed to open up more groundnut lands, as was the branch running north-west from Zaria to Kaura Namoda, which also serves a cotton-growing area. The Eastern Division main line running from Port Harcourt joins with the Western line at Kaduna, a distance of 569 miles. A bridge, second only to that over the Zambezi in length, crosses the Benue at Makurdi. With the exception of the Zaria–Jos branch line the gauge throughout is 3 ft. 6 in.

There are, in effect, three routes for produce from the north to the sea— by rail to the two ports, Lagos and Port Harcourt, and by river transport on the Niger. By tapping the Niger river the Minna–Baro line permits of some competition between rail and river transport, since it allows produce to be brought down by rail to the Niger and thence forwarded by a River Transport Company. The railway system belongs to the State and comprises in all some 2,200 miles of line. The system had by 1936 become a

[1] R. J. Harrison Church, 'The Evolution of Railways in French and British West Africa', extract from *Compte Rendu du XVIe Congrès International de Géographie, Lisbonne, 1949*, Lisbon, 1952, p. 112.

heavy charge on the general revenues of the territory. The bulk of its traffic was low-rate produce, and the Eastern section between Kaduna, Kafanchan, and Enugu in particular showed a deficit which had to be carried by the system as a whole. In 1936 it was decided to reorganize the railway on commercial lines, and until 1943 the railway budget was relieved of interest charges on the Kaduna–Enugu section. The total sum at charge on capital account was adjusted in accordance with the Report of a Committee which had been appointed to deal with the question of wasting assets.[1] The railway thus became self-contained in the matter of finance, with a Reserve Fund designed to meet losses such as those which had in the past followed on the failure of the main export crop.

Before the Second World War the railway suffered from competition by road transport in the coastal areas, but after the war it was often unable to carry all the traffic offered. Of all the African railways which suffered during that period from shortage of rolling-stock and locomotives, the Nigerian system probably fared worse than any. In some years heavy stocks of groundnuts accumulated in Northern Nigeria, owing to the lack of rolling-stock to evacuate them. At the beginning of 1953, for instance, over 300,000 tons were awaiting transport, and six months later the total had been reduced by only 49,000 tons. Debates in the United Kingdom Parliament revealed that serious errors had been made in the arrangements for obtaining renewal of locomotives and rolling-stock. There commenced in 1954 a considerable measure of re-equipment,[2] and it is proposed to spend £16 million in the Five-year Development Programme largely on locomotives and rolling-stock.

It was decided in 1953 that the railway should be reorganized as a Government Corporation, whilst the railway-operated ports of Apapa and Port Harcourt and all other Nigerian ports were to be put under a Nigerian Port Authority.

The railways of the Gold Coast, like those of Nigeria, also reveal the lack of any comprehensive planning of communications. Construction was begun in 1898 of a line from Sekondi, in order to serve the gold-mining developments at Tarkwa,[3] and it was continued to Kumasi in 1903. A line starting from Accra, begun in 1909, was designed to provide for the carriage of cocoa, but for various reasons it did not reach Kumasi until 1923. A branch line from Dunkwa to Awaso was completed in 1942–3 in order to make possible the export of bauxite. The total length of line in the territory in 1954 was 535 miles. When the Volta Power Scheme comes into operation, new branches will be required, and in

[1] *Memorandum on the Nigerian Government Railway Estimates for 1936–37*, January 1936.
[2] *Annual Report of the Government Railway, 1953–54.*
[3] F. D. Hammond, *Report on the Railway System of the Gold Coast*, 1922. R. J. Harrison Church, 'The Pattern of Communications in British West Africa', *Geographical Essays on British Tropical Lands*, 1953.

particular a branch from the Eastern line to the aluminium smelter at Kpong.[1] A branch from Accra to Tema, the new port now being constructed in advance of the operation of the Volta Power Scheme, was opened for traffic in 1954. An extension of the Central Province line to Kotoku on the Eastern line was opened in 1956; it cuts by nearly half the travelling distance between Accra and Takoradi.

Looking at the position as a whole, there is reason for regret that the Government of the Gold Coast was for so long absorbed in its political problems or in social developments as to neglect the need for a systematic planning of its railways. The whole of the Northern Territories, for example, has hitherto been left without adequate traffic facilities.[2] The Ten-year Development Plan now includes an estimate of £8 million for communications, in which a provision will also be made for a railway to Tamale, in the Northern Territories.

The hinterland of Sierra Leone was not at an early stage regarded as offering a favourable field for railway development, and when it was decided in 1895 to construct a light line with a gauge of 2ft. 6 in. from Freetown to Pendembu (a trading centre near the boundaries of Liberia and French Guinea) the main purpose was only to open up the country. The line did not reach its terminus till 1906; its total length, including a branch from Bauya to Makeni, is 227 miles. The high operational costs of the railway, and the fact that its traffic depends largely on one commodity (palm kernels), have resulted in its maintenance involving a net loss to the Government, which during the years 1899 to 1935 had to provide nearly £2 million (an amount exceeding the whole of the capital cost of the line) in order to make up the deficits in its earnings.[3] In 1927 the railway finance was separated from general revenue and organized as a self-contained account; but the average loss to the Government on this account continued. In the years 1950–2 it amounted to £167,000, in addition to a special contribution of £164,000 in 1952.[4] After some hesitation about the retention of this narrow-gauge railway, it was decided in 1949 to undertake a major reconditioning of the track and equipment, especially as far as Bauya Junction. A railway of 3 ft. 6 in. gauge, owned by the Sierra Leone Development Company, connects the iron-ore deposit at Marampa with the port at Pepel, a distance of 57 miles, but this is not available for public use.

The French Territories

It is not unnatural that French West Africa, with its great area and diversity of physical conditions, should have four separate railway systems.

[1] See above, pp. 1001, 1511. [2] F. M. Bourret, *The Gold Coast*, 1952, p. 214.
[3] S. H. Frankel, *Capital Investment in Africa*, 1938, p. 405.
[4] *Colonial Reports, Sierra Leone, 1952*, p. 17.

It is, moreover, of interest that some of these lines have not had a purely economic purpose, but were originally constructed in order to further military objectives. The earlier railways were designed as part of a connected river-rail system in which full use was to be made of the Senegal and Niger rivers as waterways, but in the result the Senegal railways have now supplanted the use of the Senegal river for the carriage of traffic; the Ivory Coast and Dahomey lines do not actually reach the Niger. The plans made for the routing of the railways in the Niger territory were also influenced at one stage by the vision of a Trans-Saharan line, a conception which for long dominated French views of West African development. It is, however, doubtful if this scheme will ever come to fruition; its value would be almost entirely military, in that it would enable troops raised in the West African Colonies to take a land route to Algiers. It projected a line from Colomb Béchar which, after crossing the Sahara, would divide into two branches, one to join with the Senegal system via Koulikoro, the other proceeding to Gao and Niamey.[1] The great length of track involved, passing through an area which could contribute no wayside traffic, would deprive such a line of any commercial value.

The existing four railways and their branches now have a total length of a little over 2,400 miles, all on the metre gauge. The railway system of Senegal consists of the Dakar–Niger main line from Dakar to Koulikoro, a distance of 805 miles. There are branch lines, 299 miles in length, from Thiès to St. Louis, Louga to Linguéré, Diourbel to Touba, and Guinguinéo to Kaolack. In French Guinea a main line of 414 miles runs from Conakry to Kankan. In the Ivory Coast a main line runs north to Bobo-Dioulasso, 521 miles in length, and is about to be extended another 220 miles to Ouagadougou. In Dahomey a main line, the Central Dahoméen, runs to Parakou, a distance of 274 miles, with branch lines of 94 miles.

The first section of the main Dakar–Niger line to be constructed, namely, the line from Kayes to Koulikoro, was begun in 1881, in order to unite the Senegal and Niger rivers; but, owing to the difficulties encountered, it was not completed to Koulikoro until 1904. The section to Thiès, designed to connect the Sudan with the sea, was finished in 1923; the branch to Kaolack, a port on the Saloum river, shortens by 126 miles the route for shipment of goods by sea. The Dakar–St. Louis Railway, which was opened in 1885, was constructed by a concessionary company, but is now worked from Thiès as a branch of the Dakar–Niger Railway. Construction of the Conakry–Kankan line began in 1900, and was completed in 1914. The Ivory Coast Railway was begun in 1903, and reached Bouaké in 1913; it was extended in 1923 northwards to Bobo-Dioulasso, which was reached in 1934. The Central Dahoméen Railway was constructed in

---

[1] 'Trans-Saharan Railway Projects: a Study of their History and of their Geographical Setting', *London Essays in Geography*, eds. L. D. Stamp and S. W. Wooldridge, 1951, pp. 135 ff.

1900 by a concessionary company, from which it was acquired by the Government in 1930.[1]

In his study of investment in Africa, Professor S. H. Frankel estimated that up to 1934 the railways in French West Africa represented a capital investment of roughly £11 million, but remarked that their method of accounting made it difficult to estimate either their original cost or the working results; he concluded, however, that few of them had at any time been self-supporting. The railways are now being re-equipped with Diesel-electric locomotives. In 1954 the International Bank advanced a loan of $7·5 million for the purchase of equipment for the lines running from Dakar to the Sudan and from Abidjan to the Upper Volta.

In French Togo, railways run from Lomé to Anécho, a distance of 30 miles; to Palimé, 74 miles; and to Blita, 173 miles. The first two were constructed during the German régime, and the Blita line had been taken by them in 1911 as far as Atakpamé. Beyond that town the last section was constructed by the French in 1934.

In French Equatorial Africa a State railway line, with a gauge of 3ft. 6in., runs from Brazzaville, on the right bank of the Congo river, to Pointe Noire, a distance of 320 miles. Exports from the territory had previously been dependent on the Belgian Leopoldville–Matadi Railway and on the use of the Belgian port at Matadi, but, apart from political considerations, the French complained that they had to contend with a constant state of congestion on the Belgian railway.[2] The difficulties of constructing an alternative route through the Chrystal Mountains of Mayumbe proved, however, to be formidable. The project of the *Congo–Océan* Railway, now known by the initials C.F.C.O., was first formed in 1886;[3] construction began only in 1922 and was not completed until 1934.[4] The *Société de Construction des Batignolles*, which had the contract for construction, had great difficulty in securing labour. The story of the efforts made by the Administration to provide the necessary manpower for the railway is still quoted as one of the outstanding proofs of the evils attending the use of compulsory labour in Africa. It is all the more striking because it relates to a relatively late period of African history, and because it appears to have involved action by the Administration which ran counter to the formal provisions of the legislation regarding compulsory labour. By an *arrêté* issued in 1925 the quota of labour was distributed over the different provinces on a system which amounted in effect to conscription. Health conditions were inadequately safeguarded, and the rate of mortality is alleged to have been without parallel in any part of Africa.[5] The work

---

[1] Gouvernement Général de l'Afrique Occidentale Française, *Le Chemin de fer de Thiès au Niger*, 1931, pp. 124–36.   [2] W. Fitzgerald, *Africa*, 1950 ed., p. 299.
[3] A. Sarraut, *La Mise en valeur des colonies*, 1923, p. 421.
[4] *Enc. A.E.F.*, pp. 442–8.
[5] Buell, op. cit., vol. ii, 1928, pp. 260–3. See also above, p. 1363.

eventually involved the employment of 120,000 *recrutés*, as against a force of 28,000 *volontaires*.[1] The recent Development Plan contemplates the equipment of the railway with Diesel-electric locomotives. Pointe Noire, the terminus of the line, has few natural advantages as a port, but the considerable expenditure undertaken between 1934 and 1942 has provided it with an adequate equipment for dealing with overseas traffic.

The Cameroons under French trusteeship is served by two metre-gauge railway lines: the Northern line from Bonabéri (opposite Douala) to N'Kongsamba, 100 miles in length, and the Central line running south-east from Douala to Yaoundé, 192 miles in length, with a short branch line joining Otélé to Mbalmayo on the navigable Nyong river.[3] It has been estimated that the Germans expended about £4 million on the railways subsequently taken over by the French in Togoland and the Cameroons. It appears that, as in the case of Tanganyika, practically nothing was paid by the Mandatory Power on this account.[3] When the French occupied the Cameroons the Central line had been constructed for a distance of 113 miles; the northern line has not so far been extended by the French. The extension of the Central line and the construction of the branch line were financed from a loan for the general development of the territory. The Cameroons system is, in consequence, treated as free from interest charges, and the rates for passengers and for goods are kept at a low level. In 1921 a Reserve Fund was formed, financed from profits, but the published accounts show that it is only since 1947 that the receipts have exceeded the expenditure.

The Germans had proposed to extend the Central line farther north to Garoua, but abandoned the scheme owing to the cost of traversing the hilly region of Dschang. The scheme for a northern extension has since been revived in the form of a project for a line from Yaoundé, taking a route through the centre of the territory towards Maroua and eventually arriving at the neighbourhood of Fort Lamy and Lake Chad. It would thus tap an extensive agricultural and pastoral area of which the products have now to find their way by road transport towards Bangui in French Equatorial Africa.

The Belgian Congo

As has already been observed, the railways of the Belgian Congo were originally designed to supplement the means of transport provided by the great river system of the Congo Basin. A resolution of the Berlin Convention of 1885 described them as being required 'dans le but spécial de suppléer à l'innavigabilité ou aux imperfections de la voie fluviale sur certaines sections du Congo'. Though the existing lines continue to fulfil

---

[1] *Enc. A.E.F.*, p. 442.   [2] *Enc. C.-T.*, pp. 299 ff.
[3] Minutes of Ninth Session, Permanent Mandates Commission, 1928.

this purpose, the modern expansion of road transport and the opening up of new sources of production in areas distant from the navigable rivers have created a somewhat different outlook on the function of the railways. They are now regarded as providing the major arterial lines of communication in the territory.[1] This can best be appreciated by considering the chief components in the comprehensive scheme of communications envisaged for the Colony. This has two 'axes'; these radiate from Leopoldville, which is the collecting point for traffic entering or leaving the country at the port of Matadi. The first of these two 'axes' is designed to serve the gold-mining areas in the north-east; the second line of communications has its terminus in the copper-mining areas of the southern Katanga. On the first axis the Congo river provides the chief line of transport from Leopoldville to Stanleyville. From Stanleyville a mixed line of river and rail transport exists via Kindu, Kongolo, and Kabalo up to Albertville on Lake Tanganyika. The second axis is formed by the Kasai river route to Port Francqui, whence the Bas-Congo–Katanga line runs south-east to Bukama (where a connexion on the Lualaba river links up with Kabalo on the Stanleyville–Albertville system just referred to). Thence the line runs to Tenke, where a connexion runs west to join the Benguela Railway near Dilolo on the Angola border. From Tenke the line then proceeds through the Katanga copper-fields to link up with the Rhodesian railway system at Sakania, a short distance south-east of Elisabethville.[2]

The railway system covered in 1953 a total distance of 2,966 miles. It consisted of the following lines: (1) the *Chemin de Fer du Mayumbe* from Boma to Tshela, 88 miles in length, constructed between 1900 and 1902; (2) the *Chemin de Fer du Congo* (C.C.F.C.), from Matadi to Leopoldville, 229 miles in length, of which the construction began in 1890; (3) the *Chemins de Fer du Congo Supérieur aux Grands Lacs Africains* (C.F.L.), from Stanleyville to Ponthierville, 78 miles in length, finished in 1906, with a further 445 miles from Kindu to Kongolo, Kabalo, and Albertville, completed in 1915; (4) the *Chemin de Fer du Bas-Congo au Katanga* (the B.C.K.) from Port Francqui to Sakania, which has 1,146 miles of 3ft. 6in. gauge, constructed between 1909 and 1931, with a branch line 326 miles long, starting at Tenke and forming the connexion with Dilolo and the Angola borders;[3] (5) the *Chemins de Fer Vicinaux du Congo* (VICICONGO) which have 534 miles of 60 cm. gauge railway; the lines run from Bondo, on the Uele river, and Aketi, on the Itimbiri, to Paulis-Mungbere (in the extreme north-east of the territory), and there is also a short line which carries traffic between Lakes Tanganyika and Kivu.

An important international link will be provided by the railway under construction from Kamina, north-west of Elisabethville on the

---

[1] Fitzgerald, op. cit. p. 298.   [2] See map facing p. 1598.
[3] *Compagnie du Chemin de Fer du Bas-Congo au Katanga, 1906–1956*, Brussels, 1956.

Katanga system, to Kabalo, at the headwaters of the Lualaba (Congo), near Albertville on Lake Tanganyika. It will be 277 miles in length and will provide a rail connexion from the Atlantic to the Indian Ocean starting from Lobito Bay in Angola and terminating at Dar-es-Salaam in Tanganyika Territory. Even more important from many points of view would be a line running direct from Leopoldville through Kikwit to Luluabourg on the B.C.K. Railway, but this project is apparently still far from realization.[1]

Among the existing lines of railway, the Leopoldville–Matadi line has a special place. The railway is sometimes known as the Kinshasa–Matadi line; Kinshasa is the industrial town, Leopoldville the administrative. As already explained, the river steamers plying on the Middle Congo were denied access to the port of Matadi because of the gorges and rapids of the Lower Congo river, and the provision of the necessary line of communication between Leopoldville and Matadi was therefore one of the earliest preoccupations of the Congo Free State. Like the French *Congo–Océan* line, the Leopoldville–Matadi line has had its place in the history of the use of forced labour.[2] The work involved, among other things, the cutting of 17 tunnels through the Mayumbe plateau.[3] Efforts were made to import labour from countries as far apart as Annam, Barbados, and Liberia. Resort was had at one stage to the employment of the second section of the annual levy of the militia, but the greater part of the labour was secured by a form of recruitment which had most of the elements of impressment.[4] The railway forms part of Belgian Congo history for another reason. In order to secure land for the reconstruction of the track and for extending the facilities at Matadi the Belgian Government was driven in 1927 to conclude an Agreement with Portugal whereby the Belgian zone at Matadi was slightly widened in return for the cession to Portugal of the 'Dilolo Boot', an area of nearly 1,350 square miles on the outer extremity of the south-west Katanga. The need for acquiring space for the reconstruction of the Leopoldville–Matadi line was also a factor in the conclusion of the convention by which Belgium agreed to provide a connexion between the Katanga line and the Benguela Railway within five years of its arrival at the international boundary.

The State has taken a leading part in the formation of the railway system, though the actual construction has usually been carried out by private companies.[5] In most instances the Government has retained an interest in the finance of the railway, as in the instance of the *Chemins de Fer du Congo Supérieur aux Grands Lacs Africains*, or holds the majority of the

---

[1] *Enc. C.B.*, vol. iii, p. 433.
[2] See above, p. 1363.
[3] R. J. Cornet, *La Bataille du rail: La Construction du chemin de fer de Matadi au Stanley-Pool*, 1947.
[4] Buell, op. cit. vol. ii, pp. 423, 502 ff.
[5] S. H. Frankel, *Capital Investment in Africa*, 1938, pp. 407 ff.

shares of the operating company, as is the case with the *Compagnie du Chemin de Fer du Bas-Congo au Katanga*. Since 1928, however, the assistance given has usually taken the form of a guarantee of interest. Only two small local lines are run by companies without the financial assistance of the State. The importance attached to the system of transport is shown by the readiness of the Belgian Administration to grant Concessions of land in order to stimulate the outlay of capital by private companies. The *Compagnie du Chemin de Fer du Congo* has received grants of nearly 2½ million acres of land, and other railway companies have also had substantial grants. The gauges of the railways vary from 2 ft. to 3 ft. 6 in. Through connexion with the Rhodesian system necessitated the use of the 3 ft. 6 in. gauge in the construction of the Bas-Congo–Katanga line, and it is understood that future construction will be authorized only in this gauge for main lines or in the 60 cm. gauge for secondary lines.

According to Professor Frankel,[1] up to 1932 about £38 million had been invested in the railways of the Congo, and the Colony had in addition advanced up to that time roughly £2¼ million from revenue. The returns in the way of dividend had on the whole been small, in spite of the high rates charged; the *Chemin de Fer du Bas-Congo au Katanga* was the only line which had been able to attain financial independence. The Belgian Senate expressed at one period the opinion that the development of the Congo had been hampered by the rates charged on freight, while the Administration had suffered direct losses from the grant of guarantees which it could have avoided under a system of State construction and management. In view of the interdependence of the river, railway, and road systems a *Comité Permanent de Co-ordination des Transports au Congo* was instituted by the Government in 1929. It was composed of heads of the public utility companies and Government representatives. Part of the functions of this Committee have since been taken over by the *Office d'Exploitation des Transports Coloniaux* (OTRACO), which was established in 1935.

The Portuguese Territories

Critics of the attitude of Portugal towards its overseas territories were in past years accustomed to comment on the lack of activity shown by the Government in developing railway communications in Angola. There was much substance in their criticism. Until the completion of the Benguela Railway in 1929 this large territory had only two railways, namely, that running from Luanda to Malange and that running from Mossâmedes to Sá da Bandeira. The small line running from Amboim was a private concern. The Luanda–Malange Railway has a length (including branch lines) of 378 miles on the metre gauge and 19 miles on the 60 cm.

---

[1] Ibid. p. 408.

gauge. The line from the port of Mossâmedes to Sá da Bandeira has (with its recent extension to Chibia and Chiengi) a length of 195 miles on the 60 cm. gauge. The private railway running inland from the port of Amboim has a length of 77 miles of 60 cm. gauge. It is characteristic that the Mossâmedes Railway, which was sanctioned in 1890, was only commenced in 1905, and did not reach Sá da Bandeira until 1928.

The position has been materially altered by the opening of the Benguela Railway, which connects the port of Lobito with Dilolo on the Belgian Congo border. The total length of the line is 1,163 miles, of which 838 miles lie in Portuguese territory and 325 in the Belgian Congo. But the railway is only to a limited extent a Portuguese enterprise. It owed its inception to a scheme put forward in 1902 by Sir Robert Williams and Tanganyika Concessions Limited, in order to find an outlet for the production of the new copper-mining area of the southern Katanga. When the Concession was signed in 1902, Tanganyika Concessions took up 90 per cent. of the share capital and Portugal the remainder. As the result of this and subsequent transactions the great bulk of the capital has actually been provided from British sources.[1] Construction was begun in 1903, but progress was much delayed. It was not completed until 1929, nearly half of the whole length of line having been built during the three years 1926–9. The gauge is 3 ft. 6 in.,[2] the same as that in use in the Rhodesian, South African, and Belgian Congo systems. The total cost has amounted to approximately £13 million.

Viewed as a means for the transport of the production of the Katanga copper-mines, the Benguela Railway has obvious advantages over the rail-river connexion of the Bas-Congo–Katanga line with Leopoldville and Matadi, and it is slightly shorter than the route from the Katanga via Rhodesia to Beira, besides giving a saving of some 3,000 miles by sea. How far the route will actually be utilized depends on the result of negotiations on the question of rates. In 1952 some 47,000 tons of copper were shipped to Lobito Bay, besides considerable quantities of cobalt and manganese.[3] The total production of copper in the Katanga is roughly 200,000 tons a year. There is at the same time no question of the value of the railway in the development of Angola. From a settlement of a few African huts, Lobito (which possesses far greater advantages as a port than Benguela)[4] has become a township with 20,000 inhabitants, and there has been a considerable influx of European colonists to the plateau area of Angola. But besides the natural obstacles usually encountered in African railway construction, the Benguela Railway had also to contend with certain political difficulties. In 1913 the failure to negotiate a loan with Germany,

---

[1] Frankel, op. cit. p. 149.   [2] Equivalent to 1·067 metres.
[3] J. d'Almada, *The Benguela Railway, 1902–1952*, 1953, p. 50, gives a table of distances over different routes.   [4] Lobito is distant some 40 miles from Benguela.

required in order to finance a further stage in its construction, resulted in the revision of the Anglo-German Colonial Pact of 1898. This Pact had been based on certain agreements regarding the demarcation of European spheres of interest in Mozambique and Angola.[1] The terms of the new Pact, though nominally secret, were equally disturbing to Belgium and to Portugal, both of whom felt that it constituted a menace to their Colonies. The First World War made the new Pact nugatory, but the war also postponed the construction of the line for a number of years. Construction was again suspended when in 1922 application for a loan was made to Britain under the Trade Facilities Act. The reaction of the Union of South Africa in regard to the proposal was unfavourable, for the Union was apprehensive of the possible competition by the Benguela Railway with the South African Railways.[2] The loan was, however, eventually granted. Tanganyika Concessions Limited is now holder of the whole of the railway's debenture capital.

The construction of the Benguela Railway may be viewed as having opened a second stage in the development of communications in Angola. A third stage opened with the formation of the Development Plan for the Portuguese African territories, to which reference has been made in a previous chapter.[3] Under this scheme the Mossâmedes Railway will be enlarged to the metre gauge, and will be continued to Vila Serpa Pinto, a distance of 282 miles. Reference has also been made elsewhere to some of the irrigation and other schemes which this extension is designed to serve in the first instance,[4] but it is also contemplated that the line may at some future date be extended to the borders of Northern Rhodesia. This project, however, has not yet been accepted as part of the programme of development. On the other hand, the Development Plan has made a definite provision for the extension of the Luanda line to serve the important cotton area of Cassange, and plans are being considered for a northern extension of the line in the direction of the Congo river.

The position in Portuguese East Africa differs materially from that in Angola. Railway development in Mozambique has from an early date been determined by the demand for access to the Indian Ocean on behalf of traffic originating in the Union or in the Central African territories. The port of Lourenço Marques, in particular, has been treated as being for this purpose within the economic system of the Union of South Africa, and its equipment owes much to the initiative of the South African Railways Administration.[5] Owing to the comparative narrowness of the territory in relation to the length of its coastline, there are few contiguous railways or connexions between their systems.[6] The lines, which had in

---

[1] Buell, op. cit. vol. ii, pp. 474–5.   [2] D'Almada, op. cit. pp. 43–44.
[3] See above, p. 1342.   [4] See above, p. 1008.   [5] W. Fitzgerald, *Africa*, 1950 ed., p. 162.
[6] C. F. Spence, *The Portuguese Colony of Moçambique*, 1951, pp. 97 ff.

1953 a total length of 1,412 miles, are now owned by the State. The only exceptions are the Dondo–Nyasaland stretch of line owned by the Trans-Zambezia Railway and a small private line serving the Sena sugar estates near Tete. The State lines are now managed through an official organization termed the *Caminhos de Ferro de Moçambique*. The earliest and best-developed line (though not the most extensive in mileage) is that which connects the Transvaal railway at Ressano Garcia (on the Transvaal border) with the port of Lourenço Marques. Constructed in 1894, it is 56 miles in length, and handles a great volume of traffic from Johannesburg and the Rand. A branch, 47 miles in length, diverges to the border of Swaziland at Goba, where it maintains a connexion with the motor-coach services operating in that territory. A short branch line serves the banana plantations at the estuary of the Incomati river. Reference has already been made to the new line, also having its terminus at Lourenço Marques, which was opened to traffic in 1955. This line, passing along the Limpopo Valley, is connected with the new Southern Rhodesia line starting from Bannockburn on the Bulawayo–Salisbury main line. It will thus provide a new route to the coast which may afford some relief from the situation created by the congestion of traffic at Beira.[1]

A project has been discussed for a connexion (in the neighbourhood of Vila Pery) between this line and the existing Umtali–Beira Railway. This would bring for the first time the two ports of Beira and Lourenço Marques into rail communication. From the small port of Vila de João Belo a line of some 90 miles in length serves a densely populated section of the interior, which is so sandy that roads suitable for motor traffic cannot be maintained. From Inhambane a line of 62 miles follows the coast southwards to Vila de João Belo. These two short lines are connected with a well-developed system of motor services.

The railway, 240 miles in length, which runs from Umtali in Southern Rhodesia to Beira via Vila de Manica transports to the coast the heavy traffic originating in the Rhodesias and the Belgian Congo. Built in 1899 with British capital, it was owned by the Beira and Mashonaland Railway until it was acquired by the Portuguese Government in 1949. At the junction of Dondo, near Beira, it is joined by the line, owned by the Trans-Zambezia Railway, which proceeds via the bridge over the Zambezi to Blantyre and Nyasaland. Although the line has opened up valuable forests, which were exploited during the Second World War, and carries agricultural produce from Nyasaland as well as from the Zambezi Valley, the heavy capital expenditure on the track and on the construction of the Zambezi bridge makes it unremunerative, and its scale of tariffs is said to be one of the highest in the world.[2] From Dona Ana on the Zambezi a branch diverges up the river to Tete, primarily with the object of utilizing

[1] See above, p. 1552.   [2] Spence, op. cit. p. 100.

the coal deposits of Moatize and thus rendering the railways of the Portuguese territories independent of the Rhodesian coalfields at Wankie. The extension of this line to Missale and to the highlands of Angonia, where climatic conditions are held to be conducive to European settlement, remains a project of the future. A line from the port of Quelimane, north of Beira, extends for 90 miles into a region which is rich in sisal and cotton.

The most recently constructed line in the territory, but one which seems likely to be of increasing importance in the future, is that which serves the port of Nacala, lying north of the old port of Lumbo, the port of Mozambique; some reference has already been made to the value of Nacala as a port. The new line runs a distance of 370 miles to Cuamba. It has opened up a rich hinterland, producing tobacco, cotton, and groundnuts; good-quality coal is said to have been found near the railhead of Cuamba. Surveys are being completed for continuing the line to Vila Cabral in the highlands bordering Lake Nyasa. These have an altitude of 4,000 ft. and may offer possibilities for European settlement. All the lines referred to are now on the 3 ft. 6 in. gauge, except the short line from Vila de João Belo and the private line serving the Sena sugar estates.[1]

Liberia

Liberia had until 1951 no railway, but in that year a narrow-gauge line, 45 miles in length, was constructed by the Liberia Mining Company in order to bring down to the port of Monrovia the haematite now being worked by the Company in the Bomi hills.[2]

THE ROADS AND ROAD SERVICES

The advent of the railways undoubtedly involved in certain cases much hardship on the manpower conscripted for their construction. When completed, however, they were everywhere welcomed, for they not only provided means for the conveyance of passengers at a speed hitherto undreamed of, but they furnished the only means for the economic transport of the heavier or bulkier articles which formed the major part of the exports from Africa. It is, however, probable that for the African population the advent of motor transport has created a greater revolution than that of the railways. It is a revolution of which the social effects have been as pronounced as the economic. Given roads of even a moderate standard, the motor as a means of conveyance has a range which far exceeds that commanded by the railway. But the wide expansion in the use of the motor and motor services has created problems which have proved to be of much

---

[1] *Anuário estatístico do Ultramar, 1952*, p. 164.
[2] E. Anderson, *Liberia*, 1952, pp. 179–89.

concern to some of the Administrations. The motor services have shown that within certain limits they can not merely supplement but can under-bid the railway as a means of transport. The majority of the railways in Africa have been developed wholly or in part as State undertakings, and some of the Administrations have found it necessary to enact a considerable volume of legislation designed to safeguard the interests of the railways. This has been essential not merely because of the effect of competition on their finances, but because it may be necessary to maintain them in being as the only form of transport available for certain classes of heavy goods.

There is a further point which touches the Administrations closely. The motor has created a demand not merely for more roads, but for roads of a standard which imposes an increasing strain on the public revenues. At an early period the Administrations could be content to provide 'fair-weather' earth roads which ceased to be available in the rainy season. The motor services began by demanding 'all-weather' earth roads, but this demand has given place to pressure for a type of surfacing capable of standing up to fast-moving traffic or the passage of heavy lorries. The expense involved in some areas is not far short of that which would at one period have been incurred by the provision of a light railway track. The issue which may arise is not merely financial. The African taxpayer could not reasonably object to the heavy expenditure on special surfacing if it could be justified by the benefits which it might bring to the community as a whole. But he might not unreasonably object if the chief benefit were felt to accrue either to the European section of the community or to the promoters of an industrial undertaking which would benefit mainly non-African interests.

The Union of South Africa and the High Commission Territories

In the Cape Province road construction and maintenance was at the outset in the charge of the *Landdrosts* and *Heemraden*, who compiled rolls of Europeans liable for service. Once a year these supplied their labour without payment, working under elected overseers, but were permitted to offer a substitute. The service of the *corvée* was, however, irregularly performed and the roads ill maintained. There were in addition certain roads which were made by contractors, who received as part payment the right to collect tolls. As the settlers moved inland, they encountered the mountain barriers of the South African highlands. The farmers performed extraordinary feats in taking their ox-wagons over the Hottentots Holland Mountains and other hill ranges, but at the expense of much damage to vehicles and not infrequently some loss of life. In 1807 a turnpike road was made through the Tulbagh Kloof Pass with convict labour. The Franschhoek Pass was negotiated in 1824; the Sir Lowry Pass followed in 1830, this being designed to make the eastern districts directly accessible for heavy traffic, which had formerly made a detour to the north via Worcester.

The immediate perimeter of mountains was thus penetrated, but it was left to the pioneers of the Great Trek of 1835 to overcome the formidable barrier of the Drakensberg. Settlement in the Eastern Province and the growth of commerce created a strong demand for better roads, and eventually the Central Road Board of 1843 was established, together with Divisional Road Boards. The road policy formulated by the Central Board was put into effect with the aid of State grants, local rates, and loans secured on the revenue from tolls. A general use was also made of convict labour which largely replaced the *corvée*. Between 1845 and 1853 convicts and English workers, introduced at Government expense, completed the Montagu Pass, connecting the Little Karroo to George and the coast, and Mitchell's Pass and Bain's Kloof, which opened the way through the Bokkeveld to the interior plateau.[1] The Central Road Board, which had some 1,650 miles under its control, was much criticized for over-centralization, and was abolished in 1858. The Government then assumed direct responsibility. In 1864 this policy was reversed, and the maintenance of roads was placed under Divisional Councils, the intention being to revive the measure of local self-government which had existed under the régime of the *Landdrosts* and *Heemraden*.

At present the upkeep and construction of roads, excluding those in urban areas, is a function of the Provincial Administrations. In Cape Province the Divisional Councils receive subsidies for road maintenance; in Natal and the Transvaal the maintenance of Government roads is purely departmental. In the Transvaal proclaimed main and district roads are maintained departmentally and some attention is given to an extensive system of farm roads. There is in consequence a marked difference between the quality of the roads in different Provinces. In 1951 the total mileage of provincial main roads was 80,715, one-third of the maintenance costs being subsidized by the Union Government.[2]

A National Road Board was established in 1935, in order to control the construction and maintenance of a national network of bituminized roads throughout the Union. These were to be built and maintained by the Provincial Road Authorities under a Five-year Plan. A National Road Fund, derived mainly from a Customs tax on petrol and an initial grant of £500,000 from the Union Parliament, was instituted in order to finance projects embracing a little over 5,000 miles of national roads. In 1948 the functions of the National Road Board passed to the National Transport Commission, an authority placed under the direct control of the Depart-

---

[1] L. C. A. and C. M. Knowles, *The Economic Development of the British Overseas Empire*, vol. iii, 1936, pp. 256–7. *Cambridge History of the British Empire*, vol. viii, 1936, p. 765.
[2] *Year Book and Guide to Southern Africa, 1954*, p. 75.

ment of Transport.[1] This has continued to supervise the building of
national roads by the Provinces. By the end of 1954 there were completed
some 3,627 miles built to bituminous standards, and 833 miles built to
gravel standards. More than 600 bridges had been erected.[2] The new
National Highway from Durban to the interior was completed in 1952.
In the Orange Free State and Klerksdorp gold-field areas the National
Resources Development Council has planned a series of roads which
will be completed according to a priority laid down by the Council.[3]

The rapid growth of motor transport since 1930 has resulted in the
enactment of a considerable volume of statutory regulations to ensure that
road motor services are treated as strictly complementary to rail services.
Under the Motor Carrier Transportation Act of 1930,[4] amended from time
to time, the Union and South-West Africa have been divided into Local
Transportation Areas, each under the control of a Local Board.[5] These
Boards are authorized to grant carrier and exemption certificates, subject
to various restrictions. The carrier had the right to appeal to a Central
Transportation Board, but the functions of this Board have since 1948
been absorbed by the National Transport Commission.[6] Certificates are
now granted to private hauliers only when they do not conflict with
services provided by the South African Railways and their road services.
The increase in the provision of the latter has been striking; they now
cover more than 26,000 route miles of scheduled services in the Union,
South-West Africa, and the High Commission Territories. In 1952 some
17 million passengers, besides nearly 2 million tons of goods, were conveyed
by a Road Motor Service fleet of 1,050 vehicles.[7] Tourist buses run by the
South African Railways have become increasingly popular since 1945.

In South-West Africa two main roads run from within the Union to
Lüderitz, Walvis Bay, and the Angola border. Little recent road construction appears to have been done. Provision has been made for the
election in each magisterial district of a Roads Board with power to levy
local rates; the Government contributes two-thirds of the amount expended
on proclaimed roads. The territory has recently been proclaimed a Local
Transportation Area under the Transport (Co-ordination) Act of 1948.

The mountainous terrain of Basutoland does not lend itself readily to
roads, and in the hill area goods are still largely conveyed by pack animals,
of which there are said to be about 165,000. In the western agricultural

---

[1] Transport (Co-ordination) Act no. 44, 1948.

[2] *Year Book and Guide to Southern Africa, 1954.* See also *S.A.S.,* no. 90, 30 September 1954, p. 4.

[3] Department of Commerce and Industries, *Third Annual Report of the Natural Resources Development Council,* 1950, p. 23.

[4] Motor Carrier Transportation Act no. 39, 1930; Act no. 31, 1932; Act no. 15, 1941; Act
no. 50, 1949.

[5] Proclamation no. 334, 1948; amended by Proclamation no. 55, 1951.

[6] Transport (Co-ordination) Act no. 44, 1948.

[7] *Overseas Economic Surveys, Union of South Africa, 1953,* p. 106.

area the roads have been more systematically developed, and there are now 500 miles of road suitable in all seasons for motor vehicles and ox-wagons. In the eastern districts roads communicate from Qacha's Nek to Griqualand, and a low-level bridge has been built over the Orange river with the aid of a grant made under the Colonial Development and Welfare Act. The problem presented by the Maluti Mountains, which rise to an altitude of 10,000 ft. where they merge in the heights of the Drakensberg, has not yet been surmounted, but the Basutoland Development Plan includes provision for a road 87 miles in length connecting the capital Maseru with the interior. This road, after ascending passes some 9,000 ft. high, will ultimately extend to Natal. It has an added significance in the fact that it will penetrate those isolated areas where the notorious Medicine Murders of 1947 and the following years found a congenial ground.[1] The closer administrative control which the road will make possible may prove to be the best precaution against their recurrence. For pack transport 1,600 miles of bridle paths are maintained by the Basuto Administration.[2]

In the Bechuanaland Protectorate a single road, 400 miles in length, follows the railway line from south to north. Its route corresponds closely to that of the 'Missionaries' Road' to the north, the preservation of which from Boer encroachment was so important a feature in British policy in the middle years of the nineteenth century.[3] Near Francistown the road bifurcates, one branch entering Southern Rhodesia, the other, 950 miles in length, proceeding to Kazungula, an important ford over the Zambezi, used by immigrant labour and exported livestock. This route had been in intermittent use since 1870 as the point of entry into Barotseland and the Batoka plateau in Northern Rhodesia. It is actually little more than a sand track, but has been maintained by the Witwatersrand Labour Association for the transport of labour from Barotseland and Angola to the Rand mines. Only the roads in some of the townships are tarred, and less than 1 per cent. of the roads have been treated with a gravelled surface.[4]

Swaziland possesses neither railway nor navigable waterways. But there are over 1,000 miles of roads, of which 205 miles are trunk roads and are adequately maintained by the Administration, the most important of them being the inter-territorial road which forms part of the connexion between Johannesburg and Lourenço Marques. Some 492 miles of road are classified as 'first grade', but these are by no means of the same standard as the trunk roads, and their relatively poor quality adds considerably to the heavy cost of local transport. Swaziland is well served by

[1] *N.A.*, Part V, pp. 130 ff.   [2] *Colonial Reports, Basutoland, 1953*, p. 74.
[3] *N.A.*, Part V, pp. 187–8, 190–1.
[4] *Colonial Reports, Bechuanaland Protectorate, 1953*, p. 52.

motor-coach services, organized by the South African Railway and the Portuguese Railway Administrations. Several subsidiary services have also been opened, mainly by the enterprise of Africans. Projects have at various times been put forward for a railway connexion between Piet Retief in the Union and Gollel, the terminus of a branch line running to Durban; other proposals have been made to join up Goba, on the Union railway system, with Lourenço Marques. The future of these projects, however, involves a number of political considerations, and the uncertainty regarding the future of railway extensions has in some measure affected the attention paid by the Local Administration to the improvement of the road system.

The Federation of Rhodesia and Nyasaland

In Southern Rhodesia a stumped track and an earth or sand surface sufficed for the ox-wagons and buck-boards of the Chartered Company's era. But the advent of the motor-car has demanded improved roads and the creation of authorities responsible for constructing and maintaining them. In 1953 the Southern Rhodesia Roads Department controlled some 3,000 miles of main and 2,000 miles of subsidiary roads, but the new Constitution now provides that the Federal Government shall take over control of the section of the roads defined as inter-territorial by the Johannesburg Conference of 1950.[1] A further 10,000 miles of roadways of various grades are maintained by District Road Councils, financed by a subsidy from the Territorial Government and by the wheel tax collected in their respective areas. For the improvement of her main communications Southern Rhodesia owes much to grants made from the Beit Trust. The Trustees have defrayed the cost of the Beit bridge over the Limpopo, the Birchenough bridge over the Sabi, the new bridge over the Zambezi at Chirundu, and a large number of minor bridges. The Native Development Fund, which is financed mainly by levies on Native products, has expended during the last five years over £3 million on development schemes which include roads, bridges, and similar improvements.

An unusual feature of Southern Rhodesian road construction is the use of concrete or asphalt strips superimposed on a gravelled surface, with the object of providing a track for motor traffic serviceable throughout the wet season. In 1952 no less than 2,300 miles had been successfully treated by this process, which is now being imitated elsewhere. The Rhodesia Railways maintain in Southern Rhodesia a fleet of motor coaches serving 39 routes, covering a distance of some 3,000 miles. Statistics for the year 1950–1 illustrate the popularity, especially with Africans, of this mode of transport, 225,000 passengers and 211,000 tons of freight having been conveyed by these vehicles. Under the Five-year Plan, completed in 1954,

[1] Federation of Rhodesia and Nyasaland, Order in Council, 1953, p. 51 (Schedule II, item 19).

some 271 miles of double-lane tarmac were laid and 415 miles of single-lane tarmac; 51 high-level bridges with double carriage way and 13 low-level bridges were also built. It is proposed to expend a total of £15 million on roads by the end of 1960.

In Northern Rhodesia the single railway line bisecting the Protectorate from its boundary with Southern Rhodesia up to the Belgian Congo border offers ample scope for a road system which will feed, but not compete with, the railway. But the country is not well adapted for road construction. On the west of the railway lies the sand belt of the Barotse plain, and on the east an undulating plateau is intersected by watercourses which in the wet season flow in torrential spate. Of the 18,600 miles of roadway in the Protectorate, some 300 have been treated with a bituminous surface at a cost of over £7,000 per mile, about 220 with compacted gravel, 3,600 with drainage to an earth surface, and the remainder are ungazetted rural roads or township streets.[1]

The arterial system comprises three routes, which, in so far as they come within the definition of the Johannesburg Conference of 1950, became in 1954 the responsibility of the Federal Government. Their total length is a little short of 2,000 miles, of which 600 miles had already been reconstructed and 400 miles were included in the programme for 1954–5. The first of them, the Great North Road, 506 miles in length, connects the railway line with Lake Tanganyika and the Tanganyika road system at Abercorn. It originated in 1915 as a means of conveying troops and stores to the front in the German East African campaign. It was, as one observer has recorded, 'used by a few motor cars, the chassis of which lay derelict beside the road for years afterwards; by wagons hauled by teams of oxen, which, as the victims of tsetse fly, provided carcass meat for the troops; alongside it ran a telegraph line, suspended from trees, which elephants nightly tore down in tangled coils for Bantu maids to turn into bangles and ear-rings'. The route was later realigned and its surface improved, and, although today the road is regarded as only of second-class standard, it carries a considerable traffic in all seasons of the year.

The Great East Road, 394 miles in length, is the means of communication between the capitals of Northern Rhodesia and Nyasaland. It was begun about 1925 and encountered two formidable obstacles, the Luangwa river and its western escarpment. The opening of this road reduced from 14 to five days the time of transit of mails from the line of rail to Fort Jameson. Across the Nyasaland border the road joins near Lilongwe the main road traversing Nyasaland, which passes through Blantyre and links up with the Trans-Zambezia Railway. The third main road, a continuation of the Southern Rhodesia road from Bulawayo which reaches the Zambezi near Livingstone, continues through Lusaka to the Belgian

[1] *Public Works Department, Annual Report, 1953*, p. 14.

Congo border below Elisabethville; it now carries the heaviest traffic of any road in the territory. A fourth main road was completed in 1954, connecting Lusaka with Salisbury in Southern Rhodesia via the Chirundu bridge over the Zambezi. This road affords a short alternative to the long detour by rail through Bulawayo. There still remains one outstanding road problem for Northern Rhodesia: the provision of an adequate road connexion with Barotseland. This problem has for over half a century defied the efforts of road engineers.

Motor transport has increased greatly in volume, and since it operates in an orbit untouched by the railway, there is little competition with it. The Fort Jameson tobacco crop, which in 1952 amounted to 10 million lb., was exported almost entirely by motor transport. A number of private transport companies operate over nine scheduled routes, chiefly in the north-eastern part of the Protectorate and in the Copperbelt.

Nyasaland was in early days the corridor through which officials, missionaries, and traders approached not only north-eastern Rhodesia, but also Lakes Tanganyika, Mweru, and Bangweulu, and even the Belgian Congo. The consequence of the continuing desiccation of the Shire river and the increase in the production of tobacco was seen in a remarkable development in the road system. Today Nyasaland has 4,852 miles of roads,[1] of which 1,726 are classified as main roads and, in so far as these are inter-territorial, they will be maintained by the Federal Government. Some 706 miles of secondary roads are maintained by the Public Works Department of the Protectorate, and 2,381 miles of lower standard, mostly unreliable in the wet season, are provided by the Provincial Administrations. The principal main road runs from Port Herald near the Mozambique border to near Tunduma on the Tanganyika boundary, with branches leading from the main ports on Lake Nyasa. A second main road connects (as already mentioned) with the Great East Road in Northern Rhodesia via Lilongwe and Fort Manning. It formerly carried much of the tobacco crop of both territories, but since Salisbury became the auction floor for the three constituent territories of the Federation, the shorter direct routes from Fort Jameson and Blantyre respectively have borne most of this traffic.

Three good roads lead out of the Protectorate into Mozambique: one from Blantyre to Tete on the Zambezi, and two others from Mlanje and Fort Johnston to ports on the east coast. A Five-year Development Programme was drawn up in 1951, financed by Protectorate funds and grants made under the Colonial Development and Welfare Acts; this includes provision for laying a tarmac surface on many of the main roads, and providing bridges on the Great North Road. In 1953 licensed motor coaches carried over a million passengers. In parts of the Protectorate

[1] *Colonial Reports, Nyasaland, 1953*, pp. 116 ff.

they form feeders to the railway, and thus avoid competition with it. In the Southern Province, however, motor traffic enters into direct competition with rail transport. The Roads Transport Ordinance of 1934 and the Motor Traffic Ordinance of 1950 contain provisions designed to restrict uneconomic competition.

The Federation of Rhodesia and Nyasaland has now assumed responsibility for 4,400 miles of main trunk roads in the three constituent territories. In 1954 a total of £6½ million was allocated for reconstruction work in the following three years.[1]

The East Africa High Commission Territories

Though the control of the East African Railways and Harbours Administration is now the concern of the East Africa High Commission, this does not extend to the financing or control of the inter-territorial road communications. The functions of the High Commission organization in respect of the roads are limited to the control of the road services maintained by the Railways and Harbours Administration in Tanganyika and Uganda.[2] The Royal Commission to East Africa 1953–5 has recommended that an East African Road Corporation, operating as an autonomous body under the High Commission, should now be established, and that it should be financed from loans raised from the East African territories and grants from the Colonial Transport Development Fund.[3] Until this has been constituted, the position in regard to the road communications in each of the territories must, therefore, be surveyed separately.

The Tanganyika road system was in design primarily strategic, and it was only after the First World War that roads were constructed with a view to commercial development. Some 6,931 miles of main or Grade 'A' roads are now maintained by the Public Works Department, 10,423 miles of Grade 'B' roads by the Provincial Administrations, about 8,000 miles of village roads by the Native Authorities, and 545 miles by Township Boards. Until recently, however, only a few miles had been treated with bitumen; only 400 miles had a gravelled surface, and the remainder were earth tracks. Improvements to render the main and Grade 'A' roads suitable in all weathers have now been undertaken; the road running from Arusha to join the Kenya border at Namanga and also the road from Moshi to Himo and Taveta in Kenya Colony have already been macadamized. The roads from Dar-es-Salaam to Morogoro, from Tanga to Korogwe, and from Tanga to join the route through Digo to Mombasa were opened to traffic in 1954. A gravelled surface is being laid between Morogoro and Iringa.

[1] *F.N.*, 29 November 1954.
[2] *Annual Report on the East Africa High Commission, 1953*, Col. no. 305, 1954, pp. 24, 93 ff.
[3] *East Africa Royal Commission 1953–1955, Report*, Cmd. 9475, 1955, p. 135.

The Ten-year Development Plan initiated in 1946 contemplated an expenditure of a little over £3¼ million, raised in the revised plan of 1950 to £8½ million, of which about 30 per cent. is provided under the Colonial Development and Welfare Act. It has, however, been estimated that £20 million would be required to bring the road system of the territory up to a first-class standard.

The main road from Dar-es-Salaam via Dodoma and Iringa connects at a point south-east of Mbeya with the main systems in Northern Rhodesia and Nyasaland. Another road from Lindi via Tunduru and Songea to Mbamba Bay forms a connexion between the eastern littoral of Lake Nyasa and Portuguese East Africa. In the Northern Province direct communication by road with Uganda proceeds from Tabora to Bukoba, and with Kenya from Mwanza to Musoma. Road transport services are operated over 1,583 miles by the East African Railways and Harbours Administration. In 1937 an inquiry was made into the problem of competition between rail and road services,[1] and provision was made for a measure of general control in a Transport Ordinance enacted in 1937.[2] This has not been fully implemented, but restriction on roads on which the Railway Administration maintains services is now enforced under the Use of Motor Vehicles (Restriction) Ordinance enacted in 1941.

In Kenya the construction of roads may be said to have begun in 1905 with the provision of feeders to the railway. One of the first roads built was from Fort Hall to Nairobi, formerly connected by a track of 80 miles, impassable for wheeled traffic. As the traffic did not warrant any considerable expenditure, the surface was formed of blocks of *murram* which could be so treated as to form a hard brick-like surface. This became the standard class of road for communication between the more important centres not connected by railway. In Nairobi itself, and generally in the black cotton soil region, the soil proved to be unsuitable as a foundation for roads, a fact which has added materially to the difficulty and cost of road making in the Colony. In Native areas road making was in the earlier stages carried out under the supervision of Administrative Officers and followed existing Native paths. Such roads sufficed for administrative needs, until the motor-car gave rise among settlers and others to a demand for all-weather roads.

Road construction and maintenance is now placed under a Road Authority, financed from a Road Fund, which derives its revenue from the petrol-consumption tax, motor-vehicle taxation, and drivers' licences, supplemented by a special grant from general revenue. The income of

[1] H. O. Mance, *Report on the Co-ordination of Transport in Kenya, Uganda and Tanganyika Territory*, 1937.
[2] *Report of Committee to Inquire into Competition between Road Transport and Railways in Tanganyika Territory*, 1937, pp. 9–16.

the Fund in 1952 amounted to £784,000. It employs as its agents the Public Works Department, which is responsible for about 10,000 miles of road, the European District Councils, which maintain about 2,800 miles, and the African District Councils, which are responsible for about 6,500 miles. It is calculated that, in addition, there are about 480 miles of roads in National Parks and an equal mileage in Forest areas. Some 340 miles have so far been surfaced with bitumen. The Fifteen-year Development Programme envisages the construction or reconstruction of 1,700 miles of bitumen roads and 650 miles of gravel roads, at a cost of £20 million. This does not include £2¼ million to be expended on the secondary system and £1¾ million on roads in townships and municipalities. Among the more important roads to benefit from this programme are the main road from Mombasa to Nairobi, the Great Trunk Road realigned via Eldoret, and the road from Thika to Sagana. It is likely, however, that the Colony will find it difficult to implement the whole of this programme. It is noteworthy that 43,000 motor vehicles of all types have been licensed.[1] To protect the Kenya–Uganda Railway from competition by road, the conveyance of goods along roads running parallel with the railways is prohibited subject to specified exceptions.[2]

Uganda is credited with having some of the best roads in Africa. This may be due in part to the fact that in the past so large a body of labour was made available by the traditional custom of *Luwalo*.[3] But it is also a fact that the road-maker in Uganda owes a debt to the wide presence of laterite ironstone, which provides excellent material for roads.[4] The maintenance engineer owes, moreover, his debt to a distribution of rainfall in Uganda which greatly favours the maintenance of 'waterbound' roads. The Public Works Department maintains 2,847 miles of roads, serviceable in all weathers and capable of carrying vehicles up to a weight of five tons. The Buganda Government and the African Administrations elsewhere maintain roughly 8,300 miles, of which only a part is reliable in the wet season; they received in 1954 a grant of £93,411 for this purpose. About 225 miles, including the important Kampala–Entebbe–Masaka road, have been laid with a double-way bituminized surface. But the recent expansion of agricultural production, the shortage of labour, and the high cost of maintenance have created a serious problem for the Administration. The laterite surface, though adequate for ordinary motor traffic, is unable to support heavy lorry traffic without rapid deterioration, and it is noteworthy that the registrations of 'commercial vehicles' have increased from 1,929 in 1939 to 7,706 in 1954; to these must be added the large number of

---

[1] *Colonial Reports, Kenya, 1952*, p. 117.
[2] Kenya Transport Licensing Ordinance, 1937.
[3] See above, p. 661. See also R. L. Buell, *The Native Problem in Africa*, vol. i, 1928, pp. 584 ff.
[4] H. B. Thomas and R. Scott, *Uganda*, 1935, pp. 60, 238–9.

vehicles licensed in the Belgian Congo and Ruanda Urundi which use the Protectorate roads.[1] Incidentally, there is probably no part of Africa in which the popular use of the bicycle is more highly developed than in Uganda. The cost of maintaining the roads constructed by the Public Works Department averaged in 1954 about £77 a mile, varying between £108 for those capable of bearing heavy traffic and £31 for those carrying only light vehicles.[2] The cost of laying a bitumen surface, however, may be as much as £3,500 per mile.[3] The present Five-year Programme, which began in 1954, envisages an expenditure of £8 million on the roads.

The British West African Territories

Road construction is more difficult and more expensive in West Africa than in East Africa, partly owing to the scarcity of good metalling material, but largely owing to the relatively high cost of unskilled labour. In Nigeria the roads were for some time confined to the coastal area and the railway line, traffic to the interior being conveyed by the rivers or by head porterage. Today the total length of all the roads of Nigeria is about 28,000 miles, of which over 1,000 miles are treated with a bituminous surface, and about 2,300 miles with gravel or earth. Of the remainder about 20,000 miles of roads of various quality are maintained by the Native Administrations. About 300 are in Townships. There has been a significant increase in the provision made in the budget for road construction and maintenance; the budget of 1952, for instance, contemplated the expenditure of £4 million on providing bituminous surfacing and the construction of 800 miles of new roadway. In 1955 £1½ million was made available from grants made under the Colonial Development and Welfare Acts for improving and extending the system of federal trunk roads and the links by road with the British Cameroons. The main road structure consists of a trunk road running north and south and another running east and west, to one or the other of which all other roads are feeders. Stations on the railways are also well connected by roads, some of which, notably that from Lagos to Ibadan, come into direct competition with the rail system. Each of the Regions has an extensive Development Programme. In 1952 Nigeria had 8,800 commercial and 10,400 private vehicles.[4]

In the British Cameroons there were in 1951 950 miles of all-weather motor roads and 520 miles of dry-season tracks, but the latter are sometimes impassable during the rains. The completion of the Mamfe–Ikom–Enugu road has now linked the territory with Eastern Nigeria. The Bamenda roads are linked to the road system of the French Cameroons,

---

[1] *Colonial Reports, Uganda, 1953*, pp. 98–99.
[2] *Background to Uganda*, no. 89, February 1955.
[3] Cmd. 9475, 1955, p. 133.　　　　[4] *Colonial Reports, Nigeria, 1952*, p. 112.

providing access to the Douala Railway. The maintenance of roads in the southern section of the Trust Territory is specially onerous owing to the high contours and the damage done by heavy rainfall. Road communications are even less developed in the northern than in the southern sector of the territory.[1]

In the Gold Coast the roads are of special importance owing to the demands of the cocoa industry. The Gold Coast Railway has only 535 miles of open line, and there is a heavy pressure on the numerous road motor services for the carriage both of passengers and goods. The number of registered vehicles reached 20,674 at the end of 1953; the total imports of motor spirit and Diesel fuel were of the order of 28 million gallons. The Public Works Department is responsible for the maintenance of 3,563 miles of roads, and there is a very considerable mileage of roads of varying quality maintained by the Local Government bodies.[2]

Although there have been many discussions as to the construction of a railway connexion with the Northern Territories, it is held in some quarters that conditions favour the further development of the road system. On the eastern side of the Northern Territories first-class roads now run from Kumasi through Tamale to Navrongo, and on the west side from Kumasi via Bole to Wa and Lawra. The attention of the Administration is directed to the improvement of road surfacing rather than to the extension of mileage. It was estimated in 1952 that some £10½ million would have been expended on this programme by the end of 1956. Of the total length of 3,563 miles maintained by the Public Works Department, 1,098 miles had been surfaced with bitumen by the end of 1953, and work was in progress on the main roads from Accra to Kumasi and the coastal road from Accra to Takoradi.

There are no railways in British Togoland, and the communications maintained by the Administration in the southern section consist of 594 miles of all-weather roads, and in the northern section of 299 miles; in addition the Local Authorities maintain 171 miles of roads classed as 'all-weather' in the southern section, and 360 miles of 'dry-weather' roads in the northern. The main trunk road from Accra into the Trust Territory, a distance of 102 miles, is maintained by the Government as a Class I trunk road with a bitumen surface. There was at one time considerable competition for traffic between the road and railway, and in 1936 legislation was passed to prevent the carriage of certain goods over roads competing with the railways.[3]

The configuration of Sierra Leone does not readily lend itself to the

[1] *Cameroons, Report for the Year 1952*, Col. no. 299, p. 95.

[2] *Colonial Reports, Gold Coast, 1953*, pp. 94 ff.

[3] Ordinance no. 38, 1936 and L. N. 378, Carriage of Goods by Road (Amendment of Schedule) (no. 3) Order, 17 September 1954.

development of communications and, moreover, the Government has in the past had relatively small resources available for this purpose. The lack of communications has not merely formed an obstacle to the economic advance of the Protectorate, but it has also stood in the way of combination of the Tribal Authorities into more effective agencies of Local Government.[1] The Public Works Department maintained in 1952 some 1,501 miles of roads which were described as serviceable throughout the year, but of these only 95 miles were bituminized. The 847 miles maintained by District Councils or Tribal Authorities were for the most part of a low standard. It is noteworthy that only 375 lorries were registered; a considerable number of passengers were, however, transported by the road services maintained by the Government Road Transport Department. Some advance is now likely to be made in the improvement of communications as the result of the provision contained in the Economic Development Plan, which includes not only the surfacing of roads but the replacement of ferries by bridges.[2]

In Gambia the waterway provided by the Gambia river practically dispenses with the need for roads other than the short lengths used as feeders to the river; these are, however, open to heavy traffic only in the dry season. Roads technically described as 'all-weather' are maintained for the purpose of communication with Dakar via Karrang and via Brikama with Sélèty and Ziguinchor. There are no regular bus services, but there are a number of lorries which ply between Bathurst and the towns in the French territory.

The French Territories

There was at an early stage a marked preference for waterways and afterwards for the railways as the agency for the penetration and development of the interior of the country. It was not till about 1914 that serious attention was given to the improvement of road communications, largely as the result of the demand created by the growing use of motor vehicles.[3] The major routes in the Ivory Coast date from the period of the First World War; in Senegal and the Sudan the construction of roads of a modern type dates from about 1924. In Dahomey a beginning had been made before 1914, but the more important roads date in their present form from about the year 1925. In the Niger territory there was until 1934 only one road practicable throughout the year, namely that between Niamey and Zinder.

In the development both of the railway and road systems the Administrations of French West Africa have experienced much difficulty in devising a system of communications which would link together the separate terri-

---

[1] See above, pp. 535 ff.   [2] *Colonial Reports, Sierra Leone, 1952*, pp. 5, 68.
[3] O. Bigorgne, in *Enc. A.O.F.*, vol. ii, pp. 207 ff.

tories, such as Senegal, the French Cameroons, Dahomey, or Togoland, without crossing the boundaries of British territories.[1] The desire to achieve this was partly strategic, but it was also sought to confine the transport of produce to conveyances based on French territory. This has often involved a circuitous detour into the interior. A great amount of work has been done in the last few years in the improvement of the road systems, particularly those leading to Dakar or Abidjan. But for this, the standards maintained would be regarded in most British territories as very inadequate. In the more sandy regions of Senegal and in the mountainous areas of French Guinea the work of construction has been especially difficult.

The extension of the road system has, however, now linked all the interior of French West Africa to the railways by a network of roads passable by motor-cars, at all events during the dry season. Of the total of 47,374 miles shown as existing in 1949, only 72 were bituminized, 395 were metalled, and 14,823 miles were earth roads classed as 'all-season', though not in fact reliable for this purpose. The road system centres on a main axis formed by the Dakar–Bamako road and linked to the territorial capitals and other towns by inter-territorial routes. These routes are the concern of the Central Government; but the territorial governments have been responsible for carrying out the work on an agreed scheme. Among the works which are calculated to improve the transport of goods, one of the most important is the provision of bridges in place of existing ferries (bacs). A number of these works are being undertaken as the result of the Franco-British Conference on Road Communications held at Dakar in April 1947. It was then estimated that the total programme of work involved, and which was to be supported mainly from Development Funds,[2] would amount roughly to 7,000 million francs and take ten or twelve years in execution.[3]

In French Togo there were in 1951 some 1,500 miles of roads, of which 740 miles were classed as 'all-season'. The coast road was then being macadamized.

In the matter of communications, as in many other respects, French Equatorial Africa is less advanced than French West Africa, and up to about 1920 it had hardly any road capable of bearing ordinary traffic. A programme of road construction was undertaken in the Gabon territory in that year, but it was not until 1936 that some 375 miles of roads of improved standard were completed. The extension of road communications received, however, a marked stimulus during the Second World War. In the Middle Congo the construction of modern roads may be said to date from 1932. The existence of laterite deposits in Oubangui

[1] See map in ibid. p. 215.
[2] See above, pp. 1338 ff.   [3] Enc. A.O.F., vol. ii, p. 217.

Chari encouraged the commencement of a road leading from Bangui towards Lake Chad in 1914, and this territory is today the part of French Equatorial Africa which is best equipped with roads. The road system in the Chad region itself owes its origin to the routes constructed by the military authorities, as for instance that between Fort Lamy and Fort Archambault, 362 miles in length. French Equatorial Africa had in 1950 roads of a total length of 11,085 miles, but only 5,654 miles could be regarded as of even moderate standard. There is still an obstacle to traffic in the existence, particularly in the Oubangui Chari region, of numbers of unbridged rivers, crossed by ferries which are frequently no more than a raft supported on canoes.

It has been estimated that it may be necessary to remake in French Equatorial Africa a length of 8,438 miles of roads, of which 3,122 miles are of major importance.[1] The Development Plan inaugurated in 1946 forecast that it might be necessary to expend a total amount of 16,440 million francs on road communications, or approximately one-third of the total expenditure on development. The first claim is made for the improvement of the main routes connecting Brazzaville with Bangui, the cross route connecting Bangui with the French Cameroons, and the road connecting Brazzaville, Pointe Noire, and Libreville.

In the Cameroons under French Trusteeship the first stimulus for the improvement of the road system came, as in French Equatorial Africa, from the use of motor vehicles. It was not, however, until 1929–30 that a road capable of use for this purpose was completed between Yaoundé and Garoua, the northern end of the 'dorsal' route which bisects the territory. The territory has now a total length of some 5,500 miles of roads described as 'all-season' earth roads, and about 1,125 miles of roads which are classed as usable only in the dry season.[2] Attention is at present concentrated on bringing up to modern standards the two axial routes, firstly, Bonabéri–Foumban–N'gaoundéré–Maroua, and, secondly, Douala–Edéa–Yaoundé–Bertoua, terminating at Bangui or alternatively at Fort Archambault. The work on these routes, which forms part of the Ten-year Development Plan, has been estimated to cost 4,470 million francs. Other subsidiary road projects were estimated in 1948 to involve a cost of 400 million francs.[3]

The Belgian Congo and Ruanda Urundi

In the Belgian Congo policy was directed in the first instance to the development of the Congo river waterways as the main avenues of transport, the railways being subsequently constructed as an ancillary service to the waterways. But nothing is more characteristic of the realistic out-

---

[1] C. Brisson, in *Enc. A.E.F.*, pp. 434–8.
[2] *Enc. C.-T.*, p. 290.   [3] Ibid. p. 297.

look of the Belgians than the attention which has been paid in later years to the improvement of road communications. The demands made for this development have been intensified by the use of heavy lorries or tractors carrying machinery and other mechanical equipment. There have, for some years, been on the roads a number of vehicles which carry weights of 16 tons, and in 1952 use was being made of the *trains Marmont*, involving a gross weight of 25 tons.[1] There were in 1953 some 35,000 vehicles of various classes operating in the Colony—three times the number which were operating six years previously.

The Colony had in 1952 over 66,500 miles of *routes publiques*, apart from over 8,400 miles classified as *routes privées*. The former are divided into arterial roads (19,562 miles) and secondary roads (46,938 miles).[2] Even more than in French Equatorial Africa, the development of road usage has been hampered by the large number of rivers and streams, the bridging of which involves heavy additional expenditure. Some of this difficulty has lately been met by large purchases of Bailey-bridge material.

Systematic road development has been promoted by the formulation in recent years of a comprehensive scheme providing for the needs of the whole Colony, and linking up the existing river and rail communications. Reference has already been made to this scheme in a previous paragraph. The road section involves the maintenance of five trunk routes. The first of these, running through the centre of the Colony, links up Costermansville (Bukavu) and Stanleyville; the second connects Matadi, Leopoldville, and Costermansville; the third links up Elisabethville with the Costermansville–Stanleyville route; the fourth connects Libenge with Buta and Aba; the fifth runs roughly from north to south in the centre of the Colony, connecting Malonga with Luluabourg, Lusambo, and Stanleyville. The programme of road construction (including the provision of bridges) contemplates the expenditure of 6,100 million francs out of a total estimated expenditure of 13,300 million francs on transport and communications generally, including the waterways and railways. Provision has been made for this sum in the Ten-year Development Plan of the Colony.

In the Trust Territory of Ruanda Urundi the road system is less well developed, and there are not the same number of road services providing both for passenger and goods traffic. There were in 1953 some 5,104 miles of 'public' roads of various standards. Of these 1,967 were classed as arterial.

The Portuguese Territories

In the Portuguese territory of Mozambique the soil in the coastal areas is unsuitable for earth roads. In one instance, indeed, it has been found

---

[1] J. Frederick and G. Gielen, in *Enc. C.B.*, vol. iii, pp. 435–43.
[2] *Rapport sur l'administration de la colonie du Congo Belge, 1952*, p. 304.

more economical to build a railway line than to maintain a road.[1] Again, the Sul do Save Province is liable to exceptional rainfall, and roads are annually destroyed by floods. The annual inundation of the Pungue Flats at one time completely isolated Beira from communication by road, until the Flats were traversed by a causeway above flood level. In the interior of the territory, however, good roads can be maintained at a relatively low cost. The main road from Lourenço Marques to Johannesburg has a tarmac surface as far as the Swaziland border, and most other roads radiating from the capital have at least a sector of their distance treated with tar. The roads leading to Southern Rhodesia and Nyasaland are liable to severe corrugation due to the heavy volume of traffic. There is, on these roads, a growing degree of competition with the railway. About 3,000 miles of roadways are classified as first-class, 4,500 as second-class, and 8,000 as third-class, but the third-class roads are little more than tracks.[2] In 1953 the Government expended 66,000 *contos* on the construction of roads and bridges, of which there are 422 in Mozambique. The Southern Rhodesian plan of laying concrete strips has been introduced on some roads with good results.

The network of roads in Angola covers about 13,000 miles, but only 54 miles have been treated with bitumen or asphalt.[3] They are classified in three grades, not, however, so much according to the condition of the roads, as to their relative importance as a means of communication. Three first-class or 'national' roads run from north to south; one runs along the coast, a second through the centre of the territory, and a third along its eastern border. Four roads of the same class proceed from west to east, namely, two from the port of Luanda, one from Lobito Bay, and the fourth from Mossâmedes.[4] Owing to the severe damage to temporary structures from floods and torrents, bridge construction takes a prominent place in the Development Programme. In 1952 some 17,000 motor vehicles of all types were registered; there is a motor-bus service on 22 scheduled routes.

Liberia

It is a characteristic feature in the record of Liberia that before the First World War there was no road leading into the hinterland of the country; all transportation was by head porterage along footpaths. Even the streets of Monrovia were not metalled. After the war, however, the Government projected a chain of roads connecting the interior with the coast, and by 1925 about 130 miles of the chief of these roads, running

[1] G. F. Spence, *The Portuguese Colony of Moçambique*, 1951, p. 99.
[2] *Anuário estatístico do Ultramar, 1952*, p. 163.
[3] *Angola* (Institute Edition), Luanda, 1953, pp. 147 ff.
[4] A. J. A. Cardoso, *Angola, Your Neighbour*, 1950, p. 44.

from Monrovia to Sanokwele (Sanniquellie), had been completed. The work at this stage is alleged to have been carried out mainly by compulsory unpaid labour; there are said to have been instances in which such labour had been obliged to work on the roads for as much as four months in the year.[1] Since about 1943 there has been an increased stimulus given to the work of road making, and apparently also a substantial improvement in the methods used.[2] The main road running from Monrovia to Ganta and Sanokwele has been continued up to the French frontier at Nzérékoré, with a branch to Tappita (in the Central Province), making a total length of nearly 400 miles. A number of shorter roads have been completed in the Western Province. Some progress has also been made in providing what is intended ultimately to form a coastal road from Monrovia to Barclayville and Cape Palmas. The development of the road programme was assisted in 1951 by the grant of a loan of $5 million from the Export-Import Bank in Washington. It should be noted that, apart from the roads comprised in the Government programme, the Firestone Company has made earth roads totalling some hundreds of miles in its rubber plantations. It was announced in 1955 that the Export-Import Bank had provided a credit of $15 million towards transportation projects in Liberia. These include the opening of road communications to the agricultural area of the Western Province and to the extensive timber areas in the Central and Eastern Provinces.

AIR TRANSPORT

The active interest in the extension of civil aviation in Africa began some years after the end of the First World War. The credit of the establishment of the first series of internal air flights appears to belong to Belgium, for the *Société Nationale pour l'Étude des Transports Aériens* (S.N.E.T.A.) instituted in 1920 a service of flying boats between Leopoldville and Stanleyville.[3] But the major impetus has been derived from the development of regular communication by air between Europe and Africa. The demonstration flight of Sir Alan Cobham in 1928 was succeeded by numerous aspirants competing for the record from London to Cape Town. In 1930 the British Government joined with other interested Governments in an agreement with British Imperial Airways to provide a subsidized weekly service between London and Cape Town. In 1931 this service reached Kisumu, and in 1932 it reached Cape Town. The

[1] R. L. Buell, *The Native Problem in Africa*, vol. ii, 1928, pp. 747, 771–3.
[2] *Seventh Annual Message of the President*, 1950, pp. 13–14. C. M. Wilson, *Liberia, 1847–1947*, 1947, pp. 4, 91–94, 209. R. L. Buell, *Liberia, A Century of Survival*, 1947, pp. 47–55. E. Anderson, *Liberia*, 1952, pp. 155, 272–81.
[3] G. Perier, 'La Navigation aérienne au Congo Belge et au Ruanda-Urundi', *Enc. C.B.*, vol. iii, pp. 444 ff.

journey occupied 11 days in 1932, but was reduced to 6½ days in 1937. It used the flying boat down the east coast to Durban. In 1956 the journey from London to Cape Town took roughly 28 hours. In the thirties French companies, and notably *Air France*, instituted a service to French West and French Equatorial Africa, the journey from France to Dakar being scheduled in 1938 to take 20 hours.

During the Second World War Africa south of the Sahara became the reception zone for supplies sent by air for the use of the North African armies. New aerodromes were built and a great advance was made in the study of air conditions.[1] After the war, the shortage of aircraft made it difficult at first to meet the demands for the expansion of air services, and recourse was had to converted military machines. The Union of South Africa and the Belgian Congo were alone able to place orders for immediate delivery. In 1946 the Pan American World Airways established regular services from New York to West and South Africa. By 1952 the first jet airliner was put into service on the London–Johannesburg route by the British Overseas Air Corporation; it has been temporarily interrupted but may be renewed. Africa is now accessible from all other continents in two or three days. In 1955 a regular air freight service was instituted by Hunting Clan Air Transport Service to all the British dependencies in Africa. But while intercontinental services are pre-eminent for speed and frequency, the development of local services is perhaps of more immediate concern to residents in Africa.

In the Union of South Africa the State-owned South African Airways acquired in 1934 and 1935 the services conducted by a number of private companies,[2] including the South-West African Airways, and it also took over the feeder lines serving the former Imperial Airways. It operates internal services between the principal towns of the Union and those in adjoining territories, as notably Salisbury in Southern Rhodesia and Lourenço Marques in Mozambique. The Jan Smuts International Airport is now one of the most efficiently equipped in the world. In the High Commission Territories it is only in Bechuanaland that air transport has been regularly developed, and there only on a small scale. The Witwatersrand Native Labour Association has made an interesting innovation by using the air for transporting labour recruits from Northern Rhodesia and Angola to join the railway at Francistown.

In the British Central African territories the present organization developed out of the Rhodesia and Nyasaland Airways (R.A.N.A.), whose fleet of small planes was acquired by the Southern Rhodesia Government in 1945. The Central African Airways Corporation was formed in 1946, each of the three territories which now comprise the Federation of Rhodesia

---

[1] *Air Affairs*, vol. i, no. 4, Washington D.C., 1947, pp. 441–51.
[2] *O.Y.S.A.*, *1949*, p. 565; ibid. *1950*, pp. 572 ff.

and Nyasaland contributing towards the capital required. When civil aviation became the concern of the Federal Government of Rhodesia and Nyasaland in 1953,[1] it was decided to employ a considerable amount of fresh capital in improving the air fleet of the Corporation. All the principal towns in the Federation are inter-connected, and services are maintained to Johannesburg and Lourenço Marques in the south and to Nairobi and Tabora in the north. Aviation in its early stages owed much to the financial assistance of the Beit Trustees. The aerodromes at Salisbury, Bulawayo, Lusaka, Livingstone, Ndola, and Kasama are international airports, and each of the first three has one runway surfaced with bitumen. The airport at Salisbury has been reconstructed at a cost of about £1¼ million; the reconstruction of that at Bulawayo has been estimated to cost nearly £1 million. In Nyasaland the international airport at Chileka, near Blantyre, has been completed; Mzimba, Salima, and Lilongwe now have services more than once a week. An organization, similar to that above mentioned in Bechuanaland, is undertaken by Africair, a Charter Company of Johannesburg, which operates from Lilongwe to Francistown for the purpose of transporting Nyasaland labour recruits for the Rand mines.

In East Africa the East African Airways Corporation succeeded the undertaking known as Wilson Airways, which had obtained the contract for carriage of mail in 1929. It serves the chief centres in Uganda, Kenya, Tanganyika, and Zanzibar; the Central African Airways co-operate by calling at Tabora for Northern Rhodesian passengers and at Dar-es-Salaam for Nyasaland destinations. S.A.B.E.N.A. Airways conduct a weekly service from the Belgian Congo. The Entebbe Airport has been described as the Charing Cross of Africa, lying as it does at the intersection of the north–south route from Europe to South Africa and the east–west route from the East African Protectorates to British West Africa. Its meteorological conditions are unusually equable. Adjacent to the airport is a flying-boat base of seven miles of water on Lake Victoria. In Tanganyika the airport at Dar-es-Salaam, which has been improved to international standard, was formally opened in 1954. Nairobi has two aerodromes, Eastleigh for main airline traffic, and Nairobi West, mostly for internal and local traffic. But a new airport, which will be capable of accommodating the largest aircraft, will take over most of the Eastleigh traffic.

Aviation in West Africa developed later than elsewhere; it was said of Nigeria that in 1935 there still seemed 'to be no demand for air facilities of an elaborate nature'.[2] The West African Airways Corporation—evolved

---

[1] Federation of Rhodesia and Nyasaland (Constitution) Order in Council no. 1199, 1953, p. 51, item 22.

[2] *Annual Report on the Social and Economic Progress of the People of Nigeria, 1935.*

in 1946 out of a number of independent private companies—now provides services to the chief towns in Nigeria, Sierra Leone, the Gold Coast, and Gambia; it runs a service to Dakar to connect with the British Overseas Airways Corporation and also with *Air France*. The chief airports of the Corporation are at Lagos and Kano in Nigeria, at Freetown in Sierra Leone, at Accra, Takoradi, Kumasi, and Tamale in the Gold Coast, and at Yundum near Bathurst in Gambia. The large airport at Robertsfield, in the neighbourhood of Monrovia, is maintained largely in the interests of Pan American Airways.

In the French territories the airport at Dakar was originally founded by Latécoère Airways as an intermediary point on the route from France to South America. The first stage from Toulouse to Dakar via Casablanca was accomplished in 1925, but it was not until 1930 that the second stage, from Dakar to South America, was achieved. This route was designed originally for conveyance of post, but a regular service between Dakar and Natal in Brazil was begun in 1936; by this time the Latécoère Company had been absorbed by *Air France*. In 1937 the *Compagnie Aéro-maritime* at Dakar began to operate services of 'amphibious' aircraft along the 5,000 miles of coastline between Senegal and the Belgian Congo. At the present time French West Africa is traversed by two main routes of air traffic. The first links the chief European capitals with French West and French Equatorial Africa, the Belgian Congo, and South Africa by routes operated by *Air France* and Trans-Sahara Airways, and by the British, Dutch, and Belgian 'international' companies. The other system passing through Dakar is operated by various continental and American corporations over routes which link Europe, the Americas, and South Africa. Dakar's airport at Yoff was constructed for military purposes, but is now used solely for civilian traffic. There are other airports at Port Étienne (for sea-planes), Conakry, Bamako, Abidjan, Lomé, and Niamey, together with numerous subsidiary aerodromes.[1]

Aviation has been less developed in French Equatorial than in French West Africa, but the Development Programme designed for execution in the next ten years provides for the improvement of existing airports and the construction of others. Of the seven larger airports that at Brazzaville has been improved to international standard; the service of *Air France* has now brought Brazzaville within a 22 hours' journey to Paris. Other aerodromes are situated at Pointe Noire, Bangui, and Port Gentil.

In the Belgian Congo the flying-boat service operated by S.N.E.T.A. between Leopoldville and Stanleyville above referred to was taken over in 1923 by the *Société Anonyme Belge d'Exploitation de la Navigation Aérienne* (S.A.B.E.N.A.) and a local network of aircraft routes, said to be the densest in Africa, was rapidly established. The S.A.B.E.N.A. service

---

[1] *Enc. A.O.F.*, vol. ii, pp. 303–8.

operating in Europe was linked up with the local service in Africa in 1935. External communications are maintained from the airport at Leopoldville to Brussels, Rome, Lisbon, and Johannesburg; from the airport at Stanleyville to Brussels, Cairo, and Khartoum; Usumbara serves the routes to Entebbe and Nairobi, and Elisabethville serves Johannesburg. There are numerous subsidiary landing grounds.

In Angola air communication with Portugal is maintained by a weekly service operated between Lisbon and Luanda by Portuguese Aerial Transports. Pan American Airways and S.A.B.E.N.A. maintain external services to Johannesburg, to Leopoldville, Brazzaville, and also to Mozambique. Internal services are organized by the *Divisão de Exploração dos Transportes Aéreos* and are routed along three lines. The northern flight is from Luanda via Cabinda to Pointe Noire in French Equatorial Africa, the southern line is from Luanda via Lobito to Mossâmedes, and the eastern from Lobito to Nova Lisboa along the route of the Benguela Railway. The most important airport is at Luanda, which is being improved by a second asphalted runway.

The *Divisão de Exploração dos Transportes Aéreos* (known in this case as D.E.T.A.) organizes aviation in Mozambique. Flights are arranged to external destinations such as Johannesburg, Durban, and Salisbury. Within the territory a weekly service is maintained from Lourenço Marques to Beira and the principal commercial towns. The largest and most modern airport is at Lourenço Marques, but Beira also has an airport and that at Lumbo is now being developed.

The Pan American Airways furnish a service between Liberia and New York, and *Air France* provides a service between Dakar and the southern West African towns. The two principal Liberian airports are at Robertsfield, near Monrovia, which was constructed in 1941 as a base for United States planes during the Second World War, and at James Spriggs Payne Airfield, completed in 1952. During the war the United States Air Force made an extensive use of the Liberian air bases.

A CONCLUDING NOTE

If the preceding pages go to some length in giving details of systems of transport in Africa, there is some justification for this. There seems to be no other type of development which can effect so speedy a change in the economic or social conditions of a backward country. That this view is now well appreciated is shown by the high proportion which expenditure on communications bears to the total amount provided in the post-war Development Plans of the different territories. There are, however, in these projects three points which call for comment here. There is, in the first place, only very occasional evidence of the formulation in any territory of a comprehensive plan of transport facilities, assigning their due place to railway and road systems, or the use of waterways where these are available. The extension of the railway system seems, in particular, to be a matter for *ad hoc* decision, usually determined by the need for transport of the product of a new mining or industrial enterprise. In the second place, little more than a beginning has been made to the co-ordination of the rail and road policies of the different territories concerned.

In the third place, there is a significant contrast between the position as we see it today and that envisaged by Lord Lugard in 1921. He looked on the building of a railway as the first step in any comprehensive system of transport. The railway was, in his words, 'a necessary precursor of roads'. It should, where possible, have some definite objective—the shore of a great body of water like Lake Victoria, or a mineralized area like the Katanga, or the linking of the navigable sections of a great river, like the Matadi–Leopoldville line. Failing that, however, 'any railway built reasonably cheaply through a populous country is bound to be remunerative'.[1] But the great increase in the cost of labour and of mechanical equipment in the last 30 years has forced us to revise our conception of the railway as a remunerative or, at all events, a self-supporting investment. It is true that its rival, the road, remains a charge on public revenues, for which there can be a little direct return in the form of licence or registration fees, but it has shown itself to be a much more flexible agency of transport than Lord Lugard thought possible. Moreover, even where circumstances compel the State to undertake road surfacing of an expensive type, its cost is still less than that of constructing a railway track and providing the mechanical equipment of a railway. Where physical conditions vary as widely as they do in different regions of Africa it is not possible to reduce to a general formula the relative cost involved in the construction of railways and roads, but it is worth noting that the line in Southern Rhodesia under construction in 1954 has cost £22,000 a mile, exclusive of bridges and culverts. The projected continuation of the Northern Rhodesian system to Tanganyika has been estimated to cost from £25,000 a mile in Northern Rhodesia to £57,000 a mile in the most difficult parts in Tanganyika. There are a growing number of instances in which the decision has been reached that road transport must be allowed to carry the burden for which a low-cost line was at one period considered to be the appropriate solution. This is, for instance, the conclusion recently arrived at in the northern part of Nyasaland, in the Gold Coast, and in Mozambique.

The preparation of a comprehensive scheme for the development of transport facilities consequently represents today an embarrassing choice

---

[1] F. D. Lugard, *The Dual Mandate in British Tropical Africa*, 1926, pp. 461–76.

of alternatives. It is possible only to summarize here certain considerations based on the survey of transport organization made in the preceding pages. Transport in Africa is still largely concerned with the carriage of bulky and relatively low-value loads over great distances. For this type of traffic, railways are in most territories essential to full development. Mining activities on a large scale can hardly ever be maintained without rail transport, as is demonstrated by the history of iron-mining in Sierra Leone and Liberia, tin-mining in Nigeria, and the exploitation of the Belgian Katanga or the Copperbelt in Northern Rhodesia. Equally, railways have been vital for the cultivation of groundnuts in Northern Nigeria, 700 miles from the coast, and of cotton in Uganda at roughly a similar distance. There is another argument which is, in the long view, in favour of the railway. Though Africa is by no means prolific in the supply of coal, it is nevertheless found in the Union of South Africa, in Southern Rhodesia, Tanganyika, Mozambique, and Nigeria. The future extension of hydroelectric installations may further assist in easing the problem of the supply of fuel on the railway. No natural source of oil for use in motors has yet been discovered, and experiments in the use of vegetable oils have not so far proved successful.

On the other side, it is clear that the road, as the basis both of a system of haulage and of passenger services, has many advantages over the railway. We have in truth arrived at a position which is the reverse of that in which the railway was envisaged as 'the precursor of the road'. By a natural logic, the road is now the pioneer and is normally the precursor of the railway. But one cannot envisage a period when the road will (as has sometimes been assumed) entirely replace the railway. It is one of the outstanding difficulties of the present situation that the railway comes on occasion under severe competition from roads, and that Governments have found it necessary to pass legislation to bring such competition under control. The effects of competition are particularly felt when there is a wide differentiation between import and export rates. Some exports can compete in the world market only if railway rates are eased, and there is at times no other way of effecting this save by increasing the rates on imports. In such cases, free competition by road transport may, by undercutting railway rates, entail a loss of revenue which the taxpayer must make good. But, while the prohibition of the transport of goods (other than that of local produce) on roads competing with railways may be a legitimate procedure, yet when roads expand and follow more circuitous routes such prohibition can only be enforced to the prejudice of the economic development of the country.

Attempts at a solution have been made in various ways. A State monopoly both of rail and road services has been adopted by the Union of South Africa. Elsewhere the two services have been kept separate, but their financial interests have been pooled, road transport paying in the form of a toll what the railway loses from competition. A third method followed has been to protect the railway monopoly by the drastic controlling of road transport. The Government of the Federation of Rhodesia and Nyasaland found itself in an unprecedented position when in 1954 it had to obtain legislative sanction in order to permit the roads to carry part of the goods normally conveyed by rail. This situation arose when the coalfields at Wankie produced more coal than the railways could carry, while at the same time the mines in the Copperbelt were so short of coal that they were burning wood fuel and importing American coal over the Benguela Railway. The difficulty was only temporary, but it illustrates the complications into which Governments may be led by the necessity for legislating in matters of this kind.

The present trends of railway construction do not differ appreciably from those in the past. The object of attaining the coast by the shortest route has generally been achieved, and the motive for railway construction today is rather to secure alternative routes which will afford relief to lines overburdened with goods and harbours congested with freight. This is the reason for the line recently constructed from Southern Rhodesia to Lourenço Marques; it is also, in large part, the ground for the projected line from Rhodesia to Walvis Bay.

As already remarked, the air services have not as yet entered into active competition with the railways. But there is no doubt of the convenience they have provided for certain purposes. A flight of two hours from Livingstone to Mongu in the Barotse Protectorate has replaced a fortnight's voyage up the Zambezi in a man-paddled barge. Muslims in West Africa can now make the pilgrimage to Mecca by air. In Nigeria a number of Hausa leather merchants, having sold their stock, return by air to their base at Kano, and instances have been cited above where labour recruits for the Rand or the Katanga mines have been carried to their work by charter planes. Though air services cannot as yet compete with railways or roads for the transport of bulky commercial produce, it is noteworthy that in October 1954 an air service was organized between Northern and Southern Rhodesia primarily for the carriage of freight.

The preceding pages have invited attention to a number of instances of the lack of co-operation between neighbouring countries in the designing of roads or railroads. Some measure of co-operation has, however, been promoted during recent years by the regional conferences convened to consider problems of transportation. The Conference held at Dakar in 1947 gave birth to the *route trans-Gambienne*, which by traversing Gambia afforded intercommunication between the two French dependencies of Senegal and Guinea, and to another route from the Ivory Coast to the Gold Coast for the transportation of seasonal labourers migrating for the

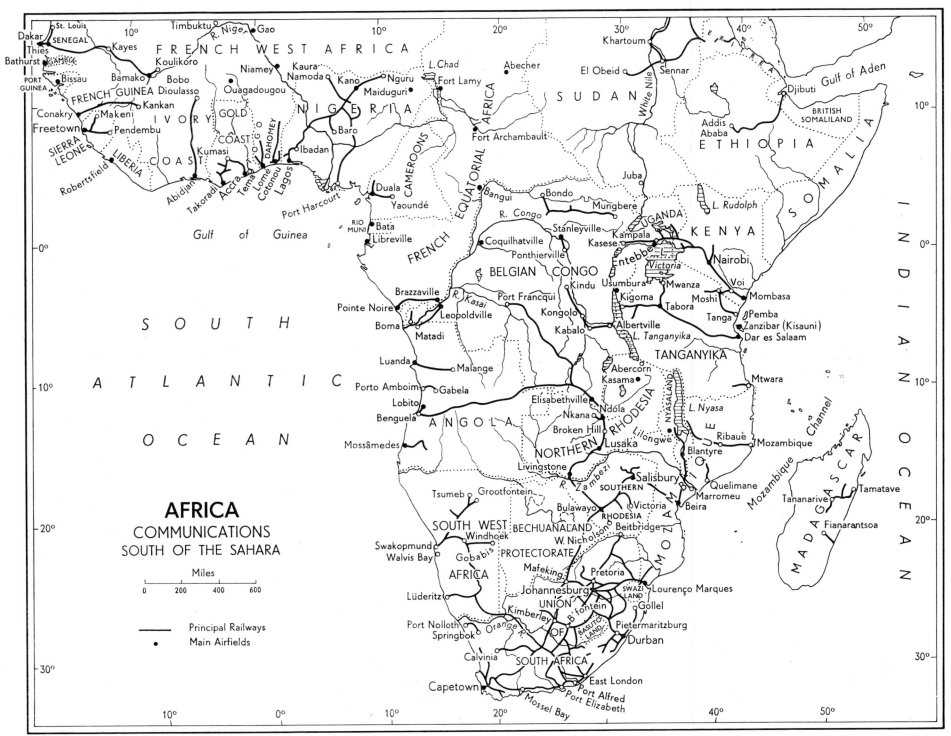

AFRICA
COMMUNICATIONS
SOUTH OF THE SAHARA

Miles

0	200	400	600

—————— Principal Railways

• Main Airfields

Since the preparation of this map, the rail link between the Rhodesian railway system and the coast at Lourenço Marques has been completed

groundnut harvest. The Lisbon Conference of 1949 was largely preparatory for the plenary conference to be held the following year at Johannesburg,[1] but it drew attention to the shortage of equipment at the port of
Beira and advocated the construction of the railway between Southern
Rhodesia and Lourenço Marques. The Conference was also signalized
by the agreement to adopt the 3 ft. 6 in. gauge as standard for all international railways in Africa.[2] The recent intervention of the Export-Import
Bank has also produced some degree of international and inter-Colonial
co-operation in railway construction.

[1] *Central and Southern Africa Transport Conference, Final Act and Related Documents*, Johannesburg,
1950, pp. 52 ff.
[2] Ibid. p. 31.

CHAPTER XXIV

THE ORGANIZATION OF RESEARCH

IT is only in relatively recent years that the Colonial Powers have realized the need to provide for a comprehensive system of research into the problems involved in the administration of their African territories. It may, indeed, be said that this new outlook is a corollary of the changing conceptions of the obligations of Colonial rule, of which the most typical result is to be seen in the various Colonial Development Programmes described in preceding chapters. Up to the end of the Second World War, the acquisition of specialized knowledge bearing on the work of the administrative, economic, or social services had been largely regarded as the function of the local institutions of research which were growing up in different territories. These had not unnaturally tended to concentrate, in the first instance, on investigations bearing on the problems with which the health, agricultural, and animal husbandry services had to deal. The new emphasis on the general improvement of the standards of life of the African peoples, and an appreciation of the growth of political consciousness shown in many sections of the indigenous community, demanded not merely an extension of the range of these studies but a more definite co-ordination of their direction. The range of the studies made by local agencies has already been illustrated, usually towards the end of each of the preceding chapters. It is now important to notice certain of the tendencies shown in the measures taken for the co-ordination of research by the Colonial Powers, either singly, or on an intercolonial basis.

Here there are three points which call for notice. It would seem, in the first place, that the character of the local institutions had at an early stage reflected the feeling that research conducted in a Colonial territory should be largely confined to the investigation of local conditions or to the examination of the results obtained by field workers. What is usually described as 'long-term' research should, in other words, be entrusted to metropolitan institutions, whether autonomous or incorporated in university or other academic bodies. But experience has shown the difficulty of maintaining in practice any definite line of distinction between 'long-term' and 'short-term' research or between the fields of 'pure' and 'applied' science. Again and again workers in 'pure' science have been responsible for discoveries of great practical value, and conversely workers in the 'applied' sciences have been able to indicate to workers in the 'pure' sciences a line of inquiry which has led to most fruitful results. It is now generally recognized that the organization of research within the Colonial territories should, if possible, include the establishment of regional centres which can work in association with localized institutions and take part in the investigation of problems demanding more 'long-term' research.

In the second place, it is doubtful whether there was at a previous period sufficient recognition of the close interrelation of many of the most insistent problems of Colonial development. Here, also, it is unnecessary to enlarge on a point which has been amply illustrated in the course of preceding chapters. One outstanding example will suffice. The elimination of the tsetse fly, which remains a major scourge of tropical Africa, is not merely a problem for the entomologist or, indeed, for the worker in any single branch of the natural sciences. It demands the co-operation of the botanist, the agronomist, medical and veterinary officers, the chemist, the engineer, and the game warden, who are all involved at one point or another with the processes by which the fly is to be attacked. They, too, must join in devising methods by which the fly can be prevented from returning to the lands from which it has been ejected.

In the third place, research cannot be confined to the field of the natural sciences. The prominence now given to the development of African production as a factor in the improvement of the general standards of living has emphasized the need for a closer study of the indigenous economy. It has become a matter of first importance to study the processes by which the system of subsistence production can be adjusted to the needs of the exchange economy. Too little is known of the nature of the incentives which will bring workers from rural communities into the field of industry to meet the increasing demand for skilled labour. It is no less necessary to acquire a closer understanding of the social structure of the African peoples in order to ascertain what adjustments can best be made in the unfamiliar political institutions to which Africa is now being introduced.

The Metropolitan Organization

The reorientation of the organization of research which has accompanied the adoption by the Colonial Powers of a more dynamic policy of African development is best exemplified in the course taken in Great Britain after the passing of the Colonial Development and Welfare Act of 1940. The organization of research had up to this date engaged a certain measure of attention, though not on a comprehensive basis. A fund for research on tropical diseases had been created in 1899, and the United Kingdom paid half the cost of the study of insect pests initiated in 1909 by the Entomological Research Committee attached to the Natural History Museum in London. A sum of £10,000 a year was voted for general research in 1919 and 1920, but the amount was reduced in 1921 to £2,000. Out of

the total of £1 million a year authorized for expenditure by the Colonial
Development Act of 1929, about £600,000 was spent on research of
various types in the Colonial Empire as a whole. The Empire Marketing
Board, which was set up in 1926, financed research on Colonial forest
products, on a number of entomological and mycological problems, and
on nutrition. But when in 1940 the United Kingdom Government published its statement of the policy to be embodied in the Colonial Development and Welfare Act of that year, it announced its intention to place the
organization of research on a wider and more regular basis. It is of
interest to note in this connexion that the Government took the occasion
to acknowledge the assistance which it had received from the recommendations for the extension of research made in 1938 in the first edition of
this Survey.[1] Out of the total provision of £5 million a year to be made
available for expenditure on Colonial Development and Welfare, up to
£500,000 a year was to be set aside in order to constitute a separate
Colonial Research Fund; this sum was increased to £1 million a year by
the amending Act of 1945. A total of £9,224,342 was actually issued for
expenditure on research schemes up to the end of 1955. The cumulative allocation for research schemes during this period amounted to
£13,474,742.[2]

Advice on the expenditure of the fund thus provided is rendered to the
Government by the Colonial Research Council (designated up to 1948
as the Colonial Research Committee), which was specially constituted for
this purpose. The Council does not itself undertake research nor directly
control its operation. Its influence has been shown most prominently in
the constitution of a number of bodies, some of which are advisory to the
Secretary of State, while others are of a more direct functional character.[3]
Thus the Colonial Products Research Council (originally constituted as a
separate body) is directly responsible for research into the use of Colonial
products, and the Colonial Geological Surveys and the Colonial Geodetic
and Topographical Surveys supplement and help to co-ordinate the work
carried out in those Colonial territories which maintain their own Survey
Departments. The Anti-Locust Research Centre combines advisory and
research activities, as do also the Colonial Insecticides and Colonial Fly
and Trypanosomiasis Research Committees. The Social Science Council,
which is mainly an advisory body, deals as such with a wide range of
anthropological, social, historical, and linguistic research. The Colonial
Medical Research Committee and the Committee for Colonial Agricultural Animal Health and Forestry Research, which are in effect branches

[1] *Statement of Policy on Colonial Development and Welfare*, Cmd. 6175, 1940, para. 8.
[2] *Colonial Research, 1954–1955*, Cmd. 9626, 1955, p. 17.
[3] See the series of Annual Reports on Colonial Research commencing with that of 1943–4:
Colonial Research Committee, First Annual Report, 1943–44, Cmd. 6535, 1944. For a full list of the
research agencies constituted, see *Colonial Research 1954–1955*, Cmd. 9626, 1955.

of the important bodies concerned with research in these subjects in the United Kingdom, advise on the studies directly affecting Colonial territories. The Colonial Economic Research Committee provides advice on problems demanding investigation in this particular field.

The research funds thus provided by Parliament for Colonial research schemes have been expended only to a minor extent on grants to metropolitan institutions of research, nor have the Advisory Committees exercised any direct control over the research carried on by institutions overseas. Their activity has consisted primarily in assisting to co-ordinate and supplement work done in the Colonies or in awarding grants to individual students. One result of the discussions which originated in the Colonial Research Council has been the creation of a unified Overseas Research Service for all Colonial dependencies, the members of which receive standard rates of pay similar to those of the United Kingdom Scientific Civil Service. Persons appointed to the Overseas Research Services are liable to work in any one of the dependencies and may be required from time to time to serve for periods in the United Kingdom or elsewhere, but are employed on research throughout the tenure of their appointment. When appointed to the Research Service, they must have the appropriate professional qualifications, but they need not necessarily have received special training for work in the tropics or in Colonial conditions.

Another expression of the enhanced interest in research has been the creation of an African Studies Branch within the Colonial Office. Its members collect and distribute information on certain particularly important problems of administrative policy, most notably the development of representative Local Government institutions and the modification of African customary law, special attention being given in the latter field to the development of systems of land tenure. The African Studies Branch produces a useful quarterly, the *Journal of African Administration*.

The major metropolitan institutions in the United Kingdom which are concerned, directly or indirectly, with research on African problems have been described in detail in previous chapters. Only a small minority of these institutions are under direct Government control. For example, the International African Institute,[1] though it receives a small subsidy from the Government, is an autonomous organization. The School of Oriental and African Studies and the London School of Hygiene and Tropical Medicine are constituent bodies of the University of London; the Liverpool School of Tropical Medicine is a constituent body of the University of Liverpool, and the School of Forestry is a constituent body of the University of Oxford. Among the few research institutions dealing largely with Colonial problems and directly controlled by the Government of the United Kingdom are the Imperial College of Tropical Agriculture

[1] See above, pp. 55, 62, 113.

at Trinidad and the Entomological Research Committee attached to the British Museum of Natural History. An important function is also performed under Government auspices by the Commonwealth Agricultural Bureaux, which analyse and disseminate the results of research in several branches of agriculture.[1] Of the funds expended on the advice of the Colonial Research Council, the major part has consisted of grants made to the Governments of territories within the Colonial Empire.

Whereas British policy has in this respect avoided the exercise of direct control over research carried out in the Colonies, and has confined itself largely to attempts to co-ordinate the efforts of their local institutions and to provide them with financial assistance, that of the French has involved from the first a greater degree of centralization. In the earlier days research in their African territories was carried out by *missions* from the *Institut Pasteur* in Paris, and the first local research organizations were the branches of this institute, established at St. Louis in 1896 and Brazzaville in 1910. Since 1943 central direction has become the responsibility of the *Office de la Recherche Scientifique d'Outre-Mer* (O.R.S.O.M.), which is attached to the Ministry for Overseas France.[2] Its function is to organize fundamental research, while leaving the investigation of immediate problems to the research organs of the specialist Government services, and to create research centres in areas in which adequate provision has not previously existed. The capital cost of these centres is met from the *Fonds d'Investissement pour le Développement Économique et Social de la France d'Outre-Mer* (F.I.D.E.S.);[3] the recurrent cost is divided between the *Office de la Recherche Scientifique d'Outre-Mer* and the Government of the territory concerned. Since there were already a number of research centres in French West Africa, the African activities of the *Office Scientifique* have been concentrated in Equatorial Africa and the Cameroons. It is responsible for the *Institut d'Études Centrafricaines* at Brazzaville, the *Institut de Recherches du Cameroun* at Yaoundé, a geophysical centre at Bangui, and a laboratory of oceanography at Pointe Noire. The Bangui centre is an example of the activities of the *Office Scientifique* in co-ordinating research in different territories; it forms one of a chain of geophysical stations, the others being at M'Bour in Senegal, in Madagascar, and in New Caledonia.

The *Office Scientifique* is also responsible for the training of scientific personnel. For this purpose it maintains two centres, one at Bondy near Paris and one at Adiopodoumé near Abidjan. Students are selected with a general grounding in the sciences, and receive a year's specialized instruction at Bondy, followed by a year at Adiopodoumé, where they are trained in research techniques. The training thus given to persons who are to be employed on research by the *Office Scientifique* is similar to that

---

[1] See above, p. 913.   [2] For further details see *Enc. A.O.F.*, vol. i, pp. 328 ff.
[3] See above, pp. 214, 337, 339.

given to those who are to join the specialist Government services. It is claimed that research workers within and outside the Government service thus share a common outlook on the relevance of research and on the appropriate methods to be followed.[1] A total of 134 specialists had been trained by 1950; of these 29 were employed in Government services, 80 by the *Office Scientifique*, and 25 in other research institutions.

The *Institut des Fruits et Agrumes Coloniaux* was set up in 1941, and the *Institut de Recherches pour les Huiles de Palme et les Oléagineux* in 1942. Both of these have functions which, to some extent, resemble those of the Commonwealth Bureaux in the United Kingdom. The *Union Cotonnière de l'Empire Français*, which succeeded the *Association Cotonnière Coloniale* in 1942, became in 1946 the *Institut de Recherches du Coton et des Textiles Exotiques*; it discharges functions similar to those of the Empire Cotton Growing Corporation of Great Britain. The *Académie des Sciences Coloniales*, now attached to the Ministry for Overseas France, was created in 1926. It has a hundred members, representing all the branches of natural and social science concerned in the overseas territories. It holds regular meetings for discussion, and may be called upon for advice by the Minister responsible for the overseas territories.

An Encyclopedia of the French Union is in preparation under the direction of M. E. Guernier of the *Institut d'Études Politiques* of the University of Paris. The volumes dealing with the African territories had been completed by 1951, and have been frequently utilized as sources of information in the present Survey.

The Belgian approach to the organization of research has shown a similar tendency to that of France. In Belgium the senior institution concerned with Colonial research is the *Musée Royal du Congo Belge* at Tervueren, founded by Leopold II in 1902. It organizes investigations in zoology, anthropology, and archaeology, and also in social and economic problems, the results of which are published in the *Annales du Musée du Congo Belge* and in the *Revue de Zoologie et de Botanique Africaines*. The centre in Belgium for the study of tropical medicine is the *Institut Prince Leopold* at Antwerp, which in 1931 replaced an institution founded in Brussels in 1906. The *Institut Royal Colonial Belge* (now the *Académie Royale des Sciences Coloniales*), established in 1930, has sections concerned with the natural, applied, and social sciences, and publishes a quarterly *Bulletin*, as well as separate volumes embodying the results of research. It directly organizes investigations in the Belgian Congo and also offers research fellowships. Other studies have been organized by the *Institut Royal des Sciences Naturelles* and the *Jardin Botanique de l'État*.

The Ministry for Colonies subsidizes travelling fellowships, and some

---

[1] See R. Combes, *Exposé des activités de l'Office de la Recherche Scientifique d'Outre-Mer pour les années 1948-1949-1950*, Paris, 1951.

of the resources of the *Fonds National de la Recherche Scientifique* and the *Institut pour l'Encouragement de la Recherche Scientifique dans l'Industrie et dans l'Agriculture* are allocated to research in the Colony. As regards other than metropolitan institutions, the *Institut pour la Recherche Scientifique en Afrique Centrale* (I.R.S.A.C.) derives its funds primarily from the budget of the Belgian Congo, but its own budget is subject to the approval of the Minister for Colonies. Its governing body meets in Brussels and consists of persons nominated by the King on the recommendation of the Minister. At least 15 of the 24 members, in addition to the president and vice-president, must be Belgian. As at present constituted, it includes a British, a French, and an American subject.

The central organization for agricultural research in the Belgian Congo, the *Institut National pour l'Étude Agronomique du Congo Belge* (I.N.E.A.C.), is administered by a committee representing the Ministry for Colonies and the Belgian Universities. An *Encyclopédie du Congo Belge* in three volumes, the third of which appeared in 1954, contains articles by specialists summarizing the present state of knowledge on flora, fauna, climate, natural resources, agriculture, and diseases of plants and animals. In addition, it gives a full description of the administrative and educational institutions and of other important aspects of the life of the Belgian Congo.

Belgium is also the headquarters of a non-governmental organization, the *Institut International des Civilisations Différentes* (INCIDI), the successor of the International Colonial Institute founded at Brussels in 1894. The Institute was reorganized under its present name in 1949. Its international conferences are a focus of discussion on research in the social sciences, and it publishes a quarterly review entitled *Civilisations*. Its scope is not, however, confined to Africa. Its membership is drawn primarily from Belgium, France (including various parts of the French Union), the Netherlands, Spain, Portugal, the United Kingdom, and the United States.

In Portugal a central council for certain aspects of Colonial research, the *Junta das Missões Geográficas e de Investigações do Ultramar*, was set up to advise the Portuguese Colonial Ministry in 1936. It is supported by both the metropolitan and Colonial budgets and has separate sections for geography and for the natural sciences. Its members are university professors and other specialists, particularly those who have worked in the overseas territories. It has been instrumental in the production of a Colonial atlas, and it has also organized research expeditions in a number of subjects. Medical research in the overseas territories is directed by the Institute of Tropical Medicine in Lisbon or by the territorial Governments in co-operation with it. Some ethnographic research has been done under the auspices of the *Escola Nacional do Ultramar*, to which an Institute of African Languages was attached in 1949.

The Colonial Institutes

The numerous research institutions situated in the different African territories have been discussed in the appropriate chapters, and it is not necessary to repeat here the details given in them. It is, however, important to note the increasing tendency to make provision for long-term investigations in a number of territorial centres, to which the local institutions are affiliated.[1] In some cases several territories may combine in this manner. The system of co-ordination of research in groups of adjacent territories has been carried furthest in British East Africa. Here the central research organizations, with the exception of the East African Institute of Social Research at Makerere, are now under the control of the East African High Commission and are carried on its budget.

In 1948 three such research organizations were created. Two of these, designed to co-ordinate the scientific direction of investigations in agriculture, forestry, and veterinary science, have adjoining headquarters at Muguga near Nairobi.[2] The third, dealing with investigations regarding tsetse infestation and trypanosomiasis, now has its headquarters at Sukulu (Tororo), Uganda. Trypanosomiasis research has since 1955 been centred at two main laboratories, Shinyanga in Tanganyika, and Sukulu (Tororo) in Uganda. An East African Bureau of Research in Medicine and Hygiene was established in Nairobi in 1949, and is responsible for a health survey extending over the whole of the East African territories. The High Commission in 1949 took over from the Rockefeller Institute the East African Virus Research Station at Entebbe. The High Commission is also responsible for organizing investigations in meteorology and locust control; it maintains units dealing with filariasis, malaria, and leprosy, and makes provision for fishery research in all three territories.[3]

As regards the social sciences, an East African Institute of Social Research was established at Makerere in 1945. This does not, however, come under the control of the High Commission. The policy of the Institute is to organize joint studies by groups of research workers in adjacent areas. It has already made a study of labour immigration in Buganda,[4] and has projected studies of changes in land rights and in the rise of new forms of African leadership.

In West Africa, where the four British territories are not contiguous, the problem of co-ordination is more complicated. Co-operation with adjacent territories under the administration of other Powers is held to be at least as important as that between the West African British dependencies. There are, however, in addition to the Cocoa Research Station in the

---

[1] See, in particular, above, pp. 915 ff., and also pp. 1072 ff.
[2] See above, p. 915.
[3] *Annual Report on the East Africa High Commission, 1954*, Col. no. 316, 1955, pp. 27–57.
[4] A. I. Richards, ed., *Economic Development and Tribal Change*, 1954.

Gold Coast,[1] the following organizations: a West African Institute for Trypanosomiasis Research (1951), a West African Fisheries Research Station, and a West African Institute of Social and Economic Research, which is associated with the West African University College at Ibadan in Nigeria. The Institute of Social and Economic Research has since 1952 held annual conferences at which papers have been submitted by persons doing research under its auspices. The conference of 1954 was held in two sections, one on sociology at Ibadan, and the other on economics at the University College of the Gold Coast. A West African Council designed to secure the co-ordination of the policy of the four territories in all matters of common concern was set up in 1945, with its secretariat at Accra. This was superseded in 1951 by the West African Interterritorial Conference, which meets annually and reviews the progress made in interterritorial co-operation in research as well as in social and economic policy.

In Central Africa the co-ordination of research was one of the functions allotted to the Central African Council which was created in 1945.[2] A committee of two members from each of the three territories recommended in 1946 that a Central African Research Council should be set up in Salisbury; a Director was appointed in 1947 and made a survey of existing facilities for research. In 1949 the Governments concerned agreed to maintain in being an interterritorial advisory board, but did not consider that financial support could be secured for other developments which the Committee had recommended. Specialist consultative committees were, however, set up to deal with a number of problems in the natural and applied sciences. The Constitution of the Federation of Rhodesia and Nyasaland has made research a Federal subject and so places it unequivocally under central direction. It is probable, therefore, that a more operative measure of co-ordination will be achieved in the future.

The one interterritorial organization already in existence is not under Government control, though it receives a Government grant. This is the Rhodes-Livingstone Institute, which was founded in 1937 to organize sociological research throughout Central Africa. Its headquarters were originally at Livingstone, but in 1952 were moved to Lusaka. Up to the present time its chief activities have been concentrated on the problems of Northern Rhodesia and Nyasaland.

In the French territories a general institution for research into all African problems, including those of the social sciences, was founded at Dakar in French West Africa in 1938, with the title *Institut Français d'Afrique Noire* (I.F.A.N.). Some reference has already been made in an earlier chapter to the activities of this institution,[3] which now has subsidiary centres in the French Cameroons, Ivory Coast, and Upper Volta.

---

[1] See above, p. 917.   [2] See above, p. 277.   [3] See above, p. 65.

A special section for sociological research was added in 1952. Of somewhat similar character is the *Institut d'Études Centrafricaines* (I.E.C.) at Brazzaville, referred to in an earlier paragraph of the present chapter, which has initiated the work of co-operating research in French Equatorial Africa. Reference has also been made in the present chapter to the *Institut pour la Recherche Scientifique en Afrique Centrale* (I.R.S.A.C.) in the Belgian Congo, which is not, however, entirely a local institute, as its governing body meets in Brussels.[1] It remains to be seen how far the direction of local research in the French and Belgian territories will be influenced by such territorial institutions, rather than by the metropolitan organizations situated in France and Belgium.

INTERCOLONIAL AND INTERNATIONAL CO-OPERATION

Some of the earlier examples of intercolonial co-operation in research are to be found in the record presented in previous chapters regarding particular fields of governmental activities. Thus the first Inter-African Forestry Conference was assembled at Abidjan in 1941. The organization established by the League of Nations for dealing with health questions carried out important investigations into problems of public health which were shared by a number of African Colonies.[2] There are again a number of instances of joint consultation on agricultural or pastoral problems, but the development of definite agencies for intercolonial co-operation in research may be said to be one of the fruits of the Second World War.

In 1945 formal discussions were held between representatives of the Ministry for Overseas France and the British Colonial Office in the hope of achieving some general co-ordination of policy in Colonial affairs. As these discussions proceeded it became apparent that a first and most promising field for co-operation lay in the joint study of technical rather than political problems. An early example of co-operation of this kind had been provided by the International Convention on Air Navigation of 1933. Again, in the year 1938 the French Government had put forward a scheme for joint action in the control of locust swarms which was accepted by the British Government, though it had barely been implemented before the outbreak of the Second World War. The obvious need for regional co-operation in this particular field led to the creation in 1943 of the *Office National Anti-Acridien* covering French North and West Africa, and the East African Locust Directorate for North Eastern Africa, which during the war years organized co-operative measures throughout the Middle East.

The establishment of formal institutions for co-operation in research

---

[1] See above, p. 1606.   [2] See above, p. 1103.

was preceded by some years of discussion between the French, British, and Belgian Governments.[1] A number of specialist conferences were held and though the membership varied on different occasions, the British and French territories were represented in all. A veterinary conference was held at Dakar in 1946 which resulted in the establishment of a closer liaison between the British and French Veterinary Departments. In the same year a medical conference was held at Accra. In 1947 a conference at Dakar drew up a list of projects to improve the communications between French and British territories. French, Belgian, and British experts discussed mass education in London and nutrition in Paris. A forestry conference in Brussels, attended by United Kingdom, French, Belgian, South African, and Portuguese experts, discussed methods of control of plant diseases and the adoption of a uniform system of nomenclature for forest products. Attended by representatives from almost all territories south of the Sahara, a conference on trypanosomiasis was held at Brazzaville in 1948. It led to the establishment in the Belgian Congo of the permanent bureau of the World Health Organization dealing with the problems of tsetse and trypanosomiasis. An inter-African conference on rinderpest was held in the same year. An international committee for locust control, representing French and British territories in West Africa, was also set up in 1948, with the object of preparing an international convention on the subject.

A proposal to create a permanent advisory body on scientific research, which would cover all Africa south of the Sahara, was adopted at a British Commonwealth Conference in 1946. In 1949 the South African Government organized a conference at Johannesburg, at which were represented the Governments of all territories south of the Sahara, with the exception of Liberia and the Spanish Colonies. The conference adopted a number of resolutions on the lines of research which were considered most urgent in each of the fields covered, and also recommended the establishment of a permanent advisory organization, with the general function of recommending research projects of common interest and facilitating the exchange of scientific workers as well as of information on the findings of research. It was to convene periodic conferences of a general scientific character and to arrange meetings of groups of specialists.[2]

There were accordingly constituted in 1950 the Commission for Technical Co-operation in Africa South of the Sahara (*Commission de Coopération Technique en Afrique au Sud du Sahara*, or C.C.T.A.), an organization of Government representatives with executive powers, and an expert advisory body, the Scientific Council for Africa South of the Sahara (*Conseil Scien-*

---

[1] See P. M. Henry, 'A Functional Approach to Regional Co-operation', *African Affairs*, October 1953, pp. 308–15.

[2] *African Regional Scientific Conference, 1949*, vol. i, pp. 101–2.

tifique pour l'Afrique au Sud du Sahara, or C.S.A.). The C.C.T.A. consists of two representatives of each of the Governments of Belgium, France, Portugal, the Federation of Rhodesia and Nyasaland, the Union of South Africa, and the United Kingdom. It has been instrumental in establishing a number of permanent specialist bureaux to collect and disseminate information and facilitate liaison in particular fields. These include the *Bureau Permanent Interafricain de la Tsétsé et de la Trypanosomiase* (B.P.I.T.T.) at Leopoldville; the Inter-African Bureau for Soils and Rural Economy in Paris; the Inter-African Bureau of Epizootic Diseases (I.B.E.D.) at Muguga near Nairobi; the Inter-African Labour Institute at Bamako, French Sudan; and the African Pedological Service at Yangambi in the Belgian Congo. An African Research Fund has been formed to finance joint projects, the first of which was a climatological atlas of Africa. Conferences have been held in the fields of medicine and health, labour, nutrition, indigenous rural economics, animal health, soil science, forestry, housing, statistics, co-operation in rural welfare, the protection of flora and fauna, water biology, and inland fisheries. The creation of regional committees which can meet more frequently is envisaged as the next development. Such meetings have already been held in the field of soil science.

The members of the C.S.A. are appointed by the C.C.T.A. as a body and are not Government representatives nor are they necessarily in Government service. The central headquarters of the Council are situated at Costermansville (Bukavu) in the Belgian Congo. One of its main functions is to recommend to the C.C.T.A. subjects appropriate for discussion by conferences or for the creation of specialist bureaux. It bases its detailed recommendations on the conclusions reached at meetings of specialist research workers, which are of a different character from those organized by the C.C.T.A., in so far that the members of the latter consist mainly of technicians in Government service. In the case of the 1952 meeting on water biology and fisheries in East Africa the cost of publication of the proceedings was defrayed by the East Africa High Commission.[1] The social sciences were first considered by a specialist committee in 1953, which recommended the appointment of an inter-African liaison officer, but no agreement was reached on the creation of a permanent bureau.[2]

Various international organizations with a comprehensive membership also concern themselves with investigation into African problems. The World Health Organization has a regional committee for Africa and a

[1] *Record of Symposium on African Hydrobiology and Inland Fisheries, 1952*, C.S.A. Publication no. 6, 1954.
[2] For a provisional programme up to 1957, see *Forthcoming Conferences and Meetings of Interest to Scientists in Africa*, C.S.A. Publication B.P. 5175, n.d. See also *African Affairs*, April 1954, p. 113, and for a list of publications see *Directory of Scientific and Technical Libraries in Africa South of the Sahara*, C.S.A. Publication no. 10, 1954.

regional office at Brazzaville. This body and the Food and Agriculture Organization of the United Nations were represented at the C.C.T.A. Conference on Nutrition in 1952, and immediately afterwards held a conference of their own at which the C.S.A. was represented by its medical member. Similarly, an international soils conference was held immediately after the Inter-African Soils Conference at Leopoldville in 1954. A regional body of narrower scope is the International Conference on Field Studies in West Africa. This was originally convened, by the *Institut Français d'Afrique Noire*, in 1945. A permanent committee was set up, representing the principal research institutions, but not the Governments, of the four nations concerned, with the function of organizing further conferences at intervals of two years. The fifth of the series was held at Abidjan in the Ivory Coast in December 1953.

A detailed account has been given in a previous chapter[1] of the international organization for dealing with the migration of locusts.

It has been mentioned that grants made by the Rockefeller Foundation constituted one of the earliest sources of finance for research in Africa in the fields both of medicine and of the social sciences.[2] There was, however, no widespread interest in African problems in the United States until the African continent became a theatre of war in which large American forces were engaged. The University of Pennsylvania then issued a series of *African Handbooks*, though these could not claim to be described as contributions to research since they were all based on material already published. At the close of the Second World War the strategic and economic importance of Africa was sufficiently obvious for the newly developed interest to be maintained. It has been manifested in a marked increase in the attention given to Africa in the universities and by the great philanthropic foundations of the United States. As a result of this, study grants have enabled a growing number of American students to undertake research in Africa.

Two of the universities have special courses of African studies, with the aim of preparing students to carry out research in the social sciences in Africa. These are Northwestern University, Illinois, and the University of Boston, both of which provide instruction on contemporary African problems for graduate students. The Program of African Studies at Northwestern University has been developed since 1948, with the assistance of grants from the Carnegie Corporation. An African Research and Studies Program was inaugurated at Boston University in 1953, with the assistance of the Ford Foundation. It is concerned primarily with the social sciences, and study is concentrated on the problems of contemporary Africa.

---

[1] See above, pp. 897 ff.
[2] See above, pp. 63, 1132.

THE FUTURE OF COLONIAL RESEARCH

The probability that material changes will take place in the constitutional status of many of the existing Colonial territories makes it difficult to foresee the future of the organization of research. As regards the British dependencies, the financial provision for research made under the terms of the Colonial Development and Welfare Act of 1940 and the amending Acts, ceases to be available in the year 1960. Furthermore, any territory which should before that date achieve the status of Responsible Government ceases to be eligible for any grant under these Acts.[1] But even if the British Parliament should decide to modify these provisions there are certain general considerations which are likely to affect materially the attitude of autonomous African Governments to schemes for the organization of research.

It is doubtful if the new political elements will take the same view as the British Government regarding the value of 'long-term' or 'fundamental' research, for it may well seem to them that the results it can promise are not commensurate with the cost involved. Even should they retain an interest in investigations of this character, it would not for many years be possible for them to secure from local sources a personnel suitable for the purpose. It is more likely that research, particularly in the natural sciences, will be largely of an *ad hoc* nature, dealing with matters demanding immediate investigation, more especially in connexion with the activities of the health, agricultural, or veterinary services.

In regard to the social sciences, the approach of the dominant political elements is likely to be affected in the future by considerations of a different order. The incentive which has in the past prompted Colonial Administrations to give support to schemes for sociological or anthropological research seems unlikely to appeal to the more advanced political element among Africans. They will, for example, be less interested in investigations directed to ascertain the actual seat of indigenous authority, or to devise the means by which traditional usages can best be adjusted to the requirements of modern political institutions. For them the indigenous Chief and the traditional Native Authority will not have the same significance as units in the new political structure. Nor will they be greatly interested in the contribution which sociological studies in Africa can make to the general volume of our knowledge of the more primitive stages of human society. They are likely, indeed, to view such studies as a reminder of a past which they have outgrown and are not anxious to recall. If there is interest in research in the social sciences, it is likely to be rather in investigations which will throw light on matters such as the preparation of a cost-of-

[1] Colonial Development and Welfare Act, 1940, c. 40, s. 1(5).

living index, the regulation of terms of employment, or the means by which a rural community can best adjust itself to the exigencies of urban life.

In the French territories the influence exercised by constitutional change on the organization of research is likely to be less marked, at all events for some time to come. In the more centralized system of the French the procedure of social or scientific investigation is effectively controlled by metropolitan influences and less liable to be affected by local fashions of thought. Moreover, research organizations in French territories have from the first shown less interest in sociological studies than in investigations bearing on the application of the natural sciences. The French philosophy of rule has not attached the same practical importance as the British to studies of indigenous institutions; they may have been valued as an addition to the store of general knowledge, but have not been regarded as an essential contribution to the successful practice of administration. The same observation applies to studies of a purely linguistic or ethnological character.

Looking to the future of research as a whole, it would seem to be likely that a considerable part of the research at present regarded as a necessary corollary of Colonial rule may in the future receive its chief support from international sources rather than from the Colonial territories themselves or from Powers which are interested in them. This is equally true both of the natural and the social sciences. Studies having a bearing on agricultural productivity or on problems of health which may now appear to be of primary importance in relation to the welfare of dependent or Colonial territories, will come to be recognized as having in fact a far wider range. Some of them have their basis in factors which are characteristic of all tropical countries; others are of almost world-wide application. The problems connected with the conservation of the soil or the prevention of erosion are not confined to the African environment; they are fundamental problems of all arid or semi-arid regions. The pests which have affected the production of cotton, coffee, or cocoa had all left their mark in other parts of the world before they became the subject of special concern in Africa. The history of research into yellow fever forms an interesting illustration of the process by which investigations which were at one time centred in certain Colonial areas have become a subject of international study, largely as the result of the institution of the special organization financed by the contributions from the Rockefeller Foundation.[1]

The problems which engaged the attention of students of the social sciences in Africa during the last generation were largely peculiar to African society. But this is no longer the case, for the problems which will now call for study have their counterpart in many other regions of the

[1] See above, p. 1132.

world. The European peoples who have extended their authority over so many parts of the African continent have introduced to it their own pattern of political institutions. Western capital and technical knowledge are in process of transforming the economic life of the African peoples, and the new problems which have resulted provide a subject for study in every branch of the social sciences. In the political field Africa now presents the problem of securing a satisfactory balance of representation in a 'multi-racial' State, and of developing centralized organs of government which will supplant the small political units of indigenous tradition. In the social sphere there are the problems created by the growth of an economic differentiation, by the rapid increase of urbanization, or by the clash between old and new types of social leadership. In the economic field there are the issues arising from African dependence on foreign capital and export markets for the development of local resources, from the adjustment of the balance between industrial and agricultural activity, or from the need for stimulating local capital formation in areas of low productivity. In yet another field of the social sciences there have arisen the educational problems created by the change in the type of skill demanded by the new phases in the economic life of the continent.

These questions are fundamental. Those which arise from a history of economic or political dependence are shared with many of the tropical and sub-tropical countries, and constitutional changes in Africa have done little, if anything, to reduce their vital importance to the communities immediately concerned. Their problems are not merely those of the Colonial areas, for they have their analogies in many of the independent countries of the East and in the countries of Central America. Not only so, but the results of a rapid transformation from a peasant to an industrial economy have been written deep into the social history of many European countries, and in some of them this type of transformation can still be seen in progress.

Whereas the more insistent of the problems challenging research in the natural sciences have often been set by local conditions of soil, climate, or insect or bacterial life, many of the factors that have created the problems of the social sciences tend to be world wide. The social anthropologists who at one period used to take non-European peoples as their chosen field for research now find that small-scale social groups in Europe and America (both in the cities and in rural areas) are equally interesting and essentially comparable. Workers in the economic field who at one time saw highly industrialized countries as practically their only subject of study are extending their view to embrace also the under-developed regions of the world. In proportion as the subjects of research are thus recognized to be of more general concern, it is likely that those studies which are not of urgent practical significance may come increasingly to be regarded as no longer dependent on the support given to them by the Colonial Powers or the Administrations of Colonial territories. In that case the local institutions of research would tend to devote themselves mainly to the investigation of problems pressing for early inquiry or demanding a special type of experience for their solution.

INDEX

Abeokuta Province (Nigeria), 790, 842.
Abercrombie, Dr. John, 1065.
Abidjan (French Ivory Coast), 331, 582, 583, 923.
Abrahams, Sir Sidney, Nyasaland Inquiry of, 711.
Abusa system, 793–4.
Acacia trees, 961, 963.
Académie Royale des Sciences Coloniales (Belgian), 16, 110, 347, 1605.
Académie des Sciences Coloniales (French), 1605.
Accra (Gold Coast), 325, 582.
   Agricultural Faculties, 892.
   Gold Coast University College, 1181.
   nursing training at, 1100.
   Prince of Wales College (Achimota), 1177, 1179–80.
Achimota College. *See under* Accra.
Acholi language, 100.
Acts:
   Act of Union, South Africa (1909), 176, 177, 179, 181, 182, 265–6, 268, 431.
   education and, 1135–6.
   'entrenched clauses', 157, 161, 164, 166–7.
   railways and harbours and, 1549.
   Bantu Authorities Act, South Africa (1951), 162, 166, 430.
   Bantu Education Act, South Africa (1954), 166, 168, 266, 1148–53.
   opposition to, 1151–2.
   British Settlement Act (1843), 324.
   Citizenship Act, South Africa (1954), 154.
   Colonial Laws Validity Act (1865), 153, 286.
   Constitution of the Senate Act, South Africa (1955), 167.
   Foreign Jurisdiction Acts, British, 285, 286 and n. 1, 305, 327, 713; (1890), 301, 305, 327, 500.
   Glen Grey Act, South Africa (1894), 159–60, 421–2, 1400.
   Amendment Act (1905), 422.
   dual purpose, 422.
   land tenure and, 761, 776, 803.
   Group Areas Act, South Africa (1950), 165, 395–6, 397.
   Immigration Act (1913) and Asians, 389–90.
   Indian Relief Act (1914), 390.
   Land Act, South Africa (1913), 158.
   Masters and Servants Acts, 1399, 1415, 1416, 1418.
   Native (Urban Areas) Accommodation and Registration Act, Southern Rhodesia (1946), 573.
   Native Administration Act, South Africa (1927), 428, 432.
   Native law and, 594, 608.
   Native Affairs, Southern Rhodesia (1927), 441.

Acts *(cont.)*
   Native Taxation and Development Act, South Africa (1925), 651.
   Native Trust and Land Act, South Africa (1936), 158.
   Natives (Urban Areas) Act, South Africa (1923), 567, 568.
   Overseas Resources Development Act (1948), 1337.
   'Pegging Act', South Africa (1943), 395, 396.
   Representation of Natives Act, South Africa (1936), 161–2.
   Separate Representation of Voters Act, South Africa (1951), 164.
   Soil Conservation Act, South Africa (1946), 1018, 1020.
   South-West Africa Affairs (Amendment) Act (1949), 175, 270–1.
   South-West Africa Native Affairs Administration Act (1954), 435.
   Suppression of Communism Act, South Africa (1950), 164, 165.
Adamawa Province (Nigeria), 470.
Adams Institution (Natal), 1152.
Addo Bush National Park, South Africa, 931.
Adeoyo Hospital (Nigeria), 462.
Adiopodoumé (French Ivory Coast), palm oil research at, 854.
   research centre, 918, 1604.
Administrative (Civil) Officers and Services, 262, 320, 359–79, 494, 541.
   anthropology and, 61.
   Belgian, 375–7.
   Buganda, 480, 484.
   Courts and, 618, 619, 620.
     Native courts and, 450, 616, 634–5, 636.
   French, 372–3, 374–5.
   grades of, 374.
   Gold Coast, 367, 368, 371, 522.
   High Commission Territories, 368–9.
   Kenya land policy and, 715.
   Nigeria, 367–8, 370–1, 457, 462, 467.
   Northern Rhodesia, 486.
   Portuguese, grades of, 356–7, 379.
   retirement and training, British, 366.
   Sierra Leone, 368.
   South Africa, 359–61.
   taxation and, 662–3, 665, 680.
   Zanzibar, 369.
   See also Colonial Services.
Advisers, Native Courts, 451, 476, 631, 635–6.
   Gold Coast, 522.
   Kenya, 451, 635.
   Northern Rhodesia, 488.
   Nyasaland, 496.
   See also Judicial Advisers.
Advisory Boards, Native, 442.
   South Africa, 265, 428–9.
   Southern Rhodesia, 442, 443.

O

3 H